Official

BASEBALL REGISTER

1990 EDITION

Editor/Baseball Register
BARRY SIEGEL

Contributing Editors/Baseball Register
CRAIG CARTER
JOHN DUXBURY
DAVE SLOAN

President-Chief Executive Officer
THOMAS G. OSENTON

Book Publisher
GREGORY WILEY

Editorial Director of Books and Periodicals
RON SMITH

Published by

The Sporting News

1212 North Lindbergh Boulevard
P.O. Box 56 — St. Louis, MO 63166

Copyright © 1990
The Sporting News Publishing Company

▼▼ A Times Mirror
◣ Company

ISBN 0-89204-336-9   ISSN 0067-4281

Table
of
CONTENTS

Players included are those who played in at least one game in the major leagues in 1989, those who were part of a team's 40-man roster and selected invitees to spring training.

ON THE COVER: San Francisco outfielder Kevin Mitchell enjoyed an outstanding 1989 season, pounding out 47 homers and driving in 125 runs en route to National League Most Valuable Player and The Sporting News Major League Player of the Year honors.

— Photo by Photo Editor Rich Pilling

EXPLANATION OF ABBREVIATIONS

G—Games played. Pos.—Position. AB—At Bats. R—Runs. H—Hits. 2B—Two-Base Hits. 3B—Three-Base Hits. HR—Home Runs. RBI—Runs Batted In. B.A.—Batting Average. PO—Putouts. A—Assists. E—Errors. F.A.—Fielding Average. IP—Innings Pitched. W—Won. L—Lost. Pct.—Winning percentage. ER—Earned Runs. SO—Strikeouts. BB—Bases on Balls. ERA—Earned-Run Average.

Players

Please note for statistical comparisons: In 1972, 10 days were missed, as well as 50 days in 1981, due to the cancellation of games because of players' strike.
*Denotes led league. ●Tied for lead. Mark before position (where more than one position is given) denotes where played as leader in department shown.

DONALD WILLIAM AASE
Name pronounced AH-see.

(Don)

Born September 8, 1954, at Orange, Calif.
Height, 6.03. Weight, 222.
Throws and bats righthanded.
Attended California State University, Fullerton, Calif.

Major League saves: 1979 (2), 1980 (2), 1981 (11), 1982 (4), 1984 (8), 1985 (14),·1986 (34), 1987 (2), 1989 (2). Total—79.
Led International League pitchers in games started with 29 in 1975.
Led Carolina League pitchers in games started with 30, complete games with 18 and tied for lead in shutouts with 4 in 1974.
Named Carolina League Pitcher of the Year, 1974.

Year Club	League	G.	IP.	W.	L.	Pct.	H.	R.	ER.	SO.	BB.	ERA.
1972—Williamsport	NYP	12	62	0	*10	.000	60	48	40	40	34	5.81
1973—Winter Haven	Florida St.	29	170	12	●15	.444	153	82	68	127	73	3.60
1974—Winston-Salem	Carolina	32	*230	*17	8	.680	185	72	62	*176	84	*2.43
1975—Pawtucket	Int'national	29	186	8	13	.381	173	85	75	125	88	3.63
1976—Rhode Island†	Int'national	10	54	5	2	.714	42	23	20	40	34	3.33
1977—Pawtucket	Int'national	18	109	6	6	.500	118	67	61	64	60	5.04
1977—Boston‡	American	13	92	6	2	.750	85	36	32	49	19	3.13
1978—California	American	29	179	11	8	.579	185	88	80	93	80	4.02
1979—California	American	37	185	9	10	.474	200	104	99	96	77	4.82
1980—California	American	40	175	8	13	.381	193	83	79	74	66	4.06
1981—California§	American	39	65	4	4	.500	56	17	17	38	24	2.35
1982—California§	American	24	52	3	3	.500	45	20	20	40	23	3.46
1983—California x	American					(Did not play)						
1984—Redwood y	California	4	12⅓	0	1	.000	9	9	7	10	7	5.11
1984—California z	American	23	39	4	1	.800	30	7	7	28	19	1.62
1985—Baltimore	American	54	88	10	6	.625	83	44	37	67	35	3.78
1986—Baltimore	American	66	81⅔	6	7	.462	71	29	27	67	28	2.98
1987—Baltimore a	American	7	8	1	0	1.000	8	2	2	3	4	2.25
1988—Rochester b	Int'national	7	7⅓	0	0	.000	5	1	1	6	3	1.23
1988—Baltimore c	American	35	46⅔	0	0	.000	40	22	21	28	37	4.05
1989—New York d	National	49	59⅓	1	5	.167	56	27	26	34	26	3.94
American League Totals—11 Years		367	1011⅓	62	54	.534	996	452	421	583	412	3.75
National League Totals—1 Year		49	59⅓	1	5	.167	56	27	26	34	26	3.94
Major League Totals—12 Years		416	1070⅔	63	59	.516	1052	479	447	617	438	3.76

Selected by Boston Red Sox' organization in 6th round of free-agent draft, June 6, 1972.
†On disabled list, June 23, 1976 through remainder of season.
‡Traded with cash to California Angels for Second Baseman Jerry Remy, December 8, 1977.
§On disabled list, June 3 to June 27 and July 20 to September 7, 1982.
xOn disabled list, March 30, 1983 through remainder of season.
yOn California disabled list, March 27 to June 13, 1984; included rehabilitation disability assignment to Redwood, May 10 to May 30, 1984.
zGranted free agency, November 8, 1984; signed by Baltimore Orioles, December 13, 1984.
aOn disabled list, April 15 to May 13 and May 27, 1987 through remainder of season.
bOn Baltimore disabled list, March 30 to May 10, 1988; included rehabilitation disability assignment to Rochester, April 21 to May 10, 1988.
cReleased, October 3, 1988; signed by Tidewater (New York Mets' organization), February 20, 1989.
dGranted free agency, November 13, 1989.

CHAMPIONSHIP SERIES RECORD

Year Club	League	G.	IP.	W.	L.	Pct.	H.	R.	ER.	SO.	BB.	ERA.
1979—California	American	2	5	1	0	1.000	4	1	1	6	2	1.80

ALL-STAR GAME RECORD

Year League		IP.	W.	L.	Pct.	H.	R.	ER.	SO.	BB.	ERA.
1986—American		⅔	0	0	.000	0	0	0	0	0	0.00

JAMES ANTHONY ABBOTT
(Jim)

Born September 19, 1967, at Flint, Mich.
Height, 6.03. Weight, 200.
Throws and bats lefthanded.
Attended University of Michigan, Ann Arbor, Mich.

Member of 1988 U.S. Olympic baseball team.
Named lefthanded pitcher on THE SPORTING NEWS College Baseball All-America Team, 1988.

Year Club	League	G.	IP.	W.	L.	Pct.	H.	R.	ER.	SO.	BB.	ERA.
1989—California	American	29	181⅓	12	12	.500	190	95	79	115	74	3.92
Major League Totals—1 Year		29	181⅓	12	12	.500	190	95	79	115	74	3.92

Selected by Toronto Blue Jays' organization in 36th round of free-agent draft, June 3, 1985.
Selected by California Angels' organization in 1st round (eighth player selected) of free-agent draft, June 1, 1988.

⚔ PAUL DAVID ABBOTT

Born September 15, 1967, at Van Nuys, Calif.
Height, 6.03. Weight, 185.
Throws and bats righthanded.

Pitched 3-0 no-hit victory against Palm Springs, June 26, 1988 (seven innings).
Tied for California League lead in games started by pitchers with 28 in 1988.

Year Club	League	G.	IP.	W.	L.	Pct.	H.	R.	ER.	SO.	BB.	ERA.
1985—Elizabethton	Ap'lachian	10	35	1	5	.167	33	32	27	34	32	6.94
1986—Kenosha	Midwest	25	98	6	10	.375	102	62	49	73	73	4.50
1987—Kenosha	Midwest	26	145⅓	13	6	.684	102	76	59	138	103	3.65
1988—Visalia	California	28	172⅓	11	9	.550	141	95	80	*205	*143	4.18
1989—Orlando	Southern	17	90⅔	9	3	.750	71	48	44	102	48	4.37

Selected by Minnesota Twins' organization in 3rd round of free-agent draft, June 3, 1985.

SHAWN WESLEY ABNER

Born June 17, 1966, at Hamilton, O.
Height, 6.01. Weight, 190.
Throws and bats righthanded.
Brother of Ben Abner, outfielder in Montreal Expos' and Pittsburgh Pirates' organizations, 1984 through 1987.

Major League stolen bases: 1987 (1), 1989 (1). Total—2.
Tied for Texas League lead in being hit by pitch with 7 in 1986.
Led Texas League outfielders in total chances with 352 in 1986.
Led Carolina League outfielders in total chances with 352 in 1985.
Named Carolina League Player of the Year, 1985.

Year Club	League	Pos.	G.	AB.	R.	H.	2B.	3B.	HR.	RBI.	B.A.	PO.	A.	E.	F.A.
1984—Kingsport	Appal.	OF	46	183	32	50	8	0	10	35	.273	87	1	1	.989
1984—Little Falls	NYP	OF	18	68	7	18	2	0	1	5	.265	40	2	1	.977
1985—Lynchburg	Carol.	OF	139	*542	71	*163	*30	*11	16	*89	.301	*332	8	12	.966
1986—Jackson†	Texas	OF	*134	511	80	136	29	●8	14	76	.266	*338	10	4	.989
1987—Las Vegas	P. C.	OF	105	406	60	122	14	11	11	85	.300	238	9	4	.984
1987—San Diego	Nat.	OF	16	47	5	13	3	1	2	7	.277	23	2	2	.926
1988—San Diego	Nat.	OF	37	83	6	15	3	0	2	5	.181	55	1	1	.982
1988—Las Vegas	P. C.	OF	63	252	35	64	16	2	4	34	.254	147	1	6	.961
1989—Las Vegas	P. C.	OF	56	223	31	60	11	2	8	31	.269	129	6	1	.993
1989—San Diego	Nat.	OF	57	102	13	18	4	0	2	14	.176	67	0	0	1.000
Major League Totals—3 Years			110	232	24	46	10	1	6	26	.198	67	0	0	1.000

Selected by New York Mets' organization in 1st round (first player selected) of free-agent draft, June 4, 1984.
†Traded with Outfielders Stanley Jefferson and Kevin Mitchell and Pitchers Kevin Armstrong and Kevin Brown to San Diego Padres for Outfielder Kevin McReynolds, Pitcher Gene Walter and Infielder Adam Ging, December 11, 1986.

JAMES JUSTIN ACKER
(Jim)

Born September 24, 1958, at Freer, Tex.
Height, 6.02. Weight, 212.
Throws and bats righthanded.
Attended University of Texas, Austin, Tex.
Brother of Bill Acker, nose tackle with St. Louis Cardinals, Kansas City Chiefs, Cincinnati Bengals and Buffalo Bills, 1980 through 1984.

Major League saves: 1983 (1), 1984 (1), 1985 (10), 1987 (14), 1989 (2). Total—28.

Year Club	League	G.	IP.	W.	L.	Pct.	H.	R.	ER.	SO.	BB.	ERA.
1980—Bradenton Braves	Gulf Coast	1	5	1	0	1.000	1	0	0	5	0	0.00
1980—Savannah	Southern	13	95	5	5	.500	84	33	28	47	29	2.65
1981—Savannah	Southern	10	77	5	5	.500	57	34	23	37	34	2.69
1981—Richmond	Int'national	21	118	8	7	.533	112	63	55	72	74	4.19
1982—Savannah†‡	Southern	26	142	9	14	.391	120	96	70	96	86	4.44
1983—Toronto	American	38	97⅔	5	1	.833	103	52	47	44	38	4.33
1984—Toronto§	American	32	72	3	5	.375	79	39	35	33	25	4.38
1985—Toronto	American	61	86⅓	7	2	.778	86	35	31	42	43	3.23
1986—Toronto x	American	23	60	2	4	.333	63	34	29	32	22	4.35
1986—Atlanta	National	21	95	3	8	.273	100	47	40	37	26	3.79
1987—Atlanta	National	68	114⅔	4	9	.308	109	57	53	68	51	4.16
1988—Atlanta y	National	21	42	0	4	.000	45	26	22	25	14	4.71
1988—Greenville z	Southern	8	15⅔	0	0	.000	7	3	3	5	3	1.72
1989—Atlanta a	National	59	97⅔	0	6	.000	84	29	29	68	20	2.67
1989—Toronto	American	14	28⅓	2	1	.667	24	7	5	24	12	1.59
American League Totals—5 Years		168	344½	19	13	.594	355	167	147	175	140	3.84
National League Totals—4 Years		169	349½	7	27	.206	338	159	144	198	111	3.71
Major League Totals—7 Years		337	693⅔	26	40	.394	693	326	291	373	251	3.78

Selected by Atlanta Braves' organization in 1st round (21st player selected) of free-agent draft, June 3, 1980.
†On disabled list, April 9 to April 20, 1982.
‡Drafted by Toronto Blue Jays, December 6, 1982.
§On disabled list, August 16 to September 1, 1984.
xTraded to Atlanta Braves for Pitcher Joe Johnson, July 6, 1986.
yOn disabled list, May 9 to August 19, 1988; included rehabilitation disability assignment to Greenville, July 30 to August 18, 1988.
zGranted free agency, November 4, 1988; re-signed by Richmond (Atlanta Braves' organization), January 6, 1989.
aTraded to Toronto Blue Jays for Pitcher Tony Castillo and a player to be named later, August 24, 1989; Atlanta Braves' organization acquired Catcher Francisco Cabrera to complete deal, August 24, 1989.

CHAMPIONSHIP SERIES RECORD

Shares Championship Series record for most games pitched, series (5), 1989.

Year Club	League	G.	IP.	W.	L.	Pct.	H.	R.	ER.	SO.	BB.	ERA.
1985—Toronto	American	2	6	0	0	.000	2	0	0	5	0	0.00
1989—Toronto	American	5	6⅓	0	0	.000	4	2	1	4	1	1.42
Championship Series Totals—2 Years		7	12⅓	0	0	.000	6	2	1	9	1	0.73

⚡ JAMES DAVID ADDUCI
Name pronounced Uh-DOO-see.
(Jim)

Born August 9, 1959, at Chicago, Ill.
Height, 6.04. Weight, 200.
Throws and bats lefthanded.
Attended Southern Illinois University, Carbondale, Ill.

Led American Association batters in game-winning RBIs with 14 and tied for lead in strikeouts with 103 in 1983.
Led Texas League in game-winning RBIs with 14 in 1982.
Tied for Pacific Coast League lead in errors by first basemen with 15 in 1985.

Year Club	League	Pos.	G.	AB.	R.	H.	2B.	3B.	HR.	RBI.	B.A.	PO.	A.	E.	F.A.
1980—Johnson City	Appal.	OF	17	63	15	21	4	0	5	16	.333	27	2	1	.967
1980—St. Petersburg	Fla. St.	OF	37	118	29	32	4	0	2	13	.271	62	3	2	.970
1981—St. Petersburg	Fla. St.	OF	92	321	44	87	12	7	7	45	.271	185	4	7	.964
1981—Arkansas	Texas	OF	40	131	16	36	8	3	5	14	.275	55	3	1	.983
1982—Arkansas	Texas	OF	121	392	64	117	28	5	22	92	.298	178	6	3	.984
1983—Louisville	A. A.	OF-1B	129	467	81	131	29	7	25	⋆101	.281	327	17	14	.961
1983—St. Louis	Nat.	1B-OF	10	20	0	1	0	0	0	0	.050	47	4	0	1.000
1984—Louisville†‡	A. A.	OF-1B	113	412	62	119	25	6	12	58	.289	252	13	5	.981
1985—Vancouver	P. C.	1B-OF	112	393	63	109	28	2	20	77	.277	788	65	16	.982
1986—Vancouver	P. C.	OF-1B	113	425	71	144	26	5	4	53	.339	418	31	7	.985
1986—Milwaukee	Amer.	1B	3	11	2	1	1	0	0	0	.091	25	3	0	1.000
1987—Denver§x	A. A.	OF-1B	16	59	9	17	3	0	2	15	.288	25	4	0	1.000
1987—Taiyo y	Japan	OF	82	280	....	75	....	....	13	48	.268	Figures Unavailable			
1988—Milwaukee	Amer.	OF-1B	44	94	8	25	6	1	1	15	.266	40	3	1	.977
1988—Denver	A. A.	OF-1B	13	49	3	13	4	0	0	5	.265	43	4	1	.979
1989—Scr./Wil.-Barre	Int.	1B-OF	74	251	31	58	9	2	6	30	.231	416	24	3	.993
1989—Philadelphia z	Nat.	1B-OF	13	19	1	7	1	0	0	0	.368	25	3	0	1.000
American League Totals—2 Years			47	105	10	26	7	1	1	15	.248	65	6	1	.986
National League Totals—2 Years			23	39	1	8	1	0	0	0	.205	72	7	0	1.000
Major League Totals—4 Years			70	144	11	34	8	1	1	15	.236	137	13	1	.993

Selected by Philadelphia Phillies' organization in 28th round of free-agent draft, June 7, 1977.
Selected by St. Louis Cardinals' organization in 7th round of free-agent draft, June 3, 1980.
†On disabled list, April 25 to May 22, 1984.
‡Traded with Outfielder Paul Householder to Milwaukee Brewers for Pitchers Rich Buonantony and Jim Koontz and Infielder Ron Koenigsfeld, October 3, 1984.
§Sold to San Francisco Giants' organization, April 19, 1987; returned, April 26, 1987.
xReleased, June 4, 1987; signed by Taiyo Whales of Japanese Baseball League.
yReleased by Taiyo Whales; re-signed by Milwaukee Brewers, January 18, 1988.
zGranted free agency, October 15, 1989.

STEVEN THOMAS ADKINS
(Steve)

Born October 26, 1964, at Chicago, Ill.
Height, 6.06. Weight, 210.
Throws left and bats righthanded.
Received bachelor of science degree in mechanical
engineering from University of Pennsylvania in 1986.

Tied for Eastern League lead in shutouts with 5 in 1989.

Year Club	League	G.	IP.	W.	L.	Pct.	H.	R.	ER.	SO.	BB.	ERA.
1986—Oneonta	NYP	14	80⅓	8	2	.800	59	23	15	74	36	1.68
1987—Fort Lauderdale	Florida St.	5	21⅓	1	1	.500	26	11	11	7	8	4.64
1987—Prince William	Carolina	21	115⅔	9	8	.529	120	72	62	84	70	4.82
1988—Prince William	Carolina	31	94⅓	6	4	.600	88	44	35	92	40	3.34
1989—Fort Lauderdale	Florida St.	11	45⅔	3	3	.600	40	15	12	48	14	2.36
1989—Albany	Eastern	16	117⅔	12	1	⋆.923	67	31	27	132	58	⋆2.07

Selected by New York Yankees' organization in 15th round of free-agent draft, June 2, 1986.

MICHAEL TROY AFENIR

(Known by middle name.)
Name pronounced AFF-nur.
Born September 21, 1963, at Escondido, Calif.
Height, 6.04. Weight, 200.
Throws and bats righthanded.
Attended Palomar College, San Marcos, Calif.

Led South Atlantic League in passed balls with 32 in 1984.

Year	Club	League	Pos.	G.	AB.	R.	H.	2B.	3B.	HR.	RBI.	B.A.	PO.	A.	E.	F.A.
1983—Sarasota Astros....	Gulf C.	C	27	89	16	26	5	1	5	24	.292	101	19	3	.976
1983—Auburn	NYP	C	7	26	2	3	0	0	0	0	.115	48	2	0	1.000
1984—Asheville	S. Atl.	C-1B	115	358	44	69	16	0	16	69	.193	656	61	12	.984
1985—Osceola	Fla. St.	★C-SS	99	323	38	80	19	1	6	41	.248	557	72	★16	.975
1986—Columbus†	South.	C-1B	91	313	50	68	15	3	14	45	.217	492	38	14	.974
1987—Osceola	Fla. St.	C-1B	79	294	60	81	20	1	14	68	.276	353	30	5	.987
1987—Columbus	South.	C-1B	31	99	15	20	8	0	2	11	.202	142	16	3	.981
1987—Houston	Nat.	C	10	20	1	6	1	0	0	1	.300	35	2	1	.974
1988—Columbus‡	South.	OF-C-1B	137	494	61	122	21	5	16	66	.247	313	29	9	.974
1989—Huntsville§	South.	OF-C-1B	65	225	31	57	15	1	13	45	.253	142	11	3	.981
Major League Totals—1 Year..................			10	20	1	6	1	0	0	1	.300	35	2	1	.974

Selected by Chicago Cubs' organization in 1st round (second player selected) of free-agent draft, January 12, 1982.
Selected by Baltimore Orioles' organization in secondary phase of free-agent draft, June 7, 1982.
Selected by Houston Astros' organization in secondary phase of free-agent draft, January 11, 1983.
†On disabled list, June 21 to July 7, 1986.
‡Traded to Huntsville (Oakland Athletics' organization) for Catcher Matt Sinatro, April 6, 1989.
§On disabled list, April 22 to May 1 and May 9 to June 14, 1989.

JUAN ROBERTO AGOSTO

Born February 23, 1958, at Rio Piedras, P.R.
Height, 6.02. Weight, 190.
Throws and bats lefthanded.

Major League saves: 1983 (7), 1984 (7), 1985 (1), 1986 (1), 1987 (?), 1988 (4), 1989 (1). Total—23.
Led Carolina League in balks with 4 in 1977 and 5 in 1978.

Year	Club	League	G.	IP.	W.	L.	Pct.	H.	R.	ER.	SO.	BB.	ERA.
1975—Winter Haven..............................	Florida St.	6	28	0	4	.000	35	23	18	19	24	5.79
1975—Elmira...............................	NYP	9	23	1	4	.200	27	37	22	22	34	8.61
1976—Winter Haven..............................	Florida St.	28	107	5	11	.313	97	70	55	80	69	4.63
1977—Winston-Salem	Carolina	30	119	4	9	.308	128	106	79	98	★111	5.97
1978—Winter Haven..............................	Florida St.	1	1	0	0	.000	5	2	2	0	0	27.00
1978—Winston-Salem†	Carolina	23	120	5	11	.313	114	76	51	74	89	3.83
1979—Puerto Rico‡..............................	Int.-Amer.	10	31	3	2	.600	31	13	9	9	17	2.61
1980—Glens Falls......................	Eastern	8	22	1	0	1.000	26	18	17	8	18	6.95
1980—Appleton	Midwest	23	144	11	6	.647	118	60	43	93	52	2.69
1981—Edmonton	P. Coast	48	120	7	10	.412	128	61	52	57	49	3.90
1981—Chicago	American	2	6	0	0	.000	5	3	3	3	0	4.50
1982—Edmonton	P. Coast	50	95⅓	3	4	.429	101	63	53	39	49	5.00
1982—Chicago	American	1	2	0	0	.000	7	4	4	1	0	18.00
1983—Denver	Am. Assoc.	19	26	4	1	.800	19	8	6	19	10	2.08
1983—Chicago	American	39	41⅔	4	2	.500	41	20	19	29	11	4.10
1984—Chicago	American	49	55⅓	2	1	.667	54	20	19	26	34	3.09
1985—Chicago	American	54	60⅓	4	3	.571	45	27	24	39	23	3.58
1985—Buffalo...........................	Am. Assoc.	6	12⅔	0	0	.000	13	3	3	11	2	2.13
1986—Chicago§-Minnesota	American	26	25	1	4	.200	49	30	24	12	18	8.64
1986—Toledo x...............................	Int'national	21	35	4	3	.571	33	11	9	29	14	2.31
1987—Tucson...............................	P. Coast	44	50	4	2	.667	48	16	11	31	19	1.98
1987—Houston...............................	National	27	27⅓	1	1	.500	26	12	8	6	10	2.63
1988—Houston...............................	National	75	91⅔	10	2	.833	74	27	23	33	30	2.26
1989—Houston...............................	National	71	83	4	5	.444	81	32	27	46	32	2.93
American League Totals—6 Years.....................		171	190⅓	9	10	.474	201	104	93	110	86	4.40
National League Totals—3 Years.....................		173	202	15	8	.652	181	71	58	85	72	2.58
Major League Totals—9 Years.............................		344	392⅓	24	18	.571	382	175	151	195	158	3.46

Signed as free agent by Boston Red Sox' organization, August 29, 1974.
†Released, September 21, 1978; signed by Puerto Rico of Inter-American League, March 10, 1979.
‡Declared free agent when Inter-American League folded, June 15, 1979; signed by Chicago White Sox' organization, January 18, 1980.
§Sold to Minnesota Twins in exchange for loaning Pitcher Pete Filson to Buffalo (Chicago White Sox' organization), April 30, 1986; Filson was returned to Minnesota and traded to Chicago White Sox for Pitcher Kurt Walker, September 3, 1986.
xReleased, December 20, 1986; signed by Tucson (Houston Astros' organization), February 13, 1987.

CHAMPIONSHIP SERIES RECORD

Year	Club	League	G.	IP.	W.	L.	Pct.	H.	R.	ER.	SO.	BB.	ERA.
1983—Chicago..	American	1	⅓	0	0	.000	0	0	0	0	0	0.00

—DID YOU KNOW—
That no major league pitcher threw a no-hitter last season?

LUIS AGUAYO (MURIEL)

Name pronounced Uh-GWY-oh.

Born March 13, 1959, at Vega Baja, P.R.
Height, 5.09. Weight, 195.
Throws and bats righthanded

Major League stolen bases: 1980 (1), 1981 (1), 1982 (1), 1985 (1), 1986 (1), 1988 (2). Total—7.
Led Carolina League second basemen in assists with 365, errors with 30 and fielding percentage with .953 in 1977.

Year Club	League	Pos.	G.	AB.	R.	H.	2B.	3B.	HR.	RBI.	B.A.	PO.	A.	E.	F.A.
1976—Spartanburg	W. Car.	2B	3	11	0	1	0	0	0	0	.091	5	2	1	.875
1976—Auburn	NYP	2B-3B-SS	51	197	27	49	9	2	0	23	.249	79	99	10	.947
1977—Peninsula	Carol.	2B-SS	130	497	73	127	28	2	9	41	.256	271	409	34	.952
1978—Reading	East.	SS-2B	115	378	49	74	19	5	4	33	.196	198	341	25	.956
1979—Oklahoma City	A. A.	SS-2B	113	370	54	101	21	1	8	46	.273	191	320	27	.950
1980—Philadelphia†	Nat.	2B-SS	20	47	7	13	1	2	1	8	.277	44	44	3	.967
1980—Oklahoma City‡	A. A.	SS	84	291	37	71	19	2	9	40	.244	154	268	*28	.938
1981—Philadelphia	Nat.	2B-SS-3B	45	84	11	18	4	0	1	7	.214	39	63	5	.953
1982—Philadelphia	Nat.	2B-SS-3B	50	56	11	15	1	2	3	7	.268	27	49	4	.950
1983—Philadelphia§	Nat.	SS	2	4	1	1	0	0	0	0	.250	3	0	0	1.000
1983—Portland	P. C.	SS-2B	71	229	38	65	14	3	5	33	.284	121	216	10	.971
1984—Philadelphia	Nat.	3B-2B-SS	58	72	15	20	4	0	3	11	.278	18	55	3	.961
1984—Portland	P. C.	SS	3	13	3	7	1	0	1	2	.538	6	7	1	.929
1985—Philadelphia	Nat.	SS-2B-3B	91	165	27	46	7	3	6	21	.279	92	158	9	.965
1986—Philadelphia	Nat.	2B-SS-3B	62	133	17	28	6	1	4	13	.211	57	90	5	.967
1987—Philadelphia x	Nat.	SS-2B-3B	94	209	25	43	9	1	12	21	.206	86	172	7	.974
1988—Philadelphia y	Nat.	SS-3B-2B	49	97	9	24	3	0	3	5	.247	47	75	7	.946
1988—New York z	Amer.	3B-SS	50	140	12	35	4	0	3	8	.250	36	81	6	.951
1989—Cleveland ab	Amer.	3B-SS-2B	47	97	7	17	4	1	1	8	.175	34	80	5	.958
National League Totals—9 Years			471	867	123	208	35	9	33	93	.240	413	706	43	.963
American League Totals—2 Years			97	237	19	52	8	1	4	16	.219	70	161	11	.955
Major League Totals—10 Years			568	1104	142	260	43	10	37	109	.236	483	867	54	.962

Signed as free agent by Philadelphia Phillies' organization, December 27, 1975.
†On disabled list, May 7 to May 22, 1980.
‡On disabled list, May 22 to August 30, 1980.
§On disabled list, March 23 to June 13, 1983.
xOn disabled list, June 1 to June 16, 1987.
yTraded to New York Yankees for Pitcher Amalio Carreno, July 15, 1988.
zGranted free agency, November 4, 1988; signed by Cleveland Indians, December 2, 1988.
aOn disabled list, August 8 to September 1, 1989.
bReleased, October 4, 1989.

DIVISION SERIES RECORD

Year Club	League	Pos.	G.	AB.	R.	H.	2B.	3B.	HR.	RBI.	B.A.	PO.	A.	E.	F.A.
1981—Philadelphia	Nat.	PR	2	0	1	0	0	0	0	0	.000	0	0	0	.000

RICHARD WARREN AGUILERA

Name pronounced Ag-ah-lair-uh.

(Rick)

Born December 31, 1961, at San Gabriel, Calif.
Height, 6.05. Weight, 200.
Throws and bats righthanded.
Attended Brigham Young University, Provo, Utah.

Major League saves: 1989 (7).
Tied for Carolina League lead in shutouts with 3 in 1984.
Tied for New York-Pennsylvania League lead in shutouts with 2 in 1983.

Year Club	League	G.	IP.	W.	L.	Pct.	H.	R.	ER.	SO.	BB.	ERA.
1983—Little Falls	NYP	16	104	5	6	.455	*109	55	43	84	26	3.72
1984—Lynchburg	Carolina	13	88⅓	8	3	.727	72	29	23	101	28	2.34
1984—Jackson†	Texas	11	67	4	4	.500	68	37	34	71	19	4.57
1985—Tidewater	Int'national	11	79	6	4	.600	64	24	22	55	17	2.51
1985—New York	National	21	122⅓	10	7	.588	118	49	44	74	37	3.24
1986—New York	National	28	141⅔	10	7	.588	145	70	61	104	36	3.88
1987—New York‡	National	18	115	11	3	.786	124	53	46	77	33	3.60
1987—Tidewater	Int'national	3	13	1	1	.500	8	2	1	10	1	0.69
1988—New York§	National	11	24⅔	0	4	.000	29	20	19	16	10	6.93
1988—St. Lucie	Florida St.	2	7	0	0	.000	8	1	1	5	1	1.29
1988—Tidewater	Int'national	1	6	0	0	.000	6	1	1	4	1	1.50
1989—New York x	National	36	69½	6	6	.500	59	19	18	80	21	2.34
1989—Minnesota	American	11	75⅔	3	5	.375	71	32	27	57	17	3.21
National League Totals—5 Years		114	473	37	27	.578	475	211	188	351	137	3.58
American League Totals—1 Year		11	75⅔	3	5	.375	71	32	27	57	17	3.21
Major League Totals—5 Years		125	548⅔	40	32	.556	546	243	215	408	154	3.53

Selected by St. Louis Cardinals' organization in 37th round of free-agent draft, June 3, 1980.
Selected by New York Mets' organization in 3rd round of free-agent draft, June 6, 1983.
†On disabled list, September 3 to September 15, 1985.
‡On disabled list, May 23 to August 24, 1987; included rehabilitation disability assignment to Tidewater, August 10 to August 24, 1987.

§On disabled list, April 19 to June 19 and July 12 to September 7, 1988; included rehabilitation disability assignment to St. Lucie, June 7 to June 14, 1988; and Tidewater, June 15 to June 19, 1988.

xTraded with Pitcher David West and three players to be named later to Minnesota Twins for Pitcher Frank Viola, July 31, 1989; Portland (Minnesota Twins' organization) acquired Pitchers Kevin Tapani and Tim Drummond on August 1, 1989, and Minnesota acquired Pitcher Jack Savage to complete deal, October 16, 1989.

CHAMPIONSHIP SERIES RECORD

Year Club	League	G.	IP.	W.	L.	Pct.	H.	R.	ER.	SO.	BB.	ERA.
1986—New York	National	2	5	0	0	.000	2	1	0	2	2	0.00
1988—New York	National	3	7	0	0	.000	3	1	1	4	2	1.29
Championship Series Totals—2 Years		5	12	0	0	.000	5	2	1	6	4	0.75

WORLD SERIES RECORD

Year Club	League	G.	IP.	W.	L.	Pct.	H.	R.	ER.	SO.	BB.	ERA.
1986—New York	National	2	3	1	0	1.000	8	4	4	4	1	12.00

⚹ DARREL WAYNE AKERFELDS

Born June 12, 1962, at Denver, Colo.
Height, 6.02. Weight, 210.
Throws and bats righthanded.
Attended Mesa College, Grand Junction, Colo., and
University of Arkansas, Fayetteville, Ark.

Tied for Midwest League lead in wild pitches with 19 in 1984.

Year Club	League	G.	IP.	W.	L.	Pct.	H.	R.	ER.	SO.	BB.	ERA.
1983—Bellingham†	Northwest	12	68⅓	5	3	.625	62	36	34	85	36	4.48
1984—Madison	Midwest	24	151	11	6	.647	156	86	74	137	74	4.41
1985—Huntsville‡	Southern	17	96⅓	9	6	.600	75	42	37	56	64	3.46
1986—Tacoma	P. Coast	25	150	8	12	.400	158	91	79	91	62	4.74
1986—Oakland	American	2	5⅓	0	0	.000	7	5	4	5	3	6.75
1987—Tacoma§	P. Coast	19	129⅔	10	3	.769	117	52	51	84	57	3.54
1987—Cleveland	American	16	74⅔	2	6	.250	84	60	56	42	38	6.75
1988—Colorado Springs x	P. Coast	49	58	3	7	.300	70	43	28	50	26	4.34
1989—Oklahoma City	Am. Assoc.	33	108	5	5	.500	89	45	40	75	59	3.33
1989—Texas	American	6	11	0	1	.000	11	6	4	9	5	3.27
Major League Totals—3 Years		24	91	2	7	.222	102	71	64	56	46	6.33

Selected by Atlanta Braves' organization in 9th round of free-agent draft, June 3, 1980.

Selected by Seattle Mariners' organization in 1st round (seventh player selected) of free-agent draft, June 6, 1983.

†Traded to Oakland A's, December 7, 1983, completing deal in which Seattle Mariners traded Pitcher Bill Caudill and a player to be named later to Oakland for Pitcher Dave Beard and Catcher Bob Kearney, November 21, 1983.

‡On disabled list, May 22 to June 13 and July 5 to August 20, 1985.

§Traded with Catcher Brian Dorsett to Cleveland Indians for Second Baseman Tony Bernazard, July 15, 1987.

xDrafted by Texas Rangers, December 5, 1988.; deal settled with future considerations.

SCOTT PHILLIP ALDRED

Born June 12, 1968, at Flint, Mich.
Height, 6.04. Weight, 195.
Throws and bats lefthanded.

Year Club	League	G.	IP.	W.	L.	Pct.	H.	R.	ER.	SO.	BB.	ERA.
1987—Fayetteville	S. Atlantic	21	110	4	9	.308	101	56	44	91	69	3.57
1988—Lakeland	Florida St.	25	131⅓	8	7	.533	122	61	52	102	72	3.56
1989—London	Eastern	20	122	10	6	.625	98	55	52	97	59	3.84

Selected by Detroit Tigers' organization in 16th round of free-agent draft, June 2, 1986.

MICHAEL PETER ALDRETE

Name pronounced Owl-DRET-ee.

(Mike)

Born January 29, 1961, at Carmel, Calif.
Height, 5.11. Weight, 185.
Throws and bats lefthanded.
Received bachelor of arts degree in communication from
Stanford University, Stanford, Calif.
Brother of Rich Aldrete, first baseman in San Francisco Giants' organization.

Major League stolen bases: 1986 (1), 1987 (6), 1988 (6), 1989 (1). Total—14.

Led California League in total bases with 225 in 1984.

Year Club	League	Pos.	G.	AB.	R.	H.	2B.	3B.	HR.	RBI.	B.A.	PO.	A.	E.	F.A.
1983—Great Falls	Pion.	1B-OF	38	132	30	55	11	2	4	31	.417	257	17	4	.986
1983—Fresno	Calif.	1B	20	68	5	14	4	0	1	12	.206	189	9	2	.990
1984—Fresno	Calif.	1B	136	457	89	155	28	3	12	72	.339	1180	74	8	*.994
1985—Shreveport	Texas	1B-OF	127	441	80	147	32	1	15	77	.333	854	41	9	.990
1985—Phoenix	P. C.	OF	3	8	0	1	1	0	0	1	.125	3	0	0	1.000
1986—Phoenix	P. C.	OF-1B	47	159	36	59	14	0	6	35	.371	131	8	1	.993
1986—San Francisco	Nat.	1B-OF	84	216	27	54	18	3	2	25	.250	317	36	1	.997
1987—San Francisco	Nat.	OF-1B	126	357	50	116	18	2	9	51	.325	328	18	3	.991
1988—San Francisco†	Nat.	OF-1B	139	389	44	104	15	0	3	50	.267	272	8	4	.986

Year	Club	League	Pos.	G.	AB.	R.	H.	2B.	3B.	HR.	RBI.	B.A.	PO.	A.	E.	F.A.
1989—Montreal‡		Nat.	OF-1B	76	136	12	30	8	1	1	12	.221	109	9	1	.992
1989—Indianapolis		A. A.	1B-OF	10	31	4	4	1	0	0	2	.129	41	3	0	1.000
Major League Totals—4 Years				425	1098	133	304	59	6	15	138	.277	1026	71	9	.992

Selected by San Francisco Giants' organization in 7th round of free-agent draft, June 6, 1983.

†Traded to Montreal Expos for Outfielder Tracy Jones, December 8, 1988.

‡On disabled list, August 16 to September 1, 1989; included rehabilitation disability assignment to Indianapolis, August 21 to September 1, 1989.

CHAMPIONSHIP SERIES RECORD

Year	Club	League	Pos.	G.	AB.	R.	H.	2B.	3B.	HR.	RBI.	B.A.	PO.	A.	E.	F.A.
1987—San Francisco		Nat.	PH-OF	5	10	0	1	0	0	0	1	.100	5	0	0	1.000

⚑ JAY ROBERT ALDRICH

Born April 14, 1961, at Alexandria, La.
Height, 6.03. Weight, 210.
Throws and bats righthanded.
Attended Monclair State College, Upper Montclair, N.J.

Major League saves: 1989 (1).
Tied for California League lead in intentional bases on balls issued with 10 in 1984.

Year	Club	League	G.	IP.	W.	L.	Pct.	H.	R.	ER.	SO.	BB.	ERA.
1982—Pikeville	Ap'lachian	11	53⅔	1	2	.333	44	33	25	37	28	4.19
1983—Beloit	Midwest	28	103⅔	7	4	.636	114	59	48	96	35	4.17
1984—Stockton	California	54	105⅔	11	●14	.440	107	46	34	78	44	2.90
1985—El Paso	Texas	42	63⅓	4	1	.800	61	28	25	35	13	3.55
1986—El Paso	Texas	40	54⅓	3	3	.500	60	24	21	34	18	3.48
1987—Denver	Am. Assoc.	20	29	1	0	1.000	26	13	11	16	6	3.41
1987—Milwaukee	American	31	58⅓	3	1	.750	71	33	32	22	13	4.94
1988—Denver	Am. Assoc.	50	72	3	7	.300	83	40	37	53	20	4.63
1989—Denver	Am. Assoc.	31	42⅔	2	4	.333	44	15	13	24	13	2.74
1989—Milwaukee†	American	16	26	1	0	1.000	24	11	11	12	13	3.81
1989—Atlanta‡	National	8	12⅓	1	2	.333	7	5	3	7	6	2.19
American League Totals—2 Years		47	84⅓	4	1	.800	95	44	43	34	26	4.59
National League Totals—1 Year		8	12⅓	1	2	.333	7	5	3	7	6	2.19
Major League Totals—2 Years		55	96⅔	5	3	.625	102	49	46	41	32	4.28

Selected by Milwaukee Brewers' organization in 10th round of free-agent draft, June 7, 1982.

†Traded to Atlanta Braves, September 1, 1989, completing deal in which Atlanta traded Infielder Ed Romero to Milwaukee Brewers for a player to be named later, August 23, 1989.

‡Released, November 15, 1989; signed by Rochester (Baltimore Orioles' organization), December 5, 1989.

DOYLE LAFAYETTE ALEXANDER

Born September 4, 1950, at Cordova, Ala.
Height, 6.03. Weight, 200.
Throws and bats righthanded.
Attended Jefferson State Junior College, Birmingham, Ala.

Shares National League record for most consecutive home runs allowed, inning (3), July 26, 1987, eighth inning.
Tied for American League lead in home runs allowed with 28 in 1989.
Major League saves: 1972 (2), 1975 (1). Total—3.

Year	Club	League	G.	IP.	W.	L.	Pct.	H.	R.	ER.	SO.	BB.	ERA.
1968—Tri-City	Northwest	13	70	3	*9	.250	66	47	32	58	47	4.11
1969—Daytona Beach	Florida St.	30	185	13	9	.591	154	75	56	140	100	2.72
1969—Albuquerque	Texas	3	15	0	3	.000	19	10	10	3	12	6.00
1970—Albuquerque	Texas	10	80	4	3	.571	72	29	28	60	20	3.15
1970—Spokane	P. Coast	19	137	9	7	.563	137	66	55	78	26	3.61
1971—Spokane	P. Coast	15	110	6	3	.667	114	49	42	65	31	3.44
1971—Los Angeles†	National	17	92	6	6	.500	105	45	39	30	18	3.82
1972—Baltimore	American	35	106	6	8	.429	78	36	29	49	30	2.46
1973—Baltimore‡	American	29	175	12	8	.600	169	85	75	63	52	3.86
1974—Baltimore	American	30	114	6	9	.400	127	65	51	40	43	4.03
1975—Baltimore	American	32	133	8	8	.500	127	47	45	46	47	3.05
1976—Baltimore§-New York x	American	30	201	13	9	.591	172	81	75	58	63	3.36
1977—Texas	American	34	237	17	11	.607	221	103	96	82	82	3.65
1978—Texas	American	31	191	9	10	.474	198	84	82	81	71	3.86
1979—Texas y	American	23	113	5	7	.417	114	65	56	50	69	4.46
1980—Atlanta z	National	35	232	14	11	.560	227	120	108	114	74	4.19
1981—San Francisco a	National	24	152	11	7	.611	156	51	49	77	44	2.90
1982—Fort Lauderdale	Florida St.	2	11	0	1	1.000	12	5	5	4	2	4.09
1982—New York bc	American	16	66⅔	1	7	.125	81	52	45	26	14	6.08
1982—Columbus	Int'national	1	3⅔	0	0	.000	5	4	4	1	2	9.82
1983—New York d-Toronto	American	25	145	7	8	.467	157	76	71	63	33	4.41
1983—Kinston	Carolina	1	6	0	0	.000	3	0	0	4	0	0.00
1984—Toronto	American	36	261⅔	17	6	*.739	238	99	91	139	59	3.13
1985—Toronto	American	36	260⅔	17	10	.630	268	105	100	142	67	3.45
1986—Toronto e	American	17	111	5	4	.556	120	56	55	65	20	4.46
1986—Atlanta f	National	17	117⅓	6	6	.500	135	58	50	74	17	3.84
1987—Atlanta g	National	16	117⅔	5	10	.333	115	57	54	64	27	4.13
1987—Detroit	American	11	88⅓	9	0	1.000	63	16	15	44	26	1.53

Year Club	League	G.	IP.	W.	L.	Pct.	H.	R.	ER.	SO.	BB.	ERA.
1988—Detroit h	American	34	229	14	11	.560	260	122	110	126	46	4.32
1989—Detroit	American	33	223	6	*18	.250	245	118	110	95	76	4.44
National League Totals—5 Years		109	711	42	40	.512	738	331	300	359	180	3.80
American League Totals—16 Years		452	2655⅓	152	134	.531	2638	1210	1106	1169	798	3.75
Major League Totals—19 Years		561	3366⅓	194	174	.527	3376	1541	1406	1528	978	3.76

Selected by Los Angeles Dodgers' organization in 44th round of free-agent draft, June 7, 1968.

†Traded with Pitcher Bob O'Brien, Catcher Sergio Robles and First Baseman-Outfielder Royle Stillman to Baltimore Orioles for Pitcher Pete Richert and Outfielder Frank Robinson, December 2, 1971.

‡On disabled list, July 10 to August 6, 1973.

§Traded with Pitchers Ken Holtzman and Grant Jackson, Catcher Elrod Hendricks and Pitcher Jimmy Freeman to New York Yankees for Pitchers Rudy May, Tippy Martinez, Dave Pagan, Scott McGregor and Catcher Rick Dempsey, June 15, 1976.

xPlayed out option year and granted free agency, November 1, 1976; signed as free agent by Texas Rangers, November 23, 1976.

yTraded with Shortstop Larvell Blanks to Atlanta Braves for Pitcher Adrian Devine, Shortstop Pepe Frias and a player to be named later, December 7, 1979; Atlanta received $50,000 to complete deal when Outfielder Jeff Burroughs exercised no-trade clause.

zTraded to San Francisco Giants for Pitcher John Montefusco and Outfielder Craig Landis, December 12, 1980.

aTraded to New York Yankees for Pitcher Andy McGaffigan and Outfielder Ted Wilborn, March 30, 1982.

bOn disabled list, May 10 to July 8, 1982; included rehabilitation disability assignment to Columbus, June 22 to July 8, 1982.

cOn disabled list, August 11 to September 10, 1982.

dReleased, May 31, 1983; signed by Toronto Blue Jays' organization, June 21, 1983.

eTraded to Atlanta Braves for Pitcher Duane Ward, July 6, 1986.

fGranted free agency, November 12, 1986; re-signed by Braves, May 5, 1987.

gTraded to Detroit Tigers for Pitcher John Smoltz, August 12, 1987.

hGranted free agency, October 24, 1988; re-signed by Tigers, January 13, 1989.

CHAMPIONSHIP SERIES RECORD

Shares Championship Series record for most games lost, series (2), 1987.

Holds American League Championship Series record for most games lost and most consecutive games lost, total series (4).

Year Club	League	G	IP.	W.	L.	Pct.	H.	R.	ER.	SO.	BB.	ERA.
1973—Baltimore	American	1	3⅔	0	1	.000	5	3	2	1	0	4.91
1985—Toronto	American	2	10⅓	0	1	.000	14	10	10	9	3	8.71
1987—Detroit	American	2	9	0	2	.000	14	10	10	5	1	10.00
Championship Series Total—3 Years		5	23	0	4	.000	33	23	22	15	4	8.61

WORLD SERIES RECORD

Year Club	League	G.	IP.	W.	L.	Pct.	H.	R.	ER.	SO.	BB.	ERA.
1976—New York	American	1	6	0	1	.000	9	5	5	1	2	7.50

ALL-STAR GAME RECORD

Member of American League All-Star Team in 1988; did not play.

ANDREW NEAL ALLANSON
(Andy)

Born December 22, 1961, at Richmond, Va.
Height, 6.05. Weight, 225.
Throws and bats righthanded.
Attended University of Richmond, Richmond, Va.

Major League stolen bases: 1986 (10), 1987 (1), 1988 (5), 1989 (4). Total—20.

Led American League catchers in total chances with 762 and double plays with 11 in 1988.

Year Club	League	Pos.	G.	AB.	R.	H.	2B.	3B.	HR.	RBI.	B.A.	PO.	A.	E.	F.A.
1983—Waterloo	Midw.	C	17	50	4	10	0	0	0	0	.200	99	8	3	.973
1983—Batavia	NYP	C	51	145	27	38	3	0	0	6	.262	372	27	5	.988
1984—Buffalo†	East.	C	39	111	12	28	4	0	0	11	.252	154	15	3	.983
1984—Waterloo	Midw.	C	46	144	14	39	5	0	0	10	.271	68	9	1	.987
1985—Waterbury	East.	C	120	420	69	131	17	1	0	47	*.312	578	64	10	.985
1986—Cleveland	Amer.	C	101	293	30	66	7	3	1	29	.225	446	33	*20	.960
1987—Buffalo	A.A.	C	76	276	21	75	8	0	4	39	.272	428	30	●12	.974
1987—Cleveland	Amer.	C	50	154	17	41	6	0	3	16	.266	252	22	4	.986
1988—Cleveland‡	Amer.	C	133	434	44	114	11	0	5	50	.263	*691	60	●11	.986
1989—Cleveland	Amer.	C	111	323	30	75	9	1	3	17	.232	570	53	9	.986
Major League Totals—4 Years			395	1204	121	296	33	4	12	112	.246	1959	168	44	.980

Selected by Cleveland Indians' organization in 2nd round of free-agent draft, June 6, 1983.

†On disabled list, June 19 to June 29, 1984.

‡On disabled list, July 16 to August 5, 1988.

HAROLD WILLIAM ALLEN JR.

Born October 10, 1965, at Terre Haute, Ind.
Height, 6.00. Weight, 210.
Throws and bats lefthanded.
Attended Indiana State University, Terre Haute, Ind.

Year Club	League	G.	IP.	W.	L.	Pct.	H.	R.	ER.	SO.	BB.	ERA.
1987—Auburn	NYP	14	68⅔	2	8	.200	71	47	36	68	38	4.72

Year Club	League	G.	IP.	W.	L.	Pct.	H.	R.	ER.	SO.	BB.	ERA.
1988—Asheville	S. Atlantic	26	159	11	8	.579	152	68	50	115	69	2.83
1989—Osceola	Florida St.	26	159	12	11	.522	157	78	59	123	57	3.34

Selected by Houston Astros' organization in 5th round of free-agent draft, June 2, 1987.

NEIL PATRICK ALLEN

Born January 24, 1958, at Kansas City, Kan.
Height, 6.02. Weight, 190.
Throws and bats righthanded.

Major League saves: 1979 (8), 1980 (22), 1981 (18), 1982 (19), 1983 (2), 1984 (3), 1985 (3). Total—75.
Tied for Carolina League lead in complete games with 11 in 1977.

Year Club	League	G.	IP.	W.	L.	Pct.	H.	R.	ER.	SO.	BB.	ERA.
1976—Marion	Ap'lachian	6	33	2	0	1.000	23	8	7	29	6	1.91
1976—Wausau	Midwest	6	48	4	2	.667	51	27	20	34	20	3.75
1977—Lynchburg†	Carolina	20	142	10	2	.833	136	55	44	★126	43	2.79
1978—Jackson	Texas	16	120	5	9	.357	88	38	28	111	38	★2.10
1978—Tidewater	Int'national	10	57	2	7	.222	65	35	28	30	12	4.42
1979—New York‡	National	50	99	6	10	.375	100	46	39	65	47	3.55
1980—New York	National	59	97	7	10	.412	87	43	40	79	40	3.71
1981—New York	National	43	67	7	6	.538	64	26	22	50	26	2.96
1982—New York	National	50	64⅔	3	7	.300	65	22	22	59	30	3.06
1983—New York§-St. Louis	National	46	175⅔	12	13	.480	179	84	77	106	84	3.94
1984—St. Louis	National	57	119	9	6	.600	105	54	47	66	49	3.55
1985—St. Louis x	National	23	29	1	4	.200	32	22	18	10	17	5.59
1985—New York y	American	17	29⅓	1	0	1.000	26	9	9	16	13	2.76
1986—Chicago z	American	22	113	7	2	.778	101	50	48	57	38	3.82
1987—Chicago ab-New York	American	23	74⅓	0	8	.000	97	52	49	42	36	5.93
1987—Daytona Beach	Florida St.	4	18	0	1	.000	17	6	4	17	7	2.00
1988—Fort Lauderdale c	Florida St.	3	9	0	0	.000	2	0	0	5	1	0.00
1988—Columbus	Int'national	2	15	0	1	.000	7	2	1	7	0	0.60
1988—New York de	American	41	117⅓	5	3	.625	121	51	50	61	37	3.84
1989—Colorado Springs	P. Coast	21	100	5	3	.625	105	57	38	52	27	3.42
1989—Cleveland fg	American	3	3	0	1	.000	8	5	5	0	0	15.00
National League Totals—7 Years		328	651⅓	45	56	.446	632	297	265	435	293	3.66
American League Totals—5 Years		106	337	13	14	.481	353	167	161	176	124	4.30
Major League Totals—11 Years		434	988⅓	58	70	.453	985	464	426	611	417	3.88

Selected by New York Mets' organization in 11th round of free-agent draft, June 8, 1976.
†On disabled list, July 26 to September 1, 1977.
‡On disabled list, June 1 to June 25, 1979.
§Traded with Pitcher Rick Ownbey to St. Louis Cardinals for First Baseman Keith Hernandez, June 15, 1983.
xTraded to New York Yankees for a player to be named later, July 17, 1985; deal settled with cash.
yTraded with Catcher Scott Bradley, Outfielder Glen Braxton and cash to Chicago White Sox for Catchers Ron Hassey and Chris Alvarez, Pitcher Eric Schmidt and Outfielder Matt Winters, February 13, 1986.
zOn disabled list, August 6 to September 10, 1986.
aOn disabled list, April 19 to May 26 and June 17 to July 20, 1987; included rehabilitation disability assignment to Daytona Beach, May 6 to May 26, 1987.
bReleased, August 29, 1987; signed by New York Yankees, September 4, 1987.
cOn New York disabled list, March 21 to May 10, 1988; included rehabilitation disability assignment to Fort Lauderdale, April 16 to May 6, 1988.
dGranted free agency, November 4, 1988; signed by Cleveland Indians, January 17, 1989.
eReleased, March 27, 1989; re-signed by Indians' organization, April 1, 1989.
fOn disabled list, June 30 to September 3, 1989; included rehabilitation disability assignment to Colorado Springs, August 14 to September 3, 1989.
gReleased, October 4, 1989.

DALE LeBEAU ALLRED
(Beau)

Born June 4, 1965, at Mesa, Ariz.
Height, 6.00. Weight, 195.
Throws and bats lefthanded.
Attended Cochise County Community College, Douglas,
Ariz., and Lamar University, Beaumont, Tex.

Year Club	League	Pos.	G.	AB.	R.	H.	2B.	3B.	HR.	RBI.	B.A.	PO.	A.	E.	F.A.
1987—Burlington	W. Car.	OF	54	167	39	57	14	1	10	38	★.341	61	2	4	.940
1988—Kinston	Carol.	OF	126	397	66	100	23	3	15	74	.252	187	10	10	.952
1989—Canton-Akron	East.	OF	118	412	67	125	23	5	14	75	.303	204	7	8	.963
1989—Colorado Springs	P. C.	OF	11	47	8	13	3	0	1	4	.277	27	1	0	1.000
1989—Cleveland	Amer.	OF	13	24	0	6	3	0	0	1	.250	11	1	0	1.000
Major League Totals—1 Year			13	24	0	6	3	0	0	1	.250	11	1	0	1.000

Selected by Cleveland Indians' organization in 25th round of free-agent draft, June 2, 1987.

—DID YOU KNOW—

That the Yankees' Roberto Kelly and the Brewers' Jim Gantner each reached first base on catcher's interference twice in 1989?

ROBERTO ALOMAR (VELAZQUEZ)

Born February 5, 1968, at Salinas, Puerto Rico.
Height, 6.00. Weight, 155.
Throws right and bats left and righthanded.
Son of Sandy Alomar Sr., infielder with Milwaukee-Atlanta Braves, New York Mets, Chicago White Sox, California Angels, New York Yankees and Texas Rangers, 1964 through 1978; minor league instructor, San Diego Padres' organization, 1985; and coach with San Diego Padres since 1986; and brother of Sandy Alomar, Jr., catcher with Cleveland Indians.

Major League stolen bases: 1988 (24), 1989 (42). Total—66.
Led National League in sacrifice hits with 17 in 1989.
Led Texas League shortstops in putouts with 167 and errors with 34 in 1987.
Led South Atlantic League second basemen in errors with 35 in 1985.

Year Club	League	Pos.	G.	AB.	R.	H.	2B.	3B.	HR.	RBI.	B.A.	PO.	A.	E.	F.A.
1985—Charleston	S. Atl.	2B-SS	*137	*546	89	160	14	3	0	54	.293	298	339	36	.947
1986—Reno	Calif.	2B	90	356	53	123	16	4	4	49	*.346	198	265	18	.963
1987—Wichita	Texas	SS-2B	130	536	88	171	41	4	12	68	.319	188	309	36	.932
1988—Las Vegas	P. C.	2B	9	37	5	10	1	0	2	14	.270	22	29	1	.981
1988—San Diego	Nat.	2B	143	545	84	145	24	6	9	41	.266	319	459	16	.980
1989—San Diego	Nat.	2B	158	623	82	184	27	1	7	56	.295	341	472	*28	.967
Major League Totals—2 Years			301	1168	166	329	51	7	16	97	.282	660	931	44	.973

Signed as free agent by San Diego Padres' organization, February 16, 1985.

❉ SANTOS ALOMAR JR. (VELAZQUEZ)
(Sandy)

Born June 18, 1966, at Salinas, Puerto Rico.
Height, 6.05. Weight, 200.
Throws and bats righthanded.
Son of Sandy Alomar, Sr., infielder with Milwaukee-Atlanta Braves, New York Mets, Chicago White Sox, California Angels, New York Yankees and Texas Rangers, 1964 through 1978; minor league instructor, San Diego Padres' organization, 1985; and coach with San Diego Padres since 1986; and brother of Roberto Alomar, second baseman with San Diego Padres.

Led Pacific Coast League catchers in putouts with 573 in 1988 and 702 in 1989.
Led Pacific Coast League catchers in total chances with 633 in 1988 and 761 in 1989.
Led Northwest League catchers in putouts with 421 in 1984.
Named Minor League Player of the Year by THE SPORTING NEWS, 1989.
Named Minor League Co-Player of the Year by THE SPORTING NEWS, 1988.
Named Pacific Coast League Player of the Year, 1988 and 1989.

Year Club	League	Pos.	G.	AB.	R.	H.	2B.	3B.	HR.	RBI.	B.A.	PO.	A.	E.	F.A.
1984—Spokane†	N'west	*C-1B	59	219	13	47	5	0	0	21	.215	465	51	8	*.985
1985—Charleston†	S. Atl.	C-OF	100	352	38	73	7	0	3	43	.207	779	75	18	.979
1986—Beaumont†	Texas	C	100	346	36	83	15	1	4	27	.240	505	60	*18	.969
1987—Wichita	Texas	C	103	375	50	115	19	1	8	65	.307	*606	50	*15	.978
1988—Las Vegas	P. C.	C-OF	93	337	59	100	9	5	16	71	.297	574	46	*14	.978
1988—San Diego	Nat.	PH	1	1	0	0	0	0	0	0	.000	0	0	0	.000
1989—Las Vegas	P. C.	C-OF	131	*523	88	160	33	8	13	101	.306	706	47	12	.984
1989—San Diego‡	Nat.	C	7	19	1	4	1	0	1	6	.211	33	1	0	1.000
Major League Totals—2 Years			8	20	1	4	1	0	1	6	.200	33	1	0	1.000

Signed as free agent by San Diego Padres' organization, October 21, 1983.
†Batted left and righthanded.
‡Traded with Outfielder Chris James and Third Baseman Carlos Baerga to Cleveland Indians for Outfielder Joe Carter, December 6, 1989.

MOISES ALOU

Born July 3, 1966, at Atlanta, Ga.
Height, 6.03. Weight, 185.
Throws and bats righthanded.
Attended Canada College, Redwood City, Calif.
Son of Felipe Alou, outfielder with San Francisco, Milwaukee-Atlanta Braves, Oakland, New York Yankees, Montreal and Milwaukee Brewers, 1958 through 1974; coach with Montreal Expos, 1979, 1980 and 1984; and minor league manager in Montreal Expos' organization, 1977, 1978, 1981 through 1983 and since 1985; Nephew of Jesus Alou, outfielder with San Francisco, Houston, Oakland and New York Yankees, 1963 through 1975, 1978 and 1979, and scout with Montreal Expos since 1983; Nephew of Matty Alou, outfielder with San Francisco, Pittsburgh, St. Louis, Oakland, New York Yankees and San Diego, 1960 through 1974; and brother of Jose Alou, outfielder in Montreal Expos' organization.

Year Club	League	Pos.	G.	AB.	R.	H.	2B.	3B.	HR.	RBI.	B.A.	PO.	A.	E.	F.A.
1986—Watertown	NYP	OF	69	254	30	60	9	*8	6	35	.236	134	6	7	.952
1987—Macon	S. Atl.	OF	4	8	1	1	0	0	0	0	.125	6	0	0	1.000
1987—Watertown	NYP	OF	39	117	20	25	6	2	4	8	.214	43	1	2	.957
1988—Augusta	S. Atl.	OF	105	358	58	112	23	5	7	62	.313	220	10	9	.962
1989—Salem	Carol.	OF	86	321	50	97	29	2	14	53	.302	166	12	10	.947
1989—Harrisburg	East.	OF	54	205	36	60	5	2	3	19	.293	89	1	2	.978

Selected by Pittsburgh Pirates' organization in 1st round (second player selected) of free agent draft, January 14, 1986.

JOSE LINO ALVAREZ

Born April 12, 1956, at Tampa, Fla.
Height, 5.11. Weight, 175.
Throws and bats righthanded.
Attended Hillsborough Junior College, Tampa, Fla., and
University of Southwestern Louisiana, Lafayette, La.

Major League saves: 1988 (3), 1989 (2). Total—5.
Tied for International League lead in shutouts with 2 in 1987.

Year Club	League	G.	IP.	W.	L.	Pct.	H.	R.	ER.	SO.	BB.	ERA.
1978—Kingsport	Ap'lachian	8	54	3	3	.500	38	15	8	45	22	1.33
1978—Greenwood	W. Carolina	7	34	3	1	.750	25	15	13	28	22	3.44
1979—Savannah	Southern	29	186	11	11	.500	165	87	62	120	73	3.00
1980—Savannah†	Southern	12	31	2	2	.500	15	5	4	35	11	1.16
1980—Bradenton	Gulf Coast	4	21	1	0	1.000	16	4	3	16	7	1.29
1980—Durham	Carolina	2	18	2	0	1.000	14	6	4	12	5	2.00
1981—Richmond	Int'national	39	71	7	5	.583	51	29	17	61	31	2.15
1981—Atlanta	National	1	2	0	0	.000	0	0	0	2	0	0.00
1982—Richmond	Int'national	36	111	5	5	.500	111	54	49	91	50	3.97
1982—Atlanta	National	7	7⅔	0	0	.000	8	4	4	6	2	4.70
1983—Richmond‡§	Int'national	33	81⅔	8	2	.800	67	50	48	61	53	5.29
1984—Tucson x	P. Coast	33	87	4	3	.571	91	56	52	69	48	5.38
1985—Memphis y-Jacksonville z	Southern	23	101	3	7	.300	90	59	51	78	63	4.54
1986—Greenville	Southern	36	149⅔	11	6	.647	123	70	59	133	63	3.55
1986—Richmond	Int'national	5	9⅓	0	0	.000	9	5	3	6	4	2.89
1987—Greenville	Southern	9	21⅓	1	0	1.000	14	2	2	20	8	0.84
1987—Richmond	Int'national	22	145	9	●13	.409	142	80	70	108	53	4.34
1988—Richmond	Int'national	10	14⅓	2	1	.667	13	2	2	10	6	1.26
1988—Atlanta	National	60	102⅓	5	6	.455	88	34	34	81	53	2.99
1989—Atlanta ab	National	30	50⅓	3	3	.500	44	18	16	45	24	2.86
Major League Totals—4 Years		98	162⅓	8	9	.471	140	56	54	134	79	2.99

Selected by Atlanta Braves' organization in 8th round of free-agent draft, June 6, 1978.
†On disabled list, April 11 to June 19, 1980.
‡On disabled list, July 10 to August 3, 1983.
§Traded to Houston Astros' organization for Pitcher Ron Meridith, February 16, 1984.
xGranted free agency, October 15, 1984; signed by Memphis (Kansas City Royals' organization), May 6, 1985.
yReleased, July 5, 1985; signed by Jacksonville (Montreal Expos' organization), July 19, 1985.
zReleased, March 31, 1986; signed by Greenville (Atlanta Braves' organization), April 4, 1986.
aOn disabled list, June 25, 1989 through remainder of season.
bDrafted by San Francisco Giants, December 4, 1989.

✴ WILSON E. ALVAREZ

Born March 24, 1970, at Maracaibo, Venezuela.
Height, 6.01. Weight, 175.
Throws and bats lefthanded.

Tied for Gulf Coast League lead in home runs allowed with 6 in 1987.

Year Club	League	G.	IP.	W.	L.	Pct.	H.	R.	ER.	SO.	BB.	ERA.
1987—Gastonia	S. Atlantic	8	32	1	5	.167	39	24	23	19	23	6.47
1987—Sarasota Rangers	Gulf Coast	10	44⅔	2	5	.286	41	29	26	46	21	5.24
1988—Gastonia	S. Atlantic	23	127	4	11	.267	113	63	42	134	49	2.98
1988—Oklahoma City	Am. Assoc.	5	16⅔	1	1	.500	17	8	7	9	6	3.78
1989—Tulsa	Texas	7	48	2	2	.500	40	14	11	29	16	2.06
1989—Texas†	American	1	0	0	1	.000	3	3	3	0	2	....
1989—Birmingham	Southern	6	35⅔	2	1	.667	32	12	12	18	16	3.03
Major League Totals—1 Year		1	0	0	1	.000	3	3	3	0	2	....

Signed as free agent by Texas Rangers' organization, September 23, 1986.
†Traded with Infielder Scott Fletcher and Outfielder Sammy Sosa to Chicago White Sox for Outfielder Harold Baines and Infielder Fred Manrique, July 29, 1989.

LARRY EUGENE ANDERSEN

Born May 6, 1953, at Portland, Ore.
Height, 6.03. Weight, 205.
Throws and bats righthanded.
Attended Bellevue Community College, Bellevue, Wash.

Pitched 6-0 no-hit victory against Victoria, June 1, 1974.
Major League saves: 1981 (5), 1982 (1), 1984 (4), 1985 (3), 1986 (1), 1987 (5), 1988 (5), 1989 (3). Total—27.
Led Pacific Coast League in saves with 25 in 1978 and 22 in 1983.
Led American Association in balks with 4 in 1975.

Year Club	League	G.	IP.	W.	L.	Pct.	H.	R.	ER.	SO.	BB.	ERA.
1971—Reno	California	7	24	1	0	1.000	37	20	18	10	9	6.75
1971—Sarasota Indians	Gulf Coast	4	15	0	3	.000	15	7	5	10	7	3.00
1972—Reno	California	27	124	4	14	.222	166	102	90	79	57	6.53
1973—Reno	California	29	164	10	8	.556	173	91	72	115	67	3.95
1974—San Antonio	Texas	25	169	10	6	.625	176	84	72	64	51	3.83
1975—Oklahoma City	Am. Assoc.	25	156	10	11	.476	179	87	73	64	52	4.21
1975—Cleveland	American	3	6	0	0	.000	4	3	3	4	2	4.50
1976—Toledo	Int'national	6	23	0	2	.000	47	33	33	8	6	12.91
1976—Williamsport	Eastern	21	133	9	6	.600	117	47	40	74	34	2.71

Year Club	League	G.	IP.	W.	L.	Pct.	H.	R.	ER.	SO.	BB.	ERA.
1977—Toledo†	Int'national	45	65	5	6	.455	52	20	14	40	37	1.94
1977—Cleveland	American	11	14	0	1	.000	10	7	5	8	9	3.21
1978—Portland	P. Coast	57	99	10	7	.588	92	42	38	65	45	3.45
1979—Tacoma	P. Coast	27	112	10	6	.625	124	59	50	52	32	4.02
1979—Cleveland‡	American	8	17	0	0	.000	25	14	14	7	4	7.41
1980—Portland§	P. Coast	52	93	5	7	.417	78	24	18	65	16	1.74
1981—Seattle	American	41	68	3	3	.500	57	27	20	40	18	2.65
1982—Seattle x	American	40	79⅔	0	0	.000	100	56	53	32	23	5.99
1982—Salt Lake City y	P. Coast	5	6⅔	1	0	1.000	2	0	0	8	3	0.00
1983—Portland	P. Coast	52	70⅓	7	8	.467	63	35	16	64	30	2.05
1983—Philadelphia	National	17	26⅓	1	0	1.000	19	7	7	14	9	2.39
1984—Philadelphia	National	64	90⅔	3	7	.300	85	32	24	54	25	2.38
1985—Philadelphia	National	57	73	3	3	.500	78	41	35	50	26	4.32
1986—Philadelphia z-Houston a	National	48	77⅓	2	1	.667	83	30	26	42	26	3.03
1987—Houston b	National	67	101⅔	9	5	.643	95	46	39	94	41	3.45
1988—Houston c	National	53	82⅔	2	4	.333	82	29	27	66	20	2.94
1989—Houston d	National	60	87⅔	4	4	.500	63	19	15	85	24	1.54
American League Totals—5 Years		103	184⅔	3	4	.429	196	107	95	91	56	4.63
National League Totals—7 Years		366	539⅓	24	24	.500	505	204	173	405	171	2.89
Major League Totals—12 Years		469	724	27	28	.491	701	311	268	496	227	3.33

Selected by Cleveland Indians' organization in 7th round of free-agent draft, June 8, 1971.
†Appeared as first baseman with no chances.
‡Traded to Pittsburgh Pirates for Outfielder Larry Littleton and Pitcher John Burden, December 21, 1979.
§Traded to Seattle Mariners, October 29, 1980, completing deal in which Seattle traded Pitcher Odell Jones to Pittsburgh Pirates for a player to be named later, April 1, 1980.
xOn disabled list, August 11 to September 1, 1982; included rehabilitation disability assignment to Salt Lake City, August 11 to August 31, 1982.
yLoaned to Portland (Philadelphia Phillies' organization), April 1, 1983; sold to Philadelphia Phillies, July 29, 1983.
zReleased, May 13, 1986; signed by Houston Astros, May 16, 1986.
aGranted free agency, November 12, 1986; re-signed by Astros, December 21, 1986.
bGranted free agency, November 9, 1987; re-signed by Astros, January 8, 1988.
cOn disabled list, April 26 to May 11, 1988.
dOn disabled list, April 25 to May 10 and August 20 to September 4, 1980.

CHAMPIONSHIP SERIES RECORD

Year Club	League	G.	IP.	W.	L.	Pct.	H.	R.	ER.	SO.	BB.	ERA.
1986—Houston	National	2	5	0	0	.000	1	0	0	3	2	0.00

WORLD SERIES RECORD

Year Club	League	G.	IP.	W.	L.	Pct.	H.	R.	ER.	SO.	BB.	ERA.
1983—Philadelphia	National	2	4	0	0	.000	4	1	1	1	0	2.25

ALLAN LEE ANDERSON

Born January 7, 1964, at Lancaster, O.
Height, 6.00. Weight, 194.
Throws and bats lefthanded.
Led California League in shutouts with 5 in 1984.

Year Club	League	G.	IP.	W.	L.	Pct.	H.	R.	ER.	SO.	BB.	ERA.
1983—Wisconsin Rapids	Midwest	7	30⅓	0	4	.000	36	28	23	46	17	6.82
1983—Elizabethton	Ap'lachian	6	12⅔	1	3	.250	17	12	12	12	7	8.53
1984—Visalia	California	26	188⅔	12	7	.632	152	80	60	151	105	2.86
1985—Toledo	Int'national	27	176	7	11	.389	176	81	67	94	79	3.43
1986—Toledo	Int'national	11	67	2	5	.286	78	39	34	37	31	4.57
1986—Minnesota†	American	21	84⅓	3	6	.333	106	54	52	51	30	5.55
1987—Portland	P. Coast	19	98	4	8	.333	127	77	61	45	49	5.60
1987—Minnesota	American	4	12⅓	1	0	1.000	20	15	15	3	10	10.95
1988—Portland	P. Coast	3	14⅓	1	1	.500	11	4	2	9	5	1.26
1988—Minnesota	American	30	202⅓	16	9	.640	199	70	55	83	37	★2.45
1989—Minnesota	American	33	196⅔	17	10	.630	214	97	83	69	53	3.80
Major League Totals—4 Years		88	495⅔	37	25	.597	539	236	205	206	130	3.72

Selected by Minnesota Twins' organization in 2nd round of free-agent draft, June 7, 1982.
†Appeared in one game as a pinch-runner.

BRADY KEVIN ANDERSON

Born January 18, 1964, at Silver Spring, Md.
Height, 6.01. Weight, 186.
Throws and bats lefthanded.
Attended University of California, Irvine, Calif.
Major League stolen bases: 1988 (10), 1989 (16). Total—26.
Led New York-Pennsylvania League in bases on balls received with 67 in 1985.
Led Florida State League in bases on balls received with 107 in 1986.

Year Club	League	Pos.	G.	AB.	R.	H.	2B.	3B.	HR.	RBI.	B.A.	PO.	A.	E.	F.A.
1985—Elmira	NYP	OF	71	215	36	55	7	•6	5	21	.256	119	5	3	.976
1986—Winter Haven	Fla. St.	OF	126	417	86	133	19	11	12	87	.319	280	5	1	★.997
1987—New Britain	East.	OF	52	170	30	50	4	3	6	35	.294	127	2	2	.985
1987—Pawtucket	Int.	OF	23	79	18	30	4	0	2	8	.380	48	1	0	1.000

— 14 —

Year	Club	League	Pos.	G.	AB.	R.	H.	2B.	3B.	HR.	RBI.	B.A.	PO.	A.	E.	F.A.
1988—Bos.†-Balt.	Amer.		OF	94	325	31	69	13	4	1	21	.212	243	4	4	.984
1988—Pawtucket	Int.		OF	49	167	27	48	6	1	4	19	.287	115	4	2	.983
1989—Baltimore	Amer.		OF	94	266	44	55	12	2	4	16	.207	191	3	3	.985
1989—Rochester	Int.		OF	21	70	14	14	1	2	1	8	.200	1	0	0	1.000
Major League Totals—2 Years				188	591	75	124	25	6	5	37	.210	434	7	7	.984

Selected by Boston Red Sox' organization in 10th round of free-agent draft, June 3, 1985.

†Traded with Pitcher Curt Schilling to Baltimore Orioles for Pitcher Mike Boddicker, July 29, 1988.

DAVID CARTER ANDERSON
(Dave)

Born August 1, 1960, at Louisville, Ky.
Height, 6.02. Weight, 191.
Throws and bats righthanded.
Attended Memphis State University, Memphis, Tenn.

Major League stolen bases: 1983 (6), 1984 (15), 1985 (5), 1986 (5), 1987 (9), 1988 (4), 1989 (2). Total—46.
Led Pacific Coast League shortstops in double plays with 81 in 1982.

Year	Club	League	Pos.	G.	AB.	R.	H.	2B.	3B.	HR.	RBI.	B.A.	PO.	A.	E.	F.A.
1981—Vero Beach	Fla. St.		SS	65	200	44	54	8	1	0	18	.270	109	218	23	.934
1982—Albuquerque	P. C.		SS	132	507	100	174	19	7	5	76	.343	223	397	★34	.948
1983—Albuquerque	P. C.		SS	9	27	10	11	1	1	0	3	.407	17	26	1	.977
1983—Los Angeles	Nat.		SS-3B	61	115	12	19	4	2	1	2	.165	56	100	5	.969
1984—Los Angeles	Nat.		SS-3B	121	374	51	94	16	2	3	34	.251	176	359	19	.966
1985—Los Angeles†	Nat.		3B-SS-2B	77	221	24	44	6	0	4	18	.199	61	187	9	.965
1985—Albuquerque	P. C.		SS-3B-2B	28	97	23	28	7	0	3	16	.289	29	62	11	.892
1986—Los Angeles‡	Nat.		3B-SS-2B	92	216	31	53	9	0	1	15	.245	77	159	11	.955
1987—Los Angeles§	Nat.		SS-3B-2B	108	265	32	62	12	3	1	13	.234	103	207	7	.978
1988—Los Angeles	Nat.		SS-3B-2B	116	285	31	71	10	2	2	20	.249	139	244	5	.987
1989—Los Angeles x	Nat.		SS-3B-2B	87	140	15	32	2	0	1	14	.229	73	1	.993
Major League Totals—7 Years				662	1616	196	375	59	9	13	116	.232	673	1329	57	.972

Selected by Los Angeles Dodgers' organization in 1st round (22nd player selected) of free-agent draft, June 8, 1981.

†On disabled list, April 29 to June 2 and July 31 to September 1, 1985; included rehabilitation disability assignment to Albuquerque, May 17 to June 1 and August 17 to August 31, 1985.

‡On disabled list, June 22 to August 19, 1986.

§On disabled list, August 11 to September 2, 1987.

xGranted free agency, November 13, 1989; signed by San Francisco Giants, November 29, 1989.

CHAMPIONSHIP SERIES RECORD

Year	Club	League	Pos.	G.	AB.	R.	H.	2B.	3B.	HR.	RBI.	B.A.	PO.	A.	E.	F.A.
1985—Los Angeles	Nat.		PR-SS-3B	4	5	1	0	0	0	0	0	.000	3	4	0	1.000

WORLD SERIES RECORD

Year	Club	League	Pos.	G.	AB.	R.	H.	2B.	3B.	HR.	RBI.	B.A.	PO.	A.	E.	F.A.
1988—Los Angeles	Nat.		PH-DH	1	1	0	0	0	0	0	0	.000	0	0	0	.000

KENT McKAY ANDERSON

Born August 12, 1963, at Florence, S.C.
Height, 6.01. Weight, 180.
Throws and bats righthanded.
Attended University of South Carolina, Columbia, S.C.

Major League stolen bases: 1989 (1).

Year	Club	League	Pos.	G.	AB.	R.	H.	2B.	3B.	HR.	RBI.	B.A.	PO.	A.	E.	F.A.
1984—Peoria	Midw.		SS	67	223	24	50	9	1	1	16	.224	124	189	18	.946
1985—Redwood	Calif.		SS	117	420	53	105	17	1	1	47	.250	182	316	29	★.945
1986—Palm Springs†	Calif.		SS-OF-3B	69	240	37	67	14	0	2	35	.279	131	166	19	.940
1987—Edmonton	P. C.		SS	57	181	27	42	4	5	3	20	.232	112	154	9	.967
1988—Edmonton	P. C.		SS	113	374	50	94	22	3	2	39	.251	175	283	30	.939
1989—Edmonton	P. C.		SS	4	12	3	4	0	0	0	1	.333	7	17	1	.960
1989—California	Amer.		S-2-3-O	86	223	27	51	6	1	0	17	.229	102	233	10	.971
Major League Totals—1 Year				86	223	27	51	6	1	0	17	.229	102	233	10	.971

Selected by California Angels' organization in 4th round of free-agent draft, June 4, 1984.

†On disabled list, May 12 to June 23, 1986.

ERIC TODD ANTHONY

Born November 8, 1967, at San Diego, Calif.
Height, 6.02. Weight, 195.
Throws and bats lefthanded.

Led Southern League in slugging percentage with .558 in 1989.
Led South Atlantic League in slugging percentage with .558 in 1988.
Led Gulf Coast League in total bases with 110 in 1987.
Named Southern League Most Valuable Player, 1989.

Year	Club	League	Pos.	G.	AB.	R.	H.	2B.	3B.	HR.	RBI.	B.A.	PO.	A.	E.	F.A.
1986—Sarasota Astros	Gulf C.		OF	13	12	2	3	0	0	0	0	.250	2	1	0	1.000
1987—Sarasota Astros	Gulf C.		OF	60	216	38	57	11	6	★10	★46	.264	100	●11	5	.957
1988—Asheville	S. Atl.		OF	115	439	73	120	★36	1	★29	89	.273	152	8	14	.920

Year Club League	Pos.	G.	AB.	R.	H.	2B.	3B.	HR.	RBI.	B.A.	PO.	A.	E.	F.A.
1989—Columbus............ South.	OF	107	403	67	121	16	2	*28	79	.300	178	17	8	.961
1989—Houston............... Nat.	OF	25	61	7	11	2	0	4	7	.180	34	1	0	1.000
1989—Tucson................. P. C.	OF	12	46	10	10	3	0	3	11	.217	21	0	0	1.000
Major League Totals—1 Year..............		25	61	7	11	2	0	4	7	.180	34	1	0	1.000

Selected by Houston Astros' organization in 34th round of free-agent draft, June 2, 1986.

ROBERT KEVIN APPIER
(Known by middle name.)

Born December 6, 1967, at Lancaster, Calif.
Height, 6.02. Weight, 180.
Throws and bats righthanded.
Attended Fresno State University, Fresno, Calif.,
and Antelope Valley College, Lancaster, Calif.
Tied for Northwest League lead in games started by pitchers with 15 in 1987.

Year Club League	G.	IP.	W.	L.	Pct.	H.	R.	ER.	SO.	BB.	ERA.
1987—Eugene............... Northwest	15	77	5	2	.714	81	43	26	72	29	3.04
1988—Baseball City .... Florida St.	24	147⅓	10	9	.526	134	58	45	112	39	2.75
1988—Memphis.................. Southern	3	19⅔	2	0	1.000	11	5	4	18	7	1.83
1989—Omaha................. Am. Assoc.	22	139	8	8	.500	141	70	61	109	42	3.95
1989—Kansas City.................... American	6	21⅔	1	4	.200	34	22	22	10	12	9.14
Major League Totals—1 Year...............	6	21⅔	1	4	.200	34	22	22	10	12	9.14

Selected by Kansas City Royals' organization in 1st round (ninth player selected) of free-agent draft, June 2, 1987.

LUIS ANTONIO AQUINO (COLON)
Name pronounced A-Keno.

Born May 19, 1965, at Rio Piedras, Puerto Rico.
Height, 6.01. Weight, 175.
Throws and bats righthanded.
Pitched 2-0 no-hit victory against Columbus, June 20, 1988.
Led Southern League in saves with 20 and tied for lead in games finished in relief with 42 in 1985.
Led Carolina League in games finished in relief with 42 in 1984.

Year Club League	G.	IP.	W.	L.	Pct.	H.	R.	ER.	SO.	BB.	ERA.
1982—Bradenton Blue Jays.................. Gulf Coast	13	73⅓	4	7	.364	60	33	27	52	17	3.31
1983—Florence.............. S. Atlantic	29	133⅔	7	9	.438	128	91	78	104	61	5.25
1984—Kinston.............. Carolina	*53	70	5	6	.455	50	21	21	78	37	2.70
1984—Knoxville.............. Southern	3	4	0	0	.000	3	4	4	7	3	9.00
1985—Knoxville.............. Southern	50	83	5	7	.417	58	29	24	82	32	2.60
1986—Syracuse.............. Int'national	43	84⅓	3	7	.300	70	30	27	60	34	2.88
1986—Toronto.............. American	7	11⅓	1	1	.500	14	8	8	5	3	6.35
1987—Syracuse†.............. Int'national	26	84⅔	6	7	.462	75	46	45	68	51	4.78
1987—Omaha.............. Am. Assoc.	14	50⅔	3	2	.600	42	15	13	29	16	2.31
1988—Omaha.............. Am. Assoc.	25	129⅓	8	3	.727	106	43	41	93	50	2.85
1988—Kansas City.............. American	7	29	1	0	1.000	33	15	9	11	17	2.79
1989—Kansas City‡.............. American	34	141⅓	6	8	.429	148	62	55	68	35	3.50
Major League Totals—3 Years...........................	48	181⅔	8	9	.471	195	85	72	84	55	3.57

Signed as free agent by Toronto Blue Jays' organization, June 15, 1981.
†Traded to Kansas City Royals' organization for Outfielder Juan Beniquez, July 14, 1987.
‡On disabled list, May 31 to June 15, 1989.

ALEJANDRO ARIAS
(Alex)

Born November 20, 1967, at New York, N.Y.
Height, 6.03. Weight, 185.
Throws and bats righthanded.
Led Midwest League shortstops in total chances with 655 and double plays with 83 in 1989.

Year Club League	Pos.	G.	AB.	R.	H.	2B.	3B.	HR.	RBI.	B.A.	PO.	A.	E.	F.A.
1987—Wytheville............ Appal.	SS-3B-2B	61	233	41	69	7	0	0	24	.296	86	162	20	.925
1988—Charleston, W.Va. S. Atl.	SS-2B-3B	127	472	57	122	12	1	0	33	.258	184	396	32	.948
1989—Peoria.................... Midw.	SS	*136	506	74	140	10	*11	2	64	.277	*210	*408	37	.944

Selected by Chicago Cubs' organization in 3rd round of free-agent draft, June 2, 1987.

ANTONIO RAFAEL ARMAS (MACHADO)
(Tony)

Born July 2, 1953, at Anzoatequi, Venezuela.
Height, 6.01. Weight, 224.
Throws and bats righthanded.
Brother of Marcos Armas, first baseman in Oakland Athletics' organization.
Holds major league records for most putouts (11) and chances accepted by right fielder, game (12), June 12, 1982.
Shares major league records for most doubles, inning (2), July 8, 1988, fourth inning; fewest double plays by outfielder, season, for leader in most double plays (4), 1977.
Major League stolen bases: 1977 (1), 1978 (1), 1979 (1), 1980 (5), 1981 (5), 1982 (2), 1984 (1), 1987 (1), 1988 (1). Total—18.

Led American League in total bases with 339 in 1984.
Led American League batters in strikeouts with 115 in 1981 and 156 in 1984.
Tied for American League lead in grounding into double plays with 31 in 1983.
Tied for American League lead in double plays by outfielders with 4 in 1977.
Named American League Player of the Year by THE SPORTING NEWS, 1981.
Named outfielder on THE SPORTING NEWS American League All-Star Team, 1981 and 1984.
Named outfielder on THE SPORTING NEWS American League Silver Slugger team, 1984.

Year Club League	Pos.	G.	AB.	R.	H.	2B.	3B.	HR.	RBI.	B.A.	PO.	A.	E.	F.A.
1971—Monroe................. W. Car.	OF	31	88	7	20	3	0	1	10	.227	37	3	6	.870
1971—Bradenton Pir...... Gulf C.	OF	43	169	12	39	3	3	0	17	.231	★98	5	3	.972
1972—Gastonia .... W. Car.	OF	117	399	50	106	18	4	9	51	.266	165	7	8	.956
1973—Sherbrooke†......... East.	OF	84	302	46	91	15	5	11	45	.301	150	6	8	.951
1974—Thetford Mines.... East.	OF	★137	476	64	132	26	3	15	81	.277	★329	18	10	.972
1975—Charleston............ Int.	OF	128	450	65	135	28	4	12	72	.300	220	●14	3	.987
1976—Charleston............ Int.	OF-1B	114	409	62	96	24	1	21	67	.235	210	8	7	.969
1976—Pittsburgh‡ .... Nat.	OF	4	6	0	2	0	0	0	1	.333	3	0	0	1.000
1977—Oakland§.............. Amer.	OF-SS	118	363	26	87	8	2	13	53	.240	294	9	6	.981
1978—Oakland x .... Amer.	OF	91	239	17	51	6	1	2	13	.213	214	3	2	.991
1979—Oakland y .... Amer.	OF	80	278	29	69	9	3	11	34	.248	194	7	5	.976
1980—Oakland................ Amer.	OF	158	628	87	175	18	8	35	109	.279	374	17	10	.975
1981—Oakland................ Amer.	OF	●109	440	51	115	24	3	●22	76	.261	259	8	2	.993
1982—Oakland za .... Amer.	OF	138	536	58	125	19	2	28	89	.233	333	9	6	.983
1983—Boston................... Amer.	OF	145	574	77	125	23	2	36°	107	.218	326	5	5	.985
1984—Boston................... Amer.	OF	157	639	107	171	29	5	★43	★123	.268	329	4	9	.974
1985—Boston b .... Amer.	OF	103	385	50	102	17	5	23	64	.265	173	3	3	.983
1986—Boston cd.............. Amer.	OF	121	425	40	112	21	4	11	58	.264	247	4	8	.969
1987—Edmonton............. P. C.	OF	29	108	11	27	4	1	3	16	.250	60	1	0	1.000
1987—California............. Amer.	OF	28	81	8	16	3	1	3	9	.198	36	0	0	1.000
1988—California............. Amer.	OF	120	368	42	100	20	2	13	49	.272	212	5	3	.986
1989—California e .... Amer.	OF-1B	60	202	22	52	7	1	11	30	.257	101	5	2	.981
National League Totals—1 Year..............		4	6	0	2	0	0	0	1	.333	3	0	0	1.000
American League Totals—13 Years		1428	5158	614	1300	204	39	251	814	.252	3092	79	61	.981
Major League Totals—14 Years..............		1432	5164	614	1302	204	39	251	815	.252	3095	79	61	.981

Signed as free agent by Pittsburgh Pirates' organization, January 18, 1971.
†On disabled list, May 27 to July 12, 1973.
‡Traded with Pitchers Dave Giusti, Doc Medich, Doug Bair and Rick Langford and Outfielder Mitchell Page to Oakland A's for Infielders Tommy Helms and Phil Garner and Pitcher Chris Batton, March 15, 1977.
§On disabled list, August 5 to September 1, 1977.
xOn disabled list, April 28 to June 2, 1978.
yOn disabled list, April 15 to June 5, 1979.
zOn disabled list, May 13 to May 28, 1982.
aTraded with Catcher Jeff Newman to Boston Red Sox for Third Baseman Carney Lansford, Outfielder Garry Hancock and a player to be named later, December 6, 1982; Oakland A's acquired Pitcher Jerry King to complete deal, December 20, 1982.
bOn disabled list, June 17 to July 26, 1985.
cOn disabled list, July 12 to July 27, 1986.
dGranted free agency, November 12, 1986; signed by California Angels' organization, July 1, 1987.
eOn disabled list, April 10 to May 15 and May 16 to June 19, 1989.

DIVISION SERIES RECORD

Year Club League	Pos.	G.	AB.	R.	H.	2B.	3B.	HR.	RBI.	B.A.	PO.	A.	E.	F.A.
1981—Oakland................. Amer.	OF	3	11	1	6	2	0	0	3	.545	6	0	1	.857

CHAMPIONSHIP SERIES RECORD

Year Club League	Pos.	G.	AB.	R.	H.	2B.	3B.	HR.	RBI.	B.A.	PO.	A.	E.	F.A.
1981—Oakland................. Amer.	OF	3	12	0	2	0	0	0	0	.167	5	2	0	1.000
1986—Boston................... Amer.	OF	5	16	1	2	1	0	0	0	.125	12	0	0	1.000
Championship Series Totals—2 Years.....		8	28	1	4	1	0	0	0	.143	17	2	0	1.000

WORLD SERIES RECORD

Year Club League	Pos.	G.	AB.	R.	H.	2B.	3B.	HR.	RBI.	B.A.	PO.	A.	E.	F.A.
1986—Boston................... Amer.	PH	1	1	0	0	0	0	0	0	.000	0	0	0	.000

ALL-STAR GAME RECORD

Year League	Pos.	AB.	R.	H.	2B.	3B.	HR.	RBI.	B.A.	PO.	A.	E.	F.A.
1981—American	OF	1	0	0	0	0	0	0	.000	0	0	0	.000

Member of American League All-Star Team in 1984; did not play.

✈ JACK WILLIAM ARMSTRONG

Born March 7, 1965, at Englewood, N.J.
Height, 6.05. Weight, 220.
Throws and bats righthanded.
Attended Rider College, Lawrenceville, N.J., and received degree in economics
from University of Oklahoma, Norman, Okla., in 1987.

Pitched 4-0 no-hit victory against Indianapolis, August 7, 1988.
Led American Association in shutouts with 6 and complete games with 12 in 1989.

Year Club League	G.	IP.	W.	L.	Pct.	H.	R.	ER.	SO.	BB.	ERA.
1987—Billings .... Pioneer	5	20⅓	2	1	.667	16	7	6	29	12	2.66

Year Club	League	G.	IP.	W.	L.	Pct.	H.	R.	ER.	SO.	BB.	ERA.
1987—Vermont	Eastern	5	35⅔	1	2	.333	24	12	12	39	23	3.03
1988—Nashville	Am. Assoc.	17	120	5	5	.500	84	44	40	116	38	3.00
1988—Cincinnati	National	14	65⅓	4	7	.364	63	44	42	45	38	5.79
1989—Nashville	Am. Assoc.	25	182⅔	●13	9	.591	144	63	59	152	58	2.91
1989—Cincinnati	National	9	42⅔	2	3	.400	40	24	22	23	21	4.64
Major League Totals—2 Years		23	108	6	10	.375	103	68	64	68	59	5.33

Selected by San Francisco Giants' organization in 3rd round of free-agent draft, June 2, 1986.
Selected by Cincinnati Reds' organization in 1st round (18th player selected) of free-agent draft, June 2, 1987.

LARRY WAYNE ARNDT

Born February 25, 1963, at Fremont, O.
Height, 6.02. Weight, 200.
Throws and bats righthanded.
Attended Bowling Green State University, Bowling Green, O.
Led Pacific Coast League in sacrifice hits with 9 in 1988.
Led Pacific Coast League third basemen in errors with 29 in 1988.
Led Midwest League third basemen in fielding percentage with .938 in 1986.

Year Club	League	Pos.	G.	AB.	R.	H.	2B.	3B.	HR.	RBI.	B.A.	PO.	A.	E.	F.A.
1985—Medford	N'west	3-1-2-O	69	266	47	77	11	★6	6	48	.289	141	86	14	.942
1986—Madison	Midw.	3B-1B	125	445	70	125	20	1	16	65	.281	99	252	22	.941
1987—Huntsville	South.	3B-1B-2B	124	422	48	103	18	1	3	31	.244	134	232	30	.924
1988—Huntsville	South.	OF-3B-2B	19	75	13	26	6	1	1	8	.347	11	1	0	1.000
1988—Tacoma	P. C.	3B-1B-SS	102	326	45	89	10	0	3	37	.273	87	182	30	.900
1989—Tacoma	P. C.	3-2-S-1	130	489	62	137	23	4	2	50	.280	115	258	21	.947
1989—Oakland	Amer.	1B-3B	2	6	1	1	0	0	0	0	.167	8	2	0	1.000
Major League Totals—1 Year			2	6	1	1	0	0	0	0	.167	8	2	0	1.000

Selected by Oakland A's organization in 26th round of free-agent draft, June 3, 1985.

BRADLEY JAMES ARNSBERG
(Brad)

Born August 20, 1963, at Seattle, Wash.
Height, 6.04. Weight, 215.
Throws and bats righthanded.
Attended Merced College, Merced, Calif.
Brother of Tim Arnsberg, pitcher in Houston Astros' organization, 1985 through 1987.
Major League saves: 1989 (1).
Pitched 5-0 no-hit victory against Savannah, May 24, 1984.
Led International League in complete games with 9 and tied for lead in shutouts with 2 in 1987.
Led International League pitchers in games started with 28 and balks with 5 in 1986.
Tied for South Atlantic League lead in complete games with 10 and shutouts with 4 in 1984.
Named International League Pitcher of the Year, 1987.
Named Eastern League Pitcher of the Year, 1985.

Year Club	League	G.	IP.	W.	L.	Pct.	H.	R.	ER.	SO.	BB.	ERA.
1984—Greensboro	S. Atlantic	23	158⅔	12	5	.706	121	61	52	112	59	2.95
1985—Albany†	Eastern	20	141⅓	●14	2	★.875	105	34	25	82	35	★1.59
1986—Columbus	Int'national	28	★177⅓	8	●12	.400	168	★106	●83	96	53	4.21
1986—New York	American	2	8	0	0	.000	13	3	3	3	1	3.38
1987—Columbus	Int'national	19	144	12	5	.706	140	55	46	83	37	2.88
1987—New York‡§	American	6	19⅓	1	3	.250	22	12	12	14	13	5.59
1988—Texas x	American					(Did not play)						
1989—Texas	American	16	48	2	1	.667	45	27	22	26	22	4.13
1989—Oklahoma City	Am. Assoc.	18	115⅓	6	8	.429	117	58	52	61	34	4.06
Major League Totals—3 Years		24	75⅓	3	4	.429	80	42	37	43	36	4.42

Selected by Cleveland Indians' organization in 19th round of free-agent draft, June 8, 1981.
Selected by St. Louis Cardinals' organization in secondary phase of free-agent draft, January 12, 1982.
Selected by Baltimore Orioles' organization in secondary phase of free-agent draft, June 7, 1982.
Selected by California Angels' organization in secondary phase of free-agent draft, January 11, 1983.
Selected by New York Yankees' organization in secondary phase of free-agent draft, June 6, 1983.
†On disabled list, May 12 to May 24 and June 23 to July 22, 1985.
‡On disabled list, August 23 to September 14, 1987.
§Traded to Texas Rangers, November 10, 1987, completing deal in which Texas traded Catcher Don Slaught to New York Yankees for a player to be named later, November 2, 1987.
xOn disabled list, March 29 to September 1, 1988.

ALAN DEAN ASHBY

Born July 8, 1951, at Long Beach, Calif.
Height, 6.02. Weight, 195.
Throws right and bats left and righthanded.
Attended Los Angeles Harbor Junior College, Wilmington, Calif.
Shares National League record for most no-hit games caught, lifetime (3).
Major League stolen bases: 1975 (3), 1978 (1), 1982 (2), 1986 (1). Total—7.
Led National League in passed balls with 14 in 1980.
Led California League catchers in double plays with 12 in 1971.

Year Club	League	Pos.	G.	AB.	R.	H.	2B.	3B.	HR.	RBI.	B.A.	PO.	A.	E.	F.A.
1969—Sarasota Indians	Gulf C.	C	48	117	10	28	3	1	0	14	.239	219	20	2	★.992
1970—Reno†	Calif.	C	40	121	15	23	5	1	3	18	.190	321	27	7	.980

Year	Club	League	Pos.	G.	AB.	R.	H.	2B.	3B.	HR.	RBI.	B.A.	PO.	A.	E.	F.A.
1971—Jacksonville		South.	C	13	35	4	7	2	0	0	8	.200	76	6	1	.988
1971—Reno‡		Calif.	C-3B	77	239	52	70	14	1	18	60	.293	492	59	10	.982
1972—Portland		P. C.	C	95	291	33	65	9	2	9	28	.223	601	50	8	.988
1973—Ok.C.§-Evan.		A. A.	C-OF	41	124	20	28	8	0	3	16	.226	253	26	2	.993
1973—Cleveland		Amer.	C	11	29	4	5	1	0	1	3	.172	45	0	1	.978
1974—Oklahoma City		A. A	C	66	211	26	60	19	1	2	24	.284	405	33	8	.982
1974—Cleveland		Amer.	C	10	7	1	1	0	0	0	0	.143	12	0	0	1.000
1975—Cleveland		Amer.	C-1B-3B	90	254	32	57	10	1	5	32	.224	450	43	6	.988
1976—Cleveland xy		Amer.	C-1B-3B	89	247	26	59	5	1	4	32	.239	476	52	7	.987
1977—Toronto		Amer.	C	124	396	25	83	16	3	2	29	.210	619	71	11	.984
1978—Toronto z		Amer.	C	81	264	27	69	15	0	9	29	.261	399	38	6	.986
1979—Houston a		Nat.	C	108	336	25	68	15	2	2	35	.202	548	57	8	.987
1980—Houston		Nat.	C	116	352	30	90	19	2	3	48	.256	608	60	6	.991
1981—Houston		Nat.	C	83	255	20	69	13	0	4	33	.271	434	58	9	.982
1982—Houston b		Nat.	C	100	339	40	87	14	2	12	49	.257	530	55	14	.977
1983—Houston c		Nat.	C	87	275	31	63	18	1	8	34	.229	435	56	13	.974
1984—Houston d		Nat.	C	66	191	16	50	7	0	4	27	.262	303	42	5	.986
1985—Houston e		Nat.	C	65	189	20	53	8	0	8	25	.280	312	37	8	.978
1986—Houston f		Nat.	C	120	315	24	81	15	0	7	38	.257	632	43	10	.985
1987—Houston		Nat.	C	125	386	53	111	16	0	14	63	.288	778	46	6	*.993
1988—Houston g		Nat.	C	73	227	19	54	10	0	7	33	.238	414	23	4	.991
1988—Tucson		P. C.	C	2	4	1	0	0	0	0	0	.000	6	2	0	1.000
1989—Houston h		Nat.	C	22	61	4	10	1	1	0	3	.164	101	4	0	1.000
American League Totals—6 Years				405	1197	115	274	47	5	21	125	.229	2001	204	31	.986
National League Totals—11 Years				965	2926	282	736	136	8	69	388	.252	5095	481	83	.985
Major League Totals—17 Years				1370	4123	397	1010	183	13	90	513	.245	7096	685	114	.986

Selected by Cleveland Indians' organization in 3rd round of free-agent draft, June 5, 1969.

†On military list, January 1 to May 23, 1970.

‡On temporary inactive list, August 27 to September 13, 1971.

§Loaned to Evansville (Milwaukee Brewers' organization), May 22, 1973; returned, July 2, 1973.

xOn disabled list, August 9, 1976 through remainder of season.

yTraded with Outfielder-First Baseman Doug Howard to Toronto Blue Jays for Pitcher Al Fitzmorris, November 5, 1976.

zTraded to Houston Astros for Pitcher Mark Lemongello, Outfielder Joe Cannon and Shortstop Pedro Hernandez, November 27, 1978.

aOn disabled list, August 30 to September 17, 1979.

bGranted free agency, November 10, 1982; re-signed by Astros, December 21, 1982.

cOn disabled list, June 27 to July 24, 1983.

dOn disabled list, April 25 to May 31, 1984.

eOn disabled list, July 29 to September 7, 1985.

fGranted free agency, November 12, 1986; re-signed by Astros, December 19, 1986.

gOn disabled list, June 22 to August 30, 1988; included rehabilitation disability assignment to Tucson, August 28 and 29, 1988.

hReleased, May 11, 1989.

DIVISION SERIES RECORD

Year	Club	League	Pos.	G.	AB.	R.	H.	2B.	3B.	HR.	RBI.	B.A.	PO.	A.	E.	F.A.
1981—Houston		Nat.	C	3	9	1	1	0	0	1	2	.111	24	2	0	1.000

CHAMPIONSHIP SERIES RECORD

Year	Club	League	Pos.	G.	AB.	R.	H.	2B.	3B.	HR.	RBI.	B.A.	PO.	A.	E.	F.A.
1980—Houston		Nat.	C-PH	2	8	0	1	0	0	0	1	.125	11	2	0	1.000
1986—Houston		Nat.	C	6	23	2	3	1	0	1	2	.130	59	1	0	1.000
Championship Series Totals—2 Years				8	31	2	4	1	0	1	3	.129	70	3	0	1.000

ANDREW JASON ASHBY
(Andy)

Born July 11, 1967, at Kansas City, Mo.
Height, 6.05. Weight, 180.
Throws and bats righthanded.
Attended Crowder College, Neosho, Mo.

Year	Club	League	G.	IP.	W.	L.	Pct.	H.	R.	ER.	SO.	BB.	ERA.
1986—Bend		Northwest	16	60	1	2	.333	56	40	33	45	34	4.95
1987—Spartanburg		S. Atlantic	13	64⅓	4	6	.400	73	45	40	52	38	5.60
1987—Utica		NYP	13	60	3	7	.300	56	38	27	51	36	4.05
1988—Spartanburg†		S. Atlantic	3	16⅔	1	1	.500	13	7	5	16	7	2.70
1988—Batavia		NYP	6	44⅔	3	1	.750	25	11	8	32	16	1.61
1989—Spartanburg		S. Atlantic	17	106⅔	5	9	.357	95	48	34	100	49	2.87
1989—Clearwater‡		Florida St.	6	43⅔	1	4	.200	28	9	6	44	21	1.24

Signed as free agent by Philadelphia Phillies' organization, May 4, 1986.

†On disabled list, April 7 to July 10, 1988.

‡On disabled list, April 6 to April 26, 1989.

PAUL ANDRE ASSENMACHER

Born December 10, 1960, at Detroit, Mich.
Height, 6.03. Weight, 200.
Throws and bats lefthanded.
Received degree in business administration from Aquinas College, Grand Rapids, Mich.

Shares major league record for most strikeouts, inning (4), August 22, 1989, fifth inning.
Major League saves: 1986 (7), 1987 (2), 1988 (5). Total—14.

Year Club	League	G.	IP.	W.	L.	Pct.	H.	R.	ER.	SO.	BB.	ERA.
1983—Bradenton Braves	Gulf Coast	10	36⅔	1	0	1.000	35	14	9	44	4	2.21
1984—Durham	Carolina	26	147⅓	6	11	.353	153	78	70	147	52	4.28
1985—Durham	Carolina	14	38⅓	3	2	.600	38	16	14	36	13	3.29
1985—Greenville	Southern	29	52⅔	6	0	1.000	47	16	15	59	11	2.56
1986—Atlanta	National	61	68⅓	7	3	.700	61	23	19	56	26	2.50
1987—Atlanta†	National	52	54⅔	1	1	.500	58	41	31	39	24	5.10
1987—Richmond	Int'national	4	24⅔	1	2	.333	30	11	10	21	8	3.65
1988—Atlanta‡	National	64	79½	8	7	.533	72	28	27	71	32	3.06
1989—Atlanta§-Chicago	National	63	76⅔	3	4	.429	74	37	34	79	28	3.99
Major League Totals—4 Years		240	279	19	15	.559	265	129	111	245	110	3.58

Signed as free agent by Atlanta Braves' organization, July 10, 1983.
†On disabled list, April 29 to May 9, 1987.
‡On disabled list, August 10 to August 25, 1988.
§Traded to Chicago Cubs for two players to be named later, August 24, 1989; Atlanta Braves acquired Catcher Kelly Mann and Pitcher Pat Gomez to complete deal, September 1, 1989.

CHAMPIONSHIP SERIES RECORD

Year Club	League	G.	IP.	W.	L.	Pct.	H.	R.	ER.	SO.	BB.	ERA.
1989—Chicago	National	2	⅔	0	0	.000	3	1	1	0	0	13.50

KEITH ROWE ATHERTON

Born February 19, 1959, at Mathews, Va.
Height, 6.04. Weight, 200.
Throws and bats righthanded.

Major League saves: 1983 (4), 1984 (2), 1985 (3), 1986 (10), 1987 (2), 1988 (3), 1989 (2). Total—26.
Led Eastern League in complete games with 13 in 1980.
Tied for Northwest League lead in shutouts with 2 in 1978.

Year Club	League	G.	IP.	W.	L.	Pct.	H.	R.	ER.	SO.	BB.	ERA.
1978—Bend	Northwest	12	92	7	3	.700	86	44	35	81	40	3.42
1979—Waterbury	Eastern	4	21	0	3	.000	28	23	13	7	13	5.57
1979—Modesto	California	21	146	9	8	.529	190	107	97	103	51	5.98
1980—West Haven	Eastern	27	190	11	12	.478	185	101	87	117	58	4.12
1981—West Haven	Eastern	27	175	11	13	.458	174	83	70	116	64	3.60
1982—Tacoma	P. Coast	28	★200	12	9	.571	214	108	97	128	54	4.37
1983—Tacoma	P. Coast	26	120⅓	3	8	.273	117	60	53	93	44	3.96
1983—Oakland†	American	29	68⅓	2	5	.286	53	22	21	40	23	2.77
1984—Oakland	American	57	104	7	6	.538	110	51	50	58	39	4.33
1985—Oakland‡	American	56	104⅔	4	7	.364	89	51	50	77	42	4.30
1986—Oakland§-Minnesota	American	60	97	6	10	.375	100	47	44	67	46	4.08
1987—Minnesota	American	59	79⅓	7	5	.583	81	46	40	51	30	4.54
1988—Minnesota x	American	49	74	7	5	.583	65	29	28	43	22	3.41
1989—Cleveland	American	32	39	0	3	.000	48	22	18	13	13	4.15
1989—Colorado Spring y	P. Coast	4	10⅔	0	1	.000	20	11	11	6	5	9.28
1989—Toledo z	Int'national	6	13	1	2	.333	7	4	2	12	1	1.38
Major League Totals—7 Years		342	566⅓	33	41	.446	546	268	251	349	215	3.99

Selected by Oakland A's organization in 2nd round of free-agent draft, June 6, 1978.
†Struck out in only at bat during season when designated hitter took the field.
‡On disabled list, July 24 to August 13, 1985.
§Traded to Minnesota Twins for a player to be named later and cash, May 20, 1986; Oakland A's organization acquired Pitcher Eric Broersma to complete deal, May 23, 1986.
xTraded to Cleveland Indians for Outfielder Carmen Castillo, March 26, 1989.
yReleased, August 7, 1989; signed by Toledo (Detroit Tigers' organization), August 17, 1989.
zGranted free agency, October 15, 1989; signed by Indianapolis (Montreal Expos' organization), December 7, 1989.

CHAMPIONSHIP SERIES RECORD

Year Club	League	G.	IP.	W.	L.	Pct.	H.	R.	ER.	SO.	BB.	ERA.
1987—Minnesota	American	1	⅓	0	0	.000	1	0	0	0	0	0.00

WORLD SERIES RECORD

Year Club	League	G.	IP.	W.	L.	Pct.	H.	R.	ER.	SO.	BB.	ERA.
1987—Minnesota	American	2	1⅓	0	0	.000	0	1	1	0	1	6.75

DONALD GLENN AUGUST
(Don)

Born July 3, 1963, at Inglewood, Calif.
Height, 6.03. Weight, 190.
Throws and bats righthanded.
Attended Chapman College, Orange, Calif.

Tied for Pacific Coast League lead in games started by pitchers with 27 in 1986.
Member of 1984 U.S. Olympic baseball team.

Year Club	League	G.	IP.	W.	L.	Pct.	H.	R.	ER.	SO.	BB.	ERA.
1985—Columbus	Southern	27	176⅓	14	8	.636	183	77	58	78	49	2.96
1986—Tucson†-Vancouver	P. Coast	27	179	10	10	.500	192	88	67	70	51	3.37

Year Club	League	G.	IP.	W.	L.	Pct.	H.	R.	ER.	SO.	BB.	ERA.
1987—Denver	Am. Assoc.	28	179⅓	10	9	.526	★220	★124	★111	91	55	5.57
1988—Denver	Am. Assoc.	10	71⅔	4	1	.800	79	37	28	58	14	3.52
1988—Milwaukee	American	24	148⅓	13	7	.650	137	55	51	66	48	3.09
1989—Milwaukee	American	31	142⅓	12	12	.500	175	93	84	51	58	5.31
1989—Denver	Am. Assoc.	4	23⅔	1	1	.500	35	18	13	12	5	4.94
Major League Totals—2 Years		55	290⅔	25	19	.568	312	148	135	117	106	4.18

Selected by Houston Astros' organization in 1st round (17th player selected) of free-agent draft, June 4, 1984.

†Traded with a player to be named later to Milwaukee Brewers for Pitcher Danny Darwin, August 15, 1986; Milwaukee organization acquired Pitcher Mark Knudson to complete deal, August 21, 1986.

STEVEN THOMAS AVERY
(Steve)

Born April 14, 1970, at Trenton, Mich.
Height, 6.04. Weight, 180.
Throws and bats lefthanded.

Tied for Appalachian League lead in shutouts with 2 in 1988.

Year Club	League	G.	IP.	W.	L.	Pct.	H.	R.	ER.	SO.	BB.	ERA.
1988—Pulaski	Ap'lachian	10	66	7	1	.875	38	16	11	80	19	1.50
1989—Durham	Carolina	13	86⅔	6	4	.600	59	22	14	90	20	1.45
1989—Greenville	Southern	13	84⅓	6	3	.667	68	32	26	75	34	2.77

Selected by Atlanta Braves' organization in 1st round (third player selected) of free-agent draft, June 1, 1988.

WALTER WAYNE BACKMAN
(Wally)

Born September 22, 1959, at Hillsboro, Ore.
Height, 5.09. Weight, 168.
Throws right and bats right and lefthanded.

Major League stolen bases: 1980 (2), 1981 (1), 1982 (8), 1984 (32), 1985 (30), 1986 (13), 1987 (11), 1988 (9), 1989 (1). Total—107.

Tied for National League lead in sacrifice hits with 14 in 1985.
Led International League in bases on balls received with 87 in 1980.
Led Carolina League in caught stealing with 17 in 1978.

Year Club	League	Pos.	G.	AB.	R.	H.	2B.	3B.	HR.	RBI.	B.A.	PO.	A.	E.	F.A.
1977—Little Falls	NYP	SS-3B	69	255	44	83	10	2	6	30	.325	96	185	19	.937
1978—Lynchburg	Carol.	SS	132	494	86	149	19	●9	3	38	.302	★202	★329	30	★.947
1979—Jackson	Texas	SS-2B	110	404	63	114	11	5	2	19	.282	184	259	31	.935
1980—Tidewater	Int.	2B-SS	125	400	53	117	15	5	1	51	.293	237	320	22	.962
1980—New York	Nat.	2B-SS	27	93	12	30	1	1	0	9	.323	62	55	1	.992
1981—New York	Nat.	2B-3B	26	36	5	10	2	0	0	0	.278	14	21	2	.946
1981—Tidewater†‡	Int.	SS-3B-2B	21	59	6	9	3	1	0	6	.153	12	38	1	.980
1982—New York§	Nat.	2B-3B-SS	96	261	37	71	13	2	3	22	.272	173	209	16	.960
1983—New York	Nat.	2B-3B	26	42	6	7	0	1	0	3	.167	16	15	2	.939
1983—Tidewater	Int.	2D-SS 3B	101	361	69	114	11	3	1	28	.316	175	278	13	.972
1984—New York	Nat.	2B-SS	128	436	68	122	10	2	1	26	.280	223	306	10	.981
1985—New York	Nat.	★2B-SS	145	520	77	142	24	5	1	38	.275	273	370	7	★.989
1986—New York	Nat.	2B	124	387	67	124	18	2	1	27	.320	186	290	17	.966
1987—New Yorkxx	Nat.	2B	94	300	43	75	6	1	1	23	.250	131	210	6	.983
1988—New York yz	Nat.	2B	99	294	44	89	12	0	0	17	.303	128	219	4	.989
1989—Minnesota ab	Amer.	2B	87	299	33	69	9	2	1	26	.231	146	187	6	.982
National League Totals—9 Years			765	2369	359	670	95	14	7	165	.283	1206	1695	65	.978
American League Totals—1 Year			87	299	33	69	9	2	1	26	.231	146	187	6	.982
Major League Totals—10 Years			852	2668	392	739	104	16	8	191	.277	1352	1882	71	.979

Selected by New York Mets' organization in 1st round (16th player selected) of free-agent draft, June 7, 1977.

†On suspended list, June 18 to June 20, 1981.
‡On disabled list, July 9 to September 1, 1981.
§On disabled list, August 15 to September 8, 1982.
xOn disabled list, June 9 to June 29, 1987.
yOn disabled list, August 27 to September 11, 1988.
zTraded with Pitcher Mike Santiago to Minnesota Twins for Pitchers Jeff Bumgarner, Steve Gasser and Toby Nivens, December 7, 1988.
aOn disabled list, May 8 to May 25 and July 9 to August 14, 1989.
bGranted free agency, November 13, 1989.

CHAMPIONSHIP SERIES RECORD

Year Club	League	Pos.	G.	AB.	R.	H.	2B.	3B.	HR.	RBI.	B.A.	PO.	A.	E.	F.A.
1986—New York	Nat.	2B-PH	6	21	5	5	0	0	0	2	.238	9	17	0	1.000
1988—New York	Nat.	2B	7	22	2	6	1	0	0	2	.273	7	19	2	.929
Championship Series Totals—2 Years			13	43	7	11	1	0	0	4	.256	16	36	2	.963

WORLD SERIES RECORD

Year Club	League	Pos.	G.	AB.	R.	H.	2B.	3B.	HR.	RBI.	B.A.	PO.	A.	E.	F.A.
1986—New York	Nat.	PR-2B	6	18	4	6	0	0	0	1	.333	9	13	0	1.000

CARLOS O. BAERGA (ORTIZ)

Born November 4, 1968, at San Juan, Puerto Rico.
Height, 5.11. Weight, 165.
Throws right and bats left and righthanded.
Led Pacific Coast League third basemen in total chances with 380 in 1989.
Led Texas League shortstops in double plays with 61 in 1988.
Led South Atlantic League second basemen in errors with 29 in 1987.

Year Club	League	Pos.	G.	AB.	R.	H.	2B.	3B.	HR.	RBI.	B.A.	PO.	A.	E.	F.A.
1986—Charleston	S. Atl.	2B-SS	111	378	57	102	14	4	7	41	.270	202	245	27	.943
1987—Charleston, S. C.	S. Atl.	2B-SS	134	515	83	157	23	•9	7	50	.305	253	341	36	.943
1988—Wichita	Texas	SS-2B	122	444	67	121	28	1	12	65	.273	221	325	33	.943
1989—Las Vegas†	P. C.	3B	132	520	63	143	28	2	10	74	.275	★92	256	★32	.916

Signed as free agent by San Diego Padres' organization, November 4, 1985.
†Traded with Catcher Sandy Alomar and Outfielder Chris James to Cleveland Indians for Outfielder Joe Carter, December 6, 1989.

SCOTT BAILES

Born December 18, 1962, at Chillicothe, O.
Height, 6.02. Weight, 175.
Throws and bats lefthanded.
Attended St. Louis Community College at Meramec, St. Louis, Mo.
Major League saves: 1986 (7), 1987 (6). Total—13.

Year Club	League	G.	IP.	W.	L.	Pct.	H.	R.	ER.	SO.	BB.	ERA.
1982—Greenwood†	S. Atlantic	3	13⅔	0	1	.000	17	12	11	8	6	7.24
1983—Alexandria	Carolina	52	75	5	2	.714	67	38	28	101	45	3.36
1984—Nashua	Eastern	54	87	6	8	.429	80	43	33	61	46	3.41
1985—Nashua‡-Waterbury	Eastern	42	126⅓	9	6	.600	123	58	38	93	43	2.71
1986—Cleveland	American	62	112⅔	10	10	.500	123	70	62	60	43	4.95
1987—Cleveland	American	39	120⅓	7	8	.467	145	75	62	65	47	4.64
1988—Cleveland	American	37	145	9	14	.391	149	89	79	53	46	4.90
1989—Cleveland§	American	34	113⅔	5	9	.357	116	57	54	47	29	4.28
Major League Totals—4 Years		172	491⅔	31	41	.431	533	291	257	225	165	4.70

Selected by Texas Rangers' organization in 7th round of free-agent draft, January 12, 1982.
Selected by Pittsburgh Pirates' organization in secondary phase of free-agent draft, June 7, 1982.
†On disabled list, August 12, 1982 through remainder of season.
‡Traded to Cleveland Indians' organization, July 3, 1985, completing deal in which Cleveland traded Shortstop Johnnie LeMaster to Pittsburgh Pirates for a player to be named later, May 30, 1985.
§On disabled list, August 13 to September 6, 1989.

HAROLD DOUGLAS BAINES

Born March 15, 1959, at Easton, Md.
Height, 6.02. Weight, 195.
Throws and bats lefthanded.
Shares major league record for most plate appearances, game (12), May 8, finished May 9, 1984 (25 innings).
Shares American League records for longest errorless game and most innings by outfielder, game (25), May 8, finished May 9, 1984.
Major League stolen bases: 1980 (2), 1981 (6), 1982 (10), 1983 (7), 1984 (1), 1985 (1), 1986 (2). Total—29.
Hit three home runs in a game, July 7, 1982 and September 17, 1984.
Led American League in slugging percentage with .541 in 1984.
Led American League in game-winning RBIs with 22 in 1983.
Tied for American Association lead in double plays by outfielders with 4 in 1979.
Named designated hitter on The Sporting News American League All-Star Team, 1988 and 1989.
Named outfielder on The Sporting News American League All-Star Team, 1985.
Named designated hitter on The Sporting News American League Silver Slugger team, 1989.

Year Club	League	Pos.	G.	AB.	R.	H.	2B.	3B.	HR.	RBI.	B.A.	PO.	A.	E.	F.A.
1977—Appleton	Midw.	OF	69	222	37	58	11	2	5	29	.261	94	10	7	.937
1978—Knoxville	South.	OF-1B	137	502	70	138	16	6	13	72	.275	291	22	13	.960
1979—Iowa	A. A.	OF	125	466	87	139	25	8	22	87	.298	222	●16	11	.956
1980—Chicago	Amer.	OF	141	491	55	125	23	6	13	49	.255	229	6	9	.963
1981—Chicago	Amer.	OF	82	280	42	80	11	7	10	41	.286	120	10	2	.985
1982—Chicago	Amer.	OF	161	608	89	165	29	8	25	105	.271	326	10	7	.980
1983—Chicago	Amer.	OF	156	596	76	167	33	2	20	99	.280	312	10	9	.973
1984—Chicago	Amer.	OF	147	569	72	173	28	10	29	94	.304	307	8	6	.981
1985—Chicago	Amer.	OF	160	640	86	198	29	3	22	113	.309	318	8	2	.994
1986—Chicago	Amer.	OF	145	570	72	169	29	2	21	88	.296	295	15	5	.984
1987—Chicago†	Amer.	OF	132	505	59	148	26	4	20	93	.293	13	0	0	1.000
1988—Chicago	Amer.	OF	158	599	55	166	39	1	13	81	.277	14	1	2	.882
1989—Chicago‡-Texas	Amer.	OF	146	505	73	156	29	1	16	72	.309	54	0	2	.964
Major League Totals—10 Years		1428	5363	679	1547	276	44	189	835	.288	1988	68	44	.979

Selected by Chicago White Sox' organization in 1st round (first player selected) of free-agent draft, June 7, 1977.
†On disabled list, April 7 to May 8, 1987.
‡Traded with Infielder Fred Manrique to Texas Rangers for Shortstop Scott Fletcher, Outfielder Sammy Sosa and Pitcher Wilson Alvarez, July 29, 1989.

CHAMPIONSHIP SERIES RECORD

Year Club	League	Pos.	G.	AB.	R.	H.	2B.	3B.	HR.	RBI.	B.A.	PO.	A.	E.	F.A.
1983—Chicago	Amer.	OF	4	16	0	2	0	0	0	0	.125	5	1	0	1.000

Year League	Pos.	AB.	R.	H.	2B.	3B.	HR.	RBI.	B.A.	PO.	A.	E.	F.A.
1985—American	PH	1	0	1	0	0	0	0	1.000	0	0	0	.000
1986—American	PH	1	0	0	0	0	0	0	.000	0	0	0	.000
1987—American	PH	1	0	0	0	0	0	0	.000	0	0	0	.000
1989—American	DH	3	1	1	0	0	0	1	.333	0	0	0	.000
All-Star Game Totals—4 Years		6	1	2	0	0	0	1	.333	0	0	0	.000

CHARLES DOUGLAS BAIR
(Doug)

Born August 22, 1949, at Defiance, O.
Height, 6.00. Weight, 185.
Throws and bats righthanded.
Received bachelor of science degree in industrial education from
Bowling Green State University, Bowling Green, O.

Major League saves: 1977 (8), 1978 (28), 1979 (16), 1980 (6), 1981 (1), 1982 (8), 1983 (5), 1984 (4), 1986 (4), 1989 (1) Total—81.

Led Carolina League in complete games with 15 in 1972.
Named Carolina League Pitcher of the Year, 1972.

Year Club	League	G.	IP.	W.	L.	Pct.	H.	R.	ER.	SO.	BB.	ERA.
1971—Salem†	Carolina	6	29	2	3	.400	35	22	19	18	26	5.90
1971—Waterbury	Eastern	1	7	1	0	1.000	5	0	0	2	0	0.00
1972—Salem	Carolina	24	180	15	7	.682	170	●86	57	186	★95	2.85
1972—Charleston	Int'national	1	4	0	1	.000	5	3	3	5	0	6.75
1973—Charleston	Int'national	26	158	7	11	.389	173	103	77	94	87	4.39
1974—Charleston‡	Int'national	26	170	7	★16	.304	166	87	77	117	91	4.08
1975—Charleston	Int'national	26	167	9	12	.429	157	72	56	113	58	3.02
1976—Charleston§	Int'national	45	122	7	10	.412	102	48	43	108	57	3.17
1976—Pittsburgh§	National	4	6	0	0	.000	4	4	4	4	5	6.00
1977—San Jose	P. Coast	20	33	5	2	.714	24	8	8	49	17	2.18
1977—Oakland x	American	45	83	4	6	.400	78	39	32	68	57	3.47
1978—Cincinnati	National	70	100	7	6	.538	87	23	22	91	38	1.98
1979—Cincinnati	National	65	94	11	7	.611	93	47	45	86	51	4.31
1980—Cincinnati	National	61	85	3	6	.333	91	42	40	62	39	4.24
1981—Cincinnati y-St. Louis	National	35	55	4	2	.667	55	34	31	30	19	5.07
1982—St. Louis	National	63	91⅔	5	3	.625	69	27	26	68	36	2.55
1983—St. Louis z	National	26	29⅔	1	1	.500	24	11	10	21	13	3.03
1983—Detroit a	American	27	55⅔	7	3	.700	51	27	24	39	19	3.88
1984—Detroit	American	47	93⅔	5	3	.625	82	42	39	57	36	3.75
1985—Detroit b	American	21	49	2	0	1.000	54	38	34	30	25	6.24
1985—St. Louis c	National	2	2	0	0	.000	1	0	0	0	2	0.00
1986—Tacoma	P. Coast	8	12	3	1	.750	8	3	0	13	6	0.00
1986—Oakland d	American	31	45	2	3	.400	37	15	15	40	18	3.00
1987—Maine	Int'national	45	72⅓	6	3	.667	56	27	24	63	32	2.99
1987—Philadelphia e	National	11	13⅔	2	0	1.000	17	9	9	10	5	5.93
1988—Syracuse	Int'national	39	65⅓	3	4	.429	41	19	17	60	20	2.34
1988—Toronto f	American	10	13⅓	0	0	.000	14	6	6	8	3	4.05
1989—Syracuse g	Int'national	19	25	2	0	1.000	11	3	2	16	8	0.72
1989—Pittsburgh h	National	44	67⅓	2	3	.400	52	19	17	56	28	2.27
National League Totals—10 Years		381	544⅓	35	28	.556	493	216	204	428	236	3.37
American League Totals—6 Years		181	339⅔	20	15	.571	316	167	150	242	158	3.97
Major League Totals—14 Years		562	884	55	43	.561	809	383	354	670	394	3.60

Selected by Pittsburgh Pirates' organization in 2nd round of free-agent draft, June 8, 1971.

†On temporary inactive list, June 23 to July 22, 1971.

‡Conditionally released to Detroit Tigers' organization, December 17, 1974; returned, March 28, 1975.

§Traded with Pitchers Doc Medich, Dave Giusti and Rick Langford, Outfielders Mitchell Page and Tony Armas to Oakland A's for Infielders Phil Garner and Tommy Helms, and Pitcher Chris Batton, March 15, 1977.

xTraded to Cincinnati Reds for First Baseman Dave Revering and cash, February 25, 1978.

yTraded to St. Louis Cardinals for Pitcher Joe Edelen and Second Baseman Neil Fiala, September 10, 1981.

zTraded to Detroit Tigers for a player to be named later, June 21, 1983; St. Louis Cardinals acquired Pitcher Dave Rucker to complete deal, July 5, 1983.

aGranted free agency, November 7, 1983; re-signed by Tigers, December 23, 1983.

bReleased, August 22, 1985; signed by St. Louis Cardinals, September 2, 1985.

cGranted free agency, November 12, 1985; signed by Oakland A's organization, May 19, 1986.

dGranted free agency, November 10, 1986; signed by Maine (Philadelphia Phillies' organization), July 23, 1987.

eReleased, March 26, 1988; signed by Syracuse (Toronto Blue Jays' organization), April 7, 1988.

fReleased, October 31, 1988; re-signed by Blue Jays' organization, February 17, 1989.

gSold to Pittsburgh Pirates, June 16, 1989.

bGranted free agency, November 13, 1989; re-signed by Pirates, November 14, 1989.

CHAMPIONSHIP SERIES RECORD

Year Club	League	G.	IP.	W.	L.	Pct.	H.	R.	ER.	SO.	BB.	ERA.
1979—Cincinnati	National	1	1	0	1	.000	2	1	1	0	1	9.00
1982—St. Louis	National	1	1	0	0	.000	2	0	0	0	3	0.00
Championship Series Totals—2 Years		2	2	0	1	.000	4	1	1	0	4	4.50

WORLD SERIES RECORD

Year Club	League	G.	IP.	W.	L.	Pct.	H.	R.	ER.	SO.	BB.	ERA.
1982—St. Louis	National	3	2	0	1	.000	2	2	2	3	2	9.00

Year Club	League	G.	IP.	W.	L.	Pct.	H.	R.	ER.	SO.	BB.	ERA.
1984—Detroit...	American	1	⅔	0	0	.000	0	0	0	1	0	0.00
World Series Totals—2 Years		4	2⅔	0	1	.000	2	2	2	4	2	6.75

DOUGLAS LEE BAKER
(Doug)

Born April 3, 1961, at Fullerton, Calif.
Height, 5.09. Weight, 165.
Throws right and bats left and righthanded.
Attended Arizona State University, Tempe, Ariz.
Brother of Dave Baker, third baseman with Toronto Blue Jays, 1982.
Major League stolen bases: 1984 (3).
Led Southern League in sacrifice hits with 18 and being hit by pitch with 13 in 1983.
Led Pacific Coast League shortstops in double plays with 80 in 1988.
Led Southern League shortstops in total chances with 747 in 1983.

Year Club	League	Pos.	G.	AB.	R.	H.	2B.	3B.	HR.	RBI.	B.A.	PO.	A.	E.	F.A.
1982—Birmingham	South.	SS	70	213	28	48	3	4	1	21	.225	115	190	14	.956
1983—Birmingham	South.	SS	★146	452	72	109	18	3	5	51	.241	238	★482	27	.964
1984—Evansville†	A. A.	SS	77	243	34	63	21	1	8	30	.259	152	270	16	.963
1984—Detroit	Amer.	SS-2B	43	108	15	20	4	1	0	12	.185	56	86	5	.966
1985—Detroit	Amer.	SS-2B	15	27	4	5	1	0	0	1	.185	12	12	1	.960
1985—Nashville	A. A.	SS	107	325	42	71	9	4	2	30	.218	179	318	22	.958
1986—Detroit	Amer.	SS-2B	13	24	1	3	1	0	0	0	.125	17	21	1	.974
1986—Nashville	A. A.	SS	112	369	46	101	14	6	2	40	.274	★208	291	15	★.971
1987—Toledo	Int.	SS	117	376	40	93	14	2	2	27	.247	190	342	★24	.957
1987—Detroit‡	Amer.	SS-2B-3B	8	1	0	0	0	0	0	0	.000	2	8	0	1.000
1988—Portland	P. C.	★SS-3B	121	417	52	102	17	4	2	45	.245	194	340	21	★.962
1988—Minnesota	Amer.	SS-3B-2B	11	7	1	0	0	0	0	0	.000	5	7	0	1.000
1989—Portland	P. C.	SS-OF-1B	84	312	38	74	10	4	2	27	.237	143	295	13	.971
1989—Minnesota	Amer.	2B-SS	43	78	17	23	5	1	0	9	.295	42	63	2	.981
Major League Totals—6 Years			133	245	38	51	11	2	0	22	.208	134	197	9	.974

Selected by Oakland A's organization in 9th round of free-agent draft, January 13, 1981.
Selected by Detroit Tigers' organization in 9th round of free-agent draft, June 7, 1982.
†On disabled list, June 10 to June 21, 1984.
‡Traded to Minnesota Twins for Shortstop Julius McDougal, February 24, 1988.

CHAMPIONSHIP SERIES RECORD

Year Club	League	Pos.	G.	AB.	R.	H.	2B.	3B.	HR.	RBI.	B.A.	PO.	A.	E.	F.A.
1984—Detroit	Amer.	SS	1	0	0	0	0	0	0	0	.000	0	0	0	.000

WORLD SERIES RECORD
Eligible for 1984 World Series with Detroit Tigers; did not play.

STEPHEN CHARLES BALBONI
(Steve)

Born January 16, 1957, at Brockton, Mass.
Height, 6.03. Weight, 235.
Throws and bats righthanded.
Attended Eckerd College, St. Petersburg, Fla.
Major League stolen bases: 1985 (1).
Led American League batters in strikeouts with 166 in 1985.
Led American League first basemen in total chances with 1,686 in 1985.
Led International League batters in strikeouts with 146 in 1981.
Led Southern League in total bases with 288 and intentional bases on balls received with 17 in 1980.
Led Florida State League batters in strikeouts with 154 in 1979.
Led Florida State League first basemen in double plays with 106 in 1979 and Southern League first basemen with 125 in 1980.
Named Southern League Most Valuable Player, 1980.
Named Florida State League Most Valuable Player, 1980.
Named designated hitter on The Sporting News College Baseball All-America Team, 1978.

Year Club	League	Pos.	G.	AB.	R.	H.	2B.	3B.	HR.	RBI.	B.A.	PO.	A.	E.	F.A.
1978—West Haven	East.	DH	2	2	0	0	0	0	0	0	.000	0	0	0	.000
1978—Fort Lauderdale ..	Fla. St.	1B	60	176	19	36	5	0	1	19	.205	475	19	4	.992
1979—Fort Lauderdale ..	Fla. St.	1B	★140	★504	69	127	19	2	★26	★91	.252	★1297	★97	11	★.992
1980—Nashville	South.	1B	141	521	★101	157	25	2	★34	★122	.301	★1218	76	13	★.990
1981—Columbus	Int.	1B	125	434	68	107	21	2	★33	★98	.247	631	55	★14	.980
1981—New York	Amer.	1B	4	7	2	2	1	1	0	2	.286	14	1	0	1.000
1982—Columbus	Int.	1B	83	313	57	89	17	1	★32	86	.284	426	38	8	.983
1982—New York	Amer.	1B	33	107	8	20	2	1	2	4	.187	194	13	2	.990
1983—Columbus	Int.	1B	84	317	72	87	14	0	27	81	.274	479	47	11	.980
1983—New York†	Amer.	1B	32	86	8	20	2	0	5	17	.233	178	9	3	.984
1984—Kansas City	Amer.	1B	126	438	58	107	23	2	28	77	.244	1102	79	●15	.987
1985—Kansas City	Amer.	1B	160	600	74	146	28	2	36	88	.243	★1573	101	12	.993
1986—Kansas City‡	Amer.	1B	138	512	54	117	25	1	29	88	.229	1236	98	★18	.987
1987—Kansas City§	Amer.	1B	121	386	44	80	11	1	24	60	.207	521	41	6	.989

Year	Club	League	Pos.	G.	AB.	R.	H.	2B.	3B.	HR.	RBI.	B.A.	PO.	A.	E.	F.A.
1988—K.C.x-Sea.y		Amer.	1B	118	413	46	97	17	1	23	66	.235	428	30	4	.991
1989—New York		Amer.	1B	110	300	33	71	12	2	17	59	.237	150	7	1	.994
Major League Totals—9 Years				842	2849	327	660	121	11	164	461	.232	5396	379	61	.990

Selected by New York Yankees' organization in 4th round of free-agent draft, June 6, 1978.

†Traded with Pitcher Roger Erickson to Kansas City Royals for Pitcher Mike Armstrong and Catcher Duane Dewey, December 8, 1983.

‡Released, December 18, 1986; re-signed by Royals, February 25, 1987.

§Released, December 21, 1987; re-signed by Royals, February 18, 1988.

xReleased, May 27, 1988; signed by Seattle Mariners, June 1, 1988.

yTraded to New York Yankees for Pitcher Dana Ridenour, March 27, 1989.

CHAMPIONSHIP SERIES RECORD

Shares American League Championship Series record for most strikeouts, series (8), 1985.

Year	Club	League	Pos.	G.	AB.	R.	H.	2B.	3B.	HR.	RBI.	B.A.	PO.	A.	E.	F.A.
1984—Kansas City		Amer.	1B	3	11	0	1	0	0	0	0	.091	20	3	1	.958
1985—Kansas City		Amer.	1B	7	25	1	3	0	0	0	1	.120	72	7	2	.975
Championship Series Totals—2 Years				10	36	1	4	0	0	0	1	.111	92	10	3	.971

WORLD SERIES RECORD

Shares World Series record for most at-bats, inning (2), October 27, 1985, fifth inning.

Year	Club	League	Pos.	G.	AB.	R.	H.	2B.	3B.	HR.	RBI.	B.A.	PO.	A.	E.	F.A.
1985—Kansas City		Amer.	1B	7	25	2	8	0	0	0	3	.320	70	3	0	1.000

JEFFREY SCOTT BALLARD
(Jeff)

Born August 13, 1963, at Billings, Mont.
Height, 6.02. Weight, 198.
Throws and bats lefthanded.
Received degree in geophysics from Stanford University, Stanford, Calif.
Tied for New York-Pennsylvania League lead in shutouts with 3 in 1985.

Year	Club	League	G.	IP.	W.	L.	Pct.	H.	R.	ER.	SO.	BB.	ERA.
1985—Newark		NYP	13	96	•10	2	.833	78	20	15	91	20	1.41
1986—Hagerstown		Carolina	17	112	9	5	.643	106	39	23	115	32	•1.85
1986—Charlotte		Southern	10	59⅔	5	2	.714	70	29	22	35	20	3.32
1986—Rochester		Int'national	2	6⅓	0	2	.000	11	6	5	7	3	7.11
1987—Rochester		Int'national	23	160⅓	13	4	.765	151	60	55	114	35	3.09
1987—Baltimore		American	14	69⅔	2	8	.200	100	60	51	27	35	6.59
1988—Rochester		Int'national	9	60⅔	4	3	.571	56	26	20	32	11	2.97
1988—Baltimore		American	25	153⅓	8	12	.400	167	83	75	41	42	4.40
1989—Baltimore		American	35	215⅓	18	8	.692	240	95	82	62	57	3.43
Major League Totals—3 Years			74	438⅓	28	28	.500	507	238	208	130	134	4.27

Selected by Milwaukee Brewers' organization in 16th round of free-agent draft, June 8, 1981.

Selected by Baltimore Orioles' organization in 27th round of free-agent draft, June 4, 1984.

Selected by Baltimore Orioles' organizaton in 7th round of free-agent draft, June 3, 1985.

CHRISTOPHER MICHAEL BANDO
(Chris)

Born February 4, 1956, at Cleveland, O.
Height, 6.00. Weight, 195.
Throws right and bats left and righthanded
Attended Arizona State University, Tempe, Ariz.
Brother of Sal Bando, infielder with Kansas City Athletics, Oakland A's and
Milwaukee Brewers, 1966 through 1981; Milwaukee Brewers' Special Assistant
to the General Manager since 1982; and coach with Milwaukee Brewers, 1983.

Major League stolen bases: 1984 (1).

Received reported $25,000 bonus to sign with Cleveland Indians, 1978.

Year	Club	League	Pos.	G.	AB.	R.	H.	2B.	3B.	HR.	RBI.	B.A.	PO.	A.	E.	F.A.
1978—Chattanooga		South.	C	76	241	30	55	12	0	4	21	.228	285	51	10	.971
1979—Chattanooga†		South.	C-3B	21	62	5	15	4	1	0	7	.242	61	13	0	1.000
1980—Chattanooga‡		South.	C-3B	121	404	78	141	31	3	12	73	•.349	480	97	12	.980
1981—Charleston		Int.	C-3B	96	320	47	98	16	2	11	45	.306	414	51	10	.979
1981—Cleveland		Amer.	C	21	47	3	10	3	0	0	6	.213	53	5	2	.967
1982—Cleveland§		Amer.	C-3B	66	184	13	39	6	1	3	16	.212	268	23	3	.990
1983—Cleveland		Amer.	C	48	121	15	31	3	0	4	15	.256	170	19	1	.995
1984—Maine x		Int.	C-1B	29	92	18	24	2	0	3	13	.261	138	12	5	.968
1984—Cleveland		Amer.	C-1B-3B	75	220	38	64	11	0	12	41	.291	307	30	6	.983
1985—Cleveland		Amer.	C	73	173	11	24	4	1	0	13	.139	251	28	4	.986
1986—Cleveland		Amer.	C	92	254	28	68	9	0	2	26	.268	359	30	4	.990
1987—Cleveland y		Amer.	C	89	211	20	46	9	0	5	16	.218	351	34	4	.990
1988—Clev.z-Det.a		Amer.	C	33	72	6	9	1	0	1	8	.125	123	14	3	.979
1989—Tacoma b		P. C.	C	31	84	11	21	4	0	3	18	.250	134	16	2	.987
1989—Oakland c		Amer.	C	1	2	0	1	0	0	0	1	.500	8	0	0	1.000
Major League Totals—9 Years				498	1284	134	292	46	2	27	142	.227	1890	183	27	.987

Selected by Milwaukee Brewers' organization in 22nd round of free-agent draft, June 7, 1977.

Selected by Cleveland Indians' organization in 2nd round of free-agent draft, June 6, 1978.
†On disabled list, April 16 to August 9, 1979.
‡On disabled list, April 24 to May 6, 1980.
§On disabled list, May 2 to June 17, 1982.
xOn Cleveland disabled list, March 28 to April 20, 1984.
yGranted free agency, November 9, 1987; re-signed by Indians, December 7, 1987.
zReleased, August 14, 1988; signed by Detroit Tigers, September 2, 1988.
aReleased, October 7, 1988; signed by Tacoma (Oakland Athletics' organization), January 13, 1989.
bOn disabled list, May 28 to August 7, 1989.
cGranted free agency, November 13, 1989.

MICHAEL SCOTT BANKHEAD
(Known by middle name.)

Born July 31, 1963, at Raleigh, N.C.
Height, 5.10. Weight, 185.
Throws and bats righthanded.
Attended University of North Carolina, Chapel Hill, N.C.
Member of 1984 U.S. Olympic baseball team.

Year Club	League	G.	IP.	W.	L.	Pct.	H.	R.	ER.	SO.	BB.	ERA.
1985—Memphis	Southern	24	140⅓	8	6	.571	117	63	56	●128	56	3.59
1986—Omaha	Am. Assoc.	7	48⅓	2	2	.500	31	11	8	34	14	1.49
1986—Kansas City†	American	24	121	8	9	.471	121	66	62	94	37	4.61
1987—Seattle‡	American	27	149⅓	9	8	.529	168	96	90	95	37	5.42
1988—San Bernardino§	California	2	11	0	0	.000	6	3	2	6	4	1.64
1988—Calgary	P. Coast	2	11	1	1	.500	15	9	9	5	5	7.36
1988—Seattle	American	21	135	7	9	.438	115	53	46	102	38	3.07
1989—Seattle	American	33	210⅓	14	6	.700	187	84	78	140	63	3.34
Major League Totals—4 Years		105	615⅔	38	32	.543	591	299	276	431	175	4.03

Selected by Pittsburgh Pirates' organization in 17th round of free-agent draft, June 8, 1981.
Selected by Kansas City Royals' organization in 1st round (16th player selected) of free-agent draft, June 4, 1984.
†Traded with Pitcher Steve Shields and Outfielder Mike Kingery to Seattle Mariners for Outfielder Danny Tartabull and Pitcher Rick Luecken, December 10, 1986.
‡On disabled list, June 24 to July 13, 1987.
§On Seattle disabled list, March 20 to May 14, 1988; included rehabilitation disability assignment to San Bernardino April 23 to May 2, 1988, and Calgary, May 3 to May 10, 1988.

WILLIE ANTHONY BANKS

Born February 27, 1969, at Jersey City, N.J.
Height, 6.01. Weight, 190.
Throws and bats righthanded.
Pitched 1-0 no-hit victory against Palm Springs, May 24, 1989.
Led California League in wild pitches with 22 and tied for lead in shutouts with 4 in 1989.
Led Appalachian League in wild pitches with 28 and tied for lead in balks with 3 in 1987.
Received reported $160,000 bonus to sign with Minnesota Twins, 1987.

Year Club	League	G.	IP.	W.	L.	Pct.	H.	R.	ER.	SO.	BB.	ERA.
1987—Elizabethton	Ap'lachian	13	65⅔	1	8	.111	73	★71	★51	71	★62	6.99
1988—Kenosha	Midwest	24	125⅔	10	10	.500	109	73	52	113	★107	3.72
1989—Visalia	California	27	174	12	9	.571	122	70	50	★173	85	2.59
1989—Orlando	Southern	1	7	1	0	1.000	10	4	4	9	0	5.14

Selected by Minnesota Twins' organization in 1st round (third player selected) of free-agent draft, June 2, 1987.

FLOYD FRANKLIN BANNISTER

Born June 10, 1955, at Pierre, S. Dakota.
Height, 6.01. Weight, 190.
Throws and bats lefthanded.
Attended Arizona State University, Tempe, Ariz.
Brother-in-law of Greg Cochran, pitcher in Oakland A's and New York Yankees'
organizations, 1975 through 1982.
Named College Player of the Year by THE SPORTING NEWS, 1976.
Named lefthanded pitcher on THE SPORTING NEWS College Baseball All-America Team, 1975 and 1976.

Year Club	League	G.	IP.	W.	L.	Pct.	H.	R.	ER.	SO.	BB.	ERA.
1976—Covington	Ap'lachian	3	13	0	0	.000	3	0	0	27	2	0.00
1976—Columbus	Southern	3	24	1	0	1.000	16	4	4	20	14	1.50
1976—Memphis	Int'national	1	6	1	0	1.000	7	1	1	6	3	1.50
1977—Houston†	National	24	143	8	9	.471	138	70	64	112	68	4.03
1978—Houston‡	National	28	110	3	9	.250	120	59	59	94	63	4.83
1979—Seattle	American	30	182	10	15	.400	185	92	82	115	68	4.05
1980—Seattle	American	32	218	9	13	.409	200	96	84	155	66	3.47
1981—Seattle§	American	21	121	9	9	.500	128	62	60	85	39	4.46
1982—Seattle x	American	35	247	12	13	.480	225	112	94	★209	77	3.43
1983—Chicago	American	34	217⅓	16	10	.615	191	88	81	193	71	3.35
1984—Chicago y	American	34	218	14	11	.560	211	127	117	152	80	4.83
1985—Chicago	American	34	210⅔	10	14	.417	211	121	114	198	100	4.87
1986—Chicago z	American	28	165⅓	10	14	.417	162	81	65	92	48	3.54
1987—Chicago a	American	34	228⅔	16	11	.593	216	100	91	124	49	3.58

Year—Club	League	G.	IP.	W.	L.	Pct.	H.	R.	ER.	SO.	BB.	ERA.
1988—Kansas City	American	31	189⅓	12	13	.480	182	102	91	113	68	4.33
1989—Kansas City bc	American	14	75⅓	4	1	.800	87	40	39	35	18	4.66
National League Totals—2 Years		52	253	11	18	.379	258	129	123	206	131	4.38
American League Totals—11 Years		327	2072⅔	122	124	.496	1998	1021	918	1471	684	3.99
Major League Totals—13 Years		379	2325⅔	133	142	.484	2256	1150	1041	1677	815	4.03

Selected by Oakland A's organization in 3rd round of free-agent draft, June 5, 1973.
Selected by Houston Astros' organization in 1st round (first player selected) of free-agent draft, June 8, 1976.
†On disabled list, July 26 to August 22, 1977.
‡Traded to Seattle Mariners for Shortstop Craig Reynolds, December 8, 1978.
§On disabled list, August 8 to August 29, 1981.
xGranted free agency, November 10, 1982; signed by Chicago White Sox, December 13, 1982.
yHad one at-bat with no hits.
zOn disabled list, May 19 to June 17, 1986.
aTraded with Infielder Dave Cochrane to Kansas City Royals for Pitchers John Davis, Melido Perez, Chuck Mount and Greg Hibbard, December 10, 1987.
bOn disabled list, June 12, 1989 through remainder of season.
cGranted free agency, November 13, 1989; signed by Yakult Swallows of Japanese Baseball League, December 4, 1989.

CHAMPIONSHIP SERIES RECORD

Year—Club	League	G.	IP.	W.	L.	Pct.	H.	R.	ER.	SO.	BB.	ERA.
1983—Chicago	American	1	6	0	1	.000	5	4	3	5	1	4.50

ALL-STAR GAME RECORD

Year—League		IP.	W.	L.	Pct.	H.	R.	ER.	SO.	BB.	ERA.
1982—American		1	0	0	.000	1	0	0	0	0	0.00

JESSE LEE BARFIELD

Born October 29, 1959, at Joliet, Ill.
Height, 6.01. Weight, 200.
Throws and bats righthanded.

Major League stolen bases: 1981 (4), 1982 (1), 1983 (2), 1984 (8), 1985 (22), 1986 (8), 1987 (3), 1988 (7), 1989 (5). Total—60.
Led American League outfielders in double plays with 8 in 1985 and 1986.
Led Florida State League batters in strikeouts with 125 in 1978.
Named outfielder on THE SPORTING NEWS American League All-Star fielding team, 1986 and 1987.
Named outfielder on THE SPORTING NEWS American League Silver Slugger team, 1986.

Year—Club	League	Pos.	G.	AB.	R.	H.	2B.	3B.	HR.	RBI.	B.A.	PO.	A.	E.	F.A.
1977—Utica	NYP	OF	70	234	37	53	9	3	5	35	.226	122	6	●13	.908
1978—Dunedin	Fla. St.	OF	133	441	40	91	12	3	2	34	.206	229	★22	★15	.944
1979—Kinston	Carol.	OF	136	477	66	126	24	5	8	71	.264	284	19	17	.947
1980—Knoxville†	South.	OF	124	433	63	104	12	8	14	65	.240	309	14	12	.964
1981—Knoxville	South.	OF	141	524	83	137	24	13	16	70	.261	270	★23	6	.980
1981—Toronto	Amer.	OF	25	95	7	22	3	2	2	9	.232	71	2	0	1.000
1982—Toronto	Amer.	OF	139	394	54	97	13	2	18	58	.246	217	15	9	.963
1983—Toronto	Amer.	OF	128	388	58	98	13	3	27	68	.253	213	16	8	.966
1984—Toronto	Amer.	OF	110	320	51	91	14	1	14	49	.284	190	9	10	.952
1985—Toronto	Amer.	OF	155	539	94	156	34	9	27	84	.289	349	★22	4	.989
1986—Toronto	Amer.	OF	158	589	107	170	35	2	★40	108	.289	368	★20	3	.992
1987—Toronto	Amer.	OF	159	590	89	155	25	3	28	84	.263	341	●17	3	.992
1988—Toronto‡	Amer.	OF	137	468	62	114	21	5	18	56	.244	325	12	4	.988
1989—Tor.§-N.Y.	Amer.	OF	150	521	79	122	23	1	23	67	.234	340	★20	●10	.973
Major League Totals—9 Years			1161	3904	601	1025	181	28	197	583	.263	2414	133	51	.980

Selected by Toronto Blue Jays' organization in 9th round of free-agent draft, June 7, 1977.
†On disabled list, August 15 to August 29, 1980.
‡On disabled list, May 16 to May 31, 1988.
§Traded to New York Yankees for Pitcher Al Leiter, April 30, 1989.

CHAMPIONSHIP SERIES RECORD

Year—Club	League	Pos.	G.	AB.	R.	H.	2B.	3B.	HR.	RBI.	B.A.	PO.	A.	E.	F.A.
1985—Toronto	Amer.	OF	7	25	3	7	1	0	1	4	.280	21	0	1	.955

ALL-STAR GAME RECORD

Year—League		Pos.	AB.	R.	H.	2B.	3B.	HR.	RBI.	B.A.	PO.	A.	E.	F.A.
1986—American		PH-OF	3	0	0	0	0	0	0	.000	2	0	0	1.000

JOHN DAVID BARFIELD

Born October 15, 1964, at Little Rock, Ark.
Height, 6.01. Weight, 185.
Throws and bats lefthanded.
Attended Crowder College, Neosho, Mo., and Oklahoma City University, Oklahoma City, Okla.

Year—Club	League	G.	IP.	W.	L.	Pct.	H.	R.	ER.	SO.	BB.	ERA.
1986—Daytona Beach	Florida St.	3	17⅓	1	1	.500	14	9	8	13	1	4.15
1986—Salem	Carolina	13	56	2	5	.286	71	43	31	39	22	4.98
1987—Charlotte	Florida St.	25	153⅔	10	7	.588	145	75	63	79	55	3.69
1988—Tulsa	Texas	24	169	9	9	.500	159	69	54	125	66	2.88

Year Club	League	G.	IP.	W.	L.	Pct.	H.	R.	ER.	SO.	BB.	ERA.
1989—Oklahoma City	Am. Assoc.	28	175⅓	10	8	.556	178	93	79	58	68	4.06
1989—Texas	American	4	11⅔	0	1	.000	15	10	8	9	4	6.17
Major League Totals—1 Year		4	11⅔	0	1	.000	15	10	8	9	4	6.17

Selected by Philadelphia Phillies' organization in 17th round of free-agent draft, January 9, 1985.
Selected by Texas Rangers' organization in 11th round of free-agent draft, June 2, 1986.

WILLIAM HENRY BARNES III
(Skeeter)

Born March 7, 1957, at Cincinnati, O.
Height, 5.10. Weight, 180.
Throws and bats righthanded.
Attended University of Cincinnati, Cincinnati, O.

Major League stolen bases: 1983 (2).
Tied for American Association lead in sacrifice flies with 8 in 1989.
Tied for Pioneer League lead in sacrifice flies with 6 in 1978.
Led Eastern League third basemen in fielding percentage with .947 in 1982 and putouts with 104 in 1981.

Year Club	League	Pos.	G.	AB.	R.	H.	2B.	3B.	HR.	RBI.	B.A.	PO.	A.	E.	F.A.
1978—Billings	Pion.	O-3-S-2-1	68	277	66	102	*22	5	3	*76	.368	56	50	16	.869
1979—Nashville	South.	3B	*145	500	54	133	19	4	12	77	.266	123	*291	*35	.922
1980—Waterbury	East.	OF	*138	533	62	156	27	6	4	64	.293	264	15	13	.955
1981—Indianapolis	A. A.	1B-OF-3B	36	118	10	31	6	1	1	11	.263	254	23	3	.989
1981—Waterbury	East.	3-O-1-2	96	363	45	93	17	0	6	49	.256	115	185	15	.952
1982—Waterbury	East.	3B-1B-SS	112	418	67	128	24	6	12	72	.306	252	192	19	.959
1982—Indianapolis	A. A.	3B-1B	18	59	8	18	5	1	1	3	.305	25	25	2	.962
1983—Indianapolis	A. A.	3-1-O-2	109	377	67	127	19	6	7	56	.337	203	140	16	.955
1983—Cincinnati	Nat.	1B-3B	15	34	5	7	0	0	1	4	.206	45	11	1	.982
1984—Wichita	A. A.	3-1-O-2	92	360	59	118	23	4	14	67	.328	143	122	13	.953
1984—Cincinnati	Nat.	3B-OF	32	42	5	5	0	0	1	3	.119	7	15	0	1.000
1985—Den.†-Ind.	A. A.	3-1-O-2	95	340	51	95	16	0	8	63	.279	308	154	10	.970
1985—Montreal	Nat.	3B-OF-1B	19	26	0	4	1	0	0	0	.154	13	6	0	1.000
1986—Indianapolis‡	A. A.	3B-OF-1B	85	300	40	80	18	5	5	40	.267	95	137	18	.928
1986—Portland§	P. C.	3-O-S-1	38	141	21	52	8	4	1	29	.369	44	60	6	.945
1987—Louis.-Den	A. A.	3B-1B-OF	110	431	79	131	33	5	16	76	.304	315	127	17	.963
1987—St. Louis xy	Nat.	3B	4	4	1	1	0	0	1	3	.250	0	0	0	.000
1988—Buf.z-Nash.a	A. A.	1-O-3-P	122	379	47	96	16	0	6	39	.253	461	38	3	.994
1989—Nashville	A. A.	OF-1B-3B	124	472	57	143	*39	3	6	55	.303	305	24	7	.979
1989—Cincinnati b	Nat.	PR-PH	5	3	1	0	0	0	0	0	.000	0	0	0	.000
Major League Totals—5 Years			75	109	12	17	1	0	3	10	.156	65	32	1	.990

Selected by Cincinnati Reds' organization in 16th round of free-agent draft, June 6, 1978.
†Traded to Montreal Expos' organization for Outfielder Max Venable, April 26, 1985.
‡Traded with Pitcher Dan Schatzeder to Philadelphia Phillies for Infielder Tom Foley and Pitcher Lary Sorensen, July 24, 1986.
§Granted free agency, October 15, 1986; signed by Louisville (St. Louis Cardinals' organization), January 26, 1987.
xSold to Denver (Milwaukee Brewers' organization), July 16, 1987.
yGranted free agency, October 15, 1987; signed by Buffalo (Pittsburgh Pirates' organization), November 20, 1987.
zReleased, May 7, 1988; signed by Nashville (Cincinnati Reds' organization), May 14, 1988.
aGranted free agency, October 15, 1988; re-signed by Reds' organization, November 5, 1988.
bGranted free agency, October 15, 1989.

PITCHING RECORD

Year Club	League	G.	IP.	W.	L.	Pct.	H.	R.	ER.	SO.	BB.	ERA.
1988—Nashville	Am. Assoc.	1	0	0	0	.000	4	6	6	0	3	......

MARTIN GLENN BARRETT
(Marty)

Born June 23, 1958, at Arcadia, Calif.
Height, 5.10. Weight, 175.
Throws and bats righthanded.
Attended Mesa Community College, Mesa, Ariz. and Arizona State University, Tempe, Ariz.
Brother of Charlie Barrett, pitcher in Los Angeles Dodgers' organization, 1973 through 1978;
and Tom Barrett, infielder in Philadelphia Phillies' organization.

Major League stolen bases: 1984 (5), 1985 (7), 1986 (15), 1987 (15), 1988 (7), 1989 (4). Total—53.
Led American League in sacrifice hits with 18 in 1986, 22 in 1987 and 20 in 1988.
Led American League second basemen in double plays with 110 in 1985.
Led Eastern League in sacrifice hits with 15 in 1980.
Led Florida State League in sacrifice flies with 9 in 1979.
Led International League second basemen in double plays with 99 in 1982.

Year Club	League	Pos.	G.	AB.	R.	H.	2B.	3B.	HR.	RBI.	B.A.	PO.	A.	E.	F.A.
1979—Winter Haven	Fla. St.	2B	57	178	25	53	7	0	1	28	.298	124	144	6	.978
1980—Bristol	East.	*2B-SS	128	475	72	130	17	2	1	41	.274	279	372	10	*.985
1981—Pawtucket†	Int.	2B	88	343	36	91	12	2	1	28	.265	186	254	10	.978
1982—Pawtucket	Int.	2B	131	477	72	143	27	1	5	57	.300	303	*415	11	*.985
1982—Boston	Amer.	2B	8	18	0	1	0	0	0	0	.056	11	21	0	1.000
1983—Boston	Amer.	2B	33	44	7	10	1	1	0	2	.227	32	28	1	.984
1983—Pawtucket	Int.	2B	36	119	24	41	4	2	1	18	.345	70	115	1	.995
1984—Boston	Amer.	2B	139	475	56	144	23	3	3	45	.303	245	417	9	*.987

Year Club	League	Pos.	G.	AB.	R.	H.	2B.	3B.	HR.	RBI.	B.A.	PO.	A.	E.	F.A.
1985—Boston...................	Amer.	2B	156	534	59	142	26	0	5	56	.266	*355	479	11	.987
1986—Boston...................	Amer.	2B	158	625	94	179	39	4	4	60	.286	303	*450	14	.982
1987—Boston‡..................	Amer.	2B	137	559	72	164	23	0	3	43	.293	320	438	9	*.988
1988—Boston...................	Amer.	2B	150	612	83	173	28	1	1	65	.283	312	402	7	.990
1989—Boston§.................	Amer.	2B	86	336	31	86	18	0	1	27	.256	152	245	10	.975
1989—Pawtucket............	Int.	2B	11	35	4	10	1	1	0	4	.286	22	25	2	.959
Major League Totals—8 Years.................			867	3203	402	899	158	9	17	298	.281	1730	2480	61	.986

Selected by California Angels' organization in 11th round of free-agent draft, January 11, 1977.
Selected by New York Mets' organization in 3rd round of free-agent draft, January 10, 1978.
Selected by Boston Red Sox' organization in secondary phase of free-agent draft, June 5, 1979.
†On disabled list, June 25 to July 15 and July 17 to August 4, 1981.
‡On disabled list, April 11 to April 27, 1987.
§On disabled list, June 5 to August 5, 1989; included rehabilitation disability assignment to Pawtucket, July 24 to August 5, 1989.

CHAMPIONSHIP SERIES RECORD

Shares American League Championship Series record for most singles, series (9), 1986.

Year Club	League	Pos.	G.	AB.	R.	H.	2B.	3B.	HR.	RBI.	B.A.	PO.	A.	E.	F.A.
1986—Boston...................	Amer.	2B	7	30	4	11	2	0	0	5	.367	19	21	0	1.000
1988—Boston...................	Amer.	2B	4	15	2	1	0	0	0	0	.067	6	8	0	1.000
Championship Series Totals—2 Years.....			11	45	6	12	2	0	0	5	.267	25	29	0	1.000

WORLD SERIES RECORD

Shares World Series record for most hits, series (13), 1986.

Year Club	League	Pos.	G.	AB.	R.	H.	2B.	3B.	HR.	RBI.	B.A.	PO.	A.	E.	F.A.
1986—Boston...................	Amer.	2B	7	30	1	13	2	0	0	4	.433	13	25	0	1.000

THOMAS LOREN BARRETT
(Tom)

Born April 2, 1960, at San Fernando, Calif.
Height, 5.10. Weight, 170.
Throws right and bats left and righthanded.
Attended Mesa Community College, Mesa, Ariz., and University of Arizona, Tucson, Ariz.
Brother of Charlie Barrett, pitcher in Los Angeles Dodgers' organization, 1973 through 1978;
and Marty Barrett, second baseman with Boston Red Sox.

Led International League in stolen bases with 44 and tied for lead in sacrifice hits with 10 in 1989.
Led Eastern League in bases on balls received with 95 in 1987.
Led Eastern League in caught stealing with 21 in 1986.
Tied for International League lead in sacrifice flies with 8 in 1988.
Led International League second basemen in putouts with 177 and total chances with 456 in 1988.
Led Eastern League second basemen in putouts with 248, assists with 423, fielding percentage with .991 and double plays with 93 in 1987.

Year Club	League	Pos.	G.	AB.	R.	H.	2B.	3B.	HR.	RBI.	B.A.	PO.	A.	E.	F.A.
1982—Paintsville............	Appal.	2B	61	231	59	84	5	2	0	21	.364	134	138	4	*.986
1983—Fort Lauderdale†	Fla. St.	3B-2B	103	397	80	130	21	1	0	32	*.327	99	207	25	.924
1984—Nashville...............	South.	2B	135	510	82	157	22	6	0	44	.308	325	365	*30	.958
1984—Columbus.............	Int.	3B	5	21	3	8	1	0	0	0	.381	2	3	0	1.000
1985—Columbus‡............	Int.	3-O-2-S	55	169	27	44	11	1	1	11	.260	47	66	5	.958
1985—Albany.................	East.	2B-3B-OF	57	233	40	61	8	3	1	18	.262	69	79	12	.925
1986—Albany.................	East.	2B-OF-3B	132	498	75	133	20	2	3	45	.267	162	158	15	.955
1986—Columbus§............	Int.	2B-3B	2	9	0	3	0	0	0	1	.333	3	5	0	1.000
1987—Reading................	East.	2B-SS-OF	*136	485	107	162	20	9	1	55	.334	265	444	9	.987
1988—Maine...................	Int.	2B-SS	114	390	•69	111	16	4	1	33	.285	204	305	11	.979
1988—Philadelphia	Nat.	2B	36	54	5	11	1	0	0	3	.204	16	31	2	.959
1989—Scr./Wil.-Barre....	Int.	*2-S-3	120	443	65	123	14	6	0	25	.278	253	335	9	*.985
1989—Philadelphia	Nat.	2B	14	27	3	6	0	0	0	1	.222	26	18	1	.978
Major League Totals—2 Years.................			50	81	8	17	1	0	0	4	.210	42	49	3	.968

Selected by New York Yankees' organization in 26th round of free-agent draft, June 7, 1982.
†On disabled list, July 26 to August 26, 1983.
‡On temporary inactive list, August 29, 1985 through remainder of season.
§Traded with Outfielder Mike Easler to Philadelphia Phillies for Pitchers Charles Hudson and Jeff Knox, December 11, 1986.

KEVIN CHARLES BASS

Born May 12, 1959, at Redwood City, Calif.
Height, 6.00. Weight, 180.
Throws right and bats right and lefthanded.
Brother of Richard Bass, minor league outfielder, 1976 and 1977;
cousin of James Lofton, wide receiver with Buffalo Bills.

Shares major league record for most games, switch-hit home runs, season (2), 1987.
Major League stolen bases: 1983 (2), 1984 (5), 1985 (19), 1986 (22), 1987 (21), 1988 (31), 1989 (11). Total—111.
Switch-hit home runs in one game, August 3, 1987, September 2, 1987 and August 20, 1989.
Led Midwest League in being hit by pitch with 10 in 1978.
Led Eastern League outfielders in double plays with 7 in 1980.

Year—Club	League	Pos.	G.	AB.	R.	H.	2B.	3B.	HR.	RBI.	B.A.	PO.	A.	E.	F.A.
1977—Newark	NYP	OF	48	189	30	56	11	•7	1	33	.296	56	2	3	.951
1978—Burlington	Midw.	OF	129	499	81	132	27	5	18	69	.265	★281	14	11	.964
1979—Holyoke	East.	OF	135	490	69	129	15	4	8	54	.263	280	•16	★17	.946
1980—Holyoke	East.	OF	136	490	79	147	★31	7	4	51	.300	305	14	★18	.947
1981—Vancouver†	P. C.	OF	97	339	40	87	10	5	2	30	.257	175	14	7	.964
1982—Milwaukee	Amer.	OF	18	9	4	0	0	0	0	0	.000	7	0	0	1.000
1982—Vancouver‡	P. C.	OF	102	413	70	130	23	7	17	65	.315	199	15	10	.955
1982—Houston	Nat.	OF	12	24	2	1	0	0	0	1	.042	11	0	1	.917
1983—Houston	Nat.	OF	88	195	25	46	7	3	2	18	.236	68	1	4	.945
1984—Houston§	Nat.	OF	121	331	33	86	17	5	2	29	.260	149	4	4	.975
1985—Houston	Nat.	OF	150	539	72	145	27	5	16	68	.269	328	10	1	★.997
1986—Houston	Nat.	OF	157	591	83	184	33	5	20	79	.311	303	12	5	.984
1987—Houston	Nat.	OF	157	592	83	168	31	5	19	85	.284	287	11	4	.987
1988—Houston	Nat.	OF	157	541	57	138	27	2	14	72	.255	267	7	6	.979
1989—Houston x	Nat.	OF	87	313	42	94	19	4	5	44	.300	186	6	3	.985
1989—Tucson y	P. C.	OF	6	17	1	5	1	0	0	2	.294	8	0	0	1.000
American League Totals—1 Year			18	9	4	0	0	0	0	0	.000	7	0	0	1.000
National League Totals—8 Years			929	3126	397	862	161	29	78	396	.276	1599	51	28	.983
Major League Totals—8 Years			947	3135	401	862	161	29	78	396	.275	1606	51	28	.983

Selected by Milwaukee Brewers' organization in 2nd round of free-agent draft, June 7, 1977.

†On disabled list, July 29 to September 1, 1981.

‡Traded with Pitchers Mike Madden and Frank DiPino to Houston Astros, September 3, 1982, completing deal in which Houston traded Pitcher Don Sutton to Milwaukee Brewers for three players to be named later, August 30, 1982.

§On disabled list, March 29 to April 13, 1984.

xOn disabled list, May 28 to August 11, 1989; included rehabilitation disability assignment to Tucson, August 4 to August 11, 1989.

yGranted free agency, November 13, 1989; signed by San Francisco Giants, November 16, 1989.

CHAMPIONSHIP SERIES RECORD

Shares Championship Series records for most times caught stealing, series (3), 1986 and game (2), October 15, 1986 (16 innings).

Year—Club	League	Pos.	G.	AB.	R.	H.	2B.	3B.	HR.	RBI.	B.A.	PO	A.	E.	F.A.
1986—Houston	Nat.	OF	6	24	0	7	2	0	0	0	.292	16	0	1	.941

ALL-STAR GAME RECORD

Year	League	Pos.	AB.	R.	H.	2B.	3B.	HR.	RBI.	B.A.	PO.	A.	E.	F.A.
1986—National		PH	1	0	0	0	0	0	0	.000	0	0	0	.000

WILLIAM DERRICK BATES
(Billy)

Born December 7, 1963, at Houston, Tex.
Height, 5.07. Weight, 155.
Throws right and bats lefthanded.
Attended University of Texas, Austin, Tex.

Major League stolen bases: 1989 (2).
Led American Association second basemen in total chances with 636 in 1988.
Led Texas League second basemen in double plays with 96 in 1986.
Named second baseman on THE SPORTING NEWS College Baseball All-America Team, 1984.

Year—Club	League	Pos.	G.	AB.	R.	H.	2B.	3B.	HR.	RBI.	B.A.	PO.	A.	E.	F.A.
1985—Stockton	Calif.	2B-OF	59	218	36	65	8	1	3	31	.298	117	175	8	.973
1986—El Paso†	Texas	2B	122	511	104	151	26	4	8	75	.295	★286	362	21	.969
1987—Denver†	A. A.	•2B-SS	130	506	★117	160	25	5	3	62	.316	254	•393	17	.974
1988—Denver†	A. A.	★2B-OF	119	472	74	122	16	★12	2	44	.258	★252	369	15	.976
1989—Denver	A. A.	2B-OF	95	363	50	99	11	2	1	38	.273	192	285	13	.973
1989—Milwaukee‡	Amer.	2B	7	14	3	3	0	0	0	0	.214	14	16	2	.938
Major League Totals—1 Year			7	14	3	3	0	0	0	0	.214	14	16	2	.938

Selected by Philadelphia Phillies' organization in 8th round of free-agent draft, June 7, 1982.
Selected by Milwaukee Brewers' organization in 4th round of free-agent draft, June 3, 1985.

†Switch-hitter.

‡On disabled list, August 23 to September 12, 1989.

WILLIAM DAVID BATHE
(Bill)

Born October 14, 1960, at Downey, Calif.
Height, 6.02. Weight, 200.
Throws and bats righthanded.
Attended Rio Hondo College, Whittier, Calif.; California State University,
Fullerton, Calif.; and Pepperdine University, Malibu, Calif.
Twin brother of Bob Bathe, third baseman in Oakland A's and Chicago Cubs'
organizations, 1982 through 1986.

Led Pacific Coast League catchers in total chances with 702 in 1983 and 684 in 1985.
Led Pacific Coast League catchers in putouts with 632 and tied for lead in double plays with 9 in 1983.

Year—Club	League	Pos.	G.	AB.	R.	H.	2B.	3B.	HR.	RBI.	B.A.	PO.	A.	E.	F.A.
1981—San Jose†	Calif.	C-OF	51	177	20	45	9	1	4	22	.254	234	42	8	.972
1982—West Haven	East.	C	128	370	57	104	22	0	17	57	.281	★763	55	9	★.989
1983—Tacoma	P. C.	C-1B	116	399	56	101	18	1	16	62	.253	633	55	15	.979

Year Club	League	Pos.	G.	AB.	R.	H.	2B.	3B.	HR.	RBI.	B.A.	PO.	A.	E.	F.A.
1984—Tacoma	P. C.	C-3B-1B	84	245	27	63	12	1	3	42	.257	381	29	7	.983
1985—Tacoma	P. C.	C	108	359	43	100	26	0	6	45	.279	★613	64	7	.990
1986—Oakland	Amer.	C	39	103	9	19	3	0	5	11	.184	211	11	2	.991
1986—Tacoma‡	P. C.	C	40	135	13	26	7	1	1	13	.193	120	21	2	.986
1987—Iowa	A. A.	C-1B	46	130	17	43	7	1	3	22	.331	176	10	4	.979
1988—Iowa§	A. A.	C-1B	106	385	48	120	27	2	8	49	.312	434	33	8	.983
1989—Phoenix	P. C.	C-OF-1B	76	270	30	94	21	5	6	40	.348	145	11	1	.994
1989—San Francisco	Nat.	C	30	32	3	9	1	0	0	6	.281	13	0	0	1.000
American League Totals—1 Year			39	103	9	19	3	0	5	11	.184	211	11	2	.991
National League Totals—1 Year			30	32	3	9	1	0	0	6	.281	13	0	0	1.000
Major League Totals—2 Years			69	135	12	28	4	0	5	17	.207	224	11	2	.992

Selected by Pittsburgh Pirates' organization in 10th round of free-agent draft, January 8, 1980.
Selected by Oakland A's organization in 8th round of free-agent draft, June 8, 1981.
†Loaned to San Jose (Co-op), June 23, 1981; returned, October 22, 1981.
‡Traded to Chicago Cubs for First Baseman Joe Hicks, December 17, 1986.
§Granted free agency, October 15, 1988; signed by Phoenix (San Francisco Giants' organization), November 8, 1988.

CHAMPIONSHIP SERIES RECORD

Year Club	League	Pos.	G.	AB.	R.	H.	2B.	3B.	HR.	RBI.	B.A.	PO.	A.	E.	F.A.
1989—San Francisco	Nat.	PH	2	1	0	0	0	0	0	0	.000	0	0	0	.000

WORLD SERIES RECORD

Shares World Series record for hitting home run in first series at-bat, October 27, 1989.

Year Club	League	Pos.	G.	AB.	R.	H.	2B.	3B.	HR.	RBI.	B.A.	PO.	A.	E.	F.A.
1989—San Francisco	Nat.	PH	2	2	1	1	0	0	1	3	.500	0	0	0	.000

KEVIN WADE BATISTE

Born October 21, 1966, at Galveston, Tex.
Height, 6.02. Weight, 187.
Throws and bats righthanded.

Led Florida State League batters in strikeouts with 136, stolen bases with 70 and caught stealing with 25 in 1987.
Led Pioneer League batters in strikeouts with 83 in 1985.
Led Florida State League outfielders in total chances with 368 in 1987.
Tied for Pioneer League lead in double plays by outfielders with 3 in 1985.

Year Club	League	Pos.	G.	AB.	R.	H.	2B.	3B.	HR.	RBI.	B.A.	PO.	A.	E.	F.A.
1985—Medicine Hat	Pion.	OF	●70	274	45	68	6	4	1	20	.248	★135	6	6	.959
1986—Florence	S. Atl.	OF	49	181	33	48	8	1	3	16	.265	109	3	7	.941
1986—Ventura County	Calif.	OF	78	250	29	45	6	0	0	9	.180	189	5	5	.975
1987—Dunedin	Fla. St.	OF	130	514	65	137	12	3	3	28	.267	★347	●16	5	.986
1988—Knoxville	South.	OF	112	363	44	85	14	4	3	22	.234	257	11	10	.964
1988—Syracuse	Int.	OF	34	105	10	24	6	1	1	9	.229	85	2	1	.989
1989—Knoxville†	South.	OF	81	279	36	62	8	8	1	25	.222	172	3	8	.956
1989—Toronto‡	Amer.	OF	6	8	1	2	0	0	0	0	.250	7	0	0	1.000
Major League Totals—1 Year			6	8	1	2	0	0	0	0	.250	7	0	0	1.000

Selected by Toronto Blue Jays' organization in 2nd round of free-agent draft, June 3, 1985.
†On disabled list, April 7 to April 14, 1989.
‡Traded with Catcher Ernie Whitt to Atlanta Braves for Pitcher Rick Trlicek, December 17, 1989.

KIMOTHY EMIL BATISTE
(Kim)

Born March 15, 1968, at New Orleans, La.
Height, 6.00. Weight, 175.
Throws and bats righthanded.

Year Club	League	Pos.	G.	AB.	R.	H.	2B.	3B.	HR.	RBI.	B.A.	PO.	A.	E.	F.A.
1987—Utica	NYP	SS-3B	46	150	15	26	8	1	2	10	.173	64	90	16	.906
1988—Spartanburg	S. Atl.	SS	122	430	51	107	19	6	6	52	.249	202	363	60	.904
1989—Clearwater	Fla. St.	SS-3B	114	385	36	90	12	4	3	33	.234	168	309	35	.932

Selected by Philadelphia Phillies' organization in 3rd round of free-agent draft, June 2, 1987.

JOSE JOAQUIN BAUTISTA

Name pronounced Bough-TEES-tuh.

Born July 25, 1964, at Bani, Dominican Republic.
Height, 6.02. Weight, 203.
Throws and bats righthanded.

Pitched 6-0 no-hit victory against Prince William, May 26, 1985 (first game).

Year Club	League	G.	IP.	W.	L.	Pct.	H.	R.	ER.	SO.	BB.	ERA.
1981—Kingsport	Ap'lachian	13	66	3	6	.333	84	54	34	34	17	4.64
1982—Kingsport	Ap'lachian	14	38⅓	0	4	.000	61	44	38	13	19	8.92
1983—Sarasota Mets	Gulf Coast	13	81⅔	4	3	.571	66	31	21	44	32	2.31
1984—Columbia	S. Atlantic	19	135	13	4	.765	121	52	47	96	35	3.13
1985—Lynchburg	Carolina	27	169	15	8	.652	145	49	44	109	33	2.34
1986—Jackson	Texas	7	21⅔	0	1	.000	36	22	20	13	8	8.31

Year Club	League	G.	IP.	W.	L.	Pct.	H.	R.	ER.	SO.	BB.	ERA.
1986—Lynchburg......................	Carolina	18	118⅔	8	8	.500	120	58	52	62	24	3.94
1987—Jackson†........................	Texas	28	169⅓	10	5	.667	174	76	61	95	43	3.24
1988—Baltimore	American	33	171⅔	6	15	.286	171	86	82	76	45	4.30
1989—Baltimore‡.....................	American	15	78	3	4	.429	84	46	46	30	15	5.31
1989—Rochester.......................	Int'national	15	98⅔	4	4	.500	84	41	31	47	26	2.83
Major League Totals—2 Years............................		48	249⅔	9	19	.321	255	132	128	106	60	4.61

Signed as free agent by New York Mets' organization, April 25, 1981.

†Drafted by Baltimore Orioles, December 7, 1987.

‡On disabled list, May 20 to June 11, 1989; included rehabilitation disability assignment to Rochester, May 29 to June 11, 1989.

JAMES BENTON BAXTER
(Jim)

Born August 8, 1966, at LaMesa, Calif.
Height, 6.02. Weight, 175.
Throws and bats righthanded.
Attended College of Southern Idaho, Twin Falls, Ida.,
and Southwestern College, Chula Vista, Calif.

Led Midwest League catchers in double plays with 11 in 1988.
Tied for Florida State League lead in double plays by catchers with 9 in 1989.

Year Club	League	Pos.	G.	AB.	R.	H.	2B.	3B.	HR.	RBI.	B.A.	PO.	A.	E.	F.A.
1986—Burlington	Appal.	C	32	90	14	16	3	0	0	4	.178	227	15	9	.964
1987—Burlington	Appal.	C	37	98	19	27	7	1	3	16	.276	243	33	5	.982
1988—Waterloo†	Midw.	C	66	190	18	39	5	1	1	13	.205	402	63	17	.965
1989—Lakeland................	Fla. St.	C	91	263	32	66	16	1	4	22	.251	496	61	★16	.972

Selected by Cleveland Indians' organization in 3rd round of free-agent draft, January 14, 1986.

†Drafted by Detroit Tigers' organization, December 5, 1988.

WILLIAM DARO BEAN
(Billy)

Born May 11, 1904, at Santa Ana, Calif.
Height, 6.01. Weight, 177.
Throws and bats lefthanded.
Received bachelor of arts degree in business administration
from Loyola Marymount University, Los Angeles, Calif.

Shares modern major league record for most hits, first game in major leagues (nine innings) (4), April 25, 1987.
Major League stolen bases: 1987 (1).

Year Club	League	Pos.	G.	AB.	R.	H.	2B.	3B.	HR.	RBI.	B.A.	PO.	A.	E.	F.A.
1986—Glens Falls...........	East.	OF	80	279	43	77	10	3	8	49	.277	189	4	3	.985
1987—Toledo	Int.	OF	104	357	51	98	18	2	8	43	.275	228	1	7	.970
1987—Detroit...................	Amer.	OF	26	66	6	17	2	0	0	4	.258	54	1	0	1.000
1988—Toledo	Int.	OF-1B	●138	484	59	124	19	1	6	40	.256	664	43	12	.983
1988—Detroit...................	Amer.	OF-1B	10	11	2	2	0	1	0	0	.182	8	1	0	1.000
1989—Detroit...................	Amer.	OF-1B	9	11	0	0	0	0	0	0	.000	12	0	2	.857
1989—Toledo†	Int.	OF-1B	76	267	43	84	14	2	4	29	.315	231	14	4	.984
1989—Albuquerque	P. C.	OF	3	9	1	2	0	1	0	3	.222	7	0	0	1.000
1989—Los Angeles	Nat.	OF	51	71	7	14	4	0	0	3	.197	49	0	0	1.000
American League Totals—3 Years........			45	88	8	19	2	1	0	4	.216	74	2	2	.974
National League Totals—1 Year.............			51	71	7	14	4	0	0	3	.197	49	0	0	1.000
Major League Totals—3 Years................			96	159	15	33	6	1	0	7	.208	123	2	2	.984

Selected by New York Yankees' organization in 24th round of free-agent draft, June 3, 1985.

Selected by Detroit Tigers' organization in 4th round of free-agent draft, June 2, 1986.

†Traded to Albuquerque (Los Angeles Dodgers' organization) for Outfielder Steve Green and First Baseman-Outfielder Domingo Michel, July 17, 1989.

WILLIAM LAMAR BEANE III

Name pronounced Been.

(Billy)

Born March 29, 1962, at Orlando, Fla.
Height, 6.04. Weight, 208.
Throws and bats righthanded.
Attended University of California at San Diego, La Jolla, Calif.

Major League stolen bases: 1986 (2), 1989 (3). Total—5.
Led Pacific Coast League outfielders in double plays with 5 in 1987.
Led International League batters in strikeouts with 130 in 1985.
Tied for Carolina League lead in sacrifice flies with 8 in 1981.
Led Texas League outfielders in fielding percentage with .994 in 1983.

Year Club	League	Pos.	G.	AB.	R.	H.	2B.	3B.	HR.	RBI.	B.A.	PO.	A.	E.	F.A.
1980—Little Falls............	NYP	OF	43	138	10	29	3	2	1	14	.210	93	5	3	.970
1981—Lynchburg............	Carol.	OF	114	403	47	108	13	●9	9	59	.268	233	8	11	.956
1982—Jackson	Texas	OF	126	418	39	88	13	4	5	36	.211	200	6	10	.954
1983—Jackson	Texas	OF-1B	121	423	53	104	14	1	11	75	.246	382	24	8	.981
1984—Jackson	Texas	OF	123	455	78	128	29	3	20	72	.281	180	5	7	.964

Year	Club	League	Pos.	G.	AB.	R.	H.	2B.	3B.	HR.	RBI.	B.A.	PO.	A.	E.	F.A.
1984—New York	Nat.		OF	5	10	0	1	0	0	0	0	.100	2	0	0	1.000
1985—Tidewater	Int.		OF	135	504	63	143	★34	4	19	77	.284	255	10	6	.978
1985—New York†	Nat.		OF	8	8	0	2	1	0	0	1	.250	1	0	0	1.000
1986—Minnesota‡	Amer.		OF	80	183	20	39	6	0	3	15	.213	118	0	0	1.000
1986—Toledo	Int.		OF	32	126	17	37	5	0	5	17	.294	68	0	4	.944
1987—Portland	P. C.		OF-1B	123	463	63	132	28	8	8	71	.285	259	15	9	.968
1987—Minnesota§	Amer.		OF	12	15	1	4	2	0	0	1	.267	8	0	0	1.000
1988—Detroit	Amer.		OF	6	6	1	1	0	0	0	1	.167	5	0	0	1.000
1988—Toledo x	Int.		OF	110	361	33	85	15	2	9	39	.235	130	4	3	.978
1989—Tacoma	P. C.		OF-3B-C	38	151	19	48	6	1	4	23	.318	61	8	2	.972
1989—Oakland y	Amer.		O-1-3-C	37	79	8	19	5	0	0	11	.241	58	3	1	.984
National League Totals—2 Years				13	18	0	3	1	0	0	1	.167	3	0	0	1.000
American League Totals—4 Years				135	283	30	63	13	0	3	28	.223	189	3	1	.995
Major League Totals—6 Years				148	301	30	66	14	0	3	29	.219	192	3	1	.995

Selected by New York Mets' organization in 1st round (23rd player selected) of free-agent draft, June 3, 1980.

†Traded with Pitchers Bill Latham and Joe Klink to Minnesota Twins for Second Baseman Tim Teufel and Outfielder Pat Crosby, January 16, 1986.

‡On disabled list, April 1 to April 21, 1986.

§Traded to Detroit Tigers for Pitcher Balvino Galvez, March 24, 1988.

xGranted free agency, October 15, 1988; signed by Oakland Athletics, November 30, 1988.

yOn disabled list, June 13 to July 4, 1989.

DAVID CHARLES BEARD
(Dave)

Born October 2, 1959, at Chamblee, Ga.
Height, 6.05. Weight, 215.
Throws right and bats lefthanded

Major League saves: 1980 (1), 1981 (3), 1982 (11), 1983 (10), 1984 (5). Total—30.
Led Eastern League in complete games with 20 in 1979.
Tied for Pacific Coast League lead in balks with 3 in 1980.
Tied for Eastern League lead in intentional bases on balls issued with 9 in 1979.
Tied for California League lead in shutouts with 5 in 1978.

Year	Club	League	G.	IP.	W.	L.	Pct.	H.	R.	ER.	SO.	BB.	ERA.
1977—Medicine Hat	Pioneer	11	71	4	5	.444	79	50	36	30	31	4.56
1978—Modesto	California	25	185	12	6	.667	161	94	60	142	64	2.42
1979—Waterbury	Eastern	25	★191	10	●14	.417	192	87	64	111	63	3.02
1980—Ogden†	P. Coast	16	97	7	8	.467	110	76	69	70	44	6.40
1980—Oakland	American	13	16	0	1	.000	12	6	6	12	7	3.38
1981—Tacoma	P. Coast	42	129	11	11	.500	132	67	61	114	51	4.26
1981—Oakland	American	8	13	1	1	.500	9	5	4	15	4	2.77
1982—Tacoma	P. Coast	1	1	0	0	.000	0	0	0	1	0	0.00
1982—Oakland	American	54	91⅔	10	9	.526	85	41	35	73	35	3.44
1983—Oakland‡	American	43	61	5	5	.500	55	39	38	40	36	5.61
1983—Modesto§	California	1	1	0	0	.000	0	0	0	2	0	0.00
1984—Seattle x	American	43	76	3	2	.600	88	56	49	40	33	5.80
1984—Salt Lake City y	P. Coast	2	9⅓	0	1	.000	13	7	6	0	1	5.79
1985—Maine za	Int'national	16	21⅔	1	0	1.000	21	7	6	15	11	2.49
1985—Iowa	Am. Assoc.	11	16	2	0	1.000	10	1	1	9	9	0.56
1985—Chicago b	National	9	12⅔	0	0	.000	16	9	9	4	7	6.39
1986—Richmond c	Int'national	45	64⅓	6	6	.500	65	40	28	62	29	3.92
1987—			(Out of Organized Baseball)									
1988—Glens Falls	Eastern	11	46⅓	3	3	.500	31	11	9	41	7	1.75
1988—Toledo	Int'national	21	104⅔	6	7	.462	84	37	35	76	29	3.01
1989—Toledo	Int'national	12	60	3	4	.429	49	21	17	50	14	2.55
1989—Detroit de	American	2	5⅓	0	2	.000	9	7	3	1	2	5.06
American League Totals—6 Years		163	263	19	20	.487	258	154	135	181	117	4.62
National League Totals—1 Year		9	12⅔	0	0	.000	16	9	9	4	7	6.39
Major League Totals—7 Years		172	275⅔	19	20	.487	274	144	144	185	124	4.70

Selected by Oakland A's organization in 6th round of free-agent draft, June 7, 1977.

†On disabled list, April 20 to May 2, 1980.

‡On disabled list, June 9 to July 1, 1983; included rehabilitation disability assignment to Modesto, June 28 to July 1, 1983.

§Traded with Catcher Bob Kearney to Seattle Mariners for Pitcher Bill Caudill and a player to be named later, November 21, 1983; Oakland A's acquired Pitcher Darrel Akerfelds to complete deal, December 7, 1983.

xOn disabled list, June 25 to July 29, 1984; included rehabilitation disability assignment to Salt Lake City, July 20 to July 29, 1984.

yReleased, April 1, 1985; signed by Maine (Cleveland Indians' organization), April 13, 1985.

zOn disabled list, May 27 to July 10, 1985.

aTraded to Iowa (Chicago Cubs' organization) for Outfielder Tom Grant, July 26, 1985.

bReleased, November 13, 1985; signed by Atlanta Braves, December 4, 1985.

cGranted free agency, October 15, 1986; signed by Detroit Tigers' organization, December 8, 1987.

dOn disabled list, July 24, 1989 through remainder of season.

eReleased, October 4, 1989.

DIVISION SERIES RECORD

Year	Club	League	G.	IP.	W.	L.	Pct.	H.	R.	ER.	SO.	BB.	ERA.
1981—Oakland	American	1	1⅓	0	0	.000	0	0	0	2	0	0.00

Year Club	League	G.	IP.	W.	L.	Pct.	H.	R.	ER.	SO.	BB.	ERA.
1981—Oakland	American	1	⅔	0	0	.000	5	3	3	0	0	40.50

KEVIN GERARD BEARSE

Born November 7, 1965, at Jersey City, N.J.
Height, 6.02. Weight, 195.
Throws and bats lefthanded.
Attended Old Dominion University, Norfolk, Va.

Led Carolina League in games finished in relief with 56 and saves with 22 in 1988.
Tied for Appalachian League lead in saves with 8 in 1987.
Named Carolina League co-Pitcher of the Year, 1988.

Year Club	League	G.	IP.	W.	L.	Pct.	H.	R.	ER.	SO.	BB.	ERA.
1987—Burlington	Ap'lachian	22	63	7	1	.875	45	13	12	81	15	1.71
1988—Kinston	Carolina	*62	103	10	8	.556	76	19	15	127	28	1.31
1989—Canton-Akron	Eastern	14	101	9	3	.750	90	29	23	67	16	2.05
1989—Colorado Springs	P. Coast	13	89	5	2	.714	87	44	39	51	32	3.94

Selected by Cleveland Indians' organization in 27th round of free-agent draft, June 2, 1986.
Selected by Cleveland Indians' organization in 22nd round of free-agent draft, June 2, 1987.

GORDON BLAINE BEATTY

(Known by middle name.)

Born April 25, 1964, at Victoria, Tex.
Height, 6.02. Weight, 185.
Throws and bats lefthanded.
Attended San Jacinto College, Pasadena, Tex.,
and Baylor University, Waco, Tex.

Led Texas League pitchers in shutouts with 5, complete games with 12 and tied for lead in games started with 28 in 1988.
Led New York-Pennsylvania League pitchers in complete games with 8 in 1986.
Tied for International League lead in games started by pitchers with 27 and shutouts with 3 in 1989.
Named Texas League Pitcher of the Year, 1988.
Named Carolina League Pitcher of the Year, 1987.

Year Club	League	G.	IP.	W.	L.	Pct.	H.	R.	ER.	SO.	BB.	ERA.
1986—Newark	NYP	15	*119⅓	*11	3	.786	98	37	28	93	30	2.11
1987—Hagerstown	Carolina	13	100	11	1	*.917	81	32	28	65	11	2.52
1987—Charlotte†	Southern	15	105⅔	6	5	.545	110	38	36	57	20	3.07
1988—Jackson	Texas	30	*208⅔	*16	8	.667	191	64	57	103	34	2.46
1989—Tidewater	Int'national	27	185	12	10	.545	173	86	68	90	43	3.31
1989—New York	National	2	6	0	0	.000	5	1	1	3	2	1.50
Major League Totals—1 Year		2	6	0	0	.000	5	1	1	3	2	1.50

Selected by Baltimore Orioles' organization in 5th round of free-agent draft, January 17, 1984.
Selected by Baltimore Orioles' organization in secondary phase of free-agent draft, June 4, 1984.
Selected by St. Louis Cardinals' organization in secondary phase of free-agent draft, June 3, 1985.
Selected by Baltimore Orioles' organization in 9th round of free-agent draft, June 2, 1986.
†Traded with a player to be named later to New York Mets for Pitcher Doug Sisk, December 8, 1987; New York acquired Pitcher Greg Talamantez to complete deal, December 11, 1987.

STEPHEN WAYNE BEDROSIAN

Name pronounced Bed-ROHZ-ee-un.

(Steve)

Born December 6, 1957, at Methuen, Mass.
Height, 6.03. Weight, 205.
Throws and bats righthanded.
Attended North Essex Community College, Haverhill, Mass., and
University of New Haven, New Haven, Conn.

Holds major league record for most games taken out as starting pitcher, season (37), 1985.
Major League saves: 1982 (11), 1983 (19), 1984 (11), 1986 (29), 1987 (40), 1988 (28), 1989 (23). Total—161.
Led National League in saves with 40 in 1987.
Tied for Southern League lead in games started by pitchers with 29 in 1980.
Won National League Cy Young Memorial Award, 1987.
Named National League Fireman of the Year by THE SPORTING NEWS, 1987.
Named National League Rookie Pitcher of the Year by THE SPORTING NEWS, 1982.

Year Club	League	G.	IP.	W.	L.	Pct.	H.	R.	ER.	SO.	BB.	ERA.
1978—Kingsport	Ap'lachian	6	38	2	2	.500	38	18	13	29	25	3.08
1978—Greenwood	W. Carol.	8	55	5	1	.833	45	17	13	58	34	2.13
1979—Savannah†	Southern	13	89	5	5	.500	71	36	30	73	58	3.03
1980—Savannah	Southern	29	*203	14	10	.583	167	91	72	*161	96	3.19
1981—Richmond	Int'national	26	184	10	10	.500	143	76	55	144	99	2.69
1981—Atlanta	National	15	24	1	2	.333	15	14	12	9	15	4.50
1982—Atlanta	National	64	137⅔	8	6	.571	102	39	37	123	57	2.42
1983—Atlanta	National	70	120	9	10	.474	100	50	48	114	51	3.60
1984—Atlanta‡	National	40	83⅔	9	6	.600	65	23	22	81	33	2.37
1985—Atlanta§	National	37	206⅔	7	15	.318	198	101	88	134	111	3.83
1986—Philadelphia	National	68	90⅓	8	6	.571	79	39	34	82	34	3.39

Year Club	League	G.	IP.	W.	L.	Pct.	H.	R.	ER.	SO.	BB.	ERA.
1987—Philadelphia	National	65	89	5	3	.625	79	31	28	74	28	2.83
1988—Maine x	Int'national	5	6⅔	0	0	.000	6	0	0	5	2	0.00
1988—Philadelphia	National	57	74⅓	6	6	.500	75	34	31	61	27	3.75
1989—Philadelphia y-San Francisco	National	68	84⅔	3	7	.300	56	31	27	58	39	2.87
Major League Totals—9 Years		484	910⅓	56	61	.479	769	362	327	736	395	3.23

Selected by Atlanta Braves' organization in 3rd round of free-agent draft, June 6, 1978.

†On disabled list, June 24 to September 18, 1979.

‡On disabled list, August 20 to September 4, 1984.

§Traded with Outfielder Milt Thompson to Philadelphia Phillies for Catcher Ozzie Virgil and Pitcher Pete Smith, December 10, 1985.

xOn Philadelphia disabled list, March 21 to May 20, 1988; included rehabilitation disability assignment to Maine, May 9 to May 19, 1988.

yTraded with a player to be named later to San Francisco Giants for Pitchers Dennis Cook and Terry Mulholland and Third Baseman Charlie Hayes, June 18, 1989; San Francisco organization acquired Infielder Rick Parker to complete deal, August 7, 1989.

CHAMPIONSHIP SERIES RECORD

Shares National League Championship Series record for most saves, series (3), 1989.

Year Club	League	G.	IP.	W.	L.	Pct.	H.	R.	ER.	SO.	BB.	ERA.
1982—Atlanta	National	2	1	0	0	.000	3	2	2	2	1	18.00
1989—San Francisco	National	4	3⅓	0	0	.000	4	1	1	2	2	2.70
Championship Series Totals—2 Years		6	4⅓	0	0	.000	7	3	3	4	3	6.23

WORLD SERIES RECORD

Year Club	League	G.	IP.	W.	L.	Pct.	H.	R.	ER.	SO.	BB.	ERA.
1989—San Francisco	National	2	2⅔	0	0	.000	0	0	0	2	2	0.00

ALL-STAR GAME RECORD

Year League	IP.	W.	L.	Pct.	H.	R.	ER.	SO.	BB.	ERA.
1987—National	1	0	0	.000	0	0	0	0	2	0.00

KEVIN D. BELCHER

Born August 8, 1967, at Waco, Tex.
Height, 6.00. Weight, 170.
Throws and bats righthanded.
Attended Navarro College, Corsicana, Tex.

Year Club League	Pos.	G.	AB.	R.	H.	2B.	3B.	HR.	RBI.	B.A.	PO.	A.	E.	F.A.
1987—Sarasota Rangers Gulf C.	OF	58	215	32	45	8	2	2	10	.209	89	6	●7	.931
1988—Gastonia	S. Atl.	OF	105	392	56	96	13	1	8	44	.245	190	8	7	.966
1989—Gastonia†	S. Atl.	OF	93	338	61	100	21	1	14	59	.296	172	5	4	.978

Selected by Texas Rangers' organization in 6th round of free-agent draft, June 2, 1987.

†On disabled list, July 15, 1989 through remainder of season.

TIMOTHY WAYNE BELCHER
(Tim)

Born October 19, 1961, at Mount Gilead, O.
Height, 6.03. Weight, 223.
Throws and bats righthanded.
Attended Mt. Vernon Nazarene College, Mt. Vernon, O.

Shares major league record for fewest complete games for leader, season (10), 1989.

Major League saves: 1988 (4), 1989 (1). Total—5.

Led National League in shutouts with 8 and tied for complete games with 10 in 1989.

Named National League Rookie Pitcher of the Year by THE SPORTING NEWS, 1988.

Named righhanded pitcher on THE SPORTING NEWS College Baseball All-America Team, 1983.

Year Club	League	G.	IP.	W.	L.	Pct.	H.	R.	ER.	SO.	BB.	ERA.
1984—Madison	Midwest	16	98⅓	9	4	.692	80	45	39	111	48	3.57
1984—Albany	Eastern	10	54	3	4	.429	37	30	20	40	41	3.33
1985—Huntsville	Southern	29	149⅔	11	10	.524	145	99	78	90	99	4.69
1986—Huntsville†	Southern	9	37	2	5	.286	50	28	27	25	22	6.57
1987—Tacoma‡	P. Coast	29	163	9	11	.450	143	89	80	136	★133	4.42
1987—Los Angeles	National	6	34	4	2	.667	30	11	9	23	7	2.38
1988—Los Angeles	National	36	179⅔	12	6	.667	143	65	58	152	51	2.91
1989—Los Angeles	National	39	230	15	12	.556	182	81	72	200	80	2.82
Major League Totals—3 Years		81	443⅔	31	20	.608	355	157	139	375	138	2.82

Selected by Minnesota Twins' organization in 1st round (first player selected) of free-agent draft, June 6, 1983.

Selected by New York Yankees' organization in secondary phase of free-agent draft, January 17, 1984.

Selected by Oakland A's organization in player compensation pool draft, February 8, 1984. (Oakland received compensation for Baltimore Orioles' signing of free-agent Pitcher Tom Underwood, a Type A player, February 7, 1984.)

†On disabled list, April 10 to May 4 and May 5 to July 23, 1986.

‡Traded to Los Angeles Dodgers, September 3, 1987, completing deal in which Los Angeles traded Pitcher Rick Honeycutt to Oakland Athletics for a player to be named later, August 29, 1987.

CHAMPIONSHIP SERIES RECORD

Year Club	League	G.	IP.	W.	L.	Pct.	H.	R.	ER.	SO.	BB.	ERA.
1988—Los Angeles	National	2	15⅓	2	0	1.000	12	7	7	16	4	4.11

Year	Club	League	G.	IP.	W.	L.	Pct.	H.	R.	ER.	SO.	BB.	ERA.
1988—Los Angeles		National	2	8⅔	1	0	1.000	10	7	6	10	6	6.23

STANLEY PETER BELINDA
(Stan)

Born August 6, 1966, at State College, Pa.
Height, 6.03. Weight, 195.
Throws and bats righthanded.
Attended Allegany Community College, Cumberland, Md.

Year	Club	League	G.	IP.	W.	L.	Pct.	H.	R.	ER.	SO.	BB.	ERA.
1986—Watertown		NYP	5	8	0	0	.000	5	3	3	5	2	3.38
1986—Bradenton Pirates†		Gulf Coast	17	20⅓	3	2	.600	23	12	6	17	2	2.66
1987—Macon		S. Atlantic	50	82	6	4	.600	59	26	19	75	27	2.09
1988—Salem		Carolina	53	71⅔	6	4	.600	54	33	22	63	32	2.76
1989—Harrisburg		Eastern	32	38⅔	1	4	.200	32	13	10	33	25	2.33
1989—Buffalo		Am. Assoc.	19	28⅓	2	2	.500	13	5	3	28	13	0.95
1989—Pittsburgh		National	8	10⅓	0	1	.000	13	8	7	10	2	6.10
Major League Totals—1 Year			8	10⅓	0	1	.000	13	8	7	10	2	6.10

Selected by Pittsburgh Pirates' organization in 10th round of free-agent draft, June 2, 1986.
†On disabled list, June 21 to June 30, 1986.

DAVID GUS BELL
(Buddy)

Born August 27, 1951, at Pittsburgh, Pa.
Height, 6.03. Weight, 200.
Throws and bats righthanded.
Attended Xavier University, Cincinnati, O., and Miami University, Oxford, O.
Son of Gus Bell, outfielder with Pittsburgh Pirates, Cincinnati Reds, New York Mets and Milwaukee Braves, 1950 through 1964; scout, Cleveland Indians, 1966, 1968 and 1969; and scout, Texas Rangers, 1985.

Shares major league record for most home runs, opening day of season (2), April 8, 1982.
Major League stolen bases: 1972 (5), 1973 (7), 1974 (1), 1975 (6), 1976 (3), 1977 (1), 1978 (1), 1979 (5), 1980 (3), 1981 (3) 1982 (5), 1983 (3), 1984 (2), 1985 (3), 1986 (2), 1987 (4), 1988 (1). Total—55.
Led American League in sacrifice flies with 10 in 1981.
Led American League third basemen in total chances with 495 in 1978, 361 in 1981, 540 in 1982 and 523 in 1983.
Led American League third basemen in assists with 364 in 1979 and 281 in 1981.
Led American League third basemen in putouts with 144 and double plays with 44 in 1973.
Tied for American League lead in game-winning RBIs with 16 in 1979.
Tied for American League lead in double plays by third basemen with 30 in 1978.
Led Gulf Coast League second basemen in double plays with 26 in 1969.
Named third baseman on THE SPORTING NEWS American League All-Star Team, 1981 and 1984.
Named third baseman on THE SPORTING NEWS American League All-Star fielding team, 1979 through 1984.
Named third baseman on THE SPORTING NEWS American League Silver Slugger team, 1984.

Year	Club	League	Pos.	G.	AB.	R.	H.	2B.	3B.	HR.	RBI.	B.A.	PO.	A.	E.	F.A.
1969—Sarasota Indians	Gulf C.		2B	51	170	18	39	4	●3	3	24	.229	119	108	7	★.970
1970—Sumter	W. Car.		3B-2B-SS	121	442	81	117	19	3	12	75	.265	116	189	27	.919
1971—Wichita	A. A.		★3-2-S-O	129	470	65	136	23	1	11	59	.289	★139	203	16	.955
1972—Cleveland	Amer.		OF-3B	132	466	49	119	21	1	9	36	.255	284	23	3	.990
1973—Cleveland	Amer.		3B-OF	156	631	86	169	23	7	14	59	.268	146	363	22	.959
1974—Cleveland†	Amer.		3B	116	423	51	111	15	1	7	46	.262	112	274	15	.963
1975—Cleveland	Amer.		3B	153	553	66	150	20	4	10	59	.271	★146	330	25	.950
1976—Cleveland	Amer.		3B-1B	159	604	75	170	26	2	7	60	.281	109	331	20	.957
1977—Cleveland	Amer.		3B-OF	129	479	64	140	23	4	11	64	.292	134	253	16	.960
1978—Cleveland‡	Amer.		3B	142	556	71	157	27	8	6	62	.282	125	★355	15	.970
1979—Texas	Amer.		3B-SS	●162	★670	89	200	42	3	18	101	.299	147	429	17	.971
1980—Texas§	Amer.		★3B-SS	129	490	76	161	24	4	17	83	.329	125	282	8	★.981
1981—Texas	Amer.		3B-SS	97	360	44	106	16	1	10	64	.294	67	284	14	.962
1982—Texas	Amer.		★3B-SS	148	537	62	159	27	2	13	67	.296	★131	397	13	★.976
1983—Texas	Amer.		3B	156	618	75	171	35	3	14	66	.277	123	★383	17	.967
1984—Texas x	Amer.		3B	148	553	88	174	36	5	11	83	.315	129	323	●20	.958
1985—Texas x	Amer.		3B	84	313	33	74	13	3	4	32	.236	70	192	16	.942
1985—Cincinnati	Nat.		3B	67	247	28	54	15	2	6	36	.219	54	105	9	.946
1986—Cincinnati	Nat.		3B-2B	155	568	89	158	29	3	20	75	.278	105	291	10	.975
1987—Cincinnati	Nat.		3B	143	522	74	148	19	2	17	70	.284	93	241	7	★.979
1988—Cinc.yz-Hou.ab	Nat.		3B-1B	95	323	27	78	10	1	7	40	.241	88	140	15	.938
1989—Texas cd	Amer.		3B-1B	34	82	4	15	4	0	0	3	.183	10	13	0	1.000
American League Totals—15 Years				1945	7335	933	2076	352	48	151	885	.283	1853	4231	221	.965
National League Totals—4 Years				460	1660	218	438	73	8	50	221	.264	340	777	41	.965
Major League Totals—18 Years				2405	8995	1151	2514	425	56	201	1106	.279	2193	5008	262	.965

Selected by Cleveland Indians' organization in 16th round of free-agent draft, June 5, 1969.
†On disabled list, May 27 to June 17 and August 8 to September 1, 1974.
‡Traded to Texas Rangers for Third Baseman Toby Harrah, December 8, 1978.
§On disabled list, June 9 to June 24, 1980.
xTraded to Cincinnati Reds for Outfielder Duane Walker and a player to be named later, July 19, 1985; Texas Rangers' organization acquired Pitcher Jeff Russell to complete deal, July 23, 1985.
yOn disabled list, March 26 to April 10 and April 14 to May 11, 1988.
zTraded to Houston Astros for a player to be named later, June 19, 1988; Cincinnati Reds' organization acquired

Pitcher Carl Grovom to complete deal, October 20, 1988.
aOn disabled list, August 4 to August 19, 1988.
bReleased, December 21, 1988; signed by Texas Rangers, January 9, 1989.
cOn disabled list, April 8 to April 28, 1989.
dOn voluntarily retired list, June 24, 1989; signed by Cleveland Indians to work in minor league development.

ALL-STAR GAME RECORD

Year League	Pos.	AB.	R.	H.	2B.	3B.	HR.	RBI.	B.A.	PO.	A.	E.	F.A.
1973—American	PH	1	0	1	0	1	0	0	1.000	0	0	0	.000
1980—American	3B	2	0	0	0	0	0	0	.000	0	2	0	1.000
1981—American	3B	1	0	0	0	0	0	1	.000	1	2	0	1.000
1982—American	PH-3B	3	0	0	0	0	0	0	.000	0	1	1	.500
1984—American	3B	1	0	0	0	0	0	0	.000	0	1	0	1.000
All-Star Game Totals—5 Years		8	0	1	0	1	0	1	.125	1	6	1	.875

DEREK NATHANIEL BELL

Born December 11, 1968, at Tampa, Fla.
Height, 6.02. Weight, 195.
Throws and bats righthanded.

Year Club	League	Pos.	G.	AB.	R.	H.	2B.	3B.	HR.	RBI.	B.A.	PO.	A.	E.	F.A.
1987—St. Catharines	NYP	OF	74	273	46	72	11	3	10	42	.264	126	6	2	.985
1988—Myrtle Beach	S. Atl.	OF	91	352	55	121	29	5	12	60	*.344	148	12	10	.941
1988—Knoxville	South.	OF	14	52	5	13	3	1	0	4	.250	18	2	2	.909
1989—Knoxville	South.	OF	136	513	72	124	22	6	16	75	.242	216	12	9	.962

Selected by Toronto Blue Jays' organization in 2nd round of free-agent draft, June 2, 1987.

ERIC ALVIN BELL

Born October 27, 1963, at Modesto, Calif.
Height, 6.00. Weight, 165.
Throws and bats lefthanded.

Tied for Carolina League lead in games started by pitchers with 26 in 1985.

Year Club	League	G.	IP.	W.	L.	Pct.	H.	R.	ER.	SO.	BB.	ERA.
1982—Bluefield	Ap'lachian	11	51⅓	4	1	.800	42	19	12	30	36	2.10
1983—Newark	NYP	18	60	3	2	.600	71	44	33	56	30	4.95
1984—Hagerstown†	Carolina	3	3⅔	0	0	.000	6	4	4	6	5	9.82
1984—Newark	NYP	15	102⅓	8	3	.727	82	40	28	114	26	2.46
1985—Hagerstown	Carolina	26	158⅓	11	6	.647	141	73	55	*162	63	3.13
1985—Baltimore	American	4	5⅔	0	0	.000	4	3	3	4	4	4.76
1986—Charlotte	Southern	18	129⅔	9	6	.600	109	49	44	104	66	*3.05
1986—Rochester	Int'national	11	76⅔	7	3	*.700	68	26	26	59	35	3.05
1986—Baltimore	American	4	23⅓	1	2	.333	23	14	13	18	14	5.01
1987—Baltimore	American	33	165	10	13	.435	174	113	100	111	78	5.45
1988—Rochester‡	Int'national	7	36⅓	3	1	.750	28	10	8	33	13	1.98
1989—Rochester§	Int'national	7	39⅔	1	2	.333	40	24	22	27	15	4.99
1989—Hagerstown	Eastern	9	43	4	2	.667	32	11	9	35	11	1.88
Major League Totals—3 Years		41	194	11	15	.423	201	130	116	133	96	5.38

Selected by Baltimore Orioles' organization in 9th round of free-agent draft, June 7, 1982.
†On disabled list, May 3 to June 18, 1984.
‡On disabled list, May 9, 1988 through remainder of season.
§On disabled list, April 5 to June 10, 1989.

GEORGE ANTONIO BELL (MATHEY)

Born October 21, 1959, at San Pedro de Macoris, D. R.
Height, 6.01. Weight, 202.
Throws and bats righthanded.
Brother of Juan Bell, shortstop in Baltimore Orioles' organization;
and Rolando Bell, infielder in Los Angeles Dodgers' organization, 1985 through 1987.

Major League stolen bases: 1981 (3), 1983 (1), 1984 (11), 1985 (21), 1986 (7), 1987 (5), 1988 (4), 1989 (4). Total—56.
Hit three home runs in a game, April 4, 1988.
Led American League in sacrifice flies with 14 in 1989.
Led American League in total bases with 369 in 1987.
Tied for American League lead in game-winning RBIs with 15 in 1986.
Tied for International League lead in double plays by outfielders with 4 in 1983.
Led Western Carolinas League in total bases with 270 in 1979.
Named Major League Player of the Year by THE SPORTING NEWS, 1987.
Named American League Player of the Year by THE SPORTING NEWS, 1987.
Named American League Most Valuable Player by Baseball Writers' Association of America, 1987.
Named outfielder on THE SPORTING NEWS American League All-Star Team, 1986 and 1987.
Named outfielder on THE SPORTING NEWS American League Silver Slugger team, 1985 through 1987.

Year Club	League	Pos.	G.	AB.	R.	H.	2B.	3B.	HR.	RBI.	B.A.	PO.	A.	E.	F.A.
1978—Helena	Pion.	OF	33	106	20	33	6	1	0	14	.311	39	4	4	.915
1979—Spartanburg	W. Car.	OF	130	491	78	150	24	*15	22	*102	.305	206	14	8	.965
1980—Reading†‡	East.	OF	22	55	11	17	5	2	0	11	.309	24	0	1	.960
1981—Toronto	Amer.	OF	60	163	19	38	2	1	5	12	.233	92	3	3	.969
1982—Syracuse§	Int.	OF	37	125	11	25	5	4	3	19	.200	72	3	1	.987
1983—Syracuse	Int.	OF	85	317	37	86	11	4	15	59	.271	135	12	6	.961
1983—Toronto	Amer.	OF	39	112	5	30	5	4	2	17	.268	61	1	3	.954

Year Club	League	Pos.	G.	AB.	R.	H.	2B.	3B.	HR.	RBI.	B.A.	PO.	A.	E.	F.A.
1984—Toronto	Amer.	OF-3B	159	606	85	177	39	4	26	87	.292	289	13	9	.971
1985—Toronto	Amer.	●OF-1B	157	607	87	167	28	6	28	95	.275	320	14	●11	.968
1986—Toronto	Amer.	OF-3B	159	641	101	198	38	6	31	108	.309	270	17	10	.966
1987—Toronto	Amer.	OF-2B-3B	156	610	111	188	32	4	47	★134	.308	249	14	11	.960
1988—Toronto	Amer.	OF	156	614	78	165	27	5	24	97	.269	253	8	15	.946
1989—Toronto x	Amer.	OF	153	613	88	182	41	2	18	104	.297	258	4	●10	.963
Major League Totals—8 Years			1039	3966	574	1145	212	32	181	654	.289	1792	74	72	.963

Signed as free agent by Philadelphia Phillies' organization, June 23, 1978.
†On disabled list, June 22, 1980 through remainder of season.
‡Drafted by Toronto Blue Jays, December 8, 1980.
§On disabled list, April 20 to May 1, June 14 to June 30 and July 8, 1982 through remainder of season.
xOn suspended list, July 31 to August 2, 1989.

CHAMPIONSHIP SERIES RECORD

Year Club	League	Pos.	G.	AB.	R.	H.	2B.	3B.	HR.	RBI.	B.A.	PO.	A.	E.	F.A.
1985—Toronto	Amer.	OF	7	28	4	9	3	0	0	1	.321	13	0	0	1.000
1989—Toronto	Amer.	OF-DH	5	20	2	4	0	0	1	2	.200	3	1	0	1.000
Championship Series Totals—2 Years			12	48	6	13	3	0	1	3	.271	16	1	0	1.000

ALL-STAR GAME RECORD

Year Club	League	Pos.	G.	AB.	R.	H.	2B.	3B.	HR.	RBI.	B.A.	PO.	A.	E.	F.A.
1987—Toronto	Amer.	OF	3	0	0	0	0	0	0	0	.000	1	0	0	1.000

JAY STUART BELL

Born December 11, 1965, at Pensacola, Fla.
Height, 6.01. Weight, 180.
Throws and bats righthanded.

Shares major league record by hitting home run in first major league at-bat, September 29, 1986.
Major League stolen bases: 1987 (2), 1988 (4), 1989 (5). Total—11.
Led American Association shortstops in putouts with 198, assists with 322 and total chances with 550 in 1987.
Led Eastern League shortstops in total chances with 613 in 1986.
Led California League shortstops in double plays with 84 in 1985.
Led Appalachian League shortstops in double plays with 43 and total chances with 352 in 1984.

Year Club	League	Pos.	G.	AB.	R.	H.	2B.	3B.	HR.	RBI.	B.A.	PO.	A.	E.	F.A.
1984—Elizabethton	Appal.	SS	66	245	43	54	12	1	6	30	.220	★109	★218	25	.929
1985—Visalia†	Calif.	SS	106	376	56	106	16	6	9	59	.282	176	330	53	.905
1985—Waterbury	East.	SS	29	114	13	34	11	2	1	14	.298	41	79	6	.952
1986—Waterbury	East.	SS	138	494	86	137	28	4	7	74	.277	197	★371	★45	.927
1986—Cleveland	Amer.	2B	5	14	3	5	2	0	1	4	.357	1	6	2	.778
1987—Buffalo	A. A.	★SS-2B	110	362	71	94	15	4	17	60	.260	201	325	★30	.946
1987—Cleveland	Amer.	SS	38	125	14	27	9	1	2	13	.216	67	93	9	.947
1988—Cleveland	Amer.	SS	73	211	23	46	5	1	2	21	.218	103	170	10	.965
1988—Colorado Springs‡	P. C.	SS	49	181	35	50	12	2	7	24	.276	87	171	18	.935
1989—Pittsburgh	Nat.	SS	78	271	33	70	13	3	2	27	.258	109	197	10	.968
1989—Buffalo	A. A.	SS-3B	86	298	49	85	15	3	10	54	.285	110	223	16	.954
American League Totals—3 Years			116	350	40	78	16	2	5	38	.223	171	269	21	.954
National League Totals—1 Year			78	271	33	70	13	3	2	27	.258	109	197	10	.968
Major League Totals—4 Years			194	621	73	148	29	5	7	65	.238	280	466	31	.960

Selected by Minnesota Twins' organization in 1st round (eighth player selected) of free-agent draft, June 4, 1984.
†Traded with Pitcher Curt Wardle, Outfielder Jim Weaver and a player to be named later to Cleveland Indians for Pitcher Bert Blyleven, August 1, 1985; Cleveland organization acquired Pitcher Rich Yett to complete deal, September 17, 1985.
‡Traded to Pittsburgh Pirates for Shortstop Felix Fermin, March 25, 1989.

JUAN BELL (MATHEY)

Born March 29, 1968 at San Pedro de Macoris, D. R.
Height, 5.11. Weight, 172.
Throws right and bats left and righthanded.
Brother of George Bell, outfielder with Toronto Blue Jays; and Rolando Bell, infielder in Los Angeles Dodgers' organization, 1985 through 1987.

Major League stolen bases: 1989 (1).
Led Gulf Coast League shortstops in total chances with 293 in 1986.
Led California League shortstops in total chances with 719 in 1987.

Year Club	League	Pos.	G.	AB.	R.	H.	2B.	3B.	HR.	RBI.	B.A.	PO.	A.	E.	F.A.
1985—Bradenton Dodg..	Gulf C.	SS-2B	42	106	11	17	0	0	0	8	.160	56	73	20	.866
1986—Sarasota Dodg.† ...	Gulf C.	SS	59	217	38	52	6	2	0	26	.240	78	★193	22	.925
1987—Bakersfield	Calif.	SS	134	473	54	116	15	3	4	58	.245	235	★431	★53	.926
1988—San Antonio†	Texas	SS	61	215	37	60	4	2	5	21	.279	106	182	20	.935
1988—Albuquerque‡	P. C.	SS	73	257	42	77	9	3	8	45	.300	114	249	23	.940
1989—Rochester	Int.	SS	116	408	50	107	15	6	2	32	.262	190	297	36	.931
1989—Baltimore	Amer.	2B-SS	8	4	2	0	0	0	0	0	.000	2	6	0	1.000
Major League Totals—1 Year			8	4	2	0	0	0	0	0	.000	2	6	0	1.000

Signed as free agent by Los Angeles Dodgers' organization, September 1, 1984.
†Batted righthanded only.
‡Traded with Pitchers Brian Holton and Ken Howell to Baltimore Orioles for First Baseman Eddie Murray, December 4, 1988.

MICHAEL ALLEN BELL
(Mike)

Born April 22, 1968, at Lewiston, N.J.
Height, 6.01. Weight, 175.
Throws and bats lefthanded.

Led Southern League first basemen in total chances with 1,316 in 1989.
Led Carolina League first basemen in total chances with 1,014 in 1988.

Year	Club	League	Pos.	G.	AB.	R.	H.	2B.	3B.	HR.	RBI.	B.A.	PO.	A.	E.	F.A.
1987—Sumter		S. Atl.	1B	133	443	54	108	17	3	5	51	.244	1007	70	16	.985
1988—Durham		Carol.	1B	126	440	72	113	18	3	17	84	.257	★924	76	14	★.986
1988—Greenville		South.	1B	4	12	1	3	1	0	0	4	.250	44	1	0	1.000
1989—Greenville		South.	1B	132	472	63	115	26	3	6	57	.244	★1209	★94	13	.990

Selected by Atlanta Braves' organization in 4th round of free-agent draft, June 2, 1986.

ALBERT JOJUAN BELLE
(Joey)

Born August 25, 1966, at Shreveport, La.
Height, 6.02. Weight, 200.
Throws and bats righthanded.
Attended Louisiana State University, Baton Rouge, La.

Major League stolen bases: 1989 (2).

Year	Club	League	Pos.	G.	AB.	R.	H.	2B.	3B.	HR.	RBI.	B.A.	PO.	A.	E.	F.A.
1987—Kinston		Carol.	OF	10	37	5	12	2	0	3	9	.324	5	0	0	1.000
1988—Kinston		Carol.	OF	41	153	21	46	16	0	8	39	.301	43	5	5	.906
1988—Waterloo		Midw.	OF	9	28	2	7	1	0	1	2	.250	11	1	0	1.000
1989—Canton-Akron		East.	OF	89	312	48	88	20	0	20	69	.282	136	4	3	.979
1989—Cleveland		Amer.	OF	62	218	22	49	8	4	7	37	.225	92	3	2	.979
Major League Totals—1 Year				62	218	22	49	8	4	7	37	.225	92	3	2	.979

Selected by Cleveland Indians' organization in 2nd round of free-agent draft, June 2, 1987.

RAFAEL LEONIDAS BELLIARD (MATIAS)

Name pronounced BELL-ee-ard.

Born October 24, 1961, at Pueblo Nuevo, Mao, D. R.
Height, 5.06. Weight, 150.
Throws and bats righthanded.

Major League stolen bases: 1982 (1), 1984 (4), 1986 (12), 1987 (5), 1988 (7), 1989 (5). Total—34.
Led National League shortstops in fielding percentage with .977 in 1988.
Led Carolina League in sacrifice hits with 12 and tied for lead in caught stealing with 15 in 1981.
Tied for Eastern League lead in double plays by shortstops with 69 in 1983.

Year	Club	League	Pos.	G.	AB.	R.	H.	2B.	3B.	HR.	RBI.	B.A.	PO.	A.	E.	F.A.
1980—Bradenton Pir.		Gulf C.	SS-2B-3B	12	42	6	9	1	0	0	2	.214	24	39	1	.984
1980—Shelby		S. Atl.	SS	8	24	1	3	0	0	0	2	.125	10	27	5	.881
1981—Alexandria		Carol.	SS	127	472	58	102	6	5	0	33	.216	330	330	29	.949
1982—Buffalo†		East.	SS	40	124	14	34	1	1	0	19	.274	56	87	5	.966
1982—Pittsburgh		Nat.	SS	9	2	3	1	0	0	0	0	.500	2	2	0	1.000
1983—Lynn		East.	SS-2B	127	431	63	113	13	2	2	37	.262	203	307	26	.951
1983—Pittsburgh		Nat.	SS	4	1	1	0	0	0	0	0	.000	1	3	0	1.000
1984—Pittsburgh‡		Nat.	SS-2B	20	22	3	5	0	0	0	0	.227	12	13	3	.893
1985—Pittsburgh		Nat.	SS	17	20	1	4	0	0	0	1	.200	13	23	2	.947
1985—Hawaii		P. C.	SS-2B	100	341	35	84	12	4	1	18	.246	172	289	5	.989
1986—Pittsburgh§		Nat.	SS-2B	117	309	33	72	5	2	0	31	.233	147	317	12	.975
1987—Pittsburgh x		Nat.	SS-2B	81	203	26	42	4	3	1	15	.207	113	191	6	.981
1987—Harrisburg		East.	SS	37	145	24	49	5	2	0	9	.338	59	115	7	.961
1988—Pittsburgh y		Nat.	SS-2B	122	286	28	61	0	4	0	11	.213	134	261	9	.978
1989—Pittsburgh		Nat.	SS-2B-3B	67	154	10	33	4	0	0	8	.214	71	138	3	.986
Major League Totals—8 Years				437	997	105	218	13	9	1	66	.219	493	948	35	.976

Signed as free agent by Pittsburgh Pirates' organization, July 10, 1980.
†On disabled list, April 19 to July 24, 1982.
‡On disabled list, June 28 to August 28, 1984.
§On disabled list, July 28 to August 12, 1986.
xOn disabled list, August 27, 1987 through remainder of season.
yOn disabled list, May 19 to June 3, 1988.

ALFREDO BENAVIDES III

Name pronounced Ben-un-VEE-dees.

(Freddie)

Born April 7, 1966, at Laredo, Tex.
Height, 6.02. Weight, 180.
Throws and bats righthanded.
Attended Texas Christian University, Fort Worth, Tex.

Year	Club	League	Pos.	G.	AB.	R.	H.	2B.	3B.	HR.	RBI.	B.A.	PO.	A.	E.	F.A.
1987—Cedar Rapids		Midw.	SS	5	15	2	2	1	0	0	0	.133	7	7	4	.778
1988—Cedar Rapids		Midw.	SS	88	314	38	70	9	2	1	32	.223	118	210	24	.932

Year Club League	Pos.	G.	AB.	R.	H.	2B.	3B.	HR.	RBI.	B.A.	PO.	A.	E.	F.A.
1989—Chattanooga .... South.	SS	88	284	25	71	14	3	0	27	.250	129	230	20	.947
1989—Nashville................ A. A.	SS	31	94	9	16	4	0	1	12	.170	40	73	7	.942

Selected by Cincinnati Reds' organization in 2nd round of free-agent draft, June 2, 1987.

BRUCE EDWIN BENEDICT

Born August 18, 1955, at Birmingham, Ala.
Height, 6.02. Weight, 195.
Throws and bats righthanded.
Attended University of Nebraska, Omaha, Neb.
Son of David Benedict, pitcher in New York Yankees', Washington Senators'
and St. Louis Cardinals' organizations, 1950 through 1958.
Major League stolen bases: 1979 (1), 1980 (3), 1981 (1), 1982 (4), 1983 (1), 1984 (1), 1986 (1). Total—12.

Year Club League	Pos.	G.	AB.	R.	H.	2B.	3B.	HR.	RBI.	B.A.	PO.	A.	E.	F.A.
1976—Kingsport .... Appal.	C	17	63	10	18	1	0	0	4	.286	98	25	3	.976
1976—Greenwood .... W. Car.	C	21	54	7	13	1	0	1	10	.241	93	12	5	.955
1976—Savannah.............. South.	C	24	73	10	21	1	0	0	7	.288	107	12	2	.983
1977—Savannah.............. South.	C	124	395	55	104	15	0	7	40	.263	★770	★112	13	.985
1978—Richmond............. Int.	C	111	348	41	97	13	0	2	34	.279	592	56	4	★.994
1978—Atlanta .... Nat.	C	22	52	3	13	2	0	0	1	.250	81	14	1	.990
1979—Atlanta .... Nat.	C	76	204	14	46	11	0	0	15	.225	344	35	6	.984
1980—Richmond............. Int.	C	3	10	0	3	0	0	0	0	.300	10	5	0	1.000
1980—Atlanta .... Nat.	C	120	359	18	91	14	1	2	34	.253	502	76	7	.988
1981—Atlanta .... Nat.	C	90	295	26	78	12	1	5	35	.264	404	★73	7	.986
1982—Atlanta .... Nat.	C	118	386	34	95	11	1	3	44	.246	602	73	5	★.993
1983—Atlanta .... Nat.	C	134	423	43	126	13	1	2	43	.298	738	91	7	.992
1984—Atlanta .... Nat.	C	95	300	26	67	8	1	4	25	.223	504	37	5	.991
1985—Atlanta .... Nat.	C	70	208	12	42	6	0	0	20	.202	314	35	4	.989
1986—Atlanta .... Nat.	C	64	160	11	36	10	1	0	13	.225	252	28	2	.993
1987—Atlanta .... Nat.	C	37	95	4	14	1	0	1	5	.147	165	21	2	.989
1988—Atlanta .... Nat.	C	90	236	11	57	7	0	0	19	.242	384	54	5	.989
1989—Atlanta† .... Nat.	C	66	160	12	31	3	0	1	6	.194	361	40	2	.995
Major League Totals—12 Years...............		982	2878	214	696	98	6	18	260	.242	4651	577	53	.990

Selected by Atlanta Braves' organization in 5th round of free-agent draft, June 8, 1976.
†On voluntarily retired list, October 13, 1989.

CHAMPIONSHIP SERIES RECORD

Year Club League	Pos.	G.	AB.	R.	H.	2B.	3B.	HR.	RBI.	B.A.	PO.	A.	E.	F.A.
1982—Atlanta .... Nat.	C	3	8	1	2	1	0	0	0	.250	16	2	0	1.000

ALL-STAR GAME RECORD

Year League	Pos.	AB.	R.	H.	2B.	3B.	HR.	RBI.	B.A.	PO.	A.	E.	F.A.
1981—National	C	1	0	0	0	0	0	0	.000	3	0	0	1.000
1983—National	C	1	0	1	0	0	0	0	1.000	5	0	0	1.000
All-Star Game Totals—2 Years....................		2	0	1	0	0	0	0	.500	8	0	0	1.000

ANDREW CHARLES BENES
(Andy)

Born August 20, 1967, at Evansville, Ind.
Height, 6.06. Weight, 235.
Throws and bats righthanded.
Attended University of Evansville, Evansville, Ind.
Led Texas League in shutouts with 3 in 1989.
Named National League Rookie Pitcher of the Year by THE SPORTING NEWS, 1989.
Named Texas League Pitcher of the Year, 1989.
Member of 1988 U.S. Olympic baseball team.
Received reported $230,000 bonus to sign with San Diego Padres, 1988.

Year Club League	G.	IP.	W.	L.	Pct.	H.	R.	ER.	SO.	BB.	ERA.
1989—Wichita............................. Texas	16	108⅓	8	4	.667	79	32	26	115	39	2.16
1989—Las Vegas................................. P. Coast	5	26⅔	2	1	.667	41	29	24	29	12	8.10
1989—San Diego.............................. National	10	66⅔	6	3	.667	51	28	26	66	31	3.51
Major League Totals—1 Year..............................	10	66⅔	6	3	.667	51	28	26	66	31	3.51

Selected by San Diego Padres' organization in 1st round (first player selected) of free-agent draft, June 1, 1988.

MICHAEL PAUL BENJAMIN
(Mike)

Born November 22, 1965, at Euclid, O.
Height, 6.03. Weight, 195.
Throws and bats righthanded.
Attended Cerritos College, Norwalk, Calif., and Arizona State University, Tempe, Ariz.

Year Club League	Pos.	G.	AB.	R.	H.	2B.	3B.	HR.	RBI.	B.A.	PO.	A.	E.	F.A.
1987—Fresno .... Calif.	SS	64	212	25	51	6	4	6	24	.241	89	188	21	.930
1988—Shreveport .... Texas	SS	89	309	48	73	19	5	6	37	.236	134	248	11	.972
1988—Phoenix................. P. C.	SS	37	106	13	18	4	1	0	6	.170	41	74	4	.966
1989—Phoenix................. P. C.	SS-2B	113	363	44	94	17	6	3	36	.259	149	332	15	.970

Year Club League	Pos.	G.	AB.	R.	H.	2B.	3B.	HR.	RBI.	B.A.	PO.	A.	E.	F.A.
1989—San Francisco ...... Nat.	SS	14	6	6	1	0	0	0	0	.167	4	4	0	1.000
Major League Totals—1 Year................		14	6	6	1	0	0	0	0	.167	4	4	0	1.000

Selected by Minnesota Twins' organization in 7th round of free-agent draft, January 9, 1985.
Selected by San Francisco Giants' organization in 3rd round of free-agent draft, June 2, 1987.

DAVID CHRISTOPHER BENNETT
(Chris)

Born September 8, 1965, at Yreka, Calif.
Height, 6.06. Weight, 205.
Throws and bats righthanded.
Attended California State University, Sacramento, Calif.

Year Club	League	G.	IP.	W.	L.	Pct.	H.	R.	ER.	SO.	BB.	ERA.
1988—Bradenton Expos	Gulf C.	4	5	0	0	.000	5	2	0	4	0	0.00
1988—West Palm Beach	Florida St.	20	26	0	1	.000	19	7	5	18	11	1.73
1989—West Palm Beach	Florida St.	18	29⅔	2	1	.667	20	3	3	29	5	0.91
1989—Jacksonville..................	Southern	25	63⅔	4	2	.667	42	29	17	52	20	2.40

Signed as free agent by Montreal Expos' organization, June 12, 1988.

TODD ERIC BENZINGER

Born February 11, 1963, at Dayton, Ky.
Height, 6.01. Weight, 190.
Throws right and bats left and righthanded.
Nephew of Don Gross, pitcher with Cincinnati Reds and Pittsburgh Pirates, 1955 through 1960.
Major League stolen bases: 1987 (5), 1988 (2), 1989 (3). Total—10.

Year Club League	Pos.	G.	AB.	R.	H.	2B.	3B.	HR.	RBI.	B.A.	PO.	A.	E.	F.A.
1981—Elmira.................. NYP	OF-1B	41	141	21	34	10	1	2	8	.241	131	9	2	.986
1982—Winston-Salem ..... Carol.	OF-1B	121	443	54	97	19	1	5	46	.219	438	28	8	.983
1983—Winter Haven...... Fla. St.	OF-1B-3B	125	480	56	134	34	5	7	68	.279	206	10	8	.964
1984—New Britain† .... East.	OF-1B	110	391	49	101	25	5	10	60	.258	465	29	14	.972
1985—Pawtucket‡......... Int.	OF	70	256	31	64	13	1	11	47	.250	106	3	3	.973
1986—Pawtucket§.......... Int.	OF-1B	90	314	41	79	13	2	11	32	.252	156	4	2	.988
1987—Pawtucket .... Int.	OF-1B	65	257	47	83	17	3	13	49	.323	256	16	2	.993
1987—Boston.................. Amer.	OF-1B	73	223	36	62	11	1	8	43	.278	155	7	2	.988
1988—Boston xy.............. Amer.	1B-OF	120	405	47	103	28	1	13	70	.254	602	38	6	.991
1989—Cincinnati .... Nat.	1B	161	★628	79	154	28	3	17	76	.245	1417	73	7	.995
American League Totals—2 Years		193	628	83	165	39	2	21	113	.263	757	45	8	.990
National League Totals—1 Year..............		161	628	79	154	28	3	17	76	.245	1417	73	7	.995
Major League Totals—3 Years................		354	1256	162	319	67	5	38	189	.254	2174	118	15	.993

Selected by Boston Red Sox' organization in 4th round of free-agent draft, June 8, 1981.
†On disabled list, August 10, 1984 through remainder of season.
‡On disabled list, April 10 to June 11, 1985.
§On disabled list, April 11 to April 21 and June 26 to July 17, 1986.
xOn disabled list, June 3 to June 22, 1988.
yTraded with Pitcher Jeff Sellers and a player to be named later to Cincinnati Reds for First Baseman Nick Esasky and Pitcher Rob Murphy, December 13, 1988; Cincinnati acquired Pitcher Luis Vasquez to complete deal, January 12, 1989.

CHAMPIONSHIP SERIES RECORD

Year Club League	Pos.	G.	AB.	R.	H.	2B.	3B.	HR.	RBI.	B.A.	PO.	A.	E.	F.A.
1988—Boston.................... Amer.	1B-PH	4	11	0	1	0	0	0	0	.091	21	1	0	1.000

JUAN BAUTISTA BERENGUER

Name pronounced Bare-en-GARE.

Born November 30, 1954, at Aguadulce, Panama.
Height, 5.11. Weight, 223.
Throws and bats righthanded.

Major League saves: 1983 (1), 1986 (4), 1987 (4), 1988 (2), 1989 (3). Total—14.
Led Carolina League pitchers in games started with 28 and hit batsmen with 13 in 1976.
Tied for American Association lead in complete games with 9 in 1982.
Tied for Texas League pitchers lead in games started with 26 in 1977.
Tied for Midwest League lead in hit batsmen with 8 in 1975.
Named International League Pitcher of the Year, 1978.

Year Club	League	G.	IP.	W.	L.	Pct.	H.	R.	ER.	SO.	BB.	ERA.
1975—Wausau......................	Midwest	18	95	5	4	.556	83	41	31	58	50	2.94
1976—Lynchburg................	Carolina	28	187	10	13	.435	★175	89	★75	114	★118	3.61
1977—Jackson	Texas	26	181	9	8	.529	143	89	69	★160	★126	3.43
1978—Tidewater.................	Int'national	24	147	10	7	.588	117	60	60	130	91	3.67
1978—New York†..............	National	5	13	0	2	.000	17	12	12	8	11	8.31
1979—Tacoma....................	P. Coast	26	166	8	8	.500	128	101	90	★220	129	4.88
1979—New York................	National	5	31	1	1	.500	28	13	10	25	12	2.90
1980—Tidewater.................	Int'national	27	157	9	●15	.375	122	78	67	★178	76	3.84
1980—New York‡..............	National	6	9	0	1	.000	9	9	6	7	10	6.00
1981—Kansas City§-Toronto x..............	American	20	91	2	★13	.133	84	62	53	49	51	5.24
1982—Evansville	Am. Assoc.	25	156⅓	11	10	.524	152	85	80	127	80	4.61

Year Club	League	G.	IP.	W.	L.	Pct.	H.	R.	ER.	SO.	BB.	ERA.
1982—Detroit	American	2	6⅔	0	0	.000	5	5	5	8	9	6.75
1983—Detroit	American	37	157⅔	9	5	.643	110	58	55	129	71	3.14
1984—Detroit	American	31	168⅓	11	10	.524	146	75	65	118	79	3.48
1985—Detroit y	American	31	95	5	6	.455	96	67	59	82	48	5.59
1986—San Francisco za	National	46	73⅓	2	3	.400	64	23	22	72	44	2.70
1987—Minnesota bc	American	47	112	8	1	.889	100	51	49	110	47	3.94
1988—Minnesota	American	57	100	8	4	.667	74	44	44	99	61	3.96
1989—Minnesota	American	56	106	9	3	.750	96	44	41	93	47	3.48
National League Totals—4 Years		62	126⅓	3	7	.300	118	57	50	112	77	3.56
American League Totals—8 Years		281	836⅔	52	42	.553	711	406	371	688	413	3.99
Major League Totals—12 Years		343	963	55	49	.529	829	463	421	800	490	3.93

Signed as free agent by New York Mets' organization, February 22, 197⁻.
†Loaned to Tacoma (Cleveland Indians' organization), March 24, 1979; returned August 29, 1979.
‡Traded to Kansas City for Outfielder Marvell Wynne and Pitcher John Skinner, March 31, 1981.
§Sold on waivers to Toronto Blue Jays, August 8, 1981.
xReleased, March 28, 1982; signed by Evansville (Detroit Tigers' organization), April 4, 1982.
yTraded with Catcher Bob Melvin and a player to be named later to San Francisco Giants for Pitchers Dave LaPoint and Eric King and Catcher Matt Nokes, October 7, 1985; San Francisco acquired Pitcher Scott Medvin to complete deal, December 11, 1985.
zOn disabled list, April 7 to April 28, 1986.
aReleased, December 9, 1986; signed by Minnesota Twins, January 9, 1987.
bOn disabled list, August 3 to August 22, 1987.
cGranted free agency, November 9, 1987; re-signed by Twins, December 22, 1987.

CHAMPIONSHIP SERIES RECORD

Shares American League Championship Series record for most games pitched, series (4), 1987.

Year Club	League	G.	IP.	W.	L.	Pct.	H.	R.	ER.	SO.	BB.	ERA.
1987—Minnesota	American	4	6	0	0	.000	1	1	1	6	3	1.50

WORLD SERIES RECORD

Year Club	League	G.	IP.	W.	L.	Pct.	H.	R.	ER.	SO.	BB.	ERA.
1987—Minnesota	American	3	4⅓	0	1	.000	10	5	5	1	0	10.38

Eligible for 1984 World Series with Detroit Tigers; did not play.

DAVID BRUCE BERGMAN
(Dave)

Born June 6, 1953, at Evanston, Ill.
Height, 6.02. Weight, 190.
Throws and bats lefthanded.
Received bachelor of arts degree in business administration
from Illinois State University, Normal, Ill., in 1974.

Major League stolen bases: 1978 (2), 1980 (1), 1981 (2), 1982 (3), 1983 (2), 1984 (3), 1989 (1). Total—14.
Led International League in bases on balls received with 95 in 1979.
Led International League first basemen in putouts with 1,199 in 1976.
Led Eastern League first basemen in assists with 58 in 1975.
Named Eastern League Most Valuable Player, 1975.
Named outfielder on THE SPORTING NEWS College Baseball All-America Team, 1974.

Year Club	League	Pos.	G.	AB.	R.	H.	2B.	3B.	HR.	RBI.	B.A.	PO.	A.	E.	F.A.
1974—Oneonta	NYP	1B	56	201	60	70	6	●7	10	48	*.348	494	*29	8	*.985
1975—West Haven	East.	1B-OF	124	399	76	124	15	6	11	60	*.311	610	61	5	.993
1975—New York	Amer.	OF	7	17	0	0	0	0	0	0	.000	10	1	1	.917
1976—Syracuse	Int.	*1B-OF	134	455	68	134	23	2	7	65	.295	1201	82	10	*.992
1977—Syracuse	Int.	OF-1B	132	468	88	146	29	4	16	59	.312	534	39	8	.986
1977—New York†	Amer.	OF-1B	5	4	1	1	0	0	0	1	.250	8	0	0	1.000
1978—Houston	Nat.	1B-OF	104	186	15	43	5	1	0	12	.231	328	16	4	.989
1979—Charleston	Int.	1B-OF	138	461	78	129	23	3	6	58	.280	910	61	11	.989
1979—Houston	Nat.	1B	13	15	4	6	0	0	1	2	.400	8	0	0	1.000
1980—Houston	Nat.	1B-OF	90	78	12	20	6	1	0	3	.256	187	16	1	.995
1981—Hou.‡-S.F.	Nat.	1B-OF	69	151	17	38	9	0	4	14	.252	255	25	3	.989
1982—San Francisco	Nat.	1B-OF	100	121	22	33	3	1	4	14	.273	321	20	4	.988
1983—San Francisco§	Nat.	1B-OF	90	140	16	40	4	1	6	24	.286	299	27	2	.994
1984—Detroit	Amer.	1B-OF	120	271	42	74	8	5	7	44	.273	658	75	8	.989
1985—Detroit x	Amer.	1B-OF	69	140	8	25	2	0	3	7	.179	306	25	3	.991
1985—Nashville	A. A.	1B	11	39	↑ 6	9	1	0	1	6	.231	87	8	1	.990
1986—Detroit	Amer.	1B-OF	65	130	14	30	6	1	1	9	.231	255	29	4	.986
1987—Detroit y	Amer.	1B-OF	91	172	25	47	7	3	6	22	.273	357	29	3	.992
1988—Detroit z	Amer.	1B-OF	116	289	37	85	14	0	5	35	.294	386	37	4	.991
1989—Detroit	Amer.	1B-OF	137	385	38	103	13	1	7	37	.268	912	85	7	.993
National League Totals—6 Years			466	691	86	180	27	4	15	69	.260	1398	104	14	.991
American League Totals—8 Years			610	1408	165	365	50	10	29	155	.259	2892	281	30	.991
Major League Totals—14 Years			1076	2099	251	545	77	14	44	224	.260	4290	385	44	.991

Selected by Chicago Cubs' organization in 12th round of free-agent draft, June 8, 1971.
Selected by New York Yankees' organization in 2nd round of free-agent draft, June 5, 1974.
†Traded to Houston Astros, November 23, 1977, completing deal in which Houston traded First Baseman-Catcher Cliff Johnson to New York Yankees for Infielder Mike Fischlin, Pitcher Randy Niemann and a player to be named later, June 15, 1977.

‡Traded with Outfielder Jeff Leonard to San Francisco Giants for First Baseman Mike Ivie, April 20, 1981.

§Traded to Philadelphia Phillies for Outfielder Alejandro Sanchez, March 24, 1984; Traded by Philadelphia with Pitcher Willie Hernandez to Detroit Tigers for Outfielder Glenn Wilson and Catcher-First Baseman John Wockenfuss, March 24, 1984.

xOn disabled list, April 22 to May 29, 1985; included rehabilitation disability assignment to Nashville, May 15 to May 29, 1985.

yOn disabled list, June 7 to June 22, 1987.

zGranted free agency, November 4, 1988; re-signed by Tigers, December 7, 1988.

CHAMPIONSHIP SERIES RECORD

Year	Club	League	Pos.	G.	AB.	R.	H.	2B.	3B.	HR.	RBI.	B.A.	PO.	A.	E.	F.A.
1980—Houston		Nat.	PR-1B	4	3	0	1	0	1	0	2	.333	8	2	1	.909
1984—Detroit		Amer.	PR-1B	2	1	1	1	0	0	0	0	1.000	5	0	0	1.000
1987—Detroit		Amer.	PH-DH-1	4	4	0	1	0	0	0	2	.250	6	0	0	1.000
Championship Series Totals—3 Years				10	8	1	3	0	1	0	4	.375	19	2	1	.955

WORLD SERIES RECORD

Year	Club	League	Pos.	G.	AB.	R.	H.	2B.	3B.	HR.	RBI.	B.A.	PO.	A.	E.	F.A.
1984—Detroit		Amer.	PR-1B	5	5	0	0	0	0	0	0	.000	22	4	0	1.000

GERONIMO EMILIANO BERROA

Born March 18, 1965, at Santo Domingo, D. R.
Height, 6.00. Weight, 165.
Throws and bats righthanded.

Led International League in being hit by pitch with 10 and tied for lead in sacrifice flies with 8 in 1988.
Led Southern League in total bases with 297 in 1987.

Year	Club	League	Pos.	G.	AB.	R.	H.	2B.	3B.	HR.	RBI.	B.A.	PO.	A.	E.	F.A.
1984—Bradenton Jays	Gulf C.	OF	62	235	31	59	16	1	3	34	.251	75	2	5	.939
1985—Kinston	Carol.	OF	19	43	4	8	0	0	1	4	.186	13	1	1	.933
1985—Medicine Hat	Pion.	OF	54	201	39	69	★22	2	6	45	.343	58	3	3	.953
1985—Florence	S. Atl.	OF	19	66	7	21	2	0	3	20	.318	24	0	2	.923
1986—Ventura	Calif.	OF	128	459	76	137	22	5	21	73	.298	194	9	14	.935
1986—Knoxville	South.	OF	1	4	0	0	0	0	0	0	.000	2	0	0	1.000
1987—Knoxville	South.	OF	134	523	87	150	33	3	36	108	.287	236	6	●15	.942
1988—Syracuse†	Int.	OF	131	470	55	122	●29	1	8	64	.260	243	12	5	.981
1989—Atlanta	Nat.	OF	81	136	7	36	4	0	2	9	.265	67	1	2	.971
Major League Totals—1 Year			81	136	7	36	4	0	2	9	.265	67	1	2	.971

Signed as free agent by Toronto Blue Jays' organization, September 4, 1983.
†Drafted by Atlanta Braves, December 5, 1988.

DAMON SCOTT BERRYHILL

Born December 3, 1963, at South Laguna, Calif.
Height, 6.00. Weight, 205.
Throws right and bats right and lefthanded.
Attended Orange Coast College, Costa Mesa, Calif.

Major League stolen bases: 1988 (1), 1989 (1). Total—2.
Led American Association catchers in putouts with 603, assists with 66, double plays with 11, passed balls with 15 and total chances with 676 in 1987.
Led Carolina League in passed balls with 18 in 1985.

Year	Club	League	Pos.	G.	AB.	R.	H.	2B.	3B.	HR.	RBI.	B.A.	PO.	A.	E.	F.A.
1984—Quad Cities†	Midw.	C-1B	62	217	30	60	14	0	0	31	.276	314	31	8	.977
1985—Winston-Salem	Carol.	C-1B	117	386	31	90	25	1	9	50	.233	625	71	11	.984
1986—Pittsfield	East.	C-OF	112	345	33	71	13	1	6	35	.206	449	61	12	.977
1987—Iowa	A. A.	★C-1B	121	429	54	123	22	1	18	67	.287	607	67	7	★.990
1987—Chicago	Nat.	C	12	28	2	5	1	0	0	1	.179	37	3	4	.909
1988—Iowa	A. A.	C	21	73	11	16	5	1	2	11	.219	117	15	0	1.000
1988—Chicago‡	Nat.	C	95	309	19	80	19	1	7	38	.259	448	54	9	.982
1989—Iowa§	A. A.	C	7	30	4	6	1	0	2	4	.200	40	5	2	.957
1989—Chicago	Nat.	C	91	334	37	86	13	0	5	41	.257	473	41	4	.992
Major League Totals—3 Years			198	671	58	171	33	1	12	80	.255	958	98	17	.984

Selected by Chicago White Sox' organization in 13th round of free-agent draft, January 11, 1983.
Selected by Chicago Cubs' organization in 1st round (fourth player selected) of free-agent draft, January 17, 1984.
†Batted righthanded only.
‡On disabled list, June 30 to July 15, 1988.
§On Chicago disabled list, March 9 to May 1 and August 19 to September 29, 1989; included rehabilitation disability assignment to Iowa, April 24 to May 1, 1989.

ALPHONSE DANTE BICHETTE

(Known by middle name.)
Born November 18, 1963, at West Palm Beach, Fla.
Height, 6.03. Weight, 215.
Throws and bats righthanded.
Attended Palm Beach Junior College, Lake Worth, Fla.

Major League stolen bases: 1989 (3).
Led Midwest League in game-winning RBIs with 13 in 1985.

Year Club	League	Pos.	G.	AB.	R.	H.	2B.	3B.	HR.	RBI.	B.A.	PO.	A.	E.	F.A.
1984—Salem	N'west	OF-1B-3B	64	250	27	58	9	2	4	30	.232	224	24	11	.958
1985—Quad Cities	Midw.	1B-OF-C	137	547	58	145	28	4	11	78	.265	300	21	15	.955
1986—Palm Springs	Calif.	OF-3B	68	290	39	79	15	0	10	73	.272	78	68	11	.930
1986—Midland	Texas	OF-3B	62	243	43	69	16	2	12	36	.284	131	30	11	.936
1987—Edmonton	P. C.	OF-3B	92	360	54	108	20	3	13	50	.300	169	21	9	.955
1988—Edmonton	P. C.	OF	132	509	64	136	29	•10	14	81	.267	218	*22	*15	.941
1988—California	Amer.	OF	21	46	1	12	2	0	0	8	.261	44	2	1	.979
1989—California	Amer.	OF	48	138	13	29	7	0	3	15	.210	95	6	1	.990
1989—Edmonton	P. C.	OF	61	226	39	55	11	2	11	40	.243	92	9	1	.990
Major League Totals—2 Years			69	184	14	41	9	0	3	23	.223	139	8	2	.987

Selected by California Angels' organization in 16th round of free-agent draft, June 4, 1984.

MICHAEL JOSEPH BIELECKI

Name pronounced Bill-LECK-ee.

(Mike)

Born July 31, 1959, at Baltimore, Md.
Height, 6.03. Weight, 195.
Throws and bats righthanded.
Attended Loyola College, Baltimore, Md. and Valencia Community College, Orlando, Fla.
Tied for Eastern League lead in home runs allowed with 24 in 1982.
Tied for South Atlantic League lead in games started with 28 in 1981.

Year Club	League	G.	IP.	W.	L.	Pct.	H.	R.	ER.	SO.	BB.	ERA.
1979—Bradenton Pirates	Gulf Coast	9	51	1	4	.200	48	21	13	35	21	2.29
1980—Shelby	S. Atlantic	29	99	3	5	.375	106	60	50	78	58	4.55
1981—Greenwood	S. Atlantic	28	192	12	11	.522	172	95	73	163	82	3.42
1982—Buffalo	Eastern	25	157⅓	7	12	.368	165	96	•85	135	75	4.86
1983—Lynn	Eastern	25	163⅔	•15	7	.682	126	73	58	*143	69	3.19
1984—Hawaii	P. Coast	28	187⅔	*19	3	*.864	162	70	62	*162	88	2.97
1984—Pittsburgh	National	4	4⅓	0	0	.000	4	0	0	1	0	0.00
1985—Pittsburgh	National	12	45⅔	2	3	.400	45	26	23	22	31	4.53
1985—Hawaii	P. Coast	20	129⅓	8	6	.571	117	58	55	111	56	3.83
1986—Pittsburgh	National	31	148⅔	6	11	.353	149	87	77	83	83	4.66
1987—Vancouver	P. Coast	26	181	12	10	.545	194	89	76	140	78	3.78
1987—Pittsburgh†	National	8	45⅔	2	3	.400	43	25	24	25	12	4.73
1988—Chicago	National	19	48½	2	2	.500	55	22	18	33	16	3.35
1988—Iowa	Am. Assoc.	23	54⅔	3	2	.600	34	19	16	50	20	2.63
1989—Chicago	National	33	212½	18	7	.720	187	82	74	147	81	3.14
Major League Totals—6 Years		107	505	30	26	.536	483	242	216	311	223	3.85

Selected by Kansas City Royals' organization in 6th round of free-agent draft, January 9, 1979.
Selected by Pittsburgh Pirates' organization in secondary phase of free-agent draft, June 5, 1979.
†Traded to Chicago Cubs for Pitcher Mike Curtis, March 31, 1988.

CHAMPIONSHIP SERIES RECORD

Year Club	League	G.	IP.	W.	L.	Pct.	H.	R.	ER.	SO.	BB.	ERA.
1989—Chicago	National	2	12⅓	0	1	.000	7	5	5	11	6	3.65

CRAIG ALAN BIGGIO

Born December 14, 1965, at Smithtown, N. Y.
Height, 5.11. Weight, 180.
Throws and bats righthanded.
Attended Seton Hall University, South Orange, N. J.
Major League stolen bases: 1988 (6), 1989 (21). Total—27.
Named catcher on THE SPORTING NEWS National League Silver Slugger team, 1989.
Named catcher on THE SPORTING NEWS College Baseball All-America Team, 1987.

Year Club	League	Pos.	G.	AB.	R.	H.	2B.	3B.	HR.	RBI.	B.A.	PO.	A.	E.	F.A.
1987—Asheville	S. Atl.	C-OF	64	216	59	81	17	2	9	49	.375	378	46	2	.995
1988—Tucson	P. C.	C-OF	77	281	60	90	21	4	3	41	.320	318	33	6	.983
1988—Houston	Nat.	C	50	123	14	26	6	1	3	5	.211	292	28	3	.991
1989—Houston	Nat.	C-OF	134	443	64	114	21	2	13	60	.257	742	56	9	.989
Major League Totals—2 Years			184	566	78	140	27	3	16	65	.247	1034	84	12	.989

Selected by Houston Astros' organization in 1st round (22nd player selected) of free-agent draft, June 2, 1987.

DANN JAMES BILARDELLO

Named pronounced Bill-ar-DELL-oh.

Born May 26, 1959, at Santa Cruz, Calif.
Height, 6.00. Weight, 190.
Throws and bats righthanded.
Attended Cabrillo College, Aptos, Calif.
Major League stolen bases: 1983 (2), 1986 (1), 1989 (1). Total—4.
Led Texas League catchers in double plays with 15 in 1982.
Led Pioneer League catchers in double plays with 5 in 1978.

Year Club	League	Pos.	G.	AB.	R.	H.	2B.	3B.	HR.	RBI.	B.A.	PO.	A.	E.	F.A.
1978—Lethbridge	Pion.	C	42	133	21	33	8	1	2	20	.248	210	36	7	.972
1979—Clinton†	Midw.	C	52	142	18	34	4	0	2	15	.239	283	31	3	.991

Year	Club	League	Pos.	G.	AB.	R.	H.	2B.	3B.	HR.	RBI.	B.A.	PO.	A.	E.	F.A.
1980—Lodi‡	Calif.		C	41	117	22	36	4	0	6	15	.308	169	30	8	.961
1981—Lodi	Calif.		C	105	352	72	108	19	2	21	80	.307	203	39	9	.964
1981—San Antonio	Texas		C	6	19	0	1	0	0	0	1	.053	34	2	1	.973
1982—San Antonio§	Texas		C	103	347	49	99	14	2	17	48	.285	546	*80	15	.977
1983—Cincinnati	Nat.		C	109	298	27	71	18	0	9	38	.238	494	72	5	.991
1984—Cincinnati	Nat.		C	68	182	16	38	7	0	2	10	.209	323	34	3	.992
1984—Wichita	A. A.		C	49	167	21	40	9	0	5	17	.240	290	31	3	.991
1985—Cincinnati	Nat.		C	42	102	6	17	0	0	1	9	.167	198	20	3	.986
1985—Denver x	A. A.	C-1B-3B	67	236	41	57	5	3	10	37	.242	365	50	6	.986
1986—Montreal	Nat.		C	79	191	12	37	5	0	4	17	.194	391	38	8	.982
1986—Indianapolis yz	A. A.		C	2	5	1	3	0	1	0	0	.600	6	0	0	1.000
1987—Vancouver a	P. C.		C	37	97	7	21	3	0	1	11	.216	186	30	4	.982
1987—Omaha	A. A.	C-3B	22	71	6	13	5	1	2	7	.183	96	13	1	.991
1988—Omaha b	A. A.		C	71	235	27	57	14	0	8	45	.243	395	31	5	.988
1989—Buffalo	A. A.	C-1B	66	180	11	37	8	0	3	17	.206	364	33	7	.983
1989—Pittsburgh c	Nat.		C	33	80	11	18	6	0	2	8	.225	150	14	5	.970
Major League Totals—5 Years				331	853	72	181	36	0	18	82	.212	1556	178	24	.986

Selected by Seattle Mariners' organization in 3rd round of free-agent draft, January 10, 1978.
Selected by Los Angeles Dodgers' organization in secondary phase of free-agent draft, June 6, 1978.
†On disabled list, May 9 to June 14, 1979.
‡On disabled list, June 12 to August 13, 1980.
§Drafted by Cincinnati Reds, December 6, 1982.
xTraded with Pitchers Jay Tibbs, Andy McGaffigan and John Stuper to Montreal Expos for Pitcher Bill Gullickson and Catcher Sal Butera, December 19, 1985.
yReleased, December 20, 1986; re-signed by Expos' organization, March 22, 1987.
zSold to Pittsburgh Pirates, March 22, 1987.
aSold to Omaha (Kansas City Royals' organization), July 23, 1987.
bGranted free agency, October 15, 1988; signed by Buffalo (Pittsburgh Pirates' organization), January 25, 1989.
cReleased, November 21, 1989.

MICHAEL LAURENCE BIRKBECK
(Mike)

Born March 10, 1961, at Orrville, O.
Height, 6.02. Weight, 185.
Throws and bats righthanded.
Attended University of Akron, Akron, O.

Year	Club	League	G.	IP.	W.	L.	Pct.	H.	R.	ER.	SO.	BB.	ERA.
1983—Paintsville	Ap'lachian	7	28⅔	3	1	.750	17	12	6	38	17	1.88
1983—Beloit	Midwest	7	42	2	4	.333	35	22	16	38	17	3.43
1984—Beloit	Midwest	26	177⅔	14	3	.824	134	57	43	164	64	2.18
1985—El Paso	Texas	24	155	9	9	.500	154	67	59	103	64	3.43
1986—Vancouver	P. Coast	23	134⅓	12	6	.667	160	82	69	81	39	4.62
1986—Milwaukee	American	7	22	1	1	.500	24	12	11	13	12	4.50
1987—Milwaukee†	American	10	45	1	4	.200	63	33	31	25	19	6.20
1987—Beloit	Midwest	1	4⅓	0	0	.000	4	4	1	7	1	2.08
1987—Denver	Am. Assoc.	1	4⅔	0	1	.000	9	11	5	1	3	9.64
1988—Milwaukee	American	23	124	10	8	.556	141	69	65	64	37	4.72
1988—Denver	Am. Assoc.	5	44⅔	4	1	.800	30	10	10	30	10	2.01
1989—Milwaukee‡	American	9	44⅔	0	4	.000	57	32	27	31	22	5.44
1989—Denver	Am. Assoc.	5	23⅔	2	2	.500	26	9	8	9	10	3.04
Major League Totals—4 Years		49	235⅔	12	17	.414	285	146	134	133	90	5.12

Selected by Chicago Cubs' organization in 11th round of free-agent draft, June 7, 1982.
Selected by Milwaukee Brewers' organization in 4th round of free-agent draft, June 8, 1983.
†On disabled list, June 2 to September 15, 1987; included rehabilitation disability assignment to Beloit, June 19 to June 23, 1987, and Denver, June 24 to July 1, 1987.
‡On disabled list, May 31 to August 29, 1989; included rehabilitation disability assignment to Denver, August 6 to August 25, 1989.

TIMOTHY DEAN BIRTSAS
(Tim)

Born September 5, 1960, at Clarkston, Mich.
Height, 6.07. Weight, 245.
Throws and bats lefthanded.
Received bachelor of science degree in recreation from Michigan State University, East Lansing, Mich.

Major League saves: 1989 (1).

Year	Club	League	G.	IP.	W.	L.	Pct.	H.	R.	ER.	SO.	BB.	ERA.
1982—Oneonta	NYP	6	16⅓	1	1	.500	19	13	7	24	17	3.86
1983—Fort Lauderdale	Florida St.	23	167⅔	12	8	.600	120	57	44	*160	88	2.36
1984—Fort Lauderdale†	Florida St.	11	57⅔	5	1	.833	51	23	23	62	37	3.59
1985—Tacoma	P. Coast	4	26⅔	2	2	.500	21	10	9	25	14	3.04
1985—Oakland	American	29	141⅓	10	6	.625	124	72	63	94	91	4.01
1986—Oakland	American	2	2	0	0	.000	2	5	5	1	4	22.50
1986—Tacoma‡	P. Coast	19	92⅓	3	7	.300	94	59	52	75	71	5.07
1987—Huntsville	Southern	17	114⅔	5	10	.333	109	54	46	75	53	3.61
1987—Tacoma§	P. Coast	10	66⅓	7	2	.778	46	26	23	50	54	3.12
1988—Nashville	Am. Assoc.	8	49⅔	1	3	.250	33	20	17	48	21	3.08

Year Club	League	G.	IP.	W.	L.	Pct.	H.	R.	ER.	SO.	BB.	ERA.
1988—Cincinnati	National	36	64⅓	1	3	.250	61	34	30	38	24	4.20
1989—Cincinnati	National	42	69⅔	2	2	.500	68	33	29	57	27	3.75
American League Totals—2 Years		31	143⅓	10	6	.625	126	77	68	95	95	4.27
National League Totals—2 Years		78	134	3	5	.375	129	67	59	95	51	3.96
Major League Totals—4 Years		109	277⅓	13	11	.542	255	144	127	190	146	4.12

Selected by New York Yankees' organization in 2nd round of free-agent draft, June 7, 1982.

†Traded with Outfielder Stan Javier and Pitchers Jay Howell, Eric Plunk and Jose Rijo to Oakland A's for Outfielder Rickey Henderson, Pitcher Bert Bradley and cash, December 5, 1984.

‡On disabled list, July 18 to August 26, 1986.

§Traded with Pitcher Jose Rijo to Cincinnati Reds for Outfielder Dave Parker, December 8, 1987.

JEFFREY SCOTT BITTIGER
(Jeff)

Born April 13, 1962, at Jersey City, N.J.
Height, 5.10. Weight, 175.
Throws and bats righthanded.
Attended Montclair State College, Upper Montclair, N.J., and
Jersey City State College, Jersey City, N.J.

Led Pacific Coast League in shutouts with 4 in 1989.
Tied for Pacific Coast League lead in complete games with 9 in 1987 and 6 in 1989.
Tied for International League lead in games started by pitchers with 28 in 1983.
Named Texas League Pitcher of the Year, 1982.

Year Club	League	G.	IP.	W.	L.	Pct.	H.	R.	ER.	SO.	BB.	ERA.
1980—Little Falls	NYP	7	26	0	1	.000	10	6	3	33	20	1.04
1981—Lynchburg	Carolina	24	137	11	7	.611	121	72	60	★168	79	3.94
1981—Jackson	Texas	4	33	2	1	.667	24	4	4	27	8	1.09
1982—Jackson	Texas	25	164	12	5	.706	106	59	54	★190	94	2.96
1983—Tidewater	Int'national	28	163	12	10	.545	175	90	79	110	★111	4.36
1984—Tidewater†	Int'national	24	134⅔	8	8	.500	124	72	58	70	53	3.88
1985—Tidewater‡	Int'national	24	131⅔	11	7	.611	131	62	54	66	52	3.69
1986—Portland	P. Coast	27	171⅓	13	8	.619	181	83	79	101	58	4.15
1986—Philadelphia§x	National	3	14⅔	1	1	.500	16	10	9	8	7	5.52
1987—Portland	P. Coast	26	180	12	10	.545	171	84	68	94	57	3.40
1987—Minnesota y	American	3	8⅓	1	0	1.000	11	5	5	5	0	5.40
1988—Vancouver	P. Coast	7	52	4	1	.800	35	9	6	49	6	1.04
1988—Chicago z	American	25	61⅔	2	4	.333	59	31	29	33	29	4.23
1989—Vancouver	P. Coast	17	123	9	5	.643	93	31	29	122	40	★2.12
1989—Chicago a	American	2	9⅔	0	1	.000	9	7	7	7	6	6.52
1989—Sarasota White Sox	Gulf Coast	2	12	1	1	.500	7	3	1	10	0	0.75
National League Totals—1 Year		3	14⅔	1	1	.500	16	10	9	8	7	5.52
American League Totals—3 Years		30	79⅔	3	5	.375	79	43	41	45	35	4.63
Major League Totals—4 Years		33	94⅓	4	6	.400	95	53	50	53	42	4.77

Selected by New York Mets' organization in 7th round of free-agent draft, June 3, 1980.

†On disabled list, June 13 to June 24, 1984.

‡Traded with Catcher Ronn Reynolds to Philadelphia Phillies for Pitcher Rodger Cole and First Baseman Ronnie Gideon, January 16, 1986.

§Released, December 8, 1986; signed by Richmond (Atlanta Braves' organization), December 20, 1986.

xReleased, April 4, 1987; signed by Portland (Minnesota Twins' organization), April 15, 1987.

yReleased, November 12, 1987; signed by Chicago White Sox, January 22, 1988.

zOn disabled list, July 20 to August 9, 1988.

aOn disabled list, May 31 to July 14, 1989; included rehabilitation disability assignment to Sarasota, July 3 to July 9, 1989.

bTraded to Los Angeles Dodgers for Infielder Tracy Woodson, November 9, 1989.

RECORD AS THIRD BASEMAN

Year Club	League	Pos.	G.	AB.	R.	H.	2B.	3B.	HR.	RBI.	B.A.	PO.	A.	E.	F.A.
1980—Little Falls	NYP	3B-P	22	37	4	7	0	1	0	3	.189	11	24	8	.814

HARRY RALSTON BLACK
(Bud)

Born June 30, 1957, at San Mateo, Calif.
Height, 6.02. Weight, 185.
Throws and bats lefthanded.
Attended Lower Columbia College, Longview, Wash. and received bachelor of arts degree
in finance from San Diego State University, San Diego, Calif. in 1979.
Son of Harry Black, Sr., former minor league hockey player.

Major League saves: 1986 (9), 1987 (1), 1988 (1). Total—11.
Led American League in balks with 7 in 1982.

Year Club	League	G.	IP.	W.	L.	Pct.	H.	R.	ER.	SO.	BB.	ERA.
1979—Bellingham	Northwest	2	5	0	0	.000	3	0	0	8	5	0.00
1979—San Jose	California	17	27	0	1	.000	17	11	9	24	16	3.00
1980—San Jose	California	32	86	5	3	.625	67	34	33	73	49	3.45
1981—Lynn	Eastern	22	87	2	6	.250	78	38	29	86	23	3.00
1981—Spokane	P. Coast	4	8	1	0	1.000	12	4	4	4	2	4.50
1981—Seattle†	American	2	1	0	0	.000	2	0	0	0	3	0.00

Year Club	League	G.	IP.	W.	L.	Pct.	H.	R.	ER.	SO.	BB.	ERA.
1982—Kansas City	American	22	88⅓	4	6	.400	92	48	45	40	34	4.58
1982—Omaha	Am. Assoc.	4	29	3	1	.750	23	9	8	20	10	2.48
1983—Omaha	Am. Assoc.	5	35	3	1	.750	31	13	13	32	13	3.34
1983—Kansas City	American	24	161⅓	10	7	.588	159	75	68	58	43	3.79
1984—Kansas City	American	35	257	17	12	.586	226	99	89	140	64	3.12
1985—Kansas City	American	33	205⅔	10	15	.400	216	111	99	122	59	4.33
1986—Kansas City	American	56	121	5	10	.333	100	49	43	68	43	3.20
1987—Kansas City‡	American	29	122⅓	8	6	.571	126	63	49	61	35	3.60
1988—Kansas City§-Cleveland x	American	33	81	4	4	.500	82	47	45	63	34	5.00
1988—Williamsport y	Eastern	1	5	1	0	1.000	0	0	0	5	0	0.00
1989—Cleveland	American	33	222⅓	12	11	.522	213	95	83	88	52	3.36
Major League Totals—9 Years		267	1260	70	71	.496	1216	587	521	640	367	3.72

Selected by San Francisco Giants' organization in 3rd round of free-agent draft, January 11, 1977.
Selected by New York Mets' organization in secondary phase of free-agent draft, June 7, 1977.
Selected by Seattle Mariners' organization in 17th round of free-agent draft, June 5, 1979.
†Traded to Kansas City Royals, March 2, 1982, completing deal in which Kansas City traded Infielder Manny Castillo to Seattle Mariners for a player to be named later, October 23, 1981.
‡On disabled list, June 8 to July 4, 1987.
§Traded to Cleveland Indians for First Baseman Pat Tabler, June 3, 1988.
xOn disabled list, July 19 to August 21, 1988; included rehabilitation disability assignment to Williamsport, August 16 to August 21, 1988.
yGranted free agency, November 4, 1988; re-signed by Indians, December 5, 1988.

CHAMPIONSHIP SERIES RECORD

Year Club	League	G.	IP.	W.	L.	Pct.	H.	R.	ER.	SO.	BB.	ERA.
1984—Kansas City	American	1	5	0	1	.000	7	4	4	3	1	7.20
1985—Kansas City	American	3	10⅔	0	0	.000	11	3	2	8	4	1.69
Championship Series Totals—2 Years		4	15⅔	0	1	.000	18	7	6	11	5	3.45

WORLD SERIES RECORD

Year Club	League	G.	IP.	W.	L.	Pct.	H.	R.	ER.	SO.	BB.	ERA.
1985—Kansas City	American	2	5⅓	0	1	.000	4	3	3	4	5	5.06

WILLIAM ALLEN BLAIR
(Willie)

Born December 18, 1965, at Paintsville, Ky.
Height, 6.01. Weight, 185.
Throws and bats righthanded.
Attended Morehead State University, Morehead, Ky.
Led New York-Pennsylvania League in saves with 12 in 1986.

Year Club	League	G.	IP.	W.	L.	Pct.	H.	R.	ER.	SO.	BB.	ERA.
1986—St. Catharines	NYP	21	53⅔	5	0	1.000	32	10	10	55	20	1.68
1987—Dunedin	Florida St.	50	85⅓	2	9	.182	99	51	42	72	29	4.43
1988—Dunedin	Florida St.	4	6⅔	2	0	1.000	5	2	2	5	4	2.70
1988—Knoxville	Southern	34	102	5	5	.500	94	49	41	76	35	3.62
1989—Syracuse	Int'national	19	106⅔	5	6	.455	94	55	47	76	38	3.97

Selected by Toronto Blue Jays' organization in 11th round of free-agent draft, June 2, 1986.

KEVIN DeWAYNE BLANKENSHIP

Born January 26, 1963, at Anaheim, Calif.
Height, 6.00. Weight, 185.
Throws and bats righthanded.
Attended University of Arizona, Tucson, Ariz.

Year Club	League	G.	IP.	W.	L.	Pct.	H.	R.	ER.	SO.	BB.	ERA.
1984—Bradenton Braves	Gulf Coast	19	53⅔	3	1	.750	48	20	8	27	16	1.34
1985—Durham	Carolina	29	116⅔	8	8	.500	124	63	49	89	53	3.78
1986—Greenville	Southern	38	123	6	7	.462	132	78	67	83	84	4.90
1987—Greenville	Southern	40	102⅓	4	7	.364	96	51	47	78	53	4.13
1988—Greenville	Southern	28	177	13	9	.591	132	58	46	127	83	2.34
1988—Atlanta†-Chicago	National	3	15⅔	1	1	.500	14	8	8	9	8	4.60
1989—Iowa	Am. Assoc.	35	162	●13	7	.650	155	79	67	110	79	3.72
1989—Chicago	National	2	5⅓	0	0	.000	4	1	1	2	2	1.69
Major League Totals—2 Years		5	21	1	1	.500	18	9	9	11	10	3.86

Signed as free agent by Atlanta Braves' organization, June 19, 1984.
†Traded with Pitcher Kevin Coffman to Chicago Cubs for Catcher Jody Davis, September 29, 1988.

LANCE ROBERT BLANKENSHIP

Born December 6, 1963, at Portland, Ore.
Height, 6.00. Weight, 185.
Throws and bats righthanded.
Attended University of California, Berkeley, Calif.
Major League stolen bases: 1989 (5).
Led Pacific Coast League in bases on balls received with 96 in 1988.
Led Pacific Coast League second basemen in total chances with 682 in 1988.
Named third baseman on THE SPORTING NEWS College Baseball All-America Team, 1985.

Year Club	League	Pos.	G.	AB.	R.	H.	2B.	3B.	HR.	RBI.	B.A.	PO.	A.	E.	F.A.
1986—Medford	N'west	OF	14	52	22	21	3	0	2	17	.404	22	1	1	.958
1986—Modesto	Calif.	OF-3B	55	171	47	50	5	3	6	25	.292	88	27	7	.943
1987—Modesto	Calif.	3-O-S-2	22	84	14	23	9	2	0	17	.274	26	30	8	.875
1987—Huntsville	South.	OF-2B-3B	107	390	64	99	21	3	4	39	.254	185	99	8	.973
1988—Tacoma	P. C.	2B-OF	131	437	84	116	21	8	9	52	.265	272	★390	21	.969
1988—Oakland	Amer.	2B	10	3	1	0	0	0	0	0	.000	1	1	0	1.000
1989—Tacoma	P. C.	2B	25	98	25	29	8	2	2	9	.296	39	81	2	.984
1989—Oakland	Amer.	OF-2B	58	125	22	29	5	1	1	4	.232	69	49	1	.992
Major League Totals—2 Years			68	128	23	29	5	1	1	4	.227	70	50	1	.992

Selected by Oakland Athletics' organization in 10th round of free-agent draft, June 2, 1986.

CHAMPIONSHIP SERIES RECORD

Year Club	League	Pos.	G.	AB.	R.	H.	2B.	3B.	HR.	RBI.	B.A.	PO.	A.	E.	F.A.
1989—Oakland	Amer.	2B	1	0	0	0	0	0	0	0	.000	0	1	0	1.000

WORLD SERIES RECORD

Year Club	League	Pos.	G.	AB.	R.	H.	2B.	3B.	HR.	RBI.	B.A.	PO.	A.	E.	F.A.
1989—Oakland	Amer.	PH-2B	1	2	1	1	0	0	0	0	.500	1	0	0	1.000

JEFFREY MICHAEL BLAUSER
(Jeff)

Born November 8, 1965, at Los Gatos, Calif.
Height, 6.00. Weight, 170.
Throws and bats righthanded.
Attended Sacramento City College, Sacramento, Calif.

Major League stolen bases: 1987 (7), 1989 (5). Total—12.
Led Carolina League shortstops in total chances with 506 in 1986.

Year Club	League	Pos.	G.	AB.	R.	H.	2B.	3B.	HR.	RBI.	B.A.	PO.	A.	E.	F.A.
1984—Pulaski	Appal.	SS	62	217	41	54	6	1	3	24	.249	61	162	24	.903
1985—Sumter	S. Atl.	SS	125	422	74	99	19	0	5	49	.235	150	306	35	.929
1986—Durham	Carol.	SS	123	447	94	128	27	3	13	52	.286	167	★314	25	★.951
1987—Richmond	Int.	SS 2B	33	113	11	20	1	0	1	12	.177	56	106	9	.947
1987—Atlanta	Nat.	SS	51	165	11	40	6	3	2	15	.242	65	166	9	.962
1987—Greenville	South.	SS	72	265	35	66	13	3	4	32	.249	101	225	8	.976
1988—Richmond	Int.	SS	69	271	40	77	19	1	5	23	.284	93	156	15	.943
1988—Atlanta	Nat.	2B-SS	18	67	7	16	3	1	2	7	.239	35	59	4	.959
1989—Atlanta	Nat.	3-2-S-O	142	456	63	123	24	2	12	46	.270	137	254	21	.949
Major League Totals—3 Years			211	688	81	179	33	6	16	68	.260	237	479	34	.955

Selected by St. Louis Cardinals' organization in 1st round (eighth player selected) of free-agent draft, January 17, 1984.
Selected by Atlanta Braves' organization in secondary phase of free-agent draft, June 4, 1984.

TERRY FENNELL BLOCKER

Born August 18, 1960, at Columbia, S.C.
Height, 6.02. Weight, 195.
Throws and bats lefthanded.
Received degree in health and recreation from Tennessee State University, Nashville, Tenn. in 1981.

Major League stolen bases: 1988 (1), 1989 (1). Total—2.
Tied for International League lead in double plays by outfielders with 6 in 1987 and 4 in 1988.

Year Club	League	Pos.	G.	AB.	R.	H.	2B.	3B.	HR.	RBI.	B.A.	PO.	A.	E.	F.A.
1981—Little Falls	NYP	OF	36	135	28	46	8	1	7	16	.341	72	6	7	.918
1982—Jackson	Texas	OF	118	438	69	114	20	2	5	38	.260	248	7	3	★.988
1983—Jackson	Texas	OF	66	263	38	81	16	7	3	54	.308	92	5	5	.951
1983—Tidewater	Int.	OF	72	239	26	73	7	2	2	32	.305	133	4	6	.958
1984—Tidewater	Int.	OF	115	386	45	85	10	1	3	31	.220	215	2	6	.973
1985—New York†	Nat.	OF	18	15	1	1	0	0	0	0	.067	4	0	0	1.000
1985—Tidewater	Int.	OF	75	267	40	82	8	4	5	38	.307	183	5	5	.974
1986—Tidewater	Int.	OF	117	434	53	125	13	5	9	47	.288	249	11	7	.974
1987—Tidewater‡	Int.	OF	124	525	89	164	21	5	6	37	.312	286	8	7	.977
1988—Atlanta	Nat.	OF	66	198	13	42	4	2	2	10	.212	164	1	1	.994
1988—Richmond	Int.	OF	69	266	34	60	3	1	2	9	.226	175	6	0	1.000
1989—Richmond	Int.	OF	8	26	3	5	0	0	1	1	.192	20	1	1	.955
1989—Atlanta	Nat.	OF-P	26	31	1	7	1	0	0	1	.226	7	0	0	1.000
1989—Greenville§	South.	OF	59	205	33	55	7	4	5	22	.268	92	5	2	.980
Major League Totals—3 Years			110	244	15	50	5	2	2	11	.205	175	1	1	.994

Selected by New York Mets' organization in 1st round (fourth player selected) of free-agent draft, June 8, 1981.
†On disabled list, June 10 to June 25, 1985.
‡Traded to Atlanta Braves for a player to be named later, November 11, 1987; New York Mets acquired Pitcher Kevin Dewayne Brown, December 8, 1987.
§Granted free agency, October 15, 1989.

PITCHING RECORD

Year Club	League	G.	IP.	W.	L.	Pct.	H.	R.	ER.	SO.	BB.	ERA.
1989—Atlanta	National	1	1	0	0	.000	0	0	0	0	2	0.00

MICHAEL ROY BLOWERS
(Mike)

Born April 24, 1965, at Wurzburg, West Germany.
Height, 6.02. Weight, 190.
Throws and bats righthanded.
Attended Tacoma Community College, Tacoma, Wash.,
and University of Washington, Seattle, Wash.

Led Southern League third basemen in double plays with 27 in 1988.
Led Florida State League third basemen in double plays with 27 and fielding percentage with .944 in 1987.

Year Club	League	Pos.	G.	AB.	R.	H.	2B.	3B.	HR.	RBI.	B.A.	PO.	A.	E.	F.A.
1986—Jamestown............	NYP	SS-3B	32	95	13	24	9	2	1	6	.253	48	73	16	.883
1986—Bradenton Expos	Gulf C.	SS	31	115	14	25	3	1	2	17	.217	50	84	15	.899
1987—W. Palm Beach....	Fla. St.	3B-SS-1B	136	491	68	124	30	3	16	71	.253	75	239	18	.946
1988—Jacksonville.........	South.	⋆3B-SS-2B	137	460	58	115	20	6	15	60	.250	⋆125	241	34	.915
1989—Indianapolis†	A. A.	⋆3B-SS	131	461	49	123	29	6	14	56	.267	91	214	23	⋆.930
1989—New York.............	Amer.	3B	13	38	2	10	0	0	0	3	.263	9	14	4	.852
Major League Totals—1 Year..................			13	38	2	10	0	0	0	3	.263	9	14	4	.852

Selected by Seattle Mariners' organization in 8th round of free-agent draft, January 17, 1984.
Selected by San Francisco Giants' organization in secondary phase of free-agent draft, June 4, 1984.
Selected by Baltimore Orioles' organization in secondary phase of free-agent draft, January 9, 1985.
Selected by Montreal Expos' organization in 10th round of free-agent draft, June 2, 1986.
†Traded to New York Yankees, August 31, 1989, completing deal in which New York traded Pitcher John Candelaria to Montreal Expos for a player to be named later, August 29, 1989.

RIK AALBERT BLYLEVEN
(Bert)

Born April 6, 1951, at Zeist, The Netherlands.
Height, 6.03. Weight, 205.
Throws and bats righthanded.

Holds major league record for most home runs allowed, season (50), 1986.
Shares major league record for most putouts by pitcher, nine-inning game (6), June 24, 1984.
Shares American League records for longest one-hit complete game (10 innings), June 21, 1976; most seasons, 200 or more strikeouts (8).
Pitched 6-0 no-hit victory against California Angels, September 22, 1977.
Led American League in home runs allowed with 50 in 1986 and 46 in 1987.
Led American League pitchers in complete games with 24 and tied for lead in games started with 37 in 1985.
Led American League in hit batsmen with 12 in 1976 and 16 in 1988.
Led American League in shutouts with 9 in 1973 and 5 in both 1985 and 1989.
Tied for American League lead in balks with 3 in 1970.
Named American League Comeback Player of the Year by THE SPORTING NEWS, 1989.
Named American League Rookie Pitcher of the Year by THE SPORTING NEWS, 1970.

Year Club	League	G.	IP.	W.	L.	Pct.	H.	R.	ER.	SO.	BB.	ERA.
1969—Sarasota Twins..............................	Gulf Coast	7	32	2	2	.500	31	13	10	39	11	2.81
1969—Orlando	Florida St.	6	37	5	0	1.000	36	6	6	41	14	1.46
1970—Evansville................................	Am. Assoc.	8	54	4	2	.667	48	18	15	63	12	2.50
1970—Minnesota	American	27	164	10	9	.526	143	66	58	135	47	3.18
1971—Minnesota	American	38	278	16	15	.516	267	95	87	224	59	2.82
1972—Minnesota	American	39	287	17	17	.500	247	93	87	228	69	2.73
1973—Minnesota	American	40	325	20	17	.541	296	109	91	258	67	2.52
1974—Minnesota	American	37	281	17	17	.500	244	99	83	249	77	2.66
1975—Minnesota	American	35	276	15	10	.600	219	104	92	233	84	3.00
1976—Minnesota†-Texas	American	36	298	13	16	.448	283	106	95	219	81	2.87
1977—Texas‡	American	30	235	14	12	.538	181	81	71	182	69	2.72
1978—Pittsburgh................................	National	34	244	14	10	.583	217	94	82	182	66	3.02
1979—Pittsburgh................................	National	37	237	12	5	.706	238	102	95	172	92	3.61
1980—Pittsburgh§................................	National	34	217	8	13	.381	219	102	92	168	59	3.82
1981—Cleveland x	American	20	159	11	7	.611	145	52	51	107	40	2.89
1982—Cleveland x	American	4	20⅓	2	2	.500	16	14	11	19	11	4.87
1983—Cleveland	American	24	156⅓	7	10	.412	160	74	68	123	44	3.91
1984—Cleveland y	American	33	245	19	7	.731	204	86	78	170	74	2.87
1985—Cleveland z-Minnesota	American	37	⋆293⅔	17	16	.515	264	121	103	⋆206	75	3.16
1986—Minnesota	American	36	⋆271⅔	17	14	.548	262	134	121	215	58	4.01
1987—Minnesota	American	37	267	15	12	.556	249	132	119	196	101	4.01
1988—Minnesota ab................................	American	33	207⅓	10	⋆17	.370	240	128	⋆125	145	51	5.43
1989—California................................	American	33	241	17	5	.773	225	76	73	131	44	2.73
National League Totals—3 Years......................		105	698	34	28	.548	674	298	269	522	217	3.47
American League Totals—17 Years...................		539	4005⅓	237	203	.539	3645	1570	1413	3040	1051	3.18
Major League Totals—20 Years......................		644	4703⅓	271	231	.540	4319	1868	1682	3562	1268	3.22

Selected by Minnesota Twins' organization in 3rd round of free-agent draft, June 5, 1969.
†Traded with Shortstop Danny Thompson to Texas Rangers for Pitcher Bill Singer, Infielders Roy Smalley and Mike Cubbage, Pitcher Jim Gideon and a reported $250,000 cash, June 1, 1976.
‡Traded with First Baseman-Outfielder John Milner to Pittsburgh Pirates for Outfielder-First Baseman Al Oliver and Infielder Nelson Norman, December 8, 1977.
§Traded with Catcher Manny Sanguillen to Cleveland Indians for Pitchers Bob Owchinko, Rafael Vasquez and Victor Cruz and Catcher Gary Alexander, December 9, 1980.
xOn disabled list, May 2, 1982 through remainder of season.
yOn disabled list, May 23 to June 10, 1984.
zTraded to Minnesota Twins for Pitcher Curt Wardle, Outfielder Jim Weaver, Infielder Jay Bell and a player to be

named later, August 1, 1985; Cleveland Indians' organization acquired Pitcher Rich Yett to complete deal, September 17, 1985.

aOn disabled list, July 30 to August 15, 1988.

bTraded with Pitcher Kevin Trudeau to California Angels for Pitchers Mike Cook and Rob Wassenaar and First Baseman Paul Sorrento, November 3, 1988.

CHAMPIONSHIP SERIES RECORD

Year Club	League	G.	IP.	W.	L.	Pct.	H.	R.	ER.	SO.	BB.	ERA.
1970—Minnesota	American	1	2	0	0	.000	2	1	0	2	0	0.00
1979—Pittsburgh	National	1	9	1	0	1.000	8	1	1	9	0	1.00
1987—Minnesota	American	2	13⅓	2	0	1.000	12	6	6	9	3	4.05
Championship Series Totals—3 Years		4	24⅓	3	0	1.000	22	8	7	20	3	2.59

WORLD SERIES RECORD

Year Club	League	G.	IP.	W.	L.	Pct.	H.	R.	ER.	SO.	BB.	ERA.
1979—Pittsburgh	National	2	10	1	0	1.000	8	2	2	4	3	1.80
1987—Minnesota	American	2	13	1	1	.500	13	5	4	12	2	2.77
World Series Totals—2 Years		4	23	2	1	.667	21	7	6	16	5	2.35

ALL-STAR GAME RECORD

Year League	IP.	W.	L.	Pct.	H.	R.	ER.	SO.	BB.	ERA.
1973—American	1	0	1	.000	2	2	2	0	2	18.00
1985—American	2	0	0	.000	3	2	2	1	1	9.00
All-Star Game Totals—2 Years	3	0	1	.000	5	4	4	1	3	12.00

RANDY WALTER BOCKUS

Born October 5, 1960, at Canton, O.
Height, 6.03. Weight, 205.
Throws right and bats lefthanded.
Attended Kent State University, Kent, O.

Led Texas League pitchers in complete games with 15 and tied for lead in games started with 27 in 1985.
Led California League pitchers in games started with 30 in 1983.
Tied for Texas League in shutouts with 3 in 1984.

Year Club	League	G.	IP.	W.	L.	Pct.	H.	R.	ER.	SO.	BB.	ERA.
1982—Great Falls	Pioneer	18	53	2	0	1.000	60	38	27	42	22	4.58
1983—Fresno	California	30	196	14	6	.700	185	89	78	*144	78	3.58
1984—Shreveport	Texas	18	128⅓	8	5	.615	106	44	40	93	54	2.81
1985—Shreveport	Texas	28	*201	*14	11	.560	196	85	61	126	44	*2.73
1986—Phoenix	P. Coast	42	122⅔	11	6	.647	139	69	58	55	54	4.26
1986—San Francisco†	National	5	7	0	0	.000	7	5	2	4	6	2.57
1987—Phoenix	P. Coast	36	108⅓	7	5	.583	133	60	54	64	41	4.49
1987—San Francisco	National	12	17⅓	1	0	1.000	17	8	7	9	4	3.63
1988—Phoenix†	P. Coast	23	51⅓	4	3	.571	63	36	34	27	22	5.96
1988—San Francisco‡	National	20	32	1	1	.500	35	19	17	18	13	4.78
1989—Toledo	Int'national	32	119⅔	6	4	.600	124	63	52	58	52	3.91
1989—Detroit§	American	2	5⅓	0	0	.000	7	3	3	2	2	5.06
National League Totals—3 Years		37	56⅓	2	1	.667	59	32	26	31	23	4.15
American League Totals—1 Year		2	5⅓	0	0	.000	7	3	3	2	2	5.06
Major League Totals—4 Years		39	61⅔	2	1	.667	66	35	29	33	25	4.23

Selected by San Francisco Giants' organization in 34th round of free-agent draft, June 7, 1982.

†Appeared in one game as an outfielder with no chances.

‡Granted free agency, October 15, 1988; signed by Detroit Tigers, November 30, 1988.

§Granted free agency, October 15, 1989.

MICHAEL JAMES BODDICKER

Name pronounced BOD-dick-er

(Mike)

Born August 23, 1957, at Cedar Rapids, Iowa.
Height, 5.11. Weight, 186.
Throws and bats righthanded.
Attended University of Iowa, Iowa City, Iowa.

Shares modern major league record for most putouts by pitcher, season (49), 1984.
Led American League in shutouts with 5 in 1983.
Named American League Rookie Pitcher of the Year by THE SPORTING NEWS, 1983.
Named righthanded pitcher on THE SPORTING NEWS American League All-Star Team, 1984.

Year Club	League	G.	IP.	W.	L.	Pct.	H.	R.	ER.	SO.	BB.	ERA.
1978—Bluefield	Ap'lachian	8	19	2	1	.667	9	2	1	28	10	0.47
1978—Charlotte	Southern	10	65	4	3	.571	42	15	14	48	17	1.94
1978—Rochester	Int'national	1	5	1	0	1.000	4	1	1	3	2	1.80
1979—Charlotte	Southern	14	102	9	3	.750	82	40	34	89	36	3.00
1979—Rochester	Int'national	15	72	4	6	.400	88	48	48	48	27	6.00
1980—Rochester	Int'national	25	190	12	9	.571	149	57	46	109	35	2.18
1980—Baltimore	American	1	7	0	1	.000	6	6	5	4	5	6.43
1981—Rochester	Int'national	30	182	10	10	.500	182	91	85	109	66	4.20
1981—Baltimore	American	2	6	0	0	.000	6	4	3	2	2	4.50
1982—Rochester	Int'national	20	133⅓	10	5	.667	121	59	53	82	36	3.58

— 50 —

Year	Club	League	G.	IP.	W.	L.	Pct.	H.	R.	ER.	SO.	BB.	ERA.
1982—Baltimore	American	7	25⅔	1	0	1.000	25	10	10	20	12	3.51
1983—Rochester	Int'national	4	23⅔	3	1	.750	17	6	5	18	13	1.90
1983—Baltimore	American	27	179	16	8	.667	141	65	55	120	52	2.77
1984—Baltimore†	American	34	261⅓	*20	11	.645	218	95	81	128	81	*2.79
1985—Baltimore‡	American	32	203⅓	12	17	.414	227	104	92	135	89	4.07
1986—Baltimore§	American	33	218⅓	14	12	.538	214	125	114	175	74	4.70
1987—Baltimore	American	33	226	10	12	.455	212	114	105	152	78	4.18
1988—Baltimore x-Boston	American	36	236	13	15	.464	234	102	89	156	77	3.39
1989—Boston	American	34	211⅔	15	11	.577	217	101	94	145	71	4.00
Major League Totals—10 Years		239	1574⅓	101	87	.537	1500	726	648	1037	541	3.70

Selected by Montreal Expos' organization in 8th round of free-agent draft, June 4, 1975.
Selected by Baltimore Orioles' organization in 6th round of free-agent draft, June 6, 1978.
†Appeared in one game as a pinch-runner.
‡Appeared in two games as a pinch-runner.
§On disabled list, April 20 to May 10, 1986.
xTraded to Boston Red Sox for Outfielder Brady Anderson and Pitcher Curt Schilling, July 29, 1988.

CHAMPIONSHIP SERIES RECORD

Shares Championship Series record for most strikeouts, game (14), October 6, 1983.

Year	Club	League	G.	IP.	W.	L.	Pct.	H.	R.	ER.	SO.	BB.	ERA.
1983—Baltimore	American	1	9	1	0	1.000	5	0	0	14	3	0.00
1988—Boston	American	1	2⅔	0	1	.000	8	6	6	2	1	20.25
Championship Series Totals—2 Years		2	11⅔	1	1	.500	13	6	6	16	4	4.63

WORLD SERIES RECORD

Year	Club	League	G.	IP.	W.	L.	Pct.	H.	R.	ER.	SO.	BB.	ERA.
1983—Baltimore	American	1	9	1	0	1.000	3	1	0	6	0	0.00

ALL-STAR GAME RECORD

Member of American League All-Star Team in 1984; did not play.

JOSEPH MARTIN BOEVER

Name pronounced BAY-vur.

(Joe)

Born October 4, 1960, at St. Louis, Mo.
Height, 6.01. Weight, 200.
Throws and bats righthanded.
Attended Crowder College, Neosho, Mo., St. Louis Community College at
Meramec, St. Louis, Mo., and University of Nevada, Las Vegas, Nev.

Major League saves: 1988 (1), 1989 (21). Total—22.
Led International League in saves with 22 in 1988.
Led American Association in saves with 21 in 1987.
Led Florida State League in games finished in relief with 38 and tied for lead in saves with 14 in 1984.
Led Florida State League in games finished in relief with 46, saves with 26 and intentional bases on balls issued with 12 in 1983.
Tied for New York-Pennsylvania League lead in intentional bases on balls issued with 5 in 1982.

Year	Club	League	G.	IP.	W.	L.	Pct.	H.	R.	ER.	SO.	BB.	ERA.
1982—Erie	NYP	19	32⅔	2	3	.400	20	8	7	63	12	1.93
1982—Springfield	Midwest	3	4	0	0	.000	3	1	1	7	2	2.25
1983—St. Petersburg	Florida St.	53	80⅓	5	6	.455	61	29	27	57	37	3.02
1984—Arkansas	Texas	8	11	0	1	.000	10	11	10	12	12	8.18
1984—St. Petersburg	Florida St.	48	77⅔	6	4	.600	52	31	26	81	45	3.01
1985—Arkansas	Texas	27	37⅔	3	1	.750	21	5	5	45	23	1.19
1985—Louisville	Am. Assoc.	21	35⅓	3	2	.600	28	11	8	37	22	2.04
1985—St. Louis	National	13	16⅓	0	0	.000	17	8	8	20	4	4.41
1986—St. Louis	National	11	21⅔	0	1	.000	19	5	4	8	11	1.66
1986—Louisville	Am. Assoc.	51	88	4	5	.444	71	25	22	75	48	2.25
1987—Louisville†	Am. Assoc.	43	59	3	2	.600	52	22	22	79	27	3.36
1987—Atlanta	National	14	18⅓	1	0	1.000	29	15	15	18	12	7.36
1987—Richmond	Int'national	6	9	1	0	1.000	8	1	1	8	4	1.00
1988—Richmond‡	Int'national	48	71⅓	6	3	.667	47	17	17	71	22	2.14
1988—Atlanta	National	16	20⅓	0	2	.000	12	4	4	7	1	1.77
1989—Atlanta	National	66	82⅓	4	11	.267	78	37	36	68	34	3.94
Major League Totals—5 Years		120	159	5	14	.263	155	69	67	121	62	3.79

Signed as free agent by St. Louis Cardinals' organization, June 25, 1982.
†Traded to Atlanta Braves for Pitcher Randy O'Neal, July 25, 1987.

WADE ANTHONY BOGGS

Born June 15, 1958, at Omaha, Neb.
Height, 6.02. Weight, 197.
Throws right and bats lefthanded.
Attended Hillsborough Community College, Tampa, Fla.

Shares major league record for most games, one or more hits, season (135), 1985.
Holds American League records for highest batting average, rookie season, 100 or more games (.349), 1982; most consecutive years with 200 or more hits (7); most singles, season (187), 1985.

Shares American League records for most seasons and most consecutive seasons leading league, intentional bases on balls (3); fewest double plays, third baseman, season, 150 or more games (17), 1988.

Major League stolen bases: 1982 (1), 1983 (3), 1984 (3), 1985 (2), 1987 (1), 1988 (2), 1989 (2). Total—14.

Led American League in intentional bases on balls received with 19 in both 1987 and 1989 and tied for lead with 18 in 1988.

Led American League in bases on balls received with 105 in 1986 and 125 in 1988.

Led American League in grounding into double plays with 23 in 1988.

Led American league third basemen in total chances with 486 in 1985.

Led American League third basemen in double plays with 30 in 1984, 37 in 1987 and 29 in 1989.

Named third baseman on THE SPORTING NEWS American League All-Star Team, 1983 and 1985 through 1988.

Named third baseman on THE SPORTING NEWS American League Silver Slugger team, 1983 and 1986 through 1989.

Year Club	League	Pos.	G.	AB.	R.	H.	2B.	3B.	HR.	RBI.	B.A.	PO.	A.	E.	F.A.
1976—Elmira	NYP	3B	57	179	29	47	6	0	0	15	.263	36	75	16	.874
1977—Winston-Salem	Carol.	3B-2B-SS	117	422	67	140	13	1	2	55	.332	145	223	27	.932
1978—Bristol	East.	3-S-2-O	109	354	63	110	14	2	1	32	.311	62	107	7	.960
1979—Bristol†	East.	*3-S-2	113	406	56	132	17	2	0	41	.325	94	213	15	*.953
1980—Pawtucket	Int.	3B-1B	129	418	51	128	21	0	1	45	.306	108	156	12	.957
1981—Pawtucket	Int.	3B-1B	137	498	67	*167	*41	3	5	60	*.335	359	238	26	.958
1982—Boston	Amer.	1B-3B-OF	104	338	51	118	14	1	5	44	.349	489	168	8	.988
1983—Boston	Amer.	3B	153	582	100	210	44	7	5	74	*.361	118	368	*27	.947
1984—Boston	Amer.	3B	158	625	109	203	31	4	6	55	.325	141	330	●20	.959
1985—Boston	Amer.	3B	161	653	107	*240	42	3	8	78	*.368	134	335	17	.965
1986—Boston	Amer.	3B	149	580	107	207	47	2	8	71	*.357	*121	267	19	.953
1987—Boston	Amer.	3B-1B	147	551	108	200	40	6	24	89	*.363	112	277	14	.965
1988—Boston	Amer.	3B	155	584	*128	214	*45	6	5	58	*.366	*122	250	11	.971
1989—Boston	Amer.	3B	156	621	●113	205	*51	7	3	54	.330	*123	264	17	.958
Major League Totals—8 Years			1183	4534	823	1597	314	36	64	523	.352	1360	2259	133	.965

Selected by Boston Red Sox' organization in 7th round of free-agent draft, June 8, 1976.

†On disabled list, April 20 to May 2, 1979.

CHAMPIONSHIP SERIES RECORD

Shares Championship Series record for most sacrifice flies, series (2), 1988.

Year Club	League	Pos.	G.	AB.	R.	H.	2B.	3B.	HR.	RBI.	B.A.	PO.	A.	E.	F.A.
1986—Boston	Amer.	3B	7	30	3	7	1	1	0	2	.233	7	13	2	.909
1988—Boston	Amer.	3B	4	13	2	5	0	0	0	3	.385	6	6	0	1.000
Championship Series Totals—2 Years			11	43	5	12	1	1	0	5	.279	13	19	2	.941

WORLD SERIES RECORD

Year Club	League	Pos.	G.	AB.	R.	H.	2B.	3B.	HR.	RBI.	B.A.	PO.	A.	E.	F.A.
1986—Boston	Amer.	3B	7	31	3	9	3	0	0	3	.290	4	15	0	1.000

ALL-STAR GAME RECORD

Year	League	Pos.	AB.	R.	H.	2B.	3B.	HR.	RBI.	B.A.	PO.	A.	E.	F.A.
1985—American		3B	0	0	0	0	0	0	0	.000	0	0	0	.000
1986—American		3B	3	0	1	0	0	0	0	.333	0	1	0	1.000
1987—American		3B	3	0	0	0	0	0	0	.000	0	3	0	1.000
1988—American		3B	3	0	1	0	0	0	0	.333	0	1	0	1.000
1989—American		3B	3	1	1	0	0	1	1	.333	1	1	0	1.000
All-Star Game Totals—5 Years			12	1	3	0	0	1	1	.250	1	6	0	1.000

BRIAN EDWARD BOHANON

Born August 1, 1968, at Denton, Tex.
Height, 6.02. Weight, 210.
Throws and bats lefthanded.

Year Club	League	G.	IP.	W.	L.	Pct.	H.	R.	ER.	SO.	BB.	ERA.
1987—Sarasota Rangers	Gulf Coast	5	21	0	2	.000	15	13	11	21	5	4.71
1988—Port Charlotte†	Florida St.	2	6⅔	0	1	.000	6	4	4	9	5	5.40
1989—Charlotte‡	Florida St.	11	54⅔	0	3	.000	40	16	11	33	20	1.81
1989—Tulsa	Texas	11	73⅔	5	0	1.000	59	20	18	44	27	2.20

Selected by Texas Rangers' organization in 1st round (19th player selected) of free-agent draft, June 2, 19__.

†On disabled list, April 17, 1988 through remainder of season.

‡On disabled list, April 7 to May 2, 1989.

THOMAS EDWARD BOLTON

(Tom)

Born May 6, 1962, at Nashville, Tenn.
Height, 6.03. Weight, 175.
Throws and bats lefthanded.

Major League saves: 1988 (1).

Year Club	League	G.	IP.	W.	L.	Pct.	H.	R.	ER.	SO.	BB.	ERA.
1980—Elmira	NYP	23	56	6	2	.750	43	26	15	43	22	2.41
1981—Winter Haven	Florida St.	24	92	2	9	.182	125	62	46	47	41	4.50
1982—Winter Haven	Florida St.	28	162⅔	9	8	.529	161	67	54	77	63	2.99
1983—New Britain†	Eastern	16	99⅔	7	3	.700	93	36	32	62	41	2.89
1983—Pawtucket	Int'national	6	29	0	5	.000	33	26	21	20	25	6.52
1984—New Britain	Eastern	33	87	4	5	.444	87	54	40	66	34	4.14

Year Club	League	G	IP	W	L	Pct.	H	R	ER.	SO.	BB.	ERA.
1985—New Britain	Eastern	34	101	5	6	.455	106	53	48	74	40	4.28
1986—Pawtucket‡	Int'national	29	86	3	4	.429	80	30	26	58	25	2.72
1987—Pawtucket	Int'national	5	21⅔	2	1	.667	25	14	13	8	12	5.40
1987—Boston	American	29	61⅔	1	0	1.000	83	33	30	49	27	4.38
1988—Pawtucket	Int'national	18	19⅓	3	0	1.000	17	7	6	15	10	2.79
1988—Boston	American	28	30⅓	1	3	.250	35	17	16	21	14	4.75
1989—Pawtucket	Int'national	25	143⅓	12	5	.706	140	57	46	99	47	2.89
1989—Boston	American	4	17½	0	4	.000	21	18	16	9	10	8.31
Major League Totals—3 Years		61	109⅓	2	7	.222	139	68	62	79	51	5.10

Selected by Boston Red Sox organization in 20th round of free-agent draft, June 3, 1980.
†On disabled list, June 27 to July 9, 1983.
‡On disabled list, April 11 to May 26, 1986.

BARRY LAMAR BONDS

Born July 24, 1964, at Riverside, Calif.
Height, 6.01. Weight, 185.
Throws and bats lefthanded.
Attended Arizona State University, Tempe, Ariz.
Son of Bobby Bonds, outfielder with San Francisco, New York Yankees, California,
Chicago White Sox, Texas, Cleveland, St. Louis and Chicago Cubs,
1968 through 1981; and coach with Cleveland Indians, 1984 through 1987.

Major League stolen bases: 1986 (36), 1987 (32), 1988 (17), 1989 (32). Total—117.
Named outfielder on THE SPORTING NEWS College Baseball All-America Team, 1985.

Year Club	League	Pos.	G.	AB.	R.	H.	2B.	3B.	HR.	RBI.	B.A.	PO.	A.	E.	F.A.
1985—Prince William	Carol.	OF	71	254	49	76	16	4	13	37	.299	202	4	5	.976
1986—Hawaii	P. C.	OF	44	148	30	46	7	2	7	37	.311	109	4	2	.983
1986—Pittsburgh	Nat.	OF	113	413	72	92	26	3	16	48	.223	280	9	5	.983
1987—Pittsburgh	Nat.	OF	150	551	99	144	34	9	25	59	.261	330	15	5	.986
1988—Pittsburgh	Nat.	OF	144	538	97	152	30	5	24	58	.283	292	5	6	.980
1989—Pittsburgh	Nat.	OF	159	580	96	144	34	6	19	58	.248	365	14	6	.984
Major League Totals—4 Years			566	2082	364	532	124	23	84	223	.256	1267	43	22	.983

Selected by San Francisco Giants' organization in 2nd round of free-agent draft, June 7, 1982.
Selected by Pittsburgh Pirates' organization in 1st round (sixth player selected) of free-agent draft, June 3, 1985.

RICARDO BONES

Name pronounced Bo-NAY.

(Ricky)

Born April 7, 1969, at Salinas, Puerto Rico.
Height, 5.10. Weight, 175.
Throws and bats righthanded.

Led Texas League in home runs allowed with 22 in 1989.

Year Club	League	G.	IP.	W.	L.	Pct.	H.	R.	ER.	SO.	BB.	ERA.
1986—Spokane	Northwest	18	58	1	3	.250	63	44	36	46	29	5.59
1987—Charleston, S.C.	S. Atlantic	26	170⅓	12	5	.706	★183	81	69	130	45	3.65
1988—Riverside	California	25	175½	15	6	.714	162	80	71	129	64	3.64
1989—Wichita	Texas	24	136⅓	10	9	.526	162	103	87	88	47	5.74

Signed as free agent by San Diego Padres' organization, May 13, 1986.

ROBERTO MARTIN ANTONIO BONILLA

Name pronounced Boh-NEE-yah.

(Bobby)

Born February 23, 1963, at New York, N.Y.
Height, 6.03. Weight, 230.
Throws right and bats left and righthanded.
Attended New York Technical College, Westbury, N.Y.

Major League stolen bases: 1986 (8), 1987 (3), 1988 (3), 1989 (8). Total—22.
Switch-hit home runs in one game, July 3, 1987 and April 6, 1988.
Led National League third basemen in double plays with 31 in 1989.
Led National League third basemen in total chances with 489 in 1988.
Named third baseman on THE SPORTING NEWS National League All-Star Team, 1988.
Named third baseman on THE SPORTING NEWS National League Silver Slugger team, 1988.

Year Club	League	Pos.	G.	AB.	R.	H.	2B.	3B.	HR.	RBI.	B.A.	PO.	A.	E.	F.A.
1981—Bradenton Pir.	Gulf C.	1B-C-3B	22	69	6	15	5	0	0	7	.217	124	23	5	.967
1982—Bradenton Pir.	Gulf C.	1B	47	167	20	38	3	0	5	26	.228	318	36	★14	.962
1983—Alexandria	Carol.	OF-1B	●136	504	88	129	19	7	11	59	.256	259	12	15	.948
1984—Nashua	East.	★OF-1B	136	484	74	128	19	5	11	71	.264	312	8	★15	.955
1985—Prince William†‡	Carol.	1B-3B	39	130	15	34	4	1	3	11	.262	180	9	2	.990
1986—Chicago§	Amer.	OF-1B	75	234	27	63	10	2	2	26	.269	361	22	2	.995
1986—Pittsburgh	Nat.	OF-1B-3B	63	192	28	46	6	2	1	17	.240	90	16	3	.972
1987—Pittsburgh	Nat.	3B-OF-1B	141	466	58	140	33	3	15	77	.300	142	139	16	.946
1988—Pittsburgh	Nat.	3B	159	584	87	160	32	7	24	100	.274	121	★336	★32	.935

Year Club League	Pos.	G.	AB.	R.	H.	2B.	3B.	HR.	RBI.	B.A.	PO.	A.	E.	F.A.
1989—Pittsburgh.............. Nat.	★3-1-0	●163	616	96	173	37	10	24	86	.281	190	334	★35	.937
American League Totals—1 Year		75	234	27	63	10	2	2	26	.269	361	22	2	.995
National League Totals—4 Years............		526	1858	269	519	108	22	64	280	.279	543	825	86	.941
Major League Totals—4 Years................		601	2092	296	582	118	24	66	306	.278	904	847	88	.952

Signed as free agent by Pittsburgh Pirates' organization, July 11, 1981.
†On Pittsburgh disabled list, March 25 to July 19, 1985.
‡Drafted by Chicago White Sox, December 10, 1985.
§Traded to Pittsburgh Pirates for Pitcher Jose DeLeon, July 23, 1986.

ALL-STAR GAME RECORD

Year League	Pos.	AB.	R.	H.	2B.	3B.	HR.	RBI.	B.A.	PO.	A.	E.	F.A.
1988—National..................................	3B	4	0	0	0	0	0	0	.000	0	2	0	1.000
1989—National..................................	DH	2	0	2	0	0	0	0	1.000	0	0	0	.000
All-Star Game Totals—2 Years..................		6	0	2	0	0	0	0	.333	0	2	0	1.000

GREGORY SCOTT BOOKER
(Greg)

Born June 22, 1960, at Lynchburg, Va.
Height, 6.06. Weight, 245.
Throws and bats righthanded.
Attended Elon College, Elon College, N.C.
Son-in-law of Jack McKeon, manager of San Diego Padres; and related to Richard (Buddy) Booker,
catcher with Cleveland Indians and Chicago White Sox, 1966 and 1968.

Major League saves: 1987 (1).
Led California League in wild pitches with 20 in 1982.

Year Club League	G.	IP.	W.	L.	Pct.	H.	R.	ER.	SO.	BB.	ERA.
1981—Walla Walla .... Northwest	11	53	2	3	.400	55	41	31	25	35	5.26
1982—Reno .... California	27	161⅔	8	★13	.381	160	★133	★114	81	★157	6.35
1983—Las Vegas .... P. Coast	46	102⅓	5	6	.455	120	77	63	58	68	5.54
1983—San Diego .... National	6	11⅔	0	1	.000	18	10	10	5	9	7.71
1984—Las Vegas .... P. Coast	9	55⅔	4	3	.571	66	39	34	23	24	5.50
1984—San Diego .... National	32	57⅓	1	1	.500	67	27	21	28	27	3.30
1985—San Diego .... National	17	22⅓	0	1	.000	20	17	17	7	17	6.85
1985—Las Vegas† .... P. Coast	10	45	1	1	.500	46	34	27	16	34	5.40
1986—Las Vegas .... P. Coast	36	128⅔	8	9	.471	148	89	75	71	65	5.25
1986—San Diego .... National	9	11	1	0	1.000	10	5	2	7	4	1.64
1987—San Diego‡ .... National	44	68⅓	1	1	.500	62	29	24	17	30	3.16
1988—San Diego .... National	34	63⅔	2	2	.500	68	31	24	43	19	3.39
1989—San Diego§ .... National	11	19	0	1	.000	15	10	9	8	10	4.26
1989—Portland .... P. Coast	14	46	0	3	.000	57	35	31	23	22	6.07
1989—Minnesota x .... American	6	8⅔	0	0	.000	11	4	4	3	2	4.15
National League Totals—7 Years	153	253⅓	5	7	.417	260	129	107	115	116	3.80
American League Totals—1 Year	6	8⅔	0	0	.000	11	4	4	3	2	4.15
Major League Totals—7 Years................	159	262	5	7	.417	271	133	111	118	118	3.81

Selected by Oakland A's organization in 32nd round of free-agent draft, June 6, 1978.
Selected by San Diego Padres' organization in 10th round of free-agent draft, June 8, 1981.
†On disabled list, July 18 to August 21, 1985.
‡On disabled list, March 29 to April 15, 1987.
§Traded to Portland (Minnesota Twins' organization) for Pitcher Fred Toliver, June 29, 1989.
xGranted free agency, October 15, 1989.

CHAMPIONSHIP SERIES RECORD

Year Club League	G.	IP.	W.	L.	Pct.	H.	R.	ER.	SO.	BB.	ERA.
1984—San Diego .... National	1	2	0	0	.000	2	0	0	2	1	0.00

WORLD SERIES RECORD

Year Club League	G.	IP.	W.	L.	Pct.	H.	R.	ER.	SO.	BB.	ERA.
1984—San Diego .... National	1	1	0	0	.000	0	1	1	0	4	9.00

RECORD AS INFIELDER

Year Club League	Pos.	G.	AB.	R.	H.	2B.	3B.	HR.	RBI.	B.A.	PO.	A.	E.	F.A.
1981—Walla Walla .... N'west	★P-1B	31	64	8	12	0	0	4	15	.188	26	14	0	★1.000

RODERICK STEWART BOOKER
(Rod)

Born September 4, 1958, at Los Angeles, Calif.
Height, 6.00. Weight, 175.
Throws right and bats lefthanded.
Attended Pasadena City College, Pasadena, Calif., and
University of California, Berkeley, Calif.

Major League stolen bases: 1987 (2), 1988 (2). Total—4.

Year Club League	Pos.	G.	AB.	R.	H.	2B.	3B.	HR.	RBI.	B.A.	PO.	A.	E.	F.A.
1980—Visalia .... Calif.	SS	69	242	45	68	5	4	0	26	.281	91	198	18	.941
1981—Orlando .... South.	SS-3B	111	331	56	85	8	3	0	33	.257	145	304	30	.937

Year—Club	League	Pos.	G.	AB.	R.	H.	2B.	3B.	HR.	RBI.	B.A.	PO.	A.	E.	F.A.
1982—Toledo†	Int.	SS-2B-3B	104	292	38	73	8	1	0	19	.250	177	272	36	.926
1983—Arkansas	Texas	SS-3B-2B	127	469	75	128	15	3	3	60	.273	153	343	19	.963
1984—Louisville	A. A.	2B-SS-3B	63	185	19	47	3	1	0	14	.254	100	167	8	.971
1984—Arkansas	Texas	SS	52	209	10	43	4	3	0	22	.206	87	160	15	.943
1985—Arkansas	Texas	SS	129	466	59	123	18	3	1	47	.264	198	362	26	★.956
1986—Arkansas	Texas	SS	36	151	20	48	7	2	0	20	.318	66	121	10	.949
1986—Louisville	A. A.	2B-SS-3B	78	289	51	81	11	5	1	30	.280	151	205	10	.973
1987—Louisville	A. A.	2B-SS-3B	34	135	25	47	3	1	1	21	.348	50	95	5	.967
1987—St. Louis	Nat.	2B-3B-SS	44	47	9	13	1	1	0	8	.277	25	28	2	.964
1988—St. Louis	Nat.	3B-2B	18	35	6	12	3	0	0	3	.343	3	15	2	.900
1988—Louisville	A. A.	2B-SS-OF	111	370	50	96	12	1	4	31	.259	197	330	20	.963
1989—St. Louis	Nat.	2B-3B	10	8	1	2	0	0	0	0	.250	4	9	2	.867
1989—Louisville‡	A. A.	SS-3B-2B	94	276	37	64	9	2	2	30	.232	123	232	14	.962
Major League Totals—3 Years			72	90	16	27	4	1	0	11	.300	32	52	6	.933

Selected by Detroit Tigers' organization in 14th round of free-agent draft, June 8, 1976.
Selected by Baltimore Orioles' organization in 10th round of free-agent draft, June 5, 1979.
Selected by Minnesota Twins' organization in 4th round of free-agent draft, June 3, 1980.
†Sold to St. Louis Cardinals' organization, April 5, 1983.
‡Released, October 5, 1989; signed by Scranton/Wilkes-Barre (Philadelphia Phillies' organization), December 14, 1989.

ROBERT RAYMOND BOONE
(Bob)

Born November 19, 1947, at San Diego, Calif.
Height, 6.02. Weight, 207.
Throws and bats righthanded.
Received bachelor of arts degree in psychology from Stanford University, Palo Alto, Calif. in 1969.
Son of Ray Boone, infielder with Cleveland, Detroit, Chicago A.L., Kansas City,
Milwaukee and Boston, 1948 through 1960; and scout with Boston Red Sox since 1961;
brother of Rodney Alan Boone, catcher-outfielder in Kansas City Royals' and
Houston Astros' organization, 1972 through 1975; and father of Bret Boone,
second baseman at University of Southern California.

Holds major league records for most games (2,185), putouts (11,017) and chances accepted (12,172) by catcher, lifetime; most years, 100 or more games, catcher (15).
Major League stolen bases: 1972 (1), 1973 (3), 1974 (3), 1975 (1), 1976 (2), 1977 (5), 1978 (2), 1979 (1), 1980 (3), 1981 (2), 1983 (4), 1984 (3), 1985 (1), 1986 (1), 1988 (2), 1989 (3). Total—37.
Led American League catchers in double plays with 12 in 1983, 15 in 1985 and 16 in 1986.
Led American League catchers in total chances with 745 in 1982 and 823 in 1989.
Led National League catchers in fielding percentage with .991 in 1978.
Led National League catchers in total chances with 924 in 1974.
Led Pacific Coast League catchers in passed balls with 18 and double plays with 13 in 1972.
Tied for Carolina League lead in double plays by third basemen with 18 in 1969.
Named catcher on THE SPORTING NEWS National League All-Star Team, 1976.
Named catcher on THE SPORTING NEWS American League All-Star fielding team, 1982 and 1986 through 1989.
Named catcher on THE SPORTING NEWS National League All-Star fielding team, 1978 and 1979.

Year—Club	League	Pos.	G.	AB.	R.	H.	2B.	3B.	HR.	RBI.	B.A.	PO.	A.	E.	F.A.
1969—Raleigh-Durham	Carol.	3B	80	300	45	90	13	1	5	46	.300	71	160	20	.920
1970—Reading|	East	3B	20	80	12	23	2	0	2	10	.288	28	38	7	.904
1971—Reading‡	East.	3B-C-SS	92	328	41	87	14	3	4	37	.265	206	138	17	.953
1972—Eugene	P. C.	C	138	513	77	158	32	4	17	67	.308	★699	★77	★24	.970
1972—Philadelphia	Nat.	C	16	51	4	14	1	0	1	4	.275	66	7	5	.936
1973—Philadelphia	Nat.	C	145	521	42	136	20	2	10	61	.261	868	★89	10	.990
1974—Philadelphia	Nat.	C	146	488	41	118	24	3	3	52	.242	★825	77	★22	.976
1975—Philadelphia	Nat.	C-3B	97	289	28	71	14	2	2	20	.246	459	48	5	.990
1976—Philadelphia	Nat.	C-1B	121	361	40	98	18	2	4	54	.271	587	39	6	.990
1977—Philadelphia	Nat.	C-3B	132	440	55	125	26	4	11	66	.284	654	83	8	.989
1978—Philadelphia	Nat.	C-1B-OF	132	435	48	123	18	4	12	62	.283	650	55	8	.989
1979—Philadelphia	Nat.	C-3B	119	398	38	114	21	3	9	58	.286	527	66	8	.987
1980—Philadelphia	Nat.	C	141	480	34	110	23	1	9	55	.229	741	88	★18	.979
1981—Philadelphia§	Nat.	C	76	227	19	48	7	0	4	24	.211	365	32	6	.985
1982—California	Amer.	C	143	472	42	121	17	0	7	58	.256	★650	★87	8	.989
1983—California	Amer.	C	142	468	46	120	18	0	9	52	.256	606	★83	★14	.980
1984—California	Amer.	C	139	450	33	91	16	1	3	32	.202	660	★71	12	.984
1985—California	Amer.	C	150	460	37	114	17	0	5	55	.248	670	71	10	.987
1986—California x	Amer.	C	144	442	48	98	12	2	7	49	.222	812	★84	11	.988
1987—Palm Springs	Calif.	C	3	9	0	1	1	0	0	0	.111	17	4	1	.955
1987—California	Amer.	C	128	389	42	94	18	0	3	33	.242	684	56	★13	.983
1988—California y	Amer.	C	122	352	38	104	17	0	5	39	.295	506	★66	8	.986
1989—Kansas City	Amer.	C	131	405	33	111	13	2	1	43	.274	★752	64	7	.991
National League Totals—10 Years			1125	3690	349	957	172	21	65	456	.259	5742	584	96	.958
American League Totals—8 Years			1099	3438	319	853	128	5	40	361	.248	5340	582	83	.986
Major League Totals—18 Years			2224	7128	668	1810	300	26	105	817	.254	11082	1166	179	.986

Selected by Philadelphia Phillies' organization in 20th round of free-agent draft, June 5, 1969.
†On military list, May 26, 1970 through remainder of season.
‡On disabled list, April 10 to June 4, 1971.
§Sold to California Angels, December 6, 1981.
xGranted free agency, November 12, 1986; re-signed by Angels, May 1, 1987.
yGranted free agency, October 24, 1988; signed by Kansas City Royals, November 30, 1988.

DIVISION SERIES RECORD

Year Club League	Pos.	G.	AB.	R.	H.	2B.	3B.	HR.	RBI.	B.A.	PO.	A.	E.	F.A.
1981—Philadelphia .... Nat.	C	3	5	0	0	0	0	0	0	.000	10	2	0	1.000

CHAMPIONSHIP SERIES RECORD

Holds Championship Series record for most sacrifice hits, total series (5).

Shares Championship Series records for most consecutive hits, series (5) and most singles, series (9), 1986; most sacrifice hits, series (2), 1982.

Shares American League Championship Series record for most consecutive hits, total series (5).

Year Club League	Pos.	G.	AB.	R.	H.	2B.	3B.	HR.	RBI.	B.A.	PO.	A.	E.	F.A.
1976—Philadelphia .... Nat.	C	3	7	0	2	0	0	0	1	.286	8	2	0	1.000
1977—Philadelphia .... Nat.	C	4	10	1	4	0	0	0	0	.400	18	2	0	1.000
1978—Philadelphia .... Nat.	C	3	11	0	2	0	0	0	0	.182	16	2	1	.947
1980—Philadelphia .... Nat.	C	5	18	1	4	0	0	0	2	.222	22	3	0	1.000
1982—California............. Amer.	C	5	16	3	4	0	0	1	4	.250	30	3	0	1.000
1986—California............. Amer.	C	7	22	4	10	0	0	1	2	.455	33	3	0	1.000
Championship Series Totals—6 Years.....		27	84	9	26	0	0	2	9	.310	127	15	1	.993

WORLD SERIES RECORD

Year Club League	Pos.	G.	AB.	R.	H.	2B.	3B.	HR.	RBI.	B.A.	PO.	A.	E.	F.A.
1980—Philadelphia .... Nat.	C	6	17	3	7	2	0	0	4	.412	49	3	0	1.000

ALL-STAR GAME RECORD

Year League	Pos.	AB.	R.	H.	2B.	3B.	HR.	RBI.	B.A.	PO.	A.	E.	F.A.
1976—National	C	2	0	0	0	0	0	0	.000	5	0	0	1.000
1978—National	C	1	1	1	0	0	0	2	1.000	3	1	0	1.000
1979—National	C	2	1	1	0	0	0	0	.500	0	0	0	.000
1983—American	C	0	0	0	0	0	0	0	.000	1	0	0	1.000
All-Star Game Totals—4 Years....................		5	2	2	0	0	0	2	.400	9	1	0	1.000

PATRICK LANCE BORDERS
(Pat)

Born May 14, 1963, at Columbus, O.
Height, 6.02. Weight, 205.
Throws and bats righthanded.
Brother of Todd Borders, catcher in Chicago Cubs' organization.

Major League stolen bases: 1989 (2).
Tied for Southern League in passed balls with 16 in 1987.

Year Club League	Pos.	G.	AB.	R.	H.	2B.	3B.	HR.	RBI.	B.A.	PO.	A.	E.	F.A.
1982—Medicine Hat....... Pion.	3B	61	217	30	66	12	2	5	33	.304	23	96	★25	.826
1983—Florence .... S. Atl.	3B	131	457	62	125	31	4	5	54	.274	70	233	★41	.881
1984—Florence .... S. Atl.	1B-3B-OF	131	467	69	129	32	5	12	85	.276	650	77	25	.967
1985—Kinston.................. Carol.	1B	127	460	43	120	16	1	10	60	.261	854	42	★20	.978
1986—Florence .... S. Atl.	C-OF	16	40	8	15	7	0	3	9	.375	22	1	0	1.000
1986—Knoxville .... South.	C-1B	12	34	3	12	1	0	2	5	.353	45	5	3	.943
1986—Kinston.................. Carol.	C-1B-OF	49	174	24	57	10	0	6	26	.328	211	26	7	.971
1987—Dunedin .... Fla. St.	1B	3	11	0	4	0	0	0	1	.364	21	1	0	1.000
1987—Knoxville .... South.	C-3B	94	349	44	102	14	1	11	51	.292	432	49	12	.976
1988—Toronto† .... Amer.	C-2B-3B	56	154	15	42	6	3	5	21	.273	205	19	7	.970
1988—Syracuse .... Int.	C	35	120	11	29	8	0	3	14	.242	202	17	2	.991
1989—Toronto .... Amer.	C	94	241	22	62	11	1	3	29	.257	261	27	6	.980
Major League Totals—2 Years.................		150	395	37	104	17	4	8	50	.263	466	46	13	.975

Selected by Toronto Blue Jays' organization in sixth round of free-agent draft, June 7, 1982.

†On disabled list, July 5 to August 19, 1988; included rehabilitation disability assignment to Syracuse, July 30 to August 19, 1988.

CHAMPIONSHIP SERIES RECORD

Year Club League	Pos.	G.	AB.	R.	H.	2B.	3B.	HR.	RBI.	B.A.	PO.	A.	E.	F.A.
1989—Toronto .... Amer.	PH-C	1	1	0	1	0	0	0	1	1.000	1	0	0	1.000

CHRISTOPHER LOUIS BOSIO
Name pronounced Boz-e-o.
(Chris)

Born April 3, 1963, at Carmichael, Calif.
Height, 6.03. Weight, 210.
Throws and bats righthanded.
Attended Sacramento City College, Sacramento, Calif.

Major League saves: 1987 (2), 1988 (6). Total—8.
Tied for Pacific Coast League lead in saves with 16 in 1986.

Year Club League	G.	IP.	W.	L.	Pct.	H.	R.	ER.	SO.	BB.	ERA.
1982—Pikeville............................... Ap'lachian	13	51⅓	3	2	.600	60	31	28	53	17	4.91
1983—Beloit .... Midwest	17	107⅔	3	10	.231	125	82	67	71	41	5.60
1983—Paintsville .... Ap'lachian	7	44⅓	2	2	.500	30	18	14	43	18	2.84
1984—Beloit .... Midwest	26	181	★17	6	.739	159	83	55	156	56	2.73
1985—El Paso .... Texas	28	181⅓	11	6	.647	186	108	77	★155	49	3.82
1986—Vancouver............................ P. Coast	44	67	7	3	.700	47	18	17	60	13	2.28

Year	Club	League	G.	IP.	W.	L.	Pct.	H.	R.	ER.	SO.	BB.	ERA.
1986—Milwaukee	American	10	34⅔	0	4	.000	41	27	27	29	13	7.01
1987—Milwaukee	American	46	170	11	8	.579	187	102	99	150	50	5.24
1988—Milwaukee	American	38	182	7	15	.318	190	80	68	84	38	3.36
1988—Denver	Am. Assoc.	2	14	1	0	1.000	13	6	6	12	4	3.86
1989—Milwaukee	American	33	234⅔	15	10	.600	225	90	77	173	48	2.95
Major League Totals—4 Years		127	621⅓	33	37	.471	643	299	271	436	149	3.93

Selected by Pittsburgh Pirates' organization in 29th round of free-agent draft, June 8, 1981.
Selected by Milwaukee Brewers' organization in secondary phase of free-agent draft, January 12, 1982.

SHAWN KEALOHA BOSKIE

Born March 28, 1967, at Hawthorne, Nev.
Height, 6.03. Weight, 205.
Throws and bats righthanded.
Attended Modesto Junior College, Modesto, Calif.

Led Southern League in hit batsmen with 19 in 1989.
Led Carolina League in hit batsmen with 17 in 1988.
Led Appalachian League in wild pitches with 15 in 1986.

Year	Club	League	G.	IP.	W.	L.	Pct.	H.	R.	ER.	SO.	BB.	ERA.
1986—Wytheville	Ap'lachian	14	54	4	4	.500	42	41	32	40	57	5.33
1987—Peoria	Midwest	26	149	9	11	.450	149	91	72	100	56	4.35
1988—Winston-Salem	Carolina	27	186	12	7	.632	176	83	70	164	89	3.39
1989—Charlotte	Southern	28	181	11	8	.579	*196	105	88	*164	84	4.38

Selected by Chicago Cubs' organization in 1st round (10th player selected) of free-agent draft, January 14, 1986.

THADDIS BOSLEY JR.

Name pronounced BAHZ-lee.

(Thad)

Born September 17, 1956, at Oceanside, Calif.
Height, 6.03. Weight, 175.
Throws and bats lefthanded.
Attended Mira Costa Community College, Oceanside, Calif.

Major League stolen bases: 1977 (5), 1978 (12), 1979 (4), 1980 (3), 1981 (2), 1982 (3), 1983 (1), 1984 (5), 1985 (5), 1986 (3), 1988 (1), 1989 (2). Total—46.
Led California League in stolen bases with 90 and caught stealing with 17 in 1976.
Led Pioneer League in bases on balls received with 71 in 1974.
Named California League Most Valuable Player, 1976.

Year	Club	League	Pos.	G.	AB.	R.	H.	2B.	3B.	HR.	RBI.	B.A.	PO.	A.	E.	F.A.
1974—Idaho Falls	Pion.	OF	68	223	55	54	3	4	0	14	.242	101	4	*11	.905
1975—Quad Cities†	Midw.	OF	108	379	67	113	12	3	1	50	.298	206	2	4	*.981
1976—Salinas	Calif.	OF	134	527	105	171	26	4	2	72	*.324	285	13	7	*.977
1977—Salt Lake City	P. C.	OF	69	298	55	97	22	2	2	38	.326	169	6	5	.972
1977—California‡§	Amer.	OF	58	212	19	63	10	2	0	19	.297	130	1	5	.963
1978—Iowa	A. A.	OF	47	179	27	52	3	0	3	15	.291	77	5	2	.976
1978—Chicago x	Amer.	OF	66	219	25	59	5	1	2	13	.269	155	3	4	.975
1979—Iowa y	A. A.	OF	95	382	62	101	14	5	1	24	.264	140	6	5	.967
1979—Chicago	Amer.	OF	36	77	13	24	1	1	1	8	.312	57	2	2	.967
1980—Chicago za	Amer.	OF	70	147	12	33	2	0	2	14	.224	91	1	4	.958
1981—Vancouver	P. C.	OF	34	122	15	39	5	2	0	14	.320	75	0	5	.938
1981—Milwaukee b	Amer.	OF	42	105	11	24	2	0	0	3	.229	55	1	2	.966
1982—Seattle	Amer.	OF	22	46	3	8	1	0	0	2	.174	12	1	0	1.000
1982—Salt Lake C. cdef	P. C.	OF	22	84	15	25	2	2	3	9	.298	24	2	0	1.000
1983—Mexico City	Mex.	OF	31	107	24	35	7	3	4	18	.327	24	1	0	1.000
1983—Iowa	A. A.	OF	39	124	22	36	11	0	7	24	.290	3	0	1	.750
1983—Chicago	Nat.	OF	43	72	12	21	4	1	2	12	.292	27	1	0	1.000
1984—Iowa	A. A.	OF	51	162	23	58	16	1	6	43	.358	31	4	2	.946
1984—Chicago	Nat.	OF	55	98	17	29	2	2	2	14	.296	39	2	1	.976
1985—Chicago	Nat.	OF	108	180	25	59	6	3	7	27	.328	84	0	1	.988
1986—Chicago g	Nat.	OF	87	120	15	33	4	1	1	9	.275	31	0	1	.969
1987—Kansas City h	Amer.	OF	80	140	13	39	6	1	1	16	.279	28	0	1	.966
1988—K.C. ij-Calif.	Amer.	OF	50	96	10	25	5	0	0	9	.260	59	0	2	.967
1988—Edmonton k	P. C.	OF	18	52	13	16	5	1	0	9	.308	20	1	0	1.000
1989—Oklahoma City l	A. A.	OF	30	101	17	31	7	0	2	12	.307	35	2	1	.974
1989—Texas l	Amer.	OF	37	40	5	9	2	0	1	9	.225	12	1	0	1.000
American League Totals—9 Years		461	1082	111	284	34	5	7	93	.262	599	10	20	.968
National League Totals—4 Years		293	470	69	142	16	7	12	62	.302	181	3	3	.984
Major League Totals—13 Years		754	1552	180	426	50	12	19	155	.274	780	13	23	.972

Selected by California Angels' organization in 4th round of free-agent draft, June 5, 1974.
†On disabled list, April 19 to May 6, 1975.
‡On disabled list, June 29 to July 10, 1977.
§Traded with Outfielder Bobby Bonds and Pitcher Richard Dotson to Chicago White Sox for Pitchers Chris Knapp and Dave Frost and Catcher Brian Downing, December 5, 1977.
xOn disabled list, June 29 to July 17, 1978.
yOn disabled list, July 15 to July 25, 1979.
zOn disabled list, August 12, 1980 through remainder of season.
aTraded to Milwaukee Brewers' organization for First Baseman-Outfielder John Poff, April 1, 1981.
bTraded to Seattle Mariners for Pitcher Mike Parrott, March 5, 1982.

cOn disabled list, June 6 to July 1 and August 3 to September 2, 1982.
dGranted free agency, September 5, 1982; signed by Tacoma (Oakland A's organization), February 14, 1983.
eSold to Iowa (Chicago Cubs' organization), March 30, 1983.
fLoaned to Mexico City Tigers, April 3, 1983; returned, May 28, 1983.
gTraded with Pitcher Dave Gumpert to Kansas City Royals for Catcher Jim Sundberg, March 30, 1987.
hGranted free agency, November 9, 1987; re-signed by Royals, January 5, 1988.
iOn disabled list, May 11 to May 27, 1988.
jReleased, May 27, 1988; signed by Edmonton (California Angels' organization), June 7, 1988.
kGranted free agency, November 4, 1988; signed by Oklahoma City (Texas Rangers' organization), June 8, 1989.
lReleased, October 2, 1989.

DIVISION SERIES RECORD

Year Club	League	Pos.	G.	AB.	R.	H.	2B.	3B.	HR.	RBI.	B.A.	PO.	A.	E.	F.A.
1981—Milwaukee.............	Amer.	PR-DH	1	0	0	0	0	0	0	0	.000	0	0	0	.000

CHAMPIONSHIP SERIES RECORD

Year Club	League	Pos.	G.	AB.	R.	H.	2B.	3B.	HR.	RBI.	B.A.	PO.	A.	E.	F.A.
1984—Chicago.................	Nat.	PH	2	2	0	0	0	0	0	0	.000	0	0	0	.000

DARYL LAMONT BOSTON

Born January 4, 1963, at Cincinnati, O.
Height, 6.03. Weight, 203.
Throws and bats lefthanded.

Major League stolen bases: 1984 (6), 1985 (8), 1986 (9), 1987 (12), 1988 (9), 1989 (7). Total—51.
Led Eastern League batters in strikeouts with 133 in 1983.
Led Midwest League outfielders in total chances with 312 in 1982.
Tied for American Association lead in sacrifice flies with 11 in 1984.
Tied for American Association lead in double plays by outfielders with 4 in 1984.

Year Club	League	Pos.	G.	AB.	R.	H.	2B.	3B.	HR.	RBI.	B.A.	PO.	A.	E.	F.A.
1981—Sarasota W. S........	Gulf C.	OF	56	189	30	55	6	3	1	30	.291	84	9	3	.969
1982—Appleton	Midw.	OF	★139	512	86	143	19	9	15	77	.279	★293	9	10	.968
1983—Glens Falls...........	East.	OF	113	435	65	104	15	1	18	50	.239	271	8	13	.955
1983—Denver	A. A.	OF	14	51	11	13	4	1	2	7	.255	26	1	5	.844
1984—Denver	A. A.	OF	127	471	94	147	21	★19	15	82	.312	311	11	●10	.970
1984—Chicago	Amer.	OF	35	83	8	14	3	1	0	3	.169	59	2	6	.910
1985—Chicago	Amer.	OF	95	232	20	53	13	1	3	15	.228	179	7	2	.989
1985—Buffalo..................	A. A.	OF	63	241	45	66	12	1	10	36	.274	151	3	3	.981
1986—Buffalo..................	A. A.	OF	96	360	57	109	16	3	5	41	.303	210	1	5	.977
1986—Chicago	Amer.	OF	56	199	29	53	11	3	5	22	.266	152	3	5	.969
1987—Chicago	Amer.	OF	103	337	51	87	21	2	10	29	.258	207	3	2	.991
1987—Hawaii..................	P. C.	OF	21	77	14	23	3	0	5	13	.299	43	3	0	1.000
1988—Chicago	Amer.	OF	105	281	37	61	12	2	15	31	.217	190	4	10	.951
1989—Chicago	Amer.	OF	101	218	34	55	3	4	5	23	.252	134	2	4	.971
Major League Totals—6 Years.................			495	1350	179	323	63	13	38	123	.239	921	21	29	.970

Selected by Chicago White Sox' organization in 1st round (seventh player selected) of free-agent draft, June 8, 1981.

KENT DENNIS BOTTENFIELD

Born November 14, 1968, at Portland, Ore.
Height, 6.03. Weight, 215.
Throws right and bats left and righthanded.

Twin brother of Keven Bottenfield, catcher-infielder in Montreal Expos' organization, 1986 and 1987.

Year Club	League	G.	IP.	W.	L.	Pct.	H.	R.	ER.	SO.	BB.	ERA.
1986—Bradenton Expos	Gulf Coast	13	74⅓	5	6	.455	73	●42	27	41	30	3.27
1987—Burlington	Midwest	27	161	9	13	.409	175	98	81	103	42	4.53
1988—West Palm Beach	Florida St.	27	181	10	8	.556	165	80	67	120	47	3.33
1989—Jacksonville.................................	Southern	25	138⅔	3	★17	.150	137	101	81	91	73	5.26

Selected by Montreal Expos' organization in 4th round of free-agent draft, June 2, 1986.

RYAN EUGENE BOWEN

Born February 10, 1968, at Hanford, Calif.
Height, 6.00. Weight, 185.
Throws and bats righthanded.

Year Club	League	G.	IP.	W.	L.	Pct.	H.	R.	ER.	SO.	BB.	ERA.
1987—Asheville..	S. Atlantic	26	160⅓	12	5	.706	143	86	72	126	78	4.04
1988—Osceola...	Florida St.	4	13⅔	1	0	1.000	12	8	6	12	10	3.95
1989—Columbus..	Southern	27	139⅔	8	6	.571	123	83	66	136	116	4.25

Selected by Houston Astros' organization in 1st round (13th player selected) of free-agent draft, June 2, 1986.

DENNIS RAY BOYD
(Oil Can)

(Given nickname from beer drinking friends in Meridian, Miss.
where beer is referred to as oil.)
Born October 6, 1959, at Meridian, Miss.
Height, 6.01. Weight, 160.
Throws and bats righthanded.
Attended Jackson State University, Jackson, Miss.
Brother of Don Boyd, outfielder in St. Louis Cardinals' organization, 1973.

Led Florida State League pitchers in games started with 28 and home runs allowed with 11 in 1981.
Tied for Eastern League lead in games started by pitchers with 27 and complete games with 13 in 1982.

Year	Club	League	G.	IP.	W.	L.	Pct.	H.	R.	ER.	SO.	BB.	ERA.
1980—Elmira	NYP	12	69	7	1	.875	54	20	19	79	30	2.48
1981—Winter Haven	Florida St.	28	186	14	8	.636	*195	90	75	154	54	3.63
1982—Bristol	Eastern	27	*205	14	8	.636	190	71	64	*191	49	2.81
1982—Boston	American	3	8⅓	0	1	.000	11	5	5	2	2	5.40
1983—Pawtucket	Int'national	20	122⅔	5	8	.385	119	69	55	129	41	4.04
1983—Boston	American	15	98⅔	4	8	.333	103	46	36	43	23	3.28
1984—Boston	American	29	197⅔	12	12	.500	207	109	96	134	53	4.37
1984—Pawtucket	Int'national	5	37⅓	3	1	.750	30	12	12	45	12	2.89
1985—Boston	American	35	272⅓	15	13	.536	*273	117	112	154	67	3.70
1986—Boston	American	30	214⅓	16	10	.615	222	99	90	129	45	3.78
1987—Pawtucket†	Int'national	3	12	1	1	.500	12	6	6	8	4	4.50
1987—Boston	American	7	36⅔	1	3	.250	47	31	24	12	9	5.89
1988—Boston‡	American	23	129⅔	9	7	.563	147	82	77	71	41	5.34
1989—Boston§	American	10	59	3	2	.600	57	31	29	26	19	4.42
1989—Pawtucket	Int'national	2	7	0	0	.000	4	0	0	11	0	0.00
1989—New Britain x	Eastern	1	5	0	1	.000	3	1	1	8	1	1.80
Major League Totals—8 Years		152	1016⅔	60	56	.517	1067	520	469	571	259	4.15

Selected by Boston Red Sox' organization in 16th round of free-agent draft, June 3, 1980.

†On Boston disabled list, March 29 to June 22 and July 31, 1987 through remainder of season; included rehabilitation disability assignment to Pawtucket, June 8 to June 22, 1987.

‡On disabled list, July 27 to August 20 and August 31, 1988 through remainder of season.

§On disabled list, May 2 to September 1, 1989; included rehabilitation disability assignment to Pawtucket, August 18 to August 27, 1989; and to New Britain, August 28 to September 1, 1989.

xGranted free agency, November 13, 1989; signed by Montreal Expos, December 7, 1989.

CHAMPIONSHIP SERIES RECORD

Year	Club	League	G.	IP.	W.	L.	Pct.	H.	R.	ER.	SO.	BB.	ERA.
1986—Boston	American	2	13⅔	1	1	.500	17	7	7	8	3	4.61

WORLD SERIES RECORD

Year	Club	League	G.	IP.	W.	L.	Pct.	H.	R.	ER.	SO.	BB.	ERA.
1986—Boston	American	1	7	0	1	.000	9	6	6	3	1	7.71

PHILIP POOLE BRADLEY
(Phil)

Born March 11, 1959, at Bloomington, Ind.
Height, 6.00. Weight, 185.
Throws and bats righthanded.
Received bachelor of science degree in personnel management from
University of Missouri, Columbia, Mo., in 1982.

Shares major league records for most doubles, inning (2), August 30, 1989, first inning; most strikeouts, nine-inning game (5), September 7, 1989, first game.
Major League stolen bases: 1983 (3), 1984 (21), 1985 (22), 1986 (21), 1987 (40), 1988 (11), 1989 (20). Total—138.
Led National League in being hit by pitch with 16 in 1988.
Named outfielder on The Sporting News American League All-Star Team, 1985.

Year	Club	League	Pos.	G.	AB.	R.	H.	2B.	3B.	HR.	RBI.	B.A.	PO.	A.	E.	F.A.
1981—Bellingham	N'west	OF	53	193	38	58	12	5	1	20	.301	94	3	1	*.990
1982—Bakersfield	Calif.	OF	109	405	98	134	17	10	0	37	.331	226	13	6	.976
1983—Salt Lake City	P. Coast	OF	130	458	100	148	14	4	2	41	.323	284	13	1	*.997
1983—Seattle	Amer.	OF	23	67	8	18	2	0	0	5	.269	36	1	1	.974
1984—Seattle	Amer.	OF	124	322	49	97	12	4	0	24	.301	235	3	2	.992
1985—Seattle	Amer.	OF	159	641	100	192	33	8	26	88	.300	336	10	5	.986
1986—Seattle†	Amer.	OF	143	526	88	163	27	4	12	50	.310	250	11	1	.996
1987—Seattle‡	Amer.	OF	158	603	101	179	38	10	14	67	.297	273	13	5	.983
1988—Philadelphia§	Nat.	OF	154	569	77	150	30	5	11	56	.264	298	14	3	.990
1989—Baltimore	Amer.	OF	144	545	83	151	23	10	11	55	.277	284	4	3	.990
American League Totals—6 Years		751	2704	429	800	135	36	63	289	.296	1414	42	17	.988
National League Totals—1 Year		154	569	77	150	30	5	11	56	.264	298	14	3	.990
Major League Totals—7 Years		905	3273	506	950	165	41	74	345	.290	1712	56	20	.989

Selected by Seattle Mariners' organization in 3rd round of free-agent draft, June 8, 1981.

†On disabled list, May 26 to June 12, 1986.

‡Traded with Pitcher Tim Fortugno to Philadelphia Phillies for Outfielders Glenn Wilson and Dave Brundage and Pitcher Mike Jackson, December 9, 1987.

§Traded to Baltimore Orioles for Pitchers Ken Howell and Gordon Dillard, December 8, 1988.

ALL-STAR GAME RECORD

Year	League	Pos.	AB.	R.	H.	2B.	3B.	HR.	RBI.	B.A.	PO.	A.	E.	F.A.
1985—American		OF	1	0	0	0	0	0	0	.000	1	0	0	1.000

SCOTT WILLIAM BRADLEY

Born March 22, 1960, at Montclair, N.J.
Height, 5.11. Weight, 185.
Throws right and bats lefthanded.
Received bachelor of science degree in business administration
from University of North Carolina, Chapel Hill, N.C.

Major League stolen bases: 1986 (1), 1988 (1), 1989 (1). Total—3.
Tied for International League lead in game-winning RBIs with 14 in 1984.
Tied for Florida State League lead in game-winning RBIs with 13 in 1982.
Named International League Player of the Year, 1984.

Year Club	League	Pos.	G.	AB.	R.	H.	2B.	3B.	HR.	RBI.	B.A.	PO.	A.	E.	F.A.
1981—Oneonta	NYP	C-OF	71	276	48	85	17	4	4	54	.308	323	40	9	.976
1982—Nashville	South.	C	5	19	2	2	1	0	0	0	.105	44	2	2	.958
1982—Fort Lauderdale	Fla. St.	C-1B-3B	121	439	52	130	28	4	3	66	.296	407	57	10	.979
1983—Nashville	South.	C-3B	137	525	83	142	33	4	8	76	.270	475	88	13	.977
1984—Columbus	Int.	C-OF-3B	★138	★538	84	★180	31	2	6	●84	★.335	432	50	9	.982
1984—New York	Amer.	OF-C	9	21	3	6	1	0	0	2	.286	10	0	0	1.000
1985—New York†	Amer.	C	19	49	4	8	2	1	0	1	.163	12	0	1	.923
1985—Albany	East.	3B	6	24	2	3	1	0	0	2	.125	8	14	4	.846
1985—Columbus‡	Int.	C-3B	43	163	17	49	10	0	4	27	.301	118	53	4	.977
1986—Buffalo	A. A.	C-OF	33	126	14	42	3	3	5	20	.333	165	9	0	1.000
1986—Chicago§-Seattle	Amer.	C-OF	77	220	20	66	8	3	5	28	.300	281	21	3	.990
1987—Seattle	Amer.	C-3B-OF	102	342	34	95	15	1	5	43	.278	438	39	8	.984
1988—Seattle	Amer.	C-O-3-1	103	335	45	86	17	1	4	33	.257	543	42	6	.990
1989—Seattle	Amer.	C-1B-OF	103	270	21	74	16	0	3	37	.274	400	26	4	.988
Major League Totals—6 Years			413	1237	127	335	59	6	17	144	.271	1684	128	22	.988

Selected by Minnesota Twins' organization in 12th round of free-agent draft, June 6, 1978.
Selected by New York Yankees' organization in 3rd round of free-agent draft, June 8, 1981.
†On disabled list, April 24 to June 17, 1985; included rehabilitation disability assignment to Sarasota, June 5 and June 6, 1985, and Albany, June 7 to June 17, 1985.
‡Traded with Pitcher Neil Allen, Outfielder Glen Braxton and cash to Chicago White Sox for Catchers Ron Hassey and Chris Alvarez, Pitcher Eric Schmidt and Outfielder Matt Winters, February 13, 1986.
§Traded to Seattle Mariners for a player to be named later, June 26, 1986; Chicago White Sox' organization acquired Outfielder Ivan Calderon to complete deal, July 1, 1986.

BRIAN PHELAN BRADY

Born July 11, 1962, at Queens, N.Y.
Height, 5.11. Weight, 185.
Throws and bats lefthanded.
Attended New York Institute of Technology, Old Westbury, N.Y.

Year Club	League	Pos.	G.	AB.	R.	H.	2B.	3B.	HR.	RBI.	B.A.	PO.	A.	E.	F.A.
1984—Salem	N'west	OF	67	242	29	52	10	2	2	26	.215	110	10	7	.945
1985—Redwood†	Calif.	OF	123	441	65	128	28	6	9	56	.290	192	10	9	.957
1986—Midland‡	Texas	OF	97	355	53	103	19	1	11	53	.290	169	7	10	.946
1987—Midland	Texas	OF-1B	100	281	46	81	17	1	9	50	.288	141	11	6	.962
1988—Edmonton	P. C.	OF	119	410	68	112	30	5	10	67	.273	158	3	4	.976
1989—Edmonton§	P. C.	OF	62	203	22	48	10	2	5	28	.236	66	3	3	.958
1989—California	Amer.	OF	2	2	0	1	1	0	0	1	.500	0	0	0	.000
Major League Totals—1 Year			2	2	0	1	1	0	0	1	.500	0	0	0	.000

Selected by California Angels' organization in 6th round of free-agent draft, June 4, 1984.
†On disabled list, June 13 to June 25, 1985.
‡On disabled list, June 24 to July 10, 1986.
§On disabled list, July 23, 1989 through remainder of season.

GLENN ERICK BRAGGS

Born October 17, 1962, at San Bernardino, Calif.
Height, 6.03. Weight, 210.
Throws and bats righthanded.
Attended University of Hawaii, Honolulu, Haw.

Major League stolen bases: 1986 (1), 1987 (12), 1988 (6), 1989 (17). Total—36.
Led Texas League in being hit by pitch with 10 in 1985.
Led Appalachian League in total bases with 164, bases on balls received with 54 and intentional bases on balls received with 6 in 1983.
Named California League Most Valuable Player, 1984.
Named Appalachian League Player of the Year, 1983.
Received reported $50,000 bonus to sign with Milwaukee Brewers, 1983.

Year Club	League	Pos.	G.	AB.	R.	H.	2B.	3B.	HR.	RBI.	B.A.	PO.	A.	E.	F.A.
1983—Paintsville	Appal.	OF	●73	241	★65	★94	★20	1	●16	★74	★.390	115	8	6	.953
1984—Stockton	Calif.	OF	108	399	76	118	29	2	15	86	.296	158	4	6	.964
1985—El Paso	Texas	OF	117	448	105	139	26	4	20	103	.310	239	10	11	.958
1986—Vancouver	P. C.	OF	90	325	80	117	26	6	15	75	.360	218	8	2	.991
1986—Milwaukee	Amer.	OF	58	215	19	51	8	2	4	18	.237	116	5	12	.910
1987—Milwaukee	Amer.	OF	132	505	67	136	28	7	13	77	.269	301	6	9	.972
1988—Milwaukee†	Amer.	OF	72	272	30	71	14	0	10	42	.261	134	1	3	.978
1989—Milwaukee	Amer.	OF	144	514	77	127	12	3	15	66	.247	267	6	8	.972
Major League Totals—4 Years			406	1506	193	385	62	12	42	203	.256	818	18	32	.963

Selected by New York Yankees' organization in 6th round of free-agent draft, June 3, 1980.
Selected by Milwaukee Brewers' organization in 2nd round of free-agent draft, June 6, 1983.
†On disabled list, July 2, 1988 through remainder of season.

JEFFREY HOKE BRANTLEY
(Jeff)

Born September 5, 1963, at Florence, Ala.
Height, 5.11. Weight, 180.
Throws and bats righthanded.
Attended Mississippi State University, Mississippi State, Miss.

Major League saves: 1988 (1).
Tied for Pacific Coast League lead in hit batsmen with 11 in 1987.
Tied for Texas League lead in complete games with 8 in 1986.

Year Club	League	G.	IP.	W.	L.	Pct.	H.	R.	ER.	SO.	BB.	ERA.
1985—Fresno	California	14	94⅔	8	2	.800	83	39	35	85	37	3.33
1986—Shreveport	Texas	26	165⅔	8	10	.444	139	78	64	125	68	3.48
1987—Shreveport	Texas	2	11⅔	0	1	.000	12	7	4	7	4	3.09
1987—Phoenix	P. Coast	29	170⅓	6	11	.353	187	110	88	111	82	4.65
1988—Phoenix	P. Coast	27	122⅔	9	5	.643	130	65	59	83	39	4.33
1988—San Francisco	National	9	20⅔	0	1	.000	22	13	13	11	6	5.66
1989—San Francisco	National	59	97⅓	7	1	.875	101	50	44	69	37	4.07
1989—Phoenix	P. Coast	7	14⅓	1	1	.500	6	2	2	20	6	1.26
Major League Totals—2 Years		68	118	7	2	.778	123	63	57	80	43	4.35

Selected by Montreal Expos' organization in 13th round of free-agent draft, June 4, 1984.
Selected by San Francisco Giants' organization in 6th round of free-agent draft, June 3, 1985.

CHAMPIONSHIP SERIES RECORD

Year Club	League	G.	IP.	W.	L.	Pct.	H.	R.	ER.	SO.	BB.	ERA.
1989—San Francisco	National	3	5	0	0	.000	1	0	0	3	2	0.00

WORLD SERIES RECORD

Year Club	League	G.	IP.	W.	L.	Pct.	H.	R.	ER.	SO.	BB.	ERA.
1989—San Francisco	National	3	4⅓	0	0	.000	5	2	2	1	3	4.15

MICHAEL CHARLES BRANTLEY
(Mickey)

Born June 17, 1961, at Catskill, N.Y.
Height, 5.10. Weight, 180.
Throws and bats righthanded.
Attended Columbia-Greene Community College, Hudson, N.Y., and
Coastal Carolina Community College, Jacksonville, N.C.

Major League stolen bases: 1986 (1), 1987 (13), 1988 (18), 1989 (2). Total—34.
Hit three home runs in a game, September 14, 1987.
Tied for Southern League lead in sacrifice flies with 10 in 1984.

Year Club	League	Pos.	G.	AB.	R.	H.	2B.	3B.	HR.	RBI.	B.A.	PO.	A.	E.	F.A.
1983—Bakersfield	Calif.	OF	53	185	33	55	9	3	6	29	.297	59	3	1	.984
1984—Chattanooga	South.	OF-3B	131	472	73	149	21	9	11	76	.316	211	14	8	.966
1984—Salt Lake City	P. C.	OF	4	17	2	4	0	0	0	1	.235	8	0	0	1.000
1985—Calgary†	P. C.	OF	74	279	52	68	13	6	11	45	.244	165	1	3	.982
1986—Calgary	P. C.	OF	106	396	*104	126	18	4	30	92	.318	201	9	4	.981
1986—Seattle	Amer.	OF	27	102	12	20	3	2	3	7	.196	54	3	1	.983
1987—Seattle‡	Amer.	OF	92	351	52	106	23	2	14	54	.302	163	3	3	.982
1987—Calgary	P. C.	OF	13	50	13	12	0	1	2	6	.240	6	1	1	.875
1988—Seattle	Amer.	OF	149	577	76	152	25	4	15	56	.263	327	5	6	.982
1989—Seattle	Amer.	OF	34	108	14	17	5	0	0	8	.157	50	1	0	1.000
1989—Calgary	P. C.	OF	49	178	33	44	12	3	4	21	.247	97	5	1	.990
Major League Totals—4 Years			302	1138	154	295	56	8	32	125	.259	594	12	10	.984

Selected by Cincinnati Reds' organization in 8th round of free-agent draft, June 7, 1982.
Selected by Seattle Mariners' organization in 2nd round of free-agent draft, June 6, 1983.
†On disabled list, August 20 to September 9, 1985.
‡On disabled list, April 19 to June 4, 1987; included rehabilitation disability assignment to Calgary, May 9 to May 29, 1987.

SIDNEY EUGENE BREAM
(Sid)

Born August 3, 1960, at Carlisle, Pa.
Height, 6.04. Weight, 220.
Throws and bats lefthanded.
Attended Liberty Baptist College, Lynchburg, Va.

Holds National League record for most assists by first baseman, season (166), 1986.
Major League stolen bases: 1984 (1), 1986 (13), 1987 (9), 1988 (9). Total—32.
Led National League first basemen in total chances with 1,503 in 1986.
Led Pacific Coast League first basemen in total chances with 1,411 in 1983 and 1,200 in 1984.
Led Pacific Coast League first basemen in double plays with 106 in 1984.

Year Club	League	Pos.	G.	AB.	R.	H.	2B.	3B.	HR.	RBI.	B.A.	PO.	A.	E.	F.A.
1981—Vero Beach	Fla. St.	1B	70	260	35	85	12	5	1	47	.327	613	45	10	.985
1982—Vero Beach	Fla. St.	1B	63	226	41	70	13	5	4	43	.310	523	40	5	.991
1982—San Antonio	Texas	1B	70	259	43	83	18	0	8	50	.320	621	40	12	.982
1982—Albuquerque	P. C.	1B	3	8	3	3	1	0	1	2	.375	11	0	0	1.000

Year Club League	Pos.	G.	AB.	R.	H.	2B.	3B.	HR.	RBI.	B.A.	PO.	A.	E.	F.A.
1983—Albuquerque .... P. C.	1B	138	485	115	149	23	4	●32	★118	.307	1264	★123	24	.983
1983—Los Angeles .... Nat.	1B	15	11	0	2	0	0	0	2	.182	8	0	0	1.000
1984—Albuquerque .... P. C.	1B	114	429	82	147	25	4	20	90	.343	1071	★112	17	.986
1984—Los Angeles .... Nat.	1B	27	49	2	9	3	0	0	6	.184	95	11	0	1.000
1985—L.A.†-Pitt. .... Nat.	1B	50	148	18	34	7	0	6	21	.230	367	35	3	.993
1985—Albuquerque .... P. C.	1B-OF	85	297	51	110	25	3	17	57	.370	381	51	2	.995
1986—Pittsburgh.............. Nat.	★1B-OF	154	522	73	140	37	5	16	77	.268	1320	★166	★17	.989
1987—Pittsburgh.............. Nat.	1B	149	516	64	142	25	3	13	65	.275	1236	127	★17	.988
1988—Pittsburgh.............. Nat.	1B	148	462	50	122	37	0	10	65	.264	1118	★140	6	.995
1989—Pittsburgh‡............. Nat.	1B	19	36	3	8	3	0	0	4	.222	111	7	1	.992
Major League Totals—7 Years.................		562	1744	210	457	112	8	45	240	.262	4255	486	44	.991

Selected by Los Angeles Dodgers' organization in 2nd round of free-agent draft, June 8, 1981.

†Traded with Outfielder Cecil Espy, September 9, 1985, completing deal in which Los Angeles Dodgers acquired Third Baseman Bill Madlock for three players to be named later, August 31, 1985. Pittsburgh Pirates acquired Outfielder R. J. Reynolds as partial completion of deal, September 3, 1985.

‡On disabled list, April 16 to May 9 and May 29, 1989 through remainder of season

ROBERT EARL BRENLY
(Bob)

Born February 25, 1954, at Coshocton, O.
Height, 6.02. Weight, 205.
Throws and bats righthanded.
Received bachelor of science degree in health education from
Ohio University, Athens, O. in 1976.

Shares major league record for most errors by third baseman, inning (4), September 14, 1986, fourth inning.
Major League stolen bases: 1982 (6), 1983 (10), 1984 (6), 1985 (1), 1986 (10), 1987 (10), 1988 (1), 1989 (1). Total—45.
Led National League catchers in assists with 83 in 1987.
Led National League catchers in fielding percentage with .995 in 1986.
Led California League third basemen in double plays with 30 in 1978.
Led Midwest League third basemen in double plays with 21 in 1977.

Year Club League	Pos.	G.	AB.	R.	H.	2B.	3B.	HR.	RBI.	B.A.	PO.	A.	E.	F.A.
1976—Great Falls........... Pion.	3B	25	86	16	27	5	1	1	17	.314	10	16	2	.929
1976—Fresno.................. Calif.	3B	17	60	16	22	3	1	1	9	.367	2	6	1	.889
1977—Cedar Rapids........ Midw.	★●3B-OF	136	499	85	135	16	1	22	73	.271	90	★263	●31	.919
1978—Fresno.................. Calif.	3B	135	489	102	139	34	5	17	89	.284	★118	247	27	.931
1979—Fresno.................. Calif.	3B	56	212	49	65	11	2	9	37	.307	39	133	17	.910
1979—Shreveport .... Texas	C-3-O-1	64	193	33	57	8	1	9	30	.295	199	55	7	.973
1980—Shreveport .... Texas	3B	2	10	2	3	0	0	1	3	.300	1	2	0	1.000
1980—Phoenix................. P. C.	3-C-S-O	84	287	34	74	9	6	7	45	.258	183	110	20	.936
1981—Phoenix................. P. C.	C-OF-3B	76	257	42	75	11	3	7	41	.292	177	41	9	.960
1981—San Francisco ...... Nat.	C-3B-OF	19	45	5	15	2	1	1	4	.333	52	6	4	.935
1982—San Francisco† ..... Nat.	C-3B	65	180	26	51	4	1	4	15	.283	265	32	12	.961
1983—San Francisco ...... Nat.	C-1B-OF	104	281	36	63	12	2	7	34	.224	465	73	9	.984
1984—San Francisco ...... Nat.	C-1B-OF	145	506	74	147	28	0	20	80	.291	807	76	13	.985
1985—San Francisco ...... Nat.	C-3B-1B	133	440	41	97	16	1	19	56	.220	719	85	17	.979
1986—San Francisco ...... Nat.	C-1B-3B	149	472	60	116	26	0	16	62	.246	688	118	16	.981
1987—San Francisco ...... Nat.	C-1B-3B	123	375	55	100	19	1	18	51	.267	685	86	9	.988
1988—San Francisco‡ ..... Nat.	C	73	206	13	39	7	0	5	22	.189	334	27	6	.984
1989—Toronto§ .... Amer.	C-1B	48	88	9	15	3	1	1	6	.170	61	5	1	.985
1989—Phoenix................. P. C.	C-3B-1B	27	98	11	25	3	0	2	11	.255	78	16	4	.959
1989—San Francisco x... Nat.	C	12	22	2	4	2	0	0	3	.182	31	5	0	1.000
National League Totals—9 Years............		823	2527	312	632	116	6	90	327	.250	4046	508	86	.981
American League Totals—1 Year...........		48	88	9	15	3	1	1	6	.170	61	5	1	.985
Major League Totals—9 Years.................		871	2615	321	647	119	7	91	333	.247	4107	513	87	.982

Signed as free agent by San Francisco Giants' organization, June 21, 1976.
†On disabled list, March 25 to May 13, 1982.
‡Released, December 21, 1988; signed by Toronto Blue Jays, January 18, 1989.
§Released, July 14, 1989; signed by Phoenix (San Francisco Giants' organization), August 2, 1989.
xGranted free agency, November 13, 1989.

CHAMPIONSHIP SERIES RECORD

Year Club League	Pos.	G.	AB.	R.	H.	2B.	3B.	HR.	RBI.	B.A.	PO.	A.	E.	F.A.
1987—San Francisco ...... Nat.	C-PH	6	17	3	4	1	0	1	2	.235	28	2	0	1.000

ALL-STAR GAME RECORD

Year League	Pos.	AB.	R.	H.	2B.	3B.	HR.	RBI.	B.A.	PO.	A.	E.	F.A.
1984—National...............................	PH	1	0	0	0	0	0	0	.000	0	0	0	.000

WILLIAM RAYMOND BRENNAN

Born January 15, 1963, at Tampa, Fla.
Height, 6.03. Weight, 194.
Throws and bats righthanded.
Attended Mercer University, Macon, Ga.

Year Club League	G.	IP.	W.	L.	Pct.	H.	R.	ER.	SO.	BB.	ERA.
1985—Vero Beach.............. Florida St.	22	142	10	9	.526	121	64	45	74	59	2.85
1986—San Antonio†.................................. Texas	26	146⅔	7	9	.438	149	75	63	83	61	3.87

Year	Club	League	G.	IP.	W.	L.	Pct.	H.	R.	ER.	SO.	BB.	ERA.
1987—Albuquerque	P. Coast	28	171⅓	10	9	.526	188	95	82	95	67	4.31
1988—Albuquerque	P. Coast	29	167⅓	14	8	.636	177	85	71	83	51	3.82
1988—Los Angeles	National	4	9⅓	0	1	.000	13	7	7	7	6	6.75
1989—Albuquerque‡	P. Coast	34	129	6	9	.400	149	87	75	104	57	5.23
Major League Totals—1 Year		4	9⅓	0	1	.000	13	7	7	7	6	6.75

Signed as free agent by Los Angeles Dodgers' organization, September 1, 1984.
†On disabled list, August 14 to August 28, 1986.
‡Drafted by Houston Astros, December 4, 1989.

GEORGE HOWARD BRETT

Born May 15, 1953, at Glen Dale, W. Va.
Height, 6.00. Weight, 200.
Throws right and bats lefthanded.
Attended Longview Community College, Lee's Summit, Mo. and
El Camino College, Torrance, Calif.
Brother of Ken Brett, pitcher with Boston, Milwaukee, Philadelphia, Pittsburgh, New York AL,
Chicago AL, California, Minnesota, Los Angeles and Kansas City, 1967 and 1969 through 1981;
and manager of Utica (Co-op) in New York-Pennsylvania League, 1985;
John Brett, third baseman in Boston Red Sox' organization, 1968;
and Bob Brett, outfielder in Kansas City Royals' organization, 1972.

Holds major league record for most consecutive games, three or more hits, season (6), May 8 through 13, 1976.
Shares major league records for most consecutive seasons leading major league in triples (2), 1975 and 1976; most home runs, month of October (4), 1985.
Holds American League record for fewest putouts by third baseman for leader in most putouts, season (140), 1976.
Became sixth major-league player to collect 20 or more doubles, triples and home runs in one season, 1979.
Hit three home runs in a game, July 22, 1979 and April 20, 1983.
Hit for the cycle, May 28, 1979.
Major League stolen bases: 1974 (8), 1975 (13), 1976 (21), 1977 (14), 1978 (23), 1979 (17), 1980 (15), 1981 (14), 1982 (6), 1985 (9), 1986 (1), 1987 (6), 1988 (14), 1989 (14). Total—175.
Led American League in intentional bases on balls received with 31 in 1985 and 18 in 1986.
Led American League in slugging percentage with .664 in 1980, .563 in 1983 and .585 in 1985.
Led American League in total bases with 298 in 1976.
Led American League third basemen in double plays with 33 in 1985.
Led American League third basemen in assists with 373, errors with 30 and total chances with 532 in 1979.
Led American League third baseman in putouts with 140 in 1976.
Led California League in sacrifice hits with 8 in 1972.
Led California League third basemen in assists with 172 in 1972.
Named Man of the Year by THE SPORTING NEWS, 1980.
Named Major League Player of the Year by THE SPORTING NEWS, 1980.
Named American League Player of the Year by THE SPORTING NEWS, 1980.
Named American League Most Valuable Player by Baseball Writers' Association of America, 1980.
Named first baseman on THE SPORTING NEWS American League All-Star Team, 1988.
Named third baseman on THE SPORTING NEWS American League All-Star Team, 1976, 1979 and 1980.
Named third baseman on THE SPORTING NEWS American League All-Star fielding team, 1985.
Named first baseman on THE SPORTING NEWS American League Silver Slugger Team, 1988.
Named third baseman on THE SPORTING NEWS Silver Slugger team, 1980 and 1985.

Year	Club	League	Pos.	G.	AB.	R.	H.	2B.	3B.	HR.	RBI.	B.A.	PO.	A.	E.	F.A.
1971—Billings	Pion.	SS-3B	68	258	44	75	8	5	5	44	.291	87	140	28	.890
1972—San Jose†	Calif.	★3-S-2	117	431	66	118	13	5	10	68	.274	101	213	★30	.913
1973—Omaha	A. A.	3B-OF	117	405	66	115	16	4	8	64	.284	92	219	26	.923
1973—Kansas City	Amer.	3B	13	40	2	5	2	0	0	0	.125	9	28	1	.974
1974—Omaha	A. A.	3B	16	64	9	17	2	0	2	14	.266	8	31	4	.907
1974—Kansas City	Amer.	3B-SS	133	457	49	129	21	5	2	47	.282	102	279	21	.948
1975—Kansas City	Amer.	●3B-SS	159	★634	84	★195	35	●13	11	89	.308	132	356	●26	.949
1976—Kansas City	Amer.	3B-SS	159	★645	94	★215	34	★14	7	67	★.333	146	350	26	.950
1977—Kansas City	Amer.	3B-SS	139	564	105	176	32	13	22	88	.312	115	325	21	.954
1978—Kansas City‡	Amer.	3B-SS	128	510	79	150	★45	8	9	62	.294	104	289	16	.961
1979—Kansas City	Amer.	3B-1B	154	645	119	★212	42	★20	23	107	.329	176	378	31	.947
1980—Kansas City§	Amer.	3B-1B	117	449	87	175	33	9	24	118	★.390	107	256	17	.955
1981—Kansas City	Amer.	3B	89	347	42	109	27	7	6	43	.314	74	170	14	.946
1982—Kansas City	Amer.	3B-OF	144	552	101	166	32	9	21	82	.301	130	295	17	.962
1983—Kansas City x	Amer.	3B-1B-OF	123	464	90	144	38	2	25	93	.310	210	192	25	.941
1984—Kansas City y	Amer.	3B	104	377	42	107	21	3	13	69	.284	59	201	14	.949
1985—Kansas City	Amer.	3B	155	550	108	184	38	5	30	112	.335	107	★339	15	.967
1986—Kansas City	Amer.	3B-SS	124	441	70	128	28	4	16	73	.290	97	218	16	.952
1987—Kansas City z	Amer.	1B-3B	115	427	71	124	18	2	22	78	.290	805	69	9	.990
1988—Kansas City	Amer.	1B-SS	157	589	90	180	42	3	24	103	.306	1126	70	10	.992
1989—Kansas City a	Amer.	1B-OF	124	457	67	129	26	3	12	80	.282	898	80	2	.998
Major League Totals—17 Years			2137	8148	1300	2528	514	120	267	1311	.310	4397	3895	281	.967

Selected by Kansas City Royals' organization in 2nd round of free-agent draft, June 8, 1971.
†On disabled list, April 29 to May 11, 1972.
‡On disabled list, May 4 to May 19 and July 27 to August 14, 1978.
§On disabled list, June 11 to July 10, 1980.
xOn disabled list, June 8 to June 29, 1983.
yOn disabled list, April 1 to May 18, 1984.
zOn disabled list, April 20 to May 13 and May 16 to June 12, 1987.
aOn disabled list, April 30 to June 10, 1989.

DIVISION SERIES RECORD

Year Club	League	Pos.	G.	AB.	R.	H.	2B.	3B.	HR.	RBI.	B.A.	PO.	A.	E.	F.A.
1981—Kansas City	Amer.	3B	3	12	0	2	0	0	0	0	.167	1	6	1	.876

CHAMPIONSHIP SERIES RECORD

Holds Championship Series records for highest slugging average, 50 or more at-bats (.728), most runs (22), triples (4), home runs (9), total bases (75), long hits (18), total series; most total bases, game (12), October 6, 1978.

Shares Championship Series records for most runs, game (4), October 11, 1985; most home runs, game (3), October 6, 1978; most triples (2), 1977, game-winning RBIs (2) and bases on balls (7), 1985, series; most game-winning RBIs, total series (3).

Holds American League Championship Series record for highest slugging average, series (1.056), 1978.

Shares American League Championship Series records for most home runs, series (3), 1978 and 1985; most long hits, game (3), October 6, 1978 and October 11, 1985.

Year Club	League	Pos.	G.	AB.	R.	H.	2B.	3B.	HR.	RBI.	B.A.	PO.	A.	E.	F.A.
1976—Kansas City	Amer.	3B	5	18	4	8	1	1	1	5	.444	3	7	3	.769
1977—Kansas City	Amer.	3B	5	20	2	6	0	2	0	2	.300	5	12	2	.895
1978—Kansas City	Amer.	3B	4	18	7	7	1	1	3	3	.389	3	8	1	.917
1980—Kansas City	Amer.	3B	3	11	3	3	1	0	2	4	.273	2	7	0	1.000
1984—Kansas City	Amer.	3B	3	13	0	3	0	0	0	0	.231	2	7	0	1.000
1985—Kansas City	Amer.	3B	7	23	6	8	2	0	3	5	.348	7	8	2	.882
Championship Series Totals—6 Years			27	103	22	35	5	4	9	19	.340	22	49	8	.899

WORLD SERIES RECORD

Year Club	League	Pos.	G.	AB.	R.	H.	2B.	3B.	HR.	RBI.	B.A.	PO.	A.	E.	F.A.
1980—Kansas City	Amer.	3B	6	24	3	9	2	1	1	3	.375	4	17	1	.955
1985—Kansas City	Amer.	3B	7	27	5	10	1	0	0	1	.370	10	19	1	.967
World Series Totals—2 Years			13	51	8	19	3	1	1	4	.373	14	36	2	.962

ALL-STAR GAME RECORD

Holds All-Star Game record for most sacrifice flies, lifetime (3).

Year League	Pos.	AB.	R.	H.	2B.	3B.	HR.	RBI.	B.A.	PO.	A.	E.	F.A.
1976—American	3B	2	0	0	0	0	0	0	.000	0	1	0	1.000
1977—American	3B	2	0	0	0	0	0	0	.000	2	1	0	1.000
1978—American	3B	3	1	2	1	0	0	2	.667	0	2	0	1.000
1979—American	3B	3	1	0	0	0	0	0	.000	1	2	0	1.000
1981—American	3B	3	0	0	0	0	0	0	.000	0	1	0	1.000
1982—American	3B	2	0	2	0	0	0	0	1.000	0	0	0	.000
1983—American	3B	4	2	2	1	1	0	1	.500	1	5	0	1.000
1984—American	3B	3	1	1	0	0	1	1	.333	3	0	0	1.000
1985—American	3B	1	0	0	0	0	0	1	.000	2	1	0	1.000
1988—American	PH	1	0	0	0	0	0	0	.000	0	0	0	.000
All-Star Game Totals—10 Years		24	5	7	2	1	1	5	.292	9	13	0	1.000

Named to American League All-Star Team in 1980 game; replaced due to injury.
Named to American League All-Star Team for 1986 game; replaced due to injury by Brook Jacoby.
Named to American League All-Star Team for 1987 game; replaced due to injury by Kevin Seitzer.

RODNEY LEE BREWER
(Rod)

Born February 24, 1966, at Zellwood, Fla.
Height, 6.03. Weight, 210.
Throws and bats lefthanded.
Attended University of Florida, Gainesville, Fla.

Led Appalachian League in intentional bases on balls received with 5 in 1987.
Led Midwest League first basemen in double plays with 106 in 1988.
Led Appalachian League first basemen in putouts with 554 and total chances with 605 in 1987.
Named first baseman on THE SPORTING NEWS College Baseball All-America Team, 1987.

Year Club	League	Pos.	G.	AB.	R.	H.	2B.	3B.	HR.	RBI.	B.A.	PO.	A.	E.	F.A.
1987—Johnson City	Appal.	*1B-OF	67	238	33	60	11	2	10	42	.252	557	*45	6	*.990
1988—Springfield	Midw.	1B	133	457	57	136	25	2	8	64	.298	*1249	78	10	*.993
1989—Arkansas	Texas	1B	128	470	71	130	25	2	10	93	.277	1084	97	●12	.990

Selected by Toronto Blue Jays' organization in 25th round of free-agent draft, June 4, 1984.
Selected by St. Louis Cardinals' organization in 5th round of free-agent draft, June 2, 1987.

GREGORY BRILEY
(Greg)

Born May 24, 1965, at Bethel, N. C.
Height, 5.08. Weight, 165.
Throws right and bats lefthanded.
Attended Louisburg College, Louisburg, N. C., and
North Carolina State University, Raleigh, N. C.

Major League stolen bases: 1989 (11).

Year Club	League	Pos.	G.	AB.	R.	H.	2B.	3B.	HR.	RBI.	B.A.	PO.	A.	E.	F.A.
1986—Bellingham	N'west	2B	63	218	52	65	12	●4	7	46	.298	132	146	24	.921
1987—Chattanooga	South.	2B	137	539	81	148	21	5	7	61	.275	221	346	*29	.951
1988—Calgary	P. C.	OF-2B	112	445	74	139	29	9	11	66	.312	237	132	15	.961

Year Club	League	Pos.	G.	AB.	R.	H.	2B.	3B.	HR.	RBI.	B.A.	PO.	A.	E.	F.A.
1988—Seattle...................	Amer.	OF	13	36	6	9	2	0	1	4	.250	13	0	1	.929
1989—Seattle...................	Amer.	OF-2B	115	394	52	105	22	4	13	52	.266	197	38	9	.963
1989—Calgary	P. C.	3B-2B-OF	25	94	27	32	8	1	4	20	.340	22	44	5	.930
Major League Totals—2 Years................			128	430	58	114	24	4	14	56	.265	210	38	10	.961

Selected by Los Angeles Dodgers' organization in 3rd round of free-agent draft, January 9, 1985.
Selected by Cleveland Indians' organization in secondary phase of free-agent draft, June 3, 1985.
Selected by Seattle Mariners' organization in secondary phase of free-agent draft, June 2, 1986.

MARIO DIONISIO BRITO

Born April 9, 1966, at Bonao, Dominican Republic.
Height, 6.03. Weight, 185.
Throws and bats righthanded.

Year Club	League	G.	IP.	W.	L.	Pct.	H.	R.	ER.	SO.	BB.	ERA.
1986—Bradenton Expos	Gulf Coast	11	59⅓	5	3	.625	58	29	27	40	24	4.10
1987—Jamestown....................	NYP	15	95⅓	6	5	.545	83	50	32	89	40	3.02
1988—Rockford........................	Midwest	27	186	13	8	.619	161	83	62	144	52	3.00
1989—West Palm Beach	Florida St.	23	149⅓	11	8	.579	134	64	48	90	49	2.89

Signed as free agent by Montreal Expos' organization, March 2, 1985.

GREGORY ALLEN BROCK
(Greg)

Born June 14, 1957, at McMinnville, Ore.
Height, 6.03. Weight, 205.
Throws right and bats lefthanded.
Attended University of Wyoming, Laramie, Wyo.
Brother of Eric Brock, shortstop in Los Angeles Dodgers' organization, 1983 and 1984.

Major League stolen bases: 1983 (5), 1984 (8), 1985 (4), 1986 (2), 1987 (5), 1988 (6), 1989 (6). Total—36.
Led Pacific Coast League in bases on balls received with 105 and intentional bases on balls received with 15 in 1982.
Led Pioneer League in bases on balls received with 54 in 1979.
Led Pacific Coast League first basemen in double plays with 106 in 1982.

Year Club	League	Pos.	G.	AB.	R.	H.	2B.	3B.	HR.	RBI.	B.A.	PO.	A.	E.	F.A.
1979—Lethbridge	Pion.	1B	66	247	61	88	18	2	16	77	.356	543	*36	8	*.986
1980—Lodi......................	Calif.	1B	121	418	72	125	19	3	*29	95	.299	906	*79	5	*.995
1981—San Antonio..........	Texas	1B	128	499	86	147	25	3	*32	106	.295	1071	*90	9	.992
1982—Albuquerque	P. C.	1B	135	480	118	149	21	8	44	138	.310	*1076	*106	*20	.983
1982—Los Angeles	Nat.	1B	18	17	1	2	1	0	0	1	.118	9	0	0	1.000
1983—Los Angeles	Nat.	1B	146	455	64	102	14	2	20	66	.224	1162	106	12	.991
1984—Los Angeles†	Nat.	1B	88	271	33	61	6	0	14	34	.225	703	65	4	.995
1984—Albuquerque	P. C.	1B-3B	24	93	19	29	7	0	6	15	.312	134	38	11	.940
1985—Los Angeles	Nat.	1B	129	438	64	110	19	0	21	66	.251	1113	84	7	.994
1986—Los Angeles‡§.......	Nat.	1B	115	325	33	76	13	0	16	52	.234	726	87	3	.996
1987—Milwaukee x	Amer.	1B	141	532	81	159	29	3	13	85	.299	1065	109	8	.993
1988—Milwaukee y	Amer.	1B	115	364	53	77	16	1	6	50	.212	915	102	7	.993
1989—Beloit z	Midw.	1B	16	52	10	18	2	0	2	10	.346	80	8	2	.978
1989—Milwaukee.............	Amer.	1B	107	373	40	99	16	0	12	52	.265	850	58	5	.995
National League Totals—5 Years...........			496	1506	195	351	53	2	71	219	.233	3713	342	26	.994
American League Totals—3 Years			363	1269	174	335	61	4	31	187	.264	2830	269	20	.994
Major League Totals—8 Years................			859	2775	369	686	114	6	102	406	.247	6543	611	46	.994

Selected by Los Angeles Dodgers' organization in 13th round of free-agent draft, June 5, 1979.
†On disabled list, May 12 to June 7, 1984.
‡On disabled list, June 19 to July 10, 1986.
§Traded to Milwaukee Brewers for Pitchers Tim Leary and Tim Crews, December 10, 1986.
xOn disabled list, June 12 to June 27, 1987.
yOn disabled list, June 7 to July 23, 1988.
zOn Milwaukee disabled list, April 2 to May 31, 1989; included rehabilitation disability assignment to Beloit, May 10 to May 28, 1989.

CHAMPIONSHIP SERIES RECORD

Year Club	League	Pos.	G.	AB.	R.	H.	2B.	3B.	HR.	RBI.	B.A.	PO.	A.	E.	F.A.
1983—Los Angeles	Nat.	1B	3	9	1	0	0	0	0	0	.000	13	0	0	1.000
1985—Los Angeles	Nat.	1B-PH	5	12	2	1	0	0	1	2	.083	35	4	0	1.000
Championship Series Totals—2 Years.....			8	21	3	1	0	0	1	2	.048	48	4	0	1.000

THOMAS DALE BROOKENS
(Tom)

Born August 10, 1953, at Chambersburg, Pa.
Height, 5.10. Weight, 170.
Throws and bats righthanded.
Attended Mansfield State College, Mansfield, Pa.
Twin brother of Tim Brookens, infielder-outfielder in Detroit Tigers' organization, 1975 through 1978;
cousin of Ike Brookens, pitcher with Detroit Tigers, 1975.

Shares American League record for most errors by third baseman, game (4), September 6, 1980.

Major League stolen bases: 1979 (10), 1980 (13), 1981 (5), 1982 (5), 1983 (10), 1984 (6), 1985 (14), 1986 (11), 1987 (7), 1988 (4), 1989 (1). Total—86.

Tied for American League lead in errors by third basemen with 23 in 1985.

Year Club	League	Pos.	G.	AB.	R.	H.	2B.	3B.	HR.	RBI.	B.A.	PO.	A.	E.	F.A.
1975—Montgomery........	South.	SS	100	329	37	73	11	2	7	36	.222	139	298	31	.934
1976—Montgomery........	South.	2B	137	492	76	127	22	5	11	56	.258	310	*389	*25	.965
1977—Evansville	A. A.	3B-2B	118	440	70	127	22	5	8	52	.289	132	250	25	.939
1978—Evansville†	A. A.	3B-2B-1B	65	206	27	58	11	1	6	25	.282	76	100	20	.898
1979—Evansville	A. A.	3B-2B	77	265	51	81	23	2	14	46	.306	71	166	16	.937
1979—Detroit..................	Amer.	3B-2B	60	190	23	50	5	2	4	21	.263	76	141	11	.952
1980—Detroit..................	Amer.	*3-2-S	151	509	64	140	25	9	10	66	.275	127	307	*29	.937
1981—Detroit‡...............	Amer.	3B	71	239	19	58	10	1	4	25	.243	58	139	10	.952
1982—Detroit..................	Amer.	3-2-S-O	140	398	40	92	15	3	9	58	.231	119	276	20	.952
1983—Detroit..................	Amer.	3B-SS-2B	138	332	50	71	13	3	6	32	.214	97	254	22	.941
1984—Detroit§................	Amer.	3B-SS-2B	113	224	32	55	11	4	5	26	.246	98	187	12	.960
1985—Detroit x...............	Amer.	3-S-2-C	156	485	54	115	34	6	7	47	.237	135	277	24	.944
1986—Detroit..................	Amer.	3-2-S-O	98	281	42	76	11	2	3	25	.270	106	144	7	.973
1987—Detroit y	Amer.	3B-SS-2B	143	444	59	107	15	3	13	59	.241	119	256	19	.952
1988—Detroit..................	Amer.	3B-SS-2B	136	441	62	107	23	5	5	38	.243	101	235	17	.952
1989—New York zab......	Amer.	3-S-2-O	66	168	14	38	6	0	4	14	.226	27	85	7	.941
Major League Totals—11 Years.............			1272	3711	459	909	168	38	70	411	.245	1063	2301	178	.950

Selected by Detroit Tigers' organization in 1st round (fourth player selected) of free-agent draft, January 9, 1975.
†On disabled list, April 14 to May 9 and June 4 to June 21, 1978.
‡On disabled list, March 30 to May 4, 1981.
§On disabled list, August 19 to September 4, 1984.
xGranted free agency, November 12, 1985; re-signed by Tigers, January 8, 1986.
yGranted free agency, January 22, 1988; re-signed by Tigers, February 9, 1988.
zTraded to New York Yankees for Pitcher Charles Hudson, March 23, 1989.
aOn disabled list, July 29 to September 6, 1989.
bReleased, November 20, 1989; signed by Cleveland Indians, December 8, 1989.

CHAMPIONSHIP SERIES RECORD

Year Club	League	Pos.	G.	AB.	R.	H.	2B.	3B.	HR.	RBI.	B.A.	PO.	A.	E.	F.A.
1984—Detroit..................	Amer.	2B-3B	2	2	0	0	0	0	0	0	.000	0	2	1	.667
1987—Detroit..................	Amer.	3B	5	13	0	0	0	0	0	0	.000	3	15	0	1.000
Championship Series Totals—2 Years.....			7	15	0	0	0	0	0	0	.000	3	17	1	.952

WORLD SERIES RECORD

Year Club	League	Pos.	G.	AB.	R.	H.	2B.	3B.	HR.	RBI.	B.A.	PO.	A.	E.	F.A.
1984—Detroit..................	Amer.	PH-3B	3	3	0	0	0	0	0	0	.000	0	3	0	1.000

HUBERT BROOKS JR.
(Hubie)

Born September 24, 1956, at Los Angeles, Calif.
Height, 6.00. Weight, 200.
Throws and bats righthanded.
Attended Mesa Community College, Mesa, Ariz., and received bachelor of science degree in health science from Arizona State University, Tempe, Ariz.
Grandson of Leandrus Brooks, player with Philadelphia of Negro National League; and cousin of Donnie Moore, pitcher with Chicago Cubs, St. Louis Cardinals, Milwaukee Brewers, Atlanta Braves and California Angels, 1975 and 1977 through 1988.

Major League stolen bases: 1980 (1), 1981 (9), 1982 (6), 1983 (6), 1984 (6), 1985 (6), 1986 (4), 1987 (4), 1988 (7), 1989 (6). Total—55.

Led International League in game-winning RBIs with 12 in 1980.
Named shortstop on THE SPORTING NEWS National League Silver Slugger team, 1985 and 1986.
Named shortstop on THE SPORTING NEWS College Baseball All-America Team, 1978.
Named outfielder on THE SPORTING NEWS College Baseball All-America Team, 1977.

Year Club	League	Pos.	G.	AB.	R.	H.	2B.	3B.	HR.	RBI.	B.A.	PO.	A.	E.	F.A.
1978—Jackson.................	Texas	SS-OF-3B	45	153	19	33	8	1	3	16	.216	49	84	14	.905
1979—Jackson.................	Texas	3B-SS	112	406	68	124	21	2	3	28	.305	92	218	29	.942
1979—Tidewater.............	Int.	SS-3B-OF	5	15	1	6	1	0	1	3	.400	4	8	1	.923
1980—Tidewater.............	Int.	OF-3B-SS	113	417	50	124	18	5	3	50	.297	152	90	18	.931
1980—New York..............	Nat.	3B	24	81	8	25	2	1	1	10	.309	16	40	2	.966
1981—New York..............	Nat.	*3-O-S	98	358	34	110	21	2	4	38	.307	67	193	*21	.925
1982—New York†...........	Nat.	3B	126	457	40	114	21	2	2	40	.249	89	237	24	.931
1983—New York..............	Nat.	3B-2B	150	586	53	147	18	4	5	58	.251	116	303	21	.952
1984—New York‡...........	Nat.	3B-SS	153	561	61	159	23	2	16	73	.283	112	284	29	.932
1985—Montreal	Nat.	SS	156	605	67	163	34	7	13	100	.269	203	441	28	.958
1986—Montreal §	Nat.	SS	80	306	50	104	18	5	14	58	.340	116	222	15	.958
1987—Montreal x............	Nat.	SS	112	430	57	113	22	3	14	72	.263	131	271	20	.953
1988—Montreal	Nat.	OF	151	588	61	164	35	2	20	90	.279	261	8	9	.968
1989—Montreal y............	Nat.	OF	148	542	56	145	30	1	14	70	.268	234	6	9	.964
Major League Totals—10 Years.............			1198	4514	487	1244	224	29	103	609	.276	1345	2005	178	.950

Selected by Montreal Expos' organization in 19th round of free-agent draft, June 5, 1974.
Selected by Kansas City Royals' organization in secondary phase of free-agent draft, January 7, 1976.
Selected by Chicago White Sox' organization in secondary phase of free-agent draft, June 8, 1976.
Selected by Oakland A's organization in secondary phase of free-agent draft, January 11, 1977.
Selected by Chicago White Sox' organization in secondary phase of free-agent draft, June 7, 1977.

Selected by New York Mets' organization in 1st round (third player selected) of free-agent draft, June 6, 1978.
†On disabled list, June 28 to July 22, 1982.
‡Traded with Catcher Mike Fitzgerald, Outfielder Herm Winningham and Pitcher Floyd Youmans to Montreal Expos for Catcher Gary Carter, December 10, 1984.
§On disabled list, August 2, 1986 through remainder of season.
xOn disabled list, April 11 to May 25, 1987.
yGranted free agency, November 13, 1989.

ALL-STAR GAME RECORD

Year League	Pos.	AB.	R.	H.	2B.	3B.	HR.	RBI.	B.A.	PO.	A.	E.	F.A.
1986—National	PH-SS	2	1	0	0	0	0	0	.000	1	0	0	1.000
1987—National	SS	3	1	1	0	0	0	0	.333	1	2	0	1.000
All-Star Game Totals—2 Years		5	2	1	0	0	0	0	.200	2	2	0	1.000

TERRENCE PAUL BROSS
(Terry)

Born March 30, 1966, at El Paso, Tex.
Height, 6.09. Weight, 234.
Throws and bats righthanded.
Attended St. John's University, Jamaica, N.Y.

Year Club	League	G.	IP.	W.	L.	Pct.	H.	R.	ER.	SO.	BB.	ERA.
1987—Little Falls	NYP	10	28	2	0	1.000	22	23	12	21	20	3.86
1988—Little Falls	NYP	20	55⅓	2	1	.667	43	25	19	59	38	3.09
1989—St. Lucie†	Florida St.	35	58	8	2	●.800	39	21	18	47	26	2.79

Selected by New York Mets' organization in 13th round of free-agent draft, June 2, 1987.
†On disabled list, May 31 to June 29, 1989.

ROBERT RICHARD BROWER
(Bob)

Born January 10, 1960, at Queens, N.Y.
Height, 6.00. Weight, 190.
Throws and bats righthanded.
Attended Duke University, Durham, N.C.

Major League stolen bases: 1986 (1), 1987 (15), 1988 (10), 1989 (3). Total—29.
Led American Association in bases on balls received with 94 in 1986.
Led American Association outfielders in total chances with 382 in 1986.

Year Club	League	Pos.	G.	AB.	R.	H.	2B.	3B.	HR.	RBI.	B.A.	PO.	A.	E.	F.A.
1982—Sarasota Rangers	Gulf C.	OF	36	122	25	35	7	2	0	7	.287	53	3	0	1.000
1983—Burlington	Midw.	OF	43	138	35	43	4	6	5	28	.312	60	4	4	.941
1983—Tulsa	Texas	OF	69	252	41	59	4	1	3	17	.234	138	4	4	.973
1984—Tulsa	Texas	OF	96	344	69	98	14	9	7	30	.285	209	10	3	.986
1984—Oklahoma City	A. A.	OF	35	107	18	24	2	2	1	8	.224	69	7	2	.974
1985—Oklahoma City	A. A.	OF	133	445	56	111	13	★18	5	50	.249	282	8	3	.990
1986—Oklahoma City	A. A.	OF	●140	★550	★130	●158	25	7	13	72	.287	★366	8	8	.979
1986—Texas	Amer.	OF	21	9	3	1	1	0	0	0	.111	9	0	0	1.000
1987—Texas	Amer.	OF	127	303	63	79	10	3	14	46	.261	183	2	7	.964
1988—Texas†‡	Amer.	OF	82	201	29	45	7	0	1	11	.224	104	2	3	.972
1989—New York§	Amer.	OF	26	69	9	16	3	0	2	3	.232	62	2	2	.970
1989—Columbus	Int.	OF	26	95	15	24	3	0	2	8	.253	36	1	0	1.000
Major League Totals—4 Years			256	582	104	141	21	3	17	60	.242	358	6	12	.968

Signed as free agent by Texas Rangers' organization, July 1, 1982.
†On disabled list, April 4 to April 27, 1988.
‡Traded to New York Yankees for Shortstop Bobby Meacham, December 5, 1988.
§On disabled list, March 28 to April 16, 1989.

JAMES KEVIN BROWN

(Known by middle name.)

Born March 14, 1965, at McIntyre, Ga.
Height, 6.04. Weight, 188.
Throws and bats righthanded.
Attended Georgia Tech, Atlanta, Ga.

Named as righthanded pitcher on THE SPORTING NEWS College Baseball All-America Team, 1986.

Year Club	League	G.	IP.	W.	L.	Pct.	H.	R.	ER.	SO.	BB.	ERA.
1986—Sarasota Rangers	Gulf Coast	3	6	0	0	.000	7	4	4	1	2	6.00
1986—Tulsa	Texas	3	10	0	0	.000	9	7	5	10	5	4.50
1986—Texas	American	1	5	1	0	1.000	6	2	2	4	0	3.60
1987—Tulsa	Texas	8	42	1	4	.200	53	36	34	26	18	7.29
1987—Oklahoma City	Am. Assoc.	5	24⅓	0	5	.000	32	32	29	9	17	10.73
1987—Port Charlotte	Florida St.	6	36⅓	0	2	.000	33	14	11	21	17	2.72
1988—Tulsa	Texas	26	174⅓	12	10	.545	174	94	68	118	61	3.51
1988—Texas	American	4	23⅓	1	1	.500	33	15	11	12	8	4.24
1989—Texas	American	28	191	12	9	.571	167	81	71	104	70	3.35
Major League Totals—3 Years		33	219⅓	14	10	.583	206	98	84	120	78	3.45

Selected by Texas Rangers' organization in 1st round (fourth player selected) of free-agent draft, June 2, 1986.

JARVIS ARDEL BROWN

Born March 26, 1967, at Waukegan, Ill.
Height, 5.07. Weight, 165.
Throws and bats righthanded.
Attended Triton College, River Grove, Ill.

Led California League outfielders in double plays with 7 in 1989.
Led Midwest League outfielders in total chances with 334 in 1988.

Year Club	League	Pos.	G.	AB.	R.	H.	2B.	3B.	HR.	RBI.	B.A.	PO.	A.	E.	F.A.
1986—Elizabethton	Appal.	2B-OF-SS	49	180	28	41	4	0	3	23	.228	90	107	17	.921
1987—Kenosha	Midw.	2B-OF	43	117	22	37	4	1	3	16	.188	74	82	15	.912
1987—Elizabethton	Appal.	OF	67	258	52	63	9	1	1	15	.244	106	6	*16	.875
1988—Kenosha	Midw.	OF	138	531	*108	*156	25	7	7	45	.294	311	15	8	.976
1989—Visalia	Calif.	OF	141	545	*95	131	21	6	4	46	.240	291	16	6	.981

Selected by Minnesota Twins' organization in 1st round (ninth player selected) of free-agent draft, January 14, 1986.

JOHN CHRISTOPHER BROWN
(Chris)

Born August 15, 1961, at Jackson, Miss.
Height, 6.02. Weight, 210.
Throws and bats righthanded.

Major League stolen bases: 1984 (2), 1985 (2), 1986 (13), 1987 (4). Total—21.
Led National League in being hit by pitch with 11 in 1985.

Year Club	League	Pos.	G.	AB.	R.	H.	2B.	3B.	HR.	RBI.	B.A.	PO.	A.	E.	F.A.
1979—Great Falls	Pion.	3B	47	171	24	46	5	3	5	30	.269	31	77	11	.908
1980—Clinton	Midw.	3B-1B	103	337	38	80	5	3	7	35	.237	352	132	19	.962
1981—Fresno	Calif.	3B-OF-1B	85	291	37	84	11	2	8	44	.289	89	156	23	.914
1982—Shreveport	Texas	3B-2B	58	185	26	49	14	0	1	21	.265	51	82	9	.937
1982—Fresno	Calif.	3B-1B-SS	41	133	22	39	9	1	4	31	.293	41	71	6	.949
1983—Shreveport	Texas	3B	102	322	44	88	21	0	10	58	.273	63	182	17	.935
1984—Phoenix†	P. C.	3B	84	283	41	80	13	5	9	64	.283	43	119	17	.905
1984—San Francisco	Nat.	3B	23	84	6	24	7	0	1	11	.286	23	40	7	.900
1985—San Francisco	Nat.	3B	131	432	50	117	20	3	16	61	.271	94	243	10	*.971
1986—San Francisco	Nat.	3B-SS	116	416	57	132	16	3	7	49	.317	73	181	18	.934
1987—S.F.‡§-S.D.	Nat.	3B-SS	82	287	34	68	9	0	12	40	.237	60	132	16	.923
1988—San Diego x	Nat.	3B	80	247	14	58	6	0	2	19	.235	54	131	10	.949
1989—Detroit y	Amer.	3B	17	57	3	11	3	0	0	4	.193	15	25	4	.909
1989—Buffalo z	A. A.	3B-1B	57	181	28	62	8	0	5	32	.343	31	70	10	.910
National League Totals—5 Years			432	1466	161	399	58	6	38	180	.272	304	727	61	.944
American League Totals—1 Year			17	57	3	11	3	0	0	4	.193	15	25	4	.909
Major League Totals—6 Years			449	1523	164	410	61	6	38	184	.269	319	752	65	.943

Selected by San Francisco Giants' organization in 2nd round of free-agent draft, June 5, 1979.
†On disabled list, April 11 to April 21 and July 30 to August 11, 1984.
‡On disabled list, May 5 to June 18, 1987.
§Traded with Pitchers Keith Comstock, Mark Davis and Mark Grant to San Diego Padres for Pitchers Dave Dravecky and Craig Lefferts and Infielder Kevin Mitchell, July 4, 1987.
xTraded with Infielder Keith Moreland to Detroit Tigers for Pitcher Walt Terrell, October 28, 1988.
yReleased, May 19, 1989; signed by Buffalo (Pittsburgh Pirates' organization), June 2, 1989.
zGranted free agency, October 15, 1989.

ALL-STAR GAME RECORD

Year League	Pos.	AB.	R.	H.	2B.	3B.	HR.	RBI.	B.A.	PO.	A.	E.	F.A.
1986—National	3B	2	1	1	1	0	0	0	.500	1	0	0	1.000

KEITH EDWARD BROWN

Born February 14, 1964, at Flagstaff, Ariz.
Height, 6.04. Weight, 205.
Throws right and bats left and righthanded.
Attended College of the Siskiyous, Weed, Calif.,
and California State University, Sacramento, Calif.

Year Club	League	G.	IP.	W.	L.	Pct.	H.	R.	ER.	SO.	BB.	ERA.
1986—Sarasota Reds	Gulf Coast	7	47⅓	4	1	.800	29	15	5	26	5	0.95
1986—Billings	Pioneer	4	21⅓	2	0	1.000	18	6	5	14	7	2.11
1986—Vermont	Eastern	4	14	1	1	.500	12	10	8	11	8	5.14
1987—Cedar Rapids	Midwest	17	124⅓	13	4	.765	91	28	22	86	27	*1.59
1988—Chattanooga	Southern	10	69⅔	9	1	*.900	47	11	11	34	20	1.42
1988—Nashville	Am. Assoc.	12	85⅓	6	3	.667	72	33	18	43	28	1.90
1988—Cincinnati	National	4	16⅓	2	1	.667	14	5	5	6	4	2.76
1989—Nashville	Am. Assoc.	29	161⅓	8	13	.381	171	99	86	85	51	4.80
Major League Totals—1 Year		4	16⅓	2	1	.667	14	5	5	6	4	2.76

Selected by Cincinnati Reds' organization in 21st round of free-agent draft, June 2, 1986.

—DID YOU KNOW—

That only four American League batters hit more doubles (home and away combined)
than Boston's Wade Boggs hit at home (37) in 1989?

KEVIN DEWAYNE BROWN

Born March 5, 1966, at Oroville, Calif.
Height, 6.01. Weight, 185.
Throws and bats lefthanded.
Attended Sacramento City College, Sacramento, Calif.

Year Club	League	G.	IP.	W.	L.	Pct.	H.	R.	ER.	SO.	BB.	ERA.
1986—Idaho Falls	Pioneer	12	68	3	6	.333	65	48	38	44	41	5.03
1987—Sumter	S. Atlantic	9	56	7	1	.875	53	14	12	45	19	1.93
1987—Durham†	Carolina	13	72⅔	4	4	.500	78	46	42	48	42	5.20
1988—St. Lucie	Florida St.	20	134	5	7	.417	96	42	27	113	37	★1.81
1988—Jackson	Texas	5	32⅔	1	2	.333	24	9	8	24	11	2.20
1989—Jackson	Texas	8	51⅔	5	2	.714	51	15	13	40	11	2.26
1989—Tidewater	Int'national	13	75	6	6	.500	81	41	37	46	31	4.44

Selected by Kansas City Royals' organization in 4th round of free-agent draft, January 9, 1985.
Selected by Philadelphia Phillies' organization in secondary phase of free-agent draft, June 3, 1985.
Selected by Atlanta Braves' organization in secondary phase of free-agent draft, January 14, 1986.
†Traded to New York Mets, December 8, 1987, to complete deal in which Atlanta Braves acquired Outfielder Terry Blocker for a player to be named later, November 11, 1987.

MARTY LEO BROWN

Born January 23, 1963, at Lawton, Okla.
Height, 6.01. Weight, 195.
Throws and bats righthanded.
Attended Crowder College, Neosho, Mo., and
University of Georgia, Athens, Ga.

Tied for Midwest League lead in caught stealing with 20 in 1986.
Led Eastern League third basemen in assists with 234 and fielding percentage with .957 in 1987.
Led Pioneer League first basemen in assists with 49 in 1985.

Year Club	League	Pos.	G.	AB.	R.	H.	2B.	3B.	HR.	RBI.	B.A.	PO.	A.	E.	F.A.
1985—Billings	Pion.	1B-OF	68	248	50	84	21	3	10	45	.339	592	50	10	.985
1986—Cedar Rapids	Midw.	3B-1B	●139	508	85	152	19	8	18	83	.299	86	249	40	.893
1987—Vermont	East.	3B-1B	134	470	69	124	17	5	15	74	.264	132	237	14	.963
1988—Nashville	A. A.	3B-OF-SS	135	484	50	128	15	4	7	55	.264	93	227	22	.936
1988—Cincinnati	Nat.	3B	10	16	0	3	1	0	0	2	.188	1	9	0	1.000
1989—Nashville	A. A.	3-O-1-S	120	422	61	103	21	2	12	46	.244	202	162	28	.929
1989—Cincinnati†	Nat.	3B	16	30	2	5	1	0	0	4	.167	2	19	2	.913
Major League Totals—2 Years			26	46	2	8	2	0	0	6	.174	3	28	2	.939

Selected by Cincinnati Reds' organization in 12th round of free-agent draft, June 3, 1985.
†Drafted by Baltimore Orioles, December 4, 1989.

JEROME A. BROWNE

(Jerry)

Born February 13, 1966, at St. Croix, Virgin Islands.
Height, 5.10. Weight, 170.
Throws right and bats left and righthanded.

Holds American League record for fewest double plays, second baseman, season, 150 or more games (67), 1989.
Major League stolen bases: 1987 (27), 1988 (7), 1989 (14). Total—48.
Led Texas League second basemen in fielding percentage with .984 in 1986.
Led Carolina League second basemen in total chances with 675 in 1985.

Year Club	League	Pos.	G.	AB.	R.	H.	2B.	3B.	HR.	RBI.	B.A.	PO.	A.	E.	F.A.
1983—Sarasota Rangers	Gulf C.	2B	48	181	34	51	2	2	0	20	.282	92	123	14	.939
1984—Burlington	Midw.	SS-2B	127	420	70	99	10	1	0	18	.236	231	311	43	.926
1985—Salem	Carol.	2B	122	460	69	123	18	4	3	58	.267	★265	★390	20	.970
1986—Tulsa	Texas	2B-SS	128	491	82	149	15	7	2	57	.303	282	307	19	.969
1986—Texas	Amer.	2B	12	24	6	10	2	0	0	3	.417	9	15	2	.923
1987—Texas†	Amer.	2B	132	454	63	123	16	6	1	38	.271	258	338	12	.980
1988—Texas	Amer.	2B	73	214	26	49	9	2	1	17	.229	112	139	11	.958
1988—Oklahoma City‡	A. A.	2B	76	286	45	72	15	2	5	34	.252	190	231	10	.977
1989—Cleveland	Amer.	2B	153	598	83	179	31	4	5	45	.299	305	380	15	.979
Major League Totals—4 Years			370	1290	178	361	58	12	7	103	.280	684	872	40	.975

Signed as free agent by Texas Rangers' organization, March 3, 1983.
†On disabled list, August 24 to September 8, 1987.
‡Traded with First Baseman Pete O'Brien and Outfielder Oddibe McDowell to Cleveland Indians for Second Baseman Julio Franco, December 6, 1988.

THOMAS LEO BROWNING

(Tom)

Born April 28, 1960, at Casper, Wyo.
Height, 6.01. Weight, 190.
Throws and bats lefthanded.
Attended Tennessee Wesleyan College, Athens, Tenn., and
Le Moyne College, Syracuse, N.Y.

Pitched 1-0 perfect game against Los Angeles Dodgers, September 16, 1988.
Pitched seven-inning, 2-0 no-hit victory against Iowa, July 31, 1984.
Led National League in home runs allowed with 36 in 1988 and 31 in 1989.

Led National League pitchers in games started with 37 in 1989 and tied for lead with 39 in 1986 and 36 in 1988.
Tied for American Association lead in home runs allowed with 24 in 1984.
Named National League Rookie Pitcher of the Year by THE SPORTING NEWS, 1985.

Year Club	League	G.	IP.	W.	L.	Pct.	H.	R.	ER.	SO.	BB.	ERA.
1982—Billings	Pioneer	14	88	4	●8	.333	96	53	38	★87	41	3.89
1983—Tampa	Florida St.	11	78⅔	8	1	.889	53	19	13	101	36	1.49
1983—Waterbury	Eastern	18	117⅓	4	10	.286	100	62	46	101	63	3.53
1984—Wichita	Am. Assoc.	30	189⅓	12	10	.545	169	88	83	★160	73	3.95
1984—Cincinnati	National	3	23⅓	1	0	1.000	27	4	4	14	5	1.54
1985—Cincinnati	National	38	261⅓	20	9	.690	242	111	103	155	73	3.55
1986—Cincinnati	National	39	243⅓	14	13	.519	225	123	103	147	70	3.81
1987—Cincinnati	National	32	183	10	13	.435	201	107	102	117	61	5.02
1987—Nashville	Am. Assoc.	5	29⅔	2	3	.400	37	22	20	28	12	6.07
1988—Cincinnati	National	36	250⅔	18	5	.783	205	98	95	124	64	3.41
1989—Cincinnati	National	37	249⅔	15	12	.556	241	109	94	118	64	3.39
Major League Totals—6 Years		185	1211⅓	78	52	.600	1141	552	501	675	337	3.72

Selected by Cincinnati Reds' organization in 9th round of free-agent draft, June 7, 1982.

ANTHONY MICHAEL BRUMLEY
(Mike)

Born April 9, 1963, at Oklahoma City, Okla.
Height, 5.10. Weight, 165.
Throws right and bats left and righthanded.
Attended University of Texas, Austin, Tex.
Son of Mike Brumley, catcher with Washington Senators, 1964 through 1966.

Major League stolen bases: 1987 (7) 1989 (8). Total—15.
Led American Association shortstops in total chances with 597 in 1986.

Year Club	League	Pos.	G.	AB.	R.	H.	2B.	3B.	HR.	RBI.	B.A.	PO.	A.	E.	F.A.
1983—Winter Haven	Fla. St.	SS-OF	44	153	25	48	6	4	1	18	.314	51	92	20	.877
1984—New Britain†	East.	OF-SS	34	121	14	28	6	2	0	9	.231	71	6	6	.928
1984—Midland	Texas	OF	73	255	37	55	11	3	6	21	.216	128	4	5	.964
1985—Pittsfield	East.	SS-OF	131	460	66	127	23	★14	3	58	.276	182	333	33	.940
1986—Iowa	A. A.	SS	139	458	74	103	21	5	10	44	.225	177	★400	20	.966
1987—Iowa	A. A.	SS-2B-OF	92	319	44	81	20	5	6	42	.254	147	240	24	.942
1987—Chicago‡	Nat.	SS-2B	39	104	8	21	2	2	1	9	.202	43	93	5	.965
1988—Las Vegas§	P. C.	S-O-3-2	113	425	77	134	16	7	3	41	.315	139	322	28	.943
1989—Detroit	Amer.	S-2-3-O	92	212	33	42	5	2	1	11	.198	80	160	12	.952
1989—Toledo	Int.	SS	8	26	4	6	2	2	0	1	.231	9	14	2	.920
National League Totals—1 Year			39	104	8	21	2	2	1	9	.202	43	93	5	.965
American League Totals—1 Year			92	212	33	42	5	2	1	11	.198	80	160	12	.952
Major League Totals—2 Years			131	316	41	63	7	4	2	20	.199	123	253	17	.957

Selected by Philadelphia Phillies' organization in 16th round of free-agent draft, June 3, 1980.
Selected by Boston Red Sox' organization in 2nd round of free-agent draft, June 6, 1983.
†Traded with Pitcher Dennis Eckersley to Chicago Cubs for First Baseman-Outfielder Bill Buckner, May 25, 1984.
‡Traded with Infielder Keith Moreland to San Diego Padres for Pitchers Rich Gossage and Ray Hayward, February 12, 1988.
§Traded to Detroit Tigers for Infielder Luis Salazar, March 23, 1989.

THOMAS ANDREW BRUNANSKY
(Tom)

Born August 20, 1960, at Covina, Calif.
Height, 6.04. Weight, 216.
Throws and bats righthanded.
Attended California State Poly University, Pomona, Calif.
Brother-in-law of Dave Engle, catcher with Minnesota Twins,
Detroit Tigers, Montreal Expos and Milwaukee Brewers, 1981 through 1989.

Major League stolen bases: 1981 (1), 1982 (1), 1983 (2), 1984 (4), 1985 (5), 1986 (12), 1987 (11), 1988 (17), 1989 (5). Total—58.
Led American League outfielders in double plays with 8 in 1983 and 6 in 1984.
Tied for Texas League lead in double plays by outfielders with 4 in 1980.
Received reported $100,000 bonus to sign with California Angels, 1978.

Year Club	League	Pos.	G.	AB.	R.	H.	2B.	3B.	HR.	RBI.	B.A.	PO.	A.	E.	F.A.
1978—Idaho Falls	Pioneer	OF	48	190	55	63	14	4	6	45	.332	85	1	8	.915
1979—Salinas	Calif.	OF	★140	485	85	131	23	1	23	76	.270	279	11	6	.980
1980—El Paso	Texas	OF	128	495	103	160	24	8	24	97	.323	306	17	★14	.958
1980—Salt Lake City	P. C.	OF	9	32	7	11	2	2	1	8	.344	28	1	0	1.000
1981—Salt Lake City†	P. C.	OF	96	343	61	114	17	10	22	81	.332	250	14	5	.981
1981—California	Amer.	OF	11	33	7	5	0	0	3	6	.152	27	3	2	.938
1982—Spokane‡	P. C.	OF	25	88	12	18	6	1	1	6	.205	44	7	1	.981
1982—Minnesota	Amer.	OF	127	463	77	126	30	1	20	46	.272	343	8	5	.986
1983—Minnesota	Amer.	OF	151	542	70	123	24	5	28	82	.227	375	16	6	.985
1984—Minnesota	Amer.	OF	155	567	75	144	21	0	32	85	.254	304	13	5	.984
1985—Minnesota	Amer.	OF	157	567	71	137	28	4	27	90	.242	300	14	5	.984
1986—Minnesota	Amer.	OF	157	593	69	152	28	1	23	75	.256	315	10	6	.982
1987—Minnesota	Amer.	OF	155	532	83	138	22	2	32	85	.259	273	10	3	.990
1988—Minnesota§	Amer.	OF	14	49	5	9	1	0	1	6	.184	19	0	3	.864
1988—St. Louis	Nat.	OF	143	523	69	128	22	4	22	79	.245	267	10	1	★.996

Year Club	League	Pos.	G.	AB.	R.	H.	2B.	3B.	HR.	RBI.	B.A.	PO.	A.	E.	F.A.
1989—St. Louis..................	Nat.	OF-1B	158	556	67	133	29	3	20	85	.239	291	9	7	.977
American League Totals—8 Years			927	3346	457	834	154	13	166	475	.249	1956	74	35	.983
National League Totals—2 Years			301	1079	136	261	51	7	42	164	.242	558	19	8	.986
Major League Totals—9 Years			1228	4425	593	1095	205	20	208	639	.247	2514	93	43	.984

Selected by California Angels' organization in 1st round (14th player selected) of free-agent draft, June 6, 1978.

†On disabled list, August 8 to August 31, 1981.

‡Traded with Pitcher Mike Walters and cash to Minnesota Twins for Pitcher Doug Corbett and Second Baseman Rob Wilfong, May 12, 1982.

§Traded to St. Louis Cardinals for Second Baseman Tom Herr, April 22, 1988.

CHAMPIONSHIP SERIES RECORD

Shares Championship Series records for most doubles (4) and long hits (6), series, 1987.

Year Club	League	Pos.	G.	AB.	R.	H.	2B.	3B.	HR.	RBI.	B.A.	PO.	A.	E.	F.A.
1987—Minnesota.............	Amer.	OF	5	17	5	7	4	0	2	9	.412	10	0	0	1.000

WORLD SERIES RECORD

Year Club	League	Pos.	G.	AB.	R.	H.	2B.	3B.	HR.	RBI.	B.A.	PO.	A.	E.	F.A.
1987—Minnesota.............	Amer.	OF	7	25	5	5	0	0	0	2	.200	14	0	0	1.000

ALL-STAR GAME RECORD

Year League	Pos.	AB.	R.	H.	2B.	3B.	HR.	RBI.	B.A.	PO.	A.	E.	F.A.
1985—American	OF	1	0	0	0	0	0	0	.000	0	0	0	.000

ROBERT GORDON BUCHANAN
(Bob)

Born May 3, 1961, at Ridley Park, Pa.
Height, 6.01. Weight, 180.
Throws and bats lefthanded.

Year Club	League	G.	IP.	W.	L.	Pct.	H.	R.	ER.	SO.	BB.	ERA.
1979—Billings...............................	Pioneer	14	91	7	5	.583	82	42	34	80	25	3.36
1980—Tampa.................................	Florida St.	27	101	7	7	.500	102	53	48	62	40	4.28
1981—Cedar Rapids.............................	Midwest	25	171	10	11	.476	174	81	61	125	64	3.21
1982—Waterbury...........................	Eastern	27	165⅓	10	8	.556	174	90	71	78	68	3.86
1983—Indianapolis................................	Am. Assoc.	30	49	1	6	.143	69	42	36	22	31	6.61
1983—Waterbury...........................	Eastern	14	18	0	1	.000	19	13	13	12	9	6.50
1984—Vermont	Eastern	14	20⅔	1	2	.333	14	8	5	18	14	2.18
1984—Wichita	Am. Assoc.	39	58⅔	1	2	.333	51	21	20	35	28	3.07
1985—Denver	Am. Assoc.	29	41⅓	4	3	.571	45	20	10	36	13	2.18
1985—Cincinnati†‡................................	National	14	16	1	0	1.000	25	15	15	3	9	8.44
1986—Denver§x	Am. Assoc.	36	77	3	7	.300	95	53	46	29	37	5.38
1987—Tidewater y	Int'national	29	60	4	4	.500	60	25	24	37	16	3.60
1988—Omaha	Am. Assoc.	47	76	5	1	.833	70	21	20	44	29	2.37
1989—Omaha	Am. Assoc.	27	164	8	9	.471	150	70	61	104	49	3.35
1989—Kansas City z............................	American	2	3⅓	0	0	.000	5	6	6	3	3	16.20
National League Totals—1 Year		14	16	1	0	1.000	25	15	15	3	9	8.44
American League Totals—1 Year		2	3⅓	0	0	.000	5	6	6	3	3	16.20
Major League Totals—2 Years............................		16	19⅓	1	0	1.000	30	21	21	6	12	9.78

Selected by Cincinnati Reds' organization in 2nd round of free-agent draft, June 5, 1979.

†On disabled list, August 8 to August 29, 1985.

‡Traded to San Francisco Giants for Pitcher Colin Ward, November 11, 1985; trade voided, January 27, 1986.

§On disabled list, July 30, 1986 through remainder of season.

xGranted free agency, October 15, 1986; signed by Tidewater (New York Mets' organization), November 24, 1986.

yGranted free agency, October 15, 1987; signed by Omaha (Kansas City Royals' organization), November 18, 1987.

zGranted free agency, October 15, 1989.

WILLIAM JOSEPH BUCKNER
(Bill)

Born December 14, 1949, at Vallejo, Calif.
Height, 6.01. Weight, 195.
Throws and bats lefthanded.
Attended University of Southern California, Los Angeles, Calif., and
Arizona State University, Tempe, Ariz.
Brother of Jim Buckner, minor league outfielder, 1972 through 1981;
and Bob Buckner, minor league infielder, 1966 through 1970;
and part-time scout with Chicago Cubs, 1977 through 1979.

Holds major league record for most assists, first baseman, season (184), 1985.

Shares major league record for most games, first baseman, season (162), 1985.

Shares National League records for fewest double plays, first baseman, season, 150 or more games (89), 1982; fewest errors by first baseman for leader in errors, season (13), 1983.

Major League stolen bases: 1971 (4), 1972 (10), 1973 (12), 1974 (31), 1975 (8), 1976 (28), 1977 (7), 1978 (7), 1979 (9), 1980 (1), 1981 (5), 1982 (15), 1983 (12), 1984 (2), 1985 (18), 1986 (6), 1987 (2), 1988 (5), 1989 (1). Total—183.

Led Pioneer League first basemen in double plays with 37 in 1968.

Year Club	League	Pos.	G.	AB.	R.	H.	2B.	3B.	HR.	RBI.	B.A.	PO.	A.	E.	F.A.
1968—Ogden	Pion.	1B	★64	★256	54	★88	10	★8	4	41	★.344	468	28	4	★.992

Year Club	League	Pos.	G.	AB.	R.	H.	2B.	3B.	HR.	RBI.	B.A.	PO.	A.	E.	F.A.
1969—Albuquerque	Texas	OF-1B	70	257	44	79	7	3	7	50	.307	220	15	3	.987
1969—Spokane	P. C.	OF-1B	36	143	21	45	1	1	2	27	.315	128	12	5	.966
1969—Los Angeles	Nat.	PH	1	1	0	0	0	0	0	0	.000	0	0	0	.000
1970—Spokane	P. C.	1B-OF	111	465	78	156	33	2	3	74	.335	582	22	7	.989
1970—Los Angeles	Nat.	OF-1B	28	68	6	13	3	1	0	4	.191	37	1	0	1.000
1971—Los Angeles	Nat.	OF-1B	108	358	37	99	15	1	5	41	.277	235	11	1	.996
1972—Los Angeles	Nat.	OF-1B	105	383	47	122	14	3	5	37	.319	434	22	4	.991
1973—Los Angeles	Nat.	1B-OF	140	575	68	158	20	0	8	46	.275	981	50	3	.997
1974—Los Angeles	Nat.	OF-1B	145	580	83	182	30	3	7	58	.314	284	5	7	.976
1975—Los Angeles†	Nat.	OF	92	288	30	70	11	2	6	31	.243	138	4	2	.986
1976—Los Angeles‡	Nat.	OF-1B	154	642	76	193	28	4	7	60	.301	315	7	5	.985
1977—Chicago§	Nat.	1B	122	426	40	121	27	0	11	60	.284	966	58	10	.990
1978—Chicago x	Nat.	1B	117	446	47	144	26	1	5	74	.323	1075	83	6	.995
1979—Chicago	Nat.	1B	149	591	72	168	34	7	14	66	.284	1258	124	7	.995
1980—Chicago	Nat.	1B-OF	145	578	69	187	41	3	10	68	★.324	916	78	8	.992
1981—Chicago	Nat.	1B	106	421	45	131	★35	3	10	75	.311	996	81	★17	.984
1982—Chicago	Nat.	1B	161	★657	93	201	34	5	15	105	.306	1547	★159	12	.993
1983—Chicago	Nat.	★●1B-OF	153	626	79	175	●38	6	16	66	.280	1391	★161	●13	.992
1984—Chicago y	Nat.	1B-OF	21	43	3	9	0	0	0	2	.209	71	6	0	1.000
1984—Boston	Amer.	1B	114	439	51	122	21	2	11	67	.278	974	96	●15	.986
1985—Boston	Amer.	1B	162	673	89	201	46	3	16	110	.299	1384	★184	12	.992
1986—Boston	Amer.	1B	153	629	73	168	39	2	18	102	.267	1067	★157	14	.989
1987—Bos. za-Cal.	Amer.	1B	132	469	39	134	18	2	5	74	.286	640	60	6	.992
1988—Cal.b-K.C.c	Amer.	1B	108	285	19	71	14	0	3	43	.249	161	13	1	.994
1989—Kansas City d	Amer.	1B	79	176	7	38	4	1	1	16	.216	181	13	3	.985
National League Totals—16 Years			1747	6683	795	1973	356	39	119	793	.295	10644	850	95	.992
American League Totals—6 Years			748	2671	278	734	142	10	54	412	.275	4407	523	51	.990
Major League Totals—21 Years			2495	9354	1073	2707	498	49	173	1205	.289	15051	1373	146	.991

Selected by Los Angeles Dodgers' organization in 2nd round of free-agent draft, June 7, 1968.
†On disabled list, April 21 to May 12, 1975.
‡Traded with Infielder Ivan DeJesus and Pitcher Jeff Albert to Chicago Cubs for Outfielder Rick Monday and Pitcher Mike Garman, January 11, 1977.
§On disabled list, March 28 to April 19, 1977.
xOn disabled list, June 22 to July 7, 1978.
yTraded to Boston Red Sox for Pitcher Dennis Eckersley and Outfielder Mike Brumley, May 25, 1984.
zOn disabled list, June 10 to June 26, 1987.
aReleased, July 23, 1987; signed by California Angels, July 28, 1987.
bReleased, May 9, 1988; signed by Kansas City Royals, May 13, 1988.
cGranted free agency, November 4, 1988; re-signed by Royals, December 6, 1988.
dGranted free agency, November 13, 1989.

CHAMPIONSHIP SERIES RECORD

Year Club	League	Pos.	G.	AB.	R.	H.	2B.	3B.	HR.	RBI.	B.A.	PO.	A.	E.	F.A.
1974—Los Angeles	Nat.	OF	4	18	0	3	1	0	0	0	.167	6	0	0	1.000
1986—Boston	Amer.	1B	7	28	3	6	1	0	0	3	.214	49	5	0	1.000
Championship Series Totals—2 Years			11	46	3	9	2	0	0	3	.196	55	5	0	1.000

WORLD SERIES RECORD

Year Club	League	Pos.	G.	AB.	R.	H.	2B.	3B.	HR.	RBI.	B.A.	PO.	A.	E.	F.A.
1974—Los Angeles	Nat.	OF	5	20	1	5	1	0	1	1	.250	11	0	0	1.000
1986—Boston	Amer.	1B	7	32	2	6	0	0	0	1	.188	53	7	1	.984
World Series Totals—2 Years			12	52	3	11	1	0	1	2	.212	64	7	1	.986

ALL-STAR GAME RECORD

Year League		Pos.	AB.	R.	H.	2B.	3B.	HR.	RBI.	B.A.	PO.	A.	E.	F.A.
1981—National		PH	1	0	0	0	0	0	0	.000	0	0	0	.000

STEVEN BERNARD BUECHELE

Name pronounced BOO-shell.

(Steve)

Born September 26, 1961, at Lancaster, Calif.
Height, 6.02. Weight, 190.
Throws and bats righthanded.
Attended Stanford University, Stanford, Calif.

Major League stolen bases: 1985 (3), 1986 (5), 1987 (2), 1988 (2), 1989 (1). Total—13.
Named American Association Most Valuable Player, 1985.

Year Club	League	Pos.	G.	AB.	R.	H.	2B.	3B.	HR.	RBI.	B.A.	PO.	A.	E.	F.A.
1982—Tulsa	Texas	2B-3B	62	213	21	63	12	2	5	33	.296	111	174	8	.973
1983—Tulsa	Texas	2B-3B	117	437	62	121	12	4	14	62	.277	182	259	18	.961
1983—Oklahoma City	A. A.	2B-3B	9	34	6	9	5	0	1	4	.265	17	22	1	.975
1984—Oklahoma City	A. A.	2B-3B	131	447	48	118	25	3	7	59	.264	236	329	17	.971
1985—Oklahoma City	A. A.	3B-2B	89	350	56	104	20	7	9	64	.297	84	170	7	.973
1985—Texas	Amer.	3B-2B	69	219	22	48	6	3	6	21	.219	52	138	6	.969
1986—Texas	Amer.	3B-2B-OF	153	461	54	112	19	2	18	54	.243	174	292	12	.975
1987—Texas	Amer.	3B-2B-OF	136	363	45	86	20	0	13	50	.237	89	211	9	.971
1988—Texas	Amer.	3B-2B	155	503	68	126	21	4	16	58	.250	114	300	16	.963
1989—Texas	Amer.	3B-2B-SS	155	486	60	114	22	2	16	59	.235	128	288	12	.972
Major League Totals—5 Years			668	2032	249	486	88	11	69	242	.239	557	1229	55	.970

Selected by Chicago White Sox' organization in 1st round (ninth player selected) of free-agent draft, June 5, 1979.
Selected by Texas Rangers' organization in 5th round of free-agent draft, June 7, 1982.

JAY CAMPBELL BUHNER

Born August 13, 1964, at Louisville, Ky.
Height, 6.03. Weight, 205.
Throws and bats righthanded.
Attended McLennan Community College, Waco, Tex.

Major League stolen bases: 1988 (1), 1989 (1). Total—2.
Led Florida State League in game-winning RBIs with 15 in 1985.
Tied for International League lead in double plays by outfielders with 6 in 1987.

Year Club League	Pos.	G.	AB.	R.	H.	2B.	3B.	HR.	RBI.	B.A.	PO.	A.	E.	F.A.
1984—Watertown† ...... NYP	OF	65	229	43	74	16	3	9	●58	.323	106	8	1	.991
1985—Fort Lauderdale .. Fla. St.	OF	117	409	65	121	18	10	11	76	.296	235	12	7	.972
1986—Fort Lauderdale‡ Fla. St.	OF	36	139	24	42	9	1	7	31	.302	84	7	3	.968
1987—Columbus .... Int.	OF	134	502	83	140	23	1	*31	85	.279	275	*20	6	.980
1987—New York .... Amer.	OF	7	22	0	5	2	0	0	1	.227	11	1	0	1.000
1988—Columbus .... Int.	OF	38	129	26	33	5	0	8	18	.256	83	3	1	.989
1988—N.Y.§-Sea. .... Amer.	OF	85	261	36	56	13	1	13	38	.215	186	9	3	.985
1989—Calgary .... P. C.	OF	56	196	43	61	12	1	11	45	.311	97	8	2	.981
1989—Seattle x .... Amer.	OF	58	204	27	56	15	1	9	33	.275	106	6	4	.966
Major League Totals—3 Years		150	487	63	117	30	2	22	72	.240	303	16	7	.979

Selected by Atlanta Braves' organization in 9th round of free-agent draft, June 6, 1983.
Selected by Pittsburgh Pirates' organization in secondary phase of free-agent draft, January 17, 1984.
†Traded with Infielder Dale Berra and Pitcher Alfonso Pulido to New York Yankees for Outfielder Steve Kemp, Infielder Tim Foli and $800,000, December 20, 1984.
‡On disabled list, April 11 to July 28, 1986.
§Traded with Pitcher Rich Balabon and a player to be named later to Seattle Mariners for Designated Hitter Ken Phelps, July 21, 1988; Seattle acquired Pitcher Troy Evers to complete deal, October 12, 1988.
xOn disabled list, June 29 to August 19, 1989; included rehabilitation disability assignment to Calgary, August 16 to August 19, 1989.

DeWAYNE ALLISON BUICE

Name pronounced Byce.
Born August 20, 1957, at Lynwood, Calif.
Height, 5.11. Weight, 170.
Throws and bats righthanded.
Attended California State University at Dominguez Hills, Carson, Calif.;
Los Angeles Harbor Junior College, Wilmington, Calif.,
and Cypress College, Cypress, Calif.

Major League saves: 1987 (17), 1988 (3). Total—20.

Year Club	League	G.	IP.	W.	L.	Pct.	H.	R.	ER.	SO.	BB.	ERA.
1977—Great Falls....................	Pioneer	15	37	1	4	.200	48	34	15	30	24	3.65
1978—Cedar Rapids................	Midwest	36	74	3	5	.375	58	30	14	68	41	1.70
1979—Fresno	California	46	97	7	5	.583	83	51	40	86	44	3.71
1980—Fresno†	California	36	100	7	4	.636	101	42	37	88	38	3.33
1981—West Haven	Eastern	*58	82	8	3	.727	75	24	19	88	41	2.09
1981—Tacoma	P. Coast	2	3	1	0	1.000	0	0	0	2	3	0.00
1982—Tacoma‡	P. Coast	19	41	4	2	.667	51	22	19	36	19	4.17
1982—West Haven	Eastern	8	23⅔	1	1	.500	18	11	9	40	8	3.42
1983—Tacoma §xy	P. Coast	32	52⅓	5	3	.625	44	27	20	41	22	3.44
1984—Nuevo Laredo	Mexico	14	40	4	1	.800	26	12	10	35	17	2.25
1985—Nuevo Laredo	Mexico	24	33⅔	0	1	.000	33	13	12	37	15	3.21
1986—Midland.....................	Texas	45	78⅓	8	6	.571	70	34	30	73	22	3.45
1986—Edmonton..................	P. Coast	8	12⅓	2	1	.667	6	2	1	11	3	0.73
1987—Edmonton..................	P. Coast	5	8⅓	1	1	.500	4	5	1	7	7	1.08
1987—California...................	American	57	114	6	7	.462	87	45	43	109	40	3.39
1988—California z.................	American	32	41⅓	2	4	.333	45	29	27	38	19	5.88
1988—Edmonton a	P. Coast	9	11⅔	0	0	.000	9	4	3	17	2	2.31
1989—Syracuse....................	Int'national	31	51	4	2	.667	34	15	14	59	28	2.47
1989—Toronto bc.................	American	7	17	1	0	1.000	13	12	11	10	13	5.82
Major League Totals—3 Years............		96	172⅓	9	11	.450	145	86	81	157	72	4.23

Signed as free agent by San Francisco Giants' organization, May 19, 1977.
†Drafted by West Haven (Oakland A's organization), December 9, 1980.
‡On disabled list, July 3 to July 13 and August 12, 1982 through remainder of season.
§On disabled list, June 8 to June 28 and July 13, 1983 through remainder of season.
xGranted free agency, October 15, 1983; signed by Maine (Cleveland Indians' organization), January 14, 1984.
yReleased, April 7, 1984; signed by Edmonton (California Angels' organization), November 19, 1985.
zOn disabled list, June 16 to August 5, 1988; included rehabilitation disability assignment to Edmonton, July 17 to August 5, 1988.
aTraded to Toronto Blue Jays for Pitcher Cliff Young, March 9, 1989.
bOn disabled list, May 31 to June 15, 1989.
cGranted free agency, October 15, 1989.

—DID YOU KNOW—

That the Reds' Lenny Harris led the majors with a .400 pinch-hitting average (8 for 20) in 1989?

ERIC JERALD BULLOCK

Born February 16, 1960, at Los Angeles, Calif.
Height, 5.11. Weight, 185.
Throws and bats lefthanded.
Attended Los Angeles Harbor Junior College, Woodland Hills, Calif.
and California State University, Fullerton, Calif.
Son of Eddie Bullock, minor league outfielder, 1955.

Major League stolen bases: 1986 (2), 1988 (1). Total—3.
Led Pacific Coast League in stolen bases with 51 and caught stealing with 18 in 1988.
Tied for Pacific Coast League lead in being hit by pitch with 7 in 1985.

Year Club	League	Pos.	G.	AB.	R.	H.	2B.	3B.	HR.	RBI.	B.A.	PO.	A.	E.	F.A.
1981—Sarasota Orange..	Gulf C.	OF	56	184	38	54	8	3	1	15	.293	67	6	3	.961
1981—Daytona Beach....	Fla. St.	DH	1	2	1	1	0	0	0	1	.500	0	0	0	.000
1982—Daytona Beach....	Fla. St.	OF	117	442	90	150	24	11	5	●85	.339	180	11	5	.974
1982—Columbus...............	South.	OF	18	66	6	20	1	0	2	13	.303	21	1	0	1.000
1983—Columbus...............	South.	OF	130	475	65	131	15	6	9	59	.276	196	9	3	.986
1984—Columbus...............	South.	OF	71	265	47	77	15	2	3	41	.291	133	3	4	.971
1984—Tucson...................	P. C.	OF	60	185	22	51	6	2	1	16	.276	96	2	5	.951
1985—Tucson...................	P. C.	OF	124	467	81	149	26	8	4	57	.319	199	5	7	.967
1985—Houston.................	Nat.	OF	18	25	3	7	2	0	0	2	.280	6	0	2	.750
1986—Houston.................	Nat.	OF	6	21	0	1	0	0	0	1	.048	7	0	1	.875
1986—Tucson†.................	P. C.	OF	42	151	28	58	8	2	3	21	.384	73	2	1	.987
1987—Tuc.‡-Port.§.........	P. C.	OF	106	330	42	88	13	6	2	34	.267	145	5	2	.987
1988—Portland...............	P. C.	OF	117	434	69	134	20	8	2	46	.309	211	11	3	★.987
1988—Minnesota x.........	Amer.	OF	16	17	3	5	0	0	0	3	.294	7	0	1	.875
1989—Scr./Wil-Barre y..	Int.	OF	80	281	37	77	10	8	3	40	.274	119	4	1	.992
1989—Philadelphia z.....	Nat.	OF	6	4	1	0	0	0	0	0	.000	2	0	0	1.000
National League Totals—3 Years...........			30	50	4	8	2	0	0	3	.160	15	0	3	.833
American League Totals—1 Year..........			16	17	3	5	0	0	0	3	.294	7	0	1	.875
Major League Totals—4 Years................			46	67	7	13	2	0	0	6	.194	22	0	4	.846

Selected by Los Angeles Dodgers' organization in 18th round of free-agent draft, June 6, 1978.
Selected by San Diego Padres' organization in 1st round (fifth player selected) of free-agent draft, January 13, 1981.
Selected by Houston Astros' organization in secondary phase of free-agent draft, June 8, 1981.
†On disabled list, May 6 to July 7, 1986.
‡Traded to Minnesota Twins' organization for Pitcher Clay Christiansen, June 2, 1987.
§Granted free agency, October 15, 1987; re-signed by Twins' organization, November 7, 1987.
xTraded with Second Baseman Tom Herr and Catcher Tom Nieto to Philadelphia Phillies for Pitcher Shane Rawley and cash, October 24, 1988.
yOn disabled list, April 6 to May 27, 1989.
zGranted free agency, October 15, 1989.

DAVID ALLEN BURBA

Born July 7, 1966, at Dayton, O.
Height, 6.04. Weight, 220.
Throws and bats righthanded.
Attended Ohio State University, Columbus, O.
Nephew of Ray Hathaway, pitcher with Brooklyn Dodgers, 1945.

Year Club	League	G.	IP.	W.	L.	Pct.	H.	R.	ER.	SO.	BB.	ERA.
1987—Bellingham	Northwest	5	23⅓	3	1	.750	20	10	5	24	3	1.93
1987—Salinas............................	California	9	54⅔	1	6	.143	53	31	28	46	29	4.61
1988—San Bernardino............................	California	20	114	5	7	.417	106	41	34	102	54	2.68
1989—San Bernardino............................	California	25	156⅔	11	7	.611	138	69	55	89	55	3.16

Selected by Seattle Mariners' organization in 2nd round of free-agent draft, June 2, 1987.

TIMOTHY PHILIP BURKE
(Tim)

Born February 19, 1959, at Omaha, Neb.
Height, 6.03. Weight, 205.
Throws and bats righthanded.
Attended University of Nebraska, Lincoln, Neb.

Holds National League record for most games pitched by rookie, season (78), 1985.
Major League saves: 1985 (8), 1986 (4), 1987 (18), 1988 (9), 1989 (28). Total—76.

Year Club	League	G.	IP.	W.	L.	Pct.	H.	R.	ER.	SO.	BB.	ERA.
1980—Salem†.....................Carolina						(Did not play)						
1981—Alexandria	Carolina	23	149	8	10	.444	139	67	57	111	48	3.44
1982—Buffalo‡......................	Eastern	25	144	7	10	.412	162	93	83	93	57	5.19
1983—Columbus......................	Eastern	4	12	1	0	1.000	15	9	9	6	8	6.75
1983—Nashville§x..................	Southern	20	129	12	4	.750	124	63	46	64	37	3.21
1984—Indianapolis	Am. Assoc.	35	180⅔	11	8	.579	192	81	70	108	61	3.49
1985—Montreal......................	National	★78	120⅓	9	4	.692	86	32	32	87	44	2.39
1986—Montreal......................	National	68	101⅓	9	7	.563	103	37	33	82	46	2.93
1987—Montreal y....................	National	55	91	7	0	1.000	64	18	12	58	17	1.19
1988—Montreal......................	National	61	82	3	5	.375	84	36	31	42	25	3.40
1989—Montreal......................	National	68	84⅔	9	3	.750	68	24	24	54	22	2.55
Major League Totals—5 Years....................		330	479⅓	37	19	.661	405	147	132	323	154	2.48

Selected by Pittsburgh Pirates' organization in 2nd round of free-agent draft, June 3, 1980.

ALL-STAR GAME RECORD

Year	League	IP.	W.	L.	Pct.	H.	R.	ER.	SO.	BB.	ERA.
1989—National		2	0	0	.000	2	0	0	1	0	0.00

JOHN DAVID BURKETT

Born November 28, 1964, at New Brighton, Pa.
Height, 6.02. Weight, 180.
Throws and bats righthanded.

Tied for Pacific Coast League lead in games started by pitchers with 28 in 1989.

Year Club	League	G.	IP.	W.	L.	Pct.	H.	R.	ER.	SO.	BB.	ERA.
1983—Great Falls	Pioneer	13	50⅓	2	6	.250	73	44	35	38	30	6.26
1984—Clinton	Midwest	20	126⅔	7	6	.538	128	81	61	83	38	4.33
1985—Fresno	California	20	109⅔	7	4	.636	98	43	35	72	46	2.87
1986—Fresno	California	4	24⅔	0	3	.000	34	19	15	14	8	5.47
1986—Shreveport	Texas	22	128⅔	10	6	.625	99	46	38	73	42	2.66
1987—Shreveport	Texas	27	*177⅔	●14	8	.636	181	75	66	126	53	3.34
1987—San Francisco	National	3	6	0	0	.000	7	4	3	5	3	4.50
1988—Phoenix	P. Coast	21	114	5	11	.313	141	79	66	74	49	5.21
1988—Shreveport	Texas	7	50⅔	5	1	.833	33	15	12	34	18	2.13
1989—Phoenix	P. Coast	28	167⅔	10	11	.476	197	111	94	105	59	5.05
Major League Totals—1 Year		3	6	0	0	.000	7	4	3	5	3	4.50

Selected by San Francisco Giants' organization in 6th round of free-agent draft, June 6, 1983.

ELLIS RENA BURKS

Born September 11, 1964, at Vicksburg, Miss.
Height, 6.02. Weight, 202.
Throws and bats righthanded.
Attended Ranger Junior College, Ranger, Tex.

Major League stolen bases: 1987 (27), 1988 (25), 1989 (21). Total—73.
Tied for Florida State League lead in double plays by outfielders with 6 in 1984.

Year Club	League	Pos.	G.	AB.	R.	H.	2B.	3B.	HR.	RBI.	B.A.	PO.	A.	E.	F.A.
1983—Elmira	NYP	OF	53	174	30	42	9	0	2	23	.241	89	5	2	.979
1984—Winter Haven	Fla. St.	OF	112	375	52	96	15	4	6	43	.256	196	12	5	.977
1985—New Britain	East.	OF	133	476	66	121	25	7	10	61	.254	306	9	8	.975
1986—New Britain	East.	OF	124	462	70	126	20	3	14	55	.273	318	5	5	.985
1987—Pawtucket	Int.	OF	11	40	11	9	3	1	3	6	.225	25	0	0	1.000
1987—Boston	Amer.	OF	133	558	94	152	30	2	20	59	.272	320	15	4	.988
1988—Boston†	Amer.	OF	144	540	93	159	37	5	18	92	.294	370	9	9	.977
1989—Boston‡	Amer.	OF	97	399	73	121	19	6	12	61	.303	245	7	6	.977
1989—Pawtucket	Int.	OF	5	21	4	3	1	0	0	0	.143	16	0	0	1.000
Major League Totals—3 Years		374	1497	260	432	86	13	50	212	.289	935	31	19	.981

Selected by Boston Red Sox' organization in 1st round (20th player selected) of free agent draft, January 11, 1983.
†On disabled list, March 26 to April 12, 1988.
‡On disabled list, June 15 to August 1, 1989; included rehabilitation disability assignment to Pawtucket, July 26 to August 1, 1989.

CHAMPIONSHIP SERIES RECORD

Year Club	League	Pos.	G.	AB.	R.	H.	2B.	3B.	HR.	RBI.	B.A.	PO.	A.	E.	F.A.
1988—Boston	Amer.	OF	4	17	2	4	1	0	0	1	.235	10	0	0	1.000

TODD EDWARD BURNS

Born July 6, 1963, at Maywood, Calif.
Height, 6.02. Weight, 186.
Throws and bats righthanded.
Attended Oral Roberts University, Tulsa, Okla.

Major League saves: 1988 (1), 1989 (8). Total—9.
Tied for Southern League lead in shutouts with 3 in 1986.

Year Club	League	G.	IP.	W.	L.	Pct.	H.	R.	ER.	SO.	BB.	ERA.
1984—Medford	Northwest	22	36⅓	3	0	1.000	21	4	2	63	12	0.50
1984—Madison	Midwest	10	14	3	2	.600	11	4	4	20	3	2.57
1985—Madison	Midwest	20	123	8	8	.500	109	55	50	94	40	3.66
1985—Huntsville	Southern	4	22⅓	3	1	.750	16	6	3	8	13	1.19
1986—Huntsville	Southern	20	124⅔	7	7	.500	122	59	52	77	39	3.75
1986—Tacoma	P.Coast	11	16⅔	0	1	.000	11	4	4	14	12	2.16
1987—Huntsville	Southern	34	63⅔	3	4	.429	49	24	21	54	17	2.97
1987—Tacoma	P. Coast	21	27⅔	2	2	.500	27	16	15	30	16	4.88
1988—Tacoma	P. Coast	21	73⅓	4	3	.571	74	39	30	59	26	3.68
1988—Oakland	American	17	102⅔	8	2	.800	93	38	36	57	34	3.16
1989—Oakland	American	50	96¼	6	5	.545	66	27	24	49	28	2.24
Major League Totals—2 Years		67	199	14	7	.667	159	65	60	106	62	2.71

Selected by Oakland A's organization in 7th round of free-agent draft, June 4, 1984.

WORLD SERIES RECORD

Year	Club	League	G.	IP.	W.	L.	Pct.	H.	R.	ER.	SO.	BB.	ERA.
1988—Oakland	American	1	1/3	0	0	.000	0	0	0	0	0	0.00
1989—Oakland	American	2	1⅔	0	0	.000	1	0	0	0	1	0.00
World Series Record—2 Years		3	2	0	0	.000	1	0	0	0	1	0.00

ROBERT RANDALL BUSH
(Randy)

Born October 5, 1958, at Dover, Del.
Height, 6.01. Weight, 184.
Throws and bats lefthanded.
Attended Miami-Dade Community College (North), Miami, Fla.,
and University of New Orleans, New Orleans, La.

Shares American League record for most home runs by pinch-hitter, consecutive at-bats (2), June 20 and 23, 1986.
Major League stolen bases: 1984 (1), 1985 (3), 1986 (5), 1987 (10), 1988 (8), 1989 (5). Total—32.
Led Southern League in being hit by pitch with 8 in 1979 and 12 in 1981.

Year	Club	League	Pos.	G.	AB.	R.	H.	2B.	3B.	HR.	RBI.	B.A.	PO.	A.	E.	F.A.
1979—Orlando	South.	1B	76	243	33	62	12	2	6	34	.255	653	38	13	.982
1980—Toledo†	Int.	OF-1B	40	108	11	21	1	0	1	7	.194	112	6	1	.992
1980—Orlando	South.	1B	51	175	32	41	2	1	7	26	.234	458	28	4	.992
1981—Orlando	South.	OF-1B	136	482	98	140	26	3	22	94	.290	174	7	5	.973
1982—Toledo	Int.	OF	49	160	21	52	14	0	8	27	.325	68	0	1	.986
1982—Minnesota	Amer.	OF	55	119	13	29	6	1	4	13	.244	7	0	0	1.000
1983—Minnesota	Amer.	1B	124	373	43	93	24	3	11	56	.249	21	3	0	1.000
1984—Minnesota	Amer.	1B	113	311	46	69	17	1	11	43	.222	5	0	0	1.000
1985—Minnesota	Amer.	OF-1B	97	234	26	56	13	3	10	35	.239	79	0	2	.975
1986—Minnesota	Amer.	OF-1B	130	357	50	96	19	7	7	45	.269	182	2	4	.979
1987—Minnesota	Amer.	OF-1B	122	293	46	74	10	2	11	46	.253	164	5	4	.977
1988—Minnesota‡	Amer.	OF-1B	136	394	51	103	20	3	14	51	.261	206	5	4	.981
1989—Minnesota	Amer.	OF-1B	141	391	60	103	17	4	14	54	.263	339	14	3	.992
Major League Totals—8 Years			918	2472	335	623	126	24	82	343	.252	1003	29	17	.984

Selected by Minnesota Twins' organization in 2nd round of free-agent draft, June 5, 1979.
†On disabled list, May 25 to June 27, 1980.
‡Granted free agency, November 4, 1988; re-signed by Twins, December 12, 1988.

CHAMPIONSHIP SERIES RECORD

Shares Championship Series record for most stolen bases, inning (2), October 8, 1987, fourth inning.

Year	Club	League	Pos.	G.	AB.	R.	H.	2B.	3B.	HR.	RBI.	B.A.	PO.	A.	E.	F.A.
1987—Minnesota	Amer.	DH	4	12	4	3	0	1	0	2	.250	0	0	0	.000

WORLD SERIES RECORD

Year	Club	League	Pos.	G.	AB.	R.	H.	2B.	3B.	HR.	RBI.	B.A.	PO.	A.	E.	F.A.
1987—Minnesota	Amer.	DH-PH	4	6	1	1	1	0	0	2	.167	0	0	0	.000

BRETT MORGAN BUTLER

Born June 15, 1957, at Los Angeles, Calif.
Height, 5.10. Weight, 160.
Throws and bats lefthanded.
Attended Arizona State University, Tempe, Ariz., and received bachelor of science degree in
education from Southeastern Oklahoma State University, Durant, Okla., in 1979.

Shares major league record for fewest double plays by outfielder, season, for leader in most double plays (4), 1983.
Shares National League record for fewest assists, outfielder, season, 150 or more games (3), 1988.
Major League stolen bases: 1981 (9), 1982 (21), 1983 (39), 1984 (52), 1985 (47), 1986 (32), 1987 (33), 1988 (43), 1989 (31).
Total—307.
Led American League in caught stealing with 22 in 1984 and 20 in 1985.
Tied for National League lead in double plays by outfielders with 4 in 1983.
Led International League in bases on balls received with 103 in 1981.
Named International League Most Valuable Player, 1981.

Year	Club	League	Pos.	G.	AB.	R.	H.	2B.	3B.	HR.	RBI.	B.A.	PO.	A.	E.	F.A.
1979—Greenwood	W. Car.	OF	35	117	26	37	2	4	1	11	.316	45	2	0	1.000
1979—Bradenton	Gulf C.	OF	30	111	36	41	7	5	3	20	.369	66	5	0	1.000
1980—Anderson	S. Atl.	OF	70	255	73	76	12	6	1	26	.298	190	5	1	.995
1980—Durham	Carol.	OF	66	224	47	82	15	6	2	39	.366	156	4	3	.982
1981—Richmond	Int.	OF	125	466	*93	156	19	4	3	36	.335	286	15	3	.990
1981—Atlanta	Nat.	OF	40	126	17	32	2	3	0	4	.254	76	2	1	.987
1982—Atlanta	Nat.	OF	89	240	35	52	2	0	0	7	.217	129	2	0	1.000
1982—Richmond	Int.	OF	41	157	22	57	8	3	1	22	.363	101	2	1	.990
1983—Atlanta†	Nat.	OF	151	549	84	154	21	*13	5	37	.281	284	13	4	.987
1984—Cleveland	Amer.	OF	159	602	108	162	25	9	3	49	.269	448	13	4	.991
1985—Cleveland	Amer.	OF	152	591	106	184	28	14	5	50	.311	437	19	1	*.998
1986—Cleveland	Amer.	OF	161	587	92	163	17	*14	4	51	.278	434	9	3	.993
1987—Cleveland‡§	Amer.	OF	137	522	91	154	25	8	9	41	.295	393	4	4	.990
1988—San Francisco	Nat.	OF	157	568	*109	163	27	9	6	43	.287	395	3	5	.988

Year Club League	Pos.	G.	AB.	R.	H.	2B.	3B.	HR.	RBI.	B.A.	PO.	A.	E.	F.A.
1989—San Francisco ...... Nat.	OF	154	594	100	168	22	4	4	36	.283	407	11	6	.986
National League Totals—5 Years		591	2077	345	569	74	29	15	127	.274	1291	31	16	.988
American League Totals—4 Years		609	2302	397	663	95	45	21	191	.288	1712	45	12	.993
Major League Totals—9 Years		1200	4379	742	1232	169	74	36	318	.281	3003	76	28	.991

Selected by Atlanta Braves' organization in 23rd round of free-agent draft, June 5, 1979.

†Traded with Infielder Brook Jacoby to Cleveland Indians, October 21, 1983, completing deal in which Atlanta Braves acquired Pitcher Len Barker for three players to be named later, August 28, 1983. Cleveland acquired Pitcher Rick Behenna as partial completion of deal, September 2, 1983.

‡On disabled list, April 11 to April 30, 1987.

§Granted free agency, November 9, 1987; signed by San Francisco Giants, December 1, 1987.

CHAMPIONSHIP SERIES RECORD

Year Club League	Pos.	G.	AB.	R.	H.	2B.	3B.	HR.	RBI.	B.A.	PO.	A.	E.	F.A.
1982—Atlanta .... Nat.	OF-PH	2	1	0	0	0	0	0	0	.000	0	0	0	.000
1989—San Francisco ...... Nat.	OF	5	19	6	4	0	0	0	0	.211	9	0	0	1.000
Championship Series Totals—2 Years		7	20	6	4	0	0	0	0	.200	9	0	0	1.000

WORLD SERIES RECORD

Year Club League	Pos.	G.	AB.	R.	H.	2B.	3B.	HR.	RBI.	B.A.	PO.	A.	E.	F.A.
1989—San Francisco ...... Nat.	OF	4	14	1	4	1	0	0	1	.286	9	0	0	1.000

FRANCISCO CABRERA (PAULINO)

Born October 10, 1966, at Santo Domingo, D.R.
Height, 6.04. Weight, 195.
Throws and bats righthanded.

Led International League in sacrifice flies with 8 in 1989.
Tied for New York-Pennsylvania League lead in game-winning RBIs with 10 in 1986.
Led International League in passed balls with 13 in 1989.
Led Southern League catchers in total chances with 874 and tied for lead in double plays with 6 in 1988.
Led South Atlantic League catchers in total chances with 959 in 1987.

Year Club League	Pos.	G.	AB.	R.	H.	2B.	3B.	HR.	RBI.	B.A.	PO.	A.	E.	F.A.
1986—Ventura County ... Calif.	C	6	12	2	2	1	0	0	3	.167	26	3	1	.967
1986—St. Catherines .... NYP	C	68	246	31	73	13	2	6	35	.297	449	50	6	.988
1987—Myrtle Beach .... S. Atl.	C	129	449	61	124	27	1	14	72	.276	★849	89	●21	.978
1988—Dunedin .... Fla. St.	C	9	35	2	14	4	0	1	9	.400	74	9	3	.965
1988—Knoxville .... South.	C	119	429	59	122	19	1	20	54	.284	★783	★68	★230	.974
1989—Syr.-Rich. .... Int.	★C-1B	116	434	59	130	31	5	9	72	.300	554	35	★12	.980
1989—Toronto† .... Amer.	DH	3	12	1	2	1	0	0	0	.167	0	0	0	.000
1989—Atlanta .... Nat.	C-1B	4	14	0	3	2	0	0	0	.214	27	1	1	.966
American League Totals—1 Year		3	12	1	2	1	0	0	0	.167	0	0	0	.000
National League Totals—1 Year		4	14	0	3	2	0	0	0	.214	27	1	1	.966
Major League Totals—1 Year		7	26	1	5	3	0	0	0	.192	27	1	1	.966

Signed as free agent by Toronto Blue Jays' organization, February 28, 1986.

†Traded to Atlanta Braves' organization, August 24, 1989, completing deal in which Atlanta traded Pitcher Jim Acker to Toronto Blue Jays for Pitcher Tony Castillo and a player to be named later, August 24, 1989.

GREGORY JAMES CADARET
(Greg)

Born February 27, 1962, at Detroit, Mich.
Height, 6.03. Weight, 205.
Throws and bats lefthanded.
Attended Grand Valley State College, Allendale, Mich.

Major League saves: 1988 (3).

Year Club	League	G.	IP.	W.	L.	Pct.	H.	R.	ER.	SO.	BB.	ERA.
1983—Medford	Northwest	12	64	7	3	.700	73	36	31	51	36	4.36
1984—Modesto...............	California	26	171⅓	13	8	.619	162	79	58	138	82	3.05
1985—Huntsville...........	Southern	17	82½	3	7	.300	96	61	56	60	57	6.12
1985—Modesto...............	California	12	61⅓	3	9	.250	59	50	40	43	54	5.87
1986—Huntsville...........	Southern	28	141⅓	12	5	.706	166	106	85	113	98	5.41
1987—Huntsville...........	Southern	24	40⅓	5	2	.714	31	16	13	48	20	2.90
1987—Tacoma.................	P. Coast	7	13	1	2	.333	5	6	5	12	13	3.46
1987—Oakland................	American	29	39⅔	6	2	.750	37	22	20	30	24	4.54
1988—Oakland................	American	58	71⅔	5	2	.714	60	26	23	64	36	2.89
1989—Oakland†-New York	American	46	120	5	5	.500	130	62	54	80	57	4.05
Major League Totals—3 Years		133	231⅓	16	9	.640	227	110	97	174	117	3.77

Selected by Oakland A's organization in 11th round of free-agent draft, June 6, 1983.

†Traded with Pitcher Eric Plunk and Outfielder Luis Polonia to New York Yankees for Outfielder Rickey Henderson, June 21, 1989.

CHAMPIONSHIP SERIES RECORD

Year Club	League	G.	IP.	W.	L.	Pct.	H.	R.	ER.	SO.	BB.	ERA.
1988—Oakland................	American	1	⅓	0	0	.000	1	1	1	0	0	27.00

WORLD SERIES RECORD

Year Club	League	G.	IP.	W.	L.	Pct.	H.	R.	ER.	SO.	BB.	ERA.
1988—Oakland................	American	3	2	0	0	.000	2	0	0	3	0	0.00

IVAN CALDERON (PEREZ)

Name pronounced Call-durh-OWN.

Born March 19, 1962, at Fajardo, Puerto Rico.
Height, 6.01. Weight, 205.
Throws and bats righthanded.

Major League stolen bases: 1984 (1), 1985 (4), 1986 (3), 1987 (10), 1988 (4), 1989 (7). Total—29.
Tied for Southern League lead in total bases with 267 in 1983.

Year Club	League	Pos.	G.	AB.	R.	H.	2B.	3B.	HR.	RBI.	B.A.	PO.	A.	E.	F.A.
1980—Bellingham	N'west	OF	57	195	44	62	7	*9	4	32	.318	56	4	7	.896
1981—Wausau	Midw.	OF-SS	117	402	79	123	19	1	20	62	.306	130	17	6	.961
1982—Wausau	Midw.	S-O-3-1	126	461	91	132	22	5	24	89	.286	215	202	45	.903
1983—Chattanooga	South.	OF	139	546	92	●170	34	*15	11	80	*.311	251	10	13	.953
1984—Salt Lake City†	P. C.	OF	66	255	61	93	7	9	4	45	.365	132	9	8	.946
1984—Seattle‡	Amer.	OF	11	24	2	5	1	0	1	1	.208	22	0	0	1.000
1985—Seattle	Amer.	OF-1B	67	210	37	60	16	4	8	28	.286	108	5	2	.983
1986—Seattle§-Chicago	Amer.	OF	50	164	16	41	7	1	2	15	.250	64	4	5	.932
1986—Calgary	P. C.	OF	24	81	17	27	3	0	3	18	.333	34	2	1	.973
1986—Buffalo	A. A.	OF	27	105	11	23	9	0	5	24	.219	30	1	5	.861
1987—Chicago x	Amer.	OF	144	542	93	159	38	2	28	83	.293	295	8	5	.984
1988—Chicago y	Amer.	OF	73	264	40	56	14	0	14	35	.212	141	5	7	.954
1989—Chicago	Amer.	OF-1B	157	622	83	178	34	9	14	87	.286	384	17	9	.978
Major League Totals—6 Years			502	1826	271	499	110	16	67	249	.273	1014	39	28	.974

Signed as free agent by Seattle Mariners' organization, July 30, 1979.
†On disabled list, May 25 to July 2, 1984.
‡On disabled list, August 26 to September 12, 1984.
§Traded to Chicago White Sox' organization, July 1, 1986, completing deal in which Chicago traded Catcher Scott Bradley to Seattle Mariners for a player to be named later, June 26, 1986.
xOn disabled list, May 16 to May 31, 1987.
yOn disabled list, June 27 to July 12 and July 31, 1988 through remainder of season.

ERNIE CARLOS CAMACHO

Born February 1, 1956, at Salinas, Calif.
Height, 6.01. Weight, 180.
Throws and bats righthanded.
Attended Hartnell Junior College, Salinas, Calif.

Major League saves: 1984 (23), 1986 (20), 1987 (1), 1988 (1). Total—45.

Year Club	League	G.	IP.	W.	L.	Pct.	H.	R.	ER.	SO.	BB.	ERA.
1976—Modesto	California	10	56	3	4	.429	69	47	35	29	39	5.63
1977—Modesto†	California	5	32	2	1	.667	30	19	14	21	23	3.94
1977—Chattanooga	Southern	11	60	3	8	.273	74	50	43	20	28	6.45
1978—Modesto‡	California	1	2	0	0	.000	0	0	0	2	2	0.00
1979—Ogden	P. Coast	21	97	7	9	.438	102	86	71	60	70	6.59
1980—Ogden	P. Coast	33	64	5	3	.625	60	29	28	58	26	3.94
1980—Oakland§	American	5	12	0	0	.000	20	9	9	9	5	6.75
1981—Portland x	P. Coast	18	38	2	3	.400	45	24	20	31	22	4.74
1981—Pittsburgh y	National	7	22	0	1	.000	23	13	12	11	15	4.91
1982—Edmonton zab	P. Coast	7	19⅔	0	0	.000	10	8	7	18	16	3.20
1982—Mexico City Reds	Mexican	15	20⅓	3	1	.750	21	12	12	15	6	5.31
1982—Rochester c	Int'national	8	17⅔	0	1	.000	16	7	4	11	10	2.04
1983—Vancouver d	P. Coast	11	23⅔	0	2	.000	31	21	18	16	12	6.85
1983—Charleston	Int'national	24	33⅓	4	0	1.000	19	5	5	27	17	1.35
1983—Cleveland	American	4	5⅓	0	1	.000	5	3	3	2	2	5.06
1984—Cleveland	American	69	100	5	9	.357	83	31	27	48	37	2.43
1985—Cleveland e	American	2	3⅓	0	1	.000	4	3	3	2	1	8.10
1986—Cleveland f	American	51	57⅓	2	4	.333	60	26	26	36	31	4.08
1987—Cleveland	American	15	13⅔	0	1	.000	21	14	14	9	5	9.22
1987—Buffalo g	Am. Assoc.	23	29⅓	1	3	.250	33	14	6	18	16	1.84
1988—Tucson	P. Coast	36	42⅓	1	5	.167	47	24	20	26	27	4.25
1988—Houston h	National	13	17⅔	0	3	.000	25	15	15	13	12	7.64
1989—Phoenix	P. Coast	40	55	3	0	1.000	33	10	9	59	16	1.47
1989—San Francisco	National	13	16⅓	3	0	1.000	10	5	5	14	11	2.76
American League Totals—6 Years		146	191⅔	7	16	.304	193	86	82	106	81	3.85
National League Totals—3 Years		33	56	3	4	.429	58	33	32	38	38	5.14
Major League Totals—9 Years		179	247⅔	10	20	.333	251	119	114	144	119	4.14

Selected by Pittsburgh Pirates' organization in 12th round of free-agent draft, June 4, 1975.
Selected by California Angels' organization in secondary phase of free-agent draft, January 7, 1976.
Selected by Oakland A's organization in secondary phase of free-agent draft, June 8, 1976.
†On disabled list, April 23 to June 14, 1977.
‡On Jersey City temporary inactive list, April 14 to July 18, 1978; on Modesto temporary inactive list, July 18 to August 30, 1978.
§Traded to Pittsburgh Pirates, April 10, 1981, completing deal in which Pittsburgh traded Pitcher Bob Owchinko to Oakland A's for cash and player to be named later, April 6, 1981.
xOn disabled list, June 23 to July 15, 1981.
yTraded with Infielder Vance Law to Chicago White Sox for Pitchers Ross Baumgarten and Butch Edge, March 21, 1982.
zOn suspended list, April 5 to April 25, 1982.
aLoaned to Mexico City Reds, May 16, 1982; returned, August 2, 1982.
bLoaned to Rochester (Baltimore Orioles' organization), August 5, 1982; returned, September 17, 1982.

cGranted free agency, October 22, 1982; signed by Vancouver (Milwaukee Brewers' organization), December 19, 1982.

dTraded with Outfielder Gorman Thomas and Pitcher Jamie Easterly to Cleveland Indians for Outfielder Rick Manning and Pitcher Rick Waits, June 6, 1983.

eOn disabled list, April 13, 1985 through remainder of season.

fOn disabled list, May 14 to May 29, 1986.

gGranted free agency, October 15, 1987; signed by Houston Astros, March 10, 1988.

hGranted free agency, October 15, 1988; signed by Phoenix (San Francisco Giants' organization), February 27, 1989.

KENNETH GENE CAMINITI
(Ken)

Born April 21, 1963, at Hanford, Calif.
Height, 6.00. Weight, 200.
Throws right and bats left and righthanded.
Attended San Jose State University, San Jose, Calif.

Major League stolen bases: 1989 (4).
Led Pacific Coast League third basemen in double plays with 25 and total chances with 382 in 1988.
Led Southern League third basemen in double plays with 34 in 1986.
Named third baseman on THE SPORTING NEWS College Baseball All-America Team, 1984.

Year Club	League	Pos.	G.	AB.	R.	H.	2B.	3B.	HR.	RBI.	B.A.	PO.	A.	E.	F.A.
1985—Osceola	Fla. St.	3B	126	468	83	133	26	9	4	73	.284	53	193	20	.925
1986—Columbus	South.	3B	137	513	82	154	29	3	12	81	.300	105	*299	33	.924
1987—Columbus	South.	3B	95	375	66	122	25	2	15	69	.325	55	205	21	.925
1987—Houston	Nat.	3B	63	203	10	50	7	1	3	23	.246	50	98	8	.949
1988—Tucson	P. C.	3B	109	416	54	113	24	7	5	66	.272	*105	*250	27	.929
1988—Houston	Nat.	3B	30	83	5	15	2	0	1	7	.181	12	43	3	.948
1989—Houston	Nat.	3B	161	585	71	149	31	3	10	72	.255	126	335	22	.954
Major League Totals—3 Years			254	871	86	214	40	4	14	102	.246	188	476	33	.953

Selected by Houston Astros' organization in 3rd round of free-agent draft, June 4, 1984.

MICHAEL THOMAS CAMPBELL
(Mike)

Born February 17, 1964, at Seattle, Wash.
Height, 6.03. Weight, 210.
Throws and bats righthanded.
Attended University of Hawaii, Honolulu, Haw.

Named Pacific Coast League Player of the Year, 1987.

Year Club	League	G.	IP.	W.	L.	Pct.	H.	R.	ER.	SO.	BB.	ERA.
1985—Salinas	California	10	50	4	4	.500	41	22	18	50	22	3.24
1986—Chattanooga	Southern	12	75	9	1	*.900	69	32	29	80	22	3.48
1986—Calgary†	P. Coast	1	3	0	1	.000	1	3	3	3	2	9.00
1987—Calgary	P. Coast	24	162⅔	*15	2	*.882	136	65	48	130	72	2.66
1987—Seattle	American	9	49⅓	1	4	.200	41	29	26	35	25	4.74
1988—Seattle	American	20	114⅔	6	10	.375	128	81	75	63	43	5.89
1988—Calgary	P. Coast	10	70⅓	4	4	.500	80	35	35	38	26	4.48
1989—Seattle	American	5	21	1	2	.333	28	22	17	6	10	7.29
1989—Calgary‡	P. Coast	16	96	6	5	.545	102	48	44	61	29	4.13
1989—Indianapolis	Am. Assoc.	9	27	1	0	1.000	23	12	12	18	4	4.00
Major League Totals—3 Years		34	185	8	16	.333	197	132	118	104	78	5.74

Selected by Atlanta Braves' organization in 5th round of free-agent draft, June 7, 1982.
Selected by Seattle Mariners' organization in 1st round (seventh player selected) of free-agent draft, June 3, 1985.
†On disabled list, June 26, 1986 through remainder of season.
‡Traded to Indianapolis (Montreal Expos' organization), July 31, 1989, completing deal in which Seattle Mariners traded Pitcher Mark Langston and a player to be named later to Montreal Expos for Pitchers Randy Johnson, Brian Holman and Gene Harris, May 25, 1989.

SILVESTRE CAMPUSANO
(Sil)

Born December 31, 1966, at Mano Guayabo, D. R.
Height, 6.00. Weight, 175.
Throws and bats righthanded.

Tied for Gulf Coast League lead in stolen bases with 21 in 1984.
Tied for International League lead in caught stealing with 15 in 1987.
Led Southern League outfielders in total chances with 437 and tied for lead in double plays with 6 in 1986.
Led South Atlantic League outfielders in double plays with 5 in 1985.
Named South Atlantic League Most Valuable Player, 1985.

Year Club	League	Pos.	G.	AB.	R.	H.	2B.	3B.	HR.	RBI.	B.A.	PO.	A.	E.	F.A.
1984—Bradenton Jays	Appal.	OF	●63	236	42	63	17	2	0	22	.267	128	7	*8	.944
1985—Florence	S. Atl.	OF	88	348	80	109	31	1	15	56	.313	188	12	4	.980
1985—Knoxville	South.	OF	45	178	30	54	9	0	6	29	.303	135	3	4	.972
1986—Knoxville	South.	OF	132	493	89	126	32	6	14	59	.256	*401	21	15	.966
1987—Syracuse	Int.	OF	129	481	70	127	28	●10	14	63	.264	324	8	*11	.968
1988—Toronto†	Amer.	OF	73	142	14	31	10	2	2	12	.218	111	2	8	.934
1988—Syracuse	Int.	OF	17	62	8	13	3	0	0	3	.210	44	0	1	.978

Year Club	League	Pos.	G.	AB.	R.	H.	2B.	3B.	HR.	RBI.	B.A.	PO.	A.	E.	F.A.
1989—Syracuse‡	Int.	OF	112	356	46	86	19	4	6	30	.242	256	9	5	.981
Major League Totals—1 Year..................			73	142	14	31	10	2	2	12	.218	111	2	8	.934

Signed as free agent by Toronto Blue Jays' organization, November 14, 1983.

†On disabled list, August 4 to September 2, 1988; included rehabilitation disability assignment to Syracuse, August 19 to September 2, 1988.

‡Drafted by Philadelphia Phillies, December 4, 1989.

GEORGE ANTHONY CANALE IV

Born August 11, 1965, at Memphis, Tenn.
Height, 6.01. Weight, 190.
Throws right and bats lefthanded.
Attended Virginia Tech, Blacksburg, Va.

Led American Association batters in strikeouts with 134 and total bases with 245 in 1989.
Led Texas League batters in strikeouts with 152 in 1988.
Led Pioneer League in bases on balls received with 54 in 1986.
Led American Association first basemen in total chances with 1,391 and double plays with 122 in 1989.
Led Texas League first basemen in double plays with 106 in 1988.
Led Pioneer League first basemen in double plays with 47 in 1986.
Named first baseman on THE SPORTING NEWS College Baseball All-America Team, 1986.

Year Club	League	Pos.	G.	AB.	R.	H.	2B.	3B.	HR.	RBI.	B.A.	PO.	A.	E.	F.A.
1986—Helena	Pion.	1B	65	221	48	72	19	0	9	49	.326	★554	29	6	★.990
1987—El Paso	Texas	1B	65	253	38	65	10	2	7	36	.257	639	35	3	.996
1987—Stockton	Calif.	1B	66	246	42	69	18	1	7	48	.280	615	33	4	.994
1988—El Paso	Texas	1B-3B-OF	132	496	77	120	23	2	23	93	.242	1231	71	12	.991
1989—Denver	A. A.	★1B-3B	●144	503	80	140	33	●9	18	71	.278	★1287	★94	10	★.993
1989—Milwaukee.............	Amer.	1B	13	26	5	5	1	0	1	3	.192	86	4	1	.989
Major League Totals—1 Year..................			13	26	5	5	1	0	1	3	.192	86	4	1	.989

Selected by Milwaukee Brewers' organization in 6th round of free-agent draft, June 2, 1986.

JOHN ROBERT CANDELARIA

Born November 6, 1953, at Brooklyn, N.Y.
Height, 6.06. Weight, 225.
Throws left and bats righthanded.

Pitched 2-0 no-hit victory against Los Angeles Dodgers, August 9, 1976.
Major League saves: 1976 (1), 1978 (1), 1980 (1), 1982 (1), 1984 (2), 1985 (9), 1988 (1). Total—16.
Tied for National League lead in home runs allowed with 29 in 1977.
Led Carolina League in home runs allowed with 17 in 1974.
Named American League Comeback Player of the Year by THE SPORTING NEWS, 1986.
Received reported $40,000 bonus to sign with Pittsburgh Pirates, 1973.

Year Club	League	G.	IP.	W.	L.	Pct.	H.	R.	ER.	SO.	BB.	ERA.
1973—Charleston	W. Carol.	18	95	10	2	★.833	84	45	40	60	38	3.79
1974—Salem	Carolina	25	154	11	8	.579	146	80	63	147	63	3.68
1974—Charleston	Int'national	1	11	0	0	.000	7	2	2	10	1	1.64
1975—Charleston	Int'national	10	61	7	1	.875	53	15	12	48	17	1.77
1975—Pittsburgh..	National	18	121	8	6	.571	95	47	37	95	36	2.75
1976—Pittsburgh..	National	32	220	16	7	.696	173	87	77	138	60	3.15
1977—Pittsburgh..	National	33	231	20	5	★.800	197	64	60	133	52	★2.34
1978—Pittsburgh..	National	30	189	12	11	.522	191	73	68	94	49	3.24
1979—Pittsburgh..	National	33	207	14	9	.609	201	83	74	101	41	3.22
1980—Pittsburgh..	National	35	233	11	14	.440	246	114	104	97	50	4.02
1981—Pittsburgh†	National	6	41	2	2	.500	42	17	16	14	11	3.51
1982—Pittsburgh..	National	31	174⅔	12	7	.632	166	62	57	133	37	2.94
1983—Pittsburgh..	National	33	197⅔	15	8	.652	191	73	71	157	45	3.23
1984—Pittsburgh..	National	33	185⅓	12	11	.522	179	69	56	133	34	2.72
1985—Pittsburgh‡	National	37	54⅓	2	4	.333	57	23	22	47	14	3.64
1985—California	American	13	71	7	3	.700	70	33	30	53	24	3.80
1986—California§	American	16	91⅔	10	2	.833	68	30	26	81	26	2.55
1986—Palm Springs	California	2	7	0	0	.000	4	2	2	8	2	2.57
1987—California xy	American	20	116⅔	8	6	.571	127	70	61	74	20	4.71
1987—New York z	National	3	12⅓	2	0	1.000	17	8	8	10	3	5.84
1988—New York	American	25	157	13	7	.650	150	69	59	121	23	3.38
1989—New York a	American	10	49	3	3	.500	49	28	28	37	12	5.14
1989—Sarasota Yankees b	Gulf Coast	2	8	1	0	1.000	6	0	0	12	1	0.00
1989—Montreal	National	12	16⅓	0	2	.000	17	8	6	14	4	3.31
National League Totals—13 Years.....................		336	1882⅔	126	86	.594	1772	728	656	1166	434	3.14
American League Totals—5 Years		84	485⅓	41	21	.661	464	230	204	366	105	3.78
Major League Totals—15 Years...........................		420	2368	167	107	.609	2236	958	860	1532	539	3.27

Selected by Pittsburgh Pirates' organization in 2nd round of free-agent draft, June 6, 1972.

†On disabled list, May 11, 1981 through remainder of season.

‡Traded with Pitcher Al Holland and Outfielder George Hendrick to California Angels for Pitcher Pat Clements, Outfielder Mike Brown and a player to be named later, August 2, 1985; Pittsburgh Pirates' organization acquired Pitcher Bob Kipper to complete deal, August 16, 1985.

§On disabled list, April 15 to July 8, 1986; included rehabilitation disability assignment to Palm Springs, June 26 to July 2, 1986.

xOn disabled list, May 14 to May 29 and June 19 to August 5, 1987.

yTraded to New York Mets for Pitchers Shane Young and Jeff Richardson, September 15, 1987.

zGranted free agency, November 9, 1987; signed by New York Yankees, January 15, 1988.

aOn disabled list, May 6 to August 19, 1989; included rehabilitation disability assignment to Sarasota Yankees, August 11 to August 19, 1989.

bTraded to Montreal Expos for a player to be named later, August 29, 1989; New York Yankees acquired Third Baseman Mike Blowers to complete deal, August 31, 1989.

CHAMPIONSHIP SERIES RECORD

Shares Championship Series records for most strikeouts (14) and most consecutive strikeouts (4), game, October 7, 1975.

Year Club	League	G.	IP.	W.	L.	Pct.	H.	R.	ER.	SO.	BB.	ERA.
1975—Pittsburgh	National	1	7⅔	0	0	.000	3	3	3	14	2	3.52
1979—Pittsburgh	National	1	7	0	0	.000	5	2	2	4	1	2.57
1986—California	American	2	10⅔	1	1	.500	11	8	1	7	6	0.84
Championship Series Totals—3 Years		4	25⅓	1	1	.500	19	13	6	25	9	2.13

WORLD SERIES RECORD

Year Club	League	G.	IP.	W.	L.	Pct.	H.	R.	ER.	SO.	BB.	ERA.
1979—Pittsburgh	National	2	9	1	1	.500	14	6	5	4	2	5.00

ALL-STAR GAME RECORD

Member of National League All-Star Team in 1977; did not play.

THOMAS CAESAR CANDIOTTI
(Tom)

Born August 31, 1957, at Walnut Creek, Calif.
Height, 6.02. Weight, 200.
Throws and bats righthanded.
Received bachelor of science degree in business administration
from St. Mary's College, Moraga, Calif., in 1979.
Brother-in-law of Brad Wellman, infielder with Kansas City Royals.

Led American League in complete games with 17 in 1986.

Year Club	League	G.	IP.	W.	L.	Pct.	H.	R.	ER.	SO.	BB.	ERA.
1979—Victoria†	Northwest	12	70	5	1	.833	63	23	19	66	16	2.44
1980—Fort Myers	Florida St.	7	44	3	2	.600	32	16	11	31	9	2.25
1980—Jacksonville‡§	Southern	17	117	7	8	.467	98	45	36	93	40	2.77
1981—El Paso x	Texas	21	119	7	6	.538	137	51	37	68	27	2.80
1982—Vancouver y	P. Coast					(Did not play)						
1983—El Paso	Texas	7	24⅔	1	0	1.000	23	10	8	18	7	2.92
1983—Vancouver	P. Coast	15	99⅓	6	4	.600	87	35	31	61	16	2.81
1983—Milwaukee	American	10	55⅔	4	4	.500	62	21	20	21	16	3.23
1984—Vancouver z	P. Coast	15	96⅔	8	4	.667	96	36	31	53	22	2.89
1984—Milwaukee a	American	8	32⅓	2	2	.500	38	21	19	23	10	5.29
1984—Beloit	Midwest	2	10	0	1	.000	12	5	3	12	5	2.70
1985—El Paso	Texas	4	29⅓	1	0	1.000	29	11	9	16	7	2.76
1985—Vancouver b	P. Coast	24	150⅔	9	13	.409	178	83	66	97	36	3.94
1986—Cleveland	American	36	252⅓	16	12	.571	234	112	100	167	106	3.57
1987—Cleveland	American	32	201⅔	7	18	.280	193	132	107	111	93	4.78
1988—Cleveland c	American	31	216⅔	14	8	.636	225	86	79	137	53	3.28
1989—Cleveland d	American	31	206	13	10	.565	188	80	71	124	55	3.10
Major League Totals—6 Years		148	964⅔	56	54	.509	940	452	396	583	333	3.69

Signed as free-agent by Victoria (Independent), July 17, 1979.

†Released, January 4, 1980; signed by Ft. Myers (Kansas City Royals' organization), January 5, 1980.

‡On disabled list, June 7 to June 26, 1980.

§Drafted by Vancouver (Milwaukee Brewers' organization), December 9, 1980.

xOn disabled list, April 10 to May 12, 1981.

yOn disabled list, April 13, 1982 through remainder of season.

zOn disabled list, May 30 to June 15, 1984.

aOn disabled list, August 2 to September 1, 1984; included rehabilitation disability assignment to Beloit, August 24 to August 31, 1984.

bGranted free agency, October 15, 1985; signed by Cleveland Indians, December 12, 1985.

cOn disabled list, August 4 to August 19, 1988.

dOn disabled list, July 2 to July 17, 1989.

JOHN ANTHONY CANGELOSI

Born March 10, 1963, at Brooklyn, N.Y.
Height, 5.08. Weight, 150.
Throws left and bats right and lefthanded.
Attended Miami-Dade Community College (North), Miami, Fla.

Holds American League record for most stolen bases by rookie (50), 1986.
Major League stolen bases: 1986 (50), 1987 (21), 1988 (9), 1989 (11). Total—91.
Led Eastern League in bases on balls received with 101 in 1984.
Led Midwest League in stolen bases with 87 and caught stealing with 35 in 1983.
Tied for New York-Pennsylvania League lead in bases on balls received with 56 in 1982.

Year Club	League	Pos.	G.	AB.	R.	H.	2B.	3B.	HR.	RBI.	B.A.	PO.	A.	E.	F.A.
1982—Niagara Falls	NYP	OF	•76	277	60	80	15	4	5	38	.289	118	5	4	.969
1983—Appleton	Midw.	OF	128	439	87	124	12	4	1	48	.282	262	10	6	.978
1984—Glens Falls†	East.	OF	138	464	91	133	17	1	1	38	.287	310	11	11	.967

Year Club League	Pos.	G.	AB.	R.	H.	2B.	3B.	HR.	RBI.	B.A.	PO.	A.	E.	F.A.
1985—Mex. City Reds..... Mex.	OF	61	201	46	71	9	4	1	30	.353	127	7	6	.957
1985—Chicago .... Amer.	OF	5	2	2	0	0	0	0	0	.000	1	0	0	1.000
1985—Buffalo.................... A. A.	OF	78	244	34	58	8	5	1	21	.238	148	9	2	.987
1986—Chicago‡ .... Amer.	OF	137	438	65	103	16	3	2	32	.235	276	7	9	.969
1987—Pittsburgh.............. Nat.	OF	104	182	44	50	8	3	4	18	.275	74	3	3	.962
1988—Pittsburgh§............. Nat.	OF-P	75	118	18	30	4	1	0	8	.254	52	0	2	.963
1988—Buffalo.................... A. A.	OF	37	145	23	48	6	0	0	10	.331	89	3	0	1.000
1989—Pittsburgh.............. Nat.	OF	112	160	18	35	4	2	0	9	.219	71	1	2	.973
American League Totals—2 Years		142	440	67	103	16	3	2	32	.234	277	7	9	.969
National League Totals—3 Years............		291	460	80	115	16	6	4	35	.250	197	4	7	.966
Major League Totals—5 Years................		433	900	147	218	32	9	6	67	.242	474	11	16	.968

Selected by Chicago White Sox' organization in 4th round of free-agent draft, January 12, 1982.

†Loaned with Infielder Manny Salinas to Mexico City Reds, March 4, 1985, as part of deal in which Infielder Nelson Barrera was purchased by Chicago White Sox; returned, June 1, 1985.

‡Traded to Pittsburgh Pirates, March 30, 1987, completing deal in which Pittsburgh traded Pitcher Jim Winn to Chicago White Sox for a player to be named later, March 27, 1987.

§On disabled list, June 6 to June 27, 1988; included rehabilitation disability assignment to Buffalo, June 20 to June 27, 1988.

PITCHING RECORD

Year Club	League	G.	IP.	W.	L.	Pct.	H.	R.	ER.	SO.	BB.	ERA.
1988—Pittsburgh......................	National	1	2	0	0	.000	1	0	0	0	0	0.00

JOSELITO SORIANO CANO
(Jose)

Born March 7, 1962, at Boca de Soco, D. R.
Height, 6.03. Weight, 175.
Throws and bats righthanded.
Named Florida State League Most Valuable Player, 1987.

Year Club	League	G.	IP.	W.	L.	Pct.	H.	R.	ER.	SO.	BB.	ERA.
1980—Bradenton Yankees†‡..................	Gulf Coast	3	3	0	0	.000	8	7	6	2	3	18.00
1981-82..						(Out of Organized Baseball)						
1983—Anderson	S. Atlantic	20	111⅔	5	8	.385	112	70	51	59	33	4.11
1984—Durham§x	Carolina	20	81⅓	4	5	.444	68	35	28	53	29	3.10
1985-86..						(Out of Organized Baseball)						
1987—Osceola	Florida St.	24	167⅓	15	3	●.833	137	50	36	99	47	*1.94
1988—Tucson y	P. Coast	4	21	2	1	.667	24	11	10	11	6	4.29
1989—Columbus	Southern	3	17	1	1	.500	16	8	6	12	4	3.18
1989—Tucson	P. Coast	15	95	5	5	.500	87	37	30	57	27	2.84
1989—Houston	National	6	23	1	1	.500	24	13	13	8	7	5.09
Major League Totals—1 Year..................		6	23	1	1	.500	24	13	13	8	7	5.09

Signed as free agent by New York Yankees' organization, March 10, 1980.

†Released, August 6, 1980; signed by Bradenton (Atlanta Braves' organization), December 1, 1981.

‡Released, June 4, 1982; re-signed by Braves' organization, January 20, 1983.

§On disabled list, July 20 to July 30 and August 5, 1984 through remainder of season.

xReleased, April 4, 1985; signed by Houston Astros' organization, April 15, 1987.

yOn disabled list, April 26, 1988 through remainder of season.

JOSE CANSECO JR.
Name pronounced CON-seko.

Born July 2, 1964, at Havana, Cuba.
Height, 6.03. Weight, 230.
Throws and bats righthanded.
Identical twin of Ozzie Canseco, outfielder in Oakland Athletics' organization.
Major League stolen bases: 1985 (1), 1986 (15), 1987 (15), 1988 (40), 1989 (6). Total—77.
Hit three home runs in a game, July 3, 1988.
Led American League in slugging percentage with .569 in 1988.
Led Northwest League batters in strikeouts with 78 in 1983.
Led California League outfielders in double plays with 8 in 1984.
Named American League Player of the Year by THE SPORTING NEWS, 1988.
Named American League Most Valuable Player by Baseball Writers' Association of America, 1988.
Named outfielder on THE SPORTING NEWS American League All-Star Team, 1988.
Named outfielder on THE SPORTING NEWS American League Silver Slugger team, 1988.
Named American League Rookie Player of the Year by THE SPORTING NEWS, 1986.
Named American League Rookie of the Year by Baseball Writers' Association of America, 1986.
Named Minor League Player of the Year by THE SPORTING NEWS, 1985.
Named Southern League Most Valuable Player, 1985.

Year Club League	Pos.	G.	AB.	R.	H.	2B.	3B.	HR.	RBI.	B.A.	PO.	A.	E.	F.A.
1982—Miami .... Fla. St.	3B	6	9	0	1	0	0	0	0	.111	3	1	1	.800
1982—Idaho Falls........... Pion.	3B-OF	28	57	13	15	3	0	2	7	.263	6	17	3	.885
1983—Madison .... Midw.	OF	34	88	8	14	4	0	3	10	.159	23	2	1	.962
1983—Medford .... N'west	OF	59	197	34	53	15	2	11	40	.269	46	5	5	.911
1984—Modesto................. Calif.	OF	116	410	61	113	21	2	15	73	.276	216	17	9	.963
1985—Huntsville† .... South.	OF	58	211	47	67	10	2	25	80	.318	117	9	7	.947
1985—Tacoma.................. P.C.	OF	60	233	41	81	16	1	11	47	.348	81	7	2	.978
1985—Oakland................. Amer.	OF	29	96	16	29	3	0	5	13	.302	56	2	3	.951

Year	Club	League	Pos.	G.	AB.	R.	H.	2B.	3B.	HR.	RBI.	B.A.	PO.	A.	E.	F.A.
1986—Oakland		Amer.	OF	157	600	85	144	29	1	33	117	.240	319	4	●14	.958
1987—Oakland		Amer.	OF	159	630	81	162	35	3	31	113	.257	263	12	7	.975
1988—Oakland		Amer.	OF	158	610	120	187	34	0	★42	★124	.307	304	11	7	.978
1989—Huntsville‡		South.	OF	9	29	2	6	0	0	0	3	.207	9	0	0	1.000
1989—Oakland		Amer.	OF	65	227	40	61	9	1	17	57	.269	119	5	3	.976
Major League Totals—5 Years				568	2163	342	583	110	5	128	424	.270	1061	34	34	.970

Selected by Oakland A's organization in 15th round of free-agent draft, June 7, 1982.
†On disabled list, May 14 to June 3, 1985.
‡On Oakland disabled list, March 23 to July 13, 1989; included rehabilitation disability assignment to Huntsville, May 6, 1989 and June 28 to July 13, 1989.

CHAMPIONSHIP SERIES RECORD

Shares American League Championship Series record for most home runs, series (3), 1988.

Year	Club	League	Pos.	G.	AB.	R.	H.	2B.	3B.	HR.	RBI.	B.A.	PO.	A.	E.	F.A.
1988—Oakland		Amer.	OF	4	16	4	5	1	0	3	4	.313	6	0	0	1.000
1989—Oakland		Amer.	OF-PH	5	17	1	5	0	0	1	3	.294	6	1	1	.875
Championship Series Totals—2 Years				9	33	5	10	1	0	4	7	.303	12	1	1	.929

WORLD SERIES RECORD

Shares World Series records for hitting home run in first series at-bat, October 15, 1988; most grand slams, game (1), October 15, 1988; most runs batted in, inning (4), October 15, 1988, second inning.

Year	Club	League	Pos.	G.	AB.	R.	H.	2B.	3B.	HR.	RBI.	B.A.	PO.	A.	E.	F.A.
1988—Oakland		Amer.	OF	5	19	1	1	0	0	1	5	.053	8	0	0	1.000
1989—Oakland		Amer.	OF	4	14	5	5	0	0	1	3	.357	6	0	0	1.000
World Series Totals—2 Years				9	33	6	6	0	0	2	8	.182	14	0	0	1.000

ALL-STAR GAME RECORD

Year	League	Pos.	AB.	R.	H.	2B.	3B.	HR.	RBI.	B.A.	PO.	A.	E.	F.A.
1988—American		OF	4	0	0	0	0	0	0	.000	3	0	0	1.000

Member of American League All-Star Team in 1986; did not play.
Named to American League All-Star Team for 1989 game; did not play due to injury.

OSVALDO CAPAS CANSECO
(Ozzie)

Born July 2, 1964, at Havana, Cuba.
Height, 6.02. Weight, 210.
Throws and bats righthanded.
Attended Miami-Dade Community College (South), Miami, Fla.
Identical twin of Jose Canseco, outfielder with Oakland Athletics.

Year	Club	League	Pos.	G.	AB.	R.	H.	2B.	3B.	HR.	RBI.	B.A.	PO.	A.	E.	F.A.
1983—Greensboro		S. Atl.	P	27	0	0	0	0	0	0	0	.000	2	15	4	.810
1984—Greensboro†		S. Atl.	P-OF	8	1	1	0	0	0	0	0	.000	3	1	2	.667
1984—Oneonta		NYP	P	14	0	0	0	0	0	0	0	.000	4	6	3	.769
1985—Fort Lauderdale		Fla. St.	P	11	0	0	0	0	0	0	0	.000	0	6	3	.667
1985—Sarasota Yankees		Gulf C.	P-OF	20	39	2	7	0	1	1	5	.179	4	15	4	.826
1986—Sarasota Yanks‡		Gulf C.	P	7	15	3	2	1	0	1	3	.133	4	0	1	.800
1986—Madison		Midw.	OF-P-1B	42	128	17	20	1	1	3	17	.156	72	1	2	.973
1987—Madison		Midw.	OF	92	309	64	82	12	4	11	54	.265	131	6	13	.913
1988—Madison		Midw.	OF	99	359	63	98	17	7	12	68	.273	187	9	5	.975
1988—Huntsville		South.	OF	27	99	6	22	7	0	3	12	.222	29	0	1	.967
1989—Huntsville§		South.	OF-P	91	317	52	74	17	2	12	52	.233	148	8	4	.975

Selected by New York Yankees' organization in 2nd round of free-agent draft, January 11, 1983.
†On temporary inactive list, April 18 to May 14 and June 2 to June 6, 1984.
‡Released, July 4, 1986; signed by Oakland Athletics' organization, July 10, 1986.
§On Oakland disabled list, March 19 to April 27, 1989.

RECORD AS PITCHER

Year	Club	League	G.	IP.	W.	L.	Pct.	H.	R.	ER.	SO.	BB.	ERA.
1983—Greensboro		S. Atlantic	27	87⅓	3	6	.333	98	62	49	59	49	5.05
1984—Greensboro		S. Atlantic	6	16⅔	1	1	.500	19	13	9	9	22	4.86
1984—Oneonta		NYP	14	43⅓	1	6	.143	44	29	17	40	21	3.53
1985—Fort Lauderdale		Florida St.	11	57⅓	5	4	.556	42	33	23	37	42	3.61
1985—Sarasota Yankees		Gulf Coast	13	84⅔	5	4	.556	93	37	29	48	11	3.08
1986—Madison		Midwest	2	4	1	0	1.000	2	0	0	3	2	0.00
1989—Huntsville		Southern	3	5	0	0	.000	5	4	4	1	1	7.20

DONALD WAYNE CARMAN
(Don)

Born August 14, 1959, at Oklahoma City, Okla.
Height, 6.03. Weight, 201.
Throws and bats lefthanded.
Attended Seminole Junior College, Seminole, Okla.,
and University of Oklahoma, Norman, Okla.

Shares National League records for fewest games lost for leader, season (15), 1989; most consecutive home runs allowed, inning (3), April 17, 1989, third inning.

Major League saves: 1983 (1), 1985 (7), 1986 (1). Total—9.

Year Club	League	G.	IP.	W.	L.	Pct.	H.	R.	ER.	SO.	BB.	ERA.
1979—Spartanburg	W. Carol.	37	78	6	3	.667	72	36	34	70	28	3.92
1980—Peninsula	Carolina	27	150	14	5	.737	149	73	57	★141	53	3.42
1981—Reading	Eastern	28	176	12	13	.480	167	93	79	105	75	4.04
1982—Oklahoma City	Am. Assoc.	10	33	0	1	.000	37	29	25	29	23	6.82
1982—Reading	Eastern	20	97⅓	6	7	.462	99	58	45	81	62	4.16
1983—Reading	Eastern	★56	124⅓	8	5	.615	85	51	41	93	71	2.97
1983—Philadelphia	National	1	1	0	0	.000	0	0	0	0	0	0.00
1984—Portland	P. Coast	39	55⅔	3	3	.500	66	36	33	53	22	5.34
1984—Philadelphia	National	11	13⅓	0	1	.000	14	9	8	16	6	5.40
1985—Philadelphia	National	71	86⅓	9	4	.692	52	25	20	87	38	2.08
1986—Philadelphia	National	50	134⅓	10	5	.667	113	50	48	98	52	3.22
1987—Philadelphia	National	35	211	13	11	.542	194	110	99	125	69	4.22
1988—Philadelphia	National	36	201⅓	10	14	.417	211	101	96	116	70	4.29
1989—Philadelphia	National	49	149⅓	5	●15	.250	152	98	87	81	86	5.24
Major League Totals—7 Years		253	796⅔	47	50	.485	736	393	358	523	321	4.04

Signed as free agent by Philadelphia Phillies' organization, August 25, 1978.

GREGORIO CARMONA
(Greg)

Born May 9, 1968, at Bani, Dominican Republic.
Height, 6.00. Weight, 150.
Throws right and bats left and righthanded.
Led Appalachian League in bases on balls received with 50 in 1987.

Year Club	League	Pos.	G.	AB.	R.	H.	2B.	3B.	HR.	RBI.	B.A.	PO.	A.	E.	F.A.
1987—Johnson City	Appal.	3B-2B-SS	47	120	35	21	4	1	0	9	.175	40	87	13	.907
1988—Johnson City	Appal.	SS	21	64	15	21	1	1	1	8	.328	20	71	7	.929
1988—Savannah	S. Atl.	SS	33	100	11	16	1	0	0	4	.160	51	102	16	.905
1989—St. Petersburg	Fla. St.	SS-3B	116	348	52	78	4	3	1	30	.224	152	373	48	.916

Signed as free agent by St. Louis Cardinals' organization, October 14, 1986.

CRIS HOWELL CARPENTER

Born April 5, 1965, at St. Augustine, Fla.
Height, 6.01. Weight, 185.
Throws and bats righthanded.
Attended University of Georgia, Athens, Ga.
Received reported $160,000 bonus to sign with St. Louis Cardinals, 1987.

Year Club	League	G.	IP.	W.	L.	Pct.	H.	R.	ER.	SO.	BB.	ERA.
1988—Louisville	Am. Assoc.	13	87⅓	6	2	.750	81	28	28	45	26	2.87
1988—St. Louis	National	8	47⅔	2	3	.600	56	27	25	24	9	4.72
1989—St. Louis	National	36	68	4	4	.500	70	30	24	35	26	3.18
1989—Louisville	Am. Assoc.	27	36⅔	5	3	.625	39	17	13	29	9	3.19
Major League Totals—2 Years		44	115⅔	6	7	.462	126	57	49	59	35	3.81

Selected by Toronto Blue Jays' organization in 7th round of free-agent draft, June 2, 1986.
Selected by St. Louis Cardinals' organization in 1st round (14th player selected) of free-agent draft, June 2, 1987.

AMALIO RAFAEL CARRENO (ADRIAN)

Born April 11, 1964, at Chacachacare, Venezuela.
Height, 6.00. Weight, 170.
Throws and bats righthanded.

Year Club	League	G.	IP.	W.	L.	Pct.	H.	R.	ER.	SO.	BB.	ERA.
1984—Sarasota Yankees	Gulf Coast	9	33	1	6	.143	37	28	18	31	26	4.91
1985—Sarasota Yankees	Gulf Coast	1	2	0	0	.000	1	1	1	1	1	4.50
1986—Sarasota Yankees	Gulf Coast	7	47⅔	5	0	1.000	36	12	9	27	12	1.70
1986—Fort Lauderdale	Florida St.	3	15⅔	1	1	.500	16	11	7	8	7	4.02
1987—Prince William	Carolina	26	62⅓	5	2	.714	53	30	21	49	30	3.03
1987—Albany	Eastern	9	24	0	3	.000	32	23	21	18	15	7.88
1987—Columbus	Int'national	11	17⅓	1	1	.500	26	15	15	11	5	7.79
1988—Albany†-Reading	Eastern	14	59⅔	3	4	.429	60	32	27	31	32	4.07
1988—Columbus	Int'national	1	3⅓	0	0	.000	8	4	4	2	0	10.80
1989—Reading	Eastern	31	101⅔	5	7	.417	99	57	49	56	41	4.34

Signed as free agent by New York Yankees' organization, November 13, 1983.
†Traded to Philadelphia Phillies for Infielder Luis Aguayo, July 15, 1988.

MARK STEVEN CARREON

Born July 19, 1963, at Chicago, Ill.
Height, 6.00. Weight, 194.
Throws left and bats righthanded.
Son of Camilo Carreon, catcher with Chicago White Sox,
Cleveland Indians and Baltimore Orioles, 1959 through 1966.
Major League stolen bases: 1989 (2).
Led International League in game-winning RBIs with 19 in 1987 and tied for lead with 11 in 1988.
Led Carolina League in sacrifice flies with 11 in 1983.
Tied for South Atlantic League lead in game-winning RBIs with 12 in 1982.

Year Club	League	Pos.	G.	AB.	R.	H.	2B.	3B.	HR.	RBI.	B.A.	PO.	A.	E.	F.A.
1981—Kingsport...............	Appal.	OF-C	64	232	30	67	8	0	1	36	.289	101	7	4	.964
1982—Shelby....................	S. Atl.	OF	133	486	*120	160	29	6	2	79	.329	183	8	5	.974
1983—Lynchburg............	Carol.	OF	128	491	94	164	13	8	1	67	.334	173	8	14	.928
1984—Jackson	Texas	OF	119	435	64	122	14	3	1	43	.280	146	1	4	.974
1985—Tidewater..............	Int.	OF	7	15	1	2	1	0	1	2	.133	2	0	0	1.000
1985—Jackson	Texas	OF	123	447	96	140	23	5	6	51	.313	201	8	1	.995
1986—Tidewater..............	Int.	OF	115	426	62	123	23	2	10	64	.289	192	6	6	.971
1987—Tidewater..............	Int.	OF	133	525	83	164	*41	5	10	89	.312	237	8	5	.980
1987—New York.............	Nat.	OF	9	12	0	3	0	0	0	1	.250	4	0	1	.800
1988—Tidewater..............	Int.	OF	102	365	48	96	13	3	14	55	.263	111	6	2	.983
1988—New York.............	Nat.	OF	7	9	5	5	2	0	1	1	.556	1	0	0	1.000
1989—Tidewater†...........	Int.	OF-1B	32	122	22	34	4	0	1	21	.279	26	0	0	1.000
1989—New York.............	Nat.	OF	68	133	20	41	6	0	6	16	.308	57	0	1	.983
Major League Totals—3 Years.................			84	154	25	49	8	0	7	18	.318	62	0	2	.969

Selected by New York Mets' organization in 8th round of free-agent draft, June 8, 1981.

†On New York disabled list, March 28 to April 24, 1989; included rehabilitation disability assignment to Tidewater, April 5 to April 24, 1989.

MATIAS CARRILLO (GARCIA)

Born February 2, 1964, at Los Mochis Sinaloa, Mexico.
Height, 5.11. Weight, 185.
Throws and bats lefthanded.

Led Mexican League in stolen bases with 30 and tied for lead in intentional bases on balls received with 16 in 1984.
Tied for Mexican League lead in double plays by outfielders with 4 in 1985.

Year Club	League	Pos.	G.	AB.	R.	H.	2B.	3B.	HR.	RBI.	B.A.	PO.	A.	E.	F.A.
1982—Poza Rica	Mex.	OF-1B	99	301	59	93	9	5	0	29	.309	150	13	6	.964
1983—Poza Rica	Mex.	OF	91	360	54	112	13	11	6	39	.311	128	12	1	.993
1984—Mex. City Tigers..	Mex.	OF	113	442	100	154	32	6	14	76	.348	281	13	12	.961
1985—Mex. City Tigers†	Mex.	OF	126	465	114	164	21	8	20	102	.353	320	13	10	.971
1986—Nashua‡	East.	OF	15	52	3	8	1	0	0	0	.154	28	0	0	1.000
1986—Mex. City Tigers..	Mex.	OF	60	216	39	70	15	5	11	64	.324	123	6	1	.992
1987—Salem§x................	Carol.	OF	90	284	42	77	11	3	8	37	.271	55	3	3	.951
1988—El Paso..................	Texas	OF	106	396	76	118	17	2	12	55	.298	232	*18	2	*.992
1989—Denver	A. A.	OF-1B	125	400	46	104	14	4	10	43	.260	236	15	7	.973

†Sold to Hawaii (Pittsburgh Pirates' organization), December 15, 1985.
‡Loaned to Mexico City Tigers of Mexican League, May 8, 1986; returned, September, 1986.
§On suspended list, May 15 to May 29, 1988.
xDrafted by Milwaukee Brewers' organization, December 8, 1987.

GARY EDMUND CARTER

Born April 8, 1954, at Culver City, Calif.
Height, 6.02. Weight, 210.
Throws and bats righthanded.
Brother of Gordon Carter, outfielder in San Francisco Giants'
organization, 1972 and 1973.

Holds major league records for most putouts, catcher, lifetime (10,626); most chances accepted, catcher, lifetime (11,701); fewest passed balls, season, 150 or more games (1), 1978.

Shares major league records for most home runs, two consecutive games (5), September 3 and 4, 1985; most years leading league in chances accepted, catcher (8).

Holds National League records for most seasons leading league in games by catcher (6); most years leading league in putouts by catcher (8); most years leading league in chances accepted by catcher (7).

Major League stolen bases: 1974 (2), 1975 (5), 1977 (5), 1978 (10), 1979 (3), 1980 (3), 1981 (1), 1982 (2), 1983 (1), 1984 (2), 1985 (1), 1986 (1). Total—36.

Hit three home runs in a game, April 20, 1977 and September 3, 1985.

Led National League in sacrifice flies with 15 and tied for lead in game-winning RBIs with 16 and grounding into double plays with 21 in 1986.

Led National League catchers in assists with 107 in 1983.

Led National League catchers in total chances with 921 in 1977, 874 in 1978, 848 in 1979, 937 in 1980, 571 in 1981, 1,068 in 1982 and 860 in 1988.

Led National League in passed balls with 12 in 1979.

Led National League catchers in putouts with 811 in 1977, 781 in 1978, 509 in 1981, 956 in 1985 and 797 in 1988.

Led National League catchers in double plays with 14 in 1977, 9 in 1978, 12 in 1979, 14 in 1983 and 13 in 1987.

Led International League catchers in putouts with 794, assists with 65, double plays with 15 and fielding percentage with .990 in 1974.

Named National League Rookie Player of the Year by THE SPORTING NEWS, 1975.

Named catcher on THE SPORTING NEWS National League All-Star Team, 1980 through 1982 and 1984 through 1986.

Named catcher on THE SPORTING NEWS National League All-Star fielding team, 1980 through 1982.

Named catcher on THE SPORTING NEWS National League Silver Slugger team, 1981, 1982 and 1984 through 1986.

Year Club	League	Pos.	G.	AB.	R.	H.	2B.	3B.	HR.	RBI.	B.A.	PO.	A.	E.	F.A.
1972—Cocoa Expos.........	Fla.E.C.	C-1B-3B	18	71	6	17	3	0	2	9	.239	111	12	10	.925
1972—W. Palm Beach....	Fla. St.	C	20	50	9	16	2	2	0	5	.320	84	12	2	.980
1973—Quebec City	East.	C-1B-OF	130	439	65	111	16	1	15	68	.253	823	75	20	.978
1973—Peninsula..............	Int.	C	8	25	2	7	2	0	0	1	.280	5	1	0	1.000
1974—Memphis...............	Int.	C-1B-OF	135	441	62	118	14	7	23	83	.268	908	76	12	.988
1974—Montreal...............	Nat.	C-OF	9	27	5	11	0	1	1	6	.407	28	4	0	1.000
1975—Montreal...............	Nat.	OF-C-3B	144	503	58	136	20	1	17	68	.270	430	38	9	.981
1976—Montreal†.............	Nat.	C-OF	91	311	31	68	8	1	6	38	.219	364	42	2	.995

Year Club League	Pos.	G.	AB.	R.	H.	2B.	3B.	HR.	RBI.	B.A.	PO.	A.	E.	F.A.
1977—Montreal............ Nat.	*C-OF	154	522	86	148	29	2	31	84	.284	813	*101	9	.990
1978—Montreal............ Nat.	C-1B	157	533	76	136	27	1	20	72	.255	787	83	10	.989
1979—Montreal............ Nat.	C	141	505	74	143	26	5	22	75	.283	*751	*88	9	.989
1980—Montreal............ Nat.	C	154	549	76	145	25	5	29	101	.264	*822	*108	7	*.993
1981—Montreal............ Nat.	C-1B	100	374	48	94	20	2	16	68	.251	515	58	4	.993
1982—Montreal............ Nat.	C	154	557	91	163	32	1	29	97	.293	*954	*104	10	.991
1983—Montreal............ Nat.	*C-1B	145	541	63	146	37	3	17	79	.270	855	108	5	*.995
1984—Montreal‡ Nat.	C-1B	159	596	75	175	32	1	27	•106	.294	990	78	7	.993
1985—New York......... Nat.	C-1B-OF	149	555	83	156	17	1	32	100	.281	987	70	8	.992
1986—New York§........ Nat.	C-1-O-3	132	490	81	125	14	2	24	105	.255	943	70	9	.991
1987—New York......... Nat.	C-1B-OF	139	523	55	123	18	2	20	83	.235	886	70	9	.991
1988—New York......... Nat.	C-1B-3B	130	455	39	110	16	2	11	46	.242	842	58	10	.989
1989—New York x Nat.	C-1B	50	153	14	28	8	0	2	15	.183	266	31	6	.980
1989—Tidewater y .... Int.	C-1B	5	16	2	3	0	0	1	3	.188	26	1	1	.964
Major League Totals—16 Years..........		2008	7194	955	1907	329	30	304	1143	.265	11233	1111	114	.991

Selected by Montreal Expos' organization in 3rd round of free-agent draft, June 6, 1972.

†On disabled list, June 6 to July 22, 1976.

‡Traded to New York Mets for Infielder Hubie Brooks, Catcher Mike Fitzgerald, Outfielder Herm Winningham and Pitcher Floyd Youmans, December 10, 1984.

§On disabled list, August 17 to September 1, 1986.

xOn disabled list, May 10 to July 25, 1989; included rehabilitation disability assignment to Tidewater, July 19 to July 25, 1989.

yReleased, November 14, 1989.

DIVISION SERIES RECORD

Year Club League	Pos.	G.	AB.	R.	H.	2B.	3B.	HR.	RBI.	B.A.	PO.	A.	E.	F.A.
1981—Montreal............ Nat.	C	5	19	3	8	3	0	2	6	.421	21	5	0	1.000

CHAMPIONSHIP SERIES RECORD

Shares Championship Series records for most game-winning RBIs, total series (3) and series (2), 1986.

Year Club League	Pos.	G.	AB.	R.	H.	2B.	3B.	HR.	RBI.	B.A.	PO.	A.	E.	F.A.
1981—Montreal............ Nat.	C	5	16	3	7	1	0	0	0	.438	27	3	0	1.000
1986—New York......... Nat.	C	6	27	1	4	1	0	0	2	.148	42	5	0	1.000
1988—New York......... Nat.	C	7	27	0	6	1	1	0	4	.222	58	1	0	1.000
Championship Series Totals—3 Years.....		18	70	4	17	3	1	0	6	.243	127	9	0	1.000

WORLD SERIES RECORD

Year Club League	Pos.	G.	AB.	R.	H.	2B.	3B.	HR.	RBI.	B.A.	PO.	A.	E.	F.A.
1986—New York......... Nat.	C	7	29	4	8	2	0	2	9	.276	57	1	0	1.000

ALL-STAR GAME RECORD

Shares All-Star Game record for most home runs, game (2), August 9, 1981.

Year League	Pos.	AB.	R.	H.	2B.	3B.	HR.	RBI.	B.A.	PO.	A.	E.	F.A.
1975—National..............................	OF	0	0	0	0	0	0	0	.000	1	0	0	1.000
1979—National..............................	C	2	0	1	0	0	0	1	.500	6	1	0	1.000
1980—National..............................	C	1	0	0	0	0	0	0	.000	1	0	0	1.000
1981—National..............................	C	3	2	2	0	0	2	2	.667	5	1	0	1.000
1982—National..............................	C	3	0	1	0	0	0	1	.333	7	0	0	1.000
1983—National..............................	C	2	0	0	0	0	0	0	.000	3	0	0	1.000
1984—National..............................	C	2	1	1	0	0	1	1	.500	9	0	0	1.000
1986—National..............................	C	3	0	0	0	0	0	0	.000	9	0	0	1.000
1987—National..............................	C	1	0	0	0	0	0	0	.000	1	0	0	1.000
1988—National..............................	C	3	0	1	0	0	0	0	.333	3	0	0	1.000
All-Star Game Totals—10 Years..................		20	3	6	0	0	3	5	.300	45	2	0	1.000

Named to National League All-Star Team for 1985 game; replaced due to injury by Terry Kennedy.

JOSEPH CARTER
(Joe)

Born March 7, 1960, at Oklahoma City, Okla.
Height, 6.03. Weight, 215.
Throws and bats righthanded.
Attended Wichita State University, Wichita, Kan.
Brother of Fred Carter, outfielder in New York Yankees' and
Cleveland Indians' organizations, 1985 through 1988.

Shares major league records for most home runs, two consecutive games (5), July 18 (2), 19 (3), 1989; most games with three or more home runs, season (2), 1989.

Shares American League record for most games with three or more home runs, lifetime (4).

Major league stolen bases: 1983 (1), 1984 (2), 1985 (24), 1986 (29), 1987 (31), 1988 (27), 1989 (13). Total—127.

Hit three home runs in a game, August 29, 1986, May 28, 1987, June 24, 1989 and July 19, 1989.

Led American League first basemen in errors with 12 in 1987.

Led American Association in total bases with 265 and tied for lead in strikeouts by batters with 103 in 1983.

Named College Player of the Year by THE SPORTING NEWS, 1981.

Named outfielder on THE SPORTING NEWS College Baseball All-America Team, 1980 and 1981.

Received reported $150,000 bonus to sign with Chicago Cubs, 1981.

Year Club League	Pos.	G.	AB.	R.	H.	2B.	3B.	HR.	RBI.	B.A.	PO.	A.	E.	F.A.
1981—Midland.................. Texas	OF	67	249	42	67	15	3	5	35	.269	100	10	4	.965

Year Club	League	Pos.	G.	AB.	R.	H.	2B.	3B.	HR.	RBI.	B.A.	PO.	A.	E.	F.A.
1982—Midland†	Texas	OF	110	427	84	136	22	8	25	98	.319	182	6	5	.974
1983—Iowa	A. A.	OF	124	*522	82	160	27	6	22	83	.307	204	9	12	.947
1983—Chicago	Nat.	OF	23	51	6	9	1	1	0	1	.176	26	0	0	1.000
1984—Iowa‡	A. A.	OF	61	248	45	77	12	7	14	67	.310	142	6	2	.987
1984—Cleveland§	Amer.	OF-1B	66	244	32	67	6	1	13	41	.275	169	11	6	.968
1985—Cleveland	Amer.	O-1-2-3	143	489	64	128	27	0	15	59	.262	311	17	6	.982
1986—Cleveland	Amer.	OF-1B	162	663	108	200	36	9	29	*121	.302	800	55	10	.988
1987—Cleveland	Amer.	1B-OF	149	588	83	155	27	2	32	106	.264	782	46	17	.980
1988—Cleveland	Amer.	OF	157	621	85	168	36	6	27	98	.271	444	8	7	.985
1989—Cleveland x	Amer.	OF-1B	●162	●651	84	158	32	4	35	105	.243	443	20	9	.981
National League Totals—1 Year			23	51	6	9	1	1	0	1	.176	26	0	0	1.000
American League Totals—6 Years			839	3256	456	876	164	22	151	530	.269	2949	157	55	.983
Major League Totals—7 Years			862	3307	462	885	165	23	151	531	.268	2975	157	55	.983

Selected by Chicago Cubs' organization in 1st round (second player selected) of free-agent draft, June 8, 1981.
†On disabled list, April 9 to April 19, 1982.
‡Traded with Outfielder Mel Hall and Pitchers Don Schulze and Darryl Banks to Cleveland Indians for Catcher Ron Hassey and Pitchers Rick Sutcliffe and George Frazier, June 13, 1984.
§On disabled list, July 2 to July 17, 1984.
xTraded to San Diego Padres for Catcher Sandy Alomar, Outfielder Chris James and Third Baseman Carlos Baerga, December 6, 1989.

STEVEN JEROME CARTER
(Steve)

Born December 3, 1964, at Charlottesville, Va.
Height, 6.04. Weight, 200.
Throws right and bats lefthanded.
Attended Hagerstown Junior College, Hagerstown, Md.,
and University of Georgia, Athens, Ga.

Year Club	League	Pos.	G.	AB.	R.	H.	2B.	3B.	HR.	RBI.	B.A.	PO.	A.	E.	F.A.
1987—Watertown	NYP	OF	66	242	50	75	18	1	0	30	.310	132	4	8	.944
1988—Harrisburg	East.	OF	9	35	7	10	2	0	0	2	.286	18	1	1	.950
1988—Augusta	S. Atl.	OF	74	278	47	83	18	6	3	43	.299	89	3	4	.958
1988—Salem	Carol.	OF	6	21	4	6	0	0	0	1	.286	15	2	0	1.000
1989—Buffalo	A. A.	OF	100	356	53	105	24	6	1	43	.295	188	3	6	.970
1989—Pittsburgh	Nat.	OF	9	16	2	2	1	0	1	3	.125	4	0	0	1.000
Major League Totals—1 Year			9	16	2	2	1	0	1	3	.125	4	0	0	1.000

Selected by Pittsburgh Pirates' organization in 21st round of free-agent draft, June 6, 1983.
Selected by Kansas City Royals' organization in secondary phase of free-agent draft, January 17, 1984.
Selected by Milwaukee Brewers' organization in 3rd round of free-agent draft, January 9, 1985.
Selected by Milwaukee Brewers' organization in secondary phase of free-agent draft, June 3, 1985.
Selected by Pittsburgh Pirates' organization in 17th round of free-agent draft, June 2, 1987.

CHARLES DOUGLAS CARY
(Chuck)

Born March 3, 1960, at Whittier, Calif.
Height, 6.04. Weight, 210.
Throws and bats lefthanded.
Attended University of California, Berkeley, Calif.

Major League saves: 1985 (2), 1987 (1). Total—3.
Tied for Southern League lead in balks with 3 in 1982.

Year Club	League	G.	IP.	W.	L.	Pct.	H.	R.	ER.	SO.	BB.	ERA.
1981—Macon	S. Atlantic	13	87	5	5	.500	77	32	25	55	19	2.59
1982—Birmingham	Southern	28	166	8	14	.364	162	93	77	125	64	4.17
1983—Birmingham†	Southern	17	104⅔	6	8	.429	103	50	42	69	42	3.61
1983—Evansville	Am. Assoc.	15	16⅓	1	1	.500	21	10	8	8	8	4.41
1984—Birmingham‡	Southern	22	108⅓	6	4	.600	118	61	58	62	46	4.82
1985—Nashville	Am. Assoc.	48	66	2	1	.667	55	27	22	54	27	3.00
1985—Detroit	American	16	23⅔	0	1	.000	16	9	9	22	8	3.42
1986—Detroit	American	22	31⅔	1	2	.333	33	18	12	21	15	3.41
1986—Nashville§	Am. Assoc.	22	26⅓	1	4	.200	29	21	16	19	15	5.47
1987—Richmond	Int'nal	40	105⅔	4	6	.400	104	64	55	128	43	4.68
1987—Atlanta	National	13	16⅔	1	1	.500	17	7	7	15	4	3.78
1988—Atlanta x	National	7	8⅓	0	0	.000	8	6	6	7	4	6.48
1988—Bradenton Braves	Gulf Coast	4	12	0	2	.000	11	10	5	18	2	3.75
1988—Richmond y	Int'national	5	6⅓	0	0	.000	4	1	1	3	2	1.42
1989—Columbus	Int'national	11	23⅓	1	1	.500	17	9	8	27	13	3.09
1989—New York z	American	22	99⅓	4	4	.500	78	42	36	79	29	3.26
American League Totals—3 Years		60	154⅔	5	7	.417	127	69	57	122	52	3.32
National League Totals—2 Years		20	25	1	1	.500	25	13	13	22	8	4.68
Major League Totals—5 Years		80	179⅔	6	8	.429	152	82	70	144	60	3.51

Selected by Detroit Tigers' organization in 7th round of free-agent draft, June 8, 1981.
†On disabled list, April 18 to May 12, 1983.
‡On disabled list, June 24 to July 11 and August 4 to August 17, 1984.
§Traded with Pitcher Randy O'Neal to Atlanta Braves for Outfielders Terry Harper and Freddy Tiburcio, January 27, 1987.

xOn disabled list, April 10 to August 17, 1988; included rehabilitation disability assignment to Bradenton, July 29 to August 10, 1988, and to Richmond, August 11 to August 17, 1988.

yReleased, December 4, 1988; signed by Columbus (New York Yankees' organization), January, 1989.

zOn disabled list, June 15 to July 11, 1989; included rehabilitation disability assignment to Columbus, July 4 to July 11, 1989.

LAWRENCE PAUL CASIAN
(Larry)

Born October 28, 1965, at Lynwood, Calif.
Height, 6.00. Weight, 170.
Throws left and bats righthanded.
Attended California State University, Fullerton, Calif.

Year	Club	League	G.	IP.	W.	L.	Pct.	H.	R.	ER.	SO.	BB.	ERA.
1987—Visalia		California	18	97	10	3	.769	89	35	27	96	49	2.51
1988—Orlando		Southern	27	174	9	9	.500	165	72	57	104	62	2.95
1988—Portland		P. Coast	1	2⅔	0	0	.000	5	3	0	2	0	0.00
1989—Portland		P. Coast	28	169⅓	7	12	.368	201	97	85	65	63	4.52

Selected by Minnesota Twins' organization in 6th round of free-agent draft, June 2, 1987.

ANTONIO CASTILLO
(Tony)

Born March 1, 1963, at Lara, Venezuela.
Height, 5.10. Weight, 188.
Throws and bats lefthanded.

Major League saves: 1989 (1).

Year	Club	League	G.	IP.	W.	L.	Pct.	H.	R.	ER.	SO.	BB.	ERA.
1983—Bradenton Jays		Gulf Coast	1	3	0	0	.000	3	1	1	4	0	3.00
1984—Florence		S. Atlantic	25	137⅓	11	8	.579	123	71	52	96	50	3.41
1985—Kinston		Carolina	36	127⅔	11	7	.611	111	44	27	136	48	1.90
1986—Knoxville†		Southern					(Did not play)						
1987—Dunedin		Florida St.	39	69⅔	6	2	.750	62	30	26	62	19	3.36
1988—Dunedin		Florida St.	30	42⅔	4	3	.571	31	9	7	46	10	1.48
1988—Knoxville		Southern	5	8	1	0	1.000	2	0	0	11	1	0.00
1988—Toronto		American	14	15	1	0	1.000	10	5	5	14	2	3.00
1989—Toronto		American	17	17⅔	1	1	.500	23	14	12	10	10	6.11
1989—Syracuse‡		Int'national	27	41⅔	1	3	.250	33	15	13	37	15	2.81
1989—Atlanta		National	12	9⅓	0	1	.000	8	5	5	5	4	4.82
American League Totals—2 Years			31	32⅔	2	1	.667	33	19	17	24	12	4.68
National League Totals—1 Year			12	9⅓	0	1	.000	8	5	5	5	4	4.82
Major League Totals—2 Years			43	42	2	2	.500	41	24	22	29	16	4.71

Signed as free agent by Toronto Blue Jays' organization, February 16, 1983.

†On disabled list, April 10, 1986 through entire season.

‡Traded with a player to be named later to Atlanta Braves for Pitcher Jim Acker, August 24, 1989; Atlanta organization acquired Catcher Francisco Cabrera to complete deal, August 24, 1989.

BRAULIO ROBINSON MEDRANO CASTILLO

Born May 13, 1968, at Elias Pina, Dominican Republic.
Height, 6.00. Weight, 160.
Throws and bats righthanded.

Tied for California League lead in being hit by pitch with 15 in 1989.

Year	Club	League	Pos.	G.	AB.	R.	H.	2B.	3B.	HR.	RBI.	B.A.	PO.	A.	E.	F.A.
1987—Sarasota Dodgers	Gulf C.		OF	49	140	21	28	4	2	1	19	.200	40	2	2	.955
1988—Salem	N'west		OF	73	306	51	86	20	●5	8	40	.281	●180	40	6	.968
1989—Bakersfield	Calif.		OF	126	494	83	147	28	●8	18	82	.298	232	9	★11	.956

Signed as free agent by Los Angeles Dodgers' organization, October 10, 1985.

FRANK ANTHONY CASTILLO

Born April 1, 1969, at El Paso, Tex.
Height, 6.01. Weight, 180.
Throws and bats righthanded.

Tied for Appalachian League lead in complete games with 5 in 1987.
Named Appalachian League Player of the Year, 1987.

Year	Club	League	G.	IP.	W.	L.	Pct.	H.	R.	ER.	SO.	BB.	ERA.
1987—Wytheville		Ap'lachian	12	90⅓	★10	1	★.909	86	31	23	83	21	2.29
1987—Geneva		NYP	1	6	1	0	1.000	3	1	0	6	1	0.00
1988—Peoria†		Midwest	9	51	6	1	.857	25	5	4	58	10	0.71
1989—Winston-Salem		Carolina	18	129⅓	9	6	.600	118	42	36	114	24	2.51
1989—Charlotte		Southern	10	68	3	4	.429	73	35	29	43	12	3.84

Selected by Chicago Cubs' organization in 6th round of free-agent draft, June 2, 1987.

†On disabled list, April 1 to July 23, 1988.

—DID YOU KNOW—

That the Twins' Kirby Puckett, who led the majors with a .339 batting mark last season, hit .390 at home and .283 on the road?

JUAN CASTILLO

Name pronounced Cas-TEE-yo.
Born January 25, 1962, at San Pedro de Macoris, D. R.
Height, 5.11. Weight, 155.
Throws right and bats left and righthanded.

Major league stolen bases: 1986 (1), 1987 (15), 1988 (2). Total—18.
Led Texas League in caught stealing with 17 in 1983.
Led Texas League second basemen in assists with 359 in 1984.
Led Texas League second basemen in putouts with 247, assists with 360, errors with 27, double plays with 79 and total chances with 634 in 1983.
Led California League second basemen in double plays with 88 in 1982.

Year	Club	League	Pos.	G.	AB.	R.	H.	2B.	3B.	HR.	RBI.	B.A.	PO.	A.	E.	F.A.
1980—Burlington	Midw.		2B	30	103	12	22	0	0	0	6	.214	60	72	3	.978
1980—Butte	Pion.		2B	59	183	28	53	9	3	0	20	.290	87	99	18	.912
1981—Burlington	Midw.		2B	110	365	36	90	8	4	4	34	.247	244	284	18	*.967
1982—Stockton	Calif.		2B	134	483	60	130	9	8	0	42	.269	273	*428	23	.968
1983—El Paso	Texas		2B-SS-OF	123	461	79	125	24	2	8	62	.271	250	363	28	.956
1984—El Paso	Texas		2B-OF-SS	119	448	78	129	21	7	4	59	.288	273	360	17	.974
1984—Vancouver	P. C.		2B	8	30	6	10	0	0	0	2	.333	16	18	1	.971
1985—Vancouver	P. C.		SS-2B	118	440	71	119	17	3	1	32	.270	222	367	26	.958
1986—Milwaukee	Amer.		2-S-3-O	26	54	6	9	0	1	0	5	.167	41	46	4	.956
1986—Vancouver	P. C.		2B	26	73	10	14	3	0	0	4	.192	34	95	5	.963
1987—Milwaukee†	Amer.		2B-SS-3B	116	321	44	72	11	4	3	28	.224	190	251	12	.974
1987—Denver	A. A.		SS	1	2	2	1	0	0	0	1	.500	2	3	0	1.000
1988—Milwaukee‡	Amer.		2-3-S-O	54	90	10	20	0	0	0	2	.222	24	82	7	.938
1989—Milwaukee	Amer.		2B	3	4	0	0	0	0	0	3	.000	6	5	0	1.000
1989—Denver§x	A. A.		3B-2B	13	53	4	9	1	0	0	2	.170	12	26	1	.974
Major League Totals—4 Years				199	469	60	101	11	5	3	38	.215	261	384	23	.966

Signed as free agent by Milwaukee Brewers' organization, October 11, 1979.
†On disabled list, July 16 to July 31, 1987; included rehabiliation disability assignment to Denver, July 27 to July 31, 1987.
‡On disabled list, April 2 to May 12, 1988.
§On disabled list, May 17, 1989 through remainder of season.
xGranted free agency, October 15, 1989.

MONTE CARMELO CASTILLO

Name pronounced Cas-TEE-yo.

(Carmen)

Born June 8, 1958, at San Francisco de Macoris, D. R.
Height, 6.01. Weight, 190.
Throws and bats righthanded.

Major League stolen bases: 1983 (1), 1984 (1), 1985 (3), 1986 (2), 1987 (1), 1988 (6), 1989 (1). Total—15.

Year	Club	League	Pos.	G.	AB.	R.	H.	2B.	3B.	HR.	RBI.	B.A.	PO.	A.	E.	F.A.
1978—Auburn†	NYP		OF	53	174	37	41	10	2	4	21	.236	109	6	11	.913
1978—Helena	Pion.		OF	5	15	1	6	2	0	0	2	.400	2	0	1	.667
1979—Waterloo	Midw.		OF	49	138	25	28	5	1	3	12	.203	54	1	7	.887
1979—Batavia	NYP		OF	36	128	29	43	8	1	8	28	.336	56	4	5	.923
1980—Waterloo	Midw.		OF	117	390	69	103	14	1	11	64	.264	173	10	14	.929
1981—Chattanooga	South.		OF	119	441	63	124	17	6	11	58	.281	236	13	15	.943
1982—Charleston	Int.		OF	71	281	46	78	12	1	9	39	.278	159	10	11	.939
1982—Cleveland	Amer.		OF	47	120	11	25	4	0	2	11	.208	91	0	2	.978
1983—Charleston‡	Int.		OF	36	148	29	40	5	2	4	22	.270	85	6	6	.938
1983—Cleveland	Amer.		OF	23	36	9	10	2	1	1	3	.278	23	3	2	.929
1984—Cleveland	Amer.		OF	87	211	36	55	9	2	10	36	.261	123	2	9	.933
1985—Cleveland	Amer.		OF	67	184	27	45	5	1	11	25	.245	101	0	5	.953
1985—Maine	Int.		OF	26	96	12	23	2	2	2	18	.240	9	0	0	1.000
1986—Cleveland	Amer.		OF	85	205	34	57	9	0	8	32	.278	58	4	4	.939
1987—Cleveland	Amer.		OF	89	220	27	55	17	0	11	31	.250	29	3	0	1.000
1988—Cleveland§	Amer.		OF	66	176	12	48	8	0	4	14	.273	69	1	5	.933
1989—Minnesota x	Amer.		OF	94	218	23	56	13	3	8	33	.257	119	3	3	.976
Major League Totals—8 Years				558	1370	179	351	67	7	55	185	.256	613	16	30	.954

Signed as free agent by Philadelphia Phillies' organization, June 30, 1978.
†Drafted by Chattanooga (Cleveland Indians' organization), December 5, 1978.
‡On disabled list, May 5 to July 4, 1983.
§Traded to Minnesota Twins for Pitcher Keith Atherton, March 26, 1989.
xGranted free agency, November 13, 1989.

ANDUJAR CEDENO

Born August 21, 1969, at La Romana, Dominican Republic.
Height, 6.01. Weight, 170.
Throws and bats righthanded.

Year	Club	League	Pos.	G.	AB.	R.	H.	2B.	3B.	HR.	RBI.	B.A.	PO.	A.	E.	F.A.
1988—Sarasota Rangers	Gulf C.		SS	46	165	25	47	5	2	1	20	.285	58	145	25	.890
1989—Asheville	S. Atl.		SS-3B	126	487	76	*146	23	6	14	93	.300	182	346	62	.895

Signed as free agent by Houston Astros' organization, October 1, 1986.

RICHARD ALDO CERONE
Name pronounced Ce-RONE.
(Rick)
Born May 19, 1954, at Newark, N. J.
Height, 5.11. Weight, 195.
Throws and bats righthanded.
Received bachelor of science degree in physical education from
Seton Hall University, South Orange, N. J. in 1975.

Holds major league record for most consecutive errorless games, catcher, lifetime (159), July 5, 1987 through May 8, 1989.

Major League stolen bases: 1979 (1), 1980 (1), 1984 (1), 1985 (1). Total—4.

Named catcher on THE SPORTING NEWS American League All-Star Team, 1980.

Received reported $60,000 bonus to sign with Cleveland Indians, 1975.

Year Club	League	Pos.	G.	AB.	R.	H.	2B.	3B.	HR.	RBI.	B.A.	PO.	A.	E.	F.A.
1975—Oklahoma City	A. A.	C-OF	46	140	22	35	6	1	2	13	.250	178	30	3	.986
1975—Cleveland	Amer.	C	7	12	1	3	1	0	0	0	.250	18	1	0	1.000
1976—Toledo†	Int.	C	96	339	38	86	19	0	11	49	.254	351	50	*18	.957
1976—Cleveland‡	Amer.	C	7	16	1	2	0	0	0	1	.125	25	1	1	.963
1977—Charleston	Int.	C-OF	70	231	30	54	10	1	6	40	.234	254	32	5	.983
1977—Toronto	Amer.	C	31	100	7	20	4	0	1	10	.200	146	15	1	.944
1978—Toronto	Amer.	C	88	282	25	63	8	2	3	20	.223	426	44	4	.992
1979—Toronto§	Amer.	C	136	469	47	112	27	4	7	61	.239	560	68	13	.980
1980—New York	Amer.	C	147	519	70	144	30	4	14	85	.277	800	73	9	.990
1981—New York x	Amer.	C	71	234	23	57	13	2	2	21	.244	353	26	3	.992
1982—New York y	Amer.	C	89	300	29	68	10	0	5	28	.227	509	25	6	.989
1983—New York	Amer.	C-3B	80	246	18	54	7	0	2	22	.220	412	18	4	.991
1984—New York z	Amer.	C	38	120	8	25	3	0	2	13	.208	230	9	1	.996
1984—Columbus a	Int.	C	8	25	2	5	2	0	0	1	.200	42	5	1	.979
1985—Atlanta bc	Nat.	C	96	282	15	61	9	0	3	25	.216	384	48	6	.986
1986—Milwaukee d	Amer.	C	68	216	22	56	14	0	4	18	.259	391	44	4	.991
1987—New York e	Amer.	*C-1B-P	113	284	28	69	12	1	4	23	.243	542	38	1	*.998
1988—Boston	Amer.	C	84	264	31	71	13	1	3	27	.269	471	28	0	*1.000
1989—Boston	Amer.	C-OF	102	296	28	72	16	1	4	48	.243	579	41	10	.984
American League Totals—14 Years			1061	3358	338	816	158	15	51	377	.243	5462	431	57	.990
National League Totals—1 Year			96	282	15	61	9	0	3	25	.216	384	48	6	.986
Major League Totals—15 Years			1157	3640	353	877	167	15	54	402	.241	5846	479	63	.990

Selected by Cleveland Indians' organization in 1st round (seventh player selected) of free-agent draft, June 4, 1975.

†On disabled list, May 13 to May 24, 1976.

‡Traded with Infielder-Outfielder John Lowenstein to Toronto Blue Jays for Outfielder Rico Carty, December 6, 1976.

§Traded with Pitcher Tom Underwood and Outfielder Ted Wilborn to New York Yankees for First Baseman Chris Chambliss, Infielder Damaso Garcia and Pitcher Paul Mirabella, November 1, 1979.

xOn disabled list, April 19 to May 24, 1981.

yOn disabled list, May 12 to July 15, 1982.

zOn disabled list, May 7 to July 5, 1984; included rehabilitation disability assignment to Columbus, June 25 to July 5, 1984.

aTraded to Atlanta Braves for Pitcher Brian Fisher, December 5, 1984.

bOn disabled list, June 17 to July 2, 1985.

cTraded with Pitcher David Clay and Shortstop Flavio Alfaro to Milwaukee Brewers for Catcher Ted Simmons, March 5, 1986.

dGranted free agency, November 12, 1986; signed by New York Yankees, February 13, 1987.

eReleased, April 4, 1988; signed by Boston Red Sox, April 15, 1988.

DIVISION SERIES RECORD

Year Club	League	Pos.	G.	AB.	R.	H.	2B.	3B.	HR.	RBI.	B.A.	PO.	A.	E.	F.A.
1981—New York	Amer.	C	5	18	1	6	2	0	1	5	.333	42	1	1	.977

CHAMPIONSHIP SERIES RECORD

Shares Championship Series record for hitting home run in first series at-bat, October 8, 1980.

Year Club	League	Pos.	G.	AB.	R.	H.	2B.	3B.	HR.	RBI.	B.A.	PO.	A.	E.	F.A.
1980—New York	Amer.	C	3	12	1	4	0	0	1	2	.333	14	4	0	1.000
1981—New York	Amer.	C	3	10	1	1	0	0	0	0	.100	23	2	0	1.000
Championship Series Totals—2 Years			6	22	2	5	0	0	1	2	.227	37	6	0	1.000

WORLD SERIES RECORD

Year Club	League	Pos.	G.	AB.	R.	H.	2B.	3B.	HR.	RBI.	B.A.	PO.	A.	E.	F.A.
1981—New York	Amer.	C	6	21	2	4	1	0	1	3	.190	42	4	0	1.000

PITCHING RECORD

Year Club	League	G.	IP.	W.	L.	Pct.	H.	R.	ER.	SO.	BB.	ERA.
1987—New York	American	2	2	0	0	.000	0	0	0	1	1	0.00

JOHN JOSEPH CERUTTI
Born April 28, 1960, at Albany, N. Y.
Height, 6.02. Weight, 200.
Throws and bats lefthanded.
Received bachelor of arts degree in economics from Amherst College, Amherst, Mass.

Major League saves: 1986 (1), 1988 (1). Total—2.
Tied for Southern League lead in shutouts with 3 in 1983.
Tied for Pioneer League lead in home runs allowed with 8 and games started by pitchers with 14 in 1981.

Year Club	League	G.	IP.	W.	L.	Pct.	H.	R.	ER.	SO.	BB.	ERA.
1981—Medicine Hat	Pioneer	14	*107	8	4	.667	87	45	36	120	43	3.03
1982—Kinston	Carolina	16	113	10	5	.667	88	47	40	136	49	3.19
1982—Knoxville	Southern	4	32⅓	4	0	1.000	18	4	4	17	10	1.11
1982—Syracuse	Int'national	6	30	0	3	.000	42	25	22	20	16	6.60
1983—Knoxville	Southern	29	188⅔	9	13	.409	182	89	72	131	65	3.43
1984—Syracuse	Int'national	29	148	7	●13	.350	152	89	73	114	52	4.44
1985—Syracuse	Int'national	28	182	11	9	.550	165	84	60	110	60	2.97
1985—Toronto	American	4	6⅔	0	2	.000	10	7	4	5	4	5.40
1986—Syracuse	Int'national	7	43⅔	1	3	.250	44	27	20	22	16	4.12
1986—Toronto	American	34	145⅓	9	4	.692	150	73	67	89	47	4.15
1987—Toronto	American	44	151⅓	11	4	*.733	144	75	74	92	59	4.40
1988—Toronto	American	46	123⅔	6	7	.462	120	56	43	65	42	3.13
1989—Toronto	American	33	205⅓	11	11	.500	214	90	70	69	53	3.07
Major League Totals—5 Years		161	632⅓	37	28	.569	638	301	258	320	205	3.67

Selected by Toronto Blue Jays' organization in 1st round (21st player selected) of free-agent draft, June 8, 1981.

CHAMPIONSHIP SERIES RECORD

Year Club	League	G.	IP.	W.	L.	Pct.	H.	R.	ER.	SO.	BB.	ERA.
1989—Toronto	American	2	2⅔	0	0	.000	0	0	0	1	3	0.00

WESLEY POLK CHAMBERLAIN
(Wes)

Born April 13, 1966, at Chicago, Ill.
Height, 6.02. Weight, 210.
Throws and bats righthanded.
Attended Jackson State University, Jackson, Miss.

Led Eastern League in total bases with 239 in 1989.
Tied for New York-Pennsylvania League lead in double plays by outfielders with 3 in 1987.
Named Eastern League Most Valuable Player, 1989.

Year Club	League	Pos.	G.	AB.	R.	H.	2B.	3B.	HR.	RBI.	B.A.	PO.	A.	E.	F.A.
1987—Watertown	NYP	OF	66	258	50	67	13	4	5	35	.260	121	9	7	.949
1988—Augusta	S. Atl.	OF	27	107	22	36	7	2	1	17	.336	49	4	1	.981
1988—Salem	Carol.	OF	92	365	66	100	15	1	11	50	.274	161	11	9	.950
1989—Harrisburg	East.	OF	129	471	65	*144	26	3	21	*87	.306	205	*14	*15	.936

Selected by Pittsburgh Pirates' organization in 5th round of free-agent draft, June 4, 1984.
Selected by Pittsburgh Pirates' organization in 4th round of free-agent draft, June 2, 1987.

COLIN MARC CHARLAND

Born November 13, 1965, at New York, N.Y.
Height, 6.03. Weight, 205.
Throws and bats lefthanded.
Attended Dallas Baptist University, Dallas, Tex.

Led California League in complete games with 12 in 1988.
Named California League co-Pitcher of the Year, 1988.

Year Club	League	G.	IP.	W.	L.	Pct.	H.	R.	ER.	SO.	BB.	ERA.
1986—Salem	Northwest	5	31	4	0	1.000	16	7	5	49	15	1.45
1986—Quad Cities	Midwest	10	59⅓	3	4	.429	55	29	23	61	29	3.49
1987—Palm Springs	California	27	147⅓	6	12	.333	159	100	88	150	87	5.38
1988—Palm Springs	California	27	204	●17	5	.773	187	76	57	183	71	2.51
1989—Edmonton	P. Coast	25	136	5	10	.333	150	87	83	107	75	5.49

Selected by California Angels' organization in 6th round of free-agent draft, June 2, 1986.

NORMAN WOOD CHARLTON III
(Norm)

Born January 6, 1963, at Fort Polk, La.
Height, 6.03. Weight, 205.
Throws left and bats left and righthanded.
Received degree in political science, religion, and physical education
from Rice University, Houston, Tex.

Led American Association in wild pitches with 13 in 1988.

Year Club	League	G.	IP.	W.	L.	Pct.	H.	R.	ER.	SO.	BB.	ERA.
1984—West Palm Beach	Florida St.	8	39⅓	1	4	.200	51	27	20	27	22	4.58
1985—West Palm Beach†	Florida St.	24	128	7	10	.412	135	79	65	71	79	4.57
1986—Vermont	Eastern	22	136⅔	10	6	.625	109	55	43	96	74	2.83
1987—Nashville‡	Am. Assoc.	18	98⅓	2	8	.200	97	57	47	74	44	4.30
1988—Nashville	Am. Assoc.	27	182	11	10	.524	149	69	61	*161	56	3.02
1988—Cincinnati	National	10	61⅓	4	5	.444	60	27	27	39	20	3.96
1989—Cincinnati	National	69	95⅓	8	3	.727	67	38	31	98	40	2.93
Major League Totals—2 Years		79	156⅔	12	8	.600	127	65	58	137	60	3.33

Selected by Montreal Expos' organization in 1st round (27th player selected) of free-agent draft, June 4, 1984.
†Traded with a player to be named later to Cincinnati Reds for Infielder Wayne Krenchicki, March 31, 1986;

Cincinnati acquired Second Baseman Tim Barker to complete deal, April 2, 1986.

‡On Cincinnati disabled list, April 6 to June 26, 1987; included rehabilitation disability assignment to Nashville, June 9 to June 26, 1987.

SCOTT MICHAEL CHIAMPARINO

Born August 22, 1966, at San Mateo, Calif.
Height, 6.02. Weight, 190.
Throws and bats righthanded.
Attended Santa Clara University, Santa Clara, Calif.

Year Club	League	G.	IP.	W.	L.	Pct.	H.	R.	ER.	SO.	BB.	ERA.
1987—Medford	Northwest	13	67⅔	5	4	.556	64	29	19	65	20	2.53
1988—Modesto	California	16	106⅔	5	7	.417	89	40	32	117	56	2.70
1988—Huntsville	Southern	13	84	4	5	.444	88	36	30	49	26	3.21
1989—Huntsville	Southern	17	101⅔	8	6	.571	109	60	52	87	29	4.60

Selected by Oakland Athletics' organization in 4th round of free-agent draft, June 2, 1987.

JAMES CLANCY
(Jim)

Born December 18, 1955, at Chicago, Ill.
Height, 6.04. Weight, 220.
Throws and bats righthanded.

Major League saves: 1988 (1).
Led American League pitchers in games started with 40 in 1982 and tied for lead with 36 in 1984.
Tied for National League lead in intentional bases on balls issued with 15 in 1989.
Tied for Gulf Coast League lead in shutouts with 2 in 1974.

Year Club	League	G.	IP.	W.	L.	Pct.	H.	R.	ER.	SO.	BB.	ERA.
1974—Sarasota Rangers	Gulf Coast	9	53	3	3	.500	40	21	16	58	28	2.72
1975—Anderson	W. Carol.	23	148	6	13	.316	139	85	63	109	91	3.83
1976—San Antonio†‡	Texas	23	125	6	8	.429	133	94	★89	77	98	6.41
1977—Jersey City	Eastern	20	118	5	13	.278	116	87	64	99	75	4.88
1977—Toronto	American	13	77	4	9	.308	80	47	43	44	47	5.03
1978—Toronto	American	31	194	10	12	.455	199	96	88	106	91	4.08
1979—Toronto§	American	12	64	2	7	.222	65	44	39	33	31	5.48
1980—Toronto	American	34	251	13	16	.448	217	108	92	152	★128	3.30
1981—Toronto	American	22	125	6	12	.333	126	77	68	56	64	4.90
1982—Toronto	American	40	266⅔	16	14	.533	251	122	110	139	77	3.71
1983—Toronto	American	34	223	15	11	.577	238	115	97	99	61	3.91
1984—Toronto	American	36	219⅔	13	15	.464	249	★132	★125	118	88	5.12
1985—Toronto x	American	23	128⅔	9	6	.600	117	54	54	66	37	3.78
1985—Knoxville	Southern	2	8	1	0	1.000	7	3	3	2	2	3.38
1986—Toronto y	American	34	219⅓	14	14	.500	202	100	96	126	63	3.94
1987—Toronto	American	37	241⅓	15	11	.577	234	103	95	180	80	3.54
1988—Toronto z	American	36	196⅓	11	13	.458	207	106	98	118	47	4.49
1989—Houston	National	33	147	7	14	.333	155	100	83	91	66	5.08
American League Totals—12 Years		352	2206	128	140	.478	2185	1104	1005	1237	814	4.10
National League Totals—1 Year		33	147	7	14	.333	155	100	83	91	66	5.08
Major League Totals—13 Years		385	2353	135	154	.467	2340	1204	1088	1328	880	4.16

Selected by Texas Rangers' organization in 4th round of free-agent draft, June 5, 1974.

†On disabled list, June 15 to June 26, 1976.

‡Selected by Toronto Blue Jays from Texas Rangers in American League expansion draft, November 5, 1976.

§On disabled list, May 12 to July 4 and August 5, 1979 through remainder of season.

xOn disabled list, March 25 to April 30 and July 27 to September 2, 1985; included rehabilitation disability assignment to Knoxville, April 21 to April 30, 1985.

yGranted free agency, November 12, 1986; re-signed by Blue Jays, January 6, 1987.

zGranted free agency, October 24, 1988; signed by Houston Astros, December 16, 1988.

CHAMPIONSHIP SERIES RECORD

Year Club	League	G.	IP.	W.	L.	Pct.	H.	R.	ER.	SO.	BB.	ERA.
1985—Toronto	American	1	1	0	1	.000	2	1	1	0	1	9.00

ALL-STAR GAME RECORD

Year League	IP.	W.	L.	Pct.	H.	R.	ER.	SO.	BB.	ERA.
1982—American	1	0	0	.000	0	0	0	0	0	0.00

DAVID EARL CLARK
(Dave)

Born September 3, 1962, at Tupelo, Miss.
Height, 6.02. Weight, 210.
Throws right and bats lefthanded.
Attended Jackson State University, Jackson, Miss.
Brother of Lewis Clark, wide receiver with Seattle Seahawks.

Major League stolen bases: 1986 (1), 1987 (1). Total—2.
Named outfielder on THE SPORTING NEWS College Baseball All-America Team, 1983.

Year Club	League	Pos.	G.	AB.	R.	H.	2B.	3B.	HR.	RBI.	B.A.	PO.	A.	E.	F.A.
1983—Waterloo	Midw.	OF	58	159	20	44	8	1	4	20	.277	37	4	1	.976
1984—Waterloo	Midw.	OF	110	363	74	112	16	3	15	63	.309	128	10	4	.972

Year Club	League	Pos.	G.	AB.	R.	H.	2B.	3B.	HR.	RBI.	B.A.	PO.	A.	E.	F.A.
1984—Buffalo....................	East.	OF	17	56	12	10	1	0	3	10	.179	23	2	1	.962
1985—Waterbury............	East.	OF	132	463	75	140	24	7	12	64	.302	204	11	11	.951
1986—Maine....................	Int.	OF	106	355	56	99	17	2	19	58	.279	150	4	6	.963
1986—Cleveland..............	Amer.	OF	18	58	10	16	1	0	3	9	.276	26	0	0	1.000
1987—Buffalo....................	A. A.	OF	108	420	83	143	22	3	30	80	.340	181	*22	6	.971
1987—Cleveland..............	Amer.	OF	29	87	11	18	5	0	3	12	.207	24	1	0	1.000
1988—Cleveland..............	Amer.	OF	63	156	11	41	4	1	3	18	.263	36	0	2	.947
1988—Colorado Springs.	P. C.	OF	47	165	27	49	10	2	4	31	.297	85	6	3	.968
1989—Cleveland†............	Amer.	OF	102	253	21	60	12	0	8	29	.237	27	0	1	.964
Major League Totals—4 Years................			212	554	53	135	22	1	17	68	.244	113	1	3	.974

Selected by Cleveland Indians' organization in 1st round (11th player selected) of free-agent draft, June 6, 1983.
†Traded to Chicago Cubs for Outfielder Mitch Webster, November 20, 1989.

JACK ANTHONY CLARK

Born November 10, 1955, at New Brighton, Pa.
Height, 6.03. Weight, 205.
Throws and bats righthanded.

Shares major league records for most strikeouts, two consecutive games (9), June 11 (5) (12 innings), 13 (4), 1989; most errors by first baseman, inning (3), May 25, 1987, second inning.

Holds National League record for most consecutive games, one or more bases on balls (16), July 18 through August 10, 1987.

Shares National League record for most bases on balls, doubleheader (6), July 8, 1987 (19 innings).

Major League stolen bases: 1975 (1), 1976 (6), 1977 (12), 1978 (15), 1979 (11), 1980 (2), 1981 (1), 1982 (6), 1983 (5), 1984 (1), 1985 (1), 1986 (1), 1987 (1), 1988 (3), 1989 (6). Total—72.

Led National League in bases on balls received with 136 in 1987 and 132 in 1989.

Led National League in slugging percentage with .597 in 1987.

Led National League in game-winning RBIs with 18 in 1980 and tied for lead with 21 in 1982.

Tied for National League lead in double plays by outfielders with 5 in 1978, 7 in 1979 and 4 in 1981.

Led Texas League in total bases with 239 in 1975.

Led California League in total bases with 254 in 1974.

Led Texas League third basemen in putouts with 102, assists with 278, double plays with 29 and fielding percentage with .872 in 1975.

Named first baseman on THE SPORTING NEWS National League All-Star Team, 1987.

Named outfielder on THE SPORTING NEWS National League All-Star Team, 1978.

Named first baseman on THE SPORTING NEWS National League Silver Slugger team, 1985 and 1987.

Year Club	League	Pos.	G.	AB.	R.	H.	2B.	3B.	HR.	RBI.	B.A.	PO.	A.	E.	F.A.
1973—Great Falls............	Pion.	OF-P-3B	65	234	46	75	20	1	9	54	.321	73	9	1	.988
1974—Fresno..................	Calif.	3B	131	495	88	156	23	9	19	*117	.315	100	204	*53	.852
1975—Lafayette..............	Texas	*3B-OF	126	466	94	141	25	2	●23	77	.303	107	279	*56	.873
1975—San Francisco	Nat.	OF-3B	8	17	3	4	0	0	0	2	.235	8	1	0	1.000
1976—Phoenix.................	P. C.	OF-3B	131	470	111	152	29	*16	17	86	.323	188	23	9	.959
1976—San Francisco	Nat.	OF	26	102	14	23	6	2	2	10	.225	71	3	1	.987
1977—San Francisco	Nat.	OF	136	413	64	104	17	4	13	51	.252	226	11	6	.975
1978—San Francisco	Nat.	OF	156	592	90	181	46	8	25	98	.306	320	16	6	.982
1979—San Francisco	Nat.	OF-3B	143	527	84	144	25	2	26	86	.273	262	13	5	.971
1980—San Francisco†	Nat.	OF	127	437	77	124	20	8	22	82	.284	229	7	8	.967
1981—San Francisco	Nat.	OF	99	385	60	103	19	2	17	53	.268	193	●14	4	.981
1982—San Francisco	Nat.	OF	157	563	90	154	30	3	27	103	.274	281	10	6	.980
1983—San Francisco	Nat.	OF-1B	135	492	82	132	25	0	20	66	.268	262	20	9	.969
1984—San Francisco‡§ ..	Nat.	OF-1B	57	203	33	65	9	1	11	44	.320	120	9	2	.985
1985—St. Louis..............	Nat.	*1B-OF	126	442	71	124	26	3	22	87	.281	1128	66	*14	.988
1986—St. Louis y............	Nat.	1B	65	232	34	55	12	2	9	23	.237	623	35	3	.995
1987—St. Louis z.............	Nat.	1B-OF	131	419	93	120	23	1	35	106	.286	1152	77	14	.989
1988—New York ab........	Amer.	OF-1B	150	496	81	120	14	0	27	93	.242	129	8	5	.965
1989—San Diego	Nat.	●1B-OF	142	455	76	110	19	1	26	94	.242	1157	89	●15	.988
National League Totals—14 Years..........			1508	5279	871	1443	277	37	255	905	.273	6032	371	93	.986
American League Totals—1 Year...........			150	496	81	120	14	0	27	93	.242	129	8	5	.965
Major League Totals—15 Years..............			1658	5775	952	1563	291	37	282	998	.271	6161	379	98	.985

Selected by San Francisco Giants' organization in 13th round of free-agent draft, June 5, 1973.
†On disabled list, August 23 to September 8, 1980.
‡On disabled list, June 25 to September 5, 1984.
§Traded to St. Louis Cardinals for First Basemen David Green and Gary Rajsich, Pitcher Dave LaPoint and Shortstop Jose Gonzalez (Jose Uribe), February 1, 1985.
xOn disabled list, August 24 to September 8, 1985.
yOn disabled list, June 25, 1986 through remainder of season.
zGranted free agency, November 9, 1987; signed by New York Yankees, January 6, 1988.
aOn disabled list, March 21 to April 15, 1988.
bTraded with Pitcher Pat Clements to San Diego Padres for Pitchers Jimmy Jones and Lance McCullers and Outfielder Stan Jefferson, October 24, 1988.

CHAMPIONSHIP SERIES RECORD

Shares Championship Series records for most at-bats (2), hits (2) and singles (2), inning, October 13, 1985, second inning.

Year Club	League	Pos.	G.	AB.	R.	H.	2B.	3B.	HR.	RBI.	B.A.	PO.	A.	E.	F.A.
1985—St. Louis................	Nat.	1B	6	21	4	8	0	0	1	4	.381	55	0	0	1.000
1987—St. Louis................	Nat.	PH	1	1	0	0	0	0	0	0	.000	0	0	0	.000
Championship Series Totals—2 Years.....			7	22	4	8	0	0	1	4	.364	55	0	0	1.000

WORLD SERIES RECORD

Year Club	League	Pos.	G.	AB.	R.	H.	2B.	3B.	HR.	RBI.	B.A.	PO.	A.	E.	F.A.
1985—St. Louis	Nat.	1B	7	25	1	6	2	0	0	4	.240	49	4	0	1.000

ALL-STAR GAME RECORD

Year League	Pos.	G.	AB.	R.	H.	2B.	3B.	HR.	RBI.	B.A.	PO.	A.	E.	F.A.
1978—National	OF	1	0	0	0	0	0	0	0	.000	0	0	0	.000
1979—National	PH	1	0	0	0	0	0	0	0	.000	0	0	0	.000
1985—National	1B	1	0	0	0	0	0	0	0	.000	4	0	0	1.000
1987—National	1B	3	0	0	0	0	0	0	0	.000	7	1	0	1.000
All-Star Game Totals—4 Years		6	0	0	0	0	0	0	0	.000	11	1	0	1.000

PITCHING RECORD

Year Club	League	G.	IP.	W.	L.	Pct.	H.	R.	ER.	SO.	BB.	ERA.
1973—Great Falls	Pioneer	5	15	0	2	.000	24	24	10	17	19	6.00

JERALD DWAYNE CLARK

Born August 10, 1963, at Crockett, Tex.
Height, 6.04. Weight, 189.
Throws and bats righthanded.
Attended Lamar University, Beaumont, Tex.
Brother of Phil Clark, catcher-outfielder in Detroit Tigers' organization;
and Isaiah Clark, shortstop in Seattle Mariners' organization.

Named Northwest League Most Valuable Player, 1985.

Year Club	League	Pos.	G.	AB.	R.	H.	2B.	3B.	HR.	RBI.	B.A.	PO.	A.	E.	F.A.
1985—Spokane	N'west	OF	73	283	45	92	●24	3	2	50	.325	145	7	6	.962
1986—Reno	Calif.	OF	95	389	76	118	34	3	7	58	.303	135	6	5	.966
1986—Beaumont	Texas	OF	16	56	9	18	4	1	0	6	.321	39	1	2	.952
1987—Wichita	Texas	OF	132	531	86	165	36	8	18	95	.311	262	10	3	.989
1988—Las Vegas	P. C.	OF-3B-1B	107	408	65	123	27	7	9	67	.301	194	11	7	.967
1988—San Diego	Nat.	OF	6	15	0	3	1	0	0	3	.200	10	1	0	1.000
1989—Las Vegas	P. C.	OF-1B	107	419	84	131	27	4	22	83	.313	213	8	8	.965
1989—San Diego	Nat.	OF	17	41	5	8	2	0	1	7	.195	16	2	1	.947
Major League Totals—2 Years		23	56	5	11	3	0	1	10	.196	26	3	1	.967

Selected by Los Angeles Dodgers' organization in 23rd round of free-agent draft, June 4, 1984.
Selected by San Diego Padres' organization in 12th round of free-agent draft, June 3, 1985.

PHILLIP BENJAMIN CLARK
(Phil)

Born May 6, 1968, at Crockett, Tex.
Height, 6.00. Weight, 175.
Throws and bats righthanded.
Brother of Jerald Clark, outfielder in San Diego Padres' organization;
and Isaiah Clark, infielder in Seattle Mariners' organization.

Led South Atlantic League catchers in passed balls with 23 and tied for lead in errors with 21 in 1987.
Led Appalachian League catchers in errors with 11 in 1986.
Tied for Eastern League lead in double plays by catchers with 8 in 1989.

Year Club	League	Pos.	G.	AB.	R.	H.	2B.	3B.	HR.	RBI.	B.A.	PO.	A.	E.	F.A.
1986—Bristol	Appal.	C-OF	66	247	40	★82	4	2	4	36	★.332	354	25	11	.972
1987—Fayetteville	S. Atl.	C-OF-3B	135	★542	83	160	26	●9	8	79	.295	480	82	28	.953
1988—Lakeland	Fla. St.	C-OF	109	403	60	120	17	4	9	66	.298	413	35	8	.982
1989—London	East.	C-OF-3B	104	373	43	108	15	4	8	42	.290	505	56	7	.988

Selected by Detroit Tigers' organization in 1st round (18th player selected) of free-agent draft, June 2, 1986.

TERRY LEE CLARK

Born October 10, 1960, at Los Angeles, Calif.
Height, 6.02. Weight, 196.
Throws and bats righthanded.
Attended Mount San Antonio College, Walnut, Calif.

Led Florida State League in games finished in relief with 51 in 1982.
Led South Atlantic League in games finished in relief with 51 in 1981.
Led Appalachian League in saves with 8 in 1979.

Year Club	League	G.	IP.	W.	L.	Pct.	H.	R.	ER.	SO.	BB.	ERA.
1979—Johnson City	Ap'lachian	●23	32	4	2	.667	31	10	7	22	11	1.97
1980—Gastonia	S. Atlantic	49	88	4	7	.364	82	34	31	50	22	3.17
1981—Gastonia	S. Atlantic	★53	75	4	5	.444	56	23	18	66	25	2.16
1982—St. Petersburg	Florida St.	★58	88⅓	10	7	.588	81	32	25	61	34	2.55
1983—Arkansas	Texas	52	81⅓	6	6	.500	68	31	29	63	19	3.21
1984—Louisville†	Am. Assoc.	18	34⅓	1	3	.250	41	19	18	24	12	4.72
1985—Arkansas‡	Texas	42	96⅔	6	5	.545	102	64	53	67	38	4.93
1986—Midland	Texas	57	90⅓	9	4	.692	98	49	33	66	28	3.29
1987—Edmonton	P. Coast	33	154⅔	9	8	.471	140	79	66	88	56	3.84
1988—Edmonton	P. Coast	16	113⅔	7	6	.538	128	62	57	59	33	4.51
1988—California	American	15	94	6	6	.500	120	54	53	39	31	5.07
1989—Edmonton§	P. Coast	21	138⅓	11	5	.688	130	62	55	90	33	3.58

Year	Club	League	G.	IP.	W.	L.	Pct.	H.	R.	ER.	SO.	BB.	ERA.
1989—California x		American	4	11	0	2	.000	13	8	6	7	3	4.91
Major League Totals—2 Years			19	105	6	8	.429	133	62	59	46	34	5.06

Selected by St. Louis Cardinals' organization in 22nd round of free-agent draft, June 5, 1979.
†On disabled list, May 27 to August 22, 1984.
‡Granted free agency, October 15, 1985; signed by Midland (California Angels' organization), February 25, 1986.
§On California disabled list, March 19 to May 3, 1989; included rehabilitation disability assignment to Palm Springs, April 12 to April 20, 1989; and Edmonton, April 21 to May 1, 1989.
xReleased, October 6, 1989.

WILLIAM NUSCHLER CLARK JR.
(Will)

Born March 13, 1964, at New Orleans, La.
Height, 6.01. Weight, 190.
Throws and bats lefthanded.
Attended Mississippi State University, Starkville, Miss.

Shares major league record by hitting home run in first major league at-bat, April 8, 1986.
Major League stolen bases: 1986 (4), 1987 (5), 1988 (9), 1989 (8). Total—26.
Led National League in bases on balls received with 100 and intentional bases on balls received with 27 in 1988.
Led National League first basemen in total chances with 1,608 in 1988 and 1,566 in 1989.
Led National League first baseman in double plays with 130 in 1987 and 126 in 1988.
Named first baseman on THE SPORTING NEWS National League All-Star Team, 1988 and 1989.
Named first baseman on THE SPORTING NEWS National League Silver Slugger team, 1989.
Named first baseman on THE SPORTING NEWS College Baseball All-America Team, 1985.
Member of 1984 U.S. Olympic baseball team.
Named designated hitter on THE SPORTING NEWS College Baseball All-America Team, 1984.

Year	Club	League	Pos.	G.	AB.	R.	H.	2B.	3B.	HR.	RBI.	B.A.	PO.	A.	E.	F.A.
1985—Fresno		Calif.	1B-OF	65	217	41	67	14	0	10	48	.309	523	51	6	.990
1986—San Francisco†		Nat.	1B	111	408	66	117	27	2	11	41	.287	942	72	11	.989
1986—Phoenix		P. C.	DH	6	20	3	5	0	0	0	1	.250	0	0	0	.000
1987—San Francisco		Nat.	1B	150	529	89	163	29	5	35	91	.308	1253	103	13	.991
1988—San Francisco		Nat.	1B	*162	575	102	162	31	6	29	*109	.282	*1492	104	12	.993
1989—San Francisco		Nat.	1B	159	588	●104	196	38	9	23	111	.333	*1445	111	10	.994
Major League Totals—4 Years				582	2100	361	638	125	22	98	352	.304	5132	390	46	.992

Selected by Kansas City Royals' organization in 4th round of free-agent draft, June 7, 1982.
Selected by San Francisco Giants' organization in 1st round (second player selected) of free-agent draft, June 3, 1985.
†On disabled list, June 4 to July 24, 1986; included rehabilitation disability assignment to Phoenix, July 7 to July 24, 1986.

CHAMPIONSHIP SERIES RECORD

Holds Championship Series records for most hits (13) and total bases (24), series, 1989; most runs batted in, game (6), October 4, 1989.
Shares Championship Series records for most runs (8), consecutive hits (5) and long hits (6), series, 1989; most runs (4) and grand slams (1), game, October 4, 1989; most runs batted in, inning (4), October 4, 1989, fourth inning.
Shares National League Championship Series record for most hits, game (4), October 4, 1989.

Year	Club	League	Pos.	G.	AB.	R.	H.	2B.	3B.	HR.	RBI.	B.A.	PO.	A.	E.	F.A.
1987—San Francisco		Nat.	1B	7	25	3	9	2	0	1	3	.360	63	7	1	.986
1989—San Francisco		Nat.	1B	5	20	8	13	3	1	2	8	.650	43	6	0	1.000
Championship Series Totals—2 Years				12	45	11	22	5	1	3	11	.489	106	13	1	.992

WORLD SERIES RECORD

Year	Club	League	Pos.	G.	AB.	R.	H.	2B.	3B.	HR.	RBI.	B.A.	PO.	A.	E.	F.A.
1989—San Francisco		Nat.	1B	4	16	2	4	1	0	0	0	.250	40	2	0	1.000

ALL-STAR GAME RECORD

Year	League	Pos.	AB.	R.	H.	2B.	3B.	HR.	RBI.	B.A.	PO.	A.	E.	F.A.
1988—National		1B	2	0	0	0	0	0	0	.000	4	1	0	1.000
1989—National		1B	2	0	0	0	0	0	0	.000	5	0	0	1.000
All-Star Game Totals—2 Years			4	0	0	0	0	0	0	.000	9	1	0	1.000

STANLEY MARTEN CLARKE
(Stan)

Born August 9, 1960, at Toledo, O.
Height, 6.00. Weight, 190.
Throws and bats lefthanded.
Attended University of Toledo, Toledo, O.

Led International League in home runs allowed with 19 and balks with 16 in 1988.
Led Pioneer League in balks with 6 and tied for lead in complete games with 6 in 1981.

Year	Club	League	G.	IP.	W.	L.	Pct.	H.	R.	ER.	SO.	BB.	ERA.
1981—Medicine Hat		Pioneer	17	94	8	4	.667	96	54	42	112	35	4.02
1982—Florence		S. Atlantic	50	95	6	4	.600	60	26	20	136	52	1.89
1982—Knoxville		Southern	11	16	0	1	.000	11	3	3	12	3	1.69
1983—Knoxville		Southern	26	43⅓	2	4	.333	30	18	12	51	20	2.49
1983—Toronto		American	10	11	1	1	.500	10	4	4	7	5	3.27
1983—Syracuse		Int'national	33	53	0	3	.000	39	26	17	58	34	2.89

Year Club	League	G.	IP.	W.	L.	Pct.	H.	R.	ER.	SO.	BB.	ERA.
1984—Syracuse†	Int'national	29	56⅔	2	3	.400	40	32	26	55	46	4.13
1985—Syracuse	Int'national	43	117⅔	●14	4	★.778	106	52	44	98	66	3.37
1985—Toronto	American	4	4	0	0	.000	3	2	2	2	2	4.50
1986—Syracuse	Int'national	31	138⅔	8	9	.471	138	68	60	64	57	3.89
1986—Toronto‡	American	10	12⅔	0	1	.000	18	13	13	9	10	9.24
1987—Calgary	P. Coast	31	64⅔	4	4	.500	46	23	21	42	34	2.92
1987—Seattle§	American	22	23	2	2	.500	31	14	14	13	10	5.48
1988—Toledo x	Int'national	31	189	12	13	.480	★184	80	73	133	61	3.48
1989—Omaha	Am. Assoc.	26	171⅔	12	6	.667	157	72	67	145	31	3.51
1989—Kansas City y	American	2	7	0	2	.000	14	12	12	2	4	15.43
Major League Totals—5 Years		48	57⅔	3	6	.333	76	45	45	33	31	7.02

Selected by Toronto Blue Jays' organization in 6th round of free-agent draft, June 8, 1981.
†On disabled list, June 6 to July 3 and August 23, 1984 through remainder of season.
‡Drafted by Seattle Mariners, December 8, 1986.
§Traded to Detroit Tigers for Outfielder Bruce Fields, October 5, 1987.
xGranted free agency, October 15, 1989; signed by Omaha (Kansas City Royals' organization), November 20, 1988.
yGranted free agency, October 15, 1989.

MARTIN KEITH CLARY
(Marty)

Born April 3, 1962, at Detroit, Mich.
Height, 6.04. Weight, 195.
Throws and bats righthanded.
Attended Northwestern University, Evanston, Ill.

Led Southern League pitchers in games started with 30 in 1984.

Year Club	League	G.	IP.	W.	L.	Pct.	H.	R.	ER.	SO.	BB.	ERA.
1983—Durham	Carolina	15	89⅔	3	8	.273	101	65	50	58	39	5.02
1984—Greenville	Southern	30	186⅓	14	9	.609	172	77	66	125	82	3.19
1985—Richmond	Int'national	26	156⅔	8	12	.400	155	81	73	76	77	4.19
1986—Richmond	Int'national	24	132⅓	7	6	.538	118	72	64	56	82	4.35
1987—Richmond	Int'national	26	178	11	10	.524	180	86	74	91	75	3.74
1987—Atlanta	National	7	14⅔	0	1	.000	20	13	10	7	4	6.14
1988—Richmond	Int'national	27	143⅔	6	11	.353	142	65	54	73	37	3.38
1989—Richmond	Int'national	15	101⅔	7	5	.583	87	33	23	70	28	2.04
1989—Atlanta	National	18	108⅔	4	3	.571	103	47	38	30	31	3.15
Major League Totals—2 Years		25	123⅓	4	4	.500	123	60	48	37	35	3.50

Selected by Atlanta Braves' organization in 3rd round of free-agent draft, June 6, 1983.

WILLIAM ROGER CLEMENS
(Known by middle name.)

Born August 4, 1962, at Dayton, O.
Height, 6.04. Weight, 220.
Throws and bats righthanded.
Attended San Jacinto College (North), Houston, Tex.,
and University of Texas, Austin, Tex.

Holds major league record for most strikeouts, nine-inning game (20), April 29, 1986.
Shares American League record for most consecutive strikeouts, game (8), April 29, 1986.
Led American League in shutouts with 7 in 1987 and 8 in 1988.
Led American League in complete games with 18 in 1987 and tied for lead with 14 in 1988.
Named Major League Player of the Year by THE SPORTING NEWS, 1986.
Named American League Pitcher of the Year by THE SPORTING NEWS, 1986.
Won American League Cy Young Memorial Award, 1986 and 1987.
Named American League Most Valuable Player by Baseball Writers' Association of America, 1986.
Named righthanded pitcher on THE SPORTING NEWS American League All-Star Team, 1986 and 1987.

Year Club	League	G.	IP.	W.	L.	Pct.	H.	R.	ER.	SO.	BB.	ERA.
1983—Winter Haven	Florida St.	4	29	3	1	.750	22	4	4	36	0	1.24
1983—New Britain	Eastern	7	52	4	1	.800	31	8	8	59	12	1.38
1984—Pawtucket	Int'national	7	46⅔	2	3	.400	39	12	10	50	14	1.93
1984—Boston	American	21	133⅓	9	4	.692	146	67	64	126	29	4.32
1985—Boston†	American	15	98⅓	7	5	.583	83	38	36	74	37	3.29
1986—Boston	American	33	254	★24	4	★.857	179	77	70	238	67	★2.48
1987—Boston	American	36	281⅔	●20	9	.690	248	100	93	256	83	2.97
1988—Boston	American	35	264	18	12	.600	217	93	86	★291	62	2.93
1989—Boston	American	35	253⅓	17	11	.607	215	101	88	230	93	3.13
Major League Totals—6 Years		175	1284⅔	95	45	.679	1088	476	437	1215	371	3.06

Selected by New York Mets' organization in 12th round of free-agent draft, June 8, 1981.
Selected by Boston Red Sox' organization in 1st round (19th player selected) of free-agent draft, June 6, 1983.
†On disabled list, July 8 to August 3 and August 21, 1985 through remainder of season.

CHAMPIONSHIP SERIES RECORD

Holds Championship Series record for most hits allowed (22), series, 1986.
Shares Championship Series records for most earned runs allowed, series (11), most earned runs allowed, game (7), October 7, 1986; most consecutive strikeouts, game (4), October 6, 1988.
Holds American League Championship Series record for most innings pitched (22⅔), 1986.
Shares American League Championship Series record for most runs allowed, game (8), October 7, 1986.

Year Club	League	G.	IP.	W.	L.	Pct.	H.	R.	ER.	SO.	BB.	ERA.
1986—Boston	American	3	22⅔	1	1	.500	22	12	11	17	7	4.37
1988—Boston	American	1	7	0	0	.000	6	3	3	8	0	3.86
Championship Series Totals—2 Years		4	29⅔	1	1	.500	28	15	14	25	7	4.25

WORLD SERIES RECORD

Year Club	League	G.	IP.	W.	L.	Pct.	H.	R.	ER.	SO.	BB.	ERA.
1986—Boston	American	2	11⅓	0	0	.000	9	5	4	11	6	3.18

ALL-STAR GAME RECORD

Year League	IP.	W.	L.	Pct.	H.	R.	ER.	SO.	BB.	ERA.
1986—American	3	1	0	1.000	0	0	0	2	0	0.00
1988—American	1	0	0	.000	0	0	0	1	0	0.00
All-Star Game Totals—2 Years	4	1	0	1.000	0	0	0	3	0	0.00

PATRICK BRIAN CLEMENTS
(Pat)

Born February 2, 1962, at McCloud, Calif.
Height, 6.00. Weight, 180.
Throws left and bats righthanded.
Attended UCLA.

Major League saves: 1985 (3), 1986 (2), 1987 (7). Total—12.

Year Club	League	G.	IP.	W.	L.	Pct.	H.	R.	ER.	SO.	BB.	ERA.
1983—Peoria	Midwest	15	92⅓	4	7	.364	113	56	46	67	24	4.48
1984—Waterbury	Eastern	43	67	4	2	.667	59	28	20	44	29	2.69
1985—California†	American	41	62	5	0	1.000	47	23	23	19	25	3.34
1985—Pittsburgh	National	27	34⅓	0	2	.000	39	14	14	17	15	3.67
1986—Pittsburgh‡	National	65	61	0	4	.000	53	20	19	31	32	2.80
1987—New York	American	55	80	3	3	.500	91	45	44	36	30	4.95
1987—Columbus	Int'national	4	19	1	0	1.000	19	8	8	7	2	3.79
1988—Columbus	Int'national	32	144	6	7	.462	136	55	44	69	34	2.75
1988—New York§	American	6	8⅓	0	0	.000	12	8	6	3	4	6.48
1989—Las Vegas	P. Coast	18	55	3	1	.750	57	31	25	34	24	4.09
1989—San Diego	National	23	39	4	1	.800	39	17	17	18	15	3.92
American League Totals—2 Years		102	150⅓	8	3	.727	150	76	73	58	59	4.37
National League Totals—3 Years		115	134⅓	4	7	.364	131	51	50	66	62	3.35
Major League Totals—5 Years		217	284⅔	12	10	.545	281	127	123	124	121	3.89

Selected by New York Yankees' organization in 32nd round of free-agent draft, June 3, 1980.
Selected by California Angels' organization in 4th round of free-agent draft, June 6, 1983.

†Traded with Outfielder Mike Brown and a player to be named later to Pittsburgh Pirates for Pitchers John Candelaria and Al Holland and Outfielder George Hendrick, August 2, 1985; Pittsburgh organization acquired Pitcher Bob Kipper to complete deal, August 16, 1985.

‡Traded with Pitchers Rick Rhoden and Cecilio Guante to New York Yankees for Pitchers Doug Drabek, Brian Fisher and Logan Easley, November 26, 1986.

§Traded with First Baseman-Outfielder Jack Clark to San Diego Padres for Pitchers Jimmy Jones and Lance McCullers and Outfielder Stan Jefferson, October 24, 1988.

BRYAN RICHARD CLUTTERBUCK

Born December 17, 1959, at Detroit, Mich.
Height, 6.04. Weight, 223.
Throws and bats righthanded.
Attended Eastern Michigan University, Ypsilanti, Mich.

Tied for Texas League lead in games started by pitchers with 27 in 1983 and 1984.
Tied for Midwest League lead in shutouts with 4 in 1982.

Year Club	League	G.	IP.	W.	L.	Pct.	H.	R.	ER.	SO.	BB.	ERA.
1981—Butte	Pioneer	6	16	1	1	.500	22	13	13	4	7	7.31
1982—Beloit	Midwest	26	173⅔	13	6	.684	165	84	70	138	56	3.63
1983—El Paso	Texas	27	166⅓	11	7	.611	204	118	96	86	78	5.19
1984—El Paso	Texas	27	179	10	9	.526	★198	★103	★79	112	52	3.97
1985—Vancouver	P. Coast	29	147⅔	11	7	.611	156	68	58	101	41	3.53
1986—Vancouver	P. Coast	17	115⅓	8	5	.615	121	60	59	63	30	4.60
1986—Milwaukee	American	20	56⅔	0	1	.000	68	32	27	38	16	4.29
1987—Denver†	Am. Assoc.	7	33⅓	3	2	.600	49	24	21	14	4	5.67
1988—Denver	Am. Assoc.	20	130⅔	9	3	★.750	133	54	50	88	32	3.44
1989—Milwaukee‡	American	14	67⅓	2	5	.286	73	39	31	29	16	4.14
1989—El Paso	Texas	4	17	0	2	.000	23	14	12	8	9	6.35
Major League Totals—2 Years		34	124	2	6	.250	141	71	58	67	32	4.21

Selected by Milwaukee Brewers' organization in 7th round of free-agent draft, June 8, 1981.

†Granted free agency, October 15, 1987; re-signed by Brewers, November 11, 1987.

‡On disabled list, June 24 to September 18, 1989; included rehabilitation disability assignment to El Paso, July 20 to August 7, 1989.

—DID YOU KNOW—

That the Mets led the National League in pinch-hitting with a .255 mark in 1989 while the Astros had the lowest average at .185?

DAVID CARTER COCHRANE
(Dave)

Born January 31, 1963, at Riverside, Calif.
Height, 6.02. Weight, 180.
Throws right and bats left and righthanded.
Attended California State University, Fullerton, Calif.

Led Texas League batters in strikeouts with 133 in 1984.
Led Carolina League in game-winning RBIs with 18 in 1983.
Led New York-Pennsylvania League batters in strikeouts with 117 and intentional bases on balls received with 7 in 1982.

Year	Club	League	Pos.	G.	AB.	R.	H.	2B.	3B.	HR.	RBI.	B.A.	PO.	A.	E.	F.A.
1982—Little Falls	NYP		3B	70	269	51	81	16	2	22	62	.301	49	110	★29	.846
1983—Lynchburg	Carol.		3B	120	445	73	117	16	1	25	★102	.267	263	66	167	26	.900
1984—Jackson	Texas		3B-SS	129	454	66	121	29	3	22	77	.267	79	167	32	.885
1985—Jackson†‡§	Texas		SS	33	103	14	23	1	0	4	20	.223	39	87	14	.900
1986—Birmingham	South.		3B-SS	93	349	66	95	23	5	17	74	.272	82	201	36	.887
1986—Buffalo	A. A.		3B-SS-OF	38	124	15	28	7	0	6	16	.226	25	58	4	.954
1986—Chicago	Amer.		3B-SS	19	62	4	12	2	0	1	2	.194	10	31	6	.872
1987—Hawaii xy	P. C.		3-O-P-1	129	451	60	122	23	3	15	66	.271	106	83	15	.926
1988—Calgary	P. C.		1-O-3-C-S	120	406	55	116	27	3	15	61	.286	387	106	29	.944
1989—Calgary	P. C.		3-1-S-C-O	32	125	22	34	10	0	6	35	.272	86	43	6	.956
1989—Seattle	Amer.		I-O-C	54	102	13	24	4	1	3	7	.235	78	41	5	.960
Major League Totals—2 Years				73	164	17	36	6	1	4	9	.220	88	72	11	.936

Selected by New York Mets' organization in 4th round of free-agent draft, June 8, 1981.
†On disabled list, May 25 to July 16, 1985.
‡Traded to Chicago White Sox' organization for Outfielder Tom Paciorek, July 16, 1985.
§On Glens Falls disabled list, July 16, 1985 through remainder of season.
xTraded with Pitcher Floyd Bannister to Kansas City Royals for Pitchers John Davis, Melido Perez, Chuck Mount and Greg Hibbard, December 10, 1987.
yTraded to Calgary (Seattle Mariners' organization) for Pitcher Ken Spratke, February 3, 1988.

PITCHING RECORD

Year	Club	League	G.	IP.	W.	L.	Pct.	H.	R.	ER.	SO.	BB.	ERA.
1987—Hawaii	P. Coast		8	11⅓	1	1	.500	15	9	9	6	11	7.15

KEVIN REESE COFFMAN

Born January 19, 1965, at Austin, Tex.
Height, 6.03. Weight, 206.
Throws and bats righthanded.

Led Southern League in wild pitches with 21 in 1987.

Year	Club	League	G.	IP.	W.	L.	Pct.	H.	R.	ER.	SO.	BB.	ERA.
1983—Bradenton Braves	Gulf Coast	6	28⅔	2	4	.333	27	29	21	25	39	6.59
1984—Anderson	S. Atlantic	7	32⅔	1	4	.200	37	23	17	23	26	4.68
1984—Pulaski	Ap'lachian	11	48	1	4	.200	41	26	22	41	33	4.13
1985—Durham†	Carolina	3	4⅓	0	1	.000	4	5	5	1	11	10.38
1985—Sumter‡	S. Atlantic	24	62⅔	1	3	.250	42	25	22	43	26	3.16
1986—Durham	Carolina	3	13⅓	1	2	.333	11	12	11	7	17	7.43
1986—Sumter	S. Atlantic	18	114⅓	10	3	.769	99	56	39	120	64	3.07
1986—Greenville	Southern	8	48⅔	3	4	.429	43	24	24	43	30	4.44
1987—Greenville	Southern	30	181⅔	11	11	.500	162	102	89	153	★130	4.41
1987—Atlanta	National	5	25⅓	2	3	.400	31	14	13	14	22	4.62
1988—Atlanta	National	18	67	2	6	.250	62	52	43	24	54	5.78
1988—Durham	Carolina	8	10	1	1	.500	12	6	5	10	3	4.50
1988—Richmond§	Int'national	9	19⅓	1	1	.500	15	10	9	18	20	4.19
1989—Charlotte	Southern	7	21⅔	0	3	.000	15	15	9	12	26	3.74
1989—Iowa	Am. Assoc.	14	17⅔	0	2	.000	17	19	16	11	26	8.15
1989—Winston-Salem	Carolina	7	36	2	3	.400	23	24	18	47	34	4.50
Major League Totals—2 Years		23	92⅓	4	9	.308	93	66	56	38	76	5.46

Selected by Atlanta Braves' organization in 11th round of free-agent draft, June 6, 1983.
†On disabled list, April 24 to May 4, 1985.
‡On disabled list, May 4 to May 28, 1985.
§Traded with Pitcher Kevin Blankenship to Chicago Cubs for Catcher Jody Davis, September 29, 1988.

ALEXANDER COLE JR.
(Alex)

Born August 17, 1965, at Fayetteville, N. C.
Height, 6.02. Weight, 170.
Throws and bats lefthanded.
Attended Manatee Junior College, Bradenton, Fla.

Led American Association in stolen bases with 47 in 1989.
Led Texas League in stolen bases with 68 and caught stealing with 29 in 1987.
Led Florida State League in caught stealing with 22 in 1986.
Led Appalachian League in stolen bases with 46 and caught stealing with 8 in 1985.
Led American Association outfielders in total chances with 342 in 1989.
Led Appalachian League outfielders in total chances with 142 in 1985.
Tied for Texas League lead in double plays by outfielders with 5 in 1987.

Year Club League	Pos.	G.	AB.	R.	H.	2B.	3B.	HR.	RBI.	B.A.	PO.	A.	E.	F.A.
1985—Johnson City .... Appal.	OF	66	232	★60	61	5	1	1	13	.263	★127	★12	3	.979
1986—St. Petersburg....... Fla. St.	OF	74	286	76	98	9	1	0	26	.343	201	4	8	.962
1986—Louisville .... A. A.	OF	63	200	25	50	2	4	1	16	.250	135	6	9	.940
1987—Arkansas................. Texas	OF	125	477	68	122	12	4	2	27	.256	289	14	10	.968
1988—Louisville .... A. A.	OF	120	392	44	91	7	8	0	24	.232	276	13	1	.997
1989—St. Petersburg....... Fla. St.	OF	8	32	2	6	0	0	0	1	.188	13	0	0	1.000
1989—Louisville .... A. A.	OF	127	455	75	128	5	5	2	29	.281	★320	14	8	.977

Selected by Pittsburgh Pirates' organization in 11th round of free-agent draft, January 17, 1984.
Selected by St. Louis Cardinals' organization in 2nd round of free-agent draft, January 9, 1985.

VINCENT MAURICE COLEMAN
(Vince)

Born September 22, 1961, at Jacksonville, Fla.
Height, 6.00. Weight, 170.
Throws right and bats left and righthanded.
Received degree in physical education from Florida A&M University, Tallahassee, Fla.
Cousin of Greg Coleman, punter with Cleveland Browns, Minnesota Vikings
and Washington Redskins, 1977 through 1988.

Holds major league records for most stolen bases (110) and most caught stealing (25), rookie season, 1985; most consecutive stolen bases without caught stealing, lifetime (50), September 18, 1988 through July 26, 1989.
Shares major league records for most sacrifice flies, game (3), May 1, 1986; fewest errors by outfielder, season, for leader in errors (9), 1986.
Major League stolen bases: 1985 (110), 1986 (107), 1987 (109), 1988 (81), 1989 (65). Total—472.
Led National League in stolen bases with 110 in 1985, 107 in 1986, 109 in 1987, 81 in 1988 and 65 in 1989.
Led National League in caught stealing with 25 in 1985, 22 in 1987 and tied for lead with 27 in 1988.
Led American Association in stolen bases with 101 and caught stealing with 36 in 1984.
Led South Atlantic League in stolen bases with 145 and caught stealing with 31 in 1983.
Tied for Appalachian League lead in stolen bases with 43 in 1982.
Led American Association outfielders in total chances with 381 in 1984.
Named National League Rookie Player of the Year by THE SPORTING NEWS, 1985.
Named National League Rookie of the Year by Baseball Writers' Association of America, 1985.
Named South Atlantic League Most Valuable Player, 1983.

Year Club League	Pos.	G.	AB.	R.	H.	2B.	3B.	HR.	RBI.	B.A.	PO.	A.	E.	F.A.
1982—Johnson City .... Appal.	OF	58	212	40	53	2	1	0	16	.250	123	7	8	.942
1983—Macon.................... S. Atl.	OF	113	446	99	156	8	7	0	53	★.350	225	18	8	.968
1984—Louisville .... A. A.	OF	152	★608	★97	156	21	7	4	48	.257	357	14	●10	.974
1985—Louisville .... A. A.	OF	5	21	1	3	0	0	0	0	.143	8	0	0	1.000
1985—St. Louis................. Nat.	OF	151	636	107	170	20	10	1	40	.267	305	16	7	.979
1986—St. Louis................. Nat.	OF	154	600	94	139	13	8	0	29	.232	300	12	●9	.972
1987—St. Louis................. Nat.	OF	151	623	121	180	14	10	3	43	.289	274	16	9	.970
1988—St. Louis................. Nat.	OF	153	616	77	160	20	10	3	38	.260	290	14	9	.971
1989—St. Louis................. Nat.	OF	145	563	94	143	21	9	2	28	.254	247	5	●10	.962
Major League Totals—5 Years.................		754	3038	493	792	88	47	9	178	.261	1416	63	44	.971

Selected by Philadelphia Phillies' organization in 20th round of free-agent draft, June 8, 1981.
Selected by St. Louis Cardinals' organization in 10th round of free-agent draft, June 7, 1982.

CHAMPIONSHIP SERIES RECORD

Shares National League Championship Series record for most times caught stealing, total series (4).

Year Club League	Pos.	G.	AB.	R.	H.	2B.	3B.	HR.	RBI.	B.A.	PO.	A.	E.	F.A.
1985—St. Louis................. Nat.	OF	3	14	2	4	0	0	0	1	.286	8	0	0	1.000
1987—St. Louis................. Nat.	OF	7	26	3	7	1	0	0	4	.269	9	1	0	1.000
Championship Series Totals—2 Years.....		10	40	5	11	1	0	0	5	.275	17	1	0	1.000

WORLD SERIES RECORD

Year Club League	Pos.	G.	AB.	R.	H.	2B.	3B.	HR.	RBI.	B.A.	PO.	A.	E.	F.A.
1987—St. Louis................. Nat.	OF	7	28	5	4	2	0	0	2	.143	10	2	0	1.000

Eligible for 1985 World Series with St. Louis Cardinals; did not play.

ALL-STAR GAME RECORD

Year League	Pos.	AB.	R.	H.	2B.	3B.	HR.	RBI.	B.A.	PO.	A.	E.	F.A.
1988—National..............................	OF	2	1	1	0	0	0	0	.500	3	0	0	1.000
1989—National..............................	PR-OF	0	0	0	0	0	0	0	.000	0	0	0	.000
All-Star Game Totals—2 Years..................		2	1	1	0	0	0	0	.500	3	0	0	1.000

DARNELL COLES

First name pronounced Darr-NELL.

Born June 2, 1962, at San Bernardino, Calif.
Height, 6.01. Weight, 185.
Throws and bats righthanded.
Attended Orange Coast College, Costa Mesa, Calif.

Major League stolen bases: 1984 (2), 1986 (6), 1987 (1), 1988 (4), 1989 (5). Total—18.
Hit three home runs in a game, September 20, 1987.
Led Midwest League shortstops in double plays with 66 in 1981.

Year Club	League	Pos.	G.	AB.	R.	H.	2B.	3B.	HR.	RBI.	B.A.	PO.	A.	E.	F.A.
1980—Bellingham	N'west	SS	35	117	23	25	3	1	2	12	.214	37	80	*28	.807
1981—Wausau................	Midw.	SS	111	354	53	97	20	3	9	48	.274	154	335	52	.904
1982—Bakersfield..........	Calif.	SS	136	482	91	146	24	4	11	55	.303	200	419	*73	.895
1983—Chattanooga	South.	SS	72	261	49	75	10	4	5	24	.287	131	232	30	.924
1983—Salt Lake City.....	P. C.	SS	61	234	43	74	12	5	10	41	.316	100	178	25	.917
1983—Seattle.................	Amer.	3B	27	92	9	26	7	0	1	6	.283	17	47	4	.941
1984—Salt Lake City†.....	P. C.	3B	69	242	57	77	22	3	14	68	.318	45	164	16	.929
1984—Seattle.................	Amer.	3B-OF	48	143	15	23	3	1	0	6	.161	31	63	8	.922
1985—Calgary‡	P. C.	3B-SS-OF	31	97	16	31	8	0	4	24	.320	16	49	5	.929
1985—Seattle§...............	Amer.	SS-3B-OF	27	59	8	14	4	0	1	5	.237	25	44	6	.920
1986—Detroit x..............	Amer.	3B-OF-SS	142	521	67	142	30	2	20	86	.273	111	242	23	.939
1987—Detroit y..............	Amer.	3-1-O-S	53	149	14	27	5	1	4	15	.181	84	67	17	.899
1987—Toledo z...............	Int.	3B-OF-SS	10	37	7	12	5	0	1	8	.324	7	8	1	.938
1987—Pittsburgh............	Nat.	OF-3B-1B	40	119	20	27	8	0	6	24	.227	39	20	3	.952
1988—Pittsburgh a	Nat.	OF-1B-3B	68	211	20	49	13	1	5	36	.232	100	0	2	.980
1988—Seattle.................	Amer.	OF-1B	55	195	32	57	10	1	10	34	.292	66	3	1	.986
1989—Seattle.................	Amer.	OF-3B-1B	146	535	54	135	21	3	10	59	.252	317	76	12	.970
American League Totals—7 Years			498	1694	199	424	80	8	46	211	.250	651	542	71	.944
National League Totals—2 Years			108	330	40	76	21	1	11	60	.230	139	20	5	.970
Major League Totals—7 Years................			606	2024	239	500	101	9	57	271	.247	790	562	76	.947

Selected by Seattle Mariners' organization in 1st round (sixth player selected) of free-agent draft, June 3, 1980.

†On Seattle disabled list, March 29 to April 24, 1984; included rehabilitation disability assignment to Salt Lake City, April 12 to April 24, 1984.

‡On disabled list, August 8 to September 9, 1985.

§Traded to Detroit Tigers for Pitcher Rich Monteleone, December 12, 1985.

xOn disabled list, June 16 to July 1, 1986.

yOn disabled list, May 25 to June 27, 1987; included rehabilitation disability assignment to Toledo, June 16 to June 27, 1987.

zTraded with a player to be named later to Pittsburgh Pirates for Third Baseman Jim Morrison, August 7, 1987; Pittsburgh organization acquired Pitcher Morris Madden to complete deal, August 12, 1987.

aTraded to Seattle Mariners for Outfielder Glenn Wilson, July 22, 1988.

DAVID S. COLLINS

(Dave)

Born October 20, 1952, at Rapid City, S. D.
Height, 5.10. Weight, 175.
Throws left and bats left and righthanded.
Attended Mesa Community College, Mesa, Ariz.

Major League stolen bases: 1975 (24), 1976 (32), 1977 (25), 1978 (7), 1979 (16), 1980 (79), 1981 (26), 1982 (13), 1983 (31), 1984 (60), 1985 (29), 1986 (27), 1987 (9), 1988 (7), 1989 (3). Total—388.
Led Pioneer League outfielders in double plays with 3 in 1972.
Named Pioneer League Most Valuable Player, 1972.

Year Club	League	Pos.	G.	AB.	R.	H.	2B.	3B.	HR.	RBI.	B.A.	PO.	A.	E.	F.A.
1972—Idaho Falls...........	Pion.	*OF-1B	68	252	40	69	8	*8	1	27	.274	101	*11	3	.974
1973—Quad Cities†.........	Midw.	OF	110	387	61	100	15	7	4	49	.258	229	10	11	.956
1974—Salinas................	Calif.	OF-1B	39	143	30	49	3	5	1	21	.343	109	0	5	.956
1974—El Paso.................	Texas	1B-OF	82	324	64	114	15	4	4	49	*.352	381	14	12	.971
1975—Salt Lake City......	P. C.	OF	51	193	41	60	7	6	0	24	.311	58	2	1	.984
1975—California............	Amer.	OF	93	319	41	85	13	4	3	29	.266	159	3	2	.988
1976—Salt Lake City......	P. C.	OF	35	136	28	49	13	4	0	12	.360	50	3	2	.964
1976—California‡...........	Amer.	OF	99	365	45	96	12	1	4	28	.263	160	3	1	.994
1977—Seattle§...............	Amer.	OF	120	402	46	96	9	3	5	28	.239	124	6	2	.985
1978—Cincinnati............	Nat.	OF	102	102	13	22	1	0	0	7	.216	30	1	1	.969
1979—Cincinnati............	Nat.	OF-1B	122	396	59	126	16	4	3	35	.318	223	3	4	.983
1980—Cincinnati............	Nat.	OF	144	551	94	167	20	4	3	35	.303	337	5	5	.986
1981—Cincinnati x..........	Nat.	OF	95	360	63	98	18	6	3	23	.272	167	4	4	.977
1982—New York y	Amer.	OF-1B	111	348	41	88	12	3	3	25	.253	498	28	7	.987
1983—Toronto z	Amer.	OF-1B	118	402	55	109	12	4	1	34	.271	270	9	3	.989
1984—Toronto a.............	Amer.	OF-1B	128	441	59	136	24	●15	2	44	.308	237	11	2	.992
1985—Oakland b.............	Amer.	OF	112	379	52	95	16	4	4	29	.251	221	1	5	.978
1986—Detroit cd............	Amer.	OF	124	419	44	113	18	2	1	27	.270	211	2	1	.995
1987—Nashville..............	A. A.	DH-PH	13	40	8	8	6	0	0	9	.200	0	0	0	.000
1987—Cincinnati e..........	Nat.	OF	57	85	19	25	5	0	0	5	.294	36	0	0	1.000
1988—Cincinnati f..........	Nat.	OF-1B	99	174	12	41	6	2	0	14	.236	66	2	4	.944
1989—Cincinnati gh	Nat.	OF	78	106	12	25	4	0	0	7	.236	41	0	0	1.000
National League Totals—7 Years			697	1774	272	504	70	16	9	126	.284	900	15	18	.981
American League Totals—8 Years			905	3075	383	818	116	36	23	244	.266	1880	63	23	.988
Major League Totals—15 Years..............			1602	4849	655	1322	186	52	32	370	.273	2780	78	41	.986

Selected by Cincinnati Reds' organization in 23rd round of free-agent draft, June 8, 1971.
Selected by Kansas City Royals' organization in secondary phase of free-agent draft, January 12, 1972.
Selected by California Angels' organization in secondary phase of free-agent draft, June 6, 1972.

†On disabled list, May 21 to May 31, 1973.

‡Selected by Seattle Mariners in special American League expansion draft, November 5, 1976.

§Traded to Cincinnati Reds for Pitcher Shane Rawley, December 9, 1977.

xGranted free agency, November 13, 1981; signed by New York Yankees, December 23, 1981.

yTraded with Pitcher Mike Morgan, First Baseman Fred McGriff and a reported $400,000 to Toronto Blue Jays for Pitcher Dale Murray and Outfielder-Catcher Tom Dodd, December 9, 1982.

zOn disabled list, June 4 to June 22, 1983.

aTraded with Shortstop Alfredo Griffin and cash to Oakland A's for Pitcher Bill Caudill, December 8, 1984.
bTraded to Detroit Tigers for Infielder Barbaro Garbey, November 13, 1985.
cReleased, October 16, 1986; signed by Montreal Expos, November 13, 1986.
dReleased, March 31, 1987; signed by Nashville (Cincinnati Reds' organization), June 19, 1987.
eGranted free agency, November 9, 1987; re-signed by Reds, December 8, 1987.
fGranted free agency, November 4, 1988; re-signed by Reds, December 7, 1988.
gReleased, June 23, 1989; re-signed by Reds, July 30, 1989.
hGranted free agency, November 13, 1989.

CHAMPIONSHIP SERIES RECORD

Year Club League	Pos.	G.	AB.	R.	H.	2B.	3B.	HR.	RBI.	B.A.	PO.	A.	E.	F.A.
1979—Cincinnati.............. Nat.	OF	3	14	0	5	1	0	0	1	.357	5	0	0	1.000

PATRICK DENNIS COMBS
(Pat)

Born September 29, 1966, at Newport, R.I.
Height, 6.04. Weight, 200.
Throws and bats lefthanded.
Attended Rice University, Houston, Tex., and
Baylor University, Waco, Tex.

Led Eastern League in home runs allowed with 16 in 1989.

Year Club	League	G.	IP.	W.	L.	Pct.	H.	R.	ER.	SO.	BB.	ERA.
1989—Reading............................	Eastern	19	125	8	7	.533	104	57	47	77	40	3.38
1989—Scranton/Wilkes-Barre................	Int'national	3	24⅓	3	0	1.000	15	4	1	20	7	0.37
1989—Philadelphia	National	6	38⅔	4	0	1.000	36	10	9	30	6	2.09
Major League Totals—1 Year.....................		6	38⅔	4	0	1.000	36	10	9	30	6	2.09

Selected by Philadelphia Phillies' organization in 1st round (11th player selected) of free-agent draft, June 1, 1988.

KEITH MARTIN COMSTOCK

Born December 23, 1955, at San Francisco, Calif.
Height, 6.00. Weight, 174.
Throws and bats lefthanded.
Attended Canada College, Redwood City, Calif.
Brother of Brad Comstock, pitcher in San Francisco Giants' organization, 1987 and 1988.

Major League saves: 1987 (1).
Tied for Southern League lead in shutouts with 3 in 1983.

Year Club	League	G.	IP.	W.	L.	Pct.	H.	R.	ER.	SO.	BB.	ERA.
1976—Idaho Falls†	Pioneer	15	37	1	4	.200	33	18	16	45	32	3.89
1977—Quad Cities.........................	Midwest	18	32	1	0	1.000	22	18	18	39	18	5.06
1977—Salinas	California	23	33	1	1	.500	35	26	17	41	18	4.64
1978—Salinas	California	27	82	6	4	.600	70	31	26	71	46	2.85
1979—El Paso‡..............................	Texas	16	63	2	5	.286	95	64	50	18	35	7.14
1980—West Haven	Eastern	29	73	2	4	.333	64	40	34	52	37	4.19
1981—West Haven	Eastern	35	145	8	7	.533	123	76	66	133	80	4.10
1982—West Haven	Eastern	24	125	9	5	.643	99	48	42	132	69	3.02
1982—Tacoma§..............................	P. Coast	5	27⅔	1	2	.333	34	24	22	22	12	7.16
1983—Birmingham x.......................	Southern	37	145⅔	12	3	●.800	130	58	52	136	63	3.21
1984—Minnesota	American	4	6⅓	0	0	.000	6	6	6	2	4	8.53
1984—Toledo y..............................	Int'national	23	164⅓	12	6	.667	132	58	51	154	56	2.79
1985—Yomiuri	Central	21	124	8	8	.500	....	....	58	87	76	4.19
1986—Yomiuri z.............................	Central	3	10	0	2	.000	....	....	9	7	7	7.83
1987—Phoenix................................	P. Coast	17	39	4	2	.667	24	12	12	35	23	2.77
1987—San Francisco ab-San Diego	National	41	56⅔	2	1	.667	52	30	29	59	31	4.61
1988—Las Vegas	P. Coast	50	71⅔	5	4	.556	67	32	25	78	31	3.14
1988—San Diego	National	7	8	0	0	.000	8	6	6	9	3	6.75
1989—Las Vegas c-Calgary	P. Coast	33	55⅓	9	2	.818	45	19	18	64	21	2.93
1989—Seattle	American	31	25⅔	1	2	.333	26	8	8	22	10	2.81
American League Totals—2 Years.....................		35	32	1	2	.333	32	14	14	24	14	3.94
National League Totals—2 Years.....................		48	64⅔	2	1	.667	60	36	35	68	34	4.87
Major League Totals—4 Years.....................		83	96⅔	3	3	.500	92	50	49	92	48	4.56

Selected by California Angels' organization in 5th round of free-agent draft, January 7, 1976.
†On disabled list, July 29, 1976 through remainder of season.
‡Released, July 6, 1979; signed by West Haven (Oakland A's organization), February 29, 1980.
§Sold to Detroit Tigers' organization, March 28, 1983.
xGranted free agency, October 23, 1983; signed by Minnesota Twins' organization, October 23, 1983.
yReleased, November 6, 1984; signed by Yomiuri Giants of Japanese Baseball League.
zReleased by Yomiuri Giants; signed by San Francisco Giants, November 24, 1986.
aAppeared in one game as an outfielder with no chances.
bTraded with Third Baseman Chris Brown and Pitchers Mark Davis and Mark Grant to San Diego Padres for Pitchers Dave Dravecky and Craig Lefferts and Infielder Kevin Mitchell, July 4, 1987.
cReleased, June 18, 1989; signed by Seattle Mariners, June 20, 1989.

DAVID BRIAN CONE

Born January 2, 1963, at Kansas City, Mo.
Height, 6.01. Weight, 185.
Throws right and bats lefthanded.

Major League saves: 1987 (1).
Tied for National League lead in balks with 10 in 1988.
Led Southern League in wild pitches with 27 in 1984.

Year	Club	League	G.	IP.	W.	L.	Pct.	H.	R.	ER.	SO.	BB.	ERA.
1981—Sarasota Royals-Blue	Gulf Coast	14	67	6	4	.600	52	24	19	45	33	2.55
1982—Charleston	S. Atlantic	16	104⅔	9	2	.818	84	38	24	87	47	2.06
1982—Fort Myers	Florida St.	10	72⅓	7	1	.875	56	21	17	57	25	2.12
1983—Jacksonville†	Southern					(Did not play)						
1984—Memphis	Southern	29	178⅔	8	12	.400	162	103	85	110	114	4.28
1985—Omaha	Am. Assoc.	28	158⅔	9	15	.375	157	90	82	115	∗93	4.65
1986—Omaha	Am. Assoc.	39	71	8	4	.667	60	23	22	63	25	2.79
1986—Kansas City‡	American	11	22⅔	0	0	.000	29	14	14	21	13	5.56
1987—New York§	National	21	99⅓	5	6	.455	87	46	41	68	44	3.71
1987—Tidewater	Int'national	3	11	0	1	.000	10	8	7	7	6	5.73
1988—New York	National	35	231⅓	20	3	∗.870	178	67	57	213	80	2.22
1989—New York	National	34	219⅔	14	8	.636	183	92	86	190	74	3.52
American League Totals—1 Year		11	22⅔	0	0	.000	29	14	14	21	13	5.56
National League Totals—3 Years		90	550⅓	39	17	.696	448	205	184	471	198	3.01
Major League Totals—4 Years		101	573	39	17	.696	477	219	198	492	211	3.11

Selected by Kansas City Royals' organization in 3rd round of free-agent draft, June 8, 1981.
†On disabled list, April 8, 1983 through entire season.
‡Traded with Catcher Chris Jelic to New York Mets for Catcher Ed Hearn and Pitchers Rick Anderson and Mauro Gozzo, March 27, 1987.
§On disabled list, May 28 to August 14, 1987; included rehabilitation disability assignment to Tidewater, July 30 to August 14, 1987.

CHAMPIONSHIP SERIES RECORD

Year	Club	League	G.	IP.	W.	L.	Pct.	H.	R.	ER.	SO.	BB.	ERA.
1988—New York	National	3	12	1	1	.500	10	6	6	9	5	4.50

ALL-STAR GAME RECORD

Year	League	IP.	W.	L.	Pct.	H.	R.	ER.	SO.	BB.	ERA.
1988—National	1	0	0	.000	0	0	0	1	0	0.00

DENNIS BRYAN COOK

Born October 4, 1962, at Lamarque, Texas.
Height, 6.03. Weight, 185.
Throws and bats lefthanded.
Attended Angelina College, Lufkin, Tex., and University of Texas, Austin, Tex.
Named Texas League Pitcher of the Year, 1987.

Year	Club	League	G.	IP.	W.	L.	Pct.	H.	R.	ER.	SO.	BB.	ERA.
1985—Clinton	Midwest	13	83	5	4	.556	73	35	31	40	27	3.36
1986—Fresno	California	27	170	12	7	.632	141	92	75	∗173	100	3.97
1987—Shreveport	Texas	16	105⅔	9	2	.818	94	32	25	98	20	2.13
1987—Phoenix	P. Coast	12	62	2	5	.286	72	45	36	24	26	5.23
1988—Phoenix	P. Coast	26	141⅓	11	9	.550	138	73	61	110	51	3.88
1988—San Francisco	National	4	22	2	1	.667	9	8	7	13	11	2.86
1989—Phoenix	P. Coast	12	78	7	4	.636	73	29	27	85	19	3.12
1989—San Francisco†-Philadelphia	National	23	121	7	8	.467	110	59	50	67	38	3.72
Major League Totals—2 Years		27	143	9	9	.500	119	67	57	80	49	3.59

Selected by San Diego Padres' organization in 6th round of free-agent draft, January 11, 1983.
Selected by San Francisco Giants' organization in 18th round of free-agent draft, June 3, 1985.
†Traded with Pitcher Terry Mulholland and Third Baseman Charlie Hayes to Philadelphia Phillies for Pitcher Steve Bedrosian and a player to be named later, June 18, 1989; San Francisco Giants' organization acquired Infielder Rick Parker to complete deal, August 7, 1989.

MICHAEL HORACE COOK
(Mike)

Born August 14, 1963, at Charleston, S. C.
Height, 6.03. Weight, 225.
Throws and bats righthanded.
Attended University of South Carolina, Columbia, S. C.

Year	Club	League	G.	IP.	W.	L.	Pct.	H.	R.	ER.	SO.	BB.	ERA.
1985—Quad Cities†	Midwest	2	10	0	0	.000	6	3	2	10	7	1.80
1986—Midland	Texas	15	105⅓	4	6	.400	101	54	41	82	52	3.50
1986—California	American	5	9	0	2	.000	13	12	9	6	7	9.00
1986—Edmonton	P. Coast	9	55⅓	4	1	.800	49	42	33	35	24	5.37
1987—California	American	16	34⅓	1	2	.333	34	21	21	27	18	5.50
1987—Edmonton	P. Coast	15	83⅓	4	7	.364	81	64	60	54	54	6.48
1988—Edmonton	P. Coast	51	91	5	9	.357	93	56	49	84	41	4.85
1988—California‡	American	3	3⅔	1	0	1.000	4	2	2	2	1	4.91
1989—Minnesota	American	15	21⅓	0	1	.000	22	12	12	15	17	5.06
1989—Portland	P. Coast	42	64	5	3	.625	53	29	26	55	35	3.66
Major League Totals—4 Years		39	68⅓	1	6	.143	73	47	44	50	43	5.80

Selected by Philadelphia Phillies' organization in 6th round of free-agent draft, June 7, 1982.
Selected by California Angels' organization in 1st round (19th player selected) of free-agent draft, June 3, 1985.

‡Traded with Pitcher Rob Wassenaar and First Baseman Paul Sorrento to Minnesota Twins for Pitchers Bert Blyleven and Kevin Trudeau, November 3, 1988.

SCOTT ROBERT COOLBAUGH

Born June 13, 1966, at Binghamton, N.Y.
Height, 5.11. Weight, 185.
Throws and bats righthanded.
Attended University of Texas, Austin, Tex.

Tied for Texas League lead in sacrifice flies with 8 in 1988.
Led American Association third basemen in putouts with 105, assists with 278, total chances with 413 and double plays with 32 in 1989.
Led Texas League third basemen in double plays with 28 and total chances with 421 in 1988.

Year	Club	League	Pos.	G.	AB.	R.	H.	2B.	3B.	HR.	RBI.	B.A.	PO.	A.	E.	F.A.
1987—Charlotte	Fla. St.	3B-2B	66	233	27	64	21	0	2	20	.275	42	151	16	.923
1988—Tulsa	Texas	3B	136	470	52	127	15	4	13	75	.270	72	★324	25	.941
1989—Oklahoma City	A. A.	3B-2B	●144	★527	66	137	28	0	18	74	.260	108	279	30	.928
1989—Texas	Amer.	3B	25	51	7	14	1	0	2	7	.275	7	39	2	.958
Major League Totals—1 Year			25	51	7	14	1	0	2	7	.275	7	39	2	.958

Selected by Texas Rangers' organization in 3rd round of free-agent draft, June 2, 1987.

JAMES CARROLL COOPER
(Jamie)

Born May 31, 1966, at DeKalb, Tex.
Height, 6.03. Weight, 185.
Throws right and bats left and righthanded.
Attended Dallas Baptist University, Dallas, Tex.

Year	Club	League	Pos.	G.	AB.	R.	H.	2B.	3B.	HR.	RBI.	B.A.	PO.	A.	E.	F.A.
1987—Everett	N'west	OF	59	203	32	44	5	1	0	13	.217	111	5	●7	.943
1988—Clinton	Midw.	OF	125	502	75	149	28	2	5	50	.297	304	18	10	.970
1989—San Jose	Calif.	OF	105	418	60	107	21	3	1	36	.256	246	13	6	.977

Selected by San Francisco Giants' organization in 6th round of free-agent draft, June 2, 1987.

SCOTT KENDRICK COOPER

Born October 13, 1967, at St. Louis, Mo.
Height, 6.03. Weight, 200.
Throws right and bats lefthanded.

Led Carolina League in total bases with 234 in 1988.

Year	Club	League	Pos.	G.	AB.	R.	H.	2B.	3B.	HR.	RBI.	B.A.	PO.	A.	E.	F.A.
1986—Elmira	NYP	3B	51	191	23	55	9	0	9	43	.288	22	62	9	.903
1987—Greensboro	S. Atl.	3B-1B	119	370	52	93	21	2	15	63	.251	150	153	21	.935
1988—Lynchburg	Carol.	3B-1B-OF	130	497	90	●148	★45	7	9	73	.298	116	198	27	.921
1989—New Britain	East.	3B	124	421	50	104	24	2	7	39	.247	91	212	22	.932

Selected by Boston Red Sox' organization in 3rd round of free-agent draft, June 2, 1986.

JOSE MANUEL CORA
(Joey)

Born May 14, 1965, at Cuguas, Puerto Rico.
Height, 5.08. Weight, 150.
Throws right and bats left and righthanded.
Attended Vanderbilt University, Nashville, Tenn.

Major League stolen bases: 1987 (15), 1989 (1). Total—16.
Led Pacific Coast League in stolen bases with 40 in 1989.
Led Pacific Coast League second basemen in errors with 24 in both 1988 and 1989.

Year	Club	League	Pos.	G.	AB.	R.	H.	2B.	3B.	HR.	RBI.	B.A.	PO.	A.	E.	F.A.
1985—Spokane	N'west	2B	43	170	48	55	11	2	3	26	.324	92	123	9	.960
1986—Beaumont†	Texas	2B-SS	81	315	54	96	5	5	3	41	.305	217	267	19	.962
1987—San Diego	Nat.	2B-SS	77	241	23	57	7	2	0	13	.237	123	200	10	.970
1987—Las Vegas	P. C.	2B-SS	81	293	50	81	9	1	1	24	.276	186	249	9	.980
1988—Las Vegas	P. C.	2B-3B-OF	127	460	73	136	15	3	3	55	.296	285	346	26	.960
1989—Las Vegas	P. C.	2B-SS	119	507	79	157	25	4	0	37	.310	245	349	27	.957
1989—San Diego	Nat.	SS-3B-2B	12	19	5	6	1	0	0	1	.316	11	15	2	.929
Major League Totals—2 Years			89	260	28	63	8	2	0	14	.242	134	215	12	.967

Selected by San Diego Padres' organization in 1st round (23rd player selected) of free-agent draft, June 3, 1985.
†On disabled list, June 22 to August 15, 1986.

SHERMAN STANLEY CORBETT

Born November 3, 1962, at New Braunfels, Tex.
Height, 6.04. Weight, 203.
Throws and bats lefthanded.
Attended Texas A&M University, College Station, Tex.

Major League saves: 1988 (1).
Tied for Pacific Coast League lead in intentional bases on balls issued with 8 in 1989.
Tied for California League lead in shutouts with 3 and games started by pitchers with 28 in 1985.
Tied for Northwest League lead in shutouts with 2 in 1984.

Year Club	League	G.	IP.	W.	L.	Pct.	H.	R.	ER.	SO.	BB.	ERA.
1984—Salem	Northwest	15	100⅓	7	6	.538	75	42	35	97	43	3.14
1985—Redwood	California	28	174	11	12	.478	165	108	78	122	101	4.03
1986—Midland	Texas	26	147⅔	7	10	.412	168	94	80	82	56	4.88
1987—Edmonton	P. Coast	41	55⅔	6	6	.500	61	37	34	29	49	5.50
1988—Midland	Texas	18	47⅔	3	2	.600	48	21	18	40	11	3.40
1988—California	American	34	45⅔	2	1	.667	47	23	21	28	23	4.14
1989—Edmonton	P. Coast	52	63⅓	6	7	.462	58	33	31	43	45	4.41
1989—California	American	4	5⅓	0	0	.000	3	2	2	3	1	3.38
Major League Totals—2 Years		38	51	2	1	.667	50	25	23	31	24	4.06

Selected by California Angels' organization in 3rd round of free-agent draft, June 4, 1984.

EDWIN JOSUE CORREA
(Ed)

Born April 29, 1966, at Hato Rey, Puerto Rico.
Height, 6.02. Weight, 215.
Throws and bats righthanded.
Brother of Ramser Correa, pitcher in Milwaukee Brewers' organization.

Year Club	League	G.	IP.	W.	L.	Pct.	H.	R.	ER.	SO.	BB.	ERA.
1982—Sarasota White Sox	Gulf Coast	10	59	5	2	.714	40	23	18	53	27	2.75
1983—Appleton†	Midwest	19	95	3	9	.250	81	59	47	87	61	4.45
1984—Appleton	Midwest	26	149⅓	10	6	.625	127	71	57	135	87	3.44
1985—Glens Falls	Eastern	8	40	1	5	.167	37	41	30	34	35	6.75
1985—Appleton	Midwest	18	139	13	3	●.813	93	45	39	128	56	2.53
1985—Chicago‡	American	5	10⅓	1	0	1.000	11	9	8	10	11	6.97
1986—Texas	American	32	202⅓	12	14	.462	167	102	95	189	126	4.23
1987—Texas§	American	15	70	3	5	.375	83	63	59	61	52	7.59
1988—Texas x	American					(Did not play)						
1989—Sarasota Rangers y	Gulf Coast	4	8⅓	0	2	.000	8	9	8	10	7	8.64
Major League Totals—3 Years		52	282⅔	16	19	.457	261	174	162	260	189	5.16

Signed as free agent by Chicago White Sox' organization, July 11, 1982.
†On disabled list, May 22 to June 12, 1983.
‡Traded with Infielder Scott Fletcher and a player to be named later to Texas Rangers for Infielder Wayne Tolleson and Pitcher Dave Schmidt, November 25, 1985; Texas acquired Infielder Jose Mota to complete deal, December 12, 1985.
§On disabled list, July 9 to September 10, 1987.
xOn disabled list, March 24 to September 1, 1988.
yOn Texas disabled list, March 26 to September 1, 1989; included rehabilitation disability assignment to Sarasota Rangers, July 13 to August 1, 1989.

JAMES BERNARD CORSI
(Jim)

Born September 9, 1961, at Newton, Mass.
Height, 6.01. Weight, 210.
Throws and bats righthanded.
Received bachelor of arts degree in management from St. Leo College, St. Leo, Fla.
Led Pacific Coast League in games finished in relief with 45 in 1988.

Year Club	League	G.	IP.	W.	L.	Pct.	H.	R.	ER.	SO.	BB.	ERA.
1982—Oneonta	NYP	1	3⅓	0	0	.000	5	4	4	6	2	10.80
1982—Paintsville	Ap'lachian	8	31	0	2	.000	32	11	10	20	13	2.90
1983—Greensboro†	S. Atlantic	12	50⅔	2	2	.500	59	37	23	37	33	4.09
1983—Oneonta‡	NYP	11	59⅓	3	6	.333	76	38	28	47	21	4.25
1984—						(Out of Organized Baseball)						
1985—Greensboro§	S. Atlantic	41	78⅔	5	8	.385	94	49	37	84	23	4.23
1986—New Britain x	Eastern	29	51⅓	2	3	.400	52	13	13	38	20	2.28
1987—Modesto	California	19	30	3	1	.750	23	16	12	45	10	3.60
1987—Huntsville	Southern	28	48	8	1	.889	30	17	15	33	15	2.81
1988—Tacoma	P. Coast	50	59	2	5	.286	60	25	18	48	23	2.75
1988—Oakland	American	11	21⅓	0	1	.000	20	10	9	10	6	3.80
1989—Tacoma	P. Coast	23	28⅓	2	3	.400	40	17	13	23	9	4.13
1989—Oakland	American	22	38⅓	1	2	.333	26	8	8	21	10	1.88
Major League Totals—2 Years		33	59⅔	1	3	.250	46	18	17	31	16	2.56

Selected by New York Yankees' organization in 25th round of free-agent draft, June 7, 1982.
†On Fort Lauderdale disabled list, April 8 to May 11, 1983.
‡Released, April 3, 1984; signed by Greensboro (Boston Red Sox' organization), April 1, 1985.
§Released, January 31, 1986; re-signed by Red Sox' organization, April 5, 1986.
xReleased, April 2, 1987; signed by Modesto (Oakland Athletics' organization), April 12, 1987.

FRED MICHAEL COSTELLO

Born December 1, 1966, at Clearlake, Calif.
Height, 6.04. Weight, 190.
Throws and bats righthanded.

Year Club	League	G.	IP.	W.	L.	Pct.	H.	R.	ER.	SO.	BB.	ERA.
1986—Sarasota Astros	Gulf Coast	14	66⅓	4	5	.444	74	●42	★35	51	26	4.75
1987—Sarasota Astros	Gulf Coast	13	72⅔	5	7	.417	74	40	26	45	28	3.22
1988—Asheville	S. Atlantic	51	76	6	7	.462	76	34	30	65	31	3.55
1989—Columbus	Southern	30	54	4	5	.444	39	22	20	39	21	3.33

Selected by Houston Astros' organization in 4th round of free-agent draft, June 2, 1986.

JOHN REILLY COSTELLO

Born December 24, 1960, at New York, N. Y.
Height, 6.01. Weight, 180.
Throws and bats righthanded.
Received degree in police science from Mercyhurst College, Erie, Pa.

Major League saves: 1988 (1), 1989 (3). Total—4.

Year Club	League	G.	IP.	W.	L.	Pct.	H.	R.	ER.	SO.	BB.	ERA.
1983—Erie	NYP	15	63⅔	2	5	.286	79	51	47	41	21	6.64
1984—Savannah	S. Atlantic	26	166	13	9	.591	142	80	62	114	86	3.36
1985—Springfield	Midwest	28	188	8	13	.381	188	105	★87	127	60	4.16
1986—St. Petersburg	Florida St.	15	71⅔	8	2	.800	65	21	19	32	24	2.39
1986—Arkansas	Texas	10	15	0	0	.000	17	11	9	10	6	5.40
1987—Arkansas	Texas	44	74	5	2	.714	64	27	19	67	22	2.31
1987—Louisville	Am. Assoc.	6	10⅓	2	0	1.000	14	6	5	8	7	4.35
1988—Louisville	Am. Assoc.	20	29⅓	1	1	.500	17	7	6	34	7	1.84
1988—St. Louis	National	36	49⅔	5	2	.714	44	15	10	38	25	1.81
1989—St. Louis†	National	48	62⅓	5	4	.556	48	24	23	40	20	3.32
1989—Louisville	Am. Assoc.	4	5	0	0	.000	5	1	1	4	1	1.80
Major League Totals—2 Years		84	112	10	6	.625	92	39	33	78	45	2.65

Selected by St. Louis Cardinals' organization in 24th round of free-agent draft, June 6, 1983.

†On disabled list, April 30 to May 21, 1989; included rehabilitation disability assignment to Louisville, May 13 to May 21, 1989.

HENRY COTTO (SUAREZ)

Name pronounced KOTT-oh.

Born January 5, 1961, at New York, N. Y.
Height, 6.02. Weight, 180.
Throws and bats righthanded.

Major League stolen bases: 1984 (9), 1985 (1), 1986 (3), 1987 (4), 1988 (27), 1989 (10). Total—54.
Led Texas League in stolen bases with 52 in 1982.
Tied for American Association lead in caught stealing with 17 in 1983.
Led Texas League outfielders in total chances with 333 in 1982.
Tied for International League lead in double plays by outfielders with 3 in 1986.

Year Club	League	Pos.	G.	AB.	R.	H.	2B.	3B.	HR.	RBI.	B.A.	PO.	A.	E.	F.A.
1980—Sarasota Cubs	Gulf C.	OF	43	166	24	47	7	5	0	30	.283	93	6	3	.971
1980—Quad Cities	Midw.	OF	19	78	9	22	1	1	0	5	.282	27	2	4	.879
1981—Quad Cities	Midw.	OF	128	493	80	144	15	6	1	46	.292	249	★23	13	.954
1982—Midland	Texas	OF	130	524	103	161	12	5	1	36	.307	★310	16	7	.979
1983—Iowa†	A. A.	OF	104	426	52	111	7	10	0	35	.261	253	8	7	.974
1984—Chicago	Nat.	OF	105	146	24	40	5	0	0	8	.274	117	3	2	.984
1984—Iowa‡	A. A.	OF	8	30	3	6	2	0	0	0	.200	12	3	0	1.000
1985—New York§	Amer.	OF	34	56	4	17	1	0	1	6	.304	41	2	1	.977
1985—Columbus	Int.	OF	75	272	38	70	16	2	7	36	.257	158	5	2	.988
1986—New York	Amer.	OF	35	80	11	17	3	0	1	6	.213	59	1	0	1.000
1986—Columbus	Int.	OF	97	359	45	89	17	6	7	48	.248	215	5	8	.965
1987—Columbus	Int.	OF	34	129	26	39	13	2	3	20	.302	73	3	2	.974
1987—New York x	Amer.	OF	68	149	21	35	10	0	5	20	.235	89	2	1	.989
1988—Seattle	Amer.	OF	133	386	50	100	18	1	8	33	.259	253	6	2	.992
1989—Seattle	Amer.	OF	100	295	44	78	11	2	9	33	.264	153	9	2	.988
National League Totals—1 Year			105	146	24	40	5	0	0	8	.274	117	3	2	.984
American League Totals—5 Years			370	966	130	247	43	3	24	98	.256	595	20	6	.990
Major League Totals—6 Years			475	1112	154	287	48	3	24	106	.258	712	23	8	.989

Signed as free agent by Chicago Cubs' organization, June 7, 1980.

†On disabled list, May 10 to May 30, 1983.

‡Traded with Catcher Ron Hassey and Pitchers Rich Bordi and Porfi Altamirano to New York Yankees for Pitcher Ray Fontenot and Outfielder Brian Dayett, December 4, 1984.

§On disabled list, May 25 to July 5, 1985; included rehabilitation disability assignment to Columbus, June 19 to July 5, 1985.

xTraded with Pitcher Steve Trout to Seattle Mariners for Pitchers Lee Guetterman, Clay Parker and Wade Taylor, December 22, 1987.

CHAMPIONSHIP SERIES RECORD

Year Club	League	Pos.	G.	AB.	R.	H.	2B.	3B.	HR.	RBI.	B.A.	PO.	A.	E.	F.A.
1984—Chicago	Nat.	OF-PR	3	1	1	1	0	0	0	0	1.000	2	0	0	1.000

—DID YOU KNOW—

That the Athletics' Carney Lansford led the majors in hitting on the road with a .360 mark in 1989?

DANNY BRADFORD COX

Born September 21, 1959, at Northhampton, England.
Height, 6.04. Weight, 225.
Throws and bats righthanded.
Attended Chattahoochee Valley Community College, Phenix City, Ala.,
and Troy State University, Troy, Ala.

Pitched 11-0 no-hit victory against Bristol, August 9, 1981.
Tied for National League lead in hit batsmen with 7 in 1984.
Led Appalachian League in complete games with 10 and shutouts with 4 in 1981.
Named Appalachian League Player of the Year, 1981.

Year—Club	League	G.	IP.	W.	L.	Pct.	H.	R.	ER.	SO.	BB.	ERA.
1981—Johnson City	Ap'lachian	13	*109	9	4	.692	80	27	25	*87	36	*2.06
1982—Springfield	Midwest	15	84⅓	5	3	.625	82	46	24	68	29	2.56
1983—St. Petersburg†	Florida St.	5	32	2	2	.500	26	10	9	22	14	2.53
1983—Arkansas	Texas	11	86⅓	8	3	.727	60	31	22	73	24	2.29
1983—Louisville	Am. Assoc.	2	11	0	0	.000	10	3	3	8	0	2.45
1983—St. Louis	National	12	83	3	6	.333	92	38	30	36	23	3.25
1984—St. Louis	National	29	156⅓	9	11	.450	171	81	70	70	54	4.03
1984—Louisville	Am. Assoc.	6	42⅓	4	1	.800	34	16	10	34	7	2.13
1985—St. Louis	National	35	241	18	9	.667	226	91	77	131	64	2.88
1986—St. Louis‡	National	32	220	12	13	.480	189	85	71	108	60	2.90
1987—St. Louis§	National	31	199⅓	11	9	.550	224	99	86	101	71	3.88
1988—St. Louis x	National	13	86	3	8	.273	89	40	38	47	25	3.98
1988—Louisville	Am. Assoc.	3	11⅔	0	0	.000	11	7	4	7	6	3.09
1989—St. Louis yz	National					(Did not play)						
Major League Totals—6 Years		152	985⅔	56	56	.500	991	434	372	493	297	3.40

Selected by St. Louis Cardinals' organization in 13th round of free-agent draft, June 8, 1981.
†On Arkansas disabled list, April 8 to April 21, 1983.
‡On disabled list, March 30 to April 24, 1986; included rehabilitation disability assignment to Louisville, April 17 to April 24, 1986.
§On disabled list, July 10 to August 8, 1987.
xOn disabled list, April 30 to June 27 and August 7, 1988 through remainder of season; included rehabilitation disability assignment to Louisville, June 16 to June 27, 1988.
yOn disabled list, March 27, 1989 through entire season.
zGranted free agency, November 13, 1989; re-signed by Cardinals, November 30, 1989.

CHAMPIONSHIP SERIES RECORD

Shares Championship Series record for most complete games pitched, series (2), 1987.
Shares National League Championship Series record for most complete games pitched, total series (2).

Year—Club	League	G.	IP.	W.	L.	Pct.	H.	R.	ER.	SO.	BB.	ERA.
1985—St. Louis	National	1	6	1	0	1.000	4	1	1	4	5	1.50
1987—St. Louis	National	2	17	1	1	.500	17	4	4	11	3	2.12
Championship Series Totals—2 Years		3	23	2	1	.667	21	5	5	15	8	1.96

WORLD SERIES RECORD

Shares World Series records for most earned runs allowed, game (7), October 18, 1987; most earned runs allowed, inning (6), October 18, 1987, fourth inning.

Year—Club	League	G.	IP.	W.	L.	Pct.	H.	R.	ER.	SO.	BB.	ERA.
1985—St. Louis	National	2	14	0	0	.000	14	2	2	13	4	1.29
1987—St. Louis	National	3	11⅔	1	2	.333	13	10	10	9	8	7.71
World Series Totals—2 Years		5	25⅔	1	2	.333	27	12	12	22	12	4.21

STEVEN RAY CRAWFORD
(Steve)

Born April 29, 1958, at Pryor, Okla.
Height, 6.05. Weight, 225.
Throws and bats righthanded.
Attended Claremore Junior College, Claremore, Okla. and
Northeastern Oklahoma State University, Tahlequah, Okla.

Major League saves: 1984 (1), 1985 (12), 1986 (4). Total—17.
Led Carolina League pitchers in games started with 28 and complete games with 15 in 1979.
Tied for Carolina League lead in shutouts with 3 in 1979.

Year—Club	League	G.	IP.	W.	L.	Pct.	H.	R.	ER.	SO.	BB.	ERA.
1978—Winston-Salem	Carolina	19	110	9	5	.643	109	53	42	60	48	3.44
1979—Winston-Salem	Carolina	29	*211	11	11	.500	*208	88	●69	127	67	2.94
1980—Bristol†	Eastern	24	177	9	7	.563	170	68	52	97	64	2.64
1980—Boston	American	6	32	2	0	1.000	41	14	13	10	8	3.66
1981—Boston	American	14	58	0	5	.000	69	38	32	29	18	4.97
1982—Boston‡	American	5	9	1	0	1.000	14	3	2	2	0	2.00
1982—Pawtucket	Int'national	10	46	1	4	.200	55	25	21	20	15	4.11
1983—Pawtucket§	Int'national	27	154⅔	8	11	.421	181	98	89	104	80	5.18
1984—Pawtucket	Int'national	7	18⅓	2	1	.667	11	10	4	8	9	1.96
1984—Boston	American	35	62	5	0	1.000	69	31	23	21	21	3.34
1985—Boston x	American	44	91	6	5	.545	103	47	38	58	28	3.76
1986—Boston y	American	40	57⅓	0	2	.000	69	29	25	32	19	3.92
1986—Pawtucket	Int'national	5	6	1	1	.500	10	4	4	2	1	6.00
1987—Boston za	American	29	72⅔	5	4	.556	91	48	43	43	32	5.33
1988—San Antonio b	Texas	3	6	1	0	1.000	2	0	0	4	0	0.00

Year Club	League	G.	IP.	W.	L.	Pct.	H.	R.	ER.	SO.	BB.	ERA.
1988—Albuquerque c	P. Coast	32	54⅓	3	6	.333	59	31	23	36	25	3.81
1989—Omaha	Am. Assoc.	22	43	3	1	.750	41	18	14	32	9	2.93
1989—Kansas City d	American	25	54	3	1	.750	48	19	17	33	19	2.83
Major League Totals—8 Years		198	436	22	17	.564	504	229	193	228	145	3.98

Signed as free agent by Boston Red Sox' organization, May 6, 1978.
†On disabled list, April 14 to May 2, 1980.
‡On disabled list, April 1 to August 12, 1982; included rehabilitation disability assignment to Pawtucket, July 21 to August 9, 1982.
§On disabled list, July 26 to August 5, 1983.
xOn disabled list, May 7 to May 22 and June 23 to July 8, 1985.
yOn disabled list, July 18 to September 1, 1986; included rehabilitation disability assignment to Pawtucket, August 15 to September 1, 1986.
zOn disabled list, July 16 to July 31, 1987.
aGranted free agency, November 9, 1987; signed by San Antonio (Los Angeles Dodgers' organization), May 12, 1988.
bOn disabled list, May 12 to May 25, 1988.
cGranted free agency, October 15, 1988; signed by Omaha (Kansas City Royals' organization), March 7, 1989.
dGranted free agency, November 13, 1989; re-signed by Royals, December 5, 1989.

CHAMPIONSHIP SERIES RECORD

Year Club	League	G.	IP.	W.	L.	Pct.	H.	R.	ER.	SO.	BB.	ERA.
1986—Boston	American	1	1⅔	1	0	1.000	1	0	0	1	2	0.00

WORLD SERIES RECORD

Year Club	League	G.	IP.	W.	L.	Pct.	H.	R.	ER.	SO.	BB.	ERA.
1986—Boston	American	3	4⅓	1	0	1.000	5	3	3	4	0	6.23

STANLEY TIMOTHY CREWS
(Tim)

Born April 3, 1961, at Tampa, Fla.
Height, 6.00. Weight, 195.
Throws and bats righthanded.
Attended Valencia Community College, Orlando, Fla.

Major League saves: 1987 (3), 1989 (1). Total—4.
Led Texas League in home runs allowed with 25 and tied for lead in balks with 4 in 1983.
Tied for Midwest League lead in home runs allowed with 16 in 1981.

Year Club	League	G.	IP.	W.	L.	Pct.	H.	R.	ER.	SO.	BB.	ERA.
1981—Burlington	Midwest	21	144	10	4	.714	148	82	67	98	27	4.19
1982—Stockton	California	19	139	10	4	.714	151	66	52	83	28	3.37
1983—El Paso	Texas	27	163⅓	9	8	.529	★207	★129	★119	99	53	6.56
1984—El Paso†	Texas	8	36	2	3	.400	56	32	27	22	10	6.75
1985—Stockton‡	California	16	90	8	1	.889	101	46	33	56	17	3.30
1986—El Paso	Texas	15	90⅔	5	5	.500	114	53	48	50	18	4.76
1986—Vancouver§	P. Coast	10	33⅓	2	1	.667	39	15	15	28	14	4.05
1987—Albuquerque	P. Coast	42	72	7	2	.778	73	34	29	60	25	3.63
1987—Los Angeles	National	20	29	1	1	.500	30	9	8	20	8	2.48
1988—Albuquerque	P. Coast	10	13⅓	1	1	.500	13	5	4	7	2	2.70
1988—Los Angeles	National	42	71⅔	4	0	1.000	77	29	25	45	16	3.14
1989—Los Angeles	National	44	61⅔	0	0	.000	69	27	22	56	23	3.21
1989—Albuquerque	P. Coast	2	2⅓	0	1	.000	3	2	2	2	0	7.71
Major League Totals—3 Years		106	162⅓	5	2	.714	176	65	55	121	47	3.05

Selected by Kansas City Royals' organization in 2nd round of free-agent draft, January 8, 1980.
Selected by Milwaukee Brewers' organization in 2nd round of free-agent draft, January 13, 1981.
†On disabled list, June 9, 1984 through remainder of season.
‡On disabled list, May 17 to July 12, 1985.
§Traded with Pitcher Tim Leary to Los Angeles Dodgers for First Baseman Greg Brock, December 10, 1986.

CHARLES ROBERT CRIM
(Chuck)

Born July 23, 1961, at Van Nuys, Calif.
Height, 6.00. Weight, 185.
Throws and bats righthanded.
Attended University of Hawaii, Honolulu, Haw.

Major League saves: 1987 (12), 1988 (9), 1989 (7). Total—28.
Led Appalachian League in complete games with 8 in 1982.
Tied for Midwest League lead in complete games with 11 in 1983.

Year Club	League	G.	IP.	W.	L.	Pct.	H.	R.	ER.	SO.	BB.	ERA.
1982—Pikeville	Ap'lachian	11	77⅓	4	6	.400	62	32	22	76	18	2.56
1983—Beloit	Midwest	25	163⅓	11	10	.524	150	83	63	154	50	3.47
1984—El Paso	Texas	55	90	7	4	.636	77	20	15	69	25	1.50
1985—Vancouver	P. Coast	48	106⅔	3	6	.333	110	58	54	68	38	4.56
1986—Vancouver	P. Coast	26	45⅓	0	3	.000	64	32	25	26	15	4.96
1986—El Paso	Texas	16	39	2	4	.333	35	16	12	32	2	2.77
1987—Milwaukee	American	53	130	6	8	.429	133	60	53	56	39	3.67
1988—Milwaukee	American	★70	105	7	6	.538	95	38	34	58	28	2.91
1989—Milwaukee†	American	★76	117⅔	9	7	.563	114	42	37	59	36	2.83
Major League Totals—3 Years		199	352⅔	22	21	.512	342	140	124	173	103	3.16

Selected by Chicago Cubs' organization in 3rd round of free-agent draft, June 5, 1979.
Selected by Milwaukee Brewers' organization in 17th round of free-agent draft, June 7, 1982.
†Appeared as first baseman in one game with no chances.

NATHANIEL CROMWELL JR
(Nate)

Born August 23, 1968, at Las Vegas, Nev.
Height, 6.01. Weight, 175.
Throws and bats lefthanded.
Led Florida State League pitchers in games started with 30 and wild pitches with 25 in 1989.

Year	Club	League	G.	IP.	W.	L.	Pct.	H.	R.	ER.	SO.	BB.	ERA.
1987—Medicine Hat	Pioneer	15	54⅓	4	6	.400	54	36	26	47	37	4.31
1988—Myrtle Beach	S. Atlantic	21	124⅓	8	8	.500	88	47	40	86	67	2.90
1989—Dunedin	Florida St.	31	151⅔	12	6	.667	136	70	61	★161	84	3.62

Selected by Toronto Blue Jays' organization in 11th round of free-agent draft, June 2, 1987.

STEVEN BRENT CUMMINGS
(Steve)

Born July 15, 1964, at Houston, Tex.
Height, 6.02. Weight, 200.
Throws right and bats left and righthanded.
Attended Blinn College, Brenham, Tex.,
and University of Houston, Houston, Tex.
Led Southern League in games started by pitchers with 33 in 1988.
Led Florida State League pitchers in games started with 29 in 1987.
Tied for New York-Pennsylvania League lead in games started by pitchers with 18 in 1986.

Year	Club	League	G.	IP.	W.	L.	Pct.	H.	R.	ER.	SO.	BB.	ERA.
1986—St. Catharines	NYP	18	110⅓	9	5	.643	80	36	25	86	34	2.04
1987—Dunedin	Florida St.	32	186⅔	★18	8	.692	189	80	61	111	60	2.94
1988—Knoxville	Southern	35	★212⅔	14	11	.560	★206	88	65	131	64	2.75
1989—Syracuse	Int'national	19	106	7	5	.583	97	46	37	60	41	3.14
1989—Toronto	American	5	21	2	0	1.000	18	9	7	8	11	3.00
Major League Totals—1 Year		5	21	2	0	1.000	18	9	7	8	11	3.00

Selected by Texas Rangers' organization in 5th round of free-agent draft, January 17, 1984.
Selected by Atlanta Braves' organization in secondary phase of free-agent draft, June 4, 1984.
Selected by Toronto Blue Jays' organization in 2nd round of free-agent draft, June 2, 1986.

MILTON CUYLER JR.
(Milt)

Born October 7, 1968, at Macon, Ga.
Height, 5.10. Weight, 175.
Throws right and bats left and righthanded.
Led Florida State League in caught stealing with 25 in 1988.
Led South Atlantic League in sacrifice hits with 17 in 1987.
Led Eastern League outfielders in total chances with 293 in 1989.

Year	Club	League	Pos.	G.	AB.	R.	H.	2B.	3B.	HR.	RBI.	B.A.	PO.	A.	E.	F.A.
1986—Bristol	Appal.	OF	45	174	24	40	3	5	1	11	.230	97	0	4	.960
1987—Fayetteville	S. Atl.	OF	94	366	65	107	8	4	2	34	.292	237	13	7	.973
1988—Lakeland	Fla. St.	OF	132	483	★100	143	11	3	2	32	.296	257	8	4	.985
1989—Toledo	Int.	OF	24	83	4	14	3	2	0	6	.169	48	3	2	.962
1989—London	East.	OF	98	366	69	96	8	7	7	34	.262	★272	13	8	.973

Selected by Detroit Tigers' organization in 2nd round of free-agent draft, June 2, 1986.

PETER MARTIN DALENA
(Pete)

Born June 26, 1960, at Fresno, Calif.
Height, 5.11. Weight, 200.
Throws right and bats lefthanded.
Attended Fresno City College, Fresno, Calif., and
Fresno State University, Fresno, Calif.
Led International League first basemen in double plays with 101 in 1988.

Year	Club	League	Pos.	G.	AB.	R.	H.	2B.	3B.	HR.	RBI.	B.A.	PO.	A.	E.	F.A.
1982—Greensboro	S. Atl.	1B	71	281	27	80	15	0	10	43	.285	574	44	7	.989
1983—Fort Lauderdale	Fla. St.	1B	49	169	16	53	9	2	2	28	.314	171	17	5	.974
1983—Nashville	South.	1B	89	335	52	108	23	4	13	59	.322	823	56	7	.992
1984—Columbus	Int.	1B	10	27	1	3	0	0	0	0	.111	35	0	0	1.000
1984—Nashville	South.	1B	125	488	60	145	28	0	14	83	.297	1162	79	★17	.986
1985—Columbus	Int.	1B	114	357	34	109	21	4	9	65	.305	338	26	1	.997
1986—Columbus	Int.	1B	123	435	54	113	27	4	12	72	.260	496	37	2	.996
1987—Columbus	Int.	1B-OF	116	433	74	122	21	4	18	61	.282	744	58	6	.993
1988—Columbus†	Int.	1B	123	426	33	91	20	1	7	44	.214	1004	60	8	.993
1989—Colorado Springs	P. C.	1B-P	98	340	52	112	24	5	5	59	.329	779	54	10	.988
1989—Cleveland‡	Amer.	PH-DH	5	7	0	1	1	0	0	0	.143	0	0	0	.000
Major League Totals—1 Year		5	7	0	1	1	0	0	0	.143	0	0	0	.000

Selected by New York Yankees' organization in 27th round of free-agent draft, June 7, 1982.
†Granted free agency, October 15, 1988; signed by Colorado Springs (Cleveland Indians' organization), November 22, 1988.
‡Granted free agency, October 15, 1989.

PITCHING RECORD

Year Club	League	G.	IP.	W.	L.	Pct.	H.	R.	ER.	SO.	BB.	ERA.
1989—Colorado Springs	P. Coast	2	2⅓	0	0	.000	5	4	2	0	0	7.71

KALVOSKI DANIELS
(Kal)

Born August 20, 1963, at Vienna, Ga.
Height, 5.11. Weight, 205.
Throws right and bats lefthanded.
Attended Middle Georgia College, Cochran, Ga.

Major League stolen bases: 1986 (15), 1987 (26), 1988 (27), 1989 (9). Total—77.
Led Eastern League in slugging percentage with .525 in 1984.
Tied for Pioneer League lead in game-winning RBIs with 9 and stolen bases with 27 in 1982.

Year Club	League	Pos.	G.	AB.	R.	H.	2B.	3B.	HR.	RBI.	B.A.	PO.	A.	E.	F.A.
1982—Billings	Pion.	OF	67	240	43	88	19	4	3	38	.367	104	4	5	.956
1983—Cedar Rapids	Midw.	OF	101	342	51	86	14	5	5	28	.251	130	5	2	.985
1984—Vermont	East.	OF	122	415	81	130	29	4	17	62	.313	143	2	5	.967
1985—Denver†	A. A.	OF	76	285	59	86	12	9	15	43	.302	83	5	4	.957
1986—Cincinnati	Nat.	OF	74	181	34	58	10	4	6	23	.320	88	0	3	.967
1986—Denver	A. A.	OF	42	132	33	49	12	2	8	32	.371	78	4	3	.965
1987—Cincinnati‡	Nat.	OF	108	368	73	123	24	1	26	64	.334	178	5	6	.968
1988—Cincinnati	Nat.	OF	140	495	95	144	29	1	18	64	.291	256	10	5	.982
1989—Cinc.§x-L.A.y	Nat.	OF	55	171	33	42	13	0	4	17	.246	88	4	0	1.000
Major League Totals—4 Years			377	1215	235	367	76	6	54	168	.302	610	19	14	.978

Selected by New York Mets' organization in 3rd round of free-agent draft, January 12, 1982.
Selected by Cincinnati Reds' organization in secondary phase of free-agent draft, June 7, 1982.
†On disabled list, July 7, 1985 through remainder of season.
‡On disabled list, July 6 to August 6, 1987.
§On disabled list, May 15 to June 21, 1989.
xTraded with Infielder Lenny Harris to Los Angeles Dodgers for Pitcher Tim Leary and Shortstop Mariano Duncan, July 18, 1989.
yOn disabled list, August 7, 1989 through remainder of season.

RONALD MAURICE DARLING JR.
(Ron)

Born August 19, 1960, at Honolulu, Haw.
Height, 6.03. Weight, 195.
Throws and bats righthanded.
Attended Yale University, New Haven, Conn.
Brother of Eddie Darling, first baseman in New York Yankees' organization, 1981 and 1982.

Shares National League record for fewest assists by pitcher, season, for leader in assists (47), 1985 and 1986.
Named pitcher on THE SPORTING NEWS National League All-Star fielding team, 1989.

Year Club	League	G.	IP.	W.	L.	Pct.	H.	R.	ER.	SO.	BB.	ERA.
1981—Tulsa†	Texas	13	71	4	2	.667	72	43	35	53	33	4.44
1982—Tidewater	Int'national	26	152	7	9	.438	143	76	63	114	95	3.73
1983—Tidewater	Int'national	27	159	10	9	.526	137	83	71	107	102	4.02
1983—New York	National	5	35⅓	1	3	.250	31	11	11	23	17	2.80
1984—New York	National	33	205⅔	12	9	.571	179	97	87	136	104	3.81
1985—New York	National	36	248	16	6	.727	214	93	80	167	⋆114	2.90
1986—New York	National	34	237	15	6	.714	203	84	74	184	81	2.81
1987—New York‡	National	32	207⅔	12	8	.600	183	111	99	167	96	4.29
1988—New York	National	34	240⅔	17	9	.654	218	97	87	161	60	3.25
1989—New York	National	33	217⅓	14	14	.500	214	100	85	153	70	3.52
Major League Totals—7 Years		207	1391⅔	87	55	.613	1242	593	523	991	542	3.38

Selected by Texas Rangers' organization in 1st round (ninth player selected) of free-agent draft, June 8, 1981.
†Traded with Pitcher Walt Terrell to New York Mets' organization for Outfielder Lee Mazzilli, April 1, 1982.
‡On disabled list, September 12, 1987 through remainder of season.

CHAMPIONSHIP SERIES RECORD

Year Club	League	G.	IP.	W.	L.	Pct.	H.	R.	ER.	SO.	BB.	ERA.
1986—New York	National	1	5	0	0	.000	6	4	4	5	2	7.20
1988—New York	National	2	7	0	1	.000	11	9	6	7	4	7.71
Championship Series Totals—2 Years		3	12	0	1	.000	17	13	10	12	6	7.50

Appeared as pinch-runner for New York Mets in one game of 1988 Championship Series.

WORLD SERIES RECORD

Shares World Series record for most wild pitches, game (2), October 18, 1986.

Year Club	League	G.	IP.	W.	L.	Pct.	H.	R.	ER.	SO.	BB.	ERA.
1986—New York	National	3	17⅔	1	1	.500	13	4	3	12	10	1.53

ALL-STAR GAME RECORD

Member of National League All-Star Team in 1985; did not play.

DANIEL WAYNE DARWIN
(Danny)

Born October 25, 1955, at Bonham, Tex.
Height, 6.03. Weight, 190.
Throws and bats righthanded.
Attended Grayson County College, Denison, Tex.

Major League saves: 1980 (8), 1982 (7), 1985 (2), 1988 (3), 1989 (7). Total—27.
Tied for American League lead in home runs allowed with 34 in 1985.
Tied for Texas League lead in shutouts with 4 and hit batsmen with 8 in 1977.
Tied for Western Carolinas League lead in balks with 5 in 1976.

Year Club	League	G.	IP.	W.	L.	Pct.	H.	R.	ER.	SO.	BB.	ERA.
1976—Asheville	W. Carol.	16	102	6	3	.667	96	54	41	76	48	3.62
1977—Tulsa†	Texas	23	154	13	4	.765	130	53	43	129	72	2.51
1978—Tucson	P. Coast	23	125	8	9	.471	147	100	87	126	83	6.26
1978—Texas	American	3	9	1	0	1.000	11	4	4	8	1	4.00
1979—Tucson	P. Coast	13	95	6	6	.500	89	43	38	65	42	3.60
1979—Texas	American	20	78	4	4	.500	50	36	35	58	30	4.04
1980—Texas‡	American	53	110	13	4	.765	98	37	32	104	50	2.62
1981—Texas	American	22	146	9	9	.500	115	67	59	98	57	3.64
1982—Texas	American	56	89	10	8	.556	95	38	34	61	37	3.44
1983—Texas§	American	28	183	8	13	.381	175	86	71	92	62	3.49
1984—Texas x	American x	35	223⅔	8	12	.400	249	110	98	123	54	3.94
1985—Milwaukee y	American	39	217⅔	8	18	.308	212	112	92	125	65	3.80
1986—Milwaukee z	American	27	130½	6	8	.429	120	62	51	80	35	3.52
1986—Houston	National	12	54⅓	5	2	.714	50	19	14	40	9	2.32
1987—Houston a	National	33	195⅔	9	10	.474	184	87	78	134	69	3.59
1988—Houston	National	44	192	8	13	.381	189	86	82	129	48	3.84
1989—Houston	National	68	122	11	4	.733	92	34	32	104	33	2.36
American League Totals—9 Years		283	1186⅔	67	76	.469	1125	552	476	749	391	3.61
National League Totals—4 Years		157	564	33	29	.532	515	226	206	407	159	3.29
Major League Totals—12 Years		440	1750⅔	100	105	.488	1640	778	682	1156	550	3.51

Signed as free agent by Texas Rangers' organization, May 10, 1976.
†On disabled list, April 25 to May 4 and May 22 to June 11, 1977.
‡On disabled list, June 5 to June 26, 1980.
§On disabled list, March 25 to April 10 and August 9 to September 1, 1983.
xTraded with a player to be named later to Milwaukee Brewers as part of a six-player, four-team deal in which Kansas City Royals acquired Catcher Jim Sundberg from Milwaukee, Texas Rangers acquired Catcher Don Slaught from Kansas City, New York Mets' organization acquired Pitcher Frank Wills from Kansas City and Milwaukee organization acquired Pitcher Tim Leary from New York, January 18, 1985; Milwaukee organization acquired Catcher Bill Hance from Texas to complete deal, January 30, 1985.
yGranted free agency, November 12, 1985; re-signed by Brewers, December 22, 1985.
zTraded to Houston Astros for Pitcher Don August and a player to be named later, August 15, 1986; Milwaukee Brewers' organization acquired Pitcher Mark Knudson to complete deal, August 21, 1986.
aGranted free agency, November 9, 1987; re-signed by Astros, January 8, 1988.

DOUGLAS CRAIG DASCENZO
(Doug)

Born June 30, 1964, at Cleveland, O.
Height, 5.08. Weight, 160.
Throws left and bats left and righthanded.
Attended Florida College, Temple Terrace, Fla., and
Oklahoma State University, Stillwater, Okla.

Major League stolen bases: 1988 (6), 1989 (6). Total—12.
Led American Association in caught stealing with 21 in 1989.
Led Carolina League in sacrifice hits with 12 in 1986.
Led Eastern League outfielders in total chances with 308 in 1987.

Year Club	League	Pos.	G.	AB.	R.	H.	2B.	3B.	HR.	RBI.	B.A.	PO.	A.	E.	F.A.
1985—Geneva	NYP	OF-1B	70	252	★59	84	15	1	3	23	.333	133	7	4	.972
1986—Winston-Salem	Carol.	OF	138	545	107	★178	29	11	6	83	.327	299	15	8	.975
1987—Pittsfield	East.	OF	134	496	84	152	32	6	3	56	.306	★299	5	4	★.987
1988—Iowa	A. A.	OF	132	505	73	149	22	5	6	49	.295	261	6	4	.985
1988—Chicago	Nat.	OF	26	75	9	16	3	0	0	4	.213	55	1	0	1.000
1989—Iowa	A. A.	OF	111	431	59	121	18	4	4	33	.281	273	15	6	.980
1989—Chicago	Nat.	OF	47	139	20	23	1	0	1	12	.165	96	0	0	1.000
Major League Totals—2 Years			73	214	29	39	4	0	1	16	.182	151	1	0	1.000

Selected by Chicago Cubs' organization in 12th round of free-agent draft, June 3, 1985.

JEFFREY WILLIAM DATZ
(Jeff)

Born November 28, 1959, at Camden, N.J.
Height, 6.04. Weight, 220.
Throws and bats righthanded.
Received bachelor of arts degree in health and physical
education from Glassboro State College, Glassboro, N.J.

Tied for International League lead in double plays by catchers with 9 in 1989.
Tied for Southern League lead in passed balls with 16 in 1987.

Year Club	League	Pos.	G.	AB.	R.	H.	2B.	3B.	HR.	RBI.	B.A.	PO.	A.	E.	F.A.
1982—Auburn	NYP	C	36	116	15	26	4	0	4	15	.224	260	27	3	.990
1983—Daytona Beach	Fla. St.	C	47	143	17	39	9	0	2	19	.273	215	38	4	.984
1983—Columbus	South.	C	39	124	15	24	3	1	3	11	.194	130	35	6	.965
1984—Daytona Beach†	Fla. St.	C-1B	11	23	5	5	2	0	1	5	.217	45	6	2	.962
1984—Auburn	NYP	C	24	71	2	14	0	0	0	8	.197	147	18	4	.976
1985—Columbus	South.	C-1B	53	150	16	29	5	0	3	13	.193	214	27	6	.976
1986—Tucson	P. C.	C	2	5	0	1	0	0	0	0	.200	5	0	0	1.000
1986—Columbus‡	South.	C-1B	59	191	26	62	13	1	6	25	.325	320	39	2	.994
1987—Columbus	South.	★C-1B	121	408	55	101	21	0	8	42	.248	687	74	5	★.993
1988—Tucson§	P. C.	C	60	148	18	33	7	0	2	11	.223	239	34	7	.975
1989—Toledo	Int.	C	77	247	26	61	13	0	3	18	.247	419	55	9	.981
1989—Detroit x	Amer.	C	7	10	0	2	0	0	0	0	.200	17	1	0	1.000
Major League Totals—1 Year			7	10	0	2	0	0	0	0	.200	17	1	0	1.000

Selected by Cincinnati Reds' organization in 27th round of free-agent draft, June 8, 1981.
Selected by Houston Astros' organization in 19th round of free-agent draft, June 7, 1982.
†On disabled list, May 16 to July 23, 1984.
‡On disabled list, April 19 to April 29, 1986.
§Granted free agency, October 15, 1988; signed by Toledo (Detroit Tigers' organization), November 14, 1988.
xGranted free agency, October 15, 1989.

JOHN MICHAEL DAUGHERTY
(Jack)

Born June 3, 1960, at Hialeah, Fla.
Height, 6.00. Weight, 185.
Throws left and bats right and lefthanded.
Attended San Diego Mesa College, San Diego, Calif.,
and University of Arizona, Tucson, Ariz.

Major League stolen bases: 1989 (2).
Led Florida State League in total bases with 213 in 1985.
Led Pioneer League in total bases with 179 and intentional bases on balls received with 10 in 1984.
Tied for Pioneer League lead in bases on balls received with 52 in 1984.
Led Pioneer League first basemen in total chances with 624 in 1984.
Named Florida State League Most Valuable Player, 1985.

Year Club	League	Pos.	G.	AB.	R.	H.	2B.	3B.	HR.	RBI.	B.A.	PO.	A.	E.	F.A.
1983—San José†	Calif.	1B	116	364	46	95	17	2	2	45	.261	670	25	7	.990
1984—Helena§	Pion.	1B	66	259	★77	★104	★26	2	15	★82	★.402	★583	33	8	.987
1985—W. Palm Beach	Fla. St.	1B	133	481	76	152	25	3	10	★87	.316	1041	50	14	.987
1986—Jacksonville	South.	1B	138	502	87	159	37	4	4	63	.317	1007	64	★19	.983
1987—Indianapolis	A. A.	1B-OF	117	420	65	131	35	3	7	50	.312	754	76	7	.992
1987—Montreal	Nat.	1B	11	10	1	1	1	0	0	1	.100	1	1	0	1.000
1988—Indianapolis§	A. A.	1B-OF	137	481	82	137	33	2	6	67	.285	896	62	8	.992
1989—Oklahoma City	A. A.	1B-OF	82	311	28	78	15	3	3	32	.251	728	54	6	.992
1989—Texas	Amer.	1B-OF	52	106	15	32	4	2	1	10	.302	132	14	0	1.000
National League Totals—1 Year			11	10	1	1	1	0	0	1	.100	1	1	0	1.000
American League Totals—1 Year			52	106	15	32	4	2	1	10	.302	132	14	0	1.000
Major League Totals—2 Years			63	116	16	33	5	2	1	11	.284	133	15	0	1.000

Signed as free agent by Oakland A's organization, October 9, 1982.
†Released, January 16, 1984; signed by Helena (Independent), June 13, 1984.
§Sold to West Palm Beach (Montreal Expos' organization), December 4, 1984.
§Traded to Texas Rangers' organization, September 13, 1988, completing deal in which Texas traded Infielder Tom O'Malley to Montreal Expos for a player to be named later, September 1, 1988.

DARREN ARTHUR DAULTON

Born January 3, 1962, at Arkansas City, Kan.
Height, 6.02. Weight, 190.
Throws right and bats lefthanded.
Attended Cowley County Community College, Arkansas City, Kan.

Major League stolen bases: 1985 (3), 1986 (2), 1988 (2), 1989 (2). Total—9.
Tied for Eastern League lead in sacrifice flies with 10 in 1983.

Year Club	League	Pos.	G.	AB.	R.	H.	2B.	3B.	HR.	RBI.	B.A.	PO.	A.	E.	F.A.
1980—Helena	Pion.	C	37	100	13	20	2	1	1	10	.200	224	17	4	.984
1981—Spartanburg	S. Atl.	C-OF-3B	98	270	44	62	11	1	3	29	.230	378	34	4	.990
1982—Peninsula	Carol.	C-1B	110	324	65	78	21	2	11	44	.241	654	63	9	.990
1983—Reading	East.	C-1B-OF	113	362	77	95	16	4	19	83	.262	557	57	14	.978
1983—Philadelphia	Nat.	C	2	3	1	1	0	0	0	0	.333	8	0	0	1.000
1984—Portland†	P. C.	C	80	252	45	75	19	4	7	38	.298	322	26	6	.983
1985—Portland	P. C.	C	23	64	13	19	5	3	2	10	.297	110	9	0	1.000
1985—Philadelphia‡	Nat.	C	36	103	14	21	3	1	4	11	.204	160	15	1	.994
1986—Philadelphia§	Nat.	C	49	138	18	31	4	0	8	21	.225	244	21	4	.985
1987—Clearwater x	Fla. St.	C-1B	9	22	1	5	3	0	1	5	.227	27	5	3	.914
1987—Maine	Int.	C-1B	20	70	9	15	1	1	3	10	.214	138	12	0	1.000
1987—Philadelphia	Nat.	C-1B	53	129	10	25	6	0	3	13	.194	210	13	2	.991
1988—Philadelphia y	Nat.	C-1B	58	144	13	30	6	0	1	12	.208	205	15	6	.973
1989—Philadelphia	Nat.	C	131	368	29	74	12	2	8	44	.201	627	56	11	.984
Major League Totals—6 Years			329	885	85	182	31	3	24	101	.206	1454	120	24	.985

Selected by Philadelphia Phillies' organization in 25th round of free-agent draft, June 3, 1980.

†On disabled list, July 20 to August 28, 1984.
‡On disabled list, May 17 to August 9, 1985; included rehabilitation disability assignment to Portland, July 20 to August 7, 1985.
§On Philadelphia disabled list, June 22, 1986 through remainder of season.
xOn Philadelphia disabled list, April 1 to April 16, 1987.
yOn disabled list, August 28, 1988 through remainder of season.

JOHN MARK DAVIDSON

(Known by middle name.)

Born February 15, 1961, at Knoxville, Tenn.
Height, 6.02. Weight, 190.
Throws and bats righthanded.
Attended University of North Carolina, Charlotte, N.C.,
and Clemson University, Clemson, S.C.
Son of Max Davidson, minor league outfielder, 1947 through 1954.

Major League stolen bases: 1986 (2), 1987 (9), 1988 (3), 1989 (1). Total—15.
Led Southern League in game-winning RBIs with 16 in 1985.

Year Club	League	Pos.	G.	AB.	R.	H.	2B.	3B.	HR.	RBI.	B.A.	PO.	A.	E.	F.A.
1982—Wis. Rapids	Midw.	OF	79	247	54	74	11	0	10	41	.300	166	13	5	.973
1983—Wis. Rapids†	Midw.	OF	111	363	63	80	15	1	13	48	.220	181	6	6	.969
1984—Orlando‡	South.	OF-1B-3B	114	348	55	99	11	6	4	37	.284	243	13	3	.988
1985—Orlando	South.	OF-3B	134	453	93	137	17	2	25	106	.302	305	14	6	.982
1986—Toledo	Int.	OF	108	383	55	95	16	1	10	38	.248	290	8	8	.974
1986—Minnesota	Amer.	OF	36	68	5	8	3	0	0	2	.118	48	0	1	.980
1987—Minnesota	Amer.	OF	102	150	32	40	4	1	1	14	.267	102	3	0	1.000
1988—Minnesota	Amer.	OF-3B	100	106	22	23	7	0	1	10	.217	103	3	5	.955
1988—Portland	P. C.	OF-P	15	56	6	18	4	2	0	5	.321	35	2	0	1.000
1989—Portland§-Tucson	P. C.	OF	69	237	26	58	9	2	5	24	.245	145	9	0	1.000
1989—Houston	Nat.	OF	33	65	7	13	2	1	1	5	.200	36	0	0	1.000
American League Totals—3 Years			238	324	59	71	14	1	2	26	.219	253	6	6	.977
National League Totals—1 Year			33	65	7	13	2	1	1	5	.200	36	0	0	1.000
Major League Totals—4 Years			271	389	66	84	16	2	3	31	.216	289	6	6	.980

Selected by Minnesota Twins' organization in 11th round of free-agent draft, June 7, 1982.
†On disabled list, April 15 to May 4, 1983.
‡On disabled list, July 16 to July 26, 1984.
§Traded to Tucson (Houston Astros' organization) for a player to be named later, May 16, 1989; Minnesota Twins acquired Pitcher Greg Johnson to complete deal, September 6, 1989.

CHAMPIONSHIP SERIES RECORD

Year Club	League	Pos.	G.	AB.	R.	H.	2B.	3B.	HR.	RBI.	B.A.	PO.	A.	E.	F.A.
1987—Minnesota	Amer.	PR	1	0	0	0	0	0	0	0	.000	0	0	0	.000

WORLD SERIES RECORD

Year Club	League	Pos.	G.	AB.	R.	H.	2B.	3B.	HR.	RBI.	B.A.	PO.	A.	E.	F.A.
1987—Minnesota	Amer.	OF-PH	2	1	0	0	0	0	0	0	.000	0	0	0	.000

PITCHING RECORD

Year Club	League	G.	IP.	W.	L.	Pct.	H.	R.	ER.	SO.	BB.	ERA.
1988—Portland	P. Coast	1	1⅓	0	1	.000	2	1	1	0	2	6.75

ROBERT BANKS DAVIDSON JR.

(Bob)

Born January 6, 1963, at Bad Kurznach, West Germany.
Height, 6.00. Weight, 185.
Throws and bats righthanded.
Attended East Carolina University, Greenville, N.C.

Year Club	League	G.	IP.	W.	L.	Pct.	H.	R.	ER.	SO.	BB.	ERA.
1984—Oneonta	NYP	24	28⅔	2	5	.286	27	18	11	26	11	3.45
1985—Oneonta	NYP	29	36	1	2	.333	28	14	10	44	13	2.50
1986—Fort Lauderdale	Florida St.	16	58⅔	4	2	.667	65	36	26	37	22	3.99
1986—Albany	Eastern	24	36⅔	1	1	.500	45	23	20	25	16	4.91
1987—Prince William	Carolina	21	124⅓	3	10	.231	140	65	55	70	33	3.98
1987—Albany	Eastern	14	59⅔	1	2	.333	63	24	16	46	16	2.41
1988—Albany	Eastern	34	92⅔	6	3	.667	81	36	28	62	23	2.72
1988—Columbus	Int'national	6	19	0	0	.000	19	7	5	5	8	2.37
1989—Albany	Eastern	12	31⅓	2	0	1.000	36	20	10	26	7	2.87
1989—Columbus	Int'national	22	93⅓	8	5	.615	71	26	19	56	30	1.83
1989—New York	American	1	1	0	0	.000	1	2	2	0	1	18.00
Major League Totals—1 Year		1	1	0	0	.000	1	2	2	0	1	18.00

Selected by New York Yankees' organization in 24th round of free-agent draft, June 4, 1984.

—DID YOU KNOW—

That Bret Saberhagen of the Royals led the majors with 12 complete games in 1989, three more than the entire Chicago White Sox' staff?

ALVIN GLENN DAVIS

Born September 9, 1960, at Riverside, Calif.
Height, 6.01. Weight, 190.
Throws right and bats lefthanded.
Received bachelor of science degree in finance from Arizona State University, Tempe, Ariz.

Shares major league record for most putouts, first baseman, nine-inning game (22), May 28, 1988.
Shares American League record for most home runs, first two major league games (2), April 11 and 13, 1984.
Major League stolen bases: 1984 (5), 1985 (1), 1988 (1). Total—7.
Led Southern League in bases on balls received with 120 and sacrifice flies with 12 in 1983.
Led Southern League first basemen in total chances with 1,348 and double plays with 118 in 1983.
Named American League Rookie Player of the Year by THE SPORTING NEWS, 1984.
Named American League Rookie of the Year by Baseball Writers' Association of America, 1984.

Year	Club	League	Pos.	G.	AB.	R.	H.	2B.	3B.	HR.	RBI.	B.A.	PO.	A.	E.	F.A.
1982—Lynn		East	1B	74	225	37	64	10	1	12	56	.284	579	51	6	.991
1983—Chattanooga†		South.	★●1B-OF	131	422	87	125	24	3	18	83	.296	★1233	★99	●16	.988
1984—Salt Lake City		P. C.	1B	1	3	2	2	0	0	0	1	.667	2	0	0	1.000
1984—Seattle		Amer.	1B	152	567	80	161	34	3	27	116	.284	1271	94	11	.992
1985—Seattle		Amer.	1B	155	578	78	166	33	1	18	78	.287	1438	103	13	.992
1986—Seattle‡		Amer.	1B	135	479	66	130	18	1	18	72	.271	880	82	14	.986
1987—Seattle		Amer.	1B	157	580	86	171	37	2	29	100	.295	1386	96	9	.994
1988—Seattle§		Amer.	1B	140	478	67	141	24	1	18	69	.295	980	65	6	.994
1989—Seattle x		Amer.	1B	142	498	84	152	30	1	21	95	.305	1106	81	10	.992
Major League Totals—6 Years				881	3180	461	921	176	9	131	530	.290	7061	521	63	.992

Selected by San Francisco Giants' organization in 8th round of free-agent draft, June 6, 1978.
Selected by Oakland A's organization in 6th round of free-agent draft, June 8, 1981.
Selected by Seattle Mariners' organization in 6th round of free-agent draft, June 7, 1982.
†On disabled list, July 21 to July 31, 1983.
‡On disabled list, June 25 to July 17, 1986.
§On disabled list, June 26 to July 15, 1988.
xOn disabled list, May 21 to June 6, 1989.

ALL-STAR GAME RECORD

Year	League	Pos.	AB.	R.	H.	2B.	3B.	HR.	RBI.	B.A.	PO.	A.	E.	F.A.
1984—American		PH	1	0	0	0	0	0	0	.000	0	0	0	.000

CHARLES THEODORE DAVIS
(Chili)

(Original nickname was Chili Bowl, which was prompted by a friend who saw Davis
after he received a haircut back in the sixth grade. The nickname was later shortened to Chili.)

Born January 17, 1960, at Kingston, Jamaica.
Height, 6.03. Weight, 210.
Throws right and bats left and righthanded.

Shares major league record for fewest errors by outfielder, season, for leader in errors (9), 1986.
Holds National League record for most games, switch-hit home runs, lifetime (3).
Shares National League record for most games, switch-hit home runs, season (2), 1987.
Major League stolen bases: 1981 (2), 1982 (24), 1983 (10), 1984 (12), 1985 (15), 1986 (16), 1987 (16), 1988 (9), 1989 (3).
Total—107.
Switch-hit home runs in one game, June 5, 1983, June 27, 1987, September 15, 1987, July 30, 1988 and July 1, 1989.
Tied for American League lead in sacrifice flies with 10 in 1988.

Year	Club	League	Pos.	G.	AB.	R.	H.	2B.	3B.	HR.	RBI.	B.A.	PO.	A.	E.	F.A.
1978—Cedar Rapids		Midw.	C-OF	124	424	63	119	18	5	16	73	.281	365	45	25	.943
1979—Fresno		Calif.	OF-C	134	490	91	132	24	5	21	95	.269	339	43	20	.950
1980—Shreveport		Texas	OF-C	129	442	50	130	30	4	12	67	.294	184	20	12	.944
1981—San Francisco		Nat.	OF	8	15	1	2	0	0	0	0	.133	7	0	0	1.000
1981—Phoenix†		P. C.	OF	88	334	76	117	16	6	19	75	.350	175	7	6	.968
1982—San Francisco		Nat.	OF	154	641	86	167	27	6	19	76	.261	404	●16	12	.972
1983—San Francisco		Nat.	OF	137	486	54	113	21	2	11	59	.233	357	7	9	.976
1983—Phoenix		P. C.	OF	10	44	12	13	2	0	2	9	.295	15	0	2	.882
1984—San Francisco		Nat.	OF	137	499	87	157	21	6	21	81	.315	292	9	9	.971
1985—San Francisco		Nat.	OF	136	481	53	130	25	2	13	56	.270	279	10	6	.980
1986—San Francisco		Nat.	OF	153	526	71	146	28	3	13	70	.278	303	9	●9	.972
1987—San Francisco‡		Nat.	OF	149	500	80	125	22	1	24	76	.250	265	6	7	.975
1988—California		Amer.	OF	158	600	81	161	29	3	21	93	.268	299	10	★19	.942
1989—California		Amer.	OF	154	560	81	152	24	1	22	90	.271	270	5	6	.979
National League Totals—7 Years				874	3148	432	840	144	20	101	418	.267	1907	57	52	.974
American League Totals—2 Years				312	1160	162	313	53	4	43	183	.270	569	15	25	.959
Major League Totals—9 Years				1186	4308	594	1153	197	24	144	601	.268	2476	72	77	.971

Selected by San Francisco Giants' organization in 11th round of free-agent draft, June 7, 1977.
†On disabled list, August 19 to August 28, 1982.
‡Granted free agency, November 9, 1987; signed by California Angels, December 1, 1987.

CHAMPIONSHIP SERIES RECORD

Year	Club	League	Pos.	G.	AB.	R.	H.	2B.	3B.	HR.	RBI.	B.A.	PO.	A.	E.	F.A.
1987—San Francisco		Nat.	OF	6	20	2	3	1	0	0	0	.150	11	1	1	.923

Year League	Pos.	AB.	R.	H.	2B.	3B.	HR.	RBI.	B.A.	PO.	A.	E.	F.A.
1984—National	PH	1	0	0	0	0	0	0	.000	0	0	0	.000
1986—National	OF	1	0	0	0	0	0	0	.000	0	0	0	.000
All-Star Game Totals—2 Years		2	0	0	0	0	0	0	.000	0	0	0	.000

ERIC KEITH DAVIS

Born May 29, 1962, at Los Angeles, Calif.
Height, 6.03. Weight, 185.
Throws and bats righthanded.

Holds major league record for most strikeouts, two consecutive games (9), April 24 and 25, 1987 (21 innings).
Shares major league record for most grand slams, one month (3), May, 1987.
Major League stolen bases: 1984 (10), 1985 (16), 1986 (80), 1987 (50), 1988 (35), 1989 (21). Total—212.
Hit three home runs in a game, September 10, 1986 and May 3, 1987.
Hit for the cycle, June 2, 1989.
Led National League in game-winning RBIs with 21 in 1988.
Led National League outfielders in total chances with 394 in 1987.
Led Northwest League in stolen bases with 40 in 1981.
Named outfielder on THE SPORTING NEWS National League All-Star Team, 1987 and 1989.
Named outfielder on THE SPORTING NEWS National League All-Star fielding team, 1987 through 1989.
Named outfielder on THE SPORTING NEWS National League Silver Slugger team, 1987 and 1989.

Year Club	League	Pos.	G.	AB.	R.	H.	2B.	3B.	HR.	RBI.	B.A.	PO.	A.	E.	F.A.
1980—Eugene	N'west	SS-2B	33	73	12	16	1	0	1	11	.219	24	35	11	.843
1981—Eugene	N'west	OF	62	214	*67	69	10	4	11	39	.322	94	11	4	.963
1982—Cedar Rapids	Midw.	OF	111	434	80	120	20	5	15	56	.276	239	9	9	.965
1983—Waterbury	East.	OF	89	293	56	85	13	1	15	43	.290	214	8	2	.991
1983—Indianapolis	A. A.	OF	19	77	18	23	4	0	7	19	.299	61	1	1	.984
1984—Wichita	A. A.	OF	52	194	42	61	9	5	14	34	.314	110	5	5	.958
1984—Cincinnati†	Nat.	OF	57	174	33	39	10	1	10	30	.224	125	4	1	.992
1985—Cincinnati	Nat.	OF	56	122	26	30	3	3	8	18	.246	75	3	1	.987
1985—Denver	A. A.	OF	64	206	48	57	10	2	15	38	.277	94	5	3	.971
1986—Cincinnati	Nat.	OF	132	415	97	115	15	3	27	71	.277	274	2	7	.975
1987—Cincinnati	Nat.	OF	129	474	120	139	23	4	37	100	.293	*380	10	4	.990
1988—Cincinnati	Nat.	OF	135	472	81	129	18	3	26	93	.273	300	2	6	.981
1989—Cincinnati‡	Nat.	OF	131	462	74	130	14	2	34	101	.281	298	2	5	.984
Major League Totals—6 Years			640	2119	431	582	83	16	142	413	.275	1452	23	24	.984

Selected by Cincinnati Reds' organization in 8th round of free-agent draft, June 3, 1980.
†On disabled list, August 16 to September 1, 1984.
‡On disabled list, May 3 to May 18, 1989.

ALL-STAR GAME RECORD

Year League	Pos.	AB.	R.	H.	2B.	3B.	HR.	RBI.	B.A.	PO.	A.	E.	F.A.
1987—National	OF	3	0	0	0	0	0	0	.000	1	0	0	1.000
1989—National	OF	2	0	0	0	0	0	0	.000	1	0	0	1.000
All-Star Game Totals—2 Years		5	0	0	0	0	0	0	.000	2	0	0	1.000

GEORGE EARL DAVIS JR.

(Storm)

(Nicknamed by mother after "Dr. Storm", a character in "Dates on Trial",
a book she was reading while pregnant with Storm.)

Born December 26, 1961, at Dallas, Tex.
Height, 6.04. Weight, 200.
Throws and bats righthanded.

Major League saves: 1984 (1).
Tied for American League lead in wild pitches with 16 in 1988.
Named American League Comeback Player of the Year by THE SPORTING NEWS, 1988.

Year Club	League	G.	IP.	W.	L.	Pct.	H.	R.	ER.	SO.	BB.	ERA.
1979—Bluefield	Ap'lachian.	10	58	4	4	.500	44	34	25	54	30	3.88
1980—Miami	Florida St.	25	151	9	12	.429	157	85	59	90	55	3.52
1981—Charlotte	Southern	28	187	14	10	.583	*215	86	72	119	65	3.47
1982—Rochester	Int'national	4	26⅔	2	1	.667	25	13	11	27	7	3.71
1982—Baltimore	American	29	100⅔	8	4	.667	96	40	39	67	28	3.49
1983—Baltimore	American	34	200⅓	13	7	.650	180	90	80	125	64	3.59
1984—Baltimore	American	35	225	14	9	.609	205	86	78	105	71	3.12
1985—Baltimore	American	31	175	10	8	.556	172	92	88	93	70	4.53
1986—Baltimore†	American	25	154	9	12	.429	166	70	62	96	49	3.62
1986—Hagerstown‡	Carolina	1	4	0	0	.000	3	0	0	6	3	0.00
1987—San Diego§	National	21	62⅔	2	7	.222	70	48	43	37	36	6.18
1987—Wichita	Texas	1	4	0	1	.000	4	3	0	2	0	0.00
1987—Reno x	California	1	5	0	0	.000	2	2	2	5	6	3.60
1987—Oakland	American	5	30⅓	1	1	.500	28	13	11	28	11	3.26
1988—Oakland	American	33	201⅔	16	7	.696	211	86	83	127	91	3.70
1989—Oakland yz	American	31	169⅓	19	7	.731	187	91	82	91	68	4.36
American League Totals—8 Years		223	1256½	90	55	.621	1245	568	523	732	452	3.75
National League Totals—1 Year		21	62⅔	2	7	.222	70	48	43	37	36	6.18
Major League Totals—8 Years		244	1319	92	62	.597	1315	616	566	769	488	3.86

Selected by Baltimore Orioles' organization in 7th round of free-agent draft, June 5, 1979.

†On disabled list, July 4 to July 22, 1986; included rehabilitation disability assignment to Hagerstown, July 18 to July 22, 1986.

‡Traded to San Diego Padres for Catcher Terry Kennedy and Pitcher Mark Williamson, October 30, 1986.

§On disabled list, June 30 to August 17, 1987; included rehabilitation disability assignment to Wichita, August 7 to August 11, and Reno, August 12 to August 17, 1987.

xTraded to Oakland Athletics for two players to be named later, August 30, 1987; San Diego Padres acquired Pitcher Dave Leiper, August 31, 1987, and First Baseman Rob Nelson, September 8, 1987, to complete deal.

yOn disabled list, May 18 to June 10, 1989.

zGranted free agency, November 13, 1989; signed by Kansas City Royals, December 7, 1989.

CHAMPIONSHIP SERIES RECORD

Year Club	League	G.	IP.	W.	L.	Pct.	H.	R.	ER.	SO.	BB.	ERA.
1983—Baltimore	American	1	6	0	0	.000	5	0	0	2	2	0.00
1988—Oakland	American	1	6⅓	0	0	.000	2	2	0	4	5	0.00
1989—Oakland	American	1	6⅓	0	1	.000	5	6	5	3	2	7.11
Championship Series Totals—3 Years		3	18⅔	0	1	.000	12	8	5	9	9	2.41

WORLD SERIES RECORD

Year Club	League	G.	IP.	W.	L.	Pct.	H.	R.	ER.	SO.	BB.	ERA.
1983—Baltimore	American	1	5	1	0	1.000	6	3	3	3	1	5.40
1988—Oakland	American	2	8	0	2	.000	14	10	10	7	1	11.25
World Series Totals—2 Years		3	13	1	2	.333	20	13	13	10	2	9.00

Eligible for 1989 World Series with Oakland Athletics; did not play.

GLENN EARL DAVIS

Born March 28, 1961, at Jacksonville, Fla.
Height, 6.03. Weight, 210.
Throws and bats righthanded.
Attended Manatee Junior College, Bradenton, Fla.,
and University of Georgia, Athens, Ga.

Shares National League record for fewest double plays by first baseman, season, 150 or more games (89), 1987.
Major League stolen bases: 1986 (3), 1987 (4), 1988 (4), 1989 (4). Total—15.
Hit three home runs in a game, September 10, 1987.
Tied for National League lead in game-winning RBIs with 16 in 1986.
Led Gulf Coast League first basemen in total chances with 520 and tied for lead in double plays with 35 in 1981.
Named first baseman on THE SPORTING NEWS National League Silver Slugger team, 1986.

Year Club	League	Pos.	G.	AB.	R.	H.	2B.	3B.	HR.	RBI.	B.A.	PO.	A.	E.	F.A.
1981—Sara. Astros-Or.	Gulf C.	*1B-OF	54	188	27	49	7	1	6	35	.261	*469	*37	*14	.973
1982—Daytona Beach	Fla. St.	1B-3B	103	378	70	119	28	3	●19	79	.315	759	70	16	.981
1982—Columbus	South.	1B	26	97	14	24	6	1	4	8	.247	257	11	2	.993
1983—Columbus	South.	OF	118	445	68	133	19	3	●25	85	.299	186	17	9	.958
1983—Tucson	P. C.	OF-1B-3B	15	57	5	12	3	0	1	8	.211	52	4	2	.966
1984—Tucson	P. C.	1B-OF	131	471	66	140	28	7	16	94	.297	922	94	22	.979
1984—Houston	Nat.	1B	18	61	6	13	5	0	2	8	.213	151	15	2	.988
1985—Tucson	P. C.	1B-OF	60	220	22	67	24	2	5	35	.305	420	29	5	.989
1985—Houston	Nat.	1B-OF	100	350	51	95	11	0	20	64	.271	766	57	12	.986
1986—Houston	Nat.	1B	158	574	91	152	32	3	31	101	.265	1253	111	11	.992
1987—Houston	Nat.	1B	151	578	70	145	35	2	27	93	.251	1283	112	12	.991
1988—Houston	Nat.	1B	152	561	78	152	26	0	30	99	.271	1355	103	6	*.996
1989—Houston	Nat.	1D	158	581	87	156	26	1	34	89	.269	1347	113	12	.992
Major League Totals—6 Years			737	2705	383	713	135	6	144	454	.264	6155	511	55	.992

Selected by Baltimore Orioles' organization in 32nd round of free-agent draft, June 5, 1979.
Selected by Houston Astros' organization in secondary phase of free-agent draft, January 13, 1981.

CHAMPIONSHIP SERIES RECORD

Shares Championship Series records for most at-bats, game (7), October 15, 1986 (16 innings); hitting home run in first series at-bat, October 8, 1986.

Year Club	League	Pos.	G.	AB.	R.	H.	2B.	3B.	HR.	RBI.	B.A.	PO.	A.	E.	F.A.
1986—Houston	Nat.	1B	6	26	3	7	1	0	1	3	.269	62	3	1	.985

ALL-STAR GAME RECORD

Year League	Pos.	AB.	R.	H.	2B.	3B.	HR.	RBI.	B.A.	PO.	A.	E.	F.A.
1986—National	PH	1	0	0	0	0	0	0	.000	0	0	0	.000
1989—National	1B	1	1	1	0	0	0	0	1.000	7	0	0	1.000
All-Star Game Totals—2 Years		2	1	1	0	0	0	0	.500	7	0	0	1.000

JODY RICHARD DAVIS

Born November 12, 1956, at Gainesville, Ga.
Height, 6.03. Weight, 210.
Throws and bats righthanded.
Attended Middle Georgia College, Cochran, Ga.

Major League stolen bases: 1984 (5), 1985 (1), 1987 (1). Total—7.
Led National League catchers in total chances with 998 and double plays with 14 in 1986.
Led National League in passed balls with 21 in 1983.
Tied for National League lead in double plays by catchers with 11 in 1982.
Led Carolina League in sacrifice flies with 13 in 1978.

Led Carolina League catchers in double plays with 8 in 1978.
Named catcher on THE SPORTING NEWS National League All-Star fielding team, 1986.

Year Club	League	Pos.	G.	AB.	R.	H.	2B.	3B.	HR.	RBI.	B.A.	PO.	A.	E.	F.A.
1976—Marion	Appal.	C	50	164	20	38	5	1	5	19	.232	290	30	*13	.961
1977—Little Falls	NYP	C-1B	64	214	37	62	11	2	11	46	.290	369	50	12	.972
1978—Lynchburg	Carol.	C-1B-3B	120	408	57	107	24	2	16	94	.262	595	79	15	.978
1979—Jackson†	Texas	C-1B	132	433	57	128	23	4	21	91	.296	661	81	15	.980
1980—St. Petersburg	Fla. St.	C-1B	45	155	27	43	4	0	6	27	.277	171	20	5	.974
1980—Springfield‡§	A. A.	C-1B	13	36	3	6	1	0	0	2	.167	59	7	1	.985
1981—Chicago	Nat.	C	56	180	14	46	5	1	4	21	.256	274	44	9	.972
1982—Chicago	Nat.	C	130	418	41	109	20	2	12	52	.261	598	89	11	.984
1983—Chicago	Nat.	C	151	510	56	138	31	2	24	84	.271	730	75	13	.984
1984—Chicago	Nat.	C	150	523	55	134	25	2	19	94	.256	811	89	*15	.984
1985—Chicago	Nat.	C	142	482	47	112	30	0	17	58	.232	694	84	8	.990
1986—Chicago	Nat.	*C-1B	148	528	61	132	27	2	21	74	.250	*885	*105	4	.992
1987—Chicago	Nat.	C	125	428	57	106	12	2	19	51	.248	749	79	9	.989
1988—Chi. xy-Atl.	Nat.	C	90	257	21	59	9	0	7	36	.230	396	34	2	.995
1989—Atlanta	Nat.	C-1B	78	231	12	39	5	0	4	19	.169	376	40	6	.986
Major League Totals—9 Years			1070	3557	364	875	164	11	127	489	.246	5513	639	81	.987

Selected by New York Mets' organization in 3rd round of free-agent draft, January 7, 1976.
†Traded to St. Louis Cardinals' organization for Pitcher Ray Searage, December 10, 1979.
‡On disabled list, April 14 to June 20, 1980.
§Drafted by Chicago Cubs, December 8, 1980.
xOn disabled list, May 3 to May 19, 1988.
yTraded to Atlanta Braves for Pitchers Kevin Coffman and Kevin Blankenship, September 29, 1988.

CHAMPIONSHIP SERIES RECORD

Year Club	League	Pos.	G.	AB.	R.	H.	2B.	3B.	HR.	RBI.	B.A.	PO.	A.	E.	F.A.
1984—Chicago	Nat.	C	5	18	3	7	2	0	2	6	.389	23	2	0	1.000

ALL-STAR GAME RECORD

Year League	Pos.	AB.	R.	H.	2B.	3B.	HR.	RBI.	B.A.	PO.	A.	E.	F.A.
1984—National	C	1	0	0	0	0	0	0	.000	1	0	0	1.000
1986—National	C	1	0	1	0	0	0	0	1.000	3	0	0	1.000
All-Star Game Totals—2 Years		2	0	1	0	0	0	0	.500	4	0	0	1.000

JOHN KIRK DAVIS

Born January 5, 1963, at Chicago, Ill.
Height, 6.07. Weight 215.
Throws and bats righthanded.

Major League saves: 1987 (2), 1988 (1), 1989 (1). Total—4.
Tied for American League lead in intentional bases on balls issued with 10 in 1988.
Led Pioneer League in wild pitches with 12 in 1982.

Year Club	League	G.	IP.	W.	L.	Pct.	H.	R.	ER.	SO.	BB.	ERA.
1981—Sarasota Royals-Blue	Gulf Coast	10	30	2	2	.500	28	21	17	13	23	5.10
1982—Butte	Pioneer	14	80⅔	7	1	.875	100	62	*55	38	37	6.14
1983—Charleston	S. Atlantic	20	78	5	6	.455	104	64	57	48	40	6.58
1984—Fort Myers	Florida St.	25	153	7	11	.389	170	91	77	84	70	4.53
1985—Memphis	Southern	27	160⅓	6	15	.286	186	113	96	103	75	5.39
1986—Memphis	Southern	41	111⅓	6	6	.500	99	63	58	70	69	4.69
1986—Omaha	Am. Assoc.	2	2	0	0	.000	2	1	1	1	1	4.50
1987—Omaha	Am. Assoc.	43	50⅔	4	3	.571	34	16	15	44	27	2.66
1987—Kansas City†	American	27	43⅔	5	2	.714	29	13	11	24	26	2.27
1988—Chicago	American	34	63⅔	2	5	.286	77	58	47	37	50	6.64
1988—Vancouver	P. Coast	15	17⅓	1	0	1.000	15	7	6	9	7	3.06
1989—Vancouver	P. Coast	35	49⅓	4	3	.571	33	24	13	57	33	2.37
1989—Chicago	American	4	6	0	1	.000	5	4	3	5	2	4.50
Major League Totals—2 Years		65	113⅓	7	8	.467	111	75	61	66	78	4.84

Selected by Kansas City Royals' organization in 7th round of free-agent draft, June 8, 1981.
†Traded with Pitchers Melido Perez, Chuck Mount and Greg Hibbard to Chicago White Sox for Pitcher Floyd Bannister and Infielder Dave Cochrane, December 10, 1987.

MARK WILLIAM DAVIS

Born October 19, 1960, at Livermore, Calif.
Height, 6.04. Weight, 200.
Throws and bats lefthanded.
Attended Chabot College, Hayward, Calif.

Major League saves: 1985 (7), 1986 (4), 1987 (2), 1988 (28), 1989 (44). Total—85.
Led National League in games finished in relief with 65 and saves with 44 in 1989.
Led Western Carolinas League in shutouts with 5, home runs allowed with 18 and tied for lead in balks with 5 in 1979.
Tied for Eastern League lead in shutouts with 4 and in games started by pitchers with 28 in 1980.
Named National League Pitcher of the Year by THE SPORTING NEWS, 1989.
Won National League Cy Young Memorial Award, 1989.
Named National League Fireman of the Year by THE SPORTING NEWS, 1989.
Named lefthanded pitcher on THE SPORTING NEWS National League All-Star Team, 1989.
Named Eastern League Most Valuable Player, 1980.

Year Club	League	G.	IP.	W.	L.	Pct.	H.	R.	ER.	SO.	BB.	ERA.
1979—Spartanburg	W. Carol.	26	166	11	9	.550	147	76	59	135	49	3.20
1980—Reading	Eastern	28	*193	*19	6	*.760	140	63	53	*185	75	*2.47
1980—Philadelphia	National	2	7	0	0	.000	4	2	2	5	5	2.57
1981—Oklahoma City†	Am. Assoc.	13	65	5	2	.714	66	34	28	56	47	3.88
1981—Philadelphia	National	9	43	1	4	.200	49	37	37	29	24	7.74
1982—Oklahoma City‡§	Am. Assoc.	21	96⅔	5	12	.294	111	75	67	95	50	6.24
1983—Phoenix	P. Coast	13	72⅔	6	3	.667	89	57	51	64	33	6.32
1983—San Francisco	National	20	111	6	4	.600	93	51	43	83	50	3.49
1984—San Francisco	National	46	174⅔	5	17	.227	201	113	*104	124	54	5.36
1985—San Francisco	National	77	114⅓	5	12	.294	89	49	45	131	41	3.54
1986—San Francisco	National	67	84⅓	5	7	.417	63	33	28	90	34	2.99
1987—San Francisco x - San Diego	National	63	133	9	8	.529	123	64	59	98	59	3.99
1988—San Diego	National	62	98⅓	5	10	.333	70	24	22	102	42	2.01
1989—San Diego y	National	70	92⅔	4	3	.571	66	21	19	92	31	1.85
Major League Totals—9 Years		416	858⅓	40	65	.381	758	394	359	754	340	3.76

Selected by New York Mets' organization in 21st round of free-agent draft, June 6, 1978.
Selected by Philadelphia Phillies' organization in secondary phase of free-agent draft, January 9, 1979.
†On disabled list, April 14 to June 11, 1981.
‡On disabled list, August 3 to August 30, 1982.
§Traded with Pitcher Mike Krukow and Outfielder Charles Penigar to San Francisco Giants for Second Baseman Joe Morgan and Pitcher Al Holland, December 14, 1982.
xTraded with third Baseman Chris Brown and Pitchers Keith Comstock and Mark Grant to San Diego Padres for Pitchers Dave Dravecky and Craig Lefferts and Infielder Kevin Mitchell, July 4, 1987.
yGranted free agency, November 13, 1989; signed by Kansas City Royals, December 11, 1989.

ALL-STAR GAME RECORD

Year League	IP.	W.	L.	Pct.	H.	R.	ER.	SO.	BB.	ERA.
1988—National	⅔	0	0	.000	1	0	0	0	0	0.00
1989—National	1	0	0	.000	0	0	0	2	0	0.00
All-Star Game Totals—2 Years	1⅔	0	0	.000	1	0	0	2	0	0.00

MICHAEL DWAYNE DAVIS
(Mike)

Born June 11, 1959, at San Diego, Calif.
Height, 6.03. Weight, 201.
Throws and bats lefthanded.
Attended San Diego Mesa College, San Diego, Calif.
Brother of Mark A. Davis, outfielder in Chicago White Sox' organization; and cousin
of Dave Grayson, Sr., defensive back with Dallas Texans,
Kansas City Chiefs and Oakland Raiders, 1961 through 1970; and related to Dave Grayson, Jr.,
linebacker with Cleveland Browns.

Major League stolen bases: 1980 (2), 1982 (3), 1983 (32), 1984 (14), 1985 (24), 1986 (27), 1987 (19), 1988 (7), 1989 (6). Total—134.

Year Club	League	Pos.	G.	AB.	R.	H.	2B.	3B.	HR.	RBI.	B.A.	PO.	A.	E.	F.A.
1977—Medicine Hat	Pion.	*OF-1-2	59	213	53	67	5	3	2	18	.315	82	6	*15	.854
1978—Modesto	Calif.	OF-1B	106	406	74	136	12	4	2	35	.335	201	10	13	.942
1979—Modesto	Calif.	OF	41	161	48	63	10	4	0	19	.391	76	3	7	.919
1979—Waterbury	East.	OF	97	351	51	77	9	5	6	39	.219	208	7	15	.935
1980—Ogden	P. C.	OF	19	69	14	21	7	2	1	14	.304	34	2	1	.973
1980—Oakland	Amer.	OF-1B	51	95	11	20	2	1	1	8	.211	76	7	1	.988
1981—Tacoma	P. C.	OF-1B	133	515	84	148	28	6	6	71	.287	286	7	7	.977
1981—Oakland	Amer.	OF-1B	17	20	0	1	1	0	0	0	.050	3	0	0	1.000
1982—Tacoma†	P. C.	OF-1B	100	374	71	118	23	3	12	68	.316	197	13	9	.959
1982—Oakland	Amer.	OF-1B	23	75	12	30	4	0	1	10	.400	65	4	5	.932
1983—Oakland‡	Amer.	OF	128	443	61	122	24	4	8	62	.275	278	16	8	.974
1984—Oakland	Amer.	OF	134	382	47	88	18	3	9	46	.230	287	6	●12	.961
1985—Oakland	Amer.	OF	154	547	92	157	34	1	24	82	.287	370	6	8	.979
1986—Oakland	Amer.	OF	142	489	77	131	28	3	19	55	.268	310	9	9	.973
1987—Oakland§	Amer.	OF	139	494	69	131	32	1	22	72	.265	210	3	●13	.942
1988—Los Angeles	Nat.	OF	108	281	29	55	11	2	2	17	.196	121	3	5	.961
1989—Los Angeles x	Nat.	OF	67	173	21	43	7	1	5	19	.249	74	1	1	.987
American League Totals—8 Years			788	2545	369	680	143	13	84	335	.267	1599	51	56	.967
National League Totals—2 Years			175	454	50	98	18	3	7	36	.216	195	4	6	.971
Major League Totals—10 Years			963	2999	419	778	161	16	91	371	.259	1794	55	62	.968

Selected by Minnesota Twins' organization in 31st round of free agent draft, June 8, 1976.
Selected by Oakland A's organization in 3rd round of free agent draft, June 7, 1977.
†On disabled list, April 13 to May 24, 1982.
‡On disabled list, July 13 to July 31, 1983.
§Granted free agency, November 9, 1987; signed by Los Angeles Dodgers, December 15, 1987.
xOn disabled list, July 6 to September 6, 1989.

CHAMPIONSHIP SERIES RECORD

Year Club	League	Pos.	G.	AB.	R.	H.	2B.	3B.	HR.	RBI.	B.A.	PO.	A.	E.	F.A.
1981—Oakland	Amer.	PH	1	1	0	1	0	0	0	0	1.000	0	0	0	.000
1988—Los Angeles	Nat.	PH	4	2	0	0	0	0	0	0	.000	0	0	0	.000
Championship Series Totals—2 Years			5	3	0	1	0	0	0	0	.333	0	0	0	.000

Year	Club	League	Pos.	G.	AB.	R.	H.	2B.	3B.	HR.	RBI.	B.A.	PO.	A.	E.	F.A.
1988—Los Angeles		Nat.	PH-DH-O	4	7	3	1	0	0	1	2	.143	0	0	0	.000

STEVEN KENNON DAVIS
(Steve)

Born August 4, 1960, at San Antonio, Tex.
Height, 6.01. Weight, 185.
Throws and bats lefthanded.
Attended Texas A&M University, College Station, Tex.

Led International League in games started by pitchers with 31 in 1988.
Tied for Southern League lead in shutouts with 3 in 1985.
Named Southern League Pitcher of the Year, 1985.

Year	Club	League	G.	IP.	W.	L.	Pct.	H.	R.	ER.	SO.	BB.	ERA.
1982—Medicine Hat		Pioneer	13	36⅔	5	1	.833	38	15	14	46	17	3.44
1983—Florence		S. Atlantic	23	153⅔	10	7	.588	129	66	55	167	52	3.22
1983—Knoxville		Southern	4	22	1	3	.250	26	17	17	18	14	6.95
1984—Knoxville		Southern	27	154⅔	9	6	.600	123	71	60	77	96	3.49
1985—Knoxville		Southern	27	154	*17	6	.739	114	49	42	107	72	*2.45
1985—Syracuse		Int'national	6	36	3	2	.600	19	11	10	34	17	2.50
1985—Toronto		American	10	28	2	1	.667	23	14	11	22	13	3.54
1986—Toronto		American	3	3⅔	0	0	.000	8	7	7	5	5	17.18
1986—Syracuse†		Int'national	23	104⅔	5	7	.417	104	67	65	80	57	5.59
1987—Syracuse		Int'national	20	51	1	5	.167	71	59	55	31	44	9.71
1987—Knoxville		Southern	13	65⅔	6	2	.750	54	26	22	37	38	3.02
1988—Syracuse‡		Int'national	31	178	10	15	.400	166	94	65	130	66	3.29
1989—Colorado Springs		P. Coast	18	121	12	2	*.857	113	36	33	75	40	2.45
1989—Cleveland§		American	12	25⅔	1	1	.500	34	24	23	12	14	8.06
Major League Totals—3 Years			25	57⅓	3	2	.600	65	45	41	39	32	6.44

Selected by Toronto Blue Jays' organization in 21st round of free-agent draft, June 7, 1982.
†On disabled list, July 11 to July 26, 1986.
‡Granted free agency, October 15, 1988; signed by Colorado Springs (Cleveland Indians' organization), December 26, 1988.
§Traded to Los Angeles Dodgers for Infielder Manny Francois and Outfielder Joe Kesselmark, December 12, 1989.

WALLACE McARTHUR DAVIS
(Butch)

Born June 19, 1958, at Williamston, N.C.
Height, 6.00. Weight, 196.
Throws and bats righthanded.
Attended St. Augustine's College, Raleigh, N.C., and received
bachelor of science degree from East Carolina University, Greenville, N.C. in 1980.

Major League stolen bases: 1983 (4), 1984 (4), 1988 (1). Total—9.
Led Gulf Coast League in total bases with 105 and stolen bases with 31 in 1980.
Led International League outfielders in total chances with 272 in 1989.

Year	Club	League	Pos.	G.	AB.	R.	H.	2B.	3B.	HR.	RBI.	B.A.	PO.	A.	E.	F.A.
1980—Sarasota Royals		Gulf C.	OF	61	235	46	*74	*17	4	2	35	.315	117	5	3	.976
1981—Fort Myers		Fla. St.	OF	126	464	*89	139	17	10	13	70	.300	239	5	12	.953
1982—Jacksonville		South.	OF	122	450	64	115	18	4	10	57	.256	231	7	2	.992
1983—Jacksonville		South.	OF-1B	90	331	51	105	15	7	14	63	.317	117	4	4	.968
1983—Omaha		A. A.	OF	46	171	27	54	10	3	5	21	.316	10	0	1	.909
1983—Kansas City		Amer.	OF	33	122	13	42	2	6	2	18	.344	83	1	2	.977
1984—Kansas City		Amer.	OF	41	116	11	17	3	0	2	12	.147	69	2	3	.959
1984—Omaha		A. A.	OF-1B	83	314	45	102	15	5	7	43	.325	153	13	6	.965
1985—Omaha		A. A.	OF-1B	109	403	58	106	26	10	6	34	.263	209	3	9	.959
1986—Omaha†‡		A. A.					(Did not play)									
1987—Vancouver		P. C.	OF	111	424	58	115	17	7	7	57	.271	232	8	4	.984
1987—Pittsburgh§		Nat.	OF	7	7	3	1	1	0	0	0	.143	3	0	0	1.000
1988—Charlotte		South.	OF	101	412	62	124	23	7	13	82	*.301	116	3	3	.975
1988—Rochester		Int.	OF	8	28	4	4	0	2	0	0	.143	10	0	0	1.000
1988—Baltimore x		Amer.	OF	13	25	2	6	1	0	0	0	.240	16	1	0	1.000
1989—Rochester		Int	OF	127	479	81	145	29	9	10	64	.303	*258	8	6	.978
1989—Baltimore		Amer.	OF	5	6	1	1	1	0	0	0	.167	3	0	0	1.000
American League Totals—4 Years				92	269	27	66	7	6	4	30	.245	171	4	5	.972
National League Totals—1 Year				7	7	3	1	1	0	0	0	.143	3	0	0	1.000
Major League Totals—5 Years				99	276	30	67	8	6	4	30	.243	174	4	5	.973

Selected by Kansas City Royals' organization in 12th round of free-agent draft, June 3, 1980.
†On disabled list, April 11, 1986 through entire season.
‡Granted free agency, October 15, 1986; signed by Pittsburgh Pirates, December 4, 1986.
§Granted free agency, October 15, 1987; signed by Charlotte (Baltimore Orioles' organization), May 3, 1988.
xGranted free agency, October 15, 1988; re-signed by Orioles' organization, November 21, 1988.

—DID YOU KNOW—

That the Blue Jays have won 15 consecutive games at Boston's Fenway Park? Their last loss there was on August 10, 1987.

WILLIAM CHESTER DAWLEY
(Bill)

Born February 6, 1958, at Norwich, Conn.
Height, 6.04. Weight, 240.
Throws and bats righthanded.

Major League saves: 1983 (14), 1984 (5), 1985 (2), 1986 (2), 1987 (2). Total—25.
Led American Association pitchers in games started with 28 in 1982.

Year	Club	League	G.	IP.	W.	L.	Pct.	H.	R.	ER.	SO.	BB.	ERA.
1976—Billings		Pioneer	13	78	6	4	.600	62	42	24	80	37	2.77
1977—Tampa		Florida St.	24	181	10	8	.556	151	69	57	110	69	2.83
1978—Nashville		Southern	27	141	7	13	.350	135	78	63	86	55	4.02
1979—Nashville†		Southern	25	140	9	9	.500	144	72	62	84	41	3.99
1980—Indianapolis		Am. Assoc.	25	77	4	6	.400	90	46	39	28	31	4.56
1980—Waterbury		Eastern	7	49	2	2	.500	43	18	16	33	25	2.94
1981—Indianapolis		Am. Assoc.	26	133	6	8	.429	141	77	73	109	69	4.94
1982—Indianapolis‡§		Am. Assoc.	29	*179	11	7	.611	196	86	76	106	48	3.82
1983—Houston		National	48	79⅔	6	6	.500	51	26	25	60	22	2.82
1984—Houston		National	60	98	11	4	.733	82	24	21	47	35	1.93
1985—Houston xy		National	49	81	5	3	.625	76	35	32	48	37	3.56
1986—Chicago z		American	46	97⅔	0	7	.000	91	38	36	66	28	3.32
1987—St. Louis a		National	60	96⅔	5	8	.385	93	51	48	65	38	4.47
1988—Maine		Int'national	22	38⅔	1	2	.333	30	13	12	29	11	2.79
1988—Philadelphia bc		National	8	8⅔	0	2	.000	16	13	13	3	4	13.50
1989—Tacoma		P. Coast	22	38⅔	3	1	.750	34	11	11	44	18	2.56
1989—Oakland d		American	4	9	0	0	.000	11	5	4	3	2	4.00
1989—Denver e		Am. Assoc.	11	19⅓	0	0	.000	30	15	13	12	6	6.05
National League Totals—5 Years			225	364	27	23	.540	318	149	139	223	136	3.44
American League Totals—2 Years			50	106⅔	0	7	.000	102	43	40	69	30	3.38
Major League Totals—7 Years			275	470⅔	27	30	.474	420	192	179	292	166	3.42

Selected by Cincinnati Reds' organization in 7th round of free-agent draft, June 8, 1976.

†On temporary inactive list, May 21 to May 31, 1979.

‡Appeared in one game as an outfielder with no chances.

§Traded with Outfielder Anthony Walker to Houston Astros' organization for Catcher Alan Knicely, March 31, 1983.

xOn disabled list, July 6 to July 24, 1985.

yReleased, April 1, 1986; signed by Chicago White Sox, April 15, 1986.

zTraded to St. Louis Cardinals for Infielder Fred Manrique, December 22, 1986.

aReleased, December 21, 1987; signed by Philadelphia Phillies' organization, February 10, 1988.

bOn disabled list, May 11 to August 19, 1988; included rehabilitation disability assignment to Maine, July 27 to August 16, 1988.

cReleased, October 7, 1988; signed by Tacoma (Oakland Athletics' organization), January, 1989.

dReleased, July 27, 1989; signed by El Paso (Milwaukee Brewers' organization), July 28, 1989.

eGranted free agency, October 15, 1989.

ALL-STAR GAME RECORD

Year	League	IP.	W.	L.	Pct.	H.	R.	ER.	SO.	BB.	ERA.
1983—National		1⅓	0	0	.000	1	0	0	1	0	0.00

ANDRE FERNANDO DAWSON

Born July 10, 1954, at Miami, Fla.
Height, 6.03. Weight, 195.
Throws and bats righthanded.
Attended Florida A&M University, Tallahassee, Fla.
Nephew of Theodore Taylor, third baseman-outfielder in Pittsburgh Pirates'
organization, 1967 through 1969.

Shares major league records for most total bases, inning (8); most home runs, inning (2), July 30, 1978, third inning, and September 24, 1985, fifth inning; most runs batted in, inning (6), September 24, 1985, fifth inning; fewest double plays by outfielder, season, 150 or more games (0), 1987.

Major League stolen bases: 1976 (1), 1977 (21), 1978 (28), 1979 (35), 1980 (34), 1981 (26), 1982 (39), 1983 (25), 1984 (13), 1985 (13), 1986 (18), 1987 (11), 1988 (12), 1989 (8). Total—284.

Hit for the cycle, April 29, 1987.

Hit three home runs in a game, September 24, 1985 and August 1, 1987.

Led National League in total bases with 341 in 1983 and 353 in 1987.

Led National League in sacrifice flies with 18 in 1983.

Led National League in being hit by pitch with 12 in 1978, 7 in 1981 and tied for lead with 6 in 1980 and 9 in 1983.

Tied for National League lead in game-winning RBIs with 16 in 1987.

Led National League outfielders in total chances with 344 in 1981, 435 in 1982 and 450 in 1983.

Led Pioneer League in total bases with 166, in being hit by pitch with 6 and tied for lead in sacrifice flies with 5 in 1975.

Named National League Player of the Year by THE SPORTING NEWS, 1981 and 1987.

Named National League Most Valuable Player by Baseball Writers' Association of America, 1987.

Named National League Rookie Player of the Year by THE SPORTING NEWS, 1977.

Named National League Rookie of the Year by Baseball Writers' Association of America, 1977.

Named outfielder on THE SPORTING NEWS National League All-Star Team, 1981, 1983 and 1987.

Named outfielder on THE SPORTING NEWS National League All-Star fielding team, 1980 through 1985, 1987 and 1988.

Named outfielder on THE SPORTING NEWS National League Silver Slugger team, 1980, 1981, 1983 and 1987.

Year	Club	League	Pos.	G.	AB.	R.	H.	2B.	3B.	HR.	RBI.	B.A.	PO.	A.	E.	F.A.
1975—Lethbridge		Pion.	OF	●72	*300	52	*99	14	7	*13	50	.330	*142	7	*10	.937

Year Club	League	Pos.	G.	AB.	R.	H.	2B.	3B.	HR.	RBI.	B.A.	PO.	A.	E.	F.A.
1976—Quebec City	East.	OF	40	143	27	51	6	0	8	27	.357	89	3	6	.939
1976—Denver	A. A.	OF	74	240	51	84	19	4	20	46	.350	97	2	2	.980
1976—Montreal	Nat.	OF	24	85	9	20	4	1	0	7	.235	61	1	2	.969
1977—Montreal	Nat.	OF	139	525	64	148	26	9	19	65	.282	352	9	4	.989
1978—Montreal	Nat.	OF	157	609	84	154	24	8	25	72	.253	411	17	5	.988
1979—Montreal	Nat.	OF	155	639	90	176	24	12	25	92	.275	394	7	5	.988
1980—Montreal	Nat.	OF	151	577	96	178	41	7	17	87	.308	410	14	6	.986
1981—Montreal	Nat.	OF	103	394	71	119	21	3	24	64	.302	★327	10	7	.980
1982—Montreal	Nat.	OF	148	608	107	183	37	7	23	83	.301	★419	8	8	.982
1983—Montreal	Nat.	OF	159	633	104	●189	36	10	32	113	.299	★435	6	9	.980
1984—Montreal	Nat.	OF	138	533	73	132	23	6	17	86	.248	297	11	8	.975
1985—Montreal	Nat.	OF	139	529	65	135	27	2	23	91	.255	248	9	7	.973
1986—Montreal†‡	Nat.	OF	130	496	65	141	32	2	20	78	.284	200	11	3	.986
1987—Chicago	Nat.	OF	153	621	90	178	24	2	★49	★137	.287	271	12	4	.986
1988—Chicago	Nat.	OF	157	591	78	179	31	8	24	79	.303	267	7	3	.989
1989—Chicago§	Nat.	OF	118	416	62	105	18	6	21	77	.252	227	4	3	.987
Major League Totals—14 Years			1871	7256	1058	2037	368	83	319	1131	.281	4319	126	74	.984

Selected by Montreal Expos' organization in 11th round of free-agent draft, June 4, 1975.

†On disabled list, June 5 to June 30, 1986.

‡Granted free agency, November 12, 1986; signed by Chicago Cubs, March 9, 1987.

§On disabled list, May 7 to June 12, 1989.

DIVISION SERIES RECORD

Year Club	League	Pos.	G.	AB.	R.	H.	2B.	3B.	HR.	RBI.	B.A.	PO.	A.	E.	F.A.
1981—Montreal	Nat.	OF	5	20	1	6	0	1	0	0	.300	12	1	1	.929

CHAMPIONSHIP SERIES RECORD

Year Club	League	Pos.	G.	AB.	R.	H.	2B.	3B.	HR.	RBI.	B.A.	PO.	A.	E.	F.A.
1981—Montreal	Nat.	OF	5	20	2	3	0	0	0	0	.150	12	0	0	1.000
1989—Chicago	Nat.	OF	5	19	0	2	1	0	0	3	.105	4	0	0	1.000
Championship Series Totals—2 Years			10	39	2	5	1	0	0	3	.128	16	0	0	1.000

ALL-STAR GAME RECORD

Year League	Pos.	AB.	R.	H.	2B.	3B.	HR.	RBI.	B.A.	PO.	A.	E.	F.A.
1981—National	OF	4	0	1	0	0	0	0	.250	4	0	0	1.000
1982—National	OF	4	0	1	0	0	0	0	.250	4	0	0	1.000
1983—National	OF	3	0	0	0	0	0	0	.000	3	0	0	1.000
1987—National	OF	3	0	1	1	0	0	0	.333	3	0	0	1.000
1988—National	OF	2	0	1	0	0	0	0	.500	0	0	0	1.000
1989—National	OF	1	0	0	0	0	0	0	.000	1	0	0	1.000
All-Star Game Totals—6 Years		17	0	4	1	0	0	0	.235	15	0	0	1.000

KENNETH GRANT DAYLEY II
(Ken)

Born February 25, 1959, at Jerome, Ida.
Height, 6.00. Weight, 180.
Throws and bats lefthanded.
Attended University of Portland, Portland, Ore.

Major League saves: 1985 (11), 1986 (5), 1987 (4), 1988 (5), 1989 (12). Total—37.
Led International League pitchers in games started with 31 in 1981.
Received reported $100,000 bonus to sign with Atlanta Braves, 1980.
Named lefthanded pitcher on THE SPORTING NEWS College Baseball All-America Team, 1980.

Year Club	League	G.	IP.	W.	L.	Pct.	H.	R.	ER.	SO.	BB.	ERA.
1980—Savannah	Southern	16	105	8	3	.727	86	38	30	104	54	2.57
1981—Richmond	Int'national	31	★200	●13	8	.619	180	82	74	★162	★117	3.33
1982—Richmond	Int'national	13	98⅓	8	3	.727	89	43	34	79	47	3.11
1982—Atlanta	National	20	71⅓	5	6	.455	79	39	36	34	25	4.54
1983—Richmond	Int'national	14	90⅔	9	3	.750	79	39	33	74	49	3.28
1983—Atlanta	National	24	104⅔	5	8	.385	100	59	50	70	39	4.30
1984—Atlanta†-St. Louis	National	7	23⅔	0	5	.000	44	28	21	10	11	7.99
1984—Richmond	Int'national	9	62⅓	5	1	.833	66	31	28	45	24	4.04
1984—Louisville	Am. Assoc.	13	96⅓	4	6	.400	86	42	35	79	22	3.27
1985—St. Louis	National	57	65⅓	4	4	.500	65	24	20	62	18	2.76
1986—St. Louis‡§	National	31	38⅔	0	3	.000	42	19	14	33	11	3.26
1987—Louisville	Am. Assoc.	1	2	0	0	.000	1	1	1	1	1	4.50
1987—Springfield	Midwest	2	3⅔	0	0	.000	1	0	0	3	1	0.00
1987—St. Louis x	National	53	61	9	5	.643	52	21	18	63	33	2.66
1988—St. Louis y	National	54	55⅓	2	7	.222	48	20	17	38	19	2.77
1989—St. Louis	National	71	75⅓	4	3	.571	63	26	24	40	30	2.87
Major League Totals—8 Years		317	495⅓	29	41	.414	493	236	200	350	186	3.63

Selected by Atlanta Braves' organization in 1st round (third player selected) of free-agent draft, June 3, 1980.

†Traded with First Baseman Mike Jorgensen to St. Louis Cardinals for Third Baseman Ken Oberkfell, June 15, 1984.

‡On disabled list, July 13, 1986 through remainder of season.

§Released, December 20, 1986; re-signed by Cardinals, January 19, 1987.

xOn St. Louis disabled list, April 5 to May 21, 1987; included rehabilitation disability assignment to Louisville, May 12 to May 21, 1987.

yOn disabled list, April 5 to May 9, 1988.

Shares Championship Series record for most games pitched, series (5), 1985.

Year Club	League	G.	IP.	W.	L.	Pct.	H.	R.	ER.	SO.	BB.	ERA.
1985—St. Louis	National	5	6	0	0	.000	2	0	0	3	1	0.00
1987—St. Louis	National	3	4	0	0	.000	1	0	0	4	2	0.00
Championship Series Totals—2 Years		8	10	0	0	.000	3	0	0	7	3	0.00

WORLD SERIES RECORD

Year Club	League	G.	IP.	W.	L.	Pct.	H.	R.	ER.	SO.	BB.	ERA.
1985—St. Louis	National	4	6	1	0	1.000	1	0	0	5	3	0.00
1987—St. Louis	National	4	4⅔	0	0	.000	2	1	1	3	0	1.93
World Series Totals—2 Years		8	10⅔	1	0	1.000	3	1	1	8	3	0.84

BRIAN LOUIS DEAK

Born October 25, 1967, at Harrisburg, Pa.
Height, 6.00. Weight, 183.
Throws and bats righthanded.
Attended Yavapai College, Prescott, Ariz.

Led Midwest League in slugging percentage with .481 in 1988.
Led Appalachian League catchers in total chances with 419 in 1986.
Tied for Carolina League lead in double plays by catchers with 8 in 1989.
Named Appalachian League Player of the Year, 1986.

Year Club	League	Pos.	G.	AB.	R.	II.	2B.	3B.	HR.	RBI.	B.A.	PO.	A.	E.	F.A.
1986—Pulaski	Appal.	C	62	197	45	64	15	2	12	43	.325	★391	24	4	.990
1987—Sumter	S. Atl.	C	92	252	50	51	6	0	15	49	.202	576	55	11	.983
1988—Burlington	Midw.	C	119	345	58	85	19	1	20	59	.246	604	87	12	.983
1989—Durham†	Carol.	C	113	327	44	77	10	0	21	64	.235	599	60	9	.987

Selected by Atlanta Braves' organization in 3rd round of free-agent draft, January 14, 1986.
†On disabled list, August 25, 1989 through remainder of season.

DEAN ANTHONY DeCILLIS

Born July 9, 1967, at New York, N.Y.
Height, 5.11. Weight, 170.
Throws and bats righthanded.
Attended Miami-Dade Community College (South), Miami, Fla.

Year Club	League	Pos.	G.	AB.	R.	H.	2B.	3B.	HR.	RBI.	B.A.	PO.	A.	E.	F.A.
1987—Fayetteville	S. Atl.	SS-3B	49	160	24	38	6	1	0	10	.238	69	106	18	.907
1988—Lakeland	Fla. St.	SS	122	436	43	113	14	4	5	61	.259	175	366	★46	.922
1989—London†	East.	2-S-3-1-O	98	375	47	92	14	1	5	46	.245	149	243	14	.966

Selected by Toronto Blue Jays' organization in 10th round of free-agent draft, January 14, 1986.
Selected by Detroit Tigers' organization in 6th round of free-agent draft, June 2, 1987.
†On disabled list, May 20 to June 3, 1989.

ROBERT GEORGE DEER
(Rob)

Born September 29, 1960, at Orange, Calif.
Height, 6.03. Weight, 210.
Throws and bats righthanded.
Attended Fresno City College, Fresno, Calif.

Shares major league records for most grand slams, two consecutive games (2), August 19 and 20, 1987; most strikeouts, nine-inning game (5), August 8, first game, 1987.
Holds American League record for most strikeouts, season (186), 1987.
Major League stolen bases: 1984 (1), 1986 (5), 1987 (12), 1988 (9), 1989 (4). Total—31.
Led American League batters in strikeouts with 186 in 1987 and tied for lead with 153 in 1988.
Led Pacific Coast League batters in strikeouts with 175 in 1984.
Led Texas League batters in strikeouts with 177 in 1982 and 185 in 1983.
Tied for Texas League lead in game-winning RBIs with 13 in 1983.
Led California League batters in strikeouts with 146 in 1981.

Year Club	League	Pos.	G.	AB.	R.	H.	2B.	3B.	HR.	RBI.	B.A.	PO.	A.	E.	F.A.
1978—Great Falls	Pion.	OF	48	137	20	34	6	5	0	18	.248	83	3	4	.956
1979—Cedar Rapids	Midw.	OF	29	86	7	18	0	1	1	16	.209	35	1	4	.900
1979—Great Falls	Pion.	OF	63	218	49	69	18	7	7	44	.317	95	10	5	.955
1980—Clinton	Midw.	OF	127	434	60	114	31	5	13	58	.263	184	●17	11	.948
1981—Fresno	Calif.	OF	135	479	86	137	24	4	★33	107	.286	211	14	6	.974
1982—Shreveport	Texas	OF-1B	128	410	58	85	26	0	27	73	.207	184	10	11	.946
1983—Shreveport	Texas	OF	132	448	89	97	15	1	★35	99	.217	252	13	7	.974
1984—Phoenix	P. C.	OF	133	449	88	102	21	1	★31	69	.227	251	★19	9	.968
1984—San Francisco	Nat.	OF	13	24	5	4	0	0	3	3	.167	19	0	2	.905
1985—San Francisco†	Nat.	OF-1B	78	162	22	30	5	1	8	20	.185	127	2	2	.985
1986—Milwaukee	Amer.	OF-1B	134	466	75	108	17	3	33	86	.232	312	8	8	.976
1987—Milwaukee	Amer.	OF-1B	134	474	71	113	15	2	28	80	.238	304	16	8	.976
1988—Milwaukee‡	Amer.	OF	135	492	71	124	24	0	23	85	.252	284	10	3	.990

Year Club	League	Pos.	G.	AB.	R.	H.	2B.	3B.	HR.	RBI.	B.A.	PO.	A.	E.	F.A.
1989—Milwaukee§	Amer.	OF	130	466	72	98	18	2	26	65	.210	267	10	8	.972
National League Totals—2 Years			91	186	27	34	5	1	11	23	.183	146	2	4	.974
American League Totals—4 Years			533	1898	289	443	74	7	110	316	.233	1167	44	27	.978
Major League Totals—6 Years			624	2084	316	477	79	8	121	339	.229	1313	46	31	.978

Selected by San Francisco Giants' organization in 4th round of free-agent draft, June 6, 1978.
†Traded to Milwaukee Brewers for Pitchers Dean Freeland and Eric Pilkington, December 18, 1985.
‡On disabled list, July 4 to July 27, 1988.
§On disabled list, August 9 to August 25, 1989.

JOSE LUIS DeJESUS (VELAZQUEZ)

Born January 6, 1965, at Brooklyn, N.Y.
Height, 6.05. Weight, 175.
Throws and bats righthanded.

Year Club	League	G.	IP.	W.	L.	Pct.	H.	R.	ER.	SO.	BB.	ERA.
1983—Sarasota Royals	Gulf Coast	10	24	1	2	.333	17	18	11	10	17	4.13
1984—Charleston	S. Atlantic	27	163	11	12	.478	152	98	80	85	69	4.42
1985—Fort Myers†	Florida St.	27	129⅔	8	10	.444	119	70	62	94	59	4.30
1986—Fort Myers	Florida St.	22	110	4	9	.308	87	64	42	97	82	3.44
1987—Memphis	Southern	25	130⅓	4	11	.267	106	78	65	79	99	4.49
1988—Memphis	Southern	20	116	9	9	.500	88	56	50	149	70	3.88
1988—Omaha	Am. Assoc.	7	49⅔	2	3	.400	44	22	19	57	14	3.44
1988—Kansas City	American	2	2⅔	0	1	.000	6	10	8	2	5	27.00
1989—Omaha	Am. Assoc.	31	145⅓	8	11	.421	112	78	61	158	*98	3.78
1989—Kansas City	American	3	8	0	0	.000	7	4	4	2	8	4.50
Major League Totals—2 Years		5	10⅔	0	1	.000	13	14	12	4	13	10.13

Signed as free agent by Kansas City Royals' organization, May 9, 1983.
†Drafted by Toronto Blue Jays, December 10, 1985; returned, April 3, 1986.

JOSE DeLEON (CHESTARO)

Born December 20, 1960, at Rancho Viejo, LaVega, D.R.
Height, 6.03. Weight, 211.
Throws and bats righthanded.

Major League saves: 1985 (3), 1986 (1). Total—4.
Led Gulf Coast League in home runs allowed with 7 in 1979.
Tied for South Atlantic League lead in home runs allowed with 19 in 1980.
Tied for Gulf Coast League lead in wild pitches with 9 in 1979.

Year Club	League	G.	IP.	W.	L.	Pct.	H.	R.	ER.	SO.	BB.	ERA.
1979—Bradenton Pirates	Gulf Coast	11	59	2	4	.333	76	47	42	33	38	6.41
1980—Shelby	S. Atlantic	26	168	10	15	.400	160	108	*90	118	69	4.82
1981—Buffalo	Eastern	25	159	12	6	.667	136	72	55	158	94	3.11
1982—Portland†	P. Coast	24	119	10	7	.588	138	81	79	94	65	5.97
1983—Hawaii	P. Coast	20	127⅓	11	6	.647	90	50	43	128	68	*3.04
1983—Pittsburgh	National	15	108	7	3	.700	75	36	34	118	47	2.83
1984—Pittsburgh	National	30	192⅓	7	13	.350	147	86	80	153	92	3.74
1985—Pittsburgh	National	31	162⅔	2	*19	.095	138	93	85	149	89	4.70
1985—Hawaii	P. Coast	5	41	4	0	1.000	15	4	4	45	10	0.88
1986—Hawaii	P. Coast	15	106	5	8	.385	87	32	29	83	44	2.46
1986—Pittsburgh‡	National	9	16⅓	1	3	.250	17	16	15	11	17	8.27
1986—Chicago	American	13	79	4	5	.444	49	30	26	68	42	2.96
1987—Chicago§	American	33	206	11	12	.478	177	106	92	153	97	4.02
1988—St. Louis x	National	34	225⅓	13	10	.565	198	95	92	208	86	3.67
1989—St. Louis	National	36	244⅔	16	12	.571	173	96	83	*201	80	3.05
National League Totals—6 Years		155	949⅓	46	60	.434	748	422	389	840	411	3.69
American League Totals—2 Years		46	285	15	17	.469	226	136	118	221	139	3.73
Major League Totals—7 Years		201	1234⅓	61	77	.442	974	558	507	1061	550	3.70

Selected by Pittsburgh Pirates' organization in 3rd round of free-agent draft June 5, 1979.
†On disabled list, July 5 to July 29, 1982.
‡Traded to Chicago White Sox for Outfielder Bobby Bonilla, July 23, 1986.
§Traded to St. Louis Cardinals for Pitcher Rick Horton, Outfielder Lance Johnson and cash, February 9, 1988.
xAppeared in one game as an outfielder with one putout.

LUIS ANTONIO DeLEON (TRICOCHE)

Born August 19, 1958, at Ponce, Puerto Rico.
Height, 6.01. Weight, 159.
Throws and bats righthanded.
Son of Luis A. DeLeon, minor league pitcher, 1957, 1958 and 1960; brother of Luis A. DeLeon, shortstop in
Boston Red Sox' and Cleveland Indians' organizations, 1974 through 1984;
and Desiderio DeLeon, minor league pitcher, 1977.
Major Leagues saves: 1982 (15), 1983 (13), 1985 (3), 1987 (1). Total—32.
Tied for International League lead in intentional bases on balls issued with 7 in 1987.
Tied for Florida State League lead in saves with 14 and intentional bases on balls issued with 10 in 1979.
Tied for Appalachian League lead in shutouts with 2 in 1978.

Year Club	League	G.	IP.	W.	L.	Pct.	H.	R.	ER.	SO.	BB.	ERA.
1978—Johnson City	Ap'lachian	13	84	7	6	.538	84	37	31	74	26	3.32
1979—St. Petersburg	Florida St.	*59	92	8	3	.727	63	20	15	100	28	1.47

Year	Club	League	G.	IP.	W.	L.	Pct.	H.	R.	ER.	SO.	BB.	ERA.
1979—Arkansas	Texas		2	3	0	0	.000	1	2	2	4	2	6.00
1980—Arkansas	Texas		*76	107	7	6	.538	85	46	39	92	49	3.28
1981—Springfield	Am. Assoc.		52	99	8	7	.533	73	34	28	96	35	2.55
1981—St. Louis†	National		10	15	0	1	.000	11	4	4	8	3	2.40
1982—San Diego	National		61	102	9	5	.643	77	25	23	60	16	2.03
1983—San Diego	National		63	111	6	6	.500	89	34	33	90	27	2.68
1984—San Diego‡	National		32	42⅔	2	2	.500	44	34	26	44	12	5.48
1984—Las Vegas	P. Coast		6	20⅔	1	1	.500	24	11	11	11	5	4.79
1984—San Diego	National		29	38⅔	0	3	.000	39	18	18	31	10	4.19
1985—Las Vegas §x	P. Coast		9	23⅓	2	1	.667	27	14	14	19	8	5.40
1986—Rochester	Int'national		49	75	4	8	.333	68	31	29	53	32	3.48
1987—Rochester	Int'national		33	47⅓	3	3	.500	41	17	14	47	22	2.66
1987—Baltimore y	American		11	20⅔	0	2	.000	19	15	11	13	8	4.79
1988—Tucson z	P. Coast		48	65⅓	4	9	.308	68	40	38	59	22	5.23
1989—Calgary	P. Coast		33	71⅔	4	4	.500	83	50	41	63	36	5.15
1989—Seattle a	American		1	4	0	0	.000	5	1	1	2	1	2.25
National League Totals—5 Years			195	309⅓	17	17	.500	260	115	104	233	68	3.03
American League Totals—2 Years			12	24⅔	0	2	.000	24	16	12	15	9	4.38
Major League Totals—7 Years			207	334	17	19	.472	284	131	116	248	77	3.13

Signed as free agent by St. Louis Cardinals' organization, November 21, 1977.

†Traded to San Diego Padres for Pitcher Al Olmsted, February 19, 1982, completing deal in which San Diego traded Pitcher Steve Mura and a player to be named later to St. Louis Cardinals for Outfielder Sixto Lezcano and a player to be named later, December 10, 1981.

‡On disabled list, May 6 to June 28 and July 21 to September 1, 1984; included rehabilitation disability assignment to Las Vegas, June 8 to June 27, 1984.

§On disabled list, August 1 to August 13, 1985.

xGranted free agency, December 20, 1985; signed by Baltimore Orioles' organization, February 20, 1986.

yReleased, October 8, 1987; signed by Houston Astros, December 29, 1987.

zGranted free agency, October 15, 1988; signed by Seattle Mariners, November 15, 1988.

aGranted free agency, October 15, 1989.

RAFAEL ALONZO DeLIMA

Born December 21, 1967, at Valencia, Venezuela.
Height, 5.11. Weight, 175.
Throws and bats lefthanded.

Led Appalachian League in sacrifice flies with 6 in 1986.
Tied for Appalachian League lead in double plays by outfielders with 2 in 1986.

Year	Club	League	Pos.	G.	AB.	R.	H.	2B.	3B.	HR.	RBI.	B.A.	PO.	A.	E.	F.A.
1986—Kenosha	Midw.		OF	20	35	2	1	0	0	0	0	.029	23	0	0	1.000
1986—Elizabethton	Appal.		OF	49	136	20	31	7	0	2	21	.228	82	5	2	.978
1987—Kenosha	Midw.		OF	131	494	75	135	24	9	9	67	.273	*272	6	10	.965
1988—Orlando	South.		OF	137	500	66	143	25	3	3	46	.286	330	8	5	*.985
1989—Portland	P. C.		OF	127	464	54	127	19	3	3	33	.274	245	9	7	.973

Signed as free agent by Minnesota Twins' organization, October 10, 1985.

PETER DELKUS
(Pete)

Born September 4, 1965, at Centerville, Ill.
Height, 6.03. Weight, 185.
Throws and bats righthanded.
Attended Southern Illinois University, Edwardsville, Ill.

Led Midwest League in saves with 33 and games finished in relief with 56 in 1988.
Tied for Appalachian League lead in saves with 8 in 1987.

Year	Club	League	G.	IP.	W.	L.	Pct.	H.	R.	ER.	SO.	BB.	ERA.
1987—Elizabethton	Ap'lachian		21	37⅔	3	2	.600	29	6	5	44	7	1.19
1988—Kenosha	Midwest		61	68	4	2	.667	43	13	2	58	13	0.26
1989—Orlando	Southern		76	139⅔	8	8	.500	119	40	29	63	28	*1.87

Signed as free agent by Minnesota Twins' organization, June 21, 1987.

LUIS MANUEL de los SANTOS

Born December 29, 1966, at San Cristobal, D.R.
Height, 6.05. Weight, 190.
Throws and bats righthanded.

Led American Association in grounding into double plays with 20 in 1987, 17 in 1988 and 19 in 1989.
Led American Association first basemen in total chances with 1,050 in 1988.
Named American Association Most Valuable Player, 1988.

Year	Club	League	Pos.	G.	AB.	R.	H.	2B.	3B.	HR.	RBI.	B.A.	PO.	A.	E.	F.A.
1984—Eugene	N'west		3B	67	257	27	69	10	2	2	30	.268	67	93	22	.879
1985—Fort Myers	Fla. St.		3B	123	454	44	120	18	2	0	48	.264	87	141	32	.877
1986—Memphis	South.		3B	135	525	72	159	21	5	3	84	.303	*136	244	*50	.884
1987—Omaha	A. A.		3B-1B	135	518	53	152	29	6	2	67	.293	401	116	27	.950
1988—Omaha	A. A.		1B	136	*535	62	*164	25	4	6	●87	.307	*971	68	*11	.990
1988—Kansas City	Amer.		1B	11	22	1	2	1	1	0	1	.091	31	1	0	1.000
1989—Omaha	A. A.		1B-3B	99	387	45	115	31	3	3	62	.297	842	57	9	.990

Year	Club	League	Pos.	G.	AB.	R.	H.	2B.	3B.	HR.	RBI.	B.A.	PO.	A.	E.	F.A.
1989—Kansas City	Amer.		1B	28	87	6	22	3	1	0	6	.253	203	16	3	.986
Major League Totals—2 Years				39	109	7	24	4	2	0	7	.220	234	17	3	.988

Selected by Kansas City Royals' organization in 2nd round of free-agent draft, June 4, 1984.

JOHN RIKARD DEMPSEY
(Rick)

Born September 13, 1949, at Fayetteville, Tenn.
Height, 6.00. Weight, 199.
Throws and bats righthanded.
Attended Pierce Junior College, Woodland Hills, Calif.
Brother of Pat Dempsey, catcher in Oakland A's, Baltimore Orioles', New York Yankees', Cleveland Indians' and Minnesota Twins' organizations, 1977 through 1987.

Shares major league record for most double plays by catcher, game (3), June 1, 1977.
Major League stolen bases: 1974 (1), 1976 (1), 1977 (2), 1978 (7), 1980 (3), 1983 (1), 1984 (1), 1986 (1), 1988 (1), 1989 (1). Total—19.
Tied for American League lead in double plays by catchers with 14 in 1978.
Led International League in passed balls with 14 in 1973.
Led New York-Pennsylvania League catchers in putouts with 468, assists with 35, fielding percentage with .990 and tied for lead in double plays with 4 in 1968.

Year	Club	League	Pos.	G.	AB.	R.	H.	2B.	3B.	HR.	RBI.	B.A.	PO.	A.	E.	F.A.
1967—Sarasota Twins	Gulf C.		C-OF-1B	40	102	9	21	4	3	0	9	.206	133	16	2	.987
1968—Wisconsin Rapids.	Midw.		C	11	35	12	8	2	0	1	6	.229	68	2	1	.986
1968—Auburn	NYP		C-1B-OF	73	270	48	79	10	7	7	61	.293	505	38	7	.987
1969—Wisconsin Rapids.	Midw.		C	50	151	35	55	11	2	6	31	.364	341	30	●13	.966
1969—Minnesota	Amer.		C	5	6	1	3	1	0	0	0	.500	5	0	1	.833
1970—Charlotte	South		C-OF-2B	105	351	28	86	20	6	4	42	.245	506	76	18	.970
1970—Minnesota	Amer.		C	5	7	1	0	0	0	0	0	.000	12	0	1	.923
1971—Charlotte	South		C-OF	105	338	39	82	16	2	8	47	.243	599	65	8	.988
1971—Minnesota	Amer.		C	6	13	2	4	1	0	0	0	.308	30	4	2	.944
1972—Minnesota†	Amer.		C	25	40	0	8	1	0	0	0	.200	67	5	1	.986
1972—Tacoma	P. C.		C-OF	48	161	13	38	6	2	3	18	.236	284	33	5	.984
1973—Syracuse	Int.		C-OF-3B	122	387	53	96	14	4	6	47	.248	585	69	9	.986
1973—New York	Amer.		C	6	11	0	2	0	0	0	0	.182	9	0	2	.818
1974—New York	Amer.		C-OF	43	109	12	26	3	0	2	12	.239	152	22	4	.978
1975—New York	Amer.		C-OF-3B	71	145	18	38	8	0	1	11	.262	92	9	3	.971
1976—N.Y.‡-Balt.	Amer.		C-OF	80	216	12	42	2	0	0	12	.194	302	39	4	.988
1977—Baltimore§	Amer.		C	91	270	27	61	7	4	3	34	.226	416	52	11	.977
1978—Baltimore	Amer.		C	136	441	41	114	25	0	6	32	.259	636	79	11	.985
1979—Baltimore	Amer.		C	124	368	48	88	23	0	6	41	.239	615	★81	7	.990
1980—Baltimore	Amer.		C-OF-1B	119	362	51	95	26	3	9	40	.262	544	55	8	.987
1981—Baltimore	Amer.		C	92	251	24	54	10	1	6	25	.215	384	35	1	★.998
1982—Baltimore	Amer.		C	125	344	35	88	15	1	5	36	.256	491	46	5	.991
1983—Baltimore	Amer.		C	128	347	33	80	16	2	4	32	.231	591	65	2	★.997
1984—Baltimore	Amer.		C	109	330	37	76	11	0	11	34	.230	453	43	4	.992
1985—Baltimore	Amer.		C	132	362	54	92	19	0	12	52	.254	575	49	8	.987
1986—Baltimore x	Amer.		C	122	327	42	68	15	1	13	29	.208	659	53	7	.990
1987—Cleveland yz	Amer.		C	60	141	16	25	10	0	1	9	.177	293	18	5	.984
1988—Los Angeles	Nat.		C	77	167	25	42	13	0	7	30	.251	333	29	4	.989
1989—Los Angeles	Nat.		C	79	151	16	27	7	0	4	16	.179	265	35	5	.984
American League Totals—19 Years				1479	4090	454	964	193	12	79	389	.236	6326	655	87	.988
National League Totals—2 Years				156	318	41	69	20	0	11	46	.217	598	64	9	.987
Major League Totals—21 Years				1635	4408	495	1033	213	12	90	435	.234	6924	719	96	.988

Selected by Minnesota Twins' organization in 12th round of free-agent draft, June 6, 1967.
†Traded to New York Yankees' organization for Outfielder Danny Walton, October 27, 1972.
‡Traded with Pitchers Rudy May, Tippy Martinez, Dave Pagan and Scott McGregor to Baltimore Orioles for Pitchers Ken Holtzman, Doyle Alexander and Grant Jackson, Catcher Ellie Hendricks and Pitcher Jimmy Freeman, June 15, 1976.
§On disabled list, July 9 to August 21, 1977.
xGranted free agency, November 12, 1986; signed by Cleveland Indians, February 6, 1987.
yOn disabled list, July 22 to September 11, 1987.
zReleased, October 29, 1987; signed by Los Angeles Dodgers, March 30, 1988.

CHAMPIONSHIP SERIES RECORD

Year	Club	League	Pos.	G.	AB.	R.	H.	2B.	3B.	HR.	RBI.	B.A.	PO.	A.	E.	F.A.
1979—Baltimore	Amer.		C	3	10	3	4	2	0	0	2	.400	10	1	0	1.000
1983—Baltimore	Amer.		C	4	12	1	2	0	0	0	0	.167	29	5	1	.971
1988—Los Angeles	Nat.		PH-C	4	5	1	2	2	0	0	2	.400	7	0	0	1.000
Championship Series Totals—3 Years				11	27	5	8	4	0	0	4	.296	46	6	1	.981

WORLD SERIES RECORD

Year	Club	League	Pos.	G.	AB.	R.	H.	2B.	3B.	HR.	RBI.	B.A.	PO.	A.	E.	F.A.
1979—Baltimore	Amer.		C-PR	7	21	3	6	2	0	0	0	.286	38	2	0	1.000
1983—Baltimore	Amer.		C	5	13	3	5	4	0	1	2	.385	27	4	0	1.000
1988—Los Angeles	Nat.		C	2	5	0	1	1	0	0	1	.200	13	1	0	1.000
World Series Totals—3 Years				14	39	6	12	7	0	1	3	.308	78	7	0	1.000

ANDREW DENSON JR.

Born November 16, 1965, at Cincinnati, O.
Height, 6.05. Weight, 210.
Throws right and bats left and righthanded.

Major League stolen bases: 1989 (1).
Led International League batters in strikeouts with 116 in 1989.
Led Gulf Coast League in total bases with 133 and slugging percentage with .556 in 1984.
Led International League first basemen in putouts with 1,111, total chances with 1,203 and double plays with 126 in 1989.
Led Southern League first basemen in double plays with 111 in 1988.

Year	Club	League	Pos.	G.	AB.	R.	H.	2B.	3B.	HR.	RBI.	B.A.	PO.	A.	E.	F.A.
1984—Bradenton Brav.†	Gulf C.		OF	62	239	43	★77	★20	3	●10	★45	★.322	65	6	2	.973
1985—Sumter†‡	S. Atl.		OF	111	383	59	115	18	4	14	74	.300	119	5	3	.976
1986—Durham†§	Carol.		OF	72	231	31	54	6	3	4	23	.234	86	3	11	.890
1987—Greenville†	South.		1B	128	447	54	98	23	1	14	55	.219	998	50	10	.991
1988—Greenville	South.		1B-OF	140	507	85	136	26	4	13	78	.268	1148	73	18	.985
1989—Richmond	Int.		★1B-OF	138	463	50	118	32	0	9	59	.255	1116	78	★14	.988
1989—Atlanta	Nat.		1B	12	36	1	9	1	0	0	5	.250	71	11	1	.988
Major League Totals—1 Year				12	36	1	9	1	0	0	5	.250	71	11	1	.988

Selected by Atlanta Braves' organization in 1st round (19th player selected) of free-agent draft, June 4, 1984.
†Batted righthanded only.
‡On disabled list, April 24 to May 4, 1985.
§On disabled list, May 3 to May 24 and July 8 to August 8, 1986.

ROBERT EUGENE DERNIER

Name pronounced Dur-NEER.

(Bob)

Born January 5, 1957, at Kansas City, Mo.
Height, 6.00. Weight, 165.
Throws and bats righthanded.
Attended Longview Community College, Lee's Summit, Mo.

Major League stolen bases: 1980 (3), 1981 (2), 1982 (42), 1983 (35), 1984 (45), 1985 (31), 1986 (27), 1987 (16), 1988 (13), 1989 (4). Total—218.
Led Carolina League in stolen bases with 77 in 1979, Eastern League with 71 in 1980 and American Association with 72 in 1981.
Led Carolina League outfielders in putouts with 315 in 1979.
Tied for Carolina League lead in sacrifice hits with 12 in 1979.
Tied for Pioneer League lead in double plays by third basemen with 9 in 1978.
Named outfielder on THE SPORTING NEWS National League All-Star fielding team, 1984.
Named Carolina League Most Valuable Player, 1979.

Year	Club	League	Pos.	G.	AB.	R.	H.	2B.	3B.	HR.	RBI.	B.A.	PO.	A.	E.	F.A.
1978—Spartanburg	W. Car.		SS	22	57	9	8	1	0	0	5	.140	23	61	16	.840
1978—Helena	Pion.		3B	53	186	49	56	6	2	4	27	.301	38	104	22	.866
1979—Peninsula	Carol.		OF-3B	135	491	102	143	19	2	4	42	.291	331	23	10	.973
1980—Reading	East.		OF	136	★536	★111	160	29	4	10	57	.299	★325	9	9	.974
1980—Philadelphia	Nat.		OF	10	7	5	4	0	0	0	1	.571	9	0	0	1.000
1981—Oklahoma City	A. A.		OF	127	497	★105	150	26	7	5	35	.302	★317	7	5	.985
1981—Philadelphia	Nat.		OF	10	4	0	3	0	0	0	0	.750	2	0	0	1.000
1982—Philadelphia	Nat.		OF	122	370	56	92	10	2	4	21	.249	255	5	5	.981
1983—Philadelphia	Nat.		OF	122	221	41	51	10	0	1	15	.231	164	3	2	.988
1983—Reading†	East.		OF	14	56	8	13	1	1	1	4	.232	36	0	0	1.000
1984—Chicago	Nat.		OF	143	536	94	149	26	5	3	32	.278	355	5	5	.986
1985—Chicago‡	Nat.		OF	121	469	63	119	20	3	1	21	.254	310	4	9	.972
1986—Chicago§	Nat.		OF	108	324	32	73	14	1	4	18	.225	222	3	3	.987
1987—Chicago x	Nat.		OF	93	199	38	63	4	4	8	21	.317	86	2	1	.989
1988—Philadelphia y	Nat.		OF	68	166	19	48	3	1	1	10	.289	98	2	2	.980
1989—Philadelphia z	Nat.		OF	107	187	26	32	5	0	1	13	.171	95	1	3	.970
Major League Totals—10 Years				904	2483	374	634	92	16	23	152	.255	1596	25	30	.982

Selected by Cincinnati Reds' organization in 12th round of free-agent draft, January 11, 1977.
Signed as free agent by Philadelphia Phillies' organization, August 5, 1977.
†Traded with Outfielder Gary Matthews and Pitcher Porfi Altamirano to Chicago Cubs for Pitcher Bill Campbell and Catcher Mike Diaz, March 27, 1984.
‡On disabled list, June 15 to July 7, 1985.
§On disabled list, June 15 to July 23, 1986.
xGranted free agency, November 9, 1987; signed by Philadelphia Phillies, December 8, 1987.
yOn disabled list, May 29 to June 16 and July 8 to July 29, 1988.
zGranted free agency, November 13, 1989.

CHAMPIONSHIP SERIES RECORD

Shares Championship Series record for hitting home run in first series at-bat, October 2, 1984.

Year	Club	League	Pos.	G.	AB.	R.	H.	2B.	3B.	HR.	RBI.	B.A.	PO.	A.	E.	F.A.
1983—Philadelphia	Nat.		OF	1	0	0	0	0	0	0	0	.000	0	0	0	.000
1984—Chicago	Nat.		OF	5	17	5	4	2	0	1	1	.235	12	1	0	1.000
Championship Series Totals—2 Years				6	17	5	4	2	0	1	1	.235	12	1	0	1.000

WORLD SERIES RECORD

Year	Club	League	Pos.	G.	AB.	R.	H.	2B.	3B.	HR.	RBI.	B.A.	PO.	A.	E.	F.A.
1983—Philadelphia	Nat.		PR	1	0	1	0	0	0	0	0	.000	0	0	0	.000

JAMES JOSEPH DESHAIES
Name pronounced Duh-SHAYS.
(Jim)

Born June 23, 1960, at Massena, N.Y.
Height, 6.04. Weight, 222.
Throws and bats lefthanded.
Received bachelor of arts degree from Le Moyne College, Syracuse, N.Y., in 1982.

Holds modern major league record for most consecutive strikeouts at start of game (8), September 23, 1986.
Pitched seven-inning, 5-1 no-hit victory for Nashville against Columbus, May 4, 1984.
Led National League in balks with 7 in 1986.
Led International League in balks with 4 in 1985.
Tied for International League lead in shutouts with 4 in 1984.

Year Club	League	G.	IP.	W.	L.	Pct.	H.	R.	ER.	SO.	BB.	ERA.
1982—Oneonta	NYP	15	108⅓	6	5	.545	93	50	40	★137	40	3.32
1983—Fort Lauderdale	Florida St.	20	117⅔	11	3	.786	105	44	33	128	58	2.52
1984—Nashville	Southern	7	45	3	2	.600	33	20	14	42	29	2.80
1984—Columbus	Int'national	18	135⅔	10	5	.667	99	45	36	117	62	★2.39
1984—New York	American	2	7	0	1	.000	14	9	9	5	7	11.57
1985—Columbus†‡	Int'national	21	131⅔	8	6	.571	124	67	63	106	59	4.31
1985—Houston	National	2	3	0	0	.000	1	0	0	2	0	0.00
1986—Houston§	National	26	144	12	5	.706	124	58	52	128	59	3.25
1987—Houston x	National	26	152	11	6	.647	149	81	78	104	57	4.62
1988—Houston	National	31	207	11	14	.440	164	77	69	127	72	3.00
1989—Houston	National	34	225⅔	15	10	.600	180	80	73	153	79	2.91
American League Totals—1 Year		2	7	0	1	.000	14	9	9	5	7	11.57
National League Totals—5 Years		119	731⅔	49	35	.583	618	296	272	514	267	3.35
Major League Totals—6 Years		121	738⅔	49	36	.576	632	305	281	519	274	3.42

Selected by Montreal Expos' organization in 13th round of free-agent draft, June 6, 1978.
Selected by New York Yankees' organization in 21st round of free-agent draft, June 7, 1982.
†On disabled list, April 10 to April 26 and August 4 to August 14, 1985.
‡Traded with a player to be named later to Houston Astros for Pitcher Joe Niekro, September 15, 1985; Houston organization acquired Infielder Neder Horta, September 24, 1985, and Pitcher Dody Rather, January 11, 1986, to complete deal.
§On disabled list, April 21 to May 7, 1986.
xOn disabled list, July 26 to August 16, 1987.

DELINO LAMONT DeSHIELDS

Born January 15, 1969, at Seaford, Del.
Height, 6.01. Weight, 170.
Throws right and bats lefthanded.
Attended Villanova University, Villanova, Pa.

Year Club	League	Pos.	G.	AB.	R.	H.	2B.	3B.	HR.	RBI.	B.A.	PO.	A.	E.	F.A.
1987—Bradenton Expos	Gulf C.	★SS-3B	31	111	17	24	5	2	1	4	.216	47	90	★22	.862
1987—Jamestown	NYP	SS	34	96	16	21	1	2	1	5	.219	25	57	21	.796
1988—Rockford	Midw.	SS	129	460	97	116	26	6	12	46	.252	173	344	42	.925
1989—Jacksonville	South.	SS	93	307	55	83	10	6	3	35	.270	127	218	34	.910
1989—Indianapolis	A. A.	SS	47	181	29	47	8	4	2	14	.260	73	101	13	.930

Selected by Montreal Expos' organization in 1st round (12th player selected) of free-agent draft, June 2, 1987.

MICHAEL DEVEREAUX
(Mike)

Born April 10, 1963, at Casper, Wyo.
Height, 6.00. Weight, 195.
Throws and bats righthanded.
Attended Mesa Community College, Mesa, Ariz., and received bachelor of arts degree in finance from Arizona State University, Tempe, Ariz.

Major League stolen bases: 1987 (3), 1989 (22). Total—25.
Led Texas League in sacrifice flies with 11 in 1987.
Led Pioneer League in total bases with 152 and stolen bases with 40 in 1985.
Led Texas League outfielders in total chances with 349 in 1987.

Year Club	League	Pos.	G.	AB.	R.	H.	2B.	3B.	HR.	RBI.	B.A.	PO.	A.	E.	F.A.
1985—Great Falls	Pion.	OF	●70	★289	★73	★103	17	10	4	★67	.356	100	4	5	.954
1986—San Antonio	Texas	OF	115	431	69	130	22	2	10	53	.302	292	13	4	.987
1987—San Antonio	Texas	OF	★135	★562	90	169	28	9	26	91	.301	★339	7	3	★.991
1987—Albuquerque	P. C.	OF	3	11	2	3	1	0	1	1	.273	4	1	0	1.000
1987—Los Angeles	Nat.	OF	19	54	7	12	3	0	0	4	.222	21	1	0	1.000
1988—Albuquerque	P. C.	OF	109	423	88	144	26	4	13	76	.340	211	5	7	.969
1988—Los Angeles†	Nat.	OF	30	43	4	5	1	0	0	2	.116	29	0	0	1.000
1989—Baltimore	Amer.	OF	122	391	55	104	14	3	8	46	.266	288	1	5	.983
National League Totals—2 Years		49	97	11	17	4	0	0	6	.175	50	1	0	1.000
American League Totals—1 Year		122	391	55	104	14	3	8	46	.266	288	1	5	.983
Major League Totals—3 Years		171	488	66	121	18	3	8	52	.248	338	2	5	.986

Selected by Cleveland Indians' organization in 26th round of free-agent draft, June 4, 1984.
Selected by Los Angeles Dodgers' organization in 5th round of free-agent draft, June 3, 1985.
†Traded to Baltimore Orioles for Pitcher Mike Morgan, March 12, 1989.

BAUDILIO JOSE DIAZ (SEIJAS)
Name pronounced DEE-az.
(Bo)
Born March 23, 1953, at Cua, Miranda, Venezuela.
Height, 5.11. Weight, 205.
Throws and bats righthanded.

Major League stolen bases: 1980 (1), 1981 (2), 1982 (3), 1983 (1), 1986 (1), 1987 (1). Total—9.
Tied for International League lead in double plays by catchers with 7 in 1977.

Year Club	League	Pos.	G.	AB.	R.	H.	2B.	3B.	HR.	RBI.	B.A.	PO.	A.	E.	F.A.
1971—Winter Haven	Fla. St.	C	4	10	1	0	0	0	0	0	.000	25	1	0	1.000
1971—Williamsport	NYP	PH	1	1	0	0	0	0	0	0	.000	0	0	0	.000
1971—Pawtucket	East.	C	1	2	0	0	0	0	0	0	.000	4	0	0	1.000
1971—Greenville	W. Car.	C	10	25	2	5	1	0	0	0	.200	35	2	2	.949
1972—Winter Haven	Fla. St.	C	14	44	3	7	1	0	0	0	.159	72	7	0	1.000
1973—Elmira	NYP	C	25	69	3	17	3	0	0	9	.246	107	16	1	.992
1974—Winter Haven	Fla. St.	C-3B	97	327	31	79	20	1	1	38	.242	476	75	14	.975
1975—Winston-Salem	Carol.	C	59	179	22	47	8	1	6	29	.263	271	45	9	.972
1976—Rhode Island	Int.	C-OF	62	117	10	29	1	0	4	18	.248	222	28	3	.988
1977—Pawtucket	Int.	★C-3B	105	308	37	81	14	1	7	54	.263	459	67	6	★.989
1977—Boston†	Amer.	C	2	1	0	0	0	0	0	0	.000	5	0	0	1.000
1978—Cleveland‡	Amer.	C	44	127	12	30	4	0	2	11	.236	183	18	6	.971
1979—Tacoma	P. C.	C	34	115	5	28	7	0	2	11	.243	223	24	5	.980
1979—Cleveland§	Amer.	C	15	32	0	5	2	0	0	1	.156	63	6	3	.958
1980—Cleveland	Amer.	C	76	207	15	47	11	2	3	32	.227	317	35	4	.989
1981—Cleveland x	Amer.	C	63	182	25	57	19	0	7	38	.313	247	27	7	.975
1982—Philadelphia	Nat.	C	144	525	69	151	29	1	18	85	.288	850	80	10	.989
1983—Philadelphia	Nat.	C	136	471	49	111	17	0	15	64	.236	903	97	★14	.986
1984—Philadelphia y	Nat.	C	27	75	5	16	4	0	1	9	.213	114	9	1	.992
1984—Reading	East.	C	3	7	2	3	0	0	1	3	.429	11	4	1	.938
1985—Phil. za-Cinc.	Nat.	C	77	237	21	58	13	1	5	31	.245	428	42	8	.983
1986—Cincinnati	Nat.	C	134	474	50	129	21	0	10	56	.272	732	83	13	.984
1987—Cincinnati	Nat.	C	140	496	49	134	28	1	15	82	.270	747	70	7	.992
1988—Cincinnati b	Nat.	C	92	315	26	69	9	0	10	35	.219	468	44	5	.990
1989—Cincinnati cd	Nat.	C	43	132	6	27	5	0	1	8	.205	237	14	4	.984
American League Totals—5 Years			200	549	52	139	36	2	12	82	.253	815	86	20	.978
National League Totals—8 Years			793	2725	275	695	126	3	75	370	.255	4479	439	62	.988
Major League Totals—13 Years			993	3274	327	834	162	5	87	452	.255	5294	525	82	.986

Signed as free agent by Boston Red Sox' organization, November 25, 1970.

†Traded with Pitchers Rick Wise and Mike Paxton and Third Baseman Ted Cox to Cleveland Indians for Pitcher Dennis Eckersley and Catcher Fred Kendall, March 30, 1978.

‡On disabled list, April 16 to June 16, 1978.

§On disabled list, March 31 to April 17 and June 8 to July 20, 1979.

xTraded to Philadelphia Phillies for Outfielder Lonnie Smith and a player to be named later, November 20, 1981; Cleveland organization acquired Pitcher Scott Munninghoff to complete deal, December 9, 1981.

yOn disabled list, May 1 to May 31, June 21 to July 16 and August 20, 1984 through remainder of season; included rehabilitation disability assignment to Reading, July 11 to July 16, 1984.

zOn disabled list, April 19 to June 1, 1985.

aTraded with Pitcher Greg Simpson to Cincinnati Reds for Shortstop Tom Foley, Catcher Alan Knicely, a player to be named later and cash, August 8, 1985; Philadelphia Phillies acquired Pitcher Freddie Toliver to complete deal, August 27, 1985.

bOn disabled list, June 17 to July 2, 1988.

cOn disabled list, March 26 to April 19 and July 14 to September 1, 1989.

dGranted free agency, November 13, 1989.

CHAMPIONSHIP SERIES RECORD

Year Club	League	Pos.	G.	AB.	R.	H.	2B.	3B.	HR.	RBI.	B.A.	PO.	A.	E.	F.A.
1983—Philadelphia	Nat.	C	4	13	0	2	1	0	0	0	.154	32	2	0	1.000

WORLD SERIES RECORD

Year Club	League	Pos.	G.	AB.	R.	H.	2B.	3B.	HR.	RBI.	B.A.	PO.	A.	E.	F.A.
1983—Philadelphia	Nat.	C	5	15	1	5	1	0	0	0	.333	37	1	1	.974

ALL-STAR GAME RECORD

Year League	Pos.	AB.	R.	H.	2B.	3B.	HR.	RBI.	B.A.	PO.	A.	E.	F.A.
1981—American	C	1	0	0	0	0	0	0	.000	2	0	0	1.000
1987—National	C	1	0	0	0	0	0	0	.000	1	0	0	1.000
All-Star Game Totals—2 Years		2	0	0	0	0	0	0	.000	3	0	0	1.000

EDGAR SERRANO DIAZ
Name pronounced DEE-az.

Born February 8, 1964, at Santurce, Puerto Rico.
Height, 6.00. Weight, 160.
Throws and bats righthanded.

Led Texas League shortstops in total chances with 743 and double plays with 101 in 1985.

Year Club	League	Pos.	G.	AB.	R.	H.	2B.	3B.	HR.	RBI.	B.A.	PO.	A.	E.	F.A.
1982—Pikeville	Appal.	SS	15	24	4	2	0	0	0	0	.083	12	30	3	.933
1983—Beloit	Midw.	SS	107	307	29	64	2	0	0	15	.208	173	258	42	.911

Year Club League	Pos.	G.	AB.	R.	H.	2B.	3B.	HR.	RBI.	B.A.	PO.	A.	E.	F.A.
1984—Stockton .... Calif.	SS	123	419	58	108	1	7	0	35	.258	189	381	40	.934
1985—El Paso.................. Texas	SS	132	501	90	134	14	4	0	55	.267	★217	★489	37	.950
1986—Vancouver†.......... P. C.	★SS-2B	108	346	44	109	2	4	0	43	.315	173	311	★31	.940
1986—Milwaukee.......... Amer.	SS	5	13	0	3	0	0	0	0	.231	6	8	2	.875
1987—Denver‡................ A. A.	SS	48	162	24	44	10	2	0	15	.272	95	144	10	.960
1988—Denver§ .... A. A.	SS	79	278	44	65	7	0	0	21	.234	161	221	18	.955
1989—Denver .... A. A.	SS	105	316	29	68	8	1	1	22	.215	198	307	24	.955
1989—El Paso.................. Texas	SS	23	78	16	24	0	0	0	6	.308	49	78	8	.941
Major League Totals—1 Year..................		5	13	0	3	0	0	0	0	.231	6	8	2	.875

Signed as free agent by Milwaukee Brewers' organization, March 3, 1982.

†On disabled list, July 3 to July 17, 1986.

‡On Milwaukee disabled list, March 29 to June 3, 1987; included rehabilitation disability assignment to Denver, May 15 to June 3, 1987.

§On restricted list, July 28, 1988 through remainder of season.

MARIO RAFAEL DIAZ (TORRES)

Born January 10, 1962, at Humacao, P. R.
Height, 5.10. Weight, 160.
Throws and bats righthanded.

Led Southern League in sacrifice hits with 14 in 1985.

Year Club League	Pos.	G.	AB.	R.	H.	2B.	3B.	HR.	RBI.	B.A.	PO.	A.	E.	F.A.
1979—Bellingham .... N'west	SS-3B-2B	32	96	12	19	2	0	1	5	.198	28	69	8	.924
1980—Wausau.................. Midw.	SS-2B	110	349	28	63	5	0	3	21	.181	172	328	41	.924
1981—Lynn...................... East.	SS	106	314	16	63	8	1	1	22	.201	163	318	18	★.964
1982—Lynn...................... East.	SS-1B	53	162	19	35	7	1	1	13	.216	384	172	18	.969
1982—Salt Lake City...... P. C.	SS	5	19	2	7	1	0	0	2	.368	4	15	1	.950
1982—Wausau.................. Midw.	SS	56	187	15	49	8	1	1	23	.262	78	148	16	.934
1983—Bakersfield........... Calif.	SS-2B	51	171	23	41	5	1	0	10	.240	92	146	22	.915
1983—Chattanooga .... South.	SS	33	111	18	30	6	5	2	13	.270	48	80	10	.928
1984—Chattanooga .... South.	SS-2B	108	322	23	67	7	1	1	19	.208	179	313	26	.950
1985—Chattanooga .... South.	SS	115	400	38	101	6	7	0	38	.253	186	314	31	.942
1986—Calgary .... P. C.	SS	109	379	40	107	17	6	1	41	.282	194	302	16	.969
1987—Calgary .... P. C.	SS	108	376	52	106	17	3	4	52	.282	195	280	21	.958
1987—Seattle.................. Amer.	SS	11	23	4	7	0	1	0	3	.304	10	25	1	.972
1988—Calgary .... P. C.	SS	46	164	16	54	18	0	1	30	.329	65	138	12	.944
1988—Seattle†................ Amer.	S-2-1-3	28	72	6	22	5	0	0	9	.306	31	47	1	.987
1989—Seattle.................. Amer.	SS-2B-3B	52	74	9	10	0	0	1	7	.135	35	54	5	.947
1989—Calgary .... P. C.	2B-SS-1B	37	127	22	43	8	1	2	9	.339	64	73	9	.938
Major League Totals—3 Years		91	169	19	39	5	1	1	19	.231	76	126	7	.967

Signed as free agent by Seattle Mariners' organization, December 21, 1978.

†On disabled list, May 6 to May 23, 1988; included rehabilitation disability assignment to Calgary, May 16 to May 23, 1988.

ROBERT KEITH DIBBLE
(Rob)

Born January 24, 1964, at Bridgeport, Conn.
Height, 6.04. Weight, 235.
Throws right and bats lefthanded.
Attended Florida Southern College, Lakeland, Fla.

Major League saves: 1989 (2).

Year Club League	G.	IP.	W.	L.	Pct.	H.	R.	ER.	SO.	BB.	ERA.
1983—Billings............................ Pioneer	5	12⅔	0	1	.000	18	13	11	7	11	7.82
1983—Eugene............................ Northwest	7	37⅔	3	2	.600	38	28	24	17	18	5.73
1984—Tampa............................. Florida St.	15	64⅔	5	2	.714	59	31	21	39	29	2.92
1985—Cedar Rapids................... Midwest	45	65⅔	5	5	.500	67	37	28	73	28	3.84
1986—Vermont.......................... Eastern	31	55⅓	3	2	.600	53	29	19	37	28	3.09
1986—Denver............................ Am. Assoc.	5	6⅔	1	0	1.000	9	4	4	3	2	5.40
1987—Nashville......................... Am. Assoc.	44	61	2	4	.333	72	34	32	51	27	4.72
1988—Nashville......................... Am. Assoc.	31	35	2	1	.667	21	9	9	41	14	2.31
1988—Cincinnati....................... National	37	59⅓	1	1	.500	43	12	12	59	21	1.82
1989—Cincinnati†‡................... National	74	99	10	5	.667	62	23	23	141	39	2.09
Major League Totals—2 Years............................	111	158⅓	11	6	.647	105	35	35	200	60	1.99

Selected by St. Louis Cardinals' organization in 11th round of free-agent draft, June 7, 1982.

Selected by Cincinnati Reds' organization in secondary phase of free-agent draft, June 6, 1983.

†On suspended list, May 31 to June 2 and July 25 to July 28, 1989.

‡On disabled list, July 10 to July 25, 1989.

GORDON LEE DILLARD

Born May 20, 1964, at Salinas, Calif.
Height, 6.01. Weight, 180.
Throws and bats lefthanded.
Attended Hartnell Community College, Salinas, Calif., Connors State College,
Warner, Okla. and Oklahoma State University, Stillwater, Okla.

Led International League in home runs allowed with 20 in 1989.

Year	Club	League	G.	IP.	W.	L.	Pct.	H.	R.	ER.	SO.	BB.	ERA.
1986—Newark	NYP	27	63⅓	5	6	.455	55	37	30	77	34	4.26
1987—Hagerstown	Carolina	14	22	2	1	.667	12	5	5	26	11	2.05
1987—Charlotte	Southern	36	49	5	2	.714	44	18	18	53	19	3.31
1988—Charlotte	Southern	38	131⅔	7	5	.583	97	42	32	100	67	2.19
1988—Rochester	Int'national	5	11	0	2	.000	9	5	3	6	9	2.45
1988—Baltimore†	American	2	3	0	0	.000	3	2	2	2	4	6.00
1989—Scranton/Wilkes-Barre	Int'national	28	157⅔	6	★16	.273	174	★92	★88	96	64	5.02
1989—Philadelphia‡	National	5	4	0	0	.000	7	3	3	2	0	6.75
American League Totals—1 Year		2	3	0	0	.000	3	2	2	2	4	6.00
National League Totals—1 Year		5	4	0	0	.000	7	3	3	2	0	6.75
Major League Totals—2 Years		7	7	0	0	.000	10	5	5	4	4	6.43

Selected by Texas Rangers' organization in 2nd round of free-agent draft, January 17, 1984.
Selected by Pittsburgh Pirates' organization in secondary phase of free-agent draft, June 4, 1984.
Selected by New York Mets' organization in secondary phase of free-agent draft, June 5, 1985.
Selected by Baltimore Orioles' organization in 14th round of free-agent draft, June 2, 1986.
†Traded with Pitcher Ken Howell to Philadelphia Phillies for Outfielder Phil Bradley, December 8, 1988.
‡Drafted by Buffalo (Pittsburgh Pirates' organization), December 5, 1989.

FRANK MICHAEL DiPINO

Born October 22, 1956, at Syracuse, N.Y.
Height, 6.00. Weight, 180.
Throws and bats lefthanded.
Attended St. Leo College, St. Leo, Fla.

Pitched seven-inning, 6-0 no-hit victory against Reading, June 8, 1980 (second game).
Major League saves: 1983 (20), 1984 (14), 1985 (6), 1986 (3), 1987 (4), 1988 (6). Total—53.

Year	Club	League	G.	IP.	W.	L.	Pct.	H.	R.	ER.	SO.	BB.	ERA.
1977—Newark	NYP	14	29	1	3	.250	14	12	8	41	22	2.48
1978—Burlington	Midwest	15	88	5	4	.556	98	58	46	68	36	4.70
1979—Stockton†	California	16	99	5	3	.625	92	45	38	67	46	3.45
1980—Holyoke	Eastern	16	76	7	0	1.000	46	13	11	58	27	1.30
1980—Vancouver	P. Coast	24	28	3	1	.750	24	10	7	32	14	2.25
1981—Vancouver‡	P. Coast	27	81	3	5	.375	83	45	39	81	39	4.33
1981—Milwaukee	American	2	2	0	0	.000	0	0	0	3	3	0.00
1982—Vancouver§	P. Coast	26	189⅔	13	9	.591	187	102	85	115	86	4.03
1982—Houston	National	6	28⅓	2	2	.500	32	20	19	25	11	6.04
1983—Houston	National	53	71⅓	3	4	.429	52	21	21	67	20	2.65
1984—Houston	National	57	75⅓	4	9	.308	74	32	28	65	36	3.35
1985—Houston	National	54	76	3	7	.300	69	44	34	49	43	4.03
1986—Houston x-Chicago	National	61	80⅓	3	7	.300	74	45	39	70	30	4.37
1987—Chicago	National	69	80	3	3	.500	75	31	28	61	34	3.15
1988—Chicago y	National	63	90⅓	2	3	.400	102	54	50	69	32	4.98
1989—St. Louis z	National	67	88⅓	9	0	1.000	73	26	24	44	20	2.45
American League Totals—1 Year		2	2	0	0	.000	0	0	0	3	3	0.00
National League Totals—8 Years		430	590	29	35	.453	551	273	243	450	226	3.71
Major League Totals—9 Years		432	592	29	35	.453	551	273	243	453	229	3.69

Signed as free agent by Milwaukee Brewers' organization, July 11, 1977.
†On disabled list, May 19 to June 11, 1979.
‡On disabled list, May 9 to June 10, 1981.
§Traded with Outfielder Kevin Bass and Pitcher Mike Madden to Houston Astros, September 3, 1982, completing deal in which Houston traded Pitcher Don Sutton to Milwaukee Brewers for three players to be named later, August 30, 1982.
xTraded to Chicago Cubs for Outfielder Davey Lopes, July 21, 1986.
yGranted free agency, November 4, 1988; signed by St. Louis Cardinals, December 21, 1988.
zGranted free agency, November 13, 1989; re-signed by Cardinals, December 13, 1989.

GARY THOMAS DISARCINA

Born November 19, 1967, at Malden, Mass.
Height, 6.01. Weight, 170.
Throws and bats righthanded.
Attended University of Massachusetts, Amherst, Mass.

Year	Club	League	Pos.	G.	AB.	R.	H.	2B.	3B.	HR.	RBI.	B.A.	PO.	A.	E.	F.A.
1988—Bend	N'west	SS	71	295	40	90	11	●5	2	39	.305	104	★237	27	.927
1989—Midland	Texas	SS	126	441	65	126	18	7	4	54	.286	206	★411	30	★.954
1989—California	Amer.	SS	2	0	0	0	0	0	0	0	.000	0	0	0	.000
Major League Totals—1 Year			2	0	0	0	0	0	0	0	.000	0	0	0	.000

Selected by California Angels' organization in 6th round of free-agent draft, June 1, 1988.

BENITO JAMES DISTEFANO JR.

Name pronounced Dis-tuh-FAHN-oh.

(Benny)

Born January 23, 1962, at Brooklyn, N.Y.
Height, 6.01. Weight, 200.
Throws and bats lefthanded.
Attended Alvin Community College, Alvin, Tex.

Major League stolen bases: 1989 (1).
Led American Association in being hit by pitch with 12 in 1988.
Led Pacific Coast League in being hit by pitch with 15 in 1987.

Year	Club	League	Pos.	G.	AB.	R.	H.	2B.	3B.	HR.	RBI.	B.A.	PO.	A.	E.	F.A.
1982—Greenwood	S. Atl.		1B	136	477	74	138	23	●8	15	89	.289	★1184	★104	19	.985
1983—Lynn	East.		OF-1B	★137	480	71	130	19	7	25	92	.271	271	13	13	.956
1984—Hawaii	P. C.		1B-OF	66	240	40	73	13	8	6	33	.304	334	30	0	1.000
1984—Pittsburgh	Nat.		OF-1B	45	78	10	13	1	2	3	9	.167	88	9	3	.970
1985—Hawaii	P. C.		OF-1B	136	480	74	114	27	8	14	67	.238	375	18	8	.980
1986—Hawaii	P. C.		OF-1B	111	402	58	104	25	9	13	57	.259	564	37	9	.985
1986—Pittsburgh	Nat.		OF-1B	31	39	3	7	1	0	1	5	.179	13	0	0	1.000
1987—Vancouver	P. C.		★1B-OF	130	431	67	120	20	4	15	77	.278	1042	67	6	★.995
1988—Buffalo	A. A.		OF-1B	135	482	69	127	26	1	19	63	.263	234	15	3	.988
1988—Pittsburgh	Nat.		1B-OF	16	29	6	10	3	1	1	6	.345	41	3	0	1.000
1989—Pittsburgh†	Nat.		1B-C-OF	96	154	12	38	8	0	2	15	.247	305	16	6	.982
1989—Buffalo‡	A. A.		1B	5	17	2	4	1	0	0	3	.235	37	3	1	.976
Major League Totals—4 Years				188	300	31	68	13	3	7	35	.227	447	28	9	.981

Selected by Los Angeles Dodgers' organization in 16th round of free-agent draft, January 13, 1981.
Selected by Toronto Blue Jays' organization in secondary phase of free-agent draft, June 8, 1981.
Selected by Pittsburgh Pirates' organization in secondary phase of free-agent draft, January 12, 1982.
†On disabled list, April 11 to April 26, 1989; included rehabilitation disability assignment to Buffalo, April 21 to April 26, 1989.
‡Released, December 6, 1989.

CHRIS BARTON DONNELS

Born April 21, 1966, at Los Angeles, Calif.
Height, 6.00. Weight, 185.
Throws right and bats lefthanded.
Attended Loyola Marymount University, Los Angeles, Calif.

Led Florida State League in slugging percentage with .510 and intentional bases on balls received with 15 in 1989.
Led Florida State League third basemen in putouts with 93, assists with 202 and total chances with 320 in 1989.
Named Florida State League Most Valuable Player, 1989.

Year	Club	League	Pos.	G.	AB.	R.	H.	2B.	3B.	HR.	RBI.	B.A.	PO.	A.	E.	F.A.
1987—Kingsport	Appal.		3B	26	86	18	26	4	0	3	16	.302	16	44	6	.909
1987—Columbia	S. Atl.		3B	41	136	20	35	7	0	2	17	.257	32	86	10	.922
1988—St. Lucie	Fla. St.		3B	65	198	25	43	14	2	3	22	.217	40	116	15	.912
1988—Columbia	S. Atl.		3B	42	133	19	32	6	0	2	13	.241	29	84	7	.942
1989—St. Lucie	Fla. St.		3B-1B	117	386	70	121	23	1	17	★78	.313	242	209	28	.942

Selected by New York Mets' organization in 1st round (24th player selected) of free agent draft, June 2, 1987.

JOHN ROBERT DOPSON JR.

Born July 14, 1963, at Baltimore, Md.
Height, 6.04. Weight, 225.
Throws right and bats lefthanded.

Led American League in balks with 15 in 1989.

Year	Club	League	G.	IP.	W.	L.	Pct.	H.	R.	ER.	SO.	BB.	ERA.
1982—Jamestown	NYP	15	106⅔	6	●8	.429	117	58	47	62	34	3.97
1983—West Palm Beach	Florida St.	23	146⅔	13	6	.684	141	82	56	69	38	3.44
1984—Jacksonville†	Southern	26	170⅔	10	8	.556	198	83	70	76	41	3.69
1985—Jacksonville	Southern	5	32⅓	3	0	1.000	27	5	4	20	10	1.11
1985—Indianapolis‡	Am. Assoc.	18	95⅓	4	7	.364	88	44	40	48	44	3.78
1985—Montreal	National	4	13	0	2	.000	25	17	16	4	4	11.08
1986—West Palm Beach§	Florida St.	2	10⅔	2	0	1.000	8	0	0	8	4	0.00
1986—Indianapolis	Am. Assoc.	4	16	0	3	.000	18	12	8	6	11	4.50
1987—Jacksonville	Southern	21	118⅓	7	5	.583	123	58	50	75	30	3.80
1988—Indianapolis	Am. Assoc.	3	18	0	0	.000	19	7	7	15	5	3.50
1988—Montreal x	National	26	168⅔	3	11	.214	150	69	57	101	58	3.04
1989—Boston y	American	29	169⅓	12	8	.600	166	84	75	95	69	3.99
1989—Pawtucket	Int'national	2	8⅔	0	2	.000	13	9	7	9	1	7.27
National League Totals—2 Years		30	181⅔	3	13	.188	175	86	73	105	62	3.62
American League Totals—1 Year		29	169⅓	12	8	.600	166	84	75	95	69	3.99
Major League Totals—3 Years		59	351	15	21	.417	341	170	148	200	131	3.79

Selected by Montreal Expos' organization in 2nd round of free-agent draft, June 7, 1982.
†On suspended list, May 24 to May 31, 1984.
‡On disabled list, June 24 to July 15, 1985.
§On Indianapolis disabled list, April 10 to May 12, May 29 to June 23 and July 7, 1986 through remainder of season.
xTraded with Shortstop Luis Rivera to Boston Red Sox for Shortstop Spike Owen and Pitcher Dan Gakeler, December 8, 1988.
yOn disabled list, August 2 to August 28, 1989; included rehabilitation disability assignment to Pawtucket, August 18 to August 28, 1989.

—DID YOU KNOW—

That Atlanta, St. Louis and Pittsburgh were the only clubs in the majors last year that did not hit a grand slam?

WILLIAM DONALD DORAN
Name pronounced DOOR-un.
(Bill)
Born May 28, 1958, at Cincinnati, O.
Height, 6.00. Weight, 175.
Throws right and bats right and lefthanded.
Attended Miami University, Oxford, O.

Major League stolen bases: 1982 (5), 1983 (12), 1984 (21), 1985 (23), 1986 (42), 1987 (31), 1988 (17), 1989 (22). Total—173.
Led National League in caught stealing with 19 in 1986.
Led National League second basemen in fielding percentage with .992 in 1987.
Led Pacific Coast League second basemen in double plays with 123 in 1982.
Led Gulf Coast League second basemen in double plays with 33 in 1979.

Year Club	League	Pos.	G.	AB.	R.	H.	2B.	3B.	HR.	RBI.	B.A.	PO.	A.	E.	F.A.
1979—Sarasota Astros....	Gulf C.	2B	44	164	21	42	6	0	1	16	.256	107	★144	11	.958
1980—Daytona Beach....	Fla. St.	2B-SS	102	369	62	90	11	3	2	45	.244	232	259	21	.959
1981—Columbus..............	South.	2B-SS	124	427	83	120	17	7	5	56	.281	263	355	17	.973
1982—Tucson..................	P. C.	2B	★142	559	100	169	32	7	1	65	.302	★361	★424	★23	.972
1982—Houston................	Nat.	2B	26	97	11	27	3	0	0	6	.278	41	78	3	.975
1983—Houston................	Nat.	2B	154	535	70	145	12	7	8	39	.271	★347	461	17	.979
1984—Houston................	Nat.	2B-SS	147	548	92	143	18	11	4	41	.261	274	440	12	.983
1985—Houston................	Nat.	2B	148	578	84	166	31	6	14	59	.287	345	440	16	.980
1986—Houston................	Nat.	2B	145	550	92	152	29	3	6	37	.276	262	329	16	.974
1987—Houston................	Nat.	2B-SS	★162	625	82	177	23	3	16	79	.283	300	432	7	.991
1988—Houston................	Nat.	2B	132	480	66	119	18	1	7	53	.248	260	371	8	★.987
1989—Houston................	Nat.	2B	142	507	65	111	25	2	8	58	.219	254	345	12	.980
Major League Totals—8 Years................			1056	3920	562	1040	159	33	63	372	.265	2083	2896	91	.982

Selected by Houston Astros' organization in 6th round of free-agent draft, June 5, 1979.

CHAMPIONSHIP SERIES RECORD
Shares Championship Series record for most at-bats, game (7), October 15, 1986 (16 innings).

Year Club	League	Pos.	G.	AB.	R.	H.	2B.	3B.	HR.	RBI.	B.A.	PO.	A.	E.	F.A.
1986—Houston................	Nat.	2B	6	27	3	6	0	0	1	3	.222	9	17	0	1.000

BRIAN RICHARD DORSETT
Born April 9, 1961, at Terre Haute, Ind.
Height, 6.03. Weight, 215.
Throws and bats righthanded.
Attended Indiana State University, Terre Haute, Ind.

Year Club	League	Pos.	G.	AB.	R.	H.	2B.	3B.	HR.	RBI.	B.A.	PO.	A.	E.	F.A.
1983—Medford................	N'west	C	14	48	11	13	2	1	1	10	.271	85	8	2	.979
1983—Madison................	Midw.	C	58	204	16	52	7	0	3	27	.255	337	51	6	.985
1984—Modesto†..............	Calif.	C-1B	99	375	39	99	19	0	8	52	.264	511	76	13	.978
1985—Madison................	Midw.	C	40	161	15	43	11	0	2	30	.267	194	40	5	.979
1985—Huntsville.............	South.	C	88	313	38	84	18	3	11	43	.268	437	51	10	.980
1986—Tacoma.................	P. C.	C	117	426	49	111	33	1	10	51	.261	420	54	18	.963
1987—Tacoma‡...............	P. C.	C	78	282	31	66	14	1	6	39	.234	341	51	4	.990
1987—Buffalo.................	A. A.	C	26	86	9	22	5	1	4	14	.256	119	9	1	.992
1987—Cleveland..............	Amer.	C	5	11	2	3	0	0	1	3	.273	12	0	0	1.000
1988—C. S. §x -Edm........	P. C.	C-1B	53	163	21	43	7	0	11	32	.264	283	37	5	.985
1988—California y..........	Amer.	C	7	11	0	1	0	0	0	2	.091	19	3	0	1.000
1989—Columbus.............	Int.	C	110	388	45	97	21	1	17	62	.250	482	47	7	.987
1989—New York.............	Amer.	C	8	22	3	8	1	0	0	4	.364	29	3	0	1.000
Major League Totals—3 Years................			20	44	5	12	1	0	1	9	.273	60	6	0	1.000

Selected by Oakland A's organization in 10th round of free-agent draft, June 6, 1983.
†On disabled list, June 18 to July 24, 1984.
‡Traded with Pitcher Darrel Akerfelds to Cleveland Indians for Second Baseman Tony Bernazard, July 15, 1987.
§On Cleveland disabled list, March 26 to June 7, 1988.
xTraded to California Angels for a player to be named later, June 7, 1988.
yTraded to New York Yankees for Pitcher Eric Schmidt, November 17, 1988.

RICHARD ELLIOTT DOTSON
Born January 10, 1959, at Cincinnati, O.
Height, 6.00. Weight, 203.
Throws and bats righthanded.

Tied for American League lead in shutouts with 4 in 1981.

Year Club	League	G.	IP.	W.	L.	Pct.	H.	R.	ER.	SO.	BB.	ERA.
1977—Idaho Falls†....................................	Pioneer	13	66	4	5	.444	65	61	42	83	63	5.73
1978—Knoxville.......................................	Southern	26	145	11	10	.524	128	85	69	152	★105	4.28
1979—Knoxville.......................................	Southern	25	163	9	9	.500	133	81	67	133	88	3.70
1979—Chicago..	American	5	24	2	0	1.000	28	13	10	13	6	3.75
1980—Chicago..	American	33	198	12	10	.545	185	105	94	109	87	4.27
1981—Chicago..	American	24	141	9	8	.529	145	67	59	73	49	3.77
1982—Chicago..	American	34	196⅔	11	15	.423	219	97	84	109	73	3.84
1983—Chicago..	American	35	240	22	7	★.759	209	92	86	137	★106	3.23
1984—Chicago‡..	American	32	245⅔	14	15	.483	216	110	98	120	103	3.59
1985—Chicago§..	American	9	52⅓	3	4	.429	53	30	26	33	17	4.47

Year Club	League	G.	IP.	W.	L.	Pct.	H.	R.	ER.	SO.	BB.	ERA.
1986—Chicago	American	34	197	10	●17	.370	226	125	120	110	69	5.48
1987—Chicago x	American	31	211⅓	11	12	.478	201	109	98	114	86	4.17
1988—New York y	American	32	171	12	9	.571	178	103	95	77	72	5.00
1989—New York z-Chicago a	American	28	151⅓	5	12	.294	181	84	75	69	58	4.46
Major League Totals—11 Years		297	1828⅓	111	109	.505	1841	935	845	964	726	4.16

Selected by California Angels' organization in 1st round (seventh player selected) of free-agent draft, June 7, 1977.

†Traded with Outfielders Bobby Bonds and Thad Bosley to Chicago White Sox for Catcher Brian Downing and Pitchers Chris Knapp and Dave Frost, December 5, 1977.

‡Appeared in one game as a pinch-runner.

§On disabled list, April 7 to April 22 and June 11, 1985 through remainder of season.

xTraded with Pitcher Scott Nielsen to New York Yankees for Outfielder Dan Pasqua, Catcher Mark Salas and Pitcher Steve Rosenberg, November 12, 1987.

yOn disabled list, July 1 to July 18, 1988.

zReleased, June 22, 1989; signed by Chicago White Sox, July 1, 1989.

aGranted free agency, November 13, 1989; signed by Kansas City Royals, December 5, 1989.

CHAMPIONSHIP SERIES RECORD

Year Club	League	G.	IP.	W.	L.	Pct.	H.	R.	ER.	SO.	BB.	ERA.
1983—Chicago	American	1	5	0	1	.000	6	6	6	3	3	10.80

ALL-STAR GAME RECORD

Year League	IP.	W.	L.	Pct.	H.	R.	ER.	SO.	BB.	ERA.
1984—American	2	0	0	.000	2	0	0	2	1	0.00

BRIAN JAY DOWNING

Born October 9, 1950, at Los Angeles, Calif.
Height, 5.10. Weight, 194.
Throws and bats righthanded.
Attended Cypress Junior College, Cypress, Calif.

Shares major league records for highest fielding percentage by outfielder, season, 150 or more games (1.000), 1982; fewest errors by outfielder, season, 150 or more games (0), 1982; fewest double plays by outfielder, season, 150 or more games (0), 1982.

Holds American League record for most consecutive errorless games by an outfielder (244), May 25, 1981 through July 21, second game, 1983.

Major League stolen bases: 1975 (13), 1976 (7), 1977 (1), 1978 (3), 1979 (3), 1981 (1), 1982 (2), 1983 (1), 1985 (5), 1986 (4), 1987 (5), 1988 (3). Total—48.

Tied for American League lead in bases on balls received with 106 in 1987.

Year Club	League	Pos.	G.	AB.	R.	H.	2B.	3B.	HR.	RBI.	B.A.	PO.	A.	E.	F.A.
1970—Sarasota W. S.	Gulf C.	C-OF	34	96	16	21	1	1	0	14	.219	167	11	1	.994
1971—Appleton	Midw.	3B-C-OF	99	333	51	82	6	3	3	22	.246	353	98	13	.972
1972—Knoxville	South.	OF-3B-C	135	442	75	123	24	7	15	67	.278	250	123	21	.947
1973—Iowa	A. A.	3B-OF-C	68	228	34	56	6	1	7	27	.246	84	90	8	.956
1973—Chicago†	Amer.	OF-C-3B	34	73	5	13	1	0	2	4	.178	72	17	5	.947
1974—Chicago	Amer.	C-OF	108	293	41	66	12	1	10	39	.225	337	30	2	.995
1975—Chicago	Amer.	C	138	420	58	101	12	1	7	41	.240	730	84	8	.990
1976—Chicago‡	Amer.	C	104	317	38	81	14	0	3	30	.256	450	38	6	.988
1977—Chicago§	Amer.	C-OF	69	169	28	48	4	2	4	25	.284	325	28	6	.983
1978—California	Amer.	C	133	412	42	105	15	0	7	46	.255	681	82	5	.993
1979—California	Amer.	C	148	509	87	166	27	3	12	75	.326	669	35	11	.985
1980—California x	Amer.	C	30	93	5	27	6	0	2	25	.290	69	6	0	1.000
1981—California	Amer.	OF-C	93	317	47	79	14	0	9	41	.249	237	18	2	.992
1982—California	Amer.	OF	158	623	109	175	37	2	28	84	.281	321	9	0	●1.000
1983—California y	Amer.	OF	113	403	68	99	15	1	19	53	.246	160	9	1	.994
1984—California	Amer.	OF	156	539	65	148	28	2	23	91	.275	272	5	0	*1.000
1985—California	Amer.	OF	150	520	80	137	23	1	20	85	.263	244	5	2	.992
1986—California z	Amer.	OF	152	513	90	137	27	4	20	95	.267	267	5	3	.989
1987—California	Amer.	OF	155	567	110	154	29	3	29	77	.272	47	2	0	1.000
1988—California a	Amer.	DH	135	484	80	117	18	2	25	64	.242	0	0	0	.000
1989—California	Amer.	DH	142	544	59	154	25	2	14	59	.283	0	0	0	.000
Major League Totals—17 Years			2018	6796	1012	1807	307	24	234	934	.266	4881	391	51	.990

Signed as free agent by Chicago White Sox' organization, August 19, 1969.

†On disabled list, June 1 to July 9, 1973.

‡On disabled list, July 30 to August 15, 1976.

§Traded with Pitchers Chris Knapp and Dave Frost to California Angels for Outfielders Bobby Bonds and Thad Bosley and Pitcher Richard Dotson, December 5, 1977.

xOn disabled list, April 20 to September 1, 1980.

yOn disabled list, May 10 to June 20, 1983.

zGranted free agency, November 12, 1986; re-signed by Angels, January 8, 1987.

aOn disabled list, April 20 to May 6, 1988.

CHAMPIONSHIP SERIES RECORD

Year Club	League	Pos.	G.	AB.	R.	H.	2B.	3B.	HR.	RBI.	B.A.	PO.	A.	E.	F.A.
1979—California	Amer.	C	4	15	1	3	0	0	0	1	.200	27	0	0	1.000
1982—California	Amer.	C	5	19	3	3	1	0	0	0	.158	5	0	0	1.000
1986—California	Amer.	OF	7	27	2	6	0	0	1	7	.222	18	0	0	1.000
Championship Series Totals—3 Years			16	61	6	12	1	0	1	8	.197	50	0	0	1.000

ALL-STAR GAME RECORD

Year League	Pos.	AB.	R.	H.	2B.	3B.	HR.	RBI.	B.A.	PO.	A.	E.	F.A.
1979—American	C	1	0	1	0	0	0	0	1.000	3	0	0	1.000

KELLY ROBERT DOWNS

Born October 25, 1960, at Ogden, Utah.
Height, 6.04. Weight, 200.
Throws and bats righthanded.
Brother of Dave Downs, pitcher with Philadelphia Phillies, 1972.

Major League saves: 1987 (1).
Tied for Pacific Coast League lead in games started by pitchers with 29 in 1983.

Year Club	League	G.	IP.	W.	L.	Pct.	H.	R.	ER.	SO.	BB.	ERA.
1980—Spartanburg	W. Carol.	14	90	5	7	.417	85	41	26	40	17	2.60
1981—Peninsula	Carolina	25	175	13	7	.650	176	79	58	124	35	2.98
1982—Oklahoma City	Am. Assoc.	32	156⅔	2	★15	.118	182	★116	93	70	72	5.34
1983—Portland	P. Coast	29	159⅓	9	●13	.409	186	98	79	71	61	4.46
1984—Portland†	P. Coast	30	163	7	12	.368	166	106	96	104	65	5.30
1985—Phoenix	P. Coast	37	137	9	10	.474	138	69	61	109	56	4.01
1986—Phoenix	P. Coast	18	108	8	5	.615	116	54	41	68	28	3.42
1986—San Francisco	National	14	88⅓	4	4	.500	78	29	27	64	30	2.75
1987—San Francisco	National	41	186	12	9	.571	185	83	75	137	67	3.63
1988—San Francisco ‡	National	27	168	13	9	.591	140	67	62	118	47	3.32
1989—San Francisco§	National	18	82⅔	4	8	.333	82	47	44	49	26	4.79
1989—Phoenix	P. Coast	3	9⅓	1	1	.500	11	9	9	9	5	8.68
1989—San Jose	California	1	5	0	0	.000	1	0	0	7	4	0.00
Major League Totals—4 Years		100	525	33	30	.524	485	226	208	368	170	3.57

Selected by Philadelphia Phillies' organization in 26th round of free-agent draft, June 5, 1979.

†Traded with Pitcher George Riley to San Francisco Giants for First Baseman Al Oliver and a player to be named later, August 20, 1984; Philadelphia Phillies acquired Pitcher Renie Martin to complete deal, August 30, 1984.

‡On disabled list, August 31, 1988 through remainder of season.

§On disabled list, May 2 to August 13, 1989; included rehabilitation disability assignment to Phoenix, May 17 to May 23 and August 3 to August 7, 1989; and San Jose, August 8 to August 12, 1989.

CHAMPIONSHIP SERIES RECORD

Year Club	League	G.	IP.	W.	L.	Pct.	H.	R.	ER.	SO.	BB.	ERA.
1987—San Francisco	National	1	1⅓	0	0	.000	1	0	0	0	0	0.00
1989—San Francisco	National	2	8⅔	1	0	1.000	8	3	3	6	6	3.12
Championship Series Totals—2 Years		3	10	1	0	1.000	9	3	3	6	6	2.70

WORLD SERIES RECORD

Year Club	League	G.	IP.	W.	L.	Pct.	H.	R.	ER.	SO.	BB.	ERA.
1989—San Francisco	National	3	4⅔	0	0	.000	3	4	4	4	2	7.71

DOUGLAS DEAN DRABEK
(Doug)

Born July 25, 1962, at Victoria, Tex.
Height, 6.01. Weight, 185.
Throws and bats righthanded.
Attended University of Houston, Houston, Tex.

Year Club	League	G.	IP.	W.	L.	Pct.	H.	R.	ER.	SO.	BB.	ERA.
1983—Niagara Falls	NYP	16	103⅔	6	7	.462	99	52	42	103	48	3.65
1984—Appleton	Midwest	1	5	1	0	1.000	3	1	1	6	3	1.80
1984—Glens Falls†	Eastern	19	124⅔	12	5	.706	90	34	31	75	44	2.24
1984—Nashville	Southern	4	31	1	2	.333	30	11	8	22	10	2.32
1985—Albany	Eastern	26	★192⅔	13	7	.650	153	71	64	★153	55	2.99
1986—Columbus	Int'national	8	42	1	4	.200	50	36	34	23	25	7.29
1986—New York‡	American	27	131⅔	7	8	.467	126	64	60	76	50	4.10
1987—Pittsburgh§	National	29	176⅓	11	12	.478	165	86	76	120	46	3.88
1988—Pittsburgh	National	33	219⅓	15	7	.682	194	83	75	127	50	3.08
1989—Pittsburgh	National	35	244⅓	14	12	.538	215	83	76	123	69	2.80
American League Totals—1 Year		27	131⅔	7	8	.467	126	64	60	76	50	4.10
National League Totals—3 Years		97	640	40	31	.563	574	252	227	370	165	3.19
Major League Totals—4 Years		124	771⅔	47	39	.547	700	316	287	446	215	3.35

Selected by Cleveland Indians' organization in 4th round of free-agent draft, June 3, 1980.

Selected by Chicago White Sox' organization in 11th round of free-agent draft, June 6, 1983.

†Traded with Pitcher Kevin Hickey to New York Yankees' organization, August 13, 1984, completing deal in which New York traded Infielder Roy Smalley to Chicago White Sox for two players to be named later, July 18, 1984.

‡Traded with Pitchers Brian Fisher and Logan Easley to Pittsburgh Pirates for Pitchers Rick Rhoden, Cecilio Guante and Pat Clements, November 26, 1986.

§On disabled list, April 26 to May 18, 1987.

DAVID FRANCIS DRAVECKY
(Dave)

Born February 14, 1956, at Youngstown, O.
Height, 6.01. Weight, 200.
Throws left and bats righthanded.
Attended Youngstown State University, Youngstown, Ohio.

Major League saves: 1982 (2), 1983 (8). Total—10.
Led Texas League in shutouts with 4 in 1981.

Year—Club	League	G.	IP.	W.	L.	Pct.	H.	R.	ER.	SO.	BB.	ERA.
1978—Charleston	W. Carol.	20	52	4	2	.667	54	30	24	31	32	4.15
1979—Buffalo	Eastern	35	114	6	7	.462	125	71	54	81	59	4.26
1980—Buffalo†	Eastern	27	161	13	7	.650	165	76	60	64	60	3.35
1981—Amarillo	Texas	30	172	●15	5	.750	157	69	51	141	45	2.67
1982—Hawaii	P. Coast	16	36⅓	4	1	.800	28	15	10	26	14	2.48
1982—San Diego	National	31	105	5	3	.625	86	37	30	59	33	2.57
1983—San Diego	National	28	183⅔	14	10	.583	181	78	73	74	44	3.58
1984—San Diego	National	50	156⅔	9	8	.529	125	53	51	71	51	2.93
1985—San Diego	National	34	214⅔	13	11	.542	200	79	70	105	57	2.93
1986—San Diego	National	26	161⅓	9	11	.450	149	68	55	87	54	3.07
1987—San Diego‡-San Francisco	National	48	191⅓	10	12	.455	186	82	73	138	64	3.43
1988—San Francisco§	National	7	37	2	2	.500	33	19	13	19	8	3.16
1988—Phoenix	P. Coast	1	2⅔	0	1	.000	11	5	5	1	0	16.88
1989—San Jose x	California	2	16	2	0	1.000	13	3	3	8	1	1.69
1989—Phoenix	P. Coast	1	9	1	0	1.000	7	2	2	3	0	2.00
1989—San Francisco y	National	2	13	2	0	1.000	8	5	5	5	4	3.46
Major League Totals—8 Years		226	1062⅓	64	57	.529	968	421	370	558	315	3.13

Selected by Pittsburgh Pirates' organization in 21st round of free-agent draft, June 6, 1978.

†Traded to San Diego Padres' organization for Outfielder Robert D. (Bobby) Mitchell, April 5, 1981.

‡Traded with Pitcher Craig Lefferts and Infielder Kevin Mitchell to San Francisco Giants for Third Baseman Chris Brown and Pitchers Keith Comstock, Mark Davis and Mark Grant, July 4, 1987.

§On disabled list, May 3 to May 28 and May 31, 1988 through remainder of season; included rehabilitation disability assignment to Phoenix, August 10 to August 16, 1988.

xOn San Francisco disabled list, March 21 to August 10 and August 16, 1989 through remainder of season; included rehabilitation disability assignment to San Jose, July 23 to August 2, 1989; and Phoenix, August 3 to August 9, 1989.

yOn voluntarily retired list, December 4, 1989.

CHAMPIONSHIP SERIES RECORD

Shares Championship Series record for fewest hits allowed, game, nine or more innings (2), October 7, 1987.

Shares National League Championship Series record for most consecutive scoreless innings, total series (16).

Year—Club	League	G.	IP.	W.	L.	Pct.	H.	R.	ER.	SO.	BB.	ERA.
1984—San Diego	National	3	6	0	0	.000	2	0	0	5	0	0.00
1987—San Francisco	National	2	15	1	1	.500	7	1	1	14	4	0.60
Championship Series Totals—2 Years		5	21	1	1	.500	9	1	1	19	4	0.43

WORLD SERIES RECORD

Year—Club	League	G.	IP.	W.	L.	Pct.	H.	R.	ER.	SO.	BB.	ERA.
1984—San Diego	National	2	4⅔	0	0	.000	3	0	0	5	1	0.00

ALL-STAR GAME RECORD

Year—League	IP.	W.	L.	Pct.	H.	R.	ER.	SO.	BB.	ERA.
1983—National	2	0	0	.000	1	0	0	2	0	0.00

THOMAS KENT DREES
(Tom)

Born June 17, 1963, at Des Moines, Ia.
Height, 6.06. Weight, 210.
Throws left and bats left and righthanded.
Received degree from Creighton University, Omaha, Neb., in 1985.

Pitched 1-0 no-hit victory against Calgary, May 23, 1989.
Pitched 1-0 no-hit victory against Edmonton, May 28, 1989 (first game).
Pitched 5-0 no-hit victory against Las Vegas, August 16, 1989 (first game).
Led Pacific Coast League in balks with 10 in 1989.

Year—Club	League	G.	IP.	W.	L.	Pct.	H.	R.	ER.	SO.	BB.	ERA.
1985—Sarasota White Sox	Gulf Coast	12	74⅓	6	3	.667	75	29	23	75	17	2.78
1986—Peninsula	Carolina	37	94⅔	5	7	.417	108	64	50	54	61	4.75
1987—Daytona Beach	Florida St.	27	168⅔	10	●14	.417	195	87	70	76	58	3.74
1988—Birmingham	Southern	22	158	9	7	.563	149	63	49	94	52	2.79
1989—Vancouver	P. Coast	26	168⅓	12	11	.522	142	76	63	66	72	3.37

Selected by Chicago White Sox' organization in 17th round of free-agent draft, June 3, 1985.

TIMOTHY DARNELL DRUMMOND
(Tim)

Born December 24, 1964, at La Plata, Md.
Height, 6.03. Weight, 170.
Throws and bats righthanded.
Attended Charles County Community College, La Plata, Md.

Major League saves: 1989 (1).

Year—Club	League	G.	IP.	W.	L.	Pct.	H.	R.	ER.	SO.	BB.	ERA.
1983—Bradenton Pirates	Gulf Coast	14	88	7	2	.778	73	20	14	40	21	1.43
1984—Macon	S. Atlantic	27	154⅔	7	★15	.318	139	93	67	76	81	3.90
1985—Macon	S. Atlantic	27	168⅓	8	11	.421	171	100	77	91	73	4.12
1986—Prince William	Carolina	47	73⅔	6	4	.600	71	39	31	55	34	3.79
1987—Vancouver†	P. Coast	46	63⅔	2	6	.250	62	35	21	49	43	2.97
1987—Pittsburgh†	National	6	6	0	0	.000	5	3	3	5	3	4.50

Year Club	League	G.	IP.	W.	L.	Pct.	H.	R.	ER.	SO.	BB.	ERA.
1988—Tidewater	Int'national	38	82⅓	6	3	.667	71	33	30	62	28	3.28
1989—Tidewater‡	Int'national	35	63⅓	5	1	.833	63	29	23	42	26	3.27
1989—Portland	P. Coast	10	22	1	1	.500	19	9	8	21	8	3.27
1989—Minnesota	American	8	16⅓	0	0	.000	16	7	7	9	8	3.86
National League Totals—1 Year		6	6	0	0	.000	5	3	3	5	3	4.50
American League Totals—1 Year		8	16⅓	0	0	.000	16	7	7	9	8	3.86
Major League Totals—2 Years		14	22⅓	0	0	.000	21	10	10	14	11	4.03

Selected by Pittsburgh Pirates' organization in 12th round of free-agent draft, January 11, 1983.

†Traded with Catcher Mackey Sasser to New York Mets for First Baseman Randy Milligan and Pitcher Scott Henion, March 26, 1988.

‡Traded with Pitcher Kevin Tapani to Portland (Minnesota Twins' organization), August 1, 1989, as partial completion of deal in which Minnesota Twins traded Pitcher Frank Viola to New York Mets for Pitchers Rick Aguilera and David West and three players to be named later, July 31, 1989. Minnesota acquired Pitcher Jack Savage to complete deal, October 16, 1989.

BRIAN ANDREW DuBOIS

Born April 18, 1967, at Joliet, Ill.
Height, 5.10. Weight, 170.
Throws and bats lefthanded.

Major League saves: 1989 (1).
Tied for Carolina League lead in games started by pitchers with 28 and complete games with 7 in 1988.

Year Club	League	G.	IP.	W.	L.	Pct.	H.	R.	ER.	SO.	BB.	ERA.
1985—Bluefield	Ap'lachian	10	57⅔	5	4	.556	42	23	16	67	20	2.50
1986—Hagerstown†	Carolina	5	20⅓	1	2	.333	29	19	16	17	11	7.08
1986—Bluefield	Ap'lachian	3	9⅓	1	1	.500	8	2	1	8	2	0.96
1987—Hagerstown‡	Carolina	27	155	8	9	.471	162	81	67	96	73	3.89
1988—Virginia-Hagerstown	Carolina	28	183⅔	●14	9	.609	★195	★113	★85	147	50	4.17
1989—Hagerstown	Eastern	15	112	6	4	.600	93	36	31	82	18	2.49
1989—Detroit	American	6	36	0	4	.000	29	14	7	13	17	1.75
1989—Rochester§-Toledo	Int'national	7	54	4	2	.667	41	14	12	29	18	2.00
Major League Totals—1 Year		6	36	0	4	.000	29	14	7	13	17	1.75

Selected by Baltimore Orioles' organization in 4th round of free-agent draft, June 3, 1985.

†On disabled list, May 9 to June 30, 1986.

‡Loaned to Virginia (Independent), April, 1988; returned, June, 1988.

§Traded to Detroit Tigers for First Baseman Keith Moreland, July 29, 1989.

ROBERT THOMAS DUCEY
(Rob)

Born May 24, 1965, at Toronto, Canada.
Height, 6.02. Weight, 175.
Throws right and bats lefthanded.
Attended Seminole Community College, Sanford, Fla.

Major League stolen bases: 1987 (2), 1988 (1), 1989 (2). Total—5.
Tied for Southern League lead in double plays by outfielders with 6 in 1986.

Year Club	League	Pos.	G.	AB.	R.	H.	2B.	3B.	HR.	RBI.	B.A.	PO.	A.	E.	F.A.
1984—Medicine Hat	Pion.	OF-1B	63	235	49	71	10	3	12	49	.302	185	11	6	.970
1985—Florence	S. Atl.	OF-1B	134	529	78	133	22	2	13	86	.251	228	8	9	.963
1986—Ventura	Calif.	OF-1B	47	178	36	60	11	3	12	38	.337	97	3	2	.980
1986—Knoxville	South.	OF	88	344	49	106	22	3	11	58	.308	186	10	6	.970
1987—Syracuse	Int.	OF	100	359	62	102	14	●10	10	60	.284	171	13	6	.968
1987—Toronto	Amer.	OF	34	48	12	9	1	0	1	6	.188	31	0	0	1.000
1988—Syracuse	Int.	OF	90	317	40	81	14	4	7	42	.256	233	6	4	.984
1988—Toronto	Amer.	OF	27	54	15	17	4	1	0	6	.315	35	1	0	1.000
1989—Toronto†	Amer.	OF	41	76	5	16	4	0	0	7	.211	56	3	0	1.000
1989—Syracuse	Int.	OF	10	29	0	3	0	1	0	3	.103	14	0	1	.933
Major League Totals—3 Years			102	178	32	42	9	1	1	19	.236	122	4	0	1.000

Signed as free agent by Toronto Blue Jays' organization, May 16, 1984.

†On disabled list, June 9 to September 2, 1989; included rehabilitation disability assignment to Syracuse, July 5 to July 14 and August 24 to September 2, 1989.

MARIANO DUNCAN

Born March 13, 1963, at San Pedro de Macoris, D. R.
Height, 6.00. Weight, 185.
Throws right and bats left and righthanded.

Major League stolen bases: 1985 (38), 1986 (48), 1987 (11), 1989 (9). Total—106.
Led Florida State League in stolen bases with 56 in 1983.
Led Texas League second basemen in double plays with 84 in 1984.

Year Club	League	Pos.	G.	AB.	R.	H.	2B.	3B.	HR.	RBI.	B.A.	PO.	A.	E.	F.A.
1982—Lethbridge	Pion.	SS-2B	30	55	9	13	3	1	1	8	.236	23	35	15	.795
1983—Vero Beach	Fla. St.	OF-SS-2B	109	384	73	102	10	★15	0	42	.266	169	157	37	.898
1984—San Antonio	Texas	2B-OF-SS	125	502	80	127	14	●11	2	44	.253	283	335	22	.966
1985—Los Angeles	Nat.	SS-2B	142	562	74	137	24	6	6	39	.244	224	430	30	.956
1986—Los Angeles†	Nat.	SS	109	407	47	93	7	0	8	30	.229	172	317	25	.951
1987—Los Angeles‡	Nat.	★S-2-O	76	261	31	56	8	1	6	18	.215	101	213	★21	.937

Year Club	League	Pos.	G.	AB.	R.	H.	2B.	3B.	HR.	RBI.	B.A.	PO.	A.	E.	F.A.
1987—Albuquerque	P. C.	SS	6	22	6	6	0	0	0	0	.273	8	15	2	.920
1988—Albuquerque	P. C.	SS-2B	56	227	48	65	4	8	0	25	.286	104	153	18	.935
1989—L.A.§x-Cin.	Nat.	SS-2B-OF	94	258	32	64	15	2	3	21	.248	101	155	14	.948
Major League Totals—4 Years			421	1488	184	350	54	9	23	108	.235	598	1115	90	.950

Signed as free agent by Los Angeles Dodgers' organization, January 17, 1982.

†On disabled list, August 19 to September 17, 1986.

‡On disabled list, June 19 to July 4 and August 16, 1987 through remainder of season.

§On disabled list, May 28 to June 12 and July 1 to July 16, 1989.

xTraded with Pitcher Tim Leary to Cincinnati Reds for Outfielder Kal Daniels and Infielder Lenny Harris, July 18, 1989.

CHAMPIONSHIP SERIES RECORD

Year Club	League	Pos.	G.	AB.	R.	H.	2B.	3B.	HR.	RBI.	B.A.	PO.	A.	E.	F.A.
1985—Los Angeles	Nat.	SS	5	18	2	4	2	1	0	1	.222	7	16	1	.958

MICHAEL DENNIS DUNNE
(Mike)

Born October 27, 1962, at South Bend, Ind.
Height, 6.04. Weight, 200.
Throws right and bats lefthanded.
Attended Bradley University, Peoria, Ill.

Led American Association pitchers in balks with 9 and tied for lead in games started with 28 in 1986.
Named National League Rookie Pitcher of the Year by THE SPORTING NEWS, 1987.
Member of 1984 U.S. Olympic baseball team.
Named righthanded pitcher on THE SPORTING NEWS College Baseball All-America Team, 1984.

Year Club	League	G.	IP.	W.	L.	Pct.	H.	R.	ER.	SO.	BB.	ERA.
1985—Arkansas†	Texas	23	146	4	9	.308	133	72	50	91	57	3.08
1986—Louisville‡	Am. Assoc.	28	★185⅔	9	●12	.429	182	102	★94	94	82	4.56
1987—Vancouver	P. Coast	9	61⅓	3	5	.375	61	21	12	41	23	1.76
1987—Pittsburgh	National	23	163⅓	13	6	.684	143	66	55	72	68	3.03
1988—Pittsburgh§	National	30	170	7	11	.389	163	88	74	70	88	3.92
1989—Pittsburgh x	National	3	14⅓	1	1	.500	21	12	12	4	9	7.53
1989—Seattle	American	15	85⅓	2	9	.182	104	61	50	38	37	5.27
1989—Calgary y	P. Coast	9	51⅔	4	0	1.000	54	26	19	19	25	3.31
National League Totals—3 Years		56	347⅔	21	18	.538	327	166	141	146	165	3.65
American League Totals—1 Year		15	85⅓	2	9	.182	104	61	50	38	37	5.27
Major League Totals—3 Years		71	433	23	27	.460	431	227	191	184	202	3.97

Selected by St. Louis Cardinals' organization in 1st round (seventh player selected) of free-agent draft, June 4, 1984.

†On disabled list, May 31 to June 10, 1985.

‡Traded with Outfielder Andy Van Slyke and Catcher Mike LaValliere to Pittsburgh Pirates for Catcher Tony Pena, April 1, 1987.

§On disabled list, April 6 to April 28, 1988.

xTraded with Pitcher Mike Walker and Outfielder Mark Merchant to Seattle Mariners for Shortstop Rey Quinones and Pitcher Bill Wilkinson, April 21, 1989.

yDrafted by San Diego Padres, December 4, 1989.

SHAWON DONNELL DUNSTON

Born March 21, 1963, at Brooklyn, N.Y.
Height, 6.01. Weight, 175.
Throws and bats righthanded.

Major League stolen bases: 1985 (11), 1986 (13), 1987 (12), 1988 (30), 1989 (19). Total—85.
Led National League shortstops in total chances with 817 and tied for lead in double plays with 96 in 1986.
Named shortstop on THE SPORTING NEWS National League All-Star Team, 1989.
Received reported $150,000 bonus to sign with Chicago Cubs, 1982.

Year Club	League	Pos.	G.	AB.	R.	H.	2B.	3B.	HR.	RBI.	B.A.	PO.	A.	E.	F.A.
1982—Sarasota Cubs	Gulf C.	SS-3B	53	190	27	61	11	0	2	28	.321	61	129	24	.888
1983—Quad Cities†	Midw.	SS	117	455	65	141	17	8	4	62	.310	172	326	47	.914
1984—Midland	Texas	SS	73	298	44	98	13	3	3	34	.329	164	203	32	.920
1984—Iowa	A. A.	SS	61	210	25	49	11	1	7	27	.233	90	165	26	.907
1985—Chicago	Nat.	SS	74	250	40	65	12	4	4	18	.260	144	248	17	.958
1985—Iowa	A. A.	SS	73	272	24	73	9	6	2	28	.268	138	176	12	.963
1986—Chicago	Nat.	SS	150	581	66	145	36	3	17	68	.250	★320	★465	★32	.961
1987—Chicago‡	Nat.	SS	95	346	40	85	18	3	5	22	.246	160	271	14	.969
1987—Iowa	A. A.	SS	5	19	1	8	1	0	0	2	.421	6	12	1	.947
1988—Chicago	Nat.	SS	155	575	69	143	23	6	9	56	.249	★257	455	20	.973
1989—Chicago	Nat.	SS	138	471	52	131	20	6	9	60	.278	213	379	17	.972
Major League Totals—5 Years			612	2223	267	569	109	22	44	224	.256	1094	1818	100	.967

Selected by Chicago Cubs' organization in 1st round (first player selected) of free-agent draft, June 7, 1982.

†On disabled list, May 31 to June 10, 1983.

‡On disabled list, June 16 to August 21, 1987; included rehabilitation disability assignment to Iowa, August 14 to August 21, 1987.

CHAMPIONSHIP SERIES RECORD

Year Club	League	Pos.	G.	AB.	R.	H.	2B.	3B.	HR.	RBI.	B.A.	PO.	A.	E.	F.A.
1989—Chicago	Nat.	SS	5	19	2	6	0	0	0	0	.316	10	14	1	.960

Member of National League All-Star Team in 1988; did not play.

LEON DURHAM

Born July 31, 1957, at Cincinnati, O.
Height, 6.02. Weight, 210.
Throws and bats lefthanded.

Shares major league record for most assists, first baseman, inning (3), July 22, 1986, first inning.
Major League stolen bases: 1980 (8), 1981 (25), 1982 (28), 1983 (12), 1984 (16), 1985 (7), 1986 (8), 1987 (2). Total—106.
Tied for National League lead in intentional bases on balls received with 24 in 1985.
Led Texas League first basemen in double plays with 96 in 1978.
Led Gulf Coast League first basemen in errors with 10 in 1976.
Named outfielder on THE SPORTING NEWS National League Silver Slugger team, 1982.

Year—Club	League	Pos.	G.	AB.	R.	H.	2B.	3B.	HR.	RBI.	B.A.	PO.	A.	E.	F.A.
1976—Sarasota Cards	Gulf C.	1B-OF	44	156	25	35	3	5	2	18	.224	296	5	12	.962
1977—Gastonia	W. Car.	1B	63	239	45	88	18	3	4	44	.368	492	28	8	.985
1977—St. Petersburg	Fla. St.	1B	63	209	26	60	3	6	0	25	.287	533	27	9	.984
1978—Arkansas†	Texas	1B	102	367	72	116	21	5	12	70	.316	931	42	8	*.992
1979—Springfield	A. A.	OF-1B	127	449	84	139	33	4	23	88	.310	304	19	6	.982
1980—Springfield	A. A.	OF-1B	32	128	20	33	5	5	5	23	.258	96	8	4	.963
1980—St. Louis‡	Nat.	OF-1B	96	303	42	82	15	4	8	42	.271	180	22	3	.985
1981—Chicago§	Nat.	OF-1B	87	328	42	95	14	6	10	35	.290	175	4	5	.973
1982—Chicago	Nat.	OF-1B	148	539	84	168	33	7	22	90	.312	311	12	12	.964
1983—Chicago x	Nat.	OF-1B	100	337	58	87	18	8	12	55	.258	203	4	6	.972
1984—Chicago y	Nat.	1B	137	473	86	132	30	4	23	96	.279	1162	96	7	.994
1985—Chicago	Nat.	1B	153	542	58	153	32	2	21	75	.282	1421	107	7	.995
1986—Chicago	Nat.	1B	141	484	66	127	18	7	20	65	.262	1231	80	7	.995
1987—Chicago	Nat.	1B	131	439	70	120	22	1	27	63	.273	1049	57	11	.990
1988—Chi.z-Cin.ab	Nat.	1B	45	124	14	27	9	1	4	8	.218	296	21	2	.994
1989—Louisville	A. A.	1B-OF	59	178	31	51	10	0	10	30	.287	246	23	2	.993
1989—St. Louis cde	Nat.	1B	29	18	2	1	1	0	0	1	.056	44	5	2	.961
Major League Totals—10 Years			1067	3587	522	992	192	40	147	530	.277	6072	408	62	.991

Selected by St. Louis Cardinals' organization in 1st round (15th player selected) of free-agent draft, June 8, 1976.
†On disabled list, April 23 to May 25, 1978.
‡Traded with Third Baseman Ken Reitz and a player to be named later to Chicago Cubs for Pitcher Bruce Sutter, December 9, 1980; Chicago acquired Third Baseman Tye Waller to complete deal, December 22, 1980.
§On disabled list, June 2 to August 9, 1981.
xOn disabled list, June 9 to June 24, 1983.
yOn disabled list, June 24 to July 12, 1984.
zTraded with cash to Cincinnati Reds for Pitcher Pat Perry, May 19, 1988.
aOn disabled list, May 24 to June 14 and July 11 to September 16, 1988.
bReleased, November 8, 1988; signed by Louisville (St. Louis Cardinals' organization), February 15, 1989.
cOn disabled list, August 10 to September 2, 1989; included rehabilitation disability assignment to Louisville, August 17 to September 2, 1989.
dOn disqualified list, September 22, 1989 through remainder of season.
eGranted free agency, November 13, 1989.

CHAMPIONSHIP SERIES RECORD

Year—Club	League	Pos.	G.	AB.	R.	H.	2B.	3B.	HR.	RBI.	B.A.	PO.	A.	E.	F.A.
1984—Chicago	Nat.	1B	5	20	2	3	0	0	2	4	.150	47	3	1	.980

ALL-STAR GAME RECORD

Year—League	Pos.	AB.	R.	H.	2B.	3B.	HR.	RBI.	B.A.	PO.	A.	E.	F.A.
1983—National	OF	2	0	0	0	0	0	0	.000	0	0	0	.000

Member of National League All-Star Team in 1982; did not play.

JAMES EDWARD DWYER
(Jimmy)

Born January 3, 1950, at Evergreen Park, Ill.
Height, 5.10. Weight, 196.
Throws and bats lefthanded.

Received bachelor of arts degree in accounting from Southern Illinois University, Carbondale, Ill., in 1973.
Nephew of Don Dwyer, second baseman in New York Giants' organization, 1947.

Major League stolen bases: 1975 (4), 1978 (7), 1979 (3), 1980 (3), 1982 (2), 1983 (1), 1987 (4), 1989 (2). Total—26.
Tied for American Association lead in caught stealing with 13 in 1977.

Year—Club	League	Pos.	G.	AB.	R.	H.	2B.	3B.	HR.	RBI.	B.A.	PO.	A.	E.	F.A.
1971—Cedar Rapids	Midw.	OF	58	201	30	63	6	6	2	15	.313	73	3	3	.962
1972—Modesto	Calif.	OF	92	354	87	115	15	*13	9	45	.325	149	8	4	.975
1972—Arkansas	Texas	OF	44	162	16	41	1	0	2	14	.253	101	6	2	.982
1973—Tulsa	A. A.	OF	87	349	63	135	22	8	1	40	*.387	127	8	5	.964
1973—St. Louis	Nat.	OF	28	57	7	11	1	1	0	0	.193	32	0	0	1.000
1974—Tulsa	A. A.	OF-1B	36	119	20	40	7	2	1	15	.336	120	13	3	.978
1974—St. Louis	Nat.	OF-1B	74	86	13	24	1	0	2	11	.279	31	3	0	1.000
1975—Tulsa	A. A.	OF	33	109	17	44	8	2	1	17	.404	49	2	2	.962
1975—St.L.†-Mont.	Nat.	OF	81	206	26	56	8	1	3	21	.272	104	8	4	.966
1976—Mont.‡-N.Y.§	Nat.	OF-PH	61	105	9	19	3	1	0	5	.181	35	0	1	.972
1976—Tidewater	Int.	OF	8	26	0	5	1	0	0	1	.192	14	0	1	.933

Year Club	League	Pos.	G.	AB.	R.	H.	2B.	3B.	HR.	RBI.	B.A.	PO.	A.	E.	F.A.
1977—Wichita x	A. A.	OF	130	464	*113	*154	*38	12	18	70	*.332	245	6	8	.969
1977—St. Louis	Nat.	OF	13	31	3	7	1	0	0	2	.226	16	0	0	1.000
1978—St.L. y-S.F. z	Nat.	OF-1B	107	238	30	53	12	2	6	26	.223	216	15	3	.987
1979—Boston	Amer.	1B-OF	76	113	19	30	7	0	2	14	.265	167	16	4	.979
1980—Boston a	Amer.	OF-1B	93	260	41	74	11	1	9	38	.285	143	15	4	.975
1981—Baltimore	Amer.	OF-1B	68	134	16	30	0	1	3	10	.224	97	2	2	.980
1982—Baltimore	Amer.	OF-1B	71	148	28	45	4	3	6	15	.304	87	0	2	.978
1983—Baltimore	Amer.	OF-1B	100	196	37	56	17	1	8	38	.286	123	2	4	.969
1984—Baltimore b	Amer.	OF	76	161	22	41	9	1	2	21	.255	83	3	3	.966
1985—Baltimore c	Amer.	OF	101	233	35	58	8	3	7	36	.249	131	4	1	.993
1986—Baltimore d	Amer.	OF-1B	94	160	18	39	13	1	8	31	.244	33	4	0	1.000
1987—Baltimore	Amer.	OF	92	241	54	66	7	1	15	33	.274	57	1	0	1.000
1988—Balt.ef-Minn.	Amer.	OF	55	94	9	24	1	0	2	18	.255	3	0	0	1.000
1988—Rochester g	Int.	DH	8	27	7	8	3	1	0	4	.296	0	0	0	.000
1989—Minnesota h	Amer.	OF	88	225	34	71	11	0	3	23	.316	0	0	0	.000
1989—Montreal	Nat.	PH	13	10	1	3	1	0	0	2	.300	0	0	0	.000
National League Totals—7 Years			377	733	89	173	27	5	11	67	.236	434	26	8	.983
American League Totals—11 Years			914	1965	313	534	88	12	65	277	.272	924	47	20	.980
Major League Totals—17 Years			1291	2698	402	707	115	17	76	344	.262	1358	73	28	.981

Selected by St. Louis Cardinals' organization in 11th round of free-agent draft, June 8, 1971.

†Traded to Montreal Expos for Infielder Larry Lintz, July 25, 1975.

‡Traded with Outfielder Jose (Pepe) Mangual to New York Mets for Outfielder Del Unser and Infielder Wayne Garrett, July 21, 1976.

§In three-club deal, Chicago Cubs traded Outfielder-First Baseman Pete LaCock to Kansas City Royals, the New York Mets traded Outfielder Jim Dwyer to Chicago Cubs' organization, and New York received a player to be named later, December 8, 1976; New York acquired Outfielder Sheldon Mallory from Kansas City to complete deal, December 13, 1976.

xReleased, September 7, 1977, signed by St. Louis Cardinals, September 13, 1977.

yTraded to San Francisco Giants, June 15, 1978, completing deal in which San Francisco traded Pitcher Frank Riccelli to St. Louis Cardinals for a player to be named later, October 25, 1977.

zSold to Boston Red Sox, March 15, 1979.

aGranted free agency, October 22, 1980; signed by Baltimore Orioles, December 23, 1980.

bOn disabled list, July 19 to August 29, 1984.

cGranted free agency, November 12, 1985; re-signed by Orioles, February 5, 1986.

dGranted free agency, November 12, 1986; re-signed by Orioles, November 20, 1986.

eOn disabled list, April 15 to May 14 and July 11 to August 1, 1988; included rehabilitation disability assignment to Rochester, May 6 to May 14, 1988.

fTraded to Minnesota Twins for a player to be named later, August 29, 1988; Baltimore Orioles acquired Pitcher Doug Kline to complete deal, August 31, 1988.

gGranted free agency, November 4, 1988; re-signed by Twins, December 6, 1988.

hTraded to Montreal Expos for a player to be named later, August 28, 1989; Minnesota Twins acquired Outfielder Alonzo Powell to complete deal, September 16, 1989.

CHAMPIONSHIP SERIES RECORD

Year Club	League	Pos.	G.	AB.	R.	H.	2B.	3B.	HR.	RBI.	B.A.	PO.	A.	E.	F.A.
1983—Baltimore	Amer.	PH-OF	2	4	1	1	1	0	0	0	.250	4	0	0	1.000

WORLD SERIES RECORD

Shares World Series record for hitting home run in first series at-bat, October 11, 1983.

Year Club	League	Pos.	G.	AB.	R.	H.	2B.	3B.	HR.	RBI.	B.A.	PO.	A.	E.	F.A.
1983—Baltimore	Amer.	OF	2	8	3	3	1	0	1	1	.375	2	0	0	1.000

MICHAEL LAWRENCE DYER

(Mike)

Born September 8, 1966, at Upland, Calif.
Height, 6.03. Weight, 195.
Throws and bats righthanded.
Attended Citrus College, Glendora, Calif.

Tied for Appalachian League lead in games started by pitchers with 14 in 1986.

Year Club	League	G.	IP.	W.	L.	Pct.	H.	R.	ER.	SO.	BB.	ERA.
1986—Elizabethton	Ap'lachian	14	72⅓	5	7	.417	70	50	28	62	42	3.48
1987—Kenosha	Midwest	27	167	16	5	.762	124	72	57	163	84	3.07
1988—Orlando	Southern	27	162⅓	11	13	.458	155	84	72	125	86	3.99
1989—Portland	P. Coast	15	89⅓	3	6	.333	80	56	44	63	51	4.43
1989—Minnesota	American	16	71	4	7	.364	74	43	38	37	37	4.82
Major League Totals—1 Year		16	71	4	7	.364	74	43	38	37	37	4.82

Selected by Minnesota Twins' organization in 4th round of free-agent draft, January 14, 1986.

LEONARD KYLE DYKSTRA

Name pronounced DYK-struh.

(Lenny)

Born February 10, 1963, at Santa Ana, Calif.
Height, 5.10. Weight, 170.
Throws and bats lefthanded.

Grandson of Pete Leswick, forward with New York Americans and Boston Bruins of NHL,
1936-37 and 1944-45; nephew of Tony Leswick, forward with New York Rangers,
Detroit Red Wings and Chicago Black Hawks of NHL, 1945-46
through 1955-56 and 1957-58; and brother of Kevin Dykstra, umpire in Northwest League, 1988.

Major League stolen bases: 1985 (15), 1986 (31), 1987 (27), 1988 (30), 1989 (30). Total—133.
Led Carolina League in bases on balls received with 107, stolen bases with 105 and caught stealing with 23 in 1983.
Named Carolina League Player of the Year, 1983.

Year Club	League	Pos.	G.	AB.	R.	H.	2B.	3B.	HR.	RBI.	B.A.	PO.	A.	E.	F.A.
1981—Shelby..................	S. Atl.	OF-SS	48	157	34	41	7	2	0	18	.261	86	3	4	.957
1982—Shelby..................	S. Atl.	OF	120	413	95	120	13	7	3	38	.291	239	11	14	.947
1983—Lynchburg............	Carol.	OF	●136	*525	*132	*188	24	*14	8	81	*.358	268	9	7	.975
1984—Jackson	Texas	OF	131	501	*100	138	25	7	6	52	.275	256	5	2	*.992
1985—Tidewater.............	Int.	OF	58	229	44	71	8	6	1	25	.310	184	4	5	.974
1985—New York.............	Nat.	OF	83	236	40	60	9	3	1	19	.254	165	6	1	.994
1986—New York.............	Nat.	OF	147	431	77	127	27	7	8	45	.295	283	8	3	.990
1987—New York.............	Nat.	OF	132	431	86	123	37	3	10	43	.285	239	4	3	.988
1988—New York.............	Nat.	OF	126	429	57	116	19	3	8	33	.270	270	3	1	.996
1989—N.Y.†-Phi.	Nat.	OF	146	511	66	121	32	4	7	32	.237	332	10	4	.988
Major League Totals—5 Years................			634	2038	326	547	124	20	34	172	.268	1289	31	12	.991

Selected by New York Mets' organization in 12th round of free-agent draft, June 8, 1981.
†Traded with Pitcher Roger McDowell and a player to be named later to Philadelphia Phillies for Outfielder Juan
Samuel, June 18, 1989; Philadelphia organization acquired Pitcher Tom Edens to complete deal, July 27, 1989.

CHAMPIONSHIP SERIES RECORD

Shares Championship Series record for most times hit by pitch, series (2), 1988.

Year Club	League	Pos.	G.	AB.	R.	H.	2B.	3B.	HR.	RBI.	B.A.	PO.	A.	E.	F.A.
1986—New York.............	Nat.	OF-PH	6	23	3	7	1	1	3	3	.304	10	0	0	1.000
1988—New York.............	Nat.	PH-OF	7	14	6	6	3	0	1	3	.429	9	0	0	1.000
Championship Series Totals—2 Years.....			13	37	9	13	4	1	2	6	.351	19	0	0	1.000

WORLD SERIES RECORD

Year Club	League	Pos.	G.	AB.	R.	H.	2B.	3B.	HR.	RBI.	B.A.	PO.	A.	E.	F.A.
1986—New York.............	Nat.	OF-PH	7	27	4	8	0	0	2	3	.296	14	0	0	1.000

KENNETH LOGAN EASLEY

(Known by middle name.)
Born November 4, 1961, at Salt Lake City, Utah.
Height, 6.01. Weight, 185.
Throws and bats righthanded.
Attended College of Southern Idaho, Twins Falls, Ida.

Major League saves: 1987 (1), 1989 (1). Total—2.
Led Eastern League in games finished in relief with 45 and tied for lead in saves with 18 in 1986.
Led South Atlantic League in shutouts with 4 in 1983.

Year Club	League	G.	IP.	W.	L.	Pct.	H.	R.	ER.	SO.	BB.	ERA.
1981—Paintsville	Ap'lachian	22	53	2	2	.500	60	36	23	26	24	3.91
1982—Paintsville	Ap'lachian	13	84⅓	7	4	.636	77	31	24	59	28	2.56
1983—Greensboro..................	S. Atlantic	29	158⅓	14	8	.636	157	82	71	116	62	4.04
1984—Fort Lauderdale..........	Florida St.	32	131	5	7	.417	150	76	56	57	44	3.85
1985—Fort Lauderdale..........	Florida St.	17	19	1	1	.500	19	6	2	16	6	0.95
1985—Albany..........................	Eastern	29	85	5	3	.625	85	40	30	58	38	3.18
1986—Albany†........................	Eastern	49	77⅔	8	7	.533	70	25	13	73	20	1.51
1987—Pittsburgh....................	National	17	26½	1	1	.500	23	17	16	21	17	5.47
1987—Vancouver‡.................	P. Coast	9	28⅓	2	2	.500	20	16	12	17	19	3.81
1988—Buffalo.........................	Am. Assoc.	28	68⅔	1	5	.167	69	36	30	32	28	3.93
1989—Buffalo.........................	Am. Assoc.	28	33⅔	4	1	.800	37	16	16	19	7	4.28
1989—Pittsburgh§.................	National	10	12⅓	1	0	1.000	8	6	6	6	7	4.38
Major League Totals—2 Years...........................		27	38⅔	2	1	.667	31	23	22	27	24	5.12

Selected by New York Yankees' organization in 20th round of free-agent draft, June 8, 1981.
†Traded with Pitchers Doug Drabek and Brian Fisher to Pittsburgh Pirates for Pitchers Rick Rhoden, Cecilio
Guante and Pat Clements, November 26, 1986.
‡Released, November 12, 1987; signed by Buffalo (Pittsburgh Pirates' organization), December 3, 1987.
§Released, November 16, 1989.

GARY LOUIS EAVE

Born July 22, 1963, at Monroe, La.
Height, 6.04. Weight, 190.
Throws and bats righthanded.
Attended Grambling State University, Grambling, La.

Year Club	League	G.	IP.	W.	L.	Pct.	H.	R.	ER.	SO.	BB.	ERA.
1985—Bradenton Braves.......................	Gulf Coast	6	30⅔	2	1	.667	28	7	6	21	8	1.76
1986—Sumter...	S. Atlantic	25	47	4	1	.800	34	18	15	61	21	2.87
1987—Durham	Carolina	16	87⅓	5	4	.556	90	51	47	82	35	4.84
1987—Greenville	Southern	25	54⅓	2	5	.286	39	19	17	52	23	2.82
1988—Richmond......................................	Int'national	34	101	5	9	.357	100	49	40	81	31	3.56
1988—Atlanta	National	5	5	0	0	.000	7	5	5	0	3	9.00
1989—Richmond......................................	Int'national	23	141⅓	●13	3	*.813	111	48	44	93	57	2.80

Year Club	League	G.	IP.	W.	L.	Pct.	H.	R.	ER.	SO.	BB.	ERA.
1989—Atlanta	National	3	20⅔	2	0	1.000	15	3	3	9	12	1.31
Major League Totals—2 Years		8	25⅔	2	0	1.000	22	8	8	9	15	2.81

Selected by Atlanta Braves' organization in 12th round of free-agent draft, June 3, 1985.

DENNIS LEE ECKERSLEY

Born October 3, 1954, at Oakland, Calif.
Height, 6.02. Weight, 195.
Throws and bats righthanded.
Son-in-law of Al Jacinto, second baseman in Chicago White Sox' organization, 1947 through 1954.
Pitched 1-0 no-hit victory against California Angels, May 30, 1977.
Major League saves: 1975 (2), 1976 (1), 1987 (16), 1988 (45), 1989 (33). Total—97.
Led American League in saves with 45 in 1988.
Led American League in home runs allowed with 30 in 1978.
Tied for American League lead in intentional bases on balls issued with 11 in 1977.
Led Texas League in hit batsmen with 10 in 1974.
Led California League pitchers in games started with 31 and tied for lead in shutouts with 5 in 1973.
Named American League Fireman of the Year by THE SPORTING NEWS, 1988.
Named American League Rookie Pitcher of the Year by THE SPORTING NEWS, 1975.
Received reported $32,000 bonus to sign with Cleveland Indians, 1972.

Year Club	League	G.	IP.	W.	L.	Pct.	H.	R.	ER.	SO.	BB.	ERA.
1972—Reno	California	12	75	5	5	.500	87	46	40	56	33	4.80
1973—Reno	California	31	202	12	8	.600	182	97	82	218	91	3.65
1974—San Antonio	Texas	23	167	●14	3	*.824	141	66	63	*163	60	3.40
1975—Cleveland	American	34	187	13	7	.650	147	61	54	152	90	2.60
1976—Cleveland	American	36	199	13	12	.520	155	82	76	200	78	3.44
1977—Cleveland†	American	33	247	14	13	.519	214	100	97	191	54	3.53
1978—Boston	American	35	268	20	8	.714	258	99	89	162	71	2.99
1979—Boston	American	33	247	17	10	.630	234	89	82	150	59	2.99
1980—Boston	American	30	198	12	14	.462	188	101	94	121	44	4.27
1981—Boston	American	23	154	9	8	.529	160	82	73	79	35	4.27
1982—Boston	American	33	224⅓	13	13	.500	228	101	93	127	43	3.73
1983—Boston	American	28	176⅓	9	13	.409	223	119	110	77	39	5.61
1984—Boston‡	American	9	64⅔	4	4	.500	71	38	36	33	13	5.01
1984—Chicago§	National	24	160⅓	10	8	.556	152	59	54	81	36	3.03
1985—Chicago x	National	25	169⅓	11	7	.611	145	61	58	117	19	3.08
1986—Chicago y	National	33	201	6	11	.353	226	109	102	137	43	4.57
1987—Oakland	American	54	115⅔	6	8	.429	99	41	39	113	17	3.03
1988—Oakland	American	60	72⅔	4	2	.667	52	20	19	70	11	2.35
1989—Oakland z	American	51	57⅔	4	0	1.000	32	10	10	55	3	1.56
American League Totals—13 Years		459	2211⅓	138	112	.552	2061	943	872	1530	557	3.55
National League Totals—3 Years		82	530⅔	27	26	.509	523	229	214	335	98	3.63
Major League Totals—15 Years		541	2742	165	138	.545	2584	1172	1086	1865	655	3.56

Selected by Cleveland Indians' organization in 3rd round of free-agent draft, June 6, 1972.
†Traded with Catcher Fred Kendall to Boston Red Sox for Pitchers Rick Wise and Mike Paxton, Third Baseman Ted Cox and Catcher Bo Diaz, March 30, 1978.
‡Traded with Outfielder Mike Brumley to Chicago Cubs for First Baseman-Outfielder Bill Buckner, May 25, 1984.
§Granted free agency, November 8, 1984; re-signed by Cubs, November 28, 1984.
xOn disabled list, August 11 to September 7, 1985.
yTraded with Infielder Dan Rohn to Oakland Athletics for Outfielder Dave Wilder, Infielder Brian Guinn and Pitcher Mark Leonette, April 3, 1987.
zOn disabled list, May 29 to July 13, 1989.

CHAMPIONSHIP SERIES RECORD

Holds Championship Series record for most saves, lifetime (7) and series (4), 1988.
Holds American League Championship Series record for most saves, total series (4).
Shares American League Championship Series record for most games pitched, series (4), 1988.

Year Club	League	G.	IP.	W.	L.	Pct.	H.	R.	ER.	SO.	BB.	ERA.
1984—Chicago	National	1	5⅓	0	1	.000	9	5	5	0	0	8.44
1988—Oakland	American	4	6	0	0	.000	1	0	0	5	2	0.00
1989—Oakland	American	4	5⅔	0	0	.000	4	1	1	2	0	1.59
Championship Series Totals—3 Years		9	17	0	1	.000	14	6	6	7	2	3.18

WORLD SERIES RECORD

Year Club	League	G.	IP.	W.	L.	Pct.	H.	R.	ER.	SO.	BB.	ERA.
1988—Oakland	American	2	1⅔	0	1	.000	2	2	2	2	1	10.80
1989—Oakland	American	2	1⅔	0	0	.000	0	0	0	0	0	0.00
World Series Totals—2 Years		4	3⅓	0	1	.000	2	2	2	2	1	5.40

ALL-STAR GAME RECORD

Year League		IP.	W.	L.	Pct.	H.	R.	ER.	SO.	BB.	ERA.
1977—American		2	0	0	.000	0	0	0	1	0	0.00
1982—American		3	0	1	.000	2	3	3	1	2	9.00
1988—American		1	0	0	.000	0	0	0	1	0	0.00
All-Star Game Totals—3 Years		6	0	1	.000	2	3	3	3	2	4.50

WAYNE MAURICE EDWARDS

Born March 7, 1964, at Burbank, Calif.
Height, 6.05. Weight, 185.
Throws and bats lefthanded.
Attended Azusa Pacific University, Azusa, Calif.

Led Southern League in wild pitches with 16 in 1988.
Led Florida State League in complete games with 15 and tied for lead in wild pitches with 17 in 1987.

Year Club	League	G.	IP.	W.	L.	Pct.	H.	R.	ER.	SO.	BB.	ERA.
1985—Sarasota White Sox	Gulf Coast	11	68⅔	•7	3	.700	52	26	19	61	18	2.49
1986—Peninsula	Carolina	24	128⅓	8	8	.500	149	80	60	86	68	4.21
1987—Daytona Beach	Florida St.	29	★199⅔	16	8	.667	★211	91	80	121	68	3.61
1988—Birmingham	Southern	27	167	9	12	.429	176	108	91	136	92	4.90
1988—Vancouver	P. Coast	2	3	0	0	.000	0	0	0	2	0	0.00
1989—Birmingham	Southern	24	158	10	4	.714	131	69	56	122	65	3.19
1989—Chicago	American	7	7⅓	0	0	.000	7	3	3	9	3	3.68
Major League Totals—1 Year		7	7⅓	0	0	.000	7	3	3	9	3	3.68

Selected by Chicago White Sox' organization in 10th round of free agent draft, June 3, 1985.

MARK ANTHONY EICHHORN

Name pronounced IKE-horn

Born November 21, 1960, at San Jose, Calif.
Height, 6.03. Weight, 200.
Throws and bats righthanded.
Attended Cabrillo Junior College, Aptos, Calif.

Shares American League record for most games, relief pitcher, season (89), 1987.
Major League saves: 1986 (10), 1987 (4), 1988 (1). Total—15.
Led American League in intentional bases on balls issued with 14 in 1986.
Tied for International League lead in saves with 19 in 1989.
Tied for Southern League lead in games started by pitchers with 29 in 1981.
Named American League Rookie Pitcher of the Year by THE SPORTING NEWS, 1986.

Year Club	League	G.	IP.	W.	L.	Pct.	H.	R.	ER.	SO.	BB.	ERA.
1979—Medicine Hat	Pioneer	16	93	7	6	.538	101	62	35	66	26	3.39
1980—Kinston	Carolina	26	183	14	10	.583	158	72	59	119	56	2.90
1981—Knoxville	Southern	30	192	10	14	.417	202	112	85	99	57	3.98
1982—Syracuse	Int'national	27	156⅔	10	11	.476	158	92	79	71	83	4.54
1982—Toronto	American	7	38	0	3	.000	40	28	23	16	14	5.45
1983—Syracuse	Int'national	7	30⅔	0	5	.000	36	32	27	12	21	7.92
1983—Knoxville	Southern	21	120⅔	6	12	.333	124	65	58	54	47	4.33
1984—Syracuse	Int'national	36	117⅔	5	9	.357	147	92	78	54	51	5.97
1985—Knoxville	Southern	26	116⅓	5	1	.833	101	49	39	76	34	3.02
1985—Syracuse	Int'national	8	37⅓	2	5	.286	38	24	20	27	7	4.82
1986—Toronto†	American	69	157	14	6	.700	105	32	30	166	45	1.72
1987—Toronto	American	★89	127⅔	10	6	.625	110	47	45	96	52	3.17
1988—Toronto	American	37	66⅔	0	3	.000	79	32	31	28	27	4.19
1988—Syracuse‡	Int'national	18	38⅓	4	4	.500	35	9	5	34	15	1.17
1989—Atlanta	National	45	68⅓	5	5	.500	70	36	33	49	19	4.35
1989—Richmond§	Int'national	25	41	1	0	1.000	29	6	6	33	6	1.32
American League Totals—4 Years		202	389⅓	24	18	.571	334	139	129	306	138	2.98
National League Totals—1 Year		45	68⅓	5	5	.500	70	36	33	49	19	4.35
Major League Totals—5 Years		247	457⅔	29	23	.558	404	175	162	355	157	3.19

Selected by Toronto Blue Jays' organization in 2nd round of free-agent draft, January 9, 1979.
†On disabled list, June 16 to July 1, 1986.
‡Sold to Atlanta Braves, March 29, 1989.
§Released, November 20, 1989.

DAVID WILLIAM EILAND
(Dave)

Born July 5, 1966, at Dade City, Fla.
Height, 6.03. Weight, 210.
Throws and bats righthanded.
Attended University of Florida, Gainesville, Fla., and
University of South Florida, Tampa, Fla.

Tied for Eastern League lead in complete games with 7 in 1988.

Year Club	League	G.	IP.	W.	L.	Pct.	H.	R.	ER.	SO.	BB.	ERA.
1987—Oneonta	NYP	5	29⅓	4	0	1.000	20	6	6	16	3	1.84
1987—Fort Lauderdale	Florida St.	8	62⅓	5	3	.625	57	17	13	28	8	1.88
1988—Albany	Eastern	18	119⅓	9	5	.643	95	39	34	66	22	2.56
1988—Columbus	Int'national	4	24⅓	1	1	.500	25	8	7	13	6	2.59
1988—New York	American	3	12⅔	0	0	.000	15	9	9	7	4	6.39
1989—Columbus	Int'national	18	103	9	4	.692	107	47	43	45	21	3.76
1989—New York	American	6	34⅓	1	3	.250	44	25	22	11	13	5.77
Major League Totals—2 Years		9	47	1	3	.250	59	34	31	18	17	5.94

Selected by New York Yankees' organization in 7th round of free-agent draft, June 2, 1987.

JAMES MICHAEL EISENREICH

Name pronounced EYES-en-rike.

(Jim)

Born April 18, 1959, at St. Cloud, Minn.
Height, 5.11. Weight, 195.
Throws and bats lefthanded.
Attended St. Cloud State University, St. Cloud, Minn.

Major League stolen bases: 1984 (2), 1987 (1), 1988 (9), 1989 (27). Total—39.
Named Appalachian League Co-Player of the Year, 1980.

Year Club	League	Pos.	G.	AB.	R.	H.	2B.	3B.	HR.	RBI.	B.A.	PO.	A.	E.	F.A.
1980—Elizabethton .... Appal.		OF	67	258	47	77	12	●4	3	41	.298	151	7	3	.981
1980—Wis. Rapids .... Midw.		DH	5	16	4	7	0	0	0	5	.438	0	0	0	.000
1981—Wis. Rapids .... Midw.		OF	*134	489	101	●152	*27	0	23	99	.311	*295	17	9	.972
1982—Minnesota† .... Amer.		OF	34	99	10	30	6	0	2	9	.303	72	0	2	.973
1983—Minnesota‡ .... Amer.		OF	2	7	1	2	1	0	0	0	.286	6	1	0	1.000
1984—Minnesota§x .... Amer.		OF	12	32	1	7	1	0	0	3	.219	5	0	0	1.000
1985-86—y...........................							(Out of Organized Baseball)								
1987—Memphis .... South.		DH	70	275	60	105	36	●10	11	57	.382	0	0	0	.000
1987—Kansas City z........ Amer.		DH	44	105	10	25	8	2	4	21	.238	0	0	0	.000
1988—Kansas City .... Amer.		OF	82	202	26	44	8	1	1	19	.218	109	0	4	.965
1988—Omaha .... A. A.		OF	36	142	28	41	8	3	4	14	.289	73	1	1	.987
1989—Kansas City a .... Amer.		OF	134	475	64	139	33	7	9	59	.293	273	4	3	.989
Major League Totals—6 Years			308	920	112	247	57	10	16	111	.268	465	5	9	.981

Selected by Minnesota Twins' organization in 16th round of free-agent draft, June 3, 1980.
†On disabled list, May 6 to May 28 and June 18 to September 1, 1982.
‡On disabled list, April 7, 1983; then transferred to voluntarily retired list, May 27, 1983 through remainder of season.
§On disabled list, April 26 to May 18, 1984.
xOn voluntarily retired list, June 4, 1984 through September 29, 1986.
yClaimed on waivers by Kansas City Royals, October 2, 1986.
zOn disabled list, August 25 to September 9, 1987.
aOn disabled list, July 22 to August 6, 1989.

STEVEN CLARK ELLSWORTH

(Steve)

Born July 30, 1960, at Chicago, Ill.
Height, 6.08. Weight, 220.
Throws and bats righthanded.
Attended Fresno City College, Fresno, Calif., and
California State University, Northridge, Calif.
Son of Dick Ellsworth, pitcher with Chicago Cubs, Philadelphia Phillies, Boston Red Sox,
Cleveland Indians and Milwaukee Brewers, 1958 and 1960 through 1971.

Tied for Carolina League lead in complete games with 7 in 1984.

Year Club	League	G.	IP.	W.	L.	Pct.	H.	R.	ER.	SO.	BB.	ERA.
1981—Elmira..............................	NYP	1	1	0	1	.000	0	2	2	0	2	18.00
1982—Elmira†............................	NYP					(Did not play)						
1983—Winter Haven..................	Florida State	20	83⅓	1	11	.083	119	81	70	47	34	7.56
1984—Wintson-Salem	Carolina	26	164⅓	13	8	.619	158	79	60	104	68	3.29
1984—New Britain	Eastern	3	21⅓	1	1	.500	18	8	7	12	5	2.95
1985—New Britain	Eastern	20	120⅓	7	8	.467	136	66	57	63	31	4.26
1986—New Britain	Eastern	9	73	5	3	.625	57	19	16	41	18	1.97
1986—Pawtucket.......................	Int'national	15	83	6	2	.750	82	33	31	43	19	3.36
1987—Pawtucket.......................	Int'national	27	165⅔	11	8	.579	182	85	79	89	46	4.29
1988—Boston............................	American	8	36	1	6	.143	47	29	27	16	16	6.75
1988—Pawtucket.......................	Int'national	18	108⅓	7	7	.500	105	49	45	58	23	3.74
1989—Pawtucket‡.....................	Int'national	14	66⅓	1	8	.111	73	45	37	35	29	5.02
Major League Totals—1 Year..............................		8	36	1	6	.143	47	29	27	16	16	6.75

Selected by Minnesota Twins' organization in 7th round of free-agent draft, January 8, 1980.
Selected by Cleveland Indians' organization in secondary phase of free-agent draft, June 8, 1980.
Selected by Boston Red Sox' organization in secondary phase of free-agent draft, June 8, 1981.
†On disabled list, June 10, 1982 through entire season.
‡On disabled list, July 7, 1989 through remainder of season.

KEVIN DANIEL ELSTER

Born August 3, 1964, at San Pedro, Calif.
Height, 6.02. Weight, 195.
Throws and bats righthanded.
Attended Golden West College, Huntington Beach, Calif.

Holds major league records for most consecutive errorless games, shortstop, lifetime (88), July 20, 1988 through May 8, 1989; fewest putouts for leader, shortstop, season (235), 1989.
Holds National League record for most consecutive errorless games, shortstop, season (60), July 20 through October 2, 1988.
Major League stolen bases: 1988 (2), 1989 (4). Total—6.
Led Texas League shortstops in total chances with 589 and double plays with 83 in 1986.
Led New York-Pennsylvania League shortstops in double plays with 45 and total chances with 358 in 1984.

Year Club League	Pos.	G.	AB.	R.	H.	2B.	3B.	HR.	RBI.	B.A.	PO.	A.	E.	F.A.
1984—Little Falls............ NYP	SS	71	257	35	66	7	3	3	35	.257	*128	214	16	*.955
1985—Lynchburg............ Carol.	SS	59	224	41	66	9	0	7	26	.295	82	195	16	.945
1985—Jackson†.............. Texas	SS	59	214	30	55	13	0	2	22	.257	107	220	10	.970
1986—Jackson............... Texas	SS	127	435	69	117	19	3	2	52	.269	*196	*365	28	*.952
1986—New York............ Nat.	SS	19	30	3	5	1	0	0	0	.167	16	35	2	.962
1987—Tidewater............. Int.	SS	134	*549	83	*170	33	7	8	74	.310	219	419	21	.968
1987—New York............ Nat.	SS	5	10	1	4	2	0	0	1	.400	4	6	1	.909
1988—New York............ Nat.	SS	149	406	41	87	11	1	9	37	.214	196	345	14	.977
1989—New York............ Nat.	SS	151	458	52	106	25	2	10	55	.231	*235	374	15	.976
Major League Totals—4 Years..............		324	904	97	202	39	3	19	93	.223	451	760	31	.975

Selected by New York Mets' organization in 2nd round of free-agent draft, January 17, 1984.

†On disabled list, August 11, 1985 through remainder of season.

CHAMPIONSHIP SERIES RECORD

Year Club League	Pos.	G.	AB.	R.	H.	2B.	3B.	HR.	RBI.	B.A.	PO.	A.	E.	F.A.
1986—New York............ Nat.	PR-SS	4	3	0	0	0	0	0	0	.000	2	3	0	1.000
1988—New York............ Nat.	SS-PR	5	8	1	2	1	0	0	1	.250	7	7	2	.875
Championship Series Totals—2 Years.....		9	11	1	2	1	0	0	1	.182	9	10	2	.905

WORLD SERIES RECORD

Year Club League	Pos.	G.	AB.	R.	H.	2B.	3B.	HR.	RBI.	B.A.	PO.	A.	E.	F.A.
1986—New York............ Nat.	SS	1	1	0	0	0	0	0	0	.000	3	3	1	.857

NARCISO ELVIRA

Born October 29, 1967, at Vera Cruz, Mexico.
Height, 5.10. Weight, 160.
Throws and bats lefthanded.

Year Club	League	G.	IP.	W.	L.	Pct.	H.	R.	ER.	SO.	BB.	ERA.
1986—Leon†......................................	Mexican	31	127⅓	8	5	.615	128	81	68	86	84	4.81
1987—Beloit‡....................................	Midwest	4	27	3	0	1.000	15	5	4	29	12	1.33
1987—Leon.......................................	Mexican	33	109⅓	6	8	.429	104	75	64	80	62	5.27
1988—Stockton.................................	California	25	135⅓	7	6	.538	87	49	44	161	79	2.93
1989—El Paso...................................	Texas	7	33	2	2	.500	48	34	28	18	23	7.64
1989—Stockton.................................	California	17	115⅓	8	5	.615	92	45	39	135	43	3.04

†Sold to Milwaukee Brewers' organization, December, 1986.

‡Loaned to Leon of Mexican League.

RALPH DAVID ENGLE
(Dave)

Born November 30, 1956, at San Diego, Calif.
Height, 6.03. Weight, 216.
Throws and bats righthanded.
Attended University of Southern California, Los Angeles, Calif.
Brother-in-law of Tom Brunansky, outfielder with St. Louis Cardinals.

Major League stolen bases: 1983 (2), 1985 (2), 1987 (1). Total—5.

Year Club League	Pos.	G.	AB.	R.	H.	2B.	3B.	HR.	RBI.	B.A.	PO.	A.	E.	F.A.
1978—Salinas†.................. Calif.	3B	53	203	34	62	11	0	6	40	.305	20	65	10	.895
1979—Toledo .... Int.	3B	106	363	46	104	17	1	7	51	.287	72	197	23	.921
1980—Toledo .... Int.	OF	133	489	74	150	27	3	7	73	*.307	225	16	5	.980
1981—Minnesota............ Amer.	OF-3B	82	248	29	64	14	4	5	32	.258	144	4	3	.980
1982—Minnesota............ Amer.	OF	58	186	20	42	7	2	4	16	.226	63	3	1	.985
1982—Toledo .... Int.	OF	9	34	14	15	1	1	5	12	.441	15	4	0	1.000
1983—Minnesota............ Amer.	C-OF	120	374	46	114	22	4	8	43	.305	306	26	9	.974
1984—Minnesota............ Amer.	C	109	391	56	104	20	1	4	38	.266	376	34	8	.981
1985—Minnesota‡.......... Amer.	C-OF	70	172	28	44	8	2	7	25	.256	66	4	1	.986
1986—Detroit§............. Amer.	1B-OF-C	35	86	6	22	7	0	0	4	.256	185	14	0	1.000
1986—Nashville x........... A. A.	OF-C	8	24	5	4	0	0	2	7	.167	17	2	0	1.000
1987—Montreal y............ Nat.	O-C-1-3	59	84	7	19	4	0	1	14	.226	33	3	0	1.000
1988—Montreal z............ Nat.	C-OF-3B	34	37	4	8	3	0	0	1	.216	25	1	0	1.000
1989—Milwaukee a........ Amer.	1B-C	27	65	5	14	3	0	2	8	.215	134	12	4	.973
American League Totals—7 Years		501	1522	190	404	81	13	30	166	.265	1274	97	26	.981
National League Totals—2 Years............		93	121	11	27	7	0	1	15	.223	58	4	0	1.000
Major League Totals—9 Years................		594	1643	201	431	88	13	31	181	.262	1332	101	26	.982

Selected by California Angels' organization in 2nd round of free-agent draft, June 6, 1978.

†Traded with Outfielder Ken Landreaux and Pitchers Paul Hartzell and Brad Havens to Minnesota Twins for First Baseman Rod Carew, February 3, 1979.

‡Traded to Detroit Tigers for Infielder Chris Pittaro and Outfielder Alex Sanchez, January 16, 1986.

§On disabled list, April 29 to August 10, 1986; included rehabilitation disability assignment to Nashville, May 28 to June 6, 1986.

xReleased, August 10, 1986; signed by Montreal Expos' organization, January 19, 1987.

yGranted free agency, November 9, 1987; signed by Indianapolis (Montreal Expos' organization), December 7, 1987.

zReleased, July 14, 1988; signed by Milwaukee Brewers, March 30, 1989.

aReleased, August 2, 1989.

ALL-STAR GAME RECORD

Member of American League All-Star Team in 1984; did not play.

JAMES GERHARD EPPARD
(Jim)

Born April 27, 1960, at South Bend, Ind.
Height, 6.02. Weight, 180.
Throws and bats lefthanded.
Attended Citrus College, Azusa, Calif., and University of California, Berkeley, Calif.

Tied for California League lead in grounding into double plays with 19 in 1985.
Led California League first basemen in total chances with 1,341 in 1985.

Year Club	League	Pos.	G.	AB.	R.	H.	2B.	3B.	HR.	RBI.	B.A.	PO.	A.	E.	F.A.
1982—Medford	N'west	*1B-OF	64	242	58	*91	13	2	1	41	*.376	459	*38	10	.980
1983—Modesto	Calif.	1B	134	488	68	138	18	4	4	45	.283	1086	74	10	*.991
1984—Albany	East.	OF-1B	118	417	58	130	14	6	0	51	.312	551	41	4	.993
1985—Modesto	Calif.	1B	141	531	97	*183	23	4	3	88	*.345	1204	*125	12	.991
1986—Tacoma†‡	P. C.	OF-1B	95	321	39	88	15	1	0	34	.274	204	11	2	.991
1987—Edmonton	P. C.	1B-OF	132	446	68	152	*33	3	3	94	*.341	947	85	11	.989
1987—California	Amer.	OF	8	9	2	3	0	0	0	0	.333	1	0	0	1.000
1988—Edmonton	P. C.	1B	41	141	18	37	6	1	0	16	.262	322	31	4	.989
1988—California	Amer.	OF-1B	56	113	7	32	3	1	0	14	.283	63	4	2	.971
1989—Edmonton	P. C.	1B-OF	90	292	40	80	16	1	2	34	.274	599	52	6	.991
1989—California§	Amer.	1B	12	12	0	3	0	0	0	2	.250	12	0	0	1.000
Major League Totals—3 Years			76	134	9	38	3	1	0	16	.284	76	4	2	.976

Selected by Chicago Cubs' organization in 11th round of free-agent draft, January 8, 1980.
Selected by Oakland A's organization in 13th round of free-agent draft, June 7, 1982.
†On disabled list, April 11 to April 21, 1986.
‡Sold to California Angels' organization, January 12, 1987.
§Released, October 6, 1989.

MICHAEL WILLIAM ERB
(Mike)

Born March 19, 1966, at San Diego, Calif.
Height, 6.04. Weight, 210.
Throws and bats righthanded.
Attended San Diego State University, San Diego, Calif.

Year Club	League	G.	IP.	W.	L.	Pct.	H.	R.	ER.	SO.	BB.	ERA.
1987—Salem	Northwest	12	85	6	3	.667	65	33	23	98	20	2.44
1988—Palm Springs	California	19	108⅓	10	7	.588	102	66	53	86	62	4.40
1989—Quad City	Midwest	25	147⅓	11	4	.733	113	57	44	161	43	2.69

Selected by Milwaukee Brewers' organization in 17th round of free-agent draft, June 4, 1984.
Selected by California Angels' organization in 2nd round of free-agent draft, June 2, 1987.

NICHOLAS ANDREW ESASKY

Name pronounced Ee-SASS-kee.

(Nick)

Born February 24, 1960, at Hialeah, Fla.
Height, 6.03. Weight, 215.
Throws and bats righthanded.

Major League stolen bases: 1983 (6), 1984 (1), 1985 (3), 1988 (7), 1989 (1). Total—18.
Led Eastern League batters in strikeouts with 131 and game-winning RBIs with 14 in 1980.

Year Club	League	Pos.	G.	AB.	R.	H.	2B.	3B.	HR.	RBI.	B.A.	PO.	A.	E.	F.A.
1978—Billings	Pion.	3B	64	213	38	65	10	5	4	48	.305	*62	88	22	.872
1979—Tampa	Fla. St.	3B	124	439	52	118	16	3	10	66	.269	91	234	27	.923
1980—Waterbury	East.	3B	135	425	79	115	18	4	*30	79	.271	98	241	23	.936
1981—Indianapolis	A. A.	3B	121	423	55	112	22	4	17	62	.265	99	220	*37	.896
1982—Indianapolis	A. A.	3B	105	341	59	90	15	3	27	62	.264	77	150	21	*.915
1983—Indianapolis	A. A.	3B	49	158	33	44	5	0	14	37	.278	27	71	14	.875
1983—Cincinnati	Nat.	3B	85	302	41	80	10	5	12	46	.265	53	133	13	.935
1984—Cincinnati	Nat.	3B-1B	113	322	30	62	10	5	10	45	.193	220	137	18	.952
1985—Cincinnati	Nat.	3B-OF-1B	125	413	61	108	21	0	21	66	.262	169	106	8	.972
1986—Cincinnati†	Nat.	1B-OF-3B	102	330	35	76	17	2	12	41	.230	585	33	5	.992
1987—Nashville‡	A. A.	1B	13	52	13	23	6	0	5	18	.442	102	7	0	1.000
1987—Cincinnati	Nat.	1B-3B-OF	100	346	48	94	19	2	22	59	.272	773	41	6	.993
1988—Cincinnati§x	Nat.	1B	122	391	40	95	17	2	15	62	.243	982	52	6	.994
1989—Boston y	Amer.	1B-OF	154	564	79	156	26	5	30	108	.277	1319	107	6	.996
National League Totals—6 Years			647	2104	255	515	94	16	92	319	.245	2782	502	56	.983
American League Totals—1 Year			154	564	79	156	26	5	30	108	.277	1319	107	6	.996
Major League Totals—7 Years			801	2668	334	671	120	21	122	427	.251	4101	609	62	.987

Selected by Cincinnati Reds' organization in 1st round (17th player selected) of free-agent draft, June 6, 1978.
†On disabled list, June 15 to July 17, 1986.
‡On Cincinnati disabled list, March 23 to May 19, 1987; included rehabilitation disability assignment to Nashville, May 5 to May 19, 1987.
§On disabled list, May 11 to June 3, 1988.
xTraded with Pitcher Rob Murphy to Boston Red Sox for First Baseman Todd Benzinger, Pitcher Jeff Sellers and a player to be named later, December 13, 1988; Cincinnati Reds acquired Pitcher Luis Vasquez to complete deal, January 12, 1989.
yGranted free agency, November 13, 1989; signed by Atlanta Braves, November 17, 1989.

ALVARO ALBERTO ESPINOZA (RAMIREZ)

Name pronounced Ess-pin-OH-zuh.

Born February 19, 1962, at Valencia, Carabobo, Venezuela.
Height, 6.00. Weight, 170.
Throws and bats righthanded.

Major League stolen bases: 1989 (3).
Tied for International League lead in sacrifice hits with 16 in 1984.
Led International League shortstops in putouts with 159 in 1986.
Led California League shortstops in total chances with 660 in 1983.
Led Gulf Coast League shortstops in assists with 217, double plays with 33 and total chances with 356 in 1980.

Year Club	League	Pos.	G.	AB.	R.	H.	2B.	3B.	HR.	RBI.	B.A.	PO.	A.	E.	F.A.
1979—Sarasota Astros....	Gulf C.	SS-2B-3B	11	32	3	7	0	0	0	5	.219	18	27	1	.978
1980—Sara. Astros-O.†....	Gulf C.	*SS-3B	59	200	24	43	5	0	0	14	.215	*114	219	*25	.930
1981—						(Out of Organized Baseball)									
1982—Wis. Rapids..........	Midw.	SS-3B-1B	112	379	41	101	9	0	5	29	.266	237	241	33	.935
1983—Visalia	Calif.	SS	130	486	57	155	20	1	4	57	.319	*256	364	40	.939
1984—Toledo‡	Int.	SS	104	344	22	80	12	5	0	30	.233	157	293	19	.959
1984—Minnesota	Amer.	SS	1	0	0	0	0	0	0	0	.000	0	0	0	.000
1985—Toledo§	Int.	SS	82	266	24	61	11	0	1	33	.229	132	245	16	.959
1985—Minnesota	Amer.	SS	32	57	5	15	2	0	0	9	.263	25	69	5	.949
1986—Toledo	Int.	SS-2B	73	253	18	71	8	1	2	27	.281	170	205	12	.969
1986—Minnesota	Amer.	2B-SS	37	42	4	9	1	0	0	1	.214	23	52	4	.949
1987—Portland x	P. C.	SS-3B-1B	91	291	28	80	3	2	4	28	.275	158	236	20	.952
1988—Columbus	Int.	SS-2B-3B	119	435	42	107	10	5	2	30	.246	221	404	19	.970
1988—New York	Amer.	2B-SS	3	3	0	0	0	0	0	0	.000	5	2	0	1.000
1989—New York	Amer.	SS	146	503	51	142	23	1	0	41	.282	237	471	22	.970
Major League Totals—4 Years................			218	605	60	166	26	1	0	51	.274	290	594	31	.966

Signed as free agent by Houston Astros' organization, October 30, 1978.
†Released, September 30, 1980; signed by Wisconsin Rapids (Minnesota Twins' organization), March 18, 1982.
‡On disabled list, June 7 to June 25, 1984.
§On disabled list, June 6 to July 2, 1985.
xGranted free agency, October 15, 1987; signed by Columbus (New York Yankees' organization), November 17, 1987.

CECIL EDWARD ESPY

Born January 20, 1963, at San Diego, Calif.
Height, 6.03. Weight, 195.
Throws right and bats left and righthanded.
Son of Cecil Espy, scout with St. Louis Cardinals since 1979.

Major League stolen bases: 1987 (2), 1988 (33), 1989 (45). Total—80.
Led American League in caught stealing with 20 in 1989.
Led Florida State League in stolen bases with 74 in 1982.
Tied for Texas League lead in caught stealing with 17 in 1985.
Led Texas League shortstops in errors with 50 in 1985.
Led Texas League outfielders in total chances with 365 in 1984.

Year Club	League	Pos.	G.	AB.	R.	H.	2B.	3B.	HR.	RBI.	B.A.	PO.	A.	E.	F.A.
1980—Sarasota W. Sox...	Gulf C.	OF	58	212	33	58	7	3	0	26	.274	138	4	7	.953
1981—Appleton	Midw.	OF	72	273	37	55	2	2	1	19	.201	143	5	5	.967
1981—Sarasota W. Sox†.	Gulf C.	OF	43	142	24	40	3	1	0	16	.282	54	1	4	.932
1982—Vero Beach..........	Fla. St.	OF	131	*523	*100	*166	14	7	1	34	.317	275	9	10	.966
1983—San Antonio..........	Texas	OF	133	*564	88	151	16	11	4	38	.268	258	12	10	.964
1983—Los Angeles	Nat.	OF	20	11	4	3	1	0	0	1	.273	11	0	0	1.000
1984—San Antonio..........	Texas	*O-2-S	*133	*535	99	146	19	8	8	60	.273	*348	16	5	.986
1985—San Antonio‡........	Texas	SS-OF	124	461	64	129	24	3	5	49	.280	183	346	51	.912
1986—Hawaii§	P. C.	OF-2B-SS	106	384	49	101	19	3	4	38	.263	172	8	5	.973
1987—Oklahoma City	A. A.	OF-SS	118	443	76	134	18	6	1	37	.302	195	161	16	.957
1987—Texas.....................	Amer.	OF	14	8	1	0	0	0	0	0	.000	8	1	0	1.000
1988—Texas x	Amer.	O-S-C-1-2	123	347	46	86	17	6	2	39	.248	200	11	7	.968
1989—Texas.....................	Amer.	OF	142	475	65	122	12	7	3	31	.257	281	5	3	.990
National League Totals—1 Year.............			20	11	4	3	1	0	0	1	.273	11	0	0	1.000
American League Totals—3 Years.........			279	830	112	208	29	13	5	70	.251	489	17	10	.981
Major League Totals—4 Years.............			299	841	116	211	30	13	5	71	.251	500	17	10	.981

Selected by Chicago White Sox' organization in 1st round (eighth player selected) of free-agent draft, June 3, 1980.
†Traded with Pitcher Burt Geiger to Los Angeles Dodgers' organization for Outfielder Rudy Law, March 30, 1982.
‡Traded with First Baseman Sid Bream to Pittsburgh Pirates, September 9, 1985, completing deal in which Los Angeles Dodgers acquired Third Baseman Bill Madlock for three players to be named later, R. J. Reynolds as partial completion of deal, September 3, 1985.
§Drafted by Texas Rangers, December 8, 1986.
xOn disabled list, May 3 to May 18, 1988.

RAUL ANTONIO EUSEBIO

Born April 27, 1967, at Boca Chica, Dominican Republic.
Height, 6.02. Weight, 175.
Throws and bats righthanded.

Tied for Southern League lead in double plays by catchers with 8 in 1989.

Year Club	League	Pos.	G.	AB.	R.	H.	2B.	3B.	HR.	RBI.	B.A.	PO.	A.	E.	F.A.
1985—Sarasota Astros....	Gulf C.	C	1	1	0	0	0	0	0	0	.000	4	0	0	1.000

Year Club	League	Pos.	G.	AB.	R.	H.	2B.	3B.	HR.	RBI.	B.A.	PO.	A.	E.	F.A.
1986—															
1987—Sarasota Astros....	Gulf C.				(Played in Dominican Summer League)										
1988—Osceola	Fla. St.	C-1B	42	125	26	26	1	2	1	15	.208	204	24	4	.983
1989—Columbus	South.	C-OF	118	392	45	96	6	3	0	40	.245	611	66	8	.988
1989—Osceola	Fla. St.	C	65	203	20	38	6	1	0	18	.187	355	46	7	.983
		C	52	175	22	50	6	3	0	30	.286	290	40	5	.985

Signed as free agent by Houston Astros' organization, May 30, 1985.

DARRELL WAYNE EVANS

Born May 26, 1947, at Pasadena, Calif.
Height, 6.02. Weight, 205.
Throws right and bats lefthanded.
Attended Pasadena City College, Pasadena, Calif. and
California State University, Los Angeles, Calif.
Grandson of David Salazar, former minor league player.

Holds National League records for most double plays, third baseman, (45), 1974; most consecutive games, one or more bases on balls (15), April 9 through 27, 1976.

Shares modern National League record for most errors in inning by third baseman (3), April 11, 1980, seventh inning.

Major League stolen bases: 1971 (2), 1972 (4), 1973 (6), 1974 (4), 1975 (12), 1976 (9), 1977 (9), 1978 (4), 1979 (6), 1980 (17), 1981 (2), 1982 (5), 1983 (6), 1984 (2), 1986 (3), 1987 (6), 1988 (1). Total—98.

Hit three home runs in a game, June 15, 1983.

Led National League in bases on balls received with 124 in 1973 and 126 in 1974.

Led National League third basemen in putouts with 161 and assists with 381 in 1975.

Led National League third basemen in double plays with 45 in 1974 and 41 in 1975.

Led National League third basemen in total chances with 471 in 1973, 578 in 1974, 578 in 1975, 520 in 1978 and 528 in 1979.

Led International League third basemen in fielding percentage with .951 in 1970.

Named third baseman on THE SPORTING NEWS National League All-Star Team, 1973.

Named Player of the Year in Gulf Coast League, 1967.

Year Club	League	Pos.	G.	AB.	R.	H.	2B.	3B.	HR.	RBI.	B.A.	PO.	A.	E.	F.A.
1967—Peninsula	Carol.	3B	8	28	4	11	1	1	0	6	.393	6	13	2	.905
1967—Bradenton A's	Gulf C.	3B-SS	14	45	13	22	3	3	2	11	.489	25	30	2	.965
1967—Leesburg	Fla. St.	3B-SS	39	142	18	37	4	2	0	12	.261	49	81	11	.922
1968—Birmingham†	South.	3B-1B-2B	56	187	18	45	6	3	3	25	.241	103	101	10	.953
1969—Richmond	Int.	3B	59	211	43	76	12	4	7	45	.360	51	103	19	.890
1969—Shreveport	Texas	3B-SS-OF	24	79	14	22	5	4	2	14	.278	25	40	3	.956
1969—Atlanta	Nat.	3B	12	26	3	6	0	0	0	1	.231	4	7	1	.917
1970—Richmond	Int.	3B-1B-OF	120	447	92	134	20	7	20	83	.300	99	220	16	.952
1970—Atlanta	Nat.	3B	12	44	4	14	1	1	0	9	.318	6	26	2	.941
1971—Richmond	Int.	OF-3B	31	101	20	31	2	2	6	30	.307	59	11	1	.986
1971—Atlanta	Nat.	3B-OF	89	260	42	63	11	1	12	38	.242	77	138	14	.939
1972—Atlanta‡	Nat.	3B	125	418	67	106	12	0	19	71	.254	126	273	25	.941
1973—Atlanta	Nat.	3B-1B	161	595	114	167	25	8	41	104	.281	266	335	24	.962
1974—Atlanta	Nat.	3B	160	571	99	137	21	3	25	79	.240	*185	367	26	.955
1975—Atlanta	Nat.	*3B-1B	156	567	82	138	22	2	22	73	.243	164	382	*36	.938
1976—Atl.§-S.F.	Nat.	1B-3B	136	396	53	81	9	1	11	46	.205	978	110	10	.991
1977—San Francisco	Nat.	OF-1B-3B	144	461	64	117	18	3	17	72	.254	324	83	13	.969
1978—San Francisco x	Nat.	3B	159	547	82	133	24	2	20	78	.243	*147	*348	*25	.952
1979—San Francisco	Nat.	3B	160	562	68	142	23	2	17	70	.253	*129	*369	*30	.943
1980—San Francisco	Nat.	3B-1B	154	556	69	147	23	0	20	78	.264	232	340	27	.955
1981—San Francisco	Nat.	3B-1B	102	357	51	92	13	4	12	48	.258	188	202	14	.965
1982—San Francisco	Nat.	3B-1B-SS	141	465	64	119	20	4	16	61	.256	471	233	21	.971
1983—San Francisco y	Nat.	1B-3B-SS	142	523	94	145	29	3	30	82	.277	1001	164	19	.984
1984—Detroit	Amer.	1B-3B	131	401	60	93	11	1	16	63	.232	331	62	2	.995
1985—Detroit	Amer.	1B-3B	151	505	81	125	17	0	*40	94	.248	831	125	20	.980
1986—Detroit z	Amer.	1B-3B	151	507	78	122	15	0	29	85	.241	809	109	2	.998
1987—Detroit	Amer.	1B-3B	150	499	90	128	20	0	34	99	.257	815	108	4	.996
1988—Detroit a	Amer.	1B	144	437	48	91	9	0	22	64	.208	509	58	4	.993
1989—Atlanta b	Nat.	1B-3B	107	276	31	57	6	1	11	39	.207	371	90	10	.979
National League Totals—16 Years			1960	6624	987	1664	257	35	273	949	.251	4669	3467	297	.965
American League Totals—5 Years			727	2349	357	559	72	1	141	405	.238	3295	462	32	.992
Major League Totals—21 Years			2687	8973	1344	2223	329	36	414	1354	.248	7964	3929	329	.973

Selected by Chicago Cubs' organization in 8th round of free-agent draft, June 22, 1965.
Selected by New York Yankees' organization in secondary phase of free-agent draft, January 29, 1966.
Selected by Detroit Tigers' organization in 5th round of free-agent draft, June 6, 1966.
Selected by Philadelphia Phillies' organization in 3rd round of free-agent draft, January 28, 1967.
Selected by Kansas City A's organization in secondary phase of free-agent draft, June 7, 1967.
†Drafted by Atlanta Braves, December 2, 1968.
‡On military list, June 17 to July 3, 1972.
§Traded with Shortstop Marty Perez to San Francisco Giants for First Baseman-Outfielder Willie Montanez, Shortstop Craig Robinson, Infielder Mike Eden and Outfielder Jake Brown, June 13, 1976.
xGranted free agency, November 2, 1978; re-signed by Giants, December 5, 1978.
yGranted free agency, November 7, 1983; signed by Detroit Tigers, December 17, 1983.
zReleased, December 20, 1986; re-signed by Tigers, February 24, 1987.
aGranted free agency, November 4, 1988; signed by Richmond (Atlanta Braves' organization), December 23, 1988.
bGranted free agency, November 13, 1989.

Year	Club	League	Pos.	G.	AB.	R.	H.	2B.	3B.	HR.	RBI.	B.A.	PO.	A.	E.	F.A.
1984—Detroit	Amer.		1B-3B	3	10	1	3	1	0	0	1	.300	22	4	0	1.000
1987—Detroit	Amer.		1B-3B	5	17	0	5	0	0	0	0	.294	43	4	3	.940
Championship Series Totals—2 Years				8	27	1	8	1	0	0	1	.296	65	8	3	.961

WORLD SERIES RECORD

Year	Club	League	Pos.	G.	AB.	R.	H.	2B.	3B.	HR.	RBI.	B.A.	PO.	A.	E.	F.A.
1984—Detroit	Amer.		1B-3B	5	15	1	1	0	0	0	1	.067	18	5	0	1.000

ALL-STAR GAME RECORD

Year	League	Pos.	AB.	R.	H.	2B.	3B.	HR.	RBI.	B.A.	PO.	A.	E.	F.A.
1973—National		PH	0	0	0	0	0	0	0	.000	0	0	0	.000
1983—National		1B	1	0	0	0	0	0	0	.000	2	1	0	1.000
All-Star Game Totals—2 Years			1	0	0	0	0	0	0	.000	2	1	0	1.000

DWIGHT MICHAEL EVANS

Born November 3, 1951, at Santa Monica, Calif.
Height, 6.03. Weight, 208.
Throws and bats righthanded.

Major League stolen bases: 1973 (5), 1974 (4), 1975 (3), 1976 (6), 1977 (4), 1978 (8), 1979 (6), 1980 (3), 1981 (3), 1982 (3), 1983 (3), 1984 (3), 1985 (7), 1986 (3), 1987 (4), 1988 (5), 1989 (3). Total—73.
Hit for the cycle, June 28, 1984.
Led American League in bases on balls received with 85 in 1981, 114 in 1985 and tied for lead with 106 in 1987.
Led American League in total bases with 215 in 1981.
Led American League outfielders in double plays with 8 in 1975 and 7 in 1980.
Tied for American League lead in errors by first basemen with 12 in 1987.
Led Western Carolinas League in sacrifice flies with 8 in 1970.
Tied for Carolina League lead in double plays by outfielders with 3 in 1971.
Named outfielder on The Sporting News American League All-Star Team, 1982, 1984 and 1987.
Named outfielder on The Sporting News American League All-Star fielding team, 1976, 1978, 1979 and 1981 through 1985.
Named outfielder on The Sporting News American League Silver Slugger team, 1981 and 1987.
Named International League Most Valuable Player, 1972.

Year	Club	League	Pos.	G.	AB.	R.	H.	2B.	3B.	HR.	RBI.	B.A.	PO.	A.	E.	F.A.
1969—Jamestown	NYP		OF-3B	34	100	13	28	3	2	1	12	.280	44	10	3	.947
1970—Greenville	W. Car.		OF-3B	108	355	69	98	14	*11	7	68	.276	130	11	7	.953
1971—Winston-Salem	Carol.		OF-1B	118	402	63	115	20	4	12	63	.286	219	17	10	.959
1972—Louisville	Int.		OF	●144	496	90	149	23	8	17	*95	.300	270	12	6	.979
1972—Boston	Amer.		OF	18	57	2	15	3	1	1	6	.263	25	3	0	1.000
1973—Boston	Amer.		OF	119	282	46	63	13	1	10	32	.223	178	4	1	.995
1974—Boston	Amer.		OF	133	463	60	130	19	8	10	70	.281	294	8	3	.990
1975—Boston	Amer.		OF	128	412	61	113	24	6	13	56	.274	281	15	4	.987
1976—Boston	Amer.		OF	146	501	61	121	34	5	17	62	.242	324	15	2	*.994
1977—Boston†	Amer.		OF	73	230	39	66	9	2	14	36	.287	126	2	1	.992
1978—Boston	Amer.		OF	147	497	75	123	24	2	24	63	.247	305	14	6	.982
1979—Boston	Amer.		OF	152	489	69	134	24	1	21	58	.274	307	15	4	.988
1980—Boston	Amer.		OF	148	463	72	123	37	5	18	60	.266	268	11	5	.982
1981—Boston	Amer.		OF	108	412	84	122	19	4	●22	71	.296	259	9	2	.993
1982—Boston	Amer.		OF	●162	609	122	178	37	7	32	98	.292	346	9	10	.973
1983—Boston‡	Amer.		OF	126	470	74	112	19	4	22	58	.238	222	6	3	.987
1984—Boston	Amer.		OF	●162	630	*121	186	37	8	32	104	.295	311	7	2	.994
1985—Boston	Amer.		OF	159	617	110	162	29	1	29	78	.263	291	9	3	.990
1986—Boston	Amer.		OF	152	529	86	137	33	2	26	97	.250	280	10	5	.983
1987—Boston	Amer.		1B-OF	154	541	109	165	37	2	34	123	.305	753	46	13	.984
1988—Boston	Amer.		OF-1B	149	559	96	164	31	7	21	111	.293	611	34	9	.986
1989—Boston	Amer.		OF	146	520	82	148	27	3	20	100	.285	153	5	3	.981
Major League Totals—18 Years				2382	8281	1369	2262	456	69	366	1283	.273	5334	222	76	.987

Selected by Boston Red Sox' organization in 5th round of free-agent draft, June 5, 1969.
†On disabled list, June 21 to July 8 and August 25 to September 21, 1977.
‡On disabled list, August 13 to September 1, 1983.

CHAMPIONSHIP SERIES RECORD

Year	Club	League	Pos.	G.	AB.	R.	H.	2B.	3B.	HR.	RBI.	B.A.	PO.	A.	E.	F.A.
1975—Boston	Amer.		OF	3	10	1	1	1	0	0	0	.100	7	0	0	1.000
1986—Boston	Amer.		OF	7	28	2	6	1	0	1	4	.214	11	0	0	1.000
1988—Boston	Amer.		OF	4	12	1	2	1	0	0	1	.167	11	0	0	1.000
Championship Series Totals—3 Years				14	50	4	9	3	0	1	5	.180	29	0	0	1.000

WORLD SERIES RECORD

Year	Club	League	Pos.	G.	AB.	R.	H.	2B.	3B.	HR.	RBI.	B.A.	PO.	A.	E.	F.A.
1975—Boston	Amer.		OF	7	24	3	7	1	1	1	5	.292	23	1	0	1.000
1986—Boston	Amer.		OF	7	26	4	8	2	0	2	9	.308	16	1	1	.944
World Series Totals—2 Years				14	50	7	15	3	1	3	14	.300	39	2	1	.976

ALL-STAR GAME RECORD

Year	League	Pos.	AB.	R.	H.	2B.	3B.	HR.	RBI.	B.A.	PO.	A.	E.	F.A.
1978—American		OF	1	0	0	0	0	0	0	.000	3	0	0	1.000
1981—American		PH-OF	2	1	1	0	0	0	0	.500	2	0	0	1.000
1987—American		OF	2	0	2	0	0	0	0	1.000	2	0	0	1.000
All-Star Game Totals—3 Years			5	1	3	0	0	0	0	.600	7	0	0	1.000

HOWARD EARL FARMER

Born January 18, 1966, at Gary, Ind.
Height, 6.03. Weight, 185.
Throws and bats righthanded.
Attended Utica Junior College, Utica, Miss., and
Jackson State University, Jackson, Miss.

Tied for Southern League lead in shutouts with 2 in 1989.

Year Club	League	G.	IP.	W.	L.	Pct.	H.	R.	ER.	SO.	BB.	ERA.
1987—Jamestown	NYP	15	96⅓	9	6	.600	93	42	35	63	30	3.27
1988—Rockford	Midwest	27	193⅔	15	7	.682	153	70	54	145	58	2.51
1989—Jacksonville	Southern	26	184	12	9	.571	122	59	45	151	50	2.20
1989—Indianapolis	Am. Assoc.	1	7	1	0	1.000	3	1	0	3	3	0.00

Selected by Toronto Blue Jays' organization in 1st round (25th player selection) of free-agent draft, January 9, 1985.
Selected by Montreal Expos' organization in 7th round of free-agent draft, June 2, 1987.

STEVEN MICHAEL FARR
(Steve)

Born December 12, 1956, at Cheverly, Md.
Height, 5.11. Weight, 200.
Throws and bats righthanded.
Attended American University, Washington, D. C.,
and Charles County Community College, La Plata, Md.

Major League saves: 1984 (1), 1985 (1), 1986 (8), 1987 (1), 1988 (20), 1989 (18). Total—49.

Year Club	League	G.	IP.	W.	L.	Pct.	H.	R.	ER.	SO.	BB.	ERA.
1977—Niagara Falls	NYP	10	52	1	5	.167	53	30	23	43	30	3.98
1978—Charleston	W. Carol.	21	77	5	3	.625	72	45	36	54	63	4.21
1978—Salem	Ap'lachian	2	16	2	0	1.000	13	2	1	12	1	0.56
1979—Salem†	Carolina	26	119	3	10	.231	138	81	66	105	47	4.99
1980—Buffalo	Eastern	23	161	11	6	.647	158	84	71	71	64	3.97
1980—Portland	P. Coast	2	7	0	1	.000	11	9	8	0	2	10.29
1981—Buffalo	Eastern	29	106	8	3	.727	102	50	44	82	48	3.74
1981—Portland	P. Coast	4	23	0	3	.000	39	28	20	19	12	7.83
1982—Buffalo‡§	Eastern	25	76⅓	5	8	.385	72	40	34	84	38	4.01
1983—Buffalo	Eastern	18	112	13	1	*.929	88	28	20	108	50	*1.61
1984—Maine	Int'national	6	45	4	0	1.000	37	14	13	40	8	2.60
1984—Cleveland xy	American	31	116	3	11	.214	106	61	59	83	46	4.58
1985—Omaha	Am. Assoc.	17	133⅔	10	4	.714	105	36	30	98	41	*2.02
1985—Kansas City	American	16	37⅔	2	1	.667	34	15	13	36	20	3.11
1986—Kansas City	American	56	109⅓	8	4	.667	90	39	38	83	39	3.13
1987—Kansas City	American	47	91	4	3	.571	97	47	42	88	44	4.15
1987—Omaha	Am. Assoc.	8	12⅔	0	0	.000	6	3	2	15	6	1.42
1988—Kansas City	American	62	82⅔	5	4	.556	74	25	23	72	30	2.50
1989—Kansas City z	American	51	63⅓	2	5	.286	75	35	29	56	22	4.12
Major League Totals—6 Years		263	500	24	28	.462	476	222	204	418	201	3.67

Signed as a free agent by Pittsburgh Pirates' organization, December 13, 1976.
†On disabled list, June 6 to June 22, 1979.
‡On Lynn suspended list, April 16, 1983; then transferred to restricted list, April 27 to June 8, 1983.
§Traded to Buffalo (Cleveland Indians' organization) for Catcher John Malkin, June 8, 1983.
xOn disabled list, June 20 to July 5, 1984.
yReleased, March 31, 1985; signed by Kansas City Royals' organization, May 9, 1985.
zOn disabled list, August 21 to September 13, 1989.

CHAMPIONSHIP SERIES RECORD

Year Club	League	G.	IP.	W.	L.	Pct.	H.	R.	ER.	SO.	BB.	ERA.
1985—Kansas City	American	2	6⅓	1	0	1.000	4	1	1	3	1	1.42

WORLD SERIES RECORD

Eligible for 1985 World Series with Kansas City Royals; did not play.

JOHN EDWARD FARRELL

Born August 4, 1962, at Monmouth Park, N. J.
Height, 6.04. Weight, 210.
Throws and bats righthanded.
Attended Oklahoma State University, Stillwater, Okla.

Led American Association in home runs allowed with 26 in 1987.
Tied for Eastern League lead in shutouts with 3 and hit batsmen with 10 in 1986.

Year Club	League	G.	IP.	W.	L.	Pct.	H.	R.	ER.	SO.	BB.	ERA.
1984—Waterloo	Midwest	9	43⅓	0	5	.000	59	34	31	29	33	6.44
1984—Maine	Int'national	5	26⅓	2	1	.667	20	11	11	12	20	3.76
1985—Waterbury	Eastern	25	149	7	13	.350	161	*106	86	75	76	5.19
1986—Waterbury	Eastern	26	173⅓	9	10	.474	158	82	59	104	54	3.06
1987—Buffalo	Am. Assoc.	25	156	6	12	.333	155	109	101	91	64	5.83
1987—Cleveland	American	10	69	5	1	.833	68	29	26	28	22	3.39
1988—Cleveland†	American	31	210⅓	14	10	.583	216	106	99	92	67	4.24
1989—Cleveland‡	American	31	208	9	14	.391	196	97	84	132	71	3.63
Major League Totals—3 Years		72	487⅓	28	25	.528	480	232	209	252	160	3.86

Selected by Oakland A's organization in 9th round of free-agent draft, June 3, 1980.
Selected by Cleveland Indians' organization in 16th round of free-agent draft, June 6, 1983.
Selected by Cleveland Indians' organization in 2nd round of free-agent draft, June 4, 1984.
†On disabled list, August 28 to September 20, 1988.
‡On disabled list, March 19 to April 16, 1989.

MICHAEL OTIS FELDER
(Mike)

Born November 18, 1962, at Richmond, Calif.
Height, 5.08. Weight, 160.
Throws right and bats left and righthanded.
Attended Contra Costa College, San Pablo, Calif.

Major League stolen bases: 1985 (4), 1986 (16), 1987 (34), 1988 (8), 1989 (26). Total—88.
Led Pacific Coast League in stolen bases with 61 in 1985.
Led Texas League in sacrifice flies with 9 in 1984.
Led Texas League in stolen bases with 71 in 1983 and 58 in 1984.
Led California League in stolen bases with 92 in 1982.
Led Texas League outfielders in putouts with 332, total chances with 363 and tied for lead in assists with 18 in 1983.

Year Club	League	Pos.	G.	AB.	R.	H.	2B.	3B.	HR.	RBI.	B.A.	PO.	A.	E.	F.A.
1981—Stockton	Calif.	2B-OF	91	338	66	91	8	1	3	30	.269	172	162	13	.963
1982—Stockton	Calif.	OF	137	524	102	138	18	11	7	47	.263	314	9	10	.970
1983—El Paso	Texas	●OF-2B	133	554	108	156	23	10	9	78	.282	334	24	●13	.965
1984—El Paso†	Texas	OF	122	496	98	144	19	2	9	72	.290	321	13	6	.982
1985—Vancouver	P. C.	OF-2B	137	563	91	177	16	11	2	43	.314	294	15	4	.987
1985—Milwaukee	Amer.	OF	15	56	8	11	1	0	0	0	.196	32	1	0	1.000
1986—Milwaukee‡	Amer.	OF	44	155	24	37	2	4	1	13	.239	98	0	0	1.000
1986—El Paso	Texas	OF	8	31	10	14	3	0	0	2	.452	14	0	0	1.000
1986—Vancouver	P. C.	OF	39	153	21	40	3	4	1	15	.261	83	4	4	.956
1987—Milwaukee	Amer.	OF-2B	108	289	48	77	5	7	2	31	.266	190	10	5	.976
1987—Denver	A. A.	OF-2B	27	113	26	41	6	2	2	20	.363	75	3	1	.987
1988—Milwaukee§	Amer.	OF-2B	50	81	14	14	1	0	0	5	.173	40	1	1	.976
1988—Denver	A. A.	OF	20	78	10	21	4	1	0	5	.269	55	1	1	.982
1989—Milwaukee	Amer.	OF-2B	117	315	50	76	11	3	3	23	.241	203	24	4	.983
Major League Totals—5 Years			334	896	144	215	20	14	6	72	.240	563	36	10	.984

Selected by Milwaukee Brewers' organization in 3rd round of free-agent draft, January 13, 1981.
†On disabled list, April 15 to April 26, 1984.
‡On disabled list, May 3 to June 5, 1986; included rehabilitation disability assignment to El Paso, May 23 to June 5, 1986.
§On disabled list, May 31 to August 2, 1988; included rehabilitation disability assignment to Denver, June 24 to July 1 and July 15 to July 28, 1988.

JUNIOR FRANCISCO FELIX (SANCHEZ)

Born October 3, 1967, at Laguna Sabada, Dominican Republic.
Height, 5.11. Weight, 170.
Throws right and bats left and righthanded.

Shares major league record by hitting home run in first major league at-bat, May 4, 1989.
Major League stolen bases: 1989 (18).
Led South Atlantic League in caught stealing with 28 in 1987.
Led Pioneer League batters in strikeouts with 84, stolen bases with 37, caught stealing with 9 and tied for lead in being hit by pitch with 6 in 1986.
Led Pioneer League outfielders in total chances with 165 in 1986.

Year Club	League	Pos.	G.	AB.	R.	H.	2B.	3B.	HR.	RBI.	B.A.	PO.	A.	E.	F.A.
1986—Medicine Hat	Pion.	OF	67	263	57	75	9	3	4	28	.285	★152	8	5	.970
1987—Myrtle Beach	S. Atl.	OF	124	466	70	135	15	●9	12	51	.290	188	8	9	.956
1988—Knoxville†	South.	OF	93	360	52	91	16	5	3	25	.253	190	13	11	.949
1989—Syracuse	Int.	OF	21	87	17	24	4	2	1	10	.276	42	0	1	.977
1989—Toronto	Amer.	OF	110	415	62	107	14	8	9	46	.258	243	9	9	.966
Major League Totals—1 Year			110	415	62	107	14	8	9	46	.258	243	9	9	.966

Signed as free agent by Toronto Blue Jays' organization, September 15, 1985.
†On suspended list, July 15, 1988 through remainder of season.

CHAMPIONSHIP SERIES RECORD

Year Club	League	Pos.	G.	AB.	R.	H.	2B.	3B.	HR.	RBI.	B.A.	PO.	A.	E.	F.A.
1989—Toronto	Amer.	OF	3	11	0	3	1	0	0	3	.273	8	0	0	1.000

FELIX JOSE FERMIN

Born October 9, 1963, at Mao, Valverde, D. R.
Height, 5.11 Weight, 170.
Throws and bats righthanded.

Shares major league record for most sacrifice hits, game (4), August 22, 1989 (10 innings).
Holds American League records for fewest long hits (10) and runs batted in (21), season, 150 or more games.
Major League stolen bases: 1988 (3), 1989 (6). Total—9.
Led American League in sacrifice hits with 32 in 1989.
Led Eastern League shortstops in fielding percentage with .968 in 1987.
Led Eastern League shortstops in total chances with 661 in 1985.
Tied for New York-Pennsylvania League lead in double plays by shortstops with 38 in 1983.

Year Club	League	Pos.	G.	AB.	R.	H.	2B.	3B.	HR.	RBI.	B.A.	PO.	A.	E.	F.A.
1983—Watertown	NYP	SS	67	234	27	46	6	1	0	14	.197	94	223	30	.914
1983—Bradenton Pir.	Gulf C.	SS	1	4	1	1	0	0	0	1	.250	1	4	0	1.000
1984—Prince William	Carol.	SS	119	382	34	94	13	1	0	41	.246	181	376	23	★.960
1985—Nashua	East.	★SS-2B	137	443	32	100	10	2	0	27	.226	★251	387	24	★.964
1986—Hawaii	P.C.	SS-2B	39	125	13	32	5	0	0	9	.256	60	99	7	.958
1986—Prince William	Carol.	SS	84	322	58	90	10	1	0	26	.280	158	205	19	.950
1987—Harrisburg	East.	SS-2B	100	399	62	107	9	5	0	35	.268	177	288	15	.969
1987—Pittsburgh†	Nat.	SS	23	68	6	17	0	0	0	4	.250	36	62	2	.980
1988—Buffalo	A. A.	SS	87	352	38	92	11	1	0	31	.261	131	268	10	.976
1988—Pittsburgh‡	Nat.	SS	43	87	9	24	0	2	0	2	.276	51	76	6	.955
1989—Cleveland	Amer.	SS-2B	156	484	50	115	9	1	0	21	.238	253	517	★26	.967
National League Totals—2 Years			66	155	15	41	0	2	0	6	.265	87	138	8	.966
American League Totals—1 Year			156	484	50	115	9	1	0	21	.238	253	517	26	.967
Major League Totals—3 Years			222	639	65	156	9	3	0	27	.244	340	655	34	.967

Signed as free agent by Pittsburgh Pirates' organization, June 11, 1983.
†On disabled list, July 19 to August 24, 1987; included rehabilitation disability assignment to Harrisburg, August 12 to August 24, 1987.
‡Traded to Cleveland Indians for Shortstop Jay Bell, March 25, 1989.

CHARLES SIDNEY FERNANDEZ
(Sid)

Born October 12, 1962, at Honolulu, Haw.
Height, 6.01. Weight, 230.
Throws and bats lefthanded.

Pitched 1-0 no-hit victory against Fort Lauderdale, June 8, 1982.
Pitched 5-0 no-hit victory against Winter Haven, April 24, 1982.
Major League saves: 1986 (1).
Named Texas League Pitcher of the Year, 1983.

Year Club	League	G.	IP.	W.	L.	Pct.	H.	R.	ER.	SO.	BB.	ERA.
1981—Lethbridge	Pioneer	11	76	5	1	.833	43	21	13	★128	31	★1.54
1982—Vero Beach	Florida St.	12	84⅔	8	1	.889	38	19	18	★137	38	1.91
1982—Albuquerque	P. Coast	13	88	6	5	.545	76	54	53	86	52	5.42
1983—San Antonio	Texas	24	153	●13	4	.765	111	61	48	★209	96	2.82
1983—Los Angeles†	National	2	6	0	1	.000	7	4	4	9	7	6.00
1984—Tidewater	Int'national	17	105⅔	6	5	.545	69	39	30	123	63	2.56
1984—New York	National	15	90	6	6	.500	74	40	35	62	34	3.50
1985—Tidewater	Int'national	5	35⅓	4	1	.800	17	8	8	42	21	2.04
1985—New York	National	26	170⅓	9	9	.500	108	56	53	180	80	2.80
1986—New York	National	32	204⅓	16	6	.727	161	82	80	200	91	3.52
1987—New York‡	National	28	156	12	8	.600	130	75	66	134	67	3.81
1988—New York	National	31	187	12	10	.545	127	69	63	189	70	3.03
1989—New York	National	35	219⅓	14	5	★.737	157	73	69	198	75	2.83
Major League Totals—7 Years		169	1033	69	45	.605	764	399	370	972	424	3.22

Selected by Los Angeles Dodgers' organization in 3rd round of free-agent draft, June 8, 1981.
†Traded with Infielder Ross Jones to New York Mets for Pitcher Carlos Diaz and a player to be named later, December 8, 1983; Los Angeles Dodgers acquired Infielder Bob Bailor to complete deal, December 12, 1983.
‡On disabled list, August 4 to August 22, 1987.

CHAMPIONSHIP SERIES RECORD

Year Club	League	G.	IP.	W.	L.	Pct.	H.	R.	ER.	SO.	BB.	ERA.
1986—New York	National	1	6	0	1	.000	3	3	3	5	1	4.50
1988—New York	National	1	4	0	1	.000	7	6	6	5	1	13.50
Championship Series Totals—2 Years		2	10	0	2	.000	10	9	9	10	2	8.10

WORLD SERIES RECORD

Year Club	League	G.	IP.	W.	L.	Pct.	H.	R.	ER.	SO.	BB.	ERA.
1986—New York	National	3	6⅔	0	0	.000	6	1	1	10	1	1.35

ALL-STAR GAME RECORD

Year League	IP.	W.	L.	Pct.	H.	R.	ER.	SO.	BB.	ERA.
1986—National	1	0	0	.000	0	0	0	3	2	0.00
1987—National	1	0	0	.000	0	0	0	1	1	0.00
All-Star Game Totals—2 Years	2	0	0	.000	0	0	0	4	3	0.00

OCTAVIO ANTONIO FERNANDEZ (CASTRO)
(Tony)

Born June 30, 1962, at San Pedro de Macoris, D. R.
Height, 6.02. Weight, 175.
Throws right and bats right and lefthanded.

Holds major league record for highest fielding average, shortstop, season, 100 or more games (.992), 1989.
Holds American League record for most games by shortstop, season (163), 1986.
Shares American League record for most games by switch-hitter, season (163), 1986.
Major League stolen bases: 1984 (5), 1985 (13), 1986 (25), 1987 (32), 1988 (15), 1989 (22). Total—112.
Led American League shortstops in total chances with 791 in 1985.
Led International League shortstops in double plays with 87 in 1983.

Named shortstop on THE SPORTING NEWS American League All-Star Team, 1986.
Named shortstop on THE SPORTING NEWS American League All-Star fielding team, 1986 through 1989.

Year Club	League	Pos.	G.	AB.	R.	H.	2B.	3B.	HR.	RBI.	B.A.	PO.	A.	E.	F.A.
1980—Kinston..................	Carol.	SS	62	187	28	52	6	2	0	12	.278	93	205	28	.914
1981—Kinston..................	Carol.	SS	75	280	57	89	10	6	1	13	.318	121	227	19	.948
1981—Syracuse†..............	Int.	SS	31	115	13	32	6	2	1	9	.278	69	80	3	.980
1982—Syracuse	Int.	SS	134	523	78	158	21	6	4	56	.302	★246	364	23	★.964
1983—Syracuse	Int.	SS	117	437	65	131	18	6	5	38	.300	★211	361	26	.957
1983—Toronto	Amer.	SS	15	34	5	9	1	1	0	2	.265	16	17	0	1.000
1984—Syracuse	Int.	SS	26	94	12	24	1	0	0	6	.255	46	72	5	.959
1984—Toronto	Amer.	SS-3B	88	233	29	63	5	3	3	19	.269	119	195	9	.972
1985—Toronto	Amer.	SS	161	564	71	163	31	10	2	51	.289	283	★478	30	.962
1986—Toronto	Amer.	SS	★163	★687	91	213	33	9	10	65	.310	★294	445	13	★.983
1987—Toronto	Amer.	SS	146	578	90	186	29	8	5	67	.322	★270	396	14	.979
1988—Toronto	Amer.	SS	154	648	76	186	41	4	5	70	.287	247	470	14	.981
1989—Toronto‡	Amer.	SS	140	573	64	147	25	9	11	64	.257	260	475	6	★.992
Major League Totals—7 Years................			867	3317	426	967	165	44	36	338	.292	1489	2476	86	.979

Signed as free agent by Toronto Blue Jays' organization, April 24, 1979.
†On disabled list, August 10 to August 27, 1981.
‡On disabled list, April 8 to May 2, 1989.

CHAMPIONSHIP SERIES RECORD

Year Club	League	Pos.	G.	AB.	R.	H.	2B.	3B.	HR.	RBI.	B.A.	PO.	A.	E.	F.A.
1985—Toronto	Amer.	SS	7	24	2	8	2	0	0	2	.333	11	15	2	.929
1989—Toronto	Amer.	SS	5	20	6	7	3	0	0	1	.350	9	15	0	1.000
Championship Series Totals—2 Years.....			12	44	8	15	5	0	0	3	.341	20	30	2	.962

ALL-STAR GAME RECORD

Year League	Pos.	AB.	R.	H.	2B.	3B.	HR.	RBI.	B.A.	PO.	A.	E.	F.A.
1986—American	SS	0	0	0	0	0	0	0	.000	0	0	0	.000
1987—American	SS	2	0	0	0	0	0	0	.000	1	3	0	1.000
1989—American	PR-SS	1	0	0	0	0	0	0	.000	2	2	0	1.000
All-Star Game Totals—3 Years....................		3	0	0	0	0	0	0	.000	3	5	0	1.000

MICHAEL LEE FETTERS
(Mike)

Born December 19, 1964, at Van Nuys, Calif.
Height, 6.04. Weight, 200.
Throws and bats righthanded.
Attended Pepperdine University, Malibu, Calif.

Tied for Pacific Coast League lead in complete games with 6 in 1989.

Year Club	League	G.	IP.	W.	L.	Pct.	H.	R.	ER.	SO.	BB.	ERA.
1986—Salem...	Northwest	12	72	4	2	.667	60	39	27	72	51	3.38
1987—Palm Springs...................................	California	19	116	9	7	.563	106	62	46	105	73	3.57
1988—Midland...	Texas	20	114	8	8	.500	116	78	75	101	67	5.92
1988—Edmonton.......................................	P. Coast	2	14	2	0	1.000	8	3	3	11	10	1.93
1989—Edmonton.......................................	P. Coast	26	168	12	8	.600	160	80	71	★144	72	3.80
1989—California..	American	1	3⅓	0	0	.000	5	4	3	4	1	8.10
Major League Totals—1 Year.............................		1	3⅓	0	0	.000	5	4	3	4	1	8.10

Selected by Los Angeles Dodgers' organization in 22nd round of free-agent draft, June 6, 1983.
Selected by California Angels' organization in 1st round (compensation selection) of free-agent draft, June 2, 1986.

BRUCE ALAN FIELDS

Born October 6, 1960, at Cleveland, O.
Height, 6.00. Weight, 185.
Throws right and bats lefthanded.
Attended Lansing Community College, Lansing, Mich.

Major League stolen bases: 1986 (1).

Year Club	League	Pos.	G.	AB.	R.	H.	2B.	3B.	HR.	RBI.	B.A.	PO.	A.	E.	F.A.
1978—Bristol....................	Appal.	OF-3B	46	159	15	32	6	2	0	11	.201	77	4	3	.964
1979—Lakeland...............	Fla. St.	OF	70	220	30	52	4	2	0	17	.236	120	2	3	.976
1979—Bristol....................	Appal.	OF-2B	41	138	23	32	4	1	1	7	.232	81	5	2	.977
1980—Lakeland...............	Fla. St.	OF	53	162	22	37	5	2	1	15	.228	113	1	4	.966
1980—Macon..................	S. Atl.	OF	67	240	40	71	7	1	2	27	.296	118	2	2	.984
1981—Lakeland...............	Fla. St.	OF	103	377	54	112	14	3	1	37	.297	225	11	4	★.983
1982—Birmingham	South.	OF	43	162	26	37	3	2	0	14	.228	102	0	6	.944
1982—Macon†................	S. Atl.	OF	80	312	61	105	13	3	6	38	.337	162	4	3	.982
1983—San Jose	Calif.	OF	123	450	80	123	21	6	2	45	.273	234	6	7	.972
1984—Birmingham	South.	OF	93	307	49	92	11	3	4	38	.300	169	8	4	.978
1985—Birmingham‡	South.	OF	114	421	59	136	24	4	2	41	★.323	228	10	5	.979
1986—Nashville...............	A. A.	OF	116	383	57	141	31	5	1	53	★.368	177	10	4	.979
1986—Detroit..................	Amer.	OF	16	43	4	12	1	1	0	6	.279	25	0	1	.962
1987—Toledo§	Int.	OF	123	446	75	136	32	4	3	51	.305	194	8	5	.976
1988—Seattle.................	Amer.	OF	39	67	8	18	5	0	1	5	.269	23	0	0	1.000
1988—Calgary	P. C.	OF	42	168	31	54	6	1	4	19	.321	73	2	1	.987
1989—Calgary	P. C.	OF	101	407	88	143	36	4	10	48	★.351	201	5	7	.967
1989—Seattle x...............	Amer.	OF	3	3	2	1	1	0	0	0	.333	0	0	0	.000
Major League Totals—3 Years................			58	113	14	31	7	1	1	11	.274	48	0	1	.980

THOMAS CARSON FILER III
(Tom)

Born December 1, 1956, at Philadelphia, Pa.
Height, 6.01. Weight, 198.
Throws and bats righthanded.
Received bachelor of science degree in marketing from
La Salle College, Philadelphia, Pa., in 1978.

Tied for American Association lead in wild pitches with 11 in 1981.

Year Club	League	G.	IP.	W.	L.	Pct.	H.	R.	ER.	SO.	BB.	ERA.
1978—Oneonta	NYP	9	43	2	3	.400	30	14	8	34	14	1.67
1979—West Haven	Eastern	24	154	12	8	.600	132	73	62	80	53	3.62
1980—Nashville†	Southern	27	187	13	9	.591	168	94	61	112	86	2.94
1981—Columbus‡	Int'national	1	3	0	1	.000	6	5	5	3	4	15.00
1981—Iowa	Am. Assoc.	21	109	4	9	.308	123	64	58	61	57	4.79
1982—Iowa	Am. Assoc.	17	92⅓	6	7	.462	109	74	69	51	31	6.73
1982—Chicago	National	8	40⅔	1	2	.333	50	25	25	15	18	5.53
1983—Iowa	Am. Assoc.	27	108	5	6	.455	128	56	50	56	44	4.17
1984—Iowa §x	Am. Assoc.	26	123⅓	9	7	.563	149	86	67	80	48	4.89
1985—Syracuse y	Int'national	12	78⅓	7	2	.778	67	24	22	31	22	2.53
1985—Toronto z	American	11	48⅔	7	0	1.000	38	21	21	24	18	3.88
1986—Toronto a	American					(Did not play)						
1987—Syracuse	Int'national	8	24⅔	1	0	1.000	23	6	4	9	6	1.46
1987—Knoxville	Southern	6	20⅔	2	0	1.000	13	2	2	14	4	0.87
1987—Dunedin b	Florida St.	6	23	0	0	.000	20	5	2	13	0	0.78
1988—Denver	Am. Assoc.	8	55⅔	4	2	.667	40	14	13	34	9	2.10
1988—Milwaukee	American	19	101⅔	5	8	.385	108	54	50	39	33	4.43
1989—Denver c	Am. Assoc.	12	83⅔	5	1	.833	77	28	26	34	14	2.80
1989—Milwaukee	American	13	72⅓	7	3	.700	74	30	29	20	23	3.61
National League Totals—1 Year		8	40⅔	1	2	.333	50	25	25	15	18	5.53
American League Totals—3 Years		43	222⅔	19	11	.633	220	105	100	83	74	4.04
Major League Totals—4 Years		51	263⅓	20	13	.606	270	130	125	98	92	4.27

CHARLES EDWARD FINLEY
(Chuck)

Born November 26, 1962 at Monroe, La.
Height, 6.06. Weight, 215.
Throws and bats lefthanded.
Attended Northeast Louisiana State University, Monroe, La.

Named lefthanded pitcher on THE SPORTING NEWS American League All-Star Team, 1989.

Year Club	League	G.	IP.	W.	L.	Pct.	H.	R.	ER.	SO.	BB.	ERA.
1985—Salem	Northwest	18	29	3	1	.750	34	21	15	32	10	4.66
1986—Quad Cities	Midwest	10	12	1	0	1.000	4	0	0	16	3	0.00
1986—California	American	25	46⅓	3	1	.750	40	17	17	37	23	3.30
1987—California	American	35	90⅔	2	7	.222	102	54	47	63	43	4.67
1988—California	American	31	194⅓	9	15	.375	191	95	90	111	82	4.17
1989—California†	American	29	199⅔	16	9	.640	171	64	57	156	82	2.57
Major League Totals—4 Years		120	531	30	32	.484	504	230	211	367	230	3.58

CHAMPIONSHIP SERIES RECORD

Year Club	League	G.	IP.	W.	L.	Pct.	H.	R.	ER.	SO.	BB.	ERA.
1986—California	American	3	2	0	0	.000	1	0	0	1	0	0.00

ALL-STAR GAME RECORD

Member of American League All-Star Team in 1989; did not play.

STEVEN ALLEN FINLEY
(Steve)

Born May 12, 1965, at Union City, Tenn.
Height, 6.02. Weight, 175.
Throws and bats lefthanded.
Attended Southern Illinois University, Carbondale, Ill.

Major League stolen bases: 1989 (17).
Led International League outfielders in total chances with 315 in 1988.

Year	Club	League	Pos.	G.	AB.	R.	H.	2B.	3B.	HR.	RBI.	B.A.	PO.	A.	E.	F.A.
1987—Newark		NYP	OF	54	222	40	65	13	2	3	33	.293	122	7	4	.970
1987—Hagerstown		Carol.	OF	15	65	9	22	3	2	1	5	.338	32	3	0	1.000
1988—Hagerstown		Carol.	OF	8	28	2	6	2	0	0	3	.214	17	0	0	1.000
1988—Charlotte		South.	OF	10	40	7	12	4	2	1	6	.300	14	0	0	1.000
1988—Rochester		Int.	OF	120	456	61	★143	19	7	5	54	★.314	★289	14	★12	.962
1989—Baltimore†		Amer.	OF	81	217	35	54	5	2	2	25	.249	144	1	2	.986
1989—Rochester		Int.	OF	7	25	2	4	0	0	0	2	.160	17	2	0	1.000
1989—Hagerstown		East.	OF	11	48	11	20	3	1	0	7	.417	35	2	3	.925
Major League Totals—1 Year				81	217	35	54	5	2	2	25	.249	144	1	2	.986

Selected by Atlanta Braves' organization in 11th round of free-agent draft, June 2, 1986.
Selected by Baltimore Orioles' organization in 13th round of free-agent draft, June 2, 1987.
†On disabled list, April 4 to April 22 and July 29 to September 1, 1989; included rehabilitation disability assignment to Hagerstown, August 21 to August 23, 1989.

JEFFREY THOMAS FISCHER
(Jeff)

Born August 17, 1963, at West Palm Beach, Fla.
Height, 6.03. Weight, 187.
Throws and bats righthanded.
Attended University of Florida, Gainesville, Fla.

Year	Club	League	G.	IP.	W.	L.	Pct.	H.	R.	ER.	SO.	BB.	ERA.
1985—West Palm Beach		Florida St.	13	84⅔	6	5	.545	92	40	33	40	18	3.51
1986—West Palm Beach		Florida St.	14	93⅔	10	2	●.833	74	24	15	64	20	1.44
1986—Jacksonville		Southern	11	70⅔	5	2	.714	70	35	29	39	16	3.69
1987—Indianapolis		Am. Assoc.	24	145⅔	7	9	.438	179	101	88	76	55	5.44
1987—Montreal		National	4	13⅔	0	1	.000	21	14	13	6	5	8.56
1988—Indianapolis†		Am. Assoc.	28	177⅓	13	8	.619	162	63	53	110	32	2.69
1989—Albuquerque		P. Coast	28	171	12	10	.545	186	78	66	112	35	3.47
1989—Los Angeles		National	2	3⅓	0	0	.000	7	5	5	2	0	13.50
Major League Totals—2 Years			6	17	0	1	.000	28	19	18	8	5	9.53

Selected by Montreal Expos' organization in 7th round of free-agent draft, June 3, 1985.
†Drafted by Los Angeles Dodgers, December 5, 1988.

BRIAN KEVIN FISHER

Born March 18, 1962, at Honolulu, Haw.
Height, 6.04. Weight, 210.
Throws and bats righthanded.
Attended Columbia College, Aurora, Colo.

Major League saves: 1985 (14), 1986 (6), 1988 (1), 1989 (1). Total—22.
Led International League pitchers in games started with 29 in 1984.
Tied for South Atlantic League lead in balks with 4 in 1981.

Year	Club	League	G.	IP.	W.	L.	Pct.	H.	R.	ER.	SO.	BB.	ERA.
1980—Bradenton Braves		Gulf Coast	12	61	5	3	.625	55	34	26	48	★53	3.84
1981—Anderson		S. Atlantic	25	152	6	8	.429	139	96	72	152	94	4.26
1982—Durham†		Carolina	18	104	6	6	.500	72	43	32	129	43	2.77
1983—Savannah		Southern	27	150	8	11	.421	172	101	87	103	56	5.22
1984—Richmond‡		Int'national	29	183	9	11	.450	188	●101	★87	122	●100	4.28
1985—Columbus		Int'national	7	11⅓	0	0	.000	8	4	3	12	7	2.38
1985—New York		American	55	98⅓	4	4	.500	77	32	26	85	29	2.38
1986—New York		American	62	96⅔	9	5	.643	105	61	53	67	37	4.93
1986—Columbus§		Int'national	6	8⅔	0	0	.000	8	4	4	4	3	4.15
1987—Pittsburgh		National	37	185⅓	11	9	.550	185	99	93	117	72	4.52
1988—Pittsburgh x		National	33	146⅓	8	10	.444	157	78	75	66	57	4.61
1989—Buffalo y		Am. Assoc.	5	28	3	0	1.000	30	17	16	15	7	5.14
1989—Pittsburgh z		National	9	17	0	3	.000	25	17	15	8	10	7.94
American League Totals—2 Years			117	195	13	9	.591	182	93	79	152	66	3.65
National League Totals—3 Years			79	348⅔	19	22	.463	367	194	183	191	139	4.72
Major League Totals—5 Years			196	543⅔	32	31	.508	549	287	262	343	205	4.34

Selected by Atlanta Braves' organization in 2nd round of free-agent draft, June 3, 1980.
†On disabled list, May 18 to July 1, 1982.
‡Traded to New York Yankees for Catcher Rick Cerone, December 5, 1984.
§Traded with Pitchers Doug Drabek and Logan Easley to Pittsburgh Pirates for Pitchers Rick Rhoden, Cecilio Guante and Pat Clements, November 26, 1986.
xOn disabled list, April 30 to May 15, 1988.
yOn Pittsburgh disabled list, March 30 to April 16, June 12 to July 13 and July 25 to September 20, 1989; included rehabilitation disability assignment to Buffalo, June 16 to July 4, 1989.
zReleased, November 29, 1989.

CARLTON ERNEST FISK

Born December 26, 1947, at Bellows Falls, Vt.
Height, 6.02. Weight, 225.
Throws and bats righthanded.
Attended University of New Hampshire, Durham, N. H.
Brother of Calvin Fisk, former catcher in Baltimore Orioles' organization;
brother-in-law of Rick Miller, outfielder with Boston Red Sox and California Angels, 1971 through 1985;
and cousin of Dave Jennings, punter with New York Giants and New York Jets, 1974 through 1987.

Holds major league records for longest game with no passed balls (25 innings), and most innings played by catcher, game (25), May 8, finished May 9, 1984.

Shares major league records for most at-bats (11) and plate appearances (12), game, May 8, finished May 9, 1984 (25 innings); most home runs, opening game of season (2), April 6, 1973.

Shares modern major league record for most long hits, inning (2), May 15, 1975, eighth inning; and June 30, 1977, eighth inning.

Holds American League records for most home runs (315), games (1,928), chances accepted (10,746), catcher, lifetime; home runs, catcher, season (33), 1985.

Shares American League records for most seasons, catcher (20); fewest passed balls, season, 150 or more games (4), 1977.

Major League stolen bases: 1972 (5), 1973 (7), 1974 (5), 1975 (4), 1976 (12), 1977 (7), 1978 (7), 1979 (3), 1980 (11), 1981 (3), 1982 (17), 1983 (9), 1984 (6), 1985 (17), 1986 (2), 1987 (1), 1989 (1). Total—117.

Hit for the cycle, May 16, 1984.
Led American League in being hit by pitch with 13 in 1980.
Led American League in passed balls with 11 in 1983.
Led American League catchers in double plays with 10 in 1981 and 15 in 1987.
Led American League catches in putouts with 470 in 1981.
Led American League in errors with 10 in 1980.
Led American League catchers in total chances with 933 in 1972, 803 in 1973, 519 in 1981 and 871 in 1985.
Led International League catchers in double plays with 12 in 1971.
Named THE SPORTING NEWS American League Rookie Player of the Year, 1972.
Named American League Rookie of the Year by Baseball Writers' Association of America, 1972.
Named catcher on THE SPORTING NEWS American League All-Star Team, 1972, 1977, 1983 and 1985.
Named catcher on THE SPORTING NEWS American League All-Star fielding team, 1972.
Named catcher on THE SPORTING NEWS American League Silver Slugger team, 1981, 1985 and 1988.

Year Club	League	Pos.	G.	AB.	R.	H.	2B.	3B.	HR.	RBI.	B.A.	PO.	A.	E.	F.A.
1967—Greenville†	W. Car.					(In Military Service)									
1968—Waterloo‡	Midw.	C	62	195	31	66	11	2	12	34	.338	385	42	8	.982
1969—Pittsfield	East.	C	97	309	38	75	18	3	10	41	.243	551	65	★22	.966
1969—Boston	Amer.	C	2	5	0	0	0	0	0	0	.000	2	0	0	1.000
1970—Pawtucket	East.	C-OF-1B	93	284	43	65	18	1	12	44	.229	482	50	7	.987
1971—Louisville	Int.	C-OF-3B	94	308	45	81	10	4	10	43	.263	588	51	13	.980
1971—Boston	Amer.	C	14	48	7	15	2	1	2	6	.313	72	6	2	.975
1972—Boston	Amer.	C	131	457	74	134	28	●9	22	61	.293	★846	★72	●15	.984
1973—Boston	Amer.	C	135	508	65	125	21	0	26	71	.246	★739	50	★14	.983
1974—Boston§	Amer.	C	52	187	36	56	12	1	11	26	.299	267	26	6	.980
1975—Boston x	Amer.	C	79	263	47	87	14	4	10	52	.331	347	30	8	.979
1976—Boston	Amer.	C	134	487	76	124	17	5	17	58	.255	649	73	12	.984
1977—Boston	Amer.	C	152	536	106	169	26	3	26	102	.315	779	69	11	.987
1978—Boston	Amer.	★C-OF	157	571	94	162	39	5	20	88	.284	734	90	★17	.980
1979—Boston y	Amer.	C-OF	91	320	49	87	23	2	10	42	.272	155	8	3	.982
1980—Boston z	Amer.	C-1-O-3	131	478	73	138	25	3	18	62	.289	543	56	11	.982
1981—Chicago	Amer.	C-1-3-O	96	338	44	89	12	0	7	45	.263	479	46	6	.989
1982—Chicago	Amer.	C-1B	135	476	66	127	17	3	14	65	.267	648	63	5	.993
1983—Chicago	Amer.	C	138	488	85	141	26	4	26	86	.289	★709	46	7	.991
1984—Chicago a	Amer.	C	102	359	54	83	20	1	21	43	.231	421	38	6	.987
1985—Chicago b	Amer.	C	153	543	85	129	23	1	37	107	.238	★801	60	10	.989
1986—Chicago	Amer.	C-OF	125	457	42	101	11	0	14	63	.221	455	44	8	.984
1987—Chicago c	Amer.	C-1B-OF	135	454	68	116	22	1	23	71	.256	597	66	7	.990
1988—Chicago d	Amer.	C	76	253	37	70	8	1	19	50	.277	338	36	2	.995
1989—Chicago e	Amer.	C	103	375	47	110	25	2	13	68	.293	419	37	3	★.993
Major League Totals—20 Years			2141	7603	1155	2063	371	46	336	1166	.271	10000	916	153	.993

Selected by Baltimore Orioles' organization in 36th round of free-agent draft, June, 1965.
Selected by Boston Red Sox' organization in 1st round (fourth player selected) of free-agent draft, January, 1967.
†On temporary inactive list, April 17, 1967; transferred to military list, May 18, 1967 through April 9, 1968.
‡On temporary inactive list, August 5 to August 20, 1968.
§On disabled list, March 21 to April 26 and June 28, 1974 through remainder of season.
xOn disabled list, March 24 to June 23, 1975.
yOn disabled list, April 14 to May 21, 1979.
zGranted free agency by arbitrator's ruling, February 12, 1981; signed by Chicago White Sox, March 18, 1981.
aOn disabled list, June 13 to July 5, 1984.
bGranted free agency, November 12, 1985; re-signed by White Sox, January 8, 1986.
cGranted free agency, January 22, 1988; re-signed by White Sox, February 9, 1988.
dOn disabled list, May 11 to July 28, 1988.
eOn disabled list, April 11 to June 1, 1989.

CHAMPIONSHIP SERIES RECORD

Year Club	League	Pos.	G.	AB.	R.	H.	2B.	3B.	HR.	RBI.	B.A.	PO.	A.	E.	F.A.
1975—Boston	Amer.	C	3	12	4	5	1	0	0	2	.417	15	0	0	1.000
1983—Chicago	Amer.	C	4	17	0	3	1	0	0	0	.176	27	3	0	1.000
Championship Series Totals—2 Years			7	29	4	8	2	0	0	2	.276	42	3	0	1.000

Shares World Series record for most at-bats, inning (2), October 15, 1975, fourth inning.

Year Club	League	Pos.	G.	AB.	R.	H.	2B.	3B.	HR.	RBI.	B.A.	PO.	A.	E.	F.A.
1975—Boston .... Amer.		C	7	25	5	6	0	0	2	4	.240	37	3	2	.952

ALL-STAR GAME RECORD

Year League	Pos.	AB.	R.	H.	2B.	3B.	HR.	RBI.	B.A.	PO.	A.	E.	F.A.
1972—American...	C	2	1	1	0	0	0	0	.500	2	0	0	1.000
1973—American...	C	2	0	0	0	0	0	0	.000	3	0	0	1.000
1976—American...	C	1	0	0	0	0	0	0	.000	1	0	0	1.000
1977—American...	C	2	0	0	0	0	0	0	.000	6	1	0	1.000
1978—American...	C	2	0	0	0	0	0	1	.000	4	0	0	1.000
1980—American...	C	2	0	0	0	0	0	0	.000	5	0	0	1.000
1981—American	C	3	1	1	0	0	0	0	.333	4	0	0	1.000
1982—American...	C	2	0	0	0	0	0	0	.000	2	0	0	1.000
1985—American	C	2	0	0	0	0	0	0	.000	2	0	0	1.000
All-Star Game Totals—9 Years....................		18	2	2	0	0	0	1	.111	29	1	0	1.000

Named to American League All-Star Team for 1974 game; replaced due to injury.

MICHAEL ROY FITZGERALD
(Mike)

Born July 13, 1960, at Long Beach, Calif.
Height, 5.11. Weight, 190.
Throws and bats righthanded.
Nephew of Dan Gausepohl, outfielder in San Diego
Padres' organization, 1979 through 1982.

Shares major league record by hitting home run in first major league at-bat, September 13, 1983.
Major League stolen bases: 1984 (1), 1985 (5), 1986 (3), 1987 (3), 1988 (2), 1989 (3). Total—17.
Led Carolina League in sacrifice flies with 11 in 1979.

Year Club	League	Pos.	G.	AB.	R.	H.	2B.	3B.	HR.	RBI.	B.A.	PO.	A.	E.	F.A.
1978—Little Falls.............	NYP	C	48	140	25	36	10	0	5	21	.257	230	37	1	.996
1979—Lynchburg.............	Carol.	C	117	368	55	93	16	4	13	★75	.253	424	60	10	.980
1980—Alex.†-Lynch.........	Carol.	C-1B-OF	105	338	36	71	10	2	10	44	.210	438	45	7	.986
1981—Jackson	Texas	C-1-O-3	66	218	28	68	14	2	4	29	.312	344	52	3	.992
1981—Tidewater.............	Int.	C-OF	24	58	9	9	2	0	1	3	.155	124	9	2	.985
1982—Tidewater.............	Int.	C-1-O-3	94	302	33	74	9	2	4	36	.245	451	34	7	986
1983—Tidewater.............	Int.	C-1-3-O	111	370	64	105	17	1	14	65	.284	588	62	8	.988
1983—New York.............	Nat.	C	8	20	1	2	0	0	1	2	.100	37	8	2	.957
1984—New York‡............	Nat.	C	112	360	20	87	15	1	2	33	.242	715	47	4	★.995
1985—Montreal	Nat.	C	108	295	25	61	7	1	5	34	.207	542	46	8	.987
1986—Indianapolis	A. A.	C	10	32	4	11	3	0	0	4	.344	58	5	1	.984
1986—Montreal§.............	Nat.	C	73	209	20	59	13	1	6	37	.282	415	35	3	.993
1987—Montreal x	Nat.	C-1B-2B	107	287	32	69	11	0	3	36	.240	603	27	12	.981
1988—Montreal...............	Nat.	C-OF	63	155	17	42	6	1	5	23	.271	262	21	6	.979
1988—Indianapolis	A. A.	C	32	96	12	24	6	1	1	13	.250	234	11	2	.992
1989—Montreal...............	Nat.	C-3B-OF	100	290	33	69	18	2	7	42	.238	465	44	8	.985
Major League Totals—7 Years................			571	1616	148	389	70	6	29	207	.241	3039	228	43	.987

Selected by New York Mets' organization in 6th round of free-agent draft, June 6, 1978.
†Loaned to Alexandria (Co-op), April 8, 1980; returned, May 31, 1980.
‡Traded with Infielder Hubie Brooks, Outfielder Herm Winningham and Pitcher Floyd Youmans to Montreal Expos for Catcher Gary Carter, December 10, 1984.
§On disabled list, August 2, 1986 through remainder of season.
xOn disabled list, March 28 to April 20, 1987.

MICHAEL KENDALL FLANAGAN
(Mike)

Born December 16, 1951, at Manchester, N. H.
Height, 6.00. Weight, 195.
Throws and bats lefthanded.
Attended University of Massachusetts, Amherst, Mass.
Son of Ed Flanagan, Jr., minor league pitcher, 1947 through 1952.

Major League saves: 1977 (1).
Tied for American League lead in shutouts with 5 in 1979.
Tied for American League lead in games started by pitchers with 40 in 1978.
Tied for International League lead in shutouts with 4 in 1975.
Tied for Southern League lead in shutouts with 3 in 1974.
Named American League Pitcher of the Year by THE SPORTING NEWS, 1979.
Won American League Cy Young Memorial Award, 1979.
Named lefthanded pitcher on THE SPORTING NEWS American League All-Star Team, 1979.

Year Club	League	G.	IP.	W.	L.	Pct.	H.	R.	ER.	SO.	BB.	ERA.
1973—Miami	Florida St.	11	61	4	1	.800	39	21	15	61	25	2.21
1974—Miami	Florida St.	14	103	6	6	.500	67	32	24	119	48	2.10
1974—Asheville	Southern	11	84	6	4	.600	61	19	17	62	18	1.82
1975—Rochester	Int'national	27	173	13	4	★.765	155	58	48	135	56	2.50
1975—Baltimore	American	2	10	0	1	.000	9	4	3	7	6	2.70
1976—Baltimore	American	20	85	3	5	.375	83	41	39	56	33	4.13

Year Club	League	G.	IP.	W.	L.	Pct.	H.	R.	ER.	SO.	BB.	ERA.
1976—Rochester	Int'national	7	51	6	1	.857	40	16	12	24	14	2.12
1977—Baltimore	American	36	235	15	10	.600	235	100	95	149	70	3.64
1978—Baltimore	American	40	281	19	15	.559	271	128	*126	167	87	4.04
1979—Baltimore	American	39	266	*23	9	.719	245	107	91	190	70	3.08
1980—Baltimore	American	37	251	16	13	.552	*278	121	115	128	71	4.12
1981—Baltimore	American	20	116	9	6	.600	108	55	54	72	37	4.19
1982—Baltimore	American	36	236	15	11	.577	233	110	104	103	76	3.97
1983—Baltimore†	American	20	125⅓	12	4	.750	135	53	46	50	31	3.30
1984—Baltimore	American	34	226⅔	13	13	.500	213	103	89	115	81	3.53
1985—Hagerstown‡	Carolina	1	6	0	0	.000	1	0	0	5	4	0.00
1985—Baltimore	American	15	86	4	5	.444	101	49	49	42	28	5.13
1986—Baltimore§	American	29	172	7	11	.389	179	95	81	96	66	4.24
1987—Baltimore xy-Toronto	American	23	144	6	8	.429	148	72	65	93	51	4.06
1987—Rochester	Int'national	3	12	0	0	.000	12	5	4	10	3	3.00
1988—Toronto z	American	34	211	13	13	.500	220	106	98	99	80	4.18
1989—Toronto	American	30	171⅔	8	10	.444	186	82	75	47	47	3.93
Major League Totals—15 Years		415	2616⅔	163	134	.549	2644	1226	1130	1414	834	3.89

Selected by Houston Astros' organization in 15th round of free-agent draft, June 8, 1971.
Selected by Baltimore Orioles' organization in 7th round of free-agent draft, June 5, 1973.
†On disabled list, May 18 to August 7, 1983.
‡On Baltimore disabled list, March 26 to July 20, 1985; included rehabilitation disability assignment to Hagerstown, July 10 to July 20, 1985.
§On disabled list, May 31 to June 19, 1986.
xOn disabled list, May 18 to July 17, 1987; included rehabilitation disability assignment to Rochester, July 3 to July 17, 1987.
yTraded to Toronto Blue Jays for Pitcher Oswald Peraza and a player to be named later, August 31, 1987; Baltimore Orioles acquired Pitcher Jose Mesa to complete deal, September 4, 1987.
zGranted free agency, November 4, 1988; re-signed by Blue Jays, December 24, 1988.

CHAMPIONSHIP SERIES RECORD

Year Club	League	G.	IP.	W.	L.	Pct.	H.	R.	ER.	SO.	BB.	ERA.
1979—Baltimore	American	1	7	1	0	1.000	6	6	4	2	1	5.14
1983—Baltimore	American	1	5	1	0	1.000	5	1	1	1	0	1.80
1989—Toronto	American	1	4⅓	0	1	.000	7	5	5	3	1	10.38
Championship Series Totals—3 Years		3	16⅓	2	1	.667	18	12	10	6	2	5.51

WORLD SERIES RECORD

Year Club	League	G.	IP.	W.	L.	Pct.	H.	R.	ER.	SO.	BB.	ERA.
1979—Baltimore	American	3	15	1	1	.500	18	7	5	13	2	3.00
1983—Baltimore	American	1	4	0	0	.000	6	2	2	1	1	4.50
World Series Totals—2 Years		4	19	1	1	.500	24	9	7	14	3	3.32

ALL-STAR GAME RECORD
Named to American League All-Star Team for 1978 game; did not play.

TIMOTHY EARL FLANNERY
(Tim)

Born September 29, 1957, at Tulsa, Okla.
Height, 5.11. Weight, 181.
Throws right and bats lefthanded.
Attended Chapman College, Orange, Calif.
Nephew of Hal Smith, catcher with St. Louis Cardinals and Pittsburgh Pirates, 1956 through 1961 and 1965; minor league manager, 1966; coach, Pittsburgh Pirates, 1967; coach, Cincinnati Reds, 1968 and 1969; and scout with St. Louis Cardinals, 1970 through 1975 and since 1978.
Major League stolen bases: 1980 (2), 1981 (1), 1982 (1), 1983 (2), 1984 (4), 1985 (2), 1986 (3), 1987 (2), 1988 (3), 1989 (2). Total—22.

Year Club	League	Pos.	G.	AB.	R.	H.	2B.	3B.	HR.	RBI.	B.A.	PO.	A.	E.	F.A.
1978—Reno	Calif.	2B-P	84	340	65	119	11	5	2	49	.350	213	269	19	.962
1979—Amarillo	Texas	2B-SS	125	524	88	●181	23	6	6	71	.345	287	374	28	.959
1979—San Diego	Nat.	2B	22	65	2	10	0	1	0	4	.154	45	60	1	.991
1980—Hawaii	P. C.	2B	47	182	27	63	10	3	1	16	.346	102	146	5	.980
1980—San Diego	Nat.	2B-3B	95	292	15	70	12	0	0	25	.240	140	204	8	.977
1981—Hawaii	P. C.	2B	21	78	16	22	3	1	0	10	.282	47	62	2	.982
1981—San Diego	Nat.	3B-2B	37	67	4	17	4	1	0	6	.254	16	32	2	.960
1982—San Diego	Nat.	2B-3B-SS	122	379	40	100	11	7	0	30	.264	226	278	14	.973
1983—San Diego	Nat.	3B-2B-SS	92	214	24	50	7	3	3	19	.234	63	156	4	.982
1984—San Diego	Nat.	2B-SS-3B	86	128	24	35	3	3	2	10	.273	36	69	5	.955
1985—San Diego	Nat.	2B-3B	126	384	50	108	14	3	1	40	.281	261	287	13	.977
1986—San Diego	Nat.	2B-3B-SS	134	368	48	103	11	2	3	28	.280	226	275	5	.990
1987—San Diego†	Nat.	2B-3B-SS	106	276	23	63	5	1	0	20	.228	142	226	7	.981
1988—San Diego‡	Nat.	3B-2B-SS	79	170	16	45	5	4	0	19	.265	28	76	3	.972
1988—Riverside	Calif.	DH	4	11	2	3	1	0	0	1	.273	0	0	0	.000
1989—San Diego§x	Nat.	3B-2B	73	130	9	30	5	0	0	8	.231	14	56	6	.921
Major League Totals—11 Years			972	2473	255	631	77	25	9	209	.255	1197	1719	68	.977

Selected by San Diego Padres' organization in 6th round of free-agent draft, June 6, 1978.
†On disabled list, May 6 to May 31, 1987.

‡On disabled list, April 29 to May 23, 1988; included rehabilitation disability assignment to Riverside, May 18 to May 23, 1988.
§On disabled list, June 12 to June 27, 1989.
xOn voluntarily retired list, October 2, 1989.

CHAMPIONSHIP SERIES RECORD

Year	Club	League	Pos.	G.	AB.	R.	H.	2B.	3B.	HR.	RBI.	B.A.	PO.	A.	E.	F.A.
1984—San Diego		Nat.	PH	3	2	2	1	0	0	0	0	.500	0	0	0	.000

WORLD SERIES RECORD

Year	Club	League	Pos.	G.	AB.	R.	H.	2B.	3B.	HR.	RBI.	B.A.	PO.	A.	E.	F.A.
1984—San Diego		Nat.	PH-2B	1	1	0	1	0	0	0	0	1.000	1	0	0	1.000

PITCHING RECORD

Year	Club	League	G.	IP.	W.	L.	Pct.	H.	R.	ER.	SO.	BB.	ERA.
1978—Reno		California	1	⅓	0	1	.000	3	6	5	0	1	135.00

DARRIN GLEN FLETCHER

Born October 3, 1966, at Elmhurst, Ill.
Height, 6.02. Weight, 195.
Throws right and bats lefthanded.
Attended University of Illinois, Champaign, Ill.
Son of Tom Fletcher, pitcher with Detroit Tigers, 1962.

Tied for Texas League lead in double plays by catchers with 9 in 1988.

Year	Club	League	Pos.	G.	AB.	R.	H.	2B.	3B.	HR.	RBI.	B.A.	PO.	A.	E.	F.A.
1987—Vero Beach		Fla. St.	C	43	124	13	33	7	0	0	15	.266	212	35	3	.988
1988—San Antonio		Texas	C	89	279	19	58	8	0	1	20	.208	529	64	5	*.992
1989—Albuquerque		P. C.	C	100	315	34	86	16	1	5	44	.273	632	63	9	.987
1989—Los Angeles		Nat.	C	5	8	1	4	0	0	1	2	.500	16	1	0	1.000
Major League Totals—1 Year				5	8	1	4	0	0	1	2	.500	16	1	0	1.000

Selected by Los Angeles Dodgers' organization in 6th round of free-agent draft, June 2, 1987.

SCOTT BRIAN FLETCHER

Born July 30, 1958, at Fort Walton Beach, Fla.
Height, 5.11. Weight, 173.
Throws and bats righthanded.
Attended University of Toledo, Toledo, O.; Valencia Community College,
Orlando, Fla., and Georgia Southern College, Statesboro, Ga.
Son of Richard W. Fletcher, minor league pitcher, 1952 through 1959.

Major League stolen bases: 1982 (1), 1983 (5), 1984 (10), 1985 (5), 1986 (12), 1987 (13), 1988 (8), 1989 (2). Total—56.
Led American Association in being hit by pitch with 9 and grounding into double plays with 20 in 1981.
Led American Association shortstops in total chances with 607 in 1982.
Led Texas League second basemen in double plays with 112 in 1980.

Year	Club	League	Pos.	G.	AB.	R.	H.	2B.	3B.	HR.	RBI.	B.A.	PO.	A.	E.	F.A.
1979—Geneva		NYP	SS	67	261	59	81	12	3	4	43	.310	99	195	18	*.942
1980—Midland		Texas	*2B-SS	130	501	*111	164	16	*11	6	65	.327	*354	*390	*29	.962
1981—Iowa		A. A.	SS	119	458	66	117	26	4	4	33	.255	*222	337	28	.952
1981—Chicago		Nat.	2B-SS-3B	19	46	6	10	4	0	0	1	.217	34	44	3	.963
1982—Iowa		A. A.	SS	129	502	90	157	26	3	4	60	.313	224	●357	26	.957
1982—Chicago†		Nat.	SS	11	24	4	4	0	0	0	1	.167	11	23	0	1.000
1983—Chicago		Amer.	SS-2B-3B	114	262	42	62	16	5	3	31	.237	126	308	16	.964
1984—Chicago		Amer.	SS-2B-3B	149	456	46	114	13	3	3	35	.250	234	439	19	.973
1985—Chicago‡		Amer.	3B-SS-2B	119	301	38	77	8	1	2	31	.256	123	208	8	.976
1986—Texas		Amer.	SS-3B-2B	147	530	82	159	34	5	3	50	.300	216	388	16	.974
1987—Texas		Amer.	SS	156	588	82	169	28	4	5	63	.287	249	413	23	.966
1988—Texas§		Amer.	SS	140	515	59	142	19	4	0	47	.276	215	414	11	.983
1989—Texas xy-Chicago		Amer.	SS-2B	142	546	77	138	25	2	1	43	.253	241	362	15	.976
National League Totals—2 Years				30	70	10	14	4	0	0	2	.200	45	67	3	.974
American League Totals—7 Years				967	3198	426	861	143	24	17	300	.269	1404	2532	108	.973
Major League Totals—9 Years				997	3268	436	875	147	24	17	302	.268	1449	2599	111	.973

Selected by Los Angeles Dodgers' organization in 33rd round of free-agent draft, June 8, 1976.
Selected by Oakland A's organization in secondary phase of free-agent draft, January 10, 1978.
Selected by Houston Astros' organization in secondary phase of free-agent draft, June 6, 1978.
Selected by Chicago Cubs' organization in secondary phase of free-agent draft, June 5, 1979.
†Traded with Pitchers Dick Tidrow and Randy Martz and Infielder Pat Tabler to Chicago White Sox for Pitchers Steve Trout and Warren Brusstar, January 25, 1983.
‡Traded with Pitcher Ed Correa and a player to be named later to Texas Rangers for Infielder Wayne Tolleson and Pitcher Dave Schmidt, November 25, 1985; Texas acquired Infielder Jose Mota to complete deal, December 12, 1985.
§Granted free agency, November 4, 1988; re-signed by Rangers, November 30, 1988.
xOn disabled list, July 5 to July 20, 1989.
yTraded with Outfielder Sammy Sosa and Pitcher Wilson Alvarez to Chicago White Sox for Outfielder Harold Baines and Infielder Fred Manrique, July 29, 1989.

CHAMPIONSHIP SERIES RECORD

Year	Club	League	Pos.	G.	AB.	R.	H.	2B.	3B.	HR.	RBI.	B.A.	PO.	A.	E.	F.A.
1983—Chicago		Amer.	SS	3	7	0	0	0	0	0	0	.000	3	8	0	1.000

THOMAS MICHAEL FOLEY
(Tom)

Born September 9, 1959, at Columbus, Ga.
Height, 6.01. Weight, 180.
Throws right and bats lefthanded.
Attended Miami-Dade Community College (South), Miami, Fla.

Major League stolen bases: 1983 (1), 1984 (3), 1985 (2), 1986 (10), 1987 (6), 1988 (2), 1989 (2). Total—26.
Led Pioneer League in caught stealing with 10 in 1977.
Led Florida State League shortstops in double plays with 71 in 1979.
Led Western Carolinas League shortstops in double plays with 98 in 1978.

Year Club	League	Pos.	G.	AB.	R.	H.	2B.	3B.	HR.	RBI.	B.A.	PO.	A.	E.	F.A.
1977—Billings	Pion.	3B-SS	59	209	37	53	7	1	2	21	.254	53	109	24	.871
1978—Shelby	W. Car.	SS	124	424	55	98	19	1	2	41	.231	*217	•352	30	*.950
1979—Tampa	Fla. St.	SS	125	414	38	95	12	6	0	37	.229	223	*394	35	.946
1980—Waterbury	East.	2B	131	477	49	119	16	4	4	41	.249	*222	329	31	.947
1981—Indianapolis	A. A.	SS	103	347	47	81	12	2	6	27	.233	175	267	27	.942
1982—Indianapolis	A. A.	SS	129	427	65	115	20	9	8	63	.269	*227	343	27	.955
1983—Cincinnati	Nat.	SS-2B	68	98	7	20	4	1	0	9	.204	54	76	2	.985
1984—Cincinnati	Nat.	SS-2B-3B	106	277	26	70	8	3	5	27	.253	119	228	11	.969
1985—Cinc.† - Phil.	Nat.	SS-2B-3B	89	250	24	60	13	1	3	23	.240	127	202	7	.979
1986—Reading‡	East.	SS-2B	3	11	2	2	2	0	0	0	.182	2	11	0	1.000
1986—Phil.§ - Mon.	Nat.	SS-2B-3B	103	263	26	70	15	3	1	23	.266	117	190	6	.981
1987—Montreal x	Nat.	SS-2B-3B	106	280	35	82	18	3	5	28	.293	134	190	9	.973
1988—Montreal	Nat.	2B-SS-3B	127	377	33	100	21	3	5	43	.265	204	324	15	.972
1989—Montreal y	Nat.	2-3-S-P	122	375	34	86	19	2	7	39	.229	203	317	8	.985
Major League Totals—7 Years			721	1920	185	488	98	16	26	192	.254	958	1527	58	.977

Selected by Cincinnati Reds' organization in 7th round of free-agent draft, June 7, 1977.

†Traded with Catcher Alan Knicely, a player to be named later and cash to Philadelphia Phillies for Catcher Bo Diaz and Pitcher Greg Simpson, August 8, 1985; Philadelphia acquired Pitcher Freddie Toliver to complete deal, August 27, 1985.

‡On Philadelphia disabled list, March 23 to April 29, 1986; included rehabilitation disability assignment to Reading, April 25 to April 29, 1986.

§Traded with Pitcher Lary Sorensen to Montreal Expos for Pitcher Dan Schatzeder and Infielder Skeeter Barnes, July 24, 1986.

xOn disabled list, May 17 to June 2, 1987.

yOn disabled list, July 26 to August 12, 1989.

PITCHING RECORD

Year Club	League	G.	IP.	W.	L.	Pct.	H.	R.	ER.	SO.	BB.	ERA.
1989—Montreal	National	1	⅓	0	0	.000	1	1	1	0	0	27.00

CURTIS GLENN FORD
(Curt)

Born October 11, 1960, at Jackson, Miss.
Height, 5.10. Weight, 158.
Throws right and bats lefthanded.
Attended Jackson State University, Jackson, Miss.

Major League stolen bases: 1985 (1), 1986 (13), 1987 (11), 1988 (6), 1989 (5). Total—36.
Led American Association in stolen bases with 45 and tied for lead in caught stealing with 17 in 1985.
Led Midwest League in total bases with 236 in 1983.
Named Midwest League Most Valuable Player, 1983.

Year Club	League	Pos.	G.	AB.	R.	H.	2B.	3B.	HR.	RBI.	B.A.	PO.	A.	E.	F.A.
1981—Johnson City	Appal.	*2B-1B	63	218	36	65	11	2	5	38	.298	115	149	*18	.936
1982—St. Petersburg	Fla. St.	2B-OF	133	447	59	123	18	8	1	49	.275	292	294	22	.964
1983—Springfield	Midw.	OF-2B	126	465	80	135	27	7	20	*91	.290	181	7	8	.960
1984—Arkansas	Texas	OF-2B-3B	118	442	62	143	23	1	10	78	.324	224	102	8	.976
1984—Louisville	A. A.	OF-2B	13	38	5	10	2	0	0.	1	.263	13	2	0	1.000
1985—Louisville	A. A.	OF-3B	127	475	73	121	20	6	7	45	.255	243	25	8	.971
1985—St. Louis	Nat.	OF	11	12	2	6	2	0	0	3	.500	3	0	1	.750
1986—Louisville	A. A.	OF	53	200	47	59	9	2	4	31	.295	120	2	1	.992
1986—St. Louis	Nat.	OF	85	214	30	53	15	2	2	29	.248	109	7	3	.975
1987—St. Louis†	Nat.	OF	89	228	32	65	9	5	3	26	.285	157	2	3	.981
1988—St. Louis‡	Nat.	OF-1B	91	128	11	25	6	0	1	18	.195	95	6	2	.981
1989—Philadelphia	Nat.	OF-1B-2B	108	142	13	31	5	1	1	13	.218	46	5	0	1.000
Major League Totals—5 Years			384	724	88	180	37	8	7	89	.249	410	20	9	.979

Selected by St. Louis Cardinals' organization in 4th round of free-agent draft, June 8, 1981.

†On disabled list, August 10 to September 18, 1987.

‡Traded with Catcher Steve Lake to Philadelphia for Outfielder Milt Thompson, December 16, 1988.

CHAMPIONSHIP SERIES RECORD

Year Club	League	Pos.	G.	AB.	R.	H.	2B.	3B.	HR.	RBI.	B.A.	PO.	A.	E.	F.A.
1987—St. Louis	Nat.	OF-PH	4	9	2	3	0	0	0	0	.333	6	0	0	1.000

WORLD SERIES RECORD

Year Club	League	Pos.	G.	AB.	R.	H.	2B.	3B.	HR.	RBI.	B.A.	PO.	A.	E.	F.A.
1987—St. Louis	Nat.	OF-PH	5	13	1	4	0	0	0	2	.308	5	0	0	1.000

ROBERT HERBERT FORSCH
(Bob)

Born January 13, 1950, at Sacramento, Calif.
Height, 6.03. Weight, 215.
Throws and bats righthanded.
Attended Sacramento City College, Sacramento, Calif.
Brother of Ken Forsch, pitcher with Houston Astros and California Angels, 1970 through 1984 and 1986.

Shares National League record for most consecutive hits allowed, game (9), August 3, 1989, first inning.
Pitched 3-0 no-hit victory against Montreal Expos, September 26, 1983.
Pitched 5-0 no-hit victory against Philadelphia Phillies, April 16, 1978.
Pitched 5-0 no-hit victory against Denver, May 25, 1973.
Pitched seven-inning, 4-0 no-hit victory against Memphis, May 13, 1972.
Major League saves: 1982 (1), 1985 (2). Total—3.
Led Midwest League in hit batsmen with 11 in 1971.
Tied for Texas League lead in hit batsmen with 10 in 1972.
Named pitcher on THE SPORTING NEWS National League Silver Slugger team, 1980 and 1987.
Received reported $25,000 bonus to sign with St. Louis Cardinals, 1968.

Year Club	League	G.	IP.	W.	L.	Pct.	H.	R.	ER.	SO.	BB.	ERA.
1970—Cedar Rapids	Midwest	1	3	0	0	.000	6	4	4	1	2	12.00
1970—Lewiston	Northwest	7	28	2	3	.400	32	22	13	15	17	4.18
1971—Cedar Rapids	Midwest	23	158	11	7	.611	140	74	55	134	41	3.13
1972—Arkansas	Texas	24	153	8	10	.444	158	85	★74	109	47	4.35
1973—Tulsa	Am. Assoc.	27	166	12	12	.500	169	91	81	124	66	4.36
1974—Tulsa	Am. Assoc.	15	103	8	5	.615	95	49	42	71	33	3.67
1974—St. Louis	National	19	100	7	4	.636	84	38	33	39	34	2.97
1975—St. Louis	National	34	230	15	10	.600	213	89	73	108	70	2.86
1976—St. Louis	National	33	194	8	10	.444	209	112	85	76	71	3.94
1977—St. Louis	National	35	217	20	7	.741	210	97	84	95	69	3.48
1978—St. Louis	National	34	234	11	17	.393	205	110	96	114	97	3.69
1979—St. Louis	National	33	219	11	11	.500	215	102	93	92	52	3.82
1980—St. Louis	National	31	215	11	10	.524	225	102	90	87	33	3.77
1981—St. Louis	National	20	124	10	5	.667	106	47	44	41	29	3.19
1982—St. Louis	National	36	233	15	9	.625	238	95	90	69	54	3.48
1983—St. Louis	National	34	187	10	12	.455	190	104	89	56	54	4.28
1984—St. Louis†	National	16	52⅓	2	5	.286	64	38	35	21	19	6.02
1985—St. Louis	National	34	136	9	6	.600	132	63	59	48	47	3.90
1986—St. Louis‡	National	33	230	14	10	.583	211	91	83	104	68	3.25
1987—St. Louis§	National	33	179	11	7	.611	189	90	86	89	45	4.32
1988—St. Louis x-Houston y	National	36	136⅓	10	8	.556	153	73	65	54	44	4.29
1989—Houston z	National	37	108⅓	4	5	.444	133	68	64	40	46	5.32
Major League Totals—16 Years		498	2795	168	136	.553	2777	1319	1169	1133	832	3.76

Selected by St. Louis Cardinals' organization in 38th round of free-agent draft, June 7, 1968.
†On disabled list, June 1 to September 3, 1984.
‡Granted free agency, November 12, 1986; re-signed by Cardinals, December 19, 1986.
§Released, December 21, 1987; re-signed by Cardinals, January 27, 1988.
xTraded to Houston Astros for Denny Walling, August 31, 1988.
yGranted free agency, November 4, 1988; re-signed by Astros, December 21, 1988.
zGranted free agency, November 13, 1989.

CHAMPIONSHIP SERIES RECORD

Year Club	League	G.	IP.	W.	L.	Pct.	H.	R.	ER.	SO.	BB.	ERA.
1982—St. Louis	National	1	9	1	0	1.000	3	0	0	6	0	0.00
1985—St. Louis	National	1	3⅓	0	0	.000	3	2	2	0	2	5.40
1987—St. Louis	National	3	3	1	1	.500	4	4	4	3	1	12.00
Championship Series Totals—3 Years		5	15⅓	2	1	.667	10	6	6	9	3	3.52

WORLD SERIES RECORD

Year Club	League	G.	IP.	W.	L.	Pct.	H.	R.	ER.	SO.	BB.	ERA.
1982—St. Louis	National	2	12⅔	0	2	.000	18	10	7	4	3	4.97
1985—St. Louis	National	2	3	0	1	.000	6	4	4	3	1	12.00
1987—St. Louis	National	3	6⅓	1	0	1.000	8	7	7	3	5	9.95
World Series Totals—3 Years		7	22	1	3	.250	32	21	18	10	9	7.36

RECORD AS INFIELDER

Year Club	League	Pos.	G.	AB.	R.	H.	2B.	3B.	HR.	RBI.	B.A.	PO.	A.	E.	F.A.
1968—Sarasota Cards	Gulf C.	3B	44	143	17	32	5	0	0	16	.224	29	80	12	★.901
1969—Lewiston	N'west	3B-OF-2B	26	74	11	15	3	0	3	10	.203	12	45	13	.814
1969—Modesto	Calif.	3B-OF	33	119	8	28	2	0	1	7	.235	33	58	6	.938
1970—Modesto	Calif.	3B-OF	20	47	4	7	3	0	1	1	.149	19	20	3	.929
1970—Cedar Rapids	Midw.	3B-1B-P	19	34	2	3	2	0	0	1	.088	9	19	3	.903
1970—Lewiston	N'west	P-S-2-3	18	30	5	4	0	1	0	3	.133	9	13	6	.786

—DID YOU KNOW—

That the Albany (Eastern) Yankees played a tripleheader against the Williamsport Bills on August 8, 1989? The teams completed the final two innings of a suspended game and then played a scheduled doubleheader.

EMILO ANTHONY FOSSAS
(Tony)

Born September 23, 1958, at Havana, Cuba.
Height, 6.00. Weight, 195.
Throws and bats lefthanded.
Attended University of South Florida, Tampa, Fla.

Major League saves: 1989 (1).
Tied for South Atlantic League in games started by pitchers with 27 in 1980.

Year	Club	League	G.	IP.	W.	L.	Pct.	H.	R.	ER.	SO.	BB.	ERA.
1979—Sarasota Rangers	Gulf Coast	10	60	6	3	.667	54	28	20	49	26	3.00
1979—Tulsa	Texas	2	11	1	1	.500	14	10	8	3	4	6.55
1980—Asheville	S. Atlantic	30	★197	8	2	.600	★187	84	69	140	69	3.15
1981—Tulsa†‡§	Texas	38	106	5	6	.455	113	65	49	57	44	4.16
1982—Burlington	Midwest	25	146⅓	8	9	.471	121	63	50	115	33	3.08
1983—Tulsa	Texas	24	133	8	7	.533	123	77	62	103	46	4.20
1983—Oklahoma City	Am. Assoc.	10	35⅓	1	2	.333	55	33	31	23	12	7.90
1984—Tulsa	Texas	4	10	0	1	.000	12	5	5	7	3	4.50
1984—Oklahoma City	Am. Assoc.	29	121	5	9	.357	143	65	58	74	34	4.31
1985—Oklahoma City x	Am. Assoc.	30	110	7	6	.538	121	65	58	49	36	4.75
1986—Edmonton y	P. Coast	7	43⅓	3	3	.500	53	23	22	15	12	4.57
1987—Edmonton z	P. Coast	40	117⅓	6	8	.429	152	76	65	54	29	4.99
1988—Oklahoma City	Am. Assoc.	52	66⅔	3	0	1.000	64	21	21	42	16	2.84
1988—Texas a	American	5	5⅔	0	0	.000	11	3	3	0	2	4.76
1989—Denver	Am. Assoc.	24	35⅓	5	1	.833	27	9	8	35	11	2.04
1989—Milwaukee	American	51	61	2	2	.500	57	27	24	42	22	3.54
Major League Totals—2 Years		56	66⅔	2	2	.500	68	30	27	42	24	3.65

Selected by Minnesota Twins' organization in 9th round of free-agent draft, June 6, 1978.
Selected by Texas Rangers' organization in 12th round of free-agent draft, June 5, 1979.
†Released, February 18, 1982; signed by Midland (Chicago Cubs' organization), March 11, 1982.
‡Loaned to Tabasco of Mexican League, March 15, 1982; returned, April 7, 1982.
§Released, April 7, 1982; signed by Burlington (Texas Rangers' organization), May 3, 1982.
xGranted free agency, October 15, 1985; signed by Edmonton (California Angels' organization), December 13, 1985.
yOn disabled list, June 2, 1986 through remainder of season.
zGranted free agency, October 15, 1987; signed by Oklahoma City (Texas Rangers' organization), December 1, 1987.
aGranted free agency, October 15, 1988; signed by Denver (Milwaukee Brewers' organization), January 21, 1989.

JOHN ANTHONY FRANCO

Born September 17, 1960, at Brooklyn, N.Y.
Height, 5.10. Weight, 185.
Throws and bats lefthanded.
Attended St. John's University, Jamaica, N.Y.

Major League saves: 1984 (4), 1985 (12), 1986 (29), 1987 (32), 1988 (39), 1989 (32). Total—148.
Led National League in saves with 39 in 1988.
Led National League in games finished in relief with 60 in 1987 and 61 in 1988.
Named National League Fireman of the Year by The Sporting News, 1988.

Year	Club	League	G.	IP.	W.	L.	Pct.	H.	R.	ER.	SO.	BB.	ERA.
1981—Vero Beach	Florida St.	13	79	7	4	.636	78	41	31	60	41	3.53
1982—Albuquerque	P. Coast	5	27⅓	1	2	.333	41	22	22	24	15	7.24
1982—San Antonio	Texas	17	105⅓	10	5	.667	137	70	58	76	46	4.96
1983—Albuquerque†	P. Coast	11	15	0	0	.000	10	11	9	8	11	5.40
1983—Indianapolis	Am. Assoc.	23	115	6	10	.375	148	69	62	54	42	4.85
1984—Wichita	Am. Assoc.	6	9⅓	1	0	1.000	8	6	6	11	4	5.79
1984—Cincinnati	National	54	79⅓	6	2	.750	74	28	23	55	36	2.61
1985—Cincinnati	National	67	99	12	3	.800	83	27	24	61	40	2.18
1986—Cincinnati	National	74	101	6	6	.500	90	40	33	84	44	2.94
1987—Cincinnati	National	68	82	8	5	.615	76	26	23	61	27	2.52
1988—Cincinnati	National	70	86	6	6	.500	60	18	15	46	27	1.57
1989—Cincinnati‡	National	60	80⅔	4	8	.333	77	35	28	60	36	3.12
Major League Totals—6 Years		393	528	42	30	.583	460	174	146	367	210	2.49

Selected by Los Angeles Dodgers' organization in 5th round of free-agent draft, June 8, 1981.
†Traded with Pitcher Brett Wise to Cincinnati Reds' organization for Infielder Rafael Landestoy, May 9, 1983.
‡Traded with Outfielder Don Brown to New York Mets for Pitchers Randy Myers and Kip Gross, December 6, 1989.

ALL-STAR GAME RECORD

Year	League	IP.	W.	L.	Pct.	H.	R.	ER.	SO.	BB.	ERA.
1987—National		⅔	0	0	.000	0	0	0	0	0	0.00

Member of National League All-Star Team in 1986; did not play.
Member of National League All-Star Team in 1989; did not play.

JULIO CESAR FRANCO

Name pronounced FRANHK-oh.

Born August 23, 1961, at San Pedro de Macoris, D. R.
Height, 6.00. Weight, 170.
Throws and bats righthanded.

Major League stolen bases: 1983 (32), 1984 (19), 1985 (13), 1986 (10), 1987 (32), 1988 (25), 1989 (21). Total—152.
Led American League in grounding into double plays with 28 in 1986 and 27 in 1989.
Led American League shortstops in errors with 35 in 1985.
Led Northwest League in total bases with 153 in 1979.
Led Carolina League shortstops in double plays with 73 in 1980.
Led Northwest League shortstops in double plays with 45 in 1979.
Named second baseman on THE SPORTING NEWS American League All-Star Team, 1989.
Named second baseman on THE SPORTING NEWS American League Silver Slugger team, 1988 and 1989.
Named Carolina League Most Valuable Player, 1980.

Year	Club	League	Pos.	G.	AB.	R.	H.	2B.	3B.	HR.	RBI.	B.A.	PO.	A.	E.	F.A.
1978—Butte		Pion.	SS	47	141	34	43	5	2	3	28	.305	37	52	25	.781
1979—Central Oregon		N'west	SS	•71	299	57	*98	15	5	•10	45	.328	103	*256	31	.921
1980—Peninsula		Carol.	SS	•140	*555	105	178	25	6	11	*99	.321	179	*412	42	.934
1981—Reading		East.	SS	*139	*532	70	160	17	3	8	74	.301	246	437	30	.958
1982—Oklahoma City		A. A.	*SS-3B	120	463	80	139	19	5	21	66	.300	211	350	*42	.930
1982—Philadelphia†		Nat.	SS-3B	16	29	3	8	1	0	0	3	.276	8	25	0	1.000
1983—Cleveland		Amer.	SS	149	560	68	153	24	8	8	80	.273	247	438	28	.961
1984—Cleveland		Amer.	SS	160	*658	82	188	22	5	3	79	.286	280	481	*36	.955
1985—Cleveland		Amer.	SS-2B	160	636	97	183	33	4	6	90	.288	252	437	36	.950
1986—Cleveland		Amer.	SS-2B	149	599	80	183	30	5	10	74	.306	248	413	19	.972
1987—Cleveland‡		Amer.	SS-2B	128	495	86	158	24	3	8	52	.319	175	313	18	.964
1988—Cleveland§		Amer.	2B	152	613	88	186	23	6	10	54	.303	310	434	14	.982
1989—Texas		Amer.	2B	150	548	80	173	31	5	13	92	.316	256	386	13	.980
National League Totals—1 Year				16	29	3	8	1	0	0	3	.276	8	25	0	1.000
American League Totals—7 Years				1048	4109	581	1224	187	36	58	521	.298	1768	2902	164	.966
Major League Totals—8 Years				1064	4138	584	1232	188	36	58	524	.298	1776	2927	164	.966

Signed as free agent by Philadelphia Phillies' organization, June 23, 1978.
†Traded with Second Baseman Manny Trillo, Outfielder George Vukovich, Pitcher Jay Baller and Catcher Jerry Willard to Cleveland Indians for Outfielder Von Hayes, December 9, 1982.
‡On disabled list, July 13 to August 8, 1987.
§Traded to Texas Rangers for First Baseman Pete O'Brien, Outfielder Oddibe McDowell and Second Baseman Jerry Browne, December 6, 1988.

ALL-STAR GAME RECORD

Year	League	Pos.	AB.	R.	H.	2B.	3B.	HR.	RBI.	B.A.	PO.	A.	E.	F.A.
1989—American		2B	3	0	1	0	0	0	0	.333	1	1	0	1.000

TERRY JON FRANCONA

Born April 22, 1959, at New Brighton, Pa.
Height, 6.01. Weight, 175.
Throws and bats lefthanded.
Attended University of Arizona, Tucson, Ariz.
Son of John (Tito) Francona, outfielder-first baseman with Baltimore, Chicago A.L., Detroit, Cleveland, St. Louis, Philadelphia, Atlanta, Oakland and Milwaukee, 1956 through 1970.

Major League stolen bases: 1981 (1), 1982 (2), 1985 (5), 1987 (2), 1989 (2). Total—12.
Named College Player of the Year by THE SPORTING NEWS.
Named outfielder on THE SPORTING NEWS College Baseball All-America Team, 1980.

Year	Club	League	Pos.	G.	AB.	R.	H.	2B.	3B.	HR.	RBI.	B.A.	PO.	A.	E.	F.A.
1980—Memphis		South.	OF	60	210	20	63	13	2	1	23	.300	59	4	4	.940
1981—Memphis		South.	OF-1B	41	161	20	56	8	1	0	18	.348	102	7	5	.956
1981—Denver		A. A.	OF	93	355	53	125	17	*9	1	58	.352	158	7	3	.982
1981—Montreal		Nat.	OF-1B	34	95	11	26	0	1	1	8	.274	41	5	0	1.000
1982—Montreal†		Nat.	OF-1B	46	131	14	42	3	0	0	9	.321	65	0	3	.956
1983—Montreal		Nat.	OF-1B	120	230	21	59	11	1	3	22	.257	172	10	3	.984
1984—Montreal‡		Nat.	1B-OF	58	214	18	74	19	2	1	18	.346	431	50	3	.994
1985—Montreal§		Nat.	1B-OF-3B	107	281	19	75	15	1	2	31	.267	431	40	6	.987
1986—Chicago		Nat.	OF-1B	86	124	13	31	3	0	2	8	.250	123	7	0	1.000
1986—Iowa x		A. A.	1B-OF	17	60	7	15	3	2	0	8	.250	82	3	1	.988
1987—Cincinnati y		Nat.	1B-OF	102	207	16	47	5	0	3	12	.227	377	45	2	.995
1988—Colorado Springs		P. C.	OF-1B	68	235	29	76	15	5	0	32	.329	115	11	3	.977
1988—Cleveland z		Amer.	1B-OF	62	212	24	66	8	0	1	12	.311	47	5	1	.981
1989—Milwaukee a		Amer.	1B-OF-P	90	233	26	54	10	1	3	23	.232	339	26	4	.989
National League Totals—7 Years				553	1282	112	354	56	5	12	108	.276	1640	157	17	.991
American League Totals—2 Years				152	445	50	120	18	1	4	35	.270	386	31	5	.988
Major League Totals—9 Years				705	1727	162	474	74	6	16	143	.274	2026	188	22	.990

Selected by Chicago Cubs' organization in 2nd round of free-agent draft, June 7, 1977.
Selected by Montreal Expos' organization in 1st round (22nd player selected) of free-agent draft, June 3, 1980.
†On disabled list, June 17 to September 27, 1982.
‡On disabled list, June 15 to September 5, 1984.
§Released, April 1, 1986; signed by Chicago Cubs' organization, May 2, 1986.
xGranted free agency, October 18, 1986; signed by Cincinnati Reds, March 23, 1987.
yGranted free agency, November 12, 1987; signed by Colorado Springs (Cleveland Indians' organization), February 28, 1988.
zGranted free agency, November 4, 1988; signed by Milwaukee Brewers, March 30, 1989.
aGranted free agency, November 13, 1989; re-signed by Brewers, December 12, 1989.

DIVISION SERIES RECORD

Year	Club	League	Pos.	G.	AB.	R.	H.	2B.	3B.	HR.	RBI.	B.A.	PO.	A.	E.	F.A.
1981—Montreal		Nat.	OF	5	12	0	4	0	0	0	0	.333	8	0	0	1.000

Year	Club	League	Pos.	G.	AB.	R.	H.	2B.	3B.	HR.	RBI.	B.A.	PO.	A.	E.	F.A.
1981—Montreal		Nat.	PH-OF	2	1	0	0	0	0	0	0	.000	0	0	0	.000

PITCHING RECORD

Year	Club	League	G.	IP.	W.	L.	Pct.	H.	R.	ER.	SO.	BB.	ERA.
1989—Milwaukee		American	1	1	0	0	.000	0	0	0	1	0	0.00

WILLIAM PATRICK FRASER
(Willie)

Born May 26, 1964, at New York, N.Y.
Height, 6.01. Weight, 208.
Throws and bats righthanded.
Attended Concordia College, Bronxville, N.Y.

Major League saves: 1987 (1), 1989 (2). Total—3.
Led American League in home runs allowed with 33 in 1988.

Year	Club	League	G.	IP.	W.	L.	Pct.	H.	R.	ER.	SO.	BB.	ERA.
1985—Quad Cities		Midwest	13	81⅔	2	6	.250	95	53	49	72	32	5.40
1986—Palm Springs		California	19	124⅓	9	2	.818	115	60	49	99	29	3.55
1986—Edmonton		P. Coast	6	40	4	1	.800	25	15	14	24	8	3.15
1986—California		American	1	4⅓	0	0	.000	6	4	4	2	1	8.31
1987—California		American	36	176⅔	10	10	.500	160	85	77	106	63	3.92
1988—California		American	34	194⅔	12	13	.480	203	129	117	86	80	5.41
1989—California		American	44	91⅔	4	7	.364	80	33	33	46	23	3.24
Major League Totals—4 Years			115	467⅓	26	30	.464	449	251	231	240	167	4.45

Selected by California Angels' organization in 1st round (15th player selected) of free-agent draft, June 3, 1985.

LaVEL MAURICE FREEMAN

Born February 18, 1963, at Oakland, Calif.
Height, 5.09. Weight, 170.
Throws and bats lefthanded.
Attended Sacramento City College, Sacramento, Calif.

Led Texas League in total bases with 330 and slugging percentage with .627 in 1987.
Led Appalachian League in game-winning RBIs with 9 in 1983.

Year	Club	League	Pos.	G.	AB.	R.	H.	2B.	3B.	HR.	RBI.	B.A.	PO.	A.	E.	F.A.
1983—Paintsville		Appal.	OF	71	264	64	81	17	0	7	50	.307	96	5	6	.944
1984—Stockton		Calif.	OF	80	290	41	68	10	4	0	22	.234	136	5	8	.946
1984—Beloit		Midw.	OF	49	170	29	50	14	1	2	33	.294	65	2	3	.957
1985—Stockton		Calif.	OF-P	137	544	89	171	25	2	7	92	.314	189	11	9	.957
1986—El Paso		Texas	OF	128	★515	101	166	31	5	14	91	.322	165	9	4	.978
1987—Paso		Texas	OF	129	526	★117	★208	42	4	24	96	★.395	212	9	8	.965
1988—Denver		A. A.	OF	111	384	54	122	26	7	5	59	★.318	176	7	5	.973
1989—Milwaukee		Amer.	DH-PR	2	3	1	0	0	0	0	0	.000	0	0	0	.000
1989—Den.†Okla.C‡		A. A.	OF-1B	98	302	32	72	14	3	3	27	.238	112	10	6	.953
Major League Totals—1 Year				2	3	1	0	0	0	0	0	.000	0	0	0	.000

Selected by Chicago White Sox' organization in 30th round of free-agent draft, June 8, 1981.
Selected by Milwaukee Brewers' organization in 1st round (26th player selected) of free-agent draft, January 11, 1983.

†Traded with Pitcher Todd Simmons to Oklahoma City (Texas Rangers' organization) for Pitcher Scott May and Outfielder Mike Wilson, June 29, 1989.

‡Granted free agency, October 15, 1989.

PITCHING RECORD

Year	Club	League	G.	IP.	W.	L.	Pct.	H.	R.	ER.	SO.	BB.	ERA.
1985—Stockton		California	1	2	0	0	.000	4	2	2	2	0	9.00

MARVIN FREEMAN

Born April 10, 1963, at Chicago, Ill.
Height, 6.06. Weight, 222.
Throws and bats righthanded.
Attended Jackson State University, Jackson, Miss.

Pitched 6-0 no-hit victory against Richmond, July 28, 1988 (second game).
Tied for Eastern League lead in games started by pitchers with 27 in 1986.
Tied for Northwest League lead in games started by pitchers with 15 in 1984.

Year	Club	League	G.	IP.	W.	L.	Pct.	H.	R.	ER.	SO.	BB.	ERA.
1984—Bend		Northwest	15	89⅔	8	5	.615	64	41	26	79	52	2.61
1985—Clearwater		Florida St.	14	88⅓	6	5	.545	72	32	30	55	36	3.06
1985—Reading		Eastern	11	65⅓	1	7	.125	51	41	39	35	52	5.37
1986—Reading		Eastern	27	163	13	6	.684	130	89	73	113	★111	4.03
1986—Philadelphia		National	3	16	2	0	1.000	6	4	4	8	10	2.25
1987—Maine		Int'national	10	46	0	7	.000	56	38	32	29	30	6.26
1987—Reading		Eastern	9	49⅔	3	3	.500	45	30	28	40	32	5.07
1988—Maine		Int'national	18	74	5	5	.500	62	43	38	37	46	4.62
1988—Philadelphia		National	11	51⅔	2	3	.400	55	36	35	37	43	6.10

Year Club	League	G.	IP.	W.	L.	Pct.	H.	R.	ER.	SO.	BB.	ERA.
1989—Scranton/Wilkes-Barre...............Int'national		5	14	1	1	.500	11	8	7	8	5	4.50
1989—Philadelphia† .... National		1	3	0	0	.000	2	2	2	0	5	6.00
Major League Totals—3 Years............................		15	70⅔	4	3	.571	63	42	41	45	58	5.22

Selected by Montreal Expos' organization in 9th round of free-agent draft, June 8, 1981.
Selected by Philadelphia Phillies' organization in 2nd round of free-agent draft, June 4, 1984.
†On disabled list, April 25, 1989 through remainder of season; included rehabilitation disability assignment to Scranton/Wilkes-Barre, August 24 to September 1, 1989.

STEVEN FRANCIS FREY
(Steve)

Born July 29, 1963, at Meadowbrook, Pa.
Height, 5.09. Weight, 170.
Throws left and bats righthanded.
Attended Bucks County Community College, Newton, Pa.

Year Club	League	G.	IP.	W.	L.	Pct.	H.	R.	ER.	SO.	BB.	ERA.
1983—Oneonta...................	NYP	28	72⅓	4	6	.400	47	27	22	86	35	2.74
1984—Fort Lauderdale	Florida St.	47	64⅔	4	2	.667	46	26	15	66	34	2.09
1985—Fort Lauderdale	Florida St.	19	22⅓	1	1	.500	11	4	3	15	12	1.21
1985—Albany................................	Eastern	40	61⅓	4	7	.364	53	30	26	54	25	3.82
1986—Albany................................	Eastern	40	73	3	4	.429	50	25	17	62	18	2.10
1986—Columbus................................	Int'national	11	19	0	2	.000	29	17	17	11	10	8.05
1987—Albany................................	Eastern	14	28	0	2	.000	20	6	6	19	7	1.93
1987—Columbus†	Int'national	23	47⅓	2	1	.667	45	19	16	35	10	3.04
1988—Tidewater‡	Int'national	58	54⅔	6	3	.667	38	23	19	58	25	3.13
1989—Indianapolis	Am. Assoc.	21	25⅓	2	1	.667	18	7	5	23	6	1.78
1989—Montreal	National	20	21⅓	3	2	.600	29	15	13	15	11	5.48
Major League Totals—1 Year................................		20	21⅓	3	2	.600	29	15	13	15	11	5.48

Selected by New York Yankees' organization in 15th round of free-agent draft, June 6, 1983.
†Traded with Outfielder Darren Reed and Catcher Phil Lombardi to New York Mets for Shortstop Rafael Santana and Pitcher Victor Garica, December 11, 1987.
‡Traded to Indianapolis (Montreal Expos' organization) for Catcher Mark Bailey and Third Baseman Tom O'Malley, March 28, 1989.

TODD GERALD FROHWIRTH

Born September 28, 1962, at Milwaukee, Wis.
Height, 6.04. Weight, 204.
Throws and bats righthanded.
Attended Northwest Missouri State University, Maryville, Mo.

Led Eastern League in saves with 19 in 1987.
Led Carolina League in games finished in relief with 48 and saves with 18 in 1985.
Led Northwest League in games finished in relief with 25 and tied for lead in saves with 11 in 1984.
Tied for International League lead in intentional bases on balls issued with 7 in 1987.

Year Club	League	G.	IP.	W.	L.	Pct.	H.	R.	ER.	SO.	BB.	ERA.
1984—Bend................................	Northwest	29	49⅔	4	4	.500	26	17	9	60	31	1.63
1985—Peninsula................................	Carolina	★54	82	7	5	.583	70	33	20	74	48	2.20
1986—Clearwater................................	FloridaSt.	32	52	3	3	.500	54	29	23	39	18	3.98
1986—Reading................................	Eastern	29	42	0	4	.000	39	20	15	23	10	3.21
1987—Reading................................	Eastern	36	58	2	4	.333	36	14	12	44	13	1.86
1987—Maine................................	Int'national	27	32⅓	1	4	.200	30	12	9	21	15	2.51
1987—Philadelphia	National	10	11	1	0	1.000	12	0	0	9	2	0.00
1988—Philadelphia	National	12	12	1	2	.333	16	11	11	11	11	8.25
1988—Maine................................	Int'national	49	62⅔	7	3	.700	52	21	17	39	19	2.44
1989—Scranton/Wilkes-Barre...............Int'national		21	32⅓	3	2	.600	29	11	8	29	11	2.23
1989—Philadelphia	National	45	62⅔	1	0	1.000	56	26	25	39	18	3.59
Major League Totals—3 Years............................		67	85⅔	3	2	.600	84	37	36	59	31	3.78

Selected by Philadelphia Phillies' organization in 13th round of free-agent draft, June 4, 1984.

DAVID TRAVIS FRYMAN
(Known by middle name.)

Born April 25, 1969, at Lexington, Ky.
Height, 6.01. Weight, 180.
Throws and bats righthanded.

Led Appalachian League shortstops in total chances with 313 in 1987.

Year Club	League	Pos.	G.	AB.	R.	H.	2B.	3B.	HR.	RBI.	B.A.	PO.	A.	E.	F.A.
1987—Bristol...................	Appal.	SS	67	248	25	58	9	0	2	20	.234	★103	187	●23	.927
1988—Fayetteville...........	S. Atl.	SS-2B	123	411	44	96	17	4	0	47	.234	174	390	32	.946
1989—London	East.	SS	118	426	52	113	★30	1	9	56	.265	192	346	★27	.952

Selected by Detroit Tigers' organization in 1st round (30th player selected) of free-agent draft, June 2, 1987.

—DID YOU KNOW—

That pitcher Ben McDonald, the No. 1 overall choice in the June 1989 free-agent draft, was involved in a triple play with the Orioles' Class A farm team in Frederick, Md. (Carolina) last season? He had just two fielding chances in the league.

GARY JOSEPH GAETTI

Name pronounced Guy-ETT-ee.

Born August 19, 1958, at Centralia, Ill.
Height, 6.00. Weight, 200.
Throws and bats righthanded.
Attended Lake Land College, Mattoon, Ill., and Northwest
Missouri State University, Maryville, Mo.

Shares major league records by hitting home run in first major league at-bat, September 20, 1981; most home runs, opening day of season (2), April 6, 1982; most sacrifice flies, rookie season (13), 1982.
Major League stolen bases: 1983 (7), 1984 (11), 1985 (13), 1986 (14), 1987 (10), 1988 (7), 1989 (6). Total—68.
Led American League in grounding into double plays with 25 in 1987.
Led American League in sacrifice flies with 13 in 1982.
Led American League third basemen in putouts with 142 in 1984 and 146 in 1985.
Led American League third basemen in total chances with 496 in 1984 and 473 in 1986.
Led American League third basemen in assists with 334 in 1984 and 1986.
Led American League third basemen in double plays with 46 in 1983 and 36 in 1986.
Tied for American League lead in errors by third basemen with 20 in 1984.
Led Southern League third basemen in putouts with 122 and assists with 281 in 1981.
Led Midwest League third basemen in double plays with 35 in 1980.
Tied for Appalachian League lead in errors by third basemen with 18 in 1979.
Named third baseman on THE SPORTING NEWS American League All-Star fielding team, 1986 through 1989.

Year	Club	League	Pos.	G.	AB.	R.	H.	2B.	3B.	HR.	RBI.	B.A.	PO.	A.	E.	F.A.
1979—Elizabethton	....	Appal.	3B-SS	66	230	50	59	15	2	14	42	.257	70	134	21	.907
1980—Wisconsin Rapids		Midw.	3B	138	503	77	134	27	3	★22	82	.266	★94	★363	●35	.929
1981—Orlando	....	South.	★3B-1B	137	495	92	137	19	2	30	93	.277	143	283	★32	.930
1981—Minnesota	....	Amer.	3B	9	26	4	5	0	0	2	3	.192	5	17	0	1.000
1982—Minnesota	....	Amer.	3B-SS	145	508	59	117	25	4	25	84	.230	106	291	17	.959
1983—Minnesota	....	Amer.	3B-SS	157	584	81	143	30	3	21	78	.245	★131	361	17	.967
1984—Minnesota	....	Amer.	3B-OF-1B	●162	588	55	154	29	4	5	65	.262	163	335	21	.960
1985—Minnesota	....	Amer.	3B-OF-1B	160	560	71	138	31	0	20	63	.246	162	316	18	.964
1986—Minnesota	....	Amer.	3-S-O-2	157	596	91	171	34	1	34	108	.287	120	335	21	.956
1987—Minnesota†	....	Amer.	3B	154	584	95	150	36	2	31	109	.257	●134	261	11	.973
1988—Minnesota	....	Amer.	3B-SS	133	468	66	141	29	2	28	88	.301	105	191	7	.977
1989—Minnesota§	....	Amer.	3B-1B	130	498	63	125	11	4	19	75	.251	115	253	10	.974
Major League Totals—9 Years	....			1207	4412	585	1144	225	20	185	673	.259	1041	2360	122	.965

Selected by St. Louis Cardinals' organization in 4th round of free-agent draft, January 10, 1978.
Selected by Chicago White Sox' organization in secondary phase of free-agent draft, June 6, 1978.
Selected by Minnesota Twins' organization in secondary phase of free-agent draft, June 5, 1979.
†Granted free agency, November 9, 1987; re-signed by Twins, January 7, 1988.
‡On disabled list, August 21 to September 5, 1988.
§On disabled list, August 26 to September 13, 1989.

CHAMPIONSHIP SERIES RECORD

Shares Championship Series record for hitting home run in first at-bat, October 7, 1987.

Year	Club	League	Pos.	G.	AB.	R.	H.	2B.	3B.	HR.	RBI.	B.A.	PO.	A.	E.	F.A.
1987—Minnesota	....	Amer.	3B	5	20	5	6	1	0	2	5	.300	8	7	0	1.000

WORLD SERIES RECORD

Shares World Series records for most at-bats (2) and most hits (2), inning, October 17, 1987, fourth inning.

Year	Club	League	Pos.	G.	AB.	R.	H.	2B.	3B.	HR.	RBI.	B.A.	PO.	A.	E.	F.A.
1987—Minnesota	....	Amer.	3B	7	27	4	7	2	1	1	4	.259	6	15	0	1.000

ALL-STAR GAME RECORD

Year	League	Pos.	AB.	R.	H.	2B.	3B.	HR.	RBI.	B.A.	PO.	A.	E.	F.A.
1988—American	....	PH	1	0	0	0	0	0	0	.000	0	0	0	.000
1989—American	....	3B	1	0	0	0	0	0	0	.000	1	0	0	1.000
All-Star Game Totals—2 Years	....		2	0	0	0	0	0	0	.000	1	0	0	1.000

GREGORY CARPENTER GAGNE

Name pronounced GAG-nee.

(Greg)

Born November 12, 1961, at Fall River, Mass.
Height, 5.11. Weight, 172.
Throws and bats righthanded.

Shares Major League record for most inside-the-park home runs, game (2), October 4, 1986.
Major League stolen bases: 1985 (10), 1986 (12), 1987 (6), 1988 (15), 1989 (11). Total—54.
Led International League shortstops in total chances with 599 in 1983.

Year	Club	League	Pos.	G.	AB.	R.	H.	2B.	3B.	HR.	RBI.	B.A.	PO.	A.	E.	F.A.
1979—Paintsville	....	Appal.	SS	41	106	10	19	2	3	0	7	.179	28	62	14	.865
1980—Greensboro†		S. Atl.	SS-3B-2B	98	337	39	91	20	5	3	32	.270	133	233	35	.913
1981—Greensboro	....	S. Atl.	2B-SS-3B	104	364	71	108	21	3	9	48	.297	172	280	25	.948
1982—Fort Lauderdale‡		Fla. St.	SS	1	3	0	1	0	0	0	0	.333	3	5	0	1.000
1982—Orlando	....	South.	SS-2B	136	504	73	117	23	5	11	57	.232	185	403	39	.938
1983—Toledo	....	Int.	SS	119	392	61	100	22	4	17	66	.255	201	★364	★34	.943
1983—Minnesota	....	Amer.	SS	10	27	2	3	1	0	0	3	.111	10	14	2	.923
1984—Toledo§	....	Int.	3B-SS-2B	70	236	31	66	7	2	9	27	.280	58	168	20	.926

Year Club	League	Pos.	G.	AB.	R.	H.	2B.	3B.	HR.	RBI.	B.A.	PO.	A.	E.	F.A.
1984—Minnesota............ Amer.		PR-PH	2	1	0	0	0	0	0	0	.000	0	0	0	.000
1985—Minnesota x .... Amer.		SS	114	293	37	66	15	3	2	23	.225	149	269	14	.968
1986—Minnesota............ Amer.		★SS-2B	156	472	63	118	22	6	12	54	.250	228	381	★26	.959
1987—Minnesota............ Amer.		SS-OF-2B	137	437	68	116	28	7	10	40	.265	196	391	18	.970
1988—Minnesota............ Amer.		S-O-2-3	149	461	70	109	20	6	14	48	.236	202	373	18	.970
1989—Minnesota............ Amer.		SS-OF	149	460	69	125	29	7	9	48	.272	218	389	18	.971
Major League Totals—7 Years................			717	2151	309	537	115	29	47	216	.250	1003	1817	96	.967

Selected by New York Yankees' organization in 5th round of free-agent draft, June 5, 1979.
†On disabled list, September 4 to September 22, 1980.
‡Traded with Pitchers Ron Davis and Paul Boris and a reported $400,000 to Minnesota Twins for Shortstop Roy Smalley, April 10, 1982.
§On disabled list, June 13 to July 18, 1984.
xOn disabled list, August 10 to September 1, 1985.

CHAMPIONSHIP SERIES RECORD

Year Club	League	Pos.	G.	AB.	R.	H.	2B.	3B.	HR.	RBI.	B.A.	PO.	A.	E.	F.A.
1987—Minnesota.............. Amer.		SS	5	18	5	5	3	0	2	3	.278	9	13	2	.917

WORLD SERIES RECORD

Shares World Series record for most at-bats, inning (2), October 18, 1987, fourth inning.

Year Club	League	Pos.	G.	AB.	R.	H.	2B.	3B.	HR.	RBI.	B.A.	PO.	A.	E.	F.A.
1987—Minnesota.............. Amer.		SS	7	30	5	6	1	0	1	3	.200	6	20	2	.929

ANDRES JOSE GALARRAGA

Name pronounced Gahl-ah-RAH-guh.

Born June 18, 1961, at Caracas, Venezuela.
Height, 6.03. Weight, 235.
Throws and bats righthanded.

Major League stolen bases: 1985 (1), 1986 (6), 1987 (7), 1988 (13), 1989 (12). Total—39.
Led National League batters in strikeouts with 153 in 1988 and 158 in 1989.
Led National League in total bases with 329 in 1988.
Led National League in being hit by pitch with 10 in 1987 and tied for lead with 13 in 1989.
Led Southern League in total bases with 271, slugging percentage with .508, intentional bases on balls received with 10 and tied for lead in being hit by pitch with 9 in 1984.
Tied for American Association lead in game-winning RBIs with 13 in 1985.
Led Southern League first basemen in total chances with 1,428 and double plays with 130 in 1984.
Named first baseman on THE SPORTING NEWS National League All-Star fielding team, 1989.
Named first baseman on THE SPORTING NEWS National League Silver Slugger team, 1988.
Named Southern League Most Valuable Player, 1984.

Year Club	League	Pos.	G.	AB.	R.	H.	2B.	3B.	HR.	RBI.	B.A.	PO.	A.	E.	F.A.
1979—W. Palm Beach.... Fla. St.		1B	7	23	3	3	0	0	0	1	.130	2	1	0	1.000
1979—Calgary .... Pion.		1B-3B-C	42	112	14	24	3	1	4	16	.214	187	21	5	.976
1980—Calgary .... Pion.		1-3-C-O	59	190	27	50	11	4	4	22	.263	287	52	21	.942
1981—Jamestown............ NYP		C-1-O-3	47	154	24	40	5	4	6	26	.260	154	15	0	1.000
1982—W. Palm Beach.... Fla. St.		1B-OF	105	338	39	95	20	2	14	51	.281	462	36	9	.982
1983—W. Palm Beach.... Fla. St.		1B-OF-3B	104	401	55	116	18	3	10	66	.289	861	77	13	.986
1984—Jacksonville......... South.		1B	143	533	81	154	28	4	27	87	.289	★1302	★110	16	.989
1985—Indianapolis......... A. A.		1B-OF	121	439	★75	118	15	8	25	87	.269	930	63	14	.986
1985—Montreal............... Nat.		1B	24	75	9	14	1	0	2	4	.187	173	22	1	.995
1986—Montreal†.............. Nat.		1B	105	321	39	87	13	0	10	42	.271	805	40	4	.995
1987—Montreal............... Nat.		1B	147	551	72	168	40	3	13	90	.305	★1300	103	10	.993
1988—Montreal............... Nat.		1B	157	609	99	★184	★42	8	29	92	.302	1464	103	15	.991
1989—Montreal............... Nat.		1B	152	572	76	147	30	1	23	85	.257	1335	91	11	.992
Major League Totals—5 Years.................			585	2128	295	600	126	12	77	313	.282	5077	359	41	.993

Signed as free agent by Montreal Expos' organization, January 19, 1979.
†On disabled list, July 10 to August 19 and August 20 to September 4, 1986.

ALL-STAR GAME RECORD

Year League	Pos.	AB.	R.	H.	2B.	3B.	HR.	RBI.	B.A.	PO.	A.	E.	F.A.
1988—National......................	1B	2	0	0	0	0	0	0	.000	6	0	0	1.000

DAVID THOMAS GALLAGHER
(Dave)

Born September 20, 1960, at Trenton, N.J.
Height, 6.00. Weight, 180.
Throws and bats righthanded.
Attended Mercer County Community College, Trenton, N.J.

Major League stolen bases: 1987 (2), 1988 (5), 1989 (5). Total—12.
Led International League in sacrifice hits with 12 in 1986.
Led Midwest League in sacrifice hits with 21 in 1982.
Led International League outfielders in total chances with 369 in 1985.
Tied for Eastern League lead in double plays by outfielders with 4 in 1983.

Year Club	League	Pos.	G.	AB.	R.	H.	2B.	3B.	HR.	RBI.	B.A.	PO.	A.	E.	F.A.
1980—Batavia................... NYP		OF	69	241	33	66	6	3	5	36	.274	114	4	2	.983
1981—Waterloo................ Midw.		OF-3B	127	435	55	102	22	1	3	34	.234	224	22	7	.972
1982—Chattanooga......... South.		OF	15	54	10	12	2	1	0	4	.222	32	1	0	1.000

Year Club League	Pos.	G.	AB.	R.	H.	2B.	3B.	HR.	RBI.	B.A.	PO.	A.	E.	F.A.
1982—Waterloo Midw.	OF	110	409	61	118	25	7	6	47	.289	232	15	4	*.984
1983—Buffalo† East.	OF-3B	107	376	64	127	21	3	2	47	*.338	223	13	5	.979
1984—Maine Int.	OF	116	380	49	94	19	5	6	49	.247	208	7	3	.986
1985—Maine Int.	OF	132	488	71	118	22	3	9	55	.242	*357	9	3	*.992
1986—Maine Int.	OF	132	497	59	145	23	5	8	44	.292	341	*14	1	*.997
1987—Cleveland Amer.	OF	15	36	2	4	1	1	0	1	.111	34	1	1	.972
1987—Buffalo‡ A. A.	OF	12	46	10	12	4	0	0	6	.261	34	1	0	1.000
1987—Calgary§ P. C.	OF	75	268	45	82	27	2	3	46	.306	143	5	4	.974
1988—Vancouver P. C.	OF	34	131	23	44	8	1	4	27	.336	79	2	0	1.000
1988—Chicago Amer.	OF	101	347	59	105	15	3	5	31	.303	228	5	0	1.000
1989—Chicago Amer.	OF	161	601	74	160	22	2	1	46	.266	390	8	3	.993
Major League Totals—3 Years		277	984	135	269	38	6	6	78	.273	652	14	4	.994

Selected by Oakland A's organization in 1st round (third player selected) of free-agent draft, January 8, 1980.
Selected by Cleveland Indians' organization in secondary phase of free-agent draft, June 3, 1980.
†On disabled list, May 2 to June 6, 1983.
‡Traded to Seattle Mariners' organization for Pitcher Mark Huismann, May 12, 1987.
§Released, September 30, 1987; signed by Vancouver (Chicago White Sox' organization), December 7, 1987.

MICHAEL ANTHONY GALLEGO
(Mike)

Born October 31, 1960, at Whittier, Calif.
Height, 5.08. Weight, 160.
Throws and bats righthanded.
Attended University of California, Los Angeles, Calif.

Major League stolen bases: 1985 (1), 1988 (2), 1989 (7). Total—10.
Led Pacific Coast League in being hit by pitch with 8 in 1986.

Year Club League	Pos.	G.	AB.	R.	H.	2B.	3B.	HR.	RBI.	B.A.	PO.	A.	E.	F.A.
1981—Modesto Calif.	2B	60	202	38	55	9	3	0	23	.272	127	161	13	.957
1982—West Haven East.	2B-SS	54	139	17	25	1	0	0	5	.180	85	111	4	.980
1982—Tacoma P. C.	2B-3B-SS	44	136	12	30	3	1	0	11	.221	73	111	8	.958
1983—Tacoma† P. C.	2B	2	2	0	0	0	0	0	0	.000	0	1	0	1.000
1983—Albany East.	2B-SS-3B	90	274	31	61	6	0	0	18	.223	184	260	4	.991
1984—Tacoma P. C.	2B-SS-3B	101	288	29	70	8	1	0	18	.243	167	231	13	.968
1985 Oakland Amer.	2B-SS-3B	76	77	13	16	5	1	1	9	.208	57	94	1	.993
1985—Modesto Calif.	2B-SS-3B	6	25	1	5	1	0	0	2	.200	12	11	1	.958
1986—Tacoma P. C.	SS-3B-2B	132	443	58	122	16	5	4	46	.275	197	417	23	.964
1986—Oakland Amer.	2B-SS	20	37	2	10	2	0	0	4	.270	24	51	1	.987
1987—Tacoma P. C.	2B	10	41	6	11	0	2	0	6	.268	15	25	1	.976
1987—Oakland‡ Amer.	2B-3B-SS	72	124	18	31	6	0	2	14	.250	75	122	8	.961
1988—Oakland Amer.	2B-SS-3B	129	277	38	58	8	0	2	20	.209	155	254	8	.981
1989—Oakland Amer.	SS-2B-3B	133	357	45	90	14	2	3	30	.252	211	363	19	.968
Major League Totals—5 Years		430	872	116	205	35	3	8	77	.235	522	884	37	.974

Selected by Oakland A's organization in 2nd round of free-agent draft., June 8, 1981.
†On temporary inactive list, April 10 to May 20, 1983.
‡On disabled list, June 13 to July 29, 1987.

CHAMPIONSHIP SERIES RECORD
Shares American League Championship Series record for most sacrifice hits, series (2), 1989.

Year Club League	Pos.	G.	AB.	R.	H.	2B.	3B.	HR.	RBI.	B.A.	PO.	A.	E.	F.A.
1988—Oakland Amer.	2B	4	12	1	1	0	0	0	0	.083	7	6	0	1.000
1989—Oakland Amer.	SS-2B	4	11	3	3	1	0	0	1	.273	6	14	0	1.000
Championship Series Totals—2 Years		8	23	4	4	1	0	0	1	.174	13	20	0	1.000

WORLD SERIES RECORD

Year Club League	Pos.	G.	AB.	R.	H.	2B.	3B.	HR.	RBI.	B.A.	PO.	A.	E.	F.A.
1988—Oakland Amer.	PR-2B	1	0	0	0	0	0	0	0	.000	0	0	0	.000
1989—Oakland Amer.	2B-3B	2	1	0	0	0	0	0	0	.000	0	0	0	.000
World Series Totals—2 Years		3	1	0	0	0	0	0	0	.000	0	0	0	.000

RONALD EDWIN GANT
(Ronnie)

Born March 2, 1965, at Victoria, Tex.
Height, 6.00. Weight, 172.
Throws and bats righthanded.

Major League stolen bases: 1987 (4), 1988 (19), 1989 (9). Total—32.
Led National League second baseman in errors with 26 in 1988.
Led Carolina League in total bases with 271 in 1986.
Led Southern League second basemen in double plays with 108 and total chances with 783 in 1987.
Led South Atlantic League second basemen in double plays with 75 in 1984.

Year Club League	Pos.	G.	AB.	R.	H.	2B.	3B.	HR.	RBI.	B.A.	PO.	A.	E.	F.A.
1983—Bradenton Brav. Gulf C.	SS	56	193	32	45	2	2	1	14	.233	68	134	22	.902
1984—Anderson S. Atl.	2B	105	359	44	85	14	6	3	38	.237	248	263	31	.943
1985—Sumter S. Atl.	2B-SS	102	305	46	78	14	4	7	37	.256	160	200	10	.973
1986—Durham Carol.	2B	137	512	108	142	31	10	*26	102	.277	240	384	26	.960
1987—Greenville South.	2B	140	527	78	130	27	3	14	82	.247	*328	*434	21	*.973

Year Club	League	Pos.	G.	AB.	R.	H.	2B.	3B.	HR.	RBI.	B.A.	PO.	A.	E.	F.A.
1987—Atlanta .... Nat.		2B	21	83	9	22	4	0	2	9	.265	45	59	3	.972
1988—Richmond............. Int.		2B	12	45	3	14	2	2	0	4	.311	22	23	5	.900
1988—Atlanta .... Nat.		2B-3B	146	563	85	146	28	8	19	60	.259	316	417	31	.959
1989—Atlanta .... Nat.		3B-OF	75	260	26	46	8	3	9	25	.177	70	103	17	.911
1989—Sumter.................... S. Atl.		OF	12	39	13	15	4	1	1	5	.385	19	1	2	.909
1989—Richmond............. Int.		OF-3B	63	225	42	59	13	2	11	27	.262	111	14	5	.962
Major League Totals—3 Years.................			242	906	120	214	40	11	30	94	.236	431	579	51	.952

Selected by Atlanta Braves' organization in 4th round of free-agent draft, June 6, 1983.

JAMES ELMER GANTNER
(Jim)

Born January 5, 1954, at Eden, Wis.
Height, 5.11. Weight, 175.
Throws right and bats lefthanded.
Attended University of Wisconsin, Oshkosh, Wis.

Shares major league record for longest errorless game by second baseman (25 innings), May 8, finished May 9, 1984; fielded 24½ innings.
Holds American League record for highest fielding average, second baseman, lifetime (.985).
Shares American League record for most innings played by second baseman, game (25), May 8, finished May 9, 1984; fielded 24½ innings.
Major League stolen bases: 1976 (1), 1977 (2), 1978 (2), 1979 (3), 1980 (11), 1981 (3), 1982 (6), 1983 (5), 1984 (6), 1985 (11), 1986 (13), 1987 (6), 1988 (20), 1989 (20). Total—109.
Led American League in being hit by pitch with 10 in 1989.
Led American League second basemen in total chances with 613 in 1981, 900 in 1983 and 844 in 1984.
Led American League second basemen in double plays with 95 in 1981 and 128 in 1983.
Led Pacific Coast League third basemen in putouts with 136 and in fielding percentage with .936 in 1977.
Led Eastern League third basemen in fielding percentage with .953 in 1976.
Led Eastern League third basemen in putouts with 118 and assists with 310 in 1975.

Year Club	League	Pos.	G.	AB.	R.	H.	2B.	3B.	HR.	RBI.	B.A.	PO.	A.	E.	F.A.
1974—Newark .... NYP		SS-3B	62	177	35	54	6	2	5	21	.305	64	134	14	.934
1975—Thetford Mines.... East.		3B-SS	●138	456	61	117	17	0	12	48	.257	129	317	33	.931
1976—Berkshire.............. East.		3B-SS	126	403	56	118	21	1	6	53	.293	120	294	20	.954
1976—Milwaukee............. Amer.		3B	26	69	6	17	1	0	0	7	.246	17	37	1	.982
1977—Spokane .... P. C.		★3B-OF	●143	541	98	152	35	5	15	80	.281	137	★321	31	.937
1977—Milwaukee............. Amer.		3B	14	47	4	14	1	0	1	2	.298	8	29	4	.902
1978—Milwaukee............. Amer.		2-3-S-1	43	97	14	21	1	0	1	8	.216	46	82	5	.962
1979—Milwaukee............. Amer.		3-2-S-P	70	208	29	59	10	3	2	22	.284	80	161	7	.972
1980—Milwaukee............. Amer.		3B-2B-SS	132	415	47	117	21	3	4	40	.282	159	335	15	.971
1981—Milwaukee............. Amer.		2B	107	352	35	94	14	1	2	33	.267	251	352	10	.984
1982—Milwaukee............. Amer.		2B	132	447	48	132	17	2	4	43	.295	307	398	13	.982
1983—Milwaukee............. Amer.		2B	161	603	85	170	23	8	11	74	.282	374	★512	14	.984
1984—Milwaukee............. Amer.		2B	153	613	61	173	27	1	3	56	.282	★362	469	13	.985
1985—Milwaukee............. Amer.		2B-3B-SS	143	523	63	133	15	4	5	44	.254	278	436	11	.985
1986—Milwaukee............. Amer.		2B-3B-SS	139	497	58	136	25	1	7	38	.274	309	353	10	.985
1987—Milwaukee†........... Amer.		2B-3B	81	265	37	72	14	0	4	30	.272	119	193	6	.981
1988—Milwaukee‡........... Amer.		★2B-3B	155	539	67	149	28	2	0	47	.276	★325	430	11	.986
1989—Milwaukee§........... Amer.		2B	116	409	51	112	18	3	0	34	.274	241	362	8	.987
Major League Totals—14 Years..............			1472	5084	605	1399	215	28	44	478	.275	2876	4149	128	.982

Selected by Milwaukee Brewers' organization in 12th round of free-agent draft, June 5, 1974.
†On disabled list, July 31 to September 3, 1987.
‡Granted free agency, November 4, 1988; re-signed by Brewers, December 20, 1988.
§On disabled list, August 16, 1989 through remainder of season.

DIVISION SERIES RECORD

Year Club	League	Pos.	G.	AB.	R.	H.	2B.	3B.	HR.	RBI.	B.A.	PO.	A.	E.	F.A.
1981—Milwaukee............. Amer.		2B	4	14	1	2	1	0	0	0	.143	3	15	2	.900

CHAMPIONSHIP SERIES RECORD

Year Club	League	Pos.	G.	AB.	R.	H.	2B.	3B.	HR.	RBI.	B.A.	PO.	A.	E.	F.A.
1982—Milwaukee............. Amer.		2B	5	16	1	3	0	0	0	2	.188	12	8	0	1.000

WORLD SERIES RECORD

Year Club	League	Pos.	G.	AB.	R.	H.	2B.	3B.	HR.	RBI.	B.A.	PO.	A.	E.	F.A.
1982—Milwaukee............. Amer.		2B	7	24	5	8	4	1	0	4	.333	9	33	5	.894

PITCHING RECORD

Year Club	League	G.	IP.	W.	L.	Pct.	H.	R.	ER.	SO.	BB.	ERA.
1979—Milwaukee.. American		1	1	0	0	.000	2	0	0	0	0	0.00

CARLOS JESUS GARCIA

Born October 15, 1967, at Tachira, Venezuela.
Height, 6.01. Weight, 185.
Throws and bats righthanded.

Year Club	League	Pos.	G.	AB.	R.	H.	2B.	3B.	HR.	RBI.	B.A.	PO.	A.	E.	F.A.
1987—Macon..................... S. Atl.		SS	110	373	44	95	14	3	3	38	.255	161	262	42	.910
1988—Augusta .... S. Atl.		SS	73	269	32	78	13	2	1	45	.290	138	207	29	.922

Year Club League	Pos.	G.	AB.	R.	H.	2B.	3B.	HR.	RBI.	B.A.	PO.	A.	E.	F.A.
1988—Salem.................Carol.	SS	62	236	21	65	9	3	1	28	.275	131	151	24	.922
1989—Salem.................Carol.	SS	81	304	45	86	12	4	7	49	.283	137	262	32	.926
1989—Harrisburg...........East.	SS	54	188	28	53	5	5	3	25	.282	84	131	7	.968

Signed as free agent by Pittsburgh Pirates' organization, January 9, 1987.

DAMASO DOMINGO GARCIA

First name pronounced Da-MAH-so.

Born February 7, 1957, at Moca, Dominican Republic.
Height, 6.00. Weight, 185.
Throws and bats righthanded.
Attended Madre y Maestra University, Santiago, Dominican Republic.

Shares major league record for most doubles, game (4), June 27, 1986.
Major League stolen bases: 1978 (1), 1979 (2), 1980 (13), 1981 (13), 1982 (54), 1983 (31), 1984 (46), 1985 (28), 1986 (9), 1988 (1), 1989 (5). Total—203.
Led Florida State League second baseman in double plays with 83 in 1976.
Tied for New York-Pennsylvania League lead in double plays by second basemen with 33 in 1975.
Named second baseman on THE SPORTING NEWS American League All-Star Team, 1982 and 1985.
Named second baseman on THE SPORTING NEWS American League Silver Slugger team, 1982.

Year Club League	Pos.	G.	AB.	R.	H.	2B.	3B.	HR.	RBI.	B.A.	PO.	A.	E.	F.A.
1975—Oneonta .... NYP	2B	50	157	28	42	4	2	0	17	.268	103	118	★17	.929
1976—Fort Lauderdale† .Fla.St.	2B	124	412	55	109	●22	4	1	41	.265	★273	353	21	★.968
1977—West Haven .... East.	2B	129	445	62	118	13	9	0	53	.265	263	382	19	.971
1978—Tacoma................. P. C.	2B-SS	102	385	51	103	18	6	1	53	.268	217	345	25	.957
1978—New York .... Amer.	2B-SS	18	41	5	8	0	0	0	1	.195	36	35	4	.947
1979—Columbus ‡ .... Int.	SS-1B	39	118	18	32	1	0	1	3	.271	53	85	6	.958
1979—New York § .... Amer.	SS-3B	11	38	3	10	1	0	0	4	.263	9	28	4	.902
1980—Toronto .... Amer.	2B	140	543	50	151	30	7	4	46	.278	316	471	16	.980
1981—Toronto x .... Amer.	2B	64	250	24	63	8	1	1	13	.252	132	181	9	.972
1982—Toronto .... Amer.	2B	147	597	89	185	32	3	5	42	.310	273	461	15	.980
1983—Toronto .... Amer.	2B	131	525	84	161	23	6	3	38	.307	266	360	12	.981
1984—Toronto .... Amer.	2B	152	633	79	180	32	5	5	46	.284	267	427	14	.980
1985—Toronto .... Amer.	2B	146	600	70	169	25	4	8	65	.282	302	371	13	.981
1986—Toronto y .... Amer.	2B-1B	122	424	57	119	22	0	6	46	.281	225	286	8	.985
1987—Richmond z .... Int.	2B	1	1	0	0	0	0	0	0	.000	0	0	0	.000
1988—Atlanta a .... Nat.	2B	21	60	3	7	1	0	1	4	.117	26	35	1	.984
1988—Albuquerque b...... P. C.	2B	3	5	1	2	1	0	0	1	.400	1	1	1	.667
1989—Montreal cd.......... Nat.	2B-3B	80	203	26	55	9	1	3	18	.271	86	157	7	.972
National League Totals—2 Years...........		101	263	29	62	10	1	4	22	.236	112	192	8	.974
American League Totals—9 Years		931	3651	461	1046	173	26	32	301	.286	1826	2620	95	.979
Major League Totals—11 Years...............		1032	3914	490	1108	183	27	36	323	.283	1938	2812	103	.979

Signed as free agent by New York Yankees' organization, March 10, 1975.
†On suspended list, June 4 to June 7, 1976.
‡On disabled list, May 14 to July 24 and July 31 to August 13, 1979.
§Traded with First Baseman Chris Chambliss and Pitcher Paul Mirabella to Toronto Blue Jays for Catcher Rick Cerone, Pitcher Tom Underwood and Outfielder Ted Wilborn, November 1, 1979.
xOn disabled list, August 22, 1981 through remainder of season.
yTraded with Pitcher Luis Leal to Atlanta Braves for Pitcher Craig McMurtry, February 2, 1987.
zOn Atlanta disabled list, March 29 to September 1, 1987; included rehabilitation disability assignment to Richmond, June 29 and June 30, 1987.
aReleased, May 17, 1988; signed by Albuquerque (Los Angeles Dodgers' organization), June 29, 1988.
bReleased, July, 1988; signed by Indianapolis (Montreal Expos' organization), January 19, 1989.
cOn disabled list, May 7 to May 26, 1989.
dGranted free agency, November 13, 1989; signed by New York Yankees, December 22, 1989.

CHAMPIONSHIP SERIES RECORD

Shares Championship Series record for most doubles, series (4), 1985.

Year Club League	Pos.	G.	AB.	R.	H.	2B.	3B.	HR.	RBI.	B.A.	PO.	A.	E.	F.A.
1985—Toronto .... Amer.	2B	7	30	4	7	4	0	0	1	.233	10	12	0	1.000

ALL-STAR GAME RECORD

Year League	Pos.	AB.	R.	H.	2B.	3B.	HR.	RBI.	B.A.	PO.	A.	E.	F.A.
1984—American	2B	1	0	0	0	0	0	0	.000	1	0	0	1.000
1985—American	2B	2	0	1	0	0	0	0	.500	0	3	0	1.000
All-Star Game Totals—2 Years....................		3	0	1	0	0	0	0	.333	1	3	0	1.000

MIGUEL ANGEL GARCIA

Born April 3, 1967, at Caracas, Venezuela.
Height, 6.01. Weight, 170.
Throws and bats lefthanded.

Year Club League	G.	IP.	W.	L.	Pct.	H.	R.	ER.	SO.	BB.	ERA.
1985—Quad City................. Midwest	29	65½	3	2	.600	60	25	21	50	21	2.89
1986—Palm Springs........... California	43	72⅔	8	3	.727	59	18	13	75	26	1.61
1987—Midland..................... Texas	50	87	10	6	.625	86	35	25	67	34	2.59
1987—California†................ American	1	1⅔	0	0	.000	3	4	3	0	3	16.20
1987—Pittsburgh................. National	1	⅔	0	0	.000	0	0	0	0	0	0.00
1988—Buffalo....................... Am. Assoc.	25	66⅓	6	2	.750	71	26	19	34	21	2.58

Year Club	League	G.	IP.	W.	L.	Pct.	H.	R.	ER.	SO.	BB.	ERA.
1988—Pittsburgh	National	1	2	0	0	.000	3	2	1	2	2	4.50
1989—Buffalo	Am. Assoc.	31	59⅔	6	2	.750	64	39	29	54	29	4.37
1989—Pittsburgh	National	11	16	0	2	.000	25	15	15	9	7	8.44
American League Totals—1 Year		1	1⅔	0	0	.000	3	4	3	0	3	16.20
National League Totals—3 Years		13	18⅔	0	2	.000	28	17	16	11	9	7.71
Major League Totals—3 Years		14	20⅓	0	2	.000	31	21	19	11	12	8.41

Signed as free agent by California Angels' organization, January 22, 1985.

†Traded to Pittsburgh Pirates, September 3, 1987, completing deal in which Pittsburgh traded Second Baseman Johnny Ray to California Angels for Third Baseman Billie Merrifield and a player to be named later, August 29, 1987.

MARK ALLAN GARDNER

Born March 1, 1962, at Clovis, Calif.
Height, 6.01. Weight, 190.
Throws and bats righthanded.
Attended Fresno City College, Fresno, Calif., and Fresno State University, Fresno, Calif.

Named American Association Pitcher of the Year, 1989.

Year Club	League	G.	IP.	W.	L.	Pct.	H.	R.	ER.	SO.	BB.	ERA.
1985—Jamestown	NYP	3	13	0	0	.000	9	4	4	16	4	2.77
1985—West Palm Beach	Florida St.	10	60⅔	5	4	.556	54	24	16	44	18	2.37
1986—Jacksonville	Southern	29	168⅔	10	11	.476	144	88	72	140	90	3.84
1987—Indianapolis	Am. Assoc.	9	46	3	3	.500	48	32	29	41	28	5.67
1987—Jacksonville	Southern	17	101	4	6	.400	101	50	47	78	42	4.19
1988—Jacksonville	Southern	15	112½	6	3	.667	72	24	20	130	36	1.60
1988—Indianapolis	Am. Assoc.	13	84½	4	2	.667	65	30	26	71	32	2.77
1989—Indianapolis	Am. Assoc.	24	163⅓	12	4	★.750	122	51	43	★175	59	2.37
1989—Montreal	National	7	26⅓	0	3	.000	26	16	15	21	11	5.13
Major League Totals—1 Year		7	26⅓	0	3	.000	26	16	15	21	11	5.13

Selected by California Angels' organization in 6th round of free-agent draft, January 11, 1983.
Selected by Cleveland Indians' organization in 17th round of free-agent draft, June 4, 1984.
Selected by Montreal Expos' organization in 8th round of free-agent draft, June 3, 1985.

WESLEY BRIAN GARDNER
(Wes)

Born April 29, 1961, at Benton, Ark.
Height, 6.04. Weight, 203.
Throws and bats righthanded.
Attended University of Central Arkansas, Conway, Ark.

Major League saves: 1984 (1), 1987 (10), 1988 (2). Total—13.
Led International League in saves with 20 in 1984 and tied for lead with 18 in 1985.
Led International League in games finished in relief with 37 in 1984.

Year Club	League	G.	IP.	W.	L.	Pct.	H.	R.	ER.	SO.	BB.	ERA.
1982—Little Falls	NYP	23	77⅔	3	6	.333	73	48	32	77	29	3.71
1983—Lynchburg	Carolina	49	62⅔	6	3	.667	55	16	13	67	32	1.87
1984—Tidewater	Int'national	40	56	1	2	.333	40	11	10	36	19	1.61
1984—New York	National	21	25⅓	1	1	.500	34	19	18	19	8	6.39
1985—Tidewater	Int'national	53	76⅔	7	6	.538	57	31	24	75	34	2.82
1985—New York†	National	9	12	0	2	.000	18	14	7	11	8	5.25
1986—Boston‡	American	1	1	0	0	.000	1	1	1	1	0	9.00
1987—Boston	American	49	89⅔	3	6	.333	98	55	54	70	42	5.42
1987—Pawtucket	Int'national	5	8⅔	1	0	1.000	8	3	3	9	3	3.12
1988—Boston§	American	36	149	8	6	.571	119	61	58	106	64	3.50
1989—Boston x	American	22	86	3	7	.300	97	64	57	81	47	5.97
National League Totals—2 Years		30	37⅓	1	3	.250	52	33	25	30	16	6.03
American League Totals—4 Years		108	325⅔	14	19	.424	315	181	170	258	153	4.70
Major League Totals—6 Years		138	363	15	22	.405	367	214	195	288	169	4.83

Selected by New York Mets' organization in 22nd round of free-agent draft, June 7, 1982.

†Traded with Pitcher Calvin Schiraldi and Outfielders John Christensen and LaSchelle Tarver to Boston Red Sox for Pitchers Bob Ojeda, Tom McCarthy, John Mitchell and Chris Bayer, November 13, 1985.

‡On disabled list, April 14, 1986 through remainder of season; included rehabilitation disability assignment to Pawtucket, June 24 to July 1, 1986.

§On disabled list, May 29 to June 13, 1988.

xOn disabled list, May 21 to June 12 and August 28, 1989 through remainder of season.

CHAMPIONSHIP SERIES RECORD

Year Club	League	G.	IP.	W.	L.	Pct.	H.	R.	ER.	SO.	BB.	ERA.
1988—Boston	American	1	4⅔	0	0	.000	6	3	3	8	2	5.79

KEVIN WAYNE GARNER

Born October 21, 1965, at Freeport, Tex.
Height, 6.02. Weight, 205.
Throws right and bats lefthanded.
Attended University of Texas, Austin, Tex.

Led Texas League outfielders in double plays with 4 in 1989.
Named outfielder on THE SPORTING NEWS College Baseball All-America Team, 1987.

Year Club	League	Pos.	G.	AB.	R.	H.	2B.	3B.	HR.	RBI.	B.A.	PO.	A.	E.	F.A.
1987—Spokane	N'west	P-DH	36	106	19	29	7	1	5	25	.274	4		5	1	.900
1988—Riverside	Calif.	OF-P	124	445	66	106	18	3	15	72	.238	26	2	1	.966
1989—Wichita..................	Texas	OF	103	350	51	87	17	2	19	63	.249	113	7	4	.968

Selected by Montreal Expos' organization in 3rd round of free-agent draft, June 4, 1984.
Selected by San Diego Padres' organization in 1st round (10th player selected) of free-agent draft, June 2, 1987.

RECORD AS PITCHER

Year Club	League	G.	IP.	W.	L.	Pct.	H.	R.	ER.	SO.	BB.	ERA.
1987—Spokane	Northwest	6	35⅔	3	1	.750	18	8	8	42	16	2.02
1988—Riverside	California	2	2⅔	0	0	.000	0	2	1	3	4	3.38

SCOTT WILLIAM GARRELTS

Name pronounced Guh-RELTZ.

Born October 30, 1961, at Urbana, Ill.
Height, 6.04. Weight, 205.
Throws and bats righthanded.

Pitched seven-inning, 1-0 no-hit victory against Tacoma, August 20, 1983.
Major League saves: 1985 (13), 1986 (10), 1987 (12), 1988 (13). Total—48.
Tied for Midwest League lead in games started by pitchers with 27 in 1980.

Year Club	League	G.	IP.	W.	L.	Pct.	H.	R.	ER.	SO.	BB.	ERA.
1979—Great Falls.....................	Pioneer	8	43	1	4	.200	45	37	28	26	40	5.86
1980—Clinton	Midwest	27	176	11	11	.500	155	98	76	*159	*149	3.89
1981—Shreveport†	Texas	14	71	3	8	.273	56	43	35	73	43	4.44
1982—Shreveport	Texas	27	151⅓	9	10	.474	131	76	64	159	90	3.81
1982—San Francisco	National	1	2	0	0	.000	3	3	3	4	2	13.50
1983—Phoenix‡......................	P. Coast	21	97⅔	5	5	.500	86	64	50	89	81	4.61
1983—San Francisco	National	5	35⅔	2	2	.500	33	11	10	16	19	2.52
1984—Phoenix	P. Coast	21	97⅔	5	7	.417	97	75	64	69	82	5.90
1984—San Francisco	National	21	43	2	3	.400	45	33	27	32	34	5.65
1985—San Francisco	National	74	105⅔	9	6	.600	76	37	27	106	58	2.30
1986—San Francisco	National	53	173⅔	13	9	.591	144	65	60	125	74	3.11
1987—San Francisco	National	64	106⅓	11	7	.611	70	41	38	127	55	3.22
1988—San Francisco§	National	65	98	5	9	.357	80	42	39	86	46	3.58
1989—San Francisco§	National	30	193⅓	14	5	*.737	149	58	49	119	46	*2.28
Major League Totals—8 Years		313	757⅔	56	41	.577	600	290	253	615	334	3.01

Selected by San Francisco Giants' organization in 1st round (15th player selected) of free-agent draft, June 5, 1979.
†On disabled list, July 15 to August 16, 1981.
‡On disabled list, May 12 to June 6 and July 8 to July 24, 1983.
§On disabled list, June 30 to July 16, 1989.

CHAMPIONSHIP SERIES RECORD

Year Club	League	G.	IP.	W.	L.	Pct.	H.	R.	ER.	SO.	BB.	ERA.
1987—San Francisco	National	2	2⅔	0	0	.000	2	2	2	4	4	6.75
1989—San Francisco	National	2	11⅔	1	0	1.000	16	7	7	8	2	5.40
Championship Series Totals—2 Years		4	14⅓	1	0	1.000	18	9	9	12	6	5.65

WORLD SERIES RECORD

Year Club	League	G.	IP.	W.	L.	Pct.	H.	R.	ER.	SO.	BB.	ERA.
1989—San Francisco	National	2	7⅓	0	2	.000	13	9	8	8	1	9.82

ALL-STAR GAME RECORD

Member of National League All-Star Team in 1985; did not play.

RICHARD LEO GEDMAN JR.

(Rich)

Born September 26, 1959, at Worcester, Mass.
Height, 6.00. Weight, 222.
Throws right and bats lefthanded.

Holds major league records for most putouts (36) and chances accepted (37) by catcher, two consecutive nine-in-ning games, April 29, 30, 1986.
Shares major league record for most putouts by catcher, nine-inning game (20), April 29, 1986.
Shares American League record for most chances accepted by catcher, nine-inning game (20), April 29, 1986.
Major League stolen bases: 1985 (2), 1986 (1). Total—3.
Hit for the cycle, September 18, 1985.
Led American League catchers in total chances with 937 and passed balls with 14 in 1986.
Led International League catchers in double plays with 13 in 1980.
Named catcher on THE SPORTING NEWS American League All-Star Team, 1986.
Named American League Rookie Player of the Year by THE SPORTING NEWS, 1981.

Year Club	League	Pos.	G.	AB.	R.	H.	2B.	3B.	HR.	RBI.	B.A.	PO.	A.	E.	F.A.
1978—Winter Haven.......	Fla. St.	C	98	297	35	89	17	3	3	32	.300	377	39	2	*.995
1979—Bristol....................	East.	C	130	470	48	129	25	1	12	63	.274	497	58	11	*.981
1980—Pawtucket	Int.	C	111	347	43	82	18	2	11	29	.236	367	*65	7	.984
1980—Boston....................	Amer.	C	9	24	2	5	0	0	0	1	.208	13	0	2	.867
1981—Pawtucket	Int.	C	25	81	8	24	3	0	2	11	.296	176	20	6	.969
1981—Boston....................	Amer.	C	62	205	22	59	15	0	5	26	.288	275	30	3	.990

Year Club	League	Pos.	G.	AB.	R.	H.	2B.	3B.	HR.	RBI.	B.A.	PO.	A.	E.	F.A.
1982—Boston	Amer.	C	92	289	30	72	17	2	4	26	.249	397	29	10	.977
1983—Boston	Amer.	C	81	204	21	60	16	1	2	18	.294	274	26	6	.980
1984—Boston	Amer.	C	133	449	54	121	26	4	24	72	.269	693	58	★18	.977
1985—Boston	Amer.	C	144	498	66	147	30	5	18	80	.295	768	★78	★15	.983
1986—Boston†	Amer.	C	135	462	49	119	29	0	16	65	.258	★866	65	6	.994
1987—Boston‡	Amer.	C	52	151	11	31	8	0	1	13	.205	306	14	8	.976
1988—Boston§	Amer.	C	95	299	33	69	14	0	9	39	.231	570	40	5	.992
1988—Pawtucket	Int.	C	4	15	2	7	1	0	1	1	.467	13	1	1	.933
1989—Boston	Amer.	C	93	260	24	55	9	0	4	16	.212	486	36	10	.981
Major League Totals—10 Years			896	2841	312	738	164	12	83	356	.260	4648	376	83	.984

Signed as free agent by Boston Red Sox' organization, August 5, 1977.
†Granted free agency, November 12, 1986; re-signed by Red Sox, May 2, 1987.
‡On disabled list, July 7 to July 22 and July 30, 1987 through remainder of season.
§On disabled list, April 26 to May 20, 1988; included rehabilitation disability assignment to Pawtucket, May 14 to May 20, 1988.

CHAMPIONSHIP SERIES RECORD

Year Club	League	Pos.	G.	AB.	R.	H.	2B.	3B.	HR.	RBI.	B.A.	PO.	A.	E.	F.A.
1986—Boston	Amer.	C	7	28	4	10	1	0	1	6	.357	45	4	0	1.000
1988—Boston	Amer.	C	4	14	1	5	0	0	1	1	.357	34	5	0	1.000
Championship Series Totals—2 Years			11	42	5	15	1	0	2	7	.357	79	9	0	1.000

WORLD SERIES RECORD

Year Club	League	Pos.	G.	AB.	R.	H.	2B.	3B.	HR.	RBI.	B.A.	PO.	A.	E.	F.A.
1986—Boston	Amer.	C	7	30	1	6	1	0	1	1	.200	46	3	2	.961

ALL-STAR GAME RECORD

Year	League	Pos.	AB.	R.	H.	2B.	3B.	HR.	RBI.	B.A.	PO.	A.	E.	F.A.
1985—American		C	1	0	0	0	0	0	0	.000	4	0	0	1.000
1986—American		C	0	0	0	0	0	0	0	.000	1	1	0	1.000
All-Star Game Totals—2 Years			1	0	0	0	0	0	0	.000	5	1	0	1.000

ROBERT PETER GEREN III
(Bob)

Born September 22, 1961, at San Diego, Calif.
Height, 6.03. Weight, 205.
Throws and bats righthanded.

Led Eastern League catchers in fielding percentage with .994 in 1987.
Led Texas League catchers in fielding percentage with .996 in 1985.
Led Midwest League catchers in putouts with 826, assists with 102 and total chances with 939 in 1983.

Year Club	League	Pos.	G.	AB.	R.	H.	2B.	3B.	HR.	RBI.	B.A.	PO.	A.	E.	F.A.
1979—Walla Walla	N'west	C	54	151	19	26	5	0	0	16	.172	183	23	9	.958
1980—Reno	Calif.	C	48	157	24	45	7	1	4	23	.287	89	17	4	.964
1980—Walla Walla†	N'west	C	51	177	19	45	8	1	2	28	.254	306	40	10	.972
1981—St. Petersburg	Fla. St.	C	64	167	15	37	9	1	0	13	.222	204	24	3	.987
1982—St. Petersburg	Fla. St.	★C-OF-1B	110	352	38	86	24	1	1	45	.244	500	★72	10	.983
1983—Springfield	Midw.	C-1B	124	434	67	115	21	3	24	73	.265	829	104	11	.988
1984—Arkansas	Texas	C-1B-3B	86	292	39	72	12	0	15	40	.247	545	56	8	.987
1984—Louisville	A. A.	C	15	40	3	7	1	0	0	3	.175	80	6	1	.989
1985—Arkansas	Texas	C-1B-OF	103	315	38	71	18	1	5	40	.225	562	60	4	.994
1985—Louisville‡	A. A.	C	5	14	2	5	2	0	1	3	.357	27	1	0	1.000
1986—Albany	East.	C-1B	11	27	3	4	1	0	0	0	.148	51	7	0	1.000
1986—Columbus	Int.	C-1B	68	205	24	52	15	3	7	25	.254	270	36	5	.984
1987—Albany	East.	C-1B-3B	78	213	33	47	7	2	11	31	.221	319	45	3	.992
1987—Columbus	Int.	C	5	20	1	3	0	0	1	3	.150	20	3	1	.958
1988—Columbus	Int.	C	95	321	37	87	13	2	8	35	.271	478	72	8	.986
1988—New York	Amer.	C	10	10	0	1	0	0	0	0	.100	18	3	0	1.000
1989—Columbus	Int.	C	27	95	11	24	4	1	2	13	.253	137	18	2	.987
1989—New York	Amer.	C	65	205	26	59	5	1	9	27	.288	308	24	3	.991
Major League Totals—2 Years			75	215	26	60	5	1	9	27	.279	326	27	3	.992

Selected by San Diego Padres' organization in 1st round (24th player selected) of free-agent draft, June 5, 1979.
†Traded to St. Louis Cardinals' organization, December 10, 1980, completing deal in which San Diego Padres traded Pitchers Rollie Fingers and Bob Shirley, Catcher-First Baseman Gene Tenace and a player to be named later to St. Louis Cardinals for Catchers Terry Kennedy and Steve Swisher, Pitchers John Littlefield, Al Olmsted, Kim Seaman and John Urrea and Infielder Mike Phillips, December 8, 1980.
‡Granted free agency, October 15, 1985; signed by Columbus (New York Yankees' organization), November 7, 1985.

KIRK HAROLD GIBSON

Born May 28, 1957, at Pontiac, Mich.
Height, 6.03. Weight, 215.
Throws and bats lefthanded.
Attended Michigan State University, East Lansing, Mich.

Shares major league record for most home runs, opening day of season (2), April 7, 1986.
Major League stolen bases: 1979 (3), 1980 (4), 1981 (17), 1982 (9), 1983 (14), 1984 (29), 1985 (30), 1986 (34), 1987 (26), 1988 (31), 1989 (12). Total—209.

Named National League Most Valuable Player by Baseball Writers' Association of America, 1988.
Named outfielder on THE SPORTING NEWS National League Silver Slugger team, 1988.
Received reported $200,000 bonus to sign with Detroit Tigers, 1978.
Named outfielder on THE SPORTING NEWS College Baseball All-America Team, 1978.
Selected by St. Louis Cardinals in 7th round (173rd player selected) of 1979 NFL draft.
Named as wide receiver on THE SPORTING NEWS College Football All-America Team, 1978.

Year Club	League	Pos.	G.	AB.	R.	H.	2B.	3B.	HR.	RBI.	B.A.	PO.	A.	E.	F.A.
1978—Lakeland†	Fla. St.	OF	54	175	27	42	5	4	8	40	.240	115	2	6	.951
1979—Evansville‡	A. A.	OF	89	327	50	80	13	5	9	42	.245	100	5	9	.921
1979—Detroit	Amer.	OF	12	38	3	9	3	0	1	4	.237	15	0	0	1.000
1980—Detroit§	Amer.	OF	51	175	23	46	2	1	9	16	.263	122	1	1	.992
1981—Detroit	Amer.	OF	83	290	41	95	11	3	9	40	.328	142	1	4	.973
1982—Detroit x	Amer.	OF	69	266	34	74	16	2	8	35	.278	167	4	1	.994
1983—Detroit	Amer.	OF	128	401	60	91	12	9	15	51	.227	116	2	3	.975
1984—Detroit	Amer.	OF	149	531	92	150	23	10	27	91	.282	245	4	•12	.954
1985—Detroit y	Amer.	OF	154	581	96	167	37	5	29	97	.287	286	1	•11	.963
1986—Detroit z	Amer.	OF	119	441	84	118	11	2	28	86	.268	190	2	2	.990
1987—Toledo	Int.	DH	6	17	2	4	0	0	0	3	.235	0	0	0	.000
1987—Detroit ab	Amer.	OF	128	487	95	135	25	3	24	79	.277	253	6	7	.974
1988—Los Angeles	Nat.	OF	150	542	106	157	28	1	25	76	.290	311	6	•12	.964
1989—Los Angeles c	Nat.	OF	71	253	35	54	8	2	9	28	.213	146	3	3	.980
American League Totals—9 Years			893	3210	528	885	140	35	150	499	.276	1536	21	41	.974
National League Totals—2 Years			221	795	141	211	36	3	34	104	.265	457	9	15	.969
Major League Totals—11 Years			1114	4005	669	1096	176	38	184	603	.274	1993	30	56	.973

Selected by Detroit Tigers' organization in 1st round (12th player selected) of free-agent draft, June 6, 1978.
†On restricted list, August 15, 1978, to March 1, 1979.
‡On disabled list, April 13 to May 21, 1979.
§On disabled list, June 18 to October 6, 1980.
xOn disabled list, July 11, 1982 through remainder of season.
yGranted free agency, November 12, 1985; re-signed by Tigers, January 8, 1986.
zOn disabled list, April 23 to June 2, 1986.
aOn Detroit disabled list, March 30 to May 5, 1987; included rehabilitation disability assignment to Toledo, April 28 to May 5, 1987.
bGranted free agency, January 22, 1988; signed by Los Angeles Dodgers, January 29, 1988.
cOn disabled list, April 26 to May 23 and July 23, 1989 through remainder of season.

CHAMPIONSHIP SERIES RECORD

Shares Championship Series record for most game-winning RBIs, series (2), 1988.
Shares American League Championship Series record for most strikeouts, series (8), 1987.

Year Club	League	Pos.	G.	AB.	R.	H.	2B.	3B.	HR.	RBI.	B.A.	PO.	A.	E.	F.A.
1984—Detroit	Amer.	OF	3	12	2	5	1	0	1	2	.417	7	0	0	1.000
1987—Detroit	Amer.	OF	5	21	4	6	1	0	1	4	.286	10	1	0	1.000
1988—Los Angeles	Nat.	OF	7	26	2	4	0	0	2	6	.154	17	1	1	.947
Championship Series Totals—3 Years			15	59	8	15	2	0	4	12	.254	34	2	1	.973

WORLD SERIES RECORD

Year Club	League	Pos.	G.	AB.	R.	H.	2B.	3B.	HR.	RBI.	B.A.	PO.	A.	E.	F.A.
1984—Detroit	Amer.	OF	5	18	4	6	0	0	2	7	.333	5	1	2	.750
1988—Los Angeles	Nat.	PH	1	1	1	1	0	0	1	2	1.000	0	0	0	.000
World Series Totals—2 Years			6	19	5	7	0	0	3	9	.368	5	1	2	.750

PAUL MARSHALL GIBSON

Born January 4, 1960, at Southampton, N.Y.
Height, 6.00. Weight, 185.
Throws left and bats righthanded.
Attended Suffolk County Community College, Selden, N.Y.

Tied for International League lead in shutouts with 2 in 1987.

Year Club	League	G.	IP.	W.	L.	Pct.	H.	R.	ER.	SO.	BB.	ERA.
1978—Shelby	W. Carol.	24	140	9	6	.600	106	57	47	71	71	3.02
1979—Tampa	Florida St.	24	129	3	8	.273	121	56	44	58	46	3.07
1980—Cedar Rapids†	Midwest	28	146	6	•15	.286	171	97	80	74	53	4.93
1981—Lakeland	Florida St.	20	64	4	3	.571	64	25	21	38	21	2.95
1982—Birmingham‡	Southern	44	77⅓	3	3	.500	60	25	23	71	39	2.68
1983—Orlando§	Southern	40	76⅔	1	7	.125	91	59	52	45	56	6.10
1984—Orlando x	Southern	27	121	7	7	.500	125	71	52	64	54	3.87
1985—Birmingham	Southern	36	144½	8	8	.500	135	73	66	79	63	4.12
1986—Glens Falls	Eastern	9	19⅔	3	1	.750	16	3	3	21	7	1.37
1986—Nashville	Am. Assoc.	30	113⅓	5	6	.455	121	58	50	91	40	3.97
1987—Toledo	Int'national	27	179	•14	7	.667	173	83	69	118	57	3.47
1988—Detroit	American	40	92	4	2	.667	83	33	30	50	34	2.93
1989—Detroit	American	45	132	4	8	.333	129	71	68	77	57	4.64
Major League Totals—2 Years		85	224	8	10	.444	212	104	98	127	91	3.94

Selected by Cincinnati Reds' organization in 3rd round of free-agent draft, January 10, 1978.
†Released, April 8, 1981; signed by Lakeland (Detroit Tigers' organization), May 23, 1981.
‡Drafted by Minnesota Twins, December 6, 1982.
§On disabled list, August 4 to August 14, 1983.
xGranted free agency, October 15, 1984; signed by Birmingham (Detroit Tigers' organization), November 9, 1984.

BYRON BRETT GIDEON
(Known by middle name.)
Born August 8, 1963, at Ozona, Tex.
Height, 6.02. Weight, 195.
Throws and bats righthanded.
Attended Bee County College, Beeville, Tex., and University of Mary Hardin-Baylor, Belton, Tex.

Major League saves: 1987 (3).

Year Club	League	G.	IP.	W.	L.	Pct.	H.	R.	ER.	SO.	BB.	ERA.
1985—Macon	S. Atlantic	15	82⅓	4	7	.364	71	38	30	62	46	3.28
1986—Prince William	Carolina	26	55⅔	1	6	.143	60	43	34	41	37	5.50
1986—Macon	S. Atlantic	6	48	5	1	.833	33	16	14	38	35	2.63
1986—Nashua	Eastern	4	11⅔	0	1	.000	13	6	4	6	5	3.09
1987—Harrisburg	Eastern	26	36⅓	4	3	.571	27	10	8	39	10	1.98
1987—Pittsburgh	National	29	36⅔	1	5	.167	34	22	19	31	10	4.66
1988—Harrisburg	Eastern	25	39⅔	3	2	.600	27	8	6	30	21	1.36
1988—Buffalo†	Am. Assoc.	24	42	1	6	.143	33	17	17	41	19	3.64
1989—Indianapolis	Am. Assoc.	47	71⅔	7	2	.778	41	24	18	71	23	2.26
1989—Montreal	National	4	4⅔	0	0	.000	5	1	1	2	5	1.93
Major League Totals—2 Years		33	41⅓	1	5	.167	39	23	20	33	15	4.35

Selected by Houston Astros' organization in 8th round of free-agent draft, January 11, 1983.
Selected by Pittsburgh Pirates' organization in 6th round of free-agent draft, June 3, 1985.
†Traded to Montreal Expos, March 30, 1989, completing deal in which Montreal traded Pitcher Neal Heaton to Pittsburgh Pirates for a player to be named later, March 28, 1989.

OTIS BERNARD GILKEY
(Known by middle name.)

Born September 24, 1966, at St. Louis, Mo.
Height, 6.00. Weight, 170.
Throws and bats righthanded.
Led Texas League in stolen bases with 53 and caught stealing with 22 in 1989.
Led New York-Pennsylvania League outfielders in total chances with 185 in 1985.

Year Club	League	Pos.	G.	AB.	R.	H.	2B.	3B.	HR.	RBI.	B.A.	PO.	A.	E.	F.A.
1985—Erie	NYP	OF	•77	★294	57	60	9	1	7	27	.204	★164	★13	★8	.957
1986—Savannah†	S. Atl.	OF	105	374	64	88	15	4	6	36	.235	220	7	5	.978
1987—Springfield‡	Midw.	OF	46	162	30	37	5	0	0	9	.228	79	5	4	.955
1988—Springfield	Midw.	OF	125	491	84	120	18	7	6	36	.244	165	10	6	.967
1989—Arkansas	Texas	OF	131	500	★104	139	25	3	6	57	.278	236	★22	9	.966

Signed as free agent by St. Louis Cardinals' organization, August 22, 1984.
†On disabled list, April 10 to April 25, 1986.
‡On disabled list, May 29, 1987 through remainder of season.

JOSEPH ELLIOTT GIRARDI
(Joe)

Born October 14, 1964, at Peoria, Ill.
Height, 5.11. Weight, 195.
Throws and bats righthanded.
Received degree in industrial engineering from Northwestern University, Evanston, Ill., in 1986.

Major League stolen bases: 1989 (2).
Led Eastern League catchers in putouts with 448, fielding percentage with .992, total chances with 528 and tied for lead in double plays with 5 in 1988.
Led Carolina League catchers in total chances with 661 and tied for lead in passed balls with 17 in 1987.

Year Club	League	Pos.	G.	AB.	R.	H.	2B.	3B.	HR.	RBI.	B.A.	PO.	A.	E.	F.A.
1986—Peoria†	Midw.	C	68	230	36	71	13	1	3	28	.309	405	34	5	.989
1987—Winston-Salem	Carol.	C	99	364	51	102	9	8	8	46	.280	★569	★74	18	.973
1988—Pittsfield‡	East.	★C-OF	104	357	44	97	14	1	7	41	.272	460	★76	6	.989
1989—Chicago	Nat.	C	59	157	15	39	10	0	1	14	.248	332	28	7	.981
1989—Iowa	A. A.	C	32	110	12	27	4	2	2	11	.245	172	21	1	.995
Major League Totals—1 Year		59	157	15	39	10	0	1	14	.248	332	28	7	.981

Selected by Chicago Cubs' organization in 5th round of free-agent draft, June 2, 1986.
†On disabled list, August 27, 1986 through remainder of season.
‡On disabled list, August 7, 1988 through remainder of season.

CHAMPIONSHIP SERIES RECORD

Year Club	League	Pos.	G.	AB.	R.	H.	2B.	3B.	HR.	RBI.	B.A.	PO.	A.	E.	F.A.
1989—Chicago	Nat.	C	4	10	1	1	0	0	0	0	.100	20	0	0	1.000

CLINTON DANIEL GLADDEN III
(Dan)

Born July 7, 1957, at San Jose, Calif.
Height, 5.11. Weight, 181.
Throws and bats righthanded.
Attended DeAnza College, Cupertino, Calif., and
Fresno State University, Fresno, Calif.
Brother of Jeff Gladden, pitcher in Kansas City Royals' and
San Francisco Giants' organization, 1980 through 1984.

Major League stolen bases: 1983 (4), 1984 (31), 1985 (32), 1986 (27), 1987 (25), 1988 (28), 1989 (23). Total—170.
Tied for American League lead in double plays by outfielders with 5 in 1988.
Led Texas League in stolen bases with 52 and caught stealing with 26 in 1981.

Year	Club	League	Pos.	G.	AB.	R.	H.	2B.	3B.	HR.	RBI.	B.A.	PO.	A.	E.	F.A.
1979—Fresno	Calif.	OF-2B-SS	60	228	41	70	9	1	3	31	.307	56	16	3	.960
1980—Fresno	Calif.	OF	62	237	46	72	10	2	9	41	.304	68	3	1	.986
1980—Shreveport	Texas	OF-SS	74	292	51	86	11	2	9	35	.295	169	14	5	.973
1981—Shreveport	Texas	OF-SS-2B	124	472	81	148	23	9	8	44	.314	211	12	3	.987
1982—Phoenix	P. C.	OF	130	503	93	155	40	5	10	74	.308	264	16	7	.976
1983—Phoenix	P. C.	OF	127	505	113	153	30	9	12	80	.303	319	6	7	.979
1983—San Francisco	Nat.	OF	18	63	6	14	2	0	1	9	.222	53	0	0	1.000
1984—Phoenix†	P. C.	OF	59	234	70	93	11	7	3	27	.397	130	4	2	.985
1984—San Francisco	Nat.	OF	86	342	71	120	17	2	4	31	.351	232	8	3	.988
1985—San Francisco	Nat.	OF	142	502	64	122	15	8	7	41	.243	273	3	7	.975
1986—San Francisco‡	Nat.	OF	102	351	55	97	16	1	4	29	.276	226	7	3	.987
1986—Phoenix§ x	P. C.	OF	7	27	5	9	4	0	0	0	.333	11	0	0	1.000
1987—Minnesota	Amer.	OF	121	438	69	109	21	2	8	38	.249	223	9	3	.987
1988—Minnesota	Amer.	O-2-3-P	141	576	91	155	32	6	11	62	.269	319	12	3	.991
1989—Minnesota y	Amer.	OF-P	121	461	69	136	23	3	8	46	.295	245	8	9	.966
National League Totals—4 Years			348	1258	196	353	50	11	16	110	.281	784	18	13	.984
American League Totals—3 Years			383	1475	229	400	76	11	27	146	.271	787	29	15	.982
Major League Totals—7 Years			731	2733	425	753	126	22	43	256	.276	1571	47	28	.983

Signed as free agent by San Francisco Giants' organization, June 17, 1979.
†On disabled list, April 19 to May 1, 1984.
‡On disabled list, June 4 to July 23, 1986; included rehabilitation disability assignment to Phoenix, July 14 to July 23, 1986.
§Batted left and righthanded.
xTraded with Pitcher David Blakley to Minnesota Twins for Pitchers Jose Dominguez and Ray Velasquez and a player to be named later, March 31 1987; San Francisco Giants' organization acquired Pitcher Bryan Hickerson to complete deal, June 15, 1987.
yOn disabled list, June 25 to July 10 and July 17 to August 7, 1989.

CHAMPIONSHIP SERIES RECORD

Shares Championship Series records for most times hit by pitch, series (2), 1987 and game (2), October 11, 1987.

Year	Club	League	Pos.	G.	AB.	R.	H.	2B.	3B.	HR.	RBI.	B.A.	PO	A.	E.	F.A.
1987—Minnesota	Amer.	OF	5	20	5	7	2	0	0	5	.350	12	0	0	1.000

WORLD SERIES RECORD

Shares World Series records for most grand slams, game (1), October 17, 1987; most runs batted in, inning (4), October 17, 1987, fourth inning.

Year	Club	League	Pos.	G.	AB.	R.	H.	2B.	3B.	HR.	RBI.	B.A.	PO.	A.	E.	F.A.
1987—Minnesota	Amer.	OF	7	31	3	9	2	1	1	7	.290	12	0	0	1.000

PITCHING RECORD

Year	Club	League	G.	IP.	W.	L.	Pct.	H.	R.	ER.	SO.	BB.	ERA.
1988—Minnesota	American	1	1	0	0	.000	0	0	0	0	0	0.00
1989—Minnesota	American	1	1	0	0	.000	2	1	1	0	1	9.00
Major League Totals—2 Years		2	2	0	0	.000	2	1	1	0	1	4.50

THOMAS MICHAEL GLAVINE

Name pronounced GLA-vin.

(Tom)

Born March 25, 1966, at Concord, Mass.
Height, 6.01. Weight, 190.
Throws and bats lefthanded.

Led Gulf Coast League in wild pitches with 12 in 1984.
Drafted by Los Angeles Kings in 1984 NHL entry draft. Fourth Kings pick, 69th player overall, fourth round.

Year	Club	League	G.	IP.	W.	L.	Pct.	H.	R.	ER.	SO.	BB.	ERA.
1984—Bradenton Braves	Gulf Coast	8	32⅓	2	3	.400	29	17	12	34	13	3.34
1985—Sumter	S. Atlantic	26	168⅔	9	6	.600	114	58	44	174	73	*2.35
1986—Greenville	Southern	22	145⅓	11	6	.647	129	62	55	114	70	3.41
1986—Richmond	Int'national	7	40	1	5	.167	40	29	25	12	27	5.63
1987—Richmond	Int'national	22	150⅓	6	12	.333	142	70	56	91	56	3.35
1987—Atlanta	National	9	50⅓	2	4	.333	55	34	31	20	33	5.54
1988—Atlanta	National	34	195⅓	7	*17	.292	201	111	99	84	63	4.56
1989—Atlanta	National	29	186	14	8	.636	172	88	76	90	40	3.68
Major League Totals—3 Years		72	431⅔	23	29	.442	428	233	206	194	136	4.29

Selected by Atlanta Braves' organization in 2nd round of free-agent draft, June 4, 1984.

JERRY DON GLEATON

(Jerry Don)

Born September 14, 1957, at Brownwood, Tex.
Height, 6.03. Weight, 210.
Throws and bats lefthanded.
Attended University of Texas, Austin, Tex.

Major League saves: 1984 (2), 1985 (1), 1987 (5), 1988 (3). Total—11.
Tied for Eastern League lead in complete games with 13 in 1982.
Tied for Texas League lead in home runs allowed with 17 in 1980.

Year Club	League	G.	IP.	W.	L.	Pct.	H.	R.	ER.	SO.	BB.	ERA.
1979—Tulsa	Texas	5	35	3	2	.600	37	19	19	21	15	4.89
1979—Texas	American	5	10	0	1	.000	15	7	7	2	2	6.30
1980—Tulsa	Texas	25	178	13	7	.650	179	83	72	138	68	3.64
1980—Texas†	American	5	7	0	0	.000	5	2	2	2	4	2.57
1981—Seattle	American	20	85	4	7	.364	88	50	45	31	38	4.76
1981—Spokane	P. Coast	13	91	5	7	.417	104	53	42	57	39	4.15
1982—Lynn	Eastern	24	182	15	7	.682	175	71	55	132	54	2.72
1982—Seattle	American	3	4⅔	0	0	.000	7	7	7	1	2	13.50
1983—Salt Lake City	P. Coast	24	137⅓	9	9	.500	189	112	102	73	81	6.68
1984—Salt Lake City‡	P. Coast	29	49⅔	4	1	.800	62	39	32	39	17	5.80
1984—Denver	Am. Assoc.	12	20	1	1	.500	20	5	4	10	4	1.80
1984—Chicago	American	11	18⅓	1	2	.333	20	12	7	4	6	3.44
1985—Buffalo	Am. Assoc.	38	55⅓	8	2	★.800	62	17	15	37	21	2.44
1985—Chicago	American	31	29⅔	1	0	1.000	37	19	19	22	13	5.76
1986—Buffalo§	Am. Assoc.	46	78⅓	4	3	.571	79	34	28	77	35	3.22
1987—Omaha	Am. Assoc.	6	15	2	0	1.000	14	6	5	9	6	3.00
1987—Kansas City	American	48	50⅔	4	4	.500	38	28	24	44	28	4.26
1988—Omaha	Am. Assoc.	15	37⅓	4	2	.667	30	7	6	40	14	1.45
1988—Kansas City	American	42	38	0	4	.000	33	17	15	29	17	3.55
1989—Kansas City	American	15	14⅓	0	0	.000	20	10	9	9	6	5.65
1989—Omaha	Am. Assoc.	24	56⅔	3	3	.500	40	12	7	57	22	1.11
Major League Totals—9 Years		180	257⅔	10	18	.357	263	152	135	144	116	4.72

Selected by Baltimore Orioles' organization in 2nd round of free-agent draft, June 8, 1976.
Selected by Texas Rangers' organization in 1st round (17th player selected) of free-agent draft, June 5, 1979.
†Traded with Pitchers Brian Allard, Ken Clay and Steve Finch, Shortstop Rick Auerbach and Outfielder Richie Zisk to Seattle Mariners for Catcher Larry Cox, Pitcher Rick Honeycutt, Outfielders Willie Horton and Leon Roberts and Shortstop Mario Mendoza, December 12, 1980.
‡Traded with Pitcher Gene Nelson to Chicago White Sox for Pitcher Salome Barojas, June 27, 1984.
§Granted free agency, October 15, 1986; signed by Kansas City Royals, November 15, 1986.

JERRY LEROY GOFF

Born April 12, 1964, at San Rafael, Calif.
Height. 6.03. Weight, 205.
Throws right and bats lefthanded.
Attended Marin Community College, Kentfield, Calif.,
and University of California, Berkeley, Calif.

Led Pacific Coast League in passed balls with 14 in 1989.
Led Northwest League catchers in double plays with 7 in 1986.
Led Midwest League in passed balls with 32 in 1987.

Year Club	League	Pos.	G.	AB.	R.	H.	2B.	3B.	HR.	RBI.	B.A.	PO.	A.	E.	F.A.
1986—Bellingham	N'west	C	54	168	26	32	7	2	7	25	.190	286	35	12	.964
1987—Wausau	Midw.	C-1B	109	336	51	78	17	2	13	47	.232	583	73	15	.978
1988—San Bernardino	Calif.	C	65	215	38	62	11	0	13	43	.288	383	64	6	.987
1988—Vermont	East.	★C-OF	63	195	27	41	7	1	7	23	.210	283	40	★17	..950
1989—Williamsport	East.	C-OF	33	119	9	22	5	0	3	8	.185	180	21	6	.971
1989—Calgary	P. C.	C-1-3-O	76	253	40	59	16	0	11	50	.233	346	63	12	.971

Selected by Oakland A's organization in 7th round of free-agent draft, January 11, 1983.
Selected by New York Yankees' organization in 12th round of free-agent draft, January 17, 1984.
Selected by Seattle Mariners' organization in 3rd round of free-agent draft, June 2, 1986.

LEONARDO GOMEZ

(Leo)

Born March 2, 1967, in Puerto Rico.
Height, 6.00. Weight, 180.
Throws and bats righthanded.

Led Eastern League in bases on balls received with 89 in 1989.
Led Eastern League third basemen in assists with 256 in 1989.

Year Club	League	Pos.	G.	AB.	R.	H.	2B.	3B.	HR.	RBI.	B.A.	PO.	A.	E.	F.A.
1986—Bluefield†	Appal.	3B-2B-SS	27	88	23	31	7	1	7	28	.352	15	38	7	.883
1987—Hagerstown	Carol.	3B-SS	131	466	94	152	★38	2	19	110	★.326	75	233	33	.903
1988—Charlotte‡	South.	3B-1B	24	89	6	26	5	0	1	10	.292	19	50	8	.896
1989—Hagerstown	East.	3B-SS	134	448	71	126	23	3	18	78	.281	79	257	25	.931

Signed as free agent by Baltimore Orioles' organization, December 13, 1985.
†On disabled list, July 3 to July 31, 1986.
‡On disabled list, May 3, 1988 through remainder of season.

PATRICK ALEXANDER GOMEZ

(Pat)

Born March 17, 1968, at Roseville, Calif.
Height, 5.11. Weight, 185.
Throws and bats lefthanded.

Year Club	League	G.	IP.	W.	L.	Pct.	H.	R.	ER.	SO.	BB.	ERA.
1986—Wytheville	Ap'lachian	11	54	3	6	.333	57	51	31	55	46	5.17
1987—Peoria	Midwest	20	94	3	6	.333	88	55	45	95	71	4.31
1988—Charleston, W. Va.	S. Atlantic	36	78⅔	2	7	.222	75	53	47	97	52	5.38
1989—Winston-Salem	Carolina	23	137⅔	11	6	.647	115	59	42	127	60	2.75
1989—Charlotte†	Southern	2	14⅓	1	0	1.000	14	5	4	11	3	2.51

Selected by Chicago Cubs' organization in 4th round of free-agent draft, June 2, 1986.

†Traded with Catcher Kelly Mann to Atlanta Braves, September 1, 1989, completing deal in which Atlanta traded Pitcher Paul Assenmacher to Chicago Cubs for two players to be named later, August 24, 1989.

RENE ADRIAN GONZALES

Born September 3, 1961, at Austin, Tex.
Height, 6.03. Weight, 191.
Throws and bats righthanded.
Attended Glendale College, Glendale, Calif.; and California State University, Los Angeles, Calif.

Major League stolen bases: 1987 (1), 1988 (2), 1989 (5). Total—8.
Led American Association shortstops in double plays with 79 in 1985.
Led Southern League shortstops in double plays with 102 in 1983.

Year Club	League	Pos.	G.	AB.	R.	H.	2B.	3B.	HR.	RBI.	B.A.	PO.	A.	E.	F.A.
1982—Memphis	South.	SS	56	183	10	39	3	1	1	11	.213	77	183	14	.949
1983—Memphis	South.	SS	144	476	67	128	12	2	2	44	.269	★258	449	20	★.972
1984—Indianapolis	A. A.	SS-3B-2B	114	359	41	84	12	2	2	32	.234	161	349	13	.975
1984—Montreal	Nat.	SS	29	30	5	7	1	0	0	2	.233	17	28	2	.957
1985—Indianapolis	A. A.	SS	130	340	21	77	11	1	0	25	.226	203	★345	23	.960
1986—Indianapolis	A. A.	3B-SS-2B	116	395	57	108	14	2	3	43	.273	208	297	23	.956
1986—Montreal†	Nat.	SS-3B	11	26	1	3	0	0	0	0	.115	7	19	0	1.000
1987—Baltimore	Amer.	3B-2B-SS	37	60	14	16	2	1	1	7	.267	22	43	2	.970
1987—Rochester	Int.	3-S-2-1-O	42	170	20	51	9	3	0	24	.300	72	108	3	.984
1988—Baltimore	Amer.	3-2-S-1-O	92	237	13	51	6	0	2	15	.215	66	185	8	.969
1989—Baltimore	Amer.	2B-3B-SS	71	166	16	36	4	0	1	11	.217	103	146	7	.973
National League Totals—2 Years			40	56	6	10	1	0	0	2	.179	24	47	2	.973
American League Totals—3 Years			200	463	43	103	12	1	4	33	.222	191	374	17	.971
Major League Totals—5 Years			240	519	49	113	13	1	4	35	.218	215	421	19	.971

Selected by Montreal Expos' organization in 5th round of free-agent draft, June 7, 1982.

†Traded to Baltimore Orioles, December 16, 1986, completing deals in which Baltimore traded Pitcher Dennis Martinez to Montreal Expos on June 16, 1986 and Catcher John Stefero to Montreal on December 8, 1986, both for a player to be named later.

DENIO MARIANO GONZALEZ (MANZUETA)
(Denny)

Born July 22, 1963, at Sabana Grande Boya, D.R.
Height, 5.11. Weight, 185.
Throws and bats righthanded.

Major League stolen bases: 1984 (1), 1985 (2). Total—3.

Year Club	League	Pos.	G.	AB.	R.	H.	2B.	3B.	HR.	RBI.	B.A.	PO.	A.	E.	F.A.
1981—Bradenton Pir.	Gulf C.	2B-3B	50	179	32	62	5	3	2	24	.346	102	113	14	.939
1982—Portland	P. C.	2B-3B	51	164	23	37	4	6	0	9	.226	106	133	20	.923
1982—Buffalo	East.	2B	68	252	28	70	5	4	3	21	.278	137	176	11	.966
1983—Hawaii	P. C.	SS-2B	125	449	76	121	18	8	9	48	.269	193	319	34	.938
1984—Hawaii	P. C.	OF-3B-2B	113	380	61	114	22	7	15	67	.300	121	84	5	.976
1984—Pittsburgh	Nat.	3B-SS-OF	26	82	9	15	3	1	0	4	.183	26	53	3	.963
1985—Hawaii	P. C.	3-O-2-S	106	365	68	105	21	6	12	57	.288	97	183	15	.949
1985—Pittsburgh	Nat.	3B-OF-2B	35	124	11	28	4	0	4	12	.226	44	42	8	.915
1986—Hawaii	P. C.	3B-SS	109	379	48	84	10	2	10	45	.222	64	157	18	.925
1987—Pittsburgh	Nat.	SS	5	7	1	0	0	0	0	0	.000	2	1	0	1.000
1987—Vancouver	P. C.	3B	113	413	62	108	20	0	13	57	.262	76	232	●25	.925
1988—Buffalo	A. A.	3B-2B	75	267	37	79	14	2	8	39	.296	64	166	17	.931
1988—Pittsburgh†	Nat.	SS-2B-3B	24	32	5	6	1	0	0	1	.188	20	22	2	.955
1989—Colorado Springs	P. C.	3B-2B	128	420	86	121	17	2	★27	76	.288	72	184	21	.924
1989—Cleveland	Amer.	3B	8	17	3	5	1	0	0	1	.294	0	0	1	.000
Major League Totals—5 Years			98	262	29	54	9	1	4	18	.206	92	118	14	.938

Signed as free agent by Pittsburgh Pirates' organization, June 25, 1981.

†Traded to Cleveland Indians for a player to be named later, November 28, 1988.

GERMAN JOSE GONZALEZ

Born October 3, 1965, at Rio Caribe, Venez.
Height, 6.00. Weight, 170.
Throws and bats righthanded.

Major League saves: 1988 (1).
Led Southern League in saves with 31 in 1988.
Named Southern League Pitcher of the Year, 1988.

Year Club	League	G.	IP.	W.	L.	Pct.	H.	R.	ER.	SO.	BB.	ERA.
1987—Kenosha	Midwest	47	82⅓	8	5	.615	70	26	23	72	22	2.51
1988—Orlando	Southern	50	61⅔	2	1	.667	41	9	7	69	19	1.02
1988—Minnesota	American	16	21⅓	0	0	.000	20	8	8	19	8	3.38
1989—Minnesota†	American	22	29	3	2	.600	32	17	15	25	11	4.66

Year Club	League	G.	IP.	W.	L.	Pct.	H.	R.	ER.	SO.	BB.	ERA.
1989—Portland..	P. Coast	17	25⅓	1	1	.500	26	11	11	24	5	3.91
Major League Totals—2 Years..............................		38	50⅓	3	2	.600	52	25	23	44	19	4.11

Signed as free agent by Minnesota Twins' organization, December 29, 1986.
†On disabled list, May 25 to July 2, 1989.

JOSE RAFAEL GONZALEZ

Born November 23, 1964, at Puerto Plata, Dominican Republic.
Height, 6.02. Weight, 201.
Throws and bats righthanded.

Major League stolen bases: 1985 (1), 1986 (4), 1987 (5), 1988 (3), 1989 (9). Total—22.
Tied for Texas League lead in caught stealing with 17 in 1985.
Led Texas League outfielders in total chances with 320 in 1985.

Year Club	League	Pos.	G.	AB.	R.	H.	2B.	3B.	HR.	RBI.	B.A.	PO.	A.	E.	F.A.
1981—Lethbridge	Pion.	OF	34	103	11	14	1	1	0	7	.136	65	6	5	.934
1982—Lethbridge	Pion.	OF	55	209	35	63	14	1	4	47	.301	112	7	1	.992
1983—Lodi†	Calif.	OF	76	310	48	91	17	4	6	36	.294	182	7	4	.979
1984—Bakersfield............	Calif.	OF	129	484	86	107	26	1	11	59	.221	264	13	9	.969
1985—San Antonio..........	Texas	OF	128	448	82	137	22	6	13	62	.306	★294	15	11	.966
1985—Los Angeles	Nat.	OF	23	11	6	3	2	0	0	0	.273	10	0	0	1.000
1986—Albuquerque........	P. C.	OF	89	303	39	84	20	3	6	37	.277	171	10	6	.968
1986—Los Angeles	Nat.	OF	57	93	15	20	5	1	2	6	.215	73	0	6	.924
1987—Albuquerque........	P. C.	OF	116	339	67	95	22	3	13	61	.280	225	10	9	.963
1987—Los Angeles	Nat.	OF	18	16	2	3	2	0	0	1	.188	19	1	0	1.000
1988—Albuquerque........	P. C.	OF	84	288	57	88	15	2	5	22	.306	177	7	6	.968
1988—Los Angeles	Nat.	OF	37	24	7	2	1	0	0	0	.083	15	0	1	.938
1989—Albuquerque........	P. C.	OF	50	180	32	48	12	4	4	31	.267	98	3	2	.981
1989—Los Angeles	Nat.	OF	95	261	31	70	11	2	3	18	.268	171	8	6	.968
Major League Totals—5 Years.................			230	405	61	98	21	3	5	25	.242	288	9	13	.958

Signed as free agent by Los Angeles Dodgers' organization, August 12, 1980.
†On disabled list, July 7, 1983 through remainder of season.

CHAMPIONSHIP SERIES RECORD

Year Club	League	Pos.	G.	AB.	R.	H.	2B.	3B.	HR.	RBI.	B.A.	PO.	A.	E.	F.A.
1988—Los Angeles	Nat.	OF-PR	5	0	2	0	0	0	0	0	.000	3	0	0	1.000

WORLD SERIES RECORD

Year Club	League	Pos.	G.	AB.	R.	H.	2B.	3B.	HR.	RBI.	B.A.	PO.	A.	E.	F.A.
1988—Los Angeles	Nat.	PH-OF	4	2	0	0	0	0	0	0	.000	2	0	0	1.000

JUAN A. GONZALEZ (VAZQUEZ)

Born October 16, 1969, at Vega Baja, Puerto Rico.
Height, 6.03. Weight, 190.
Throws and bats righthanded.

Led Texas League in total bases with 254 in 1989.

Year Club	League	Pos.	G.	AB.	R.	H.	2B.	3B.	HR.	RBI.	B.A.	PO.	A.	E.	F.A.
1986—Sarasota Rangers	Gulf C.	OF	60	★233	24	56	4	1	0	36	.240	89	6	●6	.941
1987—Gastonia................	S. Atl.	OF	127	509	69	135	21	2	14	74	.265	234	10	12	.953
1988—Port Charlotte†	Fla. St.	OF	77	277	25	71	14	3	8	43	.256	139	5	4	.973
1989—Tulsa	Texas	OF	133	502	73	147	30	7	21	85	.293	292	15	9	.972
1989—Texas....................	Amer.	OF	24	60	6	9	3	0	1	7	.150	53	0	2	.964
Major League Totals—1 Year..................			24	60	6	9	3	0	1	7	.150	53	0	2	.964

Signed as free agent by Texas Rangers' organization, May 30, 1986.
†On disabled list, April 27 to June 17, 1988.

DWIGHT EUGENE GOODEN

Born November 16, 1964, at Tampa, Fla.
Height, 6.03. Weight, 203.
Throws and bats righthanded.
Uncle of Gary Sheffield, infielder with Milwaukee Brewers.

Holds major league record for most strikeouts by rookie, season (276), 1984.
Shares modern major league record for most strikeouts, two consecutive games (32), September 12, 17, 1984.
Holds National League record for most strikeouts, three consecutive games (43), September 7, 12, 17, 1984.
Major League saves: 1989 (1).
Led National League in complete games with 16 in 1985.
Tied for National League lead in balks with 7 in 1984.
Led Carolina League in shutouts with 6 in 1983.
Named National League Pitcher of the Year by THE SPORTING NEWS, 1985.
Won National League Cy Young Memorial Award, 1985.
Named righthanded pitcher on THE SPORTING NEWS National League All-Star Team, 1985.
Named National League Rookie Pitcher of the Year by THE SPORTING NEWS, 1984.
Named National League Rookie of the Year by Baseball Writers' Association of America, 1984.
Named Carolina League Pitcher of the Year, 1983.
Received reported $125,000 bonus to sign with New York Mets, 1982.

Year Club	League	G.	IP.	W.	L.	Pct.	H.	R.	ER.	SO.	BB.	ERA.
1982—Kingsport	Ap'lachian	9	65⅔	5	4	.556	53	34	18	66	25	2.47
1982—Little Falls	NYP	2	13	0	1	.000	11	6	6	18	3	4.15
1983—Lynchburg	Carolina	27	191	*19	4	.826	121	58	53	*300	*112	*2.50
1984—New York	National	31	218	17	9	.654	161	72	63	*276	73	2.60
1985—New York	National	35	*276⅔	*24	4	.857	198	51	47	*268	69	*1.53
1986—New York	National	33	250	17	6	.739	197	92	79	200	80	2.84
1987—Tidewater†	Int'national	4	22	3	0	1.000	20	7	5	24	9	2.05
1987—Lynchburg	Carolina	1	4	0	0	.000	2	0	0	3	2	0.00
1987—New York	National	25	179⅔	15	7	.682	162	68	64	148	53	3.21
1988—New York	National	34	248⅓	18	9	.667	242	98	88	175	57	3.19
1989—New York‡	National	19	118⅓	9	4	.692	93	42	38	101	47	2.89
Major League Totals—6 Years		177	1291	100	39	.719	1053	423	379	1168	379	2.64

Selected by New York Mets' organization in 1st round (fifth player selected) of free-agent draft, June 7, 1982.

†On New York disabled list, April 1 to June 5, 1987; included rehabilitation disability assignment to Tidewater, May 12 to May 17 and May 21 to June 1, 1987.

‡On disabled list, July 2 to September 2, 1989.

CHAMPIONSHIP SERIES RECORD

Holds Championship Series record for most strikeouts, series (20), 1988.

Shares National League Championship Series record for most innings pitched, game (10), October 14, 1986.

Year Club	League	G.	IP.	W.	L.	Pct.	H.	R.	ER.	SO.	BB.	ERA.
1986—New York	National	2	17	0	1	.000	16	2	2	9	5	1.06
1988—New York	National	3	18⅓	0	0	.000	10	6	6	20	8	2.95
Championship Series Totals—2 Years		5	35⅓	0	1	.000	26	8	8	29	13	2.04

WORLD SERIES RECORD

Year Club	League	G.	IP.	W.	L.	Pct.	H.	R.	ER.	SO.	BB.	ERA.
1986—New York	National	2	9	0	2	.000	17	10	8	9	4	8.00

ALL-STAR GAME RECORD

Holds All-Star Game record for most balks, lifetime (2).

Shares All-Star Game record for most games lost, lifetime (2).

Year League		IP.	W.	L.	Pct.	H.	R.	ER.	SO.	BB.	ERA.
1984—National		2	0	0	.000	1	0	0	3	0	0.00
1986—National		3	0	1	.000	3	2	2	2	0	6.00
1988—National		3	0	1	.000	3	1	1	1	1	3.00
All-Star Game Totals—3 Years		8	0	2	.000	7	3	3	6	1	3.38

Member of National League All-Star Team in 1985; did not play.

THOMAS GORDON
(Tom)

Born November 18, 1967, at Sebring, Fla.
Height, 5.09. Weight, 160.
Throws and bats righthanded.

Major League saves: 1989 (1).

Tied for Northwest League lead in balks with 4 in 1987.

Named American League Rookie Pitcher of the Year by THE SPORTING NEWS, 1989.

Year Club	League	G.	IP.	W.	L.	Pct.	H.	R.	ER.	SO.	BB.	ERA.
1986—Sarasota Royals	Gulf Coast	9	44	3	1	.750	31	12	5	47	23	1.02
1986—Omaha	Am. Assoc.	1	1⅓	0	0	.000	6	7	7	3	2	47.25
1987—Eugene	Northwest	15	72⅓	●9	0	●1.000	48	33	23	91	47	2.86
1987—Fort Myers	Florida St.	3	13⅔	1	0	1.000	5	4	4	11	17	2.63
1988—Appleton	Midwest	17	118	7	5	.583	69	30	27	*172	43	2.06
1988—Memphis	Southern	6	47⅛	6	0	1.000	16	3	2	62	17	0.38
1988—Omaha	Am. Assoc.	3	20⅓	3	0	1.000	11	3	3	29	15	1.33
1988—Kansas City	American	5	15⅔	0	2	.000	16	9	9	18	7	5.17
1989—Kansas City	American	49	163	17	9	.654	122	67	66	153	86	3.64
Major League Totals—2 Years		54	178⅔	17	11	.607	138	76	75	171	93	3.78

Selected by Kansas City Royals' organization in 6th round of free-agent draft, June 2, 1986.

RICHARD MICHAEL GOSSAGE
(Rich or Goose)

Born July 5, 1951, at Colorado Springs, Colo.
Height, 6.03. Weight, 226.
Throws and bats righthanded.
Attended Southern Colorado State College, Pueblo, Colo.

Holds National League record for most strikeouts by relief pitcher, season (151), 1977.

Major League saves: 1972 (2), 1974 (1), 1975 (26), 1976 (1), 1977 (26), 1978 (27), 1979 (18), 1980 (33), 1981 (20), 1982 (30), 1983 (22), 1984 (25), 1985 (26), 1986 (21), 1987 (11), 1988 (13), 1989 (5). Total—307.

Led American League in saves with 26 in 1975 and 27 in 1978.

Led American League in games finished in relief with 55 in 1978.

Tied for American League lead in saves with 33 in 1980.

Tied for American League lead in intentional bases on balls issued with 15 in 1975.

Led Midwest League in complete games with 15 and shutouts with 7 in 1971.

Named American League Fireman of the Year by THE SPORTING NEWS, 1975 and 1978.
Named Midwest League Player of the Year, 1971.

Year Club	League	G.	IP.	W.	L.	Pct.	H.	R.	ER.	SO.	BB.	ERA.
1970—Sarasota White Sox	Gulf Coast	3	16	0	0	.000	11	6	5	21	4	2.81
1970—Appleton	Midwest	10	35	0	3	.000	41	27	23	21	19	5.91
1971—Appleton	Midwest	25	187	*18	2	*.900	141	48	38	149	50	*1.83
1972—Chicago	American	36	80	7	1	.875	72	44	38	57	44	4.28
1973—Iowa	Am. Assoc.	12	71	5	4	.556	59	32	29	66	28	3.68
1973—Chicago	American	20	50	0	4	.000	57	44	41	33	37	7.38
1974—Appleton	Midwest	2	8	0	2	.000	8	6	3	5	4	3.38
1974—Chicago	American	39	89	4	6	.400	92	45	41	64	47	4.15
1975—Chicago	American	61	142	9	8	.529	99	32	29	130	70	1.84
1976—Chicago†	American	31	224	9	17	.346	214	104	98	135	90	3.94
1977—Pittsburgh‡	National	72	133	11	9	.550	78	27	24	151	49	1.62
1978—New York	American	63	134	10	11	.476	87	41	30	122	59	2.01
1979—New York§	American	36	58	5	3	.625	48	18	17	41	19	2.64
1980—New York	American	64	99	6	2	.750	74	29	25	103	37	2.27
1981—New York	American	32	47	3	2	.600	22	6	4	48	14	0.77
1982—New York	American	56	93	4	5	.444	63	23	23	102	28	2.23
1983—New York x	American	57	87⅓	13	5	.722	82	27	22	90	25	2.27
1984—San Diego	National	62	101⅓	10	6	.625	75	34	33	84	36	2.90
1985—San Diego y	National	50	79	5	3	.625	64	21	16	52	17	1.82
1986—San Diego z	National	45	64⅔	5	7	.417	69	36	32	63	20	4.45
1987—San Diego ab	National	40	52	5	4	.556	47	18	18	44	19	3.12
1988—Chicago cd	National	46	43⅔	4	4	.500	50	23	21	30	15	4.33
1989—San Francisco e	National	31	43⅔	2	1	.667	32	16	13	24	27	2.68
1989—New York f	American	11	14⅓	1	0	1.000	14	6	6	6	3	3.77
National League Totals—7 Years		346	518⅓	42	34	.553	415	175	157	448	183	2.73
American League Totals—12 Years		507	1117⅔	71	64	.526	924	419	374	931	473	3.01
Major League Totals—18 Years		853	1636	113	98	.536	1339	594	531	1379	656	2.92

Selected by Chicago White Sox' organization in 9th round of free-agent draft, June 4, 1970.
†Traded with Pitcher Terry Forster to Pittsburgh Pirates for Outfielder Richie Zisk and Pitcher Silvio Martinez, December 10, 1976.
‡Granted free agency, October 28, 1977; signed by New York Yankees, November 23, 1977.
§On disabled list, April 21 to July 9, 1979.
xGranted free agency, November 7, 1983; signed by San Diego Padres, January 6, 1984.
yOn disabled list, August 8 to September 1, 1985.
zOn suspended list, August 29 to September 18, 1986.
aOn disabled list, April 15 to May 4, 1987.
bTraded with Pitcher Ray Hayward to Chicago Cubs for Infielders Keith Moreland and Mike Brumley, February 12, 1988.
cOn disabled list, June 16 to July 1, 1988.
dReleased, March 28, 1989; signed by San Francisco Giants, April 14, 1989.
eClaimed on waivers by New York Yankees, August 10, 1989.
fGranted free agency, November 13, 1989.

DIVISION SERIES RECORD

Year Club	League	G.	IP.	W.	L.	Pct.	H.	R.	ER.	SO.	BB.	ERA.
1981—New York	American	3	6⅔	0	0	.000	3	0	0	8	2	0.00

CHAMPIONSHIP SERIES RECORD

Year Club	League	G.	IP.	W.	L.	Pct.	H.	R.	ER.	SO.	BB.	ERA.
1978—New York	American	2	4	1	0	1.000	3	2	2	3	0	4.50
1980—New York	American	1	⅓	0	1	.000	3	2	2	0	0	54.00
1981—New York	American	2	2⅔	0	0	.000	1	0	0	2	0	0.00
1984—San Diego	National	3	4	0	0	.000	5	2	2	5	1	4.50
Championship Series Totals—4 Years		8	11	1	1	.500	12	6	6	10	1	4.91

WORLD SERIES RECORD

Year Club	League	G.	IP.	W.	L.	Pct.	H.	R.	ER.	SO.	BB.	ERA.
1978—New York	American	3	6	1	0	1.000	1	0	0	4	1	0.00
1981—New York	American	3	5	0	0	.000	2	0	0	5	2	0.00
1984—San Diego	National	2	2⅔	0	0	.000	3	4	4	2	1	13.50
World Series Totals—3 Years		8	13⅔	1	0	1.000	6	4	4	11	4	2.63

ALL-STAR GAME RECORD

Year League	IP.	W.	L.	Pct.	H.	R.	ER.	SO.	BB.	ERA.
1975—American	1	0	0	.000	1	1	1	0	0	9.00
1977—National	1	0	0	.000	1	2	2	2	1	18.00
1978—American	1	0	1	.000	4	4	4	1	1	36.00
1980—American	1	0	0	.000	1	0	0	0	0	0.00
1984—National	1	0	0	.000	1	0	0	2	0	0.00
1985—National	1	0	0	.000	0	0	0	2	1	0.00
All-Star Game Totals—6 Years	6	0	1	.000	8	7	7	7	3	10.50

Named to American League All-Star Team for 1981 game; replaced due to injury.
Member of American League All-Star Team in 1976 and 1982; did not play.

JAMES WILLIAM GOTT
(Jim)

Born August 3, 1959, at Hollywood, Calif.
Height, 6.04. Weight, 220.
Throws and bats righthanded.
Attended Brigham Young University, Provo, Utah.

Major League saves: 1984 (2), 1986 (1), 1987 (13), 1988 (34). Total—50.
Led Western Carolinas League in wild pitches with 21 in 1979.
Tied for Pioneer League lead in games started by pitchers with 14 in 1977.

Year Club	League	G.	IP.	W.	L.	Pct.	H.	R.	ER.	SO.	BB.	ERA.
1977—Calgary	Pioneer	14	65	3	4	.429	71	★82	★69	60	★83	9.55
1978—Gastonia	W. Carol.	22	145	9	6	.600	100	67	64	130	●113	3.97
1978—St. Petersburg	Florida St.	5	28	1	3	.250	23	9	4	15	12	1.29
1979—St. Petersburg	Florida St.	4	18	0	3	.000	18	13	13	9	13	6.50
1979—Gastonia	W. Carol.	19	77	5	5	.500	63	57	48	102	88	5.61
1979—Arkansas†	Texas	2	5	0	1	.000	3	6	3	7	13	5.40
1980—St. Petersburg	Florida St.	25	137	5	11	.313	138	96	70	103	113	4.60
1981—Arkansas‡	Texas	28	131	5	9	.357	133	68	50	93	65	3.44
1982—Toronto	American	30	136	5	10	.333	134	76	67	82	66	4.43
1983—Toronto	American	34	176⅔	9	14	.391	195	103	93	121	68	4.74
1984—Toronto§	American	35	109⅔	7	6	.538	93	54	49	73	49	4.02
1985—San Francisco	National	26	148⅓	7	10	.412	144	73	64	78	51	3.88
1986—San Francisco x	National	9	13	0	0	.000	16	12	11	9	13	7.62
1986—Phoenix y	P. Coast	2	2⅔	0	0	.000	2	2	2	2	3	6.75
1987—San Francisco z-Pittsburgh	National	55	87	1	2	.333	81	43	33	90	40	3.41
1988—Pittsburgh	National	67	77⅓	6	6	.500	68	30	30	76	22	3.49
1989—Pittsburgh ab	National	1	⅔	0	0	.000	1	0	0	1	1	0.00
American League Totals—3 Years		99	422⅓	21	30	.412	422	233	209	276	183	4.45
National League Totals—5 Years		158	326⅓	14	18	.438	310	158	138	254	127	3.81
Major League Totals—8 Years		257	748⅔	35	48	.422	732	391	347	530	310	4.17

Selected by St. Louis Cardinals' organization in 4th round of free-agent draft, June 7, 1977.
†On disabled list, August 16 to September 1, 1979.
‡Drafted by Toronto Blue Jays, December 7, 1981.
§Traded with Pitcher Jack McKnight and Infielder Augie Schmidt to San Francisco Giants for Pitcher Gary Lavelle, January 26, 1985.
xOn disabled list, May 9, 1986 through remainder of season; included rehabilitation disability assignment to Phoenix, June 9 to June 24, 1986.
yReleased, December 19, 1986; re-signed by Giants, April 7, 1987.
zClaimed on waivers by Pittsburgh Pirates, August 3, 1987.
aOn disabled list, April 7, 1989 through remainder of season.
bGranted free agency, November 13, 1989; signed by Los Angeles Dodgers, December 7, 1989.

MAURO PAUL GOZZO

Born March 7, 1966, at New Britain, Conn.
Height, 6.02. Weight, 210.
Throws and bats righthanded.

Tied for South Atlantic League lead in intentional bases on balls issued with 7 in 1985.

Year Club	League	G.	IP.	W.	L.	Pct.	H.	R.	ER.	SO.	BB.	ERA.
1984—Little Falls	NYP	24	38⅓	4	3	.571	40	27	24	30	28	5.63
1985—Columbia	S. Atlantic	49	78	11	4	.733	62	22	22	66	39	2.54
1986—Lynchburg†	Carolina	60	78½	9	4	.692	80	30	27	50	35	3.10
1987—Memphis	Southern	19	91⅓	6	5	.545	95	58	46	56	36	4.53
1988—Memphis‡	Southern	33	92⅔	4	9	.308	127	64	59	48	36	5.73
1989—Knoxville	Southern	18	60⅓	7	0	1.000	59	27	20	37	12	2.98
1989—Syracuse	Int'national	12	62	5	1	.833	56	22	19	34	19	2.76
1989—Toronto	American	9	31⅔	4	1	.800	35	19	17	10	9	4.83
Major League Totals—1 Year		9	31⅔	4	1	.800	35	19	17	10	9	4.83

Selected by New York Mets' organization in 13th round of free-agent draft, June 4, 1984.
†Traded with Catcher Ed Hearn and Pitcher Rich Anderson to Kansas City Royals for Catcher Chris Jelic and Pitcher David Cone, March 27, 1987.
‡Drafted by Toronto Blue Jays' organization, December 6, 1988.

MARK EUGENE GRACE

Born June 28, 1964, at Winston-Salem, N. C.
Height, 6.02. Weight, 190.
Throws and bats lefthanded.
Attended Saddleback College, Mission Viejo, Calif., and
San Diego State University, San Diego, Calif.

Major League stolen bases: 1988 (3), 1989 (14). Total—17.
Led Eastern League in slugging percentage with .545 in 1987.
Led Midwest League first basemen in double plays with 103 in 1986.
Named National League Rookie Player of the Year by THE SPORTING NEWS, 1988.
Named Eastern League Most Valuable Player, 1987.

Year Club	League	Pos.	G.	AB.	R.	H.	2B.	3B.	HR.	RBI.	B.A.	PO.	A.	E.	F.A.
1986—Peoria	Midw.	1B-OF	126	465	81	159	30	4	15	95	★.342	1050	69	13	.989
1987—Pittsfield	East.	1B	123	453	81	151	29	8	17	★101	.333	1054	★96	6	★.995

Year Club	League	Pos.	G.	AB.	R.	H.	2B.	3B.	HR.	RBI.	B.A.	PO.	A.	E.	F.A.
1988—Iowa	A.A.	1B	21	67	11	17	4	0	0	14	.254	189	20	1	.995
1988—Chicago	Nat.	1B	134	486	65	144	23	4	7	57	.296	1182	87	●17	.987
1989—Chicago†	Nat.	1B	142	510	74	160	28	3	13	79	.314	1230	126	6	.996
Major League Totals—2 Years			276	996	139	304	51	7	20	136	.305	2412	213	23	.991

Selected by Minnesota Twins' organization in 15th round of free-agent draft, January 17, 1984.
Selected by Chicago Cubs' organization in 24th round of free-agent draft, June 3, 1985.
†On disabled list, June 5 to June 23, 1989.

CHAMPIONSHIP SERIES RECORD

Shares Championship Series record for hitting home run in first series at-bat, October 4, 1989.

Year Club	League	Pos.	G.	AB.	R.	H.	2B.	3B.	HR.	RBI.	B.A.	PO.	A.	E.	F.A.
1989—Chicago	Nat.	1B	5	17	3	11	3	1	1	8	.647	44	3	0	1.000

MARK ANDREW GRANT

Born October 24, 1963, at Aurora, Ill.
Height, 6.02. Weight, 205.
Throws and bats righthanded.
Cousin of Rick Ramos, pitcher in Montreal Expos' organization, 1978 through 1983; and nephew
of Richard Ramos, pitcher in Chicago White Sox' organization, 1953 through 1958.

Pitched 9-0 no-hit victory against Danville, August 12, 1982.
Major League saves: 1984 (1), 1987 (1), 1989 (2). Total—4.
Led Pacific Coast League pitchers in complete games with 10 and tied for lead in games started with 27 in 1986.
Led Pacific Coast League pitchers in wild pitches with 18 and tied for league lead in games started with 29 in 1985.
Tied for Pacific Coast League lead in shutouts with 3 in 1985 and 1986.
Tied for Midwest League lead in shutouts with 4 in 1982.

Year Club	League	G.	IP.	W.	L.	Pct.	H.	R.	ER.	SO.	BB.	ERA.
1981—Great Falls	Pioneer	10	64	2	6	.250	63	36	31	50	35	4.36
1982—Clinton	Midwest	27	★198⅔	★16	5	★.762	139	63	52	★243	60	2.36
1983—Shreveport	Texas	26	★186⅔	10	8	.556	182	83	76	159	71	3.66
1984—Phoenix	P. Coast	17	111⅓	5	7	.417	102	64	49	78	61	3.96
1984—San Francisco†	National	11	53⅔	1	4	.200	56	40	38	32	19	6.37
1985—Phoenix	P. Coast	29	183	8	●15	.348	182	101	92	133	90	4.52
1986—Phoenix	P. Coast	28	181⅔	★14	7	.667	204	105	99	93	46	4.90
1986—San Francisco	National	4	10	0	1	.000	6	4	4	5	5	3.60
1987—San Francisco‡-San Diego	National	33	163⅓	7	9	.438	170	88	77	90	73	4.24
1987—Phoenix	P. Coast	3	23	2	1	.667	20	8	8	12	5	3.13
1988—San Diego	National	33	97⅔	2	8	.200	97	41	40	61	36	3.69
1989—San Diego	National	50	116⅓	8	2	.800	105	45	43	69	32	3.33
Major League Totals—5 Years		131	441	18	24	.429	434	218	202	257	165	4.12

Selected by San Francisco Giants' organization in 1st round (10th player selected) of free-agent draft, June 8, 1981.
†On disabled list, May 4 to May 23, 1984.
‡Traded with Third Baseman Chris Brown and Pitchers Keith Comstock and Mark Davis to San Diego Padres for
Pitchers Dave Dravecky and Craig Lefferts and Infielder Kevin Mitchell, July 4, 1987.

CRAIG ALLEN GREBECK

Born December 29, 1964, at Cerritos, Calif.
Height, 5.08. Weight, 160.
Throws and bats righthanded.
Attended California State University at Dominguez Hills, Carson, Calif.

Led Southern League in grounding into double plays with 15 in 1989.

Year Club	League	Pos.	G.	AB.	R.	H.	2B.	3B.	HR.	RBI.	B.A.	PO.	A.	E.	F.A.
1987—Peninsula	Carol.	SS	104	378	63	106	22	3	15	67	.280	137	278	16	.963
1988—Birmingham	South.	2B	133	450	57	126	21	1	9	53	.280	238	368	19	.970
1989—Birmingham	South.	SS-3B-2B	●143	●533	85	★153	25	4	5	80	.287	234	364	28	.955

Signed as free agent by Chicago White Sox' organization, August 13, 1986.

GARY ALLAN GREEN

Born January 14, 1962, at Pittsburgh, Pa.
Height, 6.03. Weight, 170.
Throws and bats righthanded.
Attended Oklahoma State University, Stillwater, Okla.
Son of Freddie Green, pitcher with Pittsburgh Pirates and
Washington Senators, 1959 through 1962 and 1964.

Led Pacific Coast League in sacrifice hits with 14 in 1987.
Led Texas League in sacrifice hits with 15 in 1985.
Led Pacific Coast League shortstops in double plays with 75 in 1987.
Member of 1984 U.S. Olympic baseball team.

Year Club	League	Pos.	G.	AB.	R.	H.	2B.	3B.	HR.	RBI.	B.A.	PO.	A.	E.	F.A.
1985—Beaumont†	Texas	SS	119	409	44	105	17	1	1	51	.257	157	405	30	.949
1986—Las Vegas	P. C.	SS	129	416	42	104	11	3	0	41	.250	158	390	24	.958
1986—San Diego	Nat.	SS	13	33	2	7	1	0	0	2	.212	16	35	0	1.000
1987—Las Vegas	P. C.	SS	111	337	32	80	8	2	1	32	.237	164	306	13	★.973
1988—Las Vegas	P. C.	SS-3B	88	302	39	82	16	2	0	37	.272	79	194	18	.938
1989—San Diego	Nat.	SS-3B	15	27	4	7	3	0	0	0	.259	6	29	3	.921
1989—Las Vegas‡	P. C.	SS-1B	62	191	18	40	6	0	0	18	.209	71	177	19	.929
Major League Totals—2 Years			28	60	6	14	4	0	0	2	.233	22	64	3	.966

Selected by San Francisco Giants' organization in 29th round of free-agent draft, June 3, 1980.
Selected by St. Louis Cardinals' organization in 2nd round of free-agent draft, June 6, 1983.
Selected by San Diego Padres' organization in 1st round (26th player selected) of free-agent draft, June 4, 1984.
†On disabled list, July 19 to July 28, 1985.
‡Drafted by Oklahoma City (Texas Rangers' organization), December 5, 1989.

IRA THOMAS GREENE
(Tommy)

Born April 6, 1967, at Lumberton, N. C.
Height, 6.05. Weight, 225.
Throws and bats righthanded.

Led South Atlantic League pitchers in games started with 28 and tied for lead in shutouts with 3 in 1986.
Tied for International League lead in shutouts with 3 in 1988.

Year Club	League	G.	IP.	W.	L.	Pct.	H.	R.	ER.	SO.	BB.	ERA.
1985—Pulaski	Ap'lachian	12	50⅔	2	5	.286	49	45	43	32	27	7.64
1986—Sumter	S. Atlantic	28	174⅔	11	7	.611	162	95	91	169	82	4.69
1987—Greenville	Southern	23	141⅓	11	8	.579	103	60	52	101	66	3.29
1988—Richmond	Int'national	29	177⅓	7	17	.292	169	98	94	130	70	4.77
1989—Richmond	Int'national	26	152	9	12	.429	136	74	61	125	50	3.61
1989—Atlanta	National	4	26⅓	1	2	.333	22	12	12	17	6	4.10
Major League Totals—1 Year		4	26⅓	1	2	.333	22	12	12	17	6	4.10

Selected by Atlanta Braves' organization in 1st round (14th player selected) of free-agent draft, June 3, 1985.

MICHAEL LEWIS GREENWELL
(Mike)

Born July 18, 1963, at Louisville, Ky.
Height, 6.00. Weight, 200.
Throws right and bats lefthanded.

Holds American League record for most game-winning runs batted in, season (23), 1988.
Hit for the cycle, September 14, 1988.
Major League stolen bases: 1985 (1), 1987 (5), 1988 (16), 1989 (13). Total—35.
Led American League in game-winning RBIs with 23 and tied for lead in intentional bases on balls received with 18 in 1988.
Led Carolina League in being hit by pitch with 15 in 1984.
Named outfielder on THE SPORTING NEWS American League All-Star Team, 1988.
Named outfielder on THE SPORTING NEWS American League Silver Slugger team, 1988.

Year Club	League	Pos.	G.	AB.	R.	H.	2B.	3B.	HR.	RBI.	B.A.	PO.	A.	E.	F.A.
1982—Elmira	NYP	3B-2B	72	268	57	72	10	1	6	36	.269	96	151	31	.888
1983—Winston-Salem†	Carol.	OF	48	158	23	44	8	0	3	21	.278	28	1	1	.967
1984—Winston-Salem	Carol.	3B-OF	130	454	70	139	23	6	16	84	.306	126	132	30	.896
1985—Pawtucket	Int.	OF	117	418	47	107	21	1	13	52	.256	178	8	7	.964
1985—Boston	Amer.	OF	17	31	7	10	1	0	4	8	.323	14	0	0	1.000
1986—Pawtucket	Int.	OF-3B	89	320	62	96	21	1	18	59	.300	130	20	8	.949
1986—Boston	Amer.	OF	31	35	4	11	2	0	0	4	.314	18	1	0	1.000
1987—Boston	Amer.	OF-C	125	412	71	135	31	6	19	89	.328	165	8	6	.966
1988—Boston	Amer.	OF	158	590	86	192	39	8	22	119	.325	302	6	6	.981
1989—Boston‡	Amer.	OF	145	578	87	178	36	0	14	95	.308	220	11	8	.967
Major League Totals—5 Years			476	1646	255	526	109	14	59	315	.320	719	26	20	.974

Selected by Boston Red Sox' organization in 3rd round of free-agent draft, June 7, 1982.
†On disabled list, April 21 to May 2 and May 13 to July 25, 1983.
‡On disabled list, July 30 to August 14, 1989.

CHAMPIONSHIP SERIES RECORD

Year Club	League	Pos.	G.	AB.	R.	H.	2B.	3B.	HR.	RBI.	B.A.	PO.	A.	E.	F.A.
1986—Boston	Amer.	PH	2	2	0	1	0	0	0	0	.500	0	0	0	.000
1988—Boston	Amer.	OF	4	14	2	3	1	0	1	3	.214	4	0	0	1.000
Championship Series Totals—2 Years			6	16	2	4	1	0	1	3	.250	4	0	0	1.000

WORLD SERIES RECORD

Year Club	League	Pos.	G.	AB.	R.	H.	2B.	3B.	HR.	RBI.	B.A.	PO.	A.	E.	F.A.
1986—Boston	Amer.	PH	4	3	0	0	0	0	0	0	.000	0	0	0	.000

ALL-STAR GAME RECORD

Year League	Pos.	AB.	R.	H.	2B.	3B.	HR.	RBI.	B.A.	PO.	A.	E.	F.A.
1988—American	OF	1	0	0	0	0	0	0	.000	1	0	0	1.000
1989—American	OF	0	0	0	0	0	0	0	.000	1	0	0	1.000
All-Star Game Totals—2 Years		1	0	0	0	0	0	0	.000	2	0	0	1.000

WILLIAM THOMAS GREGG JR.
(Tommy)

Born July 29, 1963, at Boone, N. C.
Height, 6.01. Weight, 190.
Throws and bats lefthanded.
Attended Wake Forest University, Winston-Salem, N. C.

Major League stolen bases: 1989 (3).
Led Eastern League in intentional bases on balls received with 14 in 1987.

Year	Club	League	Pos.	G.	AB.	R.	H.	2B.	3B.	HR.	RBI.	B.A.	PO.	A.	E.	F.A.
1985—Macon	S. Atl.	OF	72	259	43	81	14	2	1	18	.313	117	4	1	.992
1986—Nashua	East.	OF-1B	126	421	55	113	13	4	1	29	.268	216	7	4	.982
1987—Harrisburg	East.	OF	133	461	99	171	22	9	10	82	★.371	242	12	7	.973
1987—Pittsburgh	Nat.	OF	10	8	3	2	1	0	0	0	.250	1	0	0	1.000
1988—Buffalo	A. A.	OF	72	252	34	74	12	0	6	27	.294	134	3	2	.986
1988—Pitt.†-Atl.	Nat.	OF	25	44	5	13	4	0	1	7	.295	26	1	0	1.000
1989—Atlanta‡	Nat.	OF-1B	102	276	24	67	8	0	6	23	.243	321	17	2	.994
Major League Totals—3 Years			137	328	32	82	13	0	7	30	.250	348	18	2	.995

Selected by Cleveland Indians' organization in 9th round of free-agent draft, June 8, 1981.
Selected by Cleveland Indians' organization in 32nd round of free-agent draft, June 4, 1984.
Selected by Pittsburgh Pirates' organization in 7th round of free-agent draft, June 3, 1985.
†Traded to Atlanta Braves, September 1, 1988, completing deal in which Atlanta traded Infielder Ken Oberkfell and cash to Pittsburgh Pirates for a player to be named later, August 28, 1988.
‡On disabled list, April 20 to June 2, 1989.

GEORGE KENNETH GRIFFEY SR.
(Ken)

Born April 10, 1950, at Donora, Pa.
Height, 6.00. Weight, 210.
Throws and bats lefthanded.
Father of Ken Griffey Jr., outfielder with Seattle Mariners.

Shares modern major league record for most at-bats, nine inning game (7), June 13, 1975.
Major League stolen bases: 1973 (4), 1974 (9), 1975 (16), 1976 (34), 1977 (17), 1978 (23), 1979 (12), 1980 (23), 1981 (12), 1982 (10), 1983 (5), 1984 (2), 1985 (7), 1986 (14), 1987 (4), 1988 (1), 1989 (4). Total—197.
Hit three home runs in a game, July 22, 1986.
Led American Association in stolen bases with 43 in 1973.
Tied for Eastern League lead in double plays by outfielders with 6 in 1972.
Named as outfielder on THE SPORTING NEWS National League All-Star Team, 1976.

Year	Club	League	Pos.	G.	AB.	R.	H.	2B.	3B.	HR.	RBI.	B.A.	PO.	A.	E.	F.A.
1969—Bradenton Reds	Gulf C.	★OF-1B	49	153	22	43	★11	1	1	12	.281	57	4	★10	.859
1970—Sioux Falls	North.	OF	51	164	20	40	2	1	2	24	.244	76	2	7	.918
1971—Tampa	Fla. St.	OF	88	281	60	96	7	11	3	33	.342	137	13	8	.949
1971—Three Rivers	East.	OF	9	32	1	13	1	2	0	4	.406	17	0	1	.944
1972—Three Rivers	East.	●OF-SS	128	472	★96	150	21	3	14	52	.318	212	10	●15	.937
1973—Indianapolis	A. A.	OF	107	397	88	130	18	5	10	58	.327	171	11	6	.968
1973—Cincinnati	Nat.	OF	25	86	19	33	5	1	3	14	.384	25	1	0	1.000
1974—Indianapolis	A. A.	OF	43	162	34	54	6	4	5	18	.333	70	4	1	.987
1974—Cincinnati	Nat.	OF	88	227	24	57	9	5	2	19	.251	115	5	0	1.000
1975—Cincinnati	Nat.	OF	132	463	95	141	15	9	4	46	.305	202	6	7	.967
1976—Cincinnati	Nat.	OF	148	562	111	189	28	9	6	74	.336	270	10	6	.976
1977—Cincinnati	Nat.	OF	154	585	117	186	35	8	12	57	.318	298	10	3	.990
1978—Cincinnati	Nat.	OF	158	614	90	177	33	8	10	63	.288	296	13	10	.969
1979—Cincinnati†	Nat.	OF	95	380	62	120	27	4	8	32	.316	175	8	3	.984
1980—Cincinnati	Nat.	OF	146	544	89	160	28	10	13	85	.294	266	5	6	.978
1981—Cincinnati‡	Nat.	OF	101	396	65	123	21	6	2	34	.311	268	8	3	.989
1982—New York	Amer.	OF	127	484	70	134	23	2	12	54	.277	282	8	5	.983
1983—New York§	Amer.	1B-OF	118	458	60	140	21	3	11	46	.306	870	57	8	.991
1984—New York	Amer.	OF-1B	120	399	44	109	20	1	7	56	.273	422	22	16	.965
1985—New York x	Amer.	OF-1B	127	438	68	120	28	4	10	69	.274	227	8	7	.971
1986—New York y	Amer.	OF	59	198	33	60	7	0	9	26	.303	96	5	3	.971
1986—Atlanta	Nat.	OF-1B	80	292	36	90	15	3	12	32	.308	136	2	2	.986
1987—Atlanta za	Nat.	OF-1B	122	399	65	114	24	1	14	64	.286	205	8	2	.991
1988—Atl. b - Cinc. c	Nat.	OF-1B	94	243	26	62	6	0	4	23	.255	193	16	4	.981
1989—Cincinnati	Nat.	OF-1B	106	236	26	62	8	3	8	30	.263	122	2	2	.984
National League Totals—13 Years			1449	5027	825	1514	254	67	98	573	.301	2571	94	48	.982
American League Totals—5 Years			551	1977	275	563	99	10	49	251	.285	1897	100	39	.981
Major League Totals—17 Years			2000	7004	1100	2077	353	77	147	824	.297	4468	194	87	.982

Selected by Cincinnati Reds' organization in 29th round of free-agent draft, June 5, 1969.
†On disabled list, August 14 to September 7, 1979.
‡Traded to New York Yankees for Pitcher Brian Ryder and a player to be named later, November 4, 1981; Cincinnati Reds' organization acquired Pitcher Freddie Toliver to complete deal, December 10, 1981.
§On disabled list, July 2 to August 2, 1983.
xOn disabled list, May 28 to June 12, 1985.
yTraded to Atlanta Braves for Outfielder Claudell Washington and Shortstop Paul Zuvella, June 30, 1986.
zOn disabled list, May 5 to May 20, 1987.
aGranted free agency, November 9, 1987; re-signed by Braves, November 13, 1987.
bReleased, July 28, 1988; signed by Cincinnati Reds, August 2, 1988.
cReleased, December 21, 1988; re-signed by Reds, March 30, 1989.

CHAMPIONSHIP SERIES RECORD

Shares Championship Series records for most stolen bases, inning (2), October 5, 1975, sixth inning.
Shares National League Championship Series record for most stolen bases, game (3), October 5, 1975.

Year	Club	League	Pos.	G.	AB.	R.	H.	2B.	3B.	HR.	RBI.	B.A.	PO.	A.	E.	F.A.
1973—Cincinnati	Nat.	OF-PH	3	7	0	1	1	0	0	0	.143	2	0	0	1.000
1975—Cincinnati	Nat.	OF	3	12	3	4	1	0	0	4	.333	4	1	0	1.000

Year Club League	Pos.	G.	AB.	R.	H.	2B.	3B.	HR.	RBI.	B.A.	PO.	A.	E.	F.A.
1976—Cincinnati............. Nat.	OF	3	13	2	5	0	1	0	2	.385	11	0	0	1.000
Championship Series Totals—3 Years....		9	32	5	10	2	1	0	6	.313	17	1	0	1.000

WORLD SERIES RECORD

Year Club League	Pos.	G.	AB.	R.	H.	2B.	3B.	HR.	RBI.	B.A.	PO.	A.	E.	F.A.
1975—Cincinnati............. Nat.	OF	7	26	4	7	3	1	0	4	.269	10	1	0	1.000
1976—Cincinnati............. Nat.	OF	4	17	2	1	0	0		1	.059	5	0	0	1.000
World Series Totals—2 Years		11	43	6	8	3	1	0	5	.186	15	1	0	1.000

ALL-STAR GAME RECORD

Year League	Pos.	AB.	R.	H.	2B.	3B.	HR.	RBI.	B.A.	PO.	A.	E.	F.A.
1976—National...............................	OF	1	1	1	0	0	0	1	1.000	1	0	0	1.000
1980—National...............................	OF	3	1	2	0	0	1	1	.667	0	0	0	.000
All-Star Game Totals—2 Years....................		4	2	3	0	0	1	2	.750	1	0	0	1.000

Member of National League All-Star Team in 1977; did not play.

GEORGE KENNETH GRIFFEY JR.
(Ken)

Born November 21, 1969, at Donora, Pa.
Height, 6.03. Weight, 195.
Throws and bats lefthanded.
Son of Ken Griffey, Sr., outfielder-first baseman with Cincinnati Reds.

Major League stolen bases: 1989 (16).
Led American League outfielders in double plays with 6 in 1989.

Year Club League	Pos.	G.	AB.	R.	H.	2B.	3B.	HR.	RBI.	B.A.	PO.	A.	E.	F.A.
1987—Bellingham .... N'west	OF	54	182	43	57	9	1	14	40	.313	117	4	1	*.992
1988—San Bernardino†.. Calif.	OF	58	219	50	74	13	3	11	42	.338	145	3	2	.987
1988—Vermont .... East.	OF	17	61	10	17	5	1	2	10	.279	40	2	1	.977
1989—Seattle‡.................... Amer.	OF	127	455	61	120	23	0	16	61	.264	302	12	●10	.969
Major League Totals—1 Year..................		127	455	61	120	23	0	16	61	.264	302	12	10	.969

Selected by Seattle Mariners' organization in 1st round (first player selected) of free-agent draft, June 2, 1987.
†On disabled list, June 9 to August 15, 1988.
†On disabled list, July 24 to August 20, 1989.

ALFREDO CLAUDINO GRIFFIN

Born March 6, 1957, at Santo Domingo, D. R.
Height, 5.11. Weight, 165.
Throws right and bats left and righthanded.

Major League stolen bases: 1977 (2), 1979 (21), 1980 (18), 1981 (8), 1982 (10), 1983 (8), 1984 (11), 1985 (24), 1986 (33), 1987 (26), 1988 (7), 1989 (10). Total—178.
Led American League shortstops in putouts with 280 in 1983.
Led American League shortstops in total chances with 824 in 1982.
Named shortstop on THE SPORTING NEWS American League All-Star fielding team, 1985.
Named American League Co-Rookie of the Year by the Baseball Writers' Association of America, 1979.

Year Club League	Pos.	G.	AB.	R.	H.	2B.	3B.	HR.	RBI.	B.A.	PO.	A.	E.	F.A.
1974—Reno .... Calif.	SS	11	35	4	9	0	0	0	1	.257	10	22	9	.780
1974—Sarasota Indians...Gulf C.	SS	49	158	17	41	1	0	0	11	.259	67	133	*25	.889
1975—San Jose .... Calif.	SS	124	358	42	82	4	3	0	25	.229	189	281	47	.909
1976—San Jose .... Calif.	SS	64	224	40	58	3	1	0	17	.259	91	145	24	.908
1976—Williamsport......... East.	SS	58	200	22	55	3	0	0	17	.275	86	172	17	.938
1976—Toledo .... Int.	SS	22	88	5	19	7	1	0	6	.216	44	71	7	.943
1976—Cleveland............... Amer.	SS	12	4	0	1	0	0	0	0	.250	1	2	1	.750
1977—Toledo .... Int.	SS	125	457	60	114	14	5	1	32	.249	*223	398	*49	.927
1977—Cleveland............... Amer.	SS	14	41	5	6	1	0	0	3	.146	17	30	3	.940
1978—Portland .... P. C.	*SS-OF	133	474	82	138	22	10	5	48	.291	201	395	40	.937
1978—Cleveland†............. Amer.	SS	5	4	1	2	1	0	0	0	.500	4	7	1	.917
1979—Toronto .... Amer.	SS	153	624	81	179	22	10	2	31	.287	272	501	*36	.956
1980—Toronto .... Amer.	SS	155	653	63	166	26	●15	2	41	.254	295	489	*37	.955
1981—Toronto .... Amer.	*SS-3B-2B	101	388	30	81	19	6	0	21	.209	191	279	*31	.938
1982—Toronto .... Amer.	SS	●162	539	57	130	20	8	1	48	.241	*319	479	●26	.968
1983—Toronto .... Amer.	SS-2B	●162	528	62	132	22	9	4	47	.250	287	422	25	.966
1984—Toronto‡ .... Amer.	SS-2B	140	419	53	101	8	2	4	30	.241	230	320	21	.963
1985—Oakland .... Amer.	SS	162	614	75	166	18	7	2	64	.270	278	440	30	.960
1986—Oakland .... Amer.	SS	162	594	74	166	23	6	4	51	.285	282	421	25	.966
1987—Oakland§ .... Amer.	SS-2B	144	494	69	130	23	5	3	60	.263	250	389	24	.964
1988—Los Angeles xy ..... Nat.	SS	95	316	39	63	8	3	1	27	.199	145	264	15	.965
1989—Los Angeles z ...... Nat.	SS	136	506	49	125	27	2	0	29	.247	208	333	14	.975
American League Totals—12 Years		1372	4902	570	1263	183	68	22	396	.258	2426	3779	260	.960
National League Totals—2 Years		231	822	88	188	35	5	1	56	.229	353	597	29	.970
Major League Totals—14 Years		1603	5724	658	1451	218	73	23	452	.253	2779	4376	289	.961

Signed as free agent by Cleveland Indians' organization, August 22, 1973.
†Traded with Third Baseman Phil Lansford to Toronto Blue Jays for Pitcher Victor Cruz, December 6, 1978.
‡Traded with Outfielder Dave Collins and cash to Oakland A's for Pitcher Bill Caudill, December 8, 1984.
§As part of an eight-player, three-team deal, New York Mets traded Pitcher Jesse Orosco to Oakland Athletics, December 11, 1987. Oakland then traded Orosco along with Shortstop Alfredo Griffin and Pitcher Jay Howell to Los

Angeles Dodgers for Pitchers Bob Welch, Matt Young and Jack Savage. Oakland then traded Savage along with Pitchers Wally Whitehurst and Kevin Tapani to New York.
xOn disabled list, May 22 to July 25, 1988.
yGranted free agency, November 4, 1988; re-signed by Dodgers, November 7, 1988.
zOn disabled list, May 8 to May 28, 1989.

CHAMPIONSHIP SERIES RECORD

Year	Club	League	Pos.	G.	AB.	R.	H.	2B.	3B.	HR.	RBI.	B.A.	PO.	A.	E.	F.A.
1988—Los Angeles		Nat.	SS	7	25	1	4	1	0	0	3	.160	17	13	0	1.000

WORLD SERIES RECORD

Year	Club	League	Pos.	G.	AB.	R.	H.	2B.	3B.	HR.	RBI.	B.A.	PO.	A.	E.	F.A.
1988—Los Angeles		Nat.	SS	5	16	2	3	0	0	0	0	.188	7	13	1	.952

ALL-STAR GAME RECORD

Year	League	Pos.	AB.	R.	H.	2B.	3B.	HR.	RBI.	B.A.	PO.	A.	E.	F.A.
1984—American		SS	0	0	0	0	0	0	0	.000	0	1	0	1.000

MICHAEL LEROY GRIFFIN
(Mike)

Born June 26, 1957, at Colusa, Calif.
Height, 6.05. Weight, 195.
Throws and bats righthanded.
Attended American River College, Sacramento, Calif.

Major league saves: 1979 (1), 1981 (1), 1987 (1). Total—3.
Led Texas League in wild pitches with 26 in 1978.
Led Western Carolinas League pitchers in complete games with 19 and tied for lead in games started with 27 in 1977.
Tied for American Association lead in games started by pitchers with 28 in 1986.

Year	Club	League	G.	IP.	W.	L.	Pct.	H.	R.	ER.	SO.	BB.	ERA.
1976—Asheville		W. Carol.	11	65	6	3	.667	71	36	35	26	25	4.85
1977—Asheville		W. Carol.	27	*209	*17	9	.654	189	100	81	*201	75	3.49
1978—Tulsa†		Texas	27	169	6	*19	.240	*217	140	114	112	85	6.07
1979—West Haven		Eastern	17	125	8	7	.533	120	53	41	66	26	2.95
1979—Columbus		Int'national	6	41	3	1	.750	35	9	8	34	13	1.76
1979—New York		American	3	4	0	0	.000	5	2	2	5	2	4.50
1980—Columbus		Int'national	13	83	7	2	.778	88	37	32	47	22	3.47
1980—New York		American	13	54	2	4	.333	64	36	29	25	23	4.83
1981—Columbus		Int'national	17	48	3	1	.750	39	14	13	34	16	2.44
1981—New York‡		American	2	4	0	0	.000	5	1	1	4	0	2.25
1981—Chicago§		National	16	52	2	5	.286	64	27	26	20	9	4.50
1982—Wichita		Am. Assoc.	28	136⅔	8	7	.533	166	99	90	88	24	5.93
1982—Montreal x-San Diego y		National	7	10⅓	0	1	.000	9	4	4	4	3	3.48
1983—Oklahoma City		Am. Assoc.	35	144⅔	7	8	.467	155	79	68	87	43	4.23
1984—Oklahoma City z		Am. Assoc.	31	113	8	5	.615	138	67	56	69	41	4.46
1985—Omaha		Am. Assoc.	24	135	7	8	.467	115	58	49	69	43	3.27
1986—Omaha a		Am. Assoc.	28	183	8	11	.421	186	90	83	105	56	4.08
1987—Rochester		Int'national	17	74	5	1	.833	74	33	27	53	21	3.28
1987—Baltimore		American	23	74⅓	3	5	.375	78	39	36	42	33	4.36
1988—Rochester b		Int'national	43	107⅔	4	8	.333	102	54	46	68	30	3.85
1989—Nashville		Am. Assoc.	41	74½	2	3	.400	66	25	19	54	28	2.30
1989—Cincinnati c		National	3	4⅓	0	0	.000	10	6	6	1	3	12.46
American League Totals—4 Years			41	136⅓	5	9	.357	152	78	68	76	58	4.49
National League Totals—3 Years			26	66⅔	2	6	.250	83	37	36	25	15	4.86
Major League Totals—6 Years			67	203	7	15	.318	235	115	104	101	73	4.61

Selected by Texas Rangers' organization in 3rd round of free-agent draft, June 8, 1976.
†Traded with Outfielders Juan Beniquez and Greg Jemison and Pitchers Paul Mirabella and Dave Righetti to New York Yankees for Pitchers Sparky Lyle, Larry McCall and Dave Rajsich, Shortstop Domingo Ramos, Catcher Mike Heath and cash, November 10, 1978.
‡Traded to Chicago Cubs, August 5, 1981, completing deal in which New York Yankees traded Pitcher Doug Bird, $400,000 and a player to be named later to Chicago for Pitcher Rick Reuschel, June 12, 1981.
§Traded to Montreal Expos' organization, March 26, 1982, completing deal in which Montreal traded Outfielder Dan Briggs to Chicago Cubs for a player to be named later, March 15, 1982.
xTraded to San Diego Padres' organization, August 30, 1982, completing deal in which San Diego organization traded infielder Jerry Manuel to Montreal Expos' organization for a player to be named later, June 8, 1982.
yReleased, March 27, 1983; signed by Oklahoma City (Texas Rangers' organization), April 5, 1983.
zGranted free agency, October 15, 1984; signed by Omaha (Kansas City Royals' organization), December 25, 1984.
aGranted free agency, October 15, 1986; signed by Baltimore Orioles' organization, December 5, 1986.
bGranted free agency, October 15, 1988; signed by Nashville (Cincinnati Reds' organization), December 16, 1988.
cGranted free agency, October 15, 1989.

TYRONE VONTRECE GRIFFIN
(Ty)

Born September 5, 1967, at Fort Campbell, Ky.
Height, 6.00. Weight, 185.
Throws right and bats left and righthanded.
Attended Georgia Institute of Technology, Atlanta, Ga.

Tied for Midwest League lead in intentional bases on balls received with 9 in 1989.
Member of 1988 U.S. Olympic baseball team.
Named second baseman on THE SPORTING NEWS College Baseball All-America Team, 1988.
Received reported $160,000 bonus to sign with Chicago Cubs' organization, 1988.

Year Club	League	Pos.	G.	AB.	R.	H.	2B.	3B.	HR.	RBI.	B.A.	PO.	A.	E.	F.A.
1989—Peoria	Midw.	2B-3B	82	296	45	85	15	6	10	64	.287	93	176	17	.941
1989—Charlotte	South.	3B-2B	45	143	25	33	6	0	3	21	.231	39	68	12	.899

Selected by Baltimore Orioles' organization in 12th round of free-agent draft, June 3, 1985.
Selected by Chicago Cubs' organization in 1st round (ninth player selected) of free-agent draft, June 1, 1988.

JASON ALAN GRIMSLEY

Born August 7, 1967, at Cleveland, Tex.
Height, 6.03. Weight, 180.
Throws and bats righthanded.

Pitched 3-0 no-hit victory against Harrisburg, May 3, 1989 (first game).
Led New York-Pennsylvania League in hit batsmen with 11 and wild pitches with 18 in 1986.
Tied for Eastern League lead in games started by pitchers with 26 in 1989.

Year Club	League	G.	IP.	W.	L.	Pct.	H.	R.	ER.	SO.	BB.	ERA.
1985—Bend	Northwest	6	11⅓	0	1	.000	12	21	17	10	25	13.50
1986—Utica	NYP	14	64⅔	1	●10	.091	63	61	46	46	★77	6.40
1987—Spartanburg	S. Atlantic	23	88⅓	7	4	.636	59	48	31	98	54	3.16
1988—Clearwater	Florida St.	16	101⅓	4	7	.364	80	48	42	90	37	3.73
1988—Reading	Eastern	5	21⅓	1	3	.250	20	19	17	14	13	7.17
1989—Reading	Eastern	26	172	11	8	.579	121	65	57	134	★109	2.98
1989—Philadelphia	National	4	18⅓	1	3	.250	19	13	12	7	19	5.89
Major League Totals—1 Year		4	18⅓	1	3	.250	19	13	12	7	19	5.89

Selected by Philadelphia Phillies' organization in 10th round of free-agent draft, June 3, 1985.

MARQUIS DEAN GRISSOM

Born April 17, 1967, at Atlanta, Ga.
Height, 5.11. Weight, 190.
Throws and bats righthanded.
Attended Florida A&M University, Tallahassee, Fla.

Major League stolen bases: 1989 (1).
Led New York-Pennsylvania League in total bases with 146 in 1988.

Year Club	League	Pos.	G.	AB.	R.	H.	2B.	3B.	HR.	RBI.	B.A.	PO.	A.	E.	F.A.
1988—Jamestown	NYP	OF	74	★291	★69	94	14	7	8	39	.323	123	●11	3	.978
1989—Jacksonville	South.	OF	78	278	43	83	15	4	3	31	.299	141	7	3	.980
1989—Indianapolis	A. A.	OF	49	187	28	52	10	4	2	21	.278	106	5	0	1.000
1989—Montreal	Nat.	OF	26	74	16	19	2	0	1	2	.257	32	1	2	.943
Major League Totals—1 Year			26	74	16	19	2	0	1	2	.257	32	1	2	.943

Selected by Montreal Expos' organization in 3rd round of free-agent draft, June 1, 1988.

GREGORY EUGENE GROSS
(Greg)

Born August 1, 1952, at York, Pa.
Height, 5.11. Weight, 180.
Throws and bats lefthanded.

Major League stolen bases: 1973 (2), 1974 (12), 1975 (2), 1976 (2), 1978 (3), 1979 (5), 1980 (1), 1981 (2), 1982 (4), 1983 (3), 1984 (1), 1985 (1), 1986 (1). Total—39.
Tied for Appalachian League lead in double plays by outfielders with 3 in 1970.
Named National League Rookie Player of the Year by THE SPORTING NEWS, 1974.
Named Appalachian League Player of the Year, 1970.

Year Club	League	Pos.	G.	AB.	R.	H.	2B.	3B.	HR.	RBI.	B.A.	PO.	A.	E.	F.A.
1970—Covington	Appal.	OF	54	211	40	★74	8	3	2	27	.351	93	★10	3	.972
1971—Columbus	South.	OF-1B	132	494	57	144	14	4	2	33	.291	244	13	9	.966
1972—Columbus	South.	OF	101	367	55	111	14	2	0	25	.302	172	9	3	.984
1972—Oklahoma City	A. A.	OF	28	109	15	27	4	0	0	8	.248	64	4	1	.986
1973—Denver	A. A.	OF	131	528	98	★174	25	6	0	55	.330	226	11	10	.960
1973—Houston	Nat.	OF	14	39	5	9	2	1	0	1	.231	13	2	0	1.000
1974—Houston	Nat.	OF	156	589	78	185	21	8	0	36	.314	296	15	2	.994
1975—Houston†	Nat.	OF	132	483	67	142	14	10	0	41	.294	216	14	10	.958
1976—Houston‡	Nat.	OF	128	426	52	122	12	3	0	27	.286	208	13	5	.978
1977—Chicago	Nat.	OF	115	239	43	77	10	4	5	32	.322	109	3	1	.991
1978—Chicago§	Nat.	OF	124	347	34	92	12	7	1	39	.265	182	6	4	.979
1979—Philadelphia x	Nat.	OF	111	174	21	58	6	3	0	15	.333	82	5	2	.978
1980—Philadelphia	Nat.	OF-1B	127	154	19	37	7	2	0	12	.240	69	5	2	.974
1981—Philadelphia	Nat.	OF	83	102	14	23	6	1	0	7	.225	48	7	1	.982
1982—Philadelphia	Nat.	OF	119	134	14	40	4	0	0	10	.299	55	3	1	.983
1983—Philadelphia	Nat.	OF-1B	136	245	25	74	12	3	0	29	.302	105	1	1	.991
1984—Philadelphia	Nat.	OF-1B	112	202	19	65	9	1	0	16	.322	195	13	2	.990
1985—Philadelphia y	Nat.	OF-1B	93	169	21	44	5	2	0	14	.260	66	8	0	1.000
1986—Philadelphia	Nat.	OF-1B-P	87	101	11	25	5	0	0	8	.248	40	3	0	1.000
1987—Philadelphia	Nat.	OF-1B	114	133	14	38	4	1	1	12	.286	53	2	0	1.000
1988—Philadelphia z	Nat.	OF-1B	98	133	10	27	1	0	0	5	.203	108	7	1	.991
1989—Houston	Nat.	OF-1B-P	60	75	2	15	0	0	0	4	.200	37	1	1	.974

Year	Club	League	Pos.	G.	AB.	R.	H.	2B.	3B.	HR.	RBI.	B.A.	PO.	A.	E.	F.A.
1989—Tucson a		P. C.	OF	21	72	7	18	0	1	0	5	.250	11	1	0	1.000
Major League Totals—17 Years..............				1809	3745	449	1073	130	46	7	308	.287	1882	108	33	.984

Selected by Houston Astros' organization in 4th round of free-agent draft, June 4, 1970.
†On disabled list, April 2 to April 24, 1975.
‡Traded to Chicago Cubs for Infielder Julio Gonzalez, December 8, 1976.
§Traded with Second Baseman Manny Trillo and Catcher Dave Rader to Philadelphia Phillies for Outfielder Jerry Martin, Catcher Barry Foote, Second Baseman Ted Sizemore and Pitchers Derek Botelho and Henry Mack, February 23, 1979.
xGranted free agency, November 1, 1979; re-signed by Phillies, December 13, 1979.
yOn disabled list, September 6, 1985 through remainder of season.
zGranted free agency, November 4, 1988; signed by Houston Astros, April 5, 1989.
aGranted free agency, November 13, 1989.

DIVISION SERIES RECORD

Year	Club	League	Pos.	G.	AB.	R.	H.	2B.	3B.	HR.	RBI.	B.A.	PO.	A.	E.	F.A.
1981—Philadelphia		Nat.	PH-OF	4	4	0	0	0	0	0	0	.000	0	0	0	.000

CHAMPIONSHIP SERIES RECORD

Year	Club	League	Pos.	G.	AB.	R.	H.	2B.	3B.	HR.	RBI.	B.A.	PO.	A.	E.	F.A.
1980—Philadelphia		Nat.	PH-OF	4	4	2	3	0	0	0	1	.750	1	0	0	1.000
1983—Philadelphia		Nat.	OF-PH	4	5	1	0	0	0	0	0	.000	4	0	0	1.000
Championship Series Totals—2 Years.....				8	9	3	3	0	0	0	1	.333	5	0	0	1.000

WORLD SERIES RECORD

Year	Club	League	Pos.	G.	AB.	R.	H.	2B.	3B.	HR.	RBI.	B.A.	PO.	A.	E.	F.A.
1980—Philadelphia		Nat.	PH-OF	4	2	0	0	0	0	0	0	.000	1	0	0	1.000
1983—Philadelphia		Nat.	OF	2	6	0	0	0	0	0	0	.000	8	0	0	1.000
World Series Totals—2 Years				6	8	0	0	0	0	0	0	.000	9	0	0	1.000

PITCHING RECORD

Year	Club	League	G.	IP.	W.	L.	Pct.	H.	R.	ER.	SO.	BB.	ERA.
1986—Philadelphia		National	1	⅔	0	0	.000	1	0	0	2	1	0.00
1989—Houston		National	1	1	0	0	.000	3	2	2	1	1	18.00
Major League Totals—2 Years............................			2	1⅔	0	0	.000	4	2	2	3	2	10.80

KEVIN FRANK GROSS

Born June 8, 1961, at Downey, Calif.
Height, 6.05. Weight, 215.
Throws and bats righthanded.
Attended Oxnard College, Oxnard, Calif., and
California Lutheran College, Thousand Oaks, Calif.

Major League saves: 1984 (1).
Led National League in home runs allowed with 28 in 1986.
Led National League in hit batsmen with 11 in 1988 and tied for lead with 8 in 1986 and 10 in 1987.
Tied for South Atlantic League lead in games started by pitchers with 28 in 1981.

Year	Club	League	G.	IP.	W.	L.	Pct.	H.	R.	ER.	SO.	BB.	ERA.
1981—Spartanburg..................................		S. Atlantic	28	192	13	12	.520	173	94	76	123	62	3.56
1982—Reading................................		Eastern	26	151	10	15	.400	138	81	71	136	89	4.23
1983—Portland...............................		P. Coast	15	80	3	5	.375	82	60	60	61	45	6.75
1983—Philadelphia		National	17	96	4	6	.400	100	46	38	66	35	3.56
1984—Philadelphia		National	44	129	8	5	.615	140	66	59	84	44	4.12
1985—Philadelphia		National	38	205⅔	15	13	.536	194	86	78	151	81	3.41
1986—Philadelphia		National	37	241⅔	12	12	.500	240	115	108	154	94	4.02
1987—Philadelphia		National	34	200⅔	9	16	.360	205	107	97	110	87	4.35
1988—Philadelphia†		National	33	231⅔	12	14	.462	209	101	95	162	★89	3.69
1989—Montreal		National	31	201⅓	11	12	.478	188	105	★98	158	88	4.38
Major League Totals—7 Years............................			234	1306	71	78	.477	1276	626	573	885	518	3.95

Selected by Baltimore Orioles' organization in 32nd round of free-agent draft, June 5, 1979.
Selected by Philadelphia Phillies' organization in secondary phase of free-agent draft, January 13, 1981.
†Traded to Montreal Expos for Pitchers Floyd Youmans and Jeff Parrett, December 6, 1988.

WORLD SERIES RECORD

Eligible for 1983 World Series with Philadelphia Phillies; did not play.

ALL-STAR GAME RECORD

Year	League	IP.	W.	L.	Pct.	H.	R.	ER.	SO.	BB.	ERA.
1988—National...		1	0	0	.000	0	0	0	1	0	0.00

KELLY WAYNE GRUBER

Born February 26, 1962, at Bellaire, Tex.
Height, 6.00. Weight, 185.
Throws and bats righthanded.
Attended University of Texas, Austin, Tex.

Major League stolen bases: 1986 (2), 1987 (12), 1988 (23), 1989 (10). Total—47.
Hit for the cycle, April 16, 1989.
Led American League third basemen in assists with 349 and total chances with 477 in 1988.

Led International League in slugging percentage with .500 in 1984.
Led International League third basemen in total chances with 309 in 1985.
Led Southern League shortstops in errors with 43 in 1982.

Year	Club	League	Pos.	G.	AB.	R.	H.	2B.	3B.	HR.	RBI.	B.A.	PO.	A.	E.	F.A.
1980—Batavia	NYP	SS	61	212	27	46	3	2	2	19	.217	87	155	21	.920
1981—Waterloo	Midw.	SS	127	458	64	133	25	4	14	59	.290	★180	★389	★56	.910
1982—Chattanooga	South.	SS-3B	128	441	53	107	18	4	13	54	.243	161	333	44	.918
1983—Buffalo†	East.	3B-SS-OF	111	403	60	106	20	4	15	54	.263	98	170	27	.908
1984—Toronto	Amer.	3B-OF-SS	15	16	1	1	0	0	1	2	.063	6	12	2	.900
1984—Syracuse	Int.	3B-OF	97	342	53	92	12	2	21	55	.269	76	156	18	.928
1985—Syracuse	Int.	3B	121	473	71	118	16	5	21	69	.249	78	★217	14	.955
1985—Toronto	Amer.	3B-2B	5	13	0	3	0	0	0	1	.231	2	6	0	1.000
1986—Toronto	Amer.	3-2-O-S	87	143	20	28	4	1	5	15	.196	43	77	7	.945
1987—Toronto	Amer.	3-S-2-O	138	341	50	80	14	3	12	36	.235	76	200	13	.955
1988—Toronto	Amer.	3-2-O-S	158	569	75	158	33	5	16	81	.278	121	365	16	.968
1989—Toronto‡	Amer.	★3-O-S	135	545	83	158	24	4	18	73	.290	121	295	★22	.950
Major League Totals—6 Years			538	1627	229	428	75	13	52	208	.263	369	955	60	.957

Selected by Cleveland Indians' organization in 1st round (10th player selected) of free-agent draft, June 3, 1980.
†Drafted by Toronto Blue Jays, December 5, 1983.
‡On disabled list, August 10 to August 25, 1989.

CHAMPIONSHIP SERIES RECORD

Shares Championship Series record for most singles, game (4), October 7, 1989.

Year	Club	League	Pos.	G.	AB.	R.	H.	2B.	3B.	HR.	RBI.	B.A.	PO.	A.	E.	F.A.
1989—Toronto	Amer.	3B	5	17	2	5	1	0	0	1	.294	4	8	0	1.000

ALL-STAR GAME RECORD

Member of American League All-Star Team in 1989; did not play.

CECILIO GUANTE (MAGALLANES)

Name pronounced Goo-AHN-tay.

Born February 2, 1960, at Jacagua, D. R.
Height, 6.03. Weight, 205.
Throws and bats righthanded.

Major League saves: 1983 (9), 1984 (2), 1985 (5), 1986 (4), 1987 (1), 1988 (12), 1989 (2). Total—35.
Led South Atlantic League in saves with 19 in 1980.

Year	Club	League	G.	IP.	W.	L.	Pct.	H.	R.	ER.	SO.	BB.	ERA.
1980—Shelby	S. Atlantic	39	90	6	6	.500	58	32	29	114	25	2.90
1980—Salem	Carolina	6	14	0	0	.000	7	2	2	18	8	1.29
1981—Buffalo	Eastern	10	14	1	1	.500	8	3	1	17	9	0.64
1981—Portland†	P. Coast	19	104	6	6	.500	110	64	62	70	58	5.37
1982—Portland	P. Coast	21	35	3	2	.600	34	17	15	29	26	3.86
1982—Pittsburgh	National	10	27	0	0	.000	28	16	10	26	5	3.33
1983—Hawaii	P. Coast	15	25⅔	2	1	.667	22	12	10	24	12	3.51
1983—Pittsburgh	National	49	100⅓	2	6	.250	90	45	37	82	46	3.32
1984—Pittsburgh‡	National	27	41⅓	2	3	.400	32	12	12	30	16	2.61
1984—Nashua	Eastern	1	3	0	0	.000	5	1	1	2	0	3.00
1985—Pittsburgh	National	63	109	4	6	.400	84	34	33	92	40	2.72
1986—Pittsburgh§x	National	52	78	5	2	.714	65	32	29	63	29	3.35
1987—New York y	American	23	44	3	2	.600	42	30	28	46	20	5.73
1988—New York z-Texas a	American	63	79⅔	5	6	.455	67	26	25	65	26	2.82
1989—Texas bc	American	50	69	6	6	.500	66	35	30	69	36	3.91
National League Totals—5 Years		201	355⅔	13	17	.433	299	139	121	293	136	3.06
American League Totals—3 Years		136	192⅔	14	14	.500	175	91	83	180	82	3.88
Major League Totals—8 Years		337	548⅓	27	31	.466	474	230	204	473	218	3.25

Signed as free agent by Pittsburgh Pirates' organization, November 24, 1979.
†On disabled list, July 25 to August 5, 1981.
‡On disabled list, July 13 to July 30, 1984.
§On disabled list, August 25 to September 24, 1986.
xTraded with Pitchers Rick Rhoden and Pat Clements to New York Yankees for Pitchers Doug Drabek, Brian Fisher and Logan Easley, November 26, 1986.
yOn disabled list, May 25 to June 9 and July 7 to September 14, 1987.
zTraded to Texas Rangers for Pitcher Dale Mohorcic, August 30, 1988.
aGranted free agency, November 4, 1988; re-signed by Rangers, January 6, 1989.
bOn disabled list, August 19 to September 3, 1989.
cReleased, October 2, 1989; signed by Cleveland Indians, November 21, 1989.

MARK STEVEN GUBICZA

Name pronounced GOO-ba-zah.

Born August 14, 1962, at Philadelphia, Pa.
Height, 6.05. Weight, 210.
Throws and bats righthanded.
Son of Anthony F. Gubicza, minor league pitcher, 1950 and 1951.
Tied for American League lead in games started by pitchers with 36 in 1989.

Year Club	League	G.	IP.	W.	L.	Pct.	H.	R.	ER.	SO.	BB.	ERA.
1981—Sarasota Royals-Gold	Gulf Coast	11	56	●8	1	★.889	39	18	14	40	23	2.25
1982—Fort Myers†	Florida St.	11	48	2	5	.286	49	33	22	36	25	4.13
1983—Jacksonville	Southern	28	196	14	12	.538	146	81	67	★146	93	3.08
1984—Kansas City	American	29	189	10	14	.417	172	90	85	111	75	4.05
1985—Kansas City	American	29	177⅓	14	10	.583	160	88	80	99	77	4.06
1986—Kansas City‡	American	35	180⅔	12	6	.667	155	77	73	118	84	3.64
1987—Kansas City	American	35	241⅔	13	18	.419	231	114	107	166	120	3.98
1988—Kansas City	American	35	269⅔	20	8	.714	237	94	81	183	83	2.70
1989—Kansas City	American	36	255	15	11	.577	252	100	86	173	63	3.04
Major League Totals—6 Years		199	1313⅓	84	67	.556	1207	563	512	850	502	3.51

Selected by Kansas City Royals' organization in 2nd round of free-agent draft, June 8, 1981.
†On disabled list, June 29, 1982 through remainder of season.
‡On disabled list, June 6 to June 21, 1986.

CHAMPIONSHIP SERIES RECORD

Year Club	League	G.	IP.	W.	L.	Pct.	H.	R.	ER.	SO.	BB.	ERA.
1985—Kansas City	American	2	8⅓	1	0	1.000	4	3	3	4	4	3.24

WORLD SERIES RECORD

Eligible for 1985 World Series with Kansas City Royals; did not play.

ALL-STAR GAME RECORD

Year League	IP.	W.	L.	Pct.	H.	R.	ER.	SO.	BB.	ERA.
1988—American	2	0	0	.000	3	1	1	2	0	4.50
1989—American	1	0	0	.000	0	0	0	1	0	0.00
All-Star Game Totals—2 Years	3	0	0	.000	3	1	1	3	0	3.00

PEDRO GUERRERO
Name pronounced Guh-RAIR-oh.

Born June 29, 1956, at San Pedro de Macoris, D. R.
Height, 6.00. Weight, 195.
Throws and bats righthanded.
Half-brother of Domingo Michel, outfielder in Detroit Tigers' organization.

Holds National League records for most home runs, month of June (15), 1985; most consecutive times reached base safely, season (14), July 23 through 26, 1985.
Major League stolen bases: 1979 (2), 1980 (2), 1981 (5), 1982 (22), 1983 (23), 1984 (9), 1985 (12), 1987 (9), 1988 (4), 1989 (2). Total—90.
Led National League in sacrifice flies with 12 in 1989.
Led National League in slugging percentage with .577 in 1985.
Led National League third basemen in errors with 30 and tied for lead in total chances with 458 in 1983.
Led Pacific Coast League in sacrifice flies with 15 in 1978.
Tied for Northwest League lead in double plays by third basemen with 13 in 1974.
Named outfielder on THE SPORTING NEWS National League All-Star Team, 1981 and 1982.
Named outfielder on THE SPORTING NEWS National League Silver Slugger team, 1982.

Year Club	League	Pos.	G.	AB.	R.	H.	2B.	3B.	HR.	RBI.	B.A.	PO.	A.	E.	F.A.
1973—Sarasota Ind.†	Gulf C.	3B-SS	44	153	13	39	2	3	2	22	.255	32	82	11	.912
1974—Orangeburg	W. Car.	3B	19	55	3	8	1	0	0	1	.145	11	22	5	.868
1974—Bellingham	N'west	3B	82	297	49	94	●23	2	3	55	.316	★69	124	23	.894
1975—Danville	Midw.	3D-OF	104	351	81	121	25	5	10	76	★.345	111	168	31	.900
1976—Waterbury	East.	1B	132	495	73	151	★30	10	5	66	.305	1129	★96	★19	.985
1977—Albuquerque‡	P. C.	1B	32	129	30	52	11	4	4	39	.403	329	17	10	.972
1978—Albuquerque	P. C.	1B-3B	134	492	92	166	28	4	14	★116	.337	982	80	10	.991
1978—Los Angeles	Nat.	1B	5	8	3	5	0	1	0	1	.625	25	1	0	1.000
1979—Albuquerque	P. C.	OF-3B-1B	113	453	94	151	33	9	22	★103	.333	188	9	5	.975
1979—Los Angeles	Nat.	OF-1B-3B	25	62	7	15	2	0	2	9	.242	53	4	1	.983
1980—Los Angeles§	Nat.	O-2-3-1	75	183	27	59	9	1	7	31	.322	103	110	3	.986
1981—Los Angeles	Nat.	OF-3B-1B	98	347	46	104	17	2	12	48	.300	165	55	11	.952
1982—Los Angeles	Nat.	OF-3B	150	575	87	175	27	5	32	100	.304	282	53	12	.965
1983—Los Angeles	Nat.	3B-1B	160	584	87	174	28	6	32	103	.298	130	308	31	.934
1984—Los Angeles x	Nat.	3B-OF-1B	144	535	85	162	29	4	16	72	.303	271	151	22	.950
1985—Los Angeles	Nat.	OF-3B-1B	137	487	99	156	22	2	33	87	.320	251	123	13	.966
1986—Los Angeles y	Nat.	OF-1B	31	61	7	15	3	0	5	10	.246	39	1	0	1.000
1987—Los Angeles	Nat.	1B-3B	152	545	89	184	25	2	27	89	.338	482	44	12	.978
1988—L.A.zab-St.L.	Nat.	1B-3B-OF	103	364	40	104	14	2	10	65	.286	466	99	12	.979
1988—Albuquerque	P. C.	1B	5	12	3	5	0	0	1	4	.417	30	2	0	1.000
1989—St. Louis	Nat.	1B	162	570	60	177	●42	1	17	117	.311	★1445	72	●15	.990
Major League Totals—12 Years		1242	4321	637	1330	218	26	193	732	.308	3712	1021	132	.973

Signed as free agent by Cleveland Indians' organization, January 15, 1973.
†Traded to Los Angeles Dodgers for Pitcher Bruce Ellingsen, April 4, 1974.
‡On disabled list, May 19 to August 30, 1977.
§On disabled list, August 23 to September 15, 1980.
xOn disabled list, July 22 to August 6, 1984.
yOn disabled list, April 4 to July 30 and August 11 to September 3, 1986.
zOn suspended list, May 24 to May 28, 1988.

aOn disabled list, June 5 to July 29, 1988; included rehabilitation disability assignment to Albuquerque, July 23 to July 29, 1988.
bTraded to St. Louis Cardinals for Pitcher John Tudor, August 16, 1988.

Year	Club	League	Pos.	G.	AB.	R.	H.	2B.	3B.	HR.	RBI.	B.A.	PO.	A.	E.	F.A.
1981—Los Angeles		Nat.	3B	5	17	1	3	1	0	1	1	.176	3	15	0	1.000

CHAMPIONSHIP SERIES RECORD

Holds Championship Series records for most times grounded into double play, total series (5) and series (4), 1981.
Shares National League Championship Series record for most times grounded into double play (2), October 16, 1981.

Year	Club	League	Pos.	G.	AB.	R.	H.	2B.	3B.	HR.	RBI.	B.A.	PO.	A.	E.	F.A.
1981—Los Angeles		Nat.	OF	5	19	1	2	0	0	1	2	.105	9	2	0	1.000
1983—Los Angeles		Nat.	3B	4	12	1	3	1	1	0	2	.250	0	9	0	1.000
1985—Los Angeles		Nat.	OF	6	20	2	5	1	0	0	4	.250	11	0	0	1.000
Championship Series Totals—3 Years				15	51	4	10	2	1	1	8	.196	20	11	0	1.000

WORLD SERIES RECORD

Year	Club	League	Pos.	G.	AB.	R.	H.	2B.	3B.	HR.	RBI.	B.A.	PO.	A.	E.	F.A.
1981—Los Angeles		Nat.	OF	6	21	2	7	1	1	2	7	.333	17	1	0	1.000

ALL-STAR GAME RECORD

Year	League	Pos.	AB.	R.	H.	2B.	3B.	HR.	RBI.	B.A.	PO.	A.	E.	F.A.
1981—National		PH	1	0	0	0	0	0	0	.000	0	0	0	.000
1983—National		3B-OF	1	0	0	0	0	0	0	.000	0	0	1	.000
1987—National		PH	1	0	0	0	0	0	0	.000	0	0	0	.000
1989—National		DH	2	0	0	0	0	0	0	.000	0	0	0	.000
All-Star Game Totals—4 Years			5	0	0	0	0	0	0	.000	0	0	1	.000

Named to National League All-Star Team for 1985 game; replaced due to injury by Glenn Wilson.

ARTHUR LEE GUETTERMAN
(Known by middle name.)

Born November 22, 1958, at Chattanooga, Tenn.
Height, 6.08. Weight, 225.
Throws and bats lefthanded.
Received bachelor of science degree in physical education from
Liberty Baptist College, Lynchburg, Va. in 1981.

Major League saves: 1989 (13).

Year	Club	League	G.	IP.	W.	L.	Pct.	H.	R.	ER.	SO.	BB.	ERA.
1981—Bellingham		Northwest	13	84	6	4	.600	85	36	25	55	42	2.68
1982—Bakersfield		California	26	154	7	11	.389	172	100	76	82	69	4.44
1983—Bakersfield		California	25	156⅓	12	6	.667	164	72	56	93	45	3.22
1984—Chattanooga†		Southern	24	157	11	7	.611	174	68	59	47	38	3.38
1984—Seattle		American	3	4⅓	0	0	.000	9	2	2	2	2	4.15
1985—Calgary‡		P. Coast	20	110⅓	5	8	.385	138	86	71	48	44	5.79
1986—Seattle		American	41	76	0	4	.000	108	67	62	38	30	7.34
1986—Calgary		P. Coast	4	19⅓	1	0	1.000	24	12	12	8	7	5.59
1987—Calgary		P. Coast	16	44	5	1	.833	41	14	14	29	17	2.86
1987—Seattle§		American	25	113⅓	11	4	★.733	117	60	48	42	35	3.81
1988—New York		American	20	40⅔	1	2	.333	49	21	21	15	14	4.65
1988—Columbus		Int'national	18	120⅔	9	6	.600	109	46	37	49	26	2.76
1989—New York		American	70	103	5	5	.500	98	31	28	51	26	2.45
Major League Totals—5 Years			159	337⅓	17	15	.531	381	181	161	148	107	4.30

Selected by Seattle Mariners' organization in 4th round of free-agent draft, June 8, 1981.
†On disabled list, August 1 to August 15, 1984.
‡On disabled list, April 11 to May 31, 1985.
§Traded with Pitchers Clay Parker and Wade Taylor to New York Yankees for Pitcher Steve Trout and Outfielder Henry Cotto, December 22, 1987.

OSWALDO JOSE GUILLEN (BARRIOS)
Name pronounced GEY-un.

(Ozzie)

Born January 20, 1964, at Ocumare del Tuy, Miranda, Venezuela.
Height, 5.11. Weight, 153.
Throws right and bats lefthanded.

Shares major league record for fewest bases on balls received, 150 or more games, season (12), 1985, 1986.
Holds American League record for fewest putouts, shortstop, season, 150 or more games (220), 1985.
Major League stolen bases: 1985 (7), 1986 (8), 1987 (25), 1988 (25), 1989 (36). Total—101.
Led American League shortstops in total chances with 760 in 1987 and 863 in 1988.
Led American League shortstops in double plays with 105 in 1987.
Led Pacific Coast League shortstops in assists with 362 and total chances with 549 in 1984.
Tied for California League lead in sacrifice hits with 14 in 1982.
Named American League Rookie Player of the Year by THE SPORTING NEWS, 1985.
Named American League Rookie of the Year by Baseball Writers' Association of America, 1985.

Year	Club	League	Pos.	G.	AB.	R.	H.	2B.	3B.	HR.	RBI.	B.A.	PO.	A.	E.	F.A.
1981—Bradenton Padr.†	Gulf C.		SS-2B	55	189	26	49	4	1	0	16	.259	105	135	15	.941
1982—Reno†	Calif.		SS	130	528	★103	★183	33	1	2	54	.347	★240	399	41	.940
1983—Beaumont†	Texas		SS	114	427	62	126	20	4	2	48	.295	185	327	★38	.931
1984—Las Vegas†‡	P. C.		SS-2B	122	463	81	137	26	6	5	53	.296	172	364	17	.969

Year Club	League	Pos.	G.	AB.	R.	H.	2B.	3B.	HR.	RBI.	B.A.	PO.	A.	E.	F.A.
1985—Chicago	Amer.	SS	150	491	71	134	21	9	1	33	.273	220	382	12	*.980
1986—Chicago	Amer.	SS	159	547	58	137	19	4	2	47	.250	261	459	22	.970
1987—Chicago	Amer.	SS	149	560	64	156	22	7	2	51	.279	266	475	19	.975
1988—Chicago	Amer.	SS	156	566	58	148	16	7	0	39	.261	273	*570	20	.977
1989—Chicago	Amer.	SS	155	597	63	151	20	8	1	54	.253	272	512	22	.973
Major League Totals—5 Years			769	2761	314	726	98	35	6	224	.263	1292	2398	95	.975

Signed as free agent by San Diego Padres' organization, December 17, 1980.
†Switch-hitter.
‡Traded with Pitchers Tim Lollar and Bill Long and Third Baseman Luis Salazar to Chicago White Sox for Pitchers LaMarr Hoyt, Kevin Kristan and Todd Simmons, December 6, 1984.

ALL-STAR GAME RECORD
Named to American League All-Star Team for 1988 game; replaced due to injury by Kurt Stillwell.

WILLIAM LEE GULLICKSON
(Bill)

Born February 20, 1959, at Marshall, Minn.
Height, 6.03. Weight, 220.
Throws and bats righthanded.

Shares modern major league record for most wild pitches, game (6), April 10, 1982.
Led National League in home runs allowed with 27 in 1984.
Named National League Rookie Pitcher of the Year by THE SPORTING NEWS, 1980.

Year Club	League	G.	IP.	W.	L.	Pct.	H.	R.	ER.	SO.	BB.	ERA.
1977—West Palm Beach	Florida St.	10	56	3	3	.500	67	30	25	35	17	4.02
1978—West Palm Beach	Florida St.	20	148	9	9	.500	121	45	30	127	52	1.82
1978—Memphis	Southern	8	50	1	4	.200	44	19	17	43	19	3.06
1979—Denver	Am. Assoc.	11	54	3	3	.500	65	44	40	31	26	6.67
1979—Memphis	Southern	16	116	10	3	.769	110	52	47	115	42	3.65
1979—Montreal	National	1	1	0	0	.000	2	0	0	0	0	0.00
1980—Denver	Am. Assoc.	9	66	6	2	.750	47	14	14	64	29	1.91
1980—Montreal	National	24	141	10	5	.667	127	53	47	120	50	3.00
1981—Montreal	National	22	157	7	9	.438	142	54	49	115	34	2.81
1982—Montreal	National	34	236⅔	12	14	.462	231	101	94	155	61	3.57
1983—Montreal	National	34	242⅔	17	12	.586	230	108	101	120	59	3.75
1984—Montreal†	National	32	226⅔	12	9	.571	230	100	91	100	37	3.61
1985—Montreal‡§	National	29	181⅓	14	12	.538	187	78	71	68	47	3.52
1986—Cincinnati	National	37	244⅔	15	12	.556	245	103	92	121	60	3.38
1987—Cincinnati x	National	27	165	10	11	.476	172	99	89	89	39	4.85
1987—New York y	American	8	48	4	2	.667	46	29	26	28	11	4.88
1988—Yomiuri Giants	Central	26	203⅓	14	9	.609	....	....	70	134	51	3.10
1989—Yomiuri Giants z	Central	....	111	7	5	.583	....	....	45	....	....	3.65
National League Totals—9 Years		240	1595⅔	97	84	.536	1566	696	634	888	387	3.58
American League Totals—1 Year		8	48	4	2	.667	46	29	26	28	11	4.88
Major League Totals—9 Years		248	1643⅔	101	86	.540	1612	725	660	916	398	3.61

Selected by Montreal Expos' organization in 1st round (second player selected) of free-agent draft, June 7, 1977.
†On disabled list, April 20 to May 8, 1984.
‡On disabled list, June 17 to July 8, 1985.
§Traded with Catcher Sal Butera to Cincinnati Reds for Pitchers Jay Tibbs, Andy McGaffigan and John Stuper and Catcher Dann Bilardello, December 19, 1985.
xTraded to New York Yankees for Pitcher Dennis Rasmussen, August 26, 1987.
yGranted free agency, November 9, 1987; signed by Yomiuri Giants of Japanese Baseball League, January 13, 1988.
zSigned by Houston Astros, December 6, 1989.

DIVISION SERIES RECORD
Year Club	League	G.	IP.	W.	L.	Pct.	H.	R.	ER.	SO.	BB.	ERA.
1981—Montreal	National	1	7⅔	1	0	1.000	6	1	1	3	1	1.17

CHAMPIONSHIP SERIES RECORD
Shares Championship Series record for most games lost, series (2), 1981.
Year Club	League	G.	IP.	W.	L.	Pct.	H.	R.	ER.	SO.	BB.	ERA.
1981—Montreal	National	2	14⅓	0	2	.000	12	5	4	12	6	2.51

ERIC ANDREW GUNDERSON

Born March 29, 1966, at Portland, Ore.
Height, 6.00. Weight, 175.
Throws left and bats righthanded.
Attended Portland State University, Portland, Ore.

Led Northwest League pitchers in complete games with 5 and tied for lead in games started with 15 and shutouts with 3 in 1987.
Led California League in hit batsmen with 17 in 1988.

Year Club	League	G.	IP.	W.	L.	Pct.	H.	R.	ER.	SO.	BB.	ERA.
1987—Everett	Northwest	15	98⅔	8	4	.667	80	34	27	*99	34	2.46
1988—San Jose	California	20	149⅓	12	5	.706	131	56	44	151	52	2.65
1988—Shreveport	Texas	7	36⅔	1	2	.333	45	25	21	28	13	5.15

Year Club	League	G.	IP.	W.	L.	Pct.	H.	R.	ER.	SO.	BB.	ERA.
1989—Shreveport	Texas	11	72⅔	8	2	*.800	68	24	22	61	23	2.72
1989—Phoenix	P. Coast	14	85⅔	2	4	.333	93	51	48	56	36	5.04

Selected by San Francisco Giants' organization in 2nd round of free-agent draft, June 2, 1987.

MARK ANDREW GUTHRIE

Born September 22, 1965, at Buffalo, N.Y.
Height, 6.04. Weight, 205.
Throws left and bats left and righthanded.
Attended Louisiana State University, Baton Rouge, La.

Year Club	League	G.	IP.	W.	L.	Pct.	H.	R.	ER.	SO.	BB.	ERA.
1987—Visalia	California	4	12	2	1	.667	10	7	6	9	5	4.50
1988—Visalia	California	25	171⅓	12	9	.571	169	81	63	182	86	3.31
1989—Orlando	Southern	14	96	8	3	.727	75	32	21	103	38	1.97
1989—Portland	P. Coast	7	44⅓	3	4	.429	45	21	18	35	16	3.65
1989—Minnesota	American	13	57⅓	2	4	.333	66	32	29	38	21	4.55
Major League Totals—1 Year		13	57⅓	2	4	.333	66	32	29	38	21	4.55

Selected by St. Louis Cardinals' organization in 4th round of free-agent draft, June 2, 1986.
Selected by Minnesota Twins' organization in 7th round of free-agent draft, June 2, 1987.

JOSE ALBERTO GUZMAN (MIRABEL)

Born April 9, 1963, at Santa Isabel, Puerto Rico.
Height, 6.03. Weight, 198.
Throws and bats righthanded.

Year Club	League	G.	IP.	W.	L.	Pct.	H.	R.	ER.	SO.	BB.	ERA.
1981—Sarasota Rangers	Gulf Coast	14	39	3	3	.500	44	30	23	13	14	5.31
1982—Sarasota Rangers	Gulf Coast	12	66	5	4	.556	51	21	16	42	13	2.18
1983—Burlington	Midwest	25	154⅔	12	8	.600	135	68	51	146	52	2.97
1984—Tulsa	Texas	25	140⅓	7	9	.438	137	75	65	82	55	4.17
1985—Oklahoma City	Am. Assoc.	25	149⅔	10	5	.667	131	60	52	76	40	3.13
1985—Texas	American	5	32⅔	3	2	.600	27	13	10	24	14	2.76
1986—Texas	American	29	172½	9	15	.375	199	101	87	87	60	4.54
1987—Texas	American	37	208⅓	14	14	.500	196	115	108	143	82	4.67
1988—Texas	American	30	206⅔	11	13	.458	180	99	85	157	82	3.70
1989—Texas†	American					(Did not play)						
Major League Totals—4 Years		101	620	37	44	.457	602	328	290	411	238	4.21

Signed as free agent by Texas Rangers' organization, February 10, 1981.
†On disabled list, March 26 to September 1, 1989.

ANTHONY KEITH GWYNN

Name pronounced Gwin.

(Tony)

Born May 9, 1960, at Los Angeles, Calif.
Height, 5.11. Weight, 199.
Throws and bats lefthanded.
Attended San Diego State University, San Diego, Calif.
Brother of Chris Gwynn, outfielder in Los Angeles Dodgers' organization.

Holds National League record for lowest average by batting leader, season (.313), 1988.
Shares National League record for most years leading league, singles (4).
Shares modern National League record for most stolen bases, game (5), September 20, 1986.
Major League stolen bases: 1982 (8), 1983 (7), 1984 (33), 1985 (14), 1986 (37), 1987 (56), 1988 (26), 1989 (40). Total—221.
Led National League outfielders in total chances with 360 in 1986.
Named outfielder on THE SPORTING NEWS National League All-Star Team, 1984, 1986, 1987 and 1989.
Named outfielder on THE SPORTING NEWS National League All-Star fielding team, 1986, 1987 and 1989.
Named outfielder on THE SPORTING NEWS National League Silver Slugger team, 1984, 1986, 1987 and 1989.
Named Northwest League Most Valuable Player, 1981.
Drafted by San Diego Clippers in 10th round (210th player selected) of NBA draft, June 9, 1981.

Year Club	League	Pos.	G.	AB.	R.	H.	2B.	3B.	HR.	RBI.	B.A.	PO.	A.	E.	F.A.
1981—Walla Walla	N'west	OF	42	178	46	59	12	1	12	37	*.331	76	2	3	.963
1981—Amarillo	Texas	OF	23	91	22	42	8	2	4	19	.462	41	1	0	1.000
1982—Hawaii	P. C.	OF	93	366	65	120	23	2	5	46	.328	208	11	4	.982
1982—San Diego†	Nat.	OF	54	190	33	55	12	2	1	17	.289	110	1	1	.991
1983—Las Vegas‡	P. C.	OF	17	73	15	25	6	0	0	7	.342	23	2	3	.893
1983—San Diego	Nat.	OF	86	304	34	94	12	2	1	37	.309	163	9	1	.994
1984—San Diego	Nat.	OF	158	606	88	*213	21	10	5	71	*.351	345	11	4	.989
1985—San Diego	Nat.	OF	154	622	90	197	29	5	6	46	.317	337	14	4	.989
1986—San Diego	Nat.	OF	160	*642	●107	*211	33	7	14	59	.329	*337	19	4	.989
1987—San Diego	Nat.	OF	157	589	119	*218	36	13	7	54	*.370	298	13	6	.981
1988—San Diego§	Nat.	OF	133	521	64	163	22	5	7	70	*.313	264	8	5	.982
1989—San Diego	Nat.	OF	158	604	82	*203	27	7	4	62	*.336	353	13	6	.984
Major League Totals—8 Years			1060	4078	617	1354	192	51	45	416	.332	2207	88	31	.987

Selected by San Diego Padres' organization in 3rd round of free-agent draft, June 8, 1981.
†On disabled list, August 26 to September 10, 1982.
‡On San Diego disabled list, March 26 to June 21, 1983; included rehabilitation assignment to Las Vegas, May 31 to June 20, 1983.
§On disabled list, May 8 to May 29, 1988.

CHAMPIONSHIP SERIES RECORD

Year	Club	League	Pos.	G.	AB.	R.	H.	2B.	3B.	HR.	RBI.	B.A.	PO.	A.	E.	F.A.
1984—San Diego		Nat.	OF	5	19	6	7	3	0	0	3	.368	9	0	0	1.000

WORLD SERIES RECORD

Year	Club	League	Pos.	G.	AB.	R.	H.	2B.	3B.	HR.	RBI.	B.A.	PO.	A.	E.	F.A.
1984—San Diego		Nat.	OF	5	19	1	5	0	0	0	0	.263	12	1	1	.929

ALL-STAR GAME RECORD

Year	League	Pos.	AB.	R.	H.	2B.	3B.	HR.	RBI.	B.A.	PO.	A.	E.	F.A.
1984—National		OF	3	0	1	0	0	0	0	.333	0	0	0	.000
1985—National		OF	1	0	0	0	0	0	0	.000	1	0	0	1.000
1986—National		OF	3	0	0	0	0	0	0	.000	1	0	0	1.000
1987—National		PH	1	0	0	0	0	0	0	.000	0	0	0	.000
1989—National		OF	2	1	1	0	0	0	0	.500	2	0	0	1.000
All-Star Game Totals—5 Years			10	1	2	0	0	0	0	.200	4	0	0	1.000

CHRISTOPHER KARLTON GWYNN

Name pronounced Gwin.

(Chris)

Born October 13, 1964, at Los Angeles, Calif.
Height, 6.00. Weight, 216.
Throws and bats lefthanded.
Attended San Diego State University, San Diego, Calif.
Brother of Tony Gwynn, outfielder with San Diego Padres.

Major League stolen bases: 1989 (1).
Named outfielder on THE SPORTING NEWS College Baseball All-America Team, 1985.
Member of 1984 U.S. Olympic baseball team.

Year	Club	League	Pos.	G.	AB.	R.	H.	2B.	3B.	HR.	RBI.	B.A.	PO.	A.	E.	F.A.
1985—Vero Beach		Fla. St.	OF	52	179	19	46	8	6	0	17	.257	43	2	0	1.000
1986—San Antonio		Texas	OF	111	401	46	115	22	1	6	67	.287	186	11	2	.990
1987—Albuquerque		P. C.	OF	110	362	54	101	12	3	5	41	.279	141	5	1	.993
1987—Los Angeles		Nat.	OF	17	32	2	7	1	0	0	2	.219	12	0	0	1.000
1988—Albuquerque		P. C.	OF	112	411	57	123	22	●10	5	61	.299	134	3	4	.972
1988—Los Angeles		Nat.	OF	12	11	1	2	0	0	0	0	.182	0	0	0	.000
1989—Albuquerque		P. C.	OF	26	89	14	29	9	1	0	12	.326	27	0	0	1.000
1989—Los Angeles†		Nat.	OF	32	68	8	16	4	1	0	7	.235	26	1	0	1.000
Major League Totals—3 Years				61	111	11	25	5	1	0	9	.225	26	1	0	1.000

Selected by California Angels' organization in 5th round of free-agent draft, June 7, 1982.
Selected by Los Angeles Dodgers' organization in 1st round (10th player selected) of free-agent draft, June 3, 1985.
†On disabled list, June 12 to July 6 and July 16, 1989 through remainder of season; included rehabilitation disability assignment to Albuquerque, August 3 to August 11, 1989.

JERRY WAYNE HAIRSTON

Born February 16, 1952, at Birmingham, Ala.
Height, 5.10. Weight, 196.
Throws right and bats left and righthanded.
Attended Lawson State Junior College, Birmingham, Ala.
Son of Sam Hairston, Sr., catcher with Chicago White Sox, 1951; scout and minor league instructor with Chicago
White Sox, 1961 through 1982 and 1985; and minor league coach in Chicago White Sox' organization
since 1986; brother of John Hairston, catcher-outfielder with Chicago Cubs, 1969; and
Sam Hairston, Jr., second baseman in Chicago White Sox' organization, 1966.

Major League stolen bases: 1975 (1), 1976 (1), 1984 (2). Total—4.
Led Mexican League in bases on balls received with 122 in 1978, 77 in 1980 and 122 in 1981.
Led Midwest League second baseman in double plays with 77 in 1971.
Tied for Mexican League lead in double plays by outfielders with 4 in 1981.

Year	Club	League	Pos.	G.	AB.	R.	H.	2B.	3B.	HR.	RBI.	B.A.	PO.	A.	E.	F.A.
1970—Sarasota W. Sox		Gulf C.	2B	56	183	37	61	8	2	1	36	.333	129	130	★19	.932
1971—Appleton		Midw.	2B	121	448	86	120	15	4	0	39	.268	★260	★333	★31	.950
1972—Knoxville		South.	2-1-O-3	132	459	82	134	19	●9	10	64	.292	591	225	27	.968
1973—Iowa		A. A.	O-2-3-1	84	274	51	95	18	6	9	65	.347	70	36	7	.938
1973—Chicago		Amer.	OF-1B	60	210	25	57	11	1	0	23	.271	194	13	5	.976
1974—Iowa		A. A.	OF	42	140	31	53	10	2	5	42	.379	48	1	2	.961
1974—Chicago†		Amer.	OF	45	109	8	25	7	0	0	8	.229	24	1	2	.926
1975—Denver		A. A.	DH	40	139	28	51	9	0	3	31	.367	0	0	0	.000
1975—Chicago		Amer.	OF	69	219	26	62	8	0	0	23	.283	111	6	6	.951
1976—Iowa		A. A.	OF-INF	94	325	53	94	24	3	5	64	.289	199	13	5	.977
1976—Chicago		Amer.	OF	44	119	20	27	2	2	0	10	.227	71	1	2	.973
1977—Chicago‡		Amer.	OF	13	26	3	8	2	0	0	4	.308	15	1	0	1.000
1977—Pittsburgh§		Nat.	OF-2B	51	52	5	10	2	0	2	6	.192	13	0	1	.929
1978—Durango		Mex.	OF	144	488	97	177	21	7	9	77	.363	297	19	11	.966
1979—Durango		Mex.	OF	128	427	87	151	22	5	12	56	.354	295	8	6	.981
1980—Campeche		Mex.	OF-1B	77	235	50	74	15	2	7	28	.315	189	11	3	.985
1981—Mex. C. Reds x		Mex.	OF	123	536	74	118	14	8	7	73	.296	★334	11	6	.983
1981—Chicago		Amer.	OF	9	25	5	7	1	0	1	6	.280	14	0	1	.933

— 193 —

Year Club	League	Pos.	G.	AB.	R.	H.	2B.	3B.	HR.	RBI.	B.A.	PO.	A.	E.	F.A.
1982—Chicago	Amer.	OF	85	90	11	21	5	0	5	18	.233	34	2	0	1.000
1983—Chicago	Amer.	OF	101	126	17	37	9	1	5	22	.294	29	1	1	.968
1984—Chicago	Amer.	OF	115	227	41	59	13	2	5	19	.260	57	2	2	.967
1985—Chicago	Amer.	OF	95	140	9	34	8	0	2	20	.243	5	0	0	1.000
1986—Chicago	Amer.	1B-OF	101	225	32	61	15	0	5	26	.271	132	9	0	1.000
1987—Chicago y	Amer.	OF-1B	66	126	14	29	8	0	5	20	.230	82	5	1	.989
1988—Chicago z	Amer.	PH	2	2	0	0	0	0	0	0	.000	0	0	0	.000
1989—Chicago a	Amer.	PH	3	3	0	1	0	0	0	0	.333	0	0	0	.000
American League Totals—14 Years			808	1647	211	428	89	6	28	199	.260	768	41	20	.976
National League Totals—1 Year			51	52	5	10	2	0	2	6	.192	13	0	1	.929
Major League Totals—14 Years			859	1699	216	438	91	6	30	205	.258	781	41	21	.975

Selected by Chicago White Sox' organization in 3rd round of free-agent draft, June 4, 1970.
†On disabled list, June 27 to July 12, 1974.
‡Sold to Pittsburgh Pirates, June 13, 1977.
§Sold to Durango of Mexican League, March 2, 1978.
xSold to Chicago White Sox, September 10, 1981.
yReleased, March 25, 1988; signed by Chicago White Sox, August 31, 1988.
zReleased, October 19, 1988; re-signed by Chicago White Sox, September 1, 1989.
aReleased, October 2, 1989.

CHAMPIONSHIP SERIES RECORD

Year Club	League	Pos.	G.	AB.	R.	H.	2B.	3B.	HR.	RBI.	B.A.	PO.	A.	E.	F.A.
1983—Chicago	Amer.	PH-OF	2	3	0	0	0	0	0	0	.000	0	0	1	.000

WALTER WILLIAM HALE
(Chip)

Born December 2, 1964, at Santa Clara, Calif.
Height, 5.11. Weight, 180.
Throws right and bats lefthanded.
Received degree from University of Arizona, Tucson, Ariz.
Led Pacific Coast League second basemen in assists with 332 in 1989.

Year Club	League	Pos.	G.	AB.	R.	H.	2B.	3B.	HR.	RBI.	B.A.	PO.	A.	E.	F.A.
1987—Kenosha	Midw.	2B	87	339	65	117	12	7	7	65	★.345	164	233	10	.975
1988—Orlando	South.	2B	133	482	62	126	20	1	11	65	.261	254	322	★23	.962
1989—Portland	P. C.	2B-3B	108	411	49	112	16	9	2	34	.273	217	333	10	.982
1989—Minnesota	Amer.	2B-3B	28	67	6	14	3	0	0	4	.209	15	40	1	.982
Major League Totals—1 Year			28	67	6	14	3	0	0	4	.209	15	40	1	.982

Selected by Minnesota Twins' organization in 17th round of free-agent draft, June 2, 1987.

ALBERT HALL

Born March 7, 1959, at Birmingham, Ala.
Height, 5.11. Weight, 158.
Throws right and bats left and righthanded.
Major League stolen bases: 1983 (1), 1984 (6), 1985 (1), 1986 (8), 1987 (33), 1988 (15), 1989 (3). Total—67.
Hit for the cycle, September 23, 1987.
Led International League in stolen bases with 62 in 1982 and 72 in 1986.
Led International League in caught stealing with 16 in 1986.
Led Carolina League in being hit by pitch with 9, stolen bases with 100 and caught stealing with 27 in 1980.
Led Western Carolinas League in stolen bases with 66 in 1979.
Led Gulf Coast League shortstops in double plays with 23 in 1978.
Tied for Southern League lead in caught stealing with 17 in 1981.

Year Club	League	Pos.	G.	AB.	R.	H.	2B.	3B.	HR.	RBI.	B.A.	PO.	A.	E.	F.A.
1977—Kingsport	Appal.	SS	35	68	11	11	0	0	0	3	.162	10	28	10	.792
1978—Bradenton Brav...	Gulf C.	SS	34	123	15	36	4	2	0	14	.293	55	100	●15	.912
1979—Greenwood	W. Car.	SS	105	368	84	106	10	3	0	38	.288	120	288	★72	.850
1980—Durham	Carol.	OF-SS	125	491	95	139	16	7	4	41	.283	166	32	16	.925
1981—Savannah	South.	OF	133	487	83	150	28	10	5	27	.308	263	16	10	.965
1981—Atlanta	Nat.	OF	6	2	1	0	0	0	0	0	.000	0	0	0	.000
1982—Richmond	Int.	OF	129	528	97	139	18	★15	3	42	.263	297	6	7	.977
1982—Atlanta	Nat.	PR	5	0	1	0	0	0	0	0	.000	0	0	0	.000
1983—Richmond	Int.	★OF-SS	130	521	120	153	28	★11	1	42	.294	280	10	★12	.960
1983—Atlanta	Nat.	OF	10	8	2	0	0	0	0	0	.000	3	0	1	.750
1984—Atlanta	Nat.	OF	87	142	25	37	6	1	1	9	.261	64	4	5	.932
1985—Atlanta	Nat.	OF	54	47	5	7	0	1	0	3	.149	7	2	1	.900
1985—Richmond†	Int.	OF	38	98	12	22	0	3	0	5	.224	77	2	3	.963
1986—Richmond	Int.	OF	125	441	73	119	18	3	3	41	.270	264	8	7	.975
1986—Atlanta	Nat.	OF	16	50	6	12	2	0	0	1	.240	26	1	3	.900
1987—Atlanta‡	Nat.	OF	92	292	54	83	20	4	3	24	.284	148	5	3	.981
1988—Atlanta§	Nat.	OF	85	231	27	57	7	1	1	15	.247	137	7	4	.973
1988—Bradenton Brav x	Gulf C.	OF	2	8	1	2	0	0	0	1	.250	7	0	0	1.000
1989—Buffalo	A. A.	OF	90	345	63	105	13	5	4	33	.304	191	2	3	.985
1989—Pittsburgh y	Nat.	OF	20	33	4	6	2	1	0	1	.182	10	0	1	.909
Major League Totals—9 Years			375	805	125	202	37	8	5	53	.251	395	19	18	.958

Selected by Atlanta Braves' organization in 6th round of free-agent draft, June 7, 1977.
†On disabled list, July 12 to July 26, 1985.
‡On disabled list, June 19 to July 5, 1987.

xReleased, March 28, 1989; signed by Buffalo (Pittsburgh Pirates' organization), May 23, 1989.
yDrafted by Tucson (Houston Astros' organization), December 5, 1989.

ANDREW CLARK HALL
(Drew)

Born March 27, 1963, at Louisville, Ky.
Height, 6.05. Weight, 220.
Throws and bats lefthanded.
Attended Morehead State University, Morehead, Ky.

Major League saves: 1986 (1), 1988 (1). Total—2.
Tied for Eastern League lead in shutouts with 3 in 1986.
Named lefthanded pitcher on THE SPORTING NEWS College Baseball All-America Team, 1984.

Year Club	League	G.	IP.	W.	L.	Pct.	H.	R.	ER.	SO.	BB.	ERA.
1984—Lodi	California	8	48	3	3	.500	43	31	26	43	44	4.88
1985—Winston-Salem	Carolina	24	140⅔	10	7	.588	131	92	73	135	83	4.67
1986—Pittsfield	Eastern	24	158⅓	8	11	.421	130	77	63	115	84	3.58
1986—Chicago	National	5	23⅔	1	2	.333	24	12	12	21	10	4.56
1987—Iowa	Am. Assoc.	35	66½	6	3	.667	74	42	33	66	45	4.48
1987—Chicago	National	21	32⅔	1	1	.500	40	31	25	20	14	6.89
1988—Chicago	National	19	22⅓	1	1	.500	26	20	19	22	9	7.66
1988—Iowa†	Am. Assoc.	49	65½	4	3	.571	41	20	17	75	26	2.34
1989—Oklahoma City	Am. Assoc.	11	17⅔	1	0	1.000	7	3	3	18	6	1.53
1989—Texas	American	38	58⅓	2	1	.667	42	24	24	45	33	3.70
National League Totals—3 Years		45	78⅔	3	4	.429	90	63	56	63	33	6.41
American League Totals—1 Year		38	58⅓	2	1	.667	42	24	24	45	33	3.70
Major League Totals—4 Years		83	137	5	5	.500	132	87	80	108	66	5.26

Selected by Chicago Cubs' organization in 1st round (third player selected) of free-agent draft, June 4, 1984.
†Traded with Outfielder Rafael Palmeiro and Pitcher Jamie Moyer to Texas Rangers for Pitchers Mitch Williams, Paul Kilgus and Steve Wilson, Infielder Curtis Wilkerson and Luis Benitez and Outfielder Pablo Delgado, December 5, 1988.

GARDNER CARLILE HALL
(Grady)

Born May 29, 1964, at Findlay, O.
Height, 6.04. Weight, 200.
Throws left and bats righthanded.
Attended Northwestern University, Evanston, Ill.

Led Southern League in complete games with 9 in 1989.
Led Southern League in balks with 11 in 1988.

Year Club	League	G.	IP.	W.	L.	Pct.	H.	R.	ER.	SO.	BB.	ERA.
1986—Buffalo	Am. Assoc.	12	71⅓	4	5	.444	84	52	48	37	27	6.06
1987—Birmingham†	Southern	10	58	3	5	.375	54	28	24	30	20	3.72
1987—Sarasota White Sox	Gulf Coast	3	11	1	1	.500	12	7	5	11	2	4.09
1988—Birmingham	Southern	20	137	9	8	.529	132	59	45	69	42	2.96
1988—Vancouver	P. Coast	8	46	2	2	.500	43	24	21	13	21	4.11
1989—Birmingham	Southern	27	190⅔	12	8	.600	173	97	73	147	68	3.45

Selected by Boston Red Sox' organization in 27th round of free-agent draft, June 3, 1985.
Selected by Chicago White Sox' organization in 1st round (20th player selected) of free-agent draft, June 2, 1986.
†On disabled list, April 16 to July 24, 1987.

MELVIN HALL JR.
(Mel)

Born September 16, 1960, at Lyons, N. Y.
Height, 6.01. Weight, 205.
Throws and bats lefthanded.
Son of Melvin Hall Sr., minor league player in Cincinnati Reds' organization, 1949.

Major League stolen bases: 1983 (6), 1984 (3), 1986 (6), 1987 (5), 1988 (7). Total—27.
Led American Association in game-winning RBIs with 17 in 1982.
Led Texas League in total bases with 286 in 1981.
Led American Association outfielders in total chances with 339 in 1982.
Led Texas League outfielders in total chances with 324 and double plays with 5 in 1981.

Year Club	League	Pos.	G.	AB.	R.	H.	2B.	3B.	HR.	RBI.	B.A.	PO.	A.	E.	F.A.
1978—Bradenton Cubs	Gulf C.	OF	43	145	30	42	7	3	2	17	.290	★97	5	4	.962
1979—Geneva	NYP	OF	66	251	49	79	18	5	3	53	.315	113	5	7	.944
1980—Midland	Texas	OF	37	128	17	34	7	3	1	14	.266	58	3	3	.953
1980—Quad Cities	Midw.	OF	97	347	54	102	14	4	6	42	.294	171	9	5	.973
1981—Midland	Texas	OF	131	533	●98	★170	34	5	24	95	.319	★302	14	8	.975
1981—Chicago	Nat.	OF	10	11	1	1	0	0	1	2	.091	0	0	0	.000
1982—Iowa	A. A.	OF	133	502	★116	165	★34	6	32	125	.329	★317	13	●9	.973
1982—Chicago	Nat.	OF	24	80	6	21	3	2	0	4	.263	42	4	3	.939
1983—Chicago†	Nat.	OF	112	410	60	116	23	5	17	56	.283	239	8	3	.988
1983—Midland	Texas	OF	6	19	9	9	2	1	3	7	.474	8	0	0	1.000
1984—Chicago‡	Nat.	OF	48	150	25	42	11	3	4	22	.280	69	5	3	.961
1984—Cleveland	Amer.	OF	83	257	43	66	13	1	7	30	.257	143	3	1	.993

Year Club	League	Pos.	G.	AB.	R.	H.	2B.	3B.	HR.	RBI.	B.A.	PO.	A.	E.	F.A.
1985—Cleveland§	Amer.	OF	23	66	7	21	6	0	0	12	.318	18	0	0	1.000
1986—Cleveland	Amer.	OF	140	442	68	131	29	2	18	77	.296	233	7	7	.972
1987—Cleveland	Amer.	OF	142	485	57	136	21	1	18	76	.280	264	3	3	.989
1988—Cleveland x	Amer.	OF	150	515	69	144	32	4	6	71	.280	288	3	10	.967
1989—New York yz	Amer.	OF	113	361	54	94	9	0	17	58	.260	141	3	1	.993
National League Totals—4 Years			194	651	92	180	37	10	22	84	.276	350	17	9	.976
American League Totals—6 Years			651	2126	298	592	110	8	66	324	.278	1087	19	22	.980
Major League Totals—9 Years			845	2777	390	772	147	18	88	408	.278	1437	36	31	.979

Selected by Chicago Cubs' organization in 2nd round of free-agent draft, June 6, 1978.

†On disabled list, April 15 to May 31, 1983; included rehabilitation disability assignment to Midland, May 25 to May 31, 1983.

‡Traded with Outfielder Joe Carter and Pitchers Don Schulze and Darryl Banks to Cleveland Indians for Catcher Ron Hassey and Pitchers Rick Sutcliffe and George Frazier, June 13, 1984.

§On disabled list, May 10, 1985 through remainder of season.

xTraded to New York Yankees for Catcher Joel Skinner and Outfielder Turner Ward, March 19, 1989.

yOn disabled list, April 26 to May 26, 1989.

zGranted free agency, November 13, 1989; re-signed by Yankees, November 30, 1989.

DARRYL QUINN HAMILTON

Born December 3, 1964, at Baton Rouge, La.
Height, 6.01. Weight, 180.
Throws right and bats lefthanded.
Attended Nicholls State University, Thibodaux, La.

Major League stolen bases: 1988 (7).
Led California League in intentional bases on balls received with 9 in 1987.

Year Club	League	Pos.	G.	AB.	R.	H.	2B.	3B.	HR.	RBI.	B.A.	PO.	A.	E.	F.A.
1986—Helena	Pion.	OF	65	248	★72	●97	12	●6	0	35	★.391	132	9	0	★1.000
1987—Stockton	Calif.	OF	125	494	102	162	17	6	8	61	.328	221	8	1	★.996
1988—Denver	A. A.	OF	72	277	55	90	11	4	0	32	.325	160	2	2	.988
1988—Milwaukee	Amer.	OF	44	103	14	19	4	0	1	11	.184	75	1	0	1.000
1989—Denver	A. A.	OF	129	497	72	142	24	4	2	40	.286	263	11	0	★1.000
Major League Totals—1 Year			44	103	14	19	4	0	1	11	.184	75	1	0	1.000

Selected by Milwaukee Brewers' organization in 11th round of free-agent draft, June 2, 1986.

JEFFREY ROBERT HAMILTON
(Jeff)

Born March 19, 1964, at Flint, Mich.
Height, 6.03. Weight, 207.
Throws and bats righthanded.

Led Florida State League third basemen in total chances with 395 and double plays with 25 in 1984.
Led Pioneer League third basemen in double plays with 16 in 1983.

Year Club	League	Pos.	G.	AB.	R.	H.	2B.	3B.	HR.	RBI.	B.A.	PO.	A.	E.	F.A.
1983—Lodi	Calif.	3B-OF	44	141	15	28	4	0	0	10	.199	26	62	17	.838
1983—Lethbridge	Pion.	3B	68	★281	48	●94	★23	2	3	61	.335	38	118	17	.902
1984—Vero Beach	Fla. St.	3B	127	466	51	121	31	4	4	59	.260	★109	★259	★27	★.932
1985—San Antonio	Texas	3B-OF	101	377	48	125	14	3	13	59	.332	69	186	16	.941
1986—Albuquerque	P. C.	3B	71	288	40	90	21	3	10	42	.313	39	151	19	.909
1986—Los Angeles	Nat.	3B-SS	71	147	22	33	5	0	5	19	.224	40	87	4	.969
1987—Albuquerque	P. C.	3B	65	236	52	85	17	1	12	48	.360	43	102	11	.929
1987—Los Angeles†	Nat.	3B-SS	35	83	5	18	3	0	0	1	.217	27	60	6	.935
1988—Los Angeles‡	Nat.	3B-SS-1B	111	309	34	73	14	2	6	33	.236	67	160	14	.942
1989—Los Angeles	Nat.	★3-P-2-S	151	548	45	134	35	1	12	56	.245	★139	234	19	.952
Major League Totals—4 Years			368	1087	106	258	57	3	23	109	.237	273	541	43	.950

Selected by Los Angeles Dodgers' organization in 29th round of free-agent draft, June 7, 1982.

†On disabled list, August 14, 1987 through remainder of season.

‡On disabled list, July 27 to September 1, 1988.

CHAMPIONSHIP SERIES RECORD

Shares Championship Series record for most at-bats, inning (2), October 12, 1988, second inning.

Year Club	League	Pos.	G.	AB.	R.	H.	2B.	3B.	HR.	RBI.	B.A.	PO.	A.	E.	F.A.
1988—Los Angeles	Nat.	3B	7	23	2	5	0	0	0	1	.217	9	10	2	.905

WORLD SERIES RECORD

Year Club	League	Pos.	G.	AB.	R.	H.	2B.	3B.	HR.	RBI.	B.A.	PO.	A.	E.	F.A.
1988—Los Angeles	Nat.	3B	5	19	1	2	0	0	0	0	.105	2	5	1	.875

PITCHING RECORD

Year Club	League	G.	IP.	W.	L.	Pct.	H.	R.	ER.	SO.	BB.	ERA.
1989—Los Angeles	National	1	1⅔	0	1	.000	2	1	1	2	1	5.40

CHARLTON ATLEE HAMMAKER
(Known by middle name.)

Born January 24, 1958, at Carmel, Calif.
Height, 6.02. Weight, 200.
Throws left and bats right and lefthanded.
Attended East Tennessee State University, Johnson City, Tenn.

Major League saves: 1988 (5).

Year Club	League	G.	IP.	W.	L.	Pct.	H.	R.	ER.	SO.	BB.	ERA.
1979—Sarasota Royals-Gold	Gulf Coast	1	5	1	0	1.000	3	1	1	6	1	1.80
1979—Fort Myers†	Florida St.	1	5	0	1	.000	9	5	1	5	0	1.80
1980—Jacksonville‡	Southern	20	137	8	9	.471	131	64	51	88	37	3.35
1981—Omaha	Am. Assoc.	21	146	11	5	.688	147	70	59	63	40	3.64
1981—Kansas City§	American	10	39	1	3	.250	44	24	24	11	12	5.54
1982—Phoenix	P. Coast	1	5⅔	0	1	.000	13	5	4	6	2	6.35
1982—San Francisco	National	29	175	12	8	.600	189	86	80	102	28	4.11
1983—San Francisco x	National	23	172⅓	10	9	.526	147	57	43	127	32	★2.25
1984—Phoenix y	P. Coast	2	8	0	1	.000	14	7	4	5	2	4.50
1984—San Francisco	National	6	33	2	0	1.000	32	10	8	24	9	2.18
1985—San Francisco	National	29	170⅔	5	12	.294	161	81	71	100	47	3.74
1986—San Francisco za	National					(Did not play)						
1987—Phoenix b	P. Coast	3	17⅓	1	2	.333	19	9	8	8	6	4.15
1987—Shreveport	Texas	1	7	0	1	.000	6	2	1	3	0	1.29
1987—San Francisco c	National	31	168⅓	10	10	.500	159	73	67	107	57	3.58
1988—San Francisco	National	43	144⅔	9	9	.500	136	68	60	65	41	3.73
1989—San Francisco d	National	28	76⅔	6	6	.500	78	34	32	30	23	3.76
American League Totals—1 Year		10	39	1	3	.250	44	24	24	11	12	5.54
National League Totals—7 Years		189	940⅔	54	54	.500	902	409	361	555	237	3.45
Major League Totals—8 Years		199	979⅔	55	57	.491	946	433	385	566	249	3.54

Selected by Kansas City Royals' organization in 1st round (21st player selected) of free-agent draft, June 5, 1979.
†On disabled list, July 6 to October 26, 1979.
‡On disabled list, August 3 to August 22, 1980.
§Traded with Pitchers Craig Chamberlain and Renie Martin and a player to be named later to San Francisco Giants for Pitchers Vida Blue and Bob Tufts, March 30, 1982; San Francisco organization acquired Second Baseman Brad Wellman to complete deal, April 19, 1982.
xOn disabled list, July 26 to August 21, 1983.
yOn San Francisco disabled list, April 2 to June 26 and August 4 to September 1, 1984; included rehabilitation disability assignment to Phoenix, June 16 to June 25, 1984.
zOn disabled list, April 7, 1986 through entire season.
aReleased, December 9, 1986; re-signed by Giants, February 4, 1987.
bOn San Francisco disabled list, April 2 to April 30, 1987; included rehabilitation disability assignment to Phoenix April 10 to April 30, 1987.
cGranted free agency, November 9, 1987; re-signed by Giants, January 8, 1988.
dOn disabled list, June 19 to July 17 and August 3 to September 21, 1989.

CHAMPIONSHIP SERIES RECORD

Year Club	League	G.	IP.	W.	L.	Pct.	H.	R.	ER.	SO.	BB.	ERA.
1987—San Francisco	National	2	8	0	1	.000	12	7	7	7	0	7.88
1989—San Francisco	National	1	1	0	0	.000	1	0	0	0	0	0.00
Championship Series Totals—2 Years		3	9	0	1	.000	13	7	7	7	0	7.00

WORLD SERIES RECORD

Year Club	League	G.	IP.	W.	L.	Pct.	H.	R.	ER.	SO.	BB.	ERA.
1989—San Francisco	National	2	2⅓	0	0	.000	8	4	4	2	0	15.43

ALL-STAR GAME RECORD

Holds All-Star Game records for most runs and earned runs allowed, game and inning (7), July 6, 1983, third inning; most hits allowed, inning (6), July 6, 1983, third inning.
Shares All-Star Game record for most home runs allowed, inning (2), July 6, 1983, third inning.

Year League	IP.	W.	L.	Pct.	H.	R.	ER.	SO.	BB.	ERA.
1983—National	⅔	0	0	.000	6	7	7	0	1	94.50

CHRISTOPHER ANDREW HAMMOND
(Chris)

Born January 21, 1966, at Atlanta, Ga.
Height, 6.01. Weight, 190.
Throws and bats lefthanded.
Attended Gulf Coast Community College, Panama City, Fla.,
and University of Alabama, Birmingham, Ala.
Brother of Steve Hammond, outfielder with Kansas City Royals, 1982.

Year Club	League	G.	IP.	W.	L.	Pct.	H.	R.	ER.	SO.	BB.	ERA.
1986—Sarasota Reds	Gulf Coast	7	41⅔	3	2	.600	27	21	13	53	17	2.81
1986—Tampa	Florida St.	5	21⅔	0	2	.000	25	8	8	5	13	3.32
1987—Tampa	Florida St.	25	170	11	11	.500	174	81	67	126	60	3.55
1988—Chattanooga	Southern	26	182⅔	★16	5	.762	127	48	35	127	77	★1.72
1989—Nashville	Am. Assoc.	24	157⅓	11	7	.611	144	69	59	142	96	3.38

Selected by Cincinnati Reds' organization in 6th round of free-agent draft, January 14, 1986.

DAVID ANDREW HANSEN
(Dave)

Born November 24, 1968, at Long Beach, Calif.
Height, 6.00. Weight, 180.
Throws right and bats lefthanded.

Led Florida State League in total bases with 210, game-winning RBIs with 19 and tied for lead in sacrifice flies with 9 in 1988.
Led Florida State League third basemen in total chances with 383 and double plays with 24 in 1988.

Year Club	League	Pos.	G.	AB.	R.	H.	2B.	3B.	HR.	RBI.	B.A.	PO.	A.	E.	F.A.
1986—Great Falls............	Pion.	OF-3B-C	61	204	39	61	7	3	1	36	.299	54	10	7	.901
1987—Bakersfield............	Calif.	★3B-OF	132	432	68	113	22	1	3	38	.262	79	198	★45	.860
1988—Vero Beach..........	Fla. St.	3B	135	512	68	★149	●28	6	7	★81	.291	★102	★263	18	★.953
1989—San Antonio..........	Texas	3B	121	464	72	138	21	4	6	52	.297	★92	208	16	★.949
1989—Albuquerque	P. C.	3B	6	30	6	8	1	0	2	10	.267	3	8	3	.786

Selected by Los Angeles Dodgers' organization in 2nd round of free-agent draft, June 2, 1986.

ERIK B. HANSON

Born May 18, 1965, at Kinnelon, N. J.
Height, 6.06. Weight, 210.
Throws and bats righthanded.
Attended Wake Forest University, Winston-Salem, N. C.

Pitched 5-0 no-hit victory against Las Vegas, August 21, 1988 (second game).

Year Club	League	G.	IP.	W.	L.	Pct.	H.	R.	ER.	SO.	BB.	ERA.
1986—Chattanooga†	Southern	3	9⅓	0	0	.000	10	4	4	11	4	3.86
1987—Chattanooga	Southern	21	131⅓	8	10	.444	102	56	38	131	43	2.60
1987—Calgary	P. Coast	8	47⅓	1	3	.250	38	23	19	43	21	3.61
1988—Calgary	P. Coast	27	161⅔	12	7	.632	167	92	76	★154	57	4.23
1988—Seattle........................	American	6	41⅔	2	3	.400	35	17	15	36	12	3.24
1989—Seattle‡......................	American	17	113⅓	9	5	.643	103	44	40	75	32	3.18
1989—Calgary	P. Coast	8	38	4	2	.667	51	30	29	37	11	6.87
Major League Totals—2 Years............		23	155	11	8	.579	138	61	55	111	44	3.19

Selected by Montreal Expos' organization in 7th round of free-agent draft, June 6, 1983.
Selected by Seattle Mariners' organization in 2nd round of free-agent draft, June 2, 1986.
†On inactive list, June 12 to August 18, 1986.
‡On disabled list, May 25 to August 4, 1989; included rehabilitation disability assignment to Calgary, June 14 to June 22 and July 24 to August 4, 1989.

JOHN GRAYDON HARDY
(Jack)

Born October 8, 1959, at St. Petersburg, Fla.
Height, 6.02. Weight, 175.
Throws and bats righthanded.
Attended Biscayne College, Miami, Fla.

Year Club	League	G.	IP.	W.	L.	Pct.	H.	R.	ER.	SO.	BB.	ERA.
1981—Sarasota White Sox..................	Gulf Coast	13	●88	●8	2	.800	72	24	23	★78	7	2.35
1982—Glens Falls.......................	Eastern	28	146⅓	11	8	.579	140	85	58	96	32	3.57
1982—Edmonton........................	P. Coast	1	3	0	0	.000	7	5	5	1	1	15.00
1983—Glens Falls†.....................	Eastern	8	36⅓	1	1	.500	30	23	18	22	11	4.46
1983—Sarasota White Sox..............	Gulf Coast	4	19⅔	1	1	.500	19	7	4	10	2	1.83
1984—Glens Falls......................	Eastern	32	122⅓	7	8	.467	143	72	63	66	42	4.63
1985—Buffalo.........................	Am. Assoc.	3	9⅔	0	1	.000	13	7	7	4	4	6.52
1985—Glens Falls.....................	Eastern	37	59	7	3	.700	50	23	19	48	26	2.90
1986—Birmingham	Southern	34	44⅔	6	6	.500	47	22	18	34	17	3.63
1986—Buffalo.........................	Am. Assoc.	21	22	2	2	.500	26	17	14	17	20	5.73
1987—Birmingham	Southern	9	11	0	0	.000	5	2	2	12	1	1.64
1987—Hawaii.........................	P. Coast	22	39⅔	3	5	.375	35	16	15	31	18	3.40
1988—Vancouver......................	P. Coast	38	97⅓	9	5	.643	94	41	37	57	19	3.42
1989—Vancouver......................	P. Coast	36	70⅔	7	0	1.000	43	12	11	46	12	1.40
1989—Chicago........................	American	5	12⅓	0	0	.000	14	9	9	4	5	6.57
Major League Totals—1 Year............		5	12⅓	0	0	.000	14	9	9	4	5	6.57

Selected by Chicago White Sox' organization in 21st round of free-agent draft, June 8, 1981.
†On disabled list, April 16 to June 20 and August 9 to August 24, 1983.

MICHAEL ANTHONY HARKEY
(Mike)

Born October 25, 1966, at San Diego, Calif.
Height, 6.05. Weight, 220.
Throws and bats righthanded.
Attended California State University, Fullerton, Calif.

Year Club	League	G.	IP.	W.	L.	Pct.	H.	R.	ER.	SO.	BB.	ERA.
1987—Peoria...............	Midwest	12	76	2	3	.400	81	45	30	48	28	3.55
1987—Pittsfield............	Eastern	1	2	0	0	.000	1	0	0	2	0	0.00
1988—Pittsfield............	Eastern	13	85⅔	9	2	★.818	66	29	13	73	35	1.37
1988—Iowa	Am. Assoc.	12	78⅔	7	2	.778	55	36	31	62	33	3.55
1988—Chicago............	National	5	34⅔	0	3	.000	33	14	10	18	15	2.60
1989—Iowa†	Am. Assoc.	12	63	2	7	.222	67	37	31	37	35	4.43
Major League Totals—1 Year...............		5	34⅔	0	3	.000	33	14	10	18	15	2.60

Selected by San Diego Padres' organization in 18th round of free-agent draft, June 4, 1984.
Selected by Chicago Cubs' organization in 1st round (fourth player selected) of free-agent draft, June 2, 1987.
†On disabled list, April 5 to April 28 and July 4, 1989 through remainder of season.

PETER THOMAS HARNISCH
(Pete)

Born September 23, 1966, at Commack, N. Y.
Height, 6.00. Weight, 223.
Throws and bats righthanded.
Attended Fordham University, Bronx, N. Y.

Year—Club	League	G.	IP.	W.	L.	Pct.	H.	R.	ER.	SO.	BB.	ERA.
1987—Bluefield	Ap'lachian	9	52⅔	3	1	.750	38	19	15	64	26	2.56
1987—Hagerstown	Carolina	4	20	1	2	.333	17	7	5	18	14	2.25
1988—Charlotte	Southern	20	132⅓	7	6	.538	113	55	38	141	52	2.58
1988—Rochester	Int'national	7	58⅓	4	1	.800	44	16	14	43	14	2.16
1988—Baltimore	American	2	13	0	2	.000	13	8	8	10	9	5.54
1989—Baltimore	American	18	103⅓	5	9	.357	97	55	53	70	64	4.62
1989—Rochester	Int'national	12	87⅓	5	5	.500	60	27	25	59	35	2.58
Major League Totals—2 Years		20	116⅓	5	11	.313	110	63	61	80	73	4.72

Selected by Baltimore Orioles' organization in 1st round (27th player selected) of free-agent draft, June 2, 1987.

BRIAN DAVID HARPER

Born October 16, 1959, at Los Angeles, Calif.
Height, 6.02. Weight, 208.
Throws and bats righthanded.

Major League stolen bases: 1981 (1), 1989 (2). Total—3.
Led Pacific Coast League in total bases with 339 in 1981.
Led Pacific Coast League in sacrifice flies with 12 in 1987.
Led Pacific Coast League catchers in errors with 19 in 1981.
Led Texas League in passed balls with 19 in 1979.
Tied for American Association lead in errors by catchers with 13 in 1986.

Year—Club	League	Pos.	G.	AB.	R.	H.	2B.	3B.	HR.	RBI.	B.A.	PO.	A.	E.	F.A.
1977—Idaho Falls	Pion.	C	52	186	28	60	9	3	1	33	.323	352	36	13	.968
1978—Quad Cities	Midw.	C	129	508	80	149	31	2	24	★101	.293	430	46	16	.967
1979—El Paso	Texas	C	132	531	85	167	★37	3	14	90	.315	443	66	★29	.946
1979—California	Amer.	DH	1	2	0	0	0	0	0	0	.000	0	0	0	.000
1980—El Paso†	Texas	C	105	400	61	114	23	3	12	66	.285	214	30	7	.972
1981—Salt Lake City	P. C.	C-OF-1B	134	549	99	★192	45	9	28	122	.350	421	30	24	.949
1981—California‡	Amer.	OF	4	11	1	3	0	0	0	1	.273	5	0	1	.833
1982—Pittsburgh	Nat.	OF	20	29	4	8	1	0	2	4	.276	10	0	0	1.000
1982—Portland	P. C.	OF-3B-C	101	395	71	112	29	8	17	73	.284	164	36	8	.962
1983—Pittsburgh	Nat.	OF-1B	61	131	16	29	4	1	7	20	.221	40	0	0	1.000
1984—Pittsburgh§ x	Nat.	OF-C	46	112	4	29	4	0	2	11	.259	57	3	1	.984
1985—St. Louis y	Nat.	O-3-C-1	43	52	5	13	4	0	0	8	.250	15	5	0	1.000
1986—Nashville	A. A.	C-OF-1B	95	317	41	83	11	1	11	45	.262	377	55	15	.966
1986—Detroit z	Amer.	OF-1B-C	19	36	2	5	1	0	0	3	.139	25	2	1	.964
1987—San Jose a	Calif.	3B-OF-C	8	29	5	9	0	0	3	8	.310	21	12	5	.868
1987—Tacoma	P. C.	OF-C-P	94	323	41	100	17	0	9	62	.310	163	10	5	.972
1987—Oakland b	Amer.	OF	11	17	1	4	1	0	0	3	.235	0	0	0	.000
1988—Portland	P. C.	C-3-O-P	46	170	34	60	10	1	13	42	.353	181	25	5	.976
1988—Minnesota	Amer.	C-3B	60	166	15	49	11	1	3	20	.295	208	15	2	.991
1989—Minnesota	Amer.	★C-O-1-3	126	385	43	125	24	0	8	57	.325	462	36	★11	.978
American League Totals—6 Years			221	617	62	186	37	1	11	84	.301	700	53	15	.980
National League Totals—4 Years			170	324	29	79	13	1	11	43	.244	122	8	1	.992
Major League Totals—10 Years			391	941	91	265	50	2	22	127	.282	822	61	16	.982

Selected by California Angels' organization in 4th round of free-agent draft, June 7, 1977.
†On disabled list, July 1 to July 17, 1980.
‡Traded to Pittsburgh Pirates for Shortstop Tim Foli, December 11, 1981.
§On disabled list, April 12 to May 10 and May 16 to June 4, 1984.
xTraded with Pitcher John Tudor to St. Louis Cardinals for Outfielder-First Baseman George Hendrick and Catcher Steve Barnard, December 12, 1984.
yReleased, April 1, 1986; signed by Detroit Tigers, April 25, 1986.
zReleased, March 23, 1987; signed by San Jose (Independent), May 3, 1987.
aSold to Oakland Athletics' organization, May 12, 1987.
bReleased, October 12, 1987; signed by Portland (Minnesota Twins' organization), January 4, 1988.

CHAMPIONSHIP SERIES RECORD

Year—Club	League	Pos.	G.	AB.	R.	H.	2B.	3B.	HR.	RBI.	B.A.	PO.	A.	E.	F.A.
1985—St. Louis	Nat.	PH	1	1	0	0	0	0	0	0	.000	0	0	0	.000

WORLD SERIES RECORD

Year—Club	League	Pos.	G.	AB.	R.	H.	2B.	3B.	HR.	RBI.	B.A.	PO.	A.	E.	F.A.
1985—St. Louis	Nat.	PH	4	4	0	1	0	0	0	1	.250	0	0	0	.000

PITCHING RECORD

Year—Club	League	G.	IP.	W.	L.	Pct.	H.	R.	ER.	SO.	BB.	ERA.
1987—Tacoma	P. Coast	1	3	0	0	.000	3	1	1	1	0	3.00
1988—Portland	P. Coast	1	1	0	0	.000	2	1	1	0	2	9.00

GREG ALLEN HARRIS

Born November 2, 1955, at Lynwood, Calif.
Height, 6.00. Weight, 165.
Throws right and bats left and righthanded.
Attended Long Beach City College, Long Beach, Calif.

Major League saves: 1981 (1), 1982 (1), 1984 (3), 1985 (11), 1986 (20), 1988 (1), 1989 (1). Total—38.

Year Club	League	G.	IP.	W.	L.	Pct.	H.	R.	ER.	SO.	BB.	ERA.
1977—Jackson	Texas	30	83	3	6	.333	96	63	50	56	36	5.42
1978—Lynchburg	Carolina	21	154	8	9	.471	114	52	37	102	74	2.16
1978—Jackson	Texas	6	33	2	3	.400	24	13	11	18	10	3.00
1979—Jackson	Texas	25	163	9	11	.450	125	58	41	89	81	*2.26
1980—Tidewater	Int'national	39	110	2	9	.182	99	45	33	92	40	2.70
1981—Tidewater	Int'national	7	48	4	0	1.000	37	14	11	26	16	2.06
1981—New York†	National	16	69	3	5	.375	65	36	34	54	28	4.43
1982—Indianapolis	Am. Assoc.	8	48	4	1	.800	27	18	16	44	24	3.00
1982—Cincinnati	National	34	91⅓	2	6	.250	96	56	49	67	37	4.83
1983—Indianapolis	Am. Assoc.	28	152⅓	9	12	.429	155	83	70	*146	66	4.14
1983—Cincinnati‡	National	1	1	0	0	.000	2	3	3	1	3	27.00
1984—Montreal§-San Diego	National	34	54⅓	2	2	.500	38	18	15	45	25	2.48
1984—Indianapolis x	Am. Assoc.	14	44⅔	4	4	.500	44	27	22	45	29	4.43
1985—Texas	American	58	113	5	4	.556	74	35	31	111	43	2.47
1986—Texas	American	73	111⅓	10	8	.556	103	40	35	95	42	2.83
1987—Texas yz	American	42	140⅔	5	10	.333	157	92	76	106	56	4.86
1988—Maine	Int'national	3	4⅔	0	1	.000	5	3	1	5	1	1.93
1988—Philadelphia a	National	66	107	4	6	.400	80	34	28	71	52	2.36
1989—Philadelphia b	National	44	75⅓	2	2	.500	64	34	30	51	43	3.58
1989—Boston c	American	15	28	2	2	.500	21	12	8	25	15	2.57
National League Totals—6 Years		195	398	13	21	.382	345	181	159	289	188	3.60
American League Totals—4 Years		188	393	22	24	.478	355	179	150	337	156	3.44
Major League Totals—9 Years		383	791	35	45	.438	700	360	309	626	344	3.52

Selected by California Angels' organization in 10th round of free-agent draft, June 5, 1974.
Selected by New York Mets' organization in secondary phase of free-agent draft, January 9, 1975.
Selected by New York Mets' organization in 7th round of free-agent draft, January 7, 1976.
Signed as free agent by New York Mets' organization, September 17, 1976.
†Traded with Catcher Alex Trevino and Pitcher Jim Kern to Cincinnati Reds for Outfielder George Foster, February 10, 1982.
‡Claimed on waivers by Montreal Expos, September 27, 1983.
§Traded to San Diego Padres for Infielder Al Newman, July 20, 1984.
xSold to Texas Rangers, February 13, 1985.
yReleased, December 21, 1987; signed by Cleveland Indians, January 19, 1988.
zReleased, March 24, 1988; signed by Maine (Philadelphia Phillies' organization), April 1, 1988.
aGranted free agency, November 4, 1988; re-signed by Phillies, December 7, 1988.
bClaimed on waivers by Boston Red Sox, August 7, 1989.
cGranted free agency, November 13, 1989.

CHAMPIONSHIP SERIES RECORD

Shares Championship Series records for most earned runs allowed, game (7), October 2, 1984; most earned runs (6) and hits (6) allowed, inning, October 2, 1984, fifth inning.

Year Club	League	G.	IP.	W.	L.	Pct.	H.	R.	ER.	SO.	BB.	ERA.
1984—San Diego	National	1	2	0	0	.000	9	8	7	2	3	31.50

WORLD SERIES RECORD

Year Club	League	G.	IP.	W.	L.	Pct.	H.	R.	ER.	SO.	BB.	ERA.
1984—San Diego	National	1	5⅓	0	0	.000	3	0	0	5	3	0.00

GREGORY WADE HARRIS
(Greg)

Born December 1, 1963, at Greensboro, N. C.
Height, 6.02. Weight, 190.
Throws and bats righthanded.
Attended Elon College, Elon College, N. C.

Pitched 7-0 no-hit victory against Midland, August 26, 1987.
Major League saves: 1989 (6).
Led Texas League in complete games with 7, home runs allowed with 32, balks with 6 and tied for lead in shutouts with 2 in 1987.

Year Club	League	G.	IP.	W.	L.	Pct.	H.	R.	ER.	SO.	BB.	ERA.
1985—Spokane	Northwest	13	87⅓	5	4	.556	80	36	33	90	36	3.40
1986—Charleston	S. Atlantic	27	*191⅓	13	7	.650	176	69	56	176	54	2.63
1987—Wichita	Texas	27	174⅓	12	11	.522	205	103	83	170	49	4.28
1988—Las Vegas	P. Coast	26	159⅔	9	5	.643	160	84	73	147	65	4.11
1988—San Diego	National	3	18	2	0	1.000	13	3	3	15	3	1.50
1989—San Diego	National	56	135	8	9	.471	106	43	39	106	52	2.60
Major League Totals—2 Years		59	153	10	9	.526	119	46	42	121	55	2.47

Selected by San Diego Padres' organization in 10th round of free-agent draft, June 3, 1985.

LEONARD ANTHONY HARRIS
(Lenny)

Born October 28, 1964, at Miami, Fla.
Height, 5.10. Weight, 204.
Throws right and bats lefthanded.
Attended Miami-Dade Community College (North), Miami, Fla.

Major League stolen bases: 1988 (4), 1989 (14). Total—18.
Led American Association in stolen bases with 45 and caught stealing with 22 in 1988.
Led Eastern League in game-winning RBIs with 13 in 1986.
Led American Association second basemen in errors with 23 in 1988.
Led Eastern League third basemen in putouts with 116 and total chances with 360 in 1986.
Led Florida State League third basemen in double plays with 34 in 1985.

Year—Club	League	Pos.	G.	AB.	R.	H.	2B.	3B.	HR.	RBI.	B.A.	PO.	A.	E.	F.A.
1983—Billings	Pion.	3B	56	224	37	63	8	1	1	26	.281	34	95	22	.854
1984—Cedar Rapids	Midw.	3B	132	468	52	115	15	3	6	53	.246	111	204	★34	.903
1985—Tampa	Fla. St.	3B	132	499	66	129	11	8	3	51	.259	89	★277	★35	.913
1986—Vermont	East.	★3B-SS	119	450	68	114	17	2	10	52	.253	119	220	★28	.924
1987—Nashville	A. A.	SS-3B	120	403	45	100	12	3	2	31	.248	124	210	34	.908
1988—Nashville†	A. A.	2B-SS-3B	107	422	46	117	20	2	0	35	.277	203	247	25	.947
1988—Glens Falls	East.	2B	17	65	9	22	5	1	1	7	.338	40	49	5	.947
1988—Cincinnati	Nat.	3B-2B	16	43	7	16	1	0	0	8	.372	14	33	1	.979
1989—Cinc.‡-L.A.	Nat.	2-3-O-S	115	335	36	79	10	1	3	26	.236	147	168	15	.955
1989—Nashville	A. A.	2B	8	34	6	9	2	0	3	6	.265	23	20	0	1.000
Major League Totals—2 Years			131	378	43	95	11	1	3	34	.251	161	201	16	.958

Selected by Cincinnati Reds' organization in 5th round of free-agent draft, June 6, 1983.
†Loaned to Glens Falls (Detroit Tigers' organization), May 6, 1988; returned, June 26, 1988.
‡Traded with Outfielder Kal Daniels to Los Angeles Dodgers for Pitcher Tim Leary and Shortstop Mariano Duncan, July 18, 1989.

REGINALD ALLEN HARRIS
(Reggie)

Born August 12, 1968, at Waynesboro, Va.
Height, 6.01. Weight, 180.
Throws and bats righthanded.

Year—Club	League	G.	IP.	W.	L.	Pct.	H.	R.	ER.	SO.	BB.	ERA.
1987—Elmira	NYP	9	46⅔	2	3	.400	50	29	26	25	22	5.01
1988—Lynchburg	Carolina	17	64	1	8	.111	86	60	53	48	34	7.45
1988—Elmira	NYP	10	54⅓	3	6	.333	56	37	32	46	28	5.30
1989—Winter Haven†	Florida St.	29	153⅓	10	13	.435	144	81	68	85	77	3.99

Selected by Boston Red Sox' organization in 1st round (26th player selected) of free-agent draft, June 2, 1987.
†Drafted by Oakland Athletics, December 4, 1989.

TYRONE EUGENE HARRIS
(Gene)

Born December 5, 1964, at Sebring, Fla.
Height, 5.11. Weight, 190.
Throws and bats righthanded.
Attended Tulane University, New Orleans, La.

Major League saves: 1989 (1).
Led Southern League in complete games with 7 in 1988.

Year—Club	League	G.	IP.	W.	L.	Pct.	H.	R.	ER.	SO.	BB.	ERA.
1986—Jamestown	NYP	4	20⅓	0	2	.000	15	8	5	16	11	2.21
1986—Burlington	Midwest	7	53⅓	4	2	.667	37	12	8	32	15	1.35
1986—West Palm Beach	Florida St.	2	11	0	0	.000	14	7	5	5	7	4.09
1987—West Palm Beach	Florida St.	26	179	9	7	.563	178	101	87	121	77	4.37
1988—Jacksonville	Southern	18	126⅔	9	5	.643	95	43	37	103	45	2.63
1989—Montreal	National	11	20	1	1	.500	16	11	11	11	11	4.95
1989—Indianapolis†	Am. Assoc.	6	11	2	0	1.000	4	0	0	9	10	0.00
1989—Calgary	P. Coast	5	6	0	0	.000	4	0	0	4	1	0.00
1989—Seattle‡	American	10	33⅓	1	4	.200	47	27	24	14	15	6.48
National League Totals—1 Year		11	20	1	1	.500	16	11	11	11	11	4.95
American League Totals—1 Year		10	33⅓	1	4	.200	47	27	24	14	15	6.48
Major League Totals—1 Year		21	53⅓	2	5	.286	63	38	35	25	25	5.91

Selected by Montreal Expos' organization in 5th round of free-agent draft, June 2, 1986.
†Traded with Pitchers Randy Johnson and Brian Holman to Seattle Mariners for Pitcher Mark Langston and a player to be named later, May 25, 1989; Indianapolis (Montreal Expos' organization) acquired Pitcher Mike Campbell to complete deal, July 31, 1989.
‡On disabled list, July 29, 1989 through remainder of season.

MICHAEL EDWARD HARTLEY
(Mike)

Born August 31, 1961, at Hawthorne, Calif.
Height, 6.01. Weight, 197.
Throws and bats righthanded.
Attended Grossmont College, El Cajon, Calif.

Led Pacific Coast League in games finished in relief with 50 in 1989.

Year Club	League	G.	IP.	W.	L.	Pct.	H.	R.	ER.	SO.	BB.	ERA.
1982—Johnson City	Ap'lachian	8	29	3	1	.750	32	12	9	13	8	2.79
1983—St. Petersburg	Florida St.	9	29⅔	1	3	.250	25	14	11	18	24	3.34
1983—Macon	S. Atlantic	7	29	2	3	.400	36	36	33	12	30	10.24
1983—Erie	NYP	7	32	1	3	.250	36	27	24	25	31	6.75
1984—St. Petersburg	Florida St.	31	139⅓	8	14	.364	142	81	65	88	84	4.20
1985—Springfield	Midwest	33	114⅓	2	7	.222	119	77	65	100	62	5.12
1986—Springfield	Midwest	8	15	0	0	.000	22	17	16	10	14	9.60
1986—Savannah†	S. Atlantic	39	56	5	7	.417	38	31	18	55	37	2.89
1987—Bakersfield	California	33	56	5	4	.556	44	19	16	72	24	2.57
1987—San Antonio	Texas	25	41	3	4	.429	21	8	6	37	18	1.32
1987—Albuquerque	P. Coast	2	2⅔	0	1	.000	5	3	2	3	3	6.75
1988—San Antonio	Texas	30	45	5	1	.833	25	5	4	57	18	0.80
1988—Albuquerque	P. Coast	18	20⅔	2	2	.500	22	11	10	16	12	4.35
1989—Albuquerque	P. Coast	58	77⅓	7	4	.636	53	31	24	76	34	2.79
1989—Los Angeles	National	5	6	0	1	.000	2	1	1	4	0	1.50
Major League Totals—1 Year		5	6	0	1	.000	2	1	1	4	0	1.50

Signed as free agent by St. Louis Cardinals' organization, November 27, 1981.
†Drafted by San Antonio (Los Angeles Dodgers' organization), December 9, 1986.

BRYAN STANLEY HARVEY

Born June 2, 1963, at Chattanooga, Tenn.
Height, 6.02. Weight, 212.
Throws and bats righthanded.
Attended University of North Carolina, Charlotte, N. C.
Major League saves: 1988 (17), 1989 (25). Total—42.
Named American League Rookie Pitcher of the Year by THE SPORTING NEWS, 1988.

Year Club	League	G.	IP.	W.	L.	Pct.	H.	R.	ER.	SO.	BB.	ERA.
1985—Quad City†	Midwest	30	81⅔	5	6	.455	66	37	32	111	37	3.53
1986—Palm Springs	California	43	57	3	4	.429	38	24	17	68	38	2.68
1987—Midland	Texas	43	53	2	2	.500	40	14	12	78	28	2.04
1987—California	American	3	5	0	0	.000	6	0	0	3	2	0.00
1988—Edmonton	P. Coast	5	5⅔	0	0	.000	7	2	2	10	4	3.18
1988—California	American	50	76	7	5	.583	59	22	18	67	20	2.13
1989—California	American	51	55	3	3	.500	36	21	21	78	41	3.44
Major League Totals—3 Years		104	136	10	8	.556	101	43	39	148	63	2.58

Signed as free agent by California Angels' organization, August 20, 1984.
†On disabled list, April 12 to April 22, 1985.

WILLIAM JOSEPH HASELMAN
(Bill)

Born May 25, 1966, at Long Branch, N.J.
Height, 6.03. Weight, 205.
Throws and bats righthanded.
Attended UCLA.
Led Texas League in passed balls with 12 in 1989.

Year Club	League	Pos.	G.	AB.	R.	H.	2B.	3B.	HR.	RBI.	B.A.	PO.	A.	E.	F.A.
1987—Gastonia	S. Atl.	C	61	235	35	72	13	1	8	33	.306	26	2	2	.933
1988—Port Charlotte	Fla. St.	C	122	453	56	111	17	2	10	54	.245	249	30	6	.979
1989—Tulsa	Texas	C	107	352	38	95	17	2	7	36	.270	508	63	9	.984

Selected by Texas Rangers' organization in 1st round (23rd player selected) of free-agent draft, June 2, 1987.

RONALD WILLIAM HASSEY
(Ron)

Born February 27, 1953, at Tucson, Ariz.
Height, 6.02. Weight, 195.
Throws right and bats lefthanded.
Received degree in public administration from University of Arizona, Tucson, Ariz.
Son of Bill Hassey, minor league outfielder, 1949 through 1952.
Major League stolen bases: 1978 (2), 1979 (1), 1982 (3), 1983 (2), 1984 (1), 1986 (1), 1988 (2), 1989 (1). Total—13.
Led American League in passed balls with 15 in 1985.

Year Club	League	Pos.	G.	AB.	R.	H.	2B.	3B.	HR.	RBI.	B.A.	PO.	A.	E.	F.A.
1976—San Jose	Calif.	C-3B	22	62	7	19	4	0	1	7	.306	55	2	2	.966
1976—Williamsport	East.	C	21	68	6	19	3	0	0	8	.279	63	10	4	.948
1977—Toledo	Int.	C-3-1-O	129	446	50	132	21	1	10	57	.296	484	82	21	.964
1978—Portland	P. C.	C-3B	72	235	42	76	12	1	12	52	.323	312	32	7	.980
1978—Cleveland	Amer.	C	25	74	5	15	0	0	2	9	.203	130	15	1	.993
1979—Tacoma	P. C.	C-3B	44	157	25	53	10	0	3	27	.338	282	44	2	.994
1979—Cleveland	Amer.	C-1B	75	223	20	64	14	0	4	32	.287	368	29	3	.993
1980—Cleveland	Amer.	C-1B	130	390	43	124	18	4	8	65	.318	564	52	4	.994
1981—Cleveland	Amer.	C-1B	61	190	8	44	4	0	1	25	.232	327	44	3	.992
1982—Cleveland	Amer.	C-1B	113	323	33	81	18	0	5	34	.251	566	38	4	.993
1983—Cleveland	Amer.	C	117	341	48	92	21	0	6	42	.270	514	43	3	.995
1984—Cleveland†	Amer.	C-1B	48	149	11	38	5	1	0	19	.255	210	16	1	.996

Year Club League	Pos.	G.	AB.	R.	H.	2B.	3B.	HR.	RBI.	B.A.	PO.	A.	E.	F.A.
1984—Chicago‡§ .... Nat.	C-1B	19	33	5	11	0	0	2	5	.333	53	2	1	.982
1985—New York xy .... Amer.	C-1B	92	267	31	79	16	1	13	42	.296	420	20	7	.984
1986—N.Y.z-Chi............... Amer.	C	113	341	45	110	25	1	9	49	.323	318	14	4	.988
1987—Chicago a............... Amer.	C	49	145	15	31	9	0	3	12	.214	114	12	0	1.000
1987—Hawaii b................ P. C.	DH	6	21	3	3	2	0	0	4	.143	0	0	0	.000
1988—Oakland.................. Amer.	C	107	323	32	83	15	0	7	45	.257	465	31	3	.994
1989—Oakland.................. Amer.	C-1B	97	268	29	61	12	0	5	23	.228	425	25	4	.991
American League Totals—12 Years		1027	3034	320	822	157	7	63	397	.271	4421	339	37	.992
National League Totals—1 Year..............		19	33	5	11	0	0	2	5	.333	53	2	1	.982
Major League Totals—13 Years..............		1046	3067	325	833	157	7	65	402	.272	4474	341	38	.992

Selected by Cincinnati Reds' organization in 23rd round of free-agent draft, June 6, 1972.
Selected by Kansas City Royals' organization in 22nd round of free-agent draft, June 4, 1975.
Selected by Cleveland Indians' organization in 18th round of free-agent draft, June 8, 1976.
†Traded with Pitchers Rick Sutcliffe and George Frazier to Chicago Cubs for Outfielders Mel Hall and Joe Carter and Pitchers Don Schulze and Darryl Banks, June 13, 1984.
‡On disabled list, July 5 to September 1, 1984.
§Traded with Outfielder Henry Cotto and Pitchers Rich Bordi and Porfi Altamirano to New York Yankees for Pitcher Ray Fontenot and Outfielder Brian Dayett, December 4, 1984.
xTraded with Pitcher Joe Cowley to Chicago White Sox for Pitcher Britt Burns, Shortstop Mike Soper and Outfielder Glen Braxton, December 12, 1985.
yTraded with Catcher Chris Alvarez, Pitcher Eric Schmidt and Outfielder Matt Winters to New York Yankees for Pitcher Neil Allen, Catcher Scott Bradley, Outfielder Glen Braxton and cash, February 13, 1986.
zTraded with Shortstop Carlos Martinez and a player to be named later to Chicago White Sox for Outfielder Ron Kittle, Infielder Wayne Tolleson and Catcher Joel Skinner, July 30, 1986; New York Yankees traded Catcher Bill Lindsey to Chicago organization to complete deal, December 24, 1986.
aOn disabled list, June 1 to August 7, 1987; included rehabilitation disability assignment to Hawaii, June 28 to August 2, 1987.
bGranted free agency, November 30, 1987; signed by Oakland Athletics, December 9, 1987.

CHAMPIONSHIP SERIES RECORD

Year Club League	Pos.	G.	AB.	R.	H.	2B.	3B.	HR.	RBI.	B.A.	PO.	A.	E.	F.A.
1988—Oakland.................. Amer.	C	4	8	2	4	1	0	1	3	.500	13	0	0	1.000
1989—Oakland.................. Amer.	C	2	6	0	1	0	0	1	1	.167	10	0	0	1.000
Championship Series Totals—2 Years.....		6	14	2	5	1	0	1	4	.357	23	0	0	1.000

WORLD SERIES RECORD

Year Club League	Pos.	G.	AB.	R.	H.	2B.	3B.	HR.	RBI.	B.A.	PO.	A.	E.	F.A.
1988—Oakland.................. Amer.	C-PH	5	8	0	2	0	0	0	1	.250	28	1	0	1.000

Eligible for 1989 World Series with Oakland Athletics; did not play.

MICHAEL VAUGHN HATCHER JR.
(Mickey)

Born March 15, 1955, at Cleveland, O.
Height, 6.02. Weight, 202.
Throws and bats righthanded.
Attended Mesa Community College, Mesa, Ariz., and
University of Oklahoma, Norman, Okla.
Brother of Hal Hatcher, catcher in Kansas City Royals' organization, 1980 through 1985.

Major League stolen bases: 1979 (1), 1981 (3), 1983 (2), 1986 (2), 1987 (2), 1989 (1). Total—11.

Year Club League	Pos.	G.	AB.	R.	H.	2B.	3B.	HR.	RBI.	B.A.	PO.	A.	E.	F.A.
1977—Clinton................... Midw.	OF	78	288	47	89	12	4	11	53	.309	126	9	4	.971
1978—San Antonio†........ Texas	3B	83	334	60	111	12	6	8	62	.332	55	124	22	.891
1978—Albuquerque .... P. C.	3B-OF	41	155	25	51	11	5	7	39	.329	24	63	8	.916
1979—Albuquerque .... P. C.	3B-OF	103	420	88	156	29	12	10	93	★.371	127	156	12	.959
1979—Los Angeles .... Nat.	OF-3B	33	93	9	25	4	1	1	5	.269	47	24	5	.934
1980—Albuquerque .... P. C.	OF-3B	43	181	28	65	7	2	7	40	.359	52	32	9	.903
1980—Los Angeles‡ .... Nat.	3B-OF	57	84	4	19	2	0	1	5	.226	31	23	3	.947
1981—Minnesota............ Amer.	OF-1B-3B	99	377	36	96	23	2	3	37	.255	296	11	3	.990
1982—Minnesota............ Amer.	OF-3B	84	277	23	69	13	2	3	26	.249	81	17	1	.990
1983—Minnesota§........... Amer.	OF-1B-3B	106	375	50	119	15	3	9	47	.317	199	11	3	.986
1984—Minnesota............ Amer.	OF-1B-3B	152	576	61	174	35	5	5	69	.302	364	20	9	.977
1985—Minnesota x.......... Amer.	OF-1B	116	444	46	125	28	0	3	49	.282	246	7	3	.988
1986—Minnesota y......... Amer.	OF-1B-3B	115	317	40	88	13	3	3	32	.278	220	16	4	.983
1987—Los Angeles .... Nat.	3B-1B-OF	101	287	27	81	19	1	7	42	.282	277	105	11	.972
1988—Los Angeles z........ Nat.	OF-1B-3B	88	191	22	56	8	0	1	25	.293	189	19	3	.986
1989—Los Angeles a ...... Nat.	O-3-1-P	94	224	18	66	9	2	2	25	.295	89	21	4	.965
National League Totals—5 Years...........		373	879	80	247	42	4	12	102	.281	633	192	26	.969
American League Totals—6 Years		672	2366	256	671	127	15	26	260	.284	1406	82	23	.985
Major League Totals—11 Years..............		1045	3245	336	918	169	19	38	362	.283	2039	274	49	.979

Selected by Houston Astros' organization in 14th round of free-agent draft, June 5, 1974.
Selected by New York Mets' organization in 2nd round of free-agent draft, January 7, 1976.
Selected by Los Angeles Dodgers' organization in 5th round of free-agent draft, June 7, 1977.
†On disabled list, July 13 to July 23, 1978.
‡Traded with First Baseman Kelly Snider and Pitcher Matt Reeves to Minnesota Twins for Outfielder Ken Landreaux, March 30, 1981.
§On disabled list, June 21 to July 8 and August 1 to August 23, 1983.

xOn disabled list, July 10 to July 25, 1985.
yReleased, March 31, 1987; signed by Los Angeles Dodgers, April 10, 1987.
zOn disabled list, July 7 to July 22, 1988.
aOn disabled list, June 4 to June 19 and August 7 to August 22, 1989.

CHAMPIONSHIP SERIES RECORD

Year	Club	League	Pos.	G.	AB.	R.	H.	2B.	3B.	HR.	RBI.	B.A.	PO.	A.	E.	F.A.
1988—Los Angeles		Nat.	1B-OF	6	21	4	5	2	0	0	3	.238	34	1	2	.946

WORLD SERIES RECORD

Shares World Series record for hitting home run in first series at-bat, October 15, 1988.

Year	Club	League	Pos.	G.	AB.	R.	H.	2B.	3B.	HR.	RBI.	B.A.	PO.	A.	E.	F.A.
1988—Los Angeles		Nat.	OF	5	19	5	7	1	0	2	5	.368	8	0	0	1.000

PITCHING RECORD

Year	Club	League	G.	IP.	W.	L.	Pct.	H.	R.	ER.	SO.	BB.	ERA.
1989—Los Angeles		National	1	1	0	0	.000	0	1	1	0	3	9.00

WILLIAM AUGUSTUS HATCHER
(Billy)

Born October 4, 1960, at Williams, Ariz.
Height, 5.09. Weight, 175.
Throws and bats righthanded.
Attended Yavapai Community College, Prescott, Ariz.

Major League stolen bases: 1984 (2), 1985 (2), 1986 (38), 1987 (53), 1988 (32), 1989 (24). Total—151.
Tied for National League lead in double plays by outfielders with 6 in 1987.
Led American Association in being hit by pitch with 9 in 1984.
Led New York-Pennsylvania League in being hit by pitch with 8 in 1981.

Year	Club	League	Pos.	G.	AB.	R.	H.	2B.	3B.	HR.	RBI.	B.A.	PO.	A.	E.	F.A.
1981—Geneva		NYP	OF	•75	289	57	81	15	3	4	40	.280	138	7	11	.930
1982—Salinas		Calif.	OF	138	549	92	171	18	8	8	59	.311	235	10	12	.953
1983—Midland		Texas	OF	135	545	★132	163	33	11	10	80	.299	286	17	●13	.959
1984—Iowa		A. A.	OF	150	595	96	164	27	18	9	59	.276	303	15	7	.978
1984—Chicago		Nat.	OF	8	9	1	1	0	0	0	0	.111	2	1	0	1.000
1985—Iowa		A. A.	OF	67	279	39	78	14	5	5	19	.280	157	4	4	.976
1985—Chicago†‡		Nat.	OF	53	163	24	40	12	1	2	10	.245	77	2	1	.988
1986—Houston§		Nat.	OF	127	419	55	108	15	4	6	36	.258	226	7	4	.983
1987—Houston x		Nat.	OF	141	564	96	167	28	3	11	63	.296	276	16	4	.986
1988—Houston		Nat.	OF	145	530	79	142	25	4	7	52	.268	280	7	5	.983
1989—Hou.y-Pit.		Nat.	OF	135	481	59	111	19	3	4	51	.231	250	1	2	.992
Major League Totals—6 Years				609	2166	314	569	99	15	30	212	.263	1111	34	16	.986

Selected by Chicago Cubs' organization in 6th round of free-agent draft, January 13, 1981.
†On disabled list, August 19 to September 3, 1985.
‡Traded with a player to be named later to Houston Astros for Outfielder Jerry Mumphrey, December 16, 1985; Houston organization acquired Pitcher Steve Engel to complete deal, July 24, 1986.
§On disabled list, June 28 to July 13, 1986.
xOn disabled list, July 7 to July 2, 1987.
yTraded to Pittsburgh Pirates for Outfielder Glenn Wilson, August 18, 1989.

CHAMPIONSHIP SERIES RECORD

Shares Championship Series record for most at-bats, game (7), October 15, 1986 (16 innings).

Year	Club	League	Pos.	G.	AB.	R.	H.	2B.	3B.	HR.	RBI.	B.A.	PO.	A.	E.	F.A.
1986—Houston		Nat.	OF	6	25	4	7	0	0	1	2	.280	11	0	1	.917

BRADLEY DAVID HAVENS
(Brad)

Born November 17, 1959, at Highland Park, Mich.
Height, 6.01. Weight, 197.
Throws and bats lefthanded.

Major League saves: 1986 (1), 1987 (1), 1988 (1). Total—3.
Led International League in complete games with 12 in 1984.
Led California League in complete games with 12 in 1980.
Led Midwest League in complete games with 17 in 1978.
Tied for International League lead in balks with 6 in 1989.
Tied for California League lead in games started by pitchers with 28 in 1980.
Named International League Pitcher of the Year, 1984.

Year	Club	League	G.	IP.	W.	L.	Pct.	H.	R.	ER.	SO.	BB.	ERA.
1978—Quad Cities†		Midwest	26	★200	13	10	.565	171	80	59	★197	74	2.66
1979—Orlando		Southern	19	94	4	10	.286	128	85	76	63	50	7.28
1979—Wisconsin Rapids		Midwest	10	73	6	1	.857	62	35	34	80	18	4.19
1980—Visalia		California	28	195	14	9	.609	186	90	72	★179	82	3.32
1981—Orlando		Southern	11	74	6	2	.750	81	38	29	58	20	3.53
1981—Minnesota		American	14	78	3	6	.333	76	33	31	43	24	3.58
1982—Minnesota		American	33	208⅔	10	14	.417	201	112	100	129	80	4.31
1983—Minnesota		American	16	80⅓	5	8	.385	110	75	73	40	38	8.18
1983—Toledo		Int'national	11	69⅔	6	3	.667	60	34	30	64	37	3.88

Year Club	League	G.	IP.	W.	L.	Pct.	H.	R.	ER.	SO.	BB.	ERA.
1984—Toledo‡	Int'national	25	169	11	10	.524	142	56	49	*169	70	2.61
1985—Rochester	Int'national	34	133⅔	8	10	.444	135	79	72	*129	52	4.85
1985—Baltimore	American	8	14⅓	0	1	.000	20	14	14	19	10	8.79
1986—Baltimore	American	46	71	3	3	.500	64	37	36	57	29	4.56
1987—Rochester§	Int'national	9	31⅓	2	3	.400	36	22	21	16	17	6.03
1987—Los Angeles x	National	31	35⅓	0	0	.000	30	18	17	23	23	4.33
1987—Albuquerque	P. Coast	3	7	0	1	.000	5	5	4	3	7	5.14
1988—Los Angeles y	National	9	9⅔	0	0	.000	15	5	5	8	4	4.66
1988—Colorado Springs	P. Coast	9	15	0	0	.000	12	4	4	7	4	2.40
1988—Cleveland	American	28	57⅓	2	3	.400	62	22	20	30	17	3.14
1989—Cleveland z-Detroit	American	20	36	1	2	.333	46	20	20	21	21	5.00
1989—Toledo a	Int'national	16	58	5	3	.625	56	19	17	59	17	2.64
American League Totals—7 Years		165	545⅔	24	37	.393	579	313	294	339	219	4.85
National League Totals—2 Years		40	45	0	0	.000	45	23	22	31	27	4.40
Major League Totals—8 Years		205	590⅔	24	37	.393	624	336	316	370	246	4.81

Selected by California Angels' organization in 8th round of free-agent draft, June 7, 1977.

†Traded with Outfielder Ken Landreaux, Pitcher Paul Hartzell and Third Baseman Dave Engle to Minnesota Twins for First Baseman Rod Carew, February 3, 1979.

‡Traded to Baltimore Orioles' organization for Pitcher Mark Brown, March 27, 1985.

§Traded with Outfielder John Shelby to Los Angeles Dodgers for Pitcher Tom Niedenfuer, May 22, 1987.

xOn disabled list, August 3 to August 29, 1987; included rehabilitation disability assignment to Albuquerque, August 20 to August 29, 1987.

yReleased, May 13, 1988; signed by Colorado Springs (Cleveland Indians' organization), May 24, 1988.

zReleased, May 13, 1989; signed by Toledo (Detroit Tigers' organization), May 23, 1989.

aGranted free agency, October 15, 1989.

MELTON ANDREW HAWKINS
(Andy)

Born January 21, 1960, at Waco, Tex.
Height, 6.03. Weight, 217.
Throws and bats righthanded.

Led Pacific Coast League in shutouts with 6 in 1982.
Led Texas League in complete games with 14 and tied for lead in games started by pitchers with 27 in 1981.
Led Northwest League in balks with 4 in 1978.

Year Club	League	G.	IP.	W.	L.	Pct.	H.	R.	ER.	SO.	BB.	ERA.
1978—Walla Walla	Northwest	14	102	8	3	.727	95	52	24	73	45	2.12
1979—Reno	California	27	188	8	13	.381	*232	143	*117	130	97	5.60
1980—Reno	California	26	171	13	10	.565	183	108	81	124	79	4.26
1981—Amarillo	Texas	27	200	11	10	.524	*209	100	*93	144	48	4.19
1982—Hawaii	P. Coast	18	132⅔	9	7	.563	108	49	32	91	47	2.17
1982—San Diego	National	15	63⅔	2	5	.286	66	33	29	25	27	4.10
1983—Las Vegas	P. Coast	14	85½	6	4	.600	110	67	61	50	27	6.43
1983—San Diego	National	21	119⅔	5	7	.417	106	50	39	59	48	2.93
1984—San Diego	National	36	146	8	9	.471	143	90	76	77	72	4.68
1985—San Diego	National	33	228⅔	18	8	.692	229	88	80	69	65	3.15
1986—San Diego	National	37	209⅓	10	8	.556	218	111	100	117	75	4.30
1987—San Diego†	National	24	117⅔	3	10	.231	131	71	66	51	49	5.05
1988—San Diego‡	National	33	217⅔	14	11	.500	196	88	81	91	76	3.35
1989—New York	American	34	208⅓	15	15	.500	238	*127	●111	98	76	4.80
National League Totals—7 Years		199	1102⅔	60	58	.508	1089	531	471	489	412	3.84
American League Totals—1 Year		34	208⅓	15	15	.500	238	127	111	98	76	4.80
Major League Totals—8 Years		233	1311	75	73	.507	1327	658	582	587	488	4.00

Selected by San Diego Padres' organization in 1st round (fifth player selected) of free-agent draft, June 6, 1978.

†On disabled list, July 29 to September 1, 1987.

‡Granted free agency, November 4, 1988; signed by New York Yankees, December 8, 1988.

CHAMPIONSHIP SERIES RECORD

Year Club	League	G.	IP.	W.	L.	Pct.	H.	R.	ER.	SO.	BB.	ERA.
1984—San Diego	National	3	3⅔	0	0	.000	0	0	0	1	2	0.00

WORLD SERIES RECORD

Year Club	League	G.	IP.	W.	L.	Pct.	H.	R.	ER.	SO.	BB.	ERA.
1984—San Diego	National	3	12	1	1	.500	4	1	1	4	6	0.75

CHARLES DEWAYNE HAYES
(Charlie)

Born May 29, 1965, at Hattiesburg, Miss.
Height, 6.00. Weight, 205.
Throws and bats righthanded.

Major League stolen bases: 1989 (3).
Led Pacific Coast League in grounding into double plays with 19 in 1988.
Led Texas League third basemen in total chances with 334 in 1987.
Led Texas League third basemen in double plays with 27 in 1986.

Year Club League	Pos.	G.	AB.	R.	H.	2B.	3B.	HR.	RBI.	B.A.	PO.	A.	E.	F.A.
1983—Great Falls† .... Pion.	3B-OF	34	111	9	29	4	2	0	9	.261	13	32	9	.833
1984—Clinton .... Midw.	3B	116	392	41	96	17	2	2	51	.245	68	216	28	.910
1985—Fresno .... Calif.	3B	131	467	73	132	17	2	4	68	.283	*100	233	18	*.949
1986—Shreveport .... Texas	3B	121	434	52	107	23	2	5	45	.247	89	*259	25	.933
1987—Shreveport .... Texas	3B	128	487	66	148	33	3	14	75	.304	*100	*212	22	*.934
1988—Phoenix................. P. C.	OF-3B	131	492	71	151	26	4	7	71	.307	206	100	23	.930
1988—San Francisco ...... Nat.	OF-3B	7	11	0	1	0	0	0	0	.091	5	0	0	1.000
1989—Phoenix................. P. C.	3-O-1-S-2	61	229	25	65	15	1	7	27	.284	76	76	8	.950
1989—S.F.‡-Phi. .... Nat.	3B	87	304	26	78	15	1	8	43	.257	51	174	22	.911
1989—Scr./Wil.-Barre..... Int.	3B	7	27	4	11	3	1	1	3	.407	8	8	0	1.000
Major League Totals—2 Years		94	315	26	79	15	1	8	43	.251	56	174	22	.913

Selected by San Francisco Giants' organization in 4th round of free-agent draft, June 6, 1983.

†On disabled list, July 20, 1983 through remainder of season.

‡Traded with Pitchers Dennis Cook and Terry Mulholland to Philadelphia Phillies for Pitcher Steve Bedrosian and a player to be named later, June 18, 1989; San Francisco Giants' organization acquired Infielder Rick Parker to complete deal, August 7, 1989.

VON FRANCIS HAYES

Born August 31, 1958, at Stockton, Calif.
Height, 6.05. Weight, 186.
Throws right and bats lefthanded.
Attended St. Mary's College, Moraga, Calif.

Shares major league record for most home runs (2) and most total bases (8), inning, June 11, 1985, first inning.

Major League stolen bases: 1981 (8), 1982 (32), 1983 (20), 1984 (48), 1985 (21), 1986 (24), 1987 (16), 1988 (20), 1989 (28). Total—217.

Hit three home runs in a game, August 29, 1989.

Led Midwest League third basemen in fielding percentage with .930 in 1980.

Named Midwest League Most Valuable Player, 1980.

Year Club League	Pos.	G.	AB.	R.	H.	2B.	3B.	HR.	RBI.	B.A.	PO.	A.	E.	F.A.
1980—Waterloo .... Midw.	3B-SS	134	492	105	*162	*33	3	15	90	*.329	94	291	30	.928
1981—Cleveland .... Amer.	OF-3B	43	109	21	28	8	2	1	17	.257	30	4	3	.919
1981—Charleston .... Int.	3B-1B	105	382	58	120	19	6	10	73	.314	96	222	19	.944
1982—Cleveland† .... Amer.	OF-3B-1B	150	527	65	132	25	3	14	82	.250	323	17	6	.983
1983—Philadelphia‡ .... Nat.	OF	124	351	45	93	9	5	6	32	.265	165	7	5	.972
1984—Philadelphia .... Nat.	OF	152	561	85	164	27	6	16	67	.292	341	2	4	.988
1985—Philadelphia .... Nat.	OF	152	570	76	150	30	4	13	70	.263	368	9	6	.984
1986—Philadelphia .... Nat.	1B-OF	158	610	●107	186	*46	2	19	98	.305	1247	100	13	.990
1987—Philadelphia .... Nat.	1B-OF	158	556	84	154	36	5	21	84	.277	1216	80	13	.990
1988—Philadelphia§ .... Nat.	1B-OF-3B	104	367	43	100	28	2	6	45	.272	756	58	9	.989
1989—Philadelphia .... Nat.	OF-1B-3B	154	540	93	140	27	2	26	78	.259	426	47	9	.981
American League Totals—2 Years		193	636	86	160	33	5	15	99	.252	353	21	9	.977
National League Totals—7 Years		1002	3555	533	987	203	26	107	474	.278	4519	303	59	.988
Major League Totals—9 Years		1195	4191	619	1147	236	31	122	573	.274	4872	324	68	.987

Selected by Cleveland Indians' organization in 7th round of free-agent draft, June 5, 1979.

†Traded to Philadelphia Phillies for Second Baseman Manny Trillo, Outfielder George Vukovich, Infielder Julio Franco, Pitcher Jay Baller and Catcher Jerry Willard, December 9, 1982.

‡On disabled list, March 27 to April 12, 1983.

§On disabled list, July 15 to September 2, 1988.

CHAMPIONSHIP SERIES RECORD

Year Club League	Pos.	G.	AB.	R.	H.	2B.	3B.	HR.	RBI.	B.A.	PO.	A.	E.	F.A.
1983—Philadelphia .... Nat.	PH-OF	2	2	0	0	0	0	0	0	.000	0	0	0	.000

WORLD SERIES RECORD

Year Club League	Pos.	G.	AB.	R.	H.	2B.	3B.	HR.	RBI.	B.A.	PO.	A.	E.	F.A.
1983—Philadelphia .... Nat.	PH-OF	4	3	0	0	0	0	0	0	.000	1	0	0	1.000

ALL-STAR GAME RECORD

Year League	Pos.	AB.	R.	H.	2B.	3B.	HR.	RBI.	B.A.	PO.	A.	E.	F.A.
1989—National	OF	1	0	1	0	0	0	1	1.000	0	0	0	.000

MICHAEL THOMAS HEATH
(Mike)

Born February 5, 1955, at Tampa, Fla.
Height, 5.11. Weight, 180.
Throws and bats righthanded.

Major League stolen bases: 1979 (1), 1980 (3), 1981 (3), 1982 (8), 1983 (3), 1984 (7), 1985 (7), 1986 (6), 1987 (1), 1988 (1), 1989 (7). Total—47.

Led American League catchers in assists with 66 and double plays with 10 in 1989.

Led New York-Pennsylvania League shortstops in double plays with 42 in 1974.

Tied for Appalachian League lead in sacrifice hits with 7 in 1973.

Year Club League	Pos.	G.	AB.	R.	H.	2B.	3B.	HR.	RBI.	B.A.	PO.	A.	E.	F.A.
1973—Johnson City .... Appal.	SS-2B-3B	48	166	17	29	5	2	0	10	.175	83	137	24	.902
1974—Oneonta .... NYP	SS	65	234	51	66	6	3	3	34	.282	114	170	*27	.913
1975—Fort Lauderdale† .Fla. St.	SS	98	376	43	87	7	3	1	23	.231	184	256	31	.934
1976—Fort Lauderdale‡ .Fla. St.	SS-3B-C-P	80	267	28	71	16	3	2	30	.266	143	121	16	.943

Year Club League	Pos.	G.	AB.	R.	H.	2B.	3B.	HR.	RBI.	B.A.	PO.	A.	E.	F.A.
1977—West Haven .... East.	C-3B	98	352	58	94	13	5	8	42	.267	492	72	16	.972
1978—West Haven .... East.	C-SS	66	217	43	64	16	1	8	27	.295	335	53	10	.975
1978—New York§ .... Amer.	C	33	92	6	21	3	1	0	8	.228	151	11	5	.970
1979—Tucson x .... P. C.	C	54	196	21	53	8	2	1	28	.270	183	24	7	.967
1979—Oakland .... Amer.	OF-C-3B	74	258	19	66	8	0	3	27	.256	167	32	5	.975
1980—Oakland .... Amer.	C-OF	92	305	27	74	10	2	1	33	.243	292	20	4	.987
1981—Oakland .... Amer.	★C-OF	84	301	26	71	7	1	8	30	.236	399	45	★10	.978
1982—Oakland y .... Amer.	C-OF-3B	101	318	43	77	18	4	3	39	.242	368	54	12	.972
1983—Oakland z .... Amer.	C-OF-3B	96	345	45	97	17	0	6	33	.281	362	47	11	.974
1984—Oakland .... Amer.	C-O-3-S	140	475	49	118	21	5	13	64	.248	495	56	8	.986
1985—Oakland a .... Amer.	C-OF-3B	138	436	71	109	18	6	13	55	.250	539	67	12	.981
1986—St. Louis b .... Nat.	C-OF	65	190	19	39	8	1	4	25	.205	260	30	10	.967
1986—Detroit .... Amer.	C-3B	30	98	11	26	3	0	4	11	.265	145	9	3	.981
1987—Detroit c .... Amer.	C-O-I	93	270	34	76	16	0	8	33	.281	384	43	5	.988
1988—Detroit .... Amer.	C-OF	86	219	24	54	7	2	5	18	.247	361	24	6	.985
1989—Detroit .... Amer.	C-3B-OF	122	396	38	104	16	2	10	43	.263	584	68	10	.985
American League Totals—12 Years		1089	3513	393	893	144	23	74	394	.254	4247	476	91	.981
National League Totals—1 Year		65	190	19	39	8	1	4	25	.205	260	30	10	.967
Major League Totals—12 Years		1154	3703	412	932	152	24	78	419	.252	4507	506	101	.980

Selected by New York Yankees' organization in 2nd round of free-agent draft, June 5, 1973.
†On Syracuse disabled list, August 2 to September 16, 1975.
‡On disabled list, June 29 to July 13, 1976.
§Traded with Pitchers Sparky Lyle, Larry McCall and Dave Rajsich, Shortstop Domingo Ramos and cash to Texas Rangers for Outfielders Juan Beniquez and Greg Jemison and Pitchers Mike Griffin, Paul Mirabella and Dave Righetti, November 10, 1978.
xTraded with Third Baseman Dave Chalk and cash to Oakland A's for Pitcher John Henry Johnson, June 15, 1979.
yOn disabled list, March 28 to April 20, 1982.
zOn disabled list, April 25 to May 25, 1983.
aTraded with Pitcher Tim Conroy to St. Louis Cardinals for Pitcher Joaquin Andujar, December 10, 1985.
bTraded to Detroit Tigers for Pitcher Ken Hill and a player to be named later, August 10, 1986; St. Louis Cardinals acquired First Baseman Mike Laga to complete deal, September 2, 1986.
cGranted free agency, November 9, 1987; re-signed by Tigers, December 1, 1987.

DIVISION SERIES RECORD

Year Club League	Pos.	G.	AB.	R.	H.	2B.	3B.	HR.	RBI.	B.A.	PO.	A.	E.	F.A.
1981—Oakland .... Amer.	C	2	8	0	0	0	0	0	0	.000	9	1	0	1.000

CHAMPIONSHIP SERIES RECORD

Year Club League	Pos.	G.	AB.	R.	H.	2B.	3B.	HR.	RBI.	B.A.	PO.	A.	E.	F.A.
1981—Oakland .... Amer.	C-OF	3	6	1	2	0	0	0	0	.333	3	1	0	1.000
1987—Detroit .... Amer.	C	3	7	1	2	0	0	1	2	.286	14	0	0	1.000
Championship Series Totals—2 Years		6	13	2	4	0	0	1	2	.308	17	1	0	1.000

WORLD SERIES RECORD

Year Club League	Pos.	G.	AB.	R.	H.	2B.	3B.	HR.	RBI.	B.A.	PO.	A.	E.	F.A.
1978—New York .... Amer.	C	1	0	0	0	0	0	0	0	.000	0	0	0	.000

PITCHING RECORD

Year Club League	G.	IP.	W.	L.	Pct.	H.	R.	ER.	SO.	BB.	ERA.
1976—Fort Lauderdale .... Florida St.	1	1	0	0	.000	1	0	0	1	0	0.00

NEAL HEATON

Born March 3, 1960, at Jamaica, N. Y.
Height, 6.01. Weight, 195.
Throws and bats lefthanded.
Attended University of Miami, Coral Gables, Fla.

Major League saves: 1983 (7), 1986 (1), 1988 (2). Total—10.
Named lefthanded pitcher on THE SPORTING NEWS College Baseball All-America Team, 1981.

Year Club	League	G.	IP.	W.	L.	Pct.	H.	R.	ER.	SO.	BB.	ERA.
1981—Chattanooga	Southern	11	77	4	4	.500	61	42	34	50	27	3.97
1982—Charleston	Int'national	29	172⅔	10	5	.667	194	97	77	105	66	4.01
1982—Cleveland..........................	American	8	31	0	2	.000	32	21	18	14	16	5.23
1983—Cleveland..........................	American	39	149⅓	11	7	.611	157	79	69	75	44	4.16
1984—Cleveland..........................	American	38	198⅔	12	15	.444	231	128	115	75	75	5.21
1985—Cleveland..........................	American	36	207⅔	9	17	.346	244	119	113	82	80	4.90
1986—Cleveland†-Minnesota‡..........	American	33	198⅔	7	15	.318	201	102	90	90	81	4.08
1987—Montreal...........................	National	32	193⅓	13	10	.565	207	103	97	105	37	4.52
1988—Montreal§x........................	National	32	97⅓	3	10	.231	98	54	54	43	43	4.99
1989—Pittsburgh y......................	National	42	147⅓	6	7	.462	127	55	50	67	55	3.05
American League Totals—5 Years		154	785⅓	39	56	.411	865	449	405	336	296	4.64
National League Totals—3 Years		106	438	22	27	.449	432	212	201	215	135	4.13
Major League Totals—8 Years		260	1223⅓	61	83	.424	1297	661	606	551	431	4.46

Selected by New York Mets' organization in 1st round (first player selected) of free-agent draft, January 9, 1979.
Selected by Cleveland Indians' organization in 2nd round of free-agent draft, June 8, 1981.
†Traded to Minnesota Twins for Pitcher John Butcher, June 20, 1986.
‡Traded with Pitchers Al Cardwood and Yorkis Perez and Catcher Jeff Reed to Montreal Expos for Pitcher Jeff Reardon and Catcher Tom Nieto, February 3, 1987.

§On disabled list, April 8 to April 29, 1988.
xTraded to Pittsburgh Pirates for a player to be named later, March 28, 1989; Montreal Expos acquired Pitcher Brett Gideon to complete deal, March 30, 1989.
yGranted free agency, November 13, 1989; re-signed by Pirates, December 6, 1989.

DANIEL WILLIAM HEEP
(Danny)

Born July 3, 1957, at San Antonio, Tex.
Height, 5.11. Weight, 177.
Throws and bats lefthanded.
Received degree in teaching and political science from St. Mary's University, San Antonio, Tex.
Major League stolen bases: 1983 (3), 1984 (3), 1985 (2), 1986 (1), 1987 (1), 1988 (2). Total—12.
Led Southern League in total bases with 274 in 1979.
Named Southern League co-Most Valuable Player, 1979.

Year Club	League	Pos.	G.	AB.	R.	H.	2B.	3B.	HR.	RBI.	B.A.	PO.	A.	E.	F.A.
1978—Daytona Beach	Fla. St.	OF	66	212	29	72	18	2	2	24	.340	89	9	2	.980
1979—Columbus...............	South.	OF	138	523	103	*171	30	5	21	84	.327	211	12	6	.974
1979—Houston.................	Nat.	OF	14	14	0	2	0	0	0	2	.143	7	0	0	1.000
1980—Tucson..................	P. C.	1B-OF	96	376	63	129	28	5	17	69	*.343	810	53	8	.991
1980—Houston.................	Nat.	1B	33	87	6	24	8	0	0	6	.276	188	8	2	.990
1981—Houston†...............	Nat.	1B-OF	33	96	6	24	3	0	0	11	.250	198	9	2	.990
1981—Tuscon..................	P. C.	1B-OF	78	285	55	96	23	5	11	60	.337	635	44	12	.983
1982—Houston‡...............	Nat.	OF-1B	85	198	16	47	14	1	4	22	.237	192	6	1	.995
1983—New York..............	Nat.	OF-1B	115	253	30	64	12	0	8	21	.253	159	11	0	1.000
1984—New York..............	Nat.	OF-1B	99	199	36	46	9	2	1	12	.231	137	7	4	.973
1985—New York..............	Nat.	OF-1B	95	271	26	76	17	0	7	42	.280	154	5	4	.975
1986—New York§...........	Nat.	OF	86	195	24	55	8	2	5	33	.282	83	2	1	.988
1987—San Antonio..........	Texas	OF	11	47	6	16	1	0	2	9	.340	9	1	0	1.000
1987—Los Angeles........	Nat.	OF-1B	60	98	7	16	4	0	0	9	.163	52	6	1	.983
1988—Los Angeles x......	Nat.	OF-1B-P	95	149	14	36	2	0	0	11	.242	129	10	3	.979
1989—Boston..................	Amer.	OF-1B	113	320	36	96	17	0	5	49	.300	216	14	3	.987
National League Totals—10 Years.........			715	1560	165	390	77	5	25	169	.250	1299	64	18	.987
American League Totals—1 Year...........			113	320	36	96	17	0	5	49	.300	216	14	3	.987
Major League Totals—11 Years..............			828	1880	201	486	94	5	30	218	.259	1515	78	21	.987

Selected by Houston Astros' organization in 2nd round of free-agent draft, June 6, 1978.
†On disabled list, April 19 to May 4, 1981.
‡Traded to New York Mets for Pitcher Mike Scott, December 10, 1982.
§Granted free agency, November 12, 1986; signed by Los Angeles Dodgers' organization, June 12, 1987.
xReleased, December 21, 1988; signed by Boston Red Sox, February 6, 1989.

CHAMPIONSHIP SERIES RECORD

Year Club	League	Pos.	G.	AB.	R.	H.	2B.	3B.	HR.	RBI.	B.A.	PO.	A.	E.	F.A.
1980—Houston.................	Nat.	PH	1	1	0	0	0	0	0	0	.000	0	0	0	.000
1986—New York..............	Nat.	PH-OF	5	4	0	1	0	0	0	1	.250	0	0	0	.000
1988—Los Angeles	Nat.	PH	3	1	0	0	0	0	0	0	.000	0	0	0	.000
Championship Series Totals—3 Years.....			9	6	0	1	0	0	0	1	.167	0	0	0	.000

WORLD SERIES TOTALS

Year Club	League	Pos.	G.	AB.	R.	H.	2B.	3B.	HR.	RBI.	B.A.	PO.	A.	E.	F.A.
1986—New York..............	Nat.	PH-O-DH	5	11	0	1	0	0	0	2	.091	1	0	0	1.000
1988—Los Angeles	Nat.	PH-O-DH	3	8	0	2	1	0	0	0	.250	0	0	0	.000
World Series Totals—2 Years			8	19	0	3	1	0	0	2	.158	1	0	0	1.000

PITCHING RECORD

Year Club	League	G.	IP.	W.	L.	Pct.	H.	R.	ER.	SO.	BB.	ERA.
1988—Los Angeles	National	1	2	0	0	.000	2	2	2	0	0	9.00

DONALD ELLIOTT HEINKEL
(Don)

Born October 20, 1959, at Racine, Wis.
Height, 6.00. Weight, 185.
Throws right and bats lefthanded.
Received bachelor of science degree in biology from
Wichita State University, Wichita, Kan., in 1982.
Major League saves: 1988 (1).
Led Southern League pitchers in games started with 30, complete games with 13 and home runs allowed with 26 in 1983.
Tied for International League lead in home runs allowed with 24, shutouts with 2 and balks with 5 in 1987.
Tied for American Association lead in shutouts with 3 in 1984.
Named Southern League Pitcher of the Year, 1983.

Year Club	League	G.	IP.	W.	L.	Pct.	H.	R.	ER.	SO.	BB.	ERA.
1982—Bristol................................	Ap'lachian	1	9	1	0	1.000	2	1	0	11	0	0.00
1982—Lakeland............................	Florida St.	4	31⅔	3	0	1.000	27	7	6	14	12	1.71
1982—Birmingham	Southern	9	64	4	5	.444	25	20	44	15	2.81	
1983—Birmingham	Southern	30	*207⅓	*19	6	.760	*212	87	78	113	57	3.39
1984—Evansville	Am. Assoc.	30	178⅓	11	13	.458	205	101	79	75	58	3.99

— 208 —

Year Club	League	G.	IP.	W.	L.	Pct.	H.	R.	ER.	SO.	BB.	ERA.
1985—Nashville	Am. Assoc.	8	41⅔	1	3	.250	49	36	33	18	14	7.13
1985—Birmingham†	Southern	10	57	2	5	.286	77	31	31	33	18	4.89
1986—Glens Falls	Eastern	10	67	3	5	.375	61	30	21	49	22	2.82
1986—Nashville	Am. Assoc.	9	59⅓	5	2	.714	48	18	18	32	14	2.73
1987—Toledo	Int'national	29	⋆187⅓	8	10	.444	⋆208	●103	83	132	49	3.99
1988—Detroit‡	American	21	36⅓	0	0	.000	30	17	16	30	12	3.96
1988—Toledo§	Int'national	8	28⅓	1	0	1.000	25	7	6	30	8	1.91
1989—St. Louis x	National	7	26⅓	1	1	.500	40	19	17	16	7	5.81
1989—Louisville y	Am. Assoc.	2	12⅓	1	1	.500	11	7	6	12	6	4.38
American League Totals—1 Year		21	36⅓	0	0	.000	30	17	16	30	12	3.96
National League Totals—1 Year		7	26⅓	1	1	.500	40	19	17	16	7	5.81
Major League Totals—2 Years		28	62⅔	1	1	.500	70	36	33	46	19	4.74

Selected by Kansas City Royals' organization in 15th round of free-agent draft, June 6, 1978.
Selected by Detroit Tigers' organization in 30th round of free-agent draft, June 7, 1982.
†On disabled list, July 16, 1985 though remainder of season.
‡On disabled list, June 7 to July 26, 1988; included rehabilitation disability assignment to Toledo, July 6 to July 25 1988.
§Granted free agency, October 15, 1988; signed by Louisville (St. Louis Cardinals' organization), January 19, 1989.
xOn disabled list, May 21, 1989 through remainder of season.
yReleased, October 12, 1989.

SCOTT MATHEW HEMOND

Born November 18, 1965, at Taunton, Mass.
Height, 6.00. Weight, 205.
Throws and bats righthanded.
Attended University of South Florida, Tampa, Fla.

Led Southern League third basemen in assists with 299 and total chances with 427 in 1988.
Named catcher on THE SPORTING NEWS College Baseball All-America Team, 1986.

Year Club	League	Pos.	G.	AB.	R.	H.	2B.	3B.	HR.	RBI.	B.A.	PO.	A.	E.	F.A.
1986—Madison	Midw.	C	22	85	9	26	2	0	2	13	.306	121	11	2	.985
1987—Madison	Midw.	C-OF	90	343	60	99	21	4	8	52	.289	408	53	16	.966
1987—Huntsville	South.	C-3B	33	110	10	20	3	1	1	8	.182	161	32	6	.970
1988—Huntsville	South.	3B-C	133	482	51	106	22	4	9	53	.220	93	302	38	.912
1989—Huntsville	South.	3B-C	132	490	89	130	26	6	5	62	.265	272	198	31	.938
1989—Oakland	Amer.	PR	4	0	2	0	0	0	0	0	.000	0	0	0	.000
Major League Totals—1 Year			4	0	2	0	0	0	0	0	.000	0	0	0	.000

Selected by Kansas City Royals' organization in 5th round of free-agent draft, June 6, 1983.
Selected by Oakland Athletics' organization in 1st round (12th player selected) of free-agent draft, June 2, 1986.

DAVID LEE HENDERSON
(Dave)

Born July 21, 1958, at Dos Palos, Calif.
Height, 6.02. Weight, 210.
Throws and bats righthanded.
Nephew of Joe Henderson, pitcher with Chicago
White Sox and Cincinnati Reds, 1974, 1976 and 1977.

Major League stolen bases: 1981 (2), 1982 (2), 1983 (9), 1984 (5), 1985 (6), 1986 (2), 1987 (3), 1988 (2), 1989 (8). Total—39.

Year Club	League	Pos.	G.	AB.	R.	H.	2B.	3B.	HR.	RBI.	B.A.	PO.	A.	E.	F.A.
1977—Bellingham	N'west	OF	65	251	47	79	14	2	●16	63	.315	136	5	⋆11	.928
1978—Stockton	Calif.	OF	117	409	48	95	16	4	7	63	.232	204	12	14	.939
1979—San Jose	Calif.	OF	136	507	103	152	23	3	27	99	.300	264	18	4	.986
1980—Spokane†	P. C.	OF	109	341	48	95	26	1	7	50	.279	258	9	7	.974
1981—Seattle	Amer.	OF	59	126	17	21	3	0	6	13	.167	105	4	0	1.000
1981—Spokane	P. C.	OF	80	272	47	76	23	1	12	50	.279	146	7	3	.981
1982—Seattle‡	Amer.	OF	104	324	47	82	17	1	14	48	.253	249	11	4	.985
1983—Seattle	Amer.	OF	137	484	50	130	24	5	17	55	.269	304	17	6	.982
1984—Seattle§	Amer.	OF	112	350	42	98	23	0	14	43	.280	242	11	3	.988
1985—Seattle	Amer.	OF	139	502	70	121	28	2	14	68	.241	335	8	5	.986
1986—Sea. x-Bos.	Amer.	OF	139	388	59	103	22	4	15	47	.265	231	11	5	.980
1987—Boston y	Amer.	OF	75	184	30	43	10	0	8	25	.234	114	0	5	.958
1987—San Francisco z	Nat.	OF	15	21	2	5	2	0	1	1	.238	10	1	0	1.000
1988—Oakland a	Amer.	OF	146	507	100	154	38	1	24	94	.304	382	5	7	.982
1989—Oakland	Amer.	OF	152	579	77	145	24	3	15	80	.250	385	5	9	.977
American League Totals—9 Years			1063	3444	492	897	189	16	127	473	.260	2347	72	44	.982
National League Totals—1 Year			15	21	2	5	2	0	0	1	.238	10	1	0	1.000
Major League Totals—9 Years			1078	3465	494	902	191	16	127	474	.260	2357	73	44	.982

Selected by Seattle Mariners' organization in 1st round (26th player selected) of free-agent draft, June 7, 1977.
†On disabled list, June 26 to July 22, 1980.
‡On disabled list, May 3 to May 18, 1982.
§On disabled list, August 10 to August 29, 1984.
xTraded with Infielder Spike Owen to Boston Red Sox for Infielder Rey Quinones, a player to be named later and cash, August 19, 1986; as part of deal, Seattle Mariners claimed Pitchers Mike Brown and Mike Trujillo on waivers from Boston, August 22, 1986. Seattle acquired Outfielder John Christensen to complete deal, September 25, 1986.
yTraded to San Francisco Giants for a player to be named later, September 1, 1987; Boston Red Sox acquired

Outfielder Randy Kutcher to complete deal, December 9, 1987.
zGranted free agency, November 9, 1987; signed by Oakland A's, December 21, 1987.
aGranted free agency, November 4, 1988; re-signed by Athletics, December 1, 1988.

CHAMPIONSHIP SERIES RECORD

Established Championship Series record for most strikeouts, four-game Series (7), 1988.

Year Club	League	Pos.	G.	AB.	R.	H.	2B.	3B.	HR.	RBI.	B.A.	PO.	A.	E.	F.A.
1986—Boston	Amer.	OF	5	9	3	1	0	0	1	4	.111	11	0	0	1.000
1988—Oakland	Amer.	OF	4	16	2	6	1	0	1	4	.375	11	0	2	.846
1989—Oakland	Amer.	OF	5	19	4	5	3	0	1	1	.263	22	0	0	1.000
Championship Series Totals—3 Years			14	44	9	12	4	0	3	9	.273	44	0	2	.957

WORLD SERIES RECORD

Shares World Series record for most home runs, two consecutive innings (2), October 27, 1989, fourth and fifth innings.

Year Club	League	Pos.	G.	AB.	R.	H.	2B.	3B.	HR.	RBI.	B.A.	PO.	A.	E.	F.A.
1986—Boston	Amer.	OF	7	25	6	10	1	1	2	5	.400	22	0	0	1.000
1988—Oakland	Amer.	OF	5	20	1	6	2	0	1	1	.300	12	0	0	1.000
1989—Oakland	Amer.	OF	4	13	6	4	2	0	2	4	.308	13	0	0	1.000
World Series Totals—3 Years			16	58	13	20	5	1	4	10	.345	47	0	0	1.000

RICKEY HENLEY HENDERSON

Born December 25, 1958, at Chicago, Ill.
Height, 5.10. Weight, 195.
Throws left and bats righthanded.

Holds modern major league record for most stolen bases, season (130), 1982.
Holds major league record for most times caught stealing, season (42), 1982.
Shares major league record for most home runs as leadoff batter, lifetime (35).
Holds American League records for most home runs as leadoff batter, season (9), 1986; most years (9) and most consecutive years (7), 50 or more stolen bases; most times caught stealing, lifetime (201).
Shares American League records for most years leading league, stolen bases (9); most stolen bases, two consecutive games (7), July 3, 4, 1983.
Major League stolen bases: 1979 (33), 1980 (100), 1981 (56), 1982 (130), 1983 (108), 1984 (66), 1985 (80), 1986 (87), 1987 (41), 1988 (93), 1989 (77). Total—871.
Led American League in bases on balls received with 116 in 1982, 103 in 1983 and 126 in 1989.
Led American League in stolen bases with 100 in 1980, 56 in 1981, 130 in 1982, 108 in 1983, 66 in 1984, 80 in 1985, 87 in 1986, 93 in 1988 and 77 in 1989.
Led American League in caught stealing with 26 in 1980, 22 in 1981, 42 in 1982, 19 in 1983 and tied for lead with 18 in 1986.
Led American League outfielders in total chances with 341 in 1981.
Tied for American League lead in double plays by outfielders with 5 in 1988.
Led Eastern League in stolen bases with 81 and caught stealing with 28 in 1978.
Led California League in stolen bases with 95 and caught stealing with 22 in 1977.
Led Eastern League outfielders in double plays with 4 in 1978.
Won THE SPORTING NEWS Golden Shoe Award, 1983.
Won THE SPORTING NEWS Silver Shoe Award, 1982.
Named outfielder on THE SPORTING NEWS American League All-Star Team, 1981 and 1985.
Named outfielder on THE SPORTING NEWS American League All-Star fielding team, 1981.
Named outfielder on THE SPORTING NEWS American League Silver Slugger team, 1981 and 1985.

Year Club	League	Pos.	G.	AB.	R.	H.	2B.	3B.	HR.	RBI.	B.A.	PO.	A.	E.	F.A.
1976—Boise	N'west.	OF	46	140	34	47	13	2	3	23	.336	99	3	*12	.895
1977—Modesto	Calif.	OF	134	481	120	166	18	4	11	69	.345	278	15	*20	.936
1978—Jersey City	East.	OF	133	455	81	141	14	4	0	34	.310	305	●15	7	.979
1979—Ogden	P. C.	OF	71	259	66	80	11	8	3	26	.309	149	6	6	.963
1979—Oakland	Amer.	OF	89	351	49	96	13	3	1	26	.274	215	5	6	.973
1980—Oakland	Amer.	OF	158	591	111	179	22	4	9	53	.303	407	15	7	.984
1981—Oakland	Amer.	OF	108	423	*89	*135	18	7	6	35	.319	*327	7	7	.979
1982—Oakland	Amer.	OF	149	536	119	143	24	4	10	51	.267	379	2	9	.977
1983—Oakland	Amer.	OF	145	513	105	150	25	7	9	48	.292	349	9	3	.992
1984—Oakland†	Amer.	OF	142	502	113	147	27	4	16	58	.293	341	7	11	.969
1985—Fort Lauderdale‡	Fla. St.	OF	3	5	1	0	1	0	3	.167	6	0	0	1.000
1985—New York	Amer.	OF	143	547	*146	172	28	5	24	72	.314	439	7	9	.980
1986—New York	Amer.	OF	153	608	*130	160	31	5	28	74	.263	426	4	6	.986
1987—New York§	Amer.	OF	95	358	78	104	17	3	17	37	.291	189	3	4	.980
1988—New York	Amer.	OF	140	554	118	169	30	2	6	50	.305	320	7	12	.965
1989—N.Y.x-Oak.y	Amer.	OF	150	541	●113	148	26	3	12	57	.274	335	6	4	.988
Major League Totals—11 Years			1472	5524	1171	1603	261	47	138	561	.290	3727	72	78	.980

Selected by Oakland A's organization in 4th round of free-agent draft, June 8, 1976.
†Traded with Pitcher Bert Bradley and cash to New York Yankees for Outfielder Stan Javier and Pitchers Jay Howell, Jose Rijo, Eric Plunk and Tim Birtsas, December 5, 1984.
‡On New York disabled list, March 30 to April 22, 1985; included rehabilitation disability assignment to Fort Lauderdale, April 19 to April 22, 1985.
§On disabled list, June 5 to June 29 and July 26 to September 1, 1987.
xTraded to Oakland Athletics for Pitchers Greg Cadaret and Eric Plunk and Outfielder Luis Polonia, June 21, 1989.
yGranted free agency, November 13, 1989; re-signed by Athletics, November 28, 1989.

DIVISION SERIES RECORD

Year Club	League	Pos.	G.	AB.	R.	H.	2B.	3B.	HR.	RBI.	B.A.	PO.	A.	E.	F.A.
1981—Oakland	Amer.	OF	3	11	3	2	0	0	0	0	.182	8	0	0	1.000

Holds Championship Series records for most stolen bases, lifetime (10), series (8), 1989 and game (4), October 4, 1989.

Shares Championship Series records for most runs, series (8), 1989; most stolen bases, inning (2), October 4, 1989, fourth and seventh innings.

Shares American League Championship Series record for most bases on balls, series (7), 1989.

Year Club League	Pos.	G.	AB.	R.	H.	2B.	3B.	HR.	RBI.	B.A.	PO.	A.	E.	F.A.
1981—Oakland................ Amer.	OF	3	11	0	4	2	1	0	1	.364	6	0	1	.857
1989—Oakland................ Amer.	OF	5	15	8	6	1	1	2	5	.400	13	0	1	.929
Championship Series Totals—2 Years.....		8	26	8	10	3	2	2	6	.385	19	0	2	.905

WORLD SERIES RECORD

Shares World Series record for most at-bats, nine-inning game (6), October 28, 1989.

Year Club League	Pos.	G.	AB.	R.	H.	2B.	3B.	HR.	RBI.	B.A.	PO.	A.	E.	F.A.
1989—Oakland................ Amer.	OF	4	19	4	9	1	2	1	3	.474	9	0	0	1.000

ALL-STAR GAME RECORD

Shares All-Star Game record for most singles, game (3), July 13, 1982.

Year League	Pos.	AB.	R.	H.	2B.	3B.	HR.	RBI.	B.A.	PO.	A.	E.	F.A.
1980—American	OF	1	0	0	0	0	0	0	.000	0	0	0	.000
1982—American	OF	4	1	3	0	0	0	0	.750	3	0	1	.750
1983—American	OF	1	0	0	0	0	0	1	.000	0	0	0	.000
1984—American	OF	2	0	0	0	0	0	0	.000	0	0	0	.000
1985—American	OF	3	1	1	0	0	0	0	.333	1	0	0	1.000
1986—American	OF	3	0	0	0	0	0	0	.000	2	0	0	1.000
1987—American	OF	3	0	1	0	0	0	0	.333	0	0	0	.000
1988—American	OF	2	0	1	0	0	0	0	.500	1	0	0	1.000
All-Star Game Totals—8 Years....................		19	2	6	0	0	0	1	.316	7	0	1	.875

DAVID LEE HENGEL
(Dave)

Born December 18, 1961, at Oakland, Calif.
Height, 6.00. Weight, 195.
Throws and bats righthanded.
Attended University of California, Berkeley, Calif.

Led Midwest League in slugging percentage with .565 in 1984.
Led Pacific Coast League outfielders in double plays with 5 in 1986.

Year Club League	Pos.	G.	AB.	R.	H.	2B.	3B.	HR.	RBI.	B.A.	PO.	A.	E.	F.A.
1983—Bellingham .... N'west	OF	9	27	4	9	4	0	0	6	.333	10	0	0	1.000
1984—Wausau................. Midw.	OF	120	441	68	136	31	2	26	98	.308	109	9	9	.929
1985—Chattanooga .... South.	OF	122	460	71	132	30	5	17	89	.287	277	14	6	.980
1985—Calgary .... P. C.	OF	6	23	1	2	1	0	0	3	.087	13	0	0	1.000
1986—Calgary† .... P. C.	OF	113	407	73	116	22	1	27	94	.285	217	•16	8	.967
1986—Seattle.................. Amer.	OF	21	63	3	12	1	0	1	6	.190	9	1	0	1.000
1987—Calgary .... P. C.	OF	117	448	80	132	25	2	★23	★103	.295	180	10	●11	.945
1987—Seattle.................. Amer.	OF	10	19	2	6	0	0	1	4	.316	7	0	1	.875
1988—Calgary .... P. C.	OF	62	222	29	51	17	1	6	37	.230	67	4	3	.959
1988—Seattle‡................ Amer.	OF	26	60	3	10	1	0	2	7	.167	20	0	1	.952
1989—Colorado Springs. P. C.	OF	95	354	53	112	13	1	18	82	.316	138	★11	3	.980
1989—Cleveland§x .... Amer.	OF	12	25	2	3	1	0	0	1	.120	12	1	0	1.000
Major League Totals—4 Years.................		69	167	10	31	3	0	4	18	.186	48	2	2	.062

Selected by San Francisco Giants' organization in 6th round of free-agent draft, June 3, 1980.
Selected by Seattle Mariners' organization in 3rd round of free-agent draft, June 6, 1983.
†On disabled list, August 5 to August 23, 1986.
‡Traded to Cleveland Indians for Infielders Paul Noce and Chuck Baldwin, April 1, 1989.
§On disabled list, July 10 to July 28, 1989; included rehabilitation disability assignment to Colorado Springs, July 13 to July 28, 1989.
xGranted free agency, October 15, 1989.

THOMAS ANTHONY HENKE
Name pronounced HEN-key.

(Tom)

Born December 21, 1957, at Kansas City, Mo.
Height, 6.05. Weight, 225.
Throws and bats righthanded.
Attended East Central College, Union, Mo.

Major League saves: 1983 (1), 1984 (2), 1985 (13), 1986 (27), 1987 (34), 1988 (25), 1989 (20). Total—122.
Led American League in games finished in relief with 62 and saves with 34 in 1987.
Tied for International League lead in saves with 18 in 1985.
Named International League Pitcher of the Year, 1985.

Year Club League	G.	IP.	W.	L.	Pct.	H.	R.	ER.	SO.	BB.	ERA.
1980—Sarasota Rangers........................ Gulf Coast	8	38	3	3	.500	33	11	4	34	12	0.95
1980—Asheville................................. S. Atlantic	5	23	0	2	.000	25	21	20	19	20	7.83
1981—Asheville................................. S. Atlantic	28	92	8	6	.571	77	36	30	67	35	2.93
1981—Tulsa .... Texas	15	32	4	3	.571	31	16	14	37	14	3.94
1982—Tulsa .... Texas	★52	87⅔	3	6	.333	69	35	26	100	40	2.67

Year Club	League	G.	IP.	W.	L.	Pct.	H.	R.	ER.	SO.	BB.	ERA.
1982—Texas	American	8	15⅔	1	0	1.000	14	2	2	9	8	1.15
1983—Oklahoma City	Am. Assoc.	47	77⅔	9	6	.600	71	33	26	90	33	3.01
1983—Texas	American	8	16	1	0	1.000	16	6	6	17	4	3.38
1984—Texas	American	25	28⅓	1	1	.500	36	21	20	25	20	6.35
1984—Oklahoma City†	Am. Assoc.	39	64⅔	6	2	.750	59	21	19	65	25	2.64
1985—Syracuse	Int'national	39	51⅓	2	1	.667	13	5	5	60	18	0.88
1985—Toronto	American	28	40	3	3	.500	29	12	9	42	8	2.03
1986—Toronto	American	63	91⅓	9	5	.643	63	39	34	118	32	3.35
1987—Toronto	American	72	94	0	6	.000	62	27	26	128	25	2.49
1988—Toronto	American	52	68	4	4	.500	60	23	22	66	24	2.91
1989—Toronto	American	64	89	8	3	.727	66	20	19	116	25	1.92
Major League Totals—8 Years		320	442⅓	27	22	.551	346	150	138	521	146	2.81

Selected by Seattle Mariners' organization in 20th round of free-agent draft, June 5, 1979.
Selected by Chicago Cubs' organization in secondary phase of free-agent draft, January 8, 1980.
Selected by Texas Rangers' organization in secondary phase of free-agent draft, June 3, 1980.
†Selected by Toronto Blue Jays' organization in player compensation pool draft, January 24, 1985. (Toronto received compensation for Texas Rangers' signing of free agent Designated Hitter Cliff Johnson, a Type A player, December 5, 1984.

CHAMPIONSHIP SERIES RECORD

Shares American League Championship Series record for most games won, series (2), 1985.

Year Club	League	G.	IP.	W.	L.	Pct.	H.	R.	ER.	SO.	BB.	ERA.
1985—Toronto	American	3	6⅓	2	0	1.000	5	3	3	4	4	4.26
1989—Toronto	American	3	2⅔	0	0	.000	0	0	0	3	0	0.00
Championship Series Totals—2 Years		6	9	2	0	1.000	5	3	3	7	4	3.00

ALL-STAR GAME RECORD

Year League	IP.	W.	L.	Pct.	H.	R.	ER.	SO.	BB.	ERA.
1987—American	2⅔	0	0	.000	2	0	0	1	0	0.00

MICHAEL ALAN HENNEMAN
(Mike)

Born December 11, 1961, at St. Charles, Mo.
Height, 6.04. Weight, 195.
Throws and bats righthanded.
Attended Oklahoma State University, Stillwater, Okla.
Major League saves: 1987 (7), 1988 (22), 1989 (8). Total—37.
Led American League in intentional bases on balls issued with 15 in 1989 and tied for lead with 10 in 1988.
Named American League Rookie Pitcher of the Year by THE SPORTING NEWS, 1987.

Year Club	League	G.	IP.	W.	L.	Pct.	H.	R.	ER.	SO.	BB.	ERA.
1984—Birmingham	Southern	29	59⅓	4	2	.667	48	22	16	39	33	2.43
1985—Birmingham	Southern	46	70⅓	3	5	.375	88	50	45	40	28	5.76
1986—Nashville	Am. Assoc.	31	58	2	5	.286	57	27	19	39	23	2.95
1987—Toledo	Int'national	11	18⅓	1	1	.500	5	3	3	19	3	1.47
1987—Detroit†	American	55	96⅔	11	3	.786	86	36	32	75	30	2.98
1988—Detroit‡	American	65	91⅓	9	6	.600	72	23	19	58	24	1.87
1989—Detroit§	American	60	90	11	4	.733	84	46	37	69	51	3.70
Major League Totals—3 Years		180	278	31	13	.705	242	105	88	202	105	2.85

Selected by Toronto Blue Jays' organization in 27th round of free-agent draft, June 7, 1982.
Selected by Philadelphia Phillies' organization in secondary phase of free-agent draft, June 6, 1983.
Selected by Detroit Tigers' organization in 4th round of free-agent draft, June 4, 1984.
†Struck out in only at-bat.
‡On disabled list, May 22 to June 6, 1988.
§On disabled list, April 24 to May 15, 1989.

CHAMPIONSHIP SERIES RECORD

Year Club	League	G.	IP.	W.	L.	Pct.	H.	R.	ER.	SO.	BB.	ERA.
1987—Detroit	American	3	5	1	0	1.000	6	6	6	3	6	10.80

ALL-STAR GAME RECORD

Member of American League All-Star Team in 1989; did not play.

DWAYNE ALLEN HENRY

Born February 16, 1962, at Elkton, Md.
Height, 6.03. Weight, 205.
Throws and bats righthanded.
Major League saves: 1985 (3), 1988 (1), 1989 (1). Total—5.

Year Club	League	G.	IP.	W.	L.	Pct.	H.	R.	ER.	SO.	BB.	ERA.
1980—Sarasota Rangers	Gulf Coast	11	54	5	1	.833	36	23	16	47	28	2.67
1981—Asheville	S. Atlantic	25	134	8	7	.533	120	81	66	86	58	4.43
1982—Burlington†	Midwest	4	18⅔	2	0	1.000	6	0	0	25	6	0.00
1983—Tulsa‡	Texas	9	14	0	0	.000	16	14	9	14	19	5.79
1983—Sarasota Rangers	Gulf Coast	3	9	0	0	.000	10	6	4	11	1	4.00
1984—Tulsa	Texas	33	85	5	8	.385	65	42	32	79	60	3.39
1984—Texas	American	3	4⅓	0	1	.000	5	4	4	2	7	8.31

Year Club	League	G.	IP.	W.	L.	Pct.	H.	R.	ER.	SO.	BB.	ERA.
1985—Tulsa	Texas	34	81⅓	7	6	.538	51	32	24	97	44	2.66
1985—Texas	American	16	21	2	2	.500	16	7	6	20	7	2.57
1986—Texas§	American	19	19⅓	1	0	1.000	14	11	10	17	22	4.66
1986—Oklahoma City	Am. Assoc.	28	44⅓	2	1	.667	51	30	29	41	27	5.89
1987—Oklahoma City	Am. Assoc.	30	69	4	4	.500	66	39	38	55	50	4.96
1987—Texas	American	5	10	0	0	.000	12	10	10	7	9	9.00
1988—Oklahoma City	Am. Assoc.	46	75⅔	5	5	.500	57	51	47	98	54	5.59
1988—Texas x	American	11	10⅓	0	1	.000	15	10	10	10	9	8.71
1989—Richmond	Int'national	41	84⅔	11	5	.688	43	28	23	101	61	2.44
1989—Atlanta	National	12	12⅔	0	2	.000	12	6	6	16	5	4.26
American League Totals—5 Years		54	65	3	4	.429	62	42	40	56	54	5.54
National League Totals—1 Year		12	12⅔	0	2	.000	12	6	6	16	5	4.26
Major League Totals—6 Years		66	77⅔	3	6	.333	74	48	46	72	59	5.33

Selected by Texas Rangers' organization in 2nd round of free-agent draft, June 3, 1980.

†On disabled list, May 4, 1982 through remainder of season.

‡On disabled list, April 8 to July 9, 1983.

§On disabled list, May 31 to July 8, 1986; included rehabilitation disability assignment to Oklahoma City, June 18 to July 8, 1986.

xTraded to Atlanta Braves for Pitcher David Miller and cash, March 30, 1989.

FLOYD BLUFORD HENRY III
(Butch)

Born October 7, 1968, at El Paso, Tex.
Height, 6.00. Weight, 180.
Throws and bats lefthanded.

Year Club	League	G.	IP.	W.	L.	Pct.	H.	R.	ER.	SO.	BB.	ERA.
1987—Billings	Pioneer	9	35	4	0	1.000	37	21	18	38	12	4.63
1988—Cedar Rapids	Midwest	27	187	16	2	*.889	144	59	47	163	56	2.26
1989—Chattanooga†	Southern	7	26⅓	1	3	.250	22	12	10	19	12	3.42

Selected by Cincinnati Reds' organization in 15th round of free-agent draft, June 2, 1987.

†On disabled list, April 28, 1989 through remainder of season.

PATRICK GEORGE HENTGEN
(Pat)

Born November 13, 1968, at Detroit, Mich.
Height, 6.02. Weight, 190.
Throws and bats righthanded.

Led Florida State League pitchers in games started with 30 in 1988.
Led South Atlantic League pitchers in games started with 31 in 1987.

Year Club	League	G.	IP.	W.	L.	Pct.	H.	R.	ER.	SO.	BB.	ERA.
1986—St. Catharines	NYP	13	40	0	4	.000	38	27	20	30	30	4.50
1987—Myrtle Beach	S. Atlantic	32	*188	11	5	.688	145	62	49	131	60	2.35
1988—Dunedin	Florida St.	31	151⅓	3	12	.200	139	80	58	125	65	3.45
1989—Dunedin	Florida St.	29	151⅓	9	8	.529	123	53	45	148	71	2.68

Selected by Toronto Blue Jays' organization in 5th round of free-agent draft, June 2, 1986.

CARLOS ALBERTO HERNANDEZ

Born May 24, 1967, at Bolivar, Venezuela.
Height, 5.11. Weight, 185.
Throws and bats righthanded.

Led Texas League catchers in total chances with 737 in 1989.
Tied for Gulf Coast League lead in double plays by catcher with 3 in 1986.

Year Club	League	Pos.	G.	AB.	R.	H.	2B.	3B.	HR.	RBI.	B.A.	PO.	A.	E.	F.A.
1985—Braden. Dodgers	Gulf C.	3B-1B	22	49	3	12	1	0	0	0	.245	48	16	2	.970
1986—Sarasota Dodgers	Gulf C.	C-3B	57	205	19	64	7	0	1	31	.312	217	36	10	.962
1987—Bakersfield	Calif.	C	48	162	22	37	6	1	3	22	.228	181	26	8	.963
1988—Bakersfield	Calif.	C	92	333	37	103	15	2	5	52	.309	480	88	14	.976
1988—Albuquerque	P. C.	C	3	8	0	1	0	0	0	1	.125	11	0	*1	.917
1989—San Antonio	Texas	C	99	370	37	111	16	3	8	41	.300	*629	*90	*18	.976
1989—Albuquerque	P. C.	C	4	14	1	3	0	0	0	1	.214	23	3	3	.897

Signed as free agent by Los Angeles Dodgers' organization, October 10, 1984.

FRANCIS XAVIER HERNANDEZ
(Known by middle name.)

Born August 16, 1965, at Port Arthur, Tex.
Height, 6.02. Weight, 185.
Throws right and bats lefthanded.
Attended University of Southwestern Louisiana, Lafayette, La.

Year Club	League	G.	IP.	W.	L.	Pct.	H.	R.	ER.	SO.	BB.	ERA.
1986—St. Catharines	NYP	13	70⅔	5	5	.500	55	27	21	69	16	2.67
1987—St. Catharines	NYP	13	55	3	3	.500	57	39	31	49	16	5.07
1988—Myrtle Beach	S. Atlantic	23	148	13	6	.684	116	52	42	111	28	2.55
1988—Knoxville	Southern	11	68⅓	2	4	.333	73	32	22	33	15	2.90

Year Club	League	G.	IP.	W.	L.	Pct.	H.	R.	ER.	SO.	BB.	ERA.
1989—Knoxville	Southern	4	24	1	1	.500	25	11	11	17	11	4.13
1989—Syracuse	Int'national	15	99⅓	5	6	.455	95	42	39	47	22	3.53
1989—Toronto†	American	7	22⅔	1	0	1.000	25	15	12	7	8	4.76
Major League Totals—1 Year		7	22⅔	1	0	1.000	25	15	12	7	8	4.76

Selected by Toronto Blue Jays' organization in 4th round of free-agent draft, June 2, 1986.

†Drafted by Houston Astros, December 4, 1989.

GUILLERMO HERNANDEZ (VILLANUEVA)

Born November 14, 1954, at Aguada, Puerto Rico.
Height, 6.02. Weight, 185.
Throws and bats lefthanded.

Shares National League record for most consecutive strikeouts by relief pitcher, game (6), July 3, 1983.
Major League saves: 1977 (4), 1978 (3), 1981 (2), 1982 (10), 1983 (8), 1984 (32), 1985 (31), 1986 (24), 1987 (8), 1988 (10), 1989 (15). Total—147.
Led American League in games finished in relief with 68 in 1984.
Led Western Carolinas League pitchers in games started with 26 and complete games with 13 in 1977.
Named American League Most Valuable Player by Baseball Writers' Association of America, 1984.
Named American League Pitcher of the Year by THE SPORTING NEWS, 1984.
Won American League Cy Young Memorial Award, 1984.
Named lefthanded pitcher on THE SPORTING NEWS American League All-Star Team, 1984.
Received reported $25,000 bonus to sign with Philadelphia Phillies, 1974.

Year Club	League	G.	IP.	W.	L.	Pct.	H.	R.	ER.	SO.	BB.	ERA.
1974—Spartanburg	W. Carol.	26	*190	11	11	.500	169	82	58	*179	49	2.75
1975—Reading	Eastern	13	91	8	2	.800	79	32	30	46	25	2.97
1975—Toledo	Int'national	13	80	6	4	.600	86	43	29	46	26	3.26
1976—Oklahoma City†	Am. Assoc.	25	135	8	9	.471	154	82	68	88	30	4.53
1977—Chicago	National	67	110	8	7	.533	94	42	37	78	28	3.03
1978—Chicago	National	54	60	8	2	.800	57	26	25	38	35	3.75
1979—Chicago	National	51	79	4	4	.500	85	50	44	53	39	5.01
1980—Chicago	National	53	108	1	9	.100	115	58	53	75	45	4.42
1981—Iowa	Am. Assoc.	18	74	4	5	.444	84	39	32	41	27	3.89
1981—Chicago	National	12	14	0	0	.000	14	7	6	13	8	3.86
1982—Chicago	National	75	75	4	6	.400	74	26	25	54	24	3.00
1983—Chicago‡-Philadelphia§	National	74	115⅓	9	4	.692	109	47	42	93	32	3.28
1984—Detroit	American	*80	140⅓	9	3	.750	96	30	30	112	36	1.92
1985—Detroit x	American	74	106⅔	8	10	.444	82	38	32	76	14	2.70
1986—Detroit	American	64	88⅔	8	7	.533	87	35	35	77	21	3.55
1987—Detroit y	American	45	49	3	4	.429	53	27	20	30	20	3.67
1987—Toledo	Int'national	2	3	0	0	.000	4	1	1	2	1	3.00
1988—Detroit	American	63	67⅔	6	5	.545	50	24	23	59	31	3.06
1989—Detroit za	American	32	31⅓	2	2	.500	36	21	20	30	16	5.74
National League Totals—7 Years		386	561⅓	34	32	.515	548	256	232	404	211	3.72
American League Totals—6 Years		358	483⅔	36	31	.537	404	175	160	384	138	2.98
Major League Totals—13 Years		744	1045	70	63	.526	952	431	392	788	349	3.38

Signed as free agent by Philadelphia Phillies' organization, September 11, 1973.

†Drafted by Chicago Cubs, December 6, 1976.

‡Traded to Philadelphia Phillies for Pitchers Dick Ruthven and Bill Johnson, May 22, 1983.

§Traded with First Baseman Dave Bergman to Detroit Tigers for Outfielder Glenn Wilson and Catcher-First Baseman John Wockenfuss, March 24, 1984.

xGrounded out in only at-bat.

yOn disabled list, April 9 to May 5 and May 6 to May 30, 1987; included rehabilitation disability assignment to Toledo, May 1 to May 5, 1987.

zOn disabled list, July 13 to August 7 and August 19, 1989 through remainder of season.

aReleased, December 20, 1989.

CHAMPIONSHIP SERIES RECORD

Year Club	League	G.	IP.	W.	L.	Pct.	H.	R.	ER.	SO.	BB.	ERA.
1984—Detroit	American	3	4	0	0	.000	3	1	1	3	1	2.25
1987—Detroit	American	1	⅓	0	0	.000	2	0	0	0	0	0.00
Championship Series Totals—2 Years		4	4⅓	0	0	.000	5	1	1	3	1	2.08

WORLD SERIES RECORD

Year Club	League	G.	IP.	W.	L.	Pct.	H.	R.	ER.	SO.	BB.	ERA.
1983—Philadelphia	National	3	4	0	0	.000	0	0	0	4	1	0.00
1984—Detroit	American	3	5⅓	0	0	.000	4	1	1	0	0	1.69
World Series Totals—2 Years		6	9⅓	0	0	.000	4	1	1	4	1	0.96

ALL-STAR GAME RECORD

Year League	IP.	W.	L.	Pct.	H.	R.	ER.	SO.	BB.	ERA.
1984—American	1	0	0	.000	1	1	1	1	0	9.00
1985—American	⅔	0	0	.000	1	0	0	2	1	0.00
All-Star Game Totals—2 Years	1⅔	0	0	.000	2	1	1	3	1	5.40

Member of American League All-Star Team in 1986; did not play.

—DID YOU KNOW—

That in his last two 1988 starts and his first two 1989 starts, Toronto's Dave Stieb hurled three one-hitters?

JEREMY STUART HERNANDEZ

Born July 6, 1966, at Burbank, Calif.
Height, 6.05. Weight, 195.
Throws and bats righthanded.
Attended California State University, Northridge, Calif.

Year Club	League	G.	IP.	W.	L.	Pct.	H.	R.	ER.	SO.	BB.	ERA.
1987—Erie	NYP	16	99⅓	5	4	.556	87	36	31	62	41	2.81
1988—Springfield†	Midwest	24	147⅓	12	6	.667	133	73	58	97	34	3.54
1989—Charleston	S. Atlantic	10	58⅔	3	5	.375	65	37	23	39	16	3.53
1989—Riverside	California	9	67	5	2	.714	55	17	13	65	11	1.75
1989—Wichita	Texas	4	19	2	1	.667	30	18	18	9	8	8.53

Selected by St. Louis Cardinals' organization in 2nd round of free-agent draft, June 2, 1987.
†Traded to Charleston (San Diego Padres' organization) for Outfielder Randell Byers, April 24, 1989.

KEITH HERNANDEZ

Born October 20, 1953, at San Francisco, Calif.
Height, 6.00. Weight, 205.
Throws and bats lefthanded.
Attended College of San Mateo, San Mateo, Calif.
Son of John Hernandez, minor league infielder, 1941 through 1950; and brother of Gary Hernandez, first baseman-outfielder in St. Louis Cardinals' organization, 1972 through 1975.

Holds major league records for most game-winning RBIs, season (24), 1985; most game-winning RBIs, lifetime (129); most years leading league in double plays by first baseman (6); most assists by first baseman, lifetime (1,662).
Shares National League records for most grand slams, month (2), September, 1977; fewest errors by first baseman for leader in errors, season (13), 1983.
Major League stolen bases: 1976 (4), 1977 (7), 1978 (13), 1979 (11), 1980 (14), 1981 (12), 1982 (19), 1983 (9), 1984 (2), 1985 (3), 1986 (2), 1988 (2). Total—98.
Hit for the cycle, July 4, 1985.
Led National League in bases on balls received with 94 in 1986.
Led National League in intentional bases on balls received with 19 in 1982.
Led National League first basemen in putouts with 1,054 in 1981 and 1,586 in 1982.
Led National League first basemen in double plays with 146 in 1977, 145 in 1979, 146 in 1980, 99 in 1981, 147 in 1983 and 127 in 1984.
Led National League first basemen in total chances with 1,643 in 1979, 1,732 in 1982, 1,578 in 1983 and 1,457 in 1987.
Led National League in game-winning RBIs with 24 in 1985 and tied for lead with 21 in 1982.
Led Texas League first basemen in double plays with 101 in 1973.
Named National League Player of the Year by THE SPORTING NEWS, 1979.
Named National League co-Most Valuable Player by Baseball Writers' Association of America, 1979.
Named first baseman on THE SPORTING NEWS National League All-Star Team, 1979, 1980 and 1984 through 1986.
Named first baseman on THE SPORTING NEWS National League All-Star fielding team, 1978 through 1988.
Named first baseman on THE SPORTING NEWS National League Silver Slugger team, 1980 and 1984.

Year Club	League	Pos.	G.	AB.	R.	H.	2B.	3B.	HR.	RBI.	B.A.	PO.	A.	E.	F.A.
1972—St. Petersburg†	Fla. St.	1B	84	309	38	79	16	5	5	41	.256	682	52	7	.991
1972—Tulsa	A. A.	1B	11	29	5	7	1	0	0	1	.241	54	2	0	1.000
1973—Arkansas	Texas	1B	105	388	62	101	20	2	3	52	.260	960	61	9	★.991
1973—Tulsa	A. A.	1B	31	120	20	40	6	1	5	25	.333	289	15	1	.997
1974—Tulsa‡	A. A.	1B-OF	102	353	67	124	18	6	14	63	★.351	690	50	12	.984
1974—St. Louis	Nat.	1B	14	34	3	10	1	2	0	2	.294	70	1	2	.973
1975—Tulsa	A. A.	●1B-OF	85	324	70	107	29	3	10	48	.330	597	53	●13	.980
1975—St. Louis	Nat.	1B	64	188	20	47	8	2	3	20	.250	469	36	2	.996
1976—St. Louis	Nat.	1B	129	374	54	108	21	5	7	46	.289	862	●107	10	.990
1977—St. Louis	Nat.	1B	161	560	90	163	41	4	15	91	.291	1453	106	12	.992
1978—St. Louis	Nat.	1B	159	542	90	138	32	4	11	64	.255	1436	96	10	.994
1979—St. Louis	Nat.	1B	161	610	★116	210	★48	11	11	105	★.344	★1489	★146	8	.995
1980—St. Louis	Nat.	1B	159	595	★111	191	39	8	16	99	.321	1572	115	9	.995
1981—St. Louis	Nat.	1B-OF	103	376	65	115	27	4	8	48	.306	1056	86	3	.997
1982—St. Louis	Nat.	1B-OF	160	579	79	173	33	6	7	94	.299	1591	135	11	.994
1983—St.L.§-N.Y.	Nat.	1B	150	538	77	160	23	7	12	63	.297	★1418	147	●13	.992
1984—New York	Nat.	1B	154	550	83	171	31	0	15	94	.311	1214	★142	8	.995
1985—New York	Nat.	1B	158	593	87	183	34	4	10	91	.309	1310	★139	4	★.997
1986—New York	Nat.	1B	149	551	94	171	34	1	13	83	.310	1199	149	5	★.996
1987—New York	Nat.	1B	154	587	87	170	28	2	18	89	.290	1298	★149	10	.993
1988—New York x	Nat.	1B	95	348	43	96	16	0	11	55	.276	734	77	2	.998
1989—New York y	Nat.	1B	75	215	18	50	8	0	4	19	.233	405	31	4	.991
1989—Port St. Lucie z	Fla. St.	1B	4	16	1	6	1	0	0	1	.375	23	0	0	1.000
Major League Totals—16 Years			2045	7240	1117	2156	424	60	161	1063	.298	17576	1662	113	.994

Selected by St. Louis Cardinals' organization in 42nd round of free-agent draft, June 8, 1971.
†On disabled list, April 10 to May 30, 1972.
‡On disabled list, April 16 to May 20, 1974.
§Traded to New York Mets for Pitchers Neil Allen and Rick Ownbey, June 15, 1983.
xOn disabled list, June 7 to June 22 and June 24 to August 5, 1988.
yOn disabled list, May 18 to July 13, 1989; included rehabilitation disability assignment to Port St. Lucie, July 7 to July 13, 1989.
zGranted free agency, November 13, 1989; signed by Cleveland Indians, December 7, 1989.

CHAMPIONSHIP SERIES RECORD

Shares Championship Series records for most at-bats, game (7), October 15, 1986 (16 innings) and inning (2), October 7, 1982, sixth inning.

Year Club	League	Pos.	G.	AB.	R.	H.	2B.	3B.	HR.	RBI.	B.A.	PO.	A.	E.	F.A.
1982—St. Louis..................	Nat.	1B	3	12	3	4	0	0	0	1	.333	35	1	0	1.000
1986—New York.............	Nat.	1B	6	26	3	7	1	1	0	3	.269	67	12	0	1.000
1988—New York.............	Nat.	1B	7	26	2	7	0	0	1	5	.269	57	4	1	.984
Championship Series Totals—3 Years.....			16	64	8	18	1	1	1	9	.281	159	17	1	.994

WORLD SERIES RECORD

Year Club	League	Pos.	G.	AB.	R.	H.	2B.	3B.	HR.	RBI.	B.A.	PO.	A.	E.	F.A.
1982—St. Louis..................	Nat.	1B	7	27	4	7	2	0	1	8	.259	62	7	2	.972
1986—New York.............	Nat.	1B	7	26	1	6	0	0	0	4	.231	48	4	1	.981
World Series Totals—2 Years			14	53	5	13	2	0	1	12	.245	110	11	3	.976

ALL-STAR GAME RECORD

Year League	Pos.	AB.	R.	H.	2B.	3B.	HR.	RBI.	B.A.	PO.	A.	E.	F.A.
1979—National...............................	PH	1	0	0	0	0	0	0	.000	0	0	0	.000
1980—National...............................	PH-1B	2	0	2	0	0	0	0	1.000	5	0	0	1.000
1984—National...............................	1B	1	0	0	0	0	0	0	.000	1	0	0	1.000
1986—National...............................	1B	4	0	0	0	0	0	0	.000	5	0	0	1.000
1987—National...............................	1B	2	0	1	0	0	0	0	.500	4	2	0	1.000
All-Star Game Totals—5 Years..................		10	0	3	0	0	0	0	.300	15	2	0	1.000

MANUEL ANTONIO HERNANDEZ
(Manny)

Born May 7, 1961, at La Romana, Dominican Republic.
Height, 6.00. Weight, 150.
Throws and bats righthanded.

Tied for Pacific Coast League lead in games started by pitchers with 30 in 1988.
Tied for Pacific Coast League lead in balks with 5 in 1984.

Year Club	League	G.	IP.	W.	L.	Pct.	H.	R.	ER.	SO.	BB.	ERA.
1979—Sarasota Astros............................	Gulf Coast	9	14	2	0	1.000	17	6	4	10	10	2.57
1980—Sarasota Astros-Blue	Gulf Coast	11	62	5	2	.714	65	26	21	37	15	3.05
1981—Daytona Beach	Florida St.	13	79	6	5	.545	67	36	30	61	24	3.42
1982—Daytona Beach	Florida St.	21	99⅓	6	6	.500	114	70	55	50	52	4.98
1983—Daytona Beach	Florida St.	18	102⅓	10	3	.769	86	46	34	73	27	2.99
1984—Tucson......................................	P. Coast	28	146⅔	6	9	.400	153	96	80	107	65	4.91
1985—Tucson†....................................	P. Coast	11	37⅔	1	1	.500	35	19	15	25	10	3.58
1986—Tucson......................................	P. Coast	22	128	8	7	.533	139	79	67	84	27	4.71
1986—Houston....................................	National	9	27⅓	2	3	.400	33	15	12	9	12	3.90
1987—Tucson......................................	P. Coast	9	54	3	2	.600	42	21	18	42	15	3.00
1987—Houston....................................	National	6	21⅔	0	4	.000	25	15	13	12	5	5.40
1988—Tucson‡....................................	P. Coast	31	184⅔	10	9	.526	●210	99	87	122	44	4.24
1989—Portland§..................................	P. Coast	24	140⅓	9	8	.529	124	71	61	83	38	3.91
1989—Tidewater.................................	Int'national	7	42⅔	2	2	.500	32	11	8	30	7	1.69
1989—New York x...............................	National	1	1	0	0	.000	0	0	0	1	0	0.00
Major League Totals—3 Years		16	50⅓	2	7	.222	58	30	25	22	17	4.47

Signed as free agent by Houston Astros' organization, November 23, 1978.
†On disabled list, May 9 to July 18, 1985.
‡Granted free agency, October 15, 1988; signed by Portland (Minnesota Twins' organization), November 23, 1988.
§Sold to Tidewater (New York Mets' organization), August 1, 1989.
xReleased, October 3, 1989.

THOMAS MITCHELL HERR
(Tom)

Born April 4, 1956, at Lancaster, Pa.
Height, 6.00. Weight, 196.
Throws right and bats left and righthanded.
Attended University of Delaware, Newark, Del.

Shares major league record for highest fielding average, second baseman, lifetime (.989).
Shares National League record for most sacrifice flies by switch-hitter, season (13), 1985.
Major League stolen bases: 1979 (1), 1980 (9), 1981 (23), 1982 (25), 1983 (6), 1984 (13), 1985 (31), 1986 (22), 1987 (19), 1988 (13), 1989 (10). Total—172.
Led National League in sacrifice flies with 13 in 1985 and 12 in 1987.
Led National League second basemen in double plays with 74 in 1981, 106 in 1984 and 121 in 1986.
Led National League second basemen in total chances with 590 in 1981.
Led Florida State League in stolen bases with 50 in 1977.
Led Florida State League second basemen in double plays with 91 in 1977.
Named second baseman on THE SPORTING NEWS National League All-Star Team, 1985.

Year Club	League	Pos.	G.	AB.	R.	H.	2B.	3B.	HR.	RBI.	B.A.	PO.	A.	E.	F.A.
1975—Johnson City	Appal.	2B-SS	42	133	29	41	8	1	0	15	.308	74	125	5	.975
1976—St. Petersburg	Fla. St.	SS-2B	82	275	47	74	6	1	0	21	.269	133	211	18	.950
1977—St. Petersburg	Fla. St.	2B	136	★515	★80	★156	13	7	1	53	.303	★348	★430	21	★.974
1978—Arkansas................	Texas	2B	89	335	70	98	23	4	3	45	.293	207	280	13	.974
1978—Springfield............	A. A.	2B	33	86	16	24	6	1	0	8	.279	45	63	7	.939
1979—Springfield............	A. A.	2B	109	423	74	124	20	6	6	48	.293	225	324	10	★.982
1979—St. Louis................	Nat.	2B	14	10	4	2	0	0	0	1	.200	12	11	0	1.000
1980—Springfield............	A. A.	2B-3B	37	141	29	44	6	2	1	16	.312	29	52	1	.988

Year Club	League	Pos.	G.	AB.	R.	H.	2B.	3B.	HR.	RBI.	B.A.	PO.	A.	E.	F.A.
1980—St. Louis...............	Nat.	2B-SS	76	222	29	55	12	5	0	15	.248	124	184	7	.978
1981—St. Louis...............	Nat.	2B	103	411	50	110	14	9	0	46	.268	211	★374	5	★.992
1982—St. Louis...............	Nat.	2B	135	493	83	131	19	4	0	36	.266	263	427	9	.987
1983—St. Louis†.............	Nat.	2B	89	313	43	101	14	4	2	31	.323	178	245	6	.986
1983—Arkansas...............	Texas	2B	3	9	0	4	3	0	0	1	.444	4	9	0	1.000
1984—St. Louis...............	Nat.	2B	145	558	67	154	23	2	4	49	.276	328	452	6	.992
1985—St. Louis...............	Nat.	2B	159	596	97	180	38	3	8	110	.302	337	448	12	.985
1986—St. Louis...............	Nat.	2B	152	559	48	141	30	4	2	61	.252	352	414	9	.988
1987—St. Louis‡.............	Nat.	2B	141	510	73	134	29	0	2	83	.263	306	350	7	.989
1988—St. Louis§.............	Nat.	2B	15	50	4	13	0	0	1	3	.260	28	35	1	.984
1988—Minnesota xyz......	Amer.	2B-SS	86	304	42	80	16	0	1	21	.263	140	195	4	.988
1989—Philadelphia.........	Nat.	2B	151	561	65	161	25	6	2	37	.287	281	415	7	.990
National League Totals—11 Years.........			1180	4283	563	1182	204	37	21	472	.276	2420	3355	69	.988
American League Totals—1 Year..........			86	304	42	80	16	0	1	21	.263	140	195	4	.988
Major League Totals—11 Years...............			1266	4587	605	1262	220	37	22	493	.275	2560	3550	73	.988

Signed as free agent by St. Louis Cardinals' organization, August 22, 1974.

†On disabled list, March 25 to April 29 and August 9, 1983 through remainder of season; included rehabilitation disability assignment to Arkansas, April 18 to April 29, 1983.

‡On disabled list, April 24 to May 12, 1987.

§Traded to Minnesota Twins for Outfielder Tom Brunansky, April 22, 1988.

xOn disabled list, June 21 to July 22 and July 25 to August 18, 1988.

yTraded with Catcher Tom Nieto and Outfielder Eric Bullock to Philadelphia Phillies for Pitcher Shane Rawley and cash, October 24, 1988.

zGranted free agency, November 4, 1988; re-signed by Phillies, November 17, 1988.

CHAMPIONSHIP SERIES RECORD

Shares Championship Series record for most doubles, series (4), 1985.

Year Club	League	Pos.	G.	AB.	R.	H.	2B.	3B.	HR.	RBI.	B.A.	PO.	A.	E.	F.A.
1982—St. Louis...............	Nat.	2B	3	13	1	3	1	0	0	0	.231	6	10	0	1.000
1985—St. Louis...............	Nat.	2B	6	21	2	7	4	0	1	6	.333	13	12	0	1.000
1987—St. Louis...............	Nat.	2B	7	27	0	6	0	0	0	3	.222	12	11	1	.958
Championship Series Totals—3 Years.....			16	61	3	16	5	0	1	9	.262	31	33	1	.985

WORLD SERIES RECORD

Established World Series record for most double plays started, second baseman, seven-game Series (5), 1985.
Established World Series record for most runs batted in on sacrifice fly (2), October 16, 1982 (second inning).

Year Club	League	Pos.	G.	AB.	R.	H.	2B.	3B.	HR.	RBI.	B.A.	PO.	A.	E.	F.A.
1982—St. Louis...............	Nat.	2B	7	25	2	4	2	0	0	5	.160	11	19	1	.968
1985—St. Louis...............	Nat.	2B	7	26	2	4	2	0	0	0	.154	11	13	0	1.000
1987—St. Louis...............	Nat.	2B	7	28	2	7	0	0	1	1	.250	23	17	0	1.000
World Series Totals—3 Years			21	79	6	15	4	0	1	6	.190	45	49	1	.989

ALL-STAR GAME RECORD

Year League	Pos.	AB.	R.	H.	2B.	3B.	HR.	RBI.	B.A.	PO.	A.	E.	F.A.
1985—National..	2B	3	1	1	1	0	0	0	.333	0	1	0	1.000

OREL LEONARD HERSHISER IV

Name pronounced Hersh-HYZ-ur.

Born September 16, 1958, at Buffalo, N. Y.
Height, 6.03. Weight, 190.
Throws and bats righthanded.
Attended Bowling Green State University, Bowling Green, O.
Brother of Gordie Hershiser, pitcher in Los Angeles Dodgers' organization, 1987 and 1988.

Holds major league record for most consecutive scoreless innings, season (59), August 30, sixth inning, through September 28, tenth inning, 1988.

Shares National League records for fewest games lost for leader, season (15), 1989; most shutouts, month (5), September, 1988.

Major League saves: 1983 (1), 1984 (2), 1987 (1), 1988 (1). Total—5.

Led National League in shutouts with 8 in 1988 and tied for lead with 4 in 1984.

Tied for National League lead in complete games with 15 in 1988.

Tied for National League lead in sacrifice hits by batters with 19 in 1988.

Led Pacific Coast League in intentional bases on balls issued with 8 in 1983.

Named Major League Player of the Year by THE SPORTING NEWS, 1988.

Named National League Pitcher of the Year by THE SPORTING NEWS, 1988.

Won National League Cy Young Memorial Award, 1988.

Named righthanded pitcher on THE SPORTING NEWS National League All-Star Team, 1988.

Named pitcher on THE SPORTING NEWS National League All-Star fielding team, 1988.

Year Club	League	G.	IP.	W.	L.	Pct.	H.	R.	ER.	SO.	BB.	ERA.
1979—Clinton..............................	Midwest	15	43	4	0	1.000	33	15	10	33	17	2.09
1980—San Antonio.....................	Texas	49	109	5	9	.357	120	59	43	75	59	3.55
1981—San Antonio.....................	Texas	42	102	7	6	.538	94	54	53	95	50	4.68
1982—Albuquerque	P. Coast	47	123⅔	9	6	.600	121	73	51	93	63	3.71
1983—Albuquerque	P. Coast	49	134⅓	10	8	.556	132	73	61	95	57	4.09
1983—Los Angeles	National	8	8	0	0	.000	7	6	3	5	6	3.38
1984—Los Angeles	National	45	189⅔	11	8	.579	160	65	56	150	50	2.66
1985—Los Angeles	National	36	239⅔	19	3	★.864	179	72	54	157	68	2.03
1986—Los Angeles	National	35	231⅓	14	14	.500	213	112	99	153	86	3.85

Year Club	League	G.	IP.	W.	L.	Pct.	H.	R.	ER.	SO.	BB.	ERA.
1987—Los Angeles	National	37	*264⅔	16	16	.500	247	105	90	190	74	3.06
1988—Los Angeles	National	35	*267	●23	8	.742	208	73	67	178	73	2.26
1989—Los Angeles	National	35	*256⅔	15	●15	.500	226	75	66	178	77	2.31
Major League Totals—7 Years		231	1457	98	64	.605	1240	508	435	1011	434	2.69

Selected by Los Angeles Dodgers' organization in 17th round of free-agent draft, June 5, 1979.

CHAMPIONSHIP SERIES RECORD

Holds Championship Series record for most innings pitched, series (24⅔), 1988.
Shares Championship Series record for most wild pitches, total series (3).
Holds National League Championship Series record for most hit batsmen, game (2), October 12, 1988.
Shares National League Championship Series records for most complete games total series (2); most hit bastmen total series (2) and series (2), 1988.

Year Club	League	G.	IP.	W.	L.	Pct.	H.	R.	ER.	SO.	BB.	ERA.
1985—Los Angeles	National	2	15⅓	1	0	1.000	17	6	6	5	6	3.52
1988—Los Angeles	National	4	24⅔	1	0	1.000	18	5	3	15	7	1.09
Championship Series Totals—2 Years		6	40	2	0	1.000	35	11	9	20	13	2.03

WORLD SERIES RECORD

Year Club	League	G.	IP.	W.	L.	Pct.	H.	R.	ER.	SO.	BB.	ERA.
1988—Los Angeles	National	2	18	2	0	1.000	7	2	2	17	6	1.00

ALL-STAR GAME RECORD

Year League	IP.	W.	L.	Pct.	H.	R.	ER.	SO.	BB.	ERA.
1987—National	2	0	0	.000	1	0	0	0	1	0.00
1988—National	1	0	0	.000	0	0	0	0	0	0.00
All-Star Game Totals—2 Years	3	0	0	.000	1	0	0	0	1	0.00

Member of National League All-Star Team in 1989; did not play.

JOSEPH THOMAS HESKETH
(Joe)

Born February 15, 1959, at Lackawanna, N. Y.
Height, 6.02. Weight, 170
Throws and bats lefthanded.
Attended State University of New York, Buffalo, N. Y.

Major League saves: 1984 (1), 1987 (1), 1988 (9), 1989 (3). Total—14.
Tied for American Association lead in shutouts with 2 in 1983.
Named American Association Pitcher of the Year, 1984.

Year Club	League	G.	IP.	W.	L.	Pct.	H.	R.	ER.	SO.	BB.	ERA.
1980—West Palm Beach	Florida St.	11	75	8	2	.800	71	30	16	43	32	1.92
1980—Memphis	Southern	3	20	1	0	1.000	20	13	9	20	7	4.05
1981—Memphis†	Southern					(Did Not Play)						
1982—Memphis‡	Southern					(Did Not Play)						
1982—West Palm Beach	Florida St.	8	45⅔	3	2	.600	41	16	14	24	16	2.76
1983—Memphis	Southern	11	74	6	4	.600	82	38	25	22	25	3.04
1983—Wichita	Am. Assoc.	15	88⅓	5	5	.500	98	53	50	41	46	5.09
1984—Indianapolis	Am. Assoc.	22	147⅔	12	3	.800	120	60	50	135	54	3.05
1984—Montreal	National	11	45	2	2	.500	38	12	9	32	15	1.80
1985—Montreal§	National	25	155⅓	10	5	.667	125	52	43	113	45	2.49
1986—Montreal x	National	15	82⅔	6	5	.545	92	46	46	67	31	5.01
1987—Bradenton Expos	Gulf Coast	2	4⅓	0	0	.000	7	4	4	8	0	8.31
1987—Jacksonville	Southern	6	19⅔	1	0	1.000	18	6	5	22	4	2.29
1987—Montreal	National	18	28⅔	0	0	.000	23	12	10	31	15	3.14
1988—Indianapolis	Am. Assoc.	8	11	0	0	.000	10	5	4	16	5	3.27
1988—Montreal	National	60	72⅔	4	3	.571	63	30	23	64	35	2.85
1989—Montreal y	National	43	48⅓	6	4	.600	54	34	31	44	26	5.77
1989—Indianapolis	Am. Assoc.	5	9⅓	0	0	.000	11	4	4	9	5	3.86
Major League Totals—6 Years		172	432⅔	28	19	.596	395	186	162	351	167	3.37

Selected by Montreal Expos' organization in 2nd round of free-agent draft, June 3, 1980.
†On disabled list, April 9, 1981, through remainder of season.
‡On disabled list, April 8 to July 8, 1982.
§On disabled list, August 24, 1985 through remainder of season.
xOn disabled list, July 4, 1986 through remainder of season.
yOn disabled list, August 18 to September 8, 1989.

ERIC PAUL HETZEL

Born September 25, 1963, at Crowley, La.
Height, 6.03. Weight, 180.
Throws and bats righthanded.
Attended Eastern Oklahoma State College, Wilburton,
Okla., and Louisiana State University, Baton Rouge, La.

Year Club	League	G.	IP.	W.	L.	Pct.	H.	R.	ER.	SO.	BB.	ERA.
1985—Greensboro	S. Atlantic	15	76	7	5	.853	87	54	47	82	48	5.57
1986—Greensboro†	S. Atlantic					(Did not play)						
1987—Winter Haven	Florida St.	26	192⅔	10	12	.455	186	94	76	136	87	3.55
1988—Pawtucket	Int'national	22	127⅓	6	10	3.75	129	67	56	122	51	3.96

Year Club	League	G.	IP.	W.	L.	Pct.	H.	R.	ER.	SO.	BB.	ERA.
1989—Pawtucket	Int'national	12	80	4	4	.500	65	27	22	79	32	2.48
1989—Boston‡	American	12	50⅓	2	3	.400	61	39	35	33	28	6.26
Major League Totals—1 Year		12	50⅓	2	3	.400	61	39	35	33	28	6.26

Selected by Boston Red Sox' organization in 5th round of free-agent draft, January 11, 1983.
Selected by Kansas City Royals' organization in 2nd round of free-agent draft, January 17, 1984.
Selected by Pittsburgh Pirates' organization in secondary phase of free-agent draft, June 4, 1984.
Selected by Boston Red Sox' organization in secondary phase of free-agent draft, June 3, 1985.
†On disabled list, April 9, 1986 through entire season.
‡On disabled list, August 3 to August 24, 1989; included rehabilitation disability assignment to Pawtucket, August 18 to August 24, 1989.

JAMES GREGORY HIBBARD
(Greg)

Born September 13, 1964, at New Orleans, La.
Height, 6.00. Weight, 180.
Throws and bats lefthanded.
Attended Mississippi Gulf Coast Junior College, Perkinston, Miss.,
and University of Alabama, Tuscaloosa, Ala.

Year Club	League	G.	IP.	W.	L.	Pct.	H.	R.	ER.	SO.	BB.	ERA.
1986—Eugene	Northwest	26	39	5	2	.714	30	23	15	44	19	3.46
1987—Appleton	Midwest	9	64⅔	7	2	.778	53	17	8	61	18	1.11
1987—Fort Myers	Florida St.	3	24	2	1	.667	20	5	5	20	3	1.88
1987—Memphis†	Southern	16	106	7	6	.538	102	48	38	56	21	3.23
1988—Vancouver	P. Coast	25	144⅓	11	11	.500	155	74	66	65	44	4.12
1989—Vancouver	P. Coast	9	58	2	3	.400	47	24	17	45	11	2.64
1989—Chicago	American	23	137⅓	6	7	.462	142	58	49	55	41	3.21
Major League Totals—1 Year		23	137⅓	6	7	.462	142	58	49	55	41	3.21

Selected by Houston Astros' organization in 8th round of free-agent draft, January 17, 1984.
Selected by Kansas City Royals' organization in 16th round of free-agent draft, June 2, 1986.
†Traded with Pitchers Melido Perez, John Davis and Chuck Mount to Chicago White Sox for Pitcher Floyd Bannister and Third Baseman Dave Cochrane, December 10, 1987.

KEVIN JOHN HICKEY

Born February 25, 1956, at Chicago, Ill.
Height, 6.01. Weight, 200.
Throws and bats lefthanded.

Major League saves: 1981 (3), 1982 (6), 1983 (5), 1989 (2). Total—16.
Led Eastern League in home runs allowed with 20 and balks with 6 in 1980.
Led Midwest League in balks with 5 in 1979.

Year Club	League	G.	IP.	W.	L.	Pct.	H.	R.	ER.	SO.	BB.	ERA.
1978—Paintsville	Ap'lachian	9	36	2	4	.333	37	19	16	24	23	4.00
1979—Appleton	Midwest	29	121	5	10	.333	122	64	48	100	71	3.57
1980—Glens Falls	Eastern	26	169	9	7	.563	184	92	81	80	73	4.31
1981—Chicago	American	41	44	0	2	.000	38	22	18	17	18	3.68
1982—Chicago	American	60	78	4	4	.500	73	32	26	38	30	3.00
1983—Chicago†‡	American	23	20⅔	1	2	.333	23	14	12	8	11	5.23
1984—Appleton	Midwest	10	49⅔	4	3	.571	45	18	13	40	11	2.36
1984—Denver§	Am. Assoc.	16	47⅓	2	2	.500	61	39	33	20	23	6.27
1984—Int'national	Int'national	5	9⅓	1	1	.500	14	10	9	3	8	8.68
1985—Albany x-Reading	Eastern	44	60⅓	5	5	.500	53	22	18	44	22	2.69
1986—Portland y	P. Coast	33	65	1	3	.250	76	54	47	44	29	6.51
1987—Hawaii z-Phoenix a	P. Coast	46	82⅔	4	5	.444	88	52	46	48	36	5.01
1988—Charlotte	Southern	6	9⅔	1	1	.500	10	4	4	7	8	3.72
1988—Rochester	Int'national	27	37	2	0	1.000	31	7	6	24	9	1.46
1989—Baltimore	American	51	49⅓	2	3	.400	38	16	16	28	23	2.92
Major League Totals—4 Years		175	192	7	11	.389	172	84	72	91	82	3.38

Signed as free agent by Chicago White Sox' organization, August 18, 1977.
†On disabled list, August 1 to September 5, 1983.
‡Released, March 26, 1984; re-signed by Chicago White Sox' organization, April 2, 1984.
§Traded with Pitcher Doug Drabek to New York Yankees' organization, August 13, 1984, completing deal in which New York traded Infielder Roy Smalley to Chicago White Sox for two players to be named later, July 18, 1984.
xReleased, May 25, 1985; signed by Reading (Philadelphia Phillies' organization), June 1, 1985.
yReleased, September 30, 1986; signed by Hawaii (Chicago White Sox' organization), March 11, 1987.
zReleased, August 21, 1987; signed by Phoenix (San Francisco Giants' organization), August 22, 1987.
aGranted free agency, October 15, 1987; signed by Charlotte (Baltimore Orioles' organization), December 18, 1987.

MARK DOUGLAS HIGGINS

Born July 9, 1963, at Miami, Fla.
Height, 6.02. Weight, 210.
Throws and bats righthanded.
Attended Chipola Junior College, Marianna, Fla.,
and University of New Orleans, New Orleans, La.

Led New York-Pennsylvania League first basemen in total chances with 764 and double plays with 66 in 1984.

Year Club	League	Pos.	G.	AB.	R.	H.	2B.	3B.	HR.	RBI.	B.A.	PO.	A.	E.	F.A.
1984—Batavia	NYP	1B	74	279	38	76	12	0	8	39	.272	684	★46	★16	.979

Year Club	League	Pos.	G.	AB.	R.	H.	2B.	3B.	HR.	RBI.	B.A.	PO.	A.	E.	F.A.
1985—Waterloo	Midw.	1B-2B	108	355	47	90	17	2	16	55	.254	548	38	8	.986
1986—Waterloo	Midw.	1B	126	448	73	142	★34	1	23	98	.317	496	29	5	.991
1987—Williamsport	East.	1B	108	394	76	123	21	1	19	79	.312	709	80	★19	.976
1988—Williamsport	East.	1B	92	335	39	77	10	0	10	42	.230	142	17	3	.981
1988—Colorado Springs	P. C.	1B	26	80	9	16	1	0	2	7	.200	122	12	2	.985
1989—Colorado Springs	P. C.	1B	72	213	34	70	15	1	10	34	.329	408	27	8	.982
1989—Cleveland	Amer.	1B	6	10	1	1	0	0	0	0	.100	18	3	0	1.000
Major League Totals—1 Year			6	10	1	1	0	0	0	0	.100	18	3	0	1.000

Selected by Texas Rangers' organization in 13th round of free-agent draft, January 11, 1983.
Selected by Texas Rangers' organization in secondary phase of free-agent draft, June 6, 1983.
Selected by Cleveland Indians' organization in secondary phase of free-agent draft, June 4, 1984.

TEODORO HIGUERA (VALENZUELA)

Name pronounced Tea-O-door-RO Hugh-gare-a Val-en-ZWAY-luh.

(Ted)

Born November 9, 1958, at Las Mochis, Mexico.
Height, 5.10. Weight, 180.
Throws left and bats left and righthanded.

Tied for Mexican League lead in games started by pitchers with 27 and complete games with 18 in 1983.
Named lefthanded pitcher on THE SPORTING NEWS American League All-Star Team, 1986.
Named American League Rookie Pitcher of the Year by THE SPORTING NEWS, 1985.

Year Club	League	G.	IP.	W.	L.	Pct.	H.	R.	ER.	SO.	BB.	ERA.
1979—Ciudad Juarez	Mexican	2	1	0	1	.000	4	5	5	1	4	45.00
1980—Ciudad Juarez†	Mexican	19	117	8	3	.727	111	30	24	76	59	1.85
1980—Ciudad Juarez‡	Mexican	8	49	2	5	.286	44	22	20	29	17	3.67
1981—Ciudad Juarez	Mexican	28	203	16	9	.640	207	81	70	157	69	3.10
1982—Ciudad Juarez	Mexican	24	142⅓	9	12	.429	163	77	64	74	53	4.05
1983—Ciudad Juarez§	Mexican	27	★222	●17	8	.680	177	61	50	★165	68	2.03
1984—El Paso	Texas	19	121	8	7	.533	116	57	35	99	43	★2.60
1984—Vancouver	P. Coast	8	40	1	4	.200	49	26	21	29	14	4.73
1985—Milwaukee	American	32	212⅓	15	8	.652	186	105	92	127	63	3.90
1986—Milwaukee	American	34	248⅓	20	11	.645	226	84	77	207	74	2.79
1987—Milwaukee	American	35	261⅔	18	10	.643	236	120	112	240	87	3.85
1988—Milwaukee	American	31	227⅓	16	9	.640	168	66	62	192	59	2.45
1989—El Paso x	Texas	1	5	0	1	.000	5	2	1	4	1	1.80
1989—Milwaukee	American	22	135⅓	9	6	.600	125	56	52	91	48	3.46
Major League Totals—5 Years		154	1085	78	44	.639	941	431	395	857	331	3.28

†20-team season.
‡6-team season.
§Sold to Vancouver (Milwaukee Brewers' organization), September 13, 1983.
xOn Milwaukee disabled list, March 25 to May 1, 1989; included rehabilitation disability assignment to El Paso, April 9 to April 28, 1989.

ALL-STAR GAME RECORD

Year League	IP.	W.	L.	Pct.	H.	R.	ER.	SO.	BB.	ERA.
1986—American	3	0	0	.000	1	0	0	2	1	0.00

GLENALLEN HILL

Born March 22, 1965, at Santa Cruz, Calif.
Height, 6.02. Weight, 210.
Throws and bats righthanded.

Major League stolen bases: 1989 (2).
Led International League in total bases with 279 and slugging percentage with .578 in 1989.
Led International League batters in strikeouts with 152 in 1987.
Led Southern League in total bases with 287, strikeouts with 153 and tied for lead in sacrifice flies with 13 in 1986.
Led Carolina League batters in strikeouts with 211 in 1985.
Led South Atlantic League batters in strikeouts with 150 in 1984.

Year Club	League	Pos.	G.	AB.	R.	H.	2B.	3B.	HR.	RBI.	B.A.	PO.	A.	E.	F.A.
1983—Medicine Hat	Pion.	OF	46	133	34	63	3	4	6	27	.256	63	3	6	.917
1984—Florence	S. Atl.	OF	129	440	75	105	19	5	16	64	.239	281	9	16	.948
1985—Kinston	Carol.	OF	131	466	57	98	13	0	20	56	.210	234	12	13	.950
1986—Knoxville	South.	OF	141	★570	87	159	23	6	★31	96	.279	230	9	★21	.919
1987—Syracuse	Int.	OF	★137	536	65	126	25	6	16	77	.235	176	10	10	.949
1988—Syracuse	Int.	OF	51	172	21	40	7	0	4	19	.233	101	2	1	.990
1988—Knoxville	South.	OF	79	269	37	71	13	2	12	38	.264	130	6	5	.965
1989—Syracuse	Int.	OF	125	483	★86	★155	31	★15	★21	72	.321	242	3	★7	.972
1989—Toronto	Amer.	OF	19	52	4	15	0	0	1	7	.288	27	0	1	.964
Major League Totals—1 Year			19	52	4	15	0	0	1	7	.288	27	0	1	.964

Selected by Toronto Blue Jays' organization in 9th round of free-agent draft, June 6, 1983.

KENNETH WADE HILL

(Ken)

Born December 14, 1965, at Lynn, Mass.
Height, 6.02. Weight, 175.
Throws and bats righthanded.

Shares National League record for fewest games lost for leader, season (15), 1989.

Year Club	League	G.	IP.	W.	L.	Pct.	H.	R.	ER.	SO.	BB.	ERA.
1985—Gastonia	S. Atlantic	15	69	3	6	.333	60	51	38	48	57	4.96
1986—Gastonia	S. Atlantic	22	122⅔	9	5	.643	95	51	38	86	80	2.79
1986—Glens Falls†	Eastern	1	7	0	1	.000	4	4	4	4	6	5.14
1986—Arkansas	Texas	3	18	1	2	.333	18	10	9	9	7	4.50
1987—Arkansas	Texas	18	53⅔	3	5	.375	60	33	31	48	30	5.20
1988—St. Louis‡	National	4	14	0	1	.000	16	9	8	6	6	5.14
1988—Arkansas	Texas	22	115⅓	9	9	.500	129	76	63	107	50	4.92
1989—Louisville	Am. Assoc.	3	18	0	2	.000	13	8	7	18	10	3.50
1989—St. Louis	National	33	196⅔	7	●15	.318	186	92	83	112	★99	3.80
Major League Totals—2 Years		37	210⅔	7	16	.304	202	101	91	118	105	3.89

Signed as free agent by Detroit Tigers' organization, February 14, 1985.

†Traded with a player to be named later to St. Louis Cardinals for Catcher Mike Heath, August 10, 1986; St. Louis acquired First Baseman Mike Laga to complete deal, September 2, 1986.

‡On disabled list, March 26 to May 9, 1988.

SHAWN PATRICK HILLEGAS
Name pronounced HILL-uh-gus.

Born August 21, 1964, at Dos Palos, Calif.
Height, 6.02. Weight, 208.
Throws and bats righthanded.
Attended Middle Georgia College, Cochran, Ga.

Major League saves: 1989 (3).

Year Club	League	G.	IP.	W.	L.	Pct.	H.	R.	ER.	SO.	BB.	ERA.
1984—Vero Beach	Florida St.	13	93⅓	5	3	.625	71	25	19	64	33	1.83
1985—San Antonio	Texas	23	139⅓	4	10	.286	134	72	49	56	67	3.17
1986—San Antonio	Texas	17	132⅓	9	5	.643	107	60	45	97	58	3.06
1986—Albuquerque	P. Coast	9	46⅔	1	5	.167	48	35	32	43	31	6.17
1987—Albuquerque	P. Coast	24	165⅔	13	5	.722	172	79	62	105	64	3.37
1987—Los Angeles	National	12	58	4	3	.571	52	27	23	51	31	3.57
1988—Albuquerque	P. Coast	16	100⅔	6	4	.600	93	44	39	66	22	3.49
1988—Los Angeles†	National	11	56⅔	3	4	.429	54	26	26	30	17	4.13
1988—Chicago	American	6	40	3	2	.600	30	16	14	26	18	3.15
1989—Chicago	American	50	119⅔	7	11	.389	132	67	63	76	51	4.74
National League Totals—2 Years		23	114⅔	7	7	.500	106	53	49	81	48	3.85
American League Totals—2 Years		56	159⅔	10	13	.435	162	83	77	102	69	4.34
Major League Totals—3 Years		79	274⅓	17	20	.459	268	136	126	183	117	4.13

Selected by California Angels' organization in 26th round of free-agent draft, June 6, 1983.

Selected by Los Angeles Dodgers' organization in secondary phase of free-agent draft, January 17, 1984.

†Traded to Chicago White Sox, September 2, 1988, completing deal in which Chicago traded Pitcher Rick Horton to Los Angeles Dodgers for a player to be named later, August 30, 1988.

HOWARD JAMES HILTON

Born January 3, 1964, at Oxnard, Calif.
Height, 6.03. Weight, 230.
Throws and bats righthanded.
Attended Oxnard College, Oxnard, Calif., and
University of Arkansas, Fayetteville, Ark.

Led New York-Pennsylvania League in intentional bases on balls issued with 8 in 1985.

Year Club	League	G.	IP.	W.	L.	Pct.	H.	R.	ER.	SO.	BB.	ERA.
1985—Erie	NYP	24	65⅓	3	7	.300	73	46	31	66	26	4.27
1986—St. Petersburg	Florida St.	36	62⅔	4	5	.444	53	21	17	49	28	2.44
1987—Springfield	Midwest	★62	107⅓	8	6	.571	77	33	25	107	17	2.10
1988—Arkansas	Texas	66	102	8	7	.533	90	39	30	90	46	2.65
1989—Louisville	Am. Assoc.	★70	96⅓	12	5	.706	86	44	40	77	42	3.74

Selected by St. Louis Cardinals' organization in 22nd round of free-agent draft, June 3, 1985.

THOMAS LEE HINZO
(Tommy)

Born June 18, 1964, at San Diego, Calif.
Height, 5.10. Weight, 175.
Throws right and bats left and righthanded.
Attended Southwestern College, Chula Vista, Calif., and
University of Arizona, Tucson, Ariz.

Major League stolen bases: 1987 (9), 1989 (1). Total—10.
Led Pacific Coast League second basemen in double plays with 94 in 1988.

Year Club	League	Pos.	G.	AB.	R.	H.	2B.	3B.	HR.	RBI.	B.A.	PO.	A.	E.	F.A.
1986—Batavia	NYP	2B	55	219	35	73	7	3	1	15	★.333	112	135	12	.954
1987—Kinston	Carol.	2B	65	266	64	74	11	1	0	25	.278	129	186	13	.960
1987—Williamsport	East.	2B	26	99	16	24	2	1	0	9	.242	58	78	3	.978
1987—Cleveland	Amer.	2B	67	257	31	68	9	3	3	21	.265	115	204	9	.973
1988—Colorado Springs	P. C.	2B-SS	119	449	67	104	16	4	1	29	.232	236	391	19	.971

Year	Club	League	Pos.	G.	AB.	R.	H.	2B.	3B.	HR.	RBI.	B.A.	PO.	A.	E.	F.A.
1989—Colorado Springs	. P. C.		2B	102	410	65	104	13	7	1	35	.254	206	325	13	.976
1989—Cleveland†	Amer.		2B-SS	18	17	4	0	0	0	0	0	.000	9	7	3	.842
Major League Totals—2 Years				85	274	35	68	9	3	3	21	.248	124	211	12	.965

Selected by Cleveland Indians' organization in 1st round (third player selected) of free-agent draft, January 17, 1984.

Selected by New York Mets' organization in secondary phase of free-agent draft, June 4, 1984.

Selected by Pittsburgh Pirates' organization in secondary phase of free-agent draft, June 3, 1985.

Selected by Cleveland Indians' organization in 7th round of free-agent draft, June 2, 1986.

†On disabled list, August 14 to September 1, 1989.

GLENN EDWARD HOFFMAN

Born July 7, 1958, at Orange, Calif.
Height, 6.02. Weight, 190.
Throws and bats righthanded.

Major League stolen bases: 1980 (2), 1983 (1), 1985 (2). Total—5.
Led International League shortstops in putouts with 166 in 1988.
Led International League shortstops in double plays with 87 in 1978.
Tied for Florida State League lead in putouts by shortstops with 220 in 1977.

Year	Club	League	Pos.	G.	AB.	R.	H.	2B.	3B.	HR.	RBI.	B.A.	PO.	A.	E.	F.A.
1976—Elmira	NYP		SS	60	191	29	52	7	2	3	34	.272	★83	139	17	.925
1977—Winter Haven	Fla. St.		SS-3B-1B	126	425	51	123	17	2	3	61	.289	225	377	36	.944
1977—Pawtucket	Int.		SS	4	9	2	4	1	0	0	2	.444	4	10	1	.933
1978—Pawtucket	Int.		★SS-P	131	411	27	116	17	1	2	48	.282	★211	★391	45	.930
1979—Pawtucket	Int.		3B-SS-P	139	520	70	148	13	3	11	54	.285	172	286	19	.960
1980—Boston	Amer.		3B-SS-2B	114	312	37	89	15	4	4	42	.285	78	202	17	.943
1981—Boston	Amer.		SS-3B	78	242	28	56	10	0	1	20	.231	132	234	15	.961
1982—Boston	Amer.		SS	150	469	53	98	23	2	7	49	.209	246	439	20	.972
1983—Boston	Amer.		SS	143	473	56	123	24	1	4	41	.260	240	417	26	.962
1984—Boston	Amer.		SS-3B-2B	64	74	8	14	4	0	0	4	.189	43	74	5	.959
1985—Boston†	Amer.		SS-3B-2B	96	279	40	77	17	2	6	34	.276	157	232	11	.973
1986—Boston‡§	Amer.		SS-3B	12	23	1	5	2	0	0	1	.217	15	11	2	.929
1987—Pawtucket	Int.		3B-2B	46	160	18	37	7	0	2	22	.231	35	91	5	.962
1987—Boston x	Amer.		SS-3B-2B	21	55	5	11	3	0	0	6	.200	15	51	1	.985
1987—Los Angeles y	Nat.		SS	40	132	10	29	5	0	0	10	.220	70	101	6	.966
1988—Pawtucket z	Int.		SS-3B	109	366	38	88	14	0	3	33	.240	167	265	10	.977
1989—California a	Amer.		S-3-2-1	48	104	9	22	3	0	1	3	.212	45	75	3	.976
American League Totals—9 Years				726	2031	237	495	101	9	23	200	.244	971	1735	100	.964
National League Totals—1 Year				40	132	10	29	5	0	0	10	.220	70	101	6	.966
Major League Totals—9 Years				766	2163	247	524	106	9	23	210	.242	1041	1836	106	.964

Selected by Boston Red Sox' organization in 2nd round of free-agent draft, June 8, 1976.

†On disabled list, July 25 to August 21, 1985.

‡On disabled list, May 17 to September 5, 1986; included rehabilitation disability assignment to New Britain, July 13 to August 1, 1986.

§Granted free agency, November 12, 1986; re-signed by Red Sox' organization, December 20, 1986.

xTraded to Los Angeles Dodgers for a player to be named later, August 21, 1987; Boston Red Sox acquired Pitcher Billy Bartels to complete deal, December 8, 1987.

yReleased, December 16, 1987; signed by Boston Red Sox, March 10, 1988.

zReleased, December 15, 1988; signed by California Angels, January 4, 1989.

aReleased, October 31, 1989.

PITCHING RECORD

Year	Club	League	G.	IP.	W.	L.	Pct.	H.	R.	ER.	SO.	BB.	ERA.
1978—Pawtucket	Int'national		1	⅓	0	0	.000	0	0	0	0	0	0.00
1979—Pawtucket	Int'national		1	1	0	0	.000	1	1	1	0	1	9.00

CHRISTOPHER ALLEN HOILES

(Chris)

Born March 20, 1965, at Bowling Green, O.
Height, 6.00. Weight, 208.
Throws and bats righthanded.
Attended Eastern Michigan University, Ypsilanti, Mich.

Led Eastern League in slugging percentage with .500 in 1988.
Led Appalachian League in game-winning RBIs with 10 and total bases with 143 in 1986.
Led Appalachian League first basemen in putouts with 515, total chances with 551 and fielding percentage with .996 in 1986.
Tied for Eastern League lead in double plays by catchers with 5 in 1988.

Year	Club	League	Pos.	G.	AB.	R.	H.	2B.	3B.	HR.	RBI.	B.A.	PO.	A.	E.	F.A.
1986—Bristol	Appal.		1B-C	●68	253	42	81	★19	2	13	★57	.320	563	38	4	.993
1987—Glens Falls	East.		C-1B-3B	108	380	47	105	12	0	13	53	.276	406	88	11	.978
1988—Glens Falls†	East.		C-1B	103	360	67	102	21	3	●17	73	.283	438	57	7	.986
1988—Toledo	Int.		C	22	69	4	11	1	0	2	6	.159	71	2	1	.986
1989—Rochester‡	Int.		C-1B	96	322	41	79	19	1	10	51	.245	431	33	7	.985
1989—Baltimore	Amer.		C	6	9	0	1	1	0	0	1	.111	11	0	0	1.000
Major League Totals—1 Year				6	9	0	1	1	0	0	1	.111	11	0	0	1.000

Selected by Detroit Tigers' organization in 19th round of free-agent draft, June 2, 1986.

†Traded with Pitchers Cesar Mejia and Robinson Garces to Baltimore Orioles, September 9, 1988, to complete deal

in which Baltimore traded Outfielder Fred Lynn to Detroit Tigers for three players to be named later, August 31, 1988.

‡On disabled list, June 18 to July 7, 1989.

DAVID MICHAELS HOLLINS
(Dave)

Born May 25, 1966, at Buffalo, N.Y.
Height, 6.01. Weight, 195.
Throws right and bats left and righthanded.
Attended University of South Carolina, Columbia, S.C.

Led Texas League in sacrifice flies with 10 in 1989.
Led Northwest League in intentional bases on balls received with 7 in 1987.
Led Northwest League third basemen in total chances with 241 in 1987.

Year	Club	League	Pos.	G.	AB.	R.	H.	2B.	3B.	HR.	RBI.	B.A.	PO.	A.	E.	F.A.
1987—Spokane	N'west		3B	75	278	52	86	14	4	2	44	.309	★59	★167	15	★.938
1988—Riverside	Calif.		3B-1B	139	516	90	157	32	1	9	92	.304	102	248	29	.923
1989—Wichita†	Texas		3B	131	459	69	126	29	4	9	79	.275	77	209	25	.920

Selected by San Diego Padres' organization in 6th round of free-agent draft, June 2, 1987.

†Drafted by Philadelphia Phillies, December 4, 1989.

BRIAN SCOTT HOLMAN

Born January 25, 1965, at Denver, Colo.
Height, 6.04. Weight, 185.
Throws and bats righthanded.

Led Southern League in complete games with 6 in 1987.
Named Southern League Pitcher of the Year, 1987.

Year	Club	League	G.	IP.	W.	L.	Pct.	H.	R.	ER.	SO.	BB.	ERA.
1983—Jamestown†	NYP		2	5⅓	0	0	.000	7	7	7	5	4	11.81
1984—West Palm Beach	Florida St.		4	8	0	3	.000	14	19	16	14	21	18.00
1984—Gastonia	S. Atlantic		20	90⅔	5	8	.385	76	58	48	94	98	4.76
1985—West Palm Beach	Florida St.		25	143⅓	9	9	.500	124	79	63	103	90	3.96
1986—Jacksonville	Southern		27	157⅔	11	9	.550	146	111	90	118	★122	5.14
1987—Jacksonville	Southern		22	151⅓	14	5	.737	114	52	42	115	56	★2.50
1987—Indianapolis	Am. Assoc.		6	34⅔	4	0	.000	41	28	24	27	33	6.23
1988—Indianapolis	Am. Assoc.		14	91½	8	1	.889	78	26	24	70	30	2.36
1988—Montreal	National		18	100⅓	4	8	.333	101	39	36	58	34	3.23
1989—Montreal‡	National		10	31⅔	1	2	.333	34	18	17	23	15	4.83
1989—Seattle	American		23	159⅔	8	10	.444	160	68	61	82	62	3.44
National League Totals—2 Years			28	132	5	10	.333	135	57	53	81	49	3.61
American League Totals—1 Year			23	159⅔	8	10	.444	160	68	61	82	62	3.44
Major League Totals—2 Years			51	291⅔	13	20	.394	295	125	114	163	111	3.52

Selected by Montreal Expos' organization in 1st round (16th player selected) of free-agent draft, June 6, 1983.

†On disabled list, August 3, 1983 through remainder of season.

‡Traded with Pitchers Randy Johnson and Gene Harris to Seattle Mariners for Pitcher Mark Langston and a player to be named later, May 25, 1989; Indianapolis (Montreal Expos' organization) acquired Pitcher Mike Campbell to complete deal, July 31, 1989.

SHAWN LeROY HOLMAN

Born November 10, 1964, at Sewickley, Pa.
Height, 6.02. Weight, 185.
Throws and bats righthanded.

Year	Club	League	G.	IP.	W.	L.	Pct.	H.	R.	ER.	SO.	BB.	ERA.
1982—Bradenton Pirates	Gulf Coast		7	47	5	1	.833	35	20	14	33	11	2.68
1983—Greenwood	S. Atlantic		22	102⅔	5	9	.357	126	80	66	60	49	5.79
1984—Macon	S. Atlantic		9	46⅔	3	2	.600	48	19	10	32	25	1.93
1984—Prince William	Carolina		15	77⅔	7	4	.636	74	46	35	47	49	4.06
1985—Prince William	Carolina		24	142½	10	11	.476	123	69	56	65	53	3.54
1985—Nashua	Eastern		2	8	0	1	.000	10	6	4	2	7	4.50
1986—Nashua	Eastern		25	109½	4	●13	.235	108	61	58	39	67	4.77
1987—Harrisburg†-Glens Falls	Eastern		45	104½	5	6	.455	116	65	54	49	60	4.66
1988—Glens Falls	Eastern		52	91⅔	8	3	.727	82	36	19	44	26	1.87
1989—Toledo	Int'national		51	89⅔	3	1	.750	74	21	19	38	36	1.91
1989—Detroit	American		5	10	0	0	.000	8	2	2	9	11	1.80
Major League Totals—1 Year			5	10	0	0	.000	8	2	2	9	11	1.80

Selected by Pittsburgh Pirates' organization in 14th round of free-agent draft, June 7, 1982.

†Traded with First Baseman Pete Rice to Detroit Tigers for Outfielder Terry Harper, June 26, 1987.

BRIAN JOHN HOLTON

Born November 29, 1959, at McKeesport, Pa.
Height, 6.00. Weight, 207.
Throws and bats righthanded.
Attended Louisburg College, Louisburg, N. C.

Major League saves: 1987 (2), 1988 (1). Total—3.
Tied for Pacific Coast League lead in games started by pitchers with 27 in 1986.
Tied for Texas League lead in complete games with 16 in 1980.
Tied for California League lead in shutouts with 3 in 1979.

Year Club	League	G.	IP.	W.	L.	Pct.	H.	R.	ER.	SO.	BB.	ERA.
1978—Clinton†	Midwest	14	79	6	4	.600	94	51	38	54	23	4.33
1979—Lodi	California	10	72	7	0	1.000	47	26	21	72	32	2.63
1979—San Antonio	Texas	13	51	3	5	.375	50	24	21	40	25	3.71
1980—San Antonio	Texas	27	207	•15	10	.600	204	93	79	139	65	3.43
1981—Albuquerque	P. Coast	26	191	16	6	.727	215	94	73	73	51	3.44
1982—Albuquerque	P. Coast	32	161⅓	12	8	.600	191	102	92	76	60	5.13
1983—Albuquerque‡	P. Coast	20	97⅔	7	5	.583	113	76	69	70	50	6.36
1984—Albuquerque §x	P. Coast	12	32	0	0	.000	39	23	20	15	9	5.63
1985—Albuquerque	P. Coast	27	179⅔	9	10	.474	183	83	72	86	40	3.61
1985—Los Angeles	National	3	4	1	1	.500	9	7	4	1	1	9.00
1986—Albuquerque	P. Coast	27	*182⅔	10	10	.500	200	90	74	105	20	3.78
1986—Los Angeles	National	12	24⅓	2	3	.400	28	13	12	24	6	4.44
1987—Los Angeles	National	53	83⅓	3	2	.600	87	39	36	58	32	3.89
1988—Los Angeles y	National	45	84⅔	7	3	.700	69	19	16	49	26	1.70
1989—Baltimore	American	39	116⅓	5	7	.417	140	63	52	51	39	4.02
National League Totals—4 Years		113	196⅓	13	9	.591	193	78	68	132	65	3.12
American League Totals—1 Year		39	116⅓	5	7	.417	140	63	52	51	39	4.02
Major League Totals—5 Years		152	312⅔	18	16	.529	333	141	120	183	104	3.45

Selected by Los Angeles Dodgers' organization in 1st round (22nd player selected) of free-agent draft, January 10, 1978.

†On temporary inactive list, June 12 to July 7, 1978.

‡On disabled list, June 28 to July 15, 1983.

§On disabled list, April 7 to July 11, 1984.

xGranted free agency, October 15, 1984; re-signed by Dodgers' organization, October 22, 1984.

yTraded with Pitcher Ken Howell and Shortstop Juan Bell to Baltimore Orioles for First Baseman Eddie Murray, December 4, 1988.

CHAMPIONSHIP SERIES RECORD

Year Club	League	G.	IP.	W.	L.	Pct.	H.	R.	ER.	SO.	BB.	ERA.
1988—Los Angeles	National	3	4	0	0	.000	2	1	1	2	1	2.25

WORLD SERIES RECORD

Year Club	League	G.	IP.	W.	L.	Pct.	H.	R.	ER.	SO.	BB.	ERA.
1988—Los Angeles	National	1	2	0	0	.000	0	0	0	0	1	0.00

FREDERICK WAYNE HONEYCUTT
(Rick)

Born June 29, 1954, at Chattanooga, Tenn.
Height, 6.01. Weight, 190.
Throws and bats lefthanded.
Received bachelor of science degree in health education from
University of Tennessee, Knoxville, Tenn.

Major League saves: 1985 (1), 1988 (7), 1989 (12). Total—20.

Tied for New York-Pennsylvania League lead in complete games with 7 in 1976.

Year Club	League	G.	IP.	W.	L.	Pct.	H.	R.	ER.	SO.	BB.	ERA.
1976—Niagara Falls†	NYP	13	*97	5	3	.625	91	36	28	*98	20	2.60
1977—Shreveport‡§	Texas	21	135	10	6	.625	144	53	37	82	42	*2.47
1977—Seattle	American	10	29	0	1	.000	26	16	14	17	11	4.34
1978—Seattle x	American	26	134	5	11	.313	150	81	73	50	49	4.90
1979—Seattle	American	33	194	11	12	.478	201	103	87	83	67	4.04
1980—Seattle y	American	30	203	10	17	.370	221	99	89	79	60	3.95
1981—Texas	American	20	128	11	6	.647	120	49	47	40	17	3.30
1982—Texas	American	30	164	5	17	.227	201	103	96	64	54	5.27
1983—Texas z	American	25	174⅔	14	8	.636	168	59	47	56	37	*2.42
1983—Los Angeles	National	9	39	2	3	.400	46	26	25	18	13	5.77
1984—Los Angeles	National	29	183⅔	10	9	.526	180	72	58	75	51	2.84
1985—Los Angeles	National	31	142	8	12	.400	141	71	54	67	49	3.42
1986—Los Angeles	National	32	171	11	9	.550	164	71	63	100	45	3.32
1987—Los Angeles a	National	27	115⅔	2	12	.143	133	74	59	92	45	4.59
1987—Oakland	American	7	23⅔	1	4	.200	25	17	14	10	9	5.32
1988—Oakland b	American	55	79⅔	3	2	.600	74	36	31	47	25	3.50
1989—Oakland	American	64	76⅔	2	2	.500	56	26	20	52	26	2.35
American League Totals—10 Years		300	1206⅔	62	80	.437	1242	589	518	498	355	3.86
National League Totals—5 Years		128	651⅓	33	45	.423	664	314	259	352	203	3.58
Major League Totals—13 Years		428	1858	95	125	.432	1906	903	777	850	558	3.76

Selected by Baltimore Orioles' organization in 14th round of free-agent draft, June 6, 1972.

Selected by Pittsburgh Pirates' organization in 17th round of free-agent draft, June 8, 1976.

†Played two games as first baseman and one game as shortstop.

‡Traded to Seattle Mariners, August 22, 1977, completing deal in which Seattle traded Pitcher Dave Pagan to Pittsburgh Pirates for a player to be named later, July 27, 1977.

§Appeared as shortstop with no chances.

xOn disabled list, May 20 to June 26, 1978.

yTraded with Catcher Larry Cox, Outfielders Willie Horton and Leon Roberts and Shortstop Mario Mendoza to Texas Rangers for Pitchers Brian Allard, Ken Clay, Steve Finch and Jerry Don Gleaton, Shortstop Rick Auerbach and Outfielder Richie Zisk, December 12, 1980.

zTraded to Los Angeles Dodgers for Pitcher Dave Stewart and a player to be named later, August 19, 1983; Texas Rangers acquired Pitcher Ricky Wright to complete deal, September 16, 1983.

aTraded to Oakland Athletics for a player to be named later, August 29, 1987; Los Angeles Dodgers acquired Pitcher Tim Belcher to complete deal, September 3, 1987.
bGranted free agency, November 4, 1988; re-signed by Athletics, December 21, 1988.

CHAMPIONSHIP SERIES RECORD

Year	Club	League	G.	IP.	W.	L.	Pct.	H.	R.	ER.	SO.	BB.	ERA.
1983—Los Angeles		National	2	1⅔	0	0	.000	4	4	4	2	0	21.60
1985—Los Angeles		National	2	1⅓	0	0	.000	4	2	2	1	2	13.50
1988—Oakland		American	3	2	1	0	1.000	0	0	0	0	2	0.00
1989—Oakland		American	3	1⅔	0	0	.000	6	6	6	1	5	32.40
Championship Series Totals—4 Years			10	6⅔	1	0	1.000	14	12	12	4	9	16.20

WORLD SERIES RECORD

Year	Club	League	G.	IP.	W.	L.	Pct.	H.	R.	ER.	SO.	BB.	ERA.
1988—Oakland		American	3	3⅓	1	0	1.000	0	0	0	5	0	0.00
1989—Oakland		American	3	2⅔	0	0	.000	4	2	2	2	0	6.75
World Series Totals—2 Years			6	6	1	0	1.000	4	2	2	7	0	3.00

ALL-STAR GAME RECORD

Year	League	IP.	W.	L.	Pct.	H.	R.	ER.	SO.	BB.	ERA.
1983—American		2	0	0	.000	5	2	2	0	0	9.00

Member of American League All-Star Team in 1980; did not play.

DENNIS RAY HOOD

Born July 3, 1966, at Glendale, Calif.
Height, 6.02. Weight, 170.
Throws and bats righthanded.

Led Southern League batters in strikeouts with 139 in 1988.
Led South Atlantic League outfielders in total chances with 328 in 1986.

Year	Club	League	Pos.	G.	AB.	R.	H.	2B.	3B.	HR.	RBI.	B.A.	PO.	A.	E.	F.A.
1984—Bradenton Brav...	Gulf C.	OF	49	155	16	31	7	0	1	18	.200	96	3	3	.971
1985—Bradenton Brav...	Gulf C.	OF	59	204	19	49	14	0	1	17	.240	103	8	●6	.949
1986—Sumter	S. Atl.	OF	★135	★562	104	142	25	3	7	42	.253	★305	11	12	.963
1987—Durham	Carol.	OF	120	438	73	118	19	4	13	62	.269	275	15	9	.970
1988—Greenville	South.	OF	141	525	85	135	15	●8	14	47	.257	271	21	6	.980
1989—Greenville	South.	OF	136	464	68	117	20	5	11	44	.252	275	9	8	.973

Selected by Atlanta Braves' organization in 12th round of free-agent draft, June 4, 1984.

SAMUEL LEE HORN
(Sam)

Born November 2, 1963, at Dallas, Tex.
Height, 6.05. Weight, 232.
Throws and bats lefthanded.

Shares American League record for most home runs, first two major league games (2), July 25 and 26, 1987.
Led International League in slugging percentage with .649 in 1987.
Led Carolina League in slugging percentage with .538 in 1984.
Tied for International League lead in intentional bases on balls received with 10 in 1988.

Year	Club	League	Pos.	G.	AB.	R.	H.	2B.	3B.	HR.	RBI.	B.A.	PO.	A.	E.	F.A.
1982—Elmira	NYP	1B	61	213	47	64	13	1	11	48	.300	368	29	11	.973
1983—Winston-Salem† ...	Carol.	1B	68	217	33	52	9	0	9	29	.240	363	24	10	.975
1984—Winston-Salem	Carol.	1B	127	403	67	126	22	3	21	89	.313	978	★70	★29	.973
1985—New Britain	East.	1B	134	457	64	129	★32	0	11	82	.282	751	63	★23	.973
1986—New Britain	East.	1B	100	345	41	85	13	0	8	46	.246	356	28	9	.977
1986—Pawtucket	Int.	1B	20	77	8	15	2	0	3	14	.195	61	4	0	1.000
1987—Pawtucket	Int.	1B	94	333	57	107	19	0	30	84	.321	28	2	2	.938
1987—Boston	Amer.	DH	46	158	31	44	7	0	14	34	.278	0	0	0	.000
1988—Boston	Amer.	DH	24	61	4	9	0	0	2	8	.148	0	0	0	.000
1988—Pawtucket	Int.	1B	83	279	33	65	10	0	10	31	.233	6	1	1	.875
1989—Boston‡	Amer.	1B	33	54	1	8	2	0	0	4	.148	5	0	0	1.000
1989—Pawtucket§	Int.	DH	51	164	15	38	9	1	8	27	.232	0	0	0	.000
Major League Totals—3 Years			103	273	36	61	9	0	16	46	.223	5	0	0	1.000

Selected by Boston Red Sox' organization in 1st round (16th player selected) of free-agent draft, June 7, 1982.
†On disabled list, April 28 to June 23, 1983.
‡On disabled list, June 8 to July 28, 1989; included rehabilitation disability assignment to Pawtucket, July 13 to July 28, 1989.
§Released, December 20, 1989.

RICKY NEAL HORTON
(Rick)

Born July 30, 1959, at Poughkeepsie, N.Y.
Height, 6.02. Weight, 197.
Throws and bats lefthanded.
Received bachelor of science degree in engineering from
University of Virginia, Charlottesville, Va. in 1982.
Brother of David Horton, infielder in St. Louis Cardinals' organization, 1986 and 1987.

Major League saves: 1984 (1), 1985 (1), 1986 (3), 1987 (7), 1988 (2). Total—14.
Led American Association in balks with 7 in 1983.

Year Club	League	G.	IP.	W.	L.	Pct.	H.	R.	ER.	SO.	BB.	ERA.
1980—St. Petersburg	Florida St.	6	25	0	2	.000	29	18	17	13	17	6.12
1980—Gastonia	S. Atlantic	14	42	2	4	.333	30	21	17	30	25	3.64
1981—St. Petersburg	Florida St.	28	100	7	3	.700	101	52	49	66	49	4.41
1982—Arkansas	Texas	16	108⅔	9	6	.600	83	45	38	90	52	3.15
1982—Louisville	Am. Assoc.	8	36⅓	2	3	.400	47	31	27	37	11	6.69
1983—Louisville	Am. Assoc.	30	157	10	6	.625	177	99	84	92	58	4.82
1984—St. Louis	National	37	125⅔	9	4	.692	140	53	48	76	39	3.44
1985—St. Louis	National	49	89⅔	3	2	.600	84	30	29	59	34	2.91
1986—St. Louis†	National	42	100⅓	4	3	.571	77	25	25	49	26	2.24
1986—Springfield	Midwest	1	2	0	0	.000	2	0	0	2	0	0.00
1987—St. Louis‡§	National	67	125	8	3	.727	127	58	53	55	42	3.82
1988—Chicago x	American	52	109⅓	6	10	.375	120	64	59	28	36	4.86
1988—Los Angeles	National	12	9	1	1	.500	11	7	5	8	2	5.00
1989—Los Angeles y-St. Louis	National	34	72⅓	0	3	.000	85	39	39	26	21	4.85
1989—Louisville z	Am. Assoc.	2	9	1	0	1.000	8	1	1	1	2	1.00
National League Totals—6 Years		241	522	25	16	.610	524	212	199	273	164	3.43
American League Totals—1 Year		52	109⅓	6	10	.375	120	64	59	28	36	4.86
Major League Totals—6 Years		293	631⅓	31	26	.544	644	276	258	301	200	3.68

Selected by San Francisco Giants' organization in 20th round of free-agent draft, June 7, 1977.
Selected by St. Louis Cardinals' organization in 4th round of free-agent draft, June 3, 1980.
†On disabled list, May 25 to June 24, 1986; included rehabilitation disability assignment to Springfield, June 20 to June 24, 1986.
‡Appeared as an outfielder with no chances.
§Traded with Outfielder Lance Johnson and cash to Chicago White Sox for Pitcher Jose DeLeon, February 9, 1988.
xTraded to Los Angeles Dodgers for a player to be named later, August 30, 1988; Chicago White Sox acquired Pitcher Shawn Hillegas to complete deal, September 2, 1988.
yReleased, July 16, 1989; signed by Louisville (St. Louis Cardinals' organization), July 20, 1989.
zGranted free agency, November 13, 1989; re-signed by Cardinals, December 6, 1989.

CHAMPIONSHIP SERIES RECORD

Year Club	League	G.	IP.	W.	L.	Pct.	H.	R.	ER.	SO.	BB.	ERA.
1985—St. Louis	National	3	3	0	0	.000	4	4	4	1	2	12.00
1987—St. Louis	National	1	3	0	0	.000	2	0	0	2	0	0.00
1988—Los Angeles	National	4	4⅓	0	0	.000	4	0	0	3	2	0.00
Championship Series Totals—3 Years		8	10⅓	0	0	.000	10	4	4	6	4	3.48

WORLD SERIES RECORD

Year Club	League	G.	IP.	W.	L.	Pct.	H.	R.	ER.	SO.	BB.	ERA.
1985—St. Louis	National	3	4	0	0	.000	4	3	3	5	5	6.75
1987—St. Louis	National	2	3	0	0	.000	5	2	2	1	0	6.00
World Series Totals—2 Years		5	7	0	0	.000	9	5	5	6	5	6.43

CHARLES OLIVER HOUGH

Name pronounced Huff.

(Charlie)

Born January 5, 1948, at Honolulu, Haw.
Height, 6.02. Weight, 190.
Throws and bats righthanded.
Son of Dick Hough, minor league third baseman, 1933.

Shares major league record for most strikeouts, inning (4), July 4, 1988, first inning.
Holds American League record for most balks, season (9), 1987.
Major League saves: 1970 (2), 1973 (5), 1974 (1), 1975 (4), 1976 (18), 1977 (22), 1978 (7), 1980 (1), 1981 (1). Total—61.
Led American League in hit batsmen with 19 and balks with 9 in 1987.
Led American League pitchers in games started with 40 in 1987 and tied for lead with 36 in 1984.
Led American League pitchers in complete games with 17 in 1984.
Tied for American League lead in home runs allowed with 28 in 1989.
Led Pacific Coast League in intentional bases on balls issued with 13 in 1972.
Led Pacific Coast League in saves with 18 in 1970.
Led Texas League in home runs allowed with 17 in 1969.
Named Pacific Coast League Pitcher of the Year, 1972.

Year Club	League	G.	IP.	W.	L.	Pct.	H.	R.	ER.	SO.	BB.	ERA.
1966—Ogden	Pioneer	21	68	5	●7	.417	82	56	36	68	29	4.76
1967—Santa Barbara	California	20	165	14	4	*.778	129	50	41	138	43	2.24
1967—Albuquerque	Texas	7	36	2	1	.667	57	31	28	25	10	7.00
1968—Albuquerque†	Texas	27	121	6	10	.375	145	72	53	74	26	3.94
1969—Albuquerque	Texas	27	163	10	9	.526	190	87	74	113	42	4.09
1970—Spokane	P. Coast	49	134	12	8	.600	98	43	29	90	44	1.95
1970—Los Angeles	National	8	17	0	0	.000	18	11	10	8	11	5.29
1971—Spokane‡	P. Coast	47	117	10	8	.556	95	56	51	104	52	3.92
1971—Los Angeles	National	4	4	0	0	.000	3	3	2	4	3	4.50
1972—Albuquerque§	P. Coast	58	125	14	5	.737	109	47	33	95	60	2.38
1972—Los Angeles	National	2	3	0	0	.000	2	1	1	4	2	3.00
1973—Los Angeles	National	37	72	4	2	.667	52	24	22	70	45	2.75
1974—Los Angeles	National	49	96	9	4	.692	65	45	40	63	40	3.75
1975—Los Angeles	National	38	61	3	7	.300	43	25	20	34	34	2.95

Year Club	League	G.	IP.	W.	L.	Pct.	H.	R.	ER.	SO.	BB.	ERA.
1976—Los Angeles	National	77	143	12	8	.600	102	43	35	81	77	2.20
1977—Los Angeles	National	70	127	6	12	.333	98	53	47	105	70	3.33
1978—Los Angeles	National	55	93	5	5	.500	69	38	34	66	48	3.29
1979—Los Angeles	National	42	151	7	5	.583	152	88	80	76	66	4.77
1980—Los Angeles x	National	19	32	1	3	.250	37	21	20	25	21	5.63
1980—Texas	American	16	61	2	2	.500	54	30	27	47	37	3.98
1981—Texas	American	21	82	4	1	.800	61	30	27	69	31	2.96
1982—Texas	American	34	228	16	13	.552	217	111	100	128	72	3.95
1983—Texas	American	34	252	15	13	.536	219	96	89	152	95	3.18
1984—Texas	American	36	266	16	14	.533	★260	127	111	164	94	3.76
1985—Texas	American	34	250⅓	14	16	.467	198	102	92	141	83	3.31
1986—Oklahoma City y	Am. Assoc.	1	5	0	1	.000	7	5	5	3	1	9.00
1986—Texas	American	33	230⅓	17	10	.630	188	115	97	146	89	3.79
1987—Texas	American	40	★285⅓	18	13	.581	238	★159	120	223	124	3.79
1988—Texas	American	34	252	15	16	.484	202	111	93	174	★126	3.32
1989—Texas z	American	30	182	10	13	.435	168	97	88	94	95	4.35
National League Totals—11 Years		401	799	47	46	.505	641	352	311	536	417	3.50
American League Totals—10 Years		312	2089	127	111	.534	1805	978	844	1338	846	3.64
Major League Totals—20 Years		713	2888	174	157	.526	2446	1330	1155	1874	1263	3.60

Selected by Los Angeles Dodgers' organization in 8th round of free-agent draft, June 9, 1966.

†On temporary inactive list, June 19 to July 1, 1968.

‡On temporary inactive list, July 10 to July 24, 1971.

§On temporary inactive list June 12 to June 15, July 22 to July 24 and August 7 to August 12, 1972.

xSold to Texas Rangers, July 11, 1980.

yOn Texas disabled list, March 25 to May 6, 1986; included rehabilitation disability assignment to Oklahoma City, May 2 to May 6, 1986.

zOn disabled list, July 20 to August 4, 1989.

CHAMPIONSHIP SERIES RECORD

Year Club	League	G.	IP.	W.	L.	Pct.	H.	R.	ER.	SO.	BB.	ERA.
1974—Los Angeles	National	1	2⅓	0	0	.000	4	2	2	2	0	7.71
1977—Los Angeles	National	1	2	0	0	.000	2	1	1	3	0	4.50
1978—Los Angeles	National	1	2	0	0	.000	1	1	1	1	0	4.50
Championship Series Totals—3 Years		3	6⅓	0	0	.000	7	4	4	6	0	5.68

WORLD SERIES RECORD

Tied World Series record for most wild pitches, inning and game (2), October 15, 1978 (seventh inning).

Year Club	League	G.	IP.	W.	L.	Pct.	H.	R.	ER.	SO.	BB.	ERA.
1974—Los Angeles	National	1	2	0	0	.000	0	0	0	4	1	0.00
1977—Los Angeles	National	2	5	0	0	.000	3	1	1	5	0	1.80
1978—Los Angeles	National	2	5⅓	0	0	.000	10	5	5	5	2	8.44
World Series Totals—3 Years		5	12⅓	0	0	.000	13	6	6	14	3	4.38

ALL-STAR GAME RECORD

Year League	IP.	W.	L.	Pct.	H.	R.	ER.	SO.	BB.	ERA.
1986—American	1⅔	0	0	.000	2	2	1	3	0	5.40

BATTING RECORD

Year Club	League	Pos.	G.	AB.	R.	H.	2B.	3B.	HR.	RBI.	B.A.	PO.	A.	E.	F.A.
1967—Santa Barbara	Calif.	P-1B	28	72	8	14	2	0	0	4	.194	15	25	2	.953
1968—Albuquerque	Texas	P-1B-3B	56	83	10	21	4	0	0	6	.253	43	25	4	.944
1969—Albuquerque	Texas	P-3B	31	57	10	12	0	0	1	9	.211	10	19	2	.935
1970—Spokane	P. C.	P-OF-1B	49	33	1	6	0	0	1	3	.182	7	28	3	.921
1971—Spokane	P. C.	P-OF	48	36	2	10	0	0	0	3	.278	6	20	1	.963
1972—Albuquerque	P. C.	P-OF	58	34	4	9	1	0	0	5	.265	3	27	0	1.000

STEVEN BERNARD HOWARD
(Steve)

Born December 7, 1963, at Oakland, Calif.
Height, 6.02. Weight, 205.
Throws and bats righthanded.
Attended Laney College, Oakland, Calif.

Led Pacific Coast League batters in strikeouts with 135 in 1989.
Led Southern League in being hit by pitch with 12 in 1987.
Led Northwest League batters in strikeouts with 89 in 1984.
Tied for Pacific Coast League lead in double plays by outfielders with 4 in 1989.

Year Club	League	Pos.	G.	AB.	R.	H.	2B.	3B.	HR.	RBI.	B.A.	PO.	A.	E.	F.A.
1983—Idaho Falls	Pion.	OF	61	203	40	45	4	4	6	33	.222	77	2	6	.929
1984—Madison	Midw.	OF	44	123	13	21	4	0	2	14	.171	36	0	4	.900
1984—Medford	N'west	OF	53	185	26	39	4	1	4	24	.211	55	2	5	.919
1985—Modesto	Calif.	OF	110	349	59	77	15	3	14	64	.221	101	1	11	.903
1986—Modesto†	Calif.	OF	98	302	64	70	11	4	9	53	.232	156	2	12	.929
1987—Huntsville	South.	OF	133	439	79	112	17	4	13	66	.255	197	1	●15	.930
1988—Huntsville	South.	OF	128	461	70	114	19	6	17	78	.247	211	5	11	.952
1989—Tacoma	P. C.	OF	107	341	51	83	10	2	13	60	.243	170	7	6	.967

Selected by Oakland Athletics' organization in 8th round of free-agent draft, January 11, 1983.
†On disabled list, June 30 to July 22, 1986.

THOMAS SYLVESTER HOWARD
(Tom)

Born December 11, 1964, at Middletown, O.
Height, 6.00. Weight, 200.
Throws right and bats left and righthanded.
Attended Ball State University, Muncie, Ind.

Named outfielder on THE SPORTING NEWS College Baseball All-America Team, 1986.

Year	Club	League	Pos.	G.	AB.	R.	H.	2B.	3B.	HR.	RBI.	B.A.	PO.	A.	E.	F.A.
1986—Spokane	N'west	OF	13	55	16	23	3	3	2	17	.418	24	3	0	1.000
1986—Reno	Calif.	OF	61	223	35	57	7	3	10	39	.256	104	5	6	.948
1987—Wichita	Texas	OF	113	401	72	133	27	4	14	60	.332	226	6	6	.975
1988—Wichita	Texas	OF	29	103	15	31	9	2	0	16	.301	51	2	2	.964
1988—Las Vegas	P. C.	OF	44	167	29	42	9	1	0	15	.251	74	3	2	.975
1989—Las Vegas†	P. C.	OF	80	303	45	91	18	3	3	31	.300	178	7	2	.989

Selected by San Diego Padres' organization in 1st round (11th player selected) of free-agent draft, June 2, 1986.
†On disabled list, June 5 to July 17, 1989.

JACK ROBERT HOWELL

Born August 18, 1961, at Tucson, Ariz.
Height, 6.00. Weight, 201.
Throws right and bats lefthanded.
Attended Pima Community College, Tucson, Ariz., and University of Arizona, Tucson, Ariz.

Major League stolen bases: 1985 (1), 1986 (2), 1987 (4), 1988 (2). Total—9.
Led American League third basemen in total chances with 428 in 1989.
Led California League third basemen in fielding percentage with .943, assists with 259, double plays with 23 and total chances with 368 in 1984.

Year	Club	League	Pos.	G.	AB.	R.	H.	2B.	3B.	HR.	RBI.	B.A.	PO.	A.	E.	F.A.
1983—Salem	N'west	3B-2B	21	76	23	30	2	5	3	12	.395	19	32	11	.823
1984—Redwood	Calif.	3B-1B	135	451	62	111	21	5	5	64	.246	96	260	21	.944
1985—Edmonton†	P. C.	3B-SS	79	284	55	106	22	3	13	48	.373	67	130	12	.943
1985—California	Amer.	3B	43	137	19	27	4	0	5	18	.197	33	75	8	.931
1986—Edmonton	P. C.	3B	44	156	39	56	17	3	3	28	.359	28	84	8	.933
1986—California	Amer.	3B-OF	63	151	26	41	14	2	4	21	.272	38	57	2	.979
1987—California	Amer.	OF-3B-2B	138	449	64	110	18	5	23	64	.245	185	95	7	.978
1988—California	Amer.	3B-OF	154	500	59	127	32	2	16	63	.254	97	249	17	.953
1989—California	Amer.	★3B-OF	144	474	56	108	19	4	20	52	.228	97	★322	11	★.974
Major League Totals—5 Years			542	1711	224	413	87	13	68	218	.241	450	798	45	.965

Signed as free agent by California Angels' organization, August 6, 1983.
†On disabled list, June 21 to July 7, 1985.

CHAMPIONSHIP SERIES RECORD

Year	Club	League	Pos.	G.	AB.	R.	H.	2B.	3B.	HR.	RBI.	B.A.	PO.	A.	E.	F.A.
1986—California	Amer.	PH	2	1	0	0	0	0	0	0	.000	0	0	0	.000

JAY CANFIELD HOWELL

Born November 26, 1955, at Miami, Fla.
Height, 6.03. Weight, 220.
Throws and bats righthanded.
Attended University of Colorado, Boulder, Colo.

Major League saves: 1984 (7), 1985 (29), 1986 (16), 1987 (16), 1988 (21), 1989 (28). Total—117.
Tied for American Association lead in shutouts with 2 in 1982.
Tied for American Association lead in balks with 6 in 1981.
Named American Association Pitcher of the Year, 1982.

Year	Club	League	G.	IP.	W.	L.	Pct.	H.	R.	ER.	SO.	BB.	ERA.
1976—Eugene	Northwest	13	73	5	4	.556	65	30	24	79	34	2.96
1977—Tampa	Florida St.	23	158	7	13	.350	141	60	52	99	52	2.96
1978—Nashville	Southern	28	166	9	14	.391	134	70	57	★173	55	3.09
1979—Indianapolis	Am. Assoc.	24	128	10	10	.500	121	82	73	79	84	5.13
1980—Indianapolis	Am. Assoc.	25	98	5	11	.313	95	70	55	73	71	5.05
1980—Cincinnati†	National	5	3	0	0	.000	8	5	5	1	0	15.00
1981—Iowa	Am. Assoc.	23	144	5	10	.333	141	74	60	90	62	3.75
1981—Chicago	National	10	22	2	0	1.000	23	13	12	10	10	4.91
1982—Iowa‡	Am. Assoc.	20	141⅓	13	4	★.765	102	45	37	139	48	★2.36
1982—Columbus	Int'national	5	37⅓	2	1	.667	18	13	10	33	19	2.41
1982—New York	American	6	28	2	3	.400	42	25	24	21	13	7.71
1983—New York§	American	19	82	1	5	.167	89	53	49	61	35	5.38
1984—New York x	American	61	103⅔	9	4	.692	86	33	31	109	34	2.69
1985—Oakland	American	63	98	9	8	.529	98	32	31	68	31	2.85
1986—Oakland y	American	38	53⅓	3	6	.333	53	23	20	42	23	3.38
1986—Modesto	California	2	2	0	0	.000	5	3	3	1	1	13.50
1987—Oakland z	American	36	44⅓	3	4	.429	48	30	29	35	21	5.89
1988—Los Angeles b	National	50	65	5	3	.625	44	16	15	70	21	2.08
1989—Los Angeles	National	56	79⅔	5	3	.625	60	15	14	55	22	1.58
National League Totals—4 Years		121	169⅔	12	6	.667	135	49	46	136	53	2.44
American League Totals—6 Years		223	409⅓	27	30	.474	416	196	184	336	157	4.05
Major League Totals—10 Years		344	579	39	36	.520	551	245	230	472	210	3.58

Selected by Cincinnati Reds' organization in 12th round of free-agent draft, June 5, 1973.
Selected by Cincinnati Reds' organization in 31st round of free-agent draft, June 8, 1976.
†Traded to Chicago Cubs for Catcher Mike O'Berry, October 17, 1980.
‡Traded to New York Yankees' organization, August 2, 1982, completing deal in which Chicago Cubs acquired Second Baseman Pat Tabler from New York on waivers for two players to be named later, August 19, 1981; New York acquired Pitcher Bill Caudill as partial completion of deal, April 1, 1982.
§On disabled list, August 3, 1983 through remainder of season.
xTraded with Outfielder Stan Javier and Pitchers Jose Rijo, Eric Plunk and Tim Birtsas to Oakland A's for Outfielder Rickey Henderson, Pitcher Bert Bradley and cash, December 5, 1984.
yOn disabled list, April 30 to May 18 and May 27 to July 20, 1986; included rehabilitation disability assignment to Modesto, July 11 to July 16, 1986.
zOn disabled list, August 25, 1987 through remainder of season.
aAs part of an eight-player, three-team deal, New York Mets traded Pitcher Jesse Orosco to Oakland Athletics, December 11, 1987. Oakland then traded Orosco along with Shortstop Alfredo Griffin and Pitcher Jay Howell to Los Angeles Dodgers for Pitchers Bob Welch, Matt Young and Jack Savage. Oakland then traded Savage along with Pitchers Wally Whitehurst and Kevin Tapani to New York.
bOn disabled list, June 21 to July 7, 1988.

CHAMPIONSHIP SERIES RECORD

Year Club	League	G.	IP.	W.	L.	Pct.	H.	R.	ER.	SO.	BB.	ERA.
1988—Los Angeles	National	2	⅔	0	1	.000	1	2	2	1	2	27.00

WORLD SERIES RECORD

Year Club	League	G.	IP.	W.	L.	Pct.	H.	R.	ER.	SO.	BB.	ERA.
1988—Los Angeles	National	2	2⅔	0	1	.000	3	1	1	2	1	3.38

ALL-STAR GAME RECORD

Year League	IP.	W.	L.	Pct.	H.	R.	ER.	SO.	BB.	ERA.
1987—American	2	0	1	.000	3	2	2	3	0	9.00
1989—National	1	0	0	.000	1	0	0	1	0	0.00
All-Star Game Totals—2 Years	3	0	1	.000	4	2	2	4	0	6.00

Member of American League All-Star Team in 1985; did not play.

KENNETH HOWELL JR.
(Ken)

Born November 28, 1960, at Detroit, Mich.
Height, 6.03. Weight, 228.
Throws and bats righthanded.
Attended Tuskegee Institute, Tuskegee Institute, Ala.

Major League saves: 1984 (6), 1985 (12), 1986 (12), 1987 (1). Total—31.
Led National League in wild pitches with 21 in 1989.
Tied for Texas League lead in games started by pitchers with 27 in 1983.

Year Club	League	G.	IP.	W.	L.	Pct.	H.	R.	ER.	SO.	BB.	ERA.
1982—Vero Beach	Florida St.	11	59⅔	5	4	.556	58	40	28	37	36	4.22
1983—San Antonio	Texas	27	169⅓	8	11	.421	171	98	83	116	101	4.41
1983—Albuquerque	P. Coast	1	3	0	0	.000	4	3	3	1	1	9.00
1984—Albuquerque†	P. Coast	18	72½	8	2	.800	79	48	37	58	37	4.60
1984—Los Angeles	National	32	51⅓	5	5	.500	51	21	19	54	9	3.33
1985—Los Angeles	National	56	86	4	7	.364	66	41	36	85	35	3.77
1986—Los Angeles	National	62	97⅔	6	12	.333	86	48	42	104	63	3.87
1987—Los Angeles	National	40	55	3	4	.429	54	32	30	60	29	4.91
1987—Los Angeles	P. Coast	2	13	1	0	1.000	6	1	0	13	7	0.00
1988—Bakersfield‡	California	3	13⅔	0	1	.000	8	5	2	13	9	1.32
1988—Albuquerque	P. Coast	18	107⅓	10	1	*.909	92	43	39	95	42	3.27
1988—Los Angeles§x	National	4	12⅔	0	1	.000	16	10	9	12	4	6.39
1989—Philadelphia	National	33	204	12	12	.500	155	84	78	164	86	3.44
Major League Totals—6 Years		227	506⅔	30	41	.423	428	236	214	479	226	3.80

Selected by Los Angeles Dodgers' organization in 3rd round of free-agent draft, June 7, 1982.
†On disabled list, April 7 to April 17, 1984.
‡On Los Angeles disabled list, March 20 to May 25 and June 17 to July 8, 1988; included rehabilitation disability assignment to Bakersfield, May 7 to May 11 and May 17 to May 25, 1988; and to Albuquerque, May 12 to May 16 and June 24 to July 8, 1988.
§Traded with Pitcher Brian Holton and Shortstop Juan Bell to Baltimore Orioles for First Baseman Eddie Murray, December 4, 1988.
xTraded with Pitcher Gordon Dillard by Baltimore Orioles to Philadelphia Phillies for Outfielder Phil Bradley, December 8, 1988.

CHAMPIONSHIP SERIES RECORD

Year Club	League	G.	IP.	W.	L.	Pct.	H.	R.	ER.	SO.	BB.	ERA.
1985—Los Angeles	National	1	2	0	0	.000	0	0	0	2	0	0.00

DANN PAUL JOHN HOWITT

Born February 13, 1964, at Battle Creek, Mich.
Height, 6.05. Weight, 205.
Throws right and bats lefthanded.
Attended Michigan State University, East Lansing, Mich.,
and California State University, Fullerton, Calif.
Brother of Shaun Howitt, outfielder in Kansas City Royals' organization, 1972.

Led Southern League in total bases with 253 in 1989.
Led Southern League first basemen in fielding percentage with .992 in 1989.
Led California League outfielders in double plays with 6 in 1987.
Tied for Northwest League lead in double plays by outfielders with 2 in 1986.

Year	Club	League	Pos.	G.	AB.	R.	H.	2B.	3B.	HR.	RBI.	B.A.	PO.	A.	E.	F.A.
1986—Medford		N'west	OF	66	208	36	66	9	2	6	37	.317	83	5	4	.957
1987—Modesto		Calif.	OF-1B	109	336	44	70	11	2	8	42	.208	263	23	6	.979
1988—Modesto		Calif.	OF-1B	132	480	75	121	20	2	18	86	.252	475	42	12	.977
1988—Tacoma		P. C.	OF-1B	4	15	1	2	1	0	0	0	.133	14	0	0	1.000
1989—Huntsville		South.	1B-OF-P	138	509	78	143	28	2	26	111	.281	965	74	9	.991
1989—Oakland		Amer.	1B-OF	3	3	0	0	0	0	0	0	.000	2	0	0	1.000
Major League Totals—1 Year				3	3	0	0	0	0	0	0	.000	2	0	0	1.000

Selected by Oakland Athletics' organization in 18th round of free-agent draft, June 2, 1986.

PITCHING RECORD

Year	Club	League	G.	IP.	W.	L.	Pct.	H.	R.	ER.	SO.	BB.	ERA.
1989—Huntsville		Southern	2	2	0	0	.000	2	1	0	2	0	0.00

KENT ALAN HRBEK

Name pronounced HER-beck.

Born May 21, 1960, at Minneapolis, Minn.
Height, 6.04. Weight, 250.
Throws right and bats lefthanded.

Major League stolen bases: 1982 (3), 1983 (4), 1984 (1), 1985 (1), 1986 (2), 1987 (5), 1989 (3). Total—19.
Led California League in slugging percentage with .630 and tied for lead in sacrifice flies with 9 in 1981.
Named California League Most Valuable Player, 1981.

Year	Club	League	Pos.	G.	AB.	R.	H.	2B.	3B.	HR.	RBI.	B.A.	PO.	A.	E.	F.A.
1979—Elizabethton†‡		Appal.	1B	17	59	5	12	2	0	1	11	.203	126	11	2	.986
1980—Wisc. Rapids§		Midw.	1B	115	419	74	112	16	0	19	76	.267	1005	81	*20	.982
1981—Visalia		Calif.	1B	121	462	119	175	25	5	27	111	*.379	1034	53	11	*.989
1981—Minnesota		Amer.	1B	24	67	5	16	5	0	1	7	.239	124	4	0	1.000
1982—Minnesota		Amer.	1B	140	532	82	160	21	4	23	92	.301	1174	88	9	.993
1983—Minnesota		Amer.	1B	141	515	75	153	41	5	16	84	.297	1151	89	13	.990
1984—Minnesota		Amer.	1B	149	559	80	174	31	3	27	107	.311	1320	99	14	.990
1985—Minnesota		Amer.	1B	158	593	78	165	31	2	21	93	.278	1339	114	8	.995
1986—Minnesota		Amer.	1B	149	550	85	147	27	1	29	91	.267	1218	104	10	.992
1987—Minnesota		Amer.	1B	143	477	85	136	20	1	34	90	.285	1179	68	5	.996
1988—Minnesota		Amer.	1B	143	510	75	159	31	0	25	76	.312	842	57	3	.997
1989—Minnesota xy		Amer.	1B	109	375	59	102	17	0	25	84	.272	723	60	4	.995
Major League Totals—9 Years				1156	4178	624	1212	224	16	201	724	.290	9070	683	66	.993

Selected by Minnesota Twins' organization in 17th round of free-agent draft, June 6, 1978.
†On Wisconsin Rapids disabled list, April 13 to June 21, 1979.
‡On Elizabethton disabled list, July 22 to September 6, 1979.
§On disabled list, May 27 to June 6, 1980.
xOn disabled list, May 16 to June 26, 1989.
yGranted free agency, November 13, 1989; re-signed by Twins, December 6, 1989.

CHAMPIONSHIP SERIES RECORD

Year	Club	League	Pos.	G.	AB.	R.	H.	2B.	3B.	HR.	RBI.	B.A.	PO.	A.	E.	F.A.
1987—Minnesota		Amer.	1B	5	20	4	3	0	0	1	1	.150	40	3	0	1.000

WORLD SERIES RECORD

Shares World Series records for most grand slams, game (1), October 24, 1987; most runs batted in, inning (4), October 24, 1987, sixth inning.

Year	Club	League	Pos.	G.	AB.	R.	H.	2B.	3B.	HR.	RBI.	B.A.	PO.	A.	E.	F.A.
1987—Minnesota		Amer.	1B	7	24	4	5	0	0	1	6	.208	68	2	0	1.000

ALL-STAR GAME RECORD

Year	League	Pos.	AB.	R.	H.	2B.	3B.	HR.	RBI.	B.A.	PO.	A.	E.	F.A.
1982—American		PH	1	0	0	0	0	0	0	.000	0	0	0	.000

GLENN DEE HUBBARD

Born September 25, 1957, at Hahn Air Force Base, Germany.
Height, 5.07. Weight, 169.
Throws and bats righthanded.

Shares major league record for most assists by second baseman, nine-inning game (12), April 14, 1985.
Major League stolen bases: 1978 (2), 1980 (7), 1981 (4), 1982 (4), 1983 (3), 1984 (4), 1985 (4), 1986 (3), 1987 (1), 1988 (1), 1989 (2). Total—35.
Led National League in sacrifice hits with 20 in 1982.
Led National League second basemen in total chances with 888 in 1985.
Led National League second basemen in double plays with 111 in 1982, 127 in 1985 and 114 in 1987.
Led Appalachian League third basemen in fielding percentage with .932 in 1975.
Named second baseman on THE SPORTING NEWS National League All-Star Team, 1983.

Year	Club	League	Pos.	G.	AB.	R.	H.	2B.	3B.	HR.	RBI.	B.A.	PO.	A.	E.	F.A.
1975—Kingsport		Appal.	3B-SS-2B	53	136	31	39	6	4	2	21	.287	44	88	9	.936
1976—Kingsport		Appal.	2B	37	136	29	40	8	0	2	15	.294	96	122	1	.995

Year	Club	League	Pos.	G.	AB.	R.	H.	2B.	3B.	HR.	RBI.	B.A.	PO.	A.	E.	F.A.
1976—Greenwood†	W. Car.		2B	33	126	26	40	8	1	4	21	.317	62	83	6	.960
1977—Greenwood	W. Car.		2B	45	182	39	70	10	1	5	44	.385	114	133	4	.984
1977—Savannah	South.		2B	87	298	49	67	15	2	6	32	.225	209	239	10	.978
1978—Richmond	Int.		2B	80	301	58	101	12	3	14	36	.336	208	243	11	.976
1978—Atlanta‡	Nat.		2B	44	163	15	42	4	0	2	13	.258	102	130	5	.979
1979—Richmond	Int.		3B-2B	34	125	21	42	5	1	2	17	.336	83	109	7	.965
1979—Atlanta	Nat.		2B	97	325	34	75	12	0	3	29	.231	193	268	●15	.968
1980—Richmond	Int.		2B	38	143	23	45	11	2	2	25	.315	89	127	4	.982
1980—Atlanta	Nat.		2B	117	431	55	107	21	3	9	43	.248	268	405	15	.978
1981—Atlanta	Nat.		2B	99	361	39	85	13	5	6	33	.235	188	344	5	.991
1982—Atlanta	Nat.		2B	145	532	75	132	25	1	9	59	.248	312	505	14	.983
1983—Atlanta	Nat.		2B	148	517	65	136	24	6	12	70	.263	313	484	12	.985
1984—Atlanta	Nat.		2B	120	397	53	93	27	2	9	43	.234	237	405	8	.988
1985—Atlanta	Nat.		2B	142	439	51	102	21	0	5	39	.232	339	★539	10	.989
1986—Atlanta	Nat.		2B	143	408	42	94	16	1	4	36	.230	282	487	19	.976
1987—Atlanta§	Nat.		2B	141	443	69	117	33	2	5	38	.264	284	★478	11	.986
1988—Oakland x	Amer.		2B	105	294	35	75	12	2	3	33	.255	195	267	6	.987
1989—Oakland yz	Amer.		2B	53	131	12	26	6	0	3	12	.198	82	132	7	.968
National League Totals—10 Years				1196	4016	498	983	196	20	64	403	.245	2518	4045	114	.983
American League Totals—2 Years				158	425	47	101	18	2	6	45	.238	277	399	13	.981
Major League Totals—12 Years				1354	4441	545	1084	214	22	70	448	.244	2795	4444	127	.983

Selected by Atlanta Braves' organization in 20th round of free-agent draft, June 4, 1975.

†On temporary inactive list, May 17 to June 22, 1976.

‡On disabled list, July 22 to August 23, 1978.

§Granted free agency, November 9, 1987; signed by Oakland Athletics, January 11, 1988.

xOn disabled list, March 26 to April 15, 1988.

yOn disabled list, May 16 to May 31, 1989.

zReleased, July 31, 1989.

CHAMPIONSHIP SERIES RECORD

Year	Club	League	Pos.	G.	AB.	R.	H.	2B.	3B.	HR.	RBI.	B.A.	PO.	A.	E.	F.A.
1982—Atlanta	Nat.		2B	3	9	1	2	0	0	0	1	.222	4	11	0	1.000

WORLD SERIES RECORD

Year	Club	League	Pos.	G.	AB.	R.	H.	2B.	3B.	HR.	RBI.	B.A.	PO.	A.	E.	F.A.
1988—Oakland	Amer.		2B	4	12	2	3	0	0	0	0	.250	5	7	1	.923

ALL-STAR GAME RECORD

Year	League	Pos.	AB.	R.	H.	2B.	3B.	HR.	RBI.	B.A.	PO.	A.	E.	F.A.
1983—National		2B	1	0	1	0	0	0	0	1.000	0	0	0	.000

REX ALLEN HUDLER

Born September 2, 1960, at Tempe, Ariz.
Height, 6.02. Weight, 180.
Throws and bats righthanded.

Major League stolen bases: 1986 (1), 1988 (29), 1989 (15). Total—45.

Led International League second basemen in double plays with 95 in 1984.

Year	Club	League	Pos.	G.	AB.	R.	H.	2B.	3B.	HR.	RBI.	B.A.	PO.	A.	E.	F.A.
1978 Oneonta	NYP		SS	58	221	33	62	5	5	0	24	.281	123	21	22	.906
1979—Fort Lauderdale†	Fla. St.		S-3-2-O	116	414	37	104	14	1	1	25	.251	164	314	45	.914
1980—Fort Lauderdale‡	Fla. St.		3-2-O-1	37	125	14	26	4	0	0	6	.208	55	71	5	.962
1980—Greensboro	S. Atl.		2B	20	75	7	17	3	1	2	9	.227	51	52	5	.954
1981—Fort Lauderdale§	Fla. St.		2-S-S-O	79	259	35	77	11	1	2	26	.297	104	238	19	.947
1982—Nashville	South.		2B-SS-OF	89	299	27	71	14	1	0	24	.237	136	219	20	.947
1982—Fort Lauderdale	Fla. St.		2B	9	32	2	8	1	0	1	6	.250	23	25	2	.960
1983—Fort Lauderdale	Fla. St.		2B-3B-SS	91	345	55	93	15	2	2	50	.270	195	245	15	.967
1983—Columbus	Int.		2B-3B-SS	40	118	17	36	5	0	1	11	.305	55	95	4	.974
1984—Columbus	Int.		2B	114	394	49	115	26	1	1	35	.292	266	348	16	.975
1984—New York	Amer.		2B	9	7	2	1	1	0	0	0	.143	4	7	0	1.000
1985—Columbus	Int.		2-S-O-3-1	106	380	62	95	13	4	3	18	.250	192	234	17	.962
1985—New York x	Amer.		2B-1B-SS	20	51	4	8	0	1	0	1	.157	42	51	2	.979
1986—Rochester	Int.		2-3-O-S	77	219	29	57	12	3	2	13	.260	135	191	15	.956
1986—Baltimore	Amer.		2B-3B	14	1	1	0	0	0	0	0	.000	2	3	1	.833
1987—Rochester yz	Int.		OF-2B-SS	31	106	22	27	5	1	5	10	.255	51	15	2	.971
1988—Indianapolis	A. A.		O-2-S-3	67	234	36	71	11	3	7	25	.303	102	96	4	.980
1988—Montreal	Nat.		2B-SS-OF	77	216	38	59	14	2	4	14	.273	116	168	10	.966
1989—Montreal	Nat.		2B-OF-SS	92	155	21	38	7	0	6	13	.245	59	59	7	.944
American League Totals—3 Years				43	59	7	9	1	1	0	1	.153	48	61	3	.973
National League Totals—2 Years				169	371	59	97	21	2	10	27	.261	175	227	17	.959
Major League Totals—5 Years				212	430	66	106	22	3	10	28	.247	223	288	20	.962

Selected by New York Yankees' organization in 1st round (18th player selected) of free-agent draft, June 6, 1978.

†On disabled list, May 18 to May 31, 1979

‡On disabled list, May 10 to June 15, 1980.

§On disabled list, May 11 to June 11, 1981.

xTraded with Pitcher Rich Bordi to Baltimore Orioles for Oufielder Gary Roenicke and a player to be named later, December 12, 1985; New York Yankees acquired Outfielder Leo Hernandez to complete deal, December 16, 1985.

yOn Baltimore disabled list, March 23 to June 16, 1987; included rehabilitation disability assignment to Rochester,

May 28 to June 16, 1987.

zGranted free agency, October 15, 1987; signed by Indianapolis (Montreal Expos' organization) December 18, 1987.

CHARLES LYNN HUDSON

Born March 16, 1959, at Ennis, Tex.
Height, 6.03. Weight, 185.
Throws right and bats left and righthanded.
Received bachelor of business administration degree in management from
Prairie View A&M University, Prairie View, Tex., in 1981.

Major League saves: 1988 (2).
Tied for Carolina League lead in shutouts with 3 in 1982.
Tied for Carolina League lead in games started by pitchers with 14 in 1981.
Named Carolina League Pitcher of the Year, 1982.

Year Club	League	G.	IP.	W.	L.	Pct.	H.	R.	ER.	SO.	BB.	ERA.
1981—Helena	Pioneer	14	87	5	5	.500	92	53	37	67	27	3.83
1982—Peninsula	Carolina	27	185	●15	5	.750	143	56	38	147	64	*1.85
1983—Portland	P. Coast	10	64	6	3	.667	48	19	19	51	16	2.67
1983—Philadelphia	National	26	169⅓	8	8	.500	158	73	63	101	53	3.35
1984—Philadelphia†	National	30	173⅔	9	11	.450	181	101	78	94	52	4.04
1985—Philadelphia	National	38	193	8	13	.381	188	92	81	122	74	3.78
1986—Philadelphia‡	National	33	144	7	10	.412	165	87	79	82	58	4.94
1987—New York	American	35	154⅔	11	7	.611	137	63	62	100	57	3.61
1987—Columbus	Int'national	5	13⅔	0	2	.000	22	11	9	13	5	5.93
1988—New York§x	American	28	106⅓	6	6	.500	93	53	53	58	36	4.49
1989—Detroit yz	American	18	66⅔	1	5	.167	75	49	47	23	31	6.35
1989—Toledo a	Int'national	1	4	0	0	.000	3	2	2	4	1	4.50
National League Totals—4 Years		127	680	32	42	.432	692	353	301	399	237	3.98
American League Totals—3 Years		81	327⅔	18	18	.500	305	165	162	181	124	4.45
Major League Totals—7 Years		208	1007⅔	50	60	.455	997	518	463	580	361	4.14

Selected by Philadelphia Phillies' organization in 12th round of free-agent draft, June 8, 1981.

†On disabled list, August 10 to September 1, 1984.

‡Traded with Pitcher Jeff Knox to New York Yankees for Outfielder Mike Easler and Infielder Tom Barrett, December 11, 1986.

§On disabled list, July 19 to August 22, 1988.

xTraded to Detroit Tigers for Infielder Tom Brookens, March 23, 1989.

yOn disabled list, May 15 to June 14, 1989; included rehabilitation disability assignment to Toledo, June 8 to June 14, 1989.

zOn disqualified list, August 19, 1989 through remainder of season.

aGranted free agency, November 13, 1989.

CHAMPIONSHIP SERIES RECORD

Year Club	League	G.	IP.	W.	L.	Pct.	H.	R.	ER.	SO.	BB.	ERA.
1983—Philadelphia	National	1	9	1	0	1.000	4	2	2	9	2	2.00

WORLD SERIES RECORD

Year Club	League	G.	IP.	W.	L.	Pct.	H.	R.	ER.	SO.	BB.	ERA.
1983—Philadelphia	National	2	8⅓	0	2	.000	9	8	8	6	1	8.64

MICHAEL KALE HUFF
(Mike)

Born August 11, 1963, at Honolulu, Haw.
Height, 6.01. Weight, 180.
Throws and bats righthanded.
Received bachelor of science degree in industrial
engineering from Northwestern University, Evanston, Ill., in 1985.

Tied for Texas League lead in double plays by outfielders with 4 in 1988.

Year Club	League	Pos.	G.	AB.	R.	H.	2B.	3B.	HR.	RBI.	B.A.	PO.	A.	E.	F.A.
1985—Great Falls	Pion.	OF	●70	247	70	78	6	6	0	35	.316	120	5	5	.962
1986—Vero Beach	Fla. St.	OF	113	362	73	106	6	8	2	32	.293	257	10	1	.996
1987—San Antonio†	Texas	OF	31	135	23	42	5	1	3	18	.311	52	2	2	.964
1988—San Antonio	Texas	OF	102	395	68	120	18	10	2	40	.304	222	12	2	.992
1988—Albuquerque	P. C.	OF	2	4	0	1	1	0	0	0	.250	2	0	0	1.000
1989—Albuquerque	P. C.	OF-2B	115	471	75	150	29	7	10	78	.318	209	13	2	.991
1989—Los Angeles	Nat.	OF	12	25	4	5	1	0	1	2	.200	18	0	0	1.000
Major League Totals—1 Year			12	25	4	5	1	0	1	2	.200	18	0	0	1.000

Selected by Los Angeles Dodgers' organization in 16th round of free-agent draft, June 3, 1985.

†On disabled list, May 11, 1987 through remainder of season.

KEITH WILLS HUGHES

Born September 12, 1963, at Bryn Mawr, Pa.
Height, 6.03. Weight, 210.
Throws and bats lefthanded.

Major League stolen bases: 1988 (1).
Tied for South Atlantic League lead in intentional bases on balls received with 5 in 1983.

Year Club	League	Pos.	G.	AB.	R.	H.	2B.	3B.	HR.	RBI.	B.A.	PO.	A.	E.	F.A.
1982—Bend	N'west	OF	55	179	29	46	10	2	3	26	.257	90	6	5	.950
1983—Spartanburg	S. Atl.	OF-1B	131	484	80	159	31	4	15	90	.329	171	5	7	.962
1984—Reading†	East.	OF-1B	70	230	35	60	7	5	2	20	.261	117	7	9	.932
1984—Nashville	South.	OF	21	50	6	9	0	0	0	5	.180	19	0	0	1.000
1985—Albany	East.	OF-2B	104	361	53	97	22	5	10	54	.269	218	18	3	.988
1985—Columbus	Int.	OF	18	54	7	16	4	0	3	8	.296	25	0	2	.926
1986—Albany‡	East.	OF-1B	94	323	44	99	21	3	7	37	.307	247	17	7	.974
1986—Columbus	Int.	OF	2	8	0	1	0	0	0	0	.125	6	0	1	.857
1987—Columbus-Maine..	Int.	OF-1B	90	316	48	93	15	4	17	57	.294	149	2	7	.956
1987—New York§	Amer.	PH	4	4	0	0	0	0	0	0	.000	0	0	0	.000
1987—Philadelphia x	Nat.	OF	37	76	8	20	2	0	0	10	.263	26	0	1	.963
1988—Rochester	Int.	OF	77	274	44	74	13	2	7	49	.270	159	2	3	.982
1988—Baltimore	Amer.	OF	41	108	10	21	4	2	2	14	.194	59	4	2	.969
1989—Rochester yz	Int.	OF-1B	83	285	44	78	20	4	2	43	.274	180	7	5	.974
American League Totals—2 Years			45	112	10	21	4	2	2	14	.188	59	4	2	.969
National League Totals—1 Year			37	76	8	20	2	0	0	10	.263	26	0	1	.963
Major League Totals—2 Years			82	188	18	41	6	2	2	24	.218	85	4	3	.967

Signed as free agent by Philadelphia Phillies' organization, August 24, 1981.
†Traded with Pitcher Marty Bystrom to New York Yankees for Pitcher Shane Rawley, June 30, 1984.
‡On disabled list, July 22 to August 26, 1986.
§Traded with Infielder Shane Turner to Philadelphia Phillies' organization for Outfielder Mike Easler, June 10, 1987.
xTraded with Infielder Rick Schu and Outfielder Jeff Stone to Baltimore Orioles for Outfielder Mike Young and a player to be named later, March 21, 1988; Philadelphia Phillies acquired Outfielder Frank Bellino to complete deal, June 14, 1988.
yOn disabled list, July 5, 1989 through remainder of season.
zTraded with Pitcher Cesar Mejia to New York Mets for Pitcher John Mitchell and Outfielder Joaquin Contreras, December 5, 1989.

MARK LAWRENCE HUISMANN

Born May 11, 1958, at Lincoln, Neb.
Height, 6.03. Weight, 195.
Throws and bats righthanded.
Received bachelor of science degree in business and finance from
Colorado State University, Fort Collins, Colo., in 1980.

Major League saves: 1984 (3), 1986 (5), 1987 (2), 1989 (1). Total—11.
Led International League in games finished in relief with 45 in 1988.
Led American Association in saves with 33 and games finished in relief with 56 in 1985.
Named American Association Pitcher of the Year, 1985.

Year Club	League	G.	IP.	W.	L.	Pct.	H.	R.	ER.	SO.	BB.	ERA.
1980—Sarasota Royals-Blue	Gulf Coast	28	59	1	2	.333	50	20	16	46	14	2.44
1981—Charleston	S. Atlantic	28	44	3	2	.600	36	16	8	42	17	1.64
1981—Fort Myers	Florida St.	14	21	3	1	.750	15	9	8	19	16	3.43
1982—Fort Myers	Florida St.	14	23	3	1	.750	16	1	1	21	4	0.39
1982—Jacksonville	Southern	36	54⅔	4	4	.500	52	18	13	60	15	2.14
1983—Jacksonville	Southern	37	61⅓	6	3	.667	60	25	22	46	25	3.23
1983—Omaha	Am. Assoc.	17	24⅓	0	2	.000	16	7	5	25	9	1.85
1983—Kansas City	American	13	30⅔	2	1	.667	29	20	19	20	17	5.58
1984—Kansas City	American	38	75	3	3	.500	84	38	35	54	21	4.20
1984—Omaha	Am. Assoc.	15	19	2	0	1.000	11	0	0	18	5	0.00
1985—Omaha	Am. Assoc.	+59	89⅓	5	5	.500	70	20	20	70	14	2.01
1985—Kansas City	American	9	18⅔	1	0	1.000	14	4	4	9	3	1.93
1986—Kansas City†-Seattle	American	46	97⅓	3	4	.429	98	47	41	72	25	3.79
1987—Seattle‡-Cleveland	American	26	50	2	3	.400	48	32	28	38	12	5.04
1987—Buffalo§	Am. Assoc.	13	33⅓	1	1	.500	43	32	28	31	8	7.56
1988—Toledo	Int'national	48	57⅔	4	6	.400	50	20	12	61	15	1.87
1988—Detroit x	American	5	5⅓	1	0	1.000	6	3	3	6	2	5.06
1989—Rochester	Int'national	16	21	2	1	.667	9	4	4	20	3	1.71
1989—Baltimore yz	American	8	11⅓	0	0	.000	13	8	8	13	0	6.35
Major League Totals—7 Years		145	288⅓	12	11	.522	292	152	138	214	80	4.31

Selected by Chicago Cubs' organization in 23rd round of free-agent draft, June 5, 1979.
Signed as free agent by Kansas City Royals' organization, June 16, 1980.
†Traded to Seattle Mariners for Catcher Terry Bell, May 21, 1986.
‡Traded to Cleveland Indians for Outfielder Dave Gallagher, May 12, 1987.
§Released, March 17, 1988; signed by Toledo (Detroit Tigers' organization), March 23, 1988.
xReleased, February 22, 1989; signed by Rochester (Baltimore Orioles' organization), March 1, 1989.
yOn disabled list, June 11, 1989 through remainder of season.
zReleased, October 3, 1989.

CHAMPIONSHIP SERIES RECORD

Year Club	League	G.	IP.	W.	L.	Pct.	H.	R.	ER.	SO.	BB.	ERA.
1984—Kansas City	American	1	2⅔	0	0	.000	6	3	2	2	1	6.75

—DID YOU KNOW—

That the Oakland Athletics had the best record on grass (87-49) in 1989 while the Philadelphia Phillies had the worst (14-28)?

TIMOTHY CRAIG HULETT

Name pronounced HUGH-lit.

(Tim)

Born January 12, 1960, at Springfield, Ill.
Height, 6.00. Weight, 195.
Throws and bats righthanded.
Attended Miami-Dade Community College (North), Miami, Fla.,
and University of South Florida, Tampa, Fla.

Major League stolen bases: 1983 (1), 1984 (1), 1985 (6), 1986 (4). Total—12.
Tied for American League lead in errors by third basemen with 23 in 1985.
Led American Association in sacrifice flies with 9 in both 1983 and 1988.
Led International League third basemen in double plays with 23 in 1989.
Led American Association second basemen in total chances with 730 in 1983.
Led Eastern League second basemen in putouts with 343, assists with 386, double plays with 95, fielding percentage with .975 and total chances with 748 in 1982.
Led Eastern League second basemen in putouts with 332, assists with 415, double plays with 112 and total chances with 763 in 1981.

Year Club	League	Pos.	G.	AB.	R.	H.	2B.	3B.	HR.	RBI.	B.A.	PO.	A.	E.	F.A.
1980—Glens Falls	East.	SS	6	23	2	4	0	0	0	0	.174	14	13	2	.931
1980—Iowa	A. A.	3B	3	8	1	2	0	0	0	0	.250	0	6	3	.667
1980—Appleton	Midw.	2B-3B-SS	79	278	49	72	11	1	13	47	.259	162	258	17	.961
1981—Glens Falls	East.	2B-3B	134	437	59	99	27	1	10	55	.227	333	422	16	.979
1982—Glens Falls	East.	2B-SS	•140	★536	★113	145	28	5	22	87	.271	352	398	21	.973
1983—Denver	A. A.	2B	133	477	77	130	19	4	21	88	.273	★286	★424	★20	.973
1983—Chicago	Amer.	2B	6	5	0	1	0	0	0	0	.200	8	6	2	.875
1984—Chicago	Amer.	3B-2B	8	7	1	0	0	0	0	0	.000	4	15	0	1.000
1984—Denver	A. A.	2B-3B-SS	139	475	72	125	32	6	16	80	.263	269	371	28	.958
1985—Chicago	Amer.	3B-2B-OF	141	395	52	106	19	4	5	37	.268	117	256	24	.940
1986—Chicago	Amer.	3B-2B.	150	520	53	120	16	5	17	44	.231	179	331	15	.971
1987—Chicago	Amer.	3B-2B	68	240	20	52	10	0	7	28	.217	55	142	9	.956
1987—Hawaii†	P. C.	3B-2B	42	157	13	37	5	2	1	24	.236	47	81	11	.921
1988—Indianapolis‡	A. A.	3B-2B	126	427	36	100	29	2	7	59	.234	118	211	25	.929
1989—Rochester	Int.	3-S-2-P	122	461	61	129	32	12	3	50	.280	149	289	20	.956
1989—Baltimore	Amer.	2B-3B	33	97	12	27	5	0	3	18	.278	70	71	4	.972
Major League Totals—6 Years			406	1264	138	306	50	9	32	127	.242	433	821	54	.959

Selected by Texas Rangers' organization in 39th round of free-agent draft, June 6, 1978.
Selected by Chicago White Sox' organization in secondary phase of free-agent draft, January 8, 1980.
†Traded to Montreal Expos for a player to be named later, April 13, 1988; Chicago White Sox acquired Second Baseman Edgar Caceres to complete deal, June 15, 1988.
‡Granted free agency, October 15, 1988; signed by Rochester (Baltimore Orioles' organization), November 21, 1988.

PITCHING RECORD

Year Club	League	G.	IP.	W.	L.	Pct.	H.	R.	ER.	SO.	BB.	ERA.
1989—Rochester	Int'national	1	⅔	0	0	.000	0	0	0	0	0	0.00

TODD RANDOLPH HUNDLEY

Born May 27, 1969, at Martinsville, Va.
Height, 5.11. Weight, 170.
Throws right and bats left and righthanded.
Attended William Rainey Harper College, Palatine, Ill.
Son of Randy Hundley, catcher with San Francisco Giants, Chicago Cubs,
Minnesota Twins and San Diego Padres, 1964 through 1977; and minor league manager
in Chicago Cubs' organization, 1979 and 1980.

Led South Atlantic League in intentional bases on balls received with 10 and grounded into double plays with 20 in 1989.
Led South Atlantic League catchers in putouts with 826 and total chances with 930 in 1989.

Year Club	League	Pos.	G.	AB.	R.	H.	2B.	3B.	HR.	RBI.	B.A.	PO.	A.	E.	F.A.
1987—Little Falls	NYP	C	34	103	12	15	4	0	1	10	.146	181	25	7	.967
1988—Little Falls	NYP	C	52	176	23	33	8	0	2	18	.188	345	54	8	.980
1988—St. Lucie	Fla. St.	C	1	1	0	0	0	0	0	0	.000	4	0	1	.800
1989—Columbia	S. Atl.	C-OF	125	439	67	118	23	4	11	66	.269	829	91	13	.986

Selected by New York Mets' organization in 2nd round of free-agent draft, June 2, 1987.

BERTRAM O'NEAL HUNTER

(Bert)

Born August 23, 1967, at Riverside, Calif.
Height, 6.04. Weight, 200.
Throws right and bats left and righthanded.

Led Florida State League batters in strikeouts with 148 in 1988.

Year Club	League	Pos.	G.	AB.	R.	H.	2B.	3B.	HR.	RBI.	B.A.	PO.	A.	E.	F.A.
1985—Sarasota Astros†	Gulf C.	OF	56	210	17	44	4	0	1	17	.210	99	3	5	.953
1986—Asheville†	S. Atl.	OF	54	144	24	30	5	3	1	18	.208	80	4	1	.988
1986—Auburn†	NYP	OF	70	250	39	59	11	1	5	27	.236	129	4	4	.971
1987—Asheville†	S. Atl.	OF	130	473	★105	124	26	7	10	71	.262	266	15	12	.959
1988—Osceola†	Fla. St.	OF-1B	133	★524	86	122	24	4	3	50	.233	358	14	5	.987

Year Club	League	Pos.	G.	AB.	R.	H.	2B.	3B.	HR.	RBI.	B.A.	PO.	A.	E.	F.A.
1989—Columbus............... South.		1B-OF	50	154	16	28	1	1	0	13	.182	298	16	5	.984
1989—Osceola................... Fla. St.		OF	85	343	52	83	10	7	2	25	.242	168	8	5	.972

Selected by Houston Astros' organization in 2nd round of free-agent draft, June 3, 1985.
†Batted righthanded only.

BRIAN RONALD HUNTER

Born March 4, 1968, at El Toro, Calif.
Height, 6.00. Weight, 195.
Throws left and bats righthanded.
Attended Cerritos College, Norwalk, Calif.

Tied for Southern League lead in sacrifice flies with 9 in 1989.
Led Midwest League first basemen in errors with 21 in 1988.
Led Appalachian League first basemen in double plays with 43 in 1987.

Year Club	League	Pos.	G.	AB.	R.	H.	2B.	3B.	HR.	RBI.	B.A.	PO.	A.	E.	F.A.
1987—Pulaski .... Appal.		1B-OF	65	251	38	58	10	2	8	30	.231	498	29	11	.975
1988—Burlington .... Midw.		1B-OF	117	417	58	108	17	0	●22	71	.259	987	69	22	.980
1988—Durham................. Carol.		OF-1B	13	49	13	17	3	0	3	9	.347	52	6	0	1.000
1989—Greenville .... South.		OF-1B	124	451	57	114	19	2	19	82	.253	248	15	4	.985

Selected by Atlanta Braves' organization in 8th round of free-agent draft, June 2, 1987.

BRUCE VEE HURST

Born March 24, 1958, at St. George, Utah.
Height, 6.03. Weight, 215.
Throws and bats lefthanded.
Attended Dixie College, St. George, Utah.

Shares major league record for fewest complete games for leader, season (10), 1989.
Led American League in balks with 4 in 1985.
Tied for National League lead in complete games with 10 in 1989.

Year Club	League	G.	IP.	W.	L.	Pct.	H.	R.	ER.	SO.	BB.	ERA.
1976—Elmira............................... NYP		9	42	3	2	.600	25	18	14	40	38	3.00
1977—Winter Haven†........................... Florida St.		13	91	5	4	.556	77	28	21	69	25	2.08
1978—Bristol‡................................. Eastern		6	33	1	3	.250	32	15	10	35	17	2.73
1979—Winter Haven....................... Florida St.		12	84	8	2	.800	57	22	18	64	20	1.93
1979—Bristol................................... Eastern		16	113	9	4	.692	108	56	45	91	49	3.58
1980—Pawtucket .... Int'national		17	105	8	6	.571	101	52	46	54	50	3.94
1980—Boston................................. American		12	31	2	2	.500	39	33	31	16	16	9.00
1981—Pawtucket .... Int'national		32	157	12	7	.632	143	68	50	99	71	2.87
1981—Boston................................. American		5	23	2	0	1.000	23	11	11	11	12	4.30
1982—Boston................................. American		28	117	3	7	.300	161	87	75	53	40	5.77
1983—Boston................................. American		33	211⅓	12	12	.500	241	102	96	115	62	4.09
1984—Boston................................. American		33	218	12	12	.500	232	106	95	136	88	3.92
1985—Boston................................. American		35	229⅓	11	13	.458	243	123	115	189	70	4.51
1986—Boston§............................... American		25	174⅓	13	8	.619	169	63	58	167	50	2.99
1987—Boston................................. American		33	238⅔	15	13	.536	239	124	117	190	76	4.41
1988—Boston xy .... American		33	216⅔	18	6	.750	222	98	88	166	65	3.66
1989—San Diego .... National		33	244⅔	15	11	.577	214	84	73	179	66	2.69
American League Totals—9 Years		237	1459⅓	88	73	.547	1569	747	686	1043	479	4.23
National League Totals—1 Year		33	244⅔	15	11	.577	214	84	73	179	66	2.69
Major League Totals—10 Years		270	1704	103	84	.551	1783	831	759	1222	545	4.01

Selected by Boston Red Sox' organization in 1st round (22nd player selected) of free-agent draft, June 8, 1976.
†On disabled list, August 8 to September 14, 1977.
‡On disabled list, May 23 to September 21, 1978.
§On disabled list, June 3 to July 18, 1986.
xOn disabled list, July 8 to July 24, 1988.
yGranted free agency, November 4, 1988; signed by San Diego Padres, December 8, 1988.

CHAMPIONSHIP SERIES RECORD

Shares Championship Series record for most games lost, series (2), 1988.

Year Club	League	G.	IP.	W.	L.	Pct.	H.	R.	ER.	SO.	BB.	ERA.
1986—Boston................................ American		2	15	1	0	1.000	18	5	4	8	1	2.40
1988—Boston................................ American		2	13	0	2	.000	10	4	4	12	5	2.77
Championship Series Totals—2 Years................		4	28	1	2	.333	28	9	8	20	6	2.57

WORLD SERIES RECORD

Year Club	League	G.	IP.	W.	L.	Pct.	H.	R.	ER.	SO.	BB.	ERA.
1986—Boston................................ American		3	23	2	0	1.000	18	5	5	17	6	1.96

ALL-STAR GAME RECORD

Member of American League All-Star Team in 1987; did not play.

JEFFREY KENT HUSON
(Jeff)

Born August 15, 1964, at Scottsdale, Ariz.
Height, 6.03. Weight, 170.
Throws right and bats lefthanded.
Attended Glendale Community College, Glendale, Ariz., and University of Wyoming, Laramie, Wyo.

Major League stolen bases: 1988 (2), 1989 (3). Total—5.
Led Southern League in stolen bases with 56 in 1988.

Year Club League	Pos.	G.	AB.	R.	H.	2B.	3B.	HR.	RBI.	B.A.	PO.	A.	E.	F.A.
1986—Burlington .... Midw.	SS-3B-2B	133	457	85	132	19	1	16	72	.289	183	324	37	.932
1986—Jacksonville .... South.	3B	1	4	0	0	0	0	0	0	.000	0	1	0	1.000
1987—W. Palm Beach .... Fla. St.	SS-OF-2B	131	455	54	130	15	4	1	53	.286	234	347	34	.945
1988—Jacksonville .... South.	S-2-O-3	128	471	72	117	18	1	0	34	.248	217	285	26	.951
1988—Montreal .... Nat.	S-2-3-O	20	42	7	13	2	0	0	3	.310	18	41	4	.937
1989—Indianapolis .... A. A.	SS-OF-2B	102	378	70	115	17	4	3	35	.304	172	214	17	.958
1989—Montreal .... Nat.	SS-2B-3B	32	74	1	12	5	0	0	2	.162	40	65	8	.929
Major League Totals—2 Years................		52	116	8	25	7	0	0	5	.216	58	106	12	.932

Signed as free agent by Montreal Expos' organization, August 18, 1985.

BLAISE FRANCIS ILSLEY

Born April 9, 1964, at Alpena, Mich.
Height, 6.01. Weight, 185.
Throws and bats lefthanded.
Attended Indiana State University, Terre Haute, Ind.

Led South Atlantic League in complete games with 9 in 1986.
Tied for South Atlantic League lead in shutouts with 3 in 1986.
Named South Atlantic League Pitcher of the Year, 1986.

Year Club League	G.	IP.	W.	L.	Pct.	H.	R.	ER.	SO.	BB.	ERA.
1985—Auburn .... NYP	13	90	9	1	.900	55	18	14	★116	32	1.40
1986—Asheville .... S. Atlantic	15	120	12	2	.857	74	27	26	146	23	★1.95
1986—Osceola .... Florida St.	14	86⅔	8	4	.667	67	24	17	74	19	1.77
1987—Columbus .... Southern	26	167⅔	10	11	.476	162	84	72	130	63	3.86
1988—Columbus .... Southern	8	39⅓	3	1	.750	49	28	26	38	21	5.95
1989—Osceola .... Florida St.	2	7	0	0	.000	8	5	5	6	0	6.43
1989—Columbus .... Southern	4	20⅓	1	1	.500	19	10	3	11	5	1.31
1989—Tucson .... P. Coast	20	103	4	9	.308	120	68	67	49	23	5.85

Selected by Houston Astros' organization in 4th round of free-agent draft, June 3, 1985.

RODNEY CRAIG IMES

Born November 19, 1966, at Cumberland, Md.
Height, 6.05. Weight, 200.
Throws and bats righthanded.
Attended Old Dominion University, Norfolk, Va.

Led Eastern League in complete games with 9 in 1989.
Named Eastern League Pitcher of the Year, 1989.

Year Club League	G.	IP.	W.	L.	Pct.	H.	R.	ER.	SO.	BB.	ERA.
1987—Oneonta................ NYP	4	27⅔	4	0	1.000	16	1	1	10	5	0.33
1987—Prince William .... Carolina	10	68⅓	2	3	.400	68	35	30	49	20	3.95
1988—Prince William .... Carolina	11	77	4	5	.444	82	47	38	67	32	4.44
1988—Albany................ Eastern	7	49⅓	4	1	.800	46	21	15	24	16	2.74
1988—Fort Lauderdale .... Florida St.	8	57⅔	6	2	.750	48	18	11	47	17	1.72
1989—Albany† .... Eastern	24	171⅔	★17	6	.739	143	56	52	128	41	2.73

Selected by New York Yankees' organization in 16th round of free-agent draft, June 2, 1987.

†Traded with First Baseman Hal Morris to Cincinnati Reds for Pitcher Tim Leary and Outfielder Van Snider, December 12, 1989.

PETER JOSEPH INCAVIGLIA
(Pete)

Born April 2, 1964, at Pebble Beach, Calif.
Height, 6.01. Weight, 220.
Throws and bats righthanded.
Attended Oklahoma State University, Stillwater, Okla.
Son of Tom Incaviglia, minor league infielder, 1948 through 1950 and 1955; and
brother of Tony Incaviglia, minor league third baseman, 1979 through 1983.

Shares major league record for most doubles, inning (2), May 11, 1986 (second game), fourth inning.
Major League stolen bases: 1986 (3), 1987 (9), 1989 (5). Total—23.
Led American League batters in strikeouts with 185 in 1986 and tied for lead with 153 in 1988.
Received reported $175,000 bonus to sign with Texas Rangers, 1985.
Named designated hitter on THE SPORTING NEWS College Baseball All-America Team, 1985.

Year Club League	Pos.	G.	AB.	R.	H.	2B.	3B.	HR.	RBI.	B.A.	PO.	A.	E.	F.A.
1986—Texas† .... Amer.	OF	153	540	82	135	21	2	30	88	.250	157	6	●14	.921
1987—Texas .... Amer.	OF	139	509	85	138	26	4	27	80	.271	216	8	●13	.945
1988—Texas .... Amer.	OF	116	418	59	104	19	3	22	54	.249	213	12	2	.989
1989—Texas‡ .... Amer.	OF	133	453	48	107	27	4	21	81	.236	213	7	6	.973
Major League Totals—4 Years................		541	1920	274	484	93	13	100	303	.252	758	33	35	.958

Selected by San Francisco Giants' organization in 10th round of free-agent draft, June 7, 1982.
Selected by Montreal Expos' organization in 1st round (eighth player selected) of free-agent draft, June 3, 1985.
†Traded to Texas Rangers' organization for Pitcher Bob Sebra and Infielder Jim Anderson, November 2, 1985.
‡On disabled list, June 15 to June 30, 1989.

FERMIN ALEXIS INFANTE

Name pronounced En-fawn-tay.
(Known by middle name.)
Born December 4, 1961, at Barquisimeto, Venezuela.
Height, 5.10. Weight, 188.
Throws and bats righthanded.

Major League stolen bases: 1989 (1).
Led International League shortstops in errors with 23 in 1988.
Led International League shortstops in total chances with 699 and double plays with 84 in 1985.
Led South Atlantic League shortstops in total chances with 646 in 1983.

Year	Club	League	Pos.	G.	AB.	R.	H.	2B.	3B.	HR.	RBI.	B.A.	PO.	A.	E.	F.A.
1982—Bradenton Jays....	Gulf C.		SS	37	137	17	40	7	2	0	15	.292	47	117	5	.970
1983—Florence	S. Atl.		SS	128	480	88	134	25	3	4	56	.279	★197	393	★56	.913
1984—Knoxville	South.		SS	67	253	28	67	13	1	2	29	.265	92	204	18	.943
1984—Syracuse	Int.		SS	72	225	27	50	6	1	0	7	.222	88	229	21	.938
1985—Syracuse	Int.		SS	136	453	63	109	10	5	2	39	.241	★225	★432	★42	.940
1986—Syracuse†	Int.		SS	57	193	27	53	6	2	0	15	.275	73	172	14	.946
1987—Syracuse	Int.		S-3-O-2	107	319	40	72	7	4	2	30	.226	111	260	20	.949
1987—Toronto	Amer.		PR	1	0	0	0	0	0	0	0	.000	0	0	0	.000
1988—Syracuse	Int.		SS-3B-2B	97	340	48	102	15	4	2	28	.300	143	240	25	.939
1988—Toronto	Amer.		3B-SS	19	15	7	3	0	0	0	0	.200	4	6	1	.909
1989—Syracuse‡	Int.		2B-3B-SS	67	250	39	52	5	0	0	17	.208	108	166	12	.958
1989—Toronto‡	Amer.		SS-3B-2B	20	12	1	2	0	0	0	0	.167	6	13	0	1.000
Major League Totals—3 Years				40	27	8	5	0	0	0	0	.185	10	19	1	.967

Signed as free agent by Toronto Blue Jays' organization, December 8, 1981.
†On disabled list, June 18, 1986 through remainder of season.
‡Sold to Atlanta Braves, November 20, 1989.

JEFFREY DAVID INNIS
(Jeff)

Born July 5, 1962, at Decatur, Ill.
Height, 6.00. Weight, 170.
Throws and bats righthanded.
Attended University of Illinois, Champaign, Ill.

Led Texas League in saves with 25 in 1986.

Year	Club	League	G.	IP.	W.	L.	Pct.	H.	R.	ER.	SO.	BB.	ERA.
1983—Little Falls	NYP	28	46	8	0	1.000	29	8	7	68	28	1.37
1984—Jackson	Texas	42	59⅓	6	5	.545	65	34	28	63	40	4.25
1985—Lynchburg	Carolina	53	77	6	3	.667	46	26	20	91	40	2.34
1986—Jackson	Texas	56	92	4	5	.444	69	30	25	75	24	2.45
1987—Tidewater	Int'national	29	44⅓	6	1	.857	26	10	10	28	16	2.03
1987—New York	National	17	25⅔	0	1	.000	29	9	9	28	4	3.16
1988—Tidewater	Int'national	34	48⅓	0	5	.000	43	22	19	43	25	3.54
1988—New York	National	12	19	1	1	.500	19	6	4	14	2	1.89
1989—Tidewater	Int'national	25	29⅔	3	1	.750	28	9	7	14	8	2.12
1989—New York	National	29	39⅔	0	1	.000	38	16	14	16	8	3.18
Major League Totals—3 Years		58	84⅓	1	3	.250	86	31	27	58	14	2.88

Selected by New York Mets' organization in 13th round of free-agent draft, June 6, 1983.

DARYL KEITH IRVINE

Born November 15, 1964, at Harrisonburg, Va.
Height, 6.03. Weight, 195.
Throws and bats righthanded.
Attended Ferrum Junior College, Ferrum, Va.

Led Eastern League in games finished in relief with 45 in 1989.
Led Eastern League in wild pitches with 16 in 1987.

Year	Club	League	G.	IP.	W.	L.	Pct.	H.	R.	ER.	SO.	BB.	ERA.
1985—Greensboro†	S. Atlantic	8	37	4	2	.667	46	26	18	19	17	4.38
1986—Winter Haven	Florida St.	26	161	9	8	.529	162	73	57	73	67	3.19
1987—New Britain	Eastern	37	127	4	13	.235	156	101	75	70	59	5.31
1988—New Britain	Eastern	39	125⅓	5	11	.313	113	62	43	82	57	3.09
1989—New Britain	Eastern	★54	91⅓	4	6	.400	74	24	13	50	23	1.28

Selected by Boston Red Sox' organization in 3rd round of free-agent draft, January 17, 1984.
Selected by Toronto Blue Jays' organization in secondary phase of free-agent draft, June 4, 1984.
Selected by Boston Red Sox' organization in secondary phase of free-agent draft, January 9, 1985.
†On disabled list, June 2 to July 15, 1985.

CHARLES LEO JACKSON
(Chuck)

Born March 19, 1963, at Seattle, Wash.
Height, 6.00. Weight, 185.
Throws and bats righthanded.
Attended University of Hawaii, Honolulu, Haw.

Major League stolen bases: 1987 (1), 1988 (1). Total—2.
Led Southern League third basemen in errors with 30 in 1985.

Year—Club	League	Pos.	G.	AB.	R.	H.	2B.	3B.	HR.	RBI.	B.A.	PO.	A.	E.	F.A.
1984—Auburn	NYP	OF	10	38	4	14	0	2	1	4	.368	9	3	0	1.000
1984—Asheville	S. Atl.	OF	59	199	42	52	12	0	5	32	.261	98	6	4	.963
1985—Tucson	P. C.	OF	19	61	7	11	2	1	1	4	.180	43	3	1	.979
1985—Columbus	South.	3B-OF	108	361	62	112	10	8	8	46	.310	98	232	32	.912
1986—Tucson	P. C.	*3B-OF	127	448	83	137	27	5	11	62	.306	91	202	*29	.910
1987—Tucson	P. C.	3B-SS-OF	80	291	51	84	10	4	3	43	.289	79	124	20	.910
1987—Houston	Nat.	3B-OF-SS	35	71	3	15	3	0	1	6	.211	12	39	2	.962
1988—Houston	Nat.	3B-SS-OF	46	83	7	19	5	1	1	8	.229	12	51	7	.900
1988—Tucson	P. C.	SS-OF-3B	48	151	21	45	8	0	2	11	.298	55	95	9	.943
1989—Tucson†	P. C.	OF-3B-SS	69	243	33	75	14	4	3	27	.309	94	55	16	.903
1989—Omaha‡	A. A.	3B-SS	28	97	16	29	0	3	1	12	.299	14	54	7	.907
Major League Totals—2 Years			81	154	10	34	8	1	2	14	.221	24	90	9	.927

Selected by Cleveland Indians' organization in 21st round of free-agent draft, June 8, 1981.
Selected by Houston Astros' organization in 7th round of free-agent draft, June 4, 1984.
†Loaned to Omaha (Kansas City Royals' organization), July 26, 1989; returned, September 6, 1989.
‡Drafted by San Francisco Giants, December 4, 1989.

DANNY LYNN JACKSON

Born January 5, 1962, at San Antonio, Tex.
Height, 6.00. Weight, 205.
Throws left and bats righthanded.
Attended University of Oklahoma, Norman, Okla., and
Trinidad State Junior College, Trinidad, Colo.
Brother of Mike Jackson, fourth-round selection of Kansas City Kings in 1983 NBA draft.

Major League saves: 1986 (1).
Tied for National League lead in complete games with 15 in 1988.
Tied for American Association lead in complete games with 10 in 1984.
Tied for American Association lead in shutouts with 2 in 1983 and 3 in 1984.
Named lefthanded pitcher on THE SPORTING NEWS National League All-Star Team, 1988.

Year—Club	League	G.	IP.	W.	L.	Pct.	H.	R.	ER.	SO.	BB.	ERA.
1982—Charleston	S. Atlantic	13	96⅓	10	1	.909	80	37	28	62	39	2.62
1982—Jacksonville†	Southern	14	98	7	2	.778	78	30	26	74	42	2.39
1983—Omaha	Am. Assoc.	23	136	7	8	.467	126	74	60	93	73	3.97
1983—Kansas City	American	4	19	1	1	.500	26	12	11	9	6	5.21
1984—Kansas City	American	15	76	2	6	.250	84	41	36	40	35	4.26
1984—Omaha	Am. Assoc.	16	110⅓	5	8	.385	91	50	45	82	45	3.67
1985—Kansas City	American	32	208	14	12	.538	209	94	79	114	76	3.42
1986—Kansas City‡	American	32	185⅔	11	12	.478	177	83	66	115	79	3.20
1987—Kansas City§	American	36	224	9	18	.333	219	115	100	152	109	4.02
1988—Cincinnati	National	35	260⅔	●23	8	.742	206	86	79	161	71	2.73
1989—Cincinnati x	National	20	115⅔	6	11	.353	122	78	72	70	57	5.60
American League Totals—5 Years		119	712⅔	37	49	.430	715	345	292	430	305	3.69
National League Totals—2 Years		55	376⅓	29	19	.604	328	164	151	231	128	3.61
Major League Totals—7 Years		174	1089	66	68	.493	1043	509	443	661	433	3.66

Selected by Oakland A's organization in 24th round of free-agent draft, June 3, 1980.
Selected by Kansas City Royals' organization in secondary phase of free-agent draft, January 17, 1982.
†On disabled list, September 8, 1982 through remainder of season.
‡On disabled list, April 4 to April 21, 1986.
§Traded with Shortstop Angel Salazar to Cincinnati Reds for Pitcher Ted Power and Shortstop Kurt Stillwell, November 6, 1987.
xOn disabled list, June 18 to July 6 and July 25 to September 1, 1989.

CHAMPIONSHIP SERIES RECORD

Year—Club	League	G.	IP.	W.	L.	Pct.	H.	R.	ER.	SO.	BB.	ERA.
1985—Kansas City	American	2	10	1	0	1.000	10	0	0	7	1	0.00

WORLD SERIES RECORD

Year—Club	League	G.	IP.	W.	L.	Pct.	H.	R.	ER.	SO.	BB.	ERA.
1985—Kansas City	American	2	16	1	1	.500	9	3	3	12	5	1.69

ALL-STAR GAME RECORD

Member of National League All-Star Team in 1988; did not play.

DARRIN JAY JACKSON

Born August 22, 1963, at Los Angeles, Calif.
Height, 6.00. Weight, 185.
Throws and bats righthanded.

Major League stolen bases: 1988 (4), 1989 (1). Total—5.
Led Gulf Coast League outfielders in total chances with 127 in 1981.
Tied for American Association lead in double plays by outfielders with 6 in 1987.
Tied for Texas League lead in double plays with 6 in 1984.

Year—Club	League	Pos.	G.	AB.	R.	H.	2B.	3B.	HR.	RBI.	B.A.	PO.	A.	E.	F.A.
1981—Sarasota Cubs	Gulf C.	OF	62	210	29	39	5	0	1	15	.186	*121	5	1	.992
1982—Quad Cities	Midw.	OF	132	529	86	146	23	5	5	48	.276	266	9	8	.972
1983—Salinas	Calif.	OF	129	509	70	126	18	5	6	54	.248	237	15	13	.951
1984—Midland	Texas	OF	132	496	63	134	18	2	15	54	.270	286	*19	8	.974

Year Club League	Pos.	G.	AB.	R.	H.	2B.	3B.	HR.	RBI.	B.A.	PO.	A.	E.	F.A.
1985—Iowa .... A. A.	OF	10	40	0	7	2	1	0	1	.175	19	0	0	1.000
1985—Pittsfield .... East.	OF	91	325	38	82	10	1	3	30	.252	221	5	0	1.000
1985—Chicago .... Nat.	OF	5	11	0	1	0	0	0	0	.091	7	0	0	1.000
1986—Pittsfield .... East.	OF	137	•520	82	139	28	2	15	64	.267	320	*16	7	.980
1987—Iowa .... A. A.	OF	132	474	81	130	32	5	23	81	.274	290	15	6	.981
1987—Chicago .... Nat.	OF	7	5	2	4	1	0	0	0	.800	1	0	0	1.000
1988—Chicago .... Nat.	OF	100	188	29	50	11	3	6	20	.266	116	1	2	.983
1989—Chi.†-S.D. .... Nat.	OF	70	170	17	37	7	0	4	20	.218	121	5	5	.962
1989—Iowa .... A. A.	OF	30	120	18	31	4	1	7	17	.258	66	12	0	1.000
Major League Totals—4 Years...............		182	374	48	92	19	3	10	40	.246	245	6	7	.973

Selected by Chicago Cubs' organization in 2nd round of free-agent draft, June 8, 1981.

†Traded with Pitcher Calvin Schiraldi and a player to be named later to San Diego Padres for Outfielder Marvell Wynne and Infielder Luis Salazar, August 30, 1989; San Diego acquired First Baseman Phil Stephenson to complete deal, September 5, 1989.

MICHAEL RAY JACKSON
(Mike)

Born December 22, 1964, at Houston, Tex.
Height, 6.00. Weight, 185.
Throws and bats righthanded.
Attended Hill Junior College, Hillsboro, Tex.

Major League saves: 1987 (1), 1988 (4), 1989 (7). Total—12.
Tied for American League lead in intentional bases on balls issued with 10 in 1988.
Tied for National League lead in balks with 8 in 1987.
Led Carolina League in balks with 7 in 1985.

Year Club League	G.	IP.	W.	L.	Pct.	H.	R.	ER.	SO.	BB.	ERA.
1984—Spartanburg......................S. Atlantic	14	80⅔	7	2	.778	53	35	24	77	50	2.68
1985—Peninsula..........................Carolina	31	125⅓	7	9	.438	127	71	64	96	53	4.60
1986—Reading.............................Eastern	30	43⅓	2	3	.400	25	9	8	42	22	1.66
1986—Portland...........................P. Coast	17	22⅔	3	1	.750	18	8	8	23	13	3.18
1986—Philadelphia ....National	9	13⅓	0	0	.000	12	5	5	3	4	3.38
1987—Philadelphia†...................National	55	109⅓	3	10	.231	88	55	51	93	56	4.20
1987—Maine‡................................Int'national	2	11	1	0	1.000	9	2	1	13	5	0.82
1988—Seattle...............................American	62	99⅓	6	5	.545	74	37	29	76	43	2.63
1989—Seattle...............................American	65	99⅓	4	6	.400	81	43	35	94	54	3.17
National League Totals—2 Years.....................	64	122⅔	3	10	.231	100	60	56	96	60	4.11
American League Totals—2 Years	127	198⅔	10	11	.476	155	80	64	170	97	2.90
Major League Totals—4 Years............................	191	321⅓	13	21	.382	255	140	120	266	157	3.36

Selected by Philadelphia Phillies' organization in 29th round of free-agent draft, June 6, 1983.
Selected by Philadelphia Phillies' organization in secondary phase of free-agent draft, January 17, 1984.

†On disabled list, August 6 to August 21, 1987.

‡Traded with Outfielders Glenn Wilson and Dave Brundage to Seattle Mariners for Outfielder Phil Bradley and Pitcher Tim Fortugno, December 9, 1987.

VINCENT EDWARD JACKSON
(Bo)

Born November 30, 1962, at Bessemer, Ala.
Height, 6.01. Weight, 222.
Throws and bats righthanded.
Attended Auburn University, Auburn, Ala.

Shares major league records for most strikeouts, nine-inning game (5), April 18, 1987; most strikeouts, inning (2), April 8, 1987, fourth inning.
Major League stolen bases: 1986 (3), 1987 (10), 1988 (27), 1989 (26). Total—66.
Led American League batters in strikeouts with 172 in 1989.

Year Club League	Pos.	G.	AB.	R.	H.	2B.	3B.	HR.	RBI.	B.A.	PO.	A.	E.	F.A.
1986—Memphis†............South.	OF	53	184	30	51	9	3	7	25	.277	116	8	7	.947
1986—Kansas City.......... Amer.	OF	25	82	9	17	2	1	2	9	.207	29	2	4	.886
1987—Kansas City.......... Amer.	OF	116	396	46	93	17	2	22	53	.235	180	9	9	.955
1988—Kansas City‡........ Amer.	OF	124	439	63	108	16	4	25	68	.246	246	11	7	.973
1989—Kansas City§........ Amer.	OF	135	515	86	132	15	6	32	105	.256	224	11	8	.967
Major League Totals—4 Years................		400	1432	204	350	50	13	81	235	.244	679	33	28	.962

Selected by New York Yankees' organization in 2nd round of free-agent draft, June 7, 1982.
Selected by California Angels' organization in 20th round of free-agent draft, June 3, 1985.
Selected by Kansas City Royals' organization in 4th round of free-agent draft, June 2, 1986.

†On temporary inactive list, June 20 to June 30, 1986.

‡On disabled list, June 1 to July 2, 1988.

§On disabled list, July 25 to August 9, 1989.

ALL-STAR GAME RECORD

Shares All-Star Game record for hitting home run in first at-bat, July 11, 1989.

Year League	Pos.	AB.	R.	H.	2B.	3B.	HR.	RBI.	B.A.	PO.	A.	E.	F.A.
1989—American	OF	4	1	2	0	0	1	2	.500	2	0	0	1.000

RECORD AS FOOTBALL PLAYER

Heisman Trophy winner, 1985.

Named college football Player of the Year by THE SPORTING NEWS, 1985.
Named as running back on THE SPORTING NEWS College All-America Team, 1985.
Selected by Tampa Bay in 1st round (1st player selected) of 1986 NFL draft.
Selected by Birmingham in 1986 USFL territorial draft.
On reserve/did not sign entire 1986 football season through April 27, 1987.
Selected by Los Angeles Raiders in 7th round (183rd player selected) of 1987 NFL draft.
Signed by Los Angeles Raiders, July 17, 1987.
On reserve/did not report, August 27 through October 23, 1987; activated, October 24, 1987.
On reserve/did not report, August 22 through October 11, 1988; reported, October 12, 1988.
Activated from reserve/did not report, October 15, 1988.
On reserve/did not report, July 21 through October 10, 1989; activated, October 11, 1989.

Year Club	G.	Att.	Yds.	Avg.	TD.	P.C.	Yds.	Avg.	TD.	TD.	Pts.	F.
		RUSHING				PASS RECEIVING				TOTAL		
1987—Los Angeles Raiders NFL	7	81	554	6.8	4	16	136	8.5	2	6	36	2
1988—Los Angeles Raiders NFL	10	136	580	4.3	3	9	79	8.8	0	3	18	5
1989—Los Angeles Raiders NFL	11	173	950	5.5	4	9	69	7.7	0	4	24	1
Pro Totals—3 Years	28	390	2084	5.3	11	34	284	8.4	2	13	78	8

Additional pro statistics: Recovered one fumble, 1987; recovered two fumbles, 1988.

BROOK WALLACE JACOBY JR.

Born November 23, 1959, at Philadelphia, Pa.
Height, 5.11. Weight, 195.
Throws and bats righthanded.
Attended Ventura College, Ventura, Calif.
Son of Brook Jacoby Sr., minor league pitcher, 1956 through 1958.

Major League stolen bases: 1984 (3), 1985 (2), 1986 (2), 1987 (2), 1988 (2), 1989 (2). Total—13.
Hit three home runs in a game, July 3, 1987.
Tied for American League lead in putouts by third basemen with 134 in 1987.
Led International League third basemen in total chances with 331 and double plays with 22 in 1982.

Year Club	League	Pos.	G.	AB.	R.	H.	2B.	3B.	HR.	RBI.	B.A.	PO.	A.	E.	F.A.
1979—Kingsport	Appal.	OF	8	28	3	7	2	0	0	1	.250	9	0	0	1.000
1979—Bradenton	Gulf C.	OF	42	160	24	43	11	1	3	35	.269	65	7	4	.947
1980—Anderson	S. Atl.	OF-3B	132	496	82	147	★40	4	19	★108	.296	219	30	10	.961
1980—Savannah	South.	3B	3	8	0	1	0	0	0	0	.125	0	2	0	1.000
1981—Savannah	South.	3B-OF	140	507	59	148	28	3	24	82	.292	103	232	31	.915
1981—Atlanta	Nat.	3B	11	10	0	2	0	0	0	1	.200	3	4	0	1.000
1982—Richmond	Int.	3B	134	501	74	150	21	3	18	58	.299	83	★229	★19	★.943
1983—Richmond	Int.	3B	133	489	88	154	32	2	25	100	.315	62	247	18	.945
1983—Atlanta†	Nat.	3B	4	8	0	0	0	0	0	0	.000	0	2	0	1.000
1984—Cleveland‡	Amer.	3B-SS	126	439	64	116	19	3	7	40	.264	86	188	14	.951
1985—Cleveland	Amer.	3B-2B	161	606	72	166	26	3	20	87	.274	114	319	19	.958
1986—Cleveland	Amer.	3B	158	583	83	168	30	4	17	80	.288	109	292	25	.941
1987—Cleveland	Amer.	●3B-1B	155	540	73	162	26	4	32	69	.300	192	261	●22	.954
1988—Cleveland	Amer.	3B	152	552	59	133	25	0	9	49	.241	99	298	10	.975
1989—Cleveland	Amer.	3B	147	519	49	141	26	5	13	64	.272	92	268	17	.955
National League Totals—2 Years			15	18	0	2	0	0	0	1	.111	3	6	0	1.000
American League Totals—6 Years			899	3239	400	886	152	19	98	389	.274	692	1626	107	.956
Major League Totals—8 Years			914	3257	400	888	152	19	98	390	.273	695	1632	107	.956

Selected by Atlanta Braves' organization in 7th round of free-agent draft, January 9, 1979.
†Traded with Outfielder Brett Butler to Cleveland Indians, October 21, 1983, completing deal in which Atlanta Braves acquired Pitcher Len Barker for three players to be named later, August 28, 1983. Cleveland acquired Pitcher Rick Behenna as partial completion of deal, September 2, 1983.
‡On disabled list, August 20, 1984 through remainder of season.

ALL-STAR GAME RECORD

Year League	Pos.	AB.	R.	H.	2B.	3B.	HR.	RBI.	B.A.	PO.	A.	E.	F.A.
1986—American	PH-3B	1	0	0	0	0	0	0	.000	1	1	0	1.000

DION JAMES

Born November 9, 1962, at Philadelphia, Pa.
Height, 6.01. Weight, 170.
Throws and bats lefthanded.

Major League stolen bases: 1983 (1), 1984 (10), 1987 (10), 1988 (9), 1989 (2). Total—32.
Led California League outfielders in fielding percentage with .988 in 1981.

Year Club	League	Pos.	G.	AB.	R.	H.	2B.	3B.	HR.	RBI.	B.A.	PO.	A.	E.	F.A.
1980—Butte	Pion.	OF-1B	59	224	57	71	14	1	0	27	.317	80	4	7	.923
1980—Burlington	Midw.	OF	3	10	0	1	0	0	0	1	.100	8	1	0	1.000
1981—Stockton	Calif.	OF-1B	124	451	70	137	17	3	2	49	.304	250	10	3	.989
1982—El Paso†	Texas	OF	106	422	103	136	25	3	9	72	.322	237	9	7	.972
1983—Vancouver	P. C.	OF	129	467	84	157	29	5	8	68	.336	289	6	2	.993
1983—Milwaukee	Amer.	OF	11	20	1	2	0	0	0	1	.100	12	1	0	1.000
1984—Milwaukee	Amer.	OF	128	387	52	114	19	5	1	30	.295	252	7	3	.989
1985—Vancouver‡	P. C.	OF	10	37	2	4	2	0	0	5	.108	17	0	0	1.000
1985—Milwaukee	Amer.	OF	18	49	5	11	1	0	0	3	.224	20	0	0	1.000
1986—Vancouver§	P. C.	OF-1B	130	485	85	137	25	6	6	55	.282	348	7	5	.986
1987—Atlanta	Nat.	OF	134	494	80	154	37	6	10	61	.312	262	4	1	★.996
1988—Atlanta	Nat.	OF	132	386	46	99	17	5	3	30	.256	222	5	3	.987

Year Club	League	Pos.	G.	AB.	R.	H.	2B.	3B.	HR.	RBI.	B.A.	PO.	A.	E.	F.A.
1989—Atlanta x	Nat.	OF-1B	63	170	15	44	7	0	1	11	.259	126	7	0	1.000
1989—Cleveland	Amer.	OF-1B	71	245	26	75	11	0	4	29	.306	85	1	3	.966
American League Totals—4 Years			228	701	84	202	31	5	5	63	.288	369	9	6	.984
National League Totals—3 Years			329	1050	141	297	61	11	14	102	.283	610	16	4	.994
Major League Totals—6 Years			557	1751	225	499	92	16	19	165	.285	979	25	10	.990

Selected by Milwaukee Brewers' organization in 1st round (25th player selected) of free-agent draft, June 3, 1980.

†On disabled list, July 1 to August 1, 1982.

‡On Milwaukee disabled list, March 31 to April 28 and May 20 to September 1, 1985; included rehabilitation disability assignment to Vancouver, April 12 to April 28, 1985.

§Traded to Atlanta Braves for Outfielder Brad Komminsk, January 20, 1987.

xTraded to Cleveland Indians for Outfielder Oddibe McDowell, July 2, 1989.

DONALD CHRISTOPHER JAMES
(Chris)

Born October 4, 1962, at Rusk, Tex.
Height, 6.01. Weight, 190.
Throws and bats righthanded.
Attended Blinn College, Brenham, Tex.
Brother of Craig James, running back with Washington Federals
and New England Patriots, 1983 through 1988.

Major League stolen bases: 1987 (3), 1988 (7), 1989 (5). Total—15.
Tied for Pacific Coast League lead in being hit by pitch with 7 in 1985.
Led South Atlantic League in total bases with 257 and tied for lead in being hit by pitch with 12 in 1983.
Led Pacific Coast League outfielders in total chances with 351 in 1985.

Year Club	League	Pos.	G.	AB.	R.	H.	2B.	3B.	HR.	RBI.	B.A.	PO.	A.	E.	F.A.
1982—Bend	N'west	3B-OF	63	227	47	72	*19	3	12	50	.317	93	54	10	.936
1983—Spartanburg	S. Atl.	OF-3B	129	499	94	148	23	4	26	*121	.297	150	88	16	.937
1984—Reading	East.	*3B-OF	128	457	66	117	19	*12	8	57	.256	104	209	*39	.889
1985—Portland	P. C.	OF	135	507	78	160	35	8	11	73	.316	*328	16	7	.980
1986—Portland	P. C.	OF-3B	69	266	30	64	6	2	12	41	.241	83	44	8	.941
1986—Philadelphia†	Nat.	OF	16	46	5	13	3	0	1	5	.283	19	0	0	1.000
1987—Philadelphia	Nat.	OF	115	358	48	105	20	6	17	54	.293	198	5	2	.990
1987—Maine	Int.	OF-3B	13	40	5	9	2	1	0	3	.225	22	4	0	1.000
1988—Philadelphia	Nat.	OF-3B	150	566	57	137	24	1	19	66	.242	282	51	9	.974
1989—Phi.‡-S.D.§	Nat.	OF-3B	132	482	55	117	17	2	13	65	.243	215	27	7	.972
Major League Totals—4 Years			413	1452	165	372	64	9	50	190	.256	714	83	18	.978

Signed as free agent by Philadelphia Phillies' organization, October 30, 1981.

†On disabled list, May 6 to July 21, 1986; included rehabilitation disability assignment to Portland, July 3 to July 21, 1986.

‡Traded to San Diego Padres for Infielder Randy Ready and Outfielder John Kruk, June 2, 1989.

§Traded with Catcher Sandy Alomar and Third Baseman Carlos Baerga to Cleveland Indians for Outfielder Joe Carter, December 6, 1989.

STANLEY JULIAN JAVIER

Name pronounced HAAV-e-AIR.

(Stan)

Born January 9, 1965, at San Francisco Macoris, D. R.
Height, 6.00. Weight, 185.
Throws right and bats left and righthanded.
Son of Julian Javier, infielder with St. Louis Cardinals and Cincinnati Reds, 1960 through 1972.

Major League stolen bases: 1986 (8), 1987 (3), 1988 (20), 1989 (12). Total—43.
Led Southern League in bases on balls received with 112 in 1985.

Year Club	League	Pos.	G.	AB.	R.	H.	2B.	3B.	HR.	RBI.	B.A.	PO.	A.	E.	F.A.
1981—Johnson City	Appal.	OF	53	144	30	36	5	4	3	19	.250	53	2	3	.948
1982—Johnson City†	Appal.	OF	57	185	45	51	3	●4	8	36	.276	94	8	4	.962
1983—Greensboro	S. Atl.	OF	129	489	109	152	*34	6	12	77	.311	250	10	15	.945
1984—New York	Amer.	OF	7	7	1	1	0	0	0	0	.143	3	0	0	1.000
1984—Nashville‡	South.	OF	76	262	40	76	17	4	7	38	.290	202	4	7	.967
1984—Columbus	Int.	OF	32	99	12	22	3	1	0	7	.222	77	4	2	.976
1985—Huntsville	South.	OF	140	486	105	138	22	8	9	64	.284	363	8	7	.981
1986—Tacoma	P. C.	OF-1B	69	248	50	81	16	2	4	51	.327	172	9	6	.968
1986—Oakland	Amer.	OF	59	114	13	23	8	0	0	8	.202	118	1	0	1.000
1987—Oakland§	Amer.	OF-1B	81	151	22	28	3	1	2	9	.185	149	5	3	.981
1987—Tacoma	P. C.	OF-1B	15	51	6	11	2	0	0	2	.216	26	0	2	.929
1988—Oakland x	Amer.	OF-1B	125	397	49	102	13	3	2	35	.257	274	7	5	.983
1989—Oakland y	Amer.	OF-2B-1B	112	310	42	77	12	3	1	28	.248	221	8	2	.991
Major League Totals—5 Years			384	979	127	231	36	7	5	80	.236	765	21	10	.987

Signed as free agent by St. Louis Cardinals' organization, March 26, 1981.

†Traded with shortstop Bob Meacham to New York Yankees' organization for Outfielder Bob Helsom and Pitchers Marty Mason and Steve Fincher, December 14, 1982.

‡Traded with Pitchers Jay Howell, Jose Rijo, Eric Plunk and Tim Birtsas to Oakland A's for Outfielder Rickey Henderson, Pitcher Bert Bradley and cash, December 5, 1984.

§On disabled list, August 3 to September 1, 1987; included rehabilitation disability assignment to Tacoma, August 20 to September 1, 1987.

xOn disabled list, August 18 to September 2, 1988.

yOn disabled list, July 7 to July 24, 1989.

Year Club	League	Pos.	G.	AB.	R.	H.	2B.	3B.	HR.	RBI.	B.A.	PO.	A.	E.	F.A.
1988—Oakland	Amer.	OF-PR	2	4	0	2	0	0	0	1	.500	5	0	0	1.000
1989—Oakland	Amer.	OF	1	2	0	0	0	0	0	0	.000	1	0	0	1.000
Championship Series Totals—2 Years			3	6	0	2	0	0	0	1	.333	6	0	0	1.000

WORLD SERIES RECORD

Year Club	League	Pos.	G.	AB.	R.	H.	2B.	3B.	HR.	RBI.	B.A.	PO.	A.	E.	F.A.
1988—Oakland	Amer.	PR-OF	3	4	0	2	0	0	0	2	.500	1	0	0	1.000
1989—Oakland	Amer.	OF	1	0	0	0	0	0	0	0	.000	0	0	0	.000
World Series Totals—2 Years			4	4	0	2	0	0	0	2	.500	1	0	0	1.000

JAMES MICHAEL JEFFCOAT
(Mike)

Born August 3, 1959, at Pine Bluff, Ark.
Height, 6.02. Weight, 189.
Throws and bats lefthanded.
Attended Louisiana Tech University, Ruston, La.

Major League saves: 1984 (1).

Year Club	League	G.	IP.	W.	L.	Pct.	H.	R.	ER.	SO.	BB.	ERA.
1980—Waterloo	Midwest	4	6	0	0	.000	12	12	4	7	3	6.00
1980—Batavia	NYP	12	68	4	3	.571	65	40	30	71	45	3.97
1981—Waterloo	Midwest	25	147	10	8	.556	151	71	63	109	78	3.86
1982—Waterloo	Midwest	9	62	5	4	.556	58	29	28	68	15	4.06
1982—Chattanooga	Southern	18	128⅓	8	8	.500	122	49	41	107	51	2.88
1983—Charleston	Int'natonal	26	167	12	8	.600	187	95	84	96	46	4.53
1983—Cleveland	American	11	32⅓	1	3	.250	32	13	12	9	13	3.31
1984—Cleveland	American	63	75⅓	5	2	.714	82	28	25	41	24	2.99
1985—Cleveland†	American	9	9⅔	0	0	.000	8	5	3	4	6	2.79
1985—Phoenix	P. Coast	10	59⅔	4	5	.444	64	26	24	28	9	3.62
1985—San Francisco	National	19	22	0	2	.000	27	13	13	10	6	5.32
1986—Phoenix‡	P. Coast	54	75	7	2	.778	81	40	35	57	31	4.20
1987—Oklahoma City	Am. Assoc.	26	159⅓	11	8	.579	193	99	85	101	41	4.79
1987—Texas	American	2	7	0	1	.000	11	10	10	1	4	12.86
1988—Texas	American	5	10	0	2	.000	19	13	13	5	5	11.70
1988—Oklahoma City	Am. Assoc.	22	157⅓	9	5	.643	137	53	49	95	41	2.80
1989—Oklahoma City	Am. Assoc.	11	72⅔	4	4	.500	81	31	26	50	21	3.22
1989—Texas	American	22	130⅔	9	6	.600	139	65	52	64	33	3.58
American League Totals—6 Years		112	265⅓	15	14	.517	291	134	115	124	85	3.90
National League Totals—1 Year		19	22	0	2	.000	27	13	13	10	6	5.32
Major League Totals—6 Years		131	287⅓	15	16	.484	318	147	128	134	91	4.01

Selected by St. Louis Cardinals' organization in 30th round of free-agent draft, June 7, 1977.
Selected by Cleveland Indians' organization in 13th round of free-agent draft, June 3, 1980.
†Traded with Infielder Luis Quinones to San Francisco Giants' organization for Shortstop Johnnie LeMaster, May 7, 1985.

‡Released, October 21, 1986; signed by Texas Rangers' organization, December 18, 1986.

GREGORY SCOTT JEFFERIES
(Gregg)

Born August 1, 1967, at Burlingame, Calif.
Height, 5.10. Weight, 175.
Throws right and bats left and righthanded.

Major League stolen bases: 1988 (5), 1989 (21). Total—26.
Tied for International League lead in intentional bases on balls received with 10 in 1988.
Led Texas League in intentional bases on balls received with 18 in 1987.
Led Carolina League in slugging percentage with .549 in 1986.
Led International League third basemen in assists with 240 in 1988.
Named Texas League Most Valuable Player, 1987.
Named Carolina League Most Valuable Player, 1986.
Named Appalachian League Player of the Year, 1985.

Year Club	League	Pos.	G.	AB.	R.	H.	2B.	3B.	HR.	RBI.	B.A.	PO.	A.	E.	F.A.
1985—Kingsport	Appal.	SS-2B	47	166	27	57	18	2	3	29	.343	78	130	21	.908
1985—Columbia	S. Atl.	2B-SS	20	64	7	18	2	2	1	12	.281	28	26	2	.964
1986—Columbia	S. Atl.	SS	25	112	29	38	6	1	5	24	.339	36	83	7	.944
1986—Lynchburg	Carol.	SS	95	390	66	138	25	9	11	80	★.354	138	273	20	.954
1986—Jackson	Texas	SS-3B	5	19	1	8	1	1	0	7	.421	7	9	1	.941
1987—Jackson	Texas	SS-3B	134	510	81	187	★48	5	20	101	.367	167	388	35	.941
1987—New York	Nat.	PH	6	6	0	3	1	0	0	2	.500	0	0	0	.000
1988—Tidewater	Int.	3-S-2-O	132	504	62	142	28	4	7	61	.282	110	330	27	.942
1988—New York	Nat.	3B-2B	29	109	19	35	8	2	6	17	.321	33	46	2	.975
1989—New York	Nat.	2B-3B	141	508	72	131	28	2	12	56	.258	242	280	14	.974
Major League Totals—3 Years			176	623	91	169	37	4	18	75	.271	275	326	16	.974

Selected by New York Mets' organization in 1st round (20th player selected) of free-agent draft, June 3, 1985.

CHAMPIONSHIP SERIES RECORD

Year Club	League	Pos.	G.	AB.	R.	H.	2B.	3B.	HR.	RBI.	B.A.	PO.	A.	E.	F.A.
1988—New York	Nat.	3B	7	27	2	9	2	0	0	1	.333	5	8	1	.929

REGINALD JIROD JEFFERSON
(Reggie)

Born September 25, 1968, at Tallahassee, Fla.
Height, 6.04. Weight, 210.
Throws left and bats right and lefthanded.

Led Gulf Coast League first basemen in total chances with 624 in 1986.

Year Club League	Pos.	G.	AB.	R.	H.	2B.	3B.	HR.	RBI.	B.A.	PO.	A.	E.	F.A.
1986—Sarasota Reds ...... Gulf C.	1B	59	208	28	54	4	●5	3	33	.260	★581	★36	7	.989
1987—Billings .... Pion.	1B	8	22	10	8	1	0	1	9	.364	21	1	0	1.000
1987—Cedar Rapids† ...... Midw.	1B	15	54	9	12	5	0	3	11	.222	120	11	1	.992
1988—Cedar Rapids† ...... Midw.	1B	135	517	76	149	26	2	18	★90	.288	1084	91	13	.989
1989—Chattanooga .... South.	1B	135	487	66	140	19	3	17	80	.287	1004	79	16	.985

Selected by Cincinnati Reds' organization in 3rd round of free-agent draft, June 2, 1986.
†Batted lefthanded only.

STANLEY JEFFERSON
(Stan)

Born December 4, 1962, at New York, N.Y.
Height, 5.11. Weight, 180.
Throws right and bats left and righthanded.
Attended Bethune-Cookman College, Daytona Beach, Fla.

Major League stolen bases: 1987 (34), 1988 (5), 1989 (10). Total—49.
Led Texas League in stolen bases with 39 in 1985.
Led New York-Pennsylvania League in stolen bases with 35 in 1983.
Named outfielder on The Sporting News College Baseball All-America Team, 1983.

Year Club League	Pos.	G.	AB.	R.	H.	2B.	3B.	HR.	RBI.	B.A.	PO.	A.	E.	F.A.
1983—Little Falls† .... NYP	OF	71	281	57	90	5	1	9	36	.320	★153	7	4	.976
1984—Lynchburg† .... Carol.	OF	128	493	★113	142	20	●9	5	47	.288	265	11	8	.972
1985—Jackson .... Texas	OF	133	524	97	145	21	6	8	30	.277	276	9	7	.976
1986—Tidewater‡ .... Int.	OF	95	369	60	107	19	4	2	37	.290	219	5	2	.991
1986—New York§ .... Nat.	OF	14	24	6	5	1	0	1	3	.208	13	0	0	1.000
1987—San Diego x .... Nat.	OF	116	422	59	97	8	7	8	29	.230	232	3	3	.987
1988—San Diego .... Nat.	OF	49	111	16	16	1	2	1	4	.144	62	0	0	1.000
1988—Las Vegas y .... P. C.	OF	74	278	60	88	14	6	4	33	.317	163	4	7	.960
1989—N.Y.z-Bal. .... Amer.	OF	45	139	20	34	7	0	4	21	.245	82	3	1	.988
1989—Col.-Roch. .... Int.	OF	84	321	43	83	14	9	3	36	.259	150	3	4	.975
National League Totals—3 Years		179	557	81	118	10	9	10	36	.212	307	3	3	.990
American League Totals—1 Year		45	139	20	34	7	0	4	21	.245	82	3	1	.988
Major League Totals—4 Years		224	696	101	152	17	9	14	57	.218	389	6	4	.990

Selected by New York Mets' organization in 1st round (20th player selected) of free-agent draft, June 6, 1983.
†Batted righthanded only.
‡On disabled list, July 25 to August 14, 1986.
§Traded with Outfielders Shawn Abner and Kevin Mitchell and Pitchers Kevin Armstrong and Kevin Brown to San Diego Padres for Outfielder Kevin McReynolds, Pitcher Gene Walter and Infielder Adam Ging, December 11, 1986.
xOn disabled list, April 13 to May 7 and May 30 to June 14, 1987.
yTraded with Pitchers Jimmy Jones and Lance McCullers to New York Yankees for First Baseman-Outfielder Jack Clark and Pitcher Pat Clements, October 24, 1988.
zTraded to Rochester (Baltimore Orioles' organization) for Pitcher John Hayden, July 20, 1989.

LARRY STEVEN JELTZ
(Steve)

Born May 28, 1959, at Paris, France.
Height, 5.11. Weight, 190.
Throws right and bats left and righthanded.
Attended University of Kansas, Lawrence, Kan.

Major League stolen bases: 1984 (2), 1985 (1), 1986 (6), 1987 (1), 1988 (3), 1989 (4). Total—17.
Switch-hit home runs in one game, June 8, 1989.
Led Carolina League second basemen in double plays with 84 in 1981.
Tied for Carolina League lead in caught stealing with 15 in 1981.

Year Club League	Pos.	G.	AB.	R.	H.	2B.	3B.	HR.	RBI.	B.A.	PO.	A.	E.	F.A.
1980—Spartanburg† .... S. Atl.	2B	31	107	19	31	2	1	0	8	.290	51	61	4	.966
1981—Peninsula.............. Carol.	2B	133	482	81	112	18	0	2	32	.232	★293	★369	25	.964
1982—Reading.................. East.	2B-SS-3B	126	380	61	92	10	3	7	28	.242	251	297	22	.961
1983—Portland................. P. C.	3-2-S-O	71	181	34	48	6	1	0	16	.265	106	113	11	.952
1983—Philadelphia .... Nat.	2B-SS-3B	13	8	0	1	0	1	0	1	.125	4	5	0	1.000
1984—Portland................. P. C.	S-2-O-3	134	436	68	96	10	9	2	46	.220	270	349	28	.957
1984—Philadelphia .... Nat.	SS-3B	28	68	7	14	0	1	1	7	.206	37	93	1	.992
1985—Philadelphia .... Nat.	SS	89	196	17	37	4	1	0	12	.189	106	215	14	.958
1985—Portland................. P. C.	SS	21	71	6	21	4	1	1	9	.296	28	64	1	.959
1986—Philadelphia .... Nat.	SS	145	439	44	96	11	4	0	36	.219	229	406	22	.967
1987—Philadelphia .... Nat.	SS-OF	114	293	37	68	9	6	0	12	.232	192	271	14	.971
1987—Maine..................... Int.	SS	24	72	6	24	7	0	0	3	.333	45	79	6	.954
1988—Philadelphia .... Nat.	SS	148	379	39	71	11	4	0	27	.187	195	368	14	.976
1989—Philadelphia .... Nat.	S-3-2-O	116	263	28	64	7	3	4	25	.243	111	205	6	.981
Major League Totals—7 Years		653	1646	172	351	42	20	5	120	.213	874	1563	71	.972

Selected by Philadelphia Phillies' organization in 9th round of free-agent draft, June 3, 1980.
†On disabled list, July 27, 1980 through remainder of season.

JAMES DOUGLAS JENNINGS
(Doug)

Born September 30, 1964, at Atlanta, Ga.
Height, 5.10. Weight, 170.
Throws and bats lefthanded.
Attended Brevard Community College, Cocoa, Fla.

Led Pacific Coast League in bases on balls received with 93 and being hit by pitch with 16 in 1989.
Led Texas League in bases on balls received with 94 and being hit by pitch with 13 in 1987.
Led California League in bases on balls received with 117 in 1986.
Led Pacific Coast League first basemen in errors with 12 in 1989.

Year Club	League	Pos.	G.	AB.	R.	H.	2B.	3B.	HR.	RBI.	B.A.	PO.	A.	E.	F.A.
1984—Salem	N'west	OF	52	173	29	45	7	1	1	17	.260	82	5	9	.906
1985—Quad Cities	Midw.	OF	95	319	50	81	17	7	5	54	.254	187	12	11	.948
1986—Palm Springs	Calif.	OF	129	429	95	136	31	9	17	89	.317	205	10	6	.973
1987—Midland†	Texas	OF	126	464	106	157	33	1	●30	104	.338	145	6	6	.962
1988—Oakland‡	Amer.	OF-1B	71	101	9	21	6	0	1	15	.208	85	5	1	.989
1988—Tacoma	P. C.	OF-1B	16	49	12	16	1	0	0	9	.327	26	1	1	.964
1989—Tacoma	P. C.	1B-OF-P	137	497	*99	136	35	5	11	64	.274	842	34	14	.984
1989—Oakland	Amer.	OF	4	4	0	0	0	0	0	0	.000	2	0	0	1.000
Major League Totals—2 Years			75	105	9	21	6	0	1	15	.200	87	5	1	.989

Selected by California Angels' organization in 2nd round of free-agent draft, January 17, 1984.
†Drafted by Oakland Athletics, December 7, 1987.
‡On disabled list, June 27 to July 31, 1988; included rehabilitation disability assignment to Tacoma, July 15 to July 31, 1988.

PITCHING RECORD

Year Club	League	G.	IP.	W.	L.	Pct.	H.	R.	ER.	SO.	BB.	ERA.
1989—Tacoma	P. Coast	2	3	0	0	.000	4	1	1	1	0	3.00

THOMAS EDWARD JOHN
(Tommy)

Born May 22, 1943, at Terre Haute, Ind.
Height, 6.03. Weight, 203.
Throws left and bats righthanded.
Attended Indiana State College, Terre Haute, Ind.

Holds major league record for most years pitched (26).
Shares major league records for most years played (26); most errors, pitcher, inning (3), July 27, 1988, fourth inning.
Shares American League record for most hit batsmen, game, nine-innings (4), June 15, 1968.
Major League saves: 1978 (1).
Led American League in shutouts with 6 in 1980.
Tied for American League lead in shutouts with 5 in 1966 and 6 in 1967.
Tied for American League lead in wild pitches with 17 and in intentional bases on balls issued with 16 in 1970.
Named National League Comeback Player of the Year by THE SPORTING NEWS, 1976.
Named lefthanded pitcher on THE SPORTING NEWS American League All-Star Team, 1980.
Received reported $40,000 bonus to sign with Cleveland Indians, 1961.

Year Club	League	G.	IP.	W.	L.	Pct.	H.	R.	ER.	SO.	BB.	ERA.
1961—Dubuque	Midwest	14	88	10	4	.714	74	47	31	99	59	3.17
1962—Charleston	Eastern	21	128	6	8	.429	129	67	55	114	71	3.87
1962—Jacksonville	Int'national	8	34	2	2	.500	29	20	18	27	16	4.76
1963—Charleston	Eastern	12	95	9	2	.818	85	25	17	45	12	1.61
1963—Jacksonville	Int'national	18	102	6	8	.429	115	53	40	63	39	3.53
1963—Cleveland	American	6	20	0	2	.000	23	10	5	9	6	2.25
1964—Cleveland	American	25	94	2	9	.182	97	53	41	65	35	3.93
1964—Portland†	P. Coast	13	74	6	6	.500	75	38	35	72	24	4.26
1965—Chicago	American	39	184	14	7	.667	162	67	63	126	58	3.08
1966—Chicago	American	34	223	14	11	.560	195	76	65	138	57	2.62
1967—Chicago‡	American	31	178	10	13	.435	143	62	49	110	47	2.48
1968—Chicago‡	American	25	177	10	5	.667	135	45	39	117	49	1.98
1969—Chicago	American	33	232	9	11	.450	230	91	84	128	90	3.26
1970—Chicago	American	37	269	12	17	.414	253	117	98	138	101	3.28
1971—Chicago§	American	38	229	13	16	.448	244	115	92	131	58	3.62
1972—Los Angeles	National	29	187	11	5	.688	172	68	60	117	40	2.89
1973—Los Angeles	National	36	218	16	7	*.696	202	88	75	116	50	3.10
1974—Los Angeles x	National	22	153	13	3	.813	133	51	44	78	42	2.59
1975—Los Angeles y	National					(Did not play)						
1976—Los Angeles	National	31	207	10	10	.500	207	76	71	91	61	3.09
1977—Los Angeles	National	31	220	20	7	.741	225	82	68	123	50	2.78
1978—Los Angeles z	National	33	213	17	10	.630	230	95	78	124	53	3.30
1979—New York	American	37	276	21	9	.700	268	109	91	111	65	2.97
1980—New York	American	36	265	22	9	.710	270	115	101	78	56	3.43
1981—New York a	American	20	140	9	8	.529	135	50	41	50	39	2.64
1982—New York b-California	American	37	221⅔	14	12	.538	239	102	91	68	39	3.69
1983—California	American	34	234⅔	11	13	.458	*287	126	113	65	49	4.33
1984—California	American	32	181⅓	7	13	.350	223	97	91	47	56	4.52

Year Club	League	G.	IP.	W.	L.	Pct.	H.	R.	ER.	SO.	BB.	ERA.
1985—California c-Oakland	American	23	86⅓	4	10	.286	117	59	53	25	28	5.53
1985—Modesto d	California	2	4	0	0	.000	12	8	7	11	6	5.73
1985—Madison d	Midwest	1	6	0	0	.000	4	2	2	3	4	3.00
1986—New York e	American	13	70⅔	5	3	.625	73	27	23	28	15	2.93
1986—Fort Lauderdale f	Florida St.	3	13⅔	2	0	1.000	7	2	0	7	1	0.00
1987—New York g	American	33	187⅔	13	6	.684	212	95	84	63	47	4.03
1988—New York h	American	35	176⅓	9	8	.529	221	96	88	81	46	4.49
1989—New York i	American	10	63⅔	2	7	.222	87	45	41	18	22	5.80
American League Totals—20 Years		578	3509⅓	201	189	.515	3614	1557	1353	1596	963	3.47
National League Totals—6 Years		182	1198	87	42	.674	1169	460	396	649	296	2.97
Major League Totals—26 Years		760	4707⅓	288	231	.555	4783	2017	1749	2245	1259	3.34

Signed as free agent by Cleveland Indians' organization, June 12, 1961.

†Traded to Chicago White Sox with Catcher John Romano and Outfielder Tommie Agee for Catcher Camilo Carreon and Outfielder Rocky Colavito, January 20, 1965, as part of three-way deal which saw Chicago obtain Colavito from Kansas City Athletics earlier same day for Outfielders Jim Landis and Mike Hershberger and a pitcher to be named later; Kansas City acquired Pitcher Fred Talbot to complete deal, February 10, 1965.

‡On disabled list, August 22, 1968 through remainder of season.

§Traded with Infielder Steve Huntz to Los Angeles Dodgers for Infielder-Outfielder Richie Allen, December 2, 1971.

xOn disabled list, July 17, 1974 through remainder of season.

yOn disabled list, April 6, 1975 through remainder of season.

zGranted free agency, November 2, 1978; signed by New York Yankees, November 21, 1978.

aOn disabled list, June 1 to August 5, 1981.

bTraded to California Angels for a player to be named later, August 31, 1982; New York Yankees acquired Pitcher Dennis Rasmussen to complete deal, November 24 1982.

cReleased, June 19, 1985; signed by Modesto (Oakland A's organization), July 12, 1985.

dGranted free agency, November 12, 1985; signed by New York Yankees, May 2, 1986.

eOn disabled list, June 9 to August 8, 1986; included rehabilitation disability assignment to Fort Lauderdale, July 27 to August 8, 1986.

fGranted free agency, November 12, 1986; re-signed by Yankees, January 8, 1987.

gGranted free agency, November 9, 1987; re-signed by Yankees, December 18, 1987.

hReleased, November 10, 1988; re-signed by Yankees, February 13, 1989.

iReleased, May 30, 1989.

DIVISION SERIES RECORD

Year Club	League	G.	IP.	W.	L.	Pct.	H.	R.	ER.	SO.	BB.	ERA.
1981—New York	American	1	7	0	1	.000	8	5	5	0	2	6.43

CHAMPIONSHIP SERIES RECORD

Holds Championship Series records for most wild pitches, total series (4), series (3), 1982 and game (3), October 9, 1982.

Shares Championship Series records for most games won and consecutive games won (4), total series; most wild pitches, inning (2), October 9, 1982, fourth inning.

Shares National League Championship Series records for most complete games, total series (2); most hit batsmen, total series and series (2), 1977.

Year Club	League	G.	IP.	W.	L.	Pct.	H.	R.	ER.	SO.	BB.	ERA.
1977—Los Angeles	National	2	13⅔	1	0	1.000	11	5	1	11	5	0.66
1978—Los Angeles	National	1	9	1	0	1.000	4	0	0	4	2	0.00
1980—New York	American	1	6⅔	0	0	.000	8	2	2	3	1	2.70
1981—New York	American	1	6	1	0	1.000	6	1	1	3	1	1.50
1982—California	American	2	12⅓	1	1	.500	11	9	7	6	6	5.11
Championship Series Totals—5 Years		7	47⅔	4	1	.800	40	17	11	27	15	2.08

WORLD SERIES RECORD

Year Club	League	G.	IP.	W.	L.	Pct.	H.	R.	ER.	SO.	BB.	ERA.
1977—Los Angeles	National	1	6	0	1	.000	9	5	4	7	3	6.00
1978—Los Angeles	National	2	14⅔	1	0	1.000	14	8	5	6	4	3.07
1981—New York	American	3	13	1	0	1.000	11	1	1	8	0	0.69
World Series Totals—3 Years		6	33⅔	2	1	.667	34	14	10	21	7	2.67

ALL-STAR GAME RECORD

Year League		IP.	W.	L.	Pct.	H.	R.	ER.	SO.	BB.	ERA.
1968—American		⅔	0	0	.000	1	0	0	0	0	0.00
1980—American		2⅓	0	1	.000	4	3	3	1	0	11.57
All-Star Game Totals—2 Years		3	0	1	.000	5	3	3	1	0	9.00

Member of National League All-Star Team for 1978 game; did not play.
Member of American League All-Star Team for 1979 game; did not play.

DAVID WAYNE JOHNSON
(Dave)

Born October 24, 1959, at Baltimore, Md.
Height, 5.11. Weight, 179.
Throws and bats righthanded.
Attended Community College of Baltimore, Baltimore, Md.

Pitched 3-0 no-hit victory against Portland, July 23, 1987.
Led American Association pitchers in complete games with 9 and tied for games started with 29 in 1988.
Tied for Pacific Coast League lead in complete games with 9 in 1987.

Year Club	League	G.	IP.	W.	L.	Pct.	H.	R.	ER.	SO.	BB.	ERA.
1982—Greenwood	S. Atlantic	16	58⅓	4	4	.500	50	32	25	41	41	3.86
1983—Alexandria	Carolina	46	113⅔	7	5	.583	100	52	38	95	42	3.01
1984—Prince William	Carolina	13	88⅓	7	5	.583	60	22	13	48	35	1.32
1984—Nashua	Eastern	12	83⅔	1	8	.111	95	52	45	47	31	4.84
1985—Nashua	Eastern	34	153	6	9	.400	129	66	53	84	45	3.12
1986—Hawaii	P. Coast	22	150⅓	8	7	.533	150	68	53	71	35	*3.17
1987—Vancouver	P. Coast	23	153⅔	8	10	.444	133	74	60	76	68	3.51
1987—Pittsburgh	National	5	6⅓	0	0	.000	13	7	7	4	2	9.95
1988—Buffalo†‡	Am. Assoc.	29	192⅓	*15	12	.556	*213	93	75	90	55	3.51
1989—Rochester	Int'national	18	105	7	6	.538	104	45	38	60	31	3.26
1989—Baltimore	American	14	89⅓	4	7	.364	90	44	42	26	28	4.23
National League Totals—1 Year		5	6⅓	0	0	.000	13	7	7	4	2	9.95
American League Totals—1 Year		14	89⅓	4	7	.364	90	44	42	26	28	4.23
Major League Totals—2 Years		19	95⅔	4	7	.364	103	51	49	30	30	4.61

Selected by Kansas City Royals' organization in 5th round of free-agent draft, January 13, 1981.
Signed as free agent by Pittsburgh Pirates' organization, June 10, 1982.
†Granted free agency, October 15, 1988; signed by Houston Astros, December 22, 1988.
‡Traded with Outfielder Victor Hithe by Houston Astros to Baltimore Orioles for Catcher Carl Nichols, March 31, 1989.

HOWARD MICHAEL JOHNSON

Born November 29, 1960, at Clearwater, Fla.
Height, 5.10. Weight, 195.
Throws right and bats right and lefthanded.
Attended St. Petersburg Junior College, St. Petersburg, Fla.

Holds National League record for most home runs, switch-hitter, season (36), 1987, 1989.
Major League stolen bases: 1982 (7), 1984 (10), 1985 (6), 1986 (8), 1987 (32), 1988 (23), 1989 (41). Total—127.
Tied for National League lead in game-winning RBIs with 16 in 1987.
Led Florida State League in sacrifice hits with 16 in 1980.
Led American Association third basemen in double plays with 19 in 1982.
Led Florida State League third basemen in double plays with 21 in 1980.
Named third baseman on THE SPORTING NEWS National League All-Star Team, 1989.
Named third baseman on THE SPORTING NEWS National League Silver Slugger team, 1989.

Year Club	League	Pos.	G.	AB.	R.	H.	2B.	3B.	HR.	RBI.	B.A.	PO.	A.	E.	F.A.
1979—Lakeland	Fla. St.	3B-SS-OF	132	456	49	107	9	6	3	49	.235	130	240	36	.911
1980—Lakeland	Fla. St.	3B	130	474	83	135	*28	1	10	69	.285	*110	*264	13	*.966
1981—Birmingham	South.	3B	138	488	84	130	28	7	22	83	.266	103	218	26	.925
1982—Evansville	A. A.	3B-OF	98	366	70	116	16	4	23	67	.317	69	139	23	.900
1982—Detroit	Amer.	3B-OF	54	155	23	49	5	0	4	14	.316	36	40	7	.916
1983—Detroit	Amer.	3B	27	66	11	14	0	0	3	5	.212	10	30	7	.851
1983—Evansville†	A. A.	3B	3	9	1	2	1	0	0	0	.222	1	11	2	.857
1984—Detroit‡	Amer.	3-S-1-O	116	355	43	88	14	1	12	50	.248	63	150	14	.938
1985—New York§	Nat.	3B-SS-OF	126	389	38	94	18	4	11	46	.242	78	190	18	.937
1986—New York§	Nat.	3B-SS-OF	88	220	30	54	14	0	10	39	.245	52	136	20	.904
1987—New York	Nat.	3B-SS-OF	157	554	93	147	22	1	36	99	.265	118	305	26	.942
1988—New York	Nat.	3B-SS	148	495	85	114	21	1	24	68	.230	110	274	18	.955
1989—New York	Nat.	3B-SS	153	571	●104	164	41	3	36	101	.287	97	217	24	.929
American League Totals—3 Years			197	576	77	151	19	1	19	69	.262	109	220	28	.922
National League Totals—5 Years			672	2229	350	573	116	9	117	353	.257	455	1122	106	.937
Major League Totals—8 Years			869	2805	427	724	135	10	136	422	.258	564	1342	134	.934

Selected by New York Yankees' organization in 23rd round of free-agent draft, June 6, 1978.
Selected by Detroit Tigers' organization in secondary phase of free-agent draft, January 9, 1979.
†On disabled list, June 2 to August 8, 1983.
‡Traded to New York Mets for Pitcher Walt Terrell, December 7, 1984.
§On disabled list, June 2 to June 23, 1986.

CHAMPIONSHIP SERIES RECORD

Year Club	League	Pos.	G.	AB.	R.	H.	2B.	3B.	HR.	RBI.	B.A.	PO.	A.	E.	F.A.
1986—New York	Nat.	PH	2	2	0	0	0	0	0	0	.000	0	0	0	.000
1988—New York	Nat.	SS-3-PH	6	18	3	1	0	0	0	0	.056	6	9	1	.938
Championship Series Totals—2 Years			8	20	3	1	0	0	0	0	.050	6	9	1	.938

WORLD SERIES RECORD

Year Club	League	Pos.	G.	AB.	R.	H.	2B.	3B.	HR.	RBI.	B.A.	PO.	A.	E.	F.A.
1984—Detroit	Amer.	PH	1	1	0	0	0	0	0	0	.000	0	0	0	.000
1986—New York	Nat.	3B-PH-SS	2	5	0	0	0	0	0	0	.000	1	0	0	1.000
World Series Totals—2 Years			3	6	0	0	0	0	0	0	.000	1	0	0	1.000

ALL-STAR GAME RECORD

Year League	Pos.	AB.	R.	H.	2B.	3B.	HR.	RBI.	B.A.	PO.	A.	E.	F.A.
1989—National	3B	3	0	1	0	0	0	1	.333	0	0	0	.000

—DID YOU KNOW—

That the Boston Red Sox have led the American League in batting average in five of the last six years?

KENNETH LANCE JOHNSON

(Known by middle name.)
Born July 7, 1963, at Lincoln Heights, O.
Height, 5.11. Weight, 155.
Throws and bats lefthanded.
Attended Triton College, River Grove, Ill.,
and University of South Alabama, Mobile, Ala.

Major League stolen bases: 1987 (6), 1988 (6), 1989 (16). Total—28.
Led Pacific Coast League in caught stealing with 18 in 1989.
Led Texas League in stolen bases with 49 and caught stealing with 15 in 1986.
Led Pacific Coast League outfielders in total chances with 273 in 1989.
Led Pacific Coast League outfielders in double plays with 5 in 1988.
Led American Association outfielders in total chances with 333 in 1987.
Led New York-Pennsylvania League outfielders in total chances with 201 in 1984.
Named American Association Most Valuable Player, 1987.

Year	Club	League	Pos.	G.	AB.	R.	H.	2B.	3B.	HR.	RBI.	B.A.	PO.	A.	E.	F.A.
1984—Erie	NYP	OF	71	283	*63	*96	7	5	1	28	.339	*188	5	8	.960
1985—St. Petersburg	Fla. St.	OF	129	497	68	134	17	10	2	55	.270	338	16	5	.986
1986—Arkansas	Texas	OF	127	445	82	128	24	6	2	33	.288	262	11	7	.975
1987—Louisville	A. A.	OF	116	477	89	159	21	11	5	50	.333	*319	6	●8	.976
1987—St. Louis†	Nat.	OF	33	59	4	13	2	1	0	7	.220	27	0	2	.931
1988—Chicago	Amer.	OF	33	124	11	23	4	1	0	6	.185	63	1	2	.970
1988—Vancouver	P. C.	OF	100	411	71	126	12	6	2	36	.307	262	9	5	.982
1989—Vancouver	P. C.	OF	106	408	69	124	11	7	0	28	.304	*261	7	5	.982
1989—Chicago	Amer.	OF	50	180	28	54	8	2	0	16	.300	113	0	2	.983
National League Totals—1 Year			33	59	4	13	2	1	0	7	.220	27	0	2	.931
American League Totals—2 Years			83	304	39	77	12	3	0	22	.253	176	1	4	.978
Major League Totals—3 Years			116	363	43	90	14	4	0	29	.248	203	1	6	.971

Selected by Pittsburgh Pirates' organization in 30th round of free-agent draft, June 8, 1981.
Selected by Seattle Mariners' organization in 31st round of free-agent draft, June 7, 1982.
Selected by St. Louis Cardinals' organization in 6th round of free-agent draft, June 4, 1984.
†Traded with Pitcher Rick Horton and cash to Chicago White Sox for Pitcher Jose DeLeon, February 9, 1988.

CHAMPIONSHIP SERIES RECORD

Year	Club	League	Pos.	G.	AB.	R.	H.	2B.	3B.	HR.	RBI.	B.A.	PO.	A.	E.	F.A.
1987—St. Louis	Nat.	PR	1	0	1	0	0	0	0	0	.000	0	0	0	.000

WORLD SERIES RECORD

Year	Club	League	Pos.	G.	AB.	R.	H.	2B.	3B.	HR.	RBI.	B.A.	PO.	A.	E.	F.A.
1987—St. Louis	Nat.	PR	1	0	0	0	0	0	0	0	.000	0	0	0	.000

RANDALL DAVID JOHNSON

(Randy)
Born September 10, 1963, at Walnut Creek, Calif.
Height, 6.10. Weight, 225.
Throws left and bats righthanded.
Attended University of Southern California, Los Angeles, Calif.

Led American Association in balks with 20 in 1988.
Tied for Florida State League lead in games started by pitchers with 26 in 1986.

Year	Club	League	G.	IP.	W.	L.	Pct.	H.	R.	ER.	SO.	BB.	ERA.
1985—Jamestown	NYP	8	27⅓	0	3	.000	29	22	18	21	24	5.93
1986—West Palm Beach	Florida St.	26	119⅔	8	7	.533	89	49	42	133	*94	3.16
1987—Jacksonville	Southern	25	140	11	8	.579	100	63	58	*163	128	3.73
1988—Indianapolis	Am. Assoc.	20	113⅓	8	7	.533	85	52	41	111	72	3.26
1988—Montreal	National	4	26	3	0	1.000	23	8	7	25	7	2.42
1989—Montreal	National	7	29⅔	0	4	.000	29	25	22	26	26	6.67
1989—Indianapolis†	Am. Assoc.	3	18	1	1	.500	13	5	4	17	9	2.00
1989—Seattle	American	22	131	7	9	.438	118	75	64	104	70	4.40
National League Totals—2 Years		11	55⅔	3	4	.429	52	33	29	51	33	4.69
American League Totals—1 Year		22	131	7	9	.438	118	75	64	104	70	4.40
Major League Totals—2 Years		33	186⅔	10	13	.435	170	108	93	155	103	4.48

Selected by Atlanta Braves' organization in 3rd round of free-agent draft, June 7, 1982.
Selected by Montreal Expos' organization in 2nd round of free-agent draft, June 3, 1985.
†Traded with Pitchers Brian Holman and Gene Harris to Seattle Mariners for Pitcher Mark Langston and a player
to be named later, May 25, 1989; Indianapolis (Montreal Expos' organization) acquired Pitcher Mike Campbell to
complete deal, July 31, 1989.

WALLACE DARNELL JOHNSON

(Wally)
Born December 25, 1956, at Gary, Ind.
Height, 5.11. Weight, 185.
Throws right and bats right and lefthanded.
Received degree in accounting from Indiana State University, Terre Haute, Ind., in 1979.

Major League stolen bases: 1981 (1), 1982 (4), 1983 (1), 1986 (6), 1987 (5), 1989 (1). Total—18.
Led Florida State League in stolen bases with 58 and caught stealing with 22 in 1980.

Named Florida State League Southern Division Most Valuable Player, 1980.

Year	Club	League	Pos.	G.	AB.	R.	H.	2B.	3B.	HR.	RBI.	B.A.	PO.	A.	E.	F.A.
1979—Jamestown	NYP		2B	70	*284	60	96	11	6	6	42	.338	157	155	17	.948
1980—W. Palm Beach	Fla. St.		2B-OF	126	488	86	*163	17	5	3	49	*.334	294	350	31	.954
1980—Memphis	South.		2B	4	13	1	1	1	0	0	0	.077	5	12	0	1.000
1981—Memphis†	South.		2B-OF	28	102	15	37	9	0	1	18	.363	44	52	10	.906
1981—Denver	A. A.		2B-OF	59	215	39	64	13	4	0	16	.298	72	116	7	.964
1981—Montreal	Nat.		PH	11	9	1	2	0	1	0	3	.222	1	2	0	1.000
1982—Montreal	Nat.		2B	36	57	5	11	0	2	0	2	.193	22	18	2	.952
1982—Wichita	A. A.		2B-OF	76	298	62	105	12	4	6	36	.352	128	79	12	.945
1983—Wichita	A. A.		OF	16	53	7	14	3	1	0	6	.264	26	0	2	.929
1983—Mont.‡-S. F.	Nat.		2B	10	10	1	2	0	0	0	1	.200	3	2	0	1.000
1983—Phoenix§	P. C.		2B	63	229	42	66	8	2	2	26	.288	105	150	15	.944
1984—Jacksonville	South.		DH	31	117	18	35	5	0	1	12	.299	0	0	0	.000
1984—Indianapolis	A. A.		OF-1B-2B	97	357	50	101	12	2	3	38	.283	350	39	5	.987
1984—Montreal	Nat.		1B	17	24	3	5	0	0	0	4	.208	27	3	1	.968
1985—Indianapolis x	A. A.		OF-1B-2B	127	431	68	133	13	3	3	36	.309	240	14	5	.981
1986—Indianapolis	A. A.		1B-OF	61	225	27	58	15	4	0	26	.258	188	14	3	.985
1986—Montreal	Nat.		1B	61	127	13	36	3	1	1	10	.283	204	17	2	.991
1987—Montreal	Nat.		1B	75	85	7	21	5	0	1	14	.247	68	2	2	.972
1988—Montreal	Nat.		1B-2B	86	94	7	29	5	1	0	3	.309	80	9	1	.989
1989—Montreal	Nat.		1B	85	114	9	31	3	1	2	17	.272	130	7	4	.972
Major League Totals—8 Years				381	520	46	137	16	6	4	54	.263	535	60	12	.980

Selected by Montreal Expos' organization in 6th round of free-agent draft, June 5, 1979.
†On disabled list, April 29 to May 15, 1981.
‡Traded to San Francisco Giants for Outfielder Mike Vail, May 25, 1983.
§Released, March 27, 1984; signed by Jacksonville (Montreal Expos' organization), April 1, 1984.
xGranted free agency, October 15, 1985; re-signed by Expos, January 22, 1986.

DIVISION SERIES RECORD

Year	Club	League	Pos.	G.	AB.	R.	H.	2B.	3B.	HR.	RBI.	B.A.	PO.	A.	E.	F.A.
1981—Montreal	Nat.		PH	2	2	0	1	0	0	0	1	.500	0	0	0	.000

BARRY LOUIS JONES

Born February 15, 1963, at Centerville, Ind.
Height, 6.04. Weight, 225.
Throws and bats righthanded.
Attended Indiana University, Bloomington, Ind.

Major League saves: 1986 (3), 1987 (1), 1988 (3), 1989 (1). Total—8.

Year	Club	League	G.	IP.	W.	L.	Pct.	H.	R.	ER.	SO.	BB.	ERA.
1984—Watertown	NYP	14	86⅔	6	3	.667	75	41	33	61	49	3.43
1985—Prince William	Carolina	28	37⅓	3	2	.600	26	7	5	42	19	1.21
1985—Nashua	Eastern	23	29	3	2	.600	19	6	5	24	10	1.55
1985—Hawaii	P. Coast	1	3	0	0	.000	5	5	3	2	1	9.00
1986—Hawaii	P. Coast	35	48	3	6	.333	41	20	19	28	20	3.56
1986—Pittsburgh	National	26	37⅓	3	4	.429	29	16	12	29	21	2.89
1987—Pittsburgh	National	32	43⅓	2	4	.333	55	34	27	28	23	5.61
1987—Vancouver	P. Coast	20	25⅓	1	2	.333	21	9	9	27	14	3.20
1988—Pittsburgh†	National	42	56⅓	1	1	.500	57	21	19	31	21	3.04
1988—Chicago	American	17	26	2	2	.500	15	7	7	17	17	2.42
1989—Chicago†	American	22	30⅓	3	2	.600	22	12	8	17	8	2.37
1989—Sarasota White Sox	Gulf Coast	7	18⅓	0	1	.000	12	7	3	14	5	1.47
National League Totals—3 Years		100	137	6	9	.400	141	71	58	88	65	3.81
American League Totals—2 Years		39	56⅓	5	4	.556	37	19	15	34	25	2.40
Major League Totals—4 Years		139	193⅓	11	13	.458	178	89	73	122	90	3.40

Selected by Texas Rangers' organization in 6th round of free-agent draft, June 8, 1981.
Selected by Pittsburgh Pirates' organization in 3rd round of free-agent draft, June 4, 1984.
†Traded to Chicago White Sox for Pitcher Dave LaPoint, August 13, 1988.
‡On disabled list, May 4 to August 24, 1989; included rehabilitation disability assignment to Sarasota, June 29 to July 18, 1989.

DOUGLAS REID JONES
(Doug)

Born June 24, 1957, at Covina, Calif.
Height, 6.02. Weight, 195.
Throws and bats righthanded.
Attended Central Arizona College, Coolidge, Ariz., and Butler University, Indianapolis, Ind.

Major League saves: 1986 (1), 1987 (8), 1988 (37), 1989 (32). Total—78.
Led Midwest League in complete games with 16 and tied for lead in shutouts with 3 in 1979.
Tied for Eastern League lead in intentional bases on balls issued with 8 in 1985.

Year	Club	League	G.	IP.	W.	L.	Pct.	H.	R.	ER.	SO.	BB.	ERA.
1978—Newark†	NYP	15	38	2	4	.333	49	30	22	27	15	5.21
1979—Burlington	Midwest	28	*190	10	10	.500	144	63	37	115	73	*1.75
1980—Stockton	California	11	76	6	2	.750	63	32	24	54	31	2.84
1980—Vancouver	P. Coast	8	53	3	2	.600	52	19	19	28	15	3.23
1980—Holyoke	Eastern	8	62	5	3	.625	57	23	20	39	26	2.90
1981—El Paso	Texas	15	90	5	7	.417	121	67	58	62	28	5.80

Year Club	League	G.	IP.	W.	L.	Pct.	H.	R.	ER.	SO.	BB.	ERA.
1981—Vancouver	P. Coast	11	80	5	3	.625	79	29	27	38	22	3.04
1982—Milwaukee	American	4	2⅔	0	0	.000	5	3	3	1	1	10.13
1982—Vancouver	P. Coast	23	106	5	8	.385	109	48	35	60	31	2.97
1983—Vancouver‡	P. Coast	3	7	0	1	.000	10	8	8	4	5	10.29
1984—Vancouver§	P. Coast	3	8	1	0	1.000	9	9	9	2	3	10.13
1984—El Paso x	Texas	16	109⅓	6	8	.429	120	61	52	62	35	4.28
1985—Waterbury	Eastern	39	116	9	4	.692	123	59	47	113	36	3.65
1986—Maine	Int'national	43	116⅓	5	6	.455	105	35	27	98	27	★2.09
1986—Cleveland	American	11	18	1	0	1.000	18	5	5	12	6	2.50
1987—Cleveland	American	49	91½	6	5	.545	101	45	32	87	24	3.15
1987—Buffalo	Am. Assoc.	23	61⅔	5	2	.714	49	18	14	61	12	2.04
1988—Cleveland	American	51	83⅓	3	4	.429	69	26	21	72	16	2.27
1989—Cleveland	American	59	80⅔	7	10	.412	76	25	21	65	13	2.34
Major League Totals—5 Years		174	276	17	19	.472	269	104	82	237	60	2.67

Selected by Milwaukee Brewers' organization in 3rd round of free-agent draft, January 10, 1978.
†On disabled list, June 20 to July 12, 1978.
‡On disabled list, April 11 to September 1, 1983.
§On disabled list, April 25 to May 30, 1984.
xGranted free agency, October 15, 1984; signed by Waterbury (Cleveland Indians' organization), April 3, 1985.

ALL-STAR GAME RECORD

Year League	IP.	W.	L.	Pct.	H.	R.	ER.	SO.	BB.	ERA.
1988—American	⅔	0	0	.000	0	0	0	1	0	0.00
1989—American	1⅓	0	0	.000	1	0	0	0	0	0.00
All-Star Game Totals—2 Years	2	0	0	.000	1	0	0	1	0	0.00

JAMES CONDIA JONES
(Jimmy)

Born April 20, 1964, at Dallas, Tex.
Height, 6.02. Weight, 190.
Throws and bats righthanded.

Shares modern major league record for fewest hits allowed, first major league game, nine innings (1), September 21, 1986.
Tied for Pacific Coast League lead in games started by pitchers with 27 in 1986.

Year Club	League	G.	IP.	W.	L.	Pct.	H.	R.	ER.	SO.	BB.	ERA.
1982—Walla Walla	Northwest	14	78⅓	4	6	.400	64	49	28	78	71	3.22
1983—Reno	California	17	116⅔	7	5	.583	96	50	35	79	49	2.70
1984—Beaumont†	Texas	13	85⅔	7	2	.778	63	28	20	49	39	2.10
1985—Beaumont‡	Texas	16	85	7	5	.583	84	51	44	57	66	4.66
1986—Las Vegas	P. Coast	28	157⅔	9	10	.474	168	84	77	114	72	4.40
1986—San Diego	National	3	18	2	0	1.000	10	6	5	15	3	2.50
1987—Las Vegas	P. Coast	4	24⅓	2	0	1.000	24	16	16	11	8	5.92
1987—San Diego	National	30	145⅔	9	7	.563	154	85	67	51	54	4.14
1988—San Diego§	National	29	179	9	14	.391	192	98	82	82	44	4.12
1989—Columbus	Int'national	20	124	8	6	.571	110	54	52	94	31	3.77
1989—New York	American	11	48	2	1	.667	56	29	28	25	16	5.25
National League Totals—3 Years		62	342⅔	20	21	.488	356	189	154	148	101	4.04
American League Totals—1 Year		11	48	2	1	.667	56	29	28	25	16	5.25
Major League Totals—4 Years		73	390⅔	22	22	.500	412	218	182	173	117	4.19

Selected by San Diego Padres' organization in 1st round (third player selected) of free-agent draft, June 7, 1982.
†On disabled list, July 13, 1984 through remainder of season.
‡On disabled list, June 29 to July 11 and July 28, 1985 through remainder of season.
§Traded with Pitcher Lance McCullers and Outfielder Stan Jefferson to New York Yankees for First Baseman-Outfielder Jack Clark and Pitcher Pat Clements, October 24, 1988.

RONALD GLEN JONES
(Ron)

Born June 11, 1964, at Seguin, Tex.
Height, 5.10. Weight, 214.
Throws right and bats lefthanded.
Attended Wharton County Junior College, Wharton, Tex.
Nephew of Alvin Jones, outfielder in Atlanta Braves'
organization, 1973 through 1976.

Major League stolen bases: 1989 (1).
Led Florida State League in total bases with 216 and slugging percentage with .524 in 1986.
Led Northwest League in game-winning RBIs with 10 in 1985.
Tied for International League lead in game-winning RBIs with 11 and sacrifice flies with 8 in 1988.
Tied for International League lead in double plays by outfielders with 4 in 1988.
Named Florida State League Most Valuable Player, 1986.

Year Club	League	Pos.	G.	AB.	R.	H.	2B.	3B.	HR.	RBI.	B.A.	PO.	A.	E.	F.A.
1985—Bend	N'west	OF	73	286	54	90	13	1	10	60	.315	88	4	★11	.893
1986—Clearwater	Fla. St.	OF	108	412	76	●153	18	★12	7	73	★.371	196	9	2	.990
1986—Portland†	P. C.	OF	11	34	4	4	1	0	0	2	.118	11	2	0	1.000
1987—Maine	Int.	OF	90	316	33	78	13	4	7	32	.247	178	4	3	.984
1988—Maine	Int.	OF	125	445	64	119	15	3	16	★75	.267	191	14	7	.967

Year Club	League	Pos.	G.	AB.	R.	H.	2B.	3B.	HR.	RBI.	B.A.	PO.	A.	E.	F.A.
1988—Philadelphia	Nat.	OF	33	124	15	36	6	1	8	26	.290	70	1	0	1.000
1989—Philadelphia‡	Nat.	OF	12	31	7	9	0	0	2	4	.290	27	1	0	1.000
Major League Totals—2 Years................			45	155	22	45	6	1	10	30	.290	97	2	0	1.000

Selected by Toronto Blue Jays' organization in 14th round of free-agent draft, June 7, 1982.
Selected by Montreal Expos' organization in secondary phase of free-agent draft, January 11, 1983.
Signed as free agent by Philadelphia Phillies' organization, October 20, 1984.
†On disabled list, August 8, 1986 through remainder of season.
‡On disabled list, April 19, 1989 through remainder of season.

TRACY DONALD JONES

Born March 31, 1961, at Inglewood, Calif.
Height, 6.03. Weight, 220.
Throws and bats righthanded.
Attended Loyola Marymount University, Los Angeles, Calif.
Brother of Terry Jones, infielder in California Angels' and Kansas City Royals'
organizations, 1984 through 1988.
Major League stolen bases: 1986 (7), 1987 (31), 1988 (18), 1989 (3). Total—59.

Year Club	League	Pos.	G.	AB.	R.	H.	2B.	3B.	HR.	RBI.	B.A.	PO.	A.	E.	F.A.
1983—Tampa...................	Fla. St.	O-3-1-S	53	118	27	32	5	3	1	15	.271	54	12	11	.857
1983—Eugene..................	N'west	2B-3B-OF	55	203	42	54	12	0	1	26	.266	81	68	12	.925
1984—Tampa†................	Fla. St.	OF	86	307	50	95	14	3	4	41	.309	150	6	0	1.000
1985—Vermont	East.	OF	75	284	40	90	12	3	4	31	.317	117	4	1	.992
1985—Denver	A. A.	OF	51	205	43	69	12	0	10	31	.337	93	2	0	1.000
1986—Cincinnati‡...........	Nat.	OF-1B	46	86	16	30	3	0	2	10	.349	46	1	0	1.000
1987—Cincinnati.............	Nat.	OF	117	359	53	104	17	3	10	44	.290	189	2	2	.990
1988—Cinc.§x-Mon.	Nat.	OF	90	224	29	66	6	1	3	24	.295	96	2	2	.980
1988—Nashville y...........	A. A.	OF	2	6	2	3	1	0	0	1	.500	2	1	0	1.000
1989—San Francisco z ...	Nat.	OF	40	97	5	18	4	0	0	12	.186	35	0	0	1.000
1989—Detroit a	Amer.	OF	46	158	17	41	10	0	3	26	.259	72	0	1	.986
National League Totals—4 Years...........			293	766	103	218	30	4	15	90	.285	366	5	4	.989
American League Totals—1 Year			46	158	17	41	10	0	3	26	.259	72	0	1	.986
Major League Totals—4 Years...............			339	924	120	259	40	4	18	116	.280	438	5	5	.989

Selected by New York Mets' organization in 4th round of free agent draft, June 7, 1982.
Selected by Cincinnati Reds' organization in secondary phase of free-agent draft, January 11, 1983.
†On disabled list, July 18 to September 18, 1984.
‡On disabled list, May 23 to June 15 and July 10 to September 1, 1986.
§On disabled list, May 5 to May 22 and May 26 to June 20, 1988; included rehabilitation disability assignment to Nashville, June 18 and June 19, 1988.
xTraded with Pitcher Pat Pacillo to Montreal Expos for Catcher Jeff Reed, Outfielder Herm Winningham and Pitcher Randy St. Claire, July 13, 1988.
yTraded to San Francisco Giants for Outfielder Mike Aldrete, December 8, 1988.
zTraded to Detroit Tigers for Outfielder Pat Sheridan, June 18, 1989.
aOn disabled list, August 17, 1989 through remainder of season.

WILLIAM TIMOTHY JONES
(Tim)

Born December 1, 1962, at Sumter, S. C.
Height, 5.10. Weight, 172.
Throws right and bats lefthanded.
Received degree in health service from The Citadel,
Charleston, S.C., in 1985.
Major League stolen bases: 1988 (4), 1989 (1). Total—5.
Tied for Appalachian League lead in sacrifice flies with 5 in 1985.
Led Appalachian League shortstops in putouts with 105 and double plays with 30 in 1985.

Year Club	League	Pos.	G.	AB.	R.	H.	2B.	3B.	HR.	RBI.	B.A.	PO.	A.	E.	F.A.
1985—Johnson City	Appal.	SS-3B	68	∗235	33	75	10	1	3	48	.319	109	148	23	.918
1986—St. Petersburg.......	Fla. St.	SS	39	142	19	43	3	2	0	27	.254	67	125	8	.960
1986—Arkansas...............	Texas	SS	96	284	36	76	15	1	2	27	.268	142	277	24	.946
1987—Arkansas...............	Texas	SS-2B	61	176	23	58	12	0	3	26	.330	80	151	9	.963
1987—Louisville	A. A.	SS	73	276	48	78	14	3	4	43	.283	112	221	13	.962
1988—Louisville	A. A.	SS	103	370	63	95	21	2	6	38	.257	145	302	15	∗.968
1988—St. Louis.................	Nat.	SS-2B-3B	31	52	2	14	0	0	0	3	.269	26	40	1	.985
1989—St. Louis.................	Nat.	2-S-3-O-C	42	75	11	22	6	0	0	7	.293	33	48	2	.976
Major League Totals—2 Years................			73	127	13	36	6	0	0	10	.283	59	88	3	.980

Selected by St. Louis Cardinals' organization in 2nd round of free-agent draft, June 3, 1985.

PAUL SCOTT JORDAN
(Ricky)

Born May 26, 1965, at Richmond, Calif.
Height, 6.03. Weight, 210.
Throws and bats righthanded.
Major League stolen bases: 1988 (1), 1989 (4). Total—5.
Tied for Eastern League lead in sacrifice flies with 9 in 1987.
Led Eastern League first basemen in total chances with 1,255 and double plays with 110 in 1987.

Led Eastern League first basemen in double plays with 100 in 1986.

Year Club	League	Pos.	G.	AB.	R.	H.	2B.	3B.	HR.	RBI.	B.A.	PO.	A.	E.	F.A.
1983—Helena...................	Pion.	1B	60	247	32	73	7	1	5	33	.296	486	35	7	.986
1984—Spartanburg..........	S. Atl.	1B	128	490	72	143	23	4	10	76	.292	1129	69	14	.988
1985—Clearwater	Fla. St.	1B	*139	528	60	146	22	8	7	62	.277	1252	86	*20	.985
1986—Reading................	East.	*1B-OF	133	478	44	131	19	3	2	60	.274	1052	87	*17	.985
1987—Reading................	East.	1B	132	475	78	151	28	3	16	95	.318	*1193	54	8	.994
1988—Maine..................	Int.	1B	87	338	42	104	23	1	7	36	.308	809	41	4	.995
1988—Philadelphia	Nat.	1B	69	273	41	84	15	1	11	43	.308	579	35	5	.992
1989—Philadelphia	Nat.	1B	144	523	63	149	22	3	12	75	.285	1271	61	9	.993
Major League Totals—2 Years...............			213	796	104	233	37	4	23	118	.293	1850	96	14	.993

Selected by Philadelphia Phillies' organization in 1st round (22nd player selected) of free-agent draft, June 6, 1983.

TERRY ALLEN JORGENSEN

Born September 2, 1966, at Kewaunee, Wis.
Height, 6.04. Weight, 210.
Throws and bats righthanded.
Attended University of Wisconsin, Oshkosh, Wis.

Tied for Southern League lead in sacrifice flies with 9 in 1989.
Led Southern League third basemen in total chances with 406 and tied for lead in double plays with 21 in 1989.

Year Club	League	Pos.	G.	AB.	R.	H.	2B.	3B.	HR.	RBI.	B.A.	PO.	A.	E.	F.A.
1987—Kenosha................	Midw.	OF	67	254	37	80	17	0	7	33	.315	54	4	5	.921
1988—Orlando	South.	3B	135	472	53	116	27	4	3	43	.246	101	216	*39	.890
1989—Orlando	South.	3B	135	514	84	135	27	5	13	101	.263	*99	*274	33	.919
1989—Minnesota.............	Amer.	3B	10	23	1	4	1	0	0	2	.174	4	19	1	.958
Major League Totals—1 Year..................			10	23	1	4	1	0	0	2	.174	4	19	1	.958

Selected by Minnesota Twins' organization in 2nd round of free-agent draft, June 2, 1987.

DOMINGO FELIX JOSE

(Known by middle name.)

Born May 8, 1965, at Santo Domingo, D. R.
Height, 6.01. Weight, 190.
Throws right and bats left and righthanded.

Major League stolen bases: 1988 (1).

Year Club	League	Pos.	G.	AB.	R.	H.	2B.	3B.	HR.	RBI.	B.A.	PO.	A.	E.	F.A.
1984—Idaho Falls...........	Pion.	OF	45	152	16	33	6	0	1	18	.217	48	6	1	.982
1985—Madison	Midw.	OF	117	409	46	89	13	3	3	33	.218	187	9	12	.942
1986—Modesto................	Calif.	OF	127	516	77	147	22	8	14	77	.285	215	12	14	.942
1987—Huntsville	South.	OF	91	296	29	67	11	1	5	42	.226	131	7	8	.945
1988—Tacoma.................	P. C.	OF	134	508	72	161	29	5	12	83	.317	253	11	8	.971
1988—Oakland................	Amer.	OF	8	6	2	2	1	0	0	1	.333	8	0	0	1.000
1989—Tacoma.................	P. C.	OF	104	387	59	111	26	0	14	63	.287	186	7	*10	.951
1989—Oakland................	Amer.	OF	20	57	3	11	2	0	0	5	.193	35	2	1	.974
Major League Totals—2 Years.................			28	63	5	13	3	0	0	6	.206	43	2	1	.978

Signed as free agent by Oakland A's organization, January 3, 1984.

WALLACE KEITH JOYNER
(Wally)

Born June 16, 1962, at Atlanta, Ga.
Height, 6.02. Weight, 198.
Throws and bats lefthanded.
Attended Brigham Young University, Provo, Utah.

Shares major league record for most home runs, month of October (4), 1987.
Major League stolen bases: 1986 (5), 1987 (8), 1988 (8), 1989 (3). Total—24.
Hit three home runs in a game, October 3, 1987.
Led American League in sacrifice flies with 12 in 1986.
Led American League first basemen in total chances with 1,520 and double plays with 148 in 1988.
Tied for Eastern League lead in intentional bases on balls received with 8 in 1984.
Led Pacific Coast League first basemen in total chances with 1,229 and double plays with 121 in 1985.

Year Club	League	Pos.	G.	AB.	R.	H.	2B.	3B.	HR.	RBI.	B.A.	PO.	A.	E.	F.A.
1983—Peoria....................	Midw.	1B	54	192	25	63	16	2	3	33	.328	480	45	6	.989
1984—Waterbury............	East.	1B-OF	134	467	81	148	24	7	12	72	.317	906	86	9	.991
1985—Edmonton.............	P. C.	1B	126	477	68	135	29	5	12	73	.283	*1107	*107	●15	.988
1986—California...............	Amer.	1B	154	593	82	172	27	3	22	100	.290	1222	139	15	.989
1987—California...............	Amer.	1B	149	564	100	161	33	1	34	117	.285	1276	92	10	.993
1988—California...............	Amer.	1B	158	597	81	176	31	2	13	85	.295	*1369	*143	8	.995
1989—California...............	Amer.	1B	159	593	78	167	30	2	16	79	.282	*1487	99	4	*.997
Major League Totals—4 Years.................			620	2347	341	676	121	8	85	381	.288	5354	473	37	.994

Selected by California Angels' organization in 3rd round of free-agent draft, June 6, 1983.

CHAMPIONSHIP SERIES RECORD

Year Club	League	Pos.	G.	AB.	R.	H.	2B.	3B.	HR.	RBI.	B.A.	PO.	A.	E.	F.A.
1986—California................	Amer.	1B	3	11	3	5	2	0	1	2	.455	24	1	0	1.000

Year League	Pos.	AB.	R.	H.	2B.	3B.	HR.	RBI.	B.A.	PO.	A.	E.	F.A.
1986—American	1B	1	0	0	0	0	0	0	.000	3	1	0	1.000

EDWARD JAMES JURAK

Name pronounced YOU-rack.

(Ed)

Born October 24, 1957, at Los Angeles, Calif.
Height, 6.02. Weight, 187.
Throws and bats righthanded.

Major League stolen bases: 1983 (1).
Led Pacific Coast League in sacrifice flies with 10 in 1988.
Led Eastern League shortstops in double plays with 76 in 1979.

Year Club	League	Pos.	G.	AB.	R.	H.	2B.	3B.	HR.	RBI.	B.A.	PO.	A.	E.	F.A.
1975—Elmira	NYP	SS	68	250	41	63	9	3	0	25	.252	104	192	★43	.873
1976—Winston-Salem	Carol.	SS	113	401	49	88	6	2	4	35	.219	168	346	★55	.903
1977—Bristol	East.	SS	123	441	74	116	12	8	1	36	.263	173	345	26	.952
1978—Pawtucket	Int.	SS-3B	23	46	9	12	1	1	0	6	.261	11	34	8	.849
1978—Winter Haven†	Fla. St.	SS-3B-1B	38	139	14	37	0	1	0	11	.266	49	99	16	.902
1979—Bristol	East.	SS	135	435	50	96	17	2	0	41	.221	★208	★374	★40	.936
1980—Pawtucket‡	Int.	SS-3B	83	221	16	58	8	1	3	31	.262	72	130	19	.914
1981—Bristol§	East.	SS-3B-2B	87	297	63	101	19	3	1	25	★.340	114	194	29	.914
1981—Pawtucket	Int.	SS	23	90	13	27	3	2	1	9	.300	39	81	10	.923
1982—Pawtucket	Int.	3B-SS	81	284	39	84	14	1	9	43	.296	53	177	17	.931
1982—Boston	Amer.	3B-OF	12	21	3	7	0	0	0	7	.333	7	17	2	.923
1983—Boston	Amer.	S-1-3-2	75	159	19	44	8	4	0	18	.277	197	117	11	.966
1984—Boston	Amer.	1-2-3-S	47	66	6	16	3	1	1	7	.242	92	40	3	.978
1985—Pawtucket	Int.	3B-OF-1B	72	263	33	68	11	2	6	38	.259	183	75	8	.970
1985—Boston x	Amer.	3-S-1-O	26	13	4	3	0	0	0	0	.231	5	10	2	.882
1986—San Jose y	Calif.	SS-3B	28	71	14	23	0	0	3	10	.324	55	66	9	.931
1987—Tulsa	Texas	SS-3B	98	338	67	117	19	3	10	47	.346	153	247	19	.955
1987—Oklahoma City z	A. A.	3B-SS	31	94	9	29	0	1	3	8	.309	29	62	4	.958
1988—Tacoma	P. C.	SS-3B-1B	126	448	63	132	22	2	7	67	.295	188	280	23	.953
1988—Oakland a	Amer.	3B	3	1	1	0	0	0	0	0	.000	0	0	0	.000
1989—San Francisco	Nat.	S-3-2-O-1	30	42	2	10	0	0	0	1	.238	20	17	5	.881
1989—Phoenix b	P. C.	3-1-2-O-S	52	173	23	51	7	0	1	17	.295	84	67	9	.944
1989—Indianapolis c	A. A.	3B	1	3	0	0	0	0	0	0	.000	0	6	0	1.000
American League Totals—5 Years			163	260	33	70	11	5	1	32	.269	301	184	18	.964
National League Totals—1 Year			30	42	2	10	0	0	0	1	.238	20	17	5	.881
Major League Totals—6 Years			193	302	35	80	11	5	1	33	.265	321	201	23	.958

Selected by Boston Red Sox' organization in 3rd round of free-agent draft, June 4, 1975.
†On disabled list, May 4 to June 16, 1978.
‡On disabled list, April 16 to April 28 and May 28 to June 7, 1980.
§On disabled list, June 10 to July 4, 1981.
xReleased, March 19, 1986; signed by San Jose (Independent), August 2, 1986.
yReleased, December 31, 1986; signed by Tulsa (Texas Rangers' organization), February 17, 1987.
zGranted free agency, October 15, 1987; signed by Oakland Athletics' organization, November 10, 1987.
aGranted free agency, October 15, 1988; signed by San Francisco Giants, November 3, 1988.
bTraded to Indianapolis (Montreal Expos' organization) for a player to be named later, September 4, 1989.
cGranted free agency, October 15, 1989.

DAVID CHRISTOPHER JUSTICE

(Dave)

Born April 14, 1966, at Cincinnati, O.
Height, 6.03. Weight, 195.
Throws and bats lefthanded.
Attended Thomas More College, Crestview Hills, Ky.

Major League stolen bases: 1989 (2).
Tied for Appalachian League lead in sacrifice flies with 5 in 1985.

Year Club	League	Pos.	G.	AB.	R.	H.	2B.	3B.	HR.	RBI.	B.A.	PO.	A.	E.	F.A.
1985—Pulaski	Appal.	OF	66	204	39	50	8	0	●10	46	.245	86	2	4	.957
1986—Sumter	S. Atl.	OF	61	220	48	66	16	0	10	61	.300	124	7	4	.970
1986—Durham	Carol.	OF-1B	67	229	47	64	9	1	12	44	.279	163	5	1	.994
1987—Greenville	South.	OF	93	348	38	79	12	4	6	40	.227	199	4	8	.962
1988—Richmond	Int.	OF	70	227	27	46	9	1	8	28	.203	136	5	4	.972
1988—Greenville	South.	OF	58	198	34	55	13	1	9	37	.278	100	3	5	.954
1989—Richmond	Int.	OF-1B	115	391	47	102	24	3	12	58	.261	220	15	6	.975
1989—Atlanta	Nat.	OF	16	51	7	12	3	0	1	3	.235	24	0	0	1.000
Major League Totals—1 Year			16	51	7	12	3	0	1	3	.235	24	0	0	1.000

Selected by Atlanta Braves' organization in 4th round of free-agent draft, June 3, 1985.

JEFFREY PATRICK KAISER

(Jeff)

Born July 24, 1960, at Wyandotte, Mich.
Height, 6.03. Weight, 195.
Throws left and bats righthanded.

Received bachelor of arts degree in business administration from
Western Michigan University, Kalamazoo, Mich.

Year Club	League	G.	IP.	W.	L.	Pct.	H.	R.	ER.	SO.	BB.	ERA.
1982—Medford	Northwest	15	78	8	1	*.889	91	56	46	69	57	5.31
1983—Modesto	California	25	164⅔	12	9	.571	160	84	70	102	80	3.83
1984—Albany	Eastern	7	47⅔	5	1	.833	36	11	10	20	15	1.89
1984—Tacoma†	P. Coast	14	74⅔	4	7	.364	81	52	38	38	28	4.58
1985—Oakland	American	15	16⅔	0	0	.000	25	32	27	10	20	14.58
1985—Tacoma‡	P. Coast	27	46⅓	4	2	.667	33	10	9	36	18	1.75
1986—Tacoma§x	P. Coast	34	110⅔	4	4	.500	123	70	53	63	52	4.31
1987—Buffalo	Am. Assoc.	22	71⅓	5	3	.625	87	52	41	53	32	5.17
1987—Cleveland y	American	2	3⅓	0	0	.000	4	6	6	2	3	16.20
1988—Colorado Springs	P. Coast	36	53	3	2	.600	56	23	22	47	19	3.74
1988—Cleveland	American	3	2⅔	0	0	.000	2	0	0	0	1	0.00
1989—Colorado Springs	P. Coast	31	45⅓	3	6	.333	64	29	22	46	18	4.37
1989—Cleveland	American	6	3⅔	0	1	.000	5	5	3	4	5	7.36
Major League Totals—4 Years		26	26⅓	0	1	.000	36	43	36	16	29	12.30

Selected by Toronto Blue Jays' organization in 7th round of free-agent draft, June 8, 1981.
Selected by Oakland A's organization in 10th round of free-agent draft, June 7, 1982.
†On disabled list, July 20 to August 3, 1984.
‡On disabled list, June 21 to July 7, 1985.
§On disabled list, May 4 to May 14, 1986.
xTraded to Cleveland Indians for Pitcher Curt Wardle, February 23, 1987.
yOn disabled list, August 9 to August 31, 1987.

KEITH WADE KAISER

Born May 24, 1967, at San Antonio, Tex.
Height, 6.04. Weight, 205.
Throws right and bats left and righthanded.
Attended New Mexico State University, Las Cruces, N.M.

Led South Atlantic League in wild pitches with 17 in 1988.

Year Club	League	G.	IP.	W.	L.	Pct.	H.	R.	ER.	SO.	BB.	ERA.
1986—Sarasota Reds	Gulf Coast	11	28⅓	0	4	.000	28	22	10	14	25	3.18
1987—Billings	Pioneer	13	76	6	5	.545	67	37	26	71	39	3.08
1988—Greensboro	S. Atlantic	28	186	11	9	.550	135	67	52	159	*101	2.52
1989—Chattanooga	Southern	28	158	5	13	.278	169	*110	*97	105	86	5.53

Selected by Cincinnati Reds' organization in 21st round of free-agent draft, June 3, 1985.
Signed as free agent by Cincinnati Reds' organization, July 7, 1986.

SCOTT ANDREW KAMIENIECKI

Name pronounced Kam-ah-NICK-ee.
Born April 19, 1964, at Mt. Clemens, Mich.
Height, 6.00. Weight, 190.
Throws and bats righthanded.
Attended University of Michigan, Ann Arbor, Mich.

Tied for Carolina League lead in complete games with 7 in 1988.

Year Club	League	G.	IP.	W.	L.	Pct.	H.	R.	ER.	SO.	BB.	ERA.
1987—Albany	Eastern	10	37	1	3	.250	41	25	22	19	33	5.35
1987—Prince William	Carolina	19	112⅓	9	5	.643	91	61	52	84	78	4.17
1988—Prince William	Carolina	15	100⅓	6	7	.462	115	62	49	72	50	4.40
1988—Fort Lauderdale	Florida St.	12	77	3	6	.333	71	36	31	51	40	3.62
1989—Albany	Eastern	24	151	10	9	.526	142	67	62	*140	57	3.70

Selected by Detroit Tigers' organization in 2nd round of free-agent draft, June 7, 1982.
Selected by Milwaukee Brewers' organization in 23rd round of free-agent draft, June 3, 1985.
Selected by New York Yankees' organization in 14th round of free-agent draft, June 2, 1986.

RONALD JOSEPH KARKOVICE

Name pronounced CAR-koh-vice.

(Ron)

Born August 8, 1963, at Union, N. J.
Height, 6.01. Weight, 215.
Throws and bats righthanded.

Major League stolen bases: 1986 (1), 1987 (3), 1988 (4). Total—8.
Led Gulf Coast League batters in strikeouts with 73 in 1982.
Led Eastern League catchers in double plays with 13 in 1985.
Led Midwest League catchers in fielding percentage with .996 in 1983.
Led Gulf Coast League catchers in total chances with 394 and tied for lead in double plays with 5 in 1982.

Year Club	League	Pos.	G.	AB.	R.	H.	2B.	3B.	HR.	RBI.	B.A.	PO.	A.	E.	F.A.
1982—Sarasota W.S.	Gulf C.	C	60	214	34	56	6	0	7	32	.262	*331	*51	12	.970
1983—Appleton	Midw.	C-OF	97	326	54	78	17	3	13	48	.239	682	91	4	.995
1984—Glens Falls	East.	C	88	260	37	56	9	1	13	39	.215	442	*68	11	.979
1984—Denver	A. A.	C	31	86	7	19	1	0	2	10	.221	149	28	3	.983
1985—Glens Falls	East.	C	99	324	37	70	9	3	11	37	.216	573	*103	*14	.980
1986—Birmingham	South.	C	97	319	63	90	13	1	20	53	.282	463	72	10	.982
1986—Chicago	Amer.	C	37	97	13	24	7	0	4	13	.247	227	19	1	.996

Year	Club	League	Pos.	G.	AB.	R.	H.	2B.	3B.	HR.	RBI.	B.A.	PO.	A.	E.	F.A.
1987—Chicago		Amer.	C	39	85	7	6	0	0	2	7	.071	147	20	3	.982
1987—Hawaii		P. C.	C-OF	34	104	15	19	3	0	4	11	.183	108	13	3	.976
1988—Vancouver		P. C.	C	39	116	12	29	10	0	2	13	.250	202	16	3	.986
1988—Chicago		Amer.	C	46	115	10	20	4	0	3	9	.174	190	24	1	.995
1989—Chicago		Amer.	C	71	182	21	48	9	2	3	24	.264	299	47	5	.986
Major League Totals—4 Years				193	479	51	98	20	2	12	53	.205	863	110	10	.990

Selected by Chicago White Sox' organization in 1st round (14th player selected) of free-agent draft, June 7, 1982.

CHARLES PATRICK KEEDY
(Pat)

Born January 10, 1959, at Birmingham, Ala.
Height, 6.04. Weight, 215.
Throws and bats righthanded.
Received bachelor of science degree in education from
Auburn University, Auburn, Ala.

Major League stolen bases: 1987 (1).
Led Eastern League third basemen in double plays with 25 in 1981.

Year	Club	League	Pos.	G.	AB.	R.	H.	2B.	3B.	HR.	RBI.	B.A.	PO.	A.	E.	F.A.
1979—Salinas		Calif.	3B-SS	52	125	22	26	3	0	4	15	.208	47	109	9	.945
1980—El Paso		Texas	SS-3B	26	98	11	14	3	0	1	10	.143	29	87	14	.892
1980—Salinas†		Calif.	SS-3B	42	118	16	26	4	0	4	17	.220	32	89	11	.917
1981—Holyoke		East.	3B-2B-1B	107	367	45	90	14	2	6	34	.245	63	239	23	.929
1982—Holyoke		East.	3B-SS	125	437	68	108	19	6	19	73	.247	91	279	30	.925
1983—Edmonton‡		P. C.	3-O-1-2-S	66	210	38	47	13	1	14	40	.224	46	123	17	.909
1984—Edmonton		P. C.	3-O-S-1	100	348	64	90	20	4	17	53	.259	119	124	18	.931
1985—Edmonton		P. C.	I-O-P-C	107	365	59	101	24	4	17	61	.277	201	116	12	.964
1985—California		Amer.	3B-OF	3	4	1	2	1	0	1	1	.500	1	0	0	1.000
1986—Edmonton		P. C.	1-3-O-S	57	187	27	38	7	1	7	22	.203	229	72	6	.980
1986—Midland§		Texas	3B-1B-OF	60	233	41	59	8	0	11	29	.253	111	63	11	.941
1987—Hawaii		P. C.	O-1-S-3	95	302	56	85	13	3	17	55	.281	294	87	9	.977
1987—Chicago x		Amer.	3-1-S-2-O	17	41	6	7	1	0	2	2	.171	17	32	2	.961
1988—Tucson y		P. C.	3-O-S-2-1	59	171	24	46	4	0	6	22	.269	50	65	3	.975
1989—Cleveland		Amer.	O-3-1-S	9	14	3	3	2	0	1	1	.214	4	7	1	.917
1989—Colo. Springs za		P. C.	3B	3	9	1	3	1	0	0	1	.333	1	5	0	1.000
Major League Totals—3 Years				29	59	10	12	4	0	3	4	.203	22	39	3	.953

Selected by Chicago White Sox' organization in 13th round of free-agent draft, June 8, 1976.
Selected by California Angels' organization in 5th round of free-agent draft, June 5, 1979.
†On disabled list, August 13, 1980 through remainder of season.
‡On disabled list, May 17 to June 17 and July 5 to July 20, 1983.
§Granted free agency, October 15, 1986; signed by Chicago White Sox' organization, November 14, 1986.
xReleased, November 23, 1987; signed by Tucson (Houston Astros' organization), December 16, 1987.
yGranted free agency, October 15, 1988; signed by Colorado Springs (Cleveland Indians' organization), November 16, 1988.
zOn disabled list, May 30, 1989 through remainder of season.
aGranted free agency, October 15, 1989.

PITCHING RECORD

Year	Club	League	G.	IP.	W.	L.	Pct.	H.	R.	ER.	SO.	BB.	ERA.
1985—Edmonton		P. Coast	2	3	0	0	.000	1	1	1	0	2	3.00

CARL KEKOA KELIIPULEOLE

Name pronounced Ka-lee-ee-poo-lee-oh-lee.

Born January 7, 1966, at Guam.
Height, 6.00. Weight, 200.
Throws right and bats lefthanded.
Attended Brigham Young University, Provo, Utah.

Year	Club	League	G.	IP.	W.	L.	Pct.	H.	R.	ER.	SO.	BB.	ERA.
1987—Waterloo		Midwest	29	59⅓	3	3	.500	38	21	16	50	22	2.43
1988—Kinston		Carolina	31	46⅓	1	4	.200	39	16	14	63	28	2.72
1988—Williamsport		Eastern	28	31⅔	1	4	.200	35	14	9	28	17	2.56
1989—Canton-Akron		Eastern	27	89	5	5	.500	90	43	39	64	35	3.94

Selected by Cleveland Indians' organization in 4th round of free-agent draft, June 2, 1987.

ROBERTO CONRADO KELLY

Born October 1, 1964, at Panama City, Panama.
Height, 6.04. Weight, 185.
Throws and bats righthanded.
Attended Jose Dolores Moscote College, Panama.

Major League stolen bases: 1987 (9), 1988 (5), 1989 (35). Total—49.
Led International League in stolen bases with 51 in 1987.
Led International League outfielders in total chances with 345 in 1987.

Year	Club	League	Pos.	G.	AB.	R.	H.	2B.	3B.	HR.	RBI.	B.A.	PO.	A.	E.	F.A.
1982—Bradenton Yanks	Gulf C.		SS-OF	31	86	13	17	1	1	1	18	.198	47	79	19	.869
1983—Oneonta		NYP	OF-3B	48	167	17	36	1	2	2	17	.216	70	3	5	.936
1983—Greensboro		S. Atl.	OF	20	49	6	13	0	0	0	3	.265	30	2	0	1.000

Year	Club	League	Pos.	G.	AB.	R.	H.	2B.	3B.	HR.	RBI.	B.A.	PO.	A.	E.	F.A.
1984—Greensboro	S. Atl.	Of-1B	111	361	68	86	13	2	1	26	.238	228	5	4	.983
1985—Fort Lauderdale†	Fla. St.	OF	114	417	86	103	4	*13	3	38	.247	187	1	1	.995
1986—Albany‡	East.	OF	86	299	42	87	11	4	2	43	.291	206	8	7	.968
1987—Columbus	Int.	OF	118	471	77	131	19	8	13	62	.278	*331	4	10	.971
1987—New York	Amer.	OF	23	52	12	14	3	0	1	7	.269	42	0	2	.955
1988—New York§	Amer.	OF	38	77	9	19	4	1	1	7	.247	70	1	1	.986
1988—Columbus	Int.	OF	30	120	25	40	8	1	3	16	.333	51	1	0	1.000
1989—New York x	Amer.	OF	137	441	65	133	18	3	9	48	.302	353	9	6	.984
Major League Totals—3 Years			198	570	86	166	25	4	11	62	.291	465	10	9	.981

Signed as free agent by New York Yankees' organization, February 21, 1982.
†Switch-hitter.
‡On disabled list, July 10 to August 23, 1986.
§On disabled list, June 29 to September 1, 1988.
xOn disabled list, May 26 to June 12, 1989.

TERRENCE EDWARD KENNEDY
(Terry)

Born June 4, 1956, at Euclid, O.
Height, 6.04. Weight, 224.
Throws right and bats lefthanded.
Attended Florida State University, Tallahassee, Fla.

Son of Bob Kennedy, third baseman-outfielder with Chicago AL, Cleveland, Baltimore, Detroit and Brooklyn, 1939 through 1957; scout, Cleveland, 1958 through 1961; minor league manager, Chicago Cubs' organization, 1962; coach, Chicago Cubs, 1963 and 1964; Chicago Cubs executive, 1965; minor league manager, Los Angeles Dodgers' organization, 1966; coach, Atlanta Braves, 1967; manager, Oakland A's, 1968; Director of Player Development, St. Louis Cardinals, 1969 through 1976; Executive Vice President, Chicago Cubs, 1977 through 1981; Houston Astros Vice-President-Baseball Operations, 1982 through 1985; and San Francisco Giants Vice-President-Baseball Operations since 1986; brother of Bob Kennedy Jr., pitcher in St. Louis Cardinals' organization, 1971 through 1975; scout, Seattle Mariners, 1976; scout, Chicago Cubs, 1977 through 1981; scout with Houston Astros, 1982 through 1985.

Shares National League record for most doubles by catcher, season (40), 1982.
Major League stolen bases: 1982 (1), 1983 (1), 1984 (1), 1987 (1), 1989 (1). Total—5.
Led National League catchers in double plays with 12 in 1981 and tied for lead with 11 in 1982 and 12 in 1985.
Named catcher on THE SPORTING NEWS National League Silver Slugger team, 1983.
Named College Player of the Year by THE SPORTING NEWS, 1977.
Received reported $100,000 bonus to sign with St. Louis Cardinals, 1977.
Named catcher on THE SPORTING NEWS College Baseball All-America Team, 1976 and 1977.

Year	Club	League	Pos.	G.	AB.	R.	H.	2B.	3B.	HR.	RBI.	B.A.	PO.	A.	E.	F.A.
1977—Johnson City	Appal.	C-1B	12	39	14	23	7	2	3	15	.590	66	3	1	.986
1977—St. Petersburg	Fla. St.	C	45	166	22	41	8	0	4	22	.247	168	22	6	.969
1978—Arkansas	Texas	C-OF	69	239	55	69	14	0	10	54	.289	365	30	7	.983
1978—Springfield	A. A.	C-1B	64	230	35	76	13	0	10	46	.330	331	26	7	.981
1978—St. Louis	Nat.	C	10	29	0	5	0	0	0	2	.172	46	4	1	.980
1979—Springfield	A. A.	C	84	294	35	86	18	1	13	64	.293	434	38	13	.973
1979—St. Louis	Nat.	C	33	109	11	31	7	0	2	17	.284	135	7	1	.993
1980—St. Louis†	Nat.	C-OF	84	248	28	63	12	3	4	34	.254	231	22	7	.973
1981—San Diego	Nat.	C	101	382	32	115	24	1	2	41	.301	465	63	*20	.964
1982—San Diego	Nat.	C-1B	153	562	75	166	42	1	21	97	.295	777	66	9	.989
1983—San Diego	Nat.	C	149	549	47	156	27	2	17	98	.284	807	82	12	.987
1984—San Diego	Nat.	C	148	530	54	127	16	1	14	57	.240	708	54	14	.982
1985—San Diego	Nat.	C-1B	143	532	54	139	27	1	10	74	.261	662	68	10	.986
1986—San Diego‡	Nat.	C	141	432	46	114	22	1	12	57	.264	692	70	8	.990
1987—Baltimore	Amer.	C	143	512	51	128	13	1	18	62	.250	750	*58	6	.993
1988—Baltimore§	Amer.	C	85	265	20	60	10	0	3	16	.226	332	23	2	.994
1989—San Francisco x	Nat.	C-1B	125	355	19	85	15	0	5	34	.239	519	47	8	.986
National League Totals—10 Years			1087	3728	366	1001	192	10	87	511	.269	5042	483	90	.984
American League Totals—2 Years			228	777	71	188	23	1	21	78	.242	1082	81	8	.993
Major League Totals—12 Years			1315	4505	437	1189	215	11	108	589	.264	6124	564	98	.986

Selected by St. Louis Cardinals' organization in 1st round (sixth player selected) of free-agent draft, June 7, 1977.
†Traded with Catcher Steve Swisher, Pitchers John Littlefield, Al Olmsted, Kim Seaman and John Urrea and Infielder Mike Phillips to San Diego Padres for Pitchers Rollie Fingers and Bob Shirley, Catcher-First Baseman Gene Tenace and a player to be named later, December 8, 1980; St. Louis Cardinals' organization acquired catcher Bob Geren to complete deal, December 10, 1980.
‡Traded with Pitcher Mark Williamson to Baltimore Orioles for Pitcher Storm Davis, October 30, 1986.
§Traded to San Francisco Giants for Catcher Bob Melvin, January 24, 1989.
xGranted free agency, November 13, 1989; re-signed by Giants, December 8, 1989.

CHAMPIONSHIP SERIES RECORD

Year	Club	League	Pos.	G.	AB.	R.	H.	2B.	3B.	HR.	RBI.	B.A.	PO.	A.	E.	F.A.
1984—San Diego	Nat.	C	5	18	2	4	0	0	0	1	.222	28	4	0	1.000
1989—San Francisco	Nat.	C	5	16	0	3	1	0	0	0	.188	26	1	0	1.000
Championship Series Totals—2 Years			10	34	2	7	1	0	0	1	.206	54	5	0	1.000

WORLD SERIES RECORD

Year	Club	League	Pos.	G.	AB.	R.	H.	2B.	3B.	HR.	RBI.	B.A.	PO.	A.	E.	F.A.
1984—San Diego	Nat.	C	5	19	2	4	1	0	1	3	.211	30	2	0	1.000

Year Club League	Pos.	G.	AB.	R.	H.	2B.	3B.	HR.	RBI.	B.A.	PO.	A.	E.	F.A.
1989—San Francisco ...... Nat.	C	4	12	1	2	0	0	0	2	.167	23	1	1	.960
World Series Totals—2 Years		9	31	3	6	1	0	1	5	.194	53	3	1	.982

ALL-STAR GAME RECORD

Year League	Pos.	AB.	R.	H.	2B.	3B.	HR.	RBI.	B.A.	PO.	A.	E.	F.A.
1981—National	PH	1	0	0	0	0	0	0	.000	0	0	0	.000
1985—National	C	2	0	1	0	0	0	1	.500	0	0	1	.000
1987—American	C	2	0	0	0	0	0	0	.000	3	1	0	1.000
All-Star Game Totals—3 Years....................		5	0	1	0	0	0	1	.200	3	1	1	.800

Member of National League All-Star Team in 1983; did not play.

CHARLES PATRICK KERFELD
(Charley)

Born September 28, 1963, at Knob Noster, Mo.
Height, 6.07. Weight, 250.
Throws and bats righthanded.
Attended Yavapai College, Prescott, Ariz.

Major League saves: 1986 (7)
Led South Atlantic League pitchers in complete games with 12 and tied for lead in games started with 28 in 1983.
Named South Atlantic League Pitcher of the Year, 1983.

Year Club	League	G.	IP.	W.	L.	Pct.	H.	R.	ER.	SO.	BB.	ERA.
1983—Asheville	S. Atlantic	28	★192	★16	10	.615	171	84	62	189	85	2.91
1984—Columbus†	Southern	24	162⅔	14	9	.609	140	80	54	118	79	2.99
1984—Tucson	P. Coast	1	3⅔	0	1	.000	6	4	4	3	1	9.82
1985—Tucson	P. Coast	26	163⅓	10	11	.476	176	95	80	123	74	4.41
1985—Houston	National	11	44⅓	4	2	.667	44	22	20	30	25	4.06
1986—Houston‡	National	61	93⅔	11	2	.846	71	32	27	77	42	2.59
1987—Houston§	National	21	29⅓	0	2	.000	34	22	22	17	21	6.67
1987—Tucson	P. Coast	32	62⅔	4	4	.500	61	36	33	59	27	4.74
1988—Columbus x	Southern	13	64	2	7	.222	63	36	32	63	21	4.50
1989—Tucson	P. Coast	53	73⅓	3	11	.214	89	56	45	77	55	5.52
1989—Osceola......................................	Florida St.	5	7⅔	0	0	.000	4	2	1	8	3	1.17
Major League Totals—3 Years...........................		93	167⅔	15	6	.714	149	76	69	124	88	3.70

Selected by Philadelphia Phillies' organization in 24th round of free-agent draft, June 8, 1981.
Selected by Seattle Mariners' organization in secondary phase of free-agent draft, January 12, 1982.
Selected by Houston Astros' organization in secondary phase of free-agent draft, June 7, 1982.
†On disabled list, June 4 to June 28, 1984.
‡On disabled list, June 14 to July 2, 1986.
§On disabled list, July 31 to September 21, 1987.
xOn Houston disabled list, March 27 to April 21, 1988.

CHAMPIONSHIP SERIES RECORD

Year Club	League	G.	IP.	W.	L.	Pct.	H.	R.	ER.	SO.	BB.	ERA.
1986—Houston...	National	3	4	0	1	.000	2	1	1	4	1	2.25

JAMES EDWARD KEY
(Jimmy)

Born April 22, 1961, at Huntsville, Ala.
Height, 6.01. Weight, 190.
Throws left and bats righthanded.
Attended Clemson University, Clemson, S. C.

Major League saves: 1984 (10).
Named American League Pitcher of the Year by THE SPORTING NEWS, 1987.
Named lefthanded pitcher on THE SPORTING NEWS American League All-Star Team, 1987.

Year Club	League	G.	IP.	W.	L.	Pct.	H.	R.	ER.	SO.	BB.	ERA.
1982—Medicine Hat................................	Pioneer	5	31⅓	2	1	.667	27	12	8	25	10	2.30
1982—Florence	S. Atlantic	9	58	5	2	.714	59	33	24	49	18	3.72
1983—Knoxville	Southern	14	101	6	5	.545	86	35	32	57	40	2.85
1983—Syracuse	Int'national	16	89½	4	8	.333	87	58	41	71	33	4.13
1984—Toronto	American	63	62	4	5	.444	70	37	32	44	32	4.65
1985—Toronto†	American	35	212⅔	14	6	.700	188	77	71	85	50	3.00
1986—Toronto	American	36	232	14	11	.560	222	98	92	141	74	3.57
1987—Toronto	American	36	261	17	8	.680	210	93	80	161	66	★2.76
1988—Toronto‡	American	21	131⅓	12	5	.706	127	55	48	65	30	3.29
1988—Dunedin	Florida St.	4	21⅓	2	0	1.000	15	2	0	11	1	0.00
1989—Toronto§	American	33	216	13	14	.481	226	99	93	118	27	3.88
Major League Totals—6 Years.............................		224	1115	74	49	.602	1043	459	416	614	279	3.36

Selected by Chicago White Sox' organization in 10th round of free-agent draft, June 5, 1979.
Selected by Toronto Blue Jays' organization in 3rd round of free-agent draft, June 7, 1982.
†Appeared in one game as a pinch-runner.
‡On disabled list, April 15 to June 29, 1988; included rehabilitation disability assignment to Dunedin, June 10 to June 27, 1988.
§On disabled list, August 4 to August 19, 1989.

CHAMPIONSHIP SERIES RECORD

Year Club	League	G.	IP.	W.	L.	Pct.	H.	R.	ER.	SO.	BB.	ERA.
1985—Toronto	American	2	8⅔	0	1	.000	15	5	5	5	2	5.19
1989—Toronto	American	1	6	1	0	1.000	7	3	3	2	2	4.50
Championship Series Totals—2 Years		3	14⅔	1	1	.500	22	8	8	7	4	4.91

ALL-STAR GAME RECORD

Year League	IP.	W.	L.	Pct.	H.	R.	ER.	SO.	BB.	ERA.
1985—American	⅓	0	0	.000	0	0	0	0	0	0.00

DANA ERVIN KIECKER

Born February 25, 1961, at Sleepy Eye, Minn.
Height, 6.03. Weight, 180.
Throws and bats righthanded.
Attended St. Cloud State University, St. Cloud, Minn.

Led Florida State League in games started by pitchers with 29 in 1985.
Tied for Eastern League lead in balks with 5 in 1986.

Year Club	League	G.	IP.	W.	L.	Pct.	H.	R.	ER.	SO.	BB.	ERA.
1983—Elmira	NYP	16	★111⅔	11	5	.688	92	50	34	78	44	2.74
1984—Winston-Salem	Carolina	29	137⅔	6	11	.353	142	86	67	82	55	4.38
1985—Winter Haven	Florida St.	29	★193⅔	12	●12	.500	176	72	56	60	59	2.60
1986—New Britain	Eastern	24	156⅓	7	12	.368	★171	88	72	71	48	4.14
1987—New Britain	Eastern	39	153	7	10	.412	164	76	65	66	66	3.82
1988—Pawtucket	Int'national	23	132⅓	7	7	.500	120	65	54	74	46	3.67
1988—New Britain	Eastern	1	6	1	0	1.000	3	0	0	1	0	0.00
1989—Pawtucket	Int'national	28	147⅓	8	9	.471	163	83	60	87	36	3.67

Selected by Boston Red Sox' organization in 8th round of free-agent draft, June 6, 1983.

STEVEN GEORGE KIEFER

Name pronounced Key-fer.

(Steve)

Born October 18, 1960, at Chicago, Ill.
Height, 6.01. Weight, 180.
Throws and bats righthanded.
Attended Cerritos College, Norwalk, Calif. and Fullerton College, Fullerton, Calif.

Led American Association in slugging percentage with .668 in 1987.
Led Pacific Coast League shortstops in errors with 35 in 1984.
Tied for Eastern League lead in sacrifice hits with 12 in 1983.

Year Club	League	Pos.	G.	AB.	R.	H.	2B.	3B.	HR.	RBI.	B.A.	PO.	A.	E.	F.A.
1981—Medford	N'west	SS-3B	55	192	38	47	7	5	4	22	.245	68	175	17	.935
1982—Madison	Midw.	SS	124	415	72	97	24	1	15	58	.234	173	395	44	.928
1983—Albany	East.	SS-3B-OF	123	415	68	102	18	1	19	81	.246	186	306	38	.928
1984—Tacoma	P. C.	SS-3B	125	455	63	122	18	3	16	54	.268	189	328	38	.932
1984—Oakland	Amer.	SS-3B	23	40	7	7	1	2	0	2	.175	15	35	5	.909
1985—Tacoma†	P. C.	3B-SS	85	331	41	87	25	2	12	53	.263	80	171	13	.951
1985—Oakland‡	Amer.	3B	40	66	8	13	1	1	1	10	.197	15	37	7	.881
1986—Vancouver	P. C.	3B-2B-SS	126	426	67	114	22	6	15	69	.268	123	266	24	.942
1986—Milwaukee	Amer.	SS	2	6	0	0	0	0	0	0	.000	7	8	0	1.000
1987—Denver	A. A.	3B	90	361	90	119	21	4	31	95	.330	60	161	15	.936
1987—Milwaukee	Amer.	3B-2B	28	99	17	20	4	0	5	17	.202	16	50	2	.971
1988—Milwaukee	Amer.	2B-3B	7	10	2	3	1	0	1	1	.300	4	8	1	.923
1988—Denver§	A. A.	3B-2B-1B	79	294	47	63	11	8	10	45	.214	93	137	15	.929
1989—Columbus	Int.	3B	80	286	48	79	18	6	7	38	.276	53	131	17	.915
1989—New York xy	Amer.	3B	5	8	0	1	0	0	0	0	.125	1	1	0	1.000
Major League Totals—6 Years			105	229	34	44	7	3	7	30	.192	58	139	15	.929

Selected by Oakland A's organization in 1st round (16th player selected) of free-agent draft, January 13, 1981.
†On disabled list, May 6 to May 20, 1985.
‡Traded with Pitchers Mike Fulmer and Pete Kendrick and Catcher Charlie O'Brien to Milwaukee Brewers for Pitcher Moose Haas, March 30, 1986.
§Granted free agency, October 15, 1988; signed by New York Yankees, November 26, 1988.
xOn disabled list, August 23 to September 8, 1989.
yReleased, October 4, 1989; signed by Buffalo (Pittsburgh Pirates' organization), November 17, 1989.

DARRYL ANDREW KILE

Born December 2, 1968, at Garden Grove, Calif.
Height, 6.05. Weight, 185.
Throws and bats righthanded.
Attended Chaffey College, Alta Loma, Calif.

Tied for Southern League lead in shutouts with 2 in 1989.

Year Club	League	G.	IP.	W.	L.	Pct.	H.	R.	ER.	SO.	BB.	ERA.
1988—Sarasota Astros	Gulf Coast	12	59⅔	5	3	.625	48	34	21	54	33	3.17
1989—Columbus	Southern	20	125⅔	11	6	.647	74	47	36	108	68	2.58
1989—Tucson	P. Coast	6	25⅔	2	1	.667	33	20	17	18	13	5.96

Selected by Houston Astros' organization in 30th round of free-agent draft, June 2, 1987.

PAUL NELSON KILGUS

Born February 2, 1962, at Bowling Green, Ky.
Height, 6.01. Weight, 185.
Throws and bats lefthanded.
Received bachelor of science degree in biology from University of Kentucky, Lexington, Ky., in 1984.
Major League saves: 1989 (2).

Year Club	League	G.	IP.	W.	L.	Pct.	H.	R.	ER.	SO.	BB.	ERA.
1984—Tri-Cities	Northwest	14	78⅓	7	5	.583	87	38	25	60	31	2.87
1985—Salem	Carolina	38	84½	3	1	.750	69	28	19	67	26	2.03
1986—Tulsa	Texas	41	103⅔	3	7	.300	102	56	43	59	36	3.73
1987—Oklahoma City	Am. Assoc.	21	24⅔	2	0	1.000	23	12	11	14	10	4.01
1987—Texas	American	25	89½	2	7	.222	95	45	41	42	31	4.13
1988—Texas†	American	32	203⅓	12	15	.444	190	105	94	88	71	4.16
1989—Chicago	National	35	145⅔	6	10	.375	164	90	71	61	49	4.39
1989—Iowa‡	Am. Assoc.	1	9	1	0	1.000	9	3	3	5	2	3.00
American League Totals—2 Years		57	292⅔	14	22	.389	285	150	135	130	102	4.15
National League Totals—1 Year		35	145⅔	6	10	.375	164	90	71	61	49	4.39
Major League Totals—3 Years		92	438⅓	20	32	.385	449	240	206	191	151	4.23

Selected by Texas Rangers' organization in 43rd round of free-agent draft, June 4, 1984.
†Traded with Pitchers Mitch Williams and Steve Wilson, Infielders Curtis Wilkerson and Luis Benitez and Outfielder Pablo Delgado to Chicago Cubs for Outfielder Rafael Palmeiro and Pitchers Jamie Moyer and Drew Hall, December 5, 1988.
‡Traded to Toronto Blue Jays for Pitcher Jose Nunez, December 7, 1989.

CHAMPIONSHIP SERIES RECORD

Year Club	League	G.	IP.	W.	L.	Pct.	H.	R.	ER.	SO.	BB.	ERA.
1989—Chicago	National	1	3	0	0	.000	4	0	0	1	1	0.00

ERIC STEVEN KING

Born April 10, 1964, at Oxnard, Calif.
Height, 6.02. Weight, 180.
Throws and bats righthanded.
Shares major league record for most putouts by pitcher, nine-inning game (6), July 8, 1986.
Major League saves: 1986 (3), 1987 (9), 1988 (3). Total—15.

Year Club	League	G.	IP.	W.	L.	Pct.	H.	R.	ER.	SO.	BB.	ERA.
1983—Great Falls	Pioneer	20	56⅓	3	4	.429	58	31	27	61	14	4.31
1984—Clinton	Midwest	35	147⅓	5	10	.333	142	74	55	124	76	3.36
1985—Shreveport†‡	Texas	15	104⅔	5	3	.625	74	34	27	80	30	2.32
1986—Nashville	Am. Assoc.	6	38⅓	3	2	.600	29	16	15	38	16	3.52
1986—Detroit	American	33	138⅓	11	4	.733	108	54	54	79	63	3.51
1987—Detroit	American	55	116	6	9	.400	111	67	63	89	60	4.89
1988—Toledo	Int'national	10	69	3	4	.429	54	26	25	51	23	3.26
1988—Detroit	American	23	68⅔	4	1	.800	60	28	26	45	34	3.41
1989—Chicago§	American	25	159⅓	9	10	.474	144	69	60	72	64	3.39
Major League Totals—4 Years		136	482⅓	30	24	.556	423	218	203	285	221	3.79

Signed as free agent by San Francisco Giants' organization, June 11, 1983.
†On suspended list, July 3 to July 13, 1985, then transferred to disabled list, July 13 to July 27, 1985.
‡Traded with Pitcher Dave LaPoint and Catcher Matt Nokes to Detroit Tigers for Pitcher Juan Berenguer, Catcher Bob Melvin and a player to be named later, October 7, 1985; San Francisco Giants acquired Pitcher Scott Medvin to complete deal, December 11, 1985.
§Traded to Chicago White Sox for Outfielder Kenny Williams, March 23, 1989.

CHAMPIONSHIP SERIES RECORD

Year Club	League	G.	IP.	W.	L.	Pct.	H.	R.	ER.	SO.	BB.	ERA.
1987—Detroit	American	2	5⅓	0	0	.000	3	1	1	4	2	1.69

JEFFREY WAYNE KING
(Jeff)

Born December 26, 1964, at Marion, Ind.
Height, 6.01. Weight, 180.
Throws and bats righthanded.
Attended University of Arkansas, Fayetteville, Ark.
Son of Jack King, minor league catcher, 1954 and 1955; and brother of James King, shortstop drafted by Philadelphia Phillies' organization in 1982 and Seattle Mariners' organization in 1984.

Major League stolen bases: 1989 (4).
Led Carolina League in slugging percentage with .565 in 1987.
Received reported $180,000 bonus to sign with Pittsburgh Pirates, 1986.
Named College Player of the Year by THE SPORTING NEWS, 1986.
Named third baseman on THE SPORTING NEWS College Baseball All-America Team, 1986.

Year Club	League	Pos.	G.	AB.	R.	H.	2B.	3B.	HR.	RBI.	B.A.	PO.	A.	E.	F.A.
1986—Prince William	Carol.	3B	37	132	18	31	4	1	6	20	.235	25	50	8	.904
1987—Salem	Carol.	1B-3B	90	310	68	86	9	1	26	71	.277	572	106	13	.981
1987—Harrisburg	East.	1B	26	100	12	24	7	0	2	25	.240	107	10	1	.992
1988—Harrisburg	East.	3B	117	411	49	105	21	1	14	66	.255	97	208	24	.927
1989—Buffalo	A. A.	1B-3B	51	169	26	43	5	2	6	29	.254	213	61	8	.972

Year Club League	Pos.	G.	AB.	R.	H.	2B.	3B.	HR.	RBI.	B.A.	PO.	A.	E.	F.A.
1989—Pittsburgh.............. Nat.	1-3-2-S	75	215	31	42	13	3	5	19	.195	403	59	4	.991
Major League Totals—1 Year..................		75	215	31	42	13	3	5	19	.195	403	59	4	.991

Selected by Chicago Cubs' organization in 23rd round of free-agent draft, June 6, 1983.
Selected by Pittsburgh Pirates' organization in 1st round (first player selected) of free-agent draft, June 2, 1986.

MICHAEL SCOTT KINGERY
(Mike)

Born March 29, 1961, at St. James, Minn.
Height, 6.00. Weight, 180.
Throws and bats lefthanded.
Attended Willmar Community College, Willmar, Minn.;
and St. Cloud State University, St. Cloud, Minn.

Major League stolen bases: 1986 (7), 1987 (7), 1988 (3), 1989 (1). Total—18.
Led Florida State League in intentional bases on balls received with 11 in 1983.
Tied for South Atlantic League lead in double plays by outfielders with 5 in 1982.

Year Club League	Pos.	G.	AB.	R.	H.	2B.	3B.	HR.	RBI.	B.A.	PO.	A.	E.	F.A.
1980—K.C. Royals-Gold . Gulf C.	OF	44	143	12	32	3	3	0	13	.224	78	5	2	.976
1981—Charleston†.......... S. Atl.	OF	69	213	33	57	3	4	3	25	.268	80	7	4	.956
1982—Charleston............ S. Atl.	OF	140	513	65	163	19	4	8	75	.318	250	21	7	.975
1983—Fort Myers............ Fla. St.	OF	123	436	68	116	9	7	2	51	.266	200	16	5	.977
1984—Memphis................ South.	OF	139	455	65	135	19	3	4	58	.297	291	18	6	.981
1985—Omaha.................... A. A.	OF	132	444	51	113	25	6	2	49	.255	247	17	5	.981
1986—Omaha.................... A. A.	OF	79	298	47	99	14	8	3	47	.332	171	10	1	.995
1986—Kansas City‡......... Amer.	OF	62	209	25	54	8	5	3	14	.258	102	6	3	.973
1987—Seattle.................... Amer.	OF	120	354	38	99	25	4	9	52	.280	226	15	2	.992
1988—Seattle.................... Amer.	OF-1B	57	123	21	25	6	0	1	9	.203	102	6	2	.982
1988—Calgary .... P. C.	OF-1B	47	170	29	54	12	2	1	14	.318	144	4	3	.980
1989—Calgary .... P. C.	OF-1B	107	396	72	115	22	9	4	47	.290	289	10	1	.997
1989—Seattle.................... Amer.	OF	31	76	14	17	3	0	2	6	.224	70	0	0	1.000
Major League Totals—4 Years................		270	762	98	195	42	9	15	81	.256	500	27	7	.987

Signed as free agent by Kansas City Royals' organization, August 27, 1979.
†On disabled list, July 29 to August 15, 1981.
‡Traded with Pitchers Scott Bankhead and Steve Shields to Seattle Mariners for Outfielder Danny Tartabull and Pitcher Rick Luecken, December 10, 1986.

MATTHEW ROY KINZER
(Matt)

Born June 17, 1963, at Indianapolis, Ind.
Height, 6.02. Weight, 210.
Throws and bats righthanded.
Attended Purdue University, West Lafayette, Ind.

Year Club	League	G.	IP.	W.	L.	Pct.	H.	R.	ER.	SO.	BB.	ERA.
1984—Arkansas.......................	Texas	14	82⅔	5	6	.455	97	48	41	41	27	4.46
1985—Springfield†....................	Midwest	11	58⅓	5	4	.556	56	26	24	36	21	3.70
1986—St. Petersburg................	Florida St.	22	134	10	7	.588	129	49	43	80	42	2.89
1987—Arkansas.......................	Texas	17	91⅓	5	6	.455	82	57	48	74	34	4.73
1988—Arkansas.......................	Texas	16	29	3	0	1.000	26	11	10	34	3	3.10
1988—Louisville.......................	Am. Assoc.	46	80	6	2	.750	73	34	33	53	24	3.71
1989—Louisville.......................	Am. Assoc.	51	72	1	4	.200	69	28	26	62	14	3.25
1989—St. Louis‡......................	National	8	13⅓	0	2	.000	25	20	19	8	4	12.82
Major League Totals—1 Year................		8	13⅓	0	2	.000	25	20	19	8	4	12.82

Selected by Cleveland Indians' organization in 6th round of free-agent draft, June 8, 1981.
Selected by St. Louis Cardinals' organization in 2nd round of free-agent draft, June 4, 1984.
†On disabled list, August 2, 1985 through remainder of season.
‡Traded with First Baseman Jim Lindeman to Detroit Tigers for Second Baseman Pat Austin, Catcher Bill Henderson and Pitcher Marcos Betances, December 6, 1989.

RECORD AS FOOTBALL PLAYER
Signed as replacement player by Detroit Lions, September 24, 1987.
Released by Detroit Lions, October 16, 1987.

		——PUNTING——		
Year Club	G.	No.	Avg.	Blk.
1987—Detroit NFL............................	1	7	34.0	0

ROBERT WAYNE KIPPER
(Bob)

Born July 8, 1964, at Aurora, Ill.
Height, 6.02. Weight, 175.
Throws left and bats righthanded.

Pitched seven-inning, 9-0 no-hit victory against San Jose, June 10, 1984 (second game).
Major League saves: 1989 (4).
Named California League Pitcher of the Year, 1984.

Year Club	League	G.	IP.	W.	L.	Pct.	H.	R.	ER.	SO.	BB.	ERA.
1982—Salem	Northwest	13	76⅔	6	5	.545	62	46	38	65	52	4.46
1983—Peoria†	Midwest	22	127⅔	5	8	.385	112	77	66	105	52	4.65
1984—Redwood	California	26	185	*18	8	.692	147	61	42	98	65	*2.04
1985—California	American	2	3⅓	0	1	.000	7	8	8	0	3	21.60
1985—Midland‡	Texas	9	49⅔	3	3	.500	52	22	17	31	10	3.08
1985—Edmonton§x-Hawaii	P. Coast	7	49⅔	3	0	1.000	36	15	11	42	12	1.99
1985—Pittsburgh	National	5	24⅔	1	2	.333	21	16	14	13	7	5.11
1986—Pittsburgh y	National	20	114	6	8	.429	123	60	51	81	34	4.03
1986—Nashua	Eastern	4	18⅓	0	1	.000	14	7	7	19	3	3.44
1987—Pittsburgh	National	24	110⅔	5	9	.357	117	74	73	83	52	5.94
1987—Vancouver	P. Coast	6	25⅓	0	2	.000	23	7	5	22	4	1.78
1988—Pittsburgh	National	50	65	2	6	.250	54	33	27	39	26	3.74
1989—Pittsburgh z	National	52	83	3	4	.429	55	29	27	58	33	2.93
American League Totals—1 Year		2	3⅓	0	1	.000	7	8	8	0	3	21.60
National League Totals—5 Years		151	397⅓	17	29	.370	370	212	192	274	152	4.35
Major League Totals—5 Years		153	400⅔	17	30	.362	377	220	200	274	155	4.49

Selected by California Angels' organization in 1st round (eighth player selected) of free-agent draft, June 7, 1982.

†On disabled list, July 20 to August 8, 1983.

‡On disabled list, May 31 to June 10, 1985.

§Loaned to Hawaii (Pittsburgh Pirates' organization), August 2, 1985; returned, August 16, 1985.

xTraded to Pittsburgh Pirates' organization, August 16, 1985, completing deal in which Pittsburgh traded Pitchers John Candelaria and Al Holland and Outfielder George Hendrick to California Angels for Pitcher Pat Clements, Outfielder Mike Brown and a player to be named later, August 2, 1985.

yOn disabled list, June 29 to September 1, 1986; included rehabilitation disability assignment to Nashua, August 14 to September 1, 1986.

zOn disabled list, July 31 to September 1, 1989.

RONALD DALE KITTLE
(Ron)

Born January 5, 1958, at Gary, Ind.
Height, 6.04. Weight, 220.
Throws and bats righthanded.

Shares major league record for most home runs, month of October (4), 1985.

Major League stolen bases: 1983 (8), 1984 (3), 1985 (1), 1986 (4). Total—16.

Led American League batters in strikeouts with 150 in 1983.

Led Pacific Coast League in total bases with 355, slugging percentage with .752 and tied for lead in being hit by pitch with 10 in 1982.

Led Eastern League in total bases with 270 and slugging percentage with .694 in 1981.

Named American League Rookie Player of the Year by THE SPORTING NEWS, 1983.

Named American League Rookie of the Year by Baseball Writers' Association of America, 1983.

Named Minor League Player of the Year by THE SPORTING NEWS, 1982.

Named Pacific Coast League Most Valuable Player, 1982.

Named Eastern League Most Valuable Player, 1981.

Year Club	League	Pos.	G.	AB.	R.	H.	2B.	3B.	HR.	RBI.	B.A.	PO.	A.	E.	F.A.
1977—Clinton†	Midw.	OF	22	53	9	10	4	0	0	3	.189	16	0	0	1.000
1977—Lethbridge	Pion.	OF	34	100	22	25	3	0	7	21	.250	29	2	6	.838
1978—Clinton‡	Midw.	OF	13	35	2	5	2	1	0	4	.143	4	1	1	.833
1979—Knoxville	South.	OF-C	53	157	28	43	9	1	6	26	.274	44	1	6	.980
1979—Appleton	Midw.	OF-C	35	120	18	31	3	1	2	12	.258	33	1	2	.972
1980—Appleton	Midw.	C-OF	61	209	31	66	15	3	12	56	.316	56	9	1	.985
1980—Glens Falls§	East.	OF	17	65	11	20	3	1	4	9	.308	24	4	3	.903
1981—Glens Falls x	East.	OF	109	389	97	127	17	3	*40	*103	.326	28	0	3	.903
1982—Edmonton	P. C.	OF-C	127	472	*121	163	22	10	*50	*144	.345	149	15	8	.953
1982—Chicago	Amer.	OF	20	29	3	7	2	0	1	7	.241	3	0	0	1.000
1983—Chicago	Amer.	OF	145	520	75	132	19	3	35	100	.254	234	7	9	.964
1984—Chicago	Amer.	OF	139	466	67	100	15	0	32	74	.215	226	14	7	.972
1985—Chicago y	Amer.	OF	116	379	51	87	12	0	26	58	.230	88	2	1	.989
1985—Buffalo	A. A.	OF	6	21	3	7	2	0	2	5	.333	2	0	0	1.000
1986—Chi. z-N.Y.	Amer.	OF	116	376	42	82	13	0	21	60	.218	39	3	0	1.000
1987—New York a	Amer.	OF	59	159	21	44	5	0	12	28	.277	4	1	0	1.000
1987—Columbus b	Int.	DH	4	18	3	4	0	0	0	1	.222	0	0	0	.000
1988—Cleveland c	Amer.	DH	75	225	31	58	8	0	18	43	.258	0	0	0	.000
1989—Chicago d	Amer.	1B-OF	51	169	26	51	10	0	11	37	.302	216	12	4	.983
Major League Totals—8 Years			721	2323	316	561	84	3	156	407	.241	810	39	21	.976

Signed as free agent by Los Angeles Dodgers' organization, July 5, 1977.

†On disabled list, April 30 to May 14, 1977.

‡Released, July 7, 1978; signed by Knoxville (Chicago White Sox' organization), September 4, 1978.

§On disabled list, July 27 to August 31, 1980.

xOn disabled list, April 21 to May 10, 1981.

yOn disabled list, July 4 to July 25, 1985; included rehabilitation disability assignment to Buffalo, July 19 to July 25, 1985.

zTraded with Infielder Wayne Tolleson and Catcher Joel Skinner to New York Yankees for Catcher Ron Hassey, Shortstop Carlos Martinez and a player to be named later, July 30, 1986; New York traded Catcher Bill Lindsey to Chicago White Sox' organization to complete deal, December 24, 1986.

aOn disabled list, July 7 to August 16, 1987; included rehabilitation disability assignment to Columbus, August 14 to August 16, 1987.

bReleased, December 21, 1987; signed by Cleveland Indians, February 9, 1988.

cGranted free agency, November 4, 1988; signed by Chicago White Sox, November 26, 1988.

dOn disabled list, June 11, 1989 through remainder of season.

Year Club	League	Pos.	G.	AB.	R.	H.	2B.	3B.	HR.	RBI.	B.A.	PO.	A.	E.	F.A.
1983—Chicago	Amer.	OF	3	7	1	2	1	0	0	0	.286	3	0	0	1.000

ALL-STAR GAME RECORD

Year League	Pos.	AB.	R.	H.	2B.	3B.	HR.	RBI.	B.A.	PO.	A.	E.	F.A.
1983—American	OF	2	1	1	0	0	0	0	.500	1	0	0	1.000

BRENT BRADLEY KNACKERT

Born August 1, 1969, at Los Angeles, Calif.
Height, 6.03. Weight, 185.
Throws and bats righthanded.

Year Club	League	G.	IP.	W.	L.	Pct.	H.	R.	ER.	SO.	BB.	ERA.
1987—Sarasota White Sox	Gulf Coast	12	72⅔	6	2	.750	55	28	23	60	15	2.85
1988—Tampa	Florida St.	23	142	10	8	.556	132	58	50	78	46	3.17
1989—Sarasota†	Florida St.	35	98	8	5	.615	85	41	32	80	35	2.94

Selected by Chicago White Sox' organization in 2nd round of free-agent draft, June 2, 1987.
†Drafted by New York Mets, December 4, 1989.

ROBERT WESLEY KNEPPER

Name pronounced NEPP-ur.

(Bob)

Born May 25, 1954, at Akron, O.
Height, 6.02. Weight, 210.
Throws and bats lefthanded.

Shares National League record for fewest assists by pitcher, season, for leader in assists (47), 1986.
Major League saves: 1982 (1).
Led National League in shutouts with 6 in 1978 and tied for lead with 5 in 1986.
Tied for National League lead in hit batsmen with 8 in 1980.
Led California League pitchers in games started with 30 and tied for lead in complete games with 16 in 1974.
Tied for Pacific Coast League lead in shutouts with 3 in 1976.
Named National League Comeback Player of the Year by THE SPORTING NEWS, 1981.

Year Club	League	G.	IP.	W.	L.	Pct.	H.	R.	ER.	SO.	BB.	ERA.
1972—Great Falls	Pioneer	12	68	7	1	.875	53	20	11	75	19	1.46
1973—Decatur	Midwest	11	79	7	2	.778	65	28	17	68	23	1.94
1973—Fresno	California	13	71	2	8	.200	78	54	32	66	35	4.06
1974—Fresno	California	30	★238	★20	5	●.800	★239	103	84	★247	80	3.18
1975—Phoenix	P. Coast	26	155	11	11	.500	169	101	79	94	78	4.59
1976—Phoenix	P. Coast	29	205	14	10	.583	209	105	98	130	64	4.30
1976—San Francisco	National	4	25	1	2	.333	26	9	9	11	7	3.24
1977—Phoenix	P. Coast	10	51	3	6	.333	68	51	42	24	25	7.41
1977—San Francisco	National	27	166	11	9	.550	151	73	62	100	72	3.36
1978—San Francisco	National	36	260	17	11	.607	218	85	76	147	85	2.63
1979—San Francisco	National	34	207	9	12	.429	241	117	107	123	77	4.65
1980—San Francisco†	National	35	215	9	16	.360	242	114	98	103	61	4.10
1981—Houston	National	22	157	9	5	.643	128	41	38	75	38	2.18
1982—Houston	National	33	180	5	15	.250	193	100	89	108	60	4.45
1983—Houston	National	35	203	6	13	.316	202	93	72	125	71	3.19
1984—Houston	National	35	233⅔	15	10	.600	223	93	83	140	55	3.20
1985—Houston	National	37	241	15	13	.536	253	●119	95	131	54	3.55
1986—Houston	National	40	258	17	12	.586	232	100	90	143	62	3.14
1987—Houston	National	33	177⅔	8	★17	.320	226	118	104	76	54	5.27
1988—Houston	National	27	175	14	5	.737	156	70	61	103	67	3.14
1989—Houston‡-San Francisco§	National	35	165	7	12	.368	190	98	94	64	75	5.13
Major League Totals—14 Years		433	2663⅓	143	152	.485	2681	1230	1078	1449	838	3.64

Selected by San Francisco Giants' organization in 2nd round of free-agent draft, June 6, 1972.
†Traded with Outfielder Chris Bourjos to Houston Astros for Third Baseman Enos Cabell, December 8, 1980.
‡Released, July 28, 1989; signed by San Francisco Giants, August 4, 1989.
§Granted free agency, November 13, 1989.

DIVISION SERIES RECORD

Year Club	League	G.	IP.	W.	L.	Pct.	H.	R.	ER.	SO.	BB.	ERA.
1981—Houston	National	1	5	0	1	.000	6	3	3	4	2	5.40

CHAMPIONSHIP SERIES RECORD

Year Club	League	G.	IP.	W.	L.	Pct.	H.	R.	ER.	SO.	BB.	ERA.
1986—Houston	National	2	15⅓	0	0	.000	13	7	6	9	1	3.52

ALL-STAR GAME RECORD

Year League	IP.	W.	L.	Pct.	H.	R.	ER.	SO.	BB.	ERA.
1981—National	2	0	0	.000	1	0	0	3	2	0.00
1988—National	1	0	0	.000	2	1	1	0	1	9.00
All-Star Game Totals—2 Years	3	0	0	.000	3	1	1	3	3	3.00

RANDY DUANE KNORR

Born November 12, 1968, at San Gabriel, Calif.
Height, 6.02. Weight, 195.
Throws and bats righthanded.
Led South Atlantic League catchers in passed balls with 25 and total chances with 960 in 1988.

Year Club	League	Pos.	G.	AB.	R.	H.	2B.	3B.	HR.	RBI.	B.A.	PO.	A.	E.	F.A.
1986—Medicine Hat†	Pion.	1B	55	215	21	58	13	0	4	52	.270	451	29	10	.980
1987—Myrtle Beach	S. Atl.	C-1B-2B	46	129	17	34	4	0	6	21	.264	95	7	1	.990
1987—Medicine Hat	Pion.	C	26	106	21	31	7	0	10	24	.292	70	5	4	.949
1988—Myrtle Beach	S. Atl.	C	117	364	43	85	13	0	9	42	.234	★870	75	15	.984
1989—Dunedin‡	Fla. St.	C	33	122	13	32	6	0	6	23	.262	186	20	2	.990

Selected by Toronto Blue Jays' organization in 10th round of free-agent draft, June 2, 1986.
†On disabled list, June 24 to July 4, 1986.
‡On disabled list, May 10, 1989 through remainder of season.

MARK RICHARD KNUDSON

Name pronounced NOOD-sun.

Born October 28, 1960, at Denver, Colo.
Height, 6.05. Weight, 200.
Throws and bats righthanded.
Attended Colorado State University, Fort Collins, Colo.

Year Club	League	G.	IP.	W.	L.	Pct.	H.	R.	ER.	SO.	BB.	ERA.
1982—Daytona Beach	Florida St.	12	60⅓	2	6	.250	75	35	32	15	23	4.77
1983—Daytona Beach	Florida St.	12	78⅔	5	3	.625	80	29	21	47	22	2.40
1983—Columbus	Southern	13	69⅔	4	5	.444	82	40	33	28	21	4.26
1984—Columbus	Southern	14	101	4	5	.444	100	32	25	54	27	2.23
1984—Tucson	P. Coast	13	84	4	6	.400	93	41	34	42	20	3.64
1985—Tucson	P. Coast	24	146	8	5	.615	171	69	65	68	37	4.01
1985—Houston†	National	2	11	0	2	.000	21	11	11	4	3	9.00
1986—Tucson‡-Vancouver	P. Coast	17	106⅔	6	6	.500	124	54	49	63	26	4.13
1986—Houston	National	9	42⅔	1	5	.167	48	23	20	20	15	4.22
1986—Milwaukee	American	4	17⅔	0	1	.000	22	15	15	9	5	7.64
1987—Denver	Am. Assoc.	14	78⅓	7	2	.778	89	53	51	37	30	5.86
1987—Milwaukee	American	15	62	4	4	.500	88	46	37	26	14	5.37
1988—Denver	Am. Assoc.	24	164⅓	11	8	.579	180	67	62	66	33	3.40
1988—Milwaukee	American	5	16	0	0	.000	17	3	2	7	2	1.13
1989—Milwaukee	American	40	123⅔	8	5	.615	110	50	46	47	29	3.35
National League Totals—2 Years		11	53⅔	1	7	.167	69	34	31	24	18	5.20
American League Totals—4 Years		64	219⅓	12	10	.545	237	114	100	89	50	4.10
Major League Totals—5 Years		75	273	13	17	.433	306	148	131	113	68	4.32

Selected by Houston Astros' organization in 3rd round of free-agent draft, June 7, 1982.
†On disabled list, July 15 to August 5, 1985.
‡Traded to Milwaukee Brewers' organization, August 21, 1986, completing deal in which Milwaukee traded Pitcher Danny Darwin to Houston Astros for Pitcher Don August and a player to be named later, August 15, 1986.

BRAD LYNN KOMMINSK

Name pronounced KOMM-insk.

Born April 4, 1961, at Lima, O.
Height, 6.02. Weight, 205.
Throws and bats righthanded.

Major League stolen bases: 1984 (18), 1985 (10), 1987 (1), 1989 (8). Total—37.
Led American Association batters in strikeouts with 127 in 1987.
Led International League batters in strikeouts with 124 in 1986.
Led International League in slugging percentage with .596 and tied for lead in game-winning RBIs with 14 in 1983.
Led Carolina League in total bases with 278 and grounding into double plays with 24 in 1981.
Led Appalachian League batters in strikeouts with 74 and stolen bases with 20 in 1979.
Led International League third basemen in errors with 28 in 1986.
Named Carolina League Most Valuable Player, 1981.
Received reported $72,000 bonus to sign with Atlanta Braves, 1979.

Year Club	League	Pos.	G.	AB.	R.	H.	2B.	3B.	HR.	RBI.	B.A.	PO.	A.	E.	F.A.
1979—Kingsport	Appal.	OF	59	185	37	41	9	1	7	34	.222	112	1	2	.983
1980—Anderson	S. Atl.	OF	121	425	86	111	17	5	20	67	.261	217	5	12	.949
1981—Durham	Carol.	OF	132	459	108	●148	27	2	★104	★122	.322	154	7	10	.942
1982—Savannah	South.	OF	133	454	88	124	18	7	26	78	.273	158	6	10	.943
1982—Richmond	Int.	OF	5	17	4	6	1	0	2	5	.353	10	0	0	1.000
1983—Richmond	Int.	OF	117	413	94	138	24	6	24	103	.334	179	4	3	.984
1983—Atlanta	Nat.	OF	19	36	2	8	2	0	0	4	.222	16	1	1	.944
1984—Richmond	Int.	OF	42	144	23	37	11	3	5	28	.257	66	4	3	.959
1984—Atlanta	Nat.	OF	90	301	37	61	10	0	8	36	.203	135	2	1	.993
1985—Atlanta	Nat.	OF	106	300	52	68	12	3	4	21	.227	161	2	7	.959
1986—Richmond	Int.	3B-OF-1B	133	465	67	109	22	4	13	65	.234	127	200	30	.916
1986—Atlanta†	Nat.	3B-OF	5	5	1	2	0	0	0	1	.400	1	2	0	1.000
1987—Denver	A. A.	OF	135	494	110	147	31	4	★32	95	.298	269	16	5	.983
1987—Milwaukee	Amer.	OF	7	15	0	1	0	0	0	0	.067	10	0	0	1.000
1988—Denver‡	A. A.	OF	105	348	55	83	18	3	16	57	.239	210	6	4	.982
1989—Colorado Springs§	P. C.	OF	54	190	30	55	17	0	9	34	.289	119	0	1	.992

Year Club	League	Pos.	G.	AB.	R.	H.	2B.	3B.	HR.	RBI.	B.A.	PO.	A.	E.	F.A.
1989—Cleveland...............	Amer.	OF	71	198	27	47	8	2	8	33	.237	181	3	1	.995
American League Totals—2 Years			78	213	27	48	8	2	8	33	.225	191	3	1	.995
National League Totals—4 Years............			220	642	92	139	24	3	12	92	.217	313	7	9	.973
Major League Totals—6 Years.................			298	855	119	187	32	5	20	95	.219	504	10	10	.981

Selected by Atlanta Braves' organization in 1st round (fourth player selected) of free-agent draft, June 5, 1979.

†Traded to Milwaukee Brewers for Outfielder Dion James, January 20, 1987.

‡Granted free agency, October 15, 1988; signed by Colorado Springs (Cleveland Indians' organization), December 21, 1988.

§On Cleveland disabled list, April 9 to May 4, 1989.

JOSEPH WAYNE KRAEMER
(Joe)

Born September 10, 1964, at Olympia, Wash.
Height, 6.02. Weight, 185.
Throws and bats lefthanded.
Attended Lower Columbia College, Longview, Wash.,
and Portland State University, Portland, Ore.

Year Club	League	G.	IP.	W.	L.	Pct.	H.	R.	ER.	SO.	BB.	ERA.
1985—Wytheville......................................	Ap'lachian	22	45⅔	4	2	.667	33	21	17	52	36	3.35
1986—Peoria.......................................	Midwest	45	66⅓	6	3	.667	50	17	8	78	12	1.09
1987—Winston-Salem	Carolina	41	52⅔	3	2	.600	49	20	16	43	41	2.73
1987—Iowa...	Am. Assoc.	5	2⅔	1	0	1.000	8	8	8	2	5	27.00
1988—Iowa...	Am. Assoc.	20	26	3	3	.500	19	14	13	26	17	4.50
1988—Pittsfield....................................	Eastern	15	95	5	5	.500	84	37	29	47	43	2.75
1989—Iowa...	Am. Assoc.	27	181⅔	8	10	.444	180	81	70	113	50	3.47
1989—Chicago	National	1	3⅔	0	1	.000	7	6	2	5	2	4.91
Major League Totals—1 Year................................		1	3⅔	0	1	.000	7	6	2	5	2	4.91

Selected by New York Mets' organization in 2nd round of free-agent draft, January 11, 1983.
Selected by Seattle Mariners' organization in 6th round of free-agent draft, January 17, 1984.
Selected by Chicago Cubs' organization in 16th round of free-agent draft, June 3, 1985.

RANDALL JOHN KRAMER
(Randy)

Born September 20, 1960, at Palo Alto, Calif.
Height, 6.02. Weight, 180.
Throws right and bats left and righthanded.
Attended San Jose City College, San Jose, Calif.

Major League saves: 1989 (2).
Tied for Northwest League lead in games started by pitchers with 15 and wild pitches with 13 in 1984.

Year Club	League	G.	IP.	W.	L.	Pct.	H.	R.	ER.	SO.	BB.	ERA.
1982—Sarasota Rangers.........................	Gulf Coast	2	2⅔	0	0	.000	2	0	0	0	0	0.00
1983—Burlington	Midwest	26	132⅔	6	8	.429	131	97	76	113	92	5.16
1984—Salem	Carolina	12	53	2	8	.200	63	66	58	35	34	9.85
1984—Tri-Cities	Northwest	15	84	5	6	.455	83	62	47	74	*58	5.04
1985—Salem	Carolina	25	115½	7	11	.389	143	*99	*86	86	77	6.71
1986—Kinston†-Salem	Carolina	25	43⅓	3	3	.500	43	26	23	38	28	4.78
1986—Tulsa‡..	Texas	26	39	0	3	.000	40	22	19	32	19	4.38
1987—Harrisburg	Eastern	26	49⅔	4	5	.444	62	43	35	43	29	6.34
1987—Vancouver	P. Coast	11	17⅔	0	0	.000	16	14	12	16	19	6.11
1988—Buffalo.......................................	Am. Assoc.	28	*198⅓	10	8	.556	161	85	69	120	50	3.13
1988—Pittsburgh..................................	National	5	10	1	2	.333	12	6	6	7	1	5.40
1989—Buffalo.......................................	Am. Assoc.	5	14⅓	1	0	1.000	15	5	2	8	7	1.26
1989—Pittsburgh..................................	National	35	111⅓	5	9	.357	90	53	49	52	61	3.96
Major League Totals—2 Years.............................		40	121⅓	6	11	.353	102	59	55	59	62	4.08

Selected by San Diego Padres' organization in 26th round of free-agent draft, June 6, 1978.
Selected by Houston Astros' organization in 2nd round of free-agent draft, January 12, 1982.
Selected by Texas Rangers' organization in secondary phase of free-agent draft, June 7, 1982.
†Loaned to Kinston (Independent), April 2, 1986; returned, May 20, 1986.
‡Traded to Pittsburgh Pirates for Pitcher Jeff Zaske, September 30, 1986.

RAYMOND ALLEN KRAWCZYK
Name pronounced KRAH-sick.
(Ray)

Born October 9, 1959, at Pittsburgh, Pa.
Height, 6.01. Weight, 184.
Throws and bats righthanded.
Attended Golden West College, Huntington Beach, Calif., and Oral Roberts University, Tulsa, Okla.

Major League saves: 1988 (1).
Led Pacific Coast League in saves with 20 in 1985.

Year Club	League	G.	IP.	W.	L.	Pct.	H.	R.	ER.	SO.	BB.	ERA.
1981—Bradenton Pirates	Gulf Coast	4	18	0	1	.000	11	5	3	14	7	1.50
1981—Alexandria	Carolina	8	46	2	4	.333	48	32	25	41	14	4.89
1982—Alexandria	Carolina	6	18⅓	1	0	1.000	10	1	1	25	13	0.48
1982—Buffalo...	Eastern	38	101⅓	3	5	.375	93	59	53	102	59	4.71

Year Club	League	G.	IP.	W.	L.	Pct.	H.	R.	ER.	SO.	BB.	ERA.
1983—Hawaii	P. Coast	41	88⅔	5	7	.417	80	46	37	88	33	3.76
1984—Hawaii	P. Coast	43	72	4	5	.444	57	21	17	77	36	2.13
1984—Pittsburgh	National	4	5⅓	0	0	.000	7	2	2	3	4	3.38
1985—Hawaii†‡	P. Coast	38	55⅔	5	3	.625	35	15	14	54	22	2.26
1985—Pittsburgh	National	8	8⅓	0	2	.000	20	13	13	9	6	14.04
1986—Hawaii	P. Coast	32	47⅓	3	6	.333	51	29	26	40	21	4.94
1986—Pittsburgh§x	National	12	12⅓	0	1	.000	17	13	10	7	10	7.30
1987—Hawaii y	P. Coast	35	120	11	6	.647	124	59	55	78	38	4.13
1988—California	American	14	24⅓	0	1	.000	29	13	13	17	8	4.81
1988—Edmonton z	P. Coast	20	94⅔	4	9	.308	101	58	48	70	25	4.56
1989—Denver	Am. Assoc.	43	93½	2	6	.250	109	45	36	85	34	3.47
1989—Milwaukee a	American	1	2	0	0	.000	4	3	3	6	1	13.50
National League Totals—3 Years		24	26	0	3	.000	44	28	25	19	20	8.65
American League Totals—2 Years		15	26⅓	0	1	.000	33	16	16	23	9	5.47
Major League Totals—5 Years		39	52⅓	0	4	.000	77	44	41	42	29	7.05

Selected by Boston Red Sox' organization in 1st round (23rd player selected) of free-agent draft, January 8, 1980.
Selected by St. Louis Cardinals' organization in secondary phase of free-agent draft, June 3, 1980.
Selected by Pittsburgh Pirates' organization in secondary phase of free-agent draft, June 8, 1981.
†Appeared in one game as a first baseman with no chances.
‡On disabled list, June 10 to June 20, 1985.
§On disabled list, April 23 to June 18, 1986; included rehabilitation disability assignment to Prince William, June 1 to June 18, 1986.
xReleased, November 12, 1986; signed by Hawaii (Chicago White Sox' organization), April 17, 1987.
yReleased, November 22, 1987; signed by California Angels, December 22, 1987.
zGranted free agency, October 15, 1988; signed by Denver (Milwaukee Brewers' organization), December 21, 1988.
aGranted free agency, October 15, 1989.

CHAD MICHAEL KREUTER

Born August 26, 1964, in Marin County, Calif.
Height, 6.02. Weight, 190.
Throws right and bats left and righthanded.
Attended Pepperdine University, Malibu, Calif.

Shares major league record for most hits, inning, first major league game (2), September 14, 1988, fifth inning.
Led American League in passed balls with 21 in 1989.
Tied for Texas League lead in double plays by catchers with 9 in 1988.
Led Carolina League catchers in double plays with 17 and tied for lead in assists with 113 in 1986.

Year Club	League	Pos.	G.	AB.	R.	H.	2B.	3B.	HR.	RBI.	B.A.	PO.	A.	E.	F.A.
1985—Burlington†	Midw.	C	69	199	25	53	9	0	4	26	.266	349	34	8	.980
1986—Salem†	Carol.	C-OF-3B	125	387	55	85	21	2	6	49	.220	613	115	★21	.972
1987—Charlotte†	Fla. St.	C-OF-3B	85	281	36	61	18	1	9	40	.217	380	54	8	.982
1988—Tulsa	Texas	C	108	358	46	95	24	6	3	51	.265	603	71	●13	.981
1988—Texas	Amer.	C	16	51	3	14	2	1	1	5	.275	93	8	1	.990
1989—Texas	Amer.	C	87	158	16	24	3	0	5	9	.152	453	26	4	.992
1989—Oklahoma City	A. A.	C	26	87	10	22	3	0	0	6	.253	146	14	2	.988
Major League Totals—2 Years			103	209	19	38	5	1	6	14	.182	546	34	5	.991

Selected by Texas Rangers' organization in 5th round of free-agent draft, June 3, 1985.
†Batted righthanded only.

WILLIAM CULP KRUEGER

Name pronounced KREW-ger.

(Bill)

Born April 24, 1958, at Waukegan, Ill.
Height, 6.05. Weight, 205.
Throws and bats lefthanded.
Received bachelor of arts degree in business administration from
University of Portland, Portland, Ore. in 1979.

Pitched seven-inning 2-0 no-hit victory against Phoenix, August 14, 1987 (second game).
Major League saves: 1986 (1), 1989 (3). Total—4.
Led Pacific Coast League in shutouts with 4 in 1988.
Tied for Eastern League lead in games started by pitchers with 27 and shutouts with 3 in 1982.

Year Club	League	G.	IP.	W.	L.	Pct.	H.	R.	ER.	SO.	BB.	ERA.
1980—Medford	Northwest	9	44	0	4	.000	54	38	25	48	29	5.11
1981—Modesto	California	16	98	3	5	.375	87	49	40	76	52	3.67
1981—West Haven	Eastern	11	68	3	6	.333	74	36	27	36	31	3.57
1982—West Haven	Eastern	28	181	15	9	.625	160	69	57	163	81	2.83
1983—Oakland†	American	17	109⅔	7	6	.538	104	54	44	58	53	3.61
1984—Tacoma	P. Coast	5	31⅔	2	2	.500	29	17	13	20	21	3.69
1984—Oakland	American	26	142	10	10	.500	156	95	75	61	85	4.75
1985—Oakland	American	32	151⅓	9	10	.474	165	95	76	56	69	4.52
1985—Tacoma	P. Coast	2	9⅔	0	1	.000	12	10	10	10	6	9.31
1986—Oakland‡	American	11	34⅓	1	2	.333	40	25	23	10	13	6.03
1986—Madison	Midwest	1	2	0	0	.000	1	0	0	1	1	0.00
1986—Tacoma	P. Coast	8	52⅓	3	3	.500	53	32	27	41	27	4.64
1987—Oakland	American	9	5⅔	0	3	.000	9	7	6	2	8	9.53
1987—Tacoma§-Albuquerque	P. Coast	24	146½	9	7	.563	158	74	66	97	66	4.06
1987—Los Angeles x	National	2	2⅓	0	0	.000	3	2	0	2	1	0.00

Year Club	League	G.	IP.	W.	L.	Pct.	H.	R.	ER.	SO.	BB.	ERA.
1988—Albuquerque	P. Coast	27	173⅓	*15	5	.750	167	74	58	114	69	*3.01
1988—Los Angeles yz	National	1	2⅓	0	0	.000	4	3	3	1	2	11.57
1989—Denver	Am. Assoc.	2	13⅓	1	1	.500	10	4	3	9	6	2.03
1989—Milwaukee	American	34	93⅔	3	2	.600	96	43	40	72	33	3.84
American League Totals—6 Years		129	536⅔	30	33	.476	570	319	264	259	261	4.43
National League Totals—2 Years		3	4⅔	0	0	.000	7	5	3	3	3	5.79
Major League Totals—7 Years		132	541⅓	30	33	.476	577	324	267	262	264	4.44

Signed as free agent by Oakland A's organization, July 12, 1980.
†On disabled list, August 5, 1983 through remainder of season.
‡On disabled list, May 6 to August 8, 1986; included rehabilitation disability assignment to Madison, July 4 to July 8, and Tacoma, July 10 to July 18 and July 21 to July 27, 1986.
§Traded to Los Angeles Dodgers' organization for Pitcher Tim Meeks, June 23, 1987.
xReleased, November 12, 1987; re-signed by Dodgers' organization, January 1, 1988.
yTraded to Pittsburgh Pirates for Pitcher Jim Neidlinger, October 3, 1988.
zReleased, March 28, 1989; signed by Denver (Milwaukee Brewers' organization), April 7, 1989.

JOHN MARTIN KRUK

Born February 9, 1961, at Charleston, W. Va.
Height, 5.10. Weight, 204.
Throws and bats lefthanded.
Attended Allegany Community College, Cumberland, Md.

Major League stolen bases: 1986 (2), 1987 (18), 1988 (5), 1989 (3). Total—28.
Led Texas League in sacrifice flies with 13 in 1983.
Led Pacific Coast League outfielders in double plays with 4 in 1984.

Year Club	League	Pos.	G.	AB.	R.	H.	2B.	3B.	HR.	RBI.	B.A.	PO.	A.	E.	F.A.
1981—Walla Walla	N'west	OF-1B	63	157	31	38	10	0	1	13	.242	108	5	2	.983
1982—Reno	Calif.	OF-1B	125	441	82	137	30	8	11	92	.311	253	11	7	.974
1983—Beaumont	Texas	OF-1B-P	133	498	94	170	41	9	10	88	.341	304	22	8	.976
1984—Las Vegas	P. C.	OF	115	340	56	111	25	6	11	57	.326	183	7	2	.990
1985—Las Vegas	P. C.	OF-1B	123	422	61	148	29	4	7	59	*.351	356	18	7	.982
1986—San Diego	Nat.	OF-1B	122	278	33	86	16	2	4	38	.309	139	6	3	.980
1986—Las Vegas	P. C.	OF-1B	6	28	6	13	3	1	0	9	.464	22	1	0	1.000
1987—San Diego	Nat.	1B-OF	138	447	72	140	14	2	20	91	.313	911	78	5	.995
1988—San Diego	Nat.	1B-OF	120	378	54	91	17	1	9	44	.241	634	37	3	.996
1989—S.D.††‡-Phi.§	Nat.	OF-1B	112	357	53	107	13	6	8	44	.300	212	9	4	.982
Major League Totals—4 Years			492	1460	212	424	60	11	41	217	.290	1896	130	15	.993

Selected by Pittsburgh Pirates' organization in 3rd round of free-agent draft, January 13, 1981.
Selected by San Diego Padres' organization in secondary phase of free-agent draft, June 8, 1981.
†On disabled list, May 5 to May 21, 1989.
‡Traded with Infielder Randy Ready to Philadelphia Phillies for Outfielder Chris James, June 2, 1989.
§On disabled list, July 3 to July 28, 1989.

PITCHING RECORD

Year Club	League	G.	IP.	W.	L.	Pct.	H.	R.	ER.	SO.	BB.	ERA.
1983—Beaumont	Texas	3	5	0	0	.000	5	0	0	3	2	0.00

MICHAEL EDWARD KRUKOW

Name pronounced KROO-koh.

(Mike)

Born January 21, 1952, at Long Beach, Calif.
Height, 6.04. Weight, 205.
Throws and bats righthanded.
Attended California Poly State University, San Luis Obispo, Calif.

Major League saves: 1984 (1).
Tied for National League lead in games started by pitchers with 25 in 1981.
Tied for National League lead in hit batsmen with 8 in 1980.
Led Gulf Coast League in intentional bases on balls issued with 4 and tied for lead in complete games with 4 in 1973.

Year Club	League	G.	IP.	W.	L.	Pct.	H.	R.	ER.	SO.	BB.	ERA.
1973—Bradenton Cubs	Gulf Coast	13	77	4	3	.571	76	32	27	*80	28	3.16
1974—Midland	Texas	6	30	1	1	.500	42	24	17	21	19	5.10
1974—Key West	Florida St.	20	130	5	10	.333	121	66	46	94	47	3.18
1975—Midland†	Texas	24	153	13	6	.684	143	65	58	100	66	3.41
1976—Wichita	Am. Assoc.	26	144	7	9	.438	142	61	53	108	47	3.31
1976—Chicago	National	2	4	0	0	.000	6	4	4	1	2	9.00
1977—Chicago	National	34	172	8	14	.364	195	96	84	106	61	4.40
1978—Wichita	Am. Assoc.	7	53	2	3	.400	51	27	23	29	21	3.91
1978—Chicago	National	27	138	9	3	.750	125	62	60	81	53	3.91
1979—Chicago	National	28	165	9	9	.500	172	84	77	119	81	4.20
1980—Chicago	National	34	205	10	15	.400	200	117	100	130	80	4.39
1981—Chicago‡	National	25	144	9	9	.500	146	68	59	101	55	3.69
1982—Philadelphia§	National	33	208	13	11	.542	211	87	72	138	82	3.12
1983—San Francisco x	National	31	184⅓	11	11	.500	189	95	81	136	76	3.95
1984—San Francisco	National	35	199⅓	11	12	.478	*234	*117	101	141	78	4.56
1985—San Francisco	National	28	194⅔	8	11	.421	176	80	73	150	49	3.38
1986—San Francisco y	National	34	245	20	9	.690	204	90	83	178	55	3.05

Year Club	League	G.	IP.	W.	L.	Pct.	H.	R.	ER.	SO.	BB.	ERA.
1987—San Francisco z	National	30	163	5	6	.455	182	98	87	104	46	4.80
1988—San Francisco a	National	20	124⅔	7	4	.636	111	51	49	75	31	3.54
1988—Phoenix	P. Coast	1	5	1	0	1.000	0	0	0	5	0	0.00
1989—San Francisco bc	National	8	43	4	3	.571	37	20	19	18	18	3.98
Major League Totals—14 Years		369	2190	124	117	.515	2188	1069	949	1478	767	3.90

Selected by California Angels' organization in 32nd round of free-agent draft, June 4, 1970.

Selected by Chicago Cubs' organization in 8th round of free-agent draft, June 5, 1973.

†On disabled list, May 19 to June 7, 1975.

‡Traded with cash to Philadelphia Phillies for Catcher Keith Moreland and Pitchers Dan Larson and Dickie Noles, December 8, 1981.

§Traded with Pitcher Mark Davis and Outfielder Charles Penigar to San Francisco Giants for Second Baseman Joe Morgan and Pitcher Al Holland, December 14, 1982.

xOn disabled list, April 11 to May 8, 1983.

yOn disabled list, July 23 to August 7, 1986.

zOn disabled list, June 6 to June 25, 1987.

aOn disabled list, June 26 to August 13, 1988; included rehabilitation disability assignment to Phoenix, August 9 to August 13, 1988.

bOn disabled list, March 19 to April 28 and June 5, 1989 through remainder of season.

cGranted free agency, November 13, 1989.

CHAMPIONSHIP SERIES RECORD

Year Club	League	G.	IP.	W.	L.	Pct.	H.	R.	ER.	SO.	BB.	ERA.
1987—San Francisco	National	1	9	1	0	1.000	9	2	2	3	1	2.00

ALL—STAR GAME RECORD

Year League	IP.	W.	L.	Pct.	H.	R.	ER.	SO.	BB.	ERA.
1986—National	1	0	0	.000	0	0	0	0	0	0.00

JEFFREY WILLIAM KUNKEL
(Jeff)

Born March 25, 1962, at West Palm Beach, Fla.
Height, 6.02. Weight, 190.
Throws and bats righthanded
Attended Rider College, Lawrenceville, N.J.

Son of Bill Kunkel, pitcher with Kansas City A's and New York Yankees, 1961 through 1963; umpire, Florida State League, 1966; Southern League, 1967 and 1968; and American League umpire, 1968 through 1984.

Major League stolen bases: 1984 (4), 1989 (3). Total—7.

Named shortstop on THE SPORTING NEWS College Baseball All-America Team, 1983.

Year Club	League	Pos.	G.	AB.	R.	H.	2B.	3B.	HR.	RBI.	B.A.	PO.	A.	E.	F.A.
1983—Burlington	Midw.	SS	31	122	22	35	7	1	6	18	.287	38	88	13	.906
1983—Tulsa	Texas	SS-2B	37	130	21	37	14	0	5	25	.285	68	106	9	.951
1984—Tulsa†	Texas	SS	47	177	30	56	16	1	4	22	.316	64	103	16	.913
1984—Texas	Amer.	SS	50	142	13	29	2	3	3	7	.204	81	120	17	.922
1985—Oklahoma City	A. A.	SS-OF	99	370	40	72	8	6	5	43	.195	152	308	26	.947
1985—Texas	Amer.	SS	2	4	1	1	0	0	0	0	.250	2	5	0	1.000
1986—Oklahoma City	A. A.	SS	111	409	50	100	16	4	11	51	.244	135	272	19	.955
1986—Texas	Amer.	SS	8	13	3	3	0	0	1	2	.231	4	6	3	.769
1987—Oklahoma City‡	A. A.	S-O-2-3	58	193	31	49	9	3	9	34	.254	65	100	5	.971
1987—Texas	Amer.	2-3-O-1-S	15	32	1	7	0	0	1	2	.219	19	27	3	.939
1988—Oklahoma City	A. A.	SS-OF	56	203	28	44	11	4	5	21	.217	68	151	7	.969
1988—Texas	Amer.	2-S-3-O-P	55	154	14	35	8	3	2	15	.227	78	119	8	.961
1989—Texas	Amer.	S-O-2-3-P	108	293	39	79	21	2	8	29	.270	143	168	22	.934
Major League Totals—6 Years			238	638	71	154	31	8	15	55	.241	327	445	53	.936

Selected by Texas Rangers' organization in 1st round (third player selected) of free-agent draft, June 6, 1983.

†On disabled list, April 10 to May 12 and May 17 to June 4, 1984.

‡On Texas disabled list, March 25 to May 6, 1987; included rehabilitation disability assignment to Oklahoma City, April 17 to May 6, 1987.

PITCHING RECORD

Year Club	League	G.	IP.	W.	L.	Pct.	H.	R.	ER.	SO.	BB.	ERA.
1988—Texas	American	1	1	0	0	.000	0	0	0	1	0	0.00
1989—Texas	American	1	1⅔	0	0	.000	4	4	4	0	3	21.60
Major League Totals—2 Years		2	2⅔	0	0	.000	4	4	4	1	3	13.50

RANDY SCOTT KUTCHER

Born April 20, 1960, at Anchorage, Alaska.
Height, 5.11. Weight, 175.
Throws and bats righthanded

Major League stolen bases: 1986 (6), 1987 (1), 1989 (3). Total—10.

Led International League third basemen in errors with 21 in 1988.

Year Club	League	Pos.	G.	AB.	R.	H.	2B.	3B.	HR.	RBI.	B.A.	PO.	A.	E.	F.A.
1979—Great Falls	Pion.	SS	65	245	55	62	8	2	2	25	.253	79	109	29	.866
1980—Clinton	Midw.	SS-3B	138	525	72	133	17	●8	2	46	.253	204	365	39	.936
1981—Fresno	Calif.	S-O-2-3	41	161	28	44	10	2	3	26	.273	66	80	18	.890
1981—Shreveport	Texas	SS	77	249	36	71	13	4	4	20	.285	112	212	18	.947
1982—Shreveport	Texas	SS-OF	116	397	56	98	18	2	3	31	.247	183	142	18	.948

Year Club	League	Pos.	G.	AB.	R.	H.	2B.	3B.	HR.	RBI.	B.A.	PO.	A.	E.	F.A.
1983—Phoenix	P. C.	S-O-2-3-C	104	275	45	75	11	4	3	45	.273	152	138	15	.951
1984—Phoenix	P. C.	O-S-3-2-C	103	336	37	93	17	3	2	31	.277	177	80	11	.959
1985—Phoenix†	P. C.	OF-2B	97	228	36	54	15	2	1	20	.237	143	9	4	.974
1986—Phoenix	P. C.	S-O-2-3-C	55	208	47	72	14	4	11	39	.346	93	89	16	.919
1986—San Francisco	Nat.	O-S-3-2	71	186	28	44	9	1	7	16	.237	111	11	1	.992
1987—Phoenix	P. C.	O-3-2-S-1	92	349	68	89	15	5	6	53	.255	153	116	15	.947
1987—San Francisco‡	Nat.	O-2-3-S	14	16	7	3	1	1	0	1	.188	14	5	0	1.000
1988—Pawtucket	Int.	3B-OF-2B	86	331	40	77	12	2	4	27	.233	73	138	22	.906
1988—Boston	Amer.	OF-3B	19	12	2	2	1	0	0	0	.167	6	5	1	.917
1989—Boston§	Amer.	OF-3B-C	77	160	28	36	10	3	2	18	.225	112	8	3	.976
National League Totals—2 Years			85	202	35	47	10	2	7	17	.233	125	16	1	.993
American League Totals—2 Years			96	172	30	38	11	3	2	18	.221	118	13	4	.970
Major League Totals—4 Years			181	374	65	85	21	5	9	35	.227	243	29	5	.982

Selected by San Francisco Giants' organization in 4th round of free-agent draft, June 5, 1979.

†Granted free agency, October 15, 1985; re-signed by Giants, February 3, 1986.

‡Traded to Boston Red Sox, December 9, 1987, completing deal in which Boston traded Outfielder Dave Henderson to San Francisco Giants for a player to be named later, September 1, 1987.

§On disabled list, August 28 to September 12, 1989.

JERRY SCOTT KUTZLER

Born March 25, 1965, at Waukegan, Ill.
Height, 6.01. Weight, 175.
Throws right and bats lefthanded.
Attended William Penn College, Oskaloosa, Ia.

Led Florida State League pitchers in complete games with 12 in 1988.
Named Florida State League Pitcher of the Year, 1988.

Year Club	League	G.	IP.	W.	L.	Pct.	H.	R.	ER.	SO.	BB.	ERA.
1987—Sarasota White Sox	Gulf Coast	4	20	1	1	.500	14	13	11	16	7	4.95
1987—Peninsula	Carolina	10	63⅔	5	2	.714	54	34	29	30	24	4.10
1988—Tampa	Florida St.	26	184	*16	7	.696	154	73	57	100	39	2.79
1989—Birmingham	Southern	14	99⅓	9	4	.692	95	50	40	85	27	3.62
1989—Vancouver	P. Coast	12	80	5	5	.500	76	37	34	36	20	3.83

Selected by Chicago White Sox' organization in 6th round of free-agent draft, June 2, 1987.

MICHAEL JAMES LaCOSS
(Mike)

Born May 30, 1956, at Glendale, Calif.
Height, 6.04. Weight, 200.
Throws and bats righthanded.

Major League saves: 1981 (1), 1983 (1), 1984 (3), 1985 (1), 1989 (6). Total—12.
Tied for American Association lead in shutouts with 3 in 1978.

Year Club	League	G.	IP.	W.	L.	Pct.	H.	R.	ER.	SO.	BB.	ERA.
1974—Billings	Pioneer	13	87	6	5	.545	81	40	27	58	38	2.79
1975—Tampa	Florida St.	23	151	4	7	.412	131	61	48	72	41	2.86
1976—Three Rivers	Eastern	25	162	12	10	.545	148	66	53	80	53	2.94
1977—Indianapolis	Am. Assoc.	27	186	11	*13	.458	181	93	80	104	65	3.87
1978—Indianapolis	Am. Assoc.	19	130	11	5	.688	129	62	50	67	49	3.46
1978—Cincinnati	National	16	96	4	8	.333	104	56	48	31	46	4.50
1979—Cincinnati	National	35	206	14	8	.636	202	92	80	73	79	3.50
1980—Cincinnati	National	34	169	10	12	.455	207	101	87	59	68	4.63
1981—Cincinnati†	National	20	78	4	7	.364	102	55	53	22	30	6.12
1982—Houston	National	41	115	6	6	.500	107	41	37	51	54	2.90
1983—Houston‡	National	38	138	5	7	.417	142	81	68	53	56	4.43
1984—Houston§	National	39	132	7	5	.583	132	64	59	86	55	4.02
1985—Kansas City	American	21	40⅔	1	1	.500	49	25	23	26	29	5.09
1985—Omaha x	Am. Assoc.	4	22⅓	1	2	.333	23	12	8	11	15	3.22
1986—San Francisco y	National	37	204⅓	10	13	.435	179	99	81	86	70	3.57
1987—San Francisco z	National	39	171	13	10	.565	184	78	70	79	63	3.68
1988—San Francisco a	National	19	114⅓	7	7	.500	99	55	46	70	47	3.62
1989—San Francisco	National	45	150⅓	10	10	.500	143	62	53	78	65	3.17
National League Totals—11 Years		363	1574	90	93	.492	1601	784	682	688	633	3.90
American League Totals—1 Year		21	40⅔	1	1	.500	49	25	23	26	29	5.09
Major League Totals—12 Years		384	1614⅔	91	94	.492	1650	809	705	714	662	3.93

Selected by Cincinnati Reds' organization in 3rd round of free-agent draft, June 5, 1974.

†Sold on waivers to Houston Astros, April 4, 1982.

‡On disabled list, June 17 to July 8, 1983.

§Granted free agency, November 8, 1984; signed by Kansas City Royals' organization, February 19, 1985.

xReleased, November 6, 1985; signed by San Francisco Giants' organization, February 3, 1986.

yGranted free agency, November 12, 1986; re-signed by Giants, December 12, 1986.

zGranted free agency, November 9, 1987; re-signed by Giants, November 24, 1987.

aOn disabled list, July 17 to September 8, 1988.

CHAMPIONSHIP SERIES RECORD

Year Club	League	G.	IP.	W.	L.	Pct.	H.	R.	ER.	SO.	BB.	ERA.
1979—Cincinnati	National	1	1⅔	0	1	.000	1	2	2	0	4	10.80

Year Club	League	G.	IP.	W.	L.	Pct.	H.	R.	ER.	SO.	BB.	ERA.
1987—San Francisco	National	2	3⅓	0	0	.000	1	0	0	2	3	0.00
1989—San Francisco	National	1	3	0	0	.000	7	3	3	2	0	9.00
Championship Series Totals—3 Years		4	8	0	1	.000	9	5	5	4	7	5.63

WORLD SERIES RECORD

Year Club	League	G.	IP.	W.	L.	Pct.	H.	R.	ER.	SO.	BB.	ERA.
1989—San Francisco	National	2	4⅓	0	0	.000	4	3	3	2	3	6.23

ALL-STAR GAME RECORD

Year League	IP.	W.	L.	Pct.	H.	R.	ER.	SO.	BB.	ERA.
1979—National	1⅓	0	0	.000	1	0	0	0	0	0.00

MICHAEL RUSSELL LAGA
(Mike)

Born June 14, 1960, at Ridgewood, N. J.
Height, 6.02. Weight, 210.
Throws and bats lefthanded.
Attended Bergen Community College, Paramus, N. J.,
and Fairleigh Dickinson University, Teaneck, N. J.

Major League stolen bases: 1982 (1).
Led American Association in intentional bases on balls received with 12 in 1987.
Led American Association in sacrifice flies with 7 in 1985.
Led American Association in being hit by pitch with 13 in 1982.
Led American Association first basemen in double plays with 101 in 1985.
Led American Association first basemen in total chances with 1,221 in 1982 and 1,146 in 1985.

Year Club	League	Pos.	G.	AB.	R.	H.	2B.	3B.	HR.	RBI.	B.A.	PO.	A.	E.	F.A.
1980—Lakeland	Fla. St.	1B	122	407	60	111	14	6	12	74	.273	1025	84	*18	.984
1981—Birmingham	South.	1B	142	547	89	158	28	7	31	86	.289	1193	*105	*23	.983
1982—Evansville	A. A.	1B	126	444	77	111	15	3	34	90	.250	*1135	68	18	.985
1982—Detroit	Amer.	1B	27	88	6	23	9	0	3	11	.261	163	4	1	.994
1983—Evansville	A. A.	1B	105	355	46	82	24	1	16	58	.231	835	62	*11	.988
1983—Detroit	Amer.	1B	12	21	2	4	0	0	0	2	.190	9	1	0	1.000
1984—Evansville	A. A.	1B	●153	569	86	151	30	9	30	94	.265	1008	92	14	.987
1984—Detroit	Amer.	1D	9	11	1	6	0	0	0	1	.545	12	1	0	1.000
1985—Nashville	A. A.	1B	117	430	58	113	30	2	20	79	.263	*1024	*111	11	.990
1985—Detroit	Amer.	1B	9	36	3	6	1	0	2	6	.167	33	5	1	.974
1986—Detroit†	Amer.	1B	15	45	6	9	1	0	3	8	.200	98	7	0	1.000
1986—Nashville	A. A.	1B	12	41	4	9	3	0	2	7	.220	109	16	2	.984
1986—St. Louis‡	Nat.	1B	18	46	7	10	4	0	3	8	.217	109	14	0	1.000
1987—St. Louis	Nat.	1B	17	29	4	4	1	0	1	4	.138	66	7	2	.973
1987—Louisville	A. A.	1B	116	418	80	127	35	2	29	91	.304	922	67	11	.989
1988—Louisville§	A. A.	1B	13	49	4	10	2	0	1	5	.204	74	3	1	.987
1988—St. Louis x	Nat.	1B	41	100	5	13	0	0	1	4	.130	293	17	0	1.000
1989—Phoenix	P. C.	1B	126	449	55	108	20	9	23	68	.241	1064	93	6	.995
1989—San Francisco	Nat.	1B	17	20	1	4	1	0	1	7	.200	16	1	0	1.000
American League Totals—5 Years			72	201	18	48	11	0	8	28	.239	315	18	2	.994
National League Totals—4 Years			93	195	17	31	6	0	6	23	.159	484	39	2	.996
Major League Totals—8 Years			165	396	35	79	17	0	14	51	.199	799	57	4	.995

Selected by Detroit Tigers' organization in 1st round (17th player selected) of free-agent draft, January 8, 1980.

†On disabled list, May 15 to September 1, 1986; included rehabilitation disability assignment to Nashville, August 8 to August 27, 1986.

‡Traded to St. Louis Cardinals, September 2, 1986, completing deal in which St. Louis traded Catcher Mike Heath to Detroit Tigers for Pitcher Ken Hill and a player to be named later, August 10, 1986.

§On St. Louis disabled list, March 26 to July 14, 1988; included rehabilitation disability assignment to Louisville, June 28 to July 14, 1988.

xReleased, November 8, 1988; signed by Phoenix (San Francisco Giants' organization), January 25, 1989.

STEVEN MICHAEL LAKE
(Steve)

Born March 14, 1957, at Inglewood, Calif.
Height, 6.01. Weight, 190.
Throws and bats righthanded.
Cousin of Mike Lake, minor league pitcher, 1941 through 1946.

Major League stolen bases: 1985 (1).
Led Appalachian League in passed balls with 15 in 1975.

Year Club	League	Pos.	G.	AB.	R.	H.	2B.	3B.	HR.	RBI.	B.A.	PO.	A.	E.	F.A.
1975—Bluefield	Appal.	C	49	162	17	45	12	0	3	24	.278	254	*39	9	.970
1976—Miami	Fla. St.	PH	1	1	0	1	0	0	0	1	1.000	0	0	0	.000
1977—Miami	Fla. St.	C	79	232	25	55	10	1	2	24	.237	357	47	6	.985
1978—Miami†‡	Fla. St.	C	69	223	19	57	10	0	2	26	.256	300	49	6	.983
1979—Stockton§	Calif.	C	94	329	36	93	12	3	6	40	.283	504	73	8	.986
1980—Holyoke	East.	C-OF	102	325	26	84	9	2	2	44	.258	445	107	10	.982
1981—Vancouver x	P. C.	C	109	348	27	80	14	1	2	38	.230	502	102	7	.989
1982—Tucson y	P. C.	C	112	378	42	100	15	4	3	45	.265	504	91	12	.980
1983—Chicago	Nat.	C	38	85	9	22	4	1	1	7	.259	115	22	0	1.000
1984—Chicago z	Nat.	C	25	54	4	12	4	0	2	7	.222	72	13	4	.955

Year Club	League	Pos.	G.	AB.	R.	H.	2B.	3B.	HR.	RBI.	B.A.	PO.	A.	E.	F.A.
1984—Midland.................	Texas	C	9	25	2	4	0	0	0	1	.160	46	7	0	1.000
1985—Chicago.................	Nat.	C	58	119	5	18	2	0	1	11	.151	182	25	1	.995
1986—Chi. a-St.L..............	Nat.	C	36	68	8	20	2	0	2	14	.294	105	9	2	.983
1986—Iowa-Louisville.....	A. A.	C	33	98	5	24	6	0	0	13	.245	140	21	2	.988
1987—St. Louis................	Nat.	C	74	179	19	45	7	2	2	19	.251	253	21	1	.996
1988—St. Louis b.............	Nat.	C	36	54	5	15	3	0	1	4	.278	51	8	1	.983
1989—Philadelphia cd....	Nat.	C	58	155	9	39	5	1	2	14	.252	262	33	3	.990
Major League Totals—7 Years.................			325	714	59	171	27	4	11	76	.239	1040	131	12	.990

Selected by Baltimore Orioles' organization in 3rd round of free-agent draft, June 4, 1975.
†On disabled list, April 17 to May 16, 1978.
‡Sold to Milwaukee Brewers' organization, December 21, 1978.
§On disabled list, June 20 to July 6, 1979.
xLoaned to Tucson (Houston Astros' organization), April 5, 1982; returned, September 7, 1982.
yTraded to Chicago Cubs for a player to be named later, April 1, 1983; Milwaukee Brewers' organization acquired Pitcher Rich Buonantony to complete deal, October 24, 1983.
zOn disabled list, May 14 to August 3, 1984; included rehabilitation disability assignment to Midland, July 23 to August 3, 1984.
aReleased, July 15, 1986; signed by Louisville (St. Louis Cardinals' organization), July 24, 1986.
bTraded with Outfielder Curt Ford to Philadelphia Phillies for Outfielder Milt Thompson, December 16, 1988.
cOn disabled list, August 28, 1989 through remainder of season.
dGranted free agency, November 13, 1989; re-signed by Phillies, December 6, 1989.

CHAMPIONSHIP SERIES RECORD

Year Club	League	Pos.	G.	AB.	R.	H.	2B.	3B.	HR.	RBI.	B.A.	PO.	A.	E.	F.A.
1984—Chicago.................	Nat.	C	1	1	0	1	1	0	0	0	1.000	0	0	0	.000

WORLD SERIES RECORD

Year Club	League	Pos.	G.	AB.	R.	H.	2B.	3B.	HR.	RBI.	B.A.	PO.	A.	E.	F.A.
1987—St. Louis.................	Nat.	C	3	3	0	1	0	0	0	1	.333	8	1	0	1.000

DENNIS PATRICK LAMP

Born September 23, 1952, at Los Angeles, Calif.
Height, 6.03. Weight, 215.
Throws and bats righthanded.

Major League saves: 1982 (5), 1983 (15), 1984 (9), 1985 (2), 1986 (2), 1989 (2). Total—35.

Year Club	League	G.	IP.	W.	L.	Pct.	H.	R.	ER.	SO.	BB.	ERA.
1971—Caldwell...........................	Pioneer	14	46	1	2	.333	51	39	33	43	32	6.46
1972—Bradenton Cubs.............	Gulf Coast	14	70	7	2	.778	56	20	15	56	21	1.93
1973—Quincy............................	Midwest	13	89	6	4	.600	67	32	26	71	29	2.63
1973—Midland...........................	Texas	9	48	2	4	.333	54	29	25	23	11	4.69
1974—Key West........................	Florida St.	8	49	1	5	.167	39	15	8	20	14	1.47
1974—Midland...........................	Texas	24	60	1	1	.500	70	38	31	42	22	4.65
1975—Midland...........................	Texas	37	127	7	5	.583	112	52	47	71	54	3.33
1976—Wichita...........................	Am. Assoc.	30	153	8	★14	.364	182	94	69	98	52	4.06
1977—Wichita...........................	Am. Assoc.	20	129	11	4	★.733	116	54	42	52	23	2.93
1977—Chicago..........................	National	11	30	0	2	.000	43	21	21	12	8	6.30
1978—Chicago..........................	National	37	224	7	15	.318	221	96	82	73	56	3.29
1979—Chicago..........................	National	38	200	11	10	.524	223	96	78	86	46	3.51
1980—Chicago†........................	National	41	203	10	14	.417	259	★123	★117	83	82	5.19
1981—Chicago..........................	American	27	127	7	6	.538	103	41	34	71	43	2.41
1982—Chicago..........................	American	44	189⅔	11	8	.579	206	96	84	78	59	3.99
1983—Chicago‡........................	American	49	116⅓	7	7	.500	123	52	48	44	29	3.71
1984—Toronto..........................	American	56	85	8	8	.500	97	53	43	45	38	4.55
1985—Toronto..........................	American	53	105⅔	11	0	1.000	96	42	39	68	27	3.32
1986—Toronto§x......................	American	40	73	2	6	.250	93	50	41	30	23	5.05
1987—Tacoma..........................	P. Coast	6	12⅓	1	0	1.000	9	4	4	10	8	2.92
1987—Oakland y.......................	American	36	56⅔	1	3	.250	76	38	32	36	22	5.08
1988—Boston za.......................	American	46	82⅔	7	6	.538	92	39	32	49	19	3.48
1989—Boston b.........................	American	42	112⅓	4	2	.667	96	37	29	61	27	2.32
National League Totals—4 Years.............		127	657	28	41	.406	746	336	298	254	192	4.08
American League Totals—9 Years....................		393	948⅓	58	46	.558	982	448	382	482	287	3.63
Major League Totals—13 Years...........................		520	1605⅓	86	87	.497	1728	784	680	736	479	3.81

Selected by Chicago Cubs' organization in 3rd round of free-agent draft, June 8, 1971.
†Traded to Chicago White Sox for Pitcher Ken Kravec, March 28, 1981.
‡Granted free agency, November 7, 1983; signed by Toronto Blue Jays as Type A player, January 10, 1984. (Pitcher Tom Seaver selected from player compensation pool by Chicago White Sox, January 20, 1984.)
§Released, October 20, 1986; signed by Cleveland Indians, February 5, 1987.
xReleased, March 23, 1987; signed by Oakland Athletics' organization, April 27, 1987.
yGranted free agency, October 19, 1987; signed by Pawtucket (Boston Red Sox' organization), January 5, 1988.
zOn disabled list, August 9 to August 27, 1988.
aGranted free agency, November 4, 1988; re-signed by Red Sox, November 20, 1988.
bGranted free agency, November 13, 1989; re-signed by Red Sox, December 6, 1989.

CHAMPIONSHIP SERIES RECORD

Year Club	League	G.	IP.	W.	L.	Pct.	H.	R.	ER.	SO.	BB.	ERA.
1983—Chicago...........................	American	3	2	0	0	.000	0	1	0	1	2	0.00
1985—Toronto...........................	American	3	9⅓	0	0	.000	2	0	0	10	1	0.00
Championship Series Totals—2 Years................		6	11⅓	0	0	.000	2	1	0	11	3	0.00

THOMAS MICHAEL LAMPKIN
(Tom)

Born March 4, 1964, at Cincinnati, O.
Height, 5.11. Weight, 185.
Throws right and bats lefthanded.
Attended University of Portland, Portland, Ore.

Year	Club	League	Pos.	G.	AB.	R.	H.	2B.	3B.	HR.	RBI.	B.A.	PO.	A.	E.	F.A.
1986—Batavia	NYP		C	63	190	24	49	5	1	1	20	.258	323	36	8	.978
1987—Waterloo	Midw.		C	118	398	49	106	19	2	7	55	.266	689	★100	15	.981
1988—Williamsport	East.		C	80	263	38	71	10	0	3	23	.270	431	60	9	.982
1988—Colorado Springs	P. C.		C	34	107	14	30	5	0	0	7	.280	171	28	5	.975
1988—Cleveland	Amer.		C	4	4	0	0	0	0	0	0	.000	3	0	0	1.000
1989—Colorado Springs†	P. C.		C	63	209	26	67	10	3	4	32	.231	305	21	8	.976
Major League Totals—1 Year				4	4	0	0	0	0	0	0	.000	3	0	0	1.000

Selected by Cleveland Indians' organization in 11th round of free-agent draft, June 2, 1986.
†On disabled list, July 6, 1989 through remainder of season.

LESTER WAYNE LANCASTER
(Les)

Born April 21, 1962, at Dallas, Tex.
Height, 6.02. Weight, 200.
Throws and bats righthanded.
Attended Dallas Baptist College, Dallas, Tex., and University of Arkansas, Fayetteville, Ark.

Major League saves: 1988 (5), 1989 (8). Total—13.
Tied for National League lead in balks with 8 in 1987.
Led Appalachian League in complete games with 7 and intentional bases on balls issued with 5 in 1985.

Year	Club	League	G.	IP.	W.	L.	Pct.	H.	R.	ER.	SO.	BB.	ERA.
1985—Wytheville	Ap'lachian		20	★102	7	4	.636	★98	49	41	★81	24	3.62
1986—Winston-Salem	Carolina		13	97	8	3	.727	88	37	30	52	30	2.78
1986—Pittsfield	Eastern		14	88	5	6	.455	105	46	41	49	34	4.19
1987—Chicago	National		27	132⅓	8	3	.727	138	76	72	78	51	4.90
1987—Iowa	Am. Assoc.		15	67	5	3	.625	59	24	24	62	17	3.22
1988—Chicago†	National		44	85⅔	4	6	.400	89	42	36	36	34	3.78
1989—Iowa	Am. Assoc.		17	91⅓	5	7	.417	76	38	27	56	43	2.66
1989—Chicago	National		42	72⅔	4	2	.667	60	12	11	56	15	1.36
Major League Totals—3 Years			113	290⅔	16	11	.593	287	130	119	170	100	3.68

Selected by New York Yankees' organization in 24th round of free-agent draft, June 8, 1981.
Selected by Texas Rangers' organization in 39th round of free-agent draft, June 6, 1983.
Signed as free agent by Chicago Cubs' organization, June 13, 1985.
†On disabled list, July 24 to August 14 and August 20 to September 4, 1988.

CHAMPIONSHIP SERIES RECORD

Year	Club	League	G.	IP.	W.	L.	Pct.	H.	R.	ER.	SO.	BB.	ERA.
1989—Chicago	National		3	6	1	1	.500	6	4	4	3	1	6.00

THOMAS WILLIAM LANDRUM
(Bill)

Born August 17, 1958, at Columbia, S.C.
Height, 6.02. Weight, 205.
Throws and bats righthanded.
Attended Spartanburg Methodist College, Spartanburg, S.C., and received bachelor of science
degree from University of South Carolina, Columbia, S.C. in 1980.
Son of Joe Landrum, pitcher with Brooklyn Dodgers, 1950 and 1952.

Major League saves: 1987 (2), 1989 (26). Total—28.

Year	Club	League	G.	IP.	W.	L.	Pct.	H.	R.	ER.	SO.	BB.	ERA.
1980—Sarasota Cubs†	Gulf Coast		11	37	2	0	1.000	37	21	17	27	11	4.14
1981—Tampa	Florida St.		17	83	6	8	.42	87	44	35	52	22	3.80
1982—Waterbury	Eastern		★58	112⅓	10	6	.625	109	63	51	104	65	4.09
1983—Waterbury	Eastern		17	29⅔	1	1	.500	17	5	5	33	14	1.52
1983—Indianapolis‡	Am. Assoc.		15	17⅔	1	3	.250	20	6	6	21	6	3.06
1984—Wichita§	Am. Assoc.		47	130⅓	7	4	.636	12	58	50	120	52	3.45
1985—Denver	Am. Assoc.		29	138	6	6	.500	148	72	61	88	49	3.98
1986—Denver x	Am. Assoc.		24	36⅓	1	3	.250	36	20	14	36	25	3.47
1986—Cincinnati	National		10	13⅓	0	0	.000	23	11	10	14	4	6.75
1987—Cincinnati	National		44	65	3	2	.600	68	35	34	42	34	4.71
1987—Nashville y	Am. Assoc.		19	38⅔	4	0	1.000	30	9	9	47	19	2.09
1988—Iowa	Am. Assoc.		9	21⅓	1	0	1.000	13	7	7	22	6	2.95
1988—Chicago z	National		7	12⅓	1	0	1.000	19	8	8	6	3	5.84
1989—Pittsburgh	National		56	81	2	3	.400	60	18	15	51	28	1.67
1989—Buffalo	Am. Assoc.		5	25⅓	3	0	1.000	16	2	2	20	6	0.71
Major League Totals—4 Years			117	171⅔	6	5	.545	170	72	67	113	69	3.51

Signed as free agent by Chicago Cubs' organization, June 22, 1980.
†Released, October 20, 1980; signed by Billings (Cincinnati Reds' organization), February 7, 1981.
‡On disabled list, July 19 to August 4, 1983.
§Drafted by Chicago White Sox, December 3, 1984; returned, March 30, 1985.

xOn disabled list, April 29 to June 21, 1986.
yTraded to Chicago Cubs for Infielder Luis Quinones, April 1, 1988.
zGranted free agency, October 15, 1988; signed by Pittsburgh Pirates, January 12, 1989.

BRIAN CONLEY LANE

Born June 15, 1969, at Waco, Tex.
Height, 6.03. Weight, 210.
Throws and bats righthanded.

Year	Club	League	Pos.	G.	AB.	R.	H.	2B.	3B.	HR.	RBI.	B.A.	PO.	A.	E.	F.A.
1987—Billings		Pion.	3B	56	175	19	35	6	1	3	16	.200	35	107	12	.922
1988—Greensboro		S. Atl.	3B	115	451	55	127	17	3	3	52	.282	93	196	21	.932
1989—Chattanooga		South.	3B	130	464	59	117	19	4	11	89	.252	94	223	27	.922

Selected by Cincinnati Reds' organization in 3rd round of free-agent draft, June 2, 1987.

MARK EDWARD LANGSTON

Born August 20, 1960, at San Diego, Calif.
Height, 6.02. Weight, 183.
Throws left and bats righthanded.
Attended San Jose State University, San Jose, Calif.

Named pitcher on THE SPORTING NEWS American League All-Star fielding team, 1987 and 1988.
Named American League Rookie Pitcher of the Year by THE SPORTING NEWS, 1984.

Year	Club	League	G.	IP.	W.	L.	Pct.	H.	R.	ER.	SO.	BB.	ERA.
1981—Bellingham		Northwest	13	85	7	3	.700	81	37	32	97	46	3.39
1982—Bakersfield		California	26	177⅓	12	7	.632	143	71	50	161	102	2.54
1983—Chattanooga		Southern	28	198	14	9	.609	187	104	79	142	102	3.59
1984—Seattle		American	35	225	17	10	.630	188	99	85	*204	*118	3.40
1985—Seattle†		American	24	126⅔	7	14	.333	122	85	77	72	91	5.47
1986—Seattle		American	37	239⅓	12	14	.462	234	*142	*129	*245	123	4.85
1987—Seattle		American	35	272	19	13	.594	242	132	116	*262	114	3.84
1988—Seattle		American	35	261⅓	15	11	.577	222	108	97	235	110	3.34
1989—Seattle‡§		American	10	73½	4	5	.444	60	30	29	60	19	3.56
1989—Montreal§		National	24	176⅔	12	9	.571	138	57	47	175	93	2.39
American League Totals—6 Years			176	1197⅔	74	67	.525	1068	596	533	1078	575	4.01
National League Totals—1 Year			24	176⅔	12	9	.571	138	57	47	175	93	2.39
Major League Totals—6 Years			200	1374⅓	86	76	.531	1206	653	580	1253	668	3.80

Selected by Chicago Cubs' organization in 15th round of free-agent draft, June 6, 1978.
Selected by Seattle Mariners' organization in 3rd round of free-agent draft, June 8, 1981.
†On disabled list, June 7 to July 22, 1985.
‡Traded with a player to be named later to Montreal Expos for Pitchers Randy Johnson, Brian Holman and Gene Harris, May 25, 1989; Indianapolis (Montreal Expos' organization) acquired Pitcher Mike Campbell to complete deal, July 31, 1989.
§Granted free agency, November 13, 1989; signed by California Angels, December 1, 1989.

ALL-STAR GAME RECORD

Year	League	IP.	W.	L.	Pct.	H.	R.	ER.	SO.	BB.	ERA.
1987—American		2	0	0	.000	0	0	0	3	0	0.00

RAYMOND L. LANKFORD
(Ray)

Born June 5, 1967, at Modesto, Calif.
Height, 5.11. Weight, 180.
Throws and bats lefthanded.
Attended Modesto Junior College, Modesto, Calif.

Led Midwest League in total bases with 242 in 1988.
Led Appalachian League in caught stealing with 11 in 1987.
Led Texas League outfielders in total chances with 387 in 1989.
Led Appalachian League outfielders in total chances with 155 in 1987.
Named Texas League Most Valuable Player, 1989.

Year	Club	League	Pos.	G.	AB.	R.	H.	2B.	3B.	HR.	RBI.	B.A.	PO.	A.	E.	F.A.
1987—Johnson City		Appal.	OF	66	253	45	78	17	4	3	32	.308	*143	7	5	.968
1988—Springfield		Midw.	OF	135	532	90	151	28	*16	11	66	.284	284	5	7	.976
1989—Arkansas		Texas	OF	*134	498	98	*158	28	*12	11	98	.317	*367	9	11	.972

Selected by Chicago Cubs' organization in 3rd round of free-agent draft, January 14, 1986.
Selected by St. Louis Cardinals' organization in 3rd round of free-agent draft, June 2, 1987.

CARNEY RAY LANSFORD

Born February 7, 1957, at San Jose, Calif.
Height, 6.02. Weight, 195.
Throws and bats righthanded.
Brother of Phil Lansford, infielder in Cleveland Indians' and Toronto Blue Jays' organizations,
1978 through 1981; and Joe Lansford, first baseman with San Diego Padres, 1982 and 1983.

Major League stolen bases: 1978 (20), 1979 (20), 1980 (14), 1981 (15), 1982 (9), 1983 (3), 1984 (9), 1985 (2), 1986 (16), 1987 (28), 1988 (29), 1989 (37). Total—201.
Hit three home runs in a game, September 1, 1979.
Led American League in sacrifice flies with 11 in 1980.

Led American League third basemen in fielding percentage with .980 in 1987 and .979 in 1988.
Led Texas League third basemen in double plays with 16 in 1977.
Named third baseman on THE SPORTING NEWS American League All-Star Team, 1989.
Named third baseman on THE SPORTING NEWS American League Silver Slugger team, 1981.

Year Club	League	Pos.	G.	AB.	R.	H.	2B.	3B.	HR.	RBI.	B.A.	PO.	A.	E.	F.A.
1975—Idaho Falls†	Pion.	3B-SS	8	27	5	6	2	0	1	1	.222	8	14	9	.710
1976—Quad Cities	Midw.	3B-OF-SS	121	418	87	120	19	5	14	86	.287	130	215	36	.906
1977—El Paso	Texas	3B	120	443	98	147	17	3	18	94	.332	*110	*210	15	*.955
1978—California‡	Amer.	3B-SS	121	453	63	133	23	2	8	52	.294	94	186	18	.940
1979—California	Amer.	3B	157	654	114	188	30	5	19	79	.287	*135	263	7	*.983
1980—California§	Amer.	3B	151	602	87	157	27	3	15	80	.261	*151	250	19	.955
1981—Boston	Amer.	3B	102	399	61	134	23	3	4	52	*.336	70	180	13	.951
1982—Boston xy	Amer.	3B	128	482	65	145	28	4	11	63	.301	83	216	10	.968
1983—Oakland z	Amer.	3B-SS	80	299	43	92	16	2	10	45	.308	60	163	10	.957
1984—Oakland	Amer.	3B	151	597	70	179	31	5	14	74	.300	137	268	18	.957
1985—Oakland a	Amer.	3B	98	401	51	111	18	2	13	46	.277	85	119	5	.976
1986—Oakland	Amer.	3B-1B-2B	151	591	80	168	16	4	19	72	.284	480	170	6	.991
1987—Oakland	Amer.	3B-1B	151	554	89	160	27	4	19	76	.289	156	258	7	.983
1988—Oakland	Amer.	3B-1B-2B	150	556	80	155	20	2	7	57	.279	125	221	7	.980
1989—Oakland	Amer.	3B-1B	148	551	81	185	28	2	2	52	.336	195	188	13	.967
Major League Totals—12 Years			1588	6139	884	1807	287	38	141	748	.294	1771	2482	133	.970

Selected by California Angels' organization in 3rd round of free-agent draft, June 4, 1975.
†On disabled list, July 21 to September 30, 1975.
‡On disabled list, June 11 to July 7, 1978.
§Traded with Pitcher Mark Clear and Outfielder Rick Miller to Boston Red Sox for Shortstop Rick Burleson and Third Baseman Butch Hobson, December 10, 1980.
xOn disabled list, June 24 to July 21, 1982.
yTraded with Outfielder Garry Hancock and a player to be named later to Oakland A's for Outfielder Tony Armas and Catcher Jeff Newman, December 6, 1982; Oakland acquired Pitcher Jerry King to complete deal, December 20, 1982.
zOn disabled list, May 19 to June 7, 1983.
aOn disabled list, July 26 to August 28, 1985.

CHAMPIONSHIP SERIES RECORD

Year Club	League	Pos.	G.	AB.	R.	H.	2B.	3B.	HR.	RBI.	B.A.	PO.	A.	E.	F.A.
1979—California	Amer.	3B	4	17	2	5	0	0	0	3	.294	4	8	0	1.000
1988 Oakland	Amer.	3B	4	17	4	5	1	0	1	2	.294	7	8	0	1.000
1989—Oakland	Amer.	3B	3	11	2	5	0	0	0	4	.455	1	2	0	1.000
Championship Series Totals—3 Years			11	45	8	15	1	0	1	9	.333	12	18	0	1.000

WORLD SERIES RECORD

Shares World Series record for most runs, game (4), October 27, 1989.

Year Club	League	Pos.	G.	AB.	R.	H.	2B.	3B.	HR.	RBI.	B.A.	PO.	A.	E.	F.A.
1988—Oakland	Amer.	3B	5	18	2	3	0	0	0	1	.167	8	7	0	1.000
1989—Oakland	Amer.	3B	4	16'	5	7	1	0	1	4	.438	5	5	0	1.000
World Series Totals—2 Years			9	34	7	10	1	0	1	5	.294	13	12	0	1.000

ALL-STAR GAME RECORD

Year League	Pos.	AB.	R.	H.	2B.	3B.	HR.	RBI.	B.A.	PO.	A.	E.	F.A.
1988—American	3B	1	0	0	0	0	0	0	.000	0	1	0	1.000

DAVID JEFFREY LaPOINT
(Dave)

Born July 29, 1959, at Glens Falls, N. Y.
Height, 6.03. Weight, 231.
Throws and bats lefthanded.

Pitched 4-0 no-hit victory against Reno, July 25, 1979.
Major League saves: 1980 (1).
Led National League in wild pitches with 15 in 1984.
Tied for American Association lead in complete games with 9 in 1981.
Tied for California League lead in shutouts with 3 and complete games with 11 in 1979.
Tied for Midwest League lead in home runs allowed with 20 in 1978.

Year Club	League	G.	IP.	W.	L.	Pct.	H.	R.	ER.	SO.	BB.	ERA.
1977—Newark	NYP	13	69	5	2	.714	73	40	36	60	22	4.70
1978—Burlington	Midwest	25	161	12	12	.500	177	98	72	134	41	4.02
1979—Stockton	California	27	180	12	10	.545	144	74	63	*208	85	3.15
1980—Vancouver†	P. Coast	17	93	7	4	.636	71	48		64	45	2.81
1980—Milwaukee‡	American	5	15	1	0	1.000	17	14	10	5	13	6.00
1981—Springfield	Am. Assoc.	25	172	13	9	.591	160	83	61	*129	66	3.19
1981—St. Louis	National	3	11	1	0	1.000	12	5	5	4	2	4.09
1982—St. Louis	National	42	152⅔	9	3	.750	170	63	58	81	52	3.42
1983—St. Louis	National	37	191⅓	12	9	.571	191	92	84	113	84	3.95
1984—St. Louis§x	National	33	193	12	10	.545	205	94	85	130	77	3.96
1985—San Francisco y	National	31	206⅔	7	17	.292	215	99	82	122	74	3.57
1986—Detroit z	American	16	67⅔	3	6	.333	85	49	43	36	32	5.72
1986—San Diego a	National	24	61⅓	1	4	.200	67	37	29	41	24	4.26
1987—St. Louis	National	6	16	1	1	.500	26	12	12	8	5	6.75

Year	Club	League	G.	IP.	W.	L.	Pct.	H.	R.	ER.	SO.	BB.	ERA.
1987—Louisville b	Am. Assoc.	14	91⅔	5	5	.500	93	45	41	70	27	4.03
1987—Chicago c	American	14	82⅔	6	3	.667	69	29	27	43	31	2.94
1988—Chicago d	American	25	161⅓	10	11	.476	151	69	61	79	47	3.40
1988—Pittsburgh e	National	8	52	4	2	.667	54	18	16	19	10	2.77
1989—New York f	American	20	113⅔	6	9	.400	146	73	71	51	45	5.62
American League Totals—5 Years		80	440⅓	26	29	.473	468	234	212	214	168	4.33
National League Totals—8 Years		184	884	47	46	.505	940	420	371	518	328	3.78
Major League Totals—10 Years		264	1324⅓	73	75	.493	1408	654	583	732	496	3.96

Selected by Milwaukee Brewers' organization in 10th round of free-agent draft, June 7, 1977.

†On disabled list, May 6 to May 17 and June 6 to July 15, 1980.

‡Traded with Pitcher Lary Sorensen and Outfielders Sixto Lezcano and David Green to St. Louis Cardinals for Pitchers Pete Vuckovich and Rollie Fingers and Catcher Ted Simmons, December 12, 1980.

§On disabled list, June 15 to June 30, 1984.

xTraded with First Basemen David Green and Gary Rajsich and Shortstop Jose Gonzalez (Jose Uribe) to San Francisco Giants for Outfielder-First Baseman Jack Clark, February 1, 1985.

yTraded with Catcher Matt Nokes and Pitcher Eric King to Detroit Tigers for Pitcher Juan Berenguer, Catcher Bob Melvin and a player to be named later, October 7, 1985; San Francisco Giants acquired Pitcher Scott Medvin to complete deal, December 11, 1985.

zTraded to San Diego Padres for Pitcher Mark Thurmond, July 9, 1986.

aReleased, December 20, 1986; signed by St. Louis Cardinals, January 19, 1987.

bTraded to Chicago White Sox for Pitcher Bryce Hulstrom, July 30, 1987.

cGranted free agency, November 9, 1987; re-signed by White Sox, February 9, 1988.

dTraded to Pittsburgh Pirates for Pitcher Barry Jones, August 13, 1988.

eGranted free agency, November 4, 1988; signed by New York Yankees, December 3, 1988.

fOn disabled list, June 30 to July 17 and August 3, 1989 through remainder of season.

WORLD SERIES RECORD

Year	Club	League	G.	IP.	W.	L.	Pct.	H.	R.	ER.	SO.	BB.	ERA.
1982—St. Louis	National	2	8⅓	0	0	.000	10	6	3	3	2	3.24

BARRY LOUIS LARKIN

Born April 28, 1964, at Cincinnati, O.
Height, 6.00. Weight, 185.
Throws and bats righthanded.
Attended University of Michigan, Ann Arbor, Mich.

Major League stolen bases: 1986 (8), 1987 (21), 1988 (40), 1989 (10). Total—79.
Led American Association in slugging percentage with .525 in 1986.
Named shortstop on THE SPORTING NEWS National League All-Star Team, 1988.
Named shortstop on THE SPORTING NEWS National League Silver Slugger team, 1988 and 1989.
Named American Association Most Valuable Player, 1986.
Named shortstop on THE SPORTING NEWS College Baseball All-America Team, 1985.
Member of 1984 U.S. Olympic baseball team.

Year	Club	League	Pos.	G.	AB.	R.	H.	2B.	3B.	HR.	RBI.	B.A.	PO.	A.	E.	F.A.
1985—Vermont	East.	SS	72	255	42	68	13	2	1	31	.267	110	166	17	.942
1986—Denver	A. A.	SS-2B	103	413	67	136	31	10	10	51	.329	172	287	18	.962
1986—Cincinnati	Nat.	SS-2B	41	159	27	45	4	3	3	19	.283	51	125	4	.978
1987—Cincinnati†	Nat.	SS	125	439	64	107	16	2	12	43	.244	168	358	19	.965
1988—Cincinnati	Nat.	SS	151	588	91	174	32	5	12	56	.296	231	470	●29	.960
1989—Cincinnati‡	Nat.	SS	97	325	47	111	14	4	4	36	.342	142	267	10	.976
1989—Nashville	A. A.	SS	2	5	2	5	1	0	0	0	1.000	1	3	0	1.000
Major League Totals—4 Years		414	1511	229	437	66	14	31	154	.289	592	1220	62	.967

Selected by Cincinnati Reds' organization in 2nd round of free-agent draft, June 7, 1982.

Selected by Cincinnati Reds' organization in 1st round (fourth player selected) of free-agent draft, June 3, 1985.

†On disabled list, April 13 to May 2, 1987.

‡On disabled list, July 11 to September 1, 1989; included rehabilitation disability assignment to Nashville, August 27 to September 1, 1989.

ALL-STAR GAME RECORD

Year	League	Pos.	AB.	R.	H.	2B.	3B.	HR.	RBI.	B.A.	PO.	A.	E.	F.A.
1988—National	SS	2	0	0	0	0	0	0	.000	0	1	0	1.000

Member of National League All-Star Team in 1989; did not play.

EUGENE THOMAS LARKIN
(Gene)

Born October 24, 1962, at Flushing, N. Y.
Height, 6.03. Weight, 205.
Throws right and bats left and righthanded.
Received degree from Columbia University, New York, N. Y.

Major League stolen bases: 1987 (1), 1988 (3), 1989 (5). Total—9.
Led American League in being hit by pitch with 15 in 1988.
Led California League in sacrifice flies with 14 in 1985.
Tied for Southern League lead in sacrifice flies with 13 in 1986.
Led California League first basemen in double plays with 140 in 1985.
Led Appalachian League first basemen in double plays with 54 in 1984.

Year Club	League	Pos.	G.	AB.	R.	H.	2B.	3B.	HR.	RBI.	B.A.	PO.	A.	E.	F.A.
1984—Elizabethton	Appal.	1B	57	193	29	63	13	1	6	37	.326	478	19	6	★.988
1985—Visalia	Calif.	1B	●142	528	90	161	25	3	13	●106	.305	★1227	62	12	.991
1986—Orlando	South.	1B-3B	142	529	85	●170	29	6	15	104	.321	923	53	13	.987
1987—Portland	P. C.	1B-OF	35	129	17	39	9	0	1	14	.302	191	22	4	.982
1987—Minnesota	Amer.	1B	85	233	23	62	11	2	4	28	.266	165	10	2	.989
1988—Minnesota	Amer.	1B	149	505	56	135	30	2	8	70	.267	466	28	3	.994
1989—Minnesota	Amer.	1B-OF	136	446	61	119	25	1	6	46	.267	524	28	4	.993
Major League Totals—3 Years			370	1184	140	316	66	5	18	144	.267	1155	66	9	.993

Selected by Minnesota Twins' organization in 20th round of free-agent draft, June 4, 1984.

CHAMPIONSHIP SERIES RECORD

Year Club	League	Pos.	G.	AB.	R.	H.	2B.	3B.	HR.	RBI.	B.A.	PO.	A.	E.	F.A.
1987—Minnesota	Amer.	PH	1	1	0	1	1	0	0	1	1.000	0	0	0	.000

WORLD SERIES RECORD

Year Club	League	Pos.	G.	AB.	R.	H.	2B.	3B.	HR.	RBI.	B.A.	PO.	A.	E.	F.A.
1987—Minnesota	Amer.	1B-PH	5	3	1	0	0	0	0	0	.000	1	0	0	1.000

TIMOTHY JON LAUDNER

Name pronounced LAWD-ner.

(Tim)

Born June 7, 1958, at Mason City, Ia.
Height, 6.03. Weight, 218.
Throws and bats righthanded.
Attended University of Missouri, Columbia, Mo.

Shares American League record for most home runs, first two major league games (2), August 28 and 29, 1981.
Major League stolen bases: 1986 (1), 1987 (1), 1989 (1). Total—3.
Led Southern League in slugging percentage with .628 and game-winning RBIs with 14 in 1981.
Named Southern League Most Valuable Player, 1981.

Year Club	League	Pos.	G.	AB.	R.	H.	2B.	3B.	HR.	RBI.	B.A.	PO.	A.	E.	F.A.
1979—Orlando	South.	C	45	141	17	34	7	0	3	20	.241	224	29	6	.977
1980—Orlando†	South.	C	17	61	7	14	5	0	2	5	.230	81	10	1	.989
1980—Visalia	Calif.	C	56	186	23	42	13	0	10	29	.226	251	36	5	.983
1981—Orlando	South.	C-1B	130	433	87	123	21	1	★42	104	.284	631	66	15	.979
1981—Minnesota	Amer.	C	14	43	4	7	2	0	2	5	.163	49	5	0	1.000
1982—Toledo	Int.	C	20	71	4	12	2	0	2	12	.169	121	9	0	1.000
1982—Minnesota	Amer.	C	93	306	37	78	19	1	7	33	.255	454	41	★12	.976
1983—Minnesota	Amer.	C	62	168	20	31	9	0	6	18	.185	259	22	4	.986
1984—Minnesota	Amer.	C	87	262	31	54	16	1	10	35	.206	362	38	9	.978
1985—Minnesota	Amer.	C-1B	72	164	16	39	5	0	7	19	.238	236	19	8	.970
1986—Minnesota	Amer.	C	76	193	21	47	10	0	10	29	.244	299	13	5	.984
1987—Minnesota‡	Amer.	C-1B	113	288	30	55	7	1	16	43	.191	547	29	7	.988
1988—Minnesota§	Amer.	C-1B	117	375	38	94	18	1	13	54	.251	624	35	5	.992
1989—Minnesota	Amer.	C-1B	100	239	24	53	11	1	6	27	.222	347	16	3	.992
Major League Totals—9 Years			734	2038	221	458	97	5	77	263	.225	3177	218	53	.985

Selected by Cincinnati Reds' organization in 33rd round of free-agent draft, June 8, 1976.
Selected by Minnesota Twins' organization in 3rd round of free-agent draft, June 5, 1979.
†On disabled list, April 11 to April 21, 1980.
‡Granted free agency, November 9, 1987; re-signed by Twins, February 3, 1988.
§Granted free agency, November 4, 1988; re-signed by Twins, December 19, 1988.

CHAMPIONSHIP SERIES RECORD

Year Club	League	Pos.	G.	AB.	R.	H.	2B.	3B.	HR.	RBI.	B.A.	PO.	A.	E.	F.A.
1987—Minnesota	Amer.	C	5	14	1	1	1	0	0	2	.071	31	2	0	1.000

WORLD SERIES RECORD

Year Club	League	Pos.	G.	AB.	R.	H.	2B.	3B.	HR.	RBI.	B.A.	PO.	A.	E.	F.A.
1987—Minnesota	Amer.	C	7	22	4	7	1	0	1	4	.318	46	2	0	1.000

ALL-STAR GAME RECORD

Year League	Pos.	AB.	R.	H.	2B.	3B.	HR.	RBI.	B.A.	PO.	A.	E.	F.A.
1988—American	C	1	0	1	1	0	0	0	1.000	3	0	0	1.000

MICHAEL EUGENE LaVALLIERE

Name pronounced Luh-VAHL-yur.

(Mike)

Born August 18, 1960, at Charlotte, N. C.
Height, 5.10. Weight, 190.
Throws right and bats lefthanded.
Attended University of Lowell, Lowell, Mass.
Son of Guy LaValliere, minor league catcher, 1952 and 1955 through 1961.

Major League stolen bases: 1988 (3).
Named catcher on THE SPORTING NEWS National League All-Star Team, 1988.
Named catcher on THE SPORTING NEWS National League All-Star fielding team, 1987.

Year Club	League	Pos.	G.	AB.	R.	H.	2B.	3B.	HR.	RBI.	B.A.	PO.	A.	E.	F.A.
1981—Spartanburg......... S. Atl.		3B-OF	39	123	15	33	9	0	2	23	.268	16	32	5	.906
1982—Peninsula.............. Carol.		C-3B	66	178	20	49	4	2	2	23	.275	306	35	6	.983
1983—Reading................ East.		C-3B-P	81	218	24	64	16	2	4	43	.294	243	59	4	.987
1984—Reading................ East.		C-3-2-P	55	147	19	37	6	0	6	22	.252	113	45	2	.988
1984—Portland................ P. C.		C	37	122	20	38	6	3	5	21	.311	186	16	1	.995
1984—Philadelphia†‡ ..... Nat.		C	6	7	0	0	0	0	0	0	.000	20	2	0	1.000
1985—St. Louis.............. Nat.		C	12	34	2	5	1	0	0	6	.147	48	5	0	1.000
1985—Louisville§ .... A. A.		C	83	231	19	47	12	1	4	26	.203	420	53	5	.990
1986—St. Louis x........... Nat.		C	110	303	18	71	10	2	3	30	.234	468	47	6	.988
1987—Pittsburgh............. Nat.		C	121	340	33	102	19	0	1	36	.300	584	70	5	.992
1988—Pittsburgh............. Nat.		C	120	352	24	92	18	0	2	47	.261	565	55	8	.987
1989—Pittsburgh y........... Nat.		C	68	190	15	60	10	0	2	23	.316	306	24	3	.991
1989—Buffalo................. A. A.		C	7	18	0	2	0	0	0	1	.111	15	1	0	1.000
Major League Totals—6 Years.................			437	1226	92	330	58	2	8	142	.269	1991	203	22	.990

Signed as free agent by Philadelphia Phillies' organization, July 12, 1981.

†Traded to St. Louis Cardinals for a player to be named later, December 3, 1984; returned due to injured status, December 13, 1984.

‡Granted free agency, December 23, 1984; signed by Louisville (St. Louis Cardinals' organization), January 23, 1985.

§On disabled list, July 18 to July 29, 1985.

xTraded with Outfielder Andy Van Slyke and Pitcher Mike Dunne to Pittsburgh Pirates for Catcher Tony Pena, April 1, 1987.

yOn disabled list, April 17 to July 4, 1989; included rehabilitation disability assignment to Buffalo, June 26 to July 4, 1989.

PITCHING RECORD

Year Club	League	G.	IP.	W.	L.	Pct.	H.	R.	ER.	SO.	BB.	ERA.
1983—Reading.............................	Eastern	4	3⅓	0	0	.000	3	3	2	2	2	5.40
1984—Reading.............................	Eastern	1	1	0	0	.000	3	2	2	1	1	18.00

JOSEPH MICHAEL LAW
(Joe)

Born February 4, 1962, at Pittsburgh, Pa.
Height, 6.02. Weight, 200.
Throws and bats righthanded.
Attended Pensacola Junior College, Pensacola, Fla.

Pitched 1-0 no-hit victory against Stockton, August 14, 1987.
Tied for Pacific Coast League lead in games started by pitchers with 28 in 1989.

Year Club	League	G.	IP.	W.	L.	Pct.	H.	R.	ER.	SO.	BB.	ERA.
1983—Idaho Falls....................	Pioneer	14	15⅔	0	3	.000	17	12	6	20	7	3.45
1983—Albany........................	Eastern	2	3	0	0	.000	1	1	1	2	3	3.00
1984—Modesto.......................	California	29	143	11	2	*.846	114	47	41	105	71	2.58
1985—Huntsville.....................	Southern	37	106	8	8	.500	115	86	72	53	78	6.11
1986—Huntsville.....................	Southern	8	39⅓	1	4	.200	55	37	36	12	28	8.24
1986—Madison	Midwest	19	123	6	9	.400	117	58	48	80	61	3.51
1987—Modesto.......................	California	18	118⅔	10	1	*.909	87	45	38	123	40	2.88
1987—Tacoma........................	P. Coast	2	7	0	1	.000	4	5	2	7	4	2.57
1988—Tacoma........................	P. Coast	12	66⅓	5	3	.625	62	31	29	46	19	3.93
1988—Huntsville.....................	Southern	17	116	9	3	.750	100	42	33	67	33	2.56
1989—Tacoma........................	P. Coast	31	171⅓	11	8	.579	169	87	72	114	84	3.78

Signed as free agent by Oakland A's organization, July 4, 1983.

VANCE AARON LAW

Born October 1, 1956, at Boise, Ida.
Height, 6.01. Weight, 190.
Throws and bats righthanded.
Attended Brigham Young University, Provo, Utah.
Son of Vern Law, pitcher with Pittsburgh Pirates, 1950, 1951 and 1954 through 1967.

Holds American League record for longest errorless game by third baseman (25 innings), May 8, finished May 9, 1984.

Shares American League record for most innings played by third baseman, game (25), May 8, finished May 9, 1984.

Major League stolen bases: 1980 (2), 1981 (1), 1982 (4), 1983 (3), 1984 (4), 1985 (6), 1986 (3), 1987 (8), 1988 (1), 1989 (2). Total—34.

Led Pacific Coast League in sacrifice hits with 14 in 1979.

Year Club	League	Pos.	G.	AB.	R.	H.	2B.	3B.	HR.	RBI.	B.A.	PO.	A.	E.	F.A.
1978—Bradenton Pir. ..... Gulf C.		SS	1	3	0	1	0	0	0	0	.333	2	5	0	1.000
1978—Salem.................... Carol.		SS	60	213	48	68	13	7	2	30	.319	96	180	22	.926
1979—Portland................ P. C.		SS-3B-2B	131	448	62	139	16	8	2	52	.310	201	308	22	.959
1980—Portland................ P. C.		SS	96	339	59	100	23	5	5	54	.295	169	295	14	.971
1980—Pittsburgh............. Nat.		2B-SS-3B	25	74	11	17	2	2	0	3	.230	31	54	3	.966
1981—Pittsburgh............. Nat.		2B-SS-3B	30	67	1	9	0	1	0	3	.134	50	58	0	1.000
1981—Portland†‡............. P. C.		2B-SS-3B	88	310	55	86	14	9	5	43	.277	168	218	9	.977
1982—Chicago............... Amer.		S-3-2-O	114	359	40	101	20	1	5	54	.281	156	313	26	.947
1983—Chicago............... Amer.		3-2-S-O	145	408	55	99	21	5	4	42	.243	94	311	14	.967
1984—Chicago§............. Amer.		3-2-O-S	151	481	60	121	18	2	17	59	.252	119	246	16	.958
1985—Montreal .... Nat.		2-1-3-O	147	519	75	138	30	6	10	52	.266	420	402	12	.986
1986—Montreal .... Nat.		2-1-3-P-O	112	360	37	81	17	2	5	44	.225	273	299	4	.993
1987—Montreal x .... Nat.		2-1-3-P	133	436	52	119	27	1	12	56	.273	258	308	11	.981

Year Club	League	Pos.	G.	AB.	R.	H.	2B.	3B.	HR.	RBI.	B.A.	PO.	A.	E.	F.A.
1988—Chicago	Nat.	3B-OF	151	556	73	163	29	2	11	78	.293	112	272	19	.953
1989—Chicago	Nat.	3B-OF	130	408	38	96	22	3	7	42	.235	76	168	13	.949
National League Totals—7 Years			728	2420	287	623	127	17	45	278	.257	1220	1561	62	.978
American League Totals—3 Years			410	1248	155	321	59	8	26	155	.257	369	870	56	.957
Major League Totals—10 Years			1138	3668	442	944	186	25	71	433	.257	1589	2431	118	.971

Selected by Pittsburgh Pirates' organization in 38th round of free-agent draft, June 6, 1978.

†On disabled list, July 5 to July 15, 1981.

‡Traded with Pitcher Ernie Camacho to Chicago White Sox for Pitchers Ross Baumgarten and Butch Edge, March 21, 1982.

§Traded to Montreal Expos for Pitcher Bob James, December 7, 1984.

xGranted free agency, November 9, 1987; signed by Chicago Cubs, December 14, 1987.

CHAMPIONSHIP SERIES RECORD

Year Club	League	Pos.	G.	AB.	R.	H.	2B.	3B.	HR.	RBI.	B.A.	PO.	A.	E.	F.A.
1983—Chicago	Amer.	3B	4	11	0	2	0	0	1	.182	1	9	1	.909	
1989—Chicago	Nat.	PH-3B	2	3	0	0	0	0	0	0	.000	0	0	0	.000
Championship Series Totals—2 Years			6	14	0	2	0	0	0	1	.143	1	9	1	.909

ALL-STAR GAME RECORD

Year League		Pos.	AB.	R.	H.	2B.	3B.	HR.	RBI.	B.A.	PO.	A.	E.	F.A.
1988—National		2B	0	0	0	0	0	0	0	.000	0	0	0	.000

PITCHING RECORD

Year Club	League	G.	IP.	W.	L.	Pct.	H.	R.	ER.	SO.	BB.	ERA.
1986—Montreal	National	3	4	0	0	.000	3	2	1	0	2	2.25
1987—Montreal	National	3	3⅓	0	0	.000	5	2	2	2	0	5.40
Major League Totals—2 Years		6	7⅓	0	0	.000	8	4	3	2	2	3.68

THOMAS JAMES LAWLESS
(Tom)

Born December 19, 1956, at Erie, Pa.
Height, 5.11 Weight, 165.
Throws and bats righthanded.
Received bachelor of arts degree in political science from
Pennsylvania State University-Behrend, Erie, Pa.

Major League stolen bases: 1982 (16), 1984 (7), 1985 (2), 1986 (8), 1987 (2), 1988 (6), 1989 (12). Total—53.
Led American Association in stolen bases with 46 in 1983.
Led Florida State League in sacrifice hits with 13 and stolen bases with 60 in 1979.
Led Pioneer League shortstops in putouts with 116 in 1978.

Year Club	League	Pos.	G.	AB.	R.	H.	2B.	3B.	HR.	RBI.	B.A.	PO.	A.	E.	F.A.
1978—Billings	Pioneer	SS-2B	63	254	64	70	5	●7	5	35	.276	117	186	24	.927
1979—Tampa	Fla. St.	2B	131	469	66	126	9	5	1	39	.269	★296	376	17	★.975
1980—Waterbury	East.	2B	130	498	83	137	20	7	2	29	.275	★316	333	14	.979
1981—Waterbury	East.	2B	136	522	77	152	20	10	8	50	.291	323	379	15	.979
1982—Indianapolis	A. A.	2B-SS	86	351	76	108	18	6	2	28	.308	185	251	13	.971
1982—Cincinnati	Nat.	2B	49	165	19	35	6	0	0	4	.212	87	136	5	.978
1983—Indianapolis	A. A.	2B	115	423	93	118	23	3	13	35	.279	255	303	17	.970
1984—Cinc.†-Mont.	Nat.	2B-3B	54	97	11	23	3	0	1	2	.237	50	52	1	.990
1984—Wich.-Ind.‡	A. A.	3B-2B-SS	50	173	36	47	5	5	4	23	.272	53	103	4	.975
1985—Louisville	A. A.	3B-OF	31	124	16	36	9	1	1	12	.290	20	58	3	.963
1985—St. Louis	Nat.	3B-2B	47	58	8	12	3	1	0	8	.207	19	44	1	.984
1986—St. Louis	Nat.	3B-2B-OF	46	39	5	11	1	0	0	3	.282	11	15	2	.929
1987—St. Louis§	Nat.	2B-3B-OF	19	25	5	2	1	0	0	0	.080	5	15	0	1.000
1988—St. Louis x	Nat.	3-O-2-1	54	65	9	10	2	1	1	3	.154	23	29	0	1.000
1989—Toronto y	Amer.	O-3-2-C	59	70	20	16	1	0	0	3	.229	39	26	3	.956
National League Totals—6 Years			269	449	57	93	16	2	2	20	.207	195	291	9	.982
American League Totals—1 Year			59	70	20	16	1	0	0	3	.229	39	26	3	.956
Major League Totals—7 Years			328	519	77	109	17	2	2	23	.210	234	317	12	.979

Selected by Cincinnati Reds' organization in 17th round of free-agent draft, June 6, 1978.

†Traded to Montreal Expos' organization for First Baseman-Outfielder Pete Rose, August 16, 1984.

‡Sold to Louisville (St. Louis Cardinals' organization), March 25, 1985, completing deal in which St. Louis traded Pitcher Mickey Mahler to Montreal Expos for a player to be named later, February 6, 1985.

§On disabled list, August 21 to September 5, 1987.

xReleased, December 21, 1988; signed by Toronto Blue Jays, January 23, 1989.

yGranted free agency, November 13, 1989.

CHAMPIONSHIP SERIES RECORD

Year Club	League	Pos.	G.	AB.	R.	H.	2B.	3B.	HR.	RBI.	B.A.	PO.	A.	E.	F.A.
1987—St. Louis	Nat.	3B-PH-O	3	6	0	2	0	0	0	0	.333	1	4	0	1.000

WORLD SERIES RECORD

Year Club	League	Pos.	G.	AB.	R.	H.	2B.	3B.	HR.	RBI.	B.A.	PO.	A.	E.	F.A.
1985—St. Louis	Nat.	PR	1	0	0	0	0	0	0	0	.000	0	0	0	.000
1987—St. Louis	Nat.	3B	3	10	1	1	0	0	1	3	.100	3	6	1	.900
World Series Totals—2 Years			4	10	1	1	0	0	1	3	.100	3	6	1	.900

MARCUS DWAYNE LAWTON

Born August 18, 1965, at Gulfport, Miss.
Height, 6.01. Weight, 160.
Throws right and bats left and righthanded.

Major League stolen bases: 1989 (1).
Led Carolina League in bases on balls received with 102 in 1986.
Led South Atlantic League in stolen bases with 111 in 1985.
Led Carolina League outfielders in total chances with 359 in 1986.
Tied for Texas League lead in errors by outfielders with 13 in 1987.

Year	Club	League	Pos.	G.	AB.	R.	H.	2B.	3B.	HR.	RBI.	B.A.	PO.	A.	E.	F.A.
1983—Sarasota Mets†	Gulf C.		SS-3B	51	187	25	48	3	1	0	16	.257	75	128	24	.894
1984—Kingsport†	Appal.		SS	54	191	43	57	10	1	1	15	.298	86	126	20	.914
1984—Lynchburg†	Carol.		2B	3	9	3	2	0	0	0	1	.222	3	8	1	.917
1985—Columbia	S. Atl.		OF-SS-2B	128	470	113	126	11	5	1	53	.268	223	129	39	.900
1986—Lynchburg	Carol.		OF	*141	*567	*118	158	22	*16	4	66	.279	*336	17	6	*.983
1987—Jackson	Texas		OF-2B	133	530	99	159	20	*10	5	36	.300	265	18	14	.953
1988—Jackson	Texas		OF	54	205	42	61	12	0	2	20	.298	129	7	6	.958
1988—Tidewater‡	Int.		OF	94	335	46	78	16	4	0	17	.233	202	5	3	.986
1989—Tide.§-Col.	Int.		OF	112	292	39	69	12	0	4	32	.236	169	6	3	.983
1989—New York x	Amer.		OF	10	14	1	3	0	0	0	0	.214	9	0	2	.818
Major League Totals—1 Year				10	14	1	3	0	0	0	0	.214	9	0	2	.818

Selected by New York Mets' organization in 6th round of free-agent draft, June 6, 1983.
†Batted righthanded only.
‡Drafted by California Angels, December 5, 1988; returned, March 27, 1989.
§Traded to Columbus (New York Yankees' organization) for Pitcher Scott Nielsen, July 10, 1989.
xReleased, November 8, 1989.

TIMOTHY JOSEPH LAYANA
(Tim)

Born March 2, 1964, at Inglewood, Calif.
Height, 6.02. Weight, 195.
Throws and bats righthanded.
Attended Loyola Marymount University, Los Angeles, Calif.

Led Eastern League in saves with 17 in 1989.

Year	Club	League	G.	IP.	W.	L.	Pct.	H.	R.	ER.	SO.	BB.	ERA.
1986—Oneonta	NYP	3	19	2	0	1.000	10	5	5	24	5	2.37
1986—Fort Lauderdale	Florida St.	11	68⅓	5	4	.556	59	19	17	52	19	2.24
1987—Columbus	Int'national	13	70	4	5	.444	77	37	37	36	37	4.76
1987—Albany	Eastern	8	46⅓	2	4	.333	51	28	26	19	18	5.05
1987—Prince William	Carolina	7	22⅔	2	1	.667	29	22	16	17	11	6.35
1988—Columbus	Int'national	11	47⅔	1	7	.125	54	34	32	25	25	6.04
1988—Albany	Eastern	14	87	5	7	.417	90	52	42	42	30	4.34
1989—Albany†	Eastern	40	67⅔	7	4	.636	53	17	13	48	15	1.73

Selected by Chicago White Sox' organization in 28th round of free-agent draft, June 7, 1982.
Selected by New York Mets' organization in 5th round of free-agent draft, June 3, 1985.
Selected by New York Yankees' organization in 3rd round of free-agent draft, June 2, 1986.
†Drafted by Cincinnati Reds, December 4, 1989.

RICHARD MAX LEACH JR.
(Rick)

Born May 4, 1957, at Ann Arbor, Mich.
Height, 6.00. Weight, 195.
Throws and bats lefthanded.
Attended University of Michigan, Ann Arbor, Mich.

Major League stolen bases: 1982 (4), 1983 (2), 1989 (2). Total—8.
Led International League in sacrifice flies with 12 in 1985.
Tied for International League lead in assists by outfielders with 13 in 1985.
Selected by Denver Broncos in 5th round of 1979 NFL draft.
Received reported $200,000 bonus to sign with Detroit Tigers, 1979.
Named outfielder on THE SPORTING NEWS College Baseball All-America Team, 1979.

Year	Club	League	Pos.	G.	AB.	R.	H.	2B.	3B.	HR.	RBI.	B.A.	PO.	A.	E.	F.A.
1979—Lakeland†	Fla. St.		OF	48	168	21	51	10	1	2	23	.304	104	8	3	.974
1980—Evansville	A. A.		1B-OF	126	430	69	117	14	1	5	58	.272	767	62	9	.989
1981—Evansville	A. A.		1B	13	44	8	18	5	0	2	16	.409	129	16	2	.986
1981—Detroit	Amer.		1B-OF	54	83	9	16	3	1	1	11	.193	149	14	0	1.000
1982—Detroit‡	Amer.		1B-OF	82	218	23	52	7	2	3	12	.239	430	29	2	.996
1982—Evansville	A. A.		DH	11	38	6	11	2	0	0	2	.289	0	0	0	.000
1983—Detroit§	Amer.		1B-OF	99	242	22	60	17	0	3	26	.248	465	45	4	.992
1984—Syracuse	Int.		OF-1B	23	79	16	24	6	2	3	8	.304	70	4	2	.974
1984—Toronto	Amer.		OF-1B-P	65	88	11	23	6	2	0	7	.261	92	14	0	1.000
1985—Syracuse	Int.		OF-1B	136	533	77	151	24	2	15	79	.283	675	66	10	.987
1985—Toronto	Amer.		1B-OF	16	35	2	7	0	1	0	1	.200	78	6	1	.988
1986—Toronto	Amer.		OF-1B	110	246	35	76	14	1	5	39	.309	107	5	3	.974
1987—Toronto	Amer.		OF-1B	98	195	26	55	13	1	3	25	.282	57	1	1	.993
1988—Toronto x	Amer.		OF-1B	87	199	21	55	13	1	0	23	.276	93	5	0	1.000
1989—Texas y	Amer.		OF-1B	110	239	32	65	14	1	1	23	.272	74	2	3	.962
Major League Totals—9 Years				721	1545	181	409	87	10	16	167	.265	1545	121	14	.992

Selected by Philadelphia Phillies' organization in 11th round of free-agent draft, June 4, 1975.
Selected by Philadelphia Phillies' organization in 24th round of free-agent draft, June 6, 1978.
Selected by Detroit Tigers' organization in 1st round (13th player selected) of free-agent draft, June 5, 1979.
†On disabled list, June 18 to June 29, 1979.
‡On disabled list, April 12 to May 17, 1982; included rehabilitation disability assignment to Evansville, May 6 to May 17, 1982.
§Released, March 24, 1984; signed by Toronto Blue Jays' organization, April 3, 1984.
xGranted free agency, November 4, 1988; signed by Texas Rangers, January 23, 1989.
yGranted free agency, November 13, 1989.

PITCHING RECORD

Year Club	League	G.	IP.	W.	L.	Pct.	H.	R.	ER.	SO.	BB.	ERA.
1984—Toronto	American	1	1	0	0	.000	2	3	3	0	2	27.00

TERRY HESTER LEACH

Born March 13, 1954, at Selma, Ala.
Height, 6.00. Weight, 191.
Throws and bats righthanded.
Received business administration degree in personnel management-industrial relations
from Auburn University, Auburn University, Ala.

Major League saves: 1982 (3), 1985 (1), 1988 (3). Total—7.
Led Gulf States League in home runs allowed with 12 in 1976.

Year Club	League	G.	IP.	W.	L.	Pct.	H.	R.	ER.	SO.	BB.	ERA.
1976—Baton Rouge†‡	Gulf States	5	19	2	0	1.000	43	21	13	15	14	6.16
1977—Greenwood	W. Carol.	20	67	3	2	.600	47	25	19	67	24	2.55
1978—Savannah§	Southern	9	25	1	0	1.000	24	17	14	21	13	5.04
1978—Kinston	Carolina	34	66	5	4	.556	57	29	24	46	25	3.27
1979—Savannah	Southern	40	92	2	9	.182	77	33	20	68	26	1.96
1979—Richmond	Int'national	7	14	3	1	.750	14	3	3	12	4	1.93
1980—Savannah xy	Southern	22	87	5	1	.833	83	36	31	58	17	3.21
1980—Jackson	Texas	8	54	5	1	.833	50	16	9	30	15	1.50
1981—Tidewater	Int'national	15	76	5	2	.714	63	27	23	42	19	2.72
1981—Jackson	Texas	8	58	5	1	.833	47	14	11	43	12	1.71
1981—New York	National	21	35	1	1	.500	26	11	10	16	12	2.57
1982—Tidewater	Int'national	30	48⅔	4	1	.800	48	20	16	34	19	2.96
1982—New York	National	21	45⅓	2	1	.667	46	22	21	30	18	4.17
1983—Tidewater za	Int'national	37	113	5	7	.417	120	66	56	66	42	4.46
1984—Richmond b-Tidewater	Int'national	43	95	11	4	.733	98	42	32	59	30	3.03
1985—Tidewater	Int'national	24	45⅓	1	0	1.000	33	12	8	25	8	1.59
1985—New York	National	22	55⅔	3	4	.429	48	19	18	30	14	2.91
1986—Tidewater	Int'national	34	79⅔	4	4	.500	69	30	22	55	21	2.49
1986—New York	National	6	6⅔	0	0	.000	6	3	2	4	3	2.70
1987—New York c	National	44	131⅓	11	1	.917	132	54	47	61	29	3.22
1988—New York	National	52	92	7	2	.778	95	32	26	51	24	2.54
1989—New York d	National	10	21⅓	0	0	.000	19	11	10	2	4	4.22
1989—Kansas City	American	30	73⅔	5	6	.455	78	46	34	34	36	4.15
National League Totals—7 Years		176	387⅓	24	9	.727	372	152	134	194	104	3.11
American League Totals—1 Year		30	73⅔	5	6	.455	78	46	34	34	36	4.15
Major League Totals—7 Years		206	461	29	15	.659	450	198	168	228	140	3.28

Selected by Boston Red Sox' organization in 7th round of free-agent draft, January 7, 1976.
†Signed as free agent by Baton Rouge (Independent), June 29, 1976; released when Baton Rouge withdrew from league, August 13, 1976.
‡Signed by Greenwood (Atlanta Braves' organization) as free agent, May 28, 1977.
§Loaned to Kinston (Independent), June 3, 1978; returned, October 25, 1978.
xOn disabled list, June 12 to July 23, 1980.
yReleased, July 23, 1980; signed by Jackson (New York Mets' organization), July 27, 1980.
zTraded to Chicago Cubs' organization for Pitchers Jim Adamczak and Mitch Cook, September 26, 1983.
aTraded by Chicago Cubs' organization to Atlanta Braves' organization for Pitcher Ron Meridith, April 4, 1984.
bReleased, May 25, 1984; signed by New York Mets' organization, May 26, 1984.
cOn disabled list, July 12 to July 27, 1987.
dTraded to Kansas City Royals for a player to be named later, June 9, 1989; New York Mets acquired Pitcher Agueldo Vasquez to complete deal, October 1, 1989.

CHAMPIONSHIP SERIES RECORD

Year Club	League	G.	IP.	W.	L.	Pct.	H.	R.	ER.	SO.	BB.	ERA.
1988—New York	National	3	5	0	0	.000	4	0	0	4	1	0.00

TIMOTHY JAMES LEARY
(Tim)

Born December 23, 1958, at Santa Monica, Calif.
Height, 6.03. Weight, 208.
Throws and bats righthanded.
Attended UCLA.

Major League saves: 1987 (1).
Tied for National League lead in intentional bases on balls issued with 15 in 1989.
Led Texas League in shutouts with 6 in 1980.
Named National League Comeback Player of the Year by THE SPORTING NEWS, 1988.
Named pitcher on National League Silver Slugger team, 1988.

Named Texas League Most Valuable Player, 1980.
Named righthanded pitcher on THE SPORTING NEWS College Baseball All-America Team, 1979.

Year—Club	League	G.	IP.	W.	L.	Pct.	H.	R.	ER.	SO.	BB.	ERA.
1979—Jackson†	Texas					(Did not play)						
1980—Jackson	Texas	26	173	●15	8	.652	150	67	53	138	62	2.76
1981—New York‡	National	1	2	0	0	.000	0	0	0	3	1	0.00
1981—Tidewater	Int'national	6	34	1	3	.250	27	16	14	15	27	3.71
1982—Tidewater§	Int'national					(Did not play)						
1983—Tidewater	Int'national	27	160⅓	8	★16	.333	170	100	78	106	73	4.38
1983—New York	National	2	10⅔	1	1	.500	15	10	4	9	4	3.38
1984—New York	National	20	53⅔	3	3	.500	61	28	24	29	18	4.02
1984—Tidewater x	Int'national	10	53⅓	4	4	.500	47	26	24	27	42	4.05
1985—Vancouver	P. Coast	27	177⅔	10	7	.588	174	85	79	136	57	4.00
1985—Milwaukee	American	5	33⅓	1	4	.200	40	18	15	29	8	4.05
1986—Milwaukee y	American	33	188⅓	12	12	.500	216	97	88	110	53	4.21
1987—Los Angeles	National	39	107⅔	3	11	.214	121	62	57	61	36	4.76
1988—Los Angeles	National	35	228⅔	17	11	.607	201	87	74	180	56	2.91
1989—Los Angeles z-Cincinnati a	National	33	207	8	14	.364	205	84	81	123	68	3.52
National League Totals—6 Years		130	609⅔	32	40	.444	603	271	240	405	183	3.54
American League Totals—2 Years		38	221⅔	13	16	.448	256	115	103	139	61	4.18
Major League Totals—8 Years		168	831⅓	45	56	.446	859	386	343	544	244	3.71

Selected by New York Mets' organization in 1st round (second player selected) of free-agent draft, June 5, 1979.
†On disabled list, July 19 to October 1, 1979.
‡On disabled list, April 16 to August 1, 1981.
§On disabled list, April 13, 1982 through remainder of season.
xTraded to Milwaukee Brewers' organization as part of a six-player, four-team deal in which Kansas City Royals acquired Catcher Jim Sundberg from Milwaukee, Texas Rangers acquired Catcher Don Slaught from Kansas City, New York Mets' organization acquired Pitcher Frank Wills from Kansas City and Milwaukee acquired Pitcher Danny Darwin and a player to be named later from Texas, January 18, 1985; Milwaukee organization acquired Catcher Bill Hance from Texas to complete deal, January 30, 1985.
yTraded with Pitcher Tim Crews to Los Angeles Dodgers for First Baseman Greg Brock, December 10, 1986.
zTraded with Shortstop Mariano Duncan to Cincinnati Reds for Outfielder Kal Daniels and Infielder Lenny Harris, July 18, 1989.
aTraded with Outfielder Van Snider to New York Yankees for First Baseman Hal Morris and Pitcher Rodney Imes, December 12, 1989.

CHAMPIONSHIP SERIES RECORD

Year—Club	League	G.	IP.	W.	L.	Pct.	H.	R.	ER.	SO.	BB.	ERA.
1988—Los Angeles	National	2	4⅓	0	1	.000	8	4	3	3	3	6.23

WORLD SERIES RECORD

Year—Club	League	G.	IP.	W.	L.	Pct.	H.	R.	ER.	SO.	BB.	ERA.
1988—Los Angeles	National	2	6⅔	0	0	.000	6	1	1	4	2	1.35

MANUEL LORA LEE
(Manny)

Born June 17, 1965, at San Pedro de Macoris, D. R.
Height, 5.09. Weight, 161.
Throws right and bats left and righthanded.

Major League stolen bases: 1985 (1), 1987 (2), 1988 (3), 1989 (4). Total—10.

Year—Club	League	Pos.	G.	AB.	R.	H.	2B.	3B.	HR.	RBI.	B.A.	PO.	A.	E.	F.A.
1982—Kingsport	Appal.	2B-SS	16	54	2	12	1	0	0	3	.222	34	34	6	.919
1983—Sarasota Mets	Gulf C.	2B-SS	32	97	8	24	2	1	0	12	.247	44	79	8	.939
1983—Little Falls	NYP	2B	17	45	10	13	0	0	0	5	.289	34	40	3	.961
1984—Columbia†‡§	S. Atl.	SS-2B	102	346	84	114	12	5	2	33	★.329	126	277	34	.922
1985—Toronto	Amer.	2B-SS-3B	64	40	9	8	0	0	0	0	.200	34	56	3	.968
1986—Syracuse	Int.	SS-2B	76	236	34	58	6	1	1	19	.246	132	237	18	.953
1986—Knoxville	South.	SS-2B	41	158	21	43	1	2	0	11	.272	70	117	8	.959
1986—Toronto	Amer.	2B-SS-3B	35	78	8	16	0	1	1	7	.205	36	76	2	.982
1987—Toronto	Amer.	2B-SS	56	121	14	31	2	3	1	11	.256	77	110	5	.974
1987—Syracuse	Int.	SS	74	251	25	71	9	5	3	26	.283	120	177	23	.928
1988—Toronto x	Amer.	2B-SS-3B	116	381	38	111	16	3	2	38	.291	250	308	12	.979
1989—Toronto y	Amer.	2-S-3-O	99	300	27	78	9	2	3	34	.260	152	201	11	.970
Major League Totals—5 Years			370	920	96	244	27	9	7	90	.265	549	751	33	.975

Signed as free agent by New York Mets' organization, May 10, 1982.
†On disabled list, April 9 to April 22, 1984.
‡Traded with Outfielder Gerald Young to Houston Astros, August 31, 1984, as partial completion of deal in which New York Mets acquired Infielder Ray Knight for three players to be named later, August 28, 1984; Houston acquired Pitcher Mitch Cook to complete deal, September 10, 1984.
§Drafted by Toronto Blue Jays, December 3, 1984.
xOn disabled list, March 28 to April 12 and May 12 to June 1, 1988.
yOn disabled list, April 30 to June 6, 1989.

CHAMPIONSHIP SERIES RECORD

Year—Club	League	Pos.	G.	AB.	R.	H.	2B.	3B.	HR.	RBI.	B.A.	PO.	A.	E.	F.A.
1985—Toronto	Amer.	PR-2B	1	0	0	0	0	0	0	0	.000	0	0	0	.000
1989—Toronto	Amer.	2B	2	8	2	2	0	0	0	0	.250	4	1	0	1.000
Championship Series Totals—2 Years			3	8	2	2	0	0	0	0	.250	4	1	0	1.000

CRAIG LINDSAY LEFFERTS

Born September 29, 1957, in Munich, West Germany.
Height, 6.01. Weight, 210.
Throws and bats lefthanded.
Attended University of Arizona, Tucson, Ariz.

Major League saves: 1983 (1), 1984 (10), 1985 (2), 1986 (4), 1987 (6), 1988 (11), 1989 (20). Total—54.

Year Club	League	G.	IP.	W.	L.	Pct.	H.	R.	ER.	SO.	BB.	ERA.
1980—Geneva	NYP	12	94	9	1	★.900	74	35	29	★99	24	2.78
1981—Midland	Texas	26	185	12	●12	.500	203	95	85	135	36	4.14
1982—Iowa†	Am.Assoc.	18	97⅓	8	5	.615	97	50	33	71	25	3.05
1983—Chicago‡	National	56	89	3	4	.429	80	35	31	60	29	3.13
1984—San Diego	National	62	105⅔	3	4	.429	88	29	25	56	24	2.13
1985—San Diego	National	60	83⅓	7	6	.538	75	34	31	48	30	3.35
1986—San Diego	National	★83	107⅔	9	8	.529	98	41	37	72	44	3.09
1987—San Diego§-San Francisco	National	77	98⅔	5	5	.500	92	47	42	57	33	3.83
1988—San Francisco	National	64	92⅓	3	8	.273	74	33	30	58	23	2.92
1989—San Francisco x	National	70	107	2	4	.333	93	38	32	71	22	2.69
Major League Totals—7 Years		472	683⅔	32	39	.451	600	257	228	422	205	3.00

Selected by Kansas City Royals' organization in 6th round of free-agent draft, June 5, 1979.
Selected by Chicago Cubs' organization in 9th round of free-agent draft, June 3, 1980.
†On disabled list, April 24 to June 4, 1982.
‡Traded with First Baseman Carmelo Martinez and Third Baseman Fritz Connally to San Diego Padres for Pitcher Scott Sanderson, December 7, 1983.
§Traded with Pitcher Dave Dravecky and Infielder Kevin Mitchell to San Francisco Giants for Third Baseman Chris Brown and Pitchers Keith Comstock, Mark Davis and Mark Grant, July 4, 1987.
xGranted free agency, November 13, 1989; signed by San Diego Padres, December 6, 1989.

CHAMPIONSHIP SERIES RECORD

Year Club	League	G.	IP.	W.	L.	Pct.	H.	R.	ER.	SO.	BB.	ERA.
1984—San Diego	National	3	4	2	0	1.000	1	0	0	1	1	0.00
1987—San Francisco	National	3	2	0	0	.000	3	0	0	0	1	0.00
1989—San Francisco	National	2	1	0	0	.000	1	1	1	1	2	9.00
Championship Series Totals—3 Years		8	7	2	0	1.000	5	1	1	2	4	1.29

WORLD SERIES RECORD

Year Club	League	G.	IP.	W.	L.	Pct.	H.	R.	ER.	SO.	BB.	ERA.
1984—San Diego	National	3	6	0	0	.000	2	0	0	7	1	0.00
1989—San Francisco	National	3	2⅔	0	0	.000	2	1	1	1	2	3.38
World Series Totals—2 Years		6	8⅔	0	0	.000	4	1	1	8	3	1.04

CHARLES LOUIS LEIBRANDT JR.
(Charlie)

Born October 4, 1956, at Chicago, Ill.
Height, 6.03. Weight, 200.
Throws left and bats righthanded.
Received bachelor of science degree in business management from
Miami University, Oxford, O.

Holds major league record for fewest assists by pitcher, for leader in assists (43), 1986.
Major League saves: 1982 (2).
Tied for American Association lead in shutouts with 3 in 1984.
Tied for American Association lead in games started by pitchers with 26 in 1979.

Year Club	League	G.	IP.	W.	L.	Pct.	H.	R.	ER.	SO.	BB.	ERA.
1978—Eugene	Northwest	3	20	2	0	1.000	24	13	9	18	5	4.05
1978—Tampa	Florida St.	6	47	4	1	.800	26	4	4	40	17	0.77
1978—Indianapolis	Am. Assoc.	4	29	2	1	.667	20	9	9	12	12	2.79
1979—Indianapolis	Am. Assoc.	27	162	8	★14	.364	146	67	53	100	65	2.94
1979—Cincinnati	National	3	4	0	0	.000	2	2	0	1	2	0.00
1980—Cincinnati	National	36	174	10	9	.526	200	84	82	62	54	4.24
1981—Indianapolis	Am. Assoc.	25	169	9	7	.563	149	76	55	101	75	2.93
1981—Cincinnati	National	7	30	1	1	.500	28	12	12	9	15	3.60
1982—Cincinnati	National	36	107⅔	5	7	.417	130	68	61	34	48	5.10
1983—Indianapolis†-Omaha	Am. Assoc.	27	185⅓	9	10	.474	181	113	88	128	77	4.27
1984—Omaha	Am. Assoc.	9	72⅔	7	1	.875	51	14	10	38	16	1.24
1984—Kansas City	American	23	143⅔	11	7	.611	158	65	58	53	38	3.63
1985—Kansas City	American	33	237⅔	17	9	.654	223	86	71	108	68	2.69
1986—Kansas City	American	35	231⅓	14	11	.560	238	112	105	108	63	4.09
1987—Kansas City‡	American	35	240⅓	16	11	.593	235	104	91	151	74	3.41
1988—Kansas City	American	35	243	13	12	.520	244	98	86	125	62	3.19
1989—Kansas City§	American	33	161	5	11	.313	196	98	92	73	54	5.14
National League Totals—4 Years		82	315⅔	16	17	.485	360	166	155	106	119	4.42
American League Totals—6 Years		194	1257	76	61	.555	1294	563	503	618	359	3.60
Major League Totals—10 Years		276	1572⅔	92	78	.541	1654	729	658	724	478	3.77

Selected by Cincinnati Reds' organization in 9th round of free-agent draft, June 6, 1978.
†Traded to Kansas City Royals for Pitcher Bob Tufts, June 7, 1983.
‡Granted free agency, November 9, 1987; re-signed by Royals, January 7, 1988.
§Traded with Pitcher Rick Luecken to Atlanta Braves for First Baseman Gerald Perry and Pitcher Jim Lemasters, December 15, 1989.

Shares Championship Series record for most games lost, series (2), 1985.

Year Club	League	G.	IP.	W.	L.	Pct.	H.	R.	ER.	SO.	BB.	ERA.
1979—Cincinnati	National	1	⅓	0	0	.000	0	0	0	0	0	0.00
1984—Kansas City	American	1	8	0	1	.000	3	1	1	6	4	1.13
1985—Kansas City	American	3	15⅓	1	2	.333	17	9	9	6	4	5.28
Championship Series Totals—3 Years		5	23⅔	1	3	.250	20	10	10	12	8	3.80

WORLD SERIES RECORD

Year Club	League	G.	IP.	W.	L.	Pct.	H.	R.	ER.	SO.	BB.	ERA.
1985—Kansas City	American	2	16⅓	0	1	.000	10	5	5	10	4	2.76

DAVID PAUL LEIPER
(Dave)

Born June 18, 1962, at Whittier, Calif.
Height, 6.01. Weight, 160.
Throws and bats lefthanded.
Attended Fullerton College, Fullerton, Calif.

Major League saves: 1986 (1), 1987 (2), 1988 (1). Total—4.

Year Club	League	G.	IP.	W.	L.	Pct.	H.	R.	ER.	SO.	BB.	ERA.
1982—Idaho Falls	Pioneer	14	85⅓	9	3	.750	94	49	39	77	27	4.11
1983—Madison	Midwest	16	79⅓	5	4	.556	89	43	33	60	37	3.74
1984—Modesto	California	19	35⅓	5	0	1.000	12	2	1	30	14	0.25
1984—Tacoma	P. Coast	28	32⅔	2	3	.400	33	11	11	13	14	3.03
1984—Oakland	American	8	7	1	0	1.000	12	7	7	3	5	9.00
1985—Tacoma†	P. Coast	15	23⅓	0	1	.000	29	16	14	7	12	5.40
1985—Modesto	California	21	30	1	0	1.000	53	31	26	24	19	7.80
1986—Tacoma	P. Coast	20	26	2	1	.667	30	17	14	13	9	4.85
1986—Oakland	American	33	31⅔	2	2	.500	28	17	17	15	18	4.83
1987—Tacoma	P. Coast	5	9	0	0	.000	3	0	0	6	1	0.00
1987—Oakland‡	American	45	52⅓	2	1	.667	49	28	22	33	18	3.78
1987—San Diego	National	12	16	1	0	1.000	16	8	8	10	5	4.50
1988—San Diego§	National	35	54	3	0	1.000	45	19	13	33	14	2.17
1989—San Diego x	National	22	28⅔	0	1	.000	40	19	16	7	20	5.02
1989—Las Vegas y	P. Coast	11	20	2	2	.500	23	15	13	12	10	5.85
American League Totals—3 Years		86	91	5	3	.625	89	52	46	51	41	4.55
National League Totals—3 Years		69	98⅔	4	1	.800	101	46	37	50	39	3.38
Major League Totals—5 Years		155	189⅔	9	4	.692	190	98	83	101	80	3.94

Selected by Texas Rangers' organization in 2nd round of free-agent draft, January 13, 1981.
Selected by San Francisco Giants' organization in secondary phase of free-agent draft, June 8, 1981.
Selected by Oakland A's organization in secondary phase of free-agent draft, January 12, 1982.
†On disabled list, April 11 to May 13, 1985.
‡Traded to San Diego Padres, August 31, 1987, as partial completion of deal in which San Diego traded Pitcher Storm Davis to Oakland Athletics for two players to be named later, August 30, 1987. San Diego acquired First Baseman Rob Nelson to complete deal, September 8, 1987.
§On disabled list, March 27 to April 18 and May 3 to May 23, 1988.
xOn disabled list, June 14 to July 15, 1989; included rehabilitation disability assignment to Las Vegas, June 27 to July 15, 1989.
yReleased, December 19, 1989.

ALOIS TERRY LEITER
Name pronounced Li-ter.
(Al)

Born October 23, 1965, at Toms River, N. J.
Height, 6.03. Weight, 210.
Throws and bats lefthanded.
Brother of Kurt Leiter, pitcher in Baltimore Orioles' organization,
1982 through 1984; and Miami (Independent), 1986; and brother of Mark Leiter,
pitcher in Baltimore Orioles' organization, 1983 through 1985.

Year Club	League	G.	IP.	W.	L.	Pct.	H.	R.	ER.	SO.	BB.	ERA.
1984—Oneonta	NYP	10	57	3	2	.600	52	32	23	48	26	3.63
1985—Oneonta	NYP	6	38	3	2	.600	27	14	10	34	25	2.37
1985—Fort Lauderdale	Florida St.	17	82	1	6	.143	87	70	59	44	57	6.48
1986—Fort Lauderdale	Florida St.	22	117⅔	4	8	.333	96	64	53	101	90	4.05
1987—Columbus	Int'national	5	23⅓	1	4	.200	21	18	16	23	15	6.17
1987—Albany	Eastern	15	78	3	3	.500	64	34	29	71	37	3.35
1987—New York	American	4	22⅔	2	2	.500	24	16	16	28	15	6.35
1988—New York†	American	14	57⅓	4	4	.500	49	27	25	60	33	3.92
1988—Columbus	Int'national	4	13	0	2	.000	5	7	5	12	14	3.46
1989—New York‡-Toronto§	American	5	33⅓	1	2	.333	32	23	21	26	23	5.67
1989—Dunedin	Florida St.	3	8	0	2	.000	11	5	5	4	5	5.63
Major League Totals—3 Years		23	113⅓	7	8	.467	105	66	62	114	71	4.92

Selected by New York Yankees' organization in 2nd round of free-agent draft, June 4, 1984.
†On disabled list, June 22 to July 26, 1988; included rehabilitation disability assignment to Columbus, July 17 to July 25, 1988.
‡Traded to Toronto Blue Jays for Outfielder Jesse Barfield, April 30, 1989.

§On disabled list, May 11, 1989 through remainder of season; included rehabilitation disability aasignment to Dunedin, August 12 to August 29, 1989.

SCOTT THOMAS LEIUS

Born September 24, 1965, at Yonkers, N.Y.
Height, 6.03. Weight, 180.
Throws and bats righthanded.
Attended Concordia College, Bronxville, N.Y.

Led Midwest League shortstops in double plays with 74 in 1987.
Led Appalachian League shortstops in assists with 174 and double plays with 33 in 1986.

Year Club	League	Pos.	G.	AB.	R.	H.	2B.	3B.	HR.	RBI.	B.A.	PO.	A.	E.	F.A.
1986—Elizabethton	Appal.	SS-3B	61	237	37	66	14	1	4	23	.278	67	176	18	.931
1987—Kenosha	Midw.	SS	126	414	65	99	16	4	8	51	.239	183	331	31	.943
1988—Visalia	Calif.	SS	93	308	44	73	14	4	3	46	.237	154	234	15	.963
1989—Orlando†	South.	SS	99	346	49	105	22	2	4	45	*.303	148	257	22	.948

Selected by Minnesota Twins' organization in 13th round of free-agent draft, June 2, 1986.
†On disabled list, August 3, 1989 through remainder of season.

MARK ALAN LEMKE

Born August 13, 1965, at Utica, N.Y.
Height, 5.09. Weight, 165.
Throws right and bats left and righthanded.

Led Southern League in total bases with 239 in 1988.
Led International League second basemen in total chances with 731 and double plays with 105 in 1989.
Led Southern League second basemen in total chances with 739 and double plays with 105 in 1988.
Led Carolina League second basemen in double plays with 83 in 1987.
Led Gulf Coast League second basemen in assists with 207, total chances with 391 and double plays with 39 in 1984.

Year Club	League	Pos.	G.	AB.	R.	H.	2B.	3B.	HR.	RBI.	B.A.	PO.	A.	E.	F.A.
1983—Bradenton Braves	Gulf C.	2B	53	209	37	55	6	0	0	19	.263	81	101	11	.943
1984—Anderson	S. Atl.	2B-3B	42	121	18	18	2	0	0	5	.149	67	83	4	.974
1984—Bradenton Braves	Gulf C.	*2B-SS	●63	*243	41	67	11	0	3	32	.276	*175	209	9	*.977
1985—Sumter	S. Atl.	2B	90	231	25	50	6	0	0	20	.216	119	174	11	.964
1986—Sumter	S. Atl.	3B-2B	126	448	99	122	24	2	18	66	.272	134	274	16	.962
1987—Durham	Carol.	▲2B-3B	127	489	75	143	28	3	20	68	.292	248	*355	11	*.982
1987—Greenville	South.	3B	6	26	0	6	0	0	0	4	.231	4	12	1	.941
1988—Greenville	South.	2B	●143	*567	81	*153	30	4	16	80	.270	*281	*440	18	.976
1988—Atlanta	Nat.	2B	16	58	8	13	4	0	0	2	.224	47	51	3	.970
1989—Richmond..............	Int.	2B	*146	*518	69	143	22	7	5	61	.276	*299	*417	*15	.979
1989—Atlanta	Nat.	2B	14	55	4	10	2	1	2	10	.182	25	40	0	1.000
Major League Totals—2 Years................			30	113	12	23	6	1	2	12	.204	72	91	3	.982

Selected by Atlanta Braves' organization in 27th round of free-agent draft, June 6, 1983.

CHESTER EARL LEMON
(Chet)

Born February 12, 1955, at Jackson, Miss.
Height, 6.00. Weight, 190.
Throws and bats righthanded.
Attended Pepperdine University, Malibu, Calif., and Cerritos College, Norwalk, Calif.
Cousin of Eric Yarber, wide receiver-kick returner with Washington Redskins, 1986 and 1987.

Holds American League records for most chances accepted by outfielder, season (524), 1977; most putouts by outfielder, season (512), 1977; most years by outfielder, 400 or more putouts (5).
Shares American League record for most years by outfielder, 500 or more putouts (1), 1977.
Major League stolen bases: 1975 (1), 1976 (13), 1977 (8), 1978 (5), 1979 (7), 1980 (6), 1981 (5), 1982 (1), 1984 (5), 1986 (2), 1988 (1), 1989 (1). Total—55.
Led American League in being hit by pitch with 13 in 1979, 13 in 1981, 15 in 1982 and 20 in 1983.
Led American League outfielders in total chances with 536 in 1977.

Year Club	League	Pos.	G.	AB.	R.	H.	2B.	3B.	HR.	RBI.	B.A.	PO.	A.	E.	F.A.
1972—Coos Bay-N. B.	N'west	SS-3B	38	140	33	40	8	1	2	16	.286	56	94	16	.904
1972—Burlington	Midw.	3B-SS	33	129	18	33	5	0	1	8	.256	24	62	13	.869
1973—Burlington	Midw.	3B-SS	113	392	73	121	21	1	19	*88	.309	102	215	36	.898
1974—Birmingham†	South.	3B-SS	79	272	52	79	22	2	10	61	.290	84	135	23	.905
1975—Tucson‡................	P. C.	3B-OF	65	243	43	68	7	2	5	33	.280	60	70	19	.872
1975—Denver	A. A.	3B-OF	70	254	40	78	15	6	8	49	.307	39	76	19	.858
1975—Chicago	Amer.	3B-OF	9	35	2	9	2	0	0	1	.257	5	7	1	.923
1976—Chicago	Amer.	OF	132	451	46	111	15	5	4	38	.246	353	12	3	.992
1977—Chicago	Amer.	OF	150	553	99	151	38	4	19	67	.273	*512	12	12	.978
1978—Chicago§	Amer.	OF	105	357	51	107	24	6	13	55	.300	284	8	5	.983
1979—Chicago	Amer.	OF	148	556	79	177	●44	2	17	86	.318	411	10	10	.977
1980—Chicago	Amer.	OF-2B	147	514	76	150	32	6	11	51	.292	347	11	7	.981
1981—Chicago x..............	Amer.	OF	94	328	50	99	23	6	9	50	.302	240	2	4	.948
1982—Detroit..................	Amer.	OF	125	436	75	116	20	1	19	52	.266	242	11	4	.984
1983—Detroit..................	Amer.	OF	145	491	78	125	21	5	24	69	.255	406	6	5	.988
1984—Detroit..................	Amer.	OF	141	509	77	146	34	6	20	76	.287	427	6	2	.995
1985—Detroit..................	Amer.	OF	145	517	69	137	28	4	18	68	.265	411	6	4	.990
1986—Detroit..................	Amer.	OF	126	403	45	101	21	3	12	53	.251	316	6	5	.985
1987—Detroit..................	Amer.	OF	146	470	75	130	30	3	20	75	.277	350	4	3	.992

— 282 —

Year Club	League	Pos.	G.	AB.	R.	H.	2B.	3B.	HR.	RBI.	B.A.	PO.	A.	E.	F.A.
1988—Detroit..............	Amer.	OF	144	512	67	135	29	4	17	64	.264	296	8	8	.974
1989—Detroit..............	Amer.	OF	127	414	45	98	19	2	7	47	.237	189	6	3	.985
Major League Totals—15 Years..............			1884	6546	934	1792	380	57	210	852	.274	4789	115	76	.985

Selected by Oakland A's organization in 1st round (20th player selected) of free-agent draft, June 6, 1972.

†On disabled list, July 16 to September 16, 1974.

‡Traded with Pitcher Dave Hamilton to Chicago White Sox for Pitchers Stan Bahnsen and Lee (Skip) Pitlock, June 15, 1975.

§On disabled list, August 12 to August 27, 1978.

xTraded to Detroit Tigers for Outfielder Steve Kemp, November 27, 1981.

CHAMPIONSHIP SERIES RECORD

Year Club	League	Pos.	G.	AB.	R.	H.	2B.	3B.	HR.	RBI.	B.A.	PO.	A.	E.	F.A.
1984—Detroit..............	Amer.	OF	3	13	1	0	0	0	0	0	.000	9	0	0	1.000
1987—Detroit..............	Amer.	OF	5	18	4	5	0	0	2	4	.278	13	0	0	1.000
Championship Series Totals—2 Years.....			8	31	5	5	0	0	2	4	.161	22	0	0	1.000

WORLD SERIES RECORD

Year Club	League	Pos.	G.	AB.	R.	H.	2B.	3B.	HR.	RBI.	B.A.	PO.	A.	E.	F.A.
1984—Detroit..............	Amer.	OF	5	17	1	5	0	0	0	1	.294	15	0	0	1.000

ALL-STAR GAME RECORD

Year League	Pos.	AB.	R.	H.	2B.	3B.	HR.	RBI.	B.A.	PO.	A.	E.	F.A.
1978—American	OF	0	0	0	0	0	0	0	.000	0	0	1	.000
1979—American	OF	2	1	0	0	0	0	0	.000	2	0	0	1.000
1984—American	OF	2	0	1	0	0	0	0	.500	0	0	0	.000
All-Star Game Totals—3 Years...................		4	1	1	0	0	0	0	.250	2	0	1	.667

PATRICK ORLANDO LENNON

Born April 27, 1968, at Whiteville, N.C.
Height, 6.02. Weight, 200.
Throws and bats righthanded.

Led Midwest League third basemen in errors with 39 in 1987.

Year Club	League	Pos.	G.	AB.	R.	H.	2B.	3B.	HR.	RBI.	B.A.	PO.	A.	E.	F.A.
1986—Bellingham	N'west	SS-3B	51	169	35	41	5	2	3	27	.243	57	90	27	.845
1987—Wausau..................	Midw.	3B-SS	98	319	54	80	21	3	7	34	.251	73	190	40	.868
1988—Vermont	East.	3B	95	321	44	83	9	3	9	40	.259	81	143	★28	.889
1989—Williamsport.........	East.	OF-3B	66	248	32	65	14	2	3	31	.262	67	20	14	.861

Selected by Seattle Mariners' organization in 1st round (eighth player selected) of free-agent draft, June 2, 1986.

JEFFREY N. LEONARD

Born September 22, 1955, at Philadelphia, Pa.
Height, 6.04. Weight, 205.
Throws and bats righthanded.

Major League stolen bases: 1979 (23), 1980 (4), 1981 (5), 1982 (18), 1983 (26), 1984 (17), 1985 (11), 1986 (16), 1987 (16) 1988 (17), 1989 (6). Total—159.

Hit for the cycle, June 27, 1985.

Named National League Rookie Player of the Year by THE SPORTING NEWS, 1979.

Year Club	League	Pos.	G.	AB.	R.	H.	2B.	3B.	HR.	RBI.	B.A.	PO.	A.	E.	F.A.
1973—Bellingham	N'west	OF	55	187	30	52	4	3	2	20	.278	46	2	5	.906
1974—Orangeburg..........	W. Car.	OF	8	15	0	1	0	0	0	1	.067	5	1	1	.857
1974—Bellingham	N'west	OF	78	278	47	90	12	4	3	43	.324	115	7	6	.953
1975—Bakersfield...........	Calif.	OF	106	320	44	89	11	3	4	37	.278	137	5	7	.953
1976—Lodi	Calif.	OF	133	509	93	168	29	9	8	85	.330	214	13	★15	.938
1976—Albuquerque........	P. C.	OF	7	27	2	8	2	1	1	6	.296	14	0	0	1.000
1977—San Antonio.........	Texas	OF	122	468	75	147	17	10	12	70	.314	241	12	8	.969
1977—Los Angeles	Nat.	OF	11	10	1	3	0	1	0	2	.300	7	0	0	1.000
1978—Albuquerque†	P. C.	OF	133	502	111	★183	23	14	11	93	★.365	216	8	6	.974
1978—Houston	Nat.	OF	8	26	2	10	2	0	0	4	.385	16	1	0	1.000
1979—Houston	Nat.	OF	134	411	47	119	15	5	0	47	.290	227	6	10	.959
1980—Houston	Nat.	OF	88	216	29	46	7	5	3	20	.213	161	9	3	.983
1981—Hou.‡-S.F.............	OF-1B		44	145	21	42	12	4	4	29	.290	152	5	1	.994
1981—Phoenix	P. C.	OF	47	187	38	75	17	3	7	45	.401	90	2	2	.979
1982—San Francisco§	Nat.	OF-1B	80	278	32	72	16	1	9	49	.259	137	2	9	.939
1982—Phoenix	P. C.	OF	17	59	14	21	5	0	4	12	.356	5	0	0	1.000
1983—San Francisco	Nat.	OF	139	516	74	144	17	7	21	87	.279	253	17	7	.975
1984—San Francisco	Nat.	OF	136	514	76	155	27	2	21	86	.302	247	14	8	.970
1985—San Francisco	Nat.	OF	133	507	49	122	20	3	17	62	.241	203	10	5	.977
1986—San Francisco x...	Nat.	OF	89	341	48	95	11	3	6	42	.279	158	4	5	.970
1987—San Francisco	Nat.	OF	131	503	70	141	29	4	19	63	.280	193	7	7	.966
1988—San Francisco yz.	Nat.	OF	44	160	12	41	8	1	2	20	.256	74	0	1	.987
1988—Milwaukee a	Amer.	OF	94	374	45	88	19	0	8	44	.235	191	4	3	.985
1989—Seattle..................	Amer.	OF	150	566	69	144	20	1	24	93	.254	54	2	1	.982
National League Totals—12 Years..........			1037	3627	461	990	164	36	102	511	.273	1828	75	56	.971
American League Totals—2 Years			244	940	114	232	39	1	32	137	.247	245	6	4	.984
Major League Totals—13 Years..............			1281	4567	575	1222	203	37	134	648	.268	2073	81	60	.973

Signed as free agent by Los Angeles Dodgers' organization, June 7, 1973.

†Traded to Houston Astros, September 11, 1978, completing deal in which Los Angeles Dodgers acquired Catcher Joe Ferguson for two players to be named later, July 1, 1978; Houston acquired Shortstop Rafael Landestoy as partial completion of deal, July 7, 1978.

‡Traded with First Baseman-Outfielder Dave Bergman to San Francisco Giants for First Baseman Mike Ivie, April 20, 1981.

§On disabled list, May 23 to July 19, 1982; included rehabilitation disability assignment to Phoenix, July 1 to July 19, 1982.

xOn disabled list, July 31, 1986 through remainder of season.

yOn disabled list, March 29 to April 13, 1988.

zTraded to Milwaukee Brewers for Shortstop Ernest Riles, June 8, 1988.

aGranted free agency, November 4, 1988; signed by Seattle Mariners, December 7, 1988.

CHAMPIONSHIP SERIES RECORD

Shares Championship Series record for most home runs, series (4), 1987.
Shares National League Championship Series record for most total bases, series (22), 1987.

Year Club	League	Pos.	G.	AB.	R.	H.	2B.	3B.	HR.	RBI.	B.A.	PO.	A.	E.	F.A.
1980—Houston	Nat.	PH-OF	3	3	0	0	0	0	0	0	.000	2	1	0	1.000
1987—San Francisco	Nat.	OF	7	24	5	10	0	0	4	5	.417	14	1	0	1.000
Championship Series Totals—2 Years			10	27	5	10	0	0	4	5	.370	16	2	0	1.000

ALL-STAR GAME RECORD

Year League	Pos.	AB.	R.	H.	2B.	3B.	HR.	RBI.	B.A.	PO.	A.	E.	F.A.
1987—National	OF	2	0	0	0	0	0	0	.000	0	0	0	.000
1989—American	PH	1	0	0	0	0	0	0	.000	0	0	0	.000
All-Star Game Totals—2 Years		3	0	0	0	0	0	0	.000	0	0	0	.000

DEREK JANSEN LILLIQUIST

Born February 20, 1966, at Winter Park, Fla.
Height, 6.00. Weight, 210.
Throws and bats lefthanded.
Attended University of Georgia, Athens, Ga.

Named lefthanded pitcher on THE SPORTING NEWS College Baseball All-America Team, 1987.

Year Club	League	G.	IP.	W.	L.	Pct.	H.	R	ER.	SO.	BB.	ERA.
1987—Bradenton Braves	Gulf Coast	2	13	0	0	.000	3	0	0	16	2	0.00
1987—Durham	Carolina	3	25	2	1	.667	13	9	8	29	6	2.88
1988—Richmond	Int'national	28	170⅔	10	12	.455	179	70	64	80	36	3.38
1989—Atlanta	National	32	165⅔	8	10	.444	202	87	73	79	34	3.97
Major League Totals—1 Year		32	165⅔	8	10	.444	202	87	73	79	34	3.97

Selected by Boston Red Sox' organization in 15th round of free-agent draft, June 4, 1984.
Selected by Atlanta Braves in 1st round (sixth player selected) of free-agent draft, June 2, 1987.

JOSE LIND (SALGADO)

Name pronounced Leend.

Born May 1, 1964, at Toabaja, P. R.
Height, 5.11. Weight, 170.
Throws and bats righthanded.

Brother of Orlando Lind, pitcher in Pittsburgh Pirates' organization; and cousin of Onix Concepcion, infielder with Kansas City Royals and Pittsburgh Pirates, 1980 through 1985 and 1987.

Major League stolen bases: 1987 (2), 1988 (15), 1989 (15). Total—32.
Led Pacific Coast League second basemen in double plays with 84 and total chances with 764 in 1987.
Led Eastern League second basemen in total chances with 705 and double plays with 84 in 1986.

Year Club	League	Pos.	G.	AB.	R.	H.	2B.	3B.	HR.	RBI.	B.A.	PO.	A.	E.	F.A.
1983—Bradenton Pir.	Gulf C.	2B-SS	45	163	26	49	3	4	0	18	.301	102	125	9	.962
1984—Macon	S. Atl.	2B-SS	121	396	39	82	5	2	0	30	.207	271	306	32	.947
1985—Prince William	Carol.	2-S-3-O	105	377	42	104	9	4	0	28	.276	164	221	14	.965
1986—Nashua	East.	2B	134	•520	58	137	18	5	1	33	.263	★314	★378	13	★.982
1987—Vancouver	P. C.	2B	128	★533	75	143	16	3	3	30	.268	★311	★432	21	.973
1987—Pittsburgh	Nat.	2B	35	143	21	46	8	4	0	11	.322	53	139	1	.995
1988—Pittsburgh	Nat.	2B	154	611	82	160	24	4	2	49	.262	333	473	11	.987
1989—Pittsburgh	Nat.	2B	153	578	52	134	21	3	2	48	.232	309	438	18	.976
Major League Totals—3 Years			342	1332	155	340	53	11	4	108	.255	695	1050	30	.983

Signed as free agent by Pittsburgh Pirates' organization, December 3, 1982.

JAMES WILLIAM LINDEMAN
(Jim)

Born January 10, 1962, at Evanston, Ill.
Height, 6.01. Weight, 200.
Throws and bats righthanded.
Attended Bradley University, Peoria, Ill.

Major League stolen bases: 1986 (1), 1987 (3). Total—4.

Year Club	League	Pos.	G.	AB.	R.	H.	2B.	3B.	HR.	RBI.	B.A.	PO.	A.	E.	F.A.
1983—St. Petersburg	Fla. St.	3B	70	232	45	64	13	1	8	37	.276	36	98	26	.838
1984—Springfield	Midw.	3B-SS	94	354	69	169	15	2	18	66	.271	78	175	30	.894
1984—Arkansas	Texas	3B	40	137	14	26	4	3	0	13	.190	26	67	6	.939

Year Club	League	Pos.	G.	AB.	R.	H.	2B.	3B.	HR.	RBI.	B.A.	PO.	A.	E.	F.A.
1985—Arkansas...............	Texas	3B	128	450	54	127	30	6	10	63	.282	74	238	24	.929
1986—Louisville	A. A.	1B-3B-OF	139	509	82	128	38	5	20	*96	.251	718	110	19	.978
1986—St. Louis.................	Nat.	1B-3B-OF	19	55	7	14	1	0	1	6	.255	118	10	1	.992
1987—St. Louis†...............	Nat.	OF-1B	75	207	20	43	13	0	8	28	.208	196	14	3	.986
1987—Louisville.................	A. A.	OF	20	78	11	24	3	1	4	10	.308	14	1	1	.938
1988—St. Louis‡...............	Nat.	OF-1B	17	43	3	9	1	0	2	7	.209	36	2	1	.974
1988—Louisville	A. A.	OF-1B	73	261	32	66	18	4	2	30	.253	308	23	4	.988
1989—St. Louis§...............	Nat.	1B-OF	73	45	8	5	1	0	0	2	.111	93	6	1	.990
1989—Louisville x...........	A. A.	OF-1B	29	109	18	33	8	1	5	20	.303	52	5	2	.966
Major League Totals—4 Years.................			184	350	38	71	16	0	11	43	.203	443	32	6	.988

Selected by St. Louis Cardinals' organization in 1st round (24th player selected) of free-agent draft, June 6, 1983.

†On disabled list, May 12 to May 29 and June 4 to July 4, 1987; included rehabilitation disability assignment to Louisville, May 26 to May 29 and June 17 to July 4, 1987.

‡On disabled list, April 22 to July 5, 1988; included rehabilitation disability assignment to Louisville, June 16 to July 5, 1988.

§On disabled list, July 10 to August 10, 1989; included rehabilitation disability assignment to Louisville, July 26 to August 10, 1989.

xTraded with Pitcher Matt Kinzer to Detroit Tigers for Second Baseman Pat Austin, Catcher Bill Henderson and Pitcher Marcus Betances, December 6, 1989.

CHAMPIONSHIP SERIES RECORD

Year Club	League	Pos.	G.	AB.	R.	H.	2B.	3B.	HR.	RBI.	B.A.	PO.	A.	E.	F.A.
1987—St. Louis.................	Nat.	1B-PH	5	13	1	4	0	0	1	3	.308	33	2	0	1.000

WORLD SERIES RECORD

Year Club	League	Pos.	G.	AB.	R.	H.	2B.	3B.	HR.	RBI.	B.A.	PO.	A.	E.	F.A.
1987—St. Louis.................	Nat.	1B-PH-O	6	15	3	5	1	0	0	2	.333	28	2	3	.909

NELSON ARTURO LIRIANO

Name pronounced Leer-EEE-anno.
Born June 3, 1964, at Puerto Plata, D. R.
Height, 5.10. Weight, 165.
Throws right and bats left and righthanded.

Major League stolen bases: 1987 (13), 1988 (12), 1989 (16). Total—41.
Led International League second basemen in double plays with 96 and total chances with 611 in 1987.
Led Carolina League second basemen in double plays with 79 in 1985.

Year Club	League	Pos.	G.	AB.	R.	H.	2B.	3B.	HR.	RBI.	B.A.	PO.	A.	E.	F.A.
1983—Florence	S. Atl.	2B	129	478	87	124	24	5	6	57	.259	214	323	34	.940
1984—Kinston...............	Carol.	2B	132	*512	68	126	22	4	5	50	.246	260	*357	*21	.967
1985—Kinston...............	Carol.	2B	134	451	68	130	23	1	6	36	.288	*261	328	●25	.959
1986—Knoxville	South.	2B-3B-SS	135	557	88	159	25	*15	7	59	.285	239	324	22	.962
1987—Syracuse	Int.	2B	130	531	72	133	19	●10	10	55	.250	*246	*346	*19	.969
1987—Toronto	Amer.	2B	37	158	29	38	6	2	2	10	.241	83	107	1	.995
1988—Toronto	Amer.	2B-3B	99	276	36	73	6	2	3	23	.264	121	177	12	.961
1988—Syracuse	Int.	2B	8	31	2	6	1	1	0	1	.194	14	23	0	1.000
1989—Toronto	Amer.	2B	132	418	51	110	26	3	5	53	.263	267	330	12	.980
Major League Totals—3 Years.................			268	852	116	221	38	7	10	86	.259	471	614	25	.977

Signed as free agent by Toronto Blue Jays' organization, November 1, 1982.

CHAMPIONSHIP SERIES RECORD

Year Club	League	Pos.	G.	AB.	R.	H.	2B.	3B.	HR.	RBI.	B.A.	PO.	A.	E.	F.A.
1989—Toronto	Amer.	2B	3	7	1	3	0	0	0	1	.429	4	3	1	.875

DENNIS SCOTT LITTLE

(Known by middle name.)
Born January 19, 1963, at East St. Louis, Ill.
Height, 6.00. Weight, 198.
Throws and bats righthanded.
Attended Mineral Area College, Flat River, Mo.,
and University of Missouri, Columbia, Mo.

Led New York-Pennsylvania League in being hit by pitch with 9 and stolen bases with 34 in 1984.

Year Club	League	Pos.	G.	AB.	R.	H.	2B.	3B.	HR.	RBI.	B.A.	PO.	A.	E.	F.A.
1984—Little Falls.............	NYP	OF-3B	66	225	38	67	11	0	1	23	.298	107	12	7	.944
1985—Lynchburg............	Carol.	OF	*140	470	70	111	16	7	2	44	.236	252	12	6	.978
1986--Jackson	Texas	OF-1B	40	96	15	20	6	0	0	8	.208	69	5	1	.987
1986—Lynchburg†	Carol.	OF	58	172	34	42	11	4	2	31	.244	76	10	4	.956
1987—Jackson	Texas	OF	18	33	5	5	1	0	1	4	.152	20	1	1	.955
1987—Lynch.‡-Salem.......	Carol.	3B-OF	101	339	65	99	12	5	12	55	.292	105	86	15	.927
1988—Harrisburg	East.	O-3-2-S	118	410	60	119	14	6	6	52	.290	140	48	10	.949
1988—Buffalo...................	A. A.	OF	4	16	0	1	0	0	0	1	.063	6	0	0	1.000
1989—Buffalo...................	A. A.	3-O-1-C-2	107	298	38	88	11	4	3	43	.295	265	79	15	.958
1989—Pittsburgh.............	Nat.	OF	3	4	0	1	0	0	0	0	.250	1	1	0	1.000
Major League Totals—1 Year.................			3	4	0	1	0	0	0	0	.250	1	1	0	1.000

Selected by New York Mets' organization in 7th round of free-agent draft, January 17, 1984.

†On disabled list, July 30 to August 9, 1986.
‡Traded with Infielder Al Pedrique to Pittsburgh Pirates for Infielder-Outfielder Bill Almon, May 29, 1987.

JON GREGORY LITTON
(Greg)

Born July 13, 1964, at New Orleans, La.
Height, 6.00. Weight, 175.
Throws and bats righthanded.
Attended Pensacola Junior College, Pensacola, Fla.

Led Texas League second basemen in putouts with 262, assists with 369 and total chances with 655 in 1986.
Led California League second basemen in total chances with 749 in 1985.

Year Club	League	Pos.	G.	AB.	R.	H.	2B.	3B.	HR.	RBI.	B.A.	PO.	A.	E.	F.A.
1984—Everett	N'west	2B-3B	62	243	29	57	12	2	4	26	.235	135	160	17	.977
1985—Fresno	Calif.	*2B-OF	141	*564	88	150	*33	7	12	103	.266	269	*453	28	.963
1986—Shreveport	Texas	*2-S-O	131	455	46	112	30	3	10	55	.246	265	373	*24	.964
1987—Shreveport	Texas	2B-SS	72	254	34	66	6	3	8	33	.260	117	199	3	.991
1987—Phoenix	P. C.	2B-SS	60	203	24	44	8	2	1	22	.217	146	173	8	.976
1988—Shreveport	Texas	3B-2B-SS	116	432	58	120	35	5	11	64	.278	116	247	13	.965
1989—Phoenix	P. C.	2-S-3-1-C	30	89	6	16	4	2	2	6	.180	48	50	4	.961
1989—San Francisco	Nat.	3-2-S-O-C	71	143	12	36	5	3	4	17	.252	44	66	3	.973
Major League Totals—1 Year			71	143	12	36	5	3	4	17	.252	44	66	3	.973

Selected by San Francisco Giants' organization in 1st round (10th player selected) of free-agent draft, January 17, 1984.

CHAMPIONSHIP SERIES RECORD

Year Club	League	Pos.	G.	AB.	R.	H.	2B.	3B.	HR.	RBI.	B.A.	PO.	A.	E.	F.A.
1989—San Francisco	Nat.	PH-3B	1	1	0	1	0	0	0	0	1.000	0	0	0	.000

WORLD SERIES RECORD

Year Club	League	Pos.	G.	AB.	R.	H.	2B.	3B.	HR.	RBI.	B.A.	PO.	A.	E.	F.A.
1989—San Francisco	Nat.	PH-2B-3B	2	6	1	3	1	0	1	3	.500	2	3	0	1.000

KEITH VIRGIL LOCKHART

Born November 10, 1964, at Whittier, Calif.
Height, 5.10. Weight, 170.
Throws right and bats lefthanded.
Attended Mount San Antonio College, Walnut, Calif.,
and Oral Roberts University, Tulsa, Okla.

Led American Association second basemen in total chances with 631 in 1989.
Led Southern League in sacrifice flies with 11 in 1988.
Led Midwest League third basemen in double plays with 33 in 1987.

Year Club	League	Pos.	G.	AB.	R.	H.	2B.	3B.	HR.	RBI.	B.A.	PO.	A.	E.	F.A.
1986—Billings	Pion.	2B-3B	53	202	51	70	11	3	7	31	.347	81	150	17	.931
1986—Cedar Rapids	Midw.	2B-3B	13	42	4	8	2	0	0	1	.190	17	15	0	1.000
1987—Cedar Rapids	Midw.	3B-2B	*140	511	101	160	37	5	23	84	.313	85	292	28	.931
1988—Chattanooga	South.	3B-2B	139	515	74	137	27	3	12	67	.266	102	323	36	.922
1989—Nashville	A. A.	2B	131	479	77	128	21	6	14	58	.267	*279	*335	17	.973

Selected by Cincinnati Reds' organization in 11th round of free-agent draft, June 2, 1986.

MICHAEL BERNARD LOGGINS
(Mike)

Born December 21, 1963, at El Dorado, Ark.
Height, 5.08. Weight, 160.
Throws left and bats left and righthanded.
Attended University of Arkansas, Fayetteville, Ark.

Led American Association in sacrifice hits with 9 in 1988.
Led Northwest League in stolen bases with 35 in 1985.
Led American Association outfielders in total chances with 304 in 1988.

Year Club	League	Pos.	G.	AB.	R.	H.	2B.	3B.	HR.	RBI.	B.A.	PO.	A.	E.	F.A.
1985—Eugene	N'west	OF	73	289	52	90	13	2	5	31	.311	136	7	9	.941
1986—Fort Myers†	Fla. St.	OF	72	253	51	73	11	8	1	18	.289	149	6	8	.951
1986—Omaha	A. A.	OF	6	11	2	8	2	0	1	5	.727	6	0	0	1.000
1987—Memphis	South.	OF	110	440	73	124	27	7	8	49	.282	284	5	7	.976
1988—Omaha	A. A.	OF	130	425	44	104	17	8	2	42	.245	*288	10	6	.980
1989—Omaha‡	A. A.	OF	103	311	57	82	14	6	2	29	.264	209	10	4	.982

Selected by Kansas City Royals' organization in 3rd round of free-agent draft, June 3, 1985.
†On disabled list, April 24 to June 24, 1986.
‡On disabled list, July 17 to July 24 and July 26 to August 3, 1989.

PHILLIP ARDEN LOMBARDI
(Phil)

Born February 20, 1963, at Abilene, Tex.
Height, 6.02. Weight, 205.
Throws and bats righthanded.

Led Florida State League catchers in fielding percentage with .985 in 1984.

Year	Club	League	Pos.	G.	AB.	R.	H.	2B.	3B.	HR.	RBI.	B.A.	PO.	A.	E.	F.A.
1981—Bradenton Yanks	Gulf C.		C	20	53	9	13	3	0	0	6	.245	94	17	4	.965
1982—Paintsville	Appal.		C	50	180	26	45	8	0	0	14	.250	323	★50	8	.979
1983—Greensboro	S. Atl.		C-OF	94	330	63	99	15	0	7	43	.300	564	52	14	.978
1983—Fort Lauderdale	Fla. St.		C	17	49	1	11	2	0	0	3	.224	77	6	5	.943
1984—Fort Lauderdale	Fla. St.		C-O-1-3	127	393	58	115	20	2	8	70	.293	669	61	14	.990
1985—Albany†	East.		C-O-3-S	76	250	44	64	13	2	5	32	.256	390	48	11	.976
1986—Columbus‡	Int.		C-OF	75	277	43	81	12	4	8	28	.292	222	16	7	.971
1986—New York	Amer.		OF-C	20	36	6	10	3	0	2	6	.278	22	3	3	.893
1987—Columbus	Int.		3B-OF-C	67	209	32	56	13	1	6	33	.268	101	55	15	.912
1987—Albany	East.		C	20	60	9	15	3	0	3	8	.250	29	7	1	.973
1987—New York§	Amer.		C	5	8	0	1	0	0	0	0	.125	7	1	0	1.000
1988—Tidewater x	Int.		OF-1B-C	85	292	49	90	14	0	9	44	.308	383	29	5	.988
1989—Tidewater	Int.		1B-C	113	403	50	105	19	0	14	73	.261	827	77	10	.989
1989—New York	Nat.		C-1B	18	48	4	11	1	0	1	3	.229	93	5	2	.980
Major League Totals—3 Years				43	92	10	22	4	0	3	9	.239	100	6	2	.981

Selected by New York Yankees' organization in 3rd round of free-agent draft, June 8, 1981.
†On disabled list, July 20 to September 16, 1985.
‡On disabled list, June 19 to July 16, 1986.
§Traded with Outfielder Darren Reed and Pitcher Steve Frey to New York Mets for Shortstop Rafael Santana and Pitcher Victor Garcia, December 11, 1987.
xOn disabled list, July 18, 1988 through remainder of season.

STEPHEN PAUL LOMBARDOZZI
(Steve)

Born April 26, 1960, at Malden, Mass.
Height, 6.00. Weight, 183.
Throws and bats righthanded.
Attended Gulf Coast Community College, Panama City, Fla.,
and University of Florida, Gainesville, Fla.
Brother of Chris Lombardozzi, shortstop in New York Yankees' organization, 1985 through 1988.

Major League stolen bases: 1985 (3), 1986 (3), 1987 (5), 1988 (2). Total—13.
Led California League shortstops in fielding percentage with .947 in 1982.

Year	Club	League	Pos.	G.	AB.	R.	H.	2B.	3B.	HR.	RBI.	B.A.	PO.	A.	E.	F.A.
1981—Elizabethton	Appal.		SS	65	246	48	79	13	2	6	38	.321	89	192	14	★.953
1982—Visalia	Calif.		SS-OF-P	122	441	81	131	24	1	6	67	.297	185	393	33	.946
1983—Orlando	South.		SS-2B	137	492	76	143	23	6	3	52	.291	203	364	33	.945
1984—Toledo	Int.		2B-SS	119	385	57	96	15	1	9	31	.249	237	310	14	.975
1985—Toledo	Int.		2B-3B-SS	118	451	55	119	21	3	14	48	.264	272	324	17	.972
1985—Minnesota	Amer.		2B	28	54	10	20	4	1	0	6	.370	31	80	2	.982
1986—Minnesota	Amer.		2B	156	453	53	103	20	5	8	33	.227	289	407	6	★.991
1987—Minnesota	Amer.		2B	136	432	51	103	19	3	8	38	.238	245	356	14	.977
1988—Minnesota†	Amer.		2B-SS-3B	103	287	34	60	15	2	3	27	.209	152	237	5	.987
1989—Houston	Nat.		2B-3B	21	37	5	8	3	1	1	3	.216	20	28	4	.923
1989—Tucson	P. C.		2B-SS	114	401	66	103	21	2	5	46	.257	170	285	15	.968
American League Totals—4 Years				423	1226	148	286	58	11	19	104	.233	717	1080	27	.985
National League Totals—1 Year				21	37	5	8	3	1	1	3	.216	20	28	4	.923
Major League Totals—5 Years				444	1263	153	294	61	12	20	107	.233	737	1108	31	.983

Selected by Minnesota Twins' organization in 9th round of free-agent draft, June 8, 1981.
†Traded to Houston Astros for a player to be named later, March 21, 1989; Minnesota Twins acquired Outfielder Ramon Cedeno and Pitcher Gordon Farmer to complete deal, September 16, 1989.

CHAMPIONSHIP SERIES RECORD

Year	Club	League	Pos.	G.	AB.	R.	H.	2B.	3B.	HR.	RBI.	B.A.	PO.	A.	E.	F.A.
1987—Minnesota	Amer.		2B-PR	5	15	2	4	7	0	0	1	.267	8	9	1	.944

WORLD SERIES RECORD

Year	Club	League	Pos.	G.	AB.	R.	H.	2B.	3B.	HR.	RBI.	B.A.	PO.	A.	E.	F.A.
1987—Minnesota	Amer.		2B	6	17	3	7	1	0	1	4	.412	9	24	0	1.000

PITCHING RECORD

Year	Club	League	G.	IP.	W.	L.	Pct.	H.	R.	ER.	SO.	BB.	ERA.
1982—Visalia	California	1	1	0	1	.000	5	4	4	2	0	36.00

WILLIAM DOUGLAS LONG
(Bill)

Born February 29, 1960, at Cincinnati, O.
Height, 6.00. Weight, 185.
Throws and bats righthanded.
Attended Miami University, Oxford, O.

Major League saves: 1987 (1), 1988 (2), 1989 (1). Total—4.

Year	Club	League	G.	IP.	W.	L.	Pct.	H.	R.	ER.	SO.	BB.	ERA.
1981—Salem	Carolina	14	87	9	2	.818	81	31	27	80	28	2.79
1982—Amarillo	Texas	27	★198⅓	12	10	.545	★222	116	97	117	53	4.40
1983—Las Vegas	P. Coast	18	62⅓	5	5	.500	99	66	53	41	28	7.65

Year	Club	League	G.	IP.	W.	L.	Pct.	H.	R.	ER.	SO.	BB.	ERA.
1983—Beaumont	Texas	10	65⅓	2	5	.286	80	47	41	33	28	5.65
1984—Beaumont†	Texas	25	159⅔	●14	5	.737	149	56	52	114	67	2.93
1985—Buffalo	Am. Assoc.	25	151⅓	★13	6	.684	146	69	59	71	43	3.51
1985—Chicago	American	4	14	0	1	.000	25	17	16	13	5	10.29
1986—Buffalo‡	Am. Assoc.	22	146	9	9	.500	159	73	63	86	44	3.88
1987—Hawaii	P. Coast	2	13	2	0	1.000	15	7	6	6	4	4.15
1987—Chicago	American	29	169	8	8	.500	179	85	82	72	28	4.37
1988—Chicago	American	47	174	8	11	.421	187	89	78	77	43	4.03
1989—Chicago	American	30	98⅔	5	5	.500	101	49	43	51	37	3.92
1989—Vancouver	P. Coast	3	26	1	2	.333	17	8	8	14	2	2.77
Major League Totals—4 Years		110	455⅔	21	25	.457	492	240	219	213	113	4.33

Selected by San Diego Padres' organization in 2nd round of free-agent draft, June 8, 1981.

†Traded with Pitcher Tim Lollar, Third Baseman Luis Salazar and Shortstop Ozzie Guillen to Chicago White Sox for Pitchers LaMarr Hoyt, Kevin Kristan and Todd Simmons, December 6, 1984.

‡On disabled list, May 12 to June 16, 1986.

ANTHONY EUGENE LONGMIRE
(Tony)

Born August 12, 1968, at Vallejo, Calif.
Height, 6.01. Weight, 195.
Throws right and bats left and righthanded.

Year	Club	League	Pos.	G.	AB.	R.	H.	2B.	3B.	HR.	RBI.	B.A.	PO.	A.	E.	F.A.
1986—Bradenton Pir.	Gulf C.	OF	15	40	6	11	2	1	0	6	.275	19	0	2	.905
1987—Macon	S. Atl.	OF	127	445	63	117	15	4	5	62	.263	167	5	8	.956
1988—Salem†‡	Carol.	OF	64	218	46	60	12	2	11	40	.275	91	3	3	.969
1988—Harrisburg	East.	OF	32	94	7	14	2	2	0	4	.149	46	2	2	.960
1989—Salem†	Carol.	OF	14	62	8	20	3	1	1	6	.323	14	3	0	1.000
1989—Harrisburg†	East.	OF	37	127	15	37	7	0	3	22	.291	62	1	2	.969

Selected by Pittsburgh Pirates' organization in 8th round of free-agent draft, June 2, 1986.

†Batted lefthanded only.

‡On disabled list, August 27, 1988 through remainder of season.

VANCE ODELL LOVELACE

Born August 9, 1963, at Tampa, Fla.
Height, 6.05. Weight, 235.
Throws and bats lefthanded.

Led Florida State League in hit batsmen with 25, wild pitches with 25 and tied for lead in balks with 6 in 1983.

Year	Club	League	G.	IP.	W.	L.	Pct.	H.	R.	ER.	SO.	BB.	ERA.
1981—Sarasota Cubs	Gulf Coast	7	30	0	5	.000	27	22	11	31	26	3.30
1982—Quad Cities†‡	Midwest	21	94	4	6	.400	62	67	52	107	94	4.98
1983—Vero Beach	Florida St.	24	115	8	10	.444	104	80	61	95	93	4.77
1984—San Antonio§	Texas	16	65	3	7	.300	48	39	28	52	73	3.88
1985—San Antonio	Texas	7	23⅔	0	4	.000	22	27	20	12	30	7.61
1985—Vero Beach x	Florida St.	11	29⅓	1	2	.333	31	22	20	26	23	6.14
1986—Midland	Texas	23	42⅓	2	4	.333	45	46	42	27	58	8.93
1986—Palm Springs	California	6	17⅔	0	1	.000	21	23	18	16	30	9.17
1987—Midland	Texas	53	83⅔	3	3	.500	73	40	30	91	60	3.23
1988—Edmonton	P. Coast	46	69⅓	1	3	.250	79	48	47	56	57	6.10
1988—California	American	3	1⅓	0	0	.000	2	2	2	0	3	13.50
1989—California	American	1	1	0	0	.000	0	0	0	1	1	0.00
1989—Edmonton y	P. Coast	37	48⅔	0	7	.000	42	42	32	40	55	5.92
Major League Totals—2 Years		4	2⅓	0	0	.000	2	2	2	1	4	7.71

Selected by Chicago Cubs' organization in 1st round (16th player selected) of free-agent draft, June 8, 1981.

†On disabled list, April 20 to May 6, 1982.

‡Traded with Outfielder Dan Cataline to Los Angeles Dodgers' organization for Third Baseman Ron Cey, January 19, 1983.

§On disabled list, April 28 to May 24, 1984.

xDrafted by California Angels' organization, December 11, 1985.

yGranted free agency, October 15, 1989; signed by Calgary (Seattle Mariners' organization), December 18, 1989.

SALVATORE ANTHONY LOVULLO
(Torey)

Born July 25, 1965, at Santa Monica, Calif.
Height, 6.00. Weight, 180.
Throws right and bats left and righthanded.
Attended UCLA.

Tied for International League lead in intentional bases on balls received with 10 in 1989.
Named second baseman on THE SPORTING NEWS College Baseball All-America Team, 1987.

Year	Club	League	Pos.	G.	AB.	R.	H.	2B.	3B.	HR.	RBI.	B.A.	PO.	A.	E.	F.A.
1987—Fayetteville	S. Atl.	3B-2B	55	191	34	49	13	0	8	32	.257	41	133	22	.888
1987—Lakeland	Fla. St.	3B	18	60	11	16	3	0	1	16	.267	11	30	2	.953
1988—Glens Falls	East.	3B-2B	78	270	37	74	17	1	9	50	.274	63	173	21	.918
1988—Toledo	Int.	2B-3B-SS	57	177	18	41	8	1	5	20	.232	120	149	5	.982
1988—Detroit	Amer.	2B-3B	12	21	2	8	1	1	1	2	.381	12	19	0	1.000
1989—Detroit	Amer.	1B-3B	29	87	8	10	2	0	1	4	.115	134	24	1	.994

Year Club	League	Pos.	G.	AB.	R.	H.	2B.	3B.	HR.	RBI.	B.A.	PO.	A.	E.	F.A.
1989—Toledo	Int.	3-2-S-1	112	409	48	94	23	2	10	52	.230	217	257	20	.960
Major League Totals—2 Years................			41	108	10	18	3	1	2	6	.167	146	43	1	.995

Selected by Kansas City Royals' organization in 27th round of free-agent draft, June 2, 1986.
Selected by Detroit Tigers' organization in 5th round of free-agent draft, June 2, 1987.

RICHARD FRED LUECKEN
(Rick)

Born November 15, 1960, at McAllen, Tex.
Height, 6.06. Weight, 210.
Throws and bats righthanded.
Attended Texas A&M University, College Station, Tex.

Major League saves: 1989 (1).

Year Club	League	G.	IP.	W.	L.	Pct.	H.	R.	ER.	SO.	BB.	ERA.
1983—Bellingham	Northwest	14	78⅓	5	4	.556	70	39	31	83	37	3.56
1984—Chattanooga	Southern	26	163⅔	11	*13	.458	166	85	69	90	88	3.79
1985—Calgary†	P. Coast	18	111	4	8	.333	111	70	66	44	39	6.93
1986—Chattanooga‡§	Southern	17	88⅔	6	7	.462	106	57	52	55	42	5.28
1987—Memphis......................................	Southern	28	146	9	9	.500	163	86	77	88	53	4.75
1988—Memphis......................................	Southern	21	24⅔	4	1	.800	17	8	6	30	7	2.19
1988—Omaha...	Am. Assoc.	26	40	5	0	1.000	45	10	9	27	15	2.03
1989—Omaha...	Am. Assoc.	36	46⅔	4	1	.800	33	14	12	39	22	2.31
1989—Kansas City x	American	19	23⅔	2	1	.667	23	9	9	16	13	3.42
Major League Totals—1 Year................		19	23⅔	2	1	.667	23	9	9	16	13	3.42

Selected by San Francisco Giants' organization in 1st round (18th player selected) of free-agent draft, June 5, 1979.
Selected by Cincinnati Reds' organization in 12th round of free-agent draft, June 7, 1982.
Selected by Seattle Mariners' organization in 27th round of free-agent draft, June 6, 1983.
†On disabled list, April 11 to April 25, June 9 to July 2 and August 20, 1985 through remainder of season.
‡On disabled list, June 18 to August 14, 1986.
§Traded with Outfielder Danny Tartabull to Kansas City Royals for Pitchers Scott Bankhead and Steve Shields and Outfielder Mike Kingery, December 10, 1986.
xTraded with Pitcher Charlie Leibrandt to Atlanta Braves for First Baseman Gerald Perry and Pitcher Jim Lemasters, December 15, 1989.

URBANO RAFAEL LUGO

Born August 12, 1962, at Falcon, Venezuela.
Height, 5.11. Weight, 197.
Throws and bats righthanded.
Son of Urbano Lugo, pitcher in Mexican League, 1967 through 1970 and 1973.

Year Club	League	G.	IP.	W.	L.	Pct.	H.	R.	ER.	SO.	BB.	ERA.
1982—Danville	Midwest	10	24	0	2	.000	35	30	27	13	16	10.13
1982—Salem...	Northwest	14	90⅔	7	3	.700	74	45	29	62	61	2.88
1983—Peoria..	Midwest	15	107	8	5	.615	82	39	30	96	28	2.52
1983—Redwood......................................	California	11	64⅔	5	5	.500	59	36	28	58	31	3.90
1984—Waterbury....................................	Eastern	24	164⅓	13	8	.619	135	63	51	117	68	2.79
1985—Edmonton....................................	P. Coast	4	25⅔	2	0	1.000	20	14	13	19	14	4.56
1985—California†....................................	American	20	83	3	4	.429	86	36	34	42	29	3.69
1986—Midland‡......................................	Texas	2	11	1	1	.500	9	2	2	4	4	1.64
1986—Edmonton....................................	P. Coast	16	100⅓	8	6	.571	110	58	52	53	41	4.66
1986—California.....................................	American	6	21⅓	1	1	.500	21	9	9	9	6	3.80
1987—California.....................................	American	7	28	0	2	.000	42	34	29	24	18	9.32
1987—Edmonton....................................	P. Coast	15	90⅔	4	3	.571	89	46	37	47	46	3.67
1988—Edmonton....................................	P. Coast	38	116⅓	9	6	.600	148	74	68	69	47	5.26
1988—California§...................................	American	1	2	0	0	.000	2	2	2	1	1	9.00
1989—Indianapolis.................................	Am. Assoc.	22	122⅓	12	4	*.750	100	53	40	79	41	2.94
1989—Montreal x...................................	National	3	4	0	0	.000	4	3	3	3	0	6.75
American League Totals—4 Years		34	134⅓	4	7	.364	151	81	74	76	54	4.96
National League Totals—1 Year......................		3	4	0	0	.000	4	3	3	3	0	6.75
Major League Totals—5 Years............................		37	138⅓	4	7	.364	155	84	77	79	54	5.01

Signed as free agent by California Angels' organization, January 31, 1982.
†On disabled list, August 22 to September 6, 1985.
‡On California disabled list, March 31 to June 5, 1986; included rehabilitation disability assignment to Midland, May 15 to June 4, 1986.
§Released, March 31, 1989; signed by Indianapolis (Montreal Expos' organization), April 4, 1989.
xGranted free agency, October 15, 1989.

SCOTT EDWARD LUSADER

Named pronounced Loo-SAY-der.

Born September 30, 1964, at Chicago, Ill.
Height, 5.10. Weight, 165.
Throws and bats lefthanded.
Received bachelor of science degree in marketing
from University of Florida, Gainesville, Fla.

Shares major league record for most errors, outfielder, inning (3), September 9, 1989, first inning.
Major League stolen bases: 1987 (1), 1989 (3). Total—4.

Year Club	League	Pos.	G.	AB.	R.	H.	2B.	3B.	HR.	RBI.	B.A.	PO.	A.	E.	F.A.
1985—Lakeland	Fla. St.	OF	27	97	16	28	5	1	2	22	.289	47	3	3	.943
1985—Birmingham	South.	OF	21	77	13	26	3	4	2	14	.338	49	1	0	1.000
1986—Glens Falls	East.	OF	136	479	74	134	23	3	11	59	.280	275	13	●11	.963
1987—Toledo	Int.	OF	136	505	78	136	29	8	17	80	.269	274	11	6	.979
1987—Detroit	Amer.	OF	23	47	8	15	3	1	1	8	.319	29	0	1	.967
1988—Toledo	Int.	OF-1B	89	329	38	86	11	5	4	46	.261	193	0	3	.985
1988—Detroit	Amer.	OF	16	16	3	1	0	0	1	3	.063	7	0	0	1.000
1989—Toledo†	Int.	OF	44	153	17	37	9	1	2	15	.242	111	5	4	.967
1989—Detroit‡	Amer.	OF	40	103	15	26	4	0	1	8	.252	56	0	4	.933
1989—Tucson	P. C.	OF	33	121	15	30	3	1	2	13	.248	80	2	4	.953
Major League Totals—3 Years			79	166	26	42	7	1	3	19	.253	92	0	5	.948

Selected by Detroit Tigers' organization in 6th round of free-agent draft, June 3, 1985.

†On Detroit disabled list, March 27 to May 5, 1989; included rehabilitation disability assignment to Toledo, April 21 to May 5, 1989.

‡Loaned to Tucson (Houston Astros' organization), July 13, 1989; returned, September 2, 1989.

DAVID ASHLEY LYNCH

Born October 7, 1965, at Baton Rouge, La.
Height, 6.04. Weight, 210.
Throws left and bats righthanded.
Attended University of New Orleans, New Orleans, La.

Year Club	League	G.	IP.	W.	L.	Pct.	H.	R.	ER.	SO.	BB.	ERA.
1987—Sarasota Rangers	Gulf Coast	13	55	4	3	.571	38	18	14	55	29	2.29
1988—Sarasota Rangers	Gulf Coast	1	1⅔	0	0	.000	0	0	0	3	0	0.00
1988—Port Charlotte	Florida St.	36	58	6	2	.750	43	21	13	58	22	2.02
1989—Tulsa	Texas	39	51⅔	8	0	1.000	39	7	5	53	24	0.87
1989—Oklahoma City	Am. Assoc.	11	11⅔	0	2	.000	12	8	8	10	8	6.17

Selected by Philadelphia Phillies' organization in 4th round of free-agent draft, June 6, 1983.
Selected by Texas Rangers' organization in 22nd round of free-agent draft, June 2, 1987.

FREDRIC MICHAEL LYNN
(Fred)

Born February 3, 1952, at Chicago, Ill.
Height, 6.01. Weight, 190.
Throws and bats lefthanded.
Attended University of Southern California, Los Angeles, Calif.

Holds American League record for most doubles, rookie season (47), 1975.
Shares American League record for most total bases, game (16), June 18, 1975.
Major League stolen bases: 1975 (10), 1976 (14), 1977 (2), 1978 (3), 1979 (2), 1980 (12), 1981 (1), 1982 (7), 1983 (2), 1984 (2), 1985 (7), 1986 (2), 1987 (3), 1988 (2), 1989 (1). Total—70.
Hit three home runs in a game, June 18, 1975.
Hit for the cycle, May 13, 1980.
Led American League in slugging percentage with .566 in 1975 and .637 in 1979.
Named American League Player of the Year by THE SPORTING NEWS, 1975.
Named American League Most Valuable Player by Baseball Writers' Association of America, 1975.
Named American League Rookie of the Year by Baseball Writers' Association of America, 1975.
Named American League Rookie Player of the Year by THE SPORTING NEWS, 1975.
Named outfielder on THE SPORTING NEWS American League All-Star Team, 1975, 1978 and 1979.
Named outfielder on THE SPORTING NEWS American League All-Star fielding team, 1975 and 1978 through 1980.
Received reported $40,000 bonus to sign with Boston Red Sox, 1973.
Named outfielder on THE SPORTING NEWS College Baseball All-America Team, 1972 and 1973.

Year Club	League	Pos.	G.	AB.	R.	H.	2B.	3B.	HR.	RBI.	B.A.	PO.	A.	E.	F.A.
1973—Bristol	East.	OF	53	162	26	42	9	4	6	36	.259	79	3	5	.943
1974—Pawtucket	Int.	OF	124	415	65	117	19	2	21	68	.282	247	12	7	.974
1974—Boston	Amer.	OF	15	43	5	18	2	2	2	10	.419	18	2	0	1.000
1975—Boston	Amer.	OF	145	528	*103	175	*47	7	21	105	.331	404	11	7	.983
1976—Boston	Amer.	OF	132	507	76	159	32	8	10	65	.314	367	13	6	.984
1977—Boston†	Amer.	OF	129	497	81	129	29	5	18	76	.260	333	7	2	.994
1978—Boston	Amer.	OF	150	541	75	161	33	3	22	82	.298	408	11	7	.984
1979—Boston	Amer.	OF	147	531	116	177	42	1	39	122	*.333	381	10	5	.987
1980—Boston‡	Amer.	OF	110	415	67	125	32	3	12	61	.301	302	11	2	.994
1981—California	Amer.	OF	76	256	28	56	8	1	5	31	.219	176	4	4	.978
1982—California	Amer.	OF	138	472	89	141	38	1	21	86	.299	317	6	3	.991
1983—California	Amer.	OF	117	437	56	119	20	3	22	74	.272	274	8	2	.993
1984—California§	Amer.	OF	142	517	84	140	28	4	23	79	.271	321	12	6	.982
1985—Baltimore	Amer.	OF	124	448	59	118	12	1	23	68	.263	314	6	2	.994
1986—Baltimore x	Amer.	OF	112	397	67	114	13	1	23	67	.287	244	2	4	.984
1987—Baltimore y	Amer.	OF	111	396	49	100	24	0	23	60	.253	229	2	2	.991
1988—Balt. za-Det	Amer.	OF	114	391	46	96	14	1	25	56	.246	257	3	2	.992
1989—Detroit bc	Amer.	OF	117	353	44	85	11	1	11	46	.241	119	5	1	.992
Major League Totals—16 Years			1879	6729	1045	1913	385	42	300	1088	.284	4464	113	55	.988

Selected by New York Yankees' organization in 3rd round of free-agent draft, June 4, 1970.
Selected by Boston Red Sox' organization in 2nd round of free-agent draft, June 5, 1973.

†On disabled list, March 24 to May 6, 1977.

‡Traded with Pitcher Steve Renko to California Angels for Pitchers Frank Tanana and Jim Dorsey and Outfielder Joe Rudi, January 23, 1981.

§Granted free agency, November 8, 1984; signed by Baltimore Orioles, December 11, 1984. (Pitcher Donnie Moore selected from player compensation pool by California Angels, January 24, 1985.)
xOn disabled list, June 11 to June 27, 1986.
yOn disabled list, July 21 to August 5, 1987.
zOn disabled list, July 15 to August 12, 1988.
aTraded to Detroit Tigers for three players to be named later, August 31, 1988; Baltimore Orioles acquired Catcher Chris Hoiles and Pitchers Cesar Mejia and Robinson Garces to complete deal, September 9, 1988.
bOn disabled list, June 8 to June 23, 1989.
cGranted free agency, November 13, 1989; signed by San Diego Padres, December 6, 1989.

CHAMPIONSHIP SERIES RECORD

Holds American League Championship Series record for highest batting average, series (.611), 1982.
Shares Championship Series record for most hits, series (11), 1982.

Year	Club	League	Pos.	G.	AB.	R.	H.	2B.	3B.	HR.	RBI.	B.A.	PO.	A.	E.	F.A.
1975—Boston		Amer.	OF	3	11	1	4	1	0	0	3	.364	12	1	1	.929
1982—California		Amer.	OF	5	18	5	11	2	0	1	5	.611	16	0	1	.941
Championship Series Totals—2 Years				8	29	6	15	3	0	1	8	.517	28	1	2	.935

WORLD SERIES RECORD

Year	Club	League	Pos.	G.	AB.	R.	H.	2B.	3B.	HR.	RBI.	B.A.	PO.	A.	E.	F.A.
1975—Boston		Amer.	OF	7	25	3	7	1	0	1	5	.280	23	1	0	1.000

ALL-STAR GAME RECORD

Holds All-Star Game records for most grand slams, game (1), July 6, 1983; most runs batted in, inning (4), July 6, 1983, third inning.

Year	League	Pos.	AB.	R.	H.	2B.	3B.	HR.	RBI.	B.A.	PO.	A.	E.	F.A.
1975—American		PH-OF	2	0	0	0	0	0	0	.000	1	0	0	1.000
1976—American		OF	3	1	1	0	0	1	1	.333	0	0	0	1.000
1977—American		OF	1	1	0	0	0	0	0	.000	2	0	0	1.000
1978—American		OF	4	0	1	0	0	0	0	.250	3	0	0	1.000
1979—American		OF	1	1	1	0	0	1	2	1.000	0	0	0	.000
1980—American		OF	3	1	1	0	0	1	2	.333	2	0	0	1.000
1981—American		PH	1	0	1	0	0	0	1	1.000	0	0	0	.000
1982—American		OF	2	0	0	0	0	0	0	.000	0	0	0	.000
1983—American		OF	3	1	1	0	0	1	4	.333	1	0	0	1.000
All-Star Game Totals—9 Years			20	5	6	0	0	4	10	.300	9	0	0	1.000

BARRY STEPHEN LYONS

Born June 3, 1960, at Biloxi, Miss.
Height, 6.01. Weight, 205.
Throws and bats righthanded.
Attended Delta State University, Cleveland, Miss.

Led Texas League in grounding into double plays with 19 and tied for lead in game-winning RBIs with 16 in 1985.
Led Texas League catchers in errors with 19 in 1985.
Led Carolina League catchers in assists with 72 and fielding percentage with .989 in 1984.
Named Carolina League Player of the Year, 1984.

Year	Club	League	Pos.	G.	AB.	R.	H.	2B.	3B.	HR.	RBI.	B.A.	PO.	A.	E.	F.A.
1982—Shelby		S. Atl.	C-1B	45	164	23	46	12	0	4	46	.280	226	21	8	.969
1983—Lynchburg		Carol.	C	2	7	0	1	0	0	0	2	.143	21	4	0	1.000
1983—Columbia		S. Atl.	C-1B-OF	92	316	55	94	9	2	5	45	.297	387	33	17	.961
1984—Lynchburg		Carol.	C-1B-OF	115	412	59	130	17	3	12	87	.316	894	86	13	.987
1985—Jackson		Texas	C-1B	126	486	69	149	34	6	11	108	.307	834	65	23	.975
1986—New York		Nat.	C	6	9	1	0	0	0	0	2	.000	16	0	1	.941
1986—Tidewater†		Int.	1B-C	61	234	28	69	16	0	4	46	.295	423	25	6	.987
1987—New York		Nat.	C	53	130	15	33	4	1	4	24	.254	223	17	4	.984
1988—New York		Nat.	C-1B	50	91	5	21	7	1	0	11	.231	130	9	3	.979
1989—New York‡		Nat.	C	79	235	15	58	13	0	3	27	.247	463	29	10	.980
1989—Tidewater		Int.	C-1B	5	20	1	2	0	1	0	2	.100	43	5	1	.980
Major League Totals—4 Years				188	465	36	112	24	2	7	64	.241	832	55	18	.980

Selected by Detroit Tigers' organization in 25th round of free-agent draft, June 8, 1981.
Selected by New York Mets' organization in 15th round of free-agent draft, June 7, 1982.
†On disabled list, August 4, 1986 through remainder of season.
‡On disabled list, June 27 to July 25, 1989; included rehabilitation disability assignment to Tidewater, July 19 to July 25, 1989.

STEPHEN JOHN LYONS
(Steve)

Born June 3, 1960, at Tacoma, Wash.
Height, 6.03. Weight, 195.
Throws right and bats lefthanded.
Attended Oregon State University, Corvallis, Ore.

Major League stolen bases: 1985 (12), 1986 (4), 1987 (3), 1988 (1), 1989 (9). Total—29.
Led American League third basemen in double plays with 36 in 1988.
Led International League third basemen in putouts with 98, errors with 25 and total chances with 332 in 1984.

Year	Club	League	Pos.	G.	AB.	R.	H.	2B.	3B.	HR.	RBI.	B.A.	PO.	A.	E.	F.A.
1981—Winston-Salem		Carol.	OF-SS	64	252	43	61	9	3	6	40	.242	137	23	8	.952
1982—Bristol		East.	OF-SS	135	460	86	112	23	3	13	58	.243	275	11	9	.969

Year	Club	League	Pos.	G.	AB.	R.	H.	2B.	3B.	HR.	RBI.	B.A.	PO.	A.	E.	F.A.
1983—New Britain	East.	3-O-S-P	132	456	83	112	24	7	7	62	.246	145	207	17	.954
1984—Pawtucket	Int.	3B-OF-SS	131	444	80	119	21	2	17	62	.268	141	211	26	.931
1985—Boston	Amer.	OF-3B-SS	133	371	52	98	14	3	5	30	.264	253	6	7	.974
1986—Boston†-Chicago	Amer.	OF-3B-1B	101	247	30	56	9	3	1	20	.227	175	11	4	.979
1986—Buffalo	A. A.	3-S-O-1	20	74	18	22	5	1	3	8	.297	36	41	4	.951
1987—Chicago	Amer.	3B-OF-2B	76	193	26	54	11	1	1	19	.280	69	101	4	.977
1987—Hawaii	P. C.	O-2-3-S	47	167	26	48	11	0	2	16	.285	73	71	3	.980
1988—Chicago	Amer.	3-O-2-C-1	146	472	59	127	28	3	5	45	.269	128	243	29	.928
1989—Chicago	Amer.	1-O-C	140	443	51	117	21	3	2	50	.264	414	245	15	.978
Major League Totals—5 Years			596	1726	218	452	83	13	14	164	.262	1039	606	59	.965

Selected by Boston Red Sox' organization in 1st round (19th player selected) of free-agent draft, June 8, 1981.
†Traded to Chicago White Sox for Pitcher Tom Seaver, June 29, 1986.

PITCHING RECORD

Year	Club	League	G.	IP.	W.	L.	Pct.	H.	R.	ER.	SO.	BB.	ERA.
1983—New Britain	Eastern	3	3⅔	1	0	1.000	3	1	1	2	1	2.45

KEVIN CHRISTIAN MAAS

Born January 20, 1965, at Castro Valley, Calif.
Height, 6.03. Weight, 195.
Throws and bats lefthanded.
Attended University of California, Berkeley, Calif.
Brother of Jason Maas, outfielder in New York Yankees' organization.

Year	Club	League	Pos.	G.	AB.	R.	H.	2B.	3B.	HR.	RBI.	B.A.	PO.	A.	E.	F.A.
1986—Oneonta	NYP	1B	28	101	14	36	10	0	0	18	.356	222	19	1	.996
1987—Fort Lauderdale	Fla. St.	1B	116	439	77	122	28	4	11	73	.278	667	51	10	.986
1988—Prince William	Carol.	1B	29	108	24	32	7	0	12	35	.296	288	25	5	.984
1988—Albany	East.	1B	109	372	66	98	14	3	16	55	.263	902	73	12	.988
1989—Columbus†	Int.	OF	83	291	42	93	23	2	6	45	.320	78	3	3	.964

Selected by New York Yankees' organization in 22nd round of free-agent draft, June 2, 1986.
†On disabled list, April 19 to April 30 and July 27, 1989 through remainder of season.

ROBERT JOSEPH MacDONALD
(Rob)

Born April 27, 1965, at East Orange, N.J.
Height, 6.03. Weight, 200.
Throws and bats lefthanded.
Attended Rutgers University, New Brunswick, N.J.
Led South Atlantic League in games finished in relief with 48 in 1988.

Year	Club	League	G.	IP.	W.	L.	Pct.	H.	R.	ER.	SO.	BB.	ERA.
1987—St. Catharines	NYP	1	4	0	0	.000	8	4	2	4	0	4.50
1987—Myrtle Beach	S. Atlantic	10	20⅔	2	1	.667	24	18	13	12	7	5.66
1988—Myrtle Beach	S. Atlantic	52	53⅓	3	4	.429	42	13	10	43	18	1.69
1989—Knoxville	Southern	43	63	3	5	.375	52	27	23	58	23	3.29
1989—Syracuse	Int'national	12	16	1	0	1.000	16	10	10	12	6	5.63

Selected by Toronto Blue Jays' organization in 19th round of free-agent draft, June 2, 1987.

MICHAEL ANDREW MACFARLANE
(Mike)

Born April 12, 1964, at Stockton, Calif.
Height, 6.01. Weight, 200.
Throws and bats righthanded.
Attended University of Santa Clara, Santa Clara, Calif.

Year	Club	League	Pos.	G.	AB.	R.	H.	2B.	3B.	HR.	RBI.	B.A.	PO.	A.	E.	F.A.
1985—Memphis	South.	C	65	223	29	60	15	4	8	39	.269	295	24	9	.973
1986—Memphis†	South.	DH	40	141	26	34	7	2	12	29	.241	0	0	0	.000
1987—Omaha	A. A.	C	87	302	53	79	25	1	13	50	.262	408	37	6	.987
1987—Kansas City	Amer.	C	8	19	0	4	1	0	0	3	.211	29	2	0	1.000
1988—Kansas City	Amer.	C	70	211	25	56	15	0	4	26	.265	309	18	2	.994
1988—Omaha	A. A.	C	21	76	8	18	7	2	2	8	.237	85	5	1	.989
1989—Kansas City	Amer.	C	69	157	13	35	6	0	2	19	.223	249	17	1	.996
Major League Totals—3 Years			147	387	38	95	22	0	6	48	.245	587	37	3	.995

Selected by Kansas City Royals' organization in 4th round of free-agent draft, June 3, 1985.
†On disabled list, April 9 to July 9, 1986.

JULIO S. MACHADO

Born December 1, 1965, at Zulia, Venezuela.
Height, 5.09. Weight, 160.
Throws and bats righthanded.

Year	Club	League	G.	IP.	W.	L.	Pct.	H.	R.	ER.	SO.	BB.	ERA.
1985—Spartanburg	S. Atlantic	32	81⅓	4	5	.444	75	50	39	71	38	4.32
1986—Spartanburg	S. Atlantic	43	79⅔	2	5	.286	68	39	33	81	52	3.73
1987—Clearwater	Florida St.	7	34⅔	2	0	1.000	31	11	10	32	19	2.60

Year Club	League	G.	IP.	W.	L.	Pct.	H.	R.	ER.	SO.	BB.	ERA.
1987—Reading	Eastern	21	108⅓	4	5	.444	112	70	57	89	40	4.74
1988—Reading	Eastern	26	63	6	1	.857	69	41	38	52	34	5.43
1988—Clearwater†	Florida St.	13	36⅔	1	4	.200	34	13	12	45	14	2.95
1989—St. Lucie	Florida St.	4	10⅔	1	0	1.000	5	0	0	14	3	0.00
1989—Jackson	Texas	32	57	3	5	.375	42	23	18	67	27	2.84
1989—Tidewater	Int'national	14	29	1	2	.333	16	2	2	37	17	0.62
1989—New York	National	10	11	0	1	.000	9	4	4	14	3	3.27
Major League Totals—1 Year		10	11	0	1	.000	9	4	4	14	3	3.27

Signed as free agent by Philadelphia Phillies' organization, April 10, 1985.
†Released, March, 1989; signed by St. Lucie (New York Mets' organization), April, 1989.

SHANE LEE MACK

Born December 7, 1963, at Los Angeles, Calif.
Height, 6.00. Weight, 185.
Throws and bats righthanded.
Attended UCLA.

Major League stolen bases: 1987 (4), 1988 (5). Total—9.
Tied for Texas League lead in being hit by pitch with 7 in 1986.
Led Texas League outfielders in double plays with 4 in 1986.
Member of 1984 U.S. Olympic baseball team.
Named outfielder on THE SPORTING NEWS College Baseball All-America Team, 1984.

Year Club	League	Pos.	G.	AB.	R.	H.	2B.	3B.	HR.	RBI.	B.A.	PO.	A.	E.	F.A.
1985—Beaumont	Texas	OF-3B	125	430	59	112	23	3	6	55	.260	252	12	7	.974
1986—Beaumont	Texas	OF	115	452	61	127	26	3	15	68	.281	255	●14	8	.971
1986—Las Vegas	P. C.	OF	19	69	13	25	1	6	0	6	.362	43	0	2	.956
1987—Las Vegas	P. C.	OF	39	152	38	51	11	1	5	26	.336	97	3	1	.990
1987—San Diego	Nat.	OF	105	238	28	57	11	3	4	25	.239	159	1	3	.982
1988—Las Vegas	P. C.	OF	55	196	43	68	7	1	10	40	.347	116	7	3	.976
1988—San Diego	Nat.	OF	56	119	13	29	3	0	0	12	.244	110	4	2	.983
1989—Las Vegas†‡	P. C.	OF	24	80	10	18	3	1	1	8	.225	59	3	1	.984
Major League Totals—2 Years			161	357	41	86	14	3	4	37	.241	269	5	5	.982

Selected by Kansas City Royals' organization in 4th round of free-agent draft, June 8, 1981.
Selected by San Diego Padres' organization in 1st round (11th player selected) of free-agent draft, June 4, 1984.
†On San Diego disabled list, March 25 to May 4, 1989.
‡Drafted by Minnesota Twins, December 4, 1989.

MORRIS DeWAYNE MADDEN

Born August 31, 1960, at Laurens, S. C.
Height, 6.00. Weight, 165.
Throws and bats lefthanded.
Attended Spartanburg Methodist College, Spartanburg, S. C.

Year Club	League	G.	IP.	W.	L.	Pct.	H.	R.	ER.	SO.	BB.	ERA.
1979—Lethbridge	Pioneer	13	83	6	1	.857	62	44	27	106	45	2.93
1980—Vero Beach	Florida St.	27	171	11	9	.550	129	79	64	141	★127	3.37
1981—San Antonio	Texas	4	11	0	3	.000	22	17	17	6	14	13.91
1981—Vero Beach	Florida St.	21	146	6	12	.333	148	76	60	108	79	3.70
1982—San Antonio	Texas	4	19	1	1	.500	26	19	18	18	15	8.53
1982—Lodi†	California	12	72⅔	3	7	.300	67	32	21	47	36	2.60
1983—Vero Beach	Florida St.	16	46	2	4	.333	50	33	22	44	25	4.30
1983—San Antonio‡	Texas	27	72⅓	6	5	.545	77	49	44	60	59	5.47
1984—Tampa	Florida St.	29	132	6	9	.400	123	71	64	103	98	4.36
1985—Tampa	Florida St.	23	82⅓	6	8	.429	76	48	31	78	64	3.39
1985—Vermont§	Eastern	6	32⅓	1	3	.250	25	11	11	31	19	3.06
1986—Glens Falls	Eastern	35	91⅓	7	5	.583	87	52	41	64	55	4.04
1987—Toledo	Int'national	24	58⅓	4	2	.667	58	37	29	41	36	4.47
1987—Detroit x	American	2	1⅔	0	0	.000	4	3	3	0	3	16.20
1987—Vancouver	P. Coast	6	7⅓	0	0	.000	8	8	7	4	10	8.59
1988—Buffalo	Am. Assoc.	21	108⅔	5	6	.455	84	55	42	56	65	3.48
1988—Pittsburgh	National	5	5⅔	0	0	.000	5	0	0	3	7	0.00
1989—Buffalo	Am. Assoc.	26	130	12	8	.600	117	66	49	94	63	3.39
1989—Pittsburgh y	National	9	14	2	2	.500	17	14	11	6	13	7.07
American League Totals—1 Year		2	1⅔	0	0	.000	4	3	3	0	3	16.20
National League Totals—2 Years		14	19⅔	2	2	.500	22	14	11	9	20	5.03
Major League Totals—3 Years		16	21⅓	2	2	.500	26	17	14	9	23	5.91

Selected by Los Angeles Dodgers' organization in 24th round of free-agent draft, June 5, 1979.
†On disabled list, May 22 to July 4, 1982.
‡Drafted by Indianapolis (Cincinnati Reds' organization), December 6, 1983.
§Granted free agency, October 15, 1985; signed by Nashville (Detroit Tigers' organization), November 23, 1985.
xTraded to Pittsburgh Pirates' organization, August 12, 1987, completing deal in which Pittsburgh traded Third Baseman Jim Morrison to Detroit Tigers for Third Baseman Darnell Coles and a player to be named later, August 7, 1987.
yReleased, November 21, 1989.

—DID YOU KNOW—

That the Oakland Athletics were shut out the fewest times (5) while the Kansas City Royals led the majors in that category with 18 in 1989?

GREGORY ALAN MADDUX
(Greg)

Born April 14, 1966, at San Angelo, Tex.
Height, 6.00. Weight, 170.
Throws and bats righthanded.
Brother of Mike Maddux, pitcher with Philadelphia Phillies, 1986 through 1989.
Led National League in intentional bases on balls issued with 16 in 1988.
Led American Association in hit batsmen with 12 in 1986.
Led Appalachian League in hit batsmen with 8 and tied for lead in shutouts with 2 in 1984.
Tied for American Association lead in shutouts with 2 in both 1986 and 1987.

Year Club	League	G.	IP.	W.	L.	Pct.	H.	R.	ER.	SO.	BB.	ERA.
1984—Pikeville	Ap'lachian	14	85⅔	6	2	.750	63	35	25	62	41	2.63
1985—Peoria	Midland	27	186	13	9	.591	176	86	66	125	52	3.19
1986—Pittsfield	Eastern	8	62⅔	4	3	.571	49	22	19	35	15	2.69
1986—Iowa	Am. Assoc.	18	128⅓	10	1	*.909	127	49	43	65	30	3.02
1986—Chicago	National	6	31	2	4	.333	44	20	19	20	11	5.52
1987—Chicago	National	30	155⅔	6	14	.300	181	111	97	101	74	5.61
1987—Iowa	Am. Assoc.	4	27⅔	3	0	1.000	17	3	3	22	12	0.98
1988—Chicago	National	34	249	18	8	.692	230	97	88	140	81	3.18
1989—Chicago	National	35	238⅓	19	12	.613	222	90	78	135	82	2.95
Major League Totals—4 Years		105	674	45	38	.542	677	318	282	396	248	3.77

Selected by Chicago Cubs' organization in 2nd round of free-agent draft, June 4, 1984.

CHAMPIONSHIP SERIES RECORD

Shares Championship Series record for most earned runs allowed, series (11), 1989.
Holds National League Championship Series record for most runs allowed, series (12), 1989.

Year Club	League	G.	IP.	W.	L.	Pct.	H.	R.	ER.	SO.	BB.	ERA.
1989—Chicago	National	2	7⅓	0	1	.000	13	12	11	5	4	13.50

Appeared as pinch-runner for Chicago Cubs in 1989 Championship Series.

ALL-STAR GAME RECORD

Member of National League All-Star team in 1988; did not play.

MICHAEL AUSLEY MADDUX
(Mike)

Born August 27, 1961, at Dayton, O.
Height, 6.02. Weight, 180.
Throws and bats righthanded.
Attended University of Texas, El Paso, Tex.
Brother of Greg Maddux, pitcher with Chicago Cubs.
Major League saves: 1989 (1).

Year Club	League	G.	IP.	W.	L.	Pct.	H.	R.	ER.	SO.	BB.	ERA.
1982—Bend	Northwest	11	65⅓	3	6	.333	68	35	29	59	26	3.99
1983—Spartanburg	S. Atlantic	13	84⅓	4	6	.400	98	62	51	85	47	5.44
1983—Peninsula	Carolina	14	99⅓	8	4	.667	92	46	40	78	35	3.62
1983—Reading	Eastern	1	3	0	0	.000	4	2	2	2	1	6.00
1984—Reading	Eastern	20	116	3	●12	.200	143	82	65	77	49	5.04
1984—Portland	P. Coast	8	44⅔	2	4	.333	58	32	29	22	17	5.84
1985—Portland	P. Coast	27	166	9	12	.429	195	106	98	96	51	5.31
1986—Portland	P. Coast	12	84	5	2	.714	70	26	22	65	22	2.36
1986—Philadelphia	National	16	78	3	7	.300	88	56	47	44	34	5.42
1987—Maine	Int'national	18	103⅓	6	6	.500	116	58	50	71	26	4.35
1987—Philadelphia	National	7	17	2	0	1.000	17	5	5	15	5	2.65
1988—Philadelphia†	National	25	88⅔	4	3	.571	91	41	37	59	34	3.76
1988—Maine	Int'national	5	23⅔	0	2	.000	25	18	11	18	10	4.18
1989—Philadelphia	National	16	43⅔	1	3	.250	52	29	25	26	14	5.15
1989—Scranton/Wilkes-Barre‡	Int'national	19	123	7	7	.500	119	55	50	100	26	3.66
Major League Totals—4 Years		64	227⅓	10	13	.435	248	131	114	144	87	4.51

Selected by Cincinnati Reds' organization in 36th round of free-agent draft, June 5, 1979.
Selected by Philadelphia Phillies' organization in 5th round of free-agent draft, June 7, 1982.
†On disabled list, April 21 to June 1, 1988; included rehabilitation disability assignment to Maine, May 13 to May 22, 1988.
‡Released, November 20, 1989.

CHARLES SCOTT MADISON
(Scotti)

Born September 12, 1959, at Pensacola, Fla.
Height, 5.11. Weight, 185.
Throws right and bats left and righthanded.
Received bachelor of science degree in business administration from Vanderbilt University, Nashville, Tenn.
Major League stolen bases: 1988 (1).
Led American Association in slugging percentage with .590 in 1985.
Named catcher on THE SPORTING NEWS College Baseball All-America Team, 1980.

Year Club	League	Pos.	G.	AB.	R.	H.	2B.	3B.	HR.	RBI.	B.A.	PO.	A.	E.	F.A.
1980—Orlando	South.	C-1B-OF	81	282	31	65	9	4	6	32	.230	185	24	4	.981

Year Club	League	Pos.	G.	AB.	R.	H.	2B.	3B.	HR.	RBI.	B.A.	PO.	A.	E.	F.A.
1981—Visalia†	Calif.	*C-1B	133	459	109	157	*32	3	26	110	.342	542	66	11	*.982
1982—San Antonio‡........	Texas	3-C-2-O	88	294	39	69	11	2	7	35	.235	167	75	16	.938
1982—Albuquerque	P. C.	C	11	36	5	8	1	0	0	2	.222	6	0	0	1.000
1983—San Antonio..........	Texas	C-3B	80	259	54	79	11	4	11	57	.305	423	55	11	.978
1983—Albuquerque§	P. C.	C-3B	23	65	10	19	2	0	2	12	.292	103	18	7	.945
1984—Birmingham	South.	C-1-3-2	133	473	82	129	23	4	15	83	.273	773	109	18	.980
1985—Birmingham	South	C-1B-3B	37	121	28	39	8	1	5	25	.322	205	27	2	.991
1985—Nashville................	A. A.	C-3-1-O	86	317	59	108	23	4	16	54	*.341	352	74	11	.975
1985—Detroit...................	Amer.	C	6	11	0	0	0	0	0	1	.000	1	0	0	1.000
1986—Detroit x	Amer.	3B	2	7	0	0	0	0	0	1	.000	1	1	1	.667
1986—Nashville yz.........	A. A.	1-3-C-O	106	354	52	91	15	4	10	41	.257	425	95	10	.981
1987—Omaha...................	A. A.	3-1-C-O-2	125	454	68	123	31	2	22	83	.271	375	149	14	.974
1987—Kansas City..........	Amer.	1B-C	7	15	4	4	3	0	0	0	.267	28	3	3	.912
1988—Kansas City..........	Amer.	C-OF-1B	16	35	4	6	2	0	0	2	.171	23	1	0	1.000
1988—Omaha a	A. A.	O-1-C-3	36	104	14	25	4	3	2	12	.240	107	15	1	.992
1989—Nashville..............	A. A.	1B-OF-3B	79	266	26	71	14	0	6	38	.267	497	56	4	.993
1989—Cincinnati b..........	Nat.	3B	40	98	13	17	7	0	1	7	.173	19	44	0	1.000
American League Totals—4 Years			31	68	8	10	5	0	0	4	.147	53	5	4	.935
National League Totals—1 Year.............			40	98	13	17	7	0	1	7	.173	19	44	0	1.000
Major League Totals—5 Years...............			71	166	21	27	12	0	1	11	.163	72	49	4	.968

Selected by Cincinnati Reds' organization in 35th round of free-agent draft, June 8, 1976.
Selected by San Francisco Giants' organization in 10th round of free-agent draft, June 5, 1979.
Selected by Minnesota Twins' organization in 3rd round of free-agent draft, June 3, 1980.
†Traded with Pitcher Paul Voigt to Los Angeles Dodgers' organization for Pitcher Bobby Castillo and Outfielder Bobby Mitchell, January 7, 1982.
‡On disabled list, June 25 to July 16, 1982.
§Sold to Birmingham (Detroit Tigers' organization), March 19, 1984.
xOn disabled list, March 26 to April 29, 1986.
yOn suspended list, May 15 to May 17, 1986.
zGranted free agency, October 15, 1986; signed by Kansas City Royals' organization, November 14, 1986.
aGranted free agency, October 15, 1988; signed by Nashville (Cincinnati Reds' organization), January 4, 1989.
bGranted free agency, October 15, 1989.

ALEXANDER MADRID JR.
(Alex)

Born April 18, 1963, at Springerville, Ariz.
Height, 6.02. Weight, 200.
Throws and bats righthanded.
Attended Yavapai College, Prescott, Ariz.

Tied for Texas League lead in games started by pitchers with 27 and balks with 6 in 1986.

Year Club	League	G.	IP.	W.	L.	Pct.	H.	R.	ER.	SO.	BB.	ERA.
1984—Beloit†...	Midwest	22	118	6	7	.462	113	59	55	92	49	4.19
1985—Beloit...	Midwest	19	135⅔	8	5	.615	144	55	43	99	26	2.85
1985—Stockton...	California	8	59⅓	7	0	1.000	53	16	13	52	15	1.97
1986—El Paso..	Texas	27	158⅓	12	9	.571	*213	*119	*106	99	51	6.03
1987—Denver...	Am. Assoc.	27	99⅓	5	7	.417	114	64	59	50	31	5.35
1987—Milwaukee.......................................	American	3	5⅓	0	0	.000	11	9	9	1	1	15.19
1988—Denver‡...	Am. Assoc.	31	88⅔	5	2	.714	45	47	40	52	20	4.06
1988—Maine...	Int'national	2	11⅔	0	0	.000	10	3	3	9	0	2.31
1988—Philadelphia	National	5	16⅓	1	1	.500	15	5	5	2	6	2.76
1989—Scranton/Wilkes-Barre.................	Int'national	16	67	3	6	.333	64	37	36	51	30	4.84
1989—Philadelphia	National	6	24⅔	1	2	.333	32	16	15	13	14	5.47
American League Totals—1 Year......................		3	5⅓	0	0	.000	11	9	9	1	1	15.19
National League Totals—2 Years......................		11	41	2	3	.400	47	21	20	15	20	4.39
Major League Totals—3 Years............................		14	46⅓	2	3	.400	58	30	29	16	21	5.63

Selected by Chicago Cubs' organization in 2nd round of free-agent draft, January 12, 1982.
Selected by Cincinnati Reds' organization in secondary phase of free-agent draft, June 7, 1982.
Selected by Texas Rangers' organization in secondary phase of free-agent draft, January 11, 1983.
Selected by Milwaukee Brewers' organization in secondary phase of free-agent draft, June 6, 1983.
†On disabled list, June 15 to June 29, 1984.
‡Traded to Philadelphia Phillies for Outfielder Mike Young, August 24, 1988.

DAVID JOSEPH MAGADAN
(Dave)

Born September 30, 1962, at Tampa, Fla.
Height, 6.03. Weight, 195.
Throws right and bats lefthanded.
Attended University of Alabama, University, Ala.
Cousin of Lou Piniella, manager with Cincinnati Reds.

Major League stolen bases: 1989 (1).
Led Texas League in bases on balls received with 106 in 1985.
Led Carolina League in intentional bases on balls received with 10 in 1984.
Led International League third basemen in fielding percentage with .934, assists with 283 and double plays with 31 in 1986.
Led Texas League third basemen in putouts with 87, assists with 275 and total chances with 393 in 1985.
Named designated hitter on The Sporting News College Baseball All-America Team, 1983.

Year Club	League	Pos.	G.	AB.	R.	H.	2B.	3B.	HR.	RBI.	B.A.	PO.	A.	E.	F.A.
1983—Columbia	S. Atl.	1B	64	220	41	74	13	1	3	32	.336	520	37	7	.988
1984—Lynchburg†	Carol.	1B	112	371	78	130	22	4	0	62	*.350	896	64	16	.984
1985—Jackson	Texas	*3B-1B	134	466	84	144	22	0	0	76	.309	106	276	*31	.925
1986—Tidewater	Int.	3B-1B	133	473	68	147	33	6	1	64	.311	78	284	25	.935
1986—New York	Nat.	1B	10	18	3	8	0	0	0	3	.444	48	5	0	1.000
1987—New York‡	Nat.	3B-1B	85	192	21	61	13	1	3	24	.318	88	92	4	.978
1988—New York§	Nat.	1B-3B	112	314	39	87	15	0	1	35	.277	459	99	10	.982
1989—New York	Nat.	1B-3B	127	374	47	107	22	3	4	41	.286	587	89	7	.990
Major League Totals—4 Years			334	898	110	263	50	4	8	103	.293	1182	285	21	.986

Selected by Boston Red Sox' organization in 12th round of free-agent draft, June 3, 1980.
Selected by New York Mets' organization in 2nd round of free-agent draft, June 6, 1983.
†On disabled list, August 7 to September 10, 1984.
‡On disabled list, March 29 to April 17, 1987.
§On disabled list, May 5 to May 20, 1988.

CHAMPIONSHIP SERIES RECORD

Year Club	League	Pos.	G.	AB.	R.	H.	2B.	3B.	HR.	RBI.	B.A.	PO.	A.	E.	F.A.
1988—New York	Nat.	PH	3	3	0	0	0	0	0	0	.000	0	0	0	.000

JOSEPH DAVID MAGRANE
(Joe)

Born July 2, 1964, at Des Moines, Ia.
Height, 6.06. Weight, 230.
Throws left and bats righthanded.
Attended University of Arizona, Tucson, Ariz.

Tied for National League lead in hit batsmen with 10 in 1987.
Tied for American Association lead in shutouts with 2 and complete games with 8 in 1986.

Year Club	League	G.	IP.	W.	L.	Pct.	H.	R.	ER.	SO.	BB.	ERA.
1985—Johnson City	Ap'lachian	6	30	2	1	.667	15	4	2	31	11	0.60
1985—St. Petersburg	Florida St.	5	34⅔	3	1	.750	21	8	4	17	14	1.04
1986—Arkansas	Texas	13	89⅓	8	4	.667	66	29	24	66	31	2.42
1986—Louisville	Am. Assoc.	15	113⅓	9	6	.600	93	34	26	72	33	2.06
1987—Louisville	Am. Assoc.	3	23½	1	0	1.000	16	7	5	17	3	1.93
1987—St. Louis†	National	27	170⅓	9	7	.563	157	75	67	101	60	3.54
1988—St. Louis‡	National	24	165⅓	5	9	.357	133	57	40	100	51	*2.18
1988—Louisville	Am. Assoc.	4	20	2	1	.667	19	7	7	18	7	3.15
1989—St. Louis§	National	34	234⅔	18	9	.667	219	81	76	127	72	2.91
Major League Totals—3 Years		85	570⅓	32	25	.561	509	213	183	328	183	2.89

Selected by Pittsburgh Pirates' organization in 3rd round of free-agent draft, June 7, 1982.
Selected by St. Louis Cardinals' organization in 1st round (18th player selected) of free-agent draft, June 3, 1985.
†On disabled list, May 30 to June 18, 1987.
‡On disabled list, April 17 to June 11, 1988; included rehabilitation disability assignment to Louisville, May 23 to June 11, 1988.
§On disabled list, April 15 to April 30, 1989.

CHAMPIONSHIP SERIES RECORD

Year Club	League	G.	IP.	W.	L.	Pct.	H.	R.	ER.	SO.	BB.	ERA.
1987—St. Louis	National	1	4	0	0	.000	4	4	4	3	2	9.00

WORLD SERIES RECORD

Year Club	League	G.	IP.	W.	L.	Pct.	H.	R.	ER.	SO.	BB.	ERA.
1987—St. Louis	National	2	7⅓	0	1	.000	9	7	7	5	5	8.59

THOMAS JOSEPH MAGRANN
(Tom)

Born December 9, 1963, at Hollywood, Fla.
Height, 6.03. Weight, 180.
Throws and bats righthanded.
Attended Broward Community College, Fort Lauderdale, Fla.

Led Eastern League in putouts with 552, assists with 71, total chances with 632 and tied for lead in double plays with 8 in 1989.
Led Pioneer League catchers in double plays with 4 and passed balls with 16 in 1983.

Year Club	League	Pos.	G.	AB.	R.	H.	2B.	3B.	HR.	RBI.	B.A.	PO.	A.	E.	F.A.
1983—Helena	Pion.	C	43	127	17	28	4	0	2	15	.220	268	33	*18	.944
1984—Spartanburg	S. Atl.	C	68	203	32	45	4	3	2	28	.222	389	57	10	.978
1985—Peninsula†	Carol.	C-1B	31	51	2	8	2	0	0	0	.157	110	12	0	1.000
1986—Hagerstown	Carol.	C	74	210	36	64	14	2	4	32	.305	335	56	10	.975
1987—Miami	Fla. St.	C	35	99	16	18	3	0	2	6	.182	139	39	1	.952
1987—Charlotte	South.	C	57	180	23	38	6	1	3	19	.211	371	34	6	.985
1988—Charlotte	South.	C-1B-3B	20	60	6	17	0	1	1	2	.283	128	16	4	.973
1988—Rochester‡	Int.	C	7	17	1	5	2	0	0	0	.294	34	4	1	.974
1989—Canton-Akron	East.	C-1B	108	334	36	82	10	2	4	42	.246	565	75	10	.985
1989—Cleveland	Amer.	C	9	10	0	0	0	0	0	0	.000	30	2	0	1.000
Major League Totals—1 Year			9	10	0	0	0	0	0	0	.000	30	2	0	1.000

Signed as free agent by Philadelphia Phillies' organization, November 20, 1982.

RICHARD KEITH MAHLER

Name pronounced MAY-ler.

(Rick)

Born August 5, 1953, at Austin, Tex.
Height, 6.01. Weight, 202.
Throws and bats righthanded.
Attended Trinity University, San Antonio, Tex.
Brother of Mickey Mahler, pitcher with Atlanta Braves,
Pittsburgh Pirates, California Angels, Montreal Expos, Detroit Tigers,
Texas Rangers and Toronto Blue Jays, 1977 through 1982, 1985 and 1986.

Holds major league record for most game-winning runs batted in by pitcher, season (3), 1985.
Shares major league record for most years leading league in runs allowed (3).
Shares National League record for most shutouts in season openers, lifetime (3).
Major League saves: 1981 (2).
Led National League in hit batsmen with 10 in 1989.
Led National League pitchers in games started with 39 in 1985 and tied for lead with 39 in 1986.

Year Club	League	G.	IP.	W.	L.	Pct.	H.	R.	ER.	SO.	BB.	ERA.
1975—Kingsport	Ap'lachian	26	64	2	2	.500	52	23	21	58	26	2.95
1976—Greenwood	W. Carol.	31	105	6	6	.500	96	49	34	68	49	2.91
1977—Savannah	Southern	17	86	6	2	.750	71	31	22	53	38	2.30
1977—Richmond	Int'national	14	40	0	2	.000	45	29	27	25	23	6.08
1978—Richmond	Int'national	32	126	9	5	.643	130	65	55	66	53	3.93
1979—Richmond	Int'national	24	54	4	6	.400	46	26	20	40	18	3.33
1979—Atlanta	National	15	22	0	0	.000	28	16	15	12	11	6.14
1980—Atlanta	Int'national	29	188	12	6	.667	172	68	54	101	80	2.59
1980—Atlanta	National	2	4	0	0	.000	2	1	1	1	0	2.25
1981—Atlanta	National	34	112	8	6	.571	109	41	35	54	43	2.81
1982—Atlanta	National	39	205⅓	9	10	.474	213	105	96	105	62	4.21
1983—Atlanta	National	10	14⅓	0	0	.000	16	8	8	7	9	5.02
1983—Richmond	In'national	24	162⅔	12	7	.632	165	102	89	103	85	4.92
1984—Atlanta	National	38	222	13	10	.565	209	86	77	106	62	3.12
1985—Atlanta	National	39	266⅔	17	15	.531	★272	116	103	107	79	3.48
1986—Atlanta	National	39	237⅔	14	★18	.438	★283	★139	★129	137	95	4.88
1987—Atlanta	National	39	197	8	13	.381	212	118	109	95	85	4.98
1988—Atlanta†	National	39	249	9	16	.360	★279	★125	★102	131	42	3.69
1989—Cincinnati	National	40	220⅔	9	13	.409	★242	★113	94	102	51	3.83
Major League Totals—11 Years		334	1750⅔	87	101	.463	1865	868	769	857	539	3.95

Signed as free agent by Atlanta Braves' organization, June 16, 1975.
†Granted free agency, November 4, 1988; signed by Cincinnati Reds, December 2, 1988.

CHAMPIONSHIP SERIES RECORD

Year Club	League	G.	IP.	W.	L.	Pct.	H.	R.	ER.	SO.	BB.	ERA.
1982—Atlanta	National	1	1⅔	0	0	.000	3	0	0	0	2	0.00

CANDIDO MALDONADO (GUADARRAMA)

(Candy)

Born September 5, 1960, at Humacao, Puerto Rico.
Height, 6.00. Weight, 195.
Throws and bats righthanded.

Shares major league record for most sacrifice flies, game (3), August 29, 1987.
Major League stolen bases: 1985 (1), 1986 (4), 1987 (8), 1988 (6), 1989 (4). Total—23.
Hit for the cycle, May 4, 1987.
Led California League in total bases with 247 in 1980.
Tied for Pioneer League lead in sacrifice flies with 6 in 1978.
Named California League co-Most Valuable Player, 1980.

Year Club	League	Pos.	G.	AB.	R.	H.	2B.	3B.	HR.	RBI.	B.A.	PO.	A.	E.	F.A.
1978—Lethbridge	Pion.	OF	57	210	45	61	15	5	12	48	.290	112	6	8	.937
1979—Clinton	Midw.	OF	50	158	25	37	13	1	2	26	.234	81	5	2	.977
1979—Lethbridge	Pion.	OF	59	234	42	70	★20	3	5	33	.299	81	5	4	.956
1980—Lodi†	Calif.	OF	121	456	75	139	27	3	25	★102	.305	211	13	11	.953
1981—Albuquerque	P. C.	OF	126	460	96	154	40	9	21	104	.335	221	21	8	.968
1981—Los Angeles	Nat.	OF	11	12	0	1	0	0	0	0	.083	8	0	0	1.000
1982—Albuquerque	P. C.	OF	138	541	91	163	28	6	24	96	.301	303	15	10	.970
1982—Los Angeles	Nat.	OF	6	4	0	0	0	0	0	0	.000	5	0	0	1.000
1983—Los Angeles	Nat.	OF	42	62	5	12	1	1	1	6	.194	26	0	0	1.000
1983—Albuquerque	P. C.	OF-3B	38	144	23	46	6	1	4	20	.319	66	11	4	.951
1984—Los Angeles	Nat.	OF-3B	116	254	25	68	14	0	5	28	.268	124	5	8	.942
1985—Los Angeles‡	Nat.	OF	121	213	20	48	7	1	5	19	.225	121	6	2	.984
1986—San Francisco	Nat.	OF-3B	133	405	49	102	31	3	18	85	.252	161	11	3	.983
1987—San Francisco§	Nat.	OF	118	442	69	129	28	4	20	85	.292	176	7	5	.973
1988—San Francisco	Nat.	OF	142	499	53	127	23	1	12	68	.255	251	5	10	.962
1989—San Francisco x	Nat.	OF	129	345	39	75	23	0	9	41	.217	181	6	5	.974
Major League Totals—9 Years			818	2236	260	562	127	10	70	332	.251	1053	40	33	.971

Signed as free agent by Los Angeles Dodgers' organization, June 6, 1978.
†On disabled list, August 16 to September 16, 1980.
‡Traded to San Francisco Giants for Catcher Alex Trevino, December 11, 1985.
§On disabled list, June 28 to August 7, 1987.
xGranted free agency, November 13, 1989; signed by Cleveland Indians, November 28, 1989.

CHAMPIONSHIP SERIES RECORD

Year Club	League	Pos.	G.	AB.	R.	H.	2B.	3B.	HR.	RBI.	B.A.	PO.	A.	E.	F.A.
1983—Los Angeles	Nat.	PH	2	2	0	0	0	0	0	0	.000	0	0	0	.000
1985—Los Angeles	Nat.	OF-PH	4	7	0	1	0	0	0	1	.143	4	0	1	.800
1987—San Francisco	Nat.	OF	5	19	2	4	1	0	0	2	.211	7	0	0	1.000
1989—San Francisco	Nat.	PH-OF	3	3	1	0	0	0	0	1	.000	2	0	0	1.000
Championship Series Totals—4 Years			14	31	3	5	1	0	0	4	.161	13	0	1	.929

WORLD SERIES RECORD

Year Club	League	Pos.	G.	AB.	R.	H.	2B.	3B.	HR.	RBI.	B.A.	PO.	A.	E.	F.A.
1989—San Francisco	Nat.	OF-PH	4	11	1	1	0	1	0	0	.091	5	0	0	1.000

CARLOS CESAR MALDONADO

Born October 18, 1966, at Chepo, Panama.
Height, 6.02. Weight, 175.
Throws right and bats left and righthanded.

Year Club	League	G.	IP.	W.	L.	Pct.	H.	R.	ER.	SO.	BB.	ERA.
1986—Sarasota Royals	Gulf Coast	10	34⅓	0	2	.000	29	10	7	16	10	1.83
1987—Sarasota Royals	Gulf Coast	20	58	5	1	.833	32	18	16	56	19	2.48
1987—Appleton	Midwest	2	2⅓	0	0	.000	4	3	3	4	3	11.57
1988—Baseball City	Florida St.	16	52⅔	1	5	.167	46	35	31	44	39	5.30
1989—Baseball City†	Florida St.	28	76⅔	11	3	.786	47	14	10	66	24	1.17

Signed as free agent by Kansas City Royals' organization, April 28, 1986.
†On Appleton disabled list, April 7 to May 12, 1989.

CHARLES RAY MALONE JR.
(Chuck)

Born July 8, 1965, at Harrisburg, Ark.
Height, 6.07. Weight, 250.
Throws and bats righthanded.
Attended Arkansas State University, State University, Ark.,
and Three Rivers Community College, Poplar Bluff, Mo.

Year Club	League	G.	IP.	W.	L.	Pct.	H.	R.	ER.	SO.	BB.	ERA.
1986—Bend	Northwest	21	54⅔	2	6	.250	47	38	31	60	50	5.10
1987—Clearwater	Florida St.	34	120	6	8	.429	55	52	15	49	49	3.90
1988—Reading	Eastern	22	126⅔	12	7	.632	107	63	53	117	*88	3.77
1988—Maine	Int'national	6	27⅔	1	4	.200	28	27	21	38	24	6.83
1989—Reading	Eastern	33	106	5	7	.417	64	61	49	107	106	4.16

Selected by Philadelphia Phillies' organization in 5th round of free-agent draft, January 14, 1986.

KELLY JOHN MANN

Born August 17, 1967, at Santa Monica, Calif.
Height, 6.03. Weight, 215.
Throws and bats righthanded.
Tied for New York-Pennsylvania League lead in double plays by catchers with 7 in 1986.

Year Club	League	Pos.	G.	AB.	R.	H.	2B.	3B.	HR.	RBI.	B.A.	PO.	A.	E.	F.A.
1985—Wytheville	Appal.	C	26	75	6	15	3	0	1	10	.200	118	11	5	.963
1986—Geneva	NYP	C	60	191	17	37	1	0	2	15	.194	419	49	8	.983
1986—Peoria	Midw.	C	3	13	4	6	2	0	0	4	.462	26	1	1	.964
1987—Peoria	Midw.	C	95	287	24	73	16	1	4	45	.254	582	63	9	.986
1988—Winston-Salem	Carol.	C	94	307	32	84	11	0	8	40	.274	668	52	13	.982
1988—Pittsfield	East.	C	22	51	7	10	3	0	0	3	.196	95	20	4	.966
1989—Charlotte†	South.	C-1B	117	345	37	85	14	1	8	56	.246	612	84	9	.987
1989—Atlanta	Nat.	C	7	24	1	5	2	0	0	1	.208	48	5	0	1.000
Major League Totals—1 Year			7	24	1	5	2	0	0	1	.208	48	5	0	1.000

Selected by Chicago Cubs' organization in 20th round of free-agent draft, June 3, 1985.
†Traded with Pitcher Pat Gomez to Atlanta Braves, September 1, 1989, completing deal in which Atlanta traded Pitcher Paul Assenmacher to Chicago Cubs for two players to be named later, August 24, 1989.

RAMON MANON

Born January 20, 1968, at Santo Domingo, Dominican Republic.
Height, 6.00. Weight, 150.
Throws and bats righthanded.

Year Club	League	G.	IP.	W.	L.	Pct.	H.	R.	ER.	SO.	BB.	ERA.
1986—Sarasota Yankees	Gulf Coast	11	28	0	4	.000	31	22	16	13	22	5.14
1987—Prince William	Carolina	23	39⅓	2	3	.400	45	36	32	28	41	7.32
1988—Fort Lauderdale†	Florida St.	4	22⅓	2	0	1.000	13	5	5	13	12	2.01
1989—Fort Lauderdale‡	Florida St.	22	121⅓	7	9	.438	91	62	48	100	53	3.53

Signed as free agent by New York Yankees' organization, October 18, 1985.
†On disabled list, June 22, 1988 through remainder of season.
‡Drafted by Texas Rangers, December 4, 1989.

REYES FRED ELOY MANRIQUE
(Fred)

Name pronounced Man-ree-KEE.
Born November 5, 1961, at Bolivar, Venezuela.
Height, 6.01. Weight, 175.
Throws and bats righthanded.

Major League stolen bases: 1986 (1), 1987 (5), 1988 (6), 1989 (4). Total—16.
Led American Association in grounding into double plays with 19 in 1986.
Led American Association shortstops in errors with 25 and double plays with 86 in 1986.
Led International League second basemen in errors with 22 in 1983 and 24 in 1984.

Year	Club	League	Pos.	G.	AB.	R.	H.	2B.	3B.	HR.	RBI.	B.A.	PO.	A.	E.	F.A.
1979—Dunedin	Fla. St.	SS	5	15	0	2	0	0	0	0	.133	4	7	3	.786
1979—Medicine Hat	Pion.	SS	66	270	47	81	8	●10	2	30	.300	103	208	★37	.894
1980—Kinston	Carol.	SS-OF	111	390	49	108	9	5	7	50	.277	120	192	37	.894
1981—Knoxville†	South.	SS	115	469	62	131	15	6	5	42	.279	161	330	45	.916
1981—Toronto	Amer.	SS-3B	14	28	1	4	0	0	0	1	.143	10	27	3	.925
1982—Syracuse‡	Int.	2B-3B-SS	103	362	41	91	9	2	4	37	.251	186	255	24	.948
1983—Syracuse	Int.	2-S-3-O	128	485	55	130	22	8	10	50	.268	211	351	36	.940
1984—Syracuse	Int.	2B-SS-3B	129	517	63	146	15	5	6	45	.282	233	389	28	.957
1984—Toronto§	Amer.	2B	10	9	0	3	0	0	0	1	.333	5	10	1	.938
1985—Indianapolis	A. A.	3B-SS-2B	123	409	46	98	21	5	8	37	.240	126	249	19	.952
1985—Montreal x	Nat.	2B-SS-3B	9	13	5	4	1	1	1	1	.308	5	10	0	1.000
1986—Louisville	A. A.	SS-2B	133	520	79	148	19	6	9	51	.285	208	421	26	.960
1986—St. Louis y	Nat.	3B-2B	13	17	2	3	0	0	1	1	.176	1	3	0	1.000
1987—Chicago	Amer.	2B-SS	115	298	30	77	13	3	4	29	.258	176	286	7	.985
1988—Chicago	Amer.	2B-SS	140	345	43	81	10	6	5	37	.235	241	343	13	.978
1989—Chicago z-Texas	Amer.	2B-SS-3B	119	378	46	111	25	1	4	52	.294	177	250	21	.953
American League Totals—5 Years			398	1058	120	276	48	10	13	120	.261	609	916	45	.971
National League Totals—2 Years			22	30	7	7	1	1	2	2	.233	6	13	0	1.000
Major League Totals—7 Years			420	1088	127	283	49	11	15	122	.260	615	929	45	.972

Signed as free agent by Toronto Blue Jays' organization, November 24, 1978.
†On disabled list, April 9 to April 19, 1981.
‡On disabled list, June 27 to July 12, 1982.
§Sold to Montreal Expos, April 7, 1985.
xTraded to St. Louis Cardinals for Catcher Tom Nieto, March 31, 1986.
yTraded to Chicago White Sox for Pitcher Bill Dawley, December 22, 1986.
zTraded to Outfielder Harold Baines to Texas Rangers for Shortstop Scott Fletcher, Outfielder Sammy Sosa and Pitcher Wilson Alvarez, July 29, 1989.

JEFFREY PAUL MANTO
(Jeff)

Born August 23, 1964, at Bristol, Pa.
Height, 6.03. Weight, 210.
Throws and bats righthanded.
Attended Temple University, Philadelphia, Pa.

Led Texas League in grounding into double plays with 17 in 1988.
Led Pacific Coast League third basemen in assists with 265, fielding percentage with .943 and double plays with 22 in 1989.
Led California League third basemen in assists with 245 and total chances with 365 in 1987.
Named Texas League Most Valuable Player, 1988.

Year	Club	League	Pos.	G.	AB.	R.	H.	2B.	3B.	HR.	RBI.	B.A.	PO.	A.	E.	F.A.
1985—Quad Cities	Midw.	OF-3B	74	233	34	46	5	2	11	34	.197	87	8	3	.969
1986—Quad Cities†	Midw.	3B	73	239	31	59	13	0	8	49	.247	48	114	28	.853
1987—Palm Springs	Calif.	3B-1B	112	375	61	96	21	4	7	63	.256	93	246	37	.902
1988—Midland	Texas	●3B-2B-1B	120	408	88	123	23	3	24	101	.301	82	208	●32	.901
1989—Edmonton	P. C.	3B-1B	127	408	89	113	25	3	23	67	.277	140	266	21	.951

Selected by New York Yankees' organization in 35th round of free-agent draft, June 7, 1982.
Selected by California Angels' organization in 14th round of free-agent draft, June 3, 1985.
†On disabled list, July 16, 1986 through remainder of season.

KIRT DEAN MANWARING

Born July 15, 1965, at Elmira, N. Y.
Height, 5.11. Weight, 185.
Throws and bats righthanded.
Attended Coastal Carolina College, Conway, S. C.

Major League stolen bases: 1989 (2).
Led Texas League catchers in double plays with 8 and total chances with 688 in 1987.

Year	Club	League	Pos.	G.	AB.	R.	H.	2B.	3B.	HR.	RBI.	B.A.	PO.	A.	E.	F.A.
1986—Clinton	Midw.	C	49	147	18	36	7	1	2	16	.245	243	31	5	.982
1987—Shreveport	Texas	C	98	307	27	82	13	2	2	22	.267	603	★81	4	.994
1987—San Francisco	Nat.	C	6	7	0	1	0	0	0	0	.143	9	1	1	.909
1988—Phoenix	P. C.	C	81	273	29	77	12	2	2	35	.282	411	51	6	.987

Year Club League	Pos.	G.	AB.	R.	H.	2B.	3B.	HR.	RBI.	B.A.	PO.	A.	E.	F.A.
1988—San Francisco ...... Nat.	C	40	116	12	29	7	0	1	15	.250	162	24	4	.979
1989—San Francisco† .... Nat.	C	85	200	14	42	4	2	0	18	.210	289	32	6	.982
Major League Totals—3 Years		131	323	26	72	11	2	1	33	.223	460	57	11	.979

Selected by Boston Red Sox' organization in 12th round of free-agent draft, June 6, 1983.
Selected by San Francisco Giants' organization in 2nd round of free-agent draft, June 2, 1986.
†On disabled list, August 31 to September 15, 1989.

CHAMPIONSHIP SERIES RECORD

Year Club League	Pos.	G.	AB.	R.	H.	2B.	3B.	HR.	RBI.	B.A.	PO.	A.	E.	F.A.
1989—San Francisco ...... Nat.	PH-C	3	2	0	0	0	0	0	0	.000	5	0	0	1.000

WORLD SERIES RECORD

Year Club League	Pos.	G.	AB.	R.	H.	2B.	3B.	HR.	RBI.	B.A.	PO.	A.	E.	F.A.
1989—San Francisco ...... Nat.	C	1	1	1	1	1	0	0	0	1.000	0	0	0	.000

JOSIAS MANZANILLO

Born October 16, 1967, at San Pedro de Macoris, D. R.
Height, 6.00. Weight, 190.
Throws and bats righthanded.

Pitched 3-0 no-hit victory against Reading, July 12, 1989 (second game).
Led Eastern League pitchers in wild pitches with 16 and tied for lead in games started with 26 and intentional bases on balls issued with 7 in 1989.

Year Club	League	G.	IP.	W.	L.	Pct.	H.	R.	ER.	SO.	BB.	ERA.
1983—Elmira..............................	NYP	12	38⅓	1	5	.667	52	44	34	19	20	7.98
1984—Elmira..............................	NYP	14	25⅔	2	3	.400	27	24	15	15	26	5.26
1985—Greensboro....................	S. Atlantic	7	12	1	1	.500	12	13	13	10	18	9.75
1985—Elmira..............................	NYP	19	39⅔	2	4	.333	36	19	17	43	36	3.86
1986—Winter Haven................	Florida St.	23	142⅔	13	5	.722	110	51	36	102	81	2.27
1987—New Britain†..................	Eastern	2	10	2	0	1.000	8	5	5	12	8	4.50
1988—New Britain‡..................	Eastern					(Did not play)						
1989—New Britain....................	Eastern	26	147⅔	9	10	.474	129	78	60	93	85	3.66

Signed as free agent by Boston Red Sox' organization, January 10, 1983.
†On disabled list, June 8, 1987 through remainder of season.
‡On disabled list, April 8, 1988 through entire season.

CHRISTOPHER ROBERT MARCHOK
(Chris)

Born December 25, 1964, at Bristol, Pa.
Height, 6.02. Weight, 190.
Throws and bats lefthanded.
Received degree from Harvard University, Cambridge, Mass.

Year Club	League	G.	IP.	W.	L.	Pct.	H.	R.	ER.	SO.	BB.	ERA.
1987—Jamestown......................	NYP	18	48⅓	2	3	.400	43	26	13	47	17	2.42
1988—Rockford........................	Midwest	33	68⅔	2	0	1.000	57	31	23	43	28	3.01
1989—Jacksonville....................	Southern	64	76	6	6	.500	40	25	16	61	39	1.89

Selected by Montreal Expos' organization in 12th round of free-agent draft, June 2, 1987.

ISIDRO MARQUEZ (ESPINOZA)

Born May 15, 1965, at Navojoa, Sonora, Mexico.
Height, 6.03. Weight, 190.
Throws and bats righthanded.

Year Club	League	G.	IP.	W.	L.	Pct.	H.	R.	ER.	SO.	BB.	ERA.
1985—Tampico............................	Mexican	13	27⅓	0	0	.000	28	13	12	17	14	3.90
1986—San Luis..........................	Mexican	25	92	3	2	.600	96	71	60	74	69	5.87
1987—San Luis..........................	Mexican	1	4⅓	0	0	.000	5	2	1	1	5	4.15
1988—San Luis†........................	Mexican	10	72	6	3	.667	54	22	18	56	27	2.25
1988—Bakersfield......................	California	20	125⅓	8	4	.667	114	54	43	106	77	3.09
1989—Bakersfield......................	California	17	36	6	0	1.000	21	5	3	44	11	0.75
1989—San Antonio....................	Texas	39	62⅓	1	4	.200	61	33	30	52	34	4.33

Signed as free agent by Tampico (Mexican League), March 8, 1985.
†Sold to Bakersfield (Los Angeles Dodgers' organization), May 13, 1988.

MICHAEL ALLEN MARSHALL
(Mike)

Born January 12, 1960, at Libertyville, Ill.
Height, 6.05. Weight, 233.
Throws and bats righthanded.

Major League stolen bases: 1982 (2), 1983 (7), 1984 (4), 1985 (3), 1986 (4), 1988 (4), 1989 (2). Total—26.
Led California League in total bases with 301 in 1979.
Led Pacific Coast League first basemen in double plays with 136 in 1981.
Led Texas League first basemen in double plays with 120 in 1980.
Named Minor League Player of the Year by THE SPORTING NEWS, 1981.
Named Pacific Coast League Most Valuable Player, 1981.
Named California League co-Most Valuable Player, 1979.

Year Club	League	Pos.	G.	AB.	R.	H.	2B.	3B.	HR.	RBI.	B.A.	PO.	A.	E.	F.A.
1978—Lethbridge	Pion.	1B-OF	65	256	48	83	15	2	12	70	.324	308	16	7	.979
1979—Lodi	Calif.	1B	137	525	101	*186	*37	3	24	116	*.354	1173	71	20	.984
1980—San Antonio	Texas	1B	134	470	95	151	21	6	16	82	.321	*1157	64	●16	.987
1981—Albuquerque	P. C.	1B	128	467	*114	174	25	7	*34	*137	*.373	1127	54	9	.992
1981—Los Angeles	Nat.	1B-3B-OF	14	25	2	5	3	0	0	1	.200	14	2	0	1.000
1982—Albuquerque	P. C.	OF-1B-3B	66	255	74	99	20	1	14	58	.388	113	3	4	.966
1982—Los Angeles	Nat.	OF-1B	49	95	10	23	3	0	5	9	.242	122	5	2	.984
1983—Los Angeles	Nat.	OF-1B	140	465	47	132	17	1	17	65	.284	395	21	6	.986
1984—Los Angeles†	Nat.	OF-1B	134	495	68	127	27	0	21	65	.257	331	17	5	.986
1985—Los Angeles‡	Nat.	OF-1B	135	518	72	152	27	2	28	95	.293	265	12	4	.986
1986—Los Angeles§	Nat.	OF	103	330	47	77	11	0	19	53	.233	149	8	6	.963
1987—Los Angeles x	Nat.	OF	104	402	45	118	19	0	16	72	.294	147	4	2	.987
1988—Los Angeles y	Nat.	OF-1B	144	542	63	150	27	2	20	82	.277	605	49	7	.989
1989—Los Angeles za	Nat.	OF	105	377	41	98	21	1	11	42	.260	179	2	4	.978
Major League Totals—9 Years			928	3249	395	882	155	6	137	484	.271	2207	120	36	.985

Selected by Los Angeles Dodgers' organization in 6th round of free-agent draft, June 6, 1978.

†On disabled list, May 13 to June 3, 1984.

‡On disabled list, June 20 to July 18, 1985.

§On disabled list, July 20 to August 4, 1986.

xOn disabled list, May 6 to May 29 and August 21 to September 5, 1987.

yGranted free agency, November 4, 1988; re-signed by Dodgers, November 13, 1988.

zOn disabled list, May 31 to July 1, 1989.

aTraded with Pitcher Alejandro Pena to New York Mets for Outfielder Juan Samuel, December 20, 1989.

DIVISION SERIES RECORD

Year Club	League	Pos.	G.	AB.	R.	H.	2B.	3B.	HR.	RBI.	B.A.	PO.	A.	E.	F.A.
1981—Los Angeles	Nat.	PH	1	1	0	0	0	0	0	0	.000	0	0	0	.000

CHAMPIONSHIP SERIES RECORD

Shares National League Championship Series record for most at-bats, series (30), 1988.

Year Club	League	Pos.	G.	AB.	R.	H.	2B.	3B.	HR.	RBI.	B.A.	PO.	A.	E.	F.A.
1983—Los Angeles	Nat.	1B-OF	4	15	1	2	1	0	1	2	.133	22	2	0	1.000
1985—Los Angeles	Nat.	OF	6	23	1	5	2	0	1	3	.217	8	0	0	1.000
1988—Los Angeles	Nat.	OF	7	30	3	7	1	1	0	5	.233	14	0	0	1.000
Championship Series Totals—3 Years			17	68	5	14	4	1	2	10	.206	44	2	0	1.000

WORLD SERIES RECORD

Year Club	League	Pos.	G.	AB.	R.	H.	2B.	3B.	HR.	RBI.	B.A.	PO.	A.	E.	F.A.
1988—Los Angeles	Nat.	OF	5	13	2	3	0	1	1	3	.231	6	0	0	1.000

ALL-STAR GAME RECORD

Member of National League All-Star Team in 1984; did not play.

CARLOS ALBERTO MARTINEZ

Born August 11, 1965, at La Guaira, Venezuela.
Height, 6.05. Weight, 175.
Throws and bats righthanded.

Major League stolen bases: 1988 (1), 1989 (4). Total—5.

Year Club	League	Pos.	G.	AB.	R.	H.	2D.	3B.	HR.	RBI	B.A.	PO.	A.	E.	F.A.
1984—Sara. Yankees	Gulf C.	SS	31	91	9	14	1	1	0	4	.154	53	103	14	.918
1985—Fort Lauderdale	Fla. St.	SS	93	311	39	77	15	7	6	44	.248	123	254	25	.938
1986—Fort Lauderdale†	Fla. St.	SS	5	16	1	1	0	0	0	0	.063	7	18	0	1.000
1986—Albany‡	East.	SS-3B	69	253	34	70	18	2	8	39	.277	120	161	32	.898
1986—Buffalo	A. A.	SS-3B	17	54	6	16	1	0	2	6	.296	24	20	5	.898
1987—Birmingham	South.	3B	9	30	2	7	1	0	0	0	.233	5	17	2	.917
1987—Hawaii	P. C.	OF-3B-SS	83	304	32	75	15	1	3	36	.247	109	91	18	.917
1988—Birmingham	South.	OF-3B-SS	133	498	67	138	22	3	14	73	.277	196	139	20	.944
1988—Chicago	Amer.	3B	17	55	5	9	1	0	0	0	.164	7	33	4	.909
1989—Vancouver	P. C.	1B	18	64	12	25	3	1	2	9	.391	178	10	1	.995
1989—Chicago§	Amer.	3B-1B-OF	109	350	44	105	22	0	5	32	.300	283	134	20	.954
1989—South Bend	Midw.	3B	3	11	2	6	3	0	0	3	.545	0	9	3	.750
Major League Totals—2 Years			126	405	49	114	23	0	5	32	.281	290	167	24	.950

Signed as free agent by New York Yankees' organization, November 17, 1983.

†On disabled list, April 11 to May 1, 1986.

‡Traded with Catcher Ron Hassey and a player to be named later to Chicago White Sox for Catcher Joel Skinner, Infielder Wayne Tolleson and Outfielder-Designated Hitter Ron Kittle, July 30, 1986; New York Yankees traded Catcher Bill Lindsey to Chicago organization to complete deal, December 24, 1986.

§On disabled list, June 22 to July 13, 1989; included rehabilitation disability assignment to South Bend, July 8 to July 12, 1989.

CARMELO MARTINEZ (SALGADO)

Born July 28, 1960, at Dorado, Puerto Rico.
Height, 6.02. Weight, 220.
Throws and bats righthanded.
Attended Central College of Bayamon, Bayamon, Puerto Rico.
Cousin of Edgar Martinez, third baseman in Seattle Mariners' organization.

Shares major league record by hitting home run in first major league at-bat, August 22, 1983.
Major League stolen bases: 1984 (1), 1986 (1), 1987 (5), 1988 (1). Total—8.
Tied for National League lead in sacrifice flies with 10 in 1984.
Led American Association first basemen in total chances with 1,283 and tied for lead in double plays with 99 in 1983.
Led Texas League first basemen in putouts with 1,087, total chances with 1,180 and double plays with 102 in 1982.

Year Club	League	Pos.	G.	AB.	R.	H.	2B.	3B.	HR.	RBI.	B.A.	PO.	A.	E.	F.A.
1979—Sarasota Cubs	Gulf C.	OF-1B	40	143	18	29	4	0	1	23	.203	139	9	6	.961
1980—Quad Cities	Midw.	O-1-3-2-S	128	460	65	118	23	0	12	64	.257	433	99	13	.976
1981—Midland	Texas	3-O-2-1	116	392	65	116	22	1	21	84	.296	61	80	24	.855
1982—Midland	Texas	1B-OF	131	467	100	156	35	4	27	93	.334	1098	78	17	.986
1983—Iowa	A. A.	*1B-2B	123	458	76	115	25	1	*31	94	.251	*1191	*83	9	.993
1983—Chicago†	Nat.	1B-3B-OF	29	89	8	23	3	0	6	16	.258	233	17	2	.992
1984—San Diego	Nat.	OF-1B	149	488	64	122	28	2	13	66	.250	317	15	8	.976
1985—San Diego‡	Nat.	OF-1B	150	514	64	130	28	1	21	72	.253	302	14	7	.978
1986—San Diego	Nat.	OF-1B-3B	113	244	28	58	10	0	9	25	.238	142	14	2	.987
1987—San Diego	Nat.	OF-1B	139	447	59	122	21	2	15	70	.273	591	42	9	.986
1988—San Diego	Nat.	OF-1B	121	365	48	86	12	0	18	65	.236	430	32	4	.991
1989—San Diego§	Nat.	OF-1B	111	267	23	59	12	2	6	39	.221	225	18	2	.992
Major League Totals—7 Years			812	2414	294	600	114	7	88	353	.249	2240	152	34	.986

Signed as free agent by Chicago Cubs' organization, December 9, 1978.
†Traded with Pitcher Craig Lefferts and Third Baseman Fritz Connally to San Diego Padres for Pitcher Scott Sanderson, December 7, 1983.
‡On disabled list, March 31 to April 15, 1985.
§Granted free agency, November 13, 1989; signed by Philadelphia Phillies, December 1, 1989.

CHAMPIONSHIP SERIES RECORD

Year Club	League	Pos.	G.	AB.	R.	H.	2B.	3B.	HR.	RBI.	B.A.	PO.	A.	E.	F.A.
1984—San Diego	Nat.	OF	5	17	1	3	0	0	0	0	.176	6	0	0	1.000

WORLD SERIES RECORD

Year Club	League	Pos.	G.	AB.	R.	H.	2B.	3B.	HR.	RBI.	B.A.	PO.	A.	E.	F.A.
1984—San Diego	Nat.	OF	5	17	0	3	0	0	0	0	.176	7	0	1	.875

DAVID MARTINEZ
(Dave)

Born September 26, 1964, at New York, N.Y.
Height, 5.10, Weight, 170.
Throws and bats lefthanded.
Attended Valencia Community College, Orlando, Fla.

Major League stolen bases: 1986 (4), 1987 (16), 1988 (23), 1989 (23). Total—66.

Year Club	League	Pos.	G.	AB.	R.	H.	2B.	3B.	HR.	RBI.	B.A.	PO.	A.	E.	F.A.
1983—Quad Cities	Midw.	OF	44	119	17	29	6	2	0	10	.244	47	8	1	.982
1983—Geneva	NYP	OF	64	241	35	63	15	2	5	33	.261	132	6	8	.945
1984—Quad Cities†	Midw.	OF	12	41	6	9	2	2	0	5	.220	13	2	1	.938
1985—Winston-Salem	Carol.	OF	115	386	52	132	14	4	5	54	*.342	206	11	7	.969
1986—Iowa	A. A.	OF	83	318	52	92	11	5	5	32	.289	214	7	2	.991
1986—Chicago	Nat.	OF	53	108	13	15	1	1	1	7	.139	77	2	1	.988
1987—Chicago	Nat.	OF	142	459	70	134	18	8	8	36	.292	283	10	6	.980
1988—Chi.‡-Mon.	Nat.	OF	138	447	51	114	13	6	6	46	.255	281	4	6	.979
1989—Montreal	Nat.	OF	126	361	41	99	16	7	3	27	.274	199	7	7	.967
Major League Totals—4 Years			459	1375	175	362	48	22	18	116	.263	840	23	20	.977

Selected by Texas Rangers' organization in 40th round of free-agent draft, June 7, 1982.
Selected by Chicago Cubs' organization in secondary phase of free-agent draft, January 11, 1983.
†On disabled list, April 27, 1984 through remainder of season.
‡Traded to Montreal Expos for Outfielder Mitch Webster, July 14, 1988.

EDGAR MARTINEZ

Born January 2, 1963, at New York, N. Y.
Height, 5.11. Weight, 175.
Throws and bats righthanded.
Attended American College, Puerto Rico.
Cousin of Carmelo Martinez, outfielder-first baseman with Philadelphia Phillies.

Major League stolen bases: 1989 (2).
Led Southern League in sacrifice flies with 12 in 1985.
Led Pacific Coast League first basemen in double plays with 31 and total chances with 389 in 1987.
Led Southern League third basemen in double plays with 34 and total chances with 360 in 1985.

Year Club	League	Pos.	G.	AB.	R.	H.	2B.	3B.	HR.	RBI.	B.A.	PO.	A.	E.	F.A.
1983—Bellingham	N'west	3B	32	104	14	18	1	1	0	5	.173	22	58	6	.930
1984—Wausau	Midw.	3B	126	433	72	131	32	2	15	66	.303	85	246	25	.930
1985—Chattanooga	South.	3B	111	357	43	92	15	5	3	47	.258	*94	*247	19	*.947
1985—Calgary	P. C.	3B-2B	20	68	8	24	7	1	0	14	.353	15	44	4	.937
1986—Chattanooga	South.	*3B-2B	132	451	71	119	29	5	6	74	.264	94	263	15	*.960
1987—Calgary	P. C.	3B	129	438	75	144	31	1	10	66	.329	*91	*278	20	.949
1987—Seattle	Amer.	3B	13	43	6	16	5	2	0	5	.372	13	19	0	1.000
1988—Calgary	P. C.	3B-2B	95	331	63	120	19	4	8	64	*.363	48	185	20	.921
1988—Seattle	Amer.	3B	14	32	0	9	4	0	0	5	.281	5	8	1	.929

Year Club	League	Pos.	G.	AB.	R.	H.	2B.	3B.	HR.	RBI.	B.A.	PO.	A.	E.	F.A.
1989—Seattle...................	Amer.	3B	65	171	20	41	5	0	2	20	.240	40	72	6	.949
1989—Calgary	P. C.	3B-2B	32	113	30	39	11	0	3	23	.345	22	56	12	.867
Major League Totals—3 Years................			92	246	26	66	14	2	2	30	.268	58	99	7	.957

Signed as free agent by Seattle Mariners' organization, December 19, 1982.

JOSE DENNIS MARTINEZ

(Known by middle name.)

Born May 14, 1955, at Granada, Nicaragua.
Height, 6.01.   Weight, 183.
Throws and bats righthanded.

Major League saves: 1977 (4), 1980 (1). Total—5.
Led American League pitchers in games started with 39 and complete games with 18 in 1979.
Tied for National League lead in balks with 10 in 1988.
Led International League in complete games with 16 in 1976.
Named International League Pitcher of the Year, 1976.

Year Club	League	G.	IP.	W.	L.	Pct.	H.	R.	ER.	SO.	BB.	ERA.
1974—Miami	Florida St.	25	179	15	6	.714	124	48	41	162	53	2.06
1975—Miami	Florida St.	20	145	12	4	.750	125	54	42	114	35	2.61
1975—Asheville	Southern	6	45	4	1	.800	45	16	13	18	12	2.60
1975—Rochester	Int'national	2	5	0	0	.000	7	4	3	4	2	5.40
1976—Rochester	Int'national	25	180	*14	8	.636	148	64	50	*140	50	*2.50
1976—Baltimore	American	4	28	1	2	.333	23	8	8	18	8	2.57
1977—Baltimore	American	42	167	14	7	.667	157	86	76	107	64	4.10
1978—Baltimore	American	40	276	16	11	.593	257	121	108	142	93	3.25
1979—Baltimore	American	40	*292	15	16	.484	279	129	119	132	78	3.67
1980—Baltimore†	American	25	100	6	4	.600	103	44	44	42	44	3.96
1980—Miami	Florida St.	2	12	0	0	.000	3	1	0	7	5	0.00
1981—Baltimore	American	25	179	●14	5	.737	173	84	66	88	62	3.32
1982—Baltimore	American	40	252	16	12	.571	262	123	118	111	87	4.21
1983—Baltimore	American	32	153	7	16	.304	209	108	94	71	45	5.53
1984—Baltimore	American	34	141⅔	6	9	.400	145	81	79	77	37	5.02
1985—Baltimore	American	33	180	13	11	.542	203	110	103	68	63	5.15
1986—Baltimore‡	American	4	6⅔	0	0	.000	11	5	5	2	2	6.75
1986—Rochester§	Int'national	4	19⅓	2	1	.667	18	14	13	14	9	6.05
1986—Montreal x	National	19	98	3	6	.333	103	52	50	63	28	4.59
1987—Miami y	Florida St.	3	19	1	1	.500	21	14	13	11	3	6.16
1987—Indianapolis	Am. Assoc.	7	38⅓	3	2	.600	32	20	19	30	13	4.46
1987—Montreal z	National	22	144⅔	11	4	*.733	133	59	53	84	40	3.30
1988—Montreal	National	34	235⅓	15	13	.536	215	94	71	120	55	2.72
1989—Montreal	National	34	232	16	7	.696	227	88	82	142	49	3.18
American League Totals—11 Years		319	1775⅓	108	93	.537	1822	899	820	858	583	4.16
National League Totals—4 Years		109	710	45	30	.600	678	293	256	409	172	3.25
Major League Totals—14 Years...........................		428	2485⅓	153	123	.554	2500	1192	1076	1267	755	3.90

Signed as free agent by Baltimore Orioles' organization, December 10, 1973.

†On disabled list, March 28 to April 20 and June 3 to July 10, 1980; included rehabilitation disability assignment to Miami, July 1 to July 10, 1980.

‡On disabled list, April 28 to June 16, 1986; included rehabilitation disability assignment to Rochester, May 21 to June 10, 1986.

§Traded to Montreal Expos for a player to be named later, June 16, 1986; Baltimore Orioles acquired Infielder Rene Gonzales to complete deal, December 16, 1986.

xGranted free agency, November 12, 1986; signed by Miami (Independent), April 14, 1987.

yReleased, May 6, 1987; signed by Montreal Expos' organization, May 6, 1987.

zGranted free agency, November 9, 1987; re-signed by Expos, December 18, 1987.

CHAMPIONSHIP SERIES RECORD

Year Club	League	G.	IP.	W.	L.	Pct.	H.	R.	ER.	SO.	BB.	ERA.
1979—Baltimore	American	1	8⅓	0	0	.000	8	3	3	4	0	3.24

WORLD SERIES RECORD

Year Club	League	G.	IP.	W.	L.	Pct.	H.	R.	ER.	SO.	BB.	ERA.
1979—Baltimore	American	2	2	0	0	.000	6	4	4	0	0	18.00

Eligible for 1983 World Series with Baltimore Orioles; did not play.

JULIAN M. MARTINEZ

Born June 2, 1967, at Bani, Dominican Republic.
Height, 6.00. Weight, 175.
Throws and bats righthanded.

Year Club	League	Pos.	G.	AB.	R.	H.	2B.	3B.	HR.	RBI.	B.A.	PO.	A.	E.	F.A.
1985—Johnson City	Appal.	2B-3B	21	62	4	12	2	0	1	8	.194	19	31	4	.926
1986—Savannah	S. Atl.	SS-3B-2B	70	217	31	56	5	0	2	25	.258	63	147	27	.886
1987—Savannah	S. Atl.	3-O-S-2	123	427	67	97	17	2	8	31	.227	141	243	34	.919
1988—St. Petersburg.......	Fla. St.	O-S-3-2	113	375	54	94	17	1	3	39	.251	187	147	29	.920
1989—Arkansas	Texas	SS-OF	128	451	57	115	30	3	9	59	.255	164	396	41	.932

Signed as free agent by St. Louis Cardinals' organization, August 9, 1984.

RAMON JAIME MARTINEZ

Born March 22, 1968, at Santo Domingo, D. R.
Height, 6.04. Weight, 172.
Throws and bats righthanded.
Member of 1984 Dominican Republic Olympic baseball team.

Year Club	League	G.	IP.	W.	L.	Pct.	H.	R.	ER.	SO.	BB.	ERA.
1985—Bradenton Dodgers	Gulf Coast	23	59	4	1	.800	57	30	17	42	23	2.59
1986—Bakersfield	California	20	106	4	8	.333	119	73	56	78	63	4.75
1987—Vero Beach	Florida St.	25	170⅓	16	5	.762	128	45	41	148	78	2.17
1988—San Antonio	Texas	14	95	8	4	.667	79	29	26	89	34	2.46
1988—Albuquerque	P. Coast	10	58⅔	5	2	.714	43	24	18	49	32	2.76
1988—Los Angeles	National	9	35⅔	1	3	.250	27	17	15	23	22	3.79
1989—Albuquerque	P. Coast	18	113	10	2	.833	92	40	35	127	50	2.79
1989—Los Angeles	National	15	98⅔	6	4	.600	79	39	35	89	41	3.19
Major League Totals—2 Years		24	134⅓	7	7	.500	106	56	50	112	63	3.35

Signed as free agent by Los Angeles Dodgers' organization, September 1, 1984.

JOHN ROBERT MARZANO

Born February 14, 1963, at Philadelphia, Pa.
Height, 5.11. Weight, 197.
Throws and bats righthanded.
Attended Temple University, Philadelphia, Pa.
Led Eastern League in being hit by pitch with 12 in 1986.
Member of 1984 U.S. Olympic baseball team.
Named catcher on THE SPORTING NEWS College Baseball All-America Team, 1984.

Year Club	League	Pos.	G.	AB.	R.	H.	2B.	3B.	HR.	RBI.	B.A.	PO.	A.	E.	F.A.
1985—New Britain	East.	C	103	350	36	86	14	6	4	51	.246	530	70	12	.980
1986—New Britain†	East.	C-3B	118	445	55	126	28	2	10	62	.283	509	76	14	.977
1987—Pawtucket	Int.	C	70	255	46	72	22	0	10	35	.282	326	36	8	.978
1987—Boston	Amer.	C	52	168	20	41	11	0	5	24	.244	337	24	5	.986
1988—Boston	Amer.	C	10	29	3	4	1	0	0	1	.138	77	4	0	1.000
1988—Pawtucket	Int.	C	33	111	7	22	2	1	0	5	.198	151	24	8	.956
1988—New Britain	East.	C	35	112	11	23	6	1	0	5	.205	117	11	3	.977
1989—Pawtucket	Int.	C	106	322	27	68	11	0	8	36	.211	574	62	10	.985
1989—Boston	Amer.	C	7	18	5	8	3	0	1	3	.444	29	4	0	1.000
Major League Totals—3 Years			69	215	28	53	15	0	6	28	.247	443	32	5	.990

Selected by Minnesota Twins' organization in 3rd round of free-agent draft, June 8, 1981.
Selected by Boston Red Sox' organization in 1st round (14th player selected) of free-agent draft, June 4, 1984.
†On disabled list, June 13 to June 28, 1986.

ROGER LeROY MASON

Born September 18, 1958, at Bellaire, Mich.
Height, 6.06. Weight, 220.
Throws and bats righthanded.
Attended Saginaw Valley State College, University Center, Mich.
Pitched no-hitter for nine innings vs. Las Vegas, August 20, 1989 (Tucson lost game in 11 innings, 1-0).
Tied National League record for most consecutive home runs allowed, inning (3), April 13, 1987, first inning.
Major League saves: 1984 (1).

Year Club	League	G.	IP.	W.	L.	Pct.	H.	R.	ER.	SO.	BB.	ERA.
1981—Macon	S. Atlantic	26	148	10	10	.500	153	77	64	105	50	3.89
1982—Lakeland	Florida St.	22	132⅔	7	7	.500	124	60	51	72	52	3.46
1983—Birmingham	Southern	17	126⅔	7	4	.636	116	45	29	83	43	*2.06
1983—Evansville	Am. Assoc.	11	78⅔	5	5	.500	84	39	37	43	21	4.23
1984—Evansville†	Am. Assoc.	25	151⅔	9	7	.563	175	78	64	88	64	3.80
1984—Detroit‡	American	5	22	1	1	.500	23	11	11	15	10	4.50
1985—Phoenix§	P. Coast	24	167⅓	12	1	*.923	145	67	62	120	72	3.33
1985—San Francisco	National	5	29⅔	1	3	.250	28	13	7	26	11	2.12
1986—San Francisco x	National	11	60	3	4	.429	56	35	32	43	30	4.80
1986—Phoenix	P. Coast	1	6	1	0	1.000	2	0	0	2	1	0.00
1987—San Francisco	National	5	26	1	1	.500	30	15	13	18	10	4.50
1987—Phoenix	P. Coast	10	61	5	1	.833	62	34	28	49	20	4.13
1988—Phoenix y	P. Coast	19	90⅔	2	9	.182	90	62	49	62	38	4.86
1989—Tucson	P. Coast	25	155	7	12	.368	125	71	61	105	46	3.54
1989—Houston	National	2	1⅓	0	0	.000	2	3	3	3	2	20.25
American League Totals—1 Year		5	22	1	1	.500	23	11	11	15	10	4.50
National League Totals—4 Years		23	117	5	8	.385	116	66	55	90	53	4.23
Major League Totals—5 Years		28	139	6	9	.400	139	77	66	105	63	4.27

Signed as free agent by Detroit Tigers' organization, September 21, 1980.
†On disabled list, May 3 to May 19, 1984.
‡Traded to San Francisco Giants' organization for Outfielder Alejandro Sanchez, April 5, 1985.
§On disabled list, May 2 to May 23, 1985.
xOn disabled list, May 30 to July 20 and July 26, 1986 through remainder of season; included rehabilitation disability assignment to Phoenix, July 9 to July 17, 1986.
yGranted free agency, October 15, 1988; signed by Tucson (Houston Astros' organization), February 16, 1989.

GREGORY INMAN MATHEWS
(Greg)

Born May 17, 1962, at Harbor City, Calif.
Height, 6.02. Weight, 180.
Throws left and bats righthanded.
Attended Santa Ana College, Santa Ana, Calif.; and
California State University, Fullerton, Calif.

Tied for American Association lead in shutouts with 2 in 1986 and 1987.

Year Club	League	G.	IP.	W.	L.	Pct.	H.	R.	ER.	SO.	BB.	ERA.
1984—Erie	NYP	3	15	0	1	.000	16	15	15	9	8	9.00
1984—Johnson City	Ap'lachian	5	31⅓	2	3	.400	27	12	9	21	13	2.59
1984—Savannah	S. Atlantic	6	27⅓	1	0	1.000	24	10	9	21	15	2.96
1985—St. Petersburg	Florida St.	16	122	13	1	*.929	76	17	15	96	47	*1.11
1985—Louisville	Am. Assoc.	12	74	6	4	.600	61	33	24	47	26	2.92
1986—Louisville†	Am. Assoc.	7	45⅓	3	3	.500	44	19	13	20	14	2.58
1986—St. Louis	National	23	145⅓	11	8	.579	139	61	59	67	44	3.65
1987—St. Louis	National	32	197⅔	11	11	.500	184	87	82	108	71	3.73
1987—Louisville	Am. Assoc.	3	22	3	0	1.000	18	5	5	20	3	2.05
1988—St. Louis‡	National	13	68	4	6	.400	61	34	32	31	33	4.24
1988—Louisville§	Am. Assoc.	5	16	0	1	.000	15	14	13	8	9	7.31
1989—St. Louis§	National					(Did not play)						
1989—Louisville	Am. Assoc.	1	0	0	0	.000	0	1	1	0	1	......
Major League Totals—3 Years		68	411	26	25	.510	384	182	173	206	148	3.79

Selected by Minnesota Twins' organization in 9th round of free-agent draft, January 12, 1982.
Selected by St. Louis Cardinals' organization in 10th round of free-agent draft, June 4, 1984.
†On disabled list, April 25 to May 12, 1986.
‡On disabled list, May 14 to August 16, 1988; included rehabilitation disability assignment to Arkansas, June 7 to June 13, 1988; and Louisville, July 26 to August 12, 1988.
§On disabled list, March 25, 1989 through entire season; included rehabilitation disability assignment to Louisville, April 25 to May 2, 1989.

CHAMPIONSHIP SERIES RECORD

Year Club	League	G.	IP.	W.	L.	Pct.	H.	R.	ER.	SO.	BB.	ERA.
1987—St. Louis	National	2	10⅓	1	0	1.000	6	5	4	10	3	3.48

WORLD SERIES RECORD

Year Club	League	G.	IP.	W.	L.	Pct.	H.	R.	ER.	SO.	BB.	ERA.
1987—St. Louis	National	1	3⅔	0	0	.000	2	1	1	3	2	2.45

PEDRO LUIS MATILLA

Born August 1, 1968, at Havana, Cuba.
Height, 6.00. Weight, 205.
Throws and bats righthanded.

Tied for Gulf Coast League lead in double plays by outfielders with 4 in 1989.

Year Club	League	Pos.	G.	AB.	R.	H.	2B.	3B.	HR.	RBI.	B.A.	PO.	A.	E.	F.A.
1987—Elmira†	NYP	C	25	66	4	10	4	0	0	4	.152	99	17	5	.959
1988—Elmira†	NYP	C	39	117	9	18	2	1	1	4	.154	218	42	6	.977
1989—Elmira	NYP	C	14	34	9	9	4	1	0	3	.265	83	8	3	.968
1989—Sarasota Red Sox	Gulf C.	C	41	130	18	37	5	0	5	23	.285	259	*76	8	.977
1989—Winter Haven	Fla. St.	C	22	45	3	10	3	0	1	5	.222	57	13	2	.972

Selected by Boston Red Sox' organization in 12th round of free-agent draft, June 2, 1987.
†Batted lefthanded only.

DONALD ARTHUR MATTINGLY
(Don)

Born April 20, 1961, at Evansville, Ind.
Height, 6.00. Weight, 175.
Throws and bats lefthanded.
Brother of Randy Mattingly, selected by Cleveland Browns in 4th round of 1973 NFL draft; and quarterback with Saskatchewan Roughriders and Hamilton Tiger-Cats of CFL, 1974 through 1976.

Holds major league records for most home runs, seven consecutive games (9), July 8 through 17, 1987, and eight consecutive games (10), July 8 through 18, 1987; most grand slams, season (6), 1987.
Shares major league records for most doubles, inning (2), April 11, 1987, seventh inning; most consecutive games, one or more home runs (8), July 8 through 18, 1987; most sacrifice flies, game (3), May 3, 1986; most putouts and chances accepted by first baseman, nine-inning game (22), July 20, 1987.
Holds American League record for most at-bats by lefthander, season (677), 1986; most consecutive games, one or more long hits, season (10), July 7 through 19, 1987.
Major League stolen bases: 1984 (1), 1985 (2), 1987 (1), 1988 (1), 1989 (3). Total—8.
Led American League in total bases with 370 in 1985 and 388 in 1986.
Led American League in slugging percentage with .573 in 1986.
Led American League in game-winning RBIs with 21 in 1985 and tied for lead with 15 in 1986.
Led American League in sacrifice flies with 15 in 1985.
Led American League first basemen in fielding percentage with .996 in 1984 and 1986.
Led American League first basemen in putouts with 1,377 and total chances with 1,483 in 1986.
Tied for American League lead in double plays by first basemen with 154 in 1985.
Led South Atlantic League in sacrifice flies with 12 in 1980.

Named Major League Player of the Year by THE SPORTING NEWS, 1985.
Named American League Player of the Year by THE SPORTING NEWS, 1984 through 1986.
Named American League Most Valuable Player by Baseball Writers' Association of America, 1985.
Named first baseman on THE SPORTING NEWS American League All-Star Team, 1984 through 1987.
Named first baseman on THE SPORTING NEWS American League All-Star fielding team, 1985 through 1989.
Named first baseman on THE SPORTING NEWS American League Silver Slugger team, 1985 through 1987.
Named South Atlantic League Most Valuable Player, 1980.
Received reported $22,000 bonus to sign with New York Yankees, 1979.

Year—Club	League	Pos.	G.	AB.	R.	H.	2B.	3B.	HR.	RBI.	B.A.	PO.	A.	E.	F.A.
1979—Oneonta	NYP	OF-1B	53	166	20	58	10	2	3	31	.349	29	2	2	.939
1980—Greensboro	S. Atl.	OF-1B	133	494	92	★177	32	5	9	105	★.358	205	16	8	.976
1981—Nashville	South.	OF-1B	141	547	74	173	★35	4	7	98	.316	846	69	12	.987
1982—Columbus	Int.	OF-1B	130	476	67	150	24	2	10	75	.315	271	17	5	.983
1982—New York	Amer.	OF-1B	7	12	0	2	0	0	0	1	.167	15	1	0	1.000
1983—New York	Amer.	OF-1B-2B	91	279	34	79	15	4	4	32	.283	350	15	3	.992
1983—Columbus	Int.	1B-OF	43	159	35	54	11	3	8	37	.340	325	29	1	.997
1984—New York	Amer.	1B-OF	153	603	91	★207	★44	2	23	110	★.343	1143	126	6	.995
1985—New York	Amer.	1B	159	652	107	211	★48	3	35	★145	.324	1318	87	7	★.995
1986—New York†	Amer.	1B-3B	162	677	117	★238	★53	2	31	113	.352	1378	111	7	.995
1987—New York†	Amer.	1B	141	569	93	186	38	2	30	115	.327	1239	91	5	★.996
1988—New York‡	Amer.	1B-OF	144	599	94	186	37	0	18	88	.311	1250	99	9	.993
1989—New York	Amer.	1B-OF	158	631	79	191	37	2	23	113	.303	1276	87	7	.995
Major League Totals—8 Years			1015	4022	615	1300	272	15	164	717	.323	7969	617	44	.995

Selected by New York Yankees' organization in 19th round of free-agent draft, June 5, 1979.
†On disabled list, June 9 to June 24, 1987.
‡On disabled list, May 27 to June 14, 1988.

ALL-STAR GAME RECORD

Year—League	Pos.	AB.	R.	H.	2B.	3B.	HR.	RBI.	B.A.	PO.	A.	E.	F.A.
1984—American	PH	1	0	0	0	0	0	0	.000	0	0	0	.000
1985—American	1B	1	0	0	0	0	0	0	.000	4	0	0	1.000
1986—American	PH-1B	3	0	0	0	0	0	0	.000	7	0	0	1.000
1987—American	1B	1	0	0	0	0	0	0	.000	10	0	0	1.000
1988—American	1B	2	0	0	0	0	0	0	.000	2	1	1	.750
1989—American	1B	1	0	1	1	0	0	0	1.000	4	0	0	1.000
All-Star Game Totals—6 Years		9	0	1	1	0	0	0	.111	27	1	1	.966

DERRICK BRANT MAY

Born July 14, 1968, at Rochester, N.Y.
Height, 6.04. Weight, 210.
Throws right and bats lefthanded.
Son of Dave May, outfielder with Baltimore Orioles, Milwaukee Brewers,
Atlanta Braves, Texas Rangers and Pittsburgh Pirates, 1967 through 1978.
Tied for Carolina League lead in double plays by outfielders with 4 in 1988.

Year—Club	League	Pos.	G.	AB.	R.	H.	2B.	3B.	HR.	RBI.	B.A.	PO.	A.	E.	F.A.
1986—Wytheville	Appal.	OF	54	178	25	57	6	1	0	23	.320	47	3	5	.909
1987—Peoria	Midw.	OF	128	439	60	131	19	8	9	52	.298	181	13	8	.960
1988—Winston-Salem	Carol.	OF	130	485	76	●148	29	★9	8	65	.305	209	13	10	.957
1989—Charlotte	South.	OF	136	491	72	145	26	5	9	70	.295	239	8	●13	.950

Selected by Chicago Cubs' organization in 1st round (ninth player selected) of free-agent draft, June 2, 1986.

MATTHEW SAMUEL MAYSEY
(Matt)

Born January 8, 1967, at Hamilton, Ontario, Can.
Height, 6.04. Weight, 210.
Throws and bats righthanded.
Tied for Pacific Coast League lead in games started by pitchers with 28 in 1989.
Tied for Texas League lead in games started by pitchers with 28 in 1988.

Year—Club	League	G.	IP.	W.	L.	Pct.	H.	R.	ER.	SO.	BB.	ERA.
1985—Spokane	Northwest	7	29	0	3	.000	27	18	15	18	16	4.66
1986—Charleston†	S. Atlantic	18	43	3	2	.600	43	28	24	39	24	5.02
1987—Charleston	S. Atlantic	41	150⅓	14	11	.560	112	71	53	143	59	3.17
1988—Wichita	Texas	28	187	9	9	.500	180	88	77	120	68	3.71
1989—Las Vegas	P. Coast	28	176⅓	8	12	.400	173	94	80	96	84	4.08

Selected by San Diego Padres' organization in 7th round of free-agent draft, June 3, 1985.
†On disabled list, May 4 to July 9, 1986.

LEE LOUIS MAZZILLI

Born March 25, 1955, at Brooklyn, N. Y.
Height, 6.01. Weight, 195.
Throws right and bats left and righthanded.
Son of Libero Mazzilli, former professional welterweight boxer.
Major League stolen bases: 1976 (5), 1977 (22), 1978 (20), 1979 (34), 1980 (41), 1981 (17), 1982 (13), 1983 (15), 1984 (8), 1985 (4), 1986 (4), 1987 (5), 1988 (4), 1989 (5). Total—197.
Led Texas League in bases on balls received with 111, caught stealing with 15 and tied for lead in being hit by pitch with 7 in 1976.

Led California League in caught stealing with 16 in 1975.
Received reported $50,000 bonus to sign with New York Mets, 1973.

Year	Club	League	Pos.	G.	AB.	R.	H.	2B.	3B.	HR.	RBI.	B.A.	PO.	A.	E.	F.A.
1974—Anderson	W. Car.	OF	132	472	82	127	24	3	11	48	.269	227	9	9	.963
1975—Visalia	Calif.	OF-1B	125	430	103	121	10	4	13	52	.281	185	9	9	.956
1976—Jackson	Texas	OF	131	439	91	128	21	6	13	43	.292	262	8	8	.971
1976—New York	Nat.	OF	24	77	9	15	2	0	2	7	.195	55	2	1	.983
1977—New York	Nat.	OF	159	537	66	134	24	3	6	46	.250	386	9	3	.992
1978—New York	Nat.	OF	148	542	78	148	28	5	16	61	.273	386	8	5	.987
1979—New York	Nat.	OF-1B	158	597	78	181	34	4	15	79	.303	480	24	5	.990
1980—New York	Nat.	1B-OF	152	578	82	162	31	4	16	76	.280	874	53	14	.985
1981—New York†	Nat.	OF	95	324	36	74	14	5	6	34	.228	192	5	6	.970
1982—Tex.‡§-N.Y.x	Amer.	OF-1B	95	323	43	81	10	0	10	34	.251	234	8	4	.984
1983—Pittsburgh	Nat.	OF-1B	109	246	37	59	9	0	5	24	.240	173	3	4	.978
1984—Pittsburgh y	Nat.	OF-1B	111	266	37	63	11	1	4	21	.237	103	2	1	.991
1985—Pittsburgh	Nat.	1B-OF	92	117	20	33	8	0	1	9	.282	152	6	3	.981
1986—Pit. z-N.Y.	Nat.	OF-1B	100	151	28	37	5	1	3	15	.245	128	2	0	1.000
1986—Tidewater	Int.	1B-OF	6	20	3	6	1	0	1	1	.300	28	1	0	1.000
1987—New York a	Nat.	1B-OF	88	124	26	38	8	1	3	24	.306	82	3	0	1.000
1988—New York	Nat.	OF-1B	68	116	9	17	2	0	0	12	.147	114	4	3	.975
1989—New York b	Nat.	OF-1B	48	60	10	11	2	0	2	7	.183	47	1	1	.980
1989—Toronto c	Amer.	1B-OF	28	66	12	15	3	0	4	11	.227	19	1	1	.952
National League Totals—13 Years			1352	3735	566	972	178	24	79	415	.260	3172	122	46	.986
American League Totals—2 Years			123	389	55	96	13	0	14	45	.247	253	9	5	.981
Major League Totals—14 Years			1475	4124	571	1068	191	24	93	460	.259	3425	131	51	.986

Selected by New York Mets' organization in 1st round (14th player selected) of free-agent draft, June 5, 1973.
†Traded to Texas Rangers for Pitchers Ron Darling and Walt Terrell, April 1, 1982.
‡On disabled list, May 20 to June 29, 1982.
§Traded to New York Yankees for Shortstop Bucky Dent, August 8, 1982.
xTraded to Pittsburgh Pirates for Outfielder Don Aubin, Pitcher Tim Burke, Catcher John Holland and Infielder Jose Rivera, December 22, 1982.
yOn disabled list, August 28 to September 11, 1984.
zReleased, July 23, 1986; signed by New York Mets' organization, August 3, 1986.
aGranted free agency, November 9, 1987; re-signed by Mets, December 17, 1987.
bClaimed on waivers by Toronto Blue Jays, July 31, 1989.
cGranted free agency, November 13, 1989.

CHAMPIONSHIP SERIES RECORD

Year	Club	League	Pos.	G.	AB.	R.	H.	2B.	3B.	HR.	RBI.	B.A.	PO.	A.	E.	F.A.
1986—New York	Nat.	PH	5	5	0	1	0	0	0	0	.200	0	0	0	.000
1988—New York	Nat.	PH	3	2	0	1	0	0	0	0	.500	0	0	0	.000
1989—Toronto	Amer.	DH-PH	3	8	0	0	0	0	0	0	.000	0	0	0	.000
Championship Series Totals—3 Years			11	15	0	2	0	0	0	0	.133	0	0	0	.000

WORLD SERIES RECORD

Year	Club	League	Pos.	G.	AB.	R.	H.	2B.	3B.	HR.	RBI.	B.A.	PO.	A.	E.	F.A.
1986—New York	Nat.	PH-OF	4	5	2	2	0	0	0	0	.400	1	0	0	1.000

ALL-STAR GAME RECORD

Shares All-Star Game record for hitting home run in first at-bat, July 17, 1979.

Year	League	Pos.	AB.	R.	H.	2B.	3B.	HR.	RBI.	B.A.	PO.	A.	E.	F.A.
1979—National		PH-OF	1	1	1	0	0	1	2	1.000	0	0	0	.000

LARRY RANDALL McCAMENT
(Randy)

Born July 29, 1962, at Albuquerque, N.M.
Height, 6.03. Weight, 180.
Throws and bats righthanded.
Attended Grand Canyon College, Phoenix, Ariz.

Led Northwest League in shutouts with 2 in 1985.

Year	Club	League	G.	IP.	W.	L.	Pct.	H.	R.	ER.	SO.	BB.	ERA.
1985—Everett	Northwest	14	*105⅔	7	3	.700	98	46	34	66	20	2.90
1986—Fresno	California	54	86⅔	4	4	.500	87	36	24	61	24	2.49
1986—Shreveport	Texas	8	19⅓	2	1	.667	16	7	6	16	4	2.79
1987—Shreveport	Texas	52	79⅓	4	3	.571	78	28	21	39	18	2.38
1988—Phoenix	P. Coast	19	25	0	1	.000	40	26	21	7	16	7.56
1988—Shreveport	Texas	24	42	3	4	.429	56	29	25	15	14	5.36
1989—Phoenix	P. Coast	22	37⅓	3	0	1.000	40	15	15	13	12	3.62
1989—San Francisco	National	25	36⅔	1	1	.500	32	22	16	12	23	3.93
Major League Totals—1 Year		25	36⅔	1	1	.500	32	22	16	12	23	3.93

Selected by Cleveland Indians' organization in 16th round of free-agent draft, June 4, 1984.
Selected by San Francisco Giants' organization in 15th round of free-agent draft, June 3, 1985.

THOMAS MICHAEL McCARTHY
(Tom)

Born June 18, 1961, at Lundstahl, W. Germany.
Height 6.00. Weight, 180.
Throws and bats righthanded.

Major League saves: 1988 (1).

Year Club	League	G.	IP.	W.	L.	Pct.	H.	R.	ER.	SO.	BB.	ERA.
1979—Elmira	NYP	18	46	2	6	.250	67	50	36	26	37	7.04
1980—Elmira	NYP	3	20	2	1	.667	10	7	7	14	13	3.15
1980—Winston-Salem	Carolina	11	61	4	4	.500	55	32	27	28	46	3.98
1981—Winston-Salem	Carolina	28	105	3	7	.300	123	99	85	75	99	7.29
1982—Winston-Salem	Carolina	30	103⅓	3	11	.214	128	95	75	75	65	6.53
1983—Winston-Salem	Carolina	35	98	8	6	.571	91	56	45	100	54	4.13
1984—New Britain	Eastern	38	79½	8	5	.615	71	35	27	65	56	3.06
1985—Pawtucket	Int'national	26	85⅓	5	6	.455	72	48	34	65	62	3.59
1985—Boston†	American	3	5	0	0	.000	7	6	6	2	4	10.80
1986—Tidewater‡	Int'national	22	84⅔	3	2	.600	89	43	38	30	37	4.04
1987—Tidewater	Int'national	10	19	0	2	.000	22	17	9	7	16	4.26
1987—Jackson	Texas	37	54⅓	1	4	.200	57	18	16	30	21	2.65
1988—Tidewater§	Int'national	34	57⅓	8	3	.727	49	19	17	28	29	2.67
1988—Vancouver	P. Coast	9	18⅔	1	0	1.000	11	0	0	11	4	0.00
1988—Chicago	American	6	13	2	0	1.000	9	2	2	5	2	1.38
1989—Vancouver	P. Coast	17	26⅔	2	4	.333	27	17	16	17	10	5.40
1989—Chicago	American	31	66⅔	1	2	.333	72	32	26	27	20	3.51
Major League Totals—3 Years		40	84⅔	3	2	.600	88	40	34	34	26	3.61

Selected by Boston Red Sox' organization in 7th round of free-agent draft, June 5, 1979.

†Traded with Pitchers Bob Ojeda, John Mitchell and Chris Bayer to New York Mets for Pitchers Calvin Schiraldi and West Gardner and Outfielders John Christensen and LaSchelle Tarver, November 13, 1985.

‡On disabled list, July 21, 1986 through remainder of season.

§Traded with Infielder Steve Springer to Chicago White Sox for Outfielder Vince Harris and First Baseman Mike Maksodian, August 4, 1988.

KIRK EDWARD McCASKILL

Born April 9, 1961, at Kapuskasing, Ont., Canada.
Height, 6.01. Weight, 195.
Throws and bats righthanded.
Attended University of Vermont, Burlington, Vt.
Son of Ted McCaskill, center with Minnesota North Stars (NHL)
and Los Angeles Sharks (WHA), 1967-68, 1972-73 and 1973-74.

Year Club	League	G.	IP.	W.	L.	Pct.	H.	R.	ER.	SO.	BB.	ERA.
1982—Salem	Northwest	11	71⅓	5	5	.500	63	43	34	87	51	4.29
1983—Redwood	California	16	108⅓	6	5	.545	78	39	28	100	60	2.33
1983—Nashua†	Eastern	13	87	4	8	.333	90	47	43	63	43	4.45
1984—Edmonton	P. Coast	24	143	7	11	.389	162	104	91	75	74	5.73
1985—Edmonton	P. Coast	3	17⅔	1	1	.500	17	7	4	18	6	2.04
1985—California	American	30	189⅔	12	12	.500	189	105	99	102	64	4.70
1986—California	American	34	246⅓	17	10	.630	207	98	92	202	92	3.36
1987—California‡	American	14	74⅔	4	6	.400	84	52	47	56	34	5.67
1987—Palm Springs	California	2	10	2	0	1.000	4	1	0	7	3	0.00
1987—Edmonton	P. Coast	1	6	1	0	1.000	3	2	2	4	4	3.00
1988—California§	American	23	146⅓	8	6	.571	155	78	70	98	61	4.31
1989—California	American	32	212	15	10	.600	202	73	69	107	59	2.93
Major League Totals—5 Years		133	869	56	44	.560	837	406	377	565	310	3.90

Selected by California Angels' organization in 4th round of free-agent draft, June 7, 1982.

†On suspended list, August 30, 1983; then transferred to disqualified list, September 26, 1983 through April 25, 1984.

‡On disabled list, April 24 to July 11, 1987; included rehabilitation disability assignment to Palm Springs, June 24 to July 2, and Edmonton, July 3 to July 8, 1987.

§On disabled list, August 9, 1988 through remainder of season.

CHAMPIONSHIP SERIES RECORD

Holds Championship Series record for most runs allowed, series (13), 1986.
Shares Championship Series records for most games lost, series (2), 1986; most hits allowed, inning (6), October 14, 1986, third inning.

Year Club	League	G.	IP.	W.	L.	Pct.	H.	R.	ER.	SO.	BB.	ERA.
1986—California	American	2	9⅓	0	2	.000	16	13	8	7	5	7.71

RECORD AS HOCKEY PLAYER

Year Team	League	Games	G.	A.	Pts.	Pen.
1983-84—Sherbrooke Jets (a)	AHL	78	10	12	22	21

(a)—June, 1981—Drafted by Winnipeg Jets in 1981 NHL entry draft. Fourth Jets pick, 64th overall, fourth round.

PAUL WILLIAM McCLELLAN

Born February 8, 1966, at San Mateo, Calif.
Height, 6.02. Weight, 180.
Throws and bats righthanded.
Attended College of San Mateo, San Mateo, Calif.

Led Texas League in balks with 22 in 1988.

Year Club	League	G.	IP.	W.	L.	Pct.	H.	R.	ER.	SO.	BB.	ERA.
1986—Everett	Northwest	13	86⅓	5	4	.556	71	39	32	74	46	3.34
1987—Clinton	Midwest	28	177⅓	12	10	.545	141	86	64	*209	100	3.25
1988—Shreveport	Texas	27	167	10	12	.455	146	89	75	128	62	4.04
1989—Shreveport	Texas	12	84⅓	8	3	.727	56	26	21	56	35	2.24

Year Club	League	G.	IP.	W.	L.	Pct.	H.	R.	ER.	SO.	BB.	ERA.
1989—Phoenix	P. Coast	9	56⅔	3	4	.429	56	34	31	25	29	4.92

Selected by Atlanta Braves' organization in 25th round of free-agent draft, June 3, 1985.
Selected by San Francisco Giants' organization in secondary phase of free-agent draft, January 14, 1986.

LLOYD GLENN McCLENDON

Born January 11, 1959, at Gary, Ind.
Height, 5.11. Weight, 195.
Throws and bats righthanded.
Attended Valparaiso University, Valparaiso, Ind.

Major League stolen bases: 1987 (1), 1988 (4), 1989 (6). Total—11.

Year Club	League	Pos.	G.	AB.	R.	H.	2B.	3B.	HR.	RBI.	B.A.	PO.	A.	E.	F.A.
1980—Kingsport	Appal.	C	14	46	7	15	2	0	1	9	.326	19	5	3	.889
1980—Little Falls	NYP	C	40	117	25	32	9	1	3	20	.274	203	20	7	.970
1981—Lynchburg	Carol.	C-3B	103	363	55	91	12	6	7	57	.251	437	74	17	.968
1982—Lynchburg†‡	Carol.	C-3B	108	384	61	105	25	1	18	78	.273	492	87	15	.975
1983—Waterbury	East.	C-3B-1B	123	434	58	114	19	2	15	57	.263	466	99	8	.986
1984—Vermont	East.	C-1-3-O	60	202	36	56	16	0	7	27	.277	174	24	3	.985
1984—Wichita	A.A.	3B-1B-C	48	152	28	45	13	1	6	28	.296	143	45	4	.979
1985—Denver	A.A.	1-3-C-O	114	379	57	105	18	5	16	79	.277	470	104	17	.971
1986—Denver	A.A.	1-O-C-3	132	433	75	112	30	1	⋆24	88	.259	656	45	11	.985
1987—Cincinnati	Nat.	C-1-3-O	45	72	8	15	5	0	2	13	.208	80	5	2	.977
1987—Nashville	A. A.	1B-C	26	84	11	24	6	0	3	14	.286	72	3	1	.987
1988—Cincinnati	Nat.	C-O-1-3	72	137	9	30	4	0	3	14	.219	197	13	4	.981
1988—Nashville§	A. A.	OF-C	2	7	0	1	0	0	0	0	.143	12	2	0	1.000
1989—Iowa	A. A.	1B-OF-C	34	109	18	35	10	0	4	13	.321	115	6	6	.953
1989—Chicago	Nat.	O-1-3-C	92	259	47	74	12	1	12	40	.286	310	18	6	.982
Major League Totals—3 Years			209	468	64	119	21	1	17	67	.254	587	36	12	.981

Selected by New York Mets' organization in 8th round of free-agent draft, June 3, 1980.
†On disabled list, April 4 to April 27, 1982.
‡Traded with Pitcher Charlie Puleo and Outfielder Jason Felice to Cincinnati Reds for Pitcher Tom Seaver, December 16, 1982.
§Traded to Chicago Cubs for Outfielder Rolando Roomes, December 9, 1988.

CHAMPIONSHIP SERIES RECORD

Year Club	League	Pos.	G.	AB.	R.	H.	2B.	3B.	HR.	RBI.	B.A.	PO.	A.	E.	F.A.
1989—Chicago	Nat.	PH-C-OF	3	3	0	2	0	0	0	0	.667	3	0	0	1.000

ROBERT CRAIG McCLURE
(Bob)

Born April 29, 1953, at Oakland, Calif.
Height, 5.11. Weight, 175.
Throws left and bats left and righthanded.
Attended College of San Mateo, San Mateo, Calif.

Major League saves: 1975 (1), 1977 (6), 1978 (9), 1979 (5), 1980 (10), 1984 (1), 1985 (3), 1986 (6), 1987 (5), 1988 (3), 1989 (3). Total—52.
Led American League in balks with 6 in 1983.
Tied for Pioneer League lead in shutouts with 3 in 1973.

Year Club	League	G.	IP.	W.	L.	Pct	H.	R.	ER.	SO.	BB.	ERA.
1973—Billings	Pioneer	14	94	⋆10	2	.833	64	41	22	110	67	2.11
1974—Omaha	Am. Assoc.	21	136	5	8	.385	140	71	58	88	65	3.84
1975—Jacksonville†	Southern	9	42	3	2	.600	31	18	11	39	23	2.36
1975—Kansas City	American	12	15	1	0	1.000	4	0	0	15	14	0.00
1976—Omaha	Am. Assoc.	21	133	9	8	.529	133	61	44	91	41	2.98
1976—Kansas City‡	American	8	4	0	0	.000	3	4	4	3	8	9.00
1977—Milwaukee	American	68	71	2	1	.667	64	25	20	57	34	2.54
1978—Milwaukee	American	44	65	2	6	.250	53	30	27	47	30	3.74
1979—Milwaukee	American	36	51	5	2	.714	53	29	22	37	24	3.88
1980—Milwaukee	American	52	91	5	8	.385	83	34	31	47	37	3.07
1981—Burlington	Midwest	4	14	0	2	.000	19	15	15	11	11	9.64
1981—Milwaukee§	American	4	8	0	0	.000	7	3	3	6	4	3.38
1982—Milwaukee x	American	34	172⅔	12	7	.632	160	90	81	99	74	4.22
1983—Milwaukee y	American	24	142	9	9	.500	152	75	71	68	68	4.50
1984—Milwaukee	American	39	139⅔	4	8	.333	154	76	68	68	52	4.38
1985—Milwaukee	American	38	85⅔	4	1	.800	91	43	41	57	30	4.31
1986—Milwaukee z	American	13	16⅓	2	1	.667	18	7	7	11	10	3.86
1986—Montreal	National	52	62⅔	2	5	.286	53	22	21	42	23	3.02
1987—Montreal a	National	52	52⅓	6	1	.857	47	30	20	33	20	3.44
1988—Montreal b-New York c	National	33	30	2	3	.400	35	18	18	19	8	5.40
1989—California	American	48	52⅓	6	1	.857	39	14	9	36	15	1.55
American League Totals—13 Years		420	913⅔	52	44	.542	881	430	384	551	400	3.78
National League Totals—3 Years		137	145	10	9	.526	135	70	59	94	51	3.66
Major League Totals—15 Years		557	1058⅔	62	53	.539	1016	500	443	645	451	3.77

Selected by Los Angeles Dodgers' organization in 3rd round of free-agent draft, January 10, 1973.
Selected by Kansas City Royals' organization in secondary phase of free-agent draft, June 5, 1973.
†On disabled list, April 15 to May 13 and June 5 to July 25, 1975.
‡Traded to Milwaukee Brewers, March 15, 1977; completing deal in which Kansas City Royals traded Infielder

Jamie Quirk, Outfielder Jim Wohlford and a player to be named later to Milwaukee for Pitcher Jim Colborn and Catcher Darrell Porter, December 6, 1976.

§On disabled list, March 28 to September 1, 1981; included rehabilitation disability assignment to Burlington, August 7 to August 24, 1981.

xGranted free agency, November 10, 1982; re-signed by Brewers, December 6, 1982.

yOn disabled list, August 22 to September 12, 1983.

zSold to Montreal Expos, June 8, 1986.

aGranted free agency, November 9, 1987; re-signed by Expos, December 7, 1987.

bReleased, July 2, 1988; signed by New York Mets, July 13, 1988.

cReleased, October 27, 1988; signed by California Angels, January 12, 1989.

DIVISION SERIES RECORD

Year Club	League	G.	IP.	W.	L.	Pct.	H.	R.	ER.	SO.	BB.	ERA.
1981—Milwaukee	American	3	3⅓	0	0	.000	4	0	0	2	0	0.00

CHAMPIONSHIP SERIES RECORD

Year Club	League	G.	IP.	W.	L.	Pct.	H.	R.	ER.	SO.	BB.	ERA.
1982—Milwaukee	American	1	1⅔	1	0	1.000	2	0	0	0	0	0.00

WORLD SERIES RECORD

Year Club	League	G.	IP.	W.	L.	Pct.	H.	R.	ER.	SO.	BB.	ERA.
1982—Milwaukee	American	5	4⅓	0	2	.000	5	2	2	5	3	4.15

LANCE GRAYE McCULLERS

Born March 8, 1964, at Tampa, Fla.
Height, 6.01. Weight, 218.
Throws right and bats right and lefthanded.

Major League saves: 1985 (5), 1986 (5), 1987 (16), 1988 (10), 1989 (3). Total—39.
Tied for Pacific Coast League lead in hit batsmen with 6 in 1985.

Year Club	League	G.	IP.	W.	L.	Pct.	H.	R.	ER.	SO.	BB.	ERA.
1982—Helena	Pioneer	13	87	6	4	.600	89	44	36	62	33	3.72
1983—Spartanburg†	S. Atlantic	22	136⅓	9	6	.600	139	79	61	87	57	4.03
1984—Miami	Florida St.	22	106⅓	6	4	.600	92	37	30	94	45	2.54
1984—Beaumont‡	Texas	8	55⅓	4	1	.800	38	13	13	48	35	2.11
1985—Las Vegas	P. Coast	24	149⅓	11	8	.579	135	75	66	148	83	3.98
1985—San Diego	National	21	35	0	2	.000	23	15	9	27	16	2.31
1986—San Diego	National	70	136	10	10	.500	103	46	42	92	58	2.78
1987—San Diego	National	78	123⅓	8	10	.444	115	60	51	126	59	3.72
1988—San Diego§	National	60	97⅔	3	6	.333	70	29	27	81	55	2.49
1989—New York	American	52	84⅔	4	3	.571	83	46	43	82	37	4.57
National League Totals—4 Years		229	392	21	28	.429	311	150	129	326	188	2.96
American League Totals—1 Year		52	84⅔	4	3	.571	83	46	43	82	37	4.57
Major League Totals—5 Years		281	476⅔	25	31	.446	394	196	172	408	225	3.25

Selected by Philadelphia Phillies' organization in 2nd round of free-agent draft, June 7, 1982.

†Traded with Pitchers Marty Decker, Darren Burroughs and Ed Wojna to San Diego Padres, September 20, 1983, as partial completion of deal in which San Diego traded Outfielder Sixto Lezcano and a player to be named later to Philadelphia Phillies for four players to be named later, August 31, 1983; Philadelphia organization acquired Pitcher Steve Fireovid to complete deal, October 11, 1983.

‡On disabled list, September 7, 1984 through remainder of season.

§Traded with Pitcher Jimmy Jones and Outfielder Stan Jefferson to New York Yankees for First Baseman-Outfielder Jack Clark and Pitcher Pat Clements, October 24, 1988.

TERRENCE KEITH McDANIEL
(Terry)

Born December 6, 1966, at Kansas City, Mo.
Height, 5.09. Weight, 195.
Throws and bats righthanded.

Led South Atlantic League batters in strikeouts with 173 in 1988.
Led Florida State League outfielders in double plays with 5 in 1989.
Tied for New York-Pennsylvania League lead in double plays by outfielders with 3 in 1987.

Year Club	League	Pos.	G.	AB.	R.	H.	2B.	3B.	HR.	RBI.	B.A.	PO.	A.	E.	F.A.
1986—Kingsport	Appal.	OF	41	114	24	48	5	1	6	21	.246	68	∗11	3	.963
1987—Little Falls†	NYP	OF	70	237	51	57	4	2	5	31	.241	101	∗15	∗9	.928
1988—Columbia	S. Atl.	OF	127	449	76	111	16	6	5	43	.247	211	7	11	.952
1988—St. Lucie	Fla. St.	OF	4	12	1	3	0	0	0	0	.250	5	0	1	.833
1989—St. Lucie‡	Fla. St.	OF	105	351	70	81	17	11	7	43	.231	214	∗16	4	.983

Selected by New York Mets' organization in 6th round of free-agent draft, January 14, 1986.

†Switch-hitter.

‡On disabled list, June 7 to June 17, 1989.

LARRY BENARD McDONALD
(Ben)

Born November 24, 1967, at Baton Rouge, La.
Height, 6.07. Weight, 210.
Throws and bats righthanded.
Attended Louisiana State University, Baton Rouge, La.

Member of 1988 U.S. Olympic baseball team.
Named College Player of the Year by THE SPORTING NEWS, 1989.
Named righthanded pitcher on THE SPORTING NEWS College Baseball All-America Team, 1989.
Received reported $350,000 bonus to sign with Baltimore Orioles, 1989.

Year	Club	League	G.	IP.	W.	L.	Pct.	H.	R.	ER.	SO.	BB.	ERA.
1989—Frederick		Carolina	2	9	0	0	.000	10	2	2	9	0	2.00
1989—Baltimore		American	6	7⅓	1	0	1.000	8	7	7	3	4	8.59
Major League Totals—1 Year			6	7⅓	1	0	1.000	8	7	7	3	4	8.59

Selected by Atlanta Braves' organization in 27th round of free-agent draft, June 2, 1986.
Selected by Baltimore Orioles' organization in 1st round (first player selected) of free-agent draft, June 5, 1989.

JACK BURNS McDOWELL

Born January 16, 1966, at Van Nuys, Calif.
Height, 6.05. Weight, 179.
Throws and bats righthanded.
Attended Stanford University, Stanford, Calif.

Received reported $175,000 bonus to sign with Chicago White Sox, 1987.

Year	Club	League	G.	IP.	W.	L.	Pct.	H.	R.	ER.	SO.	BB.	ERA.
1987—Sarasota White Sox		Gulf Coast	2	7	0	1	.000	4	3	2	12	1	2.57
1987—Birmingham		Southern	4	20⅔	1	2	.333	19	20	18	17	8	7.84
1987—Chicago		American	4	28	3	0	1.000	16	6	6	15	6	1.93
1988—Chicago		American	26	158⅔	5	10	.333	147	85	70	84	68	3.97
1989—Vancouver		P. Coast	16	86⅔	5	6	.455	97	60	59	65	50	6.13
1989—Sarasota White Sox		Gulf Coast	4	24	2	0	1.000	19	2	2	25	4	0.75
Major League Totals—2 Years			30	186⅔	8	10	.444	163	91	76	99	74	3.66

Selected by Boston Red Sox' organization in 20th round of free-agent draft, June 4, 1984.
Selected by Chicago White Sox' organization in 1st round (fifth player selected) of free-agent draft, June 2, 1987.

ODDIBE McDOWELL JR.

First name pronounced OH-da-bee.

Born August 25, 1962, at Hollywood, Fla.
Height, 5.09. Weight, 160.
Throws and bats lefthanded.
Attended Miami-Dade Community College (North), Miami, Fla., and
Arizona State University, Tempe, Ariz.

Shares major league record for most putouts by outfielder, game (12), July 20, 1985 (15 innings).
Shares American League record for most chances accepted by outfielder, game (12), July 20, 1985 (15 innings).
Major League stolen bases: 1985 (25), 1986 (33), 1987 (24), 1988 (33), 1989 (27). Total—142.
Hit for the cycle, July 23, 1985.
Member of 1984 U.S. Olympic baseball team.
Named outfielder on THE SPORTING NEWS College Baseball All-America Team, 1983 and 1984.

Year	Club	League	Pos.	G.	AB.	R.	H.	2B.	3B.	HR.	RBI.	B.A.	PO.	A.	E.	F.A.
1985—Oklahoma City		A. A.	OF	31	125	32	50	7	8	2	18	.400	72	4	1	.987
1985—Texas		Amer.	OF	111	406	63	97	14	5	18	42	.239	282	9	2	.993
1986—Texas		Amer.	OF	154	572	105	152	24	7	18	49	.266	325	13	3	.991
1987—Texas		Amer.	OF	128	407	65	98	26	4	14	52	.241	263	5	3	.989
1988—Texas		Amer.	OF	120	437	55	108	19	5	6	37	.247	267	2	3	.989
1988—Oklahoma City†		A. A.	OF	18	70	9	20	3	1	1	6	.286	50	1	0	1.000
1989—Cleveland‡		Amer.	OF	69	239	33	53	5	2	3	22	.222	124	5	1	.992
1989—Atlanta		Nat.	OF	76	280	56	85	18	4	7	24	.304	179	2	4	.978
American League Totals—5 Years				582	2061	321	508	88	23	59	202	.246	1261	34	12	.991
National League Totals—1 Year				76	280	56	85	18	4	7	24	.304	179	2	4	.978
Major League Totals—5 Years				658	2341	377	593	106	27	66	226	.253	1440	36	16	.989

Selected by St. Louis Cardinals' organization in 4th round of free-agent draft, January 13, 1981.
Selected by Texas Rangers' organization in secondary phase of free-agent draft, June 8, 1981.
Selected by New York Yankees' organization in secondary phase of free-agent draft, January 12, 1982.
Selected by Toronto Blue Jays' organization in secondary phase of free-agent draft, June 7, 1982.
Selected by Minnesota Twins' organization in secondary phase of free-agent draft, June 1, 1983.
Selected by Texas Rangers' organization in 1st round (12th player selected) of free-agent draft, June 4, 1984.
†Traded with First Baseman Pete O'Brien and Second Baseman Jerry Browne to Cleveland Indians for Second Baseman Julio Franco, December 6, 1988.
‡Traded to Atlanta Braves for Outfielder Dion James, July 2, 1989.

ROGER ALAN McDOWELL

Born December 21, 1960, at Cincinnati, O.
Height, 6.01. Weight, 185.
Throws and bats righthanded.
Attended Bowling Green State University, Bowling Green, O.

Major League saves: 1985 (17), 1986 (22), 1987 (25), 1988 (16), 1989 (23). Total—103.

Year	Club	League	G.	IP.	W.	L.	Pct.	H.	R.	ER.	SO.	BB.	ERA.
1982—Shelby		S. Atlantic	12	71⅓	6	4	.600	61	34	26	40	30	3.28
1982—Lynchburg		Carolina	4	29⅓	2	0	1.000	26	12	7	23	11	2.15
1983—Jackson		Texas	27	172⅓	11	12	.478	203	111	93	115	71	4.86
1984—Jackson†		Texas	3	7⅓	0	0	.000	9	3	3	8	1	3.68
1985—New York		National	62	127⅓	6	5	.545	108	43	40	70	37	2.83

Year Club	League	G.	IP.	W.	L.	Pct.	H.	R.	ER.	SO.	BB.	ERA.
1986—New York‡	National	75	128	14	9	.609	107	48	43	65	42	3.02
1987—New York§	National	56	88⅔	7	5	.583	95	41	41	32	28	4.16
1988—New York	National	62	89	5	5	.500	80	31	26	46	31	2.63
1989—New York x-Philadelphia	National	69	92	4	8	.333	79	36	20	47	38	1.96
Major League Totals—5 Years		324	525	36	32	.529	469	199	170	260	176	2.91

Selected by New York Mets' organization in 3rd round of free-agent draft, June 7, 1982.

†On disabled list, April 10 to August 14, 1984.

‡Appeared in one game as an outfielder with no chances.

§On disabled list, March 29 to May 14, 1987.

xTraded with Outfielder Lenny Dykstra and a player to be named later to Philadelphia Phillies for Outfielder Juan Samuel, June 18, 1989; Philadelphia organization acquired Pitcher Tom Edens to complete deal, July 27, 1989.

CHAMPIONSHIP SERIES RECORD

Year Club	League	G.	IP.	W.	L.	Pct.	H.	R.	ER.	SO.	BB.	ERA.
1986—New York	National	2	7	0	0	.000	1	0	0	3	0	0.00
1988—New York	National	4	6	0	1	.000	6	3	3	5	2	4.50
Championship Series Totals—2 Years		6	13	0	1	.000	7	3	3	8	2	2.08

WORLD SERIES RECORD

Year Club	League	G.	IP.	W.	L.	Pct.	H.	R.	ER.	SO.	BB.	ERA.
1986—New York	National	5	7⅓	1	0	1.000	10	5	4	2	6	4.91

CHARLES DWAYNE McELROY
(Chuck)

Born October 1, 1967, at Galveston, Tex.
Height, 6.00. Weight, 160.
Throws and bats lefthanded.

Year Club	League	G.	IP.	W.	L.	Pct.	H.	R.	ER.	SO.	BB.	ERA.
1986—Utica	NYP	14	94⅔	4	6	.400	85	40	31	91	28	2.95
1987—Spartanburg	S. Atlantic	24	130⅓	14	4	.778	117	51	45	115	48	3.11
1987—Clearwater	Florida St.	2	7⅓	1	0	1.000	1	1	0	7	4	0.00
1988—Reading	Eastern	28	160	0	12	.429	●173	89	★80	92	70	4.50
1989—Reading	Eastern	32	47	3	1	.750	39	14	14	39	14	2.68
1989—Scranton/Wilkes-Barre	Int'national	14	15⅓	1	2	.333	13	6	5	12	11	2.93
1989—Philadelphia	National	11	10⅓	0	0	.000	12	2	2	8	4	1.74
Major League Totals—1 Year		11	10⅓	0	0	.000	12	2	2	8	4	1.74

Selected by Philadelphia Phillies' organization in 8th round of free-agent draft, June 2, 1986.

ANDREW JOSEPH McGAFFIGAN
(Andy)

Born October 25, 1956, at West Palm Beach, Fla.
Height, 6.03. Weight, 190.
Throws and bats righthanded.
Attended Palm Beach Junior College, Lake Worth, Fla., and
received degree from Florida Southern College, Lakeland, Fla., in 1978.

Major League saves: 1983 (2), 1984 (1), 1986 (2), 1987 (12), 1988 (4), 1989 (2). Total—23.
Named Southern League Pitcher of the Year, 1980.

Year Club	League	G.	IP.	W.	L.	Pct.	H.	R.	ER.	SO.	BB.	ERA.
1978—Oneonta	NYP	2	12	0	1	.000	14	8	6	13	9	4.50
1978—Fort Lauderdale	Florida St.	11	66	4	5	.444	45	28	21	36	20	2.86
1979—West Haven	Eastern	23	144	10	6	.625	136	75	61	113	54	3.81
1980—Nashville†	Southern	31	170	15	5	.750	139	62	45	125	62	★2.38
1981—Columbus‡	Int'national	17	103	8	6	.571	85	45	37	57	37	3.23
1981—New York§	American	2	7	0	0	.000	5	3	2	2	3	2.57
1982—Phoenix x	P. Coast	18	96	1	6	.143	115	72	64	64	51	6.00
1982—San Francisco	National	4	8	1	0	1.000	5	1	0	4	1	0.00
1983—San Francisco y	National	43	134⅓	3	9	.250	131	67	64	93	39	4.29
1984—Montreal z-Cincinnati	National	30	69	3	6	.333	60	28	27	57	23	3.52
1985—Denver	Am. Assoc.	26	106⅔	11	5	.688	105	43	35	91	37	2.95
1985—Cincinnati a	National	15	94⅓	3	3	.500	88	40	39	83	30	3.72
1986—Montreal	National	48	142⅔	10	5	.667	114	49	42	104	55	2.65
1987—Montreal	National	69	120⅓	5	2	.714	105	38	32	100	42	2.39
1988—Montreal b	National	63	91⅓	6	0	1.000	81	31	28	71	37	2.76
1989—Montreal c	National	57	75	3	5	.375	85	40	39	40	30	4.68
American League Totals—1 Year		2	7	0	0	.000	5	3	2	2	3	2.57
National League Totals—8 Years		329	735	34	30	.531	669	294	271	552	257	3.32
Major League Totals—9 Years		331	742	34	30	.531	674	297	273	554	260	3.31

Selected by Cincinnati Reds' organization in 36th round of free-agent draft, June 5, 1974.

Selected by Chicago White Sox' organization in 5th round of free-agent draft, January 7, 1976.

Selected by New York Yankees' organization in 6th round of free-agent draft, June 6, 1978.

†On disabled list, September 1 to September 22, 1980.

‡On disabled list, April 10 to June 14, 1981.

§Traded with Outfielder Ted Wilborn to San Francisco Giants' organization for Pitcher Doyle Alexander, March 30, 1982.

xOn disabled list, June 20 to August 13, 1982.

yTraded to Montreal Expos, March 31, 1984, as compensation for the injury that Pitcher Fred Breining arrived with in trade of February 27, 1984, which sent Breining and Outfielder Max Venable to Montreal for First Baseman Al Oliver. (Breining remained with Montreal.)

zTraded with Pitcher Jim Jefferson to Cincinnati Reds for First Baseman Dan Driessen, July 26, 1984.

aTraded with Pitchers Jay Tibbs and John Stuper and Catcher Dann Bilardello to Montreal Expos for Pitcher Bill Gullickson and Catcher Sal Butera, December 19, 1985.

bOn disabled list, June 15 to July 2, 1988.

cOn disabled list, August 18 to September 2, 1989.

WILLIE DEAN McGEE

Born November 2, 1958, at San Francisco, Calif.
Height, 6.01. Weight, 195.
Throws right and bats right and lefthanded.
Attended Diablo Valley College, Pleasant Hill, Calif.

Holds modern National League record for highest batting average, switch-hitter, season, 100 or more games (.353), 1985.

Major League stolen bases: 1982 (24), 1983 (39), 1984 (43), 1985 (56), 1986 (19), 1987 (16), 1988 (41), 1989 (8). Total—246.

Hit for the cycle, June 23, 1984.

Led National League in grounding into double plays with 24 in 1987.

Named National League Player of the Year by THE SPORTING NEWS, 1985.

Named National League Most Valuable Player by Baseball Writers' Association of America, 1985.

Named outfielder on THE SPORTING NEWS National League All-Star Team, 1985.

Named outfielder on THE SPORTING NEWS National League fielding team, 1983, 1985 and 1986.

Named outfielder on THE SPORTING NEWS National League Silver Slugger team, 1985.

Year	Club	League	Pos.	G.	AB.	R.	H.	2B.	3B.	HR.	RBI.	B.A.	PO.	A.	E.	F.A.
1977—Oneonta	NYP	OF	65	225	31	53	4	3	2	22	.236	103	5	10	.915
1978—Fort Lauderdale	Fla. St.	OF	124	423	62	106	6	6	0	37	.251	243	12	9	.966
1979—West Haven	East.	OF	49	115	21	28	3	1	1	8	.243	88	3	3	.968
1979—Fort Lauderdale	Fla. St.	OF	46	176	25	56	8	3	1	18	.318	103	3	2	.981
1980—Nashville†	South.	OF	78	223	35	63	4	5	1	22	.283	127	6	6	.957
1981—Nashville‡§	South.	OF	100	388	77	125	20	5	7	63	.322	203	10	6	.973
1982—Louisville x	A. A.	OF	13	55	11	16	2	2	1	3	.291	40	0	1	.976
1982—St. Louis	Nat.	OF	123	422	43	125	12	8	4	56	.296	245	3	11	.958
1983—St. Louis y	Nat.	OF	147	601	75	172	22	8	5	75	.286	385	7	5	.987
1983—Arkansas	Texas	OF	7	29	5	8	1	1	0	2	.276	7	0	0	1.000
1984—St. Louis z	Nat.	OF	145	571	82	166	19	11	6	50	.291	374	10	6	.985
1985—St. Louis	Nat.	OF	152	612	114	★216	26	★18	10	82	★.353	382	11	9	.978
1986—St. Louis a	Nat.	OF	124	497	65	127	22	7	7	48	.256	325	9	3	★.991
1987—St. Louis	Nat.	OF-SS	153	620	76	177	37	11	11	105	.285	354	10	7	.981
1988—St. Louis	Nat.	OF	137	562	73	164	24	6	3	50	.292	348	9	9	.975
1989—St. Louis b	Nat.	OF	58	199	23	47	10	2	3	17	.236	118	2	3	.976
1989—Louisville	A. A.	OF	8	27	5	11	4	0	0	4	.407	20	1	1	.955
Major League Totals—8 Years			1039	4084	551	1194	172	71	49	483	.292	2531	61	53	.980

Selected by Chicago White Sox' organization in 7th round of free-agent draft, June 8, 1976.

Selected by New York Yankees' organization in secondary phase of free-agent draft, January 11, 1977.

†On disabled list, May 22 to June 7 and July 14 to August 7, 1980.

‡On disabled list, April 24 to June 4, 1981.

§Traded to St. Louis Cardinals' organization for Pitcher Bob Sykes, October 21, 1981.

xOn disabled list, April 13 to April 23, 1982.

yOn disabled list, March 30 to April 29, 1983; included rehabilitation disability assignment to Arkansas, April 18 to April 29, 1983.

zOn disabled list, July 12 to July 27, 1984.

aOn disabled list, August 3 to August 27, 1986.

bOn disabled list, June 7 to July 18 and July 26 to August 14, 1989; included rehabilitation disability assignment to Louisville, July 8 to July 18, 1989.

CHAMPIONSHIP SERIES RECORD

Shares Championship Series records for most triples, series (2), 1982; most times caught stealing, series (3), 1985.

Holds National League Championship Series record for most triples, total series, (3).

Shares National League Championship Series record for most times caught stealing, total series (4).

Year	Club	League	Pos.	G.	AB.	R.	H.	2B.	3B.	HR.	RBI.	B.A.	PO.	A.	E.	F.A.
1982—St. Louis	Nat.	OF	3	13	4	4	0	2	1	5	.308	12	0	1	.923
1985—St. Louis	Nat.	OF	6	26	6	7	1	0	0	3	.269	18	0	0	1.000
1987—St. Louis	Nat.	OF	7	26	2	8	1	1	0	2	.308	16	0	0	1.000
Championship Series Totals—3 Years			16	65	12	19	2	3	1	10	.292	46	0	1	.979

WORLD SERIES RECORD

Year	Club	League	Pos.	G.	AB.	R.	H.	2B.	3B.	HR.	RBI.	B.A.	PO.	A.	E.	F.A.
1982—St. Louis	Nat.	OF	6	25	6	6	0	0	2	5	.240	24	0	0	1.000
1985—St. Louis	Nat.	OF	7	27	2	7	2	0	1	2	.259	15	0	0	1.000
1987—St. Louis	Nat.	OF	7	27	2	10	2	0	0	4	.370	21	1	1	.957
World Series Totals—3 Years			20	79	10	23	4	0	3	11	.291	60	1	1	.984

ALL-STAR GAME RECORD

Year	League	Pos.	AB.	R.	H.	2B.	3B.	HR.	RBI.	B.A.	PO.	A.	E.	F.A.
1983—National		OF	2	1	1	0	0	0	0	.500	2	0	0	1.000
1985—National		OF	2	0	1	1	0	0	2	.500	1	0	0	1.000
1987—National		OF	4	0	0	0	0	0	0	.000	2	0	0	1.000
1988—National		PR-OF	2	0	0	0	0	0	0	.000	1	0	0	1.000
All-Star Game Totals—4 Years			10	0	2	1	0	0	2	.200	6	0	0	1.000

FREDERICK STANLEY McGRIFF
(Fred)

Born October 31, 1963, at Tampa, Fla.
Height, 6.03. Weight, 208.
Throws and bats lefthanded.

Major League stolen bases: 1987 (3), 1988 (6), 1989 (7). Total—16.
Led American League first basemen in total chances with 1,592 and double plays with 148 in 1989.
Tied for International League lead in intentional bases on balls received with 8 and grounding into double plays with 16 in 1986.
Led Gulf Coast League in bases on balls received with 48 and tied for lead in game-winning RBIs with 6 in 1982.
Led International League first basemen in total chances with 1,314 and double plays with 108 in 1986.
Named first baseman on THE SPORTING NEWS American League All-Star Team, 1989.
Named first baseman on THE SPORTING NEWS American League Silver Slugger team, 1989.

Year Club	League	Pos.	G.	AB.	R.	H.	2B.	3B.	HR.	RBI.	B.A.	PO.	A.	E.	F.A.
1981—Bradenton Yanks	Gulf C.	1B	29	81	6	12	2	0	0	9	.148	176	8	7	.963
1982—Braden. Yanks†	Gulf C.	1B	62	217	38	59	11	1	*9	●41	.272	514	*56	8	.986
1983—Florence	S. Atl.	1B	33	119	26	37	3	1	7	26	.311	250	14	6	.978
1983—Kinston	Carol.	1B	94	350	53	85	14	1	21	57	.243	784	57	10	.988
1984—Knoxville	South.	1B	56	189	29	47	13	2	9	25	.249	481	45	10	.981
1984—Syracuse	Int.	1B	70	238	28	56	10	1	13	28	.235	644	45	3	.996
1985—Syracuse‡	Int.	1B	51	176	19	40	8	2	5	20	.227	433	37	5	.989
1986—Syracuse	Int.	*1B-OF	133	468	69	121	23	4	19	74	.259	*1219	*85	10	*.992
1986—Toronto	Amer.	1B	3	5	1	1	0	0	0	0	.200	3	0	0	1.000
1987—Toronto	Amer.	1B	107	295	58	73	16	0	20	43	.247	108	7	2	.983
1988—Toronto	Amer.	1B	154	536	100	151	35	4	34	82	.282	1344	93	5	*.997
1989—Toronto	Amer.	1B	161	551	98	148	27	3	*36	92	.269	1460	115	*17	.989
Major League Totals—4 Years			425	1387	257	373	78	7	90	217	.269	2915	215	24	.992

Selected by New York Yankees' organization in 9th round of free-agent draft, June 8, 1981.

†Traded with Outfielder Dave Collins, Pitcher Mike Morgan and a reported $400,000 to Toronto Blue Jays for Outfielder-Catcher Tom Dodd and Pitcher Dale Murray, December 9, 1982.

‡On disabled list, June 5 to August 14, 1985.

CHAMPIONSHIP SERIES RECORD

Year Club	League	Pos.	G.	AB.	R.	H.	2B.	3B.	HR.	RBI.	B.A.	PO	A.	E.	F.A.
1989—Toronto	Amer.	1B	5	21	1	3	0	0	0	3	.143	35	2	1	.974

TERENCE ROY McGRIFF
(Terry)

Born September 23, 1963, at Fort Pierce, Fla.
Height, 6.02. Weight, 195.
Throws and bats righthanded.

Major League stolen bases: 1988 (1).
Led American Association catchers in double plays with 8 1986 and tied for lead with 10 in 1989.
Led American Association in passed balls with 10 in 1986.
Led Eastern League catchers in total chances with 731 in 1985.

Year Club	League	Pos.	G.	AB.	R.	H.	2B.	3B.	HR.	RBI.	B.A.	PO.	A.	E.	F.A.
1981—Billings	Pion.	C-1B	42	96	15	26	3	0	1	15	.271	166	14	7	.963
1982—Eugene	N'west	C	53	190	23	46	10	2	4	31	.242	320	*43	8	.978
1983—Tampa	Fla. St.	C	87	260	21	66	11	3	5	45	.254	403	67	7	.985
1984—Tampa	Fla. St.	C	110	345	48	96	19	0	7	41	.278	576	88	16	.976
1985—Vermont	East.	C	110	363	52	92	10	4	13	60	.253	*636	89	6	*.992
1986—Denver	A. A.	C	108	340	54	99	22	1	9	54	.291	411	*59	11	.977
1987—Nashville	A. A.	C	67	228	36	62	11	3	10	33	.272	343	36	3	.992
1987—Cincinnati	Nat.	C	34	89	6	20	3	0	2	11	.225	160	14	3	.983
1988—Cincinnati	Nat.	C	35	96	9	19	3	0	1	4	.198	177	14	2	.990
1988—Nashville	A. A.	C	35	97	8	21	3	1	1	12	.216	175	10	4	.979
1989—Cincinnati	Nat.	C	6	11	1	3	0	0	0	2	.273	23	3	2	.929
1989—Nashville	A. A.	C	102	335	42	94	24	1	5	28	.281	534	74	9	.985
Major League Totals—3 Years			75	196	16	42	6	0	3	17	.214	360	31	7	.982

Selected by Cincinnati Reds' organization in 8th round of free-agent draft, June 8, 1981.

WILLIAM PATRICK McGUIRE JR.
(Bill)

Born February 14, 1964, at Omaha, Neb.
Height, 6.03. Weight, 215.
Throws and bats righthanded.
Attended University of Nebraska, Lincoln, Neb.

Led California League catchers in double plays with 16 in 1986.

Year Club	League	Pos.	G.	AB.	R.	H.	2B.	3B.	HR.	RBI.	B.A.	PO.	A.	E.	F.A.
1985—Wausau	Midw.	C	56	191	24	47	9	0	3	15	.246	304	26	9	.973
1986—Salinas	Calif.	C	116	368	49	110	22	1	6	62	.299	713	83	*20	.975
1987—Chattanooga	South.	C	79	259	21	59	10	0	3	29	.228	477	43	6	.989
1988—Vermont	East.	C	49	136	16	28	3	0	5	24	.206	280	43	7	.979
1988—Calgary	P. C.	C	37	117	17	27	7	0	2	15	.231	215	19	1	.996
1988—Seattle	Amer.	C	9	16	1	3	0	0	0	2	.188	29	3	0	1.000

Year Club League	Pos.	G.	AB.	R.	H.	2B.	3B.	HR.	RBI.	B.A.	PO.	A.	E.	F.A.
1989—Calgary .... P. C.	C	83	268	39	74	17	0	7	38	.276	467	55	7	.987
1989—Seattle.................... Amer.	C	14	28	2	5	0	0	1	4	.179	62	6	0	1.000
Major League Totals—2 Years................		23	44	3	8	0	0	1	6	.182	91	9	0	1.000

Selected by Cleveland Indians' organization in 25th round of free-agent draft, June 7, 1982.
Selected by Seattle Mariners' organization in 1st round (27th player selected) of free-agent draft, June 3, 1985.

MARK DAVID McGWIRE

Born October 1, 1963, at Pomona, Calif.
Height, 6.05. Weight, 225.
Throws and bats righthanded.
Attended University of Southern California, Los Angeles, Calif.
Brother of Dan McGwire, quarterback at San Diego State University.

Holds major league records for most home runs (49) and extra bases on long hits (183) by rookie, season, 1987.
Shares major league record for most home runs, two consecutive games (5), June 27 and 28, 1987.
Shares modern major league record for most runs, two consecutive games (9), June 27 and 28, 1987.
Holds American League record for highest slugging average by rookie, season (.618), 1987.
Hit three home runs in a game, June 27, 1987.
Major League stolen bases: 1987 (1), 1989 (1). Total—2.
Led American League in slugging percentage with .618 in 1987.
Led California League third basemen in assists with 239 and total chances with 354 in 1985.
Named American League Rookie Player of the Year by THE SPORTING NEWS, 1987.
Named American League Rookie of the Year by Baseball Writers' Association of America, 1987.
Member of 1984 U.S. Olympic baseball team.
Named College Player of the Year by THE SPORTING NEWS, 1984.
Named first baseman on THE SPORTING NEWS College Baseball All-America Team, 1984.

Year Club League	Pos.	G.	AB.	R.	H.	2B.	3B.	HR.	RBI.	B.A.	PO.	A.	E.	F.A.
1984—Modesto.................. Calif.	1B	16	55	7	11	3	0	1	1	.200	107	6	1	.991
1985—Modesto.................. Calif.	3B-1B	138	489	95	134	23	3	●24	●106	.274	105	240	33	.913
1986—Huntsville .... South	3B	55	195	40	59	15	0	10	53	.303	34	124	16	.908
1986—Tacoma.................. P. C.	3B	78	280	42	89	21	5	13	59	.318	53	126	25	.877
1986—Oakland................. Amer.	3B	18	53	10	10	1	0	3	9	.189	10	20	6	.833
1987—Oakland................. Amer.	1B-3B-OF	151	557	97	161	28	4	★49	118	.289	1176	101	13	.990
1988—Oakland................. Amer.	1B-OF	155	550	87	143	22	1	32	99	.260	1228	88	9	.993
1989—Oakland†............... Amer.	1B	143	490	74	113	17	0	33	95	.231	1170	114	6	.995
Major League Totals—4 Years.................		467	1650	268	427	68	5	117	321	.259	3584	323	34	.991

Selected by Montreal Expos' organization in 8th round of free-agent draft, June 8, 1981.
Selected by Oakland A's organization in 1st round (10th player selected) of free-agent draft, June 4, 1984.
†On disabled list, April 11 to April 26, 1989.

CHAMPIONSHIP SERIES RECORD

Year Club League	Pos.	G.	AB.	R.	H.	2B.	3B.	HR.	RBI.	B.A.	PO.	A.	E.	F.A.
1988—Oakland................. Amer.	1B	4	15	4	5	0	0	1	3	.333	24	2	0	1.000
1989—Oakland................. Amer.	1B	5	18	3	7	1	0	1	3	.389	46	1	1	.979
Championship Series Totals—2 Years.....		9	33	7	12	1	0	2	6	.364	70	3	1	.986

WORLD SERIES RECORD

Year Club League	Pos.	G.	AB.	R.	H.	2B.	3B.	HR.	RBI.	B.A.	PO.	A.	E.	F.A.
1988—Oakland................. Amer.	1B	5	17	1	1	0	0	1	1	.059	40	3	0	1.000
1989—Oakland................. Amer.	1B	4	17	0	5	1	0	0	1	.294	28	2	0	1.000
World Series Totals—2 Years		9	34	1	6	1	0	1	2	.176	68	5	0	1.000

ALL-STAR GAME RECORD

Year League	Pos.	AB.	R.	H.	2B.	3B.	HR.	RBI.	B.A.	PO.	A.	E.	F.A.
1987—American	1B	3	0	0	0	0	0	0	.000	7	0	1	.875
1988—American	1B	2	0	1	0	0	0	0	.500	8	0	0	1.000
1989—American	1B	3	0	1	0	0	0	0	.333	5	0	0	1.000
All-Star Game Totals—3 Years....................		8	0	2	0	0	0	0	.250	20	0	1	.952

TIMOTHY ALLEN McINTOSH
(Tim)

Born March 21, 1965, at Crystal, Minn.
Height, 5.11. Weight, 195.
Throws and bats righthanded.
Attended University of Minnesota, Minneapolis, Minn.

Led Midwest League in game-winning RBIs with 14 in 1987.
Led California League catchers in assists with 99 and double plays with 14 in 1988.

Year Club League	Pos.	G.	AB.	R.	H.	2B.	3B.	HR.	RBI.	B.A.	PO.	A.	E.	F.A.
1986—Beloit .... Midw.	OF	49	173	26	45	3	2	4	21	.260	98	4	4	.962
1987—Beloit .... Midw.	C	130	461	83	139	30	3	20	85	.302	624	71	6	★.991
1988—Stockton .... Calif.	C-OF	138	519	81	147	32	6	15	92	.283	779	101	17	.981
1989—El Paso................. Texas	C-OF	120	463	72	139	30	3	17	93	.300	474	59	17	.969

Selected by Milwaukee Brewers' organization in 3rd round of free-agent draft, June 2, 1986.

JEFFERSON ALAN McKNIGHT
(Jeff)

Born February 18, 1963, at Conway, Ark.
Height, 6.01. Weight, 170.
Throws right and bats left and righthanded.
Attended Westark Community College, Fort Smith, Ark.
Son of Jim McKnight, infielder with Chicago Cubs, 1960 and 1962.

Led International League in bases on balls received with 79 in 1989.

Year—Club	League	Pos.	G.	AB.	R.	H.	2B.	3B.	HR.	RBI.	B.A.	PO.	A.	E.	F.A.
1983—Little Falls†	NYP	SS	39	115	10	25	3	1	0	9	.217	43	72	16	.878
1984—Columbia†	S. Atl.	S-2-3-1-O	95	251	31	64	10	1	1	27	.255	115	144	21	.925
1985—Columbia†	S. Atl.	O-1-P	67	159	26	42	6	1	1	24	.264	92	16	4	.964
1985—Lynchburg†	Carol.	S-3-2-O	49	150	19	33	6	1	0	21	.220	47	106	12	.927
1986—Jackson†	Texas	O-I-P	132	469	71	118	24	3	4	55	.252	400	154	19	.967
1987—Jackson†	Texas	O-3-1-2-S	16	59	5	12	3	0	2	8	.203	22	27	1	.980
1987—Tidewater	Int.	I-O-P	87	184	21	47	7	3	2	25	.255	141	119	9	.967
1988—Tidewater†	Int.	O-2-S-1-3	113	345	36	88	14	0	2	25	.255	180	155	15	.957
1989—Tidewater	Int.	I-O-C	116	425	84	106	19	2	9	48	.249	665	172	15	.982
1989—New York‡	Nat.	2-1-S-3	6	12	2	3	0	0	0	0	.250	4	5	1	.900
Major Leaue Totals—1 Year			6	12	2	3	0	0	0	0	.250	4	5	1	.900

Selected by Baltimore Orioles' organization in 28th round of free-agent draft, June 7, 1982.
Selected by New York Mets' organization in secondary phase of free-agent draft, January 11, 1983.
†Batted lefthanded only.
‡Released, September 29, 1989; signed by Rochester (Baltimore Orioles' organziation), December 5, 1989.

RECORD AS PITCHER

Year—Club	League	G.	IP.	W.	L.	Pct.	H.	R.	ER.	SO.	BB.	ERA.
1985—Columbia	S. Atlantic	3	4	0	0	.000	4	5	4	8	3	9.00
1986—Jackson	Texas	5	6	0	0	.000	4	1	1	1	1	1.50
1987—Tidewater	Int'national	1	2	0	0	.000	0	0	0	0	0	0.00

MARK TREMELL McLEMORE

Born October 4, 1964, at San Diego, Calif.
Height, 5.11. Weight, 195.
Throws right and bats left and righthanded.

Major League stolen bases: 1987 (25), 1988 (13), 1989 (6). Total—44.
Led Pacific Coast League second basemen in total chances with 597 and double plays with 95 in 1989.
Led California League second basemen in assists with 400 and double plays with 84 in 1984.

Year—Club	League	Pos.	G.	AB.	R.	H.	2B.	3B.	HR.	RBI.	B.A.	PO.	A.	E.	F.A.
1982—Salem	N'west	2B-SS	55	165	42	49	6	2	0	25	.297	81	125	11	.947
1983—Peoria	Midw.	2B-SS	95	329	42	79	7	3	0	18	.240	170	250	24	.946
1984—Redwood	Calif.	2B-SS	134	482	102	142	8	3	0	45	.295	274	429	25	.966
1985—Midland†	Texas	2B-SS	117	458	80	124	17	6	2	46	.271	301	339	19	.971
1986—Midland	Texas	2B	63	237	54	75	9	1	1	29	.316	155	194	13	.964
1986—Edmonton	P. C.	2B	73	286	41	79	13	1	0	23	.276	173	215	7	.982
1986—California	Amer.	2B	5	4	0	0	0	0	0	0	.000	3	10	0	1.000
1987—California	Amer.	2B-SS	138	433	61	102	13	3	3	41	.236	293	363	17	.975
1988—California‡	Amer.	2B-3B	77	233	38	56	11	2	2	16	.240	108	178	6	.979
1988—Palm Springs	Calif.	2B	11	44	9	15	3	1	0	6	.341	18	24	1	.977
1988—Edmonton	P. C.	2B	12	45	7	12	3	0	0	6	.267	35	33	1	.986
1989—Edmonton	P. C.	2B	114	430	60	105	13	2	2	34	.244	*264	323	10	*.983
1989—California	Amer.	2B	32	103	12	25	3	1	0	14	.243	55	88	5	.966
Major League Totals—4 Years			252	773	111	183	27	6	5	71	.237	459	639	28	.975

Selected by California Angels' organization in 9th round of free-agent draft, June 7, 1982.
†On disabled list, May 15 to May 27, 1985.
‡On disabled list, May 24 to August 2, 1988; included rehabilitation disability assignment to Palm Springs, July 7 to July 21, 1988; and Edmonton, July 22 to July 27, 1988.

JOE CRAIG McMURTRY

(Known by middle name.)

Born November 5, 1959, at Temple, Tex.
Height, 6.05. Weight, 195.
Throws and bats righthanded.
Attended McLennan Community College, Waco, Tex.

Major League saves: 1985 (1), 1988 (3). Total—4.
Tied for International League lead in games started by pitchers with 32 in 1982.
Named National League Rookie Pitcher of the Year by THE SPORTING NEWS, 1983.
Named International League Pitcher of the Year, 1982.

Year—Club	League	G.	IP.	W.	L.	Pct.	H.	R.	ER.	SO.	BB.	ERA.
1980—Savannah	Southern	14	86	7	4	.636	82	40	34	37	35	3.56
1981—Savannah	Southern	28	202	*15	11	.577	168	87	62	111	95	2.76
1982—Richmond	Int'national	32	*210	*17	9	.654	198	98	89	96	107	3.81
1983—Atlanta	National	36	224⅔	15	9	.625	204	86	77	105	88	3.08
1984—Atlanta	National	37	183⅓	9	17	.346	184	100	88	99	102	4.32
1985—Atlanta	National	17	45	0	3	.000	56	36	33	28	27	6.60
1985—Richmond	Int'national	16	107⅓	7	5	.583	88	43	39	74	51	3.27

Year Club	League	G.	IP.	W.	L.	Pct.	H.	R.	ER.	SO.	BB.	ERA.
1986—Atlanta†	National	37	79⅔	1	6	.143	82	46	42	50	43	4.74
1986—Greenville‡	Southern	3	15	1	1	.500	13	10	10	12	9	6.00
1987—Knoxville§	Southern	12	78	4	2	.667	64	28	24	56	20	2.77
1987—Syracuse x	Int'national	9	53⅔	5	3	.625	46	23	21	31	15	3.52
1988—Oklahoma City	Am. Assoc.	9	49⅔	2	5	.286	55	27	24	35	21	4.35
1988—Texas	American	32	60	3	3	.500	37	16	15	35	24	2.25
1989—Texas y	American	19	23	0	0	.000	29	21	19	14	13	7.43
1989—Sarasota Rangers	Gulf Coast	4	8	0	1	.000	3	2	1	10	2	1.13
1989—Oklahoma City z	Am. Assoc.	1	3	0	0	.000	2	1	1	1	1	3.00
National League Totals—4 Years		127	532⅔	25	35	.417	526	268	240	282	260	4.06
American League Totals—2 Years		51	83	3	3	.500	66	37	34	49	37	3.69
Major League Totals—6 Years		178	615⅔	28	38	.424	592	305	274	331	297	4.01

Selected by Atlanta Braves' organization in 1st round (fourth player selected) of free-agent draft, January 8, 1980.

†On disabled list, July 27 to September 1, 1986; included rehabilitation disability assignment to Greenville, August 14 to September 1, 1986.

‡Traded to Toronto Blue Jays for Second Baseman Damaso Garcia and Pitcher Luis Leal, February 2, 1987.

§On Toronto disabled list, March 30 to June 18, 1987; included rehabilitation disability assignment to Knoxville, May 29 to June 17, 1987.

xGranted free agency, November 22, 1987; signed by Texas Rangers, December 8, 1987.

yOn disabled list, April 18 to May 5 and May 25 to August 20, 1989; included rehabilitation disability assignment to Sarasota Rangers, August 5 to August 14, 1989; then transferred to Oklahoma City, August 15 to August 20, 1989.

zGranted free agency, November 13, 1989.

BRIAN WESLEY McRAE

Born June 27, 1967, at Bradenton, Fla.
Height, 6.00. Weight, 175.
Throws right and bats left and righthanded.
Son of Hal McRae, outfielder with Cincinnati Reds and Kansas City Royals, 1968 and 1970 through 1987; coach with Kansas City Royals, 1987; minor league instructor in Pittsburgh Pirates' organization, 1988 and 1989; and currently coach with Montreal Expos.
Led Northwest League second basemen in total chances with 373 in 1986.
Tied for Southern League lead in double plays by outfielders with 5 in 1989.

Year Club	League	Pos.	G.	AB.	R.	H.	2B.	3B.	HR.	RBI.	B.A.	PO.	A.	E.	F.A.
1985—Sarasota Royals	Gulf C.	2B-SS	60	217	40	58	6	5	0	23	.267	116	142	18	.935
1986—Eugene	N'west	2B	72	306	★66	82	10	3	1	29	.268	146	★214	13	★.965
1987—Fort Myers	Fla. St.	2B	131	481	62	121	14	1	1	31	.252	★284	346	18	.972
1988—Baseball City	Fla. St.	2B	30	107	18	33	2	0	1	11	.308	70	103	4	.977
1988—Memphis	South.	2B	91	288	33	58	13	1	4	15	.201	147	231	18	.955
1989—Memphis	South.	OF	138	★533	72	121	18	8	5	42	.227	249	11	5	.981

Selected by Kansas City Royals' organization in 1st round (17th player selected) of free-agent draft, June 3, 1985.

WALTER KEVIN McREYNOLDS

(Known by middle name.)
Born October 16, 1959, at Little Rock, Ark.
Height, 6.01. Weight, 215.
Throws and bats righthanded.
Attended University of Arkansas, Fayetteville, Ark.
Holds major league record for most stolen bases with no caught stealing, season (21), 1988.
Shares major league record for fewest double plays by outfielder, season, 150 or more games (0), 1987.
Major League stolen bases: 1983 (2), 1984 (3), 1985 (4), 1986 (8), 1987 (14), 1988 (21), 1989 (15). Total—67.
Hit for the cycle, August 1, 1989.
Led National League outfielders in double plays with 5 in 1988.
Led National League outfielders in total chances with 436 in 1984 and 445 in 1985.
Led Pacific Coast League in total bases with 328 in 1983.
Named outfielder on THE SPORTING NEWS National League All-Star Team, 1988.
Named Minor League Player of the Year by THE SPORTING NEWS, 1983.
Named Pacific Coast League Player of the Year, 1983.
Named California League Most Valuable Player, 1982.
Received reported $125,000 bonus to sign with San Diego Padres, 1982.
Named outfielder on THE SPORTING NEWS College Baseball All-America Team, 1981.

Year Club	League	Pos.	G.	AB.	R.	H.	2B.	3B.	HR.	RBI.	B.A.	PO.	A.	E.	F.A.
1982—Reno	Calif.	OF	90	338	83	127	17	5	★28	98	★.376	52	7	3	.952
1982—Amarillo	Texas	OF	40	162	30	57	8	3	5	39	.352	76	3	2	.975
1983—Las Vegas	P. C.	OF	113	446	98	168	★46	9	●32	116	.377	257	3	9	.967
1983—San Diego	Nat.	OF	39	140	15	31	3	1	4	14	.221	87	4	1	.989
1984—San Diego	Nat.	OF	147	525	68	146	26	6	20	75	.278	★422	10	4	.991
1985—San Diego	Nat.	OF	152	564	61	132	24	4	15	75	.234	★430	12	3	.993
1986—San Diego†	Nat.	OF	158	560	89	161	31	6	26	96	.288	332	9	8	.977
1987—New York	Nat.	OF	151	590	86	163	32	5	29	95	.276	286	8	4	.987
1988—New York	Nat.	OF	147	552	82	159	30	2	27	99	.288	252	★18	4	.985
1989—New York	Nat.	OF	148	545	74	148	25	3	22	85	.272	307	10	●10	.969
Major League Totals—7 Years			942	3476	475	940	171	27	143	539	.270	2116	71	34	.985

Selected by Milwaukee Brewers' organization in 18th round of free-agent draft, June 6, 1978.

Selected by San Diego Padres' organization in 1st round (sixth player selected) of free-agent draft, June 8, 1981.

†Traded with Pitcher Gene Walter and Infielder Adam Ging to New York Mets for Outfielders Shawn Abner, Stanley Jefferson and Kevin Mitchell and Pitchers Kevin Armstrong and Kevin Brown, December 11, 1986.

Shares National League Championship Series record for most hits, game (4), October 11, 1988.

Year Club League	Pos.	G.	AB.	R.	H.	2B.	3B.	HR.	RBI.	B.A.	PO.	A.	E.	F.A.
1984—San Diego .... Nat.	OF	4	10	2	3	0	0	1	4	.300	10	0	0	1.000
1988—New York.............. Nat.	OF	7	28	4	7	2	0	2	4	.250	19	0	0	1.000
Championship Series Totals—2 Years.....		11	38	6	10	2	0	3	8	.263	29	0	0	1.000

LARRY DEAN McWILLIAMS

Born February 10, 1954, at Wichita, Kan.
Height, 6.05. Weight, 181.
Throws and bats lefthanded.
Attended Paris Junior College, Paris, Tex.

Shares major league record for most strikeouts by batter, inning (2), April 22, 1979, fourth inning.
Major League saves: 1982 (1), 1984 (1), 1988 (1). Total—3.
Named lefthanded pitcher on THE SPORTING NEWS National League All-Star Team, 1983.

Year Club	League	G.	IP.	W.	L.	Pct.	H.	R.	ER.	SO.	BB.	ERA.
1974—Greenwood†	W. Carol.	11	64	4	3	.571	64	26	20	61	23	2.81
1975—Greenwood‡	W. Carol.	17	93	8	4	.667	83	36	29	71	18	2.81
1976—Greenwood	W. Carol.	8	48	2	2	.500	40	19	14	44	13	2.63
1976—Savannah	Southern	16	74	3	8	.273	82	41	38	37	33	4.62
1977—Savannah	Southern	26	158	8	9	.471	153	70	59	139	64	3.36
1978—Richmond	Int'national	15	108	6	5	.545	87	36	34	78	41	2.83
1978—Atlanta	National	15	99	9	3	.750	84	38	31	42	35	2.82
1979—Atlanta§	National	13	66	3	2	.600	69	41	41	32	22	5.59
1980—Atlanta	National	30	164	9	14	.391	188	97	90	77	39	4.94
1981—Richmond	Int'national	29	178	●13	10	.565	174	98	●86	157	79	4.35
1981—Atlanta	National	6	38	2	1	.667	31	13	13	23	8	3.08
1982—Atlanta x-Pittsburgh	National	46	159⅓	8	8	.500	158	79	68	118	44	3.84
1983—Pittsburgh	National	35	238	15	8	.652	205	99	86	199	87	3.25
1984—Pittsburgh	National	34	227⅓	12	11	.522	226	86	74	149	78	2.93
1985—Pittsburgh y	National	30	126⅓	7	9	.438	139	70	66	52	62	4.70
1986—Pittsburgh z	National	49	122⅓	3	11	.214	129	75	70	80	49	5.15
1987—Greenville	Southern	7	33	1	2	.333	33	24	20	27	26	5.45
1987—Atlanta a	National	9	20⅓	0	1	.000	25	15	13	13	7	5.75
1987—Oklahoma City b	Am. Assoc.	7	22⅓	1	4	.200	44	29	28	13	20	11.28
1988—St. Louis c	National	42	136	6	9	.400	130	64	59	70	45	3.90
1989—Philadelphia d	National	40	120⅔	2	11	.154	123	67	55	54	49	4.10
1989—Kansas City	American	8	32⅔	2	2	.500	31	15	15	24	8	4.13
National League Totals—12 Years		349	1517⅓	76	88	.463	1507	744	666	909	525	3.95
American League Totals—1 Year		8	32⅔	2	2	.500	31	15	15	24	8	4.13
Major League Totals—12 Years		357	1550	78	90	.464	1538	759	681	933	533	3.95

Selected by Atlanta Braves' organization in 1st round (sixth player selected) of free-agent draft, January 9, 1974.
†On disabled list, July 22 to September 25, 1974.
‡On disabled list, April 11 to June 3, 1975.
§On disabled list, May 18 to June 15 and July 7 to September 1, 1979.
xTraded to Pittsburgh Pirates for Pitcher Pascual Perez and a player to be named later, June 30, 1982; Atlanta Braves' organization acquired Shortstop Carlos Rios to complete deal, September 8, 1982.
yOn disabled list, May 17 to June 8 and August 18 to September 3, 1985.
zReleased, April 6, 1987; signed by Greenville (Atlanta Braves' organization), May 18, 1987.
aReleased, July 25, 1987; signed by Oklahoma City (Texas Rangers' organization), August 6, 1987.
bReleased, February 2, 1988; signed by St. Louis Cardinals, February 12, 1988.
cGranted free agency, November 4, 1988; signed by Philadelphia Phillies, January 30, 1989.
dTraded by Kansas City Royals for a player to be named later, September 2, 1989; Reading (Philadelphia Phillies' organization) acquired Catcher Jeff Hulse to complete deal, October 21, 1989.

MICHAEL RAY MEADOWS
(Louie)

Born April 29, 1961, in Onslow County, N. C.
Height, 5.11. Weight, 190.
Throws and bats lefthanded.
Attended North Carolina State University, Raleigh, N. C.

Major League stolen bases: 1986 (1), 1988 (4), 1989 (1). Total—6.

Year Club	League	Pos.	G.	AB.	R.	H.	2B.	3B.	HR.	RBI.	B.A.	PO.	A.	E.	F.A.
1982—Asheville	S. Atl.	OF	66	228	43	72	9	1	10	41	.316	87	4	13	.875
1983—Daytona Beach	Fla. St.	OF	112	382	68	112	25	14	9	71	.293	169	5	4	.978
1984—Daytona Beach	Fla. St.	OF-1B	70	252	49	76	14	10	6	44	.302	323	17	5	.986
1984—Columbus	South.	OF-1B	65	225	33	63	17	4	8	36	.280	150	6	3	.981
1985—Columbus	South.	OF-1B	140	476	76	111	16	8	14	67	.233	514	32	12	.978
1986—Tucson†	P. C.	OF-1B	82	290	42	87	14	8	10	52	.300	203	15	9	.960
1986—Houston	Nat.	OF	6	6	1	2	0	0	0	0	.333	0	0	0	.000
1987—Tucson	P. C.	OF-1B	129	426	70	110	21	★14	10	76	.258	252	8	7	.974
1988—Tucson	P. C.	OF-1B	85	280	42	71	16	9	5	43	.254	415	28	5	.989
1988—Houston	Nat.	OF	35	42	5	8	0	1	2	3	.190	18	1	0	1.000
1989—Tucson	P. C.	OF-1B	53	179	32	44	9	2	6	27	.246	109	5	3	.974
1989—Houston	Nat.	OF-1B	31	51	5	9	0	0	3	10	.176	13	0	0	1.000
Major League Totals—3 Years			72	99	11	19	0	1	5	13	.192	31	1	0	1.000

Selected by Houston Astros' organization in 2nd round of free-agent draft, June 7, 1982.
†On disabled list, July 21, 1986 through remainder of season.

DAVID DONALD MEADS III
(Dave)

Born January 7, 1964, at Montclair, N.J.
Height, 6.00. Weight, 175.
Throws and bats lefthanded.
Attended Middlesex County College, Edison, N.J.

Year Club	League	G.	IP.	W.	L.	Pct.	H.	R.	ER.	SO.	BB.	ERA.
1984—Sarasota Astros	Gulf Coast	7	29⅓	2	2	.500	22	11	4	28	2	1.23
1984—Auburn†	NYP	10	28	5	1	.833	31	17	16	29	12	5.14
1985—Gastonia	S. Atlantic	33	146⅓	3	10	.231	160	91	71	118	50	4.37
1986—Asheville	S. Atlantic	19	54⅓	4	3	.571	51	25	12	50	14	1.99
1986—Osceola	Florida St.	11	15⅓	2	4	.333	24	14	13	10	7	7.63
1986—Columbus	Southern	16	22⅓	1	1	.500	22	11	11	26	13	4.43
1987—Houston	National	45	48⅔	5	3	.625	60	31	30	32	16	5.55
1987—Tucson	P. Coast	10	9⅔	1	0	1.000	7	4	3	6	6	2.79
1988—Tucson	P. Coast	32	46	3	4	.429	45	12	10	46	10	1.96
1988—Houston	National	22	39⅔	3	1	.750	37	20	14	27	14	3.18
1989—Tucson‡	P. Coast	1	3	0	0	.000	1	0	0	2	1	0.00
Major League Totals—2 Years		67	88⅓	8	4	.667	97	51	44	59	30	4.48

Selected by Houston Astros' organization in 6th round of free-agent draft, January 17, 1984.
†Loaned to Gastonia (Independent), April 4, 1985; returned, October 15, 1985.
‡On Houston disabled list, March 31, 1989 through entire season; included rehabilitation disability assignment to Tucson, May 6 to May 10, 1989.

LUIS MAIN MEDINA

Born March 26, 1963, at Santa Monica, Calif.
Height, 6.03. Weight, 195.
Throws left and bats righthanded.
Attended Cerritos College, Norwalk, Calif., and Arizona State University, Tempe, Ariz.

Led Pacific Coast League in slugging percentage with .616 in 1988.
Led Midwest League in total bases with 300 in 1986.
Named Midwest League Most Valuable Player, 1986.

Year Club	League	Pos.	G.	AB.	R.	H.	2B.	3B.	HR.	RBI.	B.A.	PO.	A.	E.	F.A.
1985—Batavia	NYP	OF-1B	76	290	43	77	16	0	12	43	.266	101	3	1	.990
1986—Waterloo	Midw.	OF	136	505	★107	★160	25	5	★35	★110	.317	208	8	5	.977
1987—Williamsport	East.	OF-1B	96	341	61	109	15	6	16	68	.320	260	10	4	.985
1988—Colorado Springs	P. C.	OF-1B	111	406	81	126	28	6	★28	81	.310	374	26	10	.976
1988—Cleveland	Amer.	1B	16	51	10	13	0	0	6	8	.255	137	9	0	1.000
1989—Cleveland	Amer.	OF-1B	30	83	8	17	1	0	4	8	.205	4	0	2	.667
1989—Colorado Springs	P. C.	OF-1B	51	166	17	29	8	0	3	19	.175	141	8	5	.968
Major League Totals—2 Years			46	134	18	30	1	0	10	16	.224	141	9	2	.987

Selected by New York Mets' organization in 33rd round of free-agent draft, June 8, 1981.
Selected by New York Mets' organization in secondary phase of free-agent draft, January 12, 1982.
Selected by New York Yankees' organization in secondary phase of free-agent draft, June 7, 1982.
Selected by Cincinnati Reds' organization in secondary phase of free-agent draft, January 11, 1983.
Selected by Oakland Athletics' organization in secondary phase of free-agent draft, June 6, 1983.
Selected by Houston Astros' organization in secondary phase of free-agent draft, June 4, 1984.
Selected by Cleveland Indians' organization in 9th round of free-agent draft, June 3, 1985.

SCOTT HOWARD MEDVIN

Born September 16, 1961, at North Olmsted, O.
Height, 6.00. Weight, 190.
Throws and bats righthanded.
Received bachelor of arts degree in management from Baldwin-Wallace College, Berea, O.

Year Club	League	G.	IP.	W.	L.	Pct.	H.	R.	ER.	SO.	BB.	ERA.
1984—Wausau†	Midwest	40	65⅔	4	2	.667	62	36	26	53	35	3.56
1985—Lakeland‡	Florida St.	31	51⅔	5	4	.556	48	20	16	47	20	2.79
1985—Birmingham	Southern	13	23	3	3	.500	14	10	8	17	12	3.13
1986—Shreveport	Texas	49	93⅔	8	6	.571	71	32	25	68	42	2.40
1987—Shreveport	Texas	37	78⅔	7	1	.875	59	19	15	71	41	1.72
1987—Phoenix§-Vancouver x	P. Coast	13	22⅓	1	0	1.000	22	17	13	16	18	5.24
1988—Buffalo	Am. Assoc.	39	56	5	4	.556	38	18	15	49	25	2.41
1988—Pittsburgh	National	17	27⅔	3	0	1.000	23	16	15	16	9	4.88
1989—Buffalo	Am. Assoc.	54	86	7	6	.538	65	29	22	84	46	2.30
1989—Pittsburgh	National	6	6⅓	0	1	.000	6	5	4	4	5	5.68
Major League Totals—2 Years		23	34	3	1	.750	29	21	19	20	14	5.03

Signed as free agent by Detroit Tigers' organization, September 27, 1983.
†Loaned to Wausau (Seattle Mariners' organization), April 4, 1984; returned, September 5, 1984.
‡Traded to San Francisco Giants, December 11, 1985, completing deal in which San Francisco traded Pitchers Dave LaPoint and Eric King and Catcher Matt Nokes to Detroit Tigers for Pitcher Juan Berenguer, Catcher Bob Melvin and a player to be named later, October 7, 1985.
§Traded with Pitcher Jeff Robinson to Pittsburgh Pirates for Pitcher Rick Reuschel, August 21, 1987.
xDrafted by Houston Astros, December 7, 1987; returned, April 4, 1988.

FRANCISCO JAVIER MELENDEZ (VILLEGAS)

Born January 25, 1964, at Rio Piedras, Puerto Rico.
Height, 6.00. Weight, 191.
Throws and bats lefthanded.
Led Pacific Coast League in intentional bases on balls received with 11 in 1987.
Led Pacific Coast League first basemen in putouts with 1,085 in 1984.
Led Eastern League first basemen in putouts with 1,081, total chances with 1,166 and double plays with 99 in 1983.
Tied for Pacific Coast League lead in errors by first basemen with 13 in 1987.

Year—Club	League	Pos.	G.	AB.	R.	H.	2B.	3B.	HR.	RBI.	B.A.	PO.	A.	E.	F.A.
1981—Peninsula	Carol.	1B-OF	32	74	6	10	3	0	0	6	.135	154	13	6	.965
1981—Spartanburg	S. Atl.	1B-OF	85	306	44	82	13	1	3	36	.268	760	57	17	.980
1982—Peninsula	Carol.	1B	118	424	54	124	*33	3	4	69	.292	739	75	11	.987
1983—Reading	East.	1B-OF	126	450	81	134	17	4	5	75	.298	1082	73	12	.990
1984—Portland	P. C.	*1B-OF	128	506	63	158	36	8	3	65	.312	1090	85	11	*.991
1984—Philadelphia	Nat.	1B	21	23	0	3	0	0	0	2	.130	37	4	0	1.000
1985—Portland	P. C.	●1B-OF	130	397	41	111	25	2	2	54	.280	974	69	●15	.986
1986—Portland	P. C.	1B-OF	96	356	47	113	21	2	4	57	.318	778	68	12	.986
1986—Philadelphia†	Nat.	1B	9	8	0	2	0	0	0	0	.250	1	0	0	1.000
1987—Phoenix	P. C.	1B-OF	138	514	78	*168	20	9	3	85	.327	1036	87	14	.988
1987—San Francisco	Nat.	OF	12	16	2	5	0	0	1	1	.313	19	0	0	1.000
1988—Phoenix‡	P. C.	1B-OF	96	368	61	133	26	2	4	58	.361	752	45	12	.985
1988—San Francisco§	Nat.	1B-OF	23	26	1	5	0	0	0	3	.192	27	0	0	1.000
1989—Baltimore	Amer.	1B	9	11	1	3	0	0	0	3	.273	25	2	0	1.000
1989—Rochester	Int.	1B	126	454	59	117	24	2	9	78	.258	1063	*81	9	*.992
Major League Totals—5 Years			74	84	4	18	0	0	1	9	.214	109	6	0	1.000

Signed as free agent by Philadelphia Phillies' organization, October 4, 1980.
†Sold to Phoenix (San Francisco Giants' organization), March 22, 1987.
‡On San Francisco disabled list, March 26 to May 13, 1988; included rehabilitation disability assignment to Phoenix, May 6 to May 13, 1988.
§Traded to Rochester (Baltimore Orioles' organization) for Outfielder Ken Gerhart, March 26, 1989.

ROBERT PAUL MELVIN
(Bob)

Born October 28, 1961, at Palo Alto, Calif.
Height, 6.04. Weight, 205.
Throws and bats righthanded.
Attended University of California, Berkeley, Calif.,
and Canada College, Redwood City, Calif.

Major League stolen bases: 1986 (3), 1989 (1). Total—4.

Year—Club	League	Pos.	G.	AB.	R.	H.	2B.	3B.	HR.	RBI.	B.A.	PO.	A.	E.	F.A.
1981—Macon	S. Atl.	C	114	412	56	112	19	1	14	64	.272	456	67	2	*.996
1982—Birmingham†	South.	*C-1B-3B	98	364	33	86	12	1	13	52	.236	638	54	9	*.987
1983—Birmingham	South.	C-1B-2B	78	285	43	82	14	2	10	56	.288	404	30	2	.995
1983—Evansville	A. A.	C-1B	45	142	10	27	6	0	2	11	.190	213	16	1	.996
1984—Evansville	A. A.	C-1B	44	141	12	35	13	0	0	11	.248	214	21	1	.996
1984—Birmingham	South.	C-1B-3B	69	271	34	73	14	1	2	33	.269	341	38	4	.990
1985—Nashville	A. A.	C-1B-OF	53	177	27	48	7	1	9	24	.271	276	28	2	.993
1985—Detroit‡	Amer.	C	41	82	10	18	4	1	0	4	.220	175	13	2	.989
1986—San Francisco	Nat.	C-3B	89	268	24	60	14	2	5	25	.224	443	60	6	.988
1987—San Francisco§	Nat.	C-1B	84	246	31	49	8	0	11	31	.199	414	44	1	.998
1988—San Francisco	Nat.	C-1B	92	273	23	64	13	1	8	27	.234	406	31	7	.984
1988—Phoenix x	P. C.	C	21	75	11	23	5	0	2	9	.307	123	6	1	.992
1989—Baltimore y	Amer.	C	85	278	22	67	10	1	1	32	.241	303	20	3	.991
American League Totals—2 Years			126	360	32	85	14	2	1	36	.236	478	33	5	.990
National League Totals—3 Years			265	787	78	173	35	3	24	83	.220	1263	135	14	.990
Major League Totals—5 Years			391	1147	110	258	49	5	25	119	.225	1741	168	19	.990

Selected by Baltimore Orioles' organization in 3rd round of free-agent draft, June 5, 1979.
Selected by Detroit Tigers' organization in secondary phase of free-agent draft, January 13, 1981.
†On disabled list, May 1 to May 25, 1982.
‡Traded with Pitcher Juan Berenguer and a player to be named later to San Francisco Giants for Pitchers Dave LaPoint and Eric King and Catcher Matt Nokes, October 7, 1985; San Francisco acquired Pitcher Scott Medvin to complete deal, December 11, 1985.
§On disabled list, July 11 to July 26, 1987.
xTraded to Baltimore Orioles for Catcher Terry Kennedy, January 24, 1989.
yOn disabled list, April 22 to May 7, 1989.

CHAMPIONSHIP SERIES RECORD

Year—Club	League	Pos.	G.	AB.	R.	H.	2B.	3B.	HR.	RBI.	B.A.	PO.	A.	E.	F.A.
1987—San Francisco	Nat.	PH-C	3	7	0	3	0	0	0	0	.429	14	1	0	1.000

ORLANDO MERCADO (RODRIGUEZ)

Born November 7, 1961, at Arecibo, Puerto Rico.
Height, 6.00. Weight, 195.
Throws and bats righthanded.
Major League stolen bases: 1983 (2), 1984 (1), 1989 (1). Total—4.
Led Eastern League in passed balls with 23 in 1980.
Led California League in passed balls with 24 in 1979.

Year Club	League	Pos.	G.	AB.	R.	H.	2B.	3B.	HR.	RBI.	B.A.	PO.	A.	E.	F.A.
1978—Bellingham	N'west	C	38	49	7	6	2	0	0	5	.122	184	20	4	.981
1979—San Jose	Calif.	C-1B	110	335	53	86	18	2	10	54	.257	629	71	17	.976
1980—Lynn	East.	C-1B	117	396	55	101	25	6	11	71	.255	607	78	11	.984
1981—Spokane	P. C.	C-OF	95	312	32	67	21	2	4	31	.215	446	60	13	.975
1982—Salt Lake City	P. C.	C-O-1-3	90	321	43	90	19	2	16	66	.280	497	43	13	.976
1982—Seattle	Amer.	C	9	17	1	2	0	0	1	6	.118	31	1	0	1.000
1983—Seattle	Amer.	C	66	178	10	35	11	2	1	16	.197	342	27	2	.995
1983—Salt Lake City	P. C.	C-3B	26	88	12	20	2	1	2	12	.227	131	13	2	.986
1984—Seattle	Amer.	C	30	78	5	17	3	1	0	5	.218	118	10	1	.992
1984—Salt Lake City†	P. C.	C-1B-OF	29	109	18	39	9	2	6	22	.358	169	18	2	.989
1985—Oklahoma City‡	A. A.	C	59	206	20	52	7	1	8	29	.252	268	26	4	.987
1986—Oklahoma City	A. A.	C	48	172	20	47	11	1	3	25	.273	234	29	8	.970
1986—Texas§	Amer.	C	46	102	7	24	1	1	1	7	.235	240	25	1	.996
1987—Detroit x	Amer.	C	10	22	2	3	0	0	0	1	.136	40	8	1	.980
1987—Albuquerque	P. C.	C	69	205	22	57	18	0	2	27	.278	327	47	6	.984
1987—Los Angeles y	Nat.	C	7	5	1	3	1	0	0	1	.600	13	0	0	1.000
1988—Oakland	Amer.	C	16	24	3	3	0	0	1	1	.125	45	2	2	.959
1988—Tacoma z	P. C.	C-1B-OF	53	148	16	33	6	0	2	19	.223	228	22	2	.992
1989—Portland	P. C.	C	57	196	17	58	20	1	4	29	.296	295	19	6	.981
1989—Minnesota a	Amer.	C	19	38	1	4	0	0	0	1	.105	73	9	0	1.000
American League Totals—7 Years			196	459	29	88	15	4	4	37	.192	889	82	7	.993
National League Totals—1 Year			7	5	1	3	1	0	0	1	.600	13	0	0	1.000
Major League Totals—7 Years			203	464	30	91	16	4	4	38	.196	902	82	7	.993

Signed as free agent by Seattle Mariners' organization, January 6, 1978.
†Traded to Texas Rangers' organization for Catcher Donnie Scott, April 4, 1985.
‡On disabled list, July 10 to September 19, 1985.
§Traded to Detroit Tigers for a player to be named later, March 24, 1987; Texas Rangers' organization acquired Outfielder Ruben Guzman to complete deal, May 8, 1987.
xTraded to Los Angeles Dodgers' organization for Pitcher Balvino Galvez, May 5, 1987.
yReleased, November 12, 1987; signed by Tacoma (Oakland Athletics' organization), January 14, 1988.
zGranted free agency, October 15, 1988; signed by Portland (Minnesota Twins' organization), December 30, 1988.
aGranted free agency, October 15, 1989; signed by Tidewater (New York Mets' organization), December 13, 1989.

ORLANDO LUIS MERCED

Born November 2, 1966, at San Juan, Puerto Rico.
Height, 5.11. Weight, 170.
Throws right and bats left and righthanded.

Year Club	League	Pos.	G.	AB.	R.	H.	2B.	3B.	HR.	RBI.	B.A.	PO.	A.	E.	F.A.
1985—Bradenton Pir.	Gulf C.	SS-3B-1B	40	136	16	31	6	0	1	13	.228	46	78	28	.816
1986—Macon	S. Atl.	OF-3B	65	173	20	34	4	1	2	24	.197	53	15	13	.840
1986—Watertown	NYP	3B-1B-OF	27	89	12	16	0	1	3	9	.180	49	28	10	.885
1987—Macon†	S. Atl.	OF	4	4	1	0	0	0	0	0	.000	1	1	0	1.000
1987—Watertown‡	NYP	2B	4	12	4	5	0	1	0	3	.417	11	7	2	.900
1988—Augusta	S. Atl.	2B-3B-SS	37	136	19	36	6	3	1	17	.265	35	39	7	.914
1988—Salem	Carol.	3-2-O-1-S	80	298	47	87	12	7	7	42	.292	77	183	31	.893
1989—Harrisburg	East.	1B-OF	95	341	43	82	16	4	6	48	.240	435	32	10	.979
1989—Buffalo	A. A.	1B-OF-3B	35	129	18	44	5	3	1	16	.341	173	15	3	.984

Signed as free agent by Pittsburgh Pirates' organization, February 22, 1985.
†On disabled list, April 18 to April 28, 1987.
‡On disabled list, June 23, 1987 through remainder of season.

KENT FRANKLIN MERCKER

Born February 1, 1968, at Dublin, O.
Height, 6.02. Weight, 195.
Throws and bats lefthanded.

Tied for International League lead in games started by pitchers with 27 in 1989.
Named Carolina League co-Pitcher of the Year, 1988.

Year Club	League	G.	IP.	W.	L.	Pct.	H.	R.	ER.	SO.	BB.	ERA.
1986—Bradenton Braves	Gulf Coast	9	47⅓	4	3	.571	37	21	13	42	16	2.47
1987—Durham	Carolina	3	11⅔	0	1	.000	11	8	7	14	6	5.40
1988—Durham	Carolina	19	127⅔	11	4	.733	102	44	39	159	47	*2.75
1988—Greenville	Southern	9	48⅓	3	1	.750	36	20	18	60	26	3.35
1989—Richmond	Int'national	27	168⅔	9	12	.429	107	66	60	*144	*95	3.20
1989—Atlanta	National	2	4⅓	0	0	.000	8	6	6	4	6	12.46
Major League Totals—1 Year		2	4⅓	0	0	.000	8	6	6	4	6	12.46

Selected by Atlanta Braves' organization in 1st round (fifth player selected) of free-agent draft, June 2, 1986.

MATTHEW BATES MERULLO
(Matt)

Born August 4, 1965, at Winchester, Mass.
Height, 6.02. Weight, 200.
Throws right and bats lefthanded.
Attended University of North Carolina, Chapel Hill, N.C.
Grandson of Lennie Merullo, Sr., infielder with Chicago Cubs, 1941 through 1947;
and son of Len Merullo, Jr., minor league infielder, 1961 through 1964.

Led Southern League in passed balls with 21 in 1988.

Year Club	League	Pos.	G.	AB.	R.	H.	2B.	3B.	HR.	RBI.	B.A.	PO.	A.	E.	F.A.
1986—Peninsula	Carol.	C	64	208	21	63	12	2	3	35	.303	225	26	6	.979
1987—Daytona Beach	Fla. St.	C-1B-OF	70	250	26	65	11	6	4	47	.260	227	28	6	.977
1987—Birmingham	South.	C	48	167	13	46	7	0	2	17	.275	278	24	8	.974
1988—Birmingham	South.	C-1B	125	449	58	117	26	0	6	60	.261	640	60	14	.980
1989—Vancouver	P. C.	C	3	9	0	2	1	0	0	2	.222	19	1	1	.952
1989—Chicago	Amer.	C	31	81	5	18	1	0	1	8	.222	100	10	3	.973
1989—Birmingham	South.	C	33	119	19	35	6	0	3	23	.294	149	10	1	.994
Major League Totals—1 Year			31	81	5	18	1	0	1	8	.222	100	10	3	.973

Selected by Chicago White Sox' organization in 7th round of free-agent draft, June 2, 1986.

HENSLEY FILEMON MEULENS

Born June 23, 1967, at Curacao, Netherlands Antilles.
Height, 6.03. Weight, 190.
Throws and bats righthanded.
Led Gulf Coast League batters in strikeouts with 66 in 1986.
Tied for Eastern League lead in being hit by pitch with 9 in 1989.
Led Gulf Coast League third basemen in total chances with 178 in 1986.
Tied for Eastern League lead in double plays by third basemen with 18 in 1988.

Year Club	League	Pos.	G.	AB.	R.	H.	2B.	3B.	HR.	RBI.	B.A.	PO.	A.	E.	F.A.
1986—Sarasota Yankees	Gulf C.	3B	59	219	36	51	10	4	4	31	.233	*40	*118	20	.888
1987—Prince William	Carol.	3B	116	430	76	129	23	2	28	103	.300	96	224	*37	.896
1987—Fort Lauderdale	Fla. St.	3B	17	58	2	10	3	0	0	2	.172	18	37	7	.887
1988—Albany	East.	3B	79	278	50	68	9	1	13	40	.245	57	162	23	.905
1988—Columbus	Int.	3B	55	209	27	48	9	1	6	22	.230	39	111	14	.915
1989—Albany	East.	3B	104	335	55	86	8	2	11	45	.257	67	172	*29	.892
1989—Columbus	Int.	3B	14	45	8	13	4	0	1	3	.289	11	27	3	.927
1989—New York	Amer.	3B	8	28	2	5	0	0	0	1	.179	5	23	4	.875
Major League Totals—1 Year			8	28	2	5	0	0	0	1	.179	5	23	4	.875

Signed as free agent by New York Yankees' organization, October 31, 1985.

BRIAN S. MEYER

Born January 29, 1963, at Camden, N. J.
Height, 6.01. Weight, 190.
Throws and bats rigthanded.
Attended Rollins College, Winter Park, Fla.
Major League saves: 1989 (1).
Led Southern League in games finished in relief with 59 in 1988.
Led Florida State League in saves with 25 in 1987.
Led New York-Pennsylvania League in games finished in relief with 28 in 1986.

Year Club	League	G.	IP.	W.	L.	Pct.	H.	R.	ER.	SO.	BB.	ERA.
1986—Auburn	NYP	*32	56⅔	5	2	.714	44	14	9	66	10	1.43
1987—Osceola	Florida St.	52	77	8	9	.471	58	26	17	58	23	1.99
1988—Columbus	Southern	62	83⅓	4	3	.571	61	23	21	68	36	2.27
1988—Houston	National	8	12⅓	0	0	.000	9	2	2	10	4	1.46
1989—Tucson	P. Coast	58	80⅓	5	4	.556	81	36	25	56	33	2.80
1989—Houston	National	12	18	0	1	.000	16	13	9	13	13	4.50
Major League Totals—2 Years		20	30⅓	0	1	.000	25	15	11	23	17	3.26

Selected by Houston Astros' organization in 16th round of free-agent draft, June 2, 1986.

TANNER JOE MEYER JR.
(Joey)

Born May 10, 1962, at Honolulu, Haw.
Height, 6.03. Weight, 260.
Throws and bats righthanded.
Attended University of Hawaii, Honolulu, Haw.
Major League stolen bases: 1989 (1).
Shares major league record for most strikeouts, nine-inning game (5), September 20, 1988.
Led Midwest League in total bases with 264 in 1984.
Named Midwest League Most Valuable Player, 1984.

Year Club	League	Pos.	G.	AB.	R.	H.	2B.	3B.	HR.	RBI.	B.A.	PO.	A.	E.	F.A.
1984—Beloit	Midw.	1B	128	475	73	152	22	0	*30	*102	*.320	560	34	11	.982
1985—El Paso	Texas	1B	131	506	79	154	17	2	*37	123	.304	252	15	6	.978
1986—Vancouver	P. C.	1B	126	451	65	115	16	0	24	98	.255	784	41	15	.982
1987—Denver†	A. A.	1B	79	296	58	92	23	0	29	92	.311	392	23	8	.981
1988—Milwaukee	Amer.	1B	103	327	22	86	18	0	11	45	.263	190	18	3	.986
1989—Milwaukee	Amer.	1B	53	147	13	33	6	0	7	29	.224	100	7	2	.982
1989—Denver‡	A. A.	1B	41	146	20	41	10	0	9	37	.281	8	1	0	1.000
Major League Totals—2 Years			156	474	35	119	24	0	18	74	.251	290	25	5	.984

Selected by California Angels' organization in 8th round of free-agent draft, June 8, 1981.
Selected by Milwaukee Brewers' organization in 5th round of free-agent draft, June 6, 1983.
†On disabled list, July 8, 1987 through remainder of season.
‡Released, October 16, 1989; signed by Taiyo Giants of Japanese Baseball League.

GARY ROGER MIELKE

Born January 28, 1963, at St. James, Minn.
Height, 6.03. Weight, 199.
Throws and bats righthanded.
Attended Mankato State University, Mankato, Minn.

Major League saves: 1989 (1).

Year Club	League	G.	IP.	W.	L.	Pct.	H.	R.	ER.	SO.	BB.	ERA.
1985—Sarasota Rangers	Gulf Coast	19	37⅔	2	2	.500	25	8	4	49	14	0.96
1986—Tulsa	Texas	24	47	2	0	1.000	41	22	18	48	32	3.45
1986—Salem	Carolina	37	52⅔	4	4	.500	48	25	23	49	20	3.93
1987—Tulsa	Texas	28	45⅓	3	3	.500	34	18	15	46	10	2.98
1987—Oklahoma City	Am. Assoc.	28	37⅓	2	4	.333	36	20	17	34	16	4.10
1987—Texas	American	3	3	0	0	.000	3	2	2	3	1	6.00
1988—Oklahoma City	Am. Assoc.	38	59⅔	6	5	.545	50	21	19	42	22	2.87
1989—Oklahoma City	Am. Assoc.	18	40⅔	3	3	.500	28	7	5	40	10	1.11
1989—Texas	American	43	49⅔	1	0	1.000	52	18	18	26	25	3.26
Major League Totals—2 Years		46	52⅔	1	0	1.000	55	20	20	29	26	3.42

Selected by Texas Rangers' organization in 26th round of free-agent draft, June 3, 1985.

ROBERT MILACKI
(Bob)

Born July 28, 1964, at Trenton, N. J.
Height, 6.04. Weight, 235.
Throws and bats righthanded.
Attended Yavapai College, Prescott, Ariz.

Lost no-hitter in 12th inning against Chattanooga, May 28, 1987.
Tied for American League lead in games started by pitchers with 36 in 1989.
Led International League in complete games with 11 and tied for lead in shutouts with 3 in 1988.

Year Club	League	G.	IP.	W.	L.	Pct.	H.	R.	ER.	SO.	BB.	ERA
1984—Hagerstown†	Carolina	15	77⅔	4	5	.444	69	35	29	62	48	3.36
1985—Daytona Beach‡	Florida St.	8	38⅓	1	4	.200	32	23	17	24	26	3.99
1985—Hagerstown§	Carolina	7	40⅔	3	2	.600	32	16	12	37	22	2.66
1986—Hagerstown	Carolina	13	60⅔	4	5	.444	69	59	32	46	37	4.75
1986—Miami	Florida St.	12	67⅓	4	4	.500	70	36	28	41	27	3.74
1986—Charlotte	Southern	1	5⅓	0	1	.000	7	4	4	6	4	6.75
1987—Charlotte	Southern	29	148	11	9	.550	168	86	75	101	66	4.56
1988—Charlotte	Southern	5	37⅔	3	1	.750	26	11	10	29	12	2.39
1988—Rochester	Int'national	24	176⅔	12	8	.600	174	62	53	103	65	2.70
1988—Baltimore	American	3	25	2	0	1.000	9	2	2	18	9	0.72
1989—Baltimore	American	37	243	14	12	.538	233	105	101	113	88	3.74
Major League Totals—2 Years		40	268	16	12	.571	242	107	103	131	97	3.46

Selected by San Diego Padres' organization in 1st round (ninth player selected) of free-agent draft, January 11, 1983.
Selected by Baltimore Orioles' organization in secondary phase of free-agent draft, June 6, 1983.
†On disabled list, July 2 to August 28, 1984.
‡On disabled list, April 12 to May 11, 1985.
§On disabled list, July 5 to August 24, 1985.

KEITH ALAN MILLER

Born June 12, 1963, at Midland, Mich.
Height, 5.11. Weight, 180.
Throws and bats righthanded.
Attended Oral Roberts University, Tulsa, Okla.

Major League stolen bases: 1987 (8), 1989 (6). Total—14.
Tied for Texas League lead in being hit by pitch with 7 in 1986.

Year Club	League	Pos.	G.	AB.	R.	H.	2B.	3B.	HR.	RBI.	B.A.	PO.	A.	E.	F.A.
1985—Lynchburg	Carol.	3B-2B-OF	89	325	51	98	16	5	7	54	.302	103	203	25	.924
1985—Jackson	Texas	2B-SS	46	165	17	37	8	1	3	22	.224	108	132	8	.968
1986—Jackson†	Texas	2B	94	353	80	116	23	4	5	36	.329	198	272	19	.961
1987—Tidewater	Int.	2B-OF	53	202	29	50	9	1	6	22	.248	112	129	5	.980
1987—New York‡	Nat.	2B	25	51	14	19	2	2	0	1	.373	21	38	2	.967
1988—Tidewater	Int.	2-S-3-O	42	171	23	48	11	1	1	15	.281	81	111	12	.941
1988—New York	Nat.	2-S-3-O	40	70	9	15	1	1	1	5	.214	34	24	5	.921
1989—Tidewater	Int.	2-O-S-3	48	184	33	49	8	2	1	15	.266	89	109	8	.961
1989—New York	Nat.	2-O-S-3	57	143	15	33	7	0	1	7	.231	90	52	5	.966
Major League Totals—3 Years			122	264	38	67	10	3	2	13	.254	145	114	12	.956

Selected by Cleveland Indians' organization in 24th round of free-agent draft, June 5, 1981.
Selected by New York Yankees' organization in 2nd round of free-agent draft, June 4, 1984 (contract was later voided after it was discovered he had a pre-existing knee injury).
Signed as free agent by New York Mets' organization, September 6, 1984.
†On disabled list, April 8 to May 20, 1986.
‡On disabled list, June 29 to September 1, 1987; included rehabilitation disability assignment to Tidewater, August 21 to September 1, 1987.

MICHAEL DARREN MILLER
(Mike)

Born April 14, 1967, at Kirkwood, Mo.
Height, 6.04. Weight, 200.
Throws and bats righthanded.
Attended St. Louis Community College at Meramec, Kirkwood, Mo.

Year Club	League	G.	IP.	W.	L.	Pct.	H.	R.	ER.	SO.	BB.	ERA.
1987—Little Falls	NYP	13	76⅓	2	5	.286	87	40	34	44	12	4.01
1988—Columbia	S. Atlantic	31	163⅓	14	8	.636	146	64	50	98	28	2.76
1988—St. Lucie	Florida St.	1	7	0	1	.000	2	1	0	5	2	0.00
1989—St. Lucie	Florida St.	26	*200⅓	13	6	.684	177	64	53	130	28	2.38

Selected by New York Mets' organization in 4th round of free-agent draft, June 2, 1987.

NEAL KEITH MILLER
(Known by middle name.)

Born March 7, 1963, at Dallas, Tex.
Height, 5.11. Weight, 170.
Throws right and bats left and righthanded.
Attended Lubbock Christian College, Lubbock, Tex.

Led International League outfielders in double plays with 5 in 1989.
Led Eastern League second basemen in total chances with 657 in 1985.

Year Club	League	Pos.	G.	AB.	R.	H.	2B.	3B.	HR.	RBI.	B.A.	PO.	A.	E.	F.A.
1984—Bend	N'west	SS	3	12	1	2	0	0	0	0	.167	9	12	1	.955
1984—Peninsula	Carol.	3B-SS	65	226	44	73	8	5	0	36	.323	71	181	29	.897
1985—Reading	East.	2B	134	499	77	*147	24	7	6	59	.295	273	●355	●29	.956
1986—Portland	P. C.	2-3-O-S	36	130	15	32	8	1	0	11	.246	60	70	6	.956
1986—Reading	East.	2B	98	354	57	93	14	4	7	57	.263	220	262	*15	.970
1987—Maine	Int.	2B-OF-3B	122	383	61	112	16	4	16	54	.292	183	187	11	.971
1988—Maine	Int.	OF-2B-1B	59	200	38	56	14	1	3	23	.280	105	36	3	.979
1988—Philadelphia	Nat.	OF-3B-SS	47	48	4	8	3	0	0	6	.167	3	2	1	.833
1989—Scr./Wilkes-Barre	Int.	O-2-1-C	138	474	75	125	24	7	13	62	.264	344	60	6	.985
1989—Philadelphia	Nat.	OF	8	10	0	3	1	0	0	0	.300	2	0	0	1.000
Major League Totals—2 Years			55	58	4	11	4	0	0	6	.190	5	2	1	.875

Selected by Philadelphia Phillies' organization in 16th round of free-agent draft, June 4, 1984.

RANDALL ANDRE MILLIGAN
(Randy)

Born November 27, 1961, at San Diego, Calif.
Height, 6.01. Weight, 230.
Throws and bats righthanded.
Attended San Diego Mesa College, San Diego, Calif.

Major League stolen bases: 1988 (1), 1989 (9). Total—10.
Led International League batters in total bases with 272, bases on balls received with 91 and tied for lead in intentional bases on balls received with 10 in 1987.
Named Minor League Player of the Year by THE SPORTING NEWS, 1987.
Named International League Player of the Year, 1987.

Year Club	League	Pos.	G.	AB.	R.	H.	2B.	3B.	HR.	RBI.	B.A.	PO.	A.	E.	F.A.
1981—Shelby	S. Atl.	OF-SS	130	406	90	115	16	6	7	58	.283	174	5	14	.927
1982—Lynchburg	Carol.	OF-1B	118	420	63	113	10	6	5	55	.269	341	12	11	.970
1983—Lynchburg	Carol.	1B-OF	106	349	60	102	13	5	5	56	.292	558	41	13	.979
1984—Jackson†	Texas	1B	62	193	32	53	5	0	9	34	.275	475	67	8	.985
1985—Jackson	Texas	1B	119	391	60	121	22	2	13	77	.309	726	49	11	.986
1986—Tidewater	Int.	1B	21	60	3	5	0	0	0	3	.083	60	4	1	.985
1986—Jackson	Texas	1B	78	269	53	85	11	3	7	53	.316	684	62	6	.992
1987—Tidewater	Int.	1B-OF	136	457	*99	149	28	4	29	*103	*.326	858	88	10	.990
1987—New York‡	Nat.	PH-PR	3	1	0	0	0	0	0	0	.000	0	0	0	.000
1988—Pittsburgh	Nat.	1B-OF	40	82	10	18	5	0	3	8	.220	213	15	3	.987
1988—Buffalo§	A. A.	1B-OF	63	221	37	61	15	3	2	30	.276	551	48	5	.992
1989—Baltimore	Amer.	1B	124	365	56	98	23	5	12	45	.268	914	83	5	.995
National League Totals—2 Years			43	83	10	18	5	0	3	8	.217	213	15	3	.987
American League Totals—1 Year			124	365	56	98	23	5	12	45	.268	914	83	5	.995
Major League Totals—3 Years			167	448	66	116	28	5	15	53	.259	1127	98	8	.994

Selected by New York Mets' organization in 1st round (third player selected) of free-agent draft, January 13, 1981.
†On disabled list, July 11, 1984 through remainder of season.
‡Traded with Pitcher Scott Henion to Pittsburgh Pirates for Catcher Mackey Sasser and Pitcher Tim Drummond, March 26, 1988.
§Traded to Baltimore Orioles for a player to be named later, November 9, 1988; Pittsburgh acquired Pitcher Pete Blohm to complete deal, December 7, 1988.

ALAN BERNARD MILLS

Born October 18, 1966, at Lakeland, Fla.
Height, 6.01. Weight, 190.
Throws and bats righthanded.
Attended Polk Community College, Winter Haven, Fla.

Year Club	League	G.	IP.	W.	L.	Pct.	H.	R.	ER.	SO.	BB.	ERA.
1986—Salem†	Northwest	14	83⅔	6	6	.500	77	58	43	50	60	4.63
1987—Prince William	Carolina	35	85⅔	2	11	.154	102	75	58	53	64	6.09
1988—Prince William	Carolina	42	93⅔	3	8	.273	93	56	43	59	43	4.13
1989—Prince William	Carolina	26	39⅔	6	1	.857	22	5	4	44	13	0.91
1989—Fort Lauderdale	Florida St.	22	31	1	4	.200	40	15	13	25	9	3.77

Selected by Boston Red Sox' organization in 1st round (13th player selected) of free-agent draft, January 14, 1986.

Selected by California Angels' organization in secondary phase of free-agent draft, June 2, 1986.

†Traded to New York Yankees' organization, June 22, 1987, completing deal in which California Angels traded Pitcher Ron Romanick and a player to be named later to New York for Catcher Butch Wynegar, December 19, 1986.

GREGORY BRIAN MINTON
(Greg)

Born July 29, 1951, at Lubbock, Tex.
Height, 6.02. Weight, 207.
Throws right and bats left and righthanded.
Attended San Diego Mesa College, San Diego, Calif.

Major League saves: 1979 (4), 1980 (19), 1981 (21), 1982 (30), 1983 (22), 1984 (19), 1985 (4), 1986 (5), 1987 (11), 1988 (7), 1989 (8). Total—150.

Led National League in intentional bases on balls issued with 20 in 1984 and 18 in 1985.

Led National League in games finished in relief with 44 in 1981 and 66 in 1982.

Tied for American League lead in intentional bases on balls issued with 10 in 1988.

Led Pacific Coast League in wild pitches with 18 in 1977.

Led Pacific Coast League in balks with 6 in 1975.

Year Club	League	G.	IP.	W.	L.	Pct.	H.	R.	ER.	SO.	BB.	ERA.
1970—Billings†	Pioneer	16	40	1	4	.200	37	23	14	36	16	3.15
1971—Waterloo	Midwest	27	124	11	6	.647	118	52	42	117	55	3.05
1972—San Jose‡	California	28	178	12	12	.500	182	117	78	153	77	3.94
1973—Phoenix	P. Coast	5	13	0	0	.000	11	6	6	4	8	4.15
1973—Amarillo	Texas	38	122	5	11	.313	138	87	61	77	48	4.50
1974—Fresno	California	13	96	10	1	.909	85	32	24	81	18	2.25
1974—Amarillo	Texas	6	29	1	4	.200	42	26	19	21	10	5.90
1975—Phoenix	P. Coast	42	177	10	6	.625	178	73	51	76	76	2.59
1975—San Francisco	National	4	17	1	1	.500	19	14	13	6	11	6.88
1976—San Francisco	National	10	26	0	3	.000	32	18	14	7	12	4.85
1976—Phoenix§	P. Coast	13	74	4	5	.444	91	57	46	31	32	5.59
1977—Phoenix	P. Coast	29	161	14	6	★.700	188	93	87	77	70	4.86
1977—San Francisco	National	2	14	1	1	.500	14	8	7	5	4	4.50
1978—Phoenix	P. Coast	14	92	7	4	.636	97	54	46	32	38	4.50
1978—San Francisco x	National	11	16	0	1	.000	22	14	14	6	8	7.88
1979—San Francisco x	National	46	80	4	3	.571	59	25	16	33	27	1.80
1980—San Francisco	National	68	91	4	6	.400	81	28	25	42	34	2.47
1981—San Francisco	National	55	84	4	5	.444	84	28	27	29	36	2.89
1982—San Francisco	National	78	123	10	4	.714	108	29	25	58	42	1.83
1983—San Francisco	National	73	106⅔	7	11	.389	117	51	42	38	47	3.54
1984—San Francisco	National	74	124⅓	4	9	.308	130	60	52	48	57	3.76
1985—San Francisco	National	68	96⅔	5	4	.556	98	42	38	37	54	3.54
1986—San Francisco y	National	48	68⅔	4	4	.500	63	35	30	34	34	3.93
1987—San Francisco z	National	15	23⅓	1	0	1.000	30	9	9	9	10	3.47
1987—California a	American	41	76	5	4	.556	71	28	26	35	29	3.08
1988—Palm Springs b	California	2	4	0	0	.000	3	0	0	4	1	0.00
1988—California	American	44	79	4	5	.444	67	37	25	46	34	2.85
1989—California c	American	62	90	4	3	.571	76	22	22	42	37	2.20
National League Totals—13 Years		552	870⅔	45	52	.464	857	361	312	352	376	3.23
American League Totals—3 Years		147	245	13	12	.520	214	87	73	123	100	2.68
Major League Totals—15 Years		699	1115⅔	58	64	.475	1071	448	385	475	476	3.11

Selected by Kansas City Royals' organization in 3rd round of free-agent draft, January 17, 1970.

†Appeared in two games as an outfielder with one putout.

‡Traded to San Francisco Giants for Catcher Fran Healy, April 2, 1973.

§On disabled list, July 24 to August 5, 1976.

xOn disabled list, March 26 to May 31, 1979.

yOn disabled list, July 22 to August 14, 1986.

zReleased, May 28, 1987; signed by California Angels, June 1, 1987.

aGranted free agency, November 9, 1987; re-signed by Angels, December 3, 1987.

bOn California disabled list, March 26 to May 11, 1988; included rehabilitation disability assignment to Palm Springs, May 7 to May 11, 1988.

cOn disabled list, June 23 to July 8, 1989.

ALL-STAR GAME RECORD

Year League	IP.	W.	L.	Pct.	H.	R.	ER.	SO.	BB.	ERA.
1982—National	⅔	0	0	.000	0	0	0	0	1	0.00

PAUL THOMAS MIRABELLA

Born March 20, 1954, at Belleville, N. J.
Height, 6.02. Weight, 185.
Throws and bats lefthanded.
Attended Montclair State University, Upper Montclair, N. J.

Major League saves: 1978 (1), 1982 (3), 1984 (3), 1987 (2), 1988 (4). Total—13.
Tied for Pacific Coast League lead in balks with 4 in 1978.
Tied for Texas League lead in shutouts with 4 and games started by pitchers with 26 in 1977.
Tied for Western Carolinas League lead in balks with 5 in 1976.

Year Club	League	G.	IP.	W.	L.	Pct.	H.	R.	ER.	SO.	BB.	ERA.
1976—Asheville	W. Carol.	22	149	10	7	.588	149	77	66	*136	69	3.99
1977—Tulsa	Texas	26	176	12	7	.632	167	90	75	112	70	3.83
1978—Tucson	P. Coast	22	143	9	6	.600	158	77	63	85	68	3.97
1978—Texas†	American	10	28	3	2	.600	30	18	18	23	17	5.79
1979—Columbus	Int'national	22	144	11	7	.611	129	75	62	98	50	3.88
1979—New York‡	American	10	14	0	4	.000	16	15	14	4	10	9.00
1980—Syracuse	Int'national	4	31	1	2	.333	28	13	9	23	8	2.61
1980—Toronto	American	33	131	5	12	.294	151	73	63	53	66	4.33
1981—Syracuse	Int'national	22	153	11	7	.611	150	63	52	79	53	3.06
1981—Toronto§x	American	8	15	0	0	.000	20	16	12	9	7	7.20
1982—Texas y	American	40	50⅔	1	1	.500	46	28	27	29	22	4.80
1983—Rochester	Int'national	19	76⅓	3	5	.375	87	44	31	32	29	3.66
1983—Baltimore z	American	3	9⅔	0	0	.000	9	6	6	4	7	5.59
1983—Portland a	P. Coast	5	14⅓	0	1	.000	19	13	12	11	10	7.53
1984—Seattle	American	52	68	2	5	.286	74	39	33	41	32	4.37
1985—Calgary	P. Coast	53	68⅓	5	4	.556	84	34	31	42	29	4.08
1985—Seattle	American	10	13⅔	0	0	.000	9	4	2	8	4	1.32
1986—Seattle	American	8	6⅓	0	0	.000	13	7	6	6	3	8.53
1986—Calgary b	P. Coast	47	68⅓	3	4	.429	92	48	45	42	24	5.93
1987—Denver	Am. Assoc.	25	39	5	1	.833	39	11	10	28	10	2.31
1987—Milwaukee	American	29	29½	2	1	.667	30	20	16	14	16	4.91
1988—Denver	Am. Assoc.	8	9⅔	0	0	.000	9	3	1	7	4	0.93
1988—Milwaukee c	American	38	60	2	2	.500	44	12	11	33	21	1.65
1989—Milwaukee d	American	13	15⅓	0	0	.000	18	14	13	6	8	7.63
1989—Beloit e	Midwest	2	5	0	0	.000	3	0	0	6	0	0.00
Major League Totals—12 Years		254	441	15	27	.357	460	252	221	230	212	4.51

Selected by Minnesota Twins' organization in 16th round of free-agent draft, June 4, 1975.
Selected by Texas Rangers' organization in secondary phase of free-agent draft, January 7, 1976.
†Traded with Pitchers Mike Griffin and Dave Righetti and Outfielders Juan Beniquez and Greg Jemison to New York Yankees for Pitchers Sparky Lyle, Larry McCall and Dave Rajsich, Catcher Mike Heath, Shortstop Domingo Ramos and cash, November 10, 1978.
‡Traded with First Baseman Chris Chambliss and Infielder Damaso Garcia to Toronto Blue Jays for Catcher Rick Cerone, Pitcher Tom Underwood and Outfielder Ted Wilborn, November 1, 1979.
§Traded to Chicago Cubs' organization for a player to be named later, December 28, 1981; Toronto Blue Jays' organization acquired Pitcher Dave Geisel to complete deal, March 25, 1982.
xTraded with a player to be named later and cash to Texas Rangers for Second Baseman Bump Wills, March 26, 1982; Texas organization acquired Pitcher Paul Semall to complete deal, April 21, 1982.
yReleased, March 26, 1983; signed by Rochester (Baltimore Orioles' organization), April 16, 1983.
zSold to Portland (Philadelphia Phillies' organization), August 12, 1983.
aGranted free agency, October 20, 1983; signed by Seattle Mariners, January 23, 1984.
bGranted free agency, October 15, 1986; signed by Denver (Milwaukee Brewers' organization), February 14, 1987.
cOn disabled list, August 15 to August 30, 1988.
dOn disabled list, April 25 to May 10 and May 22 to September 1, 1989; included rehabilitation disability assignment to Beloit, August 23 to September 1, 1989.
eReleased, November 9, 1989.

ANGEL MIRANDA

Born November 9, 1969, at Arecibo, Puerto Rico.
Height, 6.01. Weight, 160.
Throws and bats lefthanded.

Year Club	League	G.	IP.	W.	L.	Pct.	H.	R.	ER.	SO.	BB.	ERA.
1987—Butte†-Helena	Pioneer	25	43⅓	1	2	.333	27	22	15	60	26	3.12
1988—Stockton	California	16	26⅓	0	1	.000	20	30	21	36	37	7.18
1988—Helena	Pioneer	14	60⅔	5	2	.714	54	32	26	75	58	3.86
1989—Beloit	Midwest	43	63	6	5	.545	39	13	6	88	32	0.86

Signed as free agent by Milwaukee Brewers' organization, March 4, 1987.
†Loaned to Butte (Co-op), March 4, 1987; returned, Summer, 1987.

JOHN KYLE MITCHELL

Born August 11, 1965, at Dickson, Tenn.
Height, 6.02. Weight, 195.
Throws and bats righthanded.
Brother of Charlie Mitchell, pitcher in Boston Red Sox' and
Minnesota Twins' organization, 1982 through 1986.

Pitched 4-0 no-hit victory against Indianapolis, June 27, 1988 (first game).
Led Florida State League in wild pitches with 21 in 1984.
Named International League Pitcher of the Year, 1986.

Year Club	League	G.	IP.	W.	L.	Pct.	H.	R.	ER.	SO.	BB.	ERA.
1983—Elmira	NYP	16	75⅓	5	6	.455	78	57	41	72	41	4.90
1984—Winter Haven	Florida St.	27	*183⅔	16	9	.640	160	84	64	109	66	3.14
1985—New Britain†	Eastern	26	190⅓	12	8	.600	143	71	57	108	61	2.70
1986—Tidewater	Int'national	27	172⅓	12	9	.571	162	78	65	83	59	3.39
1986—New York	National	4	10	0	1	.000	10	4	4	2	4	3.60

Year Club	League	G.	IP.	W.	L.	Pct.	H.	R.	ER.	SO.	BB.	ERA.
1987—Tidewater.................................	Int'national	8	48⅔	3	2	.600	44	24	18	16	20	3.33
1987—New York...................................	National	20	111⅔	3	6	.333	124	64	51	57	36	4.11
1988—Tidewater.................................	Int'national	27	⋆190	10	9	.526	164	76	60	65	45	2.84
1988—New York...................................	National	1	1	0	0	.000	2	0	0	1	1	0.00
1989—Tidewater.................................	Int'national	26	178⅓	11	11	.500	169	78	60	86	57	3.03
1989—New York‡...................................	National	2	3	0	1	.000	3	7	2	4	4	6.00
Major League Totals—4 Years..............................		27	125⅔	3	8	.273	139	75	57	64	45	4.08

Selected by Boston Red Sox' organization in 7th round of free-agent draft, June 6, 1983.

†Traded with Pitchers Bob Ojeda, Tom McCarthy and Chris Bayer to New York Mets for Pitchers Calvin Schiraldi and Wes Gardner and Outfielders John Christensen and LaSchelle Tarver, November 13, 1985.

‡Traded with Outfielder Joaquin Contreras to Baltimore Orioles for Outfielder Keith Hughes and Pitcher Cesar Mejia, December 5, 1989.

KEITH ALEXANDER MITCHELL

Born August 6, 1969, at San Diego, Calif.
Height, 5.10. Weight, 180.
Throws and bats righthanded.
Cousin of Kevin Mitchell, outfielder with San Francisco Giants.

Led Gulf Coast League outfielders in assists with 109 and tied for lead in total chances with 117 in 1987.

Year Club	League	Pos.	G.	AB.	R.	H.	2B.	3B.	HR.	RBI.	B.A.	PO.	A.	E.	F.A.
1987—Bradenton Braves	Gulf C.	OF-2B	57	208	24	50	12	1	2	21	.240	111	6	4	.967
1988—Sumter....................	S. Atl.	OF	98	341	35	85	16	1	5	33	.249	193	7	6	.971
1989—Burlington	Midw.	OF-3B	127	448	64	117	23	0	10	49	.261	250	18	8	.971

Selected by Atlanta Braves' organization in 4th round of free-agent draft, June 2, 1987.

KEVIN DARRELL MITCHELL

Born January 13, 1962, at San Diego, Calif.
Height, 5.11. Weight, 210.
Throws and bats righthanded.
Cousin of Keith Mitchell, outfielder in Atlanta Braves' organization.

Holds major league record for most intentional bases on balls, righthanded batter, season (32), 1989.
Major League stolen bases: 1986 (3), 1987 (9), 1988 (5), 1989 (3). Total—20.
Led National League in total bases with 345, intentional bases on balls received with 32 and slugging percentage with .635 in 1989.
Led International League third basemen in assists with 215 in 1984.
Named Major League Player of the Year by THE SPORTING NEWS, 1989.
Named National League Player of the Year by THE SPORTING NEWS, 1989.
Named National League Most Valuable Player by Baseball Writers' Association of America, 1989.
Named outfielder on THE SPORTING NEWS National League All-Star Team, 1989.
Named outfielder on THE SPORTING NEWS National League Silver Slugger team, 1989.

Year Club	League	Pos.	G.	AB.	R.	H.	2B.	3B.	HR.	RBI.	B.A.	PO.	A.	E.	F.A.
1981—Kingsport...............	Appal.	3B-OF	62	221	39	74	9	2	7	45	.335	44	102	18	.890
1982—Lynchburg†	Carol.	3B	29	85	19	27	5	1	1	16	.318	11	33	10	.815
1983—Jackson	Texas	⋆3B-OF	120	441	75	132	25	2	15	85	.299	81	⋆224	21	.936
1984—Tidewater..............	Int.	3B-1B-OF	120	432	51	105	21	3	10	54	.243	114	220	22	.938
1984—New York..............	Nat.	3B	7	14	0	3	0	0	0	1	.214	1	4	1	.833
1985—Tidewater‡	Int.	⋆3B-1B	95	348	44	101	24	2	9	43	.290	56	209	⋆22	.923
1986—New York§	Nat.	O-S-3-1	108	328	51	91	22	2	12	43	.277	158	69	10	.958
1987—S.D. x-S.F.............	Nat.	3B-OF-SS	131	464	68	130	20	2	22	70	.280	76	240	15	.955
1988—San Francisco	Nat.	3B-OF	148	505	60	127	25	7	19	80	.251	118	205	22	.936
1989—San Francisco	Nat.	OF-3B	154	543	100	158	34	6	⋆47	⋆125	.291	305	10	7	.978
Major League Totals—5 Years..............			548	1854	279	509	101	17	100	319	.275	658	528	55	.956

Signed as free agent by New York Mets' organization, November 16, 1980.

†On disabled list, July 21, 1982 through remainder of season.

‡On disabled list, July 12 to July 30, 1985.

§Traded with Outfielders Shawn Abner and Stanley Jefferson and Pitchers Kevin Armstrong and Kevin Brown to San Diego Padres for Outfielder Kevin McReynolds, Pitcher Gene Walter and Infielder Adam Ging, December 11, 1986.

xTraded with Pitchers Dave Dravecky and Craig Lefferts to San Francisco Giants for Third Baseman Chris Brown and Pitchers Keith Comstock, Mark Davis and Mark Grant, July 4, 1987.

CHAMPIONSHIP SERIES RECORD

Shares National League Championship Series record for most at-bats, series (30), 1987.

Year Club	League	Pos.	G.	AB.	R.	H.	2B.	3B.	HR.	RBI.	B.A.	PO.	A.	E.	F.A.
1986—New York..............	Nat.	OF	2	8	1	2	0	0	0	0	.250	3	0	0	1.000
1987—San Francisco	Nat.	3B	7	30	2	8	1	0	1	2	.267	4	11	1	.938
1989—San Francisco	Nat.	OF	5	17	5	6	0	0	2	7	.353	15	1	1	.941
Championship Series Totals—3 Years.....			14	55	8	16	1	0	3	9	.291	22	12	2	.944

WORLD SERIES RECORD

Year Club	League	Pos.	G.	AB.	R.	H.	2B.	3B.	HR.	RBI.	B.A.	PO.	A.	E.	F.A.
1986—New York..............	Nat.	PH-O-DH	5	8	1	2	0	0	0	0	.250	0	2	0	1.000
1989—San Francisco	Nat.	OF	4	17	2	5	0	0	1	2	.294	10	0	1	.909
World Series Totals—2 Years			9	25	3	7	0	0	1	2	.280	10	2	1	.923

ALL-STAR GAME RECORD

Year League	Pos.	AB.	R.	H.	2B.	3B.	HR.	RBI.	B.A.	PO.	A.	E.	F.A.
1989—National	OF	4	1	2	0	0	0	1	.500	0	0	0	.000

JOHN JOSEPH MIZEROCK

Name pronounced MIZZ-rock.
Born December 8, 1960, at Punxsutawney, Pa.
Height, 5.11. Weight, 190.
Throws right and bats lefthanded.

Led Southern League in intentional bases on balls received with 12 in 1982.
Tied for International League lead in intentional bases on balls received with 10 in 1989.
Led International League catchers in putouts with 675, total chances with 751 and tied for lead in double plays with 9 in 1989.
Led Southern League catchers in putouts with 762 and total chances with 865 in 1982.
Led Florida State League catchers in fielding percentage with .993 and passed balls with 13 in 1981.
Tied for Florida State League lead in double plays by catchers with 8 in 1980.

Year Club	League	Pos.	G.	AB.	R.	H.	2B.	3B.	HR.	RBI.	B.A.	PO.	A.	E.	F.A.
1979—Daytona Beach	Fla. St.	C	53	152	13	39	6	1	3	12	.257	255	25	5	.982
1980—Daytona Beach	Fla. St.	C	99	299	37	66	11	1	2	39	.221	532	52	9	.985
1981—Daytona Beach	Fla. St.	C-1B-OF	92	304	36	67	11	0	1	42	.220	515	50	4	.993
1981—Columbus	South.	C	11	35	6	8	2	0	0	2	.229	80	11	2	.979
1982—Columbus	South.	★C-1B	128	420	46	96	14	1	12	48	.229	785	★87	17	.981
1983—Houston†	Nat.	C	33	85	8	13	4	1	1	10	.153	154	24	6	.967
1983—Tucson	P. C.	C-1B	53	176	18	46	12	2	5	31	.261	298	29	5	.985
1984—Columbus‡	South.	C-O-1-3	61	181	19	43	7	0	4	23	.238	165	19	5	.974
1985—Tucson	P. C.	C	75	223	24	47	11	1	1	19	.211	333	43	5	.987
1985—Houston	Nat.	C	15	38	6	9	4	0	0	6	.237	77	8	3	.966
1986—Houston	Nat.	C	44	81	9	15	1	1	1	6	.185	221	12	3	.987
1986—Tucson§x	P. C.	C-1B	20	56	2	9	3	0	0	5	.161	87	10	4	.960
1987—Richmond	Int.	C	90	277	21	77	20	0	2	30	.278	504	54	●13	.977
1988—Richmond	Int.	C-3B-2B	88	238	21	52	7	0	4	29	.218	407	33	8	.982
1989—Richmond	Int.	★C-1B	112	352	36	79	11	2	2	35	.224	678	★69	7	★.991
1989—Atlanta	Nat.	C	11	27	1	6	0	0	0	2	.222	48	4	0	1.000
Major League Totals—4 Years			103	231	24	43	9	2	2	24	.186	500	48	12	.979

Selected by Houston Astros' organization in 1st round (eighth player selected) of free-agent draft, June 5, 1979.
†On disabled list, July 3 to July 26, 1983.
‡On Houston disabled list, April 1 to June 20, 1984; included rehabilitation disability assignment to Columbus, May 31 to June 19, 1984.
§Released, October 24, 1986; signed by Montreal Expos' organization, December 9, 1986.
xReleased, October 24, 1986; signed by Richmond (Atlanta Braves' organization), April 3, 1987.

KEVIN PAUL MMAHAT

Name pronounced Ma-ma-hat.
Born November 9, 1964, at Memphis, Tenn.
Height, 6.05. Weight, 220.
Throws and bats lefthanded.
Attended Tulane University, New Orleans, La.

Year Club	League	G.	IP.	W.	L.	Pct.	H.	R.	ER.	SO.	BB.	ERA.
1987—Sarasota Rangers†	Gulf Coast	12	53⅓	3	3	.500	37	22	19	60	30	3.21
1988—Albany	Eastern	6	38⅓	2	3	.400	30	19	17	32	24	3.99
1988—Fort Lauderdale	Florida St.	17	102⅓	7	7	.500	95	60	47	78	57	4.13
1989—Albany	Eastern	8	51⅓	5	1	.833	35	11	9	48	19	1.58
1989—Columbus	Int'national	15	82	3	4	.429	70	44	35	50	49	3.84
1989—New York	American	4	7⅔	0	2	.000	13	12	11	3	8	12.91
Major League Totals—1 Year		4	7⅔	0	2	.000	13	12	11	3	8	12.91

Selected by Texas Rangers' organization in 31st round of free-agent draft, June 2, 1987.
†Sold to Albany (New York Yankees' organization), June 20, 1988.

DENNIS MICHAEL MOELLER

Born September 15, 1967, at Tarzana, Calif.
Height, 6.02. Weight, 175.
Throws left and bats righthanded.
Attended Los Angeles Valley College, Van Nuys, Calif.

Year Club	League	G.	IP.	W.	L.	Pct.	H.	R.	ER.	SO.	BB.	ERA.
1986—Eugene	Northwest	14	61⅔	4	0	1.000	54	22	21	65	34	3.06
1987—Appleton	Midwest	18	55	2	5	.286	72	63	44	49	45	7.20
1988—Appleton	Midwest	20	99	3	5	.375	94	46	35	88	34	3.18
1989—Baseball City	Florida St.	12	71	9	0	1.000	59	17	14	64	20	1.77
1989—Memphis	Southern	5	25⅓	1	1	.500	16	9	8	21	10	2.84

Selected by Kansas City Royals' organization in 17th round of free-agent draft, June 2, 1986.

DALE ROBERT MOHORCIC

Name pronounced Muh-HORR-sick.
Born January 25, 1956, at Cleveland, O.
Height, 6.03. Weight, 220.
Throws and bats righthanded.

Attended Cuyahoga Community College (Metro), Cleveland, O.,
and Cleveland State University, Cleveland, O.

Shares major league record for most consecutive games pitched as relief pitcher (13), August 6 through 20, 1986.
Major League saves: 1986 (7), 1987 (16), 1988 (6), 1989 (2). Total—31.
Tied for Northwest League lead in shutouts with 2 in 1978.

Year Club	League	G.	IP.	W.	L.	Pct.	H.	R.	ER.	SO.	BB.	ERA.
1978—Victoria†	Northwest	14	98	6	5	.545	84	39	22	73	36	2.02
1979—Dunedin‡	Florida St.	23	106	4	7	.364	134	59	52	52	27	4.42
1980—Salem	Carolina	47	111	7	5	.583	91	38	27	85	32	2.18
1981—Portland	P. Coast	40	93	5	3	.625	103	54	45	39	41	4.35
1982—Buffalo§	Eastern	44	57⅔	2	8	.200	71	41	32	40	23	4.99
1983—Lynn	Eastern	18	34⅔	3	1	.750	35	20	14	13	17	3.63
1983—Hawaii	P. Coast	15	69	6	6	.500	90	42	38	30	21	4.96
1984—Hawaii x	P. Coast	9	57⅓	1	3	.250	67	29	25	21	17	3.92
1985—Oklahoma City y	Amer. Assoc.	40	84⅔	3	7	.300	72	32	27	47	21	2.87
1986—Oklahoma City	Amer. Assoc.	16	37⅔	4	4	.500	34	16	10	24	11	2.39
1986—Texas	American	58	79	2	4	.333	86	25	22	29	15	2.51
1987—Texas z	American	74	99⅓	7	6	.538	88	34	33	48	19	2.99
1988—Texas ab-New York	American	56	74⅔	4	8	.333	83	42	35	44	29	4.22
1989—New York	American	32	57⅔	2	1	.667	65	41	32	24	18	4.99
1989—Columbus c	Int'national	16	26⅔	1	2	.333	18	12	3	12	10	1.01
Major League Totals—4 Years		220	310⅔	15	19	.441	322	142	122	145	81	3.53

Signed as free agent by Victoria, June 11, 1978.
†Sold to Toronto Blue Jays' organization, September 25, 1978.
‡Released, January 8, 1980; signed by Pittsburgh Pirates' organization, April 5, 1980.
§On disabled list, May 27 through July 2, 1982.
xGranted free agency, October 15, 1984; signed by Oklahoma City (Texas Rangers' organization), May 19, 1985.
yGranted free agency, October 15, 1985; re-signed by Oklahoma City (Texas Rangers' organization), February 18, 1986.
zOn disabled list, August 12 to August 27, 1987.
aOn disabled list, March 26 to April 27, 1988.
bTraded to New York Yankees for Pitcher Cecilio Guante, August 30, 1988.
cReleased, November 8, 1989; signed by Indianapolis (Montreal Expos' organization), December 7, 1989.

PAUL LEO MOLITOR

Born August 22, 1956, at St. Paul, Minn.
Height, 6.00. Weight, 175.
Throws and bats righthanded.
Attended University of Minnesota, Minneapolis, Minn.

Shares major league record for most stolen bases, inning (3), July 26, 1987, first inning.
Hit three home runs in a game, May 12, 1982.
Major League stolen bases: 1978 (30), 1979 (33), 1980 (34), 1981 (10), 1982 (41), 1983 (41), 1984 (1), 1985 (21), 1986 (20), 1987 (45), 1988 (41), 1989 (27). Total—344.
Led American League third basemen in errors with 29 and double plays with 48 in 1982.
Named American League Rookie Player of the Year by THE SPORTING NEWS, 1978.
Named Midwest League Most Valuable Player, 1977.
Received reported $100,000 bonus to sign with Milwaukee Brewers, 1977.
Named shortstop on THE SPORTING NEWS College Baseball All-America Team, 1977.
Named designated hitter on THE SPORTING NEWS American League All-Star Team, 1987.
Named designated hitter on THE SPORTING NEWS American League Silver Slugger team, 1987 and 1988.

Year Club	League	Pos.	G.	AB.	R.	H.	2B.	3B.	HR.	RBI.	B.A.	PO.	A.	E.	F.A.
1977—Burlington	Midw.	SS	64	228	52	79	12	0	8	50	.346	83	207	28	.912
1978—Milwaukee	Amer.	2B-SS-3B	125	521	73	142	26	4	6	45	.273	253	401	22	.967
1979—Milwaukee	Amer.	2B-SS	140	584	88	188	27	16	9	62	.322	309	440	16	.979
1980—Milwaukee†	Amer.	2B-SS-3B	111	450	81	137	29	2	9	37	.304	260	336	20	.968
1981—Milwaukee‡	Amer.	OF	64	251	45	67	11	0	2	19	.267	119	4	3	.976
1982—Milwaukee	Amer.	3B-SS	160	*666	*136	201	26	8	19	71	.302	134	350	32	.938
1983—Milwaukee	Amer.	3B	152	608	95	164	28	6	15	47	.270	105	343	16	.966
1984—Milwaukee§	Amer.	3B	13	46	3	10	1	0	0	6	.217	7	21	2	.933
1985—Milwaukee x	Amer.	3B	140	576	93	171	28	3	10	48	.297	126	263	19	.953
1986—Milwaukee y	Amer.	3B-OF	105	437	62	123	24	6	9	55	.281	86	171	15	.945
1987—Milwaukee za	Amer.	3B-2B	118	465	*114	164	*41	5	16	75	.353	60	113	5	.972
1988—Milwaukee	Amer.	3B-2B	154	609	115	190	34	6	13	60	.312	87	188	17	.942
1989—Milwaukee b	Amer.	3B-2B	155	615	84	194	35	4	11	56	.315	106	287	18	.956
Major League Totals—12 Years			1437	5828	989	1751	310	60	119	581	.300	1652	2917	185	.961

Selected by St. Louis Cardinals' organization in 28th round of free-agent draft, June 5, 1974.
Selected by Milwaukee Brewers' organization in 1st round (third player selected) of free-agent draft, June 7, 1977.
†On disabled list, June 24 to July 18, 1980.
‡On disabled list, May 3 to August 12, 1981.
§On disabled list, May 2, 1984 through remainder of season.
xOn disabled list, August 13 to August 28, 1985.
yOn disabled list, May 10 to May 30, June 2 to June 17 and June 19 to July 8, 1986.
zOn disabled list, April 30 to May 26 and June 27 to July 16, 1987.
aGranted free agency, November 9, 1987, re-signed by Brewers, January 5, 1988.
bOn disabled list, March 30 to April 14, 1989.

DIVISION SERIES RECORD

Year Club	League	Pos.	G.	AB.	R.	H.	2B.	3B.	HR.	RBI.	B.A.	PO.	A.	E.	F.A.
1981—Milwaukee	Amer.	OF	5	20	2	5	0	0	1	1	.250	12	0	0	1.000

Year Club League	Pos.	G.	AB.	R.	H.	2B.	3B.	HR.	RBI.	B.A.	PO.	A.	E.	F.A.
1982—Milwaukee............ Amer.	3B	5	19	4	6	1	0	2	5	.316	4	11	2	.882

WORLD SERIES RECORD

Holds World Series records for most hits (5) and singles (5), game, October 12, 1982.
Shares World Series record for most at-bats, nine-inning game (6), October 12, 1982.

Year Club League	Pos.	G.	AB.	R.	H.	2B.	3B.	HR.	RBI.	B.A.	PO.	A.	E.	F.A.
1982—Milwaukee............ Amer.	3B	7	31	5	11	0	0	0	3	.355	4	9	0	1.000

ALL-STAR GAME RECORD

Year League	Pos.	AB.	R.	H.	2B.	3B.	HR.	RBI.	B.A.	PO.	A.	E.	F.A.
1985—American	3B-OF	1	0	0	0	0	0	0	.000	0	0	0	.000
1988—American	2B	3	0	0	0	0	0	0	.000	1	2	0	1.000
All-Star Game Totals—2 Years....................		4	0	0	0	0	0	0	.000	1	2	0	1.000

Named to American League All-Star Team in 1980; replaced due to injury.

STEVEN ALBERT MONSON
(Steve)

Born September 12, 1966, at Baltimore, Md.
Height, 6.00. Weight, 200.
Throws and bats righthanded.

Year Club	League	G.	IP.	W.	L.	Pct.	H.	R.	ER.	SO.	BB.	ERA.
1987—Beloit...............................	Midwest	11	37	0	3	.000	47	34	26	23	19	6.32
1987—Helena...........................	Pioneer	14	*96	*10	1	*.909	80	38	31	94	31	2.91
1988—Stockton........................	California	25	159⅔	14	4	.778	122	65	51	157	73	2.87
1989—Stockton........................	California	6	39⅓	3	2	.600	31	13	9	32	18	2.06
1989—El Paso...........................	Texas	20	126⅔	9	5	.643	159	91	80	104	58	5.68

RECORD AS CATCHER

Year Club League	Pos.	G.	AB.	R.	H.	2B.	3B.	HR.	RBI.	B.A.	PO.	A.	E.	F.A.
1983—Helena................... Pion.	C	21	64	4	6	0	0	1	4	.094	124	12	4	.971
1984—Sara. Phillies†‡..... Gulf C.	C	17	44	6	12	2	2	1	7	.273	79	10	4	.957
1985-86...................................						(Out of Organized Baseball)								

Selected by Philadelphia Phillies' organization in 23rd round of free-agent draft, June 6, 1983.
†Released, October 18, 1984; signed by Newark (Baltimore Orioles' organization), January 30, 1985.
‡Released, February 26, 1985; signed by Beloit (Milwaukee Brewers' organization), September 11, 1986.

RICHARD MONTELEONE
(Rich)

Born March 22, 1963, at Tampa, Fla.
Height, 6.02. Weight, 217.
Throws and bats righthanded.

Led Appalachian League pitchers in home runs allowed with 8 in 1982.

Year Club	League	G.	IP.	W.	L.	Pct.	H.	R.	ER.	SO.	BB.	ERA.
1982—Bristol...............................	Ap'lachian	12	71⅔	4	6	.400	66	41	31	52	23	3.89
1983—Lakeland...........................	Florida St.	24	142⅓	9	8	.529	146	80	65	124	80	4.11
1983—Birmingham	Southern	3	15	1	1	.500	25	12	12	9	6	7.20
1984—Birmingham	Southern	19	123⅔	7	8	.467	116	69	64	74	67	4.66
1984—Evansville	Am. Assoc.	11	64	5	3	.625	64	33	32	42	36	4.50
1985—Nashville†	Am. Assoc.	27	145⅓	6	12	.333	149	89	82	97	87	5.08
1986—Calgary.............................	P. Coast	39	158⅔	8	12	.400	177	108	93	101	*89	5.28
1987—Seattle...............................	American	3	7	0	0	.000	10	5	5	2	4	6.43
1987—Calgary.............................	P. Coast	51	65⅓	6	*13	.316	59	45	40	38	63	5.51
1988—Calgary‡-Edmonton......................	P. Coast	30	122⅓	4	7	.364	141	84	69	97	27	5.08
1988—California.........................	American	3	4⅓	0	0	.000	4	0	0	3	1	0.00
1989—Edmonton........................	P. Coast	13	57	3	6	.333	50	23	22	47	16	3.47
1989—California.........................	American	24	39⅔	2	2	.500	39	15	14	27	13	3.18
Major League Totals—3 Years...........................		30	51	2	2	.500	53	20	19	32	18	3.35

Selected by Detroit Tigers' organization in 1st round (20th player selected) of free-agent draft, June 7, 1982.
†Traded to Seattle Mariners for Third Baseman Darnell Coles, December 12, 1985.
‡Released, May 9, 1988; signed by Edmonton (California Angels' organization), May 13, 1988.

JEFFREY THOMAS MONTGOMERY
(Jeff)

Born January 7, 1962, at Wellston, O.
Height, 5.11. Weight, 180
Throws and bats righthanded.
Received bachelor of science degree in computer science from
Marshall University, Huntington, W. Va., in 1984.

Major League saves: 1988 (1), 1989 (18). Total—19.
Tied for Florida State League lead in saves with 14 in 1984.

Year Club	League	G.	IP.	W.	L.	Pct.	H.	R.	ER.	SO.	BB.	ERA.
1983—Billings..............................	Pioneer	20	44⅔	6	2	.750	31	13	12	90	13	2.42

Year Club	League	G.	IP.	W.	L.	Pct.	H.	R.	ER.	SO.	BB.	ERA.
1984—Tampa	Florida St.	31	44⅓	5	3	.625	29	15	12	56	30	2.44
1984—Vermont	Eastern	22	25⅓	2	0	1.000	14	7	6	20	24	2.13
1985—Vermont	Eastern	*53	101	5	3	.625	63	25	23	89	48	2.05
1986—Denver	Am. Assoc.	30	151⅔	11	7	.611	162	88	74	78	57	4.39
1987—Nashville	Am. Assoc.	24	139	8	5	.615	132	76	64	121	51	4.14
1987—Cincinnati†	National	14	19⅓	2	2	.500	25	15	14	13	9	6.52
1988—Omaha	Am. Assoc.	20	28⅓	1	2	.333	15	6	6	36	11	1.91
1988—Kansas City	American	45	62⅔	7	2	.778	54	25	24	47	30	3.45
1989—Kansas City	American	63	92	7	3	.700	66	16	14	94	25	1.37
National League Totals—1 Year		14	19⅓	2	2	.500	25	15	14	13	9	6.52
American League Totals—2 Years		108	154⅔	14	5	.737	120	41	38	141	55	2.21
Major League Totals—3 Years		122	174	16	7	.696	145	56	52	154	64	2.69

Selected by Cincinnati Reds' organization in 9th round of free-agent draft, June 6, 1983.
†Traded to Kansas City Royals for Outfielder Van Snider, February 15, 1988.

BRADLEY ALAN MOORE
(Brad)

Born June 21, 1964, at Loveland, Colo.
Height, 6.01. Weight, 185.
Throws and bats righthanded.
Attended Garden City Community College, Garden City, Kan.,
and Grand Canyon College, Phoenix, Ariz.

Led International League in intentional bases on balls issued with 10 in 1989.

Year Club	League	G.	IP.	W.	L.	Pct.	H.	R.	ER.	SO.	BB.	ERA.
1986—Bend	Northwest	16	33⅔	2	5	.286	32	29	22	35	22	5.88
1987—Clearwater	Florida St.	53	67⅓	4	7	.364	63	23	15	42	21	2.00
1987—Reading	Eastern	9	18⅓	0	1	.000	12	2	2	13	4	0.98
1988—Reading	Eastern	57	70⅔	4	6	.400	57	30	24	39	33	3.06
1988—Philadelphia	National	5	5⅔	0	0	.000	4	0	0	2	4	0.00
1989—Scranton/Wilkes-Barre	Int'national	*61	97	6	10	.375	86	41	36	67	49	3.34
Major League Totals—1 Year		5	5⅔	0	0	.000	4	0	0	2	4	0.00

Signed as free agent by Philadelphia Phillies' organization, June 25, 1986.

MICHAEL WAYNE MOORE
(Mike)

Born November 26, 1959, at Eakly, Okla.
Height, 6.04. Weight, 205.
Throws and bats righthanded.
Attended Oral Roberts University, Tulsa, Okla.

Major League saves: 1986 (1), 1988 (1). Total—2.
Tied for American League lead in games started by pitchers with 37 in 1986.
Received reported $100,000 bonus to sign with Seattle Mariners, 1981.
Named righthanded pitcher on THE SPORTING NEWS College Baseball All-America Team, 1981.

Year Club	League	G.	IP.	W.	L.	Pct.	H.	R.	ER.	SO.	BB.	ERA.
1981—Lynn	Eastern	13	94	6	5	.545	83	42	38	81	34	3.64
1982—Seattle	American	28	144⅓	7	14	.333	159	91	86	73	79	5.36
1982—Salt Lake City	P. Coast	1	8	0	0	.000	9	4	4	6	5	4.50
1983—Seattle	American	22	128	6	8	.429	130	75	67	108	60	4.71
1983—Salt Lake City	P. Coast	11	82⅓	4	4	.500	78	48	33	80	54	3.61
1984—Seattle	American	34	212	7	17	.292	236	127	117	158	85	4.97
1985—Seattle	American	35	247	17	10	.630	230	100	95	155	70	3.46
1986—Seattle	American	38	266	11	13	.458	*279	141	127	146	94	4.30
1987—Seattle	American	33	231	9	*19	.321	*268	145	*121	115	84	4.71
1988—Seattle†	American	37	228⅔	9	15	.375	196	104	96	182	63	3.78
1989—Oakland	American	35	241⅔	19	11	.633	193	82	70	172	83	2.61
Major League Totals—8 Years		262	1698⅔	85	107	.443	1691	865	779	1109	618	4.13

Selected by St. Louis Cardinals' organization in 3rd round of free-agent draft, June 6, 1978.
Selected by Seattle Mariners' organization in 1st round (first player selected) of free-agent draft, June 8, 1981.
†Granted free agency, November 4, 1988; signed by Oakland Athletics, November 28, 1988.

CHAMPIONSHIP SERIES RECORD

Year Club	League	G.	IP.	W.	L.	Pct.	H.	R.	ER.	SO.	BB.	ERA.
1989—Oakland	American	1	7	1	0	1.000	3	1	0	3	2	0.00

WORLD SERIES RECORD

Shares World Series record for most wild pitches, game (2), October 15, 1989.

Year Club	League	G.	IP.	W.	L.	Pct.	H.	R.	ER.	SO.	BB.	ERA.
1989—Oakland	American	2	13	2	0	1.000	9	3	3	10	3	2.08

ALL-STAR GAME RECORD

Year League	IP.	W.	L.	Pct.	H.	R.	ER.	SO.	BB.	ERA.
1989—American	1	0	0	.000	0	0	0	1	0	0.00

BOBBY KEITH MORELAND

(Known by middle name.)

Born May 2, 1954, at Dallas, Tex.
Height, 6.00. Weight, 200.
Throws and bats righthanded.
Attended University of Texas, Austin, Tex.

Major League stolen bases: 1980 (3), 1981 (1), 1984 (1), 1985 (12), 1986 (3), 1987 (3), 1988 (2), 1989 (3). Total—28.
Led American Association in sacrifice flies with 10 in 1978 and with 13 in 1979.
Led American Association catchers in double plays with 10 in 1978.
Led American Association in passed balls with 11 in 1979 and tied for lead with 10 in 1978.
Led Eastern League in passed balls with 18 in 1977.
Tied for Carolina League lead in double plays by third basemen with 19 in 1976.

Year Club	League	Pos.	G.	AB.	R.	H.	2B.	3B.	HR.	RBI.	B.A.	PO.	A.	E.	F.A.
1975—Spartanburg	W. Car.	3B	69	246	28	68	13	1	1	41	.276	52	128	17	.914
1976—Peninsula	Carol.	•3B-SS	78	294	38	83	12	2	4	47	.282	50	221	•26	.912
1976—Reading	East.	3B-2B	61	199	7	52	5	0	0	7	.261	62	99	13	.925
1977—Reading	East.	C-3B	104	401	61	131	19	1	8	55	.327	339	60	8	.980
1977—Oklahoma City	A. A.	C	7	13	3	1	0	0	0	1	.077	17	1	0	1.000
1978—Oklahoma City	A. A.	C-1-3-O	130	501	73	145	25	4	16	98	.289	641	75	13	.982
1978—Philadelphia	Nat.	C	1	2	0	0	0	0	0	0	.000	4	0	0	1.000
1979—Oklahoma City	A. A.	C-3B-OF	130	494	86	149	•34	3	20	109	.302	397	44	13	.971
1979—Philadelphia	Nat.	C	14	48	3	18	3	2	0	8	.375	71	3	0	1.000
1980—Philadelphia	Nat.	C-OF	62	159	13	50	8	0	4	29	.314	186	22	7	.967
1981—Philadelphia†	Nat.	C-3-1-O	61	196	16	50	7	0	6	37	.255	267	31	9	.971
1982—Chicago	Nat.	OF-C-3B	138	476	50	124	17	2	15	68	.261	384	38	8	.981
1983—Chicago	Nat.	OF-C	154	533	76	161	30	3	16	70	.302	244	7	6	.977
1984—Chicago	Nat.	O-1-3-C	140	495	59	138	17	3	16	80	.279	393	30	10	.977
1985—Chicago	Nat.	O-1-3-C	161	587	74	180	30	3	14	106	.307	313	29	13	.963
1986—Chicago	Nat.	O-3-C-1	156	586	72	159	30	0	12	79	.271	340	58	9	.978
1987—Chicago‡	Nat.	★3B-1B	153	563	63	150	29	1	27	88	.266	99	300	★28	.934
1988—San Diego§	Nat.	1B-OF-3B	143	511	40	131	23	0	5	64	.256	747	58	7	.991
1989—Det.x-Bal.y	Amer.	1B-3B-C	123	425	45	118	20	0	6	45	.278	243	32	4	.986
National League Totals—11 Years			1183	4156	466	1161	194	14	115	629	.279	3048	576	97	.974
American League Totals—1 Year			123	425	45	118	20	0	6	45	.278	243	32	4	.986
Major League Totals—12 Years			1306	4581	511	1279	214	14	121	674	.279	3291	608	101	.975

Selected by Philadelphia Phillies' organization in 7th round of free-agent draft, June 4, 1975.
†Traded with Pitchers Dan Larson and Dickie Noles to Chicago Cubs for Pitcher Mike Krukow and cash, December 8, 1981.
‡Traded with Infielder Mike Brumley to San Diego Padres for Pitchers Rich Gossage and Ray Hayward, February 12, 1988.
§Traded with Infielder Chris Brown to Detroit Tigers for Pitcher Walt Terrell, October 28, 1988.
xTraded to Baltimore Orioles for Pitcher Brian DuBois, July 28, 1989.
yGranted free agency, November 13, 1989.

DIVISION SERIES RECORD

Year Club	League	Pos.	G.	AB.	R.	H.	2B.	3B.	HR.	RBI.	B.A.	PO.	A.	E.	F.A.
1981—Philadelphia	Nat.	C	4	13	2	6	0	0	1	3	.462	30	2	1	.970

CHAMPIONSHIP SERIES RECORD

Year Club	League	Pos.	G.	AB.	R.	H.	2B.	3B.	HR.	RBI.	B.A.	PO.	A.	E.	F.A.
1980—Philadelphia	Nat.	C-PH	2	1	0	0	0	0	0	1	.000	0	0	0	.000
1984—Chicago	Nat.	OF	5	18	3	6	2	0	0	2	.333	9	0	0	1.000
Championship Series Totals—2 Years			7	19	3	6	2	0	0	3	.316	9	0	0	1.000

WORLD SERIES RECORD

Year Club	League	Pos.	G.	AB.	R.	H.	2B.	3B.	HR.	RBI.	B.A.	PO.	A.	E.	F.A.
1980—Philadelphia	Nat.	DH	3	12	1	4	0	0	0	1	.333	0	0	0	.000

MICHAEL THOMAS MORGAN

(Mike)

Born October 8, 1959, at Tulare, Calif.
Height, 6.02. Weight, 222.
Throws and bats righthanded.

Major League saves: 1986 (1), 1988 (1). Total—2.
Tied for International League lead in shutouts with 4 in 1984.
Received reported $50,000 bonus to sign with Oakland A's, 1978.

Year Club	League	G.	IP.	W.	L.	Pct.	H.	R.	ER.	SO.	BB.	ERA.
1978—Oakland	American	3	12	0	3	.000	19	12	10	0	8	7.50
1978—Vancouver	P. Coast	14	92	5	6	.455	109	67	57	31	54	5.58
1979—Ogden	P. Coast	13	101	5	5	.500	93	48	39	42	49	3.48
1979—Oakland	American	13	77	2	10	.167	102	57	51	17	50	5.96
1980—Ogden†‡	P. Coast	20	115	6	9	.400	135	79	69	46	77	5.40
1981—Nashville§	Southern	26	169	8	7	.533	164	97	83	100	83	4.42
1982—New York x	American	30	150⅓	7	11	.389	167	77	73	71	67	4.37
1983—Toronto y	American	16	45⅓	0	3	.000	48	26	26	22	21	5.16
1983—Syracuse	Int'national	5	19⅓	0	3	.000	20	12	12	11	13	5.59
1984—Syracuse z	Int'national	34	★185⅔	13	11	.542	167	•101	84	105	•100	4.07

Year Club	League	G.	IP.	W.	L.	Pct.	H.	R.	ER.	SO.	BB.	ERA.
1985—Seattle a	American	2	6	1	1	.500	11	8	8	2	5	12.00
1985—Calgary	P. Coast	1	2	0	0	.000	3	1	1	0	0	4.50
1986—Seattle	American	37	216⅓	11	●17	.393	243	122	109	116	86	4.53
1987—Seattle b	American	34	207	12	17	.414	245	117	107	85	53	4.65
1988—Baltimore c	American	22	71⅓	1	6	.143	70	45	43	29	23	5.43
1988—Rochester d	Int'national	3	17	0	2	.000	19	10	9	7	6	4.76
1989—Los Angeles	National	40	152⅔	8	11	.421	130	51	43	72	33	2.53
American League Totals—8 Years		157	785⅓	34	68	.333	905	464	427	342	313	4.89
National League Totals—1 Year		40	152⅔	8	11	.421	130	51	43	72	33	2.53
Major League Totals—9 Years		197	938	42	79	.347	1035	515	470	414	346	4.51

Selected by Oakland A's organizaton in 1st round (fourth player selected) of free-agent draft, June 6, 1978.

†On disabled list, May 14 to June 27, 1980.

‡Traded to New York Yankees for Shortstop Fred Stanley and a player to be named later, November 3, 1980; Oakland A's acquired Second Baseman Brian Doyle to complete deal, November 17, 1980.

§On disabled list, April 9 to April 22, 1981.

xTraded with Outfielder-First Baseman Dave Collins, First Baseman Fred McGriff and a reported $400,000 to Toronto Blue Jays for Pitcher Dale Murray and Outfielder-Catcher Tom Dodd, December 9, 1982.

yOn disabled list, July 2 to August 23, 1983; included rehabilitation disability assignment to Syracuse, August 1 to August 18, 1983.

zDrafted by Seattle Mariners, December 3, 1984.

aOn disabled list, April 17, 1985 through remainder of season; included rehabilitation disability assignment to Calgary, July 19 to July 22, 1985.

bTraded to Baltimore Orioles for Pitcher Ken Dixon, December 9, 1987.

cOn disabled list, June 9 to July 19 and August 12, 1988 through remainder of season; included rehabilitation disability assignment to Rochester, June 30 to July 17, 1988.

dTraded to Los Angeles Dodgers for Outfielder Mike Devereaux, March 12, 1989.

RUSSELL LEE MORMAN
(Russ)

Born April 28, 1962, at Independence, Mo.
Height, 6.04. Weight, 215.
Throws and bats righthanded.
Attended Iowa Western Community College, Clarinda, Ia.,
and Wichita State University, Wichita, Kan.

Shares major league record for most hits, inning, first major league game (2), August 3, 1986, fourth inning.
Major League stolen bases: 1986 (1), 1989 (1). Total—2.
Led Eastern League in slugging percentage with .512 in 1985.
Led Midwest League in game-winning RBIs with 15 in 1984.
Led American Association third basemen in double plays with 23 in 1986.
Led Eastern League first basemen in assists with 79 in 1985.
Named first baseman on THE SPORTING NEWS College Baseball All-America Team, 1983.

Year Club	League	Pos.	G.	AB.	R.	H.	2B.	3B.	HR.	RBI.	B.A.	PO.	A.	E.	F.A.
1983—Glens Falls	East.	1B	71	233	29	57	9	1	3	32	.245	591	43	7	.989
1984—Appleton	Midw.	1B-OF	122	424	68	111	17	7	7	80	.262	823	43	10	.989
1985—Glens Falls	East.	*1-3-O	119	422	64	131	24	5	17	81	.310	905	81	12	*.988
1985—Buffalo	A. A.	1B	21	64	16	19	3	1	7	14	.297	144	7	2	.987
1986—Buffalo	A. A.	3B-OF	106	365	52	97	17	2	13	57	.266	87	201	24	.923
1986—Chicago	Amer.	1B	49	159	18	40	5	0	4	17	.252	342	26	4	.989
1987—Hawaii	P. C.	1B-OF	89	294	52	79	19	2	9	53	.269	410	28	3	.993
1988—Vancouver	P. C.	1B-OF	69	257	40	77	8	1	5	45	.300	823	21	3	.992
1988—Chicago	Amer.	1B-OF	40	75	8	18	2	0	0	3	.240	114	5	2	.983
1989—Vancouver	P. C.	1B-OF	61	216	18	60	14	1	1	23	.278	163	12	3	.983
1989—Chicago†	Amer.	1B	37	58	5	13	2	0	0	8	.224	157	13	2	.988
Major League Totals—3 Years			126	292	31	71	9	0	4	28	.243	613	44	8	.988

Selected by Kansas City Royals' organization in 7th round of free-agent draft, January 13, 1981.
Selected by Chicago White Sox' organization in 1st round (28th player selected) of free-agent draft, June 6, 1983.
†Released, November 20, 1989.

JOHN DANIEL MORRIS

Born February 23, 1961, at Freeport, N.Y.
Height, 6.01. Weight, 185.
Throws and bats lefthanded.
Attended Seton Hall University, South Orange, N.J.

Major League stolen bases: 1986 (6), 1987 (5), 1989 (1). Total—12.
Led Southern League outfielders in total chances with 343 in 1985.
Named Southern League Most Valuable Player, 1983.
Named outfielder on THE SPORTING NEWS College Baseball All-America Team, 1982.

Year Club	League	Pos.	G.	AB.	R.	H.	2B.	3B.	HR.	RBI.	B.A.	PO.	A.	E.	F.A.
1982—Fort Myers	Fla. St.	OF	45	137	21	39	7	2	2	17	.285	64	2	2	.971
1983—Jacksonville	South.	OF	140	490	96	141	27	8	23	92	.288	260	8	3	*.989
1984—Omaha	A. A.	OF	148	492	77	133	24	4	15	60	.270	*359	7	4	*.989
1985—Omaha†-Louis.	A. A.	OF	130	466	64	117	25	6	5	50	.251	*330	11	2	*.994
1986—Louisville‡	A. A.	OF	60	213	30	50	13	7	1	24	.235	132	6	2	.986
1986—St. Louis	Nat.	OF	39	100	8	24	0	1	1	14	.240	68	0	1	.986
1987—Louisville	A. A.	OF	14	47	13	16	5	2	3	12	.340	20	2	0	1.000
1987—St. Louis	Nat.	OF	101	157	22	41	6	4	3	23	.261	86	0	1	.989
1988—Louisville§	A. A.	OF	13	40	3	4	0	0	0	0	.100	8	0	0	1.000

Year Club League	Pos.	G.	AB.	R.	H.	2B.	3B.	HR.	RBI.	B.A.	PO.	A.	E.	F.A.
1988—St. Louis................ Nat.	OF	20	38	3	11	2	1	0	3	.289	12	0	2	.857
1989—St. Louis................ Nat.	OF	96	117	8	28	4	1	2	14	.239	45	0	0	1.000
Major League Totals—4 Years...............		256	412	41	104	12	7	6	54	.252	211	0	4	.981

Selected by Kansas City Royals' organization in 1st round (10th player selected) of free-agent draft, June 7, 1982.
†Traded to St. Louis Cardinals' organization for Outfielder Lonnie Smith, May 17, 1985.
‡On disabled list, May 7 to June 11 and June 28 to July 8, 1986.
§On St. Louis disabled list, March 20 to September 2, 1988; included rehabilitation disability assignment to Louisville, August 17 to September 2, 1988.

CHAMPIONSHIP SERIES RECORD

Year Club League	Pos.	G.	AB.	R.	H.	2B.	3B.	HR.	RBI.	B.A.	PO.	A.	E.	F.A.
1987—St. Louis................ Nat.	OF	2	3	0	0	0	0	0	0	.000	1	0	0	1.000

WORLD SERIES RECORD

Year Club League	Pos.	G.	AB.	R.	H.	2B.	3B.	HR.	RBI.	B.A.	PO.	A.	E.	F.A.
1987—St. Louis................ Nat.	OF	1	2	0	0	0	0	0	0	.000	2	0	0	1.000

JOHN SCOTT MORRIS
(Jack)

Born May 16, 1955, at St. Paul, Minn.
Height, 6.03. Weight, 200.
Throws and bats righthanded.
Attended Brigham Young University, Provo, Utah.

Holds American League record for most consecutive starting assignments, lifetime (360).
Holds American League records for most wild pitches, season (24), 1987; most seasons leading league, wild pitches (4).
Shares American League record for most wild pitches, game (5), August 3, 1987 (10 innings).
Pitched 4-0 no-hit victory against Chicago White Sox, April 7, 1984.
Led American League in shutouts with 6 in 1986.
Led American League in wild pitches with 18 in 1983, 14 in 1984, 15 in 1985 and 24 in 1987.
Named American League Pitcher of the Year by THE SPORTING NEWS, 1981.
Named righthanded pitcher on THE SPORTING NEWS American League All-Star Team, 1981.

Year Club	League	G.	IP.	W.	L.	Pct.	H.	R.	ER.	SO.	BB.	ERA.
1976—Montgomery......................	Southern	12	36	2	3	.400	37	31	25	18	36	6.25
1977—Evansville........................	Am. Assoc.	20	135	6	7	.462	141	68	54	95	42	3.60
1977—Detroit...........................	American	7	46	1	1	.500	38	20	19	28	23	3.72
1978—Detroit...........................	American	28	106	3	5	.375	107	57	51	48	49	4.33
1979—Evansville........................	Am. Assoc.	5	34	2	2	.500	22	13	9	28	18	2.38
1979—Detroit...........................	American	27	198	17	7	.708	179	76	72	113	59	3.27
1980—Detroit...........................	American	36	250	16	15	.516	252	125	116	112	87	4.18
1981—Detroit...........................	American	25	198	●14	7	.667	153	69	67	97	★78	3.05
1982—Detroit...........................	American	37	266⅓	17	16	.515	247	131	120	135	96	4.06
1983—Detroit†..........................	American	37	★293⅔	20	13	.606	257	117	109	★232	83	3.34
1984—Detroit...........................	American	35	240⅓	19	11	.633	221	108	96	148	87	3.60
1985—Detroit§..........................	American	35	257	16	11	.593	212	102	95	191	110	3.33
1986—Detroit§..........................	American	35	267	21	8	.724	229	105	97	223	82	3.27
1987—Detroit x.........................	American	34	266	18	11	.621	227	111	100	208	93	3.38
1988—Detroit...........................	American	34	235	15	13	.536	225	115	103	168	83	3.94
1989—Detroit y.........................	American	24	170⅓	6	14	.300	189	102	92	115	59	4.86
1989—Lakeland..........................	Florida St.	3	8	0	0	.000	7	2	2	2	0	2.25
Major League Totals—13 Years...........................		394	2793⅔	183	132	.581	2536	1238	1137	1818	989	3.66

Selected by Detroit Tigers' organization in 5th round of free-agent draft, June 8, 1976.
†Appeared in seven games as a pinch-runner.
‡Appeared in one game as a pinch-runner.
§Granted free agency, November 12, 1986; re-signed by Tigers, December 19, 1986.
xGranted free agency, November 9, 1987; re-signed by Tigers, December 29, 1987.
yOn disabled list, May 25 to July 24, 1989; included rehabilitation disability assignment to Lakeland, July 10 to July 24, 1989.

CHAMPIONSHIP SERIES RECORD

Year Club	League	G.	IP.	W.	L.	Pct.	H.	R.	ER.	SO.	BB.	ERA.
1984—Detroit...............................	American	1	7	1	0	1.000	5	1	1	4	1	1.29
1987—Detroit..............................	American	1	8	0	1	.000	6	6	6	7	3	6.75
Championship Series Totals—2 Years.................		2	15	1	1	.500	11	7	7	11	4	4.20

Appeared as pinch-runner for Detroit Tigers in one game of 1987 Championship Series.

WORLD SERIES RECORD

Shares World Series record for most wild pitches, game (2), October 13, 1984.

Year Club	League	G.	IP.	W.	L.	Pct.	H.	R.	ER.	SO.	BB.	ERA.
1984—Detroit................................	American	2	18	2	0	1.000	13	4	4	13	3	2.00

ALL-STAR GAME RECORD

Year League	IP.	W.	L.	Pct.	H.	R.	ER.	SO.	BB.	ERA.
1981—American	2	0	0	.000	2	0	0	2	1	0.00
1984—American	2	0	0	.000	2	0	0	2	1	0.00
1985—American	2⅔	0	1	.000	5	2	2	1	1	6.75
1987—American	2	0	0	.000	1	0	0	2	1	0.00
All-Star Game Totals—4 Years....................................	8⅔	0	1	.000	10	2	2	7	4	2.08

WILLIAM HAROLD MORRIS
(Hal)

Born April 9, 1965, at Fort Rucker, Ala.
Height, 6.04. Weight, 200.
Throws and bats lefthanded.
Attended University of Michigan, Ann Arbor, Mich.

Year Club	League	Pos.	G.	AB.	R.	H.	2B.	3B.	HR.	RBI.	B.A.	PO.	A.	E.	F.A.
1986—Oneonta	NYP	1B	36	127	26	48	9	2	3	30	.378	317	26	3	.991
1986—Albany†	East.	1B	25	79	7	17	5	0	0	4	.215	203	19	2	.991
1987—Albany	East.	1B-OF	135	*530	65	*173	31	4	5	73	.326	1086	79	17	.986
1988—Columbus	Int.	OF-1B	121	452	41	134	19	4	3	38	.296	543	26	8	.986
1988—New York	Amer.	OF	15	20	1	2	0	0	0	0	.100	7	0	0	1.000
1989—Columbus	Int.	1B-OF	111	417	70	136	24	1	17	66	*.326	636	67	9	.987
1989—New York‡	Amer.	OF-1B	15	18	2	5	0	0	0	4	.278	12	0	0	1.000
Major League Totals—2 Years			30	38	3	7	0	0	0	4	.184	19	0	0	1.000

Selected by New York Yankees' organization in 8th round of free-agent draft, June 2, 1986.
†On disabled list, August 14, 1986 through remainder of season.
‡Traded with Pitcher Rodney Imes to Cincinnati Reds for Pitcher Tim Leary and Outfielder Van Snider, December 12, 1989.

LLOYD ANTHONY MOSEBY

Born November 5, 1959, at Portland, Ark.
Height, 6.03. Weight, 200.
Throws right and bats lefthanded.

Major League stolen bases: 1980 (4), 1981 (11), 1982 (11), 1983 (27), 1984 (39), 1985 (37), 1986 (32), 1987 (39), 1988 (31), 1989 (24). Total—255.
Led Florida State League in total bases with 237 and tied for lead in being hit by pitch with 10 in 1979.
Led Pioneer League in being hit by pitch with 11 and tied for lead in caught stealing with 7 in 1978.
Named outfielder on THE SPORTING NEWS American League All-Star Team, 1983.
Named outfielder on THE SPORTING NEWS American League Silver Slugger team, 1983.

Year Club	League	Pos.	G.	AB.	R.	H.	2B.	3B.	HR.	RBI.	B.A.	PO.	A.	E.	F.A.
1978—Medicine Hat	Pion.	OF	67	253	65	77	12	4	10	38	.304	76	3	6	.929
1979—Dunedin	Fla. St.	OF	129	446	*89	*148	23	6	18	84	.332	190	11	9	.957
1980—Syracuse	Int.	OF	37	146	28	47	8	6	3	19	.322	83	1	3	.966
1980—Toronto	Amer.	OF	114	389	44	89	24	1	9	46	.229	208	12	4	.982
1981—Toronto	Amer.	OF	100	378	36	88	16	2	9	43	.233	259	4	3	.989
1982—Toronto	Amer.	OF	147	487	51	115	20	9	9	52	.236	361	4	3	.992
1983—Toronto	Amer.	OF	151	539	104	170	31	7	18	81	.315	399	10	7	.983
1984—Toronto	Amer.	OF	158	592	97	166	28	●15	18	92	.280	473	8	5	.990
1985—Toronto	Amer.	OF	152	584	92	151	30	7	18	70	.259	394	7	8	.980
1986—Toronto	Amer.	OF	152	589	89	149	24	5	21	86	.253	371	6	6	.984
1987—Toronto	Amer.	OF	155	592	106	167	27	4	26	96	.282	294	7	6	.980
1988—Toronto†	Amer.	OF	128	472	77	113	17	7	10	42	.239	304	2	5	.984
1989—Toronto‡	Amer.	OF	135	502	72	111	25	3	11	43	.221	288	3	4	.986
Major League Totals—10 Years			1392	5124	768	1319	242	60	149	651	.257	3351	63	51	.985

Selected by Toronto Blue Jays' organization in 1st round (second player selected) of free-agent draft, June 6, 1978.
†On disabled list, July 31 to August 16, 1988.
‡Granted free agency, November 13, 1989.; signed by Detroit Tigers, December 7, 1989.

CHAMPIONSHIP SERIES RECORD

Year Club	League	Pos.	G.	AB.	R.	H.	2B.	3B.	HR.	RBI.	B.A.	PO.	A.	E.	F.A.
1985—Toronto	Amer.	OF	7	31	5	7	1	0	0	4	.226	16	0	0	1.000
1989—Toronto	Amer.	OF	5	16	4	5	0	0	1	2	.313	15	0	0	1.000
Championship Series Totals—2 Years			12	47	9	12	1	0	1	6	.255	31	0	0	1.000

ALL-STAR GAME RECORD

Year League	Pos.	AB.	R.	H.	2B.	3B.	HR.	RBI.	B.A.	PO.	A.	E.	F.A.
1986—American	OF	0	0	0	0	0	0	0	.000	0	0	0	.000

JOHN WILLIAM MOSES

Born August 9, 1957, at Los Angeles, Calif.
Height, 5.10. Weight, 170.
Throws left and bats left and righthanded.
Attended Golden West College, Huntington Beach, Calif., and
University of Arizona, Tucson, Ariz.

Major League stolen bases: 1982 (5), 1983 (11), 1984 (1), 1985 (5), 1986 (25), 1987 (23), 1988 (11), 1989 (14). Total—95.
Tied for American League lead in caught stealing with 18 in 1986.
Led Midwest League in caught stealing with 21 and bases on balls received with 103 in 1981.
Tied for Midwest League lead in sacrifice hits with 13 in 1981.
Led Eastern League outfielders in double plays with 6 in 1982.

Year Club	League	Pos.	G.	AB.	R.	H.	2B.	3B.	HR.	RBI.	B.A.	PO.	A.	E.	F.A.
1980—Bellingham	N'west	OF	60	227	55	60	5	2	2	32	.264	92	6	3	.970
1981—Wausau	Midw.	OF	123	429	*102	120	24	3	3	48	.280	204	10	5	.977
1982—Lynn	East.	OF	128	466	87	133	25	6	6	52	.285	259	*20	0	*1.000
1982—Seattle	Amer.	OF	22	44	7	14	5	1	1	3	.318	16	2	1	.947
1983—Seattle	Amer.	OF	93	130	19	27	4	1	0	6	.208	87	8	2	.979

Year	Club	League	Pos.	G.	AB.	R.	H.	2B.	3B.	HR.	RBI.	B.A.	PO.	A.	E.	F.A.
1983—Salt Lake City	P. C.	OF	16	65	14	17	4	0	0	10	.262	26	0	0	1.000
1984—Chattanooga	South.	OF	53	182	27	46	6	3	0	12	.253	107	4	2	.982
1984—Salt Lake City	P. C.	OF	70	276	45	76	11	5	0	27	.275	161	8	1	.994
1984—Seattle	Amer.	OF	19	35	3	12	1	1	0	2	.343	26	1	0	1.000
1985—Calgary	P. C.	OF-1B	113	473	75	152	★37	1	5	47	.321	316	12	4	.988
1985—Seattle	Amer.	OF	33	62	4	12	0	0	0	3	.194	35	1	0	1.000
1986—Calgary	P. C.	OF	39	148	31	48	3	1	3	18	.324	93	3	1	.990
1986—Seattle	Amer.	OF-1B	103	399	56	102	16	3	3	34	.256	249	11	5	.981
1987—Seattle†‡	Amer.	OF-1B	116	390	58	96	16	4	3	38	.246	271	7	4	.986
1988—Portland	P. C.	OF	17	66	13	23	3	1	0	6	.348	40	0	0	1.000
1988—Minnesota	Amer.	OF	105	206	33	65	10	3	2	12	.316	123	1	0	1.000
1989—Minnesota	Amer.	OF-1B-P	129	242	33	68	12	3	1	31	.281	168	3	2	.988
Major League Totals—8 Years			620	1508	213	396	64	16	10	129	.263	975	34	14	.986

Selected by Seattle Mariners' organization in 16th round of free-agent draft, June 3, 1980.

†Released, December 21, 1987; signed by Cleveland Indians, January 19, 1988.

‡Released, March 29, 1988; signed by Portland (Minnesota Twins' organization), April 5, 1988.

PITCHING RECORD

Year	Club	League	G.	IP.	W.	L.	Pct.	H.	R.	ER.	SO.	BB.	ERA.
1989—Minnesota	American	1	1	0	0	.000	0	0	0	0	1	0.00

JAMIE MOYER

Born November 18, 1962, at Sellersville, Pa.
Height, 6.00. Weight, 170.
Throws and bats lefthanded.
Attended St. Joseph's University, Philadelphia, Pa.
Son-in-law of Digger Phelps, basketball coach at University of Notre Dame.

Year	Club	League	G.	IP.	W.	L.	Pct.	H.	R.	ER.	SO.	BB.	ERA.
1984—Geneva	NYP	14	★104⅔	●9	3	.750	59	27	22	★120	31	1.89
1985—Winston-Salem	Carolina	12	94	8	2	.800	82	36	24	94	22	2.30
1985—Pittsfield	Eastern	15	96⅔	7	6	.538	99	49	40	51	32	3.72
1986—Pittsfield	Eastern	6	41	3	1	.750	27	10	4	42	16	0.88
1986—Iowa	Am. Assoc.	6	42⅓	3	2	.600	25	14	12	25	11	2.55
1986—Chicago	National	16	87⅓	7	4	.636	107	52	49	45	42	5.05
1987—Chicago	National	35	201	12	15	.444	210	127	★114	147	97	5.10
1988—Chicago†	National	34	202	9	15	.375	212	84	78	121	55	3.48
1989—Texas‡	American	15	76	4	9	.308	84	51	41	44	33	4.86
1989—Sarasota Rangers	Gulf Coast	3	11	1	0	1.000	8	4	2	18	1	1.64
1989—Tulsa	Texas	2	12⅓	1	1	.500	16	8	7	9	3	5.11
National League Totals—3 Years		85	490⅓	28	34	.452	529	263	241	313	194	4.42
American League Totals—1 Year		15	76	4	9	.308	84	51	41	44	33	4.86
Major League Totals—4 Years		100	566⅓	32	43	.427	613	314	282	357	227	4.48

Selected by Chicago Cubs' organization in 6th round of free-agent draft, June 4, 1984.

†Traded with Outfielder Rafael Palmeiro and Pitcher Drew Hall to Texas Rangers for Pitchers Mitch Williams, Paul Kilgus and Steve Wilson, Infielders Curtis Wilkerson and Luis Benitez and Outfielder Pablo Delgado, December 5 1988.

‡On disabled list, May 31 to September 1, 1989; included rehabilitation disability assignment to Sarasota Rangers August 5 to August 14, 1989; and Tulsa, August 15 to August 24, 1989.

TERENCE JOHN MULHOLLAND
(Terry)

Born March 9, 1963, at Uniontown, Pa.
Height, 6.03. Weight, 207.
Throws left and bats righthanded.
Attended Marietta College, Marietta, O.

Led Pacific Coast League pitchers in games started with 29 in 1987.
Led Texas League in shutouts with 3 in 1985.

Year	Club	League	G.	IP.	W.	L.	Pct.	H.	R.	ER.	SO.	BB.	ERA.
1984—Everett	Northwest	3	19	1	0	1.000	10	2	0	15	4	0.00
1984—Fresno	California	9	42⅔	5	2	.714	32	17	14	39	36	2.95
1985—Shreveport	Texas	26	176⅔	9	8	.529	166	79	57	122	87	2.90
1986—Phoenix	P. Coast	17	111	8	5	.615	112	60	55	77	56	4.46
1986—San Francisco	National	15	54⅔	1	7	.125	51	33	30	27	35	4.94
1987—Phoenix	P. Coast	37	172⅓	7	12	.368	200	★124	●97	94	90	5.07
1988—Phoenix	P. Coast	19	100⅔	7	3	.700	116	45	40	57	44	3.58
1988—San Francisco†	National	9	46	2	1	.667	50	20	19	18	7	3.72
1989—Phoenix	P. Coast	13	78⅓	4	5	.444	67	30	26	61	26	2.99
1989—San Francisco‡-Philadelphia	National	25	115⅓	4	7	.364	137	66	63	66	36	4.92
Major League Totals—3 Years		49	216	7	15	.318	238	119	112	111	78	4.67

Selected by San Francisco Giants' organization in 1st round (24th player selected) of free-agent draft, June 4, 1984.

†On disabled list, August 1, 1988 through remainder of season.

‡Traded with Pitchers Dennis Cook and Third Baseman Charlie Hayes to Philadelphia Phillies for Pitcher Steve Bedrosian and a player to be named later, June 18, 1989; San Francisco Giants' organization acquired Infielder Rick Parker to complete deal, August 7, 1989.

STEVEN RANCE MULLINIKS

Name pronounced MUL-in-iks.

(Known by middle name.)

Born January 15, 1956, at Tulare, Calif.
Height, 6.00. Weight, 175.
Throws right and bats lefthanded.
Son of Harvey Mulliniks, pitcher in New York Yankees' organization, 1956 and 1957.

Major League stolen bases: 1977 (1), 1978 (2), 1982 (3), 1984 (2), 1985 (2), 1986 (1), 1987 (1), 1988 (1). Total—13.
Led American League third basemen in fielding percentage with .968 in 1984.
Led Pacific Coast League shortstops in fielding percentage with .968 in 1979.

Year Club	League	Pos.	G.	AB.	R.	H.	2B.	3B.	HR.	RBI.	B.A.	PO.	A.	E.	F.A.
1974—Idaho Falls	Pion.	SS	66	202	28	44	8	3	0	24	.218	★110	★170	★33	.895
1975—Quad Cities	Midw.	SS	52	186	34	50	6	2	1	21	.269	82	136	17	.928
1975—Salinas	Calif.	SS-2B	59	209	38	54	8	0	0	10	.258	88	146	14	.944
1976—El Paso†	Texas	SS-2B	90	333	81	105	22	4	7	51	.315	140	247	20	.951
1977—Salt Lake City	P. C.	SS	58	220	48	68	17	3	11	51	.309	116	207	15	.956
1977—California	Amer.	SS	78	271	36	73	13	2	3	21	.269	112	229	13	.963
1978—Salt Lake City	P. C.	SS	34	127	34	39	6	2	3	21	.307	65	109	12	.935
1978—California	Amer.	SS	50	119	6	22	3	1	1	6	.185	68	93	8	.953
1979—Salt Lake City	P. C.	SS-2B	116	402	94	138	21	7	3	59	.343	204	331	17	.969
1979—California‡	Amer.	SS	22	68	7	10	0	0	1	8	.147	46	43	4	.957
1980—Kansas City	Amer.	SS-2B	36	54	8	14	3	0	0	6	.259	30	53	1	.988
1981—Kansas City§	Amer.	2B-SS-3B	24	44	6	10	3	0	0	5	.227	25	39	5	.928
1982—Toronto	Amer.	3B-SS	112	311	32	76	25	0	4	35	.244	69	154	14	.941
1983—Toronto	Amer.	3B-SS-2B	129	364	54	100	34	3	10	49	.275	77	185	7	.974
1984—Toronto	Amer.	3B-SS-2B	125	343	41	111	21	5	3	42	.324	67	152	8	.965
1985—Toronto	Amer.	3B	129	366	55	108	26	1	10	57	.295	75	162	7	★.971
1986—Toronto x	Amer.	★3B-2B	117	348	50	90	22	0	11	45	.259	60	176	6	★.975
1987—Toronto	Amer.	3B-SS	124	332	37	103	28	1	11	44	.310	29	137	13	.927
1988—Toronto y	Amer.	3B	119	337	49	101	21	1	12	48	.300	3	5	0	1.000
1989—Toronto	Amer.	3B	103	273	25	65	11	2	3	29	.238	15	50	1	.985
Major League Totals—13 Years			1168	3230	406	883	210	16	69	395	.273	676	1478	87	.961

Selected by California Angels' organization in 3rd round of free-agent draft, June 5, 1974.

†On disabled list, May 4 to June 9 and September 2 to September 24, 1976.

‡Traded with First Baseman Willie Aikens to Kansas City Royals for Outfielder Al Cowens, Shortstop Todd Cruz and a player to be named later, December 6, 1979; California Angels acquired Pitcher Craig Eaton to complete deal, April 1, 1980.

§Traded to Toronto Blue Jays for Pitcher Phil Huffman, March 25, 1982.

xOn disabled list, August 6 to September 1, 1986.

yOn disabled list, April 12 to May 2, 1988.

CHAMPIONSHIP SERIES RECORD

Year Club	League	Pos.	G.	AB.	R.	H.	2B.	3B.	HR.	RBI.	B.A.	PO.	A.	E.	F.A.
1985—Toronto	Amer.	PH-3B	5	11	1	4	1	0	1	3	.364	1	4	0	1.000
1989—Toronto	Amer.	PH	1	1	0	0	0	0	0	0	.000	0	0	0	.000
Championship Series Totals—2 Years			6	12	1	4	1	0	1	3	.333	1	4	0	1.000

MICHAEL ANTHONY MUNOZ
(Mike)

Born July 12, 1965, at Baldwin Park, Calif.
Height, 6.02. Weight, 190.
Throws and bats lefthanded.
Attended California State Poly University, Pomona, Calif.

Tied for Pacific Coast League lead in intentional bases on balls issued with 8 in 1989.

Year Club	League	G.	IP.	W.	L.	Pct.	H.	R.	ER.	SO.	BB.	ERA.
1986—Great Falls	Pioneer	14	81⅓	4	4	.500	85	44	29	49	38	3.21
1987—Bakersfield	California	52	118	8	7	.533	125	68	49	80	43	3.74
1988—San Antonio	Texas	56	71⅔	7	2	.778	63	18	8	71	24	1.00
1989—Albuquerque	P. Coast	60	79	6	4	.600	72	32	27	81	40	3.08
1989—Los Angeles	National	3	2⅔	0	0	.000	5	5	5	3	2	16.88
Major League Totals—1 Year		3	2⅔	0	0	.000	5	5	5	3	2	16.88

Selected by Los Angeles Dodgers' organization in 3rd round of free-agent draft, June 2, 1986.

PEDRO JAVIER MUNOZ

Born September 19, 1968, at Ponce, Puerto Rico.
Height, 5.11. Weight, 170.
Throws and bats righthanded.

Tied for South Atlantic League lead in intentional bases on balls received with 4 in 1987.

Year Club	League	Pos.	G.	AB.	R.	H.	2B.	3B.	HR.	RBI.	B.A.	PO.	A.	E.	F.A.
1985—Bradenton Jays	Gulf C.	OF	40	145	14	38	3	0	2	17	.262	46	2	1	.980
1986—Florence	S. Atl.	OF	122	445	69	131	16	5	14	82	.294	197	14	9	.959
1987—Dunedin†	Fla. St.	OF	92	341	55	80	11	5	8	44	.235	4	1	0	1.000
1988—Dunedin	Fla. St.	OF	133	481	59	141	21	7	8	73	.293	164	8	★15	.920
1989—Knoxville	South.	OF	122	442	54	118	15	4	19	65	.267	55	3	1	.983

Signed as free agent by Toronto Blue Jays' organization, May 31, 1985.

†On disabled list, July 30 to August 28, 1987.

DALE BRYAN MURPHY

Born March 12, 1956, at Portland, Ore.
Height, 6.04. Weight, 215.
Throws and bats righthanded.
Attended Portland Community College, Portland, Ore. and Brigham Young University, Provo, Utah.

Shares major league records for most home runs (2) and runs batted in (6), inning, July 27, 1989, sixth inning; most years leading league in games, outfielder (6); fewest double plays by outfielder, season, 150 or more games (0), 1983; fewest double plays by outfielder, season, for leader in double plays (4), 1981 and 1985.

Shares National League record for most intentional bases on balls by righthander, season (29), 1987.

Major League stolen bases: 1978 (11), 1979 (6), 1980 (9), 1981 (14), 1982 (23), 1983 (30), 1984 (19), 1985 (10), 1986 (7), 1987 (16), 1988 (3), 1989 (3). Total—151.

Hit three home runs in a game, May 18, 1979.

Led National League in grounding into double plays with 24 in 1988.

Led National League in intentional bases on balls received with 29 in 1987.

Led National League in bases on balls received with 90 in 1985.

Led National League in total bases with 332 in 1984.

Led National League in slugging percentage with .540 in 1983 and .547 in 1984.

Led National League batters in strikeouts with 145 in 1978, 133 in 1980 and tied for lead with 141 in 1985.

Led National League first basemen in errors with 20 in 1978.

Tied for National League lead in double plays by outfielders with 4 in 1981 and 1985.

Tied for International League lead in total bases with 249 in 1977.

Led International League catchers in putouts with 510, passed balls with 14 and tied for lead in double plays with 7 in 1977.

Named National League Player of the Year by THE SPORTING NEWS, 1982 and 1983.

Named National League Most Valuable Player by Baseball Writers' Association of America, 1982 and 1983.

Named outfielder on THE SPORTING NEWS National League All-Star Team, 1982 through 1985.

Named outfielder on THE SPORTING NEWS National League All-Star fielding team, 1982 through 1986.

Named outfielder on THE SPORTING NEWS National League Silver Slugger team, 1982 through 1985.

Year	Club	League	Pos.	G.	AB.	R.	H.	2B.	3B.	HR.	RBI.	B.A.	PO.	A.	E.	F.A.
1974—Kingsport	Appal.		C	54	181	28	46	7	0	5	31	.254	389	28	7	.983
1975—Greenwood	W. Car.		C-1B	131	443	48	101	20	1	5	48	.228	723	81	18	.978
1976—Savannah	South.		C	104	352	37	94	13	5	12	55	.267	444	40	10	.980
1976—Richmond	Int.		C-OF	18	50	10	13	1	1	4	8	.260	60	9	4	.945
1976—Atlanta	Nat.		C	19	65	3	17	6	0	0	9	.262	100	13	3	.974
1977—Richmond	Int.		C-1D	127	466	71	142	●33	4	22	★90	.305	600	50	15	.977
1977—Atlanta	Nat.		C	18	76	5	24	8	1	2	14	.316	114	11	6	.954
1978—Atlanta	Nat.		1B-C	151	530	66	120	14	3	23	79	.226	1220	105	23	.983
1979—Atlanta†	Nat.		1B-C	104	384	53	106	7	2	21	57	.276	812	57	20	.978
1980—Atlanta	Nat.		OF-1B	156	569	98	160	27	2	33	89	.281	384	15	6	.985
1981—Atlanta	Nat.		OF-1B	104	369	43	91	12	1	13	50	.247	264	11	5	.982
1982—Atlanta	Nat.		OF	●162	598	113	168	23	2	36	●109	.281	407	6	9	.979
1983—Atlanta	Nat.		OF	★162	589	131	178	24	4	36	★121	.302	373	10	6	.985
1984—Atlanta	Nat.		OF	★162	607	94	176	32	8	●36	100	.290	369	10	5	.987
1985—Atlanta	Nat.		OF	●162	616	★118	185	32	2	★37	111	.300	334	8	7	.980
1986—Atlanta	Nat.		OF	160	614	89	163	29	7	29	83	.265	303	6	6	.981
1987—Atlanta	Nat.		OF	159	566	115	167	27	1	44	105	.295	325	14	8	.977
1988—Atlanta	Nat.		OF	156	592	77	134	35	4	24	77	.226	340	15	3	.992
1989—Atlanta	Nat.		OF	154	574	60	131	16	0	20	84	.228	331	5	5	.985
Major League Totals—14 Years				1829	6749	1065	1820	292	37	354	1088	.270	5676	286	112	.982

Selected by Atlanta Braves' organization in 1st round (fifth player selected) of free-agent draft, June 5, 1974.
†On disabled list, May 25 to July 19, 1979.

CHAMPIONSHIP SERIES RECORD

Year	Club	League	Pos.	G.	AB.	R.	H.	2B.	3B.	HR.	RBI.	B.A.	PO.	A.	E.	F.A.
1982—Atlanta	Nat.		OF	3	11	1	3	0	0	0	0	.273	8	0	0	1.000

ALL-STAR GAME RECORD

Year	League	Pos.	AB.	R.	H.	2B.	3B.	HR.	RBI.	B.A.	PO.	A.	E.	F.A.
1980—National		OF	1	0	0	0	0	0	0	.000	0	0	0	.000
1982—National		OF	2	1	0	0	0	0	0	.000	2	0	0	1.000
1983—National		OF	3	0	1	0	0	0	1	.333	0	0	0	.000
1984—National		OF	3	1	2	0	0	1	1	.667	0	0	0	.000
1985—National		OF	3	0	1	1	0	0	0	.333	1	0	0	1.000
1986—National		OF	2	0	0	0	0	0	0	.000	2	0	0	1.000
1987—National		OF	1	0	0	0	0	0	0	.000	1	0	0	1.000
All-Star Game Totals—7 Years			15	2	4	1	0	1	2	.267	6	0	0	1.000

DANIEL LEE MURPHY
(Dan)

Born September 18, 1964, at Artesia, Calif.
Height, 6.02. Weight, 195.
Throws and bats righthanded.

Year	Club	League	G.	IP.	W.	L.	Pct.	H.	R.	ER.	SO.	BB.	ERA.
1983—Paintsville	Ap'lachian		11	38⅔	3	1	.750	43	22	16	29	26	3.72
1983—Beloit	Midwest		8	24⅔	0	0	.000	21	14	11	22	14	4.01
1984—Beloit	Midwest		26	112⅔	9	4	.692	116	59	45	79	44	3.59
1985—Stockton	California		24	132	9	7	.563	114	65	58	157	84	3.95
1986—El Paso†	Texas		18	116⅓	9	2	.818	126	63	57	89	40	4.41

Year Club	League	G.	IP.	W.	L.	Pct.	H.	R.	ER.	SO.	BB.	ERA.
1987—El Paso	Texas	22	135⅓	10	7	.588	152	88	77	107	69	5.12
1988—Stockton‡§	California	12	25⅔	1	4	.200	25	22	18	26	40	6.31
1989—Las Vegas	P. Coast	27	133	6	9	.400	129	75	62	93	78	4.20
1989—San Diego	National	7	6⅓	0	0	.000	6	6	4	1	4	5.68
Major League Totals—1 Year		7	6⅓	0	0	.000	6	6	4	1	4	5.68

Signed as free agent by Milwaukee Brewers' organization, December 2, 1982.

†On disabled list, June 9 to June 19 and July 20 to August 11, 1986.

‡On disabled list, April 7 to July 14, 1988.

§Traded to San Diego Padres for Pitchers Todd Simmons and James Austin, February 15, 1989.

DWAYNE KEITH MURPHY

Born March 18, 1955, at Merced, Calif.
Height, 6.01. Weight, 185.
Throws right and bats lefthanded.

Shares major league record for fewest double plays by outfielder, season, 150 or more games (0), 1980 and 1985.

Major League stolen bases: 1979 (15), 1980 (26), 1981 (10), 1982 (26), 1983 (7), 1984 (4), 1985 (4), 1986 (3), 1987 (4), 1988 (1). Total—100.

Led American League in sacrifice hits with 22 in 1980 and game-winning RBIs with 15 in 1981.

Led American League outfielders in total chances with 525 in 1980, 474 in 1982 and 494 in 1984.

Led Southern League in bases on balls received with 97 in 1977.

Tied for Southern League lead in double plays by outfielders with 4 in 1977.

Named outfielder on THE SPORTING NEWS American League All-Star Team, 1981.

Named outfielder on THE SPORTING NEWS American League All-Star fielding team, 1980 through 1985.

Year Club	League	Pos.	G.	AB.	R.	H.	2B.	3B.	HR.	RBI.	B.A.	PO.	A.	E.	F.A.
1973—Lewiston	N'west	OF	68	215	25	50	7	2	3	19	.233	102	★13	6	.950
1974—Burlington†	Midw.	OF	53	150	16	33	6	2	2	10	.220	55	2	3	.959
1975—Modesto	Calif.	OF	126	429	81	125	20	7	8	71	.291	250	7	9	.966
1976—Chattanooga	South.	OF	68	200	32	52	6	0	1	23	.260	138	6	1	.993
1976—Tucson	P. C.	OF	52	179	32	42	7	2	3	11	.235	125	6	4	.970
1977—Chattanooga	South.	OF	132	406	53	104	11	9	5	53	.256	320	14	5	★.985
1978—Vancouver	P. C.	OF-SS	42	148	35	39	4	1	7	17	.264	125	9	3	.978
1978—Oakland	Amer.	OF	60	52	15	10	2	0	0	5	.192	49	1	0	1.000
1979—Oakland‡	Amer.	OF	121	388	57	99	10	4	11	40	.255	322	10	4	.988
1980—Oakland	Amer.	OF	159	573	86	157	18	2	13	68	.274	★507	13	5	.990
1981—Oakland	Amer.	OF	107	390	58	98	10	3	15	60	.251	326	6	5	.985
1982—Oakland	Amer.	★OF-SS	151	543	84	129	15	1	27	94	.238	★452	18	8	.983
1983—Oakland§	Amer.	OF	130	471	55	107	17	2	17	75	.227	365	7	8	.979
1984—Oakland	Amer.	OF	153	559	93	143	18	2	33	88	.256	★474	14	6	.988
1985—Oakland	Amer.	OF	152	523	77	122	21	3	20	59	.233	432	6	5	.989
1986—Oakland x	Amer.	OF	98	329	50	83	11	3	9	39	.252	276	6	2	.993
1986—Modesto	Calif.	OF	2	5	1	1	1	0	0	0	.200	1	0	0	1.000
1986—Madison	Midw.	OF	1	0	0	0	0	0	0	0	.000	1	0	0	1.000
1987—Oakland y	Amer.	OF-1B-2B	82	219	39	51	7	0	8	35	.233	187	2	3	.984
1987—Tacoma z	P. C.	OF	5	15	1	4	3	0	0	2	.267	6	0	0	1.000
1988—Fresno a	Calif.	OF-1B	13	34	6	7	1	0	1	5	.206	25	4	1	.967
1988—Toledo	Int.	OF	51	173	20	38	9	0	5	15	.220	112	0	2	.982
1988—Detroit b	Amer.	OF	49	144	14	36	5	0	4	19	.250	122	1	0	1.000
1989—Philadelphia c	Nat.	OF	98	156	20	34	5	0	9	27	.218	69	1	1	.986
American League Totals—11 Years			1262	4191	628	1035	134	20	157	582	.247	3512	84	46	.987
National League Totals—1 Year			98	156	20	34	5	0	9	27	.218	69	1	1	.986
Major League Totals—12 Years			1360	4347	648	1069	139	20	166	609	.246	3581	85	47	.987

Selected by Oakland A's organization in 15th round of free-agent draft, June 5, 1973.

†On disabled list, July 16 to September 16, 1974.

‡On disabled list, June 21 to July 14, 1979.

§On disabled list, June 24 to July 11, 1983.

xOn disabled list, May 12 to July 5, 1986; included rehabilitation disability assignment to Modesto, July 1 to July 3, and to Madison, July 4, 1986.

yOn disabled list, April 24 to June 25 and July 18 to August 2, 1987; included rehabilitation disability assignment to Tacoma, June 16 to June 25, 1987.

zGranted free agency, November 9, 1987; signed by Fresno (Independent), May 20, 1988.

aReleased, June 5, 1988; signed by Detroit Tigers, June 5, 1988.

bReleased, March 27, 1989; signed by Philadelphia Phillies, April 2, 1989.

cReleased, November 20, 1989.

DIVISION SERIES RECORD

Year Club	League	Pos.	G.	AB.	R.	H.	2B.	3B.	HR.	RBI.	B.A.	PO.	A.	E.	F.A.
1981—Oakland	Amer.	OF	3	11	4	6	1	0	1	2	.545	13	0	0	1.000

CHAMPIONSHIP SERIES RECORD

Year Club	League	Pos.	G.	AB.	R.	H.	2B.	3B.	HR.	RBI.	B.A.	PO.	A.	E.	F.A.
1981—Oakland	Amer.	OF	3	8	0	2	1	0	0	1	.250	9	0	0	1.000

ROBERT ALBERT MURPHY JR.

(Rob)

Born May 26, 1960, at Miami, Fla.
Height, 6.02. Weight, 215.
Throws and bats lefthanded.
Attended University of Florida, Gainesville, Fla.

Major League saves: 1986 (1), 1987 (3), 1988 (3), 1989 (9). Total—16.
Tied for Eastern League lead in saves with 15 in 1984.

Year Club	League	G.	IP.	W.	L.	Pct.	H.	R.	ER.	SO.	BB.	ERA.
1981—Tampa	Florida St.	25	105	6	8	.429	109	73	53	58	67	4.54
1982—Cedar Rapids	Midwest	31	89	3	7	.300	92	62	40	96	61	4.04
1983—Cedar Rapids	Midwest	36	140⅔	6	10	.375	120	66	52	137	69	3.33
1984—Vermont	Eastern	45	69⅔	2	3	.400	57	23	21	69	35	2.71
1985—Denver	Am. Assoc.	41	84	5	5	.500	94	55	43	66	57	4.61
1985—Cincinnati	National	2	3	0	0	.000	2	2	2	1	2	6.00
1986—Denver	Am. Assoc.	27	42⅔	3	4	.429	33	12	9	36	24	1.90
1986—Cincinnati	National	34	50⅓	6	0	1.000	26	4	4	36	21	0.72
1987—Cincinnati	National	87	100⅔	8	5	.615	91	37	34	99	32	3.04
1988—Cincinnati†	National	★76	84⅔	0	6	.000	69	31	29	74	38	3.08
1989—Boston	American	74	105	5	7	.417	97	38	32	107	41	2.74
National League Totals—4 Years		199	238⅔	14	11	.560	188	74	69	210	93	2.60
American League Totals—1 Year		74	105	5	7	.417	97	38	32	107	41	2.74
Major League Totals—5 Years		273	343⅔	19	18	.514	285	112	101	317	134	2.65

Selected by Milwaukee Brewers' organization in 29th round of free-agent draft, June 6, 1978.
Selected by Cincinnati Reds' organization in secondary phase of free-agent draft, January 13, 1981.
†Traded with First Baseman Nick Esasky to Boston Red Sox for First Baseman Todd Benzinger, Pitcher Jeff Sellers and a player to be named later, December 13, 1988; Cincinnati Reds acquired Pitcher Luis Vasquez to complete deal, January 12, 1989.

EDDIE CLARENCE MURRAY

Born February 24, 1956, at Los Angeles, Calif.
Height, 6.02. Weight, 224.
Throws right and bats left and righthanded.
Attended California State University, Los Angeles, Calif.
Brother of Rich Murray, first baseman with San Francisco Giants, 1980 and 1983;
Leon Murray, first baseman in San Francisco Giants' organization, 1970;
Charles Murray, minor league outfielder, 1962 through 1966
and 1969; and Venice Murray, first baseman in
San Francisco Giants' organization, 1978.

Shares major league record for most games, switch-hit home runs, season (2), 1982 and 1987.
Holds American League records for most consecutive games, one or more hits by switch-hitter, season (22), 1984; most game-winning runs batted in, lifetime (117); most intentional bases on balls by switch-hitter, season (25), 1984.
Major League stolen bases: 1978 (6), 1979 (10), 1980 (7), 1981 (2), 1982 (7), 1983 (5), 1984 (10), 1985 (5), 1986 (3), 1987 (1), 1988 (5), 1989 (7). Total—68.
Hit three home runs in a game, August 29, 1979 (second game), September 14, 1980 (13 innings) and August 26, 1985.
Switch-hit home runs in one game eight times: August 3, 1977, August 29, 1979 (two righthanded and one lefthanded); August 16, 1981, April 24, 1982, August 26, 1982, August 26, 1985 (two lefthanded and one righthanded), May 8, 1987 and May 9, 1987.
Led American League in bases on balls received with 107 and game-winning RBIs with 19 in 1984.
Led American League in intentional bases on balls received with 25 in 1984 and tied for lead with 18 in 1982.
Led National League first basemen in double plays with 122 in 1989.
Led American League first basemen in double plays with 152 in 1984, 146 in 1987 and tied for lead with 154 in 1985.
Led American League first basemen in total chances with 1,615 in 1978, 1,694 in 1984 and 1,526 in 1987.
Led American League first basemen in putouts with 1,504 in 1978.
Led Florida State League in total bases with 212 in 1974.
Led Florida State League first basemen in double plays with 113 in 1974.
Named American League Rookie of the Year by Baseball Writers' Association of America, 1977.
Named first baseman on THE SPORTING NEWS American League All-Star Team, 1983.
Named first baseman on THE SPORTING NEWS American League All-Star fielding team, 1982 through 1984.
Named first baseman on THE SPORTING NEWS American League Silver Slugger team, 1983 and 1984.
Named Appalachian League Player of the Year, 1973.

Year Club	League	Pos.	G.	AB.	R.	H.	2B.	3B.	HR.	RBI.	B.A.	PO.	A.	E.	F.A.
1973—Bluefield	Appal.	1B	50	188	34	54	6	0	11	32	.287	421	14	13	.971
1974—Miami	Fla. St.	1B	131	460	64	133	★29	7	12	63	.289	★1114	★51	★25	.979
1974—Asheville	South.	1B	2	7	1	2	2	0	0	2	.286	17	0	0	1.000
1975—Asheville	South.	1B-3B	124	436	66	115	13	5	17	68	.264	637	58	15	.979
1976—Charlotte	South.	1B	88	299	46	89	15	2	12	46	.298	746	45	9	.989
1976—Rochester	Int.	1B-OF-3B	54	168	35	46	6	2	11	40	.274	291	13	5	.984
1977—Baltimore	Amer.	OF-1B	160	611	81	173	29	2	27	88	.283	482	20	4	.992
1978—Baltimore	Amer.	1B-3B	161	610	85	174	32	3	27	95	.285	1507	112	6	.996
1979—Baltimore	Amer.	1B	159	606	90	179	30	2	25	99	.295	★1456	107	10	.994
1980—Baltimore	Amer.	1B	158	621	100	186	36	2	32	116	.300	1369	77	9	.994
1981—Baltimore	Amer.	1B	99	378	57	111	21	2	●22	★78	.294	899	★91	1	★.999
1982—Baltimore	Amer.	1B	151	550	87	174	30	1	32	110	.316	1269	97	4	★.997
1983—Baltimore	Amer.	1B	156	582	115	178	30	3	33	111	.306	1393	114	10	.993
1984—Baltimore	Amer.	1B	●162	588	97	180	26	3	29	110	.306	★1538	★143	13	.992
1985—Baltimore	Amer.	1B	156	583	111	173	37	1	31	124	.297	1338	152	★19	.987
1986—Baltimore†	Amer.	1B	137	495	61	151	25	1	17	84	.305	1045	88	13	.989
1987—Baltimore	Amer.	1B	160	618	89	171	28	3	30	91	.277	1371	145	10	.993
1988—Baltimore‡	Amer.	1B	161	603	75	171	27	2	28	84	.284	867	106	11	.989
1989—Los Angeles	Nat.	★1B-3B	160	594	66	147	29	1	20	88	.247	1316	★137	6	★.996
American League Totals—12 Years			1820	6845	1048	2021	351	25	333	1190	.295	14534	1252	110	.993
National League Totals—1 Year			160	594	66	147	29	1	20	88	.247	1316	137	6	.996
Major League Totals—13 Years			1980	7439	1114	2168	380	26	353	1278	.291	15850	1389	116	.993

Selected by Baltimore Orioles' organization in 3rd round of free-agent draft, June 5, 1973.

†On disabled list, July 10 to August 7, 1986.

‡Traded to Los Angeles Dodgers for Pitchers Brian Holton and Ken Howell and Shortstop Juan Bell, December 4, 1988.

CHAMPIONSHIP SERIES RECORD

Shares Championship Series record for most runs, game (4), October 7, 1983.

Year Club League	Pos.	G.	AB.	R.	H.	2B.	3B.	HR.	RBI.	B.A.	PO.	A.	E.	F.A.
1979—Baltimore .... Amer.	1B	4	12	3	5	0	0	1	5	.417	44	3	2	.959
1983—Baltimore .... Amer.	1B	4	15	5	4	0	0	1	3	.267	34	3	1	.974
Championship Series Totals—2 Years.....	8	27	8	9	0	0	2	8	.333	78	6	3	.966

WORLD SERIES RECORD

Year Club League	Pos.	G.	AB.	R.	H.	2B.	3B.	HR.	RBI.	B.A.	PO.	A.	E.	F.A.
1979—Baltimore .... Amer.	1B	7	26	3	4	1	0	1	2	.154	60	7	0	1.000
1983—Baltimore .... Amer.	1B	5	20	2	5	0	0	2	3	.250	46	1	1	.979
World Series Totals—2 Years	12	46	5	9	1	0	3	5	.196	106	8	1	.991

ALL-STAR GAME RECORD

Year League	Pos.	AB.	R.	H.	2B.	3B.	HR.	RBI.	B.A.	PO.	A.	E.	F.A.
1981—American	PH-1B	2	0	0	0	0	0	0	.000	2	1	0	1.000
1982—American	PH-1B	1	0	0	0	0	0	0	.000	4	0	0	1.000
1983—American	1B	2	0	0	0	0	0	0	.000	4	0	0	1.000
1984—American	1B	2	0	1	1	0	0	0	.500	3	0	0	1.000
1985—American	1B	3	0	0	0	0	0	0	.000	5	2	0	1.000
All-Star Game Totals—5 Years....................	10	0	1	1	0	0	0	.100	18	3	0	1.000

Member of American League All-Star Team in 1978 and 1986; did not play.

JEFFREY JOSEPH MUSSELMAN
(Jeff)

Born June 21, 1963, at Doylestown, Pa.
Height, 6.00. Weight, 185.
Throws and bats lefthanded.
Received bachelor of arts degree in economics from Harvard University, Cambridge, Mass., in 1985.

Major League saves: 1987 (1).
Tied for Pioneer League lead in games started by pitchers with 15 in 1985.

Year Club	League	G.	IP.	W.	L.	Pct.	H.	R.	ER.	SO.	BB.	ERA.
1985—Medicine Hat................................	Pioneer	16	88	6	4	.600	75	41	39	96	44	3.99
1986—Ventura County	California	26	154⅔	7	7	.500	122	67	52	165	59	3.03
1986—Knoxville	Southern	7	41⅓	5	1	.833	33	17	13	38	25	2.83
1986—Toronto	American	6	5⅓	0	0	.000	8	7	6	4	5	10.13
1987—Toronto	American	68	89	12	5	.706	75	43	41	54	54	4.15
1988—Dunedin†	Florida St.	2	5⅔	0	0	.000	6	3	2	4	1	3.18
1988—Syracuse	Int'national	10	49	4	1	.800	42	20	16	31	17	2.94
1988—Toronto	American	15	55	8	5	.615	80	34	30	39	30	3.18
1989—Toronto‡	American	5	11	0	1	.000	19	15	13	3	9	10.64
1989—Syracuse§	Int'national	10	57⅓	5	2	.714	62	24	24	30	24	3.77
1989—New York......................................	National	20	26⅓	3	2	.600	27	11	9	11	14	3.08
American League Totals—4 Years	94	190⅓	20	11	.645	182	99	90	100	98	4.26
National League Totals—1 Year	20	26⅓	3	2	.600	27	11	9	11	14	3.08
Major League Totals—4 Years...........................	114	216⅔	23	13	.639	209	110	99	111	112	4.11

Selected by Toronto Blue Jays' organization in 6th round of free-agent draft, June 3, 1985.

†On Toronto disabled list, March 22 to June 15, 1988; included rehabilitation disability assignment to Dunedin, May 23 to May 27, 1988.

‡On disabled list, April 19 to June 27, 1989; included rehabilitation disability assignment to Syracuse, June 7 to June 26, 1989.

§Traded with Pitcher Mike Brady to New York Mets for a player to be named later, July 31, 1989; Toronto Blue Jays acquired Outfielder Mookie Wilson to complete deal, August 1, 1989.

CHRIS McCALL MYERS

Born April 14, 1969, at Tampa, Fla.
Height, 6.02. Weight, 180.
Throws and bats lefthanded.

Year Club	League	G.	IP.	W.	L.	Pct.	H.	R.	ER.	SO.	BB.	ERA.
1987—Bluefield................................	Ap'lachian	10	50⅓	3	2	.600	36	18	13	60	28	2.32
1988—Hagerstown†	Carolina	7	39⅔	1	1	.500	36	15	12	21	10	2.72
1989—Frederick	Carolina	22	140	8	10	.444	138	65	62	118	53	3.99
1989—Hagerstown	Eastern	6	45⅔	4	2	.667	41	16	13	25	12	2.56

Selected by Baltimore Orioles' organization in 1st round (seventh player selected) of free-agent draft, June 2, 1987.

†On disabled list, May 23 to July 24 and August 29, 1988 through remainder of season.

GREGORY RICHARD MYERS
(Greg)

Born April 14, 1966, at Riverside, Calif.
Height, 6.02. Weight, 205.
Throws right and bats lefthanded.

Led International League catchers in total chances with 698 in 1987.
Led California League catchers in total chances with 967 in 1986.

Year	Club	League	Pos.	G.	AB.	R.	H.	2B.	3B.	HR.	RBI.	B.A.	PO.	A.	E.	F.A.
1984—Medicine Hat	Pion.	C	38	133	20	42	9	0	2	20	.316	216	24	4	.984
1985—Florence	S. Atl.	C	134	489	52	109	19	2	5	62	.223	551	61	7	★.989
1986—Ventura	Calif.	C	124	451	65	133	23	4	20	79	.295	★849	99	19	.980
1987—Syracuse	Int.	C	107	342	35	84	19	1	10	47	.246	★637	50	11	.984
1987—Toronto	Amer.	C	7	9	1	1	0	0	0	0	.111	24	1	0	1.000
1988—Syracuse†	Int.	C	34	120	18	34	7	1	7	21	.283	63	9	1	.986
1989—Knoxville‡	South.	C	29	90	11	30	10	0	5	19	.333	130	12	1	.993
1989—Toronto	Amer.	C	17	44	0	5	2	0	0	1	.114	46	6	0	1.000
1989—Syracuse	Int.	C	24	89	8	24	6	0	1	11	.270	60	7	1	.985
Major League Totals—2 Years			24	53	1	6	2	0	0	1	.113	70	7	0	1.000

Selected by Toronto Blue Jays' organization in 3rd round of free-agent draft, June 4, 1984.
†On disabled list, June 17, 1988 through remainder of season.
‡On Toronto disabled list, March 26 to June 5, 1989; included rehabilitation disability assignment to Knoxville, May 17 to June 5, 1989.

RANDALL KIRK MYERS
(Randy)

Born September 19, 1962, at Vancouver, Wash.
Height, 6.01. Weight, 208.
Throws and bats lefthanded.
Attended Clark College, Vancouver, Wash.

Major League saves: 1987 (6), 1988 (26), 1989 (24). Total—56.
Tied for Carolina League lead in complete games with 7 in 1984.
Tied for South Atlantic League lead in games started by pitchers with 28 in 1983.
Tied for Appalachian League lead in games started by pitchers with 13 and balks with 3 in 1982.
Named Carolina League Pitcher of the Year, 1984.

Year	Club	League	G.	IP.	W.	L.	Pct.	H.	R.	ER.	SO.	BB.	ERA.
1982—Kingsport	Ap'lachian	13	74⅓	6	3	.667	68	49	34	●86	69	4.12
1983—Columbia	S. Atlantic	28	173⅓	14	10	.583	146	94	70	164	108	3.63
1984—Lynchburg	Carolina	23	157	13	5	.722	123	46	36	171	61	★2.06
1984—Jackson	Texas	5	35	2	1	.667	29	14	8	35	16	2.06
1985—Jackson	Texas	19	120⅓	4	8	.333	99	61	53	116	69	3.96
1985—Tidewater	Int'national	8	44	1	1	.500	40	13	9	25	20	1.84
1985—New York	National	1	2	0	0	.000	0	0	0	2	1	0.00
1986—Tidewater	Int'national	45	65	6	7	.462	44	19	17	79	44	2.35
1986—New York	National	10	10⅔	0	0	.000	11	5	5	13	9	4.22
1987—New York	National	54	75	3	6	.333	61	36	33	92	30	3.96
1987—Tidewater	Int'national	5	7⅓	0	0	.000	6	4	4	13	4	4.91
1988—New York	National	55	68	7	3	.700	45	15	13	69	17	1.72
1989—New York†	National	65	84⅓	7	4	.636	62	23	22	88	40	2.35
Major League Totals—5 Years		185	240	17	13	.567	179	79	73	264	97	2.74

Selected by Cincinnati Reds' organization in 3rd round of free-agent draft, January 12, 1982.
Selected by New York Mets' organization in secondary phase of free-agent draft, June 7, 1982.
†Traded with Pitcher Kip Gross to Cincinnati Reds for Pitcher John Franco and Outfielder Don Brown, December 6, 1989.

CHAMPIONSHIP SERIES RECORD

Tied Championship Series record for most games won, seven-game Series (2), 1988.

Year	Club	League	G.	IP.	W.	L.	Pct.	H.	R.	ER.	SO.	BB.	ERA.
1988—New York	National	3	4⅔	2	0	1.000	1	0	0	0	2	0.00

CHARLES HARRISON NAGY

Born May 5, 1967, at Bridgeport, Conn.
Height, 6.03. Weight, 200.
Throws right and bats lefthanded.
Attended University of Connecticut, Storrs, Conn.

Led Eastern League in shutouts with 4 in 1989.
Named Carolina League Pitcher of the Year, 1989.
Received reported $125,000 bonus to sign with Cleveland Indians' organization, 1988.
Member of 1988 U.S. Olympic baseball team.

Year	Club	League	G.	IP.	W.	L.	Pct.	H.	R.	ER.	SO.	BB.	ERA.
1989—Kinston	Carolina	13	95⅓	8	4	.667	69	22	16	99	24	1.51
1989—Canton-Akron	Eastern	15	94	4	5	.444	102	44	35	65	32	3.35

Selected by Cleveland Indians' organization in 1st round (17th player selected) of free-agent draft, June 1, 1988.

JAIME NAVARRO

Born March 27, 1967, at Bayamon, Puerto Rico.
Height, 6.04. Weight, 210.
Throws and bats righthanded.
Attended Miami-Dade Community College-New World Center, Miami, Fla.
Son of Julio Navarro, pitcher with Los Angeles Dodgers, Detroit Tigers and Atlanta Braves, 1962 through 1966 and 1970; scout in Chicago Cubs' organization, 1980 through 1985; and minor league coach with Atlanta Braves' organization, 1988.

Year	Club	League	G.	IP.	W.	L.	Pct.	H.	R.	ER.	SO.	BB.	ERA.
1987—Helena	Pioneer	13	85⅔	4	3	.571	87	37	34	95	18	3.57
1988—Stockton	California	26	174⅔	15	5	.750	148	70	60	151	74	3.09
1989—El Paso	Texas	11	76⅔	5	2	.714	61	29	21	78	35	2.47
1989—Denver	Am. Assoc.	3	20	1	1	.500	24	8	8	17	7	3.60
1989—Milwaukee	American	19	109⅔	7	8	.467	119	47	38	56	32	3.12
Major League Totals—1 Year		19	109⅔	7	8	.467	119	47	38	56	32	3.12

Selected by Baltimore Orioles' organization in 2nd round of free-agent draft, January 14, 1986.
Selected by Baltimore Orioles' organization in secondary phase of free-agent draft, June 2, 1986.
Selected by Milwaukee Brewers' organization in 3rd round of free-agent draft, June 2, 1987.

ROBERT AUGUSTUS NELSON II
(Rob)

Born May 17, 1964, at Pasadena, Calif.
Height, 6.04. Weight, 215.
Throws and bats lefthanded.
Attended Mount San Antonio College, Walnut, Calif.

Major League stolen bases: 1989 (1).
Led Pacific Coast League batters in strikeouts with 133 in 1987 and 130 in 1988.
Led Pacific Coast League in sacrifice flies with 13 in 1986.
Led Midwest League batters in strikeouts with 140 in 1984.
Led Pacific Coast League first basemen in total chances with 1,359 in 1986.
Led Midwest League first basemen in double plays with 111 and total chances with 1,279 in 1984.

Year	Club	League	Pos.	G.	AB.	R.	H.	2B.	3B.	HR.	RBI.	B.A.	PO.	A.	E.	F.A.
1983—Idaho Falls	Pion.	1B	54	196	42	57	12	2	12	38	.291	418	32	6	.986
1984—Madison	Midw.	1B	136	487	71	120	25	2	19	85	.246	★1173	★89	17	.987
1985—Huntsville	South.	1B	140	499	68	116	25	0	32	98	.232	1101	86	★23	.981
1986—Tacoma	P. C.	1B	139	508	77	140	26	4	20	108	.276	★1228	★121	10	.992
1986—Oakland	Amer.	1B	5	9	1	2	1	0	0	0	.222	3	1	1	.800
1987—Oakland	Amer.	1B	7	24	1	4	1	0	0	0	.167	49	11	2	.968
1987—Tacoma†	P. C.	1B-OF	120	413	68	89	19	3	20	74	.215	971	70	7	.993
1987—San Diego	Nat.	1B	10	11	0	1	0	0	0	1	.091	14	0	0	1.000
1988—Las Vegas	P. C.	1B-OF	116	388	68	101	23	1	23	77	.260	632	50	6	.991
1988—San Diego	Nat.	1B	7	21	4	4	0	0	1	3	.190	48	5	1	.981
1989—Las Vegas	P. C.	1B	56	185	35	49	11	1	7	26	.265	451	31	7	.986
1989—San Diego	Nat.	1B	42	82	6	16	0	1	3	7	.195	201	23	2	.991
American League Totals—2 Years			12	33	2	6	2	0	0	0	.182	52	12	3	.955
National League Totals—3 Years			59	114	10	21	0	1	4	11	.184	263	28	3	.990
Major League Totals—4 Years			71	147	12	27	2	1	4	11	.184	315	40	6	.983

Selected by Houston Astros' organization in 27th round of free-agent draft, June 7, 1982.
Selected by Atlanta Braves' organization in secondary phase of free-agent draft, January 11, 1983.
Selected by Oakland A's organization in secondary phase of free-agent draft, June 6, 1983.
†Traded to San Diego Padres, September 8, 1987, completing deal in which San Diego traded Pitcher Storm Davis to Oakland Athletics for two players to be named later, August 30, 1987. San Diego acquired Pitcher Dave Leiper as partial completion of deal, August 31, 1987.

WAYLAND EUGENE NELSON II
(Gene)

Born December 3, 1960, at Tampa, Fla.
Height, 6.00. Weight, 172.
Throws and bats righthanded.

Major League saves: 1984 (1), 1985 (2), 1986 (6), 1987 (3), 1988 (3), 1989 (3). Total—18.
Major League stolen bases: 1988 (1).
Led Florida State League in shutouts with 5 and complete games with 16 in 1980.

Year	Club	League	G.	IP.	W.	L.	Pct.	H.	R.	ER.	SO.	BB.	ERA.
1978—Sarasota Rangers	Gulf Coast	14	52	5	0	●1.000	41	18	13	28	20	2.25
1979—Asheville†	W. Carol.	33	155	13	5	★.722	149	77	62	96	44	3.60
1980—Fort Lauderdale	Florida St.	27	196	★20	3	★.870	146	51	43	130	70	1.97
1981—New York‡	American	8	39	3	1	.750	40	24	21	16	23	4.85
1981—Fort Lauderdale	Florida St.	2	10	0	0	.000	9	6	6	8	5	5.40
1981—Columbus§	Int'national	5	32	4	0	1.000	25	9	9	37	14	2.53
1982—Seattle	American	22	122⅔	6	9	.400	133	70	63	71	60	4.62
1982—Salt Lake City	P. Coast	5	37⅔	1	3	.250	36	18	14	22	28	3.35
1983—Salt Lake City x	P. Coast	16	99	9	4	.692	115	65	57	74	28	5.18
1983—Seattle	American	10	32	0	3	.000	38	29	28	11	21	7.88
1984—Salt Lake City y	P. Coast	17	112	6	8	.429	138	75	70	89	54	5.63
1984—Chicago	American	20	74⅔	3	5	.375	72	38	37	36	17	4.46
1985—Chicago z	American	46	145⅔	10	10	.500	144	74	69	101	67	4.26
1986—Chicago a	American	54	114⅔	6	6	.500	118	52	49	70	41	3.85
1987—Oakland	American	54	123⅔	6	5	.545	120	58	54	94	35	3.93
1988—Oakland b	American	54	111⅔	9	6	.600	93	42	38	67	38	3.06
1989—Oakland c	American	50	80	3	5	.375	60	33	29	70	30	3.26
Major League Totals—9 Years		318	844	46	50	.479	818	420	388	536	332	4.14

Selected by Texas Rangers' organization in 29th round of free-agent draft, June 6, 1978.
†Traded with Pitcher Ray Fontenot to New York Yankees' organization for Pitchers Bob Polinsky, Neal Mersch and Mark Softy, October 8, 1979; completing deal in which New York traded Outfielder Mickey Rivers and three

players to be named later to Texas Rangers for Third Baseman Amos Lewis and two players to be named later, August 1, 1979.

‡On disabled list, April 10 to May 4, 1981; included rehabilitation disability assignment to Ft. Lauderdale, April 17 to May 4, 1981.

§Traded with Pitcher Bill Caudill, a player to be named later and cash to Seattle Mariners for Pitcher Shane Rawley, April 1, 1982; Seattle organization acquired Outfielder Bobby Brown to complete deal, April 6, 1982.

xOn disabled list, June 25 to July 31, 1983.

yTraded with Pitcher Jerry Don Gleaton to Chicago White Sox for Pitcher Salome Barojas, June 27, 1984.

zHad one at-bat with no hits.

aTraded with a player to be named later to Oakland A's for Infielder Donnie Hill, December 11, 1986; Oakland acquired Pitcher Bruce Tanner to complete deal, December 18, 1986.

bAppeared in three games as a pinch-runner.

cOn disabled list, April 8 to April 23, 1989.

CHAMPIONSHIP SERIES RECORD

Shares American League Championship Series record for most games won, series (2), 1988.

Year Club	League	G.	IP.	W.	L.	Pct.	H.	R.	ER.	SO.	BB.	ERA.
1988—Oakland	American	2	4⅔	2	0	1.000	5	0	0	0	1	0.00
1989—Oakland	American	1	1⅓	0	0	.000	1	0	0	2	0	0.00
Championship Series Totals—2 Years		3	6	2	0	1.000	6	0	0	2	1	0.00

WORLD SERIES RECORD

Year Club	League	G.	IP.	W.	L.	Pct.	H.	R.	ER.	SO.	BB.	ERA.
1988—Oakland	American	3	6⅓	0	0	.000	4	1	1	3	3	1.42
1989—Oakland	American	2	1	0	0	.000	4	6	6	1	2	54.00
World Series Totals—2 Years		5	7⅓	0	0	.000	8	7	7	4	5	8.59

ROBERT ALLEN NEN
(Robb)

Born November 28, 1969, at San Pedro, Calif.
Height, 6.04. Weight, 190.
Throws and bats righthanded.
Son of Dick Nen, first baseman with Los Angeles Dodgers,
Washington Senators and Chicago Cubs, 1963 and 1965 through 1970.

Year Club	League	G.	IP.	W.	L.	Pct.	H.	R.	ER.	SO.	BB.	ERA.
1987—Sarasota Rangers	Gulf Coast	2	2⅓	0	0	.000	4	2	2	4	3	7.71
1988—Gastonia	S. Atlantic	14	48⅓	0	5	.000	69	57	40	36	45	7.45
1988—Butte	Pioneer	14	48⅓	4	5	.444	65	55	47	30	45	8.75
1989—Gastonia	S. Atlantic	24	138⅓	7	4	.636	96	47	37	146	76	2.41

Selected by Texas Rangers' organization in 32nd round of free-agent draft, June 2, 1987.

ALBERT DWAYNE NEWMAN
(Al)

Born June 30, 1960, at Kansas City, Mo.
Height, 5.09. Weight, 188.
Throws right and bats left and righthanded.
Attended Chaffey College, Alta Loma, Calif., and
San Diego State University, San Diego, Calif.

Major League stolen bases: 1985 (2), 1986 (11), 1987 (15), 1988 (12), 1989 (25). Total—65.
Led Southern League in sacrifice hits with 18 in 1982.
Led Texas League shortstops in double plays with 58 in 1984.
Led Southern League second basemen in total chances with 776 in 1982.

Year Club	League	Pos.	G.	AB.	R.	H.	2B.	3B.	HR.	RBI.	B.A.	PO.	A.	E.	F.A.
1982—Memphis	South.	2B	142	494	85	136	16	8	1	41	.275	★356	●388	★32	.959
1983—Wichita	A. A.	2B	38	124	20	30	6	1	0	16	.242	73	96	5	.971
1983—Memphis†‡	South.	2B	52	194	18	49	5	2	0	13	.253	111	123	14	.944
1984—Beaumont§	Texas	SS	88	318	69	80	8	0	0	23	.252	138	250	27	.935
1984—Indianapolis	A. A.	2-3-O-S	37	123	13	37	3	0	0	11	.301	49	79	2	.985
1985—Indianapolis	A. A.	2B-SS	87	301	42	85	16	2	0	23	.282	144	250	10	.975
1985—Montreal	Nat.	2B-SS	25	29	7	5	1	0	0	1	.172	19	36	0	1.000
1986—Montreal x	Nat.	2B-SS	95	185	23	37	3	0	1	8	.200	98	161	11	.959
1987—Minnesota	Amer.	S-2-3-O	110	307	44	68	15	5	0	29	.221	120	225	5	.986
1988—Minnesota	Amer.	3B-SS-2B	105	260	35	58	7	0	0	19	.223	97	155	6	.977
1989—Minnesota	Amer.	2-3-S-O	141	446	62	113	18	2	0	38	.253	191	282	16	.967
National League Totals—2 Years			120	214	30	42	4	0	1	9	.196	117	197	11	.966
American League Totals—3 Years			356	1013	141	239	40	7	0	86	.236	408	662	27	.975
Major League Totals—5 Years			476	1227	171	281	44	7	1	95	.229	525	859	38	.973

Selected by California Angels' organization in 3rd round of free-agent draft, January 9, 1979.
Selected by Texas Rangers' organization in 3rd round of free-agent draft, January 8, 1980.
Selected by New York Mets' organization in secondary phase of free-agent draft, June 3, 1980.
Selected by Montreal Expos' organization in secondary phase of free-agent draft, June 8, 1981.
†On disabled list, July 23 to August 16, 1983.
‡Traded with Pitcher Scott Sanderson to San Diego Padres for Pitcher Gary Lucas, December 7, 1983.
§Traded to Montreal Expos' organization for Pitcher Greg Harris, July 20, 1984.
xTraded to Minnesota Twins for Pitcher Mike Shade, February 20, 1987.

Year Club	League	Pos.	G.	AB.	R.	H.	2B.	3B.	HR.	RBI.	B.A.	PO.	A.	E.	F.A.
1987—Minnesota...............	Amer.	2B	1	2	0	0	0	0	0	0	.000	0	1	0	1.000

Year Club	League	Pos.	G.	AB.	R.	H.	2B.	3B.	HR.	RBI.	B.A.	PO.	A.	E.	F.A.
1987—Minnesota...............	Amer.	PR-2-PH	4	5	0	1	0	0	0	0	.200	1	2	0	1.000

FRANCIS ANDREW NEZELEK
(Andy)

Born October 24, 1965, at Endicott, N.Y.
Height, 6.06. Weight, 225.
Throws right and bats lefthanded.
Attended Bucknell University, Lewisburg, Pa.

Led International League in games finished in relief with 37 in 1989.

Year Club	League	G.	IP.	W.	L.	Pct.	H.	R.	ER.	SO.	BB.	ERA.
1986—Pulaski..................	Ap'lachian	12	66⅓	2	4	.333	69	36	20	55	22	2.71
1987—Sumter...................	S. Atlantic	12	85	6	3	.667	56	24	17	67	12	1.80
1988—Greenville	Southern	26	133⅔	7	8	.467	133	77	65	89	45	4.38
1989—Richmond.................	Int'national	48	77⅓	4	5	.444	65	25	21	30	35	2.44

Selected by Atlanta Braves' organization in 5th round of free-agent draft, June 2, 1986.

CARL EDWARD NICHOLS

Born October 14, 1962, at Los Angeles, Calif.
Height, 6.00. Weight, 192.
Throws and bats righthanded.

Led Pacific Coast League catchers in assists with 76 in 1989.
Led International League catchers in fielding percentage with .988, double plays with 9 and passed balls with 9 in 1987.
Led Southern League catchers in putouts with 693 and total chances with 818 in 1986.
Led California League catchers in total chances with 897 in 1984.
Led New York-Pennsylvania League catchers in assists with 47 and tied for lead in double plays with 6 in 1983.

Year Club	League	Pos.	G.	AB.	R.	H.	2B.	3B.	HR.	RBI.	B.A.	PO.	A.	E.	F.A.
1980—Bluefield................	Appal.	C-1B-OF	37	85	24	18	2	2	0	10	.212	129	13	2	.986
1981—Miami	Fla. St.	C-1-S-3-O	16	31	1	6	0	0	0	3	.194	34	9	6	.878
1981—Hagerstown†	Carol.	C-O-S-2	38	81	8	22	4	0	1	6	.272	131	21	3	.981
1982—Macon....................	S. Atl.	C-OF-1B	84	257	33	55	10	2	0	30	.214	391	49	21	.954
1983—San Jose	Calif.	C-OF-3B	54	152	16	31	4	0	1	12	.204	204	39	17	.935
1983—Newark	NYP	C-O-3-S	66	217	40	63	14	0	5	26	.290	348	56	10	.976
1984—S.J.‡-Red.§.............	Calif.	*C-OF	121	389	53	88	14	2	4	54	.226	*769	*112	17	.981
1985—Charlotte...............	South.	C-OF-1B	115	331	45	78	11	2	2	37	.236	496	71	15	.984
1986—Charlotte...............	South.	*C-OF	118	439	63	118	26	1	14	72	.269	700	*110	16	.981
1986—Baltimore	Amer.	C	5	5	0	0	0	0	0	0	.000	11	0	0	1.000
1987—Rochester	Int.	C-OF	108	364	45	93	15	3	11	52	.255	617	65	9	.987
1987—Baltimore	Amer.	C	13	21	4	8	1	0	0	3	.381	39	3	0	1.000
1988—Baltimore	Amer.	C-OF	18	47	2	9	1	0	0	1	.191	71	13	1	.988
1988—Rochester x	Int.	C-OF-3B	75	193	20	44	7	1	3	16	.228	335	44	8	.979
1989—Tucson.................	P. C.	C-OF	104	340	45	87	27	1	4	27	.256	553	77	11	.983
1989—Houston.................	Nat.	C	8	13	0	1	0	0	0	2	.077	16	1	0	1.000
American League Totals—3 Years			36	73	6	17	2	0	0	4	.233	121	16	1	.993
National League Totals—1 Year.............			8	13	0	1	0	0	0	2	.077	16	1	0	1.000
Major League Totals—4 Years.................			44	86	6	18	2	0	0	6	.209	137	17	1	.994

Selected by Baltimore Orioles' organization in 4th round of free-agent draft, June 3, 1980.
†Loaned to Macon (Detroit Tigers' organization), April 8, 1982; returned, September 15, 1982.
‡Loaned to San Jose (Independent), April 10, 1984; returned, June 9, 1984.
§Loaned to Redwood (California Angels' organization), June 9, 1984; returned, September 10, 1984.
xTraded to Houston Astros for Pitcher Dave Johnson and Outfielder Victor Hithe, March 31, 1989.

RODNEY LEA NICHOLS
(Rod)

Born December 29, 1964, at Burlington, Ia.
Height, 6.02. Weight, 190.
Throws and bats righthanded.
Attended University of New Mexico, Albuquerque, N.M.

Year Club	League	G.	IP.	W.	L.	Pct.	H.	R.	ER.	SO.	BB.	ERA.
1985—Batavia..................	NYP	13	84	5	5	.500	74	40	28	93	33	3.00
1986—Waterloo†	Midwest	20	115⅓	8	5	.615	128	56	52	83	21	4.06
1987—Kinston...................	Carolina	9	56	4	2	.667	53	27	25	61	14	4.02
1987—Williamsport..................	Eastern	16	100	4	3	.571	107	53	41	60	33	3.69
1988—Kinston‡....................	Carolina	4	24	3	1	.750	26	13	12	19	15	4.50
1988—Colorado Springs	P. Coast	10	58⅔	2	6	.250	69	41	37	43	17	5.74
1988—Cleveland...............	American	11	69⅓	1	7	.125	73	41	39	31	23	5.06
1989—Colorado Springs§	P. Coast	10	65⅓	8	1	.889	57	28	26	41	30	3.58
1989—Cleveland................	American	15	71⅔	4	6	.400	81	42	35	42	24	4.40
Major League Totals—2 Years............................		26	141	5	13	.278	154	83	74	73	47	4.72

Selected by Cleveland Indians' organization in 5th round of free-agent draft, June 3, 1985.
†On disabled list, July 12 to August 18, 1986.
‡On Cleveland disabled list, March 26 to May 12, 1988.
§On Cleveland disabled list, March 19 to June 12, 1989; including rehabilitation disability assignment to Colorado Springs, May 24 to June 12, 1989.

THOMAS EDWARD NIEDENFUER

Name pronounced NEED-un-fyoor.

(Tom)

Born August 13, 1959, at St. Louis Park, Minn.
Height, 6.05. Weight, 230.
Throws and bats righthanded.
Attended Washington State University, Pullman, Wash.
Husband of Judy Landers, television actress.

Major League saves: 1981 (2), 1982 (9), 1983 (11), 1984 (11), 1985 (19), 1986 (11), 1987 (14), 1988 (18). Total—95.

Year Club	League	G.	IP.	W.	L.	Pct.	H.	R.	ER.	SO.	BB.	ERA.
1981—San Antonio	Texas	36	90	13	3	*.813	61	19	18	95	34	1.80
1981—Los Angeles	National	17	26	3	1	.750	25	11	11	12	6	3.81
1982—Albuquerque	P. Coast	4	10⅔	2	0	1.000	6	0	0	15	2	0.00
1982—Los Angeles	National	55	69⅔	3	4	.429	71	22	21	60	25	2.71
1983—Los Angeles	National	66	94⅔	8	3	.727	55	22	20	66	29	1.90
1984—Los Angeles†	National	33	47⅓	2	5	.286	39	14	13	45	23	2.47
1985—Los Angeles	National	64	106⅓	7	9	.438	86	32	32	102	24	2.71
1986—Los Angeles‡	National	60	80	6	6	.500	86	35	33	55	29	3.71
1987—Los Angeles§	National	15	16⅓	1	0	1.000	13	5	5	10	9	2.76
1987—Baltimore	American	45	52⅓	3	5	.375	55	32	29	37	22	4.99
1988—Baltimore x	American	52	59	3	4	.429	59	23	23	40	19	3.51
1989—Seattle y	American	25	36⅓	0	3	.000	46	29	27	15	15	6.69
1989—Calgary	P. Coast	13	18⅔	1	2	.333	23	13	11	11	7	5.30
National League Totals—7 Years		310	440⅓	30	28	.517	375	141	135	350	145	2.76
American League Totals—3 Years		122	147⅔	6	12	.333	160	84	79	92	56	4.81
Major League Totals—9 Years		432	588	36	40	.474	535	225	214	442	201	3.28

Selected by Los Angeles Dodgers' organization in 36th round of free-agent draft, June 7, 1977.
Signed as free agent by Los Angeles Dodgers' organization, August 14, 1980.
†On disabled list, July 16 to July 31 and August 5 to September 11, 1984.
‡On disabled list, August 19 to September 3, 1986.
§Traded to Baltimore Orioles for Outfielder John Shelby and Pitcher Brad Havens, May 22, 1987.
xGranted free agency, November 4, 1988; signed by Seattle Mariners, December 7, 1988.
yOn disabled list, April 12 to May 30, 1989; included rehabilitation disability assignment to Calgary, May 21 to May 30, 1989.

DIVISION SERIES RECORD

Year Club	League	G.	IP.	W.	L.	Pct.	H.	R.	ER.	SO.	BB.	ERA.
1981—Los Angeles	National	1	⅓	0	0	.000	1	0	0	1	1	0.00

CHAMPIONSHIP SERIES RECORD

Shares Championship Series record for most games lost, series (2), 1985.

Year Club	League	G.	IP.	W.	L.	Pct.	H.	R.	ER.	SO.	BB.	ERA.
1981—Los Angeles	National	1	⅓	0	0	.000	2	0	0	0	0	0.00
1983—Los Angeles	National	2	2	0	0	.000	0	0	0	3	1	0.00
1985—Los Angeles	National	3	5⅔	0	2	.000	5	4	4	5	2	6.35
Championship Series Totals—3 Years		6	8	0	2	.000	7	4	4	8	3	4.50

WORLD SERIES RECORD

Year Club	League	G.	IP.	W.	L.	Pct.	H.	R.	ER.	SO.	BB.	ERA.
1981—Los Angeles	National	2	5	0	0	.000	3	2	0	0	1	0.00

JEFFREY SCOTT NIELSEN

(Known by middle name.)

Born December 18, 1958, at Salt Lake City, Utah.
Height, 6.01. Weight, 190.
Throws and bats righthanded.
Attended Brigham Young University, Provo, Utah.

Pitched 3-0 no-hit victory against Maine, June 8, 1988.
Major League saves: 1987 (2).
Tied for International League lead in shutouts with 3 in 1988.

Year Club	League	G.	IP.	W.	L.	Pct.	H.	R.	ER.	SO.	BB.	ERA.
1983—Bellingham	Northwest	2	13	2	0	1.000	11	4	3	13	2	2.08
1983—Chattanooga†	Southern	13	63⅓	2	4	.333	81	49	45	24	27	6.39
1984—Fort Lauderdale‡	Florida St.	4	16⅔	2	1	.667	16	8	2	7	5	1.08
1984—Nashville	Southern	10	73⅔	6	3	.667	55	34	20	27	15	2.44
1984—Columbus	Int'national	11	56⅔	5	4	.556	59	27	25	21	23	3.97
1985—Albany§	Eastern	11	73⅓	6	1	.857	60	26	24	31	14	2.95
1986—Fort Lauderdale	Florida St.	6	34⅓	4	0	1.000	32	12	8	10	9	2.10
1986—Columbus	Int'national	19	116⅔	11	7	.611	123	52	45	44	38	3.47
1986—New York x	American	10	56	4	4	.500	66	29	25	20	12	4.02

Year	Club	League	G.	IP.	W.	L.	Pct.	H.	R.	ER.	SO.	BB.	ERA.
1987—Hawaii	P. Coast	10	68	3	4	.429	74	36	30	21	30	3.97
1987—Chicago y	American	19	66⅓	3	5	.375	83	48	46	23	25	6.24
1988—Columbus	Int'national	25	172⅓	●13	6	.684	142	52	46	62	42	2.40
1988—New York	American	7	19⅔	1	2	.333	27	16	15	4	13	6.86
1989—Columbus z-Tidewater	Int'national	40	109⅓	6	11	.353	93	46	39	47	39	3.21
1989—New York a	American	2	⅔	1	0	1.000	2	1	1	0	1	13.50
Major League Totals—4 Years		38	142⅔	9	11	.450	178	94	87	47	51	5.49

Selected by Seattle Mariners' organization in 6th round of free-agent draft, June 6, 1983.

†Traded with Pitcher Eric Parent to New York Yankees' organization for Infielder Larry Milbourne, February 14, 1984.

‡On disabled list, April 6 to April 23, 1984.

§On disabled list, May 30 to June 21 and June 27 to September 16, 1985.

xTraded with Infielder Mike Soper to Chicago White Sox for Pitcher Pete Filson and Infielder Randy Velarde, January 5, 1987.

yTraded with Pitcher Richard Dotson to New York Yankees for Outfielder Dan Pasqua, Catcher Mark Salas and Pitcher Steve Rosenberg, November 12, 1987.

zTraded to Tidewater (New York Mets' organization) for Outfielder Marcus Lawton, July 10, 1989.

aGranted free agency, October 15, 1989.

THOMAS ANDREW NIETO

Name pronounced Nee-AY-toh.

(Tom)

Born October 27, 1960, at Downey, Calif.
Height, 6.01. Weight, 210.
Throws and bats righthanded.
Attended Cerritos College, Norwalk, Calif., and
Oral Roberts University, Tulsa, Okla.

Tied for American Association lead in being hit by pitch with 8 in 1983.

Year	Club	League	Pos.	G.	AB.	R.	H.	2B.	3B.	HR.	RBI.	B.A.	PO.	A.	E.	F.A.
1981—Arkansas	Texas	C	62	184	12	33	2	0	2	19	.179	270	37	8	.975
1982—Arkansas†	Texas	C	96	298	33	72	11	3	5	31	.242	466	58	3	★.994
1983—Louisville	A. A.	C	115	383	44	104	17	1	5	52	.272	605	71	★15	.978
1984—Louisville	A. A.	C	77	253	23	70	12	1	7	34	.277	446	43	8	.984
1984—St. Louis	Nat.	C	33	86	7	24	4	0	3	12	.279	135	18	1	.994
1985—St. Louis‡	Nat.	C	95	253	15	57	10	2	0	34	.225	384	28	4	.990
1986—Montreal§	Nat.	C	30	65	5	13	3	1	1	7	.200	123	11	3	.978
1986—Indianapolis x	A. A.	C	53	167	21	50	16	0	3	19	.299	295	25	9	.973
1987—Minnesota y	Amer.	C	41	105	7	21	7	1	1	12	.200	210	17	1	.996
1987—Portland	P. C.	C	38	110	10	25	5	0	0	3	.227	193	15	5	.977
1988—Minnesota	Amer.	C	24	60	1	4	0	0	0	0	.067	108	6	1	.991
1988—Portland z	P. C.	C	53	158	11	44	7	2	3	21	.278	276	25	6	.980
1989—Scr./Wil.-Barre a . Int.		C	46	136	8	26	3	0	1	7	.191	236	25	7	.974
1989—Philadelphia	Nat.	C	11	20	1	3	0	0	0	0	.150	63	2	0	1.000
National League Totals—4 Years		169	424	28	97	17	3	4	53	.229	705	59	8	.990
American League Totals—2 Years		65	165	8	25	7	1	1	12	.152	318	23	2	.994
Major League Totals—6 Years		234	589	36	122	24	4	5	65	.207	1023	82	10	.991

Selected by Minnesota Twins' organization in 31st round of free-agent draft, June 5, 1979.

Selected by Pittsburgh Pirates' organization in secondary phase of free-agent draft, January 8, 1980.

Selected by St. Louis Cardinals' organization in 3rd round of free-agent draft, June 8, 1981.

†On disabled list, June 19 to June 30, 1982.

‡Traded to Montreal Expos for Infielder Fred Manrique, March 31, 1986.

§On disabled list, August 21 to September 11, 1986; included rehabilitation disability assignment to Indianapolis, September 3 to September 10, 1986.

xTraded with Pitcher Jeff Reardon to Minnesota Twins for Pitchers Neal Heaton, Al Cardwood and Yorkis Perez and Catcher Jeff Reed, February 3, 1987.

yOn disabled list, May 18 to July 22, 1987; included rehabilitation disability assignment to Portland, July 12 to July 22, 1987.

zTraded with Second Baseman Tom Herr and Outfielder Eric Bullock to Philadelphia Phillies for Pitcher Shane Rawley and cash, October 24, 1988.

aOn Philadelphia disabled list, March 29 to June 2, 1989; included rehabilitation disability assignment to Scranton/Wilkes-Barre, May 1 to May 20, 1989.

CHAMPIONSHIP SERIES RECORD

Year	Club	League	Pos.	G.	AB.	R.	H.	2B.	3B.	HR.	RBI.	B.A.	PO.	A.	E.	F.A.
1985—St. Louis	Nat.	C	1	3	1	0	0	0	0	0	.000	7	0	0	1.000

WORLD SERIES RECORD

Year	Club	League	Pos.	G.	AB.	R.	H.	2B.	3B.	HR.	RBI.	B.A.	PO.	A.	E.	F.A.
1985—St. Louis	Nat.	C	2	5	0	0	0	0	0	1	.000	23	1	0	1.000

JUAN MANUEL NIEVES

Born January 5, 1965, at Santurce, Puerto Rico.
Height, 6.03. Weight, 190.
Throws and bats lefthanded.

Pitched 7-0 no-hit victory against Baltimore Orioles, April 15, 1987.
Major League saves: 1988 (1).

Named Texas League Pitcher of the Year, 1985.
Received reported $150,000 bonus to sign with Milwaukee Brewers, 1983.

Year Club	League	G.	IP.	W.	L.	Pct.	H.	R.	ER.	SO.	BB.	ERA.
1983—Beloit	Midwest	12	69⅓	7	1	.875	43	11	10	89	15	1.30
1984—Stockton	California	24	139⅔	10	3	.769	137	75	55	133	63	3.54
1985—El Paso	Texas	17	120	8	2	*.800	106	53	47	91	44	3.53
1985—Vancouver	P. Coast	12	68⅔	8	3	.727	56	30	29	54	44	3.80
1986—Milwaukee	American	35	184⅔	11	12	.478	224	124	101	116	77	4.92
1987—Milwaukee	American	34	195⅔	14	8	.636	199	112	106	163	100	4.88
1988—Milwaukee†	American	25	110⅓	7	5	.583	84	53	50	73	50	4.08
1988—Denver	Am. Assoc.	5	19⅔	0	2	.000	11	5	5	14	7	2.29
1989—Denver‡	Am. Assoc.	3	14	2	1	.667	9	10	10	8	11	6.43
Major League Totals—3 Years		94	490⅔	32	25	.561	507	289	257	352	227	4.71

Signed as free agent by Milwaukee Brewers' organization, July 1, 1983.

†On disabled list, May 26 to July 28, 1988; included rehabilitation disability assignment to Denver, July 8 to July 27, 1988.

‡On Milwaukee disabled list, March 19, 1989 through entire season; included rehabilitation disability assignment to Denver, May 12 to May 30, 1989.

OTIS JUNIOR NIXON

Born January 9, 1959, at Evergreen, N.C.
Height, 6.02. Weight, 180.
Throws right and bats right and lefthanded.
Attended Louisburg College, Louisburg, N.C.
Brother of Donell Nixon, outfielder with San Francisco Giants.

Major League stolen bases: 1984 (12), 1985 (20), 1986 (23), 1987 (2), 1988 (46), 1989 (37). Total—140.
Led International League in stolen bases with 94 and caught stealing with 29 in 1983.
Led Southern League in bases on balls received with 110 in 1981.
Led South Atlantic League in bases on balls received with 113 and stolen bases with 67 in 1980.
Led Appalachian League in bases on balls received with 57 in 1979.
Led International League outfielders in fielding percentage with .992, putouts with 363 and total chances with 371 in 1983.
Led Appalachian League third basemen in fielding percentage with .945, putouts with 52, assists with 120, and double plays with 12 in 1979.

Year Club	League	Pos.	G.	AB.	R.	H.	2B.	3B.	HR.	RBI.	B.A.	PO.	A.	E.	F.A.
1979—Paintsville	Appal.	3B-SS	63	203	58	58	10	3	1	25	.286	54	122	11	.941
1980—Greensboro	S. Atl.	3B-SS	136	493	*124	137	12	5	3	48	.278	164	308	36	.929
1981—Nashville	South.	SS	127	407	89	102	9	2	0	20	.251	198	348	*56	.907
1982—Nashville	South.	SS-2B	72	283	47	80	3	2	0	20	.283	126	211	23	.936
1982—Columbus	Int.	2B-SS	59	207	43	58	4	0	0	14	.280	104	169	14	.951
1983—Columbus	Int.	OF-2B	138	*557	*129	*162	11	6	0	41	.291	385	24	4	.990
1983—New York†	Amer.	OF	13	14	2	2	0	0	0	0	.143	14	1	1	.938
1984—Cleveland	Amer.	OF	49	91	16	14	0	0	0	1	.154	81	3	0	1.000
1984—Maine	Int.	OF	72	253	42	70	5	1	0	22	.277	206	7	1	.995
1985—Cleveland	Amer.	OF	104	162	34	38	4	0	3	9	.235	129	5	4	.971
1986—Cleveland	Amer.	OF	105	95	33	25	4	1	0	8	.263	90	3	3	.969
1987—Cleveland	Amer.	OF	19	17	2	1	0	0	0	1	.059	21	0	0	1.000
1987—Buffalo‡	A. A.	OF	59	249	51	71	13	4	2	23	.285	170	3	3	.983
1988—Indianapolis	A. A.	OF	67	235	52	67	6	3	0	19	.285	130	1	1	.992
1988—Montreal	Nat.	OF	90	271	47	66	8	2	0	15	.244	176	2	1	.994
1989—Montreal	Nat.	OF	126	258	41	56	7	2	0	21	.217	160	2	2	.988
American League Totals—5 Years			290	379	87	80	8	1	3	19	.211	335	12	8	.977
National League Totals—2 Years			216	529	88	122	15	4	0	36	.231	336	4	3	.991
Major League Totals—7 Years			506	908	175	202	23	5	3	55	.222	671	16	11	.984

Selected by Cincinnati Reds' organization in 21st round of free-agent draft, June 6, 1978.
Selected by California Angels' organization in secondary phase of free-agent draft, January 9, 1979.
Selected by New York Yankees' organization in secondary phase of free-agent draft, June 5, 1979.

†Traded with Pitcher George Frazier and a player to be named later to Cleveland Indians for Third Baseman Toby Harrah and a player to be named later, February 5, 1984; New York organization acquired Pitcher Rick Browne and Cleveland organization acquired Pitcher Guy Elston to complete deal, February 8, 1984.

‡Granted free agency, October 15, 1987; signed by Indianapolis (Montreal Expos' organization), March 5, 1988.

ROBERT DONELL NIXON

(Known by middle name.)
Born December 31, 1961, at Evergreen, N. C.
Height, 6.01. Weight, 185.
Throws and bats righthanded.
Attended Louisburg College, Louisburg, N. C.
Brother of Otis Nixon, outfielder with Montreal Expos.

Shares major league record for most times caught stealing, inning (2), July 6, 1988, sixth inning.
Major League stolen bases: 1987 (21), 1988 (11), 1989 (10). Total—42.
Led Pacific Coast League in stolen bases with 46 in 1987.
Led Southern League in stolen bases with 102 in 1984.
Led California League in stolen bases with 144 and caught stealing with 24 in 1983.
Led Midwest League in stolen bases with 85 in 1982.

Year Club	League	Pos.	G.	AB.	R.	H.	2B.	3B.	HR.	RBI.	B.A.	PO.	A.	E.	F.A.
1981—Wausau†	Midw.	1B-2B-OF	59	204	35	58	7	2	5	26	.284	252	9	3	.989
1982—Wausau	Midw.	*3B-1B	116	461	102	156	18	7	11	56	.338	*87	187	*49	.848

Year Club	League	Pos.	G.	AB.	R.	H.	2B.	3B.	HR.	RBI.	B.A.	PO.	A.	E.	F.A.
1982—Lynn	Midw.	3B	6	24	5	7	2	1	0	1	.292	0	2	0	1.000
1983—Bakersfield	Calif.	*3B-OF	135	542	*116	174	27	4	4	51	.321	98	249	*51	.872
1984—Chattanooga	South.	OF-3B	140	536	99	144	25	5	4	57	.269	262	6	8	.971
1985—Seattle‡	Amer.					(Did not play)									
1986—Chattanooga§	South.	OF	4	18	2	6	1	0	0	0	.333	7	0	1	.875
1986—Calgary	P. C.	OF	8	35	3	12	1	1	0	1	.343	15	2	0	1.000
1987—Seattle	Amer.	OF	46	132	17	33	4	0	3	12	.250	76	1	0	1.000
1987—Calgary	P. C.	OF-1B	82	328	72	106	18	1	5	52	.323	168	1	6	.966
1988—Calgary x	P. C.	OF	40	160	28	45	7	0	3	10	.281	0	0	0	.000
1988—San Francisco	Nat.	OF	59	78	15	27	3	0	0	6	.346	59	0	1	.983
1989—San Francisco	Nat.	OF	95	166	23	44	2	0	1	15	.265	87	0	3	.967
American League Totals—1 Year			46	132	17	33	4	0	3	12	.250	76	1	0	1.000
National League Totals—2 Years			154	244	38	71	5	0	1	21	.291	146	0	4	.973
Major League Totals—3 Years			200	376	55	104	9	0	4	33	.277	222	1	4	.982

Selected by Seattle Mariners' organization in 10th round of free-agent draft, June 3, 1980.
†On disabled list, July 7, 1981 through remainder of season.
‡On disabled list, April 8, 1985 through entire season.
§On Calgary disabled list, April 11 to August 1, 1986.
xTraded to San Francisco Giants, June 23, 1988, completing deal in which San Francisco traded Pitcher Rod Scurry to Seattle Mariners for a player to be named later, March 19, 1988.

CHAMPIONSHIP SERIES RECORD

Year Club	League	Pos.	G.	AB.	R.	H.	2B.	3B.	HR.	RBI.	B.A.	PO.	A.	E.	F.A.
1989—San Francisco	Nat.	OF-PR	3	3	0	0	0	0	0	0	.000	2	0	1	.667

WORLD SERIES RECORD

Year Club	League	Pos.	G.	AB.	R.	H.	2B.	3B.	HR.	RBI.	B.A.	PO.	A.	E.	F.A.
1989—San Francisco	Nat.	PH-OF	2	5	1	1	0	0	0	0	.200	2	0	0	1.000

MILCIADES ARTURO NOBOA JR.

Name pronounced Nah-BO-ah.

(Junior)

Born November 10, 1964, at Azua, D. R.
Height, 5.10. Weight, 180.
Throws and bats righthanded.

Major League stolen bases: 1984 (1), 1987 (1). Total—2.
Led Eastern League in sacrifice hits with 17 in 1984.
Led Midwest League in sacrifice hits with 18 in 1983.
Tied for American Association lead in sacrifice flies with 8 in 1989.
Led American Association second basemen in fielding percentage with .986 in 1989.
Led Midwest League second basemen in putouts with 257 and double plays with 81 in 1983.

Year Club	League	Pos.	G.	AB.	R.	H.	2B.	3B.	HR.	RBI.	B.A.	PO.	A.	E.	F.A.
1981—Batavia	NYP	2B	50	162	15	49	8	0	0	6	.302	82	100	*18	.910
1982—Waterloo	Midw.	SS	121	385	69	96	12	5	0	23	.249	*207	306	46	.918
1983—Waterloo	Midw.	2B-SS	132	449	64	115	22	3	1	29	.256	260	355	24	.962
1984—Buffalo	East.	2B	117	383	55	97	18	4	1	45	.253	228	305	*18	.967
1984—Cleveland	Amer.	2D	23	11	3	4	0	0	0	0	.364	7	13	0	1.000
1985—Maine	Int.	2B	122	403	62	116	11	2	5	32	.288	270	379	14	.979
1986—Maine	Int.	2B-SS-3B	108	399	44	114	21	1	4	32	.286	160	252	13	.969
1987—Buffalo	A. A.	2B-SS-3B	43	149	26	47	6	2	0	14	.315	70	108	11	.942
1987—Cleveland†	Amer.	2B-SS-3B	39	80	7	18	2	1	0	7	.225	28	66	3	.969
1988—Edmonton	P. C.	2-S-O-3	50	159	24	47	6	1	0	17	.296	86	145	7	.971
1988—California‡	Amer.	2B-SS-3B	21	16	4	1	0	0	0	0	.063	8	24	1	.970
1989—Indianapolis	A. A.	2B-SS	117	467	61	*159	21	8	2	62	*.340	170	305	10	.979
1989—Montreal	Nat.	2B-SS-3B	21	44	3	10	0	0	0	1	.227	17	45	0	1.000
American League Totals—3 Years			83	107	14	23	2	1	0	7	.215	43	103	4	.973
National League Totals—1 Year			21	44	3	10	0	0	0	1	.227	17	45	0	1.000
Major League Totals—4 Years			104	151	17	33	2	1	0	8	.219	60	148	4	.981

Signed as free agent by Cleveland Indians' organization, May 26, 1981.
†Traded to California Angels for Outfielder Ted Milner, March 30, 1988.
‡Granted free agency, October 15, 1988; signed by Indianapolis (Montreal Expos' organization), January 4, 1989.

MATTHEW DODGE NOKES

(Matt)

Born October 31, 1963, at San Diego, Calif.
Height, 6.01. Weight, 185.
Throws right and bats lefthanded.

Major League stolen bases: 1987 (2), 1989 (1). Total—3.
Led Texas League catchers in double plays with 6 in 1985.
Led California League catchers in double plays with 9 in 1983.
Led Pioneer League in passed balls with 19 in 1981.
Tied for American Association lead in errors by catchers with 13 in 1986.
Named catcher on THE SPORTING NEWS American League All-Star Team, 1987.
Named catcher on THE SPORTING NEWS American League Silver Slugger team, 1987.

Year Club	League	Pos.	G.	AB.	R.	H.	2B.	3B.	HR.	RBI.	B.A.	PO.	A.	E.	F.A.
1981—Great Falls...........	Pion.	C	44	146	14	33	6	2	0	13	.226	288	35	*13	.961
1982—Clinton...................	Midw.	C	82	247	19	53	12	0	3	23	.215	363	41	13	.969
1983—Fresno...................	Calif.	C	125	429	62	138	26	6	14	82	.322	595	62	16	.976
1984—Shreveport	Texas	C	97	308	32	89	19	2	11	61	.289	400	31	8	.982
1985—Shreveport	Texas	C	105	344	52	101	24	1	14	56	.294	520	40	12	.979
1985—San Francisco†	Nat.	C	19	53	3	11	2	0	2	5	.208	84	2	2	.977
1986—Nashville................	A. A.	C-1B-OF	125	428	55	122	25	4	10	71	.285	502	50	18	.968
1986—Detroit...................	Amer.	C	7	24	2	8	1	0	1	2	.333	43	2	0	1.000
1987—Detroit...................	Amer.	C-OF-3B	135	461	69	133	14	2	32	87	.289	600	32	5	.992
1988—Detroit...................	Amer.	C	122	382	53	96	18	0	16	53	.251	574	45	7	.989
1989—Detroit‡................	Amer.	C	87	268	15	67	10	0	9	39	.250	235	26	6	.978
National League Totals—1 Year..............			19	53	3	11	2	0	2	5	.208	84	2	2	.977
American League Totals—4 Years			351	1135	139	304	43	2	58	181	.268	1452	105	18	.989
Major League Totals—5 Years			370	1188	142	315	45	2	60	186	.265	1536	107	20	.988

Selected by San Francisco Giants' organization in 20th round of free-agent draft, June 8, 1981.

†Traded with Pitchers Dave LaPoint and Eric King to Detroit Tigers for Pitcher Juan Berenguer, Catcher Bob Melvin and a player to be named later, October 7, 1985; San Francisco Giants acquired Pitcher Scott Medvin to complete deal, December 11, 1985.

‡On disabled list, June 19 to August 3, 1989.

CHAMPIONSHIP SERIES RECORD

Year Club	League	Pos.	G.	AB.	R.	H.	2B.	3B.	HR.	RBI.	B.A.	PO.	A.	E.	F.A.
1987—Detroit...................	Amer.	PH-DH-C	5	14	2	2	0	0	1	2	.143	11	2	0	1.000

ALL-STAR GAME RECORD

Year League	Pos.	AB.	R.	H.	2B.	3B.	HR.	RBI.	B.A.	PO.	A.	E.	F.A.
1987—American	C	2	0	0	0	0	0	0	.000	8	0	0	1.000

ERIC CARL NOLTE

Born April 28, 1964, at Canoga Park, Calif.
Height, 6.03. Weight, 200.
Throws and bats lefthanded.
Attended UCLA.

Tied for Northwest League lead in balks with 2 in 1985.

Year Club	League	G.	IP.	W.	L.	Pct.	H.	R.	ER.	SO.	BB.	ERA.
1985—Spokane	Northwest	14	76⅔	3	●8	.273	79	50	34	52	46	3.99
1986—Charleston	S. Atlantic	26	164	12	9	.571	154	80	71	121	68	3.90
1987—Reno	California	11	64	3	4	.429	76	38	31	47	24	4.36
1987—Wichita..	Texas	10	75	4	2	.667	62	28	24	67	19	2.88
1987—San Diego	National	12	67⅓	2	6	.250	57	28	44	36	36	3.21
1988—San Diego	National	2	3	0	0	.000	3	2	2	1	2	6.00
1988—Las Vegas.................................	P. Coast	27	128⅓	8	7	.533	168	97	86	68	53	6.03
1989—Las Vegas†...............................	P. Coast	23	116⅓	6	9	.400	121	74	67	89	54	5.18
1989—San Diego	National	3	9	0	0	.000	15	12	11	8	7	11.00
Major League Totals—3 Years..............................		17	79⅓	2	6	.250	75	42	37	53	45	4.20

Selected by Chicago Cubs' organization in 7th round of free-agent draft, June 7, 1982.
Selected by San Diego Padres' organization in 6th round of free-agent draft, June 3, 1985.
†On San Diego disabled list, March 25 to May 8, 1989.

MICHAEL KELVIN NORRIS
(Mike)

Born March 19, 1955, at San Francisco, Calif.
Height, 6.02. Weight, 190.
Throws and bats righthanded.
Attended City College of San Francisco, San Francisco, Calif.

Pitched shutout in first major league game, April 10, 1975.
Led American League in wild pitches with 14 in 1981.
Tied for American League lead in balks with 4 in 1980 and 5 in 1981.
Named pitcher on THE SPORTING NEWS American League All-Star fielding team, 1980 and 1981.
Received reported $25,000 bonus to sign with Oakland Athletics, 1973.

Year Club	League	G.	IP.	W.	L.	Pct.	H.	R.	ER.	SO.	BB.	ERA.
1973—Burlington	Midwest	20	110	8	4	.667	81	38	27	130	40	2.21
1974—Birmingham†	Southern	21	109	7	8	.467	107	64	49	103	65	4.05
1975—Oakland‡..	American	4	17	1	0	1.000	6	2	0	5	8	0.00
1976—Tucson	P. Coast	5	33	2	1	.667	28	15	14	19	23	3.82
1976—Oakland...	American	24	96	4	5	.444	91	53	51	44	56	4.78
1977—San Jose§	P. Coast	6	46	3	2	.600	42	18	18	35	18	3.52
1977—Oakland...	American	16	77	2	7	.222	77	45	41	35	31	4.79
1978—Vancouver.....................................	P. Coast	7	42	3	3	.500	42	28	27	32	27	5.79
1978—Jersey City x.................................	Eastern	9	66	2	6	.250	58	35	25	51	36	3.41
1978—Oakland...	American	14	49	0	5	.000	46	34	30	36	35	5.51
1979—Oakland y......................................	American	29	146	5	8	.385	146	87	78	96	94	4.81
1980—Oakland...	American	33	284	22	9	.710	215	88	80	180	83	2.54
1981—Oakland...	American	23	173	12	9	.571	145	77	72	78	63	3.75
1982—Oakland z......................................	American	28	166⅓	7	11	.389	154	103	88	83	84	4.76
1983—Oakland a......................................	American	16	88⅔	4	5	.444	68	42	37	63	36	3.76

Year	Club	League	G.	IP.	W.	L.	Pct.	H.	R.	ER.	SO.	BB.	ERA.
1983—Tacoma	P. Coast	1	4	0	0	.000	6	6	4	3	1	9.00
1984—Oakland b	American					(Did not play)						
1985—Modesto cd	California	2	13	1	0	1.000	4	1	0	6	1	0.00
1986—San Jose e	California	11	56⅓	4	3	.571	48	18	9	62	8	1.44
1987-88						(Out of Organized Baseball)						
1989—Huntsville	Southern	1	5⅓	1	0	1.000	6	0	0	3	0	0.00
1989—Tacoma	P. Coast	23	82	6	6	.500	78	39	29	72	27	3.18
Major League Totals—9 Years		187	1097	57	59	.491	948	531	477	620	490	3.91

Selected by Oakland Athletics' organization in 1st round (24th player selected) of free-agent draft, January 10, 1973.

†On disabled list, June 14 to June 24, 1974.
‡On disabled list, April 28 to September 19, 1975.
§On disabled list, August 27 to September 6, 1977.
xOn suspended list, May 19 to May 28, 1978.
yOn disabled list, July 12 to August 7, 1979.
zOn disabled list, June 17 to July 8, 1982.
aOn disabled list, June 18 to July 26 and August 11, 1983 through remainder of season; included rehabilitation disability assignment to Tacoma, July 6 to July 26, 1983.
bOn disabled list, March 31, 1984 through entire season.
cOn Oakland disabled list, March 29, 1985 through entire season; included rehabilitation disability assignment to Modesto, June 13 to June 25, 1985.
dGranted free agency, November 12, 1985; signed by San Jose (Independent), March 7, 1986.
eSigned by Tacoma (Oakland Athletics' organization), April 6, 1989.

DIVISION SERIES RECORD

Year	Club	League	G.	IP.	W.	L.	Pct.	H.	R.	ER.	SO.	BB.	ERA.
1981—Oakland	American	1	9	1	0	1.000	4	0	0	2	3	0.00

CHAMPIONSHIP SERIES RECORD

Year	Club	League	G.	IP.	W.	L.	Pct.	H.	R.	ER.	SO.	BB.	ERA.
1981—Oakland	American	1	7⅓	0	1	.000	6	3	3	4	2	3.68

ALL-STAR GAME RECORD

Year	League	IP.	W.	L.	Pct.	H.	R.	ER.	SO.	BB.	ERA.
1981—American		1	0	0	.000	2	1	1	1	0	9.00

RANDALL WILLIAM NOSEK
(Randy)

Born January 8, 1967, at Omaha, Neb.
Height, 6.04. Weight, 215.
Throws and bats righthanded.

Year	Club	League	G.	IP.	W.	L.	Pct.	H.	R.	ER.	SO.	BB.	ERA.
1986—Gastonia	S. Atlantic	12	52⅓	4	5	.444	56	41	35	37	49	6.02
1986—Bristol	Ap'lachian	11	63⅓	6	4	.600	58	38	32	48	45	4.55
1987—Fayetteville	S. Atlantic	16	77⅔	4	11	.267	69	63	40	57	63	4.64
1988—Lakeland	Florida St.	8	30⅔	0	4	.000	29	17	13	11	16	3.82
1989—London	Eastern	22	123⅔	8	10	.444	113	75	68	62	100	4.95
1989—Detroit	American	2	5⅓	0	2	.000	7	8	8	4	10	13.50
1989—Toledo	Int'national	1	1	0	0	.000	2	4	4	0	4	36.00
Major League Totals—1 Year		2	5⅓	0	2	.000	7	8	8	4	10	13.50

Selected by Detroit Tigers' organization in 1st round (26th player selected) of free-agent draft, June 3, 1985.

EDWIN NUNEZ (MARTINEZ)

Name pronounced NOON-yez.

Born May 27, 1963, at Humacao, Puerto Rico.
Height, 6.05. Weight, 240.
Throws and bats righthanded.

Major League saves: 1984 (7), 1985 (16), 1987 (12), 1989 (1). Total—36.
Led Midwest League in complete games with 13 in 1981.

Year	Club	League	G.	IP.	W.	L.	Pct.	H.	R.	ER.	SO.	BB.	ERA.
1979—Bellingham	Northwest	6	39	4	1	.800	39	14	9	30	5	2.08
1980—Wausau	Midwest	22	138	9	7	.563	145	71	57	91	58	3.72
1981—Wausau	Midwest	25	*186	*16	3	.842	143	61	51	*205	58	2.47
1982—Seattle†	American	8	35⅓	1	2	.333	36	18	18	27	16	4.58
1982—Salt Lake City‡	P. Coast	11	55⅓	4	3	.571	40	26	21	42	23	3.42
1983—Seattle	American	14	37	0	4	.000	40	21	18	35	22	4.38
1983—Salt Lake City§	P. Coast	14	77⅓	4	4	.500	99	70	61	52	36	7.10
1984—Salt Lake City x	P. Coast	18	27⅔	3	2	.600	24	12	11	26	12	3.58
1984—Seattle	American	37	67⅔	2	2	.500	55	26	24	57	21	3.19
1985—Seattle	American	70	90⅓	7	3	.700	79	36	31	58	34	3.09
1986—Seattle y	American	14	21⅔	1	2	.333	25	15	14	17	5	5.82
1986—Calgary	P. Coast	6	14	1	2	.333	19	13	11	17	4	7.07
1987—Seattle z	American	48	47⅓	3	4	.429	45	20	20	34	18	3.80
1988—Seattle	American	14	29⅓	1	4	.200	45	33	26	19	14	7.98
1988—Calgary a	P. Coast	3	15⅓	2	0	1.000	15	9	8	12	4	4.70
1988—New York b	National	10	14	1	0	1.000	21	7	7	8	3	4.50

Year Club	League	G.	IP.	W.	L.	Pct.	H.	R.	ER.	SO.	BB.	ERA.
1989—Toledo	Int'national	13	59⅓	1	5	.167	47	20	17	53	18	2.58
1989—Detroit	American	27	54	3	4	.429	49	33	25	41	36	4.17
American League Totals—8 Years		232	382⅔	18	25	.419	374	202	176	288	166	4.14
National League Totals—1 Year		10	14	1	0	1.000	21	7	7	8	3	4.50
Major League Totals—8 Years		242	396⅔	19	25	.432	395	209	183	296	169	4.15

Signed as free agent by Seattle Mariners' organization, March 17, 1979.
†On disabled list, April 23 to May 15, 1982.
‡On disabled list, June 4 to June 29, 1982.
§On disabled list, June 30 to July 14, 1983.
xOn disabled list, May 12 to June 3, 1984.
yOn disabled list, April 5 to April 29 and May 1 to May 16, 1986.
zOn disabled list, May 20 to June 4, 1987.
aTraded to New York Mets for Pitcher Gene Walter, July 11, 1988.
bReleased, March 28, 1989; signed by Toledo (Detroit Tigers' organization), April 1, 1989.

JOSE NUNEZ

Born January 13, 1964, at Jarabocoa, D. R.
Height, 6.03. Weight, 185.
Throws and bats righthanded.

Year Club	League	G.	IP.	W.	L.	Pct.	H.	R.	ER.	SO.	BB.	ERA.
1984—Charleston	S. Atlantic	25	170	14	8	.636	★167	91	62	106	54	3.28
1985—Fort Myers†	Florida St.	11	44⅓	3	2	.600	32	14	12	23	12	2.44
1986—Memphis	Southern	13	48⅔	2	6	.250	52	43	29	36	51	5.36
1986—Fort Myers‡	Florida St.	14	87⅓	8	2	.800	73	31	24	59	32	2.47
1987—Toronto	American	37	97	5	2	.714	91	57	54	99	58	5.01
1988—Syracuse	Int'national	12	71⅓	5	4	.556	62	26	23	67	16	2.90
1988—Toronto§	American	13	29⅓	0	1	.000	28	11	10	18	17	3.07
1989—Syracuse	Int'national	40	134⅓	11	11	.500	116	51	33	122	55	★2.21
1989—Toronto x	American	6	10⅔	0	0	.000	8	3	3	14	2	2.53
Major League Totals—3 Years		56	137	5	3	.625	127	71	67	131	77	4.40

Signed as free agent by Kansas City Royals' organization, November 11, 1983.
†On disabled list, May 30 to June 19 and July 1 to August 24, 1985.
‡Drafted by Toronto Blue Jays, December 8, 1986.
§On disabled list, June 3 to June 18, 1988.
xTraded to Chicago Cubs for Pitcher Paul Kilgus, December 7, 1989.

KENNETH RAY OBERKFELL

Name pronounced OH-burk-fell.

(Ken)

Born May 4, 1956, at Maryville, Ill.
Height, 6.01. Weight, 210.
Throws right and bats lefthanded.
Attended Belleville Area Junior College, Belleville, Ill.

Major League stolen bases: 1979 (4), 1980 (4), 1981 (13), 1982 (11), 1983 (12), 1984 (2), 1985 (1), 1986 (7), 1987 (3), 1988 (4). Total—61.
Led National League third basemen in double plays with 23 and tied for lead in total chances with 338 in 1981.
Led National League second basemen in fielding percentage with .985 in 1979.

Year Club	League	Pos.	G.	AB.	R.	H.	2B.	3B.	HR.	RBI.	B.A.	PO.	A.	E.	F.A.
1975—Johnson City	Appal.	SS	17	54	15	19	3	0	1	8	.352	21	58	4	.952
1975—St. Petersburg	Fla. St.	SS	41	134	14	47	6	1	0	22	.351	71	107	6	.967
1976—Arkansas	Texas	2B-SS	128	456	64	131	19	2	3	47	.287	259	321	18	.970
1977—New Orleans	A. A.	2B-SS	120	418	67	105	18	5	4	32	.251	205	325	17	.969
1977—St. Louis	Nat.	2B	9	9	0	1	0	0	0	1	.111	3	4	0	1.000
1978—Springfield	A. A.	3B-2B-SS	64	242	41	69	13	4	6	38	.285	77	113	6	.969
1978—St. Louis	Nat.	2B-3B	24	50	7	6	1	0	0	0	.120	30	48	1	.987
1979—St. Louis	Nat.	2B-3B-SS	135	369	53	111	19	5	1	35	.301	223	343	9	.984
1980—St. Louis†	Nat.	2B-3B	116	422	58	128	27	6	3	46	.303	227	340	7	.988
1981—St. Louis	Nat.	3B-SS	102	376	43	110	12	6	2	45	.293	77	247	15	.956
1982—St. Louis‡	Nat.	★3B-2B	137	470	55	136	22	5	2	34	.289	80	305	11	★.972
1983—St. Louis	Nat.	★3B-2B-SS	151	488	62	143	26	5	3	38	.293	132	303	18	★.960
1984—St. L.§-Atl.x	Nat.	3B-2B-SS	100	324	38	87	19	2	1	21	.269	64	173	8	.967
1985—Atlanta	Nat.	3B-2B	134	412	30	112	19	4	3	35	.272	88	257	12	.966
1986—Atlanta	Nat.	3B-2B	151	503	62	136	24	3	5	48	.270	116	335	11	.976
1987—Atlanta y	Nat.	3B-2B	135	508	59	142	29	2	3	48	.280	89	265	7	.981
1988—Atl.z-Pit.	Nat.	3-2-S-1	140	476	49	129	22	4	3	42	.271	107	237	15	.958
1989—Pit.a-S.F.b	Nat.	3B-1B-2B	97	156	19	42	6	1	2	17	.269	131	47	4	.978
Major League Totals—13 Years			1431	4563	535	1283	226	43	28	410	.281	1367	2904	118	.973

Signed as free agent by St. Louis Cardinals' organization, May 4, 1975.
†On disabled list, May 11 to June 20, 1980.
‡On disabled list, March 31 to April 23, 1982.
§Traded to Atlanta Braves for Pitcher Ken Dayley and First Baseman Mike Jorgensen, June 15, 1984.
xOn disabled list, August 27, 1984 through remainder of season.
yOn disabled list, June 26 to July 11, 1987.
zTraded with cash to Pittsburgh Pirates for a player to be named later, August 28, 1988; Atlanta Braves acquired Outfielder Tommy Gregg to complete deal, September 1, 1988.
aTraded to San Francisco Giants for Pitcher Roger Samuels, May 10, 1989.
bGranted free agency, November 13, 1989; signed by Houston Astros, December 6, 1989.

Tied Championship Series record for most at-bats, three-game Series (15).

Year	Club	League	Pos.	G.	AB.	R.	H.	2B.	3B.	HR.	RBI.	B.A.	PO.	A.	E.	F.A.
1982—St. Louis	Nat.	3B	3	15	1	3	0	0	0	2	.200	2	4	1	.857
1989—San Francisco	Nat.	PH-3B	3	4	0	0	0	0	0	0	.000	0	1	0	1.000
Championship Series Totals—2 Years			6	19	1	3	0	0	0	2	.158	2	5	1	.875

WORLD SERIES RECORD

Year	Club	League	Pos.	G.	AB.	R.	H.	2B.	3B.	HR.	RBI.	B.A.	PO.	A.	E.	F.A.
1982—St. Louis	Nat.	3B	7	24	4	7	1	0	0	1	.292	3	21	1	.960
1989—San Francisco	Nat.	PH-3B	4	6	1	2	0	0	0	0	.333	0	5	1	.833
World Series Totals—2 Years			11	30	5	9	1	0	0	1	.300	3	26	2	.935

CHARLES HUGH O'BRIEN
(Charlie)

Born May 1, 1961, at Tulsa, Okla.
Height, 6.02. Weight, 190.
Throws and bats righthanded.
Attended McClennan Community College, Waco, Tex., and Wichita State University, Wichita, Kan.

Year	Club	League	Pos.	G.	AB.	R.	H.	2B.	3B.	HR.	RBI.	B.A.	PO.	A.	E.	F.A.
1982—Medford	N'west	C	17	60	11	17	3	0	3	14	.283	116	18	4	.971
1982—Modesto	Calif.	C	41	140	23	42	6	0	3	32	.300	239	44	5	.983
1983—Albany†	East.	C-1B	92	285	50	83	12	1	14	56	.291	478	82	11	.981
1984—Modesto‡	Calif.	C	9	32	8	9	2	0	1	5	.281	41	8	0	1.000
1984—Tacoma	P. C.	C-OF	69	195	33	44	11	0	9	22	.226	260	39	0	1.000
1985—Huntsville	South.	C	33	115	20	24	5	0	7	16	.209	182	29	5	.977
1985—Oakland	Amer.	C	16	11	3	3	1	0	0	1	.273	23	0	1	.958
1985—Modesto	Calif.	C	9	27	5	8	4	1	1	2	.296	33	8	1	.976
1985—Tacoma§	P. C.	C	18	57	5	9	4	0	0	7	.158	110	9	3	.975
1986—Vancouver	P. C.	C	6	17	1	2	0	0	0	1	.118	22	3	2	.926
1986—El Paso	Texas	C-OF-1B	92	336	72	109	20	3	15	75	.324	437	43	4	.992
1987—Denver	A. A.	C	80	266	37	75	12	1	8	35	.282	415	53	6	.987
1987—Milwaukee	Amer.	C	10	35	2	7	3	1	0	0	.200	78	11	0	1.000
1988—Denver	A. A.	C	48	153	16	43	5	0	4	25	.281	243	44	3	.990
1988—Milwaukee	Amer.	C	40	118	12	26	6	0	2	9	.220	210	20	2	.991
1989—Milwaukee	Amer.	C	62	188	22	44	10	0	6	35	.234	314	36	5	.986
Major League Totals—4 Years			128	352	39	80	20	1	8	45	.227	625	67	8	.989

Selected by Texas Rangers' organization in 14th round of free-agent draft, June 6, 1978.
Selected by Seattle Mariners' organization in 21st round of free-agent draft, June 8, 1981.
Selected by Oakland A's organization in 5th round of free-agent draft, June 7, 1982.
†On disabled list, July 31, 1983 through remainder of season.
‡On Albany disabled list, April 13 to May 15, 1984.
§Traded with Infielder Steve Kiefer and Pitchers Mike Fulmer and Pete Kendrick to Milwaukee Brewers for Pitcher Moose Haas, March 30, 1986.

PETER MICHAEL O'BRIEN
(Pete)

Born February 9, 1958, at Santa Monica, Calif.
Height, 6.02. Weight, 205.
Throws and bats lefthanded.
Attended Monterrey Peninsula College, Monterrey, Calif.; and
University of Nebraska, Lincoln, Neb.

Shares major league record for most double plays started by first baseman, nine-inning game (3), May 22, 1984.
Major League stolen bases: 1982 (1), 1983 (5), 1984 (3), 1985 (5), 1986 (4), 1988 (1), 1989 (3). Total—22.
Led American League first basemen in assists with 120 in 1983.

Year	Club	League	Pos.	G.	AB.	R.	H.	2B.	3B.	HR.	RBI.	B.A.	PO.	A.	E.	F.A.
1979—Sarasota Rangers	Gulf C.	1B	50	189	39	46	10	2	0	31	.243	★465	★44	7	.986
1980—Asheville	S. Atl.	1B	134	505	98	149	34	2	17	94	.295	★1227	★96	14	.990
1981—Tulsa	Texas	1B	110	382	57	109	19	3	17	78	.285	973	95	11	.990
1982—Denver	A. A.	OF-1B	128	477	92	148	21	1	25	102	.310	418	37	8	.983
1982—Texas	Amer.	OF-1B	20	67	13	16	4	1	4	13	.239	39	3	0	1.000
1983—Texas	Amer.	1B-OF	154	524	53	124	24	5	8	53	.237	1191	121	11	.992
1984—Texas	Amer.	1B-OF	142	520	57	149	26	2	18	80	.287	1271	105	11	.992
1985—Texas	Amer.	1B	159	573	69	153	34	3	22	92	.267	1457	98	8	.995
1986—Texas	Amer.	1B	156	551	86	160	23	3	23	90	.290	1224	115	11	.992
1987—Texas	Amer.	★1B-OF	159	569	84	163	26	1	23	88	.286	1233	★146	11	.992
1988—Texas†	Amer.	1B	156	547	57	149	24	1	16	71	.272	1346	140	8	.995
1989—Cleveland‡	Amer.	1B	155	554	75	144	24	1	12	55	.260	1359	114	9	.994
Major League Totals—8 Years			1101	3905	494	1058	185	17	126	542	.271	9120	842	69	.993

Selected by Texas Rangers' organization in 15th round of free-agent draft, June 5, 1979.
†Traded with Outfielder Oddibe McDowell and Second Baseman Jerry Browne to Cleveland Indians for Second Baseman Julio Franco, December 6, 1988.
‡Granted free agency, November 13, 1989; signed by Seattle Mariners, December 7, 1989.

RONALD JOHN OESTER

Name pronounced O-ster.

(Ron)

Born May 5, 1956, at Cincinnati, O.
Height, 6.02. Weight, 195.
Throws right and bats left and righthanded.

Major League stolen bases: 1980 (6), 1981 (2), 1982 (5), 1983 (2), 1984 (7), 1985 (5), 1986 (9), 1987 (2), 1989 (1). Total—39.

Led National League second basemen in total chances with 861 in 1986.
Led American Association shortstops in double plays with 102 in 1978.
Led Eastern League shortstops in double plays with 84 in 1976.
Led Pioneer League shortstops in double plays with 27 in 1974.

Year Club	League	Pos.	G.	AB.	R.	H.	2B.	3B.	HR.	RBI.	B.A.	PO.	A.	E.	F.A.
1974—Billings	Pion.	SS	53	167	23	52	11	1	0	21	.311	87	141	27	.894
1975—Tampa	Fla. St.	SS	117	375	40	82	3	4	0	25	.219	174	358	34	.940
1976—Three Rivers	East.	SS	138	447	57	110	14	4	0	44	.246	★233	★408	38	.944
1977—Indianapolis	A. A.	SS	134	455	60	116	16	5	3	33	.255	203	★386	39	.938
1978—Indianapolis	A. A.	SS	●135	514	78	133	21	4	7	49	.259	★300	★428	32	.958
1978—Cincinnati	Nat.	SS	6	8	1	3	0	0	0	1	.375	3	9	0	1.000
1979—Indianapolis	A. A.	SS	●136	509	62	143	19	6	2	33	.281	★244	397	31	.954
1979—Cincinnati	Nat.	SS	6	3	0	0	0	0	0	0	.000	1	2	0	1.000
1980—Cincinnati	Nat.	2B-SS-3B	100	303	40	84	16	2	2	20	.277	161	224	10	.975
1981—Cincinnati	Nat.	2B-SS	105	354	45	96	16	7	5	42	.271	213	341	11	.981
1982—Cincinnati	Nat.	2B-SS-3B	151	549	63	143	19	4	9	47	.260	304	403	22	.970
1983—Cincinnati	Nat.	2B	157	549	63	145	23	5	11	58	.264	315	413	17	.977
1984—Cincinnati	Nat.	2B-SS	150	553	54	134	26	3	3	38	.242	357	388	15	.980
1985—Cincinnati	Nat.	2B	152	526	59	155	26	3	1	34	.295	366	457	9	.989
1986—Cincinnati	Nat.	2B	153	523	52	135	23	2	8	44	.258	●367	475	19	.978
1987—Cincinnati†‡	Nat.	2B	69	237	28	60	9	6	2	23	.253	183	186	10	.974
1988—Nashville	A. A.	2B	12	37	4	7	1	0	0	3	.189	15	28	4	.915
1988—Chattanooga	South.	2B	14	46	5	14	2	0	1	6	.304	19	25	1	.978
1988—Cincinnati§	Nat.	2B-SS	54	150	20	42	7	0	0	10	.280	110	113	1	.996
1989—Cincinnati x	Nat.	2B-SS	109	305	23	75	15	0	1	14	.246	215	249	7	.985
Major League Totals—12 Years			1212	4060	448	1072	180	32	42	331	.264	2595	3260	121	.980

Selected by Cincinnati Reds' organization in 9th round of free-agent draft, June 5, 1974.
†On disabled list, July 6, 1987 through remainder of season.
‡Released, October 21, 1987; re-signed by Reds' organization, January 29, 1988.
§Granted free agency, November 4, 1988; re-signed by Reds, December 2, 1988.
xOn disabled list, June 7 to July 17, 1989.

JOSE ANTONIO OFFERMAN (DONO)

Born November 8, 1968, at San Pedro de Macoris, Dominican Republic.
Height, 6.00. Weight, 150.
Throws right and bats left and righthanded.

Led Pioneer League in stolen bases with 57 and tied for lead in caught stealing with 10 in 1988.

Year Club	League	Pos.	G.	AB.	R.	H.	2B.	3B.	HR.	RBI.	B.A.	PO.	A.	E.	F.A.
1988—Great Falls	Pion.	SS	60	251	75	83	11	5	2	28	.331	82	143	18	★.926
1989—Bakersfield	Calif.	SS	62	245	53	75	9	4	2	22	.306	94	179	30	.901
1989—San Antonio	Texas	SS	68	278	47	80	6	3	2	22	.288	106	168	20	.932

Signed as free agent by Los Angeles Dodgers' organization, July 24, 1986.

ROBERT MICHAEL OJEDA

Name pronounced Oh-HEED-a.

(Bob)

Born December 17, 1957, at Los Angeles, Calif.
Height, 6.01. Weight, 195.
Throws and bats lefthanded.
Attended College of the Sequoias, Visalia, Calif.

Major League saves: 1985 (1).
Tied for American League lead in shutouts with 5 in 1984.
Tied for International League lead in balks with 3 in 1980.
Tied for Florida State League lead in games started by pitchers with 29 in 1979.
Named International League Pitcher of the Year, 1981.

Year Club	League	G.	IP.	W.	L.	Pct.	H.	R.	ER.	SO.	BB.	ERA.
1978—Elmira	NYP	18	43	1	6	.143	45	32	23	35	43	4.81
1979—Winter Haven	Florida St.	29	200	15	7	.682	163	66	54	150	84	2.43
1980—Pawtucket	Int'national	19	123	6	7	.462	107	54	44	78	56	3.22
1980—Boston	American	7	26	1	1	.500	39	20	20	12	14	6.92
1981—Pawtucket	Int'national	25	173	12	9	.571	136	52	41	113	73	★2.13
1981—Boston	American	10	66	6	2	.750	50	25	23	28	25	3.14
1982—Boston†	American	22	78⅓	4	6	.400	95	53	49	52	29	5.63
1983—Boston	American	29	173⅔	12	7	.632	173	85	78	94	73	4.04
1984—Boston‡	American	33	216⅔	12	12	.500	211	106	96	137	96	3.99
1985—Boston§	American	39	157⅔	9	11	.450	166	74	70	102	48	4.00
1986—New York	National	32	217⅓	18	5	★.783	185	72	62	148	52	2.57
1987—New York x	National	10	46⅓	3	5	.375	45	23	20	21	10	3.88

Year Club	League	G.	IP.	W.	L.	Pct.	H.	R.	ER.	SO.	BB.	ERA.
1988—New York	National	29	190⅓	10	13	.435	158	74	61	133	33	2.88
1989—New York	National	31	192	13	11	.542	179	83	74	95	78	3.47
American League Totals—6 Years		140	718⅓	44	39	.530	734	363	336	425	285	4.21
National League Totals—4 Years		102	646	44	34	.564	567	252	217	397	173	3.02
Major League Totals—10 Years		242	1364⅓	88	73	.547	1301	615	553	822	458	3.65

Signed as free agent by Boston Red Sox' organization, May 20, 1978.

†On disabled list, August 20 to September 10, 1982.

‡On disabled list, August 16 to September 1, 1984.

§Traded with Pitchers Tom McCarthy, John Mitchell and Chris Bayer to New York Mets for Pitchers Calvin Schiraldi and Wes Gardner and Outfielders John Christensen and LaSchelle Tarver, November 13, 1985.

xOn disabled list, May 11 to September 1, 1987.

CHAMPIONSHIP SERIES RECORD

Shares National League Championship Series record for most hits allowed, game (10), October 9, 1986.

Year Club	League	G.	IP.	W.	L.	Pct.	H.	R.	ER.	SO.	BB.	ERA.
1986—New York	National	2	14	1	0	1.000	15	4	4	6	4	2.57

WORLD SERIES RECORD

Year Club	League	G.	IP.	W.	L.	Pct.	H.	R.	ER.	SO.	BB.	ERA.
1986—New York	National	2	13	1	0	1.000	13	3	3	9	5	2.08

JOHN GARRETT OLERUD

Born August 5, 1968, at Bellevue, Wash.
Height, 6.05. Weight, 205.
Throws and bats lefthanded.
Attended Washington State University, Pullman, Wash.
Son of John E. Olerud, minor league catcher, 1965 through 1970.

Year Club	League	Pos.	G.	AB.	R.	H.	2B.	3B.	HR.	RBI.	B.A.	PO.	A.	E.	F.A.
1989—Toronto	Amer.	1B	6	8	2	3	0	0	0	0	.375	19	2	0	1.000
Major League Totals—1 Year			6	8	2	3	0	0	0	0	.375	19	2	0	1.000

Selected by New York Mets' organization in 27th round of free-agent draft, June 2, 1986.

Selected by Toronto Blue Jays' organization in 3rd round of free-agent draft, June 5, 1989.

STEVEN ROBERT OLIN
(Steve)

Born October 10, 1965, at Portland, Ore.
Height, 6.02. Weight, 185.
Throws and bats righthanded.
Attended Portland State University, Portland, Ore.

Major League saves: 1989 (1).

Led Pacific Coast League in saves with 24 in 1989.

Led Appalachian League in games finished in relief with 25 in 1987.

Year Club	League	G.	IP.	W.	L.	Pct.	H.	R.	ER.	SO.	BB.	ERA.
1987—Burlington	Ap'lachian	●26	57⅓	4	4	.500	42	21	15	75	17	2.35
1988—Waterloo	Midwest	29	39⅓	3	0	1.000	26	7	6	48	14	1.37
1988—Kinston	Carolina	33	56⅔	5	2	.714	49	23	19	45	15	3.02
1989—Colorado Springs	P. Coast	42	50⅓	4	1	.800	34	18	18	40	15	3.22
1989—Cleveland	American	25	36	1	4	.200	35	16	15	24	14	3.75
Major League Totals—1 Year		25	36	1	4	.200	35	16	15	24	14	3.75

Selected by Cleveland Indians' organization in 16th round of free-agent draft, June 2, 1987.

OMAR OLIVARES (PALO)

Born July 6, 1967, at Mayaguez, Puerto Rico.
Height, 6.01. Weight, 185.
Throws and bats righthanded.

Tied for Texas League lead in hit batsmen with 10 in 1989.

Year Club	League	G.	IP.	W.	L.	Pct.	H.	R.	ER.	SO.	BB.	ERA.
1987—Charleston, S.C.	S. Atlantic	31	170⅓	4	14	.222	182	107	87	86	57	4.60
1988—Charleston, S.C.	S. Atlantic	24	185⅓	13	6	.684	166	63	46	94	43	2.23
1988—Riverside	California	4	23⅓	3	0	1.000	18	9	3	16	9	1.16
1989—Wichita	Texas	26	★185⅔	12	11	.522	175	87	70	79	61	3.39

Signed as free agent by San Diego Padres' organization, September 15, 1986.

JOSEPH MELTON OLIVER
(Joe)

Born July 24, 1965, at Memphis, Tenn.
Height, 6.03. Weight, 215.
Throws and bats righthanded.

Led Florida State League catchers in assists with 84 and passed balls with 33 in 1985.

Led Midwest League catchers in passed balls with 30 and total chances with 855 in 1984.

Led Pioneer League catchers in putouts with 425, assists with 38 and total chances with 468 in 1983.

Year Club	League	Pos.	G.	AB.	R.	H.	2B.	3B.	HR.	RBI.	B.A.	PO.	A.	E.	F.A.
1983—Billings	Pion.	*C-1B	56	186	21	40	4	0	4	28	.215	426	39	5	*.989
1984—Cedar Rapids........	Midw.	C	102	335	34	73	11	0	3	29	.218	*757	85	13	.985
1985—Tampa....................	Fla. St.	C-1B	112	386	38	104	23	2	7	62	.269	615	94	16	.978
1986—Vermont†	East.	C	84	282	32	78	18	1	6	41	.277	383	62	14	.969
1987—Vermont	East.	C-1B	66	236	31	72	13	2	10	60	.305	247	35	10	.966
1988—Nashville...............	A. A.	C	73	220	19	45	7	2	4	24	.205	413	37	7	.985
1988—Chattanooga	South.	C	28	105	9	26	6	0	3	12	.248	176	15	0	1.000
1989—Nashville...............	A. A.	*C-1B	71	233	22	68	13	0	6	31	.292	388	37	*13	.970
1989—Cincinnati	Nat.	C	49	151	13	41	8	0	3	23	.272	260	21	4	.986
Major League Totals—1 Year..................			49	151	13	41	8	0	3	23	.272	260	21	4	.986

Selected by Cincinnati Reds' organization in 2nd round of free-agent draft, June 6, 1983.
†On disabled list, April 23 to May 6, 1986.

FRANCISCO JAVIER OLIVERAS (NOA)

Born January 31, 1963, at Santurce, Puerto Rico.
Height, 5.11. Weight, 170.
Throws and bats righthanded.

Tied for Southern League lead in home runs allowed with 27 in 1986.

Year Club	League	G.	IP.	W.	L.	Pct.	H.	R.	ER.	SO.	BB.	ERA.
1981—Miami...............................	Florida St.	19	108	6	5	.545	103	55	46	80	48	3.83
1981—Charlotte............................	Southern	4	16	0	2	.000	23	10	10	10	7	5.63
1982—Charlotte†	Southern	24	162⅓	10	9	.526	132	71	64	97	64	3.55
1983—Charlotte‡	Southern	25	151⅓	8	*14	.364	173	94	78	89	73	4.64
1984—Charlotte............................	Southern	19	75	3	7	.300	68	45	35	52	39	4.20
1984—Rochester§	Int'national	12	40⅔	1	3	.250	58	37	36	39	19	7.97
1985—Charlotte x	Southern	12	57	2	1	.667	57	40	30	20	25	6.64
1985—Daytona Beach y................	Florida St.	3	23⅔	3	0	1.000	13	6	5	25	9	1.90
1985—Beaumont...........................	Texas	7	27	3	1	.750	23	17	15	24	9	5.00
1986—Charlotte............................	Southern	33	194	12	9	.571	185	112	90	127	71	4.18
1987—Charlotte............................	Southern	23	100	6	3	.667	99	43	40	67	21	3.60
1987—Rochester z.........................	Int'national	6	27	3	0	1.000	31	14	13	18	7	4.33
1988—Orlando	Southern	7	43	3	1	.750	44	24	23	42	18	4.81
1988—Portland	P. Coast	21	133⅔	11	10	.524	134	69	64	95	43	4.31
1989—Portland	P. Coast	17	97⅔	6	4	.600	108	54	54	54	24	4.98
1989—Minnesota a	American	12	55⅔	3	4	.429	64	28	28	24	15	4.53
Major League Totals—1 Year..............		12	55⅔	3	4	.429	64	28	28	24	15	4.53

Signed as free agent by Baltimore Orioles' organization, September 10, 1980.
†On disabled list, July 9 to July 23, 1982.
‡On disabled list, April 22 to May 9, 1983.
§On disabled list, July 30 to August 18, 1984.
xLoaned to Daytona Beach (Co-op), June 1, 1985; returned, July 4, 1985.
yLoaned to Beaumont (San Diego Padres' organization), July 31, 1985; returned, September 1, 1985.
zGranted free agency, October 15, 1987; signed by Portland (Minnesota Twins' organization), December, 1987.
aGranted free agency, October 15, 1989.

GREGG WILLIAM OLSON

Born October 11, 1966, at Omaha, Neb.
Height, 6.04. Weight, 219.
Throws and bats righthanded.
Attended Auburn University, Auburn, Ala.

Holds American League record for most saves by rookie (27), 1989.
Major League saves: 1989 (27).
Named American League Rookie of the Year by Baseball Writers' Association of America, 1989.
Received reported $200,000 bonus to sign with Baltimore Orioles, 1988.
Named righthanded pitcher on THE SPORTING NEWS College Baseball All-America Team, 1988.

Year Club	League	G.	IP.	W.	L.	Pct.	H.	R.	ER.	SO.	BB.	ERA.
1988—Hagerstown	Carolina	8	9	1	0	1.000	5	2	2	9	2	2.00
1988—Charlotte..	Southern	8	15⅓	0	1	.000	24	13	10	22	6	5.87
1988—Baltimore	American	10	11	1	1	.500	10	4	4	9	10	3.27
1989—Baltimore	American	64	85	5	2	.714	57	17	16	90	46	1.69
Major League Totals—2 Years............................		74	96	6	3	.667	67	21	20	99	56	1.88

Selected by Baltimore Orioles' organization in 1st round (fourth player selected) of free-agent draft, June 1, 1988.

GREGORY WILLIAM OLSON
(Greg)

Born September 6, 1960, at Marshall, Minn.
Height, 6.00. Weight, 200.
Throws and bats righthanded.
Attended University of Minnesota, Minneapolis, Minn.

Led Carolina League catchers in total chances with 973 in 1983.
Tied for International League lead in passed balls with 15 in 1988.

Year Club	League	Pos.	G.	AB.	R.	H.	2B.	3B.	HR.	RBI.	B.A.	PO.	A.	E.	F.A.
1982—Lynchburg.............	Carol.	C-3B	32	91	10	24	1	0	0	5	.264	149	26	6	.967
1983—Lynchburg.............	Carol.	C	107	318	56	73	7	0	0	22	.230	*881	*82	10	*.990

Year Club	League	Pos.	G.	AB.	R.	H.	2B.	3B.	HR.	RBI.	B.A.	PO.	A.	E.	F.A.
1984—Jackson	Texas	C	74	234	27	55	9	0	0	22	.235	511	51	9	.984
1985—Jackson	Texas	C	69	211	21	57	7	0	1	32	.270	353	56	6	.986
1986—Jackson	Texas	C	64	196	28	39	5	1	2	16	.199	347	49	4	.990
1986—Tidewater	Int.	C	19	55	11	18	1	0	0	7	.327	104	13	3	.975
1987—Tidewater	Int.	C	47	120	15	34	8	1	2	15	.283	219	12	3	.987
1988—Tidewater†	Int.	C-OF	115	344	39	92	19	1	6	48	.267	600	64	7	.990
1989—Portland	P. C.	C-3B	79	247	38	58	8	2	6	38	.235	440	32	5	.990
1989—Minnesota‡	Amer.	C	3	2	0	1	0	0	0	0	.500	4	0	0	1.000
Major League Totals—1 Year			3	2	0	1	0	0	0	0	.500	4	0	0	1.000

Selected by New York Mets' organization in 7th round of free-agent draft, June 7, 1982.
†Granted free agency, October 15, 1988; signed by Portland (Minnesota Twins' organization), November 30, 1988.
‡Granted free agency, October 15, 1989.

THOMAS PATRICK O'MALLEY
(Tom)

Born December 25, 1960, at Orange, N. J.
Height, 6.00. Weight, 190.
Throws right and bats lefthanded.

Major League stolen bases: 1983 (2).
Tied for International League lead in intentional bases on balls received with 10 in 1989.
Led American Association third basemen in fielding percentage with .955 in 1988.
Led International League third basemen in fielding percentage with .964 in 1985 and .966 in 1989.
Led International League third basemen in assists with 231 and total chances with 322 in 1989.
Led International League third basemen with putouts with 90 in 1985.
Named International League Player of the Year, 1989.

Year Club	League	Pos.	G.	AB.	R.	H.	2B.	3B.	HR.	RBI.	B.A.	PO.	A.	E.	F.A.
1979—Great Falls	Pion.	2-S-O-3	42	119	13	29	6	1	1	20	.244	41	34	9	.893
1980—Fresno	Calif.	3B	122	435	67	125	20	9	3	74	.287	69	253	22	★.936
1981—Shreveport	Texas	3B	123	467	50	135	23	6	6	53	.289	94	237	15	.957
1982—Phoenix	P. C.	3B	26	96	23	43	11	1	3	15	.448	12	44	6	.903
1982—San Francisco†	Nat.	3B-SS-2B	92	291	26	80	12	4	2	27	.275	60	161	8	.965
1983—San Francisco	Nat.	3B	135	410	40	106	16	1	5	45	.259	70	213	18	.940
1984—Phoenix	P. C.	3B-1B	105	387	44	134	20	2	5	72	.346	227	134	15	.960
1984—San Francisco‡	Nat.	3B	13	25	2	3	0	0	0	0	.120	5	8	0	1.000
1984—Chicago§	Amer.	3B	12	16	0	2	0	0	0	3	.125	2	1	0	1.000
1985—Nashville x	A. A	3B	33	128	13	39	8	0	1	12	.305	16	62	9	.897
1985—Rochester	Int.	3B-1B	102	358	62	108	13	1	10	44	.302	92	207	11	.965
1985—Baltimore	Amer.	3B	8	14	1	1	0	0	1	2	.071	2	3	1	.833
1986—Rochester	Int.	3B-2B	59	212	36	65	10	0	9	30	.307	46	111	8	.952
1986—Baltimore y	Amer.	3B	56	181	19	46	9	0	1	18	.254	37	98	9	.938
1987—Oklahoma City	A. A.	3B	109	431	83	134	27	2	12	70	.311	★112	198	9	★.972
1987—Texas	Amer.	3B-2B	45	117	10	32	8	0	1	12	.274	21	56	3	.962
1988—Oklahoma City z	A. A.	3B-1B-2B	★138	522	68	152	26	4	9	72	.291	118	246	16	.958
1988—Montreal a	Nat.	3B	14	27	3	7	0	0	0	2	.259	4	15	2	.905
1989—Tidewater	Int.	3B-1B	132	492	64	145	29	0	15	★84	.295	127	235	11	.971
1989—New York	Nat.	3B	9	11	2	6	2	0	0	8	.545	2	1	0	1.000
National League Totals—5 Years			263	764	73	202	30	5	7	82	.264	141	398	28	.951
American League Totals—4 Years			121	328	30	81	17	0	3	35	.247	62	158	13	.944
Major League Totals—8 Years			384	1092	103	283	47	5	10	117	.259	203	556	41	.949

Selected by San Francisco Giants' organization in 16th round of free-agent draft, June 5, 1979.
†On disabled list, August 16 to September 6, 1982.
‡Traded to Chicago White Sox for two players to be named later, September 1, 1984; San Francisco Giants acquired Pitcher Mike Trujillo and First Baseman Pat Adams to complete deal, September 7, 1984.
§Released, April 1, 1985; signed by Nashville (Detroit Tigers' organization), April 8, 1985.
xTraded to Rochester (Baltimore Orioles' organization) for Catcher Luis Rosado, May 21, 1985.
yGranted free agency, October 15, 1986; signed by Texas Rangers' organization, December 3, 1986.
zTraded to Montreal Expos for a player to be named later, September 1, 1988; Texas Rangers' organization acquired First Baseman Jack Daugherty to complete deal, September 13, 1988.
aTraded with Catcher Mark Bailey to New York Mets for Pitcher Steve Frey, March 28, 1989.

RANDALL JEFFREY O'NEAL
(Randy)

Born August 30, 1960, at Ashland, Ky.
Height, 6.02. Weight, 195.
Throws and bats righthanded.
Attended Palm Beach Junior College, Lake Worth, Fla.,
and University of Florida, Gainesville, Fla.

Pitched seven-inning, 4-0 no-hit victory against Winter Haven, August 23, 1981 (first game).
Major League saves: 1985 (1), 1986 (2). Total—3.
Tied for American Association lead in balks with 6 in 1984.

Year Club	League	G.	IP.	W.	L.	Pct.	H.	R.	ER.	SO.	BB.	ERA.
1981—Lakeland	Florida St.	13	69	4	5	.444	59	27	22	31	18	2.87
1982—Birmingham	Southern	27	185	11	7	.611	169	83	70	105	71	3.41
1983—Evansville	Am. Assoc.	23	140⅓	8	10	.444	159	80	66	70	45	4.23
1984—Evansville	Am. Assoc.	25	166⅓	9	10	.474	152	82	66	110	59	3.57
1984—Detroit	American	4	18⅔	2	1	.667	16	7	7	12	6	3.38

Year Club	League	G.	IP.	W.	L.	Pct.	H.	R.	ER.	SO.	BB.	ERA.
1985—Nashville	Am. Assoc.	10	67⅔	5	4	.556	57	29	27	44	19	3.59
1985—Detroit	American	28	94⅓	5	5	.500	82	42	34	52	36	3.24
1986—Detroit	American	37	122⅔	3	7	.300	121	69	59	68	44	4.33
1986—Nashville†	Am. Assoc.	4	28⅓	1	2	.333	28	16	15	15	9	4.76
1987—Atlanta-St. Louis	National	17	66	4	2	.667	81	42	39	37	26	5.32
1987—Richmond‡	Int'national	1	5	0	1	.000	4	3	2	5	1	3.60
1987—Louisville	Am. Assoc.	7	47⅓	3	1	.750	54	27	24	19	10	4.56
1988—Louisville	Am. Assoc.	10	60⅔	3	5	.375	59	30	25	33	21	3.71
1988—St. Louis§x	National	10	53	2	3	.400	57	29	27	20	10	4.58
1989—Scranton/Wilkes-Barre	Int'national	18	96	4	4	.500	82	33	27	71	23	2.53
1989—Philadelphia y	National	20	39	0	1	.000	46	28	27	29	9	6.23
American League Totals—3 Years		69	235⅔	10	13	.435	219	118	100	132	86	3.82
National League Totals—3 Years		47	158	6	6	.500	184	99	93	86	45	5.30
Major League Totals—6 Years		116	393⅔	16	19	.457	403	217	193	218	131	4.41

Selected by Montreal Expos' organization in 4th round of free-agent draft, January 9, 1979.
Selected by Minnesota Twins' organization in secondary phase of free-agent draft, June 5, 1979.
Selected by Milwaukee Brewers' organization in secondary phase of free-agent draft, January 8, 1980.
Selected by Cincinnati Reds' organization in secondary phase of free-agent draft, June 3, 1980.
Selected by Detroit Tigers' organization in secondary phase of free-agent draft, June 8, 1981.
†Traded with Pitcher Chuck Cary to Atlanta Braves for Outfielders Terry Harper and Freddy Tiburcio, January 27, 1987.
‡Traded to St. Louis Cardinals' organization for Pitcher Joe Boever, July 25, 1987.
§On disabled list, June 10 to August 11, 1988; included rehabilitation disability assignment to Louisville, July 26 to August 11, 1988.
xGranted free agency, October 15, 1988; signed by Scranton/Wilkes-Barre (Philadelphia Phillies' organization), December 2, 1988.
yReleased, October 4, 1989.

PAUL ANDREW O'NEILL

Born February 25, 1963, at Columbus, O.
Height, 6.04. Weight, 215.
Throws and bats lefthanded.
Attended Otterbein College, Westerville, O.
Son of Charles W. O'Neill, minor league pitcher, 1945 through 1948.

Major League stolen bases: 1987 (2), 1988 (8), 1989 (20). Total—30.
Tied for American Association lead in game-winning RBIs with 13 in 1985.
Led American Association outfielders in assists with 19 and double plays with 8 in 1985.

Year Club	League	Pos.	G.	AB.	R.	H.	2B.	3B.	HR.	RBI.	B.A.	PO.	A.	E.	F.A.
1981—Billings	Pion.	OF	66	241	37	76	7	2	3	29	.315	87	4	5	.948
1982—Cedar Rapids	Midw.	OF	116	386	50	105	19	2	8	71	.272	137	7	8	.947
1983—Tampa	Fla. St.	OF-1B	121	413	62	115	23	7	8	51	.278	218	14	10	.959
1983—Waterbury	East.	OF	14	43	6	12	0	0	0	6	.279	26	0	0	1.000
1984—Vermont	East.	OF	134	475	70	126	31	5	16	76	.265	246	5	7	.973
1985—Denver	A. A.	OB-1B	*137	*509	63	*155	*32	3	7	74	.305	248	20	7	.975
1985—Cincinnati	Nat.	OF	5	12	1	4	1	0	0	1	.333	3	1	0	1.000
1986—Cincinnati	Nat.	PH	3	2	0	0	0	0	0	0	.000	0	0	0	.000
1986—Denver†	A. A.	OF	55	193	20	49	9	2	5	27	.254	98	7	4	.963
1987—Cincinnati	Nat.	OF-1B-P	84	160	24	41	14	1	7	28	.256	90	2	4	.958
1987—Nashville	A. A.	OF	11	37	12	11	0	0	3	6	.297	19	1	0	1.000
1988—Cincinnati	Nat.	OF-1B	145	485	58	122	25	3	16	73	.252	410	13	6	.986
1989—Cincinnati‡	Nat.	OF	117	428	49	118	24	2	15	74	.276	223	7	4	.983
1989—Nashville	A. A.	OF	4	12	1	4	0	0	0	0	.333	7	1	0	1.000
Major League Totals—5 Years			354	1087	132	285	64	6	38	176	.262	726	23	14	.982

Selected by Cincinnati Reds' organization in 4th round of free-agent draft, June 8, 1981.
†On disabled list, May 10 to July 16, 1986.
‡On disabled list, July 21 to September 1, 1989; included rehabilitation disability assignment to Nashville, August 27 to September 1, 1989.

PITCHING RECORD

Year Club	League	G.	IP.	W.	L.	Pct.	H.	R.	ER.	SO.	BB.	ERA.
1987—Cincinnati	National	1	2	0	0	.000	2	3	3	2	4	13.50

STEVEN ONTIVEROS
(Steve)

Born March 5, 1961, at Tularosa, N.M.
Height, 6.00. Weight, 190.
Throws and bats righthanded.
Received bachelor of science degree in physical education
from University of Michigan, Ann Arbor, Mich.

Major League saves: 1985 (8), 1986 (10), 1987 (1). Total—19.

Year Club	League	G.	IP.	W.	L.	Pct.	H.	R.	ER.	SO.	BB.	ERA.
1982—Medford	Northwest	4	8	1	0	1.000	3	0	0	9	4	0.00
1982—West Haven†	Eastern	16	27	2	2	.500	34	26	19	28	12	6.33
1983—Albany	Eastern	32	129⅔	8	4	.667	131	62	54	91	36	3.75
1984—Tacoma‡	P. Coast	2	11⅓	1	1	.500	18	11	10	6	5	7.94
1985—Madison	Midwest	5	30⅔	3	1	.750	23	10	7	26	6	2.05

Year Club	League	G.	IP.	W.	L.	Pct.	H.	R.	ER.	SO.	BB.	ERA.
1985—Tacoma§	P. Coast	15	33⅔	3	0	1.000	26	13	11	30	21	2.94
1985—Oakland	American	39	74⅔	1	3	.250	45	17	16	36	19	1.93
1986—Oakland xy	American	46	72⅔	2	2	.500	72	40	38	54	25	4.71
1987—Tacoma z	P. Coast	1	3	0	0	.000	1	1	1	1	2	3.00
1987—Oakland	American	35	150⅔	10	8	.556	141	78	67	97	50	4.00
1988—Oakland abc	American	10	54⅔	3	4	.429	57	32	28	30	21	4.61
1989—Philadelphia d	National	6	30⅔	2	1	.667	34	15	13	12	15	3.82
1989—Scranton/Wilkes-Barre	Int'national	1	3⅓	0	0	.000	3	0	0	0	3	0.00
American League Totals—4 Years		130	352⅔	16	17	.485	315	167	149	217	115	3.80
National League Totals—1 Year		6	30⅔	2	1	.667	34	15	13	12	15	3.82
Major League Totals—5 Years		136	383⅓	18	18	.500	349	182	162	229	130	3.80

Selected by Oakland A's organization in 2nd round of free-agent draft, June 7, 1982.

†On temporarily inactive list, July 27 to August 6, 1982.

‡On disabled list, April 16 to August 8, 1984.

§On disabled list, April 16 to April 28, 1985.

xAppeared in one game as a pinch-runner.

yOn disabled list, July 24 to September 14, 1986.

zOn Oakland disabled list, March 30 to April 24, 1987; included rehabilitation disability assignment to Tacoma, April 21 to April 24, 1987.

aAppeared in two games as a pinch-runner.

bOn disabled list, June 12 to August 2 and August 3, 1988 through remainder of season.

cReleased, December 21, 1988; signed by Philadelphia Phillies' organization, February 16, 1989.

dOn disabled list, April 20 to June 6 and June 21, 1989 through remainder of season; included rehabilitation disability assignment to Scranton/Wilkes-Barre, May 14 to May 22 and June 28, 1989.

DANIEL CHARLES OPPERMAN
(Dan)

Born November 13, 1968, at Las Vegas, Nev.
Height, 6.02. Weight, 175.
Throws and bats righthanded.

Year Club	League	G.	IP.	W.	L.	Pct.	H.	R.	ER.	SO.	BB.	ERA.
1987—Great Falls†	Pioneer						(Did not play)					
1988—Great Falls‡	Pioneer						(Did not play)					
1989—Vero Beach§	Florida St.	19	61	0	7	.000	51	26	24	35	24	3.54

Selected by Los Angeles Dodgers' organization in 1st round (eighth player selected) of free-agent draft, June 2, 1987.

†On disabled list, July 17, 1987 through entire season.

‡On disabled list, June 16, 1988 through entire season.

§On disabled list, July 12 to August 3, 1989.

JOSE MANUEL OQUENDO

Name pronounced Oh-KEN-doh.
Born July 4, 1963, at Rio Piedras, Puerto Rico.
Height, 5.10. Weight, 156.
Throws right and bats left and righthanded.

Shares major league record for fewest errors, second basemen, season, 150 or more games (5), 1989.

Shares National League record for highest fielding average, second basemen, season, 150 or more games (.994), 1989.

Major League stolen bases: 1983 (8), 1984 (10), 1986 (2), 1987 (4), 1988 (4), 1989 (3). Total—31.

Led National League second basemen in putouts with 346, assists with 500, fielding percentage with .994, total chances with 851 and double plays with 106 in 1989.

Led American Association in sacrifice hits with 15 in 1985.

Led International League in sacrifice hits with 14 in 1982.

Led Carolina League in sacrifice hits with 13 in 1980.

Led American Association shortstops in total chances with 591 in 1985.

Led Northwest League shortstops in errors with 40 in 1979.

Year Club	League	Pos.	G.	AB.	R.	H.	2B.	3B.	HR.	RBI.	B.A.	PO.	A.	E.	F.A.
1979—Grays Harbor	N'west	*SS-2B	64	220	24	50	8	0	1	14	.227	90	177	*40	.870
1980—Lynchburg	Carol.	SS	109	301	38	51	10	3	0	26	.169	126	358	31	*.940
1981—Lynchburg	Carol.	SS	124	393	59	98	8	6	0	38	.249	169	390	23	*.961
1982—Tidewater	Int.	SS	114	337	40	72	8	3	0	22	.214	186	337	25	.954
1983—Tidewater	Int.	SS	13	34	3	4	0	0	0	3	.118	20	23	4	.915
1983—New York	Nat.	SS	120	328	29	70	7	0	1	17	.213	182	326	21	.960
1984—New York	Nat.	SS	81	189	23	42	5	0	0	10	.222	95	152	7	.972
1984—Tidewater†	Int.	SS	38	113	8	18	1	0	1	8	.159	54	111	2	.988
1985—Louisville	A. A.	SS	133	384	38	81	8	1	1	30	.211	*227	341	23	.961
1986—St. Louis	Nat.	S-2-3-O	76	138	20	41	4	1	0	13	.297	52	94	8	.948
1987—St. Louis	Nat.	I-O-P	116	248	43	71	9	0	1	24	.286	149	133	4	.986
1988—St. Louis	Nat.	I-O-C-P	148	451	36	125	10	1	7	46	.277	268	315	11	.981
1989—St. Louis	Nat.	2B-SS-1B	●163	556	59	162	28	7	1	48	.291	356	523	6	.993
Major League Totals—6 Years			704	1910	210	511	63	9	10	158	.268	1102	1543	57	.979

Signed as free agent by New York Mets' organization, April 15, 1979.

†Traded with Pitcher Mark Jason Davis to St. Louis Cardinals' organization for Shortstop Argenis Salazar and Pitcher John Young, April 2, 1985.

Year	Club	League	Pos.	G.	AB.	R.	H.	2B.	3B.	HR.	RBI.	B.A.	PO.	A.	E.	F.A.
1987—St. Louis		Nat.	O-3B-PH	5	12	3	2	0	0	1	4	.167	7	0	0	1.000

WORLD SERIES RECORD

Year	Club	League	Pos.	G.	AB.	R.	H.	2B.	3B.	HR.	RBI.	B.A.	PO.	A.	E.	F.A.
1987—St. Louis		Nat.	OF-3B	7	24	2	6	0	0	0	2	.250	8	10	0	1.000

PITCHING RECORD

Year	Club	League	G.	IP.	W.	L.	Pct.	H.	R.	ER.	SO.	BB.	ERA.
1987—St. Louis		National	1	1	0	0	.000	4	3	3	0	1	27.00
1988—St. Louis		National	1	4	0	1	.000	4	2	2	1	6	4.50
Major League Totals—2 Years			2	5	0	1	.000	8	5	5	1	7	9.00

JESSE OROSCO

Name pronounced Oh-ROSS-koh.

Born April 21, 1957, at Santa Barbara, Calif.
Height, 6.02. Weight, 185.
Throws left and bats righthanded.
Attended Santa Barbara City College, Santa Barbara, Calif.

Major League saves: 1981 (1), 1982 (4), 1983 (17), 1984 (31), 1985 (17), 1986 (21), 1987 (16), 1988 (9), 1989 (3). Total—119.
Led Appalachian League in intentional bases on balls issued with 5 in 1978.

Year	Club	League	G.	IP.	W.	L.	Pct.	H.	R.	ER.	SO.	BB.	ERA.
1978—Elizabethton†		Ap'lachian	20	40	4	4	.500	29	7	5	48	20	1.13
1979—Tidewater		Int'national	16	81	4	4	.500	82	45	35	55	43	3.89
1979—New York		National	18	35	1	2	.333	33	20	19	22	22	4.89
1980—Jackson		Texas	37	71	4	4	.500	52	36	29	85	62	3.68
1981—Tidewater		Int'national	46	87	9	5	.643	80	39	32	81	32	3.31
1981—New York		National	8	17	0	1	.000	13	4	3	18	6	1.59
1982—New York		National	54	109⅓	4	10	.286	92	37	33	89	40	2.72
1983—New York		National	62	110	13	7	.650	76	27	18	84	38	1.47
1984—New York		National	60	87	10	6	.625	58	29	25	85	34	2.59
1985—New York		National	54	79	8	6	.571	66	26	24	68	34	2.73
1986—New York‡		National	58	81	8	6	.571	64	23	21	62	35	2.33
1987—New York§		National	58	77	3	9	.250	78	41	38	78	31	4.44
1988—Los Angeles x		National	55	53	3	2	.600	41	18	16	43	30	2.72
1989—Cleveland		American	69	78	3	4	.429	54	20	18	79	26	2.08
National League Totals—9 Years			427	648⅓	50	49	.505	521	225	197	549	270	2.73
American League Totals—1 Year			69	78	3	4	.429	54	20	18	79	26	2.08
Major League Totals—10 Years			496	726⅓	53	53	.500	575	245	215	628	296	2.66

Selected by St. Louis Cardinals' organization in 7th round of free-agent draft, January 11, 1977.
Selected by Minnesota Twins' organization in 2nd round of free-agent draft, January 10, 1978.
†Traded to New York Mets, February 7, 1979, completing deal in which Minnesota Twins traded Pitcher Greg Field and a player to be named later to New York for Pitcher Jerry Koosman, December 8, 1978.
‡Appeared in one game as an outfielder with one putout.
§As part of an eight-player, three-team deal, New York Mets traded Pitcher Jesse Orosco to Oakland Athletics, December 11, 1987. Oakland then traded Orosco along with shortstop Alfredo Griffin and Pitcher Jay Howell to Los Angeles Dodgers for Pitchers Bob Welch, Matt Young and Jack Savage. Oakland then traded Savage along with Pitchers Wally Whitehurst and Kevin Tapani to New York.
xGranted free agency, November 4, 1988; signed by Cleveland Indians, December 3, 1988.

CHAMPIONSHIP SERIES RECORD

Holds Championship Series record for most games won, series (3), 1986.

Year	Club	League	G.	IP.	W.	L.	Pct.	H.	R.	ER.	SO.	BB.	ERA.
1986—New York		National	4	8	3	0	1.000	5	3	3	10	2	3.38
1988—Los Angeles		National	4	2⅓	0	0	.000	4	2	2	0	3	7.71
Championship Series Totals—2 Years			8	10⅓	3	0	1.000	9	5	5	10	5	4.35

WORLD SERIES RECORD

Year	Club	League	G.	IP.	W.	L.	Pct.	H.	R.	ER.	SO.	BB.	ERA.
1986—New York		National	4	5⅔	0	0	.000	2	0	0	6	0	0.00

ALL-STAR GAME RECORD

Year	League		IP.	W.	L.	Pct.	H.	R.	ER.	SO.	BB.	ERA.
1983—National			⅓	0	0	.000	0	0	0	1	0	0.00

Member of National League All-Star Team in 1984; did not play.

JOSEPH MICHAEL ORSULAK
(Joe)

Born May 31, 1962, at Glen Ridge, N.J.
Height, 6.01. Weight, 200.
Throws and bats lefthanded.

Major League stolen bases: 1984 (3), 1985 (24), 1986 (24), 1988 (9), 1989 (5). Total—65.
Led Pacific Coast League outfielders in total chances with 367 and double plays with 8 in 1983.
Tied for South Atlantic League lead in double plays by outfielders with 4 in 1981.

Year—Club	League	Pos.	G.	AB.	R.	H.	2B.	3B.	HR.	RBI.	B.A.	PO.	A.	E.	F.A.
1981—Greenwood†	S. Atl.	OF	118	460	80	145	18	8	6	70	.315	249	16	4	★.985
1982—Alexandria	Carol.	OF-1B	129	463	92	134	18	4	14	65	.289	286	7	10	.967
1983—Hawaii	P. C.	OF	139	538	87	154	12	●13	10	58	.286	★341	●18	8	.978
1983—Pittsburgh	Nat.	OF	7	11	0	2	0	0	0	1	.182	2	2	0	1.000
1984—Hawaii	P. C.	OF	98	388	51	110	19	12	3	53	.284	258	6	2	.992
1984—Pittsburgh	Nat.	OF	32	67	12	17	1	2	0	3	.254	41	1	0	1.000
1985—Pittsburgh‡	Nat.	OF	121	397	54	119	14	6	0	21	.300	229	10	6	.976
1986—Pittsburgh	Nat.	OF	138	401	60	100	19	6	2	19	.249	193	11	4	.981
1987—Vancouver§x	P. C.	OF	39	143	20	33	6	1	1	12	.231	58	2	2	.968
1988—Baltimore	Amer.	OF	125	379	48	109	21	3	8	27	.288	228	6	5	.979
1989—Baltimore	Amer.	OF	123	390	59	111	22	5	7	55	.285	250	10	4	.985
National League Totals—4 Years			298	876	126	238	34	14	2	44	.272	465	24	10	.980
American League Totals—2 Years			248	769	107	220	43	8	15	82	.286	478	16	9	.982
Major League Totals—6 Years			546	1645	233	458	77	22	17	126	.278	943	40	19	.981

Selected by Pittsburgh Pirates' organization in 6th round of free-agent draft, June 3, 1980.
†On temporarily inactive list, July 10 to July 27, 1981.
‡On disabled list, May 25 to June 9, 1985.
§On Pittsburgh disabled list, March 31 to May 22, 1987; included rehabilitation disability assignment to Vancouver, May 4 to May 22, 1987.
xTraded to Baltimore Orioles for Shortstop Terry Crowley Jr. and Third Baseman Rico Rossy, November 6, 1987.

ADALBERTO ORTIZ JR. (COLON)

Name pronounced Orr-TEEZ.

(Junior)

Born October 24, 1959, at Humacao, Puerto Rico.
Height, 5.11. Weight, 176.
Throws and bats righthanded.
Brother of Alexander Ortiz, minor league outfielder, 1978 and 1979.

Major League stolen bases: 1983 (1), 1984 (1), 1985 (1), 1988 (1), 1989 (2). Total—6.
Led Pacific Coast League catchers in putouts with 744 and double plays with 17 in 1982.
Led Carolina League catchers in double plays with 12 in 1979.
Tied for Western Carolinas League lead in passed balls with 22 in 1978.

Year—Club	League	Pos.	G.	AB.	R.	H.	2B.	3B.	HR.	RBI.	B.A.	PO.	A.	E.	F.A.
1977—Charleston†	W. Car.	C	21	53	2	14	3	0	0	10	.264	93	13	4	.964
1977—Bradenton Pir.	Gulf C.	C	34	118	11	24	5	1	1	12	.203	76	14	4	.957
1978—Charleston‡	W. Car.	C	41	122	12	26	4	0	1	16	.213	198	44	7	.972
1979—Salem	Carol.	★C-1B	108	396	35	112	21	2	5	66	.283	632	★84	★17	.977
1980—Buffalo	East.	C	126	515	79	★178	25	1	12	78	★.346	497	91	16	.974
1980—Portland	P. C.	C	8	27	1	3	0	1	0	3	.111	42	10	0	1.000
1981—Portland	P. C.	C	105	346	49	93	14	7	2	46	.269	606	76	15	.978
1982—Portland	P. C.	★C-O-1	124	449	46	131	22	0	6	57	.292	751	★110	★19	.978
1982—Pittsburgh	Nat.	C	7	15	1	3	1	0	0	0	.200	27	3	0	1.000
1983—Pitt.§-N.Y.	Nat.	C	73	193	11	48	5	0	0	12	.249	293	31	11	.967
1984—New York x	Nat.	C	40	91	6	18	3	0	0	11	.198	136	13	3	.980
1985—Pittsburgh	Nat.	C	23	72	4	21	2	0	1	5	.292	115	14	2	.985
1986—Pittsburgh	Nat.	C	49	110	11	37	6	0	0	14	.336	165	13	3	.983
1987—Pittsburgh	Nat.	C	75	192	16	52	8	1	1	22	.271	313	39	9	.975
1988—Pittsburgh y	Nat.	C	49	118	8	33	6	0	2	18	.280	152	23	3	.983
1989—Pittsburgh	Nat.	C	91	230	16	50	6	1	1	22	.217	334	32	2	.995
Major League Totals—8 Years			407	1021	73	262	37	2	5	104	.257	1535	168	33	.981

Signed as free agent by Pittsburgh Pirates' organization, January 18, 1977.
†On temporary inactive list, June 18 to June 22, 1977.
‡On disabled list, June 16 to September 5, 1978.
§Traded with Pitcher Art Ray to New York Mets for Outfielder Marvell Wynne and Pitcher Steve Sentency, June 14, 1983.
xDrafted by Pittsburgh Pirates, December 3, 1984.
yOn disabled list, July 28 to September 5, 1988.

JOHN ANDREW ORTON

Born December 8, 1965, at Santa Cruz, Calif.
Height, 6.01. Weight, 195.
Throws and bats righthanded.
Attended California State Poly University, San Luis Obispo, Calif.

Led Texas League catchers in fielding percentage with .994 and double plays with 12 in 1989.

Year—Club	League	Pos.	G.	AB.	R.	H.	2B.	3B.	HR.	RBI.	B.A.	PO.	A.	E.	F.A.
1987—Salem	N'west	OF-C	51	176	31	46	8	1	8	36	.261	271	15	6	.979
1987—Midland	Texas	C	5	13	1	2	1	0	0	0	.154	26	5	1	.969
1988—Palm Springs†	Calif.	C	68	230	42	46	6	1	1	28	.200	235	27	8	.970
1989—Midland	Texas	C-1B	99	344	51	80	20	6	10	53	.233	466	56	4	.992
1989—California	Amer.	C	16	39	4	7	1	0	0	4	.179	76	7	1	.988
Major League Totals—1 Year			16	39	4	7	1	0	0	4	.179	76	7	1	.988

Selected by New York Mets' organization in 17th round of free-agent draft, June 4, 1984.
Selected by California Angels' organization in 1st round (25th player selected) of free-agent draft, June 2, 1987.
†On disabled list, June 14 to August 5, 1988.

DAVID ALAN OTTO
(Dave)

Born November 12, 1964, at Chicago, Ill.
Height, 6.07. Weight, 210.
Throws and bats lefthanded.
Attended University of Missouri, Columbia, Mo.

Led Pacific Coast League pitchers in wild pitches with 18 and tied for games started with 28 in 1989.

Year Club	League	G.	IP.	W.	L.	Pct.	H.	R.	ER.	SO.	BB.	ERA.
1985—Medford	Northwest	11	42⅓	2	2	.500	42	27	19	27	22	4.04
1986—Madison	Midwest	26	169	13	7	.650	154	72	50	125	71	2.66
1987—Madison	Midwest	1	3	0	0	.000	2	0	0	2	0	0.00
1987—Huntsville	Southern	9	50	4	1	.800	36	14	13	25	11	2.34
1987—Oakland	American	3	6	0	0	.000	7	6	6	3	1	9.00
1988—Tacoma	P. Coast	21	127⅔	4	9	.308	124	71	50	80	63	3.52
1988—Oakland	American	3	10	0	0	.000	9	2	2	7	6	1.80
1989—Tacoma	P. Coast	29	169	10	13	.435	164	84	69	122	61	3.67
1989—Oakland	American	1	6⅔	0	0	.000	6	2	2	4	2	2.70
Major League Totals—3 Years		7	22⅔	0	0	.000	22	10	10	14	9	3.97

Selected by Baltimore Orioles' organization in 2nd round of free-agent draft, June 7, 1982.
Selected by Oakland A's organization in 2nd round of free-agent draft, June 3, 1985.

SPIKE DEE OWEN

Born April 19, 1961, at Cleburne, Tex.
Height, 5.10. Weight, 170.
Throws right and bats left and righthanded.
Attended University of Texas, Austin, Tex.
Brother of Dave Owen, shortstop in Chicago Cubs' organization.

Shares modern major league record for most runs, game (6), August 21, 1986.
Major League stolen bases: 1983 (10), 1984 (16), 1985 (11), 1986 (4), 1987 (11), 1989 (3). Total—55.
Led American League shortstops in total chances with 767 and double plays with 133 in 1986.
Named shortstop on THE SPORTING NEWS College Baseball All-America Team, 1982.

Year Club	League	Pos.	G.	AB.	R.	H.	2B.	3B.	HR.	RBI.	B.A.	PO.	A.	E.	F.A.
1982—Lynn	East.	SS	78	241	32	64	9	2	1	27	.266	106	207	9	.972
1983—Salt Lake City	P. C.	SS	72	256	58	68	8	9	1	32	.266	111	212	14	.958
1983—Seattle	Amer.	SS	80	306	36	60	11	3	2	21	.196	122	233	11	.970
1984—Seattle	Amer.	SS	152	530	67	130	18	8	3	43	.245	245	463	17	.977
1985—Seattle†	Amer.	SS	118	352	41	91	10	6	6	37	.259	196	361	14	.975
1986—Seattle‡-Boston	Amer.	SS	154	528	67	122	24	7	1	45	.231	279	467	21	.973
1987—Boston	Amer.	SS	132	437	50	113	17	7	2	48	.259	176	336	13	.975
1988—Boston§	Amer.	SS	89	257	40	64	14	1	5	18	.249	102	192	10	.967
1989—Montreal x	Nat.	SS	142	437	52	102	17	4	6	41	.233	232	388	13	*.979
American League Totals—6 Years			725	2410	301	580	94	32	19	212	.241	1120	2052	86	.974
National League Totals—1 Year			142	437	52	102	17	4	6	41	.233	232	388	13	.979
Major League Totals—7 Years			867	2847	353	682	111	36	25	253	.240	1352	2440	99	.975

Selected by Seattle Mariners' organization in 1st round (sixth player selected) of free-agent draft, June 7, 1982.
†On disabled list, July 15 to August 1, 1985.
‡Traded with Outfielder Dave Henderson to Boston Red Sox for Infielder Rey Quinones, a player to be named later and cash, August 19, 1986; as part of deal, Seattle Mariners claimed Pitchers Mike Brown and Mike Trujillo on waivers from Boston, August 22, 1986. Seattle acquired Outfielder John Christensen to complete deal, September 25, 1986.
§Traded with Pitcher Dan Gakeler to Montreal Expos for Pitcher John Dopson and Shortstop Luis Rivera, December 8, 1988.
xOn disabled list, July 17 to August 1, 1989.

CHAMPIONSHIP SERIES RECORD

Year Club	League	Pos.	G.	AB.	R.	H.	2B.	3B.	HR.	RBI.	B.A.	PO.	A.	E.	F.A.
1986—Boston	Amer.	SS	7	21	5	9	0	1	0	3	.429	12	21	5	.868
1988—Boston	Amer.	PH	1	0	0	0	0	0	0	0	.000	0	0	0	.000
Championship Series Totals—2 Years			8	21	5	9	0	1	0	3	.429	12	21	5	.868

WORLD SERIES RECORD

Year Club	League	Pos.	G.	AB.	R.	H.	2B.	3B.	HR.	RBI.	B.A.	PO.	A.	E.	F.A.
1986—Boston	Amer.	SS	7	20	2	6	0	0	0	2	.300	10	13	0	1.000

MICHAEL TIMOTHY PAGLIARULO
Name pronounced Pal-ya-ROO-lo.
(Mike)

Born March 15, 1960, at Medford, Mass.
Height, 6.02. Weight, 195.
Throws right and bats lefthanded.
Attended University of Miami, Coral Gables, Fla.
Son of Charles Pagliarulo, infielder in Chicago Cubs' organization, 1958.

Major League stolen bases: 1986 (4), 1987 (1), 1988 (1), 1989 (3). Total—9.
Led New York-Pennsylvania League in intentional bases on balls received with 8 in 1981.
Led Southern League third basemen in total chances with 433 in 1983.
Led New York-Pennsylvania League third basemen in total chances with 214 in 1981.

Year Club	League	Pos.	G.	AB.	R.	H.	2B.	3B.	HR.	RBI.	B.A.	PO.	A.	E.	F.A.
1981—Oneonta	NYP	3B	72	245	32	53	9	4	2	28	.216	40	*159	15	.930
1982—Greensboro	S. Atl.	3B	123	403	79	113	22	0	22	79	.280	73	*278	27	.929
1983—Nashville	South.	3B	135	450	82	117	19	4	19	80	.260	*98	*315	20	*.954
1984—Columbus	Int.	3B-SS	58	146	24	31	5	1	7	25	.212	27	95	13	.904
1984—New York	Amer.	3B	67	201	24	48	15	3	7	34	.239	44	106	7	.955
1985—New York	Amer.	3B	138	380	55	91	16	2	19	62	.239	67	187	13	.951
1986—New York	Amer.	3B-SS	149	504	71	120	24	3	28	71	.238	104	283	19	.953
1987—New York	Amer.	3B-1B	150	522	76	122	26	3	32	87	.234	97	297	17	.959
1988—New York†	Amer.	3B	125	444	46	96	20	1	15	67	.216	82	232	19	.943
1989—New York‡	Amer.	3B	74	223	19	44	10	0	4	16	.197	25	122	10	.936
1989—San Diego	Nat.	3B	50	148	12	29	7	0	3	14	.196	19	83	7	.936
American League Totals—6 Years			703	2274	291	521	111	12	105	337	.229	419	1227	85	.951
National League Totals—1 Year			50	148	12	29	7	0	3	14	.196	19	83	7	.936
Major League Totals—6 Years			753	2422	303	550	118	12	108	351	.227	438	1310	92	.950

Selected by New York Yankees' organization in 6th round of free-agent draft, June 8, 1981.

†On disabled list, July 25 to August 11, 1988.

‡Traded with Pitcher Don Schulze to San Diego Padres for Pitcher Walt Terrell and a player to be named later, July 22, 1989; New York Yankees acquired Pitcher Fred Toliver to complete deal, September 27, 1989.

THOMAS ALAN PAGNOZZI
(Tom)

Born July 30, 1962, at Tucson, Ariz.
Height, 6.01. Weight, 190.
Throws and bats righthanded.
Attended Central Arizona College, Coolidge, Ariz.,
and University of Arkansas, Fayetteville, Ark.
Brother of Tim Pagnozzi, shortstop in Philadelphia Phillies' organization, 1976;
and Mike Pagnozzi, pitcher in Baltimore Orioles' organization, 1975 through 1978.

Major League stolen bases: 1987 (1).

Year Club	League	Pos.	G.	AB.	R.	H.	2B.	3B.	HR.	RBI.	B.A.	PO.	A.	E.	F.A.
1983—Erie	NYP	C	45	168	28	52	9	1	6	22	.310	183	20	3	.985
1983—Macon	S. Atl.	C	18	57	7	14	2	1	0	6	.246	125	18	8	.947
1984—Springfield	Midw.	C	114	396	57	112	20	4	10	68	.283	667	*90	12	.984
1985—Arkansas	Texas	C-1B	41	139	15	43	7	1	5	29	.309	243	27	1	.996
1985—Louisville	A. A.	C	76	268	29	72	13	2	5	40	.269	266	25	4	.986
1986—Louisville	A. A.	C	30	106	12	31	4	0	1	18	.292	160	19	3	.984
1987—Louisville	A. A.	C-3B	84	320	53	100	20	2	14	71	.313	427	43	6	.987
1987—St. Louis	Nat.	C-1B	27	48	8	9	1	0	2	9	.188	61	5	0	1.000
1988—St. Louis	Nat.	1B-C-3B	81	195	17	55	9	0	0	15	.282	340	30	4	.989
1989—St. Louis	Nat.	C-1B-3B	52	80	3	12	2	0	0	3	.150	100	9	2	.982
Major League Totals—3 Years			160	323	28	76	12	0	2	27	.235	501	44	6	.989

Selected by Milwaukee Brewers' organization in 24th round of free-agent draft, January 12, 1982.
Selected by St. Louis Cardinals' organization in 8th round of free agent draft, June 6, 1983.

CHAMPIONSHIP SERIES RECORD

Year Club	League	Pos.	G.	AB.	R.	H.	2B.	3B.	HR.	RBI.	B.A.	PO.	A.	E.	F.A.
1987—St. Louis	Nat.	PH	1	1	0	0	0	0	0	0	.000	0	0	0	.000

WORLD SERIES RECORD

Year Club	League	Pos.	G.	AB.	R.	H.	2B.	3B.	HR.	RBI.	B.A.	PO.	A.	E.	F.A.
1987—St. Louis	Nat.	DH-PH	2	4	0	1	0	0	0	0	.250	0	0	0	.000

ROBERT REY PALACIOS

Name pronounced Pah-LAH-see-os.

(Known by middle name.)

Born November 8, 1962, at Brooklyn, N. Y.
Height, 5.10. Weight, 190.
Throws and bats righthanded.
Attended Kingsborough Community College, Brooklyn, N. Y.

Led International League in sacrifice flies with 9 in 1987.
Led International League catchers in putouts with 789, total chances with 890 and tied for lead in double plays with 7 and passed balls with 15 in 1988.
Led International League catchers in assists with 66 in 1987 and 82 in 1988.
Led International League catchers in errors with 19 in 1988 and tied for lead with 13 in 1987.
Led Eastern League catchers in putouts with 603, assists with 86, errors with 20, total chances with 709 and double plays with 8 in 1986.
Tied for Appalachian League lead in double plays by catchers with 2 in 1984.

Year Club	League	Pos.	G.	AB.	R.	H.	2B.	3B.	HR.	RBI.	B.A.	PO.	A.	E.	F.A.
1983—Bristol	Appal.	C	47	139	28	42	7	1	7	28	.302	187	22	7	.968
1984—Lakeland†	Fla. St.	3B-1B-C	107	373	44	92	21	4	2	53	.247	285	105	19	.954
1985—Lakeland	Fla. St.	C-1B	85	280	35	65	11	1	2	27	.232	410	45	13	.972
1985—Birmingham	South.	C-3B-1B	35	110	14	29	4	0	2	16	.264	153	43	8	.961
1986—Glens Falls	East.	C-3B-1B	135	461	66	116	20	4	16	66	.252	703	140	26	.970
1987—Toledo	Int.	C-3-1-O	133	449	50	116	22	2	13	60	.258	569	122	22	.969
1988—Toledo‡	Int.	C-1-O-2-3	132	409	38	94	26	1	5	27	.230	811	84	20	.978

Year Club League	Pos.	G.	AB.	R.	H.	2B.	3B.	HR.	RBI.	B.A.	PO.	A.	E.	F.A.
1988—Kansas City.......... Amer.	C-3B	5	11	2	1	0	0	0	0	.091	17	1	0	1.000
1989—Kansas City.......... Amer.	3-1-C-O	55	47	12	8	2	0	1	8	.170	96	15	2	.982
1989—Omaha................. A. A.	C-3B-OF	34	90	13	16	6	0	1	6	.178	164	20	5	.974
Major League Totals—2 Years...............		60	58	14	9	2	0	1	8	.155	113	16	2	.985

Signed as free agent by Detroit Tigers' organization, August 16, 1982.
†On disabled list, April 17 to May 21, 1984.
‡Traded with Pitcher Mark Lee to Kansas City Royals for Pitcher Ted Power, August 31, 1988.

DONN STEVEN PALL

Born January 11, 1962, at Chicago, Ill.
Height, 6.01. Weight, 180.
Throws and bats righthanded.
Received degree from University of Illinois, Champaign, Ill., in 1985.

Major League saves: 1989 (6).
Tied for Gulf Coast League lead in complete games with 4 and shutouts with 2 in 1985.

Year Club League	G.	IP.	W.	L.	Pct.	H.	R.	ER.	SO.	BB.	ERA.
1985—Sarasota White Sox.......................Gulf Coast	13	*86	●7	5	.583	68	34	16	63	10	1.67
1986—Appleton .... Midwest	11	78	5	5	.500	71	29	20	51	14	2.31
1986—Birmingham .... Southern	21	73	3	4	.429	77	38	36	41	27	4.44
1987—Birmingham .... Southern	30	158	8	11	.421	173	100	75	139	63	4.27
1988—Vancouver .... P. Coast	44	72⅔	5	2	.714	61	21	18	41	20	2.23
1988—Chicago .... American	17	28⅔	0	2	.000	39	11	11	16	8	3.45
1989—Chicago† .... American	53	87	4	5	.444	90	35	32	58	19	3.31
1989—South Bend .... Midwest	2	3⅓	0	0	.000	1	0	0	4	0	0.00
Major League Totals—2 Years............................	70	115⅔	4	7	.364	129	46	43	74	27	3.35

Selected by Chicago White Sox' organization in 23rd round of free-agent draft, June 3, 1985.
†On disabled list, May 19 to June 2, 1989; included rehabilitation disability assignment to South Bend, May 30 to June 2, 1989.

RAFAEL CORRALES PALMEIRO

Name pronounced Pal-MAIR-oh.
Born September 24, 1964, at Havana, Cuba.
Height, 6.00. Weight, 180.
Throws and bats lefthanded.
Received degree in commercial art from Mississippi State University, Starkville, Miss.

Major League stolen bases: 1986 (1), 1987 (2), 1988 (12), 1989 (4). Total—19.
Led Eastern League in total bases with 225, sacrifice flies with 13 and intentional bases on balls received with 13 in 1986.
Named outfielder on THE SPORTING NEWS College Baseball All-America Team, 1985.
Named Eastern League Most Valuable Player, 1986.

Year Club League	Pos.	G.	AB.	R.	H.	2B.	3B.	HR.	RBI.	B.A.	PO.	A.	E.	F.A.
1985—Peoria..................... Midw.	OF	73	279	34	83	22	4	5	51	.297	113	7	1	.992
1986—Pittsfield .... East.	OF	●140	509	66	*156	29	2	12	*95	.306	248	9	3	*.988
1986—Chicago .... Nat.	OF	22	73	9	18	4	0	3	12	.247	34	2	4	.900
1987—Iowa .... A. A.	OF-1B	57	214	36	64	14	3	11	41	.299	150	13	2	.988
1987—Chicago .... Nat.	OF-1B	84	221	32	61	15	1	14	30	.276	176	9	1	.995
1988—Chicago† .... Nat.	OF-1B	152	580	75	178	41	5	8	53	.307	322	11	5	.985
1989—Texas.................... Amer.	1B	156	559	76	154	23	4	8	64	.275	1167	*119	12	.991
National League Totals—3 Years............		258	874	116	257	60	6	25	95	.294	532	22	10	.982
American League Totals—1 Year		156	559	76	154	23	4	8	64	.275	1167	119	12	.991
Major League Totals—4 Years............		414	1433	192	411	83	10	33	159	.287	1699	141	22	.988

Selected by New York Mets' organization in 8th round of free-agent draft, June 7, 1982.
Selected by Chicago Cubs' organization in 1st round (22nd player selected) of free-agent draft, June 3, 1985.
†Traded with Pitchers Jamie Moyer and Drew Hall to Texas Rangers for Pitchers Mitch Williams, Paul Kilgus and Steve Wilson, Infielders Curtis Wilkerson and Luis Benitez and Outfielder Pablo Delgado, December 5, 1988.

ALL-STAR GAME RECORD

Year League	Pos.	AB.	R.	H.	2B.	3B.	HR.	RBI.	B.A.	PO.	A.	E.	F.A.
1988—National.. PH-OF	0	0	0	0	0	0	0	.000	1	0	0	1.000

DAVID WILLIAM PALMER JR.

Born October 19, 1957, at Glens Falls, N.Y.
Height, 6.01. Weight, 205.
Throws and bats righthanded.

Pitched five-inning, 4-0 perfect game against St. Louis Cardinals, April 21, 1984 (second game).
Major League saves: 1979 (2).
Tied for Pioneer League lead in home runs allowed with 6 in 1976.

Year Club League	G.	IP.	W.	L.	Pct.	H.	R.	ER.	SO.	BB.	ERA.
1976—Lethbridge .... Pioneer	13	45	0	5	.000	58	49	36	44	28	7.20
1977—West Palm Beach .... Florida St.	25	119	6	8	.429	120	49	38	88	44	2.87
1978—West Palm Beach .... Florida St.	7	51	4	2	.667	44	23	11	58	4	1.94
1978—Memphis .... Southern	19	130	8	10	.444	107	57	44	78	44	3.05
1978—Montreal .... National	5	10	0	1	.000	9	4	3	7	2	2.70
1979—Montreal .... National	36	123	10	2	.833	110	41	36	72	30	2.63

Year Club	League	G.	IP.	W.	L.	Pct.	H.	R.	ER.	SO.	BB.	ERA.
1980—Montreal†	National	24	130	8	6	.571	124	53	43	73	30	2.98
1981—West Palm Beach‡	Florida St.	3	11	0	0	.000	9	1	1	7	5	0.82
1981—Memphis	Southern	1	0	0	0	.000	0	1	1	0	1	0.00
1982—Memphis	Southern	9	51⅓	3	2	.600	38	21	20	44	33	3.51
1982—Montreal §	National	13	73⅔	6	4	.600	60	34	26	46	36	3.18
1983—West Palm Beach x	Florida St.					(Did not play)						
1984—Montreal y	National	20	105⅓	7	3	.700	101	45	45	66	44	3.84
1985—Montreal za	National	24	135⅔	7	10	.412	128	60	56	106	67	3.71
1986—Atlanta b	National	35	209⅔	11	10	.524	181	98	85	170	102	3.65
1987—Atlanta c	National	28	152⅓	8	11	.421	169	94	83	111	64	4.90
1987—Greenville d	Southern	1	5	1	0	1.000	3	0	0	6	3	0.00
1988—Philadelphia ef	National	22	129	7	9	.438	129	67	64	85	48	4.47
1989—Toledo	Int'national	10	55	2	4	.333	49	34	24	33	23	3.93
1989—Detroit g	American	5	17⅓	0	3	.000	25	19	15	12	11	7.79
1989—Colorado Springs h	P. Coast	8	38⅓	2	2	.500	35	21	18	28	21	4.23
National League Totals—9 Years		207	1068⅔	64	56	.533	1011	496	441	736	423	3.71
American League Totals—1 Year		5	17⅓	0	3	.000	25	19	15	12	11	7.79
Major League Totals—10 Years		212	1086	64	59	.520	1036	515	456	748	434	3.78

Selected by Montreal Expos' organization in 21st round of free-agent draft, June 8, 1976.

†On disabled list, July 21 to August 27, 1980.

‡On Montreal disabled list, March 25 to August 9, 1981; included rehabilitation disability assignment to West Palm Beach, May 6 to May 25, 1981.

§On disabled list, August 14 to September 27, 1982.

xOn Montreal disabled list, March 28 to September 20, 1983; included rehabilitation disability assignment to West Palm Beach, August 6 to August 26, 1983.

yOn disabled list, August 5 to September 1, 1984.

zOn disabled list, August 9 to September 1, 1985.

aGranted free agency, November 12, 1985; signed by Atlanta Braves' organizaton, February 13, 1986.

bGranted free agency, November 12, 1986; re-signed by Braves, December 19, 1986.

cOn disabled list, June 19 to July 25, 1987; included rehabilitation disability assignment to Greenville, July 21 to July 25, 1987.

dGranted free agency, November 9, 1987; signed by Philadelphia Phillies, December 18, 1987.

eOn disabled list, July 3 to July 18, 1988.

fReleased, October 13, 1988; signed by Detroit Tigers, February 25, 1989.

gReleased, July 13, 1989; signed by Colorado Springs (Cleveland Indians' organization), July 27, 1989.

hReleased, October 26, 1989.

DEAN WILLIAM PALMER

Born December 27, 1968, at Tallahassee, Fla.
Height, 6.01. Weight, 175.
Throws and bats righthanded.

Led Texas League batters in strikeouts with 152 in 1989.
Led Texas League third basemen in errors with 30 in 1989.

Year Club	League	Pos.	G.	AB.	R.	H.	2B.	3B.	HR.	RBI.	B.A.	PO.	A.	E.	F.A.
1986—Sarasota Rangers	Gulf C.	3B	50	163	19	34	7	1	0	12	.209	25	75	13	.885
1987—Gastonia	S. Atl.	3B	128	484	51	104	16	0	9	54	.215	58	209	★59	.819
1988—Port Charlotte†	Fla. St.	3B	74	305	38	81	12	1	4	35	.266	49	144	28	.873
1989—Tulsa	Texas	3B-SS	133	498	82	125	32	5	★25	90	.251	85	213	31	.906
1989—Texas	Amer.	3B-SS-OF	16	19	0	2	2	0	0	1	.105	3	4	2	.778
Major League Totals—1 Year			16	19	0	2	2	0	0	1	.105	3	4	2	.778

Selected by Texas Rangers' organization in 3rd round of free-agent draft, June 2, 1986.

†On disabled list, July 19, 1988 through remainder of season.

ALBERTO JUDAS PARDO

(Al)

Born September 8, 1962, at Oviedo, Spain.
Height, 6.02. Weight, 195.
Throws right and bats left and righthanded.
Attended Hillsborough Community College, Tampa, Fla.
Brother of Braulio Pardo, minor league catcher, 1980.

Led Southern League in game-winning RBIs with 17 in 1984.

Year Club	League	Pos.	G.	AB.	R.	H.	2B.	3B.	HR.	RBI.	B.A.	PO.	A.	E.	F.A.
1980—Bluefield	Appal.	C-1B	48	151	26	52	6	2	3	23	.344	66	8	0	1.000
1981—Miami	Fla. St.	C	91	291	25	63	9	3	3	32	.216	396	41	6	.987
1981—Hagerstown	Carol.	C	21	76	11	24	3	1	1	7	.316	37	7	2	.957
1982—Hagerstown	Carol.	C-1B-OF	130	492	76	142	24	4	17	86	.289	685	74	11	.986
1983—Rochester	Int.	C	69	220	25	56	11	2	1	31	.255	223	18	9	.964
1983—Charlotte	South.	C	37	141	20	44	11	3	4	19	.312	129	18	4	.974
1984—Charlotte	South.	C-OF-1B	138	483	72	128	23	2	13	81	.265	397	32	14	.968
1985—Rochester	Int.	C	60	194	23	49	14	1	8	35	.253	258	19	6	.979
1985—Baltimore	Amer.	C	34	75	3	10	1	0	0	1	.133	131	7	3	.979
1986—Rochester	Int.	C	76	253	34	54	12	1	8	34	.213	321	27	3	.991
1986—Baltimore†	Amer.	C	16	51	3	7	1	0	1	3	.137	70	5	1	.987
1987—Richmond‡	Int.	C	16	47	8	10	3	0	2	5	.213	72	4	0	1.000
1987—Jackson	Texas	1B-C	25	61	2	20	6	0	1	13	.328	58	7	1	.985
1988—Tide.§-Maine	Int.	C-1B	59	153	13	39	8	0	4	21	.255	127	10	1	.993

Year Club League	Pos.	G.	AB.	R.	H.	2B.	3B.	HR.	RBI.	B.A.	PO.	A.	E.	F.A.
1988—Philadelphia .... Nat.	C	2	2	0	0	0	0	0	0	.000	2	0	0	1.000
1989—Scr./Wil.-Barre..... Int.	C-1B	103	306	32	73	20	3	5	30	.239	432	22	7	.985
1989—Philadelphia x...... Nat.	C	1	1	0	0	0	0	0	0	.000	3	0	0	1.000
American League Totals—2 Years		50	126	6	17	2	0	1	4	.135	201	12	4	.982
National League Totals—2 Years...........		3	3	0	0	0	0	0	0	.000	5	0	0	1.000
Major League Totals—4 Years................		53	129	6	17	2	0	1	4	.132	206	12	4	.982

Selected by Baltimore Orioles' organization in 2nd round of free-agent draft, June 3, 1980.
†Granted free agency, October 15, 1986; signed by Atlanta Braves' organization, November 17, 1986.
‡Released, June 8, 1987; signed by Jackson (New York Mets' organization), July 24, 1987.
§Sold to Maine (Philadelphia Phillies' organization), July 30, 1988.
xReleased, October 11, 1989.

JOHNNY ALFONSO PAREDES (ISAMBERT)

Born September 2, 1962, at Maracaibo, Venezuela.
Height, 5.11. Weight, 165.
Throws and bats righthanded.

Major League stolen bases: 1988 (5).

Year Club League	Pos.	G.	AB.	R.	H.	2B.	3B.	HR.	RBI.	B.A.	PO.	A.	E.	F.A.
1982—Helena.................... Pioneer	3B-2B-SS	34	105	17	32	4	1	1	7	.305	28	63	7	.929
1983—Spartanburg†........ S. Atl.	3B-1B-2B	46	130	14	31	0	3	0	11	.238	98	59	11	.925
1984—W. Palm Beach.... Fla. St.	2B	112	438	64	111	11	1	0	32	.253	275	295	15	★.974
1985—W. Palm Beach.... Fla. St.	2B	101	322	65	84	7	4	2	34	.261	184	281	9	★.981
1985—Jacksonville.......... South.	2B	21	73	11	23	2	0	0	5	.315	47	51	2	.980
1986—Jacksonville.......... South.	O-S-2-3-1	122	472	86	135	15	5	6	34	.286	230	189	19	.957
1987—Indianapolis.......... A. A.	2B	130	493	80	154	19	6	8	47	.312	234	387	14	.978
1988—Indianapolis.......... A. A.	2B-3B	101	400	69	118	17	3	4	46	.295	220	275	10	.980
1988—Montreal................ Nat.	2B-OF	35	91	6	17	2	0	1	10	.187	46	77	3	.976
1989—Montreal‡§............. Nat.					(Did not play)									
Major League Totals—1 Year..................		35	91	6	17	2	0	1	10	.187	46	77	3	.976

Signed as free agent by Philadelphia Phillies' organization, June 22, 1982.
†Released, September 19, 1983; signed by Gastonia (Montreal Expos' organization), January 12, 1984.
‡On disabled list, March 31 to September 28, 1989.
§Drafted by Detroit Tigers, December 4, 1989.

MARK ALAN PARENT

Born September 16, 1961, at Ashland, Ore.
Height, 6.05. Weight, 224.
Throws and bats righthanded.

Major League stolen bases: 1989 (1).
Led Pacific Coast League catchers in fielding percentage with .988 in 1987.
Led Carolina League catchers in double plays with 16 in 1981.
Led Northwest League catchers in fielding percentage with .979 in 1980.

Year Club League	Pos.	G.	AB.	R.	H.	2B.	3B.	HR.	RBI.	B.A.	PO.	A.	E.	F.A.
1979—Walla Walla .... N'west	C-OF	40	126	8	24	4	0	1	11	.190	229	34	6	.978
1980—Reno .... Calif.	C	30	99	8	20	3	0	0	12	.202	128	23	2	.987
1980—Grays Harbor .... N'west	C-1B	66	230	29	55	11	2	7	32	.230	381	38	9	.979
1981—Salem..................... Carol.	C	123	438	44	103	16	3	6	47	.235	★694	87	★28	.965
1982—Amarillo................. Texas	C	26	89	12	17	3	1	1	13	.191	100	6	2	.981
1982—Salem..................... Carol.	C-1B	99	360	39	81	15	2	6	41	.225	475	64	12	.978
1983—Beaumont†........... Texas	C	81	282	38	71	22	1	7	33	.252	464	71	10	★.982
1984—Beaumont‡........... Texas	C-1B	111	380	52	109	24	3	7	60	.287	674	68	7	.991
1985—Las Vegas............. P. C.	C-1B	105	361	36	87	23	3	7	45	.241	586	54	6	.991
1986—Las Vegas............. P. C.	C-1B	86	267	29	77	10	4	5	40	.288	344	40	5	.987
1986—San Diego .... Nat.	C	8	14	1	2	0	0	0	0	.143	16	0	2	.889
1987—Las Vegas............. P. C.	C-1-3-O	105	387	50	113	23	2	4	43	.292	556	58	8	.987
1987—San Diego .... Nat.	C	12	25	0	2	0	0	0	2	.080	36	3	0	1.000
1988—San Diego .... Nat.	C	41	118	9	23	3	0	6	15	.195	203	15	3	.986
1989—San Diego .... Nat.	C-1B	52	141	12	27	4	0	7	21	.191	246	17	0	1.000
Major League Totals—4 Years................		113	298	22	54	7	0	13	38	.181	501	35	5	.991

Selected by San Diego Padres' organization in 4th round of free-agent draft, June 5, 1979.
†On suspended list, August 27, 1983 through remainder of season.
‡On disabled list, September 4, 1984 through remainder of season.

DAVID GENE PARKER
(Dave)

Born June 9, 1951, at Jackson, Miss.
Height, 6.05. Weight, 245.
Throws right and bats lefthanded.

Shares major league record for most home runs, month of October (4), 1985; fewest errors by outfielder, season, for leader in errors (9), 1986.
Major League stolen bases: 1973 (1), 1974 (3), 1975 (8), 1976 (19), 1977 (17), 1978 (20), 1979 (20), 1980 (10), 1981 (6), 1982 (7), 1983 (12), 1984 (11), 1985 (5), 1986 (1), 1987 (7). Total—147.
Led National League in grounding into double plays with 26 in 1985.
Led National League in total bases with 340 in 1978, 350 in 1985 and 304 in 1986.
Led National League in slugging percentage with .541 in 1975 and .585 in 1978.

Led National League in intentional bases on balls received with 23 in 1978 and tied for lead with 24 in 1985.
Tied for National League lead in game-winning RBIs with 16 in 1987.
Tied for National League lead in sacrifice flies with 9 in 1979.
Led National League outfielders in total chances with 430 and double plays with 9 in 1977.
Led Carolina League in total bases with 270 and stolen bases with 38 in 1972.
Tied for Gulf Coast League lead in total bases with 107 in 1970.
Named National League Player of the Year by THE SPORTING NEWS, 1978.
Named National League Most Valuable Player by Baseball Writers' Association of America, 1978.
Named outfielder on THE SPORTING NEWS National League All-Star Team, 1975, 1977, 1978, 1985 and 1986.
Named outfielder on THE SPORTING NEWS National League All-Star fielding team, 1977 through 1979.
Named outfielder on THE SPORTING NEWS National League Silver Slugger team, 1985 and 1986.
Named Carolina League Most Valuable Player, 1972.

Year—Club	League	Pos.	G.	AB.	R.	H.	2B.	3B.	HR.	RBI.	B.A.	PO.	A.	E.	F.A.
1970—Bradenton Pir.	Gulf C.	●OF-P	61	239	34	75	8	3	●6	41	.314	92	11	●8	.928
1971—Waterbury	East.	OF	30	114	10	26	4	1	0	7	.228	43	5	6	.889
1971—Monroe	W. Car.	OF	71	268	49	96	16	4	11	48	.358	104	8	10	.918
1972—Salem	Carol.	OF	135	★523	★91	★162	★30	6	22	★101	.310	★250	★20	★20	.931
1973—Charleston	Int.	OF	84	309	44	98	20	7	9	57	.317	144	11	7	.957
1973—Pittsburgh	Nat.	OF	54	139	17	40	9	1	4	14	.288	77	3	3	.964
1974—Pittsburgh†	Nat.	OF-1B	73	220	27	62	10	3	4	29	.282	154	8	4	.976
1975—Pittsburgh	Nat.	OF	148	558	75	172	35	10	25	101	.308	311	7	9	.972
1976—Pittsburgh	Nat.	OF	138	537	82	168	28	10	13	90	.313	294	13	★14	.956
1977—Pittsburgh‡	Nat.	★OF-2B	159	637	107	★215	★44	8	21	88	★.338	★389	★26	★15	.965
1978—Pittsburgh‡	Nat.	OF	148	581	102	194	32	12	30	117	★.334	302	12	★13	.960
1979—Pittsburgh	Nat.	OF	158	622	109	193	45	7	25	94	.310	341	15	★15	.960
1980—Pittsburgh	Nat.	OF	139	518	71	153	31	1	17	79	.295	235	14	9	.965
1981—Pittsburgh§	Nat.	OF	67	240	29	62	14	3	9	48	.258	110	1	7	.941
1982—Pittsburgh x	Nat.	OF	73	244	41	66	19	3	6	29	.270	108	2	5	.957
1983—Pittsburgh y	Nat.	OF	144	552	68	154	29	4	12	69	.279	282	3	8	.973
1984—Cincinnati	Nat.	OF	156	607	73	173	28	0	16	94	.285	296	6	8	.974
1985—Cincinnati	Nat.	OF	160	635	88	198	★42	4	34	★125	.312	329	12	10	.972
1986—Cincinnati	Nat.	OF	★162	637	89	174	31	3	31	116	.273	278	9	●9	.970
1987—Cincinnati z	Nat.	OF-1B	153	589	77	149	28	0	26	97	.253	354	17	11	.971
1988—Oakland a	Amer.	OF-1B	101	377	43	97	18	1	12	55	.257	63	5	3	.958
1989—Oakland b	Amer.	OF	144	553	56	146	27	0	22	97	.264	2	0	0	1.000
National League Totals—15 Years			1932	7316	1055	2173	425	69	273	1190	.297	3860	147	140	.966
American League Totals—2 Years			245	930	99	243	45	1	34	152	.261	65	5	3	.959
Major League Totals—17 Years			2177	8246	1154	2416	470	70	307	1342	.293	3925	152	143	.966

Selected by Pittsburgh Pirates' organization in 14th round of free-agent draft, June 4, 1970.
†On disabled list, June 7 to June 28 and July 5 to July 31, 1974.
‡On disabled list, July 1 to July 16, 1978.
§On disabled list, May 14 to May 29, 1981.
xOn disabled list, May 12 to June 7 and July 29 to September 7, 1982.
yGranted free agency, November 7, 1983; signed by Cincinnati Reds, December 7, 1983.
zTraded to Oakland A's for Pitchers Jose Rijo and Tim Birtsas, December 8, 1987.
aOn disabled list, July 5 to August 21, 1988.
bGranted free agency, November 13, 1989; signed by Milwaukee Brewers, December 3, 1989.

CHAMPIONSHIP SERIES RECORD

Year—Club	League	Pos.	G.	AB.	R.	H.	2B.	3B.	HR.	RBI.	B.A.	PO.	A.	E.	F.A.
1974—Pittsburgh	Nat.	OF-PH	3	8	0	1	0	0	0	0	.125	4	1	0	1.000
1975—Pittsburgh	Nat.	OF	3	10	2	0	0	0	0	0	.000	13	1	0	1.000
1979—Pittsburgh	Nat.	OF	3	12	2	4	0	0	0	2	.333	9	0	0	1.000
1988—Oakland	Amer.	DH-OF	3	12	1	3	1	0	0	0	.250	1	0	1	.500
1989—Oakland	Amer.	DH	4	16	2	3	0	0	2	3	.188	0	0	0	.000
Championship Series Totals—5 Years			16	58	7	11	1	0	2	5	.190	27	2	1	.967

WORLD SERIES RECORD

Year—Club	League	Pos.	G.	AB.	R.	H.	2B.	3B.	HR.	RBI.	B.A.	PO.	A.	E.	F.A.
1979—Pittsburgh	Nat.	OF	7	29	2	10	3	0	0	4	.345	13	1	1	.933
1988—Oakland	Amer.	OF-DH	4	15	0	3	0	0	0	0	.200	4	0	0	1.000
1989—Oakland	Amer.	DH-PH	3	9	2	2	1	0	1	2	.222	0	0	0	.000
World Series Totals—3 Years			14	53	4	15	4	0	1	6	.283	17	1	1	.947

ALL-STAR GAME RECORD

Year—League	Pos.	AB.	R.	H.	2B.	3B.	HR.	RBI.	B.A.	PO.	A.	E.	F.A.
1977—National	OF	3	1	1	0	0	0	0	.333	2	0	0	1.000
1979—National	OF	3	0	1	0	0	0	1	.333	0	2	0	1.000
1980—National	OF	2	0	0	0	0	0	0	.000	0	0	0	.000
1981—National	OF	3	1	1	0	0	1	1	.333	1	0	0	1.000
1985—National	OF	2	0	0	0	0	0	0	.000	1	0	0	1.000
1986—National	OF	2	0	1	0	0	0	0	.500	0	0	0	.000
All-Star Game Totals—6 Years		15	2	4	0	0	1	2	.267	4	2	0	1.000

PITCHING RECORD

Year—Club	League	G.	IP.	W.	L.	Pct.	H.	R.	ER.	SO.	BB.	ERA.
1970—Bradenton Pirates	Gulf Coast	1	4	0	0	.000	7	2	2	2	1	4.50

JAMES CLAYTON PARKER
(Clay)

Born December 19, 1962, at Columbia, La.
Height, 6.01. Weight, 185.
Throws and bats righthanded.
Attended Louisiana State University, Baton Rouge, La.

Year Club	League	G.	IP.	W.	L.	Pct.	H.	R.	ER.	SO.	BB.	ERA.
1985—Bellingham	Northwest	10	63⅔	6	1	★.857	40	16	11	69	16	★1.55
1986—Wausau	Midwest	26	178	8	7	.533	171	77	57	154	39	2.88
1987—Chattanooga	Southern	16	112	7	5	.583	103	47	34	60	14	2.73
1987—Calgary	P. Coast	12	86	8	1	.889	78	35	28	44	28	2.93
1987—Seattle†	American	3	7⅔	0	0	.000	15	10	9	8	4	10.57
1988—Columbus‡	Int'national	10	49⅔	2	2	.500	49	21	18	51	9	3.26
1989—Columbus	Int'national	5	38	3	0	1.000	25	9	7	25	10	1.66
1989—New York§	American	22	120	4	5	.444	123	53	49	53	31	3.68
Major League Totals—2 Years		25	127⅔	4	5	.444	138	63	58	61	35	4.09

Selected by Minnesota Twins' organization in 21st round of free-agent draft, June 4, 1984.
Selected by Seattle Mariners' organization in 15th round of free-agent draft, June 3, 1985.
†Traded with Pitchers Lee Guetterman and Wade Taylor to New York Yankees for Pitcher Steve Trout and Outfilder Henry Cotto, December 22, 1987.
‡On disabled list, April 13 to April 22, June 1 to June 23 and June 28 to August 21, 1988.
§On disabled list, June 10 to July 1, 1989.

RICHARD ALLEN PARKER
(Rick)

Born March 20, 1963, at Kansas City, Mo.
Height, 6.00. Weight, 185.
Throws and bats righthanded.
Attended Southwest Missouri State University, Springfield, Mo.,
and University of Texas, Austin, Tex.

Year Club	League	Pos.	G.	AB.	R.	H.	2B.	3B.	HR.	RBI.	B.A.	PO.	A.	E.	F.A.
1985—Bend	N'west	SS	55	205	45	51	9	1	2	20	.249	79	143	25	.899
1986—Spartanburg	S. Atl.	SS	62	233	39	69	7	3	5	28	.296	87	169	18	.934
1986—Clearwater	Fla. St.	SS	63	218	24	51	10	2	0	15	.234	94	197	21	.933
1987—Clearwater	Fla. St.	2B-SS-3B	101	330	56	83	13	3	3	34	.252	130	234	27	.931
1988—Reading	East.	3-O-1-2-S	116	362	50	93	13	3	3	47	.257	174	114	18	.941
1989—Reading†	East.	3B-OF-SS	103	388	59	92	7	★9	3	32	.237	123	91	22	.907
1989—Phoenix	P. C.	3B-OF-SS	18	68	5	18	2	2	0	11	.265	25	32	1	.983

Selected by Philadelphia Phillies' organization in 16th round of free-agent draft, June 3, 1985.
†Traded to Phoenix (San Francisco Giants' organization), August 7, 1989, completing deal in which Philadelphia Phillies traded Pitcher Steve Bedrosian and a player to be named later to San Francisco Giants for Pitchers Dennis Cook and Terry Mulholland and Third Baseman Charlie Hayes, June 18, 1989.

DEREK GAVIN PARKS

Born September 29, 1968, at Covina, Calif.
Height, 6.01. Weight, 205.
Throws and bats righthanded.

Led Southern League in being hit by pitch with 15 in 1988.
Led Appalachian League in passed balls with 17 in 1986.

Year Club	League	Pos.	G.	AB.	R.	H.	2B.	3B.	HR.	RBI.	B.A.	PO.	A.	E.	F.A.
1986—Elizabethton	Appal.	C	62	224	39	53	10	1	10	40	.237	297	36	7	.979
1987—Kenosha	Midw.	C	129	466	70	115	19	2	24	94	.247	800	85	14	.984
1988—Orlando	South.	C	118	400	52	94	15	0	7	42	.235	616	66	7	.990
1989—Orlando†	South.	C	31	95	16	18	3	0	2	10	.189	135	12	3	.980

Selected by Minnesota Twins' organization in 1st round (10th player selected) of free-agent draft, June 2, 1986.
†On disabled list, June 12 to August 31, 1989.

JEFFREY DALE PARRETT
(Jeff)

Born August 26, 1961, at Indianapolis, Ind.
Height, 6.03. Weight, 193.
Throws and bats righthanded.
Attended University of Kentucky, Lexington, Ky.

Major League saves: 1987 (6), 1988 (6), 1989 (6). Total—18.

Year Club	League	G.	IP.	W.	L.	Pct.	H.	R.	ER.	SO.	BB.	ERA.
1983—Paintsville	Ap'lachian	3	17	2	0	1.000	12	6	4	21	8	2.12
1983—Beloit	Midwest	10	47	2	2	.500	40	26	21	34	29	4.02
1984—Beloit	Midwest	29	91⅔	4	3	.571	76	50	46	95	71	4.52
1985—Stockton†	California	45	127⅔	7	4	.636	97	50	39	120	75	★2.75
1986—Montreal	National	12	20⅓	0	1	.000	19	11	11	21	13	4.87
1986—Indianapolis	Am. Assoc.	25	69	2	5	.286	54	44	38	76	35	4.96
1987—Montreal	National	45	62	7	6	.538	53	33	29	56	30	4.21
1987—Indianapolis	Am. Assoc.	20	22⅓	2	1	.667	15	5	5	17	13	2.01
1988—Montreal‡§	National	61	91⅔	12	4	.750	66	29	27	62	45	2.65
1989—Philadelphia x	National	72	105⅔	12	6	.667	90	43	35	98	44	2.98
Major League Totals—4 Years		190	279⅔	31	17	.646	228	116	102	237	132	3.28

Selected by Milwaukee Brewers' organization in 9th round of free-agent draft, June 6, 1983.
†Drafted by Montreal Expos, December 10, 1985.
‡On disabled list, July 16 to August 14, 1988.
§Traded with Pitcher Floyd Youmans to Philadelphia Phillies for Pitcher Kevin Gross, December 6, 1988.
xOn disabled list, April 29 to May 22, 1989.

LANCE MICHAEL PARRISH

Born June 15, 1956, at McKeesport, Pa.
Height, 6.03. Weight, 220.
Throws and bats righthanded.

Major League stolen bases: 1979 (6), 1980 (6), 1981 (2), 1982 (3), 1983 (1), 1984 (2), 1985 (2), 1989 (1). Total—23.
Led American League in sacrifice flies with 13 in 1983.
Led American League catchers in double plays with 11 in 1984.
Led American League catchers in total chances with 772 in 1983.
Led American League in passed balls with 21 in 1979.
Led National League catchers in passed balls with 12 and tied for lead in double plays with 11 in 1988.
Tied for American League lead in passed balls with 17 in 1980.
Led Appalachian League batters in strikeouts with 92 in 1974.
Led American Association in double plays with 10 and passed balls with 21 in 1977.
Led Southern League in passed balls with 22 in 1976.
Led Florida State League catchers in double plays with 8 and passed balls with 31 in 1975.
Named catcher on THE SPORTING NEWS American League All-Star Team, 1982 and 1984.
Named catcher on THE SPORTING NEWS American League All-Star fielding team, 1983 through 1985.
Named catcher on THE SPORTING NEWS American League Silver Slugger team, 1980, 1982 through 1984 and 1986.

Year Club	League	Pos.	G.	AB.	R.	H.	2B.	3B.	HR.	RBI.	B.A.	PO.	A.	E.	F.A.
1974—Bristol	Appal.	3B-OF	68	253	45	54	11	1	11	46	.213	36	83	22	.844
1975—Lakeland	Fla. St.	C	100	341	30	75	15	2	5	37	.220	460	50	7	.986
1976—Montgomery	South.	C	107	340	46	75	9	2	14	55	.221	★600	★79	11	★.984
1977—Evansville	A. A.	C	115	416	74	116	21	2	25	90	.279	★722	★82	11	★.987
1977—Detroit	Amer.	C	12	46	10	9	2	0	3	7	.196	76	6	0	1.000
1978—Detroit	Amer.	C	85	288	37	63	11	3	14	41	.219	353	39	5	.987
1979—Detroit	Amer.	C	143	493	65	136	26	3	19	65	.276	707	★79	9	.989
1980—Detroit	Amer.	C-1B-OF	144	553	79	158	34	6	24	82	.286	607	67	7	.990
1981—Detroit	Amer.	C	96	348	39	85	18	2	10	46	.244	407	40	3	.993
1982—Detroit	Amer.	C-OF	133	486	75	138	19	2	32	87	.284	627	76	8	.989
1983—Detroit	Amer.	C	155	605	80	163	42	3	27	114	.269	695	73	4	.995
1984—Detroit	Amer.	C	147	578	75	137	16	2	33	98	.237	720	67	7	.991
1985—Detroit	Amer.	C	140	549	64	150	27	1	28	98	.273	695	53	5	.993
1986—Detroit†‡	Amer.	C	91	327	53	84	6	1	22	62	.257	483	48	6	.989
1987—Philadelphia	Nat.	C	130	466	42	114	21	0	17	67	.245	724	66	9	.989
1988—Philadelphia§x	Nat.	C-1B	123	424	44	91	17	2	15	60	.215	640	73	9	.988
1989—California	Amer.	C	124	433	48	103	12	1	17	50	.238	638	63	5	.993
American League Totals—11 Years			1270	4706	625	1226	213	24	229	750	.261	6008	611	59	.991
National League Totals—2 Years			253	890	86	205	38	2	32	127	.230	1364	139	18	.988
Major League Totals—13 Years			1523	5596	711	1431	251	26	261	877	.256	7372	750	77	.991

Selected by Detroit Tigers' organization in 1st round (16th player selected) of free-agent draft, June 5, 1974.
†On disabled list, July 31 to September 29, 1986.
‡Granted free agency, November 12, 1986; signed by Philadelphia Phillies, March 13, 1987.
§On disabled list, July 13 to July 28, 1988.
xTraded to California Angels for Pitcher David Holdridge, October 3, 1988.

CHAMPIONSHIP SERIES RECORD

Year Club	League	Pos.	G.	AB.	R.	H.	2B.	3B.	HR.	RBI.	B.A.	PO.	A.	E.	F.A.
1984—Detroit	Amer.	C	3	12	1	3	1	0	1	3	.250	21	2	0	1.000

WORLD SERIES RECORD

Year Club	League	Pos.	G.	AB.	R.	H.	2B.	3B.	HR.	RBI.	B.A.	PO.	A.	E.	F.A.
1984—Detroit	Amer.	C	5	18	3	5	1	0	1	2	.278	30	3	1	.971

ALL-STAR GAME RECORD

Year League	Pos.	AB.	R.	H.	2B.	3B.	HR.	RBI.	B.A.	PO.	A.	E.	F.A.
1980—American	C	1	0	0	0	0	0	0	.000	0	0	0	.000
1982—American	C	2	0	1	1	0	0	0	.500	2	3	0	1.000
1983—American	C	2	0	0	0	0	0	0	.000	1	0	0	1.000
1984—American	C	2	0	0	0	0	0	0	.000	3	1	1	.800
1986—American	C	3	0	0	0	0	0	0	.000	4	0	0	1.000
1988—National	C	1	0	0	0	0	0	0	.000	0	0	0	.000
All-Star Game Totals—6 Years		11	0	1	1	0	0	0	.091	10	4	1	.933

Named to American League All-Star Team for 1985 game; replaced due to injury by Rich Gedman.

DANIEL ANTHONY PASQUA

Name Pronounced PASS-quah.

(Dan)

Born October 17, 1961, at Yonkers, N. Y.
Height, 6.00. Weight, 205.
Throws and bats lefthanded.
Attended William Paterson College, Wayne, N.J.

Major League stolen bases: 1986 (2), 1988 (1), 1989 (1). Total—4.
Led American League outfielders in fielding percentage with .996 in 1988.
Led International League in slugging percentage with .599 in 1985.
Led Southern League batters in strikeouts with 148 in 1984.
Named International League Player of the Year, 1985.
Named Appalachian League Player of the Year, 1982.

Year	Club	League	Pos.	G.	AB.	R.	H.	2B.	3B.	HR.	RBI.	B.A.	PO.	A.	E.	F.A.
1982—Paintsville		Appal.	OF	60	239	43	72	10	2	★16	●63	.301	114	4	4	.967
1982—Oneonta		NYP	OF	4	17	3	5	1	0	2	4	.294	2	1	1	.750
1983—Fort Lauderdale		Fla. St.	OF	131	451	83	123	25	10	19	84	.273	213	8	5	.978
1983—Columbus		Int.	OF	1	3	0	0	0	0	0	0	.000	5	0	0	1.000
1984—Nashville		South.	OF	136	460	78	112	14	3	★33	91	.243	244	11	★12	.955
1985—Columbus		Int.	OF	78	287	52	92	16	5	18	69	.321	141	9	4	.974
1985—New York		Amer.	OF	60	148	17	31	3	1	9	25	.209	72	2	0	1.000
1986—Columbus		Int.	OF	32	110	25	32	3	3	6	20	.291	62	0	3	.954
1986—New York		Amer.	OF-1B	102	280	44	82	17	0	16	45	.293	172	4	2	.989
1987—New York		Amer.	OF-1B	113	318	42	74	7	1	17	42	.233	214	10	2	.991
1987—Columbus†		Int.	OF	23	85	16	29	6	0	6	15	.341	55	0	1	.982
1988—Chicago		Amer.	OF-1B	129	422	48	96	16	2	20	50	.227	316	14	2	.994
1989—Chicago‡		Amer.	OF	73	246	26	61	9	1	11	47	.248	149	3	1	.993
Major League Totals—5 Years				477	1414	177	344	52	5	73	209	.243	923	33	7	.993

Selected by New York Yankees' organization in 3rd round of free-agent draft, June 7, 1982.
†Traded with Catcher Mark Salas and Pitcher Steve Rosenberg to Chicago White Sox for Pitchers Richard Dotson and Scott Nielsen, November 12, 1987.
‡On disabled list, April 6 to May 14 and August 21, 1989 through remainder of season.

KENNETH BRIAN PATTERSON
(Ken)

Born July 8, 1964, at Costa Mesa, Calif.
Height, 6.04. Weight, 210.
Throws and bats lefthanded.
Attended McLennan Community College, Waco, Tex., and Baylor University, Waco, Tex.

Major League saves: 1988 (1).
Led New York-Pennsylvania League in shutouts with 4 in 1986.

Year	Club	League	G.	IP.	W.	L.	Pct.	H.	R.	ER.	SO.	BB.	ERA.
1985—Oneonta		NYP	6	22⅓	2	2	.500	23	14	12	21	14	4.84
1986—Fort Lauderdale		Florida St.	5	18⅔	0	2	.000	30	20	16	13	16	7.71
1986—Oneonta†		NYP	15	100⅓	9	3	.750	67	25	15	102	45	★1.35
1987—Daytona Beach		Florida St.	9	42⅔	1	3	.250	46	34	30	36	31	6.33
1987—Hawaii		P. Coast	3	3⅓	0	0	.000	1	0	0	5	3	0.00
1988—Vancouver		P. Coast	55	86⅓	6	5	.545	64	37	31	89	36	3.23
1988—Chicago		American	9	20⅔	0	2	.000	25	11	11	8	7	4.79
1989—Chicago		American	50	65⅔	6	1	.857	64	37	33	43	28	4.52
1989—Vancouver		P. Coast	2	9	0	1	.000	6	2	1	17	1	1.00
Major League Totals—2 Years			59	86⅓	6	3	.667	89	48	44	51	35	4.59

Selected by Philadelphia Phillies' organization in 29th round of free-agent draft, June 7, 1982.
Selected by Baltimore Orioles' organization in secondary phase of free-agent draft, January 11, 1983.
Selected by Philadelphia Phillies' organization in secondary phase of free-agent draft, June 6, 1983.
Selected by New York Yankees' organization in 3rd round of free-agent draft, June 3, 1985.
†Traded with a player to be named later to Chicago White Sox for Infielder-Outfielder Jerry Royster and Infielder Mike Soper, August 26, 1987; White Sox acquired Pitcher Jeff Pries to complete deal, September 19, 1987.

ROBERT CHANDLER PATTERSON
(Bob)

Born May 16, 1959, at Jacksonville, Fla.
Height, 6.02. Weight, 192.
Throws left and bats righthanded.
Received degree in industrial technology from East Carolina University, Greenville, N.C.

Major League saves: 1989 (1).

Year	Club	League	G.	IP.	W.	L.	Pct.	H.	R.	ER.	SO.	BB.	ERA.
1982—Sarasota Padres		Gulf Coast	8	52	4	3	.571	60	18	17	65	7	2.94
1982—Reno		California	4	25⅓	1	0	1.000	28	11	10	10	5	3.55
1983—Beaumont		Texas	43	116⅔	8	4	.667	107	61	52	97	36	4.01
1984—Las Vegas		P. Coast	★60	143⅓	8	9	.471	129	63	52	97	37	3.27
1985—Las Vegas		P. Coast	42	186⅓	10	11	.476	187	80	65	146	52	3.14
1985—San Diego†		National	3	4	0	0	.000	13	11	11	1	3	24.75
1986—Hawaii		P. Coast	25	156	9	6	.600	146	68	59	★137	44	3.40
1986—Pittsburgh		National	11	36⅓	2	3	.400	49	20	20	20	5	4.95
1987—Pittsburgh		National	15	43	1	4	.200	49	34	32	27	22	6.70
1987—Vancouver		P. Coast	14	89	5	2	.714	62	21	21	92	30	2.12
1988—Buffalo‡		Am. Assoc.	4	31	2	0	1.000	26	12	8	20	4	2.32
1989—Buffalo		Am. Assoc.	31	177⅓	12	6	.667	177	69	66	103	35	3.35
1989—Pittsburgh		National	12	26⅔	4	3	.571	23	13	12	20	8	4.05
Major League Totals—4 Years			41	110	7	10	.412	134	78	75	68	38	6.14

Selected by San Diego Padres' organization in 21st round of free-agent draft, June 7, 1982.
†Traded to Pittsburgh Pirates for Outfielder Marvell Wynne, April 3, 1986.
‡On disabled list, April 28, 1988 through remainder of season.

WILLIAM JOSEPH PECOTA
(Bill)

Born February 16, 1960, at Redwood City, Calif.
Height, 6.02. Weight, 190.
Throws and bats righthanded.
Attended De Anza College, Cupertino, Calif.

Major League stolen bases: 1987 (5), 1988 (7), 1989 (5). Total—17.
Led American Association third basemen in assists with 217 and total chances with 337 in 1986.
Led American Association third basemen in total chances with 372 and double plays with 22 in 1985.
Led Southern League third basemen in total chances with 434 in 1984.

Year	Club	League	Pos.	G.	AB.	R.	H.	2B.	3B.	HR.	RBI.	B.A.	PO.	A.	E.	F.A.
1981—Sara.Roy.-Blue	Gulf C.		C-3B-2B	61	208	*61	66	11	4	3	22	.317	112	45	6	.963
1982—Fort Myers	Fla. St.		3B	135	482	71	115	16	6	4	49	.239	109	243	15	.959
1983—Fort Myers	Fla. St.		3B	65	234	48	63	7	2	5	33	.269	46	114	7	.958
1983—Jacksonville	South.		3B-SS	72	260	38	63	9	1	5	25	.242	54	135	19	.909
1984—Memphis	South.		3B	145	543	84	131	19	2	9	50	.241	*142	267	25	*.942
1985—Omaha	A. A.		*3-S-O	130	409	47	98	17	3	1	34	.240	*111	*247	14	*.962
1986—Omaha	A. A.		3B-SS-OF	139	474	48	125	26	2	4	54	.264	125	238	11	.971
1986—Kansas City	Amer.		3B-SS	12	29	3	6	2	0	0	2	.207	7	31	1	.974
1987—Omaha	A. A.		3B-SS-2B	35	126	31	39	8	1	2	16	.310	38	78	8	.935
1987—Kansas City	Amer.		SS-3B-2B	66	156	22	43	5	1	3	14	.276	67	135	6	.971
1988—Kansas City	Amer.		I-O-C	90	178	25	37	3	3	1	15	.208	98	145	6	.976
1989—Kansas City	Amer.		S-O-2-3-1	65	83	21	17	4	2	3	5	.205	50	79	2	.985
1989—Omaha	A. A.		S-3-2-O	64	248	34	63	12	1	3	40	.254	96	206	8	.974
Major League Totals—4 Years				233	446	71	103	14	6	7	36	.231	222	390	15	.976

Selected by Kansas City Royals' organization in 10th round of free-agent draft, January 13, 1981.

JORGE ENRIQUE PEDRE

Born October 12, 1966, at Culver City, Calif.
Height, 6.01. Weight, 215.
Throws and bats righthanded.
Attended West Los Angeles College, Culver City, Calif.,
and Los Angeles Harbor Junior College, Wilmington, Calif.

Led Midwest League in passed balls with 27 in 1988.

Year	Club	League	Pos.	G.	AB.	R.	H.	2B.	3B.	HR.	RBI.	B.A.	PO.	A.	E.	F.A.
1987—Eugene	N'west		C-1B	64	233	28	63	15	0	13	66	.270	300	28	6	.982
1988—Appleton	Midw.		C-1B	111	412	44	112	20	2	6	54	.272	561	85	15	.977
1989—Baseball City	Fla. St.		C-1B	55	208	39	68	17	2	5	40	.327	183	25	7	.967
1989—Memphis	South.		C-1B	38	141	17	33	5	0	2	16	.234	145	10	3	.981

Selected by Atlanta Braves' organization in 11th round of free-agent draft, January 14, 1986.
Selected by Kansas City Royals' organization in 33rd round of free-agent draft, June 2, 1987.

ALFREDO JOSE PEDRIQUE (GARCIA)
(Al)

Born August 11, 1960, at Aragua, Venezuela.
Height, 6.00. Weight, 155.
Throws and bats righthanded.

Major League stolen bases: 1987 (5).
Led International League shortstops in fielding percentage with .962, assists with 321, errors with 18, total chances with 478 and double plays with 74 in 1986.
Led Texas League shortstops in fielding percentage with .961 in 1984.

Year	Club	League	Pos.	G.	AB.	R.	H.	2B.	3B.	HR.	RBI.	B.A.	PO.	A.	E.	F.A.
1978—Little Falls	NYP		SS	20	54	10	12	4	0	0	2	.222	25	48	6	.924
1979—Lynchburg	Carol.		SS	19	49	2	11	2	0	0	3	.224	22	63	6	.934
1979—Little Falls	NYP		SS-2B	33	92	3	21	0	2	0	11	.228	56	90	19	.885
1980—Lynchburg	Carol.		SS-2B-3B	105	321	37	79	3	2	0	24	.246	120	234	24	.937
1981—Jackson	Texas		SS-2B	115	379	39	91	9	0	0	25	.240	184	324	34	.937
1982—Jackson	Texas		SS	121	392	38	86	13	2	2	36	.219	189	370	23	*.960
1983—Jackson	Texas		SS-2B-3B	102	326	43	78	7	1	0	27	.239	182	292	20	.960
1984—Jackson†	Texas		SS-2B-3B	109	362	47	103	15	5	1	35	.285	198	281	21	.958
1985—Tidewater	Int.		S-3-1-2	110	325	39	82	17	2	2	24	.252	170	261	12	.973
1986—Tidewater	Int.		S-1-3-2	112	379	49	111	13	2	0	41	.293	189	340	19	.965
1987—N. Y.‡-Pitt.	Nat.		SS-2B-3B	93	252	24	74	10	1	1	27	.294	118	196	11	.966
1987—Tidewater	Int.		2-3-1-S	10	27	2	7	0	0	0	3	.259	14	17	0	1.000
1988—Pittsburgh	Nat.		SS-3B	50	128	7	23	5	0	0	4	.180	65	124	5	.974
1988—Buffalo§	A. A.		2B-SS-3B	61	218	23	67	14	2	1	22	.307	101	205	12	.962
1989—Detroit	Amer.		SS-3B-2B	31	69	1	14	3	0	0	5	.203	35	62	3	.970
1989—Toledo x	Int.		SS-3B-2B	56	193	15	40	8	0	1	21	.207	93	178	11	.961
Major League Totals—3 Years				174	449	32	111	18	1	1	36	.247	218	382	19	.969

Signed as free agent by New York Mets' organization, July 21, 1978.
†Granted free agency, October 15, 1984; re-signed by Mets' organization, November 12, 1984.
‡Traded with Outfielder Scott Little to Pittsburgh Pirates for Infielder-Outfielder Bill Almon, May 29, 1987.
§Released, November 20, 1988; signed by Detroit Tigers, December 5, 1988.
xGranted free agency, October 15, 1989.

JULIO CESAR PEGUERO

Born September 7, 1968, at San Isidro, Dominican Republic.
Height, 6.00. Weight, 160.
Throws right and bats left and righthanded.

Year Club League	Pos.	G.	AB.	R.	H.	2B.	3B.	HR.	RBI.	B.A.	PO.	A.	E.	F.A.
1987—Macon.................. S. Atl.	OF-2B	132	520	88	148	11	6	4	53	.285	251	19	17	.941
1988—Salem.................... Carol.	OF-2B	128	517	89	135	17	5	5	50	.261	291	15	8	.975
1989—Harrisburg† .... East.	OF	76	284	34	70	14	1	2	21	.246	163	6	2	.988

Signed as free agent by Pittsburgh Pirates' organization, July 30, 1986.
†On disabled list, July 12, 1989 through remainder of season.

STEVEN ANTONE PEGUES
(Steve)

Born May 21, 1968, at Pontotoc, Miss.
Height, 6.02. Weight, 170.
Throws and bats righthanded.

Year Club League	Pos.	G.	AB.	R.	H.	2B.	3B.	HR.	RBI.	B.A.	PO.	A.	E.	F.A.
1987—Bristol.................... Appal.	OF	59	236	36	67	6	5	2	23	.284	114	4	10	.922
1988—Fayetteville†........ S. Atl.	OF	118	437	50	112	17	5	6	46	.256	240	13	12	.955
1989—Fayetteville.......... S. Atl.	OF	70	269	35	83	11	6	1	38	.309	127	8	2	.985
1989—Lakeland............... Fla. St.	OF	55	193	24	49	7	2	0	15	.254	115	3	2	.983

Selected by Detroit Tigers' organization in 1st round (21st player selected) of free-agent draft, June 2, 1987.
†Batted left and righthanded.

ALEJANDRO PENA (VASQUEZ)

Born June 25, 1959, at Cambiaso, Dominican Republic.
Height, 6.01. Weight, 212.
Throws and bats righthanded.

Major League saves: 1981 (2), 1983 (1), 1986 (1), 1987 (11), 1988 (12), 1989 (5). Total—32.
Tied for National League lead in shutouts with 4 in 1984.
Led Pacific Coast League in saves with 22 in 1981.

Year Club League	G.	IP.	W.	L.	Pct.	H.	R.	ER.	SO.	BB.	ERA.
1979—Clinton............................ Midwest	21	71	3	3	.500	53	39	33	57	44	4.18
1980—Vero Beach.................... Florida St.	35	73	10	3	.769	57	32	26	46	41	3.21
1981—Albuquerque .... P. Coast	38	56	2	5	.286	36	12	10	40	21	1.61
1981—Los Angeles .... National	14	25	1	1	.500	18	8	8	14	11	2.88
1982—Los Angeles .... National	29	35⅔	0	2	.000	37	24	19	20	21	4.79
1982—Albuquerque .... P. Coast	16	28⅔	1	1	.500	37	18	17	27	10	5.34
1983—Los Angeles .... National	34	177	12	9	.571	152	67	54	120	51	2.75
1984—Los Angeles .... National	28	199⅓	12	6	.667	186	67	55	135	46	★2.48
1985—Los Angeles† .... National	2	4⅓	0	1	.000	7	5	4	2	3	8.31
1986—Vero Beach‡.................... Florida St.	4	15⅔	0	2	.000	22	15	13	11	4	7.47
1986—Los Angeles .... National	24	70	1	2	.333	74	40	38	46	30	4.89
1987—Los Angeles§ .... National	37	87⅓	2	7	.222	82	41	34	76	37	3.50
1988—Los Angeles x .... National	60	94⅓	6	7	.462	75	29	20	83	27	1.91
1989—Los Angeles yz .... National	53	76	4	3	.571	62	20	18	75	18	2.13
Major League Totals—9 Years............................	281	769	38	38	.500	693	301	250	571	244	2.93

Signed as free agent by Los Angeles Dodgers' organization, September 10, 1978.
†On disabled list, April 8 to September 5, 1985.
‡On Los Angeles disabled list, March 23 to May 26, 1986; included rehabilitation disability assignment to Vero
Beach, May 2 to May 19, 1986.
§On disabled list, July 27 to August 17, 1987.
xGranted free agency, November 4, 1988; re-signed by Dodgers, November 7, 1988.
yOn disabled list, July 8 to July 23, 1989.
zTraded with Outfielder Mike Marshall to New York Mets for Outfielder Juan Samuel, December 20, 1989.

CHAMPIONSHIP SERIES RECORD

Year Club League	G.	IP.	W.	L.	Pct.	H.	R.	ER.	SO.	BB.	ERA.
1981—Los Angeles .... National	2	2⅓	0	0	.000	1	0	0	0	0	0.00
1983—Los Angeles .... National	1	2⅔	0	0	.000	4	2	2	3	1	6.75
1988—Los Angeles .... National	3	4⅓	1	1	.500	1	2	2	1	5	4.15
Championship Series Totals—3 Years................	6	9⅓	1	1	.500	6	4	4	4	6	3.86

WORLD SERIES RECORD

Year Club League	G.	IP.	W.	L.	Pct.	H.	R.	ER.	SO.	BB.	ERA.
1988—Los Angeles .... National	2	5	1	0	1.000	2	0	0	7	1	0.00

Eligible for 1981 World Series with Los Angeles Dodgers; did not play.

ANTONIO FRANCISCO PENA (PADILLA)
(Tony)

Born June 4, 1957, at Monte Cristi, Dominican Republic.
Height, 6.00. Weight, 184.
Throws and bats righthanded.
Brother of Ramon Pena, pitcher in Detroit Tigers' organization; and related
to Jose Pena, catcher in San Francisco Giants' organization.

Major League stolen bases: 1981 (1), 1982 (2), 1983 (6), 1984 (12), 1985 (12), 1986 (9), 1987 (6), 1988 (6), 1989 (5). Total—59.

Tied for National League lead in grounding into double plays with 21 in 1986.
Led National League catchers in fielding percentage with .994 in 1988.
Led National League catchers in assists with 100 in 1985.
Led National League catchers in double plays with 15 in 1984 and 13 in 1989.
Led National League catchers in total chances with 1,075 in 1983, 999 in 1984 and 1,034 in 1985.
Led Eastern League catchers in double plays with 14 in 1979.
Led Carolina League catchers in double plays with 9 in 1977.
Tied for Carolina League lead in passed balls with 16 in 1977.
Named catcher on The Sporting News National League All-Star Team, 1983.
Named catcher on The Sporting News National League All-Star fielding team, 1983 through 1985.

Year—Club	League	Pos.	G.	AB.	R.	H.	2B.	3B.	HR.	RBI.	B.A.	PO.	A.	E.	F.A.
1976—Bradenton Pir.	Gulf C.	O-1-C-3	33	110	10	23	2	2	1	11	.209	108	14	4	.968
1976—Charleston	W. Car.	C	14	49	4	11	2	0	1	8	.224	64	7	2	.973
1977—Charleston	W. Car.	C	29	101	10	24	4	0	3	16	.238	172	19	6	.970
1977—Salem	Carol.	C	84	319	36	88	15	3	7	46	.276	★470	★66	★17	.969
1978—Shreveport	Texas	C	104	348	34	80	14	0	8	42	.230	637	54	★25	.965
1979—Buffalo	East.	C	134	515	89	161	16	4	34	97	.313	★768	★120	★26	.972
1980—Portland	P. C.	C	124	452	57	148	24	13	9	77	.327	★639	85	●23	.969
1980—Pittsburgh	Nat.	C	8	21	1	9	1	1	0	1	.429	38	2	2	.952
1981—Pittsburgh	Nat.	C	66	210	16	63	9	1	2	17	.300	286	41	5	.985
1982—Pittsburgh	Nat.	C	138	497	53	147	28	4	11	63	.296	763	89	16	.982
1983—Pittsburgh	Nat.	C	151	542	51	163	22	3	15	70	.301	★976	90	9	.992
1984—Pittsburgh	Nat.	C	147	546	77	156	27	2	15	78	.286	★895	★95	9	.991
1985—Pittsburgh	Nat.	C-1B	147	546	53	136	27	2	10	59	.249	925	102	12	.988
1986—Pittsburgh†	Nat.	★C-1B	144	510	56	147	26	2	10	52	.288	824	99	★18	.981
1987—St. Louis‡	Nat.	C-1B-OF	116	384	40	82	13	4	5	44	.214	624	51	8	.988
1987—Louisville	A. A.	C	2	8	0	3	0	0	0	0	.375	7	1	0	1.000
1988—St. Louis	Nat.	C-1B	149	505	55	133	23	1	10	51	.263	796	72	6	.993
1989—St. Louis§	Nat.	C-OF	141	424	36	110	17	2	4	37	.259	675	70	2	★.997
Major League Totals—10 Years			1207	4185	438	1146	193	22	82	472	.274	6802	711	87	.989

Signed as free agent by Pittsburgh Pirates' organization, July 22, 1975.
†Traded to St. Louis Cardinals for Outfielder Andy Van Slyke, Catcher Mike LaValliere and Pitcher Mike Dunne, April 1, 1987.
‡On disabled list, April 11 to May 22, 1987; included rehabilitation disability assignment to Louisville, May 19 to May 22, 1987.
§Granted free agency, November 13, 1989; signed by Boston Red Sox, November 27, 1989.

CHAMPIONSHIP SERIES RECORD

Year—Club	League	Pos.	G.	AB.	R.	H.	2B.	3B.	HR.	RBI.	B.A.	PO.	A.	E.	F.A.
1987—St. Louis	Nat.	C	7	21	5	8	0	1	0	0	.381	55	5	0	1.000

WORLD SERIES RECORD

Year—Club	League	Pos.	G.	AB.	R.	H.	2B.	3B.	HR.	RBI.	B.A.	PO.	A.	E.	F.A.
1987—St. Louis	Nat.	C-DH	7	22	2	9	1	0	0	4	.409	32	1	1	.971

ALL-STAR GAME RECORD

Year—League	Pos.	AB.	R.	H.	2B.	3B.	HR.	RBI.	B.A.	PO.	A.	E.	F.A.
1982—National	PR-C	1	0	0	0	0	0	0	.000	3	0	0	1.000
1984—National	C	0	0	0	0	0	0	0	.000	2	0	0	1.000
1985—National	C	1	0	0	0	0	0	0	.000	4	1	0	1.000
1986—National	PR	0	0	0	0	0	0	0	.000	0	0	0	.000
1989—National	PH-C	2	0	0	0	0	0	0	.000	2	0	0	1.000
All-Star Game Totals—5 Years		4	0	0	0	0	0	0	.000	11	1	0	1.000

GERONIMO PENA

Born March 29, 1967, at Distrito Nacional, D. R.
Height, 6.01. Weight, 170.
Throws right and bats left and righthanded.

Led South Atlantic League in stolen bases with 80 in 1987.
Led Appalachian League in intentional bases on balls received with 4 in 1986.
Led Florida State League second basemen in total chances with 723 and double plays with 103 in 1988.
Led South Atlantic League shortstops in putouts with 324, assists with 342, total chances with 695 and double plays with 80 in 1987.

Year—Club	League	Pos.	G.	AB.	R.	H.	2B.	3B.	HR.	RBI.	B.A.	PO.	A.	E.	F.A.
1986—Johnson City†	Appal.	2B	56	202	★55	60	7	4	3	20	.297	108	144	7	.973
1987—Savannah†	S. Atl.	★2B-SS	134	505	95	136	28	3	9	51	.269	325	343	★29	.958
1988—St. Petersburg	Fla. St.	2B	130	484	82	125	25	10	4	35	.258	★301	★402	20	★.972
1989—St. Petersburg‡	Fla. St.	2B	6	21	2	4	1	0	0	2	.190	9	19	1	.966
1989—Arkansas	Texas	2B	77	267	61	79	16	8	9	44	.296	177	208	14	.965

Signed as free agent by St. Louis Cardinals' organization, August 9, 1984.
†Batted righthanded only.
‡On St. Louis disabled list, March 25 to June 5, 1989; included rehabilitation disability assignment to St. Petersburg, May 29 to June 5, 1989.

—DID YOU KNOW—

That the Dodgers' Tim Belcher led the majors in shutouts with eight in 1989, a figure that equaled or exceeded the total of seven other major league teams last year?

JOSE LUIS PENA

Born April 24, 1965, at Bonao, Dominican Republic.
Height, 6.00. Weight, 190.
Throws and bats righthanded.
Related to Tony Pena, catcher with Boston Red Sox;
and Ramon Pena, pitcher in Detroit Tigers' organization.

Year	Club	League	Pos.	G.	AB.	R.	H.	2B.	3B.	HR.	RBI.	B.A.	PO.	A.	E.	F.A.
1983—Great Falls	Pion.		C	30	81	7	19	0	0	0	8	.235	132	10	4	.973
1984—Clinton	Midw.		C	70	222	20	39	8	0	3	26	.176	409	40	14	.970
1985—Clinton	Midw.		C	82	262	26	69	20	0	1	24	.263	321	43	10	.973
1986—Clinton	Midw.		C	102	350	30	87	18	0	5	53	.249	483	57	5	.991
1987—Fresno	Calif.		C	80	266	43	74	11	1	4	35	.278	254	46	8	.974
1988—Shreveport	Texas		C	98	314	29	77	19	1	4	36	.245	539	50	10	.983
1989—Shreveport	Texas		C	50	177	18	43	12	1	1	7	.243	300	39	4	.988
1989—Phoenix†	P. C.		C	32	108	6	24	3	1	1	9	.222	171	18	4	.979

Signed as free agent by San Francisco Giants' organization, January 17, 1983.
†On disabled list, July 27 to August 7, 1989.

RAMON ARTURO PENA

Born May 13, 1962, at Santiago, Dominican Republic.
Height, 5.10. Weight, 155.
Throws and bats righthanded.
Brother of Tony Pena, catcher with Boston Red Sox; and related
to Jose Pena, catcher in San Francisco Giants' organization.

Tied for Eastern League lead in intentional bases on balls issued with 10 in 1986.

Year	Club	League	G.	IP.	W.	L.	Pct.	H.	R.	ER.	SO.	BB.	ERA.
1980—Bradenton Pirates	Gulf Coast		13	25	0	2	.000	23	12	9	11	9	3.24
1981—Bradenton Pirates†‡	Gulf Coast						(Did not play)						
1982-83							(Out of Organized Baseball)						
1984—Lakeland	Florida St.		20	37⅔	6	1	.857	22	8	7	41	14	1.67
1984—Birmingham	Southern		40	67⅓	3	8	.273	63	32	28	47	28	3.74
1985—Birmingham	Southern		47	95⅓	6	7	.462	95	53	46	70	44	4.34
1986—Glens Falls	Eastern		54	107¼	7	1	.875	85	35	31	63	39	2.60
1987—Glens Falls	Eastern		43	67⅔	5	6	.455	76	24	21	36	16	2.79
1987—Toledo	Int'national		18	42	0	1	.000	36	10	8	21	10	1.71
1988—Toledo	Int'national		★62	90	2	5	.286	83	38	34	78	19	3.40
1989—Toledo	Int'national		33	61	5	2	.714	57	24	17	51	15	2.51
1989—Detroit§x	American		8	18	0	0	.000	26	13	12	12	8	6.00
Major League Totals—1 Year			8	18	0	0	.000	26	13	12	12	8	6.00

Signed as free agent by Pittsburgh Pirates' organization, May 16, 1980.
†On restricted list, June 20, 1981 through remainder of season.
‡Released, April 4, 1982; signed by Birmingham (Detroit Tigers' organization), January 7, 1984.
§On disabled list, May 18 to June 8, 1984.
xGranted free agency, October 15, 1989.

RECORD AS OUTFIELDER

Year	Club	League	Pos.	G.	AB.	R.	H.	2B.	3B.	HR.	RBI.	B.A.	PO.	A.	E.	F.A.
1989—Bradenton Pir.	Gulf C.		OF-P	22	52	5	9	0	1	0	7	.173	30	3	2	.943

TERRY LEE PENDLETON

Born July 16, 1960, at Los Angeles, Calif.
Height, 5.09. Weight, 178.
Throws right and bats left and righthanded.
Attended Oxnard College, Oxnard, Calif. and Fresno State University, Fresno, Calif.

Major League stolen bases: 1984 (20), 1985 (17), 1986 (24), 1987 (19), 1988 (3), 1989 (9). Total—92.
Led National League third basemen in total chances with 524 in 1986, 512 in 1987 and 520 in 1989.
Led National League third basemen in double plays with 36 in 1986.
Led American Association third basemen in putouts with 88 and fielding percentage with .964 in 1984.
Named third baseman on THE SPORTING NEWS National League All-Star fielding team, 1987 and 1989.

Year	Club	League	Pos.	G.	AB.	R.	H.	2B.	3B.	HR.	RBI.	B.A.	PO.	A.	E.	F.A.
1982—Johnson City	Appal.		2B	43	181	38	58	14	●4	4	27	.320	79	105	17	.915
1982—St. Petersburg	Fla. St.		2B	20	69	4	18	2	1	1	7	.261	41	51	2	.979
1983—Arkansas†	Texas		2B	48	185	29	51	10	3	4	20	.276	94	135	7	.970
1984—Louisville	A. A.		3B-2B	91	330	52	98	23	5	4	44	.297	91	157	10	.961
1984—St. Louis	Nat.		3B	67	262	37	85	16	3	1	33	.324	59	155	13	.943
1985—St. Louis‡	Nat.		3B	149	559	56	134	16	3	5	69	.240	129	361	18	.965
1986—St. Louis	Nat.		★3B-OF	159	578	56	138	26	5	1	59	.239	★133	★371	20	.962
1987—St. Louis	Nat.		3B	159	583	82	167	29	4	12	96	.286	117	★369	26	.949
1988—St. Louis§	Nat.		3B	110	391	44	99	20	2	6	53	.253	75	239	12	.963
1989—St. Louis	Nat.		3B	162	613	83	162	28	5	13	74	.264	113	★392	15	★.971
Major League Totals—6 Years				806	2986	358	785	135	22	38	384	.263	626	1887	104	.960

Selected by St. Louis Cardinals' organization in 7th round of free-agent draft, June 7, 1982.
†On disabled list, April 8 to May 23 and July 16 to September 5, 1983.
‡On disabled list June 15 to June 30, 1985.
§On disabled list, May 28 to June 24, 1988.

Shares Championship Series record for most at-bats, inning (2), October 13, 1985, second inning.

Year	Club	League	Pos.	G.	AB.	R.	H.	2B.	3B.	HR.	RBI.	B.A.	PO.	A.	E.	F.A.
1985—St. Louis	Nat.		3B	6	24	2	5	1	0	0	4	.208	6	18	1	.960
1987—St. Louis	Nat.		3B	6	19	3	4	0	1	0	1	.211	3	11	0	1.000
Championship Series Totals—2 Years				12	43	5	9	1	1	0	5	.209	9	29	1	.974

WORLD SERIES RECORD

Year	Club	League	Pos.	G.	AB.	R.	H.	2B.	3B.	HR.	RBI.	B.A.	PO.	A.	E.	F.A.
1985—St. Louis	Nat.		3B	7	23	3	6	1	1	0	3	.261	6	14	1	.952
1987—St. Louis	Nat.		DH-PH	3	7	2	3	0	0	0	1	.429	0	0	0	.000
World Series Totals—2 Years				10	30	5	9	1	1	0	4	.300	6	14	1	.952

MELIDO T. PEREZ

Born February 15, 1966, at San Cristobal, D. R.
Height, 6.04. Weight, 180.
Throws and bats righthanded.
Brother of Pascual Perez, pitcher with New York Yankees; and Valerio Perez,
pitcher in Kansas City Royals' organization, 1983 and 1984.

Led Midwest League in complete games with 13 in 1986.
Tied for Northwest League lead in games started by pitchers with 15, balks with 2 and home runs allowed with 13 in 1985.

Year	Club	League	G.	IP.	W.	L.	Pct.	H.	R.	ER.	SO.	BB.	ERA.
1984—Charleston	S. Atlantic		16	89	5	7	.417	99	52	43	55	19	4.35
1985—Eugene	Northwest		17	101	6	7	.462	116	65	*61	88	35	5.44
1986—Burlington	Midwest		28	170⅓	10	12	.455	148	83	70	153	49	3.70
1987—Fort Myers	Florida St.		8	64⅓	4	3	.571	51	20	17	51	7	2.38
1987—Memphis	Southern		20	133⅔	8	5	.615	125	60	51	126	20	3.43
1987—Kansas City†	American		3	10⅓	1	1	.500	18	12	9	5	5	7.84
1988—Chicago	American		32	197	12	10	.545	186	105	83	138	72	3.79
1989—Chicago	American		31	183⅓	11	14	.440	187	106	102	141	90	5.01
Major League Totals—3 Years			66	390⅔	24	25	.490	391	223	194	284	167	4.47

Signed as free agent by Kansas City Royals' organization, July 22, 1983.
†Traded with Pitchers John Davis, Chuck Mount and Greg Hibbard to Chicago White Sox for Pitcher Floyd Bannister and Infielder Dave Cochrane, December 10, 1987.

MICHAEL IRVIN PEREZ

(Mike)

Born October 19, 1964, at Yauco, Puerto Rico.
Height, 6.00. Weight, 185.
Throws and bats righthanded.
Attended San Jose City College, San Jose, Calif.,
and Troy State University, Troy, Ala.

Led Texas League in saves with 33 and games finished in relief with 51 in 1989.
Led Midwest League in saves with 41 and games finished in relief with 51 in 1987.

Year	Club	League	G.	IP.	W.	L.	Pct.	H.	R.	ER.	SO.	BB.	ERA.
1986—Johnson City	Ap'lachian		18	72⅔	3	5	.375	69	35	24	72	22	2.97
1987—Springfield	Midwest		58	84⅓	6	2	.750	47	12	8	119	21	0.85
1988—Arkansas	Texas		11	14⅓	1	3	.250	18	18	18	17	13	11.30
1988—St. Petersburg	Florida St.		35	43⅓	2	2	.500	24	12	10	45	16	2.08
1989—Arkansas	Texas		57	76⅔	4	6	.400	68	34	31	74	32	3.64

Selected by St. Louis Cardinals' organization in 12th round of free-agent draft, June 2, 1986.

PASCUAL GROSS PEREZ

Born May 17, 1957, at San Cristobal, Dominican Republic.
Height, 6.03. Weight, 175.
Throws and bats righthanded.
Brother of Melido Perez, pitcher with Chicago White Sox; and Valerio Perez,
pitcher in Kansas City Royals' organization, 1983 and 1984.

Pitched five-inning, 1-0 no-hit victory against Philadelphia Phillies, September 24, 1988.
Tied for National League lead in balks with 10 in 1988.
Led Western Carolinas League in balks with 6 in 1977.
Tied for American Association lead in shutouts with 2 in 1987.
Tied for Carolina League lead in shutouts with 5 in 1978.
Named American Association Pitcher of the Year, 1987.

Year	Club	League	G.	IP.	W.	L.	Pct.	H.	R.	ER.	SO.	BB.	ERA.
1976—Bradenton Pirates†	Gulf Coast		10	56	2	5	.286	51	41	29	34	35	4.66
1977—Charleston	W. Carol.		25	156	10	5	.667	153	80	69	96	60	3.98
1978—Salem	Carolina		24	152	11	7	.611	133	70	44	126	51	2.61
1978—Columbus	Int'national		1	5	0	0	.000	4	0	0	4	1	0.00
1979—Portland‡	P. Coast		20	103	9	7	.563	121	70	63	51	47	5.50
1980—Portland	P. Coast		24	160	12	10	.545	172	76	72	105	48	4.05
1980—Pittsburgh	National		2	12	0	1	.000	15	6	5	7	2	3.75
1981—Portland	P. Coast		5	31	1	2	.333	40	19	17	11	14	4.94
1981—Pittsburgh	National		17	86	2	7	.222	92	50	38	46	34	3.98

Year—Club	League	G.	IP.	W.	L.	Pct.	H.	R.	ER.	SO.	BB.	ERA.
1982—Portland§	P. Coast	19	106⅓	4	9	.308	111	59	57	59	37	4.82
1982—Richmond	Int'national	5	43	5	0	1.000	32	7	6	27	8	1.26
1982—Atlanta	National	16	79⅓	4	4	.500	85	35	27	29	17	3.06
1983—Atlanta	National	33	215⅓	15	8	.652	213	88	82	144	51	3.43
1984—Atlanta x	National	30	211⅔	14	8	.636	208	96	88	145	51	3.74
1985—Atlanta yza	National	22	95⅓	1	13	.071	115	72	65	57	57	6.14
1986—						(Out of Organized Baseball)						
1987—Indianapolis	Am. Assoc.	19	133	9	7	.563	128	65	56	125	34	★3.79
1987—Montreal	National	10	70⅓	7	0	1.000	52	21	18	58	16	2.30
1988—Montreal b	National	27	188	12	8	.600	133	59	51	131	44	2.44
1988—Indianapolis	Am. Assoc.	2	7⅔	0	0	.000	4	1	1	7	4	1.17
1989—Montreal c	National	33	198⅓	9	13	.409	178	85	73	152	45	3.31
Major League Totals—9 Years		190	1156⅓	64	62	.508	1091	512	447	769	317	3.48

Signed as free agent by Pittsburgh Pirates' organization, January 27, 1976.

†On suspended list, August 26 to August 28, 1976.

‡On disabled list, July 16 to August 14, 1979.

§Traded with a player to be named later to Atlanta Braves' organization for Pitcher Larry McWilliams, June 30, 1982; Atlanta organization acquired Shortstop Carlos Rios to complete deal, September 8, 1982.

xOn suspended list, April 3 to May 1, 1984.

yOn disabled list, May 5 to May 25, June 1 to June 22 and August 13 to September 3, 1985.

zOn suspended list, July 22, 1985; then transferred to restricted list, July 25 to August 4, 1985.

aReleased, April 1, 1986; signed by Indianapolis (Montreal Expos' organization), February 16, 1987.

bOn disabled list, May 8 to June 21, 1988; included rehabilitation disability assignment to Indianapolis, June 13 to June 21, 1988.

cGranted free agency, November 13, 1989; signed by New York Yankees, November 21, 1989.

CHAMPIONSHIP SERIES RECORD

Year—Club	League	G.	IP.	W.	L.	Pct.	H.	R.	ER.	SO.	BB.	ERA.
1982—Atlanta	National	2	8⅔	0	1	.000	10	5	5	4	2	5.19

ALL-STAR GAME RECORD

Year—League		IP.	W.	L.	Pct.	H.	R.	ER.	SO.	BB.	ERA.
1983—National		⅔	0	0	.000	3	2	2	1	1	27.00

YORKIS MIGUEL PEREZ

Born September 30, 1967, at Bajos de Haina, D. R.
Height, 6.01. Weight, 160.
Throws and bats lefthanded.

Year—Club	League	G.	IP.	W.	L.	Pct.	H.	R.	ER.	SO.	BB.	ERA.
1983—Elizabethton	Ap'lachian	3	4	0	1	.000	5	9	9	6	9	20.25
1984—Elizabethton	Ap'lachian	1	1⅓	0	0	.000	1	0	0	1	1	0.00
1985—Santiago	Dom. Rep.	21	122	6	8	.429	104	58	43	69	63	3.18
1986—Kenosha†	Midwest	31	131	4	11	.267	120	81	75	144	88	5.15
1987—West Palm Beach	Florida St.	15	100	6	2	.750	78	36	26	111	46	2.34
1987—Jacksonville	Southern	12	60	2	7	.222	61	34	27	60	30	4.05
1988—Jacksonville	Southern	27	130	8	12	.400	142	96	84	105	94	5.82
1989—West Palm Beach	Florida St.	18	94⅔	7	6	.538	62	34	29	85	54	2.76
1989—Jacksonville	Southern	20	35	4	3	.571	25	16	14	50	34	3.60

Signed as free agent by Minnesota Twins' organization, February 23, 1983.

†Traded with Pitchers Neal Heaton and Al Cardwood and Catcher Jeff Reed to Montreal Expos for Pitcher Jeff Reardon and Catcher Tom Nieto, February 3, 1987.

ANTONIO LLAMAS PEREZCHICA
(Tony)

Born April 20, 1966, at Mexicali, Mex.
Height, 5.11. Weight, 175.
Throws and bats righthanded.

Led Midwest League shortstops in total chances with 599 in 1985.

Year—Club	League	Pos.	G.	AB.	R.	H.	2B.	3B.	HR.	RBI.	B.A.	PO.	A.	E.	F.A.
1984—Everett	N'west	SS	33	119	10	23	6	1	0	10	.193	45	73	18	.868
1985—Clinton	Midw.	SS	127	452	54	109	21	●8	4	40	.241	★224	332	43	.928
1986—Fresno	Calif.	SS-3B	126	452	65	126	30	8	9	54	.279	224	303	42	.926
1987—Shreveport	Texas	SS-2B	89	332	44	106	24	1	11	47	.319	144	258	16	.962
1988—Phoenix	P. C.	2B-SS-OF	134	517	79	158	18	●10	9	64	.306	255	381	29	.956
1988—San Francisco	Nat.	2B	7	8	1	1	0	0	0	1	.125	5	5	0	1.000
1989—Phoenix†	P. C.	2B-SS	94	307	40	71	11	3	8	33	.231	155	224	8	.979
Major League Totals—1 Year			7	8	1	1	0	0	0	1	.125	5	5	0	1.000

Selected by San Francisco Giants' organization in 3rd round of free-agent draft, June 4, 1984.

†On disabled list, April 21 to May 5 and August 19 to August 31, 1989.

GERALD JUNE PERRY

Born October 30, 1960, at Savannah, Ga.
Height, 6.00. Weight, 190.
Throws right and bats lefthanded.
Nephew of Dan Driessen, first baseman with Cincinnati Reds, Montreal Expos, San Francisco Giants, Houston Astros and St. Louis Cardinals, 1973 through 1987.

Major League stolen bases: 1984 (15), 1985 (9), 1987 (42), 1988 (29), 1989 (10). Total—105.
Led International League in game-winning RBIs with 17 and tied for lead in intentional bases on balls received with 8 in 1986.
Led Carolina League first basemen in double plays with 109 in 1980.
Led Gulf Coast League first basemen in double plays with 46 in 1978.

Year	Club	League	Pos.	G.	AB.	R.	H.	2B.	3B.	HR.	RBI.	B.A.	PO.	A.	E.	F.A.
1978—Bradenton Brav...	Gulf C.		1B	★55	191	32	51	★12	3	1	26	.267	★479	★37	6	★.989
1979—Greenwood	W. Car.		1B	109	400	69	133	17	4	9	71	★.333	881	59	19	.980
1980—Durham	Carol.		1B	138	497	102	124	19	5	15	92	.249	★1296	93	16	.989
1981—Savannah	South.		1B	137	476	71	132	18	3	19	84	.277	1221	86	18	.986
1982—Richmond	Int.		1B	133	492	94	146	22	4	15	92	.297	1110	94	●17	.986
1983—Richmond	Int.		1B	113	423	81	133	21	8	13	71	.314	943	88	11	.989
1983—Atlanta	Nat.		1B-OF	27	39	5	14	2	0	1	6	.359	55	0	1	.982
1984—Atlanta	Nat.		1B-OF	122	347	52	92	12	2	7	47	.265	550	28	12	.980
1985—Atlanta	Nat.		1B-OF	110	238	22	51	5	0	3	13	.214	541	37	9	.985
1986—Richmond	Int.		OF-1B	107	384	69	125	30	5	10	75	.326	394	25	7	.984
1986—Atlanta	Nat.		OF-1B	29	70	6	19	2	0	2	11	.271	24	1	2	.926
1987—Atlanta	Nat.		1B-OF	142	533	77	144	35	2	12	74	.270	1297	72	14	.990
1988—Atlanta†	Nat.		1B	141	547	61	164	29	1	8	74	.300	1282	106	●17	.988
1989—Atlanta‡§	Nat.		1B	72	266	24	67	11	0	4	21	.252	618	51	9	.987
Major League Totals—7 Years				643	2040	247	551	96	5	37	246	.270	4367	295	64	.986

Selected by Atlanta Braves' organization in 11th round of free-agent draft, June 6, 1978.
†On disabled list, June 19 to July 4, 1988.
‡On disabled list, June 6 to June 21 and July 10, 1989 through remainder of season.
§Traded with Pitcher Jim Lemasters to Kansas City Royals for Pitchers Charlie Leibrandt and Rick Luecken, December 15, 1989.

ALL-STAR GAME RECORD

Year	League	Pos.	AB.	R.	H.	2B.	3B.	HR.	RBI.	B.A.	PO.	A.	E.	F.A.
1988—National		PH	1	0	0	0	0	0	0	.000	0	0	0	.000

WILLIAM PATRICK PERRY
(Pat)

Born February 4, 1959, at Taylorville, Ill.
Height, 6.01. Weight, 190.
Throws and bats lefthanded.
Attended Lincoln Land Community College, Springfield, Ill.

Major League saves: 1986 (2), 1987 (2), 1988 (1), 1989 (1). Total—6.
Tied for Gulf Coast League lead in shutouts with 2 in 1978.

Year	Club	League	G.	IP.	W.	L.	Pct.	H.	R.	ER.	SO.	BB.	ERA.
1978—Sarasota Astros	Gulf Coast	12	35	2	4	.333	29	15	9	35	14	2.31
1979—Daytona Beach	Florida St.	12	51	2	3	.400	64	31	30	30	16	5.29
1979—Sarasota Astros	Gulf Coast	9	49	3	1	.750	55	21	20	24	16	3.67
1980—Daytona Beach	Florida St.	22	115	9	5	.643	121	51	38	54	46	2.97
1981—Columbus	Southern	27	51	3	1	.750	54	40	36	35	38	6.35
1981—Daytona Beach	Florida St.	9	20	2	0	1.000	11	6	6	22	7	2.70
1982—Columbus†	Southern	22	37⅔	4	0	1.000	32	19	17	28	18	4.06
1983—Columbus‡§	Southern	11	49	5	2	.714	60	30	22	27	21	4.04
1983—Buffalo x	Eastern	4	5⅓	0	0	.000	8	5	4	4	4	6.75
1983—Springfield	Midwest	6	24⅓	1	1	.500	17	6	6	31	5	2.22
1984—Arkansas	Texas	25	48⅔	4	2	.667	34	8	6	51	17	1.11
1984—Louisville	Am. Assoc.	21	44⅔	4	3	.571	35	12	11	43	21	2.22
1985—Louisville	Am. Assoc.	45	91	4	3	.571	56	33	24	63	39	2.37
1985—St. Louis	National	6	12⅓	1	0	1.000	3	0	0	6	3	0.00
1986—St. Louis	National	46	68⅔	2	3	.400	59	31	29	29	34	3.80
1986—Louisville	Am. Assoc.	5	11	1	0	1.000	8	6	4	7	6	3.27
1987—St. Louis y-Cincinnati	National	57	81	5	2	.714	60	34	32	39	25	3.56
1988—Cincinnati z-Chicago a	National	47	58⅔	4	4	.500	61	32	27	35	16	4.14
1988—Iowa	Am. Assoc.	2	3	0	0	.000	0	0	0	4	0	0.00
1989—Chicago b	National	19	35⅔	0	1	.000	23	8	7	20	16	1.77
1989—Iowa c	Am. Assoc.	5	4⅓	1	0	1.000	3	3	3	4	6	6.23
Major League Totals—5 Years		175	256⅓	12	10	.545	206	105	95	129	94	3.34

Selected by Houston Astros' organization in 2nd round of free-agent draft, January 10, 1978.
†On disabled list, May 6 to May 24 and August 1, 1982 through remainder of season.
‡On disabled list, May 24 to June 15, 1983.
§Released, June 24, 1983; signed by Buffalo (Cleveland Indians' organization), July 1, 1983.
xReleased, July 12, 1983; signed by Springfield (St. Louis Cardinals' organization), August 3, 1983.
yTraded to Cincinnati Reds for a player to be named later, August 31, 1987; St. Louis Cardinals acquired Pitcher Scott Terry to complete deal, September 3, 1987.
zTraded to Chicago Cubs for First Baseman Leon Durham and cash, May 19, 1988.
aOn disabled list, August 20 to September 10, 1988.
bOn disabled list, June 17 to September 29, 1989; included rehabilitation disability assignment to Iowa, July 14 to July 27, 1989.
cReleased, December 13, 1989.

—DID YOU KNOW—
That when first baseman Terry Francona of the Brewers pitched one hitless inning on May 15, 1989, he was the only Milwaukee pitcher to record a strikeout in the game?

JEFFREY ALLEN PETEREK
(Jeff)

Born Setember 22, 1963, at Michigan City, Ind.
Height, 6.02. Weight, 195.
Throws and bats righthanded.

Led American Association in shutouts with 3 in 1988.
Led California League in shutouts with 3 in 1986.
Named California League Pitcher of the Year, 1986.

Year Club	League	G.	IP.	W.	L.	Pct.	H.	R.	ER.	SO.	BB.	ERA.
1985—Beloit	Midwest	14	75	6	2	.750	68	31	24	64	24	2.88
1986—Stockton	California	25	168⅔	★15	6	★.714	153	63	54	113	56	2.88
1987—El Paso	Texas	9	49⅔	2	3	.400	80	53	47	38	16	8.52
1987—Stockton	California	17	129⅓	11	3	.786	101	43	29	105	52	2.02
1988—El Paso	Texas	9	69	7	1	.875	60	32	26	54	17	3.39
1988—Denver	Am. Assoc.	19	130	7	6	.538	140	62	57	76	34	3.95
1989—Denver	Am. Assoc.	23	149⅔	9	9	.500	146	73	60	77	52	3.61
1989—Milwaukee	American	7	31⅓	0	2	.000	31	14	14	16	14	4.02
Major League Totals—1 Year		7	31⅓	0	2	.000	31	14	14	16	14	4.02

Signed as free agent by Milwaukee Brewers' organization, June 18, 1985.

ADAM CHARLES PETERSON

Born December 11, 1965, at Long Beach, Calif.
Height, 6.03. Weight, 190.
Throws and bats righthanded.

Tied for Pacific Coast League lead in complete games with 6 in 1989.

Year Club	League	G.	IP.	W.	L.	Pct.	H.	R.	ER.	SO.	BB.	ERA.
1984—Sarasota White Sox	Gulf Coast	12	43	1	4	.200	49	39	26	31	19	5.44
1985—Niagara Falls	NYP	14	92⅓	7	6	.538	74	39	31	79	34	3.02
1986—Peninsula	Carolina	24	147	9	8	.529	150	92	75	84	58	4.59
1986—Birmingham	Southern	6	32⅓	1	3	.250	34	16	15	21	16	4.18
1987—Birmingham	Southern	26	170⅔	12	9	.571	165	79	74	124	73	3.90
1987—Chicago	American	1	4	0	0	.000	8	6	6	1	3	13.50
1988 Vancouver	P. Coast	28	171	14	7	.667	161	69	63	103	81	3.32
1988—Chicago	American	2	6	0	1	.000	6	9	9	5	6	13.50
1989—Vancouver	P. Coast	25	172	14	5	.737	141	60	52	116	71	2.72
1989—Chicago	American	3	5⅓	0	1	.000	13	9	9	3	2	15.19
Major League Totals—3 Years		6	15⅓	0	2	.000	27	24	24	9	11	14.09

Selected by Chicago White Sox' organization in 5th round of free-agent draft, June 4, 1984.

MARK JOSEPH PETKOVSEK

Born November 18, 1965, at Beaumont, Tex.
Height, 6.00. Weight, 175.
Throws and bats righthanded.
Attended University of Texas, Austin, Tex.

Tied for Florida State League lead in shutouts with 5 in 1988.

Year Club	League	G.	IP.	W.	L.	Pct.	H.	R.	ER.	SO.	BB.	ERA.
1987—Sarasota Rangers	Gulf Coast	3	5⅔	0	0	.000	4	2	2	7	2	3.18
1987—Charlotte	Florida St.	11	56	3	4	.429	67	36	25	23	17	4.02
1988—Port Charlotte	Florida St.	28	175⅔	10	11	.476	156	71	58	95	42	2.97
1989—Tulsa	Texas	21	140	8	5	.615	144	63	54	66	35	3.47
1989—Oklahoma City	Am. Assoc.	6	30⅔	0	4	.000	39	27	25	8	18	7.34

Selected by Texas Rangers' organization in 1st round (29th player selected) of free-agent draft, June 2, 1987.

EUGENE JAMES PETRALLI JR.
(Geno)

Born September 25, 1959, at Sacramento, Calif.
Height, 6.01. Weight, 180.
Throws right and bats lefthanded.
Attended Sacramento City College, Sacramento, Calif.
Son of Gene Petralli, minor league first baseman, 1948 through 1951 and 1953.

Holds modern major league record for most passed balls, season (35), 1987.
Shares modern major league record for most passed balls, game (6), August 30, 1987; most passed balls, inning (4), August 22, 1987, seventh inning.
Major League stolen bases: 1983 (1), 1985 (1), 1986 (3). Total—5.
Led American League in passed balls with 35 in 1987 and 20 in 1988.
Led International League catchers in putouts with 633, assists with 86, errors with 19, double plays with 10 and total chances with 738 in 1982.
Tied for Pioneer League lead in passed balls with 27 in 1978.

Year Club	League	Pos.	G.	AB.	R.	H.	2B.	3B.	HR.	RBI.	B.A.	PO.	A.	E.	F.A.
1978—Medicine Hat†	Pion.	C-3B	65	242	42	68	14	5	2	40	.281	238	68	19	.942
1979—Dunedin†‡	Fla. St.	C-3B-OF	52	184	18	53	13	0	1	24	.288	206	42	5	.980
1979—Syracuse†	Int.	C	18	56	6	13	0	1	0	7	.232	67	12	1	.988
1980—Knoxville†	South.	C-1B-OF	116	382	42	109	20	2	3	38	.285	569	82	18	.973
1981—Syracuse‡§	Int.	C	45	151	17	40	11	0	0	16	.265	188	30	6	.973

Year Club	League	Pos.	G.	AB.	R.	H.	2B.	3B.	HR.	RBI.	B.A.	PO.	A.	E.	F.A.
1982—Syracuse†	Int.	C-1B-3B	126	395	57	114	19	3	9	58	.289	674	89	20	.974
1982—Toronto†	Amer.	C-3B	16	44	3	16	2	0	0	1	.364	51	4	1	.982
1983—Syracuse†	Int.	C-1B	104	327	39	80	9	2	3	40	.245	541	68	7	.989
1983—Toronto†	Amer.	C	6	4	0	0	0	0	0	0	.000	7	0	0	1.000
1984—Toronto† x	Amer.	C	3	3	0	0	0	0	0	0	.000	1	1	0	1.000
1984—Maine† y	Int.	C-O-1	23	83	9	18	3	0	0	5	.217	122	11	6	.957
1985—Maine z	Int.	C	2	7	0	1	0	0	0	1	.143	12	1	1	.929
1985—Oklahoma City	A. A.	C	27	80	11	21	8	0	1	5	.263	108	14	3	.976
1985—Texas†	Amer.	C	42	100	7	27	2	0	0	11	.270	179	16	2	.990
1986—Texas†	Amer.	C-3B-2B	69	137	17	35	9	3	2	18	.255	163	14	4	.978
1987—Texas†	Amer.	C-3-1-2-O	101	202	28	61	11	2	7	31	.302	370	34	5	.988
1988—Texas	Amer.	C-3-1-2	129	351	35	99	14	2	7	36	.282	421	54	10	.979
1989—Texas a	Amer.	C	70	184	18	56	7	0	4	23	.304	258	15	3	.989
1989—Tulsa	Texas	C	5	13	2	3	0	0	1	1	.231	6	1	0	1.000
Major League Totals—8 Years			436	1025	108	294	45	7	20	120	.287	1450	138	25	.985

Selected by Toronto Blue Jays' organization in 3rd round of free-agent draft, January 10, 1978.

†Switch-hitter.

‡On suspended list, April 13 to April 27, 1979.

§On disabled list, May 6 to June 1 and June 28 to August 18, 1981.

xSold to Maine (Cleveland Indians' organization), May 8, 1984.

yOn disabled list, July 11, 1984 through remainder of season.

zReleased, April 23, 1985; signed by Oklahoma City (Texas Rangers' organization), May 17, 1985.

aOn disabled list, May 27 to June 11 and June 27 to August 19, 1989; included rehabilitation disability assignment to Tulsa, August 14 to August 19, 1989.

DANIEL JOSEPH PETRY

Name pronounced PEE-tree.

(Dan)

Born November 13, 1958, at Palo Alto, Calif.
Height, 6.04. Weight, 215.
Throws and bats righthanded.

Led American League pitchers in games started with 38 and home runs allowed with 37 in 1983.

Year Club	League	G.	IP.	W.	L.	Pct.	H.	R.	ER.	SO.	BB.	ERA.
1976—Bristol	Ap'lachian	14	79	2	3	.400	54	42	33	51	★56	3.76
1977—Lakeland	Florida St.	25	145	10	11	.476	139	68	55	68	68	3.41
1978—Montgomery	Southern	14	92	6	7	.462	70	38	25	69	41	2.45
1978—Evansville	Am. Assoc.	13	71	4	3	.571	59	38	36	50	33	4.56
1979—Evansville	Am. Assoc.	15	91	4	3	.571	92	60	49	55	37	4.85
1979—Detroit	American	15	98	6	5	.545	90	46	43	43	33	3.95
1980—Evansville	Am. Assoc.	4	30	2	0	1.000	21	11	9	16	12	2.70
1980—Detroit	American	27	165	10	9	.526	156	82	72	88	83	3.93
1981—Detroit	American	23	141	10	9	.526	115	53	47	79	57	3.00
1982—Detroit	American	35	246	15	9	.625	220	98	88	132	100	3.22
1983—Detroit	American	38	266⅓	19	11	.633	256	126	116	122	99	3.92
1984—Detroit	American	35	233⅓	18	8	.692	231	94	84	144	66	3.24
1985—Detroit	American	34	238⅔	15	13	.536	190	98	89	109	81	3.36
1986—Detroit†	American	20	116	5	10	.333	122	78	60	56	53	4.66
1986—Lakeland	Florida St.	3	10⅓	1	1	.500	13	8	8	6	1	6.97
1987—Detroit‡	American	30	134⅔	9	7	.563	148	101	84	93	76	5.61
1988—California§	American	22	139⅔	3	9	.250	139	70	68	64	59	4.38
1988—Palm Springs	California	3	15	1	2	.333	19	14	11	11	11	6.60
1989—California x	American	19	51	3	2	.600	53	32	31	21	23	5.47
Major League Totals—11 Years	...	298	1829⅔	113	92	.551	1720	878	782	951	730	3.85

Selected by Detroit Tigers' organization in 4th round of free-agent draft, June 8, 1976.

†On disabled list, June 6 to August 19, 1986; included rehabilitation disability assignment to Lakeland, July 30 to August 19, 1986.

‡Traded to California Angels for Outfielder Gary Pettis, December 5, 1987.

§On disabled list, June 26 to August 30, 1988; included rehabilitation disability assignment to Palm Springs, August 13 to August 30, 1988.

xGranted free agency, November 13, 1989.

CHAMPIONSHIP SERIES RECORD

Year Club	League	G.	IP.	W.	L.	Pct.	H.	R.	ER.	SO.	BB.	ERA.
1984—Detroit	American	1	7	0	0	.000	4	2	2	4	1	2.57
1987—Detroit	American	1	3⅓	0	0	.000	1	1	0	1	0	0.00
Championship Series Totals—2 Years	...	2	10⅓	0	0	.000	5	3	2	5	1	1.74

WORLD SERIES RECORD

Year Club	League	G.	IP.	W.	L.	Pct.	H.	R.	ER.	SO.	BB.	ERA.
1984—Detroit	American	2	8	0	1	.000	14	8	8	4	5	9.00

ALL-STAR GAME RECORD

Year League		IP.	W.	L.	Pct.	H.	R.	ER.	SO.	BB.	ERA.
1985—American		⅓	0	0	.000	0	2	2	1	3	54.00

—DID YOU KNOW—

That the Toronto Blue Jays were 13-4 in extra-inning games in 1989?

GARY GEORGE PETTIS

Born April 3, 1958, at Oakland, Calif.
Height, 6.01. Weight, 160.
Throws right and bats left and righthanded.
Attended Laney College, Oakland, Calif.
Brother of Stacey Pettis, outfielder in Pittsburgh Pirates' and California Angels' organizations, 1981 through 1987.

Shares major league record for most putouts by outfielder, game (12), June 4, 1985 (15 innings).
Shares American League record for most chances accepted by outfielder, game (12), June 4, 1985 (15 innings).
Major League stolen bases: 1983 (8), 1984 (48), 1985 (56), 1986 (50), 1987 (24), 1988 (44), 1989 (43). Total—273.
Led American League outfielders in total chances with 478 in 1986.
Led Pacific Coast League in stolen bases with 53 in 1982.
Named outfielder on THE SPORTING NEWS American League All-Star fielding team, 1985, 1986, 1988 and 1989.

Year	Club	League	Pos.	G.	AB.	R.	H.	2B.	3B.	HR.	RBI.	B.A.	PO.	A.	E.	F.A.
1979—Idaho Falls	Pion.	3B-SS-2B	50	198	39	63	10	●10	3	26	.318	59	94	24	.864
1980—Salinas	Calif.	OF-SS-3B	118	393	71	94	15	3	2	31	.239	206	36	13	.949
1981—Holyoke	East.	OF	120	421	77	112	8	9	3	36	.266	237	5	4	.984
1982—Spokane	P. C.	OF	133	528	108	152	22	★14	1	59	.288	★345	9	6	★.983
1982—California	Amer.	OF	10	5	5	1	0	0	1	1	.200	5	1	0	1.000
1983—Edmonton	P. C.	OF	132	529	★138	151	27	8	11	52	.285	325	10	5	.985
1983—California	Amer.	OF	22	85	19	25	2	3	3	6	.294	49	5	1	.982
1984—California	Amer.	OF	140	397	63	90	11	6	2	29	.227	337	11	6	.983
1985—California†	Amer.	OF	125	443	67	114	10	8	1	32	.257	368	13	4	.990
1986—California	Amer.	OF	154	539	93	139	23	4	5	58	.258	★462	9	7	.985
1987—California	Amer.	OF	133	394	49	82	13	2	1	17	.208	344	2	7	.980
1987—Edmonton‡	P. C.	OF	8	16	6	2	1	0	0	1	.125	7	1	1	.889
1988—Detroit§	Amer.	OF	129	458	65	96	14	4	3	36	.210	361	5	5	.987
1989—Toledo x	Int.	OF	6	21	6	7	1	0	1	3	.333	9	1	0	1.000
1989—Detroit y	Amer.	OF	119	444	77	114	8	6	1	18	.257	325	1	4	.988
Major League Totals—8 Years			832	2765	438	661	81	33	17	197	.239	2251	47	34	.985

Selected by California Angels' organization in 6th round of free-agent draft, January 9, 1979.
†On disabled list, July 5 to July 31, 1985.
‡Traded to Detroit Tigers for Pitcher Dan Petry, December 5, 1987.
§On disabled list, July 30 to August 15, 1988.
xOn disabled list, March 26 to May 15, 1989; included rehabilitation disability assignment to Toledo, May 6 to May 15, 1989.
yGranted free agency, November 13, 1989; signed by Texas Rangers, November 24, 1989.

CHAMPIONSHIP SERIES RECORD

Shares Championship Series record for most sacrifice hits, series (2), 1986.

Year	Club	League	Pos.	G.	AB.	R.	H.	2B.	3B.	HR.	RBI.	B.A.	PO.	A.	E.	F.A.
1986—California	Amer.	OF	7	26	4	9	1	0	1	4	.346	28	0	1	.966

MARTY A. PEVEY

Born September 18, 1961, at Statesboro, Ga.
Height, 6.01. Weight, 185.
Throws right and bats lefthanded.
Attended Georgia Southern College, Statesboro, Ga.

Year	Club	League	Pos.	G.	AB.	R.	H.	2B.	3B.	HR.	RBI.	B.A.	PO.	A.	E.	F.A.
1982—Elizabethton†	Appal.	C	24	81	9	23	6	0	1	13	.284	108	8	4	.967
1983—Macon	S. Atl.	C-OF	122	436	74	136	23	2	7	77	.312	531	51	11	.981
1984—St. Petersburg	Fla. St.	1-C-O-3	128	441	53	136	16	4	2	60	.308	731	71	11	.986
1985—St. Petersburg	Fla. St.	C-1B	104	393	48	114	12	4	3	41	.290	423	57	9	.982
1986—Louisville	A. A.	C	12	37	6	6	3	0	0	0	.162	69	1	2	.972
1986—Arkansas	Texas	C-O-3-1	55	172	28	56	11	2	2	20	.326	211	27	4	.983
1987—Arkansas	Texas	1B-C-OF	80	197	28	55	11	1	3	16	.279	283	27	6	.981
1987—Louisville‡	A. A.	C-OF	16	38	5	9	2	0	1	5	.237	35	2	0	1.000
1988—Jacksonville	South.	C-OF	31	111	21	29	11	0	4	17	.261	71	14	0	1.000
1988—Indianapolis	A. A.	C-OF-3B	48	119	16	27	4	1	3	16	.227	121	24	2	.986
1989—Indianapolis	A. A.	C-3B-1B	34	108	12	28	4	2	1	14	.259	151	17	3	.982
1989—Montreal	Nat.	C-OF	13	41	2	9	1	1	0	3	.220	58	7	1	.985
Major League Totals—1 Year			13	41	2	9	1	1	0	3	.220	58	7	1	.985

Selected by Minnesota Twins' organization in 19th round of free-agent draft, June 7, 1982.
‡Released, July 29, 1982; signed by Erie (St. Louis Cardinals' organization), March 26, 1983.
‡Traded to Montreal Expos' organization for Pitcher Bob Sudo, February 11, 1988.

KENNETH ALLEN PHELPS
(Ken)

Born August 6, 1954, at Seattle, Wash.
Height, 6.01. Weight, 204.
Throws and bats lefthanded.
Attended Washington State University, Pullman, Wash.; Mesa Community College, Mesa, Ariz., and received bachelor of science degree in physical education from Arizona State University, Tempe, Ariz.

Major League stolen bases: 1984 (3), 1985 (2), 1986 (2), 1987 (1), 1988 (1). Total—9.
Led American Association in total bases with 320 in 1982.

Led American Association in bases on balls received with 128 in 1980 and 108 in 1982.
Led Southern League in bases on balls received with 99 in 1978.
Tied for American Association lead in intentional bases on balls received with 12 in 1982.
Led American Association first basemen in double plays with 111 in 1979, 103 in 1980 and 108 in 1982.
Named American Association Most Valuable Player, 1982.

Year	Club	League	Pos.	G.	AB.	R.	H.	2B.	3B.	HR.	RBI.	B.A.	PO.	A.	E.	F.A.
1976—Sarasota Royals	Gulf C.	1B	28	98	20	29	6	3	3	28	.296	166	16	2	.989
1976—Waterloo	Midw.	1B	25	72	12	19	8	0	1	10	.264	205	12	3	.986
1977—Daytona Beach	Fla. St.	1B	40	145	22	50	7	0	5	32	.345	341	31	8	.979
1977—Jacksonville	South.	1B	81	262	30	51	6	3	5	40	.195	691	38	10	.986
1978—Jacksonville	South.	1B	124	381	65	94	20	0	16	61	.247	1028	66	16	.986
1979—Omaha	A. A.	1B	130	430	71	114	26	3	20	77	.265	*1129	80	*13	.989
1980—Omaha	A. A.	1B	133	442	80	130	30	3	23	72	.294	*1154	51	12	.990
1980—Kansas City	Amer.	1B	3	4	0	0	0	0	0	0	.000	14	0	0	1.000
1981—Kansas City	Amer.	1B	21	22	1	3	0	1	0	1	.136	4	1	0	1.000
1981—Omaha†	A. A.	1B	19	66	9	22	8	1	5	21	.333	169	15	2	.989
1982—Wichita	A. A.	1B	132	453	112	151	23	4	*46	*141	.333	1047	74	14	.988
1982—Montreal‡	Nat.	PH	10	8	0	2	0	0	0	0	.250	0	0	0	.000
1983—Seattle	Amer.	1B	50	127	10	30	4	1	7	16	.236	164	16	0	1.000
1983—Salt Lake City	P. C.	1B	74	270	81	92	29	6	24	82	.341	535	37	7	.988
1984—Seattle§	Amer.	1B	101	290	52	70	9	0	24	51	.241	72	4	1	.987
1984—Salt Lake City	P. C.	1B	12	45	7	14	3	0	3	13	.311	25	5	0	1.000
1985—Seattle	Amer.	1B	61	116	18	24	3	0	9	24	.207	31	2	0	1.000
1986—Seattle	Amer.	1B	125	344	69	85	16	4	24	64	.247	487	34	9	.983
1987—Seattle	Amer.	1B	120	332	68	86	13	1	27	68	.259	8	0	0	1.000
1988—Sea. x-N.Y.	Amer.	1B	117	297	54	78	13	0	24	54	.263	18	2	1	.952
1989—N.Y.y-Oak.z	Amer.	1B	97	194	26	47	4	0	7	29	.242	56	2	1	.983
American League Totals—9 Years			695	1726	298	423	62	7	122	307	.245	854	61	12	.987
National League Totals—1 Year			10	8	0	2	0	0	0	0	.250	0	0	0	.000
Major League Totals—10 Years			705	1734	298	425	62	7	122	307	.245	854	61	12	.987

Selected by Atlanta Braves' organization in 8th round of free-agent draft, June 6, 1972.
Selected by New York Yankees' organization in 1st round (11th player selected) of free-agent draft, January 9, 1974.
Selected by Philadelphia Phillies' organization in secondary phase of free-agent draft, June 5, 1974.
Selected by Kansas City Royals' organization in 15th round of free-agent draft, June 8, 1976.
†Traded to Montreal Expos' organization for Pitcher Grant Jackson, January 19, 1982.
‡Sold to Seattle Mariners, March 31, 1983.
§On disabled list, April 7 to May 18, 1984; included rehabilitation disability assignment to Salt Lake City, May 4 to May 18, 1984.
xTraded to New York Yankees for Outfielder Jay Buhner, Pitcher Rich Balabon and a player to be named later, July 21, 1988; Seattle Mariners acquired Pitcher Troy Evers to complete deal, October 12, 1988.
yTraded to Oakland Athletics for Pitcher Scott Holcomb, August 30, 1989.
zGranted free agency, November 13, 1989; re-signed by Athletics, December 8, 1989.

CHAMPIONSHIP SERIES RECORD

Year	Club	League	Pos.	G.	AB.	R.	H.	2B.	3B.	HR.	RBI.	B.A.	PO.	A.	E.	F.A.
1989—Oakland	Amer.	PH	1	1	0	1	1	0	0	0	1.000	0	0	0	.000

WORLD SERIES RECORD

Year	Club	League	Pos.	G.	AB.	R.	H.	2B.	3B.	HR.	RBI.	B.A.	PO.	A.	E.	F.A.
1989—Oakland	Amer.	PH	1	1	0	0	0	0	0	0	.000	0	0	0	.000

KEITH ANTHONY PHILLIPS
(Tony)

Born April 15, 1959, at Atlanta, Ga.
Height, 5.10. Weight, 175.
Throws right and bats right and lefthanded.
Attended New Mexico Military Institute, Roswell, N.M.

Shares major league record for most assists by second baseman, nine-inning game (12), July 6, 1986.
Major league stolen bases: 1982 (2), 1983 (16), 1984 (10), 1985 (3), 1986 (15), 1987 (7), 1989 (3). Total—56.
Hit for the cycle, May 16, 1986.
Led Eastern League in being hit by pitch with 10 in 1981.
Led Southern League in bases on balls received with 98 in 1980.

Year	Club	League	Pos.	G.	AB.	R.	H.	2B.	3B.	HR.	RBI.	B.A.	PO.	A.	E.	F.A.
1978—W. Palm Beach†	Fla. St.	3B-SS-2B	32	54	8	9	0	0	0	3	.167	13	33	5	.902
1978—Jamestown	NYP	SS-2B-3B	52	152	24	29	5	2	1	17	.191	73	146	16	.932
1979—W. Palm Beach	Fla. St.	2B-SS	60	203	30	47	5	1	0	18	.232	120	156	21	.929
1979—Memphis	South.	SS-2B	52	156	31	44	4	2	3	11	.282	68	134	18	.914
1980—Memphis‡§	South.	*SS-2B	136	502	100	125	18	4	5	41	.249	226	408	*42	.938
1981—West Haven	East.	SS	131	461	79	114	25	3	9	64	.247	200	391	*33	.947
1981—Tacoma	P. C.	2B-SS	4	11	1	4	1	0	0	2	.364	8	10	0	1.000
1982—Tacoma	P. C.	SS	86	300	76	89	18	5	4	47	.297	138	236	30	.926
1982—Oakland	Amer.	SS	40	81	11	17	2	2	0	8	.210	46	95	7	.953
1983—Oakland	Amer.	SS-2B-3B	148	412	54	102	12	3	4	35	.248	218	383	30	.952
1984—Oakland	Amer.	SS-2B-OF	154	451	62	120	24	3	4	37	.266	255	391	28	.958
1985—Tacoma x	P. C.	3B-2B	20	69	9	9	1	0	0	5	.130	15	36	4	.927
1985—Oakland	Amer.	3B-2B	42	161	23	45	12	2	4	17	.280	54	103	3	.981
1986—Oakland y	Amer.	2-3-O-S	118	441	76	113	14	5	5	52	.256	191	326	13	.975
1987—Oakland z	Amer.	2-3-S-O	111	379	48	91	20	0	10	46	.240	179	299	14	.972

Year Club	League	Pos.	G.	AB.	R.	H.	2B.	3B.	HR.	RBI.	B.A.	PO.	A.	E.	F.A.
1987—Tacoma a	P. C.	2B-3B	7	26	5	9	2	1	1	6	.346	8	10	0	1.000
1988—Tacoma.................	P. C.	S-O-2-3	16	59	10	16	0	0	2	8	.271	25	27	2	.963
1988—Oakland b	Amer.	3-O-2-S-1	79	212	32	43	8	4	2	17	.203	84	80	10	.943
1989—Oakland c	Amer.	2-3-S-O-1	143	451	48	118	15	6	4	47	.262	184	321	15	.971
Major League Totals—8 Years.................			835	2588	354	649	107	25	33	259	.251	1211	1998	120	.964

Selected by Seattle Mariners' organization in 16th round of free-agent draft, June 7, 1977.
Selected by Montreal Expos' organization in secondary phase of free-agent draft, January 10, 1978.
†On temporary inactive list, April 11 to May 4, 1978.
‡Traded with cash to San Diego Padres for First Baseman Willie Montanez, August 31, 1980.
§Traded with Pitcher Eric Mustad and Infielder Kevin Bell to Oakland A's organization for Pitcher Bob Lacey and Pitcher Roy Moretti, March 27, 1981.
xOn Oakland disabled list, March 26 to August 22, 1985; included rehabilitation disability assignment to Tacoma, July 30 to August 5 and August 7 to August 20, 1985.
yOn disabled list, August 14 to October 3, 1986.
zOn disabled list, July 12 to August 28, 1987; included rehabilitation disability assignment to Tacoma, August 20 to August 28, 1987.
aReleased, December 21, 1987; re-signed by Athletics, March 9, 1988.
bOn disabled list, May 18 to July 8, 1988; included rehabilitation disability assignment to Tacoma, June 16 to July 4, 1988.
cGranted free agency, November 13, 1989; signed by Detroit Tigers, December 5, 1989.

CHAMPIONSHIP SERIES RECORD

Year Club	League	Pos.	G.	AB.	R.	H.	2B.	3B.	IIR.	RBI.	B.A.	PO.	A.	E.	F.A.
1988—Oakland.................	Amer.	OF-2B	2	7	0	2	1	0	0	0	.286	10	0	0	1.000
1989—Oakland.................	Amer.	2B-3B	5	18	1	3	1	0	0	1	.167	4	14	0	1.000
Championship Series Totals—2 Years.....			7	25	1	5	2	0	0	1	.200	14	14	0	1.000

WORLD SERIES RECORD

Year Club	League	Pos.	G.	AB.	R.	H.	2B.	3B.	HR.	RBI.	B.A.	PO.	A.	E.	F.A.
1988—Oakland.................	Amer.	OF-2B	2	4	1	1	0	0	0	0	.250	3	5	0	1.000
1989—Oakland.................	Amer.	2B-3B-OF	4	17	2	4	1	0	1	3	.235	8	15	0	1.000
World Series Totals—2 Years			6	21	3	5	1	0	1	3	.238	11	20	0	1.000

JEFFREY MARK PICO
(Jeff)

Born February 12, 1966, at Antioch, Calif.
Height, 6.02. Weight, 170.
Throws and bats righthanded.

Shares major league record for pitching shutout, first major league game, May 31, 1988.
Major League saves: 1988 (1), 1989 (2). Total—3.
Tied for Appalachian League lead in games started by pitchers with 13 in 1984.

Year Club	League	G.	IP.	W.	L.	Pct.	H.	R.	ER.	SO.	BB.	ERA.
1984—Pikeville..	Ap'lachian	13	73⅓	2	3	.400	65	35	27	46	29	3.31
1985—Peoria..	Midwest	27	179⅓	11	10	.524	186	76	61	109	56	3.06
1986—Winston-Salem	Carolina	27	166	12	8	.600	165	75	59	116	54	3.20
1987—Pittsfield	Eastern	12	79	4	4	.500	74	38	34	52	23	3.87
1987—Iowa	Am. Assoc.	16	93⅔	6	5	.545	118	57	50	45	27	4.80
1988—Iowa	Am. Assoc.	10	68⅓	5	2	.714	67	28	17	40	18	2.24
1988—Chicago...	National	29	112⅔	6	7	.462	108	57	52	57	37	4.15
1989—Chicago...	National	53	90⅔	3	1	.750	99	43	38	38	31	3.77
1989—Iowa	Am. Assoc.	2	6⅓	1	0	1.000	5	0	0	2	0	0.00
Major League Totals—2 Years.............................		82	203⅓	9	8	.529	207	100	90	95	68	3.98

Selected by Chicago Cubs' organization in 13th round of free-agent draft, June 4, 1984.

JOHN JOSEPH PINA JR.
(Mickey)

Born March 8, 1966, at Boston, Mass.
Height, 6.00. Weight, 195.
Throws and bats righthanded.
Attended Eckerd College, St. Petersburg, Fla.

Led Carolina League in game-winning RBIs with 17 in 1988.
Tied for Carolina League lead in double plays by outfielders with 4 in 1988.
Named Carolina League Most Valuable Player, 1988.

Year Club	League	Pos.	G.	AB.	R.	H.	2B.	3B.	HR.	RBI.	B.A.	PO.	A.	E.	F.A.
1987—Elmira...................	NYP	OF	60	196	44	54	15	2	12	45	.276	84	8	3	.968
1988—Lynchburg............	Carol.	OF	136	472	•91	129	31	4	★21	★108	.273	237	★20	6	.977
1989—New Britain	East.	OF	46	154	22	40	10	0	2	26	.260	95	3	3	.970
1989—Pawtucket	Int.	OF	71	260	32	74	15	0	14	45	.285	134	6	4	.972

Selected by Boston Red Sox' organization in 14th round of free-agent draft, June 4, 1984.
Signed as free agent by Boston Red Sox' organization, June 12, 1987.

—DID YOU KNOW—

That the Cleveland Indians had just six hits—all home runs—in a June 24, 1989 game against Texas?

JAMES PARK PITTMAN
(Known by middle name.)

Born August 5, 1965, at Richmond, Ind.
Height, 6.00. Weight, 175.
Throws and bats righthanded.
Received degree from Ohio State University, Columbus, O.

Tied for California League lead in games started by pitchers with 29 in 1987.

Year	Club	League	G.	IP.	W.	L.	Pct.	H.	R.	ER.	SO.	BB.	ERA.
1986—Elizabethton		Ap'lachian	8	44	3	1	.750	31	19	12	65	23	2.45
1987—Visalia		California	31	161⅔	4	12	.250	109	81	59	★198	★138	3.28
1988—Orlando		Southern	24	103⅔	8	7	.533	73	50	44	103	84	3.82
1989—Orlando		Southern	34	102	5	9	.357	82	60	52	103	72	4.59

Selected by Minnesota Twins' organization in 4th round of free-agent draft, June 2, 1986.

PHILLIP ALAN PLANTIER
(Phil)

Born January 27, 1969, at Manchester, N.H.
Height, 6.00. Weight, 175.
Throws right and bats lefthanded.

Led Carolina League in total bases with 242, slugging percentage with .546 and tied for lead in intentional bases on balls received with 7 in 1989.
Named Carolina League Most Valuable Player, 1989.

Year	Club	League	Pos.	G.	AB.	R.	H.	2B.	3B.	HR.	RBI.	B.A.	PO.	A.	E.	F.A.
1987—Elmira		NYP	3B	28	80	7	14	2	0	2	9	.175	12	34	12	.793
1988—Winter Haven		Fla. St.	OF-3B-2B	111	337	29	81	13	1	4	32	.240	106	72	18	.908
1989—Lynchburg		Carol.	OF	131	443	73	133	26	1	★27	★105	.300	140	10	8	.949

Selected by Boston Red Sox' organization in 11th round of free-agent draft, June 2, 1987.

DANIEL THOMAS PLESAC
(Dan)

Born February 4, 1962, at Gary, Ind.
Height, 6.05. Weight, 215.
Throws and bats lefthanded.
Attended North Carolina State University, Raleigh, N.C.

Major League saves: 1986 (14), 1987 (23), 1988 (30), 1989 (33). Total—100.
Led Appalachian League pitchers in balks with 3 and tied for lead in games started with 14 in 1983.

Year	Club	League	G.	IP.	W.	L.	Pct.	H.	R.	ER.	SO.	BB.	ERA.
1983—Paintsville		Ap'lachian	14	82⅓	★9	1	★.900	76	44	32	★85	57	3.50
1984—Stockton		California	16	108⅓	6	6	.500	106	51	40	101	50	3.32
1984—El Paso		Texas	7	39	2	2	.500	43	19	15	24	16	3.46
1985—El Paso		Texas	25	150⅓	12	5	.706	171	91	83	128	68	4.97
1986—Milwaukee		American	51	91	10	7	.588	81	34	30	75	29	2.97
1987—Milwaukee		American	57	79⅓	5	6	.455	63	30	23	89	23	2.61
1988—Milwaukee		American	50	52⅓	1	2	.333	46	14	14	52	12	2.41
1989—Milwaukee		American	52	61⅓	3	4	.429	47	16	16	52	17	2.35
Major League Totals—4 Years			210	284	19	19	.500	237	94	83	268	81	2.63

Selected by St. Louis Cardinals' organization in 2nd round of free-agent draft, June 3, 1980.
Selected by Milwaukee Brewers' organization in 1st round (26th player selected) of free-agent draft, June 6, 1983.

ALL-STAR GAME RECORD

Year	League	IP.	W.	L.	Pct.	H.	R.	ER.	SO.	BB.	ERA.
1987—American		1	0	0	.000	0	0	0	1	0	0.00
1988—American		⅓	0	0	.000	0	0	0	1	0	0.00
1989—American		0	0	0	.000	1	0	0	0	0	....
All-Star Game Totals—3 Years		1⅓	0	0	.000	1	0	0	2	0	0.00

ERIC VAUGHN PLUNK

Born September 3, 1963, at Wilmington, Calif.
Height, 6.05. Weight, 210.
Throws and bats righthanded.
Attended California State University at Dominguez Hills, Carson, Calif.

Major League saves: 1987 (2), 1988 (5), 1989 (1). Total—8.
Led American League in balks with 6 in 1986.
Tied for Florida State League lead in shutouts with 4 in 1983 and balks with 7 in 1984.

Year	Club	League	G.	IP.	W.	L.	Pct.	H.	R.	ER.	SO.	BB.	ERA.
1981—Bradenton Yankees		Gulf Coast	11	54	3	4	.429	56	29	23	47	20	3.83
1982—Paintsville		Ap'lachian	12	64	6	3	.667	63	35	33	59	30	4.64
1983—Fort Lauderdale†		Florida St.	20	125	8	10	.444	115	55	38	109	63	2.74
1984—Fort Lauderdale‡		Florida St.	28	176⅓	12	12	.500	153	85	56	★152	★123	2.86
1985—Huntsville		Southern	13	79⅓	8	2	.800	61	36	30	68	56	3.40
1985—Tacoma		P. Coast	11	53	0	5	.000	51	41	34	43	50	5.77
1986—Tacoma		P. Coast	6	32⅔	2	3	.400	25	18	17	31	33	4.68
1986—Oakland		American	26	120⅓	4	7	.364	91	75	71	98	102	5.21
1987—Oakland		American	32	95	4	6	.400	91	53	50	90	62	4.74

Year Club	League	G.	IP.	W.	L.	Pct.	H.	R.	ER.	SO.	BB.	ERA.
1987—Tacoma	P. Coast	24	34⅔	1	1	.500	21	8	6	56	17	1.56
1988—Oakland§	American	49	78	7	2	.778	62	27	26	79	39	3.00
1989—Oakland x-New York	American	50	104⅓	8	6	.571	82	43	38	85	64	3.28
Major League Totals—4 Years		157	397⅔	23	21	.523	326	198	185	352	267	4.19

Selected by New York Yankees' organization in 4th round of free-agent draft, June 8, 1981.
†On disabled list, August 11 to August 26, 1983.
‡Traded with Outfielder Stan Javier and Pitchers Jay Howell, Jose Rijo and Tim Birtsas to Oakland A's for Outfielder Rickey Henderson, Pitcher Bert Bradley and cash, December 5, 1984.
§On disabled list, July 2 to July 17, 1988.
xTraded with Pitcher Greg Cadaret and Outfielder Luis Polonia to New York Yankees for Outfielder Rickey Henderson, June 21, 1989.

CHAMPIONSHIP SERIES RECORD

Year Club	League	G.	IP.	W.	L.	Pct.	H.	R.	ER.	SO.	BB.	ERA.
1988—Oakland	American	1	⅓	0	0	.000	1	0	0	1	0	0.00

WORLD SERIES RECORD

Year Club	League	G.	IP.	W.	L.	Pct.	H.	R.	ER.	SO.	BB.	ERA.
1988—Oakland	American	2	1⅔	0	0	.000	0	0	0	3	0	0.00

GUSTAVO POLIDOR
(Gus)

Born October 26, 1961, at Caracas, Venezuela.
Height, 6.00. Weight, 184.
Throws and bats righthanded.

Major League stolen bases: 1989 (3).
Led Pacific Coast League shortstops in fielding percentage with .986 in 1986.
Led Pacific Coast League shortstops in double plays with 93 in 1985 and tied for lead with 92 in 1986.
Led Pacific Coast League shortstops in total chances with 669 in 1985.
Tied for Eastern League lead in double plays by shortstops with 69 in 1983.

Year Club	League	Pos.	G.	AB.	R.	H.	2B.	3B.	HR.	RBI.	B.A.	PO.	A.	E.	F.A.
1981—Holyoke	East.	SS	130	479	46	119	17	3	2	47	.248	192	375	32	.947
1982—Holyoke†	East.	SS	56	208	17	47	7	0	2	23	.226	74	149	21	.914
1983—Nashua	East.	★SS-3B	105	329	32	69	7	2	0	21	.210	208	283	★37	.930
1984—Waterbury	East.	★SS-P	119	394	42	88	11	1	1	32	.223	204	322	27	★.951
1985—Edmonton	P. C.	SS	132	460	56	131	18	7	2	51	.285	★250	★396	23	.966
1985—California	Amer.	SS-OF	2	1	1	1	0	0	0	0	1.000	0	2	0	1.000
1986—Edmonton	P. C.	S-2-1-3	119	476	72	143	27	5	5	61	.300	213	316	7	.987
1986—California	Amer.	2B-SS-3B	6	19	1	5	1	0	0	1	.263	10	13	0	1.000
1987—California	Amer.	SS-3B-2B	63	137	12	36	3	0	2	15	.263	46	92	2	.986
1988—California‡	Amer.	SS-3B-2B	54	81	4	12	3	0	0	4	.148	31	54	1	.988
1988—Edmonton§	P. C.	SS-1B	11	33	6	12	4	0	0	7	.364	20	23	2	.956
1989—Milwaukee	Amer.	3B-2B-SS	79	175	15	34	7	0	0	14	.194	78	123	12	.944
Major League Totals—5 Years			204	413	33	88	14	0	2	34	.213	165	284	15	.968

Signed as free agent by California Angels' organization, January 5, 1981.
†On disabled list, June 22 to July 14 and July 26, 1982 through remainder of season.
‡On disabled list, June 14 to July 1, 1988.
§Traded to Milwaukee Brewers for Catcher Bill Schroeder, December 7, 1988.

PITCHING RECORD

Year Club	League	G.	IP.	W.	L.	Pct.	H.	R.	ER.	SO.	BB.	ERA.
1984—Waterbury	Eastern	1	1	0	0	.000	0	0	0	0	1	0.00

LUIS ANDREW POLONIA (ALMONTE)

Born October 12, 1964, at Santiago City, D. R.
Height, 5.08. Weight, 155.
Throws and bats lefthanded.

Major League stolen bases: 1987 (29), 1988 (24), 1989 (22). Total—75.
Led Pacific Coast League in caught stealing with 21 in 1986.
Led Midwest League in caught stealing with 24 in 1984.

Year Club	League	Pos.	G.	AB.	R.	H.	2B.	3B.	HR.	RBI.	B.A.	PO.	A.	E.	F.A.
1984—Madison†	Midw.	OF	135	★528	103	★162	21	10	8	64	.307	202	9	10	.955
1985—Huntsville†	South.	OF	130	515	82	149	15	★18	2	36	.289	236	13	12	.954
1986—Tacoma†	P. C.	OF	134	★549	98	★165	20	4	3	63	.301	★318	8	10	.970
1987—Tacoma†	P. C.	OF	14	56	18	18	1	2	0	8	.321	28	1	1	.967
1987—Oakland	Amer.	OF	125	435	78	125	16	10	4	49	.287	235	2	5	.979
1988—Tacoma†	P. C.	OF	65	254	58	85	13	5	2	27	.335	129	7	7	.951
1988—Oakland	Amer.	OF	84	288	51	84	11	4	2	27	.292	155	3	2	.988
1989—Oak.‡-N.Y.	Amer.	OF	125	433	70	130	17	6	3	46	.300	231	9	4	.984
Major League Totals—3 Years			334	1156	199	339	44	20	9	122	.293	621	14	11	.983

Signed as free agent by Oakland A's organization, January 3, 1984.
†Switch-hitter.
‡Traded with Pitchers Greg Cadaret and Eric Plunk to New York Yankees for Outfielder Rickey Henderson, June 21, 1989.

CHAMPIONSHIP SERIES RECORD

Year Club	League	Pos.	G.	AB.	R.	H.	2B.	3B.	HR.	RBI.	B.A.	PO.	A.	E.	F.A.
1988—Oakland	Amer.	PR-O-PH	3	5	0	2	0	0	0	0	.400	2	0	0	1.000

WORLD SERIES RECORD

Year Club	League	Pos.	G.	AB.	R.	H.	2B.	3B.	HR.	RBI.	B.A.	PO.	A.	E.	F.A.
1988—Oakland	Amer.	PH-OF	3	9	1	1	0	0	0	0	.111	2	0	0	1.000

MARK STEVEN PORTUGAL

Born October 30, 1962, at Los Angeles, Calif.
Height, 6.00. Weight, 190.
Throws and bats righthanded.

Major League saves: 1986 (1), 1988 (3). Total—4.
Led Appalachian League in wild pitches with 12, home runs allowed with 11 and tied for lead in hit batsmen with 5 in 1981.

Year Club	League	G.	IP.	W.	L.	Pct.	H.	R.	ER.	SO.	BB.	ERA.
1981—Elizabethton	Ap'lachian	14	85	7	1	.875	65	41	35	65	39	3.71
1982—Wisconsin Rapids	Midwest	36	119	9	8	.529	110	62	53	95	62	4.01
1983—Visalia	California	24	131⅓	10	5	.667	142	77	61	132	84	4.18
1984—Orlando	Southern	27	196	14	7	.667	171	80	65	110	113	2.98
1985—Toledo†	Int'national	19	128⅔	8	5	.615	129	60	54	89	60	3.78
1985—Minnesota	American	6	24⅓	1	3	.250	24	16	15	12	14	5.55
1986—Toledo	Int'national	6	45	5	1	.833	34	15	13	30	23	2.60
1986—Minnesota	American	27	112⅔	6	10	.375	112	56	54	67	50	4.31
1987—Minnesota	American	13	44	1	3	.250	58	40	38	28	24	7.77
1987—Portland	P. Coast	17	102	1	10	.091	108	75	68	69	50	6.00
1988—Portland	P. Coast	3	19⅔	2	0	1.000	15	3	3	9	8	1.37
1988—Minnesota‡§	American	26	57⅔	3	3	.500	60	30	29	31	17	4.53
1989—Tucson	P. Coast	17	116⅔	7	5	.583	107	55	49	90	32	3.78
1989—Houston	National	20	108	7	1	.875	91	34	33	86	37	2.75
American League Totals—4 Years		72	238⅔	11	19	.367	254	142	136	138	105	5.13
National League Totals—1 Year		20	108	7	1	.875	91	34	33	86	37	2.75
Major League Totals—5 Years		92	346⅔	18	20	.474	345	176	169	224	142	4.39

Signed as free agent by Minnesota Twins' organization, October 23, 1980.
†On disabled list, July 22 to August 2, 1985.
‡On disabled list, August 7 to August 28, 1988.
§Traded to Houston Astros for a player to be named later, December 4, 1988; Minnesota Twins' organization acquired Pitcher Todd McClure to complete deal, December 7, 1988.

ALONZO SIDNEY POWELL

Born December 12, 1964, at San Francisco, Calif.
Height, 6.02. Weight, 205.
Throws and bats righthanded.

Year Club	League	Pos.	G.	AB.	R.	H.	2B.	3B.	HR.	RBI.	B.A.	PO.	A.	E.	F.A.
1983—Clinton	Midw.	OF	36	113	14	22	5	1	0	9	.195	66	2	5	.932
1983—Great Falls	Pion.	OF-1B-3B	51	149	13	33	2	2	1	16	.221	127	15	8	.947
1984—Everett	N'west	1B	6	17	2	3	1	0	1	4	.176	38	2	3	.930
1984—Clinton†	Midw.	OF-1B-2B	47	149	22	37	3	2	1	10	.248	166	9	5	.972
1985—San Jose‡	Calif.	★OF-1B	136	473	79	122	27	6	9	62	.258	292	★21	10	.969
1986—W. Palm Beach	Fla. St.	OF	23	76	20	25	7	1	4	18	.329	56	1	0	1.000
1986—Jacksonville	South.	OF	105	402	67	121	21	5	15	80	.301	256	4	3	.989
1987—Montreal	Nat.	OF	14	41	3	8	3	0	0	4	.195	13	0	0	1.000
1987—Indianapolis	A. A.	OF-1B	90	331	64	99	14	10	19	74	.299	163	6	5	.971
1988—Indianapolis§	A. A.	OF	88	282	31	74	18	3	4	39	.262	148	6	1	.994
1989—W. Palm Beach	Fla. St.	DH	12	41	7	13	4	3	1	8	.317	0	0	0	.000
1989—Indianapolis x	A. A.	OF-1B	121	423	50	98	26	5	13	59	.232	300	15	5	.984
Major League Totals—1 Year		14	41	3	8	3	0	0	4	.195	13	0	0	1.000

Signed as free agent by San Francisco Giants' organization, February 3, 1983.
†Loaned to San Jose (Independent), April 9, 1985; returned, September 10, 1985.
‡Traded with Pitcher George Riley to Montreal Expos' organization for Pitcher Bill Laskey, October 24, 1985.
§On disabled list, August 8, 1988 through remainder of season.
xTraded to Minnesota Twins, September 16, 1989, completing deal in which Minnesota traded Outfielder Jim Dwyer to Montreal Expos for a player to be named later, August 28, 1989.

DENNIS CLAY POWELL

Born August 13, 1963, at Moultrie, Ga.
Height, 6.03. Weight, 200.
Throws left and bats righthanded.

Major League saves: 1985 (1), 1989 (2). Total—3.
Led Gulf Coast League in shutouts with 2 in 1983.

Year Club	League	G.	IP.	W.	L.	Pct.	H.	R.	ER.	SO.	BB.	ERA.
1983—Bradenton Dodgers	Gulf Coast	11	74	8	2	.800	52	22	12	★103	23	1.46
1984—Vero Beach	Florida St.	4	26	1	1	.500	19	7	4	14	12	1.38
1984—San Antonio	Texas	24	168	9	8	.529	153	81	63	82	87	3.38
1985—Albuquerque	P. Coast	18	111⅔	9	0	1.000	106	40	34	55	48	2.74
1985—Los Angeles	National	16	29⅓	1	1	.500	30	19	17	19	13	5.22

Year Club	League	G.	IP.	W.	L.	Pct.	H.	R.	ER.	SO.	BB.	ERA.
1986—Los Angeles†	National	27	65⅓	2	7	.222	65	32	31	31	25	4.27
1986—Albuquerque‡	P. Coast	7	41⅔	3	3	.500	45	23	19	27	15	4.10
1987—Calgary	P. Coast	20	117⅓	4	8	.333	145	80	64	65	48	4.52
1987—Seattle	American	16	34⅓	1	3	.250	32	13	12	17	15	3.15
1988—Calgary	P. Coast	21	108	6	4	.600	116	57	50	81	49	4.17
1988—Seattle	American	12	18⅔	1	3	.250	29	20	18	15	11	8.68
1989—Seattle	American	43	45	2	2	.500	49	25	25	27	21	5.00
1989—Calgary	P. Coast	18	25⅓	3	2	.600	21	10	6	15	12	2.13
National League Totals—2 Years		43	94⅔	3	8	.273	95	51	48	50	38	4.56
American League Totals—3 Years		71	98	4	8	.333	110	58	55	59	47	5.05
Major League Totals—5 Years		114	192⅔	7	16	.304	205	109	103	109	85	4.81

Signed as free agent by Los Angeles Dodgers' organization, May 17, 1983.
†On disabled list, April 30 to June 6, 1986.
‡Traded with Infielder Mike Watters to Seattle Mariners for Pitcher Matt Young, December 10, 1986.

TED HENRY POWER

Born January 31, 1955, at Guthrie, Okla.
Height, 6.04. Weight, 220.
Throws and bats righthanded.
Attended Kansas State University, Manhattan, Kan.

Major League saves: 1983 (2), 1984 (11), 1985 (27), 1986 (1). Total—41.

Year Club	League	G.	IP.	W.	L.	Pct.	H.	R.	ER.	SO.	BB.	ERA.
1976—Lodi	California	13	51	1	3	.250	46	34	26	58	44	4.59
1977—San Antonio†	Texas	12	72	5	3	.625	51	35	31	60	55	3.88
1978—San Antonio‡	Texas	25	101	6	5	.545	92	57	45	97	75	4.01
1979—San Antonio	Texas	10	64	5	1	.833	69	44	37	52	43	5.20
1979—Albuquerque	P. Coast	18	101	5	5	.500	95	59	52	69	82	4.63
1980—Albuquerque	P. Coast	26	155	13	7	.650	160	93	78	113	95	4.53
1981—Albuquerque	P. Coast	27	187	★18	3	★.857	165	84	74	111	★103	3.56
1981—Los Angeles	National	5	14	1	3	.250	16	6	5	7	7	3.21
1982—Los Angeles	National	12	33⅔	1	1	.500	38	27	25	15	23	6.68
1982—Albuquerque§	P. Coast	14	73	5	4	.556	77	51	42	54	49	5.18
1983—Cincinnati	National	49	111	5	6	.455	120	62	56	57	49	4.54
1984—Cincinnati	National	★78	108⅔	9	7	.563	93	37	34	81	46	2.82
1985—Cincinnati	National	64	80	8	6	.571	65	27	24	42	45	2.70
1986—Cincinnati	National	56	129	10	6	.625	115	59	53	95	52	3.70
1987—Cincinnati x	National	34	204	10	13	.435	213	115	102	133	71	4.50
1988—Kansas City yz-Detroit ab	American	26	99	6	7	.462	121	67	65	57	38	5.91
1989—Louisville	American	8	37	4	3	.571	29	13	13	36	15	3.16
1989—St. Louis bc	National	23	97	7	7	.500	96	47	40	43	21	3.71
National League Totals—8 Years		321	777⅓	51	49	.510	756	380	339	473	314	3.92
American League Totals—1 Year		26	99	6	7	.462	121	67	65	57	38	5.91
Major League Totals—9 Years		347	876⅓	57	56	.504	877	447	404	530	352	4.15

Selected by Los Angeles Dodgers' organization in 5th round of free-agent draft, June 8, 1976.
†On disabled list, July 18 to July 29 and August 20 to September 4, 1977.
‡On disabled list, July 5 to July 21, 1978.
§Traded to Cincinnati Reds for cash and Infielder Michael James Ramsey, October 15, 1982.
xTraded with Shortstop Kurt Stillwell to Kansas City Royals for Pitcher Danny Jackson and Shortstop Angel Salazar, November 6, 1987.
yOn disabled list, June 18 to July 4, 1988.
zTraded to Detroit Tigers for Catcher Rey Palacios and Pitcher Mark Lee, August 31, 1988.
aGranted free agency, November 4, 1988; re-signed by Tigers, December 7, 1988.
bReleased, March 25, 1989; signed by Louisville (St. Louis Cardinals' organization), March 28, 1989.
cOn disabled list, May 17 to June 19, 1989; included rehabilitation disability assignment to Louisville, June 9 to June 19, 1989.
dGranted free agency, November 13, 1989; signed by Pittsburgh Pirates, November 20, 1989.

JAMES ARTHUR PRESLEY
(Jim)

Born October 23, 1961, at Pensacola, Fla.
Height, 6.01. Weight, 190.
Throws and bats righthanded.
Attended Pensacola Junior College, Pensacola, Fla.

Holds major league record for fewest putouts by third baseman, season, 150 or more games (82), 1985.
Shares major league record for most home runs, opening day of season (2), April 8, 1986.
Major League stolen bases: 1984 (1), 1985 (2), 1987 (2), 1988 (3). Total—8.
Hit three home runs in a game, September 1, 1986.
Led American League third basemen in assists with 311 and total chances with 445 in 1987.
Led Eastern League in game-winning RBIs with 16 in 1982.
Led Midwest League in being hit by pitch with 12 in 1980.
Led Eastern League third basemen in assists with 247 and total chances with 365 in 1982.
Led Southern League third basemen in double plays with 29 in 1983.

Year Club	League	Pos.	G.	AB.	R.	H.	2B.	3B.	HR.	RBI.	B.A.	PO.	A.	E.	F.A.
1979—Bellingham	N'west	SS	48	138	20	27	4	1	1	12	.196	42	127	27	.862
1980—Wausau	Midw.	3-S-2-1	126	429	45	105	21	1	12	52	.245	161	235	22	.947
1981—Wausau	Midw.	3B	57	208	48	58	10	0	12	53	.279	32	105	9	.938

Year Club	League	Pos.	G.	AB.	R.	H.	2B.	3B.	HR.	RBI.	B.A.	PO.	A.	E.	F.A.
1981—Lynn	East.	3B-2B	64	210	32	54	7	1	8	36	.257	49	110	11	.935
1982—Lynn	East.	*3B-OF	133	462	65	123	24	0	22	79	.266	84	250	*35	.905
1983—Chattanooga	South.	3B-SS	131	461	70	122	31	5	14	90	.265	122	329	27	.944
1984—Salt Lake City	P. C.	3B	69	265	43	84	13	4	13	56	.317	53	140	12	.941
1984—Seattle	Amer.	3B	70	251	27	57	12	1	10	36	.227	48	113	7	.958
1985—Seattle	Amer.	3B	155	570	71	157	33	1	28	84	.275	82	335	17	.961
1986—Seattle	Amer.	3B	155	616	83	163	33	4	27	107	.265	110	308	15	.965
1987—Seattle	Amer.	3B-SS	152	575	78	142	23	6	24	88	.247	113	315	21	.953
1988—Seattle	Amer.	3B	150	544	50	125	26	0	14	62	.230	112	234	22	.940
1989—Seattle	Amer.	3B-1B	117	390	42	92	20	1	12	41	.236	222	169	18	.956
Major League Totals—6 Years			799	2946	351	736	147	13	115	418	.250	687	1474	100	.956

Selected by Seattle Mariners' organization in 4th round of free-agent draft, June 5, 1979.

ALL-STAR GAME RECORD
Member of American League All-Star Team in 1986; did not play.

JOSEPH WALTER PRICE
(Joe)

Born November 29, 1956, at Inglewood, Calif.
Height, 6.04. Weight, 215.
Throws left and bats righthanded.
Attended Oklahoma State University, Stillwater, Okla., and
University of Oklahoma, Norman, Okla.

Major League saves: 1981 (4), 1982 (3), 1985 (1), 1987 (1), 1988 (4). Total—13.

Year Club	League	G.	IP.	W.	L.	Pct.	H.	R.	ER.	SO.	BB.	ERA.
1977—Billings	Pioneer	15	94	6	5	.545	83	50	39	97	42	3.73
1978—Tampa	Florida St.	23	165	10	4	.714	123	40	27	128	51	1.47
1978—Nashville	Southern	2	10	0	0	.000	7	3	3	10	3	2.70
1979—Nashville	Southern	22	109	6	6	.500	101	58	48	69	41	3.96
1980—Indianapolis	Am. Assoc.	11	79	4	4	.500	64	36	34	83	30	3.87
1980—Cincinnati	National	24	111	7	3	.700	95	45	44	44	37	3.57
1981—Cincinnati	National	41	54	6	1	.857	42	19	15	41	18	2.50
1982—Cincinnati	National	59	72⅔	3	4	.429	73	26	23	71	32	2.85
1983—Cincinnati†	National	21	144	10	6	.625	118	46	46	83	46	2.88
1984—Cincinnati	National	30	171⅔	7	13	.350	176	91	80	129	61	4.19
1985—Cincinnati‡	National	26	64⅔	2	2	.500	59	35	28	52	23	3.90
1986—Cincinnati§x	National	25	41⅔	1	2	.333	49	30	25	30	22	5.40
1987—Phoenix	P. Coast	17	61⅓	6	0	1.000	45	21	17	49	40	2.49
1987—San Francisco y	National	20	35	2	2	.500	19	10	10	42	13	2.57
1988—San Francisco z	National	38	61⅔	1	6	.143	59	33	27	49	27	3.94
1989—San Francisco a	National	7	14	1	1	.500	16	9	9	10	4	5.79
1989—Boston bc	American	31	70⅓	2	5	.286	71	35	34	52	30	4.35
National League Totals—10 Years		291	770½	40	40	.500	706	344	307	547	283	3.59
American League Totals—1 Year		31	70⅓	2	5	.286	71	35	34	52	30	4.35
Major League Totals—10 Years		322	840⅔	42	45	.483	777	379	341	603	313	3.65

Selected by Cincinnati Reds' organization in 4th round of free-agent draft, June 7, 1977.
†On disabled list, August 7 to September 1, 1983.
‡On disabled list, July 23 to August 8 and August 29 to September 13, 1985.
§On disabled list, July 17 to September 1, 1986.
xGranted free agency, November 12, 1986; signed by San Francisco Giants, February 5, 1987.
yGranted free agency, November 9, 1987; re-signed by San Francisco Giants, December 14, 1987.
zOn disabled list, May 9 to June 3 and August 17 to September 2, 1988.
aReleased, May 1, 1989; signed by Boston Red Sox, May 5, 1989.
bOn suspended list, September 10 to September 14, 1989.
cGranted free agency, November 13, 1989.

CHAMPIONSHIP SERIES RECORD

Year Club	League	G.	IP.	W.	L.	Pct.	H.	R.	ER.	SO.	BB.	ERA.
1987—San Francisco	National	2	5⅔	1	0	1.000	3	0	0	7	1	0.00

THOMAS ALBERT PRINCE
(Tom)

Born August 13, 1964, at Kankakee, Ill.
Height, 5.11. Weight, 185.
Throws and bats righthanded.
Attended Kankakee Community College, Kankakee, Ill.

Major League stolen bases: 1989 (1).
Led Eastern League catchers in double plays with 9 and total chances with 721 in 1987.
Led Carolina League catchers in total chances with 954 and passed balls with 15 in 1986.
Led South Atlantic League catchers in total chances with 930, double plays with 10 and passed balls with 27 in 1985.

Year Club	League	Pos.	G.	AB.	R.	H.	2B.	3B.	HR.	RBI.	B.A.	PO.	A.	E.	F.A.
1984—Watertown	NYP	C-3B	23	69	6	14	3	0	2	13	.203	155	26	2	.989
1984—Bradenton Pir.	Gulf C.	C-1B	18	48	4	11	0	0	1	6	.229	75	16	4	.958
1985—Macon	S. Atl.	C	124	360	60	75	20	1	10	42	.208	*810	*101	*19	.980
1986—Prince William	Carol.	C	121	395	59	100	34	1	10	47	.253	*821	●113	20	.979
1987—Harrisburg	East.	C	113	365	41	112	23	2	6	54	.307	*622	*88	●11	.985

Year Club League	Pos.	G.	AB.	R.	H.	2B.	3B.	HR.	RBI.	B.A.	PO.	A.	E.	F.A.
1987—Pittsburgh.............. Nat.	C	4	9	1	2	1	0	1	2	.222	14	3	0	1.000
1988—Buffalo................... A. A.	C	86	304	35	79	16	0	14	42	.260	456	51	*12	.977
1988—Pittsburgh.............. Nat.	C	29	74	3	13	2	0	0	6	.176	108	8	2	.983
1989—Buffalo................... A. A.	C	65	183	21	37	8	1	6	33	.202	312	22	5	.985
1989—Pittsburgh.............. Nat.	C	21	52	1	7	4	0	0	5	.135	85	11	4	.960
Major League Totals—3 Years.................		54	135	5	22	7	0	1	13	.163	207	22	6	.974

Selected by Atlanta Braves' organization in 8th round of free-agent draft, January 11, 1983.
Selected by Atlanta Braves' organization in secondary phase of free-agent draft, June 6, 1983.
Selected by Pittsburgh Pirates' organization in secondary phase of free-agent draft, January 17, 1984.

KIRBY PUCKETT

Born March 14, 1961, at Chicago, Ill.
Height, 5.08. Weight, 210.
Throws and bats righthanded.
Attended Bradley University, Peoria, Ill., and Triton College, River Grove, Ill.

Shares major league records for most doubles, game (4), May 13, 1989; most doubles, two consecutive games (6), May 13 (4), 14 (2), 1989; most at-bats, season, no sacrifice flies (680), 1986.
Shares modern major league record for most hits, first game in majors, nine innings (4), May 8, 1984.
Holds American League record for most hits, two consecutive nine-inning games (10), August 29 and 30, 1987.
Shares American League record for most seasons, 400 or more putouts, outfielder (5).
Major League stolen bases: 1984 (14), 1985 (21), 1986 (20), 1987 (12), 1988 (6), 1989 (11). Total—84.
Collected six hits in one game, August 30, 1987.
Hit for the cycle, August 1, 1986.
Led American League in total bases with 358 in 1988.
Led American League outfielders in total chances with 492 in 1985, 465 in 1988 and 455 in 1989.
Led Appalachian League in total bases with 135 and tied for lead in stolen bases with 43 in 1982.
Led California League outfielders in double plays with 5 in 1983.
Named outfielder on THE SPORTING NEWS American League All-Star Team, 1986 through 1989.
Named outfielder on THE SPORTING NEWS American League All-Star fielding team, 1986 through 1989.
Named outfielder on THE SPORTING NEWS American League Silver Slugger team, 1986 through 1989.
Named California League Player of the Year, 1983.

Year Club League	Pos.	G.	AB.	R.	H.	2B.	3B.	HR.	RBI.	B.A.	PO.	A.	E.	F.A.
1982—Elizabethton .... Appal.	OF	65	*275	*65	*105	15	3	3	35	*.382	133	*11	5	.966
1983—Visalia .... Calif.	OF	138	*548	105	172	29	7	9	97	.314	253	*22	5	.982
1984—Toledo .... Int.	OF	21	80	9	21	2	0	1	5	.263	35	1	3	.923
1984—Minnesota.............. Amer.	OF	128	557	63	165	12	5	0	31	.296	438	*16	3	.993
1985—Minnesota.............. Amer.	OF	161	*691	80	199	29	13	4	74	.288	*465	19	8	.984
1986—Minnesota.............. Amer.	OF	161	680	119	223	37	6	31	96	.328	429	8	6	.986
1987—Minnesota.............. Amer.	OF	157	624	96	●207	32	5	28	99	.332	341	8	5	.986
1988—Minnesota.............. Amer.	OF	158	*657	109	*234	42	5	24	121	.356	*450	12	3	.994
1989—Minnesota.............. Amer.	OF	159	635	75	*215	45	4	9	85	*.339	*438	13	4	.991
Major League Totals—6 Years................		924	3844	542	1243	197	38	96	506	.323	2561	76	29	.989

Selected by Minnesota Twins' organization in 1st round (third player selected) of free-agent draft, January 12, 1982.

CHAMPIONSHIP SERIES RECORD

Shares American League Championship Series record for most at-bats, game (6), October 12, 1987.

Year Club League	Pos.	G.	AB.	R.	H.	2B.	3B.	HR.	RBI.	B.A.	PO.	A.	E.	F.A.
1987—Minnesota.............. Amer.	OF	5	24	3	5	1	0	1	3	.208	7	0	0	1.000

WORLD SERIES RECORD

Shares World Series records for most at-bats, inning (2), October 18, 1987, fourth inning; most runs, game (4), October 24, 1987.

Year Club League	Pos.	G.	AB.	R.	H.	2B.	3B.	HR.	RBI.	B.A.	PO.	A.	E.	F.A.
1987—Minnesota.............. Amer.	OF	7	28	5	10	1	1	0	3	.357	15	1	1	.941

ALL-STAR GAME RECORD

Year League	Pos.	AB.	R.	H.	2B.	3B.	HR.	RBI.	B.A.	PO.	A.	E.	F.A.
1986—American	OF	3	0	1	0	0	0	0	.333	5	0	0	1.000
1987—American	PH-OF	4	0	0	0	0	0	0	.000	1	0	0	1.000
1988—American	OF	1	0	0	0	0	0	0	.000	1	0	0	1.000
1989—American	OF	3	1	1	0	0	0	0	.333	0	0	0	.000
All-Star Game Totals—4 Years....................		11	1	2	0	0	0	0	.182	7	0	0	1.000

TERRANCE STEPHEN PUHL

Name pronounced Pool.

(Terry)

Born July 8, 1956, at Melville, Saskatchewan, Canada.
Height, 6.02. Weight, 197.
Throws right and bats lefthanded.

Holds major league record for highest fielding percentage by outfielder, lifetime, 1,000 or more games (.993).
Shares major league records for highest fielding percentage by outfielder, season, 150 or more games (1.000), 1979; fewest errors by outfielder, season, 150 or more games (0), 1979.
Major League stolen bases: 1977 (10), 1978 (32), 1979 (30), 1980 (27), 1981 (22), 1982 (17), 1983 (24), 1984 (13), 1985 (6), 1986 (3), 1987 (1), 1988 (22), 1989 (9). Total—216.

Year Club	League	Pos.	G.	AB.	R.	H.	2B.	3B.	HR.	RBI.	B.A.	PO.	A.	E.	F.A.
1974—Covington	Appal.	OF	59	211	42	60	11	0	0	21	.284	89	2	2	.978
1975—Dubuque	Midw.	OF-1B	104	346	57	115	10	2	0	28	.332	230	11	7	.971
1976—Columbus	South.	OF	28	98	13	28	5	0	1	14	.286	76	1	2	.975
1976—Memphis	Int.	OF	105	372	50	99	17	3	1	39	.266	191	5	3	.985
1977—Charleston	Int.	OF	78	285	53	87	12	6	4	33	.305	189	4	3	.985
1977—Houston	Nat.	OF	60	229	40	69	13	5	0	10	.301	119	3	1	.992
1978—Houston	Nat.	OF	149	585	87	169	25	6	3	35	.289	386	6	3	.992
1979—Houston	Nat.	OF	157	600	87	172	22	4	8	49	.287	352	7	0	★1.000
1980—Houston	Nat.	OF	141	535	75	151	24	5	13	55	.282	311	14	3	.991
1981—Houston	Nat.	OF	96	350	43	88	19	4	3	28	.251	185	5	0	●1.000
1982—Houston	Nat.	OF	145	507	64	133	17	9	8	50	.262	257	4	3	.989
1983—Houston	Nat.	OF	137	465	66	136	25	7	8	44	.292	220	4	2	.991
1984—Houston†	Nat.	OF	132	449	66	135	19	7	9	55	.301	213	6	3	.986
1985—Houston‡	Nat.	OF	57	194	34	55	14	3	2	23	.284	92	3	0	1.000
1986—Houston§	Nat.	OF	81	172	17	42	10	0	3	14	.244	65	0	0	1.000
1987—Houston	Nat.	OF	90	122	9	28	5	0	2	15	.230	48	0	1	.980
1988—Houston	Nat.	OF	113	234	42	71	7	2	3	19	.303	116	2	2	.983
1989—Houston	Nat.	OF-1B	121	354	41	96	25	4	0	27	.271	212	3	0	1.000
Major League Totals—13 Years			1479	4796	671	1345	225	56	62	424	.280	2576	57	18	.993

Signed as free agent by Houston Astros' organization, September 19, 1973.

†On disabled list, April 13 to April 30, 1984.

‡On disabled list, April 22 to May 7, June 13 to June 28, July 19 to August 15 and August 26, 1985 through remainder of season.

§On disabled list, March 30 to April 15 and July 2 to July 23, 1986.

DIVISION SERIES RECORD

Year Club	League	Pos.	G.	AB.	R.	H.	2B.	3B.	HR.	RBI.	B.A.	PO.	A.	E.	F.A.
1981—Houston	Nat.	OF	5	21	2	4	1	0	0	0	.190	7	1	0	1.000

CHAMPIONSHIP SERIES RECORD

Shares Championship Series record for most singles, game (4), October 12, 1980 (10 innings).

Shares National League Championship Series record for most singles, series (8), 1980.

Year Club	League	Pos.	G.	AB.	R.	H.	2B.	3B.	HR.	RBI.	B.A.	PO.	A.	E.	F.A.
1980—Houston	Nat.	PH-OF	5	19	4	10	2	0	0	3	.526	13	0	0	1.000
1986—Houston	Nat.	PH	3	3	0	2	0	0	0	0	.667	0	0	0	.000
Championship Series Totals—2 Years			8	22	4	12	2	0	0	3	.545	13	0	0	1.000

ALL-STAR GAME RECORD

Member of National League All-Star Team for 1978 game; did not play.

CHARLES MICHAEL PULEO

Name pronounced Puh-LAY-oh.

(Charlie)

Born February 7, 1955, at Glen Ridge, N. J.
Height, 6.03. Weight, 200.
Throws and bats righthanded.
Received bachelor of science degree in physical education and science from Seton Hall University, South Orange, N. J. in 1977.

Pitched seven-inning, 3-0 no-hit victory against St. Petersburg, August 13, 1979 (second game).

Major League saves: 1982 (1), 1988 (1). Total—2.

Tied International League in complete games with 9 in 1986.

Year Club	League	G.	IP.	W.	L.	Pct.	H.	R.	ER.	SO.	BB.	ERA.
1978—Utica	NYP	16	104	10	3	.769	81	46	31	★125	48	2.68
1979—Dunedin	Florida St.	22	123	10	10	.500	126	72	61	77	61	4.46
1980—Knoxville†‡	Southern	19	108	8	7	.533	87	51	34	97	66	2.83
1981—Tidewater	Int'national	26	169	12	9	.571	132	74	65	133	73	3.46
1981—New York	National	4	13	0	0	.000	8	1	0	8	8	0.00
1982—New York§	National	36	171	9	9	.500	179	99	85	98	90	4.47
1983—Cincinnati x	National	27	143⅔	6	12	.333	145	86	78	71	91	4.89
1984—Wichita	Am. Assoc.	19	104⅓	8	9	.471	117	71	62	59	59	5.35
1984—Cincinnati	National	5	22	1	2	.333	27	15	14	6	15	5.73
1985—Denver y	Am. Assoc.	11	61	1	5	.167	70	42	31	40	37	4.57
1985—Richmond	Int'national	16	71	5	4	.556	50	23	22	63	37	2.79
1986—Richmond	Int'national	27	170	★14	7	.667	166	80	66	●124	76	3.79
1986—Atlanta	National	5	24⅓	1	2	.333	13	10	8	18	12	2.96
1987—Atlanta	National	35	123⅓	6	8	.429	122	63	58	99	40	4.23
1988—Atlanta	National	53	106⅓	5	5	.500	101	46	41	70	47	3.47
1989—Greenville z	Southern	2	6	0	0	.000	6	3	3	5	3	4.50
1989—Atlanta	National	15	29	1	1	.500	26	15	15	17	16	4.66
1989—Richmond a	Int'national	11	62	5	1	.833	59	26	23	57	15	3.34
Major League Totals—8 Years		180	632⅔	29	39	.426	621	335	299	387	319	4.25

Selected by Detroit Tigers' organization in 13th round of free-agent draft, June 5, 1973.

Signed as free agent by Toronto Blue Jays' organization, March 14, 1978.

†On disabled list, April 24 to June 14, 1980.

‡Traded to New York Mets' organization, April 14, 1981; completing deal in which New York traded Pitcher Mark Bomback to Toronto Blue Jays for a player to be named later, April 6, 1981.

§Traded with Catcher Lloyd McClendon and Outfielder Jason Felice to Cincinnati Reds for Pitcher Tom Seaver, December 16, 1982.

xOn disabled list, March 20 to May 2, 1983.
ySold to Richmond (Atlanta Braves' organization), June 6, 1985.
zOn Atlanta disabled list, March 28 to April 16, 1989; included rehabilitation disability assignment to Greenville, April 9 to April 13, 1989.
aReleased, November 15, 1989.

HARVEY JEROME PULLIAM JR.

Born October 20, 1967, at San Francisco, Calif.
Height, 6.01. Weight, 190.
Throws and bats righthanded.

Year Club	League	Pos.	G.	AB.	R.	H.	2B.	3B.	HR.	RBI.	B.A.	PO.	A.	E.	F.A.
1986—Sarasota Royals...	Gulf C.	OF	48	168	14	35	3	0	4	23	.208	62	5	4	.944
1987—Appleton	Midw.	OF	110	395	54	109	20	1	9	55	.276	195	8	6	.971
1988—Baseball City	Fla. St.	OF	132	457	56	111	19	4	4	42	.243	289	9	6	.980
1989—Memphis	South.	OF	116	417	67	121	28	8	10	67	.290	157	8	5	.971
1989—Omaha	A. A.	OF	7	22	3	4	2	0	0	2	.182	12	1	0	1.000

Selected by Kansas City Royals' organization in 3rd round of free-agent draft, June 2, 1986.

THOMAS RAYMOND QUINLAN
(Tom)

Born March 27, 1968, at St. Paul, Minn.
Height, 6.03. Weight, 200.
Throws and bats righthanded.

Led South Atlantic League third basemen in putouts with 96 and double plays with 29 and tied for lead in total chances with 368 in 1987.

Tied for Southern League lead in double plays by third basemen with 21 in 1989.

Year Club	League	Pos.	G.	AB.	R.	H.	2B.	3B.	HR.	RBI.	B.A.	PO.	A.	E.	F.A.
1987—Myrtle Beach	S. Atl.	3B-1B	132	435	42	97	20	3	5	51	.223	107	232	40	.894
1988—Knoxville†	South.	3B-1B	98	326	33	71	19	1	8	47	.218	87	188	25	.917
1989—Knoxville	South.	3B	139	452	62	95	21	3	16	57	.210	81	259	34	.909

Selected by Toronto Blue Jays' organization in 27th round of free-agent draft, June 2, 1986.
†On disabled list, June 10 to July 14, 1989.

LUIS RAUL QUINONES

Name pronounced Key-NO-nez.

Born April 28, 1962, at Ponce, Puerto Rico.
Height, 5.11. Weight, 180.
Throws right and bats left and righthanded.

Shares major league record for most plate appearances, inning (3), August 3, 1989, first inning.
Major League stolen bases: 1983 (1), 1986 (3), 1988 (1), 1989 (2). Total—7.
Led Carolina League shortstops in double plays with 77 in 1981.
Tied for Northwest League lead in double plays by shortstops with 33 in 1980.

Year Club	League	Pos.	G.	AB.	R.	H.	2B.	3B.	HR.	RBI.	B.A.	PO.	A.	E.	F.A.
1980—Grays Harbor	N'west	SS	56	156	33	35	2	2	0	11	.224	70	157	24	.904
1981—Salem	Carol.	●SS-2B	123	455	64	102	10	4	7	37	.224	208	341	●53	.912
1982—Salem	Carol.	SS	41	173	32	48	1	4	5	28	.277	41	99	15	.903
1982—Amarillo†	Texas	SS	95	411	69	120	19	7	11	60	.292	164	288	31	.936
1983—Albany	East.	2B-OF-SS	56	213	35	51	5	0	6	23	.239	101	138	13	.948
1983—Oakland	Amer.	2-O-3-S	19	42	5	8	2	1	0	4	.190	22	24	1	.979
1983—Tacoma‡	P. C.	SS-OF-2B	45	133	14	35	3	1	2	14	.263	62	97	9	.946
1984—Maine	Int.	★SS-OF-2B	131	473	71	127	27	3	8	60	.268	217	330	★43	.927
1985—Maine§	Int.	SS-OF	14	45	4	8	2	1	1	2	.178	19	12	0	1.000
1985—Phoenix	P. C.	SS-2B-3B	85	304	46	78	13	7	8	47	.257	106	236	13	.963
1986—Phoenix	P. C.	SS	14	55	7	14	4	1	0	7	.255	23	37	3	.952
1986—San Francisco xy.	Nat.	SS-3B-2B	71	106	13	19	1	3	0	11	.179	28	66	8	.922
1987—Iowa	A. A.	SS-2B	77	287	44	91	14	★12	11	62	.317	93	122	14	.939
1987—Chicago z	Nat.	SS-2B-3B	49	101	12	22	6	0	0	8	.218	35	58	3	.969
1988—Nashville	A. A.	SS-3B-1B	114	417	42	115	28	6	9	53	.276	164	285	25	.947
1988—Cincinnati	Nat.	SS-3B-2B	23	52	4	12	3	0	1	11	.231	15	37	2	.963
1989—Nashville	A. A.	3B-2B-SS	45	176	19	40	9	2	4	24	.227	38	75	13	.897
1989—Cincinnati	Nat.	2B-3B-SS	97	340	43	83	13	4	12	34	.244	112	213	10	.970
American League Totals—1 Year			19	42	5	8	2	1	0	4	.190	22	24	1	.979
National League Totals—4 Years			240	599	72	136	23	7	13	64	.227	190	374	23	.961
Major League Totals—5 Years			259	641	77	144	25	8	13	68	.225	212	398	24	.962

Signed as free agent by San Diego Padres' organization, April 28, 1980.
†Drafted by Oakland A's, December 6, 1982.
‡Traded to Cleveland Indians, December 8, 1983, completing deal in which Cleveland traded Catcher Jim Essian to Oakland A's for a player to be named later, December 5, 1983.
§Traded with Pitcher Mike Jeffcoat to San Francisco Giants' organization for Shortstop Johnnie LeMaster, May 7, 1985.

xReleased, November 10, 1986; signed by Tacoma (Oakland A's organization), January 22, 1987.
yTraded to Chicago Cubs for Third Baseman Ron Cey, January 30, 1987.
zTraded to Cincinnati Reds for Pitcher Bill Landrum, April 1, 1988.

REY FRANCISCO QUINONES

Name pronounced Key-NO-nez.

Born November 11, 1963, at Rio Piedras, Puerto Rico.
Height, 5.11. Weight, 185.
Throws and bats righthanded.

Major League stolen bases: 1986 (4), 1987 (1). Total—5.
Led Eastern League in being hit by pitch with 9 in 1985.
Led Carolina League in grounding into double plays with 20 in 1984.
Led Eastern League shortstops in double plays with 75 in 1985.
Led Carolina League shortstops in total chances with 718 and double plays with 84 in 1984.

Year Club	League	Pos.	G.	AB.	R.	H.	2B.	3B.	HR.	RBI.	B.A.	PO.	A.	E.	F.A.
1983—Elmira	NYP	SS	67	234	38	69	11	0	12	55	.295	107	226	27	.925
1984—Winston-Salem	Carol.	SS	132	458	53	128	★30	6	11	69	.279	★240	★428	★50	.930
1985—New Britain	East.	SS	134	439	67	113	19	5	9	50	.257	207	★402	★34	.947
1986—Pawtucket	Int.	SS	24	87	12	23	2	0	4	18	.264	35	67	4	.962
1986—Boston†-Seattle.....	Amer.	SS	98	312	32	68	16	1	2	22	.218	143	247	24	.942
1987—Seattle...............	Amer.	SS	135	478	55	132	18	2	12	56	.276	204	384	★25	.959
1988—Seattle‡...............	Amer.	SS	140	499	63	124	30	3	12	52	.248	202	396	23	.963
1989—Seattle§x	Amer.	SS	7	19	2	2	0	0	0	0	.105	5	19	3	.889
1989—Pittsburgh y	Nat.	SS	71	225	21	47	11	0	3	29	.209	94	174	19	.934
American League Totals—4 Years			380	1308	152	326	64	6	26	130	.249	554	1046	75	.955
National League Totals—1 Year.............			71	225	21	47	11	0	3	29	.209	94	174	19	.934
Major League Totals—4 Years.................			451	1533	173	373	75	6	29	159	.243	648	1220	94	.952

Signed as free agent by Boston Red Sox' organization, September 8, 1982.

†Traded with a player to be named later and cash to Seattle Mariners for Infielder Spike Owen and Outfielder Dave Henderson, August 19, 1986; as part of deal, Seattle claimed Pitchers Mike Brown and Mike Trujillo on waivers from Boston Red Sox, August 22, 1986. Seattle acquired Outfielder John Christensen to complete deal, September 25, 1986.

‡On disqualified list, May 4 to May 8, 1988.

§On disabled list, March 26 to April 15, 1989.

xTraded with Pitcher Bill Wilkinson to Pittsburgh Pirates for Pitchers Mike Dunne and Mike Walker and Outfielder Mark Merchant, April 21, 1989.

yReleased, July 22, 1989.

CARLOS NARCIS QUINTANA

Born August 26, 1965, at Estado Miranda, Venezuela.
Height, 6.02. Weight, 195.
Throws and bats righthanded.

Led International League outfielders in assists with 15 in 1988.

Year Club	League	Pos.	G.	AB.	R.	H.	2B.	3B.	HR.	RBI.	B.A.	PO.	A.	E.	F.A.
1985—Elmira	NYP	OF	65	220	27	61	8	0	4	35	.277	55	5	3	.952
1986—Greensboro	S. Atl.	OF-1B	126	443	97	144	19	4	11	81	.325	224	12	9	.963
1987—New Britain	East.	OF	56	206	31	64	11	3	2	31	.311	100	4	2	.981
1988—Pawtucket	Int.	OF-1B	131	471	67	134	25	3	16	66	.285	525	44	11	.981
1988—Boston....................	Amer.	OF	5	6	1	2	0	0	0	2	.333	4	0	0	1.000
1989—Pawtucket	Int.	1B-OF	82	272	45	78	11	2	11	52	.287	398	27	2	.995
1989—Boston†.................	Amer.	OF-1B	34	77	6	16	5	0	0	6	.208	31	0	2	.939
Major League Totals—2 Years.................			39	83	7	18	5	0	0	8	.217	35	0	2	.946

Signed as free agent by Boston Red Sox' organization, November 26, 1984.

†On disabled list, June 22 to July 7, 1989.

JAMES PATRICK QUIRK
(Jamie)

Born October 22, 1954, at Whittier, Calif.
Height, 6.04. Weight, 200.
Throws right and bats lefthanded.
Attended Whittier College, Whittier, Calif.

Major League stolen bases: 1980 (3), 1987 (1), 1988 (1). Total—5.
Led American Association in passed balls with 23 in 1985.
Led American Association third basemen in double plays with 31 in 1975.
Led Pioneer League shortstops in double plays with 16 in 1972.

Year Club	League	Pos.	G.	AB.	R.	H.	2B.	3B.	HR.	RBI.	B.A.	PO.	A.	E.	F.A.
1972—Billings	Pion.	SS	55	208	29	53	9	4	5	37	.255	★63	★162	★28	★.889
1973—San Jose	Calif.	SS	132	429	58	99	12	7	8	45	.231	160	330	39	.926
1974—Jacksonville	South.	SS	46	163	16	37	7	2	3	21	.227	75	133	20	.912
1974—Omaha....................	A. A.	SS-3B-2B	53	203	27	57	10	2	10	31	.281	64	141	14	.936
1975—Omaha....................	A. A.	3B	127	445	62	122	23	4	13	64	.274	109	★254	16	★.958
1975—Kansas City............	Amer.	OF-3B	14	39	2	10	0	0	1	5	.256	19	3	2	.917
1976—Kansas City†..........	Amer.	SS-3B-1B	64	114	11	28	6	0	1	15	.246	9	14	2	.920
1977—Milwaukee	Amer.	OF-3B	93	221	16	48	14	1	3	13	.217	19	4	2	.920
1978—Spokane‡	P. C.	3B-1B	97	343	58	100	20	2	12	63	.292	235	142	20	.950
1978—Kansas City§..........	Amer.	3B-SS	17	29	3	6	2	0	0	2	.207	11	16	2	.931
1979—Kansas City	Amer.	C-SS-3B	51	79	8	24	6	1	1	11	.304	16	9	1	.960
1980—Kansas City	Amer.	C-3-O-1	62	163	13	45	5	0	5	21	.276	78	66	8	.947
1981—Kansas City	Amer.	C-3-2-O	46	100	8	25	7	0	0	10	.250	63	23	4	.956
1982—Kansas City xy	Amer.	C-1-3-O	36	78	8	18	3	0	1	5	.231	110	12	0	1.000

Year Club	League	Pos.	G.	AB.	R.	H.	2B.	3B.	HR.	RBI.	B.A.	PO.	A.	E.	F.A.
1983—St. Louis za	Nat.	C-3B-SS	48	86	3	18	2	1	2	11	.209	68	13	6	.931
1984—Denver	A. A.	C-3-O-1-P	70	201	23	42	6	3	2	24	.209	212	67	11	.962
1984—Chi. b-Cle. c	Amer.	3B-C	4	3	1	1	0	0	1	2	.333	1	0	0	1.000
1985—Omaha	A. A.	C-1B-3B	104	324	33	79	5	1	8	48	.244	525	67	14	.977
1985—Kansas City d	Amer.	C-1B	19	57	3	16	3	1	0	4	.281	66	8	1	.987
1986—Kansas City e	Amer.	C-3-1-O	80	219	24	47	10	0	8	26	.215	303	64	4	.989
1987—Kansas City fg......	Amer.	C-SS	109	296	24	70	17	0	5	33	.236	532	40	8	.986
1988—Kansas City h	Amer.	C-1B-3B	84	196	22	47	7	1	8	25	.240	412	34	8	.982
1989—N.Y. i-Oak j-Bal....	Amer.	C-3-1-O-S	47	85	6	15	2	0	1	10	.176	129	15	1	.993
1989—Tacoma k	P. C.	C-1B	14	47	5	8	2	0	1	5	.170	89	7	2	.980
American League Totals—14 Years			726	1679	149	400	82	4	35	182	.238	1768	308	43	.980
National League Totals—1 Year.............			48	86	3	18	2	1	2	11	.209	68	13	6	.931
Major League Totals—15 Years..............			774	1765	152	418	84	5	37	193	.237	1836	321	49	.978

Selected by Kansas City Royals' organization in 1st round (18th player selected) of free-agent draft, June 6, 1972.

†Traded with Outfielder Jim Wohlford and a player to be named later to Milwaukee Brewers for Pitcher Jim Colborn and Catcher Darrell Porter, December 6, 1976; Milwaukee acquired Pitcher Bob McClure to complete deal, March 15, 1977.

‡Traded to Kansas City Royals for Pitcher Gerry Ako and cash, August 3, 1978.

§On disabled list, August 14 to September 5, 1978.

xOn disabled list, August 10 to September 1, 1982.

yGranted free agency, November 10, 1982; signed by St. Louis Cardinals, February 16, 1983.

zReleased, March 26, 1984; named St. Louis Cardinals coach, April 13, 1984.

aSigned by Chicago White Sox' organization, May 23, 1984.

bSold to Cleveland Indians, September 24, 1984.

cReleased, October 15, 1984; signed by Kansas City Royals' organization, February 25, 1985.

dGranted free agency, November 12, 1985; re-signed by Royals, November 27, 1985.

eGranted free agency, November 12, 1986; re-signed by Royals, December 17, 1986.

fOn disabled list, July 21 to August 5, 1987.

gGranted free agency, November 9, 1987; re-signed by Royals, January 25, 1988.

hGranted free agency, November 4, 1988; signed by New York Yankees, December 20, 1988.

iReleased, May 16, 1989; signed by Tacoma (Oakland Athletics' organization), May 27, 1989.

jReleased, July 24, 1989; signed by Baltimore Orioles, August 5, 1989.

kReleased, November 2, 1989; signed by Oakland Athletics, December 13, 1989.

CHAMPIONSHIP SERIES RECORD

Year Club	League	Pos.	G.	AB.	R.	H.	2B.	3B.	HR.	RBI.	B.A.	PO.	A.	E.	F.A.
1976—Kansas City...........	Amer.	PH-DH	4	7	1	1	0	1	0	2	.143	0	0	0	.000
1985—Kansas City...........	Amer.	PH	1	1	0	0	0	0	0	0	.000	0	0	0	.000
Championship Series Totals—2 Years.....			5	8	1	1	0	1	0	2	.125	0	0	0	.000

WORLD SERIES RECORD

Eligible for 1980 and 1985 World Series with Kansas City Royals; did not play.

PITCHING RECORD

Year Club	League	G.	IP.	W.	L.	Pct.	H.	R.	ER.	SO.	BB.	ERA.
1984—Denver	Am. Assoc.	2	2	0	0	.000	6	3	3	0	0	13.50

DANIEL RAYMOND QUISENBERRY

Name pronounced QUIZ-en-berry.

(Dan)

Born February 7, 1953, at Santa Monica, Calif.
Height, 6.02. Weight, 185.
Throws and bats righthanded.
Attended Orange Coast College, Costa Mesa, Calif., LaVerne College, LaVerne, Calif.,
and Fresno Pacific College, Fresno, Calif.

Holds American League record for most saves, lifetime (238).

Major League saves: 1979 (5), 1980 (33), 1981 (18), 1982 (35), 1983 (45), 1984 (44), 1985 (37), 1986 (12), 1987 (8), 1988 (1), 1989 (6). Total—244.

Led American League in games finished in relief with 68 in both 1980 and 1982, 62 in 1983 and 76 in 1985.

Led American League in saves with 35 in 1982, 45 in 1983, 44 in 1984, 37 in 1985 and tied for lead with 33 in 1980.

Tied for Southern League lead in saves with 15 in 1978.

Named American League Fireman of the Year by THE SPORTING NEWS, 1980 and 1982 through 1985.

Year Club	League	G.	IP.	W.	L.	Pct.	H.	R.	ER.	SO.	BB.	ERA.
1975—Waterloo......................................	Midwest	20	44	3	2	.600	40	16	12	31	6	2.45
1975—Jacksonville............................	Southern	6	8	0	1	.000	5	3	2	2	4	2.25
1976—Jacksonville............................	Southern	9	12	0	1	.000	8	6	3	6	2	2.25
1976—Waterloo......................................	Midwest	34	42	2	1	.667	28	4	3	19	9	0.64
1977—Jacksonville............................	Southern	33	74	3	1	.750	61	18	11	33	11	1.34
1978—Jacksonville............................	Southern	48	64	4	2	.667	62	22	17	29	12	2.39
1979—Omaha	Am. Assoc.	26	35	2	1	.667	29	15	14	16	10	3.60
1979—Kansas City..............................	American	32	40	3	2	.600	42	16	14	13	7	3.15
1980—Kansas City..............................	American	★75	128	12	7	.632	129	47	44	37	27	3.09
1981—Kansas City..............................	American	40	62	1	4	.200	59	16	12	20	15	1.74
1982—Kansas City..............................	American	72	136⅔	9	7	.563	126	43	39	46	12	2.57
1983—Kansas City..............................	American	★69	139	5	3	.625	118	35	30	48	11	1.94
1984—Kansas City..............................	American	72	129⅓	6	3	.667	121	39	38	41	12	2.64
1985—Kansas City..............................	American	★84	129	8	9	.471	142	41	34	54	16	2.37

Year Club	League	G.	IP.	W.	L.	Pct.	H.	R.	ER.	SO.	BB.	ERA.
1986—Kansas City	American	62	81⅓	3	7	.300	92	30	25	36	24	2.77
1987—Kansas City	American	47	49	4	1	.800	58	15	15	17	10	2.76
1988—Kansas City†	American	20	25⅓	0	1	.000	32	11	10	9	5	3.55
1988—St. Louis	National	33	38	2	0	1.000	54	26	26	19	6	6.16
1989—St. Louis	National	63	78⅓	3	1	.750	78	25	23	37	14	2.64
American League Totals—10 Years		573	919⅔	51	44	.537	919	293	261	321	139	2.55
National League Totals—2 Years		96	116⅓	5	1	.833	132	51	49	56	20	3.79
Major League Totals—11 Years		669	1036	56	45	.554	1051	344	310	377	159	2.69

Signed as free agent by Kansas City Royals' organization, June 7, 1975.
†Released, July 4, 1988; signed by St. Louis Cardinals, July 14, 1988.

DIVISION SERIES RECORD

Year Club	League	G.	IP.	W.	L.	Pct.	H.	R.	ER.	SO.	BB.	ERA.
1981—Kansas City	American	1	1	0	0	.000	1	0	0	0	0	0.00

CHAMPIONSHIP SERIES RECORD

Shares American League Championship Series record for most games pitched, series (4), 1985.

Year Club	League	G.	IP.	W.	L.	Pct.	H.	R.	ER.	SO.	BB.	ERA.
1980—Kansas City	American	2	4⅔	1	0	1.000	4	1	0	1	2	0.00
1984—Kansas City	American	1	3	0	1	.000	2	2	1	1	1	3.00
1985—Kansas City	American	4	4⅔	0	1	.000	7	4	2	3	0	3.86
Championship Series Totals—3 Years		7	12⅓	1	2	.333	13	7	3	5	3	2.19

WORLD SERIES RECORD

Year Club	League	G.	IP.	W.	L.	Pct.	H.	R.	ER.	SO.	BB.	ERA.
1980—Kansas City	American	6	10⅓	1	2	.333	10	6	6	0	3	5.23
1985—Kansas City	American	4	4⅓	1	0	1.000	5	1	1	3	3	2.08
World Series Totals—2 Years		10	14⅔	2	2	.500	15	7	7	3	6	4.30

ALL-STAR GAME RECORD

Year League	IP.	W.	L.	Pct.	H.	R.	ER.	SO.	BB.	ERA.
1982—American	2	0	0	.000	3	1	1	1	0	4.50
1983—American	1	0	0	.000	1	0	0	1	0	0.00
All-Star Game Totals—2 Years	3	0	0	.000	4	1	1	2	0	3.00

Member of American League All-Star Team in 1984; did not play.

SCOTT DAVID RADINSKY

Born March 3, 1968, at Glendale, Calif.
Height, 6.03. Weight, 190.
Throws and bats lefthanded.

Year Club	League	G.	IP.	W.	L.	Pct.	H.	R.	ER.	SO.	BB.	ERA.
1986—Sarasota White Sox	Gulf Coast	7	26⅔	1	0	1.000	24	20	10	18	17	3.38
1987—Peninsula	Carolina	12	39	1	7	.125	43	30	25	37	32	5.77
1987—Sarasota White Sox	Gulf Coast	11	58⅓	3	3	.500	43	23	15	41	39	2.31
1988—Sarasota White Sox	Gulf Coast	5	3⅓	0	0	.000	2	2	2	7	4	5.40
1989—South Bend	Midwest	53	61⅔	7	5	.583	39	21	12	83	19	1.75

Selected by Chicago White Sox' organization in 3rd round of free-agent draft, June 2, 1986.

TIMOTHY RAINES
(Tim)

Born September 16, 1959, at Sanford, Fla.
Height, 5.08. Weight, 185.
Throws right and bats left and righthanded.
Brother of Ned Raines, minor league outfielder, 1978 through 1980.

Holds major league records for highest stolen base percentage, lifetime, 300 or attempts (.867); most intentional bases on balls by switch-hitter, season (26), 1987.
Shares major league record for fewest double plays by outfielder, season, for leader in double plays (4), 1985.
Major League stolen bases: 1979 (2), 1980 (5), 1981 (71), 1982 (78), 1983 (90), 1984 (75), 1985 (70), 1986 (70), 1987 (50), 1988 (33), 1989 (41). Total—585.
Switch-hit home runs in one game, July 16, 1988.
Hit for the cycle, August 16, 1987.
Led National League in stolen bases with 71 in 1981, 78 in 1982, 90 in 1983 and 75 in 1984.
Led National League outfielders in assists with 21 in 1983.
Led American Association in stolen bases with 77 in 1980.
Won THE SPORTING NEWS Gold Shoe Award, 1984.
Named outfielder on THE SPORTING NEWS National League All-Star Team, 1983 and 1986.
Named outfielder on THE SPORTING NEWS National League Silver Slugger team, 1986.
Named National League Rookie Player of the Year by THE SPORTING NEWS, 1981.
Named Minor League Player of the Year by THE SPORTING NEWS, 1980.

Year Club	League	Pos.	G.	AB.	R.	H.	2B.	3B.	HR.	RBI.	B.A.	PO.	A.	E.	F.A.
1977—Sarasota Expos	Gulf C.	2B-3B-OF	49	161	28	45	6	2	0	21	.280	79	72	13	.921
1978—W. Palm Beach†	Fla. St.	2B-SS	100	359	67	103	10	0	0	23	.287	219	273	24	.953
1979—Memphis	South.	2B	●145	552	★104	160	25	10	5	50	.290	★341	★413	★23	.970
1979—Montreal	Nat.	PR	6	0	3	0	0	0	0	0	.000	0	0	0	.000
1980—Denver	A. A.	2B	108	429	105	152	23	●11	6	64	★.354	226	338	16	.972

Year Club	League	Pos.	G.	AB.	R.	H.	2B.	3B.	HR.	RBI.	B.A.	PO.	A.	E.	F.A.
1980—Montreal	Nat.	2B-OF	15	20	5	1	0	0	0	0	.050	15	16	0	1.000
1981—Montreal	Nat.	OF-2B	88	313	61	95	13	7	5	37	.304	162	8	4	.977
1982—Montreal	Nat.	OF-2B	156	647	90	179	32	8	4	43	.277	293	126	8	.981
1983—Montreal	Nat.	OF-2B	156	615	★133	183	32	8	11	71	.298	314	23	4	.988
1984—Montreal	Nat.	OF-2B	160	622	106	192	●38	9	8	60	.309	420	8	6	.986
1985—Montreal	Nat.	OF	150	575	115	184	30	13	11	41	.320	284	8	2	.993
1986—Montreal‡	Nat.	OF	151	580	91	194	35	10	9	62	★.334	270	13	6	.979
1987—Montreal	Nat.	OF	139	530	★123	175	34	8	18	68	.330	297	9	4	.987
1988—Montreal§	Nat.	OF	109	429	66	116	19	7	12	48	.270	235	5	3	.988
1989—Montreal	Nat.	OF	145	517	76	148	29	6	9	60	.286	253	7	1	.996
Major League Totals—11 Years			1275	4848	869	1467	262	76	87	490	.303	2543	223	38	.986

Selected by Montreal Expos' organization in 5th round of free-agent draft, June 7, 1977.
†On disabled list, May 23 to June 5, 1978.
‡Granted free agency, November 12, 1986; re-signed by Expos, May 2, 1987.
§On disabled list, June 24 to July 9, 1988.

CHAMPIONSHIP SERIES RECORD

Year Club	League	Pos.	G.	AB.	R.	H.	2B.	3B.	HR.	RBI.	B.A.	PO.	A.	E.	F.A.
1981—Montreal	Nat.	OF	5	21	1	5	2	0	0	1	.238	9	0	0	1.000

ALL-STAR GAME RECORD

Year League	Pos.	AB.	R.	H.	2B.	3B.	HR.	RBI.	B.A.	PO.	A.	E.	F.A.
1981—National	PR-OF	0	0	0	0	0	0	0	.000	1	0	0	1.000
1982—National	OF	1	0	0	0	0	0	0	.000	0	0	0	.000
1983—National	OF	3	0	0	0	0	0	0	.000	2	0	0	1.000
1984—National	OF	1	0	0	0	0	0	0	.000	4	0	0	1.000
1985—National	PH-OF	0	1	0	0	0	0	0	.000	0	0	0	.000
1986—National	PH-OF	2	0	0	0	0	0	0	.000	1	0	0	1.000
1987—National	OF	3	0	3	0	1	0	2	1.000	1	0	0	1.000
All-Star Game Totals—7 Years		10	1	3	0	1	0	2	.300	9	0	0	1.000

RAFAEL EMILIO RAMIREZ (PEGUERO)

Born February 18, 1959, at San Pedro de Macoris, Dominican Republic.
Height, 5.11. Weight, 190.
Throws and bats righthanded.

Shares major league records for most doubles, game (4), May 21, 1986, 13 innings; most double plays by shortstop, extra-inning game (6), June 27, 1982 (14 innings); most years leading league, errors, shortstop (6).

Holds National League record for fewest putouts by shortstop, season, for leader in most putouts (251), 1984.

Major League stolen bases: 1980 (2), 1981 (7), 1982 (27), 1983 (16), 1984 (14), 1985 (2), 1986 (19), 1987 (6), 1988 (3), 1989 (3). Total—99.

Led National League shortstops in double plays with 130 in 1982, 116 in 1983, 115 in 1985 and tied for lead with 94 in 1984.

Led National League shortstops in total chances with 866 in 1982 and 724 in 1984.

Year Club	League	Pos.	G.	AB.	R.	H.	2B.	3B.	HR.	RBI.	B.A.	PO.	A.	E.	F.A.
1977—Brad. Braves	Gulf C.	SS-OF	49	175	20	31	2	1	4	19	.177	52	94	32	.820
1978—Greenwood	W. Car.	SS	81	282	54	77	15	3	6	46	.273	119	229	★43	.890
1978—Savannah	South.	SS	38	131	14	27	4	0	2	13	.206	61	123	15	.925
1979—Savannah†	South.	SS	113	386	47	80	17	3	10	39	.207	134	282	★38	.916
1980—Richmond‡	Int.	SS	80	281	33	79	15	3	5	38	.281	117	294	23	.947
1980—Atlanta	Nat.	SS	50	165	17	44	6	1	2	11	.267	63	140	11	.949
1981—Atlanta	Nat.	SS	95	307	30	67	16	2	2	20	.218	181	306	★30	.942
1982—Atlanta	Nat.	SS	157	609	74	169	24	4	10	52	.278	★300	528	★38	.956
1983—Atlanta	Nat.	SS	152	622	82	185	13	5	7	58	.297	232	490	★39	.949
1984—Atlanta	Nat.	SS	145	591	51	157	22	4	2	48	.266	★251	443	●30	.959
1985—Atlanta	Nat.	SS	138	568	54	141	25	4	5	58	.248	214	451	★32	.954
1986—Atlanta	Nat.	SS-3B-OF	134	496	57	119	21	1	8	33	.240	156	371	29	.948
1987—Atlanta§x	Nat.	SS-3B	56	179	22	47	12	0	1	21	.263	66	110	10	.946
1988—Houston	Nat.	SS	155	566	51	156	30	5	6	59	.276	232	408	23	.965
1989—Houston	Nat.	SS	151	537	46	132	20	2	6	54	.246	189	326	★30	.945
Major League Totals—10 Years			1233	4640	484	1217	189	28	49	414	.262	1884	3573	272	.953

Signed as free agent by Atlanta Braves' organization, September 28, 1976.
†On disabled list, April 16 to April 27, 1979.
‡On disabled list, June 23 to July 17, 1980.
§On disabled list, July 2 to September 25, 1987.
xTraded with cash to Houston Astros for Third Baseman Ed Whited and Pitcher Mike Stoker, December 8, 1987.

CHAMPIONSHIP SERIES RECORD

Year Club	League	Pos.	G.	AB.	R.	H.	2B.	3B.	HR.	RBI.	B.A.	PO.	A.	E.	F.A.
1982—Atlanta	Nat.	SS	3	11	1	2	0	0	0	1	.182	5	11	1	.941

ALL-STAR GAME RECORD

Member of National League All-Star Team in 1984; did not play.

DOMINGO ANTONIO RAMOS

Born March 29, 1958, at Santiago, Dominican Republic.
Height, 5.10. Weight, 170.
Throws and bats righthanded.

Major League stolen bases: 1983 (3), 1984 (2), 1989 (1). Total—6.
Tied for International League lead in sacrifice flies with 6 in 1981.

Year Club	League	Pos.	G.	AB.	R.	H.	2B.	3B.	HR.	RBI.	B.A.	PO.	A.	E.	F.A.
1975—Oneonta	NYP	SS-3B	49	166	29	39	4	1	0	21	.235	60	143	14	.935
1976—Fort Lauderdale	Fla. St.	SS	103	328	34	79	11	3	0	29	.241	150	343	35	.934
1976—Syracuse	Int.	SS	11	39	7	10	2	1	0	8	.256	13	20	2	.943
1977—West Haven	East.	SS	129	431	55	106	18	6	2	50	.246	222	433	23	★.966
1978—Tacoma	P. C.	SS	91	314	43	74	13	3	0	30	.236	155	290	28	.941
1978—West Haven	East.	SS	40	134	16	34	2	2	1	13	.254	40	128	6	.966
1978—New York†‡	Amer.	SS	1	0	0	0	0	0	0	0	.000	0	0	0	.000
1979—Syr.§-Colum. x	Int.	SS	115	376	38	92	11	4	1	28	.245	211	323	26	.954
1980—Syracuse	Int.	SS	84	319	45	80	8	4	4	27	.251	160	240	28	.935
1980—Toronto	Amer.	SS-2B	5	16	0	2	0	0	0	0	.125	5	10	0	1.000
1981—Syracuse y	Int.	SS-3B-2B	96	320	42	82	4	5	0	31	.256	158	248	19	.955
1982—Salt Lake City	P. C.	SS	112	427	75	134	19	8	6	56	.314	174	288	19	.960
1982—Seattle	Amer.	SS	8	26	3	4	2	0	0	1	.154	9	14	2	.920
1983—Seattle	Amer.	2B-SS-3B	53	127	14	36	4	0	2	10	.283	51	109	8	.952
1984—Seattle	Amer.	3-S-1-2	59	81	6	15	2	0	0	2	.185	51	49	5	.952
1985—Seattle	Amer.	S-2-1-3	75	168	19	33	6	0	1	15	.196	87	119	10	.954
1986—Seattle	Amer.	SS-2B-3B	49	99	8	18	2	0	0	5	.182	55	93	6	.961
1987—Seattle z	Amer.	SS-3B-2B	42	103	9	32	6	0	2	11	.311	47	88	5	.964
1988—Colo. Spr. a-Edm.	P. C.	3B-SS-2B	50	165	30	46	10	2	2	25	.279	45	107	9	.944
1988—Clev.-Calif.b	Amer.	2-3-1-S-O	32	61	10	14	1	0	0	5	.230	37	43	1	.988
1989—Chicago	Nat.	SS-3B	85	179	18	47	6	2	1	19	.263	49	142	11	.946
American League Totals—9 Years			324	681	69	154	23	0	5	49	.226	342	525	37	.959
National League Totals—1 Year			85	179	18	47	6	2	1	19	.263	49	142	11	.946
Major League Totals—10 Years			409	860	87	201	29	2	6	68	.234	391	667	48	.957

Signed as free agent by New York Yankees' organization, May 27, 1975.
†Traded with Pitchers Sparky Lyle, Larry McCall and Dave Rajsich, Catcher Mike Heath and cash to Texas Rangers for Outfielders Juan Beniquez and Greg Jemison and Pitchers Mike Griffin, Paul Mirabella and Dave Righetti, November 10, 1978.
‡Loaned to Toronto Blue Jays' organization, April 5, 1979.
§Loaned to New York Yankees' organization, July 30, 1979; returned to Texas Rangers, September 28, 1979.
xSold to Toronto Blue Jays, November 5, 1979.
yDrafted by Seattle Mariners, December 7, 1981.
zReleased, December 21, 1987; signed by Colorado Springs (Cleveland Indians' organization), February 1, 1988.
aReleased, August 5, 1988; signed by Edmonton (California Angels' organization), August 17, 1988.
bGranted free agency, November 4, 1988; signed by Iowa (Chicago Cubs' organization), December 14, 1988.

CHAMPIONSHIP SERIES RECORD

Year Club	League	Pos.	G.	AB.	R.	H.	2B.	3B.	HR.	RBI.	B.A.	PO.	A.	E.	F.A.
1989—Chicago	Nat.	PH	1	1	0	0	0	0	0	0	.000	0	0	0	.000

WILLIAM LARRY RANDOLPH JR.
(Willie)

Born July 6, 1954, at Holly Hill, S. C.
Height, 5.11. Weight, 171.
Throws and bats righthanded.
Brother of Terry Randolph, defensive back with Green Bay Packers, 1977.

Shares major league record for most assists by second baseman in extra-inning game since 1900 (13), August 25, 1976 (19 innings).
Holds American League record for most chances accepted by second baseman in extra-inning game (20), August 25, 1976 (19 innings).
Major League stolen bases: 1975 (1), 1976 (37), 1977 (13), 1978 (36), 1979 (33), 1980 (30), 1981 (14), 1982 (16), 1983 (12), 1984 (10), 1985 (16), 1986 (15), 1987 (11), 1988 (8), 1989 (7). Total—259.
Led American League in bases on balls received with 119 in 1980.
Led American League second basemen in double plays with 128 in 1979 and 112 in 1984.
Led American League second basemen in total chances with 846 in 1979.
Led Eastern League in bases on balls received with 110 in 1974.
Led Western Carolinas League in bases on balls received with 90 and tied for lead in sacrifice flies with 8 in 1973.
Named second baseman on THE SPORTING NEWS American League All-Star Team, 1977, 1980 and 1987.
Named second baseman on THE SPORTING NEWS American League Silver Slugger team, 1980.

Year Club	League	Pos.	G.	AB.	R.	H.	2B.	3B.	HR.	RBI.	B.A.	PO.	A.	E.	F.A.
1972—Bradenton Pir.	Gulf C.	SS-OF	44	167	21	53	6	5	0	10	.317	85	116	24	.893
1973—Charleston	W. Car.	2B	121	428	93	120	25	6	8	51	.280	★285	308	★24	.961
1974—Thetford Mines	East.	2B	135	461	★103	117	28	6	12	53	.254	269	319	21	.966
1975—Charleston	Int.	2B	91	313	41	106	13	5	7	42	.339	189	250	16	.965
1975—Pittsburgh†	Nat.	2B-3B	30	61	9	10	1	0	0	3	.164	34	45	6	.929
1976—New York	Amer.	2B	125	430	59	115	15	4	1	40	.267	307	415	19	.974
1977—New York	Amer.	2B	147	551	91	151	28	11	4	40	.274	350	454	16	.980
1978—New York‡	Amer.	2B	134	499	87	139	18	6	3	42	.279	296	400	16	.978
1979—New York	Amer.	2B	153	574	98	155	15	13	5	61	.270	★355	★478	13	.985
1980—New York	Amer.	2B	138	513	99	151	23	7	7	46	.294	361	401	19	.976
1981—New York	Amer.	2B	93	357	59	83	14	3	2	24	.232	205	268	★11	.977
1982—New York	Amer.	2B	144	553	85	155	21	4	3	36	.280	352	380	14	.981
1983—New York§	Amer.	2B	104	420	73	117	21	1	2	38	.279	265	298	12	.979
1984—New York	Amer.	2B	142	564	86	162	24	2	2	31	.287	334	419	13	.983
1985—New York	Amer.	2B	143	497	75	137	21	2	5	40	.276	303	425	11	.985
1986—New York x	Amer.	2B	141	492	76	136	15	2	5	50	.276	313	381	★20	.972

Year	Club	League	Pos.	G.	AB.	R.	H.	2B.	3B.	HR.	RBI.	B.A.	PO.	A.	E.	F.A.
1987—New York y		Amer.	2B	120	449	96	137	24	2	7	67	.305	286	338	12	.981
1988—New York za		Amer.	2B	110	404	43	93	20	1	2	34	.230	254	339	7	.988
1989—Los Angeles		Nat.	2B	145	549	62	155	18	0	2	36	.282	260	412	9	.987
National League Totals—2 Years				175	610	71	165	19	0	2	39	.270	294	457	15	.980
American League Totals—13 Years				1694	6303	1027	1731	259	58	48	549	.275	3981	4996	183	.980
Major League Totals—15 Years				1869	6913	1098	1896	278	58	50	588	.274	4275	5453	198	.980

Selected by Pittsburgh Pirates' organization in 7th round of free-agent draft, June 6, 1972.

†Traded with Pitchers Ken Brett and Dock Ellis to New York Yankees for Pitcher Doc Medich, December 11, 1975.

‡On disabled list, June 23 to July 14, 1978.

§On disabled list, June 27 to July 12 and July 13 to August 5, 1983.

xGranted free agency, November 12, 1986; re-signed by Yankees, January 8, 1987.

yOn disabled list, July 15 to August 14, 1987.

zOn disabled list, June 10 to June 25 and August 3 to August 28, 1988.

aGranted free agency, October 24, 1988; signed by Los Angeles Dodgers, December 10, 1988.

DIVISION SERIES RECORD

Year	Club	League	Pos.	G.	AB.	R.	H.	2B.	3B.	HR.	RBI.	B.A.	PO.	A.	E.	F.A.
1981—New York		Amer.	2B	5	20	0	4	0	0	0	1	.200	7	10	0	1.000

CHAMPIONSHIP SERIES RECORD

Shares American League Championship Series record for most times grounding into double play, total series (4).

Year	Club	League	Pos.	G.	AB.	R.	H.	2B.	3B.	HR.	RBI.	B.A.	PO.	A.	E.	F.A.
1975—Pittsburgh		Nat.	PH-PR-2	2	2	1	0	0	0	0	0	.000	0	1	0	1.000
1976—New York		Amer.	2B	5	17	0	2	0	0	0	1	.118	8	14	0	1.000
1977—New York		Amer.	2B	5	18	4	5	1	0	0	2	.278	13	9	0	1.000
1980—New York		Amer.	2B	3	13	0	5	2	0	0	1	.385	2	9	0	1.000
1981—New York		Amer.	2B	3	12	2	4	0	0	1	2	.333	12	12	0	1.000
Championship Series Totals—5 Years				18	62	7	16	3	0	1	6	.258	35	45	0	1.000

WORLD SERIES RECORD

Year	Club	League	Pos.	G.	AB.	R.	H.	2B.	3B.	HR.	RBI.	B.A.	PO.	A.	E.	F.A.
1976—New York		Amer.	2B	4	14	1	1	0	0	0	0	.071	13	8	0	1.000
1977—New York		Amer.	2B	6	25	5	4	2	0	1	1	.160	13	14	0	1.000
1981—New York		Amer.	2B	6	18	5	4	1	1	2	3	.222	13	11	0	1.000
World Series Totals—3 Years				16	57	11	9	3	1	3	4	.158	39	33	0	1.000

ALL-STAR GAME RECORD

Shares All-Star Game record for most at-bats, nine-inning game (5), July 19, 1977.

Year	League	Pos.	AB.	R.	H.	2B.	3B.	HR.	RBI.	B.A.	PO.	A.	E.	F.A.
1977—American		2B	5	0	1	0	0	0	1	.200	2	6	0	1.000
1980—American		2B	4	0	2	0	0	0	0	.500	0	3	2	.600
1981—American		2B	3	0	1	0	0	0	0	.333	0	5	0	1.000
1987—American		2B	1	0	0	0	0	0	0	.000	0	1	0	1.000
1989—National		2B	1	0	0	0	0	0	0	.000	0	0	0	.000
All-Star Game Totals—5 Years			14	0	4	0	0	0	1	.286	2	15	2	.895

Named to American League All-Star Team for 1976 game; replaced due to injury.

DENNIS LEE RASMUSSEN

Born April 18, 1959, at Los Angeles, Calif.
Height, 6.07. Weight, 233.
Throws and bats lefthanded.
Attended Creighton University, Omaha, Neb.
Grandson of Wilbur Lee (Bill) Brubaker, infielder with Pittsburgh
Pirates and Boston Braves, 1932 through 1940 and 1943.

Led Eastern League in wild pitches with 18 in 1981.

Tied for International League lead in games started by pitchers with 28 in 1983.

Year	Club	League	G.	IP.	W.	L.	Pct.	H.	R.	ER.	SO.	BB.	ERA.
1980—Salinas		California	11	76	4	6	.400	69	51	46	63	52	5.45
1981—Holyoke		Eastern	24	156	8	12	.400	134	95	69	125	99	3.98
1982—Spokane†		P. Coast	27	171⅔	11	8	.579	166	110	96	162	★113	5.03
1983—Columbus‡		Int'national	28	181	●13	10	.565	161	106	92	★187	108	4.57
1983—San Diego§		National	4	13⅔	0	0	.000	10	5	3	13	8	1.98
1984—Columbus		Int'national	6	43⅔	4	1	.800	24	15	15	30	27	3.09
1984—New York		American	24	147⅔	9	6	.600	127	79	75	110	60	4.57
1985—New York		American	22	101⅔	3	5	.375	97	56	45	63	42	3.98
1985—Columbus		Int'national	7	45	0	3	.000	41	24	19	43	25	3.80
1986—New York		American	31	202	18	6	.750	160	91	87	131	74	3.88
1987—New York		American	26	146	9	7	.563	145	78	77	89	55	4.75
1987—Columbus x		Int'national	1	7	1	0	1.000	5	1	1	4	0	1.29
1987—Cincinnati		National	7	45⅓	4	1	.800	39	22	20	39	12	3.97
1988—Cincinnati y-San Diego		National	31	204⅔	16	10	.615	199	84	78	112	58	3.43
1989—San Diego		National	33	183⅔	10	10	.500	190	100	87	87	72	4.26
National League Totals—4 Years			75	447⅓	30	21	.588	438	211	188	251	150	3.78
American League Totals—4 Years			103	597⅓	39	24	.619	529	304	284	393	231	4.28
Major League Totals—7 Years			178	1044⅔	69	45	.605	967	515	472	644	381	4.07

Selected by Pittsburgh Pirates' organization in 18th round of free-agent draft, June 7, 1977.

Selected by California Angels' organization in 1st round (17th player selected) of free-agent draft, June 3, 1980.

†Traded to New York Yankees, November 24, 1982, completing deal in which New York traded Pitcher Tommy John to California Angels for a player to be named later, August 31, 1982.

‡Traded with Second Baseman Edwin Rodriguez to San Diego Padres, September 12, 1983, completing deal in which San Diego traded Pitcher John Montefusco to New York Yankees for two players to be named later, August 26, 1983.

§Traded with a player to be named later to New York Yankees' organization for Third Baseman Graig Nettles, March 30, 1984; New York organization acquired Pitcher Darin Cloninger to complete deal, April 26, 1984.

xTraded to Cincinnati Reds for Pitcher Bill Gullickson, August 26, 1987.

yTraded to San Diego Padres for Pitcher Candy Sierra, June 8, 1988.

SHANE WILLIAM RAWLEY

Born July 27, 1955, at Racine, Wis.
Height, 6.00. Weight, 185.
Throws left and bats righthanded.
Attended Indian Hills Community College, Centerville, Ia.

Major League saves: 1978 (4), 1979 (11), 1980 (13), 1981 (8), 1982 (3), 1983 (1). Total—40.
Led American League in intentional bases on balls issued with 16 in 1980.
Tied for National League lead in games started by pitchers with 36 in 1987.

Year Club	League	G.	IP.	W.	L.	Pct.	H.	R.	ER.	SO.	BB.	ERA.
1974—Sarasota Expos	Gulf Coast	2	12	0	1	.000	12	9	3	16	4	2.25
1974—Kinston	Carolina	5	19	0	2	.000	22	15	13	11	12	6.16
1975—West Palm Beach	Florida St.	24	165	8	12	.400	148	80	56	113	73	3.05
1976—Quebec City	Eastern	25	164	11	7	.611	143	55	49	113	79	2.69
1977—Denver†-Indianapolis‡§	Am. Assoc.	26	152	6	10	.375	150	89	80	92	68	4.74
1978—Seattle	American	52	111	4	9	.308	114	57	51	66	51	4.14
1979—Seattle x	American	48	84	5	9	.357	88	40	36	48	40	3.86
1980—Seattle	American	59	114	7	7	.500	103	44	42	68	63	3.32
1981—Spokane	P. Coast	3	6	0	0	.000	3	0	0	3	3	0.00
1981—Seattle yz	American	46	68	4	6	.400	64	31	30	35	38	3.97
1982—New York	American	47	164	11	10	.524	165	79	74	111	54	4.06
1983—New York	American	34	238⅓	14	14	.500	246	111	100	124	79	3.78
1984—New York ab	American	11	42	2	3	.400	46	33	29	24	27	6.21
1984—Philadelphia	National	18	120⅓	10	6	.625	117	55	51	58	27	3.81
1985—Philadelphia	National	36	198⅔	13	8	.619	188	82	73	106	81	3.31
1986—Philadelphia c	National	23	157⅔	11	7	.611	166	67	62	73	50	3.54
1987—Philadelphia	National	36	229⅔	17	11	.607	250	118	112	123	86	4.39
1988—Philadelphia de	National	32	198	8	16	.333	220	111	92	87	78	4.18
1989—Minnesota f	American	27	145	5	12	.294	167	89	84	68	60	5.21
American League Totals—8 Years		324	966⅓	52	70	.426	993	484	446	544	412	4.15
National League Totals—5 Years		145	904⅓	59	48	.551	941	433	390	447	322	3.88
Major League Totals—12 Years		469	1870⅔	111	118	.485	1934	917	836	991	734	4.02

Selected by Los Angeles Dodgers' organization in 4th round of free-agent draft, January 9, 1974.

Selected by Montreal Expos' organization in secondary phase of free-agent draft, June 5, 1974.

†Traded with Pitcher Angel Torres to Cincinnati Reds' organization, May 27, 1977, completing deal in which Cincinnati traded Pitcher Santo Alcala to Montreal Expos for two players to be named later, May 21, 1977.

‡Appeared with Indianapolis in one game as an outfielder with no chances.

§Traded to Seattle Mariners for Outfielder Dave Collins, December 9, 1977.

xOn disabled list, June 30 to August 21, 1979.

yOn disabled list, April 1 to April 24, 1981; included rehabilitation disability assignment to Spokane, April 16 to April 24, 1981.

zTraded to New York Yankees for Pitchers Gene Nelson and Bill Caudill, a player to be named later and cash, April 1, 1982; Seattle Mariners' organization acquired Outfielder Bobby Brown to complete deal, April 6, 1982.

aOn disabled list, May 20 to June 4, 1984.

bTraded to Philadelphia Phillies for Pitcher Marty Bystrom and Outfielder Keith Hughes, June 30, 1984.

cOn disabled list, July 30, 1986 through remainder of season.

dOn disabled list, August 5 to August 28, 1988.

eTraded with cash to Minnesota Twins for Second Baseman Tom Herr, Catcher Tom Nieto and Outfielder Eric Bullock, October 24, 1988.

fGranted free agency, November 13, 1989.

ALL-STAR GAME RECORD

Member of National League All-Star Team in 1986; did not play.

JOHNNY CORNELIUS RAY

Born March 1, 1957, at Chouteau, Okla.
Height, 5.11. Weight, 189.
Throws right and bats right and lefthanded.
Attended Northeastern Oklahoma A & M, Miami, Okla.; and
University of Arkansas, Fayetteville, Ark.

Shares major league record for fewest errors by second baseman, season, 150 or more games (5), 1986.
Major League stolen bases: 1982 (16), 1983 (18), 1984 (11), 1985 (13), 1986 (6), 1987 (4), 1988 (4), 1989 (6). Total—78.
Tied for National League lead in grounding into double plays with 21 in 1986.
Led National League second basemen in total chances with 914 in 1982.
Named National League Rookie Player of the Year by THE SPORTING NEWS, 1982.
Named second baseman on THE SPORTING NEWS American League All-Star Team, 1988.
Named second baseman on THE SPORTING NEWS National League Silver Slugger team, 1983.

Year	Club	League	Pos.	G.	AB.	R.	H.	2B.	3B.	HR.	RBI.	B.A.	PO.	A.	E.	F.A.
1979—Sarasota Astros....	Gulf C.	3B-2B	37	132	25	41	8	1	3	25	.311	25	51	11	.874
1979—Daytona Beach....	Fla. St.	3B-SS-2B	24	68	6	15	1	2	1	10	.221	21	38	8	.881
1980—Columbus....	South.	2B-3B-OF	138	497	86	161	32	6	10	72	.324	203	331	24	.957
1981—Tucson†....	P. C.	2B	131	525	111	183	★50	10	5	83	.349	309	369	19	.973
1981—Pittsburgh....	Nat.	2B	31	102	10	25	11	0	0	6	.245	52	96	2	.987
1982—Pittsburgh....	Nat.	2B	●162	647	79	182	30	7	7	63	.281	★381	★512	★21	.977
1983—Pittsburgh....	Nat.	2B	151	576	68	163	●38	7	5	53	.283	319	452	13	.983
1984—Pittsburgh....	Nat.	2B	155	555	75	173	●38	6	6	67	.312	331	400	12	.984
1985—Pittsburgh....	Nat.	2B	154	594	67	163	33	3	7	70	.274	305	423	18	.976
1986—Pittsburgh....	Nat.	2B	155	579	67	174	33	0	7	78	.301	280	479	5	.993
1987—Pittsburgh‡....	Nat.	2B	123	472	48	129	19	3	5	54	.273	248	358	12	.981
1987—California....	Amer.	2B	30	127	16	44	11	0	0	15	.346	52	90	2	.986
1988—California....	Amer.	2B-OF	153	602	75	184	42	7	6	83	.306	269	328	20	.968
1989—California§....	Amer.	2B	134	530	52	153	16	3	5	62	.289	279	403	11	.984
National League Totals—7 Years			931	3525	414	1009	202	26	37	391	.286	1916	2720	83	.982
American League Totals—3 Years			317	1259	143	381	69	10	11	160	.303	600	821	33	.977
Major League Totals—9 Years			1248	4784	557	1390	271	36	48	551	.291	2516	3541	116	.981

Selected by Houston Astros' organization in 12th round of free-agent draft, June 5, 1979.

†Traded with two players to be named later to Pittsburgh Pirates for Second Baseman Phil Garner, August 31, 1981; Pittsburgh organization acquired Pitcher Randy Niemann and Outfielder Kevin Houston to complete deal, September 9, 1981.

‡Traded to California Angels for Third Baseman Billie Merrifield and a player to be named later, August 29, 1987; Pittsburgh Pirates acquired Pitcher Miguel Garcia to complete deal, September 3, 1987.

§On disabled list, April 6 to April 21, 1989.

ALL-STAR GAME RECORD

Year	League	Pos.	AB.	R.	H.	2B.	3B.	HR.	RBI.	B.A.	PO.	A.	E.	F.A.
1988—American		PH	1	0	0	0	0	0	0	.000	0	0	0	.000

RANDY MAX READY

Born January 8, 1960, at San Mateo, Calif.
Height, 5.11. Weight, 180.
Throws and bats righthanded.
Attended California State University, Hayward,
Calif., and Mesa College, Grand Junction, Colo.

Shares American League record for most innings played by third baseman, game (25), May 8, finished May 9, 1984 (fielded 24⅓ innings).
Major League stolen bases: 1986 (2), 1987 (7), 1988 (6), 1989 (4). Total—19.
Led Pacific Coast League in bases on balls received with 99 in 1983.
Led Texas League in total bases with 281 in 1982.
Led Texas League third basemen in double plays with 27 and total chances with 456 in 1982.
Led Midwest League third basemen in double plays with 22 in 1981.

Year	Club	League	Pos.	G.	AB.	R.	H.	2B.	3B.	HR.	RBI.	B.A.	PO.	A.	E.	F.A.
1980—Butte	Pion.	SS-2B-3B	61	226	★65	85	★23	4	8	50	★.376	86	174	22	.922
1981—Burlington	Midw.	3B	110	367	74	113	17	0	17	56	.308	72	216	21	★.932
1982—El Paso	Texas	3B	132	475	★122	★178	33	5	20	99	★.375	★115	★312	●29	.936
1983—Vancouver	P. C.	3B	116	407	82	134	28	1	13	59	.329	136	231	24	.939
1983—Milwaukee	Amer.	3B	12	37	8	15	3	2	1	6	.405	5	8	0	1.000
1984—Milwaukee	Amer.	3B	37	123	13	23	6	1	3	13	.187	29	76	6	.946
1984—Vancouver†	P. C.	2B-3B	43	151	48	49	7	4	3	18	.325	74	125	6	.971
1985—Milwaukee‡	Amer.	OF-3B-2B	48	181	29	48	9	5	1	21	.265	93	14	1	.991
1985—Vancouver	P. C.	OF-3B-2B	52	190	33	62	12	3	4	29	.326	60	35	7	.931
1986—Milwaukee§	Amer.	OF-2B-3B	23	79	8	15	4	0	1	4	.190	35	21	3	.949
1986—San Diego x	Nat.	3B	1	3	0	0	0	0	0	0	.000	0	2	1	.667
1986—Las Vegas y	P. C.	3B-OF	10	38	5	14	4	0	1	8	.368	12	10	0	1.000
1987—San Diego	Nat.	3B-2B-OF	124	350	69	108	26	6	12	54	.309	124	220	15	.958
1988—San Diego	Nat.	3B-2B-OF	114	331	43	88	16	2	7	39	.266	112	153	11	.960
1989—S.D.z-Phi.	Nat.	OF-3B-2B	100	254	37	67	13	2	8	26	.264	80	72	9	.944
American League Totals—4 Years			120	420	58	101	22	8	6	44	.240	162	119	10	.966
National League Totals—4 Years			339	938	149	263	55	10	27	119	.280	316	447	36	.955
Major League Totals—9 Years			459	1358	207	364	77	18	33	163	.268	478	566	46	.958

Selected by Milwaukee Brewers' organization in 5th round of free-agent draft, June 3, 1980.

†On disabled list, August 21, 1984 through remainder of season.

‡On disabled list, April 30 to June 19, 1985; included rehabilitation disability assignment to Vancouver, June 1 to June 19, 1985.

§Traded to San Diego Padres for a player to be named later, June 12, 1986; San Diego traded Infielder Tim Pyznarski to Milwaukee Brewers' organization to complete deal, October 29, 1986.

xOn disabled list, June 19 to July 7, 1986.

yOn disabled list, July 22, 1986 through remainder of season.

zTraded with Outfielder John Kruk to Philadelphia Phillies for Outfielder Chris James, June 2, 1989.

JEFFREY JAMES REARDON

(Jeff)

Born October 1, 1955, at Pittsfield, Mass.
Height, 6.00. Weight, 200.
Throws and bats righthanded.
Attended University of Massachusetts, Amherst, Mass.

Major League saves: 1979 (2), 1980 (6), 1981 (8), 1982 (26), 1983 (21), 1984 (23), 1985 (41), 1986 (35), 1987 (31), 1988 (42), 1989 (31). Total—266.

Led National League in saves with 41 in 1985.
Led Carolina League in shutouts with 3 in 1977.
Named American League Co-Fireman of the Year by THE SPORTING NEWS, 1987.
Named National League Fireman of the Year by THE SPORTING NEWS, 1985.

Year Club	League	G.	IP.	W.	L.	Pct.	H.	R.	ER.	SO.	BB.	ERA.
1977—Lynchburg	Carolina	16	101	8	3	.727	89	42	37	60	30	3.30
1978—Jackson	Texas	28	163	*17	4	*.810	128	56	46	115	65	2.53
1979—Tidewater†	Int'national	30	69	5	2	.714	46	18	16	64	21	2.09
1979—New York	National	18	21	1	2	.333	12	7	4	10	9	1.71
1980—New York	National	61	110	8	7	.533	96	36	32	101	47	2.62
1981—New York‡-Montreal	National	43	70	3	0	1.000	48	17	17	49	21	2.19
1982—Montreal	National	75	109	7	4	.636	87	28	25	86	36	2.06
1983—Montreal	National	66	92	7	9	.438	87	34	31	78	44	3.03
1984—Montreal	National	68	87	7	7	.500	70	31	28	79	37	2.90
1985—Montreal	National	63	87⅔	2	8	.200	68	31	31	67	26	3.18
1986—Montreal§	National	62	89	7	9	.438	83	42	39	67	26	3.94
1987—Minnesota	American	63	80⅓	8	8	.500	70	41	40	83	28	4.48
1988—Minnesota	American	63	73	2	4	.333	68	21	20	56	15	2.47
1989—Minnesota x	American	65	73	5	4	.556	68	33	33	46	12	4.07
National League Totals—8 Years		456	665⅔	42	46	.477	551	226	207	537	246	2.80
American League Totals—3 Years		191	226⅓	15	16	.484	206	95	93	185	55	3.70
Major League Totals—11 Years		647	892	57	62	.479	757	321	300	722	301	3.03

Selected by Montreal Expos' organization in 23rd round of free-agent draft, June 5, 1973.
Signed as free agent by New York Mets' organization, June 14, 1977.
†On disabled list, June 13 to June 24 and June 29 to July 26, 1979.
‡Traded with Outfielder Dan Norman to Montreal Expos for Outfielder Ellis Valentine, May 29, 1981.
§Traded with Catcher Tom Nieto to Minnesota Twins for Pitchers Neal Heaton, Al Cardwood and Yorkis Perez and Catcher Jeff Reed, February 3, 1987.
xGranted free agency, November 13, 1989; signed by Boston Red Sox, December 6, 1989.

DIVISION SERIES RECORD

Year Club	League	G.	IP.	W.	L.	Pct.	H.	R.	ER.	SO.	BB.	ERA.
1981—Montreal	National	3	4⅓	0	1	.000	1	1	1	2	1	2.08

CHAMPIONSHIP SERIES RECORD

Shares American League Championship Series record for most games pitched, series (4), 1987.

Year Club	League	G.	IP.	W.	L.	Pct.	H.	R.	ER.	SO.	BB.	ERA.
1981—Montreal	National	1	1	0	0	.000	3	3	3	0	0	27.00
1987—Minnesota	American	4	5⅓	1	1	.500	7	3	3	5	3	5.06
Championship Series Totals—2 Years		5	6⅓	1	1	.500	10	6	6	5	3	8.53

WORLD SERIES RECORD

Year Club	League	G.	IP.	W.	L.	Pct.	H.	R.	ER.	SO.	BB.	ERA.
1987—Minnesota	American	4	4⅔	0	0	.000	5	0	0	3	0	0.00

ALL-STAR GAME RECORD

Year League	IP.	W.	L.	Pct.	H.	R.	ER.	SO.	BB.	ERA.
1985—National	1	0	0	.000	1	0	0	1	0	0.00

Member of National League All-Star Team in 1986; did not play.
Member of American League All-Star Team in 1988; did not play.

THOMAS RICHARD REDINGTON
(Tom)

Born February 13, 1969, at Fullerton, Calif.
Height, 6.01. Weight, 190.
Throws and bats righthanded.

Led Midwest League in slugging percentage with .490 in 1989.
Led South Atlantic League third basemen in putouts with 103, assists with 243, total chances with 376 and double plays with 20 in 1988.
Named Midwest League Most Valuable Player, 1989.

Year Club	League	Pos.	G.	AB.	R.	H.	2B.	3B.	HR.	RBI.	B.A.	PO.	A.	E.	F.A.
1987—Sumter	S. Atl.	3B	18	56	9	18	2	0	0	5	.321	12	29	3	.932
1988—Sumter	S. Atl.	*3B-SS	129	429	45	84	13	1	11	60	.196	104	246	*30	.992
1989—Burlington	Midw.	3B-SS	85	298	49	89	14	0	*17	52	.299	57	183	21	.920
1989—Greenville	South.	3B	33	110	9	27	4	0	3	13	.245	19	90	7	.940

Selected by Atlanta Braves' organization in 3rd round of free-agent draft, June 2, 1987.

GARY EUGENE REDUS

Name pronounced REE-dus.

Born November 1, 1956, at Athens, Ala.
Height, 6.01. Weight, 185.
Throws and bats righthanded.

Major League stolen bases: 1982 (11), 1983 (39), 1984 (48), 1985 (48), 1986 (25), 1987 (52), 1988 (31), 1989 (25). Total—279.

Hit for the cycle, August 25, 1989.
Led American Association in stolen bases with 54 and tied for lead in sacrifice flies with 9 in 1982.
Led Florida State League in total bases with 220 in 1980.
Led Pioneer League in total bases with 199, stolen bases with 42 and tied for lead in sacrifice flies with 6 in 1978.
Tied for Western Carolinas League lead in errors by second basemen with 20 in 1979.
Named Pioneer League Player of the Year, 1978.

Year	Club	League	Pos.	G.	AB.	R.	H.	2B.	3B.	HR.	RBI.	B.A.	PO.	A.	E.	F.A.
1978—Billings		Pion.	2B	68	253	★100	★117	19	6	17	62	★.462	124	★185	★28	.917
1979—Nashville		South.	OF	36	109	7	19	2	1	0	7	.174	74	3	3	.963
1979—Greensboro		W. Car.	2B-OF	83	309	79	86	17	1	16	52	.278	172	193	21	.946
1980—Tampa		Fla. St.	OF-3B-1B	128	452	78	136	18	9	16	68	.301	213	84	27	.917
1981—Waterbury		East.	OF-1B	138	477	71	119	26	4	20	75	.249	667	34	14	.980
1982—Indianapolis		A. A.	OF	122	439	112	146	29	9	24	93	.333	223	10	7	.971
1982—Cincinnati		Nat.	OF	20	83	12	18	3	2	1	7	.217	29	3	1	.970
1983—Cincinnati		Nat.	OF	125	453	90	112	20	9	17	51	.247	235	11	7	.972
1984—Cincinnati		Nat.	OF	123	394	69	100	21	3	7	22	.254	200	6	7	.967
1985—Cincinnati†		Nat.	OF	101	246	51	62	14	4	6	28	.252	140	3	2	.986
1986—Philadelphia‡		Nat.	OF	90	340	62	84	22	4	11	33	.247	185	8	4	.980
1986—Reading§		East.	OF	6	24	4	6	1	0	0	0	.250	11	1	1	.923
1987—Chicago		Amer.	OF	130	475	78	112	26	6	12	48	.236	262	13	6	.979
1988—Chicago x		Amer.	OF	77	262	42	69	10	4	6	34	.263	140	7	2	.987
1988—Pittsburgh y		Nat.	OF	30	71	12	14	2	0	2	4	.197	42	2	2	.957
1989—Pittsburgh z		Nat.	1B-OF	98	279	42	79	18	7	6	33	.283	583	55	9	.986
National League Totals—7 Years				587	1866	338	469	100	29	50	178	.251	1414	88	32	.979
American League Totals—2 Years				207	737	120	181	36	10	18	82	.246	402	20	8	.981
Major League Totals—8 Years				794	2603	458	650	136	39	68	260	.250	1816	108	40	.980

Selected by Boston Red Sox' organization in 17th round of free-agent draft, June 7, 1977.
Selected by Cincinnati Reds' organization in 15th round of free-agent draft, June 6, 1978.
†Traded with Pitcher Tom Hume to Philadelphia Phillies for Pitchers John Denny and Jeff Gray, December 11, 1985.
‡On disabled list, April 28 to July 1, 1986; included rehabilitation disability assignment to Reading, June 23 to June 30, 1986.
§Traded to Chicago White Sox for Pitcher Joe Cowley and cash, March 26, 1987.
xTraded to Pittsburgh Pirates for Outfielder Mike Diaz, August 19, 1988.
yGranted free agency, November 4, 1988; re-signed by Pirates, November 15, 1988.
zOn disabled list, March 27 to April 11 and July 25 to August 9, 1989.

DARREN DOUGLAS REED

Born October 16, 1965, at Ventura, Calif.
Height, 6.01. Weight, 190.
Throws and bats righthanded.
Attended Ventura College, Ventura, Calif.
Led International League in grounding into double plays with 15 in 1989.

Year	Club	League	Pos.	G.	AB.	R.	H.	2B.	3B.	HR.	RBI.	B.A.	PO.	A.	E.	F.A.
1984—Oneonta		NYP	OF-C	40	113	17	26	7	0	2	9	.230	41	2	2	.956
1985—Fort Lauderdale		Fla. St.	OF	100	369	63	117	21	4	10	61	.317	191	8	7	.966
1986—Albany†		East.	OF	51	196	22	45	11	1	4	27	.230	78	2	5	.941
1987—Albany		East.	OF	107	404	68	129	23	4	20	79	.319	174	6	4	.978
1987—Columbus‡		Int.	OF	21	79	15	26	3	3	8	16	.329	33	2	1	.972
1988—Tidewater		Int.	OF-C	101	345	31	83	26	0	9	47	.241	170	5	4	.978
1989—Tidewater		Int.	OF	133	444	57	119	30	6	4	50	.268	232	★19	5	.980

Selected by Oakland A's organization in 10th round of free-agent draft, January 17, 1984.
Selected by New York Yankees' organization in secondary phase of free-agent draft, June 4, 1984.
†On disabled list, June 17, 1986 through remainder of season.
‡Traded with Catcher Phil Lombardi and Pitcher Steve Frey to New York Mets for Shortstop Rafael Santana and Pitcher Victor Garcia, December 11, 1987.

JEFFREY SCOTT REED
(Jeff)

Born November 12, 1962, at Joliet, Ill.
Height, 6.02. Weight, 190.
Throws right and bats lefthanded.
Brother of Curtis Reed, outfielder in San Diego Padres' and
Chicago White Sox' organizations, 1977 through 1984.
Holds modern National League record for most errors by catcher, inning (3), July 28, 1987, seventh inning.
Major League stolen bases: 1986 (1), 1988 (1). Total—2.
Led International League catchers in total chances with 720 in 1985.
Led Southern League catchers in total chances with 714 and double plays with 12 in 1983.
Led California League catchers in total chances with 758 and tied for lead in double plays with 9 in 1982.

Year	Club	League	Pos.	G.	AB.	R.	H.	2B.	3B.	HR.	RBI.	B.A.	PO.	A.	E.	F.A.
1980—Elizabethton		Appal.	C	65	225	39	64	15	1	1	20	.284	269	★41	9	.972
1981—Wisconsin Rapids		Midw.	C	106	312	63	73	12	1	4	34	.234	547	★93	7	.989
1981—Orlando		South.	C	3	4	0	1	0	0	0	0	.250	4	1	0	1.000
1982—Visalia		Calif.	C	125	395	69	130	19	2	5	54	.329	★642	●106	10	.987
1983—Orlando		South.	C	118	379	52	100	16	5	6	45	.264	★618	★88	8	★.989
1983—Toledo		Int.	C	14	41	5	7	1	1	0	3	.171	77	6	1	.988
1984—Minnesota		Amer.	C	18	21	3	3	0	0	1	1	.143	41	2	1	.977

Year Club League	Pos.	G.	AB.	R.	H.	2B.	3B.	HR.	RBI.	B.A.	PO.	A.	E.	F.A.
1984—Toledo .... Int.	C	94	301	30	80	16	3	3	35	.266	546	43	5	*.992
1985—Toledo .... Int.	C	122	404	53	100	15	3	5	36	.248	*627	*81	12	.983
1985—Minnesota .... Amer.	C	7	10	2	2	0	0	0	0	.200	9	3	0	1.000
1986—Minnesota .... Amer.	C	68	165	13	39	6	1	2	9	.236	332	19	2	.994
1986—Toledo† .... Int.	C	25	71	10	22	5	3	1	14	.310	108	22	2	.985
1987—Montreal‡ .... Nat.	C	75	207	15	44	11	0	1	21	.213	357	36	12	.970
1987—Indianapolis .... A. A.	C	5	17	0	3	0	0	0	0	.176	27	2	0	1.000
1988—Mont.§-Cinc. .... Nat.	C	92	265	20	60	9	2	1	16	.226	468	38	3	.994
1988—Indianapolis .... A. A.	C	8	22	1	7	3	0	0	1	.318	30	11	0	1.000
1989—Cincinnati .... Nat.	C	102	287	16	64	11	0	3	23	.223	504	50	7	.988
American League Totals—3 Years		93	196	18	44	9	1	2	10	.224	382	24	3	.993
National League Totals—3 Years		269	759	51	168	31	2	5	60	.221	1329	124	22	.985
Major League Totals—6 Years		362	955	69	212	40	3	7	70	.222	1711	148	25	.987

Selected by Minnesota Twins' organization in 1st round (12th player selected) of free-agent draft, June 3, 1980.

†Traded with Pitchers Neal Heaton, Al Cardwood and Yorkis Perez to Montreal Expos for Pitcher Jeff Reardon and Catcher Tom Nieto, February 3, 1987.

‡On disabled list, April 20 to May 25, 1987; included rehabilitation disability assignment to Indianapolis, May 19 to May 25, 1987.

§Traded with Outfielder Herm Winningham and Pitcher Randy St. Claire to Cincinnati Reds for Outfielder Tracy Jones and Pitcher Pat Pacillo, July 13, 1988.

JERRY MAXWELL REED

Born October 8, 1955, at Bryson City, N.C.
Height, 6.01. Weight, 190.
Throws and bats righthanded.
Received bachelor of science degree in education from
Western Carolina University, Cullowhee, N.C. in 1977.

Major League saves: 1985 (8), 1987 (7), 1988 (1). Total—16.
Tied for Eastern League lead in intentional bases on balls issued with 9 in 1979.

Year Club League	G.	IP.	W.	L.	Pct.	H.	R.	ER.	SO.	BB.	ERA.
1977—Auburn .... NYP	*32	56	3	5	.375	63	35	30	36	24	4.82
1978—Spartanburg .... W. Carol.	39	66	7	2	.778	36	22	10	31	34	1.36
1978—Peninsula .... Carolina	15	24	1	0	1.000	9	3	2	11	5	0.75
1979—Reading .... Eastern	45	80	11	4	.733	67	25	17	37	28	1.91
1980—Oklahoma City .... Am. Assoc.	33	97	6	5	.545	128	62	53	36	42	4.92
1980—Reading .... Eastern	8	17	1	1	.500	17	6	6	10	10	3.18
1981—Reading .... Eastern	56	80	5	4	.556	80	34	29	62	29	3.26
1981—Philadelphia .... National	4	5	0	1	.000	7	4	4	5	6	7.20
1982—Oklahoma City .... Am. Assoc.	25	131⅔	6	7	.462	135	78	64	73	59	4.37
1982—Philadelphia† .... National	7	8⅔	1	0	1.000	11	6	5	1	3	5.19
1982—Cleveland .... American	6	15⅔	1	1	.500	15	6	6	10	3	3.45
1983—Charleston .... Int'national	21	145⅓	10	6	.625	141	70	58	57	67	3.59
1983—Cleveland .... American	7	21⅓	0	0	.000	26	19	17	11	9	7.17
1984—Maine .... Int'national	27	179⅓	12	6	.667	*193	86	72	77	57	3.61
1985—Maine .... Int'national	14	95⅓	8	5	.615	88	41	36	47	37	3.40
1985—Cleveland‡ .... American	33	72⅓	3	5	.375	67	41	33	37	19	4.11
1986—Calgary .... P. Coast	19	41	2	1	.667	45	24	21	20	17	4.61
1986—Seattle§ .... American	11	34⅔	4	0	1.000	38	13	12	16	13	3.12
1987—Seattle x .... American	39	81⅔	1	2	.333	79	32	31	51	24	3.42
1987—Calgary .... P. Coast	1	3	0	0	.000	1	0	0	3	0	0.00
1988—Seattle .... American	46	86⅓	1	1	.500	82	42	38	48	33	3.96
1989—Seattle .... American	52	101⅔	7	7	.500	89	44	36	50	43	3.19
National League Totals—2 Years	11	13⅔	1	1	.500	18	10	9	6	9	5.93
American League Totals—7 Years	194	413⅓	17	16	.515	396	197	173	223	144	3.76
Major League Totals—8 Years	205	427⅓	18	17	.514	414	207	182	229	153	3.83

Selected by Minnesota Twins' organization in 11th round of free-agent draft, June 5, 1973.

Selected by Philadelphia Phillies' organization in 22nd round of free-agent draft, June 7, 1977.

†Traded with Pitcher Roy Smith and Outfielder Wil Culmer to Cleveland Indians for Pitcher John Denny, September 12, 1982.

‡Released, April 1, 1986; signed by Calgary (Seattle Mariners' organization), April 11, 1986.

§On disabled list, August 4, 1986 through remainder of season.

xOn disabled list, July 25 to August 20, 1987; included rehabilitation disability assignment to Calgary, August 16 to August 20, 1987.

JODY ERIC REED

Born July 26, 1962, at Tampa, Fla.
Height, 5.09. Weight, 165.
Throws and bats righthanded.
Attended Manatee Junior College, Bradenton, Fla., and received degree in criminology
from Florida State University, Tallahassee, Fla., in 1985.

Major League stolen bases: 1987 (1), 1988 (1), 1989 (4). Total—6.
Led Florida State League in bases on balls received with 94 in 1985.
Led International League shortstops in total chances with 683 and double plays with 86 in 1987.
Led Florida State League shortstops in double plays with 101 in 1985.

Year Club League	Pos.	G.	AB.	R.	H.	2B.	3B.	HR.	RBI.	B.A.	PO.	A.	E.	F.A.
1984—Winter Haven .... Fla. St.	SS	77	273	46	74	14	1	0	20	.271	128	271	26	.939
1985—Winter Haven .... Fla. St.	SS	134	489	*95	157	25	1	0	45	*.321	*256	*478	37	*.952

Year Club League	Pos.	G.	AB.	R.	H.	2B.	3B.	HR.	RBI.	B.A.	PO.	A.	E.	F.A.
1986—New Britain .... East.	SS	60	218	33	50	12	1	0	11	.229	114	190	14	.956
1986—Pawtucket .... Int.	SS	69	227	27	64	11	0	1	30	.282	115	222	12	.966
1987—Pawtucket .... Int.	SS	136	510	77	151	22	2	7	51	.296	★236	★427	20	.971
1987—Boston.................... Amer.	SS-2B-3B	9	30	4	9	1	1	0	8	.300	11	26	0	1.000
1988—Boston†................. Amer.	SS-2B-3B	109	338	60	99	23	1	1	28	.293	147	282	11	.975
1989—Boston.................... Amer.	S-2-3-O	146	524	76	151	42	2	3	40	.288	255	423	19	.973
Major League Totals—3 Years		264	892	140	259	66	4	4	76	.290	413	731	30	.974

Selected by Texas Rangers' organization in 3rd round of free-agent draft, January 12, 1982.
Selected by San Francisco Giants' organization in secondary phase of free-agent draft, June 7, 1982.
Selected by Texas Rangers' organization in secondary phase of free-agent draft, June 6, 1983.
Selected by Boston Red Sox' organization in 8th round of free-agent draft, June 4, 1984.
†Appeared in one game as a pinch-runner.

CHAMPIONSHIP SERIES RECORD

Year Club League	Pos.	G.	AB.	R.	H.	2B.	3B.	HR.	RBI.	B.A.	PO.	A.	E.	F.A.
1988—Boston.................... Amer.	SS	4	11	0	3	1	0	0	0	.273	3	10	0	1.000

RICHARD ALLEN REED
(Rick)

Born August 16, 1964, at Huntington, W. Va.
Height, 6.00. Weight, 195.
Throws and bats righthanded.
Attended Marshall University, Huntington, W. Va.

Year Club League	G.	IP.	W.	L.	Pct.	H.	R.	ER.	SO.	BB.	ERA.
1986—Bradenton Pirates .... Gulf Coast	8	24	0	2	.000	20	12	10	15	6	3.75
1986—Macon.. S. Atlantic	1	6⅓	0	0	.000	5	3	2	1	2	2.84
1987—Macon.. S. Atlantic	46	93⅔	8	4	.667	80	38	26	92	29	2.50
1988—Salem.. Carolina	15	72⅓	6	2	.750	56	28	22	73	17	2.74
1988—Harrisburg .... Eastern	2	16	1	0	1.000	11	2	2	17	2	1.13
1988—Buffalo.. Am. Assoc.	10	77	5	2	.714	62	15	14	50	12	1.64
1988—Pittsburgh.. National	2	12	1	0	1.000	10	4	4	6	2	3.00
1989—Buffalo.. Am. Assoc.	20	125⅔	9	8	.529	130	58	52	75	28	3.72
1989—Pittsburgh.. National	15	54⅔	1	4	.200	62	35	34	34	11	5.60
Major League Totals—2 Years...........................	17	66⅔	2	4	.333	72	39	38	40	13	5.13

Selected by Pittsburgh Pirates' organization in 26th round of free-agent draft, June 2, 1986.

DARRIN FRANCIS REICHLE

Born February 24, 1966, at Melbourne, Fla.
Height, 6.05. Weight, 215.
Throws right and bats left and righthanded.
Attended St. Leo College, St. Leo, Fla.

Pitched 9-0 no-hit victory against Charleston, W.Va., May 14, 1988.
Pitched 1-0 no-hit victory against Fayetteville, May 30, 1988 (second game).

Year Club League	G.	IP.	W.	L.	Pct.	H.	R.	ER.	SO.	BB.	ERA.
1987—Spokane .... Northwest	11	54⅔	4	1	.800	45	24	18	47	40	2.96
1987—Reno.. California	4	12⅓	0	3	.000	24	19	19	6	16	13.86
1988—Charleston, S.C................................. S. Atlantic	20	107⅔	10	3	.769	62	38	34	115	61	2.84
1989—Riverside .... California	26	149⅔	10	10	.500	121	81	69	158	★100	4.15

Selected by San Diego Padres' organization in 4th round of free-agent draft, June 2, 1987.

KEVIN MICHAEL REIMER

Born June 28, 1964, at Macon, Ga.
Height, 6.02. Weight, 215.
Throws right and bats lefthanded.
Attended Orange Coast College, Costa Mesa, Calif.,
and California State University, Fullerton, Calif.
Son of Gerry Reimer, minor league first baseman-outfielder, 1958 through 1968.

Led Texas League in game-winning RBIs with 12 and tied for intentional bases on balls received with 9 in 1988.

Year Club League	Pos.	G.	AB.	R.	H.	2B.	3B.	HR.	RBI.	B.A.	PO.	A.	E.	F.A.
1985—Burlington .... Midw.	1B-OF	80	292	25	67	12	0	8	33	.229	685	29	15	.979
1986—Salem .... Carol.	OF-1B	133	453	57	111	21	2	16	76	.245	412	27	32	.932
1987—Charlotte............... Fla. St.	OF	74	271	36	66	13	7	6	34	.244	31	0	2	.939
1988—Tulsa .... Texas	OF	133	486	74	147	30	★11	21	76	.302	63	1	7	.901
1988—Texas .... Amer.	OF	12	25	2	3	0	0	1	2	.120	0	0	0	.000
1989—Oklahoma City ..... A. A.	OF	133	514	59	137	37	7	10	73	.267	73	2	6	.926
1989—Texas .... Amer.	DH-PH	3	5	0	0	0	0	0	0	.000	0	0	0	.000
Major League Totals—2 Years................		15	30	2	3	0	0	1	2	.100	0	0	0	.000

Selected by Texas Rangers' organization in 11th round of free-agent draft, June 3, 1985.

MICHAEL JOHN REMLINGER
(Mike)

Born March 23, 1966, at Middletown, N.Y.
Height, 6.00. Weight, 195.
Throws and bats lefthanded.
Attended Dartmouth College, Hanover, N.H.

Year Club	League	G.	IP.	W.	L.	Pct.	H.	R.	ER.	SO.	BB.	ERA.
1987—Everett	Northwest	2	5	0	0	.000	1	2	2	11	5	3.60
1987—Clinton	Midwest	6	30	2	1	.667	21	12	11	43	14	3.30
1987—Shreveport	Texas	6	34⅓	4	2	.667	14	11	9	51	22	2.36
1988—Shreveport	Texas	3	13	1	0	1.000	7	4	1	18	4	0.69
1989—Shreveport	Texas	16	90⅔	4	6	.400	68	43	30	92	73	2.98
1989—Phoenix	P. Coast	11	43	1	6	.143	51	47	44	28	52	9.21

Selected by San Francisco Giants' organization in 1st round (16th player selected) of free-agent draft, June 2, 1987.

RICHARD AVINA RENTERIA

Name pronounced Ren-ter-REE-ah.

(Rich)

Born December 25, 1961, at Harbor City, Calif.
Height, 5.09. Weight, 172.
Throws and bats righthanded.

Major League stolen bases: 1987 (1), 1988 (1). Total—2.
Led South Atlantic League third basemen in errors with 39 in 1981.
Tied for Carolina League in grounding into double plays with 19 in 1982.

Year Club	League	Pos.	G.	AB.	R.	H.	2B.	3B.	HR.	RBI.	B.A.	PO.	A.	E.	F.A.
1980—Bradenton Pir.	Gulf C.	3B-SS	46	176	19	40	6	1	2	23	.227	32	87	16	.882
1981—Greenwood	S. Atl.	3B-SS	127	510	90	146	19	5	4	48	.286	87	232	39	.891
1982—Alexandria	Carol.	2B	127	508	80	*168	24	5	14	*100	*.331	196	346	28	.951
1983—Lynn†	East.	3B	115	424	47	121	25	0	4	40	.285	83	170	19	.930
1984—Nashua	East.	2B	113	443	63	121	22	7	1	34	.273	208	283	12	.976
1984—Hawaii‡	P. C.	2B	19	77	8	19	3	1	0	11	.247	22	45	2	.971
1985—Mex. C. Tigers	Mex.	3B-2B	125	484	89	169	29	11	19	*125	.349	121	241	19	.950
1985—Hawaii	P. C.	2B	7	31	2	6	2	0	0	2	.194	5	15	0	1.000
1986—Hawaii	P. C.	3B-2B	112	389	51	122	20	9	1	51	.314	112	196	13	.960
1986—Pittsburgh§	Nat.	3B	10	12	2	3	1	0	0	1	.250	1	2	2	.600
1987—Seattle x	Amer.	2B-SS	12	10	2	1	1	0	0	0	.100	3	4	1	.875
1987—Calgary	P. C.	2B-SS-3B	69	267	41	79	14	3	1	32	.296	110	187	11	.964
1988—Seattle	Amer.	SS-3B-2B	31	88	6	18	9	0	0	6	.205	33	44	3	.963
1988—Calgary	P. C.	SS-2B-3B	24	87	15	23	6	1	4	10	.264	34	64	7	.933
1989—Calgary y	P. C.	2B-3B-SS	65	234	34	69	17	0	5	36	.295	106	166	9	.968
National League Totals—1 Year			10	12	2	3	1	0	0	1	.250	1	2	2	.600
American League Totals—2 Years			43	98	8	19	10	0	0	6	.194	36	48	4	.955
Major League Totals—3 Years			53	110	10	22	11	0	0	7	.200	37	50	6	.935

Selected by Pittsburgh Pirates' organization in 1st round (20th player selected) of free-agent draft, June 3, 1980.
†On disabled list, May 10 to June 1, 1983.
‡Loaned to Mexico City Tigers, March 11, 1985; returned, August 21, 1985.
§Traded to Seattle Mariners for a player to be named later, December 5, 1986; Pittsburgh Pirates' organization acquired Pitcher Bob Siegel to complete deal, December 8, 1986.
xOn disabled list, April 2 to April 18, 1987.
yOn Seattle disabled list, March 27 to June 30, 1989; included rehabilitation disability assignment to Calgary, June 14 to June 30, 1989.

RICKY EUGENE REUSCHEL

Name pronounced RUSH-ul.

(Rick)

Born May 16, 1949, at Quincy, Ill.
Height, 6.03. Weight, 240.
Throws and bats righthanded.
Attended Western Illinois University, Macomb, Ill.
Brother of Paul Reuschel, pitcher with Chicago Cubs and Cleveland Indians, 1975 through 1978.

Shares major league record for most putouts, pitcher, inning (3), April 25, 1975, third inning.
Major League saves: 1975 (1), 1976 (1), 1977 (1), 1985 (1). Total—4.
Tied for National League lead in complete games with 12 and shutouts with 4 in 1987.
Tied for National League lead in hit batsmen with 8 in 1986.
Tied for National League lead in games started by pitchers with 38 in 1980 and 36 in 1988.
Tied for National League lead in sacrifice hits by batters with 19 in 1988.
Led Northern League pitchers in complete games with 7 and tied for lead in games started with 14 in 1970.
Named righthanded pitcher on THE SPORTING NEWS National League All-Star Team, 1977.
Named National League Comeback Player of the Year by THE SPORTING NEWS, 1985.
Named pitcher on THE SPORTING NEWS National League All-Star fielding team, 1985 and 1987.

Year Club	League	G.	IP.	W.	L.	Pct.	H.	R.	ER.	SO.	BB.	ERA.
1970—Huron	Northern	14	102	9	2	.818	96	52	40	88	22	3.52
1971—San Antonio†	Texas	16	121	8	4	.667	105	40	31	81	15	2.31
1972—Wichita	Am. Assoc.	12	102	9	2	.818	78	30	15	72	30	1.32
1972—Chicago	National	21	129	10	8	.556	127	46	42	87	29	2.93
1973—Chicago	National	36	237	14	15	.483	244	95	79	168	62	3.00
1974—Chicago	National	41	241	13	12	.520	262	130	115	160	83	4.29
1975—Chicago	National	38	234	11	*17	.393	244	116	97	155	67	3.73
1976—Chicago	National	38	260	14	12	.538	260	*117	100	146	64	3.46
1977—Chicago	National	39	252	20	10	.667	233	84	78	166	74	2.79
1978—Chicago	National	35	243	14	15	.483	235	98	92	115	54	3.41
1979—Chicago	National	36	239	18	12	.600	251	104	96	125	75	3.62
1980—Chicago	National	38	257	11	13	.458	*281	111	97	140	76	3.40

Year Club	League	G.	IP.	W.	L.	Pct.	H.	R.	ER.	SO.	BB.	ERA.
1981—Chicago‡	National	13	86	4	7	.364	87	40	33	53	23	3.45
1981—New York	American	12	71	4	4	.500	75	24	21	22	10	2.66
1982—New York§	American					(Did not play)						
1983—Columbus xy	Int'national	4	16	0	1	.000	21	9	9	7	6	5.06
1983—Quad Cities	Midwest	13	70⅔	3	4	.429	73	29	19	56	9	2.42
1983—Chicago	National	4	20⅔	1	1	.500	18	9	9	9	10	3.92
1984—Chicago za	National	19	92⅓	5	5	.500	123	57	53	43	23	5.17
1985—Hawaii	P. Coast	8	54	6	2	.750	52	18	15	46	12	2.50
1985—Pittsburgh	National	31	194	14	8	.636	153	58	49	138	52	2.27
1986—Pittsburgh	National	35	215⅔	9	16	.360	232	106	95	125	57	3.96
1987—Pittsburgh b-San Francisco	National	34	227	13	9	.591	207	91	78	107	42	3.09
1988—San Francisco	National	36	245	19	11	.633	242	88	85	92	42	3.12
1989—San Francisco c	National	32	208⅓	17	8	.680	195	75	68	111	54	2.94
National League Totals—17 Years		526	3381	207	179	.536	3394	1425	1266	1940	887	3.37
American League Totals—1 Year		12	71	4	4	.500	75	24	21	22	10	2.66
Major League Totals—17 Years		538	3452	211	183	.536	3469	1449	1287	1962	897	3.36

Selected by Chicago Cubs' organization in 3rd round of free-agent draft, June 4, 1970.

†On temporary inactive list, July 2, 1971; transferred to military list, July 8, 1971 through April 10, 1972.

‡Traded to New York Yankees for Pitcher Doug Bird, $400,000 and a player to be named later, June 12, 1981; Chicago Cubs acquired Pitcher Mike Griffin to complete deal, August 5, 1981.

§On disabled list, March 23, 1982 through remainder of season.

xOn New York disabled list, April 4 to June 9, 1983; included rehabilitation disability assignment to Columbus, May 23 to June 9, 1983.

yReleased, June 9, 1983; signed by Quad Cities (Chicago Cubs' organization), June 28, 1983.

zOn disabled list, March 27 to April 21 and August 23 to September 1, 1984.

aGranted free agency, November 8, 1984; signed by Pittsburgh Pirates' organization, February 28, 1985.

bTraded to San Francisco Giants for Pitchers Jeff Robinson and Scott Medvin, August 21, 1987.

cOn disabled list, July 30 to August 16, 1989.

DIVISION SERIES RECORD

Year Club	League	G.	IP.	W.	L.	Pct.	H.	R.	ER.	SO.	BB.	ERA.
1981—New York	American	1	6	0	1	.000	4	2	2	3	1	3.00

CHAMPIONSHIP SERIES RECORD

Tied National League Championship Series record for most earned runs allowed, seven-game Series (7), 1987.

Year Club	League	G.	IP.	W.	L.	Pct.	H.	R.	ER.	SO.	BB.	ERA.
1987—San Francisco	National	2	10	0	1	.000	15	8	7	2	2	6.30
1989—San Francisco	National	2	8⅔	1	1	.500	12	6	5	5	2	5.19
Championship Series Totals—2 Years		4	18⅔	1	2	.333	27	14	12	7	4	5.79

WORLD SERIES RECORD

Year Club	League	G.	IP.	W.	L.	Pct.	H.	R.	ER.	SO.	BB.	ERA.
1981—New York	American	2	3⅔	0	0	.000	7	3	2	2	3	4.91
1989—San Francisco	National	1	4	0	1	.000	5	5	5	2	4	11.25
World Series Totals—2 Years		3	7⅔	0	1	.000	12	8	7	4	7	8.22

ALL-STAR GAME RECORD

Shares All-Star Game record for most home runs allowed, inning (2), July 11, 1989, first inning.

Year League	IP.	W.	L.	Pct.	H.	R.	ER.	SO.	BB.	ERA.
1977—National	1	0	0	.000	1	0	0	0	0	0.00
1987—National	1⅓	0	0	.000	1	0	0	1	0	0.00
1989—National	1	0	0	.000	3	2	2	0	0	18.00
All-Star Game Totals—3 Years	3⅓	0	0	.000	5	2	2	1	0	0.00

JERRY REUSS

Name pronounced Royce.

Born June 19, 1949, at St. Louis, Mo.
Height, 6.05. Weight, 227.
Throws and bats lefthanded.
Attended Southern Illinois University, Carbondale, Ill., Central Missouri State College,
Warrensburg, Mo., and University of California, Santa Barbara, Calif.

Shares major league record for most grand slams allowed, lifetime (9).
Pitched 8-0 no-hit victory against San Francisco Giants, June 27, 1980.
Major League saves: 1972 (1), 1976 (2), 1979 (3), 1980 (3), 1984 (1), 1986 (1). Total—11.
Led National League in shutouts with 6 in 1980.
Led National League in hit batsmen with 10 in 1980.
Tied for National League lead in games started by pitchers with 40 in 1973.
Led American Association pitchers in games started with 29 in 1969.
Led Texas League in wild pitches with 16 in 1968.
Named National League Comeback Player of the Year by THE SPORTING NEWS, 1980.
Received reported $30,000 bonus to sign with St. Louis Cardinals, 1967.

Year Club	League	G.	IP.	W.	L.	Pct.	H.	R.	ER.	SO.	BB.	ERA.
1967—Sarasota Cards	Gulf Coast	2	7	0	0	.000	7	6	4	6	3	5.14
1967—Cedar Rapids	Midwest	9	58	2	5	.286	44	20	12	63	19	1.86
1967—Tulsa	P. Coast	1	1	0	0	.000	2	6	6	1	4	54.00

Year Club	League	G.	IP.	W.	L.	Pct.	H.	R.	ER.	SO.	BB.	ERA.
1968—Arkansas	Texas	17	112	7	8	.467	.75	43	27	86	45	2.17
1969—Tulsa	Am. Assoc.	30	*186	●13	11	.542	188	●112	84	*151	116	4.06
1969—St. Louis	National	1	7	1	0	1.000	2	0	0	3	3	0.00
1970—Tulsa	Am. Assoc.	11	85	7	2	.778	69	26	20	69	28	2.12
1970—St. Louis	National	20	127	7	8	.467	132	62	58	74	49	4.11
1971—St. Louis†	National	36	211	14	14	.500	228	125	112	131	109	4.78
1972—Houston	National	33	192	9	13	.409	177	101	89	174	83	4.17
1973—Houston‡	National	41	279	16	13	.552	271	123	116	177	*117	3.74
1974—Pittsburgh	National	35	260	16	11	.593	259	115	101	105	101	3.50
1975—Pittsburgh	National	32	237	18	11	.621	224	73	67	131	78	2.54
1976—Pittsburgh	National	31	209	14	9	.609	209	98	82	108	51	3.53
1977—Pittsburgh	National	33	208	10	13	.435	225	109	95	116	71	4.11
1978—Pittsburgh§	National	23	83	3	2	.600	97	48	45	42	23	4.88
1979—Los Angeles	National	39	160	7	14	.333	178	88	63	83	60	3.54
1980—Los Angeles	National	37	229	18	6	.750	193	74	64	111	40	2.52
1981—Los Angeles	National	22	153	10	4	.714	138	44	39	51	27	2.29
1982—Los Angeles	National	39	254⅔	18	11	.621	232	98	88	138	50	3.11
1983—Los Angeles	National	32	223⅓	12	11	.522	233	94	73	143	50	2.94
1984—Los Angeles x	National	30	99	5	7	.417	102	51	42	44	31	3.82
1985—Los Angeles	National	34	212⅔	14	10	.583	210	78	69	84	58	2.92
1986—Los Angeles y	National	19	74	2	6	.250	96	57	48	29	17	5.84
1987—Los Angeles z-Cincinnati	National	8	36⅔	0	5	.000	54	32	31	12	12	7.61
1987—Nashville a	Am. Assoc.	2	12	0	2	.000	16	8	8	4	6	6.00
1987—California bc	American	17	82⅓	4	5	.444	112	60	48	37	17	5.25
1988—Chicago	American	32	183	13	9	.591	183	79	70	73	43	3.44
1989—Chicago d-Milwaukee ef	American	30	140⅓	9	9	.500	171	88	80	40	34	5.13
National League Totals—19 Years		545	3255⅓	194	168	.536	3260	1470	1282	1756	1030	3.54
American League Totals—3 Years		79	405⅔	26	23	.531	466	227	198	150	94	4.39
Major League Totals—21 Years		624	3661	220	191	.535	3726	1697	1480	1906	1124	3.64

Selected by St. Louis Cardinals' organization in 2nd round of free-agent draft, June 6, 1967.
†Traded to Houston Astros for Pitchers Scipio Spinks and Lance Clemons, April 15, 1972.
‡Traded to Pittsburgh Pirates for Catcher Milt May, October 31, 1973.
§Traded to Los Angeles Dodgers for Pitcher Rick Rhoden, April 9, 1979.
xOn disabled list, June 8 to July 12, 1984.
yOn disabled list, July 17 to September 3, 1986.
zReleased, April 10, 1987; signed by Nashville (Cincinnati Reds' organization), April 18, 1987.
aReleased, June 14, 1987; signed by California Angels, June 19, 1987.
bOn disabled list, August 1 to August 16, 1987.
cGranted free agency, November 9, 1987; signed by Chicago White Sox, March 29, 1988.
dTraded to Milwaukee Brewers for Pitcher Brian Drahman, July 31, 1989.
eOn disabled list, August 25 to September 9, 1989.
fReleased, November 8, 1989.

DIVISION SERIES RECORD

Year Club	League	G.	IP.	W.	L.	Pct.	H.	R.	ER.	SO.	BB.	ERA.
1981—Los Angeles	National	2	18	1	0	1.000	10	0	0	7	5	0.00

CHAMPIONSHIP SERIES RECORD

Holds Championship Series records for most games lost and most consecutive games lost, total series (7); most runs allowed, inning (7), October 13, 1985, second inning.
Shares Championship Series records for most games lost, series (2), 1974, 1983; most runs allowed, total series (25).

Year Club	League	G.	IP.	W.	L.	Pct.	H.	R.	ER.	SO.	BB.	ERA.
1974—Pittsburgh	National	2	9⅔	0	2	.000	7	4	4	3	8	3.72
1975—Pittsburgh	National	1	2⅔	0	1	.000	4	4	4	1	4	13.50
1981—Los Angeles	National	1	7	0	1	.000	7	4	4	2	1	5.14
1983—Los Angeles	National	2	12	0	2	.000	14	6	6	4	3	4.50
1985—Los Angeles	National	1	1⅔	0	1	.000	5	7	2	0	1	10.80
Championship Series Totals—5 Years		7	33	0	7	.000	37	25	20	10	17	5.45

WORLD SERIES RECORD

Year Club	League	G.	IP.	W.	L.	Pct.	H.	R.	ER.	SO.	BB.	ERA.
1981—Los Angeles	National	2	11⅔	1	1	.500	10	5	5	8	3	3.86

ALL-STAR GAME RECORD

Year League	IP.	W.	L.	Pct.	H.	R.	ER.	SO.	BB.	ERA.
1975—National	3	0	0	.000	3	0	0	2	0	0.00
1980—National	1	1	0	1.000	0	0	0	3	0	0.00
All-Star Game Totals—2 Years	4	1	0	1.000	3	0	0	5	0	0.00

GILBERTO R. REYES (POLANCO)

Name pronounced RAY-us.

(Gil)

Born December 10, 1963, at Santo Domingo, D. R.
Height, 6.02. Weight, 200.
Throws and bats righthanded.

Tied for Pacific Coast League lead in sacrifice flies with 8 in 1985.
Led American Association catchers in total chances with 742 and tied for lead in double plays with 10 in 1989.

Led Pacific Coast League catchers in assists with 64 in 1988.
Led Pacific Coast League in passed balls with 24 in 1985 and 17 in 1986.
Led Texas League catchers in total chances with 718, double plays with 13 and passed balls with 31 in 1984.
Tied for California League lead in assists by catchers with 106 and double plays with 9 in 1982.

Year Club	League	Pos.	G.	AB.	R.	H.	2B.	3B.	HR.	RBI.	B.A.	PO.	A.	E.	F.A.
1980—Lethbridge	Pion.	1B	6	11	0	2	0	0	0	1	.182	16	0	2	.889
1981—Vero Beach	Fla. St.	1B-C	21	58	3	12	3	0	1	6	.207	71	6	2	.975
1981—Lethbridge	Pion.	C-1B	44	155	28	40	9	0	6	24	.258	240	24	4	.985
1982—Lodi	Calif.	C-3B	127	424	65	119	18	1	15	55	.281	493	106	20	.968
1983—San Antonio†	Texas	C	33	124	10	35	7	0	1	16	.282	167	30	5	.975
1983—Los Angeles	Nat.	C	19	31	1	5	2	0	0	0	.161	59	9	4	.944
1983—Albuquerque	P. C.	C	20	62	8	19	1	2	2	15	.306	103	17	8	.938
1984—San Antonio	Texas	C	120	433	55	131	16	2	10	78	.303	★598	★101	★19	.974
1984—Los Angeles	Nat.	C	4	5	0	0	0	0	0	0	.000	5	0	0	1.000
1985—Albuquerque	P. C.	★C-1B	111	366	35	97	20	0	6	54	.265	439	66	★21	.960
1985—Los Angeles	Nat.	C	6	1	0	0	0	0	0	0	.000	6	4	0	1.000
1986—Albuquerque	P. C.	C-1B	104	306	36	70	13	1	7	36	.229	423	69	14	.972
1987—Albuquerque	P. C.	C-1B-P	89	265	42	72	18	2	5	46	.272	414	66	12	.976
1987—Los Angeles	Nat.	C	1	0	0	0	0	0	0	0	.000	2	0	0	1.000
1988—Albuquerque	P. C.	C-1B-3B	98	318	40	93	14	0	12	66	.292	459	70	16	.971
1988—Los Angeles‡	Nat.	C	5	9	1	1	0	0	0	0	.111	16	0	0	1.000
1989—Indianapolis	A. A.	C	106	314	35	71	8	0	9	35	.226	★647	★86	9	.988
1989—Montreal	Nat.	C	4	5	0	1	0	0	0	1	.200	10	1	0	1.000
Major League Totals—6 Years			39	51	2	7	2	0	0	1	.137	98	14	4	.966

Signed as free agent by Los Angeles Dodgers' organization, January 15, 1980.
†On disabled list, May 11 to June 1, 1983.
‡Traded to Indianapolis (Montreal Expos' organization) for Pitcher Jeff Fischer, March 27, 1989.

PITCHING RECORD

Year Club	League	G.	IP.	W.	L.	Pct.	H.	R.	ER.	SO.	BB.	ERA.
1987—Albuquerque	P. Coast	1	⅓	0	0	.000	0	0	0	1	1	0.00

GORDON CRAIG REYNOLDS

(Known by middle name.)

Born December 27, 1952, at Houston, Tex.
Height, 6.01. Weight, 175.
Throws right and bats lefthanded.
Attended Houston Baptist College, Houston, Tex.

Shares modern major league record for most three-base hits, game (3), May 16, 1981.
Major League stolen bases: 1977 (6), 1978 (9), 1979 (12), 1980 (2), 1981 (3), 1982 (3), 1984 (7), 1985 (4), 1986 (3), 1987 (5), 1988 (3), 1989 (1). Total—58.
Led National League in sacrifice hits with 34 in 1979, 18 in 1981 and 16 in 1984.
Led National League shortstops in assists with 472 in 1984.
Tied for Gulf Coast League lead in sacrifice flies with 4 in 1971.
Led Carolina League shortstops in double plays with 81 in 1973 and tied for International League lead with 64 in 1975.

Year Club	League	Pos.	G.	AB.	R.	H.	2B.	3B.	HR.	RBI.	B.A.	PO.	A.	E.	F.A.
1971—Bradenton Pir.	Gulf C.	SS	48	192	26	61	8	0	0	16	.318	★87	112	★25	.888
1972—Gastonia†	W. Car.	SS	41	146	18	35	4	1	0	9	.240	55	94	12	.925
1973—Salem	Carol.	SS-2B	138	★558	75	★160	18	5	13	86	.287	200	395	50	.922
1973—Charleston	Int.	SS-3B	9	14	2	3	0	0	0	0	.214	4	11	1	.938
1974—Thetford Mines	East.	SS	64	234	31	66	7	0	6	29	.282	76	170	13	.950
1974—Charleston‡	Int.	SS-2B	36	107	12	36	5	0	0	5	.336	40	71	3	.974
1975—Charleston	Int.	SS	108	425	51	131	22	3	6	42	.308	151	287	26	.944
1975—Pittsburgh	Nat.	SS	31	76	8	17	3	0	0	4	.224	43	82	4	.969
1976—Charleston	Int.	SS-2B	126	497	57	144	18	1	2	47	.290	198	262	31	.937
1976—Pittsburgh§	Nat.	SS-2B	7	4	1	1	0	0	1	1	.250	2	6	1	.889
1977—Seattle	Amer.	SS	135	420	41	104	12	3	4	28	.248	197	397	28	.955
1978—Seattle x	Amer.	SS	148	548	57	160	16	7	5	44	.292	243	461	29	.960
1979—Houston	Nat.	SS	146	555	63	147	20	9	0	39	.265	208	428	23	.965
1980—Houston	Nat.	SS	137	381	34	86	9	6	3	28	.226	162	362	17	.969
1981—Houston	Nat.	SS	87	323	43	84	10	●12	4	31	.260	139	261	11	.973
1982—Houston y	Nat.	SS-3B	54	118	16	30	2	3	1	7	.254	45	98	6	.960
1983—Houston	Nat.	2-3-S-O	65	98	10	21	3	0	1	6	.214	37	57	3	.969
1984—Houston	Nat.	SS-3B	146	527	61	137	15	11	6	60	.260	212	473	25	.965
1985—Houston	Nat.	SS-2B	107	379	43	103	18	8	4	32	.272	159	319	11	.978
1986—Houston	Nat.	S-1-3-O-P	114	313	32	78	7	3	6	41	.249	124	209	7	.979
1987—Houston	Nat.	SS-3B	135	374	35	95	17	3	4	28	.254	160	292	14	.970
1988—Houston z	Nat.	S-3-2-1	78	161	20	41	7	0	1	14	.255	88	81	9	.949
1989—Houston a	Nat.	1-O-P	101	189	16	38	4	0	2	14	.201	86	136	8	.965
American League Totals—2 Years		283	968	98	264	28	10	9	72	.273	440	858	57	.958		
National League Totals—13 Years		1208	3498	382	878	115	55	33	305	.251	1465	2804	139	.968		
Major League Totals—15 Years		1491	4466	480	1142	143	65	42	377	.256	1905	3662	196	.966		

Selected by Pittsburgh Pirates' organization in 1st round (22nd player selected) of free-agent draft, June 8, 1971.
†On disabled list, June 6 to August 30, 1972.
‡On disabled list, July 31 to August 21, 1974.
§Traded with Infielder Jim Sexton to Seattle Mariners for Pitcher Grant Jackson, December 7, 1976.
xTraded to Houston Astros for Pitcher Floyd Bannister, December 8, 1978.

yOn disabled list, April 11 to May 5, 1982.
zGranted free agency, November 4, 1988; re-signed by Astros, December 16, 1988.
aOn voluntarily retired list, October 2, 1989.

DIVISION SERIES RECORD

Year	Club	League	Pos.	G.	AB.	R.	H.	2B.	3B.	HR.	RBI.	B.A.	PO.	A.	E.	F.A.
1981—Houston		Nat.	PH-SS	2	3	1	1	0	0	0	0	.333	1	0	0	1.000

CHAMPIONSHIP SERIES RECORD

Year	Club	League	Pos.	G.	AB.	R.	H.	2B.	3B.	HR.	RBI.	B.A.	PO.	A.	E.	F.A.
1975—Pittsburgh		Nat.	SS	2	1	0	0	0	0	0	0	.000	0	0	1	.000
1980—Houston		Nat.	SS	4	13	2	2	1	0	0	0	.154	8	12	1	.952
1986—Houston		Nat.	SS-PH	4	12	1	4	0	0	0	0	.333	7	8	2	.882
Championship Series Totals—3 Years				10	26	3	6	1	0	0	0	.231	15	20	4	.897

ALL-STAR GAME RECORD

Year	League	Pos.	AB.	R.	H.	2B.	3B.	HR.	RBI.	B.A.	PO.	A.	E.	F.A.
1979—National		SS	2	0	0	0	0	0	0	.000	0	1	0	1.000

Named to American League All-Star Team for 1978 game; did not play.

PITCHING RECORD

Year	Club	League	G.	IP.	W.	L.	Pct.	H.	R.	ER.	SO.	BB.	ERA.
1986—Houston		National	1	1	0	0	.000	3	3	3	1	2	27.00
1989—Houston		National	1	1	0	0	.000	3	4	3	0	1	27.00
Major League Totals—2 Years			2	2	0	0	.000	6	7	6	1	3	27.00

HAROLD CRAIG REYNOLDS

Born November 26, 1960, at Eugene, Ore.
Height, 5.11. Weight, 165.
Throws right and bats left and righthanded.
Attended San Diego State University, San Diego, Calif.; Canada College,
Redwood City, Calif., and California State University, Long Beach, Calif.
Brother of Larry Reynolds, shortstop-outfielder in Texas Rangers' and St. Louis Cardinals' organizations,
1979 through 1984; and Don Reynolds, outfielder with San Diego Padres, 1978 and 1979;
and minor league instructor in Seattle Mariners' organization, 1988.

Shares major league record for most assists by second baseman, nine-inning game (12), August 27, 1986.
Major League stolen bases: 1984 (1), 1985 (3), 1986 (30), 1987 (60), 1988 (35), 1989 (25). Total—154.
Led American League in stolen bases with 60 in 1987.
Led American League in caught stealing with 20 in 1987 and 29 in 1988.
Led American League second basemen in double plays with 111 in 1986, 1987 and 1988.
Led American League second basemen in total chances with 874 in 1987, 792 in 1988 and 834 in 1989.
Led Pacific Coast League in sacrifice hits with 14 in 1983.
Led Eastern League in caught stealing with 20 in 1982.
Led Midwest League in stolen bases with 69 in 1981.
Tied for Pacific Coast League lead in caught stealing with 17 in 1984.
Led Pacific Coast League second basemen in double plays with 104 and total chances with 747 in 1984.
Led Pacific Coast League second basemen in putouts with 286 and total chances with 723 in 1983.
Led Midwest League second basemen in double plays with 82 in 1981.
Named second baseman on THE SPORTING NEWS American League All-Star fielding team, 1988 and 1989.

Year	Club	League	Pos.	G.	AB.	R.	H.	2B.	3B.	HR.	RBI.	B.A.	PO.	A.	E.	F.A.
1981—Wausau		Midw.	2B-OF-3B	127	493	98	146	23	3	11	59	.296	259	386	27	.960
1982—Lynn		East.	2B	102	375	58	102	14	4	2	48	.272	202	232	19	.958
1983—Salt Lake City		P. C.	★2B-SS	136	534	84	165	20	9	1	72	.309	287	★410	★27	.963
1983—Seattle		Amer.	2B	20	59	8	12	4	1	0	1	.203	30	48	2	.975
1984—Salt Lake City		P. C.	2B	135	★558	94	165	22	6	3	54	.296	★326	★396	★25	★.967
1984—Seattle		Amer.	2B	10	10	3	3	0	0	0	0	.300	8	12	0	1.000
1985—Seattle		Amer.	2B	67	104	15	15	3	1	0	6	.144	69	123	8	.960
1985—Calgary		P. C.	2B	52	212	36	77	11	3	5	30	.363	119	171	13	.957
1986—Calgary		P. C.	2B	29	118	20	37	7	0	1	7	.314	64	83	4	.974
1986—Seattle		Amer.	2B	126	445	46	99	19	4	1	24	.222	278	415	16	.977
1987—Seattle		Amer.	2B	160	530	73	146	31	8	1	35	.275	★347	★507	★20	.977
1988—Seattle		Amer.	2B	158	598	61	169	26	●11	4	41	.283	303	★471	★18	.977
1989—Seattle		Amer.	2B	153	613	87	184	24	9	0	43	.300	311	★506	★17	.980
Major League Totals—7 Years				694	2359	293	628	107	34	6	150	.266	1346	2082	81	.977

Selected by San Diego Padres' organization in 5th round of free-agent draft, June 5, 1979.
Selected by Seattle Mariners' organization in secondary phase of free-agent draft, June 3, 1980.

ALL-STAR GAME RECORD

Year	League	Pos.	AB.	R.	H.	2B.	3B.	HR.	RBI.	B.A.	PO.	A.	E.	F.A.
1987—American		2B	3	0	0	0	0	0	0	.000	4	4	0	1.000
1988—American		2B	1	0	0	0	0	0	0	.000	1	1	0	1.000
All-Star Game Totals—2 Years			4	0	0	0	0	0	0	.000	5	5	0	1.000

—DID YOU KNOW—

That the Rangers' Charlie Hough pitched a one-hitter on August 15, 1989, but lost to Seattle, 2-0? The Mariners allowed 13 hits.

ROBERT JAMES REYNOLDS
(R. J.)

Born April 19, 1960, at Sacramento, Calif.
Height, 6.00. Weight, 180.
Throws right and bats left and righthanded.
Attended Cosumnes River College, Sacramento, Calif.;
and Sacramento City College, Sacramento, Calif.

Shares major league record for fewest errors by outfielder, season, for leader in errors (9), 1986.
Major League stolen bases: 1983 (5), 1984 (7), 1985 (18), 1986 (16), 1987 (14), 1988 (15), 1989 (22). Total—97.
Led Texas League outfielders in double plays with 8 in 1983.
Led Florida State League outfielders in double plays with 6 and total chances with 395 in 1981.
Led California League outfielders in double plays with 6 in 1980.

Year—Club	League	Pos.	G.	AB.	R.	H.	2B.	3B.	HR.	RBI.	B.A.	PO.	A.	E.	F.A.
1980—Lodi	Calif.	OF	86	299	33	84	6	3	4	31	.281	188	10	12	.943
1981—Vero Beach	Fla. St.	OF	132	502	62	139	9	11	2	49	.277	★368	20	7	.982
1982—Lodi	Calif.	OF	108	403	67	126	19	3	6	35	.313	212	12	6	.974
1982—San Antonio	Texas	OF	3	12	3	2	0	0	1	2	.167	10	1	0	1.000
1983—San Antonio	Texas	OF	133	504	103	170	25	3	18	89	.337	255	●18	12	.958
1983—Los Angeles	Nat.	OF	24	55	5	13	0	0	2	11	.236	25	2	2	.931
1984—Albuquerque	P. C.	OF	47	199	38	69	10	4	3	30	.347	104	4	6	.947
1984—Los Angeles†	Nat.	OF	73	240	24	62	12	2	2	24	.258	104	4	3	.973
1985—L.A.‡§-Pitt.	Nat.	OF	104	337	44	95	15	7	3	42	.282	159	6	6	.965
1986—Pittsburgh	Nat.	OF	118	402	63	108	30	2	9	48	.269	190	2	●9	.955
1987—Pittsburgh	Nat.	OF	117	335	47	87	24	1	7	51	.260	134	7	1	.993
1988—Pittsburgh	Nat.	OF	130	323	35	80	14	2	6	51	.248	142	7	4	.974
1989—Pittsburgh	Nat.	OF	125	363	45	98	16	2	6	48	.270	200	6	2	.990
Major League Totals—7 Years			691	2055	263	543	111	16	35	275	.264	954	34	27	.973

Selected by Los Angeles Dodgers' organization in 2nd round of free-agent draft, January 8, 1980.
†On disabled list, July 2 to July 17, 1984.
‡On disabled list, April 8 to April 23 and July 10 to August 2, 1985.
§Traded to Pittsburgh Pirates, September 3, 1985, as partial completion of deal in which Los Angeles Dodgers acquired Third Baseman Bill Madlock for three players to be named later, August 31, 1985; Pittsburgh acquired Outfielder Cecil Espy and First Baseman Sid Bream to complete deal, September 9, 1985.

RICHARD ALAN RHODEN
Name pronounced ROH-dun.
(Rick)

Born May 16, 1953, at Boynton Beach, Fla.
Height, 6.04. Weight, 203.
Throws and bats righthanded.

Pitched seven-inning, 1-0 no-hit victory against Phoenix, April 23, 1980 (first game).
Major League saves: 1983 (1).
Named pitcher on THE SPORTING NEWS National League Silver Slugger team, 1984 through 1986.

Year—Club	League	G.	IP.	W.	L.	Pct.	H.	R.	ER.	SO.	BB.	ERA.
1971—Daytona Beach	Florida St.	11	61	4	6	.400	59	32	27	67	29	3.98
1972—El Paso	Texas	13	87	6	4	.600	70	36	32	89	30	3.31
1972—Albuquerque	P. Coast	13	80	7	1	.875	83	41	34	55	34	3.83
1973—Albuquerque†	P. Coast	20	116	4	9	.308	117	66	58	68	70	4.50
1974—Albuquerque	P. Coast	26	178	9	10	.474	197	103	87	106	65	4.40
1974—Los Angeles	National	4	9	1	0	1.000	5	2	2	7	4	2.00
1975—Los Angeles	National	26	99	3	3	.500	94	40	34	40	32	3.09
1976—Los Angeles	National	27	181	12	3	.800	165	66	60	77	53	2.98
1977—Los Angeles	National	31	216	16	10	.615	223	98	90	122	63	3.75
1978—Los Angeles‡	National	30	165	10	8	.556	160	77	67	79	51	3.65
1979—Pittsburgh§	National	1	5	0	1	.000	5	4	4	2	2	7.20
1980—Portland	P. Coast	10	52	6	3	.667	47	22	17	24	21	2.94
1980—Pittsburgh	National	20	127	7	5	.583	133	58	54	70	40	3.83
1981—Pittsburgh	National	21	136	9	4	.692	147	66	59	76	53	3.90
1982—Pittsburgh	National	35	230⅓	11	14	.440	239	115	106	128	70	4.14
1983—Pittsburgh	National	36	241⅓	13	13	.500	256	95	84	153	68	3.09
1984—Pittsburgh	National	33	238⅓	14	9	.609	216	81	72	136	62	2.72
1985—Pittsburgh	National	35	213½	10	15	.400	254	●119	★106	128	69	4.47
1986—Pittsburgh x	National	34	253⅔	15	12	.556	211	82	80	159	76	2.84
1987—New York	American	30	181⅔	16	10	.615	184	84	78	107	61	3.86
1988—New York yza	American	30	197	12	12	.500	206	107	94	94	56	4.29
1989—Houston b	National	20	96⅔	2	6	.250	108	49	46	41	41	4.28
1989—Osceola c	Florida St.	5	27	1	1	.500	23	9	6	26	5	2.00
National League Totals—14 Years		353	2214⅔	123	103	.544	2216	952	864	1218	684	3.51
American League Totals—2 Years		60	378⅔	28	22	.560	390	191	172	201	117	4.09
Major League Totals—16 Years		413	2593⅓	151	125	.547	2606	1143	1036	1419	801	3.60

Selected by Los Angeles Dodgers' organization in 1st round (20th player selected) of free-agent draft, June 8, 1971.
†On disabled list, July 20 to August 15, 1973.
‡Traded to Pittsburgh Pirates for Pitcher Jerry Reuss, April 9, 1979.
§On disabled list, May 12 to October 4, 1979.
xTraded with Pitchers Cecilio Guante and Pat Clements to New York Yankees for Pitchers Doug Drabek, Brian Fisher and Logan Easley, November 26, 1986.
yOn disabled list, April 29 to May 21, 1988.

zAppeared in one game as starting designated hitter, grounding out and hitting sacrifice fly with a run batted in during two plate appearances.

aTraded to Houston Astros for Outfielder John Fishel and Pitchers Pedro DeLeon and Mike Hook, January 10, 1989.

bOn disabled list, May 4 to July 22, 1989; included rehabilitation disability assignment to Osceola, June 3 to June 10 and July 5 to July 16, 1989.

cGranted free agency, November 13, 1989.

CHAMPIONSHIP SERIES RECORD

Year Club	League	G.	IP.	W.	L.	Pct.	H.	R.	ER.	SO.	BB.	ERA.
1977—Los Angeles	National	1	4⅓	0	0	.000	2	0	0	0	2	0.00
1978—Los Angeles	National	1	4	0	0	.000	2	1	1	3	1	2.25
Championship Series Totals—2 Years		2	8⅓	0	0	.000	4	1	1	3	3	1.08

WORLD SERIES RECORD

Year Club	League	G.	IP.	W.	L.	Pct.	H.	R.	ER.	SO.	BB.	ERA.
1977—Los Angeles	National	2	7	0	1	.000	4	2	2	5	1	2.57

ALL-STAR GAME RECORD

Year League	IP.	W.	L.	Pct.	H.	R.	ER.	SO.	BB.	ERA.
1976—National	1	0	0	.000	1	0	0	0	0	0.00

Member of National League All-Star Team in 1986; did not play.

KARL DERRICK RHODES

Born August 21, 1968, at Cincinnati, O.
Height, 6.00. Weight, 175.
Throws and bats lefthanded.

Tied for Southern League lead in double plays by outfielders with 5 in 1989.

Year Club	League	Pos.	G.	AB.	R.	H.	2B.	3B.	HR.	RBI.	B.A.	PO.	A.	E.	F.A.
1986—Sarasota Astros	Gulf C.	OF	★62	222	36	65	10	3	0	22	.293	113	6	0	★1.000
1987—Asheville	S. Atl.	OF	129	413	62	104	16	4	3	50	.252	163	14	9	.952
1988—Osceola	Fla. St.	OF-2B	132	452	69	128	4	2	1	34	.283	232	14	2	.992
1989—Columbus	South.	OF	●143	520	81	134	25	5	4	63	.258	262	15	11	.962

Selected by Houston Astros' organization in 3rd round of free-agent draft, June 2, 1986.

JAMES EDWARD RICE
(Jim)

Born March 8, 1953, at Anderson, S. C.
Height, 6.02. Weight, 217.
Throws and bats righthanded.

Holds major league record for most times grounding into double plays, season (36), 1984.

Shares major league records for most consecutive seasons leading major leagues, total bases (2); fewest double plays by outfielder, season, 150 or more games (0), 1986.

Shares American League records for most consecutive seasons leading league, total bases (3); most years leading league in grounding into double plays (3).

Major League stolen bases: 1975 (10), 1976 (8), 1977 (5), 1978 (7), 1979 (9), 1980 (8), 1981 (2), 1984 (4), 1985 (2), 1987 (1), 1988 (1), 1989 (1). Total—58.

Hit three home runs in a game, August 29, 1977 and August 29, 1983 (second game).

Led American League in grounding into double plays with 29 in 1982, 36 in 1984, 35 in 1985 and tied for lead with 31 in 1983.

Led American League in total bases with 382 in 1977, 406 in 1978, 369 in 1979 and 344 in 1983.

Led American League in slugging percentage with .593 in 1977 and .600 in 1978.

Led American League batters in strikeouts with 123 in 1976.

Led International League in total bases with 249 in 1974.

Led Florida State League in total bases with 240 in 1972.

Named American League Player of the Year by THE SPORTING NEWS, 1978.

Named American League Most Valuable Player by Baseball Writers' Association of America, 1978.

Named outfielder on THE SPORTING NEWS American League All-Star Team, 1975, 1977 through 1979, 1983 and 1986.

Named outfielder on THE SPORTING NEWS American League Silver Slugger team, 1983 and 1984.

Named Minor League Player of the Year by THE SPORTING NEWS, 1974.

Named International League Most Valuable Player, 1974.

Received reported $45,000 bonus to sign with Boston Red Sox, 1971.

Year Club	League	Pos.	G.	AB.	R.	H.	2B.	3B.	HR.	RBI.	B.A.	PO.	A.	E.	F.A.
1971—Williamsport	NYP	OF	60	223	34	57	9	5	5	27	.256	86	2	6	.936
1972—Winter Haven	Fla. St.	OF	130	★491	★80	★143	20	13	17	87	.291	190	10	9	.957
1973—Bristol	East.	OF	119	423	66	134	25	4	27	93	★.317	169	13	12	.938
1973—Pawtucket	Int.	OF	10	37	7	14	2	0	4	10	.378	21	0	0	1.000
1974—Pawtucket	Int.	OF	117	430	69	145	21	4	★25	★93	★.337	181	10	11	.946
1974—Boston	Amer.	OF	24	67	6	18	2	1	1	13	.269	4	0	1	.800
1975—Boston	Amer.	OF	144	564	92	174	29	4	22	102	.309	162	6	0	1.000
1976—Boston	Amer.	OF	153	581	75	164	25	8	25	85	.282	199	8	7	.967
1977—Boston	Amer.	OF	160	644	104	206	29	15	★39	114	.320	83	4	4	.956
1978—Boston	Amer.	OF	★163	★677	121	★213	25	★46	★139	139	.315	245	13	3	.989
1979—Boston	Amer.	OF	158	619	117	201	39	6	39	130	.325	241	8	4	.984
1980—Boston†	Amer.	OF	124	504	81	148	22	6	24	86	.294	233	10	3	.988
1981—Boston	Amer.	OF	108	★451	51	128	18	1	17	62	.284	237	9	3	.988
1982—Boston	Amer.	OF	145	573	86	177	24	5	24	97	.309	273	10	9	.969

Year	Club	League	Pos.	G.	AB.	R.	H.	2B.	3B.	HR.	RBI.	B.A.	PO.	A.	E.	F.A.
1983—Boston		Amer.	OF	155	626	90	191	34	1	★39	●126	.305	339	21	6	.984
1984—Boston		Amer.	OF	159	657	98	184	25	7	28	122	.280	336	12	4	.989
1985—Boston		Amer.	OF	140	546	85	159	20	3	27	103	.291	236	8	9	.964
1986—Boston		Amer.	OF	157	618	98	200	39	2	20	110	.324	330	16	8	.977
1987—Boston		Amer.	OF	108	404	66	112	14	0	13	62	.277	155	12	4	.977
1988—Boston		Amer.	OF	135	485	57	128	18	3	15	72	.264	30	0	1	.968
1989—Boston‡§		Amer.	DH	56	209	22	49	10	2	3	28	.234	0	0	0	.000
Major League Totals—16 Years				2089	8225	1249	2452	373	79	382	1451	.298	3103	137	66	.980

Selected by Boston Red Sox' organization in 1st round (15th player selected) of free-agent draft, June 8, 1971.
†On disabled list, June 22 to July 27, 1980.
‡On disabled list, June 1 to July 21 and August 4 to September 5, 1989; included rehabilitation disability assignment to Winter Haven, July 8 to July 21, 1989.
§Released, November 13, 1989.

CHAMPIONSHIP SERIES RECORD

Shares Championship Series record for most runs, series (8), 1986.
Shares American League Championship Series record for most strikeouts, series (8), 1986.

Year	Club	League	Pos.	G.	AB.	R.	H.	2B.	3B.	HR.	RBI.	B.A.	PO.	A.	E.	F.A.
1986—Boston		Amer.	OF	7	31	8	5	1	0	2	6	.161	13	1	0	1.000
1988—Boston		Amer.	DH	4	13	0	2	0	0	0	1	.154	0	0	0	.000
Championship Series Totals—2 Years				11	44	8	7	1	0	2	7	.159	13	1	0	1.000

WORLD SERIES RECORD

Shares World Series record for most at-bats, nine-inning game (6), October 19, 1986.

Year	Club	League	Pos.	G.	AB.	R.	H.	2B.	3B.	HR.	RBI.	B.A.	PO.	A.	E.	F.A.
1986—Boston		Amer.	OF	7	27	6	9	1	1	0	0	.333	16	2	0	1.000

ALL-STAR GAME RECORD

Holds All-Star Game record for most at-bats, inning (2), July 6, 1983, third inning.
Shares All-Star Game record for most at-bats, nine inning game (5), July 17, 1979.

Year	League	Pos.	AB.	R.	H.	2B.	3B.	HR.	RBI.	B.A.	PO.	A.	E.	F.A.
1977—American		OF	2	0	1	0	0	0	0	.500	1	0	0	1.000
1978—American		OF	4	0	0	0	0	0	0	.000	2	0	0	1.000
1979—American		OF	5	0	1	1	0	0	0	.200	3	0	0	1.000
1983—American		OF	4	1	2	0	1	1	1	.500	1	0	0	1.000
1984—American		PH-OF	1	0	0	0	0	0	0	.000	1	0	0	1.000
1985—American		OF	3	0	0	0	0	0	0	.000	1	0	0	1.000
1986—American		PH	1	0	0	0	0	0	0	.000	0	0	0	.000
All-Star Game Totals—7 Years			20	1	4	1	0	1	1	.200	9	0	0	1.000

Named to American League All-Star Team in 1980; replaced due to injury.

DAVID TODD RICHARDS
(Dave)

Born September 18, 1967, at Rock Island, Ill.
Height, 6.03. Weight, 195.
Throws and bats lefthanded.
Attended Grossmont College, El Cajon, Calif.

Year	Club	League	G.	IP.	W.	L.	Pct.	H.	R.	ER.	SO.	BB.	ERA.
1987—Bristol		Ap'lachian	20	45	0	2	.000	49	26	22	56	22	4.40
1988—Fayetteville		S. Atlantic	47	68⅔	3	9	.250	49	17	15	86	29	1.97
1989—Lakeland		Florida St.	28	100	7	3	.700	69	24	20	76	50	1.80

Selected by Oakland Athletics' organization in 11th round of free-agent draft, June 3, 1985.
Selected by Detroit Tigers' organization in 27th round of free-agent draft, June 2, 1987.

RUSSELL EARL RICHARDS
(Rusty)

Born January 27, 1965, at Houston, Tex.
Height, 6.04. Weight, 210.
Throws right and bats lefthanded.
Attended Austin Community College, Austin, Tex.,
and University of Texas, Austin, Tex.

Tied for International League lead in games started by pitchers with 27 in 1989.

Year	Club	League	G.	IP.	W.	L.	Pct.	H.	R.	ER.	SO.	BB.	ERA.
1986—Bradenton Braves		Gulf Coast	12	19⅓	0	0	.000	17	8	5	15	7	2.33
1987—Sumter		S. Atlantic	10	48	3	3	.500	45	28	17	39	17	3.19
1987—Durham		Carolina	22	125	6	10	.375	138	73	63	62	50	4.54
1988—Durham		Carolina	1	3⅓	1	0	1.000	0	0	0	3	0	0.00
1988—Greenville		Southern	28	147	10	7	.588	125	46	43	96	42	2.63
1989—Richmond		Int'national	27	167⅔	11	11	.500	★178	76	71	85	54	3.81
1989—Atlanta		National	2	9⅓	0	0	.000	10	5	5	4	6	4.82
Major League Totals—1 Year			2	9⅓	0	0	.000	10	5	5	4	6	4.82

Selected by Philadelphia Phillies' organization in 7th round of free-agent draft, January 14, 1986.
Signed as free agent by Atlanta Braves' organization, June 19, 1986.

JEFFREY SCOTT RICHARDSON
(Jeff)

Born August 29, 1963, at Wichita, Kan.
Height, 6.03. Weight, 185.
Throws and bats righthanded.
Attended Connors State College, Warner, Okla.

Led Carolina League pitchers in games started with 28 in 1987.

Year	Club	League	G.	IP.	W.	L.	Pct.	H.	R.	ER.	SO.	BB.	ERA.
1984—Medicine Hat†	Pioneer	18	70	4	6	.400	96	67	56	39	32	7.20
1985—Little Falls	NYP	11	62⅓	4	3	.571	58	32	25	56	32	3.61
1985—Columbia	S. Atlantic	5	35⅔	3	2	.600	25	11	7	33	11	1.77
1986—Lynchburg	Carolina	32	171	13	5	.722	183	96	80	93	82	4.21
1986—Jackson	Texas	1	3	0	1	.000	6	8	6	2	4	18.00
1987—Lynchburg‡	Carolina	29	154	6	12	.333	180	103	84	79	68	4.91
1988—Palm Springs	California	44	69	0	4	.000	66	24	19	56	27	2.48
1989—Palm Springs	California	24	26⅔	4	2	.667	19	15	12	25	9	4.05
1989—Midland	Texas	19	22⅔	0	1	.000	9	4	4	12	5	1.59

Selected by New York Mets' organization in 19th round of free-agent draft, June 7, 1982.
Selected by Chicago White Sox' organization in secondary phase of free-agent draft, January 17, 1984.
Selected by Toronto Blue Jays' organization in secondary phase of free-agent draft, June 4, 1984.
†Released, April 1, 1985; signed by Little Falls (New York Mets' organization), May 9, 1985.
‡Traded with Pitcher Shane Young to California Angels for Pitcher John Candelaria, September 15, 1987.

JEFFREY SCOTT RICHARDSON
(Jeff)

Born August 26, 1965, at Grand Island, Neb.
Height, 6.02. Weight, 180.
Throws and bats righthanded.
Attended University of Arkansas, Little Rock, Ark.,
and Louisiana Tech University, Ruston, La.

Major League stolen bases: 1989 (1).

Year	Club	League	Pos.	G.	AB.	R.	H.	2B.	3B.	HR.	RBI.	B.A.	PO.	A.	E.	F.A.
1986—Billings	Pion.	2B-SS	47	162	42	51	14	4	0	20	.315	48	64	6	.949
1987—Tampa	Fla. St.	2B-3B-SS	100	374	44	112	9	2	0	37	.299	180	228	17	.960
1987—Vermont	East.	2B-3B	35	134	24	28	4	0	0	8	.209	73	76	4	.974
1988—Chattanooga	South.	SS	122	399	50	100	17	1	1	37	.251	186	321	23	★.957
1989—Nashville	A. A.	SS	88	286	36	78	19	2	1	25	.273	132	218	16	.956
1989—Cincinnati	Nat.	SS-3B	53	125	10	21	4	0	2	11	.168	50	81	4	.970
Major League Totals—1 Year			53	125	10	21	4	0	2	11	.168	50	81	4	.970

Selected by Cincinnati Reds' organization in 7th round of free-agent draft, June 2, 1986.

ROBERT EUGENE RICHIE JR.
(Rob)

Born September 5, 1965, at Reno, Nev.
Height, 6.02. Weight, 190.
Throws right and bats lefthanded.
Attended University of Nevada, Reno, Nev.

Led Eastern League in total bases with 235 in 1988.
Named Eastern League Most Valuable Player, 1988.
Named outfielder on THE SPORTING NEWS College Baseball All-America Team, 1986.

Year	Club	League	Pos.	G.	AB.	R.	H.	2B.	3B.	HR.	RBI.	B.A.	PO.	A.	E.	F.A.
1987—Bristol	Appal.	OF	3	12	2	3	0	0	0	5	.250	2	0	0	1.000
1987—Lakeland	Fla. St.	OF	60	204	31	60	8	3	1	32	.294	99	7	4	.964
1988—Glens Falls	East.	OF	137	501	75	★155	24	7	14	★82	.309	240	7	8	.969
1989—Toledo	Int.	OF	69	215	42	63	9	3	6	26	.293	96	2	1	.990
1989—Detroit	Amer.	OF	19	49	6	13	4	2	1	10	.265	21	1	2	.917
Major League Totals—1 Year			19	49	6	13	4	2	1	10	.265	21	1	2	.917

Selected by Texas Rangers' organization in 4th round of free-agent draft, June 2, 1986.
Selected by Detroit Tigers' organization in 2nd round of free-agent draft, June 2, 1987.

DAVID ALLEN RIGHETTI
Name pronounced Ri-GET-tee.
(Dave)

Born November 28, 1958, at San Jose, Calif.
Height, 6.04. Weight, 210.
Throws and bats lefthanded.
Attended San Jose City College, San Jose, Calif.
Son of Leo Righetti, minor league infielder, 1944 through 1949 and 1951 through 1957;
Brother of Steven Righetti, third baseman in Texas Rangers' organization, 1977 through 1979.

Holds major league record for most saves, season (46), 1986.
Pitched 4-0 no-hit victory against Boston Red Sox, July 4, 1983.
Major League saves: 1982 (1), 1984 (31), 1985 (29), 1986 (46), 1987 (31), 1988 (25), 1989 (25). Total—188.
Led American League in saves with 46 and games finished in relief with 68 in 1986.
Named American League Co-Fireman of the Year by THE SPORTING NEWS, 1987.

Named American League Fireman of the Year by THE SPORTING NEWS, 1986.
Named American League Rookie Pitcher of the Year by THE SPORTING NEWS, 1981.
Named American League Rookie of the Year by Baseball Writers' Association of America, 1981.

Year Club	League	G.	IP.	W.	L.	Pct.	H.	R.	ER.	SO.	BB.	ERA.
1977—Asheville	W. Carol.	17	109	11	3	*.786	98	47	38	101	53	3.14
1978—Tulsa†‡	Texas	13	91	5	5	.500	66	40	32	127	49	3.16
1979—West Haven§	Eastern	11	69	4	3	.571	45	23	15	78	45	1.96
1979—Columbus x	Int'national	8	40	3	2	.600	22	13	13	44	19	2.93
1979—New York	American	3	17	0	1	.000	10	7	7	13	10	3.71
1980—Columbus	Int'national	24	142	6	10	.375	124	79	73	139	*101	4.63
1981—Columbus	Int'national	7	45	5	0	1.000	30	8	5	50	26	1.00
1981—New York	American	15	105	8	4	.667	75	25	24	89	38	2.06
1982—New York	American	33	183	11	10	.524	155	88	77	163	*108	3.79
1982—Columbus	Int'national	4	25⅔	1	0	1.000	22	11	8	33	12	2.81
1983—New York	American	31	217	14	8	.636	194	96	83	169	67	3.44
1984—New York y	American	64	96⅓	5	6	.455	79	29	25	90	37	2.34
1985—New York‖	American	74	107	12	7	.632	96	36	33	92	45	2.78
1986—New York	American	74	106⅔	8	8	.500	88	31	29	83	35	2.45
1987—New York z	American	60	95	8	6	.571	95	45	37	77	44	3.51
1988—New York	American	60	87	5	4	.556	86	35	34	70	37	3.52
1989—New York	American	55	69	2	6	.250	73	32	23	51	26	3.00
Major League Totals—10 Years		469	1083	73	60	.549	951	424	372	897	447	3.09

Selected by Texas Rangers' organization in 1st round (ninth player selected) of free-agent draft, January 11, 1977.
†On disabled list, July 31 to September 2, 1978.
‡Traded with Pitchers Mike Griffin and Paul Mirabella and Outfielders Juan Beniquez and Greg Jemison to New York Yankees for Pitchers Sparky Lyle, Larry McCall and Dave Rajsich, Catcher Mike Heath, Shortstop Domingo Ramos and cash, November 10, 1978.
§On disabled list, May 21 to June 28, 1979.
xOn disabled list, June 28 to July 20 and August 2 to August 23, 1979.
yOn disabled list, June 17 to July 2, 1984.
zGranted free agency, November 9, 1987; re-signed by Yankees, December 23, 1987.

DIVISION SERIES RECORD

Year Club	League	G.	IP.	W.	L.	Pct.	H.	R.	ER.	SO.	BB.	ERA.
1981—New York	American	2	9	2	0	1.000	8	1	1	10	3	1.00

CHAMPIONSHIP SERIES RECORD

Year Club	League	G.	IP.	W.	L.	Pct.	H.	R.	ER.	SO.	BB.	ERA.
1981—New York	American	1	6	1	0	1.000	4	0	0	4	2	0.00

WORLD SERIES RECORD

Year Club	League	G.	IP.	W.	L.	Pct.	H.	R.	ER.	SO.	BB.	ERA.
1981—New York	American	1	2	0	0	.000	5	3	3	1	2	13.50

ALL-STAR GAME RECORD

Year League	IP.	W.	L.	Pct.	H.	R.	ER.	SO.	BB.	ERA.
1986—American	⅔	0	0	.000	2	0	0	0	0	0.00
1987—American	⅓	0	0	.000	1	0	0	0	0	0.00
All-Star Game Totals—2 Years	1	0	0	.000	3	0	0	0	0	0.00

JOSE ANTONIO RIJO (ABREAU)

Name pronounced REE-ho.
Born May 13, 1965, at San Cristobal, Dominican Republic.
Height, 6.02. Weight, 210.
Throws and bats righthanded.
Son-in-law of Juan Marichal, Hall of Fame pitcher with San Francisco Giants, Boston Red Sox and Los Angeles Dodgers, 1960 through 1975; and scout for Oakland A's, 1983 through 1985.
Major League saves: 1984 (2), 1986 (1). Total—3.
Led Pacific Coast League in balks with 11 in 1985.
Led Florida State League in complete games with 15 and tied for lead in shutouts with 4 in 1983.
Named Florida State League Most Valuable Player, 1983.

Year Club	League	G.	IP.	W.	L.	Pct.	H.	R.	ER.	SO.	BB.	ERA.
1981—Bradenton Yankees	Gulf Coast	11	22	3	3	.500	37	16	11	22	7	4.50
1982—Paintsville	Ap'lachian	13	79⅓	8	4	.667	76	33	22	66	22	2.50
1983—Fort Lauderdale	Florida St.	21	160⅓	*15	5	.750	129	38	30	152	43	*1.68
1983—Nashville	Southern	5	40⅓	3	2	.600	31	12	12	32	22	2.68
1984—New York	American	24	62⅓	2	8	.200	74	40	33	47	33	4.76
1984—Columbus†	Int'national	11	65⅓	3	3	.500	67	35	32	47	40	4.41
1985—Tacoma	P. Coast	24	149	7	10	.412	116	64	48	*179	*108	2.90
1985—Oakland	American	12	63⅔	6	4	.600	57	26	25	65	28	3.53
1986—Oakland	American	39	193⅔	9	11	.450	172	116	100	176	108	4.65
1987—Oakland	American	21	82⅓	2	7	.222	106	67	54	67	41	5.90
1987—Tacoma‡	P. Coast	9	54⅔	2	4	.333	44	27	24	67	28	3.95
1988—Cincinnati§	National	49	162	13	8	.619	120	47	43	160	63	2.39
1989—Cincinnati x	National	19	111	7	6	.538	101	39	35	86	48	2.84
American League Totals—4 Years		96	402	19	30	.388	409	249	212	355	210	4.75
National League Totals—2 Years		68	273	20	14	.588	221	86	78	246	111	2.57
Major League Totals—6 Years		164	675	39	44	.470	630	335	290	601	321	3.87

Signed as free agent by New York Yankees' organization, August 1, 1980.
†Traded with Outfielder Stan Javier and Pitchers Jay Howell, Eric Plunk and Tim Birtsas to Oakland A's for Outfielder Rickey Henderson, Pitcher Bert Bradley and cash, December 5, 1984.
‡Traded with Pitcher Tim Birtsas to Cincinnati Reds for Outfielder Dave Parker, December 8, 1987.
§On disabled list, August 18 to September 8, 1988.
xOn disabled list, July 17 to September 1, 1989.

ERNEST RILES

Born October 2, 1960, at Bainbridge, Ga.
Height, 6.01. Weight, 180.
Throws right and bats lefthanded.
Attended Middle Georgia College, Cochran, Ga.

Major League stolen bases: 1985 (2), 1986 (7), 1987 (3), 1988 (3). Total—15.
Led California League in bases on balls received with 84 in 1982.
Led Texas League shortstops in total chances with 670 and double plays with 77 in 1983.
Led California League shortstops in double plays with 95 and tied for lead in total chances with 692 in 1982.

Year	Club	League	Pos.	G.	AB.	R.	H.	2B.	3B.	HR.	RBI.	B.A.	PO.	A.	E.	F.A.
1981—Butte		Pion.	SS-3B-2B	67	256	63	89	11	2	4	43	.348	97	217	27	.921
1982—Stockton		Calif.	SS	138	447	60	128	23	6	2	56	.286	204	★451	37	.947
1983—El Paso		Texas	SS	130	476	109	166	31	3	13	91	★.349	★193	★445	32	★.952
1984—Vancouver		P. C.	SS	123	424	59	113	19	7	3	54	.267	★190	316	17	.967
1985—Vancouver		P. C.	SS	30	118	19	41	7	1	2	20	.347	47	120	6	.965
1985—Milwaukee		Amer.	SS	116	448	54	128	12	7	5	45	.286	183	310	22	.957
1986—Milwaukee		Amer.	SS	145	524	69	132	24	2	9	47	.252	212	327	20	.964
1987—El Paso†		Texas	SS	41	153	45	52	10	0	6	24	.340	70	127	10	.952
1987—Milwaukee		Amer.	3B-SS	83	276	38	72	11	1	4	38	.261	76	152	13	.946
1988—Milwaukee‡		Amer.	3B-SS	41	127	7	32	6	1	1	9	.252	36	64	4	.962
1988—San Francisco		Nat.	3B-2B-SS	79	187	26	55	7	2	3	28	.294	46	133	3	.984
1989—San Francisco		Nat.	3-2-S-O	122	302	43	84	13	2	7	40	.278	69	144	9	.959
American League Totals—4 Years				385	1375	168	364	53	11	19	139	.265	507	853	59	.958
National League Totals—2 Years				201	489	69	139	20	4	10	68	.284	115	277	12	.970
Major League Totals—5 Years				586	1864	237	503	73	15	29	207	.270	622	1130	71	.961

Selected by Seattle Mariners' organization in 21st round of free-agent draft, June 3, 1980.
Selected by Milwaukee Brewers' organization in secondary phase of free-agent draft, January 13, 1981.
†On Milwaukee disabled list, March 26 to June 3, 1987; included rehabilitation disability assignment to El Paso, May 13 to June 2, 1987.
‡Traded to San Francisco Giants for Outfielder Jeffrey Leonard, June 8, 1988.

CHAMPIONSHIP SERIES RECORD

Year	Club	League	Pos.	G.	AB.	R.	H.	2B.	3B.	HR.	RBI.	B.A.	PO.	A.	E.	F.A.
1989—San Francisco		Nat.	PH	1	1	0	0	0	0	0	0	.000	0	0	0	.000

WORLD SERIES RECORD

Year	Club	League	Pos.	G.	AB.	R.	H.	2B.	3B.	HR.	RBI.	B.A.	PO.	A.	E.	F.A.
1989—San Francisco		Nat.	DH-PH	4	8	0	0	0	0	0	0	.000	0	0	0	.000

CALVIN EDWIN RIPKEN JR.
(Cal)

Born August 24, 1960, at Havre de Grace, Md.
Height, 6.04. Weight, 225.
Throws and bats righthanded.

Son of Cal Ripken, Sr., minor league catcher, 1957 through 1962 and 1964; minor league manager, 1961 through 1974; scout, Baltimore Orioles, 1975; manager, Baltimore Orioles, 1987 through April 11, 1988; and coach with Baltimore Orioles, 1976 through 1986 and since 1989; brother of Billy Ripken, second baseman with Baltimore Orioles; and nephew of Bill Ripken, minor league outfielder, 1947 through 1949.

Holds major league records for most at-bats without a triple, season (646), 1989; most at-bats without a stolen base, season (663), 1983.
Holds American League record for most assists by shortstop, season (583), 1984.
Shares American League records for most years leading league in games (5), and putouts (4), shortstop.
Major League stolen bases: 1982 (3), 1984 (2), 1985 (2), 1986 (4), 1987 (3), 1988 (2), 1989 (3). Total—19.
Hit for the cycle, May 6, 1984.
Tied for American League lead in sacrifice flies with 10 in 1988.
Tied for American League lead in game-winning RBIs with 15 in 1986.
Led American League shortstops in total chances with 831 in 1983, 906 in 1984 and 815 in 1989.
Led American League shortstops in double plays with 113 in 1983, 122 in 1984, 123 in 1985 and 119 in 1989.
Tied for Southern League lead in sacrifice flies with 9 in 1980.
Led Southern League third basemen in fielding percentage with .933, putouts with 119, assists with 268, and double plays with 34 in 1980.
Tied for Appalachian League lead in double plays by shortstops with 31 in 1978.
Named Major League Player of the Year by THE SPORTING NEWS, 1983.
Named American League Player of the Year by THE SPORTING NEWS, 1983.
Named American League Most Valuable Player by Baseball Writers' Association of America, 1983.
Named American League Rookie Player of the Year by THE SPORTING NEWS, 1982.
Named American League Rookie of the Year by Baseball Writers' Association of America, 1982.
Named shortstop on THE SPORTING NEWS American League All-Star Team, 1983 through 1985 and 1989.
Named shortstop on THE SPORTING NEWS Silver Slugger team, 1983 through 1986 and 1989.

Year Club	League	Pos.	G.	AB.	R.	H.	2B.	3B.	HR.	RBI.	B.A.	PO.	A.	E.	F.A.
1978—Bluefield................	Appal.	SS	63	239	27	63	7	1	0	24	.264	★92	204	★33	.900
1979—Miami....................	Fla. St.	3B-SS-2B	105	393	51	119	★28	1	5	54	.303	149	260	30	.932
1979—Charlotte...............	South.	3B	17	61	6	11	0	1	3	8	.180	13	26	3	.929
1980—Charlotte...............	South.	3B-SS	●144	522	91	144	28	5	25	78	.276	151	341	35	.934
1981—Rochester.............	Int.	3B-SS	114	437	74	126	31	4	23	75	.288	128	320	21	.955
1981—Baltimore	Amer.	SS-3B	23	39	1	5	0	0	0	0	.128	13	30	3	.935
1982—Baltimore	Amer.	SS-3B	160	598	90	158	32	5	28	93	.264	221	440	19	.972
1983—Baltimore	Amer.	SS	●162	★663	★121	★211	★47	2	27	102	.318	272	★534	25	.970
1984—Baltimore	Amer.	SS	●162	641	103	195	37	7	27	86	.304	★297	★583	26	.971
1985—Baltimore	Amer.	SS	161	642	116	181	32	5	26	110	.282	★286	474	26	.967
1986—Baltimore	Amer.	SS	162	627	98	177	35	1	25	81	.282	240	★482	13	.982
1987—Baltimore	Amer.	SS	★162	624	97	157	28	3	27	98	.252	240	★480	20	.973
1988—Baltimore	Amer.	SS	161	575	87	152	25	1	23	81	.264	★284	480	21	.973
1989—Baltimore	Amer.	SS	●162	646	80	166	30	0	21	93	.257	★276	★531	8	.990
Major League Totals—9 Years................			1315	5055	793	1402	266	24	204	744	.277	2129	4034	161	.975

Selected by Baltimore Orioles' organization in 2nd round of free-agent draft, June 6, 1978.

CHAMPIONSHIP SERIES RECORD

Year Club	League	Pos.	G.	AB.	R.	H.	2B.	3B.	HR.	RBI.	B.A.	PO.	A.	E.	F.A.
1983—Baltimore	Amer.	SS	4	15	5	6	2	0	0	1	.400	7	11	0	1.000

WORLD SERIES RECORD

Year Club	League	Pos.	G.	AB.	R.	H.	2B.	3B.	HR.	RBI.	B.A.	PO.	A.	E.	F.A.
1983—Baltimore	Amer.	SS	5	18	2	3	0	0	0	1	.167	6	14	0	1.000

ALL-STAR GAME RECORD

Year League	Pos.	AB.	R.	H.	2B.	3B.	HR.	RBI.	B.A.	PO.	A.	E.	F.A.
1983—American	SS	0	0	0	0	0	0	0	.000	1	0	0	1.000
1984—American	SS	3	0	0	0	0	0	0	.000	0	0	0	.000
1985—American	SS	3	0	1	0	0	0	0	.333	2	1	0	1.000
1986—American	SS	4	0	0	0	0	0	0	.000	0	1	0	1.000
1987—American	SS	2	0	1	0	0	0	0	.500	0	5	0	1.000
1988—American	SS	3	0	0	0	0	0	0	.000	1	4	0	1.000
1989—American	SS	3	0	1	1	0	0	0	.333	0	0	0	.000
All-Star Game Totals—7 Years....................		18	0	3	1	0	0	0	.167	4	11	0	1.000

WILLIAM OLIVER RIPKEN
(Billy)

Born December 16, 1964, at Havre de Grace, Md.
Height, 6.01. Weight, 183
Throws and bats righthanded.
Son of Cal Ripken, Sr., minor league catcher, 1957 through 1962 and 1964; minor league manager,
1961 through 1974; scout, Baltimore Orioles, 1975; manager, Baltimore Orioles, 1987 through April 11, 1988;
and coach with Baltimore Orioles, 1976 through 1986 and since 1989; brother of Cal Ripken, Jr., shortstop with
Baltimore Orioles; and nephew of Bill Ripken, minor league outfielder, 1947 through 1949.

Major League stolen bases: 1987 (4), 1988 (8), 1989 (1). Total—13.
Tied for Southern League lead in grounding into double plays with 21 in 1986.
Led Southern League second basemen in total chances with 723 and double plays with 79 in 1986.

Year Club	League	Pos.	G.	AB.	R.	H.	2B.	3B.	HR.	RBI.	B.A.	PO.	A.	E.	F.A.
1982—Bluefield................	Appal.	SS-3B-2B	27	45	8	11	1	0	0	4	.244	15	17	3	.914
1983—Bluefield................	Appal.	SS-3B	48	152	24	33	6	0	0	13	.217	82	145	23	.908
1984—Hagerstown†........	Carol.	SS-2B	115	409	48	94	15	3	2	40	.230	187	358	28	.951
1985—Charlotte...............	South.	SS	18	51	2	7	1	0	0	3	.137	18	52	4	.946
1985—Daytona Beach‡..	Fla. St.	SS-3B-2B	67	222	23	51	11	0	0	18	.230	90	198	8	.973
1985—Hagerstown	Carol.	3B-2B	14	47	9	12	0	1	0	0	.255	14	37	2	.962
1986—Charlotte...............	South.	2B	141	530	58	142	20	3	5	62	.268	★305	★395	★23	.968
1987—Rochester.............	Int.	2B-SS	74	238	32	68	15	0	0	11	.286	154	200	9	.975
1987—Baltimore	Amer.	2B	58	234	27	72	9	0	2	20	.308	133	162	3	.990
1988—Baltimore	Amer.	2B-3B	150	512	52	106	18	1	2	34	.207	310	440	12	.984
1989—Baltimore§	Amer.	2B	115	318	31	76	11	2	2	26	.239	255	335	9	.985
Major League Totals—3 Years................			323	1064	110	254	38	3	6	80	.239	698	937	24	.986

Selected by Baltimore Orioles' organization in 11th round of free-agent draft, June 7, 1982.
†On disabled list, April 20 to May 3, 1984.
‡On disabled list, June 23 to July 6, 1985.
§On disabled list, March 27 to April 14 and August 23 to September 7, 1989.

KEVIN D. RITZ

Born June 8, 1965, at Eatonstown, N. J.
Height, 6.04. Weight, 195.
Throws and bats righthanded.
Attended Indian Hills Community College, Centerville, Ia.

Year Club	League	G.	IP.	W.	L.	Pct.	H.	R.	ER.	SO.	BB.	ERA.
1986—Gastonia................................	S. Atlantic	7	36⅓	1	2	.333	29	19	17	34	21	4.21
1986—Lakeland................................	Florida St.	18	85⅔	3	9	.250	114	60	53	39	45	5.57
1987—Glens Falls...........................	Eastern	25	152⅔	8	8	.500	171	95	83	78	71	4.89

Year Club	League	G.	IP.	W.	L.	Pct.	H.	R.	ER.	SO.	BB.	ERA.
1988—Glens Falls	Eastern	26	136⅔	8	10	.444	115	68	58	75	70	3.82
1989—Toledo	Int'national	16	102⅔	7	8	.467	95	48	36	74	60	3.16
1989—Detroit	American	12	74	4	6	.400	75	41	36	56	44	4.38
Major League Totals—1 Year		12	74	4	6	.400	75	41	36	56	44	4.38

Selected by San Francisco Giants' organization in 4th round of free-agent draft, January 9, 1985.
Selected by Detroit Tigers' organization in secondary phase of free-agent draft, June 3, 1985.

BIENVENIDO SANTANA RIVERA
(Ben)

Born January 11, 1969, at Dominican Republic.
Height, 6.06. Weight, 210.
Throws and bats righthanded.

Year Club	League	G.	IP.	W.	L.	Pct.	H.	R.	ER.	SO.	BB.	ERA.
1987—Bradenton Braves	Gulf Coast	16	49⅔	1	5	.167	55	26	18	29	19	3.26
1988—Sumter†	S. Atlantic	27	173⅓	9	11	.450	167	77	61	99	52	3.17
1989—Durham	Carolina	23	102⅓	5	7	.417	113	55	51	58	51	4.49

Signed as free agent by Atlanta Braves' organization, November 15, 1985.
†Drafted by Atlanta Braves, December 5, 1988.

HECTOR ANTONIO RIVERA

Born February 8, 1970, at Navojoa, Sonora, Mexico.
Height, 6.04. Weight, 225.
Throws and bats righthanded.
Tied for Gulf Coast League lead in games started by pitchers with 14 in 1987.

Year Club	League	G.	IP.	W.	L.	Pct.	H.	R.	ER.	SO.	BB.	ERA.
1987—Bradenton Expos	Gulf Coast	14	*86⅔	5	*8	.385	67	38	26	62	44	2.70
1988—Rockford†	Midwest							(Did not play)				
1989—West Palm Beach	Florida St.	16	103⅓	7	3	.700	85	25	21	61	28	1.83
1989—Jacksonville	Southern	5	27	1	2	.333	24	17	16	22	17	5.33

Signed as free agent by Montreal Expos' organization, April 30, 1987.
†On disabled list, April 1, 1988 through entire season.

LUIS ANTONIO RIVERA

Born January 3, 1964, at Cidra, Puerto Rico.
Height, 5.09. Weight, 170.
Throws and bats righthanded.
Major League stolen bases: 1986 (1), 1988 (3), 1989 (2). Total—6.
Led American Association shortstops in double plays with 84 in 1987.
Led Southern League shortstops in total chances with 643 and double plays with 107 in 1985.
Led Florida State League shortstops in assists with 436, errors with 51, total chances with 704 and double plays with 95 in 1983.
Tied for Florida State League lead in total chances by shortstops with 626 in 1984.

Year Club	League	Pos.	G.	AB.	R.	H.	2B.	3B.	HR.	RBI.	B.A.	PO.	A.	E.	F.A.
1982—San Jose	Calif.	SS	130	476	53	123	20	3	3	49	.258	226	389	55	.918
1983—W. Palm Beach	Fla. St.	SS	129	419	63	95	18	5	5	53	.227	217	436	51	.928
1984—W. Palm Beach	Fla. St.	SS	124	439	54	100	23	0	6	43	.228	*198	*389	39	.938
1985—Jacksonville	South.	SS	138	*538	74	129	20	2	16	72	.240	*198	*412	33	.949
1986—Indianapolis	A. A.	SS	108	407	60	100	17	5	7	43	.246	178	330	24	.955
1986—Montreal	Nat.	SS	55	166	20	34	11	1	0	13	.205	64	119	9	.953
1987—Indianapolis	A. A.	SS	108	433	73	135	26	3	8	53	.312	190	291	18	.964
1987—Montreal	Nat.	SS	18	32	0	5	2	0	0	1	.156	9	27	3	.923
1988—Montreal†	Nat.	SS	123	371	35	83	17	3	4	30	.224	160	301	18	.962
1989—Pawtucket	Int.	SS-3B	43	175	22	44	9	0	1	13	.251	53	106	9	.946
1989—Boston	Amer.	SS-2B	93	323	35	83	17	1	5	29	.257	127	240	16	.958
National League Totals—3 Years			196	569	55	122	30	4	4	44	.214	233	447	30	.958
American League Totals—1 Year			93	323	35	83	17	1	5	29	.257	127	240	16	.958
Major League Totals—4 Years			289	892	90	205	47	5	9	73	.230	360	687	46	.958

Signed as free agent by Montreal Expos' organization, September 22, 1981.
†Traded with Pitcher John Dopson to Boston Red Sox for Shortstop Spike Owen and Pitcher Dan Gakeler, December 8, 1988.

LEON JOSEPH ROBERTS III
(Bip)

Born October 27, 1963, at Berkeley, Calif.
Height, 5.07. Weight, 160.
Throws right and bats left and righthanded.
Attended Chabot College, Hayward, Calif.; and University of Nevada, Las Vegas, Nev.
Major League stolen bases: 1986 (14), 1989 (21). Total—35.
Tied for Eastern League lead in stolen bases with 40 in 1985.
Led Carolina League second basemen in total chances with 654 and double plays with 91 in 1984.
Led South Atlantic League second basemen in fielding percentage with .962 and tied for lead in double plays with 76 in 1983.

Year Club	League	Pos.	G.	AB.	R.	H.	2B.	3B.	HR.	RBI.	B.A.	PO.	A.	E.	F.A.
1982—Bradenton Pir.	Gulf C.	2B	6	23	4	7	1	0	0	1	.304	14	15	0	1.000
1982—Greenwood............	S. Atl.	2B	33	107	15	23	3	1	0	6	.215	52	82	7	.950
1983—Greenwood............	S. Atl.	2B-SS	122	438	78	140	20	5	6	63	.320	273	311	24	.961
1984—Prince William	Carol.	2B	134	498	81	★150	25	5	8	77	.301	★282	352	20	★.969
1985—Nashua†‡	East.	2B	105	401	64	109	19	5	1	23	.272	217	249	●29	.941
1986—San Diego§	Nat.	2B	101	241	34	61	5	2	1	12	.253	166	172	10	.971
1987—Las Vegas..............	P. C.	2B-OF-3B	98	359	66	110	18	10	1	38	.306	147	150	8	.974
1988—Las Vegas..............	P. C.	3B-OF-2B	100	343	73	121	21	8	7	51	.353	103	130	17	.932
1988—San Diego	Nat.	2B-3B	5	9	1	3	0	0	0	0	.333	2	3	1	.833
1989—San Diego	Nat.	O-3-S-2	117	329	81	99	15	8	3	25	.301	134	113	9	.965
Major League Totals—3 Years................			223	579	116	163	20	10	4	37	.282	302	288	20	.967

Selected by Pittsburgh Pirates' organization in 5th round of free-agent draft, June 8, 1981.
Selected by Pittsburgh Pirates' organization in secondary phase of free-agent draft, June 7, 1982.
†On suspended list, June 30 to July 3, 1985.
‡Drafted by San Diego Padres, December 10, 1985.
§On disabled list, May 21 to June 5, 1986.

DOUGLAS SCOTT ROBERTSON
(Doug)

Born April 15, 1963, at Upland, Calif.
Height, 6.01. Weight, 185.
Throws right and bats left and righthanded.
Attended California State University, Fullerton, Calif.

Led California League in games finished in relief with 51 and saves with 23 in 1988.
Led Northwest League in wild pitches with 12 in 1985.

Year Club	League	G.	IP.	W.	L.	Pct.	H.	R.	ER.	SO.	BB.	ERA.
1985—Everett...............................	Northwest	13	81⅓	4	4	.500	77	56	40	85	59	4.43
1986—Clinton...............................	Midwest	27	118⅓	3	10	.231	117	78	60	79	73	4.56
1987—Clinton...............................	Midwest	28	164	8	12	.400	185	115	93	173	95	5.10
1988—San Jose	California	57	78⅓	7	5	.583	63	18	11	103	30	1.26
1989—Shreveport†	Texas	52	63	4	2	.667	50	26	21	50	38	3.00

Selected by San Francisco Giants' organization in 3rd round of free-agent draft, June 3, 1985.
†Drafted by Cleveland Indians, December 4, 1989.

WILLIAM JOSEPH ROBIDOUX

Name pronounced ROW-ba-doe.

(Billy Jo)

Born January 13, 1964, at Ware, Mass.
Height, 6.01. Weight, 200.
Throws right and bats lefthanded.

Major League stolen bases: 1988 (1).
Led Pacific Coast League in intentional bases on balls received with 9 in 1989.
Led Texas League in total bases with 297 and slugging percentage with .577 in 1985.
Led Texas League first basemen in putouts with 1,025, assists with 68, fielding percentage with .988, total chances with 1,106 and double plays with 102 in 1985.
Named Texas League Most Valuable Player, 1985.

Year Club	League	Pos.	G.	AB.	R.	H.	2B.	3B.	HR.	RBI.	B.A.	PO.	A.	E.	F.A.
1982—Pikeville†	Appal.	3B-1B	54	167	28	48	10	1	0	13	.287	57	54	15	.881
1983—Beloit	Midw.	3B-1B-2B	126	435	70	138	30	1	10	61	.317	104	163	25	.914
1984—Stockton	Calif.	3B-1B	97	333	50	93	18	1	5	67	.279	323	98	15	.966
1985—El Paso	Texas	1B-OF-3B	133	515	★111	★176	★46	3	23	★132	★.342	1030	69	15	.987
1985—Milwaukee.............	Amer.	OF-1B	18	51	5	9	2	0	3	8	.176	64	6	0	1.000
1986—Milwaukee‡...........	Amer.	1B	56	181	15	41	8	0	1	21	.227	326	29	5	.986
1986—Beloit	Midw.	1B	7	16	3	4	2	0	0	2	.250	12	2	0	1.000
1986—El Paso	Texas	1B	30	114	30	37	9	0	10	34	.325	269	11	1	.996
1987—Milwaukee.............	Amer.	1B	23	62	9	12	0	0	0	4	.194	53	4	1	.983
1987—Denver§	A. A.	1B-3B	30	116	27	33	9	3	3	15	.284	184	14	5	.975
1988—Denver	A. A.	1B	70	240	43	70	24	0	8	42	.292	570	48	8	.987
1988—Milwaukee x	Amer.	1B	33	91	9	23	5	0	0	5	.253	212	25	4	.983
1989—Chicago	Amer.	1B-OF	16	39	2	5	2	0	0	1	.128	93	7	1	.990
1989—Vancouver y	P. C.	1B	73	246	36	78	19	2	11	42	.317	440	41	5	.990
Major League Totals—5 Years................			146	424	40	90	17	0	4	39	.212	748	71	11	.987

Selected by Milwaukee Brewers' organization in 6th round of free-agent draft, June 7, 1982.
†On disabled list, June 21 to July 1, 1982.
‡On disabled list, May 13 to June 11 and July 8 to August 20, 1986; included rehabilitation disability assignment to Beloit, June 4 to June 11, and to El Paso, August 1 to August 20, 1986.
§On disabled list, July 16, 1987 through remainder of season.
xGranted free agency, October 15, 1988; signed by Chicago White Sox, October 30, 1988.
yGranted free agency, October 15, 1989; signed by Pawtucket (Boston Red Sox' organization), December 13, 1989.

DON ALLEN ROBINSON

Born June 8, 1957, at Ashland, Ky.
Height, 6.04. Weight, 231.
Throws and bats righthanded.

Major League saves: 1978 (1), 1980 (1), 1981 (2), 1984 (10), 1985 (3), 1986 (14), 1987 (19), 1988 (6). Total—56.
Tied for National League lead in home runs allowed with 26 in 1982.
Led Western Carolinas League in complete games with 11 in 1976.
Tied for Gulf Coast League lead in hit batsmen with 6 in 1975.
Named National League Rookie Pitcher of the Year by THE SPORTING NEWS, 1978.
Named pitcher on THE SPORTING NEWS National League Silver Slugger team, 1982 and 1989.

Year—Club	League	G.	IP.	W.	L.	Pct.	H.	R.	ER.	SO.	BB.	ERA.
1975—Bradenton Pirates	Gulf Coast	10	66	2	3	.400	51	23	18	★70	31	2.45
1976—Charleston	W. Carol.	25	★172	12	9	.571	146	79	62	132	64	3.24
1977—Shreveport	Texas	18	112	7	6	.538	113	58	51	103	41	4.06
1977—Columbus†	Int'national	1	5	1	0	1.000	7	0	0	3	1	0.00
1978—Pittsburgh	National	35	228	14	6	.700	203	98	88	135	57	3.47
1979—Pittsburgh	National	29	161	8	8	.500	171	74	69	96	52	3.86
1980—Pittsburgh‡	National	29	160	7	10	.412	157	74	71	103	45	3.99
1981—Pittsburgh§	National	16	38	0	3	.000	47	27	25	17	23	5.92
1982—Pittsburgh	National	38	227	15	13	.536	213	★123	108	165	103	4.28
1983—Pittsburgh x	National	9	36⅓	2	2	.500	43	21	18	28	21	4.46
1983—Lynn	Eastern	2	6⅔	0	1	.000	9	6	6	5	2	8.10
1984—Pittsburgh y	National	51	122	5	6	.455	99	45	41	110	49	3.02
1985—Pittsburgh	National	44	95⅓	5	11	.313	95	49	41	65	42	3.87
1986—Pittsburgh z	National	50	69⅓	3	4	.429	61	27	26	53	27	3.38
1986—Prince William	Carolina	3	12⅔	1	1	.500	13	7	1	13	1	0.71
1987—Pittsburgh a-San Francisco	National	67	108	11	7	.611	105	42	41	79	40	3.42
1988—San Francisco	National	51	176⅔	10	5	.667	152	63	48	122	49	2.45
1989—San Francisco	National	34	197	12	11	.522	184	80	75	96	37	3.43
Major League Totals—12 Years		453	1618⅔	92	86	.517	1530	723	651	1069	545	3.62

Selected by Pittsburgh Pirates' organization in 3rd round of free-agent draft, June 4, 1975.
†On disabled list, July 28 to September 6, 1977.
‡On disabled list, March 31 to May 1, 1980.
§On disabled list, May 2 to June 6 and August 2 to August 26, 1981.
xOn disabled list, March 29 to June 10 and July 29 to September 2, 1983; included rehabilitation disability assignment to Lynn, April 29 to May 18, 1983.
yAppeared in one game as an outfielder with two putouts.
zOn disabled list, April 21 to June 7, 1986; included rehabilitation disability assignment to Prince William, May 24 to June 7, 1986.
aTraded to San Francisco Giants for Catcher Mackey Sasser and $50,000, July 31, 1987.

CHAMPIONSHIP SERIES RECORD

Year—Club	League	G.	IP.	W.	L.	Pct.	H.	R.	ER.	SO.	BB.	ERA.
1979—Pittsburgh	National	2	2	1	0	1.000	0	0	0	3	1	0.00
1987—San Francisco	National	3	3	0	1	.000	3	3	3	3	0	9.00
1989—San Francisco	National	1	1⅔	1	0	1.000	3	1	0	0	0	0.00
Championship Series Totals—3 Years		6	6⅔	2	1	.667	6	4	3	6	1	4.05

WORLD SERIES RECORD

Year—Club	League	G.	IP.	W.	L.	Pct.	H.	R.	ER.	SO.	BB.	ERA.
1979—Pittsburgh	National	4	5	1	0	1.000	4	3	3	3	6	5.40
1989—San Francisco	National	1	1⅔	0	1	.000	4	4	4	0	1	21.60
World Series Totals—2 Years		5	6⅔	1	1	.500	8	7	7	3	7	9.45

JEFFREY DANIEL ROBINSON
(Jeff)

Born December 13, 1960, at Santa Ana, Calif.
Height, 6.04. Weight, 200.
Throws and bats righthanded.
Attended California State University, Fullerton, Calif.

Shares major league record by striking out side on 9 pitches, September 7, 1987, eighth inning.
Major League saves: 1986 (8), 1987 (14), 1988 (9), 1989 (4). Total—35.
Tied for National League lead in hit batsmen with 7 in 1984.
Tied for Pacific Coast League lead in games started by pitchers with 29 in 1985.

Year—Club	League	G.	IP.	W.	L.	Pct.	H.	R.	ER.	SO.	BB.	ERA.
1983—Fresno	California	14	94⅔	7	6	.538	88	35	24	78	21	2.28
1984—San Francisco	National	34	171⅔	7	15	.318	195	99	87	102	52	4.56
1985—Phoenix	P. Coast	29	161	9	9	.500	192	107	92	80	60	5.14
1985—San Francisco	National	8	12⅓	0	0	.000	16	11	7	8	10	5.11
1986—San Francisco†	National	64	104⅓	6	3	.667	92	46	39	90	32	3.36
1987—San Francisco‡-Pittsburgh	National	81	123⅓	8	9	.471	89	43	39	101	54	2.85
1988—Pittsburgh	National	75	124⅔	11	5	.688	113	44	42	87	39	3.03
1989—Pittsburgh§	National	50	141⅓	7	13	.350	161	92	72	95	59	4.58
Major League Totals—6 Years		312	677⅔	39	45	.464	666	335	286	483	246	3.80

Selected by Toronto Blue Jays' organization in 17th round of free-agent draft, June 5, 1979.
Selected by Detroit Tigers' organization in 14th round of free-agent draft, June 7, 1982.
Selected by San Francisco Giants' organization in 2nd round of free-agent draft, June 6, 1983.
†Appeared in one game as an outfielder with no chances.
‡Traded with Pitcher Scott Medvin to Pittsburgh Pirates for Pitcher Rick Reuschel, August 21, 1987.
§Traded with Pitcher Willie Smith to New York Yankees for Catcher Don Slaught, December 4, 1989.

JEFFREY MARK ROBINSON
(Jeff)

Born December 14, 1961, at Ventura, Calif.
Height, 6.06. Weight, 240.
Throws and bats righthanded.
Attended Azusa Pacific University, Azusa, Calif.

Year Club	League	G.	IP.	W.	L.	Pct.	H.	R.	ER.	SO.	BB.	ERA.
1983—Lakeland	Florida St.	11	50	2	5	.286	61	38	33	23	19	5.94
1984—Lakeland	Florida St.	10	61⅔	2	3	.400	62	30	23	33	26	3.36
1984—Birmingham	Southern	20	113	6	6	.500	111	64	59	47	56	4.70
1985—Birmingham†	Southern	22	115	4	8	.333	142	79	65	67	59	5.09
1986—Nashville	Am. Assoc.	25	150	10	7	.588	162	85	73	72	72	4.38
1987—Detroit	American	29	127⅓	9	6	.600	132	86	76	98	54	5.37
1988—Detroit‡	American	24	172	13	6	.684	121	61	57	114	72	2.98
1989—Detroit§	American	16	78	4	5	.444	76	47	41	40	46	4.73
1989—Lakeland	Florida St.	4	11	0	0	.000	12	8	8	5	4	6.55
Major League Totals—3 Years		69	377⅓	26	17	.605	329	194	174	252	172	4.15

Selected by San Diego Padres' organization in 40th round of free-agent draft, June 3, 1980.
Selected by Detroit Tigers' organization in 3rd round of free-agent draft, June 6, 1983.
†On disabled list, June 28 to July 10, 1985.
‡On disabled list, August 24, 1988 through remainder of season.
§On disabled list, May 15 to May 31 and June 11 to July 26, 1989; included rehabilitation disability assignment to Lakeland, July 10 to July 26, 1989.

CHAMPIONSHIP SERIES RECORD

Year Club	League	G.	IP.	W.	L.	Pct.	H.	R.	ER.	SO.	BB.	ERA.
1987—Detroit	American	1	⅓	0	0	.000	1	0	0	0	0	0.00

RONALD DEAN ROBINSON
(Ron)

Born March 24, 1962, at Exeter, Calif.
Height, 6.04. Weight, 235.
Throws and bats righthanded.

Major League saves: 1985 (1), 1986 (14), 1987 (4). Total—19.

Year Club	League	G.	IP.	W.	L.	Pct.	H.	R.	ER.	SO.	BB.	ERA.
1980—Tampa	Florida St.	13	76	4	6	.400	76	32	28	44	16	3.32
1981—Cedar Rapids	Midwest	24	169	10	8	.556	136	58	42	165	55	2.24
1982—Waterbury	Eastern	32	178⅓	13	7	.650	166	78	65	149	65	3.28
1983—Waterbury	Eastern	20	142⅔	7	9	.438	132	66	57	82	60	3.60
1983—Indianapolis	Am. Assoc.	4	30⅔	4	0	1.000	22	13	11	20	7	3.23
1984—Wichita	Am. Assoc.	25	150⅓	9	6	.600	168	86	77	98	60	4.61
1984—Cincinnati	National	12	39⅔	1	2	.333	35	18	12	24	13	2.72
1985—Denver	Am. Assoc.	6	39⅔	2	1	.667	39	17	12	24	12	2.72
1985—Cincinnati	National	33	108⅓	7	7	.500	107	53	48	76	32	3.99
1986—Cincinnati	National	70	116⅔	10	3	.769	110	44	42	117	43	3.24
1987—Cincinnati	National	48	154	7	5	.583	148	71	63	99	43	3.68
1988—Cincinnati†	National	17	78⅔	3	7	.300	88	47	36	38	26	4.12
1988—Nashville	Am. Assoc.	2	3⅔	0	0	.000	4	3	3	4	3	7.36
1989—Nashville‡	Am. Assoc.	3	19	2	0	1.000	12	5	4	11	6	1.89
1989—Chattanooga	Southern	1	5	0	0	.000	3	1	1	5	1	1.80
1989—Cincinnati	National	15	83⅓	5	3	.625	80	36	31	36	28	3.35
Major League Totals—6 Years		195	580⅔	33	27	.550	568	269	232	390	185	3.60

Selected by Cincinnati Reds' organization in 1st round (19th player selected) of free-agent draft, June 3, 1980.
†On disabled list, June 25 to July 18 and July 20 to September 2, 1988; included rehabilitation disability assignment to Nashville, August 15 to September 2, 1988.
‡On Cincinnati disabled list, March 19 to July 17, 1989; included rehabilitation disability assignment to Nashville, June 26 to July 2, 1989; then transferred to Chattanooga, July 3, 1989.

MICHAEL JOSEPH ROCHFORD
(Mike)

Born March 14, 1963, at Methuen, Mass.
Height, 6.04. Weight, 205.
Throws and bats lefthanded.
Attended Santa Fe Community College, Gainsville, Fla.

Led International League in balks with 5 in 1984.
Tied for International League lead in complete games with 9 in 1989.
Tied for Carolina League lead in games started by pitchers with 29 in 1983.

Year Club	League	G.	IP.	W.	L.	Pct.	H.	R.	ER.	SO.	BB.	ERA.
1982—Elmira	NYP	16	85⅔	6	4	.600	99	53	40	66	26	4.20
1983—Winston-Salem	Carolina	29	210⅓	16	11	.593	182	85	70	165	57	3.00
1984—Pawtucket	Int'national	31	141⅓	8	10	.444	156	88	77	73	59	4.90
1985—New Britain	Eastern	14	93⅓	8	5	.615	84	39	31	42	41	2.99
1985—Pawtucket	Int'national	12	72	5	2	.714	74	34	33	47	32	4.13
1986—Pawtucket	Int'national	28	170⅔	11	10	.524	178	76	67	70	50	3.53
1987—Pawtucket	Int'national	22	123⅔	8	8	.500	144	65	63	42	38	4.58
1988—Pawtucket	Int'national	52	81⅔	1	5	.167	68	30	28	47	29	3.09

Year	Club	League	G.	IP.	W.	L.	Pct.	H.	R.	ER.	SO.	BB.	ERA.
1988—Boston	American	2	2⅓	0	0	.000	4	0	0	1	1	0.00
1989—Pawtucket	Int'national	37	163⅓	9	6	.600	139	52	43	76	43	2.37
1989—Boston	American	4	4	0	0	.000	4	7	3	1	4	6.75
Major League Totals—2 Years		6	6⅓	0	0	.000	8	7	3	2	5	4.26

Selected by Boston Red Sox' organization in 1st round (17th player selected) of free-agent draft, January 12, 1982.

ROSARIO RODRIGUEZ

Born July 8, 1969 at Los Moches, Mexico.
Height, 6.00. Weight, 195.
Throws left and bats righthanded.

Year	Club	League	G.	IP.	W.	L.	Pct.	H.	R.	ER.	SO.	BB.	ERA.
1987—Sarasota Reds	Gulf Coast	17	64⅓	1	5	.167	64	32	22	33	21	3.08
1988—Greensboro	S. Atlantic	23	65⅓	6	4	.600	49	15	11	53	24	1.52
1988—Cedar Rapids	Midwest	13	70	3	4	.429	73	41	31	47	25	3.99
1989—Chattanooga	Southern	28	44⅓	3	0	1.000	48	24	22	36	18	4.47
1989—Cincinnati	National	7	4⅓	1	1	.500	3	2	2	0	3	4.15
Major League Totals—1 Year		7	4⅓	1	1	.500	3	2	2	0	3	4.15

Signed as free agent by Cincinnati Reds' organization, March 16, 1987.

VICTOR MANUEL RODRIGUEZ (RIVERA)
(Vic)

Born July 14, 1961, at New York, N.Y.
Height, 5.11. Weight, 173.
Throws and bats righthanded.

Led International League in grounding into double plays with 23 in 1984.
Led Pacific Coast League third basemen in fielding percentage with .937 in 1988.
Led International League second basemen in total chances with 689 in 1984.

Year	Club	League	Pos.	G.	AB.	R.	H.	2B.	3B.	HR.	RBI.	B.A.	PO.	A.	E.	F.A.
1977—Bluefield	Appal.	3B-SS	53	188	28	55	10	4	3	23	.293	1	6	1	.875
1978—Bluefield	Appal.	OF-3B-SS	59	209	26	67	4	2	2	28	.321	39	14	5	.914
1979—Miami	Fla. St.	2B-3B-OF	67	228	23	70	10	2	1	31	.307	71	105	11	.941
1980—Alexandria†	Carol.	2B	33	130	20	39	4	2	2	15	.300	62	94	6	.963
1980—Charlotte	South.	3B	19	65	4	15	0	0	0	4	.231	14	37	2	.962
1980—Miami	Fla. St.	2B	50	184	21	60	10	2	2	21	.326	103	144	14	.946
1981—Charlotte	South.	2B	138	553	68	169	22	1	9	65	.306	337	357	18	.975
1982—Rochester	Int.	2B	87	300	26	74	10	2	0	18	.247	189	273	17	.965
1982—Charlotte	South.	2B	47	165	17	48	13	0	3	18	.291	95	116	10	.955
1983—Charlotte	South.	2B-3B	140	★571	80	●170	26	1	14	77	.298	291	386	19	.973
1984—Rochester	Int.	2B	132	478	54	131	22	●6	6	46	.274	★272	★403	14	.980
1984—Baltimore‡	Amer.	2B	11	17	4	7	3	0	0	2	.412	8	15	1	.958
1985—Las Vegas§	P. C.	2B-3B-SS	127	462	56	144	31	3	11	58	.312	183	311	16	.969
1986—Louisville x	A. A.	3B-2B	56	191	13	52	9	0	1	18	.272	19	45	10	.865
1987—Louisville y	A. A.	3-S-2-1	116	422	44	124	33	2	3	54	.294	97	218	19	.943
1988—Portland	P. C.	3B-2B-SS	★139	★562	67	★162	27	8	9	69	.288	105	240	21	.943
1989—Portland	P. C.	3B-SS-2B	120	465	63	146	34	3	10	50	.314	78	230	17	.948
1989—Minnesota	Amer.	3B	6	11	2	5	2	0	0	0	.455	3	6	1	.900
Major League Totals—2 Years		17	28	6	12	5	0	0	2	.429	11	21	2	.941

Signed as free agent by Baltimore Orioles' organization, February 11, 1977.
†Loaned to Alexandria (Co-op), April 6, 1980; returned, May 23, 1980.
‡Traded to San Diego Padres' organization for Third Baseman Fritz Connally, February 7, 1985.
§Granted free agency, October 15, 1985; signed by St. Louis Cardinals, January 13, 1986.
xOn disabled list, April 11 to June 12, 1986.
yGranted free agency, October 15, 1987; signed by Portland (Minnesota Twins' organization), January, 1988.

MICHAEL JOSEPH ROESLER

Name pronounced RESS-ler.

(Mike)

Born September 12, 1963, at Fort Wayne, Ind.
Height, 6.05. Weight, 205.
Throws and bats righthanded.
Attended Ball State University, Muncie, Ind.

Year	Club	League	G.	IP.	W.	L.	Pct.	H.	R.	ER.	SO.	BB.	ERA.
1985—Billings	Pioneer	13	88⅔	8	2	.800	72	32	23	73	28	2.33
1986—Cedar Rapids	Midwest	32	163	9	13	.409	165	95	83	135	80	4.58
1987—Tampa	Florida St.	28	36⅓	7	2	.778	30	14	9	29	15	2.23
1987—Vermont	Eastern	22	27⅓	4	2	.667	28	10	10	19	10	3.29
1988—Chattanooga	Southern	16	20⅓	1	1	.500	16	5	5	13	8	2.21
1988—Nashville	Am. Assoc.	32	41⅓	3	2	.600	44	25	23	31	27	5.01
1989—Nashville	Am. Assoc.	40	69⅓	6	4	.600	63	30	25	53	39	3.25
1989—Cincinnati	National	17	25	0	1	.000	22	11	11	14	9	3.96
Major League Totals—1 Year		17	25	0	1	.000	22	11	11	14	9	3.96

Selected by Cincinnati Reds' organization in 17th round of free-agent draft, June 3, 1985.

JAMES RANDALL ROGERS
(Jimmy)

Born January 3, 1967, at Tulsa, Okla.
Height, 6.02. Weight, 185.
Throws and bats righthanded.
Attended Seminole Junior College, Seminole, Okla.

Led Southern League in games started by pitchers with 30 in 1989.
Tied for South Atlantic League lead in games started by pitchers with 32 in 1988.
Named South Atlantic League Pitcher of the Year, 1988.

Year Club	League	G.	IP.	W.	L.	Pct.	H.	R.	ER.	SO.	BB.	ERA.
1987—St. Catharines	NYP	13	56⅓	2	4	.333	46	33	21	60	24	3.36
1988—Myrtle Beach	S. Atlantic	33	188⅓	*18	4	*.818	145	84	70	*198	95	3.35
1989—Knoxville	Southern	32	158	12	10	.545	136	89	80	120	*132	4.56

Selected by Toronto Blue Jays' organization in 16th round of free-agent draft, June 2, 1986.

KENNETH SCOTT ROGERS
(Kenny)

Born November 10, 1964, at Savannah, Ga.
Height, 6.01. Weight, 200.
Throws and bats lefthanded.

Major League saves: 1989 (2).

Year Club	League	G.	IP.	W.	L.	Pct.	H.	R.	ER.	SO.	BB.	ERA.
1982—Sarasota Rangers	Gulf Coast	2	3	0	0	.000	0	0	0	4	0	0.00
1983—Sarasota Rangers	Gulf Coast	15	53⅓	4	1	.800	40	21	14	36	20	2.36
1984—Burlington	Midwest	39	92⅔	4	7	.364	87	52	41	93	33	3.98
1985—Daytona Beach	Florida St.	6	10	0	1	.000	12	9	8	9	11	7.20
1985—Burlington	Midwest	33	95	2	5	.286	67	34	30	96	62	2.84
1986—Tulsa†	Texas	10	26⅓	0	3	.000	39	30	29	23	18	9.91
1986—Salem	Carolina	12	66	2	7	.222	75	54	46	46	26	6.27
1987—Charlotte	Florida St.	5	17	0	3	.000	17	13	9	14	8	4.76
1987—Tulsa	Texas	28	69	1	5	.167	80	51	41	59	35	5.35
1988—Tulsa	Texas	13	83⅓	4	6	.400	73	43	37	76	34	4.00
1988—Port Charlotte	Florida St.	8	35⅓	2	0	1.000	22	8	5	26	11	1.27
1989—Texas	American	73	73⅔	3	4	.429	60	28	24	63	42	2.93
Major League Totals—1 Year		73	73⅔	3	4	.429	60	28	24	63	42	2.93

Selected by Texas Rangers' organization in 39th round of free-agent draft, June 7, 1982.
†On disabled list, April 12 to April 30, 1986.

DAVID GRANT ROHDE
(Dave)

Born May 8, 1964, at Los Altos, Calif.
Height, 6.02. Weight, 180.
Throws and bats righthanded.
Attended Saddleback Community College, Mission Viejo, Calif.,
and University of Arizona, Tucson, Ariz.

Led Southern League second basemen in fielding percentage with .987 in 1988.

Year Club	League	Pos.	G.	AB.	R.	H.	2B.	3B.	HR.	RBI.	B.A.	PO.	A.	E.	F.A.
1986—Auburn	NYP	SS	61	207	41	54	6	4	2	22	.261	90	158	16	.939
1987—Osceola	Fla. St.	2B-SS	103	377	57	108	15	1	5	42	.286	165	305	20	.959
1988—Columbus	South.	2B-SS	142	486	76	130	20	2	4	53	.267	251	356	25	.960
1989—Columbus†	South.	3B-2B-SS	67	254	40	71	5	2	2	27	.280	70	127	17	.921
1989—Tucson†	P. C.	SS-3B	75	234	35	68	7	3	1	30	.291	108	232	13	.963

Selected by Houston Astros' organization in 5th round of free-agent draft, June 2, 1986.
†Switch-hitter.

MELQUIADES ROJAS
(Mel)

Born December 10, 1966, at Haina, Dominican Republic.
Throws and bats righthanded.
Height, 5.11. Weight, 175.

Nephew of Felipe Alou, outfielder with San Francisco, Milwaukee-Atlanta Braves, Oakland, New York Yankees, Montreal and Milwaukee Brewers, 1958 through 1974; coach with Montreal Expos, 1979, 1980 and 1984; and minor league manager in Montreal Expos' organization, 1977, 1978, 1981 through 1983 and since 1985; nephew of Jesus Alou, outfielder with San Francisco, Houston, Oakland and New York Yankees, 1963 through 1975, 1978 and 1979, and scout with Montreal Expos since 1983; nephew of Matty Alou, outfielder with San Francisco, Pittsburgh, St. Louis, Oakland, New York Yankees and San Diego, 1960 through 1974; nephew of Jose Alou, outfielder in Montreal Expos' organization; and brother of Francisco Rojas, outfielder in San Francisco Giants' organization, 1978 and 1979.

Year Club	League	G.	IP.	W.	L.	Pct.	H.	R.	ER.	SO.	BB.	ERA.
1986—Bradenton Expos	Gulf Coast	13	55¼	4	5	.444	63	39	30	34	37	4.88
1987—Burlington	Midwest	25	158⅔	8	9	.471	146	84	67	100	67	3.80
1988—Rockford†	Midwest	12	73⅓	6	4	.600	52	30	20	72	29	2.45
1988—West Palm Beach‡	Florida St.	2	5	1	0	1.000	4	2	2	4	1	3.60
1989—Jacksonville	Southern	34	112	10	7	.588	62	39	31	104	57	2.49

Signed as free agent by Montreal Expos' organization, November 7, 1985.
†On disabled list, May 7 to June 14, 1988.
‡On disabled list, August 8, 1988 through remainder of season.

EDGARDO ROMERO
(Ed)

Born December 9, 1957, at Santurce, Puerto Rico.
Height, 5.11. Weight, 180.
Throws and bats righthanded.
Attended Engineer College, Mayaquez, Puerto Rico.

Major League stolen bases: 1980 (2), 1983 (1), 1984 (3), 1985 (1), 1986 (2). Total—9.
Led Pacific Coast League shortstops in double plays with 97 in 1979.
Led Midwest League shortstops in total chances with 647 and double plays with 64 in 1976.

Year	Club	League	Pos.	G.	AB.	R.	H.	2B.	3B.	HR.	RBI.	B.A.	PO.	A.	E.	F.A.
1976—Burlington	Midwest		SS	●129	462	58	101	23	1	1	32	.219	187	★419	41	.937
1977—Holyoke	East.		SS	121	457	63	118	19	6	1	38	.258	203	372	41	.933
1977—Milwaukee	Amer.		SS	10	25	4	7	1	0	0	2	.280	9	24	1	.971
1978—Spokane	P. C.		SS-3B	129	440	73	123	27	2	4	52	.280	221	349	32	.947
1979—Vancouver	P. C.		SS	139	515	65	134	26	6	0	39	.260	215	★414	26	.960
1980—Vancouver	P. C.		SS-2B	50	172	19	47	7	1	0	16	.273	72	153	6	.974
1980—Milwaukee	Amer.		SS-2B-3B	42	104	20	27	7	0	1	10	.260	60	102	12	.931
1981—Milwaukee	Amer.		SS-3B-2B	44	91	6	18	3	0	1	10	.198	61	102	6	.964
1982—Milwaukee	Amer.		2-S-3-O	52	144	18	36	8	0	1	7	.250	103	113	7	.969
1983—Milwaukee	Amer.		S-O-3-2	59	145	17	46	7	0	1	18	.317	59	58	5	.959
1984—Milwaukee	Amer.		3-S-2-1-O	116	357	36	90	12	0	1	31	.252	141	256	18	.957
1985—Milwaukee†	Amer.		S-2-O-3	88	251	24	63	11	1	0	21	.251	157	219	8	.979
1986—Boston	Amer.		S-3-2-O	100	233	41	49	11	0	2	23	.210	111	159	12	.957
1987—Boston	Amer.		2-S-3-1	88	235	23	64	5	0	0	14	.272	122	151	6	.978
1988—Boston‡	Amer.		3-S-2-1	31	75	3	18	3	0	0	5	.240	21	42	0	1.000
1989—Bos.§-Milw.	Amer.		2B-3B-SS	61	163	17	34	7	0	0	9	.209	82	127	4	.981
1989—Atlanta xy	Nat.		2B-SS-3B	7	19	1	5	1	0	1	1	.263	7	25	1	.970
American League Totals—11 Years				691	1823	209	452	75	1	7	150	.248	926	1353	79	.966
National League Totals—1 Year				7	19	1	5	1	0	1	1	.263	7	25	1	.970
Major League Totals—11 Years				698	1842	210	457	76	1	8	151	.248	933	1378	80	.967

Signed as free agent by Milwaukee Brewers' organization, November 14, 1975.
†Traded to Boston Red Sox for Pitcher Mark Clear, December 11, 1985.
‡On disabled list, June 6 to July 21, 1988.
§Released, August 5, 1989; signed by Atlanta Braves, August 12, 1989.
xTraded by Milwaukee Brewers for a player to be named later, August 23, 1989; Atlanta Braves acquired Pitcher Jay Aldrich to complete deal, September 1, 1989.
yGranted free agency, November 13, 1989.

DIVISION SERIES RECORD

Year	Club	League	Pos.	G.	AB.	R.	H.	2B.	3B.	HR.	RBI.	B.A.	PO.	A.	E.	F.A.
1981—Milwaukee	Amer.		2B	1	2	1	1	0	0	0	0	.500	2	2	0	1.000

CHAMPIONSHIP SERIES RECORD

Year	Club	League	Pos.	G.	AB.	R.	H.	2B.	3B.	HR.	RBI.	B.A.	PO.	A.	E.	F.A.
1986—Boston	Amer.		PR-SS	1	2	0	0	0	0	0	0	.000	0	0	0	.000
1988—Boston	Amer.		PR	1	0	0	0	0	0	0	0	.000	0	0	0	.000
Championship Series Totals—2 Years				2	2	0	0	0	0	0	0	.000	0	0	0	.000

WORLD SERIES RECORD

Year	Club	League	Pos.	G.	AB.	R.	H.	2B.	3B.	HR.	RBI.	B.A.	PO.	A.	E.	F.A.
1986—Boston	Amer.		PR-SS	3	1	0	0	0	0	0	0	.000	0	1	0	1.000

Eligible for 1982 World Series with Milwaukee Brewers; did not play.

KEVIN ANDREW ROMINE
Name pronounced Ro-MINE.

Born May 23, 1961, at Exeter, N.H.
Height, 5.11. Weight, 204.
Throws and bats righthanded.
Attended Orange Coast College, Costa Mesa, Calif., and
Arizona State University, Tempe, Ariz.

Major League stolen bases: 1985 (1), 1986 (2), 1988 (2), 1989 (1). Total—6.
Tied for Eastern League lead in double plays by outfielders with 4 in 1983.
Named outfielder on The Sporting News College Baseball All-America Team, 1982.

Year	Club	League	Pos.	G.	AB.	R.	H.	2B.	3B.	HR.	RBI.	B.A.	PO.	A.	E.	F.A.
1982—Winter Haven	Fla. St.		OF	55	201	24	51	4	4	3	22	.254	97	6	3	.972
1983—New Britain	East.		OF	132	467	74	122	26	5	11	80	.261	211	12	4	.982
1984—Pawtucket†	Int.		OF	113	336	62	85	10	1	12	72	.253	202	12	5	.977
1985—Pawtucket‡	Int.		OF	106	403	43	98	20	1	5	33	.243	246	9	8	.970
1985—Boston	Amer.		OF	24	28	3	6	2	0	0	1	.214	20	1	0	1.000
1986—Pawtucket	Int.		OF	71	257	30	75	8	3	4	32	.292	162	2	2	.988
1986—Boston	Amer.		OF	35	35	6	9	2	0	0	2	.257	45	1	0	1.000
1987—Pawtucket	Int.		OF	129	491	72	131	24	1	11	52	.267	311	6	3	.991
1987—Boston	Amer.		OF	9	24	5	7	2	0	0	2	.292	10	1	0	1.000

Year	Club	League	Pos.	G.	AB.	R.	H.	2B.	3B.	HR.	RBI.	B.A.	PO.	A.	E.	F.A.
1988—Boston	Amer.	OF	57	78	17	15	2	1	1	6	.192	44	0	2	.957
1988—Pawtucket	Int.	OF	41	148	18	53	6	1	4	26	.358	71	5	0	1.000
1989—Pawtucket	Int.	OF-1B	27	90	9	27	3	0	2	7	.300	49	4	1	.981
1989—Boston	Amer.	OF	92	274	30	75	13	0	1	23	.274	157	9	3	.982
Major League Totals—5 Years			217	439	61	112	21	1	2	34	.255	276	12	5	.983

Selected by California Angels' organization in 3rd round of free-agent draft, January 8, 1980.
Selected by Philadelphia Phillies' organization in secondary phase of free-agent draft, June 3, 1980.
Selected by Boston Red Sox' organization in second round of free-agent draft, June 7, 1982.
†On disabled list, July 18 to July 31, 1984.
‡On disabled list, July 6 to July 17, 1985.

CHAMPIONSHIP SERIES RECORD

Year	Club	League	Pos.	G.	AB.	R.	H.	2B.	3B.	HR.	RBI.	B.A.	PO.	A.	E.	F.A.
1988—Boston	Amer.	PR	2	0	1	0	0	0	0	0	.000	0	0	0	.000

ROLANDO AUDLEY ROOMES

Born February 15, 1962, in Jamaica, West Indies.
Height, 6.03. Weight, 180.
Throws and bats righthanded.

Holds major league record for most putouts, rightfielder, game (12), July 28, 1989 (17 innings).
Major League stolen bases: 1989 (12).
Led American Association batters in strikeouts with 134 in 1988.
Led Eastern League batters in strikeouts with 135 in 1987.
Led Midwest League batters in strikeouts with 167 in 1983.
Led New York-Pennsylvania League outfielders in double plays with 4 in 1982.

Year	Club	League	Pos.	G.	AB.	R.	H.	2B.	3B.	HR.	RBI.	B.A.	PO.	A.	E.	F.A.
1980—Sarasota Cubs	Gulf C.	OF	19	48	11	7	1	0	2	3	.146	19	1	4	.833
1981—Sarasota Cubs	Gulf C.	OF	63	207	31	48	4	9	2	25	.232	80	7	5	.946
1982—Quad Cities	Midw.	OF	31	80	11	12	1	0	3	8	.150	50	1	3	.944
1982—Geneva	NYP	OF	65	251	57	80	11	3	22	59	.319	129	8	8	.945
1983—Quad Cities	Midw.	OF	122	416	47	89	6	4	9	40	.214	216	★22	14	.944
1984—Lodi	Calif.	OF	116	377	52	100	12	2	13	52	.265	194	11	8	.962
1985—Winston-Salem	Carol.	OF	131	433	57	105	19	6	13	51	.242	254	14	6	.978
1986—Winston-Salem	Carol.	OF	19	68	10	15	3	0	6	14	.238	22	0	0	1.000
1986—Pittsfield	East.	OF	79	191	24	52	5	3	7	42	.272	91	4	7	.931
1987—Pittsfield	East.	OF	129	503	100	155	19	★12	21	95	.308	268	13	6	.979
1988—Chicago	Nat.	OF	17	16	3	3	0	0	0	0	.188	5	0	1	.833
1988—Iowa†	A. A.	OF	112	419	65	126	19	5	16	66	.301	247	12	9	.966
1989—Nashville	A. A.	OF	25	92	13	25	3	1	4	10	.272	57	2	1	.983
1989—Cincinnati	Nat.	OF	107	315	36	83	18	5	7	34	.263	201	4	4	.981
Major League Totals—2 Years			124	331	39	86	18	5	7	34	.260	206	4	5	.977

Signed as free agent by Chicago Cubs' organization, July 14, 1980.
†Traded to Cincinnati Reds for Catcher Lloyd McClendon, December 9, 1988.

VICTOR MANUEL ROSARIO

Born August 26, 1966, at Hato Mayor del Rey, Dominican Republic.
Height, 5.11. Weight, 155.
Throws and bats righthanded.

Year	Club	League	Pos.	G.	AB.	R.	H.	2B.	3B.	HR.	RBI.	B.A.	PO.	A.	E.	F.A.
1984—Elmira	NYP	SS	23	27	2	3	0	0	0	0	.111	8	22	4	.882
1985—Elmira	NYP	SS	59	177	11	36	8	1	1	14	.203	70	130	24	.893
1986—Greensboro†	S. Atl.	SS	26	93	12	28	5	1	4	19	.301	37	65	9	.919
1986—Day.B.‡-Win.Hav.	Fla. St.	SS-2B	20	55	6	12	2	0	0	5	.218	25	30	6	.902
1987—Greensboro	S. Atl.	SS	109	370	43	81	9	0	10	48	.219	155	303	44	.912
1988—New Britain§x	East.	SS	101	347	28	90	14	1	1	26	.259	159	274	25	.945
1989—Reading	East.	SS	64	213	16	50	8	0	3	16	.235	91	171	13	.953
1989—Scr./Wil.-Barre	Int.	SS	56	151	16	39	7	0	0	16	.258	58	127	11	.944

Signed as free agent by Boston Red Sox' organization, December 5, 1983.
†Switch-hitter
‡Loaned to Daytona Beach (Texas Rangers' organization), July, 1986; returned, July, 1986.
§Traded to Jacksonville (Montreal Expos' organization) for Pitcher John Trautwein, August 31, 1988.
xTraded by Montreal Expos' organization to Philadelphia Phillies' organization for Pitcher Tim Sossamon, March 28, 1989.

ROBERT RICHARD ROSE
(Bobby)

Born March 15, 1967, at Covina, Calif.
Height, 5.11. Weight, 170.
Throws and bats righthanded.

Led Texas League in slugging percentage with .541 in 1989.

Year	Club	League	Pos.	G.	AB.	R.	H.	2B.	3B.	HR.	RBI.	B.A.	PO.	A.	E.	F.A.
1985—Salem	N'west	SS-1B	50	167	15	37	6	2	0	16	.222	58	112	22	.885
1986—Quad Cities	Midw.	SS-2B	129	467	67	118	21	5	7	56	.253	176	297	40	.922
1987—				(Out of Organized Baseball)												
1988—Quad City	Midw.	3B-1B	135	483	75	137	23	3	13	78	.284	127	179	30	.911
1988—Palm Springs	Calif.	DH	1	3	0	1	0	0	0	1	.333	0	0	0	.000

Year	Club	League	Pos.	G.	AB.	R.	H.	2B.	3B.	HR.	RBI.	B.A.	PO.	A.	E.	F.A.
1989—Midland		Texas	3B-2B	99	351	64	126	21	5	11	73	★.359	102	203	17	.947
1989—California		Amer.	3B-2B	14	38	4	8	1	2	1	3	.211	10	21	2	.939
Major League Totals—1 Year				14	38	4	8	1	2	1	3	.211	10	21	2	.939

Selected by California Angels' organization in 5th round of free-agent draft, June 3, 1985.

JAIME THOMAS ROSEBORO

Born May 27, 1966, at Los Angeles, Calif.
Height, 6.02. Weight, 190.
Throws and bats righthanded.
Attended Los Angeles City College, Los Angeles, Calif., and
California State University, Los Angeles, Calif.
Son of John Roseboro , catcher with Brooklyn/Los Angeles Dodgers,
Minnesota Twins and Washington Senators, 1957 through 1970; coach with Washington Senators, 1970;
coach with California Angels, 1973 and 1974, and minor league instructor with Los Angeles Dodgers, 1978.

Year	Club	League	Pos.	G.	AB.	R.	H.	2B.	3B.	HR.	RBI.	B.A.	PO.	A.	E.	F.A.
1986—Little Falls		NYP	OF	68	234	26	63	5	2	2	17	.269	90	2	6	.939
1987—Columbia		S.Atl.	OF	113	340	41	84	8	1	5	40	.247	184	8	6	.970
1988—Columbia		S.Atl.	OF	125	486	53	132	24	4	2	72	.272	201	11	9	.959
1989—St. Lucie†		Fla. St.	OF	95	337	60	104	17	4	1	48	.309	208	5	3	.986

Selected by New York Mets' organization in 11th round of free-agent draft, June 2, 1986.
†On disabled list, May 23 to June 13, 1989.

STEVEN ALAN ROSENBERG
(Steve)

Born October 31, 1964, at Brooklyn, N.Y.
Height, 6.00. Weight, 185.
Throws and bats lefthanded.
Attended University of Florida, Gainesville, Fla.

Major League saves: 1988 (1).

Year	Club	League	G.	IP.	W.	L.	Pct.	H.	R.	ER.	SO.	BB.	ERA.
1986—Oneonta		NYP	4	9	0	0	.000	4	1	1	10	2	1.00
1986—Fort Lauderdale		Florida St.	25	29⅔	6	1	.857	24	7	7	26	18	2.12
1987—Albany		Eastern	32	40	4	4	.500	33	11	10	24	12	2.25
1987—Columbus†		Int'national	21	35⅓	4	1	.800	43	17	16	27	18	4.08
1988—Vancouver		P. Coast	20	24⅓	2	0	1.000	15	9	9	17	11	3.33
1988—Chicago		American	33	46	0	1	.000	53	22	22	28	19	4.30
1989—Chicago		American	38	142	4	13	.235	148	92	78	77	58	4.94
Major League Totals—2 Years			71	188	4	14	.222	201	114	100	105	77	4.79

Selected by New York Yankees' organization in 4th round of free-agent draft, June 2, 1986.
†Traded with Outfielder Dan Pasqua and Catcher Mark Salas to Chicago White Sox for Pitchers Richard Dotson and Scott Nielsen, November 12, 1987.

BRUCE WAYNE RUFFIN

Born October 4, 1963, at Lubbock, Tex.
Height, 6.02. Weight, 213.
Throws and bats lefthanded.
Attended University of Texas, Austin, Tex.

Major League stolen bases: 1988 (3).

Year	Club	League	G.	IP.	W.	L.	Pct.	H.	R.	ER.	SO.	BB.	ERA.
1985—Clearwater		Florida St.	14	97	5	5	.500	87	33	31	74	34	2.88
1986—Reading		Eastern	16	90⅓	8	4	.667	89	41	33	68	26	3.29
1986—Philadelphia		National	21	146⅓	9	4	.692	138	53	40	70	44	2.46
1987—Philadelphia		National	35	204⅔	11	14	.440	236	118	99	93	73	4.35
1988—Philadelphia		National	55	144⅓	6	10	.375	151	86	71	82	80	4.43
1989—Philadelphia		National	24	125⅔	6	10	.375	152	69	62	70	62	4.44
1989—Scranton/Wilkes-Barre		Int'national	9	50	5	1	.833	44	28	26	44	39	4.68
Major League Totals—4 Years			135	621	32	38	.457	677	326	272	315	259	3.94

Selected by Philadelphia Phillies' organization in 31st round of free-agent draft, June 7, 1982.
Selected by Philadelphia Phillies' organization in 2nd round of free-agent draft, June 3, 1985.

SCOTT DREW RUSKIN

Born June 8, 1963, at Jacksonville, Fla.
Height, 6.02. Weight, 185.
Throws left and bats left and righthanded.
Attended University of Florida, Gainesville, Fla.

Year	Club	League	G.	IP.	W.	L.	Pct.	H.	R.	ER.	SO.	BB.	ERA.
1989—Salem		Carolina	14	84⅔	4	5	.444	71	35	21	92	33	2.23
1989—Harrisburg		Eastern	12	63	2	3	.400	64	38	34	56	32	4.86

RECORD AS OUTFIELDER

Year	Club	League	Pos.	G.	AB.	R.	H.	2B.	3B.	HR.	RBI.	B.A.	PO.	A.	E.	F.A.
1986—Bradenton Pir.		Gulf C.	DH	11	31	3	11	1	0	0	4	.355	0	0	0	.000
1987—Macon†		S. Atl.	OF-1B	81	239	37	71	9	2	9	42	.297	183	11	6	.970

Year	Club	League	Pos.	G.	AB.	R.	H.	2B.	3B.	HR.	RBI.	B.A.	PO.	A.	E.	F.A.
1987—Salem	Carol.	1B-OF	23	83	16	25	3	1	3	11	.301	154	16	1	.994
1988—Salem	Carol.	OF-1B	26	96	16	28	8	2	4	16	.292	83	6	4	.957
1988—Harrisburg	East.	OF-1B	90	309	27	69	14	3	3	32	.223	233	12	8	.968

Selected by Cincinnati Reds' organization in 14th round of free-agent draft, June 8, 1981.
Selected by Texas Rangers' organization in 4th round of free-agent draft, June 4, 1984.
Selected by Cleveland Indians' organization in 3rd round of free-agent draft, June 3, 1985.
Selected by Montreal Expos' organization in secondary phase of free-agent draft, January 14, 1986.
Selected by Pittsburgh Pirates' organization in secondary phase of free-agent draft, June 2, 1986.
†On disabled list, April 7 to April 28, 1987.

JEFFREY LEE RUSSELL
(Jeff)

Born September 2, 1961, at Cincinnati, O.
Height, 6.03. Weight, 210.
Throws and bats righthanded.
Attended Gulf Coast Community College, Panama City, Fla.

Major League saves: 1986 (2), 1987 (3), 1989 (38). Total—43.
Led American League in saves with 38 and games finished in relief with 66 in 1989.
Named American League Fireman of the Year by THE SPORTING NEWS, 1989.

Year	Club	League	G.	IP.	W.	L.	Pct.	H.	R.	ER.	SO.	BB.	ERA.
1980—Eugene	Northwest	13	90	6	5	.545	80	47	30	75	50	3.00
1981—Tampa	Florida St.	22	143	10	4	.714	109	51	32	92	48	2.01
1982—Waterbury†	Eastern	14	79⅔	6	4	.600	67	27	21	88	23	2.37
1983—Indianapolis	Am. Assoc.	18	119	5	5	.500	106	51	47	98	44	3.55
1983—Cincinnati	National	10	68⅓	4	5	.444	58	30	23	40	22	3.03
1984—Cincinnati	National	33	181⅔	6	★18	.250	186	97	86	101	65	4.26
1985—Denver‡§-Oklahoma City	Am. Assoc.	18	115⅓	7	4	.636	105	55	52	94	51	4.06
1985—Texas	American	13	62	3	6	.333	85	55	52	44	27	7.55
1986—Oklahoma City	Am. Assoc.	11	70⅔	4	1	.800	63	32	31	34	38	3.95
1986—Texas	American	37	82	5	2	.714	74	40	31	54	31	3.40
1987—Port Charlotte x	Florida St.	2	11	0	0	.000	8	3	3	3	5	2.45
1987—Oklahoma City	Am. Assoc.	4	6⅓	0	0	.000	5	1	1	5	1	1.42
1987—Texas	American	52	97⅓	5	4	.556	109	56	48	56	52	4.44
1988—Texas y	American	34	188⅔	10	9	.526	183	86	80	88	66	3.82
1989—Texas	American	71	72⅔	6	4	.600	45	21	16	77	24	1.98
National League Totals—2 Years		43	250	10	23	.303	244	127	109	141	87	3.92
American League Totals—5 Years		207	502⅔	29	25	.537	496	258	227	319	200	4.06
Major League Totals—7 Years		250	752⅔	39	48	.448	740	385	336	460	287	4.02

Selected by Cincinnati Reds' organization in 5th round of free-agent draft, June 5, 1979.
†On disabled list, May 5 to June 10 and July 28, 1982 through remainder of season.
‡On disabled list, May 22 to June 10, 1985.
§Traded to Texas Rangers' organization, July 23, 1985, completing deal in which Texas traded Third Baseman Buddy Bell to Cincinnati Reds for Outfielder Duane Walker and a player to be named later, July 19, 1985.
xOn Texas disabled list, March 25 to May 15, 1987; included rehabilitation disability assignment to Port Charlotte, April 26 to May 4, and to Oklahoma City, May 5 to May 15, 1987.
yMade an out in only appearance as a pinch-hitter.

ALL-STAR GAME RECORD

Year	League	IP.	W.	L.	Pct.	H.	R.	ER.	SO.	BB.	ERA.
1988—American		1	0	0	.000	1	0	0	0	1	0.00
1989—American		1	0	0	.000	1	1	1	0	1	9.00
All-Star Game Totals—2 Years		2	0	0	.000	2	1	1	0	2	4.50

JOHN WILLIAM RUSSELL

Born January 5, 1961, at Oklahoma City, Okla.
Height, 6.00. Weight, 195.
Throws and bats righthanded.
Attended University of Oklahoma, Norman, Okla.

Major League stolen bases: 1985 (2).
Led National League in passed balls with 17 in 1986.
Tied for Pacific Coast League lead in passed balls with 13 in 1983.

Year	Club	League	Pos.	G.	AB.	R.	H.	2B.	3B.	HR.	RBI.	B.A.	PO.	A.	E.	F.A.
1982—Reading	East.	C-OF-1B	77	263	26	53	10	5	6	30	.202	354	44	12	.971
1983—Portland	P. C.	C-O-3	128	445	71	113	23	3	27	76	.254	551	58	12	.981
1984—Portland	P. C.	OF-1B-C	93	350	75	101	22	5	19	77	.289	182	18	5	.976
1984—Philadelphia	Nat.	OF-C	39	99	11	28	8	1	2	11	.283	51	1	0	1.000
1985—Philadelphia	Nat.	OF-1B	81	216	22	47	12	0	9	23	.218	170	9	4	.978
1985—Portland	P. C.	OF-C-1B	16	49	8	15	2	2	4	11	.306	24	1	1	.962
1986—Philadelphia	Nat.	C	93	315	35	76	21	2	13	60	.241	498	39	13	.976
1987—Philadelphia	Nat.	OF-C	24	62	5	9	1	0	3	8	.145	48	1	1	.980
1987—Maine	Int.	OF-C-3B	44	143	15	29	6	1	7	24	.203	107	14	2	.984
1988—Maine	Int.	C-O-3-1	110	394	50	90	18	0	13	52	.228	363	54	10	.977
1988—Philadelphia†	Nat.	C	22	49	5	12	1	0	2	4	.245	77	9	5	.945
1989—Atlanta	Nat.	C-O-1-3-P	74	159	14	29	2	0	2	9	.182	196	28	4	.982
Major League Totals—6 Years		333	900	92	201	45	3	31	115	.223	1040	87	27	.977

Selected by Montreal Expos' organization in 4th round of free-agent draft, June 5, 1979.
Selected by Philadelphia Phillies' organization in 1st round (13th player selected) of free-agent draft, June 7, 1982.
†Sold to Atlanta Braves, March 25, 1989.

PITCHING RECORD

Year Club	League	G.	IP.	W.	L.	Pct.	H.	R.	ER.	SO.	BB.	ERA.
1989—Atlanta	National	1	⅓	0	0	.000	0	0	0	0	0	0.00

MARK DWAYNE RYAL

Name pronounced Rile.
Born April 28, 1960, at Henryetta, Okla.
Height, 6.01. Weight, 185.
Throws and bats lefthanded.

Major League stolen bases: 1986 (1).
Led Pacific Coast League in intentional bases on balls received with 10 in 1986.
Led American Association in grounding into double plays with 21 in 1983.
Tied for American Association lead in intentional bases on balls received with 12 in 1982.

Year Club	League	Pos.	G.	AB.	R.	H.	2B.	3B.	HR.	RBI.	B.A.	PO.	A.	E.	F.A.
1978—Sarasota Royals	Gulf C.	OF	27	83	11	20	0	1	0	10	.241	37	4	0	1.000
1979—Fort Myers	Fla. St.	OF	107	360	27	79	12	1	4	34	.219	199	15	3	.986
1980—Fort Myers	Fla. St.	OF	123	440	60	117	21	3	5	51	.266	174	8	2	.989
1981—Jacksonville	South.	OF	123	457	50	122	15	2	14	69	.267	237	8	11	.957
1981—Omaha	A. A.	OF	6	19	2	4	0	0	0	1	.211	9	1	0	1.000
1982—Omaha	A. A.	★OF-1B	129	473	69	135	27	2	20	77	.285	242	★18	6	.977
1982—Kansas City	Amer.	OF	6	13	0	1	0	0	0	0	.077	9	0	1	.900
1983—Omaha	A. A.	OF-1B	132	454	61	118	28	5	9	57	.260	203	11	8	.964
1984—Omaha†	A. A.	1B-OF	131	435	56	103	18	1	13	64	.237	680	58	16	.979
1985—Buffalo	A. A.	OF	106	392	50	104	21	1	13	66	.265	175	10	2	.989
1985—Chicago‡	Amer.	OF	12	33	4	5	3	0	0	3	.152	21	0	0	1.000
1986—Edmonton	P. C.	1B-OF	127	479	72	163	33	4	14	84	.340	734	50	7	.991
1986—California	Amer.	OF-1B	13	32	6	12	0	0	2	5	.375	32	2	1	.971
1987—California	Amer.	OF-1B	58	100	7	20	6	0	5	18	.200	50	1	3	.944
1987—Edmonton§	P. C.	OF-1B	16	49	10	21	3	2	0	12	.429	44	0	0	1.000
1988—Louisville x	A. A.	OF-1B	94	336	35	86	25	1	11	62	.256	153	16	1	.994
1989—Philadelphia	Nat.	1B-OF	29	33	2	8	2	0	0	5	.242	17	0	0	1.000
1989—Scr./Wil.-Barre y	Int.	OF-1B	59	210	16	59	14	0	2	21	.281	117	4	0	1.000
American League Totals—4 Years			89	178	17	38	9	0	7	26	.213	112	3	5	.958
National League Totals—1 Year			29	33	2	8	2	0	0	5	.242	17	0	0	1.000
Major League Totals—5 Years			118	211	19	46	11	0	7	31	.218	129	3	5	.964

Selected by Kansas City Royals' organization in 3rd round of free-agent draft, June 6, 1978.
†Released, September 4, 1984; signed by Chicago White Sox' organization, December 28, 1984.
‡Granted free agency, October 15, 1985; signed by California Angels, January 21, 1986.
§Released, March 29, 1988. signed by Louisville (St. Louis Cardinals' organization), April 30, 1988.
xGranted free agency, October 15, 1988; signed by Scranton/Wilkes-Barre (Philadelphia Phillies' organization), November 11, 1988.
yGranted free agency, October 15, 1989.

LYNN NOLAN RYAN JR.

(Known by middle name.)

Born January 31, 1947, at Refugio, Tex.
Height, 6.02. Weight, 210.
Throws and bats righthanded.
Attended Alvin Junior College, Alvin, Tex.

Holds major league records for most strikeouts, lifetime (5,076); most games, 15 or more strikeouts, lifetime (23); most games, 10 or more strikeouts, lifetime (199); most seasons, 300 or more strikeouts (6); most seasons, 200 or more strikeouts (13); most games, 10 or more strikeouts, season (23), 1973; most strikeouts, three consecutive games (including extra innings—27⅓) (47), August 12, 16 and 20, 1974; most strikeouts by losing pitcher, extra-inning game (19), August 20, 1974 (11 innings); most seasons leading league, bases on balls allowed (8); most bases on balls, lifetime (2,540); most no-hit games, lifetime (5); most low-hit (one or zero) games, lifetime (16).
Holds modern major league records for most consecutive seasons, 300 or more strikeouts (3); most strikeouts, season (383), 1973.
Shares major league records for striking out side on nine pitches, April 19, 1968, third inning and July 9, 1972, second inning; most seasons, 100 or more strikeouts (21); most no-hit games, season (2), 1973; most clubs shut out, season (8), 1972; most consecutive seasons leading major leagues, bases on balls allowed (3); most strikeouts, three consecutive nine-inning games (41), August 7, 12 and 16, 1974.
Holds American League record for most games, 10 or more strikeouts, lifetime (132); most games, 15 or more strikeouts, lifetime (20).
Shares American League records for most seasons, 200 or more strikeouts (8); most consecutive strikeouts, game (8), July 9, 1972 and July 15, 1973; most strikeouts, two consecutive games (32), August 7 (13), 12 (19), 1974; most low-hit (no-hit and one-hit) games, season (3), 1973; most seasons leading league, errors by pitcher (4).
Pitched 5-0 no-hit victory against Los Angeles Dodgers, September 26, 1981.
Pitched 1-0 no-hit victory against Baltimore Orioles, June 1, 1975.
Pitched 4-0 no-hit victory against Minnesota Twins, September 28, 1974.
Pitched 6-0 no-hit victory against Detroit Tigers, July 15, 1973.
Pitched 3-0 no-hit victory against Kansas City Royals, May 15, 1973.
Major League saves: 1969 (1), 1970 (1), 1973 (1). Total—3.
Led National League in hit batsmen with 8 in 1982.
Led National League in wild pitches with 16 in 1981 and 15 in 1986.

Led American League in shutouts with 9 in 1972, 7 in 1976, and tied for lead with 5 in 1979.
Led American League in wild pitches with 18 in 1972, 21 in 1977, 13 in 1978 and 19 in 1989.
Tied for American League lead in complete games with 22 in 1977.
Tied for National League lead in sacrifice hits by hitters with 14 in 1985.
Led Western Carolinas League pitchers in games started with 28 in 1966.
Tied for Appalachian League lead in hit batsmen with 8 in 1965.
Named American League Pitcher of the Year by THE SPORTING NEWS, 1977.
Named righthanded pitcher on THE SPORTING NEWS American League All-Star Team, 1977.
Named Western Carolinas Pitcher of the Year, 1966.

Year Club	League	G.	IP.	W.	L.	Pct.	H.	R.	ER.	SO.	BB.	ERA.
1965—Marion	Ap'lachian	13	78	3	6	.333	61	47	38	115	56	4.38
1966—Greenville	W. Carol.	29	183	★17	2	.895	109	59	51	★272	★127	2.51
1966—Williamsport	Eastern	3	19	0	2	.000	9	6	2	35	12	0.95
1966—New York	National	2	3	0	1	.000	5	5	5	6	3	15.00
1967—Winter Haven†	Florida St.	1	4	0	0	.000	1	1	1	5	2	2.25
1967—Jacksonville‡	Int'national	3	7	1	0	1.000	3	1	0	18	3	0.00
1968—New York§	National	21	134	6	9	.400	93	50	46	133	75	3.09
1969—New York	National	25	89	6	3	.667	60	38	35	92	53	3.54
1970—New York	National	27	132	7	11	.389	86	59	50	125	97	3.41
1971—New York x	National	30	152	10	14	.417	125	78	67	137	116	3.97
1972—California	American	39	284	19	16	.543	166	80	72	★329	★157	2.28
1973—California	American	41	326	21	16	.568	238	113	104	★383	★162	2.87
1974—California	American	42	★333	22	16	.579	221	127	107	★367	★202	2.89
1975—California	American	28	198	14	12	.538	152	90	76	186	132	3.45
1976—California	American	39	284	17	★18	.486	193	117	106	★327	★183	3.36
1977—California	American	37	299	19	16	.543	198	110	92	★341	★204	2.77
1978—California y	American	31	235	10	13	.435	183	106	97	★260	★148	3.71
1979—California z	American	34	223	16	14	.533	169	104	89	★223	114	3.59
1980—Houston	National	35	234	11	10	.524	205	100	87	200	★98	3.35
1981—Houston	National	21	149	11	5	.688	99	34	28	140	68	★1.69
1982—Houston a	National	35	250⅓	16	12	.571	196	100	88	245	★109	3.16
1983—Houston	National	29	196⅓	14	9	.609	134	74	65	183	101	2.98
1984—Houston b	National	30	183⅔	12	11	.522	143	78	62	197	69	3.04
1985—Houston	National	35	232	10	12	.455	205	108	98	209	95	3.80
1986—Houston c	National	30	178	12	8	.600	119	72	66	194	82	3.34
1987—Houston	National	34	211⅔	8	16	.333	154	75	65	★270	87	★2.76
1988—Houston d	National	33	220	12	11	.522	186	98	86	★228	87	3.52
1989—Texas	American	32	239⅓	16	10	.615	162	96	85	★301	98	3.20
National League Totals—14 Years		387	2365	135	132	.506	1810	969	848	2359	1140	3.23
American League Totals—9 Years		323	2421⅓	154	131	.540	1682	943	828	2717	1400	3.08
Major League Totals—23 Years		710	4786⅔	289	263	.524	3492	1912	1676	5076	2540	3.15

Selected by New York Mets' organization in 8th round of free-agent draft, June, 1965.
†On military list, January 3 to May 13, 1967.
‡On disabled list, July 16 to August 30, 1967.
§On disabled list, July 30 to August 30, 1968.
xTraded with Pitcher Don Rose, Outfielder Leroy Stanton and Catcher Francisco Estrada to California Angels for Infielder Jim Fregosi, December 10, 1971.
yOn disabled list, June 14 to July 5, 1978.
zGranted free agency, November 1, 1979; signed by Houston Astros, November 19, 1979.
aOn disabled list, March 25 to April 17 and May 3 to June 6, 1983.
bOn disabled list, June 2 to June 17 and June 18 to July 3, 1984.
cOn disabled list, June 1 to June 24 and July 28 to August 12, 1986.
dGranted free agency, November 4, 1988; signed by Texas Rangers, December 7, 1988.

DIVISION SERIES RECORD

Year Club	League	G.	IP.	W.	L.	Pct.	H.	R.	ER.	SO.	BB.	ERA.
1981—Houston	National	2	15	1	1	.500	6	4	3	14	3	1.80

CHAMPIONSHIP SERIES RECORD

Shares Championship Series records for most strikeouts, total series (46); most consecutive strikeouts, game (4), October 3, 1979.

Year Club	League	G.	IP.	W.	L.	Pct.	H.	R.	ER.	SO.	BB.	ERA.
1969—New York	National	1	7	1	0	1.000	3	2	2	7	2	2.57
1979—California	American	1	7	0	0	.000	4	3	1	8	3	1.29
1980—Houston	National	2	13⅓	0	0	.000	16	8	8	14	3	5.40
1986—Houston	National	2	14	0	1	.000	9	6	6	17	1	3.86
Championship Series Totals—4 Years		6	41⅓	1	1	.500	32	19	17	46	9	3.70

WORLD SERIES RECORD

Year Club	League	G.	IP.	W.	L.	Pct.	H.	R.	ER.	SO.	BB.	ERA.
1969—New York	National	1	2⅓	0	0	.000	1	0	0	3	2	0.00

ALL-STAR GAME RECORD

Year League	IP.	W.	L.	Pct.	H.	R.	ER.	SO.	BB.	ERA.
1973—American	2	0	0	.000	2	2	2	2	2	9.00
1979—American	2	0	0	.000	5	3	3	2	1	13.50
1981—National	1	0	0	.000	0	0	0	1	0	0.00
1985—National	3	0	0	.000	2	0	0	2	0	0.00
1989—American	2	1	0	1.000	1	0	0	3	0	0.00
All-Star Game Totals—5 Years	10	1	0	1.000	10	5	5	10	5	4.50

Member of American League All-Star Team for the 1972 and 1975 games; did not play.
Named to American League All-Star Team to replace Frank Tanana for 1977 game; declined.

BRET WILLIAM SABERHAGEN

Born April 11, 1964, at Chicago Heights, Ill.
Height, 6.01. Weight, 185.
Throws and bats righthanded.

Holds American League record for fewest complete games for leader, season (12), 1989.
Major League saves: 1984 (1).
Led American League in complete games with 12 in 1989.
Named American League Pitcher of the Year by THE SPORTING NEWS, 1985 and 1989.
Won American League Cy Young Memorial Award, 1985 and 1989.
Named righthanded pitcher on THE SPORTING NEWS American League All-Star Team, 1985 and 1989.
Named pitcher on THE SPORTING NEWS American League All-Star fielding team, 1989.
Named American League Comeback Player of the Year by THE SPORTING NEWS, 1987.

Year Club	League	G.	IP.	W.	L.	Pct.	H.	R.	ER.	SO.	BB.	ERA.
1983—Fort Myers	Florida St.	16	109⅔	10	5	.667	98	34	28	82	19	2.30
1983—Jacksonville	Southern	11	77⅓	6	2	.750	66	31	25	48	29	2.91
1984—Kansas City†	American	38	157⅔	10	11	.476	138	71	61	73	36	3.48
1985—Kansas City	American	32	235⅓	20	6	.769	211	79	75	158	38	2.87
1986—Kansas City‡	American	30	156	7	12	.368	165	77	72	112	29	4.15
1987—Kansas City	American	33	257	18	10	.643	246	99	96	163	53	3.36
1988—Kansas City	American	35	260⅔	14	16	.467	★271	122	110	171	59	3.80
1989—Kansas City	American	36	★262⅓	★23	6	★.793	209	74	63	193	43	★2.16
Major League Totals—6 Years		204	1329	92	61	.601	1240	522	477	870	258	3.23

Selected by Kansas City Royals' organization in 19th round of free-agent draft, June 7, 1982.
†Appeared in one game as a pinch-runner.
‡On disabled list, August 10 to September 1, 1986.

CHAMPIONSHIP SERIES RECORD

Year Club	League	G.	IP.	W.	L.	Pct.	H.	R.	ER.	SO.	BB.	ERA.
1984—Kansas City	American	1	8	0	0	.000	6	3	2	5	1	2.25
1985—Kansas City	American	2	7⅓	0	0	.000	12	5	5	6	2	6.14
Championship Series Totals—2 Years		3	15⅓	0	0	.000	18	8	7	11	3	4.11

WORLD SERIES RECORD

Year Club	League	G.	IP.	W.	L.	Pct.	H.	R.	ER.	SO.	BB.	ERA.
1985—Kansas City	American	2	18	2	0	1.000	11	1	1	10	1	0.50

ALL-STAR GAME RECORD

Year League	IP.	W.	L.	Pct.	H.	R.	ER.	SO.	BB.	ERA.
1987—American	3	0	0	.000	1	0	0	0	0	0.00

CHRISTOPHER ANDREW SABO
(Chris)

Born January 19, 1962, at Detroit, Mich.
Height, 6.00. Weight, 185.
Throws and bats righthanded.
Attended University of Michigan, Ann Arbor, Mich.

Shares major league record for most assists, third baseman, nine-inning game (11), April 7, 1988.
Major League stolen bases: 1988 (46), 1989 (14). Total—60.
Led National League third basemen in double plays with 31 in 1988.
Led Eastern League third basemen in assists with 236 in 1985.
Led Eastern League third basemen in fielding percentage with .943 in 1984.
Named National League Rookie of the Year by Baseball Writers' Association of America, 1988.
Named third baseman on THE SPORTING NEWS College Baseball All-America Team, 1983.

Year Club	League	Pos.	G.	AB.	R.	H.	2B.	3B.	HR.	RBI.	B.A.	PO.	A.	E.	F.A.
1983—Cedar Rapids	Midw.	3B	77	274	43	75	11	6	12	37	.274	43	130	9	.951
1984—Vermont	East.	3B-2B	125	441	44	94	19	1	5	38	.213	80	210	21	.932
1985—Vermont	East.	3B-SS	124	428	66	119	19	0	11	46	.278	97	236	18	.949
1986—Denver	A. A.	3B	129	432	83	118	26	2	10	60	.273	83	202	9	★.969
1987—Nashville	A. A.	3B	91	315	56	92	19	3	7	51	.292	43	137	12	.938
1988—Cincinnati	Nat.	★3B-SS	137	538	74	146	40	2	11	44	.271	75	318	14	★.966
1989—Cincinnati†	Nat.	3B	82	304	40	79	21	1	6	29	.260	36	145	11	.943
1989—Nashville	A. A.	3B	7	30	0	5	2	0	0	3	.167	7	5	1	.923
Major League Totals—2 Years			219	842	114	225	61	3	17	73	.267	111	463	25	.958

Selected by Montreal Expos' organization in 30th round of free-agent draft, June 3, 1980.
Selected by Cincinnati Reds' organization in 2nd round of free-agent draft, June 6, 1983.
†On disabled list, June 27 to September 1, 1989; included rehabilitation disability assignment to Nashville, August 7 to August 11, 1989.

ALL-STAR GAME RECORD

Year League	Pos.	AB.	R.	H.	2B.	3B.	HR.	RBI.	B.A.	PO.	A.	E.	F.A.
1988—National	PR	0	0	0	0	0	0	0	.000	0	0	0	.000

ALAN JOE SADLER

Born September 6, 1961, at Salina, Kan.
Height, 6.04. Weight, 215.
Throws and bats righthanded.
Attended University of Maryland, College Park, Md.

Tied for Appalachian League lead in shutouts with 2 in 1984.

Year Club	League	G.	IP.	W.	L.	Pct.	H.	R.	ER.	SO.	BB.	ERA.
1984—Paintsville	Ap'lachian	11	70⅔	★9	1	★.900	43	21	15	78	29	★1.91
1985—Beloit	Midwest	13	57	5	2	.714	49	23	17	52	27	2.68
1986—Stockton	California	12	79⅓	8	2	.800	82	39	32	45	26	3.63
1986—El Paso	Texas	8	35⅓	1	3	.250	53	34	30	14	14	7.64
1987—El Paso	Texas	10	43	1	5	.167	57	52	40	17	35	8.37
1987—Stockton	California	4	15	0	0	.000	21	13	11	8	12	6.60
1988—Stockton	California	5	24	2	2	.500	21	12	9	13	11	3.38
1988—El Paso	Texas	9	51⅓	4	2	.667	44	19	11	19	26	1.93
1989—Denver	Am. Assoc.	28	171⅓	8	10	.444	169	96	81	113	85	4.25

Selected by Milwaukee Brewers' organization in 17th round of free-agent draft, June 6, 1983.
Selected by Milwaukee Brewers' organization in 11th round of free-agent draft, June 4, 1984.

MARK BRUCE SALAS

Name pronounced SAL-us.
Born March 8, 1961, at Montebello, Calif.
Height, 6.00. Weight, 205.
Throws right and bats lefthanded.

Major League stolen bases: 1986 (3).
Tied for Florida State League lead in sacrifice flies with 10 in 1981.
Tied for Appalachian League lead in passed balls with 10 in 1979.

Year Club	League	Pos.	G.	AB.	R.	H.	2B.	3B.	HR.	RBI.	B.A.	PO.	A.	E.	F.A.
1979—Johnson City	Appal.	C	53	144	23	35	4	2	5	23	.243	194	19	6	.973
1980—Gastonia	S. Atl.	C	98	267	42	67	8	3	9	46	.251	452	41	5	★.990
1981—St. Petersburg	Fla St.	●C-1B	100	321	26	78	9	2	2	52	.243	387	66	●13	.972
1982—Arkansas	Texas	C	27	76	4	17	4	0	0	5	.224	88	15	1	.990
1982—Louisville†	A. A.	C	7	22	1	4	0	0	0	1	.182	16	3	1	.950
1982—Nashville	South.	C	43	137	19	35	7	0	6	20	.255	267	24	7	.977
1983—Arkansas	Texas	C-OF	131	473	76	144	25	4	20	82	.304	334	41	4	.989
1984—Louisville	A. A.	C-OF	95	316	28	77	20	2	12	48	.244	260	28	7	.976
1984—St. Louis‡	Nat.	C-OF	14	20	1	2	1	0	0	1	.100	13	2	0	1.000
1985—Minnesota	Amer.	C	120	360	51	108	20	5	9	41	.300	529	39	5	.991
1986—Minnesota§	Amer.	C	91	258	28	60	7	4	8	33	.233	358	32	8	.980
1987—Minn. x-N. Y.	Amer.	C-OF	72	160	21	40	6	0	6	21	.250	258	16	1	.996
1987—Columbus y	Int.	C	12	43	5	10	1	0	2	4	.233	46	5	0	1.000
1988—Chicago z	Amer.	C	75	196	17	49	7	0	3	9	.250	251	35	6	.979
1989—Colorado Springs	P. C.	C-1B-OF	46	146	27	46	10	2	6	20	.315	86	5	1	.989
1989—Cleveland a	Amer.	C	30	77	4	17	4	1	2	7	.221	3	1	0	1.000
National League Totals—1 Year			14	20	1	2	1	0	0	1	.100	13	2	0	1.000
American League Totals—5 Years			388	1051	121	274	44	10	28	111	.261	1399	123	20	.987
Major League Totals—6 Years			402	1071	122	276	45	10	28	112	.258	1412	125	20	.987

Selected by St. Louis Cardinals' organization in 18th round of free-agent draft, June 5, 1979.
†Loaned to Nashville (New York Yankees' organization), June 30, 1982; returned, September 13, 1982.
‡Drafted by Minnesota Twins, December 3, 1984.
§On disabled list, May 24 to June 17, 1986.
xTraded to New York Yankees for Pitcher Joe Niekro and cash, June 7, 1987.
yTraded with Outfielder Dan Pasqua and Pitcher Steve Rosenberg to Chicago White Sox for Pitchers Richard Dotson and Scott Nielsen, November 12, 1987.
zReleased, March 28, 1989; signed by Cleveland Indians, April 1, 1989.
aReleased, December 1, 1989.

LUIS ERNESTO GARCIA SALAZAR

Born May 19, 1956, at Barcelona, Venezuela.
Height, 5.09. Weight, 180.
Throws and bats righthanded.

Major League stolen bases: 1980 (11), 1981 (11), 1982 (32), 1983 (24), 1984 (11), 1985 (14), 1987 (3), 1988 (6), 1989 (1). Total—113.
Led National League third basemen in errors with 26 and tied for lead in double plays with 28 in 1982.
Led Eastern League outfielders in putouts with 312 and tied for lead in double plays with 3 in 1979.

Year Club	League	Pos.	G.	AB.	R.	H.	2B.	3B.	HR.	RBI.	B.A.	PO.	A.	E.	F.A.
1974—Sarasota Royals†	Gulf C.	SS	2	4	0	1	0	0	0	1	.250	0	2	0	1.000
1976—Niagara Falls	NYP	SS-OF	42	151	18	36	3	4	1	17	.238	71	49	17	.876
1977—Salem	Carol.	SS-3B-2B	116	433	72	117	17	5	11	48	.270	157	294	45	.909
1978—Salem	Carol.	OF-3B-SS	126	472	55	138	20	4	3	49	.292	160	77	19	.926
1979—Buffalo	East.	OF-3B	★139	★561	★108	★181	17	5	27	86	.323	321	42	13	.965
1980—Port.‡-Hawaii	P. C.	OF	127	497	91	157	23	15	9	64	.316	304	11	8	.975
1980—San Diego	Nat.	3B-OF	44	169	28	57	4	7	1	25	.337	39	88	7	.948
1981—San Diego	Nat.	3B-OF	109	400	37	121	19	6	3	38	.303	108	191	14	.955
1982—San Diego	Nat.	3B-SS-OF	145	524	55	127	15	5	8	62	.242	133	326	29	.941
1983—San Diego	Nat.	3B-SS	134	481	52	124	16	2	14	45	.258	122	274	21	.950
1984—San Diego§x	Nat.	3B-OF-SS	93	228	20	55	7	2	3	17	.241	87	97	6	.968
1985—Chicago	Amer.	OF-3B-1B	122	327	39	80	18	2	10	45	.245	180	57	10	.960
1986—Appleton y	Midw.	3B	21	79	9	16	1	0	2	4	.203	9	39	5	.906
1986—Chicago z	Amer.	DH-PH	4	7	1	1	0	0	0	0	.143	0	0	0	.000
1987—Las Vegas	P. C.	OF	4	17	2	5	2	0	1	3	.294	5	0	0	1.000
1987—San Diego a	Nat.	3-S-O-P-1	84	189	13	48	5	0	3	17	.254	56	95	9	.944
1988—Detroit b	Amer.	O-S-3-2-1	130	452	61	122	14	1	12	62	.270	199	151	10	.972

Year Club League	Pos.	G.	AB.	R.	H.	2B.	3B.	HR.	RBI.	B.A.	PO.	A.	E.	F.A.
1989—S.D.c-Chi.................. Nat.	3-O-S-1	121	326	34	92	12	2	9	34	.282	79	154	10	.959
National League Totals—7 Years...........		730	2317	239	624	78	24	41	238	.269	624	1225	96	.951
American League Totals—3 Years........		256	786	101	203	32	3	22	107	.258	379	208	20	.967
Major League Totals—10 Years..............		986	3103	340	827	110	27	63	345	.267	1003	1433	116	.955

Signed as free agent by Kansas City Royals' organization, November 29, 1973.

†Released, July 8, 1974; signed by Pittsburgh Pirates' organization, November 23, 1975.

‡Traded with Outfielder Rick Lancellotti to San Diego Padres' organization for Infielder Kurt Bevacqua and a player to be named later, August 4, 1980; Pittsburgh Pirates' organization acquired Pitcher Mark Lee to complete deal, August 12, 1980.

§On disabled list, May 15 to June 11, 1984.

xTraded with Pitchers Tim Lollar and Bill Long and Shortstop Ozzie Guillen to Chicago White Sox for Pitchers LaMarr Hoyt, Kevin Kristan and Todd Simmons, December 6, 1984.

yOn Chicago disabled list, April 4 to August 8, August 16 to September 1 and September 8, 1986 through remainder of season; included rehabilitation disability assignment to Appleton, July 17 to August 6, 1986.

zReleased, December 19, 1986; signed by San Diego Padres' organization, April 2, 1987.

aGranted free agency, October 20, 1987; signed by Toledo (Detroit Tigers' organization), February 20, 1988.

bTraded to San Diego Padres for Shortstop Mike Brumley, March 23, 1989.

cTraded with Outfielder Marvell Wynne to Chicago Cubs for Pitcher Calvin Schiraldi, Outfielder Darrin Jackson and a player to be named later, August 30, 1989; San Diego Padres acquired First Baseman Phil Stephenson to complete deal, September 5, 1989.

CHAMPIONSHIP SERIES RECORD

Year Club League	Pos.	G.	AB.	R.	H.	2B.	3B.	HR.	RBI.	B.A.	PO.	A.	E.	F.A.
1984—San Diego .... Nat.	3B-PH-OF	3	5	0	1	0	1	0	0	.200	1	3	0	1.000
1989—Chicago .... Nat.	3B	5	19	2	7	0	1	1	2	.368	4	5	1	.900
Championship Series Totals—2 Years.....		8	24	2	8	0	2	1	2	.333	5	8	1	.929

WORLD SERIES RECORD

Year Club League	Pos.	G.	AB.	R.	H.	2B.	3B.	HR.	RBI.	B.A.	PO.	A.	E.	F.A.
1984—San Diego† .... Nat.	3B-OF	4	3	0	1	0	0	0	0	.333	1	0	0	1.000

†Also appeared as a pinch-runner and pinch-hitter.

PITCHING RECORD

Year Club	League	G.	IP.	W.	L.	Pct.	H.	R.	ER.	SO.	BB.	ERA.
1987—San Diego	National	2	2	0	0	.000	2	1	1	0	1	4.50

WILLIAM ALBERT SAMPEN
(Bill)

Born January 18, 1963, at Lincoln, Ill.
Height, 6.01. Weight, 185.
Throws and bats righthanded.
Attended McMurray College, Jacksonville, Ill.

Tied for Eastern League lead in games started by pitchers with 26 in 1989.

Year Club	League	G.	IP.	W.	L.	Pct.	H.	R.	ER.	SO.	BB.	ERA.
1985—Watertown	NYP	5	10	0	0	.000	9	3	2	11	7	1.80
1986—Watertown	NYP	9	29⅔	0	3	.000	27	18	14	29	13	4.25
1987—Salem	Carolina	26	152⅓	9	8	.529	126	77	65	137	72	3.84
1988—Harrisburg†	Eastern	13	82⅔	6	3	.667	72	38	34	65	27	3.70
1988—Salem...	Carolina	8	51⅓	3	3	.500	47	22	19	59	14	3.33
1989—Harrisburg‡	Eastern	26	165⅔	11	9	.550	148	75	59	134	40	3.21

Selected by Pittsburgh Pirates' organization in 12th round of free-agent draft, June 3, 1985.

†On disabled list, April 6 to May 5, 1988.

‡Drafted by Montreal Expos, December 4, 1989.

JUAN MILTON SAMUEL

Name pronounced SAHM-well.

Born December 9, 1960, at San Pedro de Macoris, D.R.
Height, 5.11. Weight, 170.
Throws and bats righthanded.

Holds major league records for most at-bats by righthander, season (701), 1984; fewest sacrifice hits, most at-bats, season (0 and 701), 1984.

Shares major league records for most consecutive seasons leading league in strikeouts (4), 1984 through 1987; most assists by second baseman, nine-inning game (12), April 20, 1985.

Holds National League record for most at-bats, season (701), 1984.

Major League stolen bases: 1983 (3), 1984 (72), 1985 (53), 1986 (42), 1987 (35), 1988 (33), 1989 (42). Total—280.

Led National League batters in strikeouts with 168 in 1984, 142 in 1986, 162 in 1987 and tied for lead with 141 in 1985.

Led National League second basemen in putouts with 343 and double plays with 92 in 1988.

Led National League second basemen in total chances with 826 in 1987.

Led Carolina League in total bases with 283 and tied for lead in being hit by pitch with 15 in 1982.

Led Northwest League batters in strikeouts with 87 and caught stealing with 10 in 1980.

Led Carolina League second basemen in double plays with 82 and total chances with 721 in 1982.

Led South Atlantic League second basemen in double plays with 82 and total chances with 737 in 1981.

Named second baseman on The Sporting News National League All-Star Team, 1987.

Named second baseman on The Sporting News National League Silver Slugger team, 1987.

Named National League Rookie Player of the Year by The Sporting News, 1984.

Named Carolina League Most Valuable Player, 1982.

Year — Club	League	Pos.	G.	AB.	R.	H.	2B.	3B.	HR.	RBI.	B.A.	PO.	A.	E.	F.A.
1980—Central Oregon	N'west	2B	69	*298	66	84	11	2	17	44	.282	162	188	*30	.921
1981—Spartanburg	S. Atl.	2B	135	512	88	127	22	8	11	74	.248	*280	*409	*50	.932
1982—Peninsula	Carol.	2B	135	494	*111	158	29	6	28	94	.320	*244	*442	*35	.951
1983—Reading	East.	2B	47	184	36	43	10	0	11	39	.234	121	127	14	.947
1983—Portland	P. C.	2B	65	261	59	86	14	8	15	52	.330	110	168	15	.949
1983—Philadelphia	Nat.	2B	18	65	14	18	1	2	2	5	.277	44	54	9	.916
1984—Philadelphia	Nat.	2B	160	*701	105	191	36	●19	15	69	.272	388	438	*33	.962
1985—Philadelphia	Nat.	2B	161	*663	101	175	31	13	19	74	.264	*389	463	15	.983
1986—Philadelphia†	Nat.	2B	145	591	90	157	36	12	16	78	.266	290	440	*25	.967
1987—Philadelphia	Nat.	2B	160	*655	113	178	37	*15	28	100	.272	*374	434	*18	.978
1988—Philadelphia	Nat.	2B-OF-3B	157	629	68	153	32	9	12	67	.243	351	387	16	.979
1989—Phi.‡§-N.Y.x	Nat.	OF	137	532	69	125	16	2	11	48	.235	339	6	4	.989
Major League Totals—7 Years			938	3836	560	997	189	72	103	441	.260	2175	2222	120	.973

Signed as free agent by Philadelphia Phillies' organization, April 29, 1980.
†On disabled list, April 13 to May 2, 1986.
‡On disabled list, April 1 to April 19, 1989.
§Traded to New York Mets for Outfielder Lenny Dykstra, Pitcher Roger McDowell and a player to be named later, June 18, 1989; Philadelphia Phillies' organization acquired Pitcher Tom Edens to complete deal, July 27, 1989.
xTraded to Los Angeles Dodgers for Pitcher Alejandro Pena and Outfielder Mike Marshall, December 20, 1989.

CHAMPIONSHIP SERIES RECORD

Year — Club	League	Pos.	G.	AB.	R.	H.	2B.	3B.	HR.	RBI.	B.A.	PO.	A.	E.	F.A.
1983—Philadelphia	Nat.	PR	1	0	0	0	0	0	0	0	.000	0	0	0	.000

WORLD SERIES RECORD

Year — Club	League	Pos.	G.	AB.	R.	H.	2B.	3B.	HR.	RBI.	B.A.	PO.	A.	E.	F.A.
1983—Philadelphia	Nat.	PR-PH	3	1	0	0	0	0	0	0	.000	0	0	0	.000

ALL-STAR GAME RECORD

Established All-Star Game record for most putouts by second baseman, game (7), July 14, 1987.
Tied All-Star Game record for most chances accepted by second baseman, game (9), July 14, 1987.

Year — League	Pos.	AB.	R.	H.	2B.	3B.	HR.	RBI.	B.A.	PO.	A.	E.	F.A.
1987—National	2B	4	0	0	0	0	0	0	.000	7	2	0	1.000

Member of National League All-Star Team in 1984; did not play.

ROGER HOWARD SAMUELS

Born January 3, 1961, at San Jose, Calif.
Height, 6.05. Weight, 210.
Throws and bats lefthanded.
Attended Santa Clara University, Santa Clara, Calif.

Year — Club	League	G.	IP.	W.	L.	Pct.	H.	R.	ER.	SO.	BB.	ERA.
1983—Auburn	NYP	6	33⅔	3	2	.600	33	19	13	21	19	3.48
1983—Asheville	S. Atlantic	10	60	3	4	.429	60	33	27	47	30	4.05
1984—Asheville	S. Atlantic	15	88⅓	4	5	.444	82	38	33	82	44	3.36
1984—Daytona Beach	Florida St.	13	68⅓	5	4	.556	67	40	32	44	37	4.21
1985—Columbus	Southern	33	147⅔	10	9	.526	132	73	65	85	82	3.96
1986—Columbus†	Southern	38	77⅔	2	3	.400	76	49	44	56	46	5.10
1987—Fresno	California	27	42⅔	1	2	.333	29	11	4	64	18	0.84
1987—Shreveport	Texas	21	33⅓	3	1	.750	24	10	6	35	10	1.62
1988—Phoenix	P. Coast	30	48	3	2	.600	34	16	14	33	15	2.63
1988—San Francisco	National	15	23⅓	1	2	.333	17	10	9	22	7	3.47
1989—Phoenix‡	P. Coast	14	19⅔	0	3	.000	14	7	7	18	4	3.20
1989—Buffalo	Am. Assoc.	19	26⅔	1	1	.500	23	11	7	18	8	2.36
1989—Pittsburgh	National	5	3⅔	0	0	.000	9	4	4	2	4	9.82
Major League Totals—2 Years		20	27	1	2	.333	26	14	13	24	11	4.33

Selected by Toronto Blue Jays' organization in 2nd round of free-agent draft, January 8, 1980.
Selected by Houston Astros' organization in 10th round of free-agent draft, June 6, 1983.
†Released, January 19, 1987; signed by Phoenix (San Francisco Giants' organization), February 6, 1987.
‡Traded to Pittsburgh Pirates for Infielder Ken Oberkfell, May 10, 1989.

ALEX ANTHONY SANCHEZ

Born April 8, 1966, at Antioch, Calif.
Height, 6.02. Weight, 185.
Throws and bats righthanded.
Attended UCLA.

Led New York-Pennsylvania League in games started by pitchers with 17 in 1987.
Tied for International League lead in games started by pitchers with 27 in 1989.
Named International League Pitcher of the Year, 1989.

Year — Club	League	G.	IP.	W.	L.	Pct.	H.	R.	ER.	SO.	BB.	ERA.
1987—St. Catharines	NYP	17	95⅓	8	3	.727	72	33	28	*116	38	2.64
1987—Myrtle Beach	S. Atlantic	1	3	0	0	.000	2	1	1	4	0	3.00
1988—Knoxville	Southern	24	149⅓	12	5	.706	100	56	42	166	74	2.53
1988—Syracuse	Int'national	10	57⅔	4	3	.571	47	26	23	57	43	3.59
1989—Syracuse	Int'national	28	169⅔	●13	7	.650	125	68	59	141	74	3.13
1989—Toronto	American	4	11⅔	0	1	.000	16	13	13	4	14	10.03
Major League Totals—1 Year		4	11⅔	0	1	.000	16	13	13	4	14	10.03

Selected by Chicago Cubs' organization in 20th round of free-agent draft, June 4, 1984.
Selected by Toronto Blue Jays' organization in 1st round (17th player selected), June 2, 1987.

ISRAEL SANCHEZ JR.

Born August 20, 1963, at Falcon, Cuba.
Height, 5.09. Weight, 170.
Throws and bats lefthanded.

Major League saves: 1988 (1).

Year Club	League	G.	IP.	W.	L.	Pct.	H.	R.	ER.	SO.	BB.	ERA.
1982—Sarasota Royals	Gulf Coast	12	61	3	5	.375	63	41	31	49	36	4.57
1983—Charleston	S. Atlantic	30	163	10	6	.625	172	92	65	130	70	3.59
1984—Fort Myers†	Florida St.	14	66⅔	3	3	.500	62	30	27	63	29	3.65
1985—Fort Myers‡	Florida St.	28	98⅓	8	6	.571	72	32	23	86	27	2.11
1986—Memphis	Southern	28	184⅓	13	7	.650	190	97	71	141	55	3.47
1986—Omaha	Am. Assoc.	1	3	0	1	.000	4	3	3	2	2	9.00
1987—Omaha	Am. Assoc.	23	124⅔	5	12	.294	162	74	64	74	46	4.62
1988—Omaha	Am. Assoc.	15	102	7	4	.636	102	36	33	85	36	2.91
1988—Kansas City	American	19	35⅔	3	2	.600	36	20	18	14	18	4.54
1989—Baseball City§	Florida St.	3	8	1	0	1.000	7	3	0	4	2	0.00
Major League Totals—1 Year		19	35⅔	3	2	.600	36	20	18	14	18	4.54

Selected by Kansas City Royals' organization in 9th round of free-agent draft, June 7, 1982.
†On disabled list, May 26 to June 18 and June 29 to August 22, 1984.
‡On disabled list, April 12 to May 1, 1985.
§On Kansas City disabled list, March 21, 1989 through entire season; included rehabilitation disability assignment to Baseball City, July 22 to August 4, 1989.

RYNE DEE SANDBERG

Born September 18, 1959, at Spokane, Wash.
Height, 6.02. Weight, 180.
Throws and bats righthanded.

Most consecutive errorless games, second baseman, season (90), June 21 through October 1, 1989.
Shares major league records for highest fielding average, second baseman, lifetime (.989); most assists by second baseman, nine-inning game (12), June 12, 1983; fewest errors by second baseman, season, 150 or more games (5), 1986.
Holds National League record for highest fielding average by second baseman, season (.994), 1986.
Major League stolen bases: 1982 (32), 1983 (37), 1984 (32), 1985 (54), 1986 (34), 1987 (21), 1988 (25), 1989 (15). Total—250.
Led National League second basemen in total chances with 914 in 1983, 870 in 1984 and 824 in 1988.
Led National League second basemen in assists with 571 and double plays with 126 in 1983.
Led Eastern League shortstops in fielding percentage with .964, assists with 386 and double plays with 81 in 1980.
Led Western Carolinas League shortstops in double plays with 80 in 1979.
Led Pioneer League shortstops in double plays with 39 in 1978.
Named Major League Player of the Year by THE SPORTING NEWS, 1984.
Named National League Player of the Year by THE SPORTING NEWS, 1984.
Named National League Most Valuable Player by Baseball Writers' Association of America, 1984.
Named second baseman on THE SPORTING NEWS National League All-Star Team, 1984, 1988 and 1989.
Named second baseman on THE SPORTING NEWS National League All-Star fielding team, 1983 through 1989.
Named second baseman on THE SPORTING NEWS National League Silver Slugger team, 1984, 1985, 1988 and 1989.
Received reported $30,000 bonus to sign with Philadelphia Phillies, 1978.

Year Club	League	Pos.	G.	AB.	R.	H.	2B.	3B.	HR.	RBI.	B.A.	PO.	A.	E.	F.A.
1978—Helena	Pion.	SS	56	190	34	59	6	6	1	23	.311	92	★200	24	.924
1979—Spartanburg	W. Car.	SS	★138	★539	83	133	21	7	4	47	.247	134	★467	35	★.945
1980—Reading	East.	SS-3B	129	490	95	152	21	12	11	79	.310	156	388	20	.965
1981—Oklahoma City	A. A.	SS-2B	133	519	78	152	17	5	9	62	.293	229	396	21	.967
1981—Philadelphia†	Nat.	SS-2B	13	6	2	1	0	0	0	0	.167	7	7	0	1.000
1982—Chicago	Nat.	3B-2B	156	635	103	172	33	5	7	54	.271	136	373	12	.977
1983—Chicago	Nat.	★2B-SS	158	633	94	165	25	4	8	48	.261	330	572	13	★.986
1984—Chicago	Nat.	2B	156	636	★114	200	36	●19	19	84	.314	314	★550	6	★.993
1985—Chicago	Nat.	2B-SS	153	609	113	186	31	6	26	83	.305	353	501	12	.986
1986—Chicago	Nat.	2B	154	627	68	178	28	5	14	76	.284	309	★492	5	★.994
1987—Chicago‡	Nat.	2B	132	523	81	154	25	2	16	59	.294	294	375	10	.985
1988—Chicago	Nat.	2B	155	618	77	163	23	8	19	69	.264	291	★522	11	.987
1989—Chicago	Nat.	2B	157	606	●104	176	25	5	30	76	.290	294	466	6	.992
Major League Totals—9 Years			1234	4893	756	1395	226	54	139	549	.285	2328	3858	75	.988

Selected by Philadelphia Phillies' organization in 20th round of free-agent draft, June 6, 1978.
†Traded with Shortstop Larry Bowa to Chicago Cubs for Shortstop Ivan DeJesus, January 27, 1982.
‡On disabled list, June 14, to July 11, 1987.

CHAMPIONSHIP SERIES RECORD

Year Club	League	Pos.	G.	AB.	R.	H.	2B.	3B.	HR.	RBI.	B.A.	PO.	A.	E.	F.A.
1984—Chicago	Nat.	2B	5	19	3	7	2	0	0	2	.368	13	18	1	.969
1989—Chicago	Nat.	2B	5	20	6	8	3	1	1	4	.400	7	11	0	1.000
Championship Game Totals—2 Years			10	39	9	15	5	1	1	6	.385	20	29	1	.980

ALL-STAR GAME RECORD

Year League		Pos.	AB.	R.	H.	2B.	3B.	HR.	RBI.	B.A.	PO.	A.	E.	F.A.
1984—National		2B	4	0	1	0	0	0	0	.250	0	0	0	.000
1985—National		2B	1	1	0	0	0	0	0	.000	0	3	0	1.000
1986—National		2B	3	0	0	0	0	0	0	.000	0	2	1	.667

Year League	Pos.	AB.	R.	H.	2B.	3B.	HR.	RBI.	B.A.	PO.	A.	E.	F.A.
1987—National	2B	2	0	0	0	0	0	0	.000	0	2	0	1.000
1988—National	2B	4	0	1	0	0	0	0	.250	2	2	0	1.000
1989—National	2B	3	0	0	0	0	0	0	.000	2	4	0	1.000
All-Star Game Totals—6 Years		17	1	2	0	0	0	0	.118	4	13	1	.944

DEION LUWYNN SANDERS

Born August 9, 1967, at Fort Myers, Fla.
Height, 6.01. Weight, 195.
Throws and bats lefthanded.
Attended Florida State University, Tallahassee, Fla.

Major League stolen bases: 1989 (1).

Year Club	League	Pos.	G.	AB.	R.	H.	2B.	3B.	HR.	RBI.	B.A.	PO.	A.	E.	F.A.
1988—Sarasota Yanks....	Gulf C.	OF	17	75	7	21	4	2	0	6	.280	33	1	2	.944
1988—Fort Lauderdale ..	Fla. St.	OF	6	21	5	9	2	0	0	2	.429	22	2	0	1.000
1988—Columbus	Int.	OF	5	20	3	3	1	0	0	0	.150	13	0	0	1.000
1989—Albany	East.	OF	33	119	28	34	2	2	1	6	.286	79	3	0	1.000
1989—New York	Amer.	OF	14	47	7	11	2	0	2	7	.234	30	1	1	.969
1989—Columbus	Int.	OF	70	259	38	72	12	7	5	30	.278	165	0	4	.976
Major League Totals—1 Year			14	47	7	11	2	0	2	7	.234	30	1	1	.969

Selected by Kansas City Royals' organization in 6th round of free-agent draft, June 3, 1985.
Selected by New York Yankees' organization in 30th round of free-agent draft, June 1, 1988.

RECORD AS FOOTBALL PLAYER

Named as defensive back on THE SPORTING NEWS College Football All-America Team, 1986 through 1988.
Selected by Atlanta in 1st round (5th player selected) of 1989 NFL draft.
Signed by Atlanta Falcons, September 7, 1989.

		INTERCEPTIONS				—PUNT RETURNS—				—KICKOFF RET.—				—TOTAL—		
Year Club	G.	No.	Yds.	Avg.	TD.	No.	Yds.	Avg.	TD.	No.	Yds.	Avg.	TD.	TD.	Pts.	F.
1989—Atlanta NFL	16	5	52	10.4	0	28	307	11.0	1	35	725	20.7	0	1	6	2

Additional pro statistics: Recovered one fumble and caught one pass for minus eight yards, 1989.

SCOTT DOUGLAS SANDERSON

Born July 22, 1956, at Dearborn, Mich.
Height, 6.05. Weight, 198.
Throws and bats righthanded.
Attended Vanderbilt University, Nashville, Tenn.

Shares National League record for most consecutive home runs allowed, inning (3), July 11, 1982, second inning.
Major League saves: 1979 (1), 1983 (1), 1986 (1), 1987 (2). Total—5.

Year Club	League	G.	IP.	W.	L.	Pct.	H.	R.	ER.	SO.	BB.	ERA.
1977—West Palm Beach	Florida St.	10	57	5	2	.714	58	22	17	37	23	2.68
1978—Memphis	Southern	9	58	5	3	.625	55	32	26	44	19	4.03
1978—Denver	Am. Assoc.	9	49	4	2	.667	47	35	33	36	30	6.06
1978—Montreal	National	10	61	4	2	.667	52	20	17	50	21	2.51
1979—Montreal	National	34	168	9	8	.529	148	69	64	138	54	3.43
1980—Montreal	National	33	211	16	11	.593	206	76	73	125	56	3.11
1981—Montreal	National	22	137	9	7	.563	122	50	45	77	31	2.96
1982—Montreal	National	32	224	12	12	.500	212	98	86	158	58	3.46
1983—Montreal†‡	National	18	81⅓	6	7	.462	98	50	42	55	20	4.65
1984—Chicago§	National	24	140⅔	8	5	.615	140	54	49	76	24	3.14
1984—Lodi x	California	1	5	0	1	.000	7	2	2	2	0	3.60
1985—Chicago x	National	19	121	5	6	.455	100	49	42	80	27	3.12
1986—Chicago	National	37	169⅔	9	11	.450	165	85	79	124	37	4.19
1987—Chicago y	National	32	144⅔	8	9	.471	156	72	69	106	50	4.29
1988—Peoria z	Midwest	1	5	0	0	.000	4	1	0	3	0	0.00
1988—Iowa	Am. Assoc.	3	13⅓	1	0	1.000	13	7	7	4	2	4.73
1988—Chicago a	National	11	15⅓	1	2	.333	13	9	9	6	3	5.28
1989—Chicago b	National	37	146⅓	11	9	.550	155	69	64	86	31	3.94
Major League Totals—12 Years		309	1620	98	89	.524	1567	701	639	1081	412	3.55

Selected by Kansas City Royals' organization in 11th round of free-agent draft, June 5, 1974.
Selected by Montreal Expos' organization in 3rd round of free-agent draft, June 7, 1977.
  †On disabled list, July 5 to September 1, 1983.
  ‡Traded with Infielder Al Newman to San Diego Padres for Pitcher Gary Lucas, December 7, 1983; Traded by San Diego to Chicago Cubs for First Baseman Carmelo Martinez, Pitcher Craig Lefferts and Third Baseman Fritz Connally, December 7, 1983.
  §On disabled list, June 1 to July 5, 1984; included rehabilitation disability assignment to Lodi, June 29 to July 5, 1984.
  xOn disabled list, August 14, 1985 through remainder of season.
  yOn disabled list, March 29 to April 24 and June 22 to July 7, 1987.
  zOn Chicago disabled list, April 5 to August 23, 1988; included rehabilitation disability assignment to Peoria, June 25 to June 29, 1988; and Iowa, June 30 to July 11, 1988.
  aGranted free agency, November 4, 1988; re-signed by Cubs, December 7, 1988.
  bGranted free agency, November 13, 1989; signed by Oakland Athletics, December 13, 1989.

DIVISION SERIES RECORD

Year Club	League	G.	IP.	W.	L.	Pct.	H.	R.	ER.	SO.	BB.	ERA.
1981—Montreal	National	1	2⅔	0	0	.000	4	4	2	2	2	6.75

CHAMPIONSHIP SERIES RECORD

Year Club	League	G.	IP.	W.	L.	Pct.	H.	R.	ER.	SO.	BB.	ERA.
1984—Chicago	National	1	4⅔	0	0	.000	6	3	3	2	1	5.79
1989—Chicago	National	1	2	0	0	.000	2	0	0	1	0	0.00
Championship Series Totals—2 Years		2	6⅔	0	0	.000	8	3	3	3	1	4.05

ANDRES CONFESOR SANTANA

Born March 19, 1968, at San Pedro de Macoris, D.R.
Height, 5.11. Weight, 150.
Throws right and bats left and righthanded.
Led Pioneer League in stolen bases with 45 and caught stealing with 10 in 1987.
Led Midwest League in caught stealing with 23 in 1988.
Led Pioneer League shortstops in total chances with 337 in 1987.

Year Club	League	Pos.	G.	AB.	R.	H.	2B.	3B.	HR.	RBI.	B.A.	PO.	A.	E.	F.A.
1987—Pocatello	Pion.	SS	67	256	51	67	2	3	0	9	.262	94	★202	★41	.878
1988—Clinton	Midw.	SS	118	450	77	126	4	1	0	24	.280	154	301	50	.901
1988—Shreveport	Texas	SS	11	36	3	6	0	0	0	3	.167	20	29	1	.980
1989—San Jose	Calif.	SS	18	69	14	18	3	0	0	3	.261	22	46	8	.895

Signed as free agent by San Francisco Giants' organization, November 22, 1985.

BENITO SANTIAGO (RIVERA)

Born March 9, 1965, at Ponce, P.R.
Height, 6.01. Weight, 185.
Throws and bats righthanded.
Holds major league record for most consecutive games batted safely by rookie, season (34), August 25 through October 2, 1987.
Major League stolen bases: 1987 (21), 1988 (15), 1989 (11). Total—47.
Led National League in passed balls with 14 in 1989.
Tied for National League lead in double plays by catchers with 11 in 1988.
Led Pacific Coast League catchers in total chances with 655 in 1986.
Led Texas League in passed balls with 16 in 1985.
Led Florida State League catchers in double plays with 12 and passed balls with 26 in 1983.
Led National League in passed balls with 22 in 1987.
Named catcher on THE SPORTING NEWS National League All-Star Team, 1987 and 1989.
Named catcher on THE SPORTING NEWS National League All-Star fielding team, 1988 and 1989.
Named catcher on THE SPORTING NEWS National League Silver Slugger team, 1987 and 1988.
Named National League Rookie Player of the Year by THE SPORTING NEWS, 1987.
Named National League Rookie of the Year by Baseball Writers' Association of America, 1987.

Year Club	League	Pos.	G.	AB.	R.	H.	2B.	3B.	HR.	RBI.	B.A.	PO.	A.	E.	F.A.
1983—Miami	Fla. St.	C	122	429	34	106	25	3	5	56	.247	471	★69	★21	.963
1984—Reno	Calif.	C	114	416	64	116	20	6	16	83	.279	692	96	25	.969
1985—Beaumont†	Texas	★C-1B-3B	101	372	55	111	16	6	5	52	.298	525	★78	15	.976
1986—Las Vegas	P. C.	C	117	437	55	125	26	3	17	71	.286	★563	71	★21	.968
1986—San Diego	Nat.	C	17	62	10	18	2	0	3	6	.290	80	7	5	.946
1987—San Diego	Nat.	C	146	546	64	164	33	2	18	79	.300	817	80	★22	.976
1988—San Diego	Nat.	C	139	492	49	122	22	2	10	46	.248	725	★75	★12	.985
1989—San Diego	Nat.	C	129	462	50	109	16	3	16	62	.236	685	81	★20	.975
Major League Totals—4 Years			431	1562	173	413	73	7	47	193	.264	2307	243	59	.977

Signed as free agent by San Diego Padres' organization, September 1, 1982.
†On disabled list, June 21 to July 2, 1985.

ALL-STAR GAME RECORD

Year League	Pos.	AB.	R.	H.	2B.	3B.	HR.	RBI.	B.A.	PO.	A.	E.	F.A.
1989—National	C	1	0	0	0	0	0	0	.000	0	0	1	.000

NELSON GIL SANTOVENIA

Born July 27, 1961, at Pino del Rio, Cuba.
Height, 6.03. Weight, 215.
Throws and bats righthanded.
Attended Miami-Dade Community College (South), Miami, Fla.,
and University of Miami, Coral Gables, Fla.
Major League stolen bases: 1988 (2), 1989 (2). Total—4.
Led Southern League catchers in putouts with 785 and total chances with 867 in 1987.
Led Southern League in passed balls with 21 in 1983.
Tied for Southern League lead in double plays by catchers with 9 in 1984.

Year Club	League	Pos.	G.	AB.	R.	H.	2B.	3B.	HR.	RBI.	B.A.	PO.	A.	E.	F.A.
1982—W. Palm Beach	Fla. St.	C	40	118	8	29	4	0	1	12	.246	127	21	5	.967
1983—Memphis	South.	C	94	318	27	77	13	0	3	44	.242	490	69	★15	.974
1984—Jacksonville†	South.	C	90	255	27	55	9	0	5	29	.216	464	●64	4	.992
1985—Jacksonville	South.	C	57	184	15	40	6	0	2	15	.217	281	20	9	.971
1985—Indianapolis	A. A.	C	28	75	5	16	2	0	0	4	.213	135	20	1	.994
1986—Jacksonville	South.	C-OF	31	72	15	22	7	0	4	11	.306	97	14	1	.991

Year	Club	League	Pos.	G.	AB.	R.	H.	2B.	3B.	HR.	RBI.	B.A.	PO.	A.	E.	F.A.
1986—Indianapolis	A. A.		C	18	57	6	12	1	0	1	2	.211	80	14	1	.989
1987—Jacksonville	South.		C-1B	117	394	56	110	17	0	19	63	.279	790	71	11	.987
1987—Montreal	Nat.		C	2	1	0	0	0	0	0	0	.000	1	0	0	1.000
1988—Indianapolis	A. A.		C	27	91	9	28	5	0	2	13	.308	198	23	3	.987
1988—Montreal‡	Nat.		C-1B	92	309	26	73	20	2	8	41	.236	465	63	9	.983
1989—Montreal§	Nat.		C-1B	97	304	30	76	14	1	5	31	.250	564	66	12	.981
Major League Totals—3 Years				191	614	56	149	34	3	13	72	.243	1030	129	21	.982

Selected by Philadelphia Phillies' organization in 29th round of free-agent draft, June 5, 1979.
Selected by Montreal Expos' organization in 3rd round of free-agent draft, June 8, 1981.
Selected by Montreal Expos' organization in secondary phase of free-agent draft, June 7, 1982.
†On suspended list, May 24 to May 31, 1984.
‡On disabled list, June 4 to June 20, 1988.
§On disabled list, May 13 to June 13, 1989.

MACK DANIEL SASSER JR.
(Mackey)

Born August 3, 1962, at Fort Gaines, Ga.
Height, 6.01. Weight, 210.
Throws right and bats lefthanded.
Attended George C. Wallace Community College, Dothan, Ala.,
and Troy State University, Troy, Ala.

Led Texas League in intentional bases on balls received with 13 in 1986.
Led California League in total bases with 245 and tied for lead in game-winning RBIs with 16 in 1985.
Led Pacific Coast League catchers in putouts with 584, errors with 16 and total chances with 663 in 1987.
Led California League in passed balls with 19 in 1985.

Year	Club	League	Pos.	G.	AB.	R.	H.	2B.	3B.	HR.	RBI.	B.A.	PO.	A.	E.	F.A.
1984—Clinton	Midw.		1-3-O-C	118	428	57	125	20	5	6	65	.292	526	95	17	.973
1984—Fresno	Calif.		OF-3B-1B	16	62	8	17	1	1	0	6	.274	24	15	4	.907
1985—Fresno	Calif.		O-C-1-3	133	497	79	168	27	4	14	102	.338	402	42	14	.969
1986—Shreveport	Texas		C-1B-OF	120	441	52	129	29	5	5	72	.293	577	66	10	.985
1987—Phoe.†-Vanc.	P. C.		C-3B-1B	115	400	53	127	24	1	3	56	.318	588	72	18	.973
1987—S.F.-Pitt.‡	Nat.		C	14	27	2	5	0	0	0	2	.185	29	0	0	1.000
1988—New York	Nat.		C-3B-OF	60	123	9	35	10	1	1	17	.285	235	17	6	.977
1989—New York	Nat.		C-3B	72	182	17	53	14	2	1	22	.291	335	19	3	.992
Major League Totals—3 Years				146	332	28	93	24	3	2	41	.280	599	36	9	.986

Selected by San Francisco Giants' organization in 5th round of free-agent draft, January 17, 1984.
†Traded with $50,000 to Pittsburgh Pirates' organization for Pitcher Don Robinson, July 31, 1987.
‡Traded with Pitcher Tim Drummond to New York Mets for First Baseman Randy Milligan and Pitcher Scott Henion, March 26, 1988.

CHAMPIONSHIP SERIES RECORD

Year	Club	League	Pos.	G.	AB.	R.	H.	2B.	3B.	HR.	RBI.	B.A.	PO.	A.	E.	F.A.
1988—New York	Nat.		PH-C	4	5	0	1	0	0	0	0	.200	2	0	0	1.000

JOHN JOSEPH SAVAGE
(Jack)

Born April 22, 1964, at Louisville, Ky.
Height, 6.00. Weight, 185.
Throws and bats righthanded.
Attended University of Kentucky, Lexington, Ky.

Led Texas League in intentional bases on balls issued with 12 in 1987.
Led California League in intentional bases on balls with 11 in 1986.
Tied for Pioneer League lead in saves with 8 in 1985.

Year	Club	League	G.	IP.	W.	L.	Pct.	H.	R.	ER.	SO.	BB.	ERA.
1985—Great Falls	Pioneer		24	44⅔	5	1	.833	26	5	5	51	18	1.01
1986—Bakersfield	California		44	77⅔	5	8	.385	82	45	39	77	45	4.52
1987—San Antonio	Texas		49	69⅓	5	6	.455	64	22	20	67	31	2.60
1987—Albuquerque	P. Coast		13	15	0	4	.000	20	15	7	13	11	4.20
1987—Los Angeles†	National		3	3⅓	0	0	.000	4	1	1	0	0	2.70
1988—Tidewater	Int'national		43	88½	5	8	.385	67	37	31	46	37	3.16
1989—Tidewater‡	Int'national		33	42⅔	3	2	.600	41	21	17	28	21	3.59
Major League Totals—1 Year			3	3⅓	0	0	.000	4	1	1	0	0	2.70

Selected by New York Yankees' organization in 6th round of free-agent draft, June 6, 1983.
Selected by Los Angeles Dodgers' organization in 8th round of free-agent draft, June 3, 1985.
†As part of an eight-player three-team deal, New York Mets traded Pitcher Jesse Orosco to Oakland Athletics, December 11, 1987. Oakland then traded Orosco along with Shortstop Alfredo Griffin and Pitcher Jay Howell to Los Angeles Dodgers for Pitchers Bob Welch, Matt Young and Jack Savage. Oakland then traded Savage along with Pitchers Wally Whitehurst and Kevin Tapani to New York.
‡Traded to Minnesota Twins, October 16, 1989, completing deal in which Minnesota traded Pitcher Frank Viola to New York Mets for Pitchers Rick Aguilera and David West and three players to be named later, July 31, 1989. Portland (Minnesota Twins' organization) acquired Pitchers Kevin Tapani and Tim Drummond as partial completion of deal, August 1, 1989.

—DID YOU KNOW—
That there were 145 shutout games played in the majors in 1989?

STEPHEN LOUIS SAX
(Steve)

Born January 29, 1960, at Sacramento, Calif.
Height, 5.11. Weight, 179.
Throws and bats righthanded.
Brother of David Sax, catcher in New York Yankees' organization.

Major League stolen bases: 1981 (5), 1982 (49), 1983 (56), 1984 (34), 1985 (27), 1986 (40), 1987 (37), 1988 (42), 1989 (43). Total—333.
Led National League in caught stealing with 30 in 1983.
Led American League second basemen in double plays with 117 in 1989.
Led Florida State League second basemen in double plays with 91 in 1980.
Named second baseman on The Sporting News National League All-Star Team, 1986.
Named second baseman on The Sporting News National League Silver Slugger team, 1986.
Named National League Rookie of the Year by Baseball Writers' Association of America, 1982.
Named Texas League Most Valuable Player, 1981.

Year	Club	League	Pos.	G.	AB.	R.	H.	2B.	3B.	HR.	RBI.	B.A.	PO.	A.	E.	F.A.
1978—Lethbridge	Pion.	SS	39	131	24	43	6	3	0	21	.328	21	40	9	.871
1979—Clinton	Midw.	OF-2B-3B	115	386	64	112	15	2	2	52	.290	111	75	18	.912
1980—Vero Beach	Fla. St.	★2B-OF	●139	●530	78	150	18	8	3	61	.283	★360	★438	20	★.976
1981—San Antonio	Texas	2B	115	485	94	168	23	3	8	52	★.346	255	298	17	.970
1981—Los Angeles	Nat.	2B	31	119	15	33	2	0	2	9	.277	64	93	4	.975
1982—Los Angeles	Nat.	2B	150	638	88	180	23	7	4	47	.282	347	452	19	.977
1983—Los Angeles	Nat.	2B	155	623	94	175	18	5	5	41	.281	331	399	★30	.961
1984—Los Angeles	Nat.	2B	145	569	70	138	24	4	1	35	.243	318	450	21	.973
1985—Los Angeles†	Nat.	★2B-3B	136	488	62	136	8	4	1	42	.279	330	358	★22	.969
1986—Los Angeles	Nat.	2B	157	633	91	210	43	4	6	56	.332	●367	432	16	.980
1987—Los Angeles	Nat.	2B-OF-3B	157	610	84	171	22	7	6	46	.280	343	420	14	.982
1988—Los Angeles‡	Nat.	2B	160	★632	70	175	19	4	5	57	.277	276	429	14	.981
1989—New York	Amer.	2B	158	●651	88	205	26	3	5	63	.315	312	460	10	★.987
National League Totals—8 Years			1091	4312	574	1218	159	35	30	333	.282	2376	3033	140	.975
American League Totals—1 Year			158	651	88	205	26	3	5	63	.315	312	460	10	.987
Major League Totals—9 Years			1249	4963	662	1423	185	38	35	396	.287	2688	3493	150	.976

Selected by Los Angeles Dodgers' organization in 9th round of free-agent draft, June 6, 1978.
†On disabled list, April 19 to May 4, 1985.
‡Granted free agency, November 4, 1988; signed by New York Yankees, November 23, 1988.

DIVISION SERIES RECORD

Year	Club	League	Pos.	G.	AB.	R.	H.	2B.	3B.	HR.	RBI.	B.A.	PO.	A.	E.	F.A.
1981—Los Angeles	Nat.	2B	1	0	0	0	0	0	0	0	.000	0	0	0	.000

CHAMPIONSHIP SERIES RECORD

Shares Championship Series record for most stolen bases, inning (2), October 9, 1988, third inning.
Holds National League Championship Series records for most runs, series (7), 1988.
Shares National League Championship Series records for most at-bats (30), singles (8) and stolen bases (5), series, 1988; most stolen bases, game (3), October 9, 1988 (12 innings).

Year	Club	League	Pos.	G.	AB.	R.	H.	2B.	3B.	HR.	RBI.	B.A.	PO.	A.	E.	F.A.
1981—Los Angeles	Nat.	2B	1	0	0	0	0	0	0	0	.000	0	1	0	1.000
1983—Los Angeles	Nat.	2B	4	16	0	4	0	0	0	0	.250	11	12	0	1.000
1985—Los Angeles	Nat.	2B	6	20	1	6	3	0	0	1	.300	11	21	0	1.000
1988—Los Angeles	Nat.	2B	7	30	7	8	0	0	0	3	.267	12	22	0	1.000
Championship Series Totals—4 Years			18	66	8	18	3	0	0	4	.273	34	56	0	1.000

WORLD SERIES RECORD

Year	Club	League	Pos.	G.	AB.	R.	H.	2B.	3B.	HR.	RBI.	B.A.	PO.	A.	E.	F.A.
1981—Los Angeles	Nat.	PH-PR-2	2	1	0	0	0	0	0	0	.000	0	0	0	.000
1988—Los Angeles	Nat.	2B	5	20	3	6	0	0	0	0	.300	11	11	0	1.000
World Series Totals—2 Years			7	21	3	6	0	0	0	0	.286	11	11	0	1.000

ALL-STAR GAME RECORD

Year	League	Pos.	AB.	R.	H.	2B.	3B.	HR.	RBI.	B.A.	PO.	A.	E.	F.A.
1982—National		PR-2B	1	0	1	0	0	0	0	1.000	2	0	1	.667
1983—National		2B	3	1	1	0	0	0	1	.333	2	0	1	.667
1986—National		2B	1	0	1	0	0	0	1	1.000	0	1	0	1.000
1989—American		2B	1	0	0	0	0	0	0	.000	1	3	0	1.000
All-Star Game Totals—4 Years			6	1	3	0	0	0	2	.500	5	4	2	.818

JEFFREY SCOTT SCHAEFER
(Jeff)

Born May 31, 1960, at Patchogue, N. Y.
Height, 5.10. Weight, 165.
Throws and bats righthanded.
Attended University of Maryland, College Park, Md.

Major League stolen bases: 1989 (1).
Led Pacific Coast League shortstops in total chances with 679 in 1988.
Led Texas League shortstops in total chances with 521 and double plays with 73 in 1987.
Led Southern League second basemen in fielding percentage with .982 in 1984.
Led Appalachian League second basemen in total chances with 365 and double plays with 56 in 1981.

Year Club League	Pos.	G.	AB.	R.	H.	2B.	3B.	HR.	RBI.	B.A.	PO.	A.	E.	F.A.
1981—Bluefield................. Appal.	2B	62	250	45	67	7	2	1	31	.268	★170	★189	6	.984
1982—Hagerstown .... Carol.	2B	18	60	4	6	0	0	0	7	.100	39	41	3	.964
1982—Charlotte.............. South	2-3-O-S	106	331	35	83	15	0	3	32	.251	231	232	22	.955
1983—Hagerstown .... Carol.	2B-SS	68	229	32	61	15	4	1	16	.266	145	197	7	.980
1983—Charlotte.............. South.	2B-SS	51	182	20	43	7	2	2	28	.236	102	166	11	.961
1984—Rochester............. Int.	SS-3B-2B	31	91	10	24	5	1	0	3	.264	44	84	2	.985
1984—Charlotte.............. South.	2B-SS	99	383	47	90	8	0	4	31	.235	249	264	9	.983
1985—Charlotte.............. South.	S-2-3-O	49	181	19	47	7	1	2	19	.260	84	112	7	.966
1985—Rochester†............ Int.	2B-SS	68	187	17	37	4	0	2	12	.198	134	195	5	.985
1986—Midland‡§.............. Texas	SS-2B	114	406	50	109	17	1	6	41	.268	192	342	31	.945
1987—San Antonio x ...... Texas	SS	101	368	39	112	18	2	0	37	.304	165	★330	26	.950
1988—Vancouver............ P. C.	SS	131	450	53	111	30	2	1	59	.247	★227	★417	★35	.948
1989—Vancouver............ P. C.	2B-SS-OF	88	294	32	67	13	2	3	22	.228	177	232	10	.976
1989—Chicago y.............. Amer.	SS-2B-3B	15	10	2	1	0	0	0	0	.100	5	7	2	.857
Major League Totals—1 Year..................		15	10	2	1	0	0	0	0	.100	5	7	2	.857

Selected by Baltimore Orioles' organization in 12th round of free-agent draft, June 8, 1981.

†Sold to Edmonton (California Angels' organization), January 21, 1986.

‡On disabled list, May 21 to May 31, 1986.

§Drafted by San Antonio (Los Angeles Dodgers' organization), December 9, 1986.

xGranted free agency, October 15, 1987; signed by Vancouver (Chicago White Sox' organization), November 16, 1987.

yGranted free agency, October 15, 1989.

DANIEL ERNEST SCHATZEDER
Name pronounced SHOT-zay-dur.

(Dan)

Born December 1, 1954, at Elmhurst, Ill.
Height, 6.00. Weight, 195.
Throws and bats lefthanded.
Received degree in business administration from University of Denver, Denver, Colo., in 1976.

Major League saves: 1979 (1), 1983 (2), 1984 (1), 1986 (2), 1988 (3), 1989 (1). Total—10.

Year Club	League	G.	IP.	W.	L.	Pct.	H.	R.	ER.	SO.	BB.	ERA.
1976—West Palm Beach.........................	Florida St.	10	64	5	3	.625	49	22	19	49	20	2.67
1976—Quebec City....................................	Eastern	5	28	2	3	.400	38	16	14	19	10	4.50
1977—Quebec City....................................	Eastern	8	62	5	3	.625	39	20	19	59	15	2.76
1977—Denver†...	Am. Assoc.	9	36	2	2	.500	45	25	24	28	14	6.00
1977—Montreal	National	6	22	2	1	.667	16	6	6	14	13	2.45
1978—Denver	Am. Assoc.	4	28	3	0	1.000	24	11	9	19	11	2.89
1978—Montreal	National	29	144	7	7	.500	108	54	49	69	68	3.06
1979—Montreal‡......................................	National	32	162	10	5	.667	136	57	51	106	59	2.83
1980—Detroit§..	American	32	193	11	13	.458	178	88	86	94	58	4.01
1981—Detroit x.......................................	American	17	71	6	8	.429	74	49	48	20	29	6.08
1982—San Francisco y-Montreal..........	National	39	69⅓	1	6	.143	84	46	41	33	24	5.23
1982—Phoenix..	P. Coast	1	3⅔	0	0	.000	10	6	5	1	3	12.27
1983—Montreal z.....................................	National	58	87	5	2	.714	88	34	31	48	25	3.21
1984—Montreal	National	36	136	7	7	.500	112	44	41	89	36	2.71
1985—Montreal a....................................	National	24	104⅓	3	5	.375	101	52	44	64	31	3.80
1985—Indianapolis..................................	Am. Assoc.	1	3	0	0	.000	2	0	0	3	1	0.00
1986—Montreal b-Philadelphia	National	55	88⅓	6	5	.545	81	43	32	47	35	3.26
1987—Philadelphia c...............................	National	26	37⅔	3	1	.750	40	21	17	28	14	4.06
1987—Minnesota d.................................	American	30	43⅔	3	1	.750	64	37	31	30	18	6.39
1988—Cleveland e-Minnesota	American	25	26⅓	0	3	.000	34	21	19	17	7	6.49
1988—Portland f.....................................	P. Coast	13	86⅔	6	4	.600	82	26	25	55	24	2.60
1989—Tucson	P. Coast	11	16	0	2	.000	15	8	7	15	10	3.94
1989—Houston gh	National	36	56⅔	4	1	.800	64	33	28	46	28	4.45
National League Totals—10 Years.....................		341	907⅓	48	40	.545	830	390	340	544	333	3.37
American League Totals—4 Years		104	334	20	25	.444	350	195	184	161	112	4.96
Major League Totals—13 Years		445	1241⅓	68	65	.511	1180	585	524	705	445	3.80

Selected by Montreal Expos' organization in 3rd round of free-agent draft, June 8, 1976.

†On disabled list, July 5 to August 30, 1977.

‡Traded to Detroit Tigers for Outfielder Ron LeFlore, December 7, 1979.

§On disabled list, May 27 to June 17, 1980.

xTraded with Pitcher Mike Chris to San Francisco Giants for Outfielder Larry Herndon, December 9, 1981.

ySold to Montreal Expos, June 15, 1982.

zGranted free agency, November 7, 1983; re-signed by Expos, December 19, 1983.

aOn disabled list, June 21 to July 23 and August 7 to September 1, 1985; included rehabilitation disability assignment to Indianapolis, July 19 to July 23, 1985.

bTraded with Infielder Skeeter Barnes to Philadelphia Phillies for Infielder Tom Foley and Pitcher Lary Sorensen, July 24, 1986.

cTraded with cash to Minnesota Twins for Pitcher Danny Clay and Third Baseman Tom Schwarz, June 24, 1987.

dReleased, December 21, 1987; signed by Cleveland Indians, February 9, 1988.

eReleased, June 22, 1988; signed by Portland (Minnesota Twins' organization), June 27, 1988.

fGranted free agency, November 4, 1988; signed by Houston Astros, January 30, 1989.

gOn disabled list, July 19 to September 6, 1989; included rehabilitation disability assignment to Tucson, August 18 to August 31, 1989.

hGranted free agency, November 13, 1989; re-signed by Astros, December 19, 1989.

CHAMPIONSHIP SERIES RECORD

Year Club	League	G.	IP.	W.	L.	Pct.	H.	R.	ER.	SO.	BB.	ERA.
1987—Minnesota	American	2	4⅓	0	0	.000	2	0	0	5	0	0.00

WORLD SERIES RECORD

Year Club	League	G.	IP.	W.	L.	Pct.	H.	R.	ER.	SO.	BB.	ERA.
1987—Minnesota	American	3	4⅓	1	0	1.000	4	3	3	3	3	6.23

CURTIS MONTAGUE SCHILLING

Born November 14, 1966, at Phoenix, Ariz.
Height, 6.04. Weight, 215.
Throws and bats righthanded.
Attended Yavapai College, Prescott, Ariz.

Tied for International League lead in games started by pitchers with 27, shutouts with 3, complete games with 9 and balks with 6 in 1989.

Year Club	League	G.	IP.	W.	L.	Pct.	H.	R.	ER.	SO.	BB.	ERA.
1986—Elmira	NYP	16	93⅔	7	3	.700	92	34	27	75	30	2.59
1987—Greensboro	S. Atlantic	29	184	8	★15	.348	179	96	78	★189	65	3.82
1988—New Britain†	Eastern	21	106	8	5	.615	91	44	35	62	40	2.97
1988—Charlotte	Southern	7	45⅓	5	2	.714	36	19	16	32	23	3.18
1988—Baltimore	American	4	14⅔	0	3	.000	22	19	16	4	10	9.82
1989—Rochester	Int'national	27	★185⅓	●13	11	.542	176	76	66	109	59	3.21
1989—Baltimore	American	5	8⅔	0	1	.000	10	6	6	6	3	6.23
Major League Totals—2 Years		9	23⅓	0	4	.000	32	25	22	10	13	8.49

Selected by Boston Red Sox' organization in 2nd round of free-agent draft, January 14, 1986.
†Traded with Outfielder Brady Anderson to Baltimore Orioles for Pitcher Mike Boddicker, July 29, 1988.

CALVIN DREW SCHIRALDI

Born June 16, 1962, at Houston, Tex.
Height, 6.05. Weight, 215.
Throws and bats righthanded.
Attended University of Texas, Austin, Tex.

Major League saves: 1986 (9), 1987 (6), 1988 (1), 1989 (4). Total—20.
Named Texas League Pitcher of the Year, 1984.

Year Club	League	G.	IP.	W.	L.	Pct.	H.	R.	ER.	SO.	BB.	ERA.
1983—Jackson	Texas	7	38⅔	3	3	.500	41	28	25	26	29	5.82
1983—Lynchburg	Carolina	6	30⅓	4	1	.800	28	16	15	41	17	4.45
1984—Jackson	Texas	23	156⅓	●14	3	★.824	118	58	50	131	69	2.88
1984—Tidewater	Int'national	4	31⅓	3	1	.750	18	6	4	24	10	1.15
1984—New York	National	5	17⅓	0	2	.000	20	13	11	16	10	5.71
1985—Jackson	Int'national	17	100⅓	4	5	.444	91	50	39	76	56	3.50
1985—New York†‡	National	10	26⅓	2	1	.667	43	27	26	21	11	8.89
1986—Pawtucket	Int'national	31	44	4	3	.571	32	19	14	59	20	2.86
1986—Boston	American	25	51	4	2	.667	36	8	8	55	15	1.41
1987—Boston§	American	62	83⅔	8	5	.615	75	45	41	93	40	4.41
1988—Chicago x	National	29	166⅓	9	13	.409	166	87	81	140	63	4.38
1989—Chicago y-San Diego	National	59	100	6	7	.462	72	40	39	71	63	3.51
National League Totals—4 Years		103	310	17	23	.425	301	167	157	248	147	4.56
American League Totals—2 Years		87	134⅔	12	7	.632	111	53	49	148	55	3.27
Major League Totals—6 Years		190	444⅔	29	30	.492	412	220	206	396	202	4.17

Selected by Chicago White Sox' organization in 17th round of free-agent draft, June 3, 1980.
Selected by New York Mets' organization in 1st round (27th player selected) of free-agent draft, June 6, 1983.
†On disabled list, May 15 to May 30, 1985.
‡Traded with Pitcher Wes Gardner and Outfielders John Christensen and LaSchelle Tarver to Boston Red Sox for Pitchers Bob Ojeda, Tom McCarthy, John Mitchell and Chris Bayer, November 13, 1985.
§Traded with Pitcher Al Nipper to Chicago Cubs for Pitcher Lee Smith, December 8, 1987.
xOn disabled list, May 13 to May 28 and August 5 to August 20, 1988.
yTraded with Outfielder Darrin Jackson and a player to be named later to San Diego Padres for Outfielder Marvell Wynne and Infielder Luis Salazar, August 30, 1989; San Diego acquired First Baseman Phil Stephenson to complete deal, September 5, 1989.

CHAMPIONSHIP SERIES RECORD

Shares American League Championship Series record for most games pitched, series (4), 1986.

Year Club	League	G.	IP.	W.	L.	Pct.	H.	R.	ER.	SO.	BB.	ERA.
1986—Boston	American	4	6	0	1	.000	5	2	1	9	3	1.50

WORLD SERIES RECORD

Year Club	League	G.	IP.	W.	L.	Pct.	H.	R.	ER.	SO.	BB.	ERA.
1986—Boston	American	3	4	0	2	.000	7	7	6	2	3	13.50

DAVID JOSEPH SCHMIDT
(Dave)

Born April 22, 1957, at Niles, Mich.
Height, 6.01. Weight, 194.
Throws and bats righthanded.
Attended Los Angeles Valley College, Van Nuys, Calif., and University of California, Los Angeles, Calif.

Major League saves: 1981 (1), 1982 (6), 1983 (2), 1984 (12), 1985 (5), 1986 (8), 1987 (1), 1988 (2). Total—37.

Year Club	League	G.	IP.	W.	L.	Pct.	H.	R.	ER.	SO.	BB.	ERA.
1979—Sarasota Rangers	Gulf Coast	7	30	2	2	.500	30	19	14	27	8	4.20
1980—Asheville	S. Atlantic	12	91	8	1	.889	76	32	20	67	13	1.98
1980—Tulsa	Texas	12	73	4	6	.400	90	42	36	46	28	4.44
1981—Tulsa	Texas	3	24	1	1	.500	17	5	5	17	6	1.88
1981—Texas	American	14	32	0	1	.000	31	11	11	13	11	3.09
1981—Wichita	Am. Assoc.	12	87	2	5	.286	90	47	47	49	26	4.86
1982—Texas	American	33	109⅔	4	6	.400	118	45	39	69	25	3.20
1983—Texas†	American	31	46⅓	3	3	.500	42	20	20	29	14	3.88
1984—Texas	American	43	70⅓	6	6	.500	69	30	20	46	20	2.56
1985—Texas‡	American	51	85⅔	7	6	.538	81	36	30	46	22	3.15
1986—Chicago§	American	49	92⅓	3	6	.333	94	37	34	67	27	3.31
1987—Baltimore	American	35	124	10	5	.667	128	57	52	70	26	3.77
1988—Baltimore	American	41	129⅔	8	5	.615	129	58	49	67	38	3.40
1989—Baltimore x	American	38	156⅔	10	13	.435	196	102	99	46	36	5.69
Major League Totals—9 Years		335	846⅔	51	51	.500	888	396	354	453	219	3.76

Selected by Texas Rangers' organization in 26th round of free-agent draft, June 5, 1979.

†On disabled list, March 25 to May 1, 1983.

‡Traded with Infielder Wayne Tolleson to Chicago White Sox for Pitcher Ed Correa, Infielder Scott Fletcher and a player to be named later, November 25, 1985; Texas Rangers acquired Infielder Jose Mota to complete deal, December 12, 1985.

§Released, December 19, 1986; signed by Baltimore Orioles, January 22, 1987.

xGranted free agency, November 13, 1989; signed by Montreal Expos, December 13, 1989.

MICHAEL JACK SCHMIDT
(Mike)

Born September 27, 1949, at Dayton, O.
Height, 6.02. Weight, 203.
Throws and bats righthanded.
Received bachelor of arts degree in business administration from Ohio University, Athens, O. in 1971.

Holds major league records for most total bases, extra-inning game (17), April 17, 1976 (10 innings); most home runs by third baseman, season (48), 1980; most home runs by third baseman, lifetime (509).

Shares major league records for most home runs, extra-inning game (4), April 17, 1976 (10 innings); most consecutive home runs, extra-inning game (4), April 17, 1976 (10 innings); most home runs, consecutive plate appearances (4), April 17, 1976 and July 6 and 7, 1979; most extra bases on long hits, game (12), April 17, 1976 (10 innings); most home runs, two consecutive games (5), April 17 and 18, 1976; most home runs, three consecutive games (6), April 17-20, 1976; most home runs, month of April (11), 1976; most consecutive seasons leading major leagues in strikeouts (3), 1974 through 1976; most home runs, month of October (4), 1980; most years leading league in double plays by third baseman (6).

Holds National League records for most years, third baseman (18); most years leading league in home runs (8); most years leading league in extra bases on long hits (7); most assists, third baseman, season (404), 1974; fewest singles, season, 150 or more games (63), 1979; most games, third baseman, lifetime (2,212); most assists by third baseman, lifetime (5,045); most chances accepted, third baseman, lifetime (6,636); most double plays by third baseman, lifetime (450).

Shares National League records for most years leading league in runs batted in (4); most home runs, bases full, one month, 2, June, 1973; most home runs through July 31 (36), 1979; most home runs, five consecutive games, one or more homer each game (7), July 6 through 10, 1979; most consecutive years leading league in extra bases on long hits (3, performed twice); most consecutive years leading league in bases on balls (3); most years leading league in assists by third baseman (7).

Hit three home runs in a game, July 7, 1979 and June 14, 1987.

Hit home runs in all 12 National League parks, 1979.

Major League stolen bases: 1973 (8), 1974 (23), 1975 (29), 1976 (14), 1977 (15), 1978 (19), 1979 (9), 1980 (12), 1981 (12), 1982 (14), 1983 (7), 1984 (5), 1985 (1), 1986 (1), 1987 (2), 1988 (3). Total—174.

Led National League in intentional bases on balls received with 18 in 1981 and 25 in 1986.

Led National League in total bases with 306 in 1976, 342 in 1980 and 228 in 1981.

Led National League in slugging percentage with .546 in 1974, .624 in 1980, .644 in 1981 and .547 in 1982 and 1986.

Led National League batters in strikeouts with 138 in 1974, 180 in 1975, 149 in 1976 and 148 in 1983.

Led National League in bases on balls received with 120 in 1979, 73 in 1981, 107 in 1982 and 128 in 1983.

Led National League in sacrifice flies with 13 in 1980 and tied for lead with 9 in 1979.

Tied for National League lead in being hit by pitch with 11 in 1976.

Led National League third basemen in fielding percentage with .980 in 1986.

Led National League third basemen in total chances with 537 in 1976, 521 in 1977, 497 in 1980, 457 in 1982 and tied for lead with 338 in 1981 and 458 in 1983.

Led National League third basemen in double plays with 34 in 1978, 36 in 1979, 31 in 1980, 29 in 1983, 28 in 1987 and tied for lead with 28 in 1982.

Led National League third basemen in assists with 396 in 1977 and 332 in 1983.

Led Pacific Coast League batters in strikeouts with 145 in 1972.

Named National League Player of the Year by THE SPORTING NEWS, 1980 and 1986.

Named National League Most Valuable Player by Baseball Writers' Association of America, 1980, 1981 and 1986.

Named third baseman on THE SPORTING NEWS National League All-Star Team, 1974, 1976, 1977 and 1979 through 1984 and 1986.

Named third baseman on THE SPORTING NEWS National League All-Star fielding team, 1976 through 1984 and 1986.

Named third baseman on THE SPORTING NEWS National League Silver Slugger team, 1980 through 1984 and 1986.

Named shortstop on THE SPORTING NEWS College Baseball All-America Team, 1971.

Year Club	League	Pos.	G.	AB.	R.	H.	2B.	3B.	HR.	RBI.	B.A.	PO.	A.	E.	F.A.
1971—Reading	East.	SS-3B	74	237	27	50	7	1	8	31	.211	100	224	23	.934
1972—Eugene	P. C.	2B-3B-SS	131	436	80	127	23	6	26	91	.291	271	324	25	.960
1972—Philadelphia†	Nat.	3B-2B	13	34	2	7	0	0	1	3	.206	10	25	2	.946
1973—Philadelphia‡	Nat.	3-2-1-S	132	367	43	72	11	0	18	52	.196	119	256	18	.954
1974—Philadelphia	Nat.	3B	162	568	108	160	28	7	*36	116	.282	134	*404	26	.954

Year Club League	Pos.	G.	AB.	R.	H.	2B.	3B.	HR.	RBI.	B.A.	PO.	A.	E.	F.A.
1975—Philadelphia .... Nat.	3B-SS	158	562	93	140	34	3	*38	95	.249	139	390	26	.953
1976—Philadelphia .... Nat.	3B	160	584	112	153	31	4	*38	107	.262	139	*377	21	.961
1977—Philadelphia .... Nat.	3B-SS-2B	154	544	114	149	27	11	38	101	.274	109	401	20	.962
1978—Philadelphia .... Nat.	3B-SS	145	513	93	129	27	2	21	78	.251	98	325	16	.964
1979—Philadelphia .... Nat.	3B-SS	160	541	109	137	25	4	45	114	.253	115	363	23	.954
1980—Philadelphia .... Nat.	3B	150	548	104	157	25	8	*48	*121	.286	98	*372	27	.946
1981—Philadelphia .... Nat.	3B	102	354	*78	112	19	2	*31	*91	.316	74	*249	15	.956
1982—Philadelphia§ .... Nat.	3B	148	514	108	144	26	3	35	87	.280	110	*324	23	.950
1983—Philadelphia .... Nat.	3B-SS	154	534	104	136	16	4	*40	109	.255	108	333	19	.959
1984—Philadelphia .... Nat.	3B-1B-SS	151	528	93	146	23	3	●36	●106	.277	93	330	26	.942
1985—Philadelphia .... Nat.	1B-3B-SS	158	549	89	152	31	5	33	93	.277	911	193	18	.984
1986—Philadelphia .... Nat.	3B-1B	160	552	97	160	29	1	*37	*119	.290	347	238	8	.987
1987—Philadelphia x...... Nat.	3B-1B-SS	147	522	88	153	28	0	35	113	.293	138	319	13	.972
1988—Philadelphia yz.. Nat.	3B-1B	108	390	52	97	21	2	12	62	.249	76	223	19	.940
1989—Philadelphia a...... Nat.	3B	42	148	19	30	7	0	6	28	.203	18	71	8	.918
Major League Totals—18 Years		2404	8352	1506	2234	408	59	548	1595	.267	2836	5193	328	.961

Selected by Philadelphia Phillies' organization in 2nd round of free-agent draft, June 8, 1971.
†On disabled list, August 21 to September 2, 1972.
‡On disabled list, March 28 to April 21, 1973.
§On disabled list, April 14 to April 29, 1982.
xOn disabled list, May 26 to June 10, 1987.
yOn disabled list, August 13, 1988 through remainder of season.
zGranted free agency, November 4, 1988; re-signed by Phillies, December 7, 1988.
aOn voluntarily retired list, May 29, 1989.

DIVISION SERIES RECORD

Year Club League	Pos.	G.	AB.	R.	H.	2B.	3B.	HR.	RBI.	B.A.	PO.	A.	E.	F.A.
1981—Philadelphia .... Nat.	3B	5	16	3	4	1	0	1	2	.250	6	10	1	.941

CHAMPIONSHIP SERIES RECORD

Shares Championship Series record for most doubles, total series (7).

Year Club League	Pos.	G.	AB.	R.	H.	2B.	3B.	HR.	RBI.	B.A.	PO.	A.	E.	F.A.
1976—Philadelphia .... Nat.	3B	3	13	1	4	2	0	0	2	.308	4	9	1	.929
1977—Philadelphia .... Nat.	3B	4	16	2	1	0	0	0	1	.063	4	15	0	1.000
1978—Philadelphia .... Nat.	3B	4	15	1	3	2	0	0	1	.200	3	18	2	.913
1980—Philadelphia .... Nat.	3B	5	24	1	5	1	0	0	1	.208	3	17	1	.952
1983—Philadelphia .... Nat.	3B	4	15	5	7	2	0	1	2	.467	6	7	1	.929
Championship Series Totals—5 Years....		20	83	10	20	7	0	1	7	.241	20	66	5	.945

WORLD SERIES RECORD

Year Club League	Pos.	G.	AB.	R.	H.	2B.	3B.	HR.	RBI.	B.A.	PO.	A.	E.	F.A.
1980—Philadelphia .... Nat.	3B	6	21	6	8	1	0	2	7	.381	9	8	0	1.000
1983—Philadelphia .... Nat.	3B	5	20	0	1	0	0	0	0	.050	1	10	1	.917
World Series Totals—2 Years		11	41	6	9	1	0	2	7	.220	10	18	1	.966

ALL-STAR GAME RECORD

Year League	Pos.	AB.	R.	H.	2B.	3B.	HR.	RBI.	B.A.	PO.	A.	E.	F.A.
1974—National	PH-3B	0	1	0	0	0	0	0	.000	0	1	0	1.000
1976—National	3B	1	0	0	0	0	0	0	.000	0	0	0	.000
1977—National	PR	0	0	0	0	0	0	0	.000	0	0	0	.000
1979—National	3B	3	2	2	1	1	0	1	.667	1	1	1	.667
1981—National	3B	4	1	2	1	0	1	2	.500	0	2	1	.667
1982—National	3B	1	0	0	0	0	0	0	.000	0	0	0	.000
1983—National	3B	3	0	0	0	0	0	0	.000	0	0	1	.000
1984—National	3B	3	0	0	0	0	0	0	.000	0	4	0	1.000
1986—National	3B	1	0	0	0	0	0	0	.000	0	0	0	.000
1987—National	3B	2	0	1	0	0	0	0	.500	0	1	0	1.000
All-Star Game Totals—10 Years..................		18	4	5	2	1	1	3	.278	1	9	3	.769

Named to National League All-Star Team for 1980 game; replaced due to injury by Ray Knight.
Named to National League All-Star Team for 1989 game; did not play due to retirement.

RICHARD CRAIG SCHOFIELD
(Dick)

Born November 21, 1962, at Springfield, Ill.
Height, 5.10. Weight, 175.
Throws and bats righthanded.
Son of John Richard (Dick) Schofield, infielder with St. Louis Cardinals, Pittsburgh, San Francisco, New York Yankees, Los Angeles Dodgers, Boston and Milwaukee Brewers, 1953 through 1971.
Major League stolen bases: 1984 (5), 1985 (11), 1986 (23), 1987 (19), 1988 (20), 1989 (9). Total—87.
Led American League shortstops in double plays with 125 in 1988.
Led Pioneer League in bases on balls received with 68 in 1981.
Received reported $100,000 bonus to sign with California Angels, 1981.

Year Club League	Pos.	G.	AB.	R.	H.	2B.	3B.	HR.	RBI.	B.A.	PO.	A.	E.	F.A.
1981—Idaho Falls .... Pion.	*SS-2B	66	226	59	63	10	1	6	31	.279	*102	201	22	.932
1982—Danville .... Midw.	SS	92	308	80	111	21	*10	12	53	*.360	129	249	23	.943
1982—Redwood................ Calif.	SS	33	102	15	25	3	3	1	8	.245	35	103	3	.979

Year Club	League	Pos.	G.	AB.	R.	H.	2B.	3B.	HR.	RBI.	B.A.	PO.	A.	E.	F.A.
1982—Spokane	P. C.	SS-3B	7	30	4	9	4	1	1	12	.300	7	20	0	1.000
1983—Edmonton	P. C.	SS-3B	139	521	91	148	30	7	16	94	.284	220	402	30	.954
1983—California	Amer.	SS	21	54	4	11	2	0	3	4	.204	24	67	7	.929
1984—California†	Amer.	SS	140	400	39	77	10	3	4	21	.193	218	420	12	*.982
1985—California	Amer.	SS	147	438	50	96	19	3	8	41	.219	261	397	25	.963
1986—California	Amer.	SS	139	458	67	114	17	6	13	57	.249	246	389	18	.972
1987—California‡	Amer.	*SS-2B	134	479	52	120	17	3	9	46	.251	205	351	9	*.984
1988—California	Amer.	SS	155	527	61	126	11	6	6	34	.239	278	492	13	*.983
1989—California§	Amer.	SS	91	302	42	69	11	2	4	26	.228	118	276	7	.983
Major League Totals—7 Years			827	2658	315	613	87	23	47	229	.231	1350	2392	91	.976

Selected by California Angels' organization in 1st round (third player selected) of free-agent draft, June 8, 1981.
†On disabled list, July 1 to July 24, 1984.
‡On disabled list, July 13 to August 11, 1987.
§On disabled list, April 12 to May 6 and August 11 to September 21, 1989.

CHAMPIONSHIP SERIES RECORD

Year Club	League	Pos.	G.	AB.	R.	H.	2B.	3B.	HR.	RBI.	B.A.	PO.	A.	E.	F.A.
1986—California	Amer.	SS	7	30	4	9	1	0	1	2	.300	13	23	2	.947

MICHAEL RALPH SCHOOLER
(Mike)

Born August 10, 1962, at Anaheim, Calif.
Height, 6.03. Weight, 220.
Throws and bats righthanded.
Attended Golden West College, Huntington, Beach, Calif.,
and California State University, Fullerton, Calif.

Major League saves: 1988 (15), 1989 (33). Total—48.

Year Club	League	G.	IP.	W.	L.	Pct.	H.	R.	ER.	SO.	BB.	ERA.
1985—Bellingham	Northwest	10	55⅓	4	3	.571	42	24	18	48	15	2.93
1986—Wausau	Midwest	26	166⅓	12	10	.545	166	83	62	171	44	3.35
1987—Chattanooga	Southern	28	175	13	8	.619	183	87	77	144	48	3.96
1988—Calgary	P. Coast	26	33⅔	4	4	.500	33	19	12	47	6	3.21
1088 Seattle	American	40	48⅓	5	8	.385	45	21	19	54	24	3.54
1989—Seattle	American	67	77	1	7	.125	81	27	24	69	19	2.81
Major League Totals—2 Years		107	125⅓	6	15	.286	126	48	43	123	43	3.09

Selected by Seattle Mariners' organization in 2nd round of free-agent draft, June 3, 1985.

PETER ALAN SCHOUREK
(Pete)

Born May 10, 1969, at Austin, Tex.
Height, 6.05. Weight, 195.
Throws and bats lefthanded.

Year Club	League	G.	IP.	W.	L.	Pct.	H.	R.	ER.	SO.	BB.	ERA.
1987—Kingsport	Ap'lachian	12	78⅓	4	5	.444	70	37	32	57	34	3.68
1988—Little Falls†	Ap'lachian					(Did not play)						
1989—Columbia	S. Atlantic	27	136	5	9	.357	120	66	43	131	66	2.85
1989—St. Lucie	Florida St.	2	4	0	0	.000	3	1	1	4	2	2.25

Selected by New York Mets' organization in 2nd round of free-agent draft, June 2, 1987.
†On disabled list, June 17, 1988 through entire season.

ALFRED WILLIAM SCHROEDER III
Name pronounced SHRO-der.
(Bill)

Born September 7, 1958, at Baltimore, Md.
Height, 6.02. Weight, 200.
Throws and bats righthanded.
Attended Clemson University, Clemson, S. C.

Major League stolen bases: 1986 (1), 1987 (5). Total—6.
Led Pacific Coast League batters in strikeouts with 136 and game-winning RBIs with 15 in 1982.
Led California League batters in strikeouts with 141 in 1980.
Led Pioneer League in total bases with 170 in 1979.
Led California League catchers in total chances with 759 in 1980.
Tied for Pacific Coast League lead in passed balls with 13 in 1983.

Year Club	League	Pos.	G.	AB.	R.	H.	2B.	3B.	HR.	RBI.	B.A.	PO.	A.	E.	F.A.
1979—Butte	Pion.	C-1B	65	242	73	86	16	7	18	77	.355	474	50	9	.983
1980—Stockton	Calif.	*C-1B	123	437	68	117	20	3	18	97	.268	669	96	7	*.991
1981—El Paso	Texas	C-OF	95	335	41	87	20	2	15	61	.260	511	49	10	.982
1982—Vancouver	P. C.	C	116	425	66	113	16	3	22	77	.266	569	77	7	*.989
1983—Vancouver	P. C.	C	82	304	51	87	13	3	20	70	.286	399	68	6	*.987
1983—Milwaukee	Amer.	C	23	73	7	13	2	1	3	7	.178	92	5	2	.980
1984—Milwaukee	Amer.	C-1B	61	210	29	54	6	0	14	25	.257	277	24	4	.987
1985—Milwaukee†	Amer.	C-1B	53	194	18	47	8	0	8	25	.242	216	23	3	.988
1986—El Paso‡	Texas	C	8	26	5	6	3	0	1	2	.231	26	2	0	1.000
1986—Milwaukee	Amer.	C-1B	64	217	32	46	14	0	7	19	.212	307	25	1	.997

Year—Club	League	Pos.	G.	AB.	R.	H.	2B.	3B.	HR.	RBI.	B.A.	PO.	A.	E.	F.A.
1987—Milwaukee............	Amer.	C-1B	75	250	35	83	12	0	14	42	.332	373	27	2	.995
1988—Milwaukee§..........	Amer.	C-1B	41	122	9	19	2	0	5	10	.156	197	21	0	1.000
1988—Denver x...............	A. A.	C	6	17	4	4	2	1	0	3	.235	16	3	0	1.000
1989—California y..........	Amer.	C-1B	41	138	16	28	2	0	6	15	.203	252	32	3	.990
Major League Totals—7 Years...............			358	1204	146	290	46	1	57	143	.241	1714	157	15	.992

Selected by Milwaukee Brewers' organization in 8th round of free-agent draft, June 5, 1979.

†On disabled list, May 15 to June 14 and June 22 to July 19, 1985.

‡On Milwaukee disabled list, March 29 to May 4, 1986; included rehabilitation disability assignment to El Paso, April 24 to May 4, 1986.

§On disabled list, July 27 to August 15, 1988; included rehabilitation disability assignment to Denver, August 5 to August 12, 1988.

xTraded to California Angels for Infielder Gus Polidor, December 7, 1988.

yOn disabled list, August 11 to August 29, 1989.

RICHARD SPENCER SCHU

Name pronounced Shoo.

(Rick)

Born January 26, 1962, at Philadelphia, Pa.
Height, 6.00. Weight, 194.
Throws and bats righthanded.
Attended Sacramento City College, Sacramento, Calif.
Son of Ken Schu, minor league pitcher, 1955 and 1956.

Shares major league record for most doubles, inning (2), October 3, 1985, third inning.
Major League stolen bases: 1985 (8), 1986 (2), 1988 (6), 1989 (1). Total—17.
Led Pacific Coast League third basemen in total chances with 390 in 1984.

Year—Club	League	Pos.	G.	AB.	R.	H.	2B.	3B.	HR.	RBI.	B.A.	PO.	A.	E.	F.A.
1981—Bend......................	N'west	3B-2B-SS	68	258	41	69	10	0	2	42	.267	55	137	24	.889
1982—Spartanburg..........	S. Atl.	3B-2B-SS	125	429	78	117	28	1	12	60	.273	157	257	45	.902
1983—Peninsula..............	Carol.	3B-SS-2B	122	444	69	119	22	3	14	63	.268	82	252	30	.918
1983—Portland...............	P. C.	3B-SS	9	29	7	11	2	1	1	3	.379	6	12	2	.900
1984—Portland...............	P. C.	3B	140	552	70	166	35	●14	12	82	.301	★109	★254	★27	.931
1984—Philadelphia	Nat.	3B	17	29	12	8	2	1	2	5	.276	7	13	1	.952
1985—Portland...............	P. C.	SS-3B	42	150	19	42	8	3	4	22	.280	36	91	11	.920
1985—Philadelphia	Nat.	3B	112	416	54	105	21	4	7	24	.252	86	191	20	.933
1986—Philadelphia	Nat.	3B	92	208	32	57	10	1	8	25	.274	42	94	13	.913
1987—Philadelphia†‡	Nat.	3B-1B	92	196	24	46	6	3	7	23	.235	193	71	10	.964
1988—Baltimore§	Amer.	3B-1B	89	270	22	69	9	4	4	20	.256	94	110	11	.949
1989—Balt.x-Det.	Amer.	3-2-1-S	99	266	25	57	11	0	7	21	.214	59	126	12	.939
1989—Rochester.............	Int.	3B-1B	28	94	11	21	6	1	1	10	.223	50	39	5	.947
National League Totals—4 Years...........			313	849	122	216	39	9	24	77	.254	328	369	44	.941
American League Totals—2 Years			188	536	47	126	20	4	11	41	.235	153	236	23	.944
Major League Totals—6 Years			501	1385	169	342	59	13	35	118	.247	481	605	67	.942

Signed as free agent by Philadelphia Phillies' organization, November 25, 1980.

†On disabled list, August 19 to September 3, 1987.

‡Traded with Outfielders Jeff Stone and Keith Hughes to Baltimore Orioles for Outfielder Mike Young and a player to be named later, March 21, 1988; Philadelphia Phillies acquired Outfielder Frank Bellino to complete deal, June 14, 1988.

§On disabled list, April 22 to May 7, June 6 to June 21 and August 12 to August 29, 1988.

xSold to Detroit Tigers, May 19, 1989.

JEFFREY ALAN SCHULZ

(Jeff)

Born June 2, 1961, at Evansville, Ind.
Height, 6.01. Weight, 190.
Throws right and bats lefthanded.
Attended Western Kentucky University, Bowling Green, Ky.,
and Indiana State University, Evansville, Ind.

Year—Club	League	Pos.	G.	AB.	R.	H.	2B.	3B.	HR.	RBI.	B.A.	PO.	A.	E.	F.A.
1983—Butte	Pion.	OF	61	211	44	69	12	2	7	55	.327	59	6	4	.942
1984—Charleston.............	S. Atl.	OF	69	265	52	89	14	3	5	54	.336	115	12	4	.969
1984—Fort Myers...........	Fla. St.	OF	59	204	23	64	10	0	0	26	.314	110	10	0	1.000
1985—Memphis...............	South.	OF	136	488	73	149	15	5	4	53	.305	263	12	11	.962
1986—Omaha...................	A. A.	OF	123	400	40	121	19	4	2	61	.303	119	5	5	.961
1987—Omaha...................	A. A.	OF-1B	99	316	25	81	12	7	4	36	.256	163	8	2	.988
1988—Omaha...................	A. A.	OF	101	359	37	103	20	3	5	41	.287	105	7	7	.941
1989—Omaha...................	A. A.	OF	95	331	31	92	19	5	2	37	.278	132	6	3	.979
1989—Kansas City†........	Amer.	OF	7	9	0	2	0	0	0	1	.222	6	0	0	1.000
Major League Totals—1 Year.................			7	9	0	2	0	0	0	1	.222	6	0	0	1.000

Selected by Kansas City Royals' organization in 23rd round of free-agent draft, June 6, 1983.

†Granted free agency, October 15, 1989.

—DID YOU KNOW—

That the first major-league hit by Mitch Williams of the Cubs on September 18, 1989, was a three-run homer?

DONALD ARTHUR SCHULZE
Name pronounced SHULL-zee.
(Don)

Born September 27, 1962, at Roselle, Ill.
Height, 6.03. Weight, 230.
Throws and bats righthanded.

Led Gulf Coast League in complete games with 3 in 1980.
Tied for American Association lead in shutouts with 2 in 1983.

Year Club	League	G.	IP.	W.	L.	Pct.	H.	R.	ER.	SO.	BB.	ERA.
1980—Sarasota Cubs	Gulf Coast	12	66	2	7	.222	58	38	30	30	36	4.09
1981—Quad Cities†	Midwest	17	105	8	5	.615	89	33	27	61	51	2.31
1982—Salinas	California	24	165	13	7	.650	150	61	52	122	59	2.84
1983—Iowa	Am. Assoc.	25	168⅔	11	9	.550	170	88	80	103	63	4.27
1983—Chicago	National	4	14	0	1	.000	19	11	11	8	7	7.07
1984—Iowa	Am. Assoc.	13	79	5	5	.500	79	40	38	44	29	4.33
1984—Chicago‡	National	1	3	0	0	.000	8	4	4	2	1	12.00
1984—Maine	Int'national	2	9⅓	1	1	.500	14	12	9	7	3	8.68
1984—Cleveland	American	19	85⅔	3	6	.333	105	53	46	39	27	4.83
1985—Cleveland	American	19	94⅓	4	10	.286	128	75	63	37	19	6.01
1985—Maine	Int'national	15	115½	6	4	.600	105	41	34	45	29	2.65
1986—Cleveland§	American	19	84⅔	4	4	.500	88	48	47	33	34	5.00
1986—Maine	Int'national	3	10	0	1	.000	12	7	7	7	4	6.30
1987—Buffalo x	Am. Assoc.	5	22½	0	1	.000	33	25	24	13	12	9.67
1987—Tidewater	Int'national	15	89⅓	11	1	★.917	81	37	36	45	31	3.63
1987—New York yz	National	5	21⅔	1	2	.333	24	15	15	5	6	6.23
1988—Toledo a	Int'national	27	185⅓	10	13	.435	172	72	64	107	56	3.11
1989—Columbus	Int'national	14	92	8	4	.667	71	27	21	62	28	2.05
1989—New York b	American	2	11	1	1	.500	12	5	5	5	5	4.09
1989—San Diego c	National	7	24⅓	2	1	.667	38	20	15	15	6	5.55
National League Totals—4 Years		17	63	3	4	.429	89	50	45	30	20	6.43
American League Totals—4 Years		59	275⅔	12	21	.364	333	181	161	114	85	5.26
Major League Totals—6 Years		76	338⅔	15	25	.375	422	231	206	144	105	5.47

Selected by Chicago Cubs' organization in 1st round (11th player selected) of free-agent draft, June 3, 1980.

†On disabled list, June 22 to July 10, 1981.

‡Traded with Outfielders Mel Hall and Joe Carter and Pitcher Darryl Banks to Cleveland Indians for Catcher Ron Hassey and Pitchers Rick Sutcliffe and George Frazier, June 13, 1984.

§On disabled list, July 22 to September 1, 1986; included rehabilitation disability assignment to Maine, August 20 to September 1, 1986.

xTraded to Tidewater (New York Mets' organization) for Outfielder Ricky Nelson, May 11, 1987.

yGranted free agency, October 15, 1987; signed by Minnesota Twins, December 7, 1987.

zTraded to Detroit Tigers for Pitcher Karl Best, March 28, 1988.

aGranted free agency, October 15, 1988; signed by New York Yankees, November 17, 1988.

bTraded with Third Baseman Mike Pagliarulo to San Diego Padres for Pitcher Walt Terrell and a player to be named later, July 22, 1989; New York Yankees acquired Pitcher Fred Toliver to complete deal, September 27, 1989.

cReleased, November 16, 1989.

MICHAEL SCOTT SCHWABE
(Mike)

Born July 12, 1964, at Fort Dodge, Ia.
Height, 6.04. Weight, 200.
Throws and bats righthanded.
Attended Rancho Santiago College, Santa Ana, Calif.,
and Arizona State University, Tempe, Ariz.

Year Club	League	G.	IP.	W.	L.	Pct.	H.	R.	ER.	SO.	BB.	ERA.
1987—Bristol	Ap'lachian	4	12⅔	2	1	.667	8	8	6	7	3	4.26
1987—Fayetteville	S. Atlantic	11	22	1	1	.500	18	10	6	23	2	2.45
1987—Lakeland	Florida St.	5	18	2	1	.667	12	6	6	9	8	3.00
1988—Lakeland	Florida St.	40	111⅔	9	0	1.000	88	24	20	80	14	1.61
1988—Glens Falls	Eastern	8	18	0	2	.000	16	9	7	11	5	3.50
1989—London	Eastern	8	25⅓	3	0	1.000	25	7	3	22	5	1.07
1989—Detroit	American	13	44⅔	2	4	.333	58	33	30	13	16	6.04
1989—Toledo	Int'national	13	62⅓	5	3	.625	60	20	18	32	10	2.60
Major League Totals—1 Year		13	44⅔	2	4	.333	58	33	30	13	16	6.04

Selected by Minnesota Twins' organization in 8th round of free-agent draft, January 14, 1986.

Selected by Minnesota Twins' organization in secondary phase of free-agent draft, June 2, 1986.

Selected by Detroit Tigers' organization in 21st round of free-agent draft, June 2, 1987.

MICHAEL LORRI SCIOSCIA
Name pronounced SO-sha.
(Mike)

Born November 27, 1958, at Upper Darby, Pa.
Height, 6.02. Weight, 229.
Throws right and bats lefthanded.
Attended Pennsylvania State University, University Park, Pa.

Major League stolen bases: 1980 (1), 1982 (2), 1984 (2), 1985 (3), 1986 (3), 1987 (7). Total—18.

Led National League catchers in total chances with 1,016 in 1987 and 915 in 1989.

Led National League in passed balls with 11 in 1981.
Tied for Pacific Coast League lead in being hit by pitch with 7 in 1979.
Led Pacific Coast League catchers in double plays with 19 and passed balls with 22 in 1979.
Led Midwest League catchers in errors with 20 and double plays with 12 in 1978.

Year Club	League	Pos.	G.	AB.	R.	H.	2B.	3B.	HR.	RBI.	B.A.	PO.	A.	E.	F.A.
1976—Bellingham	N'west.	C	46	151	25	42	6	0	7	26	.278	202	35	14	.944
1977—Clinton	Midw.	C-1B	121	364	58	92	20	1	7	44	.253	764	95	22	.975
1978—San Antonio†	Texas	C	58	204	29	61	16	0	2	34	.299	214	17	4	.983
1979—Albuquerque	P. C.	C	143	461	80	155	34	0	3	68	.336	★690	★86	★15	.981
1980—Albuquerque	P. C.	C	52	160	33	53	11	1	3	33	.331	207	19	5	.978
1980—Los Angeles‡	Nat.	C	54	134	8	34	5	1	1	8	.254	226	26	2	.992
1981—Los Angeles	Nat.	C	93	290	27	80	10	0	2	29	.276	493	48	7	.987
1982—Los Angeles	Nat.	C	129	365	31	80	11	1	5	38	.219	631	57	10	.986
1983—Los Angeles§	Nat.	C	12	35	3	11	3	0	1	7	.314	55	4	0	1.000
1984—Los Angeles x	Nat.	C	114	341	29	93	18	0	5	38	.273	701	64	12	.985
1985—Los Angeles y	Nat.	C	141	429	47	127	26	3	7	53	.296	818	66	●13	.986
1986—Los Angeles z	Nat.	C	122	374	36	94	18	1	5	26	.251	756	64	15	.982
1987—Los Angeles	Nat.	C	142	461	44	122	26	1	6	38	.265	★925	80	11	.989
1988—Los Angeles	Nat.	C	130	408	29	105	18	0	3	35	.257	748	63	7	.991
1989—Los Angeles	Nat.	C	133	408	40	102	16	0	10	44	.250	★822	★82	11	.988
Major League Totals—10 Years			1070	3245	294	848	151	7	45	316	.261	6175	554	88	.987

Selected by Los Angeles Dodgers' organization in 1st round (19th player selected) of free-agent draft, June 8, 1976.
†On disabled list, May 19 to August 4, 1978.
‡On disabled list, April 10 to April 20, 1980.
§On disabled list, May 15, 1983 through remainder of season.
xOn disabled list, May 6 to May 21, 1984.
yOn disabled list, June 10 to July 15, 1986.
zOn disabled list, June 1 to June 16, 1987.

DIVISION SERIES RECORD

Year Club	League	Pos.	G.	AB.	R.	H.	2B.	3B.	HR.	RBI.	B.A.	PO.	A.	E.	F.A.
1981—Los Angeles	Nat.	C	4	13	0	2	0	0	0	1	.154	21	3	0	1.000

CHAMPIONSHIP SERIES RECORD

Year Club	League	Pos.	G.	AB.	R.	H.	2B.	3B.	HR.	RBI.	B.A.	PO.	A.	E.	F.A.
1981—Los Angeles	Nat.	C	5	15	1	2	0	0	1	1	.133	27	1	0	1.000
1985—Los Angeles	Nat.	C	6	16	2	4	0	0	0	1	.250	31	4	1	.972
1988—Los Angeles	Nat.	C	7	22	3	8	1	0	1	2	.364	37	4	0	1.000
Championship Series Totals—3 Years			18	53	6	14	1	0	2	4	.264	95	9	1	.990

WORLD SERIES RECORD

Year Club	League	Pos.	G.	AB.	R.	H.	2B.	3B.	HR.	RBI.	B.A.	PO.	A.	E.	F.A.
1981—Los Angeles	Nat.	C-PH	3	4	1	1	0	0	0	0	.250	7	1	0	1.000
1988—Los Angeles	Nat.	C	4	14	0	3	0	0	0	1	.214	28	0	1	.966
World Series Totals—2 Years			7	18	1	4	0	0	0	1	.222	35	1	1	.973

ALL-STAR GAME RECORD

Year League	Pos.	AB.	R.	H.	2B.	3B.	HR.	RBI.	B.A.	PO.	A.	E.	F.A.
1989—National	C	1	0	0	0	0	0	0	.000	3	0	0	1.000

MICHAEL WARREN SCOTT
(Mike)

Born April 26, 1955, at Santa Monica, Calif.
Height, 6.03. Weight, 215.
Throws and bats righthanded.
Attended Pepperdine University, Malibu, Calif.

Shares major league record for most strikeouts, inning (4), September 3, 1986, fifth inning.
Pitched 2-0 no-hit victory against San Francisco Giants, September 25, 1986.
Major League saves: 1982 (3).
Tied for National League lead in games started by pitchers with 36 in 1987.
Tied for National League lead in shutouts with 5 in 1986.
Led Texas League in complete games with 14 and tied for lead in balks with 3 in 1977.
Tied for International League lead in games started by pitchers with 29 in 1978 and balks with 3 in 1980.
Named National League Pitcher of the Year by THE SPORTING NEWS, 1986.
Won National League Cy Young Memorial Award, 1986.
Named righthanded pitcher on THE SPORTING NEWS National League All-Star Team, 1986 and 1989.

Year Club	League	G.	IP.	W.	L.	Pct.	H.	R.	ER.	SO.	BB.	ERA.
1976—Jackson	Texas	7	44	3	3	.500	34	20	14	19	14	2.86
1977—Jackson	Texas	25	★187	★14	10	.583	132	77	61	97	55	2.94
1977—Tidewater	Int'national	2	2	0	1	.000	4	5	4	0	3	18.00
1978—Tidewater	Int'national	29	192	10	10	.500	196	105	84	93	83	3.94
1979—Tidewater	Int'national	18	99	8	4	.667	103	37	35	40	27	3.18
1979—New York	National	18	52	1	3	.250	59	35	31	21	20	5.37
1980—Tidewater	Int'national	27	170	13	7	.650	165	69	56	88	64	2.96
1980—New York	National	6	29	1	1	.500	40	14	14	13	8	4.34
1981—New York	National	23	136	5	10	.333	130	65	59	54	34	3.90
1982—New York†	National	37	147	7	13	.350	185	100	84	63	60	5.14
1983—Houston‡	National	24	145	10	6	.625	143	67	60	73	46	3.72

Year Club	League	G.	IP.	W.	L.	Pct.	H.	R.	ER.	SO.	BB.	ERA.
1984—Houston	National	31	154	5	11	.313	179	96	80	83	43	4.68
1985—Houston	National	36	221⅔	18	8	.692	194	91	81	137	80	3.29
1986—Houston	National	37	★275⅓	18	10	.643	182	73	68	★306	72	★2.22
1987—Houston	National	36	247⅔	16	13	.552	199	94	89	233	79	3.23
1988—Houston§	National	32	218⅔	14	8	.636	162	74	71	190	53	2.92
1989—Houston	National	33	229	★20	10	.667	180	87	79	172	62	3.10
Major League Totals—11 Years		313	1855⅓	115	93	.553	1653	796	716	1345	557	3.47

Selected by New York Mets' organization in 2nd round of free-agent draft, June 8, 1976.
†Traded to Houston Astros for Outfielder-First Baseman Danny Heep, December 10, 1982.
‡On disabled list, April 5 to May 4, 1983.
§On disabled list, June 22 to July 13, 1988.

CHAMPIONSHIP SERIES RECORD

Holds Championship Series record for most consecutive scoreless innings, series (16), 1986.
Shares Championship Series records for most complete games, series (2), 1986; most strikeouts (4), and consecutive strikeouts (4), game, October 8, 1986.
Shares National League Championship Series records for most complete games, total series (2); most consecutive scoreless innings, total series (16).

Year Club	League	G.	IP.	W.	L.	Pct.	H.	R.	ER.	SO.	BB.	ERA.
1986—Houston	National	2	18	2	0	1.000	8	1	1	19	1	0.50

ALL-STAR GAME RECORD

Year League	IP.	W.	L.	Pct.	H.	R.	ER.	SO.	BB.	ERA.
1986—National	1	0	0	.000	1	1	1	2	0	9.00
1987—National	2	0	0	.000	1	0	0	1	0	0.00
All-Star Game Totals—2 Years	3	0	0	.000	2	1	1	3	0	3.00

Named to National League All-Star Team for 1989 game; replaced due to injury by Rick Sutcliffe.

RICHARD EDWARD SCOTT
(Dick)

Born July 19, 1962, at Ellsworth, Me.
Height, 6.00. Weight, 170.
Throws and bats righthanded.
Led Florida State League shortstops in double plays with 73 in 1984.

Year Club	League	Pos.	G.	AB.	R.	H.	2B.	3B.	HR.	RBI.	B.A.	PO.	A.	E.	F.A.
1981—Bradenton Yanks	Gulf C.	SS	48	132	11	31	5	2	0	15	.235	66	130	17	.920
1982—Columbus	Int.	SS	5	10	2	5	0	0	1	1	.500	8	8	1	.941
1982—Fort Lauderdale	Fla. St.	SS	90	235	26	44	6	2	3	24	.187	114	238	33	.914
1983—Fort Lauderdale	Fla. St.	SS-2B	120	345	40	75	11	2	4	32	.217	178	352	34	.940
1983—Columbus	Int.	SS	1	2	0	0	0	0	0	0	.000	2	0	0	1.000
1984—Fort Lauderdale	Fla. St.	SS	111	351	43	86	20	1	6	37	.245	171	365	37	.935
1984—Nashville	South.	3B	18	63	4	14	1	1	0	4	.222	17	42	6	.908
1985—Albany†	East.	SS-1B-OF	97	299	30	64	15	4	4	34	.214	154	231	24	.941
1986—Albany‡	East.	SS	10	30	4	6	3	0	1	4	.200	20	26	6	.885
1986—Columbus	Int.	2-S-3-O	58	159	20	43	12	2	2	16	.270	81	121	14	.935
1987—Columbus	Int.	2B-3B-SS	51	166	14	33	6	0	2	15	.199	74	134	4	.981
1987—Albany	East.	2-S-3-1	18	65	10	15	3	1	0	7	.231	51	41	3	.968
1988—Albany§	East.	S-1-2-3-O	73	229	19	58	9	2	0	19	.253	138	195	15	.957
1989—Tacoma	P. C.	SS	79	256	23	48	7	1	1	23	.188	117	259	19	.952
1989—Oakland x	Amer.	SS	3	2	0	0	0	0	0	1	.000	0	0	0	.000
Major League Totals—1 Year			3	2	0	0	0	0	0	1	.000	0	0	0	.000

Selected by New York Yankees' organization in 17th round of free-agent draft, June 8, 1981.
†On disabled list, April 12 to May 24, 1985.
‡On disabled list, May 6 to May 19, 1986.
§Granted free agency, October 15, 1988; signed by Tacoma (Oakland Athletics' organization), December 15, 1988.
xGranted free agency, October 15, 1989.

WILLIAM SCOTT SCUDDER
(Known by middle name.)

Born February 14, 1968, at Paris, Tex.
Height, 6.02. Weight, 185.
Throws and bats righthanded.
Pitched 4-0 no-hit victory against Wausau, May 20, 1988.

Year Club	League	G.	IP.	W.	L.	Pct.	H.	R.	ER.	SO.	BB.	ERA.
1986—Billings	Pioneer	12	52⅔	1	3	.250	43	34	28	38	36	4.78
1987—Cedar Rapids	Midwest	26	153⅔	7	12	.368	129	86	70	128	76	4.10
1988—Cedar Rapids	Midwest	16	102⅓	7	3	.700	61	30	23	126	41	2.02
1988—Chattanooga	Southern	11	70	7	0	1.000	53	24	23	52	30	2.96
1989—Nashville	Am. Assoc.	12	80⅔	6	2	.750	54	27	24	64	48	2.68
1989—Cincinnati	National	23	100⅓	4	9	.308	91	54	50	66	61	4.49
Major League Totals—1 Year		23	100⅓	4	9	.308	91	54	50	66	61	4.49

Selected by Cincinnati Reds' organization in 1st round (17th player selected) of free-agent draft, June 2, 1986.

RUDY CABALLERO SEANEZ

Born October 20, 1968, at Brawley, Calif.
Height, 6.00. Weight, 170.
Throws and bats righthanded.

Pitched 4-0 no-hit victory against Pulaski, August 2, 1986.

Year Club	League	G.	IP.	W.	L.	Pct.	H.	R.	ER.	SO.	BB.	ERA.
1986—Burlington	Ap'lachian	13	76	5	2	.714	59	37	27	56	32	3.20
1987—Waterloo†	Midwest	10	34⅔	0	4	.000	35	29	26	23	23	6.75
1988—Waterloo	Midwest	22	113⅓	6	6	.500	98	69	59	93	68	4.69
1989—Kinston	Carolina	25	113	8	10	.444	94	66	52	149	★111	4.14
1989—Colorado Springs	P. Coast	1	1	0	0	.000	1	0	0	0	0	0.00
1989—Cleveland	American	5	5	0	0	.000	1	2	2	7	4	3.60
Major League Totals—1 Year		5	5	0	0	.000	1	2	2	7	4	3.60

Selected by Cleveland Indians' organization in 4th round of free-agent draft, June 10, 1986.
†On disabled list, May 4 to July 11 and August 9 to August 29, 1987.

RAYMOND MARK SEARAGE
(Ray)

Born May 1, 1955, at Freeport, N.Y.
Height, 6.01. Weight, 201.
Throws and bats lefthanded.
Attended West Liberty State College, West Liberty, W. Va.

Major League saves: 1981 (1), 1984 (6), 1985 (1), 1986 (1), 1987 (2). Total—11.
Led International League in wild pitches with 14 in 1982.

Year Club	League	G.	IP.	W.	L.	Pct.	H.	R.	ER.	SO.	BB.	ERA.
1976—Sara. W. Sox-Sara. Cards	Gulf Coast	11	32	1	3	.250	24	17	15	31	22	4.22
1977—St. Petersburg	Florida St.	13	19	0	0	.000	11	7	6	12	12	2.84
1977—Johnson City	Ap'lachian	8	41	3	2	.600	38	23	22	27	21	4.83
1978—Gastonia	W. Carol.	39	110	8	3	.727	86	40	34	86	68	2.78
1979—Arkansas†	Texas	42	89	10	4	.714	73	27	22	63	46	2.22
1980—Tidewater	Int'national	19	30	1	0	1.000	35	24	23	20	20	6.90
1980—Jackson	Texas	14	70	4	5	.444	54	32	26	71	26	3.34
1981—Tidewater	Int'national	18	27	2	0	1.000	29	10	7	23	13	2.33
1981—New York‡	National	26	37	1	0	1.000	34	16	15	16	17	3.65
1982—Charleston§	Int'national	38	114	2	7	.222	112	73	62	87	87	4.89
1983—Charleston x	Int'national	31	134	7	7	.500	146	94	84	77	76	5.64
1984—Vancouver	P. Coast	33	76⅓	6	3	.667	62	29	26	59	44	3.07
1984—Milwaukee	American	21	38⅓	2	1	.667	20	3	3	29	16	0.70
1985—Milwaukee	American	33	38	1	4	.200	54	27	25	36	24	5.92
1985—Vancouver	P. Coast	23	26	2	0	1.000	22	10	7	31	12	2.42
1986—Milwaukee yz-Chicago	American	46	51	1	1	.500	44	20	19	36	28	3.35
1986—Vancouver	P. Coast	20	25	2	0	1.000	12	5	4	20	8	1.44
1987—Chicago	American	58	55⅔	2	3	.400	56	28	26	33	24	4.20
1987—Hawaii a	P. Coast	3	7⅓	0	1	.000	6	5	3	5	3	3.68
1988—Albuquerque	P. Coast	51	60	2	3	.400	62	39	34	58	25	5.10
1989—Los Angeles b	National	41	35⅔	3	4	.429	29	15	14	24	18	3.53
1989—Albuquerque	P. Coast	2	8	0	1	.000	8	3	2	7	2	2.25
National League Totals—2 Years		67	72⅔	4	4	.500	63	31	29	40	35	3.59
American League Totals—4 Years		158	183	6	9	.400	174	78	73	134	92	3.59
Major League Totals—6 Years		225	255⅔	10	13	.435	237	109	102	174	127	3.59

Selected by St. Louis Cardinals' organization in 22nd round of free-agent draft, June 8, 1976.
†Traded to New York Mets' organization for Catcher Jody Davis, December 10, 1979.
‡Traded to Cleveland Indians for Shortstop Tom Veryzer, January 8, 1982.
§Traded on a conditional basis to San Diego Padres for a player to be named later, December 15, 1982; returned, March 28, 1983.
xGranted free agency, October 20, 1983; signed by Vancouver (Milwaukee Brewers' organization), November 4, 1983.
yLoaned to Buffalo (Chicago White Sox' organization), July 17, 1986; returned, July 23, 1986.
zTraded to Chicago White Sox for Pitcher Al Jones and Outfielder Tom Hartley, July 23, 1986.
aReleased, March 25, 1988; signed by Albuquerque (Los Angeles Dodgers' organization), April 5, 1988.
bOn disabled list, May 31 to July 8, 1989; included rehabilitation disability assignment to Albuquerque, June 29 to July 8, 1989.

WILLIAM STEPHEN SEARCY
(Steve)

Born June 4, 1964, at Knoxville, Tenn.
Height, 6.01. Weight, 185.
Throws and bats lefthanded.
Attended University of Tennessee, Knoxville, Tenn.

Led International League in hit batsmen with 12 in 1988.
Tied for Eastern League lead in games started by pitchers with 27 in 1986.
Named International League Pitcher of the Year, 1988.

Year Club	League	G.	IP.	W.	L.	Pct.	H.	R.	ER.	SO.	BB.	ERA.
1985—Bristol	Ap'lachian	4	22	1	1	.500	15	6	5	24	2	2.05
1985—Birmingham	Southern	7	36⅔	2	2	.500	39	17	13	19	23	3.19
1986—Glens Falls	Eastern	27	172	11	6	.647	166	79	63	★139	74	3.30

Year Club	League	G.	IP.	W.	L.	Pct.	H.	R.	ER.	SO.	BB.	ERA.
1987—Toledo	Int'national	10	53⅓	3	4	.429	49	26	25	54	32	4.22
1988—Toledo	Int'national	27	170	●13	7	.650	131	61	49	★176	79	2.59
1988—Detroit	American	2	8	0	2	.000	8	6	5	5	4	5.63
1989—Toledo†	Int'national	9	37	2	3	.400	41	36	31	26	37	7.54
1989—Lakeland	Florida St.	9	52⅔	2	3	.400	40	21	15	44	33	2.56
1989—Detroit	American	8	22⅓	1	1	.500	27	16	15	11	12	6.04
Major League Totals—2 Years		10	30⅓	1	3	.250	35	22	20	16	16	5.93

Selected by Detroit Tigers' organization in 3rd round of free-agent draft, June 3, 1985.
†On Detroit disabled list, March 27 to May 5, 1989.

ROBERT BUSH SEBRA

Name pronounced SEBB-ruh.

(Bob)

Born December 11, 1961, at Ridgewood, N.J.
Height, 6.02. Weight, 195.
Throws and bats righthanded.
Attended University of Nebraska, Lincoln, Neb.

Major League saves: 1989 (1).
Tied for American Association lead in home runs allowed with 17 in 1985.
Named American Association Pitcher of the Year, 1988.

Year Club	League	G.	IP.	W.	L.	Pct.	H.	R.	ER.	SO.	BB.	ERA.
1983—Tri-Cities	Northwest	12	58⅓	4	3	.571	48	36	26	70	29	4.01
1984—Tulsa	Texas	17	100⅓	10	5	.667	86	45	38	90	41	3.41
1984—Oklahoma City	Am. Assoc.	9	53⅓	4	4	.500	37	23	20	38	25	3.38
1985—Oklahoma City	Am. Assoc.	22	138⅔	10	6	.625	121	62	59	84	57	3.83
1985—Texas†	American	7	20⅓	0	2	.000	26	17	17	13	14	7.52
1986—Indianapolis	Am. Assoc.	20	126	9	2	.818	108	59	48	91	70	3.43
1986—Montreal	National	17	91⅓	5	5	.500	82	39	36	66	25	3.55
1987—Montreal	National	36	177⅓	6	15	.286	184	99	87	156	67	4.42
1988—Indianapolis‡	Am. Assoc.	29	174⅓	12	6	.667	154	71	57	126	59	2.94
1988—Philadelphia	National	3	11⅓	1	2	.333	15	11	10	7	10	7.94
1989—Scranton/Wilkes-Barre	Int'national	11	64⅔	3	4	.429	61	36	34	56	21	4.73
1989—Philadelphia§-Cincinnati	National	21	55⅓	2	3	.400	65	36	32	35	28	5.20
1989—Nashville	Am. Assoc.	11	18	0	0	.000	15	6	5	15	10	2.50
American League Totals—1 Year		7	20⅓	0	2	.000	26	17	17	13	14	7.52
National League Totals—4 Years		77	335⅓	14	25	.359	346	185	165	264	130	4.43
Major League Totals—5 Years		84	355⅔	14	27	.341	372	202	182	277	144	4.61

Selected by Detroit Tigers' organization in 4th round of free-agent draft, June 3, 1980.
Selected by Texas Rangers' organization in 5th round of free-agent draft, June 6, 1983.
†Traded with Infielder Jim Anderson to Montreal Expos for Outfielder Pete Incaviglia, November 2, 1985.
‡Traded to Philadelphia Phillies for Pitcher Travis Chambers, September 1, 1988.
§Traded to Cincinnati Reds for a player to be named later, July 13, 1989; Philadelphia Phillies' organization acquired Pitcher Jeff Gray to complete deal, September 6, 1989.

JOSE ALTAGRACIA SEGURA (MOTA)

Born January 26, 1963, at Fundacion Barahona, D. R.
Height, 5.11. Weight 180.
Throws and bats righthanded.

Year Club	League	G.	IP.	W.	L.	Pct.	H.	R.	ER.	SO.	BB.	ERA.
1981—Helena	Pioneer	25	35	2	3	.400	42	26	17	27	15	4.37
1982—Spartanburg	S. Atlantic	20	29	2	2	.500	32	28	25	17	18	7.76
1982—Bend	Northwest	24	36⅔	4	4	.500	27	16	7	43	28	1.72
1983—Spartanburg†	S. Atlantic	40	65⅔	1	6	.143	77	59	47	54	42	6.44
1984—Kinston	Carolina	16	97⅓	7	4	.636	88	48	43	55	35	3.98
1984—Knoxville	Southern	12	69	4	6	.400	75	47	34	26	47	4.43
1985—Kinston	Carolina	34	110⅓	4	●13	.235	109	62	51	73	69	4.16
1986—Knoxville‡	Southern	24	106⅔	4	7	.364	101	72	50	55	72	4.22
1987—Syracuse§	Int'national	43	107	9	8	.385	136	90	78	54	59	6.56
1988—Chicago	American	4	8⅔	0	0	.000	19	17	13	2	8	13.50
1988—Vancouver x	P. Coast	20	111	6	6	.500	127	69	56	39	60	4.54
1989—Vancouver	P. Coast	44	66⅔	1	2	.333	50	21	17	52	19	2.30
1989—Chicago	American	7	6	0	1	.000	13	11	10	4	3	15.00
Major League Totals—2 Years		11	14⅔	0	1	.000	32	28	23	6	11	14.11

Signed as free agent by Philadelphia Phillies' organization, June 22, 1981.
†Drafted by Syracuse (Toronto Blue Jays' organization), December 6, 1983.
‡On disabled list, July 14 to August 9, 1986.
§Granted free agency, October 15, 1987; signed by Chicago White Sox, January 29, 1988.
xReleased, November 20, 1988; re-signed by White Sox' organization, December 22, 1988.

KEVIN LEE SEITZER

Born March 26, 1962, at Springfield, Ill.
Height, 5.11. Weight, 180.
Throws and bats righthanded.
Received bachelor of science degree in industrial electronics from
Eastern Illinois University, Charleston, Ill.

Major League stolen bases: 1987 (12), 1988 (10), 1989 (17). Total—39.
Collected six hits in one game, August 2, 1987.
Led American League third basemen in errors with 22 in 1987.
Led South Atlantic League in bases on balls received with 118 in 1984.
Tied for American Association lead in being hit by pitch with 9 in 1986.
Led South Atlantic League third basemen in total chances with 409 in 1984.
Led Pioneer League third basemen in assists with 122 and total chances with 172 in 1983.
Named South Atlantic League Most Valuable Player, 1984.

Year Club	League	Pos.	G.	AB.	R.	H.	2B.	3B.	HR.	RBI.	B.A.	PO.	A.	E.	F.A.
1983—Butte	Pion.	3B-SS	68	238	60	82	14	1	2	45	.345	52	124	21	.893
1984—Charleston.............	S. Atl.	3B	●141	489	★96	★145	26	5	8	79	.297	80	★279	★50	.878
1985—Fort Myers...........	Fla. St.	1B-3B	90	290	61	91	10	5	3	46	.314	569	88	9	.986
1985—Memphis...............	South.	3B-1B-OF	52	187	26	65	6	2	1	20	.348	79	51	10	.929
1986—Memphis...............	South.	1B	4	11	4	3	0	0	0	1	.273	28	3	1	.969
1986—Omaha.................	A. A.	OF-1B-3B	129	432	86	138	20	11	13	74	.319	338	39	9	.977
1986—Kansas City..........	Amer.	1B-OF-3B	28	96	16	31	4	1	2	11	.323	224	19	3	.988
1987—Kansas City..........	Amer.	3B-1B-OF	161	641	105	●207	33	8	15	83	.323	290	315	24	.962
1988—Kansas City..........	Amer.	★3B-OF	149	559	90	170	32	5	5	60	.304	93	297	★26	.938
1989—Kansas City..........	Amer.	3-S-O-1	160	597	78	168	17	2	4	48	.281	118	277	20	.952
Major League Totals—4 Years.................			498	1893	289	576	86	16	26	202	.304	725	908	73	.957

Selected by Kansas City Royals' organization in 11th round of free-agent draft, June 6, 1983.

ALL-STAR GAME RECORD

Year League	Pos.	AB.	R.	H.	2B.	3B.	HR.	RBI.	B.A.	PO.	A.	E.	F.A.
1987—American	3B	2	0	0	0	0	0	0	.000	0	0	0	.000

DAVID SCOTT SERVICE
(Known by middle name.)

Born February 27, 1967, at Cincinnati, O.
Height, 6.06. Weight, 225.
Throws and bats righthanded.

Year Club	League	G.	IP.	W.	L.	Pct.	H.	R.	ER.	SO.	BB.	ERA.
1986—Spartanburg...................	S. Atlantic	14	58⅔	1	6	.143	68	44	38	49	34	5.83
1986—Utica	NYP	10	70½	5	4	.556	65	30	21	43	18	2.67
1986—Clearwater	Florida St.	4	25⅓	1	2	.333	20	10	9	19	15	3.20
1987—Reading........................	Eastern	5	19⅔	0	3	.000	22	19	17	12	16	7.78
1987—Clearwater	Florida St.	21	137⅔	13	4	.765	127	46	38	73	32	2.48
1988—Reading........................	Eastern	10	56⅔	3	4	.429	52	25	18	39	22	2.86
1988—Maine	Int'national	19	110½	8	8	.500	109	51	45	87	31	3.67
1988—Philadelphia	National	5	5⅓	0	0	.000	7	1	1	6	1	1.69
1989—Scranton/Wilkes-Barre................	Int'national	23	33⅓	3	1	.750	27	8	8	23	23	2.16
1989—Reading........................	Eastern	23	85⅔	6	6	.500	71	36	31	82	23	3.26
Major League Totals—1 Year............................		5	5⅓	0	0	.000	7	1	1	6	1	1.69

Signed as free agent by Philadelphia Phillies' organization, August 24, 1985.

MICHAEL TYRONE SHARPERSON
(Mike)

Born October 4, 1961, at Orangeburg, S.C.
Height, 6.03. Weight, 191.
Throws and bats righthanded.
Attended DeKalb Community College South, Decatur, Ga.

Major League stolen bases: 1987 (2).
Led International League second basemen in putouts with 286 and total chances with 666 in 1985.
Led Southern League second basemen in total chances with 775 and double plays with 103 in 1984.
Tied for International League lead in double plays by third basemen with 16 in 1987.

Year Club	League	Pos.	G.	AB.	R.	H.	2B.	3B.	HR.	RBI.	B.A.	PO.	A.	E.	F.A.
1982—Florence	S. Atl.	SS-3B	111	326	51	83	16	1	3	33	.255	136	261	33	.923
1983—Kinston†................	Carol.	S-3-2-C	90	361	55	96	8	1	5	41	.266	148	286	19	.958
1984—Knoxville	South.	2B	140	542	86	165	25	7	4	48	.304	★331	★423	21	.973
1985—Syracuse	Int.	2B-SS	134	★536	★86	★155	19	★7	1	59	.289	291	372	17	.975
1986—Syracuse	Int.	2B-3B	133	519	★86	★150	18	★9	4	45	.289	258	376	18	.972
1987—Toronto	Amer.	2B	32	96	4	20	4	1	0	9	.208	64	69	4	.971
1987—Syracuse‡	Int.	3B-2B	88	338	67	101	21	5	5	26	.299	81	152	8	.967
1987—Los Angeles	Nat.	3B-2B	10	33	7	9	2	0	0	1	.273	4	28	1	.970
1988—Albuquerque........	P. C.	2B-3B-SS	56	210	55	67	10	2	0	30	.319	88	173	12	.956
1988—Los Angeles	Nat.	2B-3B-SS	46	59	8	16	1	0	0	4	.271	19	31	2	.962
1989—Albuquerque........	P. C.	2B-3B-SS	98	359	81	111	15	7	3	48	.309	114	250	14	.963
1989—Los Angeles	Nat.	2-1-3-S	27	28	2	7	3	0	0	5	.250	11	8	0	1.000
American League Totals—1 Year..........			32	96	4	20	4	1	0	9	.208	64	69	4	.971
National League Totals—3 Years..............			83	120	17	32	6	0	0	10	.267	34	67	3	.971
Major League Totals—3 Years.................			115	216	21	52	10	1	0	19	.241	98	136	7	.971

Selected by Pittsburgh Pirates' organization in 41st round of free-agent draft, June 5, 1979.
Selected by Montreal Expos' organization in secondary phase of free-agent draft, January 8, 1980.
Selected by Detroit Tigers' organization in 4th round of free-agent draft, January 13, 1981.
Selected by Toronto Blue Jays' organization in secondary phase of free-agent draft, June 8, 1981.
†On disabled list, August 14, 1983 through remainder of season.
‡Traded to Los Angeles Dodgers for Pitcher Juan Guzman, September 22, 1987.

Year	Club	League	Pos.	G.	AB.	R.	H.	2B.	3B.	HR.	RBI.	B.A.	PO.	A.	E.	F.A.
1988—Los Angeles		Nat.	PH-S-3	2	1	0	0	0	0	0	1	.000	1	0	0	1.000

JEFFREY LEE SHAW
(Jeff)

Born July 7, 1966, at Washington Court House, O.
Height, 6.02. Weight, 185.
Throws and bats righthanded.
Attended Cuyahoga Community College-Western Campus, Parma, O.

Led Eastern League in hit batsmen with 14 in 1989.
Led Midwest League pitchers in games started with 28 and shutouts with 4 in 1987.
Tied for Eastern League lead in games started by pitchers with 27 in 1988.

Year	Club	League	G.	IP.	W.	L.	Pct.	H.	R.	ER.	SO.	BB.	ERA.
1986—Batavia		NYP	14	88⅔	8	4	.667	79	32	24	71	35	2.44
1987—Waterloo		Midwest	28	184⅓	11	11	.500	192	89	72	117	56	3.52
1988—Williamsport		Eastern	27	163⅔	5	*19	.208	●173	*94	66	61	75	3.63
1989—Canton-Akron		Eastern	30	154⅓	7	10	.412	134	84	62	95	67	3.62

Selected by Cleveland Indians' organization in 1st round (first player selected) of free-agent draft, January 14, 1986.

DANNY TODD SHEAFFER

Born August 21, 1961, at Jacksonville, Fla.
Height, 6.00. Weight, 185.
Throws and bats righthanded.
Attended Harrisburg Area Community College, Harrisburg, Pa.,
and Clemson University, Clemson, S.C.

Led Florida State League catchers in errors with 14 in 1982.

Year	Club	League	Pos.	G.	AB.	R.	H.	2B.	3B.	HR.	RBI.	B.A.	PO.	A.	E.	F.A.
1981—Elmira		NYP	C	62	198	39	57	9	0	8	29	.288	220	35	5	.981
1981—Bristol		East.	C-2B	8	12	0	0	0	0	0	1	.000	16	3	0	1.000
1982—Winter Haven†		Fla. St.	C-3B	82	260	20	65	4	0	5	25	.250	316	51	16	.958
1983—Winston-Salem		Carol.	C-1B-OF	112	380	48	105	14	2	15	63	.276	427	44	6	.987
1984—New Britain		East.	C-OF	93	303	33	73	10	0	1	27	.241	438	47	6	.988
1985—Pawtucket		Int.	C	77	243	24	63	9	0	8	33	.259	289	18	6	.981
1986—Pawtucket		Int.	C-OF	79	265	34	90	16	1	2	30	.340	380	39	5	.988
1987—Boston		Amer.	C	25	66	5	8	1	0	1	5	.121	121	5	3	.977
1987—Pawtucket		Int.	C-1B-OF	69	242	32	62	13	2	2	25	.256	346	32	5	.987
1988—Pawtucket‡		Int.	C-1-3-O	98	299	30	82	17	1	1	28	.274	509	58	6	.990
1989—Colorado Springs		P. C.	OF-3B	107	401	62	113	26	2	3	47	.282	136	11	10	.936
1989—Cleveland§		Amer.	3B-OF	7	16	1	1	0	0	0	0	.063	4	0	0	1.000
Major League Totals—2 Years				32	82	6	9	1	0	1	5	.110	125	5	3	.977

Selected by Boston Red Sox' organization in 1st round (20th player selected) of free-agent draft, January 13, 1981.
†On disabled list, May 3 to May 14, 1982.
‡Granted free agency, October 15, 1988; signed by Colorado Springs (Cleveland Indians' organization), November 15, 1988.
§Granted free agency, October 15, 1989; signed by Buffalo (Pittsburgh Pirates' organization), November 25, 1989.

LARRY KENT SHEETS

Born December 6, 1959, at Staunton, Va.
Height, 6.03. Weight, 236.
Throws right and bats lefthanded.
Received degree in health and physical education from
Eastern Mennonite College, Harrisonburg, Va. in 1986.

Major League stolen bases: 1986 (2), 1987 (1), 1988 (1), 1989 (1). Total—5.
Led International League outfielders in double plays with 5 in 1984.

Year	Club	League	Pos.	G.	AB.	R.	H.	2B.	3B.	HR.	RBI.	B.A.	PO.	A.	E.	F.A.
1978—Bluefield		Appal.	OF-1B	67	225	32	60	9	2	11	*48	.267	121	8	4	.970
1979—Miami†		Fla. St.					(Did not play)									
1979—Bluefield		Appal.	OF	3	12	2	4	2	0	0	2	.333	1	0	0	1.000
1980—Bluefield‡		Appal.	OF	37	124	29	47	9	1	*14	47	.379	40	3	2	.956
1980—Charlotte		South.	OF	13	48	1	9	4	0	0	5	.188	4	1	0	1.000
1981—Rochester§		Int.					(Did not play)									
1982—Rochester x		Int.					(Did not play)									
1982—Hagerstown y		Carol.	OF	88	324	46	96	21	0	18	59	.296	123	5	6	.955
1983—Charlotte		South.	OF-1B	138	503	72	145	*37	3	●25	87	.288	256	15	7	.975
1983—Rochester		Int.	OF	3	13	1	2	1	0	0	2	.154	5	0	1	.833
1984—Rochester		Int.	OF	134	431	76	130	26	4	13	67	.302	201	*19	2	.991
1984—Baltimore		Amer.	OF	8	16	3	7	1	0	1	2	.438	12	1	0	1.000
1985—Baltimore		Amer.	OF-1B	113	328	43	86	8	0	17	50	.262	12	1	1	.929
1986—Baltimore z		Amer.	O-1-3-C	112	338	42	92	17	1	18	60	.272	90	8	3	.970
1987—Baltimore		Amer.	OF-1B	135	469	74	148	23	0	31	94	.316	243	7	7	.973
1988—Baltimore		Amer.	OF-1B	136	452	38	104	19	1	10	47	.230	159	12	4	.977
1989—Baltimore		Amer.	DH	102	304	33	74	12	1	7	33	.243	0	0	0	.000
Major League Totals—6 Years				606	1907	233	511	80	3	84	286	.268	516	29	15	.973

Selected by Baltimore Orioles' organization in 2nd round of free-agent draft, June 6, 1978.
†On suspended list, May 1 to August 29, 1979.

‡On restricted list, June 18 to June 23, 1980.
§On restricted list, April 14 to May 28 and June 18, 1981 through remainder of season.
xOn suspended list, April 13, 1982; then transferred to restricted list, April 23 to May 13, 1982.
yOn disabled list, August 23, 1982 through remainder of season.
zOn disabled list, June 30 to July 17, 1986.

GARY ANTONIAN SHEFFIELD

Born November 18, 1968, at Tampa, Fla.
Height, 5.11. Weight, 190.
Throws and bats righthanded.
Nephew of Dwight Gooden, pitcher with New York Mets.

Major League stolen bases: 1988 (3), 1989 (10). Total—13.
Led California League shortstops in double plays with 77 in 1987.
Led Pioneer League shortstops in double plays with 34 in 1986.
Named Minor League co-Player of the Year by THE SPORTING NEWS, 1988.

Year Club	League	Pos.	G.	AB.	R.	H.	2B.	3B.	HR.	RBI.	B.A.	PO.	A.	E.	F.A.
1986—Helena	Pion.	SS	57	222	53	81	12	2	15	*71	.365	97	149	24	.911
1987—Stockton	Calif.	SS	129	469	84	130	23	3	17	*103	.277	235	345	39	.937
1988—El Paso	Texas	SS-3B-OF	77	296	70	93	19	3	19	65	.314	130	206	23	.936
1988—Denver	A. A.	3B-SS	57	212	42	73	9	5	9	54	.344	54	97	8	.950
1988—Milwaukee	Amer.	SS	24	80	12	19	1	0	4	12	.238	39	48	3	.967
1989—Milwaukee†	Amer.	SS-3B	95	368	34	91	18	0	5	32	.247	100	238	16	.955
1989—Denver	A. A.	SS	7	29	3	4	1	1	0	0	.138	2	6	0	1.000
Major League Totals—2 Years			119	448	46	110	19	0	9	44	.246	139	286	19	.957

Selected by Milwaukee Brewers' organization in 1st round (sixth player selected) of free-agent draft, June 2, 1986.
†On disabled list, July 14 to September 9, 1989.

JOHN T. SHELBY

Born February 23, 1958, at Lexington, Ky.
Height, 6.01. Weight, 175.
Throws right and bats right and lefthanded.
Attended Columbia State Community College, Columbia, Tenn.

Holds National League record for most strikeouts by switch-hitter, season (128), 1988.
Major League stolen bases: 1981 (2), 1983 (15), 1984 (12), 1985 (5), 1986 (18), 1987 (16), 1988 (16), 1989 (10). Total—94
Led Florida State League outfielders in double plays with 7 in 1979.
Led Appalachian League outfielders in double plays with 3 in 1978.

Year Club	League	Pos.	G.	AB.	R.	H.	2B.	3B.	HR.	RBI.	B.A.	PO.	A.	E.	F.A.
1977—Bluefield	Appal.	OF	60	211	28	54	9	1	0	1	.256	90	●12	7	.936
1978—Miami	Fla. St.	OF	13	26	4	6	1	0	0	3	.231	14	2	2	.889
1978—Bluefield	Appal.	OF	64	248	49	70	9	1	6	25	.282	128	*11	6	.959
1979—Miami	Fla. St.	OF	132	478	50	96	11	6	3	38	.201	*252	●22	8	.972
1980—Charlotte	South.	OF	134	*560	66	135	27	11	6	51	.241	*361	21	*16	.960
1981—Charlotte	South.	OF	62	251	40	59	11	4	2	21	.235	120	3	10	.925
1981—Rochester	Int.	OF	76	326	42	86	21	8	3	32	.264	189	8	6	.970
1981—Baltimore	Amer.	OF	7	2	2	0	0	0	0	0	.000	1	0	0	1.000
1982—Rochester	Int.	OF	133	*548	92	153	26	6	16	52	.279	331	13	8	.977
1982—Baltimore	Amer.	OF	26	35	8	11	3	0	1	2	.314	20	1	0	1.000
1983—Baltimore	Amer.	OF	126	325	52	84	15	2	5	27	.258	200	9	4	.981
1984—Baltimore	Amer.	OF	128	383	44	80	12	5	6	30	.209	261	9	2	.993
1985—Rochester	Int.	OF	52	206	31	59	16	4	8	21	.286	124	4	1	.992
1985—Baltimore	Amer.	OF-2B	69	205	28	58	6	2	7	27	.283	148	4	3	.981
1986—Baltimore	Amer.	OF	135	404	54	92	14	4	11	49	.228	222	5	5	.978
1987—Baltimore	Amer.	OF	21	32	4	6	0	0	1	3	.188	25	0	0	1.000
1987—Rochester†	Int.	OF	6	24	5	6	2	0	1	2	.250	14	0	0	1.000
1987—Los Angeles	Nat.	OF	120	476	61	132	26	0	21	69	.277	269	9	8	.972
1988—Los Angeles‡	Nat.	OF	140	494	65	130	23	6	10	64	.263	329	7	6	.982
1989—Los Angeles	Nat.	OF	108	345	28	63	11	1	1	12	.183	220	3	2	.991
1989—Albuquerque§	P. C.	OF	32	126	20	36	7	3	4	21	.286	75	2	1	.987
American League Totals—7 Years			512	1386	192	331	50	13	31	138	.239	877	28	14	.985
National League Totals—3 Years			368	1315	154	325	60	7	32	145	.247	818	19	16	.981
Major League Totals—9 Years			880	2701	346	656	110	20	63	283	.243	1695	47	30	.983

Selected by Baltimore Orioles' organization in 1st round (19th player selected) of free-agent draft, January 11, 1977.
†Traded with Pitcher Brad Havens to Los Angeles Dodgers for Pitcher Tom Niedenfuer, May 22, 1987.
‡On disabled list, April 22 to May 12, 1988.
§Granted free agency, November 13, 1989; re-signed by Dodgers, December 19, 1989.

CHAMPIONSHIP SERIES RECORD

Shares Championship Series record for most strikeouts, series (12), 1988.

Year Club	League	Pos.	G.	AB.	R.	H.	2B.	3B.	HR.	RBI.	B.A.	PO.	A.	E.	F.A.
1983—Baltimore	Amer.	OF-PH	3	9	1	2	0	0	0	0	.222	3	0	0	1.000
1988—Los Angeles	Nat.	OF	7	24	3	4	0	0	0	3	.167	19	0	0	1.000
Championship Series Totals—2 Years			10	33	4	6	0	0	0	3	.182	22	0	0	1.000

WORLD SERIES RECORD

Year Club	League	Pos.	G.	AB.	R.	H.	2B.	3B.	HR.	RBI.	B.A.	PO.	A.	E.	F.A.
1983—Baltimore	Amer.	PH-OF	5	9	1	4	0	0	0	1	.444	10	0	0	1.000
1988—Los Angeles	Nat.	OF	5	18	0	4	1	0	0	1	.222	14	0	0	1.000
World Series Totals—2 Years			10	27	1	8	1	0	0	2	.296	24	0	0	1.000

PATRICK ARTHUR SHERIDAN
(Pat)

Born December 4, 1957, at Ann Arbor, Mich.
Height, 6.03. Weight, 175.
Throws right and bats lefthanded.
Attended Eastern Michigan University, Ypsilanti, Mich.
Son of Arthur Sheridan, minor league pitcher, 1952 through 1956.

Major League stolen bases: 1983 (12), 1984 (19), 1985 (11), 1986 (9), 1987 (18), 1988 (8), 1989 (8). Total—85.

Year Club	League	Pos.	G.	AB.	R.	H.	2B.	3B.	HR.	RBI.	B.A.	PO.	A.	E.	F.A.
1979—Fort Myers	Fla. St.	OF	67	235	25	66	4	3	0	16	.281	142	8	1	.993
1980—Fort Myers	Fla. St.	OF-C	20	79	17	32	1	0	1	13	.405	37	4	1	.976
1980—Jacksonville†	South.	OF	97	367	63	112	17	7	5	42	.305	201	7	9	.959
1981—Omaha‡	A. A.	OF	86	315	49	94	15	8	5	31	.298	193	2	3	.985
1981—Kansas City	Amer.	OF	3	1	0	0	0	0	0	0	.000	2	0	0	1.000
1982—Omaha§	A. A.	OF	41	135	8	34	8	1	0	13	.252	92	3	0	1.000
1983—Omaha	A. A.	OF	20	75	16	23	4	5	4	14	.307	53	2	0	1.000
1983—Kansas City	Amer.	OF	109	333	43	90	12	2	7	36	.270	237	6	3	.988
1984—Kansas City	Amer.	OF	138	481	64	136	24	4	8	53	.283	273	8	4	.986
1985—Kansas City x	Amer.	OF	78	206	18	47	9	2	3	17	.228	116	3	2	.983
1985—Omaha y	A. A.	OF	8	28	1	10	1	0	0	1	.357	8	1	0	1.000
1986—Nashville	A. A.	OF	9	35	4	10	2	0	1	5	.286	16	0	0	1.000
1986—Detroit	Amer.	OF	98	236	41	56	9	1	6	19	.237	172	1	4	.977
1987—Detroit	Amer.	OF	141	421	57	109	19	3	6	49	.259	236	6	6	.976
1988—Detroit	Amer.	OF	127	347	47	88	9	5	11	47	.254	203	2	4	.981
1989—Detroit z	Amer.	OF	50	120	16	29	3	0	3	15	.242	52	2	1	.982
1989—San Francisco a	Nat.	OF	70	161	20	33	3	4	3	14	.205	111	2	2	.983
American League Totals—8 Years			744	2145	286	555	85	17	44	236	.259	1291	28	24	.982
National League Totals—1 Year			70	161	20	33	3	4	3	14	.205	111	2	2	.983
Major League Totals—8 Years			814	2306	306	588	88	21	47	250	.255	1402	30	26	.982

Selected by Cincinnati Reds' organization in 36th round of free-agent draft, June 8, 1976.
Selected by Kansas City Royals' organization in 3rd round of free-agent draft, June 5, 1979.
†On disabled list, May 16 to June 2, 1980.
‡On disabled list, May 25 to June 25, 1981.
§On disabled list, April 27 to June 25 and June 27 to July 19, 1982.
xOn disabled list, June 19 to July 4 and August 5 to September 3, 1985; included rehabilitation disability assignment to Omaha, August 26 to September 3, 1985.
yReleased, March 28, 1986; signed by Detroit Tigers, April 25, 1986.
zTraded to San Francisco Giants for Outfielder Tracy Jones, June 18, 1989.
aGranted free agency, November 13, 1989.

CHAMPIONSHIP SERIES RECORD

Shares Championship Series records for most times hit by pitch, series (2), 1987 and game (2), October 12, 1987.

Year Club	League	Pos.	G.	AB.	R.	H.	2B.	3B.	HR.	RBI.	B.A.	PO.	A.	E.	F.A.
1984—Kansas City	Amer.	OF	3	6	1	0	0	0	0	0	.000	9	0	1	.900
1985—Kansas City	Amer.	OF-PH	7	20	4	3	0	0	2	3	.150	13	0	0	1.000
1987—Detroit	Amer.	OF-PR	5	10	2	3	1	0	1	2	.300	7	1	0	1.000
1989—San Francisco	Nat.	OF	5	13	1	2	0	1	0	0	.154	9	1	0	1.000
Championship Series Totals—4 Years			20	49	8	8	1	1	3	5	.163	38	2	1	.976

WORLD SERIES RECORD

Year Club	League	Pos.	G.	AB.	R.	H.	2B.	3B.	HR.	RBI.	B.A.	PO.	A.	E.	F.A.
1985—Kansas City	Amer.	PH-OF	5	18	0	4	2	0	0	1	.222	6	0	0	1.000
1989—San Francisco	Nat.	OF	1	2	0	0	0	0	0	0	.000	0	0	0	.000
World Series Totals—2 Years			6	20	0	4	2	0	0	1	.200	6	0	0	1.000

STEPHEN MACK SHIELDS
(Steve)

Born November 30, 1958, in Etowah County, Ala.
Height, 6.05. Weight, 230.
Throws and bats righthanded.

Major League saves: 1987 (3).
Tied for International League lead in shutouts with 3 and hit batsmen with 8 in 1985.
Tied for Eastern League lead in complete games with 13 and shutouts with 3 in 1982.
Tied for Eastern League lead in intentional bases on balls issued with 10 in 1981.

Year Club	League	G.	IP.	W.	L.	Pct.	H.	R.	ER.	SO.	BB.	ERA.
1977—Elmira	NYP	15	81	1	6	.143	72	45	37	108	37	4.11
1978—Winter Haven†	Florida St.	14	51	3	3	.500	52	14	11	34	9	1.94
1979—Winston-Salem	Carolina	24	152	11	8	.579	149	78	51	152	80	3.02
1980—Bristol	Eastern	39	113	5	6	.455	128	79	61	63	77	4.86
1981—Bristol	Eastern	29	126	5	*14	.263	136	75	65	87	65	4.64
1982—Bristol	Eastern	29	170⅓	10	13	.435	172	100	67	125	71	3.54
1983—Pawtucket‡	Int'national	36	143	4	12	.250	171	94	74	115	63	4.66
1984—Richmond	Int'national	39	110	9	4	.692	122	69	58	101	39	4.75
1985—Richmond	Int'national	18	133	6	7	.462	110	53	39	88	54	2.64
1985—Atlanta	National	23	68	1	2	.333	86	46	39	29	32	5.16
1986—Richmond	Int'national	21	149⅓	9	8	.529	133	55	43	●124	55	2.59
1986—Atlanta§	National	6	12⅔	0	0	.000	13	10	10	6	7	7.11

Year Club	League	G.	IP.	W.	L.	Pct.	H.	R.	ER.	SO.	BB.	ERA.
1986—Kansas City x	American	3	8⅔	0	0	.000	3	3	2	2	4	2.08
1987—Seattle y	American	20	30	2	0	1.000	43	25	22	22	12	6.60
1987—Calgary z	P. Coast	16	24	3	2	.600	16	7	6	15	11	2.25
1988—Columbus	Int'national	17	25	0	1	.000	28	7	7	23	6	2.52
1988—New York a	American	39	82⅓	5	5	.500	96	44	40	55	30	4.37
1989—Portland	P. Coast	9	20	2	2	.500	23	13	11	18	7	4.95
1989—Minnesota bc	American	11	17⅓	0	1	.000	28	18	15	12	6	7.79
National League Totals—2 Years		29	80⅔	1	2	.333	99	56	49	35	39	5.47
American League Totals—4 Years		73	138⅓	7	6	.538	170	90	79	91	52	5.14
Major League Totals—5 Years		102	219	8	8	.500	269	146	128	126	91	5.26

Selected by Boston Red Sox' organization in 10th round of free-agent draft, June 7, 1977.
†On disabled list, April 10 to June 14, 1978.
‡Granted free agency, October 20, 1983; signed by Richmond (Atlanta Braves' organization), October 26, 1983.
§Traded to Kansas City Royals for Outfielder Darryl Motley, September 23, 1986.
xTraded with Pitcher Scott Bankhead and Outfielder Mike Kingery to Seattle Mariners for Outfielder Danny Tartabull and Pitcher Rick Luecken, December 19, 1986.
yOn disabled list, April 12 to May 12, 1987.
zGranted free agency, October 15, 1987; signed by New York Yankees, November 11, 1987.
aTraded to Minnesota Twins for Pitcher Balvino Galvez, March 20, 1989.
bOn disabled list, June 20, 1989 through remainder of season.
cReleased, October 3, 1989.

ZAKARY SEBASTIEN SHINALL
(Zak)

Born October 14, 1968, at St. Louis, Mo.
Height, 6.04. Weight, 220.
Throws and bats righthanded.
Attended El Camino College, Torrance, Calif.

Year Club	League	G.	IP.	W.	L.	Pct.	H.	R.	ER.	SO.	BB.	ERA.
1987—Sarasota Dodgers	Gulf Coast	8	30⅓	1	2	.333	29	17	17	29	15	5.04
1988—Bakersfield	California	28	113	7	8	.467	90	65	53	63	104	4.22
1989—Vero Beach	Florida St.	47	86	5	7	.417	71	32	24	69	29	2.51

Selected by Los Angeles Dodgers' organization in 29th round of free-agent draft, June 2, 1987.

CRAIG BARRY SHIPLEY

Born January 7, 1963, at Parramatta, Australia.
Height, 6.00. Weight, 170.
Throws and bats righthanded.
Attended University of Alabama, University, Ala.

Year Club	League	Pos.	G.	AB.	R.	H.	2B.	3B.	HR.	RBI.	B.A.	PO.	A.	E.	F.A.
1984—Vero Beach	Fla. St.	SS	85	293	56	82	11	2	0	28	.280	137	216	17	.954
1985—Albuquerque†	P. C.	SS	124	414	50	100	9	2	0	30	.242	202	367	21	.964
1986—Albuquerque†‡	P. C.	SS	61	203	33	59	8	2	0	16	.291	99	173	18	.938
1986—Los Angeles	Nat.	SS-2B-3B	12	27	3	3	1	0	0	4	.111	16	18	3	.919
1987—Albuquerque†	P. C.	SS	49	139	17	31	6	1	1	15	.223	70	101	9	.950
1987—San Antonio	Texas	3B	33	127	14	30	5	3	2	9	.236	19	56	3	.962
1987—Los Angeles§	Nat.	SS-3B	26	35	3	9	1	0	0	2	.257	15	28	3	.935
1988—Jackson	Texas	SS	89	335	41	88	14	3	6	41	.263	141	266	16	.962
1988—Tidewater	Int.	2B-SS-3B	40	151	12	41	5	0	1	13	.272	54	110	2	.988
1989—Tidewater†	Int.	SS-3B-2B	44	131	6	27	1	0	2	9	.206	48	110	6	.963
1989—New York	Nat.	SS-3B	4	7	3	1	0	0	0	0	.143	0	4	0	1.000
Major League Totals—3 Years			42	69	9	13	2	0	0	6	.188	31	50	6	.931

Signed as a free agent by Los Angeles Dodgers' organization, May 28, 1984.
†Switch-hitter.
‡On disabled list, May 5 to June 6, 1986.
§Traded to New York Mets for Catcher John Gibbons, April 1, 1988.

ERIC VAUGHN SHOW
Name rhymes with Chow.

Born May 19, 1956, at Riverside, Calif.
Height, 6.01. Weight, 182.
Throws and bats righthanded.
Attended University of California, Riverside, Calif.

Major League saves: 1981 (3), 1982 (3). Total—6.
Led Texas League in hit batsmen with 10 in 1980.

Year Club	League	G.	IP.	W.	L.	Pct.	H.	R.	ER.	SO.	BB.	ERA.
1978—Walla Walla	Northwest	11	60	5	2	.714	47	28	19	43	20	2.85
1979—Reno	California	28	169	13	9	.591	144	79	67	186	92	3.57
1980—Amarillo	Texas	26	166	12	6	.667	141	81	69	144	81	3.74
1981—Hawaii	P. Coast	34	85	7	3	.700	67	30	24	70	35	2.54
1981—San Diego	National	15	23	1	3	.250	17	9	8	22	9	3.13
1982—San Diego	National	47	150	10	6	.625	117	49	44	88	48	2.64
1983—San Diego	National	35	200⅔	15	12	.556	201	97	93	120	74	4.17
1984—San Diego	National	32	206⅔	15	9	.625	175	88	78	104	88	3.40
1985—San Diego	National	35	233	12	11	.522	212	95	80	141	87	3.09

Year	Club	League	G.	IP.	W.	L.	Pct.	H.	R.	ER.	SO.	BB.	ERA.
1986—San Diego†	National	24	136⅓	9	5	.643	109	47	45	94	69	2.97
1987—San Diego	National	34	206⅓	8	16	.333	188	99	88	117	85	3.84
1988—San Diego	National	32	234⅔	16	11	.593	201	86	85	144	53	3.26
1989—San Diego‡	National	16	106⅓	8	6	.571	113	59	50	66	39	4.23
Major League Totals—9 Years		270	1497	94	79	.543	1333	629	571	896	552	3.43

Selected by Minnesota Twins' organization in 36th round of free-agent draft, June 5, 1974.
Selected by San Diego Padres' organization in 18th round of free-agent draft, June 6, 1978.
†On disabled list, July 8 to July 31 and August 28, 1986 through remainder of season.
‡On disabled list, July 6, 1989 through remainder of season.

CHAMPIONSHIP SERIES RECORD

Year	Club	League	G.	IP.	W.	L.	Pct.	H.	R.	ER.	SO.	BB.	ERA.
1984—San Diego	National	2	5⅓	0	1	.000	8	8	8	2	4	13.50

WORLD SERIES RECORD

Year	Club	League	G.	IP.	W.	L.	Pct.	H.	R.	ER.	SO.	BB.	ERA.
1984—San Diego	National	1	2⅔	0	1	.000	4	4	3	2	1	10.13

TERRANCE DARNELL SHUMPERT
(Terry)

Born August 16, 1966, at Paducah, Ky.
Height, 6.01. Weight, 190.
Throws and bats righthanded.
Attended University of Kentucky, Lexington, Ky.

Year	Club	League	Pos.	G.	AB.	R.	H.	2B.	3B.	HR.	RBI.	B.A.	PO.	A.	E.	F.A.
1987—Eugene	N'west	2B	48	186	38	54	16	1	4	22	.290	81	107	11	.945
1988—Appleton	Midw.	2B-OF	114	422	64	102	★37	2	7	38	.242	235	266	20	.962
1989—Omaha	A. A.	2B	113	355	54	88	29	2	4	22	.248	218	295	★22	.959

Selected by Kansas City Royals' organization in 2nd round of free-agent draft, June 2, 1987.

RUBEN ANGEL SIERRA (GARCIA)

Born October 6, 1965, at Rio Piedras, Puerto Rico.
Height, 6.01. Weight, 195.
Throws right and bats left and righthanded.

Major League stolen bases: 1986 (7), 1987 (16), 1988 (18), 1989 (8). Total—49.
Switch-hit home runs in one game, September 13, 1986, August 27, 1988 and June 8, 1989.
Led American League in total bases with 344 and slugging percentage with .543 in 1989.
Led American League in sacrifice flies with 12 in 1987.
Led American League outfielders in double plays with 6 in 1987.
Named American League Player of the Year by THE SPORTING NEWS, 1989.
Named outfielder on THE SPORTING NEWS American League All-Star Team, 1989.
Named outfielder on THE SPORTING NEWS American League Silver Slugger team, 1989.

Year	Club	League	Pos.	G.	AB.	R.	H.	2B.	3B.	HR.	RBI.	B.A.	PO.	A.	E.	F.A.
1983—Sarasota Ran.†	Gulf C.	OF	48	182	26	44	7	3	1	26	.242	67	6	4	.948
1984—Burlington	Midw.	OF	●138	482	55	127	33	5	6	75	.263	239	18	★20	.928
1985—Tulsa	Texas	OF	★137	★545	63	138	34	★8	13	74	.253	234	12	★15	.943
1986—Oklahoma City	A. A.	OF	46	189	31	56	11	2	9	41	.296	114	4	2	.983
1986—Texas	Amer.	OF	113	382	50	101	13	10	16	55	.264	200	7	6	.972
1987—Texas	Amer.	OF	158	★643	97	169	35	4	30	109	.263	272	●17	11	.963
1988—Texas	Amer.	OF	156	615	77	156	32	2	23	91	.254	310	11	7	.979
1989—Texas	Amer.	OF	●162	634	101	194	35	★14	29	★119	.306	313	13	9	.973
Major League Totals—4 Years		589	2274	325	620	115	30	98	374	.273	1095	48	33	.972

Signed as free agent by Texas Rangers' organization, November 21, 1982.
†Batted righthanded only.

ALL-STAR GAME RECORD

Year	League	Pos.	AB.	R.	H.	2B.	3B.	HR.	RBI.	B.A.	PO.	A.	E.	F.A.
1989—American		OF	3	1	2	0	0	0	1	.667	1	0	0	1.000

MICHAEL HOWARD SIMMS
(Mike)

Born January 12, 1967, at Orange, Calif.
Height, 6.04. Weight, 185.
Throws and bats righthanded.

Led South Atlantic League batters in total bases with 264 and strikeouts with 167 in 1987.
Led South Atlantic League first basemen in total chances with 1,158 in 1987.

Year	Club	League	Pos.	G.	AB.	R.	H.	2B.	3B.	HR.	RBI.	B.A.	PO.	A.	E.	F.A.
1985—Sarasota Astros	Gulf C.	1B	21	70	10	19	2	1	3	18	.271	186	7	5	.975
1986—Sarasota Astros	Gulf C.	1B	54	181	33	47	14	1	4	37	.260	433	28	7	.985
1987—Asheville	S. Atl.	★1B-3B	133	469	93	128	19	0	★39	100	.273	★1089	52	★19	.984
1988—Osceola	Fla. St.	1B	123	428	63	104	19	1	16	73	.243	1143	41	22	.982
1989—Columbus	South.	1B	109	378	64	97	21	3	20	81	.257	938	44	10	.990

Selected by Houston Astros' organization in 6th round of free-agent draft, June 3, 1985.

MATTHEW STEPHEN SINATRO
(Matt)

Born March 22, 1960, at West Hartford, Conn.
Height, 5.09. Weight, 174.
Throws and bats righthanded.

Major League stolen bases: 1981 (1).
Tied for Western Carolinas League lead in caught stealing with 15 in 1979.
Led Southern League catchers in total chances with 537 in 1984.
Led International League catchers in total chances with 710 in 1983.
Led Southern League catchers in double plays with 10 in 1980.

Year Club	League	Pos.	G.	AB.	R.	H.	2B.	3B.	HR.	RBI.	B.A.	PO.	A.	E.	F.A.
1978—Kingsport...............	Appal.	C	35	112	15	23	7	0	0	6	.205	198	26	2	.991
1979—Greenwood...........	W. Car.	C	120	385	54	97	16	4	7	57	.252	639	69	11	.985
1980—Savannah...............	South.	C	122	449	76	125	16	1	11	50	.278	514	70	15	.975
1981—Richmond..............	Int.	C	121	430	43	101	13	2	6	53	.235	738	78	12	.986
1981—Atlanta	Nat.	C	12	32	4	9	1	1	0	4	.281	56	10	0	1.000
1982—Atlanta	Nat.	C	37	81	10	11	2	0	1	4	.136	112	25	0	1.000
1982—Richmond..............	Int.	C	72	246	39	62	7	1	8	29	.252	423	53	5	.990
1983—Richmond..............	Int.	C	110	365	36	77	11	1	4	41	.211	★642	60	8	.989
1983—Atlanta	Nat.	C	7	12	0	2	0	0	0	2	.167	24	5	1	.967
1984—Atlanta	Nat.	C	2	4	0	0	0	0	0	0	.000	4	0	0	1.000
1984—Greenville†............	South.	C	101	352	36	80	16	1	5	49	.227	★466	●64	7	.987
1985—Greenville	South.	C	49	172	25	48	4	1	6	28	.279	265	49	7	.978
1985—Richmond‡............	Int.	C	24	67	7	19	3	0	1	8	.284	89	8	3	.970
1986—Richmond§x	Int.	C-3B	28	66	8	13	2	0	2	7	.197	124	18	2	.986
1986—Buffalo y	A. A.	C	11	32	4	8	3	0	0	3	.250	60	7	4	.944
1987—Tacoma................	P. C.	C-3B-OF	79	215	30	54	13	0	5	32	.251	370	50	12	.972
1987—Oakland z..............	Amer.	C	6	3	0	0	0	0	0	0	.000	4	0	0	1.000
1988—Tacoma................	P. C.	C-OF	77	234	28	54	8	1	2	23	.231	361	48	7	.983
1988—Oakland ab............	Amer.	C	10	9	1	3	2	0	0	5	.333	21	2	0	1.000
1989—Tuc.cd-Cal.	P. C.	C	46	128	13	33	6	0	0	12	.258	224	28	6	.977
1989—Detroit...................	Amer.	C	13	25	2	3	0	0	0	1	.120	42	2	0	1.000
National League Totals—4 Years............			58	129	14	22	3	1	1	10	.171	196	40	1	.996
American League Totals—3 Years..........			29	37	3	6	2	0	0	6	.162	67	4	0	1.000
Major League Totals—7 Years................			87	166	17	28	5	1	1	16	.169	263	44	1	.997

Selected by Atlanta Braves' organization in 2nd round of free-agent draft, June 6, 1978.
†Granted free agency, October 15, 1984; re-signed by Atlanta Braves' organization, December 11, 1984.
‡On disabled list, July 2 to August 1, 1985.
§On suspended list, July 6 to August 15, 1986.
xReleased, August 15, 1986; signed by Buffalo (Chicago White Sox' organization), August 20, 1986.
yGranted free agency, October 15, 1986; signed by Tacoma (Oakland Athletics' organization), April 1, 1987.
zReleased, October 15, 1987; re-signed by Athletics' organization, January 5, 1988.
aOn disabled list, August 19 to September 3, 1988.
bTraded to Tucson (Houston Astros' organization) for Catcher-Outfielder Troy Afenir, April 6, 1989.
cSold to Detroit Tigers, June 19, 1989.
dSold to Calgary (Seattle Mariners' organization), August 5, 1989.

JOSEPH DOUGLAS SKALSKI
(Joe)

Born September 26, 1964, at Chicago, Ill.
Height, 6.03. Weight, 190.
Throws and bats righthanded.
Attended St. Xavier College, Chicago, Ill.

Led Pacific Coast League in home runs allowed with 30 and wild pitches with 14 in 1988.

Year Club	League	G.	IP.	W.	L.	Pct.	H.	R.	ER.	SO.	BB.	ERA.
1986—Batavia.............................	NYP	14	104⅔	7	6	.538	79	34	23	★130	29	1.98
1986—Waterloo...........................	Midwest	2	12⅔	2	0	1.000	15	8	8	16	1	5.68
1987—Williamsport†...................	Eastern	18	113⅔	8	7	.533	105	62	53	76	35	4.20
1987—Buffalo.............................	Am. Assoc.	5	18⅔	0	3	.000	30	21	21	18	12	10.13
1988—Colorado Springs..............	P. Coast	29	159½	10	13	.435	186	★125	★116	117	64	6.55
1989—Cleveland.........................	American	2	6⅔	0	2	.000	7	6	5	3	4	6.75
1989—Colorado Springs..............	P. Coast	10	44⅓	2	6	.250	43	30	29	32	25	5.89
Major League Totals—1 Year.............................		2	6⅔	0	2	.000	7	6	5	3	4	6.75

Selected by Cleveland Indians' organization in 3rd round of free-agent draft, June 2, 1986.
†On disabled list, June 21 to July 17, 1987.

JOEL PATRICK SKINNER

Born February 21, 1961, at La Jolla, Calif.
Height, 6.04. Weight, 205.
Throws and bats righthanded.
Attended San Diego Mesa College, San Diego, Calif.
Son of Bob Skinner, outfielder-first baseman with Pittsburgh Pirates, Cincinnati Reds and St. Louis
Cardinals, 1954 through 1966; manager, Philadelphia Phillies, 1968 and 1969, manager,
San Diego Padres, 1977; coach, San Diego Padres, 1977; coach, California Angels, 1978;
coach with Pittsburgh Pirates, 1979 through 1985; and coach with Atlanta Braves, 1986 through May 22, 1988.

Major League stolen bases: 1984 (1), 1986 (1), 1989 (1). Total—3.
Led American Association batters in strikeouts with 115 and tied for lead in grounding into double plays with 16 in 1985.
Led American Association catchers in total chances with 698 and double plays with 13 in 1985.
Tied for South Atlantic League lead in double plays by catchers with 7 in 1980.

Year Club League	Pos.	G.	AB.	R.	H.	2B.	3B.	HR.	RBI.	B.A.	PO.	A.	E.	F.A.
1980—Shelby.................... S. Atl.	C	100	324	36	73	15	2	7	27	.225	536	63	18	.971
1981—Greenwood†‡........ S. Atl.	C	117	428	48	114	25	2	11	63	.266	766	42	*22	.974
1982—Glens Falls............ East.	C	120	422	49	107	11	6	7	65	.254	726	80	12	.985
1983—Denver .... A. A.	C	108	361	55	94	15	5	12	50	.260	550	54	5	.992
1983—Chicago .... Amer.	C	6	11	2	3	0	0	0	1	.273	20	4	1	.960
1984—Denver§ .... A. A.	C	42	141	27	40	6	0	10	27	.284	255	24	5	.982
1984—Chicago .... Amer.	C	43	80	4	17	2	0	0	3	.213	171	11	2	.989
1985—Buffalo .... A. A.	C	115	390	47	94	13	0	12	59	.241	*623	*65	10	.986
1985—Chicago .... Amer.	C	22	44	9	15	4	1	1	5	.341	94	8	3	.971
1986—Chi. x-N.Y. .... Amer.	C	114	315	23	73	9	1	5	37	.232	507	37	9	.984
1987—New York .... Amer.	C	64	139	9	19	4	0	3	14	.137	232	18	4	.984
1987—Columbus.............. Int.	C	49	178	19	43	10	2	6	27	.242	226	25	4	.984
1988—New York .... Amer.	C-OF-1B	88	251	23	57	15	0	4	23	.227	396	16	4	.990
1989—Cleveland y .... Amer.	C	79	178	10	41	10	0	1	13	.230	280	22	3	.990
Major League Totals—7 Years................		416	1018	80	225	44	2	14	96	.221	1700	116	26	.986

Selected by Pittsburgh Pirates' organization in 36th round of free-agent draft, June 5, 1979.
†On disabled list, June 1 to June 13, 1981.
‡Selected by Chicago White Sox' organization in player compensation pool draft, February 2, 1982. (Chicago received compensation for Philadelphia Phillies' signing of free agent Pitcher Ed Farmer, a Type A player, January 28, 1982.)
§On disabled list, July 23, 1984 through remainder of season.
xTraded with Outfielder-Designated Hitter Ron Kittle and Infielder Wayne Tolleson to New York Yankees for Catcher Ron Hassey, Shortstop Carlos Martinez and a player to be named later, July 30, 1986; New York traded Catcher Bill Lindsey to Chicago White Sox' organization to complete deal, December 24, 1986.
yTraded with Outfielder Turner Ward to Cleveland Indians for Outfielder Mel Hall, March 19, 1989.

DONALD MARTIN SLAUGHT
(Don)

Born September 11, 1958, at Long Beach, Calif.
Height, 6.01. Weight, 190.
Throws and bats righthanded.
Attended El Camino College, Torrance, Calif., and received bachelor of science degree in economics from UCLA in 1983.
Major League stolen bases: 1983 (3), 1985 (5), 1986 (3), 1988 (1), 1989 (1). Total—13.

Year Club League	Pos.	G.	AB.	R.	H.	2B.	3B.	HR.	RBI.	B.A.	PO.	A.	E.	F.A.
1980—Fort Myers......... Fla. St.	C	50	176	13	46	9	0	2	16	.261	175	34	4	.981
1981—Jacksonville......... South.	C-1B	96	379	45	127	21	2	6	44	.335	482	61	9	.984
1981—Omaha†................. A. A.	C	22	71	10	21	4	0	2	8	.296	91	7	3	.970
1982—Omaha‡................. A. A.	C	53	206	29	55	10	1	4	16	.267	216	25	5	.980
1982—Kansas City .... Amer.	C	43	115	14	32	6	0	3	8	.278	156	7	1	.994
1983—Kansas City§ .... Amer.	C	83	276	21	86	13	4	0	28	.312	299	18	12	.964
1984—Kansas City x ...... Amer.	C	124	409	48	108	27	4	4	42	.264	547	44	11	.982
1985—Texas y .... Amer.	C	102	343	34	96	17	4	8	35	.280	550	33	6	.990
1986—Texas z .... Amer.	C	95	314	39	83	17	1	13	46	.264	533	40	4	.993
1986—Oklahoma City ..... A. A.	C	3	12	2	4	1	0	0	1	.333	6	1	0	1.000
1987—Texas a................. Amer.	C	95	237	25	53	15	2	8	16	.224	429	39	7	.985
1988—New York b .... Amer.	C	97	322	33	91	25	1	9	43	.283	496	24	•11	.979
1989—New York c .... Amer.	C	117	350	34	88	21	3	5	38	.251	493	44	5	.991
Major League Totals—8 Years................		756	2366	248	637	141	19	50	256	.269	3503	249	57	.985

Selected by Milwaukee Brewers' organization in 19th round of free-agent draft, June 5, 1979.
Selected by Kansas City Royals' organization in 7th round of free-agent draft, June 3, 1980.
†On disabled list, August 16 to September 29, 1981.
‡On disabled list, April 21 to May 15, 1982.
§On disabled list, May 16 to June 1, 1983.
xTraded to Texas Rangers as part of a six-player, four-team deal in which Kansas City Royals acquired Catcher Jim Sundberg from Milwaukee Brewers, New York Mets' organization acquired Pitcher Frank Wills from Kansas City, Milwaukee acquired Pitcher Danny Darwin and a player to be named later from Texas and Pitcher Tim Leary from New York, January 18, 1985; Milwaukee organization acquired Catcher Bill Hance from Texas to complete deal, January 30, 1985.
yOn disabled list, August 9 to August 26, 1985.
zOn disabled list, May 18 to July 4, 1986; included rehabilitation disability assignment to Oklahoma City, July 1 to July 4, 1986.
aTraded to New York Yankees for a player to be named later, November 2, 1987; Texas Rangers acquired Pitcher Brad Arnsberg to complete deal, November 10, 1987.
bOn disabled list, May 15 to June 20, 1988.
cTraded to Pittsburgh Pirates for Pitchers Jeff Robinson and Willie Smith, December 4, 1989.

CHAMPIONSHIP SERIES RECORD

Year Club League	Pos.	G.	AB.	R.	H.	2B.	3B.	HR.	RBI.	B.A.	PO.	A.	E.	F.A.
1984—Kansas City.......... Amer.	C	3	11	0	4	0	0	0	0	.364	17	0	3	.850

JOHN PATRICK SMILEY

Born March 17, 1965 at Phoenixville, Pa.
Height, 6.04. Weight, 195.
Throws and bats lefthanded.

Major League saves: 1987 (4).
Tied for Gulf Coast League lead in home runs allowed with 5 in 1983.

Year Club	League	G.	IP.	W.	L.	Pct.	H.	R.	ER.	SO.	BB.	ERA.
1983—Bradenton Pirates	Gulf Coast	12	65⅓	3	4	.429	69	45	43	42	27	5.92
1984—Macon†	S. Atlantic	21	130	5	11	.313	119	73	57	73	41	3.95
1985—Prince William	Carolina	10	56	2	2	.500	64	36	32	45	27	5.14
1985—Macon	S. Atlantic	16	88⅔	3	8	.273	84	55	46	70	37	4.67
1986—Prince William	Carolina	48	90	2	4	.333	64	35	31	93	40	3.10
1986—Pittsburgh	National	12	11⅔	1	0	1.000	4	6	5	9	4	3.86
1987—Pittsburgh	National	63	75	5	5	.500	69	49	48	58	50	5.76
1988—Pittsburgh	National	34	205	13	11	.542	185	81	74	129	46	3.25
1989—Pittsburgh	National	28	205⅓	12	8	.600	174	78	64	123	49	2.81
Major League Totals—4 Years		137	497	31	24	.564	432	214	191	319	149	3.46

Selected by Pittsburgh Pirates' organization in 12th round of free-agent draft, June 6, 1983.
†On disabled list, April 27 to May 27, 1984.

BRYN NELSON SMITH

First name pronounced Brin.

Born August 11, 1955, at Marietta, Ga.
Height, 6.02. Weight, 205.
Throws and bats righthanded.
Attended Allan Hancock College, Santa Maria, Calif.

Major League saves: 1982 (3), 1983 (3). Total—6.
Tied for American Association lead in complete games with 9 in 1981.
Tied for Southern League lead in complete games with 16 in 1977 and 12 in 1980.
Named American Association Pitcher of the Year, 1981.

Year Club	League	G.	IP.	W.	L.	Pct.	H.	R.	ER.	SO.	BB.	ERA.
1975—Miami	Florida St.	26	139	11	7	.611	117	48	33	93	59	2.14
1976—Miami	Florida St.	23	164	10	10	.500	140	72	51	119	62	2.80
1977—Charlotte†	Southern	27	★206	★15	11	.577	★195	78	63	103	57	2.75
1978—Denver	Am. Assoc.	11	54	0	6	.000	79	48	41	25	14	6.83
1978—Memphis‡	Southern	11	69	4	6	.400	53	28	19	48	31	2.48
1979—Memphis	Southern	27	184	11	10	.524	175	80	69	115	74	3.38
1980—Memphis	Southern	27	181	10	9	.526	179	75	56	110	54	2.78
1981—Denver	Am. Assoc.	29	★183	★15	5	★.750	166	80	62	127	42	3.05
1981—Montreal	National	7	13	1	0	1.000	14	4	4	9	3	2.77
1982—Wichita	Am. Assoc.	3	23⅔	2	0	1.000	21	5	5	15	2	1.90
1982—Montreal	National	47	79⅓	2	4	.333	81	43	37	50	23	4.20
1983—Montreal	National	49	155⅓	6	11	.353	142	51	43	101	43	2.49
1984—Montreal	National	28	179	12	13	.480	178	72	66	101	51	3.32
1985—Montreal	National	32	222⅓	18	5	.783	193	85	72	127	41	2.91
1986—Montreal§	National	30	187⅓	10	8	.556	182	101	82	105	63	3.94
1987—West Palm Beach x	Florida St.	4	17⅔	0	2	.000	19	10	8	16	1	4.08
1987—Montreal y	National	26	150⅓	10	9	.526	164	81	73	94	31	4.37
1988—Montreal	National	32	198	12	10	.545	179	79	66	122	32	3.00
1989—Montreal z	National	33	215⅔	10	11	.476	177	76	68	129	54	2.84
Major League Totals—9 Years		284	1400⅓	81	71	.533	1310	592	511	838	341	3.28

Selected by St. Louis Cardinals' organization in the 49th round of free-agent draft, June 5, 1973.
Signed as free agent by Baltimore Orioles' organization, December 18, 1974.
†Traded with Pitchers Rudy May and Randy Miller by Baltimore Orioles' organization to Montreal Expos' organization for Pitchers Don Stanhouse and Joe Kerrigan and Outfielder Gary Roenicke, December 7, 1977.
‡On disabled list, August 5 to August 17, 1978.
§Released, December 20, 1986; re-signed by Expos, February 27, 1987.
xOn Montreal disabled list, March 23 to May 1, 1987; included rehabilitation disability assignment to West Palm Beach, April 10, 1987.
yGranted free agency, November 9, 1987; re-signed by Expos, December 16, 1987.
zGranted free agency, November 13, 1989; signed by St. Louis Cardinals, November 28, 1989.

DAVID STANLEY SMITH JR.
(Dave)

Born January 21, 1955, at San Francisco, Calif.
Height, 6.01. Weight, 195.
Throws and bats righthanded.
Attended San Diego State University, San Diego, Calif.

Major League saves: 1980 (10), 1981 (8), 1982 (11), 1983 (6), 1984 (5), 1985 (27), 1986 (33), 1987 (24), 1988 (27), 1989 (25). Total—176.

Year Club	League	G.	IP.	W.	L.	Pct.	H.	R.	ER.	SO.	BB.	ERA.
1976—Covington	Ap'lachian	15	97	5	5	.500	80	40	29	71	28	2.69
1977—Cocoa	Florida St.	14	93	7	5	.583	97	40	32	81	31	3.10
1977—Columbus	Southern	9	54	3	5	.375	52	2	21	29	24	3.50
1978—Columbus	Southern	26	181	10	13	.435	170	89	70	114	88	3.48
1979—Charleston	Int'national	34	160	7	8	.467	159	80	65	90	44	3.66

Year Club	League	G.	IP.	W.	L.	Pct.	H.	R.	ER.	SO.	BB.	ERA.
1980—Houston	National	57	103	7	5	.583	90	24	22	85	32	1.92
1981—Houston	National	42	75	5	3	.625	54	26	23	52	23	2.76
1982—Houston†	National	49	63⅓	5	4	.556	69	30	27	28	31	3.84
1983—Houston	National	42	72⅔	3	1	.750	72	32	25	41	36	3.10
1984—Houston	National	53	77⅓	5	4	.556	60	22	19	45	20	2.21
1985—Houston	National	64	79⅓	9	5	.643	69	26	20	40	17	2.27
1986—Houston	National	54	56	4	7	.364	39	17	17	46	22	2.73
1987—Houston‡	National	50	60	2	3	.400	39	13	11	73	21	1.65
1988—Houston	National	51	57⅓	4	5	.444	60	26	17	38	19	2.67
1989—Houston	National	52	58	3	4	.429	49	20	17	31	19	2.64
Major League Totals—10 Years		514	702	47	41	.534	601	236	198	479	240	2.54

Selected by Houston Astros' organization in 8th round of free-agent draft, June 8, 1976.
†On disabled list, June 27 to July 18, 1982.
‡Granted free agency, November 9, 1987; re-signed by Astros, January 8, 1988.

DIVISION SERIES RECORD

Year Club	League	G.	IP.	W.	L.	Pct.	H.	R.	ER.	SO.	BB.	ERA.
1981—Houston	National	2	2⅓	0	0	.000	2	1	1	4	0	3.86

CHAMPIONSHIP SERIES RECORD

Year Club	League	G.	IP.	W.	L.	Pct.	H.	R.	ER.	SO.	BB.	ERA.
1980—Houston	National	3	2⅓	1	0	1.000	4	1	1	4	2	3.86
1986—Houston	National	2	2	0	1	.000	2	2	2	2	3	9.00
Championship Series Totals—2 Years		5	4⅓	1	1	.500	6	3	3	6	5	6.23

ALL-STAR GAME RECORD

Member of National League All-Star Team in 1986; did not play.

GREGORY ALLEN SMITH
(Greg)

Born April 5, 1967, at Baltimore, Md.
Height, 5.11. Weight, 170.
Throws right and bats left and righthanded.

Led Southern League second basemen in total chances with 621 and double plays with 59 in 1989.
Led Midwest League shortstops in errors with 48 and tied for lead in putouts with 189 in 1987.

Year Club	League	Pos.	G.	AB.	R.	H.	2B.	3B.	HR.	RBI.	B.A.	PO.	A.	E.	F.A.
1985—Wytheville	Appal.	SS	51	179	28	42	6	2	0	15	.235	56	160	24	.900
1986—Peoria	Midw.	SS-2B	53	170	24	43	6	3	2	26	.253	65	101	15	.917
1987—Peoria	Midw.	SS-2B	124	444	69	120	23	5	6	56	.270	193	347	49	.917
1988—Winston-Salem	Carol.	2B-1B	95	361	62	101	12	2	4	29	.280	162	236	16	.961
1989—Charlotte	South.	2B	126	467	59	138	23	6	5	64	.296	★253	★348	20	.968
1989—Chicago	Nat.	2B	4	5	1	2	0	0	0	2	.400	4	3	2	.778
Major League Totals—1 Year			4	5	1	2	0	0	0	2	.400	4	3	2	.778

Selected by Chicago Cubs' organization in 2nd round of free-agent draft, June 3, 1985.

JOHN DWIGHT SMITH
(Known by middle name.)

Born November 8, 1963, at Tallahassee, Fla.
Height, 5.11. Weight, 175.
Throws right and bats lefthanded.
Attended Spartanburg Methodist College, Spartanburg, S.C.

Major League stolen bases: 1989 (9).
Led Eastern League in total bases with 270, stolen bases with 60 and tied for lead in caught stealing with 18 in 1987.
Led Appalachian League in stolen bases with 47 in 1984.
Led Midwest League outfielders in total chances with 296 in 1986.
Tied for Appalachian League lead in double plays by outfielders with 3 in 1984.

Year Club	League	Pos.	G.	AB.	R.	H.	2B.	3B.	HR.	RBI.	B.A.	PO.	A.	E.	F.A.
1984—Pikeville	Appal.	OF	61	195	42	46	6	2	1	17	.236	77	8	●9	.904
1985—Geneva	NYP	OF	73	232	44	67	11	2	4	32	.289	81	4	7	.924
1986—Peoria	Midw.	OF	124	471	92	146	22	★11	11	57	.310	★272	11	13	.956
1987—Pittsfield	East.	OF	130	498	★111	168	28	10	18	72	.337	214	8	●14	.941
1988—Iowa	A. A.	OF	129	505	76	148	26	3	9	48	.293	216	11	★15	.938
1989—Iowa	A. A.	OF	21	83	11	27	7	3	2	7	.325	39	2	4	.911
1989—Chicago	Nat.	OF	109	343	52	111	19	6	9	52	.324	188	7	5	.975
Major League Totals—1 Year			109	343	52	111	19	6	9	52	.324	188	7	5	.975

Selected by Toronto Blue Jays' organization in 3rd round of free-agent draft, January 17, 1984.
Selected by Chicago Cubs' organization in secondary phase of free-agent draft, June 4, 1984.

CHAMPIONSHIP SERIES RECORD

Shares Championship Series record for most at-bats, inning (2), October 5, 1989, first inning.

Year Club	League	Pos.	G.	AB.	R.	H.	2B.	3B.	HR.	RBI.	B.A.	PO.	A.	E.	F.A.
1989—Chicago	Nat.	OF	4	15	2	3	1	0	0	0	.200	10	0	0	1.000

LEE ARTHUR SMITH

Born December 4, 1957, at Jamestown, La.
Height, 6.06. Weight, 250.
Throws and bats righthanded.
Attended Northwestern State University, Natchitoches, La.

Major League saves: 1981 (1), 1982 (17), 1983 (29), 1984 (33), 1985 (33), 1986 (31), 1987 (36), 1988 (29), 1989 (25).
Total—234.
Led National League in games finished in relief with 57 in 1985 and tied for lead with 56 in 1983.
Led National League in saves with 29 in 1983.
Tied for American Association lead in wild pitches with 16 in 1980.
Named National League co-Fireman of the Year by THE SPORTING NEWS, 1983.

Year Club	League	G.	IP.	W.	L.	Pct.	H.	R.	ER.	SO.	BB.	ERA.
1975—Bradenton Cubs	Gulf Coast	10	62	3	5	.375	35	23	16	35	★49	2.32
1976—Pompano Beach	Florida St.	26	101	4	8	.333	120	76	60	52	74	5.35
1977—Pompano Beach	Florida St.	26	130	10	4	.714	131	67	62	82	85	4.29
1978—Midland	Texas	30	155	8	10	.444	161	122	103	71	★128	5.98
1979—Midland	Texas	35	104	9	5	.643	122	65	57	46	85	4.93
1980—Wichita	Am. Assoc.	50	90	4	7	.364	70	49	37	63	56	3.70
1980—Chicago	National	18	22	2	0	1.000	21	9	7	17	14	2.86
1981—Chicago	National	40	67	3	6	.333	57	31	26	50	31	3.49
1982—Chicago	National	72	117	2	5	.286	105	38	35	99	37	2.69
1983—Chicago	National	66	103⅓	4	10	.286	70	23	19	91	41	1.65
1984—Chicago	National	69	101	9	7	.563	98	42	41	86	35	3.65
1985—Chicago	National	65	97⅔	7	4	.636	87	35	33	112	32	3.04
1986—Chicago†	National	66	90⅓	9	9	.500	69	32	31	93	42	3.09
1987—Chicago‡	National	62	83⅔	4	10	.286	84	30	29	96	32	3.12
1988—Boston	American	64	83⅔	4	5	.444	72	34	26	96	37	2.80
1989—Boston	American	64	70⅔	6	1	.857	53	30	28	96	33	3.57
National League Totals—8 Years		458	682	40	51	.440	591	240	221	644	264	2.92
American League Totals—2 Years		128	154⅓	10	6	.625	125	64	54	192	70	3.15
Major League Totals—10 Years		586	836⅓	50	57	.467	716	304	275	836	334	2.96

Selected by Chicago Cubs' organization in 2nd round of free-agent draft, June 4, 1975.
†On disabled list, April 21 to May 6, 1986.
‡Traded to Boston Red Sox for Pitchers Al Nipper and Calvin Schiraldi, December 8, 1987.

CHAMPIONSHIP SERIES RECORD

Year Club	League	G.	IP.	W.	L.	Pct.	H.	R.	ER.	SO.	BB.	ERA.
1984—Chicago	National	2	2	0	1	.000	3	2	2	3	0	9.00
1988—Boston	American	2	3⅓	0	1	.000	6	3	3	4	1	8.10
Championship Series Totals—2 Years		4	5⅓	0	2	.000	9	5	5	7	1	8.44

ALL-STAR GAME RECORD

Year League	IP.	W.	L.	Pct.	H.	R.	ER.	SO.	BB.	ERA.
1983—National	1	0	0	.000	2	2	1	1	0	9.00
1987—National	3	1	0	1.000	2	0	0	4	0	0.00
All-Star Game Totals—2 Years	4	1	0	1.000	4	2	1	5	0	2.25

LEROY PURDY SMITH III
(Roy)

Born September 6, 1961, at Mt. Vernon, N.Y.
Height, 6.03. Weight, 212.
Throws and bats righthanded.
Attended Fordham University, Bronx, N.Y.

Major League saves: 1989 (1).
Tied for Carolina League lead in shutouts with 3 in 1980.
Named Carolina League Pitcher of the Year, 1980.

Year Club	League	G.	IP.	W.	L.	Pct.	H.	R.	ER.	SO.	BB.	ERA.
1979—Helena	Pioneer	5	36	5	0	1.000	21	16	10	42	16	2.50
1980—Peninsula	Carolina	27	163	★17	6	.739	101	54	47	134	63	2.60
1981—Reading	Eastern	27	161	11	8	.579	123	92	79	117	97	4.42
1982—Reading†	Eastern	26	166	10	8	.556	141	81	71	122	82	3.85
1983—Charleston	Int'national	27	155⅓	6	8	.429	166	101	89	95	75	5.16
1984—Maine	Int'national	12	80⅔	5	4	.556	77	47	39	48	29	4.35
1984—Cleveland	American	22	86⅓	5	5	.500	91	49	44	55	40	4.59
1985—Maine	Int'national	15	109⅓	10	4	.714	84	33	29	65	29	2.39
1985—Cleveland‡§	American	12	62⅓	1	4	.200	84	40	37	28	17	5.34
1986—Minnesota	American	5	10⅓	0	2	.000	13	8	8	8	5	6.97
1986—Toledo xy	Int'national	9	53⅔	2	1	.667	42	12	9	39	16	1.51
1987—Portland	P. Coast	24	166⅓	9	12	.429	176	84	70	106	41	3.79
1987—Minnesota	American	7	16⅓	1	0	1.000	20	10	9	8	6	4.96
1988—Portland	P. Coast	22	150	12	9	.571	152	82	72	110	31	4.32
1988—Minnesota	American	9	37	3	0	1.000	29	12	11	17	12	2.68
1989—Minnesota	American	32	172⅓	10	6	.625	180	82	75	92	51	3.92
Major League Totals—6 Years		87	384⅔	20	17	.541	417	201	184	208	131	4.31

Selected by Philadelphia Phillies' organization in 3rd round of free-agent draft, June 5, 1979.
†Traded with Pitcher Jerry Reed and Outfielder Wil Culmer to Cleveland Indians for Pitcher John Denny,
September 12, 1982.

§Traded with Pitcher Ramon Romero to Minnesota Twins for Pitchers Ken Schrom and Bryan Oelkers, January 7, 1986.

xOn disabled list, June 7 to July 3, 1986.

yReleased, December 20, 1986; re-signed by Minnesota Twins' organization, February 24, 1987.

LONNIE SMITH

Born December 22, 1955, at Chicago, Ill.
Height, 5.09. Weight, 170.
Throws and bats righthanded.

Shares major league record for fewest double plays by outfielder, season, for leader in double plays (4), 1983.
Shares modern National League record for most stolen bases, game, (5), September 4, 1982.
Major League stolen bases: 1978 (4), 1979 (2), 1980 (33), 1981 (21), 1982 (68), 1983 (43), 1984 (50), 1985 (52), 1986 (26), 1987 (9), 1988 (4), 1989 (25). Total—337.
Led National League in being hit by pitch with 9 in 1982 and 1984 and tied for lead with 9 in 1983.
Tied for National League lead in caught stealing with 26 in 1982.
Tied for National League lead in double plays by outfielders with 4 in 1983.
Led International League in bases on balls received with 66 in 1988.
Led American Association in stolen bases with 66 and caught stealing with 19 in 1978.
Led Western Carolinas League in stolen bases with 56 and tied for lead in caught stealing with 14 in 1975.
Led American Association outfielders in double plays with 5 in 1978.
Named National League Comeback Player of the Year by THE SPORTING NEWS, 1989.
Named National League Rookie Player of the Year by THE SPORTING NEWS, 1980.
Named outfielder on THE SPORTING NEWS National League All-Star Team, 1982.

Year	Club	League	Pos.	G.	AB.	R.	H.	2B.	3B.	HR.	RBI.	B.A.	PO.	A.	E.	F.A.
1974—Auburn	NYP	OF	61	210	48	60	10	4	5	27	.286	143	6	•9	.943
1975—Spartanburg	W. Car.	OF	131	465	*114	*150	23	4	7	40	.323	*317	9	11	.967
1976—Oklahoma City	A. A.	OF	134	483	*93	149	24	9	8	54	.308	200	4	*14	.936
1977—Oklahoma City	A. A.	OF	125	477	91	132	14	10	4	41	.277	231	8	*13	.948
1978—Oklahoma City†	A. A.	OF	125	480	103	151	20	5	7	43	.315	274	*21	*12	.961
1978—Philadelphia	Nat.	OF	17	4	6	0	0	0	0	0	.000	5	1	0	1.000
1979—Oklahoma City	A. A.	OF	110	451	*106	149	26	9	7	44	.330	268	13	*12	.959
1979—Philadelphia	Nat.	OF	17	30	4	5	2	0	0	3	.167	19	1	0	1.000
1980—Philadelphia	Nat.	OF	100	298	69	101	14	4	3	20	.339	121	2	4	.969
1981—Philadelphia‡	Nat.	OF	62	176	40	57	14	3	2	11	.324	91	10	3	.971
1982—St. Louis§	Nat.	OF	156	592	*120	182	35	8	8	69	.307	303	•16	10	.970
1983—St. Louis	Nat.	OF	130	492	83	158	31	5	8	45	.321	225	14	*15	.941
1984—St. Louis	Nat.	OF	145	504	77	126	20	4	6	49	.250	184	*18	•11	.948
1985—St. Louis x	Nat.	OF	28	96	15	25	2	2	0	7	.260	43	1	0	1.000
1985—Kansas City	Amer.	OF	120	448	77	115	23	4	6	41	.257	195	10	9	.958
1986—Kansas City yz	Amer.	OF	134	508	80	146	25	7	8	44	.287	245	5	9	.965
1987—Omaha	A. A.	OF	40	149	36	49	9	1	7	33	.329	51	1	3	.945
1987—Kansas City a	Amer.	OF	48	167	26	42	7	1	3	8	.251	52	2	5	.915
1988—Richmond	Int.	OF	93	290	58	87	13	5	9	51	.300	120	6	2	.984
1988—Atlanta	Nat.	OF	43	114	14	27	3	0	3	9	.237	59	2	2	.968
1989—Atlanta b	Nat.	OF	134	482	89	152	34	4	21	79	.315	289	3	2	.993
National League Totals—10 Years			832	2788	517	833	155	30	51	292	.299	1339	68	47	.968
American League Totals—3 Years			302	1123	183	303	55	12	17	93	.270	492	17	23	.957
Major League Totals—12 Years			1134	3911	700	1136	210	42	68	385	.290	1831	85	70	.965

Selected by Philadelphia Phillies' organization in 1st round (third player selected) of free-agent draft, June 5, 1974.
†On disabled list, April 14 to April 25, 1978.
‡Traded with a player to be named later to Cleveland Indians for Catcher Bo Diaz, November 20, 1981; Traded by Cleveland to St. Louis Cardinals for Pitchers Lary Sorensen and Silvio Martinez, November 20, 1981. Cleveland organization acquired Pitcher Scott Munninghoff to complete first deal, December 9, 1981.
§On disabled list, June 11 to July 8, 1983.
xTraded to Kansas City Royals for Outfielder John Morris, May 17, 1985.
yOn disabled list, April 13 to May 4, 1986.
zGranted free agency, November 12, 1986; re-signed by Royals' organization, May 18, 1987.
aReleased, December 15, 1987; signed by Richmond (Atlanta Braves' organization), March 12, 1988.
bOn disabled list, May 20 to June 13, 1989.

DIVISION SERIES RECORD

Year	Club	League	Pos.	G.	AB.	R.	H.	2B.	3B.	HR.	RBI.	B.A.	PO.	A.	E.	F.A.
1981—Philadelphia	Nat.	OF	5	19	1	5	1	0	0	0	.263	6	1	0	1.000

CHAMPIONSHIP SERIES RECORD

Year	Club	League	Pos.	G.	AB.	R.	H.	2B.	3B.	HR.	RBI.	B.A.	PO.	A.	E.	F.A.
1980—Philadelphia	Nat.	PR-OF	3	5	2	3	0	0	0	0	.600	2	1	0	1.000
1982—St. Louis	Nat.	OF	3	11	1	3	0	0	1	.273	2	0	0	1.000
1985—Kansas City	Amer.	OF	7	28	2	7	2	0	1	.250	8	3	1	.917
Championship Series Totals—3 Years			13	44	5	13	2	0	0	2	.295	12	4	1	.941

WORLD SERIES RECORD

Year	Club	League	Pos.	G.	AB.	R.	H.	2B.	3B.	HR.	RBI.	B.A.	PO.	A.	E.	F.A.
1980—Philadelphia	Nat.	PR-O-DH	6	19	2	5	1	0	0	1	.263	4	1	0	1.000
1982—St. Louis	Nat.	OF-DH	7	28	6	9	4	1	0	1	.321	11	0	0	1.000
1985—Kansas City	Amer.	OF	7	27	4	9	3	0	0	4	.333	7	2	0	1.000
World Series Totals—3 Years			20	74	12	23	8	1	0	6	.311	22	3	0	1.000

Year	League	Pos.	AB.	R.	H.	2B.	3B.	HR.	RBI.	B.A.	PO.	A.	E.	F.A.
1982—National		OF	0	0	0	0	0	0	0	.000	1	0	0	1.000

MICHAEL ANTHONY SMITH
(Mike)

Born February 23, 1961, at Jackson, Miss.
Height, 6.01. Weight, 195.
Throws right and bats right and lefthanded.
Attended Utica Junior College, Utica, Miss.

Major League saves: 1988 (1).
Led Florida State League in saves with 21 in 1982.

Year	Club	League	G.	IP.	W.	L.	Pct.	H.	R.	ER.	SO.	BB.	ERA.
1981—Billings	Pioneer	22	46	5	5	.500	39	21	7	52	19	1.37
1982—Tampa	Florida St.	48	80⅓	7	1	.875	55	17	11	80	42	1.23
1983—Waterbury†	Eastern	22	28⅔	2	5	.286	18	13	9	16	25	2.83
1984—Cincinnati	National	8	10⅓	1	0	1.000	12	6	6	7	5	5.23
1984—Wichita	Am. Assoc.	12	18	3	2	.600	17	8	8	20	13	4.00
1984—Vermont	Eastern	35	51	3	3	.500	51	28	19	49	20	3.35
1985—Denver	Am. Assoc.	47	68⅔	5	4	.556	65	40	37	67	38	4.85
1985—Cincinnati	National	2	3⅓	0	0	.000	2	2	2	2	1	5.40
1986—Denver‡-Indianapolis	Am. Assoc.	40	76⅔	6	3	.667	95	54	46	50	44	5.40
1986—Cincinnati§	National	2	3⅓	0	0	.000	7	5	5	1	1	13.50
1987—Indianapolis	Am. Assoc.	45	86⅓	4	4	.500	85	51	45	90	43	4.69
1988—Indianapolis	Am. Assoc.	32	63	5	1	.833	40	22	18	55	14	2.57
1988—Montreal x	National	5	8⅔	0	0	.000	6	3	3	4	5	3.12
1989—Rochester y	Int'national	11	20⅓	1	4	.200	29	13	13	14	11	5.75
1989—Buffalo	Am. Assoc.	9	17	0	0	.000	15	5	5	11	5	2.65
1989—Pittsburgh z	National	16	24	0	1	.000	28	12	10	12	10	3.75
Major League Totals—5 Years		33	49⅔	1	1	.500	55	28	26	26	22	4.71

Signed as free agent by Cincinnati Reds' organization, May 11, 1981.
†On disabled list, June 28, 1983 through remainder of season.
‡Loaned to Indianapolis (Montreal Expos' organization), July 24, 1986; returned, September 10, 1986.
§Traded to Montreal Expos for a player to be named later, December 1, 1986; Cincinnati Reds' organization acquired Pitcher Bill Cutshall to complete deal, December 9, 1986.
xTraded to Baltimore Orioles for a player to be named later, November 14, 1988; Montreal Expos acquired Pitcher Doug Kline to complete deal, December 7, 1988.
yTraded to Buffalo (Pittsburgh Pirates' organization) for Outfielder Tony Chance, June 22, 1989.
zReleased, November 16, 1989.

MICHAEL ANTHONY SMITH
(Mike)

Born October 31, 1963, at San Antonio, Tex.
Height, 6.03. Weight, 190.
Throws and bats righthanded.
Attended Ranger Junior College, Ranger, Tex.

Led Southern League in hit batsmen with 10 in 1988.
Tied for Eastern League lead in games started by pitchers with 27 in 1987.
Tied for Midwest League lead in wild pitches with 19 in 1986.

Year	Club	League	G.	IP.	W.	L.	Pct.	H.	R.	ER.	SO.	BB.	ERA.
1984—Sarasota Reds	Gulf Coast	11	67	2	4	.333	65	33	27	65	24	3.63
1985—Billings	Pioneer	7	33⅔	2	2	.500	24	15	11	24	24	2.94
1985—Cedar Rapids	Midwest	8	44⅓	5	1	.833	38	20	16	28	22	3.25
1986—Cedar Rapids	Midwest	28	★191	10	10	.500	155	88	71	172	106	3.35
1987—Vermont	Eastern	27	171⅓	8	12	.400	152	78	64	104	★117	3.36
1988—Chattanooga†	Southern	28	194⅓	9	10	.474	160	90	69	141	★98	3.20
1989—Rochester	Int'national	36	56	2	4	.333	45	23	20	48	22	3.21
1989—Baltimore	American	13	20	2	0	1.000	25	19	17	12	14	7.65
Major League Totals—1 Year		13	20	2	0	1.000	25	19	17	12	14	7.65

Selected by San Diego Padres' organization in 4th round of free-agent draft, January 11, 1983.
Selected by Cincinnati Reds' organization in 5th round of free-agent draft, January 17, 1984.
†Drafted by Baltimore Orioles, December 5, 1988; Cincinnati Reds turned down right to reclaim.

OSBORNE EARL SMITH
(Ozzie)

Born December 26, 1954, at Mobile, Ala.
Height, 5.10. Weight, 160.
Throws right and bats left and righthanded.
Received degree from California Polytechnic State University, San Luis Obispo, Calif.

Holds major league records for most assists by shortstop, season (621), 1980; most years with 500 or more assists by shortstop (8); fewest chances accepted for leader, shortstop, season (692), 1989; most years leading league in assists and chances accepted, shortstop (8).
Shares major league record for most double plays by shortstop, extra-inning game (6), August 25, 1979 (19 innings).
Shares National League records for most consecutive years leading league in assists by shortstop (4), 1979 through 1982; most years leading league in fielding average by shortstop, 100 or more games (6); highest fielding average by shortstop, season, 150 or more games (.987), 1987.

Shares modern National League record for most consecutive years leading league in fielding average by short-stop, 100 or more games (4), 1984 through 1987.

Major League stolen bases: 1978 (40), 1979 (28), 1980 (57), 1981 (22), 1982 (25), 1983 (34), 1984 (35), 1985 (31), 1986 (31), 1987 (43), 1988 (57), 1989 (29). Total—432.

Led National League in sacrifice hits with 28 in 1978 and 23 in 1980.

Led National League shortstops in total chances with 933 in 1980, 658 in 1981, 844 in 1983, 827 in 1985, 771 in 1987, 775 in 1988 and 709 in 1989.

Led National League shortstops in double plays with 113 in 1980, 111 in 1987 and tied for lead with 94 in 1984 and 96 in 1986.

Led Northwest League in stolen bases with 30 in 1977.

Led Northwest League shortstops in double plays with 40 in 1977.

Named shortstop on THE SPORTING NEWS National League All-Star Team, 1982 and 1984 through 1987.

Named shortstop on THE SPORTING NEWS National League All-Star fielding team, 1980 through 1989.

Named shortstop on THE SPORTING NEWS National League Silver Slugger team, 1987.

Year Club	League	Pos.	G.	AB.	R.	H.	2B.	3B.	HR.	RBI.	B.A.	PO.	A.	E.	F.A.
1977—Walla Walla	N'west	SS	•68	*287	*69	87	10	2	1	35	.303	130	*254	23	*.943
1978—San Diego	Nat.	SS	159	590	69	152	17	6	1	46	.258	264	548	25	.970
1979—San Diego	Nat.	SS	156	587	77	124	18	6	0	27	.211	256	*555	20	.976
1980—San Diego	Nat.	SS	158	609	67	140	18	5	0	35	.230	*288	*621	24	.974
1981—San Diego†	Nat.	SS	•110	*450	53	100	11	2	0	21	.222	220	*422	16	*.976
1982—St. Louis	Nat.	SS	140	488	58	121	24	1	2	43	.248	279	*535	13	*.984
1983—St. Louis‡	Nat.	SS	159	552	69	134	30	6	3	50	.243	*304	519	21	.975
1984—St. Louis‡	Nat.	SS	124	412	53	106	20	5	1	44	.257	233	437	12	*.982
1985—St. Louis	Nat.	SS	158	537	70	148	22	3	6	54	.276	264	*549	14	*.983
1986—St. Louis	Nat.	SS	153	514	67	144	19	4	0	54	.280	229	453	15	*.978
1987—St. Louis	Nat.	SS	158	600	104	182	40	4	0	75	.303	245	*516	10	*.987
1988—St. Louis	Nat.	SS	153	575	80	155	27	1	3	51	.270	234	*519	22	.972
1989—St. Louis§	Nat.	SS	155	593	82	162	30	8	2	50	.273	209	*483	17	.976
Major League Totals—12 Years			1783	6507	849	1668	276	51	18	550	.256	3025	6157	209	.978

Selected by Detroit Tigers' organization in 7th round of free-agent draft, June 8, 1976.

Selected by San Diego Padres' organization in 4th round of free-agent draft, June 7, 1977.

†Traded to St. Louis Cardinals for Shortstop Garry Templeton, February 11, 1982.

‡On disabled list, July 14 to August 19, 1984.

§On disabled list, March 31 to April 15, 1989.

CHAMPIONSHIP SERIES RECORD

Year Club	League	Pos.	G.	AB.	R.	H.	2B.	3B.	HR.	RBI.	B.A.	PO.	A.	E.	F.A.
1982—St. Louis	Nat.	SS	3	9	0	5	0	0	0	3	.556	4	11	0	1.000
1985—St. Louis	Nat.	SS	6	23	4	10	1	1	1	3	.435	6	16	0	1.000
1987—St. Louis	Nat.	SS	7	25	2	5	0	1	0	1	.200	10	19	1	.967
Championship Series Totals—3 Years			16	57	6	20	1	2	1	7	.351	20	46	1	.985

WORLD SERIES RECORD

Year Club	League	Pos.	G.	AB.	R.	H.	2B.	3B.	HR.	RBI.	B.A.	PO.	A.	E.	F.A.
1982—St. Louis	Nat.	SS	7	24	3	5	0	0	0	1	.208	22	17	0	1.000
1985—St. Louis	Nat.	SS	7	23	1	2	0	0	0	0	.087	10	16	1	.963
1987—St. Louis	Nat.	SS	7	28	3	6	0	0	0	2	.214	7	19	0	1.000
World Series Totals—3 Years			21	75	7	13	0	0	0	3	.173	39	52	1	.989

ALL-STAR GAME RECORD

Year League	Pos.	AB.	R.	H.	2B.	3B.	HR.	RBI.	B.A.	PO.	A.	E.	F.A.
1981—National	SS	0	0	0	0	0	0	0	.000	1	0	0	1.000
1982—National	PR-SS	0	0	0	0	0	0	0	.000	0	1	0	1.000
1983—National	SS	2	1	1	0	0	0	0	.500	0	0	0	.000
1984—National	SS	3	0	0	0	0	0	0	.000	3	0	0	1.000
1985—National	SS	4	0	0	0	0	0	0	.000	1	3	0	1.000
1986—National	SS	1	0	0	0	0	0	0	.000	3	2	0	1.000
1987—National	SS	2	0	0	0	0	0	0	.000	3	2	1	.833
1988—National	SS	2	0	0	0	0	0	0	.000	1	4	0	1.000
1989—National	SS	4	0	1	0	0	0	0	.250	1	3	0	1.000
All-Star Game Totals—9 Years		18	1	2	0	0	0	0	.111	13	15	1	.966

PETER JOHN SMITH
(Pete)

Born February 27, 1966, at Abington, Mass.
Height, 6.02. Weight, 200.
Throws and bats righthanded.

Led National League in balks with 7 in 1989.

Year Club	League	G.	IP.	W.	L.	Pct.	H.	R.	ER.	SO.	BB.	ERA.
1984—Sarasota Phillies	Gulf Coast	8	37	1	2	.333	28	11	6	35	16	1.46
1985—Clearwater†	Florida St.	26	153	12	10	.545	135	68	56	86	80	3.29
1986—Greenville	Southern	24	104⅔	1	8	.111	117	88	68	64	78	5.85
1987—Greenville	Southern	29	177⅓	9	9	.500	162	76	66	119	67	3.35
1987—Atlanta	National	6	31⅔	1	2	.333	39	21	17	11	14	4.83
1988—Atlanta	National	32	195⅓	7	15	.318	183	89	80	124	88	3.69
1989—Atlanta	National	28	142	5	14	.263	144	83	75	115	57	4.75
Major League Totals—3 Years		66	369	13	31	.295	366	193	172	250	159	4.20

Selected by Philadelphia Phillies' organization in 1st round (21st player selected) of free-agent draft, June 4, 1984.

†Traded with Catcher Ozzie Virgil to Atlanta Braves for Pitcher Steve Bedrosian and Outfielder Milt Thompson, December 10, 1985.

WILLIE EVERETT SMITH

Born January 27, 1967, at Savannah, Ga.
Height, 6.05. Weight, 225.
Throws and bats righthanded.

Year Club	League	G.	IP.	W.	L.	Pct.	H.	R.	ER.	SO.	BB.	ERA.
1986—Bradenton Pirates	Gulf Coast	7	21⅔	1	0	1.000	16	8	6	13	6	2.49
1987—Bradenton Pirates	Gulf Coast	10	19⅓	2	1	.667	12	4	2	27	11	1.40
1987—Watertown	NYP	5	20⅓	2	0	1.000	15	13	10	24	10	4.43
1988—Augusta	S. Atlantic	30	48⅓	1	4	.200	35	20	16	48	29	2.98
1989—Salem	Carolina	23	64⅓	4	5	.444	46	26	21	58	40	2.94
1989—Harrisburg†	Eastern	12	18⅓	3	0	1.000	11	5	5	21	10	2.45

Signed as free agent by Pittsburgh Pirates' organization, July 13, 1986.
†Traded with Pitcher Jeff Robinson to New York Yankees for Catcher Don Slaught, December 4, 1989.

ZANE WILLIAM SMITH

Born December 28, 1960, at Madison, Wis.
Height, 6.02. Weight, 195.
Throws and bats lefthanded.
Attended Indiana State University, Terre Haute, Ind.

Major League saves: 1986 (1), 1989 (2). Total—3.
Led National League hitters in sacrifice hits with 14 in 1987.
Tied for National League lead in games started by pitchers with 36 in 1987.
Named lefthanded pitcher on THE SPORTING NEWS National League All-Star Team, 1987.

Year Club	League	G.	IP.	W.	L.	Pct.	H.	R.	ER.	SO.	BB.	ERA.
1982—Anderson	S. Atlantic	12	63	5	3	.625	65	53	48	32	34	6.86
1983—Durham	Carolina	27	170⅔	9	●15	.375	183	109	93	126	83	4.90
1984—Greenville	Southern	9	60	7	0	1.000	47	13	11	35	23	1.65
1984—Richmond	Int'national	19	123⅔	7	4	.636	113	62	57	68	65	4.15
1984—Atlanta	National	3	20	1	0	1.000	16	7	5	16	13	2.25
1985—Atlanta†	National	42	147	9	10	.474	135	70	62	85	80	3.80
1986—Atlanta	National	38	204⅔	8	16	.333	209	109	92	139	105	4.05
1987—Atlanta	National	36	242	15	10	.600	245	★130	110	130	91	4.09
1988—Atlanta‡	National	23	140⅓	5	10	.333	159	72	67	59	44	4.30
1989—Atlanta§-Montreal	National	48	147	1	13	.071	141	76	57	93	52	3.49
Major League Totals—6 Years		190	901	39	59	.398	905	464	393	522	385	3.93

Selected by Atlanta Braves' organization in 3rd round of free-agent draft, June 7, 1982.
†On disabled list, August 5 to September 1, 1985.
‡On disabled list, August 25, 1988 through remainder of season.
§Traded to Montreal Expos for Pitchers Sergio Valdez and Nate Minshey and Outfielder Kevin Dean, July 2, 1989.

BILLY MIKE SMITHSON

(Known by middle name.)

Born January 21, 1955, at Centerville, Tenn.
Height, 6.08. Weight, 215.
Throws right and bats lefthanded.
Attended University of Tennessee, Knoxville, Tenn.

Major League saves: 1989 (2).
Led American League in hit batsmen with 15 in 1985.
Led American League in home runs allowed with 35 in 1984.
Tied for American League lead in games started by pitchers with 36 in 1984 and 37 in 1985.
Tied for International League lead in intentional bases on balls issued with 13 in 1980.

Year Club	League	G.	IP.	W.	L.	Pct.	H.	R.	ER.	SO.	BB.	ERA.
1976—Winter Haven	Florida St.	11	64	4	3	.571	63	27	22	29	20	3.09
1977—Winter Haven	Florida St.	25	172	13	8	.619	170	56	53	92	41	2.77
1977—Bristol	Eastern	1	3	0	1	.000	8	7	7	1	0	21.00
1978—Bristol	Eastern	27	160	11	10	.524	178	92	81	86	76	4.56
1979—Bristol	Eastern	★48	132	8	12	.400	128	82	69	89	53	4.70
1980—Pawtucket	Int'national	★50	99	5	9	.357	95	50	32	73	45	2.91
1981—Pawtucket†	Int'national	34	91	2	4	.333	74	44	39	82	45	3.86
1982—Denver	Am. Assoc.	29	152⅔	11	7	.611	149	82	77	★144	47	4.54
1982—Texas	American	8	46⅔	3	4	.429	51	26	26	24	13	5.01
1983—Texas‡	American	33	223⅓	10	14	.417	233	102	97	135	71	3.91
1984—Minnesota	American	36	252	15	13	.536	246	113	103	144	54	3.68
1985—Minnesota	American	37	257	15	14	.517	264	134	★124	127	78	4.34
1986—Minnesota	American	34	198	13	14	.481	234	123	105	114	57	4.77
1987—Minnesota§	American	21	109	4	7	.364	126	76	72	53	38	5.94
1987—Portland x	P. Coast	6	38	2	3	.400	36	22	21	31	17	4.97
1988—Boston	American	31	126⅔	9	6	.600	149	87	84	73	37	5.97
1988—Pawtucket y	Int'national	2	7	1	0	1.000	6	0	0	5	2	0.00
1989—Boston z	American	40	143⅔	7	14	.333	170	84	79	61	35	4.95
Major League Totals—8 Years		240	1356⅓	76	86	.469	1473	745	690	731	383	4.58

Selected by Boston Red Sox' organization in 5th round of free-agent draft, June 8, 1976.
†Traded to Texas Rangers' organization for Pitcher John Henry Johnson, April 9, 1982.
‡Traded with Pitcher John Butcher and Catcher Sam Sorce to Minnesota Twins for Outfielder Gary Ward, December 7, 1983.
§On disabled list, May 11 to June 8, 1987.

xReleased, December 21, 1987; signed by Pawtucket (Boston Red Sox' organization), January 18, 1988.
yGranted free agency, November 4, 1988; re-signed by Red Sox, December 19, 1988.
zGranted free agency, November 13, 1989; signed by California Angels, December 21, 1989.

CHAMPIONSHIP SERIES RECORD

Year	Club	League	G.	IP.	W.	L.	Pct.	H.	R.	ER.	SO.	BB.	ERA.
1988—Boston		American	1	2⅓	0	0	.000	3	0	0	1	0	0.00

JOHN ANDREW SMOLTZ

Born May 15, 1967, at Detroit, Mich.
Height, 6.03. Weight, 185.
Throws and bats righthanded.

Tied for Florida State League lead in balks with 6 in 1986.

Year	Club	League	G.	IP.	W.	L.	Pct.	H.	R.	ER.	SO.	BB.	ERA.
1986—Lakeland†		Florida St.	17	96	7	8	.467	86	44	38	47	31	3.56
1987—Glens Falls		Eastern	21	130	4	10	.286	131	89	82	86	81	5.68
1987—Richmond		Int'national	3	16	0	1	.000	17	11	11	5	11	6.19
1988—Richmond		Int'national	20	135⅓	10	5	.667	118	49	42	115	37	2.79
1988—Atlanta		National	12	64	2	7	.222	74	40	39	37	33	5.48
1989—Atlanta		National	29	208	12	11	.522	160	79	68	168	72	2.94
Major League Totals—2 Years			41	272	14	18	.438	234	119	107	205	105	3.54

Selected by Detroit Tigers' organization in 22nd round of free-agent draft, June 3, 1985.
†Traded to Atlanta Braves for pitcher Doyle Alexander, August 12, 1987.

ALL-STAR GAME RECORD

Year	League	IP.	W.	L.	Pct.	H.	R.	ER.	SO.	BB.	ERA.
1989—National		1	0	1	.000	2	1	1	0	0	9.00

VAN VOORHEES SNIDER

Born August 11, 1963, at Birmingham, Ala.
Height, 6.03. Weight, 205.
Throws right and bats lefthanded.
Attended Gadsden State Junior College, Gadsden, Ala.

Led American Association in total bases with 259 and tied for lead in intentional bases on balls received with 9 in 1988.
Tied for American Association lead in sacrifice flies with 8 in 1989.
Tied for Southern League lead in intentional bases on balls received with 9 in 1986.
Led American Association outfielders in double plays with 5 in 1989.
Led South Atlantic League outfielders in double plays with 7 in 1983.
Tied for Pioneer League lead in double plays by outfielder with 2 in 1982.

Year	Club	League	Pos.	G.	AB.	R.	H.	2B.	3B.	HR.	RBI.	B.A.	PO.	A.	E.	F.A.
1982—Butte		Pion.	OF	67	237	46	71	13	5	9	53	.300	99	★14	9	.926
1983—Charleston		S. Atl.	OF	123	467	86	136	26	2	20	94	.291	207	17	★22	.911
1983—Jacksonville		South.	OF	13	33	2	6	3	0	0	2	.182	28	0	2	.933
1984—Memphis		South.	OF	132	488	52	120	23	9	7	62	.246	319	★24	4	★.988
1985—Memphis†		South.	OF	85	292	43	69	15	4	8	39	.236	166	9	★13	.931
1986—Memphis		South.	OF	134	492	79	133	27	5	26	81	.270	276	★23	6	.980
1986—Omaha		A. A.	OF	4	13	5	4	2	1	0	3	.308	7	0	0	1.000
1987—Omaha		A. A.	OF	70	244	26	50	9	1	9	27	.205	105	7	3	.974
1987—Memphis‡		South.	OF	45	174	25	57	10	7	9	40	.328	95	6	4	.962
1988—Nashville		A. A.	OF	135	525	72	152	22	8	★23	73	.290	263	14	4	.986
1988—Cincinnati		Nat.	OF	11	28	4	6	1	0	1	6	.214	15	0	0	1.000
1989—Nashville		A. A.	OF	119	442	48	98	17	●9	12	64	.222	244	15	8	.970
1989—Cincinnati§		Nat.	OF	8	7	1	1	0	0	0	0	.143	6	0	0	1.000
Major League Totals—2 Years				19	35	5	7	1	0	1	6	.200	21	0	0	1.000

Signed as free agent by Kansas City Royals' organization, November 2, 1981.
†On disabled list, May 3 to July 1, 1985.
‡Traded to Cincinnati Reds' organization for Pitcher Jeff Montgomery, February 15, 1988.
§Traded with Pitcher Tim Leary to New York Yankees for First Baseman Hal Morris and Pitcher Rodney Imes, December 12, 1989.

BRIAN ROBERT SNYDER

Born February 20, 1958, at Flemington, N.J.
Height, 6.03. Weight, 185.
Throws and bats lefthanded.
Attended Clemson University, Clemson, S.C.

Pitched 4-0 no-hit victory against Modesto, June 24, 1980.
Major League saves: 1985 (1).
Led Pacific Coast League in intentional bases on balls issued with 11 in 1982.

Year	Club	League	G.	IP.	W.	L.	Pct.	H.	R.	ER.	SO.	BB.	ERA.
1979—Alexandria		Carolina	6	31	3	3	.500	23	11	7	20	22	2.03
1980—San Jose		California	25	127	7	5	.583	139	96	80	97	92	5.67
1981—Wausau†		Midwest	27	67	3	1	.750	34	21	11	77	37	1.48
1982—Salt Lake City		P. Coast	●51	57⅓	4	3	.571	64	32	30	56	45	4.71
1983—Salt Lake City‡		P. Coast	28	49⅓	5	2	.714	53	25	24	37	31	4.38
1984—Salt Lake City		P. Coast	27	129⅔	8	9	.471	155	105	90	83	80	6.25

Year Club	League	G.	IP.	W.	L.	Pct.	H.	R.	ER.	SO.	BB.	ERA.
1985—Calgary	P. Coast	20	69⅔	4	2	.667	76	36	31	46	26	4.00
1985—Seattle§	American	15	35⅓	1	2	.333	44	28	25	23	19	6.37
1986—Las Vegas	P. Coast	45	72⅔	4	3	.571	87	56	45	62	35	5.57
1987—Las Vegas x	P. Coast	39	72⅔	5	4	.556	60	24	21	60	49	2.60
1988—Tacoma	P. Coast	54	109⅔	7	8	.467	94	37	32	86	54	2.63
1989—Tacoma	P. Coast	48	72	6	0	1.000	59	21	17	48	28	2.13
1989—Oakland y	American	2	⅔	0	0	.000	2	2	2	1	2	27.00
Major League Totals—2 Years		17	36	1	2	.333	46	30	27	24	21	6.75

Selected by Texas Rangers' organization in 16th round of free-agent draft, June 8, 1976.
Selected by Seattle Mariners' organization in 7th round of free-agent draft, June 5, 1979.
†On disabled list, April 15 to May 5, 1981.
‡On disabled list, July 30, 1983 through remainder of season.
§Released, November 1, 1985; signed by Las Vegas (San Diego Padres' organization), December 22, 1985.
xGranted free agency, October 15, 1987; signed by Oakland Athletics, December 23, 1987.
yGranted free agency, October 15, 1989.

JAMES CORY SNYDER

(Known by middle name.)

Born November 11, 1962, at Englewood, Calif.
Height, 6.03. Weight, 185.
Throws and bats righthanded.
Attended Brigham Young University, Provo, Utah.
Son of Jim Snyder, infielder in Milwaukee Braves' organization, 1961 and 1962.

Major League stolen bases: 1986 (2), 1987 (5), 1988 (5), 1989 (6). Total—18.
Hit three home runs in a game, May 21, 1987.
Led Eastern League in total bases with 255, game-winning RBIs with 14 and sacrifice flies with 12 in 1985.
Led Eastern League third basemen in putouts with 132, total chances with 391 and double plays with 26 in 1985.
Named Eastern League Most Valuable Player, 1985.
Member of 1984 U.S. Olympic baseball team.
Named shortstop on THE SPORTING NEWS College Baseball All-America Team, 1984.

Year Club	League	Pos.	G.	AB.	R.	H.	2B.	3B.	HR.	RBI.	B.A.	PO.	A.	E.	F.A.
1985—Waterbury	East.	3B-SS	★139	512	77	144	25	1	★28	★94	.281	134	231	33	.917
1986—Maine	Int.	3B-SS	49	192	25	58	19	0	9	32	.302	46	87	8	.943
1986—Cleveland	Amer.	OF-SS-3B	103	416	58	113	21	1	24	69	.272	213	84	10	.967
1987—Cleveland	Amer.	OF-SS	157	577	74	136	24	2	33	82	.236	313	53	15	.961
1988—Cleveland	Amer.	OF	142	511	71	139	24	3	26	75	.272	314	★16	5	.985
1989—Cleveland†	Amer.	★OF-SS	132	489	49	105	17	0	18	59	.215	297	32	1	★.997
1989—Canton-Akron	East.	OF	4	11	3	5	0	0	0	2	.455	5	2	0	1.000
Major League Totals—4 Years			534	1993	252	493	86	6	101	285	.247	1137	185	31	.977

Selected by Cleveland Indians' organization in 1st round (fourth player selected) of free-agent draft, June 4, 1984.
†On disabled list, July 14 to July 30, 1989; included rehabilitation disability assignment to Canton-Akron, July 24 to July 30, 1989.

LUIS SOJO

Born January 3, 1966, at Barquisimeto, Venezuela.
Height, 5.11. Weight, 165.
Throws and bats righthanded.

Year Club	League	Pos.	G.	AB.	R.	H.	2B.	3B.	HR.	RBI.	B.A.	PO.	A.	E.	F.A.
1986—				(Played in Dominican Republic League)											
1987—Myrtle Beach	S. Atl.	S-2-3-O	72	223	23	47	5	4	2	15	.211	104	123	14	.942
1988—Myrtle Beach	S. Atl.	SS	135	★536	83	★155	22	5	5	56	.289	191	407	28	.955
1989—Syracuse	Int.	★SS-2B	121	482	54	133	20	5	3	54	.276	170	348	23	★.957

Signed as free agent by Toronto Blue Jays' organization, January 3, 1986.

JULIO CESAR SOLANO

Born January 8, 1960, at Agua Blanca, Dominican Republic.
Height, 6.01. Weight, 170.
Throws and bats righthanded.

Major League saves: 1988 (3).
Led South Atlantic League in hit batsmen with 11 and tied for lead in games started by pitchers with 27 and shutouts with 3 in 1982.

Year Club	League	G.	IP.	W.	L.	Pct.	H.	R.	ER.	SO.	BB.	ERA.
1980—Sarasota Astros-Orange	Gulf Coast	18	38	5	2	.714	31	16	11	29	23	2.61
1981—Sarasota Astros-Blue	Gulf Coast	17	74	4	4	.500	71	47	32	45	36	3.89
1982—Asheville	S. Atlantic	28	178	10	7	.588	165	89	70	163	116	3.54
1983—Houston	National	4	6	0	2	.000	5	5	4	3	4	6.00
1983—Tucson	P. Coast	29	161⅔	10	7	.588	183	104	89	123	71	4.95
1984—Tucson	P. Coast	17	80⅔	3	5	.375	74	41	23	55	37	2.57
1984—Houston	National	31	50⅔	1	3	.250	31	13	11	33	18	1.95
1985—Houston	National	20	33⅔	2	2	.500	34	13	13	17	13	3.48
1985—Tucson	P. Coast	23	31⅔	2	3	.400	25	16	14	23	21	3.98
1986—Tucson	P. Coast	27	71⅓	6	4	.600	64	24	15	54	27	1.89
1986—Houston	National	16	32	3	1	.750	39	28	27	21	22	7.59
1987—Tucson†	P. Coast	42	69	5	5	.500	71	40	34	45	45	4.43
1987—Houston‡	National	11	20	0	0	.000	25	17	17	12	9	7.65
1988—Seattle	American	17	22	0	0	.000	22	13	10	10	12	4.09

Year Club	League	G.	IP.	W.	L.	Pct.	H.	R.	ER.	SO.	BB.	ERA.
1988—Calgary	P. Coast	25	35	3	2	.600	32	19	19	23	17	4.89
1989—Calgary	P. Coast	43	52⅔	5	5	.500	63	28	23	36	24	3.93
1989—Seattle§	American	7	9⅔	0	0	.000	6	8	6	6	4	5.59
National League Totals—5 Years		82	142⅓	6	8	.429	134	76	72	86	66	4.55
American League Totals—2 Years		24	31⅔	0	0	.000	28	21	16	16	16	4.55
Major League Totals—7 Years		106	174	6	8	.429	162	97	88	102	82	4.55

Signed as free agent by Houston Astros' organization, November 21, 1979.
†Played one game as an outfielder with no chances.
‡Traded to Seattle Mariners for Pitcher Doug Givler, September 30, 1987.
§Granted free agency, October 15, 1989.

PAUL ANTHONY SORRENTO

Born November 17, 1965, at Somerville, Mass.
Height, 6.02. Weight, 210.
Throws right and bats lefthanded.
Attended Florida State University, Tallahassee, Fla.

Led Southern League first basemen in double plays with 103 in 1989.

Year Club	League	Pos.	G.	AB.	R.	H.	2B.	3B.	HR.	RBI.	B.A.	PO.	A.	E.	F.A.
1986—Quad Cities	Midw.	OF	53	177	33	63	11	2	6	34	.356	83	7	1	.989
1986—Palm Springs	Calif.	OF	16	62	5	15	3	0	1	7	.242	16	1	1	.944
1987—Palm Springs	Calif.	OF	114	370	66	83	14	2	8	45	.224	123	10	4	.971
1988—Palm Springs†	Calif.	1B-OF	133	465	91	133	30	6	14	99	.286	719	55	18	.977
1989—Orlando	South.	1B	140	509	81	130	★35	2	27	★112	.255	1070	41	★24	.979
1989—Minnesota	Amer.	1B	14	21	2	5	0	0	1	1	.238	13	0	0	1.000
Major League Totals—1 Year			14	21	2	5	0	0	1	1	.238	13	0	0	1.000

Selected by California Angels' organization in 4th round of free-agent draft, June 2, 1986.
†Traded with Pitchers Mike Cook and Rob Wassenaar to Minnesota Twins for Pitchers Bert Blyleven and Kevin Trudeau, November 3, 1988.

SAMUEL SOSA
(Sammy)

Born November 10, 1968, at San Pedro de Macoris, D.R.
Height, 6.00. Weight, 175.
Throws and bats righthanded.

Major League stolen bases: 1989 (7).
Led Gulf Coast League in total bases with 96 in 1986.
Tied for South Atlantic League lead in double plays by outfielders with 4 in 1987.

Year Club	League	Pos.	G.	AB.	R.	H.	2B.	3B.	HR.	RBI.	B.A.	PO.	A.	E.	F.A.
1986—Sarasota Rangers	Gulf C.	OF	61	229	38	63	★19	1	4	28	.275	92	9	●6	.944
1987—Gastonia	S. Atl.	OF	129	519	73	145	27	4	11	59	.279	183	12	17	.920
1988—Port Charlotte	Fla. St.	OF	131	507	70	116	13	★12	9	51	.229	227	11	7	.971
1989—Tulsa	Texas	OF	66	273	45	81	15	4	7	31	.297	110	7	4	.967
1989—Texas†-Chicago	Amer.	OF	58	183	27	47	8	0	4	13	.257	94	2	4	.960
1989—Oklahoma City	A. A.	OF	10	39	2	4	2	0	0	3	.103	22	0	2	.917
1989—Vancouver	P. C.	OF	13	49	7	18	3	0	1	5	.367	43	1	0	1.000
Major League Totals—1 Year			58	183	27	47	8	0	4	13	.257	94	2	4	.960

Signed as free agent by Texas Rangers' organization, July 30, 1985.
†Traded with Shortstop Scott Fletcher and Pitcher Wilson Alvarez to Chicago White Sox for Outfielder Harold Baines and Infielder Fred Manrique, July 29, 1989.

CHRIS EDWARD SPEIER

Name pronounced Spire.

Born June 28, 1950, at Alameda, Calif.
Height, 6.01. Weight, 180.
Throws and bats righthanded.
Attended University of Santa Barbara, Santa Barbara, Calif.

Tied modern National League record for most years, shortstop (19).
Major League stolen bases: 1971 (4), 1972 (9), 1973 (4), 1974 (3), 1975 (4), 1976 (2), 1977 (1), 1978 (1), 1981 (1), 1982 (1), 1983 (2), 1985 (1), 1986 (2), 1987 (4), 1988 (3). Total—42.
Hit for the cycle, July 20, 1978 and July 9, 1988.
Led Texas League shortstops in putouts with 223 and assists with 325 in 1970.
Named shortstop on THE SPORTING NEWS National League All-Star Team, 1972.

Year Club	League	Pos.	G.	AB.	R.	H.	2B.	3B.	HR.	RBI.	B.A.	PO.	A.	E.	F.A.
1970—Amarillo	Texas	SS-3B-OF	129	460	44	130	20	5	6	66	.283	224	327	38	.935
1971—San Francisco	Nat.	SS	157	601	74	141	17	6	8	46	.235	239	517	●33	.953
1972—San Francisco	Nat.	SS	150	562	74	151	25	2	15	71	.269	243	★517	20	.974
1973—San Francisco	Nat.	●SS-2B	153	542	58	135	17	4	11	71	.249	255	471	●33	.957
1974—San Francisco	Nat.	SS-2B	141	501	55	125	19	5	9	53	.250	215	453	21	.970
1975—San Francisco	Nat.	★SS-3B	141	487	60	132	30	5	10	69	.271	247	421	12	★.982
1976—San Francisco	Nat.	S-2-3-1	145	495	51	112	18	4	3	40	.226	241	464	19	.974
1977—S.F.†-Mont.	Nat.	SS	145	548	59	128	31	6	5	38	.234	239	455	23	.968
1978—Montreal	Nat.	SS	150	501	47	126	18	3	5	51	.251	245	467	18	.975
1979—Montreal‡	Nat.	SS	113	344	31	78	13	1	7	26	.227	194	355	17	.970
1980—Montreal	Nat.	SS-3B	128	388	35	103	14	4	1	32	.265	187	397	21	.965

Year Club League	Pos.	G.	AB.	R.	H.	2B.	3B.	HR.	RBI.	B.A.	PO.	A.	E.	F.A.
1981—Montreal§ .... Nat.	SS	96	307	33	69	10	2	2	25	.225	175	280	17	.964
1982—Montreal .... Nat.	SS	156	530	41	136	26	4	7	60	.257	291	405	13	.982
1983—Montreal x .... Nat.	SS-3B-2B	88	261	31	67	12	2	2	22	.257	117	203	14	.958
1984—Mont. y-St.L. z.... Nat.	SS-3B	63	158	10	27	7	1	3	9	.171	56	152	4	.981
1984—Minnesota ab........ Amer.	SS	12	33	2	7	0	0	0	1	.212	14	28	1	.977
1985—Chicago .... Nat.	SS-3B-2B	106	218	16	53	11	0	4	24	.243	87	177	11	.960
1986—Chicago c.............. Nat.	3B-SS-2B	95	155	21	44	8	0	6	23	.284	62	106	3	.982
1987—San Francisco ...... Nat.	2B-3B-SS	111	317	39	79	13	0	11	39	.249	118	229	4	.989
1988—San Francisco ...... Nat.	2B-3B-SS	82	171	26	37	9	1	3	18	.216	70	142	3	.986
1989—San Francisco d... Nat.	S-3-2-1	28	37	7	9	4	0	0	2	.243	19	20	1	.975
1989—Phoenix e .... P. C.	SS-2B-3B	9	22	5	6	1	0	0	4	.273	10	12	1	.957
National League Totals—19 Years		2248	7123	768	1752	302	50	112	719	.246	3300	6231	287	.971
American League Totals—1 Year		12	33	2	7	0	0	0	1	.212	14	28	1	.977
Major League Totals—19 Years		2260	7156	770	1759	302	50	112	720	.246	3314	6259	288	.971

Selected by Washington Senators' organization in 11th round of free-agent draft, June 7, 1968.
Selected by San Francisco Giants' organization in secondary phase of free-agent draft, January 17, 1970.
†Traded to Montreal Expos for Shortstop Tim Foli, April 27, 1977.
‡On disabled list, July 8 to July 27, 1979.
§Granted free agency, November 13, 1981; re-signed by Expos, January 12, 1982.
xOn disabled list, May 29 to June 13, 1983.
yTraded with cash to St. Louis Cardinals for Infielder Mike Ramsey, July 1, 1984.
zTraded to Minnesota Twins for a player to be named later and cash, August 19, 1984; St. Louis Cardinals' organization acquired Pitcher Jay Pettibone to complete deal, October 2, 1984.
aOn disabled list, August 22 to September 7, 1984.
bGranted free agency, November 8, 1984; signed by Chicago Cubs, April 8, 1985.
cGranted free agency, November 12, 1986; signed by San Francisco Giants, December 12, 1986.
dOn disabled list, April 27 to May 13, May 13 to May 29 and June 5 to September 1, 1989; included rehabilitation disability assignment to Phoenix, August 16 to September 1, 1989.
eGranted free agency, November 13, 1989.

DIVISION SERIES RECORD

Year Club League	Pos.	G.	AB.	R.	H.	2B.	3B.	HR.	RBI.	B.A.	PO.	A.	E.	F.A.
1981—Montreal .... Nat.	SS	5	15	4	6	2	0	0	3	.400	16	15	0	1.000

CHAMPIONSHIP SERIES RECORD

Year Club League	Pos.	G.	AB.	R.	H.	2B.	3B.	HR.	RBI.	B.A.	PO.	A.	E.	F.A.
1971—San Francisco ...... Nat.	SS	4	14	4	5	1	0	1	1	.357	3	14	1	.944
1981—Montreal .... Nat.	SS	5	16	0	3	0	0	0	0	.188	15	16	2	.939
1987—San Francisco ...... Nat.	PH-2B	3	5	0	0	0	0	0	0	.000	1	3	0	1.000
Championship Series Totals—3 Years.....		12	35	4	8	1	0	1	1	.229	19	33	3	.945

ALL-STAR GAME RECORD

Year League	Pos.	AB.	R.	H.	2B.	3B.	HR.	RBI.	B.A.	PO.	A.	E.	F.A.
1972—National	SS	2	0	0	0	0	0	0	.000	1	5	0	1.000
1973—National	SS	2	0	0	0	0	0	0	.000	1	1	0	1.000
All-Star Game Totals—2 Years....................		4	0	0	0	0	0	0	.000	2	6	0	1.000

Member of National League All-Star Team in 1974 game; did not play.

WILLIAM JAMES SPIERS III
(Bill)

Born June 5, 1966, at Orangeburg, S.C.
Height, 6.02. Weight, 190.
Throws right and bats lefthanded.
Attended Clemson University, Clemson, S.C.

Major League stolen bases: 1989 (10).
Named shortstop on THE SPORTING NEWS College Baseball All-America Team, 1987.

Year Club League	Pos.	G.	AB.	R.	H.	2B.	3B.	HR.	RBI.	B.A.	PO.	A.	E.	F.A.
1987—Helena .... Pion.	SS	6	22	4	9	1	0	0	3	.409	8	6	6	.700
1987—Beloit .... Midw.	SS	64	258	43	77	10	1	3	26	.298	111	160	20	.931
1988—Stockton .... Calif.	SS	84	353	68	95	17	3	5	52	.269	140	240	19	.952
1988—El Paso .... Texas	SS	47	168	22	47	5	2	3	21	.280	73	141	13	.943
1989—Milwaukee............ Amer.	S-3-2-1	114	345	44	88	9	3	4	33	.255	164	295	21	.956
1989—Denver .... A. A.	SS	14	47	9	17	2	1	2	8	.362	32	33	2	.970
Major League Totals—1 Year..................		114	345	44	88	9	3	4	33	.255	164	295	21	.956

Selected by Milwaukee Brewers' organization in 1st round (13th player selected) of free-agent draft, June 2, 1987.

WILLIAM HARRY SPILMAN
(Known by middle name.)

Born July 18, 1954, at Albany, Ga.
Height, 6.01. Weight, 190.
Throws right and bats lefthanded.
Son of Harry Spilman, catcher in Los Angeles Dodgers' organization, 1952.

Major League stolen bases: 1987 (1).
Led Eastern League in total bases with 277 and intentional bases on balls received with 19 in 1977.
Named Eastern League Most Valuable Player, 1977.

Year Club	League	Pos.	G.	AB.	R.	H.	2B.	3B.	HR.	RBI.	B.A.	PO.	A.	E.	F.A.
1974—Billings	Pion.	1B-3B	54	178	29	55	12	2	2	30	.309	92	8	3	.971
1975—Tampa	Fla. St.	1B	115	348	33	90	13	1	1	38	.259	946	56	●17	.983
1976—Tampa	Fla. St.	1B	118	361	50	90	12	5	6	35	.249	986	70	16	.985
1977—Three Rivers	East.	1B	133	493	*94	*184	*39	3	16	78	.373	1095	78	7	.994
1978—Indianapolis	A. A.	3B-1B	133	488	95	144	26	4	13	79	.295	262	184	23	.951
1978—Cincinnati	Nat.	PH	4	4	1	1	0	0	0	0	.250	0	0	0	.000
1979—Indianapolis	A. A.	3B-1B	71	267	42	77	13	3	3	27	.288	154	92	8	.969
1979—Cincinnati	Nat.	1B-3B-OF	43	56	7	12	3	0	0	5	.214	64	11	0	1.000
1980—Cincinnati	Nat.	1-3-O-C	65	101	14	27	4	0	4	19	.267	132	15	2	.987
1981—Cinc.†-Hou.	Nat.	1B	51	58	9	14	1	0	0	4	.241	62	5	1	.985
1982—Tucson	P. C.	1B-3B	53	190	34	63	16	3	6	33	.332	307	13	3	.991
1982—Houston	Nat.	1B	38	61	7	17	2	0	3	11	.279	86	5	1	.989
1983—Houston	Nat.	1B-C	42	78	7	13	3	0	1	9	.167	138	8	0	1.000
1984—Houston‡	Nat.	1B-C	32	72	14	19	2	0	2	15	.264	143	9	3	.981
1985—Houston§	Nat.	1B-C	44	66	3	9	1	0	1	4	.136	134	4	0	1.000
1986—Detroit x	Amer.	3B-1B-C	24	49	6	12	2	0	3	8	.245	7	1	0	1.000
1986—San Francisco y	Nat.	1-3-2-O-C	58	94	12	27	7	0	2	22	.287	140	17	2	.987
1987—San Francisco	Nat.	3B-1B-C	83	90	5	24	5	0	1	14	.267	40	7	2	.959
1988—S. F. z-Hou.	Nat.	1B-C-OF	47	45	4	7	1	1	1	3	.156	24	3	1	.964
1988—Phoe.-Tucs. a	P. C.	1B	20	64	12	21	4	1	4	17	.328	121	9	1	.992
1989—Tucson	P. C.	1B	69	230	29	63	12	1	5	38	.274	164	11	3	.983
1989—Houston b	Nat.	1B-C	32	36	7	10	3	0	0	3	.278	47	4	0	1.000
National League Totals—12 Years			539	761	90	180	32	1	15	109	.237	1010	88	12	.989
American League Totals—1 Year			24	49	6	12	2	0	3	8	.245	7	1	0	1.000
Major League Totals—12 Years			563	810	96	192	34	1	18	117	.237	1017	89	12	.989

Signed as free agent by Cincinnati Reds' organization, June 25, 1974.

†Traded to Houston Astros for Second Baseman Rafael Landestoy, June 8, 1981.

‡On disabled list, July 16, 1984 through remainder of season.

§Granted free agency, November 12, 1985; signed with Nashville (Detroit Tigers' organization), February 18, 1986.

xReleased, June 12, 1986; signed by San Francisco Giants, June 13, 1986.

yGranted free agency, November 12, 1986; re-signed by Giants, December 12, 1986.

zReleased, August 11, 1988; signed by Tucson (Houston Astros' organization), August 17, 1988.

aGranted free agency, November 4, 1988; re-signed by Astros' organization, February 7, 1989.

bGranted free agency, November 13, 1989; re-signed by Astros, December 19, 1989.

DIVISION SERIES RECORD

Year Club	League	Pos.	G.	AB.	R.	H.	2B.	3B.	HR.	RBI.	B.A.	PO.	A.	E.	F.A.
1981—Houston	Nat.	PH	1	1	0	0	0	0	0	0	.000	0	0	0	.000

CHAMPIONSHIP SERIES RECORD

Year Club	League	Pos.	G.	AB.	R.	H.	2B.	3B.	HR.	RBI.	B.A.	PO.	A.	E.	F.A.
1979—Cincinnati	Nat.	PH	2	2	0	0	0	0	0	0	.000	0	0	0	.000
1987—San Francisco	Nat.	PH	3	2	1	1	0	0	1	1	.500	0	0	0	.000
Championship Series Totals—2 Years			5	4	1	1	0	0	1	1	.250	0	0	0	.000

STEPHEN BLAIR STANICEK

Name pronounced Stan-i-sek.

(Steve)

Born June 19, 1961, at Lake Forest, Ill.
Height, 6.00. Weight, 190.
Throws and bats righthanded.
Attended University of Nebraska, Lincoln, Neb.
Brother of Pete Stanicek, second baseman in Baltimore Orioles' organization.

Led American Association in total bases with 292 in 1987.

Led Texas League batters in total bases with 284, game-winning RBIs with 15 and bases on balls received with 88 in 1986.

Named Texas League Most Valuable Player, 1986.

Named designated hitter on THE SPORTING NEWS College Baseball All-America Team, 1982.

Year Club	League	Pos.	G.	AB.	R.	H.	2B.	3B.	HR.	RBI.	B.A.	PO.	A.	E.	F.A.
1982—Fresno	Calif.	1B-3B	22	69	9	17	3	0	3	6	.246	122	11	2	.985
1983—Fresno	Calif.	1B	126	438	68	106	15	3	16	77	.242	596	63	15	.978
1984—Shreveport	Texas	1B	94	271	36	63	12	2	5	34	.232	609	43	11	.983
1985—Shreveport†	Texas	1B-3B	119	401	57	113	17	2	13	54	.282	516	140	35	.949
1986—El Paso	Texas	1-3-O-S	127	487	*116	*167	*40	1	25	93	*.343	683	102	26	.968
1987—Denver	A. A.	OF-1B-3B	117	474	90	*167	*40	5	25	106	.352	226	30	10	.962
1987—Milwaukee	Amer.	DH	4	7	2	2	0	0	0	0	.286	0	0	0	.000
1988—Denver‡§	A. A.	OF-1B	27	92	18	28	6	0	2	19	.304	48	2	1	.980
1989—Scr./Wil.-Barre	Int.	1B	103	368	43	105	25	3	9	54	.285	557	43	10	.984
1989—Philadelphia x	Nat.	PH	9	9	0	1	0	0	0	1	.111	0	0	0	.000
National League Totals—1 Year			9	9	0	1	0	0	0	1	.111	0	0	0	.000
American League Totals—1 Year			4	7	2	2	0	0	0	0	.286	0	0	0	.000
Major League Totals—2 Years			13	16	2	3	0	0	0	1	.188	0	0	0	.000

Selected by St. Louis Cardinals' organization in 16th round of free-agent draft, June 5, 1979.

Selected by San Francisco Giants' organization in 1st round (11th player selected) of free-agent draft, June 7, 1982.

†Traded to Milwaukee Brewers' organization for Outfielder Rob DeWolf, March 26, 1986.

‡On Milwaukee disabled list, March 26 to June 9, 1988; included rehabiliation disability assignment to Denver, May 27 to June 9, 1988.
§Released, October 26, 1988; signed by Scranton/Wilkes-Barre (Philadelphia Phillies' organization), January 11, 1989.
xReleased, October 11, 1989.

ROBERT MICHAEL STANLEY
(Mike)

Born June 25, 1963, at Fort Lauderdale, Fla.
Height, 6.01. Weight, 185.
Throws and bats righthanded.
Attended University of Florida, Gainesville, Fla.

Major League stolen bases: 1986 (1), 1987 (3), 1989 (1). Total—5.

Year Club	League	Pos.	G.	AB.	R.	H.	2B.	3B.	HR.	RBI.	B.A.	PO.	A.	E.	F.A.
1985—Salem	Carol.	1B-C	4	9	2	5	0	0	0	3	.556	19	1	1	.952
1985—Burlington	Midw.	C-1B-OF	13	42	8	13	2	0	1	6	.310	45	2	0	1.000
1985—Tulsa	Texas	C-1-O-2	46	165	24	51	10	0	3	17	.309	289	18	6	.981
1986—Tulsa	Texas	C-1B-3B	67	235	41	69	16	2	6	35	.294	379	45	2	.995
1986—Texas	Amer.	3B-C-OF	15	30	4	10	3	0	1	1	.333	14	8	1	.957
1986—Oklahoma City	A. A.	C-3B-1B	56	202	37	74	13	3	5	49	.366	206	55	9	.967
1987—Oklahoma City	A. A.	C-1B	46	182	43	61	8	3	13	54	.335	277	32	2	.994
1987—Texas	Amer.	C-1B-OF	78	216	34	59	8	1	6	37	.273	389	26	7	.983
1988—Texas†	Amer.	C-1B-3B	94	249	21	57	8	0	3	27	.229	342	17	4	.989
1989—Texas‡	Amer.	C-1B-3B	67	122	9	30	3	1	1	11	.246	117	8	3	.977
Major League Totals—4 Years			254	617	68	156	22	2	11	76	.253	862	59	15	.984

Selected by Texas Rangers' organization in 16th round of free-agent draft, June 3, 1985.
†On disabled list, July 24 to August 14, 1988.
‡On disabled list, August 18 to September 2, 1989.

ROBERT WILLIAM STANLEY
(Bob)

Born November 10, 1954, at Portland, Me.
Height, 6.04. Weight, 225.
Throws and bats righthanded.

Holds American League record for most innings pitched by relief pitcher, season (168⅓), 1982.
Major League saves: 1977 (3), 1978 (10), 1979 (1), 1980 (14), 1982 (14), 1983 (33), 1984 (22), 1985 (10), 1986 (16), 1988 (5), 1989 (4). Total—132.
Led Eastern League in hit batsmen with 11 and tied for lead in games started by pitchers with 27 in 1976.
Led New York-Pennsylvania League pitchers in games started with 15 in 1974.
Tied for Florida State League lead in games started by pitchers with 26 in 1975.

Year Club	League	G.	IP.	W.	L.	Pct.	H.	R.	ER.	SO.	BB.	ERA.
1974—Elmira	NYP	15	86	6	6	.500	94	57	44	45	40	4.60
1975—Winter Haven	Florida St.	27	169	5	*17	.227	136	76	55	73	74	2.93
1976—Bristol†	Eastern	27	186	15	9	.625	176	76	55	78	83	2.66
1977—Boston	American	41	151	8	7	.533	176	74	67	44	43	3.99
1978—Boston	American	52	142	15	2	.882	142	50	41	38	34	2.60
1979—Boston	American	40	217	16	12	.571	250	110	96	56	44	3.98
1980—Boston	American	52	175	10	8	.556	186	75	66	71	52	3.39
1981—Boston	American	35	99	10	8	.556	110	46	42	28	38	3.82
1982—Boston	American	48	168⅓	12	7	.632	161	60	58	83	50	3.10
1983—Boston	American	64	145⅓	8	10	.444	145	56	46	65	38	2.85
1984—Boston	American	57	106⅔	9	10	.474	113	57	42	52	23	3.54
1985—Boston	American	48	87⅔	6	6	.500	76	30	28	46	30	2.87
1986—Boston	American	66	82⅓	6	6	.500	109	48	40	54	22	4.37
1987—Boston‡	American	34	152⅔	4	15	.211	198	96	85	67	42	5.01
1988—Boston§	American	57	101⅔	6	4	.600	90	41	36	57	29	3.19
1988—Winter Haven	Florida St.	2	10	0	1	.000	13	9	8	3	3	7.20
1988—Pawtucket	Int'national	4	11	1	0	1.000	7	1	1	6	5	0.82
1989—Boston x	American	43	79⅓	5	2	.714	102	54	43	32	26	4.88
Major League Totals—13 Years		637	1708	115	97	.542	1858	797	690	693	471	3.64

Selected by Los Angeles Dodgers' organization in 9th round of free-agent draft, June 5, 1973.
Selected by Boston Red Sox' organization in secondary phase of free-agent draft, January 9, 1974.
†On disabled list, June 19 to June 24, 1976.
‡On disabled list, June 28 to July 16, 1987.
§On Boston disabled list, March 26 to May 12, 1988; included rehabilitation disability assignment to Winter Haven, April 20 to May 10, 1988.
xReleased, December 20, 1989.

CHAMPIONSHIP SERIES RECORD

Year Club	League	G.	IP.	W.	L.	Pct.	H.	R.	ER.	SO.	BB.	ERA.
1986—Boston	American	3	5⅔	0	0	.000	7	4	3	1	3	4.76
1988—Boston	American	2	1	0	0	.000	2	1	1	0	1	9.00
Championship Series Totals—2 Years		5	6⅔	0	0	.000	9	5	4	1	4	5.40

WORLD SERIES RECORD

Year Club	League	G.	IP.	W.	L.	Pct.	H.	R.	ER.	SO.	BB.	ERA.
1986—Boston	American	5	6⅓	0	0	.000	5	0	0	4	1	0.00

Year League	IP.	W.	L.	Pct.	H.	R.	ER.	SO.	BB.	ERA.
1979—American	2	0	0	.000	1	1	1	0	0	4.50
1983—American	2	0	0	.000	2	0	0	0	0	0.00
All-Star Game Totals—2 Years	4	0	0	.000	3	1	1	0	0	2.25

WILLIAM MICHAEL STANTON
(Mike)

Born June 2, 1967, at Houston, Tex.
Height, 6.01. Weight, 190.
Throws and bats lefthanded.
Attended Alvin Community College, Alvin, Tex.

Major League saves: 1989 (7).

Year Club	League	G.	IP.	W.	L.	Pct.	H.	R.	ER.	SO.	BB.	ERA.
1987—Pulaski	Ap'lachian	15	83⅓	4	8	.333	64	37	30	82	42	3.24
1988—Burlington	Midwest	30	154	11	5	.688	154	86	62	160	69	3.62
1988—Durham	Carolina	2	12⅓	1	0	1.000	14	3	2	14	5	1.46
1989—Greenville	Southern	47	51⅓	4	1	.800	32	10	9	58	31	1.58
1989—Richmond	Int'national	13	20	2	0	1.000	6	0	0	20	13	0.00
1989—Atlanta	National	20	24	0	1	.000	17	4	4	27	8	1.50
Major League Totals—1 Year		20	24	0	1	.000	17	4	4	27	8	1.50

Selected by Atlanta Braves' organization in 13th round of free-agent draft, June 2, 1987.

RANDY ANTHONY ST. CLAIRE

Born August 23, 1960, at Glens Falls, N.Y.
Height, 6.02. Weight, 190.
Throws and bats righthanded.
Son of Ebba St. Claire, catcher with Boston Braves,
Milwaukee Braves and New York Giants, 1951 through 1954;
and brother of Steve St. Claire, pitcher-outfielder in Montreal Expos' organization, 1984 through 1988.
Major League saves: 1986 (1), 1987 (7), 1989 (1). Total—9.
Led Southern League in intentional bases on balls issued with 14 in 1984.

Year Club	League	G.	IP.	W.	L.	Pct.	H.	R.	ER.	SO.	BB.	ERA.
1979—Calgary	Pioneer	6	33	1	2	.333	30	22	16	17	15	4.36
1980—Calgary	Pioneer	21	57	5	7	.417	65	36	27	51	23	4.26
1981—Jamestown	NYP	13	51	4	1	.800	53	22	11	36	17	1.94
1982—San Jose	California	9	61	2	5	.286	58	32	28	44	20	4.13
1982—West Palm Beach	Florida St.	19	65	3	8	.273	74	41	38	38	17	5.26
1983—West Palm Beach	Florida St.	42	98	5	7	.417	72	33	23	77	31	2.11
1984—Jacksonville	Southern	48	75	10	7	.588	64	35	24	56	29	2.88
1984—Indianapolis	Am. Assoc.	13	17⅔	1	1	.500	15	2	2	17	6	1.02
1984—Montreal	National	4	8	0	0	.000	11	4	4	4	2	4.50
1985—Indianapolis†	Am. Assoc.	11	19⅔	0	1	1.000	21	5	4	11	3	1.83
1985—Montreal	National	42	68⅔	5	3	.625	69	32	30	25	26	3.93
1986—Indianapolis	Am. Assoc.	⋆57	99⅓	5	7	.417	105	49	44	72	29	3.99
1986—Montreal	National	11	19	2	0	1.000	13	5	5	21	6	2.37
1987—Montreal	National	44	67	3	3	.500	64	31	30	43	20	4.03
1987—Indianapolis	Am. Assoc.	18	20⅔	0	1	.000	12	5	5	15	12	3.82
1988—Montreal‡-Cincinnati	National	16	21	1	0	1.000	24	13	9	14	10	3.86
1988—Indianapolis-Nashville§	Am. Assoc.	36	40⅓	0	3	.000	35	15	12	27	9	2.68
1989—Portland	P. Coast	27	45⅓	4	0	1.000	39	21	16	48	17	3.18
1989—Minnesota x	American	14	22⅓	1	0	1.000	19	13	13	14	10	5.24
National League Totals—5 Years		117	183⅔	11	6	.647	181	85	78	107	64	3.82
American League Totals—1 Year		14	22⅓	1	0	1.000	19	13	13	14	10	5.24
Major League Totals—6 Years		131	206	12	6	.667	200	98	91	121	74	3.98

Signed as free agent by Montreal Expos' organization, September 9, 1978.
†On disabled list, May 7 to May 17, 1985.
‡Traded with Catcher Jeff Reed and Outfielder Herm Winningham to Cincinnati Reds for Outfielder Tracy Jones and Pitcher Pat Pacillo, July 13, 1988.
§Released, March 28, 1989; signed by Portland (Minnesota Twins' organization), April 1, 1989.
xGranted free agency, October 15, 1989.

JAMES EARL STEELS
(Jim)

Born May 30, 1961, at Jackson, Miss.
Height, 5.10. Weight, 185.
Throws and bats lefthanded.
Attended Allan Hancock College, Santa Maria, Calif.

Major League stolen bases: 1987 (3), 1988 (2). Total—5.
Named Texas League Most Valuable Player, 1984.

Year Club	League	Pos.	G.	AB.	R.	H.	2B.	3B.	HR.	RBI.	B.A.	PO.	A.	E.	F.A.
1980—Reno†	Calif.	OF	73	285	42	86	8	4	3	27	.302	78	9	5	.946
1981—Amarillo	Texas	OF-1B	127	485	58	138	28	5	3	59	.285	206	14	8	.965
1982—Amarillo	Texas	1B	86	371	61	118	16	8	6	57	.318	789	61	⋆20	.977
1982—Hawaii	P. C.	OF-1B	52	196	33	49	10	6	4	26	.250	103	2	4	.963

Year Club	League	Pos.	G.	AB.	R.	H.	2B.	3B.	HR.	RBI.	B.A.	PO.	A.	E.	F.A.
1983—Las Vegas.............	P. C.	OF-1B	28	95	17	23	5	1	1	14	.242	47	4	0	1.000
1983—Beaumont.............	Texas	OF-1B	83	313	57	84	17	4	10	61	.268	188	10	7	.966
1984—Beaumont.............	Texas	OF-P-1B	127	474	90	161	26	10	12	81	★.340	195	15	5	.977
1985—Las Vegas‡...........	P. C.	OF	111	394	39	103	19	4	5	46	.261	163	12	3	.983
1986—Las Vegas.............	P. C.	OF	126	482	87	148	28	9	8	64	.307	228	●16	12	.953
1987—San Diego	Nat.	OF	62	68	9	13	1	1	0	6	.191	23	1	1	.960
1987—Las Vegas§...........	P. C.	OF-1B	15	53	12	17	3	1	0	5	.321	46	4	1	.980
1988—Oklahoma City	A. A.	OF-1B	37	144	21	45	7	2	0	11	.313	92	7	6	.943
1988—Texas x	Amer.	OF-1B	36	53	4	10	1	0	0	5	.189	41	2	1	.977
1989—San Francisco	Nat.	1B-OF	13	12	0	1	0	0	0	0	.083	15	2	0	1.000
1989—Phoenix y	P. C.	OF-1B	103	368	68	100	21	4	6	45	.272	170	7	5	.973
1989—Indianapolis z	A. A.	OF	2	9	3	5	0	0	2	3	.556	4	1	0	1.000
National League Totals—2 Years............			75	80	9	14	1	1	0	6	.175	38	3	1	.976
American League Totals—1 Year			36	53	4	10	1	0	0	5	.189	41	2	1	.977
Major League Totals—3 Years.................			111	133	13	24	2	1	0	11	.180	79	5	2	.977

Selected by San Diego Padres' organization in 8th round of free-agent draft, June 5, 1979.
†On disabled list, April 29 to June 16, 1980.
‡On disabled list, July 6 to July 24, 1985.
§Granted free agency, October 15, 1987; signed by Texas Rangers, October 23, 1987.
xGranted free agency, October 15, 1988; signed by San Francisco Giants, January 17, 1989.
yTraded to Indianapolis (Montreal Expos' organization) for a player to be named later, August 3, 1989.
zGranted free agency, October 15, 1989.

PITCHING RECORD

Year Club	League	G.	IP.	W.	L.	Pct.	H.	R.	ER.	SO.	BB.	ERA.
1984—Beaumont..	Texas	3	4⅔	0	0	.000	3	4	4	2	10	7.71

TERRY LEE STEINBACH

Born March 2, 1962, at New Ulm, Minn.
Height, 6.01. Weight, 195.
Throws and bats righthanded.
Attended University of Minnesota, Minneapolis, Minn.
Brother of Tom Steinbach, outfielder in Seattle Mariners' organization, 1983.

Shares major league record by hitting home run in first major league at-bat, September 12, 1986.
Major League stolen bases: 1987 (1), 1988 (3), 1989 (1). Total—5.
Led Southern League in passed balls with 22 in 1986.
Led Midwest League third basemen in double plays with 31 in 1984.
Led Northwest League third basemen in assists with 122 and tied for lead in errors with 17 in 1983.
Named Southern League Most Valuable Player, 1986.

Year Club	League	Pos.	G.	AB.	R.	H.	2B.	3B.	HR.	RBI.	B.A.	PO.	A.	E.	F.A.
1983—Medford	N'west	3B-OF-1B	62	219	42	69	16	0	6	38	.315	105	124	21	.916
1984—Madison	Midw.	3B-1B-P	135	474	57	140	24	6	11	79	.295	107	257	27	.931
1985—Huntsville	South.	C-3-1-O-P	128	456	64	124	31	3	9	72	.272	187	43	6	.975
1986—Huntsville	South.	C-1B-3B	138	505	113	164	33	2	24	★132	.325	620	73	14	.980
1986—Oakland.................	Amer.	C	6	15	3	5	0	0	2	4	.333	21	4	1	.962
1987—Oakland.................	Amer.	C-3B-1B	122	391	66	111	16	3	16	56	.284	642	44	10	.986
1988—Oakland†...............	Amer.	C-3-1-O	104	351	42	93	19	1	9	51	.265	536	58	9	.985
1989—Oakland.................	Amer.	C-O-1-3	130	454	37	124	13	1	7	42	.273	612	47	11	.984
Major League Totals—4 Years.................			362	1211	148	333	48	5	34	153	.275	1811	153	31	.984

Selected by Cleveland Indians' organization in 16th round of free-agent draft, June 3, 1980.
Selected by Oakland A's organization in 9th round of free-agent draft, June 6, 1983.
†On disabled list, May 6 to June 1, 1988.

CHAMPIONSHIP SERIES RECORD

Year Club	League	Pos.	G.	AB.	R.	H.	2B.	3B.	HR.	RBI.	B.A.	PO.	A.	E.	F.A.
1988—Oakland.................	Amer.	C	2	4	0	1	0	0	0	0	.250	12	0	0	1.000
1989—Oakland.................	Amer.	C-DH	4	15	0	3	0	0	0	1	.200	17	0	0	1.000
Championship Series Totals—2 Years.....			6	19	0	4	0	0	0	1	.211	2	0	0	1.000

WORLD SERIES RECORD

Year Club	League	Pos.	G.	AB.	R.	H.	2B.	3B.	HR.	RBI.	B.A.	PO.	A.	E.	F.A.
1988—Oakland.................	Amer.	C-DH	3	11	0	4	1	0	0	0	.364	11	3	0	1.000
1989—Oakland.................	Amer.	C	4	16	3	4	0	1	1	7	.250	27	2	0	1.000
World Series Totals—2 Years			7	27	3	8	1	1	1	7	.296	38	5	0	1.000

ALL-STAR GAME RECORD

Shares All-Star Game record for hitting home run in first at-bat, July 12, 1988.

Year League	Pos.	AB.	R.	H.	2B.	3B.	HR.	RBI.	B.A.	PO.	A.	E.	F.A.
1988—American	C	1	1	1	0	0	1	2	1.000	3	1	1	.800
1989—American	C	3	0	1	0	0	0	0	.333	6	1	0	1.000
All-Star Game Totals—2 Years...................		4	1	2	0	0	1	2	.500	9	2	1	.917

PITCHING RECORD

Year Club	League	G.	IP.	W.	L.	Pct.	H.	R.	ER.	SO.	BB.	ERA.
1984—Madison	Midwest	2	3	0	0	.000	2	4	3	0	4	9.00
1985—Huntsville	Southern	1	1	0	0	.000	0	0	0	0	0	0.00

CARL RAY STEPHENS JR.

(Known by middle name.)
Born September 22, 1962, at Houston, Tex.
Height, 6.00. Weight, 190.
Throws and bats righthanded.
Attended Middle Georgia College, Cochran, Ga.,
and Troy State University, Troy, Ala.

Led American Association catchers in total chances with 661 and passed balls with 13 in 1988.

Year	Club	League	Pos.	G.	AB.	R.	H.'	2B.	3B.	HR.	RBI.	B.A.	PO.	A.	E.	F.A.
1985—Erie		NYP	C	9	31	3	9	1	1	1	5	.290	68	17	1	.988
1985—Savannah	S. Atl.		C	39	127	11	26	6	0	0	6	.205	229	30	4	.985
1986—Savannah	S. Atl.		C	95	325	52	71	10	0	13	56	.218	570	★70	12	.982
1986—Louisville	A. A.		C	12	31	2	6	1	0	1	2	.194	38	6	1	.978
1987—Arkansas	Texas		C	100	307	35	77	20	0	8	42	.251	553	75	5	.992
1987—Louisville	A. A.		C	9	30	1	4	0	0	0	2	.133	53	4	1	.983
1988—Louisville	A. A.		C	115	355	26	67	13	2	3	25	.189	★590	★64	7	★.989
1989—Arkansas	Texas		C	112	363	49	95	14	0	7	44	.262	545	63	9	.985

Selected by St. Louis Cardinals' organization in 6th round of free-agent draft, June 3, 1985.

PHILLIP RAYMOND STEPHENSON
(Phil)

Born September 19, 1960, at Guthrie, Okla.
Height, 6.01. Weight, 195.
Throws and bats lefthanded.
Received bachelor of arts degree in business management from Wichita State University, Wichita, Kan.
Brother of Gene Stephenson, baseball coach at Wichita State University.

Major League stolen bases: 1989 (1).
Led American Association in intentional bases on balls received with 9 in 1989 and tied for lead with 9 in 1988.
Led American Association in slugging percentage with .566 in 1988.
Led Eastern League in bases on balls received with 114 in 1983 and 129 in 1986.
Tied for Eastern League lead in sacrifice flies with 10 in 1983.
Led American Association first basemen in double plays with 103 in 1988.
Led Eastern League first basemen in putouts with 1,164 and total chances with 1,332 in 1986.
Named first baseman on THE SPORTING NEWS College Baseball All-America Team, 1981.

Year	Club	League	Pos.	G.	AB.	R.	H.	2B.	3B.	HR.	RBI.	B.A.	PO.	A.	E.	F.A.
1982—Modesto	Calif.		1B	64	212	39	60	14	2	5	26	.283	436	39	4	.992
1983—Albany	East.		●1B-OF	133	436	90	122	●30	3	19	77	.280	771	85	●14	.984
1984—Tacoma	P. C.		OF-1B	124	398	70	120	25	1	10	69	.302	418	40	9	.981
1985—Tacoma†	P. C.		OF-1B	56	171	30	36	11	0	5	24	.211	117	6	5	.961
1985—Midland‡	Texas		1B-OF	50	176	39	52	14	0	7	41	.295	340	27	3	.992
1986—Pittsfield	East.		★1B-OF-P	●140	423	72	115	29	2	12	68	.272	1165	★163	5	★.996
1987—Iowa	A. A.		1B-OF	105	298	53	91	24	2	10	56	.305	735	71	10	.988
1988—Iowa	A. A.		1B	118	426	69	125	28	11	22	81	.293	925	★88	10	.990
1989—Chi.§x-S.D.	Nat.		1B-OF	27	38	4	9	0	0	2	2	.237	42	4	1	.979
1989—Iowa	A. A.		1B-OF	84	290	52	87	17	3	13	62	.300	648	51	7	.990
Major League Totals—1 Year				27	38	4	9	0	0	2	2	.237	42	4	1	.979

Selected by Montreal Expos' organization in 5th round of free-agent draft, June 8, 1981.
Selected by Oakland A's organization in 3rd round of free-agent draft, June 7, 1982.
†Loaned to Midland (California Angels' organization), July 7, 1985; returned, September 10, 1985.
‡Traded with Third Baseman Bob Bathe to Chicago Cubs for Second Baseman Gary Jones and Pitcher John Cox, January 17, 1986.
§On disabled list, May 27 to June 11, 1989.
xTraded to San Diego Padres, September 5, 1989, completing deal in which Chicago Cubs traded Pitcher Calvin Schiraldi, Outfielder Darrin Jackson and a player to be named later to San Diego for Outfielder Marvell Wynne and Infielder Luis Salazar, August 30, 1989.

PITCHING RECORD

Year	Club	League	G.	IP.	W.	L.	Pct.	H.	R.	ER.	SO.	BB.	ERA.
1986—Pittsfield		Eastern	3	4	0	0	.000	1	0	0	1	2	0.00

DeWAIN LEE STEVENS

(Known by middle name.)

Born July 10, 1967, at Kansas City, Mo.
Height, 6.04. Weight, 205.
Throws and bats lefthanded.

Tied for Northwest League lead in game-winning RBIs with 8 in 1986.
Led Texas League outfielders in errors with 12 in 1988.
Led California League first basemen in putouts with 1,028, assists with 66 and fielding percentage with .986 in 1987.

Year	Club	League	Pos.	G.	AB.	R.	H.	2B.	3B.	HR.	RBI.	B.A.	PO.	A.	E.	F.A.
1986—Salem	N'west		OF-1B	72	267	45	75	18	2	6	47	.281	231	18	5	.980
1987—Palm Springs	Calif.		1B-OF	140	532	82	130	29	2	19	97	.244	1031	68	18	.984
1988—Midland	Texas		OF-1B	116	414	79	123	26	2	23	76	.297	217	16	14	.943
1989—Edmonton	P. C.		1B-OF	127	446	72	110	29	9	14	74	.247	635	40	7	.990

Selected by California Angels' organization in 1st round (22nd player selected) of free-agent draft, June 2, 1986.

DAVID KEITH STEWART
(Dave)

Born February 19, 1957, at Oakland, Calif.
Height, 6.02. Weight, 200.
Throws and bats righthanded.
Attended Merritt College, Oakland, Calif., and California State University, Hayward, Calif.

Major League saves: 1981 (6), 1982 (1), 1983 (8), 1985 (4). Total—19.
Led American League in balks with 16 and tied for lead in complete games with 14 in 1988.
Led American League pitchers in games started with 37 in 1988 and tied for lead with 36 in 1989.
Led Pacific Coast League pitchers in games started with 29 in 1980.
Tied for Texas League lead in games started by pitchers with 28 in 1978.
Tied for Midwest League lead in complete games with 15, shutouts with 3 and balks with 3 in 1977.
Named righthanded pitcher on THE SPORTING NEWS American League All-Star Team, 1988.

Year	Club	League	G.	IP.	W.	L.	Pct.	H.	R.	ER.	SO.	BB.	ERA.
1975—Bellingham	Northwest	22	49	0	5	.000	59	46	30	37	49	5.51
1976—Danville	Midwest	4	10	0	2	.000	17	20	18	10	16	16.20
1976—Bellingham	Northwest	24	50	1	1	.500	47	35	28	53	58	5.04
1977—Clinton	Midwest	24	176	★17	4	★.810	152	52	42	144	72	2.15
1977—Albuquerque	P. Coast	1	6	1	0	1.000	4	3	3	3	6	4.50
1978—San Antonio	Texas	28	★193	14	12	.538	181	99	79	130	97	3.68
1978—Los Angeles	National	1	2	0	0	.000	1	0	0	1	0	0.00
1979—Albuquerque	P. Coast	28	170	11	12	.478	198	112	99	105	81	5.24
1980—Albuquerque	P. Coast	31	★202	●15	10	.600	189	94	83	125	89	3.70
1981—Los Angeles	National	32	43	4	3	.571	40	13	12	29	14	2.51
1982—Los Angeles	National	45	146⅓	9	8	.529	137	72	62	80	49	3.81
1983—Los Angeles†	National	46	76	5	2	.714	67	28	25	54	33	2.96
1983—Texas	American	8	59	5	2	.714	50	15	14	24	17	2.14
1984—Texas	American	32	192⅓	7	14	.333	193	106	101	119	87	4.73
1985—Texas‡	American	42	81⅓	0	6	.000	86	53	49	64	37	5.42
1985—Philadelphia	National	4	4⅓	0	0	.000	5	4	3	2	4	6.23
1986—Philadelphia§	National	8	12⅓	0	0	.000	15	9	9	9	4	6.57
1986—Tacoma	P. Coast	1	3	0	0	.000	4	1	0	3	1	0.00
1986—Oakland	American	29	149⅓	9	5	.643	137	67	62	102	65	3.74
1987—Oakland	American	37	261⅓	●20	13	.606	224	121	107	205	105	3.68
1988—Oakland	American	37	★275⅔	21	12	.636	240	111	99	192	110	3.23
1989—Oakland	American	36	257⅔	21	9	.700	★260	105	95	155	69	3.32
National League Totals—6 Years		136	284	18	13	.581	265	126	111	175	104	3.52
American League Totals—7 Years		221	1276⅔	83	61	.576	1190	578	527	861	490	3.72
Major League Totals—10 Years		357	1560⅔	101	74	.577	1455	704	638	1036	594	3.68

Selected by Los Angeles Dodgers' organization in 16th round of free-agent draft, June 4, 1975.

†Traded with a player to be named later to Texas Rangers for Pitcher Rick Honeycutt, August 19, 1983; Texas acquired Pitcher Ricky Wright to complete deal, September 16, 1983.

‡Traded to Philadelphia Phillies for Pitcher Rick Surhoff, September 13, 1985.

§Released, May 9, 1986; signed by Tacoma (Oakland A's organization), May 23, 1986.

DIVISION SERIES RECORD

Year	Club	League	G.	IP.	W.	L.	Pct.	H.	R.	ER.	SO.	BB.	ERA.
1981—Los Angeles	National	2	⅔	0	2	.000	4	3	3	1	0	40.50

CHAMPIONSHIP SERIES RECORD

Shares American League Championship Series record for most games won, series (2), 1989.

Year	Club	League	G.	IP.	W.	L.	Pct.	H.	R.	ER.	SO.	BB.	ERA.
1988—Oakland	American	2	13⅓	1	0	1.000	9	2	2	11	6	1.35
1989—Oakland	American	2	16	2	0	1.000	13	5	5	9	3	2.81
Championship Series Totals—2 Years		4	29⅓	3	0	1.000	22	7	7	20	9	2.15

WORLD SERIES RECORD

Year	Club	League	G.	IP.	W.	L.	Pct.	H.	R.	ER.	SO.	BB.	ERA.
1981—Los Angeles	National	2	1⅔	0	0	.000	1	0	0	1	2	0.00
1988—Oakland	American	2	14⅓	0	1	.000	12	7	5	5	5	3.14
1989—Oakland	American	2	16	2	0	1.000	10	3	3	14	2	1.69
World Series Totals—3 Years		6	32	2	1	.667	23	10	8	20	9	2.25

ALL-STAR GAME RECORD

Year	League	IP.	W.	L.	Pct.	H.	R.	ER.	SO.	BB.	ERA.
1989—American		1	0	0	.000	3	2	2	0	2	18.00

DAVID ANDREW STIEB

Name pronounced Steeb.

(Dave)

Born July 22, 1957, at Santa Ana, Calif.
Height, 6.00. Weight, 195.
Throws and bats righthanded.
Attended Santa Ana College, Santa Ana, Calif., and
Southern Illinois University, Carbondale, Ill.
Brother of Steve Stieb, catcher in Atlanta Braves' organization, 1979 through 1981.

Shares major league record for most consecutive one-hit games (2), September 24 and 30, 1988.
Shares American League record for most low-hit (no-hit and one-hit) games, season (3), 1988.
Major League saves: 1986 (1).
Led American League in hit batsmen with 14 in 1983, 11 in 1984, 15 in 1986, 13 in 1989 and tied for lead with 11 in 1981.
Led American League in complete games with 19 and shutouts with 5 in 1982.
Named American League Pitcher of the Year by THE SPORTING NEWS, 1982.
Named righthanded pitcher on THE SPORTING NEWS American League All-Star Team, 1982.
Named outfielder on THE SPORTING NEWS College Baseball All-America Team, 1978.

Year	Club	League	G.	IP.	W.	L.	Pct.	H.	R.	ER.	SO.	BB.	ERA.
1978—Dunedin	Florida St.	4	26	2	0	1.000	23	10	6	8	1	2.08
1979—Dunedin	Florida St.	8	51	5	0	1.000	54	30	24	38	28	4.24
1979—Syracuse	Int'national	7	51	5	2	.714	39	15	12	20	14	2.12
1979—Toronto	American	18	129	8	8	.500	139	70	62	52	48	4.33
1980—Toronto†	American	34	243	12	15	.444	232	108	100	108	83	3.70
1981—Toronto	American	25	184	11	10	.524	148	70	65	89	61	3.18
1982—Toronto	American	38	*288⅓	17	14	.548	*271	116	104	141	75	3.25
1983—Toronto	American	36	278	17	12	.586	223	105	94	187	93	3.04
1984—Toronto	American	35	*267	16	8	.667	215	87	84	198	88	2.83
1985—Toronto	American	36	265	14	13	.519	206	89	73	167	96	*2.48
1986—Toronto‡	American	37	205	7	12	.368	239	128	108	127	87	4.74
1987—Toronto	American	33	185	13	9	.591	164	92	84	115	87	4.09
1988—Toronto‡	American	32	207⅓	16	8	.667	157	76	70	147	79	3.04
1989—Toronto	American	33	206⅔	17	8	.680	164	83	77	101	76	3.35
Major League Totals—11 Years		357	2458⅓	148	117	.558	2158	1024	921	1432	873	3.37

Selected by Toronto Blue Jays' organization in 5th round of free-agent draft, June 6, 1978.
†Appeared in one game as outfielder with no chances.
‡Appeared in one game as a pinch-runner.

CHAMPIONSHIP SERIES RECORD

Holds American League Championship Series record for most strikeouts, series (18), 1985.
Shares Championship Series record for most games lost, series (2), 1989.

Year	Club	League	G.	IP.	W.	L.	Pct.	H.	R.	ER.	SO.	BB.	ERA.
1985—Toronto	American	3	20⅓	1	1	.500	11	7	7	18	10	3.10
1989—Toronto	American	2	11⅓	0	2	.000	12	8	8	10	6	6.35
Championship Series Totals—2 Years		5	31⅔	1	3	.250	23	15	15	28	16	4.26

ALL-STAR GAME RECORD

Shares All-Star Game records for most wild pitches, game and inning (2), July 8, 1980, seventh inning.

Year	League	IP.	W.	L.	Pct.	H.	R.	ER.	SO.	BB.	ERA.
1980—American		1	0	0	.000	1	1	0	0	2	0.00
1981—American		1⅔	0	0	.000	1	0	0	1	1	0.00
1983—American		3	1	0	1.000	0	1	0	4	1	0.00
1984—American		2	0	1	.000	3	2	1	2	0	4.50
1985—American		1	0	0	.000	0	0	0	2	1	0.00
1988—American		1	0	0	.000	1	0	0	0	0	0.00
All-Star Game Totals—6 Years		9⅔	1	1	.500	6	4	1	9	5	0.93

RECORD AS OUTFIELDER

Year	Club	League	Pos.	G.	AB.	R.	H.	2B.	3B.	HR.	RBI.	B.A.	PO.	A.	E.	F.A.
1978—Dunedin	Fla. St.	OF-P	35	99	10	19	3	0	1	9	.192	85	7	3	.968

KURT ANDREW STILLWELL

Born June 4, 1965, at Glendale, Calif.
Height, 5.11. Weight, 175.
Throws right and bats left and righthanded.
Son of Ron Stillwell, infielder with Washington Senators, 1961 and 1962.
Major League stolen bases: 1986 (6), 1987 (4), 1988 (6), 1989 (9). Total—25.

Year	Club	League	Pos.	G.	AB.	R.	H.	2B.	3B.	HR.	RBI.	B.A.	PO.	A.	E.	F.A.
1983—Billings	Pion.	SS	65	250	47	81	10	1	2	44	.324	73	137	*30	.875
1984—Cedar Rapids	Midw.	SS	112	382	63	96	15	1	4	33	.251	156	245	25	.941
1985—Denver†	A. A.	SS-3B	59	182	28	48	7	4	1	22	.264	103	135	25	.905
1986—Cincinnati	Nat.	SS	104	279	31	64	6	1	0	26	.229	107	205	16	.951
1986—Denver	A. A.	SS	10	30	2	7	0	0	0	2	.233	14	21	5	.875
1987—Cincinnati‡	Nat.	SS-2B-3B	131	395	54	102	20	7	4	33	.258	144	247	23	.944
1988—Kansas City	Amer.	SS	128	459	63	115	28	5	10	53	.251	170	349	13	.976
1989—Kansas City§	Amer.	SS	130	463	52	121	20	7	7	54	.261	179	334	16	.970
National League Totals—2 Years			235	674	85	166	26	8	4	59	.246	251	452	39	.947
American League Totals—2 Years			258	922	115	236	48	12	17	107	.256	349	683	29	.973
Major League Totals—4 Years			493	1596	200	402	74	20	21	166	.252	600	1135	68	.962

Selected by Cincinnati Reds' organization in 1st round (second player selected) of free-agent draft, June 6, 1983.
†On disabled list, August 9, 1985 through remainder of season.
‡Traded with Pitcher Ted Power to Kansas City Royals for Pitcher Danny Jackson and Shortstop Angel Salazar, November 6, 1987.
§On disabled list, July 6 to August 3, 1989.

ALL-STAR GAME RECORD

Year	League	Pos.	AB.	R.	H.	2B.	3B.	HR.	RBI.	B.A.	PO.	A.	E.	F.A.
1988—American		SS	0	0	0	0	0	0	0	.000	1	0	0	1.000

TIMOTHY PAUL STODDARD
(Tim)

Born January 24, 1953, at East Chicago, Ind.
Height, 6.07. Weight, 250.
Throws and bats righthanded.
Attended North Carolina State University, Raleigh, N. C.

Major League saves: 1979 (3), 1980 (26), 1981 (7), 1982 (12), 1983 (9), 1984 (7), 1985 (1), 1987 (8), 1988 (3). Total—76.
Tied for Southern League lead in wild pitches with 17 in 1977.

Year	Club	League	G.	IP.	W.	L.	Pct.	H.	R.	ER.	SO.	BB.	ERA.
1975—Knoxville	Southern	31	66	3	4	.429	66	40	31	37	43	4.23
1975—Chicago	American	1	1	0	0	.000	2	1	1	0	0	9.00
1976—Knoxville	Southern	20	140	9	8	.529	147	55	45	62	60	2.89
1976—Iowa†	Am. Assoc.	12	29	0	2	.000	37	20	18	20	15	5.59
1977—Charlotte	Southern	36	174	10	7	.588	175	75	62	94	66	3.21
1978—Rochester‡	Int'national	45	76	7	3	.700	80	28	22	70	32	2.61
1978—Baltimore	American	8	18	0	1	.000	22	17	12	14	8	6.00
1979—Baltimore§	American	29	58	3	1	.750	44	12	11	47	19	1.71
1980—Baltimore	American	64	86	5	3	.625	72	27	24	64	38	2.51
1981—Baltimore	American	31	37	4	2	.667	38	16	16	32	18	3.89
1982—Baltimore xy	American	50	56	3	4	.429	53	26	25	42	29	4.02
1982—Rochester	Int'national	5	6	0	0	.000	2	1	1	6	2	1.50
1983—Baltimore za	American	47	57⅔	4	3	.571	65	39	39	50	29	6.09
1984—Chicago b	National	58	92	10	6	.625	77	41	39	87	57	3.82
1985—San Diego	National	44	60	1	6	.143	63	35	31	42	37	4.65
1986—San Diego c	National	30	45⅓	1	3	.250	33	20	19	47	34	3.77
1986—New York	American	24	49⅓	4	1	.800	41	23	21	34	23	3.83
1987—Fort Lauderdale d	Florida St.	2	2	0	0	.000	1	0	0	1	0	0.00
1987—New York	American	57	92⅔	4	3	.571	83	38	36	78	30	3.50
1988—New York ef	American	28	55	2	2	.500	62	41	39	33	27	6.38
1989—Canton-Akron	Eastern	5	10	0	0	.000	3	3	1	9	2	0.90
1989—Cleveland g	American	14	21⅓	0	0	.000	25	7	7	12	7	2.95
American League Totals—11 Years		353	532	29	20	.592	507	247	231	406	228	3.91
National League Totals—3 Years		132	197⅓	12	15	.444	173	96	89	176	128	4.06
Major League Totals—13 Years		485	729⅓	41	35	.539	680	343	320	582	356	3.95

Selected by Texas Rangers' organization in 24th round of free-agent draft, June 5, 1974.
Selected by Chicago White Sox' organization in secondary phase of free-agent draft, January 9, 1975.
†Released, March 28, 1977; signed by Charlotte (Baltimore Orioles' organization), April 8, 1977.
‡On disabled list, June 15 to July 9, 1978.
§On disabled list, July 21 to September 1, 1979.
xOn disabled list, March 31 to May 5, 1982; included rehabilitation disability assignment to Rochester, April 27 to May 5, 1982.
yOn disabled list, September 7, 1982 through remainder of season.
zTraded to Oakland A's for Third Baseman Wayne Gross, December 9, 1983.
aTraded to Chicago Cubs for Pitcher Stan Kyles and a player to be named later, March 26, 1984; Oakland A's acquired Outfielder Stan Boderick to complete deal, March 31, 1984.
bGranted free agency, November 8, 1984; signed by San Diego Padres, January 8, 1985.
cTraded to New York Yankees for Pitcher Ed Whitson, July 9, 1986.
dOn New York Yankees disabled list, March 28 to April 15, 1987; included rehabilitation disability assignment to Fort Lauderdale, April 10, 1987.
eOn disabled list, May 22 to June 12, 1988.
fReleased, August 14, 1988; signed by Cleveland Indians, January 18, 1989.
gReleased, July 12, 1989.

CHAMPIONSHIP SERIES RECORD

Year	Club	League	G.	IP.	W.	L.	Pct.	H.	R.	ER.	SO.	BB.	ERA.
1984—Chicago	National	2	2	0	0	.000	1	2	1	2	2	4.50

WORLD SERIES RECORD

Year	Club	League	G.	IP.	W.	L.	Pct.	H.	R.	ER.	SO.	BB.	ERA.
1979—Baltimore	American	4	5	1	0	1.000	6	3	3	3	1	5.40

Eligible for 1983 World Series with Baltimore Orioles; did not play.

JEFFERY GLEN STONE
(Jeff)

Born December 26, 1960, at Kennett, Mo.
Height, 6.00. Weight, 180.
Throws right and bats lefthanded.
Twin brother of Jerome Stone, outfielder in Philadelphia Phillies organization, 1984 through 1985.

Major League stolen bases: 1983 (4), 1984 (27), 1985 (15), 1986 (19), 1987 (3), 1988 (4), 1989 (3). Total—75.
Led Carolina League in stolen bases with 94 in 1982.
Led South Atlantic League in being hit by pitch with 15 and stolen bases with 123 in 1981.
Led South Atlantic League outfielders in total chances with 290 in 1981.
Named Eastern League Most Valuable Player, 1983.

Year	Club	League	Pos.	G.	AB.	R.	H.	2B.	3B.	HR.	RBI.	B.A.	PO.	A.	E.	F.A.
1980—Central Oregon	N'west	OF	55	241	52	63	12	4	0	19	.261	116	4	4	.968
1981—Spartanburg	S. Atl.	OF	134	516	*108	143	13	9	3	53	.277	*264	11	15	.948
1982—Peninsula	Carol.	OF	*137	*559	110	166	18	*13	2	50	.297	●276	9	8	.973

Year Club	League	Pos.	G.	AB.	R.	H.	2B.	3B.	HR.	RBI.	B.A.	PO.	A.	E.	F.A.
1983—Reading†	East.	OF	125	492	*109	156	25	10	9	67	.317	226	6	9	.963
1983—Philadelphia	Nat.	OF	9	4	2	3	0	2	0	3	.750	0	0	0	.000
1984—Portland	P. C.	OF	82	355	59	109	15	●14	7	34	.307	194	7	12	.944
1984—Philadelphia‡	Nat.	OF	51	185	27	67	4	6	1	15	.362	75	1	7	.916
1985—Philadelphia	Nat.	OF	88	264	36	70	4	3	3	11	.265	82	4	3	.966
1985—Portland	P. C.	OF	67	252	58	83	16	8	2	28	.329	103	6	6	.948
1986—Portland	P. C.	OF	31	118	25	40	4	1	2	9	.339	60	0	1	.984
1986—Philadelphia	Nat.	OF	82	249	32	69	6	4	6	19	.277	103	8	2	.982
1987—Maine	Int.	OF	40	151	22	35	6	2	1	10	.232	89	1	2	.978
1987—Philadelphia§x	Nat.	OF	66	125	19	32	7	1	1	16	.256	32	3	0	1.000
1988—Baltimore y	Amer.	OF	26	61	4	10	1	0	0	1	.164	23	3	1	.963
1988—Rochester z	Int.	OF	71	267	39	74	12	5	3	27	.277	102	9	3	.974
1989—Oklahoma City	A.A.	OF	13	39	4	7	2	0	0	1	.179	6	0	1	.857
1989—Texas a-Boston	Amer.	OF	40	51	8	9	1	2	0	6	.176	8	0	0	1.000
1989—Pawtucket b	Int.	OF	57	196	30	55	10	2	4	22	.281	70	1	2	.973
National League Totals—5 Years			296	827	116	241	21	16	11	64	.291	292	16	12	.963
American League Totals—2 Years			66	112	12	19	2	2	0	7	.170	31	3	1	.971
Major League Totals—7 Years			362	939	128	260	23	18	11	71	.277	323	19	13	.963

Signed as free agent by Philadelphia Phillies' organization, August 26, 1979.

†On disabled list, May 11 to May 21, 1983.

‡On disabled list, July 7 to August 6, 1984; included rehabilitation disability assignment to Portland, August 2 to August 6, 1984.

§On disabled list, June 16 to July 20, 1987; included rehabilitation disability assignment to Maine, July 1 to July 20, 1987.

xTraded with Infielder Rick Schu and Outfielder Keith Hughes to Baltimore Orioles for Outfielder Mike Young and a player to be named later, March 21, 1988; Philadelphia Phillies acquired Outfielder Frank Bellino to complete deal, June 14, 1988.

yOn disabled list, April 29 to June 12, 1988; included rehabilitation disability assignment to Rochester, May 24 to June 12, 1988.

zReleased, December 5, 1988; signed by Oklahoma City (Texas Rangers' organization), February 25, 1989.

aSold to Boston Red Sox, June 26, 1989.

bReleased, October 12, 1989; signed by Pawtucket (Boston Red Sox' organization), December 13, 1989.

MELVIN LEON STOTTLEMYRE JR.

(Mel)

Born December 28, 1963, at Prosser, Wash.
Height, 6.00. Weight 190.
Throws and bats righthanded.
Attended University of Nevada, Las Vegas, Nev.
Son of Mel Stottlemyre Sr., pitcher with the New York Yankees, 1964 through 1974; minor league
pitching instructor, Seattle Mariners' organization, 1977 through 1981; and coach with
the New York Mets since 1984; nephew of Jeff Stottlemyre, pitcher in Seattle Mariners'
organization, 1980 through 1983; and brother of Todd Stottlemyre, pitcher with Toronto Blue Jays.

Year Club	League	G.	IP.	W.	L.	Pct.	H.	R.	ER.	SO.	BB.	ERA.
1985—Asheville†	S. Atlantic	14	78⅔	5	4	.556	65	33	24	70	38	2.75
1986—Osceola	Florida St.	9	35⅔	0	7	.000	48	38	31	25	26	7.82
1986—Asheville	S. Atlantic	7	34⅓	3	1	.750	32	13	8	28	12	2.10
1987—Columbus‡-Memphis	Southern	20	127⅓	7	6	.538	125	68	61	85	41	4.31
1988—Memphis§	Southern	7	45	3	2	.600	41	18	12	29	14	2.40
1989—Omaha	Am. Assoc.	7	7⅔	1	1	.500	6	4	2	9	3	2.35
1989—Baseball City	Florida St.	13	23⅔	1	2	.333	30	14	13	25	9	4.94
1989—Memphis	Southern	16	22⅔	3	0	1.000	15	4	4	18	9	1.59

Selected by Seattle Mariners' organization in 28th round of free-agent draft, June 7, 1982.

Selected by Houston Astros' organization in secondary phase of free-agent draft, January 9, 1985.

†On disabled list, July 23, 1985 through remainder of season.

‡Traded to Kansas City Royals' organization for Shortstop Buddy Biancalana, July 29, 1987.

§On disabled list, May 20, 1988 through remainder of season.

TODD VERNON STOTTLEMYRE

Born May 20, 1965, at Yakima, Wash.
Height, 6.03. Weight, 190.
Throws right and bats lefthanded.
Attended Yakima Valley College, Yakima, Wash.
Son of Mel Stottlemyre Sr., pitcher with New York Yankees, 1964 through 1974; minor league
pitching instructor, Seattle Mariners' organization, 1977 through 1981; and coach with
New York Mets since 1984; nephew of Jeff Stottlemyre, pitcher in Seattle
Mariners' organization, 1980 through 1983;
and brother of Mel Stottlemyre Jr., pitcher in Kansas City Royals' organization.

Led International League pitchers in games started with 34 in 1987.

Year Club	League	G.	IP.	W.	L.	Pct.	H.	R.	ER.	SO.	BB.	ERA.
1986—Ventura County	California	17	103⅔	9	4	.692	76	39	28	104	36	2.43
1986—Knoxville	Southern	18	99	8	7	.533	93	56	46	81	49	4.18
1987—Syracuse	Int'national	34	186⅔	11	●13	.458	189	●103	*92	143	*87	4.44
1988—Toronto	American	28	98	4	8	.333	109	70	62	67	46	5.69
1988—Syracuse	Int'national	7	48⅓	5	0	1.000	36	12	11	51	8	2.05
1989—Toronto	American	27	127⅔	7	7	.500	137	56	55	63	44	3.88
1989—Syracuse	Int'national	10	55⅔	3	2	.600	46	23	20	45	15	3.23
Major League Totals—2 Years		55	225⅔	11	15	.423	246	126	117	130	90	4.67

Selected by New York Yankees' organization in 5th round of free-agent draft, June 6, 1983.
Selected by St. Louis Cardinals' organization in secondary phase of free-agent draft, January 9, 1985.
Selected by Toronto Blue Jays' organization in secondary phase of free-agent draft, June 3, 1985.

CHAMPIONSHIP SERIES RECORD

Year Club	League	G.	IP.	W.	L.	Pct.	H.	R.	ER.	SO.	BB.	ERA.
1989—Toronto	American	1	5	0	1	.000	7	4	4	3	2	7.20

JOSEPH DOUGLAS STRANGE
(Doug)

Born April 13, 1964, at Greenville, S.C.
Height, 6.02. Weight, 170.
Throws right and bats left and righthanded.
Attended North Carolina State University, Raleigh, N.C.

Major League stolen bases: 1989 (3).
Led Florida State League third basemen in putouts with 116 and tied for lead in double plays with 20 in 1986.

Year Club	League	Pos.	G.	AB.	R.	H.	2B.	3B.	HR.	RBI.	B.A.	PO.	A.	E.	F.A.
1985—Bristol	Appal.	OF-2B-3B	65	226	43	69	16	1	6	45	.305	84	59	11	.929
1986—Lakeland	Fla. St.	3B-1B	126	466	59	119	29	4	2	63	.255	202	215	37	.919
1987—Glens Falls†	East.	3-2-O-S	115	431	63	130	31	1	13	70	.302	110	214	20	.942
1987—Toledo	Int.	3B	16	45	7	11	2	0	1	5	.244	14	28	3	.933
1988—Toledo	Int.	3B-SS-1B	82	278	23	56	8	2	6	19	.201	52	126	13	.932
1988—Glens Falls	East.	3B	57	218	32	61	11	1	1	36	.280	45	112	12	.929
1989—Toledo	Int.	3B-SS	83	304	38	75	15	2	8	42	.247	108	197	17	.947
1989—Detroit	Amer.	3B-2B-SS	64	196	16	42	4	1	1	14	.214	53	118	19	.900
Major League Totals—1 Year			64	196	16	42	4	1	1	14	.214	53	118	19	.900

Selected by Detroit Tigers' organization in 7th round of free-agent draft, June 3, 1985.
†Batted righthanded only.

DARRYL EUGENE STRAWBERRY

Born March 12, 1962, at Los Angeles, Calif.
Height, 6.06. Weight, 195.
Throws and bats lefthanded.
Brother of Michael Strawberry, outfielder in Los Angeles Dodgers' organization, 1980 and 1981.

Hit three home runs in a game, August 5, 1985.
Major League stolen bases: 1983 (19), 1984 (27), 1985 (26), 1986 (28), 1987 (36), 1988 (29), 1989 (11). Total—176.
Led National League in slugging percentage with .545 in 1988.
Led Texas League in slugging percentage with .602, bases on balls received with 100 and caught stealing with 22 in 1982.
Named outfielder on THE SPORTING NEWS National League All-Star Team, 1988.
Named outfielder on THE SPORTING NEWS National League Silver Slugger team, 1988.
Named National League Rookie Player of the Year by THE SPORTING NEWS, 1983.
Named National League Rookie of the Year by Baseball Writers' Association of America, 1983.
Named Texas League Most Valuable Player, 1982.
Received reported $210,000 bonus to sign with New York Mets, 1980.

Year Club	League	Pos.	G.	AB.	R.	H.	2B.	3B.	HR.	RBI.	B.A.	PO.	A.	E.	F.A.
1980—Kingsport	Appal.	OF	44	157	27	42	5	2	5	20	.268	55	4	3	.952
1981—Lynchburg	Carol.	OF	123	420	84	107	22	6	13	78	.255	173	8	13	.933
1982—Jackson	Texas	OF	129	435	93	123	19	9	★34	97	.283	211	8	9	.961
1983—Tidewater	Int.	OF	16	57	12	19	4	1	3	13	.333	22	0	4	.846
1983—New York	Nat.	OF	122	420	63	108	15	7	26	74	.257	232	8	4	.984
1984—New York	Nat.	OF	147	522	75	131	27	4	26	97	.251	276	11	6	.980
1985—New York†	Nat.	OF	111	393	78	109	15	4	29	79	.277	211	5	2	.991
1986—New York	Nat.	OF	136	475	76	123	27	5	27	93	.259	226	10	6	.975
1987—New York	Nat.	OF	154	532	108	151	32	5	39	104	.284	272	6	8	.972
1988—New York	Nat.	OF	153	543	101	146	27	3	★39	101	.269	297	4	9	.971
1989—New York	Nat.	OF	134	476	69	107	26	1	29	77	.225	272	4	8	.972
Major League Totals—7 Years			957	3361	570	875	169	29	215	625	.260	1786	48	43	.977

Selected by New York Mets' organization in 1st round (first player selected) of free-agent draft, June 3, 1980.
†On disabled list, May 12 to June 28, 1985.

CHAMPIONSHIP SERIES RECORD

Shares Championship Series record for most strikeouts, series (12), 1986.
Shares National League Championship Series record for most at-bats, series (30), 1988.

Year Club	League	Pos.	G.	AB.	R.	H.	2B.	3B.	HR.	RBI.	B.A.	PO.	A.	E.	F.A.
1986—New York	Nat.	OF	6	22	4	5	1	0	2	5	.227	9	0	0	1.000
1988—New York	Nat.	OF	7	30	5	9	2	0	1	6	.300	11	0	0	1.000
Championship Series Totals—2 Years			13	52	9	14	3	0	3	11	.269	20	0	0	1.000

—DID YOU KNOW—

That the Padres' Tony Gwynn, who hit .336 last season, finished 85 points higher than the team's .251 average?

Year Club League	Pos.	G.	AB.	R.	H.	2B.	3B.	HR.	RBI.	B.A.	PO.	A.	E.	F.A.
1986—New York.............. Nat.	OF	7	24	4	5	1	0	1	1	.208	19	0	0	1.000

ALL-STAR GAME RECORD

Year League	Pos.	AB.	R.	H.	2B.	3B.	HR.	RBI.	B.A.	PO.	A.	E.	F.A.
1984—National.................................	OF	2	0	1	0	0	0	0	.500	0	0	0	.000
1985—National.................................	OF	1	2	1	0	0	0	0	1.000	3	0	0	1.000
1986—National.................................	OF	2	0	1	0	0	0	0	.500	1	0	0	1.000
1987—National.................................	OF	2	0	0	0	0	0	0	.000	0	0	0	.000
1988—National.................................	OF	4	0	1	0	0	0	0	.250	4	0	0	1.000
All-Star Game Totals—5 Years....................		11	2	4	0	0	0	0	.364	8	0	0	1.000

Named to National League All-Star Team for 1989 game; did not play due to injury.

FRANKLIN LEE STUBBS

Born October 21, 1960, at Laurinburg, N.C.
Height, 6.02. Weight, 209.
Throws and bats lefthanded.
Attended Virginia Tech., Blacksburg, Va.

Major League stolen bases: 1984 (2), 1986 (7), 1987 (8), 1988 (11), 1989 (3). Total—31.
Led National League first basemen in fielding percentage with .994 in 1987.
Named first baseman on THE SPORTING NEWS College Baseball All-America Team, 1982.

Year Club League	Pos.	G.	AB.	R.	H.	2B.	3B.	HR.	RBI.	B.A.	PO.	A.	E.	F.A.
1982—Vero Beach†......... Fla. St.	1B	16	54	6	11	1	1	3	5	.204	134	3	3	.979
1983—San Antonio.......... Texas	1B-OF	47	173	35	54	8	3	12	52	.312	425	23	5	.989
1983—Albuquerque .... P. C.	OF-1B	76	267	49	74	16	3	16	58	.277	106	3	6	.948
1984—Albuquerque .... P. C.	OF-1B	29	108	26	35	5	5	6	24	.324	36	4	2	.952
1984—Los Angeles .... Nat.	1B-OF	87	217	22	42	2	3	8	17	.194	417	37	4	.991
1985—Albuquerque .... P. C.	1B-OF	132	421	86	118	23	5	32	93	.280	945	87	14	.987
1985—Los Angeles .... Nat.	1B	10	9	0	2	0	0	0	2	.222	11	0	0	1.000
1986—Los Angeles .... Nat.	OF-1B	132	420	55	95	11	1	23	58	.226	244	14	7	.974
1987—Los Angeles‡ .... Nat.	1B-OF	129	386	48	90	16	3	16	52	.233	830	79	5	.995
1988—Los Angeles .... Nat.	1B-OF	115	242	30	54	13	0	8	34	.223	530	57	13	.978
1989—Los Angeles§........ Nat.	OF-1B	69	103	11	30	6	0	4	15	.291	70	5	3	.962
Major League Totals—6 Years.................		542	1377	166	313	48	7	59	178	.227	2102	192	32	.986

Selected by Los Angeles Dodgers' organization in 1st round (19th player selected) of free-agent draft, June 7, 1982.
†On disabled list, July 5, 1982 through remainder of season.
‡On disabled list, August 3 to August 24, 1987.
§On disabled list, August 20, 1989 through remainder of season.

CHAMPIONSHIP SERIES RECORD

Year Club League	Pos.	G.	AB.	R.	H.	2B.	3B.	HR.	RBI.	B.A.	PO.	A.	E.	F.A.
1988—Los Angeles .... Nat.	1B-PH	4	8	0	2	0	0	0	0	.250	16	2	0	1.000

WORLD SERIES RECORD

Year Club League	Pos.	G.	AB.	R.	H.	2B.	3B.	HR.	RBI.	B.A.	PO.	A.	E.	F.A.
1988—Los Angeles .... Nat.	1B	5	17	3	5	2	0	0	2	.294	34	0	0	1.000

JAMES HOWARD SUNDBERG
(Jim)

Born May 18, 1951, at Galesburg, Ill.
Height, 6.00. Weight, 196.
Throws and bats righthanded.
Attended University of Iowa, Iowa City, Iowa.

Shares major league records for most seasons leading league in assists by catcher (6); most assists by catcher, inning (3), September 3, 1976, fifth inning; fewest errors by catcher, season (4), 1979.
Holds American League record for highest fielding percentage by catcher, season (.995), 1979.
Shares American League record for most games, catcher, season (155), 1975.
Major League stolen bases: 1974 (2), 1975 (3), 1977 (2), 1978 (2), 1979 (3), 1980 (2), 1981 (2), 1982 (2), 1984 (1), 1986 (1). Total—20.
Led American League in passed balls with 8 in 1981 and 16 in 1982.
Led American League catchers in total chances with 909 in 1975, 822 in 1976, 909 in 1977, 863 in 1978, 833 in 1979 and 936 in 1980.
Led American League catchers in double plays with 15 in 1974, 11 in 1976 and 15 in 1982.
Tied for American League lead in passed balls with 17 in 1980.
Tied for American League lead in double plays by catchers with 12 in 1977 and 14 in 1978.
Named catcher on THE SPORTING NEWS American League All-Star Team, 1978 and 1981.
Named catcher on THE SPORTING NEWS American League All-Star fielding team, 1976 through 1981.

Year Club League	Pos.	G.	AB.	R.	H.	2B.	3B.	HR.	RBI.	B.A.	PO.	A.	E.	F.A.
1973—Pittsfield .... East.	C	91	242	39	72	14	0	5	40	.298	449	52	3	★.994
1974—Texas..................... Amer.	C	132	368	45	91	13	3	3	36	.247	722	69	8	.990
1975—Texas..................... Amer.	C	155	472	45	94	9	0	6	36	.199	★791	★101	17	.981
1976—Texas..................... Amer.	C	140	448	33	102	24	2	3	34	.228	★719	★96	7	★.991
1977—Texas..................... Amer.	C	149	453	61	132	20	3	6	65	.291	★801	★103	5	★.994
1978—Texas..................... Amer.	C	149	518	54	144	23	6	6	58	.278	★769	★91	3	★.997
1979—Texas..................... Amer.	C	150	495	50	136	23	4	5	64	.275	★754	75	4	★.995
1980—Texas..................... Amer.	C	151	505	59	138	24	1	10	63	.273	★853	★76	7	.993

Year Club	League	Pos.	G.	AB.	R.	H.	2B.	3B.	HR.	RBI.	B.A.	PO.	A.	E.	F.A.
1981—Texas	Amer.	*C-OF	102	339	42	94	17	2	3	28	.277	465	*52	2	*.996
1982—Texas	Amer.	C-OF	139	470	37	118	22	5	10	47	.251	612	69	6	.991
1983—Texas†	Amer.	C	131	378	30	76	14	0	2	28	.201	618	56	5	.993
1984—Milwaukee‡§	Amer.	C	110	348	43	91	19	4	7	43	.261	556	55	3	*.995
1985—Kansas City	Amer.	C	115	367	38	90	12	4	10	35	.245	572	41	5	.992
1986—Kansas City x	Amer.	C	140	429	41	91	9	1	12	42	.212	686	46	4	*.995
1987—Chicago y	Nat.	C	61	139	9	28	2	0	4	15	.201	273	34	2	.994
1988—Chicago y	Nat.	C	24	54	8	13	1	0	2	9	.241	88	7	0	1.000
1988—Texas z	Amer.	C	38	91	13	26	4	0	4	13	.286	141	9	0	1.000
1989—Texas a	Amer.	C	76	147	13	29	7	1	2	8	.197	353	27	3	.992
American League Totals—15 Years			1877	5828	604	1452	240	36	89	600	.249	9412	966	79	.992
National League Totals—2 Years			85	193	17	41	3	0	6	24	.212	361	41	2	.995
Major League Totals—16 Years			1962	6021	621	1493	243	36	95	624	.248	9773	1007	81	.993

Selected by Oakland A's organization in 14th round of free-agent draft, June 5, 1969.
Selected by Texas Rangers' organization in 8th round of free-agent draft, June 6, 1972.
Selected by Texas Rangers' organization in secondary phase of free-agent draft, January 10, 1973.
†Traded to Milwaukee Brewers for Catcher Ned Yost and Pitcher Dan Scarpetta, December 8, 1983.
‡On disabled list, August 6 to September 1, 1984.
§Traded to Kansas City Royals as part of a six-player, four-team deal in which Texas Rangers acquired Catcher Don Slaught from Kansas City, New York Mets' organization acquired Pitcher Frank Wills from Kansas City, Milwaukee Brewers acquired Pitcher Danny Darwin and a player to be named later from Texas and Pitcher Tim Leary from New York, January 18, 1985; Milwaukee organization acquired Catcher Bill Hance from Texas to complete deal, January 30, 1985.
xTraded to Chicago Cubs for Outfielder Thad Bosley and Pitcher Dave Gumpert, March 30, 1987.
yReleased, July 15, 1988; signed by Texas Rangers, July 21, 1988.
zGranted free agency, November 4, 1988; re-signed by Rangers, January 6, 1989.
aOn voluntarily retired list, October 2, 1989.

CHAMPIONSHIP SERIES RECORD

Year Club	League	Pos.	G.	AB.	R.	H.	2B.	3B.	HR.	RBI.	B.A.	PO.	A.	E.	F.A.
1985—Kansas City	Amer.	C	7	24	3	4	1	1	1	6	.167	41	2	1	.977

WORLD SERIES RECORD

Year Club	League	Pos.	G.	AB.	R.	H.	2B.	3B.	HR.	RBI.	B.A.	PO.	A.	E.	F.A.
1985—Kansas City	Amer.	C	7	24	6	6	2	0	0	1	.250	47	3	0	1.000

ALL-STAR GAME RECORD

Year League		Pos.	AB.	R.	H.	2B.	3B.	HR.	RBI.	B.A.	PO.	A.	E.	F.A.
1978—American		C	0	0	0	0	0	0	0	.000	2	1	0	1.000
1984—American		C	1	0	0	0	0	0	0	.000	6	0	0	1.000
All-Star Game Totals—2 Years			1	0	0	0	0	0	0	.000	8	1	0	1.000

Member of American League All-Star Team in 1974 game; did not play.

WILLIAM JAMES SURHOFF
(B. J.)

Born August 4, 1964, at Bronx, N.Y.
Height, 6.01. Weight, 190.
Throws right and bats lefthanded.
Attended University of North Carolina, Chapel Hill, N.C.
Son of Dick Surhoff, forward with New York Knicks and Milwaukee Hawks of the
National Basketball Association, 1952-53 and 1953-54; and brother of
Rich Surhoff, pitcher with Philadelphia Phillies and Texas Rangers, 1985.

Major League stolen bases: 1987 (11), 1988 (21), 1989 (14). Total—46.
Tied for Pacific Coast League lead in double plays by catchers with 10 in 1986.
Named College Player of the Year by THE SPORTING NEWS, 1985.
Member of 1984 U. S. Olympic baseball team.
Named catcher on THE SPORTING NEWS College Baseball All-America Team, 1985.

Year Club	League	Pos.	G.	AB.	R.	H.	2B.	3B.	HR.	RBI.	B.A.	PO.	A.	E.	F.A.
1985—Beloit	Midw.	C	76	289	39	96	13	4	7	58	.332	475	44	3	.994
1986—Vancouver	P. C.	C	116	458	71	141	19	3	5	59	.308	539	70	7	*.989
1987—Milwaukee	Amer.	C-3B-1B	115	395	50	118	22	3	7	68	.299	648	56	11	.985
1988—Milwaukee	Amer.	C-3-1-S-O	139	493	47	121	21	0	5	38	.245	550	94	8	.988
1989—Milwaukee	Amer.	C-3B	126	436	42	108	17	4	5	55	.248	530	58	10	.983
Major League Totals—3 Years			380	1324	139	347	60	7	17	161	.262	1728	208	29	.985

Selected by New York Yankees' organization in 5th round of free-agent draft, June 7, 1982.
Selected by Milwaukee Brewers' organization in 1st round (first player selected) of free-agent draft, June 3, 1985.

RICHARD LEE SUTCLIFFE
(Rick)

Born June 21, 1956, at Independence, Mo.
Height, 6.07. Weight, 215.
Throws right and bats lefthanded.
Brother of Terry Sutcliffe, pitcher in Los Angeles Dodgers' organization, 1979 through 1981.

Shares major league record for fewest games won, season, for leader (18), 1987.
Major League saves: 1980 (5), 1982 (1). Total—6.

Led National League in intentional bases on balls issued with 14 in 1987.
Led California League pitchers in games started with 28 in 1975.
Tied for Northwest League lead in shutouts with 2 in 1974.
Named National League Pitcher of the Year by THE SPORTING NEWS, 1984.
Won National League Cy Young Memorial Award, 1984.
Named righthanded pitcher on THE SPORTING NEWS National League All-Star Team, 1984.
Named National League Comeback Player of the Year by THE SPORTING NEWS, 1987.
Named National League Rookie Pitcher of the Year by THE SPORTING NEWS, 1979.
Named National League Rookie of the Year by Baseball Writers' Association of America, 1979.
Received reported $80,000 bonus to sign with Los Angeles Dodgers, 1974.

Year—Club	League	G.	IP.	W.	L.	Pct.	H.	R.	ER.	SO.	BB.	ERA.
1974—Bellingham	Northwest	17	95	10	3	.769	79	42	35	69	48	3.32
1975—Bakersfield	California	28	193	8	*16	.333	*214	*115	*89	91	68	4.15
1976—Waterbury	Eastern	30	187	10	11	.476	*187	90	66	121	45	3.18
1976—Los Angeles	National	1	5	0	0	.000	2	0	0	3	1	0.00
1977—Albuquerque†	P. Coast	17	77	3	10	.231	96	67	55	48	63	6.43
1978—Albuquerque	P. Coast	30	184	13	6	.684	179	101	91	99	92	4.45
1978—Los Angeles	National	2	2	0	0	.000	2	0	0	0	1	0.00
1979—Los Angeles	National	39	242	17	10	.630	217	104	93	117	97	3.46
1980—Los Angeles	National	42	110	3	9	.250	122	73	68	59	55	5.56
1981—Los Angeles‡§	National	14	47	2	2	.500	41	24	21	16	20	4.02
1982—Cleveland	American	34	216	14	8	.636	174	81	71	142	98	*2.96
1983—Cleveland	American	36	243⅓	17	11	.607	251	131	116	160	102	4.29
1984—Cleveland x	American	15	94⅓	4	5	.444	111	60	54	58	46	5.15
1984—Chicago y	National	20	150⅓	16	1	*.941	123	53	45	155	39	2.69
1985—Chicago z	National	20	130	8	8	.500	119	51	46	102	44	3.18
1986—Chicago a	National	28	176⅔	5	14	.263	166	92	91	122	96	4.64
1987—Chicago b	National	34	237⅓	*18	10	.643	223	106	97	174	106	3.68
1988—Chicago b	National	32	226	13	14	.481	232	97	97	144	70	3.86
1989—Chicago	National	35	229	16	11	.593	202	98	93	153	69	3.66
National League Totals—11 Years		267	1555⅓	98	79	.554	1449	698	651	1045	598	3.77
American League Totals—3 Years		85	553⅔	35	24	.593	536	272	241	360	246	3.92
Major League Totals—13 Years		352	2109	133	103	.564	1985	970	892	1405	844	3.81

Selected by Los Angeles Dodgers' organization in 1st round (21st player selected) of free-agent draft, June 5, 1974.
†On disabled list, May 3 to May 24, 1977.
‡On disabled list, August 14 to September 5, 1981.
§Traded with Second Baseman Jack Perconte to Cleveland Indians for Outfielder Jorge Orta, Catcher Jack Fimple and Pitcher Larry White, December 9, 1981.
xTraded with Catcher Ron Hassey and Pitcher George Frazier to Chicago Cubs for Outfielders Mel Hall and Joe Carter and Pitchers Don Schulze and Darryl Banks, June 13, 1984.
yGranted free agency, November 8, 1984; re-signed by Cubs, December 14, 1984.
zOn disabled list, May 20 to June 7, July 8 to July 23 and July 29 to September 27, 1985.
aOn disabled list, June 30 to August 3, 1986.
bOn disabled list, May 21 to June 11, 1988.

CHAMPIONSHIP SERIES RECORD

Shares Championship Series record for hitting home run in first series at-bat, October 2, 1984.

Year—Club	League	G.	IP.	W.	L.	Pct.	H.	R.	ER.	SO.	BB.	ERA.
1984—Chicago	National	2	13⅓	1	1	.500	9	6	5	10	8	3.38
1989—Chicago	National	1	6	0	0	.000	5	3	3	2	4	4.50
Championship Series Totals—2 Years		3	19⅓	1	1	.500	14	9	8	12	12	3.72

ALL-STAR GAME RECORD

Year—League		IP.	W.	L.	Pct.	H.	R.	ER.	SO.	BB.	ERA.
1987—National		2	0	0	.000	1	0	0	0	1	0.00
1989—National		1	0	0	.000	4	2	2	0	0	18.00
All-Star Game Totals—2 Years		3	0	0	.000	5	2	2	0	1	6.00

Member of American League All-Star Team in 1983; did not play.

DALE CURTIS SVEUM

Name pronounced Swaim.
Born November 23, 1963, at Richmond, Calif.
Height, 6.03. Weight, 185.
Throws right and bats left and righthanded.

Major League stolen bases: 1986 (4), 1987 (2), 1988 (1). Total—7.
Hit three home runs in a game, July 17, 1987.
Switch-hit home runs in one game, July 17, 1987 and June 12, 1988.
Led American League third basemen in errors with 26 in 1986.
Led Texas League in total bases with 256 in 1984.
Led Texas League third basemen in putouts with 111 in 1984.
Led California League third basemen in assists with 261 in 1983.

Year—Club	League	Pos.	G.	AB.	R.	H.	2B.	3B.	HR.	RBI.	B.A.	PO.	A.	E.	F.A.
1982—Pikeville	Appal.	SS-3B	58	223	29	52	13	1	2	21	.233	84	158	36	.871
1983—Stockton	Calif.	3B-SS	135	533	70	139	26	5	5	70	.261	105	281	40	.906
1984—El Paso	Texas	*3B-SS	131	523	92	*172	*41	8	9	84	.329	113	259	*30	.925
1985—Vancouver	P. C.	3B-SS	122	415	42	98	17	3	6	48	.236	81	200	26	.915
1986—Vancouver	P. C.	3B	28	105	16	31	3	2	1	23	.295	22	54	4	.950
1986—Milwaukee†	Amer.	3B-SS-2B	91	317	35	78	13	2	7	35	.246	92	179	30	.900
1987—Milwaukee	Amer.	SS-2B	153	535	86	135	27	3	25	95	.252	242	396	23	.965

Year Club	League	Pos.	G.	AB.	R.	H.	2B.	3B.	HR.	RBI.	B.A.	PO.	A.	E.	F.A.
1988—Milwaukee............	Amer.	SS-2B	129	467	41	113	14	4	9	51	.242	209	375	★27	.956
1989—Beloit‡	Midw.	DH	6	15	0	2	1	0	0	2	.133	0	0	0	.000
1989—Stockton	Calif.	DH	11	43	5	8	0	0	1	5	.186	0	0	0	.000
Major League Totals—3 Years................			373	1319	162	326	54	9	41	181	.247	543	950	80	.949

Selected by Milwaukee Brewers' organization in 1st round (25th player selected) of free-agent draft, June 7, 1982.
†On disabled list, July 23 to August 9, 1986.
‡On Milwaukee disabled list, March 19, 1989 through entire season; included rehabilitation disability assignment to Beloit, June 30 to July 5, 1989; then transferred to Stockton, July 6 to July 18, 1989.

RUSSELL HOWARD SWAN
(Russ)

Born January 3, 1964, at Fremont, Calif.
Height, 6.04. Weight, 210.
Throws and bats lefthanded.
Attended Spokane Falls Community College, Spokane, Wash.,
and Texas A&M University, College Station, Tex.

Year Club	League	G.	IP.	W.	L.	Pct.	H.	R.	ER.	SO.	BB.	ERA.
1986—Everett................	Northwest	7	46	5	0	1.000	30	17	11	45	22	2.15
1986—Clinton................	Midwest	7	43⅔	3	3	.500	36	18	15	37	8	3.09
1987—Fresno................	California	12	64	6	3	.667	54	40	27	59	29	3.80
1988—San Jose................	California	11	76⅔	7	0	1.000	53	28	19	62	26	2.23
1989—Shreveport	Texas	11	75⅓	2	3	.400	62	25	22	56	22	2.63
1989—San Francisco	National	2	6⅔	0	2	.000	11	10	8	2	4	10.80
1989—Phoenix................	P. Coast	14	83	4	3	.571	75	37	31	49	29	3.36
Major League Totals—1 Year................		2	6⅔	0	2	.000	11	10	8	2	4	10.80

Selected by Houston Astros' organization in 2nd round of free-agent draft, January 17, 1984.
Selected by Seattle Mariners' organization in secondary phase of free-agent draft, June 4, 1984.
Selected by San Francisco Giants' organization in 9th round of free-agent draft, June 2, 1986.

WILLIAM CHARLES SWIFT
(Bill)

Born December 27, 1961, at Portland, Maine.
Height, 6.00. Weight, 180.
Throws and bats righthanded.
Attended University of Maine, Orono, Maine.

Major League saves: 1989 (1).
Member of 1984 U.S. Olympic baseball team.

Year Club	League	G.	IP.	W.	L.	Pct.	H.	R.	ER.	SO.	BB.	ERA.
1985—Chattanooga†	Southern	7	39	2	1	.667	34	16	16	21	21	3.69
1985—Seattle................	American	23	120⅔	6	10	.375	131	71	64	55	48	4.77
1986—Seattle................	American	29	115⅓	2	9	.182	148	85	70	55	55	5.46
1986—Calgary................	P. Coast	10	57	4	4	.500	57	33	25	29	22	3.95
1987—Calgary‡................	P. Coast	5	18⅓	0	0	.000	32	22	18	5	13	8.84
1988—Seattle................	American	38	174⅔	8	12	.400	199	99	89	47	65	4.59
1989—San Bernardino§................	California	2	10	1	0	1.000	8	0	0	4	2	0.00
1989—Seattle................	American	37	130	7	3	.700	140	72	64	45	38	4.43
Major League Totals—4 Years................		127	540⅔	23	34	.404	618	327	287	202	206	4.78

Selected by Minnesota Twins' organization in 2nd round of free-agent draft, June 6, 1983.
Selected by Seattle Mariners' organization in 1st round (second player selected) of free-agent draft, June 4, 1984.
†On disabled list, May 6 to May 21, 1985.
‡On disabled list, April 22, 1987 through remainder of season.
§On Seattle disabled list, March 28 to April 27, 1989; included rehabilitation disability assignment to San Bernardino, April 18 to April 27, 1989.

FOREST GREGORY SWINDELL
(Greg)

Born January 2, 1965, at Fort Worth, Tex.
Height, 6.03. Weight, 225.
Throws left and bats righthanded.
Attended University of Texas, Austin, Tex.

Named lefthanded pitcher on THE SPORTING NEWS College Baseball All-America Team, 1985 and 1986.

Year Club	League	G.	IP.	W.	L.	Pct.	H.	R.	ER.	SO.	BB.	ERA.
1986—Waterloo........................	Midwest	3	18	2	1	.667	12	2	2	25	3	1.00
1986—Cleveland........................	American	9	61⅔	5	2	.714	57	35	29	46	15	4.23
1987—Cleveland†........................	American	16	102⅓	3	8	.273	112	62	58	97	37	5.10
1988—Cleveland........................	American	33	242	18	14	.563	234	97	86	180	45	3.20
1989—Cleveland‡........................	American	28	184⅓	13	6	.684	170	71	69	129	51	3.37
Major League Totals—4 Years........................		86	590⅓	39	30	.565	573	265	242	452	148	3.69

Selected by Cleveland Indians' organization in 1st round (second player selected) of free-agent draft, June 2, 1986.
†On disabled list, June 30, 1987 through remainder of season.
‡On disabled list, July 26 to August 30, 1989.

ALL-STAR GAME RECORD

Year League		IP.	W.	L.	Pct.	H.	R.	ER.	SO.	BB.	ERA.
1989—American		1⅔	0	0	.000	2	0	0	3	0	0.00

PATRICK SEAN TABLER
(Pat)

Born February 2, 1958, at Hamilton, O.
Height, 6.02. Weight, 200.
Throws and bats righthanded.

Major League stolen bases: 1983 (2), 1984 (3), 1986 (3), 1987 (5), 1988 (3). Total—16.
Led Southern League in game-winning RBIs with 13 in 1980.
Led American Association third basemen in total chances with 361 in 1982.
Tied for American Association lead in sacrifice flies with 9 in 1982.

Year—Club	League	Pos.	G.	AB.	R.	H.	2B.	3B.	HR.	RBI.	B.A.	PO.	A.	E.	F.A.
1976—Oneonta	NYP	3B-OF	65	238	27	55	3	0	1	20	.231	79	71	12	.926
1977—Fort Lauderdale	Fla. St.	3B	110	391	35	93	7	1	1	36	.238	87	209	★35	.894
1978—Fort Lauderdale	Fla. St.	1B-3B-OF	138	455	56	124	9	5	5	70	.273	855	88	15	.984
1979—Fort Lauderdale	Fla. St.	O-3-2-1	75	247	39	78	12	4	2	33	.316	102	41	11	.929
1979—West Haven	East.	2B-OF	56	190	33	57	15	3	6	36	.300	124	169	13	.958
1980—Nashville	South.	2B	136	479	82	142	38	8	16	83	.296	262	361	★27	.958
1981—Columbus†‡	Int.	2B-3B	52	179	41	53	14	3	11	33	.296	66	116	14	.929
1981—Iowa	A. A.	2B	63	222	41	68	13	3	6	37	.306	110	141	4	.984
1981—Chicago	Nat.	2B	35	101	11	19	3	1	1	5	.188	70	93	3	.982
1982—Iowa	A. A.	★3B-1B	129	441	89	151	32	★11	17	105	.342	★112	★215	★34	.906
1982—Chicago§x	Nat.	3B	25	85	9	20	4	2	1	7	.235	23	33	3	.949
1983—Charleston	Int.	3B	4	14	2	3	0	1	0	2	.214	2	4	3	.667
1983—Cleveland	Amer.	OF-3B-2B	124	430	56	125	23	5	6	65	.291	197	55	11	.958
1984—Cleveland	Amer.	1-O-3-2	144	473	66	137	21	3	10	68	.290	532	89	7	.989
1985—Cleveland	Amer.	1B-3B-2B	117	404	47	111	18	3	5	59	.275	744	77	14	.983
1986—Cleveland y	Amer.	1B	130	473	61	154	29	2	6	48	.326	846	84	9	.990
1986—Maine	Int.	DH	3	12	5	3	1	0	0	1	.250	0	0	0	.000
1987—Cleveland	Amer.	1B	151	553	66	170	34	3	11	86	.307	650	75	●12	.984
1988—Clev. z-K.C.	Amer.	OF-1B-3B	130	444	53	125	22	3	2	66	.282	182	10	5	.975
1989—Kansas City	Amer.	O-1-2-3	123	390	36	101	11	1	2	42	.259	217	25	4	.984
National League Totals—2 Years			60	186	20	39	7	3	2	12	.210	93	126	6	.973
American League Totals—7 Years			919	3167	385	923	158	20	42	434	.291	3368	415	62	.984
Major League Totals—9 Years			979	3353	405	962	165	23	44	446	.287	3461	541	68	.983

Selected by New York Yankees' organization in 1st round (16th player selected) of free-agent draft, June 8, 1976.
†Loaned to Iowa (Chicago Cubs' organization), June 12, 1981; returned, August 19, 1981.
‡Acquired on waivers by Chicago Cubs for two players to be named later, August 19, 1981; New York Yankees acquired Pitcher Bill Caudill, April 1, 1982, and New York organization acquired Pitcher Jay Howell, August 2, 1982, to complete deal.
§Traded with Pitchers Dick Tidrow and Randy Martz and Infielder Scott Fletcher to Chicago White Sox for Pitchers Steve Trout and Warren Brusstar, January 25, 1983.
xTraded to Cleveland Indians for Shortstop Jerry Dybzinski, April 1, 1983.
yOn disabled list, June 11 to June 30, 1986; included rehabilitation disability assignment to Maine, June 26 to June 30, 1986.
zTraded to Kansas City Royals for Pitcher Bud Black, June 3, 1988.

ALL-STAR GAME RECORD

Year	League	Pos.	AB.	R.	H.	2B.	3B.	HR.	RBI.	B.A.	PO.	A.	E.	F.A.
1987—American		PH	1	0	0	0	0	0	0	.000	0	0	0	.000

FRANK DARYL TANANA
Name rhymes with Banana.

Born July 3, 1953, at Detroit, Mich.
Height, 6.03. Weight, 195.
Throws and bats lefthanded.
Attended California State University, Fullerton, Calif.
Son of Frank Richard Tanana, minor league outfielder, 1952 through 1956.

Shares American League record for most consecutive hits allowed, start of game (5), May 18, 1980.
Led American League in balks with 8 in 1978 and tied for lead with 4 in 1984.
Led American League in shutouts with 7 in 1977.
Led Texas League in complete games with 15 in 1973.
Named American League Rookie Pitcher of the Year by THE SPORTING NEWS, 1974.
Named lefthanded pitcher on THE SPORTING NEWS American League All-Star Team, 1976 and 1977.
Named Texas League Pitcher of the Year, 1973.

Year—Club	League	G.	IP.	W.	L.	Pct.	H.	R.	ER.	SO.	BB.	ERA.
1971—Idaho Falls†	Pioneer	....	....	....	....	......	....	....	....	....	....	......
1972—Quad Cities	Midwest	19	129	7	2	.778	111	48	40	134	57	2.79
1973—El Paso	Texas	26	★206	16	6	.727	170	72	62	★197	63	2.71
1973—Salt Lake City	P. Coast	2	14	1	0	1.000	11	5	4	15	2	2.57
1973—California	American	4	26	2	2	.500	20	11	9	22	8	3.12
1974—California	American	39	269	14	19	.424	262	104	93	180	77	3.11
1975—California	American	34	257	16	9	.640	211	80	75	★269	73	2.63
1976—California	American	34	288	19	10	.655	212	88	78	261	73	2.44
1977—California	American	31	241	15	9	.625	201	72	68	205	61	★2.54
1978—California	American	33	239	18	12	.600	239	108	97	137	60	3.65
1979—California‡	American	18	90	7	5	.583	93	44	39	46	25	3.90
1980—California§	American	32	204	11	12	.478	223	107	94	113	45	4.15
1981—Boston x	American	24	141	4	10	.286	142	70	63	78	43	4.02
1982—Texas	American	30	194⅓	7	●18	.280	199	102	91	87	55	4.21

Year	Club	League	G.	IP.	W.	L.	Pct.	H.	R.	ER.	SO.	BB.	ERA.
1983—Texas		American	29	159⅓	7	9	.438	144	70	56	108	49	3.16
1984—Texas		American	35	246⅓	15	15	.500	234	117	89	141	81	3.25
1985—Texas y-Detroit		American	33	215	12	14	.462	220	112	102	159	57	4.27
1986—Detroit		American	32	188⅓	12	9	.571	196	95	87	119	65	4.16
1987—Detroit z		American	34	218⅔	15	10	.600	216	106	95	146	56	3.91
1988—Detroit		American	32	203	14	11	.560	213	105	95	127	64	4.21
1989—Detroit a		American	33	223⅔	10	14	.417	227	105	89	147	74	3.58
Major League Totals—17 Years			507	3403⅔	198	188	.513	3252	1496	1320	2345	966	3.49

Selected by California Angels' organization in 1st round (13th player selected) of free-agent draft, June 8, 1971.
†Appeared in one game as pinch-runner (did not pitch due to a sore arm).
‡On disabled list, July 9 to September 4, 1979.
§Traded with Pitcher Jim Dorsey and Outfielder Joe Rudi to Boston Red Sox for Outfielder Fred Lynn and Pitcher Steve Renko, January 23, 1981.
xGranted free agency, November 13, 1981; signed by Texas Rangers, January 6, 1982.
yTraded to Detroit Tigers for Pitcher Duane James, June 20, 1985.
zGranted free agency, November 9, 1987.
aGranted free agency, November 13, 1989; re-signed by Tigers, November 20, 1989.

CHAMPIONSHIP SERIES RECORD

Holds Championship Series records for most hit batsmen, total series (4) and series (3), 1987; most hit batsmen, game (3), October 11, 1987.

Year	Club	League	G.	IP.	W.	L.	Pct.	H.	R.	ER.	SO.	BB.	ERA.
1979—California		American	1	5	0	0	.000	6	2	2	3	2	3.60
1987—Detroit		American	1	5⅓	0	1	.000	6	4	3	1	4	5.06
Championship Series Totals—2 Years			2	10⅓	0	1	.000	12	6	5	4	6	4.35

ALL-STAR GAME RECORD

Year	League	IP.	W.	L.	Pct.	H.	R.	ER.	SO.	BB.	ERA.
1976—American		2	0	0	.000	3	3	3	0	1	6.00

Named to American League All-Star Team for the 1977 game; replaced due to injury.
Named to American League All-Star Team for 1978 game; did not play.

KEVIN RAY TAPANI

Born February 18, 1964, at Des Moines, Ia.
Height, 6.00. Weight, 180.
Throws and bats righthanded.
Received degree in finance from Central Michigan
University, Mt. Pleasant, Mich., in 1987.

Year	Club	League	G.	IP.	W.	L.	Pct.	H.	R.	ER.	SO.	BB.	ERA.
1986—Medford		Northwest	2	8⅓	1	0	1.000	6	3	0	9	3	0.00
1986—Modesto		California	11	69	6	1	.857	74	26	19	44	22	2.48
1986—Huntsville		Southern	1	6	1	0	1.000	8	4	4	2	1	6.00
1986—Tacoma		P. Coast	1	2⅓	0	1	.000	5	6	4	1	1	15.43
1987—Modesto†		California	24	148⅓	10	7	.588	122	74	62	121	60	3.76
1988—St. Lucie		Florida St.	3	19	1	0	1.000	17	5	3	11	4	1.42
1988—Jackson		Texas	24	62⅓	5	1	.833	46	23	19	35	19	2.74
1989—Tidewater		Int'national	17	109	7	5	.583	113	49	42	63	25	3.47
1989—New York‡		National	3	7⅓	0	0	.000	5	3	3	2	4	3.68
1989—Portland		P. Coast	6	41	4	2	.667	38	15	10	30	12	2.20
1989—Minnesota		American	5	32⅔	2	2	.500	34	15	14	21	8	3.86
National League Totals—1 Year			3	7⅓	0	0	.000	5	3	3	2	4	3.68
American League Totals—1 Year			5	32⅔	2	2	.500	34	15	14	21	8	3.86
Major League Totals—1 Year			8	40	2	2	.500	39	18	17	23	12	3.83

Selected by Chicago Cubs' organization in 9th round of free-agent draft, June 3, 1985.
Selected by Oakland Athletics' organization in 2nd round of free-agent draft, June 2, 1986.
†As part of an eight-player, three-team deal, New York Mets traded Pitcher Jesse Orosco to Oakland Athletics, December 11, 1987. Oakland then traded Orosco along with Shortstop Alfredo Griffin and Pitcher Jay Howell to Los Angeles Dodgers for Pitchers Bob Welch, Matt Young and Jack Savage. Oakland then traded Savage along with Pitchers Wally Whitehurst and Kevin Tapani to New York.
‡Traded with Pitcher Tim Drummond to Portland (Minnesota Twins' organization), August 1, 1989, as partial completion of deal in which Minnesota Twins traded Pitcher Frank Viola to New York Mets for Pitchers Rick Aguilera and David West and three players to be named later, July 31, 1989. Minnesota acquired Pitcher Jack Savage to complete deal, October 16, 1989.

DANILO TARTABULL (MORA)
(Danny)

Born October 30, 1962, at Miami, Fla.
Height, 6.01. Weight, 205.
Throws and bats righthanded.
Son of Jose Tartabull, outfielder with Kansas City A's, Boston Red Sox and Oakland A's, 1962
through 1970; and minor league manager in Houston Astros' organization, 1982
through 1984; and brother of Jose Tartabull, Jr., outfielder in Seattle Mariners' organization.

Major League stolen bases: 1985 (1), 1986 (4), 1987 (9), 1988 (8), 1989 (4). Total—26.
Led American League in game-winning RBIs with 21 in 1987.
Led Pacific Coast League in slugging percentage with .615 and total bases with 291 in 1985.

Led Pacific Coast League shortstops in errors with 35 in 1985.
Led Pacific Coast League shortstops in double plays with 68 in 1984.
Led Florida State League third basemen in errors with 29 in 1981.
Named Pacific Coast League Player of the Year, 1985.
Named Florida State League Most Valuable Player, 1981.

Year Club	League	Pos.	G.	AB.	R.	H.	2B.	3B.	HR.	RBI.	B.A.	PO.	A.	E.	F.A.
1980—Billings	Pion.	3B-OF-2B	59	157	33	47	10	0	2	27	.299	34	54	14	.863
1981—Tampa	Fla. St.	3B-2B	127	422	86	131	★28	10	14	81	★.310	150	248	39	.911
1982—Waterbury†	East.	2B	126	409	64	93	17	3	17	63	.227	237	306	★32	.944
1983—Chattanooga	South.	2B	128	481	95	145	32	7	13	66	.301	252	405	23	.966
1984—Salt Lake City	P. C.	SS	116	418	69	127	22	9	13	73	.304	181	333	24	.955
1984—Seattle	Amer.	SS-2B	10	20	3	6	1	0	2	7	.300	8	21	2	.935
1985—Calgary	P. C.	SS-3B	125	473	102	142	14	3	★43	★109	.300	181	399	36	.942
1985—Seattle	Amer.	SS-3B	19	61	8	20	7	1	1	7	.328	28	43	4	.947
1986—Seattle‡§	Amer.	OF-2B-3B	137	511	76	138	25	6	25	96	.270	233	111	18	.950
1987—Kansas City	Amer.	OF	158	582	95	180	27	3	34	101	.309	228	11	6	.976
1988—Kansas City	Amer.	OF	146	507	80	139	38	3	26	102	.274	227	8	9	.963
1989—Kansas City x	Amer.	OF	133	441	54	118	22	0	18	62	.268	108	3	2	.982
Major League Totals—6 Years			603	2122	316	601	120	13	106	375	.283	832	197	41	.962

Selected by Cincinnati Reds' organization in 3rd round of free-agent draft, June 3, 1980.

†Selected by Seattle Mariners' organization in player compensation pool draft, January 20, 1983. (Seattle received compensation for Chicago White Sox' signing of free-agent Pitcher Floyd Bannister, December 13, 1982.)

‡On disabled list, May 15 to May 30, 1986.

§Traded with Pitcher Rick Luecken to Kansas City Royals for Pitchers Scott Bankhead and Steve Shields and Outfielder Mike Kingery, December 10, 1986.

xOn disabled list, June 15 to June 30, 1989.

STUART DOUGLAS TATE
(Stu)

Born June 17, 1962, at Huntsville, Ala.
Height, 6.03. Weight, 205.
Throws and bats righthanded.
Attended Columbia State Community College, Columbia, Tenn.;
John C. Calhoun Community College, Decatur, Ala.,
and Auburn University, Auburn University, Ala.

Year Club	League	G.	IP.	W.	L.	Pct.	H.	R.	ER.	SO.	BB.	ERA.
1984—Everett	Northwest	10	10⅓	1	2	.333	9	7	7	15	11	6.10
1984—Clinton	Midwest	17	24⅔	1	1	.500	22	9	8	26	12	2.92
1985—Fresno	California	34	123	9	6	.600	112	73	59	118	86	4.32
1986—Shreveport	Texas	36	63⅔	5	1	.833	56	33	24	57	41	3.39
1987—Shreveport	Texas	34	83	5	5	.500	75	41	35	75	57	3.80
1988—Shreveport	Texas	24	40	3	2	.600	27	11	9	45	18	2.03
1988—Phoenix	P. Coast	27	47⅓	2	4	.333	50	38	31	45	30	5.89
1989—Phoenix	P. Coast	54	66⅓	3	7	.300	64	31	26	77	37	3.53
1989—San Francisco	National	2	2⅔	0	0	.000	3	3	1	4	0	3.38
Major League Totals—1 Year		2	2⅔	0	0	.000	3	3	1	4	0	3.38

Selected by San Francisco Giants' organization in 8th round of free-agent draft, June 4, 1984.

DONALD CLYDE TAYLOR
(Dorn)

Born August 11, 1958, at Abington, Pa.
Height, 6.02. Weight, 180.
Throws and bats righthanded.

Led American Association in home runs allowed with 15 in 1989.

Year Club	League	G.	IP.	W.	L.	Pct.	H.	R.	ER.	SO.	BB.	ERA.
1982—Greenwood	S. Atlantic	27	164⅔	9	8	.529	128	57	42	133	92	★2.30
1983—Alexandria	Carolina	28	35⅓	2	7	.222	38	33	31	22	30	7.90
1983—Greenwood	S. Atlantic	12	81⅔	6	3	.667	73	35	32	79	40	3.53
1984—Prince William	Carolina	25	161⅔	11	5	.688	133	68	61	148	67	3.40
1985—Nashua†	Eastern	26	112⅔	6	9	.400	101	63	54	64	57	4.31
1986—Nashua‡	Eastern	33	62⅔	2	2	.500	42	13	11	57	26	1.58
1986—Hawaii	P. Coast	5	31⅓	3	1	.750	22	10	7	29	12	2.01
1987—Vancouver	P. Coast	9	57⅔	0	3	.000	46	20	17	47	29	2.65
1987—Pittsburgh§	National	14	53⅓	2	3	.400	48	35	34	37	28	5.74
1987—Harrisburg	Eastern	3	8	1	0	1.000	6	0	0	10	1	0.00
1988—Buffalo	Am. Assoc.	22	139	10	8	.556	125	45	33	65	44	★2.14
1989—Pittsburgh	National	9	10⅔	1	1	.500	14	6	6	3	5	5.06
1989—Buffalo	Am. Assoc.	25	170⅔	10	8	.556	145	61	49	103	51	2.58
Major League Totals—2 Years		23	64	3	4	.429	62	41	40	40	33	5.63

Signed as free agent by Pittsburgh Pirates' organization, December 11, 1981.

†On disabled list, July 5 to July 21, 1985.

‡On disabled list, April 11 to April 21, 1986.

§On disabled list, July 3 to July 30, 1987; included rehabilitation disability assignment to Harrisburg, July 16 to July 30, 1987.

TERRY DERRELL TAYLOR

Born July 28, 1964, at Crestview, Fla.
Height, 6.01. Weight, 180.
Throws and bats righthanded.
Son of Tommy Taylor, pitcher in Cincinnati Reds' organization, 1957 and 1958.

Led Southern League in wild pitches with 16 in 1986.
Tied for Southern League lead in hit batsmen with 16 in 1985.

Year	Club	League	G.	IP.	W.	L.	Pct.	H.	R.	ER.	SO.	BB.	ERA.
1982—Bellingham		Northwest	14	86⅔	6	4	.600	75	53	42	61	54	4.36
1983—Wausau		Midwest	24	130⅔	9	9	.500	131	94	79	118	79	5.44
1984—Salinas		California	17	104⅓	7	6	.538	87	48	34	73	55	2.93
1985—Chattanooga		Southern	28	165⅓	4	15	.211	171	★114	★97	107	96	5.28
1986—Chattanooga		Southern	27	177	12	8	.600	164	88	79	★164	90	4.02
1987—Calgary		P. Coast	25	138	10	3	.769	131	69	56	107	90	3.65
1988—Calgary		P. Coast	24	134	11	9	.550	151	89	84	97	★90	5.64
1988—Seattle		American	5	23	0	1	.000	26	17	16	9	11	6.26
1989—Calgary†		P. Coast	10	48	2	3	.400	57	33	28	31	24	5.25
Major League Totals—1 Year			5	23	0	1	.000	26	17	16	9	11	6.26

Selected by Seattle Mariners' organization in 4th round of free-agent draft, June 7, 1982.
†On Seattle disabled list, March 27 through July 25, 1989; included rehabilitation disability assignment to Calgary, July 6 to July 25, 1989.

WILFREDO ARISTIDES TEJADA (ANDUJAR)

Named pronounced Tay-HA-duh.

(Will)

Born November 12, 1962, at Santo Domingo, D.R.
Height, 6.00, Weight, 185.
Throws and bats righthanded.
Attended Universidad Autonoma, Santo Domingo, D.R.

Tied for South Atlantic League lead in being hit by pitch with 12 in 1983.

Year	Club	League	Pos.	G.	AB.	R.	H.	2B.	3B.	HR.	RBI.	B.A.	PO.	A.	E.	F.A.
1982—Helena		Pion.	C	26	57	4	11	3	0	0	4	.193	152	17	8	.955
1983—Spartanburg		S. Atl.	C	90	273	33	68	14	2	2	29	.249	483	63	13	.977
1984—Peninsula		Carol.	C	45	127	13	34	6	1	2	16	.268	262	27	11	.963
1984—Reading		East.	C	28	72	7	24	7	0	0	15	.333	107	22	9	.935
1985—Reading†		East.	C-1B	69	210	24	57	7	0	3	25	.271	295	30	4	.988
1986—Jacksonville		South.	C	107	382	49	103	11	5	13	46	.270	576	65	★19	.971
1986—Montreal		Nat.	C	10	25	1	6	1	0	0	2	.240	40	8	0	1.000
1987—Indianapolis		A. A.	C	91	299	28	74	10	1	3	29	.247	568	53	●12	.981
1988—Indianapolis		A. A.	C	59	172	16	40	11	1	1	19	.233	339	37	3	.992
1988—Montreal‡		Nat.	C	8	15	1	4	2	0	0	2	.267	37	1	0	1.000
1989—Phoenix		P. C.	C	62	189	14	40	8	3	0	14	.212	409	38	6	.987
Major League Totals—2 Years				18	40	2	10	3	0	0	4	.250	77	9	0	1.000

Signed as free agent by Philadelphia Phillies' organization, June 10, 1982.
†Drafted by Indianapolis (Montreal Expos' organization), December 11, 1985.
‡Traded to San Francisco Giants for Shortstop Angel Escobar, November 20, 1988.

KENTON CHARLES TEKULVE

Name pronounced Tuh-KULL-vee.

(Kent)

Born March 5, 1947, at Cincinnati, O.
Height, 6.04. Weight, 190.
Throws and bats righthanded.
Received bachelor of science degree in physical education
from Marietta College, Marietta, O.

Holds major league records for most games and most consecutive appearances, relief pitcher, lifetime (1,050).
Shares major league records for most intentional bases on balls allowed, season (23), 1982; most consecutive games won by relief pitcher, three consecutive games (3), May 6, 7, 9, 1980.
Holds National League records for most games pitched, lifetime (1,050); most games finished lifetime (638); most innings by relief pitcher, lifetime (1,436⅓).
Major League saves: 1975 (5), 1976 (9), 1977 (7), 1978 (31), 1979 (31), 1980 (21), 1981 (3), 1982 (20), 1983 (18), 1984 (13), 1985 (14), 1986 (4), 1987 (3), 1988 (4), 1989 (1). Total—184.
Led National League in intentional bases on balls issued with 20 in 1979, 23 in 1982 and tied for lead with 16 in 1980.
Led National League in games finished in relief with 65 in 1978, 67 in 1979 and tied for lead with 56 in 1983.

Year	Club	League	G.	IP.	W.	L.	Pct.	H.	R.	ER.	SO.	BB.	ERA.
1969—Geneva		NYP	9	53	6	2	.750	40	15	10	60	22	1.70
1970—Salem		Carolina	41	79	4	6	.400	68	29	17	75	51	1.94
1971—Salem		Carolina	47	75	11	5	.688	77	36	29	62	31	3.48
1971—Waterbury		Eastern	2	3	0	0	.000	3	0	0	0	2	0.00
1972—Sherbrooke		Eastern	31	72	7	6	.538	61	24	21	54	22	2.63
1972—Charleston		Int'national	9	22	2	1	.667	22	10	10	9	10	4.09
1973—Sherbrooke		Eastern	★57	94	●12	4	★.750	70	24	16	89	35	1.53
1974—Charleston		Int'national	35	60	6	3	.667	50	20	15	38	21	2.25
1974—Pittsburgh		National	8	9	1	1	.500	12	6	6	6	5	6.00
1975—Charleston		Int'national	24	71	5	4	.556	47	23	14	46	19	1.77

Year Club	League	G.	IP.	W.	L.	Pct.	H.	R.	ER.	SO.	BB.	ERA.
1975—Pittsburgh	National	34	56	1	2	.333	43	20	14	28	23	2.25
1976—Pittsburgh	National	64	103	5	3	.625	91	30	28	68	25	2.45
1977—Pittsburgh	National	72	103	10	1	.909	89	41	35	59	33	3.06
1978—Pittsburgh	National	★91	135	8	7	.533	115	44	35	77	55	2.33
1979—Pittsburgh†	National	★94	134	10	8	.556	109	46	41	75	49	2.75
1980—Pittsburgh	National	78	93	8	12	.400	96	39	35	47	40	3.39
1981—Pittsburgh	National	45	65	5	5	.500	61	19	18	34	17	2.49
1982—Pittsburgh	National	★85	128⅔	12	8	.600	113	47	41	66	46	2.87
1983—Pittsburgh‡	National	76	99	7	5	.583	78	27	18	52	36	1.64
1984—Pittsburgh	National	72	88	3	9	.250	86	30	26	36	33	2.66
1985—Pittsburgh§-Philadelphia	National	61	75⅔	4	10	.286	74	35	30	40	30	3.57
1986—Philadelphia	National	73	110	11	5	.688	99	35	31	57	25	2.54
1987—Philadelphia	National	★90	105	6	4	.600	96	38	36	60	29	3.09
1988—Philadelphia xy	National	70	80	3	7	.300	87	34	32	43	22	3.60
1989—Cincinnati z	National	37	52	0	3	.000	56	35	29	31	23	5.02
Major League Totals—16 Years		1050	1436⅓	94	90	.511	1305	526	455	779	491	2.85

Signed as free agent by Pittsburgh Pirates' organization, July 16, 1969.
†Appeared in one game as an outfielder with one putout.
‡Granted free agency, November 7, 1983; re-signed by Pirates, December 22, 1983.
§Traded to Philadelphia Phillies for Pitchers Al Holland and Frankie Griffin, April 20, 1985.
xOn disabled list, June 11 to June 30, 1988.
yReleased, December 7, 1988; signed by Cincinnati Reds, March 30, 1989.
zOn voluntarily retired list, July 17, 1989.

CHAMPIONSHIP SERIES RECORD

Year Club	League	G.	IP.	W.	L.	Pct.	H.	R.	ER.	SO.	BB.	ERA.
1975—Pittsburgh	National	2	1⅓	0	0	.000	3	1	1	2	1	6.75
1979—Pittsburgh	National	2	2⅔	0	0	.000	2	1	1	2	2	3.38
Championship Series Totals—2 Years		4	4	0	0	.000	5	2	2	4	3	4.50

WORLD SERIES RECORD

Holds World Series record for most saves, series (3), 1979.

Year Club	League	G.	IP.	W.	L.	Pct.	H.	R.	ER.	SO.	BB.	ERA.
1979—Pittsburgh	National	5	9⅓	0	1	.000	4	3	3	10	3	2.89

ALL-STAR GAME RECORD

Member of National League All-Star Team in 1980; did not play.

ANTHONY CHARLES TELFORD

Born March 6, 1966, at San Jose, Calif.
Height, 6.00. Weight, 175.
Throws and bats righthanded.
Attended San Jose State University, San Jose, Calif.

Year Club	League	G.	IP.	W.	L.	Pct.	H.	R.	ER.	SO.	BB.	ERA.
1987—Newark	NYP	6	17⅔	1	0	1.000	16	2	2	27	3	1.02
1987—Hagerstown	Carolina	2	11⅓	1	0	1.000	9	2	2	10	5	1.59
1987—Rochester	Int'national	1	2	0	0	.000	0	0	0	3	3	0.00
1988—Hagerstown†	Carolina	1	7	1	0	1.000	3	0	0	10	0	0.00
1989—Frederick‡§	Carolina	9	25⅔	2	1	.667	25	15	12	19	12	4.21

Selected by Baltimore Orioles' organization in 3rd round of free-agent draft, June 2, 1987.
†On disabled list, April 20, 1988 through remainder of season.
‡On Frederick disabled list, April 7 to April 18, 1989.
§On Erie disabled list, June 16 to June 30, 1989.

GARRY LEWIS TEMPLETON

Born March 24, 1956, at Lockney, Tex.
Height, 6.00. Weight, 195.
Throws right and bats left and righthanded.
Brother of Ken Templeton, outfielder in Oakland A's organization, 1972 through 1974; son of
Spiavia Templeton, former infielder in the Negro Leagues.

Shares major league records by collecting 100 or more hits righthanded and lefthanded, season, 1979; most consecutive seasons leading league, three-base hits (3), 1977 through 1979; most intentional bases on balls, game (4), July 5, 1985 (12 innings).
Shares modern major league record for most three-base hits by switch hitter, season, (19), 1979; most intentional bases on balls, game (4), July 5, 1985 (12 innings).
Major League stolen bases: 1976 (11), 1977 (28), 1978 (34), 1979 (26), 1980 (31), 1981 (8), 1982 (27), 1983 (16), 1984 (8), 1985 (16), 1986 (10), 1987 (14), 1988 (8), 1989 (1). Total—238.
Led National League in intentional bases on balls received with 23 in 1984 and tied for lead with 24 in 1985.
Led National League shortstops in total chances with 848 in 1978 and 851 in 1979.
Led National League shortstops in double plays with 108 in 1978.
Tied for National League lead in caught stealing with 24 in 1977.
Tied for National League lead in double plays by shortstops with 102 in 1979.
Named shortstop on THE SPORTING NEWS National League All-Star Team, 1977, 1979 and 1980.
Named shortstop on THE SPORTING NEWS National League Silver Slugger team, 1980 and 1984.
Received reported $40,000 bonus to sign with St. Louis Cardinals, 1974.

Year Club	League	Pos.	G.	AB.	R.	H.	2B.	3B.	HR.	RBI.	B.A.	PO.	A.	E.	F.A.
1974—Sarasota Cards.....	Gulf C.	SS	18	71	11	19	1	0	3	10	.268	15	41	3	.949
1974—St. Petersburg	Fla. St.	SS	23	95	3	20	1	0	0	2	.211	42	64	7	.938
1975—St. Petersburg	Fla. St.	SS	82	349	50	92	7	8	1	32	.264	130	253	29	.930
1975—Arkansas................	Texas	SS	42	177	36	71	9	4	2	20	.401	60	131	18	.914
1976—Tulsa......................	A. A.	★S-3-O	106	443	65	142	24	★15	6	38	.321	★178	319	34	.936
1976—St. Louis................	Nat.	SS	53	213	32	62	8	2	1	17	.291	111	172	24	.922
1977—St. Louis................	Nat.	SS	153	621	94	200	19	★18	8	79	.322	285	453	32	.958
1978—St. Louis................	Nat.	SS	155	647	82	181	31	★13	2	47	.280	★285	523	★40	.953
1979—St. Louis................	Nat.	SS	154	672	105	★211	32	★19	9	62	.314	★292	525	★34	.960
1980—St. Louis†..............	Nat.	SS	118	504	83	161	19	9	4	43	.319	223	451	★29	.959
1981—St. Louis‡§............	Nat.	SS	80	333	47	96	16	8	1	33	.288	160	272	18	.960
1982—San Diego	Nat.	SS	141	563	76	139	25	8	6	64	.247	220	422	26	.961
1983—San Diego x..........	Nat.	SS	126	460	39	121	20	2	3	40	.263	219	355	24	.960
1984—San Diego	Nat.	SS	148	493	40	127	19	3	2	35	.258	225	407	26	.960
1985—San Diego	Nat.	SS	148	546	63	154	30	2	6	55	.282	245	460	23	.968
1986—San Diego	Nat.	SS	147	510	42	126	21	2	2	44	.247	207	358	20	.966
1987—San Diego	Nat.	SS	148	510	42	113	13	5	5	48	.222	★253	447	20	.972
1988—San Diego y..........	Nat.	SS-3B	110	362	35	90	15	7	3	36	.249	170	316	16	.968
1989—San Diego	Nat.	SS	142	506	43	129	26	3	6	40	.255	232	409	20	.970
Major League Totals—14 Years...............			1823	6940	823	1910	294	101	58	643	.275	3127	5570	352	.961

Selected by St. Louis Cardinals' organization in 1st round (13th player selected) of free-agent draft, June 5, 1974.
†On disabled list, July 24 to August 14 and August 24 to September 8, 1980.
‡On suspended list, August 26, 1981; then transferred to disabled list, August 28 to September 14, 1981.
§Traded to San Diego Padres for Shortstop Ozzie Smith, February 11, 1982.
xOn disabled list, April 28 to May 17, 1983.
yGranted free agency, November 4, 1988; re-signed by Padres, December 6, 1988.

CHAMPIONSHIP SERIES RECORD

Year Club	League	Pos.	G.	AB.	R.	H.	2B.	3B.	HR.	RBI.	B.A.	PO.	A.	E.	F.A.
1984—San Diego	Nat.	SS	5	15	2	5	1	0	0	2	.333	19	11	1	.968

WORLD SERIES RECORD

Year Club	League	Pos.	G.	AB.	R.	H.	2B.	3B.	HR.	RBI.	B.A.	PO.	A.	E.	F.A.
1984—San Diego	Nat.	SS	5	19	1	6	1	0	0	0	.316	8	11	0	1.000

ALL-STAR GAME RECORD

Year League	Pos.	AB.	R.	H.	2B.	3B.	HR.	RBI.	B.A.	PO.	A.	E.	F.A.
1977—National..	SS	1	1	1	0	0	0	0	1.000	1	2	1	.750
1985—National..	PH	1	0	1	0	0	0	0	1.000	0	0	0	.000
All-Star Game Totals—2 Years....................		2	1	2	1	0	0	0	1.000	1	2	1	.750

Named to National League All-Star Team for 1979 game; declined.

CHARLES WALTER TERRELL

Name pronounced TEAR-el.

(Walt)

Born May 11, 1958, at Jeffersonville, Ind.
Height, 6.02. Weight, 205.
Throws right and bats lefthanded.
Received degree from Morehead State University, Morehead, Ky. in 1980.
Tied for International League lead in intentional bases on balls issued with 9 in 1982.
Named International League Pitcher of the Year, 1983.

Year Club	League	G.	IP.	W.	L.	Pct.	H.	R.	ER.	SO.	BB.	ERA.
1980—Sarasota Rangers........................	Gulf Coast	7	38	3	2	.600	20	11	6	23	12	1.42
1980—Asheville..	S. Atlantic	3	8	1	1	.500	11	9	6	5	8	6.75
1981—Tulsa†...	Texas	27	174	●15	7	.682	158	74	60	123	63	3.10
1982—Tidewater‡....................................	Int'national	21	138⅔	7	8	.467	130	69	61	74	72	3.96
1982—New York......................................	National	3	21	0	3	.000	22	12	8	8	14	3.43
1983—Tidewater......................................	Int'national	12	86⅔	10	1	★.909	76	34	30	58	44	3.12
1983—New York......................................	National	21	133⅔	8	8	.500	123	57	53	59	55	3.57
1984—New York§....................................	National	33	215	11	12	.478	232	99	84	114	80	3.52
1985—Detroit...	American	34	229	15	10	.600	221	107	98	130	95	3.85
1986—Detroit...	American	34	217⅓	15	12	.556	199	116	110	93	98	4.56
1987—Detroit...	American	35	244⅔	17	10	.630	254	123	110	143	94	4.05
1988—Lakeland x....................................	Florida St.	2	9⅔	1	1	.500	13	7	7	6	1	6.52
1988—Detroit y.......................................	American	29	206⅓	7	16	.304	199	101	91	84	78	3.97
1989—San Diego z..................................	National	19	123⅓	5	13	.278	134	65	55	63	26	4.01
1989—New York a..................................	American	13	83	6	5	.545	102	52	48	30	24	5.20
National League Totals—4 Years........................		76	493	24	36	.400	511	233	200	244	175	3.65
American League Totals—5 Years		145	980⅓	60	53	.531	975	499	457	480	389	4.20
Major League Totals—8 Years............................		221	1473⅓	84	89	.486	1486	732	657	724	564	4.01

Selected by New York Mets' organization in 15th round of free-agent draft, June 5, 1979.
Selected by Texas Rangers' organization in 33rd round of free-agent draft, June 3, 1980.
†Traded with Pitcher Ron Darling to New York Mets' organization for Outfielder Lee Mazzilli, April 1, 1982.
‡On disabled list, July 19 to August 2, 1982.
§Traded to Detroit Tigers for Third Baseman Howard Johnson, December 7, 1984.

xOn Detroit disabled list, April 1 to April 30, 1988; included rehabilitation disability assignment to Lakeland, April 16 to April 26, 1988.

yTraded to San Diego Padres for Infielders Chris Brown and Keith Moreland, October 28, 1988.

zTraded with a player to be named later to New York Yankees for Third Baseman Mike Pagliarulo and Pitcher Don Schulze, July 22, 1989; New York acquired Pitcher Fred Toliver to complete deal, September 27, 1989.

aGranted free agency, November 13, 1989; signed by Pittsburgh Pirates, November 29, 1989.

CHAMPIONSHIP SERIES RECORD

Year Club	League	G.	IP.	W.	L.	Pct.	H.	R.	ER.	SO.	BB.	ERA.
1987—Detroit	American	1	6	0	0	.000	7	6	6	4	4	9.00

SCOTT RAY TERRY

Born November 21, 1959, at Hobbs, N.M.
Height, 5.11. Weight, 195.
Throws and bats righthanded.
Received degree from Southwestern University, Georgetown, Tex., in 1982.

Major League saves: 1988 (3), 1989 (2). Total—5.
Led American Association in complete games with 10 in 1987.
Led Eastern League in shutouts with 6 in 1984.
Tied for American Association lead in games started by pitchers with 28 and wild pitches with 14 in 1985.

Year Club	League	G.	IP.	W.	L.	Pct.	H.	R.	ER.	SO.	BB.	ERA.
1983—Tampa	Florida St.	30	59⅓	3	3	.500	60	34	28	52	30	4.25
1984—Vermont	Eastern	20	144	14	3	★.824	110	31	24	100	43	★1.50
1984—Wichita†	Am. Assoc.	2	9⅓	0	0	.000	13	6	6	6	7	5.79
1985—Denver	Am. Assoc.	28	178⅔	11	12	.478	★203	★105	★88	101	76	4.43
1986—Denver	Am. Assoc.	10	19⅓	1	2	.333	22	13	5	13	8	2.33
1986—Cincinnati	National	28	55⅔	1	2	.333	66	40	38	32	32	6.14
1987—Nashville‡	Am. Assoc.	27	★181⅔	11	10	.524	199	94	80	91	48	3.96
1987—St. Louis	National	11	13⅓	0	0	.000	13	5	5	9	8	3.38
1988—St. Louis§	National	51	129⅓	9	6	.600	119	48	42	65	34	2.92
1988—Louisville	Am. Assoc.	3	5	0	0	.000	2	0	0	1	1	0.00
1989—St. Louis x	National	31	148⅔	8	10	.444	142	65	59	69	43	3.57
Major League Totals—4 Years		121	347	18	18	.500	340	158	144	175	117	3.73

Selected by Cincinnati Reds' organization in 12th round of free-agent draft, June 3, 1980.

†On disabled list, August 8 to September 18, 1984.

‡Traded to St. Louis Cardinals, September 3, 1987, completing deal in which St. Louis traded Pitcher Pat Perry to Cincinnati Reds for a player to be named later, August 31, 1987.

§On disabled list, June 27 to July 24, 1988; included rehabilitation disability assignment to Louisville, July 18 to July 24, 1988.

xOn disabled list, August 14 to September 5, 1989.

RECORD AS OUTFIELDER

Year Club	League	Pos.	G.	AB.	R.	H.	2B.	3B.	HR.	RBI.	B.A.	PO.	A.	E.	F.A.
1980—Billings	Pion.	OF	67	251	39	65	9	3	4	45	.259	104	●10	5	.958
1981—Cedar Rapids	Midw.	OF	113	351	32	68	9	0	5	31	.194	147	5	5	.968
1982—Cedar Rapids	Midw.	OF	108	335	50	85	16	3	12	54	.254	156	10	8	.954
1983—Tampa	Fla. St.	OF-P	66	105	14	25	6	2	0	12	.238	60	16	3	.962

MICKEY LEE TETTLETON

Born September 16, 1960, at Oklahoma City, Okla.
Height, 6.02. Weight, 208.
Throws right and bats left and righthanded.
Attended Oklahoma State University, Stillwater, Okla.

Major League stolen bases: 1985 (2), 1986 (7), 1987 (1), 1989 (3). Total—13.
Switch-hit home runs in one game, June 13, 1988.
Tied for Eastern League lead in intentional bases on balls received with 8 in 1984.
Named catcher on THE SPORTING NEWS American League All-Star Team, 1989.
Named catcher on THE SPORTING NEWS American League Silver Slugger team, 1989.

Year Club	League	Pos.	G.	AB.	R.	H.	2B.	3B.	HR.	RBI.	B.A.	PO.	A.	E.	F.A.
1981—Modesto	Calif.	C-OF-1B	48	138	28	34	3	0	5	19	.246	235	31	14	.950
1982—Modesto†	Calif.	C-OF	88	253	44	63	18	0	8	37	.249	424	36	8	.983
1983—Modesto	Calif.	C-OF	124	378	55	92	18	2	7	62	.243	582	46	11	.983
1984—Albany	East.	★C-O-1-3-S	86	281	32	65	18	0	5	47	.231	368	42	3	★.993
1984—Oakland	Amer.	C	33	76	10	20	2	1	1	5	.263	112	10	1	.992
1985—Oakland‡	Amer.	C	78	211	23	53	12	0	3	15	.251	344	24	4	.989
1985—Modesto	Calif.	C	4	14	1	3	3	0	0	2	.214	20	1	0	1.000
1986—Oakland§	Amer.	C	90	211	26	43	9	0	10	35	.204	463	32	8	.984
1986—Modesto	Calif.	C	15	42	14	10	1	0	2	8	.238	40	3	2	.956
1987—Oakland x	Amer.	C-1B	82	211	19	41	3	0	8	26	.194	435	29	6	.987
1987—Modesto y	Calif.	C	3	11	4	4	1	0	2	2	.364	5	0	0	1.000
1988—Rochester	Int.	C-OF	19	41	9	10	3	1	1	4	.244	71	7	3	.963
1988—Baltimore	Amer.	C	86	283	31	74	11	1	11	37	.261	361	31	3	.992
1989—Baltimore z	Amer.	C	117	411	72	106	21	2	26	65	.258	297	42	2	.994
Major League Totals—6 Years			486	1403	181	337	58	4	59	183	.240	2012	168	24	.989

Selected by Oakland A's organization in 5th round of free-agent draft, June 8, 1981.

†On disabled list, July 16 to August 13, 1982.

‡On disabled list, August 4 to August 25, 1985; included rehabilitation disability assignment to Modesto, August 21 to August 25, 1985.

§On disabled list, May 9 to June 16, 1986; included rehabilitation disability assignment to Modesto, May 23 to June 13, 1986.

xOn disabled list, July 22 to August 6, 1987; included rehabilitation disability assignment to Modesto, August 2 to August 6, 1987.

yReleased, March 28, 1988; signed by Rochester (Baltimore Orioles' organization), April 5, 1988.

zOn disabled list, August 5 to September 2, 1989.

ALL-STAR GAME RECORD

Year League	Pos.	AB.	R.	H.	2B.	3B.	HR.	RBI.	B.A.	PO.	A.	E.	F.A.
1989—American	C	1	0	0	0	0	0	0	.000	2	0	0	1.000

TIMOTHY SHAWN TEUFEL

Name pronounced TUFF-el.

(Tim)

Born July 7, 1958, at Greenwich, Conn.
Height, 6.00. Weight, 175.
Throws and bats righthanded.
Attended St. Petersburg Junior College, St. Petersburg, Fla.,
and Clemson University, Clemson, S. C.

Holds American League record for fewest double plays by second baseman, season, 150 or more games (81), 1984.

Major League stolen bases: 1984 (1), 1985 (4), 1986 (1), 1987 (3), 1989 (1). Total—10.

Led International League second basemen in putouts with 304, assists with 394, total chances with 711 and double plays with 109 in 1983.

Named International League Player of the Year, 1983.

Named second baseman on THE SPORTING NEWS College Baseball All-America Team, 1980.

Year Club	League	Pos.	G.	AB.	R.	H.	2B.	3B.	HR.	RBI.	B.A.	PO.	A.	E.	F.A.
1980—Orlando	South.	2B	86	287	38	76	15	3	11	47	.265	196	246	17	.963
1981—Orlando	South.	2B	128	416	69	103	21	5	17	60	.248	312	376	20	.972
1982—Orlando	South.	2B	100	340	52	96	12	4	9	56	.282	231	185	15	.965
1982—Toledo	Int.	2B	45	149	25	42	10	4	6	20	.282	99	139	3	.988
1983—Toledo	Int.	2B-SS	136	471	103	152	27	6	27	100	.323	306	401	14	.981
1983—Minnesota	Amer.	2B-SS	21	78	11	24	7	1	3	6	.308	47	58	1	.991
1984—Minnesota	Amer.	2B	157	568	76	149	30	3	14	61	.262	315	★485	13	.984
1985—Minnesota†	Amer.	2B	138	434	58	113	24	3	10	50	.260	237	352	12	.980
1986—New York	Nat.	2B-1B-3B	93	279	35	69	20	1	4	31	.247	143	174	9	.972
1987—New York‡	Nat.	2B-1B	97	299	55	92	29	0	14	61	.308	199	214	11	.970
1988—New York§	Nat.	2B-1B	90	273	35	64	20	0	4	31	.234	175	213	7	.982
1989—New York x	Nat.	2B-1B	83	219	27	56	7	2	2	15	.256	261	112	10	.974
American League Totals—3 Years			316	1080	145	286	61	7	27	117	.265	599	895	26	.983
National League Totals—4 Years			363	1070	152	281	76	3	24	138	.263	718	713	37	.975
Major League Totals—7 Years			679	2150	297	567	137	10	51	255	.264	1317	1608	63	.979

Selected by Milwaukee Brewers' organization in 16th round of free-agent draft, June 6, 1978.

Selected by Chicago White Sox' organization in secondary phase of free-agent draft, June 5, 1979.

Selected by Minnesota Twins' organization in 2nd round of free-agent draft, June 3, 1980.

†Traded with Outfielder Pat Crosby to New York Mets for Outfielder Billy Beane and Pitchers Bill Latham and Joe Klink, January 16, 1986.

‡On disabled list, June 16 to July 1, 1987.

§On disabled list, May 17 to June 11, 1988.

xOn disabled list, June 5 to June 23, 1989.

CHAMPIONSHIP SERIES RECORD

Year Club	League	Pos.	G.	AB.	R.	H.	2B.	3B.	HR.	RBI.	B.A.	PO.	A.	E.	F.A.
1986—New York	Nat.	2B	2	6	0	1	0	0	0	0	.167	2	8	0	1.000
1988—New York	Nat.	2B	1	3	0	0	0	0	0	0	.000	1	3	0	1.000
Championship Series Totals—2 Years			3	9	0	1	0	0	0	0	.111	3	11	0	1.000

WORLD SERIES RECORD

Year Club	League	Pos.	G.	AB.	R.	H.	2B.	3B.	HR.	RBI.	B.A.	PO.	A.	E.	F.A.
1986—New York	Nat.	2B	3	9	1	4	1	0	1	1	.444	3	3	1	.857

ROBERT ALAN TEWKSBURY

(Bob)

Born November 30, 1960, at Concord, N. H.
Height, 6.04. Weight, 200.
Throws and bats righthanded.
Attended Rutgers University, New Brunswick, N.J., and St. Leo College, St. Leo, Fla.

Led Florida State League in shutouts with 5 and tied for lead in complete games with 13 in 1982.

Year Club	League	G.	IP.	W.	L.	Pct.	H.	R.	ER.	SO.	BB.	ERA.
1981—Oneonta	NYP	14	85	7	3	.700	85	43	34	62	37	3.40
1982—Fort Lauderdale	Florida St.	24	182⅓	★15	4	.789	146	46	38	92	47	★1.88
1983—Fort Lauderdale†	Florida St.	2	16	2	0	1.000	6	1	0	5	1	0.00
1983—Nashville	Southern	7	51	5	1	.833	49	20	16	15	10	2.82
1984—Nashville‡	Southern	26	172	11	9	.550	185	69	54	78	42	2.83
1985—Albany§	Eastern	17	106⅔	6	5	.545	101	48	42	63	19	3.54
1985—Columbus	Int'national	6	44	3	0	1.000	27	5	5	21	5	1.02
1986—New York	American	23	130⅓	9	5	.643	144	58	48	49	31	3.31
1986—Columbus	Int'national	2	10	1	0	1.000	6	3	3	4	2	2.70

Year Club	League	G.	IP.	W.	L.	Pct.	H.	R.	ER.	SO.	BB.	ERA.
1987—New York x	American	8	33⅓	1	4	.200	47	26	25	12	7	6.75
1987—Columbus	Int'national	11	74⅔	6	1	.857	68	23	21	32	11	2.53
1987—Chicago y	National	7	18	0	4	.000	32	15	13	10	13	6.50
1988—Iowa	Am. Assoc.	10	67	4	2	.667	73	28	28	43	10	3.76
1988—Chicago za	National	1	3⅓	0	0	.000	6	5	3	1	2	8.10
1989—Louisville	Am. Assoc.	28	★189	●13	5	.722	170	63	51	72	34	2.43
1989—St. Louis	National	7	30	1	0	1.000	25	12	11	17	10	3.30
American League Totals—2 Years		31	163⅔	10	9	.526	191	84	73	61	38	4.01
National League Totals—3 Years		15	51⅓	1	4	.200	63	32	27	28	25	4.73
Major League Totals—4 Years		46	215	11	13	.458	254	116	100	89	63	4.19

Selected by New York Yankees' organization in 19th round of free-agent draft, June 8, 1981.
†On disabled list, April 8 to June 7, 1983.
‡On disabled list, April 9 to April 27, 1984.
§On disabled list, June 10 to June 25, 1985.
xTraded with Pitchers Rich Scheid and Dean Wilkins to Chicago Cubs for Pitcher Steve Trout, July 13, 1987.
yOn disabled list, August 13, 1987 through remainder of season.
zOn disabled list, May 22 to June 12, 1988.
aGranted free agency, October 15, 1988.

ROBERT THOMAS THIGPEN
(Bobby)

Born July 17, 1963, at Tallahassee, Fla.
Height, 6.03. Weight, 195.
Throws and bats righthanded.
Attended Seminole Community College, Sanford, Fla., and
Mississippi State University, Starkville, Miss.

Major League saves: 1986 (7), 1987 (16), 1988 (34), 1989 (34). Total—91.
Led American League in games finished in relief with 59 in 1988.
Led Southern League in hit batsmen with 11 in 1986.

Year Club	League	G.	IP.	W.	L.	Pct.	H.	R.	ER.	SO.	BB.	ERA.
1985—Niagara Falls	NYP	28	52⅓	2	3	.400	30	12	10	74	19	1.72
1985—Appleton	Midwest	1	2⅔	1	0	1.000	1	0	0	4	1	0.00
1986—Birmingham	Southern	25	159⅔	8	11	.421	182	97	83	90	54	4.68
1986—Chicago	American	20	35⅔	2	0	1.000	26	7	7	20	12	1.77
1987—Chicago	American	51	89	7	5	.583	86	30	27	52	24	2.73
1987—Hawaii	P. Coast	9	52⅔	2	3	.400	72	38	36	17	14	6.15
1988—Chicago	American	68	90	5	8	.385	96	38	33	62	33	3.30
1989—Chicago	American	61	79	2	6	.250	62	34	33	47	40	3.76
Major League Totals—4 Years		200	293⅔	16	19	.457	270	109	100	181	109	3.06

Selected by Milwaukee Brewers' organization in 7th round of free-agent draft, January 11, 1983.
Selected by Chicago White Sox' organization in 4th round of free-agent draft, June 3, 1985.

ANDRES PERES THOMAS

Born November 10, 1963, at Santo Domingo, Dominican Republic.
Height, 6.01. Weight, 185.
Throws and bats righthanded.

Major League stolen bases: 1986 (4), 1987 (6), 1988 (7), 1989 (3). Total—20.
Led National League shortstops in double plays with 90 in 1988.

Year Club	League	Pos.	G.	AB.	R.	H.	2B.	3B.	HR.	RBI.	B.A.	PO.	A.	E.	F.A.
1982—Bradenton Brav...	Gulf C.	SS	44	143	18	37	2	1	1	14	.259	61	136	20	.908
1983—Anderson	S. Atl.	SS	61	251	33	79	8	4	1	20	.315	61	197	24	.915
1983—Durham	Carol.	SS	70	290	17	72	14	0	2	41	.248	107	222	32	.911
1984—Durham†	Carol.	SS	114	460	64	121	18	4	7	44	.263	156	361	34	.938
1985—Greenville	South.	SS-OF	114	458	53	114	18	4	9	59	.249	155	339	31	.941
1985—Richmond	Int.	SS	11	28	3	5	0	0	1	6	.179	15	30	3	.938
1985—Atlanta	Nat.	SS	15	18	6	5	0	0	0	2	.278	6	17	2	.920
1986—Atlanta	Nat.	SS	102	323	26	81	17	2	6	32	.251	143	290	19	.958
1987—Atlanta‡	Nat.	SS	82	324	29	75	11	0	5	39	.231	128	276	20	.953
1988—Atlanta	Nat.	SS	153	606	54	153	22	2	13	68	.252	230	456	●29	.959
1989—Atlanta	Nat.	SS	141	554	41	118	18	0	13	57	.213	231	400	29	.956
Major League Totals—5 Years			493	1825	156	432	68	4	37	198	.237	738	1439	99	.957

Signed as free agent by Atlanta Braves' organization, December 16, 1981.
†On suspended list, August 28, 1984 through remainder of season.
‡On disabled list, April 20 to May 13 and August 10, 1987 through remainder of season.

MILTON BERNARD THOMPSON
(Milt)

Born January 5, 1959, at Washington, D.C.
Height, 5.11. Weight, 170.
Throws right and bats lefthanded.
Attended Howard University, Washington, D.C.

Major League stolen bases: 1984 (14), 1985 (9), 1986 (19), 1987 (46), 1988 (17), 1989 (27). Total—132.
Led International League outfielders in total chances with 341 in 1984.
Led Southern League in stolen bases with 68 and caught stealing with 19 in 1982.
Led Southern League outfielders in total chances with 336 in 1982.

Year Club	League	Pos.	G.	AB.	R.	H.	2B.	3B.	HR.	RBI.	B.A.	PO.	A.	E.	F.A.
1979—Greenwood	W. Car.	OF	53	145	31	27	4	1	2	16	.186	85	8	3	.969
1979—Kingsport	Appal.	OF	26	94	22	31	8	4	1	11	.330	58	4	1	.984
1980—Durham	Carol.	OF	68	255	49	74	12	3	2	36	.290	159	8	5	.971
1980—Savannah	South.	OF	71	278	35	83	7	3	1	15	.299	133	11	6	.960
1981—Savannah	South.	OF	140	493	92	135	18	2	4	31	.274	226	17	8	.968
1982—Savannah	South.	OF	●144	526	83	132	20	7	6	45	.251	★312	10	14	.958
1982—Richmond	Int.	OF	3	6	2	1	0	0	0	0	.167	4	0	0	1.000
1983—Richmond	Int.	OF	12	32	12	8	1	0	0	3	.250	30	0	1	.968
1983—Savannah	South.	OF-1B	115	386	84	117	21	4	5	36	.303	295	15	7	.978
1984—Richmond	Int.	OF	134	503	●91	145	11	3	4	40	.288	★317	13	11	.968
1984—Atlanta	Nat.	OF	25	99	16	30	1	0	2	4	.303	37	6	2	.956
1985—Richmond	Int.	OF	82	312	52	98	10	1	2	22	.314	209	3	4	.981
1985—Atlanta†	Nat.	OF	73	182	17	55	7	2	0	6	.302	78	2	3	.964
1986—Philadelphia	Nat.	OF	96	299	38	75	7	1	6	23	.251	212	1	2	.991
1986—Portland	P. C.	OF	41	161	26	56	10	2	1	16	.348	101	1	1	.990
1987—Philadelphia	Nat.	OF	150	527	86	159	26	9	7	43	.302	354	4	4	.989
1988—Philadelphia‡	Nat.	OF	122	378	53	109	16	2	2	33	.288	278	5	5	.983
1989—St. Louis	Nat.	OF	155	545	60	158	28	8	4	68	.290	348	5	8	.978
Major League Totals—6 Years			621	2030	270	586	85	22	21	177	.289	1307	23	24	.982

Selected by Atlanta Braves' organization in 2nd round of free-agent draft, January 9, 1979.

†Traded with Pitcher Steve Bedrosian to Philadelphia Phillies for Catcher Ozzie Virgil and Pitcher Pete Smith, December 10, 1985.

‡Traded to St. Louis Cardinals for Catcher Steve Lake and Outfielder Curt Ford, December 16, 1988.

RICHARD NEIL THOMPSON
(Rich)

Born November 1, 1958, at New York, N.Y.
Height, 6.03. Weight, 215.
Throws right and bats left and righthanded.
Received bachelor of arts degree in economics from Amherst College, Amherst, Mass.
in 1980, and attended Baylor University School of Law, Waco, Tex.

Major League saves: 1985 (5).

Year Club	League	G.	IP.	W.	L.	Pct.	H.	R.	ER.	SO.	BB.	ERA.
1980—Batavia	NYP	7	12	2	0	1.000	12	3	1	16	6	0.75
1981—Waterloo	Midwest	28	122	5	6	.455	112	67	56	109	55	4.13
1982—Chattanooga	Southern	50	78	7	6	.538	69	39	35	55	36	4.04
1983—Buffalo	Eastern	43	78⅔	3	7	.300	67	33	25	61	46	2.86
1984—Buffalo†	Eastern	51	104⅔	9	7	.563	96	48	39	81	47	3.35
1985—Maine	Int'national	4	9	0	0	.000	6	1	1	2	2	1.00
1985—Cleveland‡	American	57	80	3	8	.273	95	63	56	30	48	6.30
1986—Vancouver§x	P. Coast	23	40⅔	1	1	.500	47	35	33	24	18	7.30
1987—Albany	Eastern	5	10⅓	0	0	.000	14	12	11	2	7	9.58
1987—Columbus y	Int'national	2	4	0	0	.000	6	2	2	3	2	4.50
1987—Jacksonville z-Memphis	Southern	15	31	1	0	1.000	35	20	18	27	11	5.23
1988—Memphis	Southern	20	80⅓	3	5	.375	87	44	37	53	17	4.15
1988—Omaha a	Am. Assoc.	17	96⅓	6	7	.462	94	36	31	46	15	2.90
1989—Indianapolis	Am. Assoc.	23	161⅓	9	6	.600	146	46	37	73	37	★2.06
1989—Montreal	National	19	33	0	2	.000	27	11	8	15	11	2.18
American League Totals—1 Year		57	80	3	8	.273	95	63	56	30	48	6.30
National League Totals—1 Year		19	33	0	2	.000	27	11	8	15	11	2.18
Major League Totals—2 Years		76	113	3	10	.231	122	74	64	45	59	5.10

Selected by Cleveland Indians' organization in 7th round of free-agent draft, June 3, 1980.

†On disabled list, August 9 to August 19, 1984.

‡Traded to Milwaukee Brewers for Pitcher Scott Roberts, December 16, 1985.

§On disabled list, July 14 to August 2, 1986.

xGranted free agency, October 15, 1986; signed by Albany (New York Yankees' organization), March 17, 1987.

yReleased, May 18, 1987; signed by Jacksonville (Montreal Expos' organization), June, 1987.

zReleased, July, 1987; signed by Memphis (Kansas City Royals' organization), August 10, 1987.

aReleased, March, 1989; signed by Indianapolis (Montreal Expos' organization), March 15, 1989.

ROBERT RANDALL THOMPSON
(Robbie)

Born May 10, 1962, at West Palm Beach, Fla.
Height, 5.11. Weight, 170.
Throws and bats righthanded.
Attended Palm Beach Junior College, Lake Worth, Fla.,
and University of Florida, Gainesville, Fla.

Major League stolen bases: 1986 (12), 1987 (16), 1988 (14), 1989 (12). Total—54.
Established major league record for most times caught stealing, game (4), June 27, 1986, 12 innings.

—DID YOU KNOW—

That when Detroit's Scott Lusader committed three errors in one inning on September 9, 1989, it was the first time an American League outfielder had done so since 1925?

Led National League in sacrifice hits with 18 in 1986.
Tied for National League lead in being hit by pitch with 13 in 1989.
Named National League Rookie Player of the Year by THE SPORTING NEWS, 1986.
Led Texas League second basemen in putouts with 291, total chances with 664 and double plays with 91 in 1985.

Year Club	League	Pos.	G.	AB.	R.	H.	2B.	3B.	HR.	RBI.	B.A.	PO.	A.	E.	F.A.
1983—Fresno	Calif.	2B	64	220	33	57	8	1	4	23	.259	118	185	11	.965
1984—Fresno	Calif.	2B-SS-3B	102	325	53	81	11	0	8	43	.249	182	280	24	.951
1985—Shreveport	Texas	★2B-SS	121	449	85	117	20	7	9	40	.261	292	366	12	★.982
1986—San Francisco	Nat.	2B-SS	149	549	73	149	27	3	7	47	.271	255	451	17	.976
1987—San Francisco†	Nat.	2B	132	420	62	110	26	5	10	44	.262	246	341	17	.972
1988—San Francisco	Nat.	2B	138	477	66	126	24	6	7	48	.264	255	365	14	.978
1989—San Francisco	Nat.	2B	148	547	91	132	26	★11	13	50	.241	307	425	8	.989
Major League Totals—4 Years			567	1993	292	517	103	25	37	189	.259	1063	1582	56	.979

Selected by Oakland A's organization in 2nd round of free-agent draft, January 12, 1982.
Selected by Seattle Mariners' organization in secondary phase of free-agent draft, June 7, 1982.
Selected by San Francisco Giants' organization in secondary phase of free-agent draft, June 6, 1983.
†On disabled list, April 28 to May 13, 1987.

CHAMPIONSHIP SERIES RECORD

Year Club	League	Pos.	G.	AB.	R.	H.	2B.	3B.	HR.	RBI.	B.A.	PO.	A.	E.	F.A.
1987—San Francisco	Nat.	2B-PH	7	20	4	2	0	1	1	2	.100	11	19	1	.968
1989—San Francisco	Nat.	2B	5	18	5	5	0	0	2	3	.278	10	13	0	1.000
Championship Series Totals—2 Years			12	38	9	7	0	1	3	5	.184	21	32	1	.981

WORLD SERIES RECORD

Year Club	League	Pos.	G.	AB.	R.	H.	2B.	3B.	HR.	RBI.	B.A.	PO.	A.	E.	F.A.
1989—San Francisco	Nat.	2B-PH	4	11	0	1	0	0	0	2	.091	4	10	0	1.000

ALL-STAR GAME RECORD

Named to National League All-Star Team for 1988 game; replaced due to injury by Bob Walk.

RICHARD WILLIAM THON
(Dickie)

Born June 20, 1958, at South Bend, Ind.
Height, 5.11. Weight, 175.
Throws and bats righthanded.
Grandson of Fred Thon, minor league pitcher, 1940.

Shares National League record for fewest triples, season, for league leader in triples (10), 1982.
Major League stolen bases: 1980 (7), 1981 (6), 1982 (37), 1983 (34), 1985 (8), 1986 (6), 1987 (3), 1988 (19), 1989 (6). Total—126.
Led National League in game-winning RBIs with 18 in 1983.
Named shortstop on THE SPORTING NEWS National League All-Star Team, 1983.
Named shortstop on THE SPORTING NEWS National League Silver Slugger team, 1983.

Year Club	League	Pos.	G.	AB.	R.	H.	2B.	3B.	HR.	RBI.	B.A.	PO.	A.	E.	F.A.
1976—Quad Cities	Midw.	SS	69	246	46	68	11	4	1	32	.276	96	193	32	.900
1977—Salinas	Calif.	SS	56	225	48	71	13	2	4	44	.316	95	162	13	.952
1977—Salt Lake City	P. C.	SS	77	274	47	79	9	3	8	43	.288	129	242	26	.935
1978—Salt Lake City	P. C.	2B-SS	130	439	67	113	17	3	1	47	.257	273	380	26	.962
1979—Salt Lake City	P. C.	SS-2B	38	162	25	47	3	1	2	21	.290	70	120	11	.945
1979—California	Amer.	2B-SS-3B	35	56	6	19	3	0	0	8	.339	38	46	8	.913
1980—Salt Lake City	P. C.	2B-SS	40	155	28	61	14	2	2	28	.394	81	107	12	.940
1980—California†	Amer.	S-2-3-1	80	267	32	68	12	2	0	15	.255	70	124	10	.951
1981—Houston	Nat.	2B-SS-3B	49	95	13	26	6	0	0	3	.274	53	63	6	.951
1982—Houston	Nat.	SS-3B-2B	136	496	73	137	31	★10	3	36	.276	183	412	17	.972
1983—Houston	Nat.	SS	154	619	81	177	28	9	20	79	.286	258	★533	28	.966
1984—Houston‡	Nat.	SS	5	17	3	6	0	1	0	1	.353	8	13	0	1.000
1985—Houston§x	Nat.	SS	84	251	26	63	6	1	6	29	.251	106	218	11	.967
1986—Houston y	Nat.	SS	106	278	24	69	13	1	3	21	.248	142	210	10	.972
1987—Tucson z	P. C.	SS	14	48	10	13	4	0	0	6	.271	22	40	7	.899
1987—Houston ab	Nat.	SS	32	66	6	14	1	0	1	3	.212	21	53	6	.925
1988—San Diego c	Nat.	SS-2B-3B	95	258	36	68	12	2	1	18	.264	84	171	12	.955
1989—Philadelphia	Nat.	SS	136	435	45	118	18	4	15	60	.271	174	380	16	.972
American League Totals—2 Years			115	323	38	87	15	2	0	23	.269	108	170	18	.939
National League Totals—9 Years			797	2515	307	678	115	28	49	250	.270	1029	2053	106	.967
Major League Totals—11 Years			912	2838	345	765	130	30	49	273	.270	1137	2223	124	.964

Signed as free agent by California Angels' organization, November 23, 1975.
†Traded to Houston Astros for Pitcher Ken Forsch, April 1, 1981.
‡On disabled list, April 9, 1984 through remainder of season.
§On disabled list, May 19 to June 8, 1985.
xGranted free agency, November 12, 1985; re-signed by Astros, January 7, 1986.
yOn disabled list, June 6 to June 23, 1986.
zOn Houston restricted list, April 3 to April 18, 1987; then transferred to disabled list, April 19 to May 10, 1987; included rehabilitation disability assignment to Tucson, April 19 to May 8, 1987.
aOn disqualified list, July 4, 1987 through remainder of season.
bGranted free agency, November 9, 1987; signed by San Diego Padres, February 18, 1988.
cSold to Philadelphia Phillies, January 27, 1989.

DIVISION SERIES RECORD

Year Club	League	Pos.	G.	AB.	R.	H.	2B.	3B.	HR.	RBI.	B.A.	PO.	A.	E.	F.A.
1981—Houston	Nat.	SS-PH	4	11	0	2	0	0	0	0	.182	5	10	1	.938

CHAMPIONSHIP SERIES RECORD

Year Club	League	Pos.	G.	AB.	R.	H.	2B.	3B.	HR.	RBI.	B.A.	PO.	A.	E.	F.A.
1979—California	Amer.	PR-SS	1	0	1	0	0	0	0	0	.000	0	0	0	.000
1986—Houston	Nat.	SS-PH	6	12	1	3	0	0	1	1	.250	6	9	0	1.000
Championship Series Totals—2 Years			7	12	2	3	0	0	1	1	.250	6	9	0	1.000

ALL-STAR GAME RECORD

Year League	Pos.	AB.	R.	H.	2B.	3B.	HR.	RBI.	B.A.	PO.	A.	E.	F.A.
1983—National	PH-SS	3	0	1	0	0	0	0	.333	0	2	0	1.000

LOUIS THORNTON JR.
(Lou)

Born April 26, 1963, at Montgomery, Ala.
Height, 6.00. Weight, 175.
Throws right and bats lefthanded.

Major League stolen bases: 1985 (1), 1989 (2). Total—3.
Led Appalachian League outfielders in errors with 9 in 1982.

Year Club	League	Pos.	G.	AB.	R.	H.	2B.	3B.	HR.	RBI.	B.A.	PO.	A.	E.	F.A.
1981—Kingsport	Appal.	1B	48	153	23	32	7	0	2	17	.209	338	43	16	.960
1982—Kingsport	Appal.	OF-1B-3B	57	210	29	44	9	2	5	29	.210	182	7	13	.940
1983—Columbia	S. Atl.	OF	119	448	80	120	24	6	11	73	.268	193	18	11	.950
1984—Lynchburg†	Carolina	OF-1B	131	505	78	139	25	7	6	67	.275	250	13	11	.960
1985—Toronto	Amer.	OF	56	72	18	17	1	1	1	8	.236	44	0	2	.957
1986—Syracuse‡	Int.	OF	64	231	34	60	4	2	2	28	.260	114	5	4	.967
1987—Syracuse	Int.	OF	122	464	64	123	10	5	9	47	.265	199	6	10	.953
1987—Toronto	Amer.	OF	12	2	5	1	0	0	0	0	.500	0	0	0	.000
1988—Syracuse	Int.	OF-3B	69	246	23	51	12	3	4	22	.207	106	31	12	.919
1988—Toronto§x	Amer.	OF	11	2	1	0	0	0	0	0	.000	1	0	0	1.000
1989—Buffalo y	A. A.	OF	28	96	8	20	3	1	1	7	.208	48	3	1	.981
1989—Tidewater	Int.	OF-1B-3B	71	229	34	62	10	2	2	20	.271	148	11	3	.981
1989—New York	Nat.	OF	13	13	5	4	1	0	0	1	.308	9	0	0	1.000
American League Totals—3 Years			79	76	24	18	1	1	1	8	.237	45	0	2	.957
National League Totals—1 Year			13	13	5	4	1	0	0	1	.308	9	0	0	1.000
Major League Totals—4 Years			92	89	29	22	2	1	1	9	.247	54	0	2	.964

Selected by New York Mets' organization in 19th round of free-agent draft, June 8, 1981.
†Drafted by Toronto Blue Jays, December 3, 1984.
‡On disabled list, May 29 to September 1, 1986.
§Granted free agency, October 15, 1988; signed by Denver (Milwaukee Brewers' organization), February, 1989.
xTraded to Pittsburgh Pirates, March 26, 1989, completing deal in which Pittsburgh traded Catcher Ruben Rodriguez to Milwaukee Brewers for a player to be named later, March 17, 1989.
yReleased, May 3, 1989; signed by Tidewater (New York Mets' organization), June 9, 1989.

CHAMPIONSHIP SERIES RECORD

Year Club	League	Pos.	G.	AB.	R.	H.	2B.	3B.	HR.	RBI.	B.A.	PO.	A.	E.	F.A.
1985—Toronto	Amer.	PR	2	0	1	0	0	0	0	0	.000	0	0	0	.000

GARY MONTEZ THURMAN JR.

Born November 12, 1964, at Indianapolis, Ind.
Height, 5.10. Weight, 175.
Throws and bats righthanded.

Shares American League record for most stolen bases with no caught stealing, season (16), 1989.
Major League stolen bases: 1987 (7), 1988 (5), 1989 (16). Total—28.
Led American Association in stolen bases with 58 in 1987.
Led Florida State League in stolen bases with 70 in 1985.
Led Gulf Coast League batters in strikeouts with 58 in 1983.
Tied for South Atlantic League lead in caught stealing with 17 in 1984.
Led Gulf Coast League outfielders in total chances with 143 in 1983, South Atlantic League outfielders with 329 in 1984 and Florida State League outfielders with 396 in 1985.
Tied for American Association lead in double plays by outfielders with 6 in 1987.

Year Club	League	Pos.	G.	AB.	R.	H.	2B.	3B.	HR.	RBI.	B.A.	PO.	A.	E.	F.A.
1983—Sarasota Royals	Gulf C.	OF	59	203	32	52	8	2	0	19	.256	★127	★13	3	.979
1984—Charleston	S. Atl.	OF	129	478	71	109	6	8	6	51	.228	★311	5	13	.960
1985—Fort Myers	Fla. St.	OF	134	453	68	137	9	9	0	45	.302	★368	18	10	.975
1986—Memphis	South.	OF	131	525	88	164	24	12	7	62	.312	277	5	11	.962
1986—Omaha	A. A.	OF	3	2	1	1	0	0	0	0	.500	2	0	0	1.000
1987—Omaha	A. A.	OF	115	450	88	132	14	9	8	39	.293	283	11	●8	.974
1987—Kansas City	Amer.	OF	27	81	12	24	2	0	0	5	.296	61	5	2	.971
1988—Omaha	A. A.	OF	106	422	77	106	12	6	3	40	.251	195	16	6	.972
1988—Kansas City	Amer.	OF	35	66	6	11	1	0	0	2	.167	36	1	2	.949
1989—Kansas City†	Amer.	OF	72	87	24	17	2	1	0	5	.195	54	2	3	.949
1989—Omaha	A. A.	OF	17	64	5	14	3	2	0	3	.219	34	1	2	.946
Major League Totals—3 Years			134	234	42	52	5	1	0	12	.222	151	8	7	.958

Selected by Kansas City Royals' organization in 1st round (21st player selected) of free-agent draft, June 6, 1983.
†On disabled list, March 26 to April 13 and May 10 to July 26, 1989; included rehabilitation disability assignment to Omaha, June 15 to July 26, 1989.

MARK ANTHONY THURMOND

Born September 12, 1956, at Houston, Tex.
Height, 6.00. Weight, 190.
Throws and bats lefthanded.
Received bachelor of science degree in finance from
Texas A&M University, College Station, Tex. in 1979.

Major League saves: 1985 (2), 1986 (3), 1987 (5), 1988 (3), 1989 (4). Total—17.
Named lefthanded pitcher on THE SPORTING NEWS National League All-Star Team, 1984.
Tied for Texas League lead in games started by pitchers with 27 in 1981.

Year Club	League	G.	IP.	W.	L.	Pct.	H.	R.	ER.	SO.	BB.	ERA.
1979—Amarillo	Texas	17	62	3	5	.375	89	52	39	46	31	5.66
1980—Amarillo†	Texas	26	156	10	9	.526	164	80	67	125	61	3.87
1981—Amarillo	Texas	27	193	12	5	.706	202	86	70	128	56	3.26
1982—Hawaii	P. Coast	28	194⅓	12	10	.545	202	88	77	106	58	3.57
1983—Las Vegas	P. Coast	19	63	6	1	.857	63	28	23	38	24	3.29
1983—San Diego	National	21	115⅓	7	3	.700	104	40	34	49	33	2.65
1984—San Diego	National	32	178⅔	14	8	.636	174	70	59	57	55	2.97
1985—San Diego	National	36	138⅓	7	11	.389	154	70	61	57	44	3.97
1986—San Diego‡	National	17	70⅔	3	7	.300	96	58	51	32	27	6.50
1986—Detroit	American	25	51⅔	4	1	.800	44	13	11	17	17	1.92
1987—Detroit§	American	48	61⅔	0	1	.000	83	32	29	21	24	4.23
1988—Baltimore	American	43	74⅔	1	8	.111	80	43	38	29	27	4.58
1988—Rochester	Int'national	8	54⅓	5	3	.625	40	22	16	25	18	2.65
1989—Baltimore x	American	49	90	2	4	.333	102	43	39	34	17	3.90
National League Totals—4 Years		106	503	31	29	.517	528	238	205	195	159	3.67
American League Totals—4 Years		165	278	7	14	.333	309	131	117	101	85	3.79
Major League Totals—7 Years		271	781	38	43	.469	837	369	322	296	244	3.71

Selected by San Diego Padres' organization in 24th round of free-agent draft, June 6, 1978.
Selected by San Diego Padres' organization in 5th round of free-agent draft, June 5, 1979.
†On disabled list, July 5 to July 16, 1980.
‡Traded to Detroit Tigers for Pitcher Dave LaPoint, July 9, 1986.
§Traded to Baltimore Orioles for Third Baseman Ray Knight, February 27, 1988.
xGranted free agency, November 13, 1989.

CHAMPIONSHIP SERIES RECORD

Year Club	League	G.	IP.	W.	L.	Pct.	H.	R.	ER.	SO.	BB.	ERA.
1984—San Diego	National	1	3⅔	0	1	.000	7	4	4	1	2	9.82
1987—Detroit	American	1	⅓	0	0	.000	0	0	0	0	0	0.00
Championship Series Totals—2 Years		2	4	0	1	.000	7	4	4	1	2	9.00

WORLD SERIES RECORD

Year Club	League	G.	IP.	W.	L.	Pct.	H.	R.	ER.	SO.	BB.	ERA.
1984—San Diego	National	2	5⅓	0	1	.000	12	6	6	2	3	10.13

JAY LINDSEY TIBBS

Born January 4, 1962, at Birmingham, Ala.
Height, 6.01. Weight, 183.
Throws and bats righthanded.

Year Club	League	G.	IP.	W.	L.	Pct.	H.	R.	ER.	SO.	BB.	ERA.
1980—Kingsport	Ap'lachian	12	76	3	7	.300	88	54	37	45	32	4.38
1981—Lynchburg	Carolina	15	72	2	7	.222	89	65	55	41	34	6.88
1981—Shelby	W. Carol.	13	89	4	8	.333	87	56	38	57	33	3.84
1982—Lynchburg†	Carolina	7	38⅓	2	4	.333	42	28	24	31	23	5.63
1982—Jackson	Texas	1	3⅓	0	0	.000	2	1	0	3	1	0.00
1983—Lynchburg‡	Carolina	28	203⅔	14	8	.636	172	94	66	170	96	2.92
1984—Jackson	Texas	6	37⅓	1	2	.333	28	15	13	31	19	3.13
1984—Tidewater§	Int'national	8	41⅓	3	5	.375	44	27	24	27	23	5.23
1984—Wichita	Am. Assoc.	4	27⅔	3	0	1.000	22	13	11	14	8	3.58
1984—Cincinnati	National	14	100⅔	6	2	.750	87	34	32	40	33	2.86
1985—Cincinnati	National	35	218	10	16	.385	216	111	95	98	83	3.92
1985—Denver x	Am. Assoc.	4	31⅔	1	2	.333	20	10	8	15	12	2.27
1986—Montreal	National	35	190⅓	7	9	.438	181	96	84	117	70	3.97
1987—Montreal	National	19	83	4	5	.444	95	55	46	54	34	4.99
1987—Indianapolis y	Am. Assoc.	12	81⅓	5	5	.500	64	31	27	55	22	2.99
1988—Rochester	Int'national	4	25⅓	3	1	.750	22	12	8	18	9	2.84
1988—Baltimore	American	30	158⅔	4	15	.211	184	103	95	82	63	5.39
1989—Rochester	Int'national	4	29	3	0	1.000	22	3	3	14	10	0.93
1989—Baltimore z	American	10	54⅓	5	0	1.000	62	17	17	30	20	2.82
National League Totals—4 Years		103	592	27	32	.458	579	296	257	309	220	3.91
American League Totals—2 Years		40	213	9	15	.375	246	120	112	112	83	4.73
Major League Totals—6 Years		143	805	36	47	.434	825	416	369	421	303	4.13

Selected by New York Mets' organization in 2nd round of free-agent draft, June 3, 1980.
†On disabled list, July 21 to August 29, 1982.

‡Drafted by Philadelphia Phillies, December 5, 1983; returned, March 29, 1984.
§Traded with Third Baseman Eddie Williams and Pitcher Matt Bullinger to Cincinnati Reds' organization for Pitcher Bruce Berenyi, June 15, 1984.
xTraded with Pitchers Andy McGaffigan and John Stuper and Catcher Dann Bilardello to Montreal Expos for Pitcher Bill Gullickson and Catcher Sal Butera, December 19, 1985.
yTraded with Pitcher Al Cardwood to Baltimore Orioles for Pitchers John Hoover, Doug Cinnella and Rick Carriger, February 16, 1988.
zOn disabled list, July 3, 1989 through remainder of season.

RONALD IRVIN TINGLEY
(Ron)

Born May 27, 1959, at Presque Isle, Maine.
Height, 6.02. Weight, 180.
Throws and bats righthanded.

Year	Club	League	Pos.	G.	AB.	R.	H.	2B.	3B.	HR.	RBI.	B.A.	PO.	A.	E.	F.A.
1977—Walla Walla	N'west		OF	21	33	8	5	0	0	1	3	.152	5	2	0	1.000
1978—Walla Walla	N'west		OF-C	43	140	22	29	2	0	2	21	.207	149	16	8	.954
1979—Santa Clara	Calif.		C-OF-P	52	143	11	29	4	1	0	17	.203	258	42	8	.974
1979—Amarillo	Texas		C-OF	30	90	16	23	4	1	1	6	.256	133	17	4	.974
1980—Reno†	Calif.		C-OF	65	204	37	61	3	3	3	35	.299	333	46	10	.974
1981—Amarillo	Texas		C-1B-OF	116	379	72	109	9	*10	13	60	.288	607	47	11	.983
1982—Hawaii	P. C.		C	115	362	45	95	13	8	6	42	.262	540	77	12	.981
1982—San Diego	Nat.		C	8	20	0	2	0	0	0	0	.100	40	4	2	.957
1983—Las Vegas	P. C.		C	92	294	44	83	15	6	10	48	.282	449	55	12	.977
1984—Salt Lake City‡§	P. C.		C	3	2	1	1	0	0	1	1	.500	3	0	0	1.000
1985—Calgary x	P. C.		C-OF	83	277	36	70	11	3	11	47	.253	399	51	10	.978
1986—Rich.y-Maine	Int.		C	58	174	13	35	2	1	3	13	.201	280	23	6	.981
1987—Buffalo	A. A.		C-1B-3B	57	167	27	45	8	5	5	30	.269	306	37	6	.983
1988—Colorado Springs	P. C.		C	44	130	11	37	5	1	3	20	.285	234	22	0	1.000
1988—Cleveland	Amer.		C	9	24	1	4	0	0	1	2	.167	48	6	0	1.000
1989—Colo. Springs z	P. C.		C-1B	66	207	28	54	8	2	6	39	.261	349	45	12	.970
1989—California	Amer.		C	4	3	0	1	0	0	0	0	.333	7	1	1	.889
National League Totals—1 Year				8	20	0	2	0	0	0	0	.100	40	4	2	.957
American League Totals—2 Years				13	27	1	5	0	0	1	2	.185	55	7	1	.984
Major League Totals—3 Years				21	47	1	7	0	0	1	2	.149	95	11	3	.972

Selected by San Diego Padres' organization in 10th round of free-agent draft, June 7, 1977.
†On disabled list, April 10 to April 29, 1980.
‡On disabled list, April 7 to August 10, 1984.
§Granted free agency, October 15, 1984; signed by Calgary (Seattle Mariners' organization), January 15, 1985.
xGranted free agency, October 15, 1985; signed by Richmond (Atlanta Braves' organization), November 19, 1985.
yReleased, June 19, 1986; signed by Maine (Cleveland Indians' organization), June 23, 1986.
zTraded to California Angels for a player to be named later, September 6, 1989.

PITCHING RECORD

Year	Club	League	G.	IP.	W.	L.	Pct.	H.	R.	ER.	SO.	BB.	ERA.
1979—Santa Clara		California	1	1	0	0	.000	4	5	1	2	2	9.00

FREDDIE LEE TOLIVER
(Fred)

Born February 3, 1961, at Natchez, Miss.
Height, 6.01. Weight, 170.
Throws and bats righthanded.

Major League saves: 1985 (1).

Year	Club	League	G.	IP.	W.	L.	Pct.	H.	R.	ER.	SO.	BB.	ERA.
1979—Oneonta	NYP		13	77	*10	2	.833	46	28	18	71	66	2.10
1980—Fort Lauderdale	Florida St.		3	8	0	2	.000	14	15	13	4	10	14.63
1980—Greensboro†	S. Atlantic		20	126	6	8	.429	98	60	40	96	89	2.86
1981—Greensboro‡§	S. Atlantic		17	80	5	3	.625	67	38	31	62	56	3.49
1982—Cedar Rapids	Midwest		23	115	6	7	.462	114	77	54	117	66	4.23
1982—Indianapolis	Am. Assoc.		4	20⅔	2	2	.500	20	10	9	19	13	3.92
1983—Indianapolis	Am. Assoc.		26	166⅔	8	10	.444	151	93	84	112	*110	4.54
1984—Wichita	Am. Assoc.		32	164	11	6	.647	142	90	88	113	*116	4.83
1984—Cincinnati	National		3	10	0	0	.000	7	2	1	4	7	0.90
1985—Denver xy	Am. Assoc.		19	121⅓	11	3	.786	113	50	44	84	56	3.24
1985—Philadelphia	National		11	25	0	4	.000	27	15	13	23	17	4.68
1986—Portland	P. Coast		6	26⅔	1	3	.250	31	23	22	15	14	7.43
1986—Philadelphia z	National		5	25⅔	0	2	.000	28	14	10	20	11	3.51
1987—Maine	Int'national		22	124⅔	6	9	.400	114	70	64	80	67	4.62
1987—Philadelphia a	National		10	30⅓	1	1	.500	34	19	19	25	17	5.64
1988—Portland	P. Coast		13	95	7	2	.778	79	42	33	54	35	3.13
1988—Minnesota	American		21	114⅔	7	6	.538	116	57	54	69	52	4.24
1989—Minnesota	American		7	29	1	3	.250	39	26	25	11	15	7.76
1989—Portland b-Las Vegas	P. Coast		13	84	8	2	.800	72	32	24	72	31	2.57
1989—San Diego c	National		9	14	0	0	.000	17	14	11	14	9	7.07
National League Totals—5 Years			38	105	1	7	.125	113	64	54	86	61	4.63
American League Totals—2 Years			28	143⅔	8	9	.471	155	83	79	80	67	4.95
Major League Totals—6 Years			66	248⅔	9	16	.360	268	147	133	166	128	4.81

Selected by New York Yankees' organization in 3rd round of free-agent draft, June 5, 1979.
†On disabled list, May 23 to June 6, 1980.
‡On disabled list, April 9 to May 27, 1981.
§Traded to Cincinnati Reds' organization, December 10, 1981, completing deal in which Cincinnati traded Outfielder Ken Griffey to New York Yankees for Pitcher Brian Ryder and a player to be named later, November 4, 1981.
xOn disabled list, July 5 to August 10, 1985.
yTraded to Philadelphia Phillies, August 27, 1985, completing deal in which Philadelphia traded Catcher Bo Diaz and Pitcher Greg Simpson to Cincinnati Reds for Shortstop Tom Foley, Catcher Alan Knicely, a player to be named later and cash, August 8, 1985.
zOn disabled list, May 30 to June 25 and July 8, 1986 through remainder of season.
aTraded to Minnesota Twins for Catcher Chris Calvert, February 5, 1988.
bTraded to San Diego Padres for Pitcher Greg Booker, June 29, 1989.
cTraded to New York Yankees, September 27, 1989, completing deal in which New York traded Third Baseman Mike Pagliarulo and Pitcher Don Schulze to San Diego Padres for Pitcher Walt Terrell and a player to be named later, July 22, 1989.

JIMMY WAYNE TOLLESON

(Known by middle name.)
Born September 22, 1955, at Spartanburg, S. C.
Height, 5.09. Weight, 160.
Throws right and bats left and righthanded.
Received degree from Western Carolina University, Cullowhee, N. C., in 1978.
Brother of Mike Tolleson, outfielder in Cleveland Indians' organization, 1984.

Major League stolen bases: 1981 (2), 1982 (1), 1983 (33), 1984 (22), 1985 (21), 1986 (17), 1987 (5), 1988 (1), 1989 (5). Total—107.

Year Club	League	Pos.	G.	AB.	R.	H.	2B.	3B.	HR.	RBI.	B.A.	PO.	A.	E.	F.A.
1978—Asheville	W. Car.	3B-SS	70	212	35	57	4	1	0	21	.269	85	175	20	.929
1979—Tulsa	Texas	SS	130	418	43	98	9	7	1	36	.234	179	413	*41	.935
1980—Tulsa	Texas	SS	131	452	69	124	19	7	1	30	.274	161	395	31	.947
1981—Wichita	A. A.	3-S-2-O	107	375	58	98	9	4	3	38	.261	96	259	15	.959
1981—Texas	Amer.	3B-SS	14	24	6	4	0	0	0	1	.167	5	8	0	1.000
1982—Texas	Amer.	SS-3B-2B	38	70	6	8	1	0	0	2	.114	47	70	5	.959
1982—Denver	A. A.	SS	71	266	48	64	9	3	4	27	.241	97	195	6	.980
1983—Texas	Amer.	2B-SS	134	470	64	122	13	2	3	20	.260	268	372	17	.974
1984—Texas	Amer.	2-S-3-O	118	338	35	72	9	2	0	9	.213	195	287	10	.980
1985—Texas†	Amer.	SS-2B-3B	123	323	45	101	9	5	1	18	.313	149	255	14	.967
1986—Chi.‡-N.Y.	Amer.	S-3-2-O	141	475	61	126	16	5	3	43	.265	147	327	14	.971
1987—New York§	Amer.	SS-3B	121	349	48	77	4	0	1	22	.221	162	326	15	.970
1988—Fort Lauderdale x	Fla. St.	SS	4	18	2	5	0	0	0	5	.278	6	13	2	.905
1988—Columbus	Int.	SS-3B	8	27	4	5	0	0	0	1	.185	7	20	1	.964
1988—New York y	Amer.	2B-3B-SS	21	59	8	15	2	0	0	5	.254	28	54	3	.965
1989—New York z	Amer.	SS-3B-2B	80	140	16	23	5	2	1	9	.164	45	107	7	.956
Major League Totals—9 Years			790	2248	289	548	59	16	9	129	.244	1046	1806	85	.971

Selected by Pittsburgh Pirates' organization in 12th round of free-agent draft, June 7, 1977.
Selected by Texas Rangers' organization in 8th round of free-agent draft, June 6, 1978.
†Traded with Pitcher Dave Schmidt to Chicago White Sox for Pitcher Ed Correa, Infielder Scott Fletcher and a player to be named later, November 25, 1985; Texas Rangers acquired Infielder Jose Mota to complete deal, December 12, 1985.
‡Traded with Outfielder-Designated Hitter Ron Kittle and Catcher Joel Skinner to New York Yankees for Catcher Ron Hassey, Shortstop Carlos Martinez and a player to be named later, July 30, 1986; New York traded Catcher Bill Lindsey to Chicago White Sox' organization to complete deal, December 24, 1986.
§On disabled list, August 19 to September 3, 1987.
xOn New York disabled list, April 4 to June 10, June 20 to July 14, July 17 to August 11 and August 14 to September 11, 1988; included rehabilitation disability assignment to Fort Lauderdale, April 16 to April 24, and to Columbus, May 19 to May 28, 1988.
yGranted free agency, November 4, 1988; re-signed by Yankees, December 18, 1988.
zOn disabled list, March 25 to April 16, 1989.

JAMES JOSEPH TRABER

(Jim)

Born December 26, 1961, at Columbus, O.
Height, 6.00. Weight, 213.
Throws and bats lefthanded.
Attended Oklahoma State University, Stillwater, Okla.

Major League stolen bases: 1988 (1), 1989 (4). Total—5.
Tied for International League lead in intentional bases on balls received with 10 in 1987.
Led Appalachian League in game-winning RBIs with 10 in 1982.
Led Carolina League first basemen in putouts with 1,006, double plays with 96 and total chances with 1,070 in 1983.
Led Appalachian League first basemen in double plays with 44 and total chances with 581 in 1982.

Year Club	League	Pos.	G.	AB.	R.	H.	2B.	3B.	HR.	RBI.	B.A.	PO.	A.	E.	F.A.
1982—Bluefield	Appal.	1B	61	235	41	76	18	3	9	●63	.323	*540	*34	7	.988
1982—Hagerstown	Carol.	OF-1B	7	26	1	9	2	0	0	2	.346	12	0	0	1.000
1983—Hagerstown	Carol.	*1B-OF	128	449	73	123	22	1	14	79	.274	1012	54	10	*.991
1984—Hagerstown†	Carol.	1B-OF	48	165	33	59	15	0	2	29	.358	361	30	7	.982
1984—Charlotte	South.	1B	75	296	50	104	17	2	16	56	.351	663	44	7	.990
1984—Baltimore	Amer.	DH-PH	10	21	3	5	0	0	0	2	.238	0	0	0	.000
1985—Rochester‡	Int.	OF-1B	80	279	32	74	13	2	7	37	.265	220	22	4	.984
1986—Rochester	Int.	1B-OF	87	323	46	90	19	2	12	55	.279	592	56	3	.995
1986—Baltimore	Amer.	1B-OF	65	212	28	54	7	0	13	44	.255	243	23	5	.982

Year Club League	Pos.	G.	AB.	R.	H.	2B.	3B.	HR.	RBI.	B.A.	PO.	A.	E.	F.A.
1987—Rochester............. Int.	OF-1B	127	482	69	132	31	3	21	71	.274	491	27	8	.985
1988—Baltimore .... Amer.	1B-OF	103	352	25	78	6	0	10	45	.222	481	59	6	.989
1988—Rochester............. Int.	1B	38	144	17	41	10	0	6	23	.285	344	31	5	.987
1989—Baltimore§ .... Amer.	1B	86	234	14	49	8	0	4	26	.209	514	54	1	.993
Major League Totals—4 Years.................		264	819	70	186	21	0	27	117	.227	1238	136	12	.991

Selected by Baltimore Orioles' organization in 21st round of free-agent draft, June 7, 1982.
†On suspended list, June 7 to June 17, 1984.
‡On disabled list, May 21 to July 8, 1985.
§Released, November 30, 1989; signed by Kintetsu Buffaloes of Japanese Baseball League, November 30, 1989.

ALAN STUART TRAMMELL
Name pronounced TRAM-mull.

Born February 21, 1958, at Garden Grove, Calif.
Height, 6.00. Weight, 175.
Throws and bats righthanded.

Major League stolen bases: 1978 (3), 1979 (17), 1980 (12), 1981 (10), 1982 (19), 1983 (30), 1984 (19), 1985 (14), 1986 (25), 1987 (21), 1988 (7), 1989 (10). Total—187.
Led American League in sacrifice hits with 16 in 1981 and 15 in 1983.
Named American League Comeback Player of the Year by THE SPORTING NEWS, 1983.
Named shortstop on THE SPORTING NEWS American League All-Star Team, 1987 and 1988.
Named shortstop on THE SPORTING NEWS American League All-Star fielding team, 1980, 1981, 1983 and 1984.
Named shortstop on THE SPORTING NEWS American League Silver Slugger team, 1987 and 1988.
Named Southern League Most Valuable Player, 1977.

Year Club League	Pos.	G.	AB.	R.	H.	2B.	3B.	HR.	RBI.	B.A.	PO.	A.	E.	F.A.
1976—Bristol..................... Appal.	SS	41	140	27	38	2	2	0	7	.271	59	131	12	.941
1976—Montgomery........ South.	SS	21	56	4	10	0	0	0	2	.179	40	64	2	.981
1977—Montgomery........ South.	SS	134	454	78	132	9	*19	3	50	.291	188	397	27	.956
1977—Detroit.................... Amer.	SS	19	43	6	8	0	0	0	0	.186	15	34	2	.961
1978—Detroit.................... Amer.	SS	139	448	49	120	14	6	2	34	.268	239	421	14	.979
1979—Detroit.................... Amer.	SS	142	460	68	127	11	4	6	50	.276	245	388	26	.961
1980—Detroit.................... Amer.	SS	146	560	107	168	21	5	9	65	.300	225	412	13	.980
1981—Detroit.................... Amer.	SS	105	392	52	101	15	3	2	31	.258	181	347	9	.983
1982—Detroit.................... Amer.	SS	157	489	66	126	34	3	9	57	.258	259	459	16	.978
1983—Detroit.................... Amer.	SS	142	505	83	161	31	2	14	66	.319	236	367	13	.979
1984—Detroit†................. Amer.	SS	139	555	85	174	34	5	14	69	.314	180	314	10	.980
1985—Detroit.................... Amer.	SS	149	605	79	156	21	7	13	57	.258	225	400	15	.977
1986—Detroit.................... Amer.	SS	151	574	107	159	33	7	21	75	.277	238	445	22	.969
1987—Detroit.................... Amer.	SS	151	597	109	205	34	3	28	105	.343	222	421	19	.971
1988—Detroit‡................. Amer.	SS	128	466	73	145	24	1	15	69	.311	195	355	11	.980
1989—Detroit§................. Amer.	SS	121	449	54	109	20	3	5	43	.243	188	396	9	.985
Major League Totals—13 Years..............		1689	6143	938	1759	292	49	138	721	.286	2648	4759	179	.976

Selected by Detroit Tigers' organization in 2nd round of free-agent draft, June 8, 1976.
†On disabled list, July 9 to July 31, 1984.
‡On disabled list, June 29 to July 17, 1988.
§On disabled list, June 4 to June 23, 1989.

CHAMPIONSHIP SERIES RECORD

Year Club League	Pos.	G.	AB.	R.	H.	2B.	3B.	HR.	RBI.	B.A.	PO.	A.	E.	F.A.
1984—Detroit.................... Amer.	SS	3	11	2	4	0	1	1	3	.364	1	8	0	1.000
1987—Detroit.................... Amer.	SS	5	20	3	4	1	0	0	2	.200	6	9	1	.938
Championship Series Totals—2 Years.....		8	31	5	8	1	1	1	5	.258	7	17	1	.960

WORLD SERIES RECORD

Tied World Series records for batting in all club's runs, game, most (4), October 13, 1984; most hits, five-game Series (9), 1984.

Year Club League	Pos.	G.	AB.	R.	H.	2B.	3B.	HR.	RBI.	B.A.	PO.	A.	E.	F.A.
1984—Detroit.................... Amer.	SS	5	20	5	9	1	0	2	6	.450	8	9	1	.944

ALL-STAR GAME RECORD

Year League	Pos.	AB.	R.	H.	2B.	3B.	HR.	RBI.	B.A.	PO.	A.	E.	F.A.
1980—American	SS	0	0	0	0	0	0	0	.000	0	0	0	.000
1985—American	SS	1	0	0	0	0	0	0	.000	0	0	0	.000
1987—American	PH	1	0	0	0	0	0	0	.000	0	0	0	.000
All-Star Game Totals—3 Years....................		2	0	0	0	0	0	0	.000	0	0	0	.000

Named to American League All-Star Team for 1984 game; replaced due to injury by Alfredo Griffin.
Named to American League All-Star Team for 1988 game; replaced due to injury by Cal Ripken Jr.

DAVID FEASTER TRAUTWEIN
(Dave)

Born June 1, 1966, at Lynn, Mass.
Height, 6.05. Weight, 210.
Throws and bats righthanded.
Attended University of North Carolina, Chapel Hill, N.C.

Year Club	League	G.	IP.	W.	L.	Pct.	H.	R.	ER.	SO.	BB.	ERA.
1987—Little Falls	NYP	25	40	3	2	.600	46	23	16	37	16	3.60
1988—St. Lucie	Florida St.	52	70⅔	1	5	.167	52	31	27	45	25	3.44
1989—Jackson	Texas	44	71	6	6	.500	50	20	13	39	18	1.65

Selected by New York Mets' organization in 22nd round of free-agent draft, June 2, 1987.

HUGH JEFFERY TREADWAY
(Jeff)

Born January 22, 1963, at Columbus, Ga.
Weight, 5.11. Weight, 170.
Throws right and bats lefthanded.
Attended Middle Georgia College, Cochran, Ga.,
and University of Georgia, Athens, Ga.

Major League stolen bases: 1987 (1), 1988 (2), 1989 (3). Total—6.

Year Club	League	Pos.	G.	AB.	R.	H.	2B.	3B.	HR.	RBI.	B.A.	PO.	A.	E.	F.A.
1984—Tampa	Fla. St.	3B-2B	119	372	44	115	16	0	0	44	.309	128	184	25	.926
1985—Vermont	East.	2B	129	431	63	130	17	1	2	49	.302	271	332	15	.976
1986—Vermont	East.	2B	33	122	18	41	8	1	1	16	.336	68	102	5	.971
1986—Denver	A. A.	2B-3B	72	204	20	67	11	4	3	23	.328	75	153	6	.974
1987—Nashville	A. A.	2B	123	409	66	129	28	5	7	59	.315	236	362	12	★.980
1987—Cincinnati	Nat.	2B	23	84	9	28	4	0	2	4	.333	44	48	4	.958
1988—Cincinnati†‡	Nat.	2B-3B	103	301	30	76	19	4	2	23	.252	189	253	8	.982
1989—Atlanta	Nat.	2B-3B	134	473	58	131	18	3	8	40	.277	273	341	12	.981
Major League Totals—3 Years			260	858	97	235	41	7	12	67	.274	506	642	24	.980

Selected by Montreal Expos' organization in 18th round of free-agent draft, January 13, 1981.
Signed as free agent by Cincinnati Reds' organization, January 29, 1984.
†On disabled list, August 28 to September 24, 1988.
‡Sold to Atlanta Braves, March 25, 1989.

ALEJANDRO TREVINO (CASTRO)
(Alex)

Born August 26, 1957, at Monterrey, Nuevo Leon, Mex.
Height, 5.11. Weight, 179.
Throws and bats righthanded.
Attended University of Nuevo Leon, Monterrey, Mex.
Brother of Bobby Trevino, outfielder with California Angels, 1968; manager, Tabasco, 1977,
Tampico, 1979, and Toluca, 1980.

Major League stolen bases: 1979 (2), 1981 (3), 1982 (3), 1984 (5), 1987 (1), 1988 (5). Total—19.
Led Midwest League catchers in putouts with 847 and assists with 102 in 1977.
Led Carolina League in passed balls with 18 in 1976.

Year Club	League	Pos.	G.	AB.	R.	H.	2B.	3B.	HR.	RBI.	B.A.	PO.	A.	E.	F.A.
1973—Victoria†	Mx. Cen.	C-OF	12	26	3	6	1	0	0	2	.231	26	5	1	.969
1974—Marion	Appal.	C-SS	12	16	0	1	0	0	0	1	.063	15	0	0	1.000
1975—Marion	Appal.	C-2B-OF	22	60	10	12	1	0	0	3	.200	96	8	6	.963
1976—Lynchburg	Carol.	C-3-2-S	94	284	17	57	11	2	0	31	.201	400	130	18	.967
1977—Wausau	Midw.	C-2-1-3	128	422	57	100	10	0	2	36	.237	865	110	15	.985
1978—Tidewater	Int.	C-3B	87	262	44	77	13	2	5	37	.294	303	68	11	.971
1978—New York	Nat.	C-3B	6	12	3	3	0	0	0	0	.250	12	4	0	1.000
1979—New York	Nat.	C-3B-2B	79	207	24	56	11	1	0	20	.271	229	71	9	.971
1980—New York	Nat.	C-3B-2B	106	355	26	91	11	2	0	37	.256	450	76	16	.970
1981—New York‡	Nat.	C-2-O-3	56	149	17	39	2	0	0	10	.262	215	25	9	.964
1982—Cincinnati	Nat.	★C-3B	120	355	24	89	10	3	1	33	.251	725	61	★17	.979
1983—Cincinnati	Nat.	C-3B-2B	74	167	14	36	8	1	1	13	.216	359	32	5	.987
1984—Cinc.§-Atl.	Nat.	C	85	272	36	66	16	0	3	28	.243	403	61	5	.989
1985—Atl. x-S.F. y	Nat.	C-3B	57	157	17	34	10	1	6	19	.217	299	19	7	.978
1986—Los Angeles	Nat.	C-1B	89	202	31	53	13	0	4	26	.262	304	46	11	.970
1987—Los Angeles z	Nat.	C-OF-3B	72	144	16	32	7	1	3	16	.222	206	22	3	.987
1988—Tucson	P. C.	C-OF-3B	15	45	5	10	3	1	0	3	.222	39	10	2	.961
1988—Houston a	Nat.	C-OF	78	193	19	48	17	0	2	13	.249	360	24	9	.977
1989—Houston	Nat.	C-1B-3B	59	131	15	38	7	1	2	16	.290	173	13	2	.989
Major League Totals—12 Years			881	2344	242	585	112	10	22	231	.250	3735	454	93	.978

Signed as free agent by Victoria, May 16, 1973.
†Sold to New York Mets' organization, May 22, 1974.
‡Traded with Pitchers Jim Kern and Greg Harris to Cincinnati Reds for Outfielder George Foster, February 10, 1982.
§Traded to Atlanta Braves for player to be named later, April 24, 1984; deal settled with reported $50,000 in July, 1984.
xTraded to San Francisco Giants for Catcher-Outfielder John Rabb, April 17, 1985.
yTraded to Los Angeles Dodgers for Outfielder Candy Maldonado, December 11, 1985.
zReleased, April 4, 1988; signed by Tucson (Houston Astros' organization), April 12, 1988.
aGranted free agency, November 4, 1988; re-signed by Astros, December 21, 1988.

—DID YOU KNOW—
That Cub rookie Jerome Walton's 30-game hitting streak was the majors' longest in 1989?

JESUS MANUEL TRILLO (MARCANO)

Name pronounced TREE-yo.

(Manny)

Born December 25, 1950, at Caritito, Monagas, Venezuela.
Height, 6.01. Weight, 164.
Throws and bats righthanded.
Attended Colegio Libertador Bolivar, Maturin, Monagas, Venz.

Holds major league records for most consecutive errorless games by second baseman, season (89), 1982; most consecutive errorless chances accepted by second baseman, season (479), 1982.

Major League stolen bases: 1975 (1), 1976 (17), 1977 (3), 1979 (4), 1980 (8), 1981 (10), 1982 (8), 1983 (1), 1985 (2), 1988 (2). Total—56.

Led National League second basemen in double plays with 99 in 1978.
Led National League second basemen in total chances with 822 in 1977 and 878 in 1978.
Led Pacific Coast League second basemen in double plays with 113 in 1973.
Named second baseman on THE SPORTING NEWS National League All-Star Team, 1980 through 1982.
Named second baseman on THE SPORTING NEWS National League All-Star fielding team, 1979, 1981 and 1982.
Named second baseman on THE SPORTING NEWS National League Silver Slugger team, 1980 and 1981.

Year	Club	League	Pos.	G.	AB.	R.	H.	2B.	3B.	HR.	RBI.	B.A.	PO.	A.	E.	F.A.
1968—Huron†	North.	SS-3B-C	35	92	8	24	2	1	0	4	.261	35	48	5	.943
1969—Spartanburg‡	W. Car.	3-C-S-2	83	275	41	77	18	0	1	26	.280	188	98	12	.960
1970—Birmingham	South.	3B-2B-SS	84	241	26	63	10	1	2	19	.261	101	130	14	.943
1971—Birmingham§	South.	3B-SS	107	371	37	104	18	1	5	44	.280	110	212	31	.912
1972—Iowa	A. A.	3B-2B-SS	133	509	67	153	27	6	9	53	.301	176	304	28	.945
1973—Tucson	P. C.	★2B-OF	135	519	76	162	25	7	8	78	.312	★304	★373	19	★.973
1973—Oakland	Amer.	2B	17	12	0	3	2	0	0	3	.250	15	17	2	.941
1974—Tucson	P. C.	2B	85	320	31	81	19	1	2	39	.253	198	256	12	.974
1974—Oakland x	Amer.	2B	21	33	3	5	0	0	0	2	.152	31	43	4	.949
1975—Chicago	Nat.	★2B-SS	154	545	55	135	12	2	7	70	.248	350	★509	★29	.967
1976—Chicago	Nat.	★2B-SS	158	582	42	139	24	3	4	59	.239	350	★527	17	.981
1977—Chicago	Nat.	2B	152	504	51	141	18	5	7	57	.280	330	★467	★25	.970
1978—Chicago y	Nat.	2B	152	552	53	144	17	5	4	55	.261	354	★505	19	.978
1979—Philadelphia z	Nat.	2B	118	431	40	112	22	1	6	42	.260	270	368	10	.985
1980—Philadelphia a	Nat.	2B	141	531	68	155	25	9	7	43	.292	★360	467	11	.987
1981—Philadelphia	Nat.	2B	94	349	37	100	14	3	6	36	.287	★245	286	7	.987
1982—Philadelphia b	Nat.	2B	149	549	52	149	24	1	0	39	.271	343	441	5	★.994
1983—Cleveland cd	Amer.	2B	88	320	33	87	13	1	1	29	.272	172	269	5	.989
1983—Montreal e	Nat.	2B	31	121	16	32	8	0	2	16	.264	57	86	3	.979
1984—San Francisco f	Nat.	2B-3B	98	401	45	102	21	1	4	36	.254	218	294	6	.988
1985—San Francisco g	Nat.	2B-3B	125	451	36	101	16	2	3	25	.224	263	361	13	.980
1986—Chicago h	Nat.	3B-1B-2B	81	152	22	45	10	0	1	19	.296	114	63	5	.973
1987—Chicago i	Nat.	1-3-2-S	108	214	27	63	8	0	8	26	.294	301	53	4	.989
1988—Chicago j	Nat.	1-3-2-S	76	164	15	41	5	0	1	14	.250	177	81	3	.989
1989—Cincinnati k	Nat.	2B-1B-SS	17	39	3	8	0	0	0	0	.205	27	18	1	.978
American League Totals—3 Years			126	365	36	95	15	1	1	34	.260	218	329	11	.980
National League Totals—15 Years			1654	5585	562	1467	224	32	60	537	.263	3759	4526	158	.981
Major League Totals—17 Years			1780	5950	598	1562	239	33	61	571	.263	3977	4855	169	.981

Signed as free agent by Philadelphia Phillies' organization, January 26, 1968.
†On disabled list, August 16 to September 3, 1968.
‡Drafted by Birmingham (Oakland Athletics' organization), December 1, 1969.
§On disabled list, May 1 to May 20, 1971.
xTraded with Pitchers Darold Knowles and Bob Locker to Chicago Cubs for First Baseman-Outfielder Billy Williams, October 23, 1974.
yTraded with Outfielder Greg Gross and Catcher Dave Rader to Philadelphia Phillies for Outfielder Jerry Martin, Catcher Barry Foote, Second Baseman Ted Sizemore and Pitchers Derek Botelho and Henry Mack, February 23, 1979.
zOn disabled list, May 4 to June 16, 1979.
aOn disabled list, April 20 to May 7, 1980.
bTraded with Outfielder George Vukovich, Infielder Julio Franco, Pitcher Jay Baller and Catcher Jerry Willard to Cleveland Indians for Outfielder Von Hayes, December 9, 1982.
cOn disabled list, July 24 to August 8, 1983.
dTraded to Montreal Expos for outfielder Don Carter and cash, August 17, 1983.
eGranted free agency, November 7, 1983; signed by San Francisco Giants, December 20, 1983.
fOn disabled list, May 13 to July 7, 1984.
gTraded to Chicago Cubs for Infielder Dave Owen, December 11, 1985.
hOn disabled list, June 3 to July 11, 1986.
iGranted free agency, November 9, 1987; re-signed by Cubs, December 7, 1987.
jGranted free agency, November 4, 1988; signed by Cincinnati Reds, December 21, 1988
kReleased, May 25, 1989.

DIVISION SERIES RECORD

Year	Club	League	Pos.	G.	AB.	R.	H.	2B.	3B.	HR.	RBI.	B.A.	PO.	A.	E.	F.A.
1981—Philadelphia	Nat.	2B	5	16	1	3	0	0	0	1	.188	15	10	0	1.000

CHAMPIONSHIP SERIES RECORD

Year	Club	League	Pos.	G.	AB.	R.	H.	2B.	3B.	HR.	RBI.	B.A.	PO.	A.	E.	F.A.
1974—Oakland	Amer.	PR	1	0	1	0	0	0	0	0	.000	0	0	0	.000
1980—Philadelphia	Nat.	2B	5	21	1	8	2	1	0	4	.381	18	25	1	.977
Championship Series Totals—2 Years			6	21	2	8	2	1	0	4	.381	18	25	1	.977

Year Club League	Pos.	G.	AB.	R.	H.	2B.	3B.	HR.	RBI.	B.A.	PO.	A.	E.	F.A.
1980—Philadelphia .... Nat.	2B	6	23	4	5	2	0	0	2	.217	14	25	1	.975

ALL-STAR GAME RECORD

Year League	Pos.	AB.	R.	H.	2B.	3B.	HR.	RBI.	B.A.	PO.	A.	E.	F.A.
1977—National...............	2B	1	0	0	0	0	0	0	.000	0	1	0	1.000
1981—National.......................	2B	2	0	0	0	0	0	0	.000	1	1	0	1.000
1982—National.......................	2B	2	0	1	0	0	0	0	.500	0	1	0	1.000
1983—American	2B	3	1	1	0	0	0	0	.333	3	1	0	1.000
All-Star Game Totals—4 Years..................		8	1	2	0	0	0	0	.250	4	4	0	1.000

RICHARD ALAN TRLICEK
(Rick)

Born April 26, 1969, at Houston, Tex.
Height, 6.02. Weight, 180.
Throws and bats righthanded.

Year Club	League	G.	IP.	W.	L.	Pct.	H.	R.	ER.	SO.	BB.	ERA.
1987—Utica...............	NYP	10	37⅓	2	5	.286	43	28	17	22	31	4.10
1988—Batavia†...........................	NYP	8	31⅔	2	3	.400	27	32	26	26	31	7.39
1989—Sumter.................................	S. Atlantic	15	93⅔	6	5	.545	73	40	27	72	40	2.59
1989—Durham‡.................................	Carolina	1	8	0	0	.000	3	2	1	4	1	1.13

Selected by Philadelphia Phillies' organization in 4th round of free-agent draft, June 2, 1987.
†Released, March 23, 1989; signed by Atlanta Braves' organization, April 2, 1989.
‡Traded to Toronto Blue Jays for Catcher Ernie Whitt and Outfielder Kevin Batiste, December 17, 1989.

STEVEN RUSSELL TROUT
(Steve)

Born July 30, 1957, at Detroit, Mich.
Height, 6.04. Weight, 190.
Throws and bats lefthanded.
Son of Paul (Dizzy) Trout, pitcher with Detroit Tigers, Boston Red Sox and
Baltimore Orioles, 1939 through 1952 and 1957.

Major League saves: 1979 (4).
Led American League in hit batsmen with 9 in 1980.

Year Club	League	G.	IP.	W.	L.	Pct.	H.	R.	ER.	SO.	BB.	ERA.
1976—Sarasota White Sox.....................Gulf Coast		9	38	1	3	.250	28	18	11	35	29	2.61
1977—Appleton	Midwest	21	111	6	8	.429	113	66	50	101	66	4.05
1977—Iowa	Am. Assoc.	5	24	0	4	.000	27	16	15	14	11	5.63
1978—Knoxville	Southern	12	71	8	3	.727	46	16	13	48	33	1.65
1978—Iowa	Am. Assoc.	9	55	3	4	.429	57	36	32	38	22	5.24
1978—Chicago	American	4	22	3	0	1.000	19	10	10	11	11	4.09
1979—Iowa	Am. Assoc.	4	27	3	1	.750	24	10	9	12	19	3.00
1979—Chicago	American	34	155	11	8	.579	165	77	67	76	59	3.89
1980—Chicago	American	32	200	9	16	.360	229	102	82	89	49	3.69
1981—Chicago	American	20	125	8	7	.533	122	53	48	54	38	3.46
1982—Chicago†	American	25	120⅓	6	9	.400	130	76	57	62	50	4.26
1983—Chicago	National	34	180	10	14	.417	217	105	93	80	59	4.65
1984—Chicago‡	National	32	190	13	7	.650	205	80	72	81	59	3.41
1985—Chicago§	National	24	140⅔	9	7	.563	142	57	53	44	63	3.39
1986—Chicago	National	37	161	5	7	.417	184	88	85	69	78	4.75
1987—Chicago x	National	11	75	6	3	.667	72	27	25	32	27	3.00
1987—Peoria y	Midwest	1	8	1	0	1.000	6	0	0	6	0	0.00
1987—New York z.....................................	American	14	46⅓	0	4	.000	51	36	34	27	37	6.60
1988—Seattle a	American	15	56⅓	4	7	.364	86	53	49	14	31	7.83
1988—Calgary	P. Coast	3	15⅔	0	2	.000	15	5	2	2	2	1.15
1989—Seattle b	American	19	30	4	3	.571	43	27	22	17	17	6.60
American League Totals—8 Years		163	755	45	54	.455	845	434	369	350	292	4.40
National League Totals—5 Years		138	746⅔	43	38	.531	820	357	328	306	286	3.95
Major League Totals—12 Years		301	1501⅔	88	92	.489	1665	791	697	656	578	4.18

Selected by Chicago White Sox' organization in 1st round (eighth player selected) of free-agent draft, June 8, 1976.
†Traded with Pitcher Warren Brusstar to Chicago Cubs for Pitchers Dick Tidrow and Randy Martz and Infielders Scott Fletcher and Pat Tabler, January 25, 1983.
‡Granted free agency, November 8, 1984; re-signed by Cubs, December 7, 1984.
§On disabled list, July 23 to August 23, 1985.
xOn disabled list, May 4 to June 16, 1987; included rehabilitation disability assignment to Peoria, June 11, 1987.
yTraded to New York Yankees for Pitchers Bob Tewksbury, Rich Scheid and Dean Wilkins, July 13, 1987.
zTraded with Outfielder Henry Cotto to Seattle Mariners for Pitchers Lee Guetterman, Clay Parker and Wade Taylor, December 22, 1987.
aOn disabled list, May 8 to June 21 and August 12 to September 2, 1988; included rehabilitation disability assignment to Calgary, June 3 to June 18, 1988.
bReleased, June 12, 1989.

CHAMPIONSHIP SERIES RECORD

Year Club	League	G.	IP.	W.	L.	Pct.	H.	R.	ER.	SO.	BB.	ERA.
1984—Chicago...............	National	2	9	1	0	1.000	5	2	2	3	3	2.00

MICHAEL ANDREW TRUJILLO

Name pronounced Tru-HEEY-O.

(Mike)

Born January 12, 1960, at Denver, Colo.
Height, 6.01. Weight, 180.
Throws and bats righthanded.
Received degree from University of Northern Colorado, Greeley, Colo., in 1984.

Major League saves: 1985 (1), 1986 (1), 1987 (1). Total—3.
Led International League in games finished in relief with 36 and tied for lead in intentional bases on balls issued with 6 in 1986.
Led Midwest League pitchers in games started with 29 and tied for lead in complete games with 11 in 1983.

Year Club	League	G.	IP.	W.	L.	Pct.	H.	R.	ER.	SO.	BB.	ERA.
1982—Sarasota White Sox	Gulf Coast	1	7⅓	0	0	.000	1	2	1	6	4	1.23
1982—Niagara Falls	NYP	12	79	5	4	.556	54	33	21	100	25	2.39
1983—Appleton	Midwest	29	*198⅔	15	8	.652	146	75	53	148	63	2.40
1984—Glens Falls	Eastern	20	121⅔	13	3	.813	107	47	32	69	25	2.37
1984—Denver†‡	Am. Assoc.	8	30	2	5	.286	38	27	26	9	20	7.80
1985—Boston	American	27	84	4	4	.500	112	55	45	19	23	4.82
1986—Pawtucket	Int'national	42	84⅔	8	9	.471	76	29	25	45	27	2.66
1986—Boston§-Seattle	American	14	47	3	2	.600	39	17	17	23	21	3.26
1987—Seattle	American	28	65⅔	4	4	.500	70	46	45	36	26	6.17
1987—Calgary x	P. Coast	5	27⅔	3	1	.750	25	8	7	21	9	2.28
1988—Toledo	Int'national	18	106⅓	4	10	.286	102	42	37	54	42	3.13
1988—Detroit	American	6	12⅓	0	0	.000	11	7	7	5	5	5.11
1989—Toledo y-Tidewater	Int'national	23	107⅔	8	5	.615	116	53	47	55	37	3.93
1989—Detroit z	American	8	25⅔	1	2	.333	35	17	17	13	13	5.96
Major League Totals—5 Years		83	234⅔	12	12	.500	267	142	131	96	88	5.02

Selected by Chicago White Sox' organization in 7th round of free-agent draft, June 7, 1982.
†Traded with First Baseman Pat Adams to San Francisco Giants, September 7, 1984, completing deal in which San Francisco traded Infielder Tom O'Malley to Chicago White Sox for two players to be named later, September 1, 1984.
‡Drafted by Boston Red Sox, December 3, 1984.
§Claimed with Pitcher Mike Brown on waivers by Seattle Mariners from Boston Red Sox, August 22, 1986, as part of deal in which Seattle traded Infielder Spike Owen and Outfielder Dave Henderson to Boston for Infielder Rey Quinones, a player to be named later and cash, August 19, 1986. Seattle acquired Outfielder John Christensen to complete deal, September 25, 1986.
xReleased, March 28, 1988; signed by Toledo (Detroit Tigers' organization), March 31, 1988.
ySold to Tidewater (New York Mets' organization), August 6, 1989.
zGranted free agency, October 15, 1989.

JOHN THOMAS TUDOR

Born February 2, 1954, at Schenectady, N.Y.
Height, 6.00. Weight, 185.
Throws and bats lefthanded.
Attended North Shore Community College, Beverly, Mass. and received bachelor of science degree in criminal justice from Georgia Southern College, Statesboro, Ga.

Pitched seven-inning, 2-0 no-hit victory against Reading, June 28, 1977.
Major League saves: 1981 (1).
Led National League in shutouts with 10 in 1985.
Named lefthanded pitcher on THE SPORTING NEWS National League All-Star Team, 1985.

Year Club	League	G.	IP.	W.	L.	Pct.	H.	R.	ER.	SO.	BB.	ERA.
1976—Winston-Salem	Carolina	25	82	5	2	.714	77	26	25	76	28	2.74
1977—Bristol	Eastern	27	115	6	5	.545	113	57	45	78	35	3.52
1977—Pawtucket	Int'national	4	4	1	1	.500	5	1	1	1	3	2.25
1978—Pawtucket	Int'national	26	105	7	4	.636	100	46	36	83	56	3.09
1979—Pawtucket	Int'national	25	163	10	11	.476	145	73	53	103	52	2.93
1979—Boston	American	6	28	1	2	.333	39	23	20	11	9	6.43
1980—Pawtucket	Int'national	12	74	4	5	.444	67	36	30	51	33	3.65
1980—Boston	American	16	92	8	5	.615	81	35	31	45	31	3.03
1981—Boston	American	18	79	4	3	.571	74	44	40	44	28	4.56
1982—Boston	American	32	195⅔	13	10	.565	215	90	79	146	59	3.63
1983—Boston†	American	34	242	13	12	.520	236	122	110	136	81	4.09
1984—Pittsburgh‡	National	32	212	12	11	.522	200	81	77	117	56	3.27
1985—St. Louis	National	36	275	21	8	.724	209	68	59	169	49	1.93
1986—St. Louis§	National	30	219	13	7	.650	197	81	71	107	53	2.92
1987—St. Louis x	National	16	96	10	2	.833	100	43	41	54	32	3.84
1987—Louisville	Am. Assoc.	2	8	1	0	1.000	11	8	7	3	1	7.88
1988—St. Louis yz-Los Angeles	National	30	197⅔	10	8	.556	189	60	51	87	41	2.32
1989—Vero Beach a	Florida St.	1	5	1	0	1.000	1	1	1	5	0	1.80
1989—Bakersfield	California	1	6⅔	0	0	.000	4	2	1	6	2	1.35
1989—Los Angeles b	National	6	14⅓	0	0	.000	17	5	5	9	6	3.14
American League Totals—5 Years		106	636⅔	39	32	.549	645	314	280	382	208	3.96
National League Totals—6 Years		150	1014	66	36	.647	912	338	304	543	237	2.70
Major League Totals—11 Years		256	1650⅔	105	68	.607	1557	652	584	925	445	3.18

Selected by New York Mets' organization in 21st round of free-agent draft, June 4, 1975.
Selected by Boston Red Sox' organization in secondary phase of free-agent draft, January 7, 1976.
†Traded to Pittsburgh Pirates for Outfielder Mike Easler, December 6, 1983.
‡Traded with Outfielder Brian Harper to St. Louis Cardinals for Outfielder-First Baseman George Hendrick and Catcher Steve Barnard, December 12, 1984.

§On disabled list, September 16, 1986 through remainder of season.
xOn disabled list, April 20 to July 30, 1987; included rehabilitation disability assignment to Louisville, July 22 to July 30, 1987.
yOn disabled list, March 26 to April 25, 1988.
zTraded to Los Angeles Dodgers for Infielder Pedro Guerrero, August 16, 1988.
aOn Los Angeles disabled list, March 31 to June 27 and July 8 to September 2, 1989; included rehabilitation disability assignment to Vero Beach, June 7 to June 17, 1989; then transferred to Bakersfield, June 18 to June 27, 1989.
bGranted free agency, November 13, 1989; signed by St. Louis Cardinals, December 14, 1989.

CHAMPIONSHIP SERIES RECORD
Shares National League Championship Series record for most hits allowed, game (10), October 7, 1987.

Year Club	League	G.	IP.	W.	L.	Pct.	H.	R.	ER.	SO.	BB.	ERA.
1985—St. Louis	National	2	12⅔	1	1	.500	10	5	4	8	3	2.84
1987—St. Louis	National	2	15⅓	1	1	.500	16	5	3	12	5	1.76
1988—Los Angeles	National	1	5	0	0	.000	8	4	4	1	1	7.20
Championship Series Totals—3 Years		5	33	2	2	.500	34	14	11	21	9	3.00

WORLD SERIES RECORD

Year Club	League	G.	IP.	W.	L.	Pct.	H.	R.	ER.	SO.	BB.	ERA.
1985—St. Louis	National	3	18	2	1	.667	15	6	6	14	7	3.00
1987—St.Louis	National	2	11	1	1	.500	15	7	7	8	3	5.73
1988—Los Angeles	National	1	1⅓	0	0	.000	0	0	0	1	0	0.00
World Series Totals—3 Years		6	30⅓	3	2	.600	30	13	13	23	10	3.86

BYRON LEE TUNNELL
Name pronounced TUNN-ul.
(Known by middle name.)
Born October 30, 1960, at Tyler, Tex.
Height, 6.01. Weight, 180.
Throws and bats righthanded.
Attended Baylor University, Waco, Tex.

Major league saves: 1984 (1).

Year Club	League	G.	IP.	W.	L.	Pct.	H.	R.	ER.	SO.	BB.	ERA.
1981—Bradenton Pirates	Gulf Coast	1	4	0	0	.000	0	0	0	6	1	0.00
1981—Buffalo	Eastern	12	71	5	5	.500	76	38	35	45	37	4.44
1982—Portland	P. Coast	28	189⅔	12	9	.571	182	93	73	112	91	3.46
1982—Pittsburgh	National	5	18⅓	1	1	.500	17	8	8	4	5	3.93
1983—Pittsburgh	National	35	177⅔	11	6	.647	167	81	72	95	58	3.65
1984—Pittsburgh†	National	26	68½	1	7	.125	81	44	40	51	40	5.27
1985—Pittsburgh	National	24	132⅓	4	10	.286	126	70	59	74	57	4.01
1985—Hawaii	P. Coast	7	46⅔	4	1	.800	32	12	12	29	24	2.31
1986—Hawaii‡§	P. Coast	27	142⅓	4	11	.267	180	106	95	95	81	6.01
1987—Louisville	Am. Assoc.	6	37	4	1	.800	33	16	14	32	19	3.41
1987—St. Louis x	National	32	74⅓	4	4	.500	90	45	40	49	34	4.84
1987—Springfield	Midwest	1	2⅔	0	1	.000	4	1	1	3	0	3.38
1988—Louisville yz	Am. Assoc.	24	135⅓	6	8	.429	136	69	58	60	55	3.86
1989—Portland	P. Coast	25	66⅓	2	4	.333	56	24	20	58	23	2.71
1989—Minnesota a	American	10	12	1	0	1.000	18	8	8	7	6	6.00
National League Totals—5 Years		122	471	21	28	.429	481	248	219	273	194	4.18
American League Totals—1 Year		10	12	1	0	1.000	18	8	8	7	6	6.00
Major League Totals—6 Years		132	483	22	28	.440	499	256	227	280	200	4.23

Selected by Pittsburgh Pirates' organization in 2nd round of free-agent draft, June 8, 1981.
†On disabled list, July 2 to July 23, 1984.
‡Released, December 20, 1986; re-signed by Pirates' organization, February 6, 1987.
§Sold to Louisville (St. Louis Cardinals' organization), April 6, 1987.
xOn disabled list, August 8 to September 1, 1987; included rehabilitation disability assignment to Springfield, August 29 to September 1, 1987.
yOn St. Louis disabled list, March 20 to April 12, 1988.
zReleased, October 4, 1988; signed by Portland (Minnesota Twins' organization), February 13, 1989.
aGranted free agency, October 15, 1989.

WORLD SERIES RECORD

Year Club	League	G.	IP.	W.	L.	Pct.	H.	R.	ER.	SO.	BB.	ERA.
1987—St. Louis	National	2	4⅓	0	0	.000	4	2	1	1	2	2.08

JOSE ALTA URIBE
(Name pronounced Yoo-REE-bay.)
(Formerly known as Jose Alta Gonzalez.)

Born January 21, 1960, at San Cristobal, D. R.
Height, 5.10. Weight, 165.
Throws right and bats left and righthanded.

Major League stolen bases: 1984 (1), 1985 (8), 1986 (22), 1987 (12), 1988 (14), 1989 (6). Total—63.
Led National League shortstops in double plays with 85 in 1989.
Led American Association in sacrifice hits with 14 in 1983.
Led American Association shortstops in total chances with 720 and double plays with 96 in 1984.
Led American Association shortstops in total chances with 664 and double plays with 90 in 1983.
Led Texas League shortstops in double plays with 88 in 1982.

Year Club League	Pos.	G.	AB.	R.	H.	2B.	3B.	HR.	RBI.	B.A.	PO.	A.	E.	F.A.
1981—St. Petersburg†..... Fla. St.	SS	128	463	54	124	15	2	0	40	.268	171	*387	32	.946
1982—Arkansas............... Texas	SS	123	465	73	115	17	7	0	41	.247	185	385	36	.941
1982—Louisville .... A. A.	SS	8	28	5	10	2	0	0	4	.357	15	18	1	.971
1983—Louisville .... A. A.	SS	122	423	64	120	19	6	3	44	.284	206	425	*33	.950
1984—Louisville .... A. A.	SS	145	484	68	135	20	2	3	46	.279	*233	*455	*32	*.956
1984—St. Louis‡............... Nat.	SS-2B	8	19	4	4	0	0	0	3	.211	7	15	1	.957
1985—San Francisco ...... Nat.	SS-2B	147	476	46	113	20	4	3	26	.237	209	438	26	.961
1986—San Francisco ...... Nat.	SS	157	453	46	101	15	1	3	43	.223	249	444	16	.977
1987—San Francisco§ .... Nat.	SS	95	309	44	90	16	5	5	30	.291	145	286	13	.971
1988—San Francisco x .... Nat.	SS	141	493	47	124	10	7	3	35	.252	212	404	19	.970
1989—San Francisco ...... Nat.	SS	151	453	34	100	12	6	1	30	.221	225	436	18	.973
Major League Totals—6 Years................		699	2203	221	532	73	23	15	167	.241	1047	2023	93	.971

Signed as free agent by New York Yankees' organization, February 18, 1977.

†Released, July 5, 1977; signed by St. Louis Cardinals' organization, August 18, 1980.

‡Traded with First Basemen David Green and Gary Rajsich and Pitcher Dave LaPoint to San Francisco Giants for Outfielder-First Baseman Jack Clark, February 1, 1985.

§On disabled list, April 11 to April 30, May 5 to May 20 and May 28 to July 4, 1987.

xOn disabled list, May 31 to June 16, 1988.

CHAMPIONSHIP SERIES RECORD

Year Club League	Pos.	G.	AB.	R.	H.	2B.	3B.	HR.	RBI.	B.A.	PO.	A.	E.	F.A.
1987—San Francisco ...... Nat.	SS	7	26	1	7	1	0	0	2	.269	11	20	1	.969
1989—San Francisco ...... Nat.	SS	5	17	2	4	1	0	0	1	.235	6	9	2	.882
Championship Series Totals—2 Years.....		12	43	3	11	2	0	0	3	.256	17	29	3	.939

WORLD SERIES RECORD

Year Club League	Pos.	G.	AB.	R.	H.	2B.	3B.	HR.	RBI.	B.A.	PO.	A.	E.	F.A.
1989—San Francisco ...... Nat.	SS	3	5	1	1	0	0	0	0	.200	1	3	0	1.000

FRANK VALDEZ

Born October 12, 1968, at Santo Domingo, Dominican Republic.
Height, 6.01. Weight, 175.
Throws and bats righthanded.

Year Club League	Pos.	G.	AB.	R.	H.	2B.	3B.	HR.	RBI.	B.A.	PO.	A.	E.	F.A.
1986—Elizabethton .... Appal.	SS	16	40	6	8	2	0	0	6	.200	13	24	8	.822
1987—Elizabethton .... Appal.	3B-SS-OF	61	227	28	52	8	0	5	28	.229	70	109	18	.909
1988—Kenosha................ Midw.	3B	115	424	49	118	30	2	8	60	.278	89	222	33	.904
1989—Visalia .... Calif.	3B	132	453	71	128	24	4	10	59	.283	80	*222	31	.907

Signed as free agent by Minnesota Twins' organization, March 19, 1986.

RAFAEL EMILIO VALDEZ (DIAZ)

Born December 17, 1967, at Nizao Boni, Dominican Republic.
Height, 5.11. Weight, 165.
Throws and bats righthanded.

Pitched 2-0 perfect game against Reno, July 20, 1989.
Led South Atlantic League shortstops in errors with 46 in 1986.

Year Club League	G.	IP.	W.	L.	Pct.	H.	R.	ER.	SO.	BB.	ERA.
1988—Charleston, S.C. .... S. Atlantic	28	152⅓	11	4	.733	117	42	38	100	46	2.25
1989—Riverside .... California	21	143⅓	10	5	.667	89	40	36	137	58	2.26
1989—Wichita............................ Texas	6	41⅔	5	0	1.000	28	10	9	26	24	1.94

Signed as free agent by San Diego Padres' organization, March 6, 1985.

RECORD AS INFIELDER

Year Club League	Pos.	G.	AB.	R.	H.	2B.	3B.	HR.	RBI.	B.A.	PO.	A.	E.	F.A.
1986—Charleston............ S. Atl.	SS-2B	90	260	25	55	15	3	3	27	.212	112	204	47	.877
1987—Charleston, S.C. ..... S. Atl.	SS	127	435	42	115	16	2	5	44	.264	145	343	53	.902

SERGIO SANCHEZ VALDEZ

Born September 7, 1965, at Elias Pina, D.R.
Height, 6.01. Weight, 190.
Throws and bats righthanded.

Tied for American Association lead in shutouts with 2 in 1987.
Tied for Florida State League lead in shutouts with 4 in 1986.
Tied for New York-Pennsylvania League lead in games started by pitchers with 15 in 1985.

Year Club League	G.	IP.	W.	L.	Pct.	H.	R.	ER.	SO.	BB.	ERA.
1983—Calgary .... Pioneer	13	72⅔	6	3	.667	88	55	45	41	31	5.57
1984—West Palm Beach† .... Florida St.	5	11⅓	0	0	.000	15	11	11	6	8	8.74
1984—Jamestown................... NYP	13	76	2	7	.222	78	47	34	46	33	4.03
1985—Utica................................ NYP	15	105⅔	6	5	.545	98	53	36	86	36	3.07
1986—West Palm Beach .... Florida St.	24	145⅔	*16	6	.727	119	48	40	108	46	2.47
1986—Montreal .... National	5	25	0	4	.000	39	20	19	20	11	6.84
1987—Indianapolis .... Am. Assoc.	27	158⅓	10	7	.588	191	108	90	*128	64	5.12
1988—Indianapolis .... Am. Assoc.	14	84	5	4	.556	80	38	32	61	28	3.43
1989—Indianapolis‡ .... Am. Assoc.	19	90⅔	6	3	.667	78	38	33	81	26	3.28
1989—Atlanta .... National	19	32⅔	1	2	.333	31	24	22	26	17	6.06
Major League Totals—2 Years............................	24	57⅔	1	6	.143	70	44	41	46	28	6.40

Signed as free agent by Montreal Expos' organizaton, June 18, 1983.

†On disabled list, May 17 to June 3, 1984.

‡Traded with Pitchers Nate Minchey and Outfielder Kevin Dean to Atlanta Braves for Pitcher Zane Smith, July 2, 1989.

FERNANDO VALENZUELA (ANGUAMEA)

Name pronounced Val-en-ZWAY-luh.

Born November 1, 1960, at Navajoa, Sonora, Mexico.
Height, 5.11. Weight, 202.
Throws and bats lefthanded.

Shares modern major league record for most shutout games won or tied, rookie year (8), 1981.
Shares National League record for fewest assists by pitcher, season, for leader in assists (47), 1986.
Major League saves: 1980 (1), 1988 (1). Total—2.
Led National League in wild pitches with 14 in 1987.
Led National League in complete games with 11 in 1981, 20 in 1986 and tied for lead with 12 in 1987.
Led National League in shutouts with 8 in 1981.
Tied for National League lead in games started by pitchers with 25 in 1981.
Led Mexican Center League in wild pitches with 13 in 1978.
Named Major League Player of the Year by THE SPORTING NEWS, 1981.
Named National League Pitcher of the Year by THE SPORTING NEWS, 1981.
Won National League Cy Young Memorial Award, 1981.
Named National League Rookie Pitcher of the Year by THE SPORTING NEWS, 1981.
Named National League Rookie of the Year by Baseball Writers' Association of America, 1981.
Named lefthanded pitcher on THE SPORTING NEWS National League All-Star Team, 1981 and 1986.
Named pitcher on THE SPORTING NEWS National League All-Star fielding team, 1986.
Named pitcher on THE SPORTING NEWS National League Silver Slugger team, 1981 and 1983.

Year Club	League	G.	IP.	W.	L.	Pct.	H.	R.	ER.	SO.	BB.	ERA.
1978—Guanajuato	Mex. Cent.	16	93	5	6	.455	88	46	23	*91	46	2.23
1979—Yucatan†	Mexican	26	181	10	12	.455	157	68	50	141	70	2.49
1979—Lodi	California	3	24	1	2	.333	21	10	3	18	3	1.13
1980—San Antonio	Texas	27	174	13	9	.591	156	70	60	*162	70	3.10
1980—Los Angeles	National	10	18	2	0	1.000	8	2	0	16	5	0.00
1981—Los Angeles	National	25	*192	13	7	.650	140	55	53	*180	61	2.48
1982—Los Angeles‡	National	37	285	19	13	.594	247	105	91	199	83	2.87
1983—Los Angeles	National	35	257	15	10	.600	245	*122	107	189	99	3.75
1984—Los Angeles	National	34	261	12	17	.414	218	109	88	240	*106	3.03
1985—Los Angeles	National	35	272⅓	17	10	.630	211	92	74	208	101	2.45
1986—Los Angeles	National	34	269⅓	*21	11	.656	226	104	94	242	85	3.14
1987—Los Angeles	National	34	251	14	14	.500	*254	120	111	190	*124	3.98
1988—Los Angeles§	National	23	142⅓	5	8	.385	142	71	67	64	76	4.24
1989—Los Angeles xy	National	31	196⅔	10	13	.435	185	89	75	116	98	3.43
Major League Totals—10 Years		298	2144⅔	128	103	.554	1876	869	760	1644	838	3.19

†Sold to Los Angeles Dodgers' organization, July 6, 1979.
‡Appeared in one game as an outfielder with no chances.
§On disabled list, July 31 to September 26, 1988.
xAppeared in one game as a first baseman with two putouts.
yGranted free agency, November 13, 1989; re-signed by Dodgers, December 15, 1989.

DIVISION SERIES RECORD

Year Club	League	G.	IP.	W.	L.	Pct.	H.	R.	ER.	SO.	BB.	ERA.
1981—Los Angeles	National	2	17	1	0	1.000	10	2	2	10	3	1.06

CHAMPIONSHIP SERIES RECORD

Holds National League Championship Series records for most bases on balls allowed, series (10), 1985; most bases on balls, game (8), October 14, 1985.
Shares National League Championship Series record for most wild pitches, total series (3).

Year Club	League	G.	IP.	W.	L.	Pct.	H.	R.	ER.	SO.	BB.	ERA.
1981—Los Angeles	National	2	14⅔	1	1	.500	10	4	4	10	5	2.45
1983—Los Angeles	National	1	8	1	0	1.000	7	1	1	5	4	1.13
1985—Los Angeles	National	2	14⅓	1	0	1.000	11	3	3	13	10	1.88
Championship Series Totals—3 Years		5	37	3	1	.750	28	8	8	28	19	1.95

WORLD SERIES RECORD

Year Club	League	G.	IP.	W.	L.	Pct.	H.	R.	ER.	SO.	BB.	ERA.
1981—Los Angeles	National	1	9	1	0	1.000	9	4	4	6	7	4.00

ALL-STAR GAME RECORD

Shares All-Star Game record for most consecutive strikeouts, game (5), July 15, 1986.

Year League		IP.	W.	L.	Pct.	H.	R.	ER.	SO.	BB.	ERA.
1981—National		1	0	0	.000	2	0	0	0	0	0.00
1982—National		⅔	0	0	.000	0	0	0	0	2	0.00
1984—National		2	0	0	.000	2	0	0	3	0	0.00
1985—National		1	0	0	.000	0	0	0	1	1	0.00
1986—National		3	0	0	.000	1	0	0	5	0	0.00
All-Star Game Totals—5 Years		7⅔	0	0	.000	5	0	0	9	3	0.00

Member of National League All-Star Team in 1983; did not play.

JULIO E. VALERA

Born October 13, 1968, at San Sebastian, Puerto Rico.
Height, 6.02. Weight, 185.
Throws and bats righthanded.

Year Club	League	G.	IP.	W.	L.	Pct.	H.	R.	ER.	SO.	BB.	ERA.
1986—Kingsport	Ap'lachian	13	76⅓	3	●10	.231	91	58	44	64	29	5.19
1987—Columbia	S. Atlantic	22	125⅓	8	7	.533	114	53	39	97	31	2.80
1988—Columbia	S. Atlantic	30	191	15	11	.577	171	77	68	144	51	3.20
1989—St. Lucie	Florida St.	6	45	4	2	.667	34	5	5	45	6	1.00
1989—Jackson	Texas	19	137⅓	10	6	.625	123	47	38	107	36	★2.49
1989—Tidewater	Int'national	2	13	1	1	.500	8	3	3	10	5	2.08

Signed as free agent by New York Mets' organization, February 6, 1986.

DAVID VALLE

Name pronounced Valley.

(Dave)

Born October 30, 1960, at Bayside, N. Y.
Height, 6.02. Weight, 200.
Throws and bats righthanded.
Brother of John Valle, minor league outfielder, 1972 through 1984.

Major League stolen bases: 1987 (2).
Led Northwest League catchers in double plays with 6 and tied for lead in passed balls with 23 in 1978.

Year Club	League	Pos.	G.	AB.	R.	H.	2B.	3B.	HR.	RBI.	B.A.	PO.	A.	E.	F.A.
1978—Bellingham	N'west	C	57	167	12	34	2	0	2	21	.204	★338	65	10	.976
1979—Alexandria†	Carol.	C	58	169	17	36	5	0	6	25	.213	290	44	11	.968
1980—San Jose	Calif.	C	119	430	81	126	14	0	12	70	.293	570	★102	17	.975
1981—Lynn‡	East.	C	93	318	38	82	16	0	11	54	.258	445	56	6	.988
1982—Salt Lake City	P. C.	C-1B	75	234	28	49	11	1	4	28	.209	347	49	11	.973
1983—Chattanooga§	South.	C-1B	53	176	20	42	11	0	3	22	.239	239	24	4	.985
1984—Salt Lake City x	P. C.	C	86	284	54	79	13	1	12	54	.278	433	34	6	.987
1984—Seattle	Amer.	C	13	27	4	8	1	0	1	4	.296	56	5	0	1.000
1985—Seattle y	Amer.	C	31	70	2	11	1	0	0	4	.157	117	7	3	.976
1985—Calgary	P. C.	C	42	131	17	45	8	0	6	26	.344	202	11	1	.995
1986—Calgary	P. C.	C	105	353	71	110	21	2	21	72	.312	404	61	6	.987
1986—Seattle	Amer.	C-1B	22	53	10	18	3	0	5	15	.340	90	3	2	.979
1987—Seattle z	Amer.	C-1B-OF	95	324	40	83	16	3	12	53	.256	422	34	5	.989
1988—Seattle a	Amer.	C-1B	93	290	29	67	15	2	10	50	.231	490	47	6	.989
1989—Seattle b	Amer.	C	94	316	32	75	10	3	7	34	.237	496	52	4	.993
1989—Calgary	P. C.	C	2	6	0	0	0	0	0	0	.000	6	0	0	1.000
Major League Totals—6 Years			348	1080	117	262	46	8	35	160	.243	1671	148	20	.989

Selected by Seattle Mariners' organization in 2nd round of free-agent draft, June 6, 1978.
†On disabled list, July 26 to August 25, 1979.
‡On disabled list, June 24 to July 3, 1981.
§On disabled list, April 13 to June 20 and June 27 to July 7, 1983.
xOn disabled list, May 4 to May 17 and June 9 to June 25, 1984.
yOn disabled list, April 26 to July 19, 1985; included rehabilitation disability assignment to Calgary, June 26 to July 12, 1985.
zOn disabled list, April 17 to May 7, 1987.
aOn disabled list, July 23 to September 2, 1988.
bOn disabled list, May 30 to July 6, 1989; included rehabilitation disability assignment to Calgary, July 4 to July 6, 1989.

PITCHING RECORD

Year Club	League	G.	IP.	W.	L.	Pct.	H.	R.	ER.	SO.	BB.	ERA.
1980—San Jose	California	1	1	0	0	.000	1	0	0	2	2	0.00

ANDREW JAMES VAN SLYKE

(Andy)

Born December 21, 1960, at Utica, N.Y.
Height, 6.02. Weight, 190.
Throws right and bats lefthanded.

Shares Major League record for fewest double plays by outfielder, season, for leader in double plays (4), 1985.
Major League stolen bases: 1983 (21), 1984 (28), 1985 (34), 1986 (21), 1987 (34), 1988 (30), 1989 (16). Total—184.
Led National League in sacrifice flies with 13 in 1988.
Led National League outfielders in total chances with 422 in 1988.
Tied for National League lead in double plays by outfielders with 4 in 1985, 6 in 1987 and 5 in 1989.
Named National League Player of the Year by THE SPORTING NEWS, 1988.
Named outfielder on THE SPORTING NEWS National League All-Star Team, 1988.
Named outfielder on THE SPORTING NEWS National League All-Star fielding team, 1988 and 1989.
Named outfielder on THE SPORTING NEWS National League Silver Slugger team, 1988.
Received reported $50,000 bonus to sign with St. Louis Cardinals, 1979.

Year Club	League	Pos.	G.	AB.	R.	H.	2B.	3B.	HR.	RBI.	B.A.	PO.	A.	E.	F.A.
1979—Johnson City†	Appal.					(Did not play)									
1980—Gastonia	S. Atl.	OF	126	426	62	115	15	4	8	59	.270	177	16	●16	.923
1981—St. Petersburg‡	Fla. St.	OF	94	282	42	62	11	3	1	25	.220	168	10	5	.973
1982—Arkansas	Texas	OF	123	416	83	116	13	★11	16	70	.279	266	17	7	.976

Year Club	League	Pos.	G.	AB.	R.	H.	2B.	3B.	HR.	RBI.	B.A.	PO.	A.	E.	F.A.
1983—Louisville	A. A.	3B-1B-OF	54	220	52	81	21	4	6	41	.368	201	78	16	.946
1983—St. Louis..................	Nat.	OF-3B-1B	101	309	51	81	15	5	8	38	.262	203	59	6	.978
1984—St. Louis..................	Nat.	OF-3B-1B	137	361	45	88	16	4	7	50	.244	357	82	8	.982
1985—St. Louis..................	Nat.	OF-1B	146	424	61	110	25	6	13	55	.259	237	13	1	.996
1986—St. Louis§...............	Nat.	OF-1B	137	418	48	113	23	7	13	61	.270	415	34	8	.982
1987—Pittsburgh..............	Nat.	OF-1B	157	564	93	165	36	11	21	82	.293	338	10	4	.989
1988—Pittsburgh..............	Nat.	OF	154	587	101	169	23	★15	25	100	.288	★406	12	4	.991
1989—Pittsburgh x	Nat.	OF-1B	130	476	64	113	18	9	9	53	.237	344	9	4	.989
Major League Totals—7 Years.................			962	3139	463	839	156	57	96	439	.267	2300	219	35	.986

Selected by St. Louis Cardinals' organization in 1st round (sixth player selected) of free-agent draft, June 5, 1979.

†On disabled list, June 8, 1979 through remainder of season.

‡On disabled list, April 10 to May 14, 1981.

§Traded with Catcher Mike LaValliere and Pitcher Mike Dunne to Pittsburgh Pirates for Catcher Tony Pena, April 1, 1987.

xOn disabled list, April 17 to May 12, 1989.

CHAMPIONSHIP SERIES RECORD

Year Club	League	Pos.	G.	AB.	R.	H.	2B.	3B.	HR.	RBI.	B.A.	PO.	A.	E.	F.A.
1985—St. Louis..................	Nat.	OF-PR	5	11	1	1	0	0	0	1	.091	6	0	0	1.000

WORLD SERIES RECORD

Year Club	League	Pos.	G.	AB.	R.	H.	2B.	3B.	HR.	RBI.	B.A.	PO.	A.	E.	F.A.
1985—St. Louis..................	Nat.	O-PH-PR	6	11	0	1	0	0	0	0	.091	8	0	0	1.000

ALL-STAR GAME RECORD

Year League	Pos.	AB.	R.	H.	2B.	3B.	HR.	RBI.	B.A.	PO.	A.	E.	F.A.
1988—National.................................	OF	2	0	0	0	0	0	0	.000	2	0	0	1.000

GARY ANDREW VARSHO

Born June 20, 1961, at Marshfield, Wis.
Height, 5.11. Weight, 190.
Throws right and bats lefthanded.
Attended University of Wisconsin, Oshkosh, Wis.

Major League stolen bases: 1988: (5), 1989 (3). Total—8.
Led American Association in caught stealing with 17 in 1987.
Led Eastern League in stolen bases with 45 in 1986 and tied for lead with 40 in 1985.
Led Texas League second basemen in total chances with 650 in 1984.
Led California League second basemen in double plays with 71 in 1983.

Year Club	League	Pos.	G.	AB.	R.	H.	2B.	3B.	HR.	RBI.	B.A.	PO.	A.	E.	F.A.
1982—Quad Cities...........	Midw.	2B	76	271	52	68	9	4	3	40	.251	190	180	14	.964
1983—Salinas...................	Calif.	2B	131	490	69	129	16	★13	3	57	.263	284	339	●33	.950
1984—Midland.................	Texas	2B	128	429	65	112	15	6	8	50	.261	★286	335	★29	.955
1985—Pittsfield	East.	1B-OF	115	418	62	101	14	6	3	37	.242	670	51	6	.992
1986—Pittsfield†	East.	OF-1B-2B	107	399	75	106	18	5	13	44	.266	213	14	6	.974
1987—Iowa	A. A.	OF	132	504	87	152	23	9	9	48	.302	227	18	6	.976
1988—Iowa	A. A.	OF	66	234	46	65	16	5	4	26	.278	120	6	2	.984
1988—Chicago	Nat.	OF	46	73	6	20	3	0	0	5	.274	29	0	3	.906
1989—Chicago	Nat.	OF	61	87	10	16	4	2	0	6	.184	25	1	2	.929
1989—Iowa	A. A.	OF	31	112	13	26	3	1	2	13	.232	67	4	3	.959
Major League Totals—2 Years.................			107	160	16	36	7	2	0	11	.225	54	1	5	.917

Selected by Chicago Cubs' organization in 5th round of free-agent draft, June 7, 1982.

†On disabled list, August 13, 1986 through remainder of season.

LUIS EDUARDO VASQUEZ

Born March 23, 1967, at Estrada Bolivar, Venezuela.
Height, 6.02. Weight, 175.
Throws and bats righthanded.

Led American Association in games started by pitchers with 29 in 1989.

Year Club	League	G.	IP.	W.	L.	Pct.	H.	R.	ER.	SO.	BB.	ERA.
1985—Elmira	NYP	18	57⅓	2	4	.333	50	28	22	42	24	3.45
1986—Winter Haven...............	Florida St.	31	159⅓	15	3	●.833	145	65	60	92	58	3.39
1987—New Britain†	Eastern	10	61	3	2	.600	63	23	19	26	19	2.80
1988—New Britain	Eastern	15	112⅓	3	9	.250	87	46	31	97	28	2.48
1988—Pawtucket‡	Int'national	12	75⅓	5	4	.556	74	37	30	73	15	3.58
1989—Nashville..........................	Am. Assoc.	29	162⅓	11	13	.458	170	91	83	115	84	4.60

Signed as free agent by Boston Red Sox' organization, January 24, 1985.

†On disabled list, July 1 to July 14 and July 17, 1987 through remainder of season.

‡Traded to Cincinnati Reds, January 12, 1989, completing deal in which Cincinnati traded First Baseman Nick Esasky and Pitcher Rob Murphy to Boston Red Sox for First Baseman Todd Benzinger, Pitcher Jeff Sellers and a player to be named later, December 13, 1988.

—DID YOU KNOW—

That when the Reds' Eric Davis hit for the cycle on June 2, 1989, it was the first time a Reds player had done so since Frank Robinson on May 2, 1959?

JAMES ERNEST VATCHER
(Jim)

Born May 27, 1966, at Santa Monica, Calif.
Height, 5.09, Weight, 165.
Throws and bats righthanded.
Attended West Los Angeles College, Culver City, Calif.,
and California State University at Northridge, Northridge, Calif.

Led South Atlantic League in bases on balls received with 89 in 1988.
Tied for New York-Pennsylvania League lead in double plays by outfielders with 3 in 1987.

Year Club	League	Pos.	G.	AB.	R.	H.	2B.	3B.	HR.	RBI.	B.A.	PO.	A.	E.	F.A.
1987—Utica	NYP	OF-SS	67	249	44	67	15	2	3	21	.269	116	12	3	.977
1988—Spartanburg	S. Atl.	OF	●137	496	★90	150	32	2	12	72	.302	224	13	4	.983
1989—Clearwater	Fla. St.	OF-2B-3B	92	349	51	105	30	5	4	46	.301	163	35	8	.961
1989—Reading	East.	OF	48	171	27	56	11	3	4	32	.327	76	5	1	.988

Selected by Philadelphia Phillies' organization in 20th round of free-agent draft, June 2, 1987.

GREGORY LAMONT VAUGHN
(Greg)

Born July 3, 1965, at Sacramento, Calif.
Height, 6.00. Weight, 195.
Throws and bats righthanded.
Attended Sacramento City College, Sacramento, Calif.,
and University of Miami, Coral Gables, Fla.

Major League stolen bases: 1989 (4).
Led American Association in slugging percentage with .548 in 1989.
Led Texas League in total bases with 279 in 1988.
Led Midwest League in total bases with 292 in 1987.
Named American Association Most Valuable Player, 1989.
Named Midwest League co-Most Valuable Player, 1987.

Year Club	League	Pos.	G.	AB.	R.	H.	2B.	3B.	HR.	RBI.	B.A.	PO.	A.	E.	F.A.
1986—Helena	Pion.	OF	66	258	64	75	13	2	16	54	.291	99	5	3	.972
1987—Beloit	Midw.	OF	139	492	★120	150	31	6	★33	105	.305	247	11	10	.963
1988—El Paso	Texas	OF	131	505	★104	152	★39	2	★28	★105	.301	216	12	7	.970
1989—Denver	A. A.	OF	110	387	74	107	17	5	★26	★92	.276	140	4	3	.980
1989—Milwaukee	Amer.	OF	38	113	18	30	3	0	5	23	.265	32	1	2	.943
Major League Totals—1 Year			38	113	18	30	3	0	5	23	.265	32	1	2	.943

Selected by St. Louis Cardinals' organization in 5th round of free-agent draft, January 17, 1984.
Selected by Milwaukee Brewers' organization in secondary phase of free-agent draft, June 4, 1984.
Selected by Pittsburgh Pirates' organization in secondary phase of free-agent draft, January 9, 1985.
Selected by California Angels' organization in secondary phase of free-agent draft, June 3, 1985.
Selected by Milwaukee Brewers' organization in secondary phase of free-agent draft, June 2, 1986.

RANDY LEE VELARDE

Born November 24, 1962, at Midland, Tex.
Height, 6.00. Weight, 185.
Throws and bats righthanded.
Attended Lubbock Christian College, Lubbock, Tex.

Major League stolen bases: 1988 (1).
Led Midwest League shortstops in errors with 52 in 1986.

Year Club	League	Pos.	G.	AB.	R.	H.	2B.	3B.	HR.	RBI.	B.A.	PO.	A.	E.	F.A.
1985—Niagara Falls	NYP	O-S-2-3	67	218	28	48	7	3	1	16	.220	124	117	15	.941
1986—Appleton	Midw.	SS-3B-OF	124	417	55	105	31	4	11	50	.252	205	300	54	.903
1986—Buffalo†	A. A.	SS	9	20	2	4	1	0	0	2	.200	9	28	3	.925
1987—Albany	East.	SS-OF	71	263	40	83	20	2	7	32	.316	128	254	17	.957
1987—Columbus	Int.	SS	49	185	21	59	10	6	5	33	.319	100	164	16	.943
1987—New York	Amer.	SS	8	22	1	4	0	0	0	1	.182	8	20	2	.933
1988—Columbus	Int.	SS-2B-3B	78	293	39	79	23	4	5	37	.270	123	271	25	.940
1988—New York	Amer.	2B-SS-3B	48	115	18	20	6	0	5	12	.174	72	98	8	.955
1989—Columbus	Int.	SS-3B	103	387	59	103	26	3	11	53	.266	150	295	22	.953
1989—New York‡	Amer.	3B-SS	33	100	12	34	4	2	2	11	.340	26	61	4	.956
Major League Totals—3 Years			89	237	31	58	10	2	7	24	.245	106	179	14	.953

Selected by Chicago White Sox' organization in 19th round of free-agent draft, June 3, 1985.
†Traded with Pitcher Pete Filson to New York Yankees for Pitcher Scott Nielsen and Infielder Mike Soper, January 5, 1987.
‡On disabled list, August 9 to August 29, 1989.

WILLIAM McKINLEY VENABLE JR.
(Max)

Born June 6, 1957, at Phoenix, Ariz.
Height, 5.10. Weight, 185.
Throws right and bats lefthanded.

Major League stolen bases: 1979 (3), 1980 (8), 1981 (3), 1982 (9), 1983 (15), 1984 (1), 1985 (11), 1986 (7). Total—57.
Led American Association in sacrifice hits with 11 in 1987.

Year	Club	League	Pos.	G.	AB.	R.	H.	2B.	3B.	HR.	RBI.	B.A.	PO.	A.	E.	F.A.
1976—Bellingham†	N'west		OF	51	162	25	35	2	0	1	16	.216	58	4	8	.886
1977—Clinton	Midw.		OF-2B	125	425	72	115	19	4	9	63	.271	149	13	13	.926
1978—Lodi‡	Calif.		OF	●140	566	134	180	30	9	17	101	.318	220	8	8	.966
1979—San Francisco	Nat.		OF	55	85	12	14	1	1	0	3	.165	30	2	3	.914
1979—Shreveport	Texas		OF	18	69	11	16	1	2	0	3	.232	28	2	1	.968
1979—Phoenix	P. C.		OF	38	150	27	46	5	4	0	11	.307	96	4	3	.971
1980—Phoenix	P. C.		OF	78	312	52	89	10	10	5	40	.285	179	7	4	.979
1980—San Francisco	Nat.		OF	64	138	13	37	5	0	0	10	.268	61	0	0	1.000
1981—Phoenix§	P. C.		OF	104	428	81	122	24	10	8	48	.285	263	6	3	.989
1981—San Francisco	Nat.		OF	18	32	2	6	0	2	0	1	.188	12	0	0	1.000
1982—San Francisco x	Nat.		OF	71	125	17	28	2	1	1	7	.224	66	6	1	.986
1982—Phoenix	P. C.		OF	8	32	5	8	1	2	0	3	.250	16	0	0	1.000
1983—San Francisco y	Nat.		OF	94	228	28	50	7	4	6	27	.219	141	5	1	.993
1984—Indianapolis	A. A.		OF	99	330	57	82	13	3	9	47	.248	183	4	4	.979
1984—Montreal	Nat.		OF	38	71	7	17	2	0	2	7	.239	33	0	0	1.000
1985—Indy. z-Den.	A. A.		OF	46	172	27	42	7	5	4	19	.244	93	2	1	.990
1985—Cincinnati	Nat.		OF	77	135	21	39	12	3	0	10	.289	60	3	0	1.000
1986—Cincinnati a	Nat.		OF	108	147	17	31	7	1	2	15	.211	63	0	2	.969
1987—Nashville	A. A.		OF	116	400	57	108	16	4	2	28	.270	212	5	5	.977
1987—Cincinnati bcd	Nat.		OF	7	7	2	1	0	0	0	2	.143	3	0	0	1.000
1988—Yucatan e	Mex.		OF	13	47	14	15	0	1	1	8	.319	31	1	0	1.000
1989—Edmonton	P. C.		OF	95	329	52	89	14	4	1	45	.271	189	9	2	.990
1989—California	Amer.		OF	20	53	7	19	4	0	0	4	.358	21	0	0	1.000
National League Totals—9 Years				532	968	119	223	36	12	11	82	.230	469	16	7	.986
American League Totals—1 Year				20	53	7	19	4	0	0	4	.358	21	0	0	1.000
Major League Totals—10 Years				552	1021	126	242	40	12	11	86	.237	490	16	7	.986

Selected by Los Angeles Dodgers' organization in 3rd round of free-agent draft, June 8, 1976.

†On disabled list, June 26 to July 10, 1976.

‡Drafted by San Francisco Giants, December 4, 1978.

§On disabled list, April 23 to May 16, 1981.

xOn disabled list, April 21 to June 1, 1982; included rehabilitation disability assignment to Phoenix, May 22 to June 1, 1982.

yTraded to Montreal Expos' organization, March 31, 1984, completing deal in which Montreal traded First Baseman Al Oliver to San Francisco Giants for Pitcher Fred Breining and a player to be named later, February 27, 1984. (San Francisco traded Pitcher Andy McGaffigan to Montreal, March 31, 1984, as compensation for the injury that Breining arrived with. Breining remained with Montreal.)

zTraded to Cincinnati Reds' organization for Infielder Skeeter Barnes, April 26, 1985.

aReleased, March 29, 1987; re-signed by Reds' organization, April 9, 1987.

bGranted free agency, October 15, 1987; signed by Baltimore Orioles, February, 1988.

cReleased, March 1988; signed by Nashville (Cincinnati Reds' organization), July 11, 1988.

dLoaned to Yucatan of Mexican League, July, 1988; returned, September, 1988.

eGranted free agency, October 15, 1988; signed by Edmonton (California Angels' organization), January 11, 1989.

ROBIN MARK VENTURA

Born July 14, 1967, at Santa Maria, Calif.
Height, 6.01. Weight, 185.
Throws right and bats lefthanded.
Attended Oklahoma State University, Stillwater, Okla.

Led Southern League in intentional bases on balls received with 12 in 1989.
Tied for Southern League lead in double plays by third basemen with 21 in 1989.
Member of 1988 U.S. Olympic baseball team.
Named College Player of the Year by THE SPORTING NEWS, 1987 and 1988.
Named third baseman on THE SPORTING NEWS College Baseball All-America Team, 1987 and 1988.

Year	Club	League	Pos.	G.	AB.	R.	H.	2B.	3B.	HR.	RBI.	B.A.	PO.	A.	E.	F.A.
1989—Birmingham	South.		★3-1-2	129	454	75	126	25	2	3	67	.278	108	249	27	★.930
1989—Chicago	Amer.		3B	16	45	5	8	3	0	0	7	.178	17	33	2	.962
Major League Totals—1 Year				16	45	5	8	3	0	0	7	.178	17	33	2	.962

Selected by Chicago White Sox' organization in 1st round (10th player selected) of free-agent draft, June 1, 1988.

RANDOLPH RUHLAND VERES
(Randy)

Born November 25, 1965, at San Francisco, Calif.
Height, 6.03. Weight, 190.
Throws and bats righthanded.
Attended Sacramento City College, Sacramento, Calif.

Year	Club	League	G.	IP.	W.	L.	Pct.	H.	R.	ER.	SO.	BB.	ERA.
1985—Helena	Pioneer		13	77⅓	7	4	.636	66	43	33	67	36	3.84
1986—Beloit†	Midwest		23	113⅓	4	12	.250	132	78	49	87	52	3.89
1987—Beloit	Midwest		21	127	10	6	.625	132	63	44	98	52	3.12
1988—Stockton	California		20	110	8	4	.667	94	54	41	96	77	3.35
1988—El Paso	Texas		6	39⅓	3	2	.600	35	18	16	31	12	3.66
1989—El Paso	Texas		8	43⅓	2	3	.400	43	29	23	41	25	4.78
1989—Denver	Am. Assoc.		17	107	6	7	.462	108	57	47	80	38	3.95
1989—Milwaukee	American		3	8⅓	0	1	.000	9	5	4	8	4	4.32
Major League Totals—1 Year			3	8⅓	0	1	.000	9	5	4	8	4	4.32

Selected by New York Mets' organization in 32nd round of free-agent draft, June 4, 1984.
Selected by Milwaukee Brewers' organization in secondary phase of free-agent draft, January 9, 1985.
†On disabled list, August 17, 1986 through remainder of season.

DONALD STEPHEN VESLING
(Don)

Born March 5, 1966, at Lorain, O.
Height, 6.04. Weight, 215.
Throws and bats lefthanded.
Attended Eastern Michigan University, Ypsilanti, Mich.

Year	Club	League	G.	IP.	W.	L.	Pct.	H.	R.	ER.	SO.	BB.	ERA.
1987—Bristol		Ap'lachian	12	80⅓	6	2	.750	83	36	28	52	11	3.14
1987—Lakeland		Florida St.	1	8	0	0	.000	5	1	1	1	0	1.13
1988—Lakeland		Florida St.	25	169⅓	10	8	.556	170	80	59	92	36	3.14
1989—London		Eastern	13	80⅓	5	4	.556	93	40	34	44	24	3.81
1989—Toledo		Int'national	11	71⅓	3	6	.333	62	29	24	34	33	3.03

Selected by Detroit Tigers' organization in 14th round of free-agent draft, June 2, 1987.

FRANK JOHN VIOLA JR.

Name pronounced Vy-OH-luh.

Born April 19, 1960, at Hempstead, N.Y.
Height, 6.04. Weight, 209.
Throws and bats lefthanded.
Attended St. John's University, Jamaica, N.Y.

Tied for American League lead in games started by pitchers with 37 in 1986.
Named American League Pitcher of the Year by THE SPORTING NEWS, 1988.
Won American League Cy Young Memorial Award, 1988.
Named lefthanded pitcher on THE SPORTING NEWS American League All-Star Team, 1988.

Year	Club	League	G.	IP.	W.	L.	Pct.	H.	R.	ER.	SO.	BB.	ERA.
1981—Orlando		Southern	17	97	5	4	.556	112	47	37	50	33	3.43
1982—Toledo		Int'national	8	58	2	3	.400	61	27	25	34	18	3.88
1982—Minnesota		American	22	126	4	10	.286	152	77	73	84	38	5.21
1983—Minnesota		American	35	210	7	15	.318	242	★141	★128	127	92	5.49
1984—Minnesota		American	35	257⅔	18	12	.600	225	101	92	149	73	3.21
1985—Minnesota		American	36	250⅔	18	14	.563	262	★136	114	135	68	4.09
1986—Minnesota		American	37	245⅔	16	13	.552	257	136	123	191	83	4.51
1987—Minnesota		American	36	251⅔	17	10	.630	230	91	81	197	66	2.90
1988—Minnesota		American	35	255⅓	★24	7	★.774	236	80	75	193	54	2.64
1989—Minnesota†		American	24	175⅔	8	12	.400	171	80	74	138	47	3.79
1989—New York		National	12	85⅓	5	5	.500	75	35	32	73	27	3.38
American League Totals—8 Years			260	1772⅔	112	93	.546	1775	842	760	1214	521	3.86
National League Totals—1 Year			12	85⅓	5	5	.500	75	35	32	73	27	3.38
Major League Totals—8 Years			272	1858	117	98	.544	1850	877	792	1287	548	3.84

Selected by Kansas City Royals' organization in 16th round of free-agent draft, June 6, 1978.
Selected by Minnesota Twins' organization in 2nd round of free-agent draft, June 8, 1981.
†Traded to New York Mets for Pitchers Rick Aguilera and David West and three players to be named later, July 31, 1989; Portland (Minnesota Twins' organization) acquired Pitchers Kevin Tapani and Tim Drummond on August 1, 1989, and Minnesota acquired Pitcher Jack Savage to complete deal, October 16, 1989.

CHAMPIONSHIP SERIES RECORD

Year	Club	League	G.	IP.	W.	L.	Pct.	H.	R.	ER.	SO.	BB.	ERA.
1987—Minnesota		American	2	12	1	0	1.000	14	8	7	9	5	5.25

WORLD SERIES RECORD

Year	Club	League	G.	IP.	W.	L.	Pct.	H.	R.	ER.	SO.	BB.	ERA.
1987—Minnesota		American	3	19⅓	2	1	.667	17	8	8	16	3	3.72

ALL-STAR GAME RECORD

Year	League	IP.	W.	L.	Pct.	H.	R.	ER.	SO.	BB.	ERA.
1988—American		2	1	0	1.000	0	0	0	1	0	0.00

OSVALDO JOSE VIRGIL JR.
(Ozzie)

Born December 7, 1956, at Mayaguez, Puerto Rico.
Height, 6.01. Weight, 195.
Throws and bats righthanded.
Son of Ozzie Virgil, infielder-catcher with New York N.L., Detroit, Kansas City, Baltimore, Pittsburgh and San Francisco, 1956 through 1958, 1960 through 1962, 1965, 1966 and 1969; coach, San Francisco Giants, 1970 through 1972, 1974 and 1975; scout, San Francisco Giants, 1973; coach, Montreal Expos, 1976 through 1981; coach, San Diego Padres, 1982 through 1985; and coach with Seattle Mariners, 1986 through June 6, 1988.

Major League stolen bases: 1984 (1), 1986 (1), 1988 (2). Total—4.
Led Carolina League in total bases with 234 in 1978.
Named Carolina League Most Valuable Player, 1978.

Year	Club	League	Pos.	G.	AB.	R.	H.	2B.	3B.	HR.	RBI.	B.A.	PO.	A.	E.	F.A.
1976—Auburn		NYP	C	39	113	10	16	1	2	1	10	.142	153	14	5	.971
1977—Spartanburg		W. Car.	C	107	365	53	103	21	1	14	54	.282	502	★68	18	.969
1978—Peninsula		Carol.	C	126	409	79	124	21	1	★29	★98	.303	581	45	8	.987
1979—Reading		East.	C	128	429	57	99	17	1	8	66	.231	532	64	12	.980

Year	Club	League	Pos.	G.	AB.	R.	H.	2B.	3B.	HR.	RBI.	B.A.	PO.	A.	E.	F.A.
1980—Reading	East.		C-1B	135	456	92	123	15	2	28	*104	.270	592	62	16	.976
1980—Philadelphia	Nat.		C	1	5	1	1	1	0	0	0	.200	4	0	0	1.000
1981—Oklahoma City†	A. A.		C	83	275	41	63	11	2	11	44	.229	201	28	4	.983
1981—Philadelphia	Nat.		C	6	6	0	0	0	0	0	0	.000	2	0	0	1.000
1982—Philadelphia	Nat.		C	49	101	11	24	6	0	3	8	.238	173	14	7	.964
1983—Philadelphia	Nat.		C	55	140	11	30	7	0	6	23	.214	228	24	9	.966
1984—Philadelphia	Nat.		C	141	456	61	119	21	2	18	68	.261	722	58	6	.992
1985—Philadelphia‡	Nat.		C	131	426	47	105	16	3	19	55	.246	667	52	4	*.994
1986—Atlanta	Nat.		C	114	359	45	80	9	0	15	48	.223	682	93	13	.984
1987—Atlanta	Nat.		C	123	429	57	106	13	1	27	72	.247	654	74	8	.989
1988—Atlanta§	Nat.		C	107	320	23	82	10	0	9	31	.256	448	45	5	.990
1989—Syracuse	Int.		C	43	146	15	38	4	0	4	18	.260	155	10	0	1.000
1989—Toronto x	Amer.		C	9	11	2	2	1	0	1	2	.182	1	0	0	1.000
National League Totals—9 Years				727	2242	256	547	83	6	97	305	.244	3580	360	52	.987
American League Totals—1 Year				9	11	2	2	1	0	1	2	.182	1	0	0	1.000
Major League Totals—10 Years				736	2253	258	549	84	6	98	307	.244	3581	360	52	.987

Selected by Philadelphia Phillies' organization in 6th round of free-agent draft, June 8, 1976.

†On disabled list, April 14 to April 27 and June 2 to June 29, 1981.

‡Traded with Pitcher Pete Smith to Atlanta Braves for Pitcher Steve Bedrosian and Outfielder Milt Thompson, December 10, 1985.

§Granted free agency, November 4, 1988; signed by Syracuse (Toronto Blue Jays' organization), June 24, 1989.

xReleased, October 20, 1989.

CHAMPIONSHIP SERIES RECORD

Year	Club	League	Pos.	G.	AB.	R.	H.	2B.	3B.	HR.	RBI.	B.A.	PO.	A.	E.	F.A.
1983—Philadelphia	Nat.		PH	1	1	0	0	0	0	0	0	.000	0	0	0	.000

WORLD SERIES RECORD

Year	Club	League	Pos.	G.	AB.	R.	H.	2B.	3B.	HR.	RBI.	B.A.	PO.	A.	E.	F.A.
1983—Philadelphia	Nat.		PH-C	3	2	0	1	0	0	0	1	.500	1	0	0	1.000

ALL-STAR GAME RECORD

Year	League	Pos.	AB.	R.	H.	2B.	3B.	HR.	RBI.	B.A.	PO.	A.	E.	F.A.
1985—National		C	1	0	1	0	0	0	2	1.000	3	0	0	1.000
1987—National		C	2	1	1	0	0	0	0	.500	7	0	0	1.000
All-Star Game Totals—2 Years			3	1	2	0	0	0	2	.667	10	0	0	1.000

JOSE LUIS VIZCAINO (PIMENTAL)

Born March 26, 1968, at Palenque, Dominican Republic.
Height, 6.01. Weight, 173.
Throws right and bats left and righthanded.

Led Pacific Coast League shortstops in total chances with 611 and double plays with 82 in 1989.
Led Gulf Coast League shortstops in double plays with 23 in 1987.

Year	Club	League	Pos.	G.	AB.	R.	H.	2B.	3B.	HR.	RBI.	B.A.	PO.	A.	E.	F.A.
1987—Sarasota Dodgers	Gulf C.		SS-1B	49	150	26	38	5	1	0	12	.253	73	107	13	.933
1988—Bakersfield	Calif.		SS	122	433	77	126	11	4	0	38	.291	185	340	30	.946
1989—Albuquerque	P. C.		SS	129	434	60	123	10	4	1	44	.283	*191	*390	*30	.951
1989—Los Angeles	Nat.		SS	7	10	2	2	0	0	0	0	.200	6	9	2	.882
Major League Totals—1 Year				7	10	2	2	0	0	0	0	.200	6	9	2	.882

Signed as free agent by Los Angeles Dodgers' organization, February 18, 1986.

OMAR ENRIQUE VIZQUEL

Born May 15, 1967, at Caracas, Venezuela.
Height, 5.09. Weight, 165.
Throws right and bats left and righthanded.

Major League stolen bases: 1989 (1).
Led Midwest League shortstops in fielding with .969 in 1986.

Year	Club	League	Pos.	G.	AB.	R.	H.	2B.	3B.	HR.	RBI.	B.A.	PO.	A.	E.	F.A.
1984—Butte†	Pion.		SS-2B	15	45	7	14	2	0	0	4	.311	13	29	5	.894
1985—Bellingham†	N'west		SS-2B	50	187	24	42	9	0	5	17	.225	85	175	19	.932
1986—Wausau†	Midw.		SS-2B	105	352	60	75	13	2	4	28	.213	153	328	16	.968
1987—Salinas†	Calif.		SS-2B	114	407	61	107	12	8	0	38	.263	81	295	25	.938
1988—Vermont†	East.		SS	103	374	54	95	18	2	2	35	.254	173	268	19	*.959
1988—Calgary	P. C.		SS	33	107	10	24	2	3	1	12	.224	43	92	6	.957
1989—Calgary	P. C.		SS	7	28	3	6	2	0	0	3	.214	15	14	0	1.000
1989—Seattle	Amer.		SS	143	387	45	85	7	3	1	20	.220	208	388	18	.971
Major League Totals—1 Year				143	387	45	85	7	3	1	20	.220	208	388	18	.971

Signed as free agent by Seattle Mariners' organization, April 1, 1984.

†Batted righthanded only.

—DID YOU KNOW—

That Dennis Martinez of the Expos had the majors' longest winning streak (11 games) in 1989?

ROBERT VERNON WALK
(Bob)

Born November 26, 1956, at Van Nuys, Calif.
Height, 6.04. Weight, 217.
Throws and bats righthanded.
Attended College of the Canyons, Valencia, Calif.

Major League saves: 1986 (2).
Led National League in wild pitches with 13 in 1988.
Led Pacific Coast League in complete games with 12 in 1985.
Led International League in complete games with 11 and tied for lead in games started by pitchers with 28 and home runs allowed with 22 in 1983.
Led Carolina League in hit batsmen with 13 in 1978.

Year Club	League	G.	IP.	W.	L.	Pct.	H.	R.	ER.	SO.	BB.	ERA.
1977—Spartanburg	W. Carol.	15	99	6	9	.400	90	55	40	66	46	3.64
1977—Peninsula	Carolina	8	36	0	2	.000	44	31	17	23	20	4.25
1978—Peninsula	Carolina	26	187	13	8	.619	147	58	44	150	64	2.12
1979—Reading	Eastern	24	185	12	7	.632	156	62	46	★135	77	★2.24
1980—Oklahoma City	Am. Assoc.	8	49	5	1	.833	39	21	16	36	17	2.94
1980—Philadelphia†	National	27	152	11	7	.611	163	82	77	94	71	4.56
1981—Atlanta‡	National	12	43	1	4	.200	41	25	22	16	23	4.60
1981—Richmond	Int'national	4	22	2	1	.667	18	7	6	13	11	2.45
1982—Atlanta	National	32	164⅓	11	9	.550	179	101	89	84	59	4.87
1983—Richmond	Int'national	28	★185	11	12	.478	179	★119	★107	123	102	5.21
1983—Atlanta§	National	1	3⅔	0	0	.000	7	3	3	4	2	7.36
1984—Hawaii	P. Coast	18	127⅓	9	5	.643	100	39	32	85	42	★2.26
1984—Pittsburgh x	National	2	10⅓	1	1	.500	8	5	3	10	4	2.61
1985—Hawaii	P. Coast	24	173	★16	5	.762	143	57	51	124	61	★2.65
1985—Pittsburgh	National	9	58⅔	2	3	.400	60	27	24	40	18	3.68
1986—Pittsburgh	National	44	141⅔	7	8	.467	129	66	59	78	64	3.75
1987—Pittsburgh	National	39	117	8	2	.800	107	52	43	78	51	3.31
1988—Pittsburgh y	National	32	212⅔	12	10	.545	183	75	64	81	65	2.71
1989—Pittsburgh z	National	33	196	13	10	.565	208	106	96	83	65	4.41
Major League Totals—9 Years		231	1099⅓	66	54	.550	1085	542	480	568	422	3.93

Selected by California Angels' organization in 5th round of free-agent draft, January 9, 1975.
Selected by Philadelphia Phillies' organization in 5th round of free-agent draft, January 7, 1976.
Selected by Philadelphia Phillies' organization in secondary phase of free-agent draft, June 8, 1976.
†Traded to Atlanta Braves for Outfielder Gary Matthews, March 25, 1981.
‡On disabled list, May 26 to August 9, 1981.
§Released, March 26, 1984; signed by Pittsburgh Pirates' organization, April 3, 1984.
xOn disabled list, July 23, 1984 through remainder of season.
yGranted free agency, November 4, 1988; re-signed by Pirates, November 27, 1988.
zOn disabled list, June 9 to June 24, 1989.

CHAMPIONSHIP SERIES RECORD

Year Club	League	G.	IP.	W.	L.	Pct.	H.	R.	ER.	SO.	BB.	ERA.
1982—Atlanta	National	1	1	0	0	.000	2	1	1	1	1	9.00

WORLD SERIES RECORD

Year Club	League	G.	IP.	W.	L.	Pct.	H.	R.	ER.	SO.	BB.	ERA.
1980—Philadelphia	National	1	7	1	0	1.000	8	6	6	3	3	7.71

ALL-STAR GAME RECORD

Year League	IP.	W.	L.	Pct.	H.	R.	ER.	SO.	BB.	ERA.
1988—National	⅓	0	0	.000	0	0	0	0	0	0.00

GREGORY LEE WALKER
(Greg)

Born October 6, 1959, at Douglas, Ga.
Height, 6.03. Weight, 210.
Throws right and bats lefthanded.

Major League stolen bases: 1983 (2), 1984 (8), 1985 (5), 1986 (1), 1987 (2). Total—18.
Led Midwest League first basemen in double plays with 108 in 1980.

Year Club	League	Pos.	G.	AB.	R.	H.	2B.	3B.	HR.	RBI.	B.A.	PO.	A.	E.	F.A.
1977—Auburn†	NYP	1B	33	98	12	25	1	2	2	8	.255	5	0	0	1.000
1978—Spartanburg	W. Car.	1B-3B-C	100	341	51	71	16	2	11	47	.208	538	50	13	.978
1979—Peninsula‡	Carol.	1B	122	446	59	125	★27	4	10	61	.280	973	53	19	.982
1980—Appleton	Midw.	1B	135	464	88	130	20	3	21	★98	.280	★1298	★88	10	★.993
1981—Glens Falls	East.	1B	135	508	★117	★163	★33	2	22	86	.321	★1215	77	11	.992
1982—Edmonton§	P. C.	1B	35	117	18	41	8	0	3	12	.350	94	11	0	1.000
1982—Chicago	Amer.	DH	11	17	3	7	2	1	2	7	.412	0	0	0	.000
1983—Chicago	Amer.	1B	118	307	32	83	16	3	10	55	.270	426	19	7	.985
1984—Chicago	Amer.	1B	136	442	62	130	29	2	24	75	.294	791	51	4	.995
1985—Chicago	Amer.	1B	★163	601	77	155	38	4	24	92	.258	1217	97	8	.994
1986—Chicago x	Amer.	1B	78	282	37	78	10	6	13	51	.277	670	57	5	.993
1987—Chicago	Amer.	1B	157	566	85	145	33	2	27	94	.256	★1402	80	9	.994
1988—Chicago y	Amer.	1B	99	377	45	93	22	1	8	42	.247	935	41	7	.993
1989—Chicago z	Amer.	1B	77	233	25	49	14	0	5	26	.210	373	17	5	.987
Major League Totals—8 Years			749	2825	366	740	164	19	113	442	.262	5814	362	45	.993

Selected by Philadelphia Phillies' organization in 20th round of free-agent draft, June 7, 1977.
†On disabled list, June 21, 1977 through remainder of season.
‡Drafted by Iowa (Chicago White Sox' organization), December 4, 1979.
§On disabled list, April 23 to July 27, 1982.
xOn disabled list, April 15 to May 14 and August 3, 1986 through remainder of season.
yOn disabled list, July 30, 1988 through remainder of season.
zOn disabled list, April 27 to May 13, 1989.

CHAMPIONSHIP SERIES RECORD

Year	Club	League	Pos.	G.	AB.	R.	H.	2B.	3B.	HR.	RBI.	B.A.	PO.	A.	E.	F.A.
1983—Chicago	Amer.	PH-1B	2	3	0	1	0	0	0	0	.333	7	1	0	1.000

LARRY KENNETH ROBERT WALKER

Born December 1, 1966, at Maple Ridge, British Columbia, Canada.
Height, 6.02. Weight, 205.
Throws right and bats lefthanded.

Major League stolen bases: 1989 (1).
Tied for Southern League lead in game-winning RBIs with 19 in 1987.

Year	Club	League	Pos.	G.	AB.	R.	H.	2B.	3B.	HR.	RBI.	B.A.	PO.	A.	E.	F.A.
1985—Utica	NYP	1B-3B	62	215	24	48	8	2	2	26	.223	354	62	8	.981
1986—Burlington	Midw.	OF-3B	95	332	67	96	12	6	29	74	.289	106	51	10	.940
1986—W. Palm Beach	Fla. St.	OF	38	113	20	32	7	5	4	16	.283	44	5	0	1.000
1987—Jacksonville	South.	OF	128	474	91	136	25	7	26	83	.287	263	9	9	.968
1988—Jacksonville†	South.						(Did not play)									
1989—Indianapolis	A.A.	OF	114	385	68	104	18	2	12	59	.270	241	★18	★11	.959
1989—Montreal	Nat.	OF	20	47	4	8	0	0	0	4	.170	19	2	0	1.000
Major League Totals—1 Year				20	47	4	8	0	0	0	4	.170	19	2	0	1.000

Signed as free agent by Montreal Expos' organization, November 14, 1984.
†On disabled list, April 4, 1988 through entire season.

MICHAEL AARON WALKER
(Mike)

Born June 23, 1965, at Houston, Tex.
Height, 6.03. Weight, 205.
Throws and bats righthanded.
Attended University of Houston, Houston, Tex.

Year	Club	League	G.	IP.	W.	L.	Pct.	H.	R.	ER.	SO.	BB.	ERA.
1986—Watertown	NYP	16	103⅓	4	●10	.286	★116	★71	★52	81	46	4.53
1987—Harrisburg	Eastern	4	15	0	2	.000	20	17	15	9	9	9.00
1987—Salem	Carolina	21	135⅔	12	5	.706	140	67	56	91	57	3.71
1988—Salem	Carolina	5	37	2	2	.500	42	17	13	29	9	3.16
1988—Harrisburg	Eastern	13	74⅓	2	7	.222	76	40	29	47	15	3.51
1988—Buffalo	Am. Assoc.	8	55	2	3	.400	52	18	17	26	8	2.78
1989—Buffalo†	Am. Assoc.	3	17	0	1	.000	12	13	10	5	13	5.29
1989—Calgary	P. Coast	18	88	6	7	.462	119	74	63	46	37	6.44

Selected by Pittsburgh Pirates' organization in 2nd round of free-agent draft, June 2, 1986.
†Traded with Pitcher Mike Dunne and Outfielder Mark Merchant to Seattle Mariners for Shortstop Rey Quinones and Pitcher Bill Wilkinson, April 21, 1989.

MICHAEL CHARLES WALKER
(Mike)

Born October 4, 1966, at Brooksville, Fla.
Height, 6.01. Weight, 175.
Throws and bats righthanded.
Attended Seminole Community College, Sanford, Fla.

Led Pacific Coast League pitchers in home runs allowed with 21, hit batsmen with 14 and tied for lead in games started with 28 in 1989.
Led Eastern League pitchers in wild pitches with 17 and tied for lead in games started with 27 in 1988.
Led Midwest League in complete games with 8 in 1987.

Year	Club	League	G.	IP.	W.	L.	Pct.	H.	R.	ER.	SO.	BB.	ERA.
1986—Burlington	Ap'lachian	14	70⅓	4	6	.400	75	★65	●46	42	45	5.89
1987—Waterloo	Midwest	23	145⅓	11	7	.611	133	74	58	144	68	3.59
1987—Kingston	Carolina	3	20⅔	3	0	1.000	17	7	6	19	14	2.61
1988—Williamsport	Eastern	28	★164⅓	★15	7	.682	162	82	68	★144	74	3.72
1988—Cleveland	American	3	8⅔	0	1	.000	8	7	7	7	10	7.27
1989—Colorado Springs	P. Coast	28	168	6	★15	.286	193	★124	★108	97	★93	5.79
Major League Totals—1 Year			3	8⅔	0	1	.000	8	7	7	7	10	7.27

Selected by Montreal Expos' organization in 14th round of free-agent draft, June 4, 1984.
Selected by Montreal Expos' organization in secondary phase of free-agent draft, January 9, 1985.
Selected by Cleveland Indians' organization in 2nd round of free-agent draft, January 14, 1986.

TIMOTHY CHARLES WALLACH
(Tim)

Born September 14, 1957, at Huntington Park, Calif.
Height, 6.03. Weight, 200.
Throws and bats righthanded.
Attended Saddleback Junior College, Mission Viejo, Calif., and
California State University, Fullerton, Calif.

Shares major league record by hitting home run in first major league at-bat, September 6, 1980.
Major League stolen bases: 1982 (6), 1984 (3), 1985 (9), 1986 (8), 1987 (9), 1988 (2), 1989 (3). Total—40.
Hit three home runs in a game, May 4, 1987.
Led National League in grounding into double plays with 21 in 1989.
Led National League in being hit by pitch with 10 in 1986.
Tied for National League lead in game-winning RBIs with 16 in 1987.
Led National League third basemen in putouts with 123 in 1988.
Led National League third basemen in total chances with 515 in 1984 and 549 in 1985.
Led National League third basemen in double plays with 29 in 1984, 34 in 1985 and tied for lead with 31 in 1988.
Led American Association in total bases with 295, game-winning RBIs with 16 and tied for lead in sacrifice flies with 9 in 1980.
Named third baseman on THE SPORTING NEWS National League All-Star Team, 1985 and 1987.
Named third baseman on THE SPORTING NEWS National League All-Star fielding team, 1985 and 1988..
Named third baseman on THE SPORTING NEWS National League Silver Slugger team, 1985 and 1987.
Named College Player of the Year by THE SPORTING NEWS College Baseball All-America Team, 1979.

Year	Club	League	Pos.	G.	AB.	R.	H.	2B.	3B.	HR.	RBI.	B.A.	PO.	A.	E.	F.A.
1979—Memphis	South.	1B-3B	75	257	50	84	16	4	18	51	.327	290	35	4	.988
1980—Denver	A. A.	3B-OF-1B	134	512	103	144	29	7	36	124	.281	222	147	21	.946
1980—Montreal	Nat.	OF-1B	5	11	1	2	0	0	1	2	.182	12	0	0	1.000
1981—Montreal	Nat.	OF-1B-3B	71	212	19	50	9	1	4	13	.236	207	31	1	.996
1982—Montreal	Nat.	★3-O-1	158	596	89	160	31	3	28	97	.268	★132	287	23	.948
1983—Montreal	Nat.	3B	156	581	54	156	33	3	19	70	.269	★151	262	19	.956
1984—Montreal	Nat.	★3B-SS	160	582	55	143	25	4	18	72	.246	★162	★332	21	.959
1985—Montreal	Nat.	3B	155	569	70	148	36	3	22	81	.260	★148	★383	18	.967
1986—Montreal	Nat.	3B	134	480	50	112	22	1	18	71	.233	94	270	16	.958
1987—Montreal	Nat.	★3B-P	153	593	89	177	★42	4	26	123	.298	★128	292	21	.952
1988—Montreal	Nat.	3B-2B	159	592	52	152	32	5	12	69	.257	124	329	18	.962
1989—Montreal	Nat.	3B-P	154	573	76	159	●42	0	13	77	.277	113	302	18	.958
Major League Totals—10 Years			1305	4789	555	1259	272	24	161	675	.263	1271	2491	155	.960

Selected by California Angels' organization in 8th round of free-agent draft, June 6, 1978.
Selected by Montreal Expos' organization in 1st round (10th player selected) of free-agent draft, June 5, 1979.

DIVISION SERIES RECORD

Year	Club	League	Pos.	G.	AB.	R.	H.	2B.	3B.	HR.	RBI.	B.A.	PO.	A.	E.	F.A.
1981—Montreal	Nat.	OF	4	4	1	1	1	0	0	0	.250	4	0	0	1.000

CHAMPIONSHIP SERIES RECORD

Year	Club	League	Pos.	G.	AB.	R.	H.	2B.	3B.	HR.	RBI.	B.A.	PO.	A.	E.	F.A.
1981—Montreal	Nat.	PH	1	1	0	0	0	0	0	0	.000	0	0	0	.000

ALL-STAR GAME RECORD

Year	League	Pos.	AB.	R.	H.	2B.	3B.	HR.	RBI.	B.A.	PO.	A.	E.	F.A.
1984—National		3B	1	0	0	0	0	0	0	.000	0	0	0	.000
1985—National		3B	2	1	1	1	0	0	0	.500	1	1	0	1.000
1987—National		3B	3	0	0	0	0	0	0	.000	0	2	0	1.000
1989—National		3B	1	0	0	0	0	0	0	.000	0	0	0	.000
All-Star Game Totals—4 Years			7	1	1	1	0	0	0	.143	1	3	0	1.000

PITCHING RECORD

Year	Club	League	G.	IP.	W.	L.	Pct.	H.	R.	ER.	SO.	BB.	ERA.
1987—Montreal	National	1	1	0	0	.000	1	0	0	0	0	0.00
1989—Montreal	National	1	1	0	0	.000	2	1	1	0	0	9.00
Major League Totals—2 Years		2	2	0	0	.000	3	1	1	0	0	4.50

DENNIS MARTIN WALLING
(Denny)

Born April 17, 1954, at Neptune, N.J.
Height, 6.01. Weight, 185.
Throws right and bats lefthanded.
Attended Brookdale Community College, Lincroft, N.J., and
Clemson University, Clemson, S.C.
Brother of Gregory Walling, minor league outfielder, 1967.

Major League stolen bases: 1978 (9), 1979 (3), 1980 (4), 1981 (2), 1982 (4), 1983 (2), 1984 (7), 1985 (5), 1986 (1), 1987 (5), 1988 (2). Total—44.
Named outfielder on THE SPORTING NEWS College Baseball All-America Team, 1975.

Year	Club	League	Pos.	G.	AB.	R.	H.	2B.	3B.	HR.	RBI.	B.A.	PO.	A.	E.	F.A.
1975—Oakland	Amer.	OF	6	8	0	1	1	0	0	2	.125	3	0	0	1.000
1976—Chattanooga	South.	OF	115	369	48	95	15	5	9	42	.257	241	8	2	★.992
1976—Oakland	Amer.	OF	3	11	1	3	0	0	0	0	.273	8	0	1	.889

Year	Club	League	Pos.	G.	AB.	R.	H.	2B.	3B.	HR.	RBI.	B.A.	PO.	A.	E.	F.A.
1977—San Jose†‡	P. C.	OF	3	10	1	3	0	0	0	4	.300	8	0	0	1.000
1977—Charleston	Int.	OF	29	89	17	31	4	1	4	14	.348	66	0	0	1.000
1977—Houston	Nat.	OF	6	21	1	6	0	1	0	6	.286	14	0	0	1.000
1978—Houston	Nat.	OF	120	247	30	62	11	3	3	36	.251	140	4	3	.980
1979—Houston	Nat.	OF	82	147	21	48	8	4	3	31	.327	65	2	1	.985
1980—Houston	Nat.	1B-OF	100	284	30	85	6	5	3	29	.299	525	31	6	.989
1981—Houston	Nat.	1B-OF	65	158	23	37	6	0	5	23	.234	226	9	2	.992
1982—Houston	Nat.	OF-1B	85	146	22	30	4	1	1	14	.205	167	11	1	.994
1983—Houston§	Nat.	1B-3B-OF	100	135	24	40	5	3	3	19	.296	134	29	6	.964
1984—Houston x	Nat.	3B-1B-OF	87	249	37	70	11	5	3	31	.281	116	102	7	.969
1985—Houston	Nat.	3B-1B-OF	119	345	44	93	20	1	7	45	.270	326	124	12	.974
1986—Houston	Nat.	3B-OF-1B	130	382	54	119	23	1	13	58	.312	108	161	9	.968
1987—Houston y	Nat.	3B-1B-OF	110	325	45	92	21	4	5	33	.283	175	119	10	.967
1988—Hou. za-St.L.	Nat.	3B-OF-1B	84	234	22	56	13	2	1	21	.239	73	112	9	.954
1988—Tucson	P. C.	3B	5	16	2	3	1	0	0	4	.188	4	10	1	.933
1989—St. Louis b	Nat.	1B-3B-OF	69	79	9	24	7	0	1	11	.304	67	9	4	.950
American League Totals—2 Years			9	19	1	4	1	0	0	2	.210	11	0	1	.917
National League Totals—13 Years			1157	2752	362	762	135	30	48	357	.277	2136	713	70	.976
Major League Totals—15 Years			1166	2771	363	766	136	30	48	359	.276	2147	713	71	.976

Selected by San Francisco Giants' organization in 8th round of free-agent draft, June 5, 1974.
Selected by Oakland A's organization in secondary phase of free-agent draft, June 4, 1975.
†On disabled list, April 18 to June 15, 1977.
‡Traded with cash to Houston Astros' organization for Outfielder Willie Crawford, June 15, 1977.
§Granted free agency, November 7, 1983; re-signed by Astros, December 20, 1983.
xOn disabled list, May 2 to May 24, 1984.
yOn disabled list, March 28 to April 17, 1987.
zOn disabled list, June 20 to August 6, 1988; included rehabilitation disability assignment to Tucson, July 29 to August 3, 1988.
aTraded to St. Louis Cardinals for Pitcher Bob Forsch, August 31, 1988.
bOn disabled list, May 24, to June 8, 1989.

DIVISION SERIES RECORD

Year	Club	League	Pos.	G.	AB.	R.	H.	2B.	3B.	HR.	RBI.	B.A.	PO.	A.	E.	F.A.
1981—Houston	Nat.	PH-1B	3	6	0	2	0	0	0	1	.333	6	1	1	.875

CHAMPIONSHIP SERIES RECORD

Year	Club	League	Pos.	G.	AB.	R.	H.	2B.	3B.	HR.	RBI.	B.A.	PO.	A.	E.	F.A.
1980—Houston	Nat.	1-O-PH	3	9	2	1	0	0	0	2	.111	6	0	0	1.000
1986—Houston	Nat.	3B-PH	5	19	1	3	1	0	0	2	.158	3	6	0	1.000
Championship Series Totals—2 Years			8	28	3	4	1	0	0	4	.143	9	6	0	1.000

JEROME O'TERRELL WALTON

Born July 8, 1965, at Newnan, Ga.
Height, 6.01. Weight, 175.
Throws and bats righthanded.
Attended Enterprise State Junior College, Enterprise, Ala.

Major League stolen bases: 1989 (24).
Led Midwest League in caught stealing with 25 in 1987.
Led Appalachian League outfielders in putouts with 128, total chances with 131 and tied for lead in double plays with 2 in 1986.
Named National League Rookie Player of the Year by THE SPORTING NEWS, 1989.
Named National League Rookie of the Year by Baseball Writers' Association of America, 1989.

Year	Club	League	Pos.	G.	AB.	R.	H.	2B.	3B.	HR.	RBI.	B.A.	PO.	A.	E.	F.A.
1986—Wytheville	Appal.	OF-3B	62	229	48	66	7	4	5	34	.288	130	7	3	.979
1987—Peoria	Midw.	OF	128	472	102	158	24	11	6	38	.335	255	9	7	.974
1988—Pittsfield	East.	OF	120	414	64	137	26	2	3	49	.331	270	11	2	*.993
1989—Chicago†	Nat.	OF	116	475	64	139	23	3	5	46	.293	289	2	3	.990
1989—Iowa	A. A.	OF	4	18	4	6	1	0	1	3	.333	8	0	0	1.000
Major League Totals—1 Year			116	475	64	139	23	3	5	46	.293	289	2	3	.990

Selected by Chicago Cubs' organization in 2nd round of free-agent draft, January 14, 1986.
†On disabled list, May 11 to June 11, 1989; included rehabilitation disability assignment to Iowa, June 6 to June 11, 1989.

CHAMPIONSHIP SERIES RECORD

Shares Championship Series records for most at-bats (2), hits (2) and singles (2), inning, October 5, 1989, first inning.

Year	Club	League	Pos.	G.	AB.	R.	H.	2B.	3B.	HR.	RBI.	B.A.	PO.	A.	E.	F.A.
1989—Chicago	Nat.	OF	5	22	4	8	0	0	0	2	.364	11	0	0	1.000

STEVEN LEE WAPNICK
(Steve)

Born September 25, 1965, at Panorama City, Calif.
Height, 6.02. Weight, 200.
Throws and bats righthanded.
Attended Moorpark College, Moorpark, Calif.,
and Fresno State University, Fresno, Calif.

Year Club	League	G.	IP.	W.	L.	Pct.	H.	R.	ER.	SO.	BB.	ERA.
1987—St. Catharines	NYP	20	65⅔	3	4	.429	53	28	22	63	21	3.02
1988—Myrtle Beach	S. Atlantic	★54	60⅓	4	3	.571	44	18	15	69	31	2.24
1989—Dunedin	Florida St.	24	66	4	0	1.000	48	19	15	59	22	2.05
1989—Knoxville	Southern	12	18⅓	1	0	1.000	12	1	1	20	7	0.49
1989—Syracuse†	Int'national	6	13	1	0	1.000	9	1	1	10	5	0.69

Selected by San Diego Padres' organization in 2nd round of free-agent draft, January 9, 1985.
Selected by Oakland Athletics' organization in secondary phase of free-agent draft, June 3, 1985.
Selected by Toronto Blue Jays' organization in 30th round of free-agent draft, June 2, 1987.
†Drafted by Detroit Tigers, December 4, 1989.

GARY LAMELL WARD

Born December 6, 1953, at Los Angeles, Calif.
Height, 6.02. Weight, 202.
Throws and bats righthanded.
Father of Agee Ward, forward at Fullerton State.

Major League stolen bases: 1981 (5), 1982 (13), 1983 (8), 1984 (7), 1985 (26), 1986 (12), 1987 (9), 1989 (1). Total—81.
Hit for the cycle, September 18, 1980 (first game).
Led American League outfielders in double plays with 4 in 1981.
Led New York-Pennsylvania League first basemen in errors with 12 in 1973.
Tied for Midwest League lead in assists by outfielders with 18 in 1974.

Year Club	League	Pos.	G.	AB.	R.	H.	2B.	3B.	HR.	RBI.	B.A.	PO.	A.	E.	F.A.
1973—Geneva	NYP	1B-OF-3B	61	211	36	57	13	1	10	38	.270	336	20	14	.962
1974—Wisconsin Rapids	Midw.	OF-1B	126	★467	★104	122	12	5	26	78	.261	184	19	11	.949
1975—Orlando	South.	OF-C	124	438	45	117	18	5	8	71	.267	204	10	4	.982
1976—Orlando	South.	OF	132	475	50	119	17	2	9	65	.251	235	●16	●10	.962
1977—Tacoma	P. C.	OF-3B	125	413	62	97	15	8	8	43	.235	212	34	10	.961
1978—Toledo	Int.	★O-1-3	139	511	82	150	20	12	14	79	.294	260	6	★13	.953
1979—Toledo	Int.	OF	134	506	75	133	16	9	13	67	.263	323	12	●11	.968
1979—Minnesota	Amer.	DH-PH	10	14	2	4	0	0	0	1	.286	0	0	0	.000
1980—Toledo†	Int.	OF-1B	128	496	82	140	22	8	13	66	.282	269	14	8	.973
1980—Minnesota	Amer.	OF	13	41	11	19	6	2	1	10	.463	14	0	0	1.000
1981—Minnesota	Amer.	OF	85	295	42	78	7	6	3	29	.264	185	8	5	.975
1982—Minnesota	Amer.	OF	152	570	85	165	33	7	28	91	.289	343	13	4	.989
1983—Minnesota‡	Amer.	OF	157	623	76	173	34	5	19	88	.278	374	★24	9	.978
1984—Texas	Amer.	OF	155	602	97	171	21	7	21	79	.284	376	11	5	.987
1985—Texas	Amer.	OF	154	593	77	170	28	7	15	70	.287	304	11	10	.969
1986—Texas§	Amer.	OF	105	380	54	120	15	2	5	51	.316	237	8	1	.996
1987—New York	Amer.	OF-1B	146	529	65	131	22	1	16	78	.248	318	10	3	.991
1988—New York	Amer.	OF-1B-3B	91	231	26	52	8	0	4	24	.225	220	5	2	.991
1989—N.Y.x-Det.	Amer.	OF-1B	113	292	27	74	11	2	9	30	.253	234	16	3	.988
Major League Totals—11 Years			1181	4170	562	1157	185	39	121	551	.277	2605	106	42	.985

Signed as free agent by Minnesota Twins' organization, August 29, 1972.
†On disabled list, April 16 to April 26, 1980.
‡Traded to Texas Rangers for Pitchers Mike Smithson and John Butcher and Catcher Sam Sorce, December 7, 1983.
§Granted free agency, November 12, 1986; signed by New York Yankees, December 24, 1986.
xReleased, April 16, 1989; signed by Detroit Tigers, April 23, 1989.

ALL-STAR GAME RECORD

Year League	Pos.	AB.	R.	H.	2B.	3B.	HR.	RBI.	B.A.	PO.	A.	E.	F.A.
1983—American	PH	1	0	0	0	0	0	0	.000	0	0	0	.000
1985—American	PH	1	0	0	0	0	0	0	.000	0	0	0	.000
All-Star Game Totals—2 Years		2	0	0	0	0	0	0	.000	0	0	0	.000

ROY DUANE WARD

(Known by middle name.)
Born May 28, 1964, at Parkview, N.M.
Height, 6.04. Weight, 210.
Throws and bats righthanded.

Major League saves: 1988 (15), 1989 (15). Total—30.

Year Club	League	G.	IP.	W.	L.	Pct.	H.	R.	ER.	SO.	BB.	ERA.
1982—Bradenton Braves	Gulf Coast	8	45⅔	2	3	.400	45	25	23	31	24	4.53
1982—Anderson	S. Atlantic	5	23⅔	1	2	.333	24	16	14	18	15	5.32
1983—Durham	Carolina	28	178⅓	11	13	.458	165	103	85	115	75	4.29
1984—Greenville†	Southern	21	104⅔	4	9	.308	108	71	58	54	57	4.99
1985—Greenville	Southern	28	150	11	10	.524	141	83	70	100	★105	4.20
1985—Richmond	Int'national	5	5⅓	0	1	.000	8	9	7	3	8	11.81
1986—Atlanta	National	10	16	0	1	.000	22	13	13	8	8	7.31
1986—Richmond‡-Syracuse	Int'national	20	117⅔	7	5	.583	125	56	52	67	52	3.98
1986—Toronto	American	2	2	0	1	.000	3	4	3	1	4	13.50
1987—Toronto	American	12	11⅔	1	0	1.000	14	9	9	10	12	6.94
1987—Syracuse	Int'national	46	76⅓	2	2	.500	59	35	33	67	42	3.89
1988—Toronto	American	64	111⅔	9	3	.750	101	46	41	91	60	3.30
1989—Toronto	American	66	114⅔	4	10	.286	94	55	48	122	58	3.77
National League Totals—1 Year		10	16	0	1	.000	22	13	13	8	8	7.31
American League Totals—4 Years		144	240	14	14	.500	212	114	101	224	134	3.79
Major League Totals—4 Years		154	256	14	15	.483	234	127	114	232	142	4.01

Selected by Atlanta Braves' organization in 1st round (ninth player selected) of free-agent draft, June 7, 1982.
†On disabled list, May 7 to May 29 and July 14 to August 7, 1984.
‡Traded to Toronto Blue Jays for Pitcher Doyle Alexander, July 6, 1986.

CHAMPIONSHIP SERIES RECORD

Year	Club	League	G.	IP.	W.	L.	Pct.	H.	R.	ER.	SO.	BB.	ERA.
1989—Toronto		American	2	3⅔	0	0	.000	6	3	3	5	3	7.36

CLAUDELL WASHINGTON

Born August 31, 1954, at Los Angeles, Calif.
Height, 6.02. Weight, 195.
Throws and bats lefthanded.
Brother of Don Washington, outfielder in Los Angeles Dodgers' and
Oakland A's organizations, 1975 through 1977.

Hit three home runs in a game, July 14, 1979 and June 22, 1980.
Major League stolen bases: 1974 (6), 1975 (40), 1976 (37), 1977 (21), 1978 (5), 1979 (19), 1980 (21), 1981 (12), 1982 (33), 1983 (31), 1984 (21), 1985 (14), 1986 (10), 1987 (10), 1988 (15), 1989 (13). Total—308.
Led Midwest League in total bases with 218 in 1973.

Year	Club	League	Pos.	G.	AB.	R.	H.	2B.	3B.	HR.	RBI.	B.A.	PO.	A.	E.	F.A.
1972—C's Bay-N. Bend		N'west.	OF	33	111	13	31	3	2	2	15	.279	37	1	6	.864
1973—Burlington		Midw.	OF	108	447	★92	144	25	5	13	81	.322	149	10	★15	.914
1974—Birmingham		South.	OF	74	294	64	106	23	3	11	55	.361	116	5	13	.903
1974—Oakland		Amer.	OF	73	221	16	63	10	5	0	19	.285	63	2	1	.985
1975—Oakland		Amer.	OF	148	590	86	182	24	7	10	77	.308	305	8	7	.978
1976—Oakland†‡		Amer.	●OF	134	490	65	126	20	6	5	53	.257	276	10	●11	.963
1977—Texas§		Amer.	OF	129	521	63	148	31	2	12	68	.284	255	11	6	.978
1978—Tex. x-Chi. y		Amer.	OF	98	356	34	90	16	5	6	33	.253	170	6	8	.957
1979—Chicago		Amer.	OF	131	471	79	132	33	5	13	66	.280	256	7	7	.974
1980—Chicago z		Amer.	OF	32	90	15	26	4	2	1	12	.289	41	1	3	.933
1980—New York a		Nat.	OF	79	284	38	78	16	4	10	42	.275	123	12	3	.978
1981—Atlanta b		Nat.	OF	85	320	37	93	22	3	5	37	.291	145	5	1	.993
1982—Atlanta		Nat.	OF	150	563	94	150	24	6	16	80	.266	221	9	12	.950
1983—Atlanta		Nat.	OF	134	496	75	138	24	8	9	44	.278	218	8	6	.974
1984—Atlanta c		Nat.	OF	120	416	62	119	21	2	17	61	.286	170	4	6	.967
1985—Atlanta de		Nat.	OF	122	398	62	110	14	6	15	43	.276	122	3	5	.962
1986—Atlanta de		Nat.	OF	40	137	17	37	11	0	5	14	.270	44	1	2	.957
1986—New York f		Amer.	OF	54	135	19	32	5	0	6	16	.237	66	0	1	.985
1987—New York g		Amer.	OF	102	312	42	87	17	0	9	44	.279	166	3	2	.988
1988—New York h		Amer.	OF	126	455	62	140	22	3	11	64	.308	309	5	5	.984
1989—California i		Amer.	OF	110	418	53	114	18	4	13	42	.273	187	6	5	.975
American League Totals—11 Years				1137	4059	534	1140	200	39	86	494	.281	2094	59	56	.975
National League Totals—7 Years				730	2614	385	725	132	29	77	321	.277	1043	42	35	.969
Major League Totals—16 Years				1867	6673	919	1865	332	68	163	815	.279	3137	101	91	.973

Signed as free agent by Oakland A's organization, July 7, 1972.
†On disabled list, August 16 to September 1, 1976.
‡Traded to Texas Rangers for Pitcher Jim Umbarger, Infielder Rodney Scott and cash estimated at $100,000, March 26, 1977.
§On disabled list, May 27 to June 11, 1977.
xTraded with Outfielder Rusty Torres and cash to Chicago White Sox for Outfielder Bobby Bonds, May 16, 1978.
yOn disabled list, May 22 to June 16, 1978.
zTraded to New York Mets for Pitcher Jesse Anderson, June 7, 1980.
aGranted free agency, October 31, 1980; signed by Atlanta Braves, November 15, 1980.
bOn disabled list, June 5 to August 9, 1981.
cOn disabled list, May 30 to June 14, 1984.
dOn disabled list, May 18 to June 16, 1986.
eTraded with Shortstop Paul Zuvella to New York Yankees for Outfielder Ken Griffey, June 30, 1986.
fGranted free agency, November 12, 1986; re-signed by Yankees, December 7, 1986.
gOn disabled list, May 18 to June 2, 1987.
hGranted free agency, October 24, 1988; signed by California Angels, January 17, 1989.
iOn disabled list, July 1 to July 18, 1989.

CHAMPIONSHIP SERIES RECORD

Year	Club	League	Pos.	G.	AB.	R.	H.	2B.	3B.	HR.	RBI.	B.A.	PO.	A.	E.	F.A.
1974—Oakland		Amer.	OF-PH	4	11	1	3	1	0	0	0	.273	11	0	0	1.000
1975—Oakland		Amer.	OF-DH	3	12	1	3	1	0	1	1	.250	1	0	2	.333
1982—Atlanta		Nat.	OF	3	9	0	3	0	0	0	0	.333	5	1	0	1.000
Championship Series Totals—3 Years				10	32	2	9	2	0	0	1	.281	17	1	2	.900

WORLD SERIES RECORD

Tied World Series record for most positions played, Series (3), 1974 (all three outfield positions).

Year	Club	League	Pos.	G.	AB.	R.	H.	2B.	3B.	HR.	RBI.	B.A.	PO.	A.	E.	F.A.
1974—Oakland		Amer.	OF-PH	5	7	1	4	0	0	0	0	.571	3	0	0	1.000

ALL-STAR GAME RECORD

Year	League	Pos.	AB.	R.	H.	2B.	3B.	HR.	RBI.	B.A.	PO.	A.	E.	F.A.
1975—American		PR-OF	1	1	0	0	0	0	0	1.000	1	0	0	1.000
1984—National		OF	2	0	1	1	0	0	0	.500	1	0	0	1.000
All-Star Game Totals—2 Years			3	0	2	1	0	0	0	.667	2	0	0	1.000

RONALD WASHINGTON
(Ron)

Born April 29, 1952, at New Orleans, La.
Height, 5.11. Weight, 160.
Throws and bats righthanded.
Attended Manatee Junior College, Bradenton, Fla.

Major League stolen bases: 1977 (1), 1981 (4), 1982 (3), 1983 (10), 1984 (1), 1985 (5), 1986 (1), 1988 (3). Total—28.

Year	Club	League	Pos.	G.	AB.	R.	H.	2B.	3B.	HR.	RBI.	B.A.	PO.	A.	E.	F.A.
1971—Sara. Royals†	Gulf C.	C	38	127	29	37	2	●6	1	23	.291	★213	23	3	★.987
1972—Waterloo	Midw.	C-OF-3B	76	241	37	55	3	1	1	30	.228	424	48	8	.983
1973—Waterloo	Midw.	SS	85	289	35	80	13	5	6	34	.277	130	198	29	.919
1974—San Jose‡	Calif.	2B-SS-C	109	425	49	104	16	3	2	41	.245	233	266	33	.938
1975—Jacksonville§	South.	2-3-S-1	96	267	22	61	7	1	0	20	.228	133	199	22	.938
1976—Waterbury x	East.	3B-2B	115	436	61	128	9	10	4	32	.294	170	249	26	.942
1977—San Antonio y	Texas	SS	39	158	24	44	8	4	0	13	.278	78	92	12	.934
1977—Albuquerque	P. C.	SS	85	359	71	116	17	8	8	59	.323	204	250	★33	.932
1977—Los Angeles	Nat.	SS	10	19	4	7	0	0	0	1	.368	4	14	3	.857
1978—Albuquerque z	P. C.	3B	31	122	26	42	10	3	5	32	.344	23	58	8	.910
1979—Aguila	Mex.	3B	42	165	22	43	3	3	0	14	.261	35	96	10	.929
1979—Tidewater a	Int.	3B-SS	83	273	18	72	13	4	1	26	.264	77	157	13	.947
1980—Toledo	Int.	3B-2B-SS	114	407	62	117	●31	5	3	36	.287	131	268	30	.930
1981—Toledo	Int.	3B-OF-SS	138	★544	84	157	27	8	15	54	.289	130	287	26	.941
1981—Minnesota	Amer.	SS-OF	28	84	8	19	3	1	0	5	.226	64	80	8	.947
1982—Minnesota	Amer.	SS-2B-3B	119	451	48	122	17	6	5	39	.271	201	269	13	.973
1983—Minnesota	Amer.	SS-2B-3B	99	317	28	78	7	3	4	26	.246	140	246	16	.960
1984—Minnesota	Amer.	SS-2B-3B	88	197	25	58	11	5	3	23	.294	77	134	4	.981
1985—Minnesota	Amer.	S-2-3-1	70	135	24	37	6	4	1	14	.274	55	100	7	.957
1986—Minnesota	Amer.	2B-SS-3B	48	74	15	19	3	0	4	11	.257	12	20	2	.941
1986—Toledo b	Int.	2B-3B-SS	49	198	22	53	6	1	3	19	.268	79	112	9	.955
1987—Rochester	Int.	2-S-3-O	70	272	50	87	17	1	15	43	.320	42	84	6	.955
1987—Baltimore c	Amer.	3-2-0-S	26	79	7	16	3	1	1	6	.203	19	42	0	1.000
1988—Cleveland d	Amer.	SS-3B-2B	69	223	30	57	14	2	2	21	.256	95	162	17	.938
1989—Tucson	P. C.	SS-3B	92	331	40	106	19	4	5	58	.320	88	212	19	.940
1989—Houston e	Nat.	3B-2B	7	7	1	1	1	0	0	0	.143	0	1	0	1.000
National League Totals—2 Years			17	26	5	8	1	0	0	1	.308	4	15	3	.864
American League Totals—8 Years			547	1560	185	406	64	22	20	145	.260	663	1053	67	.962
Major League Totals—10 Years			564	1586	190	414	65	22	20	146	.261	667	1068	70	.961

Signed as free agent by Kansas City Royals' organization, July 17, 1970.
†On military list, September 30, 1971 through March 3, 1972.
‡On temporary inactive list, July 4 to July 25, 1974.
§On disabled list, June 19 to June 30, 1975.
xTraded to Los Angeles Dodgers' organization for Catcher Steve Patchin, November 2, 1976.
yOn temporary inactive list, April 12 to April 22, 1977.
zOn disabled list, May 12 to June 26 and July 17 to September 10, 1978.
aTraded to Minnesota Twins' organization for Infielder Wayne Caughey, March 26, 1980.
bReleased, March 30, 1987; signed by Baltimore Orioles' organization, April 6, 1987.
cReleased, December 21, 1987; signed by Colorado Springs (Cleveland Indians' organization), December 28, 1987.
dGranted free agency, November 4, 1988; signed by Houston Astros' organization, February 7, 1989.
eGranted free agency, October 15, 1989; invited to Texas Rangers' spring training.

GARY ANTHONY WAYNE

Born November 30, 1962, at Dearborn, Mich.
Height, 6.03. Weight, 192.
Throws and bats lefthanded.
Attended University of Michigan, Ann Arbor, Mich.

Major League saves: 1989 (1).
Led Florida State League in saves with 25 in 1986.

Year	Club	League	G.	IP.	W.	L.	Pct.	H.	R.	ER.	SO.	BB.	ERA.
1984—West Palm Beach	Florida St.	13	74⅓	3	5	.375	70	38	32	46	49	3.87
1985—Jacksonville	Southern	21	102	3	12	.200	108	67	60	62	70	5.29
1985—West Palm Beach	Florida St.	8	30⅔	2	2	.500	37	23	19	18	22	5.58
1986—West Palm Beach	Florida St.	47	61⅓	2	5	.286	48	16	11	55	25	1.61
1987—Jacksonville	Southern	56	80⅓	5	1	.833	56	23	21	78	35	2.35
1988—Indianapolis†‡	Am. Assoc.	8	7⅓	0	0	.000	9	5	5	6	3	6.14
1989—Minnesota	American	60	71	3	4	.429	55	28	26	41	36	3.30
Major League Totals—1 Year		60	71	3	4	.429	55	28	26	41	36	3.30

Selected by Oakland A's organization in 23rd round of free-agent draft, June 6, 1983.
Selected by Montreal Expos' organization in 4th round of free-agent draft, June 4, 1984.
†On disabled list, April 7 to August 24, 1988.
‡Drafted by Minnesota Twins, December 5, 1988.

JAMES FRANCIS WEAVER
(Jim)

Born October 10, 1959, at Kingston, N.Y.
Height, 6.04. Weight, 200.
Throws and bats lefthanded.
Attended Manatee Junior College, Bradenton, Fla., and
Florida State University, Tallahassee, Fla.

Major League stolen bases: 1987 (1), 1989 (1). Total—2.
Led California League in intentional bases on balls received with 11 in 1982.
Named outfielder on THE SPORTING NEWS College Baseball All-America Team, 1980.
Tied for Southern League lead in double plays by outfielders with 4 in 1983.
Led International League outfielders in double plays with 6 in 1985.

Year	Club	League	Pos.	G.	AB.	R.	H.	2B.	3B.	HR.	RBI.	B.A.	PO.	A.	E.	F.A.
1980—Orlando	South.		OF	58	208	19	44	9	0	0	15	.212	121	3	3	.976
1981—Orlando	South.		OF	17	57	6	12	2	0	1	9	.211	21	1	2	.917
1981—Visalia	Calif.		OF	81	300	53	85	12	5	7	44	.283	110	7	4	.967
1982—Visalia	Calif.		OF	125	454	68	130	21	4	15	86	.286	261	6	9	.967
1983—Orlando	South.		OF	138	497	85	123	25	2	15	84	.247	259	20	9	.969
1984—Orlando	South.		OF	24	81	13	21	3	2	3	16	.259	38	4	0	1.000
1984—Toledo†	Int.		OF	111	409	49	94	12	5	15	64	.230	114	3	10	.921
1985—Detroit	Amer.		OF	12	7	2	1	1	0	0	0	.143	1	0	0	1.000
1985—Toledo‡-Maine	Int.		OF	91	331	54	73	10	6	12	46	.221	135	●13	7	.955
1986—Maine§x	Int.		OF-1B	100	293	42	70	11	2	11	28	.239	155	6	5	.970
1987—Calgary	P. C.		OF	124	472	95	132	25	7	17	91	.280	218	6	4	.982
1987—Seattle y	Amer.		OF	7	4	2	0	0	0	0	0	.000	4	1	0	1.000
1988—Tucson z	P. C.		OF	130	423	77	115	22	●10	8	73	.272	225	8	5	.979
1989—Vanc. a-Phoe.	P. C.		OF	115	388	44	84	19	6	8	35	.216	211	9	6	.973
1989—San Francisco	Nat.		OF	12	20	2	4	3	0	0	2	.200	7	0	0	1.000
American League Totals—2 Years				19	11	4	1	1	0	0	0	.091	5	1	0	1.000
National League Totals—1 Year				12	20	2	4	3	0	0	2	.200	7	0	0	1.000
Major League Totals—3 Years				31	31	6	5	4	0	0	2	.161	12	1	0	1.000

Selected by Montreal Expos' organization in 2nd round of free-agent draft, January 9, 1979.
Selected by Minnesota Twins' organization in 2nd round of free-agent draft, June 3, 1980.
†Drafted by Detroit Tigers, December 3, 1984; returned, May 22, 1985.
‡Traded with Pitcher Curt Wardle, Infielder Jay Bell and a player to be named later to Cleveland Indians for Pitcher Bert Blyleven, August 1, 1985; Cleveland organization acquired Pitcher Rich Yett to complete deal, September 17, 1985.
§On disabled list, April 11 to April 21, 1986.
xReleased, October 29, 1986; signed by Calgary (Seattle Mariners' organization), January 15, 1987.
yReleased, November 18, 1987; signed by Tucson (Houston Astros' organization), January 29, 1988.
zGranted free agency, October 15, 1988; signed by Vancouver (Chicago White Sox' organization), December 9, 1988.
aTraded to Phoenix (San Francisco Giants' organization) for Outfielder George Wright, August 16, 1989.

LEONARD IRELL WEBSTER
(Lenny)

Born February 10, 1965, at New Orleans, La.
Height, 5.09. Weight, 185.
Throws and bats righthanded.
Attended Grambling State University, Grambling, La.

Led Midwest League in game-winning RBIs with 14 in 1988.
Named Midwest League Most Valuable Player, 1988.

Year	Club	League	Pos.	G.	AB.	R.	H.	2B.	3B.	HR.	RBI.	B.A.	PO.	A.	E.	F.A.
1986—Kenosha	Midw.		C	22	65	2	10	2	0	0	8	.154	87	9	0	1.000
1986—Elizabethton	Appal.		C	48	152	29	35	4	0	3	14	.230	88	11	3	.971
1987—Kenosha	Midw.		C	52	140	17	35	7	0	3	17	.250	228	29	5	.981
1988—Kenosha	Midw.		C	129	465	82	134	23	2	11	87	.288	606	96	14	.980
1989—Visalia	Calif.		C	63	231	36	62	7	0	5	39	.268	352	57	4	.990
1989—Orlando	South.		C	59	191	29	45	7	0	2	17	.236	293	46	4	.988
1989—Minnesota	Amer.		C	14	20	3	6	2	0	0	1	.300	32	0	0	1.000
Major League Totals—1 Year				14	20	3	6	2	0	0	1	.300	32	0	0	1.000

Selected by Minnesota Twins' organization in 16th round of free-agent draft, June 7, 1982.
Selected by Minnesota Twins' organization in 21st round of free-agent draft, June 3, 1985.

MITCHELL DEAN WEBSTER
(Mitch)

Born May 16, 1959, at Larned, Kan.
Height, 6.01. Weight, 185.
Throws left and bats left and righthanded.

Shares major league record for fewest double plays by outfielder, season, 150 or more games (0), 1987.
Major League stolen bases: 1985 (15), 1986 (36), 1987 (33), 1988 (22), 1989 (14). Total—120.
Led International League outfielders in double plays with 5 and total chances with 385 in 1982.

Year	Club	League	Pos.	G.	AB.	R.	H.	2B.	3B.	HR.	RBI.	B.A.	PO.	A.	E.	F.A.
1977—Lethbridge	Pion		OF	55	168	45	59	4	0	0	31	.351	81	3	8	.913
1978—Clinton	Midw.		OF	45	157	18	38	3	1	0	9	.242	92	6	7	.933
1978—Lethbridge	Pion.		OF	55	182	58	58	5	1	0	18	.319	77	3	0	*1.000
1979—Clinton†	Midw.		OF	123	473	95	*154	17	7	2	40	*.326	*272	10	10	.966
1980—Syracuse	Int.		OF	49	161	23	35	4	2	1	12	.217	112	3	5	.958
1980—Kinston	Carol.		OF	65	258	43	76	7	3	0	28	.295	129	8	5	.965
1981—Knoxville	South.		OF	140	554	89	163	26	6	1	42	.294	317	7	10	.970
1982—Syracuse	Int.		OF	137	513	95	144	21	7	13	68	.281	*367	16	2	*.995
1983—Syracuse	Int.		OF-1B	135	462	77	120	26	8	9	45	.260	266	16	10	.966
1983—Toronto	Amer.		OF	11	11	2	2	0	0	0	0	.182	5	0	0	1.000
1984—Toronto	Amer.		OF-1B	26	22	9	5	2	1	0	4	.227	16	0	2	.889
1984—Syracuse	Int.		OF	95	360	60	108	22	5	3	25	.300	239	7	7	.972

Year Club	League	Pos.	G.	AB.	R.	H.	2B.	3B.	HR.	RBI.	B.A.	PO.	A.	E.	F.A.
1985—Toronto	Amer.	OF	4	1	0	0	0	0	0	0	.000	0	0	0	.000
1985—Syracuse‡	Int.	OF	47	189	32	52	5	3	3	23	.275	83	10	1	.989
1985—Montreal	Nat.	OF	74	212	32	58	8	2	11	30	.274	133	3	1	.993
1986—Montreal	Nat.	OF	151	576	89	167	31	★13	8	49	.290	325	12	8	.977
1987—Montreal	Nat.	OF	156	588	101	165	30	8	15	63	.281	266	8	5	.982
1988—Mont.§-Chi.	Nat.	OF	151	523	69	136	16	8	6	39	.260	322	3	6	.982
1989—Chicago xy	Nat.	OF	98	272	40	70	12	4	3	19	.257	161	3	6	.965
American League Totals—3 Years			41	34	11	7	2	1	0	4	.206	21	0	2	.913
National League Totals—5 Years			630	2171	331	596	97	35	43	200	.275	1207	29	26	.979
Major League Totals—7 Years			671	2205	342	603	99	36	43	204	.273	1228	29	28	.978

Selected by Los Angeles Dodgers' organization in 23rd round of free-agent draft, June 7, 1977.

†Drafted by Syracuse (Toronto Blue Jays' organization), December 4, 1979.

‡Traded to Montreal Expos for a player to be named later, June 22, 1985; Toronto Blue Jays' organization acquired Pitcher Cliff Young to complete deal, September 10, 1985.

§Traded to Chicago Cubs for Outfielder Dave Martinez, July 14, 1988.

xOn disabled list, May 14 to May 29, 1989.

yTraded to Cleveland Indians for Outfielder Dave Clark, November 20, 1989.

CHAMPIONSHIP SERIES RECORD

Year Club	League	Pos.	G.	AB.	R.	H.	2B.	3B.	HR.	RBI.	B.A.	PO.	A.	E.	F.A.
1989—Chicago	Nat.	PH-OF	3	3	0	1	0	0	0	0	.333	0	0	0	.000

WILLIAM EDWARD WEGMAN
(Bill)

Born December 19, 1962, at Cincinnati, O.
Height, 6.05. Weight, 230.
Throws and bats righthanded.

Led Pacific Coast League in home runs allowed with 21 in 1985.
Led California League in balks with 5 and tied for lead in complete games with 15 and shutouts with 4 in 1983.

Year Club	League	G.	IP.	W.	L.	Pct.	H.	R.	ER.	SO.	BB.	ERA.
1981—Butte	Pioneer	14	82	6	5	.545	94	51	38	47	44	4.17
1982—Beloit	Midwest	25	179⅔	12	6	.667	176	77	56	129	38	2.81
1983—Stockton	California	24	186⅔	★16	5	.762	149	33	27	135	45	★1.30
1984—El Paso	Texas	10	64	4	5	.444	62	25	19	42	15	2.67
1984—Vancouver†	P. Coast	6	27⅔	0	3	.000	30	11	6	16	8	1.95
1985—Vancouver	P. Coast	28	188	10	11	.476	187	93	84	113	52	4.02
1985—Milwaukee	American	3	17⅔	2	0	1.000	17	8	7	6	3	3.57
1986—Milwaukee‡	American	35	198⅓	5	12	.294	217	120	113	82	43	5.13
1987—Milwaukee§	American	34	225	12	11	.522	229	113	106	102	53	4.24
1988—Milwaukee xy	American	32	199	13	13	.500	207	104	91	84	50	4.12
1989—Milwaukee z	American	11	51	2	6	.250	69	44	38	27	21	6.71
Major League Totals—5 Years		115	691	34	42	.447	739	389	355	301	170	4.62

Selected by Milwaukee Brewers' organization in 5th round of free-agent draft, June 8, 1981.

†On disabled list, June 18 to August 11, 1984.

‡Appeared in two games as a pinch-runner.

§On disabled list, August 7 to August 22, 1987.

xAppeared in one game as a pinch-runner.

yOn disabled list, May 21 to June 7, 1988.

zOn disabled list, June 1, 1989 through remainder of season.

WALTER WILLIAM WEISS JR.
(Walt)

Born November 28, 1963, at Tuxedo, N. Y.
Height, 6.00. Weight, 175.
Throws right and bats left and righthanded.
Attended University of North Carolina, Chapel Hill, N. C.

Major League stolen bases: 1987 (1), 1988 (4), 1989 (6). Total—11.
Named American League Rookie Player of the Year by THE SPORTING NEWS, 1988.
Named American League Rookie of the Year by Baseball Writers' Association of America, 1988.

Year Club	League	Pos.	G.	AB.	R.	H.	2B.	3B.	HR.	RBI.	B.A.	PO.	A.	E.	F.A.
1985—Pocatello	Pion.	SS	40	158	19	49	9	3	0	21	.310	51	126	11	.941
1985—Modesto	Calif.	SS	30	122	17	24	4	1	0	7	.197	36	97	7	.950
1986—Madison	Midw.	SS	84	322	50	97	15	5	2	54	.301	143	251	20	.952
1986—Huntsville	South.	SS	46	160	19	40	2	1	0	13	.250	72	142	11	.951
1987—Huntsville	South.	SS	91	337	43	96	16	2	1	32	.285	152	259	17	.960
1987—Oakland	Amer.	SS	16	26	3	12	4	0	0	1	.462	8	30	1	.974
1987—Tacoma	P. C.	SS	46	179	35	47	4	3	0	17	.263	76	140	11	.952
1988—Oakland	Amer.	SS	147	452	44	113	17	3	3	39	.250	254	431	15	.979
1989—Oakland†	Amer.	SS	84	236	30	55	11	0	3	21	.233	106	195	15	.953
1989—Tacoma	P. C.	SS	2	9	1	1	1	0	0	1	.111	0	3	1	.750
1989—Modesto	Calif.	SS	5	8	1	3	0	0	0	1	.375	6	9	0	1.000
Major League Totals—3 Years			247	714	77	180	32	3	6	61	.252	368	656	31	.971

Selected by Baltimore Orioles' organization in 10th round of free-agent draft, June 7, 1982.

Selected by Oakland A's organization in 1st round (11th player selected) of free-agent draft, June 3, 1985.

†On disabled list, May 18 to July 31, 1989; included rehabilitation disability assignment to Tacoma, July 18 to July 25, 1989; and Modesto, July 26 to July 31, 1989.

CHAMPIONSHIP SERIES RECORD

Year Club	League	Pos.	G.	AB.	R.	H.	2B.	3B.	HR.	RBI.	B.A.	PO.	A.	E.	F.A.
1988—Oakland	Amer.	SS	4	15	2	5	2	0	0	2	.333	7	10	0	1.000
1989—Oakland	Amer.	SS-PR	4	9	2	1	1	0	0	0	.111	5	9	0	1.000
Championship Series Totals—2 Years			8	24	4	6	3	0	0	2	.250	12	19	0	1.000

WORLD SERIES RECORD

Year Club	League	Pos.	G.	AB.	R.	H.	2B.	3B.	HR.	RBI.	B.A.	PO.	A.	E.	F.A.
1988—Oakland	Amer.	SS	5	16	1	1	0	0	0	0	.063	5	11	1	.941
1989—Oakland	Amer.	SS	4	15	3	2	0	0	1	1	.133	7	8	0	1.000
World Series Totals—2 Years			9	31	4	3	0	0	1	1	.097	12	19	1	.969

ROBERT LYNN WELCH
(Bob)

Born November 3, 1956, at Detroit, Mich.
Height, 6.03. Weight, 195.
Throws and bats righthanded.
Attended Eastern Michigan University, Ypsilanti, Mich.

Major League saves: 1978 (3), 1979 (5). Total—8.
Tied for National League lead in shutouts with 4 in 1987.

Year	Club	League	G.	IP.	W.	L.	Pct.	H.	R.	ER.	SO.	BB.	ERA.
1977—San Antonio	Texas		14	71	4	5	.444	94	44	35	56	17	4.44
1978—Albuquerque	P. Coast		11	69	5	1	.833	72	33	29	53	19	3.78
1978—Los Angeles	National		23	111	7	4	.636	92	28	25	66	26	2.03
1979—Los Angeles	National		25	81	5	6	.455	82	42	36	64	32	4.00
1980—Los Angeles	National		32	214	14	9	.609	190	85	78	141	79	3.28
1981—Los Angeles	National		23	141	9	5	.643	141	56	54	88	41	3.45
1982—Los Angeles†	National		36	235⅔	16	11	.593	199	94	88	176	81	3.36
1983—Los Angeles	National		31	204	15	12	.556	164	73	60	156	72	2.65
1984—Los Angeles	National		31	178⅔	13	13	.500	191	86	75	126	58	3.78
1985—Los Angeles‡	National		23	167⅓	14	4	.778	141	49	43	96	35	2.31
1985—Vero Beach	Florida St.		3	17	0	0	.000	15	4	4	9	1	2.12
1986—Los Angeles	National		33	235⅔	7	13	.350	227	95	86	183	55	3.28
1987—Los Angeles§	National		35	251⅔	15	9	.625	204	94	90	196	86	3.22
1988—Oakland	American		36	244⅔	17	9	.654	237	107	99	158	81	3.64
1989—Oakland x	American		33	209⅔	17	8	.680	191	82	70	137	78	3.00
National League Totals—10 Years			292	1820	115	86	.572	1631	702	635	1292	565	3.14
American League Totals—2 Years			69	454⅓	34	17	.667	428	189	169	295	159	3.35
Major League Totals—12 Years			361	2274⅓	149	103	.591	2059	891	804	1587	724	3.18

Selected by Chicago Cubs' organization in 14th round of free-agent draft, June 5, 1974.
Selected by Los Angeles Dodgers' organization in 1st round (20th player selected) of free-agent draft, June 7, 1977.
†Appeared in one game as outfielder with no chances.
‡On disabled list, April 29 to June 5, 1985; included rehabilitation disability assignment to Vero Beach, May 21 to June 5, 1985.
§As part of an eight-player, three-team deal, New York Mets traded Pitcher Jesse Orosco to Oakland Athletics, December 11, 1987. Oakland then traded Orosco along with Shortstop Alfredo Griffin and Pitcher Jay Howell to Los Angeles Dodgers for Pitchers Bob Welch, Matt Young and Jack Savage. Oakland then traded Savage along with Pitchers Wally Whitehurst and Kevin Tapani to New York.
xOn disabled list, June 13 to June 30, 1989.

DIVISION SERIES RECORD

Year	Club	League	G.	IP.	W.	L.	Pct.	H.	R.	ER.	SO.	BB.	ERA.
1981—Los Angeles	National		1	1	0	0	.000	0	0	0	1	1	0.00

CHAMPIONSHIP SERIES RECORD

Shares Championship Series records for most series pitched (6); most bases on balls allowed, inning (4), October 12, 1985, first inning.

Year	Club	League	G.	IP.	W.	L.	Pct.	H.	R.	ER.	SO.	BB.	ERA.
1978—Los Angeles	National		1	4⅓	0	0	1.000	2	1	1	5	0	2.08
1981—Los Angeles	National		3	1⅔	0	0	.000	2	1	1	2	5	5.40
1983—Los Angeles	National		1	1⅓	0	1	.000	0	2	1	0	2	6.75
1985—Los Angeles	National		1	2⅔	0	1	.000	5	4	2	2	6	6.75
1988—Oakland	American		1	1⅔	0	0	.000	6	5	5	0	2	27.00
1989—Oakland	American		1	5⅔	1	0	1.000	8	2	2	4	1	3.18
Championship Series Totals—6 Years			8	17⅓	2	2	.500	23	15	12	13	11	6.23

WORLD SERIES RECORD

Year	Club	League	G.	IP.	W.	L.	Pct.	H.	R.	ER.	SO.	BB.	ERA.
1978—Los Angeles	National		3	4⅓	0	1	.000	4	3	3	6	2	6.23
1981—Los Angeles	National		1	0	0	0	.000	3	2	2	0	1	....
1988—Oakland	American		1	5	0	0	.000	6	1	1	8	3	1.80
World Series Totals—3 Years			5	9⅓	0	1	.000	13	6	6	14	6	5.79

Eligible for 1989 World Series with Oakland Athletics; did not play.

ALL-STAR GAME RECORD

Year	League	IP.	W.	L.	Pct.	H.	R.	ER.	SO.	BB.	ERA.
1980—National		3	0	0	.000	5	2	2	4	1	6.00

BRAD EUGENE WELLMAN

Born August 17, 1959, at Lodi, Calif.
Height, 6.00. Weight, 170.
Throws and bats righthanded.
Attended Chabot College, Hayward, Calif.
Brother-in-law of Tom Candiotti, pitcher with Cleveland Indians.

Major League stolen bases: 1983 (5), 1984 (10), 1985 (5), 1988 (1), 1989 (5). Total—26.

Year Club	League	Pos.	G.	AB.	R.	H.	2B.	3B.	HR.	RBI.	B.A.	PO.	A.	E.	F.A.
1979—Sarasota Royals...	Gulf C.	SS	48	170	24	44	6	0	2	24	.259	79	159	20	.922
1980—Fort Myers............	Fla. St.	2B-SS	105	390	67	130	15	7	1	39	.333	175	301	27	.946
1981—Jacksonville.........	South	2B-SS	135	498	72	131	25	2	6	47	.263	286	368	25	.963
1982—Omaha†.................	A. A.	2B	6	24	5	7	3	0	1	3	.292	14	23	0	1.000
1982—Phoenix.................	P. C.	2B-3B	102	339	64	110	19	7	4	42	.324	201	257	14	.970
1982—San Francisco......	Nat.	2B	6	4	1	1	0	0	0	0	.250	0	1	0	1.000
1983—Phoenix.................	P. C.	2B-SS	45	167	32	52	6	4	2	28	.311	79	123	4	.981
1983—San Francisco......	Nat.	2B-SS	82	182	15	39	3	0	1	16	.214	94	167	9	.967
1984—Phoenix.................	P. C.	2B	43	159	26	47	8	1	0	11	.296	91	123	6	.973
1984—San Francisco......	Nat.	2B-SS-3B	93	265	23	60	9	1	2	25	.226	151	258	11	.974
1985—San Francisco‡....	Nat.	2B-3B-SS	71	174	16	41	11	1	0	16	.236	66	107	9	.951
1986—San Francisco......	Nat.	SS-3B-2B	12	13	0	2	0	0	0	1	.154	3	10	0	1.000
1986—Phoenix§................	P. C.	2B-SS-3B	79	262	31	74	17	1	2	30	.282	145	221	13	.966
1987—Albuquerque........	P. C.	S-2-3-1-C	88	317	50	97	11	5	2	38	.306	123	253	18	.954
1987—Los Angeles xy....	Nat.	3B-SS-2B	3	4	1	1	0	0	0	1	.250	3	3	0	1.000
1988—Kansas City..........	Amer.	2B-SS-3B	71	107	11	29	3	0	1	6	.271	67	101	6	.966
1989—Kansas City z.......	Amer.	2B-SS-3B	103	178	30	41	4	0	2	12	.230	104	184	2	.993
National League Totals—6 Years............			267	642	56	144	23	2	3	59	.224	317	546	29	.967
American League Totals—2 Years............			174	285	41	70	7	0	3	18	.246	171	285	8	.983
Major League Totals—8 Years................			441	927	97	214	30	2	6	77	.231	488	831	37	.973

Signed as free agent by Kansas City Royals' organization, August 27, 1978.

†Traded to San Francisco Giants' organization, April 19, 1982, completing deal in which San Francisco traded Pitchers Vida Blue and Bob Tufts to Kansas City Royals for Pitchers Atlee Hammaker, Craig Chamberlain and Renie Martin and a player to be named later, March 30, 1982.

‡On disabled list, May 30 to June 28, 1985.

§Granted free agency, October 15, 1986; signed by Albuquerque (Los Angeles Dodgers' organization), December 5, 1986.

xOn disabled list, August 3 to September 2, 1987; included rehabilitation disability assignment to Albuquerque, August 18 to September 2, 1987.

yGranted free agency, October 15, 1987; signed by Kansas City Royals, October 26, 1987.

zOn disabled list, August 18 to September 2, 1989.

DAVID LEE WELLS

Born May 20, 1963, at Torrance, Calif.
Height, 6.04. Weight, 225.
Throws and bats lefthanded.

Major League saves: 1987 (1), 1988 (4), 1989 (2). Total—7.

Year Club	League	G.	IP.	W.	L.	Pct.	H.	R.	ER.	SO.	BB.	ERA.
1982—Medicine Hat..................	Pioneer	12	64⅓	4	3	.571	71	42	37	53	32	5.18
1983—Kinston............................	Carolina	25	157	6	5	.545	141	81	65	115	71	3.73
1984—Kinston............................	Carolina	7	42	1	6	.143	51	29	22	44	19	4.71
1984—Knoxville†......................	Southern	8	59	3	2	.600	58	22	17	34	17	2.59
1985—Syracuse†.......................	Int'national					(Did not play)						
1986—Florence.........................	S. Atlantic	4	12⅔	0	0	.000	7	6	5	14	9	3.55
1986—Ventura..........................	California	5	19	2	1	.667	13	5	4	26	4	1.89
1986—Knoxville§......................	Southern	10	40	1	3	.250	42	24	18	32	18	4.05
1986—Syracuse	Int'national	3	3⅔	0	1	.000	6	4	4	2	1	9.82
1987—Syracuse	Int'national	43	109⅓	4	6	.400	102	49	47	106	32	3.87
1987—Toronto	American	18	29⅓	4	3	.571	37	14	13	32	12	3.99
1988—Toronto	American	41	64⅓	3	5	.375	65	36	33	56	31	4.62
1988—Syracuse	Int'national	6	5⅔	0	0	.000	7	1	0	8	2	0.00
1989—Toronto	American	54	86⅓	7	4	.636	66	25	23	78	28	2.40
Major League Totals—3 Years.............		113	180	14	12	.538	168	75	69	166	71	3.45

Selected by Toronto Blue Jays' organization in 2nd round of free-agent draft, June 7, 1982.

†On disabled list, June 28, 1984, through remainder of season.

‡On disabled list, April 10, 1985, through entire season.

§On disabled list, July 7 to August 20, 1986.

CHAMPIONSHIP SERIES RECORD

Year Club	League	G.	IP.	W.	L.	Pct.	H.	R.	ER.	SO.	BB.	ERA.
1989—Toronto.............................	American	1	1	0	0	.000	0	1	0	1	2	0.00

TERRY WELLS

Born September 10, 1963, at Kankakee, Ill.
Height, 6.03. Weight, 205.
Throws and bats lefthanded.
Attended University of Illinois, Champaign, Ill.

Led South Atlantic League in home runs allowed with 20 in 1986.

Year—Club	League	G.	IP.	W.	L.	Pct.	H.	R.	ER.	SO.	BB.	ERA.
1985—Auburn	NYP	13	62⅓	4	4	.500	35	19	19	46	51	2.74
1986—Asheville	S. Atlantic	26	136⅔	12	6	.667	125	87	69	125	83	4.54
1987—Osceola	Florida St.	26	130⅓	7	9	.438	118	74	69	93	82	4.76
1988—Columbus	Southern	37	108⅓	5	5	.500	92	58	55	109	85	4.57
1989—Columbus	Southern	23	46⅔	2	3	.400	44	25	24	38	31	4.63
1989—Tucson	P. Coast	26	48⅓	0	5	.000	57	32	31	47	36	5.77

Selected by Cleveland Indians' organization in 11th round of free-agent draft, June 8, 1981.
Selected by Chicago White Sox' organization in 8th round of free-agent draft, June 4, 1984.
Selected by Houston Astros' organization in 8th round of free-agent draft, June 3, 1985.

DAVID LEE WEST
(Dave)

Born September 1, 1964, at Memphis, Tenn.
Height, 6.06. Weight, 220.
Throws and bats lefthanded.

Won 3-0 no-hit victory against Spartanburg, August 14, 1985.
Led New York-Pennsylvania League in wild pitches with 16 in 1984.
Tied for Texas League lead in shutouts with 2 in 1987.

Year—Club	League	G.	IP.	W.	L.	Pct.	H.	R.	ER.	SO.	BB.	ERA.
1983—Sarasota Mets	Gulf Coast	12	53⅔	2	4	.333	41	28	17	56	52	2.85
1984—Columbia	S. Atlantic	12	60⅔	3	5	.375	41	47	42	60	68	6.23
1984—Little Falls	NYP	13	62	6	4	.600	43	35	23	79	62	3.34
1985—Columbia	S. Atlantic	26	150	10	9	.526	105	97	76	194	*111	4.56
1986—Lynchburg	Carolina	13	75	1	6	.143	76	50	43	70	53	5.16
1986—Columbia	S. Atlantic	13	92⅔	10	3	.769	74	41	30	101	56	2.91
1987—Jackson	Texas	25	166⅔	10	7	.588	152	67	52	*186	*81	2.81
1988—Tidewater	Int'national	23	160⅓	12	4	*.750	106	42	32	143	*97	*1.80
1988—New York	National	2	6	1	0	1.000	6	2	2	3	3	3.00
1989—Tidewater	Int'national	12	87⅓	7	4	.636	60	31	23	69	29	2.37
1989—New York†	National	11	24⅓	0	2	.000	25	20	20	19	14	7.40
1989—Minnesota	American	10	39⅓	3	2	.600	48	29	28	31	19	6.41
National League Totals—2 Years		13	30⅓	1	2	.333	31	22	22	22	17	6.53
American League Totals—1 Year		10	39⅓	3	2	.600	48	29	28	31	19	6.41
Major League Totals—2 Years		23	69⅔	4	4	.500	79	51	50	53	36	6.46

Selected by New York Mets' organization in 4th round of free-agent draft, June 6, 1983.
†Traded with Pitcher Rick Aguilera and three players to be named later to Minnesota Twins for Pitcher Frank Viola, July 31, 1989; Portland (Minnesota Twins' organization) acquired Pitchers Kevin Tapani and Tim Drummond on August 1, 1989, and Minnesota acquired Pitcher Jack Savage to complete deal, October 16, 1989.

MICHAEL LEE WESTON
(Mickey)

Born March 26, 1961, at Flint, Mich.
Height. 6.01. Weight, 187.
Throws and bats righthanded.
Attended Eastern Michigan University, Ypsilanti, Mich.

Major League saves: 1989 (1).

Year—Club	League	G.	IP.	W.	L.	Pct.	H.	R.	ER.	SO.	BB.	ERA.
1982—Little Falls	NYP	17	92⅓	7	6	.538	105	63	52	67	22	5.07
1983—Columbia	S. Atlantic	37	74⅔	2	2	.500	87	48	36	46	22	4.34
1984—Columbia	S. Atlantic	32	63⅔	6	5	.545	58	27	13	40	27	1.84
1985—Lynchburg	Carolina	49	100⅓	6	5	.545	81	29	24	62	22	2.15
1986—Jackson†	Texas	34	70⅔	4	4	.500	73	40	34	36	27	4.33
1987—Jackson	Texas	58	82	8	4	.667	96	39	31	50	18	3.40
1988—Jackson	Texas	30	125⅓	8	5	.615	127	50	31	61	20	*2.23
1988—Tidewater‡	Int'national	4	29⅔	2	1	.667	21	6	5	16	5	1.52
1989—Rochester	Int'national	23	112	8	3	.727	103	30	26	51	19	2.09
1989—Baltimore§	American	7	13	1	0	1.000	18	8	8	7	2	5.54
Major League Totals—1 Year		7	13	1	0	1.000	18	8	8	7	2	5.54

Selected by New York Mets' organization in 12th round of free-agent draft, June 7, 1982.
†On disabled list, April 8 to April 18 and May 23 to June 25, 1986.
‡Granted free agency, October 15, 1988; signed by Rochester (Baltimore Orioles' organization.), November 28, 1988.

§On disabled list, June 23 to August 22, 1989; included rehabilitation disability assignment to Rochester, August 2 to August 21, 1989.

JEFFREY BARRETT WETHERBY
(Jeff)

Born October 18, 1963, at Granada Hills, Calif.
Height, 6.02. Weight, 195.
Throws and bats lefthanded.
Attended College of the Canyons, Valencia, Calif. and
University of Southern California, Los Angeles, Calif.

Major League stolen bases: 1989 (1).

Year	Club	League	Pos.	G.	AB.	R.	H.	2B.	3B.	HR.	RBI.	B.A.	PO.	A.	E.	F.A.
1985—Bradenton Braves	Gulf C.	1B-OF	26	88	19	32	7	0	3	18	.364	95	7	3	.971
1985—Durham	Carol.	OF	6	22	1	3	0	0	0	0	.136	7	0	0	1.000
1986—Sumter	S. Atl	OF-1B	62	212	46	63	13	3	4	34	.297	99	4	6	.945
1986—Durham	Carol.	OF	72	261	62	78	17	1	9	57	.299	139	9	4	.974
1987—Greenville	South.	OF	140	488	67	148	31	4	12	78	.303	240	10	6	.977
1988—Richmond	Int.	OF-1B	137	499	●69	134	25	4	6	61	.269	394	18	11	.974
1989—Richmond	Int.	OF-1B	50	157	19	42	9	0	1	16	.268	77	5	1	.988
1989—Atlanta	Nat.	OF	52	48	5	10	2	1	1	7	.208	8	0	0	1.000
Major League Totals—1 Year			52	48	5	10	2	1	1	7	.208	8	0	0	1.000

Selected by Philadelphia Phillies' organization in 10th round of free-agent draft, January 17, 1984.
Selected by Atlanta Braves' organization in 21st round of free-agent draft, June 3, 1985.

JOHN KARL WETTELAND

Born August 21, 1966, at San Mateo, Calif.
Height, 6.02. Weight, 195.
Throws and bats righthanded.
Attended College of San Mateo, San Mateo, Calif.

Major League saves: 1989 (1).
Led Texas League in wild pitches with 22 in 1988.
Tied for Florida State League lead in home runs allowed with 11 and wild pitches with 17 in 1987.

Year	Club	League	G.	IP.	W.	L.	Pct.	H.	R.	ER.	SO.	BB.	ERA.
1985—Great Falls	Pioneer	11	20⅔	1	1	.500	17	10	9	23	15	3.92
1986—Bakersfield	California	15	67	0	7	.000	71	50	43	38	46	5.78
1986—Great Falls	Pioneer	12	69½	4	3	.571	70	51	42	59	40	5.45
1987—Vero Beach†	Florida St.	27	175⅔	12	7	.632	150	81	61	144	92	3.13
1988—San Antonio	Texas	25	162⅓	10	8	.556	141	74	70	140	●77	3.88
1989—Albuquerque	P. Coast	10	69	5	3	.625	61	28	28	73	20	3.65
1989—Los Angeles	National	31	102⅔	5	8	.385	81	46	43	96	34	3.77
Major League Totals—1 Year		31	102⅔	5	8	.385	81	46	43	96	34	3.77

Selected by New York Mets' organization in 12th round of free-agent draft, June 4, 1984.
Selected by Los Angeles Dodgers' organization in secondary phase of free-agent draft, January 9, 1985.
†Drafted by Detroit Tigers, December 7, 1987; returned, March 29, 1988.

LOUIS RODMAN WHITAKER
(Lou)

Born May 12, 1957, at Brooklyn, N.Y.
Height, 5.11. Weight, 160.
Throws right and bats lefthanded.

Major League stolen bases: 1977 (2), 1978 (7), 1979 (20), 1980 (8), 1981 (5), 1982 (11), 1983 (17), 1984 (6), 1985 (6), 1986 (13), 1987 (13), 1988 (2), 1989 (6). Total—116.
Led American League second basemen in total chances with 811 and double plays with 120 in 1982.
Led Florida State League second basemen in double plays with 30 in 1976.
Named second baseman on THE SPORTING NEWS American League All-Star Team, 1983 and 1984.
Named second baseman on THE SPORTING NEWS American League All-Star fielding team, 1983 through 1985.
Named second baseman on THE SPORTING NEWS American League Silver Slugger team, 1983 through 1985 and 1987.
Named American League Rookie of the Year by Baseball Writers' Association of America, 1978.
Named Florida State League Most Valuable Player, 1976.

Year	Club	League	Pos.	G.	AB.	R.	H.	2B.	3B.	HR.	RBI.	B.A.	PO.	A.	E.	F.A.
1975—Bristol	Appal.	3B-SS	42	114	17	27	6	1	1	17	.237	38	82	16	.882
1976—Lakeland	Fla. St.	3B	124	343	★70	129	12	5	1	62	.297	★99	★267	★30	★.924
1977—Montgomery†	South.	2B	107	396	★81	111	13	4	3	48	.280	208	285	15	.970
1977—Detroit	Amer.	2B	11	32	5	8	1	0	0	2	.250	17	18	0	1.000
1978—Detroit	Amer.	2B	139	484	71	138	12	7	3	58	.285	301	458	17	.978
1979—Detroit‡	Amer.	2B	127	423	75	121	14	8	3	42	.286	280	369	9	.986
1980—Detroit	Amer.	2B	145	477	68	111	19	1	1	45	.233	340	428	12	.985
1981—Detroit	Amer.	2B	●109	335	48	88	14	4	5	36	.263	227	★354	9	.985
1982—Detroit	Amer.	2B	152	560	76	160	22	8	15	65	.286	331	★470	10	★.988
1983—Detroit	Amer.	2B	161	643	94	206	40	6	12	72	.320	299	447	13	.983
1984—Detroit	Amer.	2B	143	558	90	161	25	1	13	56	.289	290	405	15	.979
1985—Detroit	Amer.	2B	152	609	102	170	29	8	21	73	.279	314	414	11	.985
1986—Detroit	Amer.	2B	144	584	95	157	26	6	20	73	.269	276	421	11	.984
1987—Detroit	Amer.	2B	149	604	110	160	38	6	16	59	.265	275	416	17	.976
1988—Detroit	Amer.	2B	115	403	54	111	18	2	12	55	.275	218	284	8	.984
1989—Detroit	Amer.	2B	148	509	77	128	21	1	28	85	.251	★327	393	11	.985
Major League Totals—13 Years			1695	6221	965	1719	279	58	149	721	.276	3295	4877	143	.983

Selected by Detroit Tigers' organization in 5th round of free-agent draft, June 4, 1975.
†On disabled list, May 3 to May 14, 1977.
‡On disabled list, June 13 to June 28, 1979.

CHAMPIONSHIP SERIES RECORD

Shares Championship Series record for most bases on balls, series (7), 1987.

Year	Club	League	Pos.	G.	AB.	R.	H.	2B.	3B.	HR.	RBI.	B.A.	PO.	A.	E.	F.A.
1984—Detroit	Amer.	2B	3	14	3	2	0	0	0	0	.143	5	6	0	1.000
1987—Detroit	Amer.	2B	5	17	4	3	0	0	1	1	.176	11	14	0	1.000
Championship Series Totals—2 Years			8	31	7	5	0	0	1	1	.161	16	20	0	1.000

Year Club	League	Pos.	G.	AB.	R.	H.	2B.	3B.	HR.	RBI.	B.A.	PO.	A.	E.	F.A.
1984—Detroit...................	Amer.	2B	5	18	6	5	2	0	0	0	.278	15	18	0	1.000

ALL-STAR GAME RECORD

Year League	Pos.	AB.	R.	H.	2B.	3B.	HR.	RBI.	B.A.	PO.	A.	E.	F.A.
1983—American	PH-2B	1	1	1	0	1	0	2	1.000	1	0	0	1.000
1984—American	2B	3	0	2	1	0	0	0	.667	0	5	0	1.000
1985—American	2B	2	0	0	0	0	0	0	.000	1	1	0	1.000
1986—American	2B	2	1	1	0	0	1	2	.500	0	3	0	1.000
All-Star Game Totals—4 Years....................		8	2	4	1	1	1	4	.500	2	9	0	1.000

Named to American League All-Star Team for 1987 game; replaced due to injury by Harold Reynolds.

DEVON MARKES WHITE

First name pronounced De-VON.
Born December 29, 1962, at Kingston, Jamaica.
Height, 6.02. Weight, 178.
Throws right and bats left and righthanded.

Holds major league record for most strikeouts by switch-hitter, season (135), 1987.
Shares major league record for most stolen bases, inning (3), September 9, 1989, sixth inning.
Major League stolen bases: 1985 (3), 1986 (6), 1987 (32), 1988 (17), 1989 (44). Total—102.
Switch-hit home runs in one game, June 23, 1987.
Led American League outfielders in total chances with 449 in 1987.
Led Pacific Coast League in stolen bases with 42 in 1986.
Led Pacific Coast League outfielders in total chances with 339 in 1986.
Led California League outfielders in total chances with 351 in 1984.
Led Midwest League outfielders in total chances with 286 in 1983.
Named outfielder on THE SPORTING NEWS American League All-Star fielding team, 1988 and 1989.

Year Club	League	Pos.	G.	AB.	R.	H.	2B.	3B.	HR.	RBI.	B.A.	PO.	A.	E.	F.A.
1981—Idaho Falls...........	Pion.	OF-3B-1B	30	106	10	19	2	0	0	10	.179	33	10	3	.935
1982—Danville†	Midw.	OF	57	186	21	40	6	1	1	11	.215	89	3	8	.920
1983—Peoria	Midw.	OF	117	430	69	109	17	6	13	66	.253	267	8	11	.962
1983—Nashua	East.	OF	17	70	11	18	7	2	0	2	.257	37	0	3	.925
1984—Redwood................	Calif.	OF	138	520	101	147	25	5	7	55	.283	★322	16	13	.963
1985—Midland	Texas	OF	70	260	52	77	10	4	4	35	.296	176	10	4	.979
1985—Edmonton..............	P. C.	OF	66	277	53	70	16	5	4	39	.253	205	6	2	.991
1985—California..............	Amer.	OF	21	7	7	1	0	0	0	0	.143	10	1	0	1.000
1986—Edmonton‡..........	P. C.	OF	112	461	84	134	25	10	14	60	.291	317	●16	6	.982
1986—California..............	Amer.	OF	29	51	8	12	1	1	1	3	.235	49	0	2	.961
1987—California..............	Amer.	OF	159	639	103	168	33	5	24	87	.263	★424	16	9	.980
1988—California§............	Amer.	OF	122	455	76	118	22	2	11	51	.259	364	7	9	.976
1989—California..............	Amer.	OF	156	636	86	156	18	13	12	56	.245	430	10	5	.989
Major League Totals—5 Years.................			487	1788	280	455	74	21	48	197	.254	1277	34	25	.981

Selected by California Angels' organization in 6th round of free-agent draft, June 8, 1981.
†On suspended list, June 11 to June 12 and July 19, 1982 through remainder of season.
‡On disabled list, May 12 to May 22, 1986.
§On disabled list, May 7 to June 10, 1988.

CHAMPIONSHIP SERIES RECORD

Year Club	League	Pos.	G.	AB.	R.	H.	2B.	3B.	HR.	RBI.	B.A.	PO.	A.	E.	F.A.
1986—California..............	Amer.	OF-PR	4	2	1	1	0	0	0	0	.500	3	0	0	1.000

ALL-STAR GAME RECORD

Year League	Pos.	AB.	R.	H.	2B.	3B.	HR.	RBI.	B.A.	PO.	A.	E.	F.A.
1989—American	OF	1	0	0	0	0	0	0	.000	0	0	0	.000

FRANK WHITE JR.

Born September 4, 1950, at Greenville, Miss.
Height, 5.11. Weight, 190.
Throws and bats righthanded.
Attended Manatee Junior College, Bradenton, Fla., and
Longview Community College, Lee's Summit, Mo.

Hit for the cycle, September 26, 1979 and August 3, 1982.
Major League stolen bases: 1973 (3), 1974 (3), 1975 (11), 1976 (20), 1977 (23), 1978 (13), 1979 (28), 1980 (19), 1981 (4), 1982 (10), 1983 (13), 1984 (5), 1985 (10), 1986 (4), 1987 (1), 1988 (7), 1989 (3). Total—177.
Led American League second basemen in total chances with 849 in 1985.
Led Gulf Coast League in stolen bases with 18 in 1971.
Led Gulf Coast League shortstops in double plays with 27 in 1971.
Named second baseman on THE SPORTING NEWS American League All-Star Team, 1978.
Named second baseman on THE SPORTING NEWS American League All-Star fielding team, 1977 through 1982, 1986 and 1987.
Named second baseman on THE SPORTING NEWS American League Silver Slugger team, 1986.

Year Club	League	Pos.	G.	AB.	R.	H.	2B.	3B.	HR.	RBI.	B.A.	PO.	A.	E.	F.A.
1971—Sarasota Royals...	Gulf C.	SS	50	158	31	39	6	3	1	21	.247	70	★149	17	★.928
1972—San Jose	Calif.	SS	49	187	44	55	7	2	10	26	.294	77	138	14	.939
1972—Jacksonville..........	South.	SS	91	333	34	84	12	2	2	23	.252	124	306	31	.933
1973—Omaha....................	A. A.	2B-SS	86	348	49	92	19	2	4	32	.264	163	221	21	.948
1973—Kansas City..........	Amer.	SS-2B	51	139	20	31	6	1	0	5	.223	71	121	12	.941

Year	Club	League	Pos.	G.	AB.	R.	H.	2B.	3B.	HR.	RBI.	B.A.	PO.	A.	E.	F.A.
1974—Kansas City	Amer.	2B-SS-3B	99	204	19	45	6	3	1	18	.221	119	189	12	.963
1975—Kansas City	Amer.	2-S-3-C	111	304	43	76	10	2	7	36	.250	182	275	12	.974
1976—Kansas City	Amer.	2B-SS	152	446	39	102	17	6	2	46	.229	296	479	23	.971
1977—Kansas City	Amer.	★2B-SS	152	474	59	116	21	5	5	20	.245	310	437	8	★.989
1978—Kansas City	Amer.	2B	143	461	66	127	24	6	7	50	.275	325	385	16	.978
1979—Kansas City†	Amer.	2B	127	467	73	124	26	4	10	48	.266	317	332	12	.982
1980—Kansas City	Amer.	2B	154	560	70	148	23	4	7	60	.264	395	448	10	.988
1981—Kansas City	Amer.	2B	94	364	35	91	17	1	9	38	.250	226	263	6	.988
1982—Kansas City	Amer.	2B	145	524	71	156	45	6	11	56	.298	★361	389	★17	.978
1983—Kansas City	Amer.	2B	146	549	52	143	35	6	11	77	.260	★390	442	8	★.990
1984—Kansas City‡	Amer.	2B	129	479	58	130	22	5	17	56	.271	299	425	11	.985
1985—Kansas City	Amer.	2B	149	563	62	140	25	1	22	69	.249	342	★490	★17	.980
1986—Kansas City	Amer.	2B-SS-3B	151	566	76	154	37	3	22	84	.272	317	441	10	.987
1987—Kansas City	Amer.	2B	154	563	67	138	32	2	17	78	.245	320	458	10	.987
1988—Kansas City	Amer.	2B	150	537	48	126	25	1	8	58	.235	293	426	4	★.994
1989—Kansas City§	Amer.	2B-OF	135	418	34	107	22	1	2	36	.256	238	407	10	.985
Major League Totals—17 Years				2242	7618	892	1954	393	57	158	865	.256	4801	6407	198	.983

Signed as free agent by Kansas City Royals' organization, July 2, 1970.

†On disabled list, May 9 to June 11, 1979.

‡On disabled list, July 6 to July 21, 1984.

§Granted free agency, November 13, 1989; re-signed by Royals, December 7, 1989.

DIVISION SERIES RECORD

Year	Club	League	Pos.	G.	AB.	R.	H.	2B.	3B.	HR.	RBI.	B.A.	PO.	A.	E.	F.A.
1981—Kansas City	Amer.	2B	3	11	1	2	0	0	0	0	.182	5	6	1	.917

CHAMPIONSHIP SERIES RECORD

Year	Club	League	Pos.	G.	AB.	R.	H.	2B.	3B.	HR.	RBI.	B.A.	PO.	A.	E.	F.A.
1976—Kansas City	Amer.	2B-PR	4	8	2	1	0	0	0	0	.125	6	11	0	1.000
1977—Kansas City	Amer.	2B	5	18	1	5	1	0	0	2	.278	13	16	0	1.000
1978—Kansas City	Amer.	2B	4	13	1	3	0	0	0	2	.231	9	12	0	1.000
1980—Kansas City	Amer.	2B	3	11	3	6	1	0	1	3	.545	9	10	1	.950
1984—Kansas City	Amer.	2B	3	11	1	1	0	0	0	0	.091	7	3	0	1.000
1985—Kansas City	Amer.	2B	7	25	1	5	0	0	0	3	.200	9	28	0	1.000
Championship Series Totals—6 Years				26	86	9	21	2	0	1	10	.244	53	80	1	.993

WORLD SERIES RECORD

Year	Club	League	Pos.	G.	AB.	R.	H.	2B.	3B.	HR.	RBI.	B.A.	PO.	A.	E.	F.A.
1980—Kansas City	Amer.	2B	6	25	0	2	0	0	0	0	.080	13	21	2	.944
1985—Kansas City	Amer.	2B	7	28	4	7	3	0	1	6	.250	10	20	0	1.000
World Series Totals—2 Years				13	53	4	9	3	0	1	6	.170	23	41	2	.970

ALL-STAR GAME RECORD

Year	League	Pos.	AB.	R.	H.	2B.	3B.	HR.	RBI.	B.A.	PO.	A.	E.	F.A.
1978—American		2B	1	0	0	0	0	0	0	.000	1	2	0	1.000
1979—American		2B	2	0	0	0	0	0	0	.000	2	2	0	1.000
1981—American		PR-2B	1	0	0	0	0	0	0	.000	1	0	0	1.000
1982—American		2B	1	0	0	0	0	0	0	.000	2	1	0	1.000
1986—American		PH-2B	2	1	1	0	0	1	1	.500	1	1	0	1.000
All-Star Game Totals—5 Years			7	1	1	0	0	1	1	.143	7	6	0	1.000

EDWARD MORRIS WHITED
(Ed)

Born February 9, 1964, at Bristol, Pa.
Height, 6.03. Weight, 195.
Throws and bats righthanded.
Attended Rider College, Lawrenceville, N.J.

Major League stolen bases: 1989 (1).
Led Southern League in bases on balls received with 97 in 1988.
Led South Atlantic League in game-winning RBIs with 18 in 1987.
Led South Atlantic League third basemen in fielding percentage with .944 in 1987.
Named South Atlantic League Most Valuable Player, 1988.

Year	Club	League	Pos.	G.	AB.	R.	H.	2B.	3B.	HR.	RBI.	B.A.	PO.	A.	E.	F.A.
1986—Auburn	NYP	3B-1B	61	219	34	64	15	1	5	36	.292	286	82	15	.961
1987—Asheville†	S. Atl.	3B-1B-2B	128	440	97	142	★37	0	28	★126	★.323	107	250	19	.949
1988—Greenville	South.	3B	132	428	81	108	11	4	16	62	.252	73	264	33	.911
1989—Richmond	Int.	3B	89	298	41	73	15	1	6	32	.245	62	142	9	.958
1989—Atlanta	Nat.	3B-1B	36	74	5	12	3	0	1	4	.162	23	33	5	.918
Major League Totals—1 Year				36	74	5	12	3	0	1	4	.162	23	33	5	.918

Selected by Houston Astros' organization in 18th round of free-agent draft, June 2, 1986.

†Traded with Pitcher Mike Stoker to Atlanta Braves for Shortstop Rafael Ramirez, December 8, 1987.

WALTER RICHARD WHITEHURST
(Wally)

Born April 11, 1964, at Shreveport, La.
Height, 6.03. Weight, 180.
Throws and bats righthanded.
Attended University of New Orleans, New Orleans, La.

Tied for Southern League lead in shutouts with 3 in 1987.
Tied for Midwest League lead in shutouts with 4 in 1986.
Tied for Northwest League lead in hit batsmen with 7 and balks with 2 in 1985.

Year Club	League	G.	IP.	W.	L.	Pct.	H.	R.	ER.	SO.	BB.	ERA.
1985—Medford	Northwest	14	88	7	5	.583	92	51	35	●91	29	3.58
1985—Modesto	California	2	10	1	0	1.000	10	3	2	5	5	1.80
1986—Madison	Midwest	8	61	6	1	.857	42	8	4	57	16	0.59
1986—Huntsville	Southern	19	104⅔	9	5	.643	114	66	54	54	46	4.64
1987—Huntsville†	Southern	28	183⅓	11	10	.524	192	104	81	106	42	3.98
1988—Tidewater	Int'national	26	165	10	11	.476	145	65	56	113	32	3.05
1989—Tidewater	Int'national	21	133	8	7	.533	123	54	48	95	32	3.25
1989—New York	National	9	14	0	1	.000	17	7	7	9	5	4.50
Major League Totals—1 Year		9	14	0	1	.000	17	7	7	9	5	4.50

Selected by Oakland A's organization in 3rd round of free-agent draft, June 3, 1985.

†As part of an eight-player, three-team deal, New York Mets traded Pitcher Jesse Orosco to Oakland Athletics, December 11, 1987. Oakland then traded Orosco along with Shortstop Alfredo Griffin and Pitcher Jay Howell to Los Angeles Dodgers for Pitchers Bob Welch, Matt Young and Jack Savage. Oakland then traded Savage along with Pitchers Wally Whitehurst and Kevin Tapani to New York.

MARK ANTHONY WHITEN

Born November 25, 1966, at Pensacola, Fla.
Height, 6.03. Weight, 210.
Throws and bats righthanded.
Attended Pensacola Junior College, Pensacola, Fla.

Led Southern League in being hit by pitch with 11 in 1989.
Led South Atlantic League in being hit by pitch with 16 and tied for lead in intentional bases on balls received with 10 in 1987.
Tied for Pioneer League lead in being hit by pitch with 6 in 1986.
Led South Atlantic League outfielders in total chances with 322 and tied for lead in double plays by outfielders with 4 in 1987.

Year Club	League	Pos.	G.	AB.	R.	H.	2B.	3B.	HR.	RBI.	B.A.	PO.	A.	E.	F.A.
1986—Medicine Hat	Pion.	OF	●70	270	53	81	16	3	10	44	.300	111	9	★10	.923
1987—Myrtle Beach	S. Atl.	OF	★139	494	90	125	22	5	15	64	.253	★292	★18	12	.963
1988—Dunedin	Fla. St.	OF	99	385	61	97	8	5	7	37	.252	200	★21	9	.961
1988—Knoxville	South.	OF	28	108	20	28	3	1	2	9	.259	62	3	4	.942
1989—Knoxville	South.	OF	129	423	75	109	13	6	12	47	.258	223	17	8	.968

Selected by Toronto Blue Jays' organization in 5th round of free-agent draft, January 14, 1986.

EDDIE LEE WHITSON
(Ed)

Born May 19, 1955, at Johnson City, Tenn.
Height, 6.03. Weight, 195.
Throws and bats righthanded.

Major League saves: 1978 (4), 1979 (1), 1982 (2), 1983 (1). Total—8.
Led National League in home runs allowed with 36 in 1987.
Led Carolina League in complete games with 16 in 1976.
Led Western Carolinas League in hit batsmen with 15 in 1975.

Year Club	League	G.	IP.	W.	L.	Pct.	H.	R.	ER.	SO.	BB.	ERA.
1974—Bradenton Pirates	Gulf Coast	8	44	1	4	.200	45	28	21	25	15	4.30
1975—Charleston	W. Carol.	24	142	8	★15	.348	140	★96	★80	120	99	5.07
1976—Salem	Carolina	26	★203	●15	9	.625	168	75	57	★186	65	2.53
1977—Columbus	Int'national	26	175	8	13	.381	175	74	65	120	68	3.34
1977—Pittsburgh	National	5	16	1	0	1.000	11	6	6	10	9	3.38
1978—Columbus	Int'national	7	51	2	2	.500	56	25	21	55	10	3.71
1978—Pittsburgh	National	43	74	5	6	.455	66	31	27	64	37	3.28
1979—Pittsburgh†-San Francisco	National	37	158	7	11	.389	151	83	72	93	75	4.10
1980—San Francisco	National	34	212	11	13	.458	222	88	73	90	56	3.10
1981—San Francisco‡	National	22	123	6	9	.400	130	61	55	65	47	4.02
1982—Cleveland§	American	40	107⅔	4	2	.667	91	43	39	61	58	3.26
1983—San Diego x	National	31	144⅓	5	7	.417	143	73	69	81	50	4.30
1983—Las Vegas	P. Coast	3	12	1	0	1.000	15	9	9	11	5	6.75
1984—San Diego y	National	31	189	14	8	.636	181	72	68	103	42	3.24
1985—New York	American	30	158⅔	10	8	.556	201	100	86	89	43	4.88
1986—New York za	American	14	37	5	2	.714	54	37	31	27	23	7.54
1986—San Diego	National	17	75⅓	1	7	.125	85	48	47	46	37	5.59
1987—San Diego	National	36	205⅔	10	13	.435	197	113	108	135	64	4.73
1988—San Diego	National	34	205⅓	13	11	.542	202	93	86	118	45	3.77
1989—San Diego	National	33	227	16	11	.593	198	77	67	117	48	2.66
National League Totals—11 Years		323	1630	89	96	.481	1586	745	678	922	510	3.74
American League Totals—3 Years		84	303⅓	19	12	.613	346	180	156	177	124	4.63
Major League Totals—13 Years		407	1933⅓	108	108	.500	1932	925	834	1099	634	3.88

Selected by Pittsburgh Pirates' organization in 6th round of free-agent draft, June 5, 1974.

†Traded with Pitchers Fred Breining and Al Holland to San Francisco Giants for Infielders Bill Madlock and Lenny Randle and Pitcher Dave Roberts, June 28, 1979.

‡Traded to Cleveland Indians for Second Baseman Duane Kuiper, November 16, 1981.

§Traded to San Diego Padres for Pitcher Juan Eichelberger and First Baseman-Outfielder Broderick Perkins, November 18, 1982.

xOn disabled list, April 18 to May 28, 1983; included rehabilitation disability assignment to Las Vegas, May 10 to May 28, 1983.
yGranted free agency, November 8, 1984; signed by New York Yankees, December 27, 1984.
zOn disabled list, April 30 to May 21, 1986.
aTraded to San Diego Padres for Pitcher Tim Stoddard, July 9, 1986.

CHAMPIONSHIP SERIES RECORD

Year Club	League	G.	IP.	W.	L.	Pct.	H.	R.	ER.	SO.	BB.	ERA.
1984—San Diego	National	1	8	1	0	1.000	5	1	1	6	2	1.13

WORLD SERIES RECORD

Year Club	League	G.	IP.	W.	L.	Pct.	H.	R.	ER.	SO.	BB.	ERA.
1984—San Diego	National	1	⅔	0	0	.000	5	3	3	0	0	40.50

ALL-STAR GAME RECORD

Member of National League All-Star Team in 1980; did not play.

LEO ERNEST WHITT
(Ernie)

Born June 13, 1952, Detroit, Mich.
Height, 6.02. Weight, 205.
Throws right and bats lefthanded.
Attended Macomb County Community College, Warren, Mich.

Major League stolen bases: 1980 (1), 1981 (5), 1982 (3), 1983 (1), 1985 (3), 1988 (4), 1989 (5). Total—22.
Hit three home runs in a game, September 14, 1987.
Led American League catchers in total chances with 863 in 1987.
Led International League in passed balls with 16 in 1978.
Led Eastern League catchers in fielding percentage with .992 in 1974.
Tied for Carolina League lead in double plays by catchers with 7 in 1973.
Named catcher on THE SPORTING NEWS American League All-Star Team, 1988.

Year Club	League	Pos.	G.	AB.	R.	H.	2B.	3B.	HR.	RBI.	B.A.	PO.	A.	E.	F.A.
1972—Williamsport	NYP	1B	1	4	1	2	1	0	0	0	.500	8	1	0	1.000
1972—Winter Haven	Fla. St.	C-1B-OF	31	82	3	15	1	1	0	7	.183	151	14	5	.971
1973—Winston-Salem	Carol.	C-OF-1B	130	424	63	123	23	3	1	50	.290	686	70	15	.980
1974—Bristol	East.	C-OF-1B	111	385	55	96	10	1	9	56	.249	557	50	6	.990
1975—Bristol†	East.	C-OF	82	252	29	64	9	1	2	19	.254	357	36	7	.982
1976—Bristol	East.	C	26	87	12	19	2	3	1	10	.218	127	25	1	.993
1976—Rhode Island	Int.	C-1-O-3	90	304	33	81	16	2	7	42	.266	487	59	9	.984
1976—Boston‡	Amer.	C	8	18	4	4	2	0	1	3	.222	24	0	0	1.000
1977—Charleston	Int.	C-3B	29	94	12	24	6	0	0	7	.255	129	28	7	.957
1977—Toronto§	Amer.	C	23	41	4	7	3	0	0	6	.171	62	4	0	1.000
1978—Syracuse	Int.	C-1B-OF	121	399	50	98	16	3	12	53	.246	673	79	7	.991
1978—Toronto	Amer.	C	2	4	0	0	0	0	0	0	.000	7	1	0	1.000
1979—Syracuse	Int.	*C-OF-3B	114	382	32	95	18	4	7	43	.249	494	69	3	*.995
1980—Toronto	Amer.	C	106	295	23	70	12	2	6	34	.237	436	56	7	.986
1981—Toronto	Amer.	C	74	195	16	46	9	0	1	16	.236	297	46	3	.991
1982—Toronto	Amer.	C	105	284	28	74	14	2	11	42	.261	406	30	8	.982
1983—Toronto	Amer.	C	123	344	53	88	15	2	17	56	.256	554	50	5	.992
1984—Toronto x	Amer.	C	124	315	35	75	12	1	15	46	.238	583	40	4	.994
1985—Toronto	Amer.	C	139	412	55	101	21	2	19	64	.245	649	38	8	.988
1986—Toronto yz	Amer.	C	131	395	48	106	19	2	16	56	.268	709	41	7	.991
1987—Toronto	Amer.	C	135	446	57	120	24	1	19	75	.269	*803	55	5	.994
1988—Toronto	Amer.	C	127	398	63	100	11	2	16	70	.251	643	43	4	.994
1989—Toronto a	Amer.	C	129	385	42	101	24	1	11	53	.262	550	43	5	.992
Major League Totals—13 Years			1226	3532	428	892	166	15	132	521	.253	5723	447	56	.991

Selected by Boston Red Sox' organization in 15th round of free-agent draft, June 6, 1972.
†On disabled list, April 11 to June 13, 1975.
‡Selected by Toronto Blue Jays in American League expansion draft, November 5, 1976.
§On disabled list, August 17 to September 27, 1977.
xOn disabled list, June 16 to July 1, 1984.
yOn disabled list, April 15 to April 30, 1986; included rehabilitation disability assignment to Syracuse, April 28 to April 30, 1986.
zGranted free agency, November 12, 1986; re-signed by Blue Jays, January 8, 1987.
aTraded with Outfielder Kevin Batiste to Atlanta Braves for Pitcher Rick Trlicek, December 17, 1989.

CHAMPIONSHIP SERIES RECORD

Year Club	League	Pos.	G.	AB.	R.	H.	2B.	3B.	HR.	RBI.	B.A.	PO.	A.	E.	F.A.
1985—Toronto	Amer.	C	7	21	1	4	1	0	0	2	.190	50	3	0	1.000
1989—Toronto	Amer.	C	5	16	1	2	0	0	1	3	.125	32	2	0	1.000
Championship Series Totals—2 Years			12	37	2	6	1	0	1	5	.162	82	5	0	1.000

—DID YOU KNOW—

That the Blue Jays' Nelson Liriano spoiled two no-hit bids with ninth-inning hits in a one-week span last season?

Year League	Pos.	AB.	R.	H.	2B.	3B.	HR.	RBI.	B.A.	PO.	A.	E.	F.A.
1985—American	C	0	0	0	0	0	0	0	.000	2	0	0	1.000

KEVIN DEAN WICKANDER

Born January 4, 1965, at Fort Dodge, Ia.
Height, 6.02. Weight, 200.
Throws and bats lefthanded.
Attended Grand Canyon College, Phoenix, Ariz.

Year Club	League	G.	IP.	W.	L.	Pct.	H.	R.	ER.	SO.	BB.	ERA.
1986—Batavia	NYP	11	46⅓	3	4	.429	30	19	14	63	27	2.72
1987—Kinston	Carolina	25	147⅓	9	6	.600	128	69	56	118	75	3.42
1988—Williamsport	Eastern	24	28⅔	1	0	1.000	14	3	2	33	9	0.63
1988—Colorado Springs	P. Coast	19	32⅔	0	2	.000	44	30	26	22	27	7.16
1989—Colorado Springs	P. Coast	45	42⅔	1	3	.250	40	14	14	41	27	2.95
1989—Cleveland	American	2	2⅔	0	0	.000	6	1	1	0	2	3.38
Major League Totals—1 Year		2	2⅔	0	0	.000	6	1	1	0	2	3.38

Selected by Cleveland Indians' organization in 2nd round of free-agent draft, June 2, 1986.

CURTIS VERNON WILKERSON
(Curt)

Born April 26, 1961, at Petersburg, Va.
Height, 5.09. Weight, 173.
Throws right and bats left and righthanded.

Major League stolen bases: 1983 (3), 1984 (12), 1985 (14), 1986 (9), 1987 (6), 1988 (9), 1989 (4). Total—57.
Tied for Texas League lead in sacrifice hits with 11 in 1982.

Year Club	League	Pos.	G.	AB.	R.	H.	2B.	3B.	HR.	RBI.	B.A.	PO.	A.	E.	F.A.
1980—Sarasota Rangers	Gulf C.	SS-2B	37	105	15	20	2	0	0	8	.190	38	86	17	.879
1981—Asheville	S. Atl.	SS-2B	106	333	45	68	7	3	0	19	.204	188	372	28	.952
1982—Burlington	Midw.	SS-2B	56	198	18	50	6	0	0	13	.253	78	159	16	.937
1982—Tulsa	Texas	SS	72	266	32	71	6	3	2	14	.267	102	225	18	.948
1983—Oklahoma City†	A. A.	SS	89	343	51	107	19	4	3	31	.312	135	272	19	.955
1983—Texas	Amer.	SS-2B-3B	16	35	7	6	0	1	0	1	.171	18	31	1	.980
1984—Texas	Amer.	SS-2B	153	484	47	120	12	0	1	26	.248	227	391	30	.954
1985—Texas	Amer.	SS-2B	129	360	35	88	11	6	0	22	.244	165	328	21	.959
1986—Texas	Amer.	2B-SS	110	236	27	56	10	3	0	15	.237	125	199	13	.961
1987—Texas	Amer.	SS-2B-3B	85	138	28	37	5	3	2	14	.268	79	98	6	.967
1988—Texas‡	Amer.	2B-SS-3B	117	338	41	99	12	5	0	28	.293	186	299	15	.970
1989—Chicago	Nat.	3-2-S-O	77	160	18	39	4	2	1	10	.244	42	91	8	.943
American League Totals—6 Years			610	1591	185	406	50	18	3	106	.255	800	1346	86	.961
National League Totals—1 Year			77	160	18	39	4	2	1	10	.244	42	91	8	.943
Major League Totals—7 Years			687	1751	203	445	54	20	4	116	.254	842	1437	94	.960

Selected by Texas Rangers' organization in 4th round of free-agent draft, June 3, 1980.
†On disabled list, May 19 to June 21, 1983.
‡Traded with Pitchers Mitch Williams, Paul Kilgus and Steve Wilson, Infielder Luis Benitez and Outfielder Pablo Delgado to Chicago Cubs for Outfielder Rafael Palmeiro and Pitchers Jamie Moyer and Drew Hall, December 5, 1988.

CHAMPIONSHIP SERIES RECORD

Year Club	League	Pos.	G.	AB.	R.	H.	2B.	3B.	HR.	RBI.	B.A.	PO.	A.	E.	F.A.
1989—Chicago	Nat.	PR-3B-PH	3	2	1	1	0	0	0	0	.500	0	0	0	.000

DEAN ALLAN WILKINS

Born August 24, 1966, at Chicago, Ill.
Height, 6.01. Weight, 170.
Throws and bats righthanded.
Attended San Diego Mesa College, San Diego, Calif.

Led Eastern League in saves with 26 and games finished in relief with 49 in 1988.

Year Club	League	G.	IP.	W.	L.	Pct.	H.	R.	ER.	SO.	BB.	ERA.
1986—Oneonta	NYP	15	83⅓	9	0	★1.000	64	32	29	80	24	3.13
1987—Fort Lauderdale	Florida St.	15	105⅔	8	5	.615	95	41	32	76	39	2.73
1987—Albany†	Eastern	2	12	0	0	.000	18	11	9	8	1	6.75
1987—Winston-Salem	Carolina	13	50⅓	4	4	.500	49	31	23	29	24	4.11
1988—Pittsfield	Eastern	●59	71⅔	5	7	.417	53	25	13	59	30	1.63
1989—Iowa	Am. Assoc.	38	138	8	11	.421	149	74	65	82	58	4.24
1989—Chicago	National	11	15⅔	1	0	1.000	13	9	9	14	9	5.17
Major League Totals—1 Year		11	15⅔	1	0	1.000	13	9	9	14	9	5.17

Selected by New York Yankees' organization in 2nd round of free-agent draft, January 14, 1986.
†Traded with Pitchers Rick Scheid and Bob Tewksbury to Chicago Cubs for Pitcher Steve Trout, July 13, 1987.

RICHARD DAVID WILKINS
(Rick)

Born July 4, 1967, at Jacksonville, Fla.
Height, 6.02. Weight, 210.
Throws right and bats lefthanded.
Attended Florida Community College, Jacksonville, Fla.,
and Furman University, Greenville, S.C.

Led Appalachian League in intentional bases on balls received with 8 in 1987.
Led Carolina League catchers in total chances with 860 and tied for lead in double plays with 8 in 1989.
Led Midwest League catchers in total chances with 984 in 1988.
Led Appalachian League catchers in putouts with 483, total chances with 540 and fielding percentage with .989 and tied for lead in double plays with 6 in 1987.

Year—Club	League	Pos.	G.	AB.	R.	H.	2B.	3B.	HR.	RBI.	B.A.	PO.	A.	E.	F.A.
1987—Geneva	NYP	C-1B	75	243	35	61	8	2	8	43	.251	503	51	7	.988
1988—Peoria	Midw.	C	137	490	54	119	30	1	8	63	.243	★864	★101	★19	.981
1989—Winston-Salem	Carol.	C	132	445	61	111	24	1	12	54	.249	★764	★78	★18	.979

Selected by Chicago Cubs' organization in 23rd round of free-agent draft, June 2, 1986.

WILLIAM CARL WILKINSON
(Bill)

Born August 10, 1964, at Greybull, Wyo.
Height, 5.10. Weight, 160.
Throws left and bats righthanded.
Brother of Brian Wilkinson, pitcher in Montreal Expos' organization.

Major League saves: 1987 (10), 1988 (2). Total—12.

Year—Club	League	G.	IP.	W.	L.	Pct.	H.	R.	ER.	SO.	BB.	ERA.
1983—Bellingham	Northwest	13	63⅔	4	5	.444	54	41	24	87	54	3.39
1984—Wausau	Midwest	19	103½	6	4	.600	79	47	38	117	52	3.31
1985—Salinas	California	9	59⅔	6	1	.857	47	19	18	75	23	2.72
1985—Calgary†	P. Coast	9	57⅓	5	1	.833	44	21	17	42	25	2.67
1985—Seattle	American	2	6	0	2	.000	8	9	9	5	6	13.50
1986—Calgary‡	P. Coast	23	143	8	8	.500	146	82	76	86	51	4.78
1987—Seattle§	American	56	76⅓	3	4	.429	61	33	31	73	21	3.66
1988—Seattle x	American	30	31	2	2	.500	28	14	12	25	15	3.48
1988—Calgary	P. Coast	21	23⅔	0	4	.000	31	28	24	20	20	9.13
1989—Calgary y	P. Coast	2	6⅔	0	2	.000	8	4	4	1	7	5.40
1989—Buffalo z	Am. Assoc.	21	95⅔	4	6	.400	80	43	38	51	53	3.57
Major League Totals—3 Years		88	113⅓	5	8	.385	97	56	52	103	42	4.13

Selected by Seattle Mariners' organization in 4th round of free-agent draft, June 6, 1983.
†On disabled list, July 18, 1985 through remainder of season.
‡On disabled list, July 26, 1986 through remainder of season.
§On disabled list, July 19 to August 5, 1987.
xOn disabled list, May 13 to June 21, 1988; included rehabilitation disability assignment to Calgary, May 29 to June 15, 1988.
yTraded with Shortstop Rey Quinones to Pittsburgh Pirates for Pitchers Mike Dunne and Mike Walker and Outfielder Mark Merchant, April 21, 1989.
zDrafted by Kansas City Royals, December 4, 1989.

GERALD DUANE WILLARD JR.
(Jerry)

Born March 14, 1960, at Oxnard, Calif.
Height, 6.02. Weight, 195.
Throws right and bats lefthanded.
Attended Oxnard College, Oxnard, Calif.

Major League stolen bases: 1984 (1).
Led Pacific Coast League catchers in double plays with 12 in 1989.
Led International League catchers in assists with 78 in 1983.

Year—Club	League	Pos.	G.	AB.	R.	H.	2B.	3B.	HR.	RBI.	B.A.	PO.	A.	E.	F.A.
1980—Central Oregon	N'west	C	65	231	53	85	21	1	5	59	.368	283	37	★18	.947
1981—Peninsula	Carol.	C	107	334	43	87	17	1	12	60	.260	319	28	3	.991
1982—Reading	East.	C	81	281	43	82	10	1	12	51	.292	534	64	13	.979
1982—Oklahoma City†	A. A.	C	36	95	13	22	5	0	2	14	.232	169	35	8	.962
1983—Charleston	Int.	C-3B-OF	127	396	61	119	22	2	19	77	.301	613	79	12	.983
1984—Cleveland	Amer.	C	87	246	21	55	8	1	10	37	.224	335	35	7	.981
1985—Cleveland	Amer.	C	104	300	39	81	13	0	7	36	.270	427	52	5	.990
1985—Maine‡	Int.	C	11	40	5	9	3	0	1	4	.225	56	11	2	.971
1986—Tacoma	P. C.	C	22	62	7	16	5	0	1	12	.258	100	7	1	.991
1986—Oakland	Amer.	C	75	161	17	43	7	0	4	26	.267	300	12	2	.994
1987—Tacoma	P. C.	O-C-1-3	67	215	42	64	15	0	6	38	.298	117	14	4	.970
1987—Oakland§x	Amer.	1B-3B	7	6	1	1	0	0	0	0	.167	1	0	0	1.000
1988—							(Out of Organized Baseball)								
1989—Birmingham	South.	C	5	10	5	3	1	0	0	1	.300	38	4	2	.955
1989—Vancouver y	P. C.	C-1B	90	283	32	78	18	1	7	38	.276	435	56	1	.998
Major League Totals—4 Years		273	713	78	180	28	1	21	99	.252	1063	99	14	.988

Signed as free agent by Philadelphia Phillies' organization, December 20, 1979.
†Traded with Second Baseman Manny Trillo, Infielder Julio Franco, Outfielder George Vukovich and Pitcher Jay Baller to Cleveland Indians for Outfielder Von Hayes, December 9, 1982.
‡Released, April 1, 1986; signed by Tacoma (Oakland A's organization), April 4, 1986.
§On disabled list, May 11 to June 29, 1987.
xReleased, October 12, 1987; signed by Vancouver (Chicago White Sox' organization), February 10, 1989.
yOn disabled list, May 10 to May 24, 1989.

BERNABE WILLIAMS (FIGUEROA)
(Bernie)

Born September 13, 1968, at San Juan, Puerto Rico.
Height, 6.02. Weight, 180.
Throws right and bats left and righthanded.

Tied for Gulf Coast League lead in caught stealing with 12 in 1986.
Led Gulf Coast League outfielders in total chances with 123 in 1986.

Year Club	League	Pos.	G.	AB.	R.	H.	2B.	3B.	HR.	RBI.	B.A.	PO.	A.	E.	F.A.
1986—Sarasota Yanks† ..	Gulf C.	OF	61	230	*45	62	5	3	2	25	.270	*117	3	3	.976
1987—Fort Lauderdale†	Fla. St.	OF	25	71	11	11	3	0	0	4	.155	49	1	0	1.000
1987—Oneonta†	NYP	OF	25	93	13	32	4	0	0	15	.344	40	0	2	1.000
1988—Prince William†‡	Carol.	OF	92	337	72	113	16	7	7	45	*.335	186	8	5	.975
1989—Columbus	Int.	OF	50	162	21	35	8	1	2	16	.216	112	2	1	.991
1989—Albany	East.	OF	91	314	63	79	11	8	11	42	.252	180	5	5	.974

Signed as free agent by New York Yankees' organization, September 13, 1985.
†Batted righthanded only.
‡On disabled list, July 15, 1988 through remainder of season.

DANA LAMONT WILLIAMS

Born March 20, 1963, at Weirton, W. Va.
Height, 5.10. Weight, 170.
Throws and bats righthanded.
Attended Enterprise State Junior College, Enterprise, Ala.

Led International League in being hit by pitch with 14 in 1989.
Led Eastern League in caught stealing with 16 and tied for lead in grounding into double plays with 15 in 1985.

Year Club	League	Pos.	G.	AB.	R.	H.	2B.	3B.	HR.	RBI.	B.A.	PO.	A.	E.	F.A.
1983—Elmira	NYP	2B-SS	29	99	24	38	6	1	0	2	.384	35	46	6	.931
1983—Winston-Salem	Carol.	SS-2B-OF	24	86	10	24	4	0	0	7	.279	22	48	8	.897
1984—Winter Haven	Fla. St.	OF	135	511	65	*167	27	8	1	54	*.327	226	12	8	.967
1985—New Britain	East.	OF	115	450	56	139	16	7	1	39	.309	198	6	3	.986
1986—Pawtucket	Int.	OF	101	370	43	99	22	0	5	41	.268	183	6	1	.995
1986—New Britain	East.	OF	5	17	1	1	0	0	0	2	.059	8	0	0	1.000
1987—Pawtucket	Int.	OF	48	189	29	60	10	1	5	23	.317	115	5	2	.984
1987—New Britain	East.	OF	78	310	48	104	18	3	3	38	.335	148	7	5	.969
1988—Pawtucket	Int.	OF	120	470	53	119	●29	0	10	47	.253	226	11	5	.979
1989—Pawtucket	Int.	OF-2B	104	356	47	91	17	0	4	28	.256	226	14	2	.992
1989—Boston†	Amer.	OF	8	5	1	1	1	0	0	0	.200	0	1	0	1.000
1989—Vancouver	P. C.	OF	4	15	2	5	3	0	0	2	.333	14	0	1	.933
Major League Totals—1 Year			8	5	1	1	1	0	0	0	.200	0	1	0	1.000

Selected by Cincinnati Reds' organization in 34th round of free-agent draft, June 8, 1981.
Selected by Detroit Tigers' organization in secondary phase of free-agent draft, January 12, 1982.
Signed as free agent by Boston Red Sox' organization, May 17, 1983.
†Traded to Vancouver (Chicago White Sox' organization), August 25, 1989, completing deal in which Chicago traded Pitcher Ray Chadwick to Boston Red Sox for a player to be named later, July 31, 1989.

EDWARD LAQUAN WILLIAMS
(Eddie)

Born November 1, 1964, at Shreveport, La.
Height, 6.00. Weight, 175.
Throws and bats righthanded.

Major League stolen bases: 1989 (1).
Led Pacific Coast League in being hit by pitch with 12 in 1988.
Led American Association in being hit by pitch with 15 in 1987.
Led Midwest League in being hit by pitch with 15 in 1985.
Led American Association third basemen in total chances with 352 and double plays with 24 in 1987.
Named Midwest League Most Valuable Player, 1985.

Year Club	League	Pos.	G.	AB.	R.	H.	2B.	3B.	HR.	RBI.	B.A.	PO.	A.	E.	F.A.
1983—Little Falls	NYP	3B	50	190	30	50	6	2	6	28	.263	50	53	13	.888
1984—Columbia†	S. Atl.	3B	43	152	17	28	4	2	3	24	.184	24	76	16	.862
1984—Tampa	Fla. St.	3B	50	138	20	35	8	0	2	16	.254	25	43	11	.861
1985—Cedar Rapids‡	Midw.	3B	119	406	71	106	13	3	20	83	.261	83	204	33	.897
1986—Cleveland	Amer.	OF	5	7	2	1	0	0	0	1	.143	0	0	0	.000
1986—Waterbury	East.	3B	62	214	24	51	10	0	7	30	.238	39	100	15	.903
1987—Buffalo	A. A.	*3B-SS	131	488	90	142	29	2	22	85	.291	88	*237	*27	.923
1987—Cleveland	Amer.	3B	22	64	9	11	4	0	1	4	.172	17	37	1	.982
1988—Colorado Springs	P. C.	3B-SS-1B	101	365	53	110	24	3	12	58	.301	93	177	29	.903
1988—Cleveland§	Amer.	3B	10	21	3	4	0	0	0	1	.190	3	18	0	1.000
1989—Chicago	Amer.	3B	66	201	25	55	8	0	3	10	.274	37	123	16	.909
1989—Vancouver x	P. C.	3B-1B	35	114	12	28	4	0	1	13	.246	8	10	4	.818
Major League Totals--4 Years			103	293	39	71	12	0	4	16	.242	57	178	17	.933

Selected by New York Mets' organization in 1st round (fourth player selected) of free-agent draft, June 6, 1983.
†Traded with Pitchers Matt Bullinger and Jay Tibbs to Cincinnati Reds for Pitcher Bruce Berenyi, June 15, 1984.
‡Drafted by Cleveland Indians, December 10, 1985.
§Traded to Chicago White Sox for Pitchers Joel Davis and Ed Wojna, January 23, 1989.
xGranted free agency, October 15, 1989.

FRANK LEE WILLIAMS

Born February 13, 1958, at Seattle, Wash.
Height, 6.01. Weight, 195.
Throws and bats righthanded.
Attended Shoreline Community College, Seattle, Wash.,
and Lewis-Clark State College, Lewiston, Ida.

Major League saves: 1984 (3), 1986 (1), 1987 (2), 1988 (1), 1989 (1). Total—8.
Led California League in hit batsmen with 18 in 1980 and 13 in 1981.
Led Pioneer League in hit batsmen with 9 in 1979.
Tied for Texas League lead in hit batsmen with 13 in 1982.
Tied for California League lead in complete games with 14 in 1981.

Year—Club	League	G.	IP.	W.	L.	Pct.	H.	R.	ER.	SO.	BB.	ERA.
1979—Great Falls	Pioneer	13	91	6	•7	.462	85	53	34	81	53	3.36
1980—Fresno	California	21	114	12	3	.800	105	53	42	80	70	3.32
1981—Fresno	California	27	187	14	9	.609	170	81	70	170	85	3.37
1982—Shreveport	Texas	27	169⅔	11	9	.550	143	96	74	145	99	3.93
1983—Shreveport	Texas	21	42	7	2	.778	22	14	8	54	25	1.71
1983—Phoenix	P. Coast	25	47⅔	5	3	.625	45	22	19	37	24	3.59
1984—San Francisco	National	61	106⅓	9	4	.692	88	49	42	91	51	3.55
1985—San Francisco	National	49	73	2	4	.333	65	39	34	54	35	4.19
1985—Phoenix	P. Coast	9	13⅔	1	1	.500	10	8	6	10	14	3.95
1986—Phoenix	P. Coast	27	38	1	1	.500	28	10	9	41	17	2.13
1986—San Francisco†	National	36	52⅓	3	1	.750	35	8	7	33	21	1.20
1987—Cincinnati	National	85	105⅔	4	0	1.000	101	37	27	60	39	2.30
1988—Cincinnati	National	60	62⅔	3	2	.600	59	24	18	43	35	2.59
1988—Nashville‡	Am. Assoc.	2	3	0	0	.000	3	3	3	1	2	9.00
1989—Detroit§x	American	42	71⅔	3	3	.500	70	37	29	33	46	3.64
National League Totals—5 Years		291	400	21	11	.656	348	157	128	281	181	2.88
American League Totals—1 Year		42	71⅔	3	3	.500	70	37	29	33	46	3.64
Major League Totals—6 Years		333	471⅔	24	14	.632	418	194	157	314	227	3.00

Selected by San Francisco Giants' organization in 11th round of free-agent draft, June 5, 1979.
†Traded with Pitchers Timber Mead and Mike Villa to Cincinnati Reds for Outfielder Eddie Milner, January 8, 1987.
‡Released, December 21, 1988; signed by Detroit Tigers, January 16, 1989.
§On disabled list, June 28 to July 13 and July 26 to August 24, 1989.
xReleased, November 21, 1989.

JIMMY WILLIAMS

Born May 18, 1965, at Butler, Ala.
Height, 6.07. Weight, 232.
Throws and bats lefthanded.

Year—Club	League	G.	IP.	W.	L.	Pct.	H.	R.	ER.	SO.	BB.	ERA.
1984—Great Falls	Pioneer	8	11	0	1	.000	10	14	11	9	16	9.00
1984—Bradenton Dodgers	Gulf Coast	2	3	0	0	.000	4	4	0	1	4	0.00
1985—Bradenton Dodgers	Gulf Coast	13	66⅔	4	4	.500	54	35	28	59	★55	3.78
1986—Vero Beach†	Florida St.	30	60	1	1	.500	47	35	29	40	66	4.35
1987—Visalia	California	13	85	7	4	.636	66	38	21	81	62	2.22
1988—Visalia	California	37	51	3	4	.429	41	23	21	55	33	3.71
1989—Orlando	Southern	43	53⅓	6	4	.600	50	23	18	62	35	3.04
1989—Portland	P. Coast	16	23⅔	3	2	.600	24	15	11	22	18	4.18

Selected by Los Angeles Dodgers' organization in 10th round of free-agent draft, June 4, 1984.
†Traded with Pitcher Carl Thomas to Minnesota Twins' organization for Outfielder Tom Thomas, June 19, 1987.

KENNETH ROYAL WILLIAMS
(Kenny)

Born April 6, 1964, at Berkeley, Calif.
Height, 6.01. Weight, 187.
Throws and bats righthanded.
Attended Stanford University, Stanford, Calif.

Major League stolen bases: 1986 (1), 1987 (21), 1988 (6), 1989 (9). Total—37.
Received reported $165,000 bonus to sign with Chicago White Sox, 1982.

Year—Club	League	Pos.	G.	AB.	R.	H.	2B.	3B.	HR.	RBI.	B.A.	PO.	A.	E.	F.A.
1982—Sarasota W. Sox	Gulf C.	OF	31	104	19	31	2	1	1	11	.298	61	2	0	1.000
1983—Appleton	Midw.	OF	124	415	60	96	18	2	12	53	.231	218	10	10	.958
1984—Appleton	Midw.	OF	38	147	23	42	11	2	5	26	.286	58	5	2	.969
1984—Glens Falls	East.	OF	97	309	35	76	7	5	8	47	.246	173	10	5	.973
1985—Glens Falls	East.	OF	133	★520	★87	130	16	6	16	66	.250	296	★20	★14	.958
1986—Buffalo	A. A.	OF	50	189	21	40	4	2	4	15	.212	100	8	1	.991
1986—Birmingham	South.	OF	68	272	41	90	16	5	6	40	.331	192	3	8	.961
1986—Chicago	Amer.	OF	15	31	2	4	0	0	1	1	.129	18	1	0	1.000
1987—Hawaii	P. C.	OF	35	134	19	36	4	4	3	14	.269	75	1	2	.974
1987—Chicago	Amer.	OF	116	391	48	110	18	2	11	50	.281	303	5	6	.981
1988—Chicago†	Amer.	OF-3B	73	220	18	35	4	2	8	28	.159	87	69	17	.902
1988—Vancouver‡	P. C.	OF	16	60	8	15	2	1	1	7	.250	23	0	0	1.000
1989—Detroit§	Amer.	OF-1B	94	258	29	53	5	1	6	23	.205	180	11	4	.979
1989—Toledo	Int.	OF	14	51	8	13	2	0	3	8	.255	27	1	0	1.000
Major League Totals—4 Years			298	900	97	202	27	5	26	102	.224	588	86	27	.961

Selected by Chicago White Sox' organization in 3rd round of free-agent draft, June 7, 1982.
†On disabled list, May 25 to June 30, 1988.
‡Traded to Detroit Tigers for Pitcher Eric King, March 23, 1989.
§On disabled list, June 23 to July 29, 1989; included rehabilitation disability assignment to Toledo, July 14 to July 29, 1989.

MATTHEW DERRICK WILLIAMS
(Matt)

Born November 28, 1965, at Bishop, Calif.
Height, 6.02. Weight, 205.
Throws and bats righthanded.
Attended University of Nevada, Las Vegas, Nev.

Major League stolen bases: 1987 (4), 1989 (1). Total—5.
Named shortstop on THE SPORTING NEWS College Baseball All-America Team, 1986.

Year	Club	League	Pos.	G.	AB.	R.	H.	2B.	3B.	HR.	RBI.	B.A.	PO.	A.	E.	F.A.
1986—Everett	N'west	SS	4	17	3	4	0	1	1	10	.235	5	10	2	.882
1986—Clinton	Midw.	SS	68	250	32	60	14	3	7	29	.240	89	150	10	.960
1987—Phoenix	P. C.	3B-2B-SS	56	211	36	61	15	2	6	37	.289	53	136	14	.931
1987—San Francisco	Nat.	SS-3B	84	245	28	46	9	2	8	21	.188	110	234	9	.975
1988—Phoenix	P. C.	3-S-2-O	82	306	45	83	19	1	12	51	.271	56	173	13	.946
1988—San Francisco	Nat.	3B-SS	52	156	17	32	6	1	8	19	.205	48	108	7	.957
1989—San Francisco	Nat.	3B-SS	84	292	31	59	18	1	18	50	.202	90	168	10	.963
1989—Phoenix	P. C.	3B-SS-OF	76	284	61	91	20	2	26	61	.320	57	197	11	.958
Major League Totals—3 Years			220	693	76	137	33	4	34	90	.198	248	510	26	.967

Selected by New York Mets organization in 27th round of free-agent draft, June 6, 1983.
Selected by San Francisco Giants organization in 1st round (third player selected) of free-agent draft, June 2, 1986.

CHAMPIONSHIP SERIES RECORD

Holds National League Championship Series record for most runs batted in, series (9), 1989.

Year	Club	League	Pos.	G.	AB.	R.	H.	2B.	3B.	HR.	RBI.	B.A.	PO.	A.	E.	F.A.
1989—San Francisco	Nat.	3B-SS	5	20	2	6	1	0	2	9	.300	5	12	0	1.000

WORLD SERIES RECORD

Year	Club	League	Pos.	G.	AB.	R.	H.	2B.	3B.	HR.	RBI.	B.A.	PO.	A.	E.	F.A.
1989—San Francisco	Nat.	3B-SS	4	16	1	2	0	0	1	1	.125	4	12	0	1.000

MITCHELL STEVEN WILLIAMS
(Mitch)

Born November 17, 1964, at Santa Ana, Calif.
Height, 6.04. Weight, 205.
Throws and bats lefthanded.
Brother of Bruce Williams, pitcher in Milwaukee Brewers' organization, 1981 through 1985.

Major League saves: 1986 (8), 1987 (6), 1988 (18), 1989 (36). Total—68.
Established major league record for most games pitched by rookie (80), 1986.
Led Northwest League pitchers in wild pitches with 14 and tied for lead in games started with 14 and balks with 2 in 1983.

Year	Club	League	G.	IP.	W.	L.	Pct.	H.	R.	ER.	SO.	BB.	ERA.
1982—Walla Walla	Northwest	12	58⅓	3	4	.429	37	37	31	66	★72	4.78
1983—Reno	California	11	58	1	7	.125	58	56	46	44	60	7.14
1983—Spokane	Northwest	14	92⅓	7	6	.538	84	51	●46	87	55	4.48
1984—Reno†‡	California	26	164	9	8	.529	163	113	91	165	127	4.99
1985—Salem	Carolina	22	99	6	9	.400	57	64	60	138	★117	5.45
1985—Tulsa	Texas	6	33	2	2	.500	17	24	17	37	48	4.64
1986—Texas	American	★80	98	8	6	.571	69	39	39	90	79	3.58
1987—Texas	American	85	108⅔	8	6	.571	63	47	39	129	94	3.23
1988—Texas§x	American	67	68	2	7	.222	48	38	35	61	47	4.63
1989—Chicago	National	★76	81⅔	4	4	.500	71	27	24	67	52	2.64
American League Totals—3 Years		232	274⅔	18	19	.486	180	124	113	280	220	3.70
National League Totals—1 Year		76	81⅔	4	4	.500	71	27	24	67	52	2.64
Major League Totals—4 Years		308	356⅓	22	23	.489	251	151	137	347	272	3.46

Selected by San Diego Padres' organization in 8th round of free-agent draft, June 7, 1982.
†Drafted by Texas Rangers, December 3, 1984; returned, April 6, 1985.
‡Traded to Texas Rangers for Third Baseman Randy Asadoor, April 6, 1985.
§On suspended list, May 2 to May 4, 1988.
xTraded with Pitchers Paul Kilgus and Steve Wilson, Infielders Curtis Wilkerson and Luis Benitez and Outfielder Pablo Delgado to Chicago Cubs for Outfielder Rafael Palmeiro and Pitchers Jamie Moyer and Drew Hall, December 5, 1988.

CHAMPIONSHIP SERIES RECORD

Year	Club	League	G.	IP.	W.	L.	Pct.	H.	R.	ER.	SO.	BB.	ERA.
1989—Chicago	National	2	1	0	0	.000	1	0	0	2	0	0.00

ALL-STAR GAME RECORD

Year	League	IP.	W.	L.	Pct.	H.	R.	ER.	SO.	BB.	ERA.
1989—National		1	0	0	.000	0	0	0	1	1	0.00

MARK ALAN WILLIAMSON

Born July 21, 1959, at Corpus Christi, Tex.
Height, 6.00. Weight, 171.
Throws and bats righthanded.
Attended Grossmont College, El Cajon, Calif., and received degree in mechanical engineering from
San Diego State University, San Diego, Calif.

Major League saves: 1987 (3), 1988 (2), 1989 (9). Total—14.
Led American League in intentional bases on balls issued with 15 in 1987.
Tied for Pacific Coast League lead in saves with 16 in 1986.
Tied for California League lead in intentional bases on balls issued with 10 in 1984.

Year Club	League	G.	IP.	W.	L.	Pct.	H.	R.	ER.	SO.	BB.	ERA.
1982—Reno	California	26	41	7	5	.583	34	24	20	30	18	4.39
1983—Beaumont	Texas	47	82⅔	6	3	.667	90	45	37	39	30	4.03
1984—Reno	California	56	93	10	12	.455	105	41	30	69	23	2.90
1985—Beaumont	Texas	42	78⅔	10	9	.526	72	27	25	64	23	2.86
1986—Las Vegas†	P. Coast	★65	104⅓	10	3	★.769	103	47	39	81	36	3.36
1987—Baltimore	American	61	125	8	9	.471	122	59	56	73	41	4.03
1987—Rochester	Int'national	1	4	0	1	.000	6	3	3	1	1	6.75
1988—Baltimore	American	37	117⅔	5	8	.385	125	70	64	69	40	4.90
1988—Rochester	Int'national	12	29⅔	2	3	.400	38	11	11	25	5	3.34
1989—Baltimore	American	65	107⅓	10	5	.667	105	35	35	55	30	2.93
Major League Totals—3 Years		163	350	23	22	.511	352	164	155	197	111	3.99

Selected by Kansas City Royals' organization in 12th round of free-agent draft, June 8, 1981.
Selected by San Diego Padres' organization in 4th round of free-agent draft, June 7, 1982.
†Traded with Catcher Terry Kennedy to Baltimore Orioles for Pitcher Storm Davis, October 30, 1986.

FRANK LEE WILLS JR.

Born October 26, 1958, at New Orleans, La.
Height, 6.02. Weight, 215.
Throws and bats righthanded.
Attended Tulane University, New Orleans, La.

Pitched seven-inning, 1-0 no-hit victory against Tacoma, May 31, 1985 (first game).
Major League saves: 1985 (1), 1986 (4), 1987 (1). Total—6.
Tied for Southern League lead in wild pitches with 15 in 1981.
Named righthanded pitcher on THE SPORTING NEWS College Baseball All-America Team, 1980.

Year Club	League	G.	IP.	W.	L.	Pct.	H.	R.	ER.	SO.	BB.	ERA.
1980—Sarasota Royals-Blue	Gulf Coast	4	23	2	0	1.000	18	7	5	20	8	1.96
1980—Charleston	S. Atlantic	9	57	2	5	.286	59	33	23	48	32	3.63
1981—Jacksonville	Southern	27	192	9	14	.391	199	104	85	174	91	3.98
1982—Omaha	Am. Assoc.	41	107⅓	7	10	.412	110	71	62	77	★81	5.20
1983—Jacksonville	Southern	8	54⅓	5	2	.714	44	19	15	40	23	2.48
1983—Omaha	Am. Assoc.	16	95	4	11	.267	96	56	50	65	45	4.74
1983—Kansas City	American	6	34⅔	2	1	.667	35	17	16	23	15	4.15
1984—Omaha	Am. Assoc.	15	89⅔	7	4	.636	75	32	28	69	49	2.81
1984—Kansas City†§	American	10	37	2	3	.400	39	21	21	21	13	5.11
1985—Calgary	P. Coast	9	46⅓	4	3	.571	44	27	25	31	25	4.86
1985—Seattle x	American	24	123	5	11	.313	122	85	82	67	68	6.00
1986—Maine y	Int'national	22	31⅓	4	3	.571	37	10	10	21	10	2.87
1986—Cleveland	American	26	40⅓	4	4	.500	43	23	22	32	16	4.91
1987—Buffalo	Am. Assoc.	36	56⅔	3	2	.600	53	28	21	45	22	3.34
1987—Cleveland z	American	6	5⅓	0	1	.000	3	3	3	4	7	5.06
1988—Syracuse	Int'national	25	80⅔	6	4	.600	70	40	29	53	25	3.24
1988—Toronto a	American	10	20⅔	0	0	.000	22	12	12	19	6	5.23
1989—Syracuse	Int'national	14	17	1	0	1.000	8	7	3	13	8	1.59
1989—Toronto	American	24	71⅓	3	1	.750	65	31	29	41	30	3.66
Major League Totals—7 Years		106	332⅓	16	21	.432	329	192	185	207	155	5.01

Selected by Kansas City Royals' organization in 1st round (16th player selected) of free-agent draft, June 3, 1980.
†On disabled list, August 1 to August 16, 1984.
‡Traded to New York Mets' organization as part of a six-player, four-team deal in which Kansas City Royals acquired Catcher Jim Sundberg from Milwaukee Brewers, Texas Rangers acquired Catcher Don Slaught from Kansas City, Milwaukee acquired Pitcher Danny Darwin and a player to be named later from Texas and Pitcher Tim Leary from New York, January 18, 1985; Milwaukee organization acquired Catcher Bill Hance from Texas to complete deal, January 30, 1985.
§Traded to Seattle Mariners' organization for Pitcher Wray Bergendahl, March 29, 1985.
xReleased, March 20, 1986; signed by Maine (Cleveland Indians' organization), March 27, 1986.
yOn disabled list, May 4 to May 31, 1986.
zReleased, March 29, 1988; signed by Knoxville (Toronto Blue Jays' organization), April 7, 1988.
aReleased, October 28, 1988; re-signed by Blue Jays' organization, January 12, 1989.

PAUL RICHARD WILMET

Born November 8, 1960, at Green Bay, Wis.
Height, 5.11. Weight, 170.
Throws and bats righthanded.
Attended Des Moines Area Community College, Boone, Ia.
Brother of Steve Wilmet, pitcher in Los Angeles Dodgers' organization, 1969.

Led Midwest League in saves with 29 and games finished in relief with 46 in 1986.
Led Midwest League in intentional bases on balls issued with 10 in 1984.

Year Club	League	G	IP	W	L	Pct.	H	R	ER	SO.	BB.	ERA.
1981—Little Falls	NYP	20	39	2	2	.500	20	14	8	34	27	1.85
1981—Lynchburg	Carolina	8	22	1	1	.500	27	12	12	32	7	4.91
1982—Lynchburg†	Carolina	29	54	2	3	.400	65	46	35	48	28	5.83
1983—						(Out of Organized Baseball)						
1984—Springfield	Midwest	53	107⅔	7	7	.500	86	38	31	95	52	2.59
1985—Arkansas	Texas	9	8⅓	0	0	.000	16	11	10	2	5	10.80
1985—Springfield	Midwest	41	77⅓	7	8	.467	70	33	30	79	32	3.49
1986—Springfield‡	Midwest	*56	96⅓	9	4	.692	66	28	23	99	33	2.15
1987—Arkansas‡	Texas	17	23	0	2	.000	23	15	12	18	18	4.70
1987—Harrisburg	Eastern	5	7⅔	1	1	.500	8	8	8	3	4	9.39
1987—Salem	Carolina	22	36	2	0	1.000	17	2	2	41	8	0.50
1988—Harrisburg	Eastern	28	41	8	3	.727	34	10	9	32	16	1.98
1988—Buffalo§	Am. Assoc.	19	29	3	2	.600	25	5	4	19	11	1.24
1989—Oklahoma City	Am. Assoc.	55	100⅓	7	8	.467	71	32	26	94	40	2.33
1989—Texas x	American	3	2⅓	0	0	.000	5	4	4	1	2	15.43
Major League Totals—1 Year		3	2⅓	0	0	.000	5	4	4	1	2	15.43

Signed as free agent by New York Mets' organization, June 14, 1981.
†Released, September 15, 1982; signed by Springfield (St. Louis Cardinals' organization), March 28, 1984.
‡Sold to Harrisburg (Pittsburgh Pirates' organization), May 19, 1987.
§Granted free agency, October 15, 1988; signed by Oklahoma City (Texas Rangers' organization), November 10, 1988.
xGranted free agency, October 15, 1989.

CRAIG WILSON

Born November 28, 1964, at Anne Arundel County, Md.
Height, 5.11. Weight, 175.
Throws and bats righthanded.
Attended Anne Arundel Community College, Arnold, Md.
Led American Association third basemen in assists with 264, errors with 26, total chances with 386 and double plays with 28 in 1988.
Led Midwest League second basemen in total chances with 653 and double plays with 86 in 1986.
Led Midwest League third basemen in fielding with .932 in 1985.

Year Club	League	Pos.	G.	AB.	R.	H.	2B.	3B.	HR.	RBI.	B.A.	PO.	A.	E.	F.A.
1984—Erie	NYP	2B-3B-SS	72	282	53	83	18	4	7	46	.294	169	206	14	.964
1985—Springfield	Midw.	3B-2B	133	504	64	132	16	4	8	52	.262	156	293	27	.943
1986—Springfield	Midw.	2B	127	496	106	136	17	6	1	49	.274	*292	*343	18	*.972
1987—St. Petersburg	Fla. St.	3B-2B	38	162	35	58	6	4	0	28	.358	35	91	6	.955
1987—Louisville	A. A.	2B-3B	21	70	10	15	2	0	1	8	.214	22	51	2	.973
1987—Arkansas	Texas	2-3-S-O	66	238	37	69	13	1	1	26	.290	117	164	8	.972
1988—Louisville	A. A.	*3B-2B	133	497	59	127	27	2	1	46	.256	98	271	*26	.934
1989—Arkansas	Texas	2B-3B	55	224	41	71	12	1	1	40	.317	127	150	12	.958
1989—Louisville	A.A.	2B-3B	75	278	37	81	18	3	1	30	.291	130	151	18	.940
1989—St. Louis	Nat.	3B	6	4	1	1	0	0	0	1	.250	1	0	1	.500
Major League Totals—1 Year			6	4	1	1	0	0	0	1	.250	1	0	1	.500

Selected by St. Louis Cardinals' organization in 20th round of free-agent draft, June 4, 1984.

GLENN DWIGHT WILSON

Born December 22, 1958, at Baytown, Tex.
Height, 6.01. Weight, 190.
Throws and bats righthanded.
Attended Sam Houston State University, Huntsville, Tex.
Shares major league record for fewest double plays by outfielder, season, for leader in double plays (4), 1985.
Major League stolen bases: 1982 (2), 1983 (1), 1984 (7), 1985 (7), 1986 (5), 1987 (3), 1988 (1), 1989 (1). Total—27.
Led National League outfielders in assists with 18 in 1987.
Led National League outfielders in double plays with 5 in 1986 and tied for lead with 4 in 1985.
Received reported $60,000 bonus to sign with Detroit Tigers, 1980.
Named third baseman on THE SPORTING NEWS College Baseball All-America Team, 1980.

Year Club	League	Pos.	G.	AB.	R.	H.	2B.	3B.	HR.	RBI.	B.A.	PO.	A.	E.	F.A.
1980—Montgomery	South.	3B	77	284	36	75	16	2	7	31	.264	56	189	*33	.881
1981—Birmingham	South.	OF	124	496	77	152	24	6	18	82	.306	292	18	5	.984
1981—Evansville	A. A.	OF-1B	10	37	5	9	2	0	2	7	.243	16	2	0	1.000
1982—Detroit	Amer.	OF	84	322	39	94	15	1	12	34	.292	215	8	3	.987
1982—Evansville†	A. A.	OF	42	165	24	46	7	2	10	33	.279	96	6	3	.971
1983—Detroit‡	Amer.	OF	144	503	55	135	25	6	11	65	.268	225	12	3	.988
1984—Philadelphia	Nat.	OF-3B	132	341	28	82	21	3	6	31	.240	153	7	7	.958
1985—Philadelphia	Nat.	OF	161	608	73	167	39	5	14	102	.275	343	*18	*12	.968
1986—Philadelphia	Nat.	OF	155	584	70	158	30	4	15	84	.271	331	*20	4	.989
1987—Philadelphia§	Nat.	*OF-P	154	569	55	150	21	2	14	54	.264	315	19	*11	.968
1988—Seattle x	Amer.	OF	78	284	28	71	10	1	3	17	.250	140	4	3	.980
1988—Pittsburgh y	Nat.	OF	37	126	11	34	8	0	2	15	.270	66	1	1	.985
1989—Pitt. z-Hou.	Nat.	OF-1B	128	432	50	115	26	4	11	64	.266	249	13	6	.978
American League Totals—3 Years			306	1109	122	300	50	8	26	116	.271	580	24	9	.985
National League Totals—6 Years			767	2660	287	706	145	18	62	350	.265	1457	78	41	.974
Major League Totals—8 Years			1073	3769	409	1006	195	26	88	466	.267	2037	102	50	.977

Selected by Detroit Tigers' organization in 1st round (18th player selected) of free-agent draft, June 3, 1980.
†On disabled list, May 27 to June 9 and June 17 to June 27, 1982.
‡Traded with Catcher-First Baseman John Wockenfuss to Philadelphia Phillies for First Baseman Dave Bergman and Pitcher Willie Hernandez, March 24, 1984.

xTraded to Pittsburgh Pirates for Outfielder Darnell Coles, July 22, 1988.
yOn disabled list, August 5 to August 20, 1988.
zTraded to Houston Astros for Outfielder Billy Hatcher, August 18, 1989.

ALL-STAR GAME RECORD

Year League	Pos.	AB.	R.	H.	2B.	3B.	HR.	RBI.	B.A.	PO.	A.	E.	F.A.
1985—National	PH	1	0	0	0	0	0	0	.000	0	0	0	.000

PITCHING RECORD

Year Club	League	G.	IP.	W.	L.	Pct.	H.	R.	ER.	SO.	BB.	ERA.
1987—Philadelphia	National	1	1	0	0	.000	0	0	0	1	0	0.00

JAMES GEORGE WILSON
(Jim)

Born December 29, 1960, at Corvallis, Ore.
Height, 6.03. Weight, 230.
Throws and bats righthanded.
Attended Oregon State University, Corvallis, Ore.

Led Pacific Coast League in total bases with 271, grounding into double plays with 24 and tied for lead in sacrifice flies with 11 in 1989.
Led Eastern League in game-winning RBIs with 18 in 1988.
Led International League in total bases with 251, game-winning RBIs with 16 and grounding into double plays with 20 in 1985.
Led International League batters in strikeouts with 113 in 1984.
Led Eastern League in being hit by pitch with 10 and tied for lead in grounding into double plays with 18 in 1983.
Led International League first basemen in total chances with 1,199 and double plays with 96 in 1985.

Year Club	League	Pos.	G.	AB.	R.	H.	2B.	3B.	HR.	RBI.	B.A.	PO.	A.	E.	F.A.
1982—Chattanooga	South.	1B	11	40	3	7	1	0	0	5	.175	29	1	1	.968
1982—Waterloo	Midw.	3B-OF-1B	55	204	40	73	17	1	14	48	.358	17	32	8	.860
1983—Buffalo	East.	1B	136	496	84	144	25	0	26	★105	.290	701	57	13	.983
1984—Maine	Int.	1B	133	490	56	128	19	1	15	●84	.261	715	53	9	.988
1985—Maine	Int.	1B	★139	523	75	150	23	0	★26	★101	.287	★1104	★85	10	.992
1985—Cleveland	Amer.	1B	4	14	2	5	0	0	0	4	.357	23	0	0	1.000
1986—Maine†‡	Int.	1B	116	405	33	94	20	1	9	57	.232	723	71	8	.990
1987—Portland§	P C.	1B	45	157	16	42	7	0	3	24	.268	287	39	5	.985
1988—Vermont	East.	1B-C-P	125	439	57	125	18	1	●17	73	.285	28	4	1	.970
1989—Calgary	P. C.	1B	★138	519	79	★163	30	0	26	★133	.314	58	5	1	.984
1989—Seattle	Amer.	PH-DH	5	8	0	0	0	0	0	0	.000	0	0	0	.000
Major League Totals—2 Years			9	22	2	5	0	0	0	4	.227	23	0	0	1.000

Selected by Cleveland Indians' organization in 2nd round of free-agent draft, June 7, 1982.
†On disabled list, July 21 to July 31, 1986.
‡Released, January 26, 1987; signed by Portland (Minnesota Twins' organization), May 13, 1987.
§Granted free agency, October 15, 1987; signed by Vermont (Seattle Mariners' organization), March 1, 1988.

PITCHING RECORD

Year Club	League	G.	IP.	W.	L.	Pct.	H.	R.	ER.	SO.	BB.	ERA.
1988—Vermont	Eastern	1	1	0	0	.000	2	0	0	0	1	0.00

STEPHEN DOUGLAS WILSON
(Steve)

Born December 13, 1964, at Victoria, British Columbia, Can.
Height, 6.04. Weight, 195.
Throws and bats lefthanded.
Attended University of Portland, Portland, Ore.

Major League saves: 1989 (2).
Played semi-pro baseball with Alaska Goldpanners.

Year Club	League	G.	IP.	W.	L.	Pct.	H.	R.	ER.	SO.	BB.	ERA.
1985—Burlington	Midwest	21	72⅔	3	5	.375	71	44	37	76	27	4.58
1986—Tulsa	Texas	24	136⅔	7	13	.350	117	83	74	95	★103	4.87
1987—Charlotte	Florida St.	20	107	9	5	.643	81	41	29	80	44	2.44
1988—Tulsa	Texas	25	165⅓	15	7	.682	147	72	58	132	53	3.16
1988—Texas†	American	3	7⅔	0	0	.000	7	5	5	1	4	5.87
1989—Chicago	National	53	85⅔	6	4	.600	83	43	40	65	31	4.20
American League Totals—1 Year		3	7⅔	0	0	.000	7	5	5	1	4	5.87
National League Totals—1 Year		53	85⅔	6	4	.600	83	43	40	65	31	4.20
Major League Totals—2 Years		56	93⅓	6	4	.600	90	48	45	66	35	4.34

Selected by Texas Rangers' organization in 4th round of free-agent draft, June 3, 1985.
†Traded with Pitchers Mitch Williams and Paul Kilgus, Infielders Curtis Wilkerson and Luis Benitez and Outfielder Pablo Delgado to Chicago Cubs for Outfielder Rafael Palmeiro and Pitchers Jamie Moyer and Drew Hall, December 5, 1988.

CHAMPIONSHIP SERIES RECORD

Year Club	League	G.	IP.	W.	L.	Pct.	H.	R.	ER.	SO.	BB.	ERA.
1989—Chicago	National	2	3⅔	0	1	.000	3	5	2	4	1	4.91

TREVOR KIRK WILSON

Born June 7, 1966, at Torrance, Calif.
Height, 6.00. Weight, 175.
Throws and bats lefthanded.
Attended Oregon State University, Corvallis, Ore.

Tied for Northwest League lead in balks with 2 in 1985.

Year Club	League	G.	IP.	W.	L.	Pct.	H.	R.	ER.	SO.	BB.	ERA.
1985—Everett	Northwest	17	55⅓	2	4	.333	67	36	26	50	26	4.23
1986—Clinton	Midwest	34	130⅔	6	11	.353	126	70	62	84	64	4.27
1987—Clinton	Midwest	26	161⅓	10	6	.625	130	60	36	146	77	2.01
1988—Shreveport	Texas	12	72⅔	5	4	.556	55	19	15	53	23	1.86
1988—Phoenix	P. Coast	11	51⅔	2	3	.400	49	35	29	49	33	5.05
1988—San Francisco	National	4	22	0	2	.000	25	14	10	15	8	4.09
1989—Phoenix	P. Coast	23	115¼	7	7	.500	109	49	40	77	76	3.12
1989—San Francisco	National	14	39⅓	2	3	.400	28	20	19	22	24	4.35
Major League Totals—2 Years		18	61⅓	2	5	.286	53	34	29	37	32	4.26

Selected by San Francisco Giants' organization in 8th round of free-agent draft, June 3, 1985.

WILLIAM HAYWARD WILSON
(Mookie)

Born February 9, 1956, at Bamberg, S. C.
Height, 5.10. Weight, 170.
Throws right and bats right and lefthanded.
Attended Spartanburg Methodist College, Spartanburg, S. C.,
and University of South Carolina, Columbia, S. C.
Brother of John Wilson, outfielder in New York Mets' organization, 1982 through 1987; and
Phil Wilson, outfielder in Montreal Expos' organization.

Major League stolen bases: 1980 (7), 1981 (24), 1982 (58), 1983 (54), 1984 (46), 1985 (24), 1986 (25), 1987 (21), 1988 (15), 1989 (19). Total—293.

Led National League outfielders in double plays with 6 in 1984.

Year Club	League	Pos.	G.	AB.	R.	H.	2B.	3B.	HR.	RBI.	B.A.	PO.	A.	E.	F.A.
1977—Wausau	Midw.	OF	68	245	50	71	10	2	6	32	.290	150	8	9	.946
1978—Jackson	Texas	OF	132	497	72	145	13	★15	7	72	.292	282	10	7	.977
1979—Tidewater	Int.	OF	★141	529	84	141	22	10	5	36	.267	317	11	7	.979
1980—Tidewater	Int.	OF	132	515	★92	★152	11	★14	4	44	.295	★350	11	7	.981
1980—New York	Nat.	OF	27	105	16	26	5	3	0	4	.248	72	1	2	.973
1981—New York	Nat.	OF	92	328	49	89	8	8	3	14	.271	226	3	4	.983
1982—New York	Nat.	OF	159	639	90	178	25	9	5	55	.279	415	12	5	.988
1983—New York	Nat.	OF	152	★638	91	176	25	6	7	51	.276	422	5	7	.984
1984—New York	Nat.	OF	154	587	88	162	28	10	10	54	.276	396	8	4	.990
1985—New York†	Nat.	OF	93	337	56	93	16	8	6	26	.276	216	0	8	.964
1986—Tidewater	Int.	OF	9	31	4	8	1	0	0	4	.258	19	1	0	1.000
1986—New York‡	Nat.	OF	123	381	61	110	17	5	9	45	.289	228	7	5	.979
1987—New York	Nat.	OF	124	385	58	115	19	7	9	34	.299	205	3	8	.963
1988—New York	Nat.	OF	112	378	61	112	17	5	8	41	.296	200	4	5	.976
1989—New York§	Nat.	OF	80	249	22	51	10	1	3	18	.205	152	2	4	.975
1989—Toronto x	Amer.	OF	54	238	32	71	9	1	2	17	.298	111	2	1	.991
National League Totals—10 Years			1116	4027	592	1112	170	62	60	342	.276	2532	45	52	.980
American League Totals—1 Year			54	238	32	71	9	1	2	17	.298	111	2	1	.991
Major League Totals—10 Years			1170	4265	624	1183	179	63	62	359	.277	2643	47	53	.981

Selected by Los Angeles Dodgers' organization in 4th round of free-agent draft, January 7, 1976.
Selected by New York Mets' organization in 2nd round of free-agent draft, June 7, 1977.
†On disabled list, July 2 to September 1, 1985.
‡On New York disabled list, March 30 to May 9, 1986; included rehabilitation disability assignment to Tidewater, April 26 to May 9, 1986.
§Traded to Toronto Blue Jays, August 1, 1989, completing deal in which Toronto traded Pitcher Jeff Musselman and Pitcher Mike Brady to New York Mets for a player to be named later, July 31, 1989.
xGranted free agency, November 13, 1989; re-signed by Blue Jays, November 27, 1989.

CHAMPIONSHIP SERIES RECORD

Shares Championship Series record for most at-bats, game (7), October 15, 1986 (16 innings).

Year Club	League	Pos.	G.	AB.	R.	H.	2B.	3B.	HR.	RBI.	B.A.	PO.	A.	E.	F.A.
1986—New York	Nat.	OF	6	26	2	3	0	0	0	1	.115	16	1	0	1.000
1988—New York	Nat.	OF-PH	4	13	2	2	0	0	0	1	.154	6	0	0	1.000
1989—Toronto	Amer.	OF	5	19	2	5	0	0	0	2	.263	10	0	0	1.000
Championship Series Totals—3 Years			15	58	6	10	0	0	0	4	.172	32	1	0	1.000

WORLD SERIES RECORD

Year Club	League	Pos.	G.	AB.	R.	H.	2B.	3B.	HR.	RBI.	B.A.	PO.	A.	E.	F.A.
1986—New York	Nat.	OF	7	26	3	7	1	0	0	0	.269	15	2	0	1.000

WILLIE JAMES WILSON

Born July 9, 1955, at Montgomery, Ala.
Height, 6.03. Weight, 195.
Throws right and bats left and righthanded.

Holds major league records for most at-bats season (705), 1980; most at-bats by switch-hitter, season (705), 1980.

Shares major league records by collecting 100 or more hits righthanded and lefthanded, season, 1980; for most hits by switch-hitter, season (230), 1980.

Holds American League records for most triples by switch-hitter, season (21), 1985; highest stolen base percentage, lifetime, 300 or more attempts (.839).

Shares American League records for most years leading league in triples (5); most consecutive stolen bases without caught stealing (32), July 23 through September 23, 1980; fewest times caught stealing, season, 50 or more stolen bases (8), 1983.

Major League stolen bases: 1976 (2), 1977 (6), 1978 (46), 1979 (83), 1980 (79), 1981 (34), 1982 (37), 1983 (59), 1984 (47), 1985 (43), 1986 (34), 1987 (59), 1988 (35), 1989 (24). Total—588.

Switch-hit home runs in one game, June 15, 1979.

Led American League in stolen bases with 83 in 1979.

Led Gulf Coast League in stolen bases with 24 in 1974, Midwest League with 76 in 1975 and American Association with 74 in 1977.

Led Midwest League in being hit by pitch with 13 in 1975.

Named outfielder on THE SPORTING NEWS American League All-Star fielding team, 1980.

Named outfielder on THE SPORTING NEWS American League Silver Slugger team, 1980 and 1982.

Named Midwest League Most Valuable Player, 1975.

Received reported $90,000 bonus to sign with Kansas City Royals, 1974.

Year—Club	League	Pos.	G.	AB.	R.	H.	2B.	3B.	HR.	RBI.	B.A.	PO.	A.	E.	F.A.
1974—Sarasota Royals....	Gulf C.	OF	47	155	30	39	3	5	1	14	.252	92	8	4	.962
1975—Waterloo..............	Midw.	OF	127	486	92	★132	18	4	8	73	.272	249	●17	★17	.940
1976—Jacksonville.........	South.	OF	107	388	54	98	13	6	1	35	.253	273	5	8	.972
1976—Kansas City..........	Amer.	OF	12	6	0	1	0	0	0	0	.167	6	1	1	.875
1977—Omaha....................	A. A.	OF	132	495	67	139	10	6	4	47	.281	★278	7	11	.963
1977—Kansas City..........	Amer.	OF	13	34	10	11	2	0	0	1	.324	24	0	1	.960
1978—Kansas City..........	Amer.	OF	127	198	43	43	8	2	0	16	.217	171	6	4	.978
1979—Kansas City..........	Amer.	OF	154	588	113	185	18	13	6	49	.315	384	12	6	.985
1980—Kansas City..........	Amer.	OF	161	★705	★133	★230	28	●15	3	49	.326	482	9	6	.988
1981—Kansas City..........	Amer.	OF	102	439	54	133	10	7	1	32	.303	299	★14	4	.987
1982—Kansas City..........	Amer.	OF	136	585	87	194	19	★15	3	46	★.332	215	8	3	.987
1983—Kansas City†‡......	Amer.	OF	137	576	90	159	22	8	2	33	.276	354	3	9	.975
1984—Kansas City..........	Amer.	OF	128	541	81	163	24	9	2	44	.301	383	6	4	.990
1985—Kansas City..........	Amer.	OF	141	605	87	168	25	★21	4	43	.278	378	4	2	.995
1986—Kansas City..........	Amer.	OF	156	631	77	170	20	7	9	44	.269	408	4	3	.993
1987—Kansas City..........	Amer.	OF	146	610	97	170	18	★15	4	30	.279	342	3	1	★.997
1988—Kansas City..........	Amer.	OF	147	591	81	155	17	●11	1	37	.262	365	1	4	.989
1989—Kansas City§x......	Amer.	OF	112	383	58	97	17	7	3	43	.253	252	2	6	.977
Major League Totals—14 Years..............			1672	6492	1011	1879	228	130	38	467	.289	4063	73	54	.987

Selected by Kansas City Royals' organization in 1st round (18th player selected) of free-agent draft, June 5, 1974.

†On disabled list, August 21 to September 6, 1983.

‡On suspended list, December 15, 1983 through May 15, 1984.

§On disabled list, May 27 to June 17, 1989.

xGranted free agency, November 13, 1989; re-signed by Royals, December 7, 1989.

DIVISION SERIES RECORD

Year—Club	League	Pos.	G.	AB.	R.	H.	2B.	3B.	HR.	RBI.	B.A.	PO.	A.	E.	F.A.
1981—Kansas City..........	Amer.	OF	3	13	0	4	0	0	1	.308	6	0	0	1.000

CHAMPIONSHIP SERIES RECORD

Year—Club	League	Pos.	G.	AB.	R.	H.	2B.	3B.	HR.	RBI.	B.A.	PO.	A.	E.	F.A.
1978—Kansas City..........	Amer.	PR-OF	3	4	0	1	0	0	0	0	.250	2	0	0	1.000
1980—Kansas City..........	Amer.	OF	3	13	2	4	2	1	0	4	.308	6	1	0	1.000
1984—Kansas City..........	Amer.	OF	3	13	0	2	0	0	0	0	.154	10	0	0	1.000
1985—Kansas City..........	Amer.	OF	7	29	5	9	0	0	1	2	.310	12	0	0	1.000
Championship Series Totals—4 Years.....			16	59	7	16	2	1	1	6	.271	30	1	0	1.000

WORLD SERIES RECORD

Holds World Series record for most strikeouts, series (12), 1980.

Shares World Series record for most at-bats, inning (2), October 18, 1980, first inning.

Year—Club	League	Pos.	G.	AB.	R.	H.	2B.	3B.	HR.	RBI.	B.A.	PO.	A.	E.	F.A.
1980—Kansas City..........	Amer.	OF	6	26	3	4	1	0	0	0	.154	15	1	0	1.000
1985—Kansas City..........	Amer.	OF	7	30	2	11	0	1	0	3	.367	19	1	0	1.000
World Series Totals—2 Years			13	56	5	15	1	1	0	3	.268	34	2	0	1.000

ALL-STAR GAME RECORD

Year—League	Pos.	AB.	R.	H.	2B.	3B.	HR.	RBI.	B.A.	PO.	A.	E.	F.A.
1982—American	OF	2	0	0	0	0	0	0	.000	1	0	0	1.000
1983—American	OF	1	0	1	1	0	0	1	1.000	2	0	0	1.000
All-Star Game Totals—2 Years....................		3	0	1	1	0	0	1	.333	3	0	0	1.000

DAVID MARK WINFIELD
(Dave)

Born October 3, 1951, at St. Paul, Minn.
Height, 6.06. Weight, 220.
Throws and bats righthanded.
Received degree from University of Minnesota, Minneapolis, Minn.

Major League stolen bases: 1974 (9), 1975 (23), 1976 (26), 1977 (16), 1978 (21), 1979 (15), 1980 (23), 1981 (11), 1982 (5), 1983 (15), 1984 (6), 1985 (19), 1986 (6), 1987 (5), 1988 (9). Total—209.

Led National League in total bases with 333 and intentional bases on balls received with 24 in 1979.
Named outfielder on THE SPORTING NEWS American League All-Star Team, 1982 through 1984.
Named outfielder on THE SPORTING NEWS National League All-Star Team, 1979.
Named outfielder on THE SPORTING NEWS American League All-Star fielding team, 1982 through 1985 and 1987.
Named outfielder on THE SPORTING NEWS National League All-Star fielding team, 1979 and 1980.
Named outfielder on THE SPORTING NEWS American League Silver Slugger team, 1981 through 1985.
Received reported $100,000 bonus to sign with San Diego Padres, 1973.
Selected by Atlanta Hawks in 5th round (79th player selected) of 1973 NBA draft.
Selected by Utah Stars in 6th round (58th player selected) of 1973 ABA draft.
Selected by Minnesota Vikings in 17th round (429th player selected) of 1973 NFL draft.
Named outfielder on THE SPORTING NEWS College Baseball All-America Team, 1973.

Year Club	League	Pos.	G.	AB.	R.	H.	2B.	3B.	HR.	RBI.	B.A.	PO.	A.	E.	F.A.
1973—San Diego	Nat.	OF-1B	56	141	9	39	4	1	3	12	.277	65	1	3	.957
1974—San Diego	Nat.	OF	145	498	57	132	18	4	20	75	.265	276	11	●12	.960
1975—San Diego	Nat.	OF	143	509	74	136	20	2	15	76	.267	302	9	9	.972
1976—San Diego	Nat.	OF	137	492	81	139	26	4	13	69	.283	304	*15	6	.982
1977—San Diego	Nat.	OF	157	615	104	169	29	7	25	92	.275	368	15	11	.972
1978—San Diego	Nat.	OF-1B	158	587	88	181	30	5	24	97	.308	328	8	7	.980
1979—San Diego	Nat.	OF	159	597	97	184	27	10	34	*118	.308	344	14	5	.986
1980—San Diego†	Nat.	OF	162	558	89	154	25	6	20	87	.276	273	20	4	.987
1981—New York	Amer.	OF	105	388	52	114	25	1	13	68	.294	196	1	3	.985
1982—New York‡	Amer.	OF	140	539	84	151	24	8	37	106	.280	279	*17	8	.974
1983—New York	Amer.	OF	152	598	99	169	26	8	32	116	.283	313	5	7	.978
1984—New York§	Amer.	OF	141	567	106	193	34	4	19	100	.340	306	3	2	.994
1985—New York	Amer.	OF	155	633	105	174	34	6	26	114	.275	316	13	3	.991
1986—New York	Amer.	OF-3B	154	565	90	148	31	5	24	104	.262	292	9	5	.984
1987—New York	Amer.	OF	156	575	83	158	22	1	27	97	.275	253	6	3	.989
1988—New York	Amer.	OF	149	559	96	180	37	2	25	107	.322	276	3	3	.989
1989—New York x	Amer.							(Did not play)							
National League Totals—8 Years			1117	3997	599	1134	179	39	154	626	.284	2260	93	57	.976
American League Totals—8 Years			1152	4424	715	1287	233	35	203	812	.291	2231	57	34	.985
Major League Totals—16 Years			2269	8421	1314	2421	412	74	357	1438	.287	4491	150	91	.981

Selected by Baltimore Orioles' organization in 40th round of free-agent draft, June 5, 1969.
Selected by San Diego Padres' organization in 1st round (fourth player selected) of free-agent draft, June 5, 1973.
†Granted free agency, October 22, 1980; signed by New York Yankees, December 15, 1980.
‡On disabled list, May 20 to June 4, 1982.
§On disabled list, April 16 to May 1, 1984.
xOn disabled list, March 19, 1989 through remainder of season.

DIVISION SERIES RECORD

Year Club	League	Pos.	G.	AB.	R.	H.	2B.	3B.	HR.	RBI.	B.A.	PO.	A.	E.	F.A.
1981—New York	Amer.	OF	5	20	2	7	3	0	0	0	.350	10	1	0	1.000

CHAMPIONSHIP SERIES RECORD

Year Club	League	Pos.	G.	AB.	R.	H.	2B.	3B.	HR.	RBI.	B.A.	PO.	A.	E.	F.A.
1981—New York	Amer.	OF	3	13	2	2	1	0	0	2	.154	6	0	0	1.000

WORLD SERIES RECORD

Year Club	League	Pos.	G.	AB.	R.	H.	2B.	3B.	HR.	RBI.	B.A.	PO.	A.	E.	F.A.
1981—New York	Amer.	OF	6	22	0	1	0	0	0	1	.045	13	1	0	1.000

ALL-STAR GAME RECORD

Holds All-Star Game record for most doubles, lifetime (7).
Shares All-Star Game records for most at-bats, nine-inning game (5), July 17, 1979; most consecutive games, one or more hits (7).

Year League	Pos.	AB.	R.	H.	2B.	3B.	HR.	RBI.	B.A.	PO.	A.	E.	F.A.
1977—National	OF	2	0	2	1	0	0	2	1.000	1	0	0	1.000
1978—National	OF	2	1	1	0	0	0	1	.500	1	0	0	1.000
1979—National	OF	5	1	1	1	0	0	1	.200	3	0	0	1.000
1980—National	OF	2	0	0	0	0	0	1	.000	2	0	0	1.000
1981—American	OF	4	0	0	0	0	0	0	.000	0	1	0	1.000
1982—American	OF	2	0	1	0	0	0	0	.500	0	0	0	.000
1983—American	OF	3	2	3	1	0	0	1	1.000	3	0	0	1.000
1984—American	OF	4	0	1	1	0	0	0	.250	2	1	0	1.000
1985—American	OF	3	0	1	0	0	0	0	.333	0	0	0	.000
1986—American	OF	1	1	1	1	0	0	0	1.000	0	0	0	.000
1987—American	OF	5	0	1	1	0	0	0	.200	2	0	0	1.000
1988—American	OF	3	1	1	1	0	0	0	.333	1	0	0	1.000
All-Star Game Totals—12 Years		36	6	13	7	0	0	5	.361	15	2	0	1.000

HERMAN S. WINNINGHAM JR.
(Herm)

Born December 1, 1961, at Orangeburg, S.C.
Height, 5.11. Weight, 185.
Throws right and bats lefthanded.
Attended DeKalb Community College South, Decatur, Ga.

Major League stolen bases: 1984 (2), 1985 (20), 1986 (12), 1987 (29), 1988 (12), 1989 (14). Total—89.

Year Club League	Pos.	G.	AB.	R.	H.	2B.	3B.	HR.	RBI.	B.A.	PO.	A.	E.	F.A.
1981—Kingsport............. Appal.	OF	58	204	44	52	7	4	2	14	.255	128	3	2	★.985
1982—Lynchburg............ Carol.	OF	120	430	65	127	20	5	6	61	.295	235	6	5	.980
1983—Jackson................ Texas	OF	78	288	54	102	13	6	4	41	.354	157	5	6	.964
1983—Tidewater†........... Int.	OF	29	113	18	30	5	2	1	11	.265	70	1	3	.959
1984—Tidewater............. Int.	OF	115	406	50	114	20	3	3	47	.281	228	8	4	.983
1984—New York‡.......... Nat.	OF	14	27	5	11	1	1	0	5	.407	7	0	0	1.000
1985—Montreal§........... Nat.	OF	125	312	30	74	6	5	3	21	.237	229	6	4	.983
1985—Indianapolis......... A. A.	OF	11	35	3	6	0	0	0	2	.171	22	0	1	.957
1986—Montreal.............. Nat.	OF-SS	90	185	23	40	6	3	4	11	.216	97	2	2	.980
1986—Indianapolis......... A. A.	OF	51	201	35	54	5	7	4	24	.269	106	3	1	.991
1987—Montreal.............. Nat.	OF	137	347	34	83	20	3	4	41	.239	225	5	6	.975
1988—Mont. x-Cinc......... Nat.	OF	100	203	16	47	3	4	0	21	.232	128	1	1	.992
1988—Indianapolis......... A. A.	OF	3	10	2	2	0	1	0	1	.200	6	0	0	1.000
1989—Cincinnati y......... Nat.	OF	115	251	40	63	11	3	3	13	.251	146	3	3	.980
Major League Totals—6 Years.................		581	1325	148	318	47	19	14	112	.240	832	17	16	.982

Selected by Pittsburgh Pirates' organization in 38th round of free-agent draft, June 5, 1979.
Selected by Milwaukee Brewers' organization in secondary phase of free-agent draft, January 8, 1980.
Selected by Montreal Expos' organization in secondary phase of free-agent draft, June 3, 1980.
Selected by New York Mets' organization in secondary phase of free-agent draft, January 13, 1981.
†On disabled list, August 9 to September 20, 1983.
‡Traded with Infielder Hubie Brooks, Catcher Mike Fitzgerald and Pitcher Floyd Youmans to Montreal Expos for Catcher Gary Carter, December 10, 1984.
§On disabled list, June 24 to July 13, 1985; included rehabilitation disability assignment to Indianapolis, July 4 to July 13, 1985.
xTraded with Catcher Jeff Reed and Pitcher Randy St. Claire to Cincinnati Reds for Outfielder Tracy Jones and Pitcher Pat Pacillo, July 13, 1988.
yOn disabled list, June 6 to June 21, 1989.

MATTHEW LITTLETON WINTERS
(Matt)

Born March 18, 1960, at Buffalo, N.Y.
Height, 6.03. Weight, 200.
Throws right and bats lefthanded.

Led South Atlantic League in bases on balls received with 118 in 1982.
Led South Atlantic League in game-winning RBIs with 12 in 1980 and tied for lead with 12 in 1982.
Named Southern League Most Valuable Player, 1988.
Named South Atlantic League Most Valuable Player, 1982.

Year Club League	Pos.	G.	AB.	R.	H.	2B.	3B.	HR.	RBI.	B.A.	PO.	A.	E.	F.A.
1978—Oneonta................ NYP	OF	60	203	38	53	7	★11	2	36	.261	79	6	4	.955
1979—Fort Lauderdale .. Fla. St.	OF	34	89	8	14	2	1	1	10	.157	28	1	2	.935
1979—Oneonta................ NYP	OF-1B	62	188	40	53	6	2	●10	38	.282	79	2	4	.953
1980—Greensboro.......... S. Atl.	OF-1B	112	363	72	116	15	2	20	92	.320	165	10	7	.962
1981—Greensboro.......... S. Atl.	OF-1B	125	404	85	121	23	2	16	76	.300	109	10	5	.960
1982—Greensboro.......... S. Atl.	OF-1B	104	326	76	106	20	2	20	93	.325	163	3	3	.982
1982—Nashville.............. South.	OF	29	99	22	30	5	2	4	17	.303	40	3	0	1.000
1983—Columbus............. Int.	OF	133	431	89	126	24	3	29	99	.292	150	2	2	.987
1984—Columbus............. Int.	OF-1B	130	407	57	101	17	4	10	54	.248	206	14	3	.987
1985—Columbus†........... Int.	OF	45	130	19	40	14	1	3	19	.308	45	1	1	.979
1985—Albany‡§x............ East.	OF	14	47	7	13	2	0	2	6	.277	19	0	0	1.000
1986—Buffalo................. A. A.	OF	14	34	4	3	0	0	1	3	.088	23	1	0	1.000
1986—Columbus y........... Int.	OF	33	86	14	25	3	1	1	9	.291	56	2	0	1.000
1986—Albany z .... East.	OF	37	118	15	20	5	0	4	16	.169	61	1	1	.984
1987—Memphis............... South.	OF-1B	93	343	61	92	17	2	20	88	.268	438	28	9	.981
1987—Omaha.................. A. A.	OF	50	182	30	51	8	0	9	34	.280	90	7	3	.970
1988—Memphis............... South.	OF-1B	139	488	77	134	21	3	★25	★91	.275	444	17	7	.985
1989—Omaha.................. A. A.	OF	75	268	33	60	6	3	13	54	.224	100	3	2	.981
1989—Kansas City a .... Amer.	OF	42	107	14	25	6	0	2	9	.234	45	1	3	.939
Major League Totals—1 Year.................		42	107	14	25	6	0	2	9	.234	45	1	3	.939

Selected by New York Yankees' organization in 1st round (24th player selected) of free-agent draft, June 6, 1978.
†On disabled list, April 22 to July 7, 1985.
‡Released, November 12, 1985; signed by Chicago White Sox' organization, December 22, 1985.
§Traded with Catchers Ron Hassey and Chris Alvarez and Pitcher Eric Schmidt to New York Yankees for Pitcher Neil Allen, Catcher Scott Bradley, Outfielder Glen Braxton and cash, February 13, 1986.
xLoaned to Buffalo (Chicago White Sox' organization), March 5, 1986; returned, May 16, 1986.
yOn disabled list, June 14 to June 24, 1986.
zGranted free agency, October 15, 1986; signed by Memphis (Kansas City Royals' organization), February 13, 1987.
aGranted free agency, October 15, 1989.

MICHAEL ATWATER WITT
(Mike)

Born July 20, 1960, at Fullerton, Calif.
Height, 6.07. Weight, 198.
Throws and bats righthanded.
Attending Cypress Junior College, Cypress, Calif.

Pitched 1-0 perfect game against Texas Rangers, September 30, 1984.
Major League saves: 1983 (5).
Tied for American League lead in hit batsmen with 11 in 1981.

Year Club	League	G.	IP.	W.	L.	Pct.	H.	R.	ER.	SO.	BB.	ERA.
1978—Idaho Falls	Pioneer	13	86	7	1	.875	88	45	34	79	26	3.56
1979—Salinas	California	30	141	8	10	.444	156	96	80	94	70	5.11
1980—Salinas	California	13	90	7	3	.700	85	30	21	76	35	2.10
1980—El Paso	Texas	12	70	5	5	.500	72	53	45	64	39	5.79
1981—California	American	22	129	8	9	.471	123	60	47	75	47	3.28
1982—California	American	33	179⅔	8	6	.571	177	77	70	85	47	3.51
1983—California	American	43	154	7	14	.333	173	90	84	77	75	4.91
1984—California	American	34	246⅔	15	11	.577	227	103	95	196	84	3.47
1985—California	American	35	250	15	9	.625	228	115	99	180	98	3.56
1986—California	American	34	269	18	10	.643	218	95	85	208	73	2.84
1987—California†	American	36	247	16	14	.533	252	128	110	192	84	4.01
1988—California	American	34	249⅔	13	16	.448	263	⋆130	115	133	87	4.15
1989—California	American	33	220	9	15	.375	252	119	●111	123	48	4.54
Major League Totals—9 Years		304	1945	109	104	.512	1913	917	816	1269	643	3.78

Selected by California Angels' organization in 4th round of free-agent draft, June 6, 1978.
†Granted free agency, November 9, 1987; re-signed by Angels, December 22, 1987.

CHAMPIONSHIP SERIES RECORD

Year Club	League	G.	IP.	W.	L.	Pct.	H.	R.	ER.	SO.	BB.	ERA.
1982—California	American	1	3	0	0	.000	2	2	2	3	2	6.00
1986—California	American	2	17⅔	1	0	1.000	13	5	5	8	2	2.55
Championship Series Totals—2 Years		3	20⅔	1	0	1.000	15	7	7	11	4	3.05

ALL-STAR GAME RECORD

Member of American League All-Star Team in 1986 and 1987; did not play.

ROBERT ANDREW WITT
(Bobby)

Born May 11, 1964, at Canton, Mass.
Height, 6.02. Weight, 205.
Throws and bats righthanded.
Attended University of Oklahoma, Norman, Okla.

Shares major league record for most strikeouts, inning (4), August 2, 1987, second inning.
Led American League in wild pitches with 22 in 1986 and tied for lead with 16 in 1988.
Named as righthanded pitcher on THE SPORTING NEWS College Baseball All-America Team, 1985.
Member of 1984 U.S. Olympic baseball team.

Year Club	League	G.	IP.	W.	L.	Pct.	H.	R.	ER.	SO.	BB.	ERA.
1985—Tulsa	Texas	11	35	0	6	.000	26	26	25	39	44	6.43
1986—Texas	American	31	157⅔	11	9	.550	130	104	96	174	⋆143	5.48
1987—Texas†‡	American	26	143	8	10	.444	114	82	78	160	⋆140	4.91
1987—Oklahoma City	Am. Assoc.	1	5	1	0	1.000	5	5	5	2	3	9.00
1987—Tulsa	Texas	1	5	0	1	.000	5	9	3	2	6	5.40
1988—Texas	American	22	174⅓	8	10	.444	134	83	76	148	101	3.92
1988—Oklahoma City	Am. Assoc.	11	76⅔	4	6	.400	69	42	37	70	47	4.34
1989—Texas	American	31	194⅓	12	13	.480	182	123	●111	166	⋆114	5.14
Major League Totals—4 Years		110	669⅓	39	42	.481	560	392	361	648	498	4.85

Selected by Cincinnati Reds' organization in 7th round of free-agent draft, June 7, 1982.
Selected by Texas Rangers' organization in 1st round (third player selected) of free-agent draft, June 3, 1985.
†On disabled list, May 21 to June 20, 1987; included rehabilitation disability assignment to Oklahoma City, June 7 to June 12, and Tulsa, June 13, 1987.
‡Struck out in only at-bat.

EDWARD DAVID WOJNA
Name pronounced WOHJ-nuh.
(Ed)

Born August 20, 1960, at Bridgeport, Conn.
Height, 6.01. Weight, 187.
Throws and bats righthanded.
Attended Indian River Community College, Fort Pierce, Fla.

Led Eastern League in hit batsmen with 9 in 1983.
Tied for Pacific Coast League lead in wild pitches with 16 in 1984.

Year Club	League	G.	IP.	W.	L.	Pct.	H.	R.	ER.	SO.	BB.	ERA.
1981—Spartanburg	S. Atlantic	27	178	11	13	.458	181	●107	●82	130	69	4.15
1982—Peninsula	Carolina	27	176⅔	12	8	.600	156	79	57	116	49	2.90
1983—Reading†	Eastern	28	161⅔	13	7	.650	147	80	66	83	78	3.67
1984—Las Vegas	P. Coast	29	159⅓	14	8	.636	182	99	90	95	81	5.08
1985—Las Vegas	P. Coast	18	111⅓	5	8	.385	121	63	55	66	43	4.45
1985—San Diego	National	15	42	2	4	.333	53	35	27	18	19	5.79
1986—Las Vegas	P. Coast	25	175⅓	12	7	.632	181	81	70	102	50	3.59
1986—San Diego	National	7	39	2	2	.500	42	19	14	19	16	3.23
1987—San Diego	National	5	18⅓	0	3	.000	25	12	12	13	6	5.89
1987—Las Vegas‡	P. Coast	18	96	7	5	.583	97	50	43	47	42	4.03
1988—Vancouver§	P. Coast	21	124	10	6	.625	112	55	45	73	36	3.27
1989—Colorado Springs	P. Coast	19	122⅓	9	4	.692	116	50	39	81	36	2.87
1989—Cleveland x	American	9	33	0	1	.000	31	17	15	10	14	4.09
National League Totals—3 Years		27	99⅓	4	9	.308	120	66	53	50	41	4.80
American League Totals—1 Year		9	33	0	1	.000	31	17	15	10	14	4.09
Major League Totals—4 Years		36	132⅓	4	10	.286	151	83	68	60	55	4.62

Selected by Baltimore Orioles' organization in 6th round of free-agent draft, January 8, 1980.
Selected by Philadelphia Phillies' organization in secondary phase of free-agent draft, June 3, 1980.
†Traded with Pitchers Marty Decker, Darren Burroughs and Lance McCullers to San Diego Padres, September 20, 1983, as partial completion of deal in which San Diego traded Outfielder Sixto Lezcano and a player to be named later to Philadelphia Phillies for four players to be named later, August 31, 1983; Philadelphia organization acquired Pitcher Steve Fireovid to complete deal, October 11, 1983.
‡Traded to Chicago White Sox for a player to be named later, October 5, 1987; San Diego Padres acquired Pitcher Joel McKeon to complete deal, February 11, 1988.
§Traded with Pitcher Joel Davis to Cleveland Indians for Infielder Eddie Williams, January 23, 1989.
xReleased, December 4, 1989.

TRACY MICHAEL WOODSON

Born October 5, 1962, at Richmond, Va.
Height, 6.03. Weight, 215.
Throws and bats righthanded.
Attended North Carolina State University, Raleigh, N. C.

Major League stolen bases: 1987 (1), 1988 (1). Total—2.
Led Texas League third basemen in total chances with 413 in 1986.
Led Florida State League third basemen in putouts with 111, fielding percentage with .926 and total chances with 408 in 1985.

Year Club	League	Pos.	G.	AB.	R.	H.	2B.	3B.	HR.	RBI.	B.A.	PO.	A.	E.	F.A.
1984—Vero Beach	Fla. St.	1B	76	256	29	56	9	0	4	36	.219	630	38	9	.987
1985—Vero Beach	Fla. St.	3B-1B	138	504	55	126	30	4	9	62	.250	131	270	30	.930
1986—San Antonio	Texas	*3B-SS	131	495	65	133	27	3	18	90	.269	*135	259	22	*.947
1987—Los Angeles	Nat.	3B-1B	53	136	14	31	8	1	1	11	.228	58	58	4	.967
1987—Albuquerque	P. C.	3B-1B	67	259	37	75	13	2	5	44	.290	285	90	15	.962
1988—Albuquerque	P. C.	1-3-2-S	85	313	46	100	21	1	17	73	.319	493	131	14	.978
1988—Los Angeles	Nat.	3B-1B	65	173	15	43	4	1	3	15	.249	160	60	6	.973
1989—Albuquerque	P. C.	3B-1B	89	325	49	95	21	0	14	59	.292	296	132	13	.971
1989—Los Angeles†‡	Nat.	3B	4	6	0	0	0	0	0	0	.000	1	1	0	1.000
Major League Totals—3 Years			122	315	29	74	12	2	4	26	.235	219	119	10	.971

Selected by Los Angeles Dodgers' organization in 3rd round of free-agent draft, June 4, 1984.
†On disabled list, June 19 to July 4, 1989.
‡Traded to Chicago White Sox for Pitcher Jeff Bittiger, November 9, 1989.

CHAMPIONSHIP SERIES RECORD

Year Club	League	Pos.	G.	AB.	R.	H.	2B.	3B.	HR.	RBI.	B.A.	PO.	A.	E.	F.A.
1988—Los Angeles	Nat.	PH-1B	3	4	0	1	0	0	0	0	.250	3	0	0	1.000

WORLD SERIES RECORD

Year Club	League	Pos.	G.	AB.	R.	H.	2B.	3B.	HR.	RBI.	B.A.	PO.	A.	E.	F.A.
1988—Los Angeles	Nat.	PH-1B	4	4	0	0	0	0	0	1	.000	6	1	0	1.000

ROBERT JOHN WOODWARD
(Rob)

Born September 28, 1962, at Hanover, N.H.
Height, 6.03. Weight, 212.
Throws and bats righthanded.

Led International League in shutouts with 4 in 1986.
Led Eastern League pitchers in hit batsmen with 12 and tied for lead in games started with 27 in 1984.
Tied for Carolina League lead in games started by pitchers with 29 in 1983.

Year Club	League	G.	IP.	W.	L.	Pct.	H.	R.	ER.	SO.	BB.	ERA.
1981—Elmira	NYP	12	77	4	3	.571	77	38	29	47	23	3.39
1982—Winter Haven	Florida St.	27	126⅔	7	9	.438	140	85	72	50	62	5.12
1983—Winston-Salem	Carolina	30	197⅔	13	11	.542	177	103	91	157	100	4.14
1984—New Britain	Eastern	28	166	10	●12	.455	167	87	73	100	65	3.96
1985—New Britain	Eastern	12	86⅓	7	5	.583	71	42	34	54	36	3.54
1985—Pawtucket	Int'national	15	82⅔	3	8	.273	79	46	41	70	41	4.46
1985—Boston	American	5	26⅔	1	0	1.000	17	8	5	16	9	1.69
1986—Pawtucket	Int'national	18	127⅔	9	6	.600	114	55	45	73	42	3.17
1986—Boston	American	9	35⅔	2	3	.400	46	26	21	14	11	5.30
1987—Boston	American	9	37	1	1	.500	53	33	29	15	15	7.05
1987—Pawtucket	Int'national	21	136	12	8	.600	134	65	53	82	62	3.51
1988—Pawtucket	Int'national	47	44⅓	1	4	.200	44	20	19	53	24	3.86
1988—Boston	American	1	⅔	0	0	.000	2	1	1	0	1	13.50
1989—Pawtucket	Int'national	40	56	2	5	.286	51	30	29	58	34	4.66
Major League Totals—4 Years		24	100	4	4	.500	118	68	56	45	36	5.04

Selected by Boston Red Sox' organization in 3rd round of free-agent draft, June 8, 1981.

TODD ROLAND WORRELL

Name pronounced Wor-RELL.

Born September 28, 1959, at Arcadia, Calif.
Height, 6.05. Weight, 210.
Throws and bats righthanded.
Received bachelor of science degree in Christian education from
Biola College, La Mirada, Calif.

Holds major league record for most saves by rookie (36), 1986.
Major League saves: 1985 (5), 1986 (36), 1987 (33), 1988 (32), 1989 (20). Total—126.
Led National League in games finished in relief with 60, saves with 36 and intentional bases on balls issued with 16 in 1986.
Named National League Rookie Pitcher of the Year by THE SPORTING NEWS, 1986.
Named National League Rookie of the Year by Baseball Writers' Association of America, 1986.
Named National League Fireman of the Year by THE SPORTING NEWS, 1986.
Named righthanded pitcher on THE SPORTING NEWS College Baseball All-America Team, 1982.

Year	Club	League	G.	IP.	W.	L.	Pct.	H.	R.	ER.	SO.	BB.	ERA.
1982—Erie	NYP	9	51⅔	4	1	.800	52	23	19	57	15	3.31
1983—Louisville	Am. Assoc.	15	79⅔	4	2	.667	76	49	42	46	42	4.74
1983—Arkansas	Texas	10	70⅓	5	2	.714	57	33	24	74	37	3.07
1984—Arkansas	Texas	18	100⅓	3	10	.231	109	72	50	88	67	4.49
1984—St. Petersburg	Florida St.	8	47⅓	3	2	.600	41	22	11	33	24	2.09
1985—Louisville	Am. Assoc.	34	127⅔	8	6	.571	114	59	51	★126	47	3.60
1985—St. Louis	National	17	21⅔	3	0	1.000	17	7	7	17	7	2.91
1986—St. Louis†	National	74	103⅔	9	10	.474	86	29	24	73	41	2.08
1987—St. Louis‡	National	75	94⅔	8	6	.571	86	29	28	92	34	2.66
1988—St. Louis	National	68	90	5	9	.357	69	32	30	78	34	3.00
1989—St. Louis‡§	National	47	51⅔	3	5	.375	42	21	17	41	26	2.96
1989—Louisville	Am. Assoc.	1	1	0	0	.000	0	0	0	1	0	0.00
Major League Totals—5 Years		281	361⅔	28	30	.483	300	118	106	301	142	2.64

Selected by St. Louis Cardinals' organization in 1st round (21st player selected) of free-agent draft, June 7, 1982.
†Appeared in two games as an outfielder with no chances.
‡Appeared in one game as an outfielder with no chances.
§On disabled list, May 14 to June 7, 1989; included rehabilitation disability assignment to Louisville, June 6 and June 7, 1989.

CHAMPIONSHIP SERIES RECORD

Year	Club	League	G.	IP.	W.	L.	Pct.	H.	R.	ER.	SO.	BB.	ERA.
1985—St. Louis	National	4	6⅓	1	0	1.000	4	1	1	3	2	1.42
1987—St. Louis	National	3	4⅓	0	0	.000	4	1	1	6	1	2.08
Championship Series Totals—2 Years		7	10⅔	1	0	1.000	8	2	2	9	3	1.69

Appeared as an outfielder in one game of 1987 Championship Series.

WORLD SERIES RECORD

Shares World Series record for most consecutive strikeouts, game (6), October 24, 1985.

Year	Club	League	G.	IP.	W.	L.	Pct.	H.	R.	ER.	SO.	BB.	ERA.
1985—St. Louis	National	3	4⅔	0	1	.000	4	2	2	6	2	3.86
1987—St. Louis	National	4	7	0	0	.000	6	1	1	3	4	1.29
World Series Totals—2 Years		7	11⅔	0	1	.000	10	3	3	9	6	2.31

ALL-STAR GAME RECORD

Year	League	IP.	W.	L.	Pct.	H.	R.	ER.	SO.	BB.	ERA.
1988—National		1	0	0	.000	0	0	0	0	0	0.00

CRAIG RICHARD WORTHINGTON

Born April 17, 1965, at Los Angeles, Calif.
Height, 6.00. Weight, 202.
Throws and bats righthanded.
Attended Cerritos College, Norwalk, Calif.

Major League stolen bases: 1988 (1), 1989 (1). Total—2.
Led Carolina League in game-winning RBIs with 16 in 1986.
Led International League third basemen in total chances with 310 in 1987 and 319 in 1988.
Tied for International League lead in double plays by third basemen with 16 in 1987.
Named American League Rookie Player of the Year by THE SPORTING NEWS, 1989.
Named International League Player of the Year, 1988.

Year	Club	League	Pos.	G.	AB.	R.	H.	2B.	3B.	HR.	RBI.	B.A.	PO.	A.	E.	F.A.
1985—Bluefield	Appal.	3B	39	129	33	44	9	1	7	20	.341	32	68	12	.893
1986—Hagerstown	Carol.	3B	132	480	85	144	35	1	15	★105	.300	92	249	32	.914
1987—Rochester	Int.	3B	109	383	46	99	14	1	7	50	.258	★79	★211	★20	★.935
1988—Rochester	Int.	★3B-SS	121	430	53	105	25	1	16	73	.244	★91	209	19	.940
1988—Baltimore	Amer.	3B	26	81	5	15	2	0	2	4	.185	20	53	3	.961
1989—Baltimore	Amer.	3B	145	497	57	123	23	0	15	70	.247	113	277	20	.951
Major League Totals—2 Years		171	578	62	138	25	0	17	74	.239	133	330	23	.953

Selected by New York Mets' organization in 6th round of free-agent draft, January 17, 1984.
Selected by Houston Astros' organization in secondary phase of free-agent draft, June 4, 1984.
Selected by Chicago Cubs' organization in secondary phase of free-agent draft, January 9, 1985.
Selected by Baltimore Orioles' organization in secondary phase of free-agent draft, June 3, 1985.

RICHARD JAMES WRONA
(Rick)

Born December 10, 1963, at Tulsa, Okla.
Height, 6.01. Weight, 185.
Throws and bats righthanded.
Attended Wichita State University, Wichita, Kan.

Year Club League	Pos.	G.	AB.	R.	H.	2B.	3B.	HR.	RBI.	B.A.	PO.	A.	E.	F.A.
1985—Peoria† .... Midw.	C	6	16	2	4	1	0	0	2	.250	31	1	2	.941
1985—Winston-Salem† ... Carol.	C	20	49	4	11	4	0	0	2	.224	90	10	3	.971
1986—Winston-Salem ..... Carol.	C-O-3-1	91	267	43	68	15	0	4	32	.255	464	74	11	.980
1987—Pittsfield .... East.	C-1B	70	218	22	48	10	3	1	25	.220	299	49	9	.975
1988—Pittsfield .... East.	C	5	6	0	0	0	0	0	1	.000	11	1	0	1.000
1988—Iowa .... A. A.	C	83	193	28	51	9	0	2	23	.264	347	36	7	.982
1988—Chicago .... Nat.	C	4	6	0	0	0	0	0	0	.000	11	0	1	1.000
1989—Chicago .... Nat.	C	38	92	11	26	2	1	2	14	.283	158	15	3	.983
1989—Iowa .... A. A.	C-1B-OF	60	189	15	41	8	3	2	13	.217	340	41	6	.984
Major League Totals—2 Years................		42	98	11	26	2	1	2	14	.265	169	16	3	.984

Selected by Chicago Cubs' organization in 5th round of free-agent draft, June 3, 1985.
†Switch-hitter.

CHAMPIONSHIP SERIES RECORD

Year Club League	Pos.	G.	AB.	R.	H.	2B.	3B.	HR.	RBI.	B.A.	PO.	A.	E.	F.A.
1989—Chicago .... Nat.	C	2	5	0	0	0	0	0	0	.000	9	1	0	1.000

MARVELL WYNNE

Name pronounced Win.
Born December 17, 1959, at Chicago, Ill.
Height, 5.11. Weight, 180.
Throws and bats lefthanded.

Major League stolen bases: 1983 (12), 1984 (24), 1985 (10), 1986 (11), 1987 (11), 1988 (3), 1989 (6). Total—77.
Led South Atlantic League in total bases with 256 in 1980.
Led South Atlantic League outfielders in assists with 17 in 1980.
Tied for International League lead in game-winning RBIs with 14 in 1982.
Tied for Gulf Coast League lead in being hit by pitch with 5 in 1979.

Year Club League	Pos.	G.	AB.	R.	H.	2B.	3B.	HR.	RBI.	B.A.	PO.	A.	E.	F.A.
1979—Sarasota Royals... Gulf C.	OF	50	190	21	54	6	4	4	28	.284	108	9	4	.967
1980—Charleston† .... S. Atl.	OF-2B-3B	137	★547	106	152	20	★15	18	98	.278	281	19	13	.958
1981—Jackson .... Texas	OF	127	497	69	142	29	2	4	50	.286	267	21	6	.980
1982—Tidewater .... Int.	OF	130	512	76	118	15	7	10	65	.230	283	13	12	.961
1983—Tidewater‡ .... Int.	OF	51	175	32	50	13	1	3	29	.286	114	5	2	.983
1983—Pittsburgh............. Nat.	OF	103	366	66	89	16	2	7	26	.243	223	3	4	.983
1984—Pittsburgh............. Nat.	OF	154	653	77	174	24	11	0	39	.266	373	8	4	.990
1985—Pittsburgh§x ...... Nat.	OF	103	337	21	69	6	3	2	18	.205	229	7	3	.987
1986—San Diego .... Nat.	OF	137	288	34	76	19	2	7	37	.264	203	3	3	.986
1987—San Diego y .... Nat.	OF	98	188	17	47	8	2	2	24	.250	100	2	2	.981
1988—San Diego .... Nat.	OF	128	333	37	88	13	4	11	42	.264	216	5	3	.987
1989—S.D. z-Chi............. Nat.	OF	125	342	27	83	13	2	7	39	.243	177	7	6	.968
Major League Totals—7 Years................		848	2507	279	626	99	26	36	225	.250	1521	35	25	.984

Signed as free agent by Kansas City Royals' organization, September 3, 1978.
†Traded with Pitcher John Skinner to New York Mets' organization for Pitcher Juan Berenguer, March 31, 1981.
‡Traded with Pitcher Steve Senteney to Pittsburgh Pirates for Catcher Junior Ortiz and Pitcher Arthur Ray, June 14, 1983.
§On disabled list, April 20 to May 5 and June 3 to June 18, 1985.
xTraded to San Diego Padres for Pitcher Bob Patterson, April 3, 1986.
yOn disabled list, June 10 to June 25, 1987.
zTraded with Infielder Luis Salazar to Chicago Cubs for Pitcher Calvin Schiraldi, Outfielder Darrin Jackson and a player to be named later, August 30, 1989; San Diego Padres acquired First Baseman Phil Stephenson to complete deal, September 5, 1989.

CHAMPIONSHIP SERIES RECORD

Year Club League	Pos.	G.	AB.	R.	H.	2B.	3B.	HR.	RBI.	B.A.	PO.	A.	E.	F.A.
1989—Chicago .... Nat.	PH-OF	4	6	0	1	0	0	0	0	.167	3	0	0	1.000

ERIC GIRARD YELDING

Born February 22, 1965, at Montrose, Ala.
Height, 6.03. Weight, 180.
Thows and bats righthanded.
Attended Chipola Junior College, Marianna, Fla.

Major League stolen bases: 1989 (11).
Led International League in stolen bases with 59 and caught stealing with 23 in 1988.
Led Carolina League in stolen bases with 62 and caught stealing with 26 in 1985.
Led Pioneer League in caught stealing with 11 in 1984.
Led International League second basemen in errors with 21 in 1988.
Led California League shortstops in total chances with 573 in 1986.

Year Club League	Pos.	G.	AB.	R.	H.	2B.	3B.	HR.	RBI.	B.A.	PO.	A.	E.	F.A.
1984—Medicine Hat........ Pion.	OF	67	★304	61	94	14	6	4	29	.309	99	9	13	.893
1985—Kinston.................. Carol.	OF	135	526	59	137	14	4	2	31	.260	310	10	9	.973
1986—Ventura County ... Calif.	SS	131	★560	83	157	14	7	4	40	.280	★231	284	★58	.899
1987—Myrtle Beach .... S. Atl.	SS	88	357	53	109	12	2	1	31	.305	126	226	45	.887
1987—Knoxville .... South.	SS	39	150	23	30	6	1	0	7	.200	64	92	14	.918
1988—Syracuse† .... Int.	2B-SS	●138	★556	●69	139	15	2	1	38	.250	222	310	35	.938
1989—Houston‡ .... Nat.	SS-2B-OF	70	90	19	21	2	0	0	9	.233	37	57	3	.969
Major League Totals—1 Year..................		70	90	19	21	2	0	0	9	.233	37	57	3	.969

Selected by Toronto Blue Jays' organization in 1st round (19th player selected) of free-agent draft, January 17, 1984.

†Drafted by Chicago Cubs, December 5, 1988.

‡Claimed on waivers by Houston Astros, April 3, 1989.

RICHARD MARTIN YETT
(Rich)

Born October 6, 1962, at Pomona, Calif.
Height, 6.02. Weight, 187.
Throws and bats righthanded.

Major League saves: 1986 (1), 1987 (1). Total—2.
Led International League in wild pitches with 16 in 1985.

Year Club	League	G.	IP.	W.	L.	Pct.	H.	R.	ER.	SO.	BB.	ERA.
1980—Elizabethton	Ap'lachian	10	52	3	4	.429	46	30	25	35	19	4.33
1981—Wisconsin Rapids	Midwest	25	164	12	6	.667	147	87	67	121	77	3.68
1982—Visalia	California	27	196⅔	16	9	.640	183	98	80	121	97	3.66
1983—Orlando†	Southern	24	162	8	10	.444	153	82	68	93	78	3.78
1984—Toledo	Int'national	26	174⅔	12	9	.571	159	71	63	129	66	3.25
1985—Minnesota	American	1	⅓	0	0	.000	1	1	1	0	2	27.00
1985—Toledo‡-Maine	Int'national	25	165	9	11	.450	162	82	76	99	★101	4.15
1986—Maine	Int'national	1	6	0	0	.000	7	3	3	2	2	4.50
1986—Cleveland	American	39	78⅔	5	3	.625	84	48	45	50	37	5.15
1987—Cleveland	American	37	97⅔	3	9	.250	96	63	57	59	49	5.25
1987—Buffalo	Am. Assoc.	7	44⅓	3	3	.500	38	17	15	33	18	3.05
1988—Cleveland§	American	23	134⅓	9	6	.600	146	72	69	71	55	4.62
1988—Williamsport	Eastern	1	3⅓	0	1	.000	6	6	3	4	3	8.10
1988—Colorado Springs	P. Coast	2	8	0	1	.000	10	8	8	5	3	9.00
1989—Cleveland x	American	32	99	5	6	.455	111	56	55	47	47	5.00
Major League Totals—5 Years		132	410	22	24	.478	438	240	227	227	190	4.98

Selected by Minnesota Twins' organization in 26th round of free-agent draft, June 3, 1980.

†On disabled list, April 8 to April 25, 1983.

‡Traded to Cleveland Indians' organization, September 17, 1985, completing deal in which Cleveland traded Pitcher Bert Blyleven to Minnesota Twins for Pitcher Curt Wardle, Outfielder Jim Weaver, Infielder Jay Bell and a player to be named later, August 1, 1986.

§On disabled list, June 14 to July 18, 1988; included rehabilitation disability assignment to Williamsport, June 29 to July 18, 1988.

xReleased, December 21, 1989; signed by Minnesota Twins, December 29, 1989.

MICHAEL DAVID YORK
(Mike)

Born September 6, 1964, at Oak Park, Ill.
Height, 6.01. Weight, 187.
Throws and bats righthanded.

Year Club	League	G.	IP.	W.	L.	Pct.	H.	R.	ER.	SO.	BB.	ERA.
1983—Oneonta†	NYP	9	11	0	0	.000	19	13	10	3	8	8.18
1984—Sarasota White Sox‡	Gulf Coast	5	14⅔	1	0	1.000	18	9	6	19	9	3.68
1985—Bristol	Ap'lachian	21	38	●9	2	●.818	24	12	10	31	34	2.37
1986—Lakeland	Florida St.	16	40⅔	1	3	.250	49	42	29	29	43	6.42
1986—Gastonia§	S. Atlantic	22	34	2	2	.500	26	15	13	27	27	3.44
1987—Macon	S. Atlantic	28	165⅔	★17	6	.739	129	71	56	169	★88	3.04
1988—Salem	Carolina	13	84	9	2	●.818	65	31	25	77	52	2.68
1988—Harrisburg	Eastern	13	82⅓	0	5	.000	92	43	34	61	45	3.72
1989—Harrisburg	Eastern	18	121	11	5	.688	105	37	31	106	40	2.31
1989—Buffalo	Am. Assoc.	8	41	1	3	.250	48	29	27	28	25	5.93

Selected by New York Yankees' organization in 40th round of free-agent draft, June 7, 1982.

†Released, July 22, 1983; signed by Sarasota White Sox (Chicago White Sox' organization), July 18, 1984.

‡Released, April 8, 1985; signed by Lakeland (Detroit Tigers' organization), June 9, 1985.

§Released, August 29, 1986; signed by Pittsburgh Pirates' organization, October 11, 1986.

FLOYD EVERETT YOUMANS JR.

Name pronounced YOH-muns.

Born May 11, 1964, at Tampa, Fla.
Height, 6.01. Weight, 215.
Throws and bats righthanded.

Year Club	League	G.	IP.	W.	L.	Pct.	H.	R.	ER.	SO.	BB.	ERA.
1982—Kingsport	Ap'lachian	10	39⅓	2	4	.333	35	39	27	31	39	6.18
1983—Columbia	S. Atlantic	23	134⅓	12	3	.800	112	77	51	117	73	3.42
1984—Lynchburg	Carolina	7	39⅔	5	2	.714	31	19	16	45	27	3.63
1984—Jackson†‡	Texas	16	86	6	7	.462	75	47	44	87	74	4.60
1985—Jacksonville	Southern	14	85⅔	7	3	.700	65	35	32	86	57	3.36
1985—Montreal	National	14	77	4	3	.571	57	27	21	54	49	2.45
1985—Indianapolis	Am. Assoc.	6	37⅔	3	2	.600	19	14	13	38	26	3.11
1986—Montreal	National	33	219	13	12	.520	145	93	86	202	★118	3.53
1987—Montreal§	National	23	116⅓	9	8	.529	112	63	60	94	47	4.64
1987—Jacksonville	Southern	1	6	1	0	1.000	4	2	2	6	3	3.00
1988—Montreal x	National	14	84	3	6	.333	64	35	30	54	41	3.21
1988—Indianapolis y	Am. Assoc.	1	3	0	0	.000	2	1	1	1	1	3.00
1989—Philadelphia z	National	10	42⅔	1	5	.167	50	31	27	20	25	5.70
Major League Totals—5 Years		94	539	30	34	.469	428	249	224	424	280	3.74

Selected by New York Mets' organization in 2nd round of free-agent draft, June 7, 1982.

†On disabled list, June 11 to June 21, 1984.

‡Traded with Infielder Hubie Brooks, Catcher Mike Fitzgerald and Outfielder Herm Winningham to Montreal Expos for Catcher Gary Carter, December 10, 1984.

§On disabled list, May 4 to May 19, June 10 to June 30 and August 16 to September 1, 1987; included rehabilitation disability assignment to Jacksonville, June 26 to June 30, 1987.

xOn ineligible list, June 25 to August 24, 1988; then transferred to disabled list, August 25 to September 14, 1988; included rehabilitation disability assignment to Indianapolis, August 25 to September 13, 1988.

yTraded with Pitcher Jeff Parrett to Philadelphia Phillies for Pitcher Kevin Gross, December 6, 1988.

zOn disabled list, May 3 to June 2 and June 28, 1989 through remainder of season.

CLIFFORD RAPHAEL YOUNG
(Cliff)

Born August 2, 1964, at Willis, Tex.
Height, 6.04. Weight, 200.
Throws and bats lefthanded.

Led Southern League in games started by pitchers with 31 in 1986.
Led Florida State League in home runs allowed with 13 in 1986.

Year Club	League	G.	IP.	W.	L.	Pct.	H.	R.	ER.	SO.	BB.	ERA.
1983—Calgary	Pioneer	13	79⅓	7	1	.875	98	55	45	72	32	5.11
1984—Gastonia†	S. Atlantic	24	144⅓	8	10	.444	117	77	67	121	68	4.18
1985—West Palm Beach‡	Florida St.	25	153⅔	15	5	.750	149	77	68	112	57	3.98
1986—Knoxville§x	Southern	31	*203⅔	12	*14	.462	*232	111	88	121	71	3.89
1987—Knoxville	Southern	42	119⅓	8	9	.471	148	76	59	81	43	4.45
1988—Syracuse y	Int'national	33	147⅓	9	6	.600	133	68	56	75	32	3.42
1989—Edmonton	P. Coast	31	139	8	9	.471	158	80	74	89	32	4.79

Selected by Montreal Expos' organization in 5th round of free-agent draft, June 6, 1983.

†On suspended list, May 23 to May 30, 1984.

‡Traded to Toronto Blue Jays' organization, September 10, 1985, completing deal in which Toronto traded Outfielder Mitch Webster to Montreal Expos for a player to be named later, June 22, 1985.

§On disabled list, August 20 to August 30, 1986.

xDrafted by Oakland Athletics, December 8, 1986; returned, April 6, 1987.

yTraded to California Angels for Pitcher DeWayne Buice, March 9, 1989.

CURTIS ALLEN YOUNG
(Curt)

Born April 16, 1960, at Saginaw, Mich.
Height, 6.01. Weight, 175.
Throws left and bats righthanded.
Attended Central Michigan University, Mt. Pleasant, Mich.

Led California League pitchers in games started with 28 in 1982.

Year Club	League	G.	IP.	W.	L.	Pct.	H.	R.	ER.	SO.	BB.	ERA.
1981—Medford	Northwest	8	53	2	2	.500	45	27	25	49	32	4.25
1981—Modesto	California	5	31	2	1	.667	28	15	12	22	16	3.48
1982—Modesto	California	28	205	15	8	.652	189	90	79	162	81	3.47
1983—Tacoma	P. Coast	27	158⅔	12	9	.571	175	94	89	109	52	5.05
1983—Oakland	American.	8	9	0	1	.000	17	17	16	5	5	16.00
1984—Tacoma	P. Coast	14	95⅓	6	4	.600	88	45	40	61	28	3.78
1984—Oakland	American	20	108⅔	9	4	.692	118	53	49	41	31	4.06
1985—Oakland†	American	19	46	0	4	.000	57	38	37	19	22	7.24
1985—Modesto	California	2	5⅔	0	0	.000	7	4	3	3	6	4.76
1985—Tacoma	P. Coast	3	15	2	0	1.000	10	7	6	8	7	3.60
1986—Tacoma	P. Coast	4	27	4	0	1.000	16	7	6	28	6	2.00
1986—Oakland	American	29	198	13	9	.591	176	88	76	116	57	3.45
1987—Oakland‡§	American	31	203	13	7	.650	194	102	92	124	44	4.08
1988—Oakland	American	26	156⅓	11	8	.579	162	77	72	69	50	4.14
1989—Oakland	American	25	111	5	9	.357	117	56	46	55	47	3.73
Major League Totals—7 Years		158	832	51	42	.548	841	431	388	429	256	4.20

Selected by Oakland A's organization in 4th round of free-agent draft, June 8, 1981.

†On disabled list, May 3 to July 5, 1985; included rehabilitation disability assignment to Modesto, June 29 to July 5, 1985.

‡On disabled list, June 30 to July 20, 1987.

§Had one at-bat with no hits.

CHAMPIONSHIP SERIES RECORD

Year Club	League	G.	IP.	W.	L.	Pct.	H.	R.	ER.	SO.	BB.	ERA.
1988—Oakland	American	1	1⅓	0	0	.000	1	1	0	2	0	0.00

WORLD SERIES RECORD

Year Club	League	G.	IP.	W.	L.	Pct.	H.	R.	ER.	SO.	BB.	ERA.
1988—Oakland	American	1	1	0	0	.000	1	0	0	0	0	0.00

Eligible for 1989 World Series with Oakland Athletics; did not play.

GERALD ANTHONY YOUNG

Born October 22, 1964, in Tele, Honduras.
Height, 6.02. Weight, 185.
Throws right and bats left and righthanded.

Major League stolen bases: 1987 (26), 1988 (65), 1989 (34). Total—125.
Led National League in caught stealing with 25 in 1989 and tied for lead with 27 in 1988.
Led National League outfielders in total chances with 428 and tied for lead in double plays with 5 in 1989.
Led Southern League in stolen bases with 54 and caught stealing with 27 in 1986.
Tied for Appalachian League lead in being hit by pitch with 6 in 1982.
Led Appalachian League shortstops in errors with 38 in 1982.
Tied for Florida State League lead in double plays by outfielders with 5 in 1985.

Year	Club	League	Pos.	G.	AB.	R.	H.	2B.	3B.	HR.	RBI.	B.A.	PO.	A.	E.	F.A.
1982—Kingsport	Appal.	SS-2B-3B	59	197	27	35	6	1	0	15	.178	79	170	39	.865
1983—Sarasota Mets	Gulf C.	OF-SS	56	177	34	42	7	2	1	14	.237	88	9	7	.933
1984—Columbia†	S. Atl.	OF	124	396	69	84	14	3	1	52	.212	254	7	4	.985
1985—Osceola	Fla. St.	OF	133	474	88	121	20	9	3	48	.255	251	11	5	.981
1986—Columbus	South.	OF	136	539	101	151	30	4	9	62	.280	317	22	13	.963
1987—Tucson	P. C.	OF	86	340	59	99	15	5	2	31	.291	232	7	7	.972
1987—Houston	Nat.	OF	71	274	44	88	9	2	1	15	.321	143	5	3	.980
1988—Houston	Nat.	OF	149	576	79	148	21	9	0	37	.257	357	10	3	.992
1989—Houston	Nat.	OF	146	533	71	124	17	3	0	38	.233	★412	★15	1	★.998
Major League Totals—3 Years			366	1383	194	360	47	14	1	90	.260	912	30	7	.993

Selected by New York Mets' organization in 5th round of free-agent draft, June 7, 1982.

†Traded with Infielder Manny Lee to Houston Astros, August 31, 1984, as partial completion of deal in which New York Mets acquired Infielder Ray Knight for three players to be named later, August 28, 1984; Houston acquired Pitcher Mitch Cook to complete deal, September 10, 1984.

MATTHEW JOHN YOUNG
(Matt)

Born August 9, 1958, at Pasadena, Calif.
Height, 6.03. Weight, 205.
Throws and bats lefthanded.
Attended Pasadena City College, Pasadena, Calif., and
UCLA, Los Angeles, Calif.

Major League saves: 1985 (1), 1986 (13), 1987 (11). Total—25.

Year	Club	League	G.	IP.	W.	L.	Pct.	H.	R.	ER.	SO.	BB.	ERA.
1980—Bellingham	Northwest	12	73	4	5	.444	73	46	40	53	62	4.93
1981—Lynn	Eastern	14	81	3	9	.250	80	47	36	57	38	4.00
1982—Salt Lake City	P. Coast	29	176	12	10	.545	192	113	91	118	75	4.65
1983—Seattle	American	33	203⅔	11	15	.423	178	86	74	130	79	3.27
1984—Seattle†	American	22	113⅓	6	8	.429	141	81	72	73	57	5.72
1984—Salt Lake City	P. Coast	6	41⅔	6	0	1.000	32	9	7	37	20	1.51
1985—Seattle	American	37	218⅓	12	★19	.387	242	135	119	136	76	4.91
1986—Seattle‡	American	65	103⅔	8	6	.571	108	50	44	82	46	3.82
1987—Los Angeles§	National	47	54⅓	5	8	.385	62	30	27	42	17	4.47
1988—Oakland xy	American					(Did not play)						
1989—Modesto z	California	3	12	0	0	.000	9	1	1	13	6	0.75
1989—Tacoma	P. Coast	2	11	1	1	.500	8	4	3	6	5	2.45
1989—Oakland a	American	26	37⅓	1	4	.200	42	31	28	27	31	6.75
American League Totals—5 Years		183	676⅓	38	52	.422	711	383	337	448	289	4.48
National League Totals—1 Year		47	54⅓	5	8	.385	62	30	27	42	17	4.47
Major League Totals—6 Years		230	730⅔	43	60	.417	773	413	364	490	306	4.48

Selected by Boston Red Sox' organization in 2nd round of free-agent draft, January 10, 1978.
Selected by Seattle Mariners' organization in 2nd round of free-agent draft, June 3, 1980.

†On disabled list, July 4 to July 29, 1984.

‡Traded to Los Angeles Dodgers for Pitcher Dennis Powell and Infielder Mike Watters, December 10, 1986.

§As part of an eight-player, three-team deal, New York Mets traded Pitcher Jesse Orosco to Oakland Athletics, December 11, 1987. Oakland then traded Orosco along with Shortstop Alfredo Griffin and Pitcher Jay Howell to Los Angeles Dodgers for Pitchers Bob Welch, Matt Young and Jack Savage. Oakland then traded Savage along with Pitchers Wally Whitehurst and Kevin Tapani to New York.

xOn disabled list, April 3, 1988 through entire season.

yReleased, December 21, 1988; re-signed by Athletics, January 19, 1989.

zOn Oakland disabled list, March 19 to June 13, 1989; included rehabilitation disability assignment to Modesto, May 16 and May 25 to June 2, 1989; and Tacoma, June 3 to June 9, 1989.

aGranted free agency, November 13, 1989; signed by Seattle Mariners, December 15, 1989.

CHAMPIONSHIP SERIES RECORD

Year	Club	League	G.	IP.	W.	L.	Pct.	H.	R.	ER.	SO.	BB.	ERA.
1989—Oakland	American	1	⅓	0	0	.000	0	0	0	0	2	0.00

WORLD SERIES RECORD

Eligible for 1989 World Series with Oakland Athletics; did not play.

ALL-STAR GAME RECORD

Year	League	IP.	W.	L.	Pct.	H.	R.	ER.	SO.	BB.	ERA.
1983—American		1	0	0	.000	0	0	0	1	0	0.00

MICHAEL DARREN YOUNG
(Mike)

Born March 20, 1960, at Oakland, Calif.
Height, 6.02. Weight, 206.
Throws right and bats left and righthanded.
Attended St. Mary's College, Moraga, Calif.; and Chabot College, Hayward, Calif.

Shares major league record for most extra-inning home runs, game (2), May 28, 1987, 10th and 12th innings.
Switch-hit home runs in one game, August 13, 1985.
Major League stolen bases: 1983 (1), 1984 (6), 1985 (1), 1986 (3), 1987 (10), 1989 (1). Total—22.
Led International League batters in strikeouts with 140 in 1982.
Tied for Florida State League lead in double plays by outfielders with 4 in 1980.

Year	Club	League	Pos.	G.	AB.	R.	H.	2B.	3B.	HR.	RBI.	B.A.	PO.	A.	E.	F.A.
1980—Miami	Fla. St.	OF	115	393	72	105	13	8	5	52	.267	212	★17	7	.970
1981—Miami	Fla. St.	OF	63	235	32	81	19	6	3	34	.345	135	7	1	.993
1981—Charlotte	South.	OF	75	275	58	88	16	3	12	45	.320	190	5	5	.975
1981—Rochester	Int.	OF	1	3	0	1	0	0	0	0	.000	1	0	0	1.000
1982—Rochester	Int.	OF	137	502	86	133	22	11	16	62	.265	291	7	11	.964
1982—Baltimore	Amer.	OF	6	2	2	0	0	0	0	0	.000	1	0	0	1.000
1983—Rochester	Int.	OF	102	373	62	106	14	8	14	66	.284	198	4	6	.971
1983—Baltimore	Amer.	OF	25	36	5	6	2	1	0	2	.167	25	1	2	.929
1984—Rochester	Int.	OF	20	72	17	24	6	1	4	15	.333	39	0	3	.929
1984—Baltimore	Amer.	OF	123	401	59	101	17	2	17	52	.252	216	4	4	.982
1985—Baltimore	Amer.	OF	139	450	72	123	22	1	28	81	.273	190	6	5	.975
1986—Baltimore	Amer.	OF	117	369	43	93	15	1	9	42	.252	149	1	6	.962
1986—Rochester†	Int.	OF	32	97	14	27	2	0	5	21	.278	58	3	2	.968
1987—Rochester†	Int.	DH	7	25	4	8	0	1	2	5	.320	0	0	0	.000
1987—Baltimore‡	Amer.	OF	110	363	46	87	10	1	16	39	.240	117	0	3	.975
1988—Philadelphia§	Nat.	OF	75	146	13	33	14	0	1	14	.226	76	0	5	.938
1988—Milwaukee x	Amer.	OF	8	14	2	0	0	0	0	0	.000	0	0	0	.000
1989—Colorado Springs.	P. C.	OF	72	260	55	80	21	4	14	48	.308	39	1	0	1.000
1989—Cleveland y	Amer.	OF	32	59	2	11	0	0	1	5	.186	1	0	0	1.000
American League Totals—7 Years			450	1331	185	334	56	5	55	182	.251	582	12	17	.972
National League Totals—1 Year			75	146	13	33	14	0	1	14	.226	76	0	5	.938
Major League Totals—7 Years			525	1477	198	367	70	5	56	196	.248	658	12	22	.968

Selected by Cleveland Indians' organization in 7th round of free-agent draft, June 6, 1978.
Selected by Baltimore Orioles' organization in secondary phase of free-agent draft, January 8, 1980.
†On Baltimore disabled list, March 23 to May 13, 1987; included rehabilitation disability assignment to Rochester, May 5 to May 13, 1987.
‡Traded with a player to be named later to Philadelphia Phillies for Infielder Rick Schu and Outfielders Jeff Stone and Keith Hughes, March 21, 1988; Philadelphia acquired Outfielder Frank Bellino to complete deal, June 14, 1988.
§Traded to Milwaukee Brewers for Pitcher Alex Madrid, August 24, 1988.
xReleased, March 23, 1989; signed by Colorado Springs (Cleveland Indians' organization), April 4, 1989.
ySold to Hiroshima Toyo Carp of Japanese Baseball League, November 8, 1989.

RAYMOND CEDRICK YOUNG
(Ray)

Born May 27, 1964, at Los Angeles, Calif.
Height, 6.03. Weight, 190.
Throws and bats righthanded.
Attended Moorpark College, Moorpark, Calif.

Led Southern League in balks with 12 and tied for lead in shutouts with 2 in 1989.
Led California League in wild pitches with 28 in 1988.

Year	Club	League	G.	IP.	W.	L.	Pct.	H.	R.	ER.	SO.	BB.	ERA.
1984—Great Falls	Pioneer	13	47⅓	3	2	.600	53	46	38	47	46	7.23
1985—Bakersfield	California	19	85⅓	1	9	.100	61	73	54	81	111	5.70
1986—Bakersfield†‡	California	12	38	1	5	.167	47	43	39	27	47	9.24
1987—Dunedin§	Florida St.	34	95⅓	3	3	.600	62	34	28	69	72	2.64
1988—Modesto	California	25	98⅔	8	7	.533	70	78	61	78	142	5.56
1989—Huntsville	Southern	29	146⅔	13	6	.684	112	78	64	163	109	3.93

Signed as free agent by Los Angeles Dodgers' organization, May 16, 1984.
†On disabled list, April 11 to May 21, 1986.
‡Drafted by Toronto Blue Jays' organization, December 8, 1986.
§Released, March 30, 1988; signed by Modesto (Oakland Athletics' organization), April 7, 1988.

JOEL RANDOLPH YOUNGBLOOD III

Born August 28, 1951, at Houston, Tex.
Height, 5.11. Weight, 175.
Throws and bats righthanded.

Holds major league record for most clubs, one or more hits for, one day (2), August 4, 1982.
Shares major league record for most clubs played, one day (2), August 4, 1982.
Major League stolen bases: 1976 (1), 1977 (1), 1978 (4), 1979 (18), 1980 (14), 1981 (2), 1982 (2), 1983 (7), 1984 (5), 1985 (3), 1986 (1), 1987 (1), 1988 (1). Total—60.
Led National League third basemen in errors with 36 in 1984.
Led National League outfielders in double plays with 6 in 1980.
Led Northern League second basemen in errors with 19 in 1970.
Tied for Northern League lead in being hit by pitch with 5 in 1970.

Year Club	League	Pos.	G.	AB.	R.	H.	2B.	3B.	HR.	RBI.	B.A.	PO.	A.	E.	F.A.
1970—Tampa	Fla. St.	SS	17	54	7	12	0	0	0	3	.222	22	40	9	.873
1970—Sioux Falls	North.	2B-3B-SS	65	236	27	53	11	1	0	17	.225	110	134	26	.904
1971—Tampa	Fla. St.	3B-SS-OF	136	443	75	113	25	4	5	44	.255	159	207	26	.934
1972—Three Rivers	East.	OF-3B	104	366	57	106	15	5	12	60	.290	118	80	30	.868
1973—Indianapolis	A. A.	OF-SS-3B	124	451	88	143	24	9	11	50	.317	136	112	28	.899
1974—Indianapolis†	A. A.	OF	103	316	55	90	17	4	13	49	.285	115	6	4	.968
1975—Indianapolis	A. A.	OF-2B	123	418	65	110	21	●9	6	51	.263	201	13	7	.968
1976—Cincinnati‡	Nat.	1-O-C-2	55	57	8	11	1	1	0	1	.193	15	3	1	.947
1977—St. L.§-N.Y.	Nat.	2B-O-3B	95	209	17	51	13	1	0	12	.244	107	94	8	.962
1978—New York	Nat.	O-2-3-S	113	266	40	67	12	8	7	30	.252	160	96	13	.952
1979—New York	Nat.	OF-2B-3B	158	590	90	162	37	5	16	60	.275	337	57	9	.978
1980—New York	Nat.	OF-3B-2B	146	514	58	142	26	2	8	69	.276	318	65	13	.967
1981—New York x	Nat.	OF	43	143	16	50	10	2	4	25	.350	70	6	3	.962
1982—N.Y. y-Mont. z	Nat.	O-2-S-3	120	292	37	70	14	0	3	29	.240	149	23	7	.961
1983—San Francisco	Nat.	2B-3B-OF	124	373	59	109	20	3	17	53	.292	147	182	19	.945
1984—San Francisco	Nat.	3B-OF-2B	134	469	50	119	17	1	10	51	.254	102	206	37	.893
1985—San Francisco a	Nat.	OF-3B	95	230	24	62	6	0	4	24	.270	103	6	6	.948
1986—San Francisco b	Nat.	O-1-3-2-S	97	184	20	47	12	0	5	28	.255	68	14	3	.965
1987—San Francisco b	Nat.	OF-3B	69	91	9	23	3	0	3	11	.253	24	3	0	1.000
1988—San Francisco c	Nat.	OF	83	123	12	31	4	0	0	16	.252	48	0	1	.980
1989—Cincinnati d	Nat.	OF	76	118	13	25	5	0	3	13	.212	31	1	1	.970
Major League Totals—14 Years			1408	3659	453	969	180	23	80	422	.265	1679	756	121	.953

Selected by Cincinnati Reds' organization in 2nd round of free-agent draft, January 17, 1970.
†On disabled list, June 7 to June 19, 1974.
‡Traded to St. Louis Cardinals for Pitcher Bill Caudill, March 28, 1977.
§Traded to New York Mets for Shortstop Mike Phillips, June 15, 1977.
xOn disabled list, June 6 to August 1 and August 15 to September 15, 1981.
yTraded to Montreal Expos for a player to be named later, August 4, 1982; New York Mets' organization acquired Pitcher Tom Gorman to complete deal, August 14, 1982.
zGranted free agency, November 10, 1982; signed by San Francisco Giants, February 7, 1983.
aReleased, December 20, 1985; re-signed by Giants, March 20, 1986.
bGranted free agency, November 9, 1987; re-signed by Giants, December 1, 1987.
cGranted free agency, November 4, 1988; signed by Cincinnati Reds, December 21, 1988.
dGranted free agency, November 13, 1989.

ALL-STAR GAME RECORD

Year League	Pos.	AB.	R.	H.	2B.	3B.	HR.	RBI.	B.A.	PO.	A.	E.	F.A.
1981—National	PH	1	0	0	0	0	0	0	.000	0	0	0	.000

ROBIN R. YOUNT

Born September 16, 1955, at Danville, Ill.
Height, 6.00. Weight, 180.
Throws and bats righthanded.
Brother of Larry Yount, pitcher with Houston Astros, 1971.

Major League stolen bases: 1974 (7), 1975 (12), 1976 (16), 1977 (16), 1978 (16), 1979 (11), 1980 (20), 1981 (4), 1982 (14), 1983 (12), 1984 (14), 1985 (10), 1986 (14), 1987 (19), 1988 (22), 1989 (19). Total—226.
Hit for the cycle, June 12, 1988.
Led American League in total bases with 367 and slugging percentage with .578 in 1982.
Led American League outfielders in fielding percentage with .997 in 1986.
Led American League shortstops in double plays with 104 and total chances with 831 in 1976.
Named Major League Player of the Year by THE SPORTING NEWS, 1982.
Named American League Player of the Year by THE SPORTING NEWS, 1982.
Named American League Most Valuable Player by Baseball Writers' Association of America, 1982 and 1989.
Named outfielder on THE SPORTING NEWS American League All-Star Team, 1989.
Named shortstop on THE SPORTING NEWS American League All-Star Team, 1978, 1980 and 1982.
Named shortstop on THE SPORTING NEWS American League All-Star fielding team, 1982.
Named outfielder on THE SPORTING NEWS American League Silver Slugger team, 1989.
Named shortstop on THE SPORTING NEWS American League Silver Slugger team, 1980 and 1982.

Year Club	League	Pos.	G.	AB.	R.	H.	2B.	3B.	HR.	RBI.	B.A.	PO.	A.	E.	F.A.
1973—Newark	NYP	SS	64	242	29	69	15	3	3	25	.285	43	85	18	.877
1974—Milwaukee	Amer.	SS	107	344	48	86	14	5	3	26	.250	148	327	19	.962
1975—Milwaukee	Amer.	SS	147	558	67	149	28	2	8	52	.267	273	402	★44	.939
1976—Milwaukee	Amer.	●SS-OF	●161	638	59	161	19	3	2	54	.252	●290	510	31	.963
1972—Milwaukee	Amer.	SS	154	605	66	174	34	4	4	49	.288	256	449	29	.964
1978—Milwaukee†	Amer.	SS	127	502	66	147	23	9	9	71	.293	246	453	30	.959
1979—Milwaukee	Amer.	SS	149	577	72	154	26	5	8	51	.267	267	517	25	.969
1980—Milwaukee	Amer.	SS	143	611	121	179	★49	10	23	87	.293	239	455	28	.961
1981—Milwaukee	Amer.	SS	96	377	50	103	15	5	10	49	.273	161	370	8	★.985
1982—Milwaukee	Amer.	SS	156	635	129	★210	●46	12	29	114	.331	253	★489	24	.969
1983—Milwaukee	Amer.	SS	149	578	102	178	42	★10	17	80	.308	256	420	19	.973
1984—Milwaukee	Amer.	SS	160	624	105	186	27	7	16	80	.298	199	402	18	.971
1985—Milwaukee	Amer.	OF-1B	122	466	76	129	26	3	15	68	.277	267	5	8	.971
1986—Milwaukee	Amer.	OF-1B	140	522	82	163	31	7	9	46	.312	365	9	2	.995
1987—Milwaukee	Amer.	OF	158	635	99	198	25	9	21	103	.312	380	5	5	.987
1988—Milwaukee	Amer.	OF	★162	621	92	190	38	●11	13	91	.306	444	12	2	.996
1989—Milwaukee‡	Amer.	OF	160	614	101	195	38	9	21	103	.318	361	8	7	.981
Major League Totals—16 Years			2291	8907	1335	2602	481	111	208	1124	.292	4405	4833	296	.969

Selected by Milwaukee Brewers' organization in 1st round (third player selected) of free-agent draft, June 5, 1973.
†On disabled list, March 28 to May 3, 1978.
‡Granted free agency, November 13, 1989; re-signed by Brewers, December 19, 1989.

DIVISION SERIES RECORD

Year	Club	League	Pos.	G.	AB.	R.	H.	2B.	3B.	HR.	RBI.	B.A.	PO.	A.	E.	F.A.
1981—Milwaukee	Amer.	SS	5	19	4	6	0	1	0	1	.316	6	16	1	.957

CHAMPIONSHIP SERIES RECORD

Year	Club	League	Pos.	G.	AB.	R.	H.	2B.	3B.	HR.	RBI.	B.A.	PO.	A.	E.	F.A.
1982—Milwaukee	Amer.	SS	5	16	1	4	0	0	0	0	.250	11	12	1	.958

WORLD SERIES RECORD

Shares World Series record for most at-bats, nine-inning game (6), October 12, 1982.

Year	Club	League	Pos.	G.	AB.	R.	H.	2B.	3B.	HR.	RBI.	B.A.	PO.	A.	E.	F.A.
1982—Milwaukee	Amer.	SS	7	29	6	12	3	0	1	6	.414	20	19	3	.929

ALL-STAR GAME RECORD

Year	League	Pos.	AB.	R.	H.	2B.	3B.	HR.	RBI.	B.A.	PO.	A.	E.	F.A.
1980—American		SS	2	0	0	0	0	0	0	.000	3	2	0	1.000
1982—American		SS	3	0	0	0	0	0	0	.000	0	2	0	1.000
1983—American		SS	2	1	0	0	0	0	1	.000	0	1	0	1.000
All-Star Game Totals—3 Years			7	1	0	0	0	0	1	.000	3	5	0	1.000

CLINTON WAYNE ZAVARAS
(Clint)

Born January 4, 1967, at Denver, Colo.
Height, 6.01. Weight, 175.
Throws and bats righthanded.

Year	Club	League	G.	IP.	W.	L.	Pct.	H.	R.	ER.	SO.	BB.	ERA.
1985—Bellingham	Northwest	12	56⅓	4	7	.364	49	37	35	62	47	5.59
1986—Wausau	Midwest	17	91⅓	6	6	.500	68	45	34	98	67	3.35
1987—Salinas	California	26	139⅔	7	12	.368	102	87	69	180	101	4.45
1988—Vermont	Eastern	24	128⅔	10	7	.588	115	67	56	120	54	3.92
1989—Calgary	P. Coast	21	110⅓	6	9	.400	105	77	74	89	56	6.04
1989—Seattle	American	10	52	1	6	.143	49	33	30	31	30	5.19
Major League Totals—1 Year		10	52	1	6	.143	49	33	30	31	30	5.19

Selected by Seattle Mariners' organization in 3rd round of free-agent draft, June 3, 1985.

TODD EDWARD ZEILE

Born September 9, 1965, at Van Nuys, Calif.
Height, 6.01. Weight, 190.
Throws and bats righthanded.
Attended UCLA, Los Angeles, Calif.

Led New York-Pennsylvania League in sacrifice flies with 6 in 1986.
Led American Association catchers in fielding percentage with .992 and passed balls with 17 in 1989.
Led Texas League catchers in putouts with 687 and total chances with 761 in 1988.
Tied for New York-Pennsylvania League lead in double plays by catchers with 7 in 1986.
Named Midwest League Co-Most Valuable Player, 1987.

Year	Club	League	Pos.	G.	AB.	R.	H.	2B.	3B.	HR.	RBI.	B.A.	PO.	A.	E.	F.A.
1986—Erie	NYP	C	70	248	40	64	14	1	14	★63	.258	407	★66	8	.983
1987—Springfield	Midw.	C-3B	130	487	94	142	24	4	25	★106	.292	867	70	14	.985
1988—Arkansas	Texas	C-OF-1B	129	430	95	117	33	2	19	75	.272	697	66	10	.987
1989—Louisville	A. A.	C-3B-1B	118	453	71	131	26	3	19	85	.289	583	71	6	.991
1989—St. Louis	Nat.	C	28	82	7	21	3	1	1	8	.256	125	10	4	.971
Major League Totals—1 Year			28	82	7	21	3	1	1	8	.256	125	10	4	.971

Selected by Kansas City Royals' organization in 30th round of free-agent draft, June 6, 1983.
Selected by St. Louis Cardinals' organization in 2nd round of free-agent draft, June 2, 1986.

PAUL ZUVELLA

Name pronounced Zoo-VELL-uh.

Born October 31, 1958, at San Mateo, Calif.
Height, 6.00. Weight, 178.
Throws and bats righthanded.
Received bachelor of arts degree in communications
from Stanford University, Stanford, Calif.

Major League stolen bases: 1985 (2).
Led International League in being hit by pitch with 8 in 1984.
Led International League shortstops in total chances with 644 and double plays with 85 in 1984.
Led Southern League shortstops in total chances with 661 in 1981.

Year	Club	League	Pos.	G.	AB.	R.	H.	2B.	3B.	HR.	RBI.	B.A.	PO.	A.	E.	F.A.
1980—Bradenton Braves	Gulf C.	SS	2	8	0	1	0	0	0	1	.125	4	9	1	.929
1980—Durham†	Carol.	SS	48	149	21	47	7	0	2	19	.315	58	140	12	.943
1981—Savannah	South.	SS	138	485	61	145	17	2	11	68	.299	220	★406	35	.947
1982—Richmond	Int.	SS	133	455	63	128	15	2	9	54	.281	245	335	22	.963
1982—Atlanta	Nat.	SS	2	1	0	0	0	0	0	0	.000	0	4	1	.800
1983—Richmond	Int.	SS	117	415	53	119	13	2	6	64	.287	169	324	18	★.965
1983—Atlanta	Nat.	SS	3	5	0	0	0	0	0	0	.000	1	2	1	.750
1984—Richmond	Int.	SS	127	462	77	140	18	●6	6	55	.303	★219	★409	16	★.975

Year Club League	Pos.	G.	AB.	R.	H.	2B.	3B.	HR.	RBI.	B.A.	PO.	A.	E.	F.A.
1984—Atlanta .... Nat.	2B-SS	11	25	2	5	1	0	0	1	.200	13	21	0	1.000
1985—Richmond............. Int.	SS	8	32	3	7	0	0	1	3	.219	10	30	3	.930
1985—Atlanta .... Nat.	2B-SS-3B	81	190	16	48	8	1	0	4	.253	112	173	8	.973
1986—Rich.‡-Col. .... Int.	SS-2B	89	334	56	101	13	1	2	31	.302	149	231	10	.974
1986—New York............. Amer.	SS	21	48	2	4	1	0	0	2	.083	30	54	3	.966
1987—New York............. Amer.	2B-SS-3B	14	34	2	6	0	0	0	0	.176	20	25	0	1.000
1987—Columbus§ .... Int.	SS-2B	69	269	47	81	15	4	2	25	.301	131	178	11	.966
1988—Colorado Springs . P. C.	SS-2B	68	232	33	67	11	3	1	28	.289	105	190	16	.949
1988—Cleveland............... Amer.	SS	51	130	9	30	5	1	0	7	.231	77	112	8	.959
1989—Colorado Springs . P. C.	SS	96	387	61	128	23	3	10	66	.331	139	321	12	★.975
1989—Cleveland............... Amer.	SS-3B	24	58	10	16	2	0	2	6	.276	14	24	2	.950
National League Totals—4 Years............		97	221	18	53	9	1	0	5	.240	126	200	10	.970
American League Totals—4 Years		110	270	23	56	8	1	2	15	.207	141	215	13	.965
Major League Totals—8 Years.................		207	491	41	109	17	2	2	20	.222	267	415	23	.967

Selected by Milwaukee Brewers' organization in 11th round of free-agent draft, June 5, 1979.
Selected by Atlanta Braves' organization in 15th round of free-agent draft, June 3, 1980.
†On disabled list, August 27, 1980 through remainder of season.
‡Traded with Outfielder Claudell Washington to New York Yankees for Outfielder Ken Griffey, June 30, 1986.
§Granted free agency, October 15, 1987; signed by Colorado Springs (Cleveland Indians' organization), January 8, 1988.

PLAYER MOVES

The following player deals involve players in the Register with the transactions occurring after December 17, 1989 and through January 8, 1990:

ALEXANDER, DOYLE: Released by Detroit Tigers, December 20, 1989.

ARMAS, TONY: Released by California Angels, December 20, 1989.

BEANE, BILLY: Released by Oakland Athletics, December 21, 1989.

BOSLEY, THAD: Re-signed by Texas Rangers, December 19, 1989.

BROOKS, HUBIE: Signed by Los Angeles Dodgers, December 21, 1989.

CASTILLO, CARMEN: Re-signed by Minnesota Twins, January 8, 1990.

CERONE, RICK: Released by Boston Red Sox, December 19, 1989; signed by New York Yankees, December 20, 1989.

CLEAR, MARK: Released by California Angels, December 20, 1989.

DAVIS, BUTCH: Released by Baltimore Orioles, December 20, 1989.

DAVIS, MIKE: Released by Los Angeles Dodgers, December 20, 1989.

DEMPSEY, RICK: Re-signed by Los Angeles Dodgers, December 19, 1989.

EICHHORN, MARK: Signed by Edmonton (California Angels' organization), December 19, 1989.

EVANS, DARRELL: Re-signed by Atlanta Braves' organization, January 8, 1990.

LAW, VANCE: Released by Chicago Cubs, January 4, 1990.

LAWTON, MARCUS: Signed by Vancouver (Chicago White Sox' organization), December 18, 1989.

McMURTRY, CRAIG: Re-signed by Texas Rangers' organization, January 5, 1990.

Major League Managers

GEORGE LEE ANDERSON
(Sparky)
Detroit Tigers

Born February 22, 1934, at Bridgewater, S. D.
Height, 5.09. Weight, 168.
Threw and batted righthanded.

Major League stolen bases: 1959 (6).
Led International League in sacrifice hits with 15 in 1960.
Led Western League in sacrifice hits with 20 in 1954.
Tied for Texas League lead in sacrifice hits with 22 in 1955.
Led Texas League second basemen in double plays with 117 in 1955, Pacific Coast League with 135 in 1957 and International League with 104 in 1958 and 89 in 1960.
Led California League shortstops in double plays with 83 in 1953.

Year Club	League	Pos.	G.	AB.	R.	H.	2B.	3B.	HR.	RBI.	B.A.	PO.	A.	E.	F.A.
1953—Santa Barbara......	Calif.	SS	●141	★598	98	157	21	4	5	55	.263	★277	395	32	.955
1954—Pueblo	West.	2B	147	497	72	147	13	5	0	62	.296	★397	432	20	●.976
1955—Fort Worth	Texas	2B	158	594	86	158	24	1	0	42	.266	★456	★469	18	★.981
1956—Montreal...............	Int.	2B	140	453	65	135	17	5	0	47	.298	372	391	15	.981
1957—Los Angeles	P. C.	★●2B-SS	●168	619	74	161	15	0	2	35	.260	★524	★488	●15	★.985
1958—Montreal†	Int.	2B	●155	580	78	156	35	5	2	56	.269	★387	★464	10	★.983
1959—Philadelphia	Nat.	2B	152	477	42	104	9	3	0	34	.218	343	403	12	.984
1960—Toronto	Int.	2B	148	543	67	123	11	5	5	21	.227	319	★416	12	.984
1961—Toronto	Int.	2B	97	275	30	66	17	0	0	22	.240	189	203	6	.985
1962—Toronto	Int.	2B	124	432	56	111	18	2	2	38	.257	282	327	8	★.987
1963—Toronto	Int.	2B	116	358	56	89	12	5	3	25	.249	226	256	6	★.988
Major League Totals—1 Year..................		152	477	42	104	9	3	0	34	.218	343	403	12	.984

†Recalled by Los Angeles Dodgers; traded to Philadelphia Phillies for Pitchers Jim Golden and Gene Snyder and Outfielder Eldon (Rip) Repulski, December 23, 1958.

RECORD AS MANAGER

Named American League Manager of the Year by THE SPORTING NEWS, 1987.

Year Club	League	Position	W.	L.	Year Club	League	Position	W.	L.
1964—Toronto	Int.	Fifth	80	72	1978—Cincinnati...............	Nat.	Second(W)	92	69
1965—Rock Hill	W. Carol.	Eighth	24	40	1979—Detroit z................	Amer.	Fifth(E)	56	50
(Second Half)		†First	35	23	1980—Detroit	Amer.	Fifth(E)	84	78
1966—St. Petersburg	Fla. St.	Second	42	24	1981—Detroit a	Amer.		60	49
(Second Half)		‡First	49	21	1982—Detroit...................	Amer.	Fourth(E)	83	79
1967—Modesto	Calif.	§Second	38	32	1983—Detroit...................	Amer.	Second(E)	92	70
(Second Half)		xFirst	41	29	1984—Detroit...................	Amer.	First(E)	104	58
1968—Asheville.................	South.	First	86	54	1985—Detroit...................	Amer.	Third(E)	84	77
1970—Cincinnati...............	Nat.	First(W)	102	60	1986—Detroit...................	Amer.	Third(E)	87	75
1971—Cincinnati...............	Nat.	yFourth(W)	79	83	1987—Detroit...................	Amer.	First(E)	98	64
1972—Cincinnati...............	Nat.	First(W)	95	59	1988—Detroit...................	Amer.	Second(E)	88	74
1973—Cincinnati...............	Nat.	First(W)	99	63	1989—Detroit b.................	Amer.	Seventh(E)	59	103
1974—Cincinnati...............	Nat.	Second(W)	98	64	American League Totals—11 Years			895	777
1975—Cincinnati...............	Nat.	First(W)	108	54	National League Totals—9 Years..................			863	586
1976—Cincinnati...............	Nat.	First(W)	102	60	Major League Totals—20 Years			1758	1363
1977—Cincinnati...............	Nat.	Second(W)	88	74					

†Won playoff against Salisbury (First Half winner), two games to none.
‡Lost playoff against Leesburg (First Half winner), three games to two.
§Tied for position with Santa Barbara.
xLost playoff against San Jose (First Half winner), two games to none.
yTied for position with Houston Astros.
zReplaced Les Moss (and interim manager Dick Tracewski) with club in fifth place (record of 29-26), June 14, 1979.
aFirst Half.... Fourth (E) (record of 31-26); Second Half.... Third (E) (record of 29-23).
bTook time off and replaced by interim manager Dick Tracewski, May 19 through June 5, 1989 (record of 9-9).
Coach, San Diego Padres, 1969.
Manager, American League All-Star Team, 1985.
Manager, National League All-Star Team, 1971, 1973, 1976 and 1977.
Coach, National League All-Star Team, 1974.
Coach, American League All-Star Team, 1982 and 1984.

CHAMPIONSHIP SERIES RECORD

Year Club	League	W.	L.
1970—Cincinnati...............	National	3	0
1972—Cincinnati...............	National	3	2
1973—Cincinnati...............	National	2	3
1975—Cincinnati...............	National	3	0
1976—Cincinnati...............	National	3	0
1984—Detroit....................	American	3	0
1987—Detroit....................	American	1	4
Championship Series Totals—7 Years.............		18	9

WORLD SERIES RECORD

Year Club	League	W.	L.
1970—Cincinnati...............	National	1	4
1972—Cincinnati...............	National	3	4
1975—Cincinnati...............	National	4	3
1976—Cincinnati...............	National	4	0
1984—Detroit....................	American	4	1
World Series Totals—5 Years		16	12

ROGER LEE CRAIG
San Francisco Giants

Born February 17, 1931, at Durham, N. C.
Height, 6.04. Weight, 196.
Threw and batted righthanded.
Attended North Carolina State College, Raleigh, N. C.

Shares major league record for most 1-0 games lost, season (5), 1963.
Shares National League record for most consecutive losses, season (18), May 4 through August 4, 1963.
Tied for National League lead in shutouts with 4 in 1959.

Year Club	League	G.	IP.	W.	L.	Pct.	H.	R.	ER.	SO.	BB.	ERA.
1950—Newport News	Piedmont	6	19	0	1	.000	22	17	15	7	23	7.11
1950—Valdosta	Ga.-Fla.	23	167	14	7	.667	136	86	58	152	150	3.13
1951—Newport News	Piedmont	38	21	14	11	.560	175	109	90	119	★175	3.67
1952-53—Elmira	Eastern					(In Military Service)						
1954—Elmira	Eastern	3	2	0	0	.000	4	6	2	1	2	9.00
1954—Pueblo	Western	6	14	1	1	.500	14	17	15	8	19	9.64
1954—Newport News	Piedmont	20	125	8	3	.727	107	44	35	108	56	2.50
1955—Montreal	Int'national	22	117	10	2	.833	105	48	46	68	64	3.54
1955—Brooklyn	National	21	91	5	3	.625	81	37	28	48	43	2.77
1956—Brooklyn	National	35	199	12	11	.522	169	90	82	109	87	3.71
1957—Brooklyn	National	32	111	6	9	.400	102	58	57	69	47	4.62
1958—Los Angeles	National	9	32	2	1	.667	30	20	16	16	12	4.50
1958—St. Paul	Am. Assoc.	28	182	5	●17	.227	180	100	79	119	77	3.91
1959—Spokane	P. Coast	14	96	6	7	.462	86	39	34	46	26	3.19
1959—Los Angeles	National	29	153	11	5	.688	122	49	35	76	45	2.06
1960—Los Angeles	National	21	116	8	3	.727	99	48	42	69	43	3.26
1961—Los Angeles†	National	40	113	5	6	.455	130	87	77	63	52	6.13
1962—New York	National	42	233	10	★24	.294	261	133	117	118	70	4.52
1963—New York‡	National	46	236	5	★22	.185	249	117	99	108	58	3.78
1964—St. Louis§	National	39	166	7	9	.438	180	76	60	84	35	3.25
1965—Cincinnati x	National	40	64	1	4	.200	74	33	26	30	25	3.66
1966—Philadelphia	National	14	23	2	1	.667	31	15	14	13	5	5.48
1966—Seattle	P. Coast	6	22	0	1	.000	15	11	6	11	9	2.45
1968—Albuquerque	Texas	1	4	0	0	.000	3	0	0	2	2	0.00
Major League Totals—12 Years		368	1537	74	98	.430	1528	763	653	803	522	3.82

†Selected by New York Mets in National League expansion draft, October 10, 1961.
‡Traded to St. Louis Cardinals for Pitcher Bill Wakefield and Outfielder George Altman, November 4, 1963.
§Traded to Cincinnati Reds with Outfielder Charlie James for Pitcher Bob Purkey and a player to be named later, December 14, 1964.
xReleased by Cincinnati Reds and signed by Philadelphia Phillies, April 11, 1966.

WORLD SERIES RECORD

Year Club	League	G.	IP.	W.	L.	Pct.	H.	R.	ER.	SO.	BB.	ERA.
1955—Brooklyn	National	1	6	1	0	1.000	4	2	2	4	5	3.00
1956—Brooklyn	National	2	6	0	1	.000	10	8	8	4	3	12.00
1959—Los Angeles	National	2	9⅓	0	1	.000	15	9	9	8	5	8.68
1964—St. Louis	National	2	5	1	0	1.000	2	0	0	9	3	0.00
World Series Totals—3 Years		7	26⅓	2	2	.500	31	19	19	25	16	6.49

RECORD AS MANAGER

Year Club	League	Position	W.	L.
1968—Albuquerque	Texas	Second(W)	70	69
1978—San Diego	Nat.	Fourth(W)	84	78
1979—San Diego	Nat.	Fifth(W)	68	93
1985—San Francisco†	Nat.	Sixth(W)	6	12
1986—San Francisco	Nat.	Third(W)	83	79
1987—San Francisco	Nat.	First(W)	90	72
1988—San Francisco	Nat.	Fourth(W)	83	79
1989—San Francisco	Nat.	First(W)	92	70
Major League Totals—7 Years			506	483

†Replaced Jim Davenport with club in sixth place (record of 56-88), September 18, 1985.

Scout, Los Angeles Dodgers, 1967; coach, San Diego Padres, 1969 through 1972; minor league pitching instructor, Los Angeles Dodgers, 1973; coach, Houston Astros, 1974 and 1975; coach, San Diego Padres, 1976 and 1977; named manager of Padres (replacing Alvin Dark), March 21, 1978; coach, Detroit Tigers, 1980 through 1984; scout, Detroit Tigers, March 2, 1985 through September 18, 1985.

Coach, National League All-Star Team, 1987 and 1988.

CHAMPIONSHIP SERIES RECORD						WORLD SERIES RECORD				
Year Club	League	W.	L.			Year Club	League	W.	L.	
1987—San Francisco	National	3	4			1989—San Francisco	National	0	4	
1989—San Francisco	National	4	1							
Championship Series Totals—2 Years		7	5							

—DID YOU KNOW—

That the San Francisco Giants did not lose more than three games in a row in 1989 until being swept by Oakland in the World Series?

RUSSELL EARL DENT
(Bucky)
New York Yankees

Born November 25, 1951, at Savannah, Ga.
Height, 5.11. Weight, 180.
Threw and batted righthanded.
Attended Miami-Dade Community College (North), Miami, Fla.

Major League stolen bases: 1973 (2), 1974 (3), 1975 (2), 1976 (3), 1977 (1), 1978 (3), 1983 (3). Total—17.
Led American League in sacrifice hits with 23 in 1974.
Led American League shortstops in total chances with 838 in 1975.
Tied for American League lead in double plays by shortstops with 108 in 1974 and 105 in 1975.
Led American Association in sacrifice hits with 12 in 1973.
Led Midwest League in sacrifice hits with 12 in 1971.
Led Midwest League shortstops in double plays with 51 in 1971.
Tied for Gulf Coast League lead in sacrifice flies with 5 in 1970.

Year	Club	League	Pos.	G.	AB.	R.	H.	2B.	3B.	HR.	RBI.	B.A.	PO.	A.	E.	F.A.
1970—Sarasota W.S.	Gulf C.	3B-SS-2B	22	77	18	27	2	1	0	13	.351	30	55	11	.885
1970—Appleton	Midw.	SS-2B	39	163	23	42	4	2	3	12	.258	53	116	17	.909
1971—Appleton†	Midw.	SS-3B	83	294	34	68	16	0	1	29	.231	109	230	24	.934
1972—Knoxville	South.	SS	125	453	58	134	10	6	6	56	.296	167	437	31	.951
1973—Iowa	A. A.	*SS-3B	95	356	58	105	10	3	3	38	.295	137	308	*33	.931
1973—Chicago	Amer.	SS-2B-3B	40	117	17	29	2	0	0	10	.248	55	134	7	.964
1974—Chicago	Amer.	SS	154	496	55	136	15	3	5	45	.274	251	499	22	.972
1975—Chicago	Amer.	SS	157	602	52	159	29	4	3	58	.264	*279	*543	16	*.981
1976—Chicago‡	Amer.	SS	158	562	44	138	18	4	2	52	.246	279	468	18	.976
1977—New York	Amer.	SS	158	477	54	118	18	4	8	49	.247	250	434	18	.974
1978—New York§	Amer.	SS	123	379	40	92	11	1	5	40	.243	178	341	10	.981
1979—New York	Amer.	SS	141	431	47	99	14	2	2	32	.230	219	512	17	.977
1980—New York x	Amer.	SS	141	489	57	128	26	2	5	52	.262	224	489	13	*.982
1981—New York y	Amer.	SS	73	227	20	54	11	0	7	27	.238	104	217	10	.970
1982—N.Y. z-Tex.	Amer.	SS	105	306	27	59	10	1	1	23	.193	129	323	14	.970
1983—Texas a	Amer.	SS	131	417	36	99	15	2	2	34	.237	150	369	11	*.979
1984—Columbus b	Int.	SS	17	60	4	15	1	0	1	5	.250	23	50	3	.961
1984—Kansas City c	Amer.	SS-3B	11	9	2	3	0	0	0	1	.333	4	6	0	1.000
Major League Totals—12 Years			1392	4512	451	1114	169	23	40	423	.247	2122	4335	156	.976

Selected by St. Louis Cardinals' organization in 5th round of free-agent draft, June 5, 1969.
Selected by St. Louis Cardinals' organization in secondary phase of free-agent draft, January 17, 1970.
Selected by Chicago White Sox' organization in secondary phase of free-agent draft, June 4, 1970.
†On military list, December 31, 1970 through May 14, 1971.
‡Traded to New York Yankees for Outfielder Oscar Gamble, Pitchers Bob Polinsky and LaMarr Hoyt and cash estimated at $200,000, April 5, 1977.
§On disabled list, July 9 to July 31, 1978.
xOn disabled list, June 15 to June 30, 1980.
yOn disabled list, August 31, 1981 through remainder of season.
zTraded to Texas Rangers for Outfielder Lee Mazzilli, August 8, 1982.
aReleased, April 2, 1984; signed by New York Yankees' organization, June 7, 1984.
bReleased, July 9, 1984; signed by Kansas City Royals, August 16, 1984.
cReleased, October 10, 1984.

CHAMPIONSHIP SERIES RECORD

Year	Club	League	Pos.	G.	AB.	R.	H.	2B.	3B.	HR.	RBI.	B.A.	PO.	A.	E.	F.A.
1977—New York	Amer.	SS	5	14	1	3	1	0	0	2	.214	10	14	1	.960
1978—New York	Amer.	SS	4	15	0	3	0	0	0	4	.200	2	8	1	.909
1980—New York	Amer.	SS	3	11	0	2	0	0	0	0	.182	8	12	0	1.000
Championship Series Totals—3 Years			12	40	1	8	1	0	0	6	.200	20	34	2	.964

WORLD SERIES RECORD

Tied World Series record for one or more hits, each game, six-game Series, 1978.

Year	Club	League	Pos.	G.	AB.	R.	H.	2B.	3B.	HR.	RBI.	B.A.	PO.	A.	E.	F.A.
1977—New York	Amer.	SS	6	19	0	5	0	0	0	2	.263	2	15	1	.944
1978—New York	Amer.	SS	6	24	3	10	1	0	0	7	.417	8	16	2	.923
World Series Totals—2 Years			12	43	3	15	1	0	0	9	.349	10	31	3	.932

ALL-STAR GAME RECORD

Year	League	Pos.	AB.	R.	H.	2B.	3B.	HR.	RBI.	B.A.	PO.	A.	E.	F.A.
1975—American		SS	1	0	0	0	0	0	0	.000	0	1	0	1.000
1980—American		SS	2	0	1	0	0	0	0	.500	0	1	0	1.000
1981—American		SS	2	0	2	1	0	0	0	1.000	0	2	0	1.000
All-Star Game Totals—3 Years			5	0	3	1	0	0	0	.600	0	4	0	1.000

RECORD AS MANAGER

Year	Club	League	Position	W.	L.
1985—Fort Lauderdale	Fla. St.	†First (S)	77	63
1986—Fort Lauderdale	Fla. St.	Second (S)	80	59
1987—Columbus	Int.	‡Second	77	63
1988—Columbus	Int.	Third (W)	65	77
1989—Columbus	Int.	Third (W)	68	62
1989—New York§	Amer.	Fifth (E)	18	22
Major League Totals—1 Year			18	22

†Defeated Osceola, two games to one in semifinals, and lost to Fort Myers, three games to one for championship.
‡Defeated Rochester, three games to none in semifinals, and defeated Tidewater, three games to none for Governor's Cup.
§Replaced Dallas Green with club in sixth place (record of 56-65), August 18, 1989.

CLARENCE EDWIN GASTON
(Cito)
Toronto Blue Jays

Born March 17, 1944, at San Antonio, Tex.
Height, 6.04. Weight, 210.
Threw and batted righthanded.

Led New York-Pennsylvania League in total bases with 255 in 1966.

Year Club	League	Pos.	G.	AB.	R.	H.	2B.	3B.	HR.	RBI.	B.A.	PO.	A.	E.	F.A.
1964—Binghamton	NYP	OF	11	21	1	5	2	0	1	4	.238	8	0	1	.889
1964—Greenville	W. Car.	OF	49	165	15	38	6	3	0	16	.230	62	5	5	.931
1965—W. Palm Beach....	Fla. St.	OF	70	202	14	38	5	3	0	9	.188	111	4	5	.958
1966—Batavia..................	NYP	OF	114	433	84	143	18	5	★28	★104	.330	214	12	13	.946
1966—Austin	Texas	OF	4	10	2	3	1	1	0	4	.300	10	0	0	1.000
1967—Austin	Texas	OF	136	505	72	154	24	6	10	70	.305	274	8	12	.959
1967—Atlanta	Nat.	OF	9	25	1	3	0	1	0	1	.120	7	1	2	.800
1968—Richmond.............	Int.	OF	21	71	9	17	4	0	2	8	.239	43	0	0	1.000
1968—Shreveport†	Texas	OF	96	340	49	95	15	4	6	57	.279	203	3	9	.958
1969—San Diego	Nat.	OF	129	391	20	90	11	7	2	28	.230	243	12	11	.959
1970—San Diego	Nat.	OF	146	584	92	186	26	9	29	93	.318	310	7	8	.975
1971—San Diego	Nat.	OF	141	518	57	118	13	9	17	61	.228	271	8	5	.982
1972—San Diego‡	Nat.	OF	111	379	30	102	14	0	7	44	.269	158	10	4	.977
1973—San Diego.............	Nat.	OF	133	476	51	119	18	4	16	57	.250	198	16	●12	.947
1974—San Diego§	Nat.	OF	106	267	19	57	11	0	6	33	.213	119	7	1	.992
1975—Atlanta	Nat.	OF-1B	64	141	17	34	4	0	6	15	.241	80	2	3	.965
1976—Atlanta	Nat.	OF-1B	69	134	15	39	4	0	4	25	.291	58	2	1	.984
1977—Atlanta	Nat.	OF-1B	56	85	6	23	4	0	3	21	.271	44	4	1	.980
1978—Atl. x-Pitts. yza....	Nat.	OF-1B	62	120	6	28	1	0	1	9	.233	66	2	3	.958
1979—Leon	Mex.	OF	24	83	5	28	2	0	1	8	.337	24	0	0	1.000
1980—Leon	Mex.	1B	48	185	16	44	5	0	4	27	.238	126	3	3	.977
Major League Totals—11 Years...............			1026	3120	314	799	106	30	91	387	.256	1554	71	51	.970

†Selected by San Diego Padres from Atlanta in expansion draft, October 14, 1968.
‡On disabled list, May 17 to June 2, 1972.
§Traded to Atlanta Braves for Pitcher Danny Frisella, November 7, 1974.
xSold to Pittsburgh Pirates, September 22, 1978.
yGranted free agency, November 2, 1978; signed by Santo Domingo of Mexican League, April 10, 1979.
zOn suspended list, June 21 to July 21, 1979.
aReleased, July 22, 1979; signed by Leon of Mexican League, July 22, 1979.

ALL-STAR GAME RECORD

Year League	Pos.	AB.	R.	H.	2B.	3B.	HR.	RBI.	B.A.	PO.	A.	E.	F.A.
1970—National	OF	2	0	0	0	0	0	0	.000	2	0	0	1.000

RECORD AS MANAGER

Year Club	League	Position	W.	L.
1989—Toronto†	Amer.	First(E)	69	43
Major League Totals—1 Year........................			69	43

†Replaced Jimy Williams with club in seventh place (record of 12-24), May 15, 1989.
Minor League instructor, Atlanta Braves' organization, 1981, coach, Toronto Blue Jays, 1982 through May 15, 1989.

CHAMPIONSHIP SERIES RECORD

Year Club	League	W.	L.
1989—Toronto	American	1	4

DORREL NORMAN ELVERT HERZOG
(Relly or Whitey)

(Named "Relly" by mother from his first name; "Whitey" by Bill Speith, McAlester sportscaster, because of light hair.)

St. Louis Cardinals

Born November 9, 1931, at New Athens, Ill.
Height, 5.11. Weight, 187.
Threw and batted lefthanded.

Major League stolen bases: 1956 (8), 1957 (1), 1959 (1), 1961 (1), 1962 (2). Total—13.

Year Club	League	Pos.	G.	AB.	R.	H.	2B.	3B.	HR.	RBI.	B.A.	PO.	A.	E.	F.A.
1949—McAlester	Soo. St.	OF	96	398	53	111	19	7	0	31	.279	222	14	0	★1.000
1950—McAlester	Soo. St.	OF	132	467	107	164	36	10	4	85	.351	272	15	7	★.976
1951—Norfolk..................	Pied.	OF	5	17	5	1	0	0	0	2	.059	13	0	1	.926
1951—Joplin	W. A.	OF-1B	113	418	99	119	14	8	7	48	.285	454	19	9	.981
1952—Beaumont.............	Texas	OF	35	121	11	24	4	1	0	9	.198	83	3	5	.945
1952—Quincy..................	I. I. I.	OF	68	225	53	65	9	6	5	44	.289	131	9	5	.966
1952—Kansas City..........	A. A.	OF-1B	14	27	5	8	1	0	1	5	.296	21	1	1	.957
1953-54—						(In Military Service.)								
1955—Denver†	A. A.	OF-1B	149	515	101	149	24	7	21	98	.289	324	10	4	.988
1956—Washington	Amer.	OF-1B	117	421	49	103	13	7	4	35	.245	274	10	7	.976
1957—Washington	Amer.	OF	36	78	7	13	3	0	0	4	.167	53	0	1	.981

Year Club	League	Pos.	G.	AB.	R.	H.	2B.	3B.	HR.	RBI.	B.A.	PO.	A.	E.	F.A.
1957—Miami	Int.	OF	77	257	48	70	14	5	2	25	.272	114	5	4	.967
1958—Wash.‡-K.C.	Amer.	OF-1B	96	101	11	23	1	2	0	9	.228	146	6	3	.981
1959—Kansas City	Amer.	OF-1B	38	123	25	36	7	1	1	9	.293	87	2	3	.967
1960—Kansas City§	Amer.	OF-1B	83	252	43	67	10	2	8	38	.266	137	6	4	.973
1961—Baltimore	Amer.	OF	113	323	39	94	11	6	5	35	.291	143	2	0	1.000
1962—Baltimore x	Amer.	OF	99	263	34	70	13	1	7	35	.266	132	4	3	.978
1963—Detroit	Amer.	1B-OF	52	53	5	8	2	1	0	7	.151	44	1	1	.978
Major League Totals—8 Years			634	1614	213	414	60	20	25	172	.257	1016	31	22	.979

†Traded to Washington Senators with Pitcher Bob Wiesler, Catcher Lou Berberet, Second Baseman Herb Plews and Outfielder Dick Tettelbach for pitcher Maury McDermott and Shortstop Bob Kline (assigned to the Yankees' American Association farm club—Denver). Other players in deal assigned February 8, 1956; Herzog, April 2, 1956.

‡Sold to Kansas City Athletics, May 14, 1958.

§Traded to Baltimore Orioles with Outfielder Russ Snyder and a player to be named at later date, for Pitcher Jim Archer, Catcher Clint Courtney, First Baseman Bob Boyd, Infielder Wayne Causey and Outfielder Al Pilarcik, January 24, 1961; Courtney returned to the Orioles, April 15, 1961, to complete deal.

xTraded to Detroit Tigers with Catcher Gus Triandos for Catcher Dick Brown, November 26, 1962.

RECORD AS MANAGER

Named Man of the Year by THE SPORTING NEWS, 1982.
Named Major League Manager of the Year by THE SPORTING NEWS, 1982.

Year Club	League	Position	W.	L.	Year Club	League	Position	W.	L.
1973—Texas†	Amer.	Sixth(W)	47	91	1983—St. Louis	Nat.	Fourth(E)	79	83
1974—California‡	Amer.	Sixth(W)	2	2	1984—St. Louis	Nat.	Third(E)	84	78
1975—Kansas City§	Amer.	Second(W)	41	25	1985—St. Louis	Nat.	First(E)	101	61
1976—Kansas City	Amer.	First(W)	90	72	1986—St. Louis	Nat.	Third(E)	79	82
1977—Kansas City	Amer.	First(W)	102	60	1987—St. Louis	Nat.	First(E)	95	67
1978—Kansas City	Amer.	First(W)	92	70	1988—St. Louis	Nat.	Fifth(E)	76	86
1979—Kansas City	Amer.	Second(W)	85	77	1989—St. Louis	Nat.	Third(E)	86	76
1980—St. Louis xy	Nat.	Fourth(E)	38	35	National League Totals—10 Years			789	681
1981—St. Louis z	Nat.		59	43	American League Totals—7 Years			459	397
1982—St. Louis	Nat.	First(E)	92	70	Major League Totals—17 Years			1248	1078

†Replaced by Billy Martin, September 8, 1973 (Del Wilber served as interim manager, September 7).

‡Served as interim manager, June 27 to June 30, 1974 after Dick Williams replaced Bobby Winkles, June 26.

§Replaced Jack McKeon with club in second place (record of 50-46), July 24, 1975.

xReplaced Ken Boyer (and interim manager Jack Krol) with club in sixth place (record of 18-33), June 9, 1980.

yNamed General Manager, August 28, 1980, with Red Schoendienst serving as manager remainder of season.

zFirst Half. . . . Second(E) (record of 30-20); Second Half. . . . Second(E) (record of 29-23).

Scout, Kansas City Athletics, 1964.; coach, Kansas City Athletics, 1965; New York Mets, 1966; California Angels, 1974 and part of 1975.

Director of Player Development, New York Mets, 1967 through 1972.

Manager, National League All-Star Team, 1983, 1986 and 1988.

Coach, American League All-Star Team, 1973, 1974 and 1978.

CHAMPIONSHIP SERIES RECORD					WORLD SERIES RECORD				
Year Club	League		W.	L.	Year Club	League		W.	L.
1976—Kansas City	American		2	3	1982—St. Louis	National		4	3
1977—Kansas City	American		2	3	1985—St. Louis	National		3	4
1978—Kansas City	American		1	3	1987—St. Louis	National		3	4
1982—St. Louis	National		3	0	World Series Totals—3 Years			10	11
1985—St. Louis	National		4	2					
1987—St. Louis	National		4	3					
Championship Series Totals—6 Years			16	14					

ARTHUR HENRY HOWE JR.
(Art)
Houston Astros

Born December 15, 1946, at Pittsburgh, Pa.
Height, 6.01. Weight, 185.
Threw and batted righthanded.
Received bachelor of science degree in business administration
from University of Wyoming, Laramie, Wyo. in 1969.

Major League stolen bases: 1975 (1), 1978 (2), 1979 (3), 1980 (1), 1981 (1), 1982 (2). Total—10.

Led International League third basemen in errors with 22 and double plays with 24 in 1972.

Tied for Carolina League lead in putouts by third basemen with 95 in 1971.

Year Club	League	Pos.	G.	AB.	R.	H.	2B.	3B.	HR.	RBI.	B.A.	PO.	A.	E.	F.A.
1971—Salem	Carol.	3B-SS	114	382	77	133	27	7	12	79	*.348	110	221	21	.940
1972—Charleston†	Int.	3B-2B-SS	109	365	68	99	21	3	14	53	.271	105	248	24	.936
1973—Charleston‡	Int.	3B-2B-SS	119	372	50	85	20	1	8	44	.228	141	229	21	.946
1974—Charleston	Int.	3B	60	207	26	70	17	4	8	36	.338	35	90	9	.933
1974—Pittsburgh	Nat.	3B-SS	29	74	10	18	4	1	1	5	.243	11	49	4	.938
1975—Charleston	Int.	3B-2B	11	42	4	15	1	3	0	3	.357	15	23	1	.974
1975—Pittsburgh§	Nat.	3B-SS	63	146	13	25	9	0	1	10	.171	19	89	7	.939
1976—Memphis	Int.	3B-1B	74	259	50	92	21	3	12	59	.355	93	120	14	.934
1976—Houston	Nat.	3B-2B	21	29	0	4	1	0	0	0	.138	17	16	1	.970

Year Club	League	Pos.	G.	AB.	R.	H.	2B.	3B.	HR.	RBI.	B.A.	PO.	A.	E.	F.A.
1977—Houston	Nat.	2B-3B-SS	125	413	44	109	23	7	8	58	.264	213	333	8	.986
1978—Houston	Nat.	2B-3B-1B	119	420	46	123	33	3	7	55	.293	240	302	13	.977
1979—Houston	Nat.	2B-3B-1B	118	355	32	88	15	2	6	33	.248	188	261	7	.985
1980—Houston	Nat.	1-3-2-S	110	321	34	91	12	5	10	46	.283	598	86	10	.986
1981—Houston	Nat.	3B-1B	103	361	43	107	22	4	3	36	.296	67	206	9	.968
1982—Houston x	Nat.	3B-1B	110	365	29	87	15	1	5	38	.238	344	174	7	.987
1983—Houston yz	Nat.					(Did not play)									
1984—St. Louis	Nat.	3-1-2-S	89	139	17	30	5	0	2	12	.216	71	80	3	.981
1985—St. Louis a	Nat.	1B-3B	4	3	0	0	0	0	0	0	.000	5	1	0	1.000
Major League Totals—12 Years			891	2626	268	682	139	23	43	293	.260	1773	1597	69	.980

Signed as free agent by Pittsburgh Pirates' organization, June, 1971.
†On disabled list, August 17 to September 2, 1972.
‡On disabled list, April 13 to May 6, 1973.
§Traded to Houston Astros, January 6, 1976, completing deal in which Houston traded Second Baseman Tommy Helms to Pittsburgh Pirates for a player to be named later, December 12, 1975.
xOn disabled list, May 12 to June 19, 1982.
yOn disabled list, March 27, 1983 through remainder of season.
zGranted free agency, November 7, 1983; signed by St. Louis Cardinals, March 21, 1984.
aReleased, April 22, 1985.

DIVISION SERIES RECORD

Year Club	League	Pos.	G.	AB.	R.	H.	2B.	3B.	HR.	RBI.	B.A.	PO.	A.	E.	F.A.
1981—Houston	Nat.	3B	5	17	1	4	0	0	1	1	.235	6	9	0	1.000

CHAMPIONSHIP SERIES RECORD

Year Club	League	Pos.	G.	AB.	R.	H.	2B.	3B.	HR.	RBI.	B.A.	PO.	A.	E.	F.A.
1974—Pittsburgh	Nat.	PH	1	1	0	0	0	0	0	0	.000	0	0	0	.000
1980—Houston	Nat.	1B-PH	5	15	0	3	1	1	0	2	.200	29	3	0	1.000
Championship Series Totals—2 Years			6	16	0	3	1	1	0	2	.188	29	3	0	1.000

RECORD AS MANAGER

Year Club	League	Position	W.	L.
1989—Houston	Nat.	Third(W)	86	76
Major League Totals—1 Year			86	76

Coach, Texas Rangers, May 21, 1985 through 1988.

DAVID ALLEN JOHNSON
(Dave)
New York Mets

Born January 30, 1943, at Orlando, Fla.
Height, 6.01. Weight, 182.
Threw and batted righthanded.
Attended Texas A&M University, College Station, Tex., received bachelor of
science degree in mathematics from Trinity University, San Antonio, Tex.,
and attended Johns Hopkins University, Baltimore, Md.

Holds major league record for most home runs by second baseman, season, (42), 1973.
Shares major league records for fewest triples, season (150 or more games), (0), 1973; most grand slams by pinch-hitter, season, (2), 1978.
Major League stolen bases: 1965 (3), 1966 (3), 1967 (4), 1968 (7), 1969 (3), 1970 (2), 1971 (3), 1972 (1), 1973 (5), 1974 (1), 1977 (1). Total—33.
Tied for American League lead in sacrifice flies with 8 in 1967.
Led National League second basemen in total chances with 877 and tied for lead in double plays with 106 in 1973.
Led American League second basemen in double plays with 103 in 1971.
Led California League shortstops in double plays with 63 in 1962.
Named National League Comeback Player of the Year by THE SPORTING NEWS, 1973.
Named second baseman on THE SPORTING NEWS National League All-Star Team, 1973.
Named second baseman on THE SPORTING NEWS American League All-Star Team, 1970.
Named second baseman on THE SPORTING NEWS American League All-Star fielding team, 1969 through 1971.

Year Club	League	Pos.	G.	AB.	R.	H.	2B.	3B.	HR.	RBI.	B.A.	PO.	A.	E.	F.A.
1962—Stockton	Calif.	SS	97	343	58	106	18	●12	10	63	.309	135	307	40	★.917
1963—Elmira	East.	SS-2B	63	233	47	76	11	6	13	42	.326	115	155	12	.957
1963—Rochester	Int.	2B-OF	63	211	31	52	9	3	6	22	.246	141	138	11	.962
1964—Rochester	Int.	2B-SS	●155	590	87	156	29	14	19	73	.264	326	445	39	.952
1965—Baltimore	Amer.	3B-2B-SS	20	47	5	8	3	0	0	1	.170	11	37	3	.941
1965—Rochester	Int.	SS	52	193	29	58	9	3	4	22	.301	96	161	10	.963
1966—Baltimore	Amer.	★2B-SS	131	501	47	129	20	3	7	56	.257	294	357	★20	.970
1967—Baltimore	Amer.	2B-3B	148	510	62	126	30	3	10	64	.247	344	351	14	.980
1968—Baltimore	Amer.	2B-SS	145	504	50	122	24	4	9	56	.242	294	370	15	.978
1969—Baltimore	Amer.	2B-SS	142	511	52	143	34	1	7	57	.280	358	370	12	.984
1970—Baltimore	Amer.	●2B-SS	149	530	68	149	27	1	10	53	.281	●382	391	8	.990
1971—Baltimore	Amer.	2B	142	510	67	144	26	1	18	72	.282	361	367	12	.984
1972—Baltimore†	Amer.	2B	118	376	31	83	22	3	5	32	.221	286	307	6	★.990
1973—Atlanta	Nat.	2B	157	559	84	151	25	0	43	99	.270	383	464	★30	.966
1974—Atlanta	Nat.	1B-2B	136	454	56	114	18	0	15	62	.251	789	231	11	.989
1975—Atlanta‡	Nat.	PH	1	1	0	1	1	0	0	1	1.000	0	0	0	.000

Year Club	League	Pos.	G.	AB.	R.	H.	2B.	3B.	HR.	RBI.	B.A.	PO.	A.	E.	F.A.
1975—Yomiuri.................	Central	3B-SS	91	289	29	57	7	0	13	38	.197	85	157	11	.957
1976—Yomiuri§..............	Central	2B-3B-1B	108	371	48	102	16	2	26	74	.275	226	28	11	.979
1977—Philadelphia x......	Nat.	1B-2B-3B	78	156	23	50	9	1	8	36	.321	299	31	0	1.000
1978—Phil. y-Chi. z..........	Nat.	3B-2B-1B	68	138	19	32	3	1	4	20	.232	61	63	11	.919
1979—Miami	Int.-Am.	1B	10	25	7	6	2	0	1	2	.240	Figures	Unavailable		
American League Totals—8 Years			995	3489	382	904	186	16	66	391	.259	2330	2550	90	.982
National League Totals—5 Years............			440	1308	182	348	56	2	70	218	.266	1532	789	52	.978
Major League Totals—13 Years........			1435	4797	564	1252	242	18	136	609	.261	3862	3339	142	.981

†Traded with Pitchers Pat Dobson and Roric Harrison and Catcher Johnny Oates to Atlanta Braves for Catcher Earl Williams and Infielder Taylor Duncan, November 30, 1972.
‡Released, April 11, 1975; signed by Yomiuri Giants of Japanese Baseball League.
§Released, January 21, 1977; signed as free agent with Philadelphia Phillies, February 3, 1977.
xOn disabled list, June 15 to July 1, 1977.
yTraded to Chicago Cubs for Pitcher Larry Anderson, August 6, 1978.
zReleased, October 17, 1978.

CHAMPIONSHIP SERIES RECORD

Year Club	League	Pos.	G.	AB.	R.	H.	2B.	3B.	HR.	RBI.	B.A.	PO.	A.	E.	F.A.
1969—Baltimore	Amer.	2B	3	13	2	3	0	0	0	0	.231	5	11	0	1.000
1970—Baltimore	Amer.	2B	3	11	4	4	0	0	2	4	.364	11	4	0	1.000
1971—Baltimore	Amer.	2B	3	10	2	3	2	0	0	0	.300	5	6	1	.917
1977—Philadelphia	Nat.	1B	1	4	0	1	0	0	0	2	.250	8	0	0	1.000
Championship Series Totals—4 Years.....			10	38	8	11	2	0	2	6	.289	29	21	1	.980

WORLD SERIES RECORD

Year Club	League	Pos.	G.	AB.	R.	H.	2B.	3B.	HR.	RBI.	B.A.	PO.	A.	E.	F.A.
1966—Baltimore	Amer.	2B	4	14	1	4	1	0	0	1	.286	12	12	0	1.000
1969—Baltimore	Amer.	2B	5	16	1	1	0	0	0	0	.063	8	15	0	1.000
1970—Baltimore	Amer.	2B	5	16	2	5	2	0	0	2	.313	15	9	0	1.000
1971—Baltimore	Amer.	2B	7	27	1	4	0	0	0	3	.148	18	12	0	1.000
World Series Totals—4 Years			21	73	5	14	3	0	0	6	.192	53	48	0	1.000

ALL-STAR GAME RECORD

Year League	Pos.	AB.	R.	H.	2B.	3B.	HR.	RBI.	B.A.	PO.	A.	E.	F.A.
1968—American	2B	1	0	0	0	0	0	0	.000	1	1	0	1.000
1970—American	2B	5	0	1	0	0	0	0	.200	5	1	0	1.000
1973—National	2B	1	0	0	0	0	0	0	.000	1	1	0	1.000
All-Star Game Totals—3 Years....................		7	0	1	0	0	0	0	.143	7	3	0	1.000

Named to American League All-Star Team for 1969 game; replaced due to injury.

RECORD AS MANAGER

Year Club	League	Position	W.	L.	Year Club	League	Position	W.	L.
1979—Miami	Inter-Amer.	First	43	17	1985—New York...............	Nat.	Second(E)	98	64
(Second Half)		First	8	4	1986—New York...............	Nat.	First(E)	108	54
1981—Jackson	Texas	†First(E)	39	27	1987—New York...............	Nat.	Second(E)	92	70
(Second Half)		Third(E)	29	39	1988—New York...............	Nat.	First(E)	100	60
1983—Tidewater...............	Int.	‡Fourth	71	68	1989—New York...............	Nat.	Second(E)	87	75
1984—New York...............	Nat.	Second(E)	90	72	Major League Totals—6 Years.........................			575	395

†Defeated Tulsa, two games to one, and San Antonio (finals), three games to none, for championship.
‡Defeated Columbus, three games to two, and Richmond (finals), three games to one, for championship.
Manager, National League All-Star Team, 1987.
Coach, National League All-Star Team, 1986.
Instructor, New York Mets' organization, 1982.

CHAMPIONSHIP SERIES RECORD					WORLD SERIES RECORD				
Year Club	League		W.	L.	Year Club	League		W.	L.
1986—New York..................	National		4	2	1986—New York...................	National		4	3
1988—New York..................	National		3	4					
Championship Series Totals—2 Years...........			7	6					

JAY THOMAS KELLY
(Tom)
Minnesota Twins

Born August 15, 1950, at Graceville, Minn.
Height, 5.11. Weight, 185.
Threw and batted lefthanded.
Attended Mesa Community College, Mesa, Ariz., and Monmouth College, West Long Branch, N. J.
Son of Joe Kelly, former pitcher in St. Louis Cardinals'
and New York Giants' organizations.

Led International League in bases on balls received with 91 in 1978.
Led New York-Pennsylvania League in stolen bases with 16 in 1968.
Led Pacific Coast League outfielders in double plays with 6 in 1972.

Year Club	League	Pos.	G.	AB.	R.	H.	2B.	3B.	HR.	RBI.	B.A.	PO.	A.	E.	F.A.
1968—Newark	NYP	OF	65	218	50	69	11	4	2	10	.317	★144	★9	3	.981
1969—Clinton....................	Midw.	OF	100	269	47	60	10	2	6	35	.223	158	15	4	.977

Year Club	League	Pos.	G.	AB.	R.	H.	2B.	3B.	HR.	RBI.	B.A.	PO.	A.	E.	F.A.
1970—Jacksonville†‡...... South.	OF-1B	93	266	33	64	10	1	8	38	.241	204	19	4	.982
1971—Charlotte.............. South.	1B-OF	100	303	50	89	17	0	6	41	.294	508	38	9	.984
1972—Tacoma................ P. C.	OF-1B	132	407	76	114	19	2	10	52	.280	282	19	10	.968
1973—Tacoma................ P. C.	OF-1B	114	337	67	87	10	2	17	49	.258	200	20	6	.973
1974—Tacoma................ P. C.	OF-1B	115	357	68	110	16	0	18	69	.308	514	41	3	.985
1975—Tacoma................ P. C.	OF-1B	62	202	38	51	5	0	9	29	.252	185	12	6	.970
1975—Minnesota§........... Amer.	1B-OF	49	127	11	23	5	0	1	11	.181	360	28	6	.985
1976—Rochester....... Int.	OF-1B	127	405	71	117	19	3	18	70	.289	323	28	4	.989
1977—Tacoma xyz......... P. C.	1B-OF-P	113	363	80	99	12	1	12	64	.273	251	15	6	.978
1978—Toledo ab.............. Int.	1B-OF	119	325	47	74	13	0	10	49	.228	556	46	5	.992
Major League Totals—1 Year..................		49	127	11	23	5	0	1	11	.181	360	28	6	.985

†On temporary inactive list, April 16 to April 20, April 25 to April 30 and August 21, 1970 through remainder of season.

‡Released, April 6, 1971; signed by Charlotte (Minnesota Twins' organization), April 28, 1971.

§Loaned to Rochester (Baltimore Orioles' organization), April 5, 1976; returned, September 22, 1976.

xOn temporary inactive list, April 15 to April 19, 1977.

yPlayer-manager.

zOn disabled list, July 25 to August 4, 1977.

aPlayer-coach.

bReleased, December 18, 1978.

PITCHING RECORD

Year Club	League	G.	IP.	W.	L.	Pct.	H.	R.	ER.	SO.	BB.	ERA.
1977—Tacoma....................................	P. Coast	1	3	0	0	.000	2	2	2	0	3	6.00

RECORD AS MANAGER

Named Southern League Manager of the Year, 1981.
Named California League Co-Manager of the Year, 1980.
Named California League Manager of the Year, 1979.

Year Club	League	Position	W.	L.
1977—Tacoma†................. P. Coast	Third(W)	28	26
1979—Visalia .... Calif.	‡First(S)	44	26
(Second Half)	Second(S)	42	28
1980—Visalia .... Calif.	Fourth(S)	27	43
(Second Half)	§First(S)	44	26
1981—Orlando .... South.	xFirst(E)	42	27
(Second Half)	Third(E)	37	36
1982—Orlando .... South.	Fifth(E)	31	38
(Second Half)	Second(E)	43	32
1986—Minnesota y .... Amer.	Sixth(W)	12	11
1987—Minnesota.............. Amer.	First(W)	85	77
1988—Minnesota.............. Amer.	Second(W)	91	71
1989—Minnesota.............. Amer.	Fifth(W)	80	82
Major League Totals—4 Years........................		268	241

†Replaced Del Wilber (record of 40-49), June, 1977.

‡Lost to San Jose, two games to one in semifinals.

§Defeated Fresno, two games to none in semifinals, and lost to Stockton, three games to none for championship.

xDefeated Savannah, three games to one in semifinals, and defeated Nashville, three games to one for championship.

yReplaced Ray Miller with club in seventh place (record of 59-80), September 12, 1986.

Manager, American League All-Star Team, 1988.

Coach, Minnesota Twins, 1983 through September 11, 1986.

CHAMPIONSHIP SERIES RECORD					WORLD SERIES RECORD				
Year Club	League		W.	L.	Year Club	League		W.	L.
1987—Minnesota................... American			4	1	1987—Minnesota.................... American			4	3

ANTHONY La RUSSA JR.
(Tony)
Oakland Athletics

Born October 4, 1944, at Tampa, Fla.
Height, 6.00. Weight, 185.
Threw and batted righthanded.
Attended University of Tampa, Tampa, Fla., and received degree in industrial management from
University of Southern Florida, Tampa, Fla.; and received law degree from
Florida State University, Tallahassee, Fla. in 1980.

Led International League in being hit by pitch with 11 in 1972.
Received reported $50,000 bonus to sign with Kansas City A's, 1962.

Year Club	League	Pos.	G.	AB.	R.	H.	2B.	3B.	HR.	RBI.	B.A.	PO.	A.	E.	F.A.
1962—Daytona Beach .... Fla. St.	SS	64	225	37	58	7	0	1	32	.258	135	173	38	.890
1962—Binghamton .... East.	SS-2B	12	43	3	8	0	0	0	4	.186	20	27	8	.855
1963—Kansas City........... Amer.	SS-2B	34	44	4	11	1	1	0	1	.250	29	25	2	.964
1964—Lewiston† .... N'west	2B-SS	90	329	50	77	22	1	1	25	.234	188	218	18	.958

Year Club League	Pos.	G.	AB.	R.	H.	2B.	3B.	HR.	RBI.	B.A.	PO.	A.	E.	F.A.
1965—Birmingham‡ .... South.	2B	75	259	24	50	11	2	1	18	.193	202	161	21	.945
1966—Modesto................. Calif.	2B	81	316	67	92	20	1	7	54	.291	201	212	20	.954
1966—Mobile.................... South.	2B	51	170	20	50	9	4	4	26	.294	117	133	10	.962
1967—Birmingham§ .... South.	2B	41	139	12	32	6	1	5	22	.230	88	120	5	.977
1968—Oakland.............. Amer.	PH	5	3	0	1	0	0	0	0	.333	0	0	0	.000
1968—Vancouver........... P. C.	2B	122	455	55	109	16	8	5	29	.240	249	321	14	★.976
1969—Iowa .... A. A.	2B	67	235	37	72	11	1	4	27	.306	177	222	15	.964
1969—Oakland................ Amer.	PH	8	8	0	0	0	0	0	0	.000	0	0	0	.000
1970—Iowa .... A. A.	2B	22	88	13	22	5	0	2	5	.250	52	59	3	.974
1970—Oakland................ Amer.	2B	52	106	6	21	4	1	0	6	.198	67	89	5	.969
1971—Iowa .... A. A.	2-3-S-O	28	107	21	31	5	1	2	11	.290	70	85	2	.987
1971—Oakland x .... Amer.	2B-SS-3B	23	8	3	0	0	0	0	0	.000	8	7	2	.882
1971—Atlanta .... Nat.	2B	9	7	1	2	0	0	0	0	.286	8	6	1	.933
1972—Richmond y .... Int.	2B	122	389	68	120	13	2	10	42	.308	305	289	20	.967
1973—Wichita .... A. A.	2B-1B-3B	106	392	82	123	16	0	5	75	.314	423	213	26	.961
1973—Chicago z .... Nat.	PR	1	0	1	0	0	0	0	0	.000	0	0	0	.000
1974—Charleston a .... Int.	2B	139	457	50	119	17	1	8	35	.260	262	★378	17	.974
1975—Denver .... A. A.	3-O-S-2	118	354	87	99	23	2	7	46	.280	95	91	10	.949
1976—Iowa bc .... A. A.	INF-O-P	107	332	53	86	11	0	4	34	.259	132	160	22	.930
1977—New Orleans de ... A. A.	2B-3B	50	128	17	24	2	2	3	6	.188	66	87	7	.956
American League Totals—5 Years		122	169	13	33	5	2	0	7	.195	104	121	9	.962
National League Totals—2 Years...........		10	7	2	2	0	0	0	0	.286	8	6	1	.933
Major League Totals—6 Years................		132	176	15	35	5	2	0	7	.199	112	127	10	.960

†On disabled list, May 9 to September 8, 1964.
‡On disabled list, June 3 to July 15, 1965.
§On disabled list, April 12 to May 6 and July 3 to September 5, 1967.
xSold to Atlanta Braves, August 14, 1971.
yTraded to Chicago Cubs for Pitcher Tom Phoebus, October 20, 1972.
zSold to Pittsburgh Pirates' organization.
aReleased, April 4, 1975; signed by Chicago White Sox' organization, April 7, 1975.
bOn disabled list, August 8 to August 16, 1976.
cSold to St. Louis Cardinals' organization, December 13, 1976.
dNamed coach, June 20, 1977.
eReleased, September 29, 1977.

PITCHING RECORD

Year Club	League	G.	IP.	W.	L.	Pct.	H.	R.	ER.	SO.	BB.	ERA.
1976—Iowa	Am. Assoc.	3	3	0	0	.000	3	1	1	0	0	3.00

RECORD AS MANAGER

Shares major league record for most clubs managed, season (2), 1986.
Named Major League Manager of the Year by THE SPORTING NEWS, 1983.
Named American League Manager of the Year, 1988.

Year Club League	Position	W.	L.	Year Club League	Position	W.	L.
1978—Knoxville .... South.	First(W)	49	21	1984—Chicago .... Amer.	yFifth(W)	74	88
(Second Half)†	Third(W)	4	4	1985—Chicago .... Amer.	Third(W)	85	77
1979—Iowa‡ .... A. A.	Second(E)	54	52	1986—Chicago z .... Amer.	Sixth(W)	26	38
1979—Chicago§ .... Amer.	Fifth(W)	27	27	1986—Oakland a .... Amer.	bThird(W)	45	34
1980—Chicago .... Amer.	Fifth(W)	70	90	1987—Oakland................... Amer.	Third(W)	81	81
1981—Chicago x............... Amer.		54	52	1988—Oakland................... Amer.	First(W)	104	58
1982—Chicago .... Amer.	Third(W)	87	75	1989—Oakland................... Amer.	First(W)	99	63
1983—Chicago ...., Amer.	First(W)	99	63	Major League Totals—11 Years		851	746

†Replaced by Joe Jones, July 3, 1978.
‡Replaced by Joe Sparks, August 3, 1979.
§Replaced Don Kessinger with club in fifth place (record of 46-60), August 3, 1979.
xFirst Half. . . . Third (W) (record 31-22); Second Half. . . . Sixth (W) (record of 23-30).
yTied for position with Seattle Mariners.
zReplaced by interim manager Doug Rader, June 20, 1986.
aReplaced manager Jackie Moore (record of 29-44) and interim manager Jeff Newman (record of 2-8) with club in
seventh place (combined record of 31-52), July 7, 1986.
bTied for position with Kansas City Royals.
Manager, American League All-Star Team, 1989.
Coach, Chicago White Sox, July 3 through remainder of 1978 season.
Coach, American League All-Star Team, 1984 and 1987.

CHAMPIONSHIP SERIES RECORD

Year Club	League	W.	L.
1983—Chicago .... American		1	3
1988—Oakland...................... American		4	0
1989—Oakland...................... American		4	1
Championship Series Totals—3 Years...........		9	4

WORLD SERIES RECORD

Year Club	League	W.	L.
1988—Oakland...................... American		1	4
1989—Oakland...................... American		4	0
World Series Totals—2 Years		5	4

THOMAS CHARLES LASORDA

Name pronounced Luh-SORR-duh.

(Tom)

Los Angeles Dodgers

Born September 22, 1927, at Norristown, Pa.
Height, 5.09. Weight, 195.
Threw and batted lefthanded.

Shares National League record for most wild pitches, inning (3), May 5, 1955, first inning.
Led International League in complete games with 16 and tied for lead in shutouts with 5 in 1958.
Led Canadian-American League in wild pitches with 20 in 1948 and led International League with 14 in 1953.
Named International League Pitcher of the Year, 1958.

Year Club	League	G.	IP.	W.	L.	Pct.	H.	R.	ER.	SO.	BB.	ERA.
1945—Concord	N. C. State	27	121	3	12	.200	115	84	55	91	100	4.09
1946-47—†	E. Shore					(In Military Service)						
1948—Schenectady‡§	Can.-Am.	32	192	9	12	.429	180	122	99	195	153	4.64
1949—Greenville	Sally	45	178	7	7	.500	141	81	58	151	138	2.93
1950—Montreal	Int'national	31	146	9	4	.692	136	73	60	85	82	3.70
1951—Montreal	Int'national	31	165	12	8	.600	145	75	64	80	87	3.49
1952—Montreal	Int'national	33	182	14	5	.737	156	90	74	77	93	3.66
1953—Montreal	Int'national	36	208	17	8	.680	171	77	65	122	94	2.81
1954—Montreal	Int'national	23	154	14	5	.737	142	66	60	75	79	3.51
1954—Brooklyn	National	4	9	0	0	.000	8	5	5	5	5	5.00
1955—Brooklyn	National	4	4	0	0	.000	5	6	6	4	6	13.50
1955—Montreal x	Int'national	22	143	9	8	.529	125	58	52	92	62	3.27
1956—Kansas City y	American	18	45	0	4	.000	40	38	31	28	45	6.20
1956—Denver	Am. Assoc.	16	83	3	4	.429	94	54	46	54	34	4.99
1957—Denver z	Am. Assoc.	6	17	0	2	.000	29	25	23	8	6	12.18
1957—Los Angeles	P. Coast	29	132	7	10	.412	134	73	57	72	59	3.90
1958—Montreal	Int'national	34	★230	★18	6	.750	191	77	64	126	76	2.50
1959—Montreal	Int'national	29	188	12	8	.600	192	93	80	64	77	3.83
1960—Montreal a	Int'national	12	45	2	5	.286	79	48	41	17	24	8.20
American League Totals—1 Year		18	45	0	4	.000	40	38	31	28	45	6.20
National League Totals—2 Years		8	13	0	0	.000	13	11	11	9	11	7.62
Major League Totals—3 Years		26	58	0	4	.000	53	49	42	37	56	6.52

†On National Defense list, May 14, 1946 through February 2, 1948.
‡On disabled list, July 9 to July 19, 1948.
§Drafted by Nashua (Brooklyn Dodgers' organization) from Philadelphia Phillies' organization, November 24, 1948.

xSold by Brooklyn Dodgers' organization to Kansas City Athletics for an estimated $35,000, March 2, 1956.
yTraded to New York Yankees for Pitcher Wally Burnette and cash, July 11, 1956.
zSold by New York Yankees' organization to Brooklyn Dodgers' organization, May 26, 1957.
aReleased, July 9, 1960.

RECORD AS MANAGER

Named National League co-Manager of the Year, 1988.
Named Minor League Manager of the Year by THE SPORTING NEWS, 1970.
Named Pacific Coast League co-Manager of the Year, 1970.
Named Pioneer League Manager of the Year, 1967.

Year Club	League	Position	W.	L.	Year Club	League	Position	W.	L.
1965—Pocatello	Pion.	†Second	33	33	1979—Los Angeles	Nat.	Third(W)	79	83
1966—Ogden	Pion.	First	39	27	1980—Los Angeles	Nat.	Second(W)	92	71
1967—Ogden	Pion.	First	41	25	1981—Los Angeles y	Nat.		63	47
1968—Ogden	Pion.	First	39	25	1982—Los Angeles	Nat.	Second(W)	88	74
1969—Spokane	P. C.	Second(N)	71	73	1983—Los Angeles	Nat.	First(W)	91	71
1970—Spokane	P. C.	‡First(N)	94	52	1984—Los Angeles	Nat.	Fourth(W)	79	83
1971—Spokane	P. C.	Third(N)	69	76	1985—Los Angeles	Nat.	First(W)	95	67
1972—Albuquerque	P. C.	§First(E)	92	56	1986—Los Angeles	Nat.	Fifth(W)	73	89
1976—Los Angeles x	Nat.	Second(W)	2	2	1987—Los Angeles	Nat.	Fourth(W)	73	89
1977—Los Angeles	Nat.	First(W)	98	64	1988—Los Angeles	Nat.	First(W)	94	67
1978—Los Angeles	Nat.	First(W)	95	67	1989—Los Angeles	Nat.	Fourth(W)	77	83
					Major League Totals—14 Years			1099	957

†Tied for position with Magic Valley.
‡Won championship playoff against Hawaii, four games to none.
§Won championship playoff against Eugene, three games to one.
xReplaced retiring Walter Alston with club in second place (record of 90-68), September 29, 1976.
yFirst Half. . . . First(W) (record of 36-21); Second Half. . . . Fourth(W) (record of 27-26).
Scout, Los Angeles Dodgers, 1961 through 1965; manager Los Angeles farm team in Arizona Instructional League, 1969; coach, Los Angeles Dodgers, 1973 through 1976.
Manager, National League All-Star Team, 1978, 1979, 1982 and 1989.
Coach, National League All-Star Team, 1977, 1983, 1984 and 1986.

DIVISION SERIES RECORD

Year Club	League	W.	L.
1981—Los Angeles	National	3	2

CHAMPIONSHIP SERIES RECORD

Year	Club	League	W.	L.
1977—Los Angeles		National	3	1
1978—Los Angeles		National	3	1
1981—Los Angeles		National	3	2
1983—Los Angeles		National	1	3
1985—Los Angeles		National	2	4
1988—Los Angeles		National	4	3
Championship Series Totals—6 Years			16	14

WORLD SERIES RECORD

Year	Club	League	W.	L.
1977—Los Angeles		National	2	4
1978—Los Angeles		National	2	4
1981—Los Angeles		National	4	2
1988—Los Angeles		National	4	1
World Series Totals—4 Years			12	11

JAMES KENNETH LEFEBVRE

Name pronounced Luh-FEE-ver.

(Jim)

Seattle Mariners

Born January 7, 1943, at Inglewood, Calif.
Height, 6.00. Weight, 185.
Threw right and batted right and lefthanded.

Led California League second basemen in double plays with 79 in 1962.
Led Northwest League second basemen in double plays with 109 in 1963.
Named National League Rookie of the Year by Baseball Writers' Association of America, 1965.

Year	Club	League	Pos.	G.	AB.	R.	H.	2B.	3B.	HR.	RBI.	B.A.	PO.	A.	E.	F.A.
1962—Reno		Calif.	2B	138	541	139	177	33	4	39	130	.327	345	313	27	.961
1963—Salem		N'west	2B	139	474	82	134	29	9	17	92	.283	★316	327	★35	.948
1964—Spokane†		P. C.	2B	55	200	26	53	10	1	6	31	.265	123	126	8	.969
1965—Los Angeles		Nat.	2B	157	544	57	136	21	4	12	69	.250	349	429	24	.970
1966—Los Angeles		Nat.	2B-3B	152	544	69	149	23	3	24	74	.274	268	389	16	.976
1967—Los Angeles		Nat.	3B-2B-1B	136	494	51	129	18	5	8	50	.261	173	321	18	.965
1968—Los Angeles		Nat.	2-3-O-1	84	286	23	69	12	1	5	31	.241	179	161	8	.977
1969—Los Angeles		Nat.	3B-2B-1B	95	275	29	65	15	2	4	44	.236	154	185	6	.983
1970—Los Angeles		Nat.	2B-3B-1B	109	314	33	79	15	1	4	44	.252	168	212	6	.984
1971—Los Angeles		Nat.	2B-3B	119	388	40	95	14	2	12	68	.245	247	274	9	.983
1972—Los Angeles‡		Nat.	2B-3B	70	169	11	34	8	0	5	24	.201	70	99	4	.977
1973—Lotte		Pac.	1-2-3-O	111	400	50	106	12	2	29	63	.265	763	77	7	.992
1974—Lotte		Pac.	1B-3B	82	279	37	79	12	2	14	52	.283	580	32	4	.994
1975—Lotte		Pac.	1B	47	151	13	39	5	0	9	24	.258	252	13	0	1.000
1976—Lotte		Pac.	1B	90	268	22	65	8	0	8	37	.243	506	32	3	.994
Major League Totals—8 Years				922	3014	313	756	126	18	74	404	.251	1608	2070	91	.976

†On military list, March 15 to July 18, 1964.
‡Released, November 27, 1972; signed with Lotte Orions of Japanese Baseball League.

WORLD SERIES RECORD

Year	Club	League	Pos.	G.	AB.	R.	H.	2B.	3B.	HR.	RBI.	B.A.	PO.	A.	E.	F.A.
1965—Los Angeles		Nat.	2B	3	10	2	4	0	0	0	0	.400	3	7	1	.909
1966—Los Angeles		Nat.	2B	4	12	1	2	0	0	1	1	.167	10	10	0	1.000
World Series Totals—2 Years				7	22	3	6	0	0	1	1	.273	13	17	1	.968

ALL-STAR GAME RECORD

Year	League	Pos.	AB.	R.	H.	2B.	3B.	HR.	RBI.	B.A.	PO.	A.	E.	F.A.
1966—National		2B	2	0	0	0	0	0	0	.000	2	0	0	1.000

RECORD AS MANAGER

Named Pacific Coast League Manager of the Year, 1985 and 1986.

Year	Club	League	Position	W.	L.	Year	Club	League	Position	W.	L.
1978—Lethbridge		Pion.	Fifth	33	35	1986—Phoenix		P. C.	‡First(S)	43	28
1985—Phoenix		P. C.	Second(S)	37	33				Second(S)	38	33
(Second Half)			†First(S)	43	29	1989—Seattle		Amer.	Sixth(W)	73	89
						Major League Totals—1 Year				73	89

†Defeated Hawaii, three games to none in semifinals; lost to Vancouver, three games to none, for championship.
‡Lost to Las Vegas, three games to two in semifinals.
Coach, Lotte Orions, 1977; coach, Los Angeles Dodgers, September 24, 1978 through 1979; coach, San Francisco Giants, 1980 and 1982; Director of Player Development, San Francisco Giants, 1983 and 1984; coach, Oakland Athletics, 1987 and 1988.

JAMES RICHARD LEYLAND

Named pronounced LEE-lund.

(Jim)

Pittsburgh Pirates

Born December 15, 1944, at Toledo, O.
Height, 5.11. Weight, 170.
Threw and batted righthanded.

Year	Club	League	Pos.	G.	AB.	R.	H.	2B.	3B.	HR.	RBI.	B.A.	PO.	A.	E.	F.A.
1964—Lakeland†		Fla. St.	C	52	129	8	25	0	1	0	8	.194	268	17	6	.979
1964—Cocoa Tigers		Rookie	C	24	52	2	12	1	1	0	4	.231	122	15	3	.979
1965—Jamestown		NYP	C-3B-P	82	211	18	50	7	2	1	21	.237	318	36	6	.983

Year	Club	League	Pos.	G.	AB.	R.	H.	2B.	3B.	HR.	RBI.	B.A.	PO.	A.	E.	F.A.
1966—Rocky Mount	Carol.		C	67	173	24	42	6	0	0	16	.243	369	23	1	.997
1967—Montgomery	South.		C	62	171	11	40	3	0	1	16	.234	350	25	6	.984
1968—Montgomery	South.		C-3B-SS	81	264	19	51	3	0	1	20	.193	511	43	7	.988
1969—Montgomery	South.		C	16	39	1	8	0	0	0	1	.205	64	6	3	.959
1969—Lakeland	Fla. St.		C-P	60	179	20	43	8	0	1	16	.240	321	28	4	.989
1970—Montgomery‡	South.		C	2	3	0	0	0	0	0	0	.000	6	0	1	.857

Signed as free agent by Detroit Tigers' organization, September 21, 1963.
†On disabled list, June 15 to June 27, 1964.
‡Player-coach.

PITCHING RECORD

Year	Club	League	G.	IP.	W.	L.	Pct.	H.	R.	ER.	SO.	BB.	ERA.
1965—Jamestown	NYP		1	2	0	0	.000	2	0	0	1	0	0.00
1969—Lakeland	Florida St.		1	2	0	0	.000	4	2	2	1	0	9.00

RECORD AS MANAGER

Named National League co-Manager of the Year, 1988.
Named American Association Manager of the Year, 1979.
Named Florida State League Manager of the Year, 1977 and 1978.

Year	Club	League	Position	W.	L.	Year	Club	League	Position	W.	L.
1971—Bristol	Appal.		Third(S)	31	35		(Second Half)		xFirst(N)	47	22
1972—Clinton	Midw.		Fifth(N)	22	41	1979—Evansville	A. A.		yFirst(E)	78	58
(Second Half)			Fourth(N)	27	36	1980—Evansville	A. A.		Second(E)	61	74
1973—Clinton	Midw.		Second(N)	36	26	1981—Evansville	A. A.		zFirst(E)	73	63
(Second Half)			†First(N)	37	25	1985—Chicago	Amer.		aFourth(W)	1	1
1974—Montgomery	South.		Third(W)	61	76	1986—Pittsburgh	Nat.		Sixth(E)	64	98
1975—Clinton	Midw.		Fourth(S)	29	31	1987—Pittsburgh	Nat.		bFourth(E)	80	82
(Second Half)			Second(S)	38	30	1988—Pittsburgh	Nat.		Second(E)	85	75
1976—Lakeland	Fla. St.		‡Second(N)	74	64	1989—Pittsburgh	Nat.		Fifth(E)	74	88
1977—Lakeland	Fla. St.		§First(N)	85	53	Major League Totals—5 Years				304	344
1978—Lakeland	Fla. St.		Fourth(N)	31	38						

†Lost playoff to Wisconsin Rapids, two games to none.
‡Defeated Miami, two games to none in semifinals, and defeated Tampa, two games to none for championship.
§Defeated Miami, two games to none in semifinals, and defeated St. Petersburg, three games to one for championship.
xDefeated St. Petersburg, one game to none for Northern Division championship, and lost to Miami, two games to one for championship.
yDefeated Oklahoma City, four games to two for championship.
zLost to Denver, three games to one in semifinals.
aNamed interim manager, replacing Tony La Russa who was suspended, with club in fourth place, August 10 and 11, 1985.
bTied for position with Philadelphia Phillies.
Coach, Detroit Tigers' organization, 1970 through June 5, 1971; Coach, Chicago White Sox, 1982 through 1985.

NICOLAS TOMAS LEYVA
(Nick)
Philadelphia Phillies

Born August 16, 1953, at Ontario, Calif.
Height, 5.11. Weight, 165.
Threw and batted righthanded.
Attended University of La Verne, La Verne, Calif.

Year	Club	League	Pos.	G.	AB.	R.	H.	2B.	3B.	HR.	RBI.	B.A.	PO.	A.	E.	F.A.
1975—Sarasota Cards	Gulf C.		3B-SS	4	18	3	5	2	0	0	4	.278	8	11	4	.826
1975—St. Petersburg	Fla. St.		3B-SS	47	157	16	42	8	2	0	21	.268	48	105	7	.956
1976—St. Petersburg	Fla. St.		3B-SS	70	237	32	66	11	0	2	28	.278	69	128	7	.966
1976—Arkansas	Texas		2B-3B-SS	48	153	16	38	4	1	3	26	.248	60	87	6	.961
1977—Arkansas†	Texas		I-O-P	84	213	24	57	4	2	3	30	.268	102	119	11	.953

Selected by St. Louis Cardinals' organization in 24th round of free-agent draft, June 4, 1975.
†Released, December 12, 1977.

PITCHING RECORD

Year	Club	League	G.	IP.	W.	L.	Pct.	H.	R.	ER.	SO.	BB.	ERA.
1977—Arkansas	Texas		2	4	0	0	.000	6	5	0	0	0	0.00

RECORD AS MANAGER

Named Texas League Manager of the Year, 1983.

Year	Club	League	Position	W.	L.	Year	Club	League	Position	W.	L.
1978—Johnson City	Appal.		Second	37	33	1982—Arkansas§	Texas		Third(E)	12	7
1979—Johnson City	Appal.		Fifth	25	43	(Second Half)			Second(E)	38	31
1980—Gastonia†	S. Atl.		Third(N)	37	33	1983—Arkansas	Texas		Fourth(E)	30	38
(Second Half)			Second(N)	37	33	(Second Half)x			First(E)	39	29
1981—St. Petersburg	Fla. St.		Third(N)	33	36	1989—Philadelphia	Nat.		Sixth(E)	67	95
(Second Half)			Second(N)	36	27	Major League Totals—1 Year				67	95
1982—St. Petersburg‡	Fla. St.		Fourth(N)	26	30						

†Lost playoffs to Greensboro, two games to one.
‡Manager through May 31, 1982.
§Shared first half managing duties with Gaylen Pitts.
xLost playoffs to Jackson, two games to none.
Coach, St. Louis Cardinals, 1984 through 1988.

JOHN ALOYSIUS McKEON
(Jack)
San Diego Padres

Born November 23, 1930, at South Amboy, N. J.
Height, 5.08. Weight, 205.
Threw and batted righthanded.
Attended Holy Cross College, Worcester, Mass., Seton Hall University, South Orange, N.J., and
received bachelor of arts degree in physical education and science from Elon College, Elon, N.C.
Brother of Bill McKeon, minor league catcher, 1952 through 1954, 1956 and 1957; scout,
Kansas City Royals, 1969 and 1970; and scout, San Diego Padres since 1981; and father-in-law of Greg Booker,
pitcher with San Diego Padres and Minnesota Twins, 1983 through 1989.

Led Carolina League catchers in double plays with 17 in 1953.
Led Alabama State League catchers in double plays with 9 in 1949.

Year—Club	League	Pos.	G.	AB.	R.	H.	2B.	3B.	HR.	RBI.	B.A.	PO.	A.	E.	F.A.
1949—Greenville	Ala. St.	C	116	390	54	98	12	1	1	49	.251	★806	65	13	★.985
1950—York	Int.	C	1	3	....	1	....	....	....	....	.333	figures unavailable			
1950—Gloversville	C.-Am.	C	72	209	18	45	5	0	0	14	.215	281	30	15	.954
1951—					(In Military Service)										
1952—Hutchinson	W. Assn.	C	116	358	42	78	10	1	4	40	.218	756	68	11	.987
1953—Burlington	Carol.	C	140	474	46	86	19	2	6	52	.181	★836	★82	21	.978
1954—Burlington	Carol.	C	17	30	1	4	0	0	0	2	.133	60	9	0	1.000
1954—Hutchinson†	W. Assn.	C	46	140	18	29	5	0	1	13	.207	273	33	4	.987
1955—Fay.-Greens‡	Carol.	C	59	172	20	29	3	0	1	17	.169	292	20	6	.981
1956—Missoula§	Pion.	C	113	370	44	63	8	0	0	29	.170	630	78	9	.987
1957—Missoula§	Pion.	C	102	299	37	65	7	0	4	40	.217	645	55	10	.986
1958—Missoula§	Pion.	C	108	354	49	93	16	0	8	51	.263	739	64	12	.985
1959—Fox Cities	Three-I	C	11	20	1	2	0	0	0	1	1.000	figures unavailable			

†Released by Pittsburgh Pirates' organization, September 28, 1954.
‡Played 10 games with Fayetteville, 5 games with Greensboro, and was a player-manager with Fayetteville for 44
games.
§Player-manager.

PITCHING RECORD

Year—Club	League	G.	IP.	W.	L.	Pct.	H.	R.	ER.	SO.	BB.	ERA.
1956—Missoula	Pioneer	8	....	0	0	.000	....	....	....	....	....	....
1957—Missoula	Pioneer	6	....	0	0	.000	....	....	....	....	....	....
1958—Missoula	Pioneer	2	....	0	0	.000	....	....	....	....	....	....

RECORD AS MANAGER

Named American Association Manager of the Year, 1969 and 1970.
Named Carolina League Manager of the Year, 1961.
Named Pioneer League Manager of the Year, 1958.

Year—Club	League	Position	W.	L.	Year—Club	League	Position	W.	L.
1955—Fayetteville†	Carol.	Third	70	67	1970—Omaha	A. A.	xFirst(E)	73	65
1956—Missoula	Pion.	Seventh	61	71	1971—Omaha	A. A.	Third(E)	69	70
1957—Missoula	Pion.	Sixth	26	35	1972—Omaha	A. A.	Second (E)	71	69
(Second Half)		Third	36	29	1973—Kansas City	Amer.	Second(W)	88	74
1958—Missoula	Pion.	Fourth	34	29	1974—Kansas City	Amer.	Fifth(W)	77	85
(Second Half)		Third	36	30	1975—Kansas City y	Amer.	Second(W)	50	46
1959—Fox Cities	Three-I	Seventh	26	39	1976—Richmond	Int.	Fourth	69	71
(Second Half)		Fourth	33	28	1977—Oakland z	Amer.	aFifth(W)	26	27
1960—Wilson	Carol.	Third	36	34	1978—Oakland b	Amer.	Fourth(W)	45	78
(Second Half)		Second	37	31	1980—Denver	A. A.	Third	62	73
1961—Wilson	Carol.	First	41	28	1988—San Diego c	Nat.	Third(W)	67	48
(Second Half)		First	42	28	1989—San Diego	Nat.	Second(W)	89	73
1962—Vancouver	P. C.	Seventh	72	79	American League Totals—5 Years			286	310
1963—Dallas-Ft. W	P. C.	Third(S)	79	79	National League Totals—2 Years			156	121
1964—Atlanta‡	Int.	Eighth	19	42	Major League Totals—7 Years			442	431
1968—H. Pt.-Thom.	Carol.	§Second(W)	69	71					
1969—Omaha	A. A.	First	85	55					

†Replaced Aaron Robinson on June 11, 1955, and replaced by John Sanford on August 6, 1955 because of hand
injury with team tied for first (record is for full season).
‡Replaced by Peter Appleton, June 21, 1964.
§Defeated Greensboro, one game to none in quarterfinals; defeated Lynchburg, two games to none in semifinals;
and defeated Raleigh-Durham, two games to one for championship.
xDefeated Denver, four games to one for championship; lost Junior World Series to Syracuse, four games to one.
yReplaced by Whitey Herzog, July 24, 1975.
zReplaced by Bobby Winkles, June 10, 1977.
aTied for position with Kansas City Royals.
bReplaced Bobby Winkles with club in first place (record of 24-15), May 23, 1978.
cReplaced Larry Bowa with club in fifth place (record of 16-30), May 28, 1988.
Coach, National League All-Star Team, 1989.
Managed Sampson Air Force Base team to Air Force Championship, 1951.
Scout, Minnesota Twins, 1965 through 1967; coach, Oakland A's, beginning of 1978 season through May 22, 1978;
scout and Assistant to General Manager, San Diego Padres, 1980; and Vice-President of Baseball Operations, San Diego
Padres, 1981 through 1988.

JOHN FRANCIS McNAMARA
Cleveland Indians

Born June 4, 1932, at Sacramento, Calif.
Height, 5.10. Weight, 175.
Threw and batted righthanded.
Attended Sacramento State College, Sacramento, Calif.

Led Northwest League in sacrifice hits with 18 in 1959.
Led Northwest League catchers in double plays with 15 in 1958, 10 in 1959 and 14 in 1962.

Year	Club	League	Pos.	G.	AB.	R.	H.	2B.	3B.	HR.	RBI.	B.A.	PO.	A.	E.	F.A.
1951—Fresno	Calif.		C	60	182	20	38	2	0	0	12	.209	284	46	11	.968
1952—Houston	Texas		....	6	13	0	1	0	0	0	0	.077	....	....	....	....
1952—Lynchburg	Pied.		C	102	303	25	54	8	0	0	19	.178	489	57	8	★.986
1953—Winston-Salem	Carol.						(In Military Service)									
1954—Omaha†	West.						(In Military Service)									
1955—Lewiston	N'west		C	129	427	49	102	24	4	1	54	.239	544	★93	●15	.977
1956—Sacramento	P. C.		C	76	181	22	31	5	1	1	18	.171	256	25	0	1.000
1956—Albuquerque	West.		C	29	83	11	23	2	2	1	9	.277	191	23	1	.995
1957—Tulsa	Texas		C	19	47	5	7	2	0	0	5	.149	92	9	2	.981
1957—Amarillo	West.		C	43	93	17	26	8	0	0	21	.280	177	13	3	.984
1958—Lewiston	N'west		C	133	439	62	117	20	2	2	63	.276	★892	★76	9	★.991
1959—Lewiston	N'west		C	141	491	74	122	25	4	1	44	.248	714	★84	8	.990
1960—Lewiston	N'west		C	120	387	62	98	19	2	0	42	.253	★726	48	7	★.991
1961—Lewiston	N'west		C	77	204	28	54	6	0	0	27	.265	368	37	4	.990
1962—Lewiston	N'west		C	93	281	41	77	11	2	1	33	.274	670	74	8	★.989
1963—Binghamton	East.		C	69	199	19	45	10	1	0	24	.226	483	34	2	.996
1964—Dallas	P. C.		C-3B	13	13	1	6	0	0	0	1	.194	58	7	0	1.000
1965—Birmingham	South.						(Did Not Play)									
1966—Mobile	South.		C	8	17	3	4	0	0	0	0	.235	44	1	0	1.000
1967—Birmingham	South.		C	2	6	1	0	0	0	0	1	.000	10	1	0	1.000

†Released by St. Louis Cardinals' organization, April 16, 1955.

PITCHING RECORD

Year	Club	League	G.	IP.	W.	L.	Pct.	H.	R.	ER.	SO.	BB.	ERA.
1960—Lewiston	Northwest		5	....	0	0	.000	....	....	....	....	....	....
1961—Lewiston	Northwest		4	....	0	0	.000	....	....	....	....	....	....
1962—Lewiston	Northwest		4	9	0	0	.000	13	6	6	3	2	6.00
1963—Binghamton	Eastern		1	1	0	0	.000	0	0	0	0	0	0.00

RECORD AS MANAGER

Named Major League Co-Manager of the Year by THE SPORTING NEWS, 1986.

Year	Club	League	Position	W.	L.	Year	Club	League	Position	W.	L.
1959—Lewiston	N'west	Second	36	34	1976—San Diego	Nat.	Fifth(W)	73	89
(Second Half)		Third	39	32	1977—San Diego§	Nat.	Fifth(W)	20	28
1960—Lewiston	N'west	Third	38	29	1979—Cincinnati	Nat.	First(W)	90	71
(Second Half)		Third	40	34	1980—Cincinnati	Nat.	Third(W)	89	73
1961—Lewiston	N'west	†First	41	25	1981—Cincinnati x	Nat.		66	42
(Second Half)		Second	43	31	1982—Cincinnati y	Nat.	Sixth(W)	34	58
1962—Lewiston	N'west	Fifth	31	38	1983—California	Amer.	zFifth	70	92
(Second Half)		Fourth	35	37	1984—California	Amer.	zSecond(W)	81	81
1963—Binghamton	East.	Fourth	65	75	1985—Boston	Amer.	Fifth(E)	81	81
1964—Dallas	P. C.	Sixth(E)	53	104	1986—Boston	Amer.	First(E)	95	66
1965—Birmingham	South.	Eighth	54	85	1987—Boston	Amer.	Fifth(E)	78	84
1966—Mobile	South.	First	88	52	1988—Boston a	Amer.	Fourth(E)	43	42
1967—Birmingham	South.	First	84	55	American League Totals—8 Years			545	524
1969—Oakland‡	Amer.	Second(W)	8	5	National League Totals—8 Years			503	554
1970—Oakland	Amer.	Second(W)	89	73	Major League Totals—16 Years			1048	1078
1974—San Diego	Nat.	Sixth(W)	60	102					
1975—San Diego	Nat.	Fourth(W)	71	91					

†Won playoff by defeating Yakima (Second Half winner), four games to one.
‡Replaced Hank Bauer with club in second place (record of 80-69), September 19, 1969.
§Replaced by Alvin Dark, May 30, 1977 (Bob Skinner served as interim manager, May 29).
xFirst Half....Second (W) (record of 35-21); Second Half....Second (W) (record of 31-21).
yReplaced by Russ Nixon, July 21, 1982.
zTied for position with Minnesota Twins.
aReplaced by Joe Morgan, July 14, 1988.
Coach, Oakland Athletics, 1968 and 1969; San Francisco Giants, 1971 through 1973; California Angels, 1978.
Manager, American League All-Star Team, 1987.
Coach, American League All-Star Team, 1986.
Coach, National League All-Star Team, 1976, 1980 and 1982.

CHAMPIONSHIP SERIES RECORD

Year	Club	League	W.	L.
1979—Cincinnati	National		0	3
1986—Boston	American		4	3
Championship Series Totals—2 Years			4	6

WORLD SERIES RECORD

Year	Club	League	W.	L.
1986—Boston	American		3	4

JOSEPH MICHAEL MORGAN
(Joe)
Boston Red Sox

Born November 19, 1930, at Walpole, Mass.
Height, 5.10. Weight, 180.
Threw and batted lefthanded.
Received bachelor of science degree in history and government
from Boston College, Chestnut Hill, Mass., in 1953.

Named International League Player of the Year, 1964.

Year	Club	League	Pos.	G.	AB.	R.	H.	2B.	3B.	HR.	RBI.	B.A.	PO.	A.	E.	F.A.
1952—Hartford	East.	SS-3B	72	258	23	59	6	0	3	18	.228	141	237	22	.945
1953—Evansville†	I.I.I.	SS	78	301	53	74	10	5	4	29	.246	157	228	24	.941
1954-55—‡							(In U. S. Army)									
1956—Jacksonville	S. Atl.	SS	132	476	85	143	24	8	9	45	.300	209	421	37	.945
1957—Atlanta	S. A.	SS	149	551	111	174	31	8	12	77	.316	278	446	29	.961
1958—Wichita	A. A.	3B-SS	133	442	60	111	22	4	11	49	.251	120	271	23	.944
1959—Milwaukee	Nat.	2B	13	23	2	5	1	0	0	1	.217	9	12	2	.913
1959—Louisville§	A. A.	OF-3B	82	305	54	96	26	6	8	47	.315	134	22	5	.969
1959—Kansas City	Amer.	3B	20	21	2	4	0	1	0	3	.190	1	2	0	1.000
1960—Louisville x	A. A.	3B	55	174	35	49	5	2	4	29	.282	39	96	4	.971
1960—Philadelphia y	Nat.	3B	26	83	5	11	2	2	0	2	.133	24	42	2	.971
1960—Cleveland	Amer.	3B-OF	22	47	6	14	2	0	2	4	.298	11	22	4	.892
1961—Cleveland z	Amer.	OF	4	10	0	2	0	0	0	0	.200	6	0	0	1.000
1961—Charleston	Int.	3B	118	405	59	117	21	2	8	46	.289	79	184	15	.946
1962—Atlanta	Int.	3B-OF	142	474	70	132	15	4	16	70	.278	183	105	15	.950
1963—Atlanta	Int.	1B-OF-3B	131	406	61	114	12	3	12	70	.281	507	101	12	.981
1964—Jacksonville	Int.	3B-1B	143	476	77	138	24	4	16	66	.290	283	220	19	.964
1964—St. Louis	Nat.	PH	3	3	0	0	0	0	0	0	.000	0	0	0	.000
1965—J'cks'nv'lle abcde	Int.	3B-OF	93	270	31	56	8	2	5	24	.207	81	71	7	.956
1966—Raleigh	Carol.	3B	112	331	48	90	10	3	9	62	.272	66	169	10	.959
National League Totals—3 Years			42	109	7	16	3	2	0	3	.147	33	54	4	.956
American League Totals—3 Years			46	78	8	20	2	1	2	7	.256	18	24	4	.913
Major League Totals—4 Years			88	187	15	36	5	3	2	10	.193	51	78	8	.942

Signed as free agent by Boston Braves' organization, June 20, 1952.

†On restricted list, February 5 to June 12, 1953.

‡On National Defense Service list, November 17, 1953 through December 2, 1955.

§Sold to Kansas City A's, August 20, 1959; returned to Milwaukee Braves, April 15, 1960.

xTraded to Philadelphia Phillies for Shortstop Alvin Dark, June 23, 1960.

ySold to Cleveland Indians, August 9, 1960.

zTraded with cash and a player to be named later to St. Louis Cardinals for Outfielder Bob Nieman, May 10, 1961; St. Louis acquired Pitcher Mike Lee to complete deal, September 25, 1961.

aOn disabled list, April 17 to July 27, 1965.

bNon-player-coach, July 9 to July 16, 1965.

cPlayer-coach, July 17, 1965 through remainder of season.

dOn temporary inactive list, August 20, 1965 through remainder of season.

eReleased, January 11, 1966; signed by Raleigh (Pittsburgh Pirates' organization) as a player-manager, January 12, 1966.

RECORD OF MANAGER

Named Minor League Manager of the Year by THE SPORTING NEWS, 1973.
Named International League Manager of the Year, 1973 and 1977.
Named Eastern League Manager of the Year, 1969.
Named Carolina League Manager of the Year, 1966.

Year	Club	League	Position	W.	L.
1966—Raleigh	Carol.	Third (W)	71	66
1967—Raleigh	Carol.	†First(E)	77	65
1968—York	East.	Fifth	58	82
1969—York	East.	‡First	89	50
1970—Columbus	Int.	§Second	81	59
1971—Charleston	Int.	xThird	78	62
1973—Charleston	Int.	yFirst(N)	85	60
1974—Pawtucket	Int.	Fourth(N)	57	87
1975—Pawtucket	Int.	Eighth	53	87
1976—Pawtucket	Int.	Fifth	68	70
1977—Pawtucket	Int.	zFirst	80	60
1978—Pawtucket	Int.	aSecond	81	59
1979—Pawtucket	Int.	Fifth	66	74
1980—Pawtucket	Int.	Seventh	62	77
1981—Pawtucket	Int.	Sixth	67	73
1982—Pawtucket	Int.	Fifth	67	71
1988—Boston b	Amer.	First(E)	46	31
1989—Boston	Amer.	Third(E)	83	79
Major League Totals—2 Years			129	110

†Defeated Rocky Mount, one game to none in quarterfinals, and lost to Tidewater, two games to none in semifinals.

‡Losing to Pittsfield, one game to none in semifinals when playoffs were cancelled.

§Defeated Rochester, three games to two in semifinals, and lost to Syracuse, three games to one for championship.

xLost to Tidewater, three games to none in semifinals.

yDefeated Rochester, three games to none for championship, and lost to Pawtucket, three games to two for Governor's Cup.

zDefeated Richmond, three games to one in semifinals, and lost to Charleston, four games to none in Governor's Cup.

aDefeated Toledo, three games to two in semifinals, and lost to Richmond, four games to three for Governor's Cup.

bReplaced John McNamara with club in fourth place (record of 43-42), July 14, 1988.

Coach, American League All-Star Team, 1989.

Scout, Boston Red Sox, 1983 and 1984; coach, Pittsburgh Pirates, 1972; coach, Boston Red Sox, 1985 through July 13, 1988.

CHAMPIONSHIP SERIES RECORD

Year	Club	League	W	L.
1988—Boston	American	0	4

RUSSELL EUGENE NIXON
(Russ)
Atlanta Braves

Born February 19, 1935, at Cleves, O.
Height, 6.01. Weight, 185.
Threw right and batted lefthanded.
Attended University of Cincinnati, Cincinnati, O.
Twin brother of Roy Nixon, first baseman in Cleveland Indians' organization, 1953 through 1957.

Led Florida State League catchers in double plays with 14 and passed balls with 23 in 1954.

Year Club	League	Pos.	G.	AB.	R.	H.	2B.	3B.	HR.	RBI.	B.A.	PO.	A.	E.	F.A.
1953—Green Bay	Wis. St.	C-OF	43	137	17	46	6	5	0	30	.336	213	22	6	.975
1954—Jack'ville Beach	Fla. St.	C	125	465	114	180	*36	12	6	96	*.387	*821	*95	22	.977
1955—Keokuk	I.I.I.	C	94	358	66	138	29	2	5	77	*.385	*718	47	10	●.987
1956—Indianapolis	A. A.	C	105	320	38	102	19	5	4	44	.319	402	37	9	.980
1957—Cleveland	Amer.	C	62	185	15	52	7	1	2	18	.281	268	31	5	.984
1958—Cleveland	Amer.	C	113	376	42	113	17	4	9	46	.301	499	31	5	.991
1959—Cleveland	Amer.	C	82	258	23	62	10	3	1	29	.240	374	31	6	.985
1960—Clev.†-Boston	Amer.	C	105	354	30	101	22	3	6	39	.285	488	34	6	.989
1961—Boston	Amer.	C	87	242	24	70	12	2	1	19	.289	330	21	9	.975
1962—Boston‡	Amer.	C	65	151	11	42	7	2	1	19	.278	201	7	0	1.000
1963—Boston	Amer.	C	98	287	27	77	18	1	5	30	.268	483	22	4	.992
1964—Boston	Amer.	C	81	163	10	38	7	0	1	20	.233	273	11	3	.990
1965—Boston	Amer.	C	59	137	11	37	5	1	0	11	.270	200	10	4	.981
1965—Toronto§	Int.	C	31	93	10	30	3	2	0	14	.323	195	11	3	.986
1966—Minnesota	Amer.	C	51	90	5	25	2	1	0	7	.260	137	5	2	.986
1967—Minnesota x	Amer.	C	74	170	16	40	6	1	1	22	.235	306	26	2	.994
1968—Pittsfield y	East.	C-OF	41	137	15	29	3	2	0	13	.212	214	23	3	.988
1968—Boston za	Amer.	C	29	85	1	13	2	0	0	6	.153	147	6	1	.994
Major League Totals—12 Years			906	2504	215	670	115	19	27	266	.268	3708	238	47	.988

Signed as free agent by Cleveland Indians' organization, June 18, 1953.

†Traded with Outfielder Carroll Hardy to Boston Red Sox for Pitcher Ted Bowsfield and Outfielder Marty Keough, June 13, 1960. (Indians had traded Nixon to Red Sox for First Baseman Jim Marshall and Catcher Stan White, March 16, 1960, but deal was cancelled by Commissioner Ford Frick on March 25 because of White's request for voluntary retirement.)

‡On disabled list, May 20 to June 20, 1962.

§Traded with Infielder Chuck Schilling to Minnesota Twins for Pitcher Dick Stigman and a player to be named later, April 6, 1966; Boston Red Sox acquired First Baseman Jose Calero to complete deal, April 17, 1966.

xReleased, April 8, 1968; signed as free agent by Pittsfield (Boston Red Sox' organization), April 8, 1968.

yOn disabled list, June 25 to July 16, 1968.

zDrafted by Chicago White Sox, December 2, 1968.

aReleased, April 5, 1969.

RECORD AS MANAGER

Year Club	League	Position	W.	L.
1970—Sioux Falls	North.	Sixth	24	46
1971—Tampa	Fla. St.	Second(W)	79	61
1972—Tampa	Fla. St.	Second(W)	66	64
1973—Tampa	Fla. St.	Fourth(N)	73	71
1974—Tampa	Fla. St.	†First(N)	68	64
1975—Tampa	Fla. St.	Second(N)	72	59
1982—Cincinnati‡	Nat.	Sixth(W)	27	43
1983—Cincinnati	Nat.	Sixth(W)	74	88
1988—Greenville	South.	First§	22	21
1988—Atlanta x	Nat.	Sixth(W)	42	79
1989—Atlanta	Nat.	Sixth(W)	63	97
Major League Totals—4 Years			206	307

†Lost to West Palm Beach, two games to none in semifinals.

‡Replaced John McNamara with club in sixth place (record of 34-58), July 21, 1982.

§Tied for position.

xReplaced Chuck Tanner with club in sixth place (record of 12-27), May 22, 1988.

Coach, Cincinnati Reds' organization, April 15 to June 1, 1970; coach, Cincinnati Reds, 1976 through July 20, 1982; coach, Montreal Expos, 1984; coach, Pittsburgh Pirates, 1985; coach, Atlanta Braves, 1986 and 1987.

LOUIS VICTOR PINIELLA
Name pronounced Pin-ELLA.

(Lou)
Cincinnati Reds

Born August 28, 1943, at Tampa, Fla.
Height, 6.02. Weight, 199.
Threw and batted righthanded.
Attended University of Tampa, Tampa, Fla.
Cousin of Dave Magadan, infielder with New York Mets.

Tied major league record for most assists by outfielder, inning (2), May 27, 1974 (third inning).

Major League stolen bases: 1969 (2), 1970 (3), 1971 (5), 1972 (7), 1973 (5), 1974 (1), 1977 (2), 1978 (3), 1979 (3), 1983 (1). Total—32.

Led American League in grounding into double plays with 25 in 1972.

Named American League Rookie of the Year by Baseball Writers' Association of America, 1969.

Year Club	League	Pos.	G.	AB.	R.	H.	2B.	3B.	HR.	RBI.	B.A.	PO.	A.	E.	F.A.
1962—Selma†	Ala.-Fl.	OF	70	278	40	75	10	5	8	44	.270	94	6	9	.917
1963—Peninsula	Carol.	OF	143	548	71	170	29	4	16	77	.310	271	*23	8	.974

Year	Club	League	Pos.	G.	AB.	R.	H.	2B.	3B.	HR.	RBI.	B.A.	PO.	A.	E.	F.A.
1964—Aberdeen‡§	....	North.	OF	20	74	8	20	8	3	0	12	.270	37	1	1	.974
1964—Baltimore	....	Amer.	PH	4	1	0	0	0	0	0	0	.000	0	0	0	.000
1965—Elmira x	....	East.	OF	126	490	64	122	29	6	11	64	.249	176	5	7	.963
1966—Portland	....	P. C.	OF	133	457	47	132	22	3	7	52	.289	177	11	11	.945
1967—Portland	....	P. C.	OF	113	396	46	122	20	1	8	56	.308	199	7	6	.972
1968—Portland	....	P. C.	OF	88	331	49	105	15	3	13	62	.317	167	6	7	.961
1968—Cleveland yz	....	Amer.	OF	6	5	1	0	0	0	0	1	.000	1	0	0	1.000
1969—Kansas City	....	Amer.	OF	135	493	43	139	21	6	11	68	.282	278	13	7	.977
1970—Kansas City	....	Amer.	OF-1B	144	542	54	163	24	5	11	88	.301	250	6	4	.985
1971—Kansas City a	....	Amer.	OF	126	448	43	125	21	5	3	51	.279	201	6	3	.986
1972—Kansas City	....	Amer.	OF	151	574	65	179	*33	4	11	72	.312	275	8	7	.976
1973—Kansas City b	....	Amer.	OF	144	513	53	128	28	1	9	69	.250	196	9	3	.986
1974—New York	....	Amer.	OF-1B	140	518	71	158	26	0	9	70	.305	270	16	3	.990
1975—New York c	....	Amer.	OF	74	199	7	39	4	1	0	22	.196	65	5	1	.986
1976—New York	....	Amer.	OF	100	327	36	92	16	6	3	38	.281	199	10	4	.981
1977—New York	....	Amer.	OF-1B	103	339	47	112	19	3	12	45	.330	86	3	2	.978
1978—New York	....	Amer.	OF	130	472	67	148	34	5	6	69	.314	213	4	7	.969
1979—New York	....	Amer.	OF	130	461	49	137	22	2	11	69	.297	204	13	4	.982
1980—New York	....	Amer.	OF	116	321	39	92	18	0	2	27	.287	157	8	5	.971
1981—New York d	....	Amer.	OF	60	159	16	44	9	0	5	18	.277	69	2	1	.986
1982—New York e	....	Amer.	OF	102	261	33	80	17	1	6	37	.307	68	2	0	1.000
1983—New York e	....	Amer.	OF	53	148	19	43	9	1	2	16	.291	67	4	3	.959
1984—New York f	....	Amer.	OF	29	86	8	26	4	1	1	6	.302	40	3	0	1.000
Major League Totals—18 Years	....			1747	5867	651	1705	305	41	102	766	.291	2639	112	54	.981

Signed as free agent by Cleveland Indians' organization, June 9, 1962.
†Drafted by Washington Senators, November 26, 1962.
‡On military list, March 9 to July 20, 1964.
§Traded to Baltimore Orioles' organization, August 4, 1964, completing deal in which Baltimore traded Pitcher Lester (Buster) Narum to Washington Senators for cash and a player to be named later, March 31, 1964.
xTraded to Cleveland Indians' organization for Catcher Cam Carreon, March 10, 1966.
ySelected by Seattle Pilots in expansion draft, October 15, 1968.
zTraded by Seattle Pilots to Kansas City Royals for Outfielder Steve Whitaker and Pitcher John Gelnar, April 1, 1969.
aOn disabled list, May 5 to June 8, 1971.
bTraded with Pitcher Ken Wright to New York Yankees for Pitcher Lindy McDaniel, December 7, 1973.
cOn disabled list, June 17 to July 6, 1975.
dOn disabled list, August 23 to September 7, 1981.
eOn disabled list, March 30 to April 22, 1983.
fOn voluntarily retired list, June 17, 1984.

DIVISION SERIES RECORD

Year	Club	League	Pos.	G.	AB.	R.	H.	2B.	3B.	HR.	RBI.	B.A.	PO.	A.	E.	F.A.
1981—New York	....	Amer.	DH-PH	4	10	1	2	1	0	1	3	.200	0	0	0	.000

CHAMPIONSHIP SERIES RECORD

Year	Club	League	Pos.	G.	AB.	R.	H.	2B.	3B.	HR.	RBI.	B.A.	PO.	A.	E.	F.A.
1976—New York	....	Amer.	DH-PH	4	11	1	3	1	0	0	0	.273	0	0	0	.000
1977—New York	....	Amer.	OF-DH	5	21	1	7	3	0	0	2	.333	9	1	0	1.000
1978—New York	....	Amer.	OF	4	17	2	4	0	0	0	0	.235	13	0	0	1.000
1980—New York	....	Amer.	OF	2	5	1	1	0	0	1	1	.200	5	0	0	1.000
1981—New York	....	Amer.	PH-D-O	3	5	2	3	0	0	1	3	.600	0	0	0	.000
Championship Series Totals—5 Years	....			18	59	7	18	4	0	2	6	.305	27	1	0	1.000

WORLD SERIES RECORD

Tied World Series record for one or more hits, each game, six-game Series, 1978.

Year	Club	League	Pos.	G.	AB.	R.	H.	2B.	3B.	HR.	RBI.	B.A.	PO.	A.	E.	F.A.
1976—New York	....	Amer.	D-O-PH	4	9	1	3	1	0	0	0	.333	1	0	0	1.000
1977—New York	....	Amer.	OF	6	22	1	6	0	0	0	3	.273	16	1	1	.944
1978—New York	....	Amer.	OF	6	25	3	7	0	0	0	4	.280	14	1	0	1.000
1981—New York	....	Amer.	OF-PH	6	16	2	7	1	0	0	3	.438	7	0	0	1.000
World Series Totals—4 Years	....			22	72	7	23	2	0	0	10	.319	38	2	1	.976

ALL-STAR GAME RECORD

Year	League	Pos.	AB.	R.	H.	2B.	3B.	HR.	RBI.	B.A.	PO.	A.	E.	F.A.
1972—American	....	PH	1	0	0	0	0	0	0	.000	0	0	0	.000

RECORD AS MANAGER

Year	Club	League	Position	W.	L.
1986—New York	....	Amer.	Second(E)	90	72
1987—New York	....	Amer.	Fourth(E)	89	73
1988—New York†	....	Amer.	Fifth(E)	45	48
Major League Totals—3 Years	....			224	193

†Replaced Billy Martin with club in second place (record of 40-28), June 23, 1988.
Coach, New York Yankees, June 25, 1984 through 1985; Vice-President and General Manager, New York Yankees, beginning of 1988 season through June 22, 1988; and special advisor, New York Yankees, 1989.

DOUGLAS LEE RADER
(Doug)
California Angels

Born July 30, 1944, at Chicago, Ill.
Height, 6.03. Weight, 230.
Threw and batted righthanded.
Attended Illinois Wesleyan University, Bloomington, Ill.

Led National League third basemen in total chances with 479 in 1972.
Led National League third basemen in putouts with 147 in 1970.
Led National League third basemen in double plays with 39 in 1970 and tied for lead with 31 in 1972.
Named third baseman on THE SPORTING NEWS National League All-Star fielding team, 1970 through 1973.
Received reported $25,000 bonus to sign with Houston Astros, 1964.

Year	Club	League	Pos.	G.	AB.	R.	H.	2B.	3B.	HR.	RBI.	B.A.	PO.	A.	E.	F.A.
1965—Durham		Carol.	3B-OF	112	330	44	69	14	1	14	38	.209	111	185	21	.934
1966—Amarillo		Texas	3B	138	527	85	★153	21	12	16	74	.290	102	240	27	.927
1967—Oklahoma City		P. C.	3B	75	273	40	80	23	5	9	44	.293	47	110	12	.929
1967—Houston		Nat.	1B-3B	47	162	24	54	10	4	2	26	.333	270	33	8	.974
1968—Houston		Nat.	3B-1B	98	333	42	89	16	4	6	43	.267	130	171	22	.932
1969—Houston		Nat.	3B-1B	155	569	62	140	25	3	11	83	.246	140	307	26	.945
1970—Houston		Nat.	★3B-1B	156	576	90	145	25	3	25	87	.252	149	★357	18	★.966
1971—Houston		Nat.	3B	135	484	51	118	21	4	12	56	.244	93	275	●21	.946
1972—Houston		Nat.	3B	152	533	70	131	24	7	22	90	.237	119	★340	20	.958
1973—Houston		Nat.	3B	154	574	79	146	26	0	21	89	.254	★134	296	★25	.945
1974—Houston		Nat.	3B	152	533	61	137	27	3	17	78	.257	128	347	17	.965
1975—Houston†		Nat.	★3B-SS	129	448	41	100	23	2	12	48	.223	114	259	11	★.971
1976—San Diego		Nat.	3B	139	471	45	121	22	4	9	55	.257	109	318	20	.955
1977—San Diego‡		Nat.	3B	52	170	19	46	8	3	5	27	.271	43	104	6	.961
1977—Toronto§		Amer.	3B-1B-OF	96	313	47	75	18	2	13	40	.240	97	106	7	.967
National League Totals—11 Years				1369	4873	584	1227	227	37	142	682	.252	1429	2807	194	.956
American League Totals—1 Year				96	313	47	75	18	2	13	40	.240	97	106	7	.967
Major League Totals—11 Years				1465	5186	631	1302	245	39	155	722	.251	1526	2913	201	.957

Signed as free agent by Houston Colt .45s' organization, September 13, 1964.
†Traded to San Diego Padres for Pitchers Joe McIntosh and Larry Hardy, December 11, 1975.
‡Sold to Toronto Blue Jays, June 8, 1977.
§Released, March 18, 1978.

RECORD AS MANAGER

Year	Club	League	Position	W.	L.	Year	Club	League	Position	W.	L.
1980—Hawaii		P. C.	First(N)	40	25	1983—Texas		Amer.	Third(W)	77	85
	(Second Half)		Third(N)	36	40	1984—Texas		Amer.	Seventh(W)	69	92
1981—Hawaii		P. C.	First(N)	35	31	1985—Texas†		Amer.	Seventh(W)	9	23
	(Second Half)		Third(N)	37	34	1986—Chicago‡		Amer.	Fifth(W)	1	1
1982—Hawaii		P. C.	Second(S)	36	35	1989—California		Amer.	Third(W)	91	71
	(Second Half)		Third(S)	37	36	Major League Totals—5 Years				247	272

†Replaced by Bobby Valentine, May 16, 1985.
‡Served as interim manager, June 20 and June 21, 1986 before Jim Fregosi replaced Tony La Russa, June 22, 1986.
Coach, American League All-Star Team, 1989.
Coach, San Diego Padres, 1979; Coach, Chicago White Sox, 1986 and 1987; scout, California Angels, 1988.

FRANK ROBINSON
Baltimore Orioles

Born August 31, 1935, at Beaumont, Tex.
Height, 6.01. Weight, 194.
Threw and batted righthanded.
Attended Xavier University, Cincinnati, O.

Holds major league record for most consecutive seasons leading league, intentional bases on balls (4), 1961 through 1964 (tied in 1962).
Holds modern major league record for most times hit by pitch, rookie season (20), 1956.
Shares major league records for most home runs, bases filled, game (2), June 26, 1970; most home runs, bases filled, two successive at bats (2), June 26, 1970; most runs batted in, two successive innings (8), June 26, 1970, fifth and sixth innings; fewest putouts, first baseman, game (0), July 1, 1971; most home runs, rookie season (38), 1956; most years leading league, intentional bases on balls, since 1955 (4).
Hit three home runs in a game, August 22, 1959.
Hit for the cycle, May 2, 1959.
Won American League Triple Crown, 1966.
Led National League in slugging percentage with .595 in 1960, .611 in 1961 and .624 in 1962.
Led American League in total bases with 367 and in slugging percentage with .637 in 1966.
Led American League in being hit by pitch with 13 in 1969.
Led National League in being hit by pitch with 20 in 1956, 8 in 1959, 9 in 1960, 11 in 1962, 14 in 1963 and 18 in 1965.
Led National League in intentional bases on balls received with 23 in 1961, 20 in 1963, 20 in 1964 and tied for lead with 16 in 1962.
Led National League in sacrifice flies with 10 in 1961.
Led National League first basemen in double plays with 111 in 1959.
Tied for American League lead in sacrifice flies with 7 in 1966.
Named Major League Player of the Year by THE SPORTING NEWS, 1966.
Named American League Player of the Year by THE SPORTING NEWS, 1966.

Named American League Most Valuable Player by Baseball Writers' Association of America, 1966.
Named National League Player of the Year by THE SPORTING NEWS, 1961.
Named National League Most Valuable Player by Baseball Writers' Association of America, 1961.
Named National League Rookie of the Year by THE SPORTING NEWS, 1956.
Named National League Rookie of the Year by Baseball Writers' Association of America, 1956.
Named outfielder on THE SPORTING NEWS American League All-Star Team, 1966 and 1967.
Named outfielder on THE SPORTING NEWS National League All-Star Team, 1961 and 1962.
Named outfielder on THE SPORTING NEWS National League All-Star fielding team, 1958.
Elected to Hall of Fame, 1982.

Year Club	League	Pos.	G.	AB.	R.	H.	2B.	3B.	HR.	RBI.	B.A.	PO.	A.	E.	F.A.
1953—Ogden	Pion.	OF-3B-1B	72	270	70	94	20	6	17	83	.348	105	28	18	.881
1954—Tulsa	Texas	2B-3B	8	30	4	8	0	0	0	1	.267	17	15	1	.970
1954—Columbia	Sally	OF-3B-2B	132	491	*112	165	32	9	25	110	.336	258	63	18	.947
1955—Columbia	Sally	OF-1B	80	243	50	64	15	7	12	52	.263	203	3	4	.981
1956—Cincinnati	Nat.	OF	152	572	*122	166	27	6	38	83	.290	323	5	8	.976
1957—Cincinnati	Nat.	OF-1B	150	611	97	197	29	5	29	75	.322	487	36	6	.989
1958—Cincinnati	Nat.	OF-3B	148	554	90	149	25	6	31	83	.269	314	24	6	.983
1959—Cincinnati	Nat.	1B-OF	146	540	106	168	31	4	36	125	.311	1049	78	18	.984
1960—Cincinnati	Nat.	1B-OF-3B	139	464	86	138	33	6	31	83	.297	775	62	10	.988
1961—Cincinnati	Nat.	OF-3B	153	545	117	176	32	7	37	124	.323	284	15	3	.990
1962—Cincinnati	Nat.	OF	162	609	*134	208	*51	2	39	136	.342	315	10	2	.994
1963—Cincinnati	Nat.	OF-1B	140	482	79	125	19	3	21	91	.259	238	13	4	.984
1964—Cincinnati	Nat.	OF	156	568	103	174	38	6	29	96	.306	279	7	4	.986
1965—Cincinnati†	Nat.	OF	156	582	109	172	33	5	33	113	.296	282	5	3	.990
1966—Baltimore	Amer.	OF-1B	155	576	*122	182	34	2	*49	*122	*.316	282	6	5	.983
1967—Baltimore	Amer.	OF-1B	129	479	83	149	23	7	30	94	.311	207	8	2	.991
1968—Baltimore	Amer.	OF-1B	130	421	69	113	27	1	15	52	.268	193	5	7	.966
1969—Baltimore	Amer.	OF-1B	148	539	111	166	19	5	32	100	.308	367	19	5	.987
1970—Baltimore	Amer.	OF-1B	132	471	88	144	24	1	25	78	.306	262	11	4	.986
1971—Baltimore‡	Amer.	OF-1B	133	455	82	128	16	2	28	99	.281	449	20	11	.977
1972—Los Angeles§	Nat.	OF	103	342	41	86	6	1	19	59	.251	168	6	6	.967
1973—California	Amer.	OF	147	534	85	142	29	0	30	97	.266	38	3	1	.976
1974—Calif. x-Cleve.	Amer.	1B-OF	144	477	81	117	27	3	22	68	.245	23	0	1	.958
1975—Cleveland yz	Amer.	DH-PH	49	118	19	28	5	0	9	24	.237	0	0	0	.000
1976—Cleveland yab	Amer.	1B-OF	36	67	5	15	0	0	3	10	.224	11	0	0	1.000
National League Totals—11 Years			1605	5869	1084	1759	324	51	343	1068	.300	4514	261	70	.986
American League Totals—10 Years			1203	4137	745	1184	204	21	243	744	.286	1832	72	36	.981
Major League Totals—21 Years			2808	10006	1829	2943	528	72	586	1812	.294	6346	333	106	.984

†Traded to Baltimore Orioles for Outfielder Dick Simpson and Pitchers Milt Pappas and Jack Baldschun, December 9, 1965.

‡Traded with Pitcher Pete Richert to Los Angeles Dodgers for Pitchers Doyle Alexander and Bob O'Brien, Catcher Sergio Robles and First Baseman-Outfielder Royle Stillman, December 2, 1971.

§Traded with Infielders Billy Grabarkewitz and Bob Valentine and Pitchers Bill Singer and Mike Strahler to California Angels for Third Baseman Ken McMullen and Pitcher Andy Messersmith, November 28, 1972.

xReleased on waivers to Cleveland Indians, September 12, 1974; Indians assigned Outfielder Rusty Torres and Catcher Ken Suarez to Angels, December 4, 1974, to complete deal.

yPlayer-manager.

zOn disabled list, July 4 to July 23, 1975.

aOn disabled list, April 4 to April 26, 1976.

bReleased October 5, 1976.

CHAMPIONSHIP SERIES RECORD

Shares Championship Series records for hitting home runs in first at-bat, October 4, 1969; most at-bats, inning (2), October 3, 1970, fourth inning.

Year Club	League	Pos.	G.	AB.	R.	H.	2B.	3B.	HR.	RBI.	B.A.	PO.	A.	E.	F.A.
1969—Baltimore	Amer.	OF	3	12	1	4	2	0	1	2	.333	2	0	1	.667
1970—Baltimore	Amer.	OF	3	10	3	2	0	0	1	2	.200	2	0	0	1.000
1971—Baltimore	Amer.	OF	3	12	2	1	1	0	0	1	.083	7	0	0	1.000
Championship Series Totals—3 Years			9	34	6	7	3	0	2	5	.206	11	0	1	.917

WORLD SERIES RECORD

Shares World Series record for most times hit by pitcher, total series (3), and game (2), October 8, 1961.

Year Club	League	Pos.	G.	AB.	R.	H.	2B.	3B.	HR.	RBI.	B.A.	PO.	A.	E.	F.A.
1961—Cincinnati	Nat.	OF	5	15	3	3	2	0	1	4	.200	5	0	0	1.000
1966—Baltimore	Amer.	OF	4	14	4	4	0	1	2	3	.286	6	0	0	1.000
1969—Baltimore	Amer.	OF	5	16	2	3	0	0	1	1	.188	13	0	0	1.000
1970—Baltimore	Amer.	OF	5	22	5	6	0	0	2	4	.273	7	0	0	1.000
1971—Baltimore	Amer.	OF	7	25	5	7	0	0	2	2	.280	12	0	0	1.000
World Series Totals—5 Years			26	92	19	23	2	1	8	14	.250	43	0	0	1.000

ALL-STAR GAME RECORD

Year League	Pos.	AB.	R.	H.	2B.	3B.	HR.	RBI.	B.A.	PO.	A.	E.	F.A.
1956—National	OF	2	0	0	0	0	0	0	.000	1	0	0	1.000
1957—National	OF	2	0	1	0	0	0	0	.500	5	0	0	1.000
1959—National (second game)	1B	3	1	3	0	0	1	1	1.000	3	0	1	.750
1961—National (first game)	OF	1	0	1	0	0	0	0	1.000	2	0	0	1.000
1962—National (second game)	OF	3	0	0	0	0	0	0	.000	1	0	0	1.000
1965—National	PH	1	0	0	0	0	0	0	.000	0	0	0	.000
1966—American	OF	4	0	0	0	0	0	0	.000	2	0	0	1.000
1969—American	OF	2	0	0	0	0	0	0	.000	0	0	0	.000

Year League	Pos.	AB.	R.	H.	2B.	3B.	HR.	RBI.	B.A.	PO.	A.	E.	F.A.
1970—American	OF	3	0	0	0	0	0	0	.000	1	0	0	1.000
1971—American	OF	2	1	1	0	0	1	2	.500	2	0	0	1.000
1974—American	PH	1	0	0	0	0	0	0	.000	0	0	0	.000
All-Star Game Totals—11 Years		24	2	6	0	0	2	3	.250	17	0	1	.944

Member of National League All-Star Team in 1959 (first game) and 1961 (second game); did not play.
Named to American League Team for 1967 game; replaced due to injury.

RECORD AS MANAGER

Named American League Manager of the Year by THE SPORTING NEWS, 1989.

Year Club	League	Position	W.	L.
1975—Cleveland	Amer.	Fourth(E)	79	80
1976—Cleveland	Amer.	Fourth(E)	81	78
1977—Cleveland†	Amer.	Sixth(E)	26	31
1978—Rochester‡	Int.	Sixth	58	64
1981—San Francisco§	Nat.		56	55
1982—San Francisco	Nat.	Third(W)	87	75
1983—San Francisco	Nat.	Fifth(W)	79	83

Year Club	League	Position	W.	L.
1984—San Francisco x	Nat.	Sixth(W)	42	64
1988—Baltimore y	Amer.	Seventh(E)	54	101
1989—Baltimore	Amer.	Second(E)	87	75
National League Totals—4 Years			264	277
American League Totals—5 Years			327	365
Major League Totals—9 Years			591	642

†Replaced by Jeff Torborg, June 19, 1977.
‡Replaced interim manager Al Widmar (replacing Ken Boyer), May 8, 1978.
§First Half . . . Fifth (W) (record of 27-32); Second Half . . . Third (W) (record of 29-23).
xReplaced by interim manager Danny Ozark, August 5, 1984.
yReplaced Cal Ripken with club in seventh place (record of 0-6), April 12, 1988.
Coach, California Angels, July 11 through remainder of 1977 season; Coach, Baltimore Orioles, beginning of 1978 season through May 8, 1978, 1979, 1980 and 1985 through 1987; and Special Assistant to the President, Baltimore Orioles, beginning of 1988 through April 11, 1988.
Coach, American League All-Star Team, 1980.

ROBERT LEROY RODGERS
(Bob or Buck)
Montreal Expos

Born August 16, 1938, at Delaware, O.
Height, 6.01. Weight, 190.
Threw right and batted left and righthanded.
Attended Ohio Wesleyan University, Delaware, O., and Ohio Northern
University, Ada, O.

Holds American League record for most games, by catcher, rookie season (150), 1962.
Shares American League record for fewest assists by catcher, season, 150 or more games (73), 1962.
Major League stolen bases: 1962 (1), 1963 (2), 1964 (4), 1965 (4), 1966 (3), 1967 (1), 1968 (2). Total—17.
Led American League catchers in double plays with 14 in 1962 and 14 in 1964.

Year Club	League	Pos.	G.	AB.	R.	H.	2B.	3B.	HR.	RBI.	B.A.	PO.	A.	E.	F.A.
1956—Jamestown	Pony	OF	48	153	28	36	8	1	6	26	.235	43	6	3	.942
1957—Erie	NYP	★C-OF	114	430	79	127	26	4	12	80	.295	568	★77	★25	.963
1958—Lancaster	East.	C	19	63	8	16	3	0	3	8	.254	111	11	2	.984
1958—Idaho Falls	Pion.	★C-OF	99	378	73	115	15	6	12	74	.304	524	45	★20	.966
1959—Birmingham	South.	C	3	13	1	1	0	1	0	2	.077	28	0	1	.966
1959—Knoxville	Sally	★C-OF	105	355	53	102	18	6	7	55	.287	565	60	★13	.980
1960—Denver	A. A.	C	23	84	12	20	7	1	3	12	.238	127	15	4	.973
1960—Birmingham	South.	C	93	313	36	77	14	1	5	38	.246	456	★68	7	.987
1961—Dallas-Ft. W.†	A. A.	C	124	427	55	122	22	3	3	62	.286	★595	★70	11	.984
1961—Los Angeles	Amer.	C	16	56	8	18	2	0	2	13	.321	71	11	3	.965
1962—Los Angeles	Amer.	C	155	565	65	146	34	6	6	61	.258	826	73	●10	.989
1963—Los Angeles	Amer.	C	100	300	24	70	6	0	4	23	.233	416	48	★10	.979
1964—Los Angeles	Amer.	C	148	514	38	125	18	3	4	54	.243	884	★87	★13	.987
1965—California	Amer.	C	132	411	33	86	14	3	1	32	.209	682	52	7	.991
1966—California	Amer.	C	133	454	45	107	20	3	7	48	.236	662	★69	6	.992
1967—California	Amer.	★C-OF	139	429	29	94	13	3	6	41	.219	728	★73	7	.991
1968—California	Amer.	C	91	258	13	49	6	0	1	14	.190	407	50	7	.985
1969—Hawaii	P. C.	C-3B	44	145	15	37	5	0	0	12	.255	215	26	4	.984
1969—California	Amer.	C	18	49	4	9	1	0	0	2	.196	74	9	0	1.000
1975—Salinas‡	Calif.	PH	4	3	1	1	0	0	0	0	.333	0	0	0	.000
1977—El Paso§	Texas	PH	1	0	0	0	0	0	0	0	.000	0	0	0	.000
Major League Totals—9 Years			932	3033	259	704	114	18	31	288	.232	4750	472	63	.988

†Selected by Los Angeles Angels from Detroit Tigers in American League expansion draft, December 14, 1960.
‡Player-manager, August 24 through September 15, 1975.
§Player-manager, July 15 through August 14, 1977.

RECORD AS MANAGER
Named National League Manager of the Year by THE SPORTING NEWS, 1987.
Named Minor League Manager of the Year by THE SPORTING NEWS, 1984.

Named American Association Manager of the Year, 1984.
Named Texas League Manager of the Year, 1977.

Year	Club	League	Position	W.	L.
1975—Salinas	Calif.		Fifth	35	35
(Second Half)			Sixth	32	38
1977—El Paso	Texas		First(W)	38	24
(Second Half)			†First(W)	40	28
1980—Milwaukee‡	Amer.		Third(E)	39	31
1981—Milwaukee§	Amer.			62	47
1982—Milwaukee x	Amer.		yFifth(E)	23	24
1984—Indianapolis	A. A.		zFirst	91	63
1985—Montreal	Nat.		Third(E)	84	77
1986—Montreal	Nat.		Fourth(E)	78	83
1987—Montreal	Nat.		Third(E)	91	71
1988—Montreal	Nat.		Third(E)	81	81
1989—Montreal	Nat.		Fourth(E)	81	81
American League Totals—3 Years				124	102
National League Totals—5 Years				415	393
Major League Totals—8 Years				539	495

†Lost league championship to Arkansas, two games to none.
‡Began season as interim manager for ill George Bamberger who returned June 6, 1980, with club in second place (record of 26-21); named manager when Bamberger retired with club tied for fourth place (record of 73-66), September 7, 1980.
§First Half . . . Third (E) (record of 31-25); Second Half . . . First (E) (record of 31-22).
xReplaced by Harvey Kuenn, June 2, 1982.
yTied for position with Baltimore Orioles.
zLost semifinal playoff series to Louisville, four games to two.
Coach, National League All-Star Team, 1988 and 1989.
Coach, Minnesota Twins, 1970 through 1974; San Francisco Giants, 1976; Milwaukee Brewers, 1978 through 1980.

DIVISION SERIES RECORD

Year	Club	League	W.	L.
1981—Milwaukee	American		2	3

JEFFREY ALLEN TORBORG
(Jeff)
Chicago White Sox

Born November 26, 1941, at Westfield, N. J.
Height, 6.00. Weight, 195.
Threw and batted righthanded.
Received bachelor of science degree in education from Rutgers University, New Brunswick, N. J.; and received master's degree in athletic administration from Montclair State College, Montclair, N. J.
Father of Doug Torborg, pitcher in Pittsburgh Pirates' organization, 1987 and 1988.

Received reported $100,000 bonus to sign with Los Angeles Dodgers, 1963.

Year	Club	League	Pos.	G.	AB.	R.	H.	2B.	3B.	HR.	RBI.	B.A.	PO.	A.	E.	F.A.
1963—Albuquerque	Texas	C	64	184	19	41	10	3	1	18	.223	349	27	6	.984
1964—Los Angeles	Nat.	C	28	43	4	10	1	1	0	4	.233	80	4	2	.977
1965—Los Angeles	Nat.	C	56	150	8	36	5	1	3	13	.240	300	19	3	.991
1966—Los Angeles	Nat.	C	46	120	4	27	3	0	1	13	.225	269	17	4	.986
1967—Los Angeles	Nat.	C	76	196	11	42	4	1	2	12	.214	413	30	5	.989
1968—Los Angeles	Nat.	C	37	93	2	15	2	0	0	4	.161	206	20	2	.991
1969—Los Angeles	Nat.	C	51	124	7	23	4	0	0	7	.185	251	26	1	.996
1970—Los Angeles†	Nat.	C	64	134	11	31	8	0	1	17	.231	275	16	5	.983
1971—California‡	Amer.	C	55	123	6	25	5	0	0	5	.203	208	17	3	.987
1972—California§	Amer.	C	59	153	5	32	3	0	0	8	.209	383	28	1	.998
1973—California xyz	Amer.	C	102	255	20	56	7	0	1	18	.220	611	37	6	.991
National League Totals—7 Years			358	860	47	184	27	3	7	70	.214	1794	132	22	.989
American League Totals—3 Years			216	531	31	113	15	0	1	31	.213	1202	82	10	.990
Major League Totals—10 Years			574	1391	78	297	42	3	8	101	.214	2996	214	32	.990

†Sold to California Angels, March 13, 1971.
‡On disabled list, June 25 to July 27, 1971.
§On disabled list, May 21 to June 13, 1972.
xOn disabled list, July 13 to August 10, 1973.
yTraded to St. Louis Cardinals for Pitcher John Andrews, December 6, 1973.
zReleased, March 25, 1974.

RECORD AS MANAGER

Year	Club	League	Position	W.	L.
1977—Cleveland†	Amer.		Fifth(E)	45	59
1978—Cleveland	Amer.		Sixth(E)	69	90
1979—Cleveland‡	Amer.		Sixth(E)	43	52
1989—Chicago	Amer.		Seventh(W)	69	92
Major League Totals—4 Years				226	293

†Replaced Frank Robinson with club in sixth place (record of 26-31), June 19, 1977.
‡Replaced by Dave Garcia, July 23, 1979.
Coach, Cleveland Indians, 1975 to June 18, 1977; coach, New York Yankees, July 26, 1979 through 1988.

THOMAS LYNN TREBELHORN
(Tom)
Milwaukee Brewers

Born January 27, 1948, at Portland, Ore.
Height, 5.11. Weight, 178.
Threw right and batted lefthanded.
Received bachelor of science degree in history and teaching
from Portland State University, Portland, Ore. in 1970.
Led Northwest League catchers in fielding percentage with .997 in 1971.
Led National League catchers in double plays with 5 in 1970.
Tied for Northwest League lead in double plays by catchers with 3 in 1972.

Year Club	League	Pos.	G.	AB.	R.	H.	2B.	3B.	HR.	RBI.	B.A.	PO.	A.	E.	F.A.
1970—Bend	N'west	C-3-2-O	68	198	33	48	4	1	4	32	.242	296	48	12	.966
1971—Bend	N'west	C-OF	51	149	28	47	13	3	3	38	.315	282	33	2	.994
1972—Walla Walla†	N'west	C	42	124	17	25	5	1	2	20	.202	272	19	4	.986
1973—Birmingham	South.	3B-C-1B	33	89	9	18	5	0	2	13	.202	87	31	8	.937
1973—Burlington	Midw.	C-1B	43	146	23	33	6	0	2	20	.226	298	25	5	.985
1974—Birmingham	South.	C-3B	8	9	1	2	1	0	0	0	.222	13	1	1	.933
1974—Lewiston‡§	N'west	P	7	2	0	0	0	0	0	0	.000	1	2	0	1.000

Signed as free agent by Hawaii (Pacific Coast League), June 4, 1970.
†Sold to Oakland A's organization, September 2, 1972.
‡Player-coach.
§Released, June 17, 1975.

PITCHING RECORD

Year Club	League	G.	IP.	W.	L.	Pct.	H.	R.	ER.	SO.	BB.	ERA.
1974—Lewiston	Northwest	5	12	1	0	1.000	7	1	1	2	2	0.75

RECORD AS MANAGER

Year Club	League	Position	W.	L.	Year Club	League	Position	W.	L.
1975—Boise	N'west	Third(S)	39	39	1985—Vancouver‡	P. C.	Second(N)	38	34
1976—Boise	N'west	Third(S)	33	38			First(N)	41	30
1977—Modesto	Calif.	Fourth	31	39	(Second Half)				
(Second Half)		Sixth	22	48	1986—Milwaukee§	Amer.	Sixth(E)	6	3
1979—Batavia	NYP	Third(W)	37	34	1987—Milwaukee	Amer.	Third(E)	91	71
1982—Portland	P. C.	Fifth(N)	32	39	1988—Milwaukee	Amer.	xThird(E)	87	75
(Second Half)		Fifth(N)	33	40	1989—Milwaukee	Amer.	Fourth(E)	81	81
1983—Hawaii	P. C.	†Fourth(S)	32	40	Major League Totals—4 Years			265	230
(Second Half)		Second(S)	40	31					

†Tied for position with Phoenix.
‡Won division championship from Calgary, three games to none; won league championship from Phoenix, three games to none.
§Replaced retiring manager George Bamberger with club in sixth place (record of 71-81), September 26, 1986.
xTied for position with Toronto Blue Jays.
Coach, American League All-Star Team, 1988.
Coach, Cleveland Indians' organization, 1978; coach, Pittsburgh Pirates' organization, 1980 and 1981; coach, Milwaukee Brewers, 1984 and beginning of 1986 season through September 25, 1986.

ROBERT JOHN VALENTINE
(Bobby)
Texas Rangers

Born May 13, 1950, at Stamford, Conn.
Height, 5.10. Weight, 185.
Threw and batted righthanded.
Attended Arizona State University, Tempe, Ariz., and University of Southern California, Los Angeles, Calif.
Son-in-law of Ralph Branca, pitcher with Brooklyn Dodgers, Detroit Tigers
and New York Yankees, 1944 through 1954 and 1956.
Major League stolen bases: 1971 (5), 1972 (5), 1973 (6), 1974 (8), 1975 (1), 1978 (1), 1979 (1). Total—27.
Led Pioneer League in stolen bases with 20 in 1968.
Led Pacific Coast League in total bases with 324, sacrifice flies with 10 and double plays by shortstops with 106 in 1970.
Led Pioneer League outfielders in putouts with 107 and tied for lead in assists with 8 in 1987.
Named Pacific Coast League Player of the Year, 1970.

Year Club	League	Pos.	G.	AB.	R.	H.	2B.	3B.	HR.	RBI.	B.A.	PO.	A.	E.	F.A.
1968—Odgen	Pion.	OF-SS	62	224	★62	63	14	4	6	26	.281	111	10	6	.953
1969—Spokane	P. C.	★SS-OF	111	402	61	104	19	5	3	35	.259	166	254	★38	.917
1969—Los Angeles	Nat.	PR	5	0	3	0	0	0	0	0	.000	0	0	0	.000
1970—Spokane	P. C.	★SS-2B	●146	★621	★122	★211	★39	★16	14	80	★.340	★217	474	★54	.928
1971—Spokane	P. C.	SS	7	30	7	10	2	0	1	2	.333	13	18	3	.912
1971—Los Angeles	Nat.	S-3-2-O	101	281	32	70	10	2	1	25	.249	123	176	16	.949
1972—Los Angeles†	Nat.	2-3-O-S	119	391	42	107	11	2	3	32	.274	178	245	23	.948
1973—California‡	Amer.	SS-OF	32	126	12	38	5	2	1	13	.302	63	75	6	.958
1974—California§x	Amer.	OF-SS-3B	117	371	39	97	10	3	3	39	.261	160	116	17	.942
1975—Charleston	Int.	3B	56	175	27	41	4	0	1	17	.234	44	74	6	.952
1975—Salt Lake City	P. C.	1-O-3-2	46	147	29	45	6	1	0	17	.306	92	14	3	.972
1975—California y	Amer.	1B-3B-OF	26	57	5	16	2	0	0	5	.281	27	1	2	.933

Year Club	League	Pos.	G.	AB.	R.	H.	2B.	3B.	HR.	RBI.	B.A.	PO.	A.	E.	F.A.
1975—San Diego	Nat.	OF	7	15	1	2	0	0	1	1	.133	4	0	0	1.000
1976—Hawaii....................	P. C.	1-O-3-S	120	395	67	120	23	2	13	89	.304	578	47	4	.994
1976—San Diego	Nat.	OF-1B	15	49	3	18	4	0	0	4	.367	55	6	0	1.000
1977—S.D.z-N.Y..............	Nat.	SS-1B-3B	86	150	13	23	4	0	2	13	.153	119	64	3	.984
1978—New York a	Nat.	2B-3B	69	160	17	43	7	0	1	18	.269	78	109	6	.969
1979—Seattle b	Amer.	S-O-2-3-C	62	98	9	27	6	0	0	7	.276	32	38	2	.972
National League Totals—7 Years...........			402	1046	111	263	36	4	8	93	.251	557	600	48	.960
American League Totals—4 Years			237	652	65	178	23	5	4	64	.273	282	230	27	.950
Major League Totals—10 Years..............			639	1698	176	441	59	9	12	157	.260	839	830	75	.957

Selected by Los Angeles Dodgers' organization in 1st round (fifth player selected) of free-agent draft, June 7, 1968.

†Traded with Infielder Billy Grabarkewitz, Outfielder Frank Robinson and Pitchers Bill Singer and Mike Strahler to California Angels for Pitcher Andy Messersmith and Third Baseman Ken McMullen, November 28, 1972.

‡On disabled list, May 17, 1973 through remainder of season.

§On disabled list, May 29 to June 13, 1974.

xLoaned to Charleston (Pittsburgh Pirates' organization), April 4, 1975; returned, June 20, 1975.

yTraded with a player to be named later to San Diego Padres for Pitcher Gary Ross, September 17, 1975; San Diego acquired Infielder Rudy Meoli to complete deal, November 4, 1975.

zTraded with Pitcher Paul Siebert to New York Mets for Infielder-Outfielder Dave Kingman, June 15, 1977.

aReleased, March 26, 1979; signed by Seattle Mariners, April 10, 1979.

bGranted free agency, November 1, 1979.

RECORD AS MANAGER

Year Club	League	Position	W.	L.
1985—Texas†	Amer.	Seventh(W)	53	76
1986—Texas......................	Amer.	Second(W)	87	75
1987—Texas......................	Amer.	‡Sixth(W)	75	87
1988—Texas......................	Amer.	Sixth(W)	70	91
1989—Texas......................	Amer.	Fourth(W)	83	79
Major League Totals—5 Years...........			368	408

†Replaced Doug Rader with club in seventh place (record of 9-23), May 16, 1985.

‡Tied for position with California Angels.

Coach, American League All-Star Team, 1988.

Scout and minor league instructor, San Diego Padres, 1981; minor league instructor, New York Mets, 1982; coach, New York Mets, 1983 through May 15, 1985.

JOHN DAVID WATHAN
Kansas City Royals

Born October 4, 1949, at Cedar Rapids, Ia.
Height, 6.02. Weight, 205.
Threw and batted righthanded.
Attended University of San Diego, San Diego, Calif., and
Mount Mercy College, Cedar Rapids, Ia.

Major League stolen bases: 1977 (2), 1978 (2), 1979 (2), 1980 (17), 1981 (11), 1982 (36), 1983 (28), 1984 (6), 1985 (1). Total—105.

Year Club	League	Pos.	G.	AB.	R.	H.	2B.	3B.	HR.	RBI.	B.A.	PO.	A.	E.	F.A.
1971—San Jose	Calif.	C-OF	64	215	37	56	11	2	1	29	.260	438	31	14	.971
1971—Waterloo	Midw.	C-OF-1B	43	147	31	41	4	4	3	21	.279	282	18	1	.997
1972—San Jose†	Calif.	C-1B-3B	48	148	25	40	8	0	4	15	.270	324	31	3	.992
1972—Omaha	A. A.	C	18	51	8	15	1	1	0	2	.294	94	5	1	.990
1972—Jacksonville	South.	C	16	54	6	17	3	1	0	3	.315	111	7	4	.967
1973—Jacksonville‡........	South.	C-1B-3B	65	233	20	58	8	3	5	34	.249	294	28	4	.988
1974—Jacksonville.........	South.	1B-OF-C	120	428	63	105	14	2	7	47	.245	760	50	7	.991
1975—Omaha	A. A.	C-OF	104	360	42	109	14	4	8	46	.303	532	45	10	.983
1976—Omaha§..................	A. A.	C-OF	24	84	4	13	5	0	0	6	.155	128	14	4	.973
1976—Kansas City..........	Amer.	C-1B	27	42	5	12	1	0	0	5	.286	63	4	1	.985
1977—Kansas City..........	Amer.	C-1B	55	119	18	39	5	3	2	21	.328	156	9	2	.988
1978—Kansas City x	Amer.	1B-C	67	190	19	57	10	1	2	28	.300	385	28	2	.995
1979—Kansas City..........	Amer.	1B-C-OF	90	199	26	41	7	3	2	28	.206	336	24	3	.992
1980—Kansas City..........	Amer.	C-OF-1B	126	453	57	138	14	7	6	58	.305	472	33	8	.984
1981—Kansas City..........	Amer.	C-OF-1B	89	301	24	76	9	3	1	19	.252	316	28	7	.980
1982—Kansas City y........	Amer.	C-1B	121	448	79	121	11	3	3	51	.270	482	40	10	.981
1983—Kansas City..........	Amer.	C-1B-OF	128	437	49	107	18	3	2	32	.245	615	58	9	.987
1984—Kansas City..........	Amer.	C-1B-OF	97	171	17	31	7	1	2	10	.181	304	31	6	.982
1985—Kansas City z........	Amer.	C-1B	60	145	11	34	8	1	1	9	.234	259	29	4	.986
Major League Totals—10 Years..............			860	2505	305	656	90	25	21	261	.262	3388	284	52	.986

Selected by Kansas City Royals' organization in 4th round of free-agent draft, January 13, 1971.

†On disabled list, May 5 to May 30, 1972.

‡On disabled list, May 25 to June 28, 1973.

§On disabled list, July 29 to September 1, 1976.

xOn disabled list, June 16 to July 7, 1978.

yOn disabled list, July 6 to August 10, 1982.

zReleased and signed as coach, April 7, 1986.

DIVISION SERIES RECORD

Year Club	League	Pos.	G.	AB.	R.	H.	2B.	3B.	HR.	RBI.	B.A.	PO.	A.	E.	F.A.
1981—Kansas City..........	Amer.	C	3	10	1	3	0	0	0	0	.300	11	4	1	.938

CHAMPIONSHIP SERIES RECORD

Year Club League	Pos.	G.	AB.	R.	H.	2B.	3B.	HR.	RBI.	B.A.	PO.	A.	E.	F.A.
1976—Kansas City........... Amer.	C	1	0	0	0	0	0	0	0	.000	0	0	0	.000
1977—Kansas City........... Amer.	C-1-D-PH	4	6	0	0	0	0	0	0	.000	19	0	0	1.000
1978—Kansas City.......... Amer.	1B	1	3	0	0	0	0	0	0	.000	7	0	0	1.000
1980—Kansas City........... Amer.	OF-PH	3	6	1	0	0	0	0	0	.000	7	0	0	1.000
1984—Kansas City........... Amer.	PR-DH	1	1	0	0	0	0	0	0	.000	0	0	0	.000
Championship Series Totals—5 Years....		10	16	1	0	0	0	0	0	.000	33	0	0	1.000

WORLD SERIES RECORD

Year Club League	Pos.	G.	AB.	R.	H.	2B.	3B.	HR.	RBI.	B.A.	PO.	A.	E.	F.A.
1980—Kansas City........... Amer.	PH-OF-C	3	7	1	2	0	0	0	1	.286	7	1	0	1.000
1985—Kansas City........... Amer.	PH-PR	2	1	0	0	0	0	0	0	.000	0	0	0	.000
World Series Totals—2 Years		5	8	1	2	0	0	0	1	.250	7	1	0	1.000

RECORD AS MANAGER

Year Club	League	Position	W.	L.
1987—Omaha..................... A. A.		Seventh†	64	76
1987—Kansas City‡.......... Amer.		Second(W)	21	15
1988—Kansas City............. Amer.		Third(W)	84	77
1989—Kansas City............. Amer.		Second(W)	92	70
Major League Totals—3 Years			197	162

†Tied for position with Nashville.
‡Replaced manager Billy Gardner with club in fourth place (record of 62-64), August 27, 1987.
Coach, Kansas City Royals, 1986.

DONALD WILLIAM ZIMMER
(Don)
Chicago Cubs

Born January 17, 1931, at Cincinnati, O.
Height, 5.10. Weight, 188.
Threw and batted righthanded.
Father of Tom Zimmer, minor league catcher in St. Louis Cardinals' organization, 1971 through 1975;
coach, St. Louis Cardinals' organization, 1975; coach, St. Louis Cardinals, 1976;
player-manager with Victoria in Lone Star League (Independent), 1977; manager with Butte in
Pioneer League (Co-op), 1978; manager in Pittsburgh Pirates' organization, 1979;
manager in California Angels' organization, 1980; and scout for San Francisco Giants since 1981.

Named American Association Rookie of the Year, 1953.

Year Club League	Pos.	G.	AB.	R.	H.	2B.	3B.	HR.	RBI.	B.A.	PO.	A.	E.	F.A.
1949—Cambridge .... E. Shore	SS	71	304	56	69	14	3	4	30	.227	162	171	27	.925
1950—Hornell .... Pony	*SS-3B	123	518	*146	163	34	5	*23	122	.315	*269	*367	45	*.934
1951—Elmira .... East.	SS	137	546	94	149	28	2	9	70	.273	*326	414	38	*.951
1952—Mobile .... South.	SS	153	613	107	190	32	7	17	91	.310	*355	*517	*52	.944
1953—St. Paul† .... A. A.	SS	81	320	57	96	14	4	23	63	.300	165	264	21	.953
1954—St. Paul .... A. A.	SS	73	268	54	78	9	6	17	53	.291	152	200	16	.957
1954—Brooklyn .... Nat.	SS	24	33	3	6	0	1	0	0	.182	14	32	3	.939
1955—Brooklyn .... Nat.	2B-SS-3B	88	280	38	67	10	1	15	50	.239	184	207	12	.970
1956—Brooklyn‡ .... Nat.	SS-3B-2B	17	20	4	6	1	0	0	2	.300	10	11	1	.955
1957—Brooklyn .... Nat.	3B-SS-2B	84	269	23	59	9	1	6	19	.219	114	186	15	.952
1958—Los Angeles .... Nat.	S-3-2-O	127	455	52	119	15	2	17	60	.262	281	395	26	.963
1959—Los Angeles§ .... Nat.	SS-3B-2B	97	249	21	41	7	1	4	28	.165	120	240	10	.973
1960—Chicago .... Nat.	2-3-S-O	132	368	37	95	16	7	6	35	.258	211	274	16	.968
1961—Chicago x.............. Nat.	2B-3B-OF	128	477	57	120	25	4	13	40	.252	284	332	20	.969
1962—N.Y. y-Cinn. z........ Nat.	3B-2B-SS	77	244	19	52	12	2	2	17	.213	77	129	11	.949
1963—Los Angeles a .... Nat.	3B-2B-SS	22	23	4	5	1	0	1	2	.217	3	14	2	.895
1963—Washington .... Amer.	3B-2B	83	298	37	74	12	1	13	44	.248	90	177	18	.937
1964—Washington .... Amer.	3-O-C-2	121	341	38	84	16	2	12	38	.246	72	144	10	.956
1965—Washington b........ Amer.	C-3B-2B	95	226	20	45	6	0	2	17	.199	181	81	12	.956
1966—Toei....................... Pacific	3B-SS	87	203	14	37	2	0	9	20	.182	101	143	11	.957
1967—Knoxville .... South	P-3-1-C	25	49	2	10	3	0	0	5	.204	21	12	6	.846
1967—Buffalo .... Int.	3B-OF	16	33	2	6	2	0	1	2	.182	4	9	3	.813
American League Totals—3 Years		299	865	95	203	34	3	27	99	.235	343	402	40	.949
National League Totals—10 Years		796	2418	258	570	96	19	64	253	.236	1298	1820	116	.964
Major League Totals—12 Years		1095	3283	353	773	130	22	91	352	.235	1641	2222	156	.961

†On disabled list, July 7, 1953 through remainder of season.
‡On disabled list, June 23, 1956 through remainder of season.
§Traded to Chicago Cubs for Pitcher Ron Perranoski, Infielder John Goryl, Outfielder Lee Handley and reported $25,000, April 8, 1960.
xSelected by New York Mets in Expansion Draft, October 10, 1961.
yTraded to Cincinnati Reds for Pitcher Robert G. Miller and Third Baseman Cliff Cook, May 6, 1962.
zTraded to Los Angeles Dodgers for Pitcher Scott Breeden, January 24, 1963.
aSold to Washington Senators, June 24, 1963.
bReleased, November 19, 1965; signed by Toei Flyers of Japanese Baseball League.

WORLD SERIES RECORD

Year Club	League	Pos.	G.	AB.	R.	H.	2B.	3B.	HR.	RBI.	B.A.	PO.	A.	E.	F.A.
1955—Brooklyn	Nat.	2B	4	9	0	2	0	0	0	2	.222	4	8	2	.857
1959—Los Angeles	Nat.	SS	1	1	0	0	0	0	0	0	.000	0	1	0	1.000
World Series Totals—2 Years			5	10	0	2	0	0	0	2	.200	4	9	2	.867

ALL-STAR GAME RECORD

Year League	Pos.	AB.	R.	H.	2B.	3B.	HR.	RBI.	B.A.	PO.	A.	E.	F.A.
1961—National (first game)	2B	1	0	0	0	0	0	0	.000	0	0	1	.000

PITCHING RECORD

Year Club	League	G.	IP.	W.	L.	Pct.	H.	R.	ER.	SO.	BB.	ERA.
1967—Knoxville	Southern	12	27	0	0	.000	33	15	14	8	7	4.67

RECORD AS MANAGER

Named National League Manager of the Year by THE SPORTING NEWS, 1989.

Year Club	League	Position	W.	L.
1967—Knoxville	South.	†Sixth	26	46
1967—Buffalo	Int.	Seventh	33	40
1968—Indianapolis	P. C.	Fifth(E)	66	78
1969—Key West	Fla. St.	‡Third(S)	67	63
1972—San Diego§	Nat.	Sixth(W)	54	88
1973—San Diego	Nat.	Sixth(W)	60	102
1976—Boston x	Amer.	Third(E)	42	34
1977—Boston	Amer.	ySecond(E)	97	64
1978—Boston	Amer.	Second(E)	99	64
1979—Boston	Amer.	Third (E)	91	69
1980—Boston z	Amer.	aThird(E)	82	73
1981—Texas b	Amer.		57	48
1982—Texas c	Amer.	Sixth(W)	38	58
1988—Chicago	Nat.	Fourth(E)	77	85
1989—Chicago	Nat.	First(E)	93	69
American League Totals—7 Years			506	410
National League Totals—4 Years			284	344
Major League Totals—11 Years			790	754

†Transferred by Cincinnati Reds' organization from Knoxville to Buffalo, July 5, 1967.
‡Tied for position with Pompano Beach.
§Replaced Preston Gomez with club in fourth place (record of 4-7), April 27, 1972.
xReplaced Darrell Johnson with club in fifth place (record of 41-45), July 19, 1976.
yTied for position with Baltimore Orioles.
zReplaced by interim manager Johnny Pesky, October 1, 1980.
aTied for position with Milwaukee Brewers.
bFirst Half. . . . Second (W) (record of 33-22); Second Half. . . . Third (W) (record of 24-26).
cReplaced by Darrell Johnson, July 29, 1982.
Coach, Montreal Expos, 1971; San Diego Padres, 1972; Boston Red Sox, 1974 to July, 1976; coach, New York Yankees, 1983 and June 16, 1986 through remainder of season; coach, Chicago Cubs, 1984 through June 12, 1986; coach, San Francisco Giants, 1987.
Coach, American League All-Star Team, 1978 and 1981.

CHAMPIONSHIP SERIES RECORD

Year Club	League	W.	L.
1989—Chicago	National	1	4

1990 Hall of Fame Enshrinees

JOE LEONARD MORGAN

Born September 19, 1943, at Bonham, Tex.
Height, 5.07. Weight, 155.
Threw right and batted lefthanded.
Attended Oakland City College, Oakland, Calif., Merritt College, Oakland, Calif.
and California State University, Hayward, Calif.
Cousin of Marsh White, running back with New York Giants, 1975 through 1977.

Established major league records for most seasons by second baseman (22); most consecutive errorless games by second baseman, lifetime (91); most home runs by second baseman, lifetime (266).

Tied major league record for fewest errors by second baseman, season, 150 or more games (5), 1977.

Established National League records for most bases on balls received, lifetime (1,799); most games by second baseman, lifetime (2,427); most putouts by second baseman, lifetime (5,541); most assists by second baseman, lifetime (6,738); most chances accepted by second baseman, lifetime (12,279).

Tied National League records for most runs batted in, two consecutive innings (7), August 19, 1974 (second and third innings).

Tied modern National League record for most bases on balls, game (5), June 2, 1966.

First player to steal 60 or more bases and hit 25 or more home runs in the same season, 1973 and 1976; and one of two players in major league history to steal 50 or more bases and hit 20 or more home runs in same season (67 stolen bases and 26 home runs in 1973, 58 stolen bases and 22 home runs in 1974, and 60 stolen bases and 27 home runs in 1976).

Collected six hits in one game, July 8, 1965, (12 innings).

Major League stolen bases: 1963 (1), 1965 (20), 1966 (11), 1967 (29), 1968 (3), 1969 (49), 1970 (42), 1971 (40), 1972 (58), 1973 (67), 1974 (58), 1975 (67), 1976 (60), 1977 (49), 1978 (19), 1979 (28), 1980 (24), 1981 (14), 1982 (24), 1983 (18), 1984 (8). Total—689.

Led National League in slugging percentage with .576 in 1976.

Led National League in sacrifice flies with 12 in 1976.

Led National League in bases on balls received with 97 in 1965, 115 in 1972 and 132 in 1975.

Led National League second basemen in total chances with 814 in 1972.

Tied for National League lead in bases on balls received with 93 in 1980.

Tied for National League lead in double plays by second basemen with 106 in 1973.

Led Texas League second basemen in double plays with 106 in 1964.

Named Major League Player of the Year by THE SPORTING NEWS, 1975 and 1976.

Named National League Player of the Year by THE SPORTING NEWS, 1975.

Named National League Most Valuable Player by Baseball Writers' Association of America, 1975 and 1976.

Named National League Comeback Player of the Year by THE SPORTING NEWS, 1982.

Named National League Rookie Player of the Year by THE SPORTING NEWS, 1965.

Named second baseman on THE SPORTING NEWS National League All-Star Team, 1972 and 1974 through 1977.

Named second baseman on THE SPORTING NEWS National League All-Star fielding team, 1973 through 1977.

Named second baseman on THE SPORTING NEWS National League Silver Slugger team, 1982.

Named Texas League Most Valuable Player, 1964.

Named to Hall of Fame, 1990.

Year	Club	League	Pos.	G.	AB.	R.	H.	2B.	3B.	HR.	RBI.	B.A.	PO.	A.	E.	F.A.
1963—Modesto		Calif.	2B	45	152	42	40	5	3	5	27	.263	81	104	15	.925
1963—Durham		Carol.	2B	95	322	74	107	20	2	13	43	.332	217	273	24	.953
1963—Houston		Nat.	2B	8	25	5	6	0	1	0	3	.240	15	15	3	.909
1964—San Antonio		Texas	2B	●140	496	113	160	★42	8	12	90	.323	319	405	25	★.967
1964—Houston		Nat.	2B	10	37	4	7	0	0	0	0	.189	31	25	3	.949
1965—Houston		Nat.	2B	157	601	100	163	22	12	14	40	.271	348	492	★27	.969
1966—Houston†		Nat.	2B	122	425	60	121	14	8	5	42	.285	256	316	21	.965
1967—Houston		Nat.	2B-OF	133	494	73	136	27	11	6	42	.275	299	344	14	.979
1968—Houston‡§		Nat.	2B-OF	10	20	6	5	0	1	0	0	.250	10	6	2	.889
1969—Houston		Nat.	2B-OF	147	535	94	126	18	5	15	43	.236	315	328	18	.973
1970—Houston x		Nat.	2B	144	548	102	147	28	9	8	52	.268	349	430	17	.979
1971—Houston y		Nat.	2B	160	583	87	149	27	●11	13	56	.256	336	★482	12	.986
1972—Cincinnati		Nat.	2B	149	552	★122	161	23	4	16	73	.292	★370	436	8	★.990
1973—Cincinnati		Nat.	2B	157	576	116	167	35	2	26	82	.290	★417	440	9	.990
1974—Cincinnati		Nat.	2B	149	512	107	150	31	3	22	67	.293	344	385	13	.982
1975—Cincinnati		Nat.	2B	146	498	107	163	27	6	17	94	.327	356	425	11	★.986
1976—Cincinnati		Nat.	2B	141	472	113	151	30	5	27	111	.320	342	335	13	.981
1977—Cincinnati		Nat.	2B	153	521	113	150	21	6	22	78	.288	★351	359	5	★.993
1978—Cincinnati		Nat.	2B	132	441	68	104	27	0	13	75	.236	252	290	11	.980
1979—Cincinnati z		Nat.	2B	127	436	70	109	26	1	9	32	.250	259	329	12	.980
1980—Houston a		Nat.	2B	141	461	66	112	17	5	11	49	.243	244	348	7	.988
1981—San Francisco		Nat.	2B	90	308	47	74	16	1	8	31	.240	177	258	4	.991
1982—San Francisco b		Nat.	2B-3B	134	463	68	134	19	4	14	61	.289	255	366	8	.987
1983—Philadelphia cd		Nat.	2B	123	404	72	93	20	1	16	59	.230	231	331	17	.971
1984—Oakland e		Amer.	2B	116	365	50	89	21	0	6	43	.244	201	229	10	.977
National League Totals—21 Years				2533	8912	1600	2428	428	96	262	1090	.272	5557	6740	235	.981
American League Totals—1 Year				116	365	50	89	21	0	6	43	.244	201	229	10	.977
Major League Totals—22 Years				2649	9277	1650	2517	449	96	268	1133	.271	5758	6969	245	.981

Signed as free agent by Houston Colt .45s' organization, November 1, 1962.
†On disabled list, June 26 to August 5, 1966.
‡On military list, April 27 to April 29, 1968.
§On disabled list, May 18 to September 14, 1968.
xOn military list, June 6 to June 20, 1970.
yTraded with Pitcher Jack Billingham, Infielder Denis Menke and Outfielders Cesar Geronimo and Ed Armbrister to Cincinnati Reds for First Baseman Lee May, Second Baseman Tommy Helms and Outfielder Jim Stewart, November 29, 1971.

zGranted free agency, November 1, 1979; signed by Houston Astros, January 31, 1980.
aReleased, December 8, 1980; signed by San Francisco Giants, February 9, 1981.
bTraded with Pitcher Al Holland to Philadelphia Phillies for Pitchers Mike Krukow and Mark Davis and Outfielder Charles Penigar, December 14, 1982.
cOn disabled list, May 13 to May 28, 1983.
dReleased, October 31, 1983; signed by Oakland A's, December 13, 1983.
eOn voluntarily retired list, November 20, 1984.

CHAMPIONSHIP SERIES RECORD

Established Championship Series records for most bases on balls, total Series (23).
Tied Championship Series records for hitting home run in first Series at bat, October 7, 1972; most clubs, total Series (3); most bases on balls, three-game Series (6), 1976; most two-base hits, three-game Series (3), 1975; most stolen bases, game (3), October 4, 1975; most stolen bases, Series (4), 1975.

Year	Club	League	Pos.	G.	AB.	R.	H.	2B.	3B.	HR.	RBI.	B.A.	PO.	A.	E.	F.A.
1972—Cincinnati	Nat.	2B	5	19	5	5	0	0	2	3	.263	11	18	0	1.000
1973—Cincinnati	Nat.	2B	5	20	1	2	1	0	0	1	.100	12	27	0	1.000
1975—Cincinnati	Nat.	2B	3	11	2	3	3	0	0	1	.273	2	9	0	1.000
1976—Cincinnati	Nat.	2B	3	7	2	0	0	0	0	0	.000	9	5	0	1.000
1979—Cincinnati	Nat.	2B	3	11	0	0	0	0	0	0	.000	12	11	0	1.000
1980—Houston	Nat.	2B	4	13	1	2	1	1	0	0	.154	9	8	0	1.000
1983—Philadelphia	Nat.	2B	4	15	1	1	0	0	0	0	.067	8	7	0	1.000
Championship Series Totals—7 Years			27	96	12	13	5	1	2	5	.135	63	85	0	1.000

WORLD SERIES RECORD

Tied World Series record for most stolen bases, four-game Series (2), 1976; most putouts by second baseman, four-game Series (13), 1976; most errors by second baseman, four-game Series (2), 1976; one or more hits, each game, four-game Series, 1976.

Year	Club	League	Pos.	G.	AB.	R.	H.	2B.	3B.	HR.	RBI.	B.A.	PO.	A.	E.	F.A.
1972—Cincinnati	Nat.	2B	7	24	4	3	2	0	0	1	.125	18	18	1	.973
1975—Cincinnati	Nat.	2B	7	27	4	7	1	0	0	3	.259	17	28	0	1.000
1976—Cincinnati	Nat.	2B	4	15	3	5	1	1	1	2	.333	13	10	2	.920
1983—Philadelphia	Nat.	2B	5	19	3	5	0	1	2	2	.263	8	10	0	1.000
World Series Totals—4 Years			23	85	14	20	4	2	3	8	.235	56	66	3	.976

ALL-STAR GAME RECORD

Tied All-Star Game records for most consecutive games batted safely (7); most times home run as leadoff batter, start of game (1), July 19, 1977.

Year	League	Pos.	AB.	R.	H.	2B.	3B.	HR.	RBI.	B.A.	PO.	A.	E.	F.A.
1970—National		2B	2	1	1	0	0	0	0	.500	1	2	0	1.000
1972—National		2B	4	0	1	0	0	0	1	.250	3	5	0	1.000
1973—National		2B	3	2	1	1	0	0	0	.333	2	2	0	1.000
1974—National		2B	2	0	1	1	0	0	1	.500	3	4	0	1.000
1975—National		2B	4	0	1	0	0	0	0	.250	0	1	0	1.000
1976—National		2B	3	1	1	0	0	0	0	.333	2	3	0	1.000
1977—National		2B	4	1	1	0	0	1	1	.250	1	0	0	1.000
1978—National		2B	3	1	0	0	0	0	0	.000	2	1	0	1.000
1979—National		PH-2B	1	1	0	0	0	0	0	.000	1	1	0	1.000
All-Star Game Totals—9 Years			26	7	7	2	0	1	3	.269	15	19	0	1.000

Named to National League All-Star Team for the 1966 game; replaced due to injury.

JAMES ALVIN PALMER
(Jim)

Born October 15, 1945, at New York City, N.Y.
Height, 6.03. Weight, 194.
Threw and batted righthanded.
Attended Arizona State University, Tempe, Ariz., and
Towson State College, Towson, Md.

Established American League record for most putouts by pitcher, lifetime (292).
Pitched 8-0 no-hit victory against Oakland A's, August 13, 1969.
Pitched 8-0 no-hit victory against Duluth-Superior, June 19, 1964.
Major League saves: 1973 (1), 1975 (1), 1982 (1). Total—3.
Led American League in shutouts with 10 in 1975 and tied for lead with 5 in 1970.
Led American League pitchers in games started with 40 in 1976 and tied for lead with 39 in 1977.
Tied for American League lead in complete games with 22 in 1977.
Tied for American League lead in balks with 3 in 1970.
Led Northern League in wild pitches with 23 in 1964.
Named American League Pitcher of the Year by THE SPORTING NEWS, 1973, 1975 and 1976.
Won American League Cy Young Memorial Award, 1973, 1975 and 1976.
Named righthanded pitcher on THE SPORTING NEWS American League All-Star Team, 1971, 1973, 1975, 1976 and 1978.
Named pitcher on THE SPORTING NEWS American League All-Star fielding team, 1976 through 1979.
Received reported $60,000 bonus to sign with Baltimore Orioles, 1963.
Named to Hall of Fame, 1990.

Year	Club	League	G.	IP.	W.	L.	Pct.	H.	R.	ER.	SO.	BB.	ERA.
1964—Aberdeen	Northern	19	129	11	3	.786	75	42	36	107	*130	2.51
1965—Baltimore	American	27	92	5	4	.556	75	49	38	75	56	3.72
1966—Baltimore	American	30	208	15	10	.600	176	83	80	147	91	3.46
1967—Baltimore	American	9	49	3	1	.750	34	18	16	23	20	2.94

Year Club	League	G.	IP.	W.	L.	Pct.	H.	R.	ER.	SO.	BB.	ERA.
1967—Rochester†	Int'national	2	7	0	0	.000	12	9	9	6	5	11.57
1967—Miami	Florida St.	5	27	1	1	.500	20	6	6	16	10	2.00
1968—Miami	Florida St.	2	8	0	0	.000	4	2	0	5	9	0.00
1968—Rochester	Int'national	2	4	0	0	.000	4	6	6	6	8	13.50
1968—Elmira‡	Eastern	6	25	0	2	.000	18	13	12	26	19	4.32
1969—Baltimore§	American	26	181	16	4	⋆.800	131	48	47	123	64	2.34
1970—Baltimore	American	39	●305	20	10	.667	263	98	92	199	100	2.71
1971—Baltimore	American	37	282	20	9	.690	231	94	84	184	106	2.68
1972—Baltimore	American	36	274	21	10	.677	219	73	63	184	70	2.07
1973—Baltimore	American	38	296	22	9	.710	225	86	79	153	113	⋆2.40
1974—Baltimore x	American	26	179	7	12	.368	176	78	65	84	69	3.27
1975—Baltimore	American	39	323	●23	11	.676	253	87	75	193	80	⋆2.09
1976—Baltimore	American	40	⋆315	⋆22	13	.629	255	101	88	159	84	2.51
1977—Baltimore	American	39	⋆319	●20	11	.645	263	106	103	193	99	2.91
1978—Baltimore	American	38	⋆296	21	12	.636	246	94	81	138	97	2.46
1979—Baltimore y	American	23	156	10	6	.625	144	66	57	67	43	3.29
1980—Baltimore	American	34	224	16	10	.615	238	108	99	109	74	3.98
1981—Baltimore	American	22	127	7	8	.467	117	60	53	35	46	3.76
1982—Baltimore	American	36	227	15	5	●.750	195	85	79	103	63	3.13
1983—Baltimore z	American	14	76⅔	5	4	.556	86	42	36	34	19	4.23
1983—Hagerstown	Carolina	2	13	2	0	1.000	13	6	5	11	2	3.46
1984—Baltimore a	American	5	17⅔	0	3	.000	22	19	18	4	17	9.17
Major League Totals—19 Years		558	3947⅓	268	152	.638	3349	1395	1253	2212	1311	2.86

Signed as free agent by Baltimore Orioles' organization, August 16, 1963.
†On disabled list, from July 3 to August 8, 1967.
‡On Baltimore disabled list, August 28, 1968 through remainder of season.
§On disabled list, June 29 to August 9, 1969.
xOn disabled list, June 20 to August 13, 1974.
yOn disabled list, July 16 to August 11, 1979.
zOn disabled list, April 29 to June 14 and June 30 to August 21, 1983; included rehabilitation disability assignment to Hagerstown, August 6 to August 21, 1983.
aReleased, May 17, 1984.

CHAMPIONSHIP SERIES RECORD

Established Championship Series records for most Series played, one club (7); most strikeouts, total Series (46); most complete games, total Series (5).
Tied Championship Series records for most series pitched (6); most games won, total Series (4); most bases on balls, five-game Series (8), 1973.
Established American League Championship Series records for most strikeouts, five-game Series (15), 1973; most strikeouts, three-game Series (12), 1970; most bases on balls, total Series (19).

Year Club	League	G.	IP.	W.	L.	Pct.	H.	R.	ER.	SO.	BB.	ERA.
1969—Baltimore	American	1	9	1	0	1.000	10	2	2	4	2	2.00
1970—Baltimore	American	1	9	1	0	1.000	7	1	1	12	3	1.00
1971—Baltimore	American	1	9	1	0	1.000	7	3	3	8	3	3.00
1973—Baltimore	American	3	14⅔	1	0	1.000	11	3	3	15	8	1.84
1974—Baltimore	American	1	9	0	1	.000	4	1	1	4	1	1.00
1979—Baltimore	American	1	9	0	0	.000	7	3	3	3	2	3.00
Championship Series Totals—6 Years		8	59⅔	4	1	.800	46	13	13	46	19	1.96

WORLD SERIES RECORD

Established World Series record for most bases on balls with bases loaded, game (2), October 11, 1971.
Youngest pitcher to win complete World Series shutout game (20 years, 11 months), October 6, 1966.

Year Club	League	G.	IP.	W.	L.	Pct.	H.	R.	ER.	SO.	BB.	ERA.
1966—Baltimore	American	1	9	1	0	1.000	4	0	0	6	3	0.00
1969—Baltimore	American	1	6	0	1	.000	5	4	4	5	4	6.00
1970—Baltimore	American	2	15⅔	1	0	1.000	11	8	8	9	9	4.60
1971—Baltimore	American	2	17	1	0	1.000	15	5	5	15	9	2.65
1979—Baltimore	American	2	15	0	1	.000	18	6	6	8	5	3.60
1983—Baltimore	American	1	2	1	0	1.000	2	0	0	1	1	0.00
World Series Totals—6 Years		9	64⅔	4	2	.667	55	23	23	44	31	3.20

ALL-STAR GAME RECORD

Established All-Star Game records for most bases on balls, total games (7); most home runs allowed, game (3), July 19, 1977.
Tied All-Star Game record for most home runs allowed, inning (2), July 19, 1977 (first inning).

Year League		IP.	W.	L.	Pct.	H.	R.	ER.	SO.	BB.	ERA.
1970—American		3	0	0	.000	1	0	0	3	1	0.00
1971—American		2	0	0	.000	1	0	0	2	0	0.00
1972—American		3	0	0	.000	1	0	0	2	1	0.00
1977—American		2	0	1	.000	5	5	5	3	1	22.50
1978—American		2⅔	0	0	.000	3	3	3	4	4	10.11
All-Star Game Totals—5 Years		12⅔	0	1	.000	11	8	8	14	7	5.68

Member of American League All-Star Team for 1975 game; did not play.

Thank you for your purchase! We appreciate your support of *The Sporting News* books. We would like to know more about you and your interests so that we can continue to provide you with books that meet as many of your needs as possible. . . . Please take a few minutes and fill out our questionnaire. Thanks for your help!

Greg Wiley
Book Publisher

*Which *TSN* titles have you purchased?

In 1990 _____ _____ _____

In 1989 _____ _____ _____

In 1988 _____ _____ _____

*Have you purchased any of the following titles from other publishers?

☐ The Baseball Encyclopedia ☐ Diamond Appraised
☐ Bill James Abstract 1988 ☐ Total Baseball
☐ Dickson Baseball Dictionary ☐ The Babe—Life in Pictures
☐ The Elias Baseball Analyst ☐ The Baseball Hall Of Fame
☐ The Heart Of The Order ⠀⠀50th Anniversary Issue
☐ Summer Of 1949

*How do you purchase *TSN* books?

☐ Waldenbooks ☐ *TSN* Ads
☐ B. Dalton ☐ *TSN* Mailings
☐ Crown ☐ Other Book Stores

*Could you make some suggestions for improving *TSN* books or services?

_____

_____

*What's your favorite *TSN* book(s)? _____

_____

*What's your favorite section? _____

_____

*What's your least favorite section? _____

_____

*Do you subscribe to *The Sporting News*? ☐ Yes ☐ No

*Education: ☐ High School ☐ Graduate Degree
⠀⠀⠀⠀⠀⠀⠀⠀ ☐ Some College ☐ Attending High School
⠀⠀⠀⠀⠀⠀⠀⠀ ☐ College Graduate ☐ Attending College

*Age: ☐ Under 15 ☐ 19-23 ☐ 31-42 ☐ 56+
⠀⠀⠀⠀ ☐ 15-18 ☐ 24-30 ☐ 43-55

*Would you like to receive our book mailings announcing new titles? If so please provide us with your name and address.

Name _____

Address _____

City/State/Zip _____

Call **1-800-669-5700** if you would like subscription information.

FOLD ALONG DOTTED LINE AND STAPLE. NO POSTAGE IS NECESSARY.